PAN BOOKS EDITION

Cassell's Compact French-English English-French Dictionary

The emphasis of the dictionary is on the language of the modern Frenchman, with the sole inclusion of words and phrases in common usage.
Phonetic pronunciation, using the symbols of the International Phonetic Association, is given in brackets after each word with a key to pronunciation at the front of the book.
There is detailed advice to the user together with tables of French and English verbs. New features in the 'Compact' edition include notes at the head of the verb tables and the increased use of French in the explanatory parentheses in the English-French section.

'Within the limits of its size, the most comprehensive dictionary available.'

The Times Educational Supplement

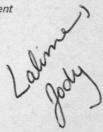

L'EDITION PAN BOOKS DE

Petit Dictionnaire Cassell Français-Anglais

Anglais-Français

Rédigé par

J. H. Douglas

BA (Lond.), Chevalier dans l'Ordre des Palmes Académiques,
Headmaster, Caldew School, Dalston, Cumberland

Denis Girard

Agrégé de l'Université
Inspecteur de l'Académie de Paris

W. Thompson

MA (Edin.), Deputy Headmaster,
The White House Grammar School, Brampton, Cumberland

Pan Books Londres et Sydney

PAN BOOKS EDITION OF

Cassell's Compact French-English English-French Dictionary

Compiled by

J. H. Douglas

BA (Lond.), Chevalier dans l'Ordre des Palmes Académiques,
Headmaster, Caldew School, Dalston, Cumberland

Denis Girard

Agrégé de l'Université
Inspecteur de l'Académie de Paris

W. Thompson

MA(Edin.), Deputy Headmaster,
The White House Grammar School, Brampton, Cumberland

Pan Books London and Sydney

Also available in this series

Cassell's Compact Spanish-English, English-Spanish Dictionary
Cassell's Compact German-English, English-German Dictionary

The large Cassell Dictionaries are available only in hardbound editions and include:
Cassell's English
Cassell's French-English, English-French
Cassell's German-English, English-German
Cassell's Spanish-English, English-Spanish
Cassell's Italian-English, English-Italian
Cassell's Dutch-English, English-Dutch
Cassell's Latin-English, English-Latin

Cassell's French-English, English-French Dictionary
first published 1904 by Cassell & Co Ltd
Entirely new and revised 33rd Edition 1954
52nd Edition 1967
Cassell's Compact French-English, English-French Dictionary
first published 1968 by Cassell & Co Ltd
This edition published 1970 by Pan Books Ltd,
Cavaye Place, London SW10 9PG
12th printing 1980

ISBN 0 330 02535 X
Set, printed and bound in Great Britain by
Cox & Wyman Ltd, Reading

Contents

Preface vii

Advice to the User viii

Avis au Lecteur ix

Key to Pronunciation xii

List of Abbreviations xiv

French–English Dictionary 1

English–French Dictionary 333

French Verbs 636

English Verbs 652

Preface

This new edition of a work which appeared for the first time in 1904 represents a departure from tradition in that it is not a revised version of its immediate predecessor, but an entirely new work based on 'Cassell's New French Dictionary' compiled by Denis Girard and first published in 1962.

The availability of such a recent publication, and one moreover which has been widely accepted as a reliable work, has made the editors' task much easier than it could ever have been otherwise. The dead wood had already been cut away and many new words had been introduced, but it will come as no surprise that there are entries in the 'Compact' which do not appear in the 'New', e.g. 'escalate', and that others which were included in the 'New' for the first time in 1962 have already been discarded as obsolete, e.g. 'teddy boy'.

It is, of course, the question of selection which poses the greatest problem for anyone concerned with the compilation of a dictionary of limited size. Many uncommon words inevitably fail to find a place, as do the less frequent uses of some which have been included. We have tried wherever possible to illustrate by examples, but we have not attempted to incorporate information which properly belongs to a grammar book rather than a dictionary. It is assumed that the user will have a knowledge not only of parts of speech but also of the essential basic grammar of both languages. Although personal preference may have played a part, we have always tried to regard suitability for this type of dictionary as the primary consideration for or against the inclusion of a word, and we hope that we have, if anything, erred on the safe side.

Several features in the general layout of the 'New French Dictionary' have been incorporated for the first time in the 'Compact'. These include the use of the symbols of the International Phonetic Association throughout, the detailed information given in the 'Advice to the User' and the tables of English and French verbs. Completely new features are the notes at the head of the verb tables and the increased use of French in the explanatory parentheses in the English–French section.

J. H. D.

Advice to the User

Grouping of Words

In both sections of the dictionary alphabetical order has been strictly observed for all entries, including proper nouns.

Numbering of Identical Words

Words which are spelt alike but which differ in origin or pronunciation are numbered separately.

Punctuation

When several translations are given for one word it can generally be assumed that those which are separated by commas have much the same meaning; semi-colons are used where there is a clear difference in meaning or usage.

Words marked with an asterisk (*) are obsolete.

Pronunciation

The phonetic transcription is given in square brackets immediately after the key-word and alternative pronunciations have been given where necessary. The mark (ˈ) precedes the syllable which carries the stress.

The symbols of the International Phonetic Association have been used throughout the dictionary, and the user who is unfamiliar with these should refer to the Key to Pronunciation.

Daniel Jones' *English Pronouncing Dictionary* has usually been followed in the English–French section.

Grammatical Information

It is assumed that the user will have a reasonable knowledge of the basic grammar of the two languages. For example, when a noun merely adds **-s** for the plural or an adjective **-e** for the feminine, it has not been considered necessary to show this. Parts of speech are indicated by an abbreviation in italics (*a.*, *n.m.*, *v.t.*, *adv.* etc.) except in the case of proper nouns where in English no indication has been given and in French only the gender. For the meanings of the abbreviations the user is referred to the list on page xiv.

Nouns and Adjectives

In the French–English section French nouns are classed as ***n.m.*** for the masculine, ***n.f.*** for the feminine or ***n.*** for a noun which may be masculine or feminine according to context. In the English–French section the gender of French nouns is shown by the abbreviations ***m.*** or ***f.***; where a noun, without change of form, may be masculine or feminine both genders are given. In a list of nouns the gender is not given after each one and the user should therefore read on to the next gender mentioned, e.g. under **damage** he will find 'dommage; tort,

Groupement des Mots

Dans les deux parties du dictionnaire l'ordre alphabétique a été strictement suivi pour tous les articles, y compris les noms propres.

Numérotage de Mots Identiques

Les mots qui ont la même orthographe sont numérotés séparément lorsqu'ils ont une racine ou une prononciation différente.

Ponctuation

Quand plusieurs traductions sont données pour un même mot, celles qui ne sont séparées que par des virgules ont en règle générale des sens à peu près identiques; le point virgule est utilisé pour indiquer des différences très nettes de sens ou d'emploi.

Les mots précédés d'un astérisque (*) sont désuets.

Prononciation

La transcription phonétique est donnée entre crochets immédiatement après le mot principal. Lorsqu'il y a d'autres prononciations possibles, elles sont également indiquées. L'accent (ˈ) précède la syllabe qui porte l'accent tonique.

Les signes de l'Association Internationale de Phonétique sont utilisés dans les deux parties du dictionnaire et le lecteur qui n'est pas familiarisé avec ces signes devra consulter la Table de Prononciation.

Pour la section Anglais–Français, on a généralement suivi le dictionnaire de M. Daniel Jones, *An English Pronouncing Dictionary*.

Indications Grammaticales

Le lecteur est considéré comme ayant une connaissance suffisante de la grammaire de base des deux langues. Par exemple, quand un nom français forme son pluriel en **-s** et quand un adjectif forme son féminin en **-e**, il n'a pas paru nécessaire de l'indiquer. La nature des mots est indiquée par une abréviation en italique (*a.*, *n.m.*, *v.t.*, *adv.* etc.) excepté dans le cas des noms propres pour lesquels aucune indication n'a été donnée dans la partie Anglais–Français et seulement le genre dans la partie Français–Anglais. On trouvera la signification des abréviations à la page xiv.

Noms et adjectifs

Dans la partie Français–Anglais, les noms français sont classés en *n.m.* pour les noms masculins, en *n.f.* pour les noms féminins et *n.* pour ceux qui se modifient selon le contexte. Dans la partie Anglais–Français, le genre des noms français est indiqué par les abréviations *m.* ou *f.*; lorsqu'un nom peut, sans changer de forme, être soit du masculin soit du féminin, les deux genres sont donnés. Dans une

dégât; (*fig.*) préjudice, détriment, *m.*' and he will know from this that all these five nouns are masculine. In the English–French section the feminine forms of French adjectives and nouns (where applicable) are not normally given. The user should consult the relevant French word in the French–English section.

Where plurals or feminines of nouns or adjectives are given, abbreviated forms are used. For example the entry **cheval** (pl. **-aux**) means that the full plural word is **chevaux.** Similarly, **acteur** (*fem.* **-trice**) indicates that the feminine form is **actrice.**

Verbs
All Verbs, other than reflexive verbs, form their compound tenses with **avoir** unless there is an indication with the entry that they take **être.** For all further information on verb entries please consult notes on Verb Tables below.

Verb Tables

1. French verbs have been listed in the tables as follows:
   a. A pattern verb for each of the three regular conjugations.
   b. Pattern verbs which may best be described as 'anomalous', i.e. verbs which are basically regular but which, for one reason or another, show slight variations from the normal forms.
   c. An alphabetical list of irregular verbs, some of which are used as a reference for other verbs which show similar irregularities.

Full conjugations have been given for the regular verbs but elsewhere only where it is considered necessary or desirable.

2. An alphabetical list of all irregular English verbs included in this dictionary is given. The user is referred to the Verb Tables for a note on the following:
   a. Verbs ending in **-y** preceded by one or more consonants.
   b. Certain verbs ending in a consonant preceded by a vowel.

3. The following explanation of verb entries in the dictionary may be helpful:
   a. *irr.* See the verb in question in the list of irregular verbs.
   b. *irr.* (*conjug. like* . . . . . .) See the pattern verb in the list of irregular verbs.
   c. (*see Verb Tables*) See the verb in question in the list of anomalous verbs.
   d. (*conjug. like* . . . . . .) See the pattern verb in the list of anomalous verbs.

liste de noms, le genre n'est pas donné après chacun d'eux et le lecteur doit alors se référer au premier genre indiqué, e.g. pour **damage** il trouvera 'dommage; tort, dégât; (*fig.*) préjudice, détriment, *m.*' et il en déduira que ces cinq noms sont du masculin. Dans la partie Anglais–Français, le féminin des mots français, lorsqu'il existe, n'est en principe pas indiqué; on le trouvera dans la partie Français–Anglais.

Lorsque le pluriel ou le féminin des noms ou des adjectifs est indiqué, il est donné en abrégé. Par exemple, **cheval** (*pl.* **-aux**) signifie que la forme de ce mot au pluriel est **chevaux.** De même, **acteur** (*fem.* **-trice**) signifie que la forme du féminin est **actrice.**

Verbes

Tous les verbes, autres que les verbes réfléchis, forment leurs temps composés avec l'auxiliaire **avoir**, à moins qu'il soit indiqué qu'ils se conjuguent avec **être.** On trouvera ci-dessous des renseignements complémentaires sur les verbes.

Tables des Verbes

1. Les verbes français sont présentés de la façon suivante:

  a. un verbe type pour chacune des trois conjugaisons régulières.
  b. des verbes-types 'anomaux', c'est-à-dire, des verbes qui sont fondamentalement réguliers mais qui comportent de légères variations par rapport aux formes normales.
  c. une liste alphabétique des verbes irréguliers dont certains servent de références à d'autres verbes présentant des irrégularités analogues.

La conjugaison des verbes réguliers a été donnée en entier, mais pour les autres verbes elle ne figure que lorsque cela paraît nécessaire.

2. On trouvera une liste alphabétique de tous les verbes irréguliers anglais qui sont donnés dans ce dictionnaire, précédée par des renseignements sur les groupes suivants:

  a. Verbes qui se terminent en **-y** précédé d'une ou plus d'une consonne.
  b. Certains verbes qui se terminent en une consonne précédée d'une voyelle.

3. Les renseignements suivants concernant la présentation des verbes dans le dictionnaire pourront s'avérer utiles:

  a. *irr.* Se reporter à la liste des verbes irréguliers.
  b. *irr.* (*conjug. like* . . . . . .) Voir le verbe-type dans la liste des verbes irréguliers.
  c. (*see Verb Tables*) Voir ce verbe dans la liste des verbes anomaux.
  d. (*conjug. like* . . . . . .) Voir le verbe-type dans la liste des verbes anomaux.

Key to Pronunciation

VOWELS

French (I)

i as in cri [kri], difficile [difi'sil]
iː „ „ écrire [e'kriːr], finir [fi'niːr]
e „ „ thé [te], mélodie [melɔ'di]
ɛ „ „ réel [re'ɛl], aile [ɛl]
ɛː „ „ bête [bɛːt], dentaire [dɑ̃'tɛːr]
a „ „ patte [pat], apparat [apa'ra]
aː „ „ tard [taːr], barbare [bar'baːr]
ɑ „ „ pas [pɑ], tailler [tɑ'je]
ɑː „ „ gaz [gɑːz], pâte [pɑːt]
ɔ „ „ coter [kɔ'te], voler [vɔ'le]
ɔː „ „ confort [kɔ̃'fɔːr], porc [pɔːr]
o „ „ côté [ko'te], gros [gro], tôt [to]
oː „ „ dôme [doːm], rôle [roːl]
u „ „ coup [ku], tourner [tur'ne]
uː „ „ bourre [buːr], cour [kuːr]
y „ „ cru [kry], salut [sa'ly]
yː „ „ littérature [litera'tyːr]
ø „ „ neveu [nə'vø], rocheux [rɔ'ʃø]
øː „ „ mitrailleuse [mitrɑ'jøːz]
œ „ „ feuillet [fœ'jɛ]
œː „ „ faveur [fa'vœːr]
ə „ „ le [lə], refaire [rə'fɛːr]

English (I)

iː as in seat [siːt]
i „ „ finish ['finiʃ], physics ['fiziks]
e „ „ neck [nek], bread [bred]
æ „ „ man [mæn], malefactor ['mælifæktə]
ɑː „ „ father ['fɑːðə], task [tɑːsk]
ɔ „ „ block [blɔk], waddle [wɔdl]
ɔː „ „ shawl [ʃɔːl], tortoise ['tɔːtəs]
o „ „ domain [do'mein]
u „ „ good [gud], July [dʒu'lai]
uː „ „ moon [muːn], tooth [tuːθ]
ʌ „ „ cut [kʌt], somewhere ['sʌmwɛə]
əː „ „ search [səːtʃ], surgeon ['səːdʒən]
ə „ „ cathedral [kə'θiːdrəl], never ['nevə]

Nasal Vowels

ɛ̃ as in faim [fɛ̃], vingt [vɛ̃]
ɛ̃ː „ „ feindre [fɛ̃ːdr], poindre [pwɛ̃ːdr]
ɑ̃ „ „ ensemencement [ɑ̃smɑ̃s'mɑ̃]
ɑ̃ː „ „ défendre [de'fɑ̃ːdr]
ɔ̃ „ „ son [sɔ̃], fonder [fɔ̃'de]
ɔ̃ː „ „ contre [kɔ̃ːtr], trompe [trɔ̃ːp]
œ̃ „ „ défunt [de'fœ̃], un [œ̃]
œ̃ː „ , humble [œ̃ːbl]

Diphthongs

ei as in great [greit]
ou „ „ show [ʃou]
ai „ „ high [hai]
au „ „ crowd [kraud]
ɔi „ „ boy [bɔi]
iə „ „ steer [stiə]
ɛə „ „ hair [hɛə]
uə „ „ moor [muə]

Key to Pronunciation

CONSONANTS

French (1)

p	as in	peine [pɛn], papier [pa'pje]
b	„ „	bon [bɔ̃]
t	„ „	tâter [tɑ'te], thé [te]
d	„ „	dinde [dɛ̃:d]
k	„ „	coquelicot [kɔkli'ko]
g	„ „	gare [ga:r]
m	„ „	maman [ma'mɑ̃], même [mɛ:m]
n	„ „	nonne [nɔn]
ɲ	„ „	agneau [a'ɲo], soigner [swa'ɲe]
f	„ „	fier [fjɛ:r]
v	„ „	vivre [vi:vr]
s	„ „	sucre [sykr]
z	„ „	raser [rɑ'ze]
l	„ „	lettre [lɛtr], valise [va'li:z]
ʃ	„ „	charme [ʃarm]
ʒ	„ „	ronger [rɔ̃'ʒe], joue [ʒu]
r	„ „	arrière [a'rjɛ:r]

English (1)

p	as in	paper ['peipə]
b	„ „	ball [bɔ:l]
t	„ „	tea [ti:], till [til]
d	„ „	deed [di:d]
k	„ „	cake [keik]
g	„ „	game [geim]
m	„ „	mammoth ['mæməθ]
n	„ „	nose [nouz], nun [nʌn]
ŋ	„ „	bring [briŋ], finger ['fiŋgə]
f	„ „	fair [fɛə], far [fɑ:]
v	„ „	vine [vain]
θ	„ „	thin [θin], bath [bɑ:θ]
ð	„ „	this [ðis], bathe [beið]
s	„ „	since [sins]
z	„ „	busy ['bizi]
l	„ „	land [lænd], hill [hil]
ʃ	„ „	shield [ʃi:ld], sugar ['ʃugə]
ʒ	„ „	visionary ['viʒənəri]
r	„ „	rut [rʌt], brain [brein]
h	„ „	here [hiə], horse [hɔ:s]
x	„ „	loch [lɔx]

SEMI-CONSONANTS

French

j	as in	rien [rjɛ̃]
w	„ „	ouate [wat], oui [wi]
ɥ	„ „	huile [ɥil]

English

j	as in	yellow ['jelou], yes [jes]
w	„ „	wall [wɔ:l]

(1) When the same symbol is used in both English and French it often represents a different sound in each language.

' denotes that the stress is on the following syllable.
: denotes that the preceding vowel is long.
~ placed over a vowel-symbol shows that the vowel has a nasal sound.

List of Abbreviations

a.	adjective
abbr.	abbreviation
Adm.	Administration
adv.	adverb
adv. phr.	adverbial phrase
affirm.	affirmative
Agric.	Agriculture
Alg.	Algebra
Am.	American
Anat.	Anatomy
Ant.	Antiquities
Arch.	Architecture
Archaeol.	Archaeology
Arith.	Arithmetic
art.	article
Artill.	Artillery
Astron.	Astronomy
aux.	auxiliary
Av.	Aviation
Bibl.	Bible, Biblical
Biol.	Biology
Bookb.	Bookbinding
Bot.	Botany
Box.	Boxing
Build.	Building
(C)	Canadian usage
Carp.	Carpentry
Ch.	Church
Chem.	Chemistry
Cine.	Cinema
Civ. Eng.	Civil Engineering
Coin.	Coinage
collect.	collective
colloq.	colloquially
comb.	combination
comb. form	combining form
Comm.	Commerce
comp.	comparative
Conch.	Conchology
cond.	conditional
conj.	conjunction
conjug.	conjugated
contr.	contraction
Cook.	Cookery
Cost.	Costume
Cycl.	Cycling
dat.	dative
def.	definite
dem.	demonstrative
Dent.	Dentistry
dial.	dialect
dim.	diminutive
Dress.	Dressmaking
Eccles.	Ecclesiastical
Econ.	Economics
Elec.	Electricity
ellipt.	elliptic
emphat.	emphatic
Eng.	Engineering
Engl.	English
Engr.	Engraving
Ent.	Entomology
esp.	especially
Exam.	Examination
f.	feminine
fam.	familiarly
facet.	facetiously
fem.	feminine
Fenc.	Fencing
Feud.	Feudal
fig.	figuratively
Fin.	Financial
foll.	the following
Fort.	Fortification
Fr.	French
Ftb.	Football
fut.	future
Gard.	Gardening
Geog.	Geography
Geol.	Geology
Geom.	Geometry
Gr.	Greek
Gram.	Grammar
Gym.	Gymnastics
Her.	Heraldry
Hist.	History
Horol.	Horology
Hort.	Horticulture
Hunt.	Hunting
Hydr.	Hydrostatics
i.	intransitive
Ichth.	Ichthyology
imp.	imperfect
impers.	impersonal
Ind.	Industry
indec.	indecent
indef.	indefinite
indic.	indicative
inf.	infinitive
int.	interjection
inter.	interrogative
inv.	invariable
iron.	ironical
irr.	irregular (see table of Irregular Verbs, pp. 636–58)
It.	Italian
Jew.	Jewish
Journ.	Journalism
L.	Latin
Lit.	Literature
Log.	Logic
m.	masculine
Mach.	Machinery
Manuf.	Manufacturing
masc.	masculine
Math.	Mathematics
Mech.	Mechanics
Med.	Medicine
Metal.	Metallurgy
Meteor.	Meteorology
Mil.	Military
Min.	Mineralogy
Motor.	Motoring
Mount.	Mountaineering
Mus.	Music
Myth.	Mythology
n.	noun
Nat.	Natural
Naut.	Nautical
neg.	negative
obj.	object
obs.	obsolete
Opt.	Optics
Orn.	Ornithology
Paint.	Painting
Parl.	Parliamentary
part.	participle, participial
Path.	Pathology
pej.	pejorative
perf.	perfect
pers.	person, personal
Pharm.	Pharmacy
Phil.	Philosophy
Philol.	Philology
Phon.	Phonetics
Phot.	Photography
phr.	phrase
Phys.	Physics
Physiol.	Physiology
pl.	plural
poet.	poetical
Polit.	Politics
pop.	popular
poss.	possessive
p.p.	past participle
prec.	the preceding
pref.	prefix
prep.	preposition
pres.	present
pres. p.	present participle
Print.	Printing
pron.	pronoun
prop.	proper, properly
Pros.	Prosody
Psych.	Psychology
Pyro.	Pyrotechnics
r.	reflexive; reciprocal
Rad.	Radio
Rail.	Railway
R.C.	Roman Catholic
reg.	registered
rel.	relative
Relig.	Religion
rhet.	rhetoric
Rom.	Roman
Row.	Rowing
Sc.	Scottish
Sch.	Schools
Sci.	Science
Sculp.	Sculpture
sing.	singular
s.o.'s	someone's
Spt.	Sport
St. Exch.	Stock Exchange
subj.	subjunctive
superl.	superlative
Surg.	Surgery
Surv.	Surveying
Swim.	Swimming
t.	transitive
Tech.	Technical
Tel.	Television
Teleg.	Telegraphy
Teleph.	Telephone
Ten.	Tennis
Tex.	Textiles
Theat.	Theatrical
Theol.	Theological
Trig.	Trigonometry
Univ.	University
U.S.	United States
usu.	usually
v.	verb
Vet.	Veterinary
v.i.	intransitive verb
v.r.	reflexive *or* reciprocal verb
v.t.	transitive verb
vulg.	vulgar
Zool.	Zoology

A, a [ɑ], *n.m.* in French *a* has two sounds: (1) as in *part*, shown in this dictionary by 'a'; (2) as in *pas*, shown by 'ɑ'.

à [a], *prep.* [*see also* AU, AUX] to, at, in, into, on, by, for, from, with.

abaisse [a'bɛ:s], *n.f.* undercrust of pastry.

abaissement [abɛs'mɑ̃], *n.m.* lowering, falling, abatement, depression; humiliation, abasement.

abaisser [abɛ'se], *v.t.* to let down, to let fall, to lower; to diminish, to reduce; (*fig.*) to bring low, to humble, to depress; to roll out (*paste*). **s'abaisser,** *v.r.* to sink, to subside, to decrease, to abate, to decline; to humble oneself, to stoop, to cringe.

abajoue [aba'ʒu], *n.f.* (*Zool.*) cheek-pouch.

abalourdir [abalur'di:r], *v.t.* to make dull *or* stupid.

abalourdissement [abalurdis'mɑ̃], *n.m.* dullness, stupidity.

abandon [abɑ̃'dɔ̃], *n.m.* relinquishment, surrender, cession; abandonment, forlornness, destitution; lack of restraint; ***à l'abandon,*** at random, in confusion, at sixes and sevens; (*Naut.*) adrift.

abandonné [abɑ̃dɔ'ne], *a.* abandoned, forsaken; lost to decency, shameless, profligate.

abandonnement [abɑ̃dɔn'mɑ̃], *n.m.* abandonment; desertion; (*fig.*) dissoluteness, profligacy.

abandonnément [abɑ̃dɔne'mɑ̃], *adv.* freely, unreservedly.

abandonner [abɑ̃dɔ'ne], *v.t.* to give up, to hand over, to surrender; to renounce; to forsake, to desert, to abandon; to leave, to quit; to neglect. **s'abandonner,** *v.r.* to give oneself up, to give way (*à*); to indulge (*à*); to neglect oneself.

abaque [a'bak], *n.m.* (*Arch.*) abacus; (*Arith.*) abacus.

abasourdir [abazur'di:r], *v.t.* to stun, to dumbfound; (*fig.*) to astound.

abasourdissant [abazurdi'sɑ̃], *a.* astounding, overwhelming.

abasourdissement [abazurdis'mɑ̃], *n.m.* stupefaction, bewilderment.

***abat** [a'ba], *n.m.* killing, knocking down; heavy shower.

abâtardi [abɑtar'di], *a.* degenerate, corrupt, debased.

abâtardir [abɑtar'di:r], *v.t.* to render degenerate; to debase, to corrupt. **s'abâtardir,** *v.r.* to degenerate.

abâtardissement [abɑtardis'mɑ̃], *n.m.* degeneracy.

abatée or **abattée** [aba'te], *n.f.* swoop (*of plane*).

abat-jour [aba'ʒu:r], *n.m. inv.* sky-light; lamp-shade; shade for the eyes.

abat-son [aba'sɔ̃], *n.m.* (*pl. unchanged* or **abat-sons**) a series of sloping louvres in the window of a bell-tower for directing the sound downwards.

abattage [aba'ta:ʒ], *n.m.* cutting down, felling (*of trees*); slaughtering (*of animals*).

abattant [aba'tɑ̃], *n.m.* flap (*of a counter etc.*).

abattée [ABATÉE].

abattement [abat'mɑ̃], *n.m.* weakening; prostration; dejection, despondency, low spirits.

abatteur [aba'tœ:r], *n.m.* one who fells (*trees etc.*); slaughterer.

abattis [aba'ti], *n.m.* things *or* materials brought down (*such as houses, walls, trees*); slaughtered animals, game etc.; killing of game; giblets (*of poultry*).

abattoir [aba'twa:r], *n.m.* slaughter-house.

abattre [a'batr], *v.t.* (*conjug. like* BATTRE) to throw *or* hurl down; to knock, beat *or* batter down; to pull down; to fell; to kill, to slaughter; to overthrow, to demolish; to dishearten, to discourage, to depress. **s'abattre,** *v.r.* to throw oneself down, to fall, to tumble down; to crash (down); to abate; to be cast down *or* dejected; to pounce upon; ***le vent s'abat,*** the wind is dropping.

abattu [aba'ty], *a.* cast down, depressed, dejected; humbled, crestfallen.

abat-vent [aba'vɑ̃], *n.m. inv.* louvre boards (*of a window*); wind-cowl (*of a chimney*).

abat-voix [aba'vwa], *n.m. inv.* sounding-board (*of a pulpit*).

abbaye [abe'ji], *n.f.* monastery, abbey.

abbé [a'be], *n.m.* abbot, abbé; ***l'abbé Martin,*** Father Martin.

abbesse [a'bɛs], *n.f.* abbess.

A.B.C. [ɑbe'se], *n.m.* alphabet; primer, spelling-book.

abcéder [apse'de], *v.i.* (*conjug. like* CÉDER) to turn into an abscess, to gather.

abcès [ap'sɛ], *n.m.* abscess, gathering; ***abcès aux gencives,*** gumboil.

abdication [abdikɑ'sjɔ̃], *n.f.* abdication; renunciation (*of property etc.*); surrender (*of authority*).

abdiquer [abdi'ke], *v.t.* to abdicate, to resign, to renounce.

abdomen [abdɔ'mɛn], *n.m.* abdomen.

abdominal [abdɔmi'nal], *a.* abdominal.

abducteur [abdyk'tœ:r], *a.* (*Anat.*) abducent. —*n.m.* (*Anat.*) abductor.

abduction [abdyk'sjɔ̃], *n.f.* abduction.

abécédaire [abese'dɛ:r], *a.* alphabetical; ***ordre abécédaire,*** alphabetical order.—*n.m.* spelling-book; elementary reading-book; primer.

abecquer [abɛ'ke], *v.t.* to feed (*a bird*).

abeille [a'bɛ:j], *n.f.* bee; ***abeille mère,*** queen bee.

aberration [abɛrɑ'sjɔ̃], *n.f.* deviation from the normal *or* the correct course; (*Astron., Opt. etc.*) aberration.

abêtir [abɛ'ti:r], *v.t.* to render stupid; to dull, to blunt.—*v.i.* to become dull *or* stupid. **s'abêtir,** *v.r.* to grow stupid.

abêtissement [abɛtis'mɑ̃], *n.m.* stultification.

abhorrer [abɔ're], *v.t.* to abhor, to hate, to loathe.
abîme [a'bi:m], *n.m.* abyss, the deep, chasm; hell.
abîmé [abi'me], *a.* swallowed up, engulfed; ruined; damaged.
abîmer [abi'me], *v.t.* *to engulf, to swallow up; to ruin; to damage. **s'abîmer,** *v.r.* to fall into ruin; to be spoiled.
abject [ab'ʒɛkt], *a.* abject, base.
abjectement [abʒɛktə'mɑ̃], *adv.* abjectly.
abjection [abʒɛk'sjɔ̃], *n.f.* abasement, humiliation; vileness.
abjuration [abʒyrɑ'sjɔ̃], *n.f.* solemn renunciation, abjuration.
abjurer [abʒy're], *v.t.* to abjure, to renounce; to foreswear.
ablatif [abla'tif], *a.* (*fem.* **-tive**) ablative. —*n.m.* (*Gram.*) ablative (case).
ablation [ablɑ'sjɔ̃], *n.f.* (*Surg.*) removal (*of a part*).
able [abl], *n.m.* any small freshwater fish of the bleak family [ABLETTE].
ablette [a'blɛt], *n.f.* bleak [ABLE].
ablution [ably'sjɔ̃], *n.f.* ablution, washing, purification.
abnégation [abnegɑ'sjɔ̃], *n.f.* abnegation, renunciation, sacrifice, self-denial.
aboi [a'bwa], *n.m.* (*dog's*) bark, barking, baying; (*fig.*) desperate condition; ***aux abois,*** at bay.
aboiement [abwa'mɑ̃], *n.m.* barking, baying.
abolir [abɔ'li:r], *v.t.* to abolish, to repeal, to annul, to suppress.
abolissement [abɔlis'mɑ̃], *n.m.* abolition.
abolition [abɔli'sjɔ̃], *n.f.* abolition, repeal.
abominable [abɔmi'nabl], *a.* abominable, execrable; heinous.
abominablement [abɔminablə'mɑ̃], *adv.* abominably.
abomination [abɔminɑ'sjɔ̃], *n.f.* abomination, detestation, horror.
abominer [abɔmi'ne], *v.t.* to abominate, to detest.
abondamment [abɔ̃da'mɑ̃], *adv.* abundantly.
abondance [abɔ̃'dɑ̃:s], *n.f.* a great quantity, abundance, plenty; affluence.
abondant [abɔ̃'dɑ̃], *a.* abundant, plentiful, copious; exuberant, effusive.
abonder [abɔ̃'de], *v.i.* to abound, to be plentiful, to be in great quantity; ***abonder dans le sens de quelqu'un,*** to support somebody's views strongly.
abonné [abɔ'ne], *n.m.* (*fem.* **-ée**) subscriber (*to periodicals etc.*); season-ticket holder.
abonnement [abɔn'mɑ̃], *n.m.* subscription (*to periodicals, theatres etc.*); agreement; season-ticket; ***carte d'abonnement,*** season-ticket.
abonner (s') [sabɔ'ne], *v.r.* to become a subscriber.
abonnir [abɔ'ni:r], *v.t.* to mend, to improve (*wine*).—*v.i.* to become good. **s'abonnir,** *v.r.* to mend, to grow better.
abonnissement [abɔnis'mɑ̃], *n.m.* improvement.
abord [a'bɔ:r], *n.m.* landing; arrival; access, approach, meeting; onset, attack; (*pl.*) approaches, surroundings; ***d'abord,*** at first.
abordable [abɔr'dabl], *a.* accessible, easily approached, affable.
abordage [abɔr'da:ʒ], *n.m.* (*Naut.*) boarding; fouling, colliding.
abordée [abɔr'de], *n.f.* the act of meeting, accosting *or* beginning.
aborder [abɔr'de], *v.t.* to arrive at; to approach, to accost; to enter upon (*a subject etc.*); to grapple (*a vessel*); to run foul of (*a ship*).—*v.i.* to arrive; to land. **s'aborder,** *v.r.* to accost each other; to run foul of each other.
aborigène [abɔri'ʒɛ:n], *a.* native, original.—*n.m.* aboriginal, aborigine.
aborner [abɔr'ne], *v.t.* to mark out, to delimit.
abortif [abɔr'tif], *a.* (*fem.* **-tive**) abortive.
abouchement [abuʃ'mɑ̃], *n.m.* interview, conference.
aboucher [abu'ʃe], *v.t.* to bring (*things or persons*) together. **s'aboucher,** *v.r.* to have an interview, to confer (*with*); to get in touch (*with*).
aboutement [abut'mɑ̃], *n.m.* abutment; placing *or* fitting end to end.
abouter [abu'te], *v.t.* to join end to end.
aboutir [abu'ti:r], *v.i.* to end at *or* in, to result (*à*); (*Surg.*) to come to a head (*with aux.* ÊTRE *or* AVOIR).
aboutissant [abuti'sɑ̃], *a.* bordering upon, abutting on, ending in.
aboutissement [abutis'mɑ̃], *n.m.* result, issue.
aboyer [abwa'je], *v.i.* (*conjug. like* EMPLOYER) to bark, to bay, to yelp.
abracadabra [abrakada'bra], *n.m.* abracadabra (*magic word*).
abracadabrant [abrakada'brɑ̃], *a.* stupendous, amazing, stunning.
abrasif [abra'zif], *n.m.* abrasive.
abrégé [abre'ʒe], *a.* short, summary.—*n.m.* abridgment, résumé, précis, abstract, summary.
abrégement [abreʒ'mɑ̃], *n.m.* abridging, abridgment.
abréger [abre'ʒe], *v.t.* (*conjug. like* ASSIÉGER) to abridge, to shorten; to abbreviate.
abreuvage [abrœ'va:ʒ], **abreuvement** [abrœv'mɑ̃], *n.m.* watering, soaking, steaming.
abreuver [abrœ've], *v.t.* to water (*animals*); to water (*the ground etc.*). **s'abreuver,** *v.r.* to drink, to be watered (*of animals*).
abreuvoir [abrœ'vwa:r], *n.m.* watering-place, horse-pond; drinking-trough.
abréviation [abrevjɑ'sjɔ̃], *n.f.* abbreviation, shortening.
abri [a'bri], *n.m.* shelter, cover, refuge, dug-out.
abricot [abri'ko], *n.m.* apricot.
abricotier [abrikɔ'tje], *n.m.* apricot-tree.
abriter [abri'te], *v.t.* to shelter, to shade, to protect. **s'abriter,** *v.r.* to take refuge.
abrogation [abrɔgɑ'sjɔ̃], *n.f.* abrogation, repeal, annulment.
abroger [abrɔ'ʒe], *v.t.* (*conjug. like* MANGER) to abrogate, to repeal, to annul. **s'abroger,** *v.r.* to fall into disuse.
abrupt [a'brypt], *a.* abrupt, steep, sheer; (*fig.*) blunt, rugged, rough (*of style etc.*).
abruptement [abryptə'mɑ̃], *adv.* abruptly.
abruti [abry'ti], *a.* and *n.m.* (*fem.* **-e**) brutalized, stupid (person).
abrutir [abry'ti:r], *v.t.* to stupefy, to brutalize. **s'abrutir,** *v.r* to become brutalized *or* stupid.

abrutissant [abryti'sɑ̃], *a.* brutalizing, stupefying.

abrutissement [abrytis'mɑ̃], *n.m.* the act of brutalizing; brutishness, degradation.

absence [ap'sɑ̃:s], *n.f.* absence; want, lack; ***absence d'esprit***, absence of mind.

absent [ap'sɑ̃], *a.* absent, away from home; wandering, woolgathering.—*n.m.* (*fem.* **-e**) absentee.

absentéisme [apsɑ̃te'ism], *n.m.* absenteeism.

absenter (s') [sapsɑ̃'te], *v.r.* to absent oneself, to be away; to play truant.

abside [ap'si:d], *n.f.* apse.

absinthe [ap'sɛ̃:t], *n.f.* absinth; wormwood.

absolu [apsɔ'ly], *a.* absolute; despotic, arbitrary; unrestricted; peremptory; positive.

absolument [apsɔly'mɑ̃], *adv.* absolutely; arbitrarily.

absolution [apsɔly'sjɔ̃], *n.f.* absolution, acquittal.

absolutisme [apsɔly'tism], *n.m.* absolutism.

absorbant [apsɔr'bɑ̃], *a.* absorptive, absorbent; engrossing.—*n.m.* absorbent.

absorber [apsɔr'be], *v.t.* to absorb, to imbibe; to eat *or* drink; (*fig.*) to engross. **s'absorber**, *v.r.* to be absorbed; (*fig.*) to be entirely taken up with (***dans***).

absorption [apsɔrp'sjɔ̃], *n.f.* absorption.

absoudre [ap'sudr], *v.t. irr.* to absolve, to acquit; to exonerate, to forgive.

abstenir (s') [sapstə'ni:r], *v.r. irr.* (*conjug. like* TENIR) to abstain (*from voting*); to refrain, to forbear, to forgo.

abstention [apstɑ̃'sjɔ̃], *n.f.* abstention.

abstinence [apsti'nɑ̃:s], *n.f.* abstinence; temperance, sobriety; (*pl.*) fasts, fasting.

abstinent [apsti'nɑ̃], *a.* abstemious, sober.

abstraction [apstrak'sjɔ̃], *n.f.* abstraction, abstract question *or* idea.

abstraire [aps'trɛ:r], *v.t. irr.* (*conjug. like* TRAIRE) to abstract; to separate, to isolate.

abstrait [aps'trɛ], *a.* abstract, abstruse; absent-minded.

abstraitement [apstrɛt'mɑ̃], *adv.* abstractedly; separately; in the abstract.

abstrus [aps'try], *a.* abstruse; obscure.

absurde [ap'syrd], *a.* absurd, nonsensical, stupid, silly, preposterous.

absurdement [apsyrdə'mɑ̃], *adv.* absurdly, nonsensically.

absurdité [apsyrdi'te], *n.f.* absurdity, nonsense.

abus [a'by], *n.m.* abuse; grievance; misuse.

abuser [aby'ze], *v.t.* to deceive, to lead astray, to delude.—*v.i.* to misuse, to make ill use (***de***); to take advantage (***de***). **s'abuser**, *v.r.* to be mistaken, to deceive oneself.

abusif [aby'zif], *a.* (*fem.* **-sive**) irregular, improper.

abusivement [abyziv'mɑ̃], *adv.* irregularly, improperly.

abyssal [abi'sal], *a.* unfathomable.

abysse [a'bis], *n.m.* abyss, unfathomable gulf *or* depth.

Abyssinie [abisi'ni], **l'**, *f.* Abyssinia.

abyssinien [abisi'njɛ̃] (*fem.* **-enne**), **abyssin** [abi'sɛ̃], *a.* Abyssinian.—*n.m.* (**Abyssinien,** *fem.* **-enne**) Abyssinian (*person*).

acabit [aka'bi], *n.m.* quality (*of fruits, vegetables*); character, nature, stamp (*of persons*).

acacia [aka'sja], *n.m.* (*Bot.*) acacia.

académicien [akademi'sjɛ̃], *n.m.* academician.

académie [akade'mi], *n.f.* academy, society of learned men, *esp.* the Académie Française; school (*of dancing, fencing, riding etc.*).

académique [akade'mik], *a.* proper, appropriate *or* belonging to an academy, academic(al).

acagnarder [akaɲar'de], *v.t.* to make lazy. **s'acagnarder**, *v.r.* to drift into an idle, slothful life.

acajou [aka'ʒu], *n.m.* mahogany.

acanthe [a'kɑ̃:t], *n.f.* acanthus.

acariâtre [aka'rjɑ:tr], *a.* contrary, crabbed, cross-grained, quarrelsome, shrewish.

acariâtreté [akarjɑtrə'te], *n.f.* crabbedness, peevishness, shrewishness.

accablant [akɑ'blɑ̃], *a.* oppressive, overwhelming, crushing.

accablement [akɑblə'mɑ̃], *n.m.* prostration, oppression, extreme discouragement *or* dejection.

accabler [akɑ'ble], *v.t.* to crush, to overpower, to overcome; (*fig.*) to weigh down, to overload, to overwhelm.

accalmie [akal'mi], *n.f.* (*Naut.*) lull.

accaparant [akapa'rɑ̃], *a.* engrossing.

accaparement [akapar'mɑ̃], *n.m.* monopoly, monopolizing.

accaparer [akapa're], *v.t.* to monopolize, to hoard, to engross.

accapareur [akapa'rœ:r], *n.m.* (*fem.* **-euse**) monopolist, monopolizer, hoarder.

accéder [akse'de], *v.i.* (*conjug. like* CÉDER) to arrive, to reach, to have access; to accede, to comply with.

accélérateur [akselera'tœ:r], *a.* (*fem.* **-trice**) accelerative, with increasing speed.—*n.m.* (*Elec., Mech., Phot. etc.*) accelerator; (*fam.*) ***appuyer sur l'accélérateur***, to step on the gas.

accélération [akselerɑ'sjɔ̃], *n.f.* acceleration.

accéléré [aksele're], *a.* accelerated.

accélérer [aksele're], *v.t.* (*conjug. like* CÉDER) to accelerate, to quicken, to hasten, to press, to dispatch.

accent [ak'sɑ̃], *n.m.* pitch, accent, stress, tone; pronunciation; expression (*of the voice*).

accentuation [aksɑ̃tɥɑ'sjɔ̃], *n.f.* accentuation, stressing.

accentuer [aksɑ̃'tɥe], *v.t.* to accent, to accentuate, to stress.

acceptable [aksɛp'tabl], *a.* acceptable, worth accepting.

acceptation [aksɛptɑ'sjɔ̃], *n.f.* acceptance; acceptation.

accepter [aksɛp'te], *v.t.* to accept, to agree to, to welcome (*what is offered* or *proposed*).

acception [aksɛp'sjɔ̃], *n.f.* respect, regard, sense, meaning, acceptation.

accès [ak'sɛ], *n.m.* access, opportunity of approach, admittance; attack, fit, paroxysm.

accessibilité [aksɛsibili'te], *n.f.* accessibility.

accessible [aksɛ'sibl], *a.* accessible, approachable; within reach.

accession [aksɛ'sjɔ̃], *n.f.* accession; adhesion, union (*of a country, province etc. to another*).

accessit [aksɛ'sit], *n.m.* award of merit, honourable mention; 'proxime accessit'.

accessoire [aksɛ'swa:r], *a.* accessory, additional, subordinate.—*n.m.* an accessory; (*pl.*) (*Theat.*) properties.

accessoiriste [aksɛswa'rist], *n.m.* props man.

accident [aksi'dɑ̃], *n.m.* accident, fortuitous incident; casualty, mishap, mischance; unevenness, irregularity (*in the ground*).
accidenté [aksidɑ̃'te], *a.* varied, unequal (*of style etc.*); rough, uneven, broken, hilly (*of ground*); chequered (*of life, career etc.*).—*n.m.* (*fem.* **-ée**) one injured by an accident.
accidentel [aksidɑ̃'tɛl], *a.* (*fem.* **-elle**) accidental, adventitious, fortuitous, unexpected; ***signe accidentel,*** (*Mus.*) accidental.
accidentellement [aksidɑ̃tɛl'mɑ̃], *adv.* accidentally, casually, by chance.
accidenter [aksidɑ̃'te], *v.t.* to make irregular *or* uneven; to diversify, to chequer, to make picturesque.
accise [ak'si:z], *n.f.* (*Law*) inland duty, excise; ***préposé à l'accise,*** exciseman.
acclamation [aklamɑ'sjɔ̃], *n.f.* acclamation, cheering.
acclamer [aklɑ'me], *v.t.* to acclaim, to applaud, to cheer.
acclimatable [aklima'tabl], *a.* that may be acclimatized.
acclimatation [aklimatɑ'sjɔ̃], *n.f.* acclimatization.
acclimater [aklima'te], *v.t.* to acclimatize. **s'acclimater,** *v.r.* to become acclimatized.
accointance [akwɛ̃'tɑ̃:s], *n.f.* (*used generally in pl. and in a bad sense*) intimacy, familiarity; ***avoir des accointances*** (***avec***), to have dealings (*with*).
accointer [akwɛ̃'te], *v.t.* to make acquainted.
accolade [akɔ'lad], *n.f.* embrace; kiss; accolade (*in knighting*).
accolader (**s'**) [sakɔla'de], *v.r.* to embrace mutually.
accolage [akɔ'la:ʒ], *n.m.* tying up training (*branches etc.*).
accolement [akɔl'mɑ̃], *n.m.* joining, uniting.
accoler [akɔ'le], *v.t.* to embrace; to tie up, to fasten, to place against; (*fig.*) to couple, to join together, to bracket.
accommodable [akɔmɔ'dabl], *a.* that may be arranged; adjustable.
accommodage [akɔmɔ'da:ʒ]. *n.m.* preparation *or* dressing (*of meat*).
accommodant [akɔmɔ'dɑ̃], *a.* accommodating, easy-going, courteous.
accommodation [akɔmɔdɑ'sjɔ̃], *n.f.* accommodation.
accommodement [akɔmɔd'mɑ̃], *n.m.* accommodation, arrangement, composition; settlement, reconciliation, compromise.
accommoder [akɔmɔ'de], *v.t.* to adapt, to accommodate, to fit, to adjust; to reconcile; to conciliate; to dress, to trim; to cook, to do up; to suit, to be convenient. **s'accommoder,** *v.r.* to agree, to come to terms; to accommodate oneself, to adapt oneself (***à***); to put up with (***de***).
accompagnateur [akɔ̃paɲa'tœ:r], *n.m.* (*fem.* **-trice**) accompanist (*with instrument* or *voice*); conductor (*of a tour*).
accompagnement [akɔ̃paɲ'mɑ̃], *n.m.* accompanying; attendance, retinue; an accompaniment, an accessory; (*Mus.*) accompaniment.
accompagner [akɔ̃pa'ɲe], *v.t.* to accompany, to attend on; to go with, to escort; (*Mus.*) to accompany.
accompli [akɔ̃'pli], *a.* accomplished, performed, fulfilled; complete, faultless perfect, out and out.
accomplir [akɔ̃'pli:r], *v.t.* to fulfil, to effect, to perform; to realize, to carry out.
accomplissement [akɔ̃plis'mɑ̃], *n.m.* accomplishment, fulfilment, realization.
accon, acconier [ACON etc.].
accord [a'kɔ:r], *n.m.* accord, concurrence, unanimity, harmony; agreement, bargain; convention, settlement; (*Mus.*) chord; ***être d'accord,*** to agree; ***d'accord,*** granted, agreed.
accordable [akɔr'dabl], *a.* that may be accorded; reconcilable; (*Mus.*) tunable.
accordage [akɔr'da:ʒ], **accordement** [akɔrdə'mɑ̃], *n.m.* tuning (*of a musical instrument*).
accordailles [akɔr'dɑ:j], *n.f.* (*used only in pl.*) betrothal.
accordant [akɔr'dɑ̃], *a.* accordant, harmonious.
accordé [akɔr'de], *n.m.* (*fem.* **-ée**) fiancé, fiancée; ***les accordés,*** the bride and bridegroom.
accordéon [akɔrde'ɔ̃], *n.m.* accordion.
accordéoniste [akɔrdeɔ'nist], *n.* accordionist.
accorder [akɔr'de], *v.t.* to bring into harmony *or* accord, to make agree, to reconcile; to concede, to grant; to admit, to avow; (*Mus.*) to tune, to harmonize; to bestow (*hand in marriage*). **s'accorder,** *v.r.* to agree, to concur; to correspond; to suit, to be suited.
accordeur [akɔr'dœ:r], *n.m.* tuner (*of musical instruments*).
accordoir [akɔr'dwa:r], *n.m.* tuning-hammer, -key *or* -cone.
accore [a'kɔ:r], *a.* abrupt, sheer, vertical (*of a coast*).
accort [a'kɔ:r], *a.* gracious, courteous.
accostable [akɔs'tabl], *a.* easy of access, approachable.
accostage [akɔs'ta:ʒ], *n.m.* the act of accosting, approaching *or* drawing alongside.
accoster [akɔs'te], *v.t.* to accost, to go up to; (*Naut.*) to come alongside.
accotement [akɔt'mɑ̃], *n.m.* (*Civ. Eng.*) roadside; footpath.
accoter [akɔ'te], *v.t.* to prop up, to support, to stay. **s'accoter,** *v.r.* to lean (***contre***).
accotoir [akɔ'twa:r], *n.m.* prop, support, leaning-post.
accouardir [akwar'di:r], *v.t.* to make a coward. **s'accouardir,** *v.r.* to turn coward.
accouchée [aku'ʃe], *n.f.* woman in childbirth, woman who has just had a child.
accouchement [akuʃ'mɑ̃], *n.m.* childbirth, delivery, confinement; ***centre d'accouchement,*** maternity home.
accoucher [aku'ʃe], *v.t.* to deliver (*a woman*). —*v.i.* to lie in, to be brought to bed, to be delivered.
accoucheur [aku'ʃœ:r], *n.m.* male midwife, accoucheur.
accoucheuse [aku'ʃø:z], *n.f.* midwife.
accoudement [akud'mɑ̃], *n.m.* the act of leaning (*on*).
accouder (**s'**) [saku'de], *v.r.* to lean on one's elbow.
accoudoir [aku'dwa:r], *n.m.* elbow-rest; (*Arch.*) rail, balustrade.

accouple [a'kupl], *n.f.* leash (*for tying dogs in couples*).
accouplement [akuplə'mɑ̃], *n.m.* coupling; pairing.
accoupler [aku'ple], *v.t.* to couple; to join together in pairs; (*Elec.*) to connect, to group (*batteries etc.*).
accourci [akur'si], *n.m.* abridgement (*of a book*).
accourcir [akur'si:r], *v.t.* to shorten, to abridge, to curtail. **s'accourcir**, *v.r.* to become shorter, to decrease.
accourcissement [akursis'mɑ̃], *n.m.* shortening, diminution.
accourir [aku'ri:r], *v.i. irr.* (*conjug. like* COURIR) to run up to, to hasten, to flock.
accoutrement [akutrə'mɑ̃], *n.m.* garb, dress, *esp.* as an object of ridicule.
accoutrer [aku'tre], *v.t.* to rig out, to dress. **s'accoutrer**, *v.r.* to dress absurdly, to rig oneself out.
accoutumance [akuty'mɑ̃:s], *n.f.* habit, custom, wont, usage.
accoutumé [akuty'me], *a.* ordinary, accustomed, habitual.
accoutumer [akuty'me], *v.t.* to accustom, to habituate, to inure.—*v.i.* (*only in compound tenses*) to use, to be wont. **s'accoutumer**, *v.r.* to be accustomed, to be used (*à*).
accouvage [aku'va:ʒ], *n.m.* hatching (*esp. by artificial means*), incubation.
accouver [aku've], *v.t.* to set (*a hen etc.*).—*v.i.* to sit, to hatch.
accréditation [akreditɑ'sjɔ̃], *n.f.* accreditation, accrediting (*of an ambassador*).
accréditer [akredi'te], *v.t.* to give credit, standing *or* sanction to; to authorize; to accredit (*an ambassador etc.*); to confirm, to spread (*rumours etc.*). **s'accréditer**, *v.r.* to gain credit *or* reputation; to ingratiate oneself; to spread (*of rumours etc.*).
accréditeur [akredi'tœ:r], *n.m.* guarantor, surety.
accroc [a'kro], *n.m.* impediment, hitch; hindrance; rent, tear.
accrochage [akrɔ'ʃa:ʒ], *n.m.* hanging, hooking, hitching; catching, retarding, stopping; grazing (*vehicles*).
accroche-cœur [akrɔʃ'kœ:r], *n.m. inv.* kiss-curl.
accrochement [akrɔʃ'mɑ̃], *n.m.* hooking, catching (*in something*).
accrocher [akrɔ'ʃe], *v.t.* to hang upon a hook; to hook, to catch, to hitch, to catch and tear; to get hold of; to pick up (*a wireless station*). **s'accrocher**, *v.r.* to catch in, to be caught *or* hooked (***par***); to lay hold of, to cling (*à*).
accroire [a'krwɑ:r], *v.t. irr.* (*used only in the infinitive after* ***faire***) to believe.
accroissement [akrwɑs'mɑ̃], *n.m.* increase, growth, enlargement, extension.
accroître [a'krwɑ:tr], *v.t. irr.* (*conjug. like* CROÎTRE *but* ***p.p.*** **accru**, *without circumflex*) to increase, to augment, to enlarge, to amplify. **s'accroître**, *v.r.* to increase, to grow.
accroupi [akru'pi], *a.* crouched, crouching.
accroupir (s') [sakru'pi:r], *v.r.* to sit down on the hams *or* heels, to squat, to crouch.
accroupissement [akrupis'mɑ̃], *n.m.* cowering, squatting, crouching.
accru [a'kry], *n.m.* (*Gard.*) sucker, scion.
accrue [a'kry], *n.f.* increase of land through the retreat of waters; encroachment of a forest on adjoining land.
accu [a'ky], *n.m. abbr.* [ACCUMULATEUR].
accueil [a'kœ:j], *n.m.* reception, welcome, greeting.
accueillir [akœ'ji:r], *v.t. irr.* (*conjug. like* CUEILLIR) to receive (*well* or *ill*); to receive graciously, to welcome.
acculer [aky'le], *v.t.* to drive into a corner; to bring to a standstill. **s'acculer**, *v.r.* to set one's back against something.
accumulateur [akymyla'tœ:r], *a.* (*fem.* **-trice**) storing, heaping up, hoarding up.—*n.m.* accumulator (*person* or *thing*); (*Elec.*) storage cell *or* battery.
accumulation [akymylɑ'sjɔ̃], *n.f.* accumulation; mass, pile.
accumuler [akymy'le], *v.t.* to accumulate, to pile up, to amass. **s'accumuler**, *v.r.* to accumulate, to increase.
accusable [aky'zabl], *a.* accusable, chargeable.
accusateur [akyza'tœ:r], *a.* (*fem.* **-trice**) accusing, accusatory.—*n.m.* (*fem.* **-trice**) accuser, denouncer.
accusatif [akyza'tif], *a.* (*fem.* **-tive**) and *n.m.* (*Gram.*) accusative (case); ***à l'accusatif***, in the accusative.
accusation [akyzɑ'sjɔ̃], *n.f.* accusation, indictment, charge; (*fig.*) prosecution; ***mise en accusation***, arraignment.
accusatoire [akyza'twa:r], *a.* accusatory
accusé [aky'ze], *n.m.* (*fem.* **-ée**) the accused, prisoner, defendant; ***accusé de réception***, acknowledgment of a letter, receipt.
accuser [aky'ze], *v.t.* to impute, to charge with; to reproach, to blame; to indict, to impeach, to prosecute. **s'accuser**, *v.r.* to admit, to avow, to confess.
acéphale [ase'fal], *a.* acephalous, headless.
acérain [ase'rɛ̃], *a.* like *or* pertaining to steel, steely.
acerbe [a'sɛrb], *a.* sour, harsh, sharp, astringent; (*fig.*) bitter, acrimonious.
acerbité [asɛrbi'te], *n.f.* acerbity, harshness; (*fig.*) bitterness, severity.
acéré [ase're], *a.* steely, steeled; sharp, keen; (*fig.*) mordant, trenchant, acute.
acérer [ase're], *v.t.* (*conjug. like* CÉDER) to steel; to sharpen, to render biting, incisive *or* mordant.
acétate [ase'tat], *n.m.* (*Chem.*) acetate.
acéteux [ase'tø], *a.* (*fem.* **-euse**) acetous, sour, tasting like vinegar.
acétique [ase'tik], *a.* acetic.
acétone [ase'tɔn], *n.m.* acetone.
acétoselle [asetɔ'sɛl], *n.f.* wood-sorrel.
acétylène [aseti'lɛ:n], *n.m.* acetylene.
achalandage [aʃalɑ̃'da:ʒ], *n.m.* custom, customers; goodwill (*of a shop*).
achalandé [aʃalɑ̃'de], *a.* having plenty of custom; ***boutique bien achalandée***, a well-frequented shop.
achalander [aʃalɑ̃'de], *v.t.* to get custom, to attract customers, to draw trade.
acharné [aʃar'ne], *a.* fleshed, fierce, tenacious, implacable; stubborn, obstinate, intense.
acharnement [aʃarnə'mɑ̃], *n.m.* tenacity; rancour, animosity, fury; stubbornness, obstinacy, desperation.

acharner [aʃar'ne], *v.t.* to flesh; to set on; to excite, to madden; to embitter, to envenom. **s'acharner,** *v.r.* to be intent, bent *or* obstinately set upon; to set one's heart upon, to persist in; to be infuriated *or* implacable.
achat [a'ʃa], *n.m.* purchasing, buying; purchase; ***faire des achats,*** to go shopping; ***pouvoir d'achat,*** purchasing power.
acheminement [aʃmin'mɑ̃], *n.m.* progress, advance, conveying.
acheminer [aʃmi'ne], *v.t.* to send on (*towards a place* or *object*); to train (*a horse*). **s'acheminer,** *v.r.* to set out (***pour***), to make one's way towards.
achetable [aʃ'tabl], *a.* purchasable.
acheter [aʃ'te], *v.t.* (*conjug. like* AMENER) to buy, to purchase; (*fig.*) to bribe. **s'acheter,** *v.r.* to be bought; to be for sale, to be venal.
acheteur [aʃ'tœ:r], *n.m.* (*fem.* **-euse**) buyer, purchaser.
achevage [aʃ'va:ʒ], *n.m.* completion, finishing; finish (*of a work of art*).
achevé [aʃ've], *a.* finished, accomplished, perfect, exquisite; absolute, downright, consummate, arrant.
achèvement [aʃɛv'mɑ̃], *n.m.* completion, conclusion.
achever [aʃ've], *v.t.* (*conjug. like* AMENER) to finish, to terminate; to put the finishing touch to; to complete, to achieve; to consummate, to perfect; (*fig.*) to do for completely, to ruin, to kill.
Achille [a'ʃil], *m.* Achilles.
achoppement [aʃɔp'mɑ̃], *n.m.* obstacle, impediment; unforeseen difficulty, embarrassment; ***pierre d'achoppement,*** stumbling-block.
achopper [aʃɔ'pe], *v.i.* and **s'achopper,** *v.r.* to stumble, to knock against something; (*fig.*) to come to grief; to fail.
achromatopsie [akrɔmatɔp'si], *n.f.* achromatopsy, colour-blindness.
acide [a'sid], *a.* acid, sour, tart, sharp.—*n.m.* acid.
acidifier [asidi'fje], *v.t.* to acidify. **s'acidifier,** *v.r.* to become acidified.
acidité [asidi'te], *n.f.* acidity, sourness, sharpness, tartness.
acidule [asi'dyl], *a.* subacid, acidulous.
acidulé [asidy'le], *a.* acidulated; ***bonbons acidulés,*** acid drops.
aciduler [asidy'le], *v.t.* to acidulate.
acier [a'sje], *n.m.* steel; ***acier chromé,*** chrome steel; ***acier coulé*** or ***fondu,*** cast steel; ***acier doux,*** mild steel; ***acier inoxydable,*** stainless steel.
aciération [asjerɑ'sjɔ̃], *n.f.* steeling, plating with steel.
aciérer [asje're], *v.t.* (*conjug. like* CÉDER) to convert into steel, to cover with steel; to acierate. **s'aciérer,** *v.r.* to steel oneself.
aciéreux [asje'rø], *a.* (*fem.* **-euse**) steely, like steel.
aciérie [asje'ri], *n.f.* steel factory, steelworks.
acné [ak'ne], *n.f.* (*Med.*) acne.
acolyte [akɔ'lit], *n.m.* (*Eccles.*) acolyte; (*fig.*) assistant, confederate, associate, accomplice.
acompte [a'kɔ̃:t], *n.m.* instalment, partial payment.
acon or **accon** [a'kɔ̃], *n.m.* small lighter, punt.
aconier or **acconier** [akɔ'nje], *n.m.* lighterman.
aconit [akɔ'nit], *n.m.* aconite.
acoquinant [akɔki'nɑ̃], *a.* alluring, engaging, captivating.
acoquiner [akɔki'ne], *v.t.* to make fond, to allure, to bewitch, to captivate. **s'acoquiner,** *v.r.* (*fam.*) to be bewitched, to be greatly attached to.
Açores [a'sɔ:r], **les,** *f.pl.* the Azores.
à-côté [ako'te], *n.m.* aside; (*pl.*) little extras.
à-coup [a'ku], *n.m.* jerk, jolt; sudden stop.
acousticien [akusti'sjɛ̃], *n.m.* (*fem.* **-enne**) acoustician.
acoustique [akus'tik], *a.* acoustic.—*n.f.* acoustics.
acquéreur [ake'rœ:r], *n.m.* (*fem.* **-euse**) buyer, purchaser.
acquérir [ake'ri:r], *v.t. irr.* to purchase, to buy, to get; to earn, to win, to gain; to acquire, to obtain. **s'acquérir,** *v.r.* to get *or* win for oneself; to be acquired, obtained *or* purchased.
acquiescement [akjɛs'mɑ̃], *n.m.* acquiescence, compliance, consent, willingness.
acquiescer [akjɛ'se], *v.i.* (*conjug. like* COMMENCER) to acquiesce, to agree, to assent, to yield, to comply.
acquis [a'ki], *a.* acquired, secured.—*n.m.* acquirements, attainments, experience.
acquisitif [akizi'tif], *a.* (*fem.* **-tive**) acquisitive.
acquisition [akizi'sjɔ̃], *n.f.* acquisition, acquiring, attaining, acquirement, attainment; purchase, conquest.
acquisivité [akizivi'te], *n.f.* acquisitiveness.
acquit [a'ki], *n.m.* receipt, discharge, release, acquittance; (*Billiards*) break (*i.e. start*).
acquittement [akit'mɑ̃], *n.m.* payment, quittance; (*Law*) acquittal.
acquitter [aki'te], *v.t.* to pay; to discharge, to pay off (*a dependant*); to acquit. **s'acquitter,** *v.r.* to fulfil, to perform; to pay off one's debts, to be quits (*in gambling*); to acquit oneself (*well* or *ill*).
acre [akr], *n.f.* acre.
âcre [ɑ:kr], *a.* sour, sharp, tart, acrid; (*fig.*) bitter, pungent, caustic.
âcrement [ɑ:krə'mɑ̃], *adv.* tartly, sourly.
âcreté [ɑ:krə'te], *n.f.* sourness, acridity, sharpness, tartness, acrimony.
acrimonie [akrimɔ'ni], *n.f.* bitterness, sharpness, keenness, acrimony.
acrimonieux [akrimɔ'njø], *a.* (*fem.* **-euse**) pungent, acrimonious, ill-natured, sharp.
acrobate [akrɔ'bat], *n.* acrobat, rope-dancer.
acrobatie [akrɔba'si], *n.f.* acrobatics; (*Av.*) stunt.
acrobatique [akrɔba'tik], *a.* acrobatic.
acrobatisme [akrɔba'tism], *n.m.* acrobatics.
acrocéphale [akrɔse'fal], *a.* having a pointed head, acrocephalic, acrocephalous.—*n.* a person with such a head.
acropole [akrɔ'pɔl], *n.f.* acropolis.
acrostiche [akrɔs'tiʃ], *a.* and *n.m.* acrostic.
acrotère [akrɔ'tɛ:r], *n.m.* (*Arch.*) acroterium, ornamental summit (*of a pediment*).
acte [akt], *n.m.* action, deed; (*Law*) deed, indenture; instrument; document, charter; (*Theat.*) act; (*pl.*) records, public registers, rolls, transactions, proceedings; ***acte de naissance,*** birth certificate.
acteur [ak'tœ:r], *n.m.* (*fem.* **-trice**) actor; actress; player.

actif [ak'tif], *a.* (*fem.* **-tive**) active, busy, energetic, assiduous; nimble, brisk, agile; (*Gram. etc.*) active.—*n.m.* (*Gram.*) active voice; assets, credit balance.
action [ak'sjɔ̃], *n.f.* action, operation, work; activity, motion; deed, feat, performance; fight, engagement, battle; (*Law*) action, law-suit; (*Theat.*) gesture; (*Lit.*) subject, action, plot; (*Comm.*) share, stock.
actionnaire [aksjɔ'nɛːr], *n.* shareholder.
actionnariat [aksjɔna'rja], *n.m.* shareholding; ***actionnariat ouvrier***, industrial co-partnership.
actionner [aksjɔ'ne], *v.t.* to bring an action against, to sue at law; to bestir, to rouse up, to set going; to operate, to run, to drive. **s'actionner**, *v.r.* to bestir oneself.
activement [aktiv'mɑ̃], *adv.* actively, vigorously.
activer [akti've], *v.t.* to press, to accelerate, to forward, to expedite, to stir up (*a fire, people*).
activisme [akti'vism], *n.m.* (*Polit.*) militancy, activism.
activiste [akti'vist], *n.m.* activist.
activité [aktivi'te], *n.f.* activity, full swing; nimbleness, alacrity, promptitude, dispatch.
actrice [ak'tris], [ACTEUR].
actuaire [ak'tɥɛːr], *n.m.* actuary.
actualisation [aktɥalizɑ'sjɔ̃], *n.f.* actualization; realization.
actualiser [aktɥali'ze], *v.t.* to bring up to date. **s'actualiser**, *v.r.* to become real.
actualité [aktɥali'te], *n.f.* actuality; event of the moment, present interest; (*Cine.*) ***les actualités***, the newsreel.
actuel [ak'tɥɛl], *a.* (*fem.* **-elle**) present, of the present time.
actuellement [aktɥɛl'mɑ̃], *adv.* now, at the present time.
acuité [akɥi'te], *n.f.* sharpness, acuteness, keenness.
acutangle [aky'tɑ̃ːgl], **acutangulaire** [akytɑ̃gy'lɛːr], *a.* acute-angled (*of triangles etc.*).
acutesse [aky'tɛs], *n.f.* acuteness, sharpness.
adage [a'daːʒ], *n.m.* adage, proverb, saying.
Adam [a'dɑ̃], *m.* Adam.
adamantin [adamɑ̃'tɛ̃], *a.* adamantine.
adaptable [adap'tabl], *a.* adaptable.
adaptateur [adapta'tœːr], *n.m.* adapter, converter.
adaptation [adaptɑ'sjɔ̃], *n.f.* adaptation.
adapter [adap'te], *v.t.* to adapt, to adjust, to apply (*à*); to fit, to make suitable. **s'adapter**, *v.r.* to fit, to suit, to adapt oneself (*to*).
addition [adi'sjɔ̃], *n.f.* adding up, addition; an addition; bill, reckoning; check.
additionnel [adisjɔ̃'nɛl], *a.* (*fem.* **-elle**) additional.
additionner [adisjɔ'ne], *v.t.* to add up.
Adélaïde [adela'id], *f.* Adelaide.
Adèle [a'dɛl], *f.* Adela.
adénite [ade'nit], *n.f.* adenitis, inflammation of the glands.
adénoïde [adenɔ'id], *a.* adenoid; ***végétations adénoïdes***, adenoids.
adent [a'dɑ̃], *n.m.* dovetail, tenon.
adenter [adɑ̃'te], *v.t.* to dovetail, to join with mortise and tenon.
adepte [a'dɛpt], *n.m.* adept, initiate, follower.
adéquat [ade'kwa], *a.* adequate; (*Phil.*) equal in content; appropriate.
adhérence [ade'rɑ̃ːs], *n.f.* adhesion, adherence; (*fig.*) attachment.
adhérent [ade'rɑ̃], *a.* adherent.—*n.m.* (*fem.* **-e**) adherent, follower, partisan.
adhérer [ade're], *v.i.* (*conjug. like* CÉDER) to adhere, to cling; (*fig.*) to hold (*à*), to cleave (*to a sect etc.*).
adhésif [ade'zif], *a.* (*fem.* **-sive**) adhesive.—*n.m.* (*Phot.*) dry-mounting tissue.
adhésion [ade'zjɔ̃], *n.f.* adhesion, adherence, union; compliance; joining (*a party*).
adhésivité [adezivi'te], *n.f.* adhesiveness.
adieu [a'djø], *int.* adieu, good-bye, farewell. —*n.m.* (*pl.* **-eux**) farewell, parting, leave; ***faire ses adieux à***, to take leave of, to say good-bye to.
adipeux [adi'pø], *a.* (*fem.* **-euse**) adipose, fat.
adiposité [adipɔzi'te], *n.f.* adipose *or* fatty condition.
adjacence [adʒa'sɑ̃ːs], *n.f.* adjacency.
adjacent [adʒa'sɑ̃], *a.* adjacent, bordering upon, contiguous.
adjectif [adʒɛk'tif], *a.* (*fem.* **-tive**) (*Gram.*) adjectival.—*n.m.* adjective.
adjectivement [adʒɛktiv'mɑ̃], *adv.* adjectivally.
adjoindre [ad'ʒwɛ̃ːdr], *v.t. irr.* (*conjug. like* CRAINDRE) to adjoin, to associate, to add as an assistant. **s'adjoindre**, *v.r.* to join as a partner *or* associate; to take on.
adjoint [ad'ʒwɛ̃], *a.* adjunct, associate.—*n.m.* (*fem.* **-e**) associate, assistant, deputy; ***adjoint au maire***, deputy-mayor.
adjonction [adʒɔ̃k'sjɔ̃], *n.f.* adjunction.
adjudant [adʒy'dɑ̃], *n.m.* company sergeant-major; warrant-officer; ***adjudant-major***, adjutant.
adjudicataire [adʒydika'tɛːr], *a.* and *n.* contracting party; successful tenderer, highest bidder.
adjudicateur [adʒydika'tœːr], *n.m.* (*fem.* **-trice**) adjudicator, awarder; auctioneer.
adjudication [adʒydikɑ'sjɔ̃], *n.f.* auction; knocking down; adjudication.
adjuger [adʒy'ʒe], *v.t.* (*conjug. like* MANGER) to adjudge, to adjudicate, to knock down (*to the highest bidder*); to award; ***adjugé!*** (*at auctions*) gone!
adjuration [adʒyrɑ'sjɔ̃], *n.f.* adjuration, imprecation.
adjurer [adʒy're], *v.t.* to adjure, to conjure; to call upon, to beseech.
admettre [ad'mɛtr], *v.t. irr.* (*conjug. like* METTRE) to admit, to let in; to concede, to allow, to acknowledge.
administrateur [administra'tœːr], *n.m.* (*fem.* **-trice**) manager, director; administrator, administratrix, trustee (*of an estate*).
administratif [administra'tif], *a.* (*fem.* **-tive**) administrative.
administration [administrɑ'sjɔ̃], *n.f.* administration, management, direction, government; (*collect.*) the management, the administration.
administré [adminis'tre], *n.m.* (*fem.* **-ée**) person under one's administration *or* jurisdiction.
administrer [adminis'tre], *v.t.* to manage, to govern, to direct; to administer, to dispense.

admirable [admi'rabl], *a.* admirable; wonderful.
admirablement [admirablə'mɑ̃], *adv.* admirably; wonderfully.
admirateur [admira'tœːr], *n.m.* (*fem.* **-trice**) admirer, praiser.
admiratif [admira'tif], *a.* (*fem.* **-tive**) admiring, wondering.
admiration [admirɑ'sjɔ̃], *n.f.* admiration.
admirer [admi're], *v.t.* to admire.
admissibilité [admisibili'te], *n.f.* admissibility.
admissible [admi'sibl], *a.* admittable, admissible.
admission [admi'sjɔ̃], *n.f.* admission, admittance; ***soupape d'admission***, inlet valve.
admonestation [admɔnɛstɑ'sjɔ̃], *n.f.* admonishment, admonition.
admonester [admɔnɛs'te], *v.t.* to reprimand, to admonish.
admoniteur [admɔni'tœːr], *n.m.* (*fem.* **-trice**) admonisher.
admonitif [admɔni'tif], *a.* (*fem.* **-tive**) admonitory.
admonition [admɔni'sjɔ̃], *n.f.* (*chiefly R.-C. Ch.*) admonition, advice, reprimand.
adolescence [adɔlɛ'sɑ̃ːs], *n.f.* adolescence.
adolescent [adɔlɛ'sɑ̃], *a.* adolescent.—*n.m.* (*fem.* **-e**) adolescent, youth, teenager.
Adonis [adɔ'niːs], *n.m.* Adonis, beau.
adonné [adɔ'ne], *a.* given to, addicted, devoted. **s'adonner**, *v.r.* to give, devote *or* addict oneself (*à*).
adopté [adɔp'te], *a.* adopted *or* adoptive (*child*).
adopter [adɔp'te], *v.t.* to adopt; to embrace, to espouse; to pass, to carry (*a bill*).
adoptif [adɔp'tif], *a.* (*fem.* **-tive**) adoptive, by adoption.
adoption [adɔp'sjɔ̃], *n.f.* adoption.
adorable [adɔ'rabl], *a.* adorable, charming, delightful, exquisite.
adorablement [adɔrablə'mɑ̃], *adv.* adorably, delightfully.
adorateur [adɔra'tœːr], *n.m.* (*fem.* **-trice**) adorer, worshipper.
adoration [adɔrɑ'sjɔ̃], *n.f.* adoration, worship; admiration, respect, reverence.
adorer [adɔ're], *v.t.* to adore, to worship.
adossé [ado'se], *a.* with one's back against.
adosser [ado'se], *v.t.* to set *or* lean with the back against; to put back to back. **s'adosser**, *v.r.* to lean one's back (***à, contre***).
adoucir [adu'siːr], *v.t.* to soften, to sweeten; to mitigate, to alleviate, to smooth. **s'adoucir**, *v.r.* to grow mild *or* soft; to get milder (*of weather*).
adoucissement [adusis'mɑ̃], *n.m.* softening, sweetening; assuaging, appeasing; ease, mitigation, alleviation; consolation.
adrénaline [adrena'lin], *n.f.* adrenalin.
adresse [a'drɛs], *n.f.* address; memorial, a document addressed to an assembly *or* person in authority; skill, dexterity, cleverness.
adresser [adrɛ'se], *v.t.* to direct, to address; to turn, to direct (*one's steps etc.*). **s'adresser**, *v.r.* to be directed; to speak, to address oneself, to make application, to appeal (*à*); ***s'adresser ici***, apply within.
Adriatique [adria'tik], **l'**, *f.* the Adriatic.
adroit [a'drwɑ], *a.* ingenious, clever, skilful; artful.
adroitement [adrwɑt'mɑ̃], *adv.* skilfully, artfully, cleverly.
adulateur [adyla'tœːr], *a.* (*fem.* **-trice**) flattering, adulatory.—*n.m.* (*fem.* **-trice**) adulator, flatterer, sycophant.
adulatif [adyla'tif], *a.* (*fem.* **-tive**) flattering adulatory.
adulation [adylɑ'sjɔ̃], *n.f.* adulation, flattery sycophancy.
aduler [ady'le], *v.t.* to flatter, to fawn upon.
adulte [a'dylt], *a.* adult, grown-up.—*n.* adult.
adultère [adyl'tɛːr], *a.* adulterous; ***femme adultère***, adulteress.—*n.m.* adultery.—*n.* adulterer, adulteress.
adultérer [adylte're], *v.t.* (*conjug. like* CÉDER) (*Pharm.*) to adulterate; (*Law*) to falsify (*money*); (*fig.*) to corrupt, to pervert, to falsify.
adultérin [adylte'rɛ̃], *a.* adulterine.
advenir [advə'niːr], *v.i. irr.* (*used only in inf. and 3rd pers.*) to occur, to happen, to befall.
adventice [advɑ̃'tis], *a.* adventitious.
adventif [advɑ̃'tif], *a.* (*fem.* **-tive**) (*Bot.*) adventitious, casual.
adverbe [ad'vɛrb], *n.m.* adverb.
adverbial [advɛr'bjal], *a.* adverbial.
adverbialement [advɛrbjal'mɑ̃], *adv.* adverbially.
adversaire [advɛr'sɛːr], *n.* adversary, opponent.
adverse [ad'vɛrs], *a.* adverse, opposite, contrary; calamitous.
adversité [advɛrsi'te], *n.f.* adversity, misfortune.
aérage [ae'raːʒ], *n.m.* ventilation, airing.
aérateur [aera'tœːr], *n.m.* ventilator.
aération [aerɑ'sjɔ̃], *n.f.* ventilation, airing.
aéré [ae're], *p.p.* ventilated.—*a.* airy.
aérer [ae're], *v.t.* (*conjug. like* CÉDER) to ventilate, to air, to renew the air of; (*Chem.*) to aerate.
aérien [ae'rjɛ̃], *a.* (*fem.* **-enne**) aerial; living *or* occurring in the air, celestial; (*fig.*) light, airy; ***base aérienne***, air-base; ***fil aérien***, overhead wire; ***ligne aérienne***, airline; ***pont aérien***, air-lift; ***raid aérien***, air-raid.
aérifère [aeri'fɛːr], *a.* air-conducting.
aérification [aerifikɑ'sjɔ̃], *n.f.* gasification.
aérifier [aeri'fje], *v.t.* to gasify.
aéro-club [aerɔ'klœb], *n.m.* (*pl.* **aéro-clubs**) flying-club.
aérodrome [aerɔ'droːm], *n.m.* aerodrome, airfield.
aérodynamique [aerɔdina'mik], *a.* aerodynamic, streamlined.—*n.f.* aerodynamics.
aérogare [aero'gaːr], *n.f.* air-terminal
aérographe [aerɔ'graf], *n.m.* aerograph.
aérographie [aerɔgra'fi], *n.f.* aerography.
aérolithe [aerɔ'lit], *n.m.* aerolite.
aérolithique [aerɔli'tik], *a.* aerolitic.
aérologie [aerɔlɔ'ʒi], *n.f.* aerology.
aéromètre [aerɔ'mɛtr], *n.m.* aerometer, airpoise.
aéronaute [aerɔ'noːt], *n.* aeronaut.
aéronautique [aerɔno'tik], *a.* aeronautic.—*n.f.* aeronautics, aerial navigation.
aéronef [aerɔ'nɛf], *n.m.* air-ship.
aéroplane [aerɔ'plan], *n.m.* aeroplane.
aéroport [aerɔ'pɔːr], *n.m.* airport.
aéroporté [aerɔpɔr'te], *a.* airborne (*troops*).

aérosphère [aerɔ'sfɛːr], *n.f.* the mass of air surrounding the globe, atmosphere.
aérostat [aerɔs'ta], *n.m.* aerostat, air-balloon.
aérostation [aerɔstɑ'sjɔ̃], *n.f.* aerostation, air-navigation.
aérostatique [aerɔsta'tik], *a.* aerostatic.—*n.f.* aerostatics.
aérostier [aerɔs'tje], *n.m.* aeronaut, one directing an aerostat.
aérothérapie [aerɔtera'pi], *n.f.* aerotherapy.
affabilité [afabili'te], *n.f.* affability, kindness, courtesy.
affable [a'fabl], *a.* affable, courteous.
affadir [afa'diːr], *v.t.* to make unsavoury *or* insipid; (*fig.*) to make flat *or* dull. **s'affadir,** *v.r.* to become insipid.
affadissement [afadis'mɑ̃], *n.m.* insipidity, nausea, sickliness.
affaiblir [afɛ'bliːr], *v.t.* to enfeeble, to weaken; to lessen. **s'affaiblir,** *v.r.* to grow weak; to abate.
affaiblissement [afɛblis'mɑ̃], *n.m.* weakening; allaying, abatement.
affaire [a'fɛːr], *n.f.* affair, business, concern, matter; trouble, scrape; lawsuit; transaction, bargain; ***c'est mon affaire,*** it is my own concern; ***mêlez-vous de vos affaires!,*** mind your own business!; ***être dans les affaires,*** to be in business; ***homme d'affaires,*** business man, legal adviser.
affairé [afɛ're], *a.* busy.
affairement [afɛr'mɑ̃], *n.m.* hurry, bustle, ado.
affaissement [afɛs'mɑ̃], *n.m.* depression, subsidence, giving way, collapse.
affaisser [afɛ'se], *v.t.* to cause to sink, to weigh down, to press down; to bear down, to overwhelm. **s'affaisser,** *v.r.* to sink, to subside; to give way; to be bent down (*by age*); to collapse.
affamé [afa'me], *a.* famished, hungry, starving; greedy, craving; ***être affamé de,*** to be greedy *or* eager for.
affamer [afa'me], *v.t.* to starve, to famish, to deprive of food.
affectation [afɛktɑ'sjɔ̃], *n.f.* appropriation, destination *or* attribution (*to a certain object*); simulation, show, pretence, affectation; preference; distinction; (*Mil.*) ***recevoir une affectation,*** to be posted.
affecté [afɛk'te], *a.* affected, assumed, simulated, put on; attributed, destined (*to a certain object*); (*Path.*) affected (*by a disease etc.*); (*Mil.*) posted to.
affecter [afɛk'te], *v.t.* to affect, to make frequent *or* habitual use of, to have a predilection for; to assume (*a certain shape etc.*); to feign, to pretend; to set apart, to earmark, to destine, to appropriate (*to a certain object*); to move, to touch, to impress emotionally. **s'affecter,** *v.r.* to be affected.
affection [afɛk'sjɔ̃], *n.f.* affection, love, attachment; (*Med.*) affection, ailment.
affectionné [afɛksjɔ'ne], *a.* affectionate, loving, attached, loved, liked.
affectionner [afɛksjɔ'ne], *v.t.* to love, to be fond of, to like.
affectueusement [afɛktɥøz'mɑ̃], *adv.* affectionately, fondly.
affectueux [afɛk'tɥø], *a.* (*fem.* **-euse**) affectionate, tender, warm-hearted.
afférent [afe'rɑ̃], *a.* reverting; relating to; assignable to; accruing to.
affermage [afɛr'maːʒ], *n.m.* farming, renting.
affermataire [afɛrma'tɛːr], *n.m.* tenant farmer.
affermateur [afɛrma'tœːr], *n.m.* (*fem.* **-trice**) lessor.
affermer [afɛr'me], *v.t.* to farm *or* let out by lease; to take a lease of, to rent.
affermir [afɛr'miːr], *v.t.* to strengthen, to make firm; to confirm, to establish, to consolidate. **s'affermir,** *v.r.* to become strong, firm, *or* fast; to become established.
affermissement [afɛrmis'mɑ̃], *n.m.* strengthening, consolidation, establishment; support, prop, stay.
affété [afe'te], *a.* affected, prim, finical; canting, mincing, pretty-pretty.
afféterie [afe'tri], *n.f.* affectation, mannerisms, primness.
affichage [afi'ʃaːʒ], *n.m.* bill-sticking; placarding.
affiche [a'fiʃ], *n.f.* placard, bill, poster; ***homme affiche,*** sandwich-man; ***affiche électorale,*** election poster.
afficher [afi'ʃe], *v.t.* to post up; to publish, to divulge, to proclaim; to make a show of, to parade; ***défense d'afficher,*** stick no bills; billposting prohibited. **s'afficher,** *v.r.* to set up (*for*); to attract public notice.
afficheur [afi'ʃœːr], *n.m.* bill-sticker.
affidavit [afida'vit], *n.m.* affidavit.
affidé [afi'de], *a.* trusty, trustworthy, in the know.—*n.m.* (*fem.* **-ée**) confederate, confidential agent; spy.
affilage [afi'laːʒ], **affilement** [afil'mɑ̃], *n.m.* whetting, sharpening, setting.
affilé [afi'le], *a.* sharp; nimble, glib (*of the tongue*).
affilée (d') [dafi'le], *adv. phr.* at a stretch; ***trois heures d'affilée,*** three hours at a stretch.
affiler [afi'le], *v.t.* to sharpen, to set, to put an edge on.
affiliation [afiljɑ'sjɔ̃], *n.f.* affiliation (*to a society, company, plot etc.*).
affilié [afi'lje], *a.* affiliated, admitted a member *or* associate.—*n.m.* (*fem.* **-ée**) affiliated member, associate, confederate.
affilier [afi'lje], *v.t.* to admit, to affiliate, to receive. **s'affilier,** *v.r.* to become admitted *or* affiliated, to join.
affiloir [afi'lwaːr], *n.m.* hone, oilstone, steel, strop.
affinage [afi'naːʒ], **affinement** [afin'mɑ̃], *n.m.* refining, fining (*of metals, sugar etc.*); heckling (*of hemp*), maturing (*of a wine*), ripening (*of a cheese*).
affiner [afi'ne], *v.t.* to fine, to refine. **s'affiner,** *v.r.* to be refined, to be fined; to become finer, wittier etc. (*of the mind*).
affinerie [afin'ri], *n.f.* metal refinery.
affineur [afi'nœːr], *n.m.* metal refiner.
affinité [afini'te], *n.f.* affinity, relationship.
affinoir [afi'nwaːr], *n.m.* carding-brush.
affiquet [afi'kɛ], *n.m.* knitting-sheath; (*pl.*) gewgaws, trinkets.
affirmatif [afirma'tif], *a.* (*fem.* **-tive**) affirmative, asserting.—*n.f.* (**-tive**) affirmative statement, answer etc.; asseveration; ***répondre par l'affirmative,*** to answer in the affirmative.
affirmation [afirmɑ'sjɔ̃], *n.f.* affirmation, assertion.

affirmativement [afirmativ'mɑ̃], *adv.* affirmatively.
affirmer [afir'me], *v.t.* to affirm, to assert, to vouch, to declare; to confirm by *or* on oath. **s'affirmer,** *v.r.* to grow stronger, to assert oneself.
affixe [a'fiks], *n.m.* affix.
affleurement [aflœr'mɑ̃], *n.m.* levelling, making flush; (*Mining*) outcrop.
affleurer [aflœ're], *v.t.* to make even, to level; (*Arch.*) to make flush.—*v.i.* to be level, to be flush (*with*); (*Mining*) to crop out.
affliction [aflik'sjɔ̃], *n.f.* affliction, trouble, distress; trial, vexation.
affligé [afli'ʒe], *a.* afflicted, grieved, distressed.
affliger [afli'ʒe], *v.t.* (*conjug. like* MANGER) to afflict, to trouble, to distress, to grieve, to vex, to torment; to mortify, to chasten. **s'affliger,** *v.r.* to grieve, to be afflicted, troubled *or* cast down; to take something to heart.
afflouage [aflu'a:ʒ], *n.m.* (*Naut.*) refloating (*of a ship*).
afflouer [aflu'e], *v.t.* to refloat.
affluence [afly'ɑ̃:s], *n.f.* affluence, abundance; concourse, crowd; ***heures d'affluence,*** rush hour.
affluent [afly'ɑ̃], *a.* falling into, running into (*of rivers*).—*n.m.* tributary.
affluer [afly'e], *v.i.* to fall, run *or* flow into (*as a tributary*) (***dans***); to abound; to come in great quantity (***à, vers***).
affolant [afɔ'lɑ̃], *a.* distracting.
affolé [afɔ'le], *a.* distracted, panic-stricken; (*Mech.*) disconnected, defective.
affolement [afɔl'mɑ̃], *n.m.* distraction, panic.
affoler [afɔ'le], *v.t.* to distract; to infatuate; to bewitch; to madden, to drive crazy. **s'affoler,** *v.r.* to fall into a panic, to stampede.
afforestage [afɔrɛs'ta:ʒ], *n.m.* right of cutting firewood, estovers.
afforestation [afɔrɛstɑ'sjɔ̃], *n.f.* afforestation.
affouillable [afu'jabl], *a.* subject *or* liable to undermining.
affouillement [afuj'mɑ̃], *n.m.* undermining, washing away.
affouiller [afu'je], *v.t.* to undermine, to wash away.
affouragement or **affourragement** [afuraʒ'mɑ̃], *n.m.* foraging, foddering.
affourager or **affourrager** [afura'ʒe], *v.t.* (*conjug. like* MANGER) to fodder, to give fodder to.
affourcher [afur'ʃe], *v.t.* to seat astride; (*Carp.*) to join a tongue and groove.
affranchi [afrɑ̃'ʃi], *a.* set free, freed.—*n.m.* (*fem.* **-e**) freedman; freedwoman.
affranchir [afrɑ̃'ʃi:r], *v.t.* to free, to set free, to enfranchise; to absolve, to exempt; to frank (*a letter*), to stamp. **s'affranchir,** *v.r.* to free oneself; to rid oneself of (***de***), to shake off, to break away from.
affranchissement [afrɑ̃ʃis'mɑ̃], *n.m.* enfranchisement; exemption, discharge; deliverance; payment of postage (*of a letter*).
affranchisseur [afrɑ̃ʃi'sœ:r], *n.m.* emancipator, liberator.
affres [a:fr], *n.f.* (*used only in pl.*) dread, horror, agony; ***les affres de la mort,*** the pangs of death, death-throes.
affrètement [afrɛt'mɑ̃], *n.m.* chartering freighting.
affréter [afre'te], *v.t.* (*conjug. like* CÉDER) (*Naut.*) to charter, to freight (*a vessel*).
affréteur [afre'tœ:r], *n.m.* charterer, freighter.
affreusement [afrøz'mɑ̃], *adv.* frightfully, horribly, dreadfully.
affreux [a'frø], *a.* (*fem.* **-euse**) frightful, hideous, shocking, horrible, ghastly.
affriander [afriɑ̃'de], *v.t.* to allure, to entice to tempt.
affricher [afri'ʃe], *v.t.* to leave fallow.
affrioler [afriɔ'le], *v.t.* to allure, to entice.
affront [a'frɔ̃], *n.m.* affront, insult; disgrace.
affronter [afrɔ̃'te], *v.t.* to face, to confront, to brave; to attack boldly.
affruiter [afrɥi'te], *v.t.* to plant with fruit-trees.—*v.i.* to bear *or* supply fruit. **s'affruiter,** *v.r.* to come into fruit.
affublement [afyblə'mɑ̃], *n.m.* grotesque make-up *or* rig-out (*of dress*).
affubler [afy'ble], *v.t.* to dress up, to rig out (*grotesquely*). **s'affubler,** *v.r.* to dress up ridiculously.
affût [a'fy], *n.m.* stand *or* place for lying in wait, watch; gun-carriage; ***être à l'affût,*** to lie in wait.
affûtage [afy'ta:ʒ], *n.m.* setting *or* sharpening (*of tools*).
affûter [afy'te], *v.t.* to grind, to sharpen.
affûteur [afy'tœ:r], *n.m.* sharpener, setter, grinder; stalker.—*n.f.* (**-euse**) sharpening machine.
afghan [af'gɑ̃], *a.* Afghan.—*n.m.* (**Afghan,** *fem.* **-ane**) Afghan (*person*).
Afghanistan [afganis'tɑ̃], **l'**, *m.* Afghanistan.
afin [a'fɛ̃], *conj.* **afin de** (*with inf.*) to, in order to, so as to; **afin que** (*with subj.*) to, in order that, so that.
africain [afri'kɛ̃], *a.* African.—*n.m.* (**Africain** *fem.* **-aine**) African (*person*).
Afrique [a'frik], **l'**, *f.* Africa.
agaçant [aga'sɑ̃], *a.* irritating, worrying; provoking, provocative; alluring, enticing.
agace or **agasse** [a'gas], *n.f.* magpie.
agacement [agas'mɑ̃], *n.m.* irritation, setting on edge.
agacer [aga'se], *v.t.* (*conjug. like* COMMENCER) to worry, to irritate, to set on edge; to excite, to provoke; to entice, to allure.
agacerie [aga'sri], *n.f.* allurement, coquetry enticement.
agaillardir [agajar'di:r], *v.t.* to cheer up.
agate [a'gat], *n.f.* agate.
Agathe [a'gat], *f.* Agatha.
âge [ɑ:ʒ], *n.m.* age, years; period, epoch, era, (*pl.*) the ages, time; ***Moyen Âge,*** Middle Ages; ***d'un certain âge,*** elderly; ***entre deux âges,*** of uncertain age.
âgé [ɑ'ʒe], *a.* aged (*so many years*); old, elderly; ***âgé de vingt ans,*** twenty years old.
agence [a'ʒɑ̃:s], *n.f.* agency, bureau, branch office.
agencement [aʒɑ̃s'mɑ̃], *n.m.* arrangement, grouping, ordering; (*Arch.*) composition, layout.
agencer [aʒɑ̃'se], *v.t.* (*conjug. like* COMMENCER) to arrange, to dispose.
agenda [aʒɛ̃'da], *n.m.* note-book; diary; engagement-book.

agenouiller (s') [saʒnu'je], *v.r.* to kneel down, to fall on one's knees; (*fig.*) to bow down (***devant***).
agenouilloir [aʒnuj'wa:r], *n.m.* hassock.
agent [a'ʒɑ̃], *n.m.* agent; deputy; middleman; broker; ***agent de change***, stock-broker; ***agent électoral***, canvasser; ***agent de liaison***, liaison officer; ***agent de police***, policeman.
agglomération [aglɔmerɑ'sjɔ̃], *n.f.* agglomeration, built-up area.
aggloméré [aglɔme're], *n.m.* compressed fuel, briquette.
agglomérer [aglɔme're], *v.t.* (*conjug. like* CÉDER) to agglomerate, to mass together, to pile up, to assemble.
agglutinant [aglyti'nɑ̃], *a.* adhesive.
agglutiner [aglyti'ne], *v.t.* to bind, to cake. **s'agglutiner,** *v.r.* to unite, to cohere; to heal over (*wound*).
aggravant [agra'vɑ̃], *a.* (*Law*) aggravating, making more heinous.
aggravation [agravɑ'sjɔ̃], *n.f.* aggravation, additional penalty; ***aggravation de peine***, increase of punishment.
aggraver [agra've], *v.t.* to aggravate, to make worse. **s'aggraver,** *v.r.* to worsen (*illness, situation*).
agile [a'ʒil], *a.* agile, nimble.
agilement [aʒil'mɑ̃], *adv.* nimbly, with agility.
agilité [aʒili'te], *n.f.* agility, nimbleness, lightness.
agio [a'ʒjo], *n.m.* stock-jobbing, speculation.
agiotage [aʒjɔ'ta:ʒ], *n.m.* stock-jobbing; ***faire l'agiotage***, to deal in stocks.
agioter [aʒjɔ'te], *v.i.* to speculate, to job.
agioteur [aʒjɔ'tœ:r], *n.m.* speculator, jobber.
agir [a'ʒi:r], *v.i.* to act, to do; to operate; to have an effect (***sur***); to negotiate, to manage a business; to sue, to prosecute, to proceed (***contre***); to behave. **s'agir,** *v.r.* (*impers.*) to be in question, to be the matter; ***de quoi s'agit-il?*** what is the matter? ***il s'agit de votre vie***, your life is at stake.
agissant [aʒi'sɑ̃], *a.* active, busy; efficacious, effective.
agitateur [aʒita'tœ:r], *n.m.* (*fem* **-trice**) agitator.—*n.m.* stirring rod.
agitation [aʒitɑ'sjɔ̃], *n.f.* agitation; disturbance, tossing, shaking, tumult; trouble, emotion, uneasiness, restlessness.
agité [aʒi'te], *a.* restless (*sleep*); rough (*sea*); fretful (*child*).
agiter [aʒi'te], *v.t.* to agitate, to put in motion, to shake, to stir; to disturb, to trouble; to excite, to perturb; to debate, to discuss. **s'agiter,** *v.r.* to be agitated *or* in movement; to get rough; to be restless, disturbed *or* uneasy; to toss, to wave, to flutter; to be debated.
agneau [a'ɲo], *n.m.* (*fem.* **-elle,** *pl.* **-eaux**) lamb.
agnelage [aɲə'la:ʒ], **agnèlement** [aɲɛl'mɑ̃], *n.m.* lambing; lambing-time.
agneler [aɲə'le], *v.i.* (*conjug. like* AMENER) to lamb, to yean.
Agnès [a'ɲɛ:s], *f.* Agnes.
agnès [a'ɲɛ:s], *n.f.* raw young girl.
agnosticisme [agnɔsti'sism], *n.m.* agnosticism.
agnosticiste [agnɔsti'sist], **agnostique** [agnɔs'tik], *a.* and *n.* agnostic.
agonie [agɔ'ni], *n.f.* agony, death pangs; (*fig.*) trouble, anguish, torture; ***être à l'agonie***, to be at the point of death.
agonir [agɔ'ni:r], *v.t.* to insult grossly.
agonisant [agɔni'zɑ̃], *a.* dying, in a dying condition.—*n.m.* (*fem.* **-e**) dying person.
agoniser [agɔni'ze], *v.i.* to be at the point of death.
agoraphobie [agɔrafɔ'bi], *n.f.* agoraphobia.
agrafe [a'graf], *n.f.* fastener, clasp, clip, staple (*for papers*); ***agrafe et porte***, hook and eye.
agrafer [agra'fe], *v.t.* to hook, to clasp, to fasten with a clasp; to staple.
agrafeuse [agra'fø:z], *n.f.* stapler.
agraire [a'grɛ:r], *a.* agrarian.
agrandir [agrɑ̃'di:r], *v.t.* to make greater, to enlarge, to augment; to widen; to exaggerate; to promote, to advance; (*fig.*) to elevate. **s'agrandir,** *v.r.* to become greater *or* larger.
agrandissement [agrɑ̃dis'mɑ̃], *n.m.* enlargement, increase; aggrandizement, elevation.
agrandisseur [agrɑ̃di'sœ:r], *n.m.* (*Phot.*) enlarger.
agréable [agre'abl], *a.* agreeable, pleasing, pleasant, acceptable.
agréablement [agreablə'mɑ̃], *adv.* agreeably, pleasantly.
agréé [agre'e], *n.m.* solicitor; attorney.
agréer [agre'e], *v.t.* to accept, to approve, to allow, to receive kindly.—*v.i.* to please, to be agreeable; ***veuillez agréer mes salutations***, yours truly.
agrégat [agre'gɑ], *n.m.* aggregate, composite mass.
agrégation [agregɑ'sjɔ̃], *n.f.* (*Phys.*) aggregation, aggregate; (=***concours d'agrégation***) competitive examination for admission on the teaching staff of State secondary schools *or* of faculties of law, medicine, pharmacy.
agrégé [agre'ʒe], *a.* and *n.m.* ***professeur agrégé***, one who has passed the ***agrégation.***
agréger [agre'ʒe], *v.t.* (*conjug. like* ASSIÉGER) to admit into a society, to incorporate; (*Phys.*) to aggregate.
agrément [agre'mɑ̃], *n.m.* consent, approbation; pleasure, charm, gracefulness; amenity; (*pl.*) ornaments, embellishments, amenities (*of life*); ***arts d'agrément***, accomplishments.
agrémenter [agremɑ̃'te], *v.t.* to set off, to ornament, to adorn.
agrès [a'grɛ], *n.m.* (*used only in pl.*) rigging (*of a ship etc.*); apparatus, gear (*of a gymnasium etc.*).
agresseur [agrɛ'sœ:r], *n.m.* aggressor.
agressif [agrɛ'sif], *a.* (*fem.* **-ive**) aggressive.
agression [agrɛ'sjɔ̃], *n.f.* aggression.
agressivité [agrɛsivi'te], *n.f.* aggressiveness.
agreste [a'grɛst], *a.* rustic; countrified (*manners*).
agrestement [agrɛstə'mɑ̃], *adv.* rustically.
agricole [agri'kɔl], *a.* agricultural.
agriculteur [agrikyl'tœ:r], *n.m.* agriculturist, husbandman, farmer.
agriculture [agrikyl'ty:r], *n.f.* agriculture, husbandry, tillage.
agriffer [agri'fe], *v.t.* to claw; to clutch, to grip. **s'agriffer,** *v.r.* to claw (*at*).
agrion [agri'ɔ̃], *n.m.* dragon-fly.
agripper [agri'pe], *v.t.* to grip, to snatch. **s'agripper,** *v.r.* to cling (*to*).

agronome [agrɔ'nɔm], *n.m.* agriculturist.
aguerri [agɛ'ri], *a.* inured to war; disciplined.
aguerrir [agɛ'ri:r], *v.t.* to train *or* inure to the hardships of war; to accustom, to inure (*to hardships etc.*). **s'aguerrir,** *v.r.* to inure *or* accustom oneself (*to hardships, abstinence etc.*), to be inured.
aguerrissement [agɛris'mɑ̃], *n.m.* inuring to war, hardening.
aguets [a'gɛ], *n.m.* (*used only in pl.*) watch, look-out; ***être aux aguets***, to be on the watch.
aheurter (s') [saœr'te], *v.r.* to persist (*in*).
ahuri [ay'ri], *a.* bewildered, perplexed, flurried.
ahurir [ay'ri:r], *v.t.* to bewilder, to flurry, to stupefy.
ahurissant [ayri'sɑ̃], *a.* bewildering.
ahurissement [ayris'mɑ̃], *n.m.* bewilderment, confusion, perplexity.
aï [a'i], *n.m.* (*Zool.*) sloth.
aide [ɛ:d], *n.f.* help, relief, assistance; succour, support, protection, rescue; relief (*of the poor etc.*); helper, female assistant, help; ***à l'aide de***, with the help of.—*n.m.* a male assistant; ***aide de camp*** (*pl.* ***aides de camp***), aide-de-camp.
aide-mémoire [ɛdme'mwa:r], *n.m. inv.* précis; memorandum.
aider [ɛ'de], *v.t.* to aid, to help, to relieve, to assist, to succour; to abet; to conduce to, to further.—*v.i.* to be helpful, to be of assistance (*à*). **s'aider,** *v.r.* to make use (***de***); to avail oneself.
aïe! [aj], *int.* oh! oh dear!
aïeul [a'jœl], *n.m.* (*fem.* **aïeule,** *pl.* **aïeuls, aïeules**) grandfather, grandsire; grandmother, grandam; (*pl.* **aïeux**) forebears, ancestors.
aigle [ɛ:gl], *n.* eagle; (*fig.*) clever *or* brilliant person, genius.—*n.m.* reading-desk, lectern (*with effigy of an eagle*).
aiglefin [ɛglə'fɛ̃], **aigrefin** (1) [ɛgrə'fɛ̃], *n.m.* haddock.
aiglon [ɛ'glɔ̃], *n.m.* (*fem.* **-onne**) eaglet.
aigre [ɛgr], *a.* sour, tart; (*fig.*) harsh, bitter, shrill.—*n.m.* sourness, mustiness.
aigre-doux [ɛgrə'du], *a.* (*fem.* **-douce**) sourish, bitter-sweet.
aigrefin (2) [ɛgrə'fɛ̃], *n.m.* sharper, swindler; adventurer; [AIGLEFIN].
aigrelet [ɛgrə'lɛ], *a.* (*fem.* **-ette**) sourish.
aigrement [ɛgrə'mɑ̃], *adv.* acrimoniously, sourly, bitterly; roughly, harshly.
aigret [ɛ'grɛ], *a.* (*fem.* **-ette** (1)) sourish.
aigrette (2) [ɛ'grɛt], *n.f.* aigrette, tuft, cluster *or* plume (*of feathers, diamonds etc.*); horn (*of an owl*); crest (*of a peacock*); egret, tufted heron.
aigreur [ɛ'grœ:r], *n.f.* sourness, sharpness, tartness; (*fig.*) harshness, bitterness, surliness, animosity, spite.
aigrir [ɛ'gri:r], *v.t.* to make sour *or* sharp, to sour; (*fig.*) to irritate, to embitter, to make worse, to incense, to make ill-humoured. **s'aigrir,** *v.r.* to turn sour; (*fig.*) to grow worse, to be exasperated, to be irritated.
aigrissement [ɛgris'mɑ̃], *n.m.* souring, embittering.
aigu [e'gy], *a.* (*fem.* **aiguë**) pointed, sharp, keen, acute; (*fig.*) shrill, piercing; ***accent aigu***, acute accent.
aiguë [AIGU].
aigue-marine [ɛgma'rin], *n.f.* (*pl.* **aigues-marines**) aquamarine.
aiguière [ɛ'gjɛ:r], *n.f.* ewer.
aiguillage [egɥi'ja:ʒ], *n.m.* (*Rail.*) shunting, points.
aiguillat [egɥi'ja], *n.m.* dog-fish.
aiguille [e'gɥi:j], *n.f.* needle; index, pointer, hand (*of a dial, watch etc.*); spire (*steeple*); point (*of an obelisk, peak etc.*); rock pinnacle *or* needle-shaped peak; ***trou d'une aiguille***, eye of a needle; (*pl., Rail.*) points.
aiguiller [egɥi'je], *v.t.* (*Rail.*) to shunt.
aiguillette [egɥi'jɛt], *n.f.* aglet, point; (*Mil.*) ornamental shoulder-knot.
aiguilleur [egɥi'jœ:r], *n.m.* (*Rail.*) pointsman, shunter.
aiguillier [egɥi'je], *n.m.* (*fem.* **-ière**) needle-maker.
aiguillon [egɥi'jɔ̃], *n.m.* goad, sting; (*fig.*) spur, incentive; (*Bot.*) prickle.
aiguillonner [egɥijɔ'ne], *v.t.* to goad, to prick; (*fig.*) to incite, to spur on; to stimulate.
aiguisage [egi'za:ʒ], **aiguisement** [egiz'mɑ̃], *n.m.* whetting, sharpening.
aiguisé [egi'ze], *a.* whetted, sharpened.
aiguiser [egi'ze], *v.t.* to whet, to sharpen, to set an edge on; to point; (*fig.*) to make keen, acid, piquant etc.; to excite, to stimulate.
aiguiseur [egi'zœ:r], *n.m.* knife-grinder, sharpener.
aiguisoir [egi'zwa:r], *n.m.* sharpening-tool, whetstone.
ail [a:j], *n.m.* (*pl.* (*Cook.*) **aulx** [o:], (*Bot.*) **ails**) garlic.
aile [ɛl], *n.f.* wing; brim (*of a hat*); flipper (*of a penguin*); blade (*of a propeller*); vane, sail (*of a windmill*); flank *or* wing (*of an army, building etc.*); wing, mudguard (*of a car*).
ailé [ɛ'le], *a.* winged.
aileron [ɛl'rɔ̃], *n.m.* pinion (*of a bird*); aileron, balancing flap (*of an aircraft*); fin (*of some fish*).
ailette [ɛ'lɛt], *n.f.* small wing; vane (*of a torpedo etc.*); (*Motor.*) rib, fin, flange.
ailier [ɛ'lje], *n.m.* (*Ftb.*) wing forward, wing three-quarter.
ailleurs [a'jœ:r], *adv.* elsewhere, somewhere else; ***d'ailleurs***, besides, moreover, in other respects.
aimable [ɛ'mabl], *a.* kind, amiable, obliging.
aimablement [ɛmablə'mɑ̃], *adv.* amiably, kindly.
aimant [ɛ'mɑ̃], *a.* loving, affectionate.—*n.m.* magnet; (*fig.*) attractiveness.
aimantation [ɛmɑ̃tɑ'sjɔ̃], *n.f.* magnetization.
aimanter [ɛmɑ̃'te], *v.t.* to magnetize.
Aimée [ɛ'me], *f.* Amy.
aimer [ɛ'me], *v.t.* to love, to be fond of, to be in love with; to like; ***aimer mieux***, to prefer. **s'aimer,** *v.r.* to love oneself, to be vain; to love each other.
aine (1) [ɛ:n], *n.f.* groin.
aine (2) [ɛ:n], *n.f.* herring-stick; leather band on organ-bellows.
aîné [ɛ'ne], *a.* (*fem.* **-ée**) eldest, elder, senior.—*n.m.* (*fem.* **-ée**) eldest son *or* daughter.
aînesse [ɛ'nɛs], *n.f.* seniority, priority by age, primogeniture; ***droit d'aînesse***, birthright.

ainsi [ɛ̃'si], *adv.* thus, so, in this *or* that manner; ***ainsi de suite,*** and so on and so forth; ***ainsi soit-il,*** so be it, amen; ***pour ainsi dire,*** so to speak, as it were; ***ainsi que,*** in the same way (*as*).

air (1) [ɛ:r], *n.m.* air; wind; (*Chem. etc.*) gas; (*pl.*) atmosphere; ***chambre à air,*** inner tube; ***courant d'air,*** draught; ***en plein air,*** in the open air.

air (2) [ɛ:r], *n.m.* mien, look, expression, air, manner, appearance.

air (3) [ɛ:r], *n.m.* (*Mus.*) tune.

airain [ɛ'rɛ̃], *n.m.* bronze; (*Poet.*) cannon, bell.

aire [ɛ:r], *n.f.* area, space; threshing-floor; eyrie; ***aire d'atterrissage,*** (*Av.*) landing area, apron.

airelle [ɛ'rɛl], *n.f.* whortleberry, bilberry.

ais [ɛ], *n.m.* board, plank; stave (*of a barrel*).

aisance [ɛ'zɑ̃:s], *n.f.* ease, facility; easiness, affluence; competency; (*Mach.*) play; freedom; the comforts *or* conveniences of life; ***cabinet*** (or ***lieu***) ***d'aisances,*** public convenience.

aisceau [AISSETTE].

aise [ɛ:z], *a.* glad, well pleased; ***je suis bien aise de vous voir,*** I am very glad to see you.—*n.f.* ease, comfort, convenience; (*pl.*) comforts, comfortable circumstances; ***à l'aise,*** at ease, comfortable; ***être à son aise,*** to be well off.

aisé [ɛ'ze], *a.* easy; convenient, comfortable; in easy circumstances.

aisément [ɛze'mɑ̃], *adv.* easily, readily, freely; comfortably.

aisseau [ɛ'so], *n.m.* (*pl.* **-eaux**), **aissante** [ɛ'sɑ̃:t], *n.f.* (*Carp.*) shingle, wooden tile.

aisselier [ɛsə'lje], *n.m.* (*Carp.*) tie-beam, brace, strut.

aisselle [ɛ'sɛl], *n.f.* armpit; (*Bot.*) axil.

aissette [ɛ'sɛt], *n.f.*, **aisceau** [ɛ'so] (*pl.* **-eaux**), *n.m.* adze (*of a cooper*); hooked hammer (*of a tiler*).

Aix-la-Chapelle [ɛkslaʃa'pɛl], *f.* Aachen.

ajointer [aʒwɛ̃'te], *v.t.* to join on to, to fit.

ajonc [a'ʒɔ̃], *n.m.* furze, gorse.

ajournement [aʒurnə'mɑ̃], *n.m.* adjournment, postponement; (*Law*) summons.

ajourner [aʒur'ne], *v.t.* to adjourn; to defer; (*Law*) to summon (*for a specified day*).

ajouter [aʒu'te], *v.t.* to add, to join, to subjoin, to interpolate. **s'ajouter,** *v.r.* to be joined, to attach oneself.

ajusté [aʒys'te], *a.* close-fitting (*clothes*).

ajustement [aʒystə'mɑ̃], *n.m.* adjustment, arranging, fitting, settlement; laying out; attire, apparel.

ajuster [aʒys'te], *v.t.* to adjust, to regulate, to square, to fit, to adapt (*one thing to another*); to take aim at; to set in order; (*Mus.*) to tune; to bedeck; to settle *or* arrange (*a dispute*). **s'ajuster,** *v.r.* to accommodate oneself, to be adapted; to dress, to deck oneself out.

ajusteur [aʒys'tœ:r], *n.m.* fitter; weigher (*at the mint*).

alacrité [alakri'te], *n.f.* alacrity, cheerful briskness.

Aladin [ala'dɛ̃], *m.* Aladdin.

Alain [a'lɛ̃], *m.* Alan.

alaise [a'lɛ:z], *n.f.* rubber sheet for pram *or* cot.

alambic [alɑ̃'bik], *n.m.* alembic, still.

alambiquer [alɑ̃bi'ke], *v.t.* to distil. to refine.

alangui [alɑ̃'gi:], *a.* languid, downcast.

alanguir [alɑ̃'gi:r], *v.t.* to enfeeble, to make languid. **s'alanguir,** *v.r.* to languish, to flag, to become languid.

alanguissement [alɑ̃gis'mɑ̃], *n.m.* languor.

alarmant [alar'mɑ̃], *a.* alarming, startling.

alarme [a'larm], *n.f.* alarm, affright, sudden fear, uneasiness.

alarmer [alar'me], *v.t.* to alarm; to startle, to render anxious *or* frightened. **s'alarmer,** *v.r.* to take alarm, to be alarmed.

alarmiste [alar'mist], *a.* and *n.* alarmist.

albanais [alba'nɛ], *a.* Albanian.—*n.m.* Albanian (*language*); (**Albanais,** *fem.* **-aise**) Albanian (*person*).

Albanie [alba'ni:], **l',** *f.* Albania.

albâtre [al'bɑ:tr], *n.m.* alabaster; (*fig.*) whiteness.

albatros [alba'trɔs], *n.m.* albatross.

albinisme [albi'nism], *n.m.* albinism.

albinos [albi'nɔs], *a.* and *n.* albino.

album [al'bɔm], *n.m.* album, scrap-book, sketch-book.

albumine [alby'min], *n.f.* albumen.

alcaïque [alka'ik], *a.* alcaic (*verse*).

alcali [alka'li], *n.m.* alkali.

alcalin [alka'lɛ̃], *a.* alkaline.

alcalinité [alkalini'te], *n.f.* alkalinity.

alcaliser [alkali'ze], **alcaliniser** [alkalini'ze], *v.t.* to alkalify.

alchimie [alʃi'mi], *n.f.* alchemy.

alchimique [alʃi'mik], *a.* alchemical.

alchimiste [alʃi'mist], *n.m.* alchemist.

alcool [al'kɔl], *n.m.* alcohol, spirit(s); ***alcool à brûler, alcool dénaturé,*** methylated spirit.

alcoolique [alkɔ'lik], *a.* alcoholic.

alcoolisme [alkɔ'lism], *n.m.* alcoholism.

Alcoran [alkɔ'rɑ̃], [CORAN].

alcôve [al'ko:v], *n.f.* alcove, recess.

alcyon [al'sjɔ̃], *n.m.* halcyon; (*Orn.*) kingfisher.

alcyonien [alsjɔ'njɛ̃], *a.* (*fem.* **-enne**) halcyon, peaceful.

aléa [ale'a], *n.m.* chance, hazard.

aléatoire [alea'twa:r], *a.* hazardous, uncertain.

alêne [a'lɛn], *n.f.* awl.

alentour or **à l'entour** [alɑ̃'tu:r], *adv.* about, around, round about.

alentours, [alɑ̃'tu:r], *n.m.* (*used only in pl.*) environs, neighbourhood.

Aléoutiennes [aleu'sjɛn], **les,** *f.pl.* the Aleutian Islands.

alerte [a'lɛrt], *a.* alert, vigilant; active, lively, agile.—*n.f.* alarm, warning; ***alerte aérienne,*** air-raid warning.

alerter [alɛr'te], *v.t.* to give the alarm to, to warn.

alésage [ale'za:ʒ], *n.m.* boring, drilling; bore (*of cylinder*).

aléser [ale'ze], *v.t.* (*conjug. like* CÉDER) to smooth *or* enlarge the bore of (*a tube, gun etc*); ***aléser un canon,*** to bore a cannon.

aléseuse [ale'zø:z], *n.f.* boring-machine.

alésoir [ale'zwa:r], *n.m.* borer, boring tool.

alester [alɛs'te], **alestir** [alɛs'ti:r], *v.t.* (*Naut.*) to lighten *or* disencumber (*a vessel*).

alésure [ale'zy:r], *n.f.* metal turnings *or* filings.

alevin [al'vɛ̃], *n.m.* fry, young fish.

aleviner [alvi'ne], *v.t.* to stock with fry.

alevinier [alvi'nje], *n.m.* breeding-pond.
Alexandre [alɛk'sɑ̃:dr], *m.* Alexander.
Alexandrie [alɛksɑ̃'dri], *f.* Alexandria.
alexandrin [alɛksɑ̃'drɛ̃], *a.* and *n.m.* (*Pros.*) Alexandrine.
alezan [al'zɑ̃], *a.* and *n.m.* chestnut (horse).
alèze or **alèse** [a'lɛ:z], [ALAISE].
alfa [al'fa], *n.m.* esparto-grass.
algarade [alga'rad], *n.f.* insult, affront; rating.
algèbre [al'ʒɛbr], *n.f.* algebra.
algébrique [alʒe'brik], *a.* algebraical.
algébriquement [alʒebrik'mɑ̃], *adv.* algebraically.
Alger [al'ʒe], *m.* Algiers.
Algérie [alʒe'ri], **l'**, *f.* Algeria.
algérien [alʒe'rjɛ̃], *a.* (*fem.* **-enne**) Algerian.—*n.m.* (**Algérien,** *fem.* **-enne**) Algerian (*person*).
algie [al'ʒi:], *n.f.* ache.
algue [alg], *n.f.* sea-weed, alga.
alibi [ali'bi], *n.m.* (*Law*) alibi.
aliboron [alibɔ'rɔ̃], *n.m.* jackass, stupid *or* self-conceited fellow.
aliénable [alje'nabl], *a.* alienable, transferable.
aliénation [aljenɑ'sjɔ̃], *n.f.* (*Law*) conveyance of property to another; (*fig.*) alienation, mental derangement; estrangement, aversion.
aliéné [alje'ne], *a.* lunatic, mad.—*n.m.* (*fem.* **-ée**) lunatic.
aliéner [alje'ne], *v.t.* (*conjug. like* CÉDER) to alienate, to give away (*property*), to transfer, to make over; to estrange, to make hostile; to derange (*the mind*). **s'aliéner,** *v.r.* to become estranged (*from*).
aliéniste [alje'nist], *n.m.* alienist.
alignée [ali'ɲe], *n.f.* line, row.
alignement [aliɲə'mɑ̃], *n.m.* alignment; laying out in line; (*Mil.*) dressing; (*Print.*) ranging.
aligner [ali'ɲe], *v.t.* to align, to lay out in line; to put in a straight line; (*Mil.*) to dress; (*Print.*) to range. **s'aligner,** *v.r.* (*Mil.*) to dress.
aliment [ali'mɑ̃], *n.m.* aliment, food, nourishment, nutriment; (*Law, pl.*) alimony, maintenance.
alimentaire [alimɑ̃'tɛ:r], *a.* alimental, alimentary; (*Mech.*) ***pompe alimentaire,*** feed-pump, donkey engine.
alimentateur [alimɑ̃ta'tœ:r], *a.* (*fem.* **-trice**) alimentary.
alimentation [alimɑ̃tɑ'sjɔ̃], *n.f.* alimentation; nourishment, feeding; ***rayon d'alimentation,*** food department.
alimenter [alimɑ̃'te], *v.t.* to feed, to nourish; to maintain; to supply, to provision; to fuel, to keep up.
alimenteux [alimɑ̃'tø], *a.* (*fem.* **-euse**) nutritive.
alinéa [aline'a], *n.m.* indented line; new paragraph.
alisé [ALIZÉ].
aliter [ali'te], *v.t.* to confine to bed; ***être alité,*** to be bedridden. **s'aliter,** *v.r.* to take to one's bed.
alizé or **alisé** [ali'ze], *a.* soft (*said of the trade-winds*); ***vents alizés,*** trade-winds.—*n.m.* trade-wind.
alkali etc. [ALCALI].
Alkoran [alkɔ'rɑ̃], [CORAN].

Allah [a'la], *m.* Allah.
allaitement [alɛt'mɑ̃], *n.m.* lactation, nursing, suckling; ***allaitement artificiel,*** bottle feeding.
allaiter [alɛ'te], *v.t.* to suckle, to nurse.
alléchant [ale'ʃɑ̃], *a.* alluring, seductive.
allèchement [alɛʃ'mɑ̃], *n.m.* allurement, enticement, seduction, attraction.
allécher [ale'ʃe], *v.t.* (*conjug. like* CÉDER) to allure, to entice, to attract.
allée [a'le], *n.f.* passage, drive, alley, avenue, walk; (*pl.*) goings.
allégation [alegɑ'sjɔ̃], *n.f.* allegation, assertion.
allège [a'lɛ:ʒ], *n.f.* lighter, hopper; (*Arch.*) window basement, sill of window.
allégeance [ale'ʒɑ̃:s], *n.f.* alleviation, relief; allegiance.
allégement [aleʒ'mɑ̃], *n.m.* alleviation, relief; reduction.
alléger [ale'ʒe], *v.t.* (*conjug. like* ASSIÉGER) to ease, to unburden, to lighten; to unload (*a boat*); to alleviate, to relieve, to assuage (*pain* or *grief*).
allégorie [alegɔ'ri], *n.f.* allegory.
allégorique [alegɔ'rik], *a.* allegorical.
allégoriquement [alegɔrik'mɑ̃], *adv.* allegorically.
allégoriser [alegɔri'ze], *v.t.* to allegorize.
allégoriste [alegɔ'rist], *n.m.* allegorist.
allègre [al'lɛgr], *a.* lively, nimble, sprightly; jolly, cheerful.
allègrement [allɛgrə'mɑ̃], *adv.* briskly; joyfully, merrily, joyously.
allégresse [alle'grɛs], *n.f.* gaiety, joy, mirth, cheerfulness; sprightliness.
alléguer [alle'ge], *v.t.* (*conjug. like* CÉDER) to allege, to advance, to urge; (*Law*) to quote, to adduce, to cite, to plead.
alléluia [allely'ja], *n.m.* and *int.* Hallelujah.
Allemagne [al'maɲ], **l'**, *f.* Germany.
allemand [al'mɑ̃], *a.* German.—*n.m.* German (*language*); (**Allemand,** *fem.* **-ande**) German (*person*).
aller [a'le], *v.i. irr.* (*with aux.* ÊTRE) to go, to go on, to proceed, to progress (*well, ill etc.*); to be (*in good* or *ill health*); to act (*in a certain way*); to suit, to fit (*well* or *ill*); to be going to; ***aller au pas,*** to go at a walking pace; ***aller et venir,*** to go up and down; ***je ne ferai qu'aller et venir,*** I won't be a minute; ***cela va tout seul,*** it is plain sailing; ***cet enfant ira loin,*** this child will go far; ***comment allez-vous?*** how are you? ***je vais bien,*** I am well; (*fam.*) ***ça va!*** all right! ***cet habit vous va mal,*** this coat does not fit you; ***allons!*** come on! ***allons donc!*** surely not! ***cela va sans dire,*** it stands to reason; ***il y va de sa vie,*** his life is at stake; ***se laisser aller,*** to yield, to give way, to abandon oneself to a thing. **s'en aller,** *v.r.* to go away, to run away; to vanish, to disappear; to die, to wear out; ***va-t'en! allez-vous-en!*** go away! be off with you!—*n.m.* going, course, run; outward voyage, trip, journey; ***billet d'aller et retour,*** return ticket.
allergie [alɛr'ʒi], *n.f.* allergy.
allergique [alɛr'ʒik], *a.* allergic.
alliage [a'lja:ʒ], *n.m.* alloy, mixture; (*fig.*) impure mixture *or* combination.

alliance [a'ljɑ̃:s], *n.f.* alliance; marriage; union, league, coalition, confederacy; compact, covenant; mixture, blending; wedding-ring.
allié [a'lje], *a.* allied; related (*by marriage*); akin, kindred.—*n.m.* (*fem.* **-ée**) ally; connexion (*by marriage*).
allier [a'lje], *v.t.* to mix; to combine; to join, to unite, to ally, to marry; to reconcile; to match. **s'allier**, *v.r.* to be incorporated *or* mixed; to become allied, to join forces (**avec**); to combine (*of metals*).
alligator [aliga'tɔ:r], *n.m.* alligator.
allitération [alitera'sjɔ̃], *n.f.* alliteration.
allo! [a'lo], *int.* (*Teleph.*) hello!
allocataire [alɔka'tɛ:r], *n.* recipient of an allowance.
allocation [alɔkɑ'sjɔ̃], *n.f.* allocation, allowance; ***allocation de chômage***, unemployment benefit; ***allocations familiales***, family allowances.
allocution [alɔky'sjɔ̃], *n.f.* allocution, short address, speech.
allonge [a'lɔ̃:ʒ], *n.f.* leaf (*of a table*); fly-leaf, addendum; rider (*of a document*); reach (*in boxing*); ***allonge de boucher***, meat-hook.
allongé [alɔ̃'ʒe], *a.* lengthened, elongated, out-stretched; downcast, long (*of face*).
allongement [alɔ̃ʒ'mɑ̃], *n.m.* lengthening, elongation, protraction.
allonger [alɔ̃'ʒe], *v.t.* (*conjug. like* MANGER) to lengthen, to elongate, to eke out; to stretch; to drag out, to protract. **s'allonger**, *v.r.* to stretch out, to grow longer; to stretch, to lie down at full length.
allouer [a'lwe], *v.t.* to allow, to grant, to accord; to allocate.
alluchon [aly'ʃɔ̃], *n.m.* cog, tooth (*of a wheel*).
allumage [aly'ma:ʒ], *n.m.* lighting, kindling; ignition; ***un raté d'allumage***, misfire; ***mettre l'allumage***, to switch on; ***couper l'allumage***, to switch off.
allumé [aly'me], *a.* lighted, ignited; (*colloq.*) excited, drunk, lit-up.
allume-feu [alym'fø], *n.m. inv.* firewood, firelighter, kindling.
allume-gaz [alym'ga:z], *n.m. inv.* gas-lighter.
allumer [aly'me], *v.t.* to light; to kindle, to set on fire; (*fig.*) to inflame, to incite, to stir up. **s'allumer**, *v.r.* to light, to take *or* catch fire; to blaze, to sparkle, to glare; to flare up, to break out.
allumette [aly'mɛt], *n.f.* match.
allumeur [aly'mœ:r], *n.m.* (*fem.* **-euse**) lighter.
allure [a'ly:r], *n.f.* carriage, gait, pace, way of walking; demeanour; aspect, look; speed; (*pl.*) ways (*of a person*); ***à toute allure***, at full speed.
allusion [aly'zjɔ̃], *n.f.* allusion, hint, innuendo.
alluvial [aly'vjal], *a.* (*m. pl.* **-aux**) alluvial.
alluvion [aly'vjɔ̃], *n.f.* alluvium.
almanach [alma'na], *n.m.* almanac, calendar.
aloès [alɔ'ɛ:s], *n.m.* aloe; aloes.
aloi [a'lwa], *n.m.* the statutory degree of purity of gold and silver; (*fig.*) standard (*good* or *bad*), quality, kind (*of persons etc.*).
alors [a'lɔ:r], *adv.* then, that time; in that case; ***d'alors***, of that time; ***alors que***, while, whereas; ***jusqu'alors***, up to then, till that moment; ***alors même que***, even though.
alose [a'lo:z], *n.f.* shad.
alouette [a'lwɛt], *n.f.* (*Orn.*) lark.
alourdir [alur'di:r], *v.t.* to make heavy, dull *or* stupid. **s'alourdir**, *v.r.* to grow heavy *or* dull.
alourdissant [alurdi'sɑ̃], *a.* oppressive, burdensome.
alourdissement [alurdis'mɑ̃], *n.m.* heaviness, dullness.
aloyau [alwa'jo], *n.m.* (*pl.* **-aux**) sirloin.
alpaca [alpa'ka], **alpaga** [alpa'ga], *n.m.* alpaca.
alpenstock [alpɛn'stɔk], *n.m.* alpenstock.
Alpes [alp], **les**, *f.pl.* the Alps.
alpestre [al'pɛstr], *a.* Alpine (*scenery, flora*).
alpha [al'fa], *n.m.* alpha; (*fig.*) beginning.
alphabet [alfa'bɛ], *n.m.* alphabet.
alphabétique [alfabe'tik], *a.* alphabetical.
alphabétiquement [alfabetik'mɑ̃], *adv.* alphabetically.
alpin [al'pɛ̃], *a.* Alpine (*club etc.*).
alpinisme [alpi'nism], *n.m.* mountaineering.
alpiniste [alpi'nist], *n.m.* Alpinist, mountaineer.
Alsace [al'zas], **l'**, *f.* Alsace.
alsacien [alza'sjɛ̃], *a.* (*fem.* **-enne**) Alsatian. —*n.m.* (**Alsacien**, *fem.* **-enne**) inhabitant of Alsace.
altérable [alte'rabl], *a.* alterable, corruptible, adulterable.
altérant [alte'rɑ̃], *a.* causing thirst.
altération [alterɑ'sjɔ̃], *n.f.* deterioration; falsification, adulteration, debasing (*of money etc.*); weakening, impairing.
altercation [altɛrkɑ'sjɔ̃], *n.f.* altercation, wrangle, dispute, quarrel.
altérer [alte're], *v.t.* (*conjug. like* CÉDER) to alter for the worse; to impair, to adulterate, to corrupt, to pervert, to debase, to falsify; to disturb, to trouble, to upset; to make thirsty. **s'altérer**, *v.r.* to be impaired, to degenerate.
alternance [altɛr'nɑ̃:s], *n.f.* alternation, rotation.
alternant [altɛr'nɑ̃], *a.* alternating, rotating (*as crops*).
alternat [altɛr'na], *n.m.* rotation (*of crops etc*).
alternatif [altɛrna'tif], *a.* (*fem.* **-tive**) alternate, alternating, alternative.—*n.f.* (**-tive**) alternation; alternative, choice, option (*between two possible actions*).
alternativement [altɛrnativ'mɑ̃], *adv.* alternately, by turns.
alterne [al'tɛrn], *a.* (*Geom.*) alternate (*of angles*); (*Bot.*) alternate.
alterner [altɛr'ne], *v.t.* to grow (*crops*) in rotation.—*v.i.* to alternate, to succeed each other alternately.
Altesse [al'tɛs], *n.f.* Highness.
altier [al'tje], *a.* (*fem.* **-ière**) haughty proud, arrogant, lordly, lofty.
altimètre [alti'mɛtr], *n.m.* altimeter.
altitude [alti'tyd], *n.f.* altitude.
alto [al'to], *n.m.* alto; tenor violin; tenor saxhorn.
altruisme [altry'ism], *n.m.* altruism.
altruiste [altry'ist], *a.* altruistic.—*n.* altruist.
alumine [aly'min], *n.f.* alumina, oxide of aluminium.

aluminer [alymi'ne], *v.t.* to aluminate, to aluminize.
aluminium [alymi'njɔm], *n.m.* aluminium.
alun [a'lœ̃], *n.m.* alum.
alunage [aly'na:ʒ], *n.m.* (*Dyeing*) steeping in alum; (*Phot.*) hardening (*negatives etc.*) in an alum-bath.
aluner [aly'ne], *v.t.* (*Dyeing*) to steep in alum-water; (*Phot.*) to harden in an alum-bath.
alunière [aly'njɛ:r], *n.f.* alum-pit *or* mine, alum-works.
alunir [aly'ni:r], *v.i.* to land on the moon.
alvéole [alve'ɔl], *n.m.* alveolus, cell (*in a honey-comb*); socket (*of a tooth*).
amabilité [amabili'te], *n.f.* amiability, affability, kindness.
amadou [ama'du], *n.m.* amadou, (German) tinder; touchwood.
amadouer [ama'dwe], *v.t.* to coax, to wheedle, to cajole.
amaigrir [amɛ'gri:r], *v.t.* to make lean, meagre *or* thin, to emaciate; to reduce, to lessen (*in bulk etc.*); to impoverish; to exhaust (*soil etc.*).—*v.i.* to fall away, to grow lean *or* thin. **s'amaigrir**, *v.r.* to grow thin, to fall away.
amaigrissant [amɛgri'sɑ̃], *a.* causing emaciation; ***régime amaigrissant***, slimming diet.
amaigrissement [amɛgris'mɑ̃], *n.m.* emaciation, wasting away.
amalgamation [amalgamɑ'sjɔ̃], *n.f.* amalgamation.
amalgame [amal'gam], *n.m.* amalgam; (*fig.*) medley, heterogeneous mixture.
amalgamer [amalga'me], *v.t.* to amalgamate, to blend, to combine. **s'amalgamer**, *v.r.* to amalgamate, to blend, to combine.
amande [a'mɑ̃:d], *n.f.* almond; kernel; ***amandes lissées***, sugar-plums.
amandier [amɑ̃'dje], *n.m.* almond-tree.
amant [a'mɑ̃], *n.m.* (*fem.* **-e**) lover, suitor; sweetheart, mistress; gallant, paramour; passionate admirer.
amarante [ama'rɑ̃:t], *n.f.* amaranth.
amareilleur or **amareyeur** [amarɛ'jœ:r], *n.m.* worker on an oyster-bed.
amarinage [amari'na:ʒ], *n.m.* (*Naut.*) manning (*a prize*).
amariner [amari'ne], *v.t.* to man (*a prize*); to inure (*a crew etc.*) to sea. **s'amariner**, *v.r.* to become used to the sea.
amarrage [ama'ra:ʒ], *n.m.* (*Naut.*) mooring; anchorage; lashing.
amarre [a'ma:r], *n.f.* (*Naut.*) cable, rope, hawser.
amarrer [ama're], *v.t.* to moor, to belay, to make fast.
amaryllis [amari'lis], *n.f.* amaryllis.
amas [a'mɑ], *n.m.* mass, heap, pile, accumulation.
amasser [amɑ'se], *v.t.* to accumulate, to heap up, to amass; to hoard; to collect, to get together. **s'amasser**, *v.r.* to gather, to get together, to accumulate, to be collected, to crowd, to assemble.
amassette [amɑ'sɛt], *n.f.* small palette-knife.
amasseur [amɑ'sœ:r], *n.m.* (*fem.* **-euse**) hoarder.

amateur [ama'tœ:r], *n.m.* amateur; devotee; connoisseur.
amazone [ama'zo:n], *n.f.* Amazon, female warrior; horse-woman; riding-habit; ***habit d'amazone***, riding-habit; ***monter en amazone***, to ride side-saddle.
ambages [ɑ̃'ba:ʒ], *n.f.* (*pl.*) circumlocution; ***sans ambages***, straight out.
ambassade [ɑ̃ba'sad], *n.f.* embassy, ambassador's staff.
ambassadeur [ɑ̃basa'dœ:r], *n.m.* ambassador; (*fig.*) envoy, messenger.
ambassadrice [ɑ̃basa'dris], *n.f.* ambassadress.
ambiance [ɑ̃'bjɑ̃:s], *n.f.* surroundings, environment; atmosphere.
ambiant [ɑ̃'bjɑ̃], *a.* ambient, surrounding.
ambidextre [ɑ̃bi'dɛkstr], *a.* ambidextrous.—*n.* ambidexter.
ambigu [ɑ̃bi'gy], *a.* (*fem.* **-guë**) ambiguous, equivocal.—*n.m.* heterogeneous mixture, medley.
ambiguïté [ɑ̃bigɥi'te], *n.f.* ambiguity.
ambigument [ɑ̃bigy'mɑ̃], *adv.* ambiguously.
ambitieusement [ɑ̃bisjøz'mɑ̃], *adv.* ambitiously.
ambitieux [ɑ̃bi'sjø], *a.* (*fem.* **-euse**) ambitious.—*n.m.* (*fem.* **-euse**) ambitious person.
ambition [ɑ̃bi'sjɔ̃], *n.f.* ambition.
ambitionner [ɑ̃bisjɔ'ne], *v.t.* to desire earnestly; to be ambitious of, to aspire to.
ambivalence [ɑ̃biva'lɑ̃:s], *n.f.* ambivalence.
ambivalent [ɑ̃biva'lɑ̃], *a.* ambivalent.
amble [ɑ̃:bl], *n.m.* amble.
ambler [ɑ̃'ble], *v.i.* to amble.
ambleur [ɑ̃'blœ:r], *a.* (*fem.* **-euse**) ambling.
amblyope [ɑ̃'bljɔp], *a.* amblyopic, weak-sighted.—*n.* weak-sighted person.
ambre [ɑ̃:br], *n.m.* amber; ***ambre gris***, ambergris.
ambré [ɑ̃'bre], *a.* amber-coloured.
ambrer [ɑ̃'bre], *v.t.* to perfume with amber.
ambrette [ɑ̃'brɛt], *n.f.* amber-seed; musk-seed.
ambroisie [ɑ̃brwa'zi], *n.f.* ambrosia.
ambulance [ɑ̃by'lɑ̃:s], *n.f.* ambulance; field-hospital; peripatetic clerkship; ***chirurgien d'ambulance*** field-surgeon.
ambulancier [ɑ̃bylɑ̃'sje], *n.m.* (*fem.* **-ière**) ambulance-man, stretcher-bearer, nurse.
ambulant [ɑ̃by'lɑ̃], *a.* ambulant, ambulatory, itinerant, peripatetic; travelling (*of a railway post-office*); strolling (*players*).
ambulatoire [ɑ̃byla'twa:r], *a.* ambulatory; (*Law*) movable.
âme (1) [ɑ:m], *n.f.* soul, spirit; sentiment, sensibility; (*fig.*) inhabitant, person (*on a lost ship etc.*); core, pith, heart (*of a thing etc.*); ***rendre l'âme***, to give up the ghost.
âme (2) [ɑ:m], *n.f.* sounding-board (*of a violin etc.*); bore (*of gun*).
amélioration [ameljɔrɑ'sjɔ̃], *n.f.* amelioration, improvement; (*pl.*) repairs, decorations (*of a house etc.*).
améliorer [ameljɔ're], *v.t.* to ameliorate, to improve, to better. **s'améliorer**, *v.r.* to get better, to mend, to improve.
amen [ɑ'mɛn], *int.* and *n.m.* amen.
aménagement [amenaʒ'mɑ̃], *n.m.* arrangement; disposition (*of a house etc.*); management (*of a forest*).

aménager [amena'ʒe], *v.t.* (*conjug. like* MANGER) to dispose, to arrange, to lay out; to regulate the felling of (*a wood* or *forest*).
amendable [amɑ̃'dabl], *a.* improvable, mendable.
amende [a'mɑ̃:d], *n.f.* fine, penalty, forfeit, compensation, reparation; ***faire amende honorable***, to make a full apology; ***mettre*** or ***condamner à l'amende***, to fine.
amendement [amɑ̃d'mɑ̃], *n.m.* amendment; improvement; manuring (*of land*).
amender [amɑ̃'de], *v.t.* to amend, to better; to manure (*land*). **s'amender**, *v.r.* to mend, to grow better.
amène [a'mɛ:n], *a.* agreeable, pleasant (*site*).
amener [am'ne], *v.t.* (*see Verb Tables*) to lead (*hither*), to bring; to induce, prevail upon; to introduce; to bring about; to occasion, to lead to; (*Naut.*) to lower, to strike (*colours, sails etc.*); ***mandat d'amener***, warrant.
aménité [ameni'te], *n.f.* amenity, pleasantness, affability; grace, urbanity.
amenuiser [amənɥi'ze], *v.t.* to make thinner *or* smaller. **s'amenuiser**, *v.r.* to grow thinner *or* smaller.
amer (1) [a'mɛ:r], *a.* (*fem.* **amère**) bitter, harsh; painful, grievous; biting, galling.—*n.m.* something bitter; gall; bitterness; (*pl.*) bitters.
amer (2) [a'mɛ:r], *n.m.* (*Naut.*) any landmark *or* leading mark.
amèrement [amɛr'mɑ̃], *adv.* bitterly, grievously.
américain [ameri'kɛ̃], *a.* American.—*n.m.* (**Américain,** *fem.* **-aine**) American (*person*).
américanisme [amerika'nism], *n.m.* Americanism.
Amérique [ame'rik], **l'**, *f.* America.
amérir or **amerrir** [ame'ri:r], *v.i.* (*Av.*) to alight on the water.
amerrissage [ameri'sa:ʒ], *n.m.* alighting (*on the water*).
amertume [amɛr'tym], *n.f.* bitterness, grief; gall, venom.
améthyste [ame'tist], *n.f.* amethyst.
ameublement [amœblə'mɑ̃], *n.m.* furniture, suite of furniture.
ameublir [amœ'bli:r], *v.t.* (*Agric.*) to make (*soil*) more broken up *or* lighter.
ameublissement [amœblis'mɑ̃], *n.m.* (*Agric.*) loosening, mellowing.
ameulonner [amølɔ'ne], *v.t.* to stack (*hay, corn etc.*).
ameuter [amø'te], *v.t.* to train dogs as a pack; (*fig.*) to stir up, to rouse, to excite.
ami [a'mi], *n.m.* (*fem.* **amie**) friend; well-wisher, partisan; lover; ***chambre d'ami***, spare room.—*a.* friendly; sympathetic, favourable, kindly-disposed; kind, propitious.
amiable [a'mjabl], *a.* friendly, courteous; amicable, conciliatory; ***vente à l'amiable***, sale by private contract.
amiablement [amjablə'mɑ̃], *adv.* amicably.
amiante [a'mjɑ̃:t], *n.m.* asbestos.
amibe [a'mib], *n.f.* amoeba.
amical [ami'kal], *a.* (*m. pl.* **-aux**) amicable, friendly.
amicalement [amikal'mɑ̃], *adv.* amicably, in a friendly manner.
amidon [ami'dɔ̃], *n.m.* starch.
amidonner [amidɔ'ne], *v.t.* to starch.
amincir [amɛ̃'si:r], *v.t.* to make thinner. **s'amincir**, *v.r.* to become thinner.
amincissement [amɛ̃sis'mɑ̃], *n.m.* thinning.
amiral [ami'ral], *n.m.* (*pl.* **-aux**) admiral; ***contre-amiral***, rear-admiral; ***grand amiral***, high-admiral; ***vice-amiral***, vice-admiral; ***vaisseau amiral***, flagship.
Amirauté [amiro'te], **Îles de l'**, *f.* Admiralty Islands.
amirauté [amiro'te], *n.f.* admiralship; admiralty.
amitié [ami'tje], *n.f.* friendship, affection; favour, kindness; (*pl.*) kind regards, compliments; ***mes amitiés à tout le monde***, love to all; ***par amitié***, out of friendship.
ammoniac [amɔ'njak], *a.* (*fem.* **-iaque**) ammoniac; ***sel ammoniac***, sal ammoniac.—*n.f.* (**-iaque**) ammonia.
ammonite [amɔ'nit], *n.f.* ammonite.
amnésie [amne'zi], *n.f.* amnesia.
amnistie [amnis'ti], *n.f.* amnesty, pardon.
amnistier [amnis'tje], *v.t.* to pardon by amnesty.
amoindrir [amwɛ̃'dri:r], *v.t.* to lessen, to decrease, to diminish. **s'amoindrir**, *v.r.* to grow less.
amoindrissement [amwɛ̃dris'mɑ̃], *n.m.* lessening, decrease.
amollir [amɔ'li:r], *v.t.* to soften; (*fig.*) to mollify. **s'amollir**, *v.r.* to soften, to grow soft; to grow effeminate *or* weak.
amollissant [amɔli'sɑ̃], *a.* softening; enervating.
amollissement [amɔlis'mɑ̃], *n.m.* softening, enervation, effeminacy.
amonceler [amɔ̃s'le], *v.t.* (*conjug. like* APPELER) to heap up, to lay in a heap; (*fig.*) to accumulate. **s'amonceler**, *v.r.* to gather; to accumulate, to drift together.
amoncellement [amɔ̃sɛl'mɑ̃], *n.m.* accumulation; heap.
amont [a'mɔ̃], *n.m.* upstream water (*used chiefly in* ***en amont***, up-stream, up-river).
amoral [amɔ'ral], *a.* (*m. pl.* **-aux**) amoral.
amorçage [amɔr'sa:ʒ], *n.m.* priming (*of pumps, motors, guns etc.*); baiting (*of hook*).
amorce [a'mɔrs], *n.f.* bait; (*fig.*) allurement, charm; priming, percussion-cap (*of guns etc.*); priming (*for a pump*).
amorcer [amɔr'se], *v.t.* (*conjug. like* COMMENCER) to bait; (*fig.*) to allure, to entice, to decoy; (*Hydraulics*) to prime; (*Artill.*) to cap (*a shell*).
amorphe [a'mɔrf], *a.* amorphous.
amortir [amɔr'ti:r], *v.t.* to deaden, to allay, to moderate; to weaken, to break (*a fall, shock etc.*); to redeem, to pay off; to cool (*passions*).
amortissable [amɔrti'sabl], *a.* redeemable.
amortissement [amɔrtis'mɑ̃], *n.m.* redemption, buying up; liquidation; deadening (*of a blow etc.*); ***fonds d'amortissement***, sinking-fund.
amortisseur [amɔrti'sœ:r], *n.m.* shock absorber.
amour [a'mu:r], *n.m.* (*usu. fem. in pl.*) love, affection, passion; the object of love, flame, fancy; ***l'Amour***, (*Myth.*) Eros, Cupid.
amouracher (s') [samura'ʃe], *v.r.* to be smitten with, to become enamoured (***de***).
amourette [amu'rɛt], *n.f.* passing amour, love-affair.

amoureusement [amurøz'mɑ̃], *adv.* amorously, lovingly; tenderly.
amoureux [amu'rø], *a.* (*fem.* **-euse**) loving, in love, smitten, enamoured (*de*); amorous.—*n.m.* (*fem.* **-euse**) lover, sweetheart; fiancé *or* fiancée.
amour-propre [amur'prɔpr], *n.m.* self-respect; vanity, conceit.
amovibilité [amɔvibili'te], *n.f.* removability, liability to removal; precariousness of tenure.
amovible [amɔ'vibl], *a.* removable, revocable.
ampère [ɑ̃'pɛ:r], *n.m.* (*Elec.*) ampere.
amphibie [ɑ̃fi'bi], *a.* amphibious.—*n.m.* amphibian.
amphibiens [ɑ̃fi'bjɛ̃], *n.m. pl.* (*Zool.*) Amphibia.
amphigouri [ɑ̃figu'ri], *n.m.* rigmarole, gibberish.
amphithéâtre [ɑ̃fite'ɑ:tr], *n.m.* amphitheatre; the whole body of occupants of this; the gallery in a theatre rising above the boxes and facing the stage; lecture-room; ***en amphithéâtre***, in semi-circular tiers.
Amphitryon [ɑ̃fitri'ɔ̃], *n.m.* Amphitryon; host, entertainer.
amphore [ɑ̃'fɔ:r], *n.f.* amphora.
ample [ɑ̃:pl], *a.* ample, full; large, vast, spacious; copious.
amplement [ɑ̃plə'mɑ̃], *adv.* amply, fully; largely, plentifully.
ampleur [ɑ̃'plœ:r], *n.f.* width, fullness (*of clothes*); abundance; profusion; dignity (*of style etc.*); volume (*of voice*).
amplifiant [ɑ̃pli'fjɑ̃], *a.* magnifying (*of a lens etc.*); amplifying.
amplificateur [ɑ̃plifika'tœ:r], *a.* (*fem.* **-trice**) magnifying; amplifying.—*n.m.* (*Phot.*) enlarger.
amplification [ɑ̃plifikɑ'sjɔ̃], *n.f.* amplification; magnification, enlargement; (*fig.*) exaggeration.
amplifier [ɑ̃pli'fje], *v.t.* to amplify, to develop, to enlarge.
amplitude [ɑ̃pli'tyd], *n.f.* extent, amplitude.
ampoule [ɑ̃'pul], *n.f.* blister, swelling; (*Elec.*) bulb; (*Med.*) ampoule.
ampoulé [ɑ̃pu'le], *a.* bombastic, turgid.
amputation [ɑ̃pytɑ'sjɔ̃], *n.f.* amputation; (*fig.*) curtailment.
amputer [ɑ̃py'te], *v.t.* to amputate, to cut off.
amulette [amy'lɛt], *n.f.* amulet, charm.
amusant [amy'zɑ̃], *a.* amusing, diverting, entertaining.
amusement [amyz'mɑ̃], *n.m.* amusement, entertainment, diversion; fooling, trifling.
amuser [amy'ze], *v.t.* to amuse, to divert, to entertain; to fool, to beguile, to dupe; to detain, to delay. **s'amuser**, *v.r.* to amuse oneself, to divert oneself; to trifle; to have a good time; ***s'amuser de quelqu'un***, to make fun of someone; ***amusez-vous bien !*** enjoy yourselves, have a good time.
amusette [amy'zɛt], *n.f.* petty amusement.
amuseur [amy'zœ:r], *n.m.* (*fem.* **-euse**) amuser, entertainer.
amygdale [ami'dal], *n.f.* (*Anat.*) tonsil.
an [ɑ̃], *n.m.* year; (*pl.*) years, time, age; ***elle a quinze ans***, she is fifteen; ***le jour de l'an***, New Year's day.
anacarde [ana'kard], *n.m.* cashew-nut.
anachorète [anakɔ'rɛt], *n.* anchorite, hermit.
anachronisme [anakrɔ'nism], *n.m.* anachronism.
anaéroïde [ANÉROÏDE].
anagramme [ana'gram], *n.f.* anagram.
analgésie [analʒe'zi], **analgie** [anal'ʒi], *n.f.* (*Med.*) analgesia.
analgésique [analʒe'zik], **analgique** [anal'ʒik], *a.* and *n.m.* analgesic.
analogie [analɔ'ʒi], *n.f.* analogy.
analogique [analɔ'ʒik], *a.* analogous, analogical.
analogue [ana'lɔg], *a.* analogous, similar.
analyse [ana'li:z], *n.f.* analysis; outline, précis, abstract (*of a book etc.*); (*Gram.*) parsing, analysis.
analyser [anali'ze], *v.t.* to analyse.
analyste [ana'list], *n.m.* analyst.
analytique [anali'tik], *a.* analytic, analytical.
analytiquement [analitik'mɑ̃], *adv.* analytically.
ananas [ana'nɑ], *n.m.* pineapple.
anarchie [anar'ʃi], *n.f.* anarchy; (*fig.*) disorder, confusion.
anarchique [anar'ʃik], *a.* anarchical.
anarchiste [anar'ʃist], *n.* anarchist.
anathème [ana'tɛ:m], *n.m.* anathema; sentence of reprobation *or* excommunication, ban, curse.
anatomie [anatɔ'mi], *n.f.* anatomy; dissection; (*fam.*) body, figure.
anatomique [anatɔ'mik], *a.* anatomical.
anatomiquement [anatɔmik'mɑ̃], *adv.* anatomically.
anatomiser [anatɔmi'ze], *v.t.* to anatomize, to dissect.
anatomiste [anatɔ'mist], *n.* anatomist.
ancêtre [ɑ̃'sɛ:tr], *n.* ancestor, ancestress.—*n.m. pl.* ancestors, forefathers.
anchois [ɑ̃'ʃwa], *n.m.* anchovy.
ancien [ɑ̃'sjɛ̃], *a.* (*fem.* **-ienne**) ancient, old; former, late, ex-; antique; ***un ancien élève***, an old boy.—*n.m.* (*fem.* **-ienne**) senior; ancient; (*Eccles.*) elder; (*Mil.*) veteran; (*pl.*) the ancients; our forefathers.
anciennement [ɑ̃sjɛn'mɑ̃], *adv.* formerly; *of yore; in former times.
ancienneté [ɑ̃sjɛn'te], *n.f.* antiquity; seniority.
ancillaire [ɑ̃sil'lɛ:r], *a.* ancillary.
ancrage [ɑ̃'kra:ʒ], *n.m.* anchorage.
ancre [ɑ̃:kr], *n.f.* anchor; cramp-iron, tie-plate (*of a wall*). ***ancre de miséricorde*** (or ***de salut***), sheet anchor (*fig.*) last resource.
ancrer [ɑ̃'kre], *v.t.* to anchor; (*fig.*) to fix *or* establish firmly.—*v.i.* to anchor. **s'ancrer**, *v.r.* to establish oneself, to get a footing (*in a place*), to take deep root (*in*).
Andalousie [ɑ̃dalu'zi], **l'**, *f.* Andalusia.
Andes [ɑ̃:d], **les**, *f. pl.* the Andes.
Andorre [ɑ̃'dɔ:r], **l'**, *m.* Andorra.
andouille [ɑ̃'du:j], *n.f.* pork sausage (*made of chitterlings*); (*pop.*) imbecile, duffer.
andouiller [ɑ̃du'je], *n.m.* tine (*of antler*).
André [ɑ̃'dre], *m.* Andrew.
Andromède [ɑ̃drɔ'mɛd], *f.* Andromeda.
âne [ɑ:n], *n.m.* ass, donkey; blockhead; stupid, ignorant *or* foolish person, idiot.
anéantir [aneɑ̃'ti:r], *v.t.* to annihilate, to destroy utterly, to abolish; (*fig.*) to overwhelm.

anéantissement [aneɑ̃tis'mɑ̃], *n.m.* annihilation; destruction, ruin, overthrow; humiliation, prostration.
anecdote [anɛg'dɔt], *n.f.* anecdote.
anecdotique [anɛgdɔ'tik], *a.* anecdotic.
anémie [ane'mi], *n.f.* anaemia.
anémique [ane'mik], *a.* anaemic.
anémone [ane'mɔn], *n.f.* anemone, windflower.
ânerie [ɑn'ri], *n.f.* stupidity; gross ignorance; gross blunder.
anéroïde [anerɔ'id], **anaéroïde** [anaerɔ'id], *a.* aneroid.—*n.m.* aneroid barometer.
ânesse [ɑ'nɛs], *n.f.* she-ass.
anesthésie [anɛste'zi], *n.f.* (*Med.*) anaesthesia.
anesthésier [anɛste'zje], *v.t.* to anaesthetize.
anesthésique [anɛste'zik], *a.* and *n.m.* anaesthetic.
anesthésiste [anɛste'zist], *n.m.* anaesthetist.
anévrisme [ane'vrism], *n.m.* aneurism.
anfractueux [ɑ̃frak'tɥø], *a.* (*fem.* **-euse**) anfractuous, winding, sinuous, craggy.
anfractuosité [ɑ̃fraktɥɔzi'te], *n.f.* anfractuosity, cragginess, twist, jagged *or* rugged outlines.
ange [ɑ̃:ʒ], *n.m.* angel; (*fig.*) an adorable *or* beloved person.
Angèle [ɑ̃'ʒɛl], *f.* Angela.
angélique [ɑ̃ʒe'lik], *a.* angelic, angelical.
angélus [ɑ̃ʒe'ly:s], *n.m.* angelus.
angevin [ɑ̃ʒə'vɛ̃], *a.* of Anjou.—*n.m.* (**Angevin**, *fem.* **-ine**) native of Anjou.
angine [ɑ̃'ʒin], *n.f.* angina, quinsy, sore throat.
anglais [ɑ̃'glɛ], *a.* English; British.—*n.m.* English (*language*); (**Anglais**, *fem.* **-aise**) Englishman, English girl *or* woman; (*pl.*) the English.
angle [ɑ̃:gl], *n.m.* angle, corner; (*Arch.*) quoin; ***angle aigu***, acute angle; ***angle droit***, right angle.
Angleterre [ɑ̃glə'tɛ:r], **l'**, *f.* England.
anglican [ɑ̃gli'kɑ̃], *a.* and *n.m.* (*fem.* **-e**) Anglican.
angliciser [ɑ̃glisi'ze], *v.t.* to anglicize. **s'angliciser**, *v.r.* to become anglicized *or* English.
anglicisme [ɑ̃gli'sism], *n.m.* anglicism.
anglomanie [ɑ̃glɔma'ni], *n.f.* Anglomania.
anglo-normand [ɑ̃glonɔr'mɑ̃], *a.* and *n.m.* (*fem.* **-e**) Anglo-Norman; ***les Îles anglo-normandes***, the Channel Islands.
anglophile [ɑ̃glɔ'fil], *a.* and *n.* Anglophil.
anglo-saxon [ɑ̃glɔsak'sɔ̃], *a.* and *n.m.* (*fem.* **-saxonne**) Anglo-Saxon.
angoisse [ɑ̃'gwas], *n.f.* anguish, agony, great distress; (*Med.*) angor, anguish.
angora [ɑ̃gɔ'ra], *a.* Angora.—*n.m.* Angora cat.
anguille [ɑ̃'gi:j], *n.f.* eel; (*pl.*, *Naut.*) launching ways, slips; ***il y a anguille sous roche***, I smell a rat.
angulaire [ɑ̃gy'lɛ:r], *a.* angular.
angusture [ɑ̃gys'ty:r], *n.f.* (*Pharm.*) angostura.
anhélation [anelɑ'sjɔ̃], *n.f.* panting.
anhéler [ane'le], *v.i.* (*conjug. like* CÉDER) to pant.
anhydre [a'nidr], *a.* (*Chem.*) anhydrous.
anhydride [ani'drid], *n.m.* anhydride; ***anhydride carbonique***, carbon dioxide.
anicroche [ani'krɔʃ], *n.f.* slight obstacle.
animadversion [animadvɛr'sjɔ̃], *n.f.* animadversion, reproof, reprimand, censure.
animal [ani'mal], *n.m.* (*pl.* **-aux**) animal; beast, brute; ***société protectrice des animaux***, Royal Society for the Prevention of Cruelty to Animals.—*a.* (*m.pl.* **-aux**) animal; sensual, carnal.
animateur [anima'tœ:r], *a.* (*fem.* **-trice**) animating.
animation [animɑ'sjɔ̃], *n.f.* animation, vitality, life; liveliness; excitement; irritation.
animé [ani'me], *a.* animated; spirited, gay, sprightly; ***rue animée***, busy street.
animer [ani'me], *v.t.* to animate, to give life to; to arouse, to excite, to urge on; to enliven, to give force to (*style etc.*). **s'animer**, *v.r.* to become animated *or* lively; to cheer up; to become angry.
animosité [animozi'te], *n.f.* animosity, ill will, spite, rancour.
anis [a'ni], *n.m.* anise, aniseed.
aniser [ani'ze], *v.t.* to flavour with aniseed.
anisette [ani'zɛt], *n.f.* aniseed cordial.
ankylose [ɑ̃ki'lo:z], *n.f.* (*Path.*) anchylosis, stiffness in the joints.
annales [a'nal], *n.f.* (*used only in pl.*) annals, public records.
annaliste [ana'list], *n.m.* annalist.
anneau [a'no], *n.m.* (*pl.* **anneaux**) ring; link (*of a chain*); ringlet (*of hair*).
année [a'ne], *n.f.* year, period of twelve months; ***année bissextile***, leap-year; ***souhaiter la bonne année***, to wish a happy New Year.
année-lumière [anely'mjɛ:r], *n.f.* (*pl.* **années-lumière**) light-year.
annelé [an'le], *a.* having *or* arranged in rings, ringed; (*Zool.*) annulated.
annelet [an'lɛ], *n.m.* ringlet, small ring.
annexe [a'nɛks], *n.f.* annex; appendage; appendix, schedule, rider; chapel of ease.
annexer [anɛk'se], *v.t.* to annex, to attach.
annexion [anɛk'sjɔ̃], *n.f.* annexation.
annihilation [aniilɑ'sjɔ̃], *n.f.* annihilation; (*Law*) annulment.
annihiler [anii'le], *v.t.* to annihilate, to destroy; (*Law*) to annul.
anniversaire [anivɛr'sɛ:r], *a.* and *n.m.* anniversary, birthday.
annonce [a'nɔ̃:s], *n.f.* announcement, notification; indication, sign, mark; advertisement; ***annonce de mariage***, banns of marriage.
annoncer [anɔ̃'se], *v.t.* (*conjug. like* COMMENCER) to announce, to give notice of; to advertise; to announce (*a visitor*), to usher *or* show in; to proclaim; to foretell. **s'annoncer**, *v.r.* to present oneself; to manifest itself.
Annonciation [anɔ̃sjɑ'sjɔ̃], *n.f.* Annunciation; Lady Day (March 25).
annoncier [anɔ̃'sje], *n.m.* publicity manager.
annotateur [anɔta'tœ:r], *n.m.* (*fem.* **-trice**) annotator (*of a book etc.*).
annotation [anɔtɑ'sjɔ̃], *n.f.* annotation.
annoter [anɔ'te], *v.t.* to annotate, to make notes on (*a text etc.*).
annuaire [a'nɥɛ:r], *n.m.* annual, year-book; ***l'Annuaire des Téléphones***, the telephone directory.
annuel [a'nɥɛl], *a.* (*fem.* **-elle**) annual, yearly.
annuellement [anɥɛl'mɑ̃], *adv.* annually, yearly.

annuité [anɥi'te], *n.f.* annuity.
annulable [any'labl], *a.* revocable.
annulaire [any'lɛ:r], *a.* annular, ring-shaped. —*n.m.* ring-finger, third finger.
annulation [anylɑ'sjɔ̃], *n.f.* annulment, cancellation, repeal, abolition.
annuler [any'le], *v.t.* to annul, to rescind, to cancel, to abolish, to set aside, to make void.
anobli [anɔ'bli], *a.* ennobled.—*n.m.* newly created nobleman.
anoblir [anɔ'bli:r], *v.t.* to ennoble, to raise to the rank of the nobility.
anoblissement [anɔblis'mɑ̃], *n.m.* ennoblement.
anode [a'nɔd], *n.f.* (*Elec.*) anode, positive pole.
anodin [anɔ'dɛ̃], *a.* (*Med.*) anodyne, soothing; (*fig.*) harmless, mild, inoffensive, insignificant.
anomal [anɔ'mal], *a.* (*m. pl.* **-aux**) (*Gram.*) anomalous, irregular.
anomalie [anɔma'li], *n.f.* anomaly, irregularity.
ânon [ɑ'nɔ̃], *n.m.* ass's foal, young ass; (*fig.*) a little fool.
ânonnement [ɑnɔn'mɑ̃], *n.m.* faltering, mumbling way of reading a text.
ânonner [anɔ'ne], *v.t.* to mumble and blunder through (*a lesson etc.*).—*v.i.* to read in a faltering way.
anonymat [anɔni'ma], *n.m.* anonymity.
anonyme [anɔ'nim], *a.* anonymous, nameless; ***société anonyme***, joint-stock company. —*n.* anonymous person.
anonymement [anɔnim'mɑ̃], *adv.* anonymously.
anorak [anɔ'rak], *n.m.* (*reg. trade mark*) anorak.
anormal [anɔr'mal], *a.* (*m. pl.* **-aux**) abnormal, irregular, mentally deficient.
anormalement [anɔrmal'mɑ̃], *adv.* abnormally.
anse [ɑ̃:s], *n.f.* handle (*of a pot, basket etc.*); creek, cove.
antagonique [ɑ̃tagɔ'nik], *a.* antagonistic.
antagonisme [ɑ̃tagɔ'nism], *n.m.* antagonism.
antagoniste [ɑ̃tagɔ'nist], *a.* antagonistic.—*n.m.* antagonist, adversary, opponent; competitor, rival.
antan** [ɑ̃'tɑ̃], *n.m.* yesteryear; ***les neiges d'antan, the snows of yesteryear.
antarctique [ɑ̃tark'tik], *a.* Antarctic.
antécédent [ɑ̃tese'dɑ̃], *a.* antecedent, preceding, foregoing, previous.—*n.m.* precedent; (*Gram.*) antecedent.
antéchrist [ɑ̃te'krist], *n.m.* Antichrist.
antédiluvien [ɑ̃tedily'vjɛ̃], *a.* (*fem.* **-ienne**) antediluvian.
antenne [ɑ̃'tɛn], *n.f.* (*Rad., Tel.*) aerial; (*Ent.*) antenna, (*pl.*) antennae.
antépénultième [ɑ̃tepenyl'tjɛm], *a.* antepenultimate.
antérieur [ɑ̃te'rjœ:r], *a.* anterior, earlier, antecedent, previous, former.
antérieurement [ɑ̃terjœr'mɑ̃], *adv.* previously, before.
antériorité [ɑ̃terjɔri'te], *n.f.* anteriority, priority, precedence.
anthologie [ɑ̃tɔlɔ'ʒi], *n.f.* anthology.
anthracite [ɑ̃tra'sit], *n.m.* anthracite.
anthrax [ɑ̃'traks], *n.m.* (*Med.*) anthrax.
anthropoïde [ɑ̃trɔpɔ'id], *a.* and *n.m.* (*Zool.*) anthropoid.
anthropologie [ɑ̃trɔpɔlɔ'ʒi], *n.f.* anthropology.
anthropologiste [ɑ̃trɔpɔlɔ'ʒist], **anthropologue** [ɑ̃trɔpɔ'lɔg], *n.* anthropologist.
anthropophage [ɑ̃trɔpɔ'fa:ʒ], *n.* cannibal.
anti-aérien [ɑ̃tiae'rjɛ̃], *a.* (*fem.* **-enne**) antiaircraft.
antibiotique [ɑ̃tibiɔ'tik], *a.* and *n.m.* antibiotic.
anti-brouillard [ɑ̃tibru'ja:r], *n.m.* (*Motor.*) fog-light.
anti-buée [ɑ̃ti'bye], *a.* (*Motor.*) demisting.—*n.m.* demister.
antichambre [ɑ̃ti'ʃɑ̃:br], *n.f.* (*formerly m.*) antechamber, anteroom.
anti-char [ɑ̃ti'ʃa:r], *a.* anti-tank.
antichrétien [ɑ̃tikre'tjɛ̃], *a.* and *n.m.* (*fem.* **-ienne**) antichristian.
anticipation [ɑ̃tisipɑ'sjɔ̃], *n.f.* anticipation; encroachment, trespass; ***par anticipation***, in advance, beforehand.
anticipé [ɑ̃tisi'pe], *a.* done *or* occurring in advance.
anticiper [ɑ̃tisi'pe], *v.t.* to anticipate, to forestall.—*v.i.* to encroach *or* trespass (***sur***).
anticlimax [ɑ̃tikli'maks], *n.m.* anticlimax.
anticommunisme [ɑ̃tikɔmy'nism], *n.m.* anti-communism.
anticonstitutionnellement [ɑ̃tikɔ̃stitysjɔnɛl'mɑ̃], *adv.* (*the longest French word*) anticonstitutionally.
anticorps [ɑ̃ti'kɔ:r], *n.m.* (*Med.*) anti-body.
anticyclone [ɑ̃tisi'klo:n], *n.m.* (*Meteor.*) anticyclone.
antidate [ɑ̃ti'dat], *n.f.* antedate.
antidater [ɑ̃tida'te], *v.t.* to antedate.
antidérapant [ɑ̃tidera'pɑ̃], *a.* non-skidding; ***pneu antidérapant***, non-skid tyre.
antidote [ɑ̃ti'dɔt], *n.m.* antidote, antitoxin; (*fig.*) cure.
anti-éblouissant [ɑ̃tieblui'sɑ̃], *a.* (*Motor.*) antidazzle.
antienne [ɑ̃'tjɛn], *n.f.* antiphon; anthem.
antigel [ɑ̃ti'ʒɛl], *n.m. inv.* anti-freeze.
antillais [ɑ̃ti'jɛ], *a.* West Indian.—*n.m.* (**Antillais**, *fem.* **-aise**) West Indian (*person*).
Antilles [ɑ̃'ti:j], **les**, *f.pl.* the West Indies; ***la mer des Antilles***, the Caribbean Sea.
antilope [ɑ̃ti'lɔp], *n.f.* antelope.
anti-mite [ɑ̃ti'mit], *a.* moth-proof.
antimoine [ɑ̃ti'mwan], *n.m.* antimony.
Antioche [ɑ̃'tjɔʃ], *f.* Antioch.
antiparasite [ɑ̃tipara'zit], *n.m.* suppressor.
antiparlementaire [ɑ̃tiparləmɑ̃'tɛ:r], *a.* unparliamentary.
antipathie [ɑ̃tipa'ti], *n.f.* antipathy, aversion.
antipathique [ɑ̃tipa'tik], *a.* antipathetic, repugnant.
antiphonaire [ɑ̃tifɔ'nɛ:r], *n.m.* antiphonal.
antipode [ɑ̃ti'pɔd], *n.m.* the region of the globe diametrically opposite; (*pl.*) antipodes.
antiputride [ɑ̃tipy'trid], *a.* and *n.m.* antiseptic.
antiquaire [ɑ̃ti'kɛ:r], *n.m.* antiquary, antiquarian, antique-dealer.
antique [ɑ̃'tik], *a.* antique, ancient; old-fashioned.—*n.f.* antique, ancient work of art.
antiquité [ɑ̃tiki'te], *n.f.* antiquity; old times; (*pl.*) antiquities; ***magasin d'antiquités***, old curiosity shop.
antirouille [ɑ̃ti'ru:j], *n.m.* rust preventive.

antirrhine [ɑ̃ti'rin], *n.f.* (*Bot.*) antirrhinum, snapdragon.
antisémite [ɑ̃tise'mit], *n.* anti-Semite.
antisémitique [ɑ̃tisemi'tik], *a.* anti-Semitic.
antisemitisme [ɑ̃tisemi'tism], *n.m.* anti-Semitism.
antiseptique [ɑ̃tisɛp'tik], *a.* and *n.m.* (*Med.*) antiseptic.
antisocial [ɑ̃tisɔ'sjal], *a.* (*m. pl.* **-aux**) antisocial.
antisportif [ɑ̃tispɔr'tif], *a.* (*fem.* **-ive**) unsportsmanlike; opposed to sports.
antithèse [ɑ̃ti'tɛ:z], *n.f.* antithesis.
antitoxine [ɑ̃titɔk'sin], *n.f.* (*Med.*) antitoxin.
anti-vol [ɑ̃ti'vɔl], *a. inv.* anti-theft.—*n.m.* burglar-proof device.
antivivisection [ɑ̃tivivisɛk'sjɔ̃], *n.f.* antivivisection.
Antoine [ɑ̃'twɑn], *m.* Anthony.
antre [ɑ̃:tr], *n.m.* den, lair; cavern.
anuiter (s') [sanɥi'te], *v.r.* to be benighted.
anus [a'ny:s], *n.m.* anus.
Anvers [ɑ̃'vɛr], *m.* Antwerp.
anxiété [ɑ̃ksje'te], *n.f.* anxiety; uneasiness; (*Med.*) pain in the heart.
anxieusement [ɑ̃ksjøz'mɑ̃], *adv.* anxiously.
anxieux [ɑ̃k'sjø], *a.* (*fem.* **-euse**) anxious, uneasy, restless.
aorte [a'ɔrt], *n.f.* (*Anat.*) aorta.
août [u(t)], *n.m.* August; (*fig.*) harvest; ***la mi-août***, the middle of August.
aoûté [u'te], *a.* ripened by the heat of August.
aoûter (s') [su'te], *v.r.* to ripen (*in August*).
apache [a'paʃ], *n.m.* ruffian of the Paris streets, hooligan.
apaisement [apɛz'mɑ̃], *n.m.* appeasement; abatement, lull.
apaiser [apɛ'ze], *v.t.* to pacify, to calm, to appease; to quiet; to mitigate, to alleviate (*pain, sorrow etc.*); to stay (*hunger*); to quench (*thirst*). **s'apaiser**, *v.r.* to be appeased; to sober down; to grow quiet; to abate, to subside.
Apalaches [apa'laʃ], *m.pl.* Appalachians.
(*C*) **apalachien** [apala'ʃjɛ̃], *a.* (*fem.* **-chienne**) Appalachian.
apanage [apa'na:ʒ], *n.m.* apanage; (*fig.*) lot.
apanager [apana'ʒe], *v.t.* (*conjug. like* MANGER) to endow.
aparté [apar'te], *n.m.* aside.
apathie [apa'ti], *n.f.* apathy, indolence, listlessness.
apathique [apa'tik], *a.* apathetic, listless.
apatride [apa'trid], *a.* and *n.* stateless (person).
Apennins [apɛ'nɛ̃], **les**, *m.pl.* the Apennines.
apepsie [apɛp'si], *n.f.* (*Path.*) apepsy, indigestion.
apeptique [apɛp'tik], *a.* dyspeptic.
apercevable [apɛrsə'vabl], *a.* perceivable, perceptible.
apercevoir [apɛrsə'vwa:r], *v.t.* (*conjug. like* RECEVOIR) to catch sight of, to notice; to perceive, to understand, to comprehend. **s'apercevoir**, *v.r.* (***de quelque chose***) to remark, to notice, to be aware of; to find out, to discover; to be visible.
aperçu [apɛr'sy], *n.m.* rapid view, glance *or* survey; rough estimate *or* summary; judgment, idea.
apéritif [aperi'tif], *a.* (*fem.* **-ive**) aperient, appetizing.—*n.m.* (*Med.*) aperient, laxative; appetizer, aperitif (*e.g. vermouth, bitters*).

à peu près [apø'prɛ], *n.m.* approximation, approach; a word roughly standing for another.—*adv.* nearly, about.
apeuré [apø're], *a.* frightened, scared.
apex [a'pɛks], *n.m.* apex.
aphélie [afe'li], *n.m.* (*Astron.*) aphelion.
aphidé [afi'de], **aphidien** [afi'djɛ̃], *n.m.* (*Ent.*) aphis, greenfly.
aphone [a'fɔn], *a.* voiceless.
aphonie [afɔ'ni], *n.f.* aphony, loss of voice.
aphorisme [afɔ'rism], *n.m.* aphorism.
à-pic [a'pik], *n.m.* steep hill, cliff.
apiculteur [apikyl'tœ:r], *n.m.* bee-keeper.
apiculture [apikyl'ty:r], *n.f.* apiculture, bee-keeping.
apitoiement [apitwɑ'mɑ̃], *n.m.* pity compassion.
apitoyant [apitwa'jɑ̃], *a.* piteous.
apitoyer [apitwa'je], *v.t.* (*conjug. like* EMPLOYER) to move to pity, to soften. **s'apitoyer**, *v.r.* to pity.
aplanir [apla'ni:r], *v.t.* to smooth, to level, to make even; (*fig.*) to level down *or* remove (*obstacles, difficulties etc.*). **s'aplanir**, *v.r.* to grow easy, smooth etc.
aplanissement [aplanis'mɑ̃], *n.m.* smoothing levelling, making even; smoothness, evenness.
aplat [a'pla], *n.m.* flat tint.
aplatir [apla'ti:r], *v.t.* to flatten, to beat flat; (*fig.*) to vanquish, to silence, to floor. **s'aplatir**, *v.r.* to become flat, to be flattened; (*fig.*) to crouch, to cringe.
aplatissement [aplatis'mɑ̃], **aplatissage** [aplati'sa:ʒ], *n.m.* flattening, flatness; (*fig.*) humiliation.
aplomb [a'plɔ̃], *n.m.* perpendicularity; equilibrium; (*fig.*) assurance, self-possession, steadiness, coolness; impudence, cheek; ***d'aplomb***, perpendicularly, upright.
apocalypse [apɔka'lips], *n.f.* Apocalypse, the Book of Revelation.
apocalyptique [apɔkalip'tik], *a.* apocalyptic, obscure.
apocryphe [apɔ'krif], *a.* apocryphal, spurious.
apode [a'pɔd], *a.* (*Zool.*) apodal, footless.
apogée [apɔ'ʒe], *n.m.* apogee; (*fig.*) acme, height, zenith.
apologétique [apɔlɔʒe'tik], *a.* by way of apology, apologetic.
apologie [apɔlɔ'ʒi], *n.f.* apology, vindication, justification.
apologue [apɔ'lɔg], *n.m.* apologue, fable.
apoplectique [apɔplɛk'tik], *a.* and *n.* apoplectic.
apoplexie [apɔplɛk'si], *n.f.* apoplexy.
apostasie [apɔsta'zi], *n.f.* apostasy.
apostat [apɔs'ta], *a.* and *n.m.* (*fem.* **-e**) apostate.
aposter [apɔs'te], *v.t.* to place in ambush, to station.
apostille [apɔs'ti:j], *n.f.* marginal note, postscript, footnote.
apostiller [apɔsti'je], *v.t.* to add a postscript *or* marginal recommendation.
apostolat [apɔstɔ'la], *n.m.* apostleship.
apostolique [apɔstɔ'lik], *a.* apostolic; papal.
apostrophe [apɔs'trɔf], *n.f.* (*Rhet. and Gram.*) apostrophe; address; (*fig.*) reprimand, attack.

apostropher [apɔstrɔ'fe], *v.t.* to apostrophize, to address; (*fig.*) to reprimand.
apothéose [apɔte'o:z], *n.f.* apotheosis.
apothicaire [apɔti'kɛ:r], *n.m.* apothecary.
apôtre [a'po:tr], *n.m.* apostle; (*fig.*) leader of a cause.
apparaître [apa'rɛ:tr], *v.i. irr.* (*conjug. like* CONNAÎTRE) to appear, to become visible; to be evident.
apparat [apa'ra], *n.m.* pomp, show, ostentation, parade.
apparaux [apa'ro], *n.m.* (*used only in pl.*) (*Naut.*) gear, tackle, outfit etc.
appareil [apa'rɛ:j], *n.m.* formal preparation; pomp, display; appearance, show; apparatus, appliances, machinery, paraphernalia; (*Surg.*) dressing; ***appareil (photographique)***, camera; ***qui est à l'appareil?*** who is speaking?
appareillage [aparɛ'ja:ʒ], *n.m.* installation; (*Naut.*) act of getting under sail, weighing.
appareillement [aparɛj'mɑ̃], *n.m.* coupling, yoking; pairing (*for breeding*).
appareiller [aparɛ'je], *v.t.* to install equipment; to match; to pair (*animals*).—*v.i.* to get under way, to weigh anchor. **s'appareiller**, *v.r.* to pair (*of birds*).
appareilleur [aparɛ'jœ:r], *n.m.* (*Building*) stone dresser; ***appareilleur à gaz***, gas-fitter.
apparemment [apara'mɑ̃], *adv.* apparently.
apparence [apa'rɑ̃:s], *n.f.* appearance, look, semblance, likelihood, probability; ***en apparence***, seemingly, apparently.
apparent [apa'rɑ̃], *a.* visible, prominent.
apparenté [aparɑ̃'te], *a.* related; ***bien apparenté***, well connected.
apparentement [aparɑ̃t'mɑ̃], *n.m.* political alliance.
apparenter [aparɑ̃'te], *v.t.* to ally, to connect by marriage. **s'apparenter**, *v.r.* to ally oneself (*by marriage*).
appariement or **apparîment** [apari'mɑ̃], *n.m.* pairing, matching; coupling, mating; ***appariement d'écoles***, school linking.
apparier [apa'rje], *v.t.* to assort by pairs, to pair (*birds etc.*), to match (*horses, gloves etc.*).
apparition [apari'sjɔ̃], *n.f.* apparition, sudden appearance; phantom, ghost; ***apparition d'anges***, vision of angels.
appartement [apartə'mɑ̃], *n.m.* suite of rooms, flat.
appartenances [apartə'nɑ̃:s], *n.f.* (*used in pl.*) appurtenances.
appartenant [apartə'nɑ̃], *a.* belonging, appertaining.
appartenir [apartə'ni:r], *v.i. irr.* (*conjug. like* TENIR) to belong, to appertain; to relate, to pertain, to concern; to behove, to be the right, privilege, duty etc. of (*à*); ***il appartient***, (*v. impers.*) it is meet *or* fit; it behoves, it concerns. **s'appartenir**, *v.r.* to be master of one's own actions, to be free.
appas [a'pɑ], *n.m. pl.* feminine charms, attractions.
appât [a'pɑ], *n.m.* bait; lure, allurement, enticement.
appâter [apɑ'te] *v.t.* to attract with a bait, to allure; to fatten (*fowls etc.*).
appauvrir [apo'vri:r], *v.t.* to impoverish. **s'appauvrir**, *v.r.* to grow poor, to become impoverished.
appauvrissement [apovris'mɑ̃], *n.m.* impoverishment.
appel [a'pɛl], *n.m.* appeal, call, summons; (*Mil.*) roll-call, muster; summoning of conscripts to the colours; (*Law*) appeal to a higher court; ***battre*** or ***sonner l'appel***, (*Mil.*) to sound the fall-in.
appelé [ap'le], *a.* called up.—*n.m.* soldier called up for service.
appeler [ap'le], *v.t.* (*see Verb Tables*) to call, to send for; to call over; to call up, to call together; to summon, to cite, to invoke, to call upon, to invite; to name, to term; to challenge.—*v.i.* to appeal (*to a higher court*). **s'appeler**, *v.r.* to be called, to call oneself.
appellation [apɛlɑ'sjɔ̃], *n.f.* calling; appelation; trade name; ***appellation contrôlée***, registered trade-name.
appendice [apɑ̃'dis], *n.m.* appendix, appendage, addition.
appendicite [apɑ̃di'sit], *n.f.* (*Path.*) appendicitis.
appendre [a'pɑ̃:dr], *v.t.* to hang up, to suspend; to attach.
appentis [apɑ̃'ti], *n.m.* shed, lean-to.
appesantir [apəzɑ̃'ti:r], *v.t.* to make heavy, to weigh down; (*fig.*) to make dull. **s'appesantir**, *v.r.* to grow heavy and dull, to be weighed down; to dwell on, to expatiate (***sur***).
appesantissement [apəzɑ̃tis'mɑ̃], *n.m.* heaviness, dullness.
appétissant [apeti'sɑ̃], *a.* desirable, appetizing, tempting; dainty, delicious.
appétit [ape'ti], *n.m.* appetite, relish; desire sensuous craving (*usu. in pl.*); appetite (*for food*); (*fig.*) inclination, taste, stomach.
applaudir [aplo'di:r], *v.t., v.i.* to clap the hands, to applaud; to praise, to commend, to approve. **s'applaudir**, *v.r.* to boast, to glory (*in a thing*); to congratulate oneself (***de***); to rejoice (***de***).
applaudissement [aplodis'mɑ̃], *n.m.* (*usually pl.*) applause, public praise; cheering.
applicabilité [aplikabili'te], *n.f.* applicability, appositeness.
applicable [apli'kabl], *a.* applicable, apposite, relevant, suitable.
application [aplikɑ'sjɔ̃], *n.f.* application, applying; employment (*of a sum of money*); infliction (*of a penalty*); attention, care, diligence; appliqué lace.
applique [a'plik], *n.f.* ornamental accessories, candelabrum *or* bracket fixed to a wall.
appliqué [apli'ke], *a.* studious; ***sciences appliquées***, applied sciences.
appliquer [apli'ke], *v.t.* to apply (*à*), to stick; to apply (*one's mind*); to adapt, to employ; to inflict, to impose (*a penalty etc.*). **s'appliquer**, *v.r.* to apply oneself, to work hard.
appoint [a'pwɛ̃], *n.m.* money paying off an account, balance; change; contribution; ***faire l'appoint***, to pay the exact sum.
appointé [apwɛ̃'te], *a.* receiving a salary.
appointement [apwɛ̃t'mɑ̃], *n.m.* (*pl.*) salary (*of employee*); emoluments; (*Eccles.*) stipend.
appointer (1) [apwɛ̃'te], *v.t.* to give a salary to.
appointer (2) [apwɛ̃'te], *v.t.* to sharpen to a point, to point.
appontement [apɔ̃t'mɑ̃], *n.m.* (*Naut.*) bridge-

like structure for loading vessels; (*wooden*) wharf *or* pier.

apport [a'pɔːr], *n.m.* property brought by a husband or wife into the common stock; a shareholder's contribution to the assets of a company.

apporter [apɔr'te], *v.t.* to bring; to furnish, to supply; to bring to bear, to employ (*trouble, pains etc.*); to cause, to produce, to bring about.

apposer [apo'ze], *v.t.* to set, to put, to affix; to insert (*a clause etc.*).

apposition [apɔzi'sjɔ̃], *n.f.* setting, putting, affixing; (*Gram.*) apposition.

appréciable [apre'sjabl], *a.* appreciable, perceptible.

appréciateur [apresja'tœːr], *n.m.* (*fem.* **-trice**) valuer.

appréciatif [apresja'tif], *a.* (*fem.* **-ive**) denoting the value of; ***état*** or ***devis appréciatif***, estimate.

appréciation [apresjɑ'sjɔ̃], *n.f.* appreciation, valuation, estimation; rise in value.

apprécier [apre'sje], *v.t.* to value, to estimate, to appraise, to judge; to appreciate, to esteem.

appréhender [apreɑ̃'de], *v.t.* to arrest, to apprehend; to be apprehensive of, to fear, to dread.

appréhensible [apreɑ̃'sibl], *a.* apprehensible, comprehensible.

appréhensif [apreɑ̃'sif], *a.* (*fem.* **-ive**) apprehensive, timid.

appréhension [apreɑ̃'sjɔ̃], *n.f.* apprehension, fear, dread.

apprendre [a'prɑ̃ːdr], *v.t. irr.* (*conjug. like* PRENDRE) to learn; to hear of, to be informed of; to acquire (*a habit etc.*); to tell, to inform; to teach, to impart knowledge of (*a subject*).

apprenti [aprɑ̃'ti], *a.* apprenticed, articled.—*n.m.* (*fem.* **-e**) apprentice; (*fig.*) novice.

apprentissage [aprɑ̃ti'saːʒ], *n.m.* apprenticeship; trial, experiment.

apprêt [a'prɛ], *n.m.* preparation; cooking, dressing (*of food*); manner of preparing cloth, silk, lace etc.; the substance used in this process; (*pl.*) preparations.

apprêtage [aprɛ'taːʒ], *n.m.* dressing, application of the preliminary preparation to cloth, silk etc.

apprêté [aprɛ'te], *a.* studied, affected, stiff.

apprêter [aprɛ'te], *v.t.* to prepare, to get ready; to dress, to cook; to apply the ***apprêts*** [*q.v.*] to. **s'apprêter**, *v.r.* to prepare oneself, to get ready (*à*).

apprêteur [aprɛ'tœːr], *a.* and *n.m.* (*fem.* **-euse**) dresser, finisher.—*n.f.* (**-euse**) hat-trimmer.

apprivoisé [aprivwa'ze], *a.* tame.

apprivoisement [aprivwaz'mɑ̃], *n.m.* taming.

apprivoiser [aprivwa'ze], *v.t.* to tame (*animals*); to win (*people*) over, to make sociable *or* tractable.

apprivoiseur [aprivwa'zœːr], *n.m.* (*fem.* **-euse**) tamer.

approbateur [aprɔba'tœːr], *a.* (*fem.* **-trice**) approving.

approbatif [aprɔba'tif], *a.* (*fem.* **-tive**) approbatory; ***geste approbatif***, nod of approbation *or* approval.

approbation [aprɔbɑ'sjɔ̃], *n.f.* approbation, consent, approval.

approbativement [aprɔbativ'mɑ̃], *adv.* approvingly.

approchable [aprɔ'ʃabl], *a.* approachable, easy of access.

approchant [aprɔ'ʃɑ̃], *a.* like, much the same, something like, approximate, bordering on.

approche [a'prɔʃ], *n.f.* approach, coming, advance, nearness; (*pl.*) approaches, access.

approcher [aprɔ'ʃe], *v.t.* to bring, put *or* draw near *or* nearer; to come near *or* nearer; to approach.—*v.i.* to approach, to draw near, to come near; to be something like, to be nearly. **s'approcher**, *v.r.* to approach, to advance.

approfondir [aprɔfɔ̃'diːr], *v.t.* to deepen, to make deeper; to examine thoroughly, to investigate. **s'approfondir**, *v.r.* to become deeper.

approfondissement [aprɔfɔ̃dis'mɑ̃], *n.m.* deepening; fathoming; thorough investigation.

appropriation [aprɔpriɑ'sjɔ̃], *n.f.* adaptation, assimilation; appropriation.

approprier [aprɔpri'e], *v.t.* to make appropriate, to accommodate, to adapt; to clean, to tidy etc.; to suit, to fit, (*style to subject etc.*). **s'approprier**, *v.r.* to appropriate a thing to oneself; to conform, to adapt oneself.

approuver [apru've], *v.t.* to sanction, to consent to, to ratify, to authorize; to approve, to approve of; to pass (*accounts*).

approvisionnement [aprɔvizjɔn'mɑ̃], *n.m.* victualling, supply, stock.

approvisionner [aprɔvizjɔ'ne], *v.t.* to supply with necessaries, to victual, to stock. **s'approvisionner**, *v.r.* to supply oneself; to lay in supplies.

approvisionneur [aprɔvizjɔ'nœːr], *n.m.* (*fem.* **-euse**) caterer, purveyor.

approximatif [aprɔksima'tif], *a.* (*fem.* **-tive**) approximate.

approximation [aprɔksimɑ'sjɔ̃], *n.f.* approximation, rough estimate.

approximativement [aprɔksimativ'mɑ̃], *adv.* approximately.

appui [a'pɥi], *n.m.* support, prop, stay; any kind of mechanical support, *as* buttress, rail, handrail, sill (*of windows*); (*Mech.*) fulcrum; (*fig.*) corroboration; (*Gram.*) stress.

appui-main [apɥi'mɛ̃], *n.m.* (*pl.* **appuis-main**) painter's maulstick *or* hand-rest.

appuyer [apɥi'je], *v.t.* (*conjug. like* EMPLOYER) to prop up, to support; to lean (*something against a wall etc.*); (*fig.*) to second, to back up, to uphold, to stand by, to reinforce.—*v.i.* to weigh upon, to lay stress (***sur***); (*fig.*) to insist; ***appuyer à droite***, to bear to the right. **s'appuyer**, *v.r.* to lean, to rest (***sur***); to rely upon, to depend (***sur***); to lay stress *or* a stress on, to dwell (***sur***).

âpre [ɑːpr], *a.* hard, rough, harsh, rugged; sharp, tart, sour; bitter, biting, bleak, raw; grating (*of sound*); (*fig.*) austere; crabbed; violent, eager (*in pursuit of something*); ***âpre à la curée***, out for the kill (*of animals*); (*fig.*) on the make (*of persons*).

âprement [ɑːprə'mɑ̃], *adv.* harshly, roughly; peevishly, crabbedly; violently, eagerly.

après [a'prɛ], *prep.* after, behind (*in time, order etc.*); next to; in pursuit of; ***d'après***, after, according to.—*adv.* afterwards, later; ***et après?*** (*ellipt.*) what next? what then? so what?—*conj.* ***après que***, after, when.
après-demain [aprɛd'mɛ̃], *adv.* the day after tomorrow.
après-midi [aprɛmi'di], *n.m.* or *f. inv.* afternoon.
âpreté [ɑprə'te], *n.f.* harshness, tartness, sharpness; roughness, ruggedness; (*fig.*) acrimony, asperity; eagerness; keenness; greediness.
à-propos [aprɔ'po], *n.m.* aptness, suitability.
apside [ap'sid], *n.f.* (*Astron.*) apsis.
apte [apt], *a.* apt, fit, proper, suitable.
aptitude [apti'tyd], *n.f.* aptitude, natural disposition *or* capacity (*for*).
apurement [apyr'mɑ̃], *n.m.* verification *or* audit (*of accounts*).
apurer [apy're], *v.t.* to verify, to audit.
aquaplane [akwa'plan], *n.f.* surf-board; ***faire de l'aquaplane***, to go surf-riding.
aquarelle [akwa'rɛl], *n.f.* painting in water-colours, aquarelle.
aquarelliste [akwarɛ'list], *n.m.* painter in water-colours.
aquarium [akwa'rjɔm], *n.m.* aquarium.
aquatique [akwa'tik], *a.* aquatic.
aqueduc [akə'dyk], *n.m.* aqueduct, conduit; (*Anat.*) duct.
aqueux [a'kø], *a.* (*fem.* **-euse**) aqueous, watery.
aquilin [aki'lɛ̃], *a.* aquiline, curved, hooked, Roman (*of noses etc.*).
aquilon [aki'lɔ̃], *n.m.* north wind, cold blast.
ara [a'ra], *n.m.* (*Orn.*) ara, macaw.
arabe [a'rab], *a.* Arabic, Arabian.—*n.m.* Arabic (*language*).—*n.* (**Arabe**) Arab, Arabian.
arabesque [ara'bɛsk], *n.f.* arabesque.
Arabie [ara'bi], **l'**, *f.* Arabia; ***Arabie Séoudite***, Saudi Arabia.
arabique [ara'bik], *a.* Arabic, Arabian; ***gomme arabique***, gum arabic.
arable [a'rabl], *a.* arable, tillable.
arachide [ara'ʃid], *n.f.* pea-nut, ground-nut.
araignée [arɛ'ɲe], *n.f.* spider; a spider-like implement etc.; (*Mil.*) a series of branching galleries in a mine; (*Naut.*) crowfoot; ***toile d'araignée***, cobweb.
arasement [arɑz'mɑ̃], *n.m.* levelling, making even.
araser [arɑ'ze], *v.t.* to level (*a wall, a building etc.*).
aratoire [ara'twa:r], *a.* pertaining to farming.
arbalète [arba'lɛt], *n.f.* arbalest, cross-bow.
arbalétrier [arbale'trje], *n.m.* cross-bowman; (*Carp.*) principal rafters of a roof; strut (*of plane*); (*Orn.*) (black) swift.
arbitrage [arbi'tra:ʒ], *n.m.* arbitration; (*Banking*) arbitrage.
arbitraire [arbi'trɛ:r], *a.* arbitrary; absolute, despotic.
arbitrairement [arbitrɛr'mɑ̃], *adv.* arbitrarily; despotically.
arbitral [arbi'tral], *a.* (*m. pl.* **-aux**) by arbitration; composed of arbitrators (*of a tribunal etc.*).
arbitralement [arbitral'mɑ̃], *adv.* by arbitration.
arbitre [ar'bitr], *n.m.* arbitrator, umpire, referee; arbiter, disposer; will.
arbitrer [arbi'tre], *v.t.* to arbitrate, to judge, to settle (*a dispute etc.*), to referee *or* umpire (*a match*).
arborer [arbɔ're], *v.t.* to put up, to hoist, to unfurl (*a flag* or *as a flag*); (*fig.*) to put on.
arbre [arbr], *n.m.* tree; (*fig.*) anything resembling this (*e.g. a genealogical tree*); (*Mach.*) arbor, shaft, spindle, axle-tree; (*Naut.*) mast; (*Motor.*) ***arbre moteur***, mainshaft; ***arbre coudé***, crankshaft.
arbrisseau [arbri'so], *n.m.* (*pl.* **-eaux**) shrubby tree.
arbuste [ar'byst], *n.m.* bush, shrub.
arc [ark], *n.m.* bow, long-bow; (*Arch.*) arch; (*Geom., Phys. etc.*) arc.
arcade [ar'kad], *n.f.* arch-shaped opening; (*pl.*) arcade.
arcanes [ar'kan], *n.m. pl.* secrets, mysteries.
arc-boutant [arkbu'tɑ̃], *n.m.* (*pl.* **arcs-boutants**) (*fig.*) buttress, arched flying buttress; supporter, pillar.
arc-bouter [arkbu'te], *v.t.* to strengthen by a flying buttress; (*fig.*) to support, to buttress.
arceau [ar'so], *n.m.* (*pl.* **-eaux**) curved part of a vault *or* arch; anything shaped like an arch; (*croquet*) hoop.
arc-en-ciel [arkɑ̃'sjɛl], *n.m.* (*pl.* **arcs-en-ciel**) rainbow.
archaïque [arka'ik], *a.* archaic.
archaïsme [arka'ism], *n.m.* archaism, obsolete word etc.
archange [ar'kɑ̃:ʒ], *n.m.* archangel.
arche (1) [arʃ], *n.f.* arch (*of a bridge*).
arche (2) [arʃ], *n.f.* ark; ***l'arche de Noé***, Noah's ark.
archéologie [arkeɔlɔ'ʒi], *n.f.* archaeology.
archéologique [arkeɔlɔ'ʒik], *a.* archaeological.
archéologue [arkeɔ'lɔg], *n.m.* archaeologist.
archer [ar'ʃe], *n.m.* archer, bowman.
archet [ar'ʃɛ], *n.m.* (*Mus.*) bow, fiddle-stick.
archevêché [arʃəvɛ'ʃe], *n.m.* archbishopric; archiepiscopal diocese; archbishop's residence.
archevêque [arʃə'vɛk], *n.m.* archbishop.
archi- [ar'ʃi *or* ar'ki], *pref.* arch-, archi-, chief; extremely *as in* ***archiriche*** *etc.*
archidiacre [arʃi'djakr], *n.m.* archdeacon.
archiduc [arʃi'dyk], *n.m.* archduke.
archiduché [arʃidy'ʃe], *n.m.* archdukedom, archduchy.
archiduchesse [arʃidy'ʃɛs], *n.f.* archduchess.
archiépiscopal [arkiepiskɔ'pal], *a.* (*m. pl.* **-aux**) archiepiscopal.
archière [ar'ʃjɛ:r], *n.f.* loophole.
Archimède [arʃi'mɛd], *m.* Archimedes.
archipel [arʃi'pɛl], *n.m.* archipelago.
archiprêtre [arʃi'prɛ:tr], *n.m.* arch-priest, high-priest.
architecte [arʃi'tɛkt], *n.m.* architect; ***architecte paysagiste***, landscape-gardener.
architectural [arʃitɛkty'ral], *a.* (*m.pl.* **-aux**) architectural.
architecture [arʃitɛk'ty:r], *n.f.* architecture.
architrave [arʃi'tra:v], *n.f.* (*Arch.*) architrave.
archives [ar'ʃi:v], *n.f.* (*used only in pl.*) archives; state, civic *or* family records; record-office, muniment-room.
archiviste [arʃi'vist], *n.m.* archivist, keeper of records, registrar; filing clerk.

arçon [ar'sɔ̃], *n.m.* saddle-bow; bow-shaped tool used by hat-makers etc.
arcot [ar'ko], *n.m.* dross, slag.
arctique [ark'tik], *a.* Arctic.
ardemment [arda'mɑ̃], *adv.* ardently.
ardent [ar'dɑ̃], *a.* burning, hot, fiery, scorching; (*fig.*) violent, intense; ardent, vehement, fervent, earnest, energetic, active; red, reddish (*of hair*); ***charbons ardents***, live coals; ***buisson ardent***, the burning bush.
ardeur [ar'dœːr], *n.f.* intense heat; ardour, intense activity, fervour, earnestness; fire, spirit, mettle.
ardoise [ar'dwaːz], *n.f.* slate; (*colloq.*) score, account.
ardoisé [ardwa'ze], *a.* slate-coloured.
ardoiser [ardwa'ze], *v.t.* to cover (*a roof*) with slates.
ardoisier [ardwa'zje], *n.m.* owner of *or* workman in a slate-quarry.
ardoisière [ardwa'zjɛːr], *n.f.* slate-quarry.
ardu [ar'dy], *a.* steep, abrupt; (*fig.*) arduous, difficult.
are [aːr], *n.m.* 100 sq. metres (*approx.* 120 *sq. yds.*).
arène [a'rɛːn], *n.f.* (*poet.*) sand; arena; (*fig.*) cock-pit, battle-ground, theatre, scene; (*pl.*) the ancient Roman amphitheatres.
arénière [are'njɛːr], *n.f.* sand-pit.
aréomètre [areɔ'mɛtr], *n.m.* areometer, hydrometer.
aréopage [areɔ'paːʒ], *n.m.* areopagus.
arête [a'rɛːt], *n.f.* fish-bone; awn *or* beard of wheat etc.; (*Geog. etc.*) ridge; ***arête du nez***, bridge of the nose.
argent [ar'ʒɑ̃], *n.m.* silver; silver money; money, cash; (*fig.*) wealth, riches; (*Her.*) argent; ***argent doré***, silver-gilt; ***vif-argent***, quick-silver; ***argent comptant***, ready money.
argentage [ARGENTURE].
argenté [arʒɑ̃'te], *a.* plated, silvered over; silvery.
argenter [arʒɑ̃'te], *v.t.* to silver over, to plate; to give the appearance of silver to.
argenterie [arʒɑ̃'tri], *n.f.* plate, silver-plate.
argentin [arʒɑ̃'tɛ̃], *a.* silvery, argentine (*tint*); silver-toned (*ringing*); Argentinian, Argentine.—*n.m.* (**Argentin,** *fem.* **-ine** (1)) Argentinian (*person*).
Argentine (2) [arʒɑ̃'tin], **l'**, *f.* Argentina, the Argentine.
argenture [arʒɑ̃'tyːr], *n.f.*, **argentage** [arʒɑ̃'taːʒ], *n.m.* silvering, silver-plating.
argile [ar'ʒil], *n.f.* clay, potter's clay, argil; ***argile à porcelaine***, china-clay; ***argile réfractaire***, fire-clay.
argileux [arʒi'lø], *a.* (*fem.* **-euse**) clayey, clayish.
argilière [arʒi'ljɛːr], *n.f.* clay-pit.
argon [ar'gɔ̃], *n.m.* (*Chem.*) argon.
argonaute [argɔ'noːt], *n.m.* argonaut, nautilus.
argot [ar'go], *n.m.* slang, cant.
arguer [ar'gɥe], *v.t.* to infer, to deduce, to argue.
argument [argy'mɑ̃], *n.m.* argument, reasoning; proof, evidence; summary; theme, subject.
argumentateur [argymɑ̃ta'tœːr], *n.m.* (*fem.* **-trice**) habitual arguer *or* disputer.
argumentation, [argymɑ̃tɑ'sjɔ̃], *n.f.* argumentation, reasoning.
argumenter [argymɑ̃'te], *v.i.* to argue; to quibble.
argutie [argy'si], *n.f.* quibble, hair-splitting, cavil.
aria [a'rja], *n.m.* (*Mus.*) aria; (*pop.*) nuisance; fuss, bother.
arianisme [arja'nism], *n.m.* Arianism.
aride [a'rid], *a.* arid, dry; sterile.
aridité [aridi'te], *n.f.* aridity, dryness, barrenness, sterility.
arien [a'rjɛ̃] *a.* (*fem.* **arienne**) Arian.—*n.m.* (**Arien**, *fem.* **Arienne**) Arian (*person*).
aristocrate [aristɔ'krat], *a.* aristocratic.—*n.* aristocrat.
aristocratie [aristɔkra'si], *n.f.* aristocracy.
aristocratique [aristɔkra'tik], *a.* aristocratic.
aristocratiquement [aristɔkratik'mɑ̃], *adv.* aristocratically.
Aristote [aris'tɔt], *m.* Aristotle.
arithmétique [aritme'tik], *n.f.* arithmetic.—*a.* arithmetical.
arithmétiquement [aritmetik'mɑ̃], *adv.* arithmetically.
arlequin [arlə'kɛ̃], *n.m.* harlequin; (*fig.*) turn-coat; weathercock; ***habit d'arlequin***, patchwork, motley.
arlequinade [arləki'nad], *n.f.* harlequinade.
armagnac [armɑ'ɲak], *n.m.* brandy (*made in Armagnac, S. of France*).
armateur [arma'tœːr], *n.m.* shipowner; captain of a privateer; privateer.
armature [arma'tyːr], *n.f.* armature, iron braces, stays, casing, gear etc.
arme [arm], *n.f.* arm, weapon; branch *or* arm (*of the service*); (*Her.*) armorial bearings; ***arme blanche***, cold steel; ***aux armes!*** to arms! ***un maître d'armes***, a fencing-master.
armé [ar'me], *a.* armed, equipped; (*Her.*) armed (*with claws, horns, teeth etc.*); ***béton armé***, reinforced concrete.
armée [ar'me], *n.f.* army; forces, troops, host; (*fig.*) body (*of officials etc.*); ***l'Armée du Salut***, the Salvation Army.
armement [armə'mɑ̃], *n.m.* arming, raising of forces, warlike preparations; armament, equipment; (*Am.*) ordnance.
Arménie [arme'ni], **l'**, *f.* Armenia.
arménien [arme'njɛ̃], *a.* (*fem.* **-enne**) Armenian.—*n.m.* Armenian (*language*); (**Arménien,** *fem.* **-enne**) Armenian (*person*).
armer [ar'me], *v.t.* to equip, to arm; (*Artill.*) to load, to mount (*guns etc.*); to cock (*a gun etc.*); (*fig.*) to fortify; to strengthen; (*Naut.*) to fit out. **s'armer,** *v.r.* to arm oneself, to take up arms; to protect oneself (*against something*).
armistice [armis'tis], *n.m.* armistice.
armoire [ar'mwaːr], *n.f.* closet, cupboard; clothes-press, wardrobe.
armoiries [armwa'ri], *n.f.* (*used only in pl.*) arms, armorial bearings.
armorial [armɔ'rjal], *a.* (*m. pl.* **-aux**) armorial, pertaining to heraldry.—*n.m.* armorial, book of heraldry.
armoricain [armɔri'kɛ̃], *a.* Armorican (*of Brittany*).
armorier [armɔ'rje], *v.t.* to put *or* paint a coat of arms upon, to blazon.

Armorique [armɔ'rik], **l'**, *f.* Armorica.
armoriste [armɔ'rist], *n.m.* armorist, heraldic engraver.
armure [ar'myːr], *n.f.* armour, arms and armour; casing, wrapper; armature (*of a magnet, dynamo etc.*); (*Agric.*) tree-guard; (*Naut.*) fish (*of a mast, yard etc.*); (*fig.*) defence, protection.
armurerie [armyrə'ri], *n.f.* armoury; manufacture of arms; arms factory.
armurier [army'rje], *n.m.* armourer, gunsmith.
arnica [arni'ka], *n.m.* (*Bot.*) arnica.
aromatique [arɔma'tik], *a.* aromatic, fragrant, spicy.
aromatiser [arɔmati'ze], *v.t.* to aromatize, to perfume, to flavour.
arome [a'roːm], *n.m.* aroma, perfume, scent.
aronde [a'rɔ̃ːd], *n.f.* (*Carp.*) dove-tail, tenon.
arpège [ar'pɛːʒ], *n.m.* arpeggio.
arpéger [arpe'ʒe], *v.i.* (*conjug. like* ASSIÉGER) to play arpeggios.
arpent [ar'pɑ̃], *n.m.* acre (*French; about one and a half English acres*).
arpentage [arpɑ̃'taːʒ], *n.m.* land-measurement; survey, measurement.
arpenter [arpɑ̃'te], *v.t.* to survey, to measure (*land*); (*fig.*) to stride up and down.
arpenteur [arpɑ̃'tœːr], *n.m.* land-surveyor.
arpon [ar'pɔ̃], *n.m.* rip-saw, cross-cut saw.
arqué [ar'ke], *a.* bent, curved, arched (*of horses*).
arquebuse [arkə'byːz], *n.f.* arquebus.
arquebusier [arkəby'zje], *n.m.* arquebusier; gunsmith, armourer.
arquer [ar'ke], *v.t., v.i.* to bend, to curve, to arch.
arraché [ara'ʃe], *a.* uprooted.
arrachement [araʃ'mɑ̃], *n.m.* tearing up *or* away, pulling *or* rooting up *or* out; drawing, extraction.
arrache-pied (d') [daraʃ'pje], *adv. phr.* without interruption; ***travailler d'arrache-pied***, to work with a will.
arracher [ara'ʃe], *v.t.* to pull *or* tear away, up *or* out; to extract, to uproot, to grub up; (*fig.*) to extort. **s'arracher**, *v.r.* to tear oneself away, to get away; to break away *or* off.
arraisonner [arɛzɔ'ne], *v.t.* (*Naut.*) to hail (*a ship*); to stop and examine (*a ship*).
arrangeant [arɑ̃'ʒɑ̃], *a.* accommodating, easy to deal with *or* get on with.
arrangement [arɑ̃ʒ'mɑ̃], *n.m.* arrangement, disposition, adjustment, setting in order; order, plan, method; agreement, settlement; (*pl.*) terms; measures; (*Math.*) permutations.
arranger [arɑ̃'ʒe], *v.t.* (*conjug. like* MANGER) to arrange, to put in order; to settle, to compromise, to compose (*a difference etc.*); to manage, to regulate; to make suitable; to fit up (*a house*); to trim up; ***cela m'arrange***, that suits me; ***comme vous voilà arrangé !*** what a sight you look! **s'arranger**, *v.r.* to prepare oneself, to make arrangements (***pour***); to come to an agreement; to be satisfied (*de*); ***arrangez-vous***, that is your look-out.
arrérages [are'raːʒ], *n.m.* (*used only in pl.*) arrears.
arrestation [arɛstɑ'sjɔ̃], *n.f.* arrest, apprehension; custody.
arrêt [a'rɛ], *n.m.* stoppage, stop, check, pause, halt; suspension, cessation; (*Law*) award, judgment; arrest, apprehension; (*fig.*) decree; (*pl.*) imprisonment; ***arrêt fixe***, regular (bus) stop; ***arrêt facultatif***, request stop; ***arrêt de mort***, sentence of death; ***chien d'arrêt***, setter, pointer; ***robinet d'arrêt***, stop-cock.
arrêté (1) [arɛ'te], *a.* stopped; decreed, agreed upon, resolved; arrested; fastened.
arrêté (2) [arɛ'te], *n.m.* departmental minute, order, decree, decision; ***arrêté ministériel***, order in council.
arrêter [arɛ'te], *v.t.* to check, to stop the movement of, to throw out of gear; to delay, to detain, to hinder, to impede, to hold up; to arrest; to decide, to resolve; to settle (*an account*). **s'arrêter**, *v.r.* to stop, to pause, to hesitate; to remain, to loiter; to lag; to leave off; to be concluded, determined *or* resolved (*of bargains etc.*); to resolve upon; to dwell (*upon*), to insist (***sur***).
arrhes [ar], *n.f. pl.* earnest (*money*), deposit.
arrière [a'rjɛːr], *adv.* behind (*of time and place*); backward; (*Naut.*) aft, abaft; ***en arrière***, backward; behindhand, in arrears; at the back, at the rear (*of a train*); ***en arrière de***, behind.—*int.* away!—*n.m.* back part, rear; (*Naut.*) stern (*of a vessel*); (*Ftb.*) back.
arriéré [arje're], *a.* in arrears; behindhand, backward, poorly developed.—*n.m.* arrears.

[In *pl.* of all the following compounds ***arrière*** is *inv.* The *n.* has its normal *pl.*]

arrière-boutique [arjɛrbu'tik], *n.f.* room at the back of a shop.
arrière-cour [arjɛr'kuːr], *n.f.* back-yard.
arrière-cousin [arjɛrku'zɛ̃], *n.m.* (*fem.* **cousine**) distant cousin, cousin several times removed.
arrière-cuisine [arjɛrkɥi'zin], *n.f.* back-kitchen, scullery.
arrière-garde [arjɛr'gard], *n.f.* rear-guard.
arrière-goût [arjɛr'gu], *n.m.* after-taste.
arrière-grand-mère [arjɛrgrɑ̃'mɛːr], *n.f.* (*pl.* **-grand-mères**) great-grand-mother.
arrière-grand-père [arjɛrgrɑ̃'pɛːr], *n.m.* (*pl.* **-grands-pères**) great-grand-father.
arrière-main [arjɛr'mɛ̃], *n.f.* back of the hand; (*Ten.*) backhand (stroke).—*n.m.* hind-quarters (*of a horse*).
arrière-neveu [arjɛrnə'vø], *n.m.* (*pl.* **-eux**) grand-nephew.
arrière-nièce [arjɛr'njɛs], *n.f.* grand-niece.
arrière-pays [arjɛr'pei], *n.m. inv.* hinterland.
arrière-pensée [arjɛrpɑ̃'se], *n.f.* mental reservation, hidden motive, underlying design.
arrière-petite-fille [arjɛrpətit'fiːj], *n.f.* (*pl.* **-petites-filles**) great-grand-daughter.
arrière-petit-fils [arjɛrpəti'fis], *n.m.* (*pl.* **-petits-fils**) great-grandson.
arrière-petits-enfants [arjɛrpətizɑ̃'fɑ̃], *n.m. pl.* great-grandchildren.
arrière-plan [arjɛr'plɑ̃], *n.m.* (*Paint., Cine.*) background.
arrière-point [arjɛr'pwɛ̃], *n.m.* back-stitch.
arrière-port [arjɛr'pɔːr], *n.m.* inner harbour.

arriérer [arje're], *v.t.* (*conjug. like* CÉDER) to defer, to put off; to leave in arrears. **s'arriérer**, *v.r.* to stay behind; to be in arrears.

arrière-saison [arjɛrsɛ'zɔ̃], *n.f.* end of autumn.

arrière-train [arjɛr'trɛ̃], *n.m.* hind-quarters (*of an animal*).

arrimage [ari'ma:ʒ], *n.m.* (*Naut.*) stowage.

arrimer [ari'me], *v.t.* (*Naut.*) to stow (*cargo etc.*).

arrimeur [ari'mœ:r], *n.m.* stower, stevedore.

arrivée [ari've], *n.f.* arrival, moment of landing, coming etc., advent.

arriver [ari've], *v.i.* (*conjug. with* ÊTRE) to arrive, to come; to arrive at, to attain, to get to, to reach (*à*); to make one's way, to succeed; to happen, to occur, to take place; to veer; ***quoi qu'il arrive***, come what may.

arrivisme [ari'vism], *n.m.* push, unscrupulous ambition.

arriviste [ari'vist], *n.m.* careerist, unscrupulous person.

arrogamment [arɔga'mɑ̃], *adv.* arrogantly, haughtily; insolently.

arrogance [arɔ'gɑ̃:s], *n.f.* arrogance, haughtiness, superciliousness.

arrogant [arɔ'gɑ̃], *a.* arrogant, haughty, supercilious, overbearing.

arroger (s') [sarɔ'ʒe], *v.r.* (*conjug. like* MANGER) to assume *or* claim presumptuously.

arrondi [arɔ̃'di], *a.* rounded.—*n.m.* curve (*of shoulder, face etc.*).

arrondir [arɔ̃'di:r], *v.t.* to make round; to give a curved shape to, to round off; (*fig.*) to enlarge, to extend. **s'arrondir**, *v.r.* to grow *or* become round; to increase one's estate.

arrondissement [arɔ̃dis'mɑ̃], *n.m.* rounding, making round; roundness; division of a (*French*) department; (*in Paris*) one of the 20 wards.

arrosage [aro'za:ʒ], **arrosement** [aroz'mɑ̃], *n.m.* watering, sprinkling; irrigation.

arroser [aro'ze], *v.t.* to water, to wet, to sprinkle; to irrigate (*land*); to soak, to moisten; to flow through (*of a river*); to bathe (*with tears*).

arrosoir [aro'zwa:r], *n.m.* watering-can.

arsenal [arsə'nal], *n.m.* arsenal; ***arsenal maritime***, naval dockyard.

arsenic [arsə'nik], *n.m.* arsenic.

arsenical [arsəni'kal], *a.* (*m.pl.* **-aux**) arsenical.—*n.m. pl.* (**-aux**) arsenical compounds.

art [a:r], *n.m.* art; skill, dexterity, artifice; ***arts d'agrément***, accomplishments; ***les beaux-arts***, the fine arts.

artère [ar'tɛ:r], *n.f.* artery; (*fig.*) thoroughfare (*in a town*).

artériel [arte'rjɛl], *a.* (*fem.* **-elle**) arterial; ***tension artérielle***, blood-pressure.

artériole [arte'rjɔl], *n.f.* small artery.

artésien [arte'zjɛ̃], *a.* (*fem.* **-enne**) artesian; ***puits artésien***, artesian well.—*n.m.* (**Artésien**, *fem.* **-enne**) inhabitant *or* native of Artois.

arthrite [ar'trit], *n.f.* arthritis.

arthritique [artri'tik], *a.* arthritic.

artichaut [arti'ʃo], *n.m.* globe artichoke.

article [ar'tikl], *n.m.* article (*in all English senses*); clause, provision (*of a treaty etc.*); item; commodity; (*pl.*) goods; ***article de fond***, leading article.

articulaire [artiky'lɛ:r], *a.* articular.

articulation [artikylɑ'sjɔ̃], *n.f.* articulation, pronunciation; (*Bot., Anat.*) joint, articulation; (*Law*) enumeration of facts.

articulé [artiky'le], *a.* articulate, clear, distinct; jointed, articulated.

articuler [artiky'le], *v.t.* to articulate, to put together by the joints; to pronounce distinctly; (*Law*) to enumerate. **s'articuler**, *v.r.* to be connected by joints.

artifice [arti'fis], *n.m.* artifice, contrivance, expedient; dodge, trick, stratagem; craft, ruse; ***un feu d'artifice***, fireworks.

artificiel [artifi'sjɛl], *a.* (*fem.* **-elle**) artificial; fictitious, spurious.

artificiellement [artifisjɛl'mɑ̃], *adv.* artificially.

artificieusement [artifisjøz'mɑ̃], *adv.* cunningly, craftily, artfully, slyly.

artificieux [artifi'sjø], *a.* (*fem* **-euse**) artful, cunning.

artillerie [artij'ri], *n.f.* artillery, ordnance.

artilleur [arti'jœ:r], *n.m.* artilleryman, gunner.

artimon [arti'mɔ̃], *n.m.* mizen-mast *or* -sail.

artisan [arti'zɑ̃], *n.m.* artisan, operative, mechanic; (*fig.*) author, architect, contriver, maker.

artiste [ar'tist], *a.* artistic (*of persons*).—*n.* artist; player, performer.

artistement [artistə'mɑ̃], *adv.* in an artistic manner; skilfully, artistically.

artistique [artis'tik], *a.* artistic, pertaining to art.

as [ɑ:s], *n.m.* ace (*at cards, dice*); as (*Roman coin and weight*).

asbeste [az'bɛst], *n.m.* asbestos.

ascendance [asɑ̃'dɑ̃:s], *n.f.* ascent; ancestry.

ascendant [asɑ̃'dɑ̃], *n.m.* ascendant; ascendency, influence; (*pl.*) ancestors.—*a.* ascending, ascendant; going upward, rising.

ascenseur [asɑ̃'sœ:r], *n.m.* lift, (*Am.*) elevator.

ascension [asɑ̃'sjɔ̃], *n.f.* ascent, climbing, rising; upstroke (*of machinery*); (***Jour de l'Ascension***, Ascension Day.

ascète [a'sɛt], *n.* ascetic.

ascétique [ase'tik], *a.* ascetic, rigid, severe.

ascétisme [ase'tism], *n.m.* asceticism.

asepsie [asɛp'si], *n.f.* (*Med.*) asepsis.

aseptique [asɛp'tik], *a.* and *n.m.* aseptic.

aseptiser [asɛpti'ze], *v.t.* to render aseptic.

asexué [asɛk'sɥe], **asexuel** [asɛk'sɥɛl] (*fem.* **-elle**), *a.* asexual.

asiatique [azja'tik], *a.* Asiatic; ***grippe asiatique***, Asian flu.—*n.* (**Asiatique**) native of Asia.

Asie [a'zi], *f.* Asia; ***Asie Mineure***, Asia Minor.

asile [a'zil], *n.m.* asylum, place of refuge, sanctuary, retreat, home (*for the aged etc.*); (*fig.*) protection, refuge; ***asile d'aliénés***, mental hospital.

asine [a'zin], *a.* asinine.

aspect [as'pɛ], *n.m.* aspect, view, look; countenance; phase, bearing; point of view.

asperge [as'pɛrʒ], *n.f.* asparagus (*head of*).

aspergement [aspɛrʒə'mɑ̃], *n.m.* sprinkling.

asperger [aspɛr'ʒe], *v.t.* (*conjug. like* MANGER) to sprinkle.

aspergerie [aspɛrʒə'ri], **aspergière** [aspɛr'ʒjɛ:r], *n.f.* asparagus-bed.

aspérité [asperi'te], *n.f.* roughness, harshness; unevenness, ruggedness; (*fig.*) asperity.
aspersion [asper'sjɔ̃], *n.f.* aspersion, sprinkling.
aspersoir [aspɛr'swa:r], *n.m.* holy-water sprinkler; rose (*of a watering-can*).
asphaltage [asfal'ta:ʒ], *n.m.* asphalting.
asphalte [as'falt], *n.m.* bitumen, asphalt.
asphalter [asfal'te], *v.t.* to asphalt.
asphodèle [asfɔ'dɛl], *n.m.* asphodel.
asphyxiant [asfik'sjɑ̃], *a.* asphyxiating, suffocating; ***gaz asphyxiant***, poison-gas.
aspyhxie [asfik'si], *n.f.* (*Med.*) asphyxia, suffocation.
asphyxié [asfik'sje], *a.* asphyxiated.—*n.m.* (*fem.* **-ée**) person in a state of asphyxia.
asphyxier [asfik'sje], *v.t.* to asphyxiate, to suffocate. **s'asphyxier**, *v.r.* to commit suicide by suffocation.
aspic [as'pik], *n.m.* asp, viper; (*Bot.*) spike-lavender; (*Cook.*) cold meat *or* fish, in jelly.
aspidistra [aspidis'tra], *n.m.* aspidistra.
aspirail [aspi'ra:j], *n.m.* (*pl.* **-aux**) airhole (*in a stove, oven etc.*).
aspirant (1) [aspi'rɑ̃], *a.* suction, sucking (*of pumps*).
aspirant (2) [aspi'rɑ̃], *n.m.* aspirant, candidate; suitor; officer-cadet; midshipman.
aspirateur [aspira'tœ:r], *n.m.* ventilator; suction-pump; vacuum cleaner.
aspiration [aspirɑ'sjɔ̃], *n.f.* aspiration (*of the letter* h *etc.*); inhaling, inspiration; (*of pumps*) exhaustion, suction; (*fig.*) yearning, aspiration; (*Motor.*) suction, intake.
aspirer [aspi're], *v.t.* to inspire, to inhale; to draw in, to suck in; (*Gram.*) to aspirate. —*v.i.* to aspire, to aim at.
aspirine [aspi'rin], *n.f.* aspirin.
assagir [asa'ʒi:r], *v.t.* to make wiser, to impart wisdom to. **s'assagir**, *v.r.* to become wiser; to settle down.
assaillant [asa'jɑ̃], *a.* attacking, aggressive.—*n.m.* (*fem.* **-e**) aggressor, assailant, besieger.
assaillir [asa'ji:r], *v.t. irr.* to assault, to assail; to worry, to molest, to beset.
assainir [asɛ'ni:r], *v.t.* to render healthy; (*fig.*) to cleanse, to purify morally etc. **s'assainir**, *v.r.* to become healthy.
assainissement [asɛnis'mɑ̃], *n.m.* purification, sanitation salubrity; drainage.
assaisonnement [asɛzɔn'mɑ̃], *n.m.* condiment, seasoning, dressing.
assaisonner [asɛzɔ'ne], *v.t.* to season, to dress, to give a relish to.
assassin [asa'sɛ̃], *a.* killing, murderous.—*n.m.* (*fem.* **-e**) assassin, murderer; ruffian.
assassinat [asasi'na], *n.m.* assassination, wilful murder, homicide.
assassiner [asasi'ne], *v.t.* to assassinate, to murder; (*fig.*) to bore; to tease, to importune.
assaut [a'so], *n.m.* assault, onset, attack.
assèchement [asɛʃ'mɑ̃], *n.m.* drying up, drainage.
assécher [ase'ʃe], *v.t.* (*conjug. like* CÉDER) to drain (*a mine, pond etc.*).—*v.i.* to become dry, to be drained.
assemblage [asɑ̃'bla:ʒ], *n.m.* assemblage, collection, union, combination; (*Print.*) gathering; (*Carp.*) joint, scarf; ***chaîne d'assemblage***, assembly line.
assemblée [asɑ̃'ble], *n.f.* assembly, meeting, company, party; convocation, congregation (*of churches*); meet (*of hunters*).
assembler [asɑ̃'ble], *v.t.* to assemble, to call together; to collect, to gather; to bring together; (*Print.*) to gather; (*Carp.*) to trim, to scarf. **s'assembler**, *v.r.* to assemble, to meet, to congregate.
asséner [ase'ne], *v.t.* (*conjug. like* CÉDER) to strike *or* deal (*a blow*).
assentiment [asɑ̃ti'mɑ̃], *n.m.* assent, agreement.
asseoir [a'swa:r], *v.t. irr.* to seat, to put on a seat, to set, to place, to fix, to establish; to pitch (*a camp etc.*). **s'asseoir**, *v.r.* to sit, to sit down, to take a seat, to settle, to perch.
assermenté [asɛrmɑ̃'te], *a.* sworn in, attested.
assermenter [asɛrmɑ̃'te], *v.t.* to swear in.
assertif [asɛr'tif], *a.* (*fem.* **-tive**) assertive.
assertion [asɛr'sjɔ̃], *n.f.* assertion, affirmation.
asservir [asɛr'vi:r], *v.t.* to enslave, to reduce to servitude; to subdue, to conquer. **s'asservir**, *v.r.* to obey, to submit (*à*).
asservissant [asɛrvi'sɑ̃], *a.* enslaving, subjecting, coercive.
asservissement [asɛrvis'mɑ̃], *n.m.* bondage, servitude, slavery, subjection.
assez [a'se], *adv.* enough, sufficiently; tolerably, passably, rather.
assidu [asi'dy], *a.* assiduous, diligent, attentive; punctual; regular, constant.
assiduité [asidɥi'te], *n.f.* assiduity, application, diligence, attention.
assidûment [asidy'mɑ̃], *adv.* assiduously, diligently, constantly; punctually.
assiéger [asje'ʒe], *v.t.* (*see Verb Tables*) to besiege; to lay siege to; to surround; to importune.
assiette [a'sjɛt], *n.f.* plate; plateful; attitude *or* posture (*in sitting etc.*), pose, situation, bearing, basis; seat (*in the saddle*); position, site; tone, state, disposition (*of the mind etc.*).
assiettée [asjɛ'te], *n.f.* plateful.
assignation [asiɲɑ'sjɔ̃], *n.f.* order to pay, transfer; (*Law*) summons, subpoena, writ; appointment, rendezvous, assignation.
assigner [asi'ɲe], *v.t.* to assign (*property in payment of a debt etc.*); to cite, to summon, to subpoena; to appoint, to fix (*a rendezvous etc.*).
assimilation [asimilɑ'sjɔ̃], *n.f.* assimilation.
assimiler [asimi'le], *v.t.* to make like; to liken, to compare, to assimilate.
assis [a'si], *a.* seated, sitting; situated; established.
assise [a'si:z], *n.f.* course (*of stones etc.*), foundation, basis; (*Geol.*) stratum; (*Mining*) measure (*of coal*); (*pl.*) assizes; ***cour d'assises***, assize court.
assistance [asis'tɑ̃:s], *n.f.* audience, company, bystanders; congregation (*in a church*); assistance, help, aid; relief.
assistant [asis'tɑ̃], *n.m.* (*fem.* **-ante**) assistant (*priest, teacher etc.*); person present, bystander, witness etc.; ***assistant*(*e*) *social*(*e*)**, social welfare worker.
assisté [asis'te], *a.* receiving public assistance. —*n.m.* (*fem.* **-ée**) person in receipt of relief.

assister [asis'te], *v.t.* to assist, to help, to succour.—*v.i.* to be at, to be present (*à*), to look on, to be a witness (*à*).

association [asɔsjɑ'sjɔ̃], *n.f.* association; union; partnership, fellowship, society, order.

associé [asɔ'sje], *a.* associated, admitted (*as a member*).—*n.m.* (*fem.* **-ée**) associate, fellow, member, partner.

associer [asɔ'sje], *v.t.* to associate, to take into partnership etc.; to divide *or* share something with someone; to link together, to connect (*ideas etc.*). **s'associer**, *v.r.* to enter into partnership, to associate oneself, to combine (*with*).

assoiffé [aswa'fe], *a.* thirsty; eager (*for*).

assolement [asɔl'mɑ̃], *n.m.* (*Agric.*) rotation (*of crops*).

assoler [asɔ'le], *v.t.* to vary *or* rotate (*crops*).

assombrir [asɔ̃'bri:r], *v.t.* to darken, to throw a gloom over, to cloud. **s'assombrir**, *v.r.* to become dark *or* gloomy; to darken (*of the brow*).

assombrissement [asɔ̃bris'mɑ̃], *n.m.* darkening, gloom.

assommant [asɔ'mɑ̃], *a.* wearisome, tiresome, boring.

assommer [asɔ'me], *v.t.* to beat to death, to knock on the head; to overpower; to overwhelm, to stun; (*fig.*) to bore, to importune, to oppress.

assommeur [asɔ'mœ:r], *n.m.* (*fem.* **-euse**) slaughterer (*of oxen etc.*).

assommoir [asɔ'mwa:r], *n.m.* pole-axe; life-preserver.

Assomption [asɔ̃p'sjɔ̃], *n.f.* (*Eccles.*) Assumption of the Blessed Virgin (August 15).

assomption [asɔ̃p'sjɔ̃], *n.f.* assumption.

assonance [asɔ'nɑ̃:s], *n.f.* assonance.

assonant [asɔ'nɑ̃], *a.* assonant.

assorti [asɔr'ti], *a.* assorted, matched, paired.

assortiment [asɔrti'mɑ̃], *n.m.* suitability, match; assortment, set.

assortir [asɔr'ti:r], *v.t.* to assort, to match, to pair; to stock, to furnish (*with things that go together* or *match*).—*v.i.* to match, to suit, to go well together. **s'assortir**, *v.r.* to match, to agree, to go well together.

assortissant [asɔrti'sɑ̃], *a.* suitable, matching, going well (*with something else*).

assoupi [asu'pi], *a.* dozing; dormant (*volcano*).

assoupir [asu'pi:r], *v.t.* to make drowsy, sleepy, heavy *or* dull; (*fig.*) to assuage, to allay, to deaden. **s'assoupir**, *v.r.* to grow drowsy, sleepy, dull *or* heavy; to doze; (*fig.*) to be assuaged, to be appeased, to be stilled.

assoupissant [asupi'sɑ̃], *a.* making drowsy *or* sleepy, soporific.

assoupissement [asupis'mɑ̃], *n.m.* drowsiness, sleepiness, heaviness; (*fig.*) carelessness, sloth; (*Med.*) coma.

assouplir [asu'pli:r], *v.t.* to make supple, flexible *or* tractable; to break in (*a horse*). **s'assouplir**, *v.r.* to become supple, tractable *or* manageable.

assouplissement [asuplis'mɑ̃], *n.m.* suppleness, tractability, docility.

assourdir [asur'di:r], *v.t.* to deafen, to stun; to muffle.

assourdissant [asurdi'sɑ̃], *a.* deafening.

assourdissement [asurdis'mɑ̃], *n.m.* deafening, muffling, deadening; deafening noise; temporary deafness.

assouvir [asu'vi:r], *v.t.* to glut, to satiate, to surfeit; to gratify; to cloy. **s'assouvir**. *v.r*, to be satiated, gratified *or* cloyed.

assouvissement [asuvis'mɑ̃], *n.m.* glutting, satiating.

assujettir [asyʒe'ti:r], *v.t.* to subdue, to subjugate; to compel; to fix, to fasten. **s'assujettir**, *v.r.* to subject oneself, to submit.

assujettissant [asyʒeti'sɑ̃], *a.* binding, constraining, fettering, restrictive.

assujettissement [asyʒetis'mɑ̃], *n.m.* subjection, subjugation; obligation, fixing.

assumer [asy'me], *v.t.* to take upon oneself, to assume.

assurance [asy'rɑ̃:s], *n.f.* confidence, security, assurance; certainty, conviction; warrant, pledge; insurance, underwriting; (*fig.*) boldness; ***(les) assurances sociales***, national insurance.

assuré [asy're], *a.* assured, confident; sure, secure, positive, certain; trusty; insured.—*n.m.* (*fem.* **-ée**) insured person.

assurément [asyre'mɑ̃], *adv.* assuredly, confidently; surely, undoubtedly; certainly.

assurer [asy're], *v.t.* to fix securely, to fasten, to steady; (*Naut.* and *Mount.*) to belay; to assure, to guarantee; to insure; to underwrite; to assert, to affirm. **s'assurer**, *v.r.* to make sure of, to ascertain.

assureur [asy'rœ:r], *n.m.* underwriter, insurer, assurer.

Assyrie [asi'ri], *f.* Assyria.

assyrien [asi'rjɛ̃], *a.* (*fem.* **-enne**) Assyrian.—*n.m.* (**Assyrien**, *fem.* **-enne**) Assyrian (*person*).

aster [as'tɛ:r], *n.m.* (*Bot.*) aster.

astérie [aste'ri], *n.f.* starfish.

astérisque [aste'risk], *n.m.* asterisk.

astéroïde [asterɔ'id], *n.m.* asteroid.

asthmatique [asma'tik], *a.* asthmatic.

asthme [asm], *n.m.* asthma.

asticot [asti'ko], *n.m.* gentle (*bait for fishing*); maggot.

asticoter [astikɔ'te], *v.t.* (*colloq.*) to tease, to worry.

astigmate [astig'mat], *a.* astigmatic.

astigmatisme [astigma'tism], *n.m.* astigmatism.

astiquer [asti'ke], *v.t.* to polish, to furbish, to glaze.

astracan or **astrakan** [astra'kɑ̃], *n.m.* astrakhan, Persian lamb (*fur*).

astral [as'tral], *a.* (*m. pl.* **-aux**) astral.

astre [astr], *n.m.* star; (*fig.*) celebrity.

astreindre [as'trɛ̃:dr], *v.t. irr.* (*conjug. like* CRAINDRE) to oblige, to compel, to subject. **s'astreindre**, *v.r.* to confine oneself, to tie oneself down (*à*).

astreinte [as'trɛ̃:t], *n.f.* (*Law*) compulsion; fine for delay in the performance of a contract.

astringence [astrɛ̃'ʒɑ̃:s], *n.f.* astringency.

astringent [astrɛ̃'ʒɑ̃], *a.* and *n.m.* astringent.

astroïde [astrɔ'id], *a.* star-shaped.

astrologie [astrɔlɔ'ʒi], *n.f.* astrology.

astrologique [astrɔlɔ'ʒik], *a.* astrological.

astrologue [astrɔ'lɔg], *n.m.* astrologer.

astronaute [astrɔ'no:t], *n.m.* astronaut.

astronautique [astrɔno'tik], *n.f.* astronautics.

astronome [astrɔ'nɔm], *n.m.* astronomer.

astronomie [astrɔnɔ'mi], *n.f.* astronomy.
astronomique [astrɔnɔ'mik], *a.* astronomical, astronomic.
astrophysique [astrɔfi'zik], *a.* astrophysical. —*n.f.* astrophysics.
astuce [as'tys], *n.f.* craft, guile; cunning.
astucieusement [astysjøz'mɑ̃], *adv.* craftily, cunningly.
astucieux [asty'sjø], *a.* (*fem.* **-euse**) crafty, wily.
Asturies [asty'ri], **les**, *f. pl.* the Asturias.
asymétrie [asime'tri], *n.f.* asymmetry.
asymétrique [asime'trik], *a.* asymmetrical.
atelier [atə'lje], *n.m.* workshop, studio, atelier; (*collect.*) gang of workmen etc.; (*Freemasonry*) lodge, lodge-meeting.
atermoyer [atɛrmwa'je], *v.t.* (*conjug. like* EMPLOYER) to put off, to delay (*a payment*). —*v.i.* (*fig.*) to put off, to make shifts. **s'atermoyer,** *v.r.* to compound with one's creditors.
athée [a'te], *a.* atheistic.—*n.* atheist.
athéisme [ate'ism], *n.m.* atheism.
Athènes [a'tɛːn], *f.* Athens.
athénien [ate'njɛ̃], *a.* (*fem.* **-enne**) Athenian. —*n.m.* (**Athénien,** *fem.* **-enne**) Athenian (*person*).
athlète [a'tlɛt], *n.m.* athlete.
athlétique [atle'tik], *a.* athletic.
athlétisme [atle'tism], *n.m.* athleticism; athletics.
Atlantide [atlɑ̃'tid], *f.* Atlantis.
atlantique [atlɑ̃'tik], *a.* Atlantic.—*n.m.* (**L'Atlantique**) the Atlantic (Ocean).
atlas [a'tlɑːs], *n.m.* atlas.
atmosphère [atmɔs'fɛːr], *n.f.* atmosphere.
atmosphérique [atmɔsfe'rik], *a.* atmospheric; ***pression atmosphérique***, atmospheric pressure.
atoll [a'tɔl], *n.m.* atoll.
atome [a'toːm], *n.m.* atom, corpuscle.
atomicité [atɔmisi'te], *n.f.* (*Chem.*) atomicity, valency.
atomique [atɔ'mik], *a.* atomic(al); ***commissariat à l'énergie atomique***, atomic energy authority.
atomiser [atɔmi'ze], *v.t.* to pulverize.
atomiste [atɔ'mist], *n.m.* atomist.
atomistique [atɔmis'tik], *a.* atomic(al).
atone [a'tɔn], *a.* atonic, debilitated, dull; lack-lustre, expressionless (*of eyes*); (*Gram.*) atonic, unaccentuated.
atonie [atɔ'ni], *n.f.* atony, debility.
atonique [atɔ'nik], *a.* atonic.
atours [a'tuːr], *n.m.* (*used only in pl.*) woman's attire, dress, ornament.
atout [a'tu], *n.m.* trump; trump-card.
atoxique [atɔk'sik], *a.* non-poisonous.
atrabilaire [atrabi'lɛːr], *a.* morose, peevish.
âtre [ɑːtr], *n.m.* hearth; fire-place.
atroce [a'trɔs], *a.* atrocious, cruel, excruciating; heinous, odious, dreadful.
atrocement [atrɔs'mɑ̃], *adv.* atrociously, cruelly, outrageously.
atrocité [atrɔsi'te], *n.f.* atrociousness, heinousness; atrocity, cruelty.
atrophie [atrɔ'fi], *n.f.* (*Path.*) atrophy.
atrophié [atrɔ'fje], *a.* atrophied, wasted, withered, stunted.
atrophier [atrɔ'fje], *v.t.* to cause to waste *or* wither. **s'atrophier,** *v.r.* to waste away, to atrophy.
atrophique [atrɔ'fik], *a.* atrophic.
attablé [ata'ble], *a.* seated at table.
attabler (s') [sata'ble], *v.r.* to sit down to *or* take one's place at table.
attachant [ata'ʃɑ̃], *a.* engaging, winning, attractive.
attache [a'taʃ], *n.f.* bond, cord, leash, strap; (*fig.*) attachment, affection for.
attaché [ata'ʃe], *n.m.* attaché (*of an embassy*).
attachement [ataʃ'mɑ̃], *n.m.* attachment; affection, liaison; eagerness, zeal.
attacher [ata'ʃe], *v.t.* to fasten, to tie, to attach, to fix; (*fig.*) to apply, to affix; to connect, to associate; to engage, to endear.— **s'attacher,** *v.r.* to take hold, to attach *or* fasten oneself; to cling, to adhere; to have an affection for; to apply oneself to.
attaquable [ata'kabl], *a.* assailable; of doubtful validity.
attaquant [ata'kɑ̃], *n.m.* assailant.
attaque [a'tak], *n.f.* attack, assault, aggression; fit, stroke.
attaquer [ata'ke], *v.t.* to attack, to assail, to assault; to seize suddenly (*of illness etc.*); to criticize; ***attaquer en justice***, to sue for. **s'attaquer,** *v.r.* to make *or* conduct an attack (*à*), to set upon.
attaqueur [ata'kœːr], *n.m.* attacker.
attardé [atar'de], *a.* late, behindhand; mentally retarded (*child*).
attarder [atar'de], *v.t.* to make late, to delay. **s'attarder,** *v.r.* to be belated; to loiter, to linger.
atteindre [a'tɛ̃ːdr], *v.t. irr.* (*conjug. like* CRAINDRE) to reach, to hit, to attain; to arrive at; to overtake, to come up to.—*v.i.* to reach with difficulty, to attain (*à*); ***atteindre à la perfection***, to attain to perfection.
atteint [a'tɛ̃], *a.* hit, struck; attacked, seized, affected; reached.
atteinte [a'tɛ̃ːt], *n.f.* reach, blow, stroke, touch; attack, fit, seizure (*of disease*); injury, damage, harm, wrong.
attelage [at'laːʒ], *n.m.* harnessing, yoking; team, yoke, set, pair; carriage, horses; (*Rail.*) coupling.
atteler [at'le], *v.t.* (*conjug. like* APPELER) to put horses etc. (*to*); to harness, to yoke; (*fig.*) to subjugate. **s'atteler,** *v.r.* to settle down to (*à*); (*fig.*) to apply oneself to, to hitch one's waggon to.
attelle [a'tɛl], *n.f.* hame; (*Surg.*) splint.
attenant [at'nɑ̃], *a.* contiguous, adjoining, next door to, close by (*à*).
attendre [a'tɑ̃ːdr], *v.t.* to await, to wait for, to stay for; to look forward to, to expect; to look for, to count upon. **s'attendre,** *v.r.* to rely upon, to count upon, to trust (*à*); to expect, to look forward (*à*).
attendrir [atɑ̃'driːr], *v.t.* to make tender, to soften; to touch, to move. **s'attendrir,** *v.r.* to grow tender; to be moved, to melt, to pity, to relent.
attendrissant [atɑ̃dri'sɑ̃], *a.* moving, touching.
attendrissement [atɑ̃dris'mɑ̃], *n.m.* compassion, pity; tears, sensibility; tenderness.
attendu [atɑ̃'dy], *prep.* considering, on account of, in consideration of.—*conj.* ***attendu que***, seeing that, as, whereas, since.
attenir [at'niːr], *v.i. irr.* (*conjug. like* TENIR) to adjoin, to be contiguous (*à*); to be related.

attentat [atɑ̃'ta], *n.m.* attempt at crime; crime, attempt; outrage, violation.
attente [a'tɑ̃:t], *n.f.* waiting, expectation; hope; ***salle d'attente***, waiting-room.
attenter [atɑ̃'te], *v.i.* to make a criminal attempt.
attentif [atɑ̃'tif], *a.* (*fem.* **-tive**) attentive, heedful; considerate.
attention [atɑ̃'sjɔ̃], *n.f.* attention, notice; heed, care, vigilance; regard, respect, consideration; ***attention!*** look out! stand by!
attentionné [atɑ̃sjɔ'ne], *a.* attentive, considerate.
attentivement [atɑ̃tiv'mɑ̃], *adv.* attentively, carefully.
atténuant [ate'nɥɑ̃], *a.* mitigating; (*Law*) extenuating.
atténuation [atenɥɑ'sjɔ̃], *n.f.* attenuation, extenuation, mitigation.
atténué [ate'nɥe], *a.* attenuated, wasted, emaciated.
atténuer [ate'nɥe], *v.t.* to make smaller, thinner, feebler etc.; to attenuate; to extenuate, to mitigate.
atterrant [atɛ'rɑ̃], *a.* astounding, startling, overwhelming.
atterrement [atɛr'mɑ̃], *n.m.* overthrow; prostration, amazement.
atterré [atɛ're], *a.* horror-stricken, dumbfounded.
atterrer [atɛ're], *v.t.* to overwhelm; to astound.
atterrir [atɛ'ri:r], *v.i.* to land, to make land.
atterrissage [atɛri'sa:ʒ], *n.m.* landing; ***terrain d'atterrissage***, landing-ground.
atterrissement [atɛris'mɑ̃], *n.m.* alluvion accretion, alluvium.
attestation [atɛstɑ'sjɔ̃], *n.f.* attestation, evidence; certificate, voucher, testimonial; ***attestation sous serment***, affidavit.
attester [atɛs'te], *v.t.* to attest, to certify, to avouch, to witness, to testify.
attiédir [atje'di:r], *v.t.* to cool, to make lukewarm; to take the chill off. **s'attiédir**, *v.r.* to grow cool *or* lukewarm; to cool off.
attiédissement [atjedis'mɑ̃], *n.m.* lukewarmness, coolness; abatement.
attifage [ati'fa:ʒ], **attifement** [atif'mɑ̃], *n.m.* get-up, rig-out.
attifer [ati'fe] (*always in a bad sense*), *v.t.* to dress up. **s'attifer**, *v.r.* to dress up, to rig oneself out.
attique [a'tik], *a.* Attic; (*fig.*) witty, urbane.—*n.m.* (*Arch.*) attic.
attirail [ati'ra:j], *n.m.* (*collect.*) apparatus, implements, utensils, gear, tackle; baggage, paraphernalia; show, pomp.
attirance [ati'rɑ̃:s], *n.f.* attraction (***vers***).
attirant [ati'rɑ̃], *a.* attractive, alluring, enticing, engaging.
attirer [ati're], *v.t.* to attract, to draw; to win *or* gain over, to lure, to wheedle, to entice; to occasion. **s'attirer**, *v.r.* to draw to *or* down upon one, to bring upon one; to incur, to win.
attisage [ati'za:ʒ], **attisement** [atiz'mɑ̃], *n.m.* the act of stirring up, poking (*a fire*), fanning (*flame*).
(*C*) **attisée** [ati'ze], *n.f.* a good fire; armful (*of stove-wood*).
attiser [ati'ze], *v.t.* to make *or* stir up (*a fire*); to poke; (*fig.*) to incense, to stir up.
attisoir [ati'zwa:r], **attisonnoir** [atizɔ'nwa:r], *n.m.* poker (*especially in foundries*), fire-rake.
attitré [ati'tre], *a.* recognized, appointed, regular, ordinary; hired.
attitude [ati'tyd], *n.f.* attitude; (*Paint.*) posture; (*fig.*) attitude of mind etc.
attouchement [atuʃ'mɑ̃], *n.m.* touch, contact.
attracteur [atrak'tœ:r], *a.* (*fem.* **-trice**) attractile.
attractif [atrak'tif], *a.* (*fem.* **-tive**) attractive.
attraction [atrak'sjɔ̃], *n.f.* attraction; (*pl.*) cabaret show.
attractivement [atraktiv'mɑ̃], *adv.* attractively.
attrait [a'trɛ], *n.m.* allurement, attraction, charm; inclination, bent; (*pl.*) attractions, charms; bait.
attrape [a'trap], *n.f.* trap, gin; (*fig.*) trick, take-in, sell, hoax; (*Naut.*) hawser.
attrape-mouche or **attrape-mouches** [atrap'muʃ], *n.m. inv.* fly-catcher.
attrape-nigaud [atrapni'go], *n.m.* (*pl.* **attrape-nigauds**) booby-trap.
attraper [atra'pe], *v.t.* to catch; to entrap, to ensnare; to take in, to trick, to bamboozle; to imitate; (*fam.*) to scold; to hit; to overtake, to catch up; to get accidentally (*a cold etc.*); ***attrape!*** take that! **s'attraper**, *v.r.* to hit (*against*); to be caught (*in*); to get hold of; to seize, to stick (*à*).
attrapeur [atra'pœ:r], *n.m.* (*fem.* **-euse**) deceiver, cheat, trickster.
attrayant [atrɛ'jɑ̃], *a.* attractive, winning, engaging, charming.
attribuable [atri'bɥabl], *a.* attributable, due to.
attribuer [atri'bɥe], *v.t.* to assign, to confer; to attribute, to ascribe, to impute (*a thing to someone*). **s'attribuer**, *v.r.* to assume, to take upon oneself, to claim.
attribut [atri'by], *n.m.* attribute, prerogative; special symbol *or* emblem; (*Gram.*) predicate.
attributif [atriby'tif], *a.* (*fem.* **-tive**) (*Gram.*) attributive; predicative; (*Law*) conferring a right.
attribution [atriby'sjɔ̃], *n.f.* attribution, conferment, awarding (*of a grant*); (*usu. in pl.*) privilege, prerogative (*of a person*); province, department, jurisdiction.
attristant [atris'tɑ̃], *a.* saddening, sorrowful, melancholy, grievous.
attrister [atris'te], *v.t.* to grieve, to sadden, to trouble. **s'attrister**, *v.r.* to be sad, to become sorrowful.
attrition [atri'sjɔ̃], *n.f.* attrition, friction.
attroupement [atrup'mɑ̃], *n.m.* riotous assemblage, mob, crowd, gathering of people.
attrouper [atru'pe], *v.t.* to assemble, to gather together in troops *or* a mob. **s'attrouper**, *v.r.* to flock together, to gather in crowds.
au [o], (*contraction of* À LE) to the.
aubade [o'bad], *n.f.* aubade, dawn song; (*iron.*) hot reception.
aubaine [o'bɛn], *n.f.* (*Law*) escheat; windfall, piece of good luck.
aube [o:b], *n.f.* the dawn; alb (*priest's vestment*).

aubépine [obe'pin], *n.f.* hawthorn, white-thorn, may.
aubère [o'bɛːr], *a.* red roan (*horse*).
auberge [o'bɛrʒ], *n.f.* inn, public-house, tavern; ***auberge de (la) jeunesse,*** youth hostel.
aubergine [obɛr'ʒin], *n.f.* aubergine, egg-plant.
aubergiste [obɛr'ʒist], *n.* innkeeper, publican, landlord, host.
aubour [o'buːr], *n.m.* laburnum; guelder-rose.
aucun [o'kœ̃], *a.* and *pron.* none, no one, not one; not any; anyone; any.
aucunement [okyn'mɑ̃], *adv.* in no wise, not at all, not in the least; at all.
audace [o'das], *n.f.* audacity, daring, boldness; impudence, insolence; ***payer d'audace,*** to brazen it out.
audacieusement [odasjøz'mɑ̃], *adv.* audaciously, daringly, boldly; rashly; impudently.
audacieux [oda'sjø], *a.* (*fem.* **-euse**) audacious, bold, daring; impudent, presumptuous.
au deçà, au dedans, au dehors, au delà [DEÇÀ, DEDANS, DEHORS, DELÀ].
au-dessous [od'su], *prep.* below.
au-dessus [od'sy], *prep.* above.
au-devant [od'vɑ̃], *prep.* towards; ***aller au-devant d'un danger,*** to anticipate danger.
audibilité [odibili'te], *n.f.* audibility.
audible [o'dibl], *a.* audible.
audience [o'djɑ̃ːs], *n.f.* audience, hearing; reception; sitting, session, court, tribunal.
audiomètre [odjɔ'mɛtr], **audimètre** [odi'mɛtr], *n.m.* audiometer.
audiophone [odjɔ'fɔn], **audiphone** [odi'fɔn], *n.m.* audiphone.
audio-visuel [odjɔvi'zɥɛl], *a.* (*fem.* **-elle**) audio-visual; ***moyens audio-visuels,*** audio-visual aids.
auditeur [odi'tœːr], *n.m.* (*fem.* **-trice**) hearer, listener.
auditif [odi'tif], *a.* (*fem.* **-tive**) auditory.
audition [odi'sjɔ̃], *n.f.* hearing; (*Law*) hearing (*of a case etc.*); audition (*of a singer etc.*).
auditionner [odisjɔ'ne], *v.t.* to audition.
auditoire [odi'twaːr], *n.m.* auditory; congregation (*in church*), audience (*theatre etc.*).
auditrice [odi'tris], [AUDITEUR].
auge [oːʒ], *n.f.* trough (*for drinking etc.*); (*plasterer's*) hod; (*Elec.*) cell.
auget [o'ʒɛ], *n.m.* small trough; seed-box.
augmentation [ɔgmɑ̃tɑ'sjɔ̃], *n.f.* augmentation, increase, addition, rise (*in salary*).
augmenter [ɔgmɑ̃'te], *v.t.* to augment, to increase; to enlarge; to raise the salary of.—*v.i.* to augment, to increase, to grow, to rise (*in price*), to multiply. **s'augmenter,** *v.r.* to increase, to enlarge, to improve.
augural [ogy'ral], *a.* (*m. pl.* **-aux**) augural.
augure [o'gyːr], *n.m.* augur, soothsayer; augury, omen, sign; ***de mauvais augure,*** ominous, portentous.
augurer [ogy're], *v.t.* to augur; (*fig.*) to conjecture, to surmise.
Auguste [o'gyst], *m.* Augustus.
auguste [o'gyst], *a.* august, majestic.
augustin [ogys'tɛ̃], *n.m.* (*fem.* **-ine**) Augustinian *or* Austin friar *or* (*f.*) nun.
aujourd'hui [oʒur'dɥi], *adv.* today, during this day; nowadays, now, at present.
aulnaie [AUNAIE].
aulne [AUNE].
aulx [oː], [AIL].
aumône [o'moːn], *n.f.* alms, alms-giving; (*fig.*) charity, favour.
aumônerie [omon'ri], *n.f.* chaplaincy.
aumônier [omo'nje], *n.m.* (*Eccles.*) almoner, chaplain; ***aumônier militaire,*** army chaplain, padre.
aunaie or **aulnaie** [o'nɛ], *n.f.* grove of alders.
aune (1) or **aulne** [oːn], *n.m.* alder-tree.
aune (2) [oːn], *n.f.* ell; (*fig.*) measure, standard.
aunée [o'ne], *n.f.* length of an ell.
auparavant [opara'vɑ̃], *adv.* before, formerly previously.
auprès [o'prɛ], *adv.* near, by, close by.—*prep.* ***auprès de,*** near to, close to; in comparison with; in the service of; in the opinion of.
auquel [o'kɛl], *contraction* of À LEQUEL (*fem.* **à laquelle,** *pl.* **auxquels, auxquelles**) to whom, to which.
auréole [ɔre'ɔl], *n.f.* aureole, halo, nimbus; (*fig.*) glory, prestige.
auréoler [ɔreɔ'le], *v.t.* to crown with a halo.
auriculaire [ɔriky'lɛːr], *a.* auricular.—*n.m.* the little finger.
auricule [ɔri'kyl], *n.f.* lower lobe of the ear, auricle; (*Bot.*) auricula.
auriculiste [ɔriky'list], *n.m.* ear specialist.
aurifère [ɔri'fɛːr], *a.* auriferous.
auriste [ɔ'rist], *n.m.* ear specialist.
aurore [ɔ'rɔːr], *n.f.* dawn, morn, daybreak; (*fig.*) promise, beginning, the East; (*Astron.*) aurora.
auscultation [oskyltɑ'sjɔ̃], *n.f.* (*Med.*) auscultation.
ausculter [oskyl'te], *v.t.* to sound a patient.
auspice [os'pis], *n.m.* auspice, omen, presage; (*pl.*) protection, patronage.
aussi [o'si], *adv.* also, likewise, too, besides; as; so.—*conj.* and so, accordingly, therefore, consequently; but then.
aussière [o'sjɛːr], *n.f.* (*Naut.*) hawser.
aussitôt [osi'to], *adv.* immediately, forthwith.—*conj.* ***aussitôt que,*** as soon as.
austère [os'tɛːr], *a.* austere, severe, stern.
austèrement [ostɛr'mɑ̃], *adv.* austerely.
austérité [osteri'te], *n.f.* austerity; severity; strictness.
austral [os'tral], *a.* (*m. pl.* **-als** or **-aux**) austral, southern.
Australasie [ostrala'zi], **l',** *f.* Australasia.
australasien [ostrala'zjɛ̃], *a.* (*fem.* **-enne**) Australasian.
Australie [ostra'li], **l',** *f.* Australia.
australien [ostra'ljɛ̃], *a.* (*fem.* **-enne**) Australian.—*n.m.* (**Australien,** *fem.* **-enne**) Australian (*person*).
autant [o'tɑ̃], *adv.* as much, so much, as many, so many; ***autant de têtes, autant d'avis,*** there are as many opinions as there are men; ***autant que,*** as much as, as many as, as far as, in the same way as; ***d'autant,*** in the same proportion; ***d'autant mieux*** or ***d'autant plus,*** the more, so much the more.—*conj.* ***d'autant que,*** seeing that, since, more especially as.
autel [o'tɛl], *n.m.* altar; (*fig.*) ministry, Church, religious life.

auteur [o'tœ:r], *n.m.* author, creator, maker; writer (*of a book etc.*); perpetrator; achiever, contriver, framer; composer, sculptor; informant, authority; ***droit d'auteur***, royalty.

authenticité [otɑ̃tisi'te], *n.f.* authenticity genuineness.

authentique [otɑ̃'tik], *a.* authenticated, genuine, incontestable, positive.

authentiquement [otɑ̃tik'mɑ̃], *adv.* authentically.

authentiquer [otɑ̃ti'ke], *v.t.* to authenticate; (*Law*) to make legal and binding.

auto [o'to], *n.f. abbr.* [AUTOMOBILE].

auto-allumage [otoaly'ma:ʒ], *n.m.* pinking (*of a car*).

autobiographe [otɔbjɔ'graf], *n.m.* autobiographer.

autobiographie [otɔbjɔgra'fi], *n.f.* autobiography.

autobiographique [otɔbjɔgra'fik], *a.* autobiographical.

autobus [oto'bys], *n.m.* bus.

autocar [oto'ka:r], *n.m.* motor-coach.

autochenille [oto'ʃni:j], *n.f.* caterpillar tractor; half-track vehicle.

autoclave [otɔ'kla:v], *a.* and *n.m.* vacuum-pan, sterilizer; ***marmite autoclave***, autoclave, digester; pressure cooker.

autocopie [otɔkɔ'pi], *n.f.* cyclostyling.

autocopier [otɔkɔ'pje], *v.t.* to cyclostyle.

autocopiste [otɔkɔ'pist], *n.m.* duplicator, cyclostyle.

autocrate [otɔ'krat], *n.m.* autocrat.

autocratie [otɔkra'si], *n.f.* autocracy.

autocratique [otɔkra'tik], *a.* autocratic.

autocratiquement [otɔkratik'mɑ̃], *adv.* autocratically.

autocritique [otɔkri'tik], *n.f.* self-criticism.

auto-cuiseur [otɔkɥi'zœ:r], *n.m.* pressure-cooker.

autodidacte [otɔdi'dakt], *n.* self-taught person.

autodrome [otɔ'dro:m], *n.m.* race-track for motor-cars.

auto-école [otoe'kɔl], *n.f.* school of motoring.

autogare [otɔ'ga:r], *n.f.* bus *or* coach station.

autographe [otɔ'graf], *a.* autographic.—*n.m.* autograph.

autographie [otɔgra'fi], *n.f.* autography.

autographier [otɔgra'fje], *v.t.* to autograph.

autogyre [oto'ʒi:r], *n.m.* autogyro.

automate [otɔ'mat], *n.m.* automaton, robot.

automation [otɔma'sjɔ̃], *n.f.* automation.

automatique [otɔma'tik], *a.* automatic; ***distributeur automatique***, (penny-in-the-) slot machine; ***machine à vente automatique***, vending machine.—*n.m.* ***l'Automatique***, automatic telephone.

automatiquement [otɔmatik'mɑ̃], *adv.* automatically.

automatisme [otɔma'tism], *n.m.* automatism, purely mechanical movement.

automitrailleuse [otomitra'jø:z], *n.f.* light armoured car.

automnal [otɔ'nal], *a.* (*m. pl.* **-aux**) autumnal.

automne [o'tɔn], *n.m.* or *f.* autumn.

automobile [otɔmɔ'bil], *a.* self-moving, self-propelling; ***canot automobile***, motor-boat.—*n.f.* motor-car; ***salon de l'automobile***, motor show.

automobilisme [otɔmɔbi'lism], *n.m.* automobilism, motoring.

automobiliste [otɔmɔbi'list], *n.* motorist.

automoteur [otɔmɔ'tœ:r], *a.* (*fem.* **-trice**) self-acting, self-moving, self-propelling.

(*C*) **auto-neige** [oto'nɛ:ʒ], *n.f.* snowmobile.

autonome [otɔ'nɔm], *a.* autonomous.

autonomie [otɔnɔ'mi], *n.f.* autonomy, self-government; cruising range.

autonomiste [otɔnɔ'mist], *n.m.* autonomist.

autoplastie [otɔplas'ti], *n.f.* (*Surg.*) plastic surgery.

auto-portrait [otɔpɔr'trɛ], *n.m.* self-portrait.

auto-propulsé [otɔprɔpyl'se], *a.* self-propelled.

auto-propulsion [otɔprɔpyl'sjɔ̃], *n.f.* self-propulsion.

autopsie [otɔp'si], *n.f.* autopsy; post-mortem examination.

autorail [otɔ'ra:j], *n.m.* rail-car.

autorisation [otɔriza'sjɔ̃], *n.f.* authorization; authority, warrant; written consent *or* permission, licence (*of a preacher*).

autoriser [otɔri'ze], *v.t.* to authorize, to empower, to commission; to license, to warrant, to permit, to sanction. **s'autoriser**, *v.r.* to have, get *or* assume authority; to act on the authority (*of*), to be warranted by (*de*).

autoritaire [otɔri'tɛ:r], *a.* and *n.* authoritative, commanding, arbitrary (person).

autoritairement [otɔritɛr'mɑ̃], *adv.* authoritatively.

autorité [otɔri'te], *n.f.* authority, legal *or* legitimate power; an authority; (*fig.*) control.

autoroute [otɔ'rut], *n.f.* motorway; (*Am.*) speedway.

auto-stop [otɔ'stɔp], *n.m.* hitch-hiking; ***faire de l'auto-stop***, to hitch-hike.

autostrade [oto'strad], *n.f.* special road for motor-cars, motorway.

autosuggestion [otɔsygʒɛs'tjɔ̃], *n.f.* autosuggestion.

autour (1) [o'tu:r], *adv.* about, round about.—*prep. phr.* ***autour de***, about, round, around.

autour (2) [o'tu:r], *n.m.* (*Orn.*) goshawk.

autre [o:tr], *a.* other; second; another different, distinct (*but of the same kind*).—*pron. indef.* another person, someone else; (*pl.*) the others, the rest.

autrefois [otrə'fwa], *adv.* formerly, in former times; of old; ***d'autrefois***, former, bygone; ***des mœurs d'autrefois***, bygone customs.

autrement [otrə'mɑ̃], *adv.* otherwise, after another manner; else; or else; ***autrement dit***, in other words.

Autriche [o'triʃ], **l'**, *f.* Austria.

autrichien [otri'ʃjɛ̃], *a.* (*fem.* **-enne**) Austrian. —*n.m.* (**Autrichien**, *fem.* **-enne**) Austrian (*person*).

autruche [o'tryʃ], *n.f.* ostrich.

autrucherie [otryʃ'ri], *n.f.* ostrich-farm.

autrui [o'trɥi], *pron. indef. inv.* others, other people, one's *or* our neighbours.

auvent [o'vɑ̃], *n.m.* weather-board, porch roof; ***auvent de capot***, bonnet louvre.

aux [o], *pl.* [AU].

auxiliaire [oksi'ljɛ:r], *a.* auxiliary, aiding, subsidiary.—*n.* auxiliary; helper, assistant.

auxquels [o'kɛl], *pl.* (*fem.* **-elles**) [AUQUEL].

avachi [ava'ʃi], *a.* out of shape, worn out; (*fam.*) flabby, floppy, downcast (*of a person*).

avachir (s') [sava'ʃi:r], *v.r.* to flag; to grow fat and flabby; to get out of shape *or* down at heel.
avachissement [avaʃis'mɑ̃], *n.m.* flabbiness; lack of energy.
aval (1) [a'val], *n.m.* (*pl.* **avals**) guarantee, endorsement.
aval (2) [a'val], *n.m.* down stream; ***en aval de***, below.
avalaison [avalɛ'zɔ̃], **avalasse** [ava'las], *n.f.* sudden flood, spate; (*Naut.*) a long-continued wind from the sea.
avalanche [ava'lɑ̃:ʃ], *n.f.* avalanche.
avalasse [AVALAISON].
avalement [aval'mɑ̃], *n.m.* descent, lowering, letting down; swallowing.
avaler [ava'le], *v.t.* to swallow, to swallow down; to drink, to gulp down; to let down, to lower (*things into a cellar*); (*fig.*) to endure, to pocket (*an affront*); to believe.—*v.i.* to go down (*a river etc. with the stream*).
avaliser [avali'ze], *v.t.* to guarantee, to endorse [AVAL (1)].
avance [a'vɑ̃:s], *n.f.* part of a building etc. projecting forwards; advance; start, distance in advance; payment of money in advance; (*fig., pl.*) attentions, first steps in an acquaintanceship.
avancé [avɑ̃'se], *a.* advanced, forward, early; late (*of the hour*); over-ripe, tainted, high; liberal, progressive (*of opinions etc.*); paid in advance; put forward, enunciated.
avancement [avɑ̃s'mɑ̃], *n.m.* projection; progress, advancement; preferment, promotion, rise.
avancer [avɑ̃'se], *v.t.* (*conjug. like* COMMENCER) to move, bring, put *or* hold forward, to advance; to pay beforehand *or* in advance; to assert, to bring forward, to urge; to promote, to give promotion to; to advantage, to profit; (*fig.*) to bring nearer, to hasten, to forward; to put on (*a clock*).—*v.i.* to advance, to proceed, to keep on; to project, to jut out; to make progress, to thrive, to get on, to gain ground; to go too fast; ***l'horloge avance***, the clock is fast. **s'avancer**, *v.r.* to advance, to go on, to move forward; to get on, to improve; to get promoted, to be successful; to grow old; to project.
avanie [ava'ni], *n.f.* insult, affront; snub.
avant [a'vɑ̃], *prep.* before, in advance of (*of time and order*); ***avant J.-C.***, B.C.—*adv.* before, previously; forward, in front; farther in advance.—*conj.* ***avant que***, before; ***en avant!*** forward!—*n.m.* front; prow, head, bow (*of a ship*); (*Ftb.*) forward.
avantage [avɑ̃'ta:ʒ], *n.m.* advantage, benefit, profit, superiority, whip-hand; (*Ten.*) 'vantage.
avantager [avɑ̃ta'ʒe], *v.t.* (*conjug. like* MANGER) to advantage, to give an advantage to; to favour. **s'avantager**, *v.r.* to take advantage.
avantageusement [avɑ̃taʒøz'mɑ̃], *adv.* advantageously, to advantage; usefully, favourably.
avantageux [avɑ̃ta'ʒø], *a.* (*fem.* **-euse**) advantageous, profitable, favourable; conceited, presumptuous; (*of dress*) becoming.

[In *pl.* of the following compounds ***avant*** is *inv.* The *n.* has its normal *pl.*]

avant-bassin [avɑ̃ba'sɛ̃], *n.m.* outer-dock.
avant-bras [avɑ̃'bra], *n.m. inv.* forearm.
avant-centre [avɑ̃'sɑ̃:tr], *n.m.* (*Ftb.*) centre-forward.
avant-corps [avɑ̃'kɔ:r], *n.m. inv.* (*Arch.*) forepart (*of a building*).
avant-cour [avɑ̃'ku:r], *n.f.* fore-court.
avant-coureur [avɑ̃ku'rœ:r], *a.* going in front, preceding, presaging.—*n.m.* forerunner, precursor, harbinger.
avant-courrier [avɑ̃ku'rje], *n.m.* (*fem.* **-ière**) (*fig.*) herald, forerunner, harbinger.
avant-dernier [avɑ̃dɛr'nje], *a.* and *n.m.* (*fem.* **-ière**) the last but one.
avant-garde [avɑ̃'gard], *n.f.* vanguard, van.
avant-goût [avɑ̃'gu], *n.m.* foretaste; earnest; anticipation.
avant-guerre [avɑ̃'gɛ:r], *n.m.* the pre-war period.
avant-hier [avɑ̃'tjɛ:r], *adv.* and *n.m.* the day before yesterday.
avant-main [avɑ̃'mɛ̃], *n.m.* flat of the hand; forehand (*of a horse*); (*Ten.*) forehand (stroke); (*Cards*) lead.
avant-port [avɑ̃'pɔ:r], *n.m.* outer harbour, tide-dock.
avant-poste [avɑ̃'pɔst], *n.m.* (*Mil.*) advanced post, outpost; (*fig.*) outer defence.
avant-première [avɑ̃prə'mjɛ:r], *n.f.* dress rehearsal; (*Cine.*) preview.
avant-projet [avɑ̃prɔ'ʒɛ], *n.m.* rough draft.
avant-propos [avɑ̃prɔ'po], *n.m. inv.* preface, preamble, introduction, foreword.
avant-scène [avɑ̃'sɛ:n], *n.f.* front of the stage (*between curtain and orchestra*), proscenium.
avant-toit [avɑ̃'twɑ], *n.m.* eaves.
avant-train [avɑ̃'trɛ̃], *n.m.* fore-carriage, limber.
avant-veille [avɑ̃'vɛ:j], *n.f.* two days before.
avare [a'va:r], *a.* avaricious, miserly, covetous, stingy, close-fisted.—*n.m.* miser, niggard.
avarement [avar'mɑ̃], *adv.* stingily.
avariable [ava'rjabl], *a.* perishable, damageable.
avarice [ava'ris], *n.f.* avarice, greed, covetousness; niggardliness, stinginess.
avaricieusement [avarisjøz'mɑ̃], *adv.* avariciously.
avaricieux [avari'sjø], *a.* (*fem.* **-euse**) avaricious, covetous, stingy.
avarie [ava'ri], *n.f.* damage (*to a ship or cargo*); deterioration.
avarié [ava'rje], *a.* damaged, spoiled, deteriorated.
avarier [ava'rje], *v.t.* to damage, to spoil. **s'avarier**, *v.r.* to become damaged.
avec [a'vɛk], *prep.* with, at the same time as, along *or* together with; by means of, by; regarding; against, in spite of; ***avec ça!*** (*colloq.*) nonsense!
aveline [a'vlin], *n.f.* filbert, Kentish cob.
avelinier [avli'nje], *n.m.* filbert-tree, hazel-tree.
aven [a'vɛ̃], *n.m.* pot-hole, swallow, chasm (*in mountain limestone*).
avenant [av'nɑ̃], *a.* personable, prepossessing, comely, pleasing, taking.—*adv. phr.* ***à l'avenant***, in keeping, in the same proportions, of a piece.—*n.m.* additional clause (*to an insurance policy*); rider (*to a verdict*); codicil (*to a treaty*).

avènement [avɛn'mɑ̃], *n.m.* coming, advent; accession, succession (*to a throne etc.*).
avenir [av'ni:r], *n.m.* future, future ages; posterity; (*fig.*) prospects; ***à l'avenir***, in future, henceforth.
Avent [a'vɑ̃], *n.m.* (*Ch.*) Advent.
aventure [avɑ̃'ty:r], *n.f.* surprising *or* unexpected event *or* experience, chance, accident, luck; adventure, daring enterprise, hazardous exploit; love affair *or* intrigue; ***à l'aventure***, at random; ***d'aventure*** or ***par aventure***, by chance, perchance.
aventurer [avɑ̃ty're], *v.t.* to venture, to hazard, to risk. **s'aventurer**, *v.r.* to venture, to take one's chance, to take risks.
aventureux [avɑ̃ty'rø], *a.* (*fem.* **-euse**) venturesome, adventurous; left to chance.
aventurier [avɑ̃ty'rje], *n.m.* (*fem.* **-ière**) adventurer, adventuress.
avenue [av'ny], *n.f.* approach; avenue.
avéré [ave're], *a.* authenticated, established by evidence.
avérer [ave're], *v.t.* (*conjug. like* CÉDER) to verify, to confirm, to establish. **s'avérer**, *v.r.* (*used only in inf. and p.p.*) to appear, to be distinctly, to turn out to be, to prove.
avers [a'vɛ:r], *n.m.* obverse (*of coins etc.*).
averse [a'vɛrs], *n.f.* sudden and heavy shower of rain, downpour; (*fig.*) flood (*of talk etc.*).
aversion [avɛr'sjɔ̃], *n.f.* aversion, dislike, detestation.
averti [avɛr'ti], *a.* warned, informed; wide awake; well-informed, experienced.
avertir [avɛr'ti:r], *v.t.* to inform, to acquaint with, to give notice, to warn, to admonish (*de*).
avertissement [avɛrtis'mɑ̃], *n.m.* information, notification, advice, warning, caution; ***avertissement au lecteur***, foreword (*of a book*).
avertisseur [avɛrti'sœ:r], *n.m.* look-out man; (*Theat.*) call-boy; call-bell, hooter; ***avertisseur d'incendie***, fire-alarm.
aveu [a'vø], *n.m.* (*pl.* **-eux**) admission, avowal, confession; approbation, consent; ***homme sans aveu***, vagrant, vagabond.
aveuglant [avœ'glɑ̃], *a.* blinding, dazzling; (*fig.*) distracting, misleading.
aveugle [a'vœgl], *a.* blind, sightless; blinded by passion etc., deluded.—*n.* blind person.
aveuglement [avœglə'mɑ̃], *n.m.* blindness; (*fig.*) infatuation, delusion.
aveuglément [avœgle'mɑ̃], *adv.* blindly, rashly; implicitly.
aveugle-né [avœglə'ne], *a.* and *n.m.* (*fem.* **-née**, *pl.* **aveugles-nés**) blind from birth.
aveugler [avœ'gle], *v.t.* to blind, to make blind; (*fig.*) to dazzle; to delude. **s'aveugler**, *v.r.* to shut one's eyes (*to*); (*fig.*) to be blinded, to be infatuated.
aveuglette [avœ'glɛt], *n.f.* (*only used in*) ***à l'aveuglette***, blindly; ***aller à l'aveuglette***, to go groping along, to go blindly *or* rashly; (*Av.*) ***voler à l'aveuglette***, to fly blind.
aveulir [avœ'li:r], *v.t.* to render weak, to enfeeble, to enervate. **s'aveulir**, *v.r.* to sink into sloth.
aveulissant [avœli'sɑ̃], *a.* enfeebling, enervating.
aveulissement [avœlis'mɑ̃], *n.m.* enfeeblement, enervation.
aviateur [avja'tœ:r], *n.m.* (*fem.* **-trice**) aviator; air-man, air-woman; flyer.
aviation [avjɑ'sjɔ̃], *n.f.* aviation; ***terrain d'aviation***, flying ground, air-field.
aviculteur [avikyl'tœ:r], *n.m.* one who raises birds *or* poultry; bird fancier.
aviculture [avikyl'ty:r], *n.f.* bird-raising; poultry-farming.
avide [a'vid], *a.* greedy, voracious, rapacious; eager for, grasping.
avidement [avid'mɑ̃], *adv.* greedily, voraciously; eagerly.
avidité [avidi'te], *n.f.* avidity, greediness; eagerness.
avilir [avi'li:r], *v.t.* to debase, to depreciate, to disparage; to lower; to degrade, to disgrace. **s'avilir**, *v.r.* to degrade oneself, to stoop to (*doing something*).
avilissant [avili'sɑ̃], *a.* debasing, degrading, humiliating.
avilissement [avilis'mɑ̃], *n.m.* debasement, degradation; depreciation, disparagement.
avilisseur [avili'sœ:r], *a.* (*fem.* **-euse**) debasing, degrading.—*n.m.* (*fem.* **-euse**) one who debases, disparages *or* degrades.
aviné [avi'ne], *a.* drunk, unsteady (*from drink*); wine-soaked (*of a cask*).
aviner [avi'ne], *v.t.* to soak *or* fill with wine. **s'aviner**, *v.r.* to get drunk.
avion [a'vjɔ̃], *n.m.* aeroplane, aircraft; ***avion de bombardement***, bomber; ***avion de chasse***, fighter; ***avion de ligne***, air-liner; ***avion à réaction***, jet-plane; ***avion-fusée***, rocket-plane; ***avion-taxi***, charter-plane; ***par avion***, by air, by air mail.
aviron [avi'rɔ̃], *n.m.* oar; (*Spt.*) rowing.
avis [a'vi], *n.m.* opinion, way of thinking, judgment; vote, motion; advice, counsel; information, notice, warning, caution, intelligence; ***à mon avis***, in my opinion; ***j'ai changé d'avis***, I have changed my mind; ***avis au public***, notice.
avisé [avi'ze], *a.* shrewd, clear-sighted, wary, circumspect, prudent.
aviser [avi'ze], *v.t.* to perceive, to espy; to inform, to apprise; (*Comm.*) to advise by letter.—*v.i.* to consider, to think (*about*), to look (*to*). **s'aviser**, *v.r.* to think (*of*), to be minded (*to*); to venture to do.
avivage [avi'va:ʒ], *n.m.* brightening, reviving (*of colours*).
aviver [avi've], *v.t.* to revive, to brighten; to sharpen the edges of, to polish, to burnish; to irritate, to exacerbate (*a wound, resentment etc.*). **s'aviver**, *v.r.* to revive.
avocat (1) [avɔ'ka], *n.m.* (*fem.* **-e**) barrister, advocate, counsel; (*fig.*) pleader, intercessor, champion.
avocat (2) [avɔ'ka], *n.m.* avocado, alligator pear.
avoine [a'vwan], *n.f.* oats.
avoir [a'vwa:r], *v.t. irr.* to have, to possess; to experience, to feel (*pain, hunger etc.*); to obtain, to get, to buy etc.; to be aged (*so many years*); to have on, to wear; to ail; ***avoir à***, to have to, to be under obligation to (*do etc.*); ***y avoir*** (*impers.*), to be; ***avoir faim***, to be hungry; ***combien y a-t-il de Paris à Londres?*** how far is it from Paris to London? ***il a quarante ans***, he is forty; ***il n'y a pas de quoi***, don't mention it, no offence taken; ***il y a deux mois que je***

suis ici, I have been here two months; ***il est arrivé il y a trois semaines***, he arrived three weeks ago; ***j'ai à vous parler***, I have something to tell you; ***qu'avez-vous donc?*** what's the matter? ***quel âge avez-vous?*** how old are you? ***qu'est-ce que vous avez?*** what is the matter with you? ***la pièce a cinq mètres de large***, the room is fifteen feet wide.—*n.m.* possessions, property, what one is worth.

avoisinant [avwazi'nɑ̃], *a.* neighbouring, adjoining, close by.

avoisiner [avwazi'ne], *v.t.* to border upon, to be contiguous to.

avortement [avɔrtə'mɑ̃], *n.m.* abortion, miscarriage; failure.

avorter [avɔr'te], *v.i.* to miscarry, to have a miscarriage; to fail to develop, ripen etc. (*of plants, fruit etc.*); to prove abortive, to fail.

avorton [avɔr'tɔ̃], *n.m.* abortion; abortive child; (*fig.*) a paltry *or* miserable person *or* thing, a miserable specimen.

avoué [a'vwe], *n.m.* attorney, solicitor; ***une étude d'avoué***, a solicitor's office.

avouer [a'vwe], *v.t.* to own, to acknowledge, to confess; to approve; to recognize as one's own, to avow.

avril [a'vril], *n.m.* April.

avunculaire [avɔ̃ky'lɛ:r], *a.* avuncular.

axe [aks], *n.m.* axis; axle, axle-tree, spindle, trunnion; (*Bot.*, *Geol.*, *Anat. etc.*) axis; (*fig.*) central support *or* main axis of a system of ideas etc.; (*Polit.*) the Nazi-Fascist Axis.

axiomatique [aksjɔma'tik], *a.* axiomatic.

axiome [ak'sjo:m], *n.m.* axiom; (*fig.*) an accepted proposition, truism.

ayant [ɛ'jɑ̃], *pres. p.* [AVOIR].

ayant cause [ɛjɑ̃'ko:z], *n.m.* (*pl.* **ayants cause**) (*Law*) trustee, executor, assign.

ayant droit [ɛjɑ̃'drwɑ], *n.m.* (*pl.* **ayants droit**) beneficiary, rightful claimant.

azalée [aza'le], *n.f.* azalea.

azotate [azɔ'tat], *n.m.* nitrate.

azote [a'zɔt], *a.* nitric.—*n.m.* nitrogen.

azoté [azɔ'te], *a.* nitrogenized.

azoter [azɔ'te], *v.t.* to charge with nitrogen; to azotize.

azoteux [azɔ'tø], *a.* (*fem.* **-euse**) nitrous.

azotique [azɔ'tik], *a.* nitric.

azur [a'zy:r], *n.m.* azure, blue, sky-colour; washing blue; ***la Côte d'Azur***, the French Riviera.

azuré [azy're], *a.* azure, sky-coloured; ***la voûte azurée***, the azure skies.

azyme [a'zim], *a.* azymous, unleavened (*bread*).—*n.m.* azyme, unleavened bread; ***fête des azymes***, feast of unleavened bread.

B

B, b [be], *n.m.* the second letter of the alphabet.

baba [ba'ba], *n.m.* a sponge cake, with sultanas, steeped in rum and syrup.

Babel [ba'bɛl], *n.f.* Babel; (*fig.*) uproar, disorder.

babeurre [ba'bœ:r], *n.m.* buttermilk.

babil [ba'bi], *n.m.* babble, prattle; chit-chat, tattle; chattering, babbling.

babillage [babi'ja:ʒ], **babillement** [babij'mɑ̃], *n.m.* prattle, babbling, twaddle; tittle-tattle.

babillard [babi'ja:r], *a.* babbling, prattling, talkative, garrulous; gossiping, tell-tale.—*n.m.* (*fem.* **-e**) chatterer, babbler; tattler, blabber, gossip, tell-tale.

babillement [BABILLAGE].

babiller [babi'je], *v.i.* to babble, to prattle, to chat; to gossip, to chatter; (*fig.*) to blab, to backbite.

babine [ba'bin], **babouine** [ba'bwin], *n.f.* the pendulous lip (*of certain animals*); (*colloq.*) chops.

babiole [ba'bjɔl], *n.f.* bauble, trinket, toy; (*fig.*) trifle, trumpery affair.

bâbord [bɑ'bɔ:r], *n.m.* (*Naut.*) port (*side*).

babouche [ba'buʃ], *n.f.* Turkish heelless slipper, babouche.

babouin [ba'bwɛ̃], *n.m.* baboon, monkey.

Babylone [babi'lɔn], *f.* Babylon.

babylonien [babilɔ'njɛ̃], *a.* (*fem.* **-enne**) Babylonian.—*n.m.* (**Babylonien**, *fem.* **-enne**) Babylonian (*person*).

bac [bak], *n.m.* ferry, ferry-boat; vat; (*Elec.*) ***bac d'accumulateurs***, accumulator-jar.

baccalauréat [bakalɔre'a], *n.m.* baccalaureate, bachelorship (*of arts, science etc.*), school-leaving certificate.

bacchanal [baka'nal], *n.m.* (*colloq.*) racket, uproar.

bacchante [ba'kɑ̃:t], *n.f.* bacchante, lewd woman.

bâche [bɑ:ʃ], *n.f.* cart tilt; awning; tank, cistern; ***bâche (goudronnée)***, tarpaulin.

bachelier [baʃə'lje], *n.m.* (*fem.* **-ière**) Bachelor (***ès Lettres, ès Sciences***, *of Arts, Science*).

bachique [ba'ʃik], *a.* bacchic, jovial, convivial; ***chant bachique***, drinking-song.

bachot [ba'ʃo], *n.m.* wherry, small ferry-boat; (*Univ. slang*) baccalaureate.

bachoteur [baʃɔ'tœ:r], *n.m.* ferryman.

bacille [ba'sil], *n.m.* (*Biol.*) bacillus; ***porteur de bacilles***, germ-carrier.

bacillose [basi'lo:z], [TUBERCULOSE].

bâclage [bɑ'kla:ʒ], *n.m.* closing of a port by means of chains, booms etc.; line of boats (*in a port*) for the discharge *or* loading of cargo; (*fig.*) hasty, scamped work.

bâcle [bɑ:kl], *n.f.* bar (*for door* or *gate*).

bâcler [bɑ'kle], *v.t.* to bar, fasten *or* secure (*a door, window etc.*); to stop, obstruct *or* interrupt (*traffic, navigation etc.*); (*fig.*) to do hastily, to polish off, to scamp (*work*); to bungle.

bactérie [bakte'ri], *n.f.* bacterium, microbe.

bactérien [bakte'rjɛ̃], *a.* (*fem.* **-enne**) bacterial.

bactériologie [bakterjɔlɔ'ʒi], *n.f.* bacteriology.

bactériologique [bakterjɔlɔ'ʒik], *a.* bacteriological; ***guerre bactériologique***, germ warfare.

bactériologiste [bakterjɔlɔ'ʒist], *n.m.* bacteriologist.

bactériothérapie [bakterjɔtera'pi], *n.f.* medical treatment by means of bacteria.

badaud [ba'do], *n.m.* (*fem.* **-e**) ninny, booby star-gazer; lounger, idler, rubber-neck.
badaudage [bado'da:ʒ], *n.m.* star-gazing, lounging, loitering, idling.
badauder [bado'de], *v.i.* to go gaping about; to lounge, to saunter, to loiter.
badauderie [bado'dri], *n.f.* star-gazing, silliness; lounging, idling, sauntering.
Bade [bad], *f.* Baden.
badigeon [badi'ʒɔ̃], *n.m.* badigeon, filling-paste; whitewash; distemper.
badigeonnage [badiʒɔ'na:ʒ], *n.m.* filling up with badigeon, making up; daubing; white-washing.
badigeonner [badiʒɔ'ne], *v.t.* to fill up (*stone-work, sculpture etc.*) with badigeon; to whitewash; (*fig.*) to disguise defects with varnish, rouge etc.; (*Med.*) to anoint.
badigeonneur [badiʒɔ'nœ:r], *n.m.* white-washer; (*pej.*) dauber.
badin [ba'dɛ̃], *a.* waggish, jocular, roguish, droll.—*n.m.* (*fem.* **-e** (1)) wag, joker; buffoon.
badinage [badi'na:ʒ], *n.m.* badinage, raillery, banter; playfulness, jocularity (*of style*); mere child's-play.
badine (2) [ba'din], *n.f.* switch, light cane, wand; (*pl.*) small tongs.
badiner [badi'ne], *v.i.* to trifle, to dally, to toy; to speak *or* write banteringly *or* playfully.
badinerie [badin'ri], *n.f.* jesting, foolery, trifling; silliness, childishness.
(*C*) **bâdrant** [bɑ'drɑ̃], *a.* bothersome.
(*C*) **bâdrer** [bɑ'dre], *v.t.* to annoy, to bother.
bafouer [ba'fwe], *v.t.* to scoff at, to make game of.
bafouillage [bafu'ja:ʒ], *n.f.* gibberish, rigmarole; spluttering; bad running (*of engine*).
bafouiller [bafu'je], *v.i.* (*colloq.*) to stammer; to splutter; to miss, to chatter (*of engine*).
bafouilleur [bafu'jœ:r], *n.m.* (*fem.* **-euse**) stammerer.
bagages [ba'ga:ʒ], *n.m. pl.* luggage; ***bagages enregistrés***, registered luggage.
bagarre [ba'ga:r], *n.f.* riot; uproar; crush, squabble, scuffle.
bagatelle [baga'tɛl], *n.f.* bauble, trinket, trifle, anything frivolous; trifling sum, mere nothing.
bagne [baɲ], *n.m.* convict-prison; penal servitude.
bagnole [ba'ɲɔl], *n.f.* (*fam.*) (old) motor-car.
bague [bag], *n.f.* ring; ring band (*for birds*).
bague-agrafe [baga'graf], *n.f.* (***d'un stylo***) (fountain-pen) clip.
baguer [ba'ge], *v.t.* to baste, to tack, to stitch; to decorate *or* hang with rings; (*Hort.*) to ring (*trees*); to ring (*a bird*).
baguette [ba'gɛt], *n.f.* switch, rod, wand; pointer; clock (*of stockings*); glove-stretcher; long roll (*French bread*).
baguier [ba'gje], *n.m.* casket for rings, jewels etc., jewel-box, ring-stand.
bah! [bɑ], *int.* pooh! pshaw! nonsense! fudge!
bahut [ba'y], *n.m.* cabinet, trunk, chest; press, cupboard; (*Sch. slang*) grammar school.
bahutier [bay'tje], *n.m.* maker of trunks, chests, cabinets, etc.
bai [bɛ], *a.* bay; ***une jument baie***(1), a bay mare.
baie (2) [bɛ], *n.f.* bay, gulf; (*Arch.*) bay, opening.
baie (3) [bɛ], *n.f.* berry.
baignade [bɛ'ɲad], *n.f.* bathing; bathing-place.
baigner [bɛ'ɲe], *v.t.* to bathe, to give a bath to, to dip; (*fig.*) to wash, to water (*a coast etc.*); to wet, to suffuse.—*v.i.* to be plunged into; to welter (*in blood etc.*). **se baigner**, *v.r.* to bathe, to wash.
baigneur [bɛ'ɲœ:r], *n.m.* (*fem.* **-euse**) bather; bathkeeper *or* attendant, bathing-attendant.
baignoire [bɛ'ɲwa:r], *n.f.* bath-tub, bath; (*Theat.*) ground-floor box.
bail [ba:j], *n.m.* (*pl.* **baux** [bo]) lease.
bâillement [bɑj'mɑ̃], *n.m.* yawning, yawn.
bâiller [bɑ'je], *v.i.* to yawn, to gape; to open (*of fissures etc.*); to be ajar (*of doors*).
bailleur [ba'jœ:r], *n.m.* (*fem.* **-eresse**) one who leases, lessor.
bâilleur [bɑ'jœ:r], *n.m.* (*fem.* **-euse**) yawner; gaper.
bailli [ba'ji], *n.m.* (*Fr. Hist.*) bailiff.
bâillon [bɑ'jɔ̃], *n.m.* gag, muzzle.
bâillonnement [bɑjɔn'mɑ̃], *n.m.* gagging.
bâillonner [bɑjɔ'ne], *v.t.* to stop the mouth of, to gag, to muzzle; (*fig.*) to silence.
bain [bɛ̃], *n.m.* bath; bathing-tub; (*pl.*) baths, bathing establishment, watering-place, spa; ***la salle de bain(s)***, the bathroom.
bain-douche [bɛ̃'duʃ], *n.m.* shower-bath.
bain-marie [bɛ̃ma'ri], *n.m.* (*pl.* **bains-marie**) (*Cook.*) double saucepan for foods that burn easily; boiler (*in a kitchen-range etc.*).
baïonnette [bajɔ'nɛt], *n.f.* bayonet.
baiser [bɛ'ze], *v.t.* (*of strictly literary use, no longer decent in conversation, practically replaced by* **embrasser**) to kiss.—*n.m.* kiss, kissing; salute.
baisse [bɛ:s], *n.f.* fall, abatement, decline; reduction *or* fall (*of prices etc.*); falling off (*of credit etc.*).
baisser [bɛ'se], *v.t.* to let down, to lower; to reduce the height of; to strike (*a flag etc.*); to bow (*the head etc.*).—*v.i.* (*with aux.* ÊTRE *or* AVOIR) to go down; to ebb; to be on the decline *or* the wane; to flag, to droop; to fail, to diminish. **se baisser**, *v.r.* to stoop; to bow down; to be lowered.
bajoue [ba'ʒu] *n.f.* jowl; chap (*of pigs etc.*).
bakélite [bake'lit], *n.f.* (*reg. trade name*) bakelite.
bal [bal], *n.m.* ball, dance; ***bal costumé***, fancy-dress ball.
baladeuse [bala'dø:z], *n.f.* costermonger's barrow; portable lamp; trailer (*for cycle* or *tram*).
baladin [bala'dɛ̃], *n.m.* (*fem.* **-e**) mountebank; buffoon.
balafre [ba'lɑ:fr], *n.f.* gash, slash, cut; scar.
balafrer [balɑ'fre], *v.t.* to gash, to slash.
balai (1) [ba'lɛ], *n.m.* broom, besom; (*Elec.*) brush.
(*C*) **balai** (2) [ba'lɛ], *n.m.* cedar.
balalaïka [balalai'ka], *n.f.* balalaika.
balance [ba'lɑ̃:s], *n.f.* balance, scales, pair of scales; (*Comm.*) balance (*of an account*), balance sheet.
balancement [balɑ̃s'mɑ̃], *n.m.* balancing, poising; rocking, see-saw; (*fig.*) fluctuation, wavering, hesitation.

balancer [balɑ̃'se], *v.t.* (*conjug. like* COMMENCER) to balance, to poise, to hold in equilibrium; to swing to and fro, to rock; (*fig.*) to weigh, to consider; to square (*accounts*); to counterbalance.—*v.i.* to hesitate, to be in suspense, to waver; to fluctuate, to oscillate, to remain undecided. **se balancer,** *v.r.* to swing, to rock.
balancier [balɑ̃'sje], *n.m.* maker of weights and scales; pendulum, balance; balancing-pole.
balançoire [balɑ̃'swa:r], *n.f.* see-saw; swing.
balandre [ba'lɑ̃:dr], *n.f.* flat canal boat.
balayage [balɛ'ja:ʒ], **balayement** [balɛ'mɑ̃], *n.m.* sweeping; (*Tel.*) scanning.
balayer [balɛ'je], *v.t.* (*conjug. like* PAYER) to sweep, to clean with a broom; (*Tel.*) to scan.
balayette [balɛ'jɛt], *n.f.* small broom, whisk.
balayeur [balɛ'jœ:r], *n.m.* (*fem.* **-euse**) sweeper, scavenger.—*n.f.* (**-euse**) sweeping-machine.
balayures [balɛ'jy:r], *n.f.* (*used only in pl.*) sweepings.
balbutier [balby'sje], *v.t.* to pronounce indistinctly.—*v.i.* to stammer, to stutter; to mumble.
balbutieur [balby'sjœ:r], *n.m.* (*fem.* **-euse**) stutterer, stammerer.
balcon [bal'kɔ̃], *n.m.* balcony; (*Theat.*) dress-circle.
baldaquin [balda'kɛ̃], *n.m.* baldachin, canopy; tester (*of bed*).
Bâle [bɑ:l], *f.* Basel, Basle.
Baléares [bale'a:r], **les**, *f. pl.* the Balearic Isles.
baleine [ba'lɛ:n], *n.f.* whale; whalebone; rib of an umbrella.
baleiné [balɛ'ne], *a.* stiffened with whalebone.
baleineau [balɛ'no], *n.m.* (*pl.* **-eaux**) young whale.
baleinier [balɛ'nje], *n.m.* (*fem.* **-ière**) whaler. —*n.f.* (**-ière**) whale-boat.
balisage [bali'za:ʒ], *n.m.* (*Naut.*) buoying, signalling; (*Av.*) ground-lights.
balise [ba'li:z], *n.f.* sea-mark, buoy, beacon; (*Av.*) ground-light.
baliser [bali'ze], *v.t.* to buoy; to mark with beacons *or* ground-lights.
balistique [balis'tik], *a.* ballistic.—*n.f.* ballistics.
balivage [bali'va:ʒ], *n.m.* *staddling.
baliveau [bali'vo], *n.m.* (*pl.* **-eaux**) *staddle; sapling.
baliverne [bali'vɛrn], *n.f.* nonsense, humbug.
baliverner [balivɛr'ne], *v.i.* to talk idly, to talk twaddle.
balkanique [balka'nik], *a.* Balkan.
ballade [ba'lad], *n.f.* ballade; ballad.
ballant [ba'lɑ̃], *a.* waving, swinging, dangling.
ballast [ba'last], *n.m.* (*Rail.*) ballast.
balle [bal], *n.f.* ball; bullet, shot; bale, pack.
ballerine [bal'rin], *n.f.* ballerina.
ballet [ba'lɛ], *n.m.* ballet.
ballon [ba'lɔ̃], *n.m.* hand-ball; football; balloon; air-balloon (*child's*).
ballonné [balɔ'ne], *a.* distended, swollen.
ballonnier [balɔ'nje], *n.m.* maker *or* vendor of toy balloons.
ballon-sonde [balɔ̃'sɔ̃:d], *n.m.* sounding balloon.
ballot [ba'lo], *n.m.* small pack (*of wares for sale*).
ballottement [balɔt'mɑ̃], *n.m.* tossing, shaking.
ballotter [balɔ'te], *v.t.* to toss, to toss about; to bandy; to keep in suspense.—*v.i.* to shake, to rattle.
balnéaire [balne'ɛ:r], *a.* pertaining to baths etc.; ***station balnéaire***, watering-place; seaside resort.
balourd [ba'lu:r], *a.* dull, heavy, thick-headed.—*n.m.* (*fem.* **-e**) stupid *or* dull person, numskull, dunce.
balourdise [balur'di:z], *n.f.* gross blunder; stupidity.
balsamier [balza'mje], **baumier** [bo'mje], *n.m.* balsam-tree.
balsamine [balza'min], *n.f.* balsamine.
Baltique [bal'tik], **la**, *f.* the Baltic (Sea).
balustrade [balys'trad], *n.f.* balustrade; low railing etc.
balustre [ba'lystr], *n.m.* baluster, hand-rail.
balustrer [balys'tre], *v.t.* to rail in, to surround.
balzane [bal'zan], *n.f.* white stocking (*of a horse*).
bambin [bɑ̃'bɛ̃], *n.m.* (*fem.* **-e**) (*colloq.*) urchin; brat, tiny tot.
bambou [bɑ̃'bu], *n.m.* bamboo (cane).
ban [bɑ̃], *n.m.* ban, announcement, public order, edict *or* proclamation; banishment, proscription; (*pl.*) banns (*of matrimony*).
banal [ba'nal], *a.* (*m. pl.* **-aux**) common, commonplace, trite.
banalité [banali'te], *n.f.* vulgarity; banality, commonplace, trite expression.
banane [ba'nan], *n.f.* banana.
bananier [bana'nje], *n.m.* banana-tree; banana boat.
banc [bɑ̃], *n.m.* bench, settle, form; reef, sand-bank; shoal (*of fish*); (*Geol.*) layer, bed; dock, bar; ***banc d'essai***, (*Motor.*) test bench; (*C*) ***banc de neige***, heap of snow; ***banc d'huîtres***, oyster-bed.
bancal [bɑ̃'kal], *a.* (*m. pl.* **-als**) bandy-legged.—*n.m.* (*fem.* **-e**) bandy-legged person.
bandage [bɑ̃'da:ʒ], *n.m.* application of bandages; bandage; belt; truss; tyre (*of wheels*).
bande (1) [bɑ̃:d], *n.f.* band, belt, strip; ribbon; bandage; ***bande de papier***, slip of paper, wrapper.
bande (2) [bɑ̃:d], *n.f.* band, troop, company; gang, crew, set (*of brigands etc.*); flock, pack.
bandé [bɑ̃'de], *a.* bandaged, taut, stretched.
bandeau [bɑ̃'do], *n.m.* (*pl.* **-eaux**) headband, bandage (*for the eyes*).
bandelette [bɑ̃'dlɛt], *n.f.* little band, string fillet.
bander [bɑ̃'de], *v.t.* to bind *or* tie up; to bandage; to tighten, to bend (*a bow etc.*).—*v.i.* to be stretched, to be taut *or* too tight.
banderole [bɑ̃'drɔl], *n.f.* banderole, streamer.
bandit [bɑ̃'di], *n.m.* brigand, bandit; ruffian, blackguard; scamp.
bandoulière [bɑ̃du'ljɛ:r], *n.f.* shoulder-strap, bandolier; ***en bandoulière***, slung across the back.
banjo [bɑ̃'ʒo], *n.m.* banjo.
banlieue [bɑ̃'ljø], *n.f.* suburbs, outskirts (*of a town*).
banne [ban], *n.f.* hamper; awning; tilt, tarpaulin.

banni [ba'ni], *a.* banished, outlawed; (*fig.*) banned, forbidden.—*n.m.* (*fem.* **-e**) exile, outlaw.
bannière [ba'njɛ:r], *n.f.* banner, standard, flag.
bannir [ba'ni:r], *v.t.* to banish; (*fig.*) to expel, to dismiss.
bannissement [banis'mɑ̃], *n.m.* banishment.
banque [bɑ̃:k], *n.f.* bank, banking.
banqueroute [bɑ̃'krut], *n.f.* bankruptcy; (*fig.*) failure, collapse.
banqueroutier [bɑ̃kru'tje], *n.m.* (*fem.* **-ière**) bankrupt.
banquet [bɑ̃'kɛ], *n.m.* banquet, feast.
banquette [bɑ̃'kɛt], *n.f.* bench; towing-path; (*Fort.*) banquette.
banquier [bɑ̃'kje], *n.m.* banker.
banquise [bɑ̃'ki:z], *n.f.* ice-floe, ice-pack.
bantam [bɑ̃'tam], *n.m.* bantam.
baptême [ba'tɛ:m], *n.m.* baptism, christening; ***nom de baptême***, Christian name.
baptiser [bati'ze], *v.t.* to baptize; (*fig.*) to christen, to give a name *or* nickname to.
baptismal [batiz'mal], *a.* (*m. pl.* **-aux**) baptismal.
baptistaire [batis'tɛ:r], *a.* of baptism; ***registre baptistaire***, parish register.
Baptiste [ba'tist], *n.m.* Baptist.
baquet [ba'kɛ], *n.m.* tub; (*Av.*) cockpit.
bar (1) [ba:r], *n.m.* (*Ichth.*) bass.
bar (2) [ba:r], *n.m.* bar (*of a public-house etc.*).
baragouin [bara'gwɛ̃], *n.m.* gibberish, jargon, lingo.
baragouinage [baragwi'na:ʒ], *n.m.* talking, gibberish, jargon etc.
baragouiner [baragwi'ne], *v.t.* to sputter out (*words*).—*v.i.* to talk gibberish; to gabble.
baraque [ba'rak], *n.f.* hut, shed, shanty; (*fam.*) hovel; booth (*at a fair*).
baraquement [barak'mɑ̃], *n.m.* (*Mil.*) hutting.
barattage [bara'ta:ʒ], *n.m.* churning.
baratte [ba'rat], *n.f.* churn.
baratter [bara'te], *v.t.* to churn.
barbacane [barba'kan], *n.f.* (*Fort.*) barbican.
Barbade [bar'bad], *f.* Barbados.
barbare [bar'ba:r], *a.* barbarous, barbarian; cruel, inhuman; (*fig.*) uncouth, rude; incorrect, ungrammatical.—*n.m.* (*usu. in pl.*) barbarians.
barbarement [barbar'mɑ̃], *adv.* barbarously.
barbaresque [barba'rɛsk], *a.* of *or* pertaining to Barbary.
Barbarie [barba'ri], **la**, *f.* Barbary.
barbarie [barba'ri], *n.f.* barbarity, rudeness; (*fig.*) cruelty.
barbarisme [barba'rism], *n.m.* (*Gram.*) barbarism.
barbe (1) [barb], *n.f.* beard; whiskers (*of cats, dogs etc.*); beard (*of corn etc.*); wattles (*of fowls*).
barbe (2) [barb], *n.m.* barb, barbary horse.
barbeau [bar'bo], *n.m.* (*pl.* **-eaux**) barbel; (*Bot.*) blue-bottle, cornflower.
barbelé [barbə'le], *a.* barbed, spiked; (***fil de fer***) ***barbelé***, barbed wire.
barbiche [bar'biʃ], **barbichette** [barbi'ʃɛt], *n.f.* beard growing only on the chin, goatee.
barbier [bar'bje], *n.m.* barber.
barbiturate [barbity'rat], **barbiturique** [barbity'rik], *n.m.* (*Chem.*) barbiturate.
barboter [barbɔ'te], *v.i.* to dabble about in mud *or* water (*with the beak, like a duck*); to paddle, to flounder about in the mud; (*fig.*) to mumble.
barboteuse [barbɔ'tø:z], *n.f.* rompers.
barbotière [barbɔ'tjɛ:r], *n.f.* duck-pond; trough.
barbouillage [barbu'ja:ʒ], *n.m.* daubing; daub; scrawl; (*fig.*) twaddle.
barbouiller [barbu'je], *v.t.* to soil, to dirty, to blot; to daub, to besmear; to scrawl, to scribble; to splutter out, to mumble; to bungle.
barbouilleur [barbu'jœ:r], *n.m.* (*fem.* **-euse**) dauber, scribbler; mumbler.
barbu [bar'by], *a.* bearded.
barbue [bar'by], *n.f.* brill.
barcarolle [barka'rɔl], *n.f.* (*Mus.*) barcarolle.
Barcelone [barsə'lɔn], *f.* Barcelona.
bardane [bar'dan], *n.f.* burr, burdock.
barde (1) [bard], *n.m.* bard.
barde (2) [bard], *n.f.* bard (*iron armour for horses*); thin rasher of bacon used for larding poultry etc.
bardé [bar'de], *a.* barded; larded.
barder [bar'de], *v.t.* to barb a horse; to cover with thin slices of bacon, to lard; (*slang*) ***ça barde*** or ***ça va barder***, things are beginning to hum.
bardot or **bardeau** (*pl.* **-eaux**) [bar'do], *n.m.* hinny; pack-mule.
barème [ba'rɛ:m], *n.m.* ready-reckoner.
barguignage [bargi'ɲa:ʒ], *n.m.* (*colloq.*) hesitation, wavering, dilly-dallying.
barguigner [bargi'ɲe], *v.i.* to be irresolute, to waver, to shilly-shally.
barguigneur [bargi'ɲœ:r], *n.m.* (*fem.* **-euse**) waverer, haggler.
baril [ba'ri], *n.m.* small barrel, cask, keg.
bariolage [barjɔ'la:ʒ], *n.m.* variegation, odd medley of colours, motley.
bariolé [barjɔ'le], *a.* gaudy, motley, many-coloured.
barioler [barjɔ'le], *v.t.* to streak with several colours, to variegate.
barnache [BERNACLE].
baromètre [barɔ'mɛtr], *n.m.* barometer.
barométrique [barɔme'trik], *a.* barometrical.
baron [ba'rɔ̃], *n.m.* (*fem.* **-onne**) baron, baroness.
baronnet [barɔ'nɛ], *n.m.* baronet.
baronnial [barɔ'njal], *a.* (*m. pl.* **-aux**) baronial.
baronnie [barɔ'ni], *n.f.* barony.
baroque [ba'rɔk], *a.* irregular, grotesque odd; baroque.
barque [bark], *n.f.* bark, boat, small craft.
barquerolle [barkə'rɔl], *n.f.* small mastless barge.
barquette [bar'kɛt], *n.f.* small craft; light puff-biscuit.
barrage [ba'ra:ʒ], *n.m.* barrier; toll-bar; dam, weir, barrage.
barre [ba:r], *n.f.* bar (*of metal, wood etc.*); dash, cross, stroke (*of the pen etc.*); bar (*in courts*) of justice; (*Naut.*) helm, tiller, bar; (*Mus.*) bar; bore (*of river*).
barreau [ba'ro], *n.m.* (*pl.* **-eaux**) small bar (*of wood, metal etc.*); bench reserved for barristers; (*fig.*) lawyers, barristers; rung (*of a ladder*); ***être reçu*** or ***admis au barreau***, to be called to the bar.

barrer [ba're], *v.t.* to bar up, to fence off; to obstruct, to thwart; to cross off, to erase.
barrette (1) or **barette** [ba'rɛt], *n.f.* square flat cap, biretta; cardinal's hat.
barrette (2) [ba'rɛt], *n.m.* axle, pin, bolt, etc. (*in watches, jewellery etc.*); bar (*of medal*).
barreur [ba'rœ:r], *n.m.* helmsman, coxswain.
barricade [bari'kad], *n.f.* barricade.
barricader [barika'de], *v.t.* to barricade, to obstruct.
barrière [ba'rjɛ:r], *n.f.* railing, barrier; gateway; farm gate.
barrique [ba'rik], *n.f.* large barrel *or* cask, hogshead.
baryton [bari'tɔ̃], *n.m.* baritone.
baryum [ba'rjɔm], *n.m.* barium.
bas (1) [bɑ], *a.* (*fem.* **basse** (1)) low; in a low situation; inferior; (*fig.*) vile, base, sordid; mean; subdued (*of sounds*); decadent; ***la marée est basse***, it is low tide; ***les Pays-Bas***, the Netherlands.—*adv.* low, down; in a subdued voice, tone, etc.; ***ici bas***, here below; ***là-bas***, over there, yonder.—*n.m.* the lower part, bottom *or* foot (*of something*); ***en bas***, below, downstairs; ***le bas de l'escalier***, the foot of the stairs.
bas (2) [bɑ], *n.m. inv.* stocking.
basalte [ba'zalt], *n.m.* basalt.
basane [ba'zan], *n.f.* sheepskin.
basané [baza'ne], *a.* sunburnt, bronzed, swarthy, tawny.
bascule [bas'kyl], *n.f.* see-saw; weighing-machine.
basculer [basky'le], *v.i.* to see-saw; to rock, to swing.
base [bɑ:z], *n.f.* base, foundation; lower part, bottom; basis.
base-ball [bes'bɔl], *n.m.* baseball.
baser [bɑ'ze], *v.t.* to found, to base, to ground. **se baser**, *v.r.* to be grounded; to depend, to rely.
bas-fond [bɑ'fɔ̃], *n.m.* (*pl.* **bas-fonds**) low-lying ground, hollow, bottom; shallow, shallow water; (*fig., pl.*) underworld.
basilic [bazi'lik], *n.m.* (*Bot.*) basil, sweet basil; (*Myth.*) basilisk, cockatrice.
basilique [bazi'lik], *n.f.* basilica.
basket-ball [baskɛt'bɔl], *n.m.* basket-ball.
basketteur [baskɛ'tœ:r], *n.m.* (*fem.* **-euse**) basket-ball player.
basque (1) [bask], *n.f.* flap, skirt, tail (*of a garment*).
basque (2) [bask], *a.* Basque.—*n.m.* Basque (*language*).—*n.* (**Basque**) Basque (*person*).
bas-relief [bɑrə'ljɛf], *n.m.* (*pl.* **bas-reliefs**) bas-relief.
basse (1) [bɑ:s], [BAS (1)].
basse (2) [bɑ:s], *n.f.* bass, bass-string; saxhorn.
basse (3) [bɑ:s], *n.f.* shallow, reef.
basse-contre [bɑs'kɔ̃:tr], *n.f.* (*pl.* **basses-contre**) (*Mus.*) contra-bass, lower tenor.
basse-cour [bɑs'ku:r], *n.f.* (*pl.* **basses-cours**) farm-yard, poultry-yard.
bassement [bɑs'mɑ̃], *adv.* basely, meanly, vilely.
bassesse [bɑ'sɛs], *n.f.* baseness; lowness (*of station etc.*); meanness, vileness; mean *or* sordid action.
basset [ba'sɛ], *n.m.* basset-hound; ***basset allemand***, dachshund.
basse-taille [bɑs'tɑ:j], *n.f.* (*pl.* **basses-tailles**) (*Mus.*) baritone; (*Sculp.*) bas-relief.
bassin [ba'sɛ̃], *n.m.* basin; pond; dock; (*Anat.*) pelvis.
bassine [ba'sin], *n.f.* deep, wide pan.
bassiner [basi'ne], *v.t.* to warm (*a bed etc.*); to bathe (*with warm lotions*), to foment, to steep; to water, to sprinkle (*crops etc.*).
bassinet [basi'nɛ], *n.m.* small basin, pan, bowl.
bassinoire [basi'nwa:r], *n.f.* warming-pan; (*pop.*) bore.
bassiste [bɑ'sist], *n.m.* saxhorn-player; 'cellist.
basson [bɑ'sɔ̃], *n.m.* bassoon; bassoonist.
bastide [bas'tid], *n.f.* (*Provence*) country cottage, villa.
bastille [bas'ti:j], *n.f.* bastille, fort.
bastion [bas'tjɔ̃], *n.m.* bastion.
bastionner [bastjɔ'ne], *v.t.* to bastion, to fortify with bastions.
bastonnade [bastɔ'nad], *n.f.* bastinado; caning.
bastringue [bas'trɛ̃:g], *n.m.* (*pop.*) dance hall; (*slang*) noise.
bas-ventre [bɑ'vɑ̃:tr], *n.m.* (*pl.* **bas-ventres**) lower part of the belly.
bât [bɑ], *n.m.* pack-saddle.
bataclan [bata'klɑ̃], *n.m.* (*fam.*) paraphernalia.
bataille [ba'tɑ:j], *n.f.* battle, fight, engagement.
batailler [batɑ'je], *v.i.* to give battle; to be at war, to fight; to struggle hard, to strive.
batailleur [batɑ'jœ:r], *a.* (*fem.* **-euse**) combative, pugnacious, quarrelsome; disputatious.
bataillon [batɑ'jɔ̃], *n.m.* battalion; (*fig.*) host; (*pl.*) troops.
bâtard [bɑ'ta:r], *a.* and *n.m.* (*fem.* **-e**) bastard, illegitimate *or* natural (child).
bâté [bɑ'te], *a.* saddled with a pack; ***c'est un âne bâté***, he is an ignorant lout.
bateau [ba'to], *n.m.* (*pl.* **-eaux**) boat; ***bateau mouche***, pleasure steamer (*Paris and Lyons*).
batelage [ba'tla:ʒ], *n.m.* juggling, legerdemain; lighterage charges.
bateleur [ba'tlœ:r], *n.m.* (*fem.* **-euse**) juggler, buffoon, mountebank.
batelier [batə'lje], *n.m.* (*fem.* **-ière**) boatman boatwoman, ferryman, ferrywoman.
bâter [bɑ'te], *v.t.* to load with a pack-saddle.
bathyscaphe [batis'kaf], *n.m.* bathyscape.
bâti [bɑ'ti], *n.m.* framing, structure; basting, tacking (*of a garment*).
batifolage [batifɔ'la:ʒ], *n.m.* romping; cuddling.
batifoler [batifɔ'le], *v.i.* to play, to romp; to cuddle.
bâtiment [bɑti'mɑ̃], *n.m.* building, structure, edifice; building trade; ship, vessel.
bâtir [bɑ'ti:r], *v.t.* to build, to erect, to construct; ***faire bâtir***, to have built, to build; ***terrain à bâtir***, building site.
bâtisse [bɑ'tis], *n.f.* masonry, ramshackle building.
batiste [ba'tist], *n.f.* cambric.
bâton [bɑ'tɔ̃], *n.m.* stick, staff, cudgel, cane.
bâtonner [bɑtɔ'ne], *v.t.* to cudgel, to cane.
batracien [batra'sjɛ̃], *n.m.* (*Zool.*) batrachian.
battant (1) [ba'tɑ̃], *n.m.* clapper (*of a bell*); leaf (*of a table* or *door*); fly (*of a flag*); ***porte à deux battants***, double door.

battant (2) [ba'tɑ̃], *a.* beating, pelting, falling heavily (*of rain etc.*); ***mener tambour battant***, to hurry on (*a business*).
batte [bat], *n.f.* long wooden staff *or* beater; ***batte de blanchisseuse***, washing-board; ***batte (de cricket)***, (cricket) bat.
battée [ba'te], *n.f.* jamb of door *or* window.
battement [bat'mɑ̃], *n.m.* beating; clapping (*of hands*), stamping (*of feet*), flapping (*of wings*); beating (*of the heart*); shuffling (*of cards*).
batterie [ba'tri], *n.f.* (*Artill., Elec., Cook. etc.*) battery; ***batterie de cuisine***, complete set of kitchen utensils.
batteur [ba'tœ:r], *n.m.* (*fem.* **-euse**) beater; (*cricket etc.*) batsman; (*jazz*) drummer.—*n.f.* (**-euse**) threshing-machine.
battre [batr], *v.t.* (*see Verb Tables*) to strike upon, against etc.; to beat, to thrash, to whip (*a horse etc.*); to beat up, to mix; to defeat; to shuffle (*cards*); ***battre des mains***, to clap; ***la fête battait son plein***, the party was in full swing.—*v.i.* to beat, to knock; to pant, to throb. **se battre**, *v.r.* to fight, to combat; to hit oneself (***contre etc.***).
battu [ba'ty], *a.* beaten (*of a path, road etc.*); frequented; (*fig.*) trite, commonplace.
battue [ba'ty], *n.f.* (*Shooting*) wholesale slaughter, battue.
baudet [bo'dɛ], *n.m.* ass; (*fig.*) dolt, donkey; sawyer's trestle.
bauge [bo:ʒ], *n.f.* lair of a wild boar; squirrel's nest; (*fig.*) a dirty hovel.
baume [bo:m], *n.m.* balm; balsam; (*fig.*) consolation.
baumier [BALSAMIER].
baux [BAIL].
bauxite [bo'sit], *n.f.* bauxite.
bavard [ba'va:r], *a.* prating, talkative, loquacious.—*n.m.* (*fem.* **-e**) prater, babbler, chatterer.
bavardage [bavar'da:ʒ], *n.m.* babbling, prattling; (*fig.*) twaddle, nonsense.
bavarder [bavar'de], *v.i.* to babble, to prattle.
bavarois [bava'rwa], *a.* Bavarian.—*n.m.* (**Bavarois**, *fem.* **-oise**) Bavarian (*person*).
bave [ba:v], *n.f.* slaver, dribble; foam; (*fig.*) slime.
baver [ba've], *v.i.* to slobber, to dribble.
bavette [ba'vɛt], *n.f.* bib.
baveux [ba'vø], *a.* (*fem.* **-euse**) dribbling, slobbering.
Bavière [ba'vjɛ:r], **la**, *f.* Bavaria.
bavure [ba'vy:r], *n.f.* seam (*left by a mould*); smudge (*of a pen*).
bazar [ba'za:r], *n.m.* bazaar; ill-kept, untidy house; (*fam.*) ***mettre tout son bazar dans une malle***, to put all one's belongings in a trunk.
bazooka [bazu'ka], *n.m.* (*Artill.*) bazooka.
béant [be'ɑ̃], *a.* gaping, yawning, wide open.
béat [be'a], *a.* blessed; devout; sanctimonious.
béatement [beat'mɑ̃], *adv.* sanctimoniously.
béatification [beatifikɑ'sjɔ̃], *n.f.* beatification.
béatifier [beati'fje], *v.t.* to beatify.
béatifique [beati'fik], *a.* beatific, blissful.
béatitude [beati'tyd], *n.f.* beatitude, blessedness.
beau [bo], **bel** [bɛl] (*before nouns singular beginning with a vowel or* h *mute*), *a.* (*fem.* **belle**, *pl.* **beaux, belles**) beautiful, fine, handsome, fair; smart, spruce; glorious; lofty, noble; seemly, becoming; (*iron.*) nice, precious; ***au beau milieu***, in the very middle; ***il fait beau***, it is a fine day; ***il l'a échappé belle***, he has had a narrow escape.—*adv.* finely, promisingly; in vain; ***avoir beau dire***, to speak in vain; ***de plus belle***, with renewed ardour, worse than ever; ***tout beau***, gently, not so fast.—*n.m.* that which is beautiful, fine, excellent etc.; beauty; beau.—*n.f.* (**belle**) belle; ***la Belle et la Bête***, Beauty and the Beast.
beaucoup [bo'ku], *adv.* many, much; a great many, a great deal; ***avoir beaucoup d'argent***, to have plenty of money.
beau-fils [bo'fis], *n.m.* (*pl.* **beaux-fils**) stepson.
beau-frère [bo'frɛ:r], *n.m.* (*pl.* **beaux-frères**) brother-in-law.
beau-père [bo'pɛ:r], *n.m.* (*pl.* **beaux-pères**) father-in-law; step-father.
beaupré [bo'pre], *n.m.* (*Naut.*) bowsprit.
beauté [bo'te], *n.f.* beauty; fineness, loveliness, comeliness, elegance, agreeableness.
beaux-arts [bo'za:r], *n.m. pl.* fine arts.
beaux-parents [bopa'rɑ̃], *n.m. pl.* father-in-law and mother-in-law.
bébé [be'be], *n.m.* baby; baby-doll.
bec [bɛk], *n.m.* beak, bill; (*fig.*) mouth; snout (*of some fishes*); lip (*of a jug*), spout (*of a kettle etc.*); gas-jet, burner; mouthpiece (*of musical instrument*); nib (*pen*); ***avoir bon bec***, to have the gift of the gab.
bécane [be'kan], *n.f.* (*pop.*) bike.
bécarre [be'ka:r], *a.* and *n.m.* (*Mus.*) natural.
bécasse [be'kas], *n.f.* woodcock; (*fam.*) stupid woman.
bécassine [beka'sin], *n.f.* snipe.
bec-de-lièvre [bɛkdə'ljɛ:vr], *n.m.* (*pl.* **becs-de-lièvre**) harelip; harelipped person.
bec-fin [bɛk'fɛ̃], *n.m.* (*pl.* **becs-fins**) warbler; pipit.
béchamel [beʃa'mɛl], *n.f.* cream-sauce, béchamel sauce.
bêche [bɛ:ʃ], *n.f.* spade.
bêcher [bɛ'ʃe], *v.t.* to dig.
becquée [bɛ'ke], **béquée** [be'ke], *n.f.* billful; ***donner la becquée***, to feed.
becqueter [bɛk'te], **béqueter** [bek'te], *v.t.* (*conjug. like* AMENER) to peck; (*colloq.*) to eat. **se becqueter, se béqueter**, *v.r.* to peck one another.
bedaine [bə'dɛn], *n.f.* (*colloq.*) paunch.
bedeau [bə'do], *n.m.* (*pl.* **-eaux**) beadle, verger.
bedonnant [bədɔ'nɑ̃], *a.* stout, pot-bellied.
bedonner [bədɔ'ne], *v.i.* to get *or* grow stout.
bédouin [be'dwɛ̃], *a.* Bedouin.—*n.m.* (**Bédouin**, *fem.* **-e**) Bedouin.
bée [be], *a. only used in* **bouche bée**, gaping, open-mouthed.
beffroi [bɛ'frwɑ], *n.m.* belfry.
bégaiement [begɛ'mɑ̃], *n.m.*, **bégayant** [begɛ'jɑ̃], *a.* stammering, faltering.
bégayer [begɛ'je], *v.t.* (*conjug. like* PAYER) to stammer out, to stutter, to lisp.—*v.i.* to stammer.
bégayeur [begɛ'jœ:r], *n.m.* (*fem.* **-euse**) stammerer, stutterer.
bégonia [begɔ'ɲa], *n.m.* begonia.
bègue [bɛg], *a.* stammering, stuttering.—*n.* stammerer, stutterer.
bégueule [be'gœl], *a.* prudish, squeamish; straitlaced.—*n.f.* (*fam.*) prude.

bégueulerie [begœl'ri], *n.f.* prudery, prudish airs, squeamishness.
béguin [be'gɛ̃], *n.m.* hood, child's cap; ***avoir un béguin pour***, to be sweet on; ***c'est mon béguin***, he *or* she is my darling.
béguine [be'gin], *n.f.* beguine (*Flemish nun*); nun; bigoted person.
bégum [be'gɔm], *n.f.* begum.
beige [bɛ:ʒ], *a.* natural, undyed (*of wool*); beige.—*n.f.* unbleached serge.
beignet [bɛ'ɲɛ], *n.m.* fritter.
béjaune [be'ʒo:n], *n.m.* (*Falconry*) eyas, unfledged hawk; (*fig.*) ninny, novice; blunder, silliness, mistake.
bel [BEAU].
bêlant [bɛ'lɑ̃], *a.* bleating.
bêlement [bɛl'mɑ̃], *n.m.* bleating (*of sheep*).
bêler [bɛ'le], *v.i.* to bleat.
belette [bə'lɛt], *n.f.* weasel.
belge [bɛlʒ], *a.* Belgian.—*n.* (**Belge**) Belgian (*person*).
Belgique [bɛl'ʒik], **la**, *f.* Belgium.
bélier [be'lje], *n.m.* ram; battering-ram; Aries.
bélière [be'ljɛ:r], *n.f.* sheep-bell; clapper-ring (*of a bell*); watch-ring; sword-sling.
bélître [be'litr], *n.m.* rascal, cad.
belladone [bɛla'dɔn], *n.f.* belladonna, deadly nightshade.
bellâtre [bɛ'lɑ:tr], *a.* having insipid beauty; foppish.—*n.m.* insipid beauty; fop, coxcomb.
belle-fille [bɛl'fi:j], *n.f.* (*pl.* **belles-filles**) daughter-in-law; stepdaughter.
belle-maman [bɛlma'mɑ̃], (*colloq.*) [BELLE-MÈRE].
bellement [bɛl'mɑ̃], *adv.* prettily, charmingly, softly, gently.
belle-mère [bɛl'mɛ:r], *n.f.* (*pl.* **belles-mères**) mother-in-law; stepmother.
belles-lettres [bɛl'lɛtr], *n.f. pl.* polite literature, belles-lettres.
belle-sœur [bɛl'sœ:r], *n.f.* (*pl.* **belles-sœurs**) sister-in-law; stepsister.
belligérance [bɛliʒe'rɑ̃:s], *n.f.* belligerence, belligerency.
belligérant [bɛliʒe'rɑ̃], *a.* and *n.m.* (*fem.* **-e**) belligerent.
belliqueux [bɛli'kø], *a.* (*fem.* **-euse**) war-like, martial; bellicose, quarrelsome.
belvédère [bɛlve'dɛ:r], *n.m.* turret, terrace, belvedere, gazebo.
bémol [be'mɔl], *a.* and *n.m.* (*Mus.*) flat.
bémoliser [bemɔli'ze], *v.t.* (*Mus.*) to mark flat *or* with a flat.
bénédicité [benedisi'te], *n.m.* grace (*before meals*).
bénédictin [benedik'tɛ̃], *a.* and *n.m.* (*fem.* **-e**) Benedictine.
bénédiction [benedik'sjɔ̃], *n.f.* benediction, blessing, consecration; (*fig.*) expression of thanks.
bénéfice [bene'fis], *n.m.* benefit, gain, profit; privilege, advantage; (*Eccles.*) benefice, living.
bénéficiaire [benefi'sjɛ:r], *a.* receiving a benefit *or* benefice.—*n.* beneficiary, recipient.
bénéficial [benefi'sjal], *n.m.* beneficiary (*of ecclesiastical livings*).
bénéficier [benefi'sje], *v.i.* to gain, to profit.—*n.m.* beneficed clergyman, incumbent.
benêt [bə'nɛ], *a.* silly, foolish, simple.—*n.m* booby, fool, simpleton.
bénévole [bene'vɔl], *a.* well-disposed, kindly; unpaid.
bénévolement [benevɔl'mɑ̃], *adv.* out of good-will; voluntarily, spontaneously.
Bengale [bɛ̃'gal], **le**, *m.* Bengal.
bengali [bɛ̃ga'li], *a.* Bengali.—*n.m.* Bengali (*language*).—*n.* (**Bengali**) Bengali (*person*).
Béni-oui-oui [beniwi'wi], *n.m. inv.* (*fam.*) yes-man.
bénignement [beniɲ'mɑ̃], *adv.* benignly, kindly, graciously.
bénignité [beniɲi'te], *n.f.* benignity, kindness; mildness (*of a disease*).
bénin [be'nɛ̃], *a.* (*fem.* **bénigne**) benign, good-natured, indulgent; mild (*of attacks of disease, remedies etc.*).
bénir [be'ni:r], *v.t.* to bless, to hallow, to consecrate; to call down blessings on; to thank; to praise.
bénit [be'ni], *a.* hallowed, consecrated.
bénitier [beni'tje], *n.m.* holy-water basin; fount.
benjamin [bɛ̃ʒa'mɛ̃], *n.m.* favourite (*especially the youngest child*).
benjoin [bɛ̃'ʒwɛ̃], *n.m.* benjamin, benzoin.
benne [bɛn], *n.f.* hamper, basket; (*Mining*) hopper, bucket.
benzine [bɛ̃'zin], *n.f.* benzine.
benzol [bɛ̃'zɔl], *n.m.* benzol.
béquillard [beki'ja:r], *a.* (*pop.*) crippled, going on crutches.—*n.m.* (*fem.* **-e**) cripple.
béquille [be'ki:j], *n.f.* crutch; (*Av.*) tail-skid.
béquiller [beki'je], *v.i.* to walk on crutches.
berbère [bɛr'bɛ:r], *a.* Berber.—*n.* (**Berbère**) Berber (*person*).
berbéris [bɛrbe'ris], *n.m.* (*Bot.*) barberry, berberis.
bercail [bɛr'ka:j], *n.m.* (*used only in sing.*) sheepfold, fold.
berce [bɛrs], *n.f.* cow-parsnip.
berceau [bɛr'so], *n.m.* (*pl.* **-eaux**) cradle; (*fig.* infancy; origin, source; (*Hort.*) arbour, bower.
bercement [bɛrsə'mɑ̃], *n.m.* rocking; lulling.
bercer [bɛr'se], *v.t.* (*conjug. like* COMMENCER) to rock, to lull asleep; to lull, to soothe; (*fig.*) to delude *or* flatter with vain hopes. **se bercer**, *v.r.* to rock; (*fig.*) to delude oneself (***de***).
berceuse [bɛr'sø:z], *n.f.* woman who rocks an infant; rocking-chair; cradle that rocks; (*Mus.*) lullaby.
béret [be'rɛ], *n.m.* beret, tam-o'-shanter (*worn by the French Alpine regiments*).
berge [bɛrʒ], *n.f.* steep bank (*of a river*); side (*of a canal, ditch, roadway etc.*).
berger [bɛr'ʒe], *n.m.* (*fem.* **-ère** (1)) shepherd, shepherdess; (*poet.*) swain; (*fig.*) pastor, guardian (*of the people etc.*); (*Chess*) ***le coup du berger***, fool's mate.
bergère (2) [bɛr'ʒɛ:r], *n.f.* large and deep arm-chair.
bergerie [bɛrʒə'ri], *n.f.* sheepfold, pen; (*Lit.*) (*chiefly used in the plural*) pastoral.
bergeronnette [bɛrʒərɔ'nɛt], *n.f.* (*Orn.*) wagtail.
berlue [bɛr'ly], *n.f.* dimness of sight.
Bermudes [bɛr'myd], **les**, *f. pl.* the Bermudas.

bernacle [bɛr'nakl], **bernache** [bɛr'naʃ], **barnache** [bar'naʃ], *n.f.* barnacle-goose; barnacle (*shell-fish*).
bernard-l'ermite [bɛrnarlɛr'mit], *n.m.* hermit-crab.
berne (1) [bɛrn], *n.f.* tossing in a blanket.
berne (2) [bɛrn], *n.f.* (*Naut.*) ***mettre le pavillon en berne***, to fly the flag at half-mast.
berner [bɛr'ne], *v.t.* to toss in a blanket; (*fig.*) to ridicule, to make a fool of, to deride; to deceive, to hoax.
bernique [bɛr'nik], *int.* (*pop.*) no use; not a bit of it, no go.
berthon [bɛr'tɔ̃], *n.m.* a small collapsible boat.
béryl or **béril** [be'ril], *n.m.* beryl.
besace [bə'zas], *n.f.* beggar's wallet, scrip.
bésigue [be'zig], *n.m.* bezique (*card game*).
besogne [bə'zɔɲ], *n.f.* work, business, labour; job, piece of work.
besogner [bəzɔ'ɲe], *v.i.* to work, to labour.
besogneux [bəzɔ'ɲø], *a.* and *n.m.* (*fem.* **-euse**) necessitous, needy (person).
besoin [bə'zwɛ̃], *n.m.* need, want; necessity; poverty, distress, emergency; ***au besoin***, at a pinch, if need be.
Bessarabie [bɛsara'bi], **la**, *f.* Bessarabia.
bestial [bɛs'tjal], *a.* (*m. pl.* **-aux** (1)) bestial, brutish.
bestialement [bɛstjal'mɑ̃], *adv.* bestially, brutally, like a beast.
bestialité [bɛstjali'te], *n.f.* bestiality.
bestiaux [BESTIAL, BÉTAIL].
bestiole [bɛs'tjɔl], *n.f.* little animal.
bêta [bɛ'tɑ], *n.m.* (*fem.* **-asse**) a bit of a blockhead, rather a simpleton.
bétail [be'ta:j], *n.m.* (*pl.* **bestiaux** (2) [bɛs'tjo]) cattle, livestock; ***gros bétail***, oxen etc.; ***menu bétail***, sheep, goats etc.
bêtasse [bɛ'tɑ:s], [BÊTA].
bête [bɛ:t], *a.* silly, stupid, nonsensical.—*n.f.* animal, beast, brute; fool, blockhead, stupid creature; ***bête noire***, pet aversion; ***bête sauvage***, wild animal.
bêtement [bɛt'mɑ̃], *adv.* like a fool, foolishly, stupidly.
Bethléem [bɛtle'ɛm], *f.* Bethlehem.
bêtise [be'ti:z], *n.f.* silliness, stupidity; tomfoolery, foolish act, suggestion etc., silly thing, absurdity.
béton [be'tɔ̃], *n.m.* (*Masonry*) beton (*a kind of concrete*); ***béton armé***, reinforced concrete.
bétonnière [betɔ'njɛ:r], **bétonneuse** [betɔ'nø:z], *n.f.* concrete-mixer.
bette [bɛt], **blette** (2) [blɛt], *n.f.* beet.
betterave [bɛ'tra:v], *n.f.* beetroot; ***betterave à sucre***, sugar-beet; ***betterave fourragère***, mangel-wurzel.
beuglement [bøglə'mɑ̃], *n.m.* bellowing, lowing (*of cattle*).
beugler [bø'gle], *v.i.* to bellow, to low.
beurre [bœ:r], *n.m.* butter.
beurrée [bœ're], *n.f.* slice of bread and butter.
beurrer [bœ're], *v.t.* to butter (*bread etc.*).
beurrerie [bœr'ri], *n.f.* butter factory.
beurrier [bœ'rje], *n.m.* butter-dish.
bévue [be'vy], *n.f.* blunder, oversight, mistake; (*colloq.*) howler.
bey [bɛ], *n.m.* bey.
biais [bjɛ], *a.* slanting, sloping, askew; oblique.—*n.m.* bias, obliquity, slope; (*fig.*) shift, subterfuge.
biaisement [bjɛz'mɑ̃], *n.m.* sloping, slanting, shift, evasion.
biaiser [bje'ze], *v.i.* to be oblique, to go obliquely, to slope, to slant, to lean on one side; to use shifts *or* evasions.
bibelot [bi'blo], *n.m.* trinket, knick-knack.
biberon (1) [bi'brɔ̃], *n.m.* (*Med.*) feeding-cup; feeding-bottle (*for infants*).
biberon (2) [bi'brɔ̃], *n.m.* (*fem.* **-onne**) tippler, toper.
Bible [bibl], *n.f.* Bible.
bibliographe [bibliɔ'graf], *n.m.* bibliographer.
bibliographie [bibliɔgra'fi], *n.f.* bibliography.
bibliographique [bibliɔgra'fik], *a.* bibliographical.
bibliomane [bibliɔ'man], *n.m.* book-collector.
bibliomanie [bibliɔma'ni], *n.f.* bibliomania.
bibliophile [bibliɔ'fil], *n.m.* book-lover.
bibliothécaire [bibliɔte'kɛ:r], *n.m.* librarian.
bibliothèque [bibliɔ'tɛk], *n.f.* library; bookcase.
biblique [bi'blik], *a.* Biblical.
bicarbonate [bikarbɔ'nat], *n.m.* (*Chem.*) bicarbonate.
biceps [bi'sɛps], *n.m.* biceps.
biche [biʃ], *n.f.* hind, doe.
bichon [bi'ʃɔ̃], *n.m.* (*fem.* **-onne**) lap-dog with long, silky hair.
bichonner [biʃɔ'ne], *v.t.* to curl; (*fig.*) to caress. **se bichonner**, *v.r.* to curl one's hair; to make oneself smart.
biconcave [bikɔ̃'ka:v], *a.* bi-concave.
biconvexe [bikɔ̃'vɛks], *a.* bi-convex.
bicoque [bi'kɔk], *n.f.* (*colloq.*) ramshackle house, shanty.
bicorne [bi'kɔrn], *a.* and *n.m.* cocked (hat).
bicyclette [bisi'klɛt], *n.f.* bicycle.
bidet [bi'dɛ], *n.m.* pony, small nag; bidet (*bath*).
bidon [bi'dɔ̃], *n.m.* tin, can (*esp. petrol can*); camp-kettle; soldier's water-bottle.
bidonville [bidɔ̃'vil], *n.m.* shanty town.
bielle [bjɛl], *n.f.* (*Mach.*) connecting-rod.
Biélorussie [bjelɔry'si], **la**, *f.* Byelorussia, White Russia.
bien [bjɛ̃], *n.m.* good; that which is pleasant, useful *or* advantageous; benefit, welfare, well-being, blessing; wealth, estate, property; gift, boon, mercy; (*pl.*) goods, chattels; fruits (*of the soil etc.*); ***biens de consommation***, consumer goods; ***biens immobiliers***, real estate.—*adv.* well; rightly, finely; much, very, far, entirely, completely; about, well-nigh; favourably, successfully; well off; on good terms, in favour; certainly, truly, indeed; formally, clearly, expressly; ***aussi bien***, anyhow, in any case; ***bien de***, plenty of, many; ***bien mieux***, far better; ***bien plus***, besides, moreover; ***bien que***, although; ***c'est bien***, that's right; ***cette femme est bien***, that woman is good-looking; ***eh bien!*** well! *or* well? ***je vous l'avais bien dit***, I told you so; ***ou bien***, or else; ***si bien que***, so that; ***tant bien que mal***, so-so.—*int.* (*sometimes pronounced colloq.* [bɛ̃]) well!
bien-aimé [bjɛ̃nɛ'me], *a.* beloved, well-beloved.—*n.m.* (*fem.* **-ée**) darling, dear.
bien-dire [bjɛ̃'di:r], *n.m.* (*no pl.*) fine speaking.

bien-être [bjɛ̃'nɛːtr], *n.m.* (*no pl.*) well-being, welfare, comfort.
bienfaisance [bjɛ̃fə'zɑ̃ːs], *n.f.* beneficence, charity, munificence.
bienfaisant [bjɛ̃fə'zɑ̃], *a.* charitable, beneficent, kind, gracious; beneficial, salutary.
bienfait [bjɛ̃'fɛ], *n.m.* good turn, kindness, benefit, favour, courtesy.
bienfaiteur [bjɛ̃fɛ'tœːr], *n.m.* (*fem.* **-trice**) benefactor, benefactress, patron.
bien-fonds [bjɛ̃'fɔ̃], *n.m.* (*pl.* **biens-fonds**) real estate.
bienheureux [bjɛ̃nœ'rø], *a.* (*fem.* **-euse**) happy, fortunate; (*Eccles.*) blessed.
biennal [biɛ'nal], *a.* (*m. pl.* **-aux**) biennial.
bienséance [bjɛ̃se'ɑ̃ːs], *n.f.* propriety decency, decorum, seemliness.
bienséant [bjɛ̃se'ɑ̃], *a.* decent, becoming, seemly, decorous, fit.
bientôt [bjɛ̃'to], *adv.* soon, before long, shortly; ***à bientôt!*** see you soon!
bienveillance [bjɛ̃vɛ'jɑ̃ːs], *n.f.* benevolence, goodwill, favour, kindness.
bienveillant [bjɛ̃vɛ'jɑ̃], *a.* benevolent, kind, friendly, favourable.
bienvenu [bjɛ̃v'ny], *a.* welcome; ***soyez le bienvenu***, it's nice to have you with us.
bienvenue [bjɛ̃v'ny], *n.f.* welcome; ***souhaiter la bienvenue à quelqu'un***, to greet *or* welcome someone.
bière (1) [bjɛːr], *n.f.* beer.
bière (2) [bjɛːr], *n.f.* coffin.
biffer [bi'fe], *v.t.* to cancel, to blot out, to erase.
biflore [bi'flɔːr], *a.* (*Bot.*) biflorate.
bifocal [bifɔ'kal], *a.* (*m. pl.* **-aux**) bifocal.
bifolié [bifɔ'lje], *a.* (*Bot.*) bifoliate.
bifteck [bif'tɛk], *n.m.* beefsteak.
bifurcation [bifyrka'sjɔ̃], *n.f.* bifurcation; fork (*of a road*).
bigame [bi'gam], *a.* bigamous.—*n.* bigamist.
bigamie [biga'mi], *n.f.* bigamy.
bigarré [biga're], *a.* parti-coloured, streaked.
bigarrer [biga're], *v.t.* to chequer, to streak, to variegate.
bigarrure [biga'ryːr], *n.f.* medley, mixture, motley, variegation.
bigot [bi'go], *a.* bigoted.—*n.m.* (*fem.* **-e**) bigot.
bigoterie [bigɔ'tri], *n.f.*, **bigotisme** [bigɔ'tism], *n.m.* bigotry.
bigoudi [bigu'di], *n.m.* curling pin *or* curler (*for the hair*).
bijou [bi'ʒu], *n.m.* (*pl.* **-oux**) jewel, gem; (*fig.*) darling.
bijouterie [biʒu'tri], *n.f.* jewellery.
bijoutier [biʒu'tje], *n.m.* (*fem.* **-ière**) jeweller.
bilan [bi'lɑ̃], *n.m.* balance-sheet.
bilatéral [bilate'ral], *a.* (*m. pl.* **-aux**) bilateral.
bilboquet [bilbɔ'kɛ], *n.m.* cup-and-ball (*toy*); small weighted figure that balances itself.
bile [bil], *n.f.* bile, spleen, gall; (*fig.*) anger.
bilieux [bi'ljø], *a.* (*fem.* **-euse**) bilious; (*fig.*) choleric, passionate.
bilingue [bi'lɛ̃ːg], *a.* bilingual.
billard [bi'jaːr], *n.m.* billiards; billiard-table; billiard-room.
bille [biːj], *n.f.* billiard-ball; marble, taw; log, unworked piece of timber; ***roulement à billes***, ball-bearings.
billet [bi'jɛ], *n.m.* note, missive; bill, hand-bill; ticket, lottery-ticket; promissory note; billet (*for quartering soldiers*); ***billet de banque***, bank-note; ***billet d'aller et retour***, return ticket; ***billet doux***, love-letter.
billevesée [bilvə'ze], *n.f.* idle story, stuff, nonsense, bunkum.
billion [bi'ljɔ̃], *n.m.* (*since* 1948 = 1 *followed by* 12 *ciphers*), billion, one million million(s); (*Am.*) trillion.
billot [bi'jo], *n.m.* block; executioner's block.
bimbelot [bɛ̃'blo], *n.m.* plaything, toy, bauble.
bimensuel [bimɑ̃'sɥɛl], *a.* (*fem.* **-elle**) twice monthly, fortnightly.
bimoteur [bimɔ'tœːr], *a.* and *n.m.* twin-engined (plane).
binaire [bi'nɛːr], *a.* binary.
biner [bi'ne], *v.t.* (*Agric.*) to dig again; to hoe.
binette [bi'nɛt], *n.f.* hoe; (*colloq.*) face, phiz.
biniou [bi'nju], *n.m.* Breton bagpipe.
binôme [bi'noːm], *n.m.* (*Alg.*) binomial.
biochimie [biɔʃi'mi], *n.f.* biochemistry.
biographe [biɔ'graf], *n.m.* biographer.
biographie [biɔgra'fi], *n.f.* biography.
biographique [biɔgra'fik], *a.* biographical.
biologie [biɔlɔ'ʒi], *n.f.* biology.
biologique [biɔlɔ'ʒik], *a.* biological.
biologiste [biɔlɔ'ʒist], **biologue** [biɔ'lɔg], *n.m.* biologist.
bion [bjɔ̃], *n.m.* sucker, shoot.
bioxyde [biɔk'sid], *n.m.* dioxide.
biparti [bipar'ti], **bipartite** [bipar'tit], *a.* bipartite.
bipède [bi'pɛd], *a.* and *n.* (*Zool.*) biped.
biplan [bi'plɑ̃], *n.m.* biplane.
bipolaire [bipɔ'lɛːr], *a.* bipolar.
bique [bik], *n.f.* nanny-goat.
biréacteur [bireak'tœːr], *n.m.* twin-engined jet-plane.
birloir [bir'lwaːr], *n.m.* window-catch.
birman [bir'mɑ̃], *a.* Burmese.—*n.m.* (**Birman**, *fem.* **-ane**) Burmese (*person*).
Birmanie [birma'ni], **la**, *f.* Burma.
bis (1) [bi], *a.* brown; tawny, swarthy; ***du pain bis***, brown bread.
bis (2) [biːs], *adv.* twice.—*int.* encore!
bisaïeul [biza'jœl], *n.m.* great-grandfather.
bisaïeule [biza'jœl], *n.f.* great-grandmother.
bisannuel [biza'nɥɛl], *a.* (*fem.* **-elle**) (*Bot.*) biennial.
bisbille [biz'biːj], *n.f.* (*fam.*) petty quarrel, tiff, bickering.
biscornu [biskɔr'ny], *a.* irregular, misshapen; (*fig.*) outlandish, odd, queer.
biscotte [bis'kɔt], *n.f.* rusk.
biscuit [bis'kɥi], *n.m.* biscuit; pastry made with flour, eggs, and sugar; (*Am.*) cracker; unglazed porcelain.
bise [biːz], *n.f.* dry and cold north wind; (*colloq.*) kiss.
biseau [bi'zo], *n.m.* (*pl.* **-eaux**) bevel, chamfer; bevelling tool.
biseauter [bizo'te], *v.t.* to bevel.
bismuth [biz'myt], *n.m.* bismuth.
bison [bi'zɔ̃], *n.m.* bison, buffalo.
bisque [bisk], *n.f.* soup made of crayfish, chicken *or* game, fish etc.; (*colloq.*) ill-humour, spite.
bisquer [bis'ke], *v.i.* (*colloq.*) to be vexed *or* riled.
bissac [bi'sak], *n.m.* double wallet, sack *or* bag, haversack.
bissecter [bisɛk'te], *v.t.* to bisect.

isser [bi'se], *v.t.* to encore.
issextile [bisɛks'til], *a.* ***année bissextile***, leap-year.
issexué [bisɛk'sɥe], **bissexuel** [-sɥɛl] (*fem.* **-elle**), *a.* (*Bot.*) bisexual.
istouri [bistu'ri], *n.m.* bistoury, lancet.
istourner [bistur'ne], *v.t.* to twist, to distort; to castrate.
istre [bistr], *n.m.* bistre, sepia.
istro or **bistrot** [bis'tro], *n.m.* (*slang*) pub.
itume [bi'tym], *n.m.* bitumen.
ituminer [bitymi'ne], *v.t.* to asphalt.
itumineux [bitymi'nø], **bitumeux** [bity'mø], *a.* (*fem.* **-euse**) bituminous.
ivalent [biva'lɑ̃], *a.* divalent, bivalent.
ivalve [bi'valv], *a.* bivalvular.—*n.m.* bivalve.
ivouac [bi'vwak], *n.m.* bivouac.
ivouaquer [bivwa'ke], *v.i.* to bivouac.
izarre [bi'za:r], *a.* queer, strange, whimsical, bizarre.
izarrement [bizar'mɑ̃], *adv.* oddly, queerly, whimsically.
izarrerie [bizar'ri], *n.f.* singularity, oddness; caprice, whim.
lack-out [blak'aut], *n.m.* black-out.
lafard [bla'fa:r], *a.* pale, wan; livid.
lague [blag], *n.f.* tobacco pouch; (*slang*) chaff, humbug, hoax, fib; trick, practical joke; ***sans blague!*** you don't say!
laguer [bla'ge], *v.i.* to chaff, to hoax, to humbug.
lagueur [bla'gœ:r], *n.m.* (*fem.* **-euse**) wag, hoaxer, humbug.
laireau [blɛ'ro], *n.m.* (*pl.* **-eaux**) badger; shaving-brush; badger-hair brush.
lâmable [blɑ'mabl], *a.* blameworthy.
lâme [blɑ:m], *n.m.* blame; reproach, reprimand.
lâmer [blɑ'me], *v.t.* to blame, to criticize; to censure, to reprimand.
lanc [blɑ̃], *a.* (*fem.* **blanche** (1) [blɑ̃:ʃ]) white; hoar, hoary; clean; blank; ***gelée blanche***, hoar frost; ***passer une nuit blanche***, to have a sleepless night; ***vers blancs***, blank verse.—*n.m.* white; blank; target, mark; ***blanc de chaux***, whitewash; ***de but en blanc***, point-blank; ***en blanc***, left blank.
lanc-bec [blɑ̃'bɛk], *n.m.* (*pl.* **blancs-becs**) beardless youth, youngster; greenhorn; sucker.
lanchaille [blɑ̃'ʃɑ:j], *n.f.* whitebait.
lanchâtre [blɑ̃'ʃɑ:tr], *a.* whitish.
lanche (1) [BLANC].
lanche (2) [blɑ̃:ʃ], *n.f.* (*Mus.*) minim.
lancheur [blɑ̃'ʃœ:r], *n.f.* whiteness; cleanliness; light; (*fig.*) purity, innocence.
lanchiment [blɑ̃ʃi'mɑ̃], *n.m.* whitening, bleaching; blanching.
lanchir [blɑ̃'ʃi:r], *v.t.* to whiten; to whitewash; to wash, to bleach, to clean; to blanch.—*v.i.* to whiten.
lanchissage [blɑ̃ʃi'sa:ʒ], *n.m.* washing; refining (*of sugar etc.*).
lanchissant blɑ̃ʃi'sɑ̃], *a.* that whitens *or* grows white; [foaming.
lanchisserie [blɑ̃ʃis'ri], *n.f.* laundry, wash-house.
blanchisseuse [blɑ̃ʃi'sø:z], *n.f.* washer-woman; laundress.
blanc-manger [blɑ̃mɑ̃'ʒe], *n.m.* (*pl.* **blancs-mangers**) blancmange.

blaser [blɑ'ze], *v.t.* to blunt, to cloy, to sicken, to surfeit.
blason [blɑ'zɔ̃], *n.m.* coat of arms; blazon; heraldry, blazonry.
blasonner [blɑzɔ'ne], *v.t.* to blazon; to interpret (*coats of arms*).
blasphémateur [blasfema'tœ:r], *n.m.* (*fem.* **-trice**) blasphemer.
blasphématoire [blasfema'twa:r], *a.* blasphemous.
blasphème [blas'fɛ:m], *n.m.* blasphemy.
blasphémer [blasfe'me], *v.t.*, *v.i.* (*conjug. like* CÉDER) to blaspheme, to curse.
blatte [blat], *n.f.* cockroach, black-beetle.
blé [ble], *n.m.* corn, wheat; ***halle au blé***, corn-exchange; ***manger son blé en herbe***, to spend one's money before one has it.
blême [blɛ:m], *a.* sallow, pale, wan; ghastly.
blêmir [blɛ'mi:r], *v.i.* to turn *or* grow pale.
blèsement [blɛz'mɑ̃], *n.m.* lisping.
bléser [ble'ze], *v.i.* (*conjug. like* CÉDER) to lisp.
blessant [blɛ'sɑ̃], *a.* wounding; (*fig.*) offensive, mortifying.
blessé [blɛ'se], *a.* wounded; (*fig.*) offended.—*n.m.* (*fem.* **-ée**) (*Mil.*) casualty.
blesser [blɛ'se], *v.t.* to wound, to hurt; to offend, to injure; to shock. **se blesser**, *v.r.* to hurt oneself; (*fig.*) to take offence.
blessure [blɛ'sy:r], *n.f.* wound, hurt, injury; offence; ***coups et blessures***, assault and battery.
blet [blɛ], *a.* (*fem.* **-ette** (1)) over ripe, sleepy (*of fruit*).
blette (2) [BETTE].
bleu [blø], *a.* blue, black and blue (*as a bruise*); (*fig.*) amazed; ***cordon bleu***, first-rate cook. —*n.m.* blue, blueness; washing-blue; greenhorn, novice; (*C*) Conservative, Tory.
bleuâtre [blø'ɑ:tr], *a.* bluish.
bleuet [BLUET].
bleuir [blø'i:r], *v.t.* to make blue, to blue (*in washing*).—*v.i.* to become blue.
blindage [blɛ̃'da:ʒ], *n.m.* iron-plating, armour-plating.
blindé [blɛ̃'de], *a.* armoured, armour-plated; screened; (*slang*) drunk.
blinder [blɛ̃'de], *v.t.* to armour-plate (*a ship, fort etc.*).
bloc [blɔk], *n.m.* block, lump, the whole lot.
blocage (1) [blɔ'ka:ʒ], *n.m.* blockading; blocking; block (*of traffic*); obstruction; (*Fin.*) freezing.
blocage (2) [blɔ'ka:ʒ], *n.m.* rubble.
blockhaus [blɔ'ko:s], *n.m. inv.* blockhouse.
bloc-note(s) [blɔk'nɔt], *n.m.* writing-pad.
blocus [blɔ'ky:s], *n.m. inv.* blockade.
blond [blɔ̃], *a.* blond, fair; light (*ale*); ***blond ardent***, auburn; ***blond cendré***, ash-blond. —*n.f.* (**-e**) (*C*) sweetheart.
blondin [blɔ̃'dɛ̃], *a.* fair-haired.—*n.m.* (*fem.* **-e**) fair-haired child.—*n.m.* spark, beau.
blondir [blɔ̃'di:r], *v.i.* to grow blond *or* fair.
blondissant [blɔ̃di'sɑ̃], *a.* growing yellow *or* golden (*of corn etc.*).
bloquer [blɔ'ke], *v.t.* to block up, to fill up (*cavities in walls*) with mortar; (*Mil.*) to blockade; (*Fin.*) to freeze; to jam on (*brakes*).
blottir (**se**) [səblɔ'ti:r], *v.r.* to curl up, to snuggle, to huddle; to cower, to crouch.
blouse [blu:z], *n.f.* smock; tunic; blouse; pinafore; overall.

blouser [blu'ze], *v.t.* to mislead, to cheat. **se blouser**, *v.r.* (*Billiards*) to pocket one's own ball; (*fig.*) to blunder; to bark up the wrong tree.
blouson [blu'zɔ̃], *n.m.* lumber-jacket, wind-cheater.
bluet [bly'ɛ], **bleuet** [blœ'ɛ], *n.m.* blue-bottle, corn-flower; (*C*) blueberry.
bluette [bly'ɛt], *n.f.* spark; (*fig.*) literary trifle, novelette.
bluff [blœf], *n.m.* bluff.
bluffer [blœ'fe], *v.t.* to bluff.
blutage [bly'ta:ʒ], *n.m.* bolting, sifting (*of flour*).
bluter [bly'te], *v.t.* to bolt, to sift (*flour etc.*).
boa [bo'a], *n.m.* boa (*snake*); boa (*of feathers*).
bobèche [bɔ'bɛʃ], *n.f.* socket (*of a candlestick*); sconce.
bobine [bɔ'bin], *n.f.* bobbin, spool, reel; (*Cine.*) reel; ***bobine d'induction***, induction-coil.
bobiner [bɔbi'ne], *v.t.* to wind on a bobbin, to spool.
bobineuse [bɔbi'nø:z], *n.f.* winder, winding machine.
bobo [bo'bo], *n.m.* (*Childish*) hurt, sore, bump; ***avoir bobo*** or ***du bobo***, to have a slight pain, sore etc.; ***faire bobo***, to hurt.
bocage [bɔ'ka:ʒ], *n.m.* copse, grove.
bocager [bɔka'ʒe], *a.* (*fem.* **-ère**) of groves *or* woodlands; shady.
bocal [bɔ'kal], *n.m.* (*pl.* **-aux**) druggist's short-necked bottle; carboy; glass jar, fish-globe.
boche [bɔʃ] (*aphæresis of* **Alboche**), *n.* (*pej.*) German, Jerry.
bock [bɔk], *n.m.* bock *or* glass (*beer*).
bœuf [bœf], *n.m.* (*pl.* **bœufs** [bø]) ox; beef.
Bohême [bɔ'ɛ:m], **la**, *f.* Bohemia.
bohème [bɔ'ɛ:m], *a.* Bohemian.—*n.* Bohemian, person of careless, unconventional habits.
bohémien [bɔe'mjɛ̃], *a.* and *n.m.* (*fem.* **-enne**) Bohemian; gipsy.
boire [bwa:r], *v.t. irr.* to drink; to consume *or* waste on drink; to absorb; to swallow (*an insult etc.*).—*v.i.* to drink (*to someone's health*); to tipple; to blot (*of paper*).—*n.m.* drink; drinking.
bois [bwɑ], *n.m.* wood, forest; wood, timber; wooden part *or* object; horns (*of a deer etc.*).
boisage [bwɑ'za:ʒ], *n.m.* wood-work; timbering (*of mines etc.*); wainscotting.
(*C*) **bois-brûlé** [bwɑbry'le], *n.m.* half-breed.
(*C*) **bois-debout** [bwɑd'bu], *n.m.* standing timber.
boisé [bwa'ze], *a.* wooded, well-timbered.
boisement [bwaz'mɑ̃], *n.m.* planting land with trees.
boiser [bwa'ze], *v.t.* to put woodwork to; to timber (*a mine etc.*); to wainscot; to plant with woods.
boiserie [bwaz'ri], *n.f.* wainscot, wainscotting.
boisseau [bwa'so], *n.m.* (*pl.* **-eaux**) bushel.
boisson [bwa'sɔ̃], *n.f.* drink; beverage; (*fig.*) drinking, drunkenness; (*C*) hard liquor; ***boisson forte***, strong drink, (*Am.*) liquor.
boîte [bwat], *n.f.* box; casket, caddy, chest; case (*of a watch, rudder etc.*); (*pop.*) mouth; ***boîte à feu***, stoke-hole; (*Motor.*) ***boîte de vitesses***, gear-box; ***boîte de nuit***, night club; (*pop.*) ***ta boîte!*** shut your big mouth.
boitement [bwat'mɑ̃], *n.m.* halting, limping.
boiter [bwa'te], *v.i.* to limp; to be lame.
boiteux [bwa'tø], *a.* (*fem.* **-euse**) lame, halt limping; rickety (*furniture*).—*n.m.* (*fem.* **-euse**) lame man *or* woman.
boîtier [bwa'tje], *n.m.* surgeon's case of instruments; case (*of a watch, an electric torch*).
bol [bɔl], *n.m.* bowl, basin.
bolchevik [bɔlʃə'vik], *n.m.* Bolshevik.
bolchevisme [bɔlʃə'vism], *n.m.* Bolshevism.
bolée [bɔ'le], *n.f.* bowlful.
boléro [bɔle'ro], *n.m.* bolero (*dance and garment*).
Bolivie [bɔli'vi], **la**, *f.* Bolivia.
bolivien [bɔli'vjɛ̃], *a.* (*fem.* **-enne**) Bolivian.—*n.m.* (**Bolivien**, *fem.* **-enne**) Bolivian (*person*).
bombance [bɔ̃'bɑ̃:s], *n.f.* feasting, junketing.
bombardement [bɔ̃bardə'mɑ̃], *n.m.* bombardment, shelling; ***bombardement en piqué***, dive-bombing.
bombarder [bɔ̃bar'de], *v.t.* to bombard, to bomb; ***quartier bombardé***, bombed site.
bombardier [bɔ̃bar'dje], *n.m.* bombardier.
bombe [bɔ̃:b], *n.f.* bomb; spray flask; ***bombe atomique***, atom bomb; ***bombe à hydrogène***, H-bomb; ***bombe incendiaire***, incendiary bomb; (*colloq.*) ***faire la bombe***, to be on the razzle.
bombé [bɔ̃'be], *a.* convex, arched.
bombement [bɔ̃bə'mɑ̃], *n.m.* convexity, swelling, bulge.
bomber [bɔ̃'be], *v.t.* to cause (*something*) to bulge, jut, swell out, arch, curve *or* barrel.—*v.i.* to bulge, to jut out.
bombyx [bɔ̃'biks], *n.m.* (*Ent.*) bombyx; silk-worm.
bon (1) [bɔ̃], *a.* (*fem.* **bonne** (1)) good; kind, favourable; fine, convenient, advantageous, profitable, proper; well-executed, cleverly done etc.; easy, good-natured; (*iron.*) simple, credulous; ***à quoi bon tant de peine***, what is the good of so much trouble? ***il fait bon dans cette pièce***, this room is nice and warm; ***pour de bon***, for good and all.—*n.m.* that which is good; the best.—*adv.* well, right, properly; ***tout de bon***, seriously, truly.
bon (2) [bɔ̃], *n.m.* bond, coupon, voucher; ***bon du trésor***, treasury bond; ***bon d'essence***, petrol coupon.
bonasse [bɔ'nas], *a.* simple-minded, credulous; soft.
bon-bec [bɔ̃'bɛk], *n.m.* (*pl.* **bons-becs**) chatterbox, gossip.
bonbon [bɔ̃'bɔ̃], *n.m.* sweet, (*Am.*) candy.
bond [bɔ̃], *n.m.* bound, leap, jump, caper, ***faire faux bond***, to give (*someone*) the slip.
bonde [bɔ̃:d], *n.f.* bung-hole, bung; sluice, flood-gate.
bondé [bɔ̃'de], *a.* chock-full, packed, crammed.
bondir [bɔ̃'di:r], *v.i.* to bound, to leap, to bounce, to caper, to frisk.
bondissant [bɔ̃di'sɑ̃], *a.* bounding, skipping.
bondissement [bɔ̃dis'mɑ̃], *n.m.* bounding, skipping, frisking.
bonheur [bɔ'nœ:r], *n.m.* happiness, prosperity, welfare; good fortune, good luck, success.

bonhomie [bɔnɔ'mi], *n.f.* good nature; simplicity, credulity.
bonhomme [bɔ'nɔm], *n.m.* (*pl.* **bonshommes** [bɔ̃'zɔm]) simple, good-natured man; foolish *or* credulous person; (*fig.*) rough drawing *or* effigy of a man; ***bonhomme de neige***, snowman.
boni [bɔ'ni], *n.m.* bonus.
boniface [bɔni'fas], *a.* and *n.* (*pop.*) simple, artless (person).
bonification [bɔnifikɑ'sjɔ̃], *n.f.* amelioration, improvement (*of land*); (*Fin.*) bonus, discount.
bonifier [bɔni'fje], *v.t.* to better, to improve; (*Fin.*) to pay, to transfer.
boniment [bɔni'mɑ̃], *n.m.* quack's show; (*fig.*) humbug.
bonjour [bɔ̃'ʒu:r], *n.m.* and *int.* good morning, good afternoon, good day.
bonne (1) [BON (1)].
bonne (2) [bɔn], *n.f.* servant-maid; housemaid; ***bonne d'enfants***, nursery-maid; ***bonne à tout faire***, general maid.
bonnement [bɔn'mɑ̃], *adv.* plainly, simply, honestly; ***tout bonnement***, quite frankly.
bonnet [bɔ'nɛ], *n.m.* cap; ***c'est bonnet blanc et blanc bonnet***, it is six of one and half a dozen of the other.
bonneterie [bɔn'tri], *n.f.* hosiery business, hosiery.
bonnetier [bɔn'tje], *n.m.* (*fem.* **-ière**) hosier.
bon-prime [bɔ̃'prim], *n.m.* (*Comm.*) free-gift token.
bonsoir [bɔ̃'swa:r], *n.m.* and *int.* good evening, good night.
bonté [bɔ̃'te], *n.f.* goodness, kindness.
boom [bum], *n.m.* (*Fin.*) boom.
borax [bɔ'raks], *n.m.* borax.
bord [bɔ:r], *n.m.* edge, margin, brink, brim, border, rim; shore, bank, side; ***au bord de la mer***, at the seaside; ***à bord***, on board; ***par-dessus bord***, overboard.
bordage [bɔr'da:ʒ], *n.m.* bordering, hemming etc.; (*Naut.*) planking, bulwarks.
bordé [bɔr'de], *n.m.* hem, edging, bordering (*of a garment*); (*Naut.*) planking.
bordeaux [bɔr'do], *n.m.* Bordeaux wine; ***bordeaux rouge***, claret.
bordée [bɔr'de], *n.f.* (*Naut.*) broadside; volley, salvo; (*C*) ***une bordée de neige***, a snow-fall.
bordelais [bɔrdə'lɛ:], *a.* of Bordeaux.—*n.m.* (**Bordelais**, *fem.* **-aise**) native of Bordeaux.
border [bɔr'de], *v.t.* to border, to edge, to hem, to skirt, to bind; to tuck in (*bedclothes*); (*Naut.*) to haul (*the sheets*).
bordereau [bɔrdə'ro], *n.m.* (*pl.* **-eaux**) memorandum, note, schedule, account.
bordure [bɔr'dy:r], *n.f.* frame, edge, edging; margin, border, kerb; rim.
boréal [bɔre'al], *a.* (*m. pl.* **-aux**) boreal, northern.
borée [bɔ're], *n.m.* Boreas, north wind (*poet.*).
borgne [bɔrɲ], *a.* one-eyed; ***rue borgne***, blind alley.—*n.* one-eyed person.
borique [bɔ'rik], *a.* boric.
borne [bɔrn], *n.f.* landmark; boundary, limit, confine; milestone; (*Elec.*) terminal; ***borne kilométrique***, milestone.
borné [bɔr'ne], *a.* bounded, limited, confined; narrow, mean, hide-bound.
borne-fontaine [bɔrnfɔ̃'tɛ:n], *n.f.* (*pl.* **bornes-fontaines**) street fountain (*like a boundary-post*).
borner [bɔr'ne], *v.t.* to set landmarks to; to bound, to limit, to confine.
Bosphore [bɔs'fɔ:r], **le**, *m.* the Bosphorus.
bosquet [bɔs'kɛ], *n.m.* grove, thicket, arbour.
bosse [bɔs], *n.f.* hump, hunch; bump, bruise; knob, protuberance, lump, boss; (*Arch.*) embossment; (*Sculp.*) relief.
bosselage [bɔs'la:ʒ], *n.m.* embossing.
bosseler [bɔs'le], *v.t.* (*conjug. like* APPELER) to dent; to emboss.
bossu [bɔ'sy], *a.* hunch-backed; deformed, crooked; pigeon-breasted.—*n.m.* (*fem.* **-e**) hunch-back; ***rire comme un bossu***, to split one's sides with laughter.
bossuer [bɔ'sɥe], *v.t.* to dent, to batter.
boston [bɔs'tɔ̃], *n.m.* boston (*card-game, dance*).
bot [bo], *a.* ***pied bot***, club-foot; club-footed.
botanique [bɔta'nik], *a.* botanical.—*n.f.* botany.
botaniser [bɔtani'ze], *v.i.* to botanize.
botaniste [bɔta'nist], *n.* botanist.
botte (1) [bɔt], *n.f.* wellington boot, jack-boot.
botte (2) [bɔt], *n.f.* bunch, truss, bale.
botte (3) [bɔt], *n.f.* (*Fenc.*) pass, thrust
bottelage [bɔ'tla:ʒ], *n.m.* tying up in bundles.
botteler [bɔ'tle], *v.t.* (*conjug. like* APPELER) to put up in bundles, to truss.
botteloir [bɔt'lwa:r], *n.m.*, **botteleuse** [bɔ'tlø:z], *n.f.* sheaf-binding machine, binder.
botter [bɔ'te], *v.t.* to put boots on (*a person*).
bottier [bɔ'tje], *n.m.* bootmaker.
bottin [bɔ'tɛ̃], *n.m.* a directory published by the firm of Didot Bottin.
bottine [bɔ'tin], *n.f.* (ankle) boot.
bouc [buk], *n.m.* billy-goat; ***bouc émissaire*** scapegoat.
boucanage [buka'na:ʒ], *n.m.* smoke-drying.
boucaner [buka'ne], *v.t.* to smoke (*meat, hides etc.*).
boucanier [buka'nje], *n.m.* buccaneer; freebooter.
(*C*) **boucanière** [buka'ɲɛ:r], *n.f.* smokehouse (*for fish*).
bouchage [bu'ʃa:ʒ], *n.m.* stopping, corking.
bouche [buʃ], *n.f.* mouth; lips; tongue; voice; victuals; muzzle (*of a cannon*); ***bouche d'eau***, hydrant.
bouchée [bu'ʃe], *n.f.* mouthful.
boucher (1) [bu'ʃe], *v.t.* to stop, to choke.
boucher (2) [bu'ʃe], *n.m.* butcher.
bouchère [bu'ʃɛ:r], *n.f.* butcher's wife; woman keeping a butcher's shop.
boucherie [buʃ'ri], *n.f.* butcher's shop; butchery, slaughter.
bouche-trou [buʃ'tru], *n.m.* (*pl.* **bouche-trous**) stopgap.
bouchon [bu'ʃɔ̃], *n.m.* stopper, cork; wisp (*of straw etc.*).
bouchonner [buʃɔ'ne], *v.t.* to rub down (*a horse*).
bouchonnier [buʃɔ'nje], *n.m.* one who cuts *or* sells corks.
boucle [bukl], *n.f.* buckle; curl, lock (*of hair*); loop (*of a river etc.*).
bouclé [bu'kle], *a.* buckled, curled.

boucler [bu'kle], *v.t.* to buckle; to put a ring to; to curl (*hair*); ***boucler la boucle***, to loop the loop. **se boucler**, *v.r.* to curl one's hair.
bouclier [bu'klje], *n.m.* buckler, shield; (*fig.*) defence.
Bouddha [bu'da], *m.* Buddha.
bouddhisme [bu'dism], *n.m.* Buddhism.
bouddhiste [bu'dist], *n.* Buddhist.
bouder [bu'de], *v.i.* to sulk, to be sullen, to pout. **se bouder**, *v.r.* to be cool towards each other.
bouderie [bu'dri], *n.f.* pouting, sulkiness.
boudeur [bu'dœ:r], *a.* (*fem.* **-euse**) sulky, sullen.
boudin [bu'dɛ̃], *n.m.* black-pudding; spring (*of a coach*).
boudoir [bu'dwa:r], *n.m.* boudoir, lady's private room.
boue [bu], *n.f.* mud, mire, dirt, filth.
bouée [bu'e], *n.f.* buoy.
boueux [bu'ø], *a.* (*fem.* **-euse**) muddy, dirty, miry; foul.—*n.m.* scavenger; dustman.
bouffant [bu'fɑ̃], *a.* puffed (*sleeve*), baggy (*trousers*).
bouffe [buf], *a.* comic.—*n.m. pl.* ***Les Bouffes***, the Italian opera (*in Paris*).
bouffée [bu'fe], *n.f.* puff, gust, blast, whiff.
bouffette [bu'fɛt], *n.f.* bow of ribbon; tassel.
bouffi [bu'fi], *a.* puffed up, swollen, inflated.
bouffir [bu'fi:r], *v.t.* to puff up, to swell, to bloat.—*v.i.* to swell.
bouffissure [bufi'sy:r], *n.f.* swelling, puffing up.
bouffon [bu'fɔ̃], *a.* (*fem.* **-onne**) jocose, facetious, comical.—*n.m.* buffoon, clown, jester.
bouffonner [bufɔ'ne], *v.i.* to play the buffoon; to be jocose *or* full of jests.
bouffonnerie [bufɔn'ri], *n.f.* buffoonery, drollery, jesting.
bougainvillée [bugɛ̃vi'le], *n.f.*, **bougainvillier** [bugɛ̃vi'lje], *n.m.* bougainvillea.
bouge [bu:ʒ], *n.m.* den, dirty hole, hovel.
bougeoir [bu'ʒwa:r], *n.m.* flat candlestick.
bouger [bu'ʒe], *v.i.* (*conjug. like* MANGER) to stir, to budge, to fidget.
bougie [bu'ʒi], *n.f.* wax-candle; (*Elec.*) candle-power; ***bougie d'allumage***, (*Motor.*) sparking-plug.
bougran [bu'grɑ̃], *n.m.* buckram.
bouillabaisse [buja'bɛs], *n.f.* Provençal fish-soup with saffron etc.
bouillant [bu'jɑ̃], *a.* boiling, hot, scalding.
bouilleur [bu'jœ:r], *n.m.* brandy distiller; boiler-tube (*of an engine*).
bouilli [bu'ji], *n.m.* boiled beef.
bouillie [bu'ji], *n.f.* pap (*for infants*), porridge; pulp.
bouillir [bu'ji:r], *v.t. irr.* to boil (*milk etc.*). —*v.i.* to boil.
bouilloire [buj'wa:r], *n.f.* kettle.
bouillon [bu'jɔ̃], *n.m.* broth, beef-tea; bubble; ebullition.
bouillonnement [bujɔn'mɑ̃], *n.m.* bubbling up, spouting, gushing.
bouillonner [bujɔ'ne], *v.i.* to bubble, to boil; (*fig.*) to be in a state of excitement.
bouillotte [bu'jɔt], *n.f.* foot-warmer; hot-water bottle; small kettle.
boulanger [bulɑ̃'ʒe], *n.m.* (*fem.* **-ère**) baker, baker's wife.—*v.t.* (*conjug. like* MANGER) to make, knead *or* bake (*bread*).
boulangerie [bulɑ̃'ʒri], *n.f.* baking, baker's business; baker's shop.
boule [bul], *n.f.* ball; bowl; (*pop.*) face, pate, head.
bouleau [bu'lo], *n.m.* (*pl.* **-eaux**) birch, birch-tree.
bouledogue [bul'dɔg], *n.m.* bulldog.
boulet [bu'lɛ], *n.m.* cannon- *or* musket-ball.
boulette [bu'lɛt], *n.f.* pellet; forcemeat ball.
boulevard [bul'va:r], *n.m.* rampart; boulevard.
bouleversement [bulvɛrsə'mɑ̃], *n.m.* overthrow; commotion, confusion; destruction, ruin.
bouleverser [bulvɛr'se], *v.t.* to overthrow, to throw down; to subvert; (*fig.*) to agitate, to upset.
boulier [bu'lje], *n.m.* (*Fishing*) bag-net; scoring-board (*at billiards*).
bouline [bu'lin], *n.f.* (*Naut.*) bowline.
boulon [bu'lɔ̃], *n.m.* bolt, large iron pin.
boulonner [bulɔ'ne], *v.t.* to fasten with iron pins, to bolt.
boulot [bu'lo], *a.* (*fem.* **-otte**) fat, dumpy, squat.
bouquet [bu'kɛ], *n.m.* bunch (*of flowers*), nosegay, bouquet; aroma (*of wine*), perfume.
bouquetier [buk'tje], *n.f.* flower-vase.
bouquetière [buk'tjɛ:r], *n.f.* flower-girl.
bouquetin [buk'tɛ̃], *n.m.* ibex.
bouquin (1) [bu'kɛ̃], *n.m.* (*Zool.*) old billy-goat; old hare.
bouquin (2) [bu'kɛ̃], *n.m.* old book; second-hand book; (*colloq.*) book.
bouquiner [buki'ne], *v.i.* to hunt after old books; (*colloq.*) to read.
bouquineur [buki'nœ:r], *n.m.* (*colloq.*) lover of old books, book-fancier.
bouquiniste [buki'nist], *n.m.* dealer in second-hand books.
bourbe [burb], *n.f.* mud, mire, slush.
bourbeux [bur'bø], *a.* (*fem.* **-euse**) miry, muddy, sloshy.
bourbier [bur'bje], *n.m.* slough, puddle, mire.
bourdaine [bur'dɛn], **bourgène** [bur'ʒɛn], *n.f.* black alder.
bourdon (1) [bur'dɔ̃], *n.m.* pilgrim's staff.
bourdon (2) [bur'dɔ̃], *n.m.* humble-bee; great bell; (*Organ*) drone.
bourdonnant [burdɔ'nɑ̃], *a.* humming, buzzing.
bourdonnement [burdɔn'mɑ̃], *n.m.* buzz, buzzing; humming.
bourdonner [burdɔ'ne], *v.t.* to hum.—*v.i.* to buzz, to hum; to murmur.
bourdonneur [burdɔ'nœ:r], *a.* humming.—*n.m.* humming-bird, colibri.
bourg [bu:r], *n.m.* borough, market-town.
bourgade [bur'gad], *n.f.* small market-town.
bourgène [BOURDAINE].
bourgeois [bur'ʒwa], *a.* middle-class; plain, common, ordinary.—*n.m.* (*fem.* **-e**) citizen, townsman, townswoman; commoner; middle-class person, bourgeois.
bourgeoisie [burʒwa'zi], *n.f.* bourgeoisie, middle-class.
bourgeon [bur'ʒɔ̃], *n.m.* (*Bot.*) bud, shoot; pimple.
bourgeonnement [burʒɔn'mɑ̃], *n.m.* budding.

bourgeonner [burʒɔ'ne], *v.i.* to bud; to break out in pimples.
bourgeron [burʒə'rɔ̃], *n.m.* workman's blouse, smock-frock.
bourgmestre [burg'mɛstr], *n.m.* burgomaster.
Bourgogne [bur'gɔɲ], **la**, *f.* Burgundy.
bourguignon [burgi'ɲɔ̃], *a.* (*fem.* **-onne**) Burgundian, of Burgundy.—*n.m.* (**Bourguignon**, *fem.* **-onne**) native *or* inhabitant of Burgundy.
bourrade [bu'rad], *n.f.* blow, thrust, buffet.
bourrasque [bu'rask], *n.f.* squall, gust; fit of anger.
bourre [bu:r], *n.f.* hair, fluff (*of animals*); flock (*of wool*); floss (*of silk*); (*fig.*) stuff, trash.
bourreau [bu'ro], *n.m.* (*pl.* **-eaux**) hangman, executioner; tyrant.
bourrée [bu're], *n.f.* brushwood, faggot; an Auvergne dance.
bourreler [bur'le], *v.t.* (*conjug. like* APPELER) to torment, to rack.
bourrelet [bur'lɛ], *n.m.* pad, cushion.
bourrelier [burə'lje], *n.m.* harness-maker.
bourrellerie [burɛl'ri], *n.f.* harness-maker's shop.
bourrer [bu're], *v.t.* to tamp; to stuff, to cram; (*fig.*) to ill-treat, to thrash. **se bourrer**, *v.r.* to cram oneself; to thrash each other.
bourriche [bu'riʃ], *n.f.* game-basket, basket of game.
bourrique [bu'rik], *n.f.* she-ass; (*fig.*) stupid person, dolt.
bourriquet [buri'kɛ], *n.m.* ass's colt *or* small ass; hand-barrow.
bourru [bu'ry], *a.* cross, peevish, moody, surly.
Bourse [burs], *n.f.* Stock Exchange; ***Bourse du travail***, labour exchange.
bourse [burs], *n.f.* purse, bag; scholarship, grant, bursary; rabbit-net.
boursier [bur'sje], *a.* (*fem.* **-ière**) pertaining to the Stock Exchange.—*n.m.* (*fem.* **-ière**) speculator on the Stock Exchange, exchange broker; purse-maker; (*Univ.*) exhibitioner.
boursouflage [bursu'fla:ʒ], *n.m.* bombast.
boursouflé [bursu'fle], *a.* bloated; bombastic, swollen.
boursouflement [bursuflə'mɑ̃], *n.m.* bloatedness, puffiness; blister (*of paint*).
boursoufler [bursu'fle], *v.t.* to bloat, to puff up.
boursouflure [bursu'fly:r], *n.f.* bloatedness (*of face etc.*); (*fig.*) turgidity (*of style*).
bousculade [busky'lad], *n.m.* jostling, hustling; scrimmage.
bousculer [busky'le], *v.t.* to throw into disorder; to jostle, to hustle. **se bousculer**, *v.r.* to jostle each other.
boussole [bu'sɔl], *n.f.* compass.
bout [bu], *n.m.* end, tip, top, point; fragment, bit; ***venir à bout de***, to succeed, to get through (*something*).
boutade [bu'tad], *n.f.* whim, fit, start, caprice; witticism.
boute-en-train [butɑ̃'trɛ̃], *n.m. inv.* one who promotes gaiety in others, merry-maker; ***être le boute-en-train***, to be the life and soul of the party.
boutefeu [but'fø], *n.m.* (*pl.* **-eux**) (*fig.*) incendiary, fire-brand.
bouteille [bu'tɛ:j], *n.f.* bottle; bottleful.
bouteillerie [butɛj'ri], *n.f.* bottle-works.
boutique [bu'tik], *n.f.* shop; work-shop; (*collect.*) tools, implements.
boutiquier [buti'kje], *n.m.* (*fem.* **-ière**) shopkeeper.—*a.* (*fem.* **-ière**) shopkeeping.
bouton [bu'tɔ̃], *n.m.* bud; pimple; button, stud, knob; (*Elec. etc.*) switch.
bouton d'or [butɔ̃'dɔ:r], *n.m.* (*pl.* **boutons d'or**) (*Bot.*) buttercup.
boutonné [butɔ'ne], *a.* buttoned; pimpled.
boutonner [butɔ'ne], *v.t.* to button; (*Fenc.*) to touch.—*v.i.* to bud; to button up. **se boutonner**, *v.r.* to button one's coat.
boutonnière [butɔ'njɛ:r], *n.f.* buttonhole.
bouture [bu'ty:r], *n.f.* slip; cutting.
bouveau [bu'vo] (*pl.* **-eaux**), **bouvelet** [buv'lɛ], *n.m.* young ox.
bouverie [bu'vri], *n.f.* cattle-shed, byre.
bouvet [bu'vɛ], *n.m.* joiner's grooving-plane.
bouvetage [buv'ta:ʒ], *n.m.* grooving and tonguing.
bouveter [buv'te], *v.t.* (*conjug. like* APPELER) to groove and tongue.
bouvier [bu'vje], *n.m.* (*fem.* **-ière**) cow-herd, ox-drover.
bouvillon [buvi'jɔ̃], *n.m.* young bullock, steer.
bouvreuil [bu'vrœ:j], *n.m.* bullfinch.
bovin [bɔ'vɛ̃], *a.* bovine.
box [bɔks], *n.m.* (*pl.* **boxes**) horse-box, loose box; lock-up garage; ***le box des accusés***, the dock.
boxe [bɔks], *n.f.* boxing.
boxer [bɔk'se], *v.i.* to box, to spar.
boxeur [bɔk'sœ:r], *n.m.* boxer, prize-fighter.
boy [bɔj], *n.m.* groom; native servant.
boyau [bwa'jo], *n.m.* (*pl* **-aux**) bowel, gut; catgut; hose-pipe; (*Cycl.*) racing tyre.
brabançon [brabɑ̃'sɔ̃], *a.* (*fem.* **-onne**) Brabantine, Belgian.—*n.m.* (**Brabançon**, *fem.* **-onne**) Brabantine, Belgian (*person*).
bracelet [bras'lɛ], *n.m.* bracelet, armlet, bangle.
bracelet-montre [braslɛ'mɔ̃:tr], *n.m.* (*pl.* **bracelets-montres**) wrist-watch.
braconnage [brakɔ'na:ʒ], *n.m.* poaching.
braconner [brakɔ'ne], *v.i.* to poach, to steal game.
braconnier [brakɔ'nje], *n.m.* (*fem.* **-ière**) poacher.—*a.* (*fem.* **-ière**) poaching; pertaining to poaching.
braguette [bra'gɛt], *n.f.* fly (*of trousers*).
brahmane [bra'man], **brahme** [bram], *n.m.* Brahmin.
brahmanisme [brama'nism], *n.m.* Brahminism.
brahme [BRAHMANE].
brai [brɛ], *n.m.* resin, rosin, pitch.
braillard [brɑ'ja:r], *a.* brawling, squalling; obstreperous.—*n.m.* (*fem.* **-e**) brawler, squaller.—*n.m.* small speaking-trumpet.
braille [brɑj], *n.m.* braille.
braillement [brɑj'mɑ̃], *n.m.* squalling.
brailler [brɑ'je], *v.i.* to bawl, to shout, to be noisy.
brailleur [brɑ'jœ:r], *a.* and *n.m.* (*fem.* **-euse**) [BRAILLARD].
braiment [brɛ'mɑ̃], *n.m.* braying (*of an ass*).
braire [brɛ:r], *v.i. irr.* to bray; (*fig.*) to cry, to whine.
braise [brɛ:z], *n.f.* wood-embers, live coals.

braiser [brɛ'ze], *v.t.* to braise.
braisier [brɛ'zje], *n.m.* brazier.
braisière [brɛ'zjɛ:r], *n.f.* braising-pan.
bramer [bra'me], *v.i.* to bell (*of deer*).
brancard [brɑ̃'ka:r], *n.m.* stretcher, litter; hand-barrow; shaft (*of a cart*).
brancardier [brɑ̃kar'dje], *n.m.* stretcher-bearer, ambulance-man.
branchage [brɑ̃'ʃa:ʒ], *n.m.* (*collect.*) branches, boughs.
branche [brɑ̃:ʃ], *n.f.* branch, bough; part, division.
brancher [brɑ̃'ʃe], *v.t.* to divide into branches; (*Elec.*) to connect, to plug in; to tap (*a gas* or *water pipe*).—*v.i.* to branch off.
branchu [brɑ̃'ʃy], *a.* forked, bifurcated, ramifying.
brande [brɑ̃:d], *n.f.* heather; heath.
Brandebourg [brɑ̃d'bu:r], *m.* Brandenburg.
brandebourgs [brɑ̃d'bu:r], *n.m. pl.* braid; frogs and loops (*on a uniform*).
brandillement [brɑ̃dij'mɑ̃], *n.m.* tossing; swinging.
brandiller [brɑ̃di'je], *v.t.* to swing, to shake to and fro.—*v.i.* to swing, to move to and fro. **se brandiller**, *v.r.* to swing.
brandir [brɑ̃'di:r], *v.t.* to brandish, to flourish.
brandissement [brɑ̃dis'mɑ̃], *n.m.* brandishing, flourishing.
brandon [brɑ̃'dɔ̃], *n.m.* torch, fire-brand.
branlant [brɑ̃'lɑ̃], *a.* shaking, loose, tottering.
branle [brɑ̃:l], *n.m.* oscillation, shaking *or* tossing motion; jog; an old-fashioned dance.
branle-bas [brɑ̃l'bɑ], *n.m. inv.* (*Naut.*) clearing for action; (*fig.*) commotion, disturbance.
branlement [brɑ̃l'mɑ̃], *n.m.* oscillation, shaking, swing.
branler [brɑ̃'le], *v.t.* to shake, to wag.—*v.i.* to shake, to stagger, to rock; to move; to waver.
braquage [bra'ka:ʒ], *n.m.* aiming; steering, lock (*of a car*).
braque (1) [brak], *n.m.* French pointer.
braque (2) [brak], *a.* madcap, hare-brained.
braquer [bra'ke], *v.t.* to aim, to level, to point.
bras [bra], *n.m.* arm; bracket; branch (*of a stream etc.*); (*fig.*) power, action, assistance.
braser [brɑ'ze], *v.t.* to braze.
brasier [brɑ'zje], *n.m.* quick clear fire; brazier, furnace.
brasiller [brɑzi'je], *v.t.* to grill, to broil.—*v.i.* to glitter, to shine (*of the sea*).
brassage [bra'sa:ʒ], *n.m.* mashing, brewing.
brassard [bra'sa:r], *n.m.* brace (*armour*); armlet.
brasse [bras], *n.f.* fathom, six feet; armful; stroke (*in swimming*).
brassée [bra'se], *n.f.* armful; stroke (*in swimming*).
brassement [bras'mɑ̃], *n.m.* brewing; mixing.
brasser [bra'se], *v.t.* to mix; to brew, to mash; to stir up.
brasserie [bras'ri], *n.f.* brewery; brewing; drinking-saloon, 'pub'.
brasseur [bra'sœ:r], *n.m.* brewer.
brassière [bra'sjɛ:r], *n.f.* shoulder-strap (*of a knapsack etc.*); infant's vest *or* bodice.
brassin [bra'sɛ̃], *n.m.* brewing-tub; mash-tub; a boiling (*quantity boiled* or *brewed*).
bravache [bra'vaʃ], *n.m.* bully, swaggerer blusterer.—*a.* blustering, bullying.
bravade [bra'vad], *n.f.* bravado, boast, bluster.
brave [bra:v], *a.* brave, courageous, gallant; worthy, honest, good.—*n.m.* brave *or* courageous man; good fellow.
bravement [brav'mɑ̃], *adv.* bravely, stoutly, valiantly; skilfully, finely.
braver [bra've], *v.t.* to defy, to dare; to brave, to beard.
bravo [bra'vo], *n.m.* (*pl.* **bravos**) and *int.* bravo; hear, hear!
bravoure [bra'vu:r], *n.f.* bravery, courage, gallantry; (*pl.*) exploits.
break [brɛk], *n.m.* break (*carriage*).
brebis [brə'bi], *n.f.* ewe; (*fig.*) sheep; (*pl.*) flock.
brèche [brɛʃ], *n.f.* breach, flaw; notch, gap.
bréchet [bre'ʃɛ], *n.m.* (*Orn.*) breast-bone.
bredouillage [brədu'ja:ʒ], **bredouillement** [brəduj'mɑ̃], *n.m.* stammering, stuttering, sputtering.
bredouille [brə'du:j], *n.f.* (*Trictrac*) lurch.—*a. inv.* empty-handed; ***revenir bredouille***, to return with an empty bag (*of sportsmen*).
bredouillement [BREDOUILLAGE].
bredouiller [brədu'je], *v.t., v.i.* to stammer, to stutter.
bredouilleur [brədu'jœ:r], *a.* (*fem.* **-euse**) stammering, stuttering.—*n.m.* (*fem.* **-euse**) stammerer, stutterer.
bref [brɛf], *a.* (*fem.* **brève** (1)) short, brief, concise; brusque.—*adv.* in short, in fine, in a word.
brelan [brə'lɑ̃], *n.m.* brelan (*card game*); gaming-house.
brêler or **breller** [brɛ'le], *v.t.* to lash.
breller [BRÊLER].
breloque [brə'lɔk], *n.f.* trinket, gewgaw; charm.
Brême [brɛ:m], *m.* Bremen.
brème [brɛ:m], *n.f.* bream.
Brésil [bre'zil], **le**, *m.* Brazil.
brésil [bre'zil], *n.m.* Brazil-wood (*for dyeing*).
brésilien [brezi'ljɛ̃], *a.* (*fem.* **-enne**) Brazilian.—*n.m.* (**Brésilien**, *fem.* **-enne**) Brazilian (*person*).
Bretagne [brə'taɲ], **la**, *f.* Brittany; ***la Grande-Bretagne***, Great Britain; ***la Nouvelle-Bretagne***, New Britain.
bretelle [brə'tɛl], *n.f.* strap; brace; (*pl.*) pair of braces; (*Rail.*) points; (*rifle*) sling.
breton [brə'tɔ̃], *a.* (*fem.* **-onne**) Breton.—*n.m.* Breton (*language*); (**Breton**, *fem.* **-onne**) Breton (*person*).
bretteur [brɛ'tœ:r], *n.m.* swashbuckler, duellist.
bretzel [brɛt'sɛl], *n.m.* pretzel.
breuil [brœ:j], *n.m.* enclosed coppice, covert.
breuvage [brœ'va:ʒ], *n.m.* beverage, drink, liquor.
brève (1) [brɛ:v], [BREF].
brève (2) [brɛ:v], *n.f.* short syllable; (*Mus.*) breve.
brevet [brə'vɛ], *n.m.* warrant, brevet, certificate (*school etc.*); diploma, licence (*of printers*); patent; badge (*of boy-scouts*); (*Mil.*) commission.
breveté [brəv'te], *a.* patented; (*Mil.*) certificated—*n.m.* (*fem.* **-ée**) patentee.

breveter [brəv'te], *v.t.* (*conjug. like* APPELER) to patent; to license; to certificate.
bréviaire [bre'vjɛ:r], *n.m.* breviary.
brévité [brevi'te], *n.f.* shortness (*of syllables*).
bribes [brib], *n.f. pl.* scraps, bits; odds and ends.
bric-à-brac [brika'brak], *n.m. inv.* curios, bric-a-brac; curiosity-shop.
brick [brik], *n.m.* brig.
bricolage [brikɔ'la:ʒ], *n.m.* pottering.
bricoler [brikɔ'le], *v.i.* to potter, to do odds and ends.
bricoleur [brikɔ'lœ:r], *n.m.* (*fem.* **-euse**) odd job man, handyman *or* woman.
bride [brid], *n.f.* bridle, bridle-rein; check, curb; string (*of a woman's cap, bonnet etc.*).
brider [bri'de], *v.t.* to bridle; to restrain, to curb; to truss (*a fowl*); to tie; to check.
bridge [bridʒ], *n.m.* bridge (*card game*); bridge (*in dentistry*).
bridger [bri'dʒe], *v.i.* to play bridge.
bridgeur [bri'dʒœ:r], *n.m.* (*fem.* **-euse**) bridge-player.
bridon [bri'dɔ̃], *n.m.* snaffle-bridle.
brie [bri], *n.m.* Brie cheese.
brièvement [briɛv'mɑ̃], *adv.* briefly, succinctly, in short.
brièveté [briɛv'te], *n.f.* brevity, briefness, conciseness.
brigade [bri'gad], *n.f.* brigade; (*fig.*) troop, gang, body.
brigadier [briga'dje], *n.m.* corporal (*in cavalry, artillery*); sergeant (*of police*).
brigand [bri'gɑ̃], *n.m.* brigand; (*fig.*) robber, thief.
brigandage [brigɑ̃'da:ʒ], *n.m.* brigandage, plunder.
brigander [brigɑ̃'de], *v.i.* to rob, to plunder.
brigantin [brigɑ̃'tɛ̃], *n.m.* brigantine.
brigantine [brigɑ̃'tin], *n.f.* (*Naut.*) spanker; small vessel.
brigue [brig], *n.f.* intrigue, cabal, faction.
briguer [bri'ge], *v.t.* to canvass for, to solicit, to court.
brigueur [bri'gœ:r], *n.m.* (*fem.* **-euse**) intriguer, canvasser.
brillamment [brija'mɑ̃], *adv.* brilliantly, in a brilliant manner.
brillance [bri'jɑ̃:s], *n.f.* (*Opt.*) brilliancy.
brillant [bri'jɑ̃], *a.* brilliant, sparkling, glittering; radiant.—*n.m.* brilliance, splendour; brilliant (*diamond*).
brillanter [brijɑ̃'te], *v.t.* to cut into a brilliant.
brillantine [brijɑ̃'tin], *n.f.* brilliantine (*hair-oil*); glossy cotton-cloth.
briller [bri'je], *v.i.* to shine, to glitter, to sparkle; (*fig.*) to distinguish oneself, to stand out.
brimade [bri'mad], *n.f.* ragging; vexation; persecution.
brimborion [brɛ̃bɔ'rjɔ̃], *n.m.* knick-knack, bauble.
brimer [bri'me], *v.t.* to rag, to bully.
brin [brɛ̃], *n.m.* blade, slender stalk, shoot (*of corn etc.*); (*fig.*) bit, jot.
brindille [brɛ̃'di:j], *n.f.* sprig, twig.
brio [bri'o] [It.], *n.m.* (*Mus. etc.*) dash, spirit, go.
brioche [bri'ɔʃ], *n.f.* brioche, bun; (*fig.*) blunder.
brique [brik], *n.f.* brick; ***brique anglaise***, bath brick.
briquet [bri'kɛ], *n.m.* tinder-box; (cigarette) lighter.
briquetage [brik'ta:ʒ], *n.m.* brick-work; imitation brick-work.
briqueter [brik'te], *v.t.* (*conjug. like* APPELER) to brick, to pave with bricks.
briqueterie [brik'tri], *n.f.* brick-field, brick-making; brickworks.
briqueteur [brik'tœ:r], *n.m.* bricklayer.
briquetier [brik'tje], *n.m.* brick-maker.
briquette [bri'kɛt], *n.f.* briquette; compressed slack.
brisant [bri'zɑ̃], *n.m.* sand-bank, reef, shoal; (*pl.*) breakers.
brise [bri:z], *n.f.* breeze; strong wind.
brisé [bri'ze], *a.* broken to pieces; (*fig.*) harassed.
brise-bise [briz'bi:z], *n.m. inv.* draught excluder; sash curtain.
brisées [bri'ze], *n.f.* (*used only in pl.*) footsteps, wake; ***aller*** or ***marcher sur les brisées de quelqu'un***, to poach on someone's preserves.
brise-glace [briz'glas], *n.m.* (*pl.* **brise-glace** or **-glaces**) ice-breaker (*ship*).
brise-jet [briz'ʒɛ], *n.m. inv.* anti-splash tap-nozzle.
brise-lames [briz'lam], *n.m. inv.* break-water.
brisement [briz'mɑ̃], *n.m.* breaking, dashing (*of waves*); (*fig.*) trouble, contrition.
briser [bri'ze], *v.t.* to break to pieces, to smash, to break, to shatter; to burst; to crack; to destroy.—*v.i.* to break; to dash (*of waves*).
brise-tout [briz'tu], *n.m. inv.* person who breaks everything; rough, clumsy fellow.
briseur [bri'zœ:r], *n.m.* (*fem.* **-euse**) one who breaks *or* likes to break anything; iconoclast.
brise-vent [briz'vɑ̃], *n.m.* (*pl.* **brise-vent** or **brise-vents**) wind-screen (*for protecting plants*).
brisque [brisk], *n.f.* a card-game; (*Mil.*) stripe; war service chevron.
brisure [bri'zy:r], *n.f.* break; folding-point in a piece of joiner's work; small fragment.
britannique [brita'nik], *a.* British, Britannic; ***Les Îles Britanniques***, the British Isles.
broc [bro], *n.m.* large jug *or* quart-pot.
brocantage [brɔkɑ̃'ta:ʒ], *n.m.* dealing in second-hand goods, broker's business; bartering.
brocante [brɔ'kɑ̃:t], *n.f.* second-hand trade; article of trifling value.
brocanter [brɔkɑ̃'te], *v.i.* to deal in second-hand goods; to exchange, to barter.
brocanteur [brɔkɑ̃'tœ:r], *n.m.* (*fem.* **-euse**) dealer in second-hand goods, junk-shop owner.
brocard [brɔ'ka:r], *n.m.* taunt, jeer; lampoon.
brocarder [brɔkar'de], *v.t.* to taunt, to ridicule.
brocardeur [brɔkar'dœ:r], *n.m.* (*fem.* **-euse**) scoffer, jeerer.
brocart or **broquart** [brɔ'ka:r], *n.m.* brocade.
brochage [brɔ'ʃa:ʒ], *n.m.* stitching (*of books*).
broche [brɔʃ], *n.f.* spit; spindle; skewer; spigot; knitting-needle; brooch; (*pl.*) tusks (*of wild boars*); (*Elec.*) ***fiche à deux broches***, two-pin plug.

broché [brɔ'ʃe], *a.* embossed (*of linen*); brocaded, figured (*of other materials*); ***livre broché***, paper-bound book.
brocher [brɔ'ʃe], *v.t.* to stitch (*a book etc.*); to figure (*materials*); to emboss (*linen*).
brochet [brɔ'ʃɛ], *n.m.* pike (*fish*).
brocheter [brɔʃ'te], *v.t.* (*conjug. like* APPELER) to skewer.
brochette [brɔ'ʃɛt], *n.f.* (*Cook.*) small spit.
brocheur [brɔ'ʃœ:r], *n.m.* (*fem.* **-euse**) stitcher, esp. book-stitcher.
brochure [brɔ'ʃy:r], *n.f.* stitching; booklet, brochure, pamphlet, tract; embroidery.
brocoli [brɔkɔ'li], *n.m.* broccoli.
brodequin [brɔd'kɛ̃], *n.m.* buskin, half-boot.
broder [brɔ'de], *v.t.* to embroider; to adorn, to embellish (*a story etc.*).—*v.i.* to romance.
broderie [brɔd'ri], *n.f.* embroidery; (*fig.*) embellishment.
brodeur [brɔ'dœ:r], *n.m.* (*fem.* **-euse**) embroiderer.
broiement or **broîment** [brwɑ'mɑ̃], **broyage** [brwɑ'ja:ʒ], *n.m.* grinding, powdering.
bromure [brɔ'my:r], *n.m.* bromide.
bronche [brɔ̃:ʃ], *n.f.* (*pl.*) (*Anat.*) bronchial tubes.
bronchement [brɔ̃ʃ'mɑ̃], *n.m.* stumbling; flinching.
broncher [brɔ̃'ʃe], *v.i.* to stumble, to trip, to reel; to falter.
bronchial [brɔ̃'ʃjal], *a.* (*m. pl.* **-aux**) (*Anat.*) bronchial.
bronchique [brɔ̃'ʃik], *a.* bronchial.
bronchite [brɔ̃'ʃit], *n.f.* (*Path.*) bronchitis.
broncho-pneumonie [brɔ̃kɔpnømɔ'ni], *n.f.* broncho-pneumonia.
bronze [brɔ̃:z], *n.m.* bronze; bronze statue *or* medal.
bronzer [brɔ̃'ze], *v.t.* to bronze; to tan (*the face etc.*).
broquart [BROCART].
broquette [brɔ'kɛt], *n.f.* tack, carpet-nail.
brosse [brɔs], *n.f.* brush; painter's brush *or* pencil; ***cheveux en brosse***, crew-cut hair.
brosser [brɔ'se], *v.t.* to brush. **se brosser**, *v.r.* to brush oneself.
brosserie [brɔ'sri], *n.f.* brushmaking business; brush factory.
brou [bru], *n.m.* husk *or* peel (*of nuts, esp. walnuts*); ***brou de noix***, walnut stain, walnut liquor.
brouet [bru'ɛ], *n.m.* thin broth.
brouette [bru'ɛt], *n.f.* wheelbarrow.
brouettée [bruɛ'te], *n.f.* barrow-load.
brouetter [bruɛ'te], *v.t.* to wheel in a barrow.
brouetteur [bruɛ'tœ:r], **brouettier** [bruɛ'tje], *n.m.* barrowman.
brouhaha [brua'a], *n.m.* hubbub, uproar, hurly-burly.
brouillage [bru'ja:ʒ], *n.m.* (*Rad.*) atmospherics, jamming.
brouillard [bru'ja:r], *n.m.* fog, mist, haze; (*Comm.*) rough-book.
brouillasse [bru'jas], *n.f.* drizzle, Scotch mist.
brouillasser [bruja'se], *v.impers.* to drizzle.
brouille [bru:j], **brouillerie** [bruj'ri], *n.f.* quarrel, falling-out.
brouillé [bru'je], *a.* scrambled (*eggs*); blurred; on bad terms.
brouillement [bruj'mɑ̃], *n.m.* mixing together, jumbling.
brouiller [bru'je], *v.t.* to mix together, to jumble up, to shuffle; to embroil, to confuse; (*Rad.*) to jam. **se brouiller**, *v.r.* to fall out (*with someone*).
brouillerie [BROUILLE].
brouillon [bru'jɔ̃], *a.* (*fem.* **-onne**) mischief-making; blundering.—*n.m.* rough draft, rough copy; blunderer, bungler.
brouillonner [brujɔ'ne], *v.t.* to write in a blundering *or* confused way, to botch.
brouir [bru'i:r], *v.t.* to blight, to nip, to parch.
brouissure [brui'sy:r], *n.f.* blight, scorching.
broussailles [bru'sɑ:j], *n.f.* (*usu. in pl.*) bushes, brushwood, undergrowth.
broussailleux [brusɑ'jø], *a.* (*fem.* **-euse**) bushy, covered with bushes.
brousse [brus], *n.f.* brushwood, bush (*Australia etc.*).
brouter [bru'te], *v.t., v.i.* to browse, to graze.
broutilles [bru'ti:j], *n.f. pl.* sprigs; (*fig.*) trifles.
brownien [bro'njɛ̃], *a.* ***mouvements browniens***, molecular motion.
browning [bro'niŋ], *n.m.* automatic pistol.
broyage [brwa'ja:ʒ], *n.m.* crushing (*of ore*), grinding (*of colours*).
broyer [brwɑ'je], *v.t.* (*conjug. like* EMPLOYER) to grind, to pound, to pulverize.
broyeur [brwa'jœ:r], *a.* (*fem.* **-euse**) grinding.—*n.m.* (*fem.* **-euse**) grinding; grinder, pounder.
bru [bry], *n.f.* daughter-in-law.
brucelles [bry'sɛl], *n.f. pl.* tweezers.
brugnon [bry'ɲɔ̃], *n.m.* nectarine.
bruine [brɥin], *n.f.* light drizzling rain.
bruiner [brɥi'ne], *v.impers.* to drizzle.
bruineux [brɥi'nø], *a.* (*fem.* **-euse**) drizzly, drizzling.
bruire [brɥi:r], *v.t. irr.* to make a noise; to rustle, to rattle; to roar, to sough (*of the wind*).
bruissant [brɥi'sɑ̃], *a.* rustling, rattling; roaring.
bruissement [brɥis'mɑ̃], *n.m.* rustling noise, rattling, roaring.
bruit [brɥi], *n.m.* noise, din, uproar, clamour; fame, renown; report, talk, rumour.
bruitage [brɥi'ta:ʒ], *n.m.* sound-effects.
bruiter [brɥi'te], *v.i.* to make sound-effects.
bruiteur [brɥi'tœ:r], *n.m.* sound-effects specialist.
brûlage [bry'la:ʒ], *n.m.* burning (*of rubbish*); singeing (*of hair*); roasting (*of coffee*).
brûlant [bry'lɑ̃], *a.* burning, scorching, hot, torrid; (*fig.*) eager, ardent.
brûlé [bry'le], *n.m.* smell of burning; (*C*) burnt part of wood, burnbeat field.
brûle-gueule [bryl'gœl], *n.m. inv.* (*colloq.*) short pipe, cutty.
brûle-pourpoint, à [abrylpur'pwɛ̃], *adv.* point-blank (*of shooting*).
brûler [bry'le], *v.t.* to burn; to cauterize; to scorch, to parch; to singe (*hair*).—*v.i.* to burn, to be on fire; (*fig.*) to be eager. **se brûler**, *v.r.* to burn oneself, to be burnt.
brûleur [bry'lœ:r], *n.m.* (*fem.* **-euse**) burner; incendiary; ***brûleur à gaz***, gas-ring, gas-jet.
brûlis [bry'li], *n.m.* burnt part of a wood *or* field.
brûloir [bry'lwa:r], *n.m.* coffee-burner *or* roaster.

brûlot [bry'lo], *n.m.* fire-ship; (*fig.*) firebrand, incendiary; (*C*) kind of gnat *or* midge.
brûlure [bry'ly:r], *n.f.* burn, frost nip, scald.
brumaire [bry'mɛ:r], *n.m.* Brumaire (*second month of the calendar of the first French Republic, from Oct. 22nd to Nov. 20th*).
brume [brym], *n.f.* haze, mist.
brumeux [bry'mø], *a.* (*fem.* **-euse**) hazy, misty; (*fig.*) sombre.
brun [brœ̃], *a.* brown, dark, dusky.—*n.m.* brown (*colour*); (*fem.* **-e** (1)) dark-complexioned person.
brunâtre [bry'nɑ:tr], *a.* brownish.
brune (2) [bryn], *n.f.* dusk (*of the evening*); dark woman, dark girl, brunette.
brunet [bry'nɛ], *a.* (*fem.* **-ette**) brownish.—*n.f.* (**-ette**) dark woman, dark girl.
brunir [bry'ni:r], *v.t.* to make brown; to burnish.—*v.i.* to turn brown. **se brunir,** *v.r.* to turn dark *or* brown.
brunissage [bryni'sa:ʒ], *n.m.* burnishing.
brunisseur [bryni'sœ:r], *n.m.* (*fem.* **-euse**) burnisher.
brunissoir [bryni'swa:r], *n.m.* burnisher (*tool*).
brunissure [bryni'sy:r], *n.f.* burnishing; polish.
brusque [brysk], *a.* blunt, abrupt, rough; unexpected.
brusquement [bryskə'mɑ̃], *adv.* bluntly, abruptly; uncivilly.
brusquer [brys'ke], *v.t.* to be sharp with (*someone*); to offend; (*fig.*) to precipitate.
brusquerie [bryskə'ri], *n.f.* abruptness, bluntness; hastiness.
brut [bryt], *a.* rough, raw, unhewn; uncultured.—*adv.* (*Comm.*) gross (*as opposed to* net).
brutal [bry'tal], *a.* (*m.pl.* **-aux**) brutal; surly, churlish.—*n.m.* (*fem.* **-e**) brute, brutal person.
brutalement [brytal'mɑ̃], *adv.* brutally.
brutaliser [brytali'ze], *v.t.* to bully; to brutalize.
brutalité [brytali'te], *n.f.* brutality, brutishness.
brute [bryt], *n.f.* brute, brutal person; boor.
Bruxelles [bry'sɛl], *f.* Brussels.
bruyamment [bryja'mɑ̃], *adv.* noisily.
bruyère [bry'jɛ:r], *n.f.* heath, heather.
buanderie [bɥɑ̃'dri], *n.f.* wash-house, laundry.
buandier [bɥɑ̃'dje], *n.m.* (*fem.* **-ière**) bleacher; washerman, washerwoman.
bube [byb], *n.f.* pimple.
bubonique [bybɔ'nik], *a.* bubonic.
Bucarest [byka'rest], *m.* Bucharest.
buccin [byk'sɛ̃], *n.m.* (*Mus. Ant.*) long trumpet; (*Conch.*) whelk.
bûche [byʃ], *n.f.* log; (*fig.*) blockhead, dolt.
bûcher (1) [by'ʃe], *n.m.* wood-house; funeral-pile, pyre; stake.
bûcher (2) [by'ʃe], *v.t.* to rough-hew.—*v.i.* to cram, to swot.
bûcheron [byʃ'rɔ̃], *n.m.* (*fem.* **-onne**) wood-cutter.
bûchette [by'ʃɛt], *n.f.* stick of dry wood.
bucolique [bykɔ'lik], *a.* bucolic.
budget [by'dʒɛ], *n.m.* budget.
budgétaire [bydʒe'tɛ:r], *a.* budgetary.
buée [bɥe], *n.f.* steam (*on window-panes*).
buffet [by'fɛ], *n.m.* sideboard; buffet; refreshment-room.
buffetier [byf'tje], *n.m.* (*fem.* **-ière**) refreshment-room manager.
buffle [byfl], *n.m.* buffalo; buffalo hide; buff-leather.
buffleterie [byflə'tri], *n.f.* buff belts, straps etc. (*of a soldier*).
bugle [bygl], *n.m.* key-bugle.
buis [bɥi], *n.m.* box; box-tree, box-wood.
buissaie [bɥi'sɛ], **buissière** [bɥi'sjɛ:r], *n.f.* box-grove.
buisson [bɥi'sɔ̃], *n.m.* bush; thicket.
buissoner [bɥisɔ'ne], *v.i.* to grow into a bush.
buissonnet [bɥisɔ'nɛ], *n.m.* little bush.
buissonneux [bɥisɔ'nø], *a.* (*fem.* **-euse**) bushy.
buissonnier [bɥisɔ'nje], *a.* (*fem.* **-ière**) retiring into the bushes; ***faire l'école buissonnière***, to play truant; ***lapins buissonniers***, thicket-rabbits.—*n.m.* shrubbery.
bulbe [bylb], *n.m.* bulb.
bulbeux [byl'bø], *a.* (*fem.* **-euse**) bulbous.
bulgare [byl'ga:r], *a.* Bulgarian.—*n.m.* Bulgarian (*language*).—*n.* (**Bulgare**) Bulgarian (*person*).
Bulgarie [bylga'ri], **la,** *f.* Bulgaria.
bulle [byl], *n.f.* bubble; blister; a papal bull.
bullé [by'le], *a.* authenticated with a seal; by papal bull.
bulletin [byl'tɛ̃], *n.m.* bulletin, official report (*school etc.*); certificate, receipt; ballot paper; ***bulletin d'information*** news bulletin; ***bulletin météorologique***, weather forecast.
bulleux [by'lø], *a.* (*fem.* **-euse**) bubbly; blistery.
buraliste [byra'list], *n.* receiver of taxes; tobacconist.
bure [by:r], *n.f.* drugget; fustian, baize.
bureau [by'ro], *n.m.* (*pl.* **-eaux**) writing-table, desk; office; board; committee; ***Deuxième Bureau***, Intelligence Service, M.I.5.
bureaucrate [byrɔ'krat], *n.m.* (*pej.*) bureaucrat.
bureaucratie [byrɔkra'si], *n.f.* bureaucracy; (*fig.*) red tape.
bureaucratique [byrɔkra'tik], *a.* bureaucratic; formal.
burette [by'rɛt], *n.f.* cruet; oil-can; (*Chem.*) burette.
burin [by'rɛ̃], *n.m.* graver, graving-tool; (*fig.*) pen.
buriner [byri'ne], *v.t.* to engrave; to drill (*a tooth*).
burineur [byri'nœ:r], *n.m.* engraver.
burlesque [byr'lɛsk], *a.* burlesque, ludicrous.—*n.m.* burlesque.
burnous [byr'nus], *n.m.* burnous, hooded Arab cloak.
busard [by'za:r], *n.m.* buzzard.
buse (1) [by:z], *n.f.* buzzard; (*fig.*) blockhead.
buse (2) [by:z], *n.f.* channel, pipe; nozzle; (*Mining*) air-shaft.
busqué [bys'ke], *a.* aquiline (*nose*).
buste [byst], *n.m.* bust, head and shoulders.
but [by(t)], *n.m.* mark; object, end; purpose, design, goal, objective; ***de but en blanc,*** bluntly; (*Ftb.*) ***marquer un but***, to score.
buté [by'te], *a.* stubborn, (*fam.*) dead set on.
buter or **butter** (1) [by'te], *v.t.* to support, to prop.—*v.i.* to rest *or* abut (**contre**); to stumble *or* hit (**contre**). **se buter,** *v.r.* to be bent on, to stick (**à**).

butin [by'tɛ̃], *n.m.* booty, spoils, prize, plunder.
butiner [byti'ne], *v.t., v.i.* to pillage, to plunder.
butoir [by'twa:r], *n.m.* buffer, buffer-stop (*on railway*); tappet.
butor [by'tɔ:r], *n.m.* bittern; (*fig.*) churl, lout, booby.
butte [byt], *n.f.* rising ground; knoll, mound.
butter (1) [BUTER].
butter (2) [by'te], *v.t.* to earth up.
butteur [BUTTOIR].
buttoir [by'twa:r], **butteur** [by'tœ:r], *n.m.* ridging-plough.
buvable [by'vabl], *a.* drinkable, fit to drink.
buvard [by'va:r], *a.* ***papier buvard,*** blotting paper.—*n.m.* blotting-pad, blotter.
buvetier [byv'tje], *n.m.* (*fem.* **-ière**) innkeeper, publican.
buvette [by'vɛt], *n.f.* refreshment-room (*railway station*); pump-room (*at spa*).
buveur [by'vœ:r], *n.m.* (*fem.* **-euse**) drinker; toper; ***buveur d'eau,*** teetotaller.
buvoter [byvɔ'te], *v.i.* to sip, to tipple.
Byzance [bi'zɑ̃:s], *f.* Byzantium.
byzantin [bizɑ̃'tɛ̃], *a.* Byzantine.—*n.m.* (**Byzantin**, *fem.* **-ine**) Byzantine (*person*).

C

C, c [se], *n.m.* the third letter of the alphabet.
ça [sa], *pron.* [*contraction of* **cela**] that; ***comme ci comme ça,*** only so-so; ***donnez-moi ça,*** give me that.
çà [sa], *adv.* here; ***çà et là,*** here and there.—*int.* now; ***çà alors!*** well, I never!
cabale [ka'bal], *n.f.* cabal, faction.
cabaler [kaba'le], *v.i.* to cabal, to plot.
cabaleur [kaba'lœ:r], *n.m.* (*fem.* **-euse**) caballer, intriguer.
caban [ka'bɑ̃], *n.m.* hooded cloak, oilskins.
cabane [ka'ban], *n.f.* hut, shed, cabin, shanty; central part (*of an aeroplane*).
cabanon [kaba'nɔ̃], *n.m.* small hut; prison-cell; padded room.
cabaret [kaba'rɛ], *n.m.* inferior kind of wine-shop, tavern; night-club.
cabaretier [kabar'tje], *n.m.* (*fem.* **-ière**) publican, tavern-keeper.
cabas [ka'bɑ], *n.m.* flat two-handled basket.
cabeliau [CABILLAUD].
cabestan [kabɛs'tɑ̃], *n.m.* capstan, windlass.
cabillaud [kabi'jo], **cabeliau** [kab'ljo] (*pl.* **-aux**), *n.m.* fresh cod.
cabine [ka'bin], *n.f.* cabin; (*Av.*) ***cabine de pilotage,*** cockpit; ***cabine téléphonique,*** call-box.
cabinet [kabi'nɛ], *n.m.* closet, study; practice (*of a professional man*); office (*of a lawyer, barrister etc.*); (*Polit.*) Cabinet; ***cabinet d'aisances*** or ***les cabinets,*** lavatory.
câblage [kɑ'bla:ʒ], *n.m.* (*Elec.*) wiring.
câble [kɑ:bl], *n.m.* cable.
câbler [kɑ'ble], *v.t.* to twist into a cord; to telegraph by cable.
câblogramme [kɑblɔ'gram], *n.m.* cablegram.
cabochon [kabɔ'ʃɔ̃], *n.m.* fancy brass nail; (*Cycl.*) ***cabochon rouge,*** red reflector.
cabosse [ka'bɔs], *n.f.* (*pop.*) bruise, bump.
cabosser [kabɔ'se], *v.t.* to bump, to bruise; to dent.
cabotage [kabɔ'ta:ʒ], *n.m.* coasting, coasting-trade.
caboter [kabɔ'te], *v.i.* to coast.
caboteur [kabɔ'tœ:r], **cabotier** [kabɔ'tje], *n.m.* coasting-vessel; coaster.
cabotin [kabɔ'tɛ̃], *n.m.* strolling player; bad actor, mummer.
cabotiner [kabɔti'ne], *v.i.* to act badly; (*fig.*) to strut.
cabré [kɑ'bre], *a.* rearing (*of a horse*); tail-down (*of a plane*).
cabrer [kɑ'bre], *v.t.* to make (*a horse, a plane*) rear. **se cabrer**, *v.r.* to prance, to rear; (*fig.*) to revolt, to fly into a passion.
cabri [ka'bri], *n.m.* kid.
cabriole [kabri'ɔl], *n.f.* caper, leap.
cabrioler [kabriɔ'le], *v.i.* to caper, to cut capers.
cabriolet [kabriɔ'lɛ], *n.m.* cabriolet, cab.
cacahouète [kaka'wɛt], **cacahuète** [kaka'ɥɛt], *n.f.* peanut, monkey nut.
cacao [kaka'o], *n.m.* cacao, chocolate-nut.
cacaoyer [kakaɔ'je], **cacaotier** [kakaɔ'tje], *n.m.* cacao-tree.
cacaoyère [kakaɔ'jɛ:r], **cacaotière** [kakaɔ'tjɛ:r], *n.f.* cacao-plantation.
cacatois [kaka'twa], **cacatoès** [kakatɔ'ɛ:s], *n.m.* cockatoo.
cachalot [kaʃa'lo], *n.m.* sperm whale.
cachalotier [kaʃalɔ'tje], *n.m.* whaler.
cache [kaʃ], *n.f.* hiding-place.
cache-cache [kaʃ'kaʃ], *n.m.* hide-and-seek.
cachemire [kaʃ'mi:r], *n.m.* cashmere.
cache-nez [kaʃ'ne], *n.m.* muffler, comforter.
cacher [ka'ʃe], *v.t.* to hide, to conceal; to mask. **se cacher**, *v.r.* to hide, to lurk.
cache-sexe [kaʃ'sɛks], *n.m.* trunks; panties; (*colloq.*) G-string.
cachet [ka'ʃɛ], *n.m.* seal, stamp; signet-ring; ticket; tablet (*of aspirin*); (*fig.*) character, stamp, mark.
cacheter [kaʃ'te], *v.t.* (*conjug. like* APPELER) to seal.
cachette [ka'ʃɛt], *n.f.* hiding-place.
cachot [ka'ʃo], *n.m.* dungeon, prison.
cachotter [kaʃɔ'te], *v.t.* to make a mystery of, to conceal.
cachotterie [kaʃɔ'tri], *n.f.* mysterious ways; underhand work.
cachottier [kaʃɔ'tje], *a.* (*fem.* **-ière**) mysterious, sly.—*n.m.* (*fem.* **-ière**) one who makes a mystery of things.
cachou [ka'ʃu], *n.m.* cachou.
cacophonie [kakɔfɔ'ni], *n.f.* cacophony.
cacophonique [kakɔfɔ'nik], *a.* cacophonous.
cactier [kak'tje], **cactus** [kak'ty:s], *n.m.* cactus.
cadastral [kadas'tral], *a.* (*m. pl.* **-aux**) cadastral, referring to the register of lands.
cadastre [ka'dastr], *n.m.* cadastre, register of the survey of lands.
cadastrer [kadas'tre], *v.t.* to survey.
cadavéreux [kadave'rø], *a.* (*fem.* **-euse**) cadaverous, corpse-like, ghastly.
cadavérique [kadave'rik], *a.* of *or* pertaining to a corpse.

cadavre [ka'dɑːvr], *n.m.* corpse, dead body.
cadeau [ka'do], *n.m.* (*pl.* **-eaux**) present, gift.
cadenas [kad'nɑ], *n.m.* padlock; clasp.
cadenasser [kadna'se], *v.t.* to padlock; to snap, clasp.
cadence [ka'dɑ̃ːs], *n.f.* cadence, rhythm, time (*in dancing*).
cadencer [kadɑ̃'se], *v.t.* (*conjug. like* COMMENCER) to cadence, to harmonize.
cadène [ka'dɛːn], *n.f.* chain (*for convicts*); chain-gang.
cadenette [kad'nɛt], *n.f.* tress (*of hair*).
cadet [ka'dɛ], *a.* and *n.m.* (*fem.* **-ette**) younger, junior (*of two*).
Cadix [ka'diks], *f.* Cadiz.
cadmium [kad'mjɔm], *n.m.* cadmium.
cadrage [ka'draːʒ], *n.m.* (*Phot., Cine.*) centring.
cadran [ka'drɑ̃], *n.m.* dial-plate, dial; ***cadran solaire***, sun-dial.
cadre [kɑːdr], *n.m.* frame, framework; (*Mil.*) the staff; (*pl.*) the higher staff (*of an administration* or *a firm*).
cadrer [kɑ'dre], *v.t.* (*Phot., Cine.*) to centre.—*v.i.* to agree, to tally, to square (***à*** or ***avec***).
caduc [ka'dyk], *a.* (*fem.* **-uque**) decrepit, decayed; frail, tumble-down; lapsed, null, void (*of legacies*); (*Bot.*) deciduous.
caducité [kadysi'te], *n.f.* caducity, decrepitude.
cafard [ka'faːr], *a.* hypocritical, sanctimonious.—*n.m.* (*fem.* **-e**) hypocrite, sanctimonious person; humbug; (*Sch.*) sneak. *n.m.* cockroach.
cafarder [kafar'de], *v.i.* (*fam.*) to sneak, to tell tales (*at school*).
cafarderie [kafar'dri], *n.f.* cant, hypocrisy, sanctimoniousness.
café [ka'fe], *n.m.* coffee; café, coffee-house; coffee-berry.
caféière [kafe'jɛːr], *n.f.* coffee-plantation.
caféine [kafe'iːn], *n.f.* caffeine.
cafetan or **caftan** [kaf'tɑ̃], *n.m.* caftan.
cafetier [kaf'tje], *n.m.* (*fem.* **cafetière** (1)) coffee-house keeper.
cafetière (2) [kaf'tjɛːr], *n.f.* coffee-pot, percolator.
cafouillage [kafu'jaːʒ], *n.m.* floundering.
cafre [kɑːfr], *a.* and *n.* (**Cafre**) Kaffir, Bantu.
caftan [CAFETAN].
cage [kaːʒ], *n.f.* cage; coop.
cageot [ka'ʒo], *n.m.* little cage, hamper, crate.
cagibi [kaʒi'bi], *n.m.* small hut *or* room.
cagneux [ka'ɲø], *a.* (*fem.* **-euse**) knock-kneed, pigeon-toed.
cagnotte [ka'ɲɔt], *n.f.* kitty, pool, jackpot.
cagot [ka'go], *a.* (*fem.* **-otte**) bigoted, hypocritical.—*n.m.* (*fem.* **-otte**) bigot, hypocrite.
cagoterie [kagɔ'tri], *n.f.* an act *or* word of hypocrisy *or* bigotry.
cagotisme [kagɔ'tism], *n.m.* hypocrisy, bigotry.
cagoule [ka'gul], *n.f.* monk's cloak; penitent's cowl; hood.
cahier [ka'je], *n.m.* stitched paper-book; exercise-book; quarter of a quire of paper.
cahot [ka'o], *n.m.* jerk, jolt.
cahotage [kaɔ'taːʒ], **cahotement** [kaɔt'mɑ̃], *n.m.* jolting, jerking.
cahotant [kaɔ'tɑ̃], *a.* rough, jolting.
cahoter [kaɔ'te], *v.i.* to jolt, to be jerked about.
cahute [ka'yt], *n.f.* hut, hovel.
caïd [ka'id], *n.m.* Arab chief *or* judge.
caïeu or **cayeu** [ka'jø], *n.m.* (*pl.* **-eux**) (*Hort.*) offshoot of a bulb, clove.
caillage [kɑ'jaːʒ], *n.m.* curdling, congealing.
caille [kɑːj], *n.f.* quail.—(*C*) *a.* piebald.
caillé [kɑ'je], *n.m.* curdled milk, curds.—*a.* curdled.
caillebottage [kɑjbɔ'taːʒ], *n.m.* curdling.
caillebotte [kɑj'bɔt], *n.f.* curds.
caillebotter (se) [səkɑjbɔ'te], *v.r.* to curdle.
caille-lait [kɑj'lɛ], *n.m. inv.* rennet.
caillement [kɑj'mɑ̃], *n.m.* curdling, coagulating.
cailler [kɑ'je], *v.t.* to curdle, to clot. **se cailler**, *v.r.* to coagulate, to turn to curds.
cailleteau [kɑj'to], *n.m.* (*pl.* **-eaux**) young quail.
caillette (1) [kɑ'jɛt], *n.f.* rennet.
caillette (2) [kɑ'jɛt], *n.f.* (*Orn.*) petrel; flirt.
caillot [kɑ'jo], *n.m.* clot of blood, coagulum.
caillou [ka'ju], *n.m.* (*pl.* **-oux**) pebble, small stone, flint, flint-stone.
cailloutage [kaju'taːʒ], *n.m.* gravelling; ballasting; rough-cast, pebble-work.
caillouter [kaju'te], *v.t.* to gravel, to ballast.
caillouteux [kaju'tø], *a.* (*fem.* **-euse**) pebbly, flinty.
cailloutis [kaju'ti], *n.m.* broken stones, gravel; road metal.
caïman [kai'mɑ̃], *n.m.* American crocodile, cayman.
Caïn [ka'ɛ̃], *m.* Cain.
caïque or **caïc** [ka'ik], *n.m.* (*Naut.*) caique.
Caire [kɛːr], **Le**, *m.* Cairo.
caisse [kɛːs], *n.f.* chest, case, box, trunk; till; cash; cashier's office, pay desk; ***la grosse caisse***, the (big) drum; ***caisse d'épargne***, savings-bank.
caissette [kɛ'sɛt], *n.f.* small box.
caissier [kɛ'sje], *n.m.* (*fem.* **-ière**) treasurer, cashier.
caisson [kɛ'sɔ̃], *n.m.* ammunition-wagon; (*Naut.*) locker.
cajoler [kaʒɔ'le], *v.t.* to cajole, to coax.
cajolerie [kaʒɔl'ri], *n.f.* cajolery, coaxing.
cajoleur [kaʒɔ'lœːr], *n.m.* (*fem.* **-euse**) cajoler, coaxer.—*a.* cajoling, coaxing.
cal [kal], *n.m.* callosity, callus.
Calabre [ka'lɑːbr], **la**, *f.* Calabria.
calage [ka'laːʒ], *n.m.* lowering (*of sails etc.*) propping, wedging (*of furniture*).
calaison [kalɛ'zɔ̃], *n.f.* load-line, sea-gauge.
calaminage [kalami'naːʒ], *n.m.* (*Motor.*) carbonizing.
calamine [kala'min], *n.f.* carbon (*on plugs of a car etc.*).
calamité [kalami'te], *n.f.* calamity, misfortune.
calamiteusement [kalamitøz'mɑ̃], *adv.* calamitously.
calamiteux [kalami'tø], *a.* (*fem.* **-euse**) calamitous.
calandrage [kalɑ̃'draːʒ], *n.m.* calendering, hot-pressing.
calandre [ka'lɑ̃ːdr], *n.f.* mangle, calender; (*Motor.*) radiator grill.
calandrer [kalɑ̃'dre], *v.t.* to calender, to press, to smooth.
calandrette [kalɑ̃'drɛt], *n.f.* song-thrush.
calcaire [kal'kɛːr], *a.* calcareous.—*n.m.* limestone.
calcéolaire [kalseɔ'lɛːr], *n.f.* calceolaria.

calcination [kalsinɑ'sjɔ̃], *n.f.* calcination.
calciner [kalsi'ne], *v.t.* to calcine, to burn. **se calciner**, *v.r.* to calcine.
calcium [kal'sjɔm], *n.m.* calcium.
calcul [kal'kyl], *n.m.* calculation; arithmetic; reckoning, counting; (*Math.*) calculus; (*fig.*) design, selfish motive; (*Med.*) calculus (*stone*).
calculable [kalky'labl], *a.* computable, calculable.
calculateur [kalkyla'tœ:r], *a.* (*fem.* **-trice**) calculating, scheming.—*n.m.* (*fem.* **-trice**) calculator, reckoner; schemer.—*n.f.* (**-trice**) computer.
calculer [kalky'le], *v.t.* to calculate, to compute, to estimate; ***machine à calculer***, computer.
cale (1) [kal], *n.f.* hold (*of a ship*); stocks, slip; ducking, keel-hauling (*punishment*); ***cale sèche***, dry dock.
cale (2) [kal], *n.f.* wedge, block; prop, strut.
calebasse [kal'bas], *n.f.* calabash, gourd.
calèche [ka'lɛʃ], *n.f.* calash; barouche, open carriage.
caleçon [kal'sɔ̃], *n.m.* (*men's*) drawers, pants; ***caleçon de bain***, bathing-trunks.
Calédonie [kaledɔ'ni], **la**, *f.* Caledonia.
calédonien [kaledɔ'njɛ̃], *a.* (*fem.* **-enne**) Caledonian.—*n.m.* (**Calédonien**, *fem.* **-enne**) Caledonian (*person*).
caléfaction [kalefak'sjɔ̃], *n.f.* heating, calefaction.
calembour [kalɑ̃'bu:r], *n.m.* pun.
calembourdiste [kalɑ̃bur'dist], *n.m.* punster.
calembredaine [kalɑ̃brə'dɛn], *n.f.* quibble, subterfuge, nonsense.
calendes [ka'lɑ̃:d], *n.f. pl.* (*Ant.*) calends; convocation of the clergy of a diocese.
calendrier [kalɑ̃dri'e], *n.m.* calendar, almanac.
calendule [kalɑ̃'dyl], *n.f.* calendula.
cale-pied [kal'pje], *n.m.* toe clip.
calepin [kal'pɛ̃], *n.m.* notebook, memorandum-book.
caler (1) [ka'le], *v.t.* (*Naut.*) to lower, to strike; to draw, to have a draught of.
caler (2) [ka'le], *v.t.* to prop up, to wedge; to steady; to jam; (*Motor.*) to stall.—*v.i.* (*Motor.*) to stall.
calfeutrage [kalfø'tra:ʒ], **calfeutrement** [kalføtr'mɑ̃], *n.m.* stopping of chinks.
calfeutrer [kalfø'tre], *v.t.* to stop up the chinks of, to make air-tight. **se calfeutrer**, *v.r.* to shut oneself up.
calibre [ka'libr], *n.m.* calibre, bore (*of a gun*); size (*of a bullet*); (*fig.*) kind, sort.
calibrer [kali'bre], *v.t.* to calibrate; to give the proper calibre to (*bullets etc.*).
calice (1) [ka'lis], *n.m.* chalice, communion-cup; (*fig.*) grief, sacrifice.
calice (2) [ka'lis], *n.m.* (*Bot.*) calyx, flower, cup.
calicot [kali'ko], *n.m.* calico; (*slang*) counter-jumper.
calicule [kali'kyl], *n.m.* calicle, caliculus.
califat [kali'fa], *n.m.* caliphate.
calife [ka'lif], *n.m.* caliph.
Californie [kalifɔr'ni], **la**, *f.* California.
califourchon [kalifur'ʃɔ̃], *n.m.* ***à califourchon***, astride.
câlin [kɑ'lɛ̃], *a.* wheedling, winning, coaxing. —*n.m.* (*fem.* **-e**) wheedler, cajoler.
câliner [kɑ:li'ne], *v.t.* to cajole, to wheedle. **se câliner**, *v.r.* to coddle oneself, to take one's ease.
câlinerie [kɑ:lin'ri], *n.f.* wheedling, cajolery, caressing.
calleux [ka'lø], *a.* (*fem.* **-euse**) callous, horny.
calligraphe [kali'graf], *n.m.* calligrapher, good penman.
calligraphie [kaligra'fi], *n.f.* calligraphy, penmanship.
callisthénie [kaliste'ni], *n.f.* callisthenics.
callosité [kalozi'te], *n.f.* callosity.
calmant [kal'mɑ̃], *a.* calming, soothing, sedative.—*n.m.* (*Med.*) anodyne, sedative.
calme [kalm], *a.* tranquil, quiet, serene, calm; composed, dispassionate.—*n.m.* calm, stillness, quiet; composure.
calmer [kal'me], *v.t.* to calm, to still, to quiet, to allay, to soothe.—*v.i.* (*Naut.*) to lull, to become calm. **se calmer**, *v.r.* to become calm, to compose oneself; to blow over.
calomel [kalɔ'mɛl], *n.m.* calomel.
calomniateur [kalɔmnja'tœ:r], *a.* (*fem.* **-trice**) slanderous.—*n.m.* (*fem.* **-trice**) calumniator, slanderer.
calomnie [kalɔm'ni], *n.f.* calumny, slander.
calomnier [kalɔm'nje], *v.t.* to calumniate, to slander.
calomnieusement [kalɔmnjøz'mɑ̃], *adv.* calumniously, slanderously.
calomnieux [kalɔm'njø], *a.* (*fem.* **-euse**) calumnious, slanderous.
calorie [kalɔ'ri], *n.f.* calorie, unit of heat.
calorifère [kalɔri'fɛ:r], *n.m.* hot-air stove *or* pipe; central heating.—*a.* heat-conveying.
calorifique [kalɔri'fik], *a.* calorific.
calorifuger [kalɔrify'ʒe], *v.t.* (*conjug. like* MANGER) to insulate, to lag (*pipes*).
calorique [kalɔ'rik], *a.* and *n.m.* caloric, heat.
calotte [ka'lɔt], *n.f.* skull-cap (*esp. that worn by priests*); small dome; box on the ears.
calotter [kalɔ'te], *v.t.* to box the ears of.
calque [kalk], *n.m.* tracing; close copy.—*a.* ***papier calque***, tracing paper.
calquer [kal'ke], *v.t.* to trace; to copy, to imitate closely. **se calquer**, *v.r.* (***sur***) to model oneself (*on*).
calumet [kaly'mɛ], *n.m.* pipe, calumet.
calvados [kalva'dɔs], *n.m.* apple brandy, calvados.
calvaire [kal'vɛ:r], *n.m.* calvary; (*fig.*) torture, suffering, tribulation.
calvinisme [kalvi'nism], *n.m.* Calvinism.
calviniste [kalvi'nist], *a.* Calvinistic.—*n.* (**Calviniste**) Calvinist.
calvitie [kalvi'si], *n.f.* baldness.
camaïeu [kama'jø], *n.m.* (*pl.* **-eux**) cameo (*brooch etc.*).
camail [ka'ma:j], *n.m.* (*pl.* **-ails**) hood, capuchin; hackles (*of poultry*).
camarade [kama'rad], *n.* comrade, fellow, mate, chum, playmate.
camaraderie [kamara'dri], *n.f.* comradeship; intimacy.
camard [ka'ma:r], *a.* snub-nosed, flat.—*n.m.* (*fem.* **-e**) snub-nosed person.
Cambodge [kɑ̃'bɔdʒ], **le**, *m.* Cambodia.
cambodgien [kɑ̃bɔ'dʒjɛ̃], *a.* (*fem.* **-enne**) Cambodian.—*n.m.* (**Cambodgien**, *fem.* **-enne**) Cambodian (*person*).
cambouis [kɑ̃'bwi], *n.m.* dirty cart-grease, dirty lubricating oil.

cambrage [kɑ̃'bra:ʒ], *n.m.* cambering, bending.
cambrai [kɑ̃'brɛ], *n.m.* machine-made lace; cambric.
cambré [kɑ̃'bre], *a.* bent, cambered.
cambrement [kɑ̃brə'mɑ̃], *n.m.* arching, curving.
cambrer [kɑ̃'bre], *v.t.* to arch, to bend, to curve. **se cambrer**, *v.r.* to be cambered; to warp; to draw oneself up.
cambriolage [kɑ̃briɔ'la:ʒ], *n.m.* house-breaking, burglary.
cambrioler [kɑ̃briɔ'le], *v.t.* to break into (*a house*), to burgle.
cambrioleur [kɑ̃briɔ'lœ:r], *n.m.* house-breaker, burglar.
cambrure [kɑ̃'bry:r], *n.f.* bend, curvature, arch; the arched part in a shoe.
cambuse [kɑ̃'by:z], *n.f.* (*Naut.*) store-room, canteen.
came [kam], *n.f.* cam, wiper; ***arbre à cames*** cam-shaft.
camée [ka'me], *n.m.* cameo.
caméléon [kamele'ɔ̃], *n.m.* chameleon.
camélia [kame'lja], *n.m.* camellia.
camelot [kam'lo], *n.m.* camlet; cheap-jack, pedlar, hawker.
camelote [kam'lɔt], *n.f.* inferior merchandise, shoddy; (*fig.*) trash.
caméra [kame'ra], *n.f.* ciné camera.
camérier [kame'rje], *n.m.* chamberlain (*of the Pope etc.*).
Cameroun [kamə'run], **le**, *m.* Cameroon.
camion [ka'mjɔ̃], *n.m.* dray, low wagon, lorry.
camionnage [kamjɔ'na:ʒ], *n.m.* carting, carriage.
camionner [kamjɔ'ne], *v.t.* to convey on a dray, lorry, truck etc.
camionnette [kamjɔ'nɛt], *n.f.* light motor lorry; van.
camionneur [kamjɔ'nœ:r], *n.m.* drayman; vanman; haulage contractor.
camisole [kami'zɔl], *n.f.* woman's morning jacket; ***camisole de force***, strait jacket.
camomille [kamɔ'mi:j], *n.f.* camomile.
camouflage [kamu'fla:ʒ], **camouflement** [kamuflə'mɑ̃], *n.m.* disguise; camouflage.
camoufler [kamu'fle], *v.t.* to disguise; to camouflage. **se camoufler**, *v.r.* to disguise *or* camouflage oneself.
camouflet [kamu'flɛ], *n.m.* whiff of smoke (*in the face*); (*fig.*) affront, snub.
camp [kɑ̃], *n.m.* camp; (*fig.*) army; party; (*C*) country cottage.
campagnard [kɑ̃pa'ɲa:r], *a.* rustic, countrified, rural.—*n.m.* (*fem.* **-e**) countryman *or* countrywoman, peasant; clodhopper.
campagne [kɑ̃'paɲ], *n.f.* the country, the fields, plain; seat, estate, country-house; campaign; (*Naut.*) cruise.
campagnol [kɑ̃pa'ɲɔl], *n.m.* vole, field-mouse.
campanile [kɑ̃pa'nil], *n.m.* campanile, bell-tower.
campanule [kɑ̃pa'nyl], *n.f.* campanula, bell-flower, bluebell.
campé [kɑ̃'pe], *a.* established, firmly planted, well set up.
campement [kɑ̃p'mɑ̃], *n.m.* encamping; encampment; camp party, billeting party.
camper [kɑ̃'pe], *v.t.* to encamp (*troops etc.*); to place, to seat, to clap down.—*v.i.* to live in camp, to encamp. **se camper**, *v.r.* to encamp; to plant oneself.
campeur [kɑ̃'pœ:r], *n.m.* (*fem.* **-euse**) camper.
camphre [kɑ̃:fr], *n.m.* camphor.
camphré [kɑ̃'fre], *a.* camphorated.
camphrier [kɑ̃fri'e], *n.f.* camphor-tree.
camus [ka'my], *a.* flat-nosed, snub-nosed.
Canada [kana'da], **le**, *m.* Canada.
canadien [kana'djɛ̃], *a.* (*fem.* **-enne**) Canadian.—*n.m.* (**Canadien,** *fem.* **-enne**) Canadian (*person*).
canaille [ka'nɑ:j], *n.f.* rabble, riffraff, mob.
canaillerie [kanɑ:j'ri], *n.f.* blackguardism; vulgarity.
canal [ka'nal] *n.m.* (*pl.* **-aux**) canal; conduit, drain; pipe, tube, spout; water-course.
canalisation [kanalizɑ'sjɔ̃], *n.f.* canalization; mains; ***canalisation de gaz***, gas mains.
canaliser [kanali'ze], *v.t.* to canalize; to instal pipes (*for gas etc.*).
canamelle [kana'mɛl], *n.f.* sugar-cane.
canapé [kana'pe], *n.m.* sofa, couch.
canapé-lit [kanape'li], *n.m.* divan-bed.
canard [ka'na:r], *n.m.* duck; drake; (*fig.*) hoax.
canardeau [kanar'do], *n.m.* (*pl.* **-eaux**) young duck.
canarder [kanar'de], *v.t.* to shoot from behind a shelter; to snipe.—*v.i.* (*Naut.*) to pitch heavily.
canardière [kanar'djɛ:r], *n.f.* duck-pond; duck-gun.
canari [kana'ri], *n.m.* canary (*bird*).
Canaries [kana'ri], **les Îles**, *f. pl.* the Canary Islands.
canasta [kanas'ta], *n.f.* canasta.
cancan [kɑ̃'kɑ̃], *n.m.* tittle-tattle, scandal; French cancan.
cancaner [kɑ̃ka'ne], *v.i.* to tattle, to invent stories.
cancanier [kɑ̃ka'nje], *a.* (*fem.* **-ière**) addicted to gossip.—*n.m.* (*fem.* **-ière**) scandal-monger.
cancer [kɑ̃'sɛ:r], *n.m.* (*Astron., Geol., Med.*) cancer.
cancéreux [kɑ̃se'rø], *a.* (*fem.* **-euse**) cancerous.
cancre [kɑ̃:kr], *n.m.* crab; (*fig.*) dunce (*at school*).
cancrelat or **cancrelas** [kɑ̃krə'lɑ], *n.m.* cockroach.
candélabre [kɑ̃de'lɑ:br], *n.m.* candelabrum, sconce.
candeur [kɑ̃'dœ:r], *n.f.* artlessness, guilelessness, ingenuousness.
candi [kɑ̃'di], *a.m.* candied; ***fruits candis,*** crystallized fruits.—*n.m.* sugar-candy.
candidat [kɑ̃di'da], *n.m.* candidate.
candidature [kɑ̃dida'ty:r], *n.f.* candidature.
candide [kɑ̃'did], *a.* ingenuous, artless.
candidement [kɑ̃did'mɑ̃], *adv.* ingenuously.
candir [kɑ̃'di:r], *v.i.* or **se candir**, *v.r.* to candy, to crystallize.
cane [kan], *n.f.* (*female*) duck.
canebière [CANNEBIÈRE].
canepetière [kanpə'tjɛ:r], *n.f.* lesser bustard.
caneton [kan'tɔ̃], *n.m.* duckling.
canette (1) or **cannette** (1) [ka'nɛt], *n.f.* small duck, duckling; teal.
canette (2) or **cannette** (2) [ka'nɛt], *n.f.* measure for beer; spool (*inside shuttle*).
canevas [kan'vɑ], *n.m.* canvas; sail-cloth; outline sketch, rough draft.
caniche [ka'niʃ], *n.m.* poodle.

canichon [kani'ʃɔ̃], *n.m.* small poodle; duckling.
caniculaire [kaniky'lɛ:r], *a.* canicular.
canicule [kani'kyl], *n.f.* dog-days; (*Astron.*) dog-star.
canif [ka'nif], *n.m.* penknife.
canin [ka'nɛ̃], *a.* canine.—*n.f.* (*dent*) *canine*, canine (tooth).
canitie [kani'si], *n.f.* whiteness of the hair.
caniveau [kani'vo], *n.m.* (*pl.* **-eaux**) (*Arch.*) channel-stone, gutter.
cannage [ka'na:ʒ], *n.m.* cane-work (*in chairs etc.*).
cannaie [ka'nɛ], *n.f.* cane-plantation, cane-field.
canne [kan], *n.f.* cane, reed; walking-stick; glass-blower's pipe.
canneberge [kan'bɛrʒ], *n.f.* cranberry.
cannebière or **canebière** [kan'bjɛ:r], *n.f.* (*S.-E. France*) [CHÈNEVIÈRE].
cannelé [kan'le], *a.* fluted (*column*); grooved (*tyre*).—*n.m.* ribbed silk.
canneler [kan'le], *v.t.* (*conjug. like* APPELER) to flute, to channel, to groove.
cannelier [kanə'lje], *n.m.* cinnamon-tree.
cannelle (1) [ka'nɛl], *n.f.* cinnamon bark, cinnamon.
cannelle (2) [ka'nɛl], **cannette** (3) [ka'nɛt], *n.f.* spigot, tap.
cannelure [kan'ly:r], *n.f.* fluting, channelling.
cannette (1) [CANETTE (1)].
cannette (2) [CANETTE (2)].
cannette (3) [CANNELLE (2)].
cannibale [kani'bal], *n.m.* cannibal.
cannibalisme [kaniba'lism], *n.m.* cannibalism; (*fig.*) ferocity.
canon (1) [ka'nɔ̃], *n.m.* cannon, gun; barrel (*of a gun*); cylinder, pipe, tube (*of lock*).
canon (2) [ka'nɔ̃], *n.m.* (*Eccles.*) canon; (*Mus.*) round, canon.
cañon [ka'ɲɔ̃], *n.m.* canyon.
canonial [kanɔ'njal], *a.* (*m.pl.* **-aux**) canonical.
canonicat [kanɔni'ka], *n.m.* canonry; (*fig.*) sinecure.
canonicité [kanɔnisi'te], *n.f.* canonicity.
canonique [kanɔ'nik], *a.* canonical.
canonisation [kanɔnizɑ'sjɔ̃], *n.f.* canonization.
canoniser [kanɔni'ze], *v.t.* to canonize.
canonnade [kanɔ'nad], *n.f.* cannonading, cannonade.
canonner [kanɔ'ne], *v.t.* to attack with heavy artillery, to cannonade.
canonnier [kanɔ'nje], *n.m.* gunner.
canonnière [kanɔ'njɛ:r], *n.f.* pop-gun; gunboat.
canot [ka'no], *n.m.* small open boat, dinghy; (*C*) Canadian canoe; ***canot automobile***, motor-boat; ***canot de sauvetage***, lifeboat.
canotage [kanɔ'ta:ʒ], *n.m.* boating, rowing.
cantate [kɑ̃'tat], *n.f.* (*Mus.*) cantata.
cantatrice [kɑ̃ta'tris], *n.f.* cantatrice, (*classical*) singer.
cantharide [kɑ̃ta'rid], *n.f.* (*Ent.*) cantharis, Spanish fly.
cantilène [kɑ̃ti'lɛ:n], *n.f.* cantilena, ballad, popular song.
cantine [kɑ̃'tin], *n.f.* canteen; kit-case.
cantique [kɑ̃'tik], *n.m.* canticle, hymn.
canton [kɑ̃'tɔ̃], *n.m.* canton (*district*); (*C*) township.
cantonade [kɑ̃tɔ'nad], *n.f.* (*Theat.*) either of the wings; ***parler à la cantonade***, to speak to an actor off the stage.
cantonnement [kɑ̃tɔn'mɑ̃], *n.m.* (*Mil.*) cantonment, billet, quarters.
cantonner [kɑ̃tɔ'ne], *v.t.* (*Mil.*) to billet (*troops*). **se cantonner**, *v.r.* to take up a position, quarters *or* abode; to fortify oneself.
cantonnier [kɑ̃tɔ'nje], *n.m.* roadman; (*Rail.*) platelayer.
cantonnière [kɑ̃tɔ'njɛ:r], *n.f.* valance.
canule [ka'nyl], *n.f.* clyster-pipe, injection-tube, douche-tube.
caoutchouc [kau'tʃu], *n.m.* (India-)rubber; mackintosh; (*pl.*) galoshes.
cap [kap], *n.m.* head; bow (*of a ship*); cape, headland, promontory.
capable [ka'pabl], *a.* able, fit, capable; apt; competent.
capacité [kapasi'te], *n.f.* extent, size; ability.
caparaçon [kapara'sɔ̃], *n.m.* caparison, trappings.
caparaçonner [kaparasɔ'ne], *v.t.* to caparison (*a horse*).
cape [kap], *n.f.* cape, mantle *or* cloak with a hood.
capharnaüm [kafarna'ɔm], *n.m.* lumber-room, glory-hole.
capillaire [kapi'lɛ:r], *a.* capillary.—*n.m.* capillary; maiden-hair.
capilotade [kapilɔ'tad], *n.f.* hash, ragoût; (*fig.*) thrashing.
capitaine [kapi'tɛn], *n.m.* captain; (*fig.*) eminent commander.
capital [kapi'tal], *a.* (*m.pl.* **-aux**) capital, main, chief, principal.—*n.m.* capital, principal; property, stock.
capitale [kapi'tal], *n.f.* capital, chief city; capital letter.
capitaliser [kapitali'ze], *v.t.* to put at compound interest; to add to the capital; to realize, to capitalize.—*v.i.* to save, to lay by.
capitaliste [kapita'list], *n.* capitalist, moneyed man *or* woman.
capitan [kapi'tɑ̃], *n.m.* braggadocio, swaggerer.
capitation [kapitɑ'sjɔ̃], *n.f.* capitation, poll-tax.
capiteux [kapi'tø], *a.* (*fem.* **-euse**) heady, strong.
Capitole [kapi'tɔl], *n.m.* Capitol (*of Rome etc.*).
capitonner [kapitɔ'ne], *v.t.* to stuff, to pad.
capitulaire [kapity'lɛ:r], *a.* and *n.m.* capitulary.
capitulation [kapitylɑ'sjɔ̃], *n.f.* capitulation; compromise.
capituler [kapity'le], *v.i.* to capitulate; to compound, to compromise.
capoc [ka'pɔk], *n.m.* kapok.
capon [ka'pɔ̃], *a.* (*fem.* **-onne**) cowardly.—*n.m.* (*fem.* **-onne**) mean fellow, sneak; coward.
caponner [kapɔ'ne], *v.i.* to cheat; to be cowardly; to rat.
caporal [kapɔ'ral], *n.m.* (*pl.* **-aux**) corporal; sort of 'shag' (*tobacco*).
capot (1) [ka'po], *n.m.* (*Motor.*) bonnet, (*Am.*) hood.
capot (2) [ka'po], *a. inv.* capot (*at piquet etc.*); flabbergasted.
capote [ka'pɔt], *n.f.* capote, large cloak with a hood; (*soldier's*) great-coat; baby's bonnet.

capoter [kapɔ'te], *v.i.* (*Naut. etc.*) to capsize; to turn turtle.
câpre [kɑːpr], *n.f.* (*Bot.*) caper.
caprice [ka'pris], *n.m.* caprice, whim, humour; flight, sally.
capricieusement [kaprisjøz'mɑ̃], *adv.* capriciously, whimsically.
capricieux [kapri'sjø], *a.* (*fem.* **-euse**) capricious, whimsical, fickle.
capricorne [kapri'kɔrn], *n.m.* (*Astron.*) Capricorn.
capsule [kap'syl], *n.f.* capsule; pod; percussion-cap (*of firearms*).
captation [kaptɑ'sjɔ̃], *n.f.* captation, inveigling; intercepting.
captatoire [kapta'twaːr], *a.* inveigling.
capter [kap'te], *v.t.* to obtain by underhand methods; to win by bribery etc.
captieusement [kapsjøz'mɑ̃], *adv.* insidiously, cunningly, deceitfully.
captieux [kap'sjø], *a.* (*fem.* **-euse**) insidious, cunning, specious.
captif [kap'tif], *a.* and *n.m.* (*fem.* **-tive**) captive.
captivant [kapti'vɑ̃], *a.* captivating; enthralling.
captiver [kapti've], *v.t.* to captivate, to charm.
captivité [kaptivi'te], *n.f.* captivity, bondage.
capture [kap'tyːr], *n.f.* capture, prize, booty.
capturer [kapty're], *v.t.* to capture; to arrest.
capuchon [kapy'ʃɔ̃], *n.m.* hood, cowl.
capuchonné [kapyʃɔ'ne], *a.* cowled; hooded.
capucin [kapy'sɛ̃], *n.m.* (*fem.* **capucine (1)** [kapy'sin]) Capuchin friar *or* nun.
capucine (1) [CAPUCIN].
capucine (2) [kapy'sin], *n.f.* nasturtium.
caque [kak], *n.f.* keg, barrel.
caquet [ka'kɛ], *n.m.* cackle (*of geese etc.*); tittle-tattle, gossip, scandal.
caquetage [kak'taːʒ], *n.m.*, **caqueterie** [kak(ə)'tri], *n.f.* babbling, prattling; tattling, gossiping.
caqueter [kak'te], *v.i.* (*conjug. like* APPELER) to cackle, to chatter; to gossip.
car (1) [kaːr], *conj.* for, because.
car (2) [kaːr], *n.m.* (*fam.*) coach, long-distance bus.
carabin [kara'bɛ̃], *n.m.* (*colloq.*) saw-bones, medical student.
carabine [kara'bin], *n.f.* carbine, rifle.
carabiné [karabi'ne], *a.* rifled; (*colloq.*) strong, violent.
carabiner [karabi'ne], *v.t.* to rifle (*a gun-barrel*).
carabinier [karabi'nje], *n.m.* carabinier, rifleman.
caractère [karak'tɛːr], *n.m.* character, letter; hand-writing; nature, disposition; temper, spirit; stamp; quality.
caractériser [karakteri'ze], *v.t.* to characterize, to describe.
caractéristique [karakteris'tik], *a.* and *n.f.* characteristic.
carafe [ka'raf], *n.f.* carafe, decanter, water-bottle.
carafon [kara'fɔ̃], *n.m.* small carafe *or* decanter.
Caraïbes [kara'ib], **les**, *f.pl.* the Caribbean Isles.
carambolage [karɑ̃bɔ'laːʒ], *n.m.* (*Billiards*) cannon; (*pop.*) affray, shindy; (*fig.*) rebound (*against*).
caramboler [karɑ̃bɔ'le], *v.i.* (*Billiards*) to cannon.
caramel [kara'mɛl], *n.m.* caramel.
carapace [kara'pas], *n.f.* (*Zool.*) carapace, shell.
carat [ka'ra], *n.m.* (*Gold*) carat.
caravane [kara'van], *n.f.* caravan, convoy; caravan (*on wheels*).
carbonate [karbɔ'nat], *n.m.* (*Chem.*) carbonate.
carbone [kar'bɔn], *n.m.* carbon.
carboné [karbɔ'ne], *a.* carbonated, carbonized.
carbonique [karbɔ'nik], *a.* carbonic.
carboniser [karbɔni'ze], *v.t.* to carbonize.
carburant [karby'rɑ̃], *a.* and *n.m.* motor-fuel.
carburateur [karbyra'tœːr], *n.m.* carburettor.
carbure [kar'byːr], *n.m.* (*Chem.*) carbide.
carburé [karby're], *a.* carburetted.
carcasse [kar'kas], *n.f.* carcass, skeleton.
cardage [kar'daːʒ], *n.m.* carding.
cardan [kar'dɑ̃], *n.m.* (*Mech.*) universal joint.
carde [kard], *n.f.* (*Bot.*) cardoon.
carder [kar'de], *v.t.* to card, to comb.
cardialgie [kardjal'ʒi], *n.f.* cardialgy, heart-burn.
cardiaque [kar'djak], *a.* and *n.* cardiac (case).
cardinal [kardi'nal], *a.* (*m. pl.* **-aux**) cardinal, chief, principal.—*n.m.* (*pl.* **-aux**) (*Eccles.*) cardinal.
cardinalat [kardina'la], *n.m.* cardinalate, cardinalship.
cardiogramme [kardiɔ'gram], *n.m.* cardiogram.
cardiographe [kardiɔ'graf], *n.m.* cardiograph.
cardon [kar'dɔ̃], *n.m.* (*Bot.*) cardoon.
carême [ka'rɛːm], *n.m.* Lent; Lent-sermons.
carénage [kare'naːʒ], *n.m.* careening.
carence [ka'rɑ̃ːs], *n.f.* (*Law*) insolvency.
carène [ka'rɛːn], *n.f.* (*Naut.*) bottom (*keel and sides up to water-mark*).
caréné [kare'ne], *a.* (*Bot.*) carinate; keeled; (*Motor.*) stream-lined.
caréner [kare'ne], *v.t.* (*conjug. like* CÉDER) to careen; to stream-line.
caressant [karɛ'sɑ̃], *a.* caressing, endearing; tender.
caresse [ka'rɛs], *n.f.* caress, endearment.
caresser [karɛ'se], *v.t.* to caress, to fondle, to stroke.
caret (1) [ka'rɛ], *n.m.* rope-maker's reel.
caret (2) [ka'rɛ], *n.m.* turtle.
cargaison [kargɛ'zɔ̃], *n.f.* cargo, freight.
cargo [kar'go], *n.m.* (*Naut.*) tramp, cargo-boat.
carguer [kar'ge], *v.t.* to reef (*sails*).
cargueur [kar'gœːr], *n.m.* (*Naut.*) reefer.
cari [ka'ri], *n.m.* curry-powder.
cariatide [karja'tid], *n.f.* caryatid.
caribou [kari'bu], *n.m.* cariboo.
caricature [karika'tyːr], *n.f.* caricature; (*fam.*) fright (*person*).
caricaturer [karikaty're], *v.t.* to caricature.
caricaturiste [karikaty'rist], *n.* caricaturist.
carie [ka'ri], *n.f.* (*Path.*) caries, decay; (*Bot.*) brown rust; rot (*of timber*).
carier [ka'rje], *v.t.* to make carious, to rot.
carillon [kari'jɔ̃], *n.m.* carillon; chime, peal.
carillonnement [karijɔn'mɑ̃], *n.m.* chiming, jingling.

carillonner [karijɔ'ne], *v.i.* to chime; to ring the changes; to jingle.
carillonneur [karijɔ'nœ:r], *n.m.* bell-ringer.
carlin [kar'lɛ̃], *a.* pug; turned-up (*nose*).
carlingue [kar'lɛ̃:g], *n.f.* (*Av.*) cockpit.
carmagnole [karma'ɲɔl], *n.f.* Piedmontese jacket; carmagnole.
carme [karm], *n.m.* Carmelite friar, White friar.
carmélite [karme'lit], *n.f.* Carmelite nun.—*a.* light brown.
carmin [kar'mɛ̃], *a.* and *n.m.* carmine.
carnage [kar'na:ʒ], *n.m.* carnage, slaughter.
carnassier [karna'sje], *a.* (*fem.* **-ière**) carnivorous, flesh-eating.—*n.m.* feline animal; flesh-eater.—*n.f.* (**-ière**) game-bag.
carnation [karnɑ'sjɔ̃], *n.f.* complexion; flesh-colour.
carnaval [karna'val], *n.m.* carnival; masquerade, festival; guy.
carné [kar'ne], *a.* flesh-coloured; composed of meat.
carnet [kar'nɛ], *n.m.* notebook, log-book.
carnier [kar'nje], *n.m.* game-bag.
carnivore [karni'vɔ:r], *a.* carnivorous.—*n.* carnivore.
carogne [ka'rɔɲ], *n.f.* hag, jade, impudent slut.
carotide [karɔ'tid], *a.* and *n.f.* carotid.
carotte [ka'rɔt], *n.f.* carrot; (*slang*) fake, ruse, hoax; sign outside a tobacconist's shop.—*a.* (*inv.*) ginger (*hair*).
carotter [karɔ'te], *v.t.* to cheat, to diddle.
carotteur [karɔ'tœ:r], **carottier** [karɔ'tje], *n.m.* (*fem.* **-euse**, **-ière**) cheat, trickster; wangler.
carpe (1) [karp], *n.f.* (*Ichth.*) carp.
carpe (2) [karp], *n.m.* (*Anat.*) wrist.
carquois [kar'kwa], *n.m.* quiver.
carrare [ka'ra:r], *n.m.* Carrara marble.
carré [ka're], *a.* square; well-set; plain, straightforward.—*n.m.* square; landing, floor; (*Hort.*) plot.
carreau [ka'ro], *n.m.* (*pl.* **-eaux**) small square; square tile *or* brick, small flag-stone; pane (*of glass*); diamond (*at cards*).
carrefour [kar'fu:r], *n.m.* cross-roads.
carrelage [kar'la:ʒ], *n.m.* tile-flooring, paving-squares.
carreler [kar'le], *v.t.* (*conjug. like* APPELER) to pave (*a floor*) with square tiles, bricks, stones etc.; to cobble (*shoes etc.*).
carrelet [kar'lɛ], *n.m.* plaice.
carrelette [kar'lɛt], *n.f.* flat file.
carreleur [kar'lœ:r], *n.m.* floor-tiler.
carrément [kare'mɑ̃], *adv.* squarely; (*fig.*) bluntly, plainly.
carrer [ka're], *v.t.* to square. **se carrer**, *v.r.* to strut, to pose.
carrier [ka'rje], *n.m.* quarryman.
carrière (1) [ka'rjɛ:r], *n.f.* career, course; scope, play, vent; profession, vocation; ***la Carrière***, the diplomatic service.
carrière (2) [ka'rjɛ:r], *n.f.* quarry.
carriole [ka'rjɔl], *n.f.* light covered cart.
carrossable [karɔ'sabl], *a.* practicable for vehicles (*of roads*).
carrosse [ka'rɔs], *n.m.* state-coach, four-wheeled carriage.
carrosserie [karɔ'sri], *n.f.* coach-building; body (*of motors*).
carrossier [karɔ'sje], *n.m.* coach-maker carriage-builder.
carrousel [karu'zɛl], *n.m.* merry-go-round, roundabout; tournament.
carrure [ka'ry:r], *n.f.* breadth of shoulders.
cartable [kar'tabl], *n.m.* school-satchel.
carte [kart], *n.f.* pasteboard; card, playing-card, postcard; ticket; bill of fare; map, chart; ***avoir carte blanche***, to have full power; ***carte d'abonnement***, season ticket; ***carte d'alimentation***, ration card, ration book; ***un jeu de cartes***, a pack of cards.
cartel [kar'tɛl], *n.m.* challenge; cartel; dial-case; wall clock; frieze-panel.
carte-lettre [kartə'lɛtr], *n.f.* (*pl.* **cartes-lettres**) letter-card.
carter [kar'tɛr], *n.m.* gear-case (*of bicycle*); crank-case (*of car*).
cartésianisme [kartezja'nism], *n.m.* Cartesian philosophy.
cartésien [karte'zjɛ̃], *a.* and *n.m.* (*fem.* **-ienne**) Cartesian.
cartilage [karti'la:ʒ], *n.m.* cartilage, gristle.
cartilagineux [kartilaʒi'nø], *a.* (*fem.* **-euse**) cartilaginous, gristly.
cartographe [kartɔ'graf], *n.m.* cartographer.
cartographie [kartɔgra'fi], *n.f.* cartography.
carton [kar'tɔ̃], *n.m.* cardboard, pasteboard; cardboard box, hat-box; (*Paint.*) cartoon; (*Phot.*) mount.
cartonnage [kartɔ'na:ʒ], *n.m.* (*Bookb.*) boarding.
cartonneur [kartɔ'nœ:r], *n.m.* (*fem.* **-euse**) binder (*of books*).
carton-pâte [kartɔ̃'pɑ:t], *n.m.* millboard; papier mâché.
carton-pierre [kartɔ̃'pjɛ:r], *n.m.* pasteboard for making ornaments.
cartothèque [kartɔ'tɛk], *n.f.* card-index.
cartouche (1) [kar'tuʃ], *n.m.* escutcheon, scroll.
cartouche (2) [kar'tuʃ], *n.f.* cartridge.
cartouchier [kartu'ʃje], *n.m.*, **cartouchière** [kartu'ʃjɛ:r], *n.f.* cartridge-pouch *or* box.
cas [kɑ], *n.m.* case; instance, circumstance, state of things, conjuncture; (*Law*) cause; ***c'est le cas ou jamais***, it is now or never; ***en tout cas***, at all events.
casanier [kaza'nje], *a.* (*fem.* **-ière**) domestic stay-at-home, home-loving.
cascade [kas'kad], *n.f.* cascade, waterfall.
case [kɑ:z], *n.f.* cabin, hut, small house; division, compartment; box (*for animals*); pigeon-hole; square (*of chess* or *draught-board*); (*Naut.*) berth.
casemate [kaz'mat], *n.f.* (*Fort.*) casemate.
caser [kɑ'ze], *v.t.* to put in order, to file (*documents*), (*fam.*) to provide for; to marry off.—*v.i.* (*backgammon*) to make a point. **se caser**, *v.r.* to take up one's abode, to settle.
caserne [ka'zɛrn], *n.f.* barracks.
caserner [kazɛr'ne], *v.t.* to quarter in barracks.—*v.i.* to be in barracks.
casier [kɑ'zje], *n.m.* rack, card- *or* music-stand, set of pigeon-holes; ***casier judiciaire***, police record.
casilleux [kazi'jø], *a.* (*fem.* **-euse**) brittle.
casino [kazi'no], *n.m.* casino, club.
casque [kask], *n.m.* helmet, head-piece; (*Nat. Hist.*) crest; head-phone (*wireless*).

casquette [kas'kɛt], *n.f.* cap.

cassable [kɑ'sabl], *a.* breakable.

cassage [kɑ'saːʒ], *n.m.* breakage.

cassant [kɑ'sɑ̃], *a.* brittle; crisp; breakable; (*fig.*) abrupt, gruff.

cassation [kasɑ'sjɔ̃], *n.f.* (*Law*) cassation, annulment, repeal; ***cour de cassation***, the highest court of appeal in France.

casse (1) [kɑːs], *n.f.* breakage(s); damage, losses.

casse (2) [kɑːs], *n.f.* (*Print.*) case; ***bas de casse***, lower case.

casse-cou [kɑs'ku], *n.m. inv.* death-trap; rough-rider; dare-devil.

casse-croûte [kɑs'krut], *n.m. inv.* quick meal, snack.

casse-noisette [kɑsnwɑ'zɛt], *n.m.* (*pl.* **casse-noisettes**) nutcracker; (*Orn.*) nuthatch.

casse-noix [kɑs'nwɑ], *n.m. inv.* nutcrackers.

casse-pipes [kɑs'pip], *n.m. inv.* shooting-gallery; (*pop.*) war.

casser [kɑ'se], *v.t.* to break, to smash; to cashier (*an officer*), to reduce to the ranks; to dissolve (*Parliament etc.*); to annul, to rescind. **se casser**, *v.r.* to break, to snap; to break down.

casserole [kas'rɔl], *n.f.* saucepan, stewpan.

casse-tête [kɑs'tɛːt], *n.m. inv.* life-preserver; (*fig.*) din; conundrum.

cassette [ka'sɛt], *n.f.* casket; cash-box.

casseur [kɑ'sœːr], *n.m.* (*fem.* **-euse**) breaker, smasher.

cassis [ka'sis], *n.m.* black currant.

casson [kɑ'sɔ̃], *n.m.* piece of broken glass *or* pottery; rough lump (*of sugar*).

cassonade [kasɔ'nad], *n.f.* moist brown sugar.

cassoulet [kasu'lɛ], *n.m.* stew of beans with mutton and pork.

cassure [kɑ'syːr], *n.f.* break, crack, fracture; broken piece.

castagnette [kasta'ɲɛt], *n.f.* castanet.

caste [kast], *n.f.* caste.

castillan [kasti'jɑ̃], *a.* Castilian.—*n.m.* Castilian (*speech*); (**Castillan**, *fem.* **-ane**) Castilian (*person*).

castine [kas'tin], *n.f.* (*Metal.*) flux.

castor [kas'tɔːr], *n.m.* beaver.

casuel [ka'zɥɛl], *a.* (*fem.* **-uelle**) casual, fortuitous, accidental.—*n.m.* perquisites, fees.

casuiste [ka'zɥist], *n.m.* casuist.

cataclysme [kata'klism], *n.m.* cataclysm; (*fig.*) disaster.

catacombes [kata'kɔ̃ːb], *n.f. pl.* catacombs.

catafalque [kata'falk], *n.m.* catafalque.

cataire [ka'tɛːr], *n.f.* (*Bot.*) catmint.

catalan [kata'lɑ̃], *a.* Catalan.—*n.m.* Catalan (*language*); (**Catalan**, *fem.* **-ane**) Catalan (*person*).

catalepsie [katalɛp'si], *n.f.* catalepsy.

catalogue [kata'lɔg], *n.m.* list, catalogue.

cataloguer [katalɔ'ge], *v.t.* to catalogue.

catalyse [kata'liːz], *n.f.* (*Chem.*) catalysis.

catalyseur [katali'zœːr], *n.m.* catalyst.

catalytique [katali'tik], *a.* catalytic.

cataphote [kata'fɔt], *n.m.* cat's eye (*reflector*).

cataplasme [kata'plasm], *n.m.* cataplasm, poultice.

cataracte [kata'rakt], *n.f.* cataract, waterfall; (*Path.*) cataract.

catarrhal [kata'ral], *a.* (*m.pl.* **-aux**) catarrhal.

catarrhe [ka'taːr], *n.m.* catarrh.

catastrophe [katas'trɔf], *n.f.* catastrophe, calamity.

catastrophique [katastrɔ'fik], *a.* catastrophic.

catéchiser [kateʃi'ze], *v.t.* to catechize; (*fig.*) to reason with; to lecture.

catéchisme [kate'ʃism], *n.m.* catechism.

catégorie [kategɔ'ri], *n.f.* category.

catégorique [kategɔ'rik], *a.* categorical, explicit.

catégoriquement [kategɔrik'mɑ̃], *adv.* categorically.

catharsis [katar'sis], *n.f.* (*Med.*) catharsis.

cathédral [kate'dral], *a.* (*m.pl.* **-aux**) cathedral.

cathédrale [kate'dral], *n.f.* cathedral.

cathode [ka'tɔd], *n.f.* cathode.

cathodique [katɔ'dik], *a.* cathode.

catholicisme [katɔli'sism], *n.m.* Catholicism.

catholique [katɔ'lik], *a.* catholic; moral, orthodox.—*n.* Catholic (*person*).

cati [ka'ti], *n.m.* gloss, lustre.

catir [ka'tiːr], *v.t.* to give a gloss to.

catissage [kati'saːʒ], *n.m.* glossing, pressing.

catisseur [kati'sœːr], *a.* and *n.m.* (*fem.* **-euse**) presser.

Caucase [ko'kɑːz], **le**, *m.* the Caucasus.

caucasien [kokɑ'zjɛ̃], *a.* (*fem.* **-enne**) Caucasian.—*n.m.* (**Caucasien**, *fem.* **-enne**) Caucasian (*person*).

cauchemar [kɔʃ'maːr], *n.m.* nightmare.

caudataire [koda'tɛːr], *n.m.* train-bearer.

cauri, cauris or **coris** [ko'ri], *n.m.* cowrie.

causal [ko'zal], *a.* causal.

causant [ko'zɑ̃], *a.* chatty, talkative.

causatif [koza'tif], *a.* (*fem.* **-tive**) (*Gram.*) causative, causal.

cause [koːz], *n.f.* cause; grounds, motive; interest; case, trial, suit, action; ***à cause de***, because of; ***mettre en cause***, to sue.

causer (1) [ko'ze], *v.t.* to cause, to be the cause of.

causer (2) [ko'ze], *v.i.* to chat, to talk; to prate.

causerie [ko'zri], *n.f.* talk, chat, gossip; chatty essay, review etc.

causette [ko'zɛt], *n.f.* chit-chat, small talk.

causeur [ko'zœːr], *a.* (*fem.* **-euse**) talkative, chatty.—*n.m.* (*fem.* **-euse**) talker.—*n.f.* (**-euse**) small sofa, settee for two.

causticité [kostisi'te], *n.f.* causticity.

caustique [kos'tik], *a.* caustic, biting, cutting. —*n.m.* caustic.

caustiquement [kostik'mɑ̃], *adv.* caustically.

cauteleusement [kotløz'mɑ̃], *adv.* craftily, slyly.

cauteleux [kot'lø], *a.* (*fem.* **-euse**) cunning, crafty.

cautère [ko'tɛːr], *n.m.* (*Med.*) cautery; issue.

cautérisation [koterizɑ'sjɔ̃], *n.f.* cauterization.

cautériser [koteri'ze], *v.t.* to cauterize.

caution [ko'sjɔ̃], *n.f.* security, bail, surety; (*fig.*) pledge, guarantee; ***verser une caution***, to pay a deposit.

cautionnement [kosjɔn'mɑ̃], *n.m.* bail; security.

cautionner [kosjɔ'ne], *v.t.* to stand bail for someone.

cavage [ka'vaːʒ], *n.m.* cellarage.

cavalcade [kaval'kad], *n.f.* procession; cavalcade.

cavale [ka'val], *n.f.* mare.

cavalerie [kaval'ri], *n.f.* cavalry.

cavalier [kava'lje], *n.m.* horseman, rider, trooper; (*Dancing*) partner; (*C*) lover, sweetheart; (*Chess*) knight.—*a.* (*fem.* **-ière**) cavalier, unceremonious (*of manners etc.*); off-hand, flippant.
cavalièrement [kavaljɛr'mɑ̃], *adv.* cavalierly, bluntly.
cave (1) [kaːv], *a.* hollow.
cave (2) [kaːv], *n.f.* (*wine*) cellar, vault; cellarage.
caveau [ka'vo], *n.m.* (*pl.* **-eaux**) small cellar; burial vault.
caver [ka've], *v.t.* to hollow, to scoop out, to dig under; (*fig.*) to undermine; (*Fenc.*) to lunge. **se caver**, *v.r.* to become hollow *or* sunken.
caverne [ka'vɛrn], *n.f.* cavern, cave, hollow; (*fig.*) retreat, lair.
caverneux [kavɛr'nø], *a.* (*fem.* **-euse**) cavernous, hollow.
caviar [ka'vjaːr], *n.m.* caviare.
cavillation [kavilɑ'sjɔ̃], *n.f.* sophistry, cavil.
cavité [kavi'te], *n.f.* cavity, hollow.
ce (1) [sə], *dem. a.* (*before vowels* **cet**, *fem.* **cette**, *pl.* **ces**) this, that, (*pl.*) these, those.
ce (2) [sə], *dem. pron. inv.* it, that (*sometimes* = he, she, *or*, *with plural verb*, they); ***c'en est fait***, it is all over, it is done; ***c'est-à-dire***, that is to say; ***c'est que***, the fact is that; ***pour ce qui est de . . .***, as for . . . .
***céans** [se'ɑ̃], *adv.* within, here within, in this house, at home.
ceci [sə'si], *dem. pron.* this, this thing.
cécité [sesi'te], *n.f.* blindness.
cédant [se'dɑ̃], *a.* that grants; (*Law*) that assigns, transfers.—*n.m.* (*fem.* **-e**) (*Law*) grantor, assignor, transferrer.
céder [se'de], *v.t.* (*see Verb Tables*) to give up, to yield, to surrender, to cede; to transfer, to make over.—*v.i.* to give way; to submit.
cédille [se'diːj], *n.f.* cedilla.
cédrat [se'dra], *n.m.* citron-tree; citron.
cèdre [sɛːdr], *n.m.* cedar.
cédule [se'dyl], *n.f.* schedule, memorandum; notice; (*Law*) notification.
cégétiste [seʒe'tist], *n.m.* a member of the C.G.T. (Confédération Générale du Travail.)
ceindre [sɛ̃ːdr], *v.t. irr.* (*conjug. like* CRAINDRE) to gird, to encircle, to encompass, to surround; to bind *or* gird on. **se ceindre**, *v.r.* to bind round one, to put on (*a scarf etc.*).
ceinture [sɛ̃'tyːr], *n.f.* sash, girdle, belt, waist-band; waist; enclosure, circle; ***ceinture de sauvetage***, life-belt.
ceinturer [sɛ̃ty're], *v.t.* to girdle, to surround.
ceinturon [sɛ̃ty'rɔ̃], *n.m.* belt, sword-belt.
cela [sə'la, sla], *dem. pron.* that, that thing (*in opposition to this*, *of which we are speaking*); ***c'est cela***, that's it. *In popular speech* **cela** *becomes* **ça**; ***pas de ça***, none of that; ***comme ci comme ça***, middling.
céladon [sela'dɔ̃], *a.* and *n.m.* sea-green (*colour*).
célébrant [sele'brɑ̃], *n.m.* celebrant.
célébration [selebrɑ'sjɔ̃], *n.f.* solemn performance, celebration.
célèbre [se'lɛbr], *a.* celebrated, famous, renowned.
célébrer [sele'bre], *v.t.* (*conjug. like* CÉDER) to celebrate, to praise, to extol; to solemnize.
célébrité [selebri'te], *n.f.* celebrity.
***celer** [sə'le], *v.t.* (*conjug. like* AMENER) to conceal, to keep secret. ***se celer**, *v.r.* to conceal oneself, to hide.
céleri [sel'ri], *n.m.* celery; ***un pied de céleri***, a stick of celery.
célerin [sel'rɛ̃], *n.m.* (*Ichth.*) pilchard.
célérité [seleri'te], *n.f.* celerity, rapidity.
céleste [se'lɛst], *a.* celestial, heavenly, divine.
célibat [seli'ba], *n.m.* celibacy, single life.
célibataire [seliba'tɛːr], *a.* single.—*n.m.* bachelor.—*n.f.* spinster.
celle [sɛl], [CELUI].
cellérier [sɛle'rje], *n.m.* (*fem.* **-ière**) cellarer.
cellier [sɛ'lje], *n.m.* cellar, store-room.
cellophane [sɛlɔ'fan], *n.f.* cellophane.
cellulaire [sɛly'lɛːr], *a.* cellular.
cellule [sɛ'lyl], *n.f.* cell; ***cellule photoélectrique***, electric eye.
celluleux [sɛly'lø], *a.* (*fem.* **-euse**) cellular.
celluloïd or **celluloïde** [sɛlylo'id], *n.m.* celluloid.
cellulose [sɛly'loːz], *n.f.* cellulose.
Celte [sɛlt], *n.* Celt.
celtique [sɛl'tik], *a.* Celtic.—*n.m.* Celtic (*language*).
celui [sə'lɥi], *dem. pron. m.* (*fem.* **celle**, *pl.* **ceux, celles**) the one, that, those (*sometimes* = he *or* she). *Followed by* **-ci** or **-là** = this one, that one etc. *or* the latter *and* the former.
cément [se'mɑ̃], *n.m.* (*Metal.*) cement.
cémentation [semɑ̃tɑ'sjɔ̃], *n.f.* (*Metal.*) cementation.
cémenter [semɑ̃'te], *v.t.* (*Metal.*) to cement.
cénacle [se'nakl], *n.m.* (*Ant.*) guest-chamber; (*fig.*) literary society *or* coterie.
cendre [sɑ̃ːdr], *n.f.* ashes, embers, cinders; dust, ashes (*of the dead*).
cendré [sɑ̃'dre], *a.* ashy, ashen.
cendrée [sɑ̃'dre], *n.f.* small shot; cinders (*for track*); ***piste en cendrée***, dirt track, cinder track.
cendrer [sɑ̃'dre], *v.t.* to paint ash-grey; to mix *or* cover with ashes.
cendreux [sɑ̃'drø], *a.* (*fem.* **-euse**) ashy.
cendrier [sɑ̃dri'e], *n.m.* ash-pan, ash-pit; ash-tray.
cendrière [sɑ̃dri'ɛːr], *n.f.* peat.
Cendrillon [sɑ̃dri'jɔ̃], *n.f.* Cinderella, drudge.
Cène [sɛːn], *n.f.* The Lord's Supper, Holy Communion.
cenelle [sə'nɛl], *n.f.* haw.
cénobite [senɔ'bit], *n.m.* coenobite.
cénotaphe [senɔ'taf], *n.m.* cenotaph.
cens [sɑ̃ːs], *n.m.* census; rating.
censé [sɑ̃'se], *a.* accounted, reputed, supposed.
censeur [sɑ̃'sœːr], *n.m.* censor; critic; proctor (*of Engl. Univ.*); assistant headmaster (*in French Lycée*).
censure [sɑ̃'syːr], *n.f.* censorship; criticism, censure; audit (*of accounts*).
censurer [sɑ̃sy're], *v.t.* to find fault with, to criticize; to censure.
cent [sɑ̃], *a.* one hundred; ***faire les cent pas***, to walk up and down.—*n.m.* a hundred; ***cinq pour cent***, five per cent.
centaine [sɑ̃'tɛn], *n.f.* a hundred; a hundred or so.
centaure [sɑ̃'tɔːr], *n.m.* centaur.
centenaire [sɑ̃t'nɛːr], *a.* a hundred years old.—*n.* centenarian.—*n.m.* centenary.

centième [sɑ̃'tjɛm], *a.* hundredth.—*n.m.* hundredth part.
centigrade [sɑ̃ti'grad], *a.* centigrade.
centigramme [sɑ̃ti'gram], *n.m.* centigram, the hundredth part of a gram (·1543 grain).
centilitre [sɑ̃ti'litr], *n.m.* centilitre, hundredth part of a litre (·61028 cubic in.).
centime [sɑ̃'tim], *n.m.* centime, hundredth part of a franc.
centimètre [sɑ̃ti'mɛtr], *n.m.* centimetre, hundredth part of a metre (·39371 in.).
centipède [sɑ̃ti'pɛd], *n.m.* centipede.
central [sɑ̃'tral], *a.* (*m. pl.* **-aux**) central; chief, principal, head.—*n.m.* ***central téléphonique***, telephone exchange.—*n.f.* ***centrale électrique***, electric power station.
centralement [sɑ̃tral'mɑ̃], *adv.* centrally.
centralisateur [sɑ̃traliza'tœ:r], *a.* (*fem.* **-trice**) centralizing.
centralisation [sɑ̃tralizɑ'sjɔ̃], *n.f.* centralization.
centraliser [sɑ̃trali'ze], *v.t.* to centralize.
centre [sɑ̃:tr], *n.m.* centre, middle.
centrer [sɑ̃'tre], *v.t.* to centre.
centrifuge [sɑ̃tri'fy:ʒ], *a.* centrifugal.
centripète [sɑ̃tri'pɛt], *a.* centripetal.
centuple [sɑ̃'typl], *a.* and *n.m.* centuple, hundredfold.
centupler [sɑ̃ty'ple], *v.t.* to multiply a hundredfold.
centurion [sɑ̃ty'rjɔ̃], *n.m.* centurion.
cep [sɛp], *n.m.* vine-stock.
cépage [se'pa:ʒ], *n.m.* vine-plant.
cépée [se'pe], *n.f.* (*Agric.*) tuft of shoots from a pollarded stump; copse of one or two years' growth.
cependant [spɑ̃'dɑ̃], *adv.* in the meantime, meanwhile.—*conj.* yet, still, however, nevertheless.
céramique [sera'mik], *a.* ceramic.—*n.f.* ceramics.
Cerbère [sɛr'bɛ:r], *m.* (*Myth.*) Cerberus.
cerceau [sɛr'so], *n.m.* (*pl.* **-eaux**) hoop, ring; hoop-net.
cerclage [sɛr'kla:ʒ], *n.m.* hooping (*of casks*).
cercle [sɛrkl], *n.m.* circle, ring; circumference; club, club-house.
cercler [sɛr'kle], *v.t.* to bind with hoops, to hoop.
cercueil [sɛr'kœ:j], *n.m.* coffin; (*fig.*) the tomb.
céréale [sere'al], *n.f.* cereal, corn, grain.
cérébral [sere'bral], *a.* (*m.pl.* **-aux**) cerebral.
cérémonial [seremɔ'njal], *a.* (*m. pl.* **-aux**) ceremonial.—*n.m.* (*no pl.*) ceremonial, pomp.
cérémonie [seremɔ'ni], *n.f.* ceremony; pomp; fuss, ado.
cérémonieux [seremɔ'njø], *a.* (*fem.* **-euse**) ceremonious, formal.
cerf [sɛ:r], *n.m.* stag, hart, deer.
cerfeuil [sɛr'fœ:j], *n.m.* chervil.
cerf-volant [sɛrvɔ'lɑ̃], *n.m.* (*pl.* **cerfs-volants**) stag-beetle; kite, paper-kite.
cerisaie [səri'zɛ], *n.f.* cherry-orchard.
cerise [sə'ri:z], *n.f.* cherry.—*n.m.* cherry-colour, cerise.—*a.* cherry-coloured, cerise.
cerisier [səri'zje], *n.m.* cherry-tree, cherry-wood.
cerner [sɛr'ne], *v.t.* to cut *or* dig round (*a tree*), to ring (*a tree*); to surround, to encompass, to hem in.
certain [sɛr'tɛ̃], *a.* certain, sure, positive; fixed, determined; ***d'un certain âge***, not so young.—*n.m.* certainty; a sure thing.
certainement [sɛrtɛn'mɑ̃], *adv.* certainly.
certes [sɛrt], *adv.* indeed, most certainly.
certificat [sɛrtifi'ka], *n.m.* certificate; testimonial; diploma.
certification [sɛrtifikɑ'sjɔ̃], *n.f.* certification.
certifier [sɛrti'fje], *v.t.* to certify, to testify, to vouch for.
certitude [sɛrti'tyd], *n.f.* certitude, certainty.
cerveau [sɛr'vo], *n.m.* (*pl.* **-eaux**) brain; mind, intellect, intelligence.
cervelas [sɛrvə'lɑ], *n.m.* saveloy.
cervelle [sɛr'vɛl], *n.f.* brains; mind, intelligence.
cervin [sɛr'vɛ̃], *a.* cervine; ***le (Mont) Cervin***, the Matterhorn.
César [se'za:r], *m.* Caesar.—*n.m.* Caesar, emperor.
césarien [seza'rjɛ̃], *a.* (*fem.* **-ienne**) Caesarean.—*n.f.* (**-ienne**) Caesarean operation.
cessant [sɛ'sɑ̃], *a.* ceasing, suspended.
cessation [sɛsɑ'sjɔ̃], *n.f.* cessation, suspension, stoppage.
cesse [sɛs], *n.f.* ceasing, intermission, respite.
cesser [sɛ'se], *v.t.* to leave off, to break off, to stop.—*v.i.* to cease, to leave off, to stop.
cession [sɛ'sjɔ̃], *n.f.* transfer, assignment (*of property*).
cessionnaire [sɛsjɔ'nɛ:r], *n.m.* grantee, assignee.
césure [se'zy:r], *n.f.* caesura.
cet, cette [sɛt], [CE].
cétacé [seta'se], *a.* cetaceous.—*n.m.* cetacean.
ceux [sø:], [CELUI].
Ceylan [sɛ'lɑ̃], **le**, *m.* Ceylon.
chablis (1) [ʃɑ'bli], *n.m.* dead-wood.
chablis (2) [ʃɑ'bli], *n.m.* Chablis (*white wine*).
chacal [ʃa'kal], *n.m.* jackal.
chacun [ʃa'kœ̃], *pron. indef. sing.* each, each one, every one.
chafouin [ʃa'fwɛ̃], *a.* weasel-faced, mean-looking.
chagrin (1), [ʃa'grɛ̃], *n.m.* grief, chagrin; sorrow.—*a.* gloomy, melancholy, sad.
chagrin (2) [ʃa'grɛ̃], *n.m.* shagreen.
chagrinant [ʃagri'nɑ̃], *a.* distressing, sad.
chagriner [ʃagri'ne], *v.t.* to grieve, to afflict; to cross, to vex. **se chagriner**, *v.r.* to fret, to grieve.
chahut [ʃa'y], *n.m.* row, shindy.
chahuter [ʃay'te], *v.i.* to make a row, to kick up a shindy.
chaîne [ʃɛ:n], *n.f.* chain; shackle, fetters; bonds, bondage; (*Naut.*) cable; (*fig.*) series, range; (*Ind.*) ***chaîne de montage***, assembly-line.
chaîner [ʃɛ:'ne], *v.t.* (*Surveying*) to measure (*land*) with the chain.
chaînette [ʃɛ'nɛt], *n.f.* little chain; (*Arch.*) catenary arch.
chaînon [ʃɛ'nɔ̃], *n.m.* link.
chaintre [ʃɛ̃:tr], *n.m.* (*Agric.*) balk, headland.
chair [ʃɛ:r], *n.f.* flesh; meat; (*fig.*) the human body, the flesh; (*Paint.*, *pl.*) naked flesh.
chaire [ʃɛ:r], *n.f.* pulpit; professorship; bishop's throne.
chaise [ʃɛ:z], *n.f.* chair, seat; post-chaise.
chaland (1) [ʃa'lɑ̃], *n.m.* lighter, barge.
chaland (2) [ʃa'lɑ̃], *n.m.* (*fem.* **-e**) customer, client.

chalandeau [ʃalɑ̃'do], *n.m.* (*pl.* **-eaux**) lighterman, bargee.
chalcographe [kalkɔ'graf], *n.m.* chalcographer, engraver on metal.
chalcographie [kalkɔgra'fi], *n.f.* chalcography; engraving establishment.
chaldaïque [kalda'ik], *a.* Chaldaic.
Chaldée [kal'de], *f.* Chaldea.
chaldéen [kalde'ɛ̃], *a.* (*fem.* **-éenne**) Chaldean.—*n.m.* (**Chaldéen**, *fem.* **-éenne**) Chaldean (*person*).
châle [ʃɑ:l], *n.m.* shawl.
chalet [ʃa'lɛ], *n.m.* chalet, Swiss cottage.
chaleur [ʃa'lœ:r], *n.f.* heat; warmth, warm weather; (*fig.*) glow; zeal, ardour; **'*craint la chaleur*'**, 'store in a cool place'.
chaleureusement [ʃalœrøz'mɑ̃], *adv.* cordially, warmly.
chaleureux [ʃalœ'rø], *a.* (*fem.* **-euse**) warm, cordial.
chalicose [ʃali'ko:z], *n.f.* silicosis.
châlit [ʃɑ'li], *n.m.* bedstead.
chaloupe [ʃa'lup], *n.f.* ship's boat, launch.
chalumeau [ʃaly'mo], *n.m.* (*pl.* **-eaux**) stalk of corn, drinking-straw; flute, pipe.
chalut [ʃa'ly], *n.m.* drag-net, trawl.
chalutier [ʃaly'tje], *n.m.* trawler.
chamaillard [ʃamɑ'ja:r], *a.* squabbling, quarrelsome.
chamailler [ʃamɑ'je], *v.i.* to bicker, to squabble. **se chamailler**, *v.r.* to squabble, to wrangle.
chamaillis [ʃamɑ'ji], *n.m.* fray; squabble; uproar.
chamarrer [ʃama're], *v.t.* to bedizen, to bedeck.
chambellan [ʃɑ̃bɛ'lɑ̃], *n.m.* chamberlain.
chambranle [ʃɑ̃'brɑ̃:l], *n.m.* door-frame, window-frame.
chambre [ʃɑ̃:br], *n.f.* chamber, room; apartment; House (*of Parliament*); court (*of justice*); ***chambre à air***, inner tube (*bicycle etc.*); ***chambre à un*** (***deux***) ***lit***(***s***), single (double) room; ***chambre d'ami***, spare bedroom; ***chambre d'écluse***, lock; ***chambre noire***, camera obscura.
chambrée [ʃɑ̃'bre], *n.f.* barrack-room; roomful; (*Theat. etc.*) house.
chambrer [ʃɑ̃'bre], *v.t.* to keep (*someone*) confined; to bring wine to room temperature.—*v.i.* to lodge (*together*). **se chambrer**, *v.r.* to become pitted.
chambrette [ʃɑ̃'brɛt], *n.f.* little room.
chameau [ʃa'mo], *n.m.* (*pl.* **-eaux**) camel; (*pop.*) nasty, evil-minded person.
chamelier [ʃamə'lje], *n.m.* camel-driver.
chamelle [ʃa'mɛl], *n.f.* female camel.
chamelon [ʃam'lɔ̃], *n.m.* young camel.
chamois [ʃa'mwɑ], *n.m.* chamois; chamois leather.—*a.* chamois-coloured, buff.
chamoiseur [ʃamwɑ'zœ:r], *n.m.* chamois- *or* leather-dresser.
champ [ʃɑ̃], *n.m.* field, piece of ground; scope, range; (*poet.*) land; (*fig.*) space; ***sur-le-champ***, at once, immediately.
champagne [ʃɑ̃'paɲ], *n.m.* champagne; ***champagne frappé***, iced champagne; ***champagne mousseux***, sparkling champagne; ***fine champagne***, liqueur brandy.
champenois [ʃɑ̃pə'nwa], *a.* of Champagne.—*n.m.* (**Champenois**, *fem.* **-oise**) inhabitant of Champagne.
champêtre [ʃɑ̃'pɛ:tr], *a.* rural, rustic; ***garde champêtre***, village policeman.
champignon [ʃɑ̃pi'ɲɔ̃], *n.m.* mushroom, fungus.
champion [ʃɑ̃'pjɔ̃] *n.m.* (*fem.* **-onne**) champion.
championnat [ʃɑ̃pjɔ'na], *n.m.* championship.
chançard [ʃɑ̃'sa:r], *a.* and *n.m.* (*fem.* **-e**) (*fam.*) lucky (person).
chance [ʃɑ̃:s], *n.f.* chance; luck, good luck, good fortune; (*pl.*) chances, (*fam.*) odds.
chancelant [ʃɑ̃s'lɑ̃], *a.* staggering, tottering.
chanceler [ʃɑ̃s'le], *v.i.* (*conjug. like* APPELER) to stagger, to totter; to reel.
chancelier [ʃɑ̃sə'lje], *n.m.* chancellor.
chancellement [ʃɑ̃sɛl'mɑ̃], *n.m.* tottering, staggering.
chancellerie [ʃɑ̃sɛl'ri], *n.f.* chancellery.
chanceux [ʃɑ̃'sø], *a.* (*fem.* **-euse**) lucky, fortunate; risky, doubtful (*of things*).
chanci [ʃɑ̃'si], *a.* mouldy.
chancir [ʃɑ̃'si:r], *v.i.* to grow musty *or* mouldy.
chancissure [ʃɑ̃si'sy:r], *n.f.* mustiness, mouldiness.
chancre [ʃɑ̃:kr], *n.m.* ulcer, tumour; canker.
chancreux [ʃɑ̃'krø], *a.* (*fem.* **-euse**) ulcerous; cankered.
chandail [ʃɑ̃'da:j], *n.m.* jersey, sweater.
Chandeleur [ʃɑ̃'dlœ:r], *n.f.* Candlemas.
chandelier [ʃɑ̃də'lje], *n.m.* candlestick.
chandelle [ʃɑ̃'dɛl], *n.f.* (*tallow*) candle; (*fig.*) light; (*Tennis*) lob.
change [ʃɑ̃:ʒ], *n.m.* exchange; exchange of money; exchange office; agio; (*Hunt.*) wrong scent; ***agent de change***, stockbroker; ***cours du change***, rate of exchange.
changeant [ʃɑ̃'ʒɑ̃], *a.* changeable, fickle; unstable; unsettled (*of the weather*).
changement [ʃɑ̃ʒ'mɑ̃], *n.m.* change, alteration; (*Law*) amendment.
changer [ʃɑ̃'ʒe], *v.t.*, *v.i.* (*conjug. like* MANGER) to change, to exchange; to alter.
changeur [ʃɑ̃'ʒœ:r], *n.m.* (*fem.* **-euse**) money-changer.
chanoine [ʃa'nwan], *n.m.* canon.
chanson [ʃɑ̃'sɔ̃], *n.f.* song, ballad; (*fig.*) idle story, stuff, trash; ***chansons que tout cela!*** humbug!
chansonner [ʃɑ̃sɔ'ne], *v.t.* to lampoon.
chansonnette [ʃɑ̃sɔ'nɛt], *n.f.* little song, ditty.
chansonneur [ʃɑ̃sɔ'nœ:r], *n.m.* lampooner.
chansonnier [ʃɑ̃sɔ'nje], *n.m.* (*fem.* **-ière**) song-writer, ballad-writer; singer of satirical songs.
chant [ʃɑ̃], *n.m.* singing; song; air, tune; poem; canto; chant, hymn.
chantable [ʃɑ̃'tabl], *a.* fit to be sung, worth singing.
chantage [ʃɑ̃'ta:ʒ], *n.m.* extortion of hush-money, blackmail.
chantant [ʃɑ̃'tɑ̃], *a.* easily sung; tuneful, harmonious.
chanteau [ʃɑ̃'to], *n.m.* (*pl.* **-eaux**) hunk (*of bread*), bit (*of material etc.*), remnant; (*Dress.*) gore.
chantepleure [ʃɑ̃t'plœ:r], *n.f.* funnel with a rose.

chanter [ʃɑ̃'te], *v.t.* to extol, to praise, to celebrate; to sing.—*v.i.* to sing; to chirp, to warble, to crow; ***cela vous chante-t-il?*** how do you like the idea? **se chanter,** *v.r.* to be sung.
chanterelle [ʃɑ̃'trɛl], *n.f.* first string of a violin etc.; decoy-bird.
chanteur [ʃɑ̃'tœ:r], *a.* (*fem.* **-euse**) singing.—*n.m.* (*fem.* **-euse**) singer, vocalist.
chantier [ʃɑ̃'tje], *n.m.* timber-yard, wood-yard; stone-yard; dock-yard; site; (*C*) shanty, lumber camp.
chantonner [ʃɑ̃tɔ'ne], *v.t., v.i.* to hum.
chantourner [ʃɑ̃tur'ne], *v.t.* to cut in profile; ***scie à chantourner,*** bow saw.
chantre [ʃɑ̃:tr], *n.m.* singer, *esp.* a chorister; precentor, lay-clerk; (*fig.*) songster (*of birds*).
chanvre [ʃɑ̃:vr], *n.m.* hemp.
chanvreux [ʃɑ̃'vrø], *a.* (*fem.* **-euse**) hempen.
chaos [ka'o], *n.m.* chaos; (*fig.*) confusion, disorder.
chaotique [kaɔ'tik], *a.* chaotic.
chaparder [ʃapar'de], *v.t.* (*slang*) to steal, to scrounge.
chape [ʃap], *n.f.* cope (*ecclesiastical vestment*); tread (*of a tyre*).
chapeau [ʃa'po], *n.m.* (*pl.* **-eaux**) hat; (*Mech. etc.*) cap; ***un coup de chapeau,*** a bow.
chapelain [ʃa'plɛ̃], *n.m.* chaplain.
chapelet [ʃa'plɛ], *n.m.* rosary, beads; (*Arch. etc.*) chaplet; ***chapelet de bombes,*** stick of bombs; ***chapelet d'oignons,*** string of onions.
chapelier [ʃapə'lje], *n.m.* (*fem.* **-ière**) hatter.
chapelle [ʃa'pɛl], *n.f.* chapel; coterie, school (*of literature etc.*); church plate; living.
chapellenie [ʃapɛl'ni], *n.f.* chaplaincy.
chapellerie [ʃapɛl'ri], *n.f.* hat-making; hat trade, shop *or* business.
chapelure [ʃa'ply:r], *n.f.* grated bread-crumbs.
chaperon [ʃa'prɔ̃], *n.m.* hood; (*fig.*) chaperon; ***Le Petit Chaperon Rouge,*** Little Red Riding Hood.
chaperonner [ʃaprɔ'ne], *v.t.* to cope (*a wall*); (*fig.*) to chaperon.
chapiteau [ʃapi'to], *n.m.* (*pl.* **-eaux**) capital (*of column etc.*); cornice (*of a wardrobe etc.*); big top (*circus*).
chapitre [ʃa'pitr], *n.m.* chapter (*of a book, of knights, of a cathedral*); subject-matter of discourse.
chapitrer [ʃapi'tre], *v.t.* to reprimand, to rebuke.
chapon [ʃa'pɔ̃], *n.m.* capon; sop in broth.
chaponner [ʃapɔ'ne], *v.t.* to caponize.
chaque [ʃak], *a.* each, every.
char [ʃa:r], *n.m.* chariot, carriage, vehicle; ***char d'assaut,*** (*Mil.*) tank.
charabia [ʃara'bja], *n.m.* gibberish.
charade [ʃa'rad], *n.f.* charade.
charançon [ʃarɑ̃'sɔ̃], *n.m.* weevil.
charbon [ʃar'bɔ̃], *n.m.* coal, charcoal; (*pl.*) embers; (*Path.*) anthrax; (*Chem.*) carbon.
charbonnée [ʃarbɔ'ne], *n.f.* piece of grilled meat; charcoal-drawing.
charbonner [ʃarbɔ'ne], *v.t.* to char; to black with coal. **se charbonner,** *v.r.* to be charred, to burn black.
charbonnerie [ʃarbɔn'ri], *n.f.* coal depot.
charbonneux [ʃarbɔ'nø], *a.* (*fem.* **-euse**) coaly; affected *or* infected with anthrax.
charbonnier [ʃarbɔ'nje], *n.m.* (*fem.* **-ière**) charcoal-burner; coal-man.—*n.m.* coal-heaver; coal-hole; (*Naut.*) collier.—*n.f.* (**-ière**) charcoal-kiln; coal-scuttle; (*Orn.*) great tit.
charcuter [ʃarky'te], *v.t.* to hack and hew (*meat*); to hack, to butcher (*of a surgeon*).
charcuterie [ʃarky'tri], *n.f.* pork-butcher's meat; pork-butcher's business *or* shop.
charcutier [ʃarky'tje], *n.m.* (*fem.* **-ière**) pork-butcher; (*colloq.*) sawbones.
chardon [ʃar'dɔ̃], *n.m.* thistle; spikes (*on a wall* or *railing*).
chardonneret [ʃardɔn'rɛ], *n.m.* goldfinch.
charge [ʃarʒ], *n.f.* pack; load; expense, cost; accusation; post, employment; care, custody; charge, onset; ***à charge de revanche,*** provided that I may return the favour.
chargé [ʃar'ʒe], *a.* loaded, burdened.
chargement [ʃarʒə'mɑ̃], *n.m.* cargo, freight; bill of lading; load; charging (*of a battery*).
charger [ʃar'ʒe], *v.t.* (*conjug. like* MANGER) to load, to charge, to burden; to charge with; to register (*a letter*). **se charger,** *v.r.* to take upon oneself, to saddle oneself with (***de***).
chargeur [ʃar'ʒœ:r], *n.m.* loader, shipper; stoker; (*Phot., Cine.*) cassette.
chariot [ʃa'rjo], *n.m.* waggon, go-cart; (*Mech.*) truck, trolley.
charitable [ʃari'tabl], *a.* charitable.
charitablement [ʃaritablə'mɑ̃], *adv.* charitably.
charité [ʃari'te], *n.f.* charity; benevolence, alms.
charivari [ʃariva'ri], *n.m.* rough music; hubbub, clatter.
charlatan [ʃarla'tɑ̃], *n.m.* charlatan, mountebank, quack.
charlatanisme [ʃarlata'nism], *n.m.* quackery, charlatanism.
charlot [ʃar'lo], *n.m.* (*Orn.*) curlew.
charmant [ʃar'mɑ̃], *a.* charming, delightful.
charme (1) [ʃarm], *n.m.* charm; spell, enchantment.
charme (2) [ʃarm], *n.m.* (*Bot.*) hornbeam.
charmer [ʃar'me], *v.t.* to charm, to enchant, to bewitch, to fascinate, to captivate, to delight.
charmeur [ʃar'mœ:r], *n.m.* (*fem.* **-euse**) charmer, enchanter; bewitching woman, enchantress.
charmille [ʃar'mi:j], *n.f.* hedge of young hornbeam; bower, arbour.
charnel [ʃar'nɛl], *a.* (*fem.* **-elle**) carnal; sensual (*person*).
charnellement [ʃarnɛl'mɑ̃], *adv.* carnally.
charnier [ʃar'nje], *n.m.* charnel-house.
charnière [ʃar'njɛ:r], *n.f.* hinge; joint, articulation.
charnu [ʃar'ny], *a.* fleshy, plump; pulpy (*of fruits*).
charogne [ʃa'rɔɲ], *n.f.* carrion; (*pop.*) blackguard; slut.
charpente [ʃar'pɑ̃:t], *n.f.* frame, framework.
charpenter [ʃarpɑ̃'te], *v.t.* to square (*timber*); (*fig.*) to frame, to construct.
charpenterie [ʃarpɑ̃'tri], *n.f.* carpentry, carpenter's work *or* trade.

charpentier [ʃarpɑ̃'tje], *n.m.* carpenter.
charpie [ʃar'pi], *n.f.* lint.
charretée [ʃar'te], *n.f.* cart-load.
charretier [ʃar'tje], *n.m.* (*fem.* **-ière**) carter, waggoner.—*a.* passable for carts etc.
charrette [ʃa'rɛt], *n.f.* cart; ***charrette à bras***, hand-cart.
charriage [ʃa'ria:ʒ], *n.m.* cartage; haulage.
charrier [ʃa'rje], *v.t.* to cart.—*v.i.* to drift (*of ice*).
charroi [ʃa'rwɑ], *n.m.* cartage.
charron [ʃa'rɔ̃], *n.m.* wheelwright.
charroyer [ʃarwɑ'je], *v.t.* (*conjug. like* EMPLOYER) to cart (*heavy things*).
charrue [ʃa'ry], *n.f.* plough.
charte [ʃart], *n.f.* charter.
chartreuse [ʃar'trø:z], *n.f.* Carthusian monastery *or* convent; Carthusian nun; isolated country-house; chartreuse (*liqueur*).
chartreux [ʃar'trø], *n.m.* Carthusian friar; cat of a bluish-grey colour.
chartrier [ʃartri'e], *n.m.* keeper of charters; archives; muniment room.
Charybde [ka'ribd], *n.m.* Charybdis.
chas [ʃɑ], *n.m.* eye (*of a needle*).
chasme [kasm], *n.m.* chasm.
châsse [ʃɑ:s], *n.f.* reliquary, shrine; frame.
chasse [ʃas], *n.f.* hunting, shooting, fowling; the hunt, the chase; game preserve; play (*of machinery etc.*); flush (*of lavatory*).
chassé [ʃa'se], *n.m.* chassé (*a step in dancing*).
chassé-croisé [ʃasekrwɑ'ze], *n.m.* (*pl.* **chassés-croisés**) (*Dancing*) a dance step; (*fig.*) ***faire un chassé-croisé***, to exchange places.
chasselas [ʃas'lɑ], *n.m.* table grapes.

[In the following compounds **chasse** is *inv.*]

chasse-marée [ʃasma're], *n.m.* fish-cart.
chasse-mouches [ʃas'muʃ], *n.m.* a form of fan; fly-swatter.
chasse-neige [ʃas'nɛ:ʒ], *n.m.* snow-plough.
chasse-pierre(s) [ʃas'pjɛ:r], *n.m.* (*Rail.*) guard-iron, cow-catcher.
chasser [ʃa'se], *v.t.* to hunt; to chase, to pursue; to drive in (*a nail etc.*); to expel, to turn out, to discharge; to propel.—*v.i.* to go shooting *or* hunting; to glide along; (*Motor.*) to skid.
chasseresse [ʃas'rɛs], *n.f.* huntress.
chasseur [ʃa'sœ:r], *n.m.* (*fem.* **-euse**) hunter *or* huntress, sportsman *or* sportswoman.—*n.m.* page-boy; light infantry soldier; (*Av.*) fighter.
chassie [ʃɑ'si], *n.f.* gum on the edge of the eyelids.
chassieux [ʃa'sjø], *a.* (*fem.* **-euse**) blear-eyed.
châssis [ʃɑ'si], *n.m.* case, frame; window-sash; garden-frame; printer's chase; (*Motor.*) chassis; (*Theat.*) flat for scenery.
chaste [ʃast], *a.* chaste; pure, virtuous.
chastement [ʃastə'mɑ̃], *adv.* chastely, purely, virtuously.
chasteté [ʃastə'te], *n.f.* chastity, purity.
chasuble [ʃa'zybl], *n.f.* chasuble.
chat [ʃa], *n.m.* (*fem.* **chatte**) cat; darling, dear little thing; ***à bon chat bon rat***, set a thief to catch a thief; (*C*) ***chat sauvage***, raccoon; ***Le Chat Botté***, Puss in Boots.
châtaigne [ʃɑ'tɛɲ], *n.f.* chestnut.
châtaignier [ʃɑtɛ'ɲje], *n.m.* chestnut-tree.
châtain [ʃɑ'tɛ̃], *a. inv.* chestnut, nut-brown, auburn.
chat-cervier [ʃasɛr'vje], *n.m.* (*pl.* **chats-cerviers**) lynx.
château [ʃɑ'to], *n.m.* (*pl.* **-eaux**) castle, fortress; country-seat, mansion, hall, palace.
châteaubriant [ʃɑtobri'ɑ̃], *n.m.* large grilled rump-steak.
châtelain [ʃɑ'tlɛ̃], *n.m.* (*fem.* **-aine**) lord *or* lady of a manor, squire *or* squire's wife.
chat-huant [ʃa'ɥɑ̃], *n.m.* (*pl.* **chats-huants**) tawny owl.
châtiable [ʃɑ'tjabl], *a.* chastisable, punishable.
châtier [ʃɑ'tje], *v.t.* to chastise, to punish; (*fig.*) to correct.
chatière [ʃa'tjɛ:r], *n.f.* cat's hole (*in door etc.*).
châtiment [ʃɑti'mɑ̃], *n.m.* chastisement, punishment.
chatoiement or **chatoîment** [ʃatwa'mɑ̃], *n.m.* play of colours, changing lustre (*as of shot-silk, opals etc.*).
chaton (1) [ʃa'tɔ̃], *n.m.* kitten; catkin.
chaton (2) [ʃa'tɔ̃], *n.m.* setting of a gem; stone in a setting.
chatouillant [ʃatu'jɑ̃], *a.* tickling.
chatouillement [ʃatuj'mɑ̃], *n.m.* tickling, titillation.
chatouiller [ʃatu'je], *v.t.* to tickle, to titillate; (*fig.*) to please, to gratify, to flatter.
chatouilleux [ʃatu'jø], *a.* (*fem.* **-euse**) ticklish; (*fig.*) delicate, touchy.
chatoyant [ʃatwa'jɑ̃], *a.* shot, glistening (*of colours etc.*).
chatoyer [ʃatwa'je], *v.i.* (*conjug. like* EMPLOYER) to shimmer, to glisten.
châtrer [ʃɑ'tre], *v.t.* to castrate, to geld; (*Hort.*) to lop, to prune; (*fig.*) to expurgate.
chattée [ʃa'te], *n.f.* litter of kittens.
chatte [ʃat], [CHAT].
chatterie [ʃat'ri], *n.f.* playfulness, pretty *or* coaxing way; wheedling caress; (*pl.*) titbits.
chatterton [ʃatɛr'tɔn], *n.m.* insulating tape.
chaud [ʃo], *a.* hot, warm, burning, glowing.—*n.m.* heat, warmth; ***il fait chaud***, it is hot.—*adv.* hot, warm.
chaudeau [ʃo'do], *n.m.* (*pl.* **-eaux**) egg-flip.
chaudement [ʃod'mɑ̃], *adv.* warmly; (*fig.*) quickly, eagerly, fiercely, hotly.
chaud-froid [ʃo'frwɑ], *n.m.* cold jellied chicken *or* game with mayonnaise.
chaudière [ʃo'djɛ:r], *n.f.* copper; boiler (*of a steam-engine etc.*); (*C*) pail.
chaudron [ʃo'drɔ̃], *n.m.* cauldron.
chaudronnerie [ʃodrɔn'ri], *n.f.* boiler works.
chaudronnier [ʃodrɔ'nje], *n.m.* brazier, coppersmith, tinker.
chauffage [ʃo'fa:ʒ], *n.m.* heating, warming; stoking; fuel, firewood; ***chauffage central***, central heating.
chauffard [ʃo'fa:r], *n.m.* (*pop.*) road-hog.
chauffe [ʃo:f], *n.f.* furnace.
chauffe-bain [ʃof'bɛ̃], *n.m.* (*pl.* **chauffe-bains**) geyser.
chauffe-eau [ʃof'o], *n.m. inv.* water-heater.
chauffelinge [ʃof'lɛ̃:ʒ], *n.m. inv.* clothes-horse, airing cupboard.
chauffer [ʃo'fe], *v.t.* to heat, to warm; (*fig.*) to excite.—*v.i.* to grow hot; to be brewing; (*fig.*) to be urgent *or* pressing. **se chauffer**, *v.r.* to warm oneself.
chaufferette [ʃo'frɛt], *n.f.* foot-warmer.

chauffeur [ʃo'fœ:r], *n.m.* fireman; (*fem.* **-euse**) (*Motor.*) driver, chauffeur, chauffeuse.
chaufour [ʃo'fu:r], *n.m.* lime-kiln.
chaulage [ʃo'la:ʒ], *n.m.* (*Agric.*) liming.
chauler [ʃo'le], *v.t.* to lime (*soil*).
chaume [ʃo:m], *n.m.* stubble; stubble-field; thatch.
chaumer [ʃo'me], *v.t., v.i.* (*Agric.*) to cut stubble.
chaumière [ʃo'mjɛ:r], *n.f.* thatched house, cottage.
chausse [ʃo:s], *n.f.* shoulder-band (*worn in universities etc.*); *(*pl.*) hose (*covering the body from waist to foot*).
chaussée [ʃo'se], *n.f.* embankment, dike; causeway; roadway, (*Am.*) pavement; ***le rez-de-chaussée***, the ground floor.
chausse-pied [ʃos'pje], *n.m.* (*pl.* **chausse-pieds**) shoe-horn.
chausser [ʃo'se], *v.t.* to put on (*footwear*); to shoe, to make (*the shoes etc.*) for; (*colloq.*) to fit, to suit.—*v.i.* ***chausser du*** **40**, to take a 7 (*in shoes*). **se chausser,** *v.r.* to put on one's shoes etc.
chausse-trape [ʃos'trap], *n.f.* (*pl.* **chausse-trapes**) snare, trap.
chaussette [ʃo'sɛt], *n.f.* sock.
chausseur [ʃo'sœ:r], *n.m.* footwear dealer.
chausson [ʃo'sɔ̃], *n.m.* slipper; gym shoe; bootee (*for infants*).
chaussure [ʃo'sy:r], *n.f.* foot-wear.
chauve [ʃo:v], *a.* bald.
chauve-souris [ʃovsu'ri], *n.f.* (*pl.* **chauves-souris**) bat, flittermouse.
chauvin [ʃo'vɛ̃], *n.m.* fanatical patriot.—*a.* chauvinistic, jingoistic.
chaux [ʃo], *n.f.* lime; limestone.
chavirage [ʃavi'ra:ʒ], **chavirement** [ʃavir'mɑ̃], *n.m.* capsizing, upsetting.
chavirer [ʃavi're], *v.t., v.i.* to capsize, to upset.
chef [ʃɛf], *n.m.* chief, commander, conductor, master, principal, ringleader; chef.
chef-d'œuvre [ʃɛ'dœ:vr], *n.m.* (*pl.* **chefs-d'œuvre**) chef-d'œuvre, masterpiece.
chef-lieu [ʃɛf'ljø], *n.m.* (*pl.* **chefs-lieux**) chief town, county town.
cheik [SCHEIK].
chelem or **schelem** [ʃlɛm], *n.m. inv.* slam (*at cards*).
chemin [ʃə'mɛ̃], *n.m.* way, road, path, track; (*fig.*) means; course; ***chemin de fer***, railway, (*Am.*) railroad.
chemineau [ʃəmi'no], *n.m.* (*pl.* **-eaux**) tramp.
cheminée [ʃəmi'ne], *n.f.* chimney; funnel; fire-place; mantelpiece; nipple (*of a percussion-gun*).
cheminer [ʃəmi'ne], *v.i.* to walk, to tramp; to proceed.
cheminot [ʃəmi'no], *n.m.* railwayman; platelayer.
chemise [ʃə'mi:z], *n.f.* shirt; wrapper, cover.
chemiserie [ʃəmi'zri], *n.f.* shirt-factory; shirt-making.
chemisette [ʃəmi'zɛt], *n.f.* short-sleeved shirt (*men*).
chemisier [ʃəmi'zje], *n.m.* (*fem.* **-ière**) shirt-maker *or* seller.
chênaie [ʃɛ'nɛ], *n.f.* oak-plantation.
chenal [ʃə'nal], *n.m.* channel, fairway.
chenapan [ʃəna'pɑ̃], *n.m.* vagabond, good-for-nothing, scamp.
chêne [ʃɛ:n], *n.m.* oak.
chêneau [ʃɛ'no], *n.m.* (*pl.* **-eaux**) young oak.
chéneau [ʃe'no], *n.m.* (*pl.* **-eaux**) (eaves) gutter.
chenet [ʃə'nɛ], *n.m.* fire-dog.
chènevière [ʃɛn'vjɛ:r], *n.f.* hemp-field.
chènevis [ʃɛn'vi], *n.m.* hemp-seed.
chènevotte [ʃɛn'vɔt], *n.f.* stalk (*of hemp*).
chenil [ʃə'ni], *n.m.* dog-kennel; kennels; dirty hovel.
chenille [ʃə'ni:j], *n.f.* caterpillar; kind of silk cord, chenille; ***tracteur à chenille***, (*reg. trade name*) caterpillar tractor.
chenillère [ʃəni'jɛ:r], *n.f.* nest of caterpillars.
chenillette [ʃəni'jɛt], *n.f.* (*Mil.*) half-track.
chenu [ʃə'ny], *a.* grey-headed; snow-capped.
cheptel [ʃə'tɛl, ʃɛp'tɛl], *n.m.* live-stock (*of a country*).
chèque [ʃɛk], *n.m.* cheque, (*Am.*) check.
chéquier [ʃe'kje], *n.m.* cheque-book.
cher [ʃɛ:r], *a.* (*fem.* **chère** (1)) dear, beloved; precious; expensive.—*adv.* dear, dearly, expensively.
chercher [ʃɛr'ʃe], *v.t.* to seek, to look for, to search for; to endeavour, to try, to attempt; ***aller chercher***, to go for; to fetch.
chercheur [ʃɛr'ʃœ:r], *n.m.* (*fem.* **-euse**) seeker, searcher; research worker.
chère (1) [ʃɛ:r], [CHER].
chère (2) [ʃɛ:r], *n.f.* entertainment, fare; ***bonne chère***, good cheer, good living.
chèrement [ʃɛr'mɑ̃], *adv.* dearly, tenderly; dear, at a high price.
chéri [ʃe'ri], *a.* beloved; cherished.—*n.m.* (*fem.* **-e**) darling, dearest.
chérif [ʃe'rif], *n.m.* shereef (*Arabian prince*).
chérir [ʃe'ri:r], *v.t.* to love dearly, to cherish.
cherté [ʃɛr'te], *n.f.* dearness, high price.
chérubin [ʃery'bɛ̃], *n.m.* cherub.
chérubique [ʃery'bik], *a.* cherubic.
chester [ʃɛs'tɛr], *n.m.* Cheshire cheese.
chétif [ʃe'tif], *a.* (*fem.* **-tive**) puny, pitiful; worthless.
chétivement [ʃetiv'mɑ̃], *adv.* meanly, pitifully, poorly, feebly.
chétiveté [ʃetiv'te], *n.f.* puniness, paltriness.
cheval [ʃə'val], *n.m.* (*pl.* **-aux**) horse; nag, steed; ***aller à cheval***, to ride; ***cheval d'arçons, cheval de bois***, (*Gym.*) vaulting horse; ***cheval à bascule***, rocking-horse; ***chevaux de bois***, merry-go-round; ***cheval marin***, sea-horse; walrus.
chevaleresque [ʃəval'rɛsk], *a.* chivalrous, knightly.
chevaleresquement [ʃəvalrɛsk'mɑ̃], *adv.* chivalrously.
chevalerie [ʃəval'ri], *n.f.* knighthood, chivalry.
chevalet [ʃəva'lɛ], *n.m.* easel; bridge (*of a stringed instrument*); sawing-trestle; buttress, prop; clothes-horse.
chevalier (1) [ʃəva'lje], *n.m.* knight.
chevalier (2) [ʃəva'lje], *n.m.* (*Orn.*) sandpiper; redshank.
chevalière [ʃəva'ljɛ:r], *n.f.* knight's lady; signet-ring.
chevalin [ʃəva'lɛ̃], *a.* equine; ***boucherie chevaline***, horse butcher's shop.
cheval-vapeur [ʃəvalva'pœ:r], *n.m.* (*pl.* **chevaux-vapeur**) horse-power.
chevauchant [ʃəvo'ʃɑ̃], *a.* overlapping.
chevauchée [ʃəvo'ʃe], *n.f.* ride, excursion on horseback; cavalcade.

chevauchement [ʃəvoʃ'mɑ̃], *n.m.* overlap *or* crossing (*tiles, wires*).
chevaucher [ʃəvo'ʃe], *v.i.* to ride on horseback; to be astride; to overlap.
chevaucheur [ʃəvo'ʃœːr], *n.m.* rider, horseman.
chevauchure [ʃəvo'ʃyːr], *n.f.* overlapping.
chevelu [ʃə'vly], *a.* hairy, long-haired; (*Bot.*) fibrous.
chevelure [ʃə'vlyːr], *n.f.* hair, head of hair.
chevesne [ʃə'vɛn], *n.m.* (*Ichth.*) chub.
chevet [ʃə'vɛ], *n.m.* head (*of a bed*); bolster; pillow; bedside.
cheveu [ʃə'vø], *n.m.* (*pl.* **-eux**) a single hair; *pl.* the hair (*of the head*).
chevillage [ʃəvi'jaːʒ], *n.m.* fastening, bolting, dowelling.
cheville [ʃə'viːj], *n.f.* ankle; peg, pin, dowel, bolt; plug.
cheviller [ʃəvi'je], *v.t.* to dowel, to peg, to bolt.
cheviotte [ʃə'vjɔt], *n.f.* cheviot (*tweed*).
chèvre [ʃɛːvr], *n.f.* goat, nanny-goat.
chevreau [ʃə'vro], *n.m.* (*pl.* **-eaux**) kid (*animal* or *skin*).
chèvrefeuille [ʃɛvrə'fœːj], *n.m.* honeysuckle.
chèvrerie [ʃɛvrə'ri], *n.f.* goat-pen.
chevrette [ʃə'vrɛt], *n.f.* small goat; young roe.
chevreuil [ʃə'vrœːj], *n.m.* roe, roe-deer.
chevrier [ʃəvri'e], *n.m.* (*fem.* **-ière**) goatherd.
chevron [ʃə'vrɔ̃], *n.m.* rafter; chevron, stripe.
chevronnage [ʃəvrɔ'naːʒ], *n.m.* rafters, raftering.
chevronné [ʃəvrɔ'ne], *a.* (*fam.*) experienced
chevrotain or **chevrotin** [ʃəvrɔ'tɛ̃], *n.m.* chevrotain, musk-deer.
chevrotant [ʃəvrɔ'tɑ̃], *a.* quavering, tremulous.
chevrotement [ʃəvrɔt'mɑ̃], *n.m.* tremulous motion, trembling (*of the voice etc.*).
chevroter [ʃəvrɔ'te], *v.i.* to sing *or* speak in a tremulous voice.
chevrotin (1) [CHEVROTAIN].
chevrotin (2) [ʃəvrɔ'tɛ̃], *n.m.* fawn of roe-deer; kid (*leather*).
chevrotine [ʃəvrɔ'tin], *n.f.* buck-shot.
chez [ʃe], *prep.* at, to, in (*the house, family* or *country of*); in, with, among; in the works of, (*on letters*) care of.
chiasse [ʃjas], *n.f.* dross, scum.
chibouque or **chibouk** [ʃi'buk], *n.f.* chibouk (*Turkish pipe*).
chic [ʃik], *n.m.* style, chic; aplomb, ease and elegance.—*a. inv.* stylish, smart.
chicane [ʃi'kan], *n.f.* cavil, evasion, quibble; chicanery.
chicaner [ʃika'ne], *v.t.* to quarrel *or* wrangle with.—*v.i.* to cavil, to quibble.
chicanerie [ʃikan'ri], *n.f.* chicanery, quibbling, cavilling.
chicaneur [ʃika'nœːr], *n.m.* (*fem.* **-euse**) or **chicanier** [ʃika'nje], *n.m.* (*fem.* **-ière**) caviller, pettifogger.—*a.* litigious, cavilling, wrangling.
chiche (1) [ʃiʃ], *a.* niggardly, stingy.
chiche (2) [ʃiʃ], *a.* ***pois chiches***, chick-peas.
chichement [ʃiʃ'mɑ̃], *adv.* stingily.
chicorée [ʃikɔ're], *n.f.* endive; chicory.
chicot [ʃi'ko], *n.m.* stub *or* stump (*of tree* or *tooth*).
chicotin [ʃikɔ'tɛ̃], *n.m.* bitter juice of aloes.
chien [ʃjɛ̃], *n.m.* (*fem.* **chienne**) dog; hammer, cock (*of a gun* or *pistol*); ***chien de mer***, dog-fish.
chiendent [ʃjɛ̃'dɑ̃], *n.m.* couch-grass.
chiennée [ʃjɛ'ne], *n.f.* litter of pups.
chiffe [ʃif], *n.f.* poor stuff, rag; (*fig.*) weakling; spineless person.
chiffon [ʃi'fɔ̃], *n.m.* rag, scrap, bit; frippery.
chiffonnage [ʃifɔ'naːʒ], *n.m.* rumpled drapery, rumpling, crumpling.
chiffonner [ʃifɔ'ne], *v.t.* to rumple, to crumple; (*colloq.*) to ruffle, to tease, to vex.—*v.i.* to be a rag-collector.
chiffonnier [ʃifɔ'nje], *n.m.* (*fem.* **-ière**) rag-picker; chiffonnier.
chiffrage [ʃi'fraːʒ], **chiffrement** [ʃifr'mɑ̃], *n.m.* figuring, figures; calculation; writing in cipher, coding.
chiffre [ʃifr], *n.m.* figure, number; total amount; cipher; monogram.
chiffrer [ʃi'fre], *v.t.* to calculate, to tot up; to code.—*v.i.* to cipher.
chiffreur [ʃi'frœːr], *n.m.* (*fem.* **-euse**) reckoner, cipherer.
chignole [ʃi'ɲɔl], *n.f.* ratchet drill.
chignon [ʃi'ɲɔ̃], *n.m.* chignon, coil of hair.
Chili [ʃi'li], **le**, *m.* Chile.
chilien [ʃi'ljɛ̃], *a.* (*fem.* **-enne**) Chilean.—*n.m.* (**Chilien**, *fem.* **-enne**) Chilean (*person*).
chimère [ʃi'mɛːr], *n.f.* chimera; myth, idle fancy.
chimérique [ʃime'rik], *a.* chimerical, visionary.
chimériquement [ʃimerik'mɑ̃], *adv.* chimerically.
chimie [ʃi'mi], *n.f.* chemistry.
chimique [ʃi'mik], *a.* chemical.
chimiquement [ʃimik'mɑ̃], *adv.* chemically.
chimiste [ʃi'mist], *n.m.* chemist (*not pharmaceutical chemist*).
chimpanzé [ʃɛ̃pɑ̃'ze], *n.m.* chimpanzee.
chinchilla [ʃɛ̃ʃil'la], *n.m.* chinchilla.
Chine [ʃin], **la**, *f.* China.
chiner [ʃi'ne], *v.t.* to colour differently; to figure (*stuffs*).
chinois [ʃi'nwa], *a.* Chinese.—*n.m.* Chinese (*language*); ***un chinois***, a small green orange preserved in brandy; (**Chinois**, *fem.* **-oise**) Chinese (*person*).
chinoiserie [ʃinwa'zri], *n.f.* Chinese thing, curio; (*fig.*) trick; red tape.
chiot [ʃjo], *n.m.* puppy.
chiourme [ʃjurm], *n.f.* convict-gang.
chipolata [ʃipɔla'ta], *n.f.* onion stew; small sausage.
chipotage [ʃipɔ'taːʒ], *n.m.* dawdling; haggling.
chipoter [ʃipɔ'te], *v.i.* to dally, to dawdle; to haggle; to peck at a dish.
chipotier [ʃipɔ'tje], *n.m.* (*fem.* **-ière**) trifler dallier, shuffler.
chique [ʃik], *n.f.* quid of tobacco.
chiquement [ʃik'mɑ̃], *adv.* smartly.
chiquenaude [ʃik'noːd], *n.f.* flick.
chiquenauder [ʃikno'de], *v.t.* to flick.
chiquer [ʃi'ke], *v.i.* to chew tobacco.
chiquet [ʃi'kɛ], *n.m.*, **chiquette** [ʃi'kɛt], *n.f.* driblet, bit, shred.
chiqueur [ʃi'kœːr], *n.m.* chewer of tobacco; pretender.

chiromancie [kirɔmɑ̃'si], *n.f.* chiromancy, palmistry.

chiromancien [kirɔmɑ̃'sjɛ̃], *n.m.* (*fem.* **-ienne**) chiromancer, palmist.

chirurgical [ʃiryrʒi'kal], *a.* (*m. pl.* **-aux**) surgical.

chirurgicalement [ʃiryrʒikal'mɑ̃], *adv.* surgically.

chirurgie [ʃiryr'ʒi], *n.f.* surgery.

chirurgien [[ʃiryr'ʒjɛ̃], *n.m.* surgeon.

chirurgique [ʃiryr'ʒik], *a.* surgical.

chiure [ʃjy:r], *n.f.* fly-speck.

chlorate [klɔ'rat], *n.m.* chlorate.

chlore [klɔ:r], *n.m.* (*Chem.*) chlorine.

chloré [klɔ're], *a.* containing chlorine.

chlorhydrate [klɔri'drat], *n.m.* (*Chem.*) hydrochlorate.

chlorhydrique [klɔri'drik], *a.* hydrochloric.

chloroforme [klɔrɔ'fɔrm], *n.m.* chloroform.

chloroformer [klɔrɔfɔr'me], *v.t.* to chloroform.

chlorure [klɔ'ry:r], *n.m.* (*Chem.*) chloride.

choc [ʃɔk], *n.m.* shock; impact; clash, encounter.

chocolat [ʃɔkɔ'la], *n.m.* chocolate.—*a.* chocolate-coloured.

chocolaterie [ʃɔkɔla'tri], *n.f.* chocolate-making; chocolate-factory.

chocolatier [ʃɔkɔla'tje], *n.m.* (*fem.* **-ière**) chocolate-maker *or* seller.—*n.f.* (**-ière**) chocolate pot.

chœur [kœ:r], *n.m.* choir; chancel; (*Ant.* and *fig.*) chorus.

choir [ʃwa:r], *v.i. irr.* to fall, to drop.

choisir [ʃwa'zi:r], *v.t.* to choose, to single out, to select.

choix [ʃwa], *n.m.* choice, alternative; selection; distinction.

choléra [kɔle'ra], *n.m.* cholera.

cholérique [kɔle'rik], *a.* choleraic.—*n.* person affected with cholera.

chômable [ʃo'mabl], *a.* (*of days, fêtes etc.*) to be kept as a holiday.

chômage [ʃo'ma:ʒ], *n.m.* unemployment, enforced idleness; stoppage; ***allocation de chômage***, unemployment benefit, 'dole'.

chômer [ʃo'me], *v.i.* to be doing nothing; to be unemployed.

chômeur [ʃo'mœ:r], *n.m.* (*fem.* **-euse**) idle *or* unemployed person.

chope [ʃɔp], *n.f.* large beer-glass; mug of beer.

chopper [ʃɔ'pe], *v.i.* to stumble, to trip (***contre***).

choquant [ʃɔ'kɑ̃], *a.* offensive, unpleasant, improper.

choquer [ʃɔ'ke], *v.t.* to shock, to strike *or* dash against; to displease, to offend.—*v.i.* to clink glasses; to be offensive, to be shocking. **se choquer**, *v.r.* to take offence; to come into collision with each other.

choral [kɔ'ral], *a.* choral.—*n.m.* (*pl.* **-als**) choral(e).—*n.f.* (**chorale**) choir, choral society.

chorée [kɔ're], *n.f.* chorea, St. Vitus's dance.

chorégraphe [kɔre'graf], *n.m.* choreographer.

chorégraphie [kɔregra'fi], *n.f.* choreography.

choriste [kɔ'rist], *n.m.* chorister; (*Theat.*) member of the chorus.

chorus [kɔ'ry:s], *n.m.* chorus.

chose [ʃo:z], *n.f.* thing; matter, business, affair; (*Law*) chattel, property.

chou [ʃu], *n.m.* (*pl.* **choux**) cabbage, kale; (*colloq.*) puff-paste; darling, dear; bow, rosette; ***choux de Bruxelles***, Brussels sprouts.

chouan [ʃwɑ̃], *n.m.* Chouan, Breton royalist insurgent (*during the French Revolution*).

choucas [ʃu'kɑ], *n.m.*, **chouchette** [ʃu'ʃɛt] *n.f.* jackdaw.

choucroute [ʃu'krut], *n.f.* sauerkraut.

chouette (1) [ʃwɛt], *n.f.* owl.

chouette (2) [ʃwɛt] *int.* (*pop.*) fine, marvellous.—*a.* nice, fine, good of its kind.

chou-fleur [ʃu'flœ:r], *n.m.* (*pl.* **choux-fleurs**) cauliflower.

chou-rave [ʃu'ra:v], *n.m.* (*pl.* **choux-raves**) kohl-rabi, turnip-cabbage.

choyer [ʃwa'je], *v.t.* (*conjug. like* EMPLOYER) to take great care of, to be fond of, to pamper, to pet. **se choyer**, *v.r.* to pamper oneself.

chrême [krɛ:m], *n.m.* chrism, holy oil.

chrémeau [kre'mo], *n.m.* (*pl.* **-eaux**) chrism-cloth.

chrétien [kre'tjɛ̃], *a.* and *n.m.* (*fem.* **-enne**) Christian.

chrétiennement [kretjɛn'mɑ̃], *adv.* like a Christian.

chrétienté [kretjɛ̃'te], *n.f.* Christendom.

christ [krist], *n.m.* crucifix; representation of Christ crucified; ***le Christ***, Jesus Christ.

christianisme [kristja'nism], *n.m.* Christianity.

Christophe [kris'tɔf], *m.* Christopher.

chromage [kro'ma:ʒ], *n.m.* chromium plating.

chromate [krɔ'mat] *n.m.* (*Chem.*) chromate.

chromatique [krɔma'tik], *a.* (*Chem., Mus.*) chromatic.—*n.f.* (*Mus., Paint.*) chromatics.

chrome [kro:m], *n.m.* chromium, chrome.

chromé [kro'me], *a.* chromium-plated.

chromer [kro'me], *v.t.* to chrome.

chromique [kro'mik], *a.* chromic.

chromosome [kromo'zo:m], *n.m.* chromosome.

chronique (1) [krɔ'nik], *n.f.* chronicle, history; news-summary.

chronique (2) [krɔ'nik], *a.* (*Med.*) chronic.

chroniqueur [krɔni'kœ:r], *n.m.* (*fem.* **-euse**) chronicler; newswriter, columnist.

chronologie [krɔnɔlɔ'ʒi], *n.f.* chronology.

chronologique [krɔnɔlɔ'ʒik], *a.* chronological.

chronomètre [krɔnɔ'mɛ:tr], *n.m.* chronometer.

chronométrer [krɔnɔme'tre], *v.t.* (*conjug. like* CÉDER) to time.

chronométreur [krɔnɔme'trœ:r], *n.m.* time-keeper.

chrysalide [kriza'lid], *n.f.* chrysalis.

chrysanthème [krizɑ̃'tɛ:m], *n.m.* chrysanthemum.

chuchotement [ʃyʃɔt'mɑ̃], *n.m.* whispering, whisper, rustling.

chuchoter [ʃyʃɔ'te], *v.t.*, *v.i.* to whisper.

chuchoterie [ʃyʃɔ'tri], *n.f.* whispering.

chuchoteur [ʃyʃɔ'tœ:r], *n.m.* (*fem.* **-euse**) whisperer.

chuinter [ʃɥɛ̃'te], *v.i.* to hoot (*of owls*); to hiss (*of gas*).

chut [ʃ:t], *int.* and *n.m.* hush!

chute [ʃyt], *n.f.* fall, tumble; collapse, ruin, downfall; disaster.
chuter [ʃy'te], *v.i.* (*fam.*) to fall, to fail.
Chypre [ʃipr], *f.* Cyprus.
ci [si], *adv.* here.
cible [sibl], *n.f.* target, mark; (*fig.*) purpose.
ciboire [si'bwa:r], *n.m.* sacred vase, pyx.
ciboule [si'bul], *n.f.* Welsh onion, scallion.
ciboulette [sibu'lɛt], *n.f.* chive.
cicatrice [sika'tris], *n.f.* scar, seam, mark.
cicatrisant [sikatri'zɑ̃], *a.* cicatrizing.
cicatrisation [sikatrizɑ'sjɔ̃], *n.f.* cicatrization.
cicatriser [sikatri'ze], *v.t.* to cicatrize; to close, to heal up. **se cicatriser,** *v.r.* to skin over, to heal up.
Cicéron [sise'rɔ̃], *m.* Cicero.
cicérone [sise'rɔn], *n.m.* cicerone, guide.
cicéronien [siserɔ'njɛ̃], *a.* (*fem.* **-enne**) Ciceronian.
cidre [sidr], *n.m.* cider.
cidrerie [sidrə'ri], *n.f.* cider making; cider-factory.
ciel [sjɛl], *n.m.* (*pl.* **cieux**) the heavens, the firmament, the sky; heaven.
cierge [sjɛrʒ], *n.m.* taper, church candle.
cigale [si'gal], *n.f.* cicada.
cigare [si'ga:r], *n.m.* cigar.
cigarette [siga'rɛt], *n.f.* cigarette.
cigogne [si'gɔɲ], *n.f.* stork.
cigogneau [sigɔ'ɲo], *n.m.* (*pl.* **-eaux**) young stork.
ciguë [si'gy], *n.f.* hemlock (*plant* or *poison*).
cil [sil], *n.m.* eyelash.
cilice [si'lis], *n.m.* cilice, hair-shirt.
cillement [sij'mɑ̃], *n.m.* blink, winking.
ciller [si'je], *v.t., v.i.* to wink, to blink (*the eyes*).
cimaise or **cymaise** [si'mɛ:z], *n.f.* cyma, ogee; dado-rail, picture rail.
cime [sim], *n.f.* top, summit, peak.
ciment [si'mɑ̃], *n.m.* cement.
cimenter [simɑ̃'te], *v.t.* to cement; to strengthen, to consolidate.
cimentier [simɑ̃'tje], *n.m.* cement-maker.
cimeterre [sim'tɛ:r], *n.m.* scimitar.
cimetière [sim'tjɛ:r], *n.m.* cemetery, church-yard.
cimier [si'mje], *n.m.* crest (*of a helmet*); buttock (*of beef*).
cinéaste [sine'ast], *n.m.* film producer.
cinéma [sine'ma], *n.m.* cinema.
cinémascope [sinemas'kɔp], *n.m.* cinemascope.
cinémathèque [sinema'tɛk], *n.f.* film library.
cinématographier [sinematɔgra'fje], *v.t.* to film.
cinérama [sinera'ma], *n.m.* cinerama.
cinétique [sine'tik], *n.f.* kinetics.—*a.* kinetic, motive (*energy*).
cinétiquement [sinetik'mɑ̃], *adv.* kinetically.
cingalais [sɛ̃ga'lɛ], *a.* Sin(g)halese *or* Cingalese.—*n.m.* Sin(g)halese *or* Cingalese (*language*); (**Cingalais,** *fem.* **-aise**) Sin(g)-halese *or* Cingalese (*person*).
cinglage [sɛ̃'gla:ʒ], *n.m.* sailing, ship's course, run of a ship in twenty-four hours.
cinglement [sɛ̃gl'mɑ̃], *n.m.* lashing, slashing.
cingler (1) [sɛ̃'gle], *v.i.* to sail before the wind.
cingler (2) [sɛ̃'gle], *v.t.* to lash; (*fig.*) to chastize.
cinname [si'nam], **cinnamome** [sina'mɔm], *n.m.* cinnamon.

cinq [sɛ̃:k], *a.* five.—*n.m.* five.
cinquantaine [sɛ̃kɑ̃'tɛn], *n.f.* about fifty.
cinquante [sɛ̃'kɑ̃:t], *a.* fifty.
cinquantenaire [sɛ̃kɑ̃t'nɛ:r], *a.* and *n.* quinquagenarian.—*n.m.* fiftieth anniversary, jubilee.
cinquantième [sɛ̃kɑ̃'tjɛm], *a.* fiftieth.—*n.m.* fiftieth part.
cinquième [sɛ̃'kjɛm], *a.* fifth.—*n.m.* fifth part; fifth floor.
cintrage [sɛ̃'tra:ʒ], *n.m.* arching, curving (*of arches etc.*).
cintre [sɛ̃:tr], *n.m.* curve of an arch; coat-hanger.
cintrer [sɛ̃'tre], *v.t.* to arch, to curve.
cipaye [si'pa:j], **cipahi** [si'pai], *n.m.* sepoy.
cipolin [sipɔ'lɛ̃], *n.m.* cipollino, cipolin marble.
cippe [sip], *n.m.* cippus (*half-column*).
cirage [si'ra:ʒ], *n.m.* waxing; blacking (*composition* or *process*); boot-polish.
circoncire [sirkɔ̃'si:r], *v.t. irr.* (*conjug. like* CONFIRE *except for p.p.* **circoncis**) to circumcise.
circoncis [sirkɔ̃'si], *a.* circumcised.—*n.m.* one who is circumcised.
circoncision [sirkɔ̃si'zjɔ̃], *n.f.* circumcision.
circonférence [sirkɔ̃fe'rɑ̃:s], *n.f.* circumference.
circonflexe [sirkɔ̃'flɛks], *a.* and *n.m.* circumflex.
circonlocution [sirkɔ̃lɔky'sjɔ̃], *n.f.* circumlocution.
circonscription [sirkɔ̃skrip'sjɔ̃], *n.f.* circumscription; district; constituency.
circonscrire [sirkɔ̃s'kri:r], *v.t. irr.* (*conjug. like* ÉCRIRE) to circumscribe, to encircle; to limit.
circonspect [sirkɔ̃s'pɛkt, -spɛ], *a.* circumspect, wary, discreet, reserved.
circonspection [sirkɔ̃spɛk'sjɔ̃], *n.f.* circumspection, wariness, caution.
circonstance [sirkɔ̃s'tɑ̃:s], *n.f.* circumstance; occurrence, event.
circonstanciel [sirkɔ̃stɑ̃'sjɛl], *a.* (*fem.* **-elle**) circumstantial.
circonstancier [sirkɔstɑ̃'sje], *v.t.* to state circumstantially, to particularize.
circonvenir [sirkɔ̃v'ni:r], *v.t. irr.* (*conjug. like* TENIR) to circumvent, to outwit.
circonvention [sirkɔ̃vɑ̃'sjɔ̃], *n.f.* circumvention, fraud.
circonvoisin [sirkɔ̃vwa'zɛ̃], *a.* circumjacent, neighbouring, adjoining.
circonvolution [sirkɔ̃vɔly'sjɔ̃], *n.f.* circumvolution.
circuit [sir'kɥi], *n.m.* circuit, circumference; detour; lap; (*Elec.*) ***court circuit,*** short circuit; ***en circuit,*** switched on.
circulaire [sirky'lɛ:r], *a.* circular, round.—*n.f.* circular.
circulation [sirkylɑ'sjɔ̃], *n.f.* circulation; currency; traffic.
circulatoire [sirkyla'twa:r], *a.* circulatory, circulating.
circuler [sirky'le], *v.i.* to circulate, to revolve, to move round; to be current.
cire [si:r], *n.f.* beeswax; wax; taper.
ciré [si're], *n.m.* (*Naut.*) (suit of) oilskins.
cirer [si're], *v.t.* to wax; to black *or* to polish (*boots*).

cireur [si'rœːr], *n.m.* (*fem.* **cireuse** (1)) polisher; ***cireuse électrique***, electric polisher.
cireux [si'rø], *a.* (*fem.* **cireuse** (2)) waxy.
ciron [si'rɔ̃], *n.m.* mite.
cirque [sirk], *n.m.* circus.
cirrus [sir'ryːs], *n.m.* cirrus (*curl-cloud*).
cirure [si'ryːr], *n.f.* prepared wax.
cisaille [si'zɑːj], *n.f.* clipping *or* shearing of metals; (*pl.*) shears; (*Bookb.*) guillotine.
cisailler [sizɑ'je], *v.t.* to pare, to clip (*coins etc.*); to cut with shears.
cisalpin [sizal'pɛ̃], *a.* Cisalpine.
ciseau [si'zo], *n.m.* (*pl.* **-eaux**) chisel; (*pl.*) scissors.
ciseler [siz'le], *v.t.* (*conjug. like* AMENER) to chisel; to chase.
ciselet [siz'lɛ], *n.m.* small chisel, graver.
ciseleur [siz'lœːr], *n.m.* chaser; carver, sculptor.
ciselure [siz'lyːr], *n.f.* chasing, sculpture, carving.
cisoires [si'zwaːr], *n.f.* (*used only in pl.*) big bench-shears (*to cut sheet iron*).
ciste [sist], *n.m.* cistus, rock-rose.
citadelle [sita'dɛl], *n.f.* citadel; (*fig.*) stronghold.
citadin [sita'dɛ̃], *n.m.* (*fem.* **-e**) citizen, townsman *or* -woman.
citation [sitɑ'sjɔ̃], *n.f.* citation, quotation; summons.
cité [si'te], *n.f.* city, town.
citer [si'te], *v.t.* to cite, to quote; to summon.
citérieur [site'rjœːr], *a.* (*Geog.*) nearer, hithermost.
citerne [si'tɛrn], *n.f.* cistern, reservoir; (*Naut.*) tanker.
cithare [si'taːr], *n.f.* zither.
citoyen [sitwa'jɛ̃], *n.m.* (*fem.* **-enne**) citizen, burgess; (*fig.*) patriot.
citrate [si'trat], *n.m.* citrate.
citrin [si'trɛ̃], *a.* citrine, lemon-coloured.
citrique [si'trik], *a.* citric.
citron [si'trɔ̃], *a.* lemon-coloured.—*n.m.* lemon, citron.
citronnade [sitrɔ'nad], *n.f.* lemon-squash.
citronnat [sitrɔ'na], *n.m.* candied lemon-peel.
citronné [sitrɔ'ne], *a.* lemon-flavoured.
citronnier [sitrɔ'nje], *n.m.* citron-tree.
citrouille [si'truːj], *n.f.* pumpkin, gourd.
cive [siːv], **civette** (1) [si'vɛt], [CIBOULETTE].
civet [si'vɛ], *n.m.* wine stew (*of venison*); ***civet de lièvre***, jugged hare.
civette (1) [CIVE].
civette (2) [si'vɛt], *n.f.* civet-cat; civet.
civière [si'vjɛːr], *n.f.* hand-barrow; stretcher; bier.
civil [si'vil], *a.* civil; private; plain; polite.—*n.m.* civilian.
civilement [sivil'mɑ̃], *adv.* civilly; courteously.
civilisable [sivili'zabl], *a.* civilizable.
civilisateur [siviliza'tœːr], *a.* (*fem.* **-trice**) civilizing.
civilisation [sivilizɑ'sjɔ̃], *n.f.* civilization.
civiliser [sivili'ze], *v.t.* to civilize. **se civiliser**, *v.r.* to become civilized.
civilité [sivili'te], *n.f.* civility, good manners; (*pl.*) compliments.
civique [si'vik], *a.* civic.
civisme [si'vism], *n.m.* good citizenship.

clabaudage [klabo'daːʒ], *n.m.* barking, bawling.
clabauder [klabo'de], *v.i.* to clamour, to bawl out.
clabaudeur [klabo'dœːr], *n.m.* (*fem.* **-euse**) brawler, scandalmonger.
claie [klɛ], *n.f.* wattle, hurdle; screen (*of a sieve*).
clair [klɛːr], *a.* clear, bright, luminous; light-coloured, pure, cloudless; thin (*of liquids etc.*); plain, intelligible, obvious.—*adv.* clearly, distinctly, plainly.—*n.m.* light, clearness; (*Paint.*) highlight.
Claire [klɛːr], *f.* Clara, Cla(i)re.
clairement [klɛr'mɑ̃], *adv.* clearly, plainly, distinctly.
clairet [klɛ'rɛ], *a.* (*fem.* **clairette** (1)) palish, lightish (*of wines*).—*n.m.* light-red wine.
clairette (2) [klɛ'rɛt], *n.f.* white grape.
claire-voie [klɛr'vwɑ], *n.f.* (*pl.* **claires-voies**) wooden fencing; opening (*in garden wall*), wicket; skylight.
clairière [klɛ'rjɛːr], *n.f.* clearing, glade.
clair-obscur [klɛrɔps'kyːr], *n.m.* (*pl.* **clairs-obscurs**) chiaroscuro; light and shade.
clairon [klɛ'rɔ̃], *n.m.* clarion, bugle; bugler.
clairsemé [klɛrsə'me], *a.* thin, thinly sown, scattered.
clairvoyance [klɛrvwa'jɑ̃ːs], *n.f.* sharpness, perspicacity; clairvoyance.
clairvoyant [klɛrvwa'jɑ̃], *a.* clear-sighted, discerning; clairvoyant.
clamer [kla'me], *v.t.* to cry out, to shout.
clameur [kla'mœːr], *n.f.* clamour, outcry.
clan [klɑ̃], *n.m.* clan.
clandestin [klɑ̃dɛs'tɛ̃], *a.* clandestine, secret.
clandestinement [klɑ̃dɛstin'mɑ̃], *adv.* clandestinely, secretly.
clapement [CLAPPEMENT].
clapet [kla'pɛ], *n.m.* valve, clapper.
clapier [kla'pje], *n.m.* hutch (*for rabbits*).
clapir [kla'piːr], *v.i.* to squeak (*of rabbits*). **se clapir**, *v.r.* to hide in a hole, to squat, to cower.
clapotage [klapɔ'taːʒ], *n.m.* rippling, plashing; lapping.
clapotement [klapɔt'mɑ̃], *n.m.* [CLAPOTAGE].
clapoter [klapɔ'te], *v.i.* to plash, to chop.
clapoteux [klapɔ'tø], *a.* (*fem.* **-euse**) plashing, choppy, rough.
clapotis [klapɔ'ti], *n.m.* [CLAPOTAGE].
clappement or **clapement** [klap'mɑ̃], *n.m.* clacking, smacking.
clapper [kla'pe], *v.i.* to clack, to smack (*of the tongue*).
claque (1) [klak], *n.f.* slap, smack; claque (*paid applauders at theatres*); (*pl.*) (*C*) clogs, galoshes.
claque (2) [klak], *n.m.* opera-hat, crush-hat.
claquebois [klak'bwɑ], *n.m.* xylophone.
claquement [klak'mɑ̃], *n.m.* clapping, clap; snapping; cracking; chattering; slamming.
claquemurer [klakmy're], *v.t.* to coop up, to imprison. **se claquemurer**, *v.r.* to shut oneself up.
claquer [kla'ke], *v.t.* to slap, to crack, to slam.—*v.i.* to snap, to crack, to clap, to clack; to slam, to bang.
claqueter [klak'te], *v.i.* (*conjug. like* APPELER) to cackle (*of a hen*); to cry (*of the stork*).
claquette [kla'kɛt], *n.f.* clapper, rattle; ***danseur à claquettes***, tap-dancer.

claquoir [kla'kwa:r], *n.m.* [CLAQUETTE].
clarification [klarifika'sjɔ̃], *n.f.* clarification.
clarifier [klari'fje], *v.t.* to clarify; to purify, to fine. **se clarifier**, *v.r.* to clarify, to settle.
clarine [kla'rin], *n.f.* bell (*attached to cattle*).
clarinette [klari'nɛt], *n.f.* clarinet.
clarinettiste [klarinɛ'tist], *n.* clarinetist.
clarté [klar'te], *n.f.* light, splendour; clearness.
classe [klɑ:s], *n.f.* class, order, rank; kind, tribe; class *or* form (*in a school*); classroom; lesson; (*pl.*) school-hours; school-time.
classement [klɑs'mɑ̃], *n.m.* classing, classification, filing.
classer [klɑ'se], *v.t.* to class, to classify, to sort; to file.
classeur [klɑ'sœ:r], *n.m.* card-index; file.
classification [klasifikɑ'sjɔ̃], *n.f.* classification.
classifier [klasi'fje], *v.t.* to classify.
classique [kla'sik], *a.* classic, classical; standard (*of authors, books etc.*); conventional.—*n.m.* classic (*author, book etc.*).
claudicant [klodi'kɑ̃], *a.* lame, limping.
claudication [klodikɑ'sjɔ̃], *n.f.* lameness, limping, halting.
clause [klo:z], *n.f.* clause.
claustral [klos'tral], *a.* (*m. pl.* **-aux**) claustral; monastic.
claustration [klostrɑ'sjɔ̃], *n.f.* claustration, confinement.
claustrer [klos'tre], *v.t.* to cloister, to confine.
claustrophobie [klostrɔfɔ'bi], *n.f.* claustrophobia.
clavecin [klav'sɛ̃], *n.m.* harpsichord, clavecin.
clavette [kla'vɛt], *n.f.* (*Tech.*) peg, pin; key, cotter.
claviculaire [klaviky'lɛ:r], *a.* clavicular.
clavicule [klavi'kyl], *n.f.* clavicle, collar-bone.
clavier [kla'vje], *n.m.* clavier, key-board (*piano, typewriter*), key-frame.
clayère [klɛ'jɛ:r], *n.f.* oyster bed *or* breeding-ground.
clayon [klɛ'jɔ̃], *n.m.* wattle; stand (*for draining cheese*).
clef or **clé** [kle], *n.f.* key; plug (*of a cock*); spanner; keystone (*of arch*); (*Mus.*) clef, tuning-key.
clématite [klema'tit], *n.f.* (*Bot.*) clematis.
clémence [kle'mɑ̃:s], *n.f.* clemency, mercy.
clément [kle'mɑ̃], *a.* clement, merciful, lenient; mild (*of the weather*).
Clémentine [klemɑ̃'tin], *f.* Clementine.
clenche [klɑ̃:ʃ], **clenchette** [klɑ̃'ʃɛt], *n.f.* catch *or* latch (*of a lock*).
cleptomane [klɛptɔ'man], *n.* kleptomaniac.
cleptomanie [klɛptɔma'ni], *n.f.* kleptomania.
clerc [klɛ:r], *n.m.* clergyman; (*fig.*) scholar.
clergé [klɛr'ʒe], *n.m.* clergy.
clérical [kleri'kal], *a.* (*m. pl.* **-aux**) clerical.
cléricalisme [klerika'lism], *n.m.* clericalism.
cléricaliste [klerika'list], *n.* clericalist.
clic-clac [klik'klak], *n.m.* cracking (*of a whip*).
clichage [kli'ʃa:ʒ], *n.m.* stereotyping, stereotype.
cliché [kli'ʃe], *n.m.* stereotype plate, cliché; (*fig.*) stereotyped phrase; (*Phot.*) negative; (*Sculp.*) cast.
clicher [kli'ʃe], *v.t.* to stereotype.
client [kli'ɑ̃], *n.m.* (*fem.* **-e**) client (*of lawyers etc.*); patient (*of physicians*); customer (*of tradesmen*).
clientèle [kliɑ̃'tɛl], *n.f.* clientele; practice; connection; custom; goodwill (*of a business*).
clignement [kliɲ'mɑ̃], *n.m.* winking, blinking, wink.
cligner [kli'ɲe], *v.t., v.i.* to wink, to blink.
clignotant [kliɲɔ'tɑ̃], *a.* winking, blinking.—*n.m.* (*Motor.*) winker, flashing indicator.
clignotement [kliɲɔt'mɑ̃], *n.m.* winking, blinking.
clignoter [kliɲɔ'te], *v.i.* to wink, to blink.
climat [kli'mɑ], *n.m.* climate; region, country.
climatérique [klimate'rik], **climatique** [klima'tik], *a.* climatic.
climatisation [klimatizɑ'sjɔ̃], *n.f.* air conditioning.
climatisé [klimati'ze], *a.* air-conditioned.
climatiser [klimati'ze], *v.t.* to air-condition.
clin [klɛ̃], *n.m.* wink (*of an eye*).
clinicien [klini'sjɛ̃], *a.m.* clinical.—*n.m.* clinical physician.
clinique [kli'nik], *a.* clinical.—*n.f.* clinical surgery; clinic, nursing-home.
clinquant [klɛ̃'kɑ̃], *a.* showy, gaudy, trumpery.—*n.m.* tinsel; (*fig.*) glitter, affectation.
clip [klip], *n.m.* clip-fastened jewel.
clipper [kli'pɛr], *n.m.* (*Naut.* and *Av.*) clipper.
clique [klik], *n.f.* set, coterie, party, clique.
cliquet [kli'kɛ], *n.m.* catch, pawl.
cliqueter [klik'te], *v.i.* (*conjug. like* APPELER) to click *or* jingle; (*Motor.*) to 'pink'.
cliquetis [klik'ti], *n.m.* clanking, clash.
cliquette [kli'kɛt], *n.f.* sinker (*of net*); (*usu. pl.*) bones (*a kind of castanets*).
clissage [kli'sa:ʒ], *n.m.* wickering.
clisse [klis], *n.f.* wicker mat for draining cheese; basket-work cover for a bottle; (*Surg.*) splint.
clisser [kli'se], *v.t.* to wicker, to cover with wicker-work etc.
clivage [kli'va:ʒ], *n.m.* (*Min.*) cleavage; cleaving.
cliver [kli've], *v.t.* to cleave (*diamonds etc.*). **se cliver**, *v.r.* to split, to be cleft.
cloaque [klɔ'ak], *n.m.* drain, sewer, sink, cesspool; (*fig.*) filthy hole.
clochage [klɔ'ʃa:ʒ], *n.m.* cultivation under cloches.
clochard [klɔ'ʃa:r], *n.m.* (*fam.*) tramp, vagrant; (*Am.*) hobo.
cloche [klɔʃ], *n.f.* bell; dish-cover; blister; stew-pan; (*Gard.*) cloche.
clochement [klɔʃ'mɑ̃], *n.m.* hobbling, halting.
cloche-pied [klɔʃ'pje], *n.m.* hopping on one leg.
clocher (1) [klɔ'ʃe], *n.m.* steeple, belfry; (*fig.*) parish, native place.
clocher (2) [klɔ'ʃe], *v.t.* (*Gard.*) to cover with a cloche.
clocher (3) [klɔ'ʃe], *v.i.* to limp, to hobble; (*fig., fam.*) to go wrong somewhere, to be defective.
clocheton [klɔʃ'tɔ̃], *n.m.* bell-turret.
clochette [klɔ'ʃɛt], *n.f.* small bell, hand-bell; bell-flower.
cloison [klwa'zɔ̃], *n.f.* partition, division; compartment; (*Naut.*) bulkhead.
cloisonnage [klwazɔ'na:ʒ], **cloisonnement** [klwazɔn'mɑ̃], *n.m.* partition-work, wainscoting.

cloisonner [klwazɔ'ne], *v.t.* to partition.

cloître [klwɑ:tr], *n.m.* cloister; cathedral close.

cloîtrer [klwɑ'tre], *v.t.* to shut up in a cloister, to immure. **se cloîtrer**, *v.r.* to enter a monastery *or* convent.

cloîtrier [klwɑ'trie], *n.m.* (*fem.* **-ière**) cloistered monk *or* nun.

clopin-clopant [klɔpɛ̃klɔ'pɑ̃], *adv.* limpingly, hobbling along.

clopiner [klɔpi'ne], *v.i.* to limp, to halt, to hobble.

cloporte [klɔ'pɔrt], *n.m.* woodlouse.

cloque [klɔk], *n.f.* blister (*on skin, paint etc.*); blight, rust (*of plants*).

cloquer [klɔ'ke], *v.i.* to blister (*of paint*).

clore [klɔ:r], *v.t. irr.* (*chiefly used in p.p.*) to close, to shut; to enclose; to end.—*v.i.* to close, to shut. **se clore**, *v.r.* to close, to be closed; to end.

clos [klo], *a.* closed, sealed; completed; ***à huis clos***, in camera.—*n.m.* close; enclosure, field.

closeau [klo'zo], *n.m.* (*pl.* **-eaux**) small garden.

closerie [kloz'ri], *n.f.* small enclosed farm *or* garden.

clôture [klo'ty:r], *n.f.* enclosure, fence; closing, close; closure; (*Relig.*) enclosure (*of nuns etc.*).

clôturer [kloty're], *v.t.* to close.

clou [klu], *n.m.* nail, spike, stud; (*Path.*) carbuncle, boil; ***clou de girofle***, clove.

clouage [klu'a:ʒ], **clouement** [klu'mɑ̃] *n.m.* nailing.

clouer [klu'e], *v.t.* to nail; to fix; (*fig.*) to detain.

clouter [klu'te], *v.t.* to adorn with nails, to stud; ***passage clouté***, pedestrian crossing.

clouterie [klu'tri], *n.f.* nail-factory; nail trade.

cloutier [klu'tje], *n.m.* nail-maker, nail-dealer.

cloutière [klu'tjɛ:r], *n.f.* nail-box.

clovisse [klɔ'vis], *n.f.* winkle; cockle.

clown [klun], *n.m.* clown.

cloyère [klwa'jɛ:r], *n.f.* oyster-basket.

club [klʌb, klyb], *n.m.* club (*sporting* or *political*).

clystère [klis'tɛ:r] *n.m.* clyster, injection, enema.

coaccusé [koaky'ze], *n.m.* (*fem.* **-ée**) fellow-prisoner; co-defendant.

coacquéreur [koake'rœ:r], *n.m.* (*fem.* **-euse**) co-purchaser, joint buyer.

coacquisition [koakizi'sjɔ̃], *n.f.* joint purchase.

coactif [koak'tif], *a.* (*fem.* **-tive**) coactive.

coaction [koak'sjɔ̃], *n.f.* coercion, compulsion.

coadjuteur [koadʒy'tœ:r], *n.m.* coadjutor.

coadjutrice [koadʒy'tris], *n.f.* coadjutrix.

coagulant [koagy'lɑ̃], *a.* coagulant.

coagulation [koagylɑ'sjɔ̃], *n.f.* coagulation.

coaguler [koagy'le], *v.t.* to coagulate. **se coaguler**, *v.r.* to coagulate.

coaliser [koali'ze], *v.t.* to unite in a coalition. **se coaliser**, *v.r.* to coalesce, to league, to unite, to combine.

coalition [koali'sjɔ̃], *n.f.* coalition, union, league.

coassement [koas'mɑ̃], *n.m.* croaking (*of frogs*).

coasser [koa'se], *v.i.* to croak (*of frogs*).

coassocié [koasɔ'sje], *n.m.* (*fem.* **-ée**) co-partner.

coauteur [koo'tœ:r], *n.m.* co-author.

cobalt [kɔ'balt], *n.m.* cobalt.

cobaye [kɔ'ba:j], *n.m.* guinea-pig.

cobra [kɔ'bra], *n.m.* cobra, hooded-snake.

cocagne [kɔ'kaɲ], *n.f.* ***mât de cocagne***, greasy pole; ***pays de cocagne***, land of plenty.

cocaïne [kɔka'in], *n.f.* cocaine.

cocarde [kɔ'kard], *n.f.* cockade; rosette.

cocasse [kɔ'kas], *a.* (*fam.*) odd, laughable, comical.

cocasserie [kɔkas'ri], *n.f.* drollery, foolery, farce.

coccinelle [kɔksi'nɛl], *n.f.* lady-bird.

coche (1) [kɔʃ], *n.m.* coach; ***c'est la mouche du coche***, he is a busy-body.

coche (2) [kɔʃ], *n.f.* notch, score.

coche (3) [kɔʃ], *n.f.* sow.

cochenille [kɔʃ'ni:j], *n.f.* cochineal.

cocher (1) [kɔ'ʃe], *n.m.* coachman, driver.

cocher (2) [kɔ'ʃe], *v.t.* to notch.

cochère [kɔ'ʃɛ:r], *a.f.* for carriages; ***porte cochère***, carriage-entrance, gateway.

cochet [kɔ'ʃɛ], *n.m.* young cock, cockerel.

cochon [kɔ'ʃɔ̃], *n.m.* hog, pig; pork; ***cochon d'Inde***, guinea-pig.

cochonnée [kɔʃɔ'ne], *n.f.* litter (*of pigs*).

cochonner [kɔʃɔ'ne], *v.i.* to farrow, to pig.

cochonnerie [kɔʃɔn'ri], *n.f.* nastiness, filth.

cochonnet [kɔʃɔ'nɛ], *n.m.* young pig; jack (*at bowls*).

cocktail [kɔk'tɛl], *n.m.* cocktail; cocktail party.

coco [ko'ko], *n.m.* coco-nut.

cocon [kɔ'kɔ̃], *n.m.* cocoon.

cocotier [kɔkɔ'tje], *n.m.* coco-nut palm.

coction [kɔk'sjɔ̃], *n.f.* coction, boiling; digestion (*of food*).

code [kɔd], *n.m.* code (*digest* or *collection of laws*); law, rule.

codemandeur [kodəmɑ̃'dœ:r], *n.m.* (*fem.* **-eresse**) co-plaintiff.

coder [kɔ'de], *v.t.* to code (*telegram*).

codétenteur [kodetɑ̃'tœ:r], *n.m.* (*fem.* **-trice**) joint-holder.

codétenu [kodet'ny], *n.m.* (*fem.* **-e**) fellow-prisoner.

codicillaire [kɔdisi'lɛ:r], *a.* contained in a codicil.

codicille [kɔdi'sil], *n.m.* codicil, rider.

codifier [kɔdi'fje], *v.t.* to codify.

codirecteur [kodirɛk'tœ:r], *n.m.* (*fem.* **-trice**) joint manager.

codonataire [kodɔna'tɛ:r], *n.* joint donee.

codonateur [kodɔna'tœ:r], *n.m.* (*fem.* **-trice**) joint donor.

coéquipier [koeki'pje], *n.m.* fellow member (*of a crew, team etc.*).

coercer [koɛr'se], *v.t.* to coerce.

coercition [koɛrsi'sjɔ̃], *n.f.* coercion.

cœur [kœ:r], *n.m.* heart; (*fig.*) bosom, mind, soul; courage; core, middle; love, affection; hearts (*cards*).

coexistant [koɛgzis'tɑ̃], *a.* coexistent.

coexistence [koɛgzis'tɑ̃:s], *n.f.* coexistence.

coexister [koɛgzis'te], *v.i.* to coexist.

coffre [kɔfr], *n.m.* chest, trunk; coffer; (*Naut.*) mooring-buoy; boot (*of a car*).

coffre-fort [kɔfrə'fɔ:r], *n.m.* (*pl.* **coffres-forts**) strong-box, safe.

coffret [kɔ'frɛ], *n.m.* little chest, casket.
cogitation [kɔʒitɑ'sjɔ̃], *n.f.* cogitation, reflection.
cognac [kɔ'ɲak], *n.m.* Cognac brandy.
cognasse [kɔ'ɲas], *n.f.* wild quince.
cognassier [kɔɲa'sje], *n.m.* quince-tree.
cognée [kɔ'ɲe], *n.f.* axe, hatchet.
cogner [kɔ'ɲe], *v.t.* to knock in, to drive in; to thump.—*v.i.* to hit, to bump (***contre***); to knock (*engine*). **se cogner**, *v.r.* to knock (*against*).
cohabitant [koabi'tɑ̃], *a.* cohabiting (*with*).
cohabitation [koabitɑ'sjɔ̃], *n.f.* cohabitation.
cohabiter [koabi'te], *v.i.* to cohabit.
cohérence [kɔe'rɑ̃:s], *n.f.* coherence.
cohérent [kɔe'rɑ̃], *a.* coherent.
cohériter [koeri'te], *v.i.* to inherit conjointly.
cohéritier [koeri'tje], *n.m.* (*fem.* **-ière**) co-heir, co-heiress.
cohésif [kɔe'zif], *a.* (*fem.* **-sive**) cohesive.
cohésion [kɔe'zjɔ̃], *n.f.* cohesion.
cohorte [kɔ'ɔrt], *n.f.* cohort; (*poet.*) troop, host; (*colloq.*) crew, gang.
cohue [kɔ'y], *n.f.* throng, mob, crush.
coi [kwa], *a.* (*fem.* **coite** (1)) quiet, calm, still.
coiffe [kwaf], *n.f.* hood, head-dress.
coiffer [kwa'fe], *v.t.* to put on the head of; to dress the hair of; (*fig.*) to infatuate.—*v.i.* to dress hair; to become; to suit. **se coiffer**, *v.r.* to put one's hat on; to do one's hair.
coiffeur [kwa'fœ:r], *n.m.* (*fem.* **-euse**) hair-dresser.—*n.f.* (**-euse**) lady's dressing-table.
coiffure [kwa'fy:r], *n.f.* head-dress, hairstyle.
coin [kwɛ̃], *n.m.* corner, angle, nook; (*Coin. etc.*) stamp.
coincer [kwɛ̃'se], *v.t.* (*conjug. like* COMMENCER) to wedge. **se coincer**, *v.r.* to jam (*of machines*).
coïncidence [kɔɛ̃si'dɑ̃:s], *n.f.* coincidence.
coïncident [kɔɛ̃si'dɑ̃], *a.* coincident.
coïncider [kɔɛ̃si'de], *v.i.* to coincide, to be coincident.
coing [kwɛ̃], *n.m.* quince.
coïntéressé [kɔɛ̃terɛ'se], *a.* jointly interested. —*n.m.* (*fem.* **-ée**) associate, partner.
coite (1) [kwat], [COI].
coite (2), **coitte** [COUETTE].
cojouissance [koʒwi'sɑ̃:s], *n.f.* (*Law*) joint use.
coke [kɔk], *n.m.* coke.
cokéfier [kɔke'fje], *v.t.* to coke.
col [kɔl], *n.m.* neck (*of a bottle, dress etc.*); collar; pass, col (*of mountain*).
colback [kɔl'bak], *n.m.* busby.
colchique [kɔl'ʃik], *n.m.* (*Bot.*) meadow-saffron, colchicum.
colégataire [kolega'tɛ:r], *n.* co-legatee.
coléoptère [kɔleɔp'tɛ:r], *a.* coleopterous.—*n.m.* beetle.
colère [kɔ'lɛ:r], *n.f.* anger, wrath, rage, fury.
colérique [kɔle'rik], *a.* choleric, irascible.
colibri [kɔli'bri], *n.m.* humming-bird.
colifichet [kɔlifi'ʃɛ], *n.m.* trinket, knick-knack.
colimaçon [kɔlimɑ'sɔ̃], *n.m.* snail; ***escalier en colimaçon***, spiral staircase.
colin-maillard [kɔlɛ̃ma'ja:r], *n.m. inv.* blind-man's-buff.
colique [kɔ'lik], *n.f.* colic, stomach-ache.
colis [kɔ'li], *n.m.* package, parcel, case.
collaborateur [kɔlabɔra'tœ:r], *n.m.* (*fem.* **-trice**) collaborator.
collaboration [kɔlabɔrɑ'sjɔ̃], *n.f.* collaboration.
collaborer [kɔlabɔ're], *v.i.* to collaborate.
collage [kɔ'la:ʒ], *n.m.* pasting, gluing; paper-hanging; (*Art*) collage.
collant [kɔ'lɑ̃], *a.* sticky; tight, close-fitting.
collatéral [kɔllate'ral], *a.* (*m. pl.* **-aux**) collateral.
collatéralement [kɔllateral'mɑ̃], *adv.* collaterally.
collation [kɔllɑ'sjɔ̃], *n.f.* light meal; comparison (*of documents etc.*).
collationnement [kɔllasjɔn'mɑ̃], *n.m.* collating, comparing.
collationner [kɔllasjɔ'ne], *v.t.* to collate, to compare.—*v.i.* to have a snack.
colle [kɔl], *n.f.* paste, gum; poser; sham, fib.
collecte [kɔ'lɛkt], *n.f.* collection (*of money etc.*); collect (*prayer*).
collecteur [kɔlɛk'tœ:r], *n.m.* (*fem.* **-trice**) collector.
collectif [kɔlɛk'tif], *a.* (*fem.* **-tive**) collective.
collection [kɔlɛk'sjɔ̃], *n.f.* collection; set.
collectionner [kɔlɛksjɔ'ne], *v.t.* to collect, to make collections of things.
collectionneur [kɔlɛksjɔ'nœ:r], *n.m.* (*fem.* **-euse**) collector.
collectivement [kɔlɛktiv'mɑ̃], *adv.* collectively.
collectivisme [kɔlɛkti'vism], *n.m.* collectivism.
collectiviste [kɔlɛkti'vist], *n.* collectivist.
collectivité [kɔlɛktivi'te], *n.f.* collectivity; common ownership.
collège [kɔ'lɛʒ], *n.m.* college; grammar-school.
collégien [kɔle'ʒjɛ̃], *n.m.* (*fem.* **-enne**) high-school boy *or* girl.
collègue [kɔl'lɛg], *n.* colleague.
coller [kɔ'le], *v.t.* to paste, to glue; to stick together.—*v.i.* to stick, to adhere. **se coller,** *v.r.* to stick to.
collerette [kɔl'rɛt], *n.f.* collar (*for ladies*).
collet [kɔ'lɛ], *n.m.* collar (*of gown etc.*); cape; flange; snare.
colleter [kɔl'te], *v.t.* (*conjug. like* APPELER) to collar, to seize by the neck.—*v.i.* to set snares. **se colleter**, *v.r.* to come to grips (*with someone*).
colleur [kɔ'lœ:r], *n.m.* (*fem.* **-euse**) gluer, paster, paper-hanger; bill-sticker.
collier [kɔ'lje], *n.m.* necklace; gold chain (*of knightly orders etc.*); collar (*for animals*).
colline [kɔ'lin], *n.f.* hill, hillock.
collision [kɔli'zjɔ̃], *n.f.* collision.
collocation [kɔllɔkɑ'sjɔ̃], *n.f.* classification.
colloque [kɔl'lɔk], *n.m.* colloquy, conference.
collusion [kɔlly'zjɔ̃], *n.f.* collusion.
collusoire [kɔlly'zwa:r], *a.* collusory, collusive.
Colomb [kɔ'lɔ̃], *m.* Columbus.
colombe [kɔ'lɔ̃:b], *n.f.* (*poet.*) pigeon, dove.
Colombie [kɔlɔ̃'bi], **la**, *f.* Colombia.
colombien [kɔlɔ̃'bjɛ̃], *a.* (*fem.* **-enne**) Colombian.—*n.m.* (**Colombien,** *fem.* **-enne**) Colombian (*person*).
colombier [kɔlɔ̃'bje], *n.m.* dove-cot, pigeon-house.
colombin [kɔlɔ̃'bɛ̃], *a.* columbine; dove-colour.
colombophile [kɔlɔ̃bɔ'fil], *a.* and *n.* pigeon-fancier.

colon [kɔ'lɔ̃], *n.m.* colonist, planter; settler.

côlon [ko'lɔ̃], *n.m.* (*Anat.*) colon.

colonel [kɔlɔ'nɛl], *n.m.* colonel; (*Av.*) group captain.

colonial [kɔlɔ'njal], *a.* (*m. pl.* **-aux**) colonial.—*n.m.* (*fem.* **-e**) colonial.

colonie [kɔlɔ'ni], *n.f.* colony, settlement; ***colonie de vacances***, holiday camp.

colonisation [kɔlɔnizɑ'sjɔ̃], *n.f.* colonization.

coloniser [kɔlɔni'ze], *v.t.* to colonize.

colonnade [kɔlɔ'nad], *n.f.* (*Arch.*) colonnade.

colonne [kɔ'lɔn], *n.f.* column, pillar; column (*of units, tens etc.*).

colonnette [kɔlɔ'nɛt], *n.f.* little column.

colorant [kɔlɔ'rɑ̃], *a.* colouring.—*n.m.* dye.

coloration [kɔlɔrɑ'sjɔ̃], *n.f.* coloration, staining.

colorer [kɔlɔ're], *v.t.* to colour, to dye; to varnish. **se colorer**, *v.r.* to colour (*of a thing*).

coloriage [kɔlɔ'rja:ʒ], *n.m.* (*Paint.*) colouring.

colorier [kɔlɔ'rje], *v.t.* to colour, to stain (*a drawing etc.*).

coloris [kɔlɔ'ri], *n.m.* colouring, art of colouring.

coloriste [kɔlɔ'rist], *n.* colourer; colourist.

colossal [kɔlɔ'sal], *a.* (*m. pl.* **-aux**) colossal.

colosse [kɔ'lɔs], *n.m.* colossus, giant.

colportage [kɔlpɔr'ta:ʒ], *n.m.* hawking, peddling.

colporter [kɔlpɔr'te], *v.t.* to hawk about; to spread.

colporteur [kɔlpɔr'tœ:r], *n.m.* hawker, pedlar.

coltiner [kɔlti'ne], *v.t.* to carry heavy loads (*on head and back*).

coltineur [kɔlti'nœ:r], *n.m.* coal-heaver, load-porter.

colza [kɔl'za], *n.m.* colza, rape, rape-seed.

coma [kɔ'ma], *n.m.* coma.

comateux [kɔma'tø], *a.* (*fem.* **-euse**) comatose.

combat [kɔ̃'ba], *n.m.* combat, fight, battle, contest; struggle; ***hors de combat***, disabled.

combattant [kɔ̃ba'tɑ̃], *n.m.* combatant; champion; ***anciens combattants***, ex-service men.

combattre [kɔ̃'batr], *v.t.* (*conjug. like* BATTRE) to fight, to combat, to wage war against, to strive against.—*v.i.* to fight, to vie, to struggle. **se combattre**, *v.r.* to combat; to contend with each other.

combien [kɔ̃'bjɛ̃], *adv.* how much, how many; how; how far; how long.

combinaison [kɔ̃binɛ'zɔ̃], *n.f.* combination; contrivance, scheme; overalls; slip (*woman's undergarment*).

combiné [kɔ̃bi'ne], *n.m.* (*Chem.*) compound; (*Rad.*) radiogram.

combiner [kɔ̃bi'ne], *v.t.* to combine; (*fig.*) to contrive.

comble [kɔ̃bl], *n.m.* heaping up above a full measure; summit; (*fig.*) zenith; (*pl.*) roof-timbers.—*a.* full, heaped up, full to the top; ***salle comble***, house full.

comblement [kɔ̃blə'mɑ̃], *n.m.* filling up, heaping up.

combler [kɔ̃'ble], *v.t.* to heap up, to fill up; to complete; to overwhelm.

comburant [kɔ̃by'rɑ̃], *a.* (*Chem.*) causing burning (*of oxygen etc.*).—*n.m.* fuel.

combustibilité [kɔ̃bystibili'te], *n.f.* combustibility.

combustible [kɔ̃bys'tibl], *a.* combustible.—*n.m.* combustible; fuel, firing.

combustion [kɔ̃bys'tjɔ̃], *n.f.* combustion, flame.

comédie [kɔme'di], *n.f.* comedy; theatre; players.

comédien [kɔme'djɛ̃], *n.m.* (*fem.* **-enne**) comedian, actor, actress, player; (*fig.*) hypocrite.

comestible [kɔmɛs'tibl], *a.* edible, eatable.—*n.m.* eatable; (*pl.*) eatables.

comète [kɔ'mɛt], *n.f.* comet.

comice [kɔ'mis], *n.m.* meeting; electoral meeting; ***comice agricole***, agricultural show.

comique [kɔ'mik], *a.* comic; comical, ludicrous.—*n.m.* comic art, comedy.

comiquement [kɔmik'mɑ̃], *adv.* comically.

comité [kɔmi'te], *n.m.* committee, board.

commandant [kɔmɑ̃'dɑ̃], *a.* commanding.—*n.m.* (*fem.* **-e**) commander, commanding officer, commandant; major.

commande [kɔ'mɑ̃:d], *n.f.* order; (*Mach.*) driving-wheel.

commandement [kɔmɑ̃d'mɑ̃], *n.m.* command; authority, control; order; commandment, law.

commander [kɔmɑ̃'de], *v.t.* to command, to order; to govern; to overlook.—*v.i.* to command, to have authority. **se commander**, *v.r.* to control oneself.

commandeur [kɔmɑ̃'dœ:r], *n.m.* commander (*in orders of knighthood*).

commanditaire [kɔmɑ̃di'tɛ:r], *n.* sleeping partner.

commandite [kɔmɑ̃'dit], *n.f.* limited partnership.

commanditer [kɔmɑ̃di'te], *v.t.* to finance (*a commercial undertaking*).

commando [kɔmɑ̃'do], *n.m.* commando.

comme [kɔm], *adv.* as; like, such as; almost, nearly, as if; how, in what way, to what extent.—*conj.* as, since, because.

commémoraison [kɔmemɔrɛ'zɔ̃], *n.f.* (*R.-C. Ch.*) commemoration, remembrance.

commémoratif [kɔmemɔra'tif], *a.* (*fem.* **-tive**) commemorative.

commémoration [kɔmemɔrɑ'sjɔ̃], *n.f.* commemoration.

commémorer [kɔmemɔ're], *v.t.* to commemorate, to remember.

commençant [kɔmɑ̃'sɑ̃], *n.m.* (*fem.* **-e**) beginner, novice.

commencement [kɔmɑ̃s'mɑ̃], *n.m.* beginning, commencement.

commencer [kɔmɑ̃'se], *v.t.*, *v.i.* (*see Verb Tables*) to begin, to commence; to initiate.

commensal [kɔmɑ̃'sal], *n.m.* (*m. pl.* **-aux**) habitual guest; fellow-boarder, messmate.

commensurable [kɔmɑ̃sy'rabl], *a.* commensurable.

comment [kɔ'mɑ̃], *adv.* how, in what manner; why, wherefore.—*int.* what! indeed!—*n.m.* the why and wherefore.

commentaire [kɔmɑ̃'tɛ:r], *n.m.* commentary, exposition; (*fig.*) unfavourable comment.

commentateur [kɔmɑ̃ta'tœ:r], *n.m.* (*fem.* **-trice**) commentator, annotator.

commenter [kɔmɑ̃'te], *v.t.* to comment on, to explain, to annotate.—*v.i.* to criticize adversely.

commérage [kɔme'ra:ʒ], *n.m.* gossip, tittle-tattle.
commerçant [kɔmɛr'sɑ̃], *a.* commercial, mercantile, trading.—*n.m.* (*fem.* **-e**) merchant, tradesman, shopkeeper.
commerce [kɔ'mɛrs], *n.m.* commerce, trade, trading, traffic; intercourse, dealings.
commercer [kɔmɛr'se], *v.i.* (*conjug. like* COMMENCER) to trade, to deal.
commercial [kɔmɛr'sjal], *a.* (*m. pl.* **-aux**) commercial.
commercialement [kɔmɛrsjal'mɑ̃], *adv.* commercially.
commercialisation [kɔmɛrsjalizɑ'sjɔ̃], *n.f.* commercialization.
commercialiser [kɔmɛrsjali'ze], *v.t.* to commercialize.
commère [kɔ'mɛr], *n.f.* godmother; gossip.
commettre [kɔ'mɛtr], *v.t. irr.* (*conjug. like* METTRE) to commit, to perpetrate; to appoint, to empower; to entrust. **se commettre**, *v.r.* to commit oneself.
commis (1) [kɔ'mi], *n.m.* (*fem.* **commise**) clerk; ***commis voyageur***, commercial traveller.
commis (2) [kɔ'mi], *a.* committed, appointed.
commisération [kɔmizerɑ'sjɔ̃], *n.f.* commiseration, compassion, pity.
commissaire [kɔmi'sɛ:r], *n.m.* commissioner; manager, steward, trustee; purser (*of a vessel*).
commissaire-priseur [kɔmisɛrpri'zœ:r], *n.m.* auctioneer, valuer.
commissariat [kɔmisa'rja], *n.m.* commissaryship, trusteeship; (*Mil., Navy*) commissariat; police station.
commission [kɔmi'sjɔ̃], *n.f.* commission, charge; errand; power; (*Comm.*) percentage; warrant.
commissionnaire [kɔmisjɔ'nɛ:r], *n.m.* commission agent, commissionnaire; messenger, porter.
commissionner [kɔmisjɔ'ne], *v.t.* to empower, to commission; to order (*goods*).
commode [kɔ'mɔd], *a.* convenient, commodious, handy; comfortable, suitable; easy.—*n.f.* chest of drawers, commode.
commodément [kɔmɔde'mɑ̃], *adv.* commodiously, conveniently; comfortably suitably.
commodité [kɔmɔdi'te], *n.f.* convenience, accommodation.
commotion [kɔmo'sjɔ̃], *n.f.* commotion; shock; concussion.
commotionné [kɔmosjɔ'ne], *a.* suffering from concussion.
commuable [kɔ'mɥabl], *a.* commutable.
commun [kɔ'mœ̃], *a.* common; usual, ordinary; mean, vulgar; ***le bien commun***, the common weal; ***lieux communs***, commonplaces.—*n.m.* common people.
communal [kɔmy'nal], *a.* (*m. pl.* **-aux**) communal, parochial; common.—*n.m. pl.* (***biens***) ***communaux***, communal property.
communauté [kɔmyno'te], *n.f.* community, society, corporation.
commune [kɔ'myn], *n.f.* commune (*parish, township, in France*).
communément [kɔmyne'mɑ̃], *adv.* commonly, usually.
communiant [kɔmy'njɑ̃], *n.m.* (*fem.* **-e**) communicant.
communicatif [kɔmynika'tif], *a.* (*fem.* **-tive**) communicative, open.
communication [kɔmynikɑ'sjɔ̃], *n.f.* intercourse, communication; (*Teleph.*) call.
communicativement [kɔmynikativ'mɑ̃], *adv.* communicatively.
communier [kɔmy'nje], *v.i.* to communicate, to receive the sacrament.
communion [kɔmy'njɔ̃], *n.f.* communion, fellowship; persuasion; sacrament.
communiqué [kɔmyni'ke], *n.m.* statement, communiqué.
communiquer [kɔmyni'ke], *v.t.* to communicate, to impart; to tell, to acquaint.—*v.i.* to be in contact *or* correspondence (*with*).
communisant [kɔmyni'zɑ̃], *a.* communistic. —*n.m.* (*fem.* **-e**) fellow-traveller.
communisme [kɔmy'nism], *n.m.* communism.
communiste [kɔmy'nist], *n.* communist.
commutable [kɔmy'tabl], [COMMUABLE].
commutateur [kɔmyta'tœ:r], *n.m.* (*Elec.*) switch.
compact [kɔ̃'pakt], *a.* compact, dense.
compagne [kɔ̃'paɲ], *n.f.* female companion, consort; playmate.
compagnie [kɔ̃pa'ɲi], *n.f.* society, companionship; company; (*Comm.*) company.
compagnon [kɔ̃pa'ɲɔ̃], *n.m.* companion, comrade; playmate; mate; (*Bot.*) campion.
comparable [kɔ̃pa'rabl], *a.* comparable.
comparablement [kɔmparablə'mɑ̃], *adv.* in comparison (*with*).
comparaison [kɔ̃parɛ'zɔ̃], *n.f.* comparison; similitude.
comparaître [kɔ̃pa'rɛ:tr], *v.i. irr.* (*conjug. like* CONNAÎTRE) to appear (*before a tribunal*).
comparant [kɔ̃pa'rɑ̃], *n.m.* (*fem.* **-e**) person appearing in court on a summons.
comparatif [kɔ̃para'tif], *a.* (*fem.* **-tive**) comparative.—*n.m.* comparative degree.
comparativement [kɔmparativ'mɑ̃], *adv.* comparatively.
comparer [kɔ̃pa're], *v.t.* to compare. **se comparer**, *v.r.* to be compared.
compartiment [kɔ̃parti'mɑ̃], *n.m.* compartment, division.
compas [kɔ̃'pɑ], *n.m.* pair of compasses; mariner's compass.
compassé [kɔ̃pɑ'se], *a.* formal, stiff, starchy.
compasser [kɔ̃pɑ'se], *v.t.* to measure, set out; to proportion, to regulate; (*fig.*) to weigh, to consider.
compassion [kɔ̃pɑ'sjɔ̃], *n.f.* compassion, pity, mercy.
compatibilité [kɔ̃patibili'te], *n.f.* compatibility.
compatible [kɔmpa'tibl], *a.* compatible, consistent.
compatir [kɔ̃pɑ'ti:r], *v.i.* to sympathize; to agree, to be compatible (*with*).
compatissant [kɔ̃pɑti'sɑ̃], *a.* compassionate, tender.
compatriote [kɔ̃patri'ɔt], *n.* compatriot, fellow-countryman.
compendium [kɔ̃pɑ̃'djɔm], *n.m.* summary.
compensable [kɔ̃pɑ̃'sabl], *a.* that may be compensated.
compensation [kɔ̃pɑ̃sɑ'sjɔ̃], *n.f.* compensation, amends, reparation.

compensatoire [kõpɑ̃sa'twaːr], *a.* compensatory.
compenser [kõpɑ̃'se], *v.t.* to counterbalance, to compensate, to make up for. **se compenser**, *v.r.* to compensate each other; to be set off against.
compère [kõ'pɛːr], *n.m.* godfather; (*fig.*) gossip, crony; confederate.
compétence [kõpe'tɑ̃ːs], *n.f.* competence, cognizance; (*fig.*) department, province; proficiency.
compétent [kõpe'tɑ̃], *a.* competent, qualified; (*fig.*) suitable, requisite.
compétiteur [kõpeti'tœːr], *n.m.* (*fem.* **-trice**) competitor, candidate.
compétitif [kõpeti'tif], *a.* (*fem.* **-tive**) competitive.
compétition [kõpeti'sjõ], *n.f.* competition, rivalry.
compilateur [kõpila'tœːr], *n.m.* compiler.
compilation [kõpilɑ'sjõ], *n.f.* compilation.
compiler [kõpi'le], *v.t.* to compile.
complainte [kõ'plɛ̃ːt], *n.f.* tragic *or* plaintive ballad, lament; (*fig.*) lamentation.
complaire [kõ'plɛːr], *v.i. irr.* (*conjug. like* PLAIRE) to be pleasing (*à*). **se complaire**, *v.r.* to delight (***dans*** or *à*).
complaisamment [kõplɛza'mɑ̃], *adv.* complaisantly, obligingly.
complaisance [kõplɛ'zɑ̃ːs], *n.f.* complaisance, good-nature; complacency.
complaisant [kõplɛ'zɑ̃], *a.* affable, civil, obliging, kind.—*n.m.* (*fem.* **-e**) flatterer; go-between.
complément [kõple'mɑ̃], *n.m.* complement; (*Gram.*) object; extension (*of subject*).
complémentaire [kõplemɑ̃'tɛːr], *a.* complementary, completing.
complet [kõ'plɛ], *a.* (*fem.* **-plète**) complete, whole; full, filled.—*n.m.* complement, full number; suit (*of clothes*).
complètement [kõplɛt'mɑ̃], *adv.* completely, entirely, thoroughly.
complétement [kõplet'mɑ̃], *n.m.* finishing, completion.
compléter [kõple'te], *v.t.* (*conjug. like* CÉDER) to complete, to perfect; to fill up.
complexe [kõ'plɛks], *a.* complex, complicated.—*n.m.* ***complexe d'infériorité***, inferiority complex.
complexion [kõplɛk'sjõ], *n.f.* constitution; disposition, humour, temper.
complexité [kõplɛksi'te], *n.f.* complexity.
complication [kõplikɑ'sjõ], *n.f.* complication, intricacy.
complice [kõ'plis], *a.* accessory, privy to.—*n.* accomplice, accessory.
complicité [kõplisi'te], *n.f.* complicity, participation.
compliment [kõpli'mɑ̃], *n.m.* compliment; (*pl.*) regards, congratulations.
complimenter [kõplimɑ̃'te], *v.t.* to compliment, to congratulate.
complimenteur [kõplimɑ̃'tœːr], *a.* and *n.m.* (*fem.* **-euse**) over-complimentary; obsequious (person).
compliqué [kõpli'ke], *a.* complicated, intricate.
compliquer [kõpli'ke], *v.t.* to complicate, to entangle. **se compliquer**, *v.r.* to become complicated
complot [kõ'plo], *n.m.* plot, conspiracy; ***chef du complot***, ringleader.
comploter [kõplɔ'te], *v.t.* to plot.
comploteur [kõplɔ'tœːr], *n.m.* plotter, schemer.
componction [kõpõk'sjõ], *n.f.* compunction; solemn manners *or* expression.
comportement [kõpɔrtə'mɑ̃], *n.m.* demeanour, deportment, behaviour.
comporter [kõpɔr'te], *v.t.* to permit, to allow; to require; to comprise. **se comporter**, *v.r.* to behave; to act, to manage.
composant [kõpo'zɑ̃], *n.m.* (*Chem.*) component, constituent.
composé [kõpo'ze], *a.* composed, compound. —*n.m.* compound.
composer [kõpo'ze], *v.t.* to compose, to compound, to make up; to form, to create; to adjust, to regulate; ***composer un numéro***, to dial a number.—*v.i.* to compound, to compromise, to make up.
composeuse [kõpo'zøːz], *n.f.* type-setting machine.
composite [kõpɔ'zit], *a.* composite.
compositeur [kõpɔzi'tœːr], *n.m.* (*fem.* **-trice**) composer (*of music*); (*Print.*) compositor.
composition [kõpɔzi'sjõ], *n.f.* composition; chemical composition; settlement; (*fig.*) disposition; (*Print.*) composing.
compost [kõ'pɔst], *n.m.* (*Agric.*) compost.
composter [kõpɔs'te], *v.t.* to compost; to date *or* obliterate (*ticket etc.*).
compote [kõ'pɔt], *n.f.* stewed fruit, compote.
compotier [kõpɔ'tje], *n.m.* fruit-dish.
compréhensibilité [kõpreɑ̃sibili'te], *n.f.* comprehensibility.
compréhensible [kõpreɑ̃'sibl], *a.* understandable, intelligible.
compréhensif [kõpreɑ̃'sif], *a.* (*fem.* **-sive**) comprehensive; broadminded.
compréhension [kõpreɑ̃'sjõ], *n.f.* comprehension; (*fig.*) understanding, intelligence.
compréhensivité [kõpreɑ̃sivi'te], *n.f.* comprehensiveness, faculty of comprehending.
comprendre [kõ'prɑ̃ːdr], *v.t. irr.* (*conjug. like* PRENDRE) to include, to comprise; to understand, to conceive, to realize.
compresse [kõ'prɛːs], *n.f.* (*Surg.*) compress, pledget.
compresseur [kõprɛ'sœːr], *a.* compressive.—*n.m.* compressor, roller.
compressif [kõprɛ'sif], *a.* (*fem.* **-ssive**) compressive, repressive.
compression [kõprɛ'sjõ], *n.f.* compression; (*fig.*) constraint.
comprimable [kõpri'mabl], *a.* compressible.
comprimé [kõpri'me], *a.* compressed, condensed; kept under.—*n.m.* (*Pharm.*) tabloid, tablet.
comprimer [kõpri'me], *v.t.* to compress, to condense; to repress, to restrain.
compris [kõ'pri], *a.* understood; included.
compromettant [kõprɔmɛ'tɑ̃], *a.* compromising; damaging.
compromettre [kõprɔ'mɛtr], *v.t. irr.* (*conjug. like* METTRE) to expose, to commit, to compromise, to jeopardize.—*v.i.* to compromise; to submit to arbitration. **se compromettre**, *v.r.* to compromise oneself.
compromis [kõprɔ'mi], *n.m.* mutual agreement, compromise.

comptabilité [kɔ̃tabili'te], *n.f.* accountancy, book-keeping; accountant's department.
comptable [kɔ̃'tabl], *a.* responsible for accounts; accountable, responsible.—*n.m.* accountant, book-keeper; (*Naut.*) purser.
comptant [kɔ̃'tɑ̃], *a.m.* (*of money*) ready; (*of payment*) in cash.—*n.m.* ready money, cash.
compte [kɔ̃:t], *n.m.* reckoning; account, score, statement, report; (*fig.*) profit; esteem, value; ***se rendre compte de***, to realize.
compte-gouttes [kɔ̃t'gut], *n.m. inv.* (*Med.*) drop-tube, dropper; filler; (*fig.*) ***au compte-gouttes***, sparingly.
compte-pas [kɔ̃tə'pɑ], *n.m.* pedometer.
compter [kɔ̃'te], *v.t.* to count, to calculate, to compute; to pay down; to comprise.—*v.i.* to reckon, to count; to be reckoned; to expect; to intend; to rely (***sur***). **se compter**, *v.r.* to be reckoned *or* included.
compteur [kɔ̃'tœ:r], *a.* and *n.m.* (*fem.* **-euse**) that counts; computer.—*n.m.* meter; (*C*) ***compteur de stationnement***, parking meter.
comptoir [kɔ̃'twa:r], *n.m.* counter; cashier's desk; counting-house; branch bank; factory.
compulser [kɔ̃pyl'se], *v.t.* to inspect (*documents etc.*).
computation [kɔ̃pytɑ'sjɔ̃], *n.f.* computation.
computer [kɔ̃py'te], *v.t.* to compute.
comtal [kɔ̃'tal], *a.* (*m. pl.* **-aux**) pertaining to an earl *or* a countess.
comte [kɔ̃:t], *n.m.* count; earl.
comté [kɔ̃'te], *n.m.* county, shire; earldom.
comtesse [kɔ̃'tɛs], *n.f.* countess.
concassage [kɔ̃kɑ'sa:ʒ], *n.m.* pounding, crushing.
concasser [kɔ̃kɑ'se], *v.t.* to pound, to crush.
concasseur [kɔ̃kɑ'sœ:r], *n.m.* crushing-mill; steam-roller.
concave [kɔ̃'ka:v], *a.* concave.
concavité [kɔ̃kavi'te], *n.f.* concave; concavity.
concéder [kɔ̃se'de], *v.t.* (*conjug. like* CÉDER) to grant, to concede, to allow.
concentration [kɔ̃sɑ̃trɑ'sjɔ̃], *n.f.* concentration; condensation; ***camp de concentration***, concentration camp.
concentré [kɔ̃sɑ̃'tre], *a.* concentrated; (*fig.*) silent, reserved.—*n.m.* extract.
concentrer [kɔ̃sɑ̃'tre], *v.t.* to concentrate, to focus; (*fig.*) to repress, to smother (*anger etc.*). **se concentrer**, *v.r.* to concentrate; to withdraw within oneself.
concentrique [kɔ̃sɑ̃'trik], *a.* concentric.
concentriquement [kɔ̃sɑ̃trik'mɑ̃], *adv.* concentrically.
concept [kɔ̃'sɛpt], *n.m.* concept.
conceptibilité [kɔ̃sɛptibili'te], *n.f.* conceivability.
conceptible [kɔ̃sɛp'tibl], *a.* conceivable.
conceptif [kɔ̃sɛp'tif], *a.* (*fem.* **-tive**) conceptive.
conception [kɔ̃sɛp'sjɔ̃], *n.f.* conception; thought, notion; understanding.
concernant [kɔ̃sɛr'nɑ̃], *prep.* concerning, relating to.
concerner [kɔ̃sɛr'ne], *v.t.* to relate (*to*), to concern, to regard.
concert [kɔ̃'sɛ:r], *n.m.* harmony; concert; (*fig.*) concord.
concertant [kɔ̃sɛr'tɑ̃], *a.* in concert (*of a piece of music*).—*n.m.* (*fem.* **-e**) performer in a concert.
concerté [kɔ̃sɛr'te], *a.* concerted, united; studied, stiff.
concerter [kɔ̃sɛr'te], *v.t.* to contrive, to concert; to plan, to devise; to compose (*one's demeanour etc.*). **se concerter**, *v.r.* to plan together, to concert.
concertiste [kɔ̃sɛr'tist], *n.* performer (*at a concert*).
concerto [kɔ̃sɛr'to], *n.m.* concerto.
concession [kɔ̃sɛ'sjɔ̃], *n.f.* concession, privilege.
concessionnaire [kɔ̃sɛsjɔ'nɛ:r], *a.* concessionary.—*n.* grantee.
concevable [kɔ̃s'vabl], *a.* conceivable, imaginable.
concevoir [kɔ̃sə'vwa:r], *v.t. irr.* (*conjug. like* RECEVOIR) to become pregnant, to conceive; to imagine, to understand; to comprehend.
concierge [kɔ̃'sjɛrʒ], *n.* concierge, hall-porter, caretaker.
conciergerie [kɔ̃sjɛrʒə'ri], *n.f.* caretaker's lodge; ***La Conciergerie***, a prison in Paris (*during French Revolution*).
concile [kɔ̃'sil], *n.m.* an assembly of prelates and doctors, council, synod.
conciliable [kɔ̃si'ljabl], *a.* reconcilable.
conciliabule [kɔ̃silja'byl], *n.m.* conventicle, secret meeting.
conciliaire [kɔ̃si'ljɛ:r], *a.* of *or* belonging to a council.
conciliant [kɔ̃si'ljɑ̃], *a.* conciliating, reconciling.
conciliateur [kɔ̃silja'tœ:r], *a.* (*fem.* **-trice**) conciliatory.—*n.m.* (*fem.* **-trice**) conciliator.
conciliation [kɔ̃siljɑ'sjɔ̃], *n.f.* reconciliation.
conciliatoire [kɔ̃silja'twa:r], *a.* conciliatory.
concilier [kɔ̃si'lje], *v.t.* to conciliate, to reconcile; to gain, to win, to procure. **se concilier**, *v.r.* to gain, to win.
concis [kɔ̃'si], *a.* concise, brief, short.
concision [kɔ̃si'zjɔ̃], *n.f.* brevity, conciseness.
concitoyen [kɔ̃sitwa'jɛ̃], *n.m.* (*fem.* **-enne**) fellow-citizen.
conclave [kɔ̃'kla:v], *n.m.* conclave, assembly of all the cardinals.
concluant [kɔ̃kly'ɑ̃], *a.* conclusive, decisive.
conclure [kɔ̃'kly:r], *v.t. irr.* to conclude; to infer; to judge.
conclusif [kɔ̃kly'zif], *a.* (*fem.* **-sive**) conclusive.
conclusion [kɔ̃kly'zjɔ̃], *n.f.* conclusion, upshot.
concombre [kɔ̃'kɔ̃:br], *n.m.* cucumber.
concomitance [kɔ̃kɔmi'tɑ̃:s], *n.f.* concomitance.
concomitant [kɔ̃kɔmi'tɑ̃], *a.* concomitant.
concordance [kɔ̃kɔr'dɑ̃:s], *n.f.* agreement; (*Bibl. etc.*) concordance.
concordant [kɔ̃kɔr'dɑ̃], *a.* concordant.
concordat [kɔ̃kɔr'da], *n.m.* concordat, agreement; bankrupt's certificate.
concordataire [kɔ̃kɔrda'tɛ:r], *n.m.* certificated bankrupt.
concorde [kɔ̃'kɔrd], *n.f.* concord, agreement, harmony; good understanding.
concorder [kɔ̃kɔr'de], *v.i.* to be in accord, to agree, to concur.
concourir [kɔ̃ku'ri:r], *v.i. irr.* (*conjug. like* COURIR) to concur; to contribute to; to co-operate; to compete; to converge.

concours [kɔ̃'ku:r], *n.m.* concourse, meeting; coincidence; competition; co-operation; competitive examination; assistance.
concret [kɔ̃'krɛ], *a.* (*fem.* **-crète**) concrete, solid.
concubine [kɔ̃ky'bin], *n.f.* concubine.
concupiscence [kɔ̃kypi'sɑ̃:s], *n.f.* concupiscence, lust.
concurremment [kɔ̃kyra'mɑ̃], *adv.* concurrently; jointly, together.
concurrence [kɔ̃ky'rɑ̃:s], *n.f.* competition; rivalry, opposition.
concurrent [kɔ̃ky'rɑ̃], *n.m.* (*fem.* **-e**) competitor, rival.
concussion [kɔ̃ky'sjɔ̃], *n.f.* extortion, embezzlement.
concussionnaire [kɔ̃kysjɔ'nɛ:r], *a.* guilty of peculation, of bribery *or* of extortion.—*n.m.* extortioner, peculator, embezzler.
condamnable [kɔ̃dɑ'nabl], *a.* condemnable, blamable.
condamnation [kɔ̃danɑ'sjɔ̃], *n.f.* condemnation, judgment, sentence; penalty.
condamné [kɔ̃dɑ'ne], *a.* condemned, convicted.—*n.m.* (*fem.* **-ée**) convict.
condamner [kɔ̃dɑ'ne], *v.t.* to condemn, to sentence, to convict; (*fig.*) to blame, to censure.
condensateur [kɔ̃dɑ̃sa'tœ:r], *n.m.* (*Phys.*) condenser.
condensation [kɔ̃dɑ̃sɑ'sjɔ̃], *n.f.* condensation.
condensé [kɔ̃dɑ̃'se], *a.* condensed.—*n.m.* digest.
condenser [kɔ̃dɑ̃'se], *v.t.* to condense.
condenseur [kɔ̃dɑ̃'sœ:r], *n.m.* condenser.
condescendance [kɔ̃desɑ̃'dɑ̃:s], *n.f.* condescension.
condescendant [kɔ̃desɑ̃'dɑ̃], *a.* condescending, complying.
condescendre [kɔ̃de'sɑ̃:dr], *v.i.* to condescend, to comply.
condiment [kɔ̃di'mɑ̃], *n.m.* condiment, seasoning.
condisciple [kɔ̃di'sipl], *n.m.* schoolfellow.
condit [kɔ̃'di], *n.m.* candied fruit.
condition [kɔ̃di'sjɔ̃], *n.f.* condition; rank, station; domestic service; situation, circumstances; terms; ***à condition*** or ***sous condition***, on condition, on approval.
conditionné [kɔ̃disjɔ'ne], *a.* conditioned (***bien*** or ***mal***); well-conditioned, sound.
conditionnel [kɔ̃disjɔ'nɛl], *a.* conditional.—*n.m.* (*Gram.*) conditional.
conditionnellement [kɔ̃disjɔnɛl'mɑ̃], *adv.* conditionally, on condition.
conditionner [kɔ̃disjɔ'ne], *v.t.* to condition; to dry (*silk*); to season (*wood*).
condoléance [kɔ̃dɔle'ɑ̃:s], *n.f.* condolence.
condominium [kɔ̃dɔmi'njɔm], *n.m.* condominium.
condor [kɔ̃'dɔ:r], *n.m.* condor.
conductance [kɔ̃dyk'tɑ̃:s], *n.f.* (*Elec.*) conductance.
conducteur [kɔ̃dyk'tœ:r], *n.m.* (*fem.* **-trice**) conductor, conductress, leader, guide; driver, drover.—*a.* (*Phys.*) conducting.
conductibilité [kɔ̃dyktibili'te], *n.f.* conductibility.
conductible [kɔ̃dyk'tibl], *a.* conductible.
conduction [kɔ̃dyk'sjɔ̃], *n.f.* (*Phys.*) conduction; (*Civic Law*) hiring.
conduire [kɔ̃'dɥi:r], *v.t. irr.* to conduct, to lead, to guide; to drive; to accompany; to bring, to take; to be at the head of.—*v.i.* to lead (*à*); to drive. **se conduire**, *v.r.* to conduct *or* behave oneself.
conduit [kɔ̃'dɥi], *n.m.* conduit, duct, pipe, passage, tube, canal.
conduite [kɔ̃'dɥit], *n.f.* conducting, leading, driving, steering; management, direction, administration; conveyance, distribution; scheme, plan; water-pipe, conduit; behaviour, demeanour; prudence, discretion.
cône [ko:n], *n.m.* cone; ***en cône***, conical.
confection [kɔ̃fɛk'sjɔ̃], *n.f.* preparation, making; making of ready-made clothes; (*Pharm.*) confection; ***vêtements de confection***, ready-made clothes.
confectionner [kɔ̃fɛksjɔ'ne], *v.t.* to make, to manufacture, to finish.
confectionneur [kɔ̃fɛksjɔ'nœ:r], *n.m.* (*fem.* **-euse**) maker, finisher (*of wearing apparel*), clothier, outfitter.
confédération [kɔ̃federɑ'sjɔ̃], *n.f.* confederation, confederacy; ***la Confédération Générale du Travail*** (*abbr.* ***C.G.T.***), the French equivalent of the T.U.C.
confédéré [kɔ̃fede're], *a.* and *n.m.* (*fem.* **-ée**) confederate, associate.
confédérer (se) [səkɔ̃fede're], *v.r.* (*conjug. like* CÉDER) to combine, to enter into confederation.
conférence [kɔ̃fe'rɑ̃:s], *n.f.* conference; lecture.
conférencier [kɔ̃ferɑ̃'sje], *n.m.* (*fem.* **-ière**) lecturer.
conférer [kɔ̃fe're], *v.t.* (*conjug. like* CÉDER) to confer, to bestow, to grant; to compare.—*v.i.* to consult together, to confer.
confesse [kɔ̃'fɛs], *n.f.* (*always used with* **à** *or* **de**) ***aller à confesse***, to go to confession; ***venir de confesse***, to come from confession.
confesser [kɔ̃fɛ'se], *v.t.* to confess; to acknowledge, to admit; to shrive. **se confesser**, *v.r.* to confess one's sins, to confess (*to a priest*).
confesseur [kɔ̃fɛ'sœ:r], *n.m.* (father) confessor.
confession [kɔ̃fɛ'sjɔ̃], *n.f.* confession, acknowledgment, avowal.
confessionnal [kɔ̃fɛsjɔ'nal], *n.m.* confessional.
confetti [kɔ̃fɛt'ti], *n.m. pl.* confetti.
confiance [kɔ̃'fjɑ̃:s], *n.f.* confidence, reliance, trust.
confiant [kɔ̃'fjɑ̃], *a.* confident, unsuspecting, sanguine; self-conceited.
confidemment [kɔ̃fida'mɑ̃], *adv.* confidentially.
confidence [kɔ̃fi'dɑ̃:s], *n.f.* confidence; secret.
confident [kɔ̃fi'dɑ̃], *n.m.* (*fem.* **-ente**) confidant, confidante.
confidentiel [kɔ̃fidɑ̃'sjɛl], *a.* confidential.
confidentiellement [kɔ̃fidɑ̃sjɛl'mɑ̃], *adv.* confidentially.
confier [kɔ̃'fje], *v.t.* to confide, to entrust, to commit (*à*). **se confier**, *v.r.* to trust in; to unbosom oneself (*à*).
configuration [kɔ̃figyrɑ'sjɔ̃], *n.f.* configuration, form, shape, lie (*of the land*).
confinement [kɔ̃fin'mɑ̃], *n.m.* confinement; overcrowding.

confiner [kɔ̃fi'ne], *v.t.* to confine, to imprison; ***air confiné***, stuffy atmosphere.—*v.i.* to border upon, to be adjoining. **se confiner,** *v.r.* to confine *or* to limit oneself.
confins [kɔ'fɛ̃], *n.m.* (*used only in pl.*) confines, borders, limits.
confire [kɔ̃'fi:r], *v.t. irr.* to preserve; to candy, to pickle.
confirmatif [kɔ̃firma'tif], *a.* (*fem.* **-tive**) confirmative.
confirmation [kɔ̃firmɑ'sjɔ̃], *n.f.* confirmation, ratification.
confirmer [kɔ̃fir'me], *v.t.* to strengthen, to corroborate; to confirm; to ratify. **se confirmer,** *v.r.* to be confirmed.
confiscable [kɔ̃fis'kabl], *a.* confiscable, forfeitable.
confiscation [kɔ̃fiskɑ'sjɔ̃], *n.f.* confiscation, forfeiture.
confiserie [kɔ̃fiz'ri], *n.f.* confectionery; confectioner's shop.
confiseur [kɔ̃fi'zœ:r] *n.m.* (*fem.* **-euse**) confectioner.
confisquer [kɔ̃fis'ke], *v.t.* to confiscate, to forfeit, to impound; to seize.
confit (1) [kɔ̃'fi], *p.p.* [CONFIRE].
confit (2) [kɔ̃'fi], *n.m.* meat, poultry etc. preserved in fat; bran-mash (*for pigs etc.*).
confiture [kɔ̃fi'ty:r], *n.f.* preserve, jam.
conflagration [kɔ̃flagrɑ'sjɔ̃], *n.f.* conflagration.
conflit [kɔ̃'fli], *n.m.* conflict, collision, encounter; contention, strife, contest, rivalry; jar, clash.
confluent [kɔ̃fly'ɑ̃], *n.m.* confluence, junction (*of rivers*).
confluer [kɔ̃fly'e], *v.i.* to meet, to unite (*of streams etc.*).
confondre [kɔ̃'fɔ̃:dr], *v.t.* to confound, to confuse; to mix, to mingle; (*fig.*) to amaze, to astound. **se confondre,** *v.r.* to mingle, to be lost in; to be confounded, to be abashed.
conformation [kɔ̃fɔrmɑ'sjɔ̃], *n.f.* conformation, structure.
conforme [kɔ̃'fɔrm], *a.* conformable; congenial, consistent; ***pour copie conforme,*** certified true copy.
conformé [kɔ̃fɔr'me], *a.* formed, shaped (***bien*** or ***mal***).
conformément [kɔ̃fɔrme'mɑ̃], *adv.* suitably; according to.
conformer [kɔ̃fɔr'me], *v.t.* to give form to. **se conformer,** *v.r.* to conform, to comply (*with*).
conformisme [kɔ̃fɔr'mism], *n.m.* conformity, orthodoxy.
conformité [kɔ̃fɔrmi'te], *n.f.* likeness, conformity, compliance.
confort [kɔ̃'fɔ:r], *n.m.* comfort, ease.
confortable [kɔ̃fɔr'tabl], *a.* cosy, comfortable.
confortablement [kɔ̃fɔrtablə'mɑ̃], *adv.* comfortably.
confraternité [kɔ̃fratɛrni'te], *n.f.* fraternity, brotherhood.
confrère [kɔ̃'frɛ:r], *n.m.* colleague; fellow-member.
confrérie [kɔ̃fre'ri], *n.f.* brotherhood, fraternity.
confrontation [kɔ̃frɔ̃tɑ'sjɔ̃], *n.f.* confrontation; comparing.
confronter [kɔ̃frɔ̃'te], *v.t.* to confront; to compare.
confus [kɔ̃'fy], *a.* confused, muddled, vague, indistinct, obscure; abashed, crest-fallen.
confusément [kɔ̃fyze'mɑ̃], *adv.* confusedly, vaguely, dimly.
confusion [kɔ̃fy'zjɔ̃], *n.f.* confusion, disorder; bewilderment; embarrassment, shame, blush; misunderstanding.
congé [kɔ̃'ʒe], *n.m.* leave, permission; leave of absence, holiday; discharge, dismissal; notice (to quit); permit.
congédier [kɔ̃ʒe'dje], *v.t.* to discharge, to dismiss, to pay off; to disband.
congélateur [kɔ̃ʒela'tœ:r], *n.m.* refrigerator.
congeler [kɔ̃ʒ'le], *v.t.*, **se congeler,** *v.r.* (*conjug. like* AMENER) to congeal, to freeze; to coagulate.
congénère [kɔ̃ʒe'nɛ:r], *a.* congeneric; of same species; (*Philol.*) cognate.
congénial [kɔ̃ʒe'njal], *a.* (*m. pl.* **-aux**) congenial, of the same nature.
congénital [kɔ̃ʒeni'tal], *a.* (*m. pl.* **-aux**) congenital, hereditary.
congère [kɔ̃'ʒɛ:r], *n.f.* snow-drift.
congestion [kɔ̃ʒɛs'tjɔ̃], *n.f.* congestion.
conglomération [kɔ̃glɔmerɑ'sjɔ̃], *n.f.* conglomeration.
conglomérer [kɔ̃glɔme're], *v.t.* (*conjug. like* CÉDER) to conglomerate.
congolais [kɔ̃gɔ'lɛ], *a.* Congolese.—(**Congolais,** *fem.* **-aise**) Congolese (*person*).
congratulation [kɔ̃gratylɑ'sjɔ̃], *n.f.* congratulation.
congratulatoire [kɔ̃gratyla'twa:r], *a.* congratulatory.
congratuler [kɔ̃graty'le], *v.t.* to congratulate.
congre [kɔ̃:gr], *n.m.* conger, conger-eel.
congrégation [kɔ̃gregɑ'sjɔ̃], *n.f.* fraternity, brotherhood, general body (*of an order etc.*).
congrès [kɔ̃'grɛ], *n.m.* congress.
congressiste [kɔ̃grɛ'sist], *n.m.* (*Am.*) congressman.
congru [kɔ̃'gry], *a.* suitable, consistent, congruous, proper.
congruité [kɔ̃gryi'te], *n.f.* congruity, consistency, propriety.
congrûment [kɔ̃gry'mɑ̃], *adv.* congruously, properly.
conifère [kɔni'fɛ:r], *a.* coniferous.—*n.m.* conifer.
conique [kɔ'nik], *a.* conical.
conjecture [kɔ̃ʒɛk'ty:r], *n.f.* conjecture, surmise, guess.
conjecturer [kɔ̃ʒɛkty're], *v.t.* to conjecture, to guess, to surmise.
conjoindre [kɔ̃'ʒwɛ̃:dr], *v.t. irr.* (*conjug. like* CRAINDRE) to conjoin, to unite together; to marry.
conjoint [kɔ̃'ʒwɛ̃], *a.* conjoined, united, joint.—*n.m.* (*fem.* **-e**) spouse.
conjointement [kɔ̃ʒwɛ̃t'mɑ̃], *adv.* conjointly, unitedly.
conjoncteur [kɔ̃ʒɔ̃k'tœ:r], *n.m.* (*Elec.*) circuit-breaker, switch key.
conjonctif [kɔ̃ʒɔ̃k'tif], *a.* (*fem.* **-tive**) conjunctive.
conjonction [kɔ̃ʒɔ̃k'sjɔ̃], *n.f.* conjunction; union, connexion; coition.
conjoncture [kɔ̃ʒɔ̃k'ty:r], *n.f.* conjuncture, juncture.
conjugaison [kɔ̃ʒygɛ'zɔ̃], *n.f.* conjugation.

conjugal [kɔ̃ʒy'gal], *a.* (*m. pl.* **-aux**) conjugal.
conjugalement [kɔ̃ʒygal'mɑ̃], *adv.* conjugally.
conjugué [kɔ̃ʒy'ge], *a.* (*Mech.*) twin.
conjuguer [kɔ̃ʒy'ge], *v.t.* (*Gram.*) to conjugate.
conjuration [kɔ̃ʒyrɑ'sjɔ̃], *n.f.* conspiracy, plot.
conjuré [kɔ̃ʒy're], *a.* confederate, sworn.—*n.m.* (*fem.* **-ée**) conspirator, plotter.
conjurer [kɔ̃ʒy're], *v.t.* to implore; to conspire; to swear; to conjure up, to exorcize, to ward off.
connaissable [kɔnɛ'sabl], *a.* recognizable.
connaissance [kɔnɛ'sɑ̃:s], *n.f.* knowledge, learning; consciousness (*de*); acquaintance; intercourse; (*Law*) cognizance; (*pl.*) attainments.
connaisseur [kɔnɛ'sœ:r], *a.* (*fem.* **-euse**) expert, skilled.—*n.m.* connoisseur, expert.
connaître [kɔ'nɛ:tr], *v.t. irr.* to know, to perceive; to understand; to be acquainted with.—*v.i.* to have *or* take cognizance of; to deal with (*a matter*). **se connaître**, *v.r.* to know oneself; to know each other; to be a connoisseur.
connecter [kɔnɛk'te], *v.t.* to connect; (*Elec.*) to couple (up), to group.
connétable [kɔne'tabl], *n.m.* high constable.
connexion [kɔnɛk'sjɔ̃], *n.f.* connexion, affinity.
connexité [kɔnɛksi'te], *n.f.* connexion.
connivence [kɔni'vɑ̃:s], *n.f.* connivance.
connotation [kɔnɔtɑ'sjɔ̃], *n.f.* connotation.
connu [kɔ'ny], *a.* known, understood.—*n.m.* that which is known.
conque [kɔ̃:k], *n.f.* conch, sea-shell.
conquérant [kɔ̃ke'rɑ̃], *a.* conquering.—*n.m.* (*fem.* **-e**) conqueror.
conquérir [kɔ̃ke'ri:r], *v.t. irr.* (*conjug. like* ACQUÉRIR) to conquer, to subdue (*a country*); (*fig.*) to gain, to win over.
conquête [kɔ̃'kɛ:t], *n.f.* conquest, acquisition.
conquis [kɔ̃'ki], *a.* conquered.
consacrant [kɔ̃sa'krɑ̃], *a.* consecrating, officiating.—*n.m.* consecrator, officiant.
consacrer [kɔ̃sa'kre], *v.t.* to consecrate, to dedicate, to sanctify; to sanction; to authorize. **se consacrer**, *v.r.* to devote oneself.
consciemment [kɔ̃sja'mɑ̃], *adv.* consciously, knowingly.
conscience [kɔ̃'sjɑ̃:s], *n.f.* consciousness, perception; conscience, conscientiousness.
consciencieusement [kɔ̃sjɑ̃sjøz'mɑ̃], *adv.* conscientiously.
consciencieux [kɔ̃sjɑ̃'sjø], *a.* (*fem.* **-euse**) conscientious.
conscient [kɔ̃'sjɑ̃], *a.* conscious (*de*); self-conscious.
conscription [kɔ̃skrip'sjɔ̃], *n.f.* enlistment; conscription.
conscrit [kɔ̃'skri], *a.* conscript.—*n.m.* conscript; (raw) recruit.
consécrateur [kɔ̃sekra'tœ:r], [CONSACRANT].
consécration [kɔ̃sekrɑ'sjɔ̃], *n.f.* consecration; ordination.
consécutif [kɔ̃seky'tif], *a.* (*fem.* **-tive**) consecutive, following.
consécutivement [kɔ̃sekytiv'mɑ̃], *adv.* consecutively.
conseil [kɔ̃'sɛ:j], *n.m.* counsel, advice; resolution; council, board; (*Law*) counsel; ***conseil d'administration***, board of directors; ***Conseil d'État***, Council of State; ***Conseil de Sécurité (de l'O.N.U.)***, (U.N.) Security Council; ***conseil judiciaire***, guardian; ***conseil de guerre***, court-martial; council of war; ***conseil municipal***, town council, corporation.
conseiller [kɔ̃sɛ'je], *v.t.* to advise, to counsel; to recommend.—*n.m.* (*fem.* **-ère**) counsellor, adviser, councillor.
consensus [kɔ̃sɑ̃'sy:s], *n.m.* consent, consensus.
consentant [kɔ̃sɑ̃'tɑ̃], *a.* consenting, willing.
consentement [kɔ̃sɑ̃t'mɑ̃], *n.m.* consent, assent.
consentir [kɔ̃sɑ̃'ti:r], *v.i. irr.* (*conjug. like* SENTIR) to consent, to agree, to acquiesce (*à*).
conséquemment [kɔ̃seka'mɑ̃], *adv.* consequently, accordingly.
conséquence [kɔ̃se'kɑ̃:s], *n.f.* consequence, sequel; issue, result; inference, conclusion.
conséquent [kɔ̃se'kɑ̃], *a.* rational, consistent.—*n.m.* (*Log., Math.*) consequent; ***par conséquent***, consequently.
conservateur [kɔ̃sɛrva'tœ:r], *a.* (*fem.* **-trice**) preserving, conservative.—*n.m.* (*fem.* **-trice**) Conservative, Tory.—*n.m.* guardian, keeper, curator.
conservatif [kɔ̃sɛrva'tif], *a.* (*fem.* **-tive**) conservative, preservative.—*n.m.* preservative.
conservation [kɔ̃sɛrvɑ'sjɔ̃], *n.f.* conservation, preservation; registration (*of mortgages etc.*).
conservatisme [kɔ̃sɛrva'tism], *n.m.* conservatism.
Conservatoire [kɔ̃sɛrva'twa:r], *n.m.* academy of music and school of elocution in Paris.
conserve [kɔ̃'sɛrv], *n.f.* preserve; tinned (*Am.* canned) food.
conserver [kɔ̃sɛr've], *v.t.* to preserve; to keep. **se conserver**, *v.r.* to be preserved; to bear one's age well; to keep (*of meat, fruit etc.*).
considérable [kɔ̃side'rabl], *a.* considerable, notable, eminent; ***peu considérable***, of little importance.
considérablement [kɔ̃siderablə'mɑ̃], *adv.* considerably.
considérant [kɔ̃side'rɑ̃], *conj. phr.* ***considérant que***, whereas.
considération [kɔ̃siderɑ'sjɔ̃], *n.f.* consideration, attention; motive, grounds; regard, respect.
considérément [kɔ̃sidere'mɑ̃], *adv.* considerately, prudently.
considérer [kɔ̃side're], *v.t.* (*conjug. like* CÉDER) to consider, to look at, to view; to ponder; to value, to esteem; to pay attention to. **se considérer**, *v.r.* to esteem oneself.
consignataire [kɔ̃siɲa'tɛ:r], *n.* trustee, depositary.
consignateur [kɔ̃siɲa'tœ:r], *n.m.* (*fem.* **-trice**) (*Comm.*) consignor, shipper.
consignation [kɔ̃siɲɑ'sjɔ̃], *n.f.* (*Comm.*) deposit, consignment.
consigne [kɔ̃'siɲ], *n.f.* (*Mil.*) order, password; (*fig.*) strict command, prohibition; (*Rail.*) left-luggage office, cloak-room; (*sch.*) gating, detention.

consigner [kõsi'ɲe], *v.t.* to deposit; to consign; to record, to register; to keep in; to refuse admittance to.
consistance [kõsis'tɑ̃:s], *n.f.* consistency; firmness, stability; (*fig.*) credit, consideration.
consistant [kõsis'tɑ̃], *a.* consisting of; consistent, firm, solid.
consister [kõsis'te], *v.i.* to consist; to be composed of.
consistoire [kõsis'twa:r], *n.m.* consistory.
consolable [kõsɔ'labl], *a.* consolable.
consolant [kõsɔ'lɑ̃], *a.* consoling, comforting.
consolateur [kõsɔla'tœ:r], *a.* (*fem.* **-trice**) consoling.—*n.m.* (*fem.* **-trice**) comforter, consoler.
consolation [kõsɔlɑ'sjõ], *n.f.* consolation, comfort, solace.
console [kõ'sɔl], *n.f.* console, bracket.
consoler [kõsɔ'le], *v.t.* to console, to comfort. **se consoler**, *v.r.* to console oneself.
consolidation [kõsɔlidɑ'sjõ], *n.f.* consolidation; strengthening; funding (*of interest*).
consolidé [kõsɔli'de], *a.* funded.—*n.m.* (*Fin.*, *used only in pl.*) consols.
consolider [kõsɔli'de], *v.t.* to consolidate; to strengthen. **se consolider**, *v.r.* to consolidate, to grow firm.
consommable [kõsɔ'mabl], *a.* consumable, edible.
consommateur [kõsɔma'tœ:r], *n.m.* (*fem.* **-trice**) consumer (*as opposed to producer*), eater, drinker.
consommation [kõsɔmɑ'sjõ], *n.f.* consumption; consummation; food, drinks, refreshments.
consommé [kõsɔ'me], *a.* consumed; consummated; consummate; accomplished.—*n.m.* clear soup.
consommer [kõsɔ'me], *v.t.* to consume, to use; (*fig.*) to consummate, to accomplish.—*v.i.* (*pop.*) to have a drink.
consomption [kõsõp'sjõ], *n.f.* consumption, using up; (*Path.*) phthisis, decline.
consonance [kõsɔ'nɑ̃:s], *n.f.* consonance; (*fig.*) concord.
consonant [kõsɔ'nɑ̃], *a.* consonant.
consonne [kõ'sɔn], *n.f.* consonant.
consort [kõ'sɔ:r], *a.* consort (*of the husband or wife of a sovereign*).—*n.m.* (*used only in pl.*) consorts, confederates; (*Law*) associates.
consortium [kõsɔr'sjɔm], *n.m.* consortium.
conspirateur [kõspira'tœ:r], *n.m.* (*fem.* **-trice**) conspirator.—*a.* conspiring.
conspiration [kõspirɑ'sjõ], *n.f.* conspiracy, plot.
conspirer [kõspi're], *v.t.* to plot.—*v.i.* to conspire, to concur; to plot.
conspuer [kõs'pɥe], *v.t.* to despise, to spurn; to boo, to barrack.
constamment [kõsta'mɑ̃] *adv.* steadily; continually, constantly.
constance [kõs'tɑ̃:s], *n.f.* constancy; perseverance.
constant [kõs'tɑ̃], *a.* constant, faithful, unshaken; persevering.
constatation [kõstatɑ'sjõ], *n.f.* authentication; statement; findings.
constater [kõsta'te], *v.t.* to prove, to verify; to ascertain; to state, to declare.
constellation [kõstɛlɑ'sjõ], *n.f.* constellation.
constellé [kõstɛ'le], *a.* constellated; studded.
consteller [kõstɛ'le], *v.t.* to constellate, to stud.
consternation [kõstɛrnɑ'sjõ], *n.f.* consternation, dismay.
consterné [kõstɛr'ne], *a.* dismayed, overwhelmed.
consterner [kõstɛr'ne], *v.t.* to dismay, to dishearten; to astound, to amaze.
constipation [kõstipɑ'sjõ], *n.f.* constipation, costiveness.
constipé [kõsti'pe], *a.* costive, constipated.
constiper [kõsti'pe], *v.t.* to constipate, to bind.
constituant [kõsti'tɥɑ̃], *a.* constituent.
constituer [kõsti'tɥe], *v.t.* to constitute; to establish; to appoint; to settle, to assign. **se constituer**, *v.r.* to constitute oneself.
constitution [kõstity'sjõ], *n.f.* constitution; establishment; settlement (*of an annuity etc.*); temperament.
constitutionnel [kõstitysjɔ'nɛl], *a.* (*fem.* **-elle**) constitutional.
constitutionnellement [kõstitysjɔnɛl'mɑ̃], *adv.* constitutionally.
constriction [kõstrik'sjõ], *n.f.* constriction.
constringent [kõstrɛ̃'ʒɑ̃], *a.* constringent.
constructeur [kõstryk'tœ:r], *n.m.* constructor, builder; shipbuilder, shipwright.
construction [kõstryk'sjõ], *n.f.* building, construction; erection, structure.
constructivité [kõstryktivi'te], *n.f.* constructiveness.
construire [kõs'trɥi:r], *v.t. irr.* (*conjug. like* CONDUIRE) to construct, to build, to erect.
consul [kõ'syl], *n.m.* consul.
consulaire [kõsy'lɛ:r], *a.* consular.
consulat [kõsy'la], *n.m.* consulate, consulship.
consultant [kõsyl'tɑ̃], *a.* consulting.—*n.m.* (*fem.* **-e**) consultant, consulting physician.
consultatif [kõsylta'tif], *a.* (*fem.* **-tive**) consultative, deliberative.
consultation [kõsyltɑ'sjõ], *n.f.* consultation; opinion, advice; ***cabinet de consultation***, surgery.
consulter [kõsyl'te], *v.t.* to consult; to refer to.—*v.i.* to deliberate, to take counsel (*together*). **se consulter**, *v.r.* to consider, to reflect, to deliberate.
consumable [kõsy'mabl], *a.* consumable.
consumant [kõsy'mɑ̃], *a.* consuming, devouring, burning.
consumer [kõsy'me], *v.t.* to consume; to destroy, to wear out, to wear away, to squander, to waste. **se consumer**, *v.r.* to decay, to waste away, to wear out; to undermine one's health.
contact [kõ'takt], *n.m.* contact; touch; connexion; (*Motor.*) ***clé de contact***, ignition key; (*Opt.*) ***verres de contact***, contact lenses.
contagieux [kõta'ʒjø], *a.* (*fem.* **-euse**) contagious, infectious.
contagion [kõta'ʒjõ], *n.f.* contagion, infection.
contamination [kõtaminɑ'sjõ], *n.f.* contamination, pollution.
contaminé [kõtami'ne], *a.* polluted, contaminated.
contaminer [kõtami'ne], *v.t.* to contaminate.
conte [kõ:t], *n.m.* story, tale; (*fig.*) fib, fairy-tale.

contemplateur [kɔ̃tɑ̃pla'tœ:r], *n.m.* (*fem.* **-trice**) contemplator.

contemplatif [kɔ̃tɑ̃pla'tif], *a.* (*fem.* **-tive**) contemplative.

contemplation [kɔ̃tɑ̃plɑ'sjɔ̃], *n.f.* contemplation, meditation.

contempler [kɔ̃tɑ̃'ple], *v.t.* to contemplate, to survey, to gaze on.—*v.i.* to contemplate, to meditate, to reflect.

contemporain [kɔ̃tɑ̃pɔ'rɛ̃], *a.* and *n.m.* (*fem.* **-e**) contemporary.

contempteur [kɔ̃tɑ̃p'tœ:r], *a.* (*fem.* **-trice**) contemptuous, scornful, insolent, disdainful.—*n.m.* contemner, despiser, scorner.

contenance [kɔ̃t'nɑ̃:s], *n.f.* capacity; volume; (*fig.*) countenance, air, bearing.

contenant [kɔ̃t'nɑ̃], *a.* holding, containing.—*n.m.* holder, container.

contenir [kɔ̃t'ni:r], *v.t. irr.* (*conjug. like* TENIR) to contain, to comprise, to hold, to include; to restrain. **se contenir**, *v.r.* to keep within bounds, to be moderate; to control oneself.

content [kɔ̃'tɑ̃], *a.* content, satisfied; pleased, glad, gratified.

contentement [kɔ̃tɑ̃t'mɑ̃], *n.m.* contentment, satisfaction; comfort, pleasure.

contenter [kɔ̃tɑ̃'te], *v.t.* to content, to satisfy; to please, to gratify. **se contenter**, *v.r.* to be satisfied, to be content.

contentieusement [kɔ̃tɑ̃sjøz'mɑ̃], *adv.* contentiously, litigiously.

contentieux [kɔ̃tɑ̃'sjø], *a.* (*fem.* **-euse**) contentious, disputable; litigious; in dispute; quarrelsome.—*n.m.* debatable matter; ***bureau du contentieux***, legal department.

contention [kɔ̃tɑ̃'sjɔ̃], *n.f.* application, vehemence; contention, contest, debate, strife.

contenu [kɔ̃t'ny], *a.* contained; (*fig.*) kept in control.—*n.m.* contents; enclosure; terms (*of a letter etc.*).

conter [kɔ̃'te], *v.t.* to tell, to relate; ***en conter***, to tell fibs.

contestable [kɔ̃tɛs'tabl], *a.* disputable, debatable.

contestant [kɔ̃tɛs'tɑ̃], *a.* contending (*at law*).—*n.m.* (*fem.* **-e**) contesting party, litigant.

contestation [kɔ̃tɛstɑ'sjɔ̃], *n.f.* contestation, contest; dispute, debate; litigation.

contester [kɔ̃tɛs'te], *v.t.* to dispute, to contest; to contend, to debate.—*v.i.* to quarrel; to be contentious.

conteur [kɔ̃'tœ:r], *a.* (*fem.* **-euse**) who tells stories.—*n.m.* (*fem.* **-euse**) story-teller; (*fig.*) fibber.

contexte [kɔ̃'tɛkst], *n.m.* context; text (*of a deed*).

contexture [kɔ̃tɛks'ty:r], *n.f.* contexture (*of the muscles etc.*); texture (*of materials*).

contigu [kɔ̃ti'gy], *a.* (*fem.* **-ë**) contiguous, adjoining.

contiguïté [kɔ̃tigɥi'te], *n.f.* contiguity.

continence [kɔ̃ti'nɑ̃:s], *n.f.* continency, chastity.

continent (1) [kɔ̃ti'nɑ̃], *a.* chaste, continent.

continent (2) [kɔ̃ti'nɑ̃], *n.m.* continent, mainland.

continental [kɔ̃tinɑ̃'tal], *a.* (*m. pl.* **-aux**) continental.

contingence [kɔ̃tɛ̃'ʒɑ̃:s], *n.f.* contingency, casualty.

contingent [kɔ̃tɛ̃'ʒɑ̃], *a.* contingent, accidental, casual.—*n.m.* quota; contingent.

continu [kɔ̃ti'ny], *a.* continuous, continual, uninterrupted; incessant.

continuation [kɔ̃tinɥɑ'sjɔ̃], *n.f.* continuation.

continuel [kɔ̃ti'nɥɛl], *a.* (*fem.* **-elle**) continual, perpetual.

continuellement [kɔ̃tinɥɛl'mɑ̃], *adv.* continually, perpetually.

continuer [kɔ̃ti'nɥe], *v.t.* to continue, to proceed with; to lengthen.—*v.i.* to continue, to keep on. **se continuer**, *v.r.* to be continued, to last.

continuité [kɔ̃tinɥi'te], *n.f.* continuity; continuance.

continûment [kɔ̃tiny'mɑ̃], *adv.* unremittingly, continuously, without cessation.

contorsion [kɔ̃tɔr'sjɔ̃], *n.f.* contortion; grimace.

contorsionniste [kɔ̃tɔrsjɔ'nist], *n.* contortionist.

contour [kɔ̃'tu:r], *n.m.* circuit, circumference; contour, outline.

contourné [kɔ̃tur'ne], *a.* distorted, bizarre.

contournement [kɔ̃turnə'mɑ̃], *n.m.* outlining, tracing; winding, convolution; ***route de contournement***, by-pass (*road*).

contourner [kɔ̃tur'ne], *v.t.* to outline; to distort, to twist; to twist, turn, go *or* wind round. **se contourner**, *v.r.* to grow crooked, to become bent.

contractant [kɔ̃trak'tɑ̃], *a.* ***partie contractante***, contracting party.—*n.m.* (*fem.* **-e**) stipulator.

contracté [kɔ̃trak'te], *a.* contracted, shortened.

contracter [kɔ̃trak'te], *v.t.* to contract; to covenant, to stipulate, to bargain; to make a contract; to acquire. **se contracter**, *v.r.* to contract, to shrink; to shorten; to be settled by contract.

contraction [kɔ̃trak'sjɔ̃], *n.f.* contraction.

contractuel [kɔ̃trak'tɥɛl], *a.* (*fem.* **-elle**) stipulated, done by contract.

contractuellement [kɔ̃traktɥɛl'mɑ̃], *adv.* by contract.

contradicteur [kɔ̃tradik'tœ:r], *n.m.* contradictor; (*Law*) adversary.

contradiction [kɔ̃tradik'sjɔ̃], *n.f.* contradiction, denial; opposition; discrepancy.

contradictoire [kɔ̃tradik'twa:r], *a.* contradictory, inconsistent, conflicting; ***examen contradictoire***, cross-examination.

contraindre [kɔ̃'trɛ̃:dr], *v.t. irr.* (*conjug. like* CRAINDRE) to constrain, to compel, to coerce; to restrain; to squeeze. **se contraindre**, *v.r.* to restrain oneself, to refrain.

contraint [kɔ̃'trɛ̃], *a.* constrained, forced.

contrainte [kɔ̃'trɛ̃:t], *n.f.* constraint, compulsion, coercion; restraint; uneasiness.

contraire [kɔ̃'trɛ:r], *a.* contrary, opposite, inconsistent; adverse; prejudicial.—*n.m.* contrary, opposite, reverse.

contrairement [kɔ̃trɛr'mɑ̃], *adv.* contrarily, in opposition.

contralte [kɔ̃'tralt], **contralto** [kɔ̃tral'to], *n.m.* contralto, counter-tenor.

contrariant [kɔ̃tra'rjɑ̃], *a.* thwarting, annoying.

contrarier [kɔ̃tra'rje], *v.t.* to thwart, to counteract, to baffle; to annoy; to disappoint.

contrariété [kɔ̃trarje'te], *n.f.* contrariety, contradiction; annoyance; hindrance, disappointment; ***quelle contrariété !*** how annoying!
contrastant [kɔ̃tras'tɑ̃], *a.* contrasting.
contraste [kɔ̃'trast], *n.m.* contrast, opposition.
contraster [kɔ̃trɑs'te], *v.t., v.i.* to contrast.
contrat [kɔ̃'tra], *n.m.* contract, deed; agreement, bargain.
contravention [kɔ̃travɑ̃'sjɔ̃], *n.f.* contravention.
contre [kɔ̃:tr], *prep.* against, versus, contrary to; close up against, near; in exchange for; ***ci-contre***, opposite, in the margin; ***par contre***, on the other hand; ***pour et contre***, pro and con.—*adv.* against.—*n.m.* the opposite side of the question; ***le pour et le contre***, the pros and cons.
contre-allée [kɔ̃tra'le], *n.f.* side-walk, side-alley.
contre-amiral [kɔ̃trami'ral], *n.m.* (*pl.* **contre-amiraux**) rear-admiral.
contre-attaque [kɔ̃tra'tak], *n.f.* (*Mil.*) counter-attack.
contre-avions [kɔ̃tra'vjɔ̃], *a.* anti-aircraft.
contrebalancer [kɔ̃trəbalɑ̃'se], *v.t.* (*conjug. like* COMMENCER) to counterbalance, to counterpoise.
contrebande [kɔ̃trə'bɑ̃:d], *n.f.* contraband, smuggling; smuggled goods.
contrebandier [kɔ̃trəbɑ̃'dje], *n.m.* smuggler, gunrunner; smuggling vessel.
contre-bas (en) [ɑ̃kɔ̃trə'bɑ], *adv.* downwards.
contrebasse [kɔ̃trə'bɑ:s], *n.f.* double-bass.
contre-bord (à) [akɔ̃trə'bɔ:r], *adv.* (*Naut.*) on the opposite tack.
contre-boutant [kɔ̃trəbu'tɑ̃], **contreboutement** [kɔ̃trəbut'mɑ̃], *n.m.* abutment, buttress.
contre-bouter [kɔ̃trəbu'te], *v.t.* to buttress; to shore up.
contrecarrer [kɔ̃trəkɑ're], *v.t.* to thwart, to oppose.
contre-cœur [kɔ̃trə'kœ:r], *n.m.* chimney-back; ***à contre-cœur***, reluctantly.
contre-coup [kɔ̃trə'ku], *n.m.* rebound, repercussion; (*fig.*) consequence, result; ***par contre-coup***, as a consequence.
contredanse [kɔ̃trə'dɑ̃:s], *n.f.* quadrille.
contredire [kɔ̃trə'di:r], *v.t. irr.* (*conjug. like* MÉDIRE) to contradict, to gainsay; (*Law*) to disprove. **se contredire**, *v.r.* to contradict oneself; to be contradictory.
contredisant [kɔ̃trədi'zɑ̃], *a.* contradicting.
contredit [kɔ̃trə'di], *n.m.* contradiction; answer, reply; ***sans contredit***, incontestably.
contrée [kɔ̃'tre], *n.f.* country, region, district.
contre-échange [kɔ̃tre'ʃɑ̃:ʒ], *n.m.* mutual exchange.
contre-écrou [kɔ̃tre'kru], *n.m.* lock-nut.
contre-épreuve [kɔ̃tre'prœ:v], *n.f.* (*Engraving*) counter-proof; (*fig.*) feeble imitation.
contre-espionnage [kɔ̃trɛspjɔ'na:ʒ], *n.m.* counter-espionage.
contrefaçon [kɔ̃trəfa'sɔ̃], *n.f.* counterfeiting, forgery.
contrefacteur [kɔ̃trəfak'tœ:r], *n.m.* counterfeiter (*of coins etc.*); forger (*of bills etc.*); infringer (*of patents etc.*).
contrefaire [kɔ̃trə'fɛ:r], *v.t. irr.* (*conjug. like* FAIRE) to counterfeit, to imitate; to copy; to forge; to mimic; to disguise. **se contrefaire**, *v.r.* to dissemble, to sham.
contrefaiseur [kɔ̃trəfə'zœ:r], *n.m.* (*fem.* **-euse**) counterfeiter, mimic, imitator.
contrefait [kɔ̃trə'fɛ], *a.* counterfeit; deformed.
contre-fiche [kɔ̃trə'fiʃ], *n.f.* (*Carp.*) prop, strut.
contre-haut (en) [ɑ̃kɔ̃trə'o], *adv.* upwards.
contre-jour [kɔ̃trə'ʒu:r], *n.m.* (*Phot.*) low light; ***à contre-jour***, against the light.
contremaître [kɔ̃trə'mɛ:tr], *n.m.* overseer, foreman.
contremander [kɔ̃trəmɑ̃'de], *v.t.* to countermand.
contremarche [kɔ̃trə'marʃ], *n.f.* countermarch.
contremarcher [kɔ̃trəmar'ʃe], *v.i.* to countermarch.
contremarque [kɔ̃trə'mark], *n.f.* countermark; (*Theat.*) check ticket.
contre-mesure [kɔ̃trəmə'zy:r], *n.f.* countermeasure.
contre-offensive [kɔ̃trɔfɑ̃'si:v], *n.f.* counterattack.
contre-partie [kɔ̃trəpar'ti], *n.f.* counterpart; (*fig.*) opposite, contrary; return match.
contre-pédaler [kɔ̃trəpeda'le], *v.i.* to backpedal.
contre-pied [kɔ̃trə'pje], *n.m.* (*Hunt.*) backscent; (*fig.*) reverse way, contrary.
contre-plaqué [kɔ̃trəpla'ke], *a.* laminated. —*n.m.* two- (*or* three-) ply wood.
contrepoids [kɔ̃trə'pwɑ], *n.m. inv.* counterpoise, counter-balance; (*fig.*) equilibrium.
contre-poil [kɔ̃trə'pwal], *n.m.* wrong way of the hair *or* of the nap; ***à contre-poil***, against the grain.
contrepoint [kɔ̃trə'pwɛ̃], *n.m.* counterpoint.
contrepoison [kɔ̃trəpwa'zɔ̃], *n.m.* antidote, counter-poison.
contre-poser [kɔ̃trəpo'ze], *v.t.* to misplace; (*Comm.*) to set down wrong.
contrer [kɔ̃'tre], *v.t.* (*Bridge*) to double.
contre-ressort [kɔ̃trərə'sɔ:r], *n.m.* shock-absorber.
contre-révolution [kɔ̃trərevɔly'sjɔ̃], *n.f.* counter-revolution.
contre-saison (à) [akɔ̃trəsɛ'zɔ̃], *adv. phr.* (*flower*) produced out of season; ill-timed.
contresens [kɔ̃trə'sɑ̃:s], *n.m.* contrary sense; wrong construction *or* meaning; mistranslation; wrong side (*of material*).
contresigner [kɔ̃trəsi'ɲe], *v.t.* to countersign.
contretemps [kɔ̃trə'tɑ̃], *n.m. inv.* untoward accident, disappointment, mishap; (*Mus.*) syncopation; ***à contretemps***, at the wrong time.
contre-torpilleur [kɔ̃trətɔrpi'jœ:r], *n.m.* torpedo-boat destroyer.
contrevenant [kɔ̃trəv'nɑ̃], *n.m.* (*fem.* **-e**) contravener, infringer, offender, transgressor.
contrevenir [kɔ̃trəv'ni:r], *v.i. irr.* (*conjug. like* TENIR) to contravene, infringe.
contrevent [kɔ̃trə'vɑ̃], *n.m.* outside window-shutter.
contribuable [kɔ̃tri'bɥabl], *a.* taxable, rateable.—*n.* tax-payer, rate-payer.
contribuer [kɔ̃tri'bɥe], *v.i.* to contribute, to pay; (*fig.*) to conduce, to be an accessory (*à*).

contributaire [kɔ̃triby'tɛ:r], *a.* contributory.
contribution [kɔ̃triby'sjɔ̃], *n.f.* contribution; tax; share, portion; ***contribution foncière***, land tax.
contrister [kɔ̃tris'te], *v.t.* to grieve, to vex, to sadden.
contrit [kɔ̃'tri], *a.* contrite, penitent; afflicted.
contrition [kɔ̃tri'sjɔ̃], *n.f.* contrition.
contrôlable [kɔ̃tro'labl], *a.* that may be checked, verified.
contrôle [kɔ̃'tro:l], *n.m.* control-register; roll, list; controller's office; stamp, hall-mark; (*Theat.*) ticket-checking counter; (*fig.*) control, censure.
contrôler [kɔ̃tro'le], *v.t.* to register; to stamp; to check, to verify; to audit; to censure.
contrôleur [kɔ̃tro'lœ:r], *n.m.* (*fem.* **-euse**) controller; (*Taxes, Theat., Rail.*) inspector; time-keeper; ticket-collector; (*fig.*) critic.
controuver [kɔ̃tru've], *v.t.* to forge, to fabricate.
controversable [kɔ̃trɔvɛr'sabl], *a.* controvertible, controversial.
controverse [kɔ̃trɔ'vɛrs], *n.f.* controversy, discussion, dispute.
controverser [kɔ̃trɔvɛr'se], *v.t.* to dispute, to discuss.
contumace [kɔ̃ty'mas], *n.f.* contumacy, non-appearance *or* default, contempt of court; obstinacy.—*a.* contumacious.—*n.* defaulter.
contus [kɔ̃'ty], *a.* bruised, contused.
contusion [kɔ̃ty'zjɔ̃], *n.f.* contusion, bruise.
contusionner [kɔ̃tyzjɔ'ne], *v.t.* to contuse, to bruise.
convaincant [kɔ̃vɛ̃'kɑ̃], *a.* convincing.
convaincre [kɔ̃'vɛ̃:kr], *v.t. irr.* (*conjug. like* VAINCRE) to convince; to persuade. **se convaincre,** *v.r.* to convince oneself.
convaincu [kɔ̃vɛ̃'ky], *a.* convinced; sincere; convicted.
convalescence [kɔ̃valɛ'sɑ̃:s], *n.f.* convalescence.
convalescent [kɔ̃valɛ'sɑ̃], *a.* and *n.m.* (*fem.* **-e**) convalescent (person).
convection [kɔ̃vɛk'sjɔ̃], *n.f.* convection.
convenable [kɔ̃v'nabl], *a.* suitable, fit, proper; convenient; becoming.
convenablement [kɔ̃vənablə'mɑ̃], *adv.* suitably, becomingly, decently.
convenance [kɔ̃v'nɑ̃:s], *n.f.* fitness, propriety; seasonableness (*of time*); decency, seemliness; (*pl.*) propriety, decorum; ***mariage de convenance***, marriage of convenience.
convenir [kɔ̃v'ni:r], *v.i. irr.* (*conjug. like* TENIR, *but with aux.* ÊTRE) to agree; to admit, to own, to acknowledge (***de***); (*with aux.* AVOIR) to suit, to fit, to match; (*impers.*) to be fitting. **se convenir,** *v.r.* to suit each other, to agree.
convention [kɔ̃vɑ̃'sjɔ̃], *n.f.* agreement, treaty; (*social and other*) convention; (*pl.*) conditions (*of an agreement*).
conventionnel [kɔ̃vɑ̃sjɔ'nɛl], *a.* (*fem.* **-elle**) conventional.
conventionnellement [kɔ̃vɑ̃sjɔnɛl'mɑ̃], *adv.* by agreement.
convenu [kɔ̃v'ny], *a.* agreed; conventional, banal.
convergent [kɔ̃vɛr'ʒɑ̃], *a.* convergent.
converger [kɔ̃vɛr'ʒe], *v.i.* (*conjug. like* MANGER) to converge.
conversation [kɔ̃vɛrsɑ'sjɔ̃], *n.f.* conversation, converse, talk.
converse [kɔ̃'vɛrs], *a.* and *n.f.* (*Log.*) converse; (*Math.*) inverted.
converser [kɔ̃vɛr'se], *v.i.* to converse, to discourse.
conversible [kɔ̃vɛr'sibl], [CONVERTIBLE].
conversion [kɔ̃vɛr'sjɔ̃], *n.f.* conversion; transformation; change.
converti [kɔ̃vɛr'ti], *n.m.* (*fem.* **-e**) convert.
convertible [kɔ̃vɛr'tibl], *a.* convertible.
convertir [kɔ̃vɛr'ti:r], *v.t.* to convert, to transform, to change, to turn. **se convertir,** *v.r.* to be converted, to turn.
convertissement [kɔ̃vɛrtis'mɑ̃], *n.m.* conversion.
convexe [kɔ̃'vɛks], *a.* convex.
convexité [kɔ̃vɛksi'te], *n.f.* convexity.
conviction [kɔ̃vik'sjɔ̃], *n.f.* conviction, convincing proof.
convié [kɔ̃'vje], *a.* invited.—*n.m.* (*fem.* **-ée**) guest.
convier [kɔ̃'vje], *v.t.* to invite, to bid; (*fig.*) to urge.
convive [kɔ̃'viv], *n.* guest; fellow diner.
convocation [kɔ̃vɔkɑ'sjɔ̃], *n.f.* convocation; summons.
convoi [kɔ̃'vwa], *n.m.* (*Mil., Navy*) convoy; (*Rail. etc.*) train; ***convoi funèbre***, funeral procession.
convoiter [kɔ̃vwa'te], *v.t.* to covet, to hanker after.
convoitise [kɔ̃vwa'ti:z], *n.f.* covetousness; lust.
convolution [kɔ̃vɔly'sjɔ̃], *n.f.* convolution.
convolvulus [kɔ̃vɔlvy'ly:s], *n.m.* (*Bot.*) convolvulus.
convoquer [kɔ̃vɔ'ke], *v.t.* to convoke, to convene; to summon.
convoyer [kɔ̃vwa'je], *v.t.* (*conjug. like* EMPLOYER) to convoy, to escort.
convoyeur [kɔ̃vwa'jœ:r], *n.m.* convoy (*ship*); (*Mech.*) conveyor.
convulser [kɔ̃vyl'se], *v.t.* to convulse. **se convulser,** *v.r.* to be *or* become convulsed.
convulsif [kɔ̃vyl'sif], *a.* (*fem.* **-sive**) convulsive.
convulsion [kɔ̃vyl'sjɔ̃], *n.f.* convulsion.
convulsionner [kɔ̃vylsjɔ'ne], *v.t.* (*Med.*) to convulse.
convulsivement [kɔ̃vylsiv'mɑ̃], *adv.* convulsively.
coolie or **coulis** [ku'li], *n.m.* coolie.
coopérateur [koɔpera'tœ:r], *n.m.* (*fem.* **-trice**) co-operator, fellow-workman.—*a.* (*fem.* **-trice**) co-operating.
coopératif [koɔpera'tif], *a.* (*fem.* **-tive**) co-operative.
coopération [koɔperɑ'sjɔ̃], *n.f.* co-operation.
coopérer [koɔpe're], *v.i.* (*conjug. like* CÉDER) to co-operate.
coopter [koɔp'te], *v.t.* to co-opt.
coordination [koɔrdinɑ'sjɔ̃], *n.f.* co-ordination.
coordonné [koɔrdɔ'ne], *a.* co-ordinate.—*n.f. pl.* (**-ées**) (*Gram., Geom.*) co-ordinates.
coordonner [koɔrdɔ'ne], *v.t.* to co-ordinate.
copain [kɔ'pɛ̃], *n.m.* (*colloq.*) pal, mate.
copal [kɔ'pal], *n.m.* copal.
copeau [kɔ'po], *n.m.* (*pl.* **-eaux**) shaving, chip (*of wood*).
Copenhague [kɔpə'nag], *f.* Copenhagen.

cophte [COPTE].
copie [kɔ'pi], *n.f.* copy, transcript; reproduction; (*Print.*) 'copy'; candidate's paper.
copier [kɔ'pje], *v.t.* to copy; to imitate; to mimic.
copieusement [kɔpjøz'mɑ̃], *adv.* copiously, heartily (*of drinking, eating*).
copieux [kɔ'pjø], *a.* (*fem.* **-euse**) copious, plentiful.
co-pilote [kopi'lɔt], *n.m.* second pilot.
copiste [kɔ'pist], *n.* copier, transcriber, copyist.
copte or **cophte** [kɔpt], *a.* Coptic.—*n.* (**Copte, Cophte**) Copt.
coq [kɔk], *n.m.* cock, rooster; cock- (*as opposed to hen-*), weathercock; ***au chant du coq***, at cock-crow; ***coq de bruyère***, grouse; ***coq d'Inde***, turkey-cock; ***poids coq***, (*Box.*) bantam weight.
coq-à-l'âne [kɔka'lɑːn], *n.m. inv.* nonsense, cock-and-bull story.
coque [kɔk], *n.f.* shell (*of eggs, walnuts, fruits, snails etc.*); cocoon; cockle-shell (*small boat*); (*Naut.*) hull.
coquelicot [kɔkli'ko], *n.m.* corn-poppy.
coqueluche [kɔ'klyʃ], *n.f.* the rage, favourite; (*Med.*) whooping-cough.
coquerico [kɔkri'ko], *n.m.* cock-a-doodle-doo.
coqueriquer [kɔkri'ke], *v.i.* to crow.
coquet [kɔ'kɛ], *a.* (*fem.* **-ette**) coquettish; stylish, smart.—*n.m.* (*fem.* **-ette**) coquette, flirt; dandy.
coqueter [kɔk'te], *v.i.* (*conjug. like* APPELER) to coquet, to flirt.
coquetier [kɔk'tje], *n.m.* egg-merchant, poulterer; egg-cup.
coquetterie [kɔ̃kɛ'tri], *n.f.* coquettishness, flirtation; affectation (*in dress etc.*).
coquillage [kɔki'jaːʒ], *n.m.* shell-fish; shell.
coquille [kɔ'kiːj], *n.f.* shell (*of shell-fish, egg, fruits etc.*); (*Cook.*) Dutch oven; pat (*of butter*); (*Print.*) wrong letter; thumb (*of a latch*); (*ornament*) conch.
coquin [kɔ'kɛ̃], *a.* roguish; rascally.—*n.m.* knave, rascal, rogue, scamp.—*n.f.* **(-e)** slut, hussy, jade.
coquinerie [kɔkin'ri], *n.f.* knavery, rascality, roguery.
coquinet [kɔki'nɛ], *n.m.* little rascal.
cor (1) [kɔːr], *n.m.* horn, hunting-horn.
cor (2) [kɔːr], *n.m.* corn (*on the foot*).
cor (3) [kɔːr], *n.m.* tine (*of antler*).
corail [kɔ'raːj], *n.m.* (*pl.* **-aux**) coral.
corailleur [kɔra'jœːr], *n.m.* coral-fisher; coral-fishing boat.
Coran [kɔ'rɑ̃], *n.m.* Koran.
corbeau [kɔr'bo], *n.m.* (*pl.* **-eaux**) raven; crow.
corbeille [kɔr'bɛːj], *n.f.* flat, wide basket.
corbillard [kɔrbi'jaːr], *n.m.* hearse.
corbillon [kɔrbi'jɔ̃], *n.m.* small basket; crambo (*game*).
corbin [kɔr'bɛ̃], *n.m.* crow.
corbine [kɔr'bin], *n.f.* carrion-crow.
corbleu! [kɔr'blø], *int.* by Jove!
cordage [kɔr'daːʒ], *n.m.* cord, rope, cordage, rigging.
corde [kɔrd], *n.f.* cord, rope; twine, twist; string (*musical instrument, racquet*); line; (*Mus., Geom. etc.*) chord; tone, note; ***corde à boyau***, catgut.
cordé (1) [kɔr'de], *a.* twisted, corded.
cordé (2) [kɔr'de], *a.* cordate, heart-shaped.
cordeau [kɔr'do], *n.m.* (*pl.* **-eaux**) cord; line; fuse; tape.
cordée [kɔr'de], *n.f.* fishing-line; line of roped mountaineers.
cordeler [kɔrdə'le], *v.t.* (*conjug. like* APPELER) to twist, to twine.
cordelette [kɔrdə'lɛt], *n.f.* small cord; string.
cordelier [kɔrdə'lje], *n.m.* Franciscan friar.
cordelière [kɔrdə'ljɛːr], *n.f.* girdle (*of dressing-gown etc.*).
cordelle [kɔr'dɛl], *n.f.* towline, tow-rope.
corder [kɔr'de], *v.t.* to twist (*into cord*); to cord; to bind with a cord; to string (*racquet*). **se corder**, *v.r.* to be corded; to become stringy (*of plants etc.*).
corderie [kɔr'dri], *n.f.* rope-walk.
cordial [kɔr'djal], *a.* (*m. pl.* **-aux**) cordial, hearty, sincere.—*n.m.* cordial.
cordialement [kɔrdjal'mɑ̃], *adv.* cordially, heartily, sincerely.
cordialité [kɔrdjali'te], *n.f.* cordiality, heartiness.
cordier [kɔr'dje], *n.m.* rope-maker.
Cordillères [kɔrdi'jɛːr], **les**, *f.pl.* the Cordilleras.
cordite [kɔr'dit], *n.f.* cordite.
cordon [kɔr'dɔ̃], *n.m.* strand (*of a rope*); twist, string; cord; ribbon (*of an order*); border, edging; ***cordon bleu***, blue-ribbon, first-rate cook.
cordonner [kɔrdɔ'ne], *v.t.* to twist, to twine, to braid; to mill (*coins*).
cordonnerie [kɔrdɔn'ri], *n.f.* shoe-making; cobbler's shop.
cordonnet [kɔrdɔ'nɛ], *n.m.* twist; milled edge (*of coins*).
cordonnier [kɔrdɔ'nje], *n.m.* shoe-maker.
Corée [kɔ're], **la**, *f.* Korea.
coréen [kɔre'ɛ̃], *a.* (*fem.* **-enne**) Korean.—*n.m.* Korean (*language*); (**Coréen**, *fem.* **-enne**) Korean (*person*).
coriace [kɔ'rjas], *a.* tough, leathery; (*fig.*) close, niggardly; dogged.
coricide [kɔri'sid], *n.m.* corn cure.
corinthien [kɔrɛ̃'tjɛ̃], *a.* (*fem.* **-enne**) Corinthian.—*n.m.* (**Corinthien**, *fem.* **-enne**) Corinthian.
coris [CAURI].
corli [kɔr'li], **courlis** [kur'li], **corlieu** [kɔr'ljø], *n.m.* curlew.
cormoran [kɔrmɔ'rɑ̃], *n.m.* cormorant.
cornac [kɔr'nak], *n.m.* elephant-driver, mahout; mentor.
corne [kɔrn], *n.f.* horn, hoof; shoe-horn; dog's-ear (*on books, leaves*); ***chapeau à trois cornes***, three-cornered hat.
corné [kɔr'ne], *a.* corneous, horny.
cornée [kɔr'ne], *n.f.* cornea.
corneille [kɔr'nɛːj], *n.f.* crow; rook.
cornement [kɔrnə'mɑ̃], *n.m.* buzzing in the ears.
cornemuse [kɔrnə'myːz], *n.f.* bagpipes.
corner (1) [kɔr'ne], *v.t.* to blurt out, to trumpet; to dog-ear (*a leaf*).—*v.i.* to blow, wind *or* sound a horn; to tingle (*of the ears*).
corner (2) [kɔr'nɛr], *n.m.* (*Ftb.*) corner (-kick).
cornet [kɔr'nɛ], *n.m.* horn, hooter; ink-horn; cone.
cornette [kɔr'nɛt], *n.f.* mob-cap; pennant of cavalry.
corniche [kɔr'niʃ], *n.f.* cornice; ledge.

cornichon [kɔrni'ʃɔ̃], *n.m.* gherkin; (*fig.*) greenhorn.
corniste [kɔr'nist], *n.* horn-player.
Cornouaille [kɔr'nwɑːj], **la**, *f.* Cornwall.
cornu [kɔr'ny], *a.* horned; angular, cornered; (*fig.*) absurd.
cornue [kɔr'ny], *n.f.* (*Chem.*) retort.
corollaire [kɔrɔ'lɛːr], *n.m.* corollary.
corolle [kɔ'rɔl], *n.f.* corolla.
coronaire [kɔrɔ'nɛːr], *a.* (*Anat.*) coronary.
coronal [kɔrɔ'nal], *a.* (*m. pl.* **-aux**) (*Anat.*) coronal.
corporation [kɔrpɔrɑ'sjɔ̃], *n.f.* corporation, corporate body.
corporel [kɔrpɔ'rɛl], *a.* (*fem.* **-elle**) corporal, bodily.
corps [kɔːr], *n.m.* body; matter, substance; thickness, consistence; chief part; corporation, company; society, college; corps; fellow-creature; ***à corps perdu***, desperately; ***à son corps défendant***, (*fig.*) reluctantly; ***corps à corps***, hand to hand, (*Box.*) in-fight(ing); ***corps morts***, (*Naut.*) fixed moorings; ***garde du corps***, life-guard; ***sombrer corps et biens***, to founder with all hands.
corpulence [kɔrpy'lɑ̃ːs], *n.f.* corpulence, stoutness.
corpulent [kɔrpy'lɑ̃], *a.* corpulent, stout.
corpuscule [kɔrpys'kyl], *n.m.* corpuscule, corpuscle.
correct [kɔ'rɛkt], *a.* correct, accurate.
correctement [kɔrɛkt'mɑ̃], *adv.* correctly, accurately.
correctif [kɔrɛk'tif], *a.* (*fem.* **-tive**) corrective. —*n.m.* corrective.
correction [kɔrɛk'sjɔ̃], *n.f.* correction; correctness, accuracy; (*Print.*) reading, alteration (*of a proof etc.*); (*fig.*) reprimand, reproof; punishment; thrashing.
correctionnel [kɔrɛksjɔ'nɛl], *a.* (*fem.* **-elle**) within the jurisdiction of the ***tribunal de police correctionnelle***, court of petty sessions.
corrélation [kɔrelɑ'sjɔ̃], *n.f.* correlation.
correspondance [kɔrɛspɔ̃'dɑ̃ːs], *n.f.* correspondence; connexion; intercourse; conformity; (*Rail.*) connexion.
correspondant [kɔrɛspɔ̃'dɑ̃], *a.* correspondent, corresponding.—*n.m.* (*fem.* **-e**) correspondent, corresponding member.
correspondre [kɔrɛs'pɔ̃ːdr], *v.i.* to correspond, to communicate, to be in correspondence; to agree.
corridor [kɔri'dɔːr], *n.m.* corridor, gallery, passage.
corrigé [kɔri'ʒe], *n.m.* corrected (*schoolboy's*) exercise; key (*book*), crib.
corriger [kɔri'ʒe], *v.t.* (*conjug. like* MANGER) to correct, to rectify; to repair, to amend; to reprove, to chide, to chastise. **se corriger**, *v.r.* to correct oneself, to amend, to reform.
corroboration [kɔrɔbɔrɑ'sjɔ̃], *n.f.* corroboration, strengthening.
corroborer [kɔrɔbɔ're], *v.t.* to strengthen; to corroborate.
corrodant [kɔrɔ'dɑ̃], *a.* corroding, corrosive.
corroder [kɔrɔ'de], *v.t.* to corrode.
corrompre [kɔ'rɔ̃ːpr], *v.t.* (*conjug. like* ROMPRE) to corrupt, to infect; to spoil; to taint (*meat*); (*fig.*) to pervert; to bribe. **se corrompre**, *v.r.* to grow corrupt; to become tainted.
corrompu [kɔrɔ̃'py], *a.* corrupted, unsound; bribed.
corrosif [kɔro'zif], *a.* (*fem.* **-sive**) and *n.m.* corrosive.
corrosion [kɔro'zjɔ̃], *n.f.* corrosion.
corroyer [kɔrwɑ'je], *v.t.* (*conjug. like* EMPLOYER) to curry (*leather*); to plane (*wood*).
corroyeur [kɔrwɑ'jœːr], *n.m.* currier.
corrupteur [kɔryp'tœːr], *a.* (*fem.* **-trice**) corrupting, perverting, infectious.—*n.m.* (*fem.* **-trice**) corrupter, seducer; briber.
corruptibilité [kɔryptibili'te], *n.f.* corruptibility.
corruptible [kɔryp'tibl], *a.* corruptible.
corruptif [kɔryp'tif], *a.* (*fem.* **-tive**) corruptive.
corruption [kɔryp'sjɔ̃], *n.f.* corruption; rottenness; (*fig.*) depravity; (*Polit.*) bribery.
corsage [kɔr'saːʒ], *n.m.* chest (*of the body*); corsage, bodice.
corsaire [kɔr'sɛːr], *n.m.* privateer, corsair; (*fig.*) shark.
Corse [kɔrs], **la**, *f.* Corsica.—*n.* Corsican (*person*).
corse [kɔrs], *a.* Corsican.
corsé [kɔr'se], *a.* rich, full-bodied; (*colloq.*) strong, thick; (*of stories etc.*) spicy.
corser [kɔr'se], *v.t.* to stiffen, to thicken; to complicate.
corset [kɔr'sɛ], *n.m.* corset, stays.
corsetier [kɔrsə'tje], *n.m.* (*fem.* **-ière**) corset-maker.
cortège [kɔr'tɛːʒ], *n.m.* train, retinue, suite, procession.
corvée [kɔr've], *n.f.* (*Feud.*) forced *or* statute labour; fatigue party; (*fig.*) drudgery.
corvette [kɔr'vɛt], *n.f.* corvette, sloop of war.
Cosaque [kɔ'zak], *n.m.* Cossack.
cosinus [kɔsi'nyːs], *n.m.* cosine.
cosmétique [kɔsme'tik], *a.* and *n.m.* cosmetic.
cosmique [kɔs'mik], *a.* cosmic.
cosmographie [kɔsmɔgra'fi], *n.f.* cosmography.
cosmopolite [kɔsmɔpɔ'lit], *n.* cosmopolite. —*a.* cosmopolitan.
cosmos [kɔs'mos], *n.m.* cosmos.
cosse [kɔs], *n.f.* pod, shell, husk, rind.
cossu [kɔ'sy], *a.* substantial, wealthy.
costume [kɔs'tym], *n.m.* costume, dress; uniform.
costumer [kɔsty'me], *v.t.* to dress (*in a certain style etc.*). **se costumer**, *v.r.* to dress (*oneself*) up.
costumier [kɔsty'mje], *n.m.* (*fem.* **-ière**) costumier.
cote [kɔt], *n.f.* quota, share; letter, number, figure (*to indicate order etc.*); (*St. Exch.*) quotation; (*Comm.*) price-list; odds.
côte [koːt], *n.f.* rib (*of the body, cloth, fruit etc.*); slope, hill; shore, sea-coast; ***à mi-côte***, half-way up.
côté [ko'te], *n.m.* side; part, quarter, hand, way, direction; face, aspect; ***à côté de***, by, near; ***d'à côté***, adjoining, next.
coté [kɔ'te], *a.* marked; classed; backed; ***point coté***, (*on a map*) trig-point; ***cheval bien coté***, well-backed horse.
coteau [kɔ'to], *n.m.* (*pl.* **-eaux**) slope; little hill.

côtelette [ko'tlɛt], *n.f.* cutlet, chop.
coter [kɔ'te], *v.t.* to number; to price; (*St. Exch.*) to quote.
coterie [kɔ'tri], *n.f.* coterie, set, circle, clique.
cothurne [kɔ'tyrn], *n.m.* buskin.
côtier [ko'tje], *a.* (*fem.* **-ière**) coasting.—*n.m.* coaster (*ship*).
cotillon [kɔti'jɔ̃], *n.m.* under-petticoat; cotillion.
cotisation [kɔtizɑ'sjɔ̃], *n.f.* assessment, quota, share; subscription.
cotiser [kɔti'ze], *v.t.* to assess, to rate. **se cotiser**, *v.r.* to club together; to get up a subscription, to subscribe.
coton [kɔ'tɔ̃], *n.m.* cotton; fluff, down (*of fruit, and hair on the face*); cotton wool.
cotonnade [kɔtɔ'nad], *n.f.* cotton-cloth.
cotonné [kɔtɔ'ne], *a.* covered with *or* full of cotton; downy; woolly (*of hair*); padded.
cotonner [kɔtɔ'ne], *v.t.* to fill *or* to stuff with cotton; to pad. **se cotonner**, *v.r.* to be covered with down.
cotonneux [kɔtɔ'nø], *a.* (*fem.* **-euse**) cottony, downy; spongy, mealy.
cotonnier [kɔtɔ'nje], *n.m.* cotton-bush.
côtoyer [kotwa'je], *v.t.* (*conjug. like* EMPLOYER) to go by the side of, to skirt; to coast; (*fig.*) to keep close to.
cotre [ko:tr], *n.m.* cutter (*vessel*).
cotret [kɔ'trɛ], *n.m.* faggot; stick.
cottage [kɔ'ta:ʒ], *n.m.* cottage.
cotte [kɔt], *n.f.* short petticoat; (*engineer's*) overalls.
cotuteur [kɔty'tœ:r], *n.m.* (*fem.* **-trice**) joint-guardian.
cou [ku], *n.m.* neck.
couac [kwak], *n.m.* false note; squawk.
couard [kwa:r], *a.* coward, cowardly.—*n.m.* (*fem.* **-e**) coward.
couardise [kwar'di:z], *n.f.* cowardice.
couchage [ku'ʃa:ʒ], *n.m.* act of lying in bed; bed, night's lodging; bedding.
couchant [ku'ʃɑ̃], *a.* setting; lying; (*fig.*) fawning; ***un chien couchant***, a setter.—*n.m.* west; (*fig.*) decline.
couche [kuʃ], *n.f.* bed, couch; confinement; nappy; layer, row; (*Min.*) seam; (*Gard.*) hotbed, bed; coat (*of varnish* or *colour*); (*fig.*) social stratum.
couché [ku'ʃe], *a.* in bed, gone to bed, lying down, recumbent; (*Her.*) couchant.
couchée [ku'ʃe], *n.f.* act of lying down; sleeping place; night's lodging.
coucher [ku'ʃe], *v.t.* to put to bed; to lay down; to knock down; to lay on; to stake.—*v.i.* to sleep, to lie (down), to rest; ***coucher à la belle étoile***, to sleep in the open air. **se coucher**, *v.r.* to go to bed; to lie down; to set, to go down (*of the sun etc.*).—*n.m.* going to bed; bed-time; setting (*of the sun etc.*).
couchette [ku'ʃɛt], *n.f.* small bed, crib; berth; bunk (*on a ship*); ***wagon à couchettes***, second-class sleeper.
coucou [ku'ku], *n.m.* cuckoo; cuckoo-clock; (*Bot.*) cowslip.
coude [kud], *n.m.* elbow; bend, angle; turning.
coudé [ku'de], *a.* bent, elbowed, cranked.
coudée [ku'de], *n.f.* length of arm from elbow to tip of middle finger, cubit.
cou-de-pied [kud'pje], *n.m.* (*pl.* **cous-de-pied**) instep.
couder [ku'de] *v.t.* to bend, to make an elbow in. **se couder**, *v.r.* to elbow, to form an elbow.
coudoyer [kudwa'je], *v.t.* (*conjug. like* EMPLOYER) to elbow, to jostle. **se coudoyer**, *v.r.* to elbow *or* jostle each other.
coudraie [ku'drɛ], *n.f.* hazel-copse; filbert-orchard.
coudre [kudr], *v.t. irr.* to sew, to stitch; (*fig.*) to attach, to connect.
coudrier [ku'drje], *n.m.* hazel-tree.
couenne [kwan], *n.f.* scraped pig-skin; crackling (*of pork*); rind; (*Med.*) birthmark.
couette [kwɛt], **coit(t)e** (2) [kwat], *n.f.* feather-bed; sea-gull; (*hare's*) scut.
couguar [ku'ga:r], *n.m.* cougar, puma.
coulage [ku'la:ʒ], *n.m.* flow (*of metal in fusion*); melting, casting; leakage, waste; pilferage.
coulant [ku'lɑ̃], *a.* flowing, smooth, natural (*of style etc.*); (*fig.*) easy; ***nœud coulant***, slip knot.—*n.m.* sliding ring (*for a necktie, umbrella etc.*).
coulé [ku'le], *n.m.* (*Mus.*) slur; (*Billiards*) follow through; (*Swim.*) plunge.
coulée [ku'le], *n.f.* running-hand (*of writing*); (*Metal.*) tapping; flow, rush (*of a torrent etc.*); (*Hunt.*) track, path.
couler [ku'le], *v.t.* to cast; to strain; to slip (***dans***); to sink, to run down; (*Mus.*) to slur. —*v.i.* to flow; to glide; to trickle; to leak; to slip away (*of time etc.*); to founder (*of a ship etc.*). **se couler**, *v.r.* to slip, to creep, to steal, to glide; to be cast (*of metals*).
couleur [ku'lœ:r], *n.f.* colour; colouring-matter, paint; colouring; (*fig.*) appearance; pretence; suit (*at cards*).
couleuvre [ku'lœ:vr], *n.f.* (grass) snake.
coulis [ku'li], *n.m.* strained juice from meat etc. slowly stewed.
coulisse [ku'lis], *n.f.* groove, channel; running string; (*Theat.*) wing; (*fig.*) behind the scenes; ***porte à coulisse***, sliding door; ***faire les yeux en coulisse***, to make sheep's eyes.
coulissé [kuli'se], *a.* grooved.
coulissier [kuli'sje], *n.m.* stock-jobber outside broker.
couloir [ku'lwa:r], *n.m.* passage, corridor, lobby, gangway.
couloire [ku'lwa:r], *n.f.* colander, strainer.
coup [ku], *n.m.* blow, stroke, hit, thump, knock, stab, thrust; beat (*of a drum*); draught (*of liquids*); clap (*of thunder*); (*Artill.*) charge; gust (*of wind*); throw; shot; moment; bout; attempt; deed; event; ***à coup sûr***, unquestionably; (*Ftb.*) ***coup d'envoi***, kick-off; ***coup d'œil***, glance; ***coup de téléphone***, telephone call; ***le coup de grâce***, the finishing stroke; ***tout à coup***, all of a sudden; ***tout d'un coup***, all at once.
coupable [ku'pabl], *a.* culpable, guilty.—*n.* guilty person, culprit.
coupage [ku'pa:ʒ], *n.m.* cutting; diluting (*of wine*); blending (*of spirits*).
coupant [ku'pɑ̃], *a.* cutting, sharp.—*n.m.* edge (*of a sword etc.*)
coupe (1) [kup], *n.f.* cutting, felling (*of wood*); wood felled; the cut end; cut (*clothes etc.*); shape; (*Pros.*) cadence; (*Swim.*) overarm stroke.

coupe (2) [kup], *n.f.* cup, goblet, chalice; basin (*of a fountain etc.*).

coupé (1) [ku'pe], *a.* intersected; diluted; (*fig.*) laconic.

coupé (2) [ku'pe], *n.m.* coupé (*kind of brougham*); a dance step.

[In the following compounds ***coupe*** is *inv.*]

coupe-circuit [kupsir'kɥi], *n.m. inv.* cut-out, circuit-breaker; fuse.

coupée [ku'pe], *n.f.* (*Naut.*) gangway; ***échelle de coupée***, accommodation ladder.

coupe-file [kup'fil], *n.m. inv.* police pass.

coupe-gorge [kup'gɔrʒ], *n.m. inv.* cut-throat place, den.

coupe-jarret [kupʒa'rɛ], *n.m.* cut-throat, assassin, ruffian.

coupe-papier [kuppa'pje], *n.m. inv.* paper-knife.

couper [ku'pe], *v.t.* to cut; to dock, to strike off; to clip, to pare; to geld; (*Mil.*) to intercept; to dilute (*milk, wine, with water*); to intersect; to interrupt.—*v.i.* to make an incision; to cut, to trump (*at cards*). **se couper,** *v.r.* to cut oneself; to intersect.

couperet [ku'prɛ], *n.m.* (*butcher's*) chopper; knife (*of guillotine*).

couperose [ku'pro:z], *n.f.* copperas.

couperosé [kupro'ze], *a.* blotched.

coupeur [ku'pœ:r], *n.m.* (*fem.* **-euse**) cutter. —*n.f.* (**-euse**) cutting machine.

(*C*) **coupe-vent** [kup'vɑ̃], *n.m.* wind breaker.

couplage [ku'pla:ʒ], *n.m.* coupling.

couple [kupl], *n.f.* brace, couple.—*n.m.* married couple; pair (*of animals, male and female*); (*Naut.*) frame.

coupler [ku'ple], *v.t.* to couple, to link.

couplet [ku'plɛ], *n.m.* couplet; verse of song; (*fig.*) tirade; (*Tech.*) hinge.

coupleur [ku'plœ:r], *n.m.* (*Elec.*) make-and-break.

coupoir [ku'pwa:r], *n.m.* cutter (*instrument*).

coupole [ku'pɔl], *n.f.* cupola; (*Naut.*) revolving gun-turret.

coupon [ku'pɔ̃], *n.m.* remnant; coupon; dividend-warrant, cheque; (*Theat.*) ticket.

coupure [ku'py:r], *n.f.* cut, incision, slit; cutting; suppression; drain; (*Banking*) small note.

cour [ku:r], *n.f.* court (*of a prince, of justice etc.*); yard, courtyard; (*fig.*) courtship, suit.

courage [ku'ra:ʒ], *n.m.* courage, daring; spirit, mettle; fortitude, greatness of soul.

courageusement [kuraʒøz'mɑ̃], *adv.* courageously, bravely, resolutely.

courageux [kura'ʒø], *a.* (*fem.* **-euse**) courageous, daring, fearless, plucky.

couramment [kura'mɑ̃], *adv.* fluently, readily.

courant [ku'rɑ̃], *a.* running; current, present; usual; fair, middling (*of goods*); lineal (*of measures*).—*n.m.* stream, current, tide; course (*of time etc.*); routine; present price; present (*time*).

courbage [kur'ba:ʒ], *n.m.* bending, curving.

courbatu [kurba'ty], *a.* foundered (*of horses*); stiff in the joints; (*Med.*) affected with lumbago.

courbature [kurba'ty:r], *n.f.* foundering, lameness; (*Path.*) stiffness in the limbs, lumbago.

courbaturer [kurbaty're], *v.t.* to make (*someone*) feel stiff all over.

courbe [kurb], *a.* curved, bent, crooked.—*n.f.* curve; (*Naut., Carp.*) knee; (*Vet.*) curb; (*Math.*) graph.

courber [kur'be], *v.t.* to curve, to bend, to warp, to make crooked.—*v.i.* to bend, to sag. **se courber,** *v.r.* to bend, to stoop; to bow down.

courbette [kur'bɛt], *n.f.* curvet; (*pl.*) bowing and scraping, cringing.

courbetter [kurbɛ'te], *v.i.* to curvet.

courbure [kur'by:r], *n.f.* curvature, curve; bend; sagging.

coureur [ku'rœ:r], *a.* (*fem.* **-euse**) swift.—*n.m.* runner, racer; hunter (*horse*); light porter; rover; rake, libertine; (*Mil.*) scout.

courge [kurʒ], *n.f.* gourd; ***courge à la moelle***, vegetable marrow.

courir [ku'ri:r], *v.t. irr.* to pursue; to travel over; to hunt; to frequent; to expose oneself to.—*v.i.* to run; to hasten; to ramble, to rove; to flow; to stretch; to circulate.

courlis [kur'li], **courlieu** [kur'ljø], *n.m.* curlew.

couronne [ku'rɔn], *n.f.* crown; coronet; wreath; crown (*a coin*).

couronnement [kurɔn'mɑ̃], *n.m.* crowning, coronation; completion.

couronner [kurɔ'ne], *v.t.* to crown; to award a prize, to honour (***avec***); to consummate; to wreathe.

courre [ku:r], *v.t. only used in* ***chasse à courre***, hunting.

courrier [ku'rje], *n.m.* messenger, courier; mail, post; letters, correspondence.

courriériste [kurje'rist], *n.m.* columnist.

courroie [ku'rwɑ], *n.f.* strap, thong; driving belt *or* band.

courroucer [kuru'se], *v.t.* (*conjug. like* COMMENCER) to provoke, to anger, to incense, to irritate. **se courroucer,** *v.r.* to become angry, to rage.

courroux [ku'ru], *n.m.* wrath, anger, rage.

cours [ku:r], *n.m.* course, stream, current, flow; lapse; path, orbit; vent, scope; public drive *or* walk; vogue; currency; series of lectures; (*pl.*) classes; (*St. Exch.*) market price, rate.

course [kurs], *n.f.* running, run; course; drive, walk, excursion; career; race; errand; privateering; cruise; length of the stroke (*of a piece of machinery*).

coursier [kur'sje], *n.m.* charger; (*poet.*) steed; (*Naut.*) bow-gun.

coursive [kur'si:v], *n.f.* (*Naut.*) gangway.

court (1) [ku:r], *a.* short; brief; concise, curt; limited, scanty; fleeting.—*adv.* short, abruptly; ***demeurer court***, to stop short; ***être à court d'argent***, to be short of money.

court (2) [kɔrt, ku:r], *n.m.* tennis court.

courtage [kur'ta:ʒ], *n.m.* brokerage, commission.

courtaud [kur'to], *a.* thick-set, dumpy; docked, crop-eared.—*n.m.* (*fem.* **-e**) short, thick-set person; docked *or* crop-eared horse.

courtauder [kurto'de], *v.t.* to dock, to crop (*horses etc.*).

court-circuit [kursir'kɥi], *n.m.* (*pl.* **courts-circuits**) short-circuit.

court-circuiter [kursirkɥi'te], *v.t.* to short-circuit.
courtement [kurtə'mɑ̃], *adv.* shortly, briefly.
courtepointe [kurtə'pwɛ̃:t], *n.f.* counterpane, quilt.
courtier [kur'tje], *n.m.* (*fem.* **-ière**) broker, agent.
courtil [kur'til], *n.m.* *small garden; garth.
courtisan [kurti'zɑ̃], *n.m.* courtier; fawner.
courtisane [kurti'zan], *n.f.* courtesan.
courtisanerie [kurtizan'ri], *n.f.* court flattery, toadyism.
courtisanesque [kurtiza'nɛsk], *a.* courtier-like.
courtiser [kurti'ze], *v.t.* to court; to woo; to flatter.
courtois [kur'twa] *a.* courteous, polite.
courtoisement [kurtwaz'mɑ̃], *adv.* courteously.
courtoisie [kurtwa'zi], *n.f.* courtesy; kindness, good turn.
couseur [ku'zœ:r], *n.m.* (*fem.* **-euse**) sewer, stitcher (*of books*).
cousin [ku'zɛ̃], *n.m.* (*fem.* **-e**) cousin; (*fig.*) friend, crony.
cousinage [kuzi'na:ʒ], *n.m.* cousinhood; cousins; relationship.
cousiner [kuzi'ne], *v.t.* to call cousin; to hob-nob with.—*v.i.* to live on others; to be friends *or* cronies.
coussin [ku'sɛ̃], *n.m.* cushion, hassock; pad.
coussiner [kusi'ne], *v.t.* to pad, to cushion.
coussinet [kusi'nɛ], *n.m.* small cushion, pad; iron wedge; pillion.
cousu [ku'zy], *a.* sewn, stitched.
coût [ku], *n.m.* costs, charge; ***le coût de la vie***, the cost of living.
coûtant [ku'tɑ̃], *a.* costing; ***à prix coûtant***, at cost price.
couteau [ku'to], *n.m.* (*pl.* **-eaux**) knife.
coutelas [kut'lɑ], *n.m.* cutlass.
coutelier [kutə'lje], *n.m.* cutler.
coutelière [kutə'ljɛ:r], *n.f.* knife-case; cutler's wife.
coutellerie [kutɛl'ri], *n.f.* cutler's shop *or* business; cutlery.
coûter [ku'te], *v.t.* to cost, to cause, to occasion.—*v.i.* to cost (***cher*** *etc.*); to be expensive; (*fig.*) to be painful, troublesome.
coûteusement [kutøz'mɑ̃], *adv.* expensively.
coûteux [ku'tø], *a.* (*fem.* **-euse**) expensive, costly.
coutil [ku'ti], *n.m.* tick, ticking; (*Tex.*) drill.
coutre [kutr], *n.m.* plough-share, coulter, axe.
coutume [ku'tym], *n.f.* custom, habit, practice.
coutumier [kuty'mje], *a.* (*fem.* **-ière**) customary, common, ordinary; habitual.
couture [ku'ty:r], *n.f.* sewing, needlework; seam, suture; scar.
couturer [kuty're], *v.t.* to seam.
couturier [kuty'rje], *n.m.* ladies' tailor.—*a.* sartorial.
couturière [kuty'rjɛ:r], *n.f.* dressmaker, seamstress.
couvage [ku'va:ʒ], **couvaison** [kuvɛ'zɔ̃], *n.f.* brooding-time, sitting, incubation.
couvée [ku've], *n.f.* sitting (*of eggs*); brood, covey.
couvent [ku'vɑ̃], *n.m.* convent, monastery, nunnery; convent school.
couver [ku've], *v.t.* to sit on, to incubate, to hatch; to brood, to prepare in secret (*a plot etc.*); to brood over.—*v.i.* to lie hidden, to lurk; to smoulder.
couvercle [ku'vɛrkl], *n.m.* cover, lid, cap, shutter.
couvert [ku'vɛ:r], *a.* covered; clad, clothed; cloudy, overcast; obscure, ambiguous (*of words*).—*n.m.* cover (*plate, spoon, knife, fork*); shelter; cover, wrapper; covert, thicket; ***le vivre et le couvert***, board and lodging.
couverte [ku'vɛrt], *n.f.* glaze, glazing.
couverture [kuvɛr'ty:r], *n.f.* covering, wrapper; blanket, rug, counterpane, quilt; cover (*of a book*); (*Comm.*) guaranty, security; ***couverture chauffante***, electric blanket.
couveuse [ku'vø:z], *n.f.* broody hen; ***couveuse artificielle***, incubator.
couvi [ku'vi], *a.* addled, rotten (*egg*).
couvoir [ku'vwa:r], *n.m.* incubator.

[In the following compounds ***couvre*** is *inv.*]

couvre-chef [kuvrə'ʃɛf], *n.m.* headgear.
couvre-feu [kuvrə'fø], *n.m. inv.* curfew; curfew-bell; fire-cover, fire-plate; black-out.
couvre-plat [kuvrə'pla], *n.m.* dish-cover.
couvre-théière [kuvrəte'jɛ:r], *n.m.* tea-cosy.
couvreur [ku'vrœ:r], *n.m.* roofer.
couvrir [ku'vri:r], *v.t. irr.* (*conjug. like* OUVRIR) to cover; to wrap up; to roof; to overwhelm; to clothe; to defend, to protect; to overrun, to overflow; to excuse; to disguise; to defray (*expenses etc.*). **se couvrir**, *v.r.* to cover oneself, to put on (*one's hat*); to get under cover; to be overcast (*of the weather*); (*Comm.*) to reimburse oneself.
coyote [kɔ'jɔt], *n.m.* prairie wolf.
crabe [kra:b], *n.m.* crab.
crac! [krak], *int.* crack! pop!
crachat [kra'ʃa], *n.m.* spittle, expectoration.
crachement [kraʃ'mɑ̃], *n.m.* spitting.
cracher [kra'ʃe], *v.t.* to spit; (*fig.*) to spit out, to come out with.—*v.i.* to spit, to splutter; (*Mach. etc.*) to spark, to backfire.
crachoir [kra'ʃwa:r], *n.m.* spittoon.
crachoter [kraʃɔ'te], *v.i.* to spit often.
Cracovie [krakɔ'vi], *f.* Cracow.
craie [krɛ], *n.f.* chalk.
craillement [krɑj'mɑ̃] *n.m.* cawing (*of crows*).
crailler [krɑ'je], *v.i.* to caw.
craindre [krɛ̃:dr], *v.t. irr.* to fear; to dread; to dislike.
crainte [krɛ̃:t], *n.f.* fear, apprehension; dread, awe.
craintif [krɛ̃'tif], *a.* (*fem.* **-tive**) fearful, apprehensive, timid.
craintivement [krɛ̃tiv'mɑ̃], *adv.* fearfully timorously.
cramoisi [kramwa'zi], *a.* and *n.m.* crimson.
crampe [krɑ̃:p], *n.f.* cramp; crampon.
crampon [krɑ̃'pɔ̃], *n.m.* crampon, cramp-iron, grappling-iron.
cramponner [krɑ̃pɔ'ne], *v.t.* to cramp, to fasten with a cramp-iron. **se cramponner**, *v.r.* to hold fast, to cling like grim death.

cramponnet [krɑ̃pɔ'nɛ], *n.m.* small cramp, tack; staple (*of a lock*).

cran (1) [krɑ̃], *n.m.* notch; cog; (*Print.*) nick; (*fam.*) pluck.

cran (2) [krɑ̃], *n.m.* horse-radish.

crâne [krɑːn], *a.* bold, plucky.—*n.m.* skull, cranium.

crânement [krɑn'mɑ̃], *adv.* pluckily; in style, famously.

craner [kra'ne], *v.t.* to notch, to indent (*a clock wheel*).

crâner [krɑ'ne], *v.i.* to swagger.

cranologie [kranɔlɔ'ʒi], **craniologie** [kranjɔlɔ'ʒi], *n.f.* craniology.

crapaud [kra'po], *n.m.* toad; jumping cracker; (*fig.*) urchin, brat.

crapaudière [krapo'djɛːr], *n.f.* nest of toads; (*fig.*) low, swampy place.

crapaudine [krapo'din], *n.f.* toadstone; grating (*of an escape-pipe*); ***à la crapaudine***, cut open and broiled.

crapouillot [krapu'jo], *n.m.* trench-mortar.

crapule [kra'pyl], *n.f.* low vulgar debauchery, gluttony, drunkenness; blackguards.

crapuleusement [krapyløz'mɑ̃], *adv.* dissolutely.

crapuleux [krapy'lø], *a.* (*fem.* **-euse**) low, debauched, vicious, dissolute.

craque [krak], *n.f.* fib, humbug.

craqueler [kra'kle], *v.t.* (*conjug. like* APPELER) to crackle (*china*).

craquelot [kra'klo], *n.m.* bloater.

craquelure [kra'klyːr], *n.f.* crack (*in china*).

craquement [krak'mɑ̃], *n.m.* cracking noise, creaking, snapping (*boughs*).

craquer [kra'ke], *v.i.* to crack, to crackle, to snap, to creak, to crunch.

craquètement [krakɛt'mɑ̃], *n.m.* crackling; chattering (*of the teeth*); gabbling (*of a stork and other birds*).

craqueter [krak'te], *v.i.* (*conjug. like* APPELER) to crackle, to crepitate; to gabble (*birds*).

crasse (1) [kras], *a.* gross, thick, coarse, crass.

crasse (2) [kras], *n.f.* dirt, filth, squalor; stinginess; dross.

crasser [kra'se], *v.t.* to foul, to dirty (*fire-arms etc.*). **se crasser**, *v.r.* to become foul (*of fire-arms etc.*).

crasseux [kra'sø], *a.* (*fem.* **-euse**) dirty, filthy, nasty, squalid, sordid; stingy, mean.—*n.m.* (*fem.* **-euse**) sloven, slut; skinflint.

crassier [kra'sje], *n.m.* slag heap; rubbish dump.

cratère [kra'tɛːr], *n.m.* crater (*mouth of volcano*); (*Gr.* or *Rom.*) bowl *or* cup.

cravache [kra'vaʃ], *n.f.* riding-whip.

cravacher [krava'ʃe], *v.t.* to horsewhip.

cravate [kra'vat], *n.f.* cravat, (neck-)tie.

cravater (se) [səkrava'te], *v.r.* to put on one's (neck-)tie.

cravatier [krava'tje], *n.m.* maker *or* vendor of neckties.

crawl [krol], *n.m.* (*Swim.*) crawl.

crawleur [kro'lœːr], *n.m.* crawl-swimmer.

crayer [krɛ'je], *v.t.* (*conjug. like* PAYER) to chalk, to mark up etc. with chalk.

crayère [krɛ'jɛːr], *n.f.* chalk-pit.

crayeux [krɛ'jø], *a.* (*fem.* **-euse**) chalky.

crayon [krɛ'jɔ̃], *n.m.* pencil; drawing *or* portrait in crayon; (*fig.*) style; sketch; ***crayon à bille***, ball-point pen.

crayonnage [krɛjɔ'naːʒ], *n.m.* pencil-drawing.

crayonner [krɛjɔ'ne], *v.t.* to draw with a pencil; to mark with a pencil; (*fig.*) to sketch.

crayonneux [krɛjɔ'nø], *a.* (*fem.* **-euse**) chalky.

créance [kre'ɑ̃ːs], *n.f.* credence, trust, belief; credit; money owing; (*Hunt.*) command.

créancier [kreɑ̃'sje], *n.m.* (*fem.* **-ière**) creditor.

créateur [krea'tœːr], *a.* (*fem.* **-trice**) creative, inventive.—*n.m.* (*fem.* **-trice**) creator, maker, author.

création [krea'sjɔ̃], *n.f.* creation; universe; establishment; (*Dress.*) design.

créature [krea'tyːr], *n.f.* creature; man, as opposed to God.

crécelle [kre'sɛl], *n.f.* child's *or* hand rattle.

crécerelle [kres'rɛl], *n.f.* (*Orn.*) kestrel.

crèche [krɛːʃ], *n.f.* manger; crib; crèche.

crédence [kre'dɑ̃ːs], *n.f.* credence-table; side-board.

crédibilité [kredibili'te], *n.f.* credibility.

crédit [kre'di], *n.m.* credit; trust; authority, influence; esteem; vogue; parliamentary grant.

créditer [kredi'te], *v.t.* to credit.

créditeur [kredi'tœːr], *a.* credit.—*n.m.* (*fem.* **-trice**) creditor.

credo [kre'do], *n.m.* (*no pl.*) creed, belief.

crédule [kre'dyl], *a.* credulous.

crédulement [kredyl'mɑ̃], *adv.* credulously.

crédulité [kredyli'te], *n.f.* credulity.

créer [kre'e], *v.t.* to create, to produce; to invent, to imagine; to establish.

crémaillère [kremɑ'jɛːr], *n.f.* pot-hook.

crémation [kremɑ'sjɔ̃], *n.f.* cremation.

crématorium [kremato'rjɔm], *n.m.* (*pl.* **-ia**) crematorium.

crème [krɛːm], *n.f.* cream; custard; sweet liqueur; the best part of a thing.

crémer (1) [kre'me], *v.t.* (*conjug. like* CÉDER) to dye cream colour.—*v.i.* to cream.

crémer (2) [kre'me], *v.t.* (*conjug. like* CÉDER) to cremate.

crémerie [krem'ri], *n.f.* creamery, dairy.

crémeux [kre'mø], *a.* (*fem.* **-euse**) creamy.

crémier [kre'mje], *n.m.* (*fem.* **-ière**) milkman, dairyman *or* -woman.—*n.f.* (**-ière**) cream-jug.

créneau [kre'no], *n.m.* (*pl.* **-eaux**) battlement.

crénelage [kren'laːʒ], *n.m.* milling, milled edge (*on coins*), crenellation.

créneler [kren'le], *v.t.* (*conjug. like* APPELER) to embattle; to indent, to notch.

crénelure [kren'lyːr], *n.f.* crenellation; notching.

créole [kre'ɔl], *a.* Creole.—*n.* (**Créole**) Creole.

créosote [kreɔ'zɔt], *n.f.* creosote.

créosoter [kreɔzɔ'te], *v.t.* to creosote.

crêpe (1) [krɛːp], *n.m.* crape; (*fig.*) veil; crêpe-rubber.

crêpe (2) [krɛːp], *n.f.* pancake.

crêpelu [krɛ'ply], *a.* frizzy (*hair*).

crêper [krɛ'pe], *v.t.* to crisp, to frizz.

crépi [kre'pi], *n.m.* rough-cast, parget.

crépir [kre'piːr], *v.t.* to rough-cast, to plaster.

crépissage [krepi'saːʒ], **crépissement** [krepis'mɑ̃], *n.m.* plastering, pargeting, rough-casting.

crépissure [krepi'syːr], *n.m.* parget; rough-casting.

crépitant [krepi'tɑ̃], *a.* crepitating; crackling.
crépitation [krepitɑ'sjɔ̃], *n.f.*, **crépitement** [krepit'mɑ̃], *n.m.* crepitation; crackling.
crépiter [krepi'te], *v.i.* to crackle; to crepitate.
crépu [kre'py], *a.* crisped, frizzy; woolly.
crêpure [krɛ'py:r], *n.f.* crisping; craping.
crépusculaire [krepysky'lɛ:r], *a.* crepuscular, twilight.
crépuscule [krepys'kyl], *n.m.* twilight; dawn.
créquier [kre'kje], *n.m.* sloe-tree.
cresson [krɛ'sɔ̃], *n.m.* cress.
cressonnière [krɛsɔ'njɛ:r], *n.f.* water-cress bed.
Crésus [kre'zy:s], *m.* Croesus.
crésus [kre'zy:s], *n.m. inv.* very rich man.
crétacé [kreta'se], *a.* cretaceous, chalky.
Crète [krɛ:t], **la**, *f.* Crete.
crête [krɛ:t], *n.f.* crest, comb (*of a cock* or *hen*); tuft; ridge; coping.
crêté [krɛ'te], *a.* crested, tufted.
crételer [kre'tle], *v.i.* (*conjug. like* APPELER) to cackle (*of hens*).
crétin [kre'tɛ̃], *a.* cretinous; idiotic.—*n.m.* (*fem.* **-e**) cretin; idiot, dunce.
crétinerie [kretin'ri], *n.f.* idiotic behaviour; foolishness.
crétiniser [kretini'ze], *v.t.* to make cretinous, to brutalize, to make an idiot of.
crétinisme [kreti'nism], *n.m.* cretinism.
crétois [kre'twa], *a.* Cretan.—*n.m.* (**Crétois**, *fem.* **-oise**) Cretan (*person*).
cretonne [krə'tɔn], *n.f.* cretonne.
creusage [krø'za:ʒ], **creusement** [krøz'mɑ̃], *n.m.* deepening, hollowing; excavation.
creuser [krø'ze], *v.t.* to dig, to hollow, to excavate, to scoop out; to sink, to drive (*a well, shaft etc.*); to make hollow *or* empty. **se creuser**, *v.r.* to become hollow.
creuset [krø'zɛ], *n.m.* crucible, melting-pot; (*fig.*) test, trial.
creux [krø], *a.* (*fem.* **creuse**) hollow; cavernous; deep; empty; (*fig.*) airy, extravagant.—*n.m.* hollow, cavity; pit, hole, chasm; mould, mortar, trough.—*adv.* hollow; ***sonner creux***, to sound hollow.
crevaison [krəvɛ'zɔ̃], *n.f.* puncture (*of a tyre*).
crevant [krə'vɑ̃], *a.* (*vulg.*) tiresome; killing (*toil etc.*); killing (*funny*).
crevasse [krə'vas], *n.f.* crevice, rift, crack, chink, crevasse; gap, cranny; chap (*in the hands etc.*).
crevasser [krəva'se], *v.t.* to split; to crack; to chap. **se crevasser**, *v.r.* to crack, to become chapped.
crevé [krə've], *n.m.* (*Dress.*) opening, slash (*in sleeves*).
crève-cœur [krɛv'kœ:r], *n.m. inv.* heartbreak; heart-breaking thing.
crever [krə've], *v.t.* (*conjug. like* AMENER) to burst, to split, to break open, to rend; to stave in; to puncture.—*v.i.* to burst; to die (*animals*); (*vulg.*) to die (*human beings*). **se crever**, *v.r.* to burst; to kill oneself.
crevette [krə'vɛt], *n.f.* shrimp, prawn.
cri [kri], *n.m.* cry; scream, roar, yell, shriek, screech, wail, outcry, clamour.
criaillement [kriɑj'mɑ̃], *n.m.* shouting, wrangling, brawling; scolding.
criailler [kriɑ'je], *v.i.* to bawl, to cry, to clamour; to scold; to brawl; to gabble (*of geese*).
criaillerie [kriɑj'ri], *n.f.* brawling, clamouring, wrangling.
criailleur [kriɑ'jœ:r], *n.m.* (*fem.* **-euse**) brawler, wrangler; shrew, scold.
criant [kri'ɑ̃], *a.* crying; (*fig.*) glaring, shocking.
criard [kri'a:r], *a.* crying, noisy, clamorous; scolding; (*fig.*) shrill, discordant, crude.—*n.m.* (*fem.* **-e**) bawler, clamourer; scold, shrew.
criblage [kri'bla:ʒ], *n.m.* sifting, screening (*of coals etc.*).
crible [kribl], *n.m.* sieve, riddle.
cribler [kri'ble], *v.t.* to sift, to riddle; to pierce all over, to riddle (*with wounds etc.*); (*fig.*) to overwhelm.
cric [kri], *n.m.* jack, screw-jack, hand-screw.
cri-cri [kri'kri], *n.m. inv.* (*fam.*) cricket (*insect*); chirping.
criée [kri'e], *n.f.* (*public*) auction.
crier [kri'e], *v.t.* to cry, to proclaim, to put up for sale; to publish, to announce.—*v.i.* to cry out; to shout, to scream, to shriek; to call out; to whine; to complain loudly, to exclaim; to chirp; to creak.
crieur [kri'jœ:r], *n.m.* (*fem.* **-euse**) bawler; crier; (*Theat.*) call-boy; auctioneer; hawker; ***crieur public***, town-crier; ***crieur de journaux***, newsboy.
crime [krim], *n.m.* crime, offence.
Crimée [kri'me], **la**, *f.* the Crimea.
criminel [krimi'nɛl], *a.* (*fem.* **-elle**) criminal, felonious, guilty.—*n.m.* (*fem.* **-elle**) criminal, felon, culprit, offender.
criminellement [kriminɛl'mɑ̃], *adv.* criminally, culpably, guiltily.
crin [krɛ̃], *n.m.* horse-hair, bristles, fibres, mane.
crinière [kri'njɛ:r], *n.f.* mane (*of animal*).
crinoline [krinɔ'lin], *n.f.* crinoline.
crique [krik], *n.f.* creek, cove; flaw, crack.
criquet [kri'kɛ], *n.m.* locust; (*fig.*) bad horse.
criqueter [krik'te], *v.i.* (*conjug. like* APPELER) to rasp, to grate.
crise [kri:z], *n.f.* crisis; fit, convulsion; slump.
crispation [krispɑ'sjɔ̃], *n.f.* shrivelling, crispation; fidgets.
crisper [kris'pe], *v.t.* to shrivel; to irritate (*the nerves*), to give (*someone*) the fidgets. **se crisper**, *v.r.* to shrivel, to contract.
crissement [kris'mɑ̃], *n.m.* grating (*of teeth, of brakes etc.*).
crisser [kri'se], *v.i.* to grate, to squeak.
cristal [kris'tal], *n.m.* (*pl.* **-aux**) crystal, cut glass; (*fig.*) limpidity; ***cristal de mine***, quartz; ***cristal de roche***, rock-crystal.
cristallerie [kristal'ri], *n.f.* glass-cutting; crystal-manufactory, glass-works.
cristallier [krista'lje], *n.m.* glass-cutter; glass-cupboard.
cristallière [krista'ljɛ:r], *n.f.* rock-crystal mine; machine for glass-cutting.
cristallin [krista'lɛ̃], *a.* crystalline; pellucid.—*n.m.* (*Anat.*) crystalline lens (*of the eye*); (*Astron.*) crystalline heaven.
cristallisant [kristali'zɑ̃], *a.* crystallizing.
cristallisation [kristalizɑ'sjɔ̃], *n.f.* crystallization.

cristalliser [kristali'ze], *v.t.*, *v.i.* to crystallize. **se cristalliser**, *v.r.* to crystallize; to candy.
critère [kri'tɛːr], **critérium** [krite'rjɔm], *n.m.* criterion, standard, test.
critiquable [kriti'kabl], *a.* open to criticism, censurable, exceptionable.
critique [kri'tik], *a.* critical; censorious, carping; ticklish, momentous; critical (*in the literary sense*).—*n.m.* critic; censor, carper.—*n.f.* criticism, science of criticism; review.
critiquer [kriti'ke], *v.t.* to criticize unfavourably; to censure, to find fault with.
critiqueur [kriti'kœːr], *n.m.* (*fem.* **-euse**) criticizer, fault-finder, carper.
croassement [krɔas'mɑ̃], *n.m.* croak, croaking, cawing (*of rooks*).
croasser [krɔa'se], *v.i.* to croak, to caw (*of crows, rooks etc.*).
croate [krɔ'at], *a.* Croatian.—*n.m.* Croatian (*language*).—*n.* (**Croate**) Croat.
Croatie [krɔa'si], **la**, *f.* Croatia.
croc [kro], *n.m.* hook; fang (*of dog*), tusk (*of walrus*).
croc-en-jambe [krɔkɑ̃'ʒɑ̃ːb], *n.m.* (*pl.* **crocs-en-jambe**) trip up; dirty trick.
croche [krɔʃ], *a.* crooked, bent.—*n.f.* (*Mus.*) quaver; (*pl.*) smith's tongs; ***double croche***, semi-quaver; ***triple croche***, demi-semi-quaver.
crocher [krɔ'ʃe], *v.t.* to hook; to bend like a hook.
crochet [krɔ'ʃɛ], *n.m.* small hook; knitting-needle, crochet-hook; (*Print.*) square bracket; teeth of certain animals.
crochetable [krɔʃ'tabl], *a.* pickable (*of locks*).
crochetage [krɔʃ'taːʒ], *n.m.* lock-picking.
crocheter [krɔʃ'te], *v.t.* (*conjug. like* AMENER) to pick (*a lock*); to crochet.
crochetier [krɔʃ'tje], *n.m.* hook-maker, clasp-maker.
crochu [krɔ'ʃy], *a.* crooked, hooked.
crocodile [krɔkɔ'dil], *n.m.* crocodile; (*Rail.*) automatic stop.
crocus [krɔ'kyːs], *n.m.* (*Bot.*) crocus.
croire [krwaːr], *v.t. irr.* to believe; to have faith in; to think, to deem.—*v.i.* to believe, to have faith (*à*), to be a believer. **se croire**, *v.r.* to believe *or* think oneself, to consider oneself; to be believed, to be credible.
croisade [krwa'zad], *n.f.* crusade.
croisé [krwa'ze], *a.* crossed; twilled, double-milled (*of cloth*); cross (*of breeds of animals*); ***mots croisés***, a crossword.—*n.m.* crusader; twill; crossing (*a step in dancing*).
croisée [krwa'ze], *n.f.* crossing point; casement window (*opening inside*).
croisement [krwaz'mɑ̃], *n.m.* crossing (*of two roads etc.*); meeting; cross-breeding (*of animals*).
croiser [krwa'ze], *v.t.* to cross; to lay across; to cross (*breeds of animals*); to pass (*a person*); to thwart.—*v.i.* to overlap; to cruise. **se croiser**, *v.r.* to cross *or* pass each other; to be crossed; to thwart one another.
croiseur [krwa'zœːr], *n.m.* cruiser.
croisière [krwa'zjɛːr], *n.f.* cruise, cruising; (*Rail.*) crossing.
croissance [krwa'sɑ̃ːs], *n.f.* growth, increase.
croissant [krwa'sɑ̃], *a.* growing, increasing.—*n.m.* the moon in her increase; crescent; pruning-hook, hedging-bill; crescent roll.
croît [krwa], *n.m.* increase (*from breeding*).
croître [krwaːtr], *v.i. irr.* to grow; to increase; to wax (*moon*); to spring up, to sprout; to lengthen; to swell.
croix [krwa], *n.f.* cross; the Holy Rood; (*fig.*) affliction; (*Coin.*) obverse.
cromlech [krɔm'lɛk], *n.m.* (*Archaeol.*) stone circle.
crône [kroːn], *n.m.* crane (*on a wharf*).
croquade [krɔ'kad], *n.f.* rough sketch.
croquant [krɔ'kɑ̃], *a.* crisp, crackling, short.—*n.m.* poor wretch; clodhopper.—*n.f.* crisp almond-cake.
croque-au-sel (à la) [krɔko'sɛl], *adv. phr.* with salt only.
croque-mitaine [krɔkmi'tɛn], *n.m.* (*pl.* **croque-mitaines**) bogy-man.
croquer [krɔ'ke], *v.t.* to crunch; to devour; to draft, to sketch.—*v.i.* to crackle between the teeth, to make a scrunching noise.
croquet [krɔ'kɛ], *n.m.* crisp biscuit; croquet (*game*).
croquette [krɔ'kɛt], *n.f.* croquette.
croquignole [krɔki'ɲɔl], *n.f.* cracknel; fillip; (*C*) doughnut.
croquis [krɔ'ki], *n.m.* first sketch, rough draft, outline.
cross [krɔs], *n.m.* (*Box.*) cross-counter; cross-country running.
crosse [krɔs], *n.f.* crooked stick, crosier (*of bishops*); butt (*of rifle*); stock; hockey-stick, golf-club etc.; (*C*) ***jeu de crosse***, lacrosse.
crossé [krɔ'se], *a.* crosiered, mitred.
crosser [krɔ'se], *v.t.* to strike (*a ball etc.*).
crosseur [krɔ'sœːr], *n.m.* hockey-player, lacrosse-player.
crotale [krɔ'tal], *n.m.* rattlesnake.
crotte [krɔt], *n.f.* dung; dirt, mud, mire.
crotté [krɔ'te], *a.* dirty, muddy; (*fig.*) squalid.
crotter [krɔ'te], *v.t.* to dirty; to draggle, to bespatter. **se crotter**, *v.r.* to get dirty.
crottin [krɔ'tɛ̃], *n.m.* dung.
croulant [kru'lɑ̃], *a.* sinking, crumbling; tottering, tumbledown.
croulement [krul'mɑ̃], *n.m.* sinking, falling in, collapse.
crouler [kru'le], *v.i.* to give way, to fall in, to collapse.
croup [krup], *n.m.* (*Path.*) croup, diphtheria.
croupal [kru'pal], *a.* (*m. pl.* **-aux**) pertaining to the croup; laryngitic.
croupe [krup], *n.f.* croup, crupper, buttocks (*of a horse*), rump; top *or* brow (*of a hill*); ***monter en croupe***, to ride pillion.
croupé [kru'pe], *a.* with a rump *or* crupper.
croupi [kru'pi], *a.* stagnant, putrid; ***de l'eau croupie***, ditch-water.
croupier [kru'pje], *n.m.* croupier (*at a gaming-table*); partner (*of a financier etc.*).
croupière [kru'pjɛːr], *n.f.* saddle-tie, crupper.
croupion [kru'pjɔ̃], *n.m.* rump; ***le croupion (d'une volaille)***, the parson's nose.
croupir [kru'piːr], *v.i.* to stagnate; to wallow.
croupissant [krupi'sɑ̃], stagnant, putrescent.
croupon [kru'pɔ̃], *n.m.* square hide, butt.
croustillant [krusti'jɑ̃], *a.* crisp, crusty.
croustille [krus'tiːj], *n.f.* little crust; (*fig.*) snack.

croustiller [krusti'je], *v.i.* to bite, eat, crunch a crust, to munch.
croûte [krut], *n.f.* crust; pie-crust; scab; ***casser la croûte***, to have a snack; (*C*) crust (*of the snow*); (*fig.*) bad painting, daub.
croûton [kru'tɔ̃], *n.m.* bit of crust, crusty end; sippet.
croyable [krwɑ'jabl], *a.* credible, likely.
croyance [krwɑ'jɑ̃:s], *n.f.* belief; creed, faith.
croyant [krwɑ'jɑ̃], *a.* believing.—*n.m.* (*fem.* **-e**) believer.
cru (1) [kry], *n.m.* growth; production (*esp. of wine*).
cru (2) [kry], *a.* raw, uncooked; unwrought; (*fig.*) crude, coarse, indecent; ***à cru***, on the bare skin.
cruauté [kryo'te], *n.f.* cruelty, inhumanity.
cruche [kryʃ], *n.f.* pitcher, jar, jug; (*colloq.*) blockhead.
cruchée [kry'ʃe], *n.f.* pitcherful, jugful, jarful.
cruchon [kry'ʃɔ̃], *n.m.* little pitcher; (*stone*) hot-water bottle.
crucial [kry'sjal], *a.* (*m. pl.* **-aux**) cross-shaped, crucial; (*fig.*) decisive.
crucifiement [krysifi'mɑ̃], *n.m.* crucifixion.
crucifier [krysi'fje], *v.t.* to crucify.
crucifix [krysi'fi], *n.m.* crucifix.
crucifixion [krysifik'sjɔ̃], *n.f.* crucifixion.
cruciforme [krysi'fɔrm], *a.* cruciform, cross-shaped.
crudité [krydi'te], *n.f.* crudity, rawness; coarse expression; (*pl.*) raw vegetables *or* fruit.
crue [kry], *n.f.* growth, increase; rise, swelling (*of river etc.*); flood.
cruel [kry'ɛl], *a.* (*fem.* **-elle**) cruel, merciless; bloodthirsty; hard; grievous, sad.
cruellement [kryɛl'mɑ̃], *adv.* cruelly; unmercifully; severely.
crûment [kry'mɑ̃], *adv.* roughly, coarsely; crudely.
crustacé [krysta'se], *a.* crustaceous.—*n.m.* crustacean; shell-fish.
crypte [kript], *n.f.* crypt.
cryptogramme [kriptɔ'gram], *n.m.* cryptogram, cipher.
cryptographe [kriptɔ'graf], *n.* cryptographer.
cryptographie [kriptɔgra'fi], *n.f.* cryptography.
cryptographique [kriptɔgra'fik], *a.* cryptographic.
cubage [ky'ba:ʒ], *n.m.* cubage, cubature; cubic content.
cubain [ky'bɛ̃], *a.* Cuban.—*n.m.* (**Cubain**, *fem.* **-aine**) Cuban (*person*).
cubature (kyba'ty:r], *n.f.* cubature.
cube [kyb], *a.* cubic.—*n.m.* cube (*shape and measure*).
cuber [ky'be], *v.t.* to cube.
cubique [ky'bik], *a.* cubic; cubical.
cubisme [ky'bism], *n.m.* (*Art*) cubism.
cubiste [ky'bist], *a.* and *n.* cubist.
cueillage [kœ'ja:ʒ], *n.m.*, **cueillaison** [kœjɛ'zɔ̃], **cueille** [kœ:j], *n.f.* gathering-time, gathering.
cueillette [kœ'jɛt], *n.f.* gathering of a crop; harvesting time.
cueilleur [kœ'jœ:r], *n.m.* (*fem.* **-euse**) gatherer, picker.
cueillir [kœ'ji:r], *v.t. irr.* to gather, to cull, to pick, to pluck; to acquire.
cueilloir [kœj'wa:r], *n.m.* fruit-basket; implement for picking fruit.
cuiller [kɥi'je], **cuillère** [kɥi'jɛ:r], *n.f.* spoon; scoop.
cuillerée [kɥij're], *n.f.* spoonful.
cuilleron [kɥij'rɔ̃], *n.m.* bowl of a spoon.
cuir [kɥi:r], *n.m.* hide; leather; strop.
cuirasse [kɥi'ras], *n.f.* cuirass, breast-plate.
cuirassé [kɥira'se], *a.* armed with a cuirass; armour-plated; hardened; secret.—*n.m.* (*Naut.*) battleship.
cuirassement [kɥiras'mɑ̃], *n.m.* armour-plating.
cuirasser [kɥira'se], *v.t.* to arm with a cuirass; to armour-plate; (*fig.*) to steel, to harden. **se cuirasser**, *v.r.* to put on a cuirass; to harden *or* fortify oneself.
cuirassier [kɥira'sje], *n.m.* cuirassier.
cuire [kɥi:r], *v.t. irr.* (*conjug. like* CONDUIRE) to cook; to burn (*of the sun*); to ripen.—*v.i.* to cook, to be cooked, to be done; to bake, boil etc.; to smart.
cuisage [kɥi'za:ʒ], *n.m.* burning (*of charcoal*), charring.
cuisant [kɥi'zɑ̃], *a.* sharp, smarting; piercing.
cuiseur [kɥi'zœ:r], *n.m.* pressure cooker.
cuisine [kɥi'zin], *n.f.* kitchen; cookery; cooks; fare, living; (*Naut.*) galley.
cuisiner [kɥizi'ne], *v.t.*, *v.i.* to cook.
cuisinier [kɥizi'nje], *n.m.* (*fem.* **-ière**) cook.—*n.f.* (**-ière**) Dutch oven.
cuisse [kɥis], *n.f.* thigh; quarter (*of venison*); leg (*of poultry*).
cuisseau [kɥi'so], *n.m.* (*pl.* **-eaux**) leg (*of veal*).
cuisson [kɥi'sɔ̃], *n.f.* cooking (*baking, boiling, roasting etc.*); smart (*pain*).
cuissot [kɥi'so], *n.m.* haunch (*of venison*).
cuit [kɥi], *a.* cooked, done (*roasted, boiled, baked etc.*); (*fig.*) done for, dished.
cuite [kɥit], *n.f.* baking; burning (*of bricks etc.*); ovenful, kilnful; (*slang*) intoxication.
cuivrage [kɥi'vra:ʒ], *n.m.* coppering; copper-plating.
cuivre [kɥi:vr], *n.m.* copper; copper money; copper-plate; ***cuivre battu***, wrought copper; ***cuivre jaune***, brass; ***cuivre rouge***, copper.
cuivré [kɥi'vre], *a.* copper-coloured; (*fig.*) bronzed (*complexion*); ringing, clear.
cuivrer [kɥi'vre], *v.t.* to cover with copper.
cuivrerie [kɥivrə'ri], *n.f.* copper-works; copper wares.
cuivreux [kɥi'vrø], *a.* (*fem.* **-euse**) coppery.
cul [ky], *n.m.* (*indec.*) backside, posterior; bottom (*of bottle* or *bag*); stern (*of ship*).
culasse [ky'las], *n.f.* breech (*of a cannon etc.*); cylinder-head (*of car engine*).
culbute [kyl'byt], *n.f.* somersault; fall, tumble; (*fig.*) ruin, bankruptcy.
culbuter [kylby'te], *v.t.* to throw over, to upset violently; to overthrow.—*v.i.* to fall head over heels.
culbutis [kylby'ti], *n.m.* confused heap, jumble.
cul de bouteille [kydbu'tɛ:j], *a.* bottle-green.—*n.m.* bottom of bottle.
cul-de-jatte [kyd'ʒat], *n.m.* (*pl.* **culs-de-jatte**) legless cripple.
cul-de-lampe [kyd'lɑ̃p], *n.m.* (*Print.*) tail-piece.
cul-de-sac [kyd'sak], *n.m.* (*pl.* **culs-de-sac**) blind alley, cul-de-sac; (*fig.*) deadlock.

culée [ky'le], *n.f.* abutment (*of bridges*); (*Naut.*) stern-way.
culer [ky'le], *v.i.* to go backwards; to fall astern.
culière [ky'ljɛ:r], *n.f.* hind girth, crupper (*of harness*); gutter-stone.
culinaire [kyli'nɛ:r], *a.* culinary.
culminance [kylmi'nɑ̃:s], *n.f.* culmination, highest point.
culminant [kylmi'nɑ̃], *a.* culminating; prominent.
culmination [kylminɑ'sjɔ̃], *n.f.* culmination.
culminer [kylmi'ne], *v.i.* to culminate.
culot [ky'lo], *n.m.* bottom (*of lamps, crucibles etc.*); residuum, (*fam.*) dottle (*in a pipe*).
culottage [kylɔ'ta:ʒ], *n.m.* colouring, seasoning (*of pipes*).
culotte [ky'lɔt], *n.f.* breeches; (*pl.*) shorts; tights; (*Cook.*) rump (*of an ox*).
culotter [kylɔ'te], *v.t.* to breech, to put in breeches; to colour (*pipes*). **se culotter**, *v.r.* to put on one's breeches; to become coloured (*of pipes*).
culottier [kylɔ'tje], *n.m.* (*fem.* **-ière**) breeches-maker.
culpabilité [kylpabili'te], *n.f.* culpability; guilt.
culte [kylt], *n.m.* worship, adoration; (*fig.*) cult, religion, creed; veneration, love.
cultivable [kylti'vabl], *a.* cultivable, arable.
cultivateur [kyltiva'tœ:r], *a.* agricultural.—*n.m.* (*fem.* **-trice**) cultivator, farmer, agriculturist; cultivator (*implement*).
cultivé [kylti've], *a.* cultivated; (*of the mind*) cultured.
cultiver [kylti've], *v.t.* to cultivate; to till; to improve (*the mind*); to study, to practise; to cultivate the acquaintance of.
cultural [kylty'ral], *a.* (*m. pl.* **-aux**) cultural (*in relation to agriculture*).
culture [kyl'ty:r], *n.f.* culture, cultivation, tillage, husbandry; education, improvement.
culturel [kylty'rɛl], *a.* (*fem.* **-elle**) cultural (*in relation to intellectual culture*).
cumulatif [kymyla'tif], *a.* (*fem.* **-tive**) cumulative.
cumulativement [kymylativ'mɑ̃], *adv.* by accumulation.
cumuler [kymy'le], *v.t.* to accumulate; to hold several (*offices, salaries etc.*).
cumulus [kymy'ly:s], *n.m.* cumulus.
cupide [ky'pid], *a.* covetous, greedy, grasping.
cupidement [kypid'mɑ̃], *adv.* greedily, covetously.
cupidité [kypidi'te], *n.f.* cupidity, covetousness, greed.
Cupidon [kypi'dɔ̃], *n.m.* (*Myth.*) Cupid, Love.
curable [ky'rabl], *a.* curable.
curaçao [kyra'so], *n.m.* curaçao (*liqueur*).
curage [ky'ra:ʒ], **curement** [kyr'mɑ̃], *n.m.* cleansing.
curatelle [kyra'tɛl], *n.f.* guardianship, trusteeship.
curateur [kyra'tœ:r], *n.m.* (*fem.* **-trice**) guardian, trustee.
curatif [kyra'tif], *a.* (*fem.* **-tive**) curative.—*n.m.* curative agent.
cure [ky:r], *n.f.* medical treatment, cure, healing; living, rectorship; vicarage, rectory.
curé [ky're], *n.m.* parish priest; parson, rector, vicar.
cure-dent [kyr'dɑ̃], *n.m.* (*pl.* **cure-dents**) tooth-pick.
curée [ky're], *n.f.* (*Hunt.*) quarry, chase; (*fig.*) prey, booty.
curement [CURAGE].
cure-môle [kyr'mo:l], *n.m.* (*pl.* **cure-môles**) dredging-machine.
cure-ongles [ky'rɔ̃gl], *n.m. inv.* nail-file.
curer [ky're], *v.t.* to cleanse, to clean out (*harbours, sewers etc.*); to pick (*teeth, ears etc.*).
curial (1) [ky'rjal], *a.* (*m. pl.* **-aux**) vicarial, rectorial.
curial (2) or **curiale** [ky'rjal], *a.* (*Rom. Ant.*) curial.
curie [ky'ri], *n.f.* (*Rom. Ant.*) curia.
curieusement [kyrjøz'mɑ̃], *adv.* curiously; inquisitively; carefully; quaintly.
curieux [ky'rjø], *a.* (*fem.* **-euse**) curious; inquisitive, prying; inquiring; careful; dainty; particular; strange.—*n.m.* (*fem.* **-euse**) interested person; inquisitive person; sightseer, looker-on.—*n.m.* curious fact.
curiosité [kyrjɔzi'te], *n.f.* curiosity; inquisitiveness; curio, rarity; quaintness.
cursif [kyr'sif], *a.* (*fem.* **-sive**) cursive, running; cursory.
cursivement [kyrsiv'mɑ̃], *adv.* cursively; cursorily.
curure [ky'ry:r], *n.f.* dirt, sewage.
cussonné [kysɔ'ne], *a.* worm-eaten (*of wood*).
custode [kys'tɔd], *n.m.* warden (*among monks*); custodian, inspector.
cutané [kyta'ne], *a.* cutaneous.
cuticule [kyti'kyl], *n.f.* cuticle.
cuvage [ky'va:ʒ], *n.m.*, **cuvaison** [kyvɛ'zɔ̃], *n.f.* fermenting (*of wine*).
cuve [ky:v], *n.f.* tub, vat.
cuvée [ky've], *n.f.* tubful; vatful.
cuvelage [ky'vla:ʒ], **cuvellement** [kyvɛl'mɑ̃], *n.m.* lining, casing (*of mine-shafts*).
cuveler [ky'vle], *v.t.* (*conjug. like* APPELER) to line, to case (*mine shafts etc.*).
cuver [ky've], *v.t.* to ferment; (*fam.*) to sleep off the effects of (*wine*).—*v.i.* to work, to ferment, to settle.
cuvette [ky'vɛt], *n.f.* shallow basin; wash-hand basin; lavatory bowl.
cuvier [ky'vje], *n.m.* wash-tub.
cyanure [sja'ny:r], *n.m.* (*Chem.*) cyanide.
cybernétique [sibɛrne'tik], *n.f.* cybernetics.
cyclamen [sikla'mɛn], *n.m.* cyclamen, sow-bread.
cycle [sikl], *n.m.* cycle (*of events*); ***cycle à 4 temps*** (*d'un moteur*), 4-stroke cycle (*of an engine*).
cyclique [si'klik], *a.* cyclical.
cyclisme [si'klism], *n.m.* cycling.
cycliste [si'klist], *n.* cyclist.
cyclomoteur [siklɔmɔ'tœ:r], *n.m.* auto-cycle.
cyclonal [siklɔ'nal], *a.* (*m. pl.* **-aux**) cyclonic.
cyclone [si'klo:n], *n.m.* cyclone.
cyclonique [siklɔ'nik], *a.* cyclonic.
Cyclope [si'klɔp], *n.m.* Cyclops.
cygne [siɲ], *n.m.* swan.
cylindrage [silɛ̃'dra:ʒ], *n.m.* mangling (*of linen etc.*); rolling (*of roads*).
cylindre [si'lɛ̃:dr], *n.m.* cylinder; roller; garden-roller; mangle, calender.

cylindrée [silɛ̃'dre], *n.f.* cubic capacity of an engine.
cylindrer [silɛ̃'dre], *v.t.* to calender; to roll.
cylindrique [silɛ̃'drik], *a.* cylindrical.
cymaise [CIMAISE].
cymbale [sɛ̃'bal], *n.f.* (*Mus.*) cymbal.
cymbalier [sɛ̃ba'lje], *n.m.* cymbal-player.
cynancie [sinɑ̃'si], [ESQUINANCIE].
cynégétique [sineʒe'tik], *a.* relating to hunting and dogs.—*n.f.* the art of hunting with dogs, cynegetics.
cynique [si'nik], *a.* cynical; snarling, snappish; impudent.—*n.* cynic.
cyniquement [sinik'mɑ̃], *adv.* cynically.
cynisme [si'nism], *n.m.* cynicism; impudence.
cynodrome [sinɔ'dro:m], *n.m.* greyhound racing track.
cynosure [sinɔ'sy:r], *n.f.* (*Astron.*) Cynosure, Little Bear.
cyprès [si'prɛ], *n.m.* cypress, cypress-tree.
cyprière [si'prjɛ:r], *n.f.* cypress-grove.
cypriote [si'prjɔt], *a.* Cypriot.—*n.* (**Cypriote**) Cypriot (*person*).
cytise [si'ti:z], *n.m.* cytisus, laburnum.
czar [tsa:r], [TZAR].

D

D, d [de], *n.m.* the fourth letter of the alphabet.
d', *abbr.* [DE].
da [da], *particle* (*used after* ***oui, non***) truly, indeed; ***oui-da***, yes indeed.
d'abord [da'bɔ:r], [ABORD].
dactylo [dakti'lo], *n.f. abbr. of* [DACTYLOGRAPHE].
dactylographe [daktilɔ'graf], *n.f.* typist.
dactylographie [daktilɔgra'fi], *n.f.* typewriting.
dactylographier [daktilɔgra'fje], *v.t.* to type(write).
dactylographique [daktilɔgra'fik], *a.* typewritten (*report*); typewriting (*material*).
dactyloptère [daktilɔp'tɛ:r], *n.m.* flying-fish.
dada [da'da], *n.m.* (*childish*) horse, cock-horse; gee-gee.
dadais [da'dɛ], *n.m.* booby, clown, ninny.
dague [dag], *n.f.* dagger, dirk.
daguerréotype [dagɛreɔ'tip], *n.m.* daguerreotype.
dahlia [da'lja], *n.m.* dahlia.
daigner [dɛ'ɲe], *v.i.* to deign, to condescend.
d'ailleurs [da'jœ:r], [AILLEURS].
daim [dɛ̃], *n.m.* deer, fallow-deer; buck.
daine [dɛn], *n.f.* doe.
dais [dɛ], *n.m.* canopy.
dallage [da'la:ʒ], *n.m.* paving with flagstones.
dalle [dal], *n.f.* flag, flagstone; slab.
daller [da'le], *v.t.* to pave with flagstones, to flag.
dalleur [da'lœ:r], *n.m.* pavior.
dalmate [dal'mat], *a.* Dalmatian.—*n.* (**Dalmate**) Dalmatian (*person*).
dalmatique [dalma'tik], *n.f.* dalmatic.
daltonisme [daltɔ'nism], *n.m.* colour-blindness.
damas [da'mɑ], *n.m.* damask; damson; Damascus blade.
damasquiner [damaski'ne], *v.t.* to damascene.
damassé [damɑ'se], *n.m.* damask linen, damask cloth.
damasser [damɑ'se], *v.t.* to damask.
damassin [damɑ'sɛ̃], *n.m.* figured linen cloth, diaper.
damassure [damɑ'sy:r], *n.f.* damasking (*of linen*); damask work.
dame (1) [dam], *n.f.* (*married*) lady, dame; rowlock; beetle, rammer; (*Cards*, and *Chess*) queen.
dame (2) [dam], *int.* ***dame oui!*** why, yes!
dame-jeanne [dam'ʒɑ:n], *n.f.* (*pl.* **dames-jeannes**) demijohn, carboy.
damer [da'me], *v.t.* (*Draughts*) to crown (*a man*); (*Chess*) to queen; to ram (*earth etc.*).
damier [da'mje], *n.m.* draught-board.
damnable [dɑ'nabl], *a.* damnable.
damnablement [dɑnablə'mɑ̃], *adv.* damnably.
damnation [dɑnɑ'sjɔ̃], *n.f.* damnation.
damné [dɑ'ne], *a.* and *n.m.* (*fem.* **-ée**) damned (person).
damner [dɑ'ne], *v.t.* to damn. **se damner**, *v.r.* to damn oneself.
dancing [dɑ̃'siŋ], *n.m.* dance-hall, palais de danse.
dandin [dɑ̃'dɛ̃], *n.m.* ninny.
dandinement [dɑ̃din'mɑ̃], *n.m.* swinging (*of the body*); rolling gait.
dandiner [dɑ̃di'ne], *v.i.* to swing (*of the body*), to dandle (*of a baby*). **se dandiner**, *v.r.* to waddle.
dandy [dɑ̃'di], *n.m.* dandy.
dandysme [dɑ̃'dism], *n.m.* dandyism.
Danemark [dan'mark], **le**, *m.* Denmark.
danger [dɑ̃'ʒe], *n.m.* danger, peril, risk, hazard.
dangereusement [dɑ̃ʒrøz'mɑ̃], *adv.* dangerously.
dangereux [dɑ̃'ʒrø], *a.* (*fem.* **-euse**) dangerous.
danois [da'nwɑ], *a.* Danish.—*n.m.* Danish (*language*); Great Dane (*dog*); (**Danois**, *fem.* **-oise**) Dane (*person*).
dans [dɑ̃], *prep.* in, within; into; with, according to; during; out of.
danse [dɑ̃:s], *n.f.* dance; dancing; (*fig.*) beating, hiding; ***danse de Saint-Guy***, St. Vitus's dance.
danser [dɑ̃'se], *v.t.*, *v.i.* to dance.
danseur [dɑ̃'sœ:r], *n.m.* (*fem.* **-euse**) dancer, ballet-girl.
dard [da:r], *n.m.* dart; sting; forked tongue (*of a snake*); pistil.
darder [dar'de], *v.t.* to hurl; to spear; to shoot forth, to beam, to dart.
dardillon [dardi'jɔ̃], *n.m.* small dart; barb (*of a fish-hook*).
dare-dare [dar'da:r], *adv.* (*fam.*) in great haste, in double-quick time.
darne [darn], *n.f.* slice (*of fish*).
dartre [dartr], *n.f.* slight and dry eruption (*of the skin*), scurf.
dartreux [dar'trø], *a.* (*fem.* **-euse**) herpetic, scurfy.
date [dat], *n.f.* date.
dater [da'te], *v.t.* to date (*a letter etc.*).—*v.i.* to date (*de*); to reckon.
datif [da'tif], *n.m.* (*Gram.*) dative, dative case

datte [dat], *n.f.* date.
dattier [da'tje], *n.m.* date-palm.
datura [daty'ra], *n.m.* datura, thorn-apple.
daube [do:b], *n.f.* stew.
dauber [do'be], *v.t.* to cuff, to drub; (*fig.*) to banter, to jeer at; (*Cook.*) to stew.
daubeur [do'bœ:r], *n.m.* (*fem.* **-euse**) jeerer, banterer, sneerer.
daubière [do'bjɛ:r], *n.f.* stew-pan.
dauphin [do'fɛ̃], *n.m.* dolphin; dauphin (*eldest son of the king of France*).
dauphine [do'fin], *n.f.* wife of the dauphin.
dauphinelle [dofi'nɛl], *n.f.* (*Bot.*) larkspur, delphinium.
daurade [do'rad], *n.f.* gilt-head (*fish*).
davantage [davɑ̃'ta:ʒ], *adv.* more, any more; any longer, any further.
davier [da'vje], *n.m.* dentist's forceps; cramp; (*Naut.*) davit.
de [də], *prep.* of; out of, made of, composed of, from; by, with; at, for; concerning, about.
dé (1) [de], *n.m.* die (*for playing*); (*fig.*) throw, hazard.
dé (2) [de], *n.m.* thimble.
débâcher [deba'ʃe], *v.t.* to uncover, to untilt.
débâcle [de'bɑ:kl], *n.f.* breaking up (*of ice*); (*fig.*) downfall, collapse.
débâcler [debɑ'kle], *v.i.* to break up (*of ice*).
débâcleur [debɑ'klœ:r], *n.m.* water *or* port-bailiff.
déballage [deba'la:ʒ], *n.m.* unpacking.
déballer [deba'le], *v.t.* to unpack.
débandade [debɑ̃'dad], *n.f.* rout, stampede; ***à la débandade***, in confusion.
débander [debɑ̃'de], *v.t.* to unbind; to loosen; to remove a bandage from. **se débander**, *v.r.* to slacken, to relax; to disband.
débaptiser [debati'ze], *v.t.* to change the name of.
débarbouillage [debarbu'ja:ʒ], *n.m.* washing, cleansing.
débarbouiller [debarbu'je], *v.t.* to wash, to cleanse. **se débarbouiller,** *v.r.* to wash one's face etc.; (*fig.*) to extricate oneself.
débarcadère [debarka'dɛ:r], *n.m.* landing-place, wharf; (*Rail.*) station; arrival platform.
débardage [debar'da:ʒ], *n.m.* unloading (*of wood etc.*).
débarder [debar'de], *v.t.* to unload (*wood etc.*); to clear (*a wood etc.*) of felled trees.
débardeur [debar'dœ:r], *n.m.* stevedore, lighterman, docker.
débarquement [debarkə'mɑ̃], *n.m.* landing, disembarkation (*of persons*); unloading (*of goods*).
débarquer [debar'ke], *v.t.*, *v.i.* to disembark, to land.
débarras [deba'rɑ], *n.m.* riddance, disencumbrance; ***chambre de débarras***, lumber-room, box-room.
débarrasser [debara'se], *v.t.* to disencumber, to rid; to disentangle, to extricate; to clear (*the table*). **se débarrasser,** *v.r.* to extricate oneself, to rid oneself of, to shake off; to get clear.
débarrer [deba're], *v.t.* to unbar.
débat [de'ba], *n.m.* dispute, contest; debate, discussion; (*pl.*) parliamentary debates.
débateler [debatə'le], *v.t.* (*conjug. like* APPELER) to unlade (*boats etc.*).
débâter [debɑ'te], *v.t.* to unsaddle; to take a packsaddle off.
débâtir [debɑ'ti:r], *v.t.* to pull down, to demolish; to unbaste, to untack (*garments*).
débattre [de'batr], *v.t. irr.* (*conjug. like* BATTRE) to debate, to discuss, to argue. **se débattre,** *v.r.* to struggle, to strive; to flounder, to flutter.
débauche [de'bo:ʃ], *n.f.* debauchery; dissoluteness.
débauché [debo'ʃe], *n.m.* debauchee, rake.
débaucher [debo'ʃe], *v.t.* to debauch; to corrupt; to lead astray. **se débaucher,** *v.r.* to become debauched.
débet [de'bɛ], *n.m.* debit.
débile [de'bil], *a.* weak, feeble.
débilement [debil'mɑ̃], *adv.* feebly, weakly.
débilité [debili'te], *n.f.* debility, weakness.
débiliter [debili'te], *v.t.* to debilitate, to enfeeble.
débit [de'bi], *n.m.* sale; market; retail; retail shop; (*fig.*) delivery, utterance; (*Bookkeeping*) debit.
débitage [debi'ta:ʒ], *n.m.* cutting up (*of stones, timber etc.*).
débitant [debi'tɑ̃], *n.m.* (*fem.* **-e**) retailer, dealer.
débiter [debi'te], *v.t.* to sell; to retail; to supply; to debit; to cut up (*wood, stone etc.*); (*fig.*) to spread, to report, to utter.
débiteur (1) [debi'tœ:r], *n.m.* (*fem.* **-trice**) debtor.
débiteur (2) [debi'tœ:r], *n.m.* (*fem.* **-euse**) prattler, newsmonger.
déblai [de'blɛ], *n.m.* clearing; excavation; (*pl.*) earth, stones etc. cleared away.
déblaiement or **déblayement** [deblɛ'mɑ̃], *n.m.* clearance; cutting, excavation, digging.
déblatérer [deblate're], *v.i.* (*conjug. like* CÉDER) to utter violent abuse, to rail (**contre**).
déblayement [DÉBLAIEMENT].
déblayer [deblɛ'je], *v.t.* (*conjug. like* PAYER) to clear away; to clear; (*fig.*) to sweep away (*obstacles etc.*).
déblocage [deblɔ'ka:ʒ], *n.m.* (*Print.*) turning letters.
débloquer [deblɔ'ke], *v.t.* to raise the blockade from; (*Print.*) to turn letters; to unlock; to release.
débobiner [debɔbi'ne], *v.t.* to unwind.
déboire [de'bwa:r], *n.m.* after-taste; (*fig.*) disappointment, vexation.
déboisement [debwaz'mɑ̃], *n.m.* clearing of trees, deforestation.
déboiser [debwa'ze], *v.t.* to clear of trees.
déboîtement [debwat'mɑ̃], *n.m.* dislocation.
déboîter [debwa'te], *v.t.* to put out of joint, to dislocate; (*Elec.*) to disconnect. **se déboîter,** *v.r.* to be dislocated.
débonder [debɔ̃'de], *v.t.* to unplug, to unstopper; to loosen, to unbind.—*v.i.* or **se débonder**, *v.r.* to gush, to break out, to burst forth; to be relaxed (*of a person*).
débonnaire [debɔ'nɛ:r], *a.* good-natured, easy-tempered.
débonnairement [debɔnɛr'mɑ̃], *adv.* compliantly, easily.
débonnaireté [debɔnɛr'te], *n.f.* compliance, good-nature.
débordé [debɔr'de], *a.* overflowing (*river*); overwhelmed (*man*); outflanked (*troops*).

débordement [debɔrdə'mɑ̃], *n.m.* overflowing, flood; outburst; (*fig.*) dissoluteness.
déborder [debɔr'de], *v.t.* to take off the border from; to go beyond; to outrun.—*v.i.* to overflow, to run over; to project, to jut out. **se déborder,** *v.r.* to overflow; to run over, to burst forth.
débordoir [debɔr'dwa:r], *n.m.* edging-tool; spoke-shave.
débosseler [debɔs'le], *v.t.* (*conjug. like* APPELER) to take the dents out of.
débotté or **débotter** (1) [debɔ'te], *n.m.* the moment of taking boots off; (*fig.*) ***au débotté***, at once.
débotter (2) [debɔ'te], *v.t.* to pull off (*someone's*) boots. **se débotter,** *v.r.* to take off one's boots.
débouché [debu'ʃe], *n.m.* outlet, issue; waterway; (*Comm.*) market, sale.
débouchage [debu'ʃa:ʒ], **débouchement** [debuʃ'mɑ̃], *n.m.* uncorking; outlet; market, sale.
déboucher [debu'ʃe], *v.t.* to open, to clear; to uncork; to unplug.—*v.i.* to emerge; to empty itself (*of rivers*); (*Mil.*) to debouch.
déboucler [debu'kle], *v.t.* to unbuckle; to uncurl.
débouler [debu'le], *v.i.* to roll down (*like a ball*); to start off suddenly (*like a hare*).
déboulonner [debulɔ'ne], *v.t.* to unrivet, to unbolt.
débourrer [debu're], *v.t.* to draw the wad *or* wadding out of (*fire-arms*); to empty the tobacco out of (*a pipe*); (*fig.*) to polish (*a person's manners*).
débours [de'bu:r], **déboursé** [debur'se], *n.m.* disbursement, outlay.
déboursement [deburs'mɑ̃], *n.m.* outlay, expenditure.
débourser [debur'se], *v.t.* to disburse, to expend, to lay out.
debout [də'bu], *adv.* upright, on end, standing up; out of bed, up; in existence; (*Naut.*) ahead (*of the wind*).
déboutonner [debutɔ'ne], *v.t.* to unbutton. **se déboutonner,** *v.r.* to unbutton oneself; (*colloq.*) to unbosom oneself.
débraillé [debrɑ'je], *a.* loosely dressed, in disorder.—*n.m.* disorder, untidiness; (*fig.*) licence.
débrailler (se) [sədebrɑ'je], *v.r.* to uncover one's breast, to be untidy *or* disordered.
débrancher [debrɑ̃'ʃe], *v.t.* (*Elec.*) to disconnect.
débrayage [debrɛ'ja:ʒ], **désembrayage** [dezɑ̃brɛ'ja:ʒ], *n.m.* disengaging gear (*of motors etc.*); declutching.
débrayer [debrɛ'je], *v.t.* (*conjug. like* PAYER) to throw out of gear, to disengage, to declutch.
débridement [debrid'mɑ̃], *n.m.* unbridling; (*fig.*) dispatch, hurry.
débrider [debri'de], *v.t. v.i.* to unbridle (*horse*); to halt.
débris [de'bri], *n.m.* (*usu. in pl.*) remains, debris; rubbish.
débrouillard [debru'ja:r], *a.* and *n.m.* (*fem.* **-e**) (*colloq.*) resourceful (person).
débrouiller [debru'je], *v.t.* to disentangle, to unravel; (*fig.*) to explain. **se débrouiller,** *v.r.* to be cleared up; to get out of difficulties, to manage.
débusquement [debyskə'mɑ̃], *n.m.* driving out, dislodging.
débusquer [debys'ke], *v.t.* to turn out, to oust, to expel; (*Hunt.*) to start.
début [de'by], *n.m.* lead; outset; début.
débutant [deby'tɑ̃], *n.m.* (*fem.* **-e**) actor *or* actress appearing for the first time; beginner.
débuter [deby'te], *v.i.* to lead, to play first; to open; to start; to make one's début.
deçà [də'sa], *prep.* on this side of; short of, well within.—*adv.* here, on this side; ***deçà (et) delà***, here and there.
décachetage [dekaʃ'ta:ʒ], *n.m.* unsealing, opening.
décacheter [dekaʃ'te], *v.t.* (*conjug. like* APPELER) to unseal, to open.
décadaire [deka'dɛ:r], *a.* decadal.
décade [de'kad], *n.f.* decade, group of ten.
décadenasser [dekadnɑ'se], *v.t.* to unpadlock.
décadence [deka'dɑ̃:s], *n.f.* decadence, decline, wane.
décadent [deka'dɑ̃], *a.* and *n.m.* (*fem.* **-e**) decadent (person).
décaèdre [deka'ɛdr], *a.* decahedral.—*n.m.* decahedron.
décagonal [dekagɔ'nal], *a.* (*pl.* **-aux**) decagonal (*ten-sided*).
décagone [deka'gɔn], *n.m.* decagon.
décagramme [deka'gram], *n.m.* decagramme, ten grammes.
décaissement [dekɛs'mɑ̃], **décaissage** [dekɛ'sa:ʒ], *n.m.* uncasing, unpacking.
décaisser [dekɛ'se], *v.t.* to unpack; to pay out.
décaler [deka'le], *v.t.* to unwedge.
décalaminage [dekalami'na:ʒ], *n.m.* (*Motor.*) decarbonizing.
décalaminer [dekalami'ne], *v.t.* to decarbonize.
décalitre [deka'litr], *n.m.* decalitre (2·2 *gallons*).
décalquer [dekal'ke], *v.t.* to transfer (*a tracing*), to countertrace.
décamètre [deka'mɛtr], *n.m.* decametre.
décamper [dekɑ̃'pe], *v.i.* to decamp; (*fig.*) to bolt.
décanter [dekɑ̃'te], *v.t.* to decant, to pour off gently.
décapitation [dekapitɑ'sjɔ̃], *n.f.* decapitation, beheading.
décapiter [dekapi'te], *v.t.* to behead, to decapitate.
décapotable [dekapɔ'tabl], *a.* (*Motor.*) convertible.
décarboniser [dekarbɔni'ze], *v.t.* to decarbonize.
décarburation [dekarbyrɑ'sjɔ̃], *n.f.* decarbonization.
décarburer [dekarby're], *v.t.* to decarburize, to decarbonize.
décastère [deka'stɛ:r], *n.m.* measure of 10 steres *or* cubic metres (13·1 cubic yards).
décathlon [dekat'lɔ̃], *n.m.* (*spt.*) decathlon.
decauville [dəko'vil], *n.m.* narrow gauge railway.
décaver [deka've], *v.t.* to win the whole of the stakes from, (*fam.*) to clean out; (*fig.*) to ruin, to beggar.
décédé [dese'de], *n.m.* (*fem.* **-ée**) deceased (*person*).
décéder [dese'de], *v.i.* (*conjug. like* CÉDER) to die, to decease.

décèlement [desɛl'mɑ̃], *n.m.* disclosure, exposure, discovery.
déceler [des'le], *v.t.* (*conjug. like* AMENER) to disclose, to reveal, to betray. **se déceler,** *v.r.* to betray oneself.
déceleur [des'lœːr], *n.m.* (*fem.* **-euse**) betrayer, revealer.
décembre [de'sɑ̃ːbr], *n.m.* December.
décemment [desa'mɑ̃], *adv.* decently.
décence [de'sɑ̃ːs], *n.f.* decency, propriety.
décent [de'sɑ̃], *a.* decent, becoming; modest.
décentralisation [desɑ̃traliza'sjɔ̃], *n.f.* decentralization.
décentraliser [desɑ̃trali'ze], *v.t.* to decentralize.
déception [desɛp'sjɔ̃], *n.f.* disappointment; deception, deceit.
décernement [desɛrnə'mɑ̃], *n.m.* awarding.
décerner [desɛr'ne], *v.t.* to decree, to enact; to award, to confer (*an honour*); to issue (*a summons etc.*).
décès [de'sɛ], *n.m.* decease, demise, death.
décevant [des'vɑ̃], *a.* deceptive; disappointing.
décevoir [desə'vwaːr], *v.t. irr.* (*conjug. like* RECEVOIR) to deceive; to disappoint.
déchaînement [deʃɛn'mɑ̃], *n.m.* unbridling, bursting (*of storm*); outburst (*of passion*); fury, rage; invective.
déchaîner [deʃɛ'ne], *v.t.* to unchain, to let loose; to give vent to (*passion*). **se déchaîner,** *v.r.* to break loose; to burst out; to run wild (*of passions etc.*).
déchaler [deʃa'le], *v.i.* to ebb; to lie dry.
déchanter [deʃɑ̃'te], *v.i.* to lower one's key (*in singing*); (*fig.*) to lower one's pretensions, to sing another tune.
déchaperonner [deʃaprɔ'ne], *v.t.* to unhood (*a hawk etc.*); to uncope (*a wall*).
décharge [de'ʃarʒ], *n.f.* unloading; rebate (*on a tax*); outlet, discharge (*of water etc.*); (*Law*) discharge, acquittal; (*Mil.*) volley.
déchargement [deʃarʒə'mɑ̃], *n.m.* unloading, unlading.
décharger [deʃar'ʒe], *v.t.* (*conjug. like* MANGER) to unload; to empty; to disburden; to discharge; to fire (*fire-arms*); to acquit (*de*). **se décharger,** *v.r.* to be unloaded, to discharge; to give vent (*to*); to unburden oneself.
déchargeur [deʃar'ʒœːr], *n.m.* unloader, wharf-porter, heaver, lumper.
décharné [deʃar'ne], *a.* fleshless; lean, emaciated.
décharnement [deʃarnə'mɑ̃], *n.m.* emaciation.
décharner [deʃar'ne], *v.t.* to strip the flesh off; to emaciate.
déchaumage [deʃo'maːʒ], *n.m.* (*Agric.*) ploughing up fallow ground.
déchaumer [deʃo'me], *v.t.* to plough up the stubble on; to break up (*fallow land*).
déchaussé [deʃo'se], *a.* barefooted.
déchausser [deʃo'se], *v.t.* to pull off (*someone's*) shoes and stockings; to lay bare the root *or* base (*of trees, buildings, teeth etc.*). **se déchausser,** *v.r.* to take off one's shoes and stockings.
déchéance [deʃe'ɑ̃ːs], *n.f.* forfeiture; disgrace; deposition.
déchet [de'ʃɛ], *n.m.* loss, waste, offal.
décheveler [deʃə'vle], *v.t.* (*conjug. like* APPELER) to dishevel [ÉCHEVELER].
déchevêtrer [deʃəvɛ'tre], *v.t.* to unhalter (*a beast of burden*).
décheviller [deʃəvi'je], *v.t.* to unpeg, to unpin.
déchiffrable [deʃi'frabl], *a.* legible.
déchiffrement [deʃifrə'mɑ̃], *n.m.* deciphering; reading *or* playing at sight.
déchiffrer [deʃi'fre], *v.t.* to decipher, to unravel; to read *or* play at sight. **se déchiffrer,** *v.r.* to be deciphered.
déchiffreur [deʃi'frœːr], *n.m.* (*fem.* **-euse**) decipherer; sight-reader; ***déchiffreur de radar,*** radar scanner.
déchiqueté [deʃik'te], *a.* jagged, indented.
déchiqueter [deʃik'te], *v.t.* (*conjug. like* APPELER) to cut, to slash, to hack; to cut into long pieces.
déchiqueture [deʃik'tyːr], *n.f.* tear, slash.
déchirage [deʃi'raːʒ], *n.m.* ripping up, breaking up (*of a ship etc.*).
déchirant [deʃi'rɑ̃], *a.* heart-rending, piercing; excruciating.
déchirement [deʃir'mɑ̃], *n.m.* rending, tearing, laceration; (*fig.*) heart-break.
déchirer [deʃi're], *v.t.* to tear to pieces, to rend; (*fig.*) to torture; to revile. **se déchirer,** *v.r.* to tear, to be torn; to defame each other.
déchirure [deʃi'ryːr], *n.f.* rent, tear; fissure.
déchoir [de'ʃwaːr], *v.i. irr.* to decay, to fall off, to decline; to sink.
déchouer [deʃu'e], *v.t.* to get off, to set afloat.
déchu [de'ʃy], *a.* fallen, decayed; sunken; ***ange déchu,*** fallen angel.
décidé [desi'de], *a.* decided, determined, resolved.
décidément [decide'mɑ̃], *adv.* decidedly, positively; firmly; definitely.
décider [desi'de], *v.t.* to decide, to determine, to settle; to induce, to persuade.—*v.i.* to decide. **se décider,** *v.r.* to decide, to determine, to make up one's mind.
décigramme [desi'gram], *n.m.* decigram (*one-tenth of a gramme, 1·54 grains*).
décilitre [desi'litr], *n.m.* decilitre (*one-tenth of a litre*).
décimal [desi'mal], *a.* (*m.pl.* **-aux**) decimal.—*n.f.* (**-e**) a decimal.
décimalisation [desimaliza'sjɔ̃], *n.f.* decimalization.
décimaliser [desimali'ze], *v.t.* to decimalize.
décimateur [desima'tœːr], *n.m.* tithe-owner.
décime [de'sim], *n.f.* tithe.
décimer [desi'me], *v.t.* to decimate, to destroy, to annihilate.
décimètre [desi'mɛtr], *n.m.* decimetre (*3·937 inches*).
décimo [desi'mo], *adv.* tenthly.
décintrer [desɛ̃'tre], *v.t.* to remove the centerings from (*arches*).
décisif [desi'zif], *a.* (*fem.* **-sive**) decisive, conclusive.
décision [desi'zjɔ̃], *n.f.* decision, determination; resolution.
décisivement [desiziv'mɑ̃], *adv.* decisively; peremptorily, positively.
décistère [desi'stɛːr], *n.m.* tenth of a stere (*3·53 cubic feet*).
déciviliser [desivili'ze], *v.t.* to decivilize.

déclamateur [deklama'tœːr], *n.m.* (*fem.* **-trice**) declaimer; (*fig.*) tub-thumper.—*a.* (*fem.* **-trice**) declamatory, bombastic.
déclamation [deklamɑ'sjɔ̃], *n.f.* declamation, elocution.
déclamatoire [deklama'twaːr], *a.* declamatory.
déclamer [dekla'me], *v.t., v.i.* to declaim; to spout, to mouth.
déclarant [dekla'rɑ̃], *n.m.* (*Law*) informant.
déclaration [deklarɑ'sjɔ̃], *n.f.* declaration, proclamation; disclosure; notification; ***déclaration sous serment***, affidavit.
déclaratoire [deklara'twaːr], *a.* declaratory.
déclarer [dekla're], *v.t.* to declare, to make known; to proclaim; to certify. **se déclarer**, *v.r.* to speak one's mind; to declare oneself *or* itself; to show oneself *or* itself.
déclassé [deklɑ'se], *a.* come down in the world.—*n.m.* (*fem.* **-ée**) one who has come down in the world; one rejected by his own class *or* sphere.
déclassement [deklɑs'mɑ̃], *n.m.* loss of social position.
déclasser [deklɑ'se], *v.t.* to alter the classing of; to transfer from one class to another (*on trains, boats etc.*); to strike off the rolls, to dismiss from the service.
déclencher [deklɑ̃'ʃe], *v.t.* to unlatch (*a door*); to unhook, to detach; to release; (*Mil.*) to launch (*an attack*).
déclic [de'klik], *n.m.* pawl, catch.
déclin [de'klɛ̃], *n.m.* decline; decay; wane (*of the moon*); ebb; close (*of day etc.*).
déclinaison [deklinɛ'zɔ̃], *n.f.* (*Gram.*) declension.
déclinant [dekli'nɑ̃], *a.* declining.
décliner [dekli'ne], *v.t.* to refuse; (*Gram.*) to decline; to state.—*v.i.* to decline, to be on the wane, to fall off.
déclive [de'kliːv], *a.* declivous, sloping.
déclivité [deklivi'te], *n.f.* declivity, slope.
décloîtrer (se) [sədeklwa'tre], *v.r.* to leave the cloister, to return to the world.
déclore [de'klɔːr], *v.t. irr.* (*conjug. like* CLORE) to unclose, to throw open.
décochement [dekɔʃ'mɑ̃], *n.m.* discharge, shooting (*of arrows, shafts etc.*).
décocher [dekɔ'ʃe], *v.t.* to discharge, to dart (*arrows etc.*); to let fly (*insults etc.*).
décoiffer [dekwa'fe], *v.t.* to remove *or* undo the coiffure of, to undress the hair of. **se décoiffer**, *v.r.* to undo one's head-dress; to take off one's hat.
décoincer (se) [sədekwɛ̃'se], *v.r.* (*conjug. like* COMMENCER) to work loose.
décollage [dekɔ'laːʒ], *n.m.* (*Av.*) taking off.
décollement [dekɔl'mɑ̃], *n.m.* ungluing, unpasting; coming off; detachment (*of retina*).
décoller [dekɔ'le], *v.t.* to unglue.—*v.i.* (*Av.*) to take off. **se décoller**, *v.r.* to become unglued,to come off.
décolletage [dekɔl'taːʒ], *n.m.* lowness in the neck (*of dresses*); baring the neck and shoulders.
décolleté [dekɔl'te], *a.* (*Dress.*) low-necked.
décolleter [dekɔl'te], *v.t.* (*conjug. like* APPELER) to uncover the neck, shoulders etc., of; to cut (*a dress*) low. **se décolleter**, *v.r.* to bare one's shoulders; to wear a low dress.
décoloration [dekɔlɔrɑ'sjɔ̃], *n.f.* discoloration.
décoloré [dekɔlɔ're], *a.* discoloured, faded.
décolorer [dekɔlɔ're], *v.t.* to discolour. **se décolorer**, *v.r.* to become discoloured, to fade.
décombres [de'kɔ̃ːbr], *n.m.* (*used only in pl.*) rubbish, debris, ruins.
décommander [dekɔmɑ̃'de], *v.t.* to countermand; to cancel.
décomposé [dekɔ̃po'ze], *a.* decomposed.
décomposer [dekɔ̃po'ze], *v.t.* to decompose; to break up; to distort. **se décomposer**, *v.r.* to decompose, to rot; (*fig.*) to be distorted (*of the face etc.*).
décomposition [dekɔ̃pɔzi'sjɔ̃], *n.f.* decomposition, analysis.
décompresseur [dekɔ̃prɛ'sœːr], *n.m.* (*Motor.*) exhaust-valve.
décompte [de'kɔ̃ːt], *n.m.* deduction, discount, allowance; deficit; balance due; (*fig.*) drawback; disappointment.
décompter [dekɔ̃'te], *v.t.* to deduct.—*v.i.* (*fig.*) to be disappointed.
déconcertant [dekɔ̃sɛr'tɑ̃], *a.* disconcerting.
déconcerter [dekɔ̃sɛr'te], *v.t.* to disconcert; to baffle. **se déconcerter**, *v.r.* to be disconcerted *or* put out.
déconfiture [dekɔ̃fi'tyːr], *n.f.* discomfiture; break-down; insolvency.
décongeler [dekɔ̃'ʒle], *v.t.* (*conjug. like* AMENER) to thaw (*chilled meat*).
déconseiller [dekɔ̃sɛ'je], *v.t.* to dissuade.
déconsidération [dekɔ̃siderɑ'sjɔ̃], *n.f.* disrepute, discredit.
déconsidérer [dekɔ̃side're], *v.t.* (*conjug. like* CÉDER) to bring into disrepute, to discredit. **se déconsidérer**, *v.r.* to fall into disrepute.
décontenancement [dekɔ̃tnɑ̃s'mɑ̃], *n.m.* mortification, embarrassment.
décontenancer [dekɔ̃tnɑ̃'se], *v.t.* (*conjug. like* COMMENCER) to abash, to put out of countenance. **se décontenancer**, *v.r.* to be put out of countenance, to be abashed.
déconvenue [dekɔ̃v'ny], *n.f.* discomfiture; disappointment, set-back.
décor [de'kɔːr], *n.m.* decoration; (*Theat., pl.*) scenery.
décorateur [dekɔra'tœːr], *n.m.* (*fem.* **-trice**) ornamental painter, decorator; scene-painter.
décoratif [dekɔra'tif], *a.* (*fem.* **-tive**) decorative, ornamental.
décoration [dekɔrɑ'sjɔ̃], *n.f.* decoration, embellishment; medal, insignia (*of an order*).
décorder [dekɔr'de], *v.t.* to untwist, to untwine (*a cord etc.*); to untie the rope (*of a box*).
décoré [dekɔ're], *a.* decorated; wearing the insignia of some order *or* its ribbon in one's buttonhole.
décorer [dekɔ're], *v.t.* to decorate; to set off; to confer the Legion of Honour etc. upon.
décorner [dekɔr'ne], *v.t.* to dishorn.
décortiquer [dekɔrti'ke], *v.t.* to decorticate, to bark, to husk, to shell, to peel.
décorum [dekɔ'rɔm], *n.m.* decorum, propriety.
découcher [deku'ʃe], *v.i.* to sleep away from home; to stay out all night.

découdre [de'kudr] *v.t. irr.* (*conjug. like* COUDRE) to unsew, to unstitch; to rip up. **se découdre,** *v.r.* to come unstitched.

découler [deku'le], *v.i.* to trickle, to flow; to spring, to proceed (*from*).

découpage [deku'pa:ʒ], *n.m.* cutting out, carving out.

découpé [deku'pe], *a.* (*Bot.*) cut, denticulated.

découper [deku'pe], *v.t.* to cut up; to pink, to cut out; to punch. **se découper,** *v.r.* to stand out, to show up (*against*).

découpeur [deku'pœ:r], *n.m.* (*fem.* **-euse**) carver; pinker, cutter.

découplé [deku'ple], *a.* strapping.

découpler [deku'ple], *v.t.* to uncouple, to unleash, to let loose (*in pursuit*).

découpoir [deku'pwa:r], *n.m.* punch, stamping-machine, stamping-press.

découpure [deku'py:r], *n.f.* cutting out, pinking, work cut out; cut paper-work; indentation.

décourageant [dekura'ʒɑ̃], *a.* discouraging, disheartening.

découragement [dekuraʒ'mɑ̃], *n.m.* discouragement.

décourager [dekura'ʒe], *v.t.* (*conjug. like* MANGER) to discourage, to dishearten. **se décourager,** *v.r.* to be disheartened.

décours [de'ku:r], *n.m.* decrease; wane (*of the moon*).

décousu [deku'zy], *a.* unsewn, unstitched; (*fig.*) desultory (*of style etc.*).

décousure [deku'zy:r], *n.f.* unpicked stitching.

découvert [deku'vɛ:r], *a.* uncovered; discovered; open, unguarded; bare, bareheaded.—*n.m.* (*Comm.*) overdraft, deficit.

découverte [deku'vɛrt], *n.f.* discovery, detection; (*Mil.*) reconnoitring; (*Naut.*) look out.

découvreur [deku'vrœ:r], *n.m.* (*fem.* **-euse**) discoverer.

découvrir [deku'vri:r], *v.t.* (*conjug. like* OUVRIR) to uncover, to expose; to discover, to disclose, to detect. **se découvrir,** *v.r.* to uncover oneself, to take off one's hat; to unbosom oneself; to expose oneself; to lie open *or* bare; to clear up (*of the sky*).

décramponner (se) [sədekrɑ̃pɔ'ne], *v.r.* to let go one's hold.

décrasser [dekra'se], *v.t.* to take the dirt off, to scour; (*fig.*) to make presentable. **se décrasser,** *v.r.* to wash, to clean oneself; to become polished.

décrassoir [dekra'swa:r], *n.m.* fine tooth-comb.

décréditement [dekredit'mɑ̃], *n.m.* discrediting.

décrépi [dekre'pi], *a.* unplastered.

décrépir (se) [sədekre'pi:r], *v.r.* to lose its plaster (*of a wall etc.*).

décrépit [dekre'pi], *a.* decrepit, broken-down.

décrépitude [dekrepi'tyd], *n.f.* decrepitude.

décret [de'krɛ], *n.m.* decree, order, enactment; (*Law*) writ, warrant.

décret-loi [dekrɛ'lwɑ], *n.m.* Order in Council.

décréter [dekre'te], *v.t.* (*conjug. like* CÉDER) to decree, to order, to enact.

décri [de'kri], *n.m.* official crying down *or* depreciation (*of coinage*); (*fig.*) discredit.

décrier [dekri'e], *v.t.* to decry, to run down; (*fig.*) to discredit. **se décrier,** *v.r.* to bring oneself into disrepute; to decry one another.

décrire [de'kri:r], *v.t. irr.* (*conjug. like* ÉCRIRE) to describe, to depict. **se décrire,** *v.r.* to be described.

décrocher [dekrɔ'ʃe], *v.t.* to unhook, to take down, to disconnect.

décroiser [dekrwɑ'ze], *v.t.* to uncross (*the legs etc.*).

décroissant [dekrwɑ'sɑ̃], *a.* decreasing, diminishing; subsiding.

décroissement [dekrwɑs'mɑ̃], *n.m.*, **décroissance** [dekrwɑ'sɑ̃:s], *n.f.* decrease.

décroît [de'krwɑ], *n.m.* wane (*of the moon*).

décroître [de'krwɑ:tr], *v.i. irr.* (*conjug. like* CROÎTRE *but p.p.* **décru,** *without circumflex*) to decrease, to diminish, to wane.

décrottage [dekrɔ'ta:ʒ], *n.m.* cleaning (*of boots, trousers etc.*).

décrotter [dekrɔ'te], *v.t.* to rub the dirt off; (*fig.*) to improve the manners of. **se décrotter,** *v.r.* to clean oneself; to clean one's boots etc.

décrotteur [dekrɔ'tœ:r], *n.m.* (*fem.* **-euse**) shoe-black.

décrottoir [dekrɔ'twa:r], *n.m.* scraper (*for shoes*).

décrottoire [dekrɔ'twa:r], *n.f.* shoe-brush.

décrue [de'kry], *n.f.* decrease; fall (*of water*).

décrypter [dekrip'te], *v.t.* to decipher.

déculotter [dekylɔ'te], *v.t.* to take off (*s.o.'s*) breeches, (*a child's*) pants; (*colloq.*) to debag.

décuple [de'kypl], *a.* and *n.m.* tenfold.

décupler [deky'ple], *v.t.* to increase tenfold.

décuvage [deky'va:ʒ], *n.m.*, **décuvaison** [dekyvɛ'zɔ̃], *n.f.* tunning (*of wine*).

décuver [deky've], *v.t.* to tun.

dédaigner [dedɛ'ɲe], *v.t.* to disdain, to scorn, to despise.

dédaigneusement [dedɛɲøz'mɑ̃], *adv.* disdainfully, scornfully.

dédaigneux [dedɛ'ɲø], *a.* (*fem.* **-euse**) disdainful, scornful.

dédain [de'dɛ̃], *n.m.* disdain, scorn, disregard.

dédale [de'dal], *n.m.* labyrinth, maze.

dedans [də'dɑ̃], *adv.* within, in, inside; at home.—*n.m.* inside, interior.

dédicace [dedi'kas], *n.f.* dedication, consecration (*of a church etc.*).

dédication [dedikɑ'sjɔ̃], *n.f.* (*Law*) dedication (*of a temple etc.*).

dédier [de'dje], *v.t.* to dedicate, to consecrate; to devote; to inscribe (*a book etc.*).

dédire [de'di:r], *v.t. irr.* (*conjug. like* MÉDIRE) to disown; gainsay, to contradict. **se dédire,** *v.r.* to recant, to retract, to go back on one's word.

dédit [de'di], *n.m.* retraction; forfeit.

dédommagement [dedɔmaʒ'mɑ̃], *n.m.* indemnification; compensation, damages.

dédommager [dedɔma'ʒe], *v.t.* (*conjug. like* MANGER) to make amends for; to compensate, to make up for. **se dédommager,** *v.r.* to indemnify oneself.

dédorer [dedɔ're], *v.t.* to ungild. **se dédorer,** *v.r.* to lose its gilt (*of metal etc.*).

dédouanement [dedwan'mɑ̃], *n.m.* (*customs*) clearance.

dédouaner [dedwa'ne], *v.t.* to clear (*goods*) from the custom house.

dédoublement [dedublə'mɑ̃], **dédoublage** [dedu'bla:ʒ], *n.m.* dividing into two; unlining (*of a garment*); diluting.
dédoubler [dedu'ble], *v.t.* to take out the lining of; to divide into two; ***dédoubler un autocar*** (***un train***), to run a relief coach (train). **se dédoubler**, *v.r.* to be divided into two.
déductif [dedyk'tif], *a.* (*fem.* **-tive**) deductive.
déduction [dedyk'sjɔ̃], *n.f.* deduction, allowance; inference.
déduire [de'dɥi:r], *v.t. irr.* (*conjug. like* CONDUIRE) to deduct, to subtract; to deduce, to infer.
déesse [de'ɛs], *n.f.* goddess, female deity.
défâcher [defɑ'ʃe], *v.t.* to pacify. **se défâcher**, *v.r.* to be pacified, to cool down.
défaillance [defa'jɑ̃:s], *n.f.* fainting fit, swoon, faintness; exhaustion; extinction (*of a family etc.*).
défaillant [defa'jɑ̃], *a.* failing, falling off; decaying; without heirs; weak, feeble.—*n.m.* (*fem.* **-e**) (*Law*) defaulter.
défaillir [defa'ji:r], *v.i. irr.* (*conjug. like* ASSAILLIR) to fail, to default; to decay; to swoon, to faint away.
défaire [de'fɛ:r], *v.t. irr.* (*conjug. like* FAIRE) to undo, to unmake; to defeat; to emaciate; to embarrass; to rid. **se défaire**, *v.r.* to come undone; ***se défaire de***, to get rid of, to give up.
défait [de'fɛ], *a.* undone, defeated; meagre, wasted; worn out.
défaite [de'fɛt], *n.f.* defeat, overthrow; evasion, pretence, excuse.
défaitisme [defɛ'tism], *n.m.* defeatism.
défaitiste [defɛ'tist], *a.* and *n.* defeatist.
défalcation [defalkɑ'sjɔ̃], *n.f.* deduction.
défalquer [defal'ke], *v.t.* to take off, to deduct.
défausser [defo'se], *v.t.* to straighten.
défaut [de'fo], *n.m.* absence, lack, default; defect, fault, flaw; (*Law*) non-appearance; ***à défaut de***, instead of, for want of; ***faire défaut***, to be wanting, to be missing.
défaveur [defa'vœ:r], *n.f.* disfavour, discredit.
défavorable [defavɔ'rabl], *a.* unfavourable.
défavorablement [defavɔrɑblə'mɑ̃], *adv.* unfavourably.
défectif [defɛk'tif], *a.* (*fem.* **-tive**) (*Gram.*) defective.
défection [defɛk'sjɔ̃], *n.f.* defection, falling off, disloyalty.
défectueux [defɛk'tɥø], *a.* (*fem.* **-euse**) defective, imperfect.
défectuosité [defɛktɥɔzi'te], *n.f.* defect, imperfection, flaw.
défendable [defɑ̃'dabl], *a.* defensible, tenable.
défendeur [defɑ̃'dœ:r], *n.m.* (*fem.* **-eresse**) defendant; respondent.
défendre [de'fɑ̃:dr], *v.t.* to defend, to protect; to shield; to support; to forbid. **se défendre**, *v.r.* to defend oneself; to clear oneself; to deny.
défense [de'fɑ̃:s], *n.f.* defence, protection; prohibition; apology, plea; (*Law*) the defence; (*Fort., pl.*) outworks; tusk, fang (*of animals*); (*Naut.*) fender; ***défense de fumer***, no smoking.
défenseur [defɑ̃'sœ:r], *n.m.* defender, supporter; advocate, counsel.
défensif [defɑ̃'sif], *a.* (*fem.* **-sive**) defensive.—*n.f.* (**-sive**) defensive.
déféquer [defe'ke], *v.t.* (*conjug. like* CÉDER) to purify.—*v.i.* to defecate.
déférence [defe'rɑ̃:s], *n.f.* deference, regard, respect.
déférent [defe'rɑ̃], *a.* deferential, compliant.
déférer [defe're], *v.t.* (*conjug. like* CÉDER) * to confer, to bestow; to tender; to accuse, to inform against.—*v.i.* to defer, to yield, to comply.
déferler [defɛr'le], *v.t.* (*Naut.*) to unfurl.—*v.i.* to break into foam (*of the sea*).
déferrer [defɛ're], *v.t.* to unshoe (*a horse*). **se déferrer**, *v.r.* to come unshod, to lose a shoe.
défeuiller [defœ'je], *v.t.* to take the leaves off. **se défeuiller**, *v.r.* to shed its leaves.
défi [de'fi], *n.m.* defiance, challenge.
défiance [de'fjɑ̃:s], *n.f.* distrust, mistrust; caution.
défiant [de'fjɑ̃], *a.* distrustful, suspicious.
déficeler [defis'le], *v.t.* (*conjug. like* APPELER) to untie; to undo.
déficient [defi'sjɑ̃], *a.* deficient.
déficit [defi'sit], *n.m.* deficit, deficiency.
défier [de'fje], *v.t.* to defy, to challenge; to brave, to face; to set at defiance. **se défier**, *v.r.* to defy *or* to challenge each other; to distrust, to beware (***de***).
défiger [defi'ʒe], *v.t.* (*conjug. like* MANGER) to liquefy.
défiguration [defigyrɑ'sjɔ̃], *n.f.*, **défigurement** [defigyr'mɑ̃], *n.m.* disfigurement, defacement.
défigurer [defigy're], *v.t.* to disfigure, to mar; to distort. **se défigurer**, *v.r.* to disfigure oneself; to become deformed.
défilade [defi'lad], *n.f.* filing off *or* past, marching past; succession.
défilé [defi'le], *n.m.* defile, narrow pass, gorge; (*fig.*) strait, difficulty; (*Mil.*) filing past; ***un défilé de mannequins***, a mannequin parade.
défiler [defi'le], *v.t.* to unstring, to unthread; to untwist.—*v.i.* to file off, to march past. **se défiler**, *v.r.* to come unthreaded *or* unstrung; (*Mil.*) to take cover; to slip away.
défini [defi'ni], *a.* definite, determined, defined.
définir [defi'ni:r], *v.t.* to define; to determine; to describe.
définissable [defini'sabl], *a.* definable.
définitif [defini'tif], *a.* (*fem.* **-tive**) definitive, final; ultimate, eventual.
définition [defini'sjɔ̃], *n.f.* definition.
définitivement [definitiv'mɑ̃], *adv.* definitively, positively, decidedly; eventually.
déflation [deflɑ'sjɔ̃], *n.f.* deflation.
défléchir [defle'ʃi:r], *v.t.*, *v.i.* to turn from *or* aside, to deflect.
déflecteur [deflɛk'tœ:r], *n.m.* (*Motor.*) ventilating window; deflector.
défleuraison [DÉFLORAISON].
défleurir [deflœ'ri:r], *v.t.* to nip *or* strip off blossoms.—*v.i.* to lose its flowers.
déflexion [deflɛk'sjɔ̃], *n.f.* deviation; (*Gram.*) deflection.
défloraison [deflɔrɛ'zɔ̃], **défleuraison** [deflœrɛ'zɔ̃], *n.f.* fall *or* withering of the blossom.
déflorer [deflɔ're], *v.t.* to deflower, to seduce.

défonçage [defɔ̃'saːʒ], **défoncement** [defɔ̃s'mɑ̃], *n.m.* staving in (*of the head of casks*), breaking *or* smashing in; (*Agric.*) deep trenching.
défoncer [defɔ̃'se], *v.t.* (*conjug. like* COMMENCER) to stave in, to bilge (*a cask*); to dig deeply, to trench (*ground*). **se défoncer**, *v.r.* to give way; to break up (*of roads*); to get battered.
défonceuse [defɔ̃'søːz], *n.f.* trenching plough.
déforestation [defɔrɛstɑ'sjɔ̃], *n.f.* deforestation.
déformant [defɔr'mɑ̃], *a.* distorting (*mirror etc.*).
deformation [defɔrmɑ'sjɔ̃], *n.f.* distortion, buckling.
déformer [defɔr'me], *v.t.* to deform, to distort. **se déformer**, *v.r.* to lose its shape.
défortifier [defɔrti'fje], *v.t.* to dismantle the fortifications of.
défourner [defur'ne], *v.t.* to draw out of an oven *or* kiln.
défourrer [defu're], *v.t.* to unwrap, to take out of its cover; to thresh (*corn*).
défraîchir [defrɛ'ʃiːr], *v.t.* to tarnish, to take away the brilliancy, gloss *or* freshness of. **se défraîchir**, *v.r.* to lose its brilliancy, freshness etc., to tarnish.
défrayer [defrɛ'je], *v.t.* (*conjug. like* PAYER) to defray, to bear the cost of; to amuse.
défriche [de'friʃ], *n.f.*, **défriché** [defri'ʃe], *n.m.* piece of cleared land.
défrichement [defriʃ'mɑ̃], **défrichage** [defri'ʃaːʒ], *n.m.* clearing, breaking up (*of land for tillage*).
défricher [defri'ʃe], *v.t.* to clear, to break up (*ground*) for tillage; to reclaim.
défricheur [defri'ʃœːr], *n.m.* clearer; settler.
défriper [defri'pe], *v.t.* to smooth out.
défrisement [defriz'mɑ̃], *n.m.* uncurling.
défriser [defri'ze], *v.t.* to uncurl; (*fam.*) to disappoint, to ruffle.
défroque [de'frɔk], *n.f.* the effects left by a dying monk; *hence*, old things, effects, cast-off clothes, etc.
défroqué [defrɔ'ke], *a.* and *n.m.* unfrocked (*priest*).
défroquer [defrɔ'ke], *v.t.* to unfrock. **se défroquer**, *v.r.* to renounce one's order (*of monks*).
défunt [de'fœ̃], *a.* defunct, deceased, late.—*n.m.* (*fem.* **-e**) the deceased.
dégagé [dega'ʒe], *a.* free, easy, unconstrained; flippant; bold; slender, graceful.
dégagement [degaʒ'mɑ̃], *n.m.* disengagement, redemption; clearance; discharge (*of gas etc.*); (*fig.*) unconcern.
dégager [dega'ʒe], *v.t.* (*conjug. like* MANGER) to disengage, to extricate; to clear; to deliver, to rescue; to release, to emit (*fumes etc.*); to redeem, to take out of pawn. **se dégager**, *v.r.* to be liberated (*de*); to extricate, disengage *or* disentangle oneself; to get away; (*Chem.*) to be emitted.
dégaine [de'gɛːn], *n.f.* (*colloq.*) awkward gait.
dégainer [degɛ'ne], *v.t.* to unsheathe (*one's sword etc.*).
déganter [degɑ̃'te], *v.t.* to unglove. **se déganter**, *v.r.* to take off one's gloves.
dégarnir [degar'niːr], *v.t.* to strip; to dismantle; to thin (*trees, woods etc.*). **se dégarnir**, *v.r.* to strip oneself (*de*); to become empty; to grow thin; to lose branches etc.
dégât [de'gɑ], *n.m.* havoc, damage, ravage.
dégauchir [dego'ʃiːr], *v.t.* to smooth, to plane, to level, to straighten; (*fig.*) to polish.
dégauchissement [degoʃis'mɑ̃], **dégauchissage** [degoʃi'saːʒ], *n.m.* planing, straightening, levelling, smoothing.
dégazonner [degɑzɔ'ne], *v.t.* to remove the turf from.
dégel [de'ʒɛl], *n.m.* thaw.
dégeler [de'ʒle], *v.t.*, *v.i.* (*conjug. like* AMENER) to thaw. **se dégeler**, *v.r.* to thaw (*of persons*).
dégénération [deʒenerɑ'sjɔ̃], *n.f.* degeneration, degeneracy.
dégénéré [deʒene're], *a.* and *n.m.* (*fem.* **-ée**) degenerate (person).
dégénérer [deʒene're], *v.i.* (*conjug. like* CÉDER) to decline, to degenerate.
dégénérescence [deʒenerɛ'sɑ̃ːs], *n.f.* degeneracy, degeneration.
dégénérescent [deʒenerɛ'sɑ̃], *a.* degenerating.
dégingandé [deʒɛ̃gɑ̃'de], *a.* ungainly, gawky, awkward in one's gait; clumsy, disjointed, irregular.
dégivrer [deʒi'vre], *v.t.* to de-ice.
dégivreur [deʒi'vrœːr], *n.m.* (*Motor.*, *Av.*) de-icer.
déglutir [degly'tiːr], *v.t.* to swallow.
déglutition [deglyti'sjɔ̃], *n.f.* deglutition, swallowing.
dégommer [degɔ'me], *v.t.* to wash the gum out of; (*slang*) to sack.
dégonflement [degɔ̃flə'mɑ̃], *n.m.* deflating (*of tyre, balloon*); collapse; reduction.
dégonfler [degɔ̃'fle], *v.t.* to cause to collapse; to deflate; to reduce (*a swelling*). **se dégonfler**, *v.r.* to go down, to be reduced; to subside; (*pop.*) to sing small.
dégorgement [degɔrʒ'mɑ̃], *n.m.* breaking out, overflow; unstopping.
dégorger [degɔr'ʒe], *v.t.* (*conjug. like* MANGER) to disgorge; to unstop, to clear; to cleanse.—*v.i.* to discharge, to overflow. **se dégorger**, *v.r.* to discharge *or* empty itself *or* oneself, to be unstopped, to be cleared.
dégourdi [degur'di], *a.* quick, sharp, acute, smart; tepid (*of water*).—*n.m.* (*fem.* **-e**) a shrewd *or* forward person.
dégourdir [degur'diːr], *v.t.* to revive, to quicken; to take the chill off; (*fig.*) to sharpen, to render shrewd; to polish. **se dégourdir**, *v.r.* to lose numbness, to feel warmer; to brighten up.
dégourdissement [degurdis'mɑ̃], *n.m.* return of circulation; quickening, reviving.
dégoût [de'gu], *n.m.* dislike, distaste; disgust, aversion; mortification.
dégoûtant [degu'tɑ̃], *a.* disgusting, distasteful, nauseous; loathsome; unpleasant.
dégoûté [degu'te], *a.* disgusted; fastidious.—*n.m.* (*fem.* **-ée**) fastidious person.
dégoûter [degu'te], *v.t.* to disgust. **se dégoûter**, *v.r.* to take a dislike to.
dégouttant [degu'tɑ̃], *a.* dripping.
dégouttement [degut'mɑ̃], *n.m.* dripping, falling in drops.
dégoutter [degu'te], *v.i.* to drip, to fall in drops, to trickle.
dégradant [degra'dɑ̃], *a.* degrading, debasing.

dégradation [degradɑ'sjɔ̃], *n.f.* degradation; debasement; (*Paint.*) gradation of light and shade; (*Law*) ***dégradation nationale*** or ***civile***, loss of civil rights; ***dégradation militaire***, cashiering.
dégrader [degra'de], *v.t.* to degrade, to debase; to deface; (*Mil.*) to reduce to the ranks; to cashier; (*Paint.*) to graduate the light and shade. **se dégrader**, *v.r.* to degrade, debase *or* disgrace oneself; to become damaged *or* defaced.
dégrafer [degra'fe], *v.t.* to unclasp, to unhook. **se dégrafer**, *v.r.* to come unfastened (*of garments etc.*); to unfasten one's clothes.
dégraissage [degrɛ'sa:ʒ], **dégraissement** [degrɛs'mɑ̃], *n.m.* dry-cleaning (*garments*); scouring (*wool*).
dégraisser [degrɛ'se], *v.t.* to remove greasy stains from.
dégraisseur [degrɛ'sœ:r], *n.m.* (*fem.* **-euse**) scourer (*of wool*); dry-cleaner (*of clothes etc.*).
dégraissoir [degrɛ'swa:r], *n.m.* scraper.
degré [də'gre], *n.m.* step, stair; stage, grade, degree; point, extent, height, pitch.
dégréer [degre'e], *v.t.* to unrig; to strip a mast.
dégrèvement [degrɛv'mɑ̃], *n.m.* reduction; tax allowance, relief.
dégrever [degrə've], *v.t.* (*conjug. like* AMENER) to diminish, to reduce (*a tax etc.*); to relieve (*someone of a tax*); to disencumber (*an estate etc.*); to pay off (*a mortgage*).
dégringolade [degrɛ̃gɔ'lad], *n.f.* (*fam.*) fall, tumble.
dégringoler [degrɛ̃gɔ'le], *v.i.* to tumble down, to topple over.
dégrisement [degriz'mɑ̃], *n.m.* (*colloq.*) sobering, getting sober; (*fig.*) cooling down.
dégriser [degri'ze], *v.t.* to sober; (*fig.*) to cool down, to bring to one's senses. **se dégriser**, *v.r.* to sober down; (*fig.*) to come to one's senses; to lose one's illusions.
dégrossir [degro'si:r], *v.t.* to rough-hew; (*fig.*) to make a rough sketch of.
dégrossissage [degrosi'sa:ʒ], **dégrossissement** [degrosis'mɑ̃], *n.m.* rough-hewing; (*Carp.*) dressing, trimming.
déguenillé [degəni'je], *a.* tattered, ragged.—*n.m.* (*fem.* **-ée**) ragamuffin.
déguerpir [degɛr'pi:r], *v.i.* to move off; to be gone.
déguerpissement [degɛrpis'mɑ̃], *n.m.* quitting, giving up, abandonment.
dégueuler [degœ'le], *v.t.* (*vulg.*) to spew.
déguignonner [degiɲɔ'ne], *v.t.* to lift a curse from, to bring better luck to.
déguisable [degi'zabl], *a.* disguisable.
déguisement [degiz'mɑ̃], *n.m.* disguise, concealment; ***parlez sans déguisement***, speak openly.
déguiser [degi'ze], *v.t.* to disguise, to cloak; to misrepresent. **se déguiser**, *v.r.* to disguise oneself, to put on fancy dress.
dégustateur [degysta'tœ:r], *n.m.* (*fem.* **-trice**) taster (*of wines etc.*).
dégustation [degystɑ'sjɔ̃], *n.f.* tasting (*of wines etc.*).
déguster [degys'te], *v.t.* to taste; to sip, to savour.
déhaler [dea'le], *v.t.* (*Naut.*) to tow out; to haul off.
déhâler [deɑ'le], *v.t.* to take away sun-burn, freckles, tan etc. from. **se déhâler**, *v.r.* to clear one's complexion.
déhanché [deɑ̃'ʃe], *a.* having the hip dislocated; (*fig.*) ungainly.
déhanchement [deɑ̃ʃ'mɑ̃], *n.m.* waddling gait, waddle.
déhancher (se) [sədeɑ̃'ʃe], *v.r.* to sway one's hips; to have a waddling, loose gait.
déharnachement [dearnaʃ'mɑ̃], *n.m.* unharnessing.
déharnacher [dearna'ʃe], *v.t.* to unharness.
dehors [də'ɔ:r], *adv.* out, *without, outside; out of doors; abroad; externally; (*Naut.*) at sea; ***au dedans et au dehors***, at home and abroad; ***au dehors***, outwardly; ***de dehors***, from without; ***en dehors***, outside, *without; ***mettre quelqu'un dehors***, to turn someone out.—*n.m. inv.* outside, exterior; (*pl.*) appearances; (*Fort.*) outworks; dependencies, approaches, grounds (*of a house*); ***sauver les dehors***, to save appearances.
déification [deifikɑ'sjɔ̃], *n.f.* deification.
déifier [dei'fje], *v.t.* to deify.
déisme [de'ism], *n.m.* deism.
déiste [de'ist], *a.* deistic.—*n.* deist.
déité [dei'te], *n.f.* deity (*god, goddess*), divinity.
déjà [de'ʒa], *adv.* already, before, previously.
déjection [deʒɛk'sjɔ̃], *n.f.* (*Med.*) dejection, ejection, evacuation.
déjeté [deʒ'te], *a.* awry, lopsided, off the straight.
déjeter [deʒ'te], *v.t.* (*conjug. like* APPELER) to warp. **se déjeter**, *v.r.* to warp (*of wood etc.*); (*Path.*) to deviate.
déjettement [deʒɛt'mɑ̃], *n.m.* warping; deviation.
déjeuner [deʒœ'ne], *n.m.* lunch; ***petit déjeuner***, breakfast; ***un déjeuner de porcelaine***, a china breakfast-set.—*v.i.* to breakfast, to lunch.
déjouer [de'ʒwe], *v.t.* to baffle, to frustrate, to foil; (*Mil.*) to outmanœuvre.
déjucher [deʒy'ʃe], *v.t.* to dislodge.—*v.i.* to come down from the roost *or* from one's perch.
déjuger (se) [sədeʒy'ʒe], *v.r.* (*conjug. like* MANGER) to reverse one's opinion *or* decision.
delà [də'la], *prep.* on the other side of; beyond; ***au delà***, ***de delà***, ***par delà***, or ***en delà***, beyond; ***deçà et delà***, both here and there, both this and that; ***l'au-delà***, the hereafter.
délabré [delɑ'bre], *a.* tattered, shabby (*garments*); tumbledown, ramshackle (*building*).
délabrement [delɑbrə'mɑ̃], *n.m.* decay, dilapidation; shabbiness.
délabrer [delɑ'bre], *v.t.* to shatter, to ruin, to tear to tatters. **se délabrer**, *v.r.* to fall to pieces, to go to ruin.
délacer [dela'se], *v.t.* (*conjug. like* COMMENCER) to unlace (*shoes etc.*). **se délacer**, *v.r.* to unlace oneself; to come undone (*of shoes, strings etc.*).
délai [de'lɛ], *n.m.* delay; respite.
délaissé [delɛ'se], *a.* abandoned, friendless.

délaissement [delɛs'mɑ̃], *n.m.* desertion; destitution, helplessness.

délaisser [delɛ'se], *v.t.* to forsake, to abandon; to neglect.

délassant [delɑ'sɑ̃], *a.* refreshing, diverting.

délassement [delɑs'mɑ̃], *n.m.* relaxation; repose.

délasser [delɑ'se], *v.t.* to refresh, to relax, to divert. **se délasser**, *v.r.* to refresh oneself, to rest.

délateur [dela'tœ:r], *n.m.* (*fem.* **-trice**) informer, accuser.

délation [delɑ'sjɔ̃], *n.f.* informing.

délavage [dela'va:ʒ], *n.m.* diluting of colour; soaking.

délaver [dela've], *v.t.* to dilute *or* wash (*colour*); to soak into. **se délaver**, *v.r.* to become soaked; to lose colour.

délayable [delɛ'jabl], *a.* dilutable.

délayage [delɛ'ja:ʒ], *n.m.* diluting, dilution.

délayé [delɛ'je], *a.* watery.

délayer [delɛ'je], *v.t.* (*conjug. like* PAYER) to dilute; (*fig.*) to spin out.

délectable [delɛk'tabl], *a.* delectable, delightful.

délecter (se) [sədelɛk'te], *v.r.* to take delight.

délégation [delegɑ'sjɔ̃], *n.f.* delegation, assignment.

délégatoire [delega'twa:r], *a.* delegatory.

délégué [dele'ge], *n.m.* (*fem.* **-ée**) delegate, deputy; proxy.

déléguer [dele'ge], *v.t.* (*conjug. like* CÉDER) to delegate; to assign. **se déléguer**, *v.r.* to be delegated.

délester [delɛs'te], *v.t.* to unballast.

délétère [dele'tɛ:r], *a.* deleterious.

délibérant [delibe'rɑ̃], *a.* deliberative.

délibératif [delibera'tif], *a.* (*fem.* **-tive**) deliberative.

délibération [deliberɑ'sjɔ̃], *n.f.* deliberation; resolution.

délibéré [delibe're], *a.* deliberate, determined, resolute.

délibérément [delibere'mɑ̃], *adv.* deliberately, resolutely.

délibérer [delibe're], *v.i.* (*conjug. like* CÉDER) to deliberate; to resolve.

délicat [deli'ka], *a.* delicate, dainty; nice, fastidious; frail.—*n.m.* (*fem.* **-e**) fastidious person.

délicatement [delikat'mɑ̃], *adv.* delicately, daintily, tenderly.

délicatesse [delika'tɛs], *n.f.* delicacy, fragility; tenderness; daintiness, fastidiousness; refinement, squeamishness; nicety (*of language etc.*); considerateness; (*pl.*) dainties.

délice [de'lis], *n.m. in sing.* (*used chiefly in f.pl.*) delight, pleasure.

délicieusement [delisjøz'mɑ̃], *adv.* deliciously, delightfully.

délicieux [deli'sjø], *a.* (*fem.* **-euse**) delicious, delightful.

délié [de'lje], *a.* slender, fine; sharp, shrewd; glib, flowing (*of style etc.*); untied, loose.

délier [de'lje], *v.t.* to unbind, to untie; to liberate, to release; to absolve. **se délier**, *v.r.* to come untied, to get loose.

délimitation [delimitɑ'sjɔ̃], *n.f.* delimitation, fixing of boundaries.

délimiter [delimi'te], *v.t.* to delimit, to settle the boundaries of.

délinéation [delineɑ'sjɔ̃], *n.f.* delineation.

délinéer [deline'e], *v.t.* to delineate.

délinquance [delɛ̃'kɑ̃:s], *n.f.* delinquency.

délinquant [delɛ̃'kɑ̃], *n.m.* (*fem.* **-e**) delinquent, offender.—*a.* ***enfance délinquante***, juvenile delinquents.

délirant [deli'rɑ̃], *a.* delirious, frenzied, frantic; rapturous, ecstatic.—*n.m.* (*fem.* **-e**) a delirious *or* ecstatic person.

délire [de'li:r], *n.m.* delirium, frenzy, folly.

délirer [deli're], *v.i.* to be delirious, to rave, to wander.

délit [de'li], *n.m.* misdemeanour, offence; ***en flagrant délit***, in the very act, red-handed.

délivrance [deli'vrɑ̃:s], *n.f.* rescue, deliverance; issue (*of tickets*); delivery (*of certificates etc.*); accouchement.

délivre [de'livr], *n.m.* (*Anat.*) after-birth, placenta.

délivrer [deli'vre], *v.t.* to deliver, to release, to set free; to hand over; to issue; to deliver (*a woman of a baby*).

délogement [delɔʒ'mɑ̃], *n.m.* removal, change of quarters, decamping.

déloger [delɔ'ʒe], *v.t.* (*conjug. like* MANGER) to turn out (*of house etc.*), to oust; to drive away; (*Mil.*) to dislodge.—*v.i.* to remove, to go (*from one's house etc.*), to go away, to march off.

déloyal [delwa'jal], *a.* (*m.pl.* **-aux**) disloyal, false, treacherous, unfair; foul.

déloyalement [delwajal'mɑ̃], *adv.* disloyally, unfairly.

déloyauté [delwajo'te], *n.f.* disloyalty, treachery.

delta [dɛl'ta], *n.m.* delta.

déluge [de'ly:ʒ], *n.m.* deluge, flood.

déluré [dely're], *a.* wide-awake, sharp.

délustrer [delys'tre], *v.t.* to take the lustre *or* gloss from.

démagnétiser [demaɲeti'ze], *v.t.* to demagnetize.

démagogue [dema'gɔg], *n.* demagogue.

démailler [demɑ'je], *v.t.* to undo the meshes of (*a net etc.*).

demain [də'mɛ̃], *adv.* and *n.m.* tomorrow; ***à demain!*** see you tomorrow!

démancher [demɑ̃'ʃe], *v.t.* to take off the handle of; (*fig.*) to dislocate. **se démancher**, *v.r.* to lose its handle; to go wrong.

demande [də'mɑ̃:d], *n.f.* question; request, application, petition; claim; (*Comm.*) demand; order.

demander [dəmɑ̃'de], *v.t.* to ask, to beg, to request; to desire, to wish; to require, to call for; to need, to want; to inquire about; to ask to see; to seek in marriage; (*Comm.*) to order. **se demander**, *v.r.* to ask oneself, to wonder.

demandeur [dəmɑ̃'dœ:r], *a.* (*fem.* **-euse**) always asking.—*n.m.* (*fem.* **-eresse**) asker, applicant; (*Law*) plaintiff.

démangeaison [demɑ̃ʒɛ'zɔ̃], *n.f.* itching; longing.

démanger [demɑ̃'ʒe], *v.i.* (*conjug. like* MANGER) to itch; to long.

démantibuler [demɑ̃tiby'le], *v.t.* to break, to dislocate.

démaquiller [demaki'je], *v.t.* to take off someone's make-up. **se démaquiller**, *v.r.* to take off one's make-up.

démarcation [demarkɑ'sjɔ̃], *n.f.* demarcation; ***ligne de démarcation***, line of demarcation.
démarche [de'marʃ], *n.f.* gait, walk, bearing; proceeding, measure, step, course.
démarcheur [demar'ʃœ:r], *n.m.* canvasser.
démarier [dema'rje], *v.t.* (*fam.*) to annul the marriage of; (*Hort.*) to thin out. **se démarier,** *v.r.* to be divorced.
démarrer [dema're], *v.t.* to cast off; to unfasten.—*v.i.* to leave, to slip her moorings (*of a ship*); to move, to get away, to start.
démarreur [dema'rœ:r], *n.m.* (*Motor.*) self-starter.
démasquer [demas'ke], *v.t.* to unmask; to show up.
démâter [demɑ'te], *v.t.* to dismast.—*v.i.* to lose her masts (*of a ship*).
démêlage [demɛ'la:ʒ], *n.m.* combing (*of wool*).
démêlé [demɛ'le], *n.m.* strife, contest, quarrel.
démêler [demɛ'le], *v.t.* to unravel, to disentangle, to separate; to clear up; to distinguish, to discern; to comb out (*hair*), to tease (*wool*). **se démêler,** *v.r.* to be disentangled; to extricate oneself; to stand out (*clearly*); to comb out one's hair.
démembrement [demɑ̃brə'mɑ̃], *n.m.* dismemberment; breaking up.
démembrer [demɑ̃'bre], *v.t.* to tear limb from limb, to dismember; to break up.
déménagement [demenaʒ'mɑ̃], *n.m.* (*household*) removal.
déménager [demena'ʒe], *v.t.* (*conjug. like* MANGER) to remove (*one's furniture*).—*v.i.* to (re)move.
déménageur [demena'ʒœ:r], *n.m.* furniture-remover.
démence [de'mɑ̃:s], *n.f.* insanity, madness.
démener (se) [sədem'ne], *v.r.* (*conjug. like* AMENER) to stir, to struggle, to make a great fuss, to strive hard.
démenti [demɑ̃'ti], *n.m.* denial, flat contradiction; lie.
démentir [demɑ̃'ti:r], *v.t.* (*conjug. like* SENTIR) to give the lie to, to contradict; to deny; to belie, to refute. **se démentir,** *v.r.* to contradict oneself; to fall off, to flag.
démérite [deme'rit], *n.m.* demerit.
démériter [demeri'te], *v.i.* to lose esteem *or* favour.
démesuré [deməzy're], *a.* inordinate, excessive, enormous.
démesurément [deməzyre'mɑ̃], *adv.* inordinately, excessively.
démettre [de'mɛtr], *v.t. irr.* (*conjug. like* METTRE) to put out of joint, to dislocate; to dismiss; (*Law*) to overrule. **se démettre,** *v.r.* to be put out of joint; to resign.
démeubler [demœ'ble], *v.t.* to strip of furniture.
demeurant [dəmœ'rɑ̃], *a.* dwelling, living.—*n.m.* remainder; ***au demeurant***, after all, nevertheless.
demeure [də'mœ:r], *n.f.* abode, home, dwelling; stay; (*Law*) delay.
demeurer [dəmœ're], *v.i.* to live, to lodge, to reside; to stop, to stand; to continue, to stay.
demi [də'mi], *a.* and *adv.* half.—*n.m.* (*Arith.*) half; (*Ftb. etc.*) half-back; glass of beer.—*n.f.* (**-e**) (the) half-hour.

[In the following compounds ***demi*** is *inv.* The noun has its regular plural, unless otherwise indicated.]

demi-bain [dəmi'bɛ̃], *n.m.* hip-bath.
demi-bas [dəmi'bɑ], *n.m. inv.* knee-length stocking.
demi-botte [dəmi'bɔt], *n.f.* Wellington boot.
demi-cercle [dəmi'sɛrkl], *n.m.* semicircle.
demi-finale [dəmifi'nal], *n.f.* (*Spt.*) semi-final.
demi-fond [dəmi'fɔ̃], *n.m. inv.* middle distance (*race*).
demi-heure [dəmi'œ:r], *n.f.* half-hour; ***une demi-heure***, half an hour.
demi-jour [dəmi'ʒu:r], *n.m.* twilight.
demi-mot [dəmi'mo], *adv. phr.* ***comprendre à demi-mot,*** to take the hint.
déminage [demi'na:ʒ], *n.m.* mine clearing.
déminer [demi'ne], *v.t.* to clear of mines.
demi-pension [dəmipɑ̃'sjɔ̃], *n.f.* half-board.
demi-pensionnaire [dəmipɑ̃sjɔ'nɛ:r], *n.* day-boarder.
demi-place [dəmi'plas], *n.f.* half-fare.
demi-saison [dəmisɛ'zɔ̃], *n.f.* autumn *or* spring.
demi-sang [dəmi'sɑ̃], *n.m. inv.* half-bred horse.
demi-sel [dəmi'sɛl], *n.m.* slightly salted cream-cheese.
demi-solde [dəmi'sɔld], *n.f.* half-pay.
démission [demi'sjɔ̃], *n.f.* resignation.
démissionnaire [demisjɔ'nɛ:r], *a.* who has resigned *or* vacated his seat, outgoing.
démissionner [demisjɔ'ne], *v.i.* to resign.
demi-tour [dəmi'tu:r], *n.m.* half-turn; (*Mil.*) about turn; ***faire demi-tour***, to turn back.
démobilisation [demɔbilizɑ'sjɔ̃], *n.f.* demobilization.
démobiliser [demɔbili'ze], *v.t.* to demobilize.
démocrate [demɔ'krat], *a.* democratic.—*n.* democrat.
démocratie [demɔkra'si], *n.f.* democracy.
démocratique [demɔkra'tik], *a.* democratic.
démocratiquement [demɔkratik'mɑ̃], *adv.* democratically.
démocratiser [demɔkrati'ze], *v.t.* to democratize.
démodé [demɔ'de], *a.* old-fashioned, antiquated.
demoiselle [dəmwa'zɛl], *n.f.* young lady; unmarried woman, spinster; young girl; dragon-fly; ***demoiselle d'honneur*** bridesmaid.
démolir [demɔ'li:r], *v.t.* to demolish, to pull down.
démolisseur [demɔli'sœ:r], *n.m.* (*fem.* **-euse**) demolisher.
démolition [demɔli'sjɔ̃], *n.f.* demolition; (*pl.*) old building materials.
démon [de'mɔ̃], *n.m.* demon; (*good* or *evil*) genius; devil, fiend.
démonétisation [demɔnetizɑ'sjɔ̃], *n.f.* withdrawal from circulation (*of money*).
démonétiser [demɔneti'ze], *v.t.* to withdraw from circulation, to call in (*money*).
démoniaque [demɔ'njak], *a.* demoniac(al).—*n.* demoniac, demon, devil.
démonstrateur [demɔ̃stra'tœ:r], *n.m.* (*fem.* **-euse**) demonstrator, lecturer.
démonstratif [demɔ̃stra'tif], *a.* (*fem.* **-tive**) demonstrative.

démonstration [demɔ̃strɑ'sjɔ̃], *n.f.* demonstration, proof; exhibition.
démontable [demɔ̃'tabl], *a.* that can be taken to pieces; collapsible (*canoe*).
démontage [demɔ̃'ta:ʒ], *n.m.* taking to pieces, dismantling.
démonte-pneu [demɔ̃t'pnø], *n.m.* tyre lever.
démonter [demɔ̃'te], *v.t.* to unhorse, to dismount; to take to pieces, to dismantle; (*fig.*) to nonplus, to baffle; ***mer démontée***, very rough sea. **se démonter**, *v.r.* to take *or* come to pieces (*of machinery*); to lose countenance, to be nonplussed; to be getting out of order (*of machinery etc.*).
démontrer [demɔ̃'tre], *v.t.* to demonstrate, to prove.
démoralisant [demɔrali'zɑ̃], *a.* demoralizing.
démoralisateur [demɔraliza'tœ:r], *a.* (*fem.* **-trice**) corrupting, demoralizing.
démoralisation [demɔralizɑ'sjɔ̃], *n.f.* demoralization.
démoraliser [demɔrali'ze], *v.t.* to demoralize; to corrupt.
démordre [de'mɔrdr], *v.i.* to let go one's hold; to desist, to yield, to give in.
démoucheter [demuʃ'te], *v.t.* (*conjug. like* APPELER) to take off the button from (*a foil*), to uncap.
démoulage [demu'la:ʒ], *n.m.* taking from the mould.
démouler [demu'le], *v.t.* to take from the mould.
démunir [demy'ni:r], *v.t.* to strip (*of ammunition*), to leave unprovided. **se démunir**, *v.r.* to deprive oneself, to leave oneself unprovided for.
démuseler [demyz'le], *v.t.* (*conjug. like* APPELER) to unmuzzle; (*fig.*) to let loose.
dénatalité [denatali'te], *n.f.* fall in the birthrate.
dénationalisation [denasjɔnalizɑ'sjɔ̃], *n.f.* denationalization.
dénationaliser [denasjɔnali'ze], *v.t.* to denationalize.
dénatter [dena'te], *v.t.* to unplait (*hair etc.*).
dénaturé [denaty're], *a.* unnatural, barbarous, cruel.
dénaturer [denaty're], *v.t.* to alter the nature of; to misrepresent, to distort; to disfigure; to methylate (*alcohol*).
dénégation [denegɑ'sjɔ̃], *n.f.* denial, denegation.
déni [de'ni], *n.m.* denial, refusal.
déniaiser [denjɛ'ze], *v.t.* to sharpen the wits of; to initiate; to seduce. **se déniaiser**, *v.r.* to learn to be sharp, to grow cunning; (*fam.*) to lose one's innocence.
dénicher [deni'ʃe], *v.t.* to take out of the nest; to hunt out, to find out.—*v.i.* to forsake its nest (*of a bird*); to make off, to run away.
dénicheur [deni'ʃœ:r], *n.m.* bird's-nester.
denier [də'nje], *n.m.* (*Rom. Ant.*) denarius; (*Fr. Ant.*) denier; penny; farthing, mite; (*pl.*) state revenues.
dénier [de'nje], *v.t.* to deny, to refuse.
dénigrant [deni'grɑ̃], *a.* disparaging.
dénigrement [denigrə'mɑ̃], *n.m.* disparagement.
dénigrer [deni'gre], *v.t.* to disparage; to vilify.
dénivellation [denivɛllɑ'sjɔ̃], *n.f.*, **dénivellement** [denivɛl'mɑ̃], *n.m.* difference of level; unevenness.
dénombrement [denɔ̃brə'mɑ̃], *n.m.* enumeration; census.
dénombrer [denɔ̃'bre], *v.t.* to number, to enumerate.
dénominateur [denɔmina'tœ:r], *n.m.* (*Arith.*) denominator.
dénomination [denɔminɑ'sjɔ̃], *n.f.* denomination, name.
dénommer [denɔ'me], *v.t.* to designate.
dénoncer [denɔ̃'se], *v.t.* (*conjug. like* COMMENCER) to denounce, to inform against; to give notice of, to declare (*war etc.*). **se dénoncer**, *v.r.* to own up; to give oneself up.
dénonciateur [denɔ̃sja'tœ:r], *n.m.* (*fem.* **-trice**) informer, accuser.
dénonciation [denɔ̃sjɑ'sjɔ̃], *n.f.* denunciation, declaration.
dénoter [denɔ'te], *v.t.* to denote, to betoken.
dénouement or **dénoûment** [denu'mɑ̃], *n.m.* dénouement, unravelling (*esp. of a play etc.*).
dénouer [denu'e], *v.t.* to untie, to loosen; to solve (*difficulties etc.*); to unravel (*plots*). **se dénouer**, *v.r.* to come untied, to be unravelled; to be solved.
denrée [dɑ̃'re], *n.f.* commodity, produce, provisions.
dense [dɑ̃:s], *a.* dense, close, thick.
densité [dɑ̃si'te], *n.f.* density, thickness.
dent [dɑ̃], *n.f.* tooth; fang; notch; cog; prong; ***faire ses dents***, to cut one's teeth.
dentaire [dɑ̃'tɛ:r], *a.* dental.
dental [dɑ̃'tal], *a.* (*m.pl.* **-aux**) (*Phon.*) dental.
dent-de-lion [dɑ̃də'ljɔ̃], *n.m.* (*pl.* **dents-de-lion**) dandelion.
denté [dɑ̃'te], *a.* toothed; (*Bot.*) dentate; ***roue dentée***, cogged wheel.
dentelé [dɑ̃'tle], *a.* notched, denticulated, indented, jagged.
denteler [dɑ̃'tle], *v.t.* (*conjug. like* APPELER) to indent, to notch.
dentelle [dɑ̃'tɛl], *n.f.* lace, lace-work.
dentellier [dɑ̃tɛ'lje], *n.m.* (*fem.* **-ière**) lace-maker.
dentelure [dɑ̃'tly:r], *n.f.* denticulation, indenting; scallop.
denticule [dɑ̃ti'kyl], *n.m.* denticle.
dentier [dɑ̃'tje], *n.m.* set of teeth (*esp. artificial*), denture.
dentifrice [dɑ̃ti'fris], *n.m.* toothpaste.
dentiste [dɑ̃'tist], *n.m.* dentist.
denture [dɑ̃'ty:r], *n.f.* set of teeth; (*Horol.*) teeth of a wheel.
dénudation [denydɑ'sjɔ̃], *n.f.* denudation.
dénuder [deny'de], *v.t.* to denude; to lay bare.
dénuement or **dénûment** [deny'mɑ̃], *n.m.* destitution, penury, want.
dénuer [de'nɥe], *v.t.* to strip, to leave destitute. **se dénuer**, *v.r.* to strip oneself; to leave oneself destitute.
dépannage [depa'na:ʒ], *n.m.* (*Mach., Elec.*) repairing; ***service de dépannage***, breakdown *or* repair service.
dépanner [depa'ne], *v.t.* (*Mach., Elec.*) to repair (*a breakdown*).
dépanneuse [depa'nø:z], *n.f.* breakdown vehicle.
dépaqueter [depak'te], *v.t.* (*conjug. like* APPELER) to unpack.

dépareillé [deparɛ'je], *a.* unmatched, odd.
déparer [depa're], *v.t.* to strip (*of ornaments*); (*fig.*) to mar, to disfigure.
déparier [depa'rje], *v.t.* to take away one (*of a pair*); to separate (*a pair of animals*).
départ [de'pa:r], *n.m.* departure, start, setting out.
départager [departa'ʒe], *v.t.* (*conjug. like* MANGER) to settle by a casting-vote.
département [departə'mɑ̃], *n.m.* department; line, business.
départemental [departəmɑ̃'tal], *a.* (*m. pl.* **-aux**) departmental.
départir [depar'ti:r], *v.t. irr.* (*conjug. like* SENTIR) to separate; to distribute, to divide, to endow, to bestow. **se départir**, *v.r.* to desist; to deviate (*from*).
dépassement [depɑs'mɑ̃], *n.m.* overstepping (*of credit etc.*); (*Motor.*) overtaking.
dépasser [depɑ'se], *v.t.* to go beyond, to pass, to overtake; to exceed, to surpass; to be taller etc. than; to show; ***son jupon dépasse***, her slip is showing.
dépaver [depa've], *v.t.* to unpave, to take up the pavement of.
dépaysé [depei'ze], *a.* away from home, out of one's element.
dépayser [depei'ze], *v.t.* to send away from home; to remove from his natural sphere etc.; (*fig.*) to bewilder. **se dépayser**, *v.r.* to leave one's home; to go abroad; to get out of one's element.
dépècement [depɛs'mɑ̃], **dépeçage** [depə'sa:ʒ], *n.m.* cutting up, carving, dismemberment.
dépecer [dep'se], *v.t.* (*see Verb Tables*) to cut up (*a carcass*), to carve.
dépêche [de'pɛ:ʃ], *n.f.* dispatch (*letter on affairs of State*); communication (*esp. a telegram*).
dépêcher [depɛ'ʃe], *v.t.* to dispatch, to do quickly; to send quickly, to send by messenger; to kill. **se dépêcher**, *v.r.* to hurry, to make haste; ***dépêchez-vous***, hurry up.
dépeigner [depɛ'ɲe], *v.t.* to ruffle (*hair*).
dépeindre [de'pɛ̃:dr], *v.t. irr.* (*conjug. like* CRAINDRE) to depict, to describe; to portray, to paint.
dépelotonner [deplɔtɔ'ne], *v.t.* to unwind. **se dépelotonner**, *v.r.* to come unwound; to uncurl (*of cat*).
dépenaillé [depnɑ'je], *a.* tattered, ragged.
dépendance [depɑ̃'dɑ̃:s], *n.f.* subordination; dependence; appendage, annexe, outhouse, (*pl.*) out-buildings.
dépendant [depɑ̃'dɑ̃], *a.* dependent.
dépendre (1) [de'pɑ̃:dr], *v.t.* to take down; to unhang.
dépendre (2) [de'pɑ̃:dr], *v.i.* to depend, to be dependent (***de***).
dépens [de'pɑ̃], *n.m.* (*used only in pl.*) expense, cost.
dépense [de'pɑ̃:s], *n.f.* expense; expenditure, outlay; waste, flow.
dépenser [depɑ̃'se], *v.t.* to spend, to consume; to waste.
dépensier [depɑ̃'sje], *a.* (*fem.* **-ière**) extravagant.—*n.m.* (*fem.* **-ière**) extravagant person, spend-thrift; bursar.
déperdition [deperdi'sjɔ̃], *n.f.* loss, waste.
dépérir [depe'ri:r], *v.i.* to decline, to pine away, to wither, to dwindle, to waste away.
dépérissement [deperis'mɑ̃], *n.m.* decay, withering, wasting away.
dépêtrer [depɛ'tre], *v.t.* to disentangle, to extricate. **se dépêtrer**, *v.r.* to get clear of.
dépeuplement [depœplə'mɑ̃], *n.m.* depopulation; thinning (*of forests etc.*).
dépeupler [depœ'ple], *v.t.* to depopulate; to thin. **se dépeupler**, *v.r.* to become depopulated, to be unstocked (*of river*).
dépilage [depi'la:ʒ], *n.m.* removal of hairs, bristles, etc. (*from hides etc.*).
dépilation [depilɑ'sjɔ̃], *n.f.* depilation.
dépiquage [depi'ka:ʒ], *n.m.* threshing *or* treading out (*corn etc.*).
dépiquer (1) [depi'ke], *v.t.* to unquilt, to unstitch.
dépiquer (2) [depi'ke], *v.t.* to tread out (*corn*).
dépister [depis'te], *v.t.* to track down; to hunt out; (*fig.*) to throw off the scent.
dépit [de'pi], *n.m.* spite; vexation.
dépiter [depi'te], *v.t.* to vex, to spite. **se dépiter**, *v.r.* to be vexed, to fret.
déplacé [depla'se], *a.* displaced, misplaced, ill-timed, unbecoming.
déplacement [deplas'mɑ̃], *n.m.* removal; displacement; ***frais de déplacement***, travelling expenses.
déplacer [depla'se], *v.t.* (*conjug. like* COMMENCER) to displace; to remove, to change; to misplace. **se déplacer**, *v.r.* to move, to change one's place, to leave one's residence; to be displaced (*of things*).
déplaire [de'plɛ:r], *v.i. irr.* (*conjug. like* PLAIRE) to displease, to offend; to be disagreeable, to give offence. **se déplaire**, *v.r.* to be displeased *or* dissatisfied (*with*).
déplaisant [deplɛ'zɑ̃], *a.* unpleasant, disagreeable.
déplaisir [deple'zi:r], *n.m.* displeasure, annoyance; grief.
déplanter [deplɑ̃'te], *v.t.* to dig *or* take up (*a plant*).
déplantoir [deplɑ̃'twa:r], *n.m.* garden trowel.
dépliant [depli'ɑ̃], *n.m.* folding page; folder, prospectus, leaflet.
déplier [depli'e], *v.t.* to unfold, to open out; to lay out.
déplisser [depli'se], *v.t.* to unpleat. **se déplisser**, *v.r.* to come unpleated; to lose its pleats (*of a skirt etc.*).
déploiement or **déploîment** [deplwa'mɑ̃], *n.m.* unfolding; display, show; (*Mil.*) deployment.
déplombage [deplɔ̃'ba:ʒ], *n.m.* unsealing; unstopping.
déplomber [deplɔ̃'be], *v.t.* to take the custom-house seal off (*goods*); to unstop (*a tooth*).
déplorable [deplɔ'rabl], *a.* deplorable, lamentable.
déplorablement [deplɔrablə'mɑ̃], *adv.* deplorably, wretchedly.
déplorer [deplɔ're], *v.t.* to deplore, to bewail, to lament, to mourn.
déployer [deplwa'je], *v.t.* (*conjug. like* EMPLOYER) to unfold, to unroll, to unfurl, to spread out; to display, to show; (*Mil.*) to deploy; ***à gorge déployée***, at the top of one's voice. **se déployer**, *v.r.* to unroll; to display oneself; (*Mil.*) to deploy.
déplumer [deply'me], *v.t.* to pluck; (*fig.*) to despoil; to tear the hair from. **se déplumer**, *v.r.* to moult, to shed feathers.

dépolariser [depɔlari'ze], *v.t.* to depolarize.

dépolir [depɔ'li:r], *v.t.* to make the surface (*of metal etc.*) dull, to frost (*glass*).

dépopulation [depɔpyla'sjɔ̃], *n.m.* depopulation.

déportation [depɔrta'sjɔ̃], *n.f.* deportation.

déporté [depɔr'te], *n.m.* (*fem.* **-ée**) deported person.

déportements [depɔrtə'mɑ̃], *n.m. pl.* misconduct, evil-doings.

déporter [depɔr'te], *v.t.* to deport, to transport for life; to swerve; to carry away, to drift. **se déporter**, *v.r.* (*Law*) to desist (*from*).

déposant [depo'zɑ̃], *a.* giving evidence; depositing.—*n.m.* (*fem.* **-e**) witness; depositor.

déposer [depo'ze], *v.t.* to lay down *or* aside; to divest oneself of; to depose; to deposit; to lodge (*a complaint etc.*); ***marque déposée***, registered trademark.—*v.i.* to give evidence; to settle, to leave a sediment.

dépositaire [depɔzi'tɛ:r], *n.m.* depositary, trustee; agent.

déposition [depɔzi'sjɔ̃], *n.f.* deposition, evidence.

dépositoire [depɔzi'twa:r], *n.m.* depository, mortuary.

déposséder [depɔse'de], *v.t.* (*conjug. like* CÉDER) to dispossess, to oust.

dépossession [depɔsɛ'sjɔ̃], *n.f.* dispossession, deprivation.

dépôt [de'po], *n.m.* depositing; deposit; sediment; depository, warehouse; (*Mil.*) depot; (*Med.*) tumour, abscess; ***dépôt d'essence***, petrol station; ***en dépôt***, as a deposit in trust, (*Comm.*) on sale; ***mandat de dépôt***, writ of imprisonment.

dépotage [depɔ'ta:ʒ], **dépotement** [depɔt'mɑ̃], *n.m.* unpotting; decanting.

dépoter [depɔ'te], *v.t.* to take out of a pot; to decant.

dépouille [de'pu:j], *n.f.* slough, cast-off skin *or* hide; spoil; remains, wardrobe (*of persons deceased*); (*pl.*) spoils, booty; ***dépouille mortelle***, mortal remains.

dépouillement [depuj'mɑ̃], *n.m.* spoliation, despoiling; scrutiny (*of a ballot-box*); abstract (*of an account*).

dépouiller [depu'je], *v.t.* to strip, to skin; to unclothe; to despoil; to throw off; to cast (*of insects*); to reap (*crops*); to inspect, to count up (*a ballot-box*); to present an abstract (*of accounts*). **se dépouiller**, *v.r.* to shed its skin (*of insects and animals*), to moult; ***se dépouiller de***, to divest oneself of, to strip oneself of, to renounce (*possessions etc.*).

dépourvoir [depur'vwa:r], *v.t. irr.* (*conjug. like* POURVOIR) to leave unprovided (*with*) *or* destitute (*of*). **se dépourvoir**, *v.r.* to leave oneself unequipped.

dépourvu [depur'vy], *a.* destitute, unprovided; ***au dépourvu***, unawares, unexpectedly.

dépravation [deprava'sjɔ̃], *n.f.* vitiation, depravity.

dépravé [depra've], *a.* vitiated, depraved, corrupt.

dépraver [depra've], *v.t.* to deprave, to corrupt, to pervert. **se dépraver**, *v.r.* to become depraved *or* corrupted.

dépréciation [depresjα'sjɔ̃], *n.f.* depreciation.

déprécier [depre'sje], *v.t.* to depreciate, to undervalue, to underrate; to disparage. **se déprécier**, *v.r.* to underrate oneself; to fall in value (*of things*).

déprédateur [depreda'tœ:r], *n.m.* (*fem.* **-trice**) depredator, plunderer.

déprédation [depredα'sjɔ̃], *n.f.* plundering, depredation.

déprendre [de'prɑ̃:dr], *v.t. irr.* (*conjug. like* PRENDRE) to loosen, to detach. **se déprendre**, *v.r.* to get loose; to detach oneself (*de*).

dépression [deprɛ'sjɔ̃], *n.f.* depression, hollow; (*fig.*) recession, slump (*of business*); ***dépression nerveuse***, nervous breakdown.

déprimer [depri'me], *v.t.* to press down, to depress; (*fig.*) to discourage.

depuis [də'pɥi], *prep.* since, for; from, after; ***depuis longtemps***, for a long time; ***depuis peu***, lately; ***depuis quand?*** since when ?—*adv.* since (then), afterwards, since that time.—*conj. phr.* ***depuis que***, since.

députation [depytα'sjɔ̃], *n.f.* deputation; deputyship.

député [depy'te], *n.m.* deputy, delegate; Member of Parliament.

députer [depy'te], *v.t.* to send as representative, to depute.

déracinement [derasin'mɑ̃], *n.m.* uprooting, eradication.

déraciner [derasi'ne], *v.t.* to uproot; to eradicate, to extirpate.

déraidir [derɛ'di:r], *v.t.* to unstiffen; to make pliant. **se déraidir**, *v.r.* to grow soft *or* supple; to unbend.

déraillement [derαj'mɑ̃], *n.m.* derailment.

dérailler [derα'je], *v.i.* to run off the rails.

déraison [derɛ'zɔ̃], *n.f.* unreasonableness, folly.

déraisonnable [derɛzɔ'nabl], *a.* unreasonable, senseless.

déraisonnablement [derɛzɔnablə'mɑ̃], *adv.* unreasonably, irrationally.

déraisonner [derɛzɔ'ne], *v.i.* to reason falsely, to talk nonsense; to rave.

dérangement [derɑ̃ʒ'mɑ̃], *n.m.* derangement; trouble; disorder, disturbance.

déranger [derɑ̃'ʒe], *v.t.* (*conjug. like* MANGER) to derange, to put out of place *or* order; to discompose, to disconcert; to disturb, to upset; to unsettle. **se déranger**, *v.r.* to move; to be deranged, to get out of order; to trouble *or* disturb oneself, to put oneself out.

déraper [dera'pe], *v.i.* to skid, to side-slip (*bicycle, car etc.*).

dératé [dera'te], *n.m.* *only used in* ***courir comme un dératé***, to run like a greyhound.

derechef [dər'ʃɛf], *adv.* over again, afresh, anew.

déréglé [dere'gle], *a.* out of order; irregular; intemperate, (*fig.*) unruly, dissolute.

dérèglement [derɛglə'mɑ̃], *n.m.* irregularity, disorder; dissoluteness, licentiousness.

dérégler [dere'gle], *v.t.* (*conjug. like* CÉDER) to put out of order. **se dérégler**, *v.r.* to get out of order, to be deranged; to lead a disorderly life.

dérider [deri'de], *v.t.* to unwrinkle, to smooth; to brighten, to cheer up. **se dérider**, *v.r.* to smooth one's brow; to cheer up.
dérision [deri'zjɔ̃], *n.f.* derision, mockery, ridicule.
dérisoire [deri'zwaːr], *a.* derisive, mocking.
dérivatif [deriva'tif], *a.* (*fem.* **-tive**) derivative.—*n.m.* (*Med.*) derivative, counter-irritant.
dérivation [derivɑ'sjɔ̃], *n.f.* derivation; diversion (*of water etc.*); (*Elec.*) branching, shunting; (*Naut.*) drift, leeway; (*Av.*) windage; (*Elec.*) ***circuit en dérivation***, branch-circuit.
dérive [de'riːv], *n.f.* (*Naut.*) drift, leeway; (*Av.*) fin.
dérivé [deri've], *a.* drifted.—*n.m.* (*Gram.*) derivative.
dériver [deri've], *v.t.* to divert; to derive.—*v.i.* to be turned from its proper course; (*Naut.*) to drift (*from the shore*), to go adrift.
dermatite [dɛrma'tit], *n.f.* dermatitis.
dernier [dɛr'nje], *a.* (*fem.* **-ière**) last, latest; vilest, meanest; extreme (*highest, greatest etc.*); the one just past; youngest (*of a family of children*).—*n.m.* (*fem.* **-ière**) the last; the highest, lowest etc.
dernièrement [dɛrnjɛr'mɑ̃], *adv.* lately, recently.
dérobé [derɔ'be], *a.* stolen, hidden, secret; ***à la dérobée***, stealthily.
dérober [derɔ'be], *v.t.* to steal; to remove; to conceal; to protect, to screen. **se dérober**, *v.r.* to steal away, to escape, to disappear.
dérogation [derɔgɑ'sjɔ̃], *n.f.* derogation.
dérogatoire [derɔga'twaːr], *a.* derogatory.
déroger [derɔ'ʒe], *v.i.* (*conjug. like* MANGER) to derogate; to detract; to condescend, to stoop.
dérouillement [deruj'mɑ̃], *n.m.* removal of rust.
dérouiller [deru'je], *v.t.* to remove the rust from; (*fig.*) to polish. **se dérouiller**, *v.r.* to lose its *or* one's rust; to brighten up; to read a subject up again.
déroulement [derul'mɑ̃], *n.m.* unrolling, unfolding.
dérouler [deru'le], *v.t.* to unroll; to spread out, to display. **se dérouler**, *v.r.* to unroll; to open to the view; to roll in (*of the waves*); to take place (*of events*).
déroutant [deru'tɑ̃], *a.* baffling, confusing.
déroute [de'rut], *n.f.* rout, overthrow; ruin; disorder, confusion.
dérouter [deru'te], *v.t.* to lead astray; to embarrass, to disconcert; to baffle; to divert (*ship, train etc.*).
derrière [dɛ'rjɛːr], *prep.* behind, on the other side of.—*adv.* behind, after.—*n.m.* back, hinder part; posterior; behind; ***pattes de derrière***, hind legs; ***porte de derrière***, back-door.
derviche [dɛr'viʃ], **dervis** [dɛr'vi], *n.m.* dervish.
des [de], [*contr. of* DE LES].
dès [dɛ], *prep.* from, since, as early as.—*conj. phr.* ***dès que***, when, as soon as, since.
désabonnement [dezabɔn'mɑ̃], *n.m.* withdrawal of subscription.
désabonner (se) [sədezabɔ'ne], *v.r.* to withdraw one's subscription (*to a magazine etc.*).
désabuser [dezaby'ze], *v.t.* to disabuse, to undeceive. **se désabuser**, *v.r.* to be undeceived, to face the facts.
désaccord [deza'kɔːr], *n.m.* disagreement, discord.
désaccorder [dezakɔr'de], *v.t.* to untune; (*fig.*) to set at variance. **se désaccorder**, *v.r.* to get out of tune.
désaccouplement [dezakuplə'mɑ̃], *n.m.* uncoupling.
désaccoupler [dezaku'ple], *v.t.* to uncouple. **se désaccoupler**, *v.r.* to become uncoupled; to come asunder.
désaccoutumer [dezakuty'me], *v.t.* to disaccustom. **se désaccoutumer**, *v.r.* to break oneself of, to lose the habit of.
désaffecter [dezafɛk'te], *v.t.* to secularize (*a church*); (*Mil.*) to transfer; to put a building to another use.
désaffection [dezafɛk'sjɔ̃], *n.f.* loss of affection.
désaffectionner [dezafɛksjɔ'ne], *v.t.* to cause (*someone*) to lose his *or* her affection, to disaffect. **se désaffectionner**, *v.r.* to lose affection.
désagencement [dezaʒɑ̃s'mɑ̃], *n.m.* throwing out of gear.
désagencer [dezaʒɑ̃'se], *v.t.* (*conjug. like* COMMENCER) to throw out of gear, to disarrange.
désagréable [dezagre'abl], *a.* disagreeable, unpleasant.
désagréablement [dezagreablə'mɑ̃], *adv.* disagreeably, unpleasantly.
désagréger [dezagre'ʒe], *v.t.* (*conjug. like* ASSIÉGER) to disaggregate, to break up, to separate.
désagrément [dezagre'mɑ̃], *n.m.* disagreeableness, unpleasantness; annoyance, discomfort.
désaimanter [dezɛmɑ̃'te], *v.t.* to demagnetize.
désajustement [dezaʒystə'mɑ̃], *n.m.* disarrangement, disorder.
désajuster [dezaʒys'te], *v.t.* to disarrange, to disturb, to put out of order. **se désajuster**, *v.r.* to become disarranged, to get out of order.
désaltérant [dezalte'rɑ̃], *a.* thirst-quenching.
désaltérer [dezalte're], *v.t.* (*conjug. like* CÉDER) to quench the thirst of, to refresh. **se désaltérer**, *v.r.* to quench one's thirst.
désamorcer [dezamɔr'se], *v.t.* (*conjug. like* COMMENCER) to unprime, to uncap (*fire-arms etc.*). **se désamorcer**, *v.r.* to run down (*dynamo*); to run dry (*pump*).
désappointement [dezapwɛ̃t'mɑ̃], *n.m.* disappointment.
désappointer [dezapwɛ̃'te], *v.t.* to disappoint.
désapprendre [deza'prɑ̃ːdr], *v.t. irr.* (*conjug. like* PRENDRE) to unlearn, to forget.
désapprobateur [dezaprɔba'tœːr], *a.* (*fem.* **-trice**) disapproving, censuring, carping.—*n.m.* (*fem.* **-trice**) censurer, fault-finder.
désapprobation [dezaprɔbɑ'sjɔ̃], *n.f.* disapprobation, disapproval.
désappropriation [dezaprɔpriɑ'sjɔ̃], *n.f.* renunciation (*of property*).
désapprouver [dezapru've], *v.t.* to disapprove of, to blame.

désarçonner [dezarsɔ'ne], *v.t.* to unhorse; (*fig.*) to baffle, to floor.
désarmement [dezarmə'mɑ̃], *n.m.* disarming, disarmament; (*Naut.*) laying up.
désarmer [dezar'me], *v.t.* to disarm, to unarm; (*fig.*) to appease, to calm; to uncock (*a gun*); (*Naut.*) to lay up (*a vessel*).—*v.i.* to disarm; to give up maintaining troops.
désarroi [deza'rwɑ], *n.m.* disorder, disarray, confusion.
désarticulation [dezartikylɑ'sjɔ̃], *n.f.* disarticulation.
désarticuler [dezartiky'le], *v.t.* to disarticulate, to disjoint.
désassemblage [dezasɑ̃'blaːʒ], **désassemblement** [dezasɑ̃blə'mɑ̃], *n.m.* dismantling.
désassembler [dezasɑ̃'ble], *v.t.* to take to pieces, to separate, to dismantle.
désassocier [dezasɔ'sje], *v.t.* to disassociate, to dissociate.
désassortiment [dezasɔrti'mɑ̃], *n.m.* unmatching, ill-assortment; unstocking.
désastre [de'zastr], *n.m.* disaster.
désastreusement [dezastrøz'mɑ̃], *adv.* disastrously.
désastreux [dezas'trø], *a.* (*fem.* **-euse**) disastrous, unfortunate, very sad.
désavantage [dezavɑ̃'taːʒ], *n.m.* disadvantage; detriment, prejudice; drawback, handicap.
désavantager [dezavɑ̃ta'ʒe], *v.t.* (*conjug. like* MANGER) to disadvantage, to handicap.
désavantageusement [dezavɑ̃taʒøz'mɑ̃], *adv.* disadvantageously; disparagingly.
désavantageux [dezavɑ̃ta'ʒø], *a.* (*fem.* **-euse**) disadvantageous; detrimental, prejudicial, unfavourable.
désaveu [deza'vø], *n.m.* (*pl.* **-eux**) disavowal; denial; retractation.
désavouer [deza'vwe], *v.t.* to disown, to disclaim, to disavow; to retract.
désaxé [deza'kse], *a.* offset, out of true (*of a wheel, etc.*); (*fig.*) out of joint.
descellement [desɛl'mɑ̃], *n.m.* loosening, unsealing.
desceller [desɛ'le], *v.t.* to unseal; to loosen (*masonry etc.*). **se desceller**, *v.r.* to become loose *or* unsealed.
descendance [desɑ̃'dɑ̃ːs], *n.f.* descent, lineage.
descendant [desɑ̃'dɑ̃], *a.* descending, going down; (*Mil.*) coming off duty.—*n.m.* (*fem.* **-e**) descendant, offspring, issue.
descendre [de'sɑ̃ːdr], *v.t.* (*with aux.* AVOIR) to take down, bring *or* let down; to go *or* come down (*a staircase etc.*); to set down (*of a cab etc.*); to land.—*v.i.* (*with aux.* ÊTRE) to descend, to go down; to go downstairs; to alight, to land; to slope, to incline; to fall, to subside.
descente [de'sɑ̃ːt], *n.f.* descent; taking down; subsidence (*of waters etc.*); dismounting; disembarkation; declivity; raid; (*pop.*) rupture; ***descente de lit***, bedside rug; ***descente de bain***, bath-mat.
descriptif [deskrip'tif], *a.* (*fem.* **-tive**) descriptive.
description [deskrip'sjɔ̃], *n.f.* description; inventory.
désemballage [dezɑ̃ba'laːʒ], *n.m.* unpacking.
désemballer [dezɑ̃ba'le], *v.t.* to unpack.
désembarquement [dezɑ̃barkə'mɑ̃], *n.m.* disembarkation, landing.
désembarquer [dezɑ̃bar'ke], *v.t.* to disembark, to land; to unship, to unload.
désemboîter [dezɑ̃bwa'te], *v.t.* to dislocate. **se désemboîter**, *v.r.* to become disjointed.
désembourber [dezɑ̃bur'be], *v.t.* to draw out of the mire.
désemparé [dezɑ̃pa're], *a.* in distress, helpless.
désemparer [dezɑ̃pa're], *v.t.* (*Naut.*) to disable.—*v.i.* to quit, to go away; ***sans désemparer***, on the spot, at once.
désempeser [dezɑ̃pə'ze], *v.t.* (*conjug. like* AMENER) to unstarch. **se désempeser**, *v.r.* to become limp.
désemplir [dezɑ̃'pliːr], *v.t.* to make less full, to empty in part.—*v.i.* to become less full (*used only in negative*). **se désemplir**, *v.r.* to become less full.
désenchaîner [dezɑ̃ʃɛ'ne], *v.t.* to unchain.
désenchantement [dezɑ̃ʃɑ̃t'mɑ̃], *n.m.* disenchantment, disillusion.
désenchanter [dezɑ̃ʃɑ̃'te], *v.t.* to disenchant, to disillusion.
désenchanteur [dezɑ̃ʃɑ̃'tœːr], *a.* (*fem.* **-eresse**) disenchanting.
désencombrement [dezɑ̃kɔ̃brə'mɑ̃], *n.m.* disencumbrance; dispersal.
désencombrer [dezɑ̃kɔ̃'bre], *v.t.* to disencumber, to clear (*a road etc.*).
désenfiler [dezɑ̃fi'le], *v.t.* to unthread, to unstring. **se désenfiler**, *v.r.* to come unthreaded *or* unstrung.
désenfler [dezɑ̃'fle], *v.t.* to reduce the swelling of.—*v.i.* and **se désenfler**, *v.r.* to become less swollen.
désenflure [dezɑ̃'flyːr], *n.f.*, **désenflement** [dezɑ̃flə'mɑ̃], *n.m.* diminution *or* disappearance of a swelling.
désengager [dezɑ̃ga'ʒe], *v.t.* (*conjug. like* MANGER) to disengage, to release from an engagement.
désengrener [dezɑ̃grə'ne], *v.t.* (*conjug. like* AMENER) to throw out of gear.
désenivrer [dezɑ̃ni'vre], *v.t.*, to make sober again.—*v.i.* to sober. **se désenivrer**, *v.r.* to become sober (*again*), to sober up.
désenlaidir [dezɑ̃lɛ'diːr], *v.t.* to render less ugly.—*v.i.* to become less ugly.
désennuyer [dezɑ̃nɥi'je], *v.t.* (*conjug. like* EMPLOYER) to enliven, to cheer. **se désennuyer**, *v.r.* to find amusement, to kill time.
désenrayer [dezɑ̃rɛ'je], *v.t.* (*conjug. like* PAYER) to unlock *or* unskid (*a wheel etc.*).
désenrhumer [dezɑ̃ry'me], *v.t.* to cure (*someone*) of a cold. **se désenrhumer**, *v.r.* to get rid of a cold.
désenrôlement [dezɑ̃rol'mɑ̃], *n.m.* (*Mil.*) discharge.
désenrôler [dezɑ̃ro'le], *v.t.* to discharge.
désensevelir [dezɑ̃sə'vliːr], *v.t.* to unshroud; to exhume.
désensevelissement [dezɑ̃səvlis'mɑ̃], *n.m.* unshrouding, exhumation, disinterment.
désentortiller [dezɑ̃tɔrti'je], *v.t.* to untwist to unravel.
désentraver [dezɑ̃tra've], *v.t.* to untrammel, to unhobble (*a horse etc.*).
déséquilibre [dezeki'libr], *n.m.* lack of balance, unbalance; imbalance.

déséquilibré [dezekili'bre], *a.* and *n.m.* (*fem.* **-ée**) unbalanced (person).
déséquilibrer [dezekili'bre], *v.t.* to unbalance.
désert [de'zɛːr], *a.* uninhabited, solitary; wild, waste, deserted.—*n.m.* desert, wilderness; solitary place; (*C*) clearing in a forest.
déserter [dezɛrte], *v.t.* to desert, to abandon, to forsake; to quit, to leave; (*C*) to clear land, to break up (*ground*) for tillage.—*v.i.* to desert, to go over to the enemy.
déserteur [dezɛr'tœːr], *n.m.* deserter.
désertion [dezɛr'sjɔ̃], *n.f.* desertion.
désespérance [dezɛspe'rɑ̃ːs], *n.f.* despair.
désespérant [dezɛspe'rɑ̃], *a.* desperate, hopeless; disheartening, distressing.
désespéré [dezɛspe're], *a.* hopeless, desperate; disconsolate.—*n.m.* (*fem.* **-ée**) person in despair; madman, madwoman.
désespérément [dezɛspere'mɑ̃], *adv.* desperately, despairingly.
désespérer [dezɛspe're], *v.t.* (*conjug. like* CÉDER) to drive to despair; to dishearten; to distress.—*v.i.* to despair. **se désespérer**, *v.r.* to be in despair.
désespoir [dezɛs'pwaːr], *n.m.* despair, hopelessness, despondency, grief; ***en désespoir de cause***, as a last resource.
déshabiliter [dezabili'te], *v.t.* to disqualify.
déshabillé [dezabi'je], *n.m.* deshabille, undress; ***en déshabillé***, partly *or* scantily dressed.
déshabiller [dezabi'je], *v.t.* to undress, to strip. **se déshabiller**, *v.r.* to undress oneself.
déshabituer [dezabi'tɥe], *v.t.* to disaccustom, to break off. **se déshabituer**, *v.r.* to lose the habit of; to break oneself of.
déshérence [deze'rɑ̃ːs], *n.f.* (*Law*) escheat.
déshériter [dezeri'te], *v.t.* to disinherit.
déshonnête [dezɔ'nɛːt], *a.* immodest, indecent, unseemly.
déshonnêtement [dezɔnɛt'mɑ̃], *adv.* indecently, immodestly.
déshonnêteté [dezɔnɛt'te], *n.f.* indecency, unseemliness.
déshonneur [dezɔ'nœːr], *n.m.* dishonour, disgrace, shame.
déshonorable [dezɔnɔ'rabl], *a.* dishonourable.
déshonorablement [dezɔnɔrablə'mɑ̃], *adv.* dishonourably.
déshonorant [dezɔnɔ'rɑ̃], *a.* dishonourable, disgraceful.
déshonorer [dezɔnɔ're], *v.t.* to dishonour, to disgrace. **se déshonorer**, *v.r.* to dishonour *or* disgrace oneself.
déshydrater [dezidra'te], *v.t.* to dehydrate.
désignatif [deziɲa'tif], *a.* (*fem.* **-tive**) indicative.
désignation [deziɲɑ'sjɔ̃], *n.f.* designation, indication.
désigner [dezi'ɲe], *v.t.* to designate, to denote; to appoint, to nominate, to point out; (*Mil.*) to detail.
désillusion [dezily'zjɔ̃], *n.f.*, **désillusionnement** [dezilyzjɔn'mɑ̃], *n.m.* disillusion.
désillusionner [dezilyzjɔ'ne], *v.t.* to disillusion, to disappoint.
désinfectant [dezɛ̃fɛk'tɑ̃], *a.* disinfecting.—*n.m.* disinfectant.
désinfecter [dezɛ̃fɛk'te], *v.t.* to disinfect, to decontaminate.
désinfection [dezɛ̃fɛk'sjɔ̃], *n.f.* disinfection.
désintégration [dezɛ̃tegrɑ'sjɔ̃], *n.f.* disintegration; fission.
désintégrer [dezɛ̃te'gre], *v.t.* (*conjug. like* CÉDER) to disintegrate; to split (*atom*).
désintéressé [dezɛ̃terɛ'se], *a.* disinterested, unselfish, unbiased.
désintéressement [dezɛ̃terɛs'mɑ̃], *n.m.* disinterestedness.
désintéresser [dezɛ̃terɛ'se], *v.t.* to indemnify.
désinvestir [desɛ̃vɛs'tiːr], *v.t.* (*Mil.*) to raise the siege of.
désinvolte [dezɛ̃'vɔlt], *a.* free, easy; offhand.
désinvolture [dezɛ̃vɔl'tyːr], *n.f.* casual, easy bearing *or* gait; offhandedness.
désir [de'ziːr], *n.m.* desire, wish, longing.
désirable [dezi'rabl], *a.* desirable.
désirer [dezi're], *v.t.* to desire, to wish for, to long for, to want.
désireux [dezi'rø], *a.* (*fem.* **-euse**) desirous, anxious, eager (*to*).
désistement [dezistə'mɑ̃], *n.m.* desistance, withdrawal.
désister (se) [sədezis'te], *v.r.* to desist from, to renounce, to withdraw.
désobéir [dezɔbe'iːr], *v.i.* to disobey.
désobéissance [dezɔbei'sɑ̃ːs], *n.f.* disobedience.
désobéissant [dezɔbei'sɑ̃], *a.* disobedient.
désobligeamment [dezɔbliʒa'mɑ̃], *adv.* disobligingly; unkindly.
désobligeance [dezɔbli'ʒɑ̃ːs], *n.f.* lack of complaisance; unkindness.
désobligeant [dezɔbli'ʒɑ̃], *a.* disobliging; uncivil.
désobliger [dezɔbli'ʒe], *v.t.* (*conjug. like* MANGER) to disoblige, to displease.
désodorisant [dezɔdɔri'zɑ̃], *a.* and *n.m.* deodorant.
désœuvré [dezœ'vre], *a.* unoccupied, idle.
désœuvrement [dezœvrə'mɑ̃], *n.m.* want of occupation, idleness.
désolant [dezɔ'lɑ̃], *a.* grievous, distressing.
désolation [dezɔlɑ'sjɔ̃], *n.f.* desolation, ruin; deep affliction, grief.
désolé [dezɔ'le], *a.* afflicted, broken-hearted; very sorry, grieved; dreary, desolate (*place*).
désoler [dezɔ'le], *v.t.* to devastate, to desolate, to lay waste; to afflict, to grieve; to annoy, to torment. **se désoler**, *v.r.* to grieve, to be disconsolate.
désolidariser [desɔlidari'ze], *v.t.* to break the ties which keep together (*a party, friends etc.*).
désopilant [dezɔpi'lɑ̃], *a.* very funny, side-splitting.
désopiler [dezɔpi'le], *v.t.* (*Med.*) to clear of obstruction; (*fig.*) to cheer up, to enliven.
désordonné [dezɔrdɔ'ne], *a.* disorderly; (*fig.*) dissolute, unruly; inordinate.
désordonner [dezɔrdɔ'ne], *v.t.* to disturb; to throw into confusion.
désordre [de'zɔrdr], *n.m.* disorder, confusion; disorderly life; perturbation; (*pl.*) disturbances, riots.
désorganisation [dezɔrganizɑ'sjɔ̃], *n.f.* disorganization.
désorganiser [dezɔrgani'ze], *v.t.* to disorganize. **se désorganiser**, *v.r.* to become disorganized.

désorienter [dezɔrjɑ̃'te], *v.t.* to lead astray, to mislead, to bewilder; to put out, to disconcert.

désormais [dezɔr'mɛ], *adv.* henceforth, hereafter.

désossé [dezɔ'se], *a.* boneless, flabby.

désosser [dezɔ'se], *v.t.* to bone. **se désosser**, *v.r.* to become disjointed, limp, flabby etc.

despote [dɛs'pɔt], *n.m.* despot.

despotique [dɛspɔ'tik], *a.* despotic.

despotiquement [dɛspɔtik'mɑ̃], *adv.* despotically.

despotisme [dɛspɔ'tism], *n.m.* despotism.

desquels [de'kɛl], *m.pl.* (*fem.* **-elles**) [DUQUEL].

dessaisir [desɛ'zi:r], *v.t.* to let go; to dispossess. **se dessaisir**, *v.r.* to give up, to part with.

dessaisissement [desɛzis'mɑ̃], *n.m.* parting with, abandonment.

dessalé [desa'le], *a.* unsalted, free from salt; (*fam.*) sharp.—*n.m.* (*fem.* **-ée**) sharp person.

dessaler [desa'le], *v.t.* to remove salt from (*meat etc.*); (*fig.*) to make sharp, cunning etc.

dessangler [desɑ̃'gle], *v.t.* to loosen the girth of (*a horse etc.*).

desséchant [dese'ʃɑ̃], *a.* drying, parching.

dessèchement [desɛʃ'mɑ̃], *n.m.* drying up; dryness.

dessécher [dese'ʃe], *v.t.* to dry up; to parch; (*fig.*) to wither (*the heart etc.*); to emaciate. **se dessécher**, *v.r.* to become dry, to dry up; (*fig.*) to wither, to waste away.

dessein [de'sɛ̃], *n.m.* design, plan, scheme; intention, resolution.

desseller [desɛ'le], *v.t.* to unsaddle.

desserrer [desɛ're], *v.t.* to loosen, to relax; to ease. **se desserrer**, *v.r.* to become loose, to relax.

dessert [de'sɛ:r], *n.m.* dessert.

desserte [de'sɛrt], *n.f.* leavings, remains (*of a meal*); small sideboard; parochial duty; railway service.

desservant [desɛr'vɑ̃], *n.m.* officiating minister (*of a parish etc.*).

desservir [desɛr'vi:r], *v.t. irr.* (*conjug. like* SENTIR) to clear (*a table*); to officiate (*of clergymen*); to ply between (*of boats etc.*); (*fig.*) to do someone a disservice.

dessiller or **déciller** [desi'je], *v.t.* to open (*someone's eyes*); to undeceive.

dessin [de'sɛ̃], *n.m.* drawing; sketch; pattern, design; ***dessin animé***, (*Cine.*) cartoon.

dessinateur [desina'tœ:r], *n.m.* (*fem.* **-trice**) draughtsman; designer.

dessiner [desi'ne], *v.t.* to draw, to sketch; to set off, to indicate; to lay out. **se dessiner**, *v.r.* to be delineated, to be visible, to stand out.

dessous [də'su], *adv.* under, underneath, below.—*n.m.* lower part; under, hidden *or* wrong side; worst; lee (*of the wind*); (*pl.*) underclothing (*of women*).—*prep. phr.* ***au-dessous de***, beneath.

dessus [də'sy], *adv.* on, upon, over, above; ***là-dessus***, thereupon; ***par-dessus***, over, besides; ***sens dessus dessous***, upside down.—*n.m.* top, upper part; right side; upper hand, advantage.—*prep. phr.* ***au-dessus de***, above.

destin [dɛs'tɛ̃], *n.m.* destiny, fate; career.

destinataire [dɛstina'tɛ:r], *n.* addressee; recipient; (*Comm.*) consignee; payee.

destination [dɛstinɑ'sjɔ̃], *n.f.* destination; object, end.

destinée [dɛsti'ne], *n.f.* fate, destiny, doom.

destiner [dɛsti'ne], *v.t.* to destine, to purpose; to reserve (*for a particular fate etc.*). **se destiner**, *v.r.* to be destined.

destituer [dɛsti'tɥe], *v.t.* to dismiss, to discharge.

destitution [dɛstity'sjɔ̃], *n.f.* dismissal, removal (*from office*).

destroyer [dɛstrwa'jœ:r], *n.m.* (*Navy*) destroyer.

destructeur [dɛstryk'tœ:r], *a.* (*fem.* **-trice**) destructive, deadly, ruinous.—*n.m.* (*fem.* **-trice**) ravager, spoiler.

destructif [dɛstryk'tif], *a.* (*fem.* **-tive**) destructive, destroying.

destruction [dɛstryk'sjɔ̃], *n.f.* destruction.

désuet [desɥ'ɛ], *a.* (*fem.* **-ète**) obsolete, out-of-date.

désuétude [desɥe'tyd], *n.f.* disuse, desuetude.

désunion [dezy'njɔ̃], *n.f.* disunion; disjunction.

désunir [dezy'ni:r], *v.t.* to disunite, to disjoin, to part. **se désunir**, *v.r.* to disunite, to come asunder.

détachage [deta'ʃa:ʒ], *n.m.* cleaning, scouring.

détachant [deta'ʃɑ̃], *n.m.* cleaner, stain-remover.

détachement [detaʃ'mɑ̃], *n.m.* indifference, unconcern; (*Mil.*) detachment, draft.

détacher (1) [deta'ʃe], *v.t.* to remove stains, spots etc.

détacher (2) [deta'ʃe], *v.t.* to detach, to untie, to unfasten, to undo; to cut off; (*Mil.*) to detail. **se détacher**, *v.r.* to come unfastened, to come undone; to disengage oneself; to break away; to stand out clearly.

détail [de'ta:j], *n.m.* detail, small matter, trifle; retail.

détaillant [deta'jɑ̃], *n.m.* (*fem.* **-e**) retailer, small dealer.

détailler [deta'je], *v.t.* to cut in pieces; to retail; to relate minutely.

détaxation [detaksɑ'sjɔ̃], *n.f.* decontrol (*of prices*).

détaxer [detak'se], *v.t.* to reduce *or* take off a tax; to decontrol.

détecter [detɛk'te], *v.t.* to detect.

détecteur [detɛk'tœ:r], *n.m.* detector.

détection [detɛk'sjɔ̃], *n.f.* detection.

détective [detɛk'ti:v], *n.m.* detective.

déteindre [de'tɛ̃:dr], *v.t. irr.* (*conjug. like* CRAINDRE) to take the dye *or* colour out of.—*v.i.* to lose colour, to run, to fade.

dételage [de'tla:ʒ], *n.m.* unharnessing.

dételer [de'tle], *v.t.* (*conjug. like* APPELER) to unharness, to unyoke.

détendre [de'tɑ̃:dr], *v.t.* to slacken, to relax; to reduce the pressure of; to take down. **se détendre**, *v.r.* to slacken, to unbend, to become easier, to relax.

détenir [det'ni:r], *v.t. irr.* (*conjug. like* TENIR) to detain, to withhold; to confine.

détente [de'tɑ̃:t], *n.f.* trigger (*of a gun etc.*); cut-off (*of an engine*); relaxation, easing.

détenteur [detɑ̃'tœ:r], *n.m.* (*fem.* **-trice**) holder, detainer.

détention [detɑ̃'sjɔ̃], *n.f.* detention; imprisonment.
détenu [det'ny], *a.* detained, imprisoned.—*n.m.* (*fem.* **-e**) prisoner.
détergent [detɛr'ʒɑ̃], *a.* (*Med.*) detergent.—*n.m.* detergent.
déterger [detɛr'ʒe], *v.t.* (*conjug. like* MANGER) to cleanse, to purify.
détérioration [deterjɔrɑ'sjɔ̃], *n.f.* deterioration; wear and tear.
détériorer [deterjɔ're], *v.t.* to impair, to make worse. **se détériorer**, *v.r.* to deteriorate.
déterminable [detɛrmi'nabl], *a.* determinable.
déterminant [detɛrmi'nɑ̃], *a.* determinative, decisive.—*n.m.* (*Math.*) determinant.
détermination [detɛrminɑ'sjɔ̃], *n.f.* determination, resolution.
déterminé [detɛrmi'ne], *a.* determined, decided, fixed; resolute, firm.
déterminer [detɛrmi'ne], *v.t.* to determine, to settle; to ascertain; to decide; to cause to take a resolution. **se déterminer**, *v.r.* to resolve, to determine.
déterré [detɛ're], *n.m.* exhumed body.
déterrer [detɛ're], *v.t.* to dig up, to disinter; to unearth, to bring to light.
détestable [detɛs'tabl], *a.* detestable, hateful, odious; wretched.
détestablement [detɛstablə'mɑ̃], *adv.* detestably, abominably.
détestation [detɛstɑ'sjɔ̃], *n.f.* detestation, abhorrence.
détester [detɛs'te], *v.t.* to detest, to hate.
détirer [deti're], *v.t.* to draw out, to stretch.
détisser [deti'se], *v.t.* to unweave.
détonateur [detɔna'tœ:r], *n.m.* detonator.
détonation [detɔnɑ'sjɔ̃], *n.f.* detonation, report.
détoner [detɔ'ne], *v.t., v.i.* to detonate.
détonneler [detɔn'le], *v.t.* (*conjug. like* APPELER) to draw from a cask.
détonner [detɔ'ne], *v.i.* to be out of tune; to jar.
détordre [de'tɔrdr], *v.t.* to untwist; to unravel. **se détordre**, *v.r.* to come untwisted.
détors [de'tɔ:r], *a.* untwisted.
détortiller [detɔrti'je], *v.t.* to untwist; to unravel. **se détortiller**, *v.r.* to become untwisted; to be unravelled.
détour [de'tu:r], *n.m.* turning, change of direction; roundabout way; (*fig.*) shift, evasion, trick.
détourné [detur'ne], *a.* out of the way, unfrequented; indirect.
détournement [deturnə'mɑ̃], *n.m.* turning aside; (*Av.*) hijacking; embezzlement; ***détournement de mineur***, (*Law*) abduction.
détourner [detur'ne], *v.t.* to turn away; to lead astray; (*Av.*) to divert; to hijack; to ward off; to embezzle; to deter.—*v.i.* to turn, to turn off. **se détourner**, *v.r.* to turn aside; to abandon (*de*).
détracteur [detrak'tœ:r], *a.* (*fem.* **-trice**) detractive, detracting.—*n.m.* (*fem.* **-trice**) detractor, disparager.
détraqué [detra'ke], *a.* out of order; deranged, (*colloq.*) crazy.—*n.m.* (*fem.* **-ée**) person shattered in mind *or* body.
détraquement [detrak'mɑ̃], *n.m.* breakdown (*of mechanism, mind, health*).
détraquer [detra'ke], *v.t.* to spoil (*a horse's*) paces; (*fig.*) to put out of order. **se détraquer**, *v.r.* to lose its paces (*of a horse*); (*fig.*) to be disordered.
détrempe [de'trɑ̃:p], *n.f.* distemper (*paint*).
détremper [detrɑ̃'pe], *v.t.* to dilute, to dissolve.
détresse [de'trɛs], *n.f.* distress, grief, trouble.
détresser [detrɛ'se], *v.t.* to unravel; to unplait.
détriment [detri'mɑ̃], *n.m.* detriment, injury prejudice.
détritus [detri'tys], *n.m.* residue, refuse; offal.
détroit [de'trwɑ], *n.m.* strait, channel, sound, narrow firth.
détromper [detrɔ̃'pe], *v.t.* to undeceive. **se détromper**, *v.r.* to be undeceived.
détrônement [detron'mɑ̃], *n.m.* dethronement.
détrôner [detro'ne], *v.t.* to dethrone.
détrousser [detru'se], *v.t.* to untruss, to let down; (*fig.*) to rob.
détrousseur [detru'sœ:r], *n.m.* (*fem.* **-euse**) highwayman, robber.
détruire [de'trɥi:r], *v.t. irr.* (*conjug. like* CONDUIRE) to destroy, to demolish, to ruin; to exterminate, to do away with, to efface, to suppress. **se détruire**, *v.r.* to fall into ruin *or* decay; to destroy each other.
dette [dɛt], *n.f.* debt; obligation.
deuil [dœ:j], *n.m.* mourning; grief, sorrow; gloom; period of mourning; bereavement; mourning clothes; funeral cortège.
Deutéronome [døterɔ'nɔm], *n.m.* Deuteronomy.
deux [dø], *a.* two, both; second.—*n.m.* two; second (*of the month*); (*Cards, Dice etc.*) deuce.
deuxième [dø'zjɛm], *a.* second.—*n.m.* second; second floor.
deuxièmement [døzjɛm'mɑ̃], *adv.* secondly.
deux-pièces [dø'pjɛs], *n.m. inv.* (*women's*) two-piece (*suit*).
deux-points [dø'pwɛ̃], *n.m. inv.* (*Print.*) colon.
dévaler [deva'le], *v.t.* to descend; to lower.—*v.i.* to descend, to slope; to go *or* rush down (*of streams etc.*).
dévaliser [devali'ze], *v.t.* to rifle, to strip, to rob.
dévaliseur [devali'zœ:r], *n.m.* (*fem.* **-euse**) thief, burglar.
dévaluation [devalɥɑ'sjɔ̃], *n.f.* devaluation.
dévaluer [deva'lɥe], *v.t.* to devalue.
devancer [dəvɑ̃'se], *v.t.* (*conjug. like* COMMENCER) to precede; to outstrip; to forestall, to anticipate; to surpass.
devancier [dəvɑ̃'sje], *n.m.* (*fem.* **-ière**) predecessor; (*pl.*) ancestors, forefathers.
devant [də'vɑ̃], *prep.* before; in front of, over against.—*adv.* in front, ahead.—*n.m.* front, forepart.
devanture [dəvɑ̃'ty:r], *n.f.* front(age) (*of a building*); shop-front.
dévaser [devɑ'ze], *v.t.* to dredge.
dévastateur [devasta'tœ:r], *a.* (*fem.* **-trice**) devastating, destructive.—*n.m.* (*fem.* **-trice**) devastator.

dévastation [devastɑ'sjɔ̃], *n.f.* devastation, ravage, havoc.
dévaster [devas'te], *v.t.* to devastate, to lay waste.
développement [devlɔp'mɑ̃], *n.m.* unfolding, opening; development, progress; (*Mil.*) deployment.
développer [devlɔ'pe], *v.t.* to open, to unwrap; to expand, to explain; to develop. **se développer**, *v.r.* to expand, to unfold; to be unravelled; to extend; to develop.
devenir [dəv'ni:r], *v.i. irr.* (*conjug. like* TENIR) to become, to grow, to get, to turn into.—*n.m.* gradual development (*of beings* or *of things*).
dévergondage [devɛrgɔ̃'da:ʒ], *n.m.* shamelessness; profligacy, dissoluteness.
dévergonder (se) [sədevɛrgɔ̃'de], *v.r.* to become dissolute.
déverrouillement [devɛruj'mɑ̃], *n.m.* unbolting.
déverrouiller [devɛru'je], *v.t.* to unbolt; (*fig.*) to set free.
devers [də'vɛ:r], *prep.* towards; ***par devers,*** in the presence of.
dévers [de'vɛ:r], *a.* inclined; out of alignment. —*n.m.* inclination; warping.
déverser [devɛr'se], *v.t.* to bend; to dump; to pour out (*water etc.*).—*v.i.* to lean, to jut out; to warp. **se déverser**, *v.r.* to empty (*of rivers, canals etc.*).
déversoir [devɛr'swa:r], *n.m.* overflow (*of a canal etc.*), outfall.
dévêtir [devɛ'ti:r], *v.t. irr.* (*conjug. like* VÊTIR) to undress, to strip of clothes; (*Law*) to divest. **se dévêtir**, *v.r.* to take off one's clothes, to undress.
déviation [devjɑ'sjɔ̃], *n.f.* deviation, curvature; diversion (*of a road*).
déviationnisme [devjasjɔ'nism], *n.m.* (*Polit.*) deviationism.
déviationniste [devjasjɔ'nist], *n.* deviationist.
dévidage [devi'da:ʒ], *n.m.* winding *or* reeling off.
dévider [devi'de], *v.t.* to wind off (*into skeins etc.*); (*fig.*) to explain.
dévideur [devi'dœ:r], *n.m.* (*fem.* **-euse**) winder, reeler.
dévidoir [devi'dwa:r], *n.m.* reel, skein-winder, spool.
dévier [de'vje], *v.i.* and **se dévier**, *v.r.* to deviate; to swerve.
devin [də'vɛ̃], *n.m.* (*fem.* **devineresse**) diviner, augur; fortune-teller.
deviner [dəvi'ne], *v.t.* to divine, to predict; to guess. **se deviner**, *v.r.* to understand each other.
devinette [dəvi'nɛt], *n.f.* poser, riddle, conundrum.
devineur [dəvi'nœ:r], *n.m.* (*fem.* **-euse**) guesser.
devis [də'vi], *n.m.* estimate; specification.
dévisager [deviza'ʒe], *v.t.* (*conjug. like* MANGER) to disfigure; to stare out.
devise [də'vi:z], *n.f.* device, emblem; motto, slogan; (*Fin.*) currency; ***des devises étrangères***, foreign currency.
deviser [dəvi'ze], *v.i.* to talk casually, to chat.
dévissage [devi'sa:ʒ], **dévissement** [devis'mɑ̃], *n.m.* unscrewing.
dévisser [devi'se], *v.t.* to unscrew. **se dévisser**, *v.r.* to come unscrewed.

dévitaliser [devitali'ze], *v.t.* to kill the nerve (*of a tooth etc.*).
dévoiement [devwɑ'mɑ̃], *n.m.* looseness (*of the bowels*); (*Arch.*) inclination, slope; (*fig.*) departure from the normal path.
dévoilement [devwal'mɑ̃], *n.m.* unveiling, disclosure.
dévoiler [devwa'le], *v.t.* to unveil, to reveal, to disclose. **se dévoiler**, *v.r.* to be revealed.
dévoîment [DÉVOIEMENT].
devoir [də'vwa:r], *v.t. irr.* to owe (*money, gratitude*); to be obliged to, to be bound to, to have to, must. **se devoir**, *v.r.* to owe oneself; to owe it to oneself.—*n.m.* duty; (*Sch.*) work set, homework; (*pl.*) respects, compliments.
dévoltage [devɔl'ta:ʒ], *n.m.* (*Elec.*) reduction of voltage.
dévolter [devɔl'te], *v.t.* to reduce the voltage, to step down (*current*).
dévolteur [devɔl'tœ:r], *n.m.* reducing transformer.
dévolu [devɔ'ly], *a.* (*Law*) devolved, vested.—*n.m.* choice, preference.
dévolution [devɔly'sjɔ̃], *n.f.* devolution; escheat.
dévorant [devɔ'rɑ̃], *a.* devouring, ravenous; (*fig.*) wasting.
dévorateur [devɔra'tœ:r], *a.* (*fem.* **-trice**) devouring.—*n.m.* (*fem.* **-trice**) devourer, destroyer.
dévorer [devɔ're], *v.t.* to devour; to destroy; to squander; to gaze at eagerly.
dévot [de'vo], *a.* devout, pious; sanctimonious; holy (*of books etc.*).—*n.m.* (*fem.* **-e**) devout person, devotee; bigot.
dévotement [devɔt'mɑ̃], *adv.* devoutly, piously.
dévotion [devo'sjɔ̃], *n.f.* devotion, piety; disposal; devoutness.
dévouement or **dévoûment** [devu'mɑ̃], *n.m.* self-sacrifice; devotion, devotedness; zeal.
dévouer [de'vwe], *v.t.* to devote, to dedicate. **se dévouer**, *v.r.* to devote oneself; to dedicate oneself.
dévoyé [devwa'je], *a.* stray, gone astray.—*n.m.* (*fem.* **-ée**) (*fig.*) black sheep.
dévoyer [devwa'je], *v.t.* (*conjug. like* EMPLOYER) to corrupt, to lead astray. **se dévoyer**, *v.r.* to become corrupted.
dextérité [dɛksteri'te], *n.f.* dexterity, skill.
dextrine [dɛks'trin], *n.f.* dextrin.
dextrose [dɛks'tro:z], *n.f.* dextrose, glucose.
diabète [dja'bɛt], *n.m.* diabetes.
diabétique [djabe'tik], *a.* and *n.* diabetic.
diable [djɑ:bl], *n.m.* devil; wayward child; jack-in-the-box; luggage-truck; drag; ***un bon diable***, a good-natured fellow; ***un pauvre diable***, a poor wretch.—*int.* the devil! the deuce! confound it! hang it!
diablement [djɑblə'mɑ̃], *adv.* devilishly.
diablerie [djɑblə'ri], *n.f.* devilry, witchcraft; mischief.
diablesse [djɑ'blɛs], *n.f.* she-devil; shrew, vixen.
diablotin [djɑblɔ'tɛ̃], *n.m.* imp; (Christmas) cracker.
diabolique [djabɔ'lik], *a.* diabolical, devilish.
diaboliquement [djabɔlik'mɑ̃], *adv.* diabolically, devilishly.
diaconal [djakɔ'nal], *a.* (*m. pl.* **-aux**) diaconal.
diaconat [djakɔ'na], *n.m.* diaconate, deaconry.

diaconesse [djakɔ'nɛs], *n.f.* deaconess.
diacre [djakr], *n.m.* deacon.
diadème [dja'dɛ:m], *n.m.* diadem; coronet.
diagnose [djag'no:z], *n.f.* (*art of*) diagnosis.
diagnostic [djagnɔs'tik], *n.m.* diagnosis.
diagnostique [djagnɔs'tik], *a.* diagnostic.
diagnostiquer [djagnɔsti'ke], *v.t.* to diagnose.
diagonal [djagɔ'nal], *a.* (*m. pl.* **-aux**) diagonal.—*n.f.* (**-e**) diagonal.
diagonalement [djagɔnal'mɑ̃], *adv.* diagonally.
diagramme [dja'gram], *n.m.* diagram.
dialecte [dja'lɛkt], *n.m.* dialect.
dialecticien [djalɛkti'sjɛ̃], *n.m.* dialectician.
dialectique [djalɛk'tik], *a.* dialectical.—*n.f.* dialectics, logic.
dialogue [dja'lɔg], *n.m.* dialogue, colloquy.
dialoguer [djalɔ'ge], *v.t.* to write in dialogue form.—*v.i.* to converse, to chat.
dialoguiste [djalɔ'gist], *n.m.* (*Cine.*) script-writer.
diamant [dja'mɑ̃], *n.m.* diamond.
diamantaire [djamɑ̃'tɛ:r], *a.* of diamond brilliancy.—*n.m.* diamond-cutter *or* seller.
diamanter [djamɑ̃'te], *v.t.* to set with diamonds; to tinsel, to frost.
diamétral [djame'tral], *a.* (*m. pl.* **-aux**) diametrical.
diamétralement [djametral'mɑ̃], *adv.* diametrically.
diamètre [dja'mɛtr], *n.m.* diameter.
diane [djan], *n.f.* reveille.
diantre [djɑ̃:tr], *int.* the deuce! dash! blast!
diapason [djapa'zɔ̃], *n.m.* diapason, pitch; tuning-fork.
diaphane [dja'fan], *a.* diaphanous, transparent.
diaphragme [dja'fragm], *n.m.* diaphragm, midriff.
diapositive [djapozi'ti:v] *n.f.* transparency, slide.
diapré [djɑ'pre], *a.* dappled, variegated.
diaprer [djɑ'pre], *v.t.* to dapple, to variegate, to mottle.
diarrhée [dja're], *n.f.* diarrhoea.
diatribe [dja'trib], *n.f.* diatribe, bitter criticism *or* dissertation.
dictamen [dikta'mɛn], *n.m.* dictate (*of one's conscience*).
dictateur [dikta'tœ:r], *n.m.* dictator.
dictatorial [diktatɔ'rjal], *a.* (*m.pl.* **-aux**) dictatorial.
dictature [dikta'ty:r], *n.f.* dictatorship.
dictée [dik'te], *n.f.* act of dictating, dictation.
dicter [dik'te], *v.t.* to dictate; (*fig.*) to suggest, to inspire.
diction [dik'sjɔ̃], *n.f.* diction; delivery.
dictionnaire [diksjɔ'nɛ:r], *n.m.* dictionary.
dicton [dik'tɔ̃], *n.m.* common saying, saw, proverb.
didactique [didak'tik], *a.* didactic.—*n.f.* didactic art.
didactiquement [didaktik'mɑ̃], *adv.* didactically.
dièse [djɛ:z], *n.m.* (*Mus.*) sharp.
diesel [djɛ'zɛl], *n.m.* diesel (*engine*).
diète (1) [djɛt], *n.f.* diet (*regimen*).
diète (2) [djɛt], *n.f.* (*Hist.*) diet.
diététicien [djeteti'sjɛ̃], *n.m.* (*fem.* **-enne**) dietician, dietist.
diététique [djete'tik], *a.* dietetical.—*n.f.* dietetics.
Dieu [djø], *n.m.* God.
dieu [djø], *n.m.* (*pl.* **dieux**) god.
diffamant [difa'mɑ̃], *a.* defamatory, libellous, slanderous.
diffamateur [difama'tœ:r], *n.m.* (*fem.* **-trice**) defamer, slanderer.
diffamation [difamɑ'sjɔ̃], *n.f.* defamation, aspersion, calumny.
diffamatoire [difama'twa:r], *a.* defamatory, libellous, slanderous.
diffamer [difa'me], *v.t.* to defame, to slander, to libel.
différement [difera'mɑ̃], *adv.* differently.
différence [dife'rɑ̃:s], *n.f.* difference, diversity, contrast.
différenciation [diferɑ̃sjɑ'sjɔ̃], *n.f.* differentiation.
différencier [diferɑ̃'sje], *v.t.* to make a difference, to distinguish; (*Math.*) to differentiate.
différend [dife'rɑ̃], *n.m.* difference, quarrel, dispute.
différent [dife'rɑ̃], *a.* different, dissimilar, unlike.
différentiel [diferɑ̃s'jɛl], *a.* (*fem.* **-elle**) differential.—*n.m.* (*Motor.*) differential.
différer [dife're], *v.t.* (*conjung. like* CÉDER) to defer, to postpone, to adjourn.—*v.i.* to defer, to put off; to differ, to disagree.
difficile [difi'sil], *a.* difficult; hard, trying; hard to please, particular.
difficilement [difisil'mɑ̃], *adv.* with difficulty.
difficulté [difikyl'te], *n.f.* difficulty; obstacle; rub; objection.
difficultueux [difikyl'tɥø], *a.* (*fem.* **-euse**) prone to raise difficulties; hard to please.
difforme [di'fɔrm], *a.* deformed, misshapen.
difformité [difɔrmi'te], *n.f.* deformity; hideousness.
diffus [di'fy], *a.* diffuse, prolix, verbose.
diffusément [difyze'mɑ̃] *adv.* diffusely, wordily.
diffuser [dify'ze], *v.t.* to diffuse; (*Rad. Tel.*) to broadcast.
diffuseur [dify'zœ:r], *n.m.* diffuser, spray cone; loudspeaker.
diffusion [dify'zjɔ̃], *n.f.* diffusion; diffusiveness, wordiness; propagation; broadcasting.
digérer [diʒe're], *v.t.* (*conjug. like* CÉDER) to digest; to ponder, to discuss; to put up with.
digestible [diʒɛs'tibl], *a.* digestible.
digestif [diʒɛs'tif], *a.* (*fem.* **-tive**) and *n.m.* digestive.
digestion [diʒɛs'tjɔ̃], *n.f.* digestion.
digital [diʒi'tal], *a.* (*m. pl.* **-aux**) digital; ***empreinte digitale,*** finger-print.
digitale [diʒi'tal], *n.f.* foxglove.
digitaline [diʒita'lin], *n.f.* (*Pharm.*) digitalis.
digne [diɲ], *a.* deserving, worthy; dignified.
dignement [diɲ'mɑ̃], *adv.* worthily deservedly; with dignity.
dignitaire [diɲi'tɛ:r], *n.m.* dignitary.
dignité [diɲi'te], *n.f.* dignity, nobility, seriousness; self-respect.
digresser [digrɛ'se], *v.i.* to digress, to depart from the main subject.
digressif [digrɛ'sif], *a.* (*fem.* **-ive**) digressive.
digression [digrɛ'sjɔ̃], *n.f.* digression.

digressivement [digrɛsiv'mɑ̃], *adv.* digressively.
digue [dig], *n.f.* dike, dam, embankment; (*fig.*) limit; security.
diguer [di'ge], *v.t.* to dam, to embank.
dilacération [dilaserɑ'sjɔ̃], *n.f.* tearing, rending.
dilacérer [dilase're], *v.t.* (*conjug. like* CÉDER) to tear to pieces.
dilapidateur [dilapida'tœːr], *a.* (*fem.* **-trice**) wasteful, extravagant.—*n.m.* (*fem.* **-trice**) squanderer.
dilapidation [dilapidɑ'sjɔ̃], *n.f.* waste; embezzlement.
dilapider [dilapi'de], *v.t.* to waste, to squander (*a fortune*); to embezzle.
dilatation [dilatɑ'sjɔ̃] *n.f.* dilatation, expansion, distension.
dilater [dila'te], *v.t.* to dilate, to distend, to expand. **se dilater**, *v.r.* to dilate, to be dilated.
dilatoire [dila'twaːr], *a.* (*Law*) dilatory.
dilemme [di'lɛm], *n.m.* dilemma.
dilettante [dilɛ'tɑ̃ːt], *n.* dilettante.
dilettantisme [dilɛtɑ̃'tism], *n.m.* dilettantism, amateurism.
diligemment [diliʒa'mɑ̃], *adv.* diligently, promptly.
diligence [dili'ʒɑ̃ːs], *n.f.* diligence; dispatch, application; stage-coach.
diligent [dili'ʒɑ̃], *a.* diligent, assiduous, active.
diluer [di'lɥe], *v.t.* to dilute.
dilution [dily'sjɔ̃], *n.f.* dilution.
diluvien [dily'vjɛ̃], *a.* (*fem* **-enne**) diluvian.
dimanche [di'mɑ̃ːʃ], *n.m.* Sunday, Sabbath.
dîme [dim], *n.f.* tithe; (U.S.) dime.
dimension [dimɑ̃'sjɔ̃], *n.f.* dimension, size.
dîmer [di'me], *v.t.* to tithe.—*v.i.* to levy a tithe.
diminuer [dimi'nɥe], *v.t.* to diminish, to lessen; to impair.—*v.i.* to diminish, to abate, to fall (*in price etc.*); to draw in (*of days*).
diminutif [diminy'tif], *a.* (*fem.* **ive**) and *n.m.* diminutive.
diminution [diminy'sjɔ̃], *n.f.* diminution, reduction, abatement.
dinde [dɛ̃ːd], *n.f.* turkey-hen; turkey.
dindon [dɛ̃'dɔ̃], *n.m.* turkey-cock.
dindonneau [dɛ̃dɔ'no], *n.m.* (*pl.* **-eaux**) young turkey.
dindonner [dɛ̃dɔ'ne], *v.t.* to dupe, to take in.
dindonnier [dɛ̃dɔ'nje], *n.m.* (*fem.* **-ière**) turkey-keeper.
dîné [DÎNER].
dîner [di'ne], *v.i.* to dine, to have dinner.—*n.m.* or **dîné** [di'ne], dinner; dinner-party.
dînette [di'nɛt], *n.f.* child's *or* doll's dinner.
dîneur [di'nœːr], *n.m.* (*fem.* **-euse**) diner; diner-out.
diocésain [djɔse'zɛ̃], *a.* diocesan.
diocèse [djɔ'sɛːz], *n.m.* diocese.
diphasé [difa'ze], *a.* (*Elec.*) two-phase, diphasic.
diphtérie [difte'ri], *n.f.* diphtheria.
diphtongue [dif'tɔ̃ːg], *n.f.* diphthong.
diplomate [diplɔ'mat], *a.* diplomatic.—*n.* diplomatist, diplomat.
diplomatie [diplɔma'si], *n.f.* diplomacy; diplomatic service.
diplomatique [diplɔma'tik], *a.* diplomatic; tactful.
diplomatiquement [diplɔmatik'mɑ̃], *adv.* diplomatically.
diplôme [di'ploːm], *n.m.* diploma.
diplômé [diplo'me], *a.* (*fem.* **-ée**) qualified.—*n.m.* (*fem.* **-ée**) qualified person.
dipsomane [dipsɔ'man], *n.m.* dipsomaniac.
dipsomanie [dipsɔma'ni], *n.f.* dipsomania.
dire [diːr], *v.t. irr.* to say, to speak; to tell; to recite; to order; to express. **se dire**, *v.r.* to call oneself, to be called; to say to oneself; to be said.—*n.m.* what one says, statement; (*Law*) allegation.
direct [di'rɛkt], *a.* direct, straight, immediate.—*n.m.* (*Box.*) straight blow; ***un direct du gauche***, a straight left.
directement [dirɛktə'mɑ̃], *adv.* directly, point-blank.
directeur [dirɛk'tœːr], *n.m.* (*fem.* **-trice**) director, manager, superintendent, head; principal, head master, head mistress; conductor (*of orchestra*).
direction [dirɛk'sjɔ̃], *n.f.* directing, direction; management; directorship; (*Motor.*) steering.
directives [dirɛk'tiːv], *n.f. pl.* general rules, directives.
directoire [dirɛk'twaːr], *n.m.* (*Eccles.*) directory.
directorat [dirɛktɔ'ra], *n.m.* directorship directorate.
dirigeable [diri'ʒabl], *n.m.* dirigible ballo *or* airship.
dirigeant [diri'ʒɑ̃], *a.* directing, leading.— ruler, leader.
diriger [diri'ʒe], *v.t.* (*conjug. like* MANGER to direct; to control; to steer, to manage, to govern; to send, to aim. **se diriger**, *v.r.* to make for, to go (*towards*); to govern oneself.
dirigisme [diri'ʒism], *n.m.* (*Polit.*) state planning *or* controls.
discernement [disɛrnə'mɑ̃], *n.m.* discernment; discrimination; judgment.
discerner [disɛr'ne], *v.t.* to discern; to distinguish, to discriminate.
disciple [di'sipl], *n.m.* disciple, follower.
disciplinaire [disipli'nɛːr], *a.* disciplinary.
discipline [disi'plin], *n.f.* discipline; education, training; (*sch.*) subject.
discipliner [disipli'ne], *v.t.* to discipline. **se discipliner**, *v.r.* to be disciplined.
discontinu [diskɔ̃ti'ny], *a.* discontinuous.
discontinuation [diskɔ̃tinɥɑ'sjɔ̃], *n.f.* discontinuance, discontinuation.
discontinuer [diskɔ̃ti'nɥe], *v.t.* to discontinue, to interrupt, to suspend.—*v.i.* to cease, to leave off.
discontinuité [diskɔ̃tinɥi'te], *n.f.* discontinuity, discontinuance, interruption.
disconvenance [diskɔ̃v'nɑ̃ːs], *n.f.* incongruity, unsuitability; dissimilarity.
disconvenir [diskɔ̃v'niːr], *v.i. irr.* (*conjug. like* TENIR) to deny, to disown; to disagree.
discord [dis'kɔːr], *a.* (*Mus.*) out of tune, discordant.
discordance [diskɔr'dɑ̃ːs], *n.f.* discordancy, dissonance.
discordant [diskɔr'dɑ̃], *a.* discordant, dissonant, out of tune; inharmonious, incongruous.
discorde [dis'kɔrd], *n.f.* discord, disagreement, strife.

discorder [diskɔr'de], *v.i.* (*Mus.*) to be out of tune; to be in a state of dissension.
discothèque [diskɔ'tɛk], *n.f.* record library; discothèque.
discoureur [disku'rœ:r], *n.m.* (*fem.* **-euse**) talker, chatterer.
discourir [disku'ri:r], *v.i. irr.* (*conjug. like* COURIR) to discourse; to descant (***sur***); to babble.
discours [dis'ku:r], *n.m.* discourse; speech, address; diction; treatise.
discourtois [diskur'twa], *a.* discourteous.
discourtoisement [diskurtwaz'mɑ̃], *adv.* discourteously.
discourtoisie [diskurtwa'zi], *n.f.* discourtesy, incivility.
discrédit [diskre'di], *n.m.* discredit, disrepute.
discréditer [diskredi'te], *v.t.* to discredit.
discret [dis'krɛ], *a.* (*fem.* **-ète**) discreet; cautious, shy; secret, close.
discrètement [diskrɛt'mɑ̃], *adv.* discreetly; warily.
discrétion [diskre'sjɔ̃], *n.f.* circumspection, prudence; discretion; reserve; ***pain à discrétion***, bread ad lib.
discrétionnaire [diskresjɔ'nɛ:r], *a.* discretionary.
discrimination [diskriminɑ'sjɔ̃], *n.f.* discrimination.
discriminer [diskrimi'ne], *v.t.* to discriminate.
disculper [diskyl'pe], *v.t.* to exculpate, to vindicate, to exonerate.
discursif [diskyr'sif], *a.* (*fem.* **-sive**) discursive.
discussion [disky'sjɔ̃], *n.f.* discussion, debate; altercation, dispute.
discutable [disky'tabl], *a.* debatable, disputable, contestable.
discuter [disky'te], *v.t.* to discuss, to debate, to argue; to examine, to inquire into, to sift.
discuteur, [disky'tœ:r] *n.m.* (*fem.* **-euse**) disputant.
disert [di'zɛ:r], *a.* copious, fluent, eloquent.
disertement [dizɛrtə'mɑ̃], *adv.* copiously, fluently.
disette [di'zɛt], *n.f.* scarcity, dearth, famine; poverty, penury.
diseur [di'zœ:r], *n.m.* (*fem.* **-euse**) sayer, teller; diseuse.
disgrâce [diz'grɑ:s], *n.f.* disfavour; disgrace, misfortune; plainness (*of features*).
disgracié [dizgra'sje], *a.* out of favour; (*fig.*) ill-favoured, deformed.
disgracier [dizgra'sje], *v.t.* to disgrace, to put out of favour.
disgracieusement [dizgrasjøz'mɑ̃], *adv.* awkwardly, ungracefully.
disgracieux [dizgra'sjø], *a.* (*fem.* **-euse**) awkward, uncouth, disagreeable.
disjoindre [diz'ʒwɛ̃:dr], *v.t. irr.* (*conjug. like* CRAINDRE) to disjoin, to disunite. **se disjoindre**, *v.r.* to come apart, to disunite.
disjoncteur [dizʒɔ̃k'tœ:r], *n.m.* (*Elec.*) circuit breaker.
disjonction [dizʒɔ̃k'sjɔ̃], *n.f.* disjunction, separation.
dislocation [dislɔkɑ'sjɔ̃], *n.f.* dislocation, dismemberment.
disloquement [dislɔk'mɑ̃], *n.m.* dislocation.
disloquer [dislɔ'ke], *v.t.* to dislocate, to dismember; to take to pieces (*machines etc.*); (*Mil.*) to break up (*an army*). **se disloquer**, *v.r.* to dislocate one's arm etc.; to be taken to pieces; to come apart.
dispache [dis'paʃ], *n.f.* (*Maritime Insurance*) assessment; average adjustment.
dispacheur [dispa'ʃœ:r], **dispatcheur** [dispa'tʃœ:r], *n.m.* assessor, average adjuster.
disparaître [dispa'rɛ:tr], *v.i. irr.* (*conjug. like* CONNAÎTRE) to vanish, to disappear; to abscond; to die.
disparate [dispa'rat], *a.* dissimilar, incongruous, unlike, ill-matched.—*n.f.* incongruity, dissimilarity.
disparité [dispari'te], *n.f.* disparity, dissimilarity.
disparition [dispari'sjɔ̃], *n.f.* disappearance.
dispendieusement [dispɑ̃djøz'mɑ̃], *adv.* expensively.
dispendieux [dispɑ̃'djø], *a.* (*fem.* **-euse**) expensively, costly.
dispensaire [dispɑ̃'sɛ:r], *n.m.* dispensary; out-patients' department.
dispensateur [dispɑ̃sa'tœ:r], *n.m.* (*fem.* **-trice**) dispenser; bestower, giver.
dispensation [dispɑ̃sɑ'sjɔ̃], *n.f.* dispensation; distribution; dispensing.
dispense [dis'pɑ̃:s], *n.f.* dispensation (*from fasting*); exemption (*from military service*).
dispenser [dispɑ̃'se], *v.t.* to dispense, to bestow; to exempt; to dispense (*with*). **se dispenser**, *v.r.* to dispense with; to exempt *or* excuse oneself (*from*); to spare oneself.
disperser [dispɛr'se], *v.t.* to disperse, to scatter. **se disperser**, *v.r.* to be dispersed, to break up, to be scattered.
dispersion [dispɛr'sjɔ̃], *n.f.* dispersion, breaking up.
disponibilité [dispɔnibili'te], *n.f.* (*Law*) state of being disposable, disposal (*of property*); (*Mil.*) state of being unattached.
disponible [dispɔ'nibl], *a.* disposable, available; disengaged.—*n.m.* realizable assets.
dispos [dis'po], *a.* fit and well, in good fettle, nimble; cheerful.
disposer [dispo'ze], *v.t.* to dispose, to arrange, to prepare; to incline, to prevail upon.—*v.i.* to dispose (***de***); to prescribe, to ordain. **se disposer**, *v.r.* to dispose oneself, to be disposed; to get ready.
disposition [dispozi'sjɔ̃], *n.f.* disposition, arrangement; inclination, frame of mind; mind, intention.
disproportion [disprɔpɔr'sjɔ̃], *n.f.* disproportion.
disproportionné [disprɔpɔrsjɔ'ne], *a.* disproportionate, inadequate.
disproportionnel [disprɔpɔrsjɔ'nɛl], *a.* (*fem.* **-elle**) disproportional.
disputable [dispy'tabl], *a.* disputable, debatable, doubtful.
dispute [dis'pyt], *n.f.* dispute, debate, controversy, wrangle; quarrel.
disputer [dispy'te], *v.t.* to contend for; to dispute, to call in question.—*v.i.* to discuss, to argue, to dispute; to contend, to wrangle. **se disputer**, *v.r.* to dispute; to contend, to quarrel.
disputeur [dispy'tœ:r], *a.* (*fem.* **-euse**) contentious, quarrelsome.—*n.m.* (*fem.* **-euse**) wrangler.

disqualification [diskalifikɑ'sjɔ̃], *n.f.* disqualification.
disqualifier [diskali'fje], *v.t.* to disqualify.
disquaire [dis'kɛːr], *n.* gramophone record seller.
disque [disk], *n.m.* discus, quoit; disk; (*Rail.*) signal-disk; gramophone record; ***disque longue durée*** or ***microsillon***, long-playing record.
disruptif [disryp'tif], *a.* (*fem.* **-tive**) disruptive.
disrupteur [disryp'tœːr], *n.m.* (*Elec.*) interrupter.
dissecteur [disɛk'tœːr], *n.m.* dissector.
dissection [disɛk'sjɔ̃], *n.f.* dissection.
dissemblable [disɑ̃'blabl], *a.* dissimilar, unlike.
dissemblablement [disɑ̃blablə'mɑ̃], *adv.* dissimilarly.
dissemblance [disɑ̃'blɑ̃ːs], *n.f.* dissimilarity, difference.
dissemblant [disɑ̃'blɑ̃], *a.* dissimilar, different.
dissémination [diseminɑ'sjɔ̃], *n.f.* dissemination, scattering (*of seeds etc.*).
disséminer [disemi'ne], *v.t.* to disseminate, to scatter.
dissension [disɑ̃'sjɔ̃], *n.f.* dissension, discord, strife.
dissentiment [disɑ̃ti'mɑ̃], *n.m.* dissent, disagreement.
disséquer [dise'ke], *v.t.* (*conjug. like* CÉDER) to dissect; to analyse.
disséqueur [dise'kœːr], [DISSECTEUR].
dissertation [disɛrtɑ'sjɔ̃], *n.f.* dissertation, treatise; essay (*in schools*).
disserter [disɛr'te], *v.i.* to dissert.
dissidence [disi'dɑ̃ːs], *n.f.* dissidence, difference of opinion, dissent.
dissident [disi'dɑ̃], *a.* dissident.—*n.m.* (*fem.* **-e**) dissenter, rebel.
dissimilaire [disimi'lɛːr], *a.* dissimilar, different, unlike.
dissimilarité [disimilari'te], *n.f.* dissimilarity.
dissimilitude [disimili'tyd], *n.f.* dissimilitude, difference.
dissimulateur [disimyla'tœːr], *n.m.* (*fem.* **-trice**) dissembler; hypocrite.
dissimulation [disimylɑ'sjɔ̃], *n.f.* dissimulation; double-dealing.
dissimulé [disimy'le], *a.* two-faced, artful.—*n.m.* (*fem.* **-ée**) dissembler; hypocrite.
dissimuler [disimy'le], *v.t.* to dissemble, to conceal. **se dissimuler**, *v.r.* to hide oneself, to pass unnoticed.
dissipateur [disipa'tœːr], *a.* (*fem.* **-trice**) lavish, extravagant.—*n.m.* (*fem.* **-trice**) squanderer, spendthrift.
dissipation [disipɑ'sjɔ̃], *n.f.* dissipation, waste; idleness.
dissipé [disi'pe], *a.* dissipated, profligate; inattentive.
dissiper [disi'pe], *v.t.* to dissipate, to dispel; to scatter, to squander. **se dissiper**, *v.r.* to be dispersed; to vanish; to be squandered; to be inattentive (*in class-room*).
dissolu [disɔ'ly], *a.* dissolute, profligate, licentious.
dissolubilité [disɔlybili'te], *n.f.* dissolubility.
dissoluble [disɔ'lybl], *a.* dissoluble, dissolvable.
dissolution [disɔly'sjɔ̃], *n.f.* dissolution; solution; dissoluteness.
dissolvant [disɔl'vɑ̃], *a.* and *n.m.* dissolvent, solutive, solvent.
dissonance [disɔ'nɑ̃ːs], *n.f.* dissonance, discord.
dissonant [disɔ'nɑ̃], *a.* dissonant, discordant.
dissoudre [di'sudr], *v.t. irr.* (*conjug. like* ABSOUDRE) to dissolve; to break up; to annul. **se dissoudre**, *v.r.* to dissolve, to be dissolved; to break up.
dissous [di'su], *a.* (*fem.* **-oute**) dissolved; broken up.
dissuader [disɥa'de], *v.t.* to dissuade.
dissuasif [disɥa'zif], *a.* (*fem.* **-sive**) dissuasive.
dissymétrique [disime'trik], *a.* assymetric(al).
distance [dis'tɑ̃ːs], *n.f.* distance; interval (*of place* or *time*).
distancer [distɑ̃'se], *v.t.* (*conjug. like* COMMENCER) to out-distance, to outrun; (*fig.*) to surpass, to outdo.
distant [dis'tɑ̃], *a.* distant, remote; aloof, stand-offish.
distendre [dis'tɑ̃ːdr], *v.t.* to distend.
distension [distɑ̃'sjɔ̃], *n.f.* distension, strain.
distillable [disti'labl], *a.* distillable.
distillateur [distila'tœːr], *n.m.* distiller.
distillation [distilɑ'sjɔ̃], *n.f.* distillation.
distiller [disti'le], *v.t.* to distil; to discharge; to vent.—*v.i.* to drop, to distil, to trickle.
distillerie [distil'ri], *n.f.* distillery; distilling.
distinct [dis'tɛ̃], *a.* distinct, different, separate.
distinctement [distɛ̃ktə'mɑ̃], *adv.* distinctly, clearly, plainly.
distinctif [distɛ̃k'tif], *a.* (*fem.* **-tive**) distinctive, characteristic.
distinction [distɛ̃k'sjɔ̃], *n.f.* distinction; division, difference; eminence; refinement.
distinctivement [distɛ̃ktiv'mɑ̃], *adv.* distinctively.
distingué [distɛ̃'ge], *a.* distinguished, eminent, noted; elegant, well-bred.
distinguer [distɛ̃'ge], *v.t.* to distinguish, to discern; to discriminate; to honour. **se distinguer**, *v.r.* to be conspicuous; to gain distinction.
distique [dis'tik], *n.m.* distich; couplet.
distordre [dis'tɔrdr], *v.t.* to distort; to sprain. **se distordre**, *v.r.* to become distorted.
distorsion [distɔr'sjɔ̃], *n.f.* distortion; sprain.
distraction [distrak'sjɔ̃], *n.f.* separation; absence of mind, inattention; diversion, hobby.
distraire [dis'trɛːr], *v.t. irr.* (*conjug. like* TRAIRE) to separate; to distract, to disturb; to entertain. **se distraire**, *v.r.* to be disturbed; to be diverted (*de*); to amuse oneself.
distrait [dis'trɛ], *a.* absent-minded, heedless; vacant (*person*).—*n.m.* (*fem.* **-e**) absent-minded person.
distraitement [distrɛt'mɑ̃], *adv.* absent-mindedly.
distrayant [distrɛ'jɑ̃], *a.* diverting, pleasing.
distribuable [distri'bɥabl], *a.* distributable.
distribuer [distri'bɥe], *v.t.* to distribute, to divide; to dispose; to arrange.
distributaire [distriby'tɛːr], *n.* recipient, receiver; sharer.

distributeur [distriby'tœ:r], *a.* (*fem.* **-trice**) distributing.—*n.m.* (*fem.* **-trice**) distributer, bestower, dispenser; ***distributeur automatique***, slot machine.
distributif [distriby'tif], *a.* (*fem.* **-tive**) distributive.
distribution [distriby'sjɔ̃], *n.f.* distribution; division; disposition; delivery (*of mail*).
district [dis'trikt], *n.m.* (administrative) district; region.
dit [di], *a.* said, spoken; surnamed, called; ***aussitôt dit, aussitôt fait***, no sooner said than done; ***autrement dit***, in other words.—*n.m.* maxim; saying.
dito [di'to], *adv.* (*Comm.*) ditto, (*abbr.*) do.
diurnal [djyr'nal], *a.* (*m. pl.* **-aux**) diurnal.—*n.m.* diurnal, daily prayer-book.
diurne [djyrn], *a.* diurnal, daily.—*n.m.* diurnal insect.
divagant [diva'gɑ̃], *a.* wandering, rambling.
divagateur [divaga'tœ:r], *a.* (*fem.* **-trice**) desultory, rambling.—*n.m.* (*fem.* **-trice**) rambling speaker.
divagation [divagɑ'sjɔ̃], *n.f.* divagation, wandering.
divaguer [diva'ge], *v.i.* to ramble, to wander from the question; to be incoherent (*in writing* or *speaking*).
divan [di'vɑ̃], *n.m.* divan; couch.
divergence [divɛr'ʒɑ̃:s], *n.f.* divergence.
divergent [divɛr'ʒɑ̃], *a.* divergent; different.
diverger [divɛr'ʒe], *v.i.* (*conjug. like* MANGER) to diverge, to branch off.
divers [di'vɛ:r], *a.* diverse, miscellaneous; changing; (*pl.*) various, divers, sundry.
diversement [divɛrsə'mɑ̃], *adv.* diversely, variously.
diversifier [divɛrsi'fje], *v.t.* to diversify; to variegate. **se diversifier**, *v.r.* to be varied *or* diversified.
diversion [divɛr'sjɔ̃], *n.f.* diversion; change.
diversité [divɛrsi'te], *n.f.* diversity, variety, difference.
divertir [divɛr'ti:r], *v.t.* to amuse, to delight; to divert; to embezzle. **se divertir**, *v.r.* to amuse oneself.
divertissant [divɛrti'sɑ̃], *a.* diverting, entertaining.
divertissement [divɛrtis'mɑ̃], *n.m.* diversion, amusement, entertainment; (*Law*) embezzlement.
divette [di'vɛt], *n.f.* musical comedy actress.
dividende [divi'dɑ̃:d], *n.m.* dividend.
divin [di'vɛ̃], *a.* divine, heavenly; (*fig.*) admirable, exquisite.
divinateur [divina'tœ:r], *a.* (*fem.* **-trice**) prophetic.—*n.m.* (*fem.* **-trice**) diviner, seer.
divination [divinɑ'sjɔ̃], *n.f.* divination.
divinatoire [divina'twa:r], *a.* divinatory divining.
divinement [divin'mɑ̃], *adv.* divinely; (*fig.*) admirably, exquisitely.
diviniser [divini'ze], *v.t.* to deify; to laud to the skies.
divinité [divini'te], *n.f.* divinity, godhead, deity.
diviser [divi'ze], *v.t.* to divide, to portion out; to disunite. **se diviser**, *v.r.* to be divided; to fall (*into*), to break up (*into*).
diviseur [divi'zœ:r], *a.* divisive, dividing.—*n.m.* (*Arith.*) divisor; divider.
divisibilité [divizibili'te], *n.f.* divisibility.
divisible [divi'zibl], *a.* divisible.
division [divi'zjɔ̃], *n.f.* division, partition, dividing; (*Mil.*) division.
divisionnaire [divizjɔ'nɛ:r], *a.* divisional, divisionary.
divorce [di'vɔrs], *n.m.* divorce; (*fig.*) variance.
divorcer [divɔr'se], *v.i.* (*conjug. like* COMMENCER) to divorce oneself (*de*); to break with; to divorce *or* get a divorce from someone (***d'avec quelqu'un***).
divulgation [divylgɑ'sjɔ̃], *n.f.* divulgence; revelation.
divulguer [divyl'ge], *v.t.* to divulge, to reveal, to make public. **se divulguer**, *v.r.* to leak out (*secret*).
dix [dis], *when other words follow* [di] *or* [diz], *a.* ten; tenth.—*n.m.* ten.
dix-huit [di'zɥit], *a.* and *n.m.* eighteen.
dix-huitième [dizɥi'tjɛm], *a.* and *n.* eighteenth.
dixième [di'zjɛm], *a.* and *n.* tenth.
dixièmement [dizjɛm'mɑ̃], *adv.* tenthly.
dix-neuf [diz'nœf], *a.* and *n.m.* nineteen; nineteenth.
dix-neuvième [diznœ'vjɛm], *a.* and *n.* nineteenth.
dix-sept [dis'sɛt], *a.* and *n.m.* seventeen; seventeenth.
dix-septième [dissɛ'tjɛm], *a.* and *n.* seventeenth.
dizaine [di'zɛn], *n.f.* half a score; about ten.
djinn [dʒin], *n.m.* jinn(ee).
do [do], *n.m.* (*Mus.*) do *or* ut; (the note) C.
docile [dɔ'sil], *a.* docile, tractable, submissive.
docilement [dɔsil'mɑ̃], *adv.* with docility.
docilité [dɔsili'te], *n.f.* docility, tractability.
dock [dɔk], *n.m.* dock; warehouse.
docker [dɔ'kɛ:r], *n.m.* docker.
docte [dɔkt], *a.* erudite, learned.
doctement [dɔktə'mɑ̃], *adv.* learnedly; pedantically.
docteur [dɔk'tœ:r], *n.* doctor.
doctoral [dɔktɔ'ral], *a.* (*m. pl.* **-aux**) doctoral.
doctorat [dɔktɔ'ra], *n.m.* doctorate, doctor's degree.
doctrinaire [dɔktri'nɛ:r], *a.* stiff, formal, pedantic.—*n.m.* doctrinaire.
doctrinairement [dɔktrinɛr'mɑ̃], *adv.* stiffly, formally, pedantically.
doctrine [dɔk'trin], *n.f.* doctrine.
document [dɔky'mɑ̃], *n.m.* document; (*pl.*) records.
documentaire [dɔkymɑ̃'tɛ:r], *a.* documentary.—*n.m.* (*Cine.*) documentary film.
documentation [dɔkymɑ̃tɑ'sjɔ̃], *n.f.* documentation.
documenter [dɔkymɑ̃'te], *v.t.* to give information. **se documenter**, *v.r.* to gather evidence.
dodelinement [dɔdlin'mɑ̃], *n.m.* wagging, nodding (*of head*); dandling.
dodeliner [dɔdli'ne], *v.t.* to dandle, to rock (*a child*).—*v.i.* to wag, nod (*head*).
dodiner [dɔdi'ne], *v.t.* to rock, to dandle.—*v.i.* to oscillate. **se dodiner**, *v.r.* to rock one's body; to nurse *or* coddle oneself.
dodo [do'do], *n.m.* (*Infantile*) bye-bye; (*fig.*) sleep, bed.
dodu [dɔ'dy], *a.* plump.
dogaresse [dɔga'rɛs], *n.f.* dogaressa, wife of a doge.
doge [dɔ:ʒ], *n.m.* doge.

dogmatique [dɔgma'tik], *a.* dogmatic.
dogmatiquement [dɔgmatik'mɑ̃], *adv.* dogmatically.
dogmatiser [dɔgmɑti'ze], *v.t.* to state dogmatically.—*v.i.* to dogmatize.
dogmatisme [dɔgma'tism], *n.m.* dogmatism.
dogmatiste [dɔgma'tist], *n.* dogmatist.
dogme [dɔgm], *n.m.* dogma, tenet.
dogue [dɔg], *n.m.* mastiff; (*fig.*) bull-dog (*of a man*).
doguin [dɔ'gɛ̃], *n.m.* pug.
doigt [dwa], *n.m.* finger, digit; toe.
doigté [dwa'te], *n.m.* (*Mus.*) fingering, touch; (*fig.*) tact, adroitness.
doigtier [dwa'tje], *n.m.* finger-stall.
dol [dɔl], *n.m.* deceit, fraud.
dolage [dɔ'la:ʒ], *n.m.* planing.
doléances [dɔle'ɑ̃:s], *n.f. pl.* complaints; grievances.
dolemment [dɔla'mɑ̃], *adv.* dolefully.
dolent [dɔ'lɑ̃], *a.* doleful, piteous, plaintive.
doler [dɔ'le], *v.t.* to smooth with the adze; to plane.
dolmen [dɔl'mɛn], *n.m.* dolmen.
doloir [dɔ'lwa:r], *n.m.* paring-knife, parer.
doloire [dɔ'lwa:r], *n.f.* cooper's adze; mason's axe.
dolosif [dɔlɔ'zif], *a.* (*fem.* **-sive**) fraudulent.
domaine [dɔ'mɛ:n], *n.m.* domain, estate, property; province, sphere.
dôme [do:m], *n.m.* dome; canopy, vault.
domestication [dɔmɛstikɑ'sjɔ̃], *n.f.* domestication.
domesticité [dɔmɛstisi'te], *n.f.* domesticity; (*collect.*) domestic servants.
domestique [dɔmɛs'tik], *a.* domestic; tame, domesticated.—*n.* servant, domestic.—*n.m.* household.
domestiquer [dɔmɛsti'ke], *v.t.* to domesticate, to tame.
domicile [dɔmi'sil], *n.m.* domicile, residence.
domiciliaire [dɔmisi'ljɛ:r], *a.* domiciliary.
domicilié [dɔmisi'lje], *a.* resident, domiciled.
domicilier (se) [sədɔmisi'lje], *v.r.* to settle down in a place.
dominance [dɔmi'nɑ̃:s], *n.f.* dominance.
dominant [dɔmi'nɑ̃], *a.* dominant, predominant, prevalent.
dominateur [dɔmina'tœ:r], *a.* (*fem.* **-trice**) ruling, domineering, arrogant.—*n.m.* (*fem.* **-trice**) dominator, ruler, tyrant.
domination [dɔminɑ'sjɔ̃], *n.f.* domination; dominion, rule, sway.
dominer [dɔmi'ne], *v.t.* to dominate; to rule; to prevail over; to overlook, to tower over.—*v.i.* to rule, to control; to dominate, to prevail; to lord it; to tower. **se dominer**, *v.r.* to control oneself.
dominicain [dɔmini'kɛ̃], *a.* (*Relig.*, *Polit.*) Dominican.—*n.m.* (**Dominicain**, *fem.* **-aine**) (*Polit.*) Dominican (*person*), Dominican friar *or* nun; ***la République Dominicaine***, the Dominican Republic.
dominical [dɔmini'kal], *a.* (*m. pl.* **-aux**) dominical.
dominicale [dɔmini'kal], *n.f.* Sunday sermon.
dominion [dɔmi'njɔ̃], *n.m.* dominion.
domino [dɔmi'no], *n.m.* domino.
dommage [dɔ'ma:ʒ], *n.m.* damage, injury, loss; ***c'est dommage***, it is a pity.
dommageable [dɔma'ʒabl], *a.* hurtful, prejudicial, injurious; damageable (*goods*).
domptable [dɔ̃'tabl], *a.* tamable, manageable.
dompter [dɔ̃'te], *v.t.* to subdue, to subjugate, to tame. **se dompter**, *v.r.* to quell *or* overcome one's passions.
dompteur [dɔ̃'tœ:r], *n.m.* (*fem.* **-euse**) subduer; tamer; breaker-in.
don [dɔ̃], *n.m.* gift, donation; (*fig.*) aptitude, talent.
donataire [dɔna'tɛ:r], *n.* donee, recipient.
donateur [dɔna'tœ:r], *n.m.* (*fem.* **-trice**) donor, giver.
donation [dɔnɑ'sjɔ̃], *n.f.* donation, free gift.
donc [dɔ̃:k, dɔ̃], *conj.* then, therefore, accordingly, hence; consequently; of course, to be sure.
donjon [dɔ̃'ʒɔ̃], *n.m.* keep, castle-keep; turret.
donnant [dɔ'nɑ̃], *a.* open-handed, generous; ***donnant donnant***, give and take.
donne [dɔn], *n.f.* deal (*at cards*).
donnée [dɔ'ne], *n.f.* given fact, datum; notion; (*Math.*) known quantity; (*pl.*) data.
donner [dɔ'ne], *v.t.* to give, to bestow; to grant; to present (*a play etc.*); to deal (*at cards*).—*v.i.* to give way; to hit, to stumble (***dans***); to be addicted to (***dans***); to attack (*of troops etc.*); to yield; to overlook. **se donner**, *v.r.* to procure; to take place (*of battles etc.*); to give oneself out (***pour***).
donneur [dɔ'nœ:r], *n.m.* (*fem.* **-euse**) giver, donor; dealer (*of cards*); ***donneur de sang***, blood donor.
don Quichotte [dɔ̃ki'ʃɔt], *n.m.* Don Quixote, quixotic person.
dont [dɔ̃], *pron.* whose, of which, of whom, from whom etc.
doper [dɔ'pe], *v.t.* (*Spt.*) to dope (*a horse etc.*).
doping [dɔ'piŋ], *n.m.* dope; doping.
dorade [dɔ'rad], *n.f.* (*Ichth*). sea-bream.
doré [dɔ're], *a.* gilt, gilded, golden.
dorénavant [dɔrena'vɑ̃], *adv.* henceforth, hereafter.
dorer [dɔ're], *v.t.* to gild; to glaze (*pastry*). **se dorer**, *v.r.* to gild; to become yellow.
doreur [dɔ'rœ:r], *n.m.* (*fem.* **-euse**) gilder.
dorien [dɔ'rjɛ̃], *a.* and *n.m.* (*fem.* **-enne**) Dorian; Doric.
dorique [dɔ'rik], *a.* and *n.m.* Doric.
dorloter [dɔrlɔ'te], *v.t.* to fondle, to pamper, to coddle, to pet. **se dorloter**, *v.r.* to coddle oneself; to indulge oneself.
dormant [dɔr'mɑ̃], *a.* sleeping, asleep; dormant, stagnant.—*n.m.* fixed frame (*of window etc.*).
dormeur [dɔr'mœ:r], *a.* (*fem.* **-euse** (1) sleepy, drowsy, sluggish.—*n.m.* (*fem.* **-euse** (1)) sleeper; sluggard.—*n.f.* (**-euse** (2)) sort of chaise-longue.
dormeuse (3) [dɔr'mø:z], *n.f.* stud ear-ring.
dormir [dɔr'mi:r], *v.i. irr.* (*conjug. like* SENTIR) to sleep, to be asleep; to lie still; to lie dormant (*of money*); to be stagnant (*of water*).
dormitif [dɔrmi'tif], *a.* (*fem.* **-tive**) soporific, dormitive.
Dorothée [dɔrɔ'te], *f.* Dorothy.
dorsal [dɔr'sal], *a.* dorsal.
dortoir [dɔr'twa:r], *n.m.* dormitory.
dorure [dɔ'ry:r], *n.f.* gilding; glazing (*of pastry*).

doryphore [dɔri'fɔ:r], *n.m.* Colorado beetle.
dos [do], *n.m. inv.* back; rear; top, ridge.
dosable [do'zabl], *a.* measurable.
dosage [do'za:ʒ], *n.m.* dosage; titration.
dose [do:z], *n.f.* dose; quantity; portion.
doser [do'ze], *v.t.* to dose; to proportion.
dossier [do'sje], *n.m.* back (*of chair etc.*); brief (*of a barrister*); record, file, dossier.
dossière [do'sjɛ:r], *n.f.* back-band, ridge-band (*of harness*); back-plate (*of a cuirass*).
dot [dɔt], *n.f.* marriage portion, dowry.
dotal [dɔ'tal], *a.* (*m. pl.* **-aux**) of *or* concerning dowry.
dotation [dɔtɑ'sjɔ̃], *n.f.* endowment.
doter [dɔ'te], *v.t.* to endow; to make a grant.
douaire [dwɛ:r], *n.m.* (*widow's*) dower; jointure, marriage-settlement.
douairière [dwɛ'rjɛ:r], *n.f.* dowager.
douane [dwan], *n.f.* customs; custom-house; custom-duty.
douanier [dwa'nje], *a.* relating to the custom-house, of customs.—*n.m.* customs officer.
doublage [du'bla:ʒ], *n.m.* lining, plating; (*Cine.*) dubbing.
double [dubl], *a.* twofold, double, duplicate; (*fig.*) deceitful, downright.—*n.m.* double; carbon copy, duplicate, replica; (*Ten.*) doubles.—*adv.* double; ***voir double***, to see double.
doublé [du'ble], *n.m.* gold- *or* silver-plated ware; (*Billiards*) cannon off the cushion.
doubleau [du'blo], *n.m.* (*pl.* **-eaux**) ceiling-beam.
doublement [dublə'mɑ̃], *n.m.* doubling.—*adv.* doubly.
doubler [du'ble], *v.t.* to double; to line (*clothes etc.*); to overtake, to pass; (*Theat.*) to understudy; (*Cine.*) to dub.
doublet [du'blɛ], *n.m.* doublet.
doubleur [du'blœ:r], *n.m.* (*fem.* **-euse**) doubler, twister.
doublure [du'bly:r], *n.f.* lining; (*Theat.*) understudy.
douce-amère [dusa'mɛ:r], *n.f.* (*pl.* **douces-amères**) woody nightshade, bitter-sweet.
douceâtre [du'sɑ:tr], *a.* sweetish, sickly.
doucement [dus'mɑ̃], *adv.* gently, tenderly; slowly, quietly; mildly, calmly; so-so.
doucereux [du'srø], *a.* (*fem.* **-euse**) sweetish; mawkish, mealy-mouthed.
doucet [du'sɛ], *a.* and *n.m.* (*fem.* **-ette** (1)) demure, mild, affected (person).
doucette (2) [du'sɛt], *n.f.* corn salad.
doucette (3) [du'sɛt], *n.f.* Venus's looking-glass.
douceur [du'sœ:r], *n.f.* sweetness, softness; fragrance; kindness; peacefulness; gentleness; (*pl.*) sweets; gallantries.
douche [duʃ], *n.f.* shower-bath.
doucher [du'ʃe], *v.t.* to give someone a shower-bath; to cool down (*excitement etc.*). **se doucher**, *v.r.* to take a shower.
doucir [du'si:r], *v.t.* to polish (*looking-glasses etc.*).
doucissage [dusi'sa:ʒ], *n.m.* polishing.
doucisseur [dusi'sœ:r], *n.m.* polisher.
doué [dwe], *a.* gifted.
douer [dwe], *v.t.* to endow, to bestow upon.
douille [du:j], *n.f.* socket; case *or* shell (*of cartridges*); ***douille d'embrayage***, clutch casing; ***douille de lampe***, lamp-socket, lamp-holder.
douillet [du'jɛ], *a.* effeminate, delicate; sensitive; soft.
douillettement [dujɛt'mɑ̃], *adv.* softly; delicately; cosily.
douleur [du'lœ:r], *n.f.* pain, suffering, ache; anguish, grief, sorrow.
douloureusement [duluroz'mɑ̃], *adv.* painfully; grievously.
douloureux [dulu'rø], *a.* (*fem.* **-euse**) painful, smarting, sore; grievous, afflicting, sad.
doute [dut], *n.m.* doubt, irresolution; suspicion; scepticism; fear; ***sans doute***, no doubt.
douter [du'te], *v.i.* (**de**) to doubt, to question; to hesitate; to distrust, to fear. **se douter**, *v.r.* (**de, que**) to suspect, to conjecture.
douteur [du'tœ:r], *a.* (*fem.* **-euse** (1)) doubting.—*n.m.* (*fem.* **-euse**) doubter.
douteusement [dutøz'mɑ̃], *adv.* doubtfully.
douteux [du'tø], *a.* (*fem.* **-euse** (2)) doubtful, questionable.
douve [du:v], *n.f.* stave (*for casks*); trench, moat.
Douvres [du:vr], *m.* Dover.
doux [du], *a.* (*fem.* **douce**) sweet; fragrant; kindly, charming; easy; gentle; calm; fresh (*of water*).—*adv.* gently; submissively.
douzaine [du'zɛn], *n.f.* dozen.
douze [du:z], *a.* twelve, twelfth.—*n.m.* twelve.
douzième [du'zjɛm], *a.* and *n.* twelfth.
douzièmement [duzjɛm'mɑ̃], *adv.* twelfthly.
doyen [dwa'jɛ̃], *n.m.* (*fem.* **-enne**) senior, oldest member; dean.
doyenné [dwajɛ'ne], *n.m.* deanship, deanery.
drachme [drakm], *n.f.* drachma; (*Pharm.*) dram.
draconien [drakɔ'njɛ̃], *a.* (*fem.* **-enne**) draconian, harsh, severe.
dragage [dra'ga:ʒ], *n.m.* dredging, dragging (*of a river etc.*).
dragée [dra'ʒe], *n.f.* sugar-almond, sugar-plum; small shot.
drageoir [dra'ʒwa:r], *n.m.* comfit-dish.
drageon [dra'ʒɔ̃], *n.m.* sucker.
drageonner [draʒɔ'ne], *v.i.* to put forth suckers.
dragon [dra'gɔ̃], *a.* dragonish—*n.m.* dragon; (*fig.*) vixen; dragoon.
dragonne [dra'gɔn], *n.f.* sword-knot.
drague [drag], *n.f.* dredger; dredge-net; grappling-iron.
draguer [dra'ge], *v.t.* to drag, to dredge.
dragueur [dra'gœ:r], *n.m.* dredger; ***dragueur de mines***, minesweeper.
drain [drɛ̃], *n.m.* drain, drain-pipe.
drainage [drɛ'na:ʒ], *n.m.* drainage.
drainer [drɛ'ne], *v.t.* to drain.
dramatique [drama'tik], *a.* dramatic.
dramatiser [dramati'ze], *v.t.* to dramatize.
dramaturge [drama'tyrʒ], *n.m.* dramatist, playwright.
drame [dram], *n.m.* drama.
drap [dra], *n.m.* cloth; (*bed*) sheet; pall.
drapeau [dra'po], *n.m.* (*pl.* **-eaux**) flag, standard, ensign, streamer, colours.
draper [dra'pe], *v.t.* to cover with cloth; to drape. **se draper**, *v.r.* to wrap oneself up; to make a show, to parade.
draperie [dra'pri], *n.f.* drapery; cloth-trade, cloth-making.
drapier [dra'pje], *n.m.* draper, clothier.

drastique [dras'tik], *a.* and *n.m.* (*Med.*) drastic.
(*C*) **drave** [drav], *n.f.* drive, log-running.
(*C*) **draver** [dra've], *v.t.* to drive, to drift.
(*C*) **draveur** [dra'vœ:r], *n.m.* wood-floater, rafter.
drayage [drɛ'ja:ʒ], *n.m.* fleshing (*of hides*).
drayer [drɛ'je], *v.t.* (*conjug. like* PAYER) to flesh (*hides*).
dressage [drɛ'sa:ʒ], *n.m.* erection; training (*of animals*); pitching (*of a tent*).
dresser [drɛ'se], *v.t.* to erect, to set up, to raise; to straighten; to lay out; to lay (*a snare*); to pitch (*a tent*); to draw up (*a report*); to prick up (*the ears*); to train (*animals*). **se dresser**, *v.r.* to stand on end (*of hair*); to stand erect; to rear.
dresseur [drɛ'sœ:r], *n.m.* (*fem.* **-euse**) trainer (*of dogs etc.*).
dressoir [drɛ'swa:r], *n.m.* dresser, sideboard.
drille [dri:j], *n.f.* hand-drill, borer.
driller [dri'je], *v.t.* to drill, to bore.
drive [driv], *n.m.* (*Ten.*) drive.
drogue [drɔg], *n.f.* drug; rubbish; dope.
droguer [drɔ'ge], *v.t.* to drug, to physic. **se droguer**, *v.r.* to physic *or* doctor oneself, to dope oneself.
droguerie [drɔ'gri], *n.f.* drug-store; drug-trade, drysaltery.
droguiste [drɔ'gist], *n.* retailer in drugs and chemicals.
droguet [drɔ'gɛ], *n.m.* (*Tex.*) drugget.
droit [drwɑ], *a.* straight, right, direct; vertical, upright; just, sincere; right (*opposed to left*).—*adv.* straight, straight on.—*n.m.* right, equity; law; right (*to*), claim, title; fee; due (*tax*), duty, customs duty.
droite [drwɑt], *n.f.* right hand, right.
droitement [drwɑt'mɑ̃], *adv.* rightly; sincerely, straightforwardly.
droitier [drwɑ'tje], *a.* and *n.m.* (*fem.* **-ière**) right-handed (person).
droiture [drwɑ'ty:r], *n.f.* equity, justice; uprightness, integrity.
drolatique [drola'tik], *a.* amusing, laughable, facetious.
drôle [dro:l], *a.* funny, droll, ludicrous; strange, curious.—*n.* rogue, rascal, scoundrel.
drôlement [drol'mɑ̃], *adv.* comically, facetiously, jocosely.
drôlerie [drol'ri], *n.f.* drollery; buffoonery.
drôlesse [dro'lɛs], *n.f.* jade, hussy.
dromadaire [drɔma'dɛ:r], *n.m.* dromedary.
dru [dry], *a.* sturdy; dense (*of rain*); brisk, lively; close-planted; fledged (*of birds*).—*adv.* thick, fast, hard.
druide [drɥid], *n.m.* Druid.
druidesse [drɥi'dɛs], *n.f.* Druidess.
druidique [drɥi'dik], *a.* druidical.
druidisme [drɥi'dism], *n.m.* druidism.
dryade [dri'ad], *n.f.* dryad; (*Bot.*) dryas.
du [dy], (*contraction of* DE LE) of the, from the, by the; some, any.
dû [dy], *n.m.* due, what is owed, what is owing.
dualisme [dɥa'lism], *n.m.* dualism.
dualiste [dɥa'list], *a.* and *n.* dualist.
dualité [dɥali'te], *n.f.* duality.
duc [dyk], *n.m.* duke; horned owl.
ducal [dy'kal], *a.* (*m. pl.* **-aux**) ducal.
ducat [dy'ka], *n.m.* ducat.
duché [dy'ʃe], *n.m.* dukedom, duchy.
duchesse [dy'ʃɛs], *n.f.* duchess.
ductile [dyk'til], *a.* ductile, malleable.
ductilité [dyktili'te], *n.f.* ductility.
duègne [dɥɛɲ], *n.f.* duenna, chaperon.
duel [dɥɛl], *n.m.* duel; struggle.
duelliste [dɥɛ'list], *n.* duellist.
dulcifier [dylsi'fje], *v.t.* to dulcify.
dulcinée [dylsi'ne], *n.f.* sweetheart.
dûment [dy'mɑ̃], *adv.* duly, properly.
dumping [dʌm'piŋ], *n.m.* dumping, unfair competition.
dune [dyn], *n.f.* dune, sand-hill.
dunette [dy'nɛt], *n.f.* poop-deck.
duo [dɥo], *n.m.* duet.
duodécimal [dɥɔdesi'mal], *a.* (*m. pl.* **-aux**) duodecimal.
duodénal [dɥɔde'nal], *a.* (*m. pl.* **-aux**) duodenal.
duodénum [dɥɔde'nɔm], *n.m.* duodenum.
dupe [dyp], *n.f.* dupe.
duper [dy'pe], *v.t.* to dupe, to gull, to take in.
duperie [dy'pri], *n.f.* dupery, trickery.
dupeur [dy'pœ:r], *n.m.* (*fem.* **-euse**) cheat, trickster.
duplicata [dyplika'ta], *n.m.* duplicate.
duplicateur [dyplika'tœ:r], *n.m.* (*Elec.*) duplicator; duplicating machine.
duplicité [dyplisi'te], *n.f.* duplicity, double-dealing, deceit.
duquel [dy'kɛl], (*contraction of* DE LEQUEL) of whom, of which.
dur [dy:r], *a.* hard; tough; (*fig.*) unyielding, harsh, unkind; difficult.—*adv.* hard; firmly; ***travailler dur***, to work hard.
durabilité [dyrabili'te], *n.f.* durability.
durable [dy'rabl], *a.* durable, lasting, solid.
durablement [dyrablə'mɑ̃], *adv.* durably, lastingly.
duralumin [dyraly'mɛ̃], *n.m.* duralumin.
durant [dy'rɑ̃], *prep.* during.
durcir [dyr'si:r], *v.t.* to harden.—*v.i.* to harden, to stiffen. **se durcir**, *v.r.* to harden.
durcissement [dyrsis'mɑ̃], *n.m.* hardening, stiffening, induration.
dure [dy:r], *n.f.* hard ground *or* floor *in* ***coucher sur la dure***.
durée [dy're], *n.f.* duration; continuance.
durement [dyr'mɑ̃], *adv.* hard; harshly, roughly.
durer [dy're], *v.i.* to last, to remain; to endure.
dureté [dyr'te], *n.f.* hardness; harshness, austerity, unkindness; (*pl.*) harsh *or* offensive words.
durillon [dyri'jɔ̃], *n.m.* callosity, corn.
duvet [dy'vɛ], *n.m.* down; wool, nap; fluff.
duveté [dyv'te], *a.* downy (*of birds etc.*); like down.
duveteux [dyv'tø], *a.* (*fem.* **-euse**) downy, fluffy.
dynamique [dina'mik], *a.* dynamic.—*n.f.* dynamics.
dynamisme [dina'mism], *n.m.* dynamism.
dynamiste [dina'mist], *n.* dynamist.
dynamitage [dinami'ta:ʒ], *n.m.* blasting, blowing up.
dynamite [dina'mit], *n.f.* dynamite.
dynamiter [dinami'te], *v.t.* to dynamite, to blow up.
dynamo [dina'mo], *n.f.* dynamo.
dynastie [dinas'ti], *n.f.* dynasty.

dynastique [dinas'tik], *a.* dynastic.
dysenterie [disɑ̃'tri], *n.f.* dysentery.
dyspepsie [dispɛp'si], *n.f.* dyspepsia.
dyspepsique [dispɛp'sik], **dyspeptique** [dispɛp'tik], *a.* dyspeptic.

E

E, e [ə], *n.m.* the fifth letter of the alphabet.
eau [o], *n.f.* water; rain, flood; (*pl.*) mineral *or* thermal waters; watering-place; stream; track; gloss; ***à fleur d'eau***, on a level with the water; (*Chem.*) ***eau lourde***, heavy water.
eau-de-vie [o'dvi], *n.f.* (*pl.* **eaux-de-vie**) brandy.
ébahi [eba'i], *a.* astonished, dumbfounded.
ébahir (s') [seba'i:r], *v.r.* to wonder (at), to be amazed.
ébahissement [ebais'mɑ̃], *n.m.* amazement, astonishment.
ébats [e'ba], *n.m. pl.* pastime, sport, gambol, frolic.
ébattre (s') [se'batr], *v.r.* (*conjug. like* BATTRE) to sport, to gambol, to frolic.
ébauchage [ebo'ʃa:ʒ], *n.m.* sketching.
ébauche [e'bo:ʃ], *n.f.* rough draft, outline.
ébaucher [ebo'ʃe], *v.t.* to make the first draft of, to draw an outline of, to sketch.
ébauchoir [ebo'ʃwa:r], *n.m.* (*Sculp.*) roughing-chisel; (*Carp.*) mortise-chisel.
ébène [e'bɛ:n], *n.f.* ebony, ebony work.
ébéner [ebe'ne], *v.t.* (*conjug. like* CÉDER) to ebonize.
ébénier [ebe'nje], *n.m.* ebony-tree.
ébéniste [ebe'nist], *n.* cabinet-maker.
ébénisterie [ebenis'tri], *n.f.* cabinet-work.
ébiseler [ebi'zle], *v.t.* (*conjug. like* APPELER) to chamfer, to bevel.
éblouir [eblu'i:r], *v.t.* to dazzle; (*fig.*) to fascinate, to amaze. **s'éblouir**, *v.r.* to be dazzled *or* fascinated.
éblouissant [eblui'sɑ̃], *a.* dazzling, resplendent.
éblouissement [ebluis'mɑ̃], *n.m.* dazzle, daze; (*fig.*) bewilderment.
ébonite [ebɔ'nit], *n.f.* ebonite; vulcanite.
ébouage [ebu'a:ʒ], *n.m.* scavenging.
ébouer [ebu'e], *v.t.* to scavenge.
éboueur [ebu'œ:r], *n.m.* (*fem.* **-euse**) road-sweeper, scavenger.—*n.f.* (**-euse**) road-sweeping machine.
ébouillanter [ebujɑ̃'te], *v.t.* to dip in hot water, to scald.
éboulement [ebul'mɑ̃], *n.m.* falling in, fall; caving in, collapse; landslide, landslip.
ébouler [ebu'le], *v.i.* to fall in, to fall down, to sink. **s'ébouler**, *v.r.* to fall in, to cave in.
éboulis [ebu'li], *n.m. inv.* debris, fallen rocks.
ébourgeonner [eburʒɔ'ne], *v.t.* to disbud.
ébouriffé [eburi'fe], *a.* disordered, ruffled, in disorder; (*fig.*) in a flutter.
ébouriffer [eburi'fe], *v.t.* to ruffle, to disorder; (*fig.*) to startle, to amaze.
ébouter [ebu'te], *v.t.* to cut off (*the end*).
ébranchage [ebrɑ̃'ʃa:ʒ], **ébranchement** [ebrɑ̃ʃ'mɑ̃], *n.m.* (*Hort.*) pruning, lopping, trimming.
ébrancher [ebrɑ̃'ʃe], *v.t.* to prune, to lop, to trim.
ébranlement [ebrɑ̃l'mɑ̃], *n.m.* shock, shaking; (*fig.*) perturbation, disturbance.
ébranler [ebrɑ̃'le], *v.t.* to shake; to disturb, to unsettle. **s'ébranler**, *v.r.* to get under way, to move off.
ébrécher [ebre'ʃe], *v.t.* (*conjug. like* CÉDER) to notch, to indent; to crack, to chip; (*fig.*) to impair.
ébriété [ebrie'te], *n.f.* drunkenness, inebriety.
ébrouement [ebru'mɑ̃], *n.m.* snorting.
ébrouer (s') [sebru'e], *v.r.* to snort from fear (*of horses*).
ébruiter [ebrɥi'te], *v.t.* to make known, to spread about. **s'ébruiter**, *v.r.* to spread, to be noised abroad.
ébullition [ebyli'sjɔ̃], *n.f.* boiling, ebullition.
écaille [eka:j], *n.f.* scale; shell.
écaillé [eka'je], *a.* scaly.
écailler (1) [eka'je], *v.t.* to scale. **s'écailler** *v.r.* to peel off, to scale.
écailler (2) [eka'je], *n.m.* (*fem.* **-ère**) oyster-man, oyster-woman.
écailleux [eka'jø], *a.* (*fem.* **-euse**) scaly, squamous.
écale [e'kal], *n.f.* shell, pod (*of peas etc.*); hull, husk (*of walnut*).
écaler [eka'le], *v.t.* to shell (*beans, peas etc.*); to hull, to husk (*almonds, nuts etc.*). **s'écaler**, *v.r.* to come out of the shell.
écarlate [ekar'lat], *a.* and *n.f.* scarlet; hectic red.
écarquillement [ekarkij'mɑ̃], *n.m.* spreading out, opening wide (*of one's eyes, legs etc.*).
écarquiller [ekarki'je], *v.t.* to spread out, to open wide.
écart [e'ka:r], *n.m.* stepping aside, swerving; fault; deviation; ***à l'écart***, aside; ***faire un écart***, to step aside.
écarté (1) [ekar'te], *n.m.* écarté (*game of cards*).
écarté (2) [ekar'te], *a.* remote, lonely, secluded.
écartelé [ekartə'le], *a.* (*of mind, heart etc.*) divided, torn asunder; (*Her.*) quartered.
écartèlement [ekartɛl'mɑ̃], *n.m.* tearing to pieces, quartering.
écarteler [ekartə'le], *v.t.* (*conjug. like* AMENER) to tear to pieces; (*Her.*) to quarter.
écartement [ekartə'mɑ̃], *n.m.* putting aside; removal; spacing; spread.
écarter [ekar'te], *v.t.* to open, to throw wide apart; to set aside; to avert; to dispel, to deviate; to spread. **s'écarter**, *v.r.* to turn aside, to swerve; to stray; to make way.
ecchymose [ɛki'mo:z], *n.f.* (*Med.*) ecchymosis.
ecclésiastique [ɛklezjas'tik], *a.* ecclesiastie; clerical.—*n.m.* clergyman, ecclesiastic.
écervelé [esɛrvə'le], *a.* hare-brained, rash, giddy.—*n.m.* (*fem.* **-ée**) madcap; scatter-brain.
échafaud [eʃa'fo], *n.m.* scaffold.
échafaudage [eʃafo'da:ʒ], *n.m.* scaffolding; (*fig.*) structure.
échafauder [eʃafo'de], *v.t.* to pile up; (*fig.*) to lay out (*a plan*).—*v.i.* to erect scaffolding.

échalas [eʃa'lɑ], *n.m.* vine-prop; hop-pole.
échalassage [eʃalɑ'sa:ʒ], **échalassement** [eʃalɑs'mɑ̃], *n.m.* propping.
échalasser [eʃalɑ'se], *v.t.* to prop (*vines etc.*).
échalier [eʃa'lje], **échalis** [eʃa'li], *n.m.* stile; wooden fence.
échalote [eʃa'lɔt], *n.f.* (*Bot.*) shallot.
échancrer [eʃɑ̃'kre], *v.t.* to make a crescent-shaped cut; to indent.
échancrure [eʃɑ̃'kry:r], *n.f.* notch, cut, indentation; opening.
échandole [eʃɑ̃'dɔl], *n.f.* shingle (*for roofing*).
échange [e'ʃɑ̃:ʒ], *n.m.* exchange, barter; ***libre échange***, free trade.
échangeable [eʃɑ̃'ʒabl], *a.* exchangeable.
échanger [eʃɑ̃'ʒe], *v.t.* (*conjug. like* MANGER) to exchange, to barter; to interchange.
échanson [eʃɑ̃'sɔ̃], *n.m.* cup-bearer; butler.
échantillon [eʃɑ̃ti'jɔ̃], *n.m.* sample, pattern, specimen; (*fig.*) model.
échantillonner [eʃɑ̃tijɔ'ne], *v.t.* to sample.
échappatoire [eʃapa'twa:r], *n.f.* shift, subterfuge, loop-hole, evasion.
échappé [eʃa'pe], *a.* runaway.—*n.m.* (*fem.* **-ée** (1)) one who has escaped, runaway.
échappée (2) [eʃa'pe], *n.f.* escapade, prank; short space of time.
échappement [eʃap'mɑ̃], *n.m.* escape; leakage; (*Horol.*) escapement; exhaust.
échapper [eʃa'pe], *v.t.* to escape, to avoid; ***l'échapper belle***, to have a narrow escape. —*v.i.* to escape, to make good one's escape; to be overlooked. **s'échapper,** *v.r.* to escape; to vanish.
écharde [e'ʃard], *n.f.* prickle (*of a thistle etc.*); splinter.
écharner [eʃar'ne], *v.t.* to flesh *or* scrape (*hides*).
écharnoir [eʃar'nwa:r], *n.m.* fleshing-knife.
écharpe [e'ʃarp], *n.f.* scarf, sash; arm-sling.
écharper [eʃar'pe], *v.t.* to slash, to cut.
échasse [e'ʃɑ:s], *n.f.* stilt; long-legged plover.
échassier [eʃɑ'sje], *n.m.* (*fem.* **-ière**) stilt-walker; (*colloq.*) long-legged person.—*n.m.* (*Orn.*) wader.
échauboulure [eʃobu'ly:r], *n.f.* pimple, blotch.
échaudage [eʃo'da:ʒ], *n.m.* whitewash; white-washing; scalding.
échaudé (1) [eʃo'de], *n.m.* simnel, cracknel.
échaudé (2) [eʃo'de], *a.* scalded.
échauder [eʃo'de], *v.t.* to scald. **s'échauder,** *v.r.* to burn oneself.
échaudoir [eʃo'dwa:r], *n.m.* scalding-house; scalding-tub.
échaudure [eʃo'dy:r], *n.f.* scald.
échauffant [eʃo'fɑ̃], *a.* heating; binding (*food*).
échauffement [eʃof'mɑ̃], *n.m.* heating; over-excitement.
échauffer [eʃo'fe], *v.t.* to warm, to heat, to over-heat; to excite, to irritate. **s'échauffer,** *v.r.* to grow warm, to overheat oneself; to grow angry, to chafe.
échauffourée [eʃofu're], *n.f.* rash *or* blundering enterprise; brush, scuffle.
échauffure [eʃo'fy:r], *n.f.* red rash.
échauguette [eʃo'gɛt], *n.f.* (*Mil.*) watch-tower.
échéable [eʃe'abl], *a.* due, payable.
échéance [eʃe'ɑ̃:s], *n.f.* falling due (*of bill*); date (*of payment, of maturity*); expiration (*of tenancy*).
échéant [eʃe'ɑ̃], *a.* falling due; ***le cas échéant***, in that case, if need be.
échec [e'ʃɛk], *n.m.* check, defeat, blow, loss.
échecs [e'ʃɛk], *n.m. pl.* chess; chess-men.
échelle [e'ʃɛl], *n.f.* ladder; scale; gradation.
échelon [eʃ'lɔ̃], *n.m.* round, rung, step (*of a ladder*); degree; (*Mil.*) echelon.
échelonner [eʃlɔ'ne], *v.t.* to draw up in echelon; to arrange according to gradation; to spread (*over a period of time*); to place (*at regular intervals*); ***vacances échelonnées,*** staggered holidays. **s'échelonner,** *v.r.* to be graduated; to slope gradually; to be arranged in echelon.
écheniller [eʃni'je], *v.t.* to rid (*plants, trees etc.*) of caterpillars.
écheveau [eʃ'vo], *n.m.* (*pl.* **-eaux**) hank, skein.
échevelé [eʃə'vle], *a.* dishevelled; (*fig.*) wild, extravagant.
écheveler [eʃə'vle], *v.t.* (*conjug. like* APPELER) to dishevel.
***échevin** [eʃ'vɛ̃], *n.m.* sheriff; alderman; (*C*) municipal magistrate.
échine [e'ʃin], *n.f.* spine, backbone, chine.
échiner [eʃi'ne], *v.t.* to beat unmercifully; to tire out. **s'échiner,** *v.r.* (*pop.*) to work oneself to death.
échiqueté [eʃik'te], *a.* chequered.
échiquier [eʃi'kje], *n.m.* chess-board; exchequer; square net.
écho [e'ko], *n.m.* echo.
échoir [e'ʃwa:r], *v.i. irr.* (*aux.* ÊTRE) to expire, to fall due, to lapse; to happen, to befall.
échoppe [e'ʃɔp], *n.f.* booth, covered stall.
échopper [eʃɔ'pe], *v.t.* to gouge.
échotier [eko'tje], *n.m.* (*fem.* **-ière**) gossip-writer, columnist.
échouage [e'ʃwa:ʒ], **échouement** [eʃu'mɑ̃], *n.m.* (*Naut.*) beaching, running aground.
échouer [e'ʃwe], *v.t.* to run (*a vessel*) aground. —*v.i.* to run aground, to be stranded; (*fig.*) to miscarry, to fail.
écimer [esi'me], *v.t.* to top (*plants etc.*), to pollard (*trees*).
éclaboussement [eklabus'mɑ̃], *n.m.* splashing, bespattering.
éclabousser [eklabu'se], *v.t.* to splash, to bespatter.
éclaboussure [eklabu'sy:r], *n.f.* splash.
éclair [e'klɛ:r], *n.m.* lightning, flash of lightning; variety of chocolate cake.
éclairage [eklɛ'ra:ʒ], *n.m.* lighting, illumination, light.
éclaircie [eklɛr'si], *n.f.* opening, rift (*in clouds etc.*); glade, clearing; (*fig.*) favourable change of affairs.
éclaircir [eklɛr'si:r], *v.t.* to make clear *or* clearer, to brighten; to clarify; to make thin *or* thinner; to elucidate, to explain. **s'éclaircir,** *v.r.* to become clear, bright *or* fine; to grow light; to be explained.
éclaircissement [eklɛrsis'mɑ̃], *n.m.* clearing up, explanation, solution; hint, light.
éclaire [e'klɛ:r], *n.f.* celandine.
éclairé [eklɛ're], *a.* lighted; well-lighted; (*fig.*) well-informed; intelligent; enlightened.
éclairer [eklɛ're], *v.t.* to light, to give light to, to illuminate; to enlighten; to observe; (*Mil.*) to reconnoitre.—*v.i.* to sparkle, to shine, to glitter. **s'éclairer,** *v.r.* to become enlightened; to instruct *or* enlighten one another; to light up.

éclaireur [eklɛ'rœ:r], *n.m.* (*Mil.*) scout; boy-scout.
éclanche [e'klɑ̃:ʃ], *n.f.* shoulder of mutton.
éclat [e'kla], *n.m.* burst; crash, peal; splinter (*of wood, stone, brick etc.*); brightness, glare, glitter; lustre, pomp; renown; gaudiness (*of colours*); rumour, scandal; ***un éclat de rire***, a burst of laughter; ***un grand éclat de voix***, a loud shout; ***voler en éclats***, to fly into a thousand pieces.
éclatant [ekla'tɑ̃], *a.* bright, sparkling, brilliant; striking; piercing, shrill.
éclatement [eklat'mɑ̃], *n.m.* bursting, explosion.
éclater [ekla'te], *v.i.* to split, to burst, to explode; to cry out; to shine, to sparkle, to flash; to break out (*war etc.*); ***éclater de rire***, to burst out laughing.
éclectique [eklɛk'tik], *a.* and *n.* eclectic; dilettante.
éclectisme [eklɛk'tism], *n.m.* eclecticism.
éclipse [e'klips], *n.f.* eclipse; (*fig.*) disappearance.
éclipser [eklip'se], *v.t.* to eclipse, (*fig.*) to surpass. **s'éclipser**, *v.r.* (*fig.*) to disappear, to vanish.
écliptique [eklip'tik], *a.* and *n.f.* ecliptic.
éclisse [e'klis], *n.f.* (*Surg.*) splint.
éclisser [ekli'se], *v.t.* (*Surg.*) to splint.
éclopé [eklɔ'pe], *a.* crippled, footsore, lame.—*n.m.* (*fem.* **-ée**) cripple.
écloper [eklɔ'pe], *v.t.* to lame, to disable.
éclore [e'klɔ:r], *v.i. irr.* (*conjug. like* CLORE, *but with aux.* ÊTRE) to hatch; to open, to bloom (*of flowers*); (*fig.*) to show itself.
éclosion [eklo'zjɔ̃], *n.f.* hatching; (*fig.*) opening, blooming; appearance.
écluse [e'kly:z], *n.f.* lock (*on canals etc.*); dam, weir; ***porte d'écluse***, sluice, flood-gate.
écluser [ekly'ze], *v.t.* to furnish with locks; to take (*a boat etc.*) through a lock.
éclusier [ekly'zje], *n.m.* (*fem.* **-ière**) lock-keeper.
écœurant [ekœ'rɑ̃], *a.* disgusting, nauseating.
écœurement [ekœr'mɑ̃], *n.m.* disgust; nausea.
écœurer [ekœ're], *v.t.* to disgust, to sicken; (*fig.*) to shock, to dishearten.
école [e'kɔl], *n.f.* school, college; scholastic philosophy; sect; (*Mil.*) training; (*fig.*) manner, practice.
écolier [ekɔ'lje], *n.m.* (*fem.* **-ière**) schoolboy, schoolgirl, pupil, student.
éconduire [ekɔ̃'dɥi:r], *v.t. irr.* (*conjug. like* CONDUIRE) to show out, to dismiss; to refuse.
économat [ekɔnɔ'ma], *n.m.* stewardship, bursarship.
économe [ekɔ'nɔm], *a.* economical, saving, thrifty.—*n.* steward, housekeeper, bursar, treasurer (*of colleges, hospitals etc.*).
économie [ekɔnɔ'mi], *n.f.* economy; thrift, saving.
économique [ekɔnɔ'mik], *a.* (*applied to things only*) economic, economical, cheap.—*n.f.* economics.
économiquement [ekɔnɔmik'mɑ̃], *adv.* economically.
économiser [ekɔnɔmi'ze], *v.t, v.i.* to economize, to save (up).
économiste [ekɔnɔ'mist], *n.* economist.
écope [e'kɔp], *n.f.* scoop, ladle; (*Naut.*) bailer.
écorce [e'kɔrs], *n.f.* bark, rind, peel; shell; (*Geol.*) crust (*of the earth*).
écorcement [ekɔrs'mɑ̃], **écorçage** [ekɔr'sa:ʒ], *n.m.* barking *or* stripping (*of trees etc.*); peeling.
écorcer [ekɔr'se], *v.t.* (*conjug. like* COMMENCER) to bark, to strip (*trees etc.*), to peel.
écorchement [ekɔrʃə'mɑ̃], *n.m.* excoriation, flaying, skinning.
écorcher [ekɔr'ʃe], *v.t.* to flay, to skin; to graze (*skin*); to peel, to bark; (*fig.*) to strip, to fleece. **s'écorcher**, *v.r.* to graze oneself.
écorcheur [ekɔr'ʃœ:r], *n.m.* (*fem.* **-euse**) knacker, flayer; (*fig.*) fleecer.
écorchure [ekɔr'ʃy:r], *n.f.* scratch, graze.
écorner [ekɔr'ne], *v.t.* to break the horns of; to break the corners of, to dog-ear; to curtail, to impair.
écornifler [ekɔrni'fle], *v.t.* to sponge upon.
écornure [ekɔr'ny:r], *n.f.* broken-off corner, chip.
écossais [ekɔ'sɛ], *a.* Scottish.—*n.m.* Scots (*language*); plaid, tartan cloth; (**Écossais**, *fem.* **-aise**) Scot, Scotsman, Scotswoman.
Écosse [e'kɔs], **l'**, *f.* Scotland; ***La Nouvelle Écosse***, *f.* Nova Scotia.
écosser [ekɔ'se], *v.t.* to shell, to husk (*peas* or *beans*).
écosseur [ekɔ'sœ:r], *n.m.* (*fem.* **-euse**) sheller.
écot (1) [e'ko], *n.m.* share (*of a reckoning*); bill, reckoning, score (*usually in the expression* ***payer son écot***, *to pay one's share*).
écot (2) [e'ko], *n.m.* stump of a tree.
écoulement [ekul'mɑ̃], *n.m.* flowing, flow, running; outlet; (*Comm.*) sale, disposal; export.
écouler [eku'le], *v.t.* to dispose of, to sell. **s'écouler**, *v.r.* to run *or* flow away, to pass, to slip away; (*Comm.*) to be disposed of.
écourter [ekur'te], *v.t.* to shorten, to dock, to crop.
écoutant [eku'tɑ̃], *a.* listening; ***avocat écoutant***, briefless barrister.
écoute (1) [e'kut], *n.f.* hiding-place for listening; ***être aux écoutes***, to be on the watch.
écoute (2) [e'kut], *n.f.* (*Naut.*) sheet (*of sail*).
écouter [eku'te], *v.t.* to listen to, to hearken to; to pay attention to. **s'écouter**, *v.r.* to like the sound of one's own voice; to indulge oneself.
écouteur [eku'tœ:r], *n.m.* (*fem.* **-euse**) listener, listener-in; (*Teleph.*) receiver; (*Teleg.*) ear-phone.
écoutille [eku'ti:j], *n.f.* (*Naut.*) hatchway.
écran [e'krɑ̃], *n.m.* screen; ***vedette de l'écran***, film-star.
écrasant [ekrɑ'zɑ̃], *a.* crushing; (*fig.*) humiliating, excessive; overwhelming.
écrasé [ekrɑ'ze], *a.* crushed, ruined.
écrasement [ekrɑz'mɑ̃], *n.m.* crushing, bruising; (*fig.*) overwhelming.
écraser [ekrɑ'ze], *v.t.* to crush; to bruise; to overwhelm, to ruin; to run over.
écraseur [ekrɑ'zœ:r], *n.m.* crusher; (*Motor.*) road-hog; steam-roller.
écrémer [ekre'me], *v.t.* (*conjug. like* CÉDER) to take the cream off, to skim.
écrémeuse [ekre'mø:z], *n.f.* separator.
écrevisse [ekrə'vis], *n.f.* crayfish; (*Am.*) crawfish; (*Astron.*) Cancer.
écrier (s') [sekri'je], *v.r.* to cry out, to exclaim.

écrin [e'krɛ̃], *n.m.* casket, jewel-box *or* case.
écrire [e'kri:r], *v.t. irr.* to write; to spell. **s'écrire**, *v.r.* to be written; to be spelled; to write to each other.
écrit [e'kri], *n.m.* writing; pamphlet.
écriteau [ekri'to], *n.m.* (*pl.* **-eaux**) bill (*poster*); board.
écritoire [ekri'twa:r], *n.f.* writing-desk; inkstand.
écriture [ekri'ty:r], *n.f.* writing, handwriting; scripture; (*pl.*) accounts, documents.
écrivain [ekri'vɛ̃], *n.m.* writer, author; ***femme écrivain***, authoress, woman writer.
écrivassier [ekriva'sje], *n.m.* (*fem.* **-ière**) (*colloq.*) scribbler.
écrou [e'kru], *n.m.* screw-nut; ***écrou à oreilles***, wing-nut.
écrouelles [ekru'ɛl], *n.f. pl.* king's evil, scrofula.
écrouelleux [ekruɛ'lø], *a.* (*fem.* **-euse**) scrofulous.
écrouer [ekru'e], *v.t.* to imprison, to lock up.
écroulement [ekrul'mɑ̃], *n.m.* falling in, collapse; wreck, ruin.
écrouler (s') [sekru'le], *v.r.* to fall in, to fall to pieces, to collapse.
écru [e'kry], *a.* raw, unbleached; ***toile écrue***, (brown) holland.
ectoplasme [ɛktɔ'plasm], *n.m.* ectoplasm.
écu [e'ky], *n.m.* shield; crown (*coin*); (*fig.*) money, cash.
écueil [e'kœ:j], *n.m.* reef, rock, (*fig.*) danger, stumbling-block.
écuelle [e'kɥɛl], *n.f.* porringer, bowl, basin.
écuellée [ekɥɛ'le], *n.f.* bowlful.
éculer [eky'le], *v.t.* to tread down at heel; ***des souliers éculés***, down-at-heel shoes.
écumage [eky'ma:ʒ], *n.m.* skimming.
écumant [eky'mɑ̃], *a.* foaming, frothing, seething.
écume [e'kym], *n.f.* foam, froth; lather; (*fig.*) scum, dregs.
écumer [eky'me], *v.t.* to skim; to scour; ***écumer la marmite***, to be a sponger.—*v.i.* to foam, to froth.
écumeur [eky'mœ:r], *n.m.* (*fem.* **écumeuse** (1)) skimmer; hanger-on, parasite.
écumeux [eky'mø], *a.* (*fem.* **écumeuse (2)**) frothy, foaming.
écumoire [eky'mwa:r], *n.f.* skimmer.
écurage [eky'ra:ʒ], *n.m.* scouring, cleaning.
écurer [eky're], *v.t.* to scour, to cleanse.
écureuil [eky'rœ:j], *n.m.* squirrel.
écurie [eky'ri], *n.f.* stable, mews; stud.
écusson [eky'sɔ̃], *n.m.* escutcheon; shield.
écuyer [ekɥi'je], *n.m.* squire; equerry; riding-master; rider; wall hand-rail (*of a staircase*).
écuyère [ekɥi'jɛ:r], *n.f.* horsewoman; female equestrian performer; ***bottes à l'écuyère***, top-boots, riding-boots.
eczéma [ɛgze'ma], *n.m.* eczema.
édenté [edɑ̃'te], *a.* toothless.
édenter [edɑ̃'te], *v.t.* to break the teeth of (*combs, saws etc.*).
édicter [edik'te], *v.t.* to enact, to decree.
édicule [edi'kyl], *n.m.* small building (*pavilion, kiosk etc.*).
édifiant [edi'fjɑ̃], *a.* edifying.
édification [edifikɑ'sjɔ̃], *n.f.* building, erection; (*fig.*) edification.
édifice [edi'fis], *n.m.* edifice, building, pile.
édifier [edi'fje], *v.t.* to build, to erect, to construct; (*fig.*) to edify, to improve; to instruct, to enlighten; to satisfy.
édile [e'dil], *n.m.* ædile; town councillor.
Édimbourg [edɛ̃'bu:r], *m.* or *f.* Edinburgh.
édit [e'di], *n.m.* edict.
éditer [edi'te], *v.t.* to publish; to edit.
éditeur [edi'tœ:r], *n.m.* (*fem.* **-trice**) publisher.
édition [edi'sjɔ̃], *n.f.* edition.
éditorial [editɔ'rjal], *n.m.* (*pl.* **-aux**) leading article, leader.
éditorialiste [editɔrja'list], *n.* leader-writer.
Édouard [e'dwa:r], *m.* Edward.
édredon [edrə'dɔ̃], *n.m.* eider-down; eider-down quilt.
éducateur [edyka'tœ:r], *a.* (*fem.* **-trice**) educative, instructing.—*n.m.* (*fem.* **-trice**) educator; breeder.
éducatif [edyka'tif], *a.* (*fem.* **-tive**) educational.
éducation [edykɑ'sjɔ̃], *n.f.* education; training; rearing (*of animals*); breeding, manners.
éduquer [edy'ke], *v.t.* to bring up, to educate (*children*).
effacement [efas'mɑ̃], *n.m.* effacement, obliteration; disappearance; humility, self-effacement.
effacer [efa'se], *v.t.* (*conjug. like* COMMENCER) to efface, to erase, to rub out, to blot out, to obliterate, **s'effacer**, *v.r.* to become obliterated; to wear away; to draw aside, to give way.
effaçure [efa'sy:r], *n.f.* erasure, blotting out, obliteration.
effaré [efa're], *a.* wild, scared, bewildered; astounded.
effarement [efar'mɑ̃], *n.m.* bewilderment, terror, affright.
effarer [efa're], *v.t.* to frighten, to scare. **s'effarer**, *v.r.* to be scared, to take fright.
effarouchant [efaru'ʃɑ̃], *a.* startling, disquieting; shocking; annoying.
effaroucher [efaru'ʃe], *v.t.* to startle, to frighten away. **s'effaroucher**, *v.r.* to be scared, to be startled.
effectif [efɛk'tif], *a.* (*fem.* **-tive**) actual, real, positive.—*n.m.* effective force (*of troops etc.*); size (*of a class*).
effectivement [efɛktiv'mɑ̃], *adv.* in effect, actually, indeed, in fact; (*in answer*) that is so.
effectuer [efɛk'tɥe], *v.t.* to effect, to accomplish, to carry out. **s'effectuer**, *v.r.* to be accomplished, to take place.
effémination [efeminɑ'sjɔ̃], *n.f.* effeminacy.
efféminé [efemi'ne], *a.* effeminate, womanish.
effervescence [efɛrvɛ'sɑ̃:s], *n.f.* effervescence; (*fig.*) agitation, ferment.
effervescent [efɛrvɛ'sɑ̃], *a.* effervescent; (*fig.*) excitable, irascible.
effet [e'fɛ], *n.m.* effect, result; performance; impression; power (*transmitted by machinery etc.*); (*Comm.*) bill of exchange; (*pl.*) belongings; ***en effet***, indeed, in fact.
effeuillaison [efœjɛ'zɔ̃], *n.f.*, **effeuillement** [efœj'mɑ̃], *n.m.* fall of the leaves.
effeuiller [efœ'je], *v.t.* to strip off leaves, to pick (*a flower*) to pieces. **s'effeuiller**, *v.r.* to lose *or* shed its leaves.
efficace [efi'kas], *a.* efficacious, effective.

efficacité [efikasi'te], *n.f.* efficacy, effectiveness; efficiency.
effigie [efi'ʒi], *n.f.* effigy.
effilé [efi'le], *a.* slender, slim; sharp, keen, trenchant.—*n.m.* fringe.
effiler [efi'le], *v.t.* to unweave, to unravel; to taper. **s'effiler**, *v.r.* to unravel; to taper, to become sharp; to fray.
effiloche [efi'lɔʃ], **effiloque** [efi'lɔk], *n.f.* floss silk, light refuse silk.
effilocher [efilɔ'ʃe], **effiloquer** [efilɔ'ke], *v.t.* to unravel, to undo.
efflanqué [eflɑ̃'ke], *a.* lean, thin, lank.
efflanquer [eflɑ̃'ke], *v.t.* to make lean, to emaciate.
effleurer [eflœ're], *v.t.* to graze, to skim the surface of, to touch lightly; (*fig.*) to touch upon.
efflorescence [eflɔrɛ'sɑ̃:s], *n.f.* efflorescence.
efflorescent [eflɔrɛ'sɑ̃], *a.* efflorescent.
effluent [efly'ɑ̃], *a.* effluent.
effluve [e'fly:v], *n.m.* effluvium.
effondrement [efɔ̃drə'mɑ̃], *n.m.* (*Agric.*) trenching; falling in, sinking; collapse.
effondrer [efɔ̃'dre], *v.t.* to dig deeply; to break in; to overwhelm. **s'effondrer**, *v.r.* to fall in, to collapse.
efforcer (s') [sefɔr'se], *v.r.* (*conjug. like* COMMENCER) to exert oneself, to strain, to strive.
effort [e'fɔ:r], *n.m.* effort, exertion, endeavour; stress; (*Med.*) strain, rupture.
effraction [efrak'sjɔ̃], *n.f.* breaking into, house-breaking; ***vol avec effraction***, burglary.
effraie [e'frɛ], *n.f.* barn-owl, screech owl.
effrayant [efrɛ'jɑ̃], *a.* frightful, dreadful.
effrayer [efrɛ'je], *v.t.* (*conjug. like* PAYER) to frighten, to alarm, to terrify. **s'effrayer**, *v.r.* to be frightened, to be startled.
effréné [efre'ne], *a.* unrestrained; lawless; wild.
effritement [efrit'mɑ̃], *n.m.* crumbling into dust.
effriter (s') [sefri'te], *v.r.* to crumble.
effroi [e'frwɑ], *n.m.* fright, terror, dread.
effronté [efrɔ̃'te], *a.* and *n.m.* (*fem.* **-ée**) shameless, brazen, impudent (person).
effrontément [efrɔ̃te'mɑ̃], *adv.* impudently, shamelessly.
effronterie [efrɔ̃'tri], *n.f.* effrontery, impudence.
effroyable [efrwɑ'jabl], *a.* frightful, dreadful, hideous.
effroyablement [efrwɑjablə'mɑ̃], *adv.* frightfully, horribly, dreadfully.
effusion [efy'zjɔ̃], *n.f.* effusion; overflowing.
égal [e'gal], *a.* (*m. pl.* **-aux**) equal, alike; even, level, smooth; all the same.—*n.m.* (*fem.* **-e**) equal.
également [egal'mɑ̃], *adv.* equally, alike.
égaler [ega'le], *v.t.* to equal; to make equal; to compare. **s'égaler**, *v.r.* to equal; to compare oneself (*à*).
égalisation [egalizɑ'sjɔ̃], *n.f.* equalization.
égaliser [egali'ze], *v.t.* to equalize; to level.
égalitaire [egali'tɛ:r], *a.* and *n.* egalitarian.
égalité [egali'te], *n.f.* equality, parity; uniformity.
égard [e'ga:r], *n.m.* regard, consideration, respect.
égaré [ega're], *a.* wandering, strayed; misled; mislaid; distracted.
égarement [egar'mɑ̃], *n.m.* straying, losing one's way; mistake; ill-conduct.
égarer [ega're], *v.t.* to mislead; to lose; to lead astray; to bewilder; to impair (*intellect*). **s'égarer**, *v.r.* to lose one's way, to stray; to err.
égayer [egɛ'je], *v.t.* (*conjug. like* PAYER) to enliven, to cheer up; (*Hort.*) to prune (*trees*). **s'égayer**, *v.r.* to brighten up; to make merry.
églantier [eglɑ̃'tje], *n.m.* eglantine, briar, dog-rose (*bush*).
églantine [eglɑ̃'tin], *n.f.* eglantine, dog-rose (*flower*).
église [e'gli:z], *n.f.* church.
églogue [e'glɔg], *n.f.* eclogue.
égocentrique [egosɑ̃'trik], *a.* egocentric, self-centred.
égoïsme [egɔ'ism], *n.m.* egoism, selfishness.
égoïste [egɔ'ist], *a.* egoistic, selfish.—*n.* egoist, selfish person.
égorger [egɔr'ʒe], *v.t.* (*conjug. like* MANGER) to cut the throat of, to slaughter.
égorgeur [egɔr'ʒœ:r], *n.m.* (*fem.* **-euse**) slaughterer, murderer.
égosiller (s') [segozi'je], *v.r.* to make oneself hoarse; to bawl.
égotisme [egɔ'tism], *n.m.* egotism.
égotiste [egɔ'tist], *a.* egotistic(al).—*n.* egotist.
égout [e'gu], *n.m.* running *or* falling of water; sink, drain, sewer.
égouttage [egu'ta:ʒ], **égouttement** [egut'mɑ̃], *n.m.* drainage, draining; dripping.
égoutter [egu'te], *v.t.*, *v.i.* to drain, to drip. **s'égoutter**, *v.r.* to drip, to drain.
égouttoir [egu'twa:r], *n.m.* drainer (*plate-rack etc.*).
égrapper [egra'pe], *v.t.* to pick (*grapes, currants etc.*) from the bunch.
égratigner [egrati'ɲe], *v.t.* to scratch.
égratignure [egrati'ɲy:r], *n.f.* scratch; slight wound.
égrenage [egrə'na:ʒ], *n.m.* picking off (*of grapes etc.*).
égrener [egrə'ne], *v.t.* (*conjug. like* AMENER) to tell (*beads*); to unstring (*beads etc.*); to pick off (*grapes etc.*) from the bunch. **s'égrener**, *v.r.* to fall from the stalk, to drop one by one.
égrillard [egri'ja:r], *a.* lewd, broad, naughty; ***propos égrillards***, spicy talk.
égrilloir [egri'jwa:r], *n.m.* weir; grate (*to confine fish in a pond*).
égrisé, *n.m.* or **égrisée** [egri'ze], *n.f.* diamond-dust.
égriser [egri'ze], *v.t.* to grind, to polish (*diamonds etc.*).
égrugeoir [egry'ʒwa:r], *n.m.* mortar.
égruger [egry'ʒe], *v.t.* (*conjug. like* MANGER to pound, to grind in a mortar.
égueuler [egœ'le], *v.t.* to break off the mouth *or* neck (*of glass and other vessels*).
Égypte [e'ʒipt], **l'**, *f.* Egypt.
égyptien [eʒip'sjɛ̃], *a.* (*fem.* **-enne**) Egyptian.—*n.m.* (**Égyptien**, *fem.* **-enne**) Egyptian (*person*).
eh! [e], *int.* ah! well! hey! ***eh bien !*** well!
éhonté [eɔ̃'te], *a.* shameless.

éjaculation [eʒakylɑ'sjɔ̃], *n.f.* throwing out with force, discharge; ejaculation.
éjaculer [eʒaky'le], *v.t.* to discharge, to ejaculate.
éjecter [eʒɛk'te], *v.t.* to eject.
éjecteur [eʒɛk'tœ:r], *a.* (*fem.* **-trice**) ejecting; (*Av.*) ***siège éjecteur***, ejector seat.—*n.m.* ejector (*of firearm*).
élaboration [elabɔrɑ'sjɔ̃], *n.f.* elaboration.
élaboré [elabɔ're], *a.* wrought; elaborate.
élaborer [elabɔ're], *v.t.* to elaborate, to work out.
élaguer [ela'ge], *v.t.* to lop, to prune; (*fig.*) to curtail, to cut down.
élagueur [ela'gœ:r], *n.m.* (*Hort.*) pruner.
élan (1) [e'lɑ̃], *n.m.* start, spring, bound; flight; burst; dash.
élan (2) [e'lɑ̃], *n.m.* elk; moose, wapiti (*Canada*), eland (*S. Africa*).
élancé [elɑ̃'se], *a.* slender, slim.
élancement [elɑ̃s'mɑ̃], *n.m.* darting forward; shooting pain, twinge; (*pl.*) transports.
élancer [elɑ̃'se], *v.t.* (*conjug. like* COMMENCER) to dart, to hurl.—*v.i.* to shoot, to twitch (*of pain*). **s'élancer**, *v.r.* to bound, to shoot *or* dart forth, to rush, to dash; to soar up.
élargir [elar'ʒi:r], *v.t.* to widen, to enlarge; to release. **s'élargir**, *v.r.* to widen; to stretch; to enlarge one's estate.
élargissement [elarʒis'mɑ̃], *n.m.* widening, enlarging; discharge (*from prison etc.*).
élasticité [elastisi'te], *n.f.* elasticity, springiness.
élastique [elas'tik], *a.* elastic, springy.—*n.m.* india-rubber; elastic band.
électeur [elɛk'tœ:r], *n.m.* (*fem.* **-trice**) (*Hist.*) elector, electress; (*Polit.*) voter.
élection [elɛk'sjɔ̃], *n.f.* election, polling; choice; appointment.
électoral [elɛktɔ'ral], *a.* (*m. pl.* **-aux**) electoral.
électorat [elɛktɔ'ra], *n.m.* electorate.
électricien [elɛktri'sjɛ̃], *n.m.* electrician.
électricité [elɛktrisi'te], *n.f.* electricity.
électrification [elɛktrifikɑ'sjɔ̃], *n.f.* electrification.
électrifier [elɛktri'fje], *v.t.* to provide with current, to electrify.
électrique [elɛk'trik], *a.* electric; ***secousse électrique***, electric shock.
électriquement [elɛktrik'mɑ̃], *adv.* electrically.
électriser [elɛktri'ze], *v.t.* to electrify.
électro-aimant [elɛktrɔɛ'mɑ̃], *n.m.* (*pl.* **électro-aimants**) electro-magnet.
électrocuter [elɛktrɔky'te], *v.t.* to electrocute.
électrocution [elɛktrɔky'sjɔ̃], *n.f.* electrocution.
électron [elɛk'trɔ̃], *n.m.* electron.
électronique [elɛktrɔ'nik], *a.* electronic.
élégamment [elega'mɑ̃], *adv.* elegantly, stylishly.
élégance [ele'gɑ̃:s], *n.f.* elegance, style.
élégant [ele'gɑ̃], *a.* elegant, smart, fashionable, stylish.—*n.m.* (*fem.* **-ée**) gentleman *or* lady of fashion.
élégiaque [ele'ʒjak], *a.* elegiac.—*n.* elegist.
élégie [ele'ʒi], *n.f.* elegy.
élément [ele'mɑ̃], *n.m.* element, component part.
élémentaire [elemɑ̃'tɛ:r], *a.* elementary, elemental.
éléphant [ele'fɑ̃], *n.m.* elephant.
éléphantin [elefɑ̃'tɛ̃], *a.* elephantine.
élevage [el'va:ʒ], *n.m.* breeding, rearing (*of cattle*); stud.
élévateur [eleva'tœ:r], *a.* (*fem.* **-trice**) raising, lifting.—*n.m.* elevator, lift, hoist.
élévation [elevɑ'sjɔ̃], *n.f.* elevation, raising; eminence, height; promotion; greatness (*of soul*); rise (*in prices etc.*).
élève [e'lɛ:v], *n.* pupil; student, disciple; apprentice.
élevé [el've], *a.* raised, grand; reared; heroic, eminent; high (*of prices etc.*); exalted; ***bien élevé***, well-bred; ***mal élevé***, ill-bred.
élever [el've], *v.t.* (*conjug. like* AMENER) to raise, to lift up; to erect; to exalt; to run up (*accounts etc.*); to bring up, to rear; to educate; to foster. **s'élever**, *v.r.* to rise, to ascend, to go up; to be constructed; to increase; to break out.
éleveur [el'vœ:r], *n.m.* (*fem.* **-euse**) raiser; cattle-breeder.—*n.f.* (**-euse**) incubator.
elfe [ɛlf], *n.m.* elf, brownie.
élider [eli'de], *v.t.* (*Gram.*) to cut off, to elide. **s'élider**, *v.r.* to be elided.
éligibilité [eliʒibili'te], *n.f.* eligibility.
éligible [eli'ʒibl], *a.* eligible.
élimer [eli'me], *v.t.* to wear out. **s'élimer**, *v.r.* to wear threadbare (*of clothes etc.*).
élimination [eliminɑ'sjɔ̃], *n.f.* elimination.
éliminatoire [elimina'twa:r], *a.* and *n.f.* (*Spt.*) eliminating (heat); disqualifying.
éliminer [elimi'ne], *v.t.* to eliminate; to expel; to remove.
élire [e'li:r], *v.t. irr.* (*conjug. like* LIRE) to elect, to choose; to return, to appoint.
élision [eli'zjɔ̃], *n.f.* elision.
élite [e'lit], *n.f.* choice, pick, select few, élite.
élixir [elik'si:r], *n.m.* elixir.
elle [ɛl], *pron.* (*pl.* **elles**) she, her, it; (*pl.*) they.
ellébore [ɛle'bɔ:r], *n.m.* hellebore.
ellipse [ɛ'lips], *n.f.* ellipse; (*Gram.*) ellipsis.
elliptique [ɛlip'tik], *a.* elliptical.
élocution [elɔky'sjɔ̃], *n.f.* elocution.
éloge [e'lɔ:ʒ], *n.m.* eulogy, praise; panegyric.
élogieux [elɔ'ʒjø], *a.* (*fem.* **-euse**) laudatory, eulogistic, flattering.
éloigné [elwa'ɲe], *a.* removed, distant, remote; absent.
éloignement [elwaɲ'mɑ̃], *n.m.* removal; remoteness; dislike; unwillingness.
éloigner [elwa'ɲe], *v.t.* to remove; to dismiss; to set aside, to repudiate; to waive; to banish; to put off; to alienate. **s'éloigner**, *v.r.* to go away, to withdraw; to digress; to deviate; to be alienated.
éloquemment [elɔka'mɑ̃], *adv.* eloquently.
éloquence [elɔ'kɑ̃:s], *n.f.* eloquence, oratory.
éloquent [elɔ'kɑ̃], *a.* eloquent.
élu [e'ly], *a.* elected, chosen, elect; appointed. —*n.m.* (*fem.* **-e**) elected *or* chosen person.
élucidation [elysidɑ'sjɔ̃], *n.f.* elucidation.
élucider [elysi'de], *v.t.* to elucidate, to clear up.
éluder [ely'de], *v.t.* to elude, to evade.
Élysée [eli'ze], *n.m.* Elysium; ***l'Élysée***, the residence (*in Paris*) of the President of the Republic.
émaciation [emasjɑ'sjɔ̃], *n.f.* emaciation.
émacié [ema'sje], *a.* emaciated.

émail [e'maːj], *n.m.* (*pl.* **émaux**) enamel.
émaillage [ema'jaːʒ], *n.m.* enamelling.
émailler [ema'je], *v.t.* to enamel; (*fig.*) to adorn.
émailleur [ema'jœr], *n.m.* enameller.
émaillure [ema'jyːr], *n.f.* enamelling.
émanation [emanɑ'sjɔ̃], *n.f.* emanation.
émancipation [emɑ̃sipɑ'sjɔ̃], *n.f.* emancipation.
émanciper [emɑ̃si'pe], *v.t.* to emancipate. **s'émanciper**, *v.r.* to gain one's liberty; to overstep the mark, to forget oneself.
émaner [ema'ne], *v.i.* to emanate.
émargement [emarʒə'mɑ̃], *n.m.* writing in the margin, marginal note; signature in the margin.
émarger [emar'ʒe], *v.t.* (*conjug. like* MANGER) to write *or* sign in the margin, *esp. on receipt*; *hence*, to draw one's salary.
embâcle [ɑ̃'bɑːkl], *n.m.* ice-pack (*in a river etc.*).
emballage [ɑ̃ba'laːʒ], *n.m.* packing up, packing; package; (*Spt.*) spurt.
emballement [ɑ̃bal'mɑ̃], *n.m.* excitement; flying into a temper; burst of enthusiasm.
emballer [ɑ̃ba'le], *v.t.* to pack up, to wrap up; (*colloq.*) to pack off; to arrest; to tell (*someone*) off. **s'emballer**, *v.r.* to bolt (*of a horse etc.*); to wrap oneself up; to be carried away (*by rage, enthusiasm etc.*), to race (*of an engine*).
emballeur [ɑ̃ba'lœːr], *n.m.* packer.
embarbouiller [ɑ̃barbu'je], *v.t.* to besmear. **s'embarbouiller**, *v.r.* to get muddled.
embarcadère [ɑ̃barka'dɛːr], *n.m.* wharf, pier, landing-stage.
embarcation [ɑ̃barkɑ'sjɔ̃], *n.f.* small boat, craft.
embardée [ɑ̃bar'de], *n.f.* lurch (*of a boat, a car etc.*); ***faire une embardée***, to lurch (*of boat*); to swerve, to skid (*of car*).
embargo [ɑ̃bar'go], *n.m.* embargo.
embarquement [ɑ̃barkə'mɑ̃], *n.m.* embarkation, embarking; shipment.
embarquer [ɑ̃bar'ke], *v.t.* to embark, to take on board; to ship (*water etc.*). **s'embarquer**, *v.r.* to embark, to go on board; ***s'embarquer dans***, (*fig.*) to embark upon.
embarras [ɑ̃ba'rɑ], *n.m.* encumbrance, hindrance; difficulty, fuss; (*pl.*) embarrassing circumstances; trouble, nervousness.
embarrassant [ɑ̃bara'sɑ̃], *a.* embarrassing, puzzling, awkward; troublesome.
embarrassé [ɑ̃bara'se], *a.* embarrassed, perplexed.
embarrasser [ɑ̃bara'se], *v.t.* to embarrass, to obstruct; to trouble, to confound, to puzzle. **s'embarrasser**, *v.r.* to entangle oneself; to be embarrassed; to concern oneself (*with*).
embâter [ɑ̃bɑ'te], *v.t.* to put a pack-saddle on, to saddle.
embauchage [ɑ̃bo'ʃaːʒ], *n.m.*, **embauche** [ɑ̃'boʃ], *n.f.* hiring, engaging (*of workmen*); enlisting, recruiting (*soldiers*).
embaucher [ɑ̃bo'ʃe], *v.t.* to hire, to engage, to sign on (*workmen*); to enlist (*soldiers*).
embaucheur [ɑ̃bo'ʃœːr], *n.m.* (*fem.* **-euse**) hirer, recruiting officer.
embauchoir [ɑ̃bo'ʃwaːr], *n.m.* boot-tree, boot-last.
embaumement [ɑ̃bom'mɑ̃], *n.m.* embalming.
embaumer [ɑ̃bo'me], *v.t.* to embalm; to perfume.—*v.i.* to smell sweet.
embaumeur [ɑ̃bo'mœːr], *n.m.* embalmer.
embecquer [ɑ̃bɛ'ke], *v.t.* to feed (*a bird*); to bait (*a hook*).
embéguiner [ɑ̃begi'ne], *v.t.* to muffle up. **s'embéguiner**, *v.r.* to wrap oneself up; (*fig.*) to be infatuated with.
embellir [ɑ̃bɛ'liːr], *v.t.* to embellish, to beautify.—*v.i.* to grow more beautiful. **s'embellir,** *v.r.* to grow more beautiful; to enhance one's looks.
embellissement [ɑ̃bɛlis'mɑ̃], *n.m.* embellishment; improvement.
embêtant [ɑ̃bɛ'tɑ̃], *a.* (*colloq.*) boring, annoying.
embêtement [ɑ̃bɛt'mɑ̃], *n.m.* (*colloq.*) annoyance; nuisance, bore.
embêter [ɑ̃bɛ'te], *v.t.* to bore; to annoy, to rile; to worry. **s'embêter,** *v.r.* to feel dull *or* bored.
emblée (d') [dɑ̃'ble], *adv.* at the first, at the first attempt, directly.
emblématique [ɑ̃blema'tik], *a.* emblematical.
emblème [ɑ̃'blɛːm], *n.m.* emblem.
emboîtage [ɑ̃bwa'taːʒ], *n.m.* boards, cover (*book*).
emboîtement [ɑ̃bwat'mɑ̃], *n.m.* fitting in, jointing, clamping.
emboîter [ɑ̃bwa'te], *v.t.* to fit in, to put (*a book*) into its boards; to clamp. **s'emboîter,** *v.r.* to fit, to fit in; (*fig.*) to model oneself upon.
emboîture [ɑ̃bwa'tyːr], *n.f.* socket, clamp.
embolie [ɑ̃bɔ'li], *n.f.* (*Path.*) embolism.
embonpoint [ɑ̃bɔ̃'pwɛ̃], *n.m.* plumpness, stoutness, obesity.
emboucher [ɑ̃bu'ʃe], *v.t.* to put to one's mouth, to sound (*wind-instruments*); to bit (*a horse*).
embouchure [ɑ̃bu'ʃyːr], *n.f.* mouth (*of a river, harbour etc.*); mouth-piece (*of wind-instruments*); opening (*of a receptacle*).
embourber [ɑ̃bur'be], *v.t.* to put in the mire; (*fig.*) to implicate in a dirty affair. **s'embourber,** *v.r.* to stick in the mire, to get bogged down; (*fig.*) to be involved (*in some trouble*); to put one's foot in it.
embourser [ɑ̃bur'se], *v.t.* to receive, to pocket (*affronts etc.*).
embout [ɑ̃'bu], *n.m.* ferrule.
embouteillage [ɑ̃butɛ'jaːʒ], *n.m.* bottling; traffic-jam.
embouteiller [ɑ̃butɛ'je], *v.t.* to bottle; to bottle up; to block up.
emboutir [ɑ̃bu'tiːr], *v.t.* to beat out (*coppersmith's work etc.*); to scoop out, to stamp; (*fam.*) to bump into. **s'emboutir,** *v.r.* to crash, to cannon into.
embranchement [ɑ̃brɑ̃ʃ'mɑ̃], *n.m.* branching off; branch-road, branch-line etc.; junction.
embrancher [ɑ̃brɑ̃'ʃe], *v.t.* to put together, to join up (*roads, railways, pipes etc.*). **s'embrancher,** *v.r.* to join (*of a minor road or line joining a major one*).
embrasement [ɑ̃brɑz'mɑ̃], *n.m.* conflagration; illumination.

embraser [ɑ̃brɑ'ze], *v.t.* to fire, to set on fire; (*fig.*) to inflame; to illuminate. **s'embraser,** *v.r.* to kindle, to catch fire; to glow.
embrassade [ɑ̃bra'sad], *n.f.* embrace, hug; kissing, kiss.
embrasse [ɑ̃'bras], *n.f.* curtain-loop.
embrassement [ɑ̃bras'mɑ̃], *n.m.* embrace, embracing.
embrasser [ɑ̃bra'se], *v.t.* to embrace, to clasp; to kiss; (*fig.*) to encircle; to comprise. **s'embrasser,** *v.r.* to embrace *or* kiss one another; to be included.
embrassure [ɑ̃bras'sy:r], *n.f.* band of iron.
embrasure [ɑ̃brɑ'zy:r], *n.f.* embrasure, recess.
embrayage [ɑ̃brɛ'ja:ʒ], *n.m.* (*Motor.*) coupling-gear, clutch.
embrayer [ɑ̃brɛ'je], *v.t.* (*conjug. like* PAYER) to connect up, to throw into gear.—*v.i.* to let in the clutch.
embrèvement [ɑ̃brɛv'mɑ̃], *n.m.* (*Carp.*) mortise.
embrocation [ɑ̃brɔkɑ'sjɔ̃], *n.f.* embrocation.
embrocher [ɑ̃brɔ'ʃe], *v.t.* to put on the spit.
embrouillement [ɑ̃bruj'mɑ̃], *n.m.* embroilment, entanglement, perplexity.
embrouiller [ɑ̃bru'je], *v.t.* to embroil, to confuse; to perplex; to obscure. **s'embrouiller,** *v.r.* to become intricate *or* entangled; to get confused *or* muddled.
embrouilleur [ɑ̃bru'jœ:r], *n.m.* (*fem.* **-euse**) muddler, blunderer.
embrumer (s') [sɑ̃bry'me], *v.r.* to be covered with fog etc; to become misty *or* hazy; (*fig.*) to grow sombre *or* gloomy.
embrun [ɑ̃'brœ̃], *n.m.* (*usu. pl.*) spray, spindrift.
embrunir [ɑ̃bry'ni:r], *v.t.* to brown.
embryon [ɑ̃bri'jɔ̃], *n.m.* embryo; germ; (*fig.*) dwarf, shrimp.
embryonnaire [ɑ̃brijɔ'nɛ:r], *a.* embryonic, in embryo.
embûche [ɑ̃'byʃ], *n.f.* ambush, snare.
embuscade [ɑ̃bys'kad], *n.f.* ambuscade, ambush.
embusqué [ɑ̃bys'ke], *n.m.* (*Mil. slang*) shirker, scrimshanker.
embusquer [ɑ̃bys'ke], *v.t.* to place in ambuscade, to post. **s'embusquer,** *v.r.* to lie in wait.
émender [emɑ̃'de], *v.t.* (*Law*) to amend, to correct.
émeraude [em'ro:d], *n.f.* emerald.
émergence [emɛr'ʒɑ̃:s], *n.f.* emergence, emersion.
émergent [emɛr'ʒɑ̃], *a.* emergent.
émerger [emɛr'ʒe], *v.i.* (*conjug. like* MANGER) to emerge, to rise out.
émeri [em'ri], *n.m.* emery.
émerillon [emri'jɔ̃], *n.m.* (*Orn.*) merlin.
émeriser [emri'ze], *v.t.* to cover with emery; ***papier émerisé,*** emery-paper.
émérite [eme'rit], *a.* emeritus; practised, perfect; eminent.
émersion [emɛr'sjɔ̃], *n.f.* emersion.
émerveillement [emɛrvɛj'mɑ̃], *n.m.* wonder, astonishment.
émerveiller [emɛrvɛ'je], *v.t.* to astonish, to amaze. **s'émerveiller,** *v.r.* to marvel, to be astonished.
émétique [eme'tik], *a.* and *n.m.* emetic.
émetteur [emɛ'tœ:r] *a.* (*fem.* **-trice**) (*Rad., Tel.*) ***poste émetteur*** or ***station émettrice,*** broadcasting station.—*n.m.* transmitter; ***émetteur-récepteur,*** transmitter-receiver, (*fam.*) walkie-talkie.
émettre [e'mɛtr], *v.t. irr.* (*conjug. like* METTRE) to emit, to give out; to utter, to express; (*Rad., Tel.*) to broadcast.
émeu [e'mø], *n.m.* (*Orn.*) emu.
émeute [e'mø:t], *n.f.* riot, disturbance, tumult, rising; ***chef d'émeute,*** ringleader.
émeuter [emø'te], *v.t.* to rouse, to stir up, to excite.
émeutier [emø'tje], *n.m.* (*fem.* **-ière**) rioter.
émiettement [emjɛt'mɑ̃], *n.m.* crumbling.
émietter [emjɛ'te], *v.t.* to crumble. **s'émietter,** *v.r.* to crumble.
émigrant [emi'grɑ̃], *a.* emigrating.—*n.m.* (*fem.* **-e**) emigrant.
émigration [emigrɑ'sjɔ̃], *n.f.* emigration, migration.
émigré [emi'gre], *n.m.* (*fem.* **-ée**) emigrant; refugee.
émigrer [emi'gre], *v.i.* to emigrate; to migrate.
émincé [emɛ̃'se], *n.m.* (*Cook.*) thin slices (*of meat*).
émincer [emɛ̃'se], *v.t.* (*conjug. like* COMMENCER) to slice (*meat*).
éminemment [emina'mɑ̃], *adv.* eminently.
éminence [emi'nɑ̃:s], *n.f.* eminence, elevation, rising ground, height.
éminent [emi'nɑ̃], *a.* eminent, high, lofty.
émissaire [emi'sɛ:r], *n.m.* emissary, messenger; ***bouc émissaire,*** scapegoat.
émission [emi'sjɔ̃], *n.f.* emission; issue, uttering; broadcasting.
emmagasinage [ɑ̃magazi'na:ʒ], *n.m.* storage, warehousing.
emmagasiner [ɑ̃magazi'ne], *v.t.* to warehouse, to store.
emmaillotement [ɑ̃majɔt'mɑ̃], *n.m.* swaddling, swathing.
emmailloter [ɑ̃majɔ'te], *v.t.* to swaddle, to swathe.
emmanchement [ɑ̃mɑ̃ʃ'mɑ̃], *n.m.* hafting, helving (*putting a handle on*); (*fig.*) joining.
emmancher [ɑ̃mɑ̃'ʃe], *v.t.* to put a handle to, to haft, to helve. **s'emmancher,** *v.r.* to fit on a handle; (*fig.*) to start (*of an affair*).
emmanchure [ɑ̃mɑ̃'ʃy:r], *n.f.* armhole.
emmarchement [ɑ̃marʃə'mɑ̃], *n.m.* tread (*of stair*).
emmêlement [ɑ̃mɛl'mɑ̃], *n.m.* tangle, muddle.
emmêler [ɑ̃mɛ'le], *v.t.* to entangle. **s'emmêler,** *v.r.* to get entangled.
emménagement [ɑ̃menaʒ'mɑ̃], *n.m.* moving into (*a new house*), installation.
emménager [ɑ̃mena'ʒe], *v.t.* (*conjug. like* MANGER) to move in; to fit out (*a ship etc.*). —*v.i.* and **s'emménager,** *v.r.* to move in.
emmener [ɑ̃m'ne], *v.t.* (*conjug. like* AMENER) to take away, to lead away, to fetch away, to convey away.
emmenotter [ɑ̃mnɔ'te], *v.t.* to handcuff.
emmeuler [ɑ̃mø'le], *v.t.* to stack (*hay etc.*).
emmiellé [ɑ̃mjɛ'le], *a.* honeyed, sweet.
emmieller [ɑ̃mjɛ'le], *v.t.* to honey, to sweeten with *or* as with honey.
emmitoufler [ɑ̃mitu'fle], *v.t.* to wrap up warmly.

émoi [e'mwa], *n.m.* emotion, anxiety, flutter.
émollient [emɔ'ljɑ̃], *a.* emollient, softening. —*n.m.* emollient.
émolument [emɔly'mɑ̃], *n.m.* emolument, fee; (*pl.*) salary.
émondage [emɔ̃'da:ʒ], *n.m.* pruning, lopping, trimming.
émonder [emɔ̃'de], *v.t.* to prune, to lop.
émondeur [emɔ̃'dœ:r], *n.m.* (*fem.* **-euse**) pruner, trimmer.
émotion [emo'sjɔ̃], *n.f.* emotion; stir, commotion.
émotter [emɔ'te], *v.t.* to break up (*soil, a field etc.*).
émoucher [emu'ʃe], *v.t.* to drive flies away from. **s'émoucher**, *v.r.* to whisk away the flies.
émouchet [emu'ʃɛ], *n.m.* sparrow-hawk.
émouchette [emu'ʃɛt], *n.f.* fly-net (*for horses etc.*).
émouchoir [emu'ʃwa:r], *n.m.* fly-whisk.
émoudre [e'mudr], *v.t. irr.* (*conjug. like* MOUDRE) to grind, to sharpen.
émouleur [emu'lœ:r], *n.m.* knifegrinder.
émoulu [emu'ly], *a.* sharpened, sharp.
émousser [emu'se], *v.t.* to blunt, to take the edge off; (*fig.*) to dull; to deaden. **s'émousser**, *v.r.* to get blunt; to become dull.
émoustiller [emusti'je], *v.t.* (*colloq.*) to exhilarate, to put into good spirits; (*fam.*) to ginger up. **s'émoustiller**, *v.r.* to bestir oneself.
émouvant [emu'vɑ̃], *a.* touching, moving, stirring.
émouvoir [emu'vwa:r], *v.t. irr.* (*conjug. like* MOUVOIR) to move, to affect; to excite, to rouse. **s'émouvoir**, *v.r.* to be roused *or* moved; to be agitated.
empaillage [ɑ̃pɑ'ja:ʒ], **empaillement** [ɑ̃pɑj'mɑ̃], *n.m.* bottoming (*with straw*); stuffing (*of animals*).
empaillé [ɑ̃pɑ'je], *a.* stuffed; (*fam.*) ***avoir l'air empaillé***, to be slow *or* dull-witted.
empailler [ɑ̃pɑ'je], *v.t.* to pack in straw; to straw-bottom; to stuff (*birds etc.*).
empailleur [ɑ̃pɑ'jœ:r], *n.m.* (*fem.* **-euse**) chair-mender; bird- *or* animal-stuffer, taxidermist.
empaler [ɑ̃pa'le], *v.t.* to impale.
empanacher [ɑ̃pana'ʃe], *v.t.* to adorn with a plume; (*colloq.*) to touch up.
empaquetage [ɑ̃pak'ta:ʒ], *n.m.* packing.
empaqueter [ɑ̃pak'te], *v.t.* (*conjug. like* APPELER) to pack up, to make up into a bundle, to do up. **s'empaqueter**, *v.r.* to wrap oneself up.
emparer (s') [sɑ̃pa're], *v.r.* to possess oneself (*of*), to get hold (*of*); to seize, to secure.
empâtement [ɑ̃pɑt'mɑ̃], *n.m.* stickiness, clamminess.
empâter [ɑ̃pɑ'te], *v.t.* to make clammy *or* sticky; to cram (*fowls*).
empattement [ɑ̃pat'mɑ̃], *n.m.* footing, foundation, base; (*Motor. etc.*) wheel-base.
empaumer [ɑ̃po'me], *v.t.* to catch *or* strike (*tennis-ball etc.*) in *or* with the palm of the hand; (*fig.*) to get hold of, to grasp, to take possession of.
empêchement [ɑ̃pɛʃ'mɑ̃], *n.m.* hindrance, obstacle, impediment, objection.
empêcher [ɑ̃pɛ'ʃe], *v.t.* to oppose, to prevent; to hinder. **s'empêcher** *v.r.* (*always in the negative*) to forbear, to refrain from; ***je ne peux m'empêcher de rire***, I cannot help laughing.
empeigne [ɑ̃'pɛɲ], *n.f.* upper (leather) (*of shoe*).
empenner [ɑ̃pɛ'ne], *v.t.* to feather (*arrows*); to fit on (*fins*).
empereur [ɑ̃'prœ:r], *n.m.* emperor.
empesage [ɑ̃pə'za:ʒ], *n.m.* starching.
empesé [ɑ̃pə'ze], *a.* starched; stiff (*of style etc.*), formal.
empeser [ɑ̃pə'ze], *v.t.* (*conjug. like* AMENER) to starch.
empester [ɑ̃pɛs'te], *v.t.* to infect, to taint; to cause to stink horribly; (*fig.*) to corrupt.
empêtrer [ɑ̃pɛ'tre], *v.t.* to entangle; to embarrass. **s'empêtrer**, *v.r.* to become entangled.
emphase [ɑ̃'fɑ:z], *n.f.* grandiloquence; emphasis, stress.
emphatique [ɑ̃fa'tik], *a.* bombastic, affected; emphatic.
empiècement [ɑ̃pjɛs'mɑ̃], *n.m.* yoke (*of blouse*).
empierrement [ɑ̃pjɛr'mɑ̃], *n.m.* stoning, metalling (*a road etc.*).
empierrer [ɑ̃pjɛ're], *v.t.* to stone, to metal (*roads etc.*).
empiétement [ɑ̃pjet'mɑ̃], *n.m.* encroaching, infringement.
empiéter [ɑ̃pje'te], *v.t.* (*conjug. like* CÉDER) to encroach upon, to invade, to trespass upon.—*v.i.* to encroach (***sur***).
empilement [ɑ̃pil'mɑ̃], *n.m.* piling, stacking.
empiler [ɑ̃pi'le], *v.t.* to pile up, to stack.
empire [ɑ̃'pi:r], *n.m.* empire, sovereignty, control, authority, dominion; (*fig.*) prestige, sway, mastery.
empirer [ɑ̃pi're], *v.t.* to make worse.—*v.i.* to grow worse.
empirique [ɑ̃pi'rik], *a.* empiric(al).
empirisme [ɑ̃pi'rism], *n.m.* empiricism.
emplacement [ɑ̃plas'mɑ̃], *n.m.* site, place, piece of ground.
emplâtre [ɑ̃'plɑ:tr], *n.m.* plaster, ointment; (*fig.*) palliative; (*colloq.*) helpless creature.
emplette [ɑ̃'plɛt], *n.f.* purchase; ***faire des emplettes***, to go shopping.
emplir [ɑ'pli:r], *v.t.* to fill. **s'emplir**, *v.r.* to fill; to be filled.
emploi [ɑ̃'plwa], *n.m.* employ, employment; use, function; situation, post.
employé [ɑ̃plwa'je], *a.* employed.—*n.m.* (*fem.* **-ée**) employee, assistant, clerk.
employer [ɑ̃plwa'je], *v.t.* (*see Verb Tables*) to employ, to use; to give employment to; to spend, to invest. **s'employer**, *v.r.* to employ oneself, to exert *or* busy oneself; to use one's interest; to be used.
employeur [ɑ̃plwa'jœ:r], *n.m.* (*fem.* **-euse**) employer.
emplumer (s') [sɑ̃ply'me], *v.r.* to become fledged.
empocher [ɑ̃pɔ'ʃe], *v.t.* to pocket.
empoignade [ɑ̃pɔ'ɲad, ɑ̃pwa'ɲad], *n.f.* (*colloq.*) dispute, row, set-to.
empoignant [ɑ̃pɔ'ɲɑ̃, ɑ̃pwa'ɲɑ̃], *a.* thrilling, poignant.
empoigner [ɑ̃pɔ'ɲe, ɑ̃pwa'ɲe], *v.t.* to grasp, to seize. **s'empoigner**, *v.r.* to lay hold of each other, to grapple.
empois [ɑ̃'pwɑ], *n.m.* starch.

empoisonné [ɑ̃pwazɔ'ne], *a.* poisoned; (*fig.*) poisonous.
empoisonner [ɑ̃pwazɔ'ne], *v.t.* to poison; (*fig.*) to infect; to corrupt; to embitter; (*slang*) to bore to death. **s'empoisonner,** *v.r.* to poison oneself.
empoisonneur [ɑ̃pwazɔ'nœ:r], *a.* (*fem.* **-euse**) poisonous; (*fig.*) corrupting.—*n.m.* (*fem.* **-euse**) poisoner; (*fig.*) corrupter.
empoissonner [ɑ̃pwasɔ'ne], *v.t.* to stock with fish.
emporté [ɑ̃pɔr'te], *a.* fiery, passionate, hot-headed; runaway, unmanageable.
emportement [ɑ̃pɔrt'mɑ̃], *n.m.* transport, fit of passion, outburst (*of anger, rage etc.*).
emporte-pièce [ɑ̃pɔrtə'pjɛs], *n.m.* punch (*instrument*), cutting-out machine; ***c'est une réponse à l'emporte-pièce,*** it is a very cutting answer.
emporter [ɑ̃pɔr'te], *v.t.* to carry away, to take away; to remove (*stains etc.*); to transport (*of emotion etc.*); to entail, to involve; to gain, to obtain. **s'emporter,** *v.r.* to fly into a passion, to flare up; to declaim (***contre***); to bolt (*of horses*).
empotage [ɑ̃pɔ'ta:ʒ], *n.m.* potting (*of plants*).
empoter [ɑ̃pɔ'te], *v.t.* to pot (*plants*).
empourpré [ɑ̃pur'pre], *a.* crimson.
empourprer [ɑ̃pur'pre], *v.t.* to colour red *or* purple. **s'empourprer,** *v.r.* to turn red *or* purple; to flush, to blush.
empreindre [ɑ̃'prɛ̃:dr], *v.t. irr.* (*conjug. like* CRAINDRE) to imprint, to stamp, to impress. **s'empreindre,** *v.r.* to become tinged.
empreinte [ɑ̃'prɛ̃:t], *n.f.* stamp, print, impression; mark; ***empreintes digitales,*** finger-prints.
empressé [ɑ̃prɛ'se], *a.* eager, earnest; assiduous.
empressement [ɑ̃prɛs'mɑ̃], *n.m.* alacrity, eagerness; haste, hurry.
empresser (s') [sɑ̃prɛ'se], *v.r.* to be eager (*to*); to crowd, to press.
emprisonnement [ɑ̃prizɔn'mɑ̃], *n.m.* imprisonment.
emprisonner [ɑ̃prizɔ'ne], *v.t.* to imprison, to confine.
emprunt [ɑ̃'prœ̃], *n.m.* borrowing; loan.
emprunter [ɑ̃prœ̃'te], *v.t.* to borrow; to assume.
emprunteur [ɑ̃prœ̃'tœ:r], *a.* (*fem.* **-euse**) borrowing.—*n.m.* (*fem.* **-euse**) borrower.
empuantir [ɑ̃pɥɑ̃'ti:r], *v.t.* to give an ill smell to, to infect.
ému [e'my], *a.* moved, affected.
émulation [emylɑ'sjɔ̃], *n.f.* emulation, rivalry.
émule [e'myl], *n.* rival, competitor.
émulgent [emyl'ʒɑ̃], *a.* (*Physiol.*) emulgent.
émulsif [emyl'sif], *a.* (*fem.* **-sive**) emulsive.
émulsion [emyl'sjɔ̃], *n.f.* emulsion.
en (1) [ɑ̃], *prep.* in; to; within; into; at; like, in the form of, as; out of, by, through, from; for, on.
en (2) [ɑ̃], *pron. inv.* of him, of her, of it, its, of them, their; from him, by him, about him etc.; thence, from thence; some of it, any.
enamourer (s') [sɑ̃namu're], *v.r.* to fall in love; to be enamoured (***de***).
encadrement [ɑ̃kɑdrə'mɑ̃], *n.m.* framing, frame; border; (*fig.*) environment.
encadrer [ɑ̃kɑ'dre], *v.t.* to frame; to surround; to insert; (*Mil.*) to bracket (*target*); to officer (*troops*). **s'encadrer,** *v.r.* to be inserted *or* enclosed.
encadreur [ɑ̃kɑ'drœ:r], *n.m.* (*fem.* **-euse**) picture-frame maker.
encager [ɑ̃ka'ʒe], *v.t.* (*conjug. like* MANGER) to cage, to put in a cage.
encaissage [ɑ̃kɛ'sa:ʒ], *n.m.* encasing.
encaisse [ɑ̃'kɛs], *n.f.* cash in hand, cash-balance.
encaissé [ɑ̃kɛ'se], *a.* encased; sunk, hollow; steeply *or* deeply embanked.
encaissement [ɑ̃kɛs'mɑ̃], *n.m.* packing, putting in boxes etc.; embankment; paying in (*of money*).
encaisser [ɑ̃kɛ'se], *v.t.* to encase, to pack; to bank, pay in; to collect, to receive (*money*).
encaisseur [ɑ̃kɛ'sœ:r], *n.m.* (*fem.* **-euse**) cashier.
encan [ɑ̃'kɑ̃], *n.m.* public auction.
encapuchonner (s') [sɑ̃kapyʃɔ'ne], *v.r.* to put on a cowl; to wrap one's head up; to arch the neck (*of horses*).
encarter [ɑ̃kar'te], *v.t.* to card-index.
en-cas [ɑ̃'kɑ], *n.m. inv.* anything kept for use in emergency; small umbrella; light meal prepared in case of need.
encastrement [ɑ̃kastrə'mɑ̃], *n.m.* fitting, fitting in.
encastrer [ɑ̃kas'tre], *v.t.* to fit in, to imbed.
encaustiquage [ɑ̃kosti'ka:ʒ], *n.m.* wax-polishing.
encavement [ɑ̃kav'mɑ̃], *n.m.* storing (*in cellar*), cellaring.
encaver [ɑ̃ka've], *v.t.* to put *or* store in a cellar.
enceindre [ɑ̃'sɛ̃:dr], *v.t. irr.* (*conjug. like* CRAINDRE) to surround, to enclose.
enceinte [ɑ̃'sɛ̃:t], *n.f.* circuit, enclosure; (*Fort.*) enceinte. *a.* pregnant
encens [ɑ̃'sɑ̃], *n.m.* incense; (*fig.*) fragrance; flattery.
encensement [ɑ̃sɑ̃s'mɑ̃], *n.m.* incensing; (*fig.*) flattery.
encenser [ɑ̃sɑ̃'se], *v.t.* to incense; (*fig.*) to flatter.
encenseur [ɑ̃sɑ̃'sœ:r], *n.m.* (*fem.* **-euse**) burner of incense; (*fig.*) flatterer.
encensoir [ɑ̃sɑ̃'swa:r], *n.m.* censer; (*fig.*) flattery.
encerclement [ɑ̃sɛrklə'mɑ̃], *n.m.* encircling; (*Polit.*) encirclement.
encercler [ɑ̃sɛr'kle], *v.t.* to encircle.
enchaînement [ɑ̃ʃɛn'mɑ̃], *n.m.* chaining, linking; series, connexion.
enchaîner [ɑ̃ʃɛ'ne], *v.t.* to chain up, to bind in chains; (*Cine.*) to fade in; (*fig.*) to restrain; to captivate; to link. **s'enchaîner,** *v.r.* to be connected *or* linked together.
enchanté [ɑ̃ʃɑ̃'te], *a.* enchanted; (*fig.*) charmed, delighted.
enchantement [ɑ̃ʃɑ̃t'mɑ̃], *n.m.* enchantment, magic; (*fig.*) charm, delight.
enchanter [ɑ̃ʃɑ̃'te], *v.t.* to enchant; (*fig.*) to fascinate, to charm.
enchanteur [ɑ̃ʃɑ̃'tœ:r], *a.* (*fem.* **-eresse**) enchanting, entrancing, captivating.—*n.m.* (*fem.* **-eresse**) enchanter, enchantress, charmer.
enchâsser [ɑ̃ʃɑ'se], *v.t.* to enchase; to enshrine; to insert.
enchâssure [ɑ̃ʃɑ'sy:r], *n.f.* setting, mount; insertion.

enchère [ɑ̃'ʃɛːr], *n.f.* bid (*at an auction*); auction.
enchérir [ɑ̃ʃe'riːr], *v.t.* to bid for, to outbid; to raise (*prices etc.*).—*v.i.* to rise (*in price*); (*fig.*) to surpass, to outdo; to bid, to outbid (*sur*).
enchérissement [ɑ̃ʃeris'mɑ̃], *n.m.* rise, increase.
enchérisseur [ɑ̃ʃeri'sœːr], *n.m.* bidder (*at an auction*).
enchevêtrement [ɑ̃ʃvɛtrə'mɑ̃], *n.m.* entanglement.
enchevêtrer [ɑ̃ʃvɛ'tre], *v.t.* to halter (*a horse etc.*); to entangle. **s'enchevêtrer**, *v.r.* to get entangled, confused *or* embarrassed.
enclave [ɑ̃'klaːv], *n.f.* enclave, piece of enclosed land.
enclaver [ɑ̃kla've], *v.t.* to enclose, to hem in.
enclenchement [ɑ̃klɑ̃ʃ'mɑ̃], *n.m.* throwing into gear; automatic clutch.
enclin [ɑ̃'klɛ̃], *a.* inclined; prone, addicted, apt, given to.
enclore [ɑ̃'klɔːr], *v.t. irr.* (*conjug. like* CLORE) to enclose, to fence in, to take in, to shut in.
enclos [ɑ̃'klo], *n.m.* enclosure, close; paddock; fencing, wall.
enclume [ɑ̃'klym], *n.f.* anvil.
encoche [ɑ̃'kɔʃ], *n.f.* notch.
encoffrer [ɑ̃kɔ'fre], *v.t.* to shut in a coffer; (*fig.*) to cage.
encoignure [ɑ̃kɔ'ɲyːr], *n.f.* corner, angle (*of a street*); corner-piece; corner-cupboard.
encollage [ɑ̃kɔ'laːʒ], *n.m.* sizing, gluing; glue, size.
encoller [ɑ̃kɔ'le], *v.t.* to size, to glue.
encolure [ɑ̃kɔ'lyːr], *n.f.* neck and shoulders (*of a horse*); neck-line (*of a garment*); size (*of collars*); (*fig.*) appearance (*of a person*).
encombrant [ɑ̃kɔ̃'brɑ̃], *a.* cumbersome.
encombre [ɑ̃'kɔ̃ːbr], *n.m.* (*now only used after* ***sans***) impediment, hindrance.
encombrement [ɑ̃kɔ̃brə'mɑ̃], *n.m.* obstruction; crowding, congestion (*of traffic*).
encombrer [ɑ̃kɔ̃'bre], *v.t.* to obstruct; to crowd, to throng.
encontre (à l' . . . de) [alɑ̃'kɔ̃ːtrdə], *prep. phr.* against, counter to.
encore [ɑ̃'kɔːr], *adv.* yet, still, as yet; anew, again, once more; further, moreover, besides; even, but, only.
encorner [ɑ̃kɔr'ne], *v.t.* to gore, to toss.
encourageant [ɑ̃kura'ʒɑ̃], *a.* encouraging, cheering.
encouragement [ɑ̃kuraʒ'mɑ̃], *n.m.* encouragement.
encourager [ɑ̃kura'ʒe], *v.t.* (*conjug. like* MANGER) to encourage, to stimulate. **s'encourager**, *v.r.* to encourage each other, to take courage.
encourir [ɑ̃ku'riːr], *v.t. irr.* (*conjug. like* COURIR) to incur (*disgrace, reproach*), to fall under.
encrasser [ɑ̃kra'se], *v.t.* to make dirty, to foul. **s'encrasser**, *v.r.* to become dirty.
encre [ɑ̃ːkr], *n.f.* ink.
encrier [ɑ̃kri'e], *n.m.* ink-stand, ink-pot.
encroûté [ɑ̃kru'te], *a.* covered with a crust; (*fig.*) full of prejudices.—*n.m.* (*fem.* **-ée**) 'Blimp'.
encroûter (s') [sɑ̃kru'te], *v.r.* to crust, to get hard; to become dull, stupid *or* hide-bound.
encuvage [ɑ̃ky'vaːʒ], **encuvement** [ɑ̃kyv'mɑ̃], *n.m.* tubbing.
encuver [ɑ̃ky've], *v.t.* to put into a vat, to tub.
encyclopédie [ɑ̃siklɔpe'di], *n.f.* encyclopaedia.
endémique [ɑ̃de'mik], *a.* endemic.
endenté [ɑ̃dɑ̃'te], *a.* indented.
endenter [ɑ̃dɑ̃'te], *v.t.* to cog, to tooth.
endetter [ɑ̃dɛ'te], *v.t.* to get (*a person*) into debt. **s'endetter**, *v.r.* to run into debt.
endeuiller [ɑ̃dœ'je], *v.t.* to put into mourning; to sadden.
endiablé [ɑ̃djɑ'ble], *a.* possessed; (*fig.*) devilish.
endiabler [ɑ̃djɑ'ble], *v.i.* to be furious; ***faire endiabler***, to torment.
endiguement [ɑ̃dig'mɑ̃], *n.m.* damming up.
endiguer [ɑ̃di'ge], *v.t.* to dam up, to embank.
endimancher (s') [sɑ̃dimɑ̃'ʃe], *v.r.* to put on one's Sunday best.
endive [ɑ̃'diːv], *n.f.* (*broad-leaved*) chicory.
endoctrinement [ɑ̃dɔktrin'mɑ̃], *n.m.* indoctrination.
endoctriner [ɑ̃dɔktri'ne], *v.t.* to indoctrinate.
endolorir [ɑ̃dɔlɔ'riːr], *v.t.* to make sore; to make (*the heart etc.*) ache. **s'endolorir**, *v.r.* to become sore.
endolorissement [ɑ̃dɔlɔris'mɑ̃], *n.m.* pain, soreness.
endommagement [ɑ̃dɔmaʒ'mɑ̃], *n.m.* loss, injury, damage.
endommager [ɑ̃dɔma'ʒe], *v.t.* (*conjug. like* MANGER) to damage, to injure.
endormeur [ɑ̃dɔr'mœːr], *n.m.* (*fem.* **-euse**) cajoler, flatterer; bore.
endormi [ɑ̃dɔr'mi], *a.* asleep; sleepy; benumbed.—*n.m.* (*fem.* **-e**) sleepy-head.
endormir [ɑ̃dɔr'miːr], *v.t. irr.* (*conjug. like* SENTIR) to send to sleep, to rock to sleep; to anaesthetize; to wheedle, to deceive; to benumb; to bore. **s'endormir**, *v.r.* to fall asleep.
endos [ɑ̃'do], **endossement** [ɑ̃dos'mɑ̃], *n.m.* endorsement.
endosser [ɑ̃do'se], *v.t.* to put on one's back, to put on; to saddle oneself with (*an obligation etc.*); to endorse.
endroit [ɑ̃'drwɑ], *n.m.* place, spot; point; right side (*of a material*); part, passage (*of a book etc.*).
enduire [ɑ̃'dɥiːr], *v.t. irr.* (*conjug. like* CONDUIRE) to do over, to coat, to smear.
enduit [ɑ̃'dɥi], *n.m.* coating, layer, plaster, glaze, varnish, polish.
endurance [ɑ̃dy'rɑ̃ːs], *n.f.* endurance, fortitude; ***épreuve d'endurance***, endurance *or* reliability test.
endurant [ɑ̃dy'rɑ̃], *a.* patient, tolerant.
endurci [ɑ̃dyr'si], *a.* hardened; inured, callous.
endurcir [ɑ̃dyr'siːr], *v.t.* to harden, to toughen, to inure; to render callous. **s'endurcir**, *v.r.* to harden, to grow hard; to become callous.
endurcissement [ɑ̃dyrsis'mɑ̃], *n.m.* hardening, obduracy; callousness.
endurer [ɑ̃dy're], *v.t.* to endure, to bear; to put up with.
énergie [enɛr'ʒi], *n.f.* energy, strength, vigour, power.
énergique [enɛr'ʒik], *a.* energetic, vigorous.

énergiquement [enɛrʒik'mɑ̃], *adv.* energetically, vigorously.

énervant [enɛr'vɑ̃], *a.* enervating; debilitating, nerve-racking.

énervé [enɛr've], *a.* nerveless; nervy, fidgety.

énervement [enɛrv'mɑ̃], *n.m.* nervous tension.

énerver [enɛr've], *v.t.* to enervate, to debilitate; to weaken; to unnerve; (*fam.*) to get on the nerves. **s'énerver**, *v.r.* to become enervated, unnerved, irritable *or* fidgety.

enfance [ɑ̃'fɑ̃:s], *n.f.* infancy, childhood; childishness.

enfant [ɑ̃'fɑ̃], *n.* child; infant, baby; descendant; citizen, native.

enfantement [ɑ̃fɑ̃t'mɑ̃], *n.m.* childbirth.

enfanter [ɑ̃fɑ̃'te], *v.t.* to bring forth, to bear; (*fig.*) to beget, to give birth to.

enfantillage [ɑ̃fɑ̃ti'ja:ʒ], *n.m.* child's-play, childishness.

enfantin [ɑ̃fɑ̃'tɛ̃], *a.* infantile, childish.

enfariner [ɑ̃fari'ne], *v.t.* to flour, to sprinkle with flour.

enfer [ɑ̃'fɛ:r], *n.m.* hell; (*fig.*) torment, misery.

enfermer [ɑ̃fɛr'me], *v.t.* to shut in *or* up; to lock up; to enclose; to conceal; to comprise. **s'enfermer**, *v.r.* to lock oneself in.

enficeler [ɑ̃fis'le], *v.t.* (*conjug. like* APPELER) to tie with string etc.

enfièvrement [ɑ̃fjɛvrə'mɑ̃], *n.m.* feverishness.

enfilade [ɑ̃fi'lad], *n.f.* suite (*of chambers etc.*); string (*of phrases etc.*); (*Mil.*) enfilade.

enfiler [ɑ̃fi'le], *v.t.* to thread (*a needle*), to string (*beads*); to pierce; to pass through; (*Mil.*) to enfilade; to slip on (*clothes*). **s'enfiler**, *v.r.* to be threaded; to be pierced; to get involved in.

enfin [ɑ̃'fɛ̃], *adv.* at last, finally, at length, after all, lastly; in short, in a word.

enflammé [ɑ̃flɑ'me], *a.* on fire, in flames, ignited.

enflammer [ɑ̃flɑ'me], *v.t.* to set on fire, to kindle; (*fig.*) to incense, to provoke. **s'enflammer**, *v.r.* to catch fire, to blaze; (*fig.*) to be incensed.

enflé [ɑ̃'fle], *a.* swollen, puffed up; (*fig.*) bombastic, high-flown (*style etc.*).

enfler [ɑ̃'fle], *v.t.* to swell out, to puff up, to distend; (*fig.*) to excite; to exaggerate. **s'enfler**, *v.r.* to swell; (*fig.*) to be puffed up.

enflure [ɑ̃'fly:r], *n.f.* bloatedness, swelling; bombast.

enfoncé [ɑ̃fɔ̃'se], *a.* broken open; sunken; (*pop.*) done for.

enfoncement [ɑ̃fɔ̃s'mɑ̃], *n.m.* breaking in; sinking; recess; (*Paint.*) background.

enfoncer [ɑ̃fɔ̃'se], *v.t.* (*conjug. like* COMMENCER) to push *or* drive in, down etc.; to sink; to break in; to get the better of.—*v.i.* to sink, to founder. **s'enfoncer**, *v.r.* to sink; to bury oneself; to plunge; (*fig.*) to fail.

enfonçure [ɑ̃fɔ̃'sy:r], *n.f.* cavity, hole, hollow.

enforcir [ɑ̃fɔr'si:r], *v.t.* to strengthen.—*v.i.* and **s'enforcir**, *v.r.* to gather strength; to grow stronger.

enfouir [ɑ̃'fwi:r], *v.t.* to put *or* bury in the ground; (*fig.*) to hide. **s'enfouir**, *v.r.* to bury oneself (*in an out-of-the-way place etc.*).

enfourcher [ɑ̃fur'ʃe], *v.t.* to bestride, to straddle; to pierce with a pitch-fork etc.

enfourchure [ɑ̃fur'ʃy:r], *n.f.* fork; crotch.

enfourner [ɑ̃fur'ne], *v.t.* to put in the oven. **s'enfourner**, *v.r.* to get into a blind alley, a scrape etc.

enfreindre [ɑ̃'frɛ̃:dr], *v.t. irr.* (*conjug. like* CRAINDRE) to infringe, to break, to violate.

enfuir (s') [sɑ̃'fɥi:r], *v.r. irr.* (*conjug. like* FUIR) to run away, to escape.

enfumer [ɑ̃fy'me], *v.t.* to smoke, to fill with smoke, to smoke (*vermin etc.*) out.

enfûtage [ɑ̃fy'ta:ʒ], *n.m.* casking.

enfutailler [ɑ̃fyta'je], **enfuter** [ɑ̃fy'te], *v.t.* to cask, to barrel, to tun (*wine etc.*).

engagé [ɑ̃ga'ʒe], *a.* pledged; engaged, enlisted; in action; (*Naut.*) water-logged.

engageant [ɑ̃ga'ʒɑ̃], *a.* engaging, winning.

engagement [ɑ̃gaʒ'mɑ̃], *n.m.* engagement, commitment; pledging; mortgage; appointment; (*Mil.*) enlisting; action; entry (*for a sporting event*); (*pl.*) liabilities.

engager [ɑ̃ga'ʒe], *v.t.* (*conjug. like* MANGER) to pledge, to pawn; to engage; to begin; to invite, to induce, to urge; to involve. **s'engager**, *v.r.* to engage oneself, to undertake, to promise; to stand security; to begin; to enter; to enlist; to get involved.

engeance [ɑ̃'ʒɑ̃:s], *n.f.* breed; brood (*esp. of poultry*).

engelure [ɑ̃ʒ'ly:r], *n.f.* chilblain.

engendrer [ɑ̃ʒɑ̃'dre], *v.t.* to beget, to engender; (*fig.*) to produce.

engin [ɑ̃'ʒɛ̃], *n.m.* machine, engine; snare; tool; ***engin téléguidé***, guided missile.

englober [ɑ̃glɔ'be], *v.t.* to unite, to put together; (*fig.*) to include, to embrace.

engloutir [ɑ̃glu'ti:r], *v.t.* to swallow, to devour. **s'engloutir**, *v.r.* to be swallowed up.

engloutissement [ɑ̃glutis'mɑ̃], *n.m.* engulfing, swallowing up.

engoncé [ɑ̃gɔ̃'se], *a.* ***avoir l'air engoncé***, to look awkward and stiff.

engorgement [ɑ̃gɔrʒə'mɑ̃], *n.m.* obstruction, stopping up (*of a pipe etc.*); (*Med.*) congestion; (*Econ.*) glut.

engorger [ɑ̃gɔr'ʒe], *v.t.* (*conjug. like* MANGER) to obstruct, to block. **s'engorger**, *v.r.* to be obstructed *or* choked up.

engouement or **engoûment** [ɑ̃gu'mɑ̃], *n.m.* (*Med.*) choking, obstruction; (*fig.*) infatuation.

engouer [ɑ̃'gwe], *v.t.* to obstruct (*the throat etc.*); (*fig.*) to infatuate. **s'engouer**, *v.r.* to half choke oneself; (*fig.*) to be infatuated.

engouffrer [ɑ̃gu'fre], *v.t.* to engulf; (*fig.*) to swallow up. **s'engouffrer**, *v.r.* to be engulfed; to be swallowed up; to blow hard (*of the wind*).

engourdi [ɑ̃gur'di], *a.* torpid; benumbed.

engourdir [ɑ̃gur'di:r], *v.t.* to benumb; to dull, to enervate. **s'engourdir**, *v.r.* to get benumbed; to become sluggish.

engourdissement [ɑ̃gurdis'mɑ̃], *n.m.* numbness; torpor, enervation.

engrais [ɑ̃'grɛ], *n.m.* manure, fertilizer; fattening (*cattle*).

engraissant [ɑ̃grɛ'sɑ̃], *a.* fattening.

engraissement [ɑ̃grɛs'mɑ̃], *n.m.* fattening.

engraisser [ɑ̃grɛ'se], *v.t.* to fatten; to manure; (*fig.*) to enrich.—*v.i.* to grow fat; (*fig.*) to thrive. **s'engraisser**, *v.r.* to grow fat *or* stout.

engrenage [ɑ̃grə'na:ʒ], *n.m.* gear, gearing etc.; action of these; (*fig.*) correlation (*of circumstances etc.*).
engrener (1) [ɑ̃grə'ne], *v.t.* (*conjug. like* AMENER) to put corn into (*the mill-hopper*); to feed with corn.
engrener (2) [ɑ̃grə'ne], *v.t.* (*conjug. like* AMENER) (*Mach.*) to throw into gear. **s'engrener**, *v.r.* to work into each other (*of toothed wheels*); to be put in gear.
engrenure [ɑ̃grə'ny:r], *n.f.* engagement of teeth, cogs etc.
engrumeler (s') [sɑ̃grym'le], *v.r.* (*conjug. like* APPELER) to clot, to coagulate.
enhardir [ɑ̃ar'di:r], *v.t.* to embolden, to encourage. **s'enhardir**, *v.r.* to grow bold.
enherber [ɑ̃nɛr'be], *v.t.* to put land under grass.
énigmatique [enigma'tik], *a.* enigmatical.
énigmatiquement [enigmatik'mɑ̃], *adv.* enigmatically.
énigme [e'nigm], *n.f.* enigma, riddle.
enivrant [ɑ̃ni'vrɑ̃], *a.* intoxicating.
enivrement [ɑ̃nivrə'mɑ̃], *n.m.* intoxication; (*fig.*) elation.
enivrer [ɑ̃ni'vre], *v.t.* to intoxicate, to inebriate; (*fig.*) to elate. **s'enivrer**, *v.r.* to get intoxicated; (*fig.*) to be elated.
enjambée [ɑ̃ʒɑ̃'be], *n.f.* stride.
enjambement [ɑ̃ʒɑ̃b'mɑ̃], *n.m.* (*Pros.*) run-on line, enjambment.
enjamber [ɑ̃ʒɑ̃'be], *v.t.* to skip *or* leap over; to stride; (*fig.*) to encroach upon; (*Pros.*) to make enjambment.
enjeu [ɑ̃'ʒø], *n.m.* (*pl.* **-eux**) stake (*gaming* and *fig.*).
enjoindre [ɑ̃'ʒwɛ̃:dr], *v.t. irr.* (*conjug. like* CRAINDRE) to enjoin, to charge, to direct, to prescribe.
enjôlement [ɑ̃ʒol'mɑ̃], *n.m.* wheedling, coaxing, cajoling.
enjôler [ɑ̃ʒo'le], *v.t.* to coax, to wheedle.
enjôleur [ɑ̃ʒo'lœ:r], *n.m.* (*fem.* **-euse**) wheedler, coaxer.
enjolivement [ɑ̃ʒɔliv'mɑ̃], *n.m.* embellishment, decoration, ornament.
enjoliver [ɑ̃ʒɔli've], *v.t.* to embellish, to set off.
enjoliveur [ɑ̃ʒɔli'vœ:r], *n.m.* (*fem.* **-euse**) embellisher.
enjolivure [ɑ̃ʒɔli'vy:r], *n.f.* (small) embellishment.
enjoué [ɑ̃'ʒwe], *a.* playful, sprightly, lively, jovial, sportive.
enjouement or **enjoûment** [ɑ̃ʒu'mɑ̃], *n.m.* playfulness, sportiveness, sprightliness.
enlacement [ɑ̃las'mɑ̃], *n.m.* lacing, interlacing, entwining.
enlacer [ɑ̃la'se], *v.t.* (*conjug. kile* COMMENCER) to lace; to entwine; to clasp. **s'enlacer**, *v.r.* to entwine, to be interlaced.
enlaidir [ɑ̃lɛ'di:r], *v.t.* to make ugly; to disfigure.—*v.i.* to grow ugly, to be disfigured.
enlaidissement [ɑ̃lɛdis'mɑ̃], *n.m.* disfigurement.
enlèvement [ɑ̃lɛv'mɑ̃], *n.m.* carrying off; removal; wiping off; kidnapping.
enlever [ɑ̃lə've], *v.t.* (*conjug. like* AMENER) to remove, to take off; to carry off; to kidnap; to wipe off; to charm. **s'enlever**, *v.r.* to rise, to be lifted; to come off, to peel off; to come out; to be snapped up (*of goods on sale*); to get into a passion.
enlève-taches [ɑ̃lɛv'taʃ], *n.m. inv.* stain remover.
enliasser [ɑ̃lja'se], *v.t.* to tie up in a bundle.
enlignement [ɑ̃liɲ'mɑ̃], *n.m.* alignment.
enligner [ɑ̃li'ɲe], *v.t.* to put in line.
enlisement [ɑ̃liz'mɑ̃], *n.m.* sinking, swallowing up (*in quicksand*).
enliser [ɑ̃li'ze], *v.t.* to engulf. **s'enliser**, *v.r.* to be engulfed *or* swallowed up.
enluminer [ɑ̃lymi'ne], *v.t.* to colour; to illuminate. **s'enluminer**, *v.r.* to rouge, to paint; to flush.
enlumineur [ɑ̃lymi'nœ:r], *n.m.* (*fem.* **-euse**) colourer of maps, prints etc.
enluminure [ɑ̃lymi'ny:r], *n.f.* colouring; coloured print; tinsel (*of style*).
enneigé [ɑ̃nɛ'ʒe], *a.* snow-covered.
ennemi [ɛn'mi], *a.* hostile; injurious.—*n.m.* (*fem.* **-e**) enemy, foe.
ennoblir [ɑ̃nɔ'bli:r], *v.t.* to dignify, to exalt. **s'ennoblir**, *v.r.* to be ennobled *or* exalted.
ennoblissement [ɑ̃nɔblis'mɑ̃], *n.m.* ennoblement, exaltation.
ennui [ɑ̃'nɥi], *n.m.* trouble, worry; nuisance; boredom.
ennuyer [ɑ̃nɥi'je], *v.t.* (*conjug. like* EMPLOYER) to bore, to weary; to pester; (*fig.*) to annoy. **s'ennuyer**, *v.r.* to be bored, to feel dull; to miss.
ennuyeusement [ɑ̃nɥijøz'mɑ̃], *adv.* tediously, irksomely.
ennuyeux [ɑ̃nɥi'jø], *a.* (*fem.* **-euse**) boring, tedious, dull, tiresome; annoying.—*n.m.* (*fem.* **-euse**) tiresome person, bore.
énoncé [enɔ̃'se], *n.m.* statement.
énoncer [enɔ̃'se], *v.t.* (*conjug. like* COMMENCER) to state, to express, to enunciate. **s'énoncer**, *v.r.* to be worded *or* expressed.
éconciatif [enɔ̃sja'tif], *a.* (*fem.* **-tive**) enunciative.
énonciation [enɔ̃sjɑ'sjɔ̃], *n.f.* enunciation, delivery; statement; wording.
enorgueillir [ɑ̃nɔrgœ'ji:r], *v.t.* to make proud, to elate. **s'enorgueillir**, *v.r.* to be *or* grow proud of, to be elated, to glory in (***de***).
énorme [e'nɔrm], *a.* enormous, huge.
énormément [enɔrme'mɑ̃], *adv.* enormously, beyond measure.
énormité [enɔrmi'te], *n.f.* hugeness, vastness; enormity.
enquérir (s') [sɑ̃ke'ri:r], *v.r. irr.* (*conjug. like* ACQUÉRIR) to inquire, to make inquiries.
enquête [ɑ̃'kɛ:t], *n.f.* inquiry, investigation; inquest.
enquêter [ɑ̃kɛ'te], *v.i.* to inquire into a matter (***sur***), to conduct an inquiry.
enquêteur [ɑ̃kɛ'tœ:r], *n.m.* (*fem.* **-euse**) investigator.
enraciner [ɑ̃rasi'ne], *v.t.* to root; (*fig.*) to implant. **s'enraciner**, *v.r.* to take root.
enragé [ɑ̃ra'ʒe], *a.* mad, rabid; (*fig.*) enthusiastic.—*n.m.* (*fem.* **-ée**) madman, mad woman; desperate person.
enrageant [ɑ̃ra'ʒɑ̃], *a.* maddening, vexing.
enrager [ɑ̃ra'ʒe], *v.i.* (*conjug. like* MANGER) to be mad, to go mad; to be enraged, to fume.
enrayage [ɑ̃rɛ'ja:ʒ], *n.m.* (*Mil.*) jam (*in rifle*).

enrayement or **enraiement** [ɑ̃rɛj'mɑ̃], *n.m.* skidding, locking.
enrayer (1) [ɑ̃rɛ'je], *v.t.* (*conjug. like* PAYER) to put spokes to (*a wheel*); to skid (*a wheel*), to apply brakes to; (*fig.*) to check, to slow up (*an attack*); to stem (*an epidemic*); to jam (*a machine-gun*).
enrayer (2) [ɑ̃rɛ'je], *v.t.* (*conjug. like* PAYER) (*Agric.*) to plough the first furrow in.
enrayure (1) [ɑ̃rɛ'jy:r], *n.f.* drag, skid, lock-chain.
enrayure (2) [ɑ̃rɛ'jy:r], *n.m.* (*Agric.*) first furrow.
enrégimenter [ɑ̃reʒimɑ̃'te], *v.t.* to form into regiments; (*fig.*) to enrol.
enregistrement [ɑ̃rəʒistrə'mɑ̃], *n.m.* registration, recording; booking (*of luggage*).
enregistrer [ɑ̃rəʒis'tre], *v.t.* to register, to record; to book (*luggage*).
enregistreur [ɑ̃rəʒis'trœ:r], *n.m.* registrar; recording machine.
enrêner [ɑ̃rɛ'ne], *v.t.* to rein in; to tie up by the reins.
enrhumer [ɑ̃ry'me], *v.t.* to give a cold to (*someone*). **s'enrhumer**, *v.r.* to catch a cold.
enrichi [ɑ̃ri'ʃi], *n.m.* (*fem.* **-e**) upstart, parvenu, new rich.
enrichir [ɑ̃ri'ʃi:r], *v.t.* to enrich; (*fig.*) to embellish. **s'enrichir**, *v.r.* to enrich oneself, to thrive.
enrichissement [ɑ̃riʃis'mɑ̃], *n.m.* enrichment; (*fig.*) embellishment.
enrôlement [ɑ̃rol'mɑ̃], *n.m.* enrolment; (*Mil.*) enlistment.
enrôler [ɑ̃ro'le], *v.t.* to enlist; to enrol. **s'enrôler**, *v.r.* to enrol oneself, to enlist.
enroué [ɑ̃'rwe], *a.* hoarse, husky.
enrouement [ɑ̃ru'mɑ̃], *n.m.* hoarseness, huskiness.
enrouer [ɑ̃'rwe], *v.t.* to make hoarse. **s'enrouer**, *v.r.* to become hoarse *or* husky.
enroulement [ɑ̃rul'mɑ̃], *n.m.* rolling up; (*Arch.*) scroll.
enrouler [ɑ̃ru'le], *v.t.* to roll up, to coil. **s'enrouler**, *v.r.* to roll oneself up; to twine (*of plants etc.*).
enrubanner [ɑ̃ryba'ne], *v.t.* to deck out with ribbons. **s'enrubanner**, *v.r.* to beribbon oneself.
ensabiement [ɑ̃sɑblə'mɑ̃], *n.m.* sand-bank; ballasting; stranding (*of a ship*).
ensabler [ɑ̃sɑ'ble], *v.t.* to ballast; to run aground, to strand. **s'ensabler**, *v.r.* to run aground; to sink in sand; to silt up.
ensacher [ɑ̃sa'ʃe], *v.t.* to put in bags *or* sacks.
ensanglanter [ɑ̃sɑ̃glɑ̃'te], *v.t.* to make bloody, to stain with blood.
enseignant [ɑ̃sɛ'ɲɑ̃], *a.* teaching.—*n.m.* (*pl.*) teachers.
enseigne [ɑ̃'sɛɲ], *n.f.* sign, signboard; mark, token; ensign, flag.—*n.m.* (*Navy*) sub-lieutenant; (*U.S.*) ensign.
enseignement [ɑ̃sɛɲ'mɑ̃], *n.m.* teaching, education; teaching profession.
enseigner [ɑ̃sɛ'ɲe], *v.t.* to teach, to instruct; to inform, to direct.
ensemble [ɑ̃'sɑ̃:bl], *adv.* together, at the same time.—*n.m.* whole, general effect, mass; two- *or* three-piece (*clothing*); suite (*furniture*); (*Math.*) set.
ensemencement [ɑ̃smɑ̃s'mɑ̃], *n.m.* sowing.
ensemencer [ɑ̃smɑ̃'se], *v.t.* (*conjug. like* COMMENCER) to sow.
enserrer [ɑ̃sɛ're], *v.t.* to enclose; to lock up; to hem in.
ensevelir [ɑ̃sə'vli:r], *v.t.* to shroud; (*fig.*) to bury; to swallow up, to entomb; to absorb. **s'ensevelir**, *v.r.* to bury oneself.
ensevelissement [ɑ̃səvlis'mɑ̃], *n.m.* putting in a shroud; burial.
ensoleillé [ɑ̃sɔlɛ'je], *a.* sunny.
ensoleiller [ɑ̃sɔlɛ'je], *v.t.* to light up with sunshine; (*fig.*) to brighten.
ensommeillé [ɑ̃sɔmɛ'je], *a.* heavy with sleep; (*fig.*) torpid.
ensorceler [ɑ̃sɔrsə'le], *v.t.* (*conjug. like* APPELER) to bewitch.
ensorceleur [ɑ̃sɔrsə'lœ:r], *a.* (*fem.* **-euse**) bewitching.—*n.m.* (*fem.* **-euse**) enchanter, enchantress.
ensorcellement [ɑ̃sɔrsɛl'mɑ̃], *n.m.* bewitchment.
ensuite [ɑ̃'sɥit], *adv.* after, afterwards, then, in the next place; what then? what next? well!
ensuivre (s') [sɑ̃'sɥi:vr], *v.r. irr.* (*conjug. like* SUIVRE) to follow, to result, to ensue.
entacher [ɑ̃ta'ʃe], *v.t.* to sully; to taint, to cast a slur on.
entaille [ɑ̃'tɑ:j], *n.f.* notch; cut; gash; groove.
entailler [ɑ̃tɑ'je], *v.t.* to notch, to cut.
entamer [ɑ̃ta'me], *v.t.* to make the first cut in, to make an incision in; to broach; to break into.
entartrer (s') [sɑ̃tar'tre], *v.r.* to scale, to become furred.
entassement [ɑ̃tɑs'mɑ̃], *n.m.* accumulation; heap, pile; crowding together.
entasser [ɑ̃tɑ'se], *v.t.* to heap *or* pile up, to accumulate; to hoard up; to pack together. **s'entasser**, *v.r.* to heap up; to crowd together.
entendement [ɑ̃tɑ̃d'mɑ̃], *n.m.* understanding; judgment, sense.
entendre [ɑ̃'tɑ̃:dr], *v.t.* to hear; to understand; to know; to intend; to mean. **s'entendre**, *v.r.* to hear each other; to hear one's own voice; to be heard; to be understood; to understand one another; to act in concert; to come to terms (*avec*); to agree with; to be skilful in.
entendu [ɑ̃tɑ̃'dy], *a.* heard; understood; agreed; skilful.
enténébrer [ɑ̃tene'bre], *v.t.* (*conjug. like* CÉDER) to plunge *or* wrap in darkness.
entente [ɑ̃'tɑ̃:t], *n.f.* meaning; skill, judgment; understanding, agreement.
enter [ɑ̃'te], *v.t.* to graft upon, to engraft; to join.
entériner [ɑ̃teri'ne], *v.t.* to ratify, to confirm.
entérique [ɑ̃te'rik], *a.* enteric.
entérite [ɑ̃te'rit], *n.f.* enteritis.
enterrement [ɑ̃tɛr'mɑ̃], *n.m.* burial, interment, funeral.
enterrer [ɑ̃tɛ're], *v.t.* to bury, to inter; (*fig.*) to survive, to outlive; to end. **s'enterrer**, *v.r.* to bury oneself.
en-tête [ɑ̃'tɛ:t], *n.m.* (*pl.* **-têtes**) heading, headline.
entêté [ɑ̃tɛ'te], *a.* stubborn, obstinate.—*n.m.* (*fem.* **-ée**) stubborn person.

entêtement [ɑ̃tɛt'mɑ̃], *n.m.* stubbornness, obstinacy; infatuation.
entêter [ɑ̃tɛ'te], *v.t.* to give a headache to; to make giddy, to intoxicate. **s'entêter**, *v.r.* to be stubborn, to persist (*in*); to be infatuated (***de***).
enthousiasme [ɑ̃tu'zjasm], *n.m.* enthusiasm, rapture, ecstasy.
enthousiasmer [ɑ̃tuzjas'me], *v.t.* to render enthusiastic, to enrapture. **s'enthousiasmer**, *v.r.* to be enthusiastic, to be in raptures (***de***).
enthousiaste [ɑ̃tu'zjast], *a.* enthusiastic.—*n.* enthusiast.
entiché [ɑ̃ti'ʃe], *a.* infatuated, keen on.
entichement [ɑ̃tiʃ'mɑ̃], *n.m.* infatuation, addiction.
enticher [ɑ̃ti'ʃe], *v.t.* to infatuate. **s'enticher**, *v.r.* to be infatuated with (***de***).
entier [ɑ̃'tje], *a.* (*fem.* **-ière**) entire, whole; total; positive.—*n.m.* entirety, totality; (*Arith.*) integral.
entièrement [ɑ̃tjɛr'mɑ̃], *adv.* entirely, wholly.
entité [ɑ̃ti'te], *n.f.* entity.
entonner (1) [ɑ̃tɔ'ne], *v.t.* to tun, to put into casks.
entonner (2) [ɑ̃tɔ'ne], *v.t.* to begin to sing, to strike up.
entonnoir [ɑ̃tɔ'nwa:r], *n.m.* funnel; shell-hole.
entorse [ɑ̃'tɔrs], *n.f.* sprain; strain, twist.
entortillage [ɑ̃tɔrti'ja:ʒ], **entortillement** [ɑ̃tɔrtij'mɑ̃], *n.m.* entanglement; winding, coiling; abstruseness; subterfuge; equivocation.
entortiller [ɑ̃tɔrti'je], *v.t.* to wrap, to roll round; to distort; to entangle. **s'entortiller**, *v.r.* to twist oneself round; to twine; to be obscure.
entour [ɑ̃'tu:r], *n.m.* (*used only in pl. except in the adverbial expression* **à l'entour**, around) environs, adjacent parts.
entourage [ɑ̃tu'ra:ʒ], *n.m.* frame; entourage, friends, relations, circle, attendants.
entourer [ɑ̃tu're], *v.t.* to surround; to gather round.
entournure [ɑ̃tur'ny:r], *n.f.* arm-hole.
entracte [ɑ̃'trakt], *n.m.* interval (*between acts*); interlude.
entraide [ɑ̃'trɛd], *n.f.* (*no pl.*) mutual aid.
entraider (**s'**) or **entr'aider** (**s'**) [sɑ̃trɛ'de], *v.r.* to help one another.
entrailles [ɑ̃'trɑ:j], *n.f. pl.* intestines, entrails, bowels; (*fig.*) feelings, tenderness, pity.
entrain [ɑ̃'trɛ̃], *n.m.* warmth, heartiness; spirit, animation, life, go.
entraînant [ɑ̃trɛ'nɑ̃], *a.* captivating, seductive.
entraînement [ɑ̃trɛn'mɑ̃], *n.m.* enthusiasm, rapture; impulse, temptation; (*Spt.*) coaching, training.
entraîner [ɑ̃trɛ'ne], *v.t.* to drag along; to carry away; to win over; to involve; to train.
entraîneur [ɑ̃trɛ'nœ:r], *n.m.* (*fem.* **-euse**) trainer (*esp. of horses*); pace-maker; coach (*of teams*).
entrant [ɑ̃'trɑ̃], *a.* ingoing, incoming.—*n.m.* (*fem.* **-e**) person going *or* coming in.
entr'apercevoir [ɑ̃trapɛrsə'vwa:r], *v.t. irr.* (*conjug. like* RECEVOIR) to catch a quick glimpse of.
entr'appeler (**s'**) [sɑ̃tra'ple], *v.r.* (*conjug. like* APPELER) to call one another.
entrave [ɑ̃'tra:v], *n.f.* clog, fetter, hobble; (*fig.*) hindrance, impediment.
entraver [ɑ̃tra've], *v.t.* to shackle; to hinder, to thwart.
entre [ɑ̃:tr], *prep.* between, betwixt; among, amongst; into.
entrebâillé [ɑ̃trəbɑ'je], *a.* ajar, half-open.
entrebâillement [ɑ̃trəbɑj'mɑ̃], *n.m.* small opening, gap, chink.
entrebâiller [ɑ̃trəbɑ'je], *v.t.* to half-open.
entrechat [ɑ̃trə'ʃa], *n.m.* caper in dancing, entrechat.
entrechoquement [ɑ̃trəʃɔk'mɑ̃], *n.m.* clash, collision, conflict.
entrechoquer (**s'**) [sɑ̃trəʃɔ'ke], *v.r.* to knock, to run *or* dash against each other.
entre-clos [ɑ̃trə'klo], *a.* half-closed; half-drawn.
entr'éclos [ɑ̃tre'klo], *a.* half-opened (*flower*).
entrecôte [ɑ̃trə'ko:t], *n.f.* steak cut from between the ribs.
entrecoupé [ɑ̃trəku'pe], *a.* broken (*of words, speech etc.*).
entrecouper [ɑ̃trəku'pe], *v.t.* to intersect; to interrupt; to intersperse.
entrecroisement [ɑ̃trəkrwɑz'mɑ̃], *n.m.* intersection, crossing.
entrecroiser [ɑ̃trəkrwɑ'ze], *v.t.* to intersect. **s'entrecroiser**, *v.r.* to cross one other, to intersect.
entre-deux [ɑ̃trə'dø], *n.m. inv.* partition; insertion (*of lace etc.*).
entrée [ɑ̃'tre], *n.f.* entry, entrance; mouth; reception; beginning; first course.
entrefaites [ɑ̃trə'fɛt], *n.f. pl.* interval, meantime; ***sur ces entrefaites***, meanwhile.
entrefilet [ɑ̃trəfi'lɛ], *n.m.* (short) paragraph, note (*in a newspaper*).
entregent [ɑ̃trə'ʒɑ̃], *n.m.* tact, cleverness (*in dealing with people*).
entrelacement [ɑ̃trəlas'mɑ̃], *n.m.* interlacing, interweaving, intertwining.
entrelacer [ɑ̃trəla'se], *v.t.* (*conjug. like* COMMENCER) to interlace, to intertwine. **s'entrelacer**, *v.r.* to entwine, to twist round each other.
entrelardé [ɑ̃trəlar'de], *a.* interlarded, streaky.
entrelarder [ɑ̃trəlar'de], *v.t.* to lard.
entremêlement [ɑ̃trəmɛl'mɑ̃], *n.m.* intermixing, intermingling.
entremêler [ɑ̃trəmɛ'le], *v.t.* to intermingle, to intermix. **s'entremêler**, *v.r.* to intermingle, to meddle.
entremets [ɑ̃trə'mɛ], *n.m. inv.* side-dish, sweet.
entremetteur [ɑ̃trəmɛ'tœ:r], *n.m.* (*fem.* **-euse**) go-between, mediator.
entremettre (**s'**) [sɑ̃trə'mɛtr], *v.r. irr.* (*conjug. like* METTRE) to interpose; to interfere, to meddle.
entremise [ɑ̃trə'mi:z], *n.f.* intervention, mediation.
entrepont [ɑ̃trə'pɔ̃], *n.m.* (*Naut.*) between decks; ***passagers d'entrepont***, steerage passengers.
entreposer [ɑ̃trəpo'ze], *v.t.* to store, to warehouse; to put in bond.
entrepositaire [ɑ̃trəpɔzi'tɛ:r], *n.* bonder; depositor (*of goods*).
entrepôt [ɑ̃trə'po], *n.m.* bonded warehouse, store; mart, emporium, depot.

entreprenant [ɑ̃trəprə'nɑ̃], *a.* enterprising, adventurous; daring, bold.
entreprendre [ɑ̃trə'prɑ̃:dr], *v.t. irr.* (*conjug. like* PRENDRE) to undertake, to attempt; to contract for *or* to; to venture.—*v.i.* to encroach, to infringe (***sur***).
entrepreneur [ɑ̃trəprə'nœ:r], *n.m.* (*fem.* **-euse**) contractor; master-builder; ***entrepreneur de pompes funèbres***, undertaker.
entreprise [ɑ̃trə'pri:z], *n.f.* enterprise, undertaking; concern, company.
entrer [ɑ̃'tre], *v.i.* (*with aux.* ÊTRE) to enter, to come *or* go in; to run into.
entre-rail [ɑ̃trə'rɑ:j], *n.m.* (*pl.* **-rails**) (*Rail.*) gauge.
entresol [ɑ̃trə'sɔl], *n.m.* mezzanine, entresol (*rooms between the ground floor and the first floor*).
entre-temps [ɑ̃trə'tɑ̃], *n.m. inv.* interval; ***dans l'entre-temps***, meanwhile.—*adv.* meanwhile.
entretenir [ɑ̃trət'ni:r], *v.t. irr.* (*conjug. like* TENIR) to hold together, to keep up, to keep in good order; to maintain, to support; to entertain. **s'entretenir**, *v.r.* to be kept up, to be maintained; to subsist; to converse.
entretien [ɑ̃trə'tjɛ̃], *n.m.* maintenance, servicing (*of car etc.*); preservation; living, livelihood; conversation, interview, conference.
entrevoir [ɑ̃trə'vwa:r], *v.t. irr.* (*conjug. like* VOIR) to catch a glimpse of; to foresee confusedly.
entrevue [ɑ̃trə'vy], *n.f.* interview.
entr'ouvert [ɑ̃tru'vɛ:r], *a.* partly open, ajar; gaping.
entr'ouvrir [ɑ̃tru'vri:r], *v.t. irr.* (*conjug. like* OUVRIR) to open a little, to half-open. **s'entr'ouvrir**, *v.r.* to be ajar; to open up.
énumérateur [enymera'tœ:r], *n.m.* (*fem.* **-trice**) enumerator.
énumératif [enymera'tif], *a.* (*fem.* **-tive**) enumerative.
énumération [enymerɑ'sjɔ̃], *n.f.* enumeration.
énumérer [enyme're], *v.t.* (*conjug. like* CÉDER) to enumerate, to count, to reckon.
envahir [ɑ̃va'i:r], *v.t.* to invade, to overrun; to encroach upon.
envahissant [ɑ̃vai'sɑ̃], *a.* invading, encroaching.
envahissement [ɑ̃vais'mɑ̃], *n.m.* invasion, overrunning; encroachment.
envahisseur [ɑ̃vai'sœ:r], *a.* (*fem.* **-euse**) invading, encroaching.—*n.m.* (*fem.* **-euse**) invader.
envaser [ɑ̃vɑ'ze], *v.t.* to fill up *or* choke with silt. **s'envaser**, *v.r.* to stick fast in the mud; to silt up.
enveloppe [ɑ̃'vlɔp], *n.f.* wrapper, cover; envelope; exterior; (*Motor.*) outer cover.
enveloppement [ɑ̃vlɔp'mɑ̃], *n.m.* enveloping, wrapping up.
envelopper [ɑ̃vlɔ'pe], *v.t.* to envelop, to wrap up, to cover; to surround; to disguise. **s'envelopper**, *v.r.* to cover *or* wrap oneself up.
envenimement [ɑ̃vnimə'mɑ̃], *n.m.* poisoning; aggravation (*of a quarrel*).
envenimer [ɑ̃vni'me], *v.t.* to poison; to inflame, to exasperate. **s'envenimer**, *v.r.* to be envenomed; to fester, to rankle.
envergure [ɑ̃vɛr'gy:r], *n.f.* spread (*of sail*); spread, span (*of a bird's wings, of an aeroplane*).
envers [ɑ̃'vɛ:r], *prep.* towards, to (*in respect of*).—*n.m.* wrong side, reverse side, back; ***à l'envers***, on the wrong side, inside out.
envi (à l') [alɑ̃'vi], *adv. phr.* emulously, vying with each other.
enviable [ɑ̃'vjabl], *a.* enviable, to be envied.
envie [ɑ̃'vi], *n.f.* envy; desire, longing; birthmark; ***avoir envie de***, to have a mind to, to long for, to feel like.
envier [ɑ̃'vje], *v.t.* to envy; to long for; to grudge.
envieux [ɑ̃'vjø], *a.* and *n.m.* (*fem.* **-euse**) envious, jealous (person).
environ [ɑ̃vi'rɔ̃], *adv.* about, nearly, thereabouts.—*n.m.* (*pl.*) environs, vicinity, neighbourhood.
environnant [ɑ̃virɔ'nɑ̃], *a.* surrounding.
environner [ɑ̃virɔ'ne], *v.t.* to surround, to stand round, to encircle, to enclose.
envisager [ɑ̃viza'ʒe], *v.t.* (*conjug. like* MANGER) to look, to stare in the face, to face; to consider, to envisage.
envoi [ɑ̃'vwa], *n.m.* sending (*of thing sent*); packet, parcel, consignment, shipment; (*Pros.*) envoy.
envol [ɑ̃'vɔl], *n.m.* taking wing (*of birds*), taking off (*of aeroplanes*), start; ***piste d'envol***, runway.
envolée [ɑ̃vɔ'le], *n.f.* flight; (*fig.*) élan.
envoler (s') [sɑ̃vɔ'le], *v.r.* to fly away; to take off; (*fig.*) to be carried off (*by the wind etc.*); (*fig.*) to disappear.
envoûtement [ɑ̃vut'mɑ̃], *n.m.* spell, magical charm.
envoûter [ɑ̃vu'te], *v.t.* to cast a spell on (*someone*).
envoyé [ɑ̃vwa'je], *n.m.* (*fem.* **-ée**) envoy; delegate, messenger; ***envoyé spécial*** (*of a paper*), special correspondent.
envoyer [ɑ̃vwa'je], *v.t. irr.* to send, to forward, to dispatch.
envoyeur [ɑ̃vwa'jœ:r], *n.m.* (*fem.* **-euse**) sender.
enzyme [ɑ̃'ʒim], *n.f.* enzyme.
éon [e'ɔ̃], *n.m.* aeon.
épagneul [epa'ɲœl], *n.m.* spaniel.
épais [e'pɛ], *a.* thick, dense; thickset; (*fig.*) dull, gross.—*adv.* thick, thickly.
épaisseur [epɛ'sœ:r], *n.f.* thickness, density; stoutness; dullness.
épaissir [epɛ'si:r], *v.t.* to thicken.—*v.i.* and **s'epaissir,** *v.r.* to become thick, to grow big; to become heavy.
épaississement [epɛsis'mɑ̃], *n.m.* thickening.
épanchement [epɑ̃ʃ'mɑ̃], *n.m.* pouring out, discharge; (*fig.*) outpouring (*emotion etc.*).
épancher [epɑ̃'ʃe], *v.t.* to pour out, to shed; to discharge. **s'épancher**, *v.r.* to be discharged, to overflow; to open one's heart.
épanchoir [epɑ̃'ʃwa:r], *n.m.* outlet, overflow.
épandre [e'pɑ̃:dr], *v.t.* to scatter, to strew; to shed (*light etc.*). **s'épandre**, *v.r.* to spread; (*fig.*) to stretch (*of a sheet of water etc.*).
épanoui [epa'nwi], *a.* in full bloom; (*fig.*) beaming.
épanouir [epa'nwi:r], *v.t.* to cause to open *or* expand; (*fig.*) to gladden. **s'épanouir**, *v.r.* to blossom, to open (*of flowers*); to brighten up (*of the face etc.*).

épanouissement [epanwis'mɑ̃], *n.m.* blossoming, opening (*of flowers*); (*fig.*) brightness, glow.
épargnant [epar'ɲɑ̃], *a.* sparing, saving; parsimonious.—*n.m.* (*fem.* **-e**) small investor.
épargne [e'parɲ], *n.f.* saving, thrift; parsimony; ***caisse d'épargne***, savings bank.
épargner [epar'ɲe], *v.t.* to save; to spare; to economize.
éparpillement [eparpij'mɑ̃], *n.m.* scattering, dispersion.
éparpiller [eparpi'je], *v.t.* to scatter, to spread, to disperse; to squander.
épars [e'pa:r], *a.* scattered, dispersed, sparse; dishevelled (*of hair*).
épaté [epa'te], *a.* flat (*of noses*); (*fam.*) amazed.
épaule [e'po:l], *n.f.* shoulder.
épaulement [epol'mɑ̃], *n.m.* shoulder; (*Naut.*) bows; (*Fort.*) breast-work.
épauler [epo'le], *v.t.* to splay the shoulder (*a horse etc.*); to bring (*a rifle*) to the shoulder.
épaulette [epo'lɛt], *n.f.* shoulder-strap; epaulet.
épave [e'pa:v], *n.f.* wreck; flotsam, jetsam; waif.
épée [e'pe], *n.f.* sword; (*fig.*) brand, steel.
épeler [e'ple], *v.t.* (*conjug. like* APPELER) to spell.
épellation [epɛlɑ'sjɔ̃], *n.f.* spelling.
éperdu [epɛr'dy], *a.* distracted, bewildered.
éperdument [epɛrdy'mɑ̃], *adv.* madly, distractedly.
éperon [e'prɔ̃], *n.m.* spur; (*Arch.*) buttress, starling (*of a bridge etc.*); (*Naut.*) prow.
éperonné [eprɔ'ne], *a.* spurred.
éperonner [eprɔ'ne], *v.t.* to spur; to urge forward.
éperonnière [eprɔ'njɛ:r], *n.f.* (*Bot.*) larkspur.
épervier [epɛr'vje], *n.m.* sparrow-hawk; cast-net.
épeuré [epø're], *a.* scared.
éphélide [efe'lid], *n.f.* sunburn; freckle.
éphémère [efe'mɛ:r], *a.* ephemeral, short-lived.—*n.m.* ephemera, may-fly.
épi [e'pi], *n.m.* ear of corn; (*Rail.*) system of marshalling tracks.
épice [e'pis], *n.f.* spice.
épicé [epi'se], *a.* spiced; seasoned.
épicer [epi'se], *v.t.* (*conjug. like* COMMENCER) to spice.
épicerie [epi'sri], *n.f.* spices; grocery.
épicier [epi'sje], *n.m.* (*fem.* **-ière**) grocer.
épicurien [epiky'rjɛ̃], *a.* (*fem.* **-enne**) epicurean, voluptuous.—*n.m.* (*fem.* **-enne**) epicure.
épicurisme [epiky'rism], *n.m.* epicureanism, epicurism.
épidémie [epide'mi], *n.f.* epidemic.
épidémique [epide'mik], *a.* epidemic.
épiderme [epi'dɛrm], *n.m.* epidermis, cuticle.
épidermique [epidɛr'mik], *a.* epidermic, epidermal.
épier (1) [e'pje], *v.i.* to ear (*of grain*).
épier (2) [e'pje], *v.t.* to watch; to spy upon; to lie in wait for.
épieu [e'pjø], *n.m.* (*pl.* **-eux**) boar-spear, hunting-pole.
épigrammatique [epigrama'tik], *a.* epigrammatical.
épigrammatiste [epigrama'tist], *n.* epigrammatist.
épigramme [epi'gram], *n.f.* epigram.
épigraphe [epi'graf], *n.f.* epigraph.
épilation [epilɑ'sjɔ̃], *n.f.* depilation.
épilatoire [epila'twa:r], *a.* depilatory.
épilepsie [epilɛp'si], *n.f.* epilepsy.
épileptique [epilɛp'tik], *a.* and *n.* epileptic.
épiler [epi'le], *v.t.* to depilate. **s'épiler**, *v.r.* to pluck out one's hairs.
épileur [epi'lœ:r], *n.m.* (*fem.* **-euse**) depilator (*person*).
épilogue [epi'lɔg], *n.m.* epilogue.
épiloguer [epilɔ'ge], *v.t.* to censure, to criticize.—*v.i.* to carp, to find fault.
épilogueur [epilɔ'gœ:r], *a.* (*fem.* **-euse**) fault-finding.—*n.m.* (*fem.* **-euse**) critic, fault-finder, carper.
épiloir [epi'lwa:r], *n.m.* tweezers.
épinaie [epi'nɛ], *n.f.* brake, thorny thicket.
épinard [epi'na:r], *n.m.* spinach.
épine [e'pin], *n.f.* thorn, prickle; (*fig.*) obstacle, difficulty; (*Anat.*) spine.
épinette [epi'nɛt], *n.f.* *spinet; (*Bot.*) spruce.
épineux [epi'nø], *a.* (*fem.* **-euse**) thorny prickly; (*fig.*) irritable; ticklish, intricate.
épingle [e'pɛ̃gl], *n.f.* pin; scarf-pin, breast-pin.
épinglé [epɛ̃'gle], *a.* pinned; corded, terry.—*n.m.* terry velvet.
épingler [epɛ̃'gle], *v.t.* to pin.
épinglier [epɛ̃'glje], *n.m.* pin-tray; (*fem.* **-ière**) pin-maker.
épinière [epi'njɛ:r], *a.* (*Anat.*) spinal.
Épiphanie [epifa'ni], *n.f.* Epiphany.
épique [e'pik], *a.* epic(al).
épiscopal [episkɔ'pal], *a.* (*m.pl.* **-aux**) episcopal.
épiscopalien [episkɔpa'ljɛ̃], *a.* and *n.m.* (*fem.* **-enne**) episcopalian.
épiscopat [episkɔ'pa], *n.m.* episcopate, episcopacy.
épisode [epi'zɔd], *n.m.* episode.
épistolaire [epistɔ'lɛ:r], *a.* epistolary.
épitaphe [epi'taf], *n.f.* epitaph.
épithète [epi'tɛt], *n.f.* epithet.
épitomé [epito'me], *n.m.* epitome, abridgment.
épître [e'pi:tr], *n.f.* epistle, letter, missive.
éploré [eplɔ're], *a.* in tears, distressed.
épluchage [eply'ʃa:ʒ], **épluchement** [eplyʃ'mɑ̃], *n.m.* cleaning; picking; peeling.
éplucher [eply'ʃe], *v.t.* to pick; to clean; to peel; (*fig.*) to sift.
éplucheur [eply'ʃœ:r], *n.m.* (*fem.* **-euse**) picker; fault-finder, hair-splitter.
épluchures [eply'ʃy:r], *n.f. pl.* parings, peelings.
épointé [epwɛ̃'te], *a.* blunt (*pencil, needle*).
épointement [epwɛ̃t'mɑ̃], *n.m.* bluntness.
épointer [epwɛ̃'te], *v.t.* to break the point off, to blunt. **s'épointer**, *v.r.* to have its point broken off.
éponge [e'pɔ̃:ʒ], *n.f.* sponge.
épongeage [epɔ̃'ʒa:ʒ], *n.m.* sponging.
éponger [epɔ̃'ʒe], *v.t.* (*conjug. like* MANGER) to sponge.
épopée [epɔ'pe], *n.f.* epic.
époque [e'pɔk], *n.f.* epoch, period, era; time.
époumoner [epumɔ'ne], *v.t.* to tire the lungs of, to exhaust. **s'époumoner**, *v.r.* to tire one's lungs; (*fig.*) to shout oneself hoarse.
épouse [e'pu:z], *n.f.* spouse, bride, wife.
épouser [epu'ze], *v.t.* to marry, to wed; (*fig.*) to take up. **s'épouser**, *v.r.* to marry (*each other*).

époussetage [epus'ta:ʒ], *n.m.* dusting.
épousseter [epus'te], *v.t.* (*conjug. like* APPELER) to dust.
époussette [epu'sɛt], *n.f.* dusting-brush, duster.
épouvantable [epuvɑ̃'tabl], *a.* frightful, dreadful, horrible, appalling.
épouvantablement [epuvɑ̃tablə'mɑ̃], *adv.* frightfully; dreadfully.
épouvantail [epuvɑ̃'ta:j], *n.m.* scarecrow; (*fig.*) bugbear.
épouvante [epu'vɑ̃:t], *n.f.* terror, fright; dismay.
épouvanter [epuvɑ̃'te], *v.t.* to terrify, to frighten. **s'épouvanter**, *v.r.* to be frightened *or* terrified.
époux [e'pu], *n.m.* husband, bridegroom; (*pl.*) married couple.
épreindre [e'prɛ̃:dr], *v.t. irr.* (*conjug. like* CRAINDRE) to squeeze out, to press.
éprendre (s') [se'prɑ̃:dr], *v.r. irr.* (*conjug. like* PRENDRE) to fall in love (*de*).
épreuve [e'prœ:v], *n.f.* proof, test; ordeal; examination; (*Print.*) proof-sheet; (*Phot.*) print.
épris [e'pri], *a.* in love, taken with.
éprouvé [epru've], *a.* tried, tested; stricken with misfortune.
éprouver [epru've], *v.t.* to try, to test; to put to the proof; (*fig.*) to feel, to experience.
éprouvette [epru'vɛt], *n.f.* gauge; test-tube; eprouvette (*for testing gunpowder*); (*Surg.*) probe.
épuisable [epɥi'zabl], *a.* exhaustible.
épuisement [epɥiz'mɑ̃], *n.m.* exhaustion, draining; enervation.
épuiser [epɥi'ze], *v.t.* to exhaust, to drain; to use up; to tire out, to wear out. **s'épuiser**, *v.r.* to be exhausted; to use up one's strength.
épuisette [epɥi'zɛt], *n.f.* landing-net; scoop.
épurateur [epyra'tœ:r], *a.* (*fem.* **-trice**) purifying.—*n.m.* purifier.
épuratif [epyra'tif], *a.* (*fem.* **-tive**) purifying, refining.
épuration [epyrɑ'sjɔ̃], *n.f.* purification; refining; (*Polit.*) purge.
épuratoire [epyra'twa:r], *a.* purifying.
épurement [epyr'mɑ̃], *n.m.* purifying.
épurer [epy're], *v.t.* to purify; to clarify; to refine; to purge. **s'épurer**, *v.r.* to be purified, to become pure.
équanime [ekwa'nim], *a.* even-tempered.
équanimité [ekwanimi'te], *n.f.* equanimity.
équarrir [eka'ri:r], *v.t.* to square; to cut up (*a carcass*).
équarrissage [ekari'sa:ʒ], **équarrissement** [ekaris'mɑ̃], *n.m.* squaring; squareness; flaying and cutting up (*of horses etc.*).
équarrisseur [ekari'sœ:r], *n.m.* knacker.
Équateur [ekwa'tœ:r], **l'**, *m.* Ecuador.
équateur [ekwa'tœ:r], *n.m.* equator.
équation [ekwɑ'sjɔ̃], *n.f.* equation.
équatorial [ekwatɔ'rjal], *a.* (*m. pl.* **-aux**) equatorial.
équatorien [ekwatɔ'rjɛ̃], *a.* (*fem.* **-enne**) Ecuadorean.—*n.m.* (**Équatorien**, *fem.* **-enne**) Ecuadorean (*person*).
équerre [e'kɛ:r], *n.f.* square, set-square.
équerrer [ekɛ're], *v.t.* to square, to bevel.
équestre [e'kɛstr], *a.* equestrian.
équilibre [eki'libr], *n.m.* equilibrium, poise, balance; (*Hist.*) balance of power.
équilibrer [ekili'bre], *v.t.* to equilibrate, to balance.
équilibriste [ekili'brist], *n.* tight-rope walker, acrobat.
équin [e'kɛ̃], *a.* equine; ***pied équin***, club foot.
équinoxe [eki'nɔks], *n.m.* equinox.
équinoxial [ekinɔk'sjal], *a.* (*m. pl.* **-aux**) equinoctial.
équipage [eki'pa:ʒ], *n.m.* equipage; carriage; dress; gear, tackle; personnel, crew.
équipe [e'kip], *n.f.* train of boats; gang (*of workmen etc.*); team (*of sportsmen*).
équipement [ekip'mɑ̃], *n.m.* outfit, fitting out; equipment.
équiper [eki'pe], *v.t.* to equip, to fit out; to furnish; to man. **s'équiper**, *v.r.* to fit oneself out; to rig oneself out.
équitable [eki'tabl], *a.* equitable, just, fair.
équitablement [ekitablə'mɑ̃], *adv.* equitably, justly, fairly.
équitation [ekitɑ'sjɔ̃], *n.f.* horsemanship, riding.
équité [eki'te], *n.f.* equity, fairness.
équivalence [ekiva'lɑ̃:s], *n.f.* equivalence.
équivalent [ekiva'lɑ̃], *a.* equivalent; tantamount (to).—*n.m.* equivalent.
équivaloir [ekiva'lwa:r], *v.i. irr.* (*conjug. like* VALOIR) to be equivalent, to be tantamount (*à*).
équivoque [eki'vɔk], *a.* equivocal, ambiguous; doubtful.—*n.f.* equivocation, ambiguity; evasion.
équivoquer [ekivɔ'ke], *v.t.* to equivocate, to speak ambiguously, to quibble.
érable [e'rabl], *n.m.* maple, maple-tree.
éradication [eradikɑ'sjɔ̃], *n.f.* eradication
érafler [erɑ'fle], *v.t.* to scratch slightly, to graze.
éraflure [erɑ'fly:r], *n.f.* slight scratch, graze.
éraillé [erɑ'je], *a.* frayed; wrinkled; bloodshot (*of the eyes*); raucous, hoarse (*of the voice*).
éraillement [erɑj'mɑ̃], *n.m.* eversion of the eyelids; fraying; huskiness.
érailler [erɑ'je], *v.t.* to unravel; to fray. **s'érailler**, *v.r.* to fray; to become bloodshot (*of the eyes*); to become husky (*of the voice*).
éraillure [erɑ'jy:r], *n.f.* fret, fraying; scratch.
ère [ɛ:r], *n.f.* era, epoch.
érection [erɛk'sjɔ̃], *n.f.* erection, erecting.
éreinter [erɛ̃'te], *v.t.* to break the back (*of*); to tire out; to beat unmercifully; (*fig.*) to slate, to lash (*satire etc.*). **s'éreinter**, *v.r.* to break one's back, to tire oneself out, to drudge.
érésipèle [ERYSIPÈLE].
ergot [ɛr'go], *n.m.* spur (*of certain birds etc.*); catch, stop (*of machine*).
ergotage [ɛrgɔ'ta:ʒ], **ergotement** [ɛrgɔt'mɑ̃], *n.m.*, **ergoterie** [ɛrgɔ'tri], *n.f.* cavilling, quibbling.
ergoter [ɛrgɔ'te], *v.i.* (*colloq.*) to cavil; to wrangle.
ergoteur [ɛrgɔ'tœ:r], *a.* (*fem.* **-euse**) cavilling.—*n.m.* (*fem.* **-euse**) caviller, quibbler.
ériger [eri'ʒe], *v.t.* (*conjug. like* MANGER) to erect, to raise, to rear; to set up; to exalt. **s'ériger**, *v.r.* to set up for, to pose (*en*); to be erected.
ermitage [ɛrmi'ta:ʒ], *n.m.* hermitage.

ermite [ɛr'mit], *n.* hermit, recluse.
éroder [ero'de], *v.t.* to erode.
érosif [ero'zif], *a.* (*fem.* **-sive**) erosive.
érosion [ero'zjɔ̃], *n.f.* erosion.
érotique [erɔ'tik], *a.* erotic.
errant [ɛ'rɑ̃], *a.* wandering, roving, errant; erring; ***chevalier errant***, knight-errant.
erratique [ɛra'tik], *a.* erratic.
erre [e:r], *n.f.* course, way; (*pl.*) track (*of a stag etc.*).
errements [ɛr'mɑ̃], *n.m.* (*used only in pl.*) manner, way; vagaries, follies.
errer [ɛ're], *v.i.* to wander, to stray; to range to rove; to err, to go astray.
erreur [ɛ'rœ:r], *n.f.* error, mistake.
erroné [ɛrɔ'ne], *a.* erroneous, mistaken, false.
erronément [ɛrɔne'mɑ̃], *adv.* erroneously.
érudit [ery'di], *a.* erudite, learned.—*n.m.* (*fem.* **-e**) scholar, learned person.
érudition [erydi'sjɔ̃], *n.f.* erudition, scholarship.
éruptif [eryp'tif], *a.* (*fem.* **-tive**) eruptive.
éruption [eryp'sjɔ̃], *n.f.* eruption; cutting (*of teeth*); breaking out (*of a rash*).
érysipèle [erizi'pɛl], **érésipèle** [erezi'pɛl], *n.m.* erysipelas.
ès [ɛs], *contraction of* EN (1) LES (*survives only in a few set expressions*) in, of; ***licencié ès lettres***, bachelor of arts.
escabeau [ɛska'bo], *n.m.* (*pl.* **-eaux**) stool; step-ladder.
escabelle [ɛska'bɛl], *n.f.* three-legged stool.
escadre [ɛs'ka:dr], *n.f.* (*Naut.*) squadron; (*Av.*) wing.
escadrille [ɛska'dri:j], *n.f.* small squadron, flotilla.
escadron [ɛska'drɔ̃], *n.m.* squadron (*of horse*).
escalade [ɛska'lad], *n.f.* scaling (*a wall*); rock-climbing; escalation (*of a war etc.*).
escalader [ɛskala'de], *v.t.* to scale, to climb over.
escale [ɛs'kal], *n.f.* port of call, stopping-place.
escalier [ɛska'lje], *n.m.* staircase, stairs, steps; ***escalier roulant***, escalator.
escalope [ɛska'lɔp], *n.f.* escalope, collop (*of veal*); steak (*of fish*).
escamotable [ɛskamɔ'tabl], *a.* which can be tucked away; (*Av.*) ***train escamotable***, retractable landing-gear.
escamotage [ɛskamɔ'ta:ʒ], *n.m.* juggling, sleight of hand; (*fig.*) filching.
escamoter [ɛskamɔ'te], *v.t.* to conjure away; to pilfer, to make away with; (*Av.*) to retract (*the undercarriage*).
escamoteur [ɛskamɔ'tœ:r], *n.m.* (*fem.* **-euse**) juggler, conjurer; pilferer, pickpocket.
escapade [ɛska'pad], *n.f.* escapade, prank.
escarbille [ɛskar'bi:j], *n.f.* cinder (*of coal*).
escarboucle [ɛskar'bukl], *n.f.* carbuncle (*precious stone*).
escargot [ɛskar'go], *n.m.* snail (*edible*).
escarmouche [ɛskar'muʃ], *n.f.* skirmish; brush; (*fig.*) bickering.
escarmoucher [ɛskarmu'ʃe], *v.i.* to skirmish; (*fig.*) to bicker.
escarpé [ɛskar'pe], *a.* scarped, steep, precipitous; (*fig.*) difficult.
escarpement [ɛskarpə'mɑ̃], *n.m.* escarpment; steep face *or* slope.
escarpin [ɛskar'pɛ̃], *n.m.* pump, dancing-shoe.
escarpolette [ɛskarpɔ'lɛt], *n.f.* (*child's*) swing.
escarre or **eschare** [ɛs'ka:r], *n.f.* scab.
escient [ɛ'sjɑ̃], *n.m. used only in* ***à bon escient***, wittingly, knowingly.
esclaffer (s') [sɛskla'fe], *v.r.* to laugh noisily, to guffaw.
esclandre [ɛs'klɑ̃:dr], *n.m.* scandal, exposure, scene.
esclavage [ɛskla'va:ʒ], *n.m.* slavery; bondage.
esclave [ɛs'klɑ:v], *a.* slavish.—*n.* slave, bondsman; drudge.
escogriffe [ɛskɔ'grif], *n.m.* (*colloq.*) tall, lanky, ungainly fellow.
escompte [ɛs'kɔ̃:t], *n.m.* discount, rebate.
escompter [ɛskɔ̃'te], *v.t.* to discount; (*fig.*) to anticipate; ***escompter un billet***, to cash a bill.
escorte [ɛs'kɔrt], *n.f.* escort; (*Navy*) convoy; (*fig.*) retinue, attendants.
escorter [ɛskɔr'te], *v.t.* to escort, to accompany, to attend.
escorteur [ɛskɔr'tœ:r], *n.m.* escort vessel.
escouade [ɛs'kwad], *n.f.* squad, small party (*of soldiers*); gang (*of workmen*).
escrime [ɛs'krim], *n.f.* fencing.
escrimer [ɛskri'me], *v.i.* to fence; (*fig.*) to have a trial of skill etc. **s'escrimer**, *v.r.* (*colloq.*) to strive; to try hard.
escrimeur [ɛskri'mœ:r], *n.m.* (*fem.* **-euse**) fencer.
escroc [ɛs'kro], *n.m.* sharper, swindler.
escroquer [ɛskrɔ'ke], *v.t.* to swindle out of; to cheat.
escroquerie [ɛskrɔ'kri], *n.f.* swindling.
espace [ɛs'pɑ:s], *n.m.* space, room; duration. —*n.f.* (*Print.*) space.
espacement [ɛspɑs'mɑ̃], *n.m.* interval; (*Print.*) spacing.
espacer [ɛspɑ'se], *v.t.* (*conjug. like* COMMENCER) to leave a space between; to separate. **s'espacer**, *v.r.* to become less frequent *or* numerous.
espadrille [ɛspa'dri:j], *n.f.* canvas shoe with cord soles.
Espagne [ɛs'paɲ], **l'**, *f.* Spain.
espagnol [ɛspa'ɲɔl], *a.* Spanish.—*n.m.* Spanish (*language*); (**Espagnol**, *fem.* **-ole**) Spaniard.
espagnolette [ɛspaɲɔ'lɛt], *n.f.* bolt of french window.
espalier [ɛspɑ'lje], *n.m.* espalier (*tree* or *wall*).
espèce [ɛs'pɛs], *n.f.* species; sort, nature; (*pl.*) ready money, hard cash.
espérance [ɛspe'rɑ̃:s], *n.f.* hope, trust, expectation.
espéranto [ɛsperɑ̃'to], *n.m.* Esperanto.
espérer [ɛspe're], *v.t.* (*conjug. like* CÉDER) to hope for; to expect; to trust.—*v.i.* to hope; to put one's trust in.
espiègle [ɛs'pjɛgl], *a.* and *n.* mischievous, roguish (person).
espièglerie [ɛspjɛglə'ri], *n.f.* frolic, roguish trick, prank.
espion [ɛs'pjɔ̃], *n.m.* (*fem.* **-onne**) spy.
espionnage [ɛspjɔ'na:ʒ], *n.m.* espionage.
espionner [ɛspjɔ'ne], *v.t.* to spy, to pry into.
esplanade [ɛspla'nad], *n.f.* esplanade, parade.
espoir [ɛs'pwa:r], *n.m.* hope.
esprit [ɛs'prit], *n.m.* spirit, ghost; soul; mind, sense, intellect; wit; humour, character.
esquif [ɛs'kif], *n.m.* small boat.
esquille [ɛs'ki:j], *n.f.* splinter (*of a bone*).

esquimau [ɛski'mo], *a.* (*pl.* **-aux**) and *n.* (**Esquimau** or **Eskimo**) Eskimo.
esquinancie [ɛskinɑ̃'si], **cynancie** [sinɑ̃'si], *n.f.* quinsy.
esquisse [ɛs'kis], *n.f.* sketch, outline, rough draft *or* plan.
esquisser [ɛski'se], *v.t.* to sketch, to outline.
esquiver [ɛski've], *v.t.* to avoid, to elude; to duck; to dodge. **s'esquiver,** *v.r.* to escape; to give the slip.
essai [ɛ'sɛ], *n.m.* trial; attempt; experiment, testing; (*Rugby*) try; (*Lit.*) essay.
essaim [ɛ'sɛ̃], *n.m.* swarm; (*fig.*) crowd, host.
essaimer [ɛsɛ'me], *v.i.* to swarm; to hive off.
essarter [ɛsar'te], *v.t.* to clear, to grub (*land*).
essayage [ɛsɛ'ja:ʒ] *n.m.* trying, testing; trying-on (*of clothes*).
essayer [ɛsɛ'je], *v.t.* (*conjug. like* PAYER) to try; to try on; to attempt; to assay.—*v.i.* to try, to make an attempt. **s'essayer,** *v.r.* to try one's strength *or* skill.
essayeur [ɛsɛ'jœ:r], *n.m.* (*fem.* **-euse**) assayer; (*cloth*) fitter.
essayiste [ɛsɛ'jist], *n.* essayist.
essence [ɛ'sɑ̃:s], *n.f.* essence; petrol; attar (*of roses*).
essentiel [ɛsɑ̃'sjɛl], *a.* (*fem.* **-elle**) essential, material.—*n.m.* essential, main point.
essentiellement [ɛsɑ̃sjɛl'mɑ̃], *adv.* essentially, absolutely, above all.
essieu [ɛ'sjø], *n.m.* (*pl.* **-eux**) axle-tree; spindle; pin (*of a block*); ***écartement des essieux***, wheel base (*motor*); ***essieu moteur***, driving-shaft.
essor [ɛ'sɔ:r], *n.m.* flight, soaring; (*fig.*) impulse, vigour.
essorer [ɛsɔ're], *v.t.* to hang in the air to dry, to wring out (*washing*).
essoreuse [ɛsɔ'rø:z], *n.f.* wringer; ***essoreuse (rotative)***, spin dryer.
essoriller [ɛsɔri'je], *v.t.* to cut the ears (*of a dog etc.*); to crop.
essoufflement [ɛsuflə'mɑ̃], *n.m.* panting, breathlessness.
essouffler [ɛsu'fle], *v.t.* to wind (*horses etc.*). **s'essouffler,** *v.r.* to be out of breath; to be winded.
essuie-glaces [ɛsɥi'glas], *n.m. pl.* windscreen wipers.
essuie-main(s) [ɛsɥi'mɛ̃], *n.m. inv.* hand-towel.
essuie-pieds [ɛsɥi'pje], *n.m. inv.* doormat.
essuyage [ɛsɥi'ja:ʒ], *n.m.* wiping, drying.
essuyer [ɛsɥi'je], *v.t.* (*conjug. like* EMPLOYER) to wipe; to dry; to sustain, to endure, to undergo. **s'essuyer,** *v.r.* to dry oneself; ***s'essuyer les mains, la figure*** *etc.*, to dry one's hands, one's face etc.
est [ɛst], *n.m.* east.
estacade [ɛsta'kad], *n.f.* breakwater; pier *or* boom made of timbers.
estafette [ɛsta'fɛt], *n.f.* courier, express messenger; dispatch rider.
estafilade [ɛstafi'lad], *n.f.* cut, gash; rent.
estaminet [ɛstami'nɛ], *n.m.* coffee-house *or* room; tavern.
estampage [ɛstɑ̃'pa:ʒ], *n.m.* stamping (*of metal etc.*).
estampe [ɛs'tɑ̃:p], *n.f.* print, engraving.
estamper [ɛstɑ̃'pe], *v.t.* to stamp, to punch.
estampeur [ɛstɑ̃'pœ:r], *a.* (*fem.* **-euse**) stamping.—*n.m.* (*fem.* **-euse**) stamper.—*n.f.* (**-euse**) stamping-machine.
estampillage [ɛstɑ̃pi'ja:ʒ], *n.m.* stamping, marking.
estampille [ɛstɑ̃'pi:j], *n.f.* stamp, mark, trade-mark.
estampiller [ɛstɑ̃pi'je], *v.t.* to stamp, to mark.
esthétique [ɛste'tik], *a.* aesthetic.—*n.f.* aesthetics.
Esthonie [ɛstɔ'ni], **l'**, *f.* Estonia.
esthonien [ɛstɔ'njɛ̃], *a.* (*fem.* **-enne**) Estonian.—*n.m.* Estonian (*language*); (**Esthonien,** *fem.* **-enne**) Estonian (*person*).
estimable [ɛsti'mabl], *a.* estimable.
estimateur [ɛstima'tœ:r], *n.m.* (*fem.* **-trice**) appraiser, valuer.
estimation [ɛstimɑ'sjɔ̃], *n.f.* estimation, appraising, valuation, estimate.
estime [ɛs'tim], *n.f.* esteem, regard, estimation; (*Naut.*) reckoning.
estimer [ɛsti'me], *v.t.* to estimate, to value, to assess; to esteem; to deem. **s'estimer,** *v.r.* to esteem oneself; to deem oneself.
estival [ɛsti'val], *a.* (*m. pl.* **-aux**) aestival, summer (*plant, resort etc.*).
estivant [ɛsti'vɑ̃], *n.m.* (*fem.* **-e**) summer visitor.
estomac [ɛstɔ'ma], *n.m.* stomach; (*fig.*) pluck.
estompage [ɛstɔ̃'pa:ʒ], *n.m.* (*Drawing*) stumping.
estompe [ɛs'tɔ̃:p], *n.f.* (*Drawing*) stump.
estomper [ɛstɔ̃'pe], *v.t.* (*Drawing*) to stump; to shade off, to blur. **s'estomper,** *v.r.* to become blurred.
Estonie [ESTHONIE].
estonien [ESTHONIEN].
estrade [ɛs'trad], *n.f.* platform, stand, stage.
estragon [ɛstra'gɔ̃], *n.m.* (*Bot.*) tarragon.
estropié [ɛstrɔ'pje], *a.* crippled, lame, disabled.—*n.m.* (*fem.* **-ée**) cripple.
estropier [ɛstrɔ'pje], *v.t.* to cripple, to maim, to disable; (*fig.*) to distort, to mangle.
estuaire [ɛs'tyɛ:r], *n.m.* estuary.
esturgeon [ɛstyr'ʒɔ̃], *n.m.* sturgeon.
et [e], *conj.* and.
étable [e'tabl], *n.f.* shed (*for oxen, sheep, goats etc.*); stall; pigsty, sty.
établi [eta'bli], *n.m.* bench (*joiner's etc.*).
établir [eta'bli:r], *v.t.* to fix, to erect, to set up; to establish, to found; to assert. **s'établir,** *v.r.* to establish oneself; to take up one's residence; to settle down; to set up in business.
établissement [etablis'mɑ̃], *n.m.* establishment, setting up; placing, erecting; proving; imposition (*of taxes*).
étage [e'ta:ʒ], *n.m.* storey, floor, flight (*of stairs*); (*fig.*) stage; tier; (*Geol., Mining*) layer, stratum.
étager [eta'ʒe], *v.t.* (*conjug. like* MANGER) to dispose in tiers. **s'étager,** *v.r.* to rise tier upon tier.
étagère [eta'ʒɛ:r], *n.f.* whatnot, set of shelves, shelf.
étai [e'tɛ], *n.m.* stay, shore, prop, strut.
étaiement [ÉTAYAGE].
étain [e'tɛ̃], *n.m.* tin; pewter.
étal [e'tal], *n.m.* (*pl.* **-aux** or **-als**) butcher's stall, butcher's shop.
étalage [eta'la:ʒ], *n.m.* laying out of goods for sale; goods exposed for sale; shop window, frontage; (*fig.*) showing off.

étalager [etala'ʒe], *v.t.* (*conjug. like* MANGER) to display (*goods*) for sale.
étalagiste [etala'ʒist], *n.* stall-keeper; window-dresser.
étale [e'tal], *a.* slack (*of water* or *wind*).
étalement [etal'mɑ̃] *n.m.* display, parade; staggering (*of holidays*).
étaler [eta'le], *v.t.* to expose for sale; to spread out; to display; (*Naut.*) to stem (*current*); to weather (*gale*). **s'étaler,** *v.r.* to stretch oneself out, to sprawl; to show off.
étalon (1) [eta'lɔ̃], *n.m.* stallion.
étalon (2) [eta'lɔ̃], *n.m.* standard (*of weights and measures*).
étalonnage [etalɔ'na:ʒ], **étalonnement** [etalɔn'mɑ̃], *n.m.* standardization; stamping (*of weights etc.*); gauging.
étalonner [etalɔ'ne], *v.t.* to standardize; to gauge.
étalonneur [etalɔ'nœ:r], *n.m.* inspector of weights and measures.
étamage [eta'ma:ʒ], *n.m.* tinning; quick-silvering (*of glass*).
étamer [eta'me], *v.t.* to tin; to quicksilver.
étameur [eta'mœ:r], *n.m.* tinner; silverer (*of mirrors*).
étamine (1) [eta'min], *n.f.* sieve, strainer; (*Naut.*) bunting.
étamine (2) [eta'min], *n.f.* (*Bot.*) stamen.
étampe [e'tɑ̃:p], *n.f.* die; punch.
étamper [etɑ̃'pe], *v.t.* to punch (*horse-shoes etc.*); to stamp (*sheet metal etc.*).
étanche [e'tɑ̃:ʃ], *a.* water-tight, air-tight etc.
étanchement [etɑ̃ʃ'mɑ̃], *n.m.* stanching, stopping; slaking; quenching.
étancher [etɑ̃'ʃe], *v.t.* to stanch, to stop; to render water-tight; (*fig.*) to quench.
étang [e'tɑ̃], *n.m.* pond, mere, pool.
étape [e'tap], *n.f.* halting-place, stage, station; day's march.
état [e'ta], *n.m.* state, case, condition; circumstance, predicament; statement; list, estimate; profession.
étatique [eta'tik], *a.* nationalized.
étatiser [etati'ze], *v.t.* to nationalize.
étatisme [eta'tism], *n.m.* State-socialism, State control, nationalization.
état-major [etama'ʒɔ:r], *n.m.* (*pl.* **états-majors**) (*Mil.*) staff, general staff.
étau [e'to], *n.m.* (*pl.* **-aux**) (*Tech.*) vice.
étayage [etɛ'ja:ʒ], **étayement** [etɛj'mɑ̃], **étaiement** [etɛ'mɑ̃], *n.m.* staying, shoring, supporting.
étayer [etɛ'je], *v.t.* (*conjug. like* PAYER) to stay, to shore; to support (*a theory etc.*).
été [e'te], *n.m.* summer; (*C*) ***Été des Sauvages***, Indian summer.
éteignoir [etɛ'ɲwa:r], *n.m.* extinguisher (*for candles*).
éteindre [e'tɛ̃:dr], *v.t. irr.* (*conjug. like* CRAINDRE) to put out, to extinguish; to appease; to destroy. **s'éteindre,** *v.r.* to be extinguished, to be put out; to die out; to become extinct.
éteint [e'tɛ̃], *a.* extinguished; extinct; (*fig.*) dull.
étendard [etɑ̃'da:r], *n.m.* standard, banner, flag.
étendre [e'tɑ̃:dr], *v.t.* to extend, to spread out; to stretch; to dilute; to prolong; to lay (down) (*a person*). **s'étendre,** *v.r.* to stretch oneself out; to reach, to extend; to dwell on.
étendu [etɑ̃'dy], *a.* outstretched, outspread; extensive; diluted.
étendue [etɑ̃'dy], *n.f.* extent; scope, length.
éternel [etɛr'nɛl], *a.* (*fem.* **-elle**) eternal, everlasting.—*n.m.* (**l'Éternel**) God, the Eternal.
éternellement [etɛrnɛl'mɑ̃], *adv.* eternally.
éterniser [etɛrni'ze], *v.t.* to perpetuate. **s'éterniser,** *v.r.* to be perpetuated, to last forever.
éternité [etɛrni'te], *n.f.* eternity.
éternuement or **éternûment** [etɛrny'mɑ̃], *n.m.* sneezing, sneeze.
éternuer [etɛr'nɥe], *v.i.* to sneeze.
éternueur [etɛr'nɥœ:r], *n.m.* (*fem.* **-euse**) sneezer.
éteule [e'tø:l], *n.f.* stubble.
éther [e'tɛ:r], *n.m.* ether.
éthéré [ete're], *a.* ethereal.
éthériser [eteri'ze], *v.t.* to etherize.
Éthiopie [etjɔ'pi], **l'**, *f.* Ethiopia.
éthiopien [etjɔ'pjɛ̃], *a.* (*fem.* **-enne**) Ethiopian.—*n.m.* (**Éthiopien,** *fem.* **-enne**) Ethiopian (*person*).
éthique [e'tik], *a.* ethic(al).—*n.f.* ethics, morals.
ethnique [ɛt'nik], *a.* ethnic(al).
ethnographe [ɛtnɔ'graf], *n.* ethnographer.
ethnographie [ɛtnɔgra'fi], *n.f.* ethnography.
ethnographique [ɛtnɔgra'fik], *a.* ethnographic.
ethnologie [ɛtnɔlɔ'ʒi], *n.f.* ethnology.
ethnologique [ɛtnɔlɔ'ʒik], *a.* ethnological.
ethnologue [ɛtnɔ'lɔg], **ethnologiste** [ɛtnɔlɔ'ʒist], *n.* ethnologist.
éthologie [etɔlɔ'ʒi], *n.f.* ethology.
éthyle [e'ti:l], *n.m.* ethyl.
étiage [e'tja:ʒ], *n.m.* low-water mark; (*fig.*) level.
Étienne [e'tjɛn], *m.* Stephen.
étincelant [etɛ̃s'lɑ̃], *a.* sparkling, glittering, glistening.
étinceler [etɛ̃s'le], *v.i.* (*conjug. like* APPELER) to sparkle, to flash, to gleam, to glitter.
étincelle [etɛ̃'sɛl], *n.f.* spark, flash; brilliance.
étincellement [etɛ̃sɛl'mɑ̃], *n.m.* sparkling, twinkling, scintillation.
étiolement [etjɔl'mɑ̃], *n.m.* etiolation, sickliness (*of plants etc.*); paleness, emaciation.
étioler [etjɔ'le], *v.t.* to etiolate (*plants*); (*fig.*) to enervate. **s'étioler,** *v.r.* to become etiolated (*of plants*); (*fig.*) to waste away.
étique [e'tik], *a.* consumptive; emaciated.
étiqueter [etik'te], *v.t.* (*conjug. like* APPELER) to label, to ticket.
étiquette [eti'kɛt], *n.f.* ticket, label, tag; etiquette.
étirage [eti'ra:ʒ], *n.m.* stretching.
étirer [eti're], *v.t.* to stretch; to lengthen. **s'étirer,** *v.r.* to stretch one's limbs.
étisie [eti'zi], *n.f.* consumption.
étoffe [e'tɔf], *n.f.* material; stuff, cloth; quality, worth; (*C*) ***étoffe du pays***, home-spun.
étoffé [etɔ'fe], *a.* stuffed full; upholstered; stout, substantial.
étoffer [etɔ'fe], *v.t.* to stuff; to upholster.
étoile [e'twal], *n.f.* star; (*fig.*) fate, destiny; blaze (*on horse's head*); star (*crack in glass*).
étoilé [etwa'le], *a.* starry; star-shaped.
étoiler [etwa'le], *v.t.* to star, to stud with stars; to crack (*of glass*). **s'étoiler,** *v.r.* to star, to crack (*of glass*).

étole [e'tal], *n.f.* stole.
étonnamment [etɔna'mɑ̃], *adv.* astonishingly, wonderfully, amazingly.
étonnant [etɔ'nɑ̃], *a.* astonishing, wonderful, marvellous.
étonnement [etɔn'mɑ̃], *n.m.* astonishment, amazement; wonder; crack, fissure.
étonner [etɔ'ne], *v.t.* to astonish, to amaze, to astound; to shock; to cause to crack. **s'étonner,** *v.r.* to be astonished, to wonder; to become cracked.
étouffant [etu'fɑ̃], *a.* suffocating, sultry, close.
étouffement [etuf'mɑ̃], *n.m.* suffocation.
étouffer [etu'fe], *v.t.* to suffocate, to choke, to smother; (*fig.*) to stifle, to hush up; to deaden (*sound etc.*).—*v.i.* to choke, to suffocate. **s'étouffer,** *v.r.* to be choking, to be suffocated; to swelter.
étoupe [e'tup], *n.f.* tow, oakum.
étouper [etu'pe], *v.t.* to stop (*with tow* or *oakum*]; to caulk.
étoupiller [etupi'je], *v.t.* to prime (*a friction tube*).
étourderie [eturdə'ri], *n.f.* heedlessness, thoughtlessness; blunder.
étourdi [etur'di], *a.* giddy, thoughtless, heedless.—*n.m.* (*fem.* **-e**) madcap.
étourdiment [eturdi'mɑ̃], *adv.* heedlessly, thoughtlessly.
étourdir [etur'di:r], *v.t.* to stun, to deafen, to make giddy; to din; to astound. **s'étourdir,** *v.r.* to divert one's thoughts; to try to forget something.
étourdissant [eturdi'sɑ̃], *a.* deafening, stunning, astounding.
étourdissement [eturdis'mɑ̃], *n.m.* dizziness, giddiness; stupefaction; shock.
étourneau [etur'no], *n.m.* (*pl.* **-eaux**) starling; (*fig.*) giddy fellow.
étrange [e'trɑ̃:ʒ], *a.* strange, odd, queer.
étrangement [etrɑ̃ʒ'mɑ̃], *adv.* strangely, queerly, extraordinarily.
étranger [etrɑ̃'ʒe], *a.* (*fem.* **-ère**) foreign; strange; unknown; irrelevant.—*n.m.* (*fem.* **-ère**) foreigner, alien; stranger; ***à l'etranger***, abroad.
étrangeté [etrɑ̃ʒ'te], *n.f.* strangeness, oddness.
étranglé [etrɑ̃'gle], *a.* strangled; restricted, scanty, too narrow.
étranglement [etrɑ̃glə'mɑ̃], *n.m.* strangling; garotting; constriction.
étrangler [etrɑ̃'gle], *v.t.* to strangle, to choke, to stifle; to constrict, to confine; (*fig.*) to smother, to suppress.—*v.i.* to be choked, to be short of breath. **s'étrangler,** *v.r.* to strangle oneself; to choke.
étrangleur [etrɑ̃'glœ:r], *n.m.* (*fem.* **-euse**) strangler; garotter.
être [ɛ:tr], *v.i. irr.* to be, to exist; to belong (***à***); to stand; to take part (***à***); to be a member (***de***).—*n.m.* being, existence; creature.
étreindre [e'trɛ̃:dr], *v.t. irr.* (*conjug. like* CRAINDRE) to embrace, to clasp, to grip.
étreinte [e'trɛ̃:t], *n.f.* embrace, hug; grip.
étrenne [e'trɛn], *n.f.* New Year's gift (*usually in pl.*); gift, present.
étrenner [etrɛ'ne], *v.t.* to give a New Year's gift; to handsel; to try *or* put on for the first time; to buy the first lot from.
étrier [etri'e], *n.m.* stirrup; (*Surg.*) caliper.
étrille [e'tri:j], *n.f.* curry-comb.
étriller [etri'je], *v.t.* to curry, to comb (*a horse*); (*fig.*) to fleece; to drub.
étriper [etri'pe], *v.t.* to gut (*an animal*).
étriqué [etri'ke], *a.* scanty, narrow, curtailed.
étriquer [etri'ke], *v.t.* to shorten, to curtail, to make too small.
étrivière [etri'vjɛ:r], *n.f.* stirrup-leather.
étroit [e'trwɑ], *a.* narrow, tight, strait; limited; (*fig.*) strict, rigorous.
étroitement [etrwɑt'mɑ̃], *adv.* narrowly, tightly; intimately, closely.
étroitesse [etrwɑ'tɛs], *n.f.* narrowness, straitness; tightness, closeness.
Étrurie [etry'ri], **l',** *f.* Etruria.
étrusque [e'trysk], *a.* Etruscan.—*n.m.* Etruscan (*language*).—*n.* (**Étrusque**) Etruscan (*person*).
étude [e'tyd], *n.f.* study; room for study; time of preparation; office, practice (*of attorneys*); essay, article.
étudiant [ety'djɑ̃], *n.m.* (*fem.* **-e**) student; undergraduate.
étudié [ety'dje], *a.* studied; affected.
étudier [ety'dje], *v.t.* to study, to learn; to practise (*music*); to rehearse (*a play*); to observe.—*v.i.* to study, to learn; to practise (*music*). **s'étudier,** *v.r.* to make (*it*) one's study, to school oneself.
étui [e'tɥi], *n.m.* case, box, sheath.
étuve [e'ty:v], *n.f.* sweating-room; stove; drying room; incubator.
étuvée [ety've], *n.f.* stew.
étuver [ety've], *v.t.* to stew, (*Med.*) to bathe, to foment.
étymologie [etimɔlɔ'ʒi], *n.f.* etymology.
étymologique [etimɔlɔ'ʒik], *a.* etymological.
étymologiste [etimɔlɔ'ʒist], *n.* etymologist.
eucharistie [økaris'ti], *n.f.* eucharist.
eucharistique [økaris'tik], *a.* eucharistic.
eugénique [øʒe'nik], *n.f.*, **eugénisme** [øʒe'nism], *n.m.* eugenics.
euh [ø], *int.* aha! oh! hum!
eunuque [ø'nyk], *n.m.* eunuch.
euphémique [øfe'mik], *a.* euphemistic.
euphémisme [øfe'mism], *n.m.* euphemism.
euphonie [øfɔ'ni], *n.f.* euphony.
euphonique [øfɔ'nik], *a.* euphonious.
Euphrate [ø'frat], **l',** *m.* the Euphrates.
euphuïsme [øfy'ism], *n.m.* euphuism.
eurasien [øra'zjɛ̃], *a.* (*fem.* **-enne**) Eurasian.—*n.m.* (**Eurasien,** *fem.* **-enne**) Eurasian (*person*).
Euripide [øri'pid], *m.* Euripides.
Europe [ørɔp], *f.* (*Myth.*) Europa; ***l'Europe*** (*Geog.*) Europe.
européaniser [ørɔpeani'ze], *v.t.* to Europeanize.
européen [ørɔpe'ɛ̃], *a.* (*fem.* **-éenne**) European.—*n.m.* (**Européen,** *fem.* **-éenne**) European (person).
euthanasie [øtana'zi], *n.f.* euthanasia.
eux [ø], *pron. pers. m. pl.* (*fem.* **-elles**) they; them.
évacuant [eva'kɥɑ̃], **évacuatif** [evakɥa'tif] (*fem.* **-tive**), *a.* and *n.m.* evacuant.
évacuation [evakɥɑ'sjɔ̃], *n.f.* evacuation; ejection.
évacué [eva'kɥe], *n.m.* (*fem.* **-ée**) evacuee.
évacuer [eva'kɥe], *v.t.* to evacuate; to throw off, to eject, to clear. **s'évacuer,** *v.r.* to discharge (*into*).

évadé [eva'de], *a.* and *n.m.* (*fem.* **-ée**) escaped (*person*); escapee.
évader (s') [seva'de], *v.r.* to escape; to get away *or* out of (*de*).
évaluable [eva'lɥabl], *a.* rateable, appraisable.
évaluateur [evalɥa'tœ:r], *n.m.* (*fem.* **-trice**) valuer, appraiser.
évaluation [evalɥɑ'sjɔ̃], *n.f.* valuation, estimate.
évaluer [eva'lɥe], *v.t.* to value, to estimate, to appreciate.
évangélique [evɑ̃ʒe' lik], *a.* evangelical.
évangéliser [evɑ̃ʒeli'ze], *v.t.* to evangelize, to preach the Gospel to.
évangélisme [evɑ̃ʒe'lism], *n.m.* evangelism.
évangéliste [evɑ̃ʒe'list], *n.m.* evangelist.
évangile [evɑ̃'ʒil], *n.m.* Gospel.
évanouir (s') [seva'nwi:r], *v.r.* to faint, to swoon, to lose consciousness; (*fig.*) to vanish, to disappear.
évanouissement [evanwis'mɑ̃], *n.m.* swoon, fainting fit; disappearance; (*Math.*) cancelling out.
évaporatif [evapɔra'tif], *a.* (*fem.* **-tive**) evaporative.
évaporation [evapɔrɑ'sjɔ̃], *n.f.* evaporation.
évaporé [evapɔ're], *a.* and *n.m.* (*fem.* **-ée**) frivolous, thoughtless (person).
évaporer [evapɔ're], *v.t.* to evaporate; (*fig.*) to exhale, to give vent to; ***évaporer son chagrin***, to give vent to one's grief. **s'évaporer**, *v.r.* to evaporate; (*fig.*) to get giddy.
évasé [evɑ'ze], *a.* wide, bell-shaped; flared (*skirt*).
évasement [evɑz'mɑ̃], *n.m.* width, widening (*at the mouth of a vase etc.*); flare (*of a skirt*).
évaser [evɑ'ze], *v.t.* to widen (*an opening*); to flare (*a skirt*). **s'évaser**, *v.r.* to be widened; to extend, to spread.
évasif [evɑ'zif], *a.* (*fem.* **-sive**) evasive.
évasion [evɑ'zjɔ̃], *n.f.* escape, flight; evasion; escapism.
évasivement [evɑziv'mɑ̃], *adv.* evasively.
évêché [evɛ'ʃe], *n.m.* bishopric, episcopate, see; bishop's palace.
éveil [e'vɛ:j], *n.m.* awakening; warning, hint, alarm.
éveillé [evɛ'je], *a.* wide-awake; lively, sprightly; sharp, intelligent.
éveiller [evɛ'je], *v.t.* to awaken, to rouse; to excite, to enliven. **s'éveiller**, *v.r.* to wake up; to become animated.
événement [evɛn'mɑ̃], *n.m.* event, occurrence; result; climax; emergency.
évent [e'vɑ̃], *n.m.* open air; vent-hole, airhole; (*fig.*) flatness, vapidness.
éventail [evɑ̃'ta:j], *n.m.* (*pl.* **éventails**) fan; fan-light.
éventaire [evɑ̃'tɛ:r], *n.m.* flat tray (*carried by hawkers*); street stall.
éventé [evɑ̃'te], *a.* fanned, aired; flat, stale (*beer etc.*); (*fig.*) giddy, thoughtless.
éventer [evɑ̃'te], *v.t.* to fan; to winnow (*corn*); to air; to let (*wine etc.*) get flat; to get wind of; to divulge. **s'éventer**, *v.r.* to fan oneself; to evaporate; to become flat; to be divulged.
éventrer [evɑ̃'tre], *v.t.* to disembowel, to gut (*fish etc.*); to rip up, to break open. **s'éventrer**, *v.r.* to rip one's bowels open; to commit hara-kiri.
éventualité [evɑ̃tɥali'te], *n.f.* contingency eventuality.
éventuel [evɑ̃'tɥɛl], *a.* (*fem.* **-elle**) contingent possible.
éventuellement [evɑ̃tɥɛl'mɑ̃], *adv.* possibly on occasion.
évêque [e'vɛ:k], *n.m.* bishop.
évertuer (s') [sevɛr'tɥe], *v.r.* to strive, to exert *or* bestir oneself.
éviction [evik'sjɔ̃], *n.f.* eviction, ejectment.
évidemment [evida'mɑ̃], *adv.* evidently.
évidence [evi'dɑ̃:s], *n.f.* obviousness, clearness; conspicuousness.
évident [evi'dɑ̃], *a.* evident, plain, clear obvious.
évider [evi'de], *v.t.* to hollow, to groove, to scoop out.
évier [e'vje], *n.m.* sink.
évincer [evɛ̃'se], *v.t.* (*conjug. like* COMMENCER) to evict, to eject, to oust.
éviscérer [evise're], *v.t.* (*conjug. like* CÉDER) to disembowel.
évitable [evi'tabl], *a.* avoidable.
évitement [evit'mɑ̃], *n.m.* (*Rail.*) siding shunting; by-pass.
éviter [evi'te], *v.t.* to shun, to avoid, to evade to abstain from.
évocateur [evɔka'tœ:r], *a.* (*fem.* **-trice**) evocative.
évocation [evɔkɑ'sjɔ̃], *n.f.* evocation; recollection.
évolué [evɔ'lɥe], *a.* highly civilized.
évoluer [evɔ'lɥe], *v.i.* to evolve; to develop.
évolution [evɔly'sjɔ̃], *n.f.* evolution.
évoquer [evɔ'ke], *v.t.* to evoke; to allude to.
exacerbation [egzasɛrbɑ'sjɔ̃], *n.f.* exacerbation.
exacerber [egzasɛr'be], *v.t.* to exacerbate.
exact [eg'zakt], *a.* exact, correct; punctual.
exactement [egzaktə'mɑ̃], *adv.* exactly accurately; punctually.
exaction [egzak'sjɔ̃], *n.f.* exaction, impost extortion.
exactitude [egzakti'tyd], *n.f.* exactness accuracy; punctuality.
exagération [egzaʒerɑ'sjɔ̃], *n.f.* exaggeration overrating.
exagérer [egzaʒe're], *v.t.* (*conjug. like* CÉDER) to exaggerate, to magnify.
exaltation [ɛgzaltɑ'sjɔ̃], *n.f.* exaltation; extolling.
exalté [ɛgzal'te], *a.* exalted, feverish.—*n.m.* (*fem.* **-ée**) enthusiast, fanatic.
exalter [ɛgzal'te], *v.t.* to exalt, to magnify; to excite, to inflame. **s'exalter**, *v.r.* to become excited, to be elated.
examen [ɛgza'mɛ̃], *n.m.* examination; inspection; research.
examinateur [ɛgzamina'tœ:r], *n.m.* (*fem.* **-trice**) examiner.
examiner [ɛgzami'ne], *v.t.* to examine, to inspect, to survey; to discuss, to investigate. **s'examiner**, *v.r.* to examine *or* search oneself; to observe each other attentively.
exaspération [ɛgzasperɑ'sjɔ̃], *n.f.* exasperation, aggravation.
exaspérer [ɛgzaspe're], *v.t.* (*conjug. like* CÉDER) to exasperate, to incense, to inflame; to aggravate (*pain etc.*). **s'exaspérer**, *v.r.* to become exasperated *or* incensed; to become aggravated (*pain etc.*).

exaucer [ɛgzo'se], *v.t.* (*conjug. like* COMMENCER) to hearken to, to grant.
excavateur [ɛkskava'tœ:r], *n.m.* excavator, digging-machine.
excavation [ɛkskavɑ'sjɔ̃], *n.f.* excavation.
excaver [ɛkska've], *v.t.* to excavate, to hollow out.
excédant [ɛkse'dɑ̃], *a.* exceeding, excessive; unbearable.
excédent [ɛkse'dɑ̃], *n.m.* surplus, excess.
excéder [ɛkse'de], *v.t.* (*conjug. like* CÉDER) to exceed, to surpass, to rise above (*in level, price etc.*); (*fig.*) to wear out, to tire out.
excellemment [ɛksɛla'mɑ̃], *adv.* excellently, surpassingly.
Excellence [ɛksɛ'lɑ̃:s], *f.* (*title*) Excellency.
excellence [ɛksɛ'lɑ̃:s], *n.f.* excellence; ***par excellence***, pre-eminently, above all.
excellent [ɛksɛ'lɑ̃], *a.* excellent; delightful.
excellentissime [ɛksɛlɑ̃ti'sim], *a.* most excellent.
exceller [ɛksɛ'le], *v.i.* to excel, to be eminent; to surpass.
excentricité [ɛksɑ̃trisi'te], *n.f.* eccentricity.
excentrique [ɛksɑ̃'trik], *a.* eccentric, odd.
excepté [ɛksɛp'te], *prep.* except, excepting, but.
excepter [ɛksɛp'te], *v.t.* to except.
exception [ɛksɛp'sjɔ̃], *n.f.* exception.
exceptionnel [ɛksɛpsjɔ'nɛl], *a.* (*fem.* **-elle**) exceptional; rare, infrequent.
excès [ɛk'sɛ], *n.m. inv.* excess; (*pl.*) riot, outrages, violence.
excessif [ɛksɛ'sif], *a.* (*fem.* **-ive**) excessive, exorbitant; intemperate.
excessivement [ɛksɛsiv'mɑ̃], *adv.* excessively, to excess.
excise [ɛk'si:z], *n.f.* excise; excise-office.
excitabilité [ɛksitabili'te], *n.f.* excitability.
excitable [ɛksi'tabl], *a.* excitable.
excitant [ɛksi'tɑ̃], *a.* exciting.—*n.m.* (*Med.*) excitant.
excitateur [ɛksita'tœ:r], *a.* (*fem.* **-trice**) provocative.—*n.m.* (*fem.* **-trice**) instigator.
excitation [ɛksitɑ'sjɔ̃], *n.f.* exciting, excitation; excitement.
exciter [ɛksi'te], *v.t.* to excite, to stir up, to rouse; to stimulate, to animate; to instigate, to prompt; to irritate. **s'exciter**, *v.r.* to excite oneself, to work oneself up; to encourage each other; to be excited.
exclamation [ɛksklamɑ'sjɔ̃], *n.f.* exclamation; ***point d'exclamation***, exclamation mark.
exclamer (s') [sɛkskla'me], *v.r.* to exclaim, to cry out; to protest.
exclure [ɛks'kly:r], *v.t. irr.* (*conjug. like* CONCLURE) to exclude, to debar, to shut out; to bar; to be incompatible with.
exclusif [ɛkskly'zif], *a.* (*fem.* **-sive**) exclusive; intolerant.
exclusion [ɛkskly'zjɔ̃], *n.f.* exclusion.
exclusivement [ɛksklyziv'mɑ̃], *adv.* exclusively.
excommunication [ɛkskɔmynikɑ'sjɔ̃], *n.f.* excommunication.
excommunié [ɛkskɔmy'nje], *a.* excommunicated.—*n.m.* (*fem.* **-ée**) excommunicated person.
excommunier [ɛkskɔmy'nje], *v.t.* to excommunicate.
excrément [ɛkskre'mɑ̃], *n.m.* excrement.
excréter [ɛkskre'te], *v.t.* (*conjug. like* CÉDER) to excrete.
excrétion [ɛkskre'sjɔ̃], *n.f.* excretion.
excroissance [ɛkskrwɑ'sɑ̃:s], *n.f.* excrescence (*tumour etc.*).
excursion [ɛkskyr'sjɔ̃], *n.f.* excursion, ramble, tour, trip; raid; (*fig.*) digression.
excursionniste [ɛkskyrsjɔ'nist], *n.* tripper.
excusable [ɛksky'zabl], *a.* excusable, pardonable.
excuse [ɛks'ky:z], *n.f.* excuse, (*pl.*) apology.
excuser [ɛksky'ze], *v.t.* to excuse, to pardon; to bear with; to apologize for. **s'excuser**, *v.r.* to excuse *or* exculpate oneself; to apologize; to decline; ***qui s'excuse, s'accuse***, excuses indicate a guilty conscience.
exécrable [egze'krabl], *a.* execrable; abominable.
exécrablement [egzekrablə'mɑ̃], *adv.* execrably.
exécration [egzekrɑ'sjɔ̃], *n.f.* execration.
exécrer [egze'kre], *v.t.* (*conjug. like* CÉDER) to execrate, to abhor.
exécutable [egzeky'tabl], *a.* feasible, practicable.
exécutant [egzeky'tɑ̃], *n.m.* (*fem.* **-e**) performer, player (*esp. of music*).
exécuter [egzeky'te], *v.t.* to execute, to perform, to accomplish; to carry out, to fulfil. **s'exécuter**, *v.r.* to be performed, to be done, to take place; to yield, to comply, to submit; ***allons, exécutez-vous***, come, do the needful.
exécuteur [egzeky'tœ:r], *n.m.* (*fem.* **-trice**) executor, executrix; ***exécuteur*** (***des hautes œuvres***), executioner.
exécutif [egzeky'tif], *a.* (*fem.* **-tive**) executive.—*n.m.* the executive.
exécution [egzeky'sjɔ̃], *n.f.* execution, accomplishment, performance, fulfilment; (*St. Exch.*) hammering (*of defaulter*).
exemplaire [egzɑ̃'plɛ:r], *a.* exemplary.—*n.m.* model, pattern; copy (*of printed books, engravings etc.*); specimen.
exemplairement [egzɑ̃plɛr'mɑ̃], *adv.* in an exemplary manner.
exemple [eg'zɑ̃:pl], *n.m.* example, pattern, model; precedent, parallel, instance; ***à l'exemple de***, in imitation of; ***par exemple***, for instance; upon my word! ***sans exemple***, unparalleled.
exempt [eg'zɑ̃], *a.* exempt, free (*from*).
exempté [egzɑ̃'te], *a.* and *n.m.* (*fem.* **-ée**) exempt(ed) (person).
exempter [egzɑ̃'te], *v.t.* to exempt, to free; to dispense, to exonerate.
exemption [egzɑ̃'sjɔ̃], *n.f.* exemption, immunity; dispensation.
exercer [egzɛr'se], *v.t.* (*conjug. like* COMMENCER) to exercise, to train; to fulfil (*an office etc.*); to follow, to practise (*a trade* or *profession*); (*fig.*) to try (*one's patience etc.*). **s'exercer**, *v.r.* to exercise, to practise; to exert oneself.
exercice [egzɛr'sis], *n.m.* exercise, practice, use; (*Customs*) inspection; (*Administration*) financial year; (*Mil.*) drill.
exerciseur [egzɛrsi'zœ:r], *n.m.* (*Gym.*) chest expander.
exhalaison [egzalɛ'zɔ̃], *n.f.* exhalation, effluvium.
exhalation [egzalɑ'sjɔ̃], *n.f.* exhalation.

exhaler [egza'le], *v.t.* to send forth, to exhale; to give vent to, to emit. **s'exhaler**, *v.r.* to be emitted, to be exhaled; to give vent to.
exhausser [egzo'se], *v.t.* to raise, to make higher.
exhaustif [egzos'tif], *a.* (*fem.* **-tive**) exhaustive.
exhaustion [egzos'tjɔ̃], *n.f.* exhaustion.
exhiber [egzi'be], *v.t.* to exhibit (*in a law-court*); to produce, to show. **s'exhiber**, *v.r.* (*pej.*) to show off.
exhibition [egzibi'sjɔ̃], *n.f.* producing, show, exhibiting, exhibition.
exhilarant [egzila'rɑ̃], *a.* exhilarating.
exhortation [egzɔrtɑ'sjɔ̃], *n.f.* exhortation.
exhorter [egzɔr'te], *v.t.* to exhort, to encourage.
exhumation [egzymɑ'sjɔ̃], *n.f.* exhumation, disinterment.
exhumer [egzy'me], *v.t.* to exhume, to disinter; (*fig.*) to rake up.
exigeant [egzi'ʒɑ̃], *a.* exacting, hard to please.
exigence [egzi'ʒɑ̃:s], *n.f.* unreasonableness; exigency; demand, requirement.
exiger [egzi'ʒe], *v.t.* (*conjug. like* MANGER) to exact, to require, to demand.
exigu [egzi'gy], *a.* (*fem.* **-uë**) very small; scanty, slender, slight.
exiguïté [egzigɥi'te], *n.f.* scantiness, slenderness, slightness.
exil [eg'zil], *n.m.* exile, banishment.
exilé [egzi'le], *a.* exiled.—*n.m.* (*fem.* **-ée**) exile.
exiler [egzi'le], *v.t.* to exile, to banish. **s'exiler**, *v.r.* to go into exile.
existant [egzis'tɑ̃], *a.* existing, in being, existent; extant.
existence [egzis'tɑ̃:s], *n.f.* existence; subsistence, living; (*pl.*) (*Comm.*) stock on hand.
existentialisme [egzistɑ̃sja'lism], *n.m.* existentialism.
exister [egzis'te], *v.i.* to exist, to live; to be extant.
exocet [egzɔ'sɛ], *n.m.* flying-fish.
exode [eg'zɔd], *n.m.* exodus.
exonération [egzɔnerɑ'sjɔ̃], *n.f.* exoneration.
exonérer [egzɔne're], *v.t.* (*conjug. like* CÉDER) to exonerate, to discharge.
exorable [egzɔ'rabl], *a.* lenient, merciful.
exorbitant [egzɔrbi'tɑ̃], *a.* exorbitant.
exorciser [egzɔrsi'ze], *v.t.* to exorcize.
exorde [eg'zɔrd], *n.m.* exordium, beginning (*of a speech etc.*).
exotique [egzɔ'tik], *a.* exotic; foreign, outlandish.
expansif [ɛkspɑ̃'sif], *a.* (*fem.* **-sive**) expansive; (*fig.*) unreserved, open-hearted.
expansion [ɛkspɑ̃'sjɔ̃], *n.f.* expansion; (*fig.*) unreservedness.
expatriation [ɛkspatriɑ'sjɔ̃], *n.f.* expatriation; self-banishment.
expatrier [ɛkspatri'e], *v.t.* to expatriate, to exile. **s'expatrier**, *v.r.* to leave one's country.
expectant [ɛkspɛk'tɑ̃], *a.* expectant.
expectative [ɛkspɛkta'ti:v], *n.f.* expectation, hope, expectancy.
expectoration [ɛkspɛktɔrɑ'sjɔ̃], *n.f.* expectoration; sputum.
expectorer [ɛkspɛktɔ're], *v.t.* to expectorate, to spit.
expédient [ɛkspe'djɑ̃], *a.* expedient, fit, meet.—*n.m.* expedient, device; shift.
expédier [ɛkspe'dje], *v.t.* to dispatch, to send off, to forward; to do quickly; to clear (*at the customs*); to draw up (*a deed etc.*).
expéditeur [ɛkspedi'tœ:r], *n.m.* (*fem.* **-trice**) sender (*by post*); shipper, consigner.
expéditif [ɛkspedi'tif], *a.* (*fem.* **-tive**) expeditious, quick.
expédition [ɛkspedi'sjɔ̃], *n.f.* expedition, dispatch; shipment; thing sent; performance; (*Law*) copy (*of a deed etc.*).
expéditionnaire [ɛkspedisjɔ'nɛ:r], *a.* expeditionary.—*n.* sender, shipper; commission-agent; copying-clerk.
expérience [ɛkspe'rjɑ̃:s], *n.f.* experience; experiment, test.
expérimental [ɛksperimɑ̃'tal], *a.* (*m.pl.* **-aux**) experimental.
expérimenté [ɛksperimɑ̃'te], *a.* experienced.
expérimenter [ɛksperimɑ̃'te], *v.t.* to try out, to test; to experience.
expert [ɛks'pɛ:r], *a.* expert, skilful.—*n.m.* connoisseur; valuer, surveyor; expert; ***expert comptable***, chartered accountant.
expertement [ɛkspɛrt'mɑ̃], *adv.* expertly skilfully.
expertise [ɛkspɛr'ti:z], *n.f.* survey, valuation; appraisal.
expertiser [ɛkspɛrti'ze], *v.t.* to make a survey of; to appraise, to value, to assess.
expiation [ɛkspjɑ'sjɔ̃], *n.f.* expiation, atonement.
expiatoire [ɛkspja'twa:r], *a.* expiatory.
expier [ɛks'pje], *v.t.* to expiate, to atone for.
expirant [ɛkspi'rɑ̃], *a.* expiring, dying.
expiration [ɛkspirɑ'sjɔ̃], *n.f.* expiration.
expirer [ɛkspi're], *v.t.* to breathe out; exhale. —*v.i.* to expire, to die; to come to an end.
explicable [ɛkspli'kabl], *a.* explicable.
explicatif [ɛksplika'tif], *a.* (*fem.* **-tive**) explicative, explanatory.
explication [ɛksplikɑ'sjɔ̃], *n.f.* explanation; interpretation; meaning.
explicite [ɛkspli'sit], *a.* explicit, clear, express.
explicitement [ɛksplisit'mɑ̃], *adv.* explicitly, clearly.
expliquer [ɛkspli'ke], *v.t.* to explain, to expound; to interpret; to make known. **s'expliquer**, *v.r.* to explain oneself; to be explained.
exploit [ɛks'plwa], *n.m.* exploit, achievement, feat; (*Law*) writ, process.
exploitable [ɛksplwa'tabl], *a.* workable; (*Law*) distrainable.
exploitant [ɛksplwa'tɑ̃], *n.m.* operator (*of mines etc.*); farmer, grower.
exploitation [ɛksplwatɑ'sjɔ̃], *n.f.* working, improving (*of lands etc.*); employing, using; taking advantage of, exploitation.
exploiter [ɛksplwa'te], *v.t.* to work, to improve, to cultivate; to use; to exploit, to take (*unfair*) advantage of.
exploiteur [ɛksplwa'tœ:r], *n.m.* (*fem.* **-euse**) exploiter, person who takes advantage (*of others*).
explorateur [ɛksplɔra'tœ:r], *a.* (*fem.* **-trice** exploratory.—*n.m.* (*fem.* **-trice**) explorer.

exploration [ɛksplɔrɑ'sjɔ̃], *n.f.* exploration.

explorer [ɛksplɔ're], *v.t.* to explore.

exploser [ɛksplo'ze], *v.i.* to explode, to blow up.

explosible [ɛksplo'zibl], *a.* explosive.

explosif [ɛksplo'zif], *a.* (*fem.* **-sive**) and *n.m.* explosive.

explosion [ɛksplo'zjɔ̃], *n.f.* explosion; (*fig.*) outbreak.

exportateur [ɛkspɔrta'tœ:r], *a.* (*fem.* **-trice**) exporting.—*n.m.* (*fem.* **-trice**) exporter.

exportation [ɛkspɔrtɑ'sjɔ̃], *n.f.* exportation, export.

exporter [ɛkspɔr'te], *v.t.* to export.

exposant [ɛkspo'zɑ̃], *n.m.* (*fem.* **-e**) exhibitor; (*Law*) petitioner.—*n.m.* (*Math.*) exponent.

exposé [ɛkspo'ze], *a.* exposed, on view; dangerous (*position*).—*n.m.* statement, explanation; account, report.

exposer [ɛkspo'ze], *v.t.* to expose, to show, to exhibit; to lay bare; to state, to explain; to endanger.—*v.i.* to explain; to exhibit. **s'exposer**, *v.r.* to expose oneself; to be liable.

exposition [ɛkspozi'sjɔ̃], *n.f.* exhibition; exposure; situation, aspect; explanation, account.

exprès [ɛks'prɛs], *a.* (*fem.* **-presse**) express, formal, positive.—[ɛks'prɛ], *adv.* expressly, on purpose.—*n.m.* express (*messenger*).

express [ɛks'prɛs], *a.* (*Rail.*) express.—*n.m.* express train.

expressément [ɛksprɛse'mɑ̃], *adv.* expressly, positively.

expressif [ɛksprɛ'sif], *a.* (*fem.* **-ive**) expressive.

expression [ɛksprɛ'sjɔ̃], *n.f.* expression; expressiveness.

exprimer [ɛkspri'me], *v.t.* to express; to press *or* squeeze out; to utter; to betoken. **s'exprimer**, *v.r.* to express oneself.

expropriation [ɛksprɔpriɑ'sjɔ̃], *n.f.* expropriation, dispossession, compulsory purchase.

exproprier [ɛksprɔpri'e], *v.t.* to expropriate, to dispossess; to requisition (*buildings*).

expulser [ɛkspyl'se], *v.t.* to expel, to turn out; to evict.

expulsion [ɛkspyl'sjɔ̃], *n.f.* expulsion; (*Law*) ejection.

expurger [ɛkspyr'ʒe], *v.t.* (*conjug. like* MANGER) to expurgate, to bowdlerize (*a book*).

exquis [ɛks'ki], *a.* exquisite, nice, refined.

exquisement [ɛkskiz'mɑ̃], *adv.* exquisitely.

exsangue [ɛk'sɑ̃:g], *a.* bloodless, anaemic.

extase [ɛks'tɑ:z], *n.f.* ecstasy, rapture.

extasier (s') [sɛkstɑ'zje], *v.r.* to be enraptured, to go into raptures.

extatique [ɛksta'tik], *a.* ecstatic, rapturous.

extenseur [ɛkstɑ̃'sœ:r], *a.* extensor.—*n.m.* (*Anat.*) extensor; chest-expander.

extension [ɛkstɑ̃'sjɔ̃], *n.f.* extension, stretching; extent; increase.

exténuant [ɛkste'nɥɑ̃], *a.* extenuating.

exténuation [ɛkstenɥɑ'sjɔ̃], *n.f.* extenuation, debility.

exténuer [ɛkste'nɥe], *v.t.* to extenuate, to enfeeble.

extérieur [ɛkste'rjœ:r], *a.* exterior, external, outward; foreign.—*n.m.* exterior; outward appearance; abroad.

extérieurement [ɛksterjœr'mɑ̃], *adv.* externally, outwardly.

exterminateur [ɛkstɛrmina'tœ:r], *a.* (*fem.* **-trice**) exterminating, destroying.—*n.m.* (*fem.* **-trice**) destroyer, exterminator.

extermination [ɛkstɛrminɑ'sjɔ̃], *n.f.* extermination.

exterminer [ɛkstɛrmi'ne], *v.t.* to exterminate, to destroy.

externat [ɛkstɛr'na], *n.m.* day-school.

externe [ɛks'tɛrn], *a.* external, exterior, outer.—*n.* day-scholar.

extincteur [ɛkstɛ̃k'tœ:r], *a.* (*fem.* **-trice**) extinguishing (*fire*).—*n.m.* fire-extinguisher.

extinction [ɛkstɛ̃k'sjɔ̃], *n.f.* extinction, destruction; liquidation; quelling; quenching (*of thirst*); slaking (*of lime*).

extinguible [ɛkstɛ̃'gibl], *a.* extinguishable.

extirpateur [ɛkstirpa'tœ:r], *n.m.* extirpator, destroyer; (*Agric.*) scarifier.

extirpation [ɛkstirpɑ'sjɔ̃], *n.f.* extirpation.

extirper [ɛkstir'pe], *v.t.* to extirpate.

extorquer [ɛkstɔr'ke], *v.t.* to extort, to wrest.

extorsion [ɛkstɔr'sjɔ̃], *n.f.* extortion.

extra [ɛks'tra], *n.m. inv.* extra.

extra-conjugal [ɛkstrakɔ̃ʒy'gal], *a.* (*m.pl.* **-aux**) extra-marital.

extracteur [ɛkstrak'tœ:r], *n.m.* extractor.

extraction [ɛkstrak'sjɔ̃], *n.f.* extraction; origin, descent.

extrader [ɛkstra'de], *v.t.* to extradite.

extradition [ɛkstradi'sjɔ̃], *n.f.* extradition.

extraire [ɛks'trɛ:r], *v.t. irr.* (*conjug. like* TRAIRE) to extract, to take out; to make extracts from.

extrait [ɛks'trɛ], *n.m.* extract; selection; abstract; certificate.

extraordinaire [ɛkstraɔrdi'nɛ:r], *a.* extraordinary, unusual.—*n.m.* extraordinary thing.

extraordinairement [ɛkstraɔrdinɛr'mɑ̃], *adv.* extraordinarily, unusually; oddly.

extrapolation [ɛkstrapɔlɑ'sjɔ̃], *n.f.* (*Math.*) extrapolation.

extra-scolaire [ɛkstraskɔ'lɛ:r], *a.* out-of-school (*activities*).

extravagamment [ɛkstravaga'mɑ̃], *adv.* extravagantly, unreasonably.

extravagance [ɛkstrava'gɑ̃:s], *n.f.* extravagance, folly.

extravagant [ɛkstrava'gɑ̃], *a.* and *n.m.* (*fem.* **-e**) extravagant (person).

extravaguer [ɛkstrava'ge], *v.i.* to talk wildly.

extrême [ɛks'trɛ:m], *a.* extreme, utmost; excessive.—*n.m.* extreme *or* utmost point.

extrêmement [ɛkstrɛm'mɑ̃], *adv.* extremely.

Extrême-Orient [ɛkstrɛmɔ'rjɑ̃], **l'**, *m.* Far East.

extrémiste [ɛkstre'mist], *n.* extremist, diehard.

extrémité [ɛkstremi'te], *n.f.* extremity, end; last moment; (*fig.*) border, brink.

exubérance [egzybe'rɑ̃:s], *n.f.* exuberance.

exubérant [egzybe'rɑ̃], *a.* exuberant, luxuriant.

exultation [egzyltɑ'sjɔ̃], *n.f.* exultation, rapture.

F

F, f (1) [ɛf], *n.m.* the sixth letter of the alphabet.
f. (2) or **fr.**, (*abbr.*) franc.
fa [fa], *n.m.* (*Mus.*) fa; F.
fable [fɑ:bl], *n.f.* fable; story, tale; (*fig.*) untruth; byword.
fablier [fɑbli'e], *n.m.* book of fables; fabulist.
fabricant [fabri'kɑ̃], *n.m.* (*fem.* **-e**) manufacturer, maker.
fabricateur [fabrika'tœ:r], *n.m.* (*fem.* **-trice**) fabricator; coiner, forger.
fabrication [fabrikɑ'sjɔ̃], *n.f.* fabrication, manufacture.
fabrique [fa'brik], *n.f.* building, fabric (*esp. of churches*); factory; fabrication.
fabriquer [fabri'ke], *v.t.* to manufacture, to make; to fabricate.
fabuleusement [fabyløz'mɑ̃], *adv.* fabulously; (*fig.*) incredibly.
fabuleux [faby'lø], *a.* (*fem.* **-euse**) fabulous, fictitious; (*fig.*) incredible.
fabuliste [faby'list], *n.* fabulist.
façade [fa'sad], *n.f.* façade, front (*of an edifice*); (*fig.*) appearance.
face [fas], *n.f.* face; front; side (*of a record*); (*fig.*) state, appearance; turn (*of affairs*); ***en face de***, opposite.
facétie [fase'si], *n.f.* facetiousness; jest, joke.
facétieusement [fasesjøz'mɑ̃], *adv.* facetiously.
facétieux [fase'sjø], *a.* (*fem.* **-euse**) facetious, humorous.
facette [fa'sɛt], *n.f.* facet, face.
fâcher [fɑ'ʃe], *v.t.* to anger, to offend, to displease; ***être fâché avec***, to be on bad terms with; ***fâché*** (***contre***), angry (*with*); ***fâché*** (***de***), sorry. **se fâcher**, *v.r.* to get angry, to be offended.
fâcherie [fɑ'ʃri], *n.f.* angry feeling; quarrel.
fâcheusement [fɑʃøz'mɑ̃], *adv.* unfortunately, unpleasantly; inopportunely, disagreeably; awkwardly.
fâcheux [fɑ'ʃø], *a.* (*fem.* **-euse**) troublesome, vexatious; unfortunate; cross.—*n.m.* (*fem.* **-euse**) troublesome *or* disagreeable person *or* thing, pesterer, bore.
facial [fa'sjal], *a.* (*m. pl.* **-aux**) (*Anat.*) facial.
facile [fa'sil], *a.* easy; facile; fluent; ready, quick; weak.
facilement [fasil'mɑ̃], *adv.* easily, readily.
facilité [fasili'te], *n.f.* facility, ease; readiness; (*pl.*) easy terms (*for payment*).
faciliter [fasili'te], *v.t.* to facilitate, to make easy.
façon [fa'sɔ̃], *n.f.* make, shape, fashion; making, workmanship; (*fig.*) manner; appearance; sort; affectation; fuss; (*pl.*) ceremony.
faconde [fa'kɔ̃:d], *n.f.* talkativeness, loquacity.
façonné [fasɔ'ne], *a.* figured (*of materials*); wrought.
façonnement [fasɔn'mɑ̃], **façonnage** [fasɔ'na:ʒ], *n.m.* fashioning, making.
façonner [fasɔ'ne], *v.t.* to make, to fashion, to form; to work, to mould; to accustom, to use (*to discipline etc.*).
façonnier [fasɔ'nje], *a.* (*fem.* **-ière**) ceremonious, affected.—*n.m.* bespoke tailor.
fac-similé [faksimi'le], *n.m.* facsimile.

factage [fak'ta:ʒ], *n.m.* porterage, carriage.
facteur [fak'tœ:r], *n.m.* (*fem.* **-trice**) maker (*of musical instruments*); agent; postman; railway porter; (*Math.*, *Biol.*) factor.
factice [fak'tis], *a.* factitious, artificial; unnatural.
factieux [fak'sjø], *a.* (*fem.* **-euse**) factious, mutinous.—*n.m.* (*fem.* **-euse**) rebel.
faction [fak'sjɔ̃], *n.f.* watch, sentry-duty; faction.
factionnaire [faksjɔ'nɛ:r], *n.m.* sentry.
factorerie [faktɔrə'ri], *n.f.* trading depot, factory (*in a colony etc.*).
facture [fak'ty:r], *n.f.* composition, workmanship (*of music, verse etc.*); (*Comm.*) bill (of sale), invoice.
facturer [fakty're], *v.t.* to invoice.
facultatif [fakylta'tif], *a.* (*fem.* **-tive**) optional; ***arrêt facultatif***, request stop.
faculté [fakyl'te], *n.f.* faculty, ability, power; quality; option, right; (*pl.*) mental faculties.
fadaise [fa'dɛ:z], *n.f.* trifle, stuff, nonsense, twaddle.
fade [fad], *a.* insipid, tasteless, dull; (*fig.*) flat, stale.
fadement [fad'mɑ̃], *adv.* insipidly, tastelessly; mawkishly.
fadeur [fa'dœ:r], *n.f.* insipidity, tastelessness; (*fig.*) pointlessness.
fagot [fa'go], *n.m.* faggot, bundle of sticks etc.
fagoter [fagɔ'te], *v.t.* to tie into faggots; (*fig.*) to jumble together; to dress in a slovenly manner; ***comme le voilà fagoté***, what a sight he looks. **se fagoter**, *v.r.* to dress in a slovenly manner.
faible [fɛ:bl], *a.* and *n.* weak, feeble (person). —*n.m.* weak part; defect, failing; partiality, weakness (*for*).
faiblement [fɛblə'mɑ̃], *adv.* weakly, feebly.
faiblesse [fɛ'blɛs], *n.f.* weakness, feebleness; faintness; deficiency; backwardness; defect; partiality.
faiblir [fɛ'bli:r], *v.i.* to become weak, to flag, to yield, to abate, to relax.
faïence [fa'jɑ̃:s], *n.f.* crockery, earthenware.
faïencier [fajɑ̃'sje], *n.m.* (*fem.* **-ière**) dealer in *or* maker of crockery.
faille [fɑ:j], *n.f.* (*Geol.*) fault.
failli [fa'ji], *a.* and *n.m.* (*fem.* **-e**) bankrupt, insolvent (person).
faillibilité [fajibili'te], *n.f.* fallibility.
faillible [fa'jibl], *a.* fallible.
faillir [fa'ji:r], *v.i. irr.* to err, to transgress; to yield; to fail; to be on the point of; ***j'ai failli tomber***, I nearly fell.
faillite [fa'jit], *n.f.* bankruptcy, insolvency; ***faire faillite***, to become bankrupt.
faim [fɛ̃], *n.f.* hunger, appetite; (*fig.*) longing; ***avoir faim***, to be hungry.
faîne [fɛ:n], *n.f.* beechnut; beechmast.
fainéant [fɛne'ɑ̃], *a.* idle, lazy.—*n.m.* (*fem.* **-e**) idler.
fainéanter [fɛneɑ̃'te], *v.i.* (*colloq.*) to be idle, to loaf.
fainéantise [fɛneɑ̃'ti:z], *n.f.* idleness, laziness, sloth.
faire (1) [fɛ:r], *v. irr.* (*The most frequently used verb in the language; **faire** not only translates* to do *or* to make, *but, followed by a noun or an infinitive, it may take the place of practically any verb; followed by an adjective*

or an adverb it forms many current idioms.)
I. *v.t.* to do; to make; to form; to be; ***cela fait mon affaire***, this is exactly what I want; ***cela fait beaucoup***, that makes a great difference; ***cela ne fait rien***, that makes no difference; ***faire accueil à***, to welcome; ***faire attention***, to pay attention; ***faire bâtir***, to have built; ***faire cas de***, to have a high opinion of; (*Motor.*) ***faire du 50 à l'heure***, to do 50 kilometres an hour; ***faire le mort***, to sham dead; ***faire part de***, to inform, to announce; ***faire peu de cas de***, to set little store by; ***faire ses dents***, to cut one's teeth; ***faire une promenade***, to take a walk; ***faire venir***, to send for; ***faire voir***, to show; ***faites-le entrer***, show him in; ***il ne fait que d'arriver***, he has only just arrived; ***je n'ai que faire de lui***, I am in no way interested in him; ***qu'est-ce que cela vous fait?*** what is that to you? ***que faire?*** what is to be done? ***se laisser faire***, to offer no resistance.
II. *v.i.* to do; to mean, to signify, to look; to fit, to suit; to deal (*at cards*); to arrange, to manage; ***avoir à faire***, to have work to do; ***c'en est fait de***, it is all up with.
III. *v. impers.* to be; ***il fait beau***, it is fine; ***quel temps fait-il?*** what sort of weather is it?
IV. **se faire**, *v.r.* to be done, to be made; to happen, to become; to pretend to be; to have, make *or* get oneself; to be used (*à*), to accustom oneself (*à*); to improve; ***cela ne se fait pas***, that is not done.
faire (2) [fɛ:r], *n.m.* doing, making; (*Paint. etc.*) execution, style.
faire-part [fɛr'pa:r], *n.m. inv.* ***un faire-part*** or ***une lettre de faire-part de décès*** or ***de mariage***, notification of death, wedding-card.
faisable [fə'zabl], *a.* practicable, feasible.
faisan [fə'zɑ̃], *n.m.* pheasant.
faisandé [fəzɑ̃'de], *a.* gamy, high.
faisandeau [fəzɑ̃'do], *n.m.* (*pl.* **-eaux**) young pheasant.
faisceau [fɛ'so], *n.m.* (*pl.* **-eaux**) bundle; sheaf (*of arrows etc.*); pile (*of arms etc.*); (*fig.*) union; (*Elec.*) beam; (*Antiq., pl.*) fasces.
faiseur [fə'zœ:r], *n.m.* (*fem.* **-euse**) maker; doer; charlatan, quack.
fait [fɛ, fɛt], *a.* made; done; fit, qualified; dressed, got up; full grown; mature.—*n.m.* act, deed; fact, actual event; case, matter, point in business; ***tout à fait***, quite.
faîte [fɛ:t], *n.m.* top, pinnacle; ridge, coping (*of a building*); (*fig.*) zenith, height.
faits divers [fɛdi'vɛr], *n.m. pl.* news items, news in brief.
faix [fɛ], *n.m. inv.* weight, burden, load.
falaise [fa'lɛ:z], *n.f.* cliff.
fallacieusement [falasjøz'mɑ̃], *adv.* fallaciously, falsely.
fallacieux [fala'sjø], *a.* (*fem.* **-euse**) fallacious, deceptive.
falloir [fa'lwa:r], *v. impers. irr.* to be necessary, to be obligatory, proper *or* expedient (*should, must*); to be needful, to be wanting *or* lacking; ***comme il faut***, properly, well-bred (*of people*); ***peu s'en faut***, very nearly; ***tant s'en faut***, far from it.
falot [fa'lo], *n.m.* large hand-lantern.
falsification [falsifikɑ'sjɔ̃], *n.f.* falsification; adulteration, debasement.
falsifier [falsi'fje], *v.t.* to falsify; to alter (*texts etc.*); to adulterate (*milk, metals*); to tamper with.
faluche [fa'lyʃ], *n.f.* student's beret.
famé [fa'me], *a. used only in* **bien** or **mal** ***famé***, of good *or* evil repute.
famélique [fame'lik], *a.* starving.—*n.* starveling.
fameux [fa'mø], *a.* (*fem.* **-euse**) famous, celebrated; first-rate; (*iron. adj. before noun*) perfect.
familial [fami'ljal], *a.* (*m. pl.* **-aux**) pertaining to family.
familiariser [familjari'ze], *v.t.* to accustom to, to familiarize. **se familiariser**, *v.r.* to familiarize oneself (***avec***), to become accustomed; to grow familiar.
familiarité [familjari'te], *n.f.* familiarity, familiar terms, intimacy; (*pl.*) liberties.
familier [fami'lje], *a.* (*fem.* **-ière**) familiar, intimate; free; homely.—*n.m.* familiar.
familièrement [familjɛr'mɑ̃], *adv.* familiarly.
famille [fa'mi:j], *n.f.* family, kindred, kin; race, tribe; (*fig.*) set.
famine [fa'min], *n.f.* famine, dearth.
fanal [fa'nal], *n.m.* (*pl.* **-aux**) signal-light; ship's lantern.
fanatique [fana'tik], *a.* fanatical.—*n.* fanatic, enthusiast.
fanatiquement [fanatik'mɑ̃], *adv.* fanatically.
fanatisme [fana'tism], *n.m.* fanaticism.
faner [fa'ne] *v.t.* to toss *or* ted (*hay*); to cause to fade; to tarnish. **se faner**, *v.r.* to fade, to droop, to wither; to tarnish.
faneur [fa'nœ:r], *n.m.* (*fem.* **-euse**) haymaker. —*n.f.* (**-euse**) haymaking machine.
fanfare [fɑ̃'fa:r], *n.f.* flourish (*of trumpets*), fanfare; brass band.
fanfaron [fɑ̃fa'rɔ̃], *a.* (*fem.* **-onne**) blustering, swaggering, boasting.—*n.m.* (*fem.* **-onne**) blusterer, swaggerer; braggart.
fanfreluche [fɑ̃frə'lyʃ], *n.f.* bauble, gewgaw.
fange [fɑ̃:ʒ], *n.f.* mire, mud, dirt; vileness.
fangeux [fɑ̃'ʒø], *a.* (*fem.* **-euse**) miry, muddy, dirty.
fanon [fa'nɔ̃], *n.m.* dewlap (*oxen*); fetlock (*horse*); horny strip (*in whales*); (*Mil.*) pennon (*of lance*).
fantaisie [fɑ̃tɛ'zi], *n.f.* imagination; fancy; whim, caprice; (*Mus.*) fantasia.
fantaisiste [fɑ̃tɛ'zist], *a.* whimsical, fantastic. —*n.* whimsical painter, writer *or* other artist.
fantasmagorie [fɑ̃tasmagɔ'ri], *n.f.* phantasmagoria.
fantasque [fɑ̃'task], *a.* fantastic, whimsical; strange, odd.
fantassin [fɑ̃ta'sɛ̃], *n.m.* foot-soldier, infantryman.
fantastique [fɑ̃tas'tik], *a.* fantastic, fanciful. —*n.m.* uncanny.
fantastiquement [fɑ̃tastik'mɑ̃], *adv.* fantastically.
fantoche [fɑ̃'tɔʃ], *n.m.* marionette, puppet.
fantôme [fɑ̃'to:m], *n.m.* phantom, spectre, ghost.

faon [fɑ̃], *n.m.* fawn, calf of deer.
faquin [fa'kɛ̃], *n.m.* cad, rascal.
farandole [farɑ̃'dɔl], *n.f.* farandole (*Provençal dance*).
farce [fars], *n.f.* stuffing, force-meat; farce; buffoonery; practical joke; prank.
farceur [far'sœ:r], *a.* (*fem.* **-euse**) waggish, facetious.—*n.m.* (*fem.* **-euse**) practical joker; humbug.
farcir [far'si:r], *v.t.* to stuff with force-meat etc.; to cram.
fard [fa:r], *n.m.* paint (*for the complexion*), rouge, make-up; (*fig.*) varnish, disguise; ***sans fard***, plainly, frankly.
fardeau [far'do], *n.m.* (*pl.* **-eaux**) burden, load; mash (*for brewing*); (*Mining*) mass.
farder [far'de], *v.t.* to paint (*the face*), to make up; (*fig.*) to varnish, to gloss over. **se farder**, *v.r.* to paint one's face, to make up.
(*C*) **fardoches** [far'dɔʃ], *n.f. pl.* brushwood.
farfadet [farfa'dɛ], *n.m.* goblin, elf.
farfouiller [farfu'je], *v.i.* (*fam.*) to rummage.
faribole [fari'bɔl], *n.f.* idle story; trifle.
farine [fa'rin], *n.f.* flour; meal.
farineux [fari'nø], *a.* (*fem.* **-euse**) mealy, farinaceous; white with flour.
farouche [fa'ruʃ], *a.* wild; fierce; sullen; shy.
fascicule [fasi'kyl], *n.m.* fascicle.
fascinateur [fasina'tœ:r], *a.* (*fem.* **-trice**) fascinating.
fascination [fasinɑ'sjɔ̃], *n.f.* fascination.
fasciner [fasi'ne], *v.t.* to fascinate.
fascisme [fa'ʃism], *n.m.* Fascism.
fasciste [fa'ʃist], *a.* and *n.* Fascist.
faste [fast], *a.* favourable, lucky.—*n.m.* (*used only in sing.*) pomp, ostentation.
fastidieusement [fastidjøz'mɑ̃], *adv.* tediously.
fastidieux [fasti'djø], *a.* (*fem.* **-euse**) irksome, tedious.
fastueusement [fastɥøz'mɑ̃], *adv.* ostentatiously, pompously; splendidly.
fastueux [fas'tɥø], *a.* (*fem.* **-euse**) ostentatious, pompous, showy; stately.
fat [fat], *a.* conceited, vain, foppish.—*n.m.* fop, coxcomb.
fatal [fa'tal], *a.* fatal; inevitable; ***une femme fatale***, a vamp.
fatalement [fatal'mɑ̃], *adv.* fatally; inevitably.
fatalisme [fata'lism], *n.m.* fatalism.
fataliste [fata'list], *n.* fatalist.
fatalité [fatali'te], *n.f.* fatality.
fatigant [fati'gɑ̃], *a.* fatiguing, tiring, wearisome.
fatigue [fa'tig], *n.f.* fatigue, weariness; toil, hardship; ***habits de fatigue***, working clothes.
fatigué [fati'ge], *a.* fatigued, tired; (*fig.*) worn out.
fatiguer [fati'ge], *v.t.* to fatigue; to tire.—*v.i.* to tire; to be fatiguing. **se fatiguer**, *v.r.* to tire oneself out, to get tired, to be jaded.
fatras [fa'trɑ], *n.m.* jumble; rubbish, trash.
fatuité [fatɥi'te], *n.f.* fatuity, self-conceit.
faubourg [fo'bu:r], *n.m.* outskirts, suburb.
faubourien [fobu'rjɛ̃], *a.* (*fem.* **-enne**) suburban, working-class; common.—*n.m.* (*fem.* **-enne**) person living in the suburbs; (*pej.*) common person.
fauchage [fo'ʃa:ʒ], *n.m.* mowing.
fauchaison [foʃɛ'zɔ̃], *n.f.* mowing-time.
fauché [fo'ʃe], *a.* mown; (*slang*) broke.
faucher [fo'ʃe], *v.t.* to mow, to reap.
faucheur [fo'ʃœ:r], *n.m.* (*fem.* **-euse**) mower, reaper.—*n.f.* (**-euse**) (*mechanical*) mower.
faucille [fo'si:j], *n.f.* sickle, reaping-hook.
faucon [fo'kɔ̃], *n.m.* falcon, hawk.
fauconnerie [fokɔn'ri], *n.f.* falconry.
fauconnier [fokɔ'nje], *n.m.* falconer.
faufiler [fofi'le], *v.t.* to tack, to baste (*needlework*). **se faufiler**, *v.r.* to insinuate oneself, to sneak in; to find a way in.
faune (1) [fo:n], *n.m.* faun.
faune (2) [fo:n], *n.f.* (*Zool.*) fauna.
faussaire [fo'sɛ:r], *n.* forger.
fausse [fos], [FAUX].
faussement [fos'mɑ̃], *adv.* falsely, wrongfully.
fausser [fo'se], *v.t.* to bend; to falsify, to pervert; to break, to force *or* strain (*a lock*).
fausset [fo'sɛ], *n.m.* (*Mus.*) falsetto.
fausseté [fos'te], *n.f.* falsity, falsehood; duplicity.
faute [fo:t], *n.f.* want; defect; fault, mistake, error; ***faute de***, for want of.
fauteuil [fo'tœ:j], *n.m.* arm-chair; chair (*speaker's, president's seat*).
fauteur [fo'tœ:r], *n.m.* abettor, favourer.
fautif [fo'tif], *a.* (*fem.* **-tive**) faulty, at fault, defective.
fauve [fo:v], *a.* fawn-coloured, tawny.—*n.m.* wild animal; ***Les Fauves***, group of French painters at the beginning of this century.
fauvette [fo'vɛt], *n.f.* warbler.
faux (1) [fo], *n.f. inv.* scythe.
faux (2) [fo], *a.* (*fem.* **fausse**) false, untrue, wrong; base, counterfeit, forged (*coinage*); sham; insincere; (*Mus.*) out of tune; ***faire un faux pas***, to stumble; (*fig.*) to make a slip.—*n.m.* falsehood; error; forgery.—*adv.* falsely, erroneously; (*Mus.*) out of tune.
faux-filet [fofi'lɛ], *n.m.* sirloin.
faux-fuyant [fofɥi'jɑ̃], *n.m.* subterfuge, evasion.
faux-monnayeur [fomɔne'jœ:r], *n.m.* coiner, counterfeiter.
faveur [fa'vœ:r], *n.f.* favour, boon; grace; vogue; (*narrow*) silk ribbon; ***à la faveur de***, by means of; ***en faveur de***, on behalf of.
favorable [favɔ'rabl], *a.* favourable, propitious.
favorablement [favɔrablə'mɑ̃], *adv.* favourably.
favori [favɔ'ri], *a.* and *n.m.* (*fem.* **-ite**) favourite.—*n.m.* (*pl.*) side-whiskers.
favoriser [favɔri'ze], *v.t.* to favour, to befriend; to assist, to protect.
favoritisme [favɔri'tism], *n.m.* favouritism.
fébrile [fe'bril], *a.* febrile, feverish.
fécond [fe'kɔ̃], *a.* fruitful, prolific; copious, abundant, fertile.
fécondation [fekɔ̃dɑ'sjɔ̃], *n.f.* impregnation; fertilization.
féconder [fekɔ̃'de], *v.t.* to make fruitful, to fertilize.
fécondité [fekɔ̃di'te], *n.f.* fecundity, fruitfulness, fertility.
fécule [fe'kyl], *n.f.* faecula, starch.
féculent [feky'lɑ̃], *a.* feculent.—*n.m.* starchy food.
fédéral [fede'ral], *a.* (*m. pl.* **-aux**) federal.
fédéralisme [federa'lism], *n.m.* federalism.
fédéraliste [federa'list], *a.* and *n.* federalist.

fédération [federɑ'sjɔ̃], *n.f.* federation, alliance.
fédéré [fede're], *a.* federate, confederate; amalgamated.
fédérer (se) [səfede're], *v.r.* (*conjug. like* CÉDER) to federate, to band together.
fée [fe], *n.f.* fairy, fay.
féerie [feə'ri], *n.f.* enchantment; fairy scene; fairy-land.
féerique [feə'rik], *a.* fairy-like; wonderful.
feindre [fɛ̃:dr], *v.t. irr* (*conjug. like* CRAINDRE) to feign, to simulate, to sham, to pretend.—*v.i.* to feign, to sham.
feint [fɛ̃], *a.* feigned, pretended, sham.
feinte [fɛ̃:t], *n.f.* feint; pretence, dissimulation.
feld-maréchal [fɛldmare'ʃal], *n.m.* (*pl.* **-aux**) field-marshal.
feldspath [fɛls'pat], *n.m.* feldspar.
fêlé [fɛ'le], *a.* cracked (*of glass*); (*fig.*) crack-brained.
fêler [fɛ'le], *v.t.* and **se fêler**, *v.r.* to crack (*of glass etc.*).
félicitation [felisitɑ'sjɔ̃], *n.f.* felicitation, congratulation.
félicité [felisi'te], *n.f.* felicity, bliss.
féliciter [felisi'te], *v.t.* to congratulate, to felicitate. **se féliciter**, *v.r.* to congratulate oneself.
félin [fe'lɛ̃], *a.* and *n.m.* (*fem.* **-e**) feline.
félon [fe'lɔ̃], *a.* (*fem.* **-onne**) disloyal, traitorous.—*n.m.* (*fem.* **-onne**) traitor, caitiff.
félonie [felɔ'ni], *n.f.* (*Feud.*) felony, treason.
fêlure [fɛ'ly:r], *n.f.* crack, fissure.
femelle [fə'mɛl], *a.* female, feminine, she-.—*n.f.* female, (*pej.*) woman.
féminin [femi'nɛ̃], *a.* feminine, female, womanish, womanly, effeminate.—*n.m.* (*Gram.*) feminine.
femme [fam], *n.f.* woman; married woman; wife; female attendant; lady.
femme-agent [fama'ʒɑ̃], *n.f.* police-woman.
femmelette [fam'lɛt], *n.f.* silly, weak woman; effeminate man.
femme-soldat [famsɔl'da], *n.f.* service-woman.
fémur [fe'my:r], *n.m.* femur, thigh-bone.
fenaison [fənɛ'zɔ̃], *n.f.* hay-time, hay-making.
fendiller (se) [səfɑ̃di'je], *v.r.* to be covered with small cracks, to crack, to split.
fendre [fɑ̃:dr], *v.t.* to cleave, to split, to crack, to cut open; to plough (*the sea*). **se fendre**, *v.r.* to burst asunder, to split, to be ready to burst.
fendu [fɑ̃'dy], *a.* cleft, split, cloven.
fenêtre [fə'nɛ:tr], *n.f.* window, casement.
fenil [fə'ni], *n.m.* hayloft.
fenouil [fə'nu:j], *n.m.* fennel.
fente [fɑ̃:t], *n.f.* slit, chink, cleft; gap, crevice.
féodal [feɔ'dal], *a.* (*m. pl.* **-aux**) feudal.
féodalisme [feɔda'lism], *n.m.* feudalism.
fer [fɛ:r], *n.m.* iron; iron tool; horseshoe; head, point, etc.; (*fig.*) sword, brand; (*Golf*) club; (*pl.*) irons, chains, fetters; ***fer battu*** or ***forgé***, wrought-iron; ***fil de fer***, wire.
fer-blanc [fɛr'blɑ̃], *n.m.* (*pl.* **fers-blancs**) tin, tin-plate.
férié [fe'rje], *a.* holiday; ***jour férié***, holiday, general holiday, bank-holiday.
férir [fe'rir], *v.t. used only in* ***sans coup férir***, without striking a blow.
ferler [fɛr'le], *v.t.* to furl (*sails*).
fermage [fɛr'ma:ʒ], *n.m.* rent (*of a farm*).
fermail [fɛr'ma:j], *n.m.* clasp, buckle.
ferme (1) [fɛrm], *a.* firm; fixed, stable; strong, stout, stiff, steady; resolute.—*adv.* firmly, fast, hard.
ferme (2) [fɛrm], *n.f.* farm, farmhouse, farm-stead; farming (*of taxes*); letting out on lease.
ferme (3) [fɛrm], *n.f.* framework of beams.
fermement [fɛrmə'mɑ̃], *adv.* firmly, steadily; resolutely.
ferment [fɛr'mɑ̃], *n.m.* ferment, leaven.
fermentation [fɛrmɑ̃tɑ'sjɔ̃], *n.f.* fermentation, working; (*fig.*) ferment.
fermenter [fɛrmɑ̃'te], *v.i.* to ferment, to rise, to work.
fermer [fɛr'me], *v.t.* to shut, to close; to fasten; to turn off (*water, gas etc.*); to put an end to (*a discussion etc.*); to enclose.—*v.i.* to shut, to be shut. **se fermer**, *v.r.* to shut, to close, to be closed; to lock.
fermeté [fɛrmə'te], *n.f.* firmness; steadiness; resolution.
fermeture [fɛrmə'ty:r], *n.f.* closing, shutting; ***fermeture à glissière***, zip fastener.
fermier [fɛr'mje], *n.m.* (tenant) farmer.
fermière [fɛr'mjɛ:r], *n.f.* farmer's wife.
fermoir [fɛr'mwa:r], *n.m.* clasp, fastener.
féroce [fe'rɔs], *a.* ferocious, fierce, savage.
férocement [ferɔs'mɑ̃], *adv.* ferociously.
férocité [ferɔsi'te], *n.f.* ferocity, fierceness.
ferraille [fɛ'rɑ:j], *n.f.* old iron, scrap-iron.
ferrailler [fɛrɑ'je], *v.i.* (*Spt.*) to fence clumsily; (*fig.*) to squabble.
ferrailleur [fɛrɑ'jœ:r], *n.m.* dealer in old iron, scrap merchant; (*Spt.*) clumsy fencer.
ferrant [fɛ'rɑ̃], *a.* ***maréchal ferrant***, farrier, shoeing-smith.
ferré [fɛ're], *a.* bound, shod etc., with iron; metalled; (*colloq.*) skilled; ***voie ferrée***, railway.
ferrer [fɛ're], *v.t.* to bind, hoop, etc., with iron; to shoe (*a horse etc.*).
ferret [fɛ'rɛ], *n.m.* tag (*of a lace*).
ferronnerie [fɛrɔn'ri], *n.f.* iron-foundry; ironmongery; wrought iron.
ferronnier [fɛrɔ'nje], *n.m.* (*fem.* **-ière**) iron-monger, iron-worker.
ferroviaire [fɛrɔ'vjɛ:r], *a.* pertaining to railways.
ferrure [fɛ'ry:r], *n.f.* iron-work; shoeing (*of a horse etc.*).
fertile [fɛr'til], *a.* fertile, fruitful.
fertilement [fɛrtil'mɑ̃], *adv.* fertilely, abundantly.
fertilisant [fɛrtili'zɑ̃], *a.* fertilizing.
fertiliser [fɛrtili'ze], *v.t.* to fertilize, to manure.
fertilité [fɛrtili'te], *n.f.* fertility, fruitfulness.
féru [fe'ry], *a.* smitten; keen on (*something* or *someone*).
férule [fe'ryl], *n.f.* (*Sch.*) cane, ferule, rod; stroke, cut.
fervent [fɛr'vɑ̃], *a.* fervent.—*n.m.* (*fem.* **-e**) enthusiast, devotee, fan.
ferveur [fɛr'vœ:r], *n.f.* fervour, ardour.
fesse [fɛs], *n.f.* buttock, rump; (*pl.*) bottom.
fessée [fɛ'se], *n.f.* spanking.
fesse-mathieu [fɛsma'tjø], *n.m.* (*pl.* **fesse-mathieux**) miser, skinflint.
fesser [fɛ'se], *v.t.* to spank, to smack.

fessier [fɛ'sje], *n.m.* buttocks, bottom.
festin [fɛs'tɛ̃], *n.m.* feast, banquet.
***festiner** [fɛsti'ne], *v.i.* to banquet, to carouse.
festival [fɛsti'val], *n.m.* festival.
festivité [fɛstivi'te], *n.f.* festivity.
feston [fɛs'tɔ̃], *n.m.* festoon; scallop.
festonner [fɛstɔ'ne], *v.t.* to festoon; to cut in festoons, to scallop.
festoyer [fɛstwa'je], *v.t.* (*conjug. like* EMPLOYER) to entertain, to feast.
fête [fɛ:t], *n.f.* holiday, festival; saint's day; feast; birthday; festivity, merry-making.
fête-Dieu [fɛ:t'djø], *n.f.* Corpus Christi day.
fêter [fɛ'te], *v.t.* to keep (as a holiday); to entertain, to feast.
fétiche [fe'tiʃ], *n.m.* fetish.
fétide [fe'tid], *a.* fetid, rank, offensive.
fétidité [fetidi'te], *n.f.* fetidity, offensive smell.
fétu [fe'ty], *n.m.* straw; (*fig.*) pin, rap.
feu (1) [fø], *n.m.* (*pl.* **feux**) fire; burning; heat; discharge of fire-arms; fire-place; (*fig.*) light; brilliancy; passion; vivacity; ***crier 'au feu'***, to cry 'fire!'; ***faire feu***, to fire; ***feu d'artifice***, fireworks; ***feu de joie***, bonfire; ***feux de position***, (*Motor.*) parking lights; ***le coin du feu***, the fireside; ***prendre feu***, to catch fire.
feu (2) [fø], *a.* late, deceased.
feuillage [fœ'ja:ʒ], *n.m.* foliage, leaves.
feuille [fœ:j], *n.f.* leaf; sheet (*of paper, metal etc.*); newspaper; list; foil (*of mirrors*).
feuillet [fœ'jɛ], *n.m.* leaf (*of a book*).
feuilleter [fœj'te], *v.t.* (*conjug. like* APPELER) to turn over; to peruse rapidly; ***gâteau feuilleté***, flaky puff.
feuillu [fœ'jy], *a.* leafy.
feutrage [fø'tra:ʒ], *n.m.* felting.
feutre [fø:tr], *n.m.* felt; felt hat.
feutrer [fø'tre], *v.t.* to felt; to pad, to pack.
feutrier [føtri'e], *n.m.* (*fem.* **-ière**) felt-maker.
fève [fɛ:v], *n.f.* bean, broad bean.
février [fevri'e], *n.m.* February.
fez [fɛ:z], *n.m. inv.* fez (*Turkish cap*).
fi! [fi], *int.* fie!
fiacre [fjakr], *n.m.* hackney-coach, cab.
fiançailles [fjɑ̃'sɑ:j], *n.f.* (*used only in pl.*) betrothal, engagement.
fiancé [fjɑ̃'se], *n.m.* (*fem.* **-ée**) betrothed, fiancé, fiancée.
fiancer [fjɑ̃'se], *v.t.* (*conjug. like* COMMENCER) to betroth, to affiance. **se fiancer**, *v.r.* to become engaged to each other.
fiasco [fjas'ko], *n.m. inv.* fiasco, failure.
fibre [fibr], *n.f.* fibre, filament; (*fig.*) feeling.
fibreux [fi'brø], *a.* (*fem.* **-euse**) fibrous, stringy.
ficeler [fis'le], *v.t.* (*conjug. like* APPELER) to bind *or* tie up with string; to do up; to dress up.
ficeleur [fis'lœ:r], *n.m.* (*fem.* **-euse**) packer.
ficelle [fi'sɛl], *n.f.* string, packthread, twine; (*fig.*) dodge.
fiche [fiʃ], *n.f.* peg, pin (*for a hinge etc.*); (*Teleph.*) plug; small card; (*Whist*) booby prize; (*colloq.*) slip of paper, memo.
ficher [fi'ʃe], *v.t.* to drive in, to fasten in. **se ficher**, *v.r.* (*colloq.*) to laugh at (*de*).
fichier [fi'ʃje], *n.m.* card-index (*cabinet*).
fichoir [fi'ʃwa:r], *n.m.* peg, clothes-peg.
fichtre! [fiʃtr], *int.* (*colloq.*) dash it! hang it!
fichu (1) [fi'ʃy], *n.m.* neckerchief.
fichu (2) [fi'ʃy], *a.* sorry, pitiful; got up (*dressed*); (*slang*) done for.
fictif [fik'tif], *a.* (*fem.* **-tive**) supposed, fictitious.
fiction [fik'sjɔ̃], *n.f.* fiction; fable.
fictivement [fiktiv'mɑ̃], *adv.* fictitiously.
fidèle [fi'dɛl], *a.* faithful, loyal, true.—*n.* faithful friend etc.; (*pl.*) worshippers, faithful.
fidèlement [fidɛl'mɑ̃], *adv.* faithfully, truly.
fidélité [fideli'te], *n.f.* fidelity, faithfulness, loyalty; accuracy.
fief [fjɛf], *n.m.* fief, fee.
fieffé [fjɛ'fe], *a.* (*colloq.*) arrant, downright.
fiel [fjɛl], *n.m.* gall; (*fig.*) hatred, bitterness, rancour.
fier [fje], *v.t.* to trust, to entrust. **se fier**, *v.r.* to trust to *or* in, to depend upon (*à*).
fier [fjɛ:r], *a.* (*fem.* **fière**) proud, haughty; bold; (*colloq.*) fine, capital.
fièrement [fjɛr'mɑ̃], *adv.* proudly, arrogantly, haughtily; boldly.
fierté [fjɛr'te], *n.f.* pride, arrogance; dignity.
fièvre [fjɛ:vr], *n.f.* fever, feverishness; (*fig.*) restlessness, excitement.
fiévreux [fje'vrø], *a.* (*fem.* **-euse**) feverish; (*fig.*) restless.—*n.m.* (*fem.* **-euse**) fever-patient.
fifre [fifr], *n.m.* fife; fifer.
figé [fi'ʒe], *a.* stiff, cold, set (*features, smile etc.*).
figement [fiʒ'mɑ̃], *n.m.* congealment, coagulation, curdling.
figer [fi'ʒe], *v.t.* and **se figer**, *v.r.* (*conjug. like* MANGER) to congeal, to coagulate, to curdle.
figue [fig], *n.f.* fig.
figuier [fi'gje], *n.m.* fig-tree.
figurant [figy'rɑ̃], *n.m.* (*fem.* **-e**) (*Theat., Cine.*) figurant; extra.
figuratif [figyra'tif], *a.* (*fem.* **-tive**) figurative.
figurativement [figyrativ'mɑ̃], *adv.* figuratively.
figure [fi'gy:r], *n.f.* figure, shape; face, appearance; symbol, type.
figuré [figy're], *a.* figured; figurative.
figurer [figy're], *v.t.* to figure, to represent.—*v.i.* to figure, to appear. **se figurer**, *v.r.* to imagine, fancy *or* picture to oneself.
figurine [figy'rin], *n.f.* figurine, statuette.
fil [fil], *n.m.* thread; wire; yarn; (cutting) edge; grain, vein (*in stones etc.*); course (*of a stream etc.*); chain, series; ***de fil en aiguille***, one thing leading to another; ***donner un coup de fil***, to give a ring; ***être au bout du fil***, to be speaking (*on the phone*); ***fil à coudre***, sewing-thread; ***fil de la Vierge***, gossamer; ***laine deux fils***, two-ply wool.
filage [fi'la:ʒ], *n.m.* spinning.
filament [fila'mɑ̃], *n.m.* filament, thread.
filamenteux [filamɑ̃'tø], *a.* (*fem.* **-euse**) thready, stringy.
filandière [filɑ̃'djɛ:r], *n.f.* spinner.
filandreux [filɑ̃'drø], *a.* (*fem.* **-euse**) fibrous, stringy, thready.
filant [fi'lɑ̃], *a.* flowing; ropy; shooting (*of stars*).
filasse [fi'las], *n.f.* harl, tow (*of flax, hemp etc.*); oakum.
filateur [fila'tœ:r], *n.m.* spinning-mill owner; spinner.

filature [fila'ty:r], *n.f.* spinning-mill; spinning; shadowing (*by a detective*).

file [fil], *n.f.* file; ***à la file***, one after another; ***prendre la file***, to take one's place in the queue.

filé [fi'le], *a.* drawn out, sustained.—*n.m.* gold *or* silver thread.

filer [fi'le], *v.t.* to spin; (*fig.*) to carry on; to spin out (*a story etc.*); (*Naut.*) to pay out (*a rope*); to trail, to shadow.—*v.i.* to become ropy; to go, to travel; to shoot (*of stars*); to flare (*of a lamp etc.*); to take oneself off; ***filer à l'anglaise***, to take French leave; ***filer doux***, to sing small.

filet [fi'lɛ], *n.m.* slender thread, string; net; (*Rail.*) rack; filament, fibre; (*Bot., Arch. etc.*) fillet; drop (*of water etc.*); (*fig.*) streak; trickle, streamlet; snaffle-bridle; (*fig.*) snare.

fileur [fi'lœ:r], *n.m.* (*fem.* **-euse**) spinner; wire-drawer.

filial [fi'ljal], *a.* (*m. pl.* **-aux**) filial.

filiale [fi'ljal], *n.f.* subsidiary company, branch.

filiation [filja'sjɔ̃], *n.f.* filiation; (*fig.*) connexion, relationship.

filière [fi'ljɛ:r], *n.f.* draw-plate; screw-plate; (*Carp.*) purlin; (*fig.*) channel, series.

filigrane [fili'gran], *n.m.* filigree, filigree-work; water-mark (*in paper*); embossing.

filigraner [filigra'ne], *v.t.* to work in filigree; to emboss.

fille [fi:j], *n.f.* daughter; girl, young unmarried woman; maiden; servant-maid; ***arrière-petite-fille***, grcat-granddaughter; ***belle-fille***, daughter-in-law, stepdaughter; ***jeune fille***, girl; ***petite-fille***, granddaughter; ***vieille fille***, old maid.

fillette [fi'jɛt], *n.f.* little girl; lass.

filleul [fi'jœ:l], *n.m.* godson.

filleule [fi'jœ:l], *n.f.* goddaughter.

film [film], *n.m.* film; ***film fixe***, film strip.

filmer [fil'me], *v.t.* to film.

filon [fi'lɔ̃], *n.m.* metallic vein; (*fig.*) good job; tip.

filou [fi'lu], *n.m.* pickpocket, thief; swindler.

filouter [filu'te], *v.t.* to steal; to cheat, to swindle.

filouterie [filu'tri], *n.f.* picking pockets; swindling, cheating.

fils [fis], *n.m. inv.* son, male child; offspring; ***arrière-petit-fils***, great-grandson; ***beau-fils***, stepson, son-in-law; ***petit-fils***, grandson.

filtrage [fil'tra:ʒ], *n.m.* filtering, straining.

filtrant [fil'trɑ̃], *a.* filtering, straining; ***bout filtrant***, filter-tip.

filtration [filtrɑ'sjɔ̃], *n.f.* filtration, straining; percolation.

filtre (1) [filtr], *n.m.* filter; cup of filtered coffee; ***filtre à café***, percolator.

filtre (2) [PHILTRE].

filtrer [fil'tre], *v.t.* to filter, to strain.—*v.i.* and **se filtrer**, *v.r.* to filter; to percolate.

filure [fi'ly:r], *n.f.* texture of a spun fabric.

fin (1) [fɛ̃], *n.f.* end, conclusion, close; death; destination; aim, design.

fin (2) [fɛ̃], *a.* fine, thin, slender; delicate; refined, polite; acute; cunning.—*n.m.* sharp fellow; main point.—*n.f.* (**-e**) type of liqueur brandy.

final [fi'nal], *a.* final, last, ultimate.

finale [fi'nal], *n.m.* (*Mus.*) finale.—*n.f.* (*Spt.*) final.

finalement [final'mɑ̃], *adv.* finally, lastly.

finalité [finali'te], *n.f.* finality.

finance [fi'nɑ̃:s], *n.f.* ready money; (*pl.*) (*public*) finances, exchequer, treasury.

financer [finɑ̃'se], *v.t.* (*conjug. like* COMMENCER) to finance—*v.i.* to lay out money.

financier [finɑ̃'sje], *a.* (*fem.* **-ière**) financial. —*n.m.* financier.

financièrement [finɑ̃sjɛr'mɑ̃], *adv.* financially.

finaud [fi'no], *a.* sly, artful, cunning.—*n.m.* (*fem.* **-e**) sly, artful person.

fine [fin], [FIN (2)].

finement [fin'mɑ̃], *adv.* finely, delicately; ingeniously; artfully.

finesse [fi'nɛs], *n.f.* fineness; delicacy; ingenuity; finesse, artifice, slyness.

finette [fi'nɛt], *n.f.* thin material of wool *or* cotton, flannelette.

fini [fi'ni], *a.* finished, ended.—*n.m.* finish, high finish, perfection.

finir [fi'ni:r], *v.t.* to finish, to complete; to end, to terminate.—*v.i.* to end, to conclude, to be over; to expire.

finissage [fini'sa:ʒ], *n.m.* finishing touches.

finissant [fini'sɑ̃], *a.* declining, dying.

finlandais [fɛ̃lɑ̃'dɛ], *a.* Finnish.—*n.m.* Finnish (*language*); (**Finlandais**, *fem.* **-aise**) Finn.

Finlande [fɛ̃'lɑ̃:d], **la**, *f.* Finland.

finnois [fi'nwa], *a.* Finnish.—*n.m.* Finnish (*language*); (**Finnois**, *fem.* **-oise**) Finn.

fiole [fjɔl], *n.f.* phial.

firmament [firma'mɑ̃], *n.m.* firmament, sky.

fisc [fisk], *n.m.* public treasury, fisc.

fiscal [fis'kal], *a.* (*m. pl.* **-aux**) fiscal, financial.

fissible [fi'sibl], *a.* fissile (*of radio-active materials*).

fission [fi'sjɔ̃], *n.f.* fission, splitting (*of atom*); ***fission de l'atome***, nuclear fission.

fissure [fi'sy:r], *n.f.* fissure, crack, rent.

fissurer (se) [səfisy're], *v.r.* to become fissured.

five-o'clock [faivɔ'klɔk], *n.m.* afternoon tea.

fixation [fiksɑ'sjɔ̃], *n.f.* fixation, fixing; settlement; rating, assessment.

fixe [fiks], *a.* fixed; settled; appointed, regular. —*n.m.* fixed salary.—*int.* (*Mil.*) eyes front! steady!

fixement [fiksə'mɑ̃], *adv.* fixedly, steadily.

fixer [fik'se], *v.t.* to fix, to fasten; to settle; to establish; to stare at; to attract. **se fixer**, *v.r.* to be fixed; to settle down.

fixité [fiksi'te], *n.f.* fixity, stability.

flac [flak], *int.* slap! bang! plop!—*n.m.* anti-aircraft gunfire, flak.

flaccidité [flaksidi'te], *n.f.* flaccidity.

flacon [fla'kɔ̃], *n.m.* bottle; decanter; phial.

flagellant [flaʒɛ'lɑ̃], *n.m.* flagellant.

flagellation [flaʒɛlɑ'sjɔ̃] *n.f.* flagellation, flogging.

flageller [flaʒɛ'le], *v.t.* to flagellate, to scourge, to flog; (*fig.*) to lash with words.

flageoler [flaʒɔ'le], *v.i.* to tremble, to shake (*of legs*).

flageolet [flaʒɔ'lɛ], *n.m.* flageolet (*music*); (*small*) green kidney bean.

flagorner [flagɔr'ne], *v.t.* to flatter servilely, to toady to.

flagornerie [flagɔrnə'ri], *n.f.* sycophancy, base flattery.
flagorneur [flagɔr'nœ:r], *n.m.* (*fem.* **-euse**) sycophant, toady.
flagrant [fla'grɑ̃], *a.* flagrant, gross; ***en flagrant délit***, red-handed.
flair [flɛ:r], *n.m.* (*Hunt.*) nose; (*fig.*) perspicacity.
flairer [flɛ're], *v.t.* to smell, to scent; (*colloq.*) to smell of; to find out.
flamand [fla'mɑ̃], *a.* Flemish.—*n.m.* Flemmish (*language*); (**Flamand**, *fem.* **-ande**) Fleming.
flamant (**rose**) [fla'mɑ̃(ro:z)], *n.m.* flamingo.
flambant [flɑ̃'bɑ̃], *a.* blazing, flaming; (*pop.*) smart, flashy; ***flambant neuf***, brand new.
flambeau [flɑ̃'bo], *n.m.* (*pl.* **-eaux**) torch, link; candle, candlestick.
flambée [flɑ̃'be], *n.f.* blaze.
flamber [flɑ̃'be], *v.t.* to singe; to fumigate, to disinfect.—*v.i.* to blaze, to flame, to flare.
flamboiement [flɑ̃bwa'mɑ̃], *n.m.* flaming, blaze.
flamboyant [flɑ̃bwa'jɑ̃], *a.* flaming, blazing; flashing.
flamboyer [flɑ̃bwa'je], *v.i.* (*conjug. like* EMPLOYER) to flame, to blaze, to flare.
flamme [flɑ:m], *n.f.* flame; (*fig.*) fire; glow; ardour, passion.
flammèche [flɑ'mɛʃ], *n.f.* flake of fire, spark.
flammer [flɑ'me], *v.t.* to singe (*material*).
flan [flɑ̃], *n.m.* (*baked*) custard tart; flan.
flanc [flɑ̃], *n.m.* flank, side; (*fig.*) womb, bowels.
flancher [flɑ̃'ʃe], *v.i.* (*fam.*) to give in, to rat, to jib; (*Motor.*) to stop, to break down.
flandrin [flɑ̃'drɛ̃], *n.m.* (*colloq.*) ***un grand flandrin***, a long, lanky fellow.
flanelle [fla'nɛl], *n.f.* flannel.
flâner [flɑ'ne], *v.i.* to lounge, to stroll, to loaf.
flânerie [flɑ'nri], *n.f.* lounging; stroll; loafing.
flâneur [flɑ'nœ:r], *n.m.* (*fem.* **-euse**) stroller; lounger, loafer.
flanquer [flɑ̃'ke], *v.t.* to flank; (*Mil.*) to defend, to guard; (*colloq.*) to deal (*a blow*); to fling. **se flanquer**, *v.r.* ***se flanquer par terre***, to throw oneself down.
flaque [flak], *n.f.* small pool, puddle.
flash [flaʃ], *n.m.* (*Phot.*) flash-light; (*Cine.*) flash.
flasque (1) [flask], *a.* limp, slack, flabby, flaccid.
flasque (2) [flask], *n.f.* powder-horn.
flatter [fla'te], *v.t.* to stroke, to caress; to flatter; to soothe; to cajole. **se flatter**, *v.r.* to flatter oneself; to pride oneself; to hope, to expect.
flatterie [fla'tri], *n.f.* flattery, adulation.
flatteur [fla'tœ:r], *a.* (*fem.* **-euse**) flattering, complimentary.—*n.m.* (*fem.* **-euse**) flatterer.
flatteusement [flatøz'mɑ̃], *adv.* flatteringly.
flatulence [flaty'lɑ̃:s], *n.f.* flatulence, wind.
flatulent [flaty'lɑ̃], *a.* flatulent, windy.
fléau [fle'o], *n.m.* (*pl.* **fléaux**) flail; (*fig.*) scourge, plague; beam (*of a balance*).
flèche [flɛʃ], *n.f.* arrow, dart; shaft; (*Arch.*) slender spire; ***faire flèche de tout bois***, to leave no stone unturned.
fléchette [fle'ʃɛt], *n.f.* dart (*game*).
fléchir [fle'ʃi:r], *v.t.* to bend, to bow; (*fig.*) to move, to persuade.—*v.i.* to bend, to bow, to yield; to stagger.
fléchissement [fleʃis'mɑ̃], *n.m.* bending, giving way.
flegmatique [flɛgma'tik], *a.* (*Med.*) phlegmatic; (*fig.*) stolid, sluggish.
flegme [flɛgm], *n.m.* phlegm; (*fig.*) coolness, impassivity.
flet [fle], **flétan** [fle'tɑ̃], *n.m.* ***grand flétan***, halibut; ***petit flétan*** or ***flet***, flounder.
flétrir [fle'tri:r], *v.t.* to wither; (*fig.*) to blight, to tarnish, to blemish. **se flétrir**, *v.r.* to fade, to wither.
flétrissant [fletri'sɑ̃], *a.* dishonouring, blighting.
flétrissure [fletri'sy:r], *n.f.* fading, withering; stigma, disgrace.
fleur [flœ:r], *n.f.* flower, blossom; bloom; (*fig.*) best, pick; surface; ***à fleur d'eau***, at water level; ***à fleur de peau***, superficially; ***yeux à fleur de tête***, prominent *or* goggle eyes.
fleurer [flœ're], *v.i.* to smell, to exhale.
fleuret [flœ'rɛ], *n.m.* (*Fenc.*) foil; miner's drill.
fleurette [flœ'rɛt], *n.f.* little flower, floweret; amorous discourse, gallant speech.
fleuri [flœ'ri], *a.* flowery; florid.
fleurir [flœ'ri:r], *v.t.* to decorate with flowers. —*v.i.* to flower, to blossom; to flourish. **se fleurir**, *v.r.* to adorn oneself with flowers.
fleurissant [flœri'sɑ̃], *a.* blossoming, blooming.
fleuriste [flœ'rist], *a.* and *n.* florist; artificial flower-maker *or* seller.
fleuron [flœ'rɔ̃], *n.m.* carved *or* painted flower; (*fig.*) flower-work; jewel.
fleuve [flœ:v], *n.m.* river (*flowing into the sea*), large stream.
flexibilité [flɛksibili'te], *n.f.* flexibility, pliancy.
flexible [flɛk'sibl], *a.* flexible, pliable, supple.
flexion [flɛk'sjɔ̃], *n.f.* flexion, bending.
flibuster [flibys'te], *v.i.* to buccaneer, to filibuster, to freeboot.
flibusterie [flibys'tri], *n.f.* filibustering; robbery, theft.
flibustier [flibys'tje], *n.m.* buccaneer, pirate; filibuster.
flirt [flœrt], *n.m.* flirtation, flirting.
flirter [flœr'te], *v.i.* to flirt.
floc [flɔk], *n.m.* tuft, tassel.—*int.* flop!
floche [flɔʃ], *a.* flossy, shaggy.
flocon [flɔ'kɔ̃], *n.m.* flock, tuft; flake (*of snow*).
floconneux [flɔkɔ'nø], *a.* (*fem.* **-euse**) flaky.
floraison [flɔrɛ'zɔ̃], *n.f.* efflorescence, flowering.
floral [flɔ'ral], *a.* (*m. pl.* **-aux**) floral.
flore [flɔ:r], *n.f.* flora.
florentin [flɔrɑ̃'tɛ̃], *a.* Florentine.
florin [flɔ'rɛ̃], *n.m.* florin.
florir [flɔ'ri:r], [FLEURIR].
florissant [flɔri'sɑ̃], *a.* prosperous, flourishing.
floriste [flɔ'rist], *n.* florist.
flot [flo], *n.m.* wave, billow; (*fig.*) tide, flood; crowd; (*pl.*) sea, stream, torrent.
flottage [flɔ'ta:ʒ], *n.m.* floating of wood, rafting.
flottaison [flɔtɛ'zɔ̃], *n.f.* floating.
flottant [flɔ'tɑ̃], *a.* floating, waving; (*fig.*) irresolute.
flotte [flɔt], *n.f.* fleet; navy.
flottement [flɔt'mɑ̃], *n.m.* floating; (*fig.*) wavering, irresolution.

flotter [flɔ'te], *v.i.* to float; to flutter (*of flag*); to be irresolute.
flotteur [flɔ'tœ:r], *n.m.* raftsman; fishing-float; cable-buoy.
flottille [flɔ'ti:j], *n.f.* flotilla.
flou [flu], *a.* hazy, soft, blurred, out of focus.—*n.m.* softness, haziness (*of outlines*); (*Dress.*) looseness.
fluctuation [flyktɥɑ'sjɔ̃], *n.f.* fluctuation.
fluctuer [flyk'tɥe], *v.i.* to fluctuate.
fluctueux [flyk'tɥø], *a.* (*fem.* **-euse**) fluctuating, agitated, boisterous.
fluet [flɥ'ɛ], *a.* (*fem.* **-ette**) slender, thin, slim.
fluide [flɥ'id], *a.* fluid (*liquid*).—*n.m.* fluid.
fluidité [flyidi'te], *n.f.* fluidity.
fluorescence [flyɔrɛ'sɑ̃:s], *n.f.* fluorescence.
fluorescent [flyɔrɛ'sɑ̃], *a.* fluorescent.
fluorure [flyɔ'ry:r], *n.m.* fluoride.
flûte [flyt], *n.f.* flute; long French roll; tall glass (*for champagne*).
flûté [fly'te], *a.* soft, fluted, fluty (*of a voice*).
flûtiste [fly'tist], *n.* flautist, flute-player.
fluvial [fly'vjal], *a.* (*m. pl.* **-aux**) fluvial.
flux [fly], *n.m.* flux, flow, flood, rising.
fluxion [flyk'sjɔ̃], *n.f.* inflammation, swelling.
foc [fɔk], *n.m.* (*Naut.*) jib.
focal [fɔ'kal], *a.* (*m. pl.* **-aux**) focal.
foi [fwɑ], *n.f.* faith, belief; trust; fidelity, honour; proof, testimony.
foie [fwɑ], *n.m.* liver.
foin [fwɛ̃], *n.m.* hay.
foire [fwa:r], *n.f.* fair (*market*); fairing.
fois [fwa], *n.f. inv.* time (*turn, occasion*); ***une fois***, once; ***trois fois***, three times.
foison [fwa'zɔ̃], *n.f.* plenty, abundance.
foisonner [fwazɔ'ne], *v.i.* to abound, to increase, to multiply.
fol [fɔl], [FOU].
folâtre [fɔ'lɑ:tr], *a.* playful, gay, frolicsome.
folâtrer [fɔlɑ'tre], *v.i.* to play, to sport, to frolic.
folâtrerie [fɔlɑtrə'ri], *n.f.* frolic, prank, gambol.
foliacé [fɔlja'se], *a.* (*Bot.*) foliaceous.
foliation [fɔljɑ'sjɔ̃], *n.f.* foliation.
folichon [fɔli'ʃɔ̃], *a.* (*fam.*) frolicsome, waggish, wanton.
folie [fɔ'li], *n.f.* madness, distraction, folly; foolery, jest; mania; hobby.
folio [fɔ'ljo], *n.m.* folio.
folle [fɔl], [FOU].
follement [fɔl'mɑ̃], *adv.* madly, foolishly.
follet [fɔ'lɛ], *a.* (*fem.* **-ette**) wanton, playful, frolicsome; ***feu follet***, will o' the wisp.
fomentation [fɔmɑ̃tɑ'sjɔ̃], *n.f.* fomentation.
fomenter [fɔmɑ̃'te], *v.t.* to foment; (*fig.*) to feed, to excite.
foncé [fɔ̃'se], *a.* dark, deep (*of colour*).
foncer [fɔ̃'se], *v.t.* (*conjug. like* COMMENCER) to fit a bottom to (*a cask etc.*); to sink (*wells etc.*); to deepen (*colours*).—*v.i.* to dash, to swoop (***sur***).
foncier [fɔ̃'sje], *a.* (*fem.* **-ière**) landed; based on *or* derived from land; (*fig.*) thorough.—*n.m.* land-tax.
foncièrement [fɔ̃sjɛr'mɑ̃], *adv.* thoroughly, completely, fundamentally.
fonction [fɔ̃k'sjɔ̃], *n.f.* function, office; occupation.
fonctionnaire [fɔ̃ksjɔ'nɛ:r], *n.m.* civil servant, officer, official.
fonctionnel [fɔ̃ksjɔ'nɛl], *a.* (*fem.* **-elle**) functional.
fonctionnement [fɔ̃ksjɔn'mɑ̃], *n.m.* operation, working, action.
fonctionner [fɔ̃ksjɔ'ne], *v.i.* to work, to act, to operate.
fond [fɔ̃], *n.m.* bottom; bed, ground; farther end; foundation; (*fig.*) essence; basis; subject matter; (*Paint.*) background; (*Theat.*) back-cloth.
fondage [fɔ̃'da:ʒ], *n.m.* casting, smelting.
fondamental [fɔ̃damɑ̃'tal], *a.* (*m. pl.* **-aux**) fundamental, essential.
fondamentalement [fɔ̃damɑ̃tal'mɑ̃], *adv.* fundamentally, essentially, radically.
fondant [fɔ̃'dɑ̃], *a.* melting, dissolving, luscious.—*n.m.* fondant (*sweetmeat*); flux (*for metals*).
fondateur [fɔ̃da'tœ:r], *n.m.* (*fem.* **-trice**) founder; promoter.
fondation [fɔ̃dɑ'sjɔ̃], *n.f.* foundation; groundwork; founding; endowment.
fondé [fɔ̃'de], *a.* founded, well-founded; (*Fin.*) consolidated.—*n.m.* proxy.
fondement [fɔ̃d'mɑ̃], *n.m.* foundation; basis, ground, cause.
fonder [fɔ̃'de], *v.t.* to lay the foundation of, to establish; to institute; to base; to endow. **se fonder**, *v.r.* to rely *or* rest (*upon*), to be founded (***sur***).
fonderie [fɔ̃'dri], *n.f.* foundry; smelting-house; casting.
fondeur [fɔ̃'dœ:r], *n.m.* founder, caster, smelter.
fondre [fɔ̃:dr], *v.t.* to melt; to dissolve; to smelt; to cast.—*v.i.* to melt; to pounce (***sur***); to vanish; to blow (*of a fuse*); ***fondre en larmes***, to burst into tears. **se fondre**, *v.r.* to melt; to dissolve; to be cast; to blend; to diminish, to melt away.
fondrière [fɔ̃dri'ɛ:r], *n.f.* bog, quagmire; rut, pothole; slough.
fonds [fɔ̃], *n.m.* land, soil; landed property; funds, capital; business assets; (*pl.*) funds, stocks etc.
fondue [fɔ̃'dy], *n.f.* dish of melted cheese and eggs.
fongicide [fɔ̃ʒi'sid], *a.* fungicide.
fongoïde [fɔ̃gɔ'id], *a.* fungoid.
fongueux [fɔ̃'gø], *a.* (*fem.* **-euse**) fungous.
fongus [fɔ̃'gys], *n.m.* (*Med.*) fungus.
fontaine [fɔ̃'tɛ:n], *n.f.* fountain, spring; cistern.
fonte [fɔ̃:t], *n.f.* melting, smelting; cast-iron; casting; holster (*of saddles*).
fonts [fɔ̃], *n.m. pl.* (*no sing.*) font.
football [fut'bɔl], *n.m.* Association Football.
footballeur [futbɔ'lœ:r], *n.m.* footballer.
footing [fu'tiŋ], *n.m.* walking (*for training* or *exercise*).
forage [fɔ'ra:ʒ], *n.m.* boring, drilling; sinking (*of well*).
forain [fɔ'rɛ̃], *a.* non-resident, travelling, itinerant; ***marchand forain***, hawker, pedlar.
forban [fɔr'bɑ̃], *n.m.* pirate, corsair, free-booter.
forçat [fɔr'sa], *n.m.* convict.
force [fɔrs], *n.f.* strength, might, power; authority; violence, constraint; vigour; resolution; skill; (*pl.*) troops, forces.—**adv.* a great deal, a great many.

forcé [fɔr'se], *a.* forced, compulsory; unnatural, strained, far-fetched.
forcément [fɔrse'mɑ̃], *adv.* forcibly; necessarily, inevitably.
forcené [fɔrsə'ne], *a.* mad, furious; passionate, infuriated.—*n.m.* (*fem.* **-ée**) mad person.
forceps [fɔr'sɛps], *n.m. inv.* forceps.
forcer [fɔr'se], *v.t.* (*conjug. like* COMMENCER) to force; to compel; to impel; to strain; to break open; to storm; to outrage. **se forcer,** *v.r.* to strain oneself; to do violence to one's feelings.
forer [fɔ're], *v.t.* to bore, to drill, to perforate.
forestier [fɔrɛs'tje], *a.* (*fem.* **-ière**) pertaining to forests.—*n.m.* ranger, keeper, forester.
foret [fɔ'rɛ], *n.m.* borer, drill.
forêt [fɔ'rɛ], *n.f.* forest; woodland.
forfaire [fɔr'fɛ:r], *v.t. irr.* to forfeit (*a fief*).—*v.i.* (*used only in inf., p.p.* (**forfait** (1) *and compound tenses*) to fail (*in one's duty*); to trespass, to be false to.
forfait (2) [fɔr'fɛ], *n.m.* crime, heinous offence.
forfait (3) [fɔr'fɛ], *n.m.* contract.
forfaiture [fɔrfɛ'ty:r], *n.f.* forfeiture; breach of duty.
forfanterie [fɔrfɑ̃'tri], *n.f.* romancing, bragging, boasting.
forge [fɔrʒ], *n.f.* forge, smithy; iron-works.
forger [fɔr'ʒe], *v.t.* (*conjug. like* MANGER) to forge, to hammer; (*fig.*) to invent, to fabricate. **se forger,** *v.r.* to imagine, to conjure up, to fancy.
forgeron [fɔrʒə'rɔ̃], *n.m.* smith, blacksmith.
formaliser (se) [səfɔrmali'ze], *v.r.* to take exception *or* offence (*de*).
formalisme [fɔrma'lism], *n.m.* formalism.
formaliste [fɔrma'list], *a.* formal, precise.—*n.* formalist; quibbler.
formalité [fɔrmali'te], *n.f.* formality; form, ceremony.
format [fɔr'ma], *n.m.* format (*size, shape etc., of a book*).
formateur [fɔrma'tœ:r], *a.* (*fem.* **-trice**) formative, creative.
formation [fɔrmɑ'sjɔ̃], *n.f.* formation; education; (*Geol.*) structure.
forme [fɔrm], *n.f.* form, shape, figure; etiquette; crown (*of a hat*).
formé [fɔr'me], *a.* formed, mature.
formel [fɔr'mɛl], *a.* (*fem.* **-elle**) formal; express, precise.
formellement [fɔrmɛl'mɑ̃], *adv.* formally; expressly, precisely, strictly.
former [fɔr'me], *v.t.* to form, to frame; to make up; to bring up; to train; to mould. **se former,** *v.r.* to be formed; to take shape.
formidable [fɔrmi'dabl], *a.* formidable, fearful; (*fam.*) terrific.
Formose [fɔr'mo:z], **la,** *f.* Formosa, Taiwan.
formule [fɔr'myl], *n.f.* formula, form; model; recipe.
formuler [fɔrmy'le], *v.t.* to formulate; to detail; (*Med.*) to write (*a prescription*).
fort [fɔ:r], *a.* strong, sturdy; powerful; clever; plentiful; shocking; painful; high (*wind*); heavy (*ground, rain*).—*n.m.* strong part; stronghold, fort; strength; depth, heat, height; centre.—*adv.* very, very much, extremely; hard.
fortement [fɔrtə'mɑ̃], *adv.* strongly, vigorously; much, exceedingly.
forteresse [fɔrtə'rɛs], *n.f.* fortress, stronghold.
fortifiant [fɔrti'fjɑ̃], *a.* strengthening, bracing.—*n.m.* (*Med.*) tonic.
fortification [fɔrtifikɑ'sjɔ̃], *n.f.* fortification; fort, redoubt.
fortifier [fɔrti'fje], *v.t.* to strengthen, to invigorate; to fortify; to confirm. **se fortifier,** *v.r.* to fortify oneself, to grow strong.
fortuit [fɔr'tɥi], *a.* fortuitous, casual.
fortuitement [fɔrtɥit'mɑ̃], *adv.* fortuitously, casually, by chance.
fortune [fɔr'tyn], *n.f.* fortune, chance, hazard, risk; success, luck; wealth.
fortuné [fɔrty'ne], *a.* fortunate, lucky; happy; well-to-do.
fosse [fo:s], *n.f.* hole, pit; grave; (*Hort.*) trench.
fossé [fo'se], *n.m.* ditch, drain, trench; moat.
fossette [fɔ'sɛt], *n.f.* dimple.
fossile [fɔ'sil], *a.* fossilized.—*n.m.* fossil.
fossiliser [fɔsili'se], *v.t.* to fossilize. **se fossiliser,** *v.r.* to become fossilized.
fossoyage [foswa'ja:ʒ], *n.m.* ditching; grave-digging.
fossoyer [foswa'je], *v.t.* (*conjug. like* EMPLOYER) to ditch, to dig a trench round.
fossoyeur [foswa'jœ:r], *n.m.* grave-digger; sexton beetle.
fou [fu], *a.* (*before vowels* **fol,** *fem.* **folle**) mad, demented; wild, foolish; tremendous.—*n.m.* (*fem.* **folle**) madman, madwoman.—*n.m* jester, fool; (*Chess*) bishop.
foudre (1) [fudr], *n.f.* lightning; thunder, thunderbolt; (*fig.*) sudden calamity; ***coup de foudre***, clap of thunder.—*n.m.* (*fig.*) ***un foudre de guerre***, a great captain; ***un foudre d'éloquence***, a mighty speaker.
foudre (2) [fudr], *n.m.* large cask, tun.
foudroiement [fudrwɑ'mɑ̃], *n.m.* striking, blasting (*by thunder* or *lightning*); (*fig.*) destruction.
foudroyant [fudrwɑ'jɑ̃], *a.* thundering; terrible, crushing (*news*).
foudroyer [fudrwɑ'je], *v.t.* (*conjug. like* EMPLOYER) to strike (*thunder* or *lightning*); to riddle with shot; (*fig.*) to blast, to crush.—*v.i.* to thunder; (*fig.*) to fulminate.
fouet [fwɛ], *n.m.* whip; lash; whipping, slating (*criticism*).
fouetter [fwɛ'te], *v.t.* to whip, to flog; to whisk (*eggs etc.*); to flick; (*fig.*) to excite.—*v.i.* to beat, to patter (*of hail, rain*).
fougeraie [fuʒ'rɛ], *n.f.* fern-patch, fernery.
fougère [fu'ʒɛ:r], *n.f.* fern.
fougue [fug], *n.f.* ardour, impetuosity; fire, spirit, mettle; (*Naut.*) mizzen-top.
fougueux [fu'gø], *a.* (*fem.* **-euse**) fiery, impetuous, ardent, passionate, high-mettled.
fouille [fu:j], *n.f.* excavation, digging; search.
fouiller [fu'je], *v.t.* to excavate; (*fig.*) to pry into, to rummage, to ransack; to search; to think out (*problems etc.*).—*v.i.* to dig, to search; (*fig.*) to rummage.
fouillis [fu'ji], *n.m.* medley, jumble; confused mass (*of foliage etc.*).
fouine (1) [fwin], *n.f.* marten.

fouine (2) [fwin], *n.f.* pitchfork; fish-spear.
fouiner [fwi'ne], *v.i.* (*colloq.*) to nose about, to ferret; to slink off.
fouir [fwi:r], *v.t.* to dig; to burrow.
fouissement [fwis'mɑ̃], *n.m.* digging; burrowing.
fouisseur [fwi'sœ:r], *a.* (*fem.* **-euse**) burrowing (*animal*).
foulage [fu'la:ʒ], *n.m.* fulling; treading, pressing (*of grapes*).
foulant [fu'lɑ̃], *a.* pressing; forcing; ***pompe foulante***, force-pump.
foulard [fu'la:r], *n.m.* silk neckerchief; scarf.
foule [ful], *n.f.* crowd, throng, multitude; mob.
foulée [fu'le], *n.f.* tread (*of steps*); stride (*of a horse* or *runner*).
fouler [fu'le], *v.t.* to tread; to trample down; to press; to oppress; to sprain (*ankle*).—*v.i.* (*Print.*) to press. **se fouler**, ***v.r. se fouler le pied***, to sprain one's foot.
fouleur [fu'lœ:r], *n.m.* (*fem.* **-euse**) fuller; wine-presser.
foulure [fu'ly:r], *n.f.* sprain, wrench, strain.
four [fu:r], *n.m.* oven; bakehouse; furnace; kiln; ***des petits fours***, fancy biscuits, small cakes.
fourbe [furb], *a.* cheating, deceitful.—*n.* cheat, swindler, impostor.
fourberie [furbə'ri], *n.f.* cheating, knavery, imposture, deceit.
fourbir [fur'bi:r], *v.t.* to furbish, to polish.
fourbisseur [furbi'sœ:r], *n.m.* furbisher, sword-cutler.
fourbissure [furbi'sy:r], *n.f.* furbishing, polishing.
fourbu [fur'by], *a.* foundered, run down (*of horses*); dead tired (*of persons*).
fourbure [fur'by:r], *n.f.* foundering, inflammation of the feet.
fourche [furʃ], *n.f.* pitchfork, (garden) fork, fork (*of roads*).
fourchée [fur'ʃe], *n.f.* pitchforkful.
fourcher [fur'ʃe], *v.i.* to fork; to divide. **se fourcher**, *v.r.* to fork, to branch off.
fourchetée [furʃ'te], *n.f.* table-forkful.
fourchette [fur'ʃɛt], *n.f.* table-fork; breastbone (*of birds*).
fourchu [fur'ʃy], *a.* forked; cloven; furcate.
fourgon (1) [fur'gɔ̃], *n.m.* van, wagon, guard's van.
fourgon (2) [fur'gɔ̃], *n.m.* poker, fire-iron (*for ovens etc.*).
fourgonner [furgɔ'ne], *v.i.* to poke the fire (*of an oven*); (*colloq.*) to poke, to rummage.
fourmi [fur'mi], *n.f.* ant.
fourmilière [furmi'ljɛ:r], *n.f.* ant-hill, ants' nest; (*fig.*) swarm; crowd.
fourmillement [furmij'mɑ̃], *n.m.* tingling, pins and needles; swarming.
fourmiller [furmi'je], *v.i.* to swarm, to be full (*de*); to have pins and needles (*in one's limbs etc.*).
fournaise [fur'nɛ:z], *n.f.* (*Lit.*) furnace; (*fig.*) oven.
fourneau [fur'no], *n.m.* (*pl.* **-eaux**) stove, cooker, cooking-range; furnace.
fournée [fur'ne], *n.f.* batch, baking; kilnful (*of bricks*).
fournil [fur'ni], *n.m.* bakehouse.
fourniment [furni'mɑ̃], *n.m.* (*Mil.*) equipment.
fournir [fur'ni:r], *v.t.* to furnish, to supply, to stock, to provide; to make up (*a sum of money*).—*v.i.* to contribute (*à*); to suffice.
fournisseur [furni'sœ:r], *n.m.* army contractor; purveyor; tradesman.
fourniture [furni'ty:r], *n.f.* furnishing; supply, provision; equipment.
fourrage [fu'ra:ʒ], *n.m.* fodder; forage; foraging-party.
fourrager [fura'ʒe], *v.t.* (*conjug. like* MANGER) to ravage; to upset.—*v.i.* to forage; to plunder, to ravage; (*fig.*) to rummage.
fourrageur [fura'ʒœ:r], *n.m.* forager; (*fig.*) marauder; rummager.
fourré [fu're], *a.* thick, furry; wooded; (*fig.*) underhand (*of a blow etc.*).—*n.m.* thicket, brake.
fourreau [fu'ro], *n.m.* (*pl.* **-eaux**) sheath, case; scabbard; cover; tight-fitting *or* sheath dress.
fourrer [fu're], *v.t.* to line with fur; to poke; to cram, to stuff. **se fourrer**, *v.r.* to thrust oneself in, to intrude; to wrap oneself up warmly.
fourreur [fu'rœ:r], *n.m.* furrier.
fourrier [fu'rje], *n.m.* quartermaster-sergeant; (*fig.*) harbinger.
fourrière [fu'rjɛ:r], *n.f.* pound (*for vehicles, strayed animals*).
fourrure [fu'ry:r], *n.f.* fur, furred gown.
fourvoyer [furvwa'je], *v.t.* (*conjug. like* EMPLOYER) to lead astray, to mislead; (*fig.*) to baffle. **se fourvoyer**, *v.r.* to go astray, to lose one's way; (*fig.*) to blunder badly.
fox (1) [fɔks], *n.m.* fox-terrier.
fox (2) [fɔks], *n.m.* foxtrot.
foyer [fwa'je], *n.m.* hearth; fire; fire-box (*of an engine*); (*fig.*) home, family; (*Theat.*) foyer; focus, source.
frac [frak], *n.m.* frock-coat.
fracas [fra'kɑ], *n.m.* noise, din; disturbance; fuss.
fracasser [fraka'se], *v.t.* to break into pieces, to shatter. **se fracasser**, *v.r.* to crash to pieces.
fraction [frak'sjɔ̃], *n.f.* breaking; fraction, portion.
fractionnaire [fraksjɔ'nɛ:r], *a.* fractional.
fracture [frak'ty:r], *n.f.* breaking (*with violence*), rupture; (*Surg.*) fracture.
fracturer [frakty're], *v.t.* to break, to smash; (*Surg.*) to fracture. **se fracturer**, *v.r.* to fracture oneself; to be fractured.
fragile [fra'ʒil], *a.* fragile, brittle; frail.
fragilité [fraʒili'te], *n.f.* fragility, brittleness; frailty.
fragment [frag'mɑ̃], *n.m.* fragment, piece, remnant.
fragmentaire [fragmɑ̃'tɛ:r], *a.* fragmentary.
fragmentation [fragmɑ̃tɑ'sjɔ̃], *n.f.* fragmenting, fragmentation.
fragmenter [fragmɑ̃'te], *v.t.* to reduce to fragments.
fragrance [fra'grɑ̃:s], *n.f.* fragrance.
fragrant [fra'grɑ̃], *a.* fragrant.
frai [frɛ], *n.m.* fraying; spawning (*of fish*).
fraîche [frɛʃ], [FRAIS (1)].
fraîchement [frɛʃ'mɑ̃], *adv.* coolly, freshly; newly, recently.
fraîcheur [frɛ'ʃœ:r], *n.f.* coolness, freshness, coldness; ruddiness; brilliancy.
fraîchir [frɛ'ʃi:r], *v.i.* to freshen; to get cool.

frais (1) [frɛ], *a.* (*fem.* **fraîche**) cool; fresh; new; youthful; ruddy; new-laid (*of eggs*).—*n.m.* coolness, freshness; cool spot.—*adv.* freshly, newly, recently, just.

frais (2) [frɛ], *n.m.* (*used only in pl.*) expense, expenses; charge, charges, cost, outlay; ***menus frais***, petty expenses; ***sans frais***, free of charge.

fraise (1) [frɛ:z], *n.f.* strawberry; strawberry-mark; ruff.

fraise (2) [frɛ:z], *n.f.* fraise (*tool for enlarging a drill hole etc.*); (dentist's) drill.

fraiser [frɛ'ze], *v.t.* to plait, to ruffle; to countersink.

fraisier [frɛ'zje], *n.m.* strawberry-plant; strawberry grower.

framboise [frɑ̃'bwa:z], *n.f.* raspberry.

framboiser [frɑ̃bwa'ze], *v.t.* to give a raspberry flavour to.

framboisier [frɑ̃bwa'zje], *n.m.* raspberry-bush.

franc (1) [frɑ̃], *n.m.* franc (*French coin*); new franc (*of 1960*).

franc (2) [frɑ̃], *a.* (*fem.* **franche**) free; exempt; frank, candid, sincere; clear.—*adv.* frankly, openly, sincerely; clean; quite, completely.

franc (3) [frɑ̃], *a.* (*fem.* **franque**) Frankish.—*n.m.* Frankish (*language*); (**Franc**, *fem.* **Franque**) Frank.

français [frɑ̃'sɛ], *a.* French.—*n.m.* French (*language*); (**Français**, *fem.* **-aise**) Frenchman, Frenchwoman.

France [frɑ̃:s], **la**, *f.* France.

franche [frɑ̃ʃ], [FRANC (2)].

franchement [frɑ̃ʃ'mɑ̃], *adv.* frankly, sincerely; plainly; boldly.

franchir [frɑ̃'ʃi:r], *v.t.* to leap, to jump over; to clear; to pass over; to surmount.

franchise [frɑ̃'ʃi:z], *n.f.* exemption, immunity; freedom (*of a city*); (*fig.*) frankness, sincerity.

franchissable [frɑ̃ʃi'sabl], *a.* passable, capable of being crossed.

franchissement [frɑ̃ʃis'mɑ̃], *n.m.* leaping over, crossing.

francisation [frɑ̃sizɑ'sjɔ̃], *n.f.* gallicizing of foreign word; registration as a French ship.

franciscain [frɑ̃sis'kɛ̃], *a.* and *n.m.* (*fem.* **-e**) Franciscan, grey friar, Franciscan nun.

franciser [frɑ̃si'ze], *v.t.* to gallicize; to Frenchify. **se franciser**, *v.r.* to become French *or* Frenchified.

franc-maçon [frɑ̃ma'sɔ̃], *n.m.* (*pl.* **francs-maçons**) freemason.

franc-maçonnerie [frɑ̃masɔn'ri], *n.f.* freemasonry.

franco [frɑ̃'ko], *adv.* free of charge; prepaid.

François [frɑ̃'swa], *m.* Francis.

Françoise [frɑ̃'swa:z], *f.* Frances.

francophile [frɑ̃kɔ'fil], *a.* and *n.* Francophile.

francophobe [frɑ̃kɔ'fɔb], *a.* and *n.* Francophobe.

franc-parler [frɑ̃par'le], *n.m.* frankness *or* freedom of speech.

franc-tireur [frɑ̃ti'rœ:r], *n.m.* franc-tireur; sniper.

frange [frɑ̃:ʒ], *n.f.* fringe.

franger [frɑ̃'ʒe], *v.t.* (*conjug. like* MANGER) to fringe.

franque [frɑ̃k], [FRANC (3)].

frappant [fra'pɑ̃], *a.* striking, impressive.

frappé [fra'pe], *a.* struck, astounded; iced (*of liquids etc.*); (*fig.*) powerful.

frappement [frap'mɑ̃], *n.m.* striking, stamping; clapping (*of hands*).

frapper [fra'pe], *v.t.* to strike, to slap, to hit; to make an impression on, to affect; to surprise, to frighten; to ice (*liquids*).—*v.i.* to knock, to rap. **se frapper**, *v.r.* to strike oneself; to strike each other; to be impressed.

frappeur [fra'pœ:r], *a.* (*fem.* **-euse**) striking, rapping.—*n.m.* (*fem.* **-euse**) beater, striker.

frasque [frask], *n.f.* prank, escapade.

fraternel [fratɛr'nɛl], *a.* (*fem.* **-elle**) fraternal, brotherly.

fraternellement [fratɛrnɛl'mɑ̃], *adv.* fraternally.

fraternisation [fratɛrnizɑ'sjɔ̃], *n.f.* fraternization.

fraterniser [fratɛrni'ze], *v.t.* to fraternize.

fraternité [fratɛrni'te] *n.f.* fraternity, brotherhood.

fratricide [fratri'sid], *a.* fratricidal.—*n.m.* fratricide.

fraude [fro:d], *n.f.* fraud, deceit.

frauder [fro'de], *v.t.* to defraud.—*v.i.* to smuggle.

fraudeur [fro'dœ:r], *n.m.* (*fem.* **-euse**) defrauder; smuggler.

frauduleusement [frodyløz'mɑ̃], *adv.* fraudulently.

frauduleux [frody'lø], *a.* (*fem.* **-euse**) fraudulent.

frayer [frɛ'je], *v.t.* to trace out, to open out; to make (*a way etc.*); to rub against, to graze.—*v.i.* to wear away; to spawn (*of fish*); (*fig.*) to frequent, to be on good terms (***avec***). **se frayer**, *v.r.* to open for oneself; to prepare *or* carve out (*a way*) for oneself.

frayeur [frɛ'jœ:r], *n.f.* fright, terror, fear.

fredaine [frə'dɛn], *n.f.* (*colloq.*) frolic, prank; freak.

Frédéric [frede'rik], *m.* Frederick.

Frédérique [frede'rik], *f.* Frederica.

fredon [frə'dɔ̃], *n.m.* song, refrain.

fredonnement [frədɔn'mɑ̃], *n.m.* humming.

fredonner [frədɔ'ne], *v.t., v.i.* to hum.

frégate [fre'gat], *n.f.* frigate; frigate bird; (*Navy*) ***capitaine de frégate***, commander.

frein [frɛ̃], *n.m.* bit, bridle; curb, check; brake.

freinage [frɛ'na:ʒ], *n.m.* braking.

freiner [frɛ'ne], *v.t.* to brake; to curb.

frelatage [frəla'ta:ʒ], **frelatement** [frəlat'mɑ̃], *n.m.*, **frelaterie** [frəla'tri], **frelatation** [frəlatɑ'sjɔ̃], *n.f.* adulteration.

frelater [frəla'te], *v.t.* to adulterate.

frêle [frɛ:l], *a.* frail, fragile, weak.

frelon [frə'lɔ̃], *n.m.* hornet.

freluquet [frəly'kɛ], *n.m.* conceited young man, puppy.

frémir [fre'mi:r], *v.i.* to quiver, to shudder, to tremble; to vibrate; to rustle.

frémissant [fremi'sɑ̃], *a.* quivering, trembling.

frémissement [fremis'mɑ̃], *n.m.* quivering, trembling, shuddering; thrill, vibration; rustling.

frênaie [frɛ'nɛ], *n.f.* ash-grove.

frêne [frɛ:n], *n.m.* ash, ash-tree.

frénésie [frene'zi], *n.f.* frenzy, madness.

frénétique [frene'tik], *a.* frantic, frenzied.—*n.* raving, frantic person.
frénétiquement [frenetik'mɑ̃], *adv.* frantically.
fréquemment [freka'mɑ̃], *adv.* frequently.
fréquence [fre'kɑ̃:s], *n.f.* frequency.
fréquent [fre'kɑ̃], *a.* frequent.
fréquentation [frekɑ̃tɑ'sjɔ̃], *n.f.* frequentation, company.
fréquenter [frekɑ̃'te], *v.t.* to frequent, to keep company with; to haunt.—*v.i.* to associate (*chez*); to be a frequent caller (*at*).
frère [frɛ:r], *n.m.* brother; fellow-member; monk.
fresque [frɛsk], *n.f.* fresco.
fret [frɛ], *n.m.* freight, cargo.
fréter [fre'te], *v.t.* (*conjug. like* CÉDER) to charter; to freight; to hire (*a car*).
fréteur [fre'tœ:r], *n.m.* freighter, charterer.
frétillant [freti'jɑ̃], *a.* wriggling, lively; frisky.
frétillement [fretij'mɑ̃] *n.m.* wriggling; frisking.
frétiller [freti'je], *v.i.* to wriggle, to jump about; to frisk.
fretin [frə'tɛ̃], *n.m.* fry, young fish; (*fig.*) trash.
freudien [frø'djɛ̃], *a.* (*fem.* **-enne**) Freudian.
freux [frø], *n.m. inv.* (*Orn.*) rook.
friable [fri'abl], *a.* friable; crisp, short.
friand [fri'ɑ̃], *a.* dainty, nice; partial to; appetizing.
friandise [friɑ̃'di:z], *n.f.* daintiness; dainty, titbit.
fricassée [frika'se], *n.f.* hash.
fricasser [frika'se], *v.t.* to fricassee.
friche [friʃ], *n.f.* waste *or* fallow land.
fricot [fri'ko], *n.m.* (*colloq.*) ragout, stew.
fricoter [frikɔ'te], *v.t.* to squander.—*v.i.* to cook.
fricoteur [frikɔ'tœ:r], *n.m.* (*fem.* **-euse**) feaster; fast liver.
friction [frik'sjɔ̃], *n.f.* friction, rubbing.
frictionner [friksjɔ'ne], *v.t.* to rub.
frigide [fri'ʒid], *a.* frigid.
frigidité [friʒidi'te], *n.f.* frigidity.
frigorifier [frigɔri'fje], *v.t.* to chill, to freeze (*meat etc.*).
frileux [fri'lø], *a.* (*fem.* **-euse**) chilly; susceptible to cold.—*n.m.* redbreast, robin.
frimas [fri'mɑ], *n.m.* *rime, hoar-frost.
frime [frim], *n.f.* (*pop.*) show, pretence, sham.
fringant [frɛ̃'gɑ̃], *a.* brisk, frisky; smart.
fringuer [frɛ̃'ge], *v.i.* to skip; to prance (*of a horse*).
fripe [frip], *n.f.* rag, scrap (*of cloth etc.*).
friper [fri'pe], *v.t.* to crumple, to rumple. **se friper**, *v.r.* to become rumpled *or* shabby.
friperie [fri'pri], *n.f.* frippery, old clothes; junk shop.
fripier [fri'pje], *n.m.* (*fem.* **-ière**) dealer in old clothes, furniture etc.
fripon [fri'pɔ̃], *a.* (*fem.* **-onne**) cheating, rascally.—*n.m.* (*fem.* **-onne**) rogue, cheat.
friponnerie [fripɔn'ri], *n.f.* cheating, roguery, knavery.
friquet [fri'kɛ], *n.m.* tree-sparrow.
frire [fri:r], *v.t., v.i. irr.* to fry.
frisage [fri'za:ʒ], *n.m.* curling, frizzing (*of hair etc.*).
frise [fri:z], *n.f.* (*Arch. etc.*) frieze.
friser [fri'ze], *v.t.* to curl, to frizz (*hair*); to graze; to border upon.—*v.i.* to curl. **se friser**, *v.r.* to curl; to curl one's hair.
frisson [fri'sɔ̃], *n.m.* shiver, shudder; thrill.
frissonnant [frisɔ'nɑ̃], *a.* shuddering, shivering.
frissonnement [frisɔn'mɑ̃], *n.m.* shivering, shudder; thrill.
frissonner [frisɔ'ne], *v.i.* to shiver, to shudder; to feel a thrill; to tremble.
frisure [fri'zy:r], *n.f.* crisping; curling.
frit [fri], *a.* fried.—*n.f. pl.* ***des frites***, chips.
friture [fri'ty:r], *n.f.* frying; fried fish etc.; grease (*for frying*).
frivole [fri'vɔl], *a.* frivolous, trifling; futile.
frivolité [frivɔli'te], *n.f.* frivolity; trifle.
froc [frɔk], *n.m.* cowl, monk's gown.
froid [frwɑ], *a.* cold; (*fig.*) indifferent, lifeless; reserved.—*n.m.* cold, coldness; chilliness; (*fig.*) unconcern, dullness; reserve.
froidement [frwɑd'mɑ̃], *adv.* coldly, frigidly; dispassionately.
froideur [frwɑ'dœ:r], *n.f.* coldness; chilliness; (*fig.*) indifference, coolness.
froidure [frwɑ'dy:r], *n.f.* coldness (*of the weather*); cold; (*fig.*) winter.
froissement [frwɑs'mɑ̃], *n.m.* rumpling; bruising; (*fig.*) clash; slight, affront, annoyance.
froisser [frwɑ'se], *v.t.* to rumple; to crease; to bruise slightly; (*fig.*) to offend, to wound. **se froisser**, *v.r.* to become bruised (*of a muscle*); to take offence.
froissure [frwɑ'sy:r], *n.f.* crease; bruise.
frôlement [frol'mɑ̃], *n.m.* grazing; rustle.
frôler [fro'le], *v.t.* to graze, to touch slightly in passing; to brush past.
fromage [frɔ'ma:ʒ], *n.m.* cheese; (*fig.*) ***un (bon) fromage***, a nice soft job.
fromagerie [frɔmaʒ'ri], *n.f.* cheese farm *or* dairy; cheese-trade.
fromageux [frɔma'ʒø], *a.* (*fem.* **-euse**) cheesy.
froment [frɔ'mɑ̃], *n.m.* wheat.
fronce [frɔ̃:s], *n.f.* gather, pucker (*in needlework etc.*); crease (*in paper*).
froncement [frɔ̃s'mɑ̃], *n.m.* contraction, knitting (*of the brows etc.*); (*fig.*) frowning, frown.
froncer [frɔ̃'se], *v.t.* (*conjug. like* COMMENCER) to contract; to wrinkle; to purse (*the lips*); to gather (*needlework*); ***froncer les sourcils***, to frown. **se froncer**, *v.r.* to contract, to pucker; to wrinkle.
frondaison [frɔ̃dɛ'zɔ̃], *n.f.* foliation; foliage.
fronde [frɔ̃:d], *n.f.* sling; frond; (*Surg.*) bandage.
fronder [frɔ̃'de], *v.t.* to sling, to fling with a sling; to banter; to jeer at.
frondeur [frɔ̃'dœ:r], *n.m.* (*fem.* **-euse**) slinger; censurer, fault-finder; rioter.
front [frɔ̃], *n.m.* forehead, brow; face; (*fig.*) boldness, impudence; (*Polit.*) ***Front populaire***, Popular Front.
frontal [frɔ̃'tal], *a.* (*m. pl.* **-aux**) (*Anat.*) frontal.—*n.m.* headband.
frontière [frɔ̃'tjɛ:r], *n.f.* frontier, border.
frontispice [frɔ̃tis'pis], *n.m.* frontispiece; title-page.
fronton [frɔ̃'tɔ̃], *n.m.* (*Arch.*) fronton, pediment.
frottage [frɔ'ta:ʒ], *n.m.* rubbing; polishing.

frottée [frɔ'te], *n.f.* (*colloq.*) drubbing.
frottement [frɔt'mɑ̃], *n.m.* rubbing, friction; (*fig.*) interaction.
frotter [frɔ'te], *v.t.* to rub; to polish; (*fig.*) to pommel, to warm (*the ears of*).—*v.i.* to rub. **se frotter**, *v.r.* to rub oneself; to provoke, to meddle (*à*).
frotteur [frɔ'tœ:r], *n.m.* (*fem.* **-euse**) rubber; scrubber; floor-polisher.
frottoir [frɔ'twa:r], *n.m.* rubbing-cloth; (*Elec.*) brush (*of dynamo*).
frou-frou [fru'fru], *n.m.* (*pl.* **-frous**) rustling (*of silk etc.*).
fructification [fryktifikɑ'sjɔ̃], *n.f.* fructification.
fructifier [frykti'fje], *v.i.* to fructify, to bear fruit; (*fig.*) to thrive.
fructueusement [fryktɥøz'mɑ̃], *adv.* fruitfully profitably.
fructueux [fryk'tɥø], *a.* (*fem.* **-euse**) fruitful, profitable.
frugal [fry'gal], *a.* (*m. pl.* **-aux**) frugal.
frugalement [frygal'mɑ̃], *adv.* frugally.
frugalité [frygali'te], *n.f.* frugality.
fruit [frɥi], *n.m.* fruit; (*fig.*) offspring; advantage, utility; (*pl.*) fruits; result.
fruiterie [frɥi'tri], *n.f.* fruit-loft; fruit-trade.
fruitier [frɥi'tje], *a.* (*fem.* **-ière**) fruit-bearing.—*n.m.* (*fem.* **-ière**) fruiterer, greengrocer.
fruste [fryst], *a.* worn, defaced; unpolished (*person*).
frustration [frystrɑ'sjɔ̃], *n.f.* frustration.
frustrer [frys'tre], *v.t.* to defraud; to frustrate, to disappoint, to baffle.
fuchsia [fyk'sja], *n.m.* fuchsia.
fugace [fy'gas], *a.* fugitive, fleeting, transient.
fugitif [fyʒi'tif], *a.* (*fem.* **-tive**) fugitive, fleeting.—*n.m.* (*fem.* **-tive**) fugitive, runaway.
fugue [fyg], *n.f.* fugue; (*colloq.*) flight, escapade.
fuir [fɥi:r], *v.t. irr.* to fly, to avoid; to shun.—*v.i.* to fly, to flee, to run away; to elude; to leak. **se fuir**, *v.r.* to fly from oneself; to shun *or* avoid each other.
fuite [fɥit], *n.f.* flight, escaping; avoiding; evasion, shift; leakage.
fulgurant [fylgy'rɑ̃], *a.* flashing, vivid, sharp.
fulguration [fylgyrɑ'sjɔ̃], *n.f.* (*Chem.*) fulguration, lightning.
fuligineux [fyliʒi'nø], *a.* (*fem.* **-euse**) fuliginous.
fulminant [fylmi'nɑ̃], *a.* fulminant, fulminating.
fulminer [fylmi'ne], *v.t.* to fulminate, to send forth (*maledictions* or *religious decrees*).—*v.i.* to explode; (*fig.*) to storm, to thunder, to inveigh (*against*).
fumage [fy'ma:ʒ], *n.m.*, **fumaison** [fymɛ'zɔ̃], **fumure** [fy'my:r], *n.f.* manuring, spreading of dung on land.
fumant [fy'mɑ̃], *a.* smoking, reeking, fuming.
fumé [fy'me], *a.* smoked; manured.
fumée [fy'me], *n.f.* smoke; steam; fume, reek; phantom, dream.
fumer [fy'me], *v.t.* to smoke (*a cigarette etc.*); to smoke-dry; to manure.—*v.i.* to smoke; to reek, to steam; (*fig.*) to fret, to fume.
fumerolle [fym'rɔl], *n.f.* fumarole.
fumet [fy'mɛ], *n.m.* flavour (*of meat*); bouquet (*of wines*); (*fig.*) raciness; (*Hunt.*) scent.
fumeur [fy'mœ:r]. *n.m.* (*fem.* **-euse** (1)) smoker.
fumeux [fy'mø], *a.* (*fem.* **-euse** (2)) smoky, fumy; hazy (*of brain, ideas etc.*).
fumier [fy'mje], *n.m.* manure, dung, dunghill; (*fig.*) trash.
fumigateur [fymiga'tœ:r], *n.m.* fumigator.
fumigation [fymigɑ'sjɔ̃], *n.f.* fumigation.
fumiger [fymi'ʒe], *v.t.* (*conjug. like* MANGER) to fumigate.
fumiste [fy'mist], *n.m.* stove- *or* chimney-repairer; (*fig.*) practical joker; humbug, trickster.
fumisterie [fymis'tri], *n.f.* (*fig.*) practical joke.
fumoir [fy'mwa:r], *n.m.* smoking-shed (*for curing fish etc.*); smoking-room.
fumure [FUMAGE].
funèbre [fy'nɛbr], *a.* funeral; funereal, mournful; dismal.
funérailles [fyne'rɑ:j], *n.f. pl.* funeral ceremonies, obsequies.
funéraire [fyne'rɛ:r], *a.* funeral, funereal.
funeste [fy'nɛst], *a.* fatal, deadly; (*fig.*) disastrous; distressing.
funestement [fynɛst'mɑ̃], *adv.* fatally, disastrously.
funiculaire [fyniky'lɛ:r], *a.* funicular.—*n.m.* funicular railway.
fur [fy:r], *n.m., used only in the expression* ***au fur et à mesure*** (***que***), gradually (as), in proportion (as).
furet [fy'rɛ], *n.m.* ferret; ***jouer au furet***, to hunt the slipper.
fureter [fyr'te], *v.i.* (*conjug. like* AMENER) to ferret, to hunt with a ferret; (*fig.*) to rummage.
fureteur [fyr'tœ:r], *n.m.* (*fem.* **-euse**) ferreter; (*fig.*) Nosey Parker.
fureur [fy'rœ:r], *n.f.* rage, fury; passion, frenzy.
furibond [fyri'bɔ̃], *a.* furious, raging, wild.—*n.m.* (*fem.* **-e**) furious person.
furie [fy'ri], *n.f.* fury, rage; ardour, intensity.
furieusement [fyrjøz'mɑ̃], *adv.* furiously.
furieux [fy'rjø], *a.* (*fem.* **-euse**) furious; mad, fierce, impetuous; (*colloq.*) monstrous.—*n.m.* (*fem.* **-euse**) mad person.
furoncle [fy'rɔ̃:kl], *n.m.* (*Med.*) furuncle, boil.
furtif [fyr'tif], *a.* (*fem.* **-tive**) furtive, stealthy, secret.
furtivement [fyrtiv'mɑ̃], *adv.* furtively.
fusain [fy'zɛ̃], *n.m.* spindle-tree; charcoal (*for drawing*).
fuseau [fy'zo], *n.m.* (*pl.* **-eaux**) spindle; distaff.
fusée [fy'ze], *n.f.* spindleful; spindle (*of axle*); (*Motor.*) stub axle; (*Mil. etc.*) fuse; rocket; (*Vet.*) splint.
fuselage [fyz'la:ʒ], *n.m.* framework, fuselage (*of an aeroplane*).
fuselé [fyz'le], *a.* slender, tapering (*fingers*); streamlined.
fuser [fy'ze], *v.i.* to spirt; to liquefy, to dissolve, to fuse.
fusibilité [fyzibili'te], *n.f.* fusibility.
fusible [fy'zibl], *a.* fusible.—*n.m.* (*Elec.*) fuse.
fusil [fy'zi], *n.m.* gun, rifle; steel (*for sharpening knives*).
fusilier [fyzi'lje], *n.m.* fusilier; ***fusilier marin***, marine.
fusillade [fyzi'jad], *n.f.* discharge of musketry, fusillade; execution by shooting.

fusiller [fyzi'je], *v.t.* to shoot (down); to execute by shooting.
fusil-mitrailleur [fyzimitrɑ'jœ:r], *n.m.* sub-machine-gun.
fusion [fy'zjɔ̃], *n.f.* fusion, melting; (*fig.*) blending, merger.
fusionner [fyzjɔ'ne], *v.t., v.i.* to amalgamate, to unite, to merge; to blend.
fustigation [fystigɑ'sjɔ̃], *n.f.* fustigation, whipping, flogging.
fustiger [fysti'ʒe], *v.t.* (*conjug. like* MANGER) to flog, to whip.
fût [fy], *n.m.* stock (*of a gun* or *pistol*); shaft (*of a column*); cask; barrel (*of a drum*).
futaie [fy'tɛ], *n.f.* forest of high trees; high forest tree.
futaille [fy'tɑ:j], *n.f.* cask, barrel.
futaine [fy'tɛ:n], *n.f.* fustian.
futé [fy'te], *a.* (*colloq.*) sharp, cunning, sly.
futile [fy'til], *a.* futile, frivolous, trifling.
futilité [fytili'te], *n.f.* futility; trifle.
futur [fy'ty:r], *a.* future.—*n.m.* (*Gram.*) future. —*n.m.* (*fem.* **-e**) intended husband *or* wife.
futurisme [fyty'rism], *n.m.* futurism.
futuriste [fyty'rist], *a.* futuristic.—*n.* futurist.
fuyant [fɥi'jɑ̃], *a.* flying, fleeing, retreating; receding (*of the forehead etc.*); fleeting.—*n.m.* perspective.
fuyard [fɥi'ja:r], *a.* and *n.m.* (*fem.* **-e**) fugitive, runaway.

G

G, g [ʒe], *n.m.* the seventh letter of the alphabet.
gabardine [gabar'din], *n.f.* gabardine.
gabare [ga'ba:r], *n.f.* lighter, flat-bottomed barge; store-ship.
gabarier [gaba'rje], *n.m.* lighterman.
gabelle [ga'bɛl], *n.f.* gabelle, salt-tax.
gâche (1) [gɑ:ʃ], *n.f.* staple, wall-hook.
gâche (2) [gɑ:ʃ], *n.f.* trowel; (baker's) spatula.
gâcher [gɑ'ʃe], *v.t.* to mix (*mortar*); (*fig.*) to bungle, to botch.
gâchette [gɑ'ʃɛt], *n.f.* tumbler, sear (*of a gun-lock*); follower, catch (*of a lock*); (*fam.*) trigger.
gâcheur [gɑ'ʃœ:r], *n.m.* mason's labourer; (*fig.*) bungler.
gâchis [gɑ'ʃi], *n.m.* wet mortar; sludge; (*fig.*) mess.
gaélique [gae'lik], *a.* Gaelic.—*n.m.* Gaelic (*language*).
gaffe [gaf], *n.f.* boat-hook, gaff; (*fam.*) gross blunder, howler.
gaffer [ga'fe], *v.t.* to hook with a gaff.—*v.i.* (*fam.*) to blunder; (*Row.*) to catch a crab.
gage [ga:ʒ], *n.m.* pawn, pledge; security, deposit; stake, token; (*pl.*) wages.
gager [ga'ʒe], *v.t.* (*conjug. like* MANGER) to wager, to bet, to stake; to pay wages to; to engage.
gageur [ga'ʒœ:r], *n.m.* (*fem.* **-euse**) bettor, one who wagers, punter.
gageure [ga'ʒy:r], *n.f.* wager, stake.
gagnant [gɑ'ɲɑ̃], *a.* winning.—*n.m.* (*fem.* **-e**) winner.
gagne-pain [gɑɲ'pɛ̃], *n.m. inv.* livelihood, daily bread; bread-winner.
gagner [gɑ'ɲe], *v.t.* to gain, to earn; to win; to deserve; to prevail upon, to gain over; to allure; to seize; to overtake.—*v.i.* to spread; to gain (*à*); to improve. **se gagner**, *v.r.* to be gained; to be contagious.
gai [ge], *a.* gay, merry; exhilarating; vivid (*of colours*).
gaiement or **gaîment** [ge'mɑ̃], *adv.* gaily, merrily, cheerfully; briskly, willingly.
gaieté or **gaîté** [ge'te], *n.f.* gaiety, cheerfulness, good humour.
gaillard (1) [ga'ja:r], *n.m.* (*Naut.*) castle; ***gaillard d'arrière***, quarter-deck; ***gaillard d'avant***, forecastle.
gaillard (2) [ga'ja:r], *a.* strong; jolly, lively; wanton; gallant.—*n.m.* (*fem.* **-e**) lively, merry, strapping fellow *or* girl.
gaillardement [gajardə'mɑ̃], *adv.* joyously, merrily; boldly.
gaillardise [gajar'di:z], *n.f.* sprightliness, liveliness, jollity; broad language, risky story.
gaîment [GAIEMENT].
gain [gɛ̃], *n.m.* gain, profit; earnings; winnings.
gaine [gɛ:n], *n.f.* sheath; foundation garment; case (*of a clock etc.*).
gaîté [GAIETÉ].
gala [ga'la], *n.m.* gala.
galamment [gala'mɑ̃], *adv.* gallantly, courteously; gracefully, handsomely.
galant [ga'lɑ̃], *a.* attentive to ladies; elegant; correct, courteous; complimentary, flattering; ***c'est un galant homme***, he is a man of honour; ***femme galante***, courtesan.—*n.m.* gallant; sweetheart, suitor; ***faire le galant***, to court the ladies.
galanterie [galɑ̃'tri], *n.f.* politeness; gallantry (*towards the ladies*); intrigue, love-affair.
galantin [galɑ̃'tɛ̃], *n.m.* fop, coxcomb.
galbe [galb], *n.m.* graceful curve *or* contour.
gale [gal], *n.f.* scabies; itch; scab; mange.
galène [ga'lɛ:n], *n.f.* galena; ***poste à galène***, crystal set.
galère [ga'lɛ:r], *n.f.* galley; (*pl.*) galleys, imprisonment with hard labour.
galerie [gal'ri], *n.f.* gallery; corridor; picture-gallery; (*Theat.*) upper circle, gallery; (*fig.*) spectators; (*Mining*) drift.
galérien [gale'rjɛ̃], *n.m.* galley-slave, convict.
galet [ga'lɛ], *n.m.* pebble, shingle; friction-roller.
galetas [gal'tɑ], *n.m. inv.* garret, attic; (*fig.*) hole, hovel.
galette [ga'lɛt], *n.f.* broad thin cake; sea-biscuit.
galeux [ga'lø], *a.* (*fem.* **-euse**) itchy; scabby; mangy; ***brebis galeuse***, (*fig.*) black sheep.
Galilée [gali'le], *m.* Galileo.
Galilée [gali'le], *f.* Galilaea, Galilee.
galimatias [galima'tjɑ], *n.m.* balderdash; rigmarole.
galion [ga'ljɔ̃], *n.m.* galleon.
galiote [ga'ljɔt], *n.f.* galliot, half-galley.
galle [gal], *n.f.* gall.
Galles, le Pays de [ləpeidə'gal], *m.* Wales.

gallican [gali'kɑ̃], *a.* gallican.
gallicisme [gali'sism], *n.m.* gallicism, French idiom.
gallois [ga'lwa], *a.* Welsh.—*n.m.* Welsh (*language*); (**Gallois**, *fem.* **-oise**) Welshman, Welshwoman.
galoche [ga'lɔʃ], *n.f.* clog.
galon [ga'lɔ̃], *n.m.* braid; lace; (*pl.*) (*Mil.*) bands *or* stripes (*officers and N.C.O.s*).
galonner [galɔ'ne], *v.t.* to lace, to adorn with gold- *or* silver-lace.
galonnier [galɔ'nje], *n.m.* gold- *or* silver-lace maker.
galop [ga'lo], *n.m.* gallop, galloping.
galopade [galɔ'pad], *n.f.* galloping, gallop.
galoper [galɔ'pe], *v.t.* to gallop (*a horse etc.*); to run after.—*v.i.* to gallop; (*fig.*) to run on.
galopin [galɔ'pɛ̃], *n.m.* errand-boy; (*fig.*) urchin, rogue, imp.
galvanique [galva'nik], *a.* galvanic.
galvaniser [galvani'ze], *v.t.* to galvanize; (*fig.*) to stimulate.
galvanisme [galva'nism], *n.m.* galvanism.
galvanomètre [galvanɔ'mɛːtr], *n.m.* galvanometer.
galvanoplastie [galvanɔplas'ti], *n.f.* electroplating.
galvauder [galvo'de], *v.t.* to muddle; to lower, to dishonour.
gambade [gɑ̃'bad], *n.f.* skip, gambol.
gambader [gɑ̃ba'de], *v.i.* to skip, to gambol, to romp, to frisk about.
Gambie [gɑ̃'bi], **la**, *f.* Gambia.
gambit [gɑ̃'bi], *n.m.* gambit.
gamelle [ga'mɛl], *n.f.* (*Mil.*, *Naut.*) mess-tin, dixie; (*fig.*) company-mess.
gamète [ga'mɛt], *n.m.* (*Biol.*) gamete.
gamin [ga'mɛ̃], *n.m.* boy, youngster, urchin.
gamine [ga'min], *n.f.* hoyden, chit of a girl.
gamme [gam], *n.f.* gamut, scale.
gammée [ga'me], *a. used in* **'croix gammée'**, swastika.
ganache [ga'naʃ], *n.f.* lower jaw (*of a horse*); (*colloq.*) booby, blockhead.
gandin [gɑ̃'dɛ̃], *n.m.* dandy, swell.
gang [gɑ̃g], *n.m.* gang (*of thieves*).
Gange [gɑ̃ːʒ], **le**, *m.* Ganges.
gangrène [gɑ̃'grɛːn], *n.f.* gangrene; (*fig.*) corruption.
gangrené [gɑ̃grə'ne], *a.* gangrened; (*fig.*) cankered, corrupt.
gangrener [gɑ̃grə'ne], *v.t.* (*conjug. like* AMENER) to gangrene, to mortify; (*fig.*) to corrupt.
gangreneux [gɑ̃grə'nø], *a.* (*fem.* **-euse**) gangrenous, cankered.
gangster [gɑ̃gs'tɛːr], *n.m.* gangster.
ganse [gɑ̃ːs], *n.f.* braid; cord, twist; edging; string.
gant [gɑ̃], *n.m.* glove, gauntlet.
gantelet [gɑ̃'tlɛ], *n.m.* gauntlet; hand-leather; (*Surg.*) glove-bandage.
ganter [gɑ̃'te], *v.t.* to glove, to put gloves on; (*fig.*) to fit, to suit. **se ganter**, *v.r.* to put on one's gloves.
ganterie [gɑ̃'tri], *n.f.* glove-making; glove-trade; glove-shop.
gantier [gɑ̃'tje], *n.m.* (*fem.* **-ière**) glover.
garage [ga'raːʒ], *n.m.* parking, storing away; (*Rail.*) shunting; siding; (*on rivers, canals etc.*) putting into wet dock; (*Motor. etc.*) garage; (*Row.*) boat-house.
garagiste [gara'ʒist], *n.m.* garage keeper; garage mechanic *or* owner.
garance [ga'rɑ̃ːs], *a.* madder-coloured.—*n.f.* madder; madder-root.
garant [ga'rɑ̃], *n.m.* (*fem.* **-e**) guarantor, surety.—*n.m.* guaranty, voucher, proof.
garanti [garɑ̃'ti], *a.* guaranteed, warranted.
garantie [garɑ̃'ti], *n.f.* guarantee, guaranty; indemnity; security; voucher, pledge.
garantir [garɑ̃'tiːr], *v.t.* to guarantee, to vouch for; to ensure; to indemnify; to protect, to shield. **se garantir**, *v.r.* to secure oneself, to preserve oneself.
garantisseur [garɑ̃ti'sœːr], *n.m.* warranter.
garçon [gar'sɔ̃], *n.m.* boy, lad; bachelor; workman; porter; waiter; stable-boy; steward (*on ship*).
garçonnet [garsɔ'nɛ], *n.m.* little boy.
garçonnière [garsɔ'njɛːr], *n.f.* bachelor's flat.
garde [gard], *n.f.* keeping; defence, guard; custody, watch; heed; nurse; hilt (*of sword*).—*n.m.* guard, guardsman, keeper, warder; watchman.
garde-à-vous [garda'vu], *n.m. inv.* (*Mil.*) position at attention.
garde-barrière [gardba'rjɛːr], *n.m.* (*pl. unchanged* or **gardes-barrières**) (*Rail.*) signalman at level-crossing.
garde-boue [gard'bu], *n.m. inv.* mudguard.
garde-cendre(s) [gard'sɑ̃ːdr], *n.m. inv.* fender, fire-guard.
garde-chasse [gard'ʃas], *n.m.* (*pl. unchanged* or **gardes-chasses**) game-keeper.
garde-chiourme [gard'ʃjurm], *n.m.* (*pl. unchanged* or **gardes-chiourme**) overseer of convict-gangs; warder.
garde-corps [gard'kɔːr], *n.m. inv.* rail, hand-rail; (*Naut.*) life-line.
garde-côte(s) [gard'kot], *n.m.* (*pl.* **garde-côtes** or **gardes-côtes**) guard-ship, coast-guard.
garde-crotte [gard'krɔt], *n.m. inv.* mud-guard.
garde-feu [gard'fø], *n.m.* (*pl. unchanged* or **garde-feux**) fire-guard; fender.
garde-fou [gard'fu], *n.m.* (*pl.* **-fous**) parapet; railings.
garde-frein [gard'frɛ̃], *n.m.* (*pl.* **garde-freins** or **gardes-freins**) brakesman.
garde-magasin [gardmaga'zɛ̃], *n.m.* (*pl. unchanged* or **gardes-magasins**) warehouse-keeper, storekeeper.
garde-malade [gardma'lad], *n.* (*pl. unchanged* or **gardes-malades**) sick-nurse, attendant.
garde-manger [gardmɑ̃'ʒe], *n.m. inv.* larder, pantry, meat safe.
garde-meuble(s) [gard'mœbl], *n.m. inv.* furniture repository.
garde-pêche [gard'pɛːʃ], *n.m.* (*pl.* **gardes-pêche**) river-keeper, water-bailiff.
garde-port [gard'pɔːr], *n.m.* (*pl.* **gardes-port** or **gardes-ports**) harbour-master.
garder [gar'de], *v.t.* to keep, to preserve; to retain; to watch over, to take care of, to nurse; to guard, to defend; to observe (*silence etc.*); to keep up. **se garder**, *v.r.* to keep, to last; to beware, to take care not to; to refrain (*de*); to guard.
garderie [gardə'ri], *n.f.* day nursery.

garde-robe (1) [gard'rɔb], *n.m.* (*pl.* **-robes**) apron; overall.
garde-robe (2) [gard'rɔb], *n.f.* (*pl.* **-robes**) wardrobe (*cupboard for clothes*).
gardeur [gar'dœ:r], *n.m.* (*fem.* **-euse**) herd-boy *or* -girl, keeper.
gardien [gar'djɛ̃], *a.* (*fem.* **-enne**) tutelary, guardian.—*n.m.* (*fem.* **-enne**) guardian, keeper, door-keeper; trustee; ***gardien de but***, goalkeeper.
gardon [gar'dɔ̃], *n.m.* roach.
gare! (1) [ga:r], *int.* beware! take care! look out!
gare (2) [ga:r], *n.f.* railway-station, terminus; (*wet*) dock; ***gare routière***, coach station.
garenne [ga'rɛn], *n.f.* warren.
garer [ga're], *v.t.* to side-track (*a train*); to garage, to park. **se garer**, *v.r.* to keep *or* get out of the way; to take cover; to park.
Gargantua [gargɑ̃'tɥa], *n.m.* Gargantua; glutton.
gargantuesque [gargɑ̃'tɥɛsk], *a.* gluttonous.
gargariser (se) [səgargari'ze], *v.r.* to gargle.
gargarisme [garga'rism], *n.m.* gargle, gargling.
gargote [gar'gɔt], *n.f.* cheap eating-house, cook-shop.
gargotier [gargɔ'tje], *n.m.* (*fem.* **-ière**) keeper of a cook-shop; bad cook.
gargouille [gar'gu:j], *n.f.* gargoyle, water-spout.
gargouillement [garguj'mɑ̃], *n.m.* rumbling (*in the stomach*); gurgling, bubbling (*of water*).
gargouiller [gargu'je], *v.i.* to rumble, to gurgle.
gargouillis [gargu'ji], *n.m.* gurgling (*of water*).
gargousse [gar'gus], *n.f.* cannon-cartridge; ***papier à gargousse***, cartridge-paper.
garnement [garnə'mɑ̃], *n.m.* scapegrace, scamp, (*young*) rogue.
garni [gar'ni], *a.* furnished; trimmed, garnished.—*n.m.* furnished lodgings *or* house.
garnir [gar'ni:r], *v.t.* to furnish, to stock; to trim, to garnish, to adorn; to fill. **se garnir**, *v.r.* to furnish *or* provide oneself (*with*).
garnison [garni'zɔ̃], *n.f.* garrison, station.
garnissage [garni'sa:ʒ], **garnissement** [garnis'mɑ̃], *n.m.* trimming (*of clothes etc.*).
garnisseur [garni'sœ:r], *n.m.* (*fem.* **-euse**) trimmer.
garniture [garni'ty:r], *n.f.* furniture, trimmings; ornaments.
garrot (1) [ga'ro], *n.m.* withers (*of a horse etc.*).
garrot (2) [ga'ro], *n.m.* tightener, garrot; (*Surg.*) tourniquet.
garrotte [ga'rɔt], *n.f.* garrotting, strangulation.
garrotter [garɔ'te], *v.t.* to tie down, to pinion; to strangle.
gars [gɑ], *n.m.* lad, stripling, young fellow.
Gascogne [gas'kɔɲ], **la**, *f.* Gascony; **le Golfe de Gascogne**, the Bay of Biscay.
gascon [gas'kɔ̃], *a.* (*fem.* **-onne**) Gascon.—*n.m.* Gascon (*dialect*); (**Gascon**, *fem.* **-onne**) Gascon (*person*); (*fig.*) boaster, braggart.
gasconnade [gaskɔ'nad], *n.f.* gasconade, boast, brag.
gasconner [gaskɔ'ne], *v.i.* to speak with a Gascon accent; to brag.
gaspillage [gaspi'ja:ʒ], *n.m.* waste, squandering.
gaspiller [gaspi'je], *v.t.* to waste, to squander.
gaspilleur [gaspi'jœ:r], *a.* (*fem.* **-euse**) wasting, squandering.—*n.m.* (*fem.* **-euse**) waster, squanderer, spendthrift.
gastrique [gas'trik], *a.* gastric.
gastrite [gas'trit], *n.f.* gastritis.
gastro-entérite [gastroɑ̃te'rit], *n.f.* gastroenteritis.
gâté [gɑ'te], *a.* marred, damaged, tainted; (*fig.*) spoiled.
gâteau [gɑ'to], *n.m.* (*pl.* **-eaux**) cake.
gâte-métier [gɑtme'tje], *n.m.* (*pl. unchanged* or **gâte-métiers**) underseller.
gâte-papier [gɑtpa'pje], *n. inv.* scribbler, poor writer.
gâter [gɑ'te], *v.t.* to spoil, to damage, to injure, to mar; to corrupt. **se gâter**, *v.r.* to taint, to spoil, to get spoiled; to break up (*of weather*).
gâterie [gɑ'tri], *n.f.* spoiling (*of children*), foolish indulgence.
gâte-sauce [gɑt'so:s], *n.m.* (*pl. unchanged* or **gâte-sauces**) scullion; (*colloq.*) bad cook.
gâteux [gɑ'tø], *a.* and *n.m.* (*fem.* **-euse**) idiot.
gauche [go:ʃ], *a.* left; (*fig.*) crooked, ugly; clumsy.—*n.f.* left hand, left side; (*Mil.*) left wing, left flank.
gauchement [goʃ'mɑ̃], *adv.* awkwardly, clumsily.
gaucher [go'ʃe], *a.* and *n.m.* (*fem.* **-ère**) left-handed (person).
gaucherie [go'ʃri], *n.f.* awkwardness, clumsiness.
gauchir [go'ʃi:r], *v.t.* to warp.—*v.i.* to turn aside; to flinch; to become warped; (*fig.*) to dodge.
gaudriole [godri'ɔl], *n.f.* broad joke, coarse jest.
gaufrage [go'fra:ʒ], *n.m.* goffering.
gaufre [go:fr], *n.f.* wafer, waffle (*thin cake*); honeycomb.
gaufrer [go'fre], *v.t.* to goffer.
gaufrette [go'frɛt], *n.f.* small wafer.
gaufreur [go'frœ:r], *n.m.* (*fem.* **-euse**) gofferer.
gaufrier [gofri'e], *n.m.* waffle-iron.
gaufrure [go'fry:r], *n.f.* goffering.
Gaule [go:l], **la**, *f.* Gaul.
gaule [go:l], *n.f.* pole, switch, long stick.
gauler [go'le], *v.t.* to beat (*trees*) with a long pole; to knock down (*fruit*).
gaullisme [go'lism], *n.m.* policy *or* partisanship of General de Gaulle.
gaulliste [go'list], *a.* and *n.* follower of General de Gaulle.
gaulois [go'lwa], *a.* Gaulish, Gallic; (*fig.*) free.—*n.m.* Gallic (*language*); (**Gaulois**, *fem.* **-oise**) Gaul (*person*).
gausser (se) [səgo'se], *v.r.* (*colloq.*) to banter, to chaff.
Gauthier [go'tje], *m.* Walter.
gave (1) [ga:v], *n.m.* torrent, mountain stream (*in the Pyrenees*).
gave (2) [ga:v], *n.f.* crop (*of birds*).
gaver [ga've], *v.t.* (*colloq.*) to cram, to gorge.
gavotte [ga'vɔt], *n.f.* gavotte (*dance*).
gavroche [ga'vrɔʃ], *n.m.* Parisian urchin.
gaz [gɑ:z], *n.m.* gas; ***bec de gaz***, gas-burner.

gaze [gɑːz], *n.f.* gauze.
gazé [gɑ'ze], *a.* covered with gauze, veiled; softened, toned down; (*Mil.*) gassed (*soldier*).
gazelle [ga'zɛl], *n.f.* gazelle.
gazer (1) [gɑ'ze], *v.t.* to cover with gauze; (*fig.*) to veil, to tone down.
gazer (2) [gɑ'ze], *v.t.* (*Mil.*) to gas (*men*).
gazette [ga'zɛt], *n.f.* gazette, newspaper; (*fig.*) newsmonger.
gazeux [gɑ'zø], *a.* (*fem.* **-euse**) gaseous; aerated.
gazier (1) [gɑ'zje], *n.m.* gas-fitter.
gazier (2) [gɑ'zje], *n.m.* (*fem.* **-ière**) gauze-maker.
gazolène [gɑzɔ'lɛn], **gazoléine** [gɑzɔle'in], **gazoline** [gɑzɔ'lin], *n.f.* gasolene.
gazomètre [gɑzɔ'mɛtr], *n.m.* gasometer.
gazon [gɑ'zɔ̃], *n.m.* grass; sod, turf; lawn.
gazonnant [gɑzɔ'nɑ̃], *a.* producing grass; grassy.
gazonner [gɑzɔ'ne], *v.t.* to cover with turf, to turf.
gazonneux [gɑzɔ'nø], *a.* (*fem.* **-euse**) turfy, swarded.
gazouillement [gazuj'mɑ̃], *n.m.* chirping, warbling (*of birds*); babbling (*of a brook etc.*); prattle.
gazouiller [gazu'je], *v.i.* to chirp, to warble; to twitter; to prattle; to babble.
gazouillis [gazu'ji], *n.m.* warbling, twittering.
geai [ʒe], *n.m.* jay.
géant [ʒe'ɑ̃], *a.* gigantic.—*n.m.* (*fem.* **-e**) giant.
geignard [ʒɛ'ɲaːr], *a.* always whining, querulous.
geignement [ʒɛɲ'mɑ̃], *n.m.* moan, whine.
geindre [ʒɛ̃ːdr], *v.i. irr.* (*conjug. like* CRAINDRE) to moan, to whine, to fret, to complain.
gel [ʒɛl], *n.m.* frost, freezing.
gélatine [ʒela'tin], *n.f.* gelatine.
gélatiner [ʒelati'ne], *v.t.* to gelatinize.
gélatineux [ʒelati'nø], *a.* (*fem.* **-euse**) gelatinous.
gelé [ʒə'le], *a.* frozen, cold.
gelée [ʒə'le], *n.f.* frost; jelly; aspic.
geler [ʒə'le], *v.t.*, *v.i.* (*conjug. like* AMENER) and **se geler**, *v.r.* to freeze.
gélignite [ʒeli'ɲit], *n.f.* gelignite.
gelinotte [ʒəli'nɔt], *n.f.* grouse (*bird*).
gémir [ʒe'miːr], *v.i.* to groan, to moan; to lament; (*fig.*) to suffer.
gémissant [ʒemi'sɑ̃], *a.* groaning, moaning; lamenting.
gémissement [ʒemis'mɑ̃], *n.m.* groan, moan; (*fig.*) lament, cooing.
gemme [ʒɛm], *n.f.* gem; resin; (*Bot.*) bud.
gemmer [ʒɛ'me], *v.i.* to bud.
gênant [ʒɛ'nɑ̃], *a.* troublesome, inconvenient, embarrassing.
gencive [ʒɑ̃'siːv], *n.f.* gum (*of the teeth*).
gendarme [ʒɑ̃'darm], *n.m.* gendarme (*armed policeman*); constable; virago (*woman*).
gendarmerie [ʒɑ̃darm'ri], *n.f.* gendarmery (*armed police*); constabulary; barracks (*of gendarmes*).
gendre [ʒɑ̃ːdr], *n.m.* son-in-law.
gêne [ʒɛːn], *n.f.* constraint, uneasiness, annoyance; difficulty; financial difficulties, penury.
gêné [ʒɛ'ne], *a.* constrained, ill at ease; hard up.
généalogie [ʒenealɔ'ʒi], *n.f.* genealogy; pedigree.
généalogique [ʒenealɔ'ʒik], *a.* genealogical.
généalogiste [ʒenealɔ'ʒist], *n.m.* genealogist.
gêner [ʒɛ'ne], *v.t.* to constrain, to constrict; to impede; to obstruct; to thwart, to restrain; to inconvenience, to embarrass; to annoy. **se gêner**, *v.r.* to constrain oneself, to put oneself out.
général [ʒene'ral], *a.* (*m. pl.* **-aux**) general, universal; vague.—*adv. phr.* ***en général***, in general.—*n.m.* (*Mil.*) general.
générale [ʒene'ral], *n.f.* general's wife; drum-beat (*to give alarm of fire etc.*).
généralement [ʒeneral'mɑ̃], *adv.* generally, in general.
généralisation [ʒeneralizɑ'sjɔ̃], *n.f.* generalization.
généraliser [ʒenerali'ze], *v.t.* to generalize.
généralissime [ʒenerali'sim], *n.m.* generalissimo, commander-in-chief of allied armies.
généralité [ʒenerali'te], *n.f.* generality.
générateur [ʒenera'tœːr], *a.* (*fem.* **-trice**) generating, generative.—*n.m.* generator.
génératif [ʒenera'tif], *a.* (*fem.* **-tive**) generative.
génération [ʒenerɑ'sjɔ̃], *n.f.* generation; procreation.
générer [ʒene're], *v.t.* (*conjug. like* CÉDER) to generate.
généreusement [ʒenerøz'mɑ̃], *adv.* generously, bountifully; nobly, bravely.
généreux [ʒene'rø], *a.* (*fem.* **-euse**) generous, liberal, bountiful; noble; courageous.
générique [ʒene'rik], *a.* generic.—*n.m.* (*Cine.*) credits.
générosité [ʒenerozi'te], *n.f.* generosity, liberality; magnanimity.
Gênes [ʒɛːn], *f.* Genoa.
genèse [ʒə'nɛːz], *n.f.* genesis.
genêt [ʒə'nɛ], *n.m.* (*Bot.*) broom.
genette [ʒə'nɛt], *n.f.* genet, civet cat.
gêneur [ʒɛ'nœːr], *n.m.* (*fem.* **-euse**) intruder; spoil-sport.
Genève [ʒə'nɛv], *f.* Geneva.
genevois [ʒən'vwa], *a.* Genevese.
genévrier [ʒənevri'e], *n.m.* juniper-tree.
génie [ʒe'ni], *n.m.* genius; spirit, nature, bent, talent; (*Mil.*) corps of engineers.
genièvre [ʒə'njɛːvr], *n.m.* juniper-berry; juniper-tree; gin.
génisse [ʒe'nis], *n.f.* heifer.
génital [ʒeni'tal], *a.* (*m. pl.* **-aux**) genital.
génitif [ʒeni'tif], *n.m.* (*Gram.*) genitive.
génocide [ʒenɔ'sid], *n.m.* genocide.
génois [ʒe'nwa], *a.* Genoese.
genou [ʒə'nu], *n.m.* (*pl.* **-oux**) knee; (*Mech.*) ball and socket; (*pl.*) lap.
genouillière [ʒənu'jɛːr], *n.f.* knee-piece (*of armour*); top (*of a high boot*); knee-cap; ball-and-socket joint.
genre [ʒɑ̃ːr], *n.m.* genus; species, kind, sort; fashion, style; (*Gram.*) gender.
gens [ʒɑ̃], *n.m. pl.* (*but adjectives directly preceding the word take the feminine form*) people, persons, folk; men, hands; servants.
gent [ʒɑ̃], *n.f.* brood, race, tribe.
gentiane [ʒɑ̃'sjan], *n.f.* (*Bot.*) gentian.
gentil (1) [ʒɑ̃'ti], *n.m.* Gentile.
gentil (2) [ʒɑ̃'ti], *a.* (*fem.* **-ille**) noble, gentle; pretty, nice, graceful; amiable, pleasing.

gentilhomme [ʒɑ̃ti'jɔm], *n.m.* (*pl.* **gentilshommes**) nobleman, gentleman.
gentillesse [ʒɑ̃ti'jɛs], *n.f.* kindness, sweetness (*of temperament*); prettiness, gracefulness; pretty thing, thought etc.
gentiment [ʒɑ̃ti'mɑ̃], *adv.* prettily, gracefully, like a good boy *or* girl.
génuflexion [ʒenyflɛk'sjɔ̃], *n.f.* genuflexion.
géocentrique [ʒeosɑ̃'trik], *a.* geocentric.
Geoffroy [ʒɔ'frwɑ], *m.* Geoffrey, Jeffrey.
géographe [ʒeɔ'graf], *n.m.* geographer.
géographie [ʒeɔgra'fi], *n.f.* geography.
géographique [ʒeɔgra'fik], *a.* geographical.
geôle [ʒo:l], *n.f.* gaol, prison.
geôlier [ʒo'lje], *n.m.* gaoler.
géologie [ʒeɔlɔ'ʒi], *n.f.* geology.
géologique [ʒeɔlɔ'ʒik], *a.* geological.
géologue [ʒeɔ'lɔg], *n.m.* geologist.
géométral [ʒeɔme'tral], *a.* (*m. pl.* **-aux**) geometrical.
géomètre [ʒeɔ'mɛtr], *n.m.* geometrician; geometer.
géométrie [ʒeɔme'tri], *n.f.* geometry.
géométrique [ʒeɔme'trik], *a.* geometrical.
Georges [ʒɔrʒ], *m.* George.
gérance [ʒe'rɑ̃:s], *n.f.* management, managership; editorship.
géranium [ʒera'njɔm], *n.m.* geranium.
gérant [ʒe'rɑ̃], *n.m.* (*fem.* **-e**) manager; editor; ***rédacteur gérant***, managing editor.
gerbe [ʒɛrb], *n.f.* sheaf, bundle; bunch of flowers.
gerber [ʒɛr'be], *v.t.* to make up *or* bind into sheaves.
gerbier [ʒɛr'bje], *n.m.* cornstack.
gerce [ʒɛrs], *n.f.* chap, crack.
gercé [ʒɛr'se], *a.* chapped (*hands*).
gercer [ʒɛr'se], *v.t.*, *v.i.*, (*conjug. like* COMMENCER) and **se gercer**, *v.r.* to chap, to crack.
gerçure [ʒɛr'sy:r], *n.f.* chap, crack; chink, cleft.
gérer [ʒe're], *v.t.* (*conjug. like* CÉDER) to manage, to administer.
gerfaut [ʒɛr'fo], *n.m.* gerfalcon.
germain [ʒɛr'mɛ̃], *a.* german, first (*of cousins etc.*); (*Law*) full (*brother etc.*).
germanique [ʒɛrma'nik], *a.* Germanic.
germe [ʒɛrm], *n.m.* germ, embryo; seed; bud, sprout, shoot; (*fig.*) origin.
germer [ʒɛr'me], *v.i.* to shoot, to sprout, to germinate.
germination [ʒɛrminɑ'sjɔ̃], *n.f.* germination.
gésier [ʒe'zje], *n.m.* gizzard.
gésir** [ʒe'zi:r], *v.i. irr.* to lie; ***ci-gît, here lies.
gestation [ʒɛstɑ'sjɔ̃], *n.f.* gestation.
gestatoire [ʒɛsta'twa:r], *a.* gestatory.
geste [ʒɛst], *n.m.* gesture, action; sign.
gesticulateur [ʒɛstikyla'tœ:r], *n.m.* (*fem.* **-trice**) gesticulator.
gesticulation [ʒɛstikylɑ'sjɔ̃], *n.f.* gesticulation.
gesticuler [ʒɛstiky'le], *v.i.* to gesticulate.
gestion [ʒɛs'tjɔ̃], *n.f.* management, administration.
geyser [ge'zɛ:r], *n.m.* geyser.
Ghana [ga'na], **le**, *m.* Ghana.
ghetto [ge'to], *n.m.* Jewish quarter, ghetto.
gibbeux [ʒi'bø], *a.* (*fem.* **-euse**) gibbous, hump-backed.
gibbon [ʒi'bɔ̃], *n.m.* gibbon (*ape*).
gibbosité [ʒibozi'te], *n.f.* gibbosity; hump.
gibecière [ʒib'sjɛ:r], *n.f.* game-bag, satchel; juggler's pocket.
gibelet [ʒi'blɛ], *n.m.* gimlet.
giberne [ʒi'bɛrn], *n.f.* cartridge-box *or* pouch.
gibet [ʒi'bɛ], *n.m.* gibbet, gallows.
gibier [ʒi'bje], *n.m.* (*Hunt.*) game.
giboulée [ʒibu'le], *n.f.* sudden shower, hail-shower.
gibus [ʒi'by:s], *n.m. inv.* gibus (*crush-hat, opera-hat*).
giclage [ʒi'kla:ʒ], *n.m.* spraying; ***carburateur à giclage***, jet carburettor.
giclée [ʒi'kle], *n.f.* squirt, spirt.
gicleur [ʒi'klœ:r], *n.m.* spray nozzle, jet.
gicler [ʒi'kle], *v.i.* to spout, to squirt.
gifle [ʒifl], *n.f.* slap in the face, box on the ear.
gifler [ʒi'fle], *v.t.* to slap in the face, to box the ears of.
gigantesque [ʒigɑ̃'tɛsk], *a.* gigantic, colossal.
gigot [ʒi'go], *n.m.* leg of mutton.
gigue [ʒig], *n.f.* shank, leg, haunch (*of venison*); jig (*dance*).
gilet [ʒi'lɛ], *n.m.* waistcoat; vest.
Gilles [ʒil], *m.* Giles.
gingembre [ʒɛ̃'ʒɑ̃:br], *n.m.* ginger.
gingivite [ʒɛ̃ʒi'vit], *n.f.* gingivitis.
ginguet [ʒɛ̃'gɛ], *a.* (*fem.* **-ette**) (*colloq.*) weak, worthless, scanty.—*n.m.* thin wine.
girandole [ʒirɑ̃'dɔl], *n.f.* girandole, epergne.
giration [ʒirɑ'sjɔ̃], *n.f.* gyration.
giratoire [ʒira'twa:r], *a.* gyratory.
girofle [ʒi'rɔfl], *n.m.* clove.
giroflée [ʒirɔ'fle], *n.f.* gillyflower, stock; ***giroflée jaune***, wallflower.
giron [ʒi'rɔ̃], *n.m.* lap; (*fig.*) bosom.
girouette [ʒi'rwɛt], *n.f.* weathercock, vane.
gisant [ʒi'zɑ̃], *a.* lying (*ill, dead etc.*); outstretched [GÉSIR].
gisement [ʒiz'mɑ̃], *n.m.* (*Geol. etc.*) lie (*of strata*); layer, bed; (*Naut.*) bearing (*of coast etc.*).
gitan [ʒi'tɑ̃], *n.m.* (*fem.* **-e**) gipsy.
gîte [ʒit], *n.m.* home, lodging; refuge; lair (*of deer*); (*Min.*) seam, layer.—*n.f.* (*Naut.*) list.
gîter [ʒi'te], *v.t.* to lodge, to house, to put up, to shelter.—*v.i.* to lie, to lodge; (*Naut.*) to list; to run aground. **se gîter**, *v.r.* to lodge, to sleep.
givrage [ʒi'vra:ʒ], *n.m.* (*Av.*) frosting, icing.
givre [ʒi:vr], *n.m.* hoar-frost, *rime.
givré [ʒi'vre], *a.* rimed, rimy.
glabre [glɑ:br], *a.* (*Bot.*) glabrous, smooth, without down; hairless.
glaçage [gla'sa:ʒ], *n.m.* frosting, glazing.
glaçant [gla'sɑ̃], *a.* freezing; icy, chilling.
glace [glas], *n.f.* ice; ice-cream; glass, plate-glass; mirror; carriage window; flaw (*in a diamond etc.*); icing (*on cakes etc.*).
glacé [gla'se], *a.* frozen, freezing; icy-cold; iced; glazed; glossy (*paper*); candied.
glacer [gla'se], *v.t.* (*conjug. like* COMMENCER) to freeze; to ice; (*fig.*) to paralyse; to glaze. —*v.i.* and **se glacer**, *v.r.* to freeze.
glaciaire [gla'sjɛ:r], *a.* of glaciers, glacial.
glacial [gla'sjal], *a.* frozen, glacial, icy.
glaciale [gla'sjal], *n.f.* (*Bot.*) ice-plant.
glacier [gla'sje], *n.m.* glacier, field of ice; ice-cream vendor.
glaçon [gla'sɔ̃], *n.m.* block of ice; floe; ice-cube; ***petit glaçon***, icicle.
gladiateur [gladja'tœ:r], *n.m.* gladiator.

glaïeul [gla'jœl], *n.m.* gladiolus; iris.
glaire [glɛ:r], *n.f.* glair, white of egg; phlegm, mucus.
glaise [glɛ:z], *a.* clayey.—*n.f.* clay, loam; potter's earth.
glaiseux [glɛ'zø], *a.* (*fem.* **-euse**) clayey, loamy.
glaisière [glɛ'zjɛ:r], *n.f.* clay-pit.
glaive [glɛ:v], *n.m.* sword, blade, steel.
gland [glɑ̃], *n.m.* acorn; tassel.
glande [glɑ̃:d], *n.f.* (*Anat.*) gland; (*pop.*) tumour; kernel.
glanduleux [glɑ̃dy'lø], *a.* (*fem.* **-euse**) glandulous, glandular.
glaner [gla'ne], *v.t., v.i.* to glean.
glaneur [gla'nœ:r], *n.m.* (*fem.* **-euse**) gleaner.
glapir [gla'pi:r], *v.i.* to yelp (*of puppies etc.*); to screech, to scream (*of persons*).
glapissant [glapi'sɑ̃], *a.* yelping; screeching, shrill.
glapissement [glapis'mɑ̃], *n.m.* yelping; screeching.
glas [glɑ], *n.m.* knell.
glauque [glo:k], *a.* glaucous, sea-green.
glèbe [glɛb], *n.f.* glebe; land, soil.
glissade [gli'sad], *n.f.* sliding, slide; slipping.
glissant [gli'sɑ̃], *a.* slippery; (*fig.*) ticklish, delicate.
glissement [glis'mɑ̃], *n.m.* slipping, sliding, gliding; (*Polit.*) landslide.
glisser [gli'se], *v.t.* to slip, to slide; to insinuate.—*v.i.* to slip, to slide; to glide. **se glisser**, *v.r.* to slip, to slide, to creep, to steal, to insinuate oneself (***dans***).
glissière [gli'sjɛ:r], *n.f.* slide; ***porte à glissière***, sliding door.
glissoire [gli'swa:r], *n.f.* slide on ice.
global [glɔ'bal], *a.* (*m. pl.* **-aux**) in a mass, entire; ***somme globale***, lump sum.
globe [glɔb], *n.m.* globe, sphere, orb; glass-shade.
globulaire [glɔby'lɛ:r], *a.* globular.
globule [glɔ'byl], *n.m.* globule.
gloire [glwa:r], *n.f.* glory, fame.
gloriette [glɔ'rjɛt], *n.f.* arbour, summer-house.
glorieusement [glɔrjøz'mɑ̃], *adv.* gloriously.
glorieux [glɔ'rjø], *a.* (*fem.* **-euse**) glorious; vainglorious.—*n.m.* braggart, boaster.
glorification [glɔrifikɑ'sjɔ̃], *n.f.* glorification.
glorifier [glɔri'fje], *v.t.* to glorify, to honour. **se glorifier**, *v.r.* to glory in, to boast (***de***).
gloriole [glɔ'rjɔl], *n.f.* vainglory, petty vanity.
glose [glo:z], *n.f.* gloss; criticism; comment; parody.
gloser [glo'ze], *v.t.* to gloss; to criticize.—*v.i.* to carp, to find fault.
gloseur [glo'zœ:r], *n.m.* (*fem.* **-euse**) carper, fault-finder.
glossaire [glɔ'sɛ:r], *n.m.* glossary, vocabulary.
glouglou [glu'glu], *n.m.* gurgling, gurgle.
glouglouter [gluglu'te], *v.i.* to gurgle.
gloussement [glus'mɑ̃], *n.m.* clucking.
glousser [glu'se], *v.i.* to cluck (*of hens*).
glouton [glu'tɔ̃], *a.* (*fem.* **-onne**) gluttonous, greedy.—*n.m.* (*fem.* **-onne**) glutton.
gloutonnement [glutɔn'mɑ̃], *adv.* gluttonously, greedily.
gloutonnerie [glutɔn'ri], *n.f.* gluttony, greediness.
glu [gly], *n.f.* bird-lime, glue.
gluant [gly'ɑ̃], *a.* glutinous, sticky; slimy.
glucose [gly'ko:z], *n.m.* glucose.
glutineux [glyti'nø], *a.* (*fem.* **-euse**) glutinous, viscous.
glycérine [glise'rin], *n.f.* glycerine.
glycine [gli'sin], *n.f.* wistaria.
gnome [gno:m], *n.m.* (*fem.* **gnomide**) gnome.
gnou [gnu], *n.m.* gnu.
gobelet [gɔ'blɛ], *n.m.* goblet, mug; dice-box; ***tour de gobelet***, juggler's trick.
gobelin [gɔ'blɛ̃], *n.m.* goblin, imp.
gobe-mouches [gɔb'muʃ], *n.m. inv.* fly-catcher (*bird*); fly-trap (*plant*); (*fig.*) simpleton.
gober [gɔ'be], *v.t.* to gulp down, to swallow; (*colloq.*) to believe easily; to have a liking for (*a person*).
(*C*) **godendard** [gɔdɑ̃'da:r], *n.m.* cross-cut saw, whip-saw, two-handle saw.
goder [gɔ'de], *v.i.* to crease, to bag (*of clothes*), to pucker (*of needlework etc.*).
godiche [gɔ'diʃ], *a.* clumsy, boobyish, simple.
godille [gɔ'di:j], *n.f.* stern-oar; scull.
goéland [gɔe'lɑ̃], *n.m.* gull, sea-gull.
goélette [gɔe'lɛt], *n.f.* schooner.
goémon [gɔe'mɔ̃], *n.m.* seaweed.
gogo [go'go], (*in adv. phr.*) ***à gogo***, galore.
goguenard [gɔg'na:r], *a.* bantering, jeering, mocking, scoffing.—*n.m.* (*fem.* **-e**) banterer, jeerer, chaffer.
goguenarder [gɔgnar'de], *v.i.* to jeer, to banter, to chaff.
goguette [gɔ'gɛt], *n.f.* ***être en goguette***, to be in a merry mood, to be on the spree.
goinfre [gwɛ̃:fr], *n.m.* (*fam.*) guzzler, gormandizer.
goinfrer [gwɛ̃'fre], *v.i.* to gorge, to gormandize.
goinfrerie [gwɛ̃frə'ri], *n.f.* gluttony.
goître [gwa:tr], *n.m.* goitre, wen.
goîtreux [gwa'trø], *a.* (*fem.* **-euse**) goitrous. —*n.m.* (*fem.* **-euse**) goitrous person, (*colloq.*) imbecile, idiot.
golfe [gɔlf], *n.m.* gulf, bay.
gommage [gɔ'ma:ʒ], *n.m.* gumming.
gomme [gɔm], *n.f.* gum; rubber, eraser.
gommer [gɔ'me], *v.t.* to gum; to rub out.
gommeux [gɔ'mø], *a.* (*fem.* **-euse**) gummy.
gommier [gɔ'mje], *n.m.* gum-tree.
gond [gɔ̃], *n.m.* hinge; ***hors des gonds***, unhinged, (*fig.*) enraged, beside oneself.
gondole [gɔ̃'dɔl], *n.f.* gondola; car *or* gondola (*of a balloon etc.*); eye-bath.
gondoler [gɔ̃dɔ'le], *v.i.* to bulge; to warp (*of wood*); to buckle.
gondolier [gɔ̃dɔ'lje], *n.m.* gondolier.
gonflement [gɔ̃flə'mɑ̃], *n.m.* swelling, inflation.
gonfler [gɔ̃'fle], *v.t.* to swell, to inflate; to pump up (*a tyre*); to puff up.—*v.i.* to swell, to be swollen. **se gonfler**, *v.r.* to swell, to be swollen, to be puffed up; (*fam.*) to swank.
gonfleur [gɔ̃'flœ:r], *n.m.* air-pump, inflator.
gong [gɔ̃:g], *n.m.* gong.
gorge [gɔrʒ], *n.f.* throat, gullet; bosom, neck; defile, strait; (*Bot.*) mouth; (*Arch., Fort.*) gorge; ***avoir mal à la gorge***, to have a sore throat; ***avoir la gorge serrée***, to have a lump in one's throat; ***rendre gorge***, to refund, to stump up; ***faire des gorges chaudes***, to gloat over.
gorge-de-pigeon [gɔrʒdəpi'ʒɔ̃], *a. inv.* iridescent, shot (*of colours*).

gorgée [gɔr'ʒe], *n.f.* draught, gulp; ***petite gorgée***, sip.

gorger [gɔr'ʒe], *v.t.* (*conjug. like* MANGER) to gorge, to cram. **se gorger,** *v.r.* to gorge oneself.

gorille [gɔ'ri:j], *n.m.* gorilla.

gosier [go'zje], *n.m.* throat, gullet; (*fig.*) voice.

gosse [gɔs], *n.* (*fam.*) brat, urchin, kid.

gothique [gɔ'tik], *a.* Gothic.—*n.f.* (*Print.*) Old English.

gouache [gwaʃ], *n.f.* gouache, body-colour; painting in this.

goudron [gu'drɔ̃], *n.m.* tar.

goudronnage [gudrɔ'na:ʒ], *n.m.* tarring.

goudronner [gudrɔ'ne], *v.t.* to tar.

goudronneux [gudrɔ'nø], *a.* (*fem.* **-euse**) tarry.

gouffre [gufr], *n.m.* gulf, abyss, pit.

gouge [gu:ʒ], *n.f.* gouge.

goujat [gu'ʒɑ], *n.m.* (*fig.*) cad, vulgar fellow.

goujon [gu'ʒɔ̃], *n.m.* gudgeon (*pin* or *fish*).

goule [gul], *n.f.* ghoul.

goulet [gu'lɛ], *n.m.* narrow entrance (*to a harbour etc.*); inlet; mouth, neck (*of a bottle etc.*); gully, gorge (*between mountains etc.*).

goulot [gu'lo], *n.m.* neck (*of a bottle etc.*).

goulu [gu'ly], *a.* gluttonous, greedy.—*n.m.* (*fem.* **-e**) glutton, greedy person.

goulûment [guly'mɑ̃], *adv.* greedily.

goupille [gu'pi:j], *n.f.* pin, peg, bolt.

goupiller [gupi'je], *v.t.* to pin, to bolt.

gourd [gu:r], *a.* benumbed, numb.

gourde [gurd], *n.f.* gourd; flask, wineskin.

gourdin [gur'dɛ̃], *n.m.* cudgel, club, thick stick.

gourmade [gur'mad], *n.f.* smack in the face.

gourmand [gur'mɑ̃], *a.* greedy.—*n.m.* (*fem.* **-e**) glutton.

gourmander [gurmɑ̃'de], *v.t.* to chide, to reprimand; to prune (*trees*).

gourmandise [gurmɑ̃'di:z], *n.f.* gluttony, greediness; (*pl.*) sweetmeats.

gourmé [gur'me], *a.* stiff, stuck-up, formal, solemn.

gourmer [gur'me], *v.t.* to box, to thump; to curb (*a horse*). **se gourmer,** *v.r.* to thump, to pummel each other.

gourmet [gur'mɛ], *n.m.* connoisseur in wines etc.; epicure.

gourmette [gur'mɛt], *n.f.* curb, curb-chain.

gousse [gus], *n.f.* shell, pod, husk; ***gousse d'ail***, clove of garlic.

gousset [gu'sɛ], *n.m.* armpit; fob, (waistcoat-) pocket; gusset (*of a shirt etc.*); bracket.

goût [gu], *n.m.* taste, flavour, relish; savour; inclination, liking; style, manner; ***chacun à son goût***, every man to his taste; ***chacun son goût***, tastes differ; ***viande de haut goût***, highly seasoned meat.

goûter [gu'te], *v.t.* to taste, to try; to like; to enjoy; to feel.—*v.i.* to taste; to try; to have a snack.—*n.m.* a snack taken between lunch and dinner (*the equivalent of English tea*).

goutte (1) [gut], *n.f.* drop, small quantity; sip, dram; (*Arch., Pharm.*) drop.—*adv. phr.* ***ne . . . goutte***; ***n'entendre goutte***, not to hear *or* understand in the least; ***n'y voir goutte***, not to make it out at all.

goutte (2) [gut], *n.f.* gout.

gouttelette [gu'tlɛt], *n.f.* small drop, drip.

goutter [gu'te], *v.i.* to drip.

goutteux [gu'tø], *a.* and *n.m.* (*fem.* **-euse**) gouty (person).

gouttière [gu'tjɛ:r], *n.f.* gutter of a roof; shoot, spout (*for rain-water*); cradle splint.

gouvernable [guvɛr'nabl], *a.* governable, manageable.

gouvernail [guvɛr'na:j], *n.m.* rudder, helm.

gouvernant [guvɛr'nɑ̃], *a.* governing, ruling.—*n.m.* governor, ruler.—*n.f.* (**-e**) governor's wife; governess; housekeeper (*of bachelor*).

gouverne [gu'vɛrn], *n.f.* guidance, guide, direction; (*pl.*) (*Av.*) rudders and ailerons.

gouvernement [guvɛrnə'mɑ̃], *n.m.* government, rule, sway; management; governorship.

gouvernemental [guvɛrnəmɑ̃'tal], *a.* (*m. pl.* **-aux**) governmental.

gouverner [guvɛr'ne], *v.t.* to control, to govern, to direct, to steer; to rule, to command, to manage, to regulate.—*v.i.* to steer, to answer the helm.

gouverneur [guvɛr'nœ:r], *n.m.* governor; manager; tutor.

grabat [gra'bɑ], *n.m.* pallet, litter (*of straw etc.*), truckle-bed.

grabuge [gra'by:ʒ], *n.m.* (*fam.*) wrangling, squabble, brawl.

grâce [grɑ:s], *n.f.* grace, favour, mercy, forgiveness; gracefulness, elegance; (*pl.*) thanks; (*Myth.*) ***les Grâces***, the Graces.

graciable [gra'sjabl], *a.* pardonable.

gracier [gra'sje], *v.t.* to pardon, to reprieve.

gracieusement [grasjøz'mɑ̃], *adv.* graciously, kindly, gracefully.

gracieuseté [grasjøz'te], *n.f.* graciousness, kindness; act of courtesy; gratuity.

gracieux [gra'sjø], *a.* (*fem.* **-euse**) graceful, gracious, obliging.

gracilité [grasili'te], *n.f.* slimness, slenderness.

gradation [gradɑ'sjɔ̃], *n.f.* gradation; climax.

grade [grad], *n.m.* grade, rank; degree; ***monter en grade***, to be promoted.

gradé [gra'de], *n.m.* (*Mil.*) non-commissioned officer.

gradin [gra'dɛ̃], *n.m.* step; tier.

graduation [gradɥɑ'sjɔ̃], *n.f.* graduation; scale.

gradué [gra'dɥe], *a.* graduated; progressive (*exercises*).—*n.m.* (*fem.* **-ée**) graduate (*of a university*).

graduel [gra'dɥɛl], *a.* (*fem.* **-elle**) gradual.

graduellement [gradɥɛl'mɑ̃], *adv.* gradually.

graduer [gra'dɥe], *v.t.* to graduate, to proportion.

graillon [grɑ'jɔ̃], *n.m.* smell of burnt meat *or* fat; (*pl.*) scraps (*of meat etc.*) from a meal.

grain (1) [grɛ̃], *n.m.* grain, berry; bead; jot, bit; ***avoir un grain***, to have a bee in one's bonnet; ***grain de beauté***, mole, beauty-spot; ***grain de café***, coffee bean; ***grain de poivre***, peppercorn; ***grain de raisin***, grape.

grain (2) [grɛ̃], *n.m.* (*Naut.*) squall.

graine [grɛ:n], *n.f.* seed; breed; ***c'est une mauvaise graine***, he is a bad lot.

grainetier [grɛn'tje], **grainier** [grɛ'nje], *n.m.* (*fem.* **-ière**) seedsman, seedswoman; corn-chandler.

graissage [grɛ'sa:ʒ], *n.m.* greasing, oiling, lubrication.

graisse [grɛ:s], *n.f.* fat, grease.
graisser [grɛ'se], *v.t.* to grease; to make greasy; to lubricate, to oil.
graisseur [grɛ'sœ:r], *n.m.* greaser, oiler.
graisseux [grɛ'sø], *a.* (*fem.* **-euse**) greasy; oily; fatty.
grammaire [gra'mɛ:r], *n.f.* grammar.
grammairien [gramɛ'rjɛ̃], *n.m.* (*fem.* **-enne**) grammarian.
grammatical [gramati'kal], *a.* (*m. pl.* **-aux**) grammatical.
grammaticalement [gramatikal'mɑ̃], *adv.* grammatically.
gramme [gram], *n.m.* gramme *or* gram.
grand [grɑ̃], *a.* great; large, big; high, tall; wide, spacious; grown-up; capital (*of letters*); broad (*of daylight*); grand, noble.—*adv.* ***voir grand***, to have big ideas; ***en grand***, on a large scale; (*of portraits*) full length.—*n.m.* the grand, the sublime.—*n.m.* (*fem.* **-e**) great person; grown-up person; ***grand d'Espagne***, Spanish grandee; (*pl.*) the great, great people; (*sch.*) the big (*or* senior) boys *or* girls.
(*C*) **grand-bois** [grɑ̃'bwɑ], *n.m.* virgin forest.
grand-duc [grɑ̃'dyk], *n.m.* (*pl.* **grands-ducs**) grand duke; eagle-owl.
grand-duché [grɑ̃dy'ʃe], *n.m.* (*pl.* **grands-duchés**) grand-duchy.
grande-duchesse [grɑ̃ddy'ʃɛs], *n.f.* (*pl.* **grandes-duchesses**) grand-duchess.
grandement [grɑ̃d'mɑ̃], *adv.* greatly, extremely, very much; grandly, nobly, handsomely.
grandeur [grɑ̃'dœ:r], *n.f.* extent, size; height; length; breadth; bulk; greatness, magnitude; tallness; grandeur, magnificence; grace, highness (*titles*).
grandiose [grɑ̃'djo:z], *a.* grandiose.
grandir [grɑ̃'di:r], *v.t.* to increase; to magnify.—*v.i.* to grow; to grow (tall, big, up etc.). **se grandir**, *v.r.* to make oneself appear taller; to grow taller; to raise oneself, to rise.
grandissement [grɑ̃dis'mɑ̃], *n.m.* growth, increase; rise; (*Opt.*) magnification.
grand-maman [grɑ̃ma'mɑ̃], *n.f.* (*pl.* **-mamans**) granny.
grand-mère [grɑ̃'mɛ:r], *n.f.* (*pl.* **-mères**) grandmother.
grand-père [grɑ̃'pɛ:r], *n.m.* (*pl.* **grands-pères**) grandfather.
grand-route [grɑ̃'rut], *n.f.* (*pl.* **-routes**) high-road, main road.
grand-rue [grɑ̃'ry], *n.f.* (*pl.* **-rues**) high street, main street.
grange [grɑ̃:ʒ], *n.f.* barn.
granit [gra'nit, gra'ni], **granite** [gra'nit], *n.m.* granite.
granulaire [grany'lɛ:r], *a.* granular.
granule [gra'nyl], *n.m.* granule.
granulé [grany'le], *a.* granulated, granular.
graphique [gra'fik], *a.* graphic.—*n.m.* diagram; graph.
graphiquement [grafik'mɑ̃], *adv.* graphically.
graphite [gra'fit], *n.m.* graphite; plumbago.
grappe [grap], *n.f.* bunch (*of grapes, currants etc.*); cluster (*of fruit etc.*); (*Artill.*) grape-shot.
grappillage [grapi'ja:ʒ], *n.m.* vine-gleaning *or* pickings.
grappiller [grapi'je], *v.t.* to glean.—*v.i.* to glean; to get pickings, to make a little profit.
grappilleur [grapi'jœ:r], *n.m.* (*fem.* **-euse**) gleaner; petty thief, profiteer.
grappin [gra'pɛ̃], *n.m.* grapnel, grappling-iron; grab.
gras [grɑ], *a.* (*fem.* **grasse**) fat; fleshy, corpulent; greasy, oily, unctuous; rich; broad, indecent; ***eaux grasses***, dishwater; ***faire la grasse matinée***, to get up late; ***mardi gras***, Shrove Tuesday; ***matières grasses***, fats.—*n.m.* fat, fat part (*of meat etc.*); meat, flesh; meat diet.
gras-double [grɑ'dubl], *n.m.* tripe.
grassement [grɑs'mɑ̃], *adv.* plentifully, liberally; in affluence.
grasseyement [grasɛj'mɑ̃], *n.m.* exaggerated rolling of uvular r.
grasseyer [grasɛ'je], *v.i.* to roll one's r's.
grassouillet [grɑsu'jɛ], *a.* (*fem.* **-ette**) (*fam.*) plump, chubby.
gratification [gratifikɑ'sjɔ̃], *n.f.* gratuity, extra pay, reward.
gratifier [grati'fje], *v.t.* to confer (*a favour*) on; to ascribe.
gratin [gra'tɛ̃], *n.m.* burnt part; ***au gratin***, (*Cook.*) dressed with crust of bread-crumbs.
gratis [gra'tis], *adv.* gratis, for nothing.
gratitude [grati'tyd], *n.f.* gratitude.
gratte-ciel [grat'sjɛl], *n.m. inv.* skyscraper.
grattelle [gra'tɛl], *n.f.* rash, itching.
gratte-papier [gratpa'pje], *n.m. inv.* scribbler, pen-pusher.
gratter [gra'te], *v.t.* to scratch; to scrape. **se gratter**, *v.r.* to scratch oneself.
grattoir [gra'twa:r], *n.m.* scraper; eraser, paint-scraper.
gratuit [gra'tɥi], *a.* free (of charge); gratuitous.
gratuité [gratɥi'te], *n.f.* gratuitousness.
gratuitement [gratɥit'mɑ̃], *adv.* for nothing; gratuitously.
gravats [gra'va], *n.m. pl.* rubbish, debris (*of a building*).
grave [gra:v], *a.* heavy, grave, serious; weighty; dangerous; low, deep (*of voice*); (*Mus.*) low-pitched.
gravé [gra've], *a.* pitted; engraved.
graveleux [gra'vlø], *a.* (*fem.* **-euse**) gravelly, sandy, gritty; (*fig.*) smutty.
gravelle [gra'vɛl], *n.f.* (*Path.*) gravel.
gravement [grav'mɑ̃], *adv.* gravely, seriously.
graver [gra've], *v.t.* to engrave; to impress, to imprint. **se graver**, *v.r.* to be engraved, to be impressed *or* imprinted.
graveur [gra'vœ:r], *n.m.* engraver.
gravier [gra'vje], *n.m.* gravel, grit; (*Path.*) gravel.
gravir [gra'vi:r], *v.t.* to clamber up, to climb, to ascend.
gravitation [gravitɑ'sjɔ̃], *n.f.* gravitation.
gravité [gravi'te], *n.f.* gravity; seriousness, solemnity; weight, importance.
graviter [gravi'te], *v.i.* to gravitate.
gravure [gra'vy:r], *n.f.* engraving, print; illustration (*in book*).
gré [gre], *n.m.* will, wish; liking, pleasure; mind, taste; accord, consent ***bon gré mal gré*** or ***de gré ou de force***, willy nilly; ***de bon gré***, willingly; ***de mauvais gré***, unwillingly; ***savoir (bon) gré***, to be thankful; ***vendre de gré à gré***, to sell by private contract.

grèbe [grɛb], *n.m.* (*Orn.*) grebe.
grec [grɛk], *a.* (*fem.* **grecque**) Greek; Grecian.—*n.m.* Greek (*language*); (**Grec**, *fem.* **Grecque**) Greek (*person*).
Grèce [grɛs], **la**, *f.* Greece.
gredin [grə'dɛ̃], *n.m.* rascal, scoundrel.
gréer [gre'e], *v.t.* to rig.
greffe (1) [grɛf], *n.m.* (*Law*) registry, record-office.
greffe (2) [grɛf], *n.f.* graft; grafting.
greffer [grɛ'fe], *v.t.* to graft.
greffier [grɛ'fje], *n.m.* registrar, recorder, clerk of the court.
greffoir [grɛ'fwa:r], *n.m.* grafting-knife.
greffon [grɛ'fɔ̃], *n.m.* graft, scion, slip.
grégaire [gre'gɛ:r], **grégarien** [grega'rjɛ̃] (*fem.* **-enne**), *a.* gregarious.
grêle (1) [grɛ:l], *a.* slender, slim; shrill.
grêle (2) [grɛ:l], *n.f.* hail; hailstorm.
grêlé [grɛ'le], *a.* ravaged by hail; pock-marked.
grêler [grɛ'le], *v. impers.* to hail.—*v.t.* to ravage, ruin *or* spoil by hail.
grêlon [grɛ'lɔ̃], *n.m.* hailstone.
grelot [grə'lo], *n.m.* small (*round*) bell.
grelotter [grəlɔ'te], *v.i.* to tremble, to shake, to shiver (*with cold, fear*); to tinkle.
grenade [grə'nad], *n.f.* pomegranate; (*Mil.*) grenade.
grenadier [grəna'dje], *n.m.* pomegranate-tree; (*Mil.*) grenadier.
grenadine [grəna'din], *n.f.* grenadine (*silk* or *syrup*).
grenat [grə'na], *n.m.* garnet.—*a.* garnet-red.
grener [grə'ne], *v.t.* (*conjug. like* AMENER) to granulate; to grain (*leather etc.*); (*Engr.*) to stipple.—*v.i.* to seed, to run to seed.
grènetis [grɛn'ti], *n.m.* milling, milled edge.
grenier [grə'nje], *n.m.* loft; attic; corn-loft, granary.
grenouille [grə'nu:j], *n.f.* frog.
grenu [grə'ny], *a.* full of corn; rough-grained.
grès [grɛ], *n.m.* sandstone, stoneware.
grésil [gre'zi], *n.m.* sleet.
grésillement [grezij'mɑ̃], *n.m.* pattering (*like sleet*); shrivelling, crackling; chirping.
grésiller [grezi'je], *v. impers.* to sleet, to patter.—*v.t.* to shrivel up.—*v.i.* to crackle.
grève [grɛ:v], *n.f.* strand, beach of sand *or* shingle; strike of workmen; ***grève du zèle***, working to rule.
grever [grə've], *v.t.* (*conjug. like* AMENER) to wrong, to injure; to burden; to encumber (*with debt etc.*).
gréviste [gre'vist], *n.* striker.
gribouillage [gribu'ja:ʒ], **gribouillis** [gribu'ji], *n.m.* (*Paint.*) daub; scrawl.
gribouiller [gribu'je], *v.t., v.i.* to daub; to scrawl, to scribble.
gribouilleur [gribu'jœ:r], *n.m.* (*fem.* **-euse**) dauber; scrawler, scribbler.
grief [gri'ɛf], *n.m.* wrong, injury, grievance.
grièvement [griɛv'mɑ̃], *adv.* grievously, gravely.
grièveté [griɛv'te], *n.f.* gravity, seriousness.
griffade [gri'fad], *n.f.* clawing, scratch.
griffe [grif], *n.f.* claw, talon; (*pl.*) clutches; paper-clip, clamp; ***griffe d'asperge***, root of asparagus.
griffer [gri'fe], *v.t.* to claw, to scratch (*of cats etc.*); to stamp (*with signature etc.*).
griffon [gri'fɔ̃], *n.m.* griffin; griffon.
griffonnage [grifɔ'na:ʒ], *n.m.* scrawl, scribble.
griffonner [grifɔ'ne], *v.t.* to scrawl, to scribble.
griffonneur [grifɔ'nœ:r], *n.m.* (*fem.* **-euse**) scrawler, scribbler.
grignoter [griɲɔ'te], *v.t.* to nibble; (*fig.*) to get pickings out of.
gril [gri], *n.m.* gridiron, grill.
grillade [gri'jad], *n.f.* grilling, broiling; grill, grilled steak.
grillage [gri'ja:ʒ], *n.m.* grilling, broiling, toasting; wire guard *or* mesh; light iron railing.
grille [gri:j], *n.f.* railing, grating; grill; iron gate *or* bars; (*Elec.*) grid.
grille-pain [grij'pɛ̃], *n.m. inv.* toaster.
griller (1) [gri'je], *v.t.* to broil, to grill (*meat*); to roast (*coffee*); to toast (*bread*).—*v.i.* to broil, to be burned up *or* scorched; to burn out (*electric bulbs*); (*fig.*) to be itching (*to do something*). **se griller**, *v.r.* to be scorched, to be parched.
griller (2) [gri'je], *v.t.* to enclose with iron rails.
grillon [gri'jɔ̃], *n.m.* cricket.
grimaçant [grima'sɑ̃], *a.* grimacing, grinning; (*fig.*) gaping, ill-fitting.
grimace [gri'mas], *n.f.* grimace, wry face; (*fig.*) (*pl.*) affectations, airs and graces.
grimacer [grima'se], *v.i.* (*conjug. like* COMMENCER) to make faces, to grimace, to grin; to simper; to pucker.
grimer (se) [səgri'me], *v.r.* to make up.
grimpant [grɛ̃'pɑ̃], *a.* climbing, creeping (*of plants*).
grimper [grɛ̃'pe], *v.i.* to climb, to clamber up; to creep up (*of plants*).
grimpeur [grɛ̃'pœ:r], *a.* (*fem.* **-euse**) climbing, twining.—*n.m.* (*fem.* **-euse**) (*Orn.*) climber.
grincement [grɛ̃s'mɑ̃], *n.m.* gnashing, grinding (*of the teeth etc.*); grating.
grincer [grɛ̃'se], *v.i.* (*conjug. like* COMMENCER) to grind, to gnash, to grate.
grincheux [grɛ̃'ʃø], *a.* (*fem.* **-euse**) ill-tempered, peevish, crabbed, surly.—*n.m.* (*fem.* **-euse**) grumbler.
gringalet [grɛ̃ga'lɛ], *n.m.* weak, puny man.
griotte [gri'ɔt], *n.f.* morello cherry.
grippage [gri'pa:ʒ], **grippement** [grip'mɑ̃], *n.m.* friction (*of two surfaces*); seizing, jamming (*of bearing*).
grippe [grip], *n.f.* influenza, 'flu; (*colloq.*) dislike.
grippé [gri'pe], *a.* shrunk, contracted (*of the face*); ill with influenza; run hot, seized up (*of motors*).
gripper [gri'pe], *v.t.* to pounce upon, to clutch, to seize.—*v.i.* to run hot, to seize up, to jam. **se gripper**, *v.r.* to shrivel, to shrink.
grippe-sou [grip'su], *n.m.* (*pl. unchanged* or **grippe-sous**) miser, money-grubber.
gris [gri], *a.* grey; grey-haired; dull (*of the weather*); (*fig.*) tipsy; ***papier gris***, brown paper.—*n.m.* grey.
grisaille [gri'zɑ:j], *n.f.* sketch *or* painting in tones of grey; greyness (*of weather*).
grisâtre [gri'zɑ:tr], *a.* greyish.
griser [gri'ze], *v.t.* to give a grey tint to; to intoxicate; **se griser**, *v.r.* to get tipsy.
grisette [gri'zɛt], *n.f.* grey gown; (*Orn.*) whitethroat.

grison [gri'zɔ̃], *a.* (*fem.* **-onne**) grey, grey-haired.—*n.m.* (*colloq.*) grey-beard (*old man*); donkey.
grisonnant [grizɔ'nɑ̃], *a.* turning grey.
grisonner [grizɔ'ne], *v.i.* to grow grey (*of hair etc.*).
grisou [gri'zu], *n.m.* fire-damp.
grive [gri:v], *n.f.* thrush.
grivelé [gri'vle], *a.* speckled.
grivois [gri'vwa], *a.* loose, broad, obscene.
grivoiserie [grivwaz'ri], *n.f.* smutty story.
Groenland [grɔen'lɑ̃d], **le**, *m.* Greenland.
groenlandais [grɔenlɑ̃dɛ], *a.* of Greenland.—*n.m.* (**Groenlandais**, *fem.* **-aise**) Greenlander.
grognard [grɔ'ɲa:r], *a.* grumbling, growling.—*n.* grumbler, grouser; veteran of Napoleon's Old Guard.
grognement [grɔɲ'mɑ̃], *n.m.* grunt, grunting; growling, grumbling.
grogner [grɔ'ɲe], *v.i.* to grunt; to growl, to grumble, to grouse.
grognon [grɔ'ɲɔ̃], *a.* (*fem.* **-onne**, *but usu. unchanged*) grumbling, querulous.—*n.m.* (*fem.* **-onne**) grumbler, growler.
groin [grwɛ̃], *n.m.* snout (*of a hog*).
grommeler [grɔm'le], *v.t.*, *v.i.* (*conjug. like* APPELER) to mutter, to grumble.
grondant [grɔ̃'dɑ̃], *a.* scolding; roaring, rumbling.
grondement [grɔ̃d'mɑ̃], *n.m.* rumbling, growling, snarling; roar.
gronder [grɔ̃'de], *v.t.* to chide, to scold.—*v.i.* to growl, to mutter; to snarl, to rumble, to roar.
gronderie [grɔ̃'dri], *n.f.* scolding, chiding.
grondeur [grɔ̃'dœ:r], *a.* (*fem.* **-euse**) grumbling, scolding.—*n.m.* (*fem.* **-euse**) scold; grumbler.
grondin [grɔ̃'dɛ̃], *n.m.* (*Ichth.*) gurnard, gurnet.
groom [grum], *n.m.* page, (*U.S.*) bell-boy; stable lad.
gros [gro], *a.* (*fem.* **grosse** (1)) big, large, bulky; stout; coarse; pregnant; loud (*of laughter*); gruff (*of the voice*); substantial; foul (*of the weather*); high (*of the sea etc.*); dark, deep (*in colour*); (*Cine.*) ***gros plan***, close-up.—*n.m.* large *or* main part; bulk, mass; main body (*of an army*); ***en gros et en détail***, wholesale and retail.—*adv.* much.
groseille [gro'zɛ:j], *n.f.* currant; ***groseille à maquereau***, gooseberry.
groseillier [grozɛ'je], *n.m.* currant-bush.
grosse (1) [gros], [GROS].
grosse (2) [gros], *n.f.* gross (*twelve dozen*).
grossement [gros'mɑ̃], *adv.* grossly, coarsely.
grossesse [gro'sɛs], *n.f.* pregnancy.
grosseur [gro'sœ:r], *n.f.* size, bulk; bigness; swelling, tumour.
grossier [gro'sje], *a.* (*fem.* **-ière**) gross, coarse, thick; plain, common; rough, rude, unpolished, unmannerly, boorish.
grossièrement [grosjɛr'mɑ̃], *adv.* coarsely, rudely, roughly, uncouthly.
grossièreté [grosjɛr'te], *n.f.* coarseness, grossness; rudeness; coarse language.
grossir [gro'si:r], *v.t.* to make bigger *or* greater.—*v.i.* to grow bigger; to put on weight.
grossissant [grosi'sɑ̃], *a.* magnifying.
grossissement [grosis'mɑ̃], *n.m.* magnifying, magnifying-power; increase; exaggeration.
grosso-modo [grɔsɔmɔ'do], *adv.* summarily.
grotesque [grɔ'tɛsk], *a.* and *n.m.* grotesque.
grotte [grɔt], *n.f.* grotto, cave.
grouillant [gru'jɑ̃], *a.* stirring, swarming, crawling.
grouillement [gruj'mɑ̃], *n.m.* stirring, swarming; rumbling (*of the intestines*).
grouiller [gru'je], *v.i.* to stir, to move; to swarm; to rumble (*of the intestines*).
groupe [grup], *n.m.* group, party (*of people*); cluster (*of stars*); clump (*of trees etc.*).
groupement [grup'mɑ̃], *n.m.* grouping.
grouper [gru'pe], *v.t.* to group. **se grouper**, *v.r.* to form groups, to gather.
gruau [gry'o], *n.m.* flour of wheat; ***gruau d'avoine***, groats; oatmeal; ***tisane de gruau***, gruel.
grue [gry], *n.f.* (*Orn.*, *Eng.*) crane.
gruger [gry'ʒe], *v.t.* (*conjug. like* MANGER) to crunch; to eat, to devour.
grume [grym], *n.f.* bark (*of tree*); ***bois de*** or ***en grume***, wood with the bark on.
grumeau [gry'mo], *n.m.* (*pl.* **-eaux**) clot, small lump.
grumeler (se) [səgry'mle], *v.r.* (*conjug. like* APPELER) to clot.
grumeleux [gry'mlø], *a.* (*fem.* **-euse**) clotted, rough.
gruyère [gry'jɛ:r], *n.m.* Gruyère cheese.
guano [gwa'no], *n.m.* guano.
Guatémala [gwatema'la], **le**, *m.* Guatemala.
guatémaltèque [gwatemal'tɛk], *a.* Guatemalan.—*n.* (**Guatémaltèque**) Guatemalan (*person*).
gué [ge], *n.m.* ford.
guéable [ge'abl], *a.* fordable.
guéer [ge'e], *v.t.* to ford.
guenille [gə'ni:j], *n.f.* rag, tatter; (*pl.*) tattered clothes.
guenilleux [gəni'jø], *a.* (*fem.* **-euse**) tattered, ragged.
guenon [gə'nɔ̃], *n.f.* monkey, ape; she-monkey; (*fig.*) fright, ugly woman.
guépard [ge'pa:r], *n.m.* cheetah.
guêpe [gɛ:p], *n.f.* wasp.
guêpier [gɛ:'pje], *n.m.* wasps' nest; bee-eater (*bird*); scrape, difficulty.
guère [gɛ:r], *adv.* but little, not much, not very; not long; hardly, scarcely.
guères (*poet.*) [GUÈRE].
guéret [ge'rɛ], *n.m.* ploughed but unsown land; fallow-land; (*pl.*, *poet.*) fields.
guéridon [geri'dɔ̃], *n.m.* (small) round table.
guérilla [geri'ja], *n.f.* guerrilla war *or* troops.
guérir [ge'ri:r], *v.t.* to heal, to cure.—*v.i.* to heal, to heal up; to recover, to be cured.
guérison [geri'zɔ̃], *n.f.* recovery, healing, cure.
guérissable [geri'sabl], *a.* curable.
guérisseur [geri'sœ:r], *n.m.* (*fem.* **-euse**) healer, faith-healer; quack.
guérite [ge'rit], *n.f.* sentry-box; look-out turret.
Guernesey [gɛrnə'zɛ], *f.* Guernsey.
guerre [gɛ:r], *n.f.* war; warfare, hostilities; strife.
guerrier [gɛ'rje], *a.* (*fem.* **-ière**) warlike, martial.—*n.m.* (*fem.* **-ière**) warrior, fighting man *or* woman.

guerroyant [gɛrwɑ'jɑ̃], *a.* bellicose, pugnacious.
guerroyer [gɛrwɑ'je], *v.i.* (*conjug. like* EMPLOYER) to make war, to wage war.
guet [gɛ], *n.m.* watch; watching; ***au guet***, on the look-out.
guet-apens [gɛta'pɑ̃], *n.m.* (*pl.* **guets-apens**) ambush; trap.
guêtre [gɛ:tr], *n.f.* gaiter; ***grandes guêtres***, leggings; ***petites guêtres***, spats.
guetter [gɛ'te], *v.t.* to lie in wait for, to watch for, to waylay.
guetteur [gɛ'tœ:r], *n.m.* signalman, look-out man.
gueulard [gœ'la:r], *a.* (*pop.*) bawling, mouthing; gluttonous; hard-mouthed (*of horses*).—*n.m.* (*fem.* **-e**) bawler; glutton.—*n.m.* furnace-mouth.
gueule [gœl], *n.f.* mouth (*of animals*); (*vulg.*) mouth, face, mug (*of human*).
gueule-de-lion [gœldə'ljɔ̃], *n.f.* (*pl.* **gueules-de-lion**) antirrhinum.
gueule-de-loup [gœldə'lu], *n.f.* (*pl.* **gueules-de-loup**) snapdragon; chimney cowl.
gueuler [gœ'le], *v.i.* (*pop.*) to bawl.
gueuse (1) [gø:z], *n.f.* pig-iron.
gueuser [gø'ze], *v.t., v.i.* to beg.
gueuserie [gø'zri], *n.f.* beggary; destitution; (*fig.*) trash.
gueux [gø], *a.* (*fem.* **-euse**) poor, destitute; wretched.—*n.m.* beggar, tramp; knave, rascal.—*n.f.* (**-euse** (2)) wench, bitch.
gui [gi], *n.m.* mistletoe.
guichet [gi'ʃɛ], *n.m.* wicket-gate (*of prison*); spyhole (*of door*); position at counter (*banks, post-office*), pay-desk; booking-office (*railways*).
guichetier [giʃ'tje], *n.m.* turnkey.
guide [gid], *n.m.* guide; guide-book.—*n.f.* girl-guide; rein.
guider [gi'de], *v.t.* to guide, to lead; to direct.
guidon [gi'dɔ̃], *n.m.* (*Mil.*) guidon; (*Navy*) burgee; (fore)sight, bead (*of fire-arms*); reference-mark (*in a book*); handle-bar (*of bicycle*).
guigner [gi'ɲe], *v.t.* to peer *or* peep at; to ogle; to covet.—*v.i.* to peep, to peer.
guignol [gi'ɲɔl], *n.m.* Punch; puppet-show, Punch and Judy show.
guignolet [giɲɔ'lɛ], *n.m.* cherry-brandy.
guignon [gi'ɲɔ̃], *n.m.* bad luck, ill-luck.
Guillaume [gi'jo:m], *m.* William.
guillemet [gij'mɛ], *n.m.* quotation mark, inverted comma.
guillemot [gij'mo], *n.m.* (*Orn.*) guillemot.
guilleret [gij'rɛ], *a.* (*fem.* **-ette**) brisk, lively.
guilleri [gij'ri], *n.m.* chirping (*of sparrows*).
guillotine [gijɔ'tin], *n.f.* guillotine; ***fenêtre à guillotine***, sash-window.
guillotiner [gijɔti'ne], *v.t.* to guillotine.
guimauve [gi'mo:v], *n.f.* marsh-mallow.
guimbarde [gɛ̃'bard], *n.f.* Jew's-harp; (*colloq.*) rickety old vehicle, boneshaker.
guimpe [gɛ̃:p], *n.f.* stomacher; wimple (*for nuns etc.*).
guindé [gɛ̃'de], *a.* stiff, forced, unnatural; formal (*of style*).
guindeau [gɛ̃'do], *n.m.* (*pl.* **-eaux**) windlass.
guinder [gɛ̃'de], *v.t.* to hoist; to strain, to force. **se guinder**, *v.r.* to hoist oneself up; to be strained, to be forced.
Guinée [gi'ne], **la**, *f.* Guinea.
guinéen [gine'ɛ̃], *a.* (*fem.* **-éenne**) Guinean.—*n.m.* (**Guinéen**, *fem.* **-éenne**) Guinean (*person*).
guingan [gɛ̃'gɑ̃], *n.m.* gingham.
guingois [gɛ̃'gwa], *n.m.* crookedness; ***de guingois***, awry, askew.
guinguette [gɛ̃'gɛt], *n.f.* small suburban tavern (*usually with pleasure garden*).
guirlande [gir'lɑ̃:d], *n.f.* garland, wreath.
guise [gi:z], *n.f.* manner, way, guise; fancy; ***en guise de***, by way of.
guitare [gi'ta:r], *n.f.* guitar.
guitariste [gita'rist], *n.* guitarist, guitar-player.
gustatif [gysta'tif], *a.* (*fem.* **-tive**) gustatory.
gustation [gystɑ'sjɔ̃], *n.f.* tasting, gustation.
guttural [gyty'ral], *a.* (*m. pl.* **-aux**) guttural.
guyanais [gɥija'nɛ], *a.* (*fem.* **-aise**) Guyanese.—*n.m.* (**Guyanais**, *fem.* **-aise**) Guyanese (*person*).
Guyane [gɥi'jan], **la**, *f.* Guyana.
gymnase [ʒim'nɑ:z], *n.m.* gymnasium.
gymnaste [ʒim'nast], *n.* gymnast.
gymnastique [ʒimnas'tik], *a.* gymnastic.—*n.f.* gymnastics.
gynécologie [ʒinekɔlɔ'ʒi], *n.f.* gynaecology.
gynécologiste [ʒinekɔlɔ'ʒist], **gynécologue** [ʒinekɔ'lɔg], *n.* gynaecologist.
gypse [ʒips], *n.m.* gypsum; plaster of Paris.
gyroscope [ʒirɔs'kɔp], *n.m.* gyroscope.

H

[In words marked thus † the *h* is 'aspirated'.]

H, h [aʃ], *n.m.* or *f.* the eighth letter of the alphabet. *H* is mute *or* aspirated. The so-called aspirated *h* is a graphic symbol which indicates that there is neither elision nor liaison; *e.g.* ***la halle*** [la'al], ***les halles*** [lɛ'al]; ***l'heure H***, (*Mil.*) zero hour.
habile [a'bil], *a.* able, clever; capable; skilful; sharp, cunning.
habilement [abil'mɑ̃], *adv.* cleverly, skilfully.
habileté [abil'te], *n.f.* ability, skill, cleverness.
habilité [abili'te], *a.* entitled, qualified.—*n.f.* (*Law*) competency, qualification.
habiliter [abili'te], *v.t.* to qualify, to enable, to entitle.
habillage [abi'ja:ʒ], *n.m.* dressing; trussing (*poultry*).
habillant [abi'jɑ̃], *a.* dressy *or* suiting well (*of clothes etc.*).
habillé [abi'je], *a.* dressed, clad, decked out.
habillement [abij'mɑ̃], *n.m.* clothes, dress, attire.
habiller [abi'je], *v.t.* to dress; to make clothes for; to become, to fit; to wrap up; (*Cook.*) to truss (*fowls, fish etc.*); (*fig.*) to adorn. **s'habiller**, *v.r.* to dress; to have one's clothes made.
habilleur [abi'jœ:r], *n.m.* (*fem.* **-euse**) (*Theat.*) dresser.

habit [a'bi], *n.m.* clothes; dress-coat; ***habit complet***, suit of clothes.
habitable [abi'tabl], *a.* habitable.
habitant [abi'tã], *n.m.* (*fem.* **-e**) inhabitant, resident; occupier; denizen; (*C*) farmer.
habitation [abitɑ'sjɔ̃], *n.f.* habitation, residence, abode.
habiter [abi'te], *v.t.* to inhabit, to dwell in, to live in; to frequent; ***habiter un lieu***, to live in a place.—*v.i.* to inhabit, to dwell, to reside; ***habiter avec***, (*Law*) to cohabit.
habitude [abi'tyd], *n.f.* habit, custom, practice; ***d'habitude***, usually.
habitué [abi'tɥe], *n.m.* (*fem.* **-ée**) frequenter, customer.
habituel [abi'tɥɛl], *a.* (*fem.* **-elle**) habitual, usual.
habituellement [abitɥɛl'mã], *adv.* habitually usually.
habituer [abi'tɥe], *v.t.* to accustom. **s'habituer**, *v.r.* to accustom oneself; to get used (*à*).
†**hâbler** [ɑ'ble], *v.i.* to brag, to boast.
†**hâblerie** [ɑblə'ri], *n.f.* bragging, boasting.
†**hâbleur** [ɑ'blœ:r], *n.m.* (*fem.* **-euse**) braggart, boaster.
†**hache** [aʃ], *n.f.* axe, hatchet.
†**haché** [a'ʃe], *a.* chopped up, mixed; (*fig.*) abrupt.
†**hacher** [a'ʃe], *v.t.* to chop, to cut to pieces; to hash, to mince; to hack; to cross-hatch.
†**hachis** [a'ʃi], *n.m.* minced meat, hash.
†**hachoir** [a'ʃwa:r], *n.m.* chopping-board; chopping-knife; mincer.
†**hachure** [a'ʃy:r], *n.f.* (*Engr.*) hatching, hachure.
†**hagard** [a'ga:r], *a.* wild-looking, haggard.
†**haie** [ɛ], *n.f.* hedge, hedgerow; hurdle; row, line.
†**haillon** [ɑ'jɔ̃], *n.m.* rag, tatter.
†**haine** [ɛ:n], *n.f.* hate, hatred; dislike; spite.
†**haineusement** [ɛnøz'mã], *adv.* hatefully, spitefully.
†**haineux** [ɛ'nø], *a.* (*fem.* **-euse**) hating, spiteful.
†**haïr** [a'i:r], *v.t. irr.* to hate, to detest, to loathe.
†**haire** [ɛ:r], *n.f.* hair-shirt.
†**haïssable** [ai'sabl], *a.* hateful, odious.
†**Haïti** [ai'ti], *m.* or *f.* Haiti.
†**haïtien** [ai'sjɛ̃], *a.* (*fem.* **-enne**) Haitian.—*n.m.* (**Haïtien**, *fem.* **-enne**) Haitian (*person*).
†**halage** [a'la:ʒ], *n.m.* towage, hauling.
†**hale** [a:l], *n.m.* tow-line, tow-rope.
†**hâle** [ɑ:l], *n.m.* heat of the sun; sunburn.
†**hâlé** [ɑ'le], *a.* sunburnt; tanned; swarthy.
haleine [a'lɛn], *n.f.* breath, wind.
†**haler** [a'le], *v.t.* (*Naut.*) to haul, to tow.
†**hâler** [ɑ'le], *v.t.* to tan, to burn (*of the sun*). **se hâler**, *v.r.* to become sunburnt *or* tanned.
†**haletant** [al'tã], *a.* out of breath, panting.
†**haleter** [al'te], *v.i.* (*conjug. like* AMENER) to pant, to gasp for breath.
†**hall** [ɔl], *n.m.* large entrance hall (*of hotel, station*).
†**halle** [al], *n.f.* market; market-hall, market-place.
†**hallebarde** [al'bard], *n.f.* halberd; ***pleuvoir des hallebardes***, to rain cats and dogs.
†**hallebardier** [albar'dje], *n.m.* halberdier.
†**hallier** [a'lje], *n.m.* thicket, coppice.
hallucination [alysinɑ'sjɔ̃], *n.f.* hallucination, delusion.
halluciné [alysi'ne], *a.* hallucinated; (*fig*). deluded.—*n.m.* (*fem.* **-ée**) person suffering from delusions.
halluciner [alysi'ne], *v.t.* to hallucinate; (*fig.*) to delude.
†**halo** [a'lo], *n.m.* halo; (*Phot.*) halation.
†**halot** [a'lo], *n.m.* rabbit-burrow.
†**halte** [alt], *n.f.* halt; stand, stop; halting-place.—*int.* halt! stop!
haltère [al'tɛ:r], *n.m.* dumb-bell.
†**hamac** [a'mak], *n.m.* hammock.
†**hameau** [a'mo], *n.m.* (*pl.* **-eaux**) hamlet.
hameçon [am'sɔ̃], *n.m.* hook, fish-hook; bait.
†**hampe** [ã:p], *n.f.* staff (*of a lance, flag etc.*); stem, flower-stalk.
†**hamster** [ams'tɛ:r], *n.m.* hamster.
†**hanche** [ã:ʃ], *n.f.* hip; haunch (*of horse*).
†**handicap** [ãdi'kap], *n.m.* handicap.
†**hangar** [ã'ga:r], *n.m.* outhouse, shed, cart-shed; hangar (*for aeroplanes*).
†**hanneton** [an'tɔ̃], *n.m.* May-bug, cockchafer; (*fig.*) thoughtless person.
†**hanter** [ã'te], *v.t.* to haunt; to frequent.
†**hantise** [ã'ti:z], *n.f.* obsession.
†**happer** [a'pe], *v.t.* to snap up, to snatch; to seize.
†**happeur** [a'pœ:r], *n.m.* paper-clip.
†**haquenée** [ak'ne], *n.f.* hack, quiet horse; (*fig.*) ungainly woman.
†**haquet** [a'kɛ], *n.m.* dray.
†**harangue** [a'rã:g], *n.f.* harangue, speech; (*boring*) address.
†**haranguer** [arã'ge], *v.t.*, *v.i.* to harangue.
†**harangueur** [arã'gœ:r], *n.m.* (*fem.* **-euse**) haranguer, orator, speechifier.
†**haras** [a'rɑ], *n.m.* stud, breeding-stud.
†**harasser** [ara'se], *v.t.* to harass, to tire out, to weary.
†**harceler** [arsə'le], *v.t.* (*conjug. like* APPELER) to worry, to pester, to torment, to harass.
†**harde** [ard], *n.f.* herd (*of deer etc.*); leash (*for hounds*).
†**hardes** [ard], *n.f.* (*used only in pl.*) wearing apparel, attire; worn clothes.
†**hardi** [ar'di], *a.* bold, daring, fearless; rash; impudent.
†**hardiesse** [ar'djɛs], *n.f.* boldness, daring; rashness; assurance, impudence.
†**hardiment** [ardi'mã], *adv.* boldly, daringly; impudently.
†**harem** [a'rɛm], *n.m.* harem.
†**hareng** [a'rã], *n.m.* herring.
†**harengère** [arã'ʒɛ:r], *n.f.* fish-wife.
†**harenguet** [arã'gɛ], *n.m.* sprat.
†**hargneux** [ar'ɲø], *a.* (*fem.* **-euse**) cross, cross-grained, peevish, surly.
†**haricot** [ari'ko], *n.m.* kidney-bean; ***haricot de mouton***, Irish stew; ***haricots d'Espagne***, scarlet runners; ***haricots verts***, French beans.
†**haridelle** [ari'dɛl], *n.f.* jade, hack; (*fig.*) gawky woman.
†**harle** [arl], *n.m.* (*Orn.*) merganser.
harmonica [armɔni'ka], *n.m.* harmonica; mouth-organ.
harmonie [armɔ'ni], *n.f.* harmony; concord; (*Mus.*) harmonics.
harmonieusement [armɔnjøz'mã], *adv.* harmoniously.

harmonieux [armɔ'ɲjø], *a.* (*fem.* **-euse**) harmonious; musical, melodious; in keeping; blending (*of colours*).
harmonique [armɔ'nik], *a.* harmonic.—*n.f.* harmonics.
harmoniser [armɔni'ze], *v.t.* and **s'harmoniser**, *v.r.* to harmonize.
harmonium [armɔ'njɔm], *n.m.* harmonium.
†**harnachement** [arnaʃ'mɑ̃], *n.m.* harness, trappings.
†**harnacher** [arna'ʃe], *v.t.* to harness; to rig out.
†**harnais** [ar'nɛ], *n.m.* harness; horse-trappings; armour; equipment, tackle.
†**haro** [a'ro], *n.m.* hue and cry.
†**harpagon** [arpa'gɔ̃], *n.m.* miser, skinflint.
†**harpe** [arp], *n.f.* harp.
†**harper** [ar'pe], *v.t.* to grasp, to clutch.
†**harpie** [ar'pi], *n.f.* harpy, vixen, shrew.
†**harpiste** [ar'pist], *n.* harpist.
†**harpon** [ar'pɔ̃], *n.m.* harpoon.
†**harponner** [arpɔ'ne], *v.t.* to harpoon.
†**hasard** [a'za:r], *n.m.* chance; hazard; risk, danger; ***à tout hasard***, on the off chance; ***au hasard***, at random; ***par hasard***, by chance.
†**hasardé** [azar'de], *a.* hazarded, ventured; hazardous, bold.
†**hasarder** [azar'de], *v.t.* to hazard, to risk, to venture. **se hasarder**, *v.r.* to hazard, to venture, to take the risk.
†**hasardeusement** [azardøz'mɑ̃], *adv.* hazardously.
†**hasardeux** [azar'dø], *a.* (*fem.* **-euse**) venturesome, daring; hazardous, unsafe.
†**hâte** [ɑ:t], *n.f.* hurry, haste; ***à la hâte***, in a hurry.
†**hâter** [ɑ'te], *v.t.* to hasten, to forward, to hurry, to urge on; to expedite; to force (*fruit*). **se hâter**, *v.r.* to make haste, to hurry.
†**hâtif** [ɑ'tif], *a.* (*fem.* **-tive**) forward; precocious, premature; (*Hort.*) early.
†**hâtivement** [ɑtiv'mɑ̃], *adv.* early, prematurely; hastily.
†**hauban** [o'bɑ̃], *n.m.* (*Naut.*) shroud, guy, stay.
†**hausse** [o:s], *n.f.* lift, block (*for raising anything*); (*Comm.*) rise, advance; (back) sight (*of a rifle*).
†**haussement** [os'mɑ̃], *n.m.* raising, lifting; ***haussement d'épaules***, shrugging of the shoulders.
†**hausser** [o'se], *v.t.* to raise, to lift up; to increase; to shrug; (*Comm.*) to advance.—*v.i.* to rise; to get higher; to increase. **se hausser**, *v.r.* to be raised, to rise; to raise oneself; to clear up (*of the weather*); to increase.
†**haussier** [o'sje], *n.m.* (*St. Exch.*) bull.
†**haussière** [o'sjɛ:r], *n.f.* hawser.
†**haut** [o], *a.* high, tall, lofty; elevated; upper; principal; eminent; haughty; loud (*of sound*); ***lire à haute voix***, to read aloud; ***pousser les hauts cris***, to complain loudly.—*n.m.* height; top, summit; upper part; ***d'en haut***, from above.—*n.f.* (*colloq.*) ***la haute***, the wealthy, the upper crust.—*adv.* high; loud, aloud, loudly; haughtily; ***ainsi qu'il a été dit plus haut***, as has already been said; ***parlez plus haut***, speak louder.—*adv. phr.* ***en haut***, upstairs.
†**hautain** [o'tɛ̃], *a.* haughty, proud.
†**hautainement** [otɛn'mɑ̃], *adv.* haughtily, superciliously, proudly.
†**hautbois** [o'bwɑ], *n.m.* hautboy, oboe; oboe-player.
†**haut-de-forme** [od'fɔrm], *n.m.* (*pl.* **hauts-de-forme**) top-hat.
†**hautement** [ot'mɑ̃], *adv.* boldly, resolutely, proudly; aloud.
†**hauteur** [o'tœ:r], *n.f.* height, elevation, altitude; depth; rising ground; haughtiness, arrogance; pitch (*of the voice etc.*); (*Naut.*) bearing; ***être à la hauteur de quelqu'un***, to be a match for someone; ***être à la hauteur d'une tâche***, to be equal to a task.
†**haut-fond** [o'fɔ̃], *n.m.* (*pl.* **hauts-fonds**) shoal, shallow.
†**haut-le-corps** [ol'kɔ:r] *n.m. inv.* spring, bound; start.
†**haut-le-pied** [ol'pje], *a. inv.* ***cheval haut-le-pied***, spare horse; ***locomotive haut-le-pied***, engine running light.
†**haut-parleur** [opar'lœ:r], *n.m.* (*pl.* **-parleurs**) loud-speaker; amplifier.
†**Havane** [a'van], **la**, *f.* Havana.
†**havane** [a'van], *a.* brown, tan.—*n.m.* Havana cigar.
†**hâve** [ɑ:v], *a.* pale, wan, emaciated.
†**havre** [ɑ:vr], *n.m.* haven, harbour, port.
†**havresac** [ɑvrə'sak], *n.m.* knapsack, pack.
†**Haye** [ɛ], **La**, *f.* the Hague.
†**hé!** [e], *int.* hoy! (*for calling, warning etc.*); why! well! I say! (*emphat.*).
†**heaume** [o:m], *n.m.* helmet.
hebdomadaire [ɛbdɔma'dɛ:r], *a.* weekly.—*n.m.* weekly newspaper.
hébergement [ebɛrʒə'mɑ̃], *n.m.* lodging.
héberger [ebɛr'ʒe], *v.t.* (*conjug. like* MANGER) to lodge.
hébété [ebe'te], *a.* dazed, stupid, bewildered.
hébéter [ebe'te], *v.t.* (*conjug. like* CÉDER) to make stupid, to besot.
hébraïque [ebra'ik], *a.* Hebrew, Hebraic.
hébreu [e'brø], *a.* (*fem.* **hébraïque**) Hebrew.—*n.m.* Hebrew (*language*); (**Hébreu**, *fem.* **Juive**, *pl.* **Hébreux**) Hebrew (*person*).
hécatombe [eka'tɔ̃:b], *n.f.* hecatomb.
hectare [ɛk'ta:r], *n.m.* hectare (*2 acres, 1 rood 35 perches* or *2·4711 acres*).
hectogramme [ɛktɔ'gram], **hecto** [ɛk'to], *n.m.* hectogramme (*3·527 oz. avoirdupois*).
hectolitre [ɛktɔ'litr], *n.m.* hectolitre (*22·009668 imperial gallons*).
hectomètre [ɛktɔ'mɛtr], *n.m.* hectometre (*109·936 yds.*).
hégire [e'ʒi:r], *n.f.* Hegira (*Mohammedan era*).
†**hein!** [ɛ̃], *int.* (*before a sentence*) hey! what! (*after a sentence* = ***n'est-ce pas***) isn't it etc.?
hélas! [e'lɑ:s], *int.* alas!
Hélène [e'lɛn], *f.* Helen.
†**héler** [e'le], *v.t.* (*conjug. like* CÉDER) to hail, to call (*a taxi, a boat etc.*).
hélice [e'lis], *n.f.* screw; propeller.
hélicoptère [elikɔp'tɛ:r], *n.m.* helicopter.
héliport [eli'pɔ:r], *n.m.* heliport, helicopter landing-ground.
hélium [e'ljɔm], *n.m.* helium.
helvétique [ɛlve'tik], *a.* Helvetic, Helvetian, Swiss.
hémisphère [emis'fɛ:r], *n.m.* hemisphere.

hémisphérique [emisfe'rik], *a.* hemispheric.
hémistiche [emis'tiʃ], *n.m.* hemistich.
hémoglobine [emɔglɔ'bin], *n.f.* haemoglobin.
hémophylie [emofi'li], *n.f.* haemophilia.
hémorragie [emɔra'ʒi], *n.f.* haemorrhage.
hémorroïdes [emɔrɔ'id], *n.f. pl.* haemorrhoids, piles.
†**henné** [ɛ'ne], *n.m.* (*Bot.*) henna.
†**hennir** [ɛ'niːr], *v.i.* to neigh, to whinny.
†**hennissement** [ɛnis'mɑ̃], *n.m.* neighing.
Henri [ɑ̃'ri], *m.* Henry.
hépatique [epa'tik], *a.* hepatic.—*n.f.* (*Bot.*) liverwort.
hépatite [epa'tit], *n.f.* hepatitis (*inflammation of the liver*); (*Min.*) hepatite (*liver-stone*).
heptagone [ɛpta'gɔn], *a.* heptagonal.—*n.m.* heptagon.
héraldique [eral'dik], *a.* heraldic.—*n.f.* heraldry.
†**héraut** [e'ro], *n.m.* herald.
herbacé [ɛrba'se], *a.* (*Bot.*) herbaceous.
herbage [ɛr'baːʒ], *n.m.* herbage, grass-land; pasture.
herbager [ɛrba'ʒe] *v.t.* (*conjug. like* MANGER) to graze (*cattle*).
herbe [ɛrb], *n.f.* herb, grass, wort; ***blé en herbe***, corn in the blade; ***brin d'herbe***, blade of grass; ***fines herbes***, herbs for seasoning; ***mauvaise herbe***, weed; (*fig.*) scamp.
herbette [ɛr'bɛt], *n.f.* (*Poet.*) short grass, green-sward.
herbeux [ɛr'bø], *a.* (*fem.* **-euse**) grassy, herbous.
herbicide [ɛrbi'sid], *a.* weed-killing.—*n.m.* weed-killer.
herbivore [ɛrbi'vɔːr], *a.* herbivorous.—*n.m.* herbivore.
herboriste [ɛrbɔ'rist], *n.* herbalist, dealer in medicinal herbs.
herbu [ɛr'by], *a.* grassy, covered with grass.
Hercule [ɛr'kyl], *m.* Hercules.
hercule [ɛr'kyl], *n.m.* man of herculean strength; strong-arm man.
herculéen [ɛrkyle'ɛ̃], *a.* (*fem.* **-éenne**) herculean.
†**hère** [ɛːr], *n.m.* ***un pauvre hère***, a sorry fellow, a poor devil.
héréditaire [eredi'tɛːr], *a.* hereditary.
hérédité [eredi'te], *n.f.* hereditary transmission, inheritance *or* succession, hereditary right; heredity.
hérésie [ere'zi], *n.f.* heresy.
hérétique [ere'tik], *a.* heretical.—*n.* heretic.
†**hérissé** [eri'se], *a.* bristling, on end; rough, shaggy; (*Bot.*) hairy, prickly.
†**hérissement** [eris'mɑ̃], *n.m.* bristling, shagginess.
†**hérisser** [eri'se], *v.t.* to bristle, to erect; **se hérisser**, *v.r.* to stand on end, to bristle up; to be bristling with.
†**hérisson** [eri'sɔ̃], *n.m.* hedgehog; (*fig.*) cross-grained person; ***hérisson de mer***, sea-urchin.
héritage [eri'taːʒ], *n.m.* heritage, inheritance, legacy.
hériter [eri'te], *v.t.* to inherit.—*v.i.* to inherit, to be heir (*de*); to succeed.
héritier [eri'tje], *n.m.* (*fem.* **-ière**) heir, heiress.
hermétique [ɛrme'tik], *a.* hermetic, air-tight, water-tight.
hermétiquement [ɛrmetik'mɑ̃], *adv.* hermetically.
hermine [ɛr'min], *n.f.* ermine.
hermitage [ɛrmi'taːʒ], [ERMITAGE].
†**herniaire** [ɛr'njɛːr], *a.* hernial; ***bandage herniaire***, truss.
†**hernie** [ɛr'ni], *n.f.* hernia, rupture.
héroïne [erɔ'in], *n.f.* heroine; (*Chem.*) heroin.
héroïque [erɔ'ik], *a.* heroic.
héroïquement [erɔik'mɑ̃], *adv.* heroically.
héroïsme [erɔ'ism], *n.m.* heroism.
†**héron** [e'rɔ̃], *n.m.* heron.
†**héros** [e'ro], *n.m.* hero.
†**hersage** [ɛr'saːʒ], *n.m.* harrowing.
†**herse** [ɛrs], *n.f.* harrow; portcullis, herse; (*pl.*) (*Theat.*) battens, lights (*above stage*).
†**hersé** [ɛr'se], *a.* harrowed; (*Her.*) represented with a herse.
†**herser** [ɛr'se], *v.t.* to harrow.
hésitant [ezi'tɑ̃], *a.* hesitating, wavering.
hésitation [ezitɑ'sjɔ̃], *n.f.* hesitation.
hésiter [ezi'te], *v.i.* to hesitate, to falter, to pause, to waver.
†**hessois** [ɛ'swa], *a.* Hessian.—*n.m.* (**Hessois**, *fem.* **-oise**) Hessian (*person*).
hétéroclite [eterɔ'klit], *a.* heteroclite, anomalous; irregular.
hétérodoxe [eterɔ'dɔks], *a.* heterodox.
hétérodyne [eterɔ'din], *a.* and *n.f.* (*Rad.*) heterodyne.
hétérogène [eterɔ'ʒɛːn], *a.* heterogeneous; incongruous.
†**hêtre** [ɛːtr], *n.m.* beech, beech-tree.
heure [œːr], *n.f.* hour; o'clock; time of day; moment; (*pl.*) primer (*prayer-book*); ***heures d'affluence*** or ***de pointe***, rush hours, peak periods; (***nouvelles de la***) ***dernière heure***, latest news; ***quelle heure est-il?*** what time is it? ***tout à l'heure***, in a few minutes, just now; ***de bonne heure***, early.
heureusement [œrøz'mɑ̃], *adv.* happily, luckily, fortunately; successfully.
heureux [œ'rø], *a.* (*fem.* **-euse**) happy, blissful; blessed, lucky; successful; pleasing; delighted.
†**heurt** [œːr], *n.m.* blow; knock, shock, collision; bruise.
†**heurté** [œr'te], *a.* abrupt, harsh, jerky (*of style*).
†**heurtement** [œrtə'mɑ̃], *n.m.* clash, collision; hiatus.
†**heurter** [œr'te], *v.t.* to knock against, to strike against; to jostle; to shock, to offend; to jar with.—*v.i.* to strike, to knock, to hit. **se heurter**, *v.r.* to strike *or* hit oneself; to strike against each other; to jostle each other, to clash.
hiatus [ja'tyːs], *n.m.* hiatus; gap.
hibernal [ibɛr'nal], *a.* (*m. pl.* **-aux**) hibernal.
hibernant [ibɛr'nɑ̃], *a.* hibernating.
hibernation [ibɛrnɑ'sjɔ̃], *n.f.* hibernation.
hiberner [ibɛr'ne], *v.i.* to hibernate.
†**hibou** [i'bu], *n.m.* (*pl.* **-oux**) owl; (*fig.*) moper.
†**hic** [ik], *n.m.* knot, difficulty, rub.
†**hideur** [i'dœːr], *n.f.* hideousness.
†**hideusement** [idøz'mɑ̃], *adv.* hideously.
†**hideux** [i'dø], *a.* (*fem.* **-euse**) hideous, frightful, shocking.
hier [jɛːr], *adv.* yesterday; ***avant-hier***, the day before yesterday; ***hier matin***, yesterday morning; ***hier (au) soir***, last night.

†**hiérarchie** [jerar'ʃi], *n.f.* hierarchy.

†**hiérarchique** [jerar'ʃik], *a.* hierarchical.

hiératique [jera'tik], *a.* hieratic.

hiéroglyphe [jerɔ'glif], *n.m.* hieroglyph.

hiéroglyphique [jerɔgli'fik], *a.* hieroglyphical.

Hilaire [i'lɛ:r], *m.* Hilary.

hilarant [ila'rɑ̃], *a.* screamingly funny, rollicking; ***gaz hilarant***, laughing-gas.

hilare [i'la:r], *a.* hilarious.

hilarité [ilari'te], *n.f.* hilarity, mirth, laughter.

hindou [ɛ̃'du], *a.* Hindu; Indian (*of India*).—*n.m.* (**Hindou**, *fem.* **-oue**) Hindu; Indian (*of India*).

hindouisme [ɛ̃du'ism], *n.m.* Hinduism.

hindoustani [ɛ̃dusta'ni], *n.m.* Hindustani, Urdu (*language*).

hippique [i'pik], *a.* hippic; ***concours hippique***, horse-show.

hippodrome [ipɔ'drom], *n.m.* hippodrome, circus; race-course.

hippopotame [ipɔpɔ'tam], *n.m.* hippopotamus.

hirondelle [irɔ̃'dɛl], *n.f.* swallow.

hirsute [ir'syt], *a.* hirsute, hairy; shaggy, dishevelled; (*fig.*) boorish.

†**hisser** [i'se], *v.t.* to hoist, to lift, to run up, to raise. **se hisser**, *v.r.* to raise, hoist *or* lift oneself up.

histoire [is'twa:r], *n.f.* history; tale, story; idle story, untruth, falsehood; trifle; (*pl.*) fuss.

historien [istɔ'rjɛ̃], *n.m.* historian.

historier [istɔ'rje], *v.t.* to illustrate, to embellish, to adorn.

historiette [istɔ'rjɛt], *n.f.* little story, short tale.

historiographe [istɔriɔ'graf], *n.* historiographer.

historique [istɔ'rik], *a.* historic(al).—*n.m.* historical account.

historiquement [istɔrik'mɑ̃], *adv.* historically.

histrion [istri'jɔ̃], *n.m.* histrion, actor; mountebank.

histrionique [istriɔ'nik], *a.* histrionic.

hitlérien [itle'rjɛ̃], *a.* (*fem.* **-enne**) Hitlerite.

hitlérisme [itle'rism], *n.m.* Hitlerism.

hiver [i'vɛ:r], *n.m.* winter.

hivernage [ivɛr'na:ʒ], *n.m.* winter season, winter-time; wintering place.

hivernal [ivɛr'nal], *a.* (*m. pl.* **-aux**) wintry.

hiverner [ivɛr'ne], *v.t.* (*Agric.*) to winter-fallow.—*v.i.* to winter.

†**hobereau** [ɔ'bro], *n.m.* (*pl.* **-eaux**) hobby (*bird*); country squire, squireen.

†**hochement** [ɔʃ'mɑ̃], *n.m.* shaking, tossing, wagging (*of the head*).

†**hochequeue** [ɔʃ'kø], *n.m.* (*Orn.*) wagtail.

†**hocher** [ɔ'ʃe], *v.t.* to shake, to toss; to wag (*the tail etc.*).

†**hochet** [ɔ'ʃɛ], *n.m.* rattle (*for children*); (*fig.*) toy, bauble, plaything.

†**hockey** [ɔ'kɛ], *n.m.* hockey; (*C*) hockey, hockey stick; ***hockey sur glace*** ice-hockey.

†**holà!** [ɔ'la], *int.* stop! hold on! hallo, there! —*n.m.* stop, end; ***mettre le holà***, to put a stop to (*a quarrel*).

†**hollandais** [ɔlɑ̃'dɛ], *a.* Dutch.—*n.m.* Dutch (*language*); (**Hollandais**, *fem.* **-aise**) Dutchman, Dutchwoman.

†**Hollande** [ɔ'lɑ̃:d], **la**, *f.* Holland, the Netherlands.

holocauste [ɔlɔ'ko:st], *n.m.* holocaust, burnt-offering; sacrifice.

†**homard** [ɔ'ma:r], *n.m.* lobster.

homélie [ɔme'li], *n.f.* homily, familiar sermon.

homéopathe [ɔmeɔ'pat], *a.* homoeopathic.—*n.* homoeopath.

homéopathie [ɔmeɔpa'ti], *n.f.* homoeopathy.

homéopathique [ɔmeɔpa'tik], *a.* homoeopathic.

Homère [ɔ'mɛ:r], *m.* Homer.

homérique [ɔme'rik], *a.* Homeric.

homicide [ɔmi'sid], *a.* murderous.—*n.m.* homicide, manslaughter.—*n.* murderer.

hommage [ɔ'ma:ʒ], *n.m.* homage; respect; service; acknowledgment; token, gift; (*pl.*) respects.

homme [ɔm], *n.m.* man; (*colloq.*) husband, old man.

homme-grenouille [ɔmgrə'nu:j], *n.m.* (*pl.* **hommes-grenouilles**) frogman.

homme-sandwich [ɔmsɑ̃'dwitʃ], *n.m.* (*pl.* **hommes-sandwich(e)s**) sandwich man.

homogène [ɔmɔ'ʒɛ:n], *a.* homogeneous.

homogénéité [ɔmɔʒenei'te], *n.f.* homogeneity.

homonyme [ɔmɔ'nim], *a.* homonymous.—*n.m.* homonym; namesake,

†**Honduras** [ɔ̃dy'ras], **le**, *m.* Honduras.

†**hondurien** [ɔ̃dy'rjɛ̃], *a.* (*fem.* **-enne**) Honduran.—*n.m.* (**Hondurien**, *fem.* **-enne**) Honduran (*person*).

†**hongre** [ɔ̃:gr], *a.* gelded.—*n.m.* gelding.

†**hongrer** [ɔ̃'gre], *v.t.* to geld (*a horse*).

†**Hongrie** [ɔ̃'gri], **la**, *f.* Hungary.

†**hongrois** [ɔ̃'grwa], *a.* Hungarian.—*n.m.* Hungarian (*language*); (**Hongrois**, *fem.* **-oise**) Hungarian (*person*).

honnête [ɔ'nɛ:t], *a.* honest, upright; modest (*of women*); respectable; decorous; proper; handsome; reasonable.—*n.m.* honesty, probity.

honnêtement [ɔnɛt'mɑ̃], *adv.* honestly, honourably; virtuously; becomingly; handsomely; suitably; reasonably.

honnêteté [ɔnɛt'te], *n.f.* honesty, integrity; modesty, chastity, virtue; propriety; respectability.

honneur [ɔ'nœ:r], *n.m.* honour; virtue; integrity; repute; credit; distinction; respect; (*Cards*) honour.

†**honnir** [ɔ'ni:r], *v.t.* to dishonour, to disgrace, to cover with shame.

honorabilité [ɔnɔrabili'te], *n.f.* honour, respectability.

honorable [ɔnɔ'rabl], *a.* honourable; respectable, creditable; suitable.

honorablement [ɔnɔrablə'mɑ̃], *adv.* honourably, respectably, creditably; nobly.

honoraire [ɔnɔ'rɛ:r], *a.* honorary, titular.—*n.m.* (*pl.*) honorarium, fee.

honorer [ɔnɔ're], *v.t.* to honour; to do credit to, to be an honour to; ***honorer une traite***, to meet a bill. **s'honorer**, *v.r.* to do oneself honour; to acquire honour; to deem it an honour; to pride oneself.

honorifique [ɔnɔri'fik], *a.* honorary, titular, gratuitous.

†**honte** [ɔ̃:t], *n.f.* shame; disgrace, infamy; reproach; scandal; ***avoir honte de***, to be ashamed of; ***mauvaise honte*** or ***fausse honte***, self-consciousness, bashfulness.
†**honteusement** [ɔ̃tøz'mɑ̃], *adv.* shamefully, disgracefully; infamously.
†**honteux** [ɔ̃'tø], *a.* (*fem.* **-euse**) ashamed; bashful, shy; shameful, disgraceful.
hôpital [ɔpi'tal], *n.m.* (*pl.* **-aux**) hospital.
†**hoquet** [ɔ'kɛ], *n.m.* hiccup.
hoqueter [ɔk'te], *v.i.* (*conjug. like* APPELER) to hiccup.
horaire [ɔ'rɛ:r], *a.* hourly; horary, horal.—*n.m.* time-table, schedule.
†**horde** [ɔrd], *n.f.* horde; pack; rabble.
horizon [ɔri'zɔ̃], *n.m.* horizon, sky-line.
horizontal [ɔrizɔ̃'tal], *a.* (*m. pl.* **-aux**) horizontal.
horizontalement [ɔrizɔ̃tal'mɑ̃], *adv.* horizontally.
horloge [ɔr'lɔ:ʒ], *n.f.* clock; time-keeper.
horloger [ɔrlɔ'ʒe], *a.* (*fem.* **-ère**) pertaining to clock-making.—*n.m.* (*fem.* **-ère**) clock-maker, watch-maker.
horlogerie [ɔrlɔ'ʒri], *n.f.* watch- and clock-making; clocks and watches.
hormis [ɔr'mi], *prep.* except, excepting, but.
hormone [ɔr'mɔn], *n.f.* hormone.
horoscope [ɔrɔs'kɔp], *n.m.* horoscope.
horreur [ɔ'rœ:r], *n.f.* horror, dread; detestation; enormity.
horrible [ɔ'ribl], *a.* horrible, dreadful; hideous, frightful, shocking.
horriblement [ɔriblə'mɑ̃], *adv.* horribly, awfully.
horrifier [ɔri'fje], *v.t.* to horrify.
horrifique [ɔri'fik], *a.* hair-raising.
horripilant [ɔripi'lɑ̃], *a.* exasperating.
horripiler [ɔripi'le], *v.t.* to horripilate; to exasperate.
†**hors** [ɔ:r], *prep.* out of, outside of; beyond, past; but, except, save; ***hors d'affaire***, out of danger; ***hors de combat***, disabled; ***hors de doute***, beyond doubt; ***hors d'ici!*** away with you! out of my sight! ***hors de prix***, exorbitant; ***hors de service***, unserviceable, out of order; ***hors la loi***, outlawed.
†**hors-bord** [ɔr'bɔr], *n.m. inv.* outboard; speed-boat.
†**hors-caste** [ɔr'kast], *a.* and *n. inv.* outcaste, untouchable.
†**hors-d'œuvre** [ɔr'dœ:vr], *n.m. inv.* (*Arch.*) outwork, outbuilding; (*Lit.*) digression, episode; (*Cook.*) dish served at the beginning of a meal.
†**hors-jeu** [ɔr'ʒø], *n.m. inv.* (*Ftb.*) off-side.
†**hors-la-loi** [ɔrla'lwa], *n.m. inv.* outlaw.
hortensia [ɔrtɑ̃'sja], *n.m.* hydrangea.
horticulteur [ɔrtikyl'tœ:r], *n.m.* horticulturist.
horticultural [ɔrtikylty'ral], *a.* (*m. pl.* **-aux**) horticultural.
horticulture [ɔrtikyl'tyr], *n.f.* horticulture.
hospice [ɔs'pis], *n.m.* refuge; asylum; alms-house.
hospitalier [ɔspita'lje], *a.* (*fem.* **-ière**) hospitable.—*n.m.* (*fem.* **-ière**) hospitaller.
hospitalièrement [ɔspitaljɛr'mɑ̃], *adv.* hospitably.
hospitalité [ɔspitali'te], *n.f.* hospitality.
hostellerie [ɔstɛl'ri], *n.f.* inn.
hostie [ɔs'ti], *n.f.* (*Jewish Ant.*) offering, victim, sacrifice; (*R.-C. Ch.*) host.
hostile [ɔs'til], *a.* hostile, adverse.
hostilement [ɔstil'mɑ̃], *adv.* hostilely adversely.
hostilité [ɔstili'te], *n.f.* hostility, enmity.
hôte [o:t], *n.m.* (*fem.* **-esse**) host, hostess; landlord innkeeper; guest; lodger; occupier, inmate.
hôtel [o'tɛl], *n.m.* town mansion, large house; hotel, inn; ***hôtel de ville***, town hall; ***hôtel des ventes***, auction mart; ***hôtel meublé***, furnished lodgings, lodging-house.
hôtelier [otə'lje], *n.m.* (*fem.* **-ière**) innkeeper, host, hostess.
hôtellerie [otɛl'ri], *n.f.* inn, hotel; hotel trade.
hôtesse [o'tɛs], [HÔTE].
†**hotte** [ɔt], *n.f.* basket (*carried on the back*); dosser, hod.
†**hottée** [ɔ'te], *n.f.* basketful.
†**hottentot** [ɔtɑ̃'to], *a.* Hottentot.—*n.m.* (**Hottentot**, *fem.* **-e**) Hottentot (*person*).
†**houage** [wa:ʒ], *n.m.* hoeing.
†**houblon** [u'blɔ̃], *n.m.* (*Bot.*) hop.
†**houblonnière** [ublɔ'njɛ:r], *n.f.* hop-field.
†**houe** [u], *n.f.* hoe.
†**houer** [u'e], *v.t.* to hoe.
†**houille** [u:j], *n.f.* coal, pit-coal.
†**houiller** [u'je], *a.* (*fem.* **-ère**) coal-bearing.—*n.f.* (**-ère**) coal-mine, colliery.
†**houilleur** [u'jœ:r], *n.m.* collier, coal-miner.
†**houilleux** [u'jø], *a.* (*fem.* **-euse**) containing coal.
†**houle** [ul], *n.f.* swell, surge.
†**houlette** [u'lɛt], *n.f.* (shepherd's) crook; crosier.
†**houleux** [u'lø], *a.* (*fem.* **-euse**) swelling, rough (*of sea*).
†**houppe** [up], *n.f.* tuft; top-knot; tassel.
†**houppé** [u'pe], *a.* tufted, crested.
†**houppelande** [u'plɑ̃:d], *n.f.* great-coat, cloak.
†**houpper** [u'pe], *v.t.* to tuft; to comb (*wool*).
†**houppette** [u'pɛt], *n.f.* powder-puff.
†**hourdage** [ur'da:ʒ], †**hourdis** [ur'di], *n.m.* rough-walling; pugging.
†**hourder** [ur'de], *v.t.* to rough-wall; to pug.
†**hourdis** [HOURDAGE].
†**hourra** [u'ra], *n.m.* hurrah.
†**houspiller** [uspi'je], *v.t.* to manhandle, to rough-house; to abuse.
†**housse** [us], *n.f.* housing, horse-cloth; dust-sheet, loose cover.
†**housser** [u'se], *v.t.* to cover up.
†**houssine** [u'sin], *n.f.* switch, riding-switch.
†**houssiner** [usi'ne], *v.t.* to switch; to beat.
†**houx** [u], *n.m.* holly, holly-tree.
†**hoyau** [wa'jo], *n.m.* (*pl.* **-aux**) mattock, grubbing-hoe.
†**huard** [ɥa:r], *n.m.* osprey; sea-eagle.
†**hublot** [y'blo], *n.m.* (*Naut.*) side-light, port-hole.
†**huche** [yʃ], *n.f.* kneading-trough; bread-pan.
†**hue!** [y], *int.* gee! gee-up!
†**huée** [ɥe], *n.f.* whoop, shouting; hooting, booing.
†**huer** [ɥe], *v.t.* to shout after; to hoot at, to boo.—*v.i.* to boo.

†**huguenot** [yg'no], *a.* Huguenot.—*n.m.* (**Huguenot**, *fem.* **-e**) Huguenot (*person*).

huilage [ɥi'la:ʒ], *n.m.* oiling.

huile [ɥil], *n.f.* oil.

huiler [ɥi'le], *v.t.* to oil; to anoint with oil; to lubricate.—*v.i.* (*Bot.*) to exude oil.

huilerie [ɥil'ri], *n.f.* oil-works.

huileux [ɥi'lø], *a.* (*fem.* **-euse**) oily, greasy.

huilier [ɥi'lje], *n.m.* cruet-stand; oil-merchant.

†***huis** [ɥi], *n.m.* door; ***à huis clos***, behind closed doors, in camera.

huisserie [ɥis'ri], *n.f.* door-frame.

huissier [ɥi'sje], *n.m.* usher; gentleman-usher; door-keeper; sheriff's officer, bailiff.

†**huit** [ɥit], *a.* and *n.m.* eight; eighth.

†**huitaine** [ɥi'tɛn], *n.f.* eight days, week.

†**huitième** [ɥi'tjɛm], *a.* eighth.—*n.m.* eighth, eighth part.

†**huitièmement** [ɥitjɛm'mɑ̃], *adv.* eighthly.

huître [ɥitr], *n.f.* oyster; (*fig.*) blockhead, dunce.

huîtrier [ɥit'rje], *n.m.* (*Orn.*) oyster-catcher.

huîtrière [ɥitri'ɛ:r], *n.f.* oyster-bed.

hululer [ULULER].

humain [y'mɛ̃], *a.* human; humane, benevolent.—*n.m.* humanity, mankind.

humainement [ymɛn'mɑ̃], *adv.* humanly; humanely.

humaniser [ymani'ze], *v.t.* to humanize, to civilize. **s'humaniser**, *v.r.* to become humanized.

humanisme [yma'nism], *n.m.* humanism.

humaniste [yma'nist], *a.* and *n.* humanist; classical scholar.

humanitaire [ymani'tɛ:r], *a.* and *n.* humanitarian.

humanité [ymani'te], *n.f.* humanity; human nature; mankind.

humble [œ̃:bl], *a.* humble, meek, modest.

humblement [œ̃mblə'mɑ̃], *adv.* humbly, meekly.

humectant [ymɛk'tɑ̃], *a.* refreshing, moistening.—*n.m.* humectant.

humectation [ymɛktɑ'sjɔ̃], *n.f.* moistening.

humecter [ymɛk'te], *v.t.* to damp, to moisten, to refresh. **s'humecter**, *v.r.* to be moistened; to refresh oneself.

†**humer** [y'me], *v.t.* to inhale.

humeur [y'mœ:r], *n.f.* humour; temperament, disposition; mood, fancy; ill-humour.

humide [y'mid], *a.* damp, wet, moist, humid.

humidité [ymidi'te], *n.f.* humidity, moisture, dampness.

humiliant [ymi'ljɑ̃], *a.* humiliating, degrading.

humiliation [ymiljɑ'sjɔ̃], *n.f.* humiliation, abasement.

humilier [ymi'lje], *v.t.* to humble, to humiliate. **s'humilier**, *v.r.* to humble *or* abase oneself.

humilité [ymili'te], *n.f.* humility, meekness, lowliness.

humoriste [ymɔ'rist], *a.* humorous.—*n.* humorist.

humoristique [ymɔris'tik] *a.* humorous (*writer etc.*).

humour [y'mur], *n.m.* humour.

humus [y'mys], *n.m.* humus, mould.

†**hune** [yn], *n.f.* (*Naut.*) top.

†**hunier** [y'nje], *n.m.* topsail.

†**huppe** [yp], *n.f.* hoopoe; tuft, crest.

†**huppé** [y'pe], *a.* tufted, crested (*of birds*); (*colloq.*) well off, smartly dressed.

†**hurlement** [yrlə'mɑ̃], *n.m.* howling; howl, roar, yell.

†**hurler** [yr'le], *v.i.* to howl, to yell; to roar; ***hurler avec les loups***, to do as others do.

†**hurleur** [yr'lœ:r], *a.* (*fem.* **-euse** howling.—*n.m.* (*fem.* **-euse**) howler.

hurluberlu [yrlybɛr'ly], *n.* hare-brained person, harum-scarum.

†**hussard** [y'sa:r], *n.m.* hussar.

†**hutte** [yt], *n.f.* hut, cabin, shanty.

hyacinthe [ja'sɛ̃:t], *n.f.* jacinth; hyacinth.

hybride [i'brid], *a.* and *n.m.* hybrid, mongrel.

hydrangée [idrɑ̃'ʒe], *n.f.* (*Bot.*) hydrangea.

hydrater [idra'te], *v.t.* to hydrate.

hydraulique [idro'lik], *a.* hydraulic.—*n.f.* hydraulics.

hydravion [idra'vjɔ̃], *n.m.* flying-boat, seaplane.

hydre [idr], *n.f.* hydra.

hydro-électrique [idrɔelɛk'trik], *a.* hydro-electric.

hydrogène [idrɔ'ʒɛ:n], *n.m.* hydrogen.

hydrophobe [idrɔ'fɔb], *a.* and *n.* hydrophobic (person).

hydrophobie [idrɔfɔ'bi], *n.f.* hydrophobia, rabies.

hydropique [idrɔ'pik], *a.* and *n.* dropsical (person).

hydropisie [idrɔpi'zi], *n.f.* dropsy.

hydroplane [idrɔ'plan], *n.m.* hydroplane.

hydroscope [idrɔs'kɔp], *n.m.* water-diviner.

hyène [jɛ:n], *n.f.* hyena.

hygiène [i'ʒjɛ:n], *n.f.* hygiene.

hygiénique [iʒje'nik], *a.* hygienic; sanitary.

hymen [i'mɛn], **hyménée** [ime'ne], *n.m.* hymen, marriage, wedlock.

hymnaire [im'nɛ:r], *n.m.* hymn-book, hymnal.

hymne [imn], *n.m.* (*patriotic*) song, anthem.—*n.f.* hymn.

hyperbole [ipɛr'bɔl], *n.f.* hyperbole, exaggeration; (*Math.*) hyperbola.

hyperbolique [ipɛrbɔ'lik], *a.* hyperbolic.

hypermétrope [ipɛrme'trɔp], *a.* long-sighted.

hypersensible [ipɛrsɑ̃'sibl], *a.* over-sensitive.

hypertension [ipɛrtɑ̃'sjɔ̃], *n.f.* high blood-pressure.

hypnose [ip'no:z], *n.f.* hypnosis.

hypnotique [ipnɔ'tik], *a.* and *n.m.* hypnotic.

hypnotiser [ipnɔti'ze], *v.t.* to hypnotize; to fascinate.

hypnotiseur [ipnɔti'zœ:r], *n.m.* (*fem.* **-euse**) hypnotist.

hypnotisme [ipnɔ'tism], *n.m.* hypnotism.

hypocondriaque [ipɔkɔ̃'driak], *a.* and *n.* hypochondriac.

hypocondrie [ipɔkɔ̃'dri], *n.f.* hypochondria.

hypocrisie [ipɔkri'zi], *n.f.* hypocrisy.

hypocrite [ipɔ'krit], *a.* hypocritical.—*n.* hypocrite.

hypodermique [ipɔdɛr'mik], *a.* hypodermic, under the skin.

hypotension [ipɔtɑ̃'sjɔ̃], *n.f.* low blood-pressure.

hypothécaire [ipɔte'kɛ:r], *a.* on mortgage.

hypothèque [ipɔ'tɛk], *n.f.* mortgage.

hypothéquer [ipɔte'ke], *v.t.* (*conjug. like* CÉDER) to mortgage.

hypothèse [ipɔ'tɛ:z], *n.f.* hypothesis, supposition.

hypothétique [ipote'tik], *a.* hypothetical.
hystérie [iste'ri], *n.f.* hysteria.
hystérique [iste'rik], *a.* hysteric, hysterical.

I

I, i [i], *n.m.* the ninth letter of the alphabet.
iceberg [is'bɛrg], *n.m.* iceberg.
ici [i'si], *adv.* here, in this place; hither; now, this time.
iconoclaste [ikɔnɔ'klast], *a.* iconoclastic.—*n.* iconoclast.
iconolâtre [ikɔnɔ'lɑ:tr], *n.m.* image-worshipper.
iconolâtrie [ikɔnɔlɑ'tri], *n.f.* image-worship.
idéal [ide'al], *a.* (*m. pl.* **-aux**) ideal; unreal, imaginary.—*n.m.* (*pl.* **-als** or **-aux**) ideal.
idéalement [ideal'mɑ̃], *adv.* ideally.
idéaliser [ideali'ze], *v.t.* to idealize.
idéalisme [idea'lism], *n.m.* idealism.
idéaliste [idea'list], *a.* idealistic.—*n.* idealist.
idée [i'de], *n.f.* idea; notion; conception; opinion; plan; fancy; sketch, suggestion.
idem [i'dɛm], *adv.* idem, ditto.
identification [idɑ̃tifikɑ'sjɔ̃], *n.f.* identification.
identifier [idɑ̃ti'fje], *v.t.* to identify. **s'identifier**, *v.r.* to identify oneself.
identique [idɑ̃'tik], *a.* identical, the same.
identiquement [idɑ̃tik'mɑ̃], *adv.* identically.
identité [idɑ̃ti'te], *n.f.* identity.
idéologie [ideɔlɔ'ʒi], *n.f.* ideology.
idéologique [ideɔlɔ'ʒik], *a.* ideological.
idéologue [ideɔ'lɔg], *n.m.* ideologist.
ides [id], *n.f. pl.* Ides (15 March etc.).
idiomatique [idjɔma'tik], *a.* idiomatic.
idiome [i'djo:m], *n.m.* idiom, dialect.
idiosyncrasie [idjɔsɛ̃kra'zi], *n.f.* idiosyncrasy.
idiot [i'djo], *a.* idiotic, absurd.—*n.m.* (*fem.* **-e**) idiot, imbecile, fool.
idiotie [idjɔ'si], *n.f.* idiocy, imbecility.
idiotisme [idjɔ'tism], *n.m.* (*Gram.*) idiom; (*Path.*) idiocy.
idolâtre [idɔ'lɑ:tr], *a.* idolatrous.—*n.* idolater.
idolâtrer [idɔlɑ'tre], *v.t.* to idolize, to dote upon.
idolâtrie [idɔlɑ'tri], *n.f.* idolatry.
idole [i'dɔl], *n.f.* idol.
idylle [i'dil], *n.f.* idyll.
idyllique [idi'lik], *a.* idyllic.
if [if], *n.m.* yew, yew-tree.
igloo or **iglou** [i'glu], *n.m.* igloo.
ignare [i'ɲa:r], *a.* illiterate, ignorant.—*n.* dunce, ignoramus.
igné [ig'ne], *a.* igneous.
ignifuge [igni'fy:ʒ], *a.* fire-resisting, fireproof; ***grenade ignifuge***, fire-extinguisher.
ignifuger [ignify'ʒe], *v.t.* (*conjug. like* MANGER) to fireproof.
ignition [igni'sjɔ̃], *n.f.* ignition.
ignoble [i'ɲɔbl], *a.* ignoble; vile, base; beastly, filthy.
ignoblement [iɲɔblə'mɑ̃], *adv.* ignobly, vilely, basely.
ignominie [iɲɔmi'ni], *n.f.* ignominy, shame, dishonour.
ignominieusement [iɲɔminjøz'mɑ̃], *adv.* ignominiously.
ignominieux [iɲɔmi'njø], *a.* (*fem.* **-euse**) ignominious.
ignorance [iɲɔ'rɑ̃:s], *n.f.* ignorance; error, mistake, blunder.
ignorant [iɲɔ'rɑ̃], *a.* ignorant, illiterate, unlearned.—*n.m.* (*fem.* **-e**) ignoramus.
ignorer [iɲɔ're], *v.t.* to be ignorant of, not to know, not to be aware of. **s'ignorer**, *v.r.* not to know oneself; to be ignorant of one's own capabilities.
iguane [i'gwan], *n.m.* iguana.
il [il], *pron. m.* (*pl.* **ils**) he; it; there; (*pl.*) they.
île [il], *n.f.* island, isle.
illégal [ille'gal], *a.* (*m. pl.* **-aux**) illegal, unlawful.
illégalement [illegal'mɑ̃], *adv.* illegally.
illégalité [illegali'te], *n.f.* illegality.
illégitime [illeʒi'tim], *a.* illegitimate; unlawful, unjust.
illégitimement [illeʒitim'mɑ̃], *adv.* illegitimately, unlawfully.
illégitimité [illeʒitimi'te], *n.f.* illegitimacy; unlawfulness; spuriousness.
illettré [illɛ'tre], *a.* and *n.m.* (*fem.* **-ée**) illiterate, unlettered (person).
illicite [illi'sit], *a.* illicit, unlawful.
illicitement [illisit'mɑ̃], *adv.* illicitly, unlawfully.
illimitable [illimi'tabl], *a.* illimitable.
illimité [illimi'te], *a.* unlimited, unbounded, boundless.
illisibilité [illizibili'te], *n.f.* illegibility.
illisible [illi'zibl], *a.* illegible.
illisiblement [illiziblə'mɑ̃], *adv.* illegibly.
illogique [illɔ'ʒik], *a.* illogical.
illogiquement [illɔʒik'mɑ̃], *adv.* illogically.
illuminant [illymi'nɑ̃], *a.* illuminating.—*n.m.* illuminant.
illuminateur [illymina'tœ:r], *n.m.* illuminator, enlightener.
illumination [ilyminɑ'sjɔ̃], *n.f.* illumination.
illuminé [illymi'ne], *a.* illuminated, enlightened.—*n.m.* (*fem.* **-ée**) visionary, fanatic.
illuminer [illymi'ne], *v.t.* to illuminate, to illumine, to light up; to enlighten (*the mind etc.*). **s'illuminer**, *v.r.* to light *or* brighten up.
illusion [illy'zjɔ̃], *n.f.* illusion, self-deception, delusion; fallacy, chimera.
illusionner [illyzjɔ'ne], *v.t.* to delude, to deceive.
illusionniste [illyzjɔ'nist], *n.m.* conjurer.
illusoire [illy'zwa:r], *a.* illusive, illusory, delusive.
illusoirement [illyzwar'mɑ̃], *adv.* illusively.
illustration [illystrɑ'sjɔ̃], *n.f.* illustriousness, renown; explanation; illustration.
illustre [il'lystr], *a.* illustrious, famous.
illustrer [illys'tre], *v.t.* to do honour to; to illustrate, to make clear. **s'illustrer**, *v.r.* to win fame.
illustrissime [illystri'sim], *a.* most illustrious.
îlot [i'lo], *n.m.* islet (*in sea*); holm (*in river*); block (*of houses*).
ilote [i'lɔt], *n.m.* helot.
ils [il], *pl. pron.* [IL].
image [i'ma:ʒ], *n.f.* image; likeness; picture; statue.

imaginable [imaʒi'nabl], *a.* imaginable.
imaginaire [imaʒi'nɛ:r], *a.* imaginary, visionary, unreal, fantastic.
imaginatif [imaʒina'tif], *a.* (*fem.* **-tive**) imaginative.
imagination [imaʒinɑ'sjɔ̃], *n.f.* imagination; conception, thought; fancy.
imaginer [imaʒi'ne], *v.t.* to imagine, to conceive; to fancy, to suppose; to devise. **s'imaginer**, *v.r.* to imagine oneself; to imagine, to fancy, to surmise.
imbécile [ɛ̃be'sil], *a.* imbecile; foolish, idiotic.—*n.* imbecile, idiot; fool.
imbécilement [ɛ̃besil'mɑ̃], *adv.* foolishly.
imbécillité [ɛ̃besili'te], *n.f.* imbecility, idiocy; stupidity.
imberbe [ɛ̃'bɛrb], *a.* beardless; (*fig.*) green.
imbiber [ɛ̃bi'be], *v.t.* to imbibe; to imbue; to steep. **s'imbiber**, *v.r.* to imbibe, to drink in.
imbroglio [ɛ̃brɔ'ljo], *n.m.* imbroglio, intricacy.
imbu [ɛ̃'by], *a.* imbued, saturated.
imbuvable [ɛ̃by'vabl], *a.* undrinkable.
imitable [imi'tabl], *a.* imitable.
imitateur [imita'tœ:r], *a.* (*fem.* **-trice**) imitative.—*n.m.* (*fem.* **-trice**) imitator.
imitatif [imita'tif], *a.* (*fem.* **-tive**) imitative.
imitation [imitɑ'sjɔ̃], *n.f.* imitation.
imiter [imi'te], *v.t.* to imitate, to copy; to mimic; to resemble.
immaculé [immaky'le], *a.* immaculate, spotless.
immanent [imma'nɑ̃], *a.* immanent.
immangeable [ɛ̃mɑ̃'ʒabl, imɑ̃'ʒabl], *a.* uneatable.
immanquable [ɛ̃mɑ̃'kabl], *a.* infallible, certain, sure.
immanquablement [ɛ̃mɑ̃kablə'mɑ̃], *adv.* infallibly, certainly, without fail.
immatériel [immate'rjɛl], *a.* (*fem.* **-elle**) immaterial, incorporeal.
immatriculation [immatrikylɑ'sjɔ̃], *n.f.* matriculation; registering; enrolment; (*Motor.*) ***plaque d'immatriculation***, number plate.
immatriculé [immatriky'le], *a.* registered; matriculated.
immatriculer [immatriky'le], *v.t.* to matriculate; to register.
immaturité [immatyri'te], *n.f.* unripeness; immaturity.
immédiat [imme'dja], *a.* immediate.
immédiatement [immedjat'mɑ̃] *adv.* immediately.
immémorial [immemɔ'rjal], *a.* (*m. pl.* **-aux** immemorial.
immense [im'mɑ̃:s], *a.* immense, immeasurable; boundless, huge.
immensément [immɑ̃se'mɑ̃], *adv.* immensely.
immensité [immɑ̃si'te], *n.f.* immensity.
immerger [immɛr'ʒe], *v.t.* (*conjug. like* MANGER) to immerse, to plunge.
immérité [immeri'te], *a.* undeserved, unmerited, unjust.
immersion [immɛr'sjɔ̃], *n.f.* immersion; submergence; committal to the deep.
immesurable [imməzy'rabl], *a.* unmeasurable, immeasurable.
immeuble [im'mœbl], *a.* fixed, real (*of estate*).—*n.m.* real estate; property; premises.
immigrant [immi'grɑ̃], *a.* and *n.m.* (*fem.* **-e**) immigrant.
immigration [immigrɑ'sjɔ̃], *n.f.* immigration.
immigrer [immi'gre], *v.i.* to immigrate.
imminence [immi'nɑ̃:s], *n.f.* imminence.
imminent [immi'nɑ̃], *a.* imminent, impending.
immiscer (s') [simmi'se], *v.r.* (*conjug. like* COMMENCER) to interfere.
immobile [immɔ'bil], *a.* motionless, still; (*fig.*) firm, immovable, unshaken.
immobilier [immɔbi'lje], *a.* (*fem.* **-ière**) real, landed (*of estate*); ***agent immobilier***, estate agent; ***société immobilière***, building society.
immobilisation [immɔbilizɑ'sjɔ̃], *n.f.* immobilization; (*Law*) conversion of movable property into real estate.
immobiliser [immɔbili'ze], *v.t.* to immobilize; to convert into real estate, to tie up (*capital*).
immobilité [immɔbili'te], *n.f.* immobility, immovability.
immodération [immɔderɑ'sjɔ̃], *n.f.* immoderation.
immodéré [immɔde're], *a.* immoderate, excessive, violent.
immodérément [immɔdere'mɑ̃], *adv.* immoderately, intemperately; excessively.
immodeste [immɔ'dɛst], *a.* immodest, indecent.
immodestement [immɔdɛstə'mɑ̃], *adv.* immodestly.
immodestie [immɔdɛs'ti], *n.f.* immodesty.
immolation [immɔlɑ'sjɔ̃], *n.f.* immolation; (*fig.*) sacrifice.
immoler [immɔ'le], *v.t.* to immolate, to sacrifice; to slay. **s'immoler**, *v.r.* to immolate *or* sacrifice oneself.
immonde [im'mɔ̃:d], *a.* unclean, impure.
immondice [immɔ̃'dis], *n.f.* (*usu. in pl.*) filth, dirt; rubbish.
immoral [immɔ'ral], *a.* (*m. pl.* **-aux**) immoral.
immoralité [immɔrali'te], *n.f.* immorality.
immortaliser [immɔrtali'ze], *v.t.* to immortalize. **s'immortaliser**, *v.r.* to immortalize oneself.
immortalité [immɔrtali'te], *n.f.* immortality.
immortel [immɔr'tɛl], *a.* (*fem.* **-elle**) immortal, everlasting.
immuable [im'mɥabl], *a.* immutable, unalterable, unchangeable.
immuablement [immɥablə'mɑ̃], *adv.* immutably, unalterably, unchangeably.
immunisation [immynizɑ'sjɔ̃], *n.f.* (*Med.*) immunization.
immuniser [immyni'ze], *v.t.* to immunize.
immunité [immyni'te], *n.f.* immunity; privilege; exemption.
immutabilité [immytabili'te], *n.f.* immutability, unchangeableness, fixity.
impact [ɛ̃'pakt], *n.m.* impact; hit.
impaction [ɛ̃pak'sjɔ̃], *n.f.* (*Surg.*) impaction.
impair [ɛ̃'pɛ:r], *a.* odd, uneven.—*n.m.* blunder, bloomer.
impalpabilité [ɛ̃palpabili'te], *n.f.* impalpability.
impalpable [ɛ̃pal'pabl], *a.* impalpable.
impardonnable [ɛ̃pardɔ'nabl], *a.* unpardonable, unforgivable.

imparfait [ɛ̃par'fɛ], *a.* imperfect, incomplete, defective.—*n.m.* (*Gram.*) imperfect (tense).
imparfaitement [ɛ̃parfɛt'mɑ̃], *adv.* imperfectly.
imparité [ɛ̃pari'te], *n.f.* imparity, inequality; oddness.
impartageable [ɛ̃parta'ʒabl], *a.* indivisible.
impartial [ɛ̃par'sjal], *a.* (*m. pl.* **-aux**) impartial.
impartialement [ɛ̃parsjal'mɑ̃], *adv.* impartially, even-handedly.
impartialité [ɛ̃parsjali'te], *n.f.* impartiality.
impasse [ɛ̃'pɑːs], *n.f.* blind alley, cul-de-sac; deadlock, dilemma.
impassibilité [ɛ̃pɑsibili'te], *n.f.* impassibility, insensibility.
impassible [ɛ̃pɑ'sibl], *a.* impassive, unmoved.
impassiblement [ɛ̃pɑsiblə'mɑ̃], *adv.* impassively, impassibly.
impatiemment [ɛ̃pasja'mɑ̃], *adv.* impatiently, eagerly.
impatience [ɛ̃pa'sjɑ̃ːs], *n.f.* impatience; restlessness; eagerness, longing.
impatient [ɛ̃pa'sjɑ̃], *a.* impatient; anxious, restless, eager.
impatientant [ɛ̃pasjɑ̃'tɑ̃], *a.* provoking, vexing, tiresome.
impatienter [ɛ̃pasjɑ̃'te], *v.t.* to make impatient, to put out of patience; to provoke. **s'impatienter**, *v.r.* to lose one's patience; to fret, to worry.
impayable [ɛ̃pɛ'jabl], *a.* invaluable, priceless; inimitable, extraordinarily funny.
impayé [ɛ̃pɛ'je], *a.* unpaid.
impeccabilité [ɛ̃pɛkabili'te], *n.f.* impeccability.
impeccable [ɛ̃pɛ'kabl], *a.* impeccable, faultless.
impécunieux [ɛ̃peky'njø], *a.* (*fem.* **-euse**) impecunious.
impénétrabilité [ɛ̃penetrabili'te], *n.f.* impenetrability, imperviousness.
impénétrable [ɛ̃pene'trabl], *a.* impenetrable, impervious; inscrutable.
impénitence [ɛ̃peni'tɑ̃ːs], *n.f.* impenitence, obduracy.
impénitent [ɛ̃peni'tɑ̃], *a.* and *n.m.* (*fem.* **-e**) impenitent, obdurate (person).
impératif [ɛ̃pera'tif], *a.* (*fem.* **-tive**) imperative, peremptory.—*n.m.* (*Gram.*) imperative.
impérativement [ɛ̃perativ'mɑ̃], *adv.* imperatively.
impératrice [ɛ̃pera'tris], *n.f.* empress.
imperceptible [ɛ̃pɛrsɛp'tibl], *a.* imperceptible, unperceivable.
imperceptiblement [ɛ̃pɛrsɛptiblə'mɑ̃], *adv.* imperceptibly.
imperfectible [ɛ̃pɛrfɛk'tibl], *a.* imperfectible.
imperfection [ɛ̃pɛrfɛk'sjɔ̃], *n.f.* imperfection, defect, flaw.
impérial [ɛ̃pe'rjal], *a.* (*m. pl.* **-aux**) imperial.
impériale [ɛ̃pe'rjal], *n.f.* top, outside (*of a coach*); imperial (*small beard under the lip*).
impérieusement [ɛ̃perjøz'mɑ̃], *adv.* imperiously.
impérieux [ɛ̃pe'rjø], *a.* (*fem.* **-euse**) imperious, supercilious, haughty, lordly.
impérissable [ɛ̃peri'sabl], *a.* imperishable.
impérissablement [ɛ̃perisablə'mɑ̃], *adv.* imperishably.
impéritie [ɛ̃peri'si], *n.f.* incapacity, incompetence.
imperméabilité [ɛ̃pɛrmeabili'te], *n.f.* impermeability.
imperméable [ɛ̃pɛrme'abl], *a.* impermeable, impervious.—*n.m.* raincoat, mackintosh.
impersonnalité [ɛ̃pɛrsɔnali'te], *n.f.* impersonality.
impersonnel [ɛ̃pɛrsɔ'nɛl], *a.* (*fem.* **-elle**) impersonal.—*n.m.* (*Gram.*) impersonal verb.
impersonnellement [ɛ̃pɛrsɔnɛl'mɑ̃], *adv.* impersonally.
impertinemment [ɛ̃pɛrtina mɑ̃], *adv.* impertinently.
impertinence [ɛ̃pɛrti'nɑ̃ːs], *n.f.* impertinence, insolence; silliness.
impertinent [ɛ̃pɛrti'nɑ̃], *a.* impertinent, insolent, pert.—*n.m.* (*fem.* **-e**) impertinent, saucy person.
imperturbabilité [ɛ̃pɛrtyrbabili'te], *n.f.* imperturbability.
imperturbable [ɛ̃pɛrtyr'babl], *a.* imperturbable.
imperturbablement [ɛ̃pɛrtyrbablə'mɑ̃], *adv.* imperturbably.
impétigo [ɛ̃peti'go], *n.m.* (*Med.*) impetigo.
impétueusement [ɛ̃petɥøz'mɑ̃], *adv.* impetuously.
impétueux [ɛ̃pe'tɥø], *a.* (*fem.* **-euse**) impetuous, vehement, violent.
impétuosité [ɛ̃petɥɔzi'te], *n.f.* impetuosity, vehemence; impetus.
impie [ɛ̃'pi], *a.* impious, godless; irreligious.—*n.* impious, ungodly *or* irreligious person.
impiété [ɛ̃pje'te], *n.f.* impiety, godlessness.
impitoyable [ɛ̃pitwa'jabl], *a.* pitiless, merciless, ruthless; unrelenting.
impitoyablement [ɛ̃pitwajablə'mɑ̃], *adv.* pitilessly.
implacabilité [ɛ̃plakabili'te], *n.f.* implacability.
implacable [ɛ̃pla'kabl], *a.* implacable.
implacablement [ɛ̃plakablə'mɑ̃], *adv.* implacably.
implantation [ɛ̃plɑ̃tɑ'sjɔ̃], *n.f.* implantation.
implanter [ɛ̃plɑ̃'te], *v.t.* to implant; to plant. **s'implanter**, *v.r.* to be implanted, fixed, rooted *or* lodged.
implication [ɛ̃plikɑ'sjɔ̃], *n.f.* implication, involving; discrepancy.
implicite [ɛ̃pli'sit], *a.* implicit.
implicitement [ɛ̃plisit'mɑ̃], *adv.* implicitly.
impliquer [ɛ̃pli'ke], *v.t.* to implicate, to involve, to entangle; to imply.
implorateur [ɛ̃plɔra'tœːr], *n.m.* (*fem.* **-trice**) implorer, supplicant.
imploration [ɛ̃plɔrɑ'sjɔ̃], *n.f.* supplication, imploration.
implorer [ɛ̃plɔ're], *v.t.* to implore, to entreat, to beseech; to crave.
imployable [ɛ̃plwa'jabl], *a.* unbending.
impoli [ɛ̃pɔ'li], *a.* impolite, discourteous, uncivil, rude.
impoliment [ɛ̃pɔli'mɑ̃], *adv.* impolitely, discourteously.
impolitesse [ɛ̃pɔli'tɛs], *n.f.* impoliteness, incivility; rudeness.
impolitique [ɛ̃pɔli'tik], *a.* impolitic, ill-advised.

impolitiquement [ɛ̃pɔlitik'mɑ̃], *adv.* unwisely.
impopulaire [ɛ̃pɔpy'lɛːr], *a.* unpopular.
impopularité [ɛ̃pɔpylari'te], *n.f.* unpopularity.
importable [ɛ̃pɔr'tabl], *a.* importable.
importance [ɛ̃pɔr'tɑ̃ːs], *n.f.* importance, consequence; authority, credit; self-conceit.
important [ɛ̃pɔr'tɑ̃], *a.* important, of consequence, weighty.—*n.m.* the essential, the main point; (*fem.* **-e**) person of importance.
importateur [ɛ̃pɔrta'tœːr], *a.* (*fem.* **-trice**) importing.—*n.m.* (*fem.* **-trice**) importer.
importation [ɛ̃pɔrtɑ'sjɔ̃], *n.f.* importation; (*pl.*) imports.
importer [ɛ̃pɔr'te], *v.t.* to import; (*fig.*) to introduce.—*v.i.* to import, to be of moment, to matter; ***n'importe***, no matter, never mind; ***n'importe où***, anywhere; ***n'importe qui***, anyone; ***n'importe quoi***, anything; ***peu importe***, it does not much matter; ***venez n'importe quand***, come when you like.
importun [ɛ̃pɔr'tœ̃], *a.* importunate, tiresome, obtrusive, irksome.—*n.m.* (*fem.* **-e**) tiresome person; intruder, bore.
importuner [ɛ̃pɔrty'ne], *v.t.* to importune, to pester; to inconvenience; to tease.
importunité [ɛ̃pɔrtyni'te], *n.f.* importunity.
imposable [ɛ̃po'zabl], *a.* taxable.
imposant [ɛ̃po'zɑ̃], *a.* imposing, impressive, striking.
imposer [ɛ̃po'ze], *v.t.* to lay on (*hands*); to impose, to tax; to force (à).—*v.i.* or **en imposer**, to awe, to overawe. **s'imposer**, *v.r.* to assert oneself; to thrust oneself (*upon somebody*); to be indispensable.
imposition [ɛ̃pozi'sjɔ̃], *n.f.* imposition, laying on (*of hands*); tax, assessment.
impossibilité [ɛ̃pɔsibili'te], *n.f.* impossibility.
impossible [ɛ̃pɔ'sibl], *a.* impossible.—*n.m.* one's utmost, a great deal.
imposte [ɛ̃'pɔst], *n.f.* (*Arch.*) impost, fanlight.
imposteur [ɛ̃pɔs'tœːr], *n.m.* impostor, cheat.
imposture [ɛ̃pɔs'tyːr], *n.f.* imposture, deception.
impôt [ɛ̃'po], *n.m.* tax, duty, impost; ***percevoir les impôts***, to collect the taxes.
impotence [ɛ̃pɔ'tɑ̃ːs], *n.f.* helplessness, infirmity.
impotent [ɛ̃pɔ'tɑ̃], *a.* infirm, crippled.—*n.m.* (*fem.* **-e**) cripple, helpless invalid.
impraticabilité [ɛ̃pratikabili'te], *n.f.* impracticability.
impraticable [ɛ̃prati'kabl], *a.* impracticable; impassable; unmanageable.
imprécation [ɛ̃prekɑ'sjɔ̃], *n.f.* imprecation, curse.
imprécatoire [ɛ̃preka'twaːr], *a.* imprecatory.
imprécis [ɛ̃pre'si], *a.* unprecise, indefinite (*words*); (*Mil.*) inaccurate (*fire*).
imprécision [ɛ̃presi'zjɔ̃], *n.f.* lack of precision, vagueness (*of statement*); looseness (*of terms*); (*Mil.*) inaccuracy (*in firing*).
imprégnation [ɛ̃preɲɑ'sjɔ̃], *n.f.* impregnation.
imprégner [ɛ̃pre'ɲe], *v.t.* (*conjug. like* CÉDER) to impregnate; (*fig.*) to imbue. **s'imprégner**, *v.r.* to become impregnated; to be imbued.
imprenable [ɛ̃prə'nabl], *a.* impregnable.
impressif [ɛ̃prɛ'sif], *a.* (*fem.* **-ive**) impressive, striking.
impression [ɛ̃prɛ'sjɔ̃], *n.f.* impression; mark; stamp; print; edition; ***faute d'impression***, misprint.
impressionnable [ɛ̃prɛsjɔ'nabl], *a.* impressionable, sensitive.
impressionnant [ɛ̃prɛsjɔ'nɑ̃], *a.* impressive.
impressionner [ɛ̃prɛsjɔ'ne], *v.t.* to move, to affect, to impress.
impressionnisme [ɛ̃prɛsjɔ'nism], *n.m.* impressionism.
impressionniste [ɛ̃prɛsjɔ'nist], *a.* and *n.* impressionist.
imprévisible [ɛ̃previ'zibl], *a.* unforeseeable.
imprévoyance [ɛ̃prevwa'jɑ̃ːs], *n.f.* want of foresight, improvidence.
imprévoyant [ɛ̃prevwa'jɑ̃], *a.* improvident.
imprévu [ɛ̃pre'vy], *a.* unforeseen, unexpected.
imprimable [ɛ̃pri'mabl], *a.* fit to be printed.
imprimé [ɛ̃pri'me], *n.m.* printed book, paper, document etc.; ***service des imprimés***, book-post.
imprimer [ɛ̃pri'me], *v.t.* to imprint, to impress, to stamp; to print; to instil; to impart. **s'imprimer**, *v.r.* to be printed.
imprimerie [ɛ̃prim'ri], *n.f.* printing; printing-office, printing establishment.
imprimeur [ɛ̃pri'mœːr], *n.m.* printer; (*Print.*) press-man.
improbabilité [ɛ̃prɔbabili'te], *n.f.* improbability, unlikelihood.
improbable [ɛ̃prɔ'babl], *a.* improbable, unlikely.
improbablement [ɛ̃prɔbablə'mɑ̃], *adv.* improbably.
improbité [ɛ̃prɔbi'te], *n.f.* improbity, dishonesty.
improductible [ɛ̃prɔdyk'tibl], *a.* unproducible.
improductif [ɛ̃prɔdyk'tif], *a.* (*fem.* **-tive**) unproductive, idle.
impromptu [ɛ̃prɔ̃p'ty], *a. inv.* impromptu, extemporary.—*n.m.* impromptu.—*adv.* offhand, extempore.
imprononçable [ɛ̃prɔnɔ̃'sabl], *a.* unpronounceable (*word*).
impropre [ɛ̃'prɔpr], *a.* improper, wrong; unfit.
improprement [ɛ̃prɔprə'mɑ̃], *adv.* improperly.
impropriété [ɛ̃prɔprie'te], *n.f.* impropriety; unfitness.
improvisateur [ɛ̃prɔviza'tœːr], *n.m.* (*fem.* **-trice**) improviser, extemporary speaker.
improvisation [ɛ̃prɔvizɑ'sjɔ̃], *n.f.* improvisation; (*Mus.*) voluntary.
improviser [ɛ̃prɔvi'ze], *v.t.* to improvise, to extemporize.
improviste (à l') [alɛ̃prɔ'vist], *adv. phr.* all of a sudden, unawares, unexpectedly.
imprudemment [ɛ̃pryda'mɑ̃], *adv.* imprudently, indiscreetly.
imprudence [ɛ̃pry'dɑ̃ːs], *n.f.* imprudence, rashness; indiscretion.
imprudent [ɛ̃pry'dɑ̃], *a.* imprudent, foolhardy, unwise, incautious.
impudemment [ɛ̃pyda'mɑ̃], *adv.* impudently, shamelessly.
impudence [ɛ̃py'dɑ̃ːs], *n.f.* impudence, shamelessness.

impudent [ɛ̃py'dɑ̃], *a.* impudent, shameless, saucy.—*n.m.* (*fem.* **-e**) impudent person.
impudeur [ɛ̃py'dœːr], *n.f.* immodesty, indecency; effrontery.
impudicité [ɛ̃pydisi'te], *n.f.* impudicity, immodesty, lewdness.
impudique [ɛ̃py'dik], *a.* unchaste, lewd, immodest.
impudiquement [ɛ̃pydik'mɑ̃], *adv.* immodestly, unchastely, lewdly.
impuissance [ɛ̃pɥi'sɑ̃ːs], *n.f.* impotence, incapacity, powerlessness.
impuissant [ɛ̃pɥi'sɑ̃], *a.* impotent, powerless, unable.
impulsif [ɛ̃pyl'sif], *a.* (*fem.* **-sive**) impulsive.
impulsion [ɛ̃pyl'sjɔ̃], *n.f.* impulsion, impulse; impetus; motive.
impunément [ɛ̃pyne'mɑ̃], *adv.* with impunity.
impuni [ɛ̃py'ni], *a.* unpunished.
impunité [ɛ̃pyni'te], *n.f.* impunity.
impur [ɛ̃'pyːr], *a.* impure, foul; unchaste, immodest; unclean.
impurement [ɛ̃pyr'mɑ̃], *adv.* impurely; immodestly.
impureté [ɛ̃pyr'te], *n.f.* impurity, foulness; immodesty; obscenity.
imputabilité [ɛ̃pytabili'te], *n.f.* imputability.
imputable [ɛ̃py'tabl], *a.* imputable, chargeable; to be deducted.
imputation [ɛ̃pytɑ'sjɔ̃], *n.f.* imputation, charge; deduction.
imputer [ɛ̃py'te], *v.t.* to impute, to attribute; to deduct.
imputrescible [ɛ̃pytrɛ'sibl], *a.* not liable to putrefaction; rot-proof.
inabordable [inabor'dabl], *a.* inaccessible, unapproachable.
inabrité [inabri'te], *a.* unsheltered, open.
inabrogé [inabrɔ'ʒe], *a.* unrepealed.
inacceptable [inaksɛp'tabl], *a.* unacceptable.
inaccessibilité [inaksɛsibili'te], *n.f.* inaccessibility.
inaccessible [inaksɛ'sibl], *a.* inaccessible.
inaccordable [inakɔr'dabl], *a.* irreconcilable; unallowable, inadmissible.
inaccoutumé [inakuty'me], *a.* unaccustomed, unusual.
inachevé [inaʃ've], *a.* unfinished.
inactif [inak'tif], *a.* (*fem.* **-tive**) inactive; inert, indolent.
inaction [inak'sjɔ̃], *n.f.* inaction; indolence, inertness.
inactivement [inaktiv'mɑ̃], *adv.* inactively.
inactivité [inaktivi'te], *n.f.* inactivity.
inadaptation [inadaptɑ'sjɔ̃], *n.f.* maladjustment.
inadapté [inadap'te], *a.* maladjusted.—*n.m.* (*fem.* **-ée**) social misfit.
inadmissible [inadmi'sibl], *a.* inadmissible.
inadmission [inadmi'sjɔ̃], *n.f.* non-admission.
inadvertance [inadvɛr'tɑ̃ːs], *n.f.* inadvertence, oversight.
inaliénable [inalje'nabl], *a.* inalienable.
inaliéné [inalje'ne], *a.* unalienated.
inalliable [ina'ljabl], *a.* that cannot be alloyed; incompatible.
inaltérable [inalte'rabl], *a.* unalterable, invariable.
inamical [inami'kal], *a.* (*m. pl.* **-aux**) unfriendly.
inamovibilité [inamɔvibili'te], *n.f.* irremovability, fixity of tenure.
inamovible [inamɔ'vibl], *a.* irremovable, permanent; built in.
inanimé [inani'me], *a.* inanimate, lifeless.
inanité [inani'te], *n.f.* inanity, emptiness.
inanition [inani'sjɔ̃], *n.f.* inanition, starvation.
inapaisé [inapɛ'ze], *a.* unappeased; unquenched.
inaperçu [inapɛr'sy], *a.* unperceived, unobserved, unnoticed.
inapparent [inapa'rɑ̃], *a.* unapparent; inconspicuous.
inapplicable [inapli'kabl], *a.* inapplicable.
inappliqué [inapli'ke], *a.* inattentive, heedless.
inappréciable [inapre'sjabl], *a.* inappreciable; invaluable.
inappréciablement [inapresjablə'mɑ̃], *adv.* inappreciably.
inapprécié [inapre'sje], *a.* unappreciated.
inapprêté [inaprɛ'te], *a.* unprepared, undressed, uncooked.
inapprochable [inaprɔ'ʃabl], *a.* unapproachable.
inapte [i'napt], *a.* inapt, unfit, unqualified.
inaptitude [inapti'tyd], *n.f.* inaptitude, unfitness; disqualification.
inarticulé [inartiky'le], *a.* inarticulate.
inassouvi [inasu'vi], *a.* unsatiated.
inassouvissable [inasuvi'sabl], *a.* insatiable.
inattaquable [inata'kabl], *a.* unassailable; (*fig.*) unimpeachable, irreproachable.
inattendu [inatɑ̃'dy], *a.* unexpected, unforeseen; unhoped for.
inattentif [inatɑ̃'tif], *a.* (*fem.* **-tive**) inattentive, unmindful.
inattention [inatɑ̃'sjɔ̃], *n.f.* inattention, carelessness; ***faute d'inattention***, slip.
inaudible [ino'dibl], *a.* inaudible.
inaugural [inogy'ral], *a.* (*m. pl.* **-aux**) inaugural.
inauguration [inogyrɑ'sjɔ̃], *n.f.* inauguration.
inaugurer [inogy're], *v.t.* to inaugurate, to open; to usher in.
inavouable [ina'vwabl], *a.* unavowable; shameful.
incalculable [ɛ̃kalky'labl], *a.* incalculable, numberless.
incandescence [ɛ̃kɑ̃dɛ'sɑ̃ːs], *n.f.* incandescence.
incandescent [ɛ̃kɑ̃dɛ'sɑ̃], *a.* incandescent.
incapable [ɛ̃ka'pabl], *a.* incapable, unable (*de*); unfit, incompetent.
incapacité [ɛ̃kapasi'te], *n.f.* incapacity, incapability; inability, unfitness; incompetence, disability; disqualification, (*Mil.*) disablement; ***frapper d'incapacité*** to incapacitate.
incarcération [ɛ̃karserɑ'sjɔ̃], *n.f.* incarceration.
incarcérer [ɛ̃karse're], *v.t.* (*conjug. like* CÉDER) to incarcerate, to imprison.
incarnat [ɛ̃kar'na], *a.* flesh-coloured, rosy.—*n.m.* carnation, flesh-colour.
incarnation [ɛ̃karnɑ'sjɔ̃], *n.f.* incarnation.
incarné [ɛ̃kar'ne] *a.* incarnate; ingrowing (*nail*).

incarner [ɛ̃kar'ne], *v.t.* to incarnate, to embody. **s'incarner**, *v.r.* to become incarnate; to grow in (*of nails*).
incartade [ɛ̃kar'tad], *n.f.* thoughtless insult; prank, folly.
incassable [ɛ̃kɑ'sabl], *a.* unbreakable.
incendiaire [ɛ̃sɑ̃'djɛ:r], *a.* and *n.* incendiary.
incendie [ɛ̃sɑ̃'di], *n.m.* fire, conflagration.
incendié [ɛ̃sɑ̃'dje], *a.* burnt-out, gutted.—*n.m.* (*fem.* **-ée**) sufferer by fire.
incendier [ɛ̃sɑ̃'dje], *v.t.* to set fire to, to burn down.
incertain [ɛ̃sɛr'tɛ̃], *a.* uncertain; unsettled, inconstant; vague.
incertitude [ɛ̃sɛrti'tyd], *n.f.* uncertainty, doubt, suspense; instability, fickleness.
incessamment [ɛ̃sɛsa'mɑ̃], *adv.* immediately, at once; incessantly.
incessant [ɛ̃sɛ'sɑ̃], *a.* incessant, ceaseless, unremitting.
inceste [ɛ̃'sɛst], *a.* incestuous.—*n.m.* incest. —*n.* incestuous person.
incestueusement [ɛ̃sɛstɥøz'mɑ̃], *adv.* incestuously.
incestueux [ɛ̃sɛs'tɥø], *a.* (*fem.* **-euse**) incestuous.—*n.m.* (*fem.* **-euse**) incestuous person.
incidemment [ɛ̃sida'mɑ̃], *adv.* incidentally.
incidence [ɛ̃si'dɑ̃:s], *n.f.* incidence.
incident [ɛ̃si'dɑ̃], *a.* incidental; incident.—*n.m.* incident, occurrence.
incinération [ɛ̃sinerɑ'sjɔ̃], *n.f.* incineration; cremation.
incinérer [ɛ̃sine're], *v.t.* (*conjug. like* CÉDER) to incinerate; to cremate.
inciser [ɛ̃si'ze], *v.t.* to make an incision in, to notch, to gash; to tap (*a tree*).
incisif [ɛ̃si'zif], *a.* (*fem.* **-sive**) sharp, cutting, incisive.—*n.f.* (**-sive**) incisive tooth, incisor.
incision [ɛ̃si'zjɔ̃], *n.f.* incision.
incitation [ɛ̃sitɑ'sjɔ̃], *n.f.* incitement, instigation; (*Med.*) stimulus.
inciter [ɛ̃si'te], *v.t.* to incite; to instigate, to induce.
incivil [ɛ̃si'vil], *a.* uncivil, unmannerly.
incivilement [ɛ̃sivil'mɑ̃], *adv.* uncivilly.
incivilisé [ɛ̃sivili'ze], *a.* uncivilized.
incivilité [ɛ̃sivili'te], *n.f.* incivility; rude remark.
inclémence [ɛ̃kle'mɑ̃:s], *n.f.* inclemency.
inclément [ɛ̃kle'mɑ̃], *a.* inclement.
inclinaison [ɛ̃klinɛ'zɔ̃], *n.f.* inclination; incline, gradient; pitch, slant.
inclination [ɛ̃klinɑ'sjɔ̃], *n.f.* bow, bending; proneness, propensity; attachment, passion.
incliner [ɛ̃kli'ne], *v.t.* to incline, to slope; to bow; to bend; (*fig.*) to dispose, to turn.—*v.i.* to incline, to lean; to be inclined (*à* or *vers*). **s'incliner**, *v.r.* to incline, to lean; to bow, to bend, to yield.
inclure [ɛ̃'kly:r] *v.t. irr.* (*conjug. like* CONCLURE *but p.p.* **inclus**) to include, to enclose, to insert.
inclus [ɛ̃'kly], *a.* enclosed, included.
inclusif [ɛ̃kly'zif], *a.* (*fem.* **-sive**) inclusive.
inclusion [ɛ̃kly'zjɔ̃], *n.f.* enclosing; inclusion.
inclusivement [ɛ̃klyziv'mɑ̃], *adv.* inclusively.
incognito [ɛ̃kɔɲi'to], *adv.* incognito.
incohérence [ɛ̃kɔe'rɑ̃:s], *n.f.* incoherence.
incohérent [ɛ̃kɔe'rɑ̃], *a.* incoherent.
incolore [ɛ̃kɔ'lɔ:r], *a.* colourless.
incomber [ɛ̃kɔ̃'be], *v.i.* to be incumbent (*on anyone*).
incombustible [ɛ̃kɔ̃bys'tibl], *a.* incombustible, fire-proof.
incomestible [ɛ̃kɔmɛs'tibl], *a.* inedible.
incommode [ɛ̃kɔ'mɔd], *a.* inconvenient, uncomfortable; annoying, disagreeable.
incommodé [ɛ̃kɔmɔ'de], *a.* indisposed, unwell, poorly.
incommodément [ɛ̃kɔmɔde'mɑ̃], *adv.* incommodiously, inconveniently.
incommoder [ɛ̃kɔmɔ'de], *v.t.* to inconvenience, to trouble; to disturb, to annoy; to make unwell.
incommodité [ɛ̃kɔmɔdi'te], *n.f.* inconvenience, incommodiousness; annoyance; indisposition.
incommunicable [ɛ̃kɔmyni'kabl], *a.* incommunicable.
incomparable [ɛ̃kɔ̃pa'rabl], *a.* incomparable, unequalled, peerless.
incomparablement [ɛ̃kɔ̃parablə'mɑ̃], *adv.* incomparably.
incompatibilité [ɛ̃kɔ̃patibili'te], *n.f.* incompatibility.
incompatible [ɛ̃kɔ̃pa'tibl], *a.* incompatible, inconsistent.
incompétence [ɛ̃kɔ̃pe'tɑ̃:s], *n.f.* incompetence.
incompétent [ɛ̃kɔ̃pe'tɑ̃], *a.* imcompetent.
incomplet [ɛ̃kɔ̃'plɛ], *a.* (*fem.* **-ète**) incomplete.
incomplètement [ɛ̃kɔ̃plɛt'mɑ̃], *adv.* incompletely.
incompréhensible [ɛ̃kɔ̃preɑ̃'sibl], *a.* incomprehensible, inscrutable.
incompréhension [ɛ̃kɔ̃preɑ̃'sjɔ̃], *n.f.* lack of understanding; obtuseness.
incompressible [ɛ̃kɔ̃prɛ'sibl], *a.* incompressible.
incompris [ɛ̃kɔ̃'pri], *a.* and *n.m.* (*fem.* **-e**) misunderstood, unappreciated (person).
inconcevable [ɛ̃kɔ̃s'vabl], *a.* inconceivable, unthinkable.
inconcevablement [ɛ̃kɔ̃svablə'mɑ̃], *adv.* inconceivably.
inconciliable [ɛ̃kɔ̃si'ljabl], *a.* irreconcilable, incompatible.
inconduite [ɛ̃kɔ̃'dɥit], *n.f.* misconduct.
inconfort [ɛ̃kɔ̃'fɔ:r], *n.m.* discomfort, lack of comfort.
inconfortable [ɛ̃kɔfɔr'tabl], *a.* uncomfortable.
incongru [ɛ̃kɔ̃'gry], *a.* incongruous, improper, unseemly.
incongruité [ɛ̃kɔ̃gryi'te], *n.f.* incongruity, impropriety.
incongrûment [ɛ̃kɔ̃gry'mɑ̃], *adv.* incongruously, improperly.
inconnu [ɛ̃kɔ'ny], *a.* unknown.—*n.m.* the unknown.—*n.m.* (*fem.* **-e**) stranger. —*n.f.* (**-e**) (*Math.*) unknown quantity.
inconquis [ɛ̃kɔ̃'ki], *a.* unconquered.
inconsciemment [ɛ̃kɔ̃sja'mɑ̃], *adv.* unconsciously, unawares.
inconscience [ɛ̃kɔ̃'sjɑ̃:s], *n.f.* unconsciousness; failure to realize.
inconscient [ɛ̃kɔ̃'sjɑ̃], *a.* unconscious.—*n.m.* the unconscious.
inconséquemment [ɛ̃kɔ̃seka'mɑ̃], *adv.* inconsistently, inconsequentially.
inconséquence [ɛ̃kɔ̃se'kɑ̃:s], *n.f.* inconsistency, inconsequence.
inconséquent [ɛ̃kɔ̃se'kɑ̃], *a.* inconsistent; inconsequential.

inconsidéré [ɛ̃kɔ̃side're], *a.* inconsiderate, thoughtless.
inconsistance [ɛ̃kɔ̃sis'tɑ:s], *n.f.* inconsistency.
inconsistant [ɛ̃kɔ̃sis'tɑ̃], *a.* inconsistent.
inconsolable [ɛ̃kɔ̃sɔ'labl], *a.* disconsolate; inconsolable.
inconsolablement [ɛ̃kɔ̃sɔlablə'mɑ̃], *adv.* disconsolately, inconsolably.
inconsolé [ɛ̃kɔ̃sɔ'le], *a.* unconsoled, uncomforted.
inconstamment [ɛ̃kɔ̃sta'mɑ̃], *adv.* inconstantly; unsteadily.
inconstance [ɛ̃kɔ̃s'tɑ:s], *n.f.* inconstancy, fickleness; instability.
inconstant [ɛ̃kɔ̃'stɑ̃], *a.* inconstant, fickle; changeable; unsettled, unsteady.—*n.m.* (*fem.* **-e**) fickle person.
inconstitutionnel [ɛ̃kɔ̃stitysjɔ'nɛl], *a.* (*fem.* **-elle**) unconstitutional.
incontestable [ɛ̃kɔ̃tɛs'tabl], *a.* incontestable, indisputable.
incontestablement [ɛ̃kɔ̃tɛstablə'mɑ̃], *adv.* incontestably.
incontesté [ɛ̃kɔ̃tɛs'te], *a.* uncontested, unquestioned, undisputed.
incontinence [ɛ̃kɔ̃ti'nɑ:s], *n.f.* incontinence.
incontinent (1) [ɛ̃kɔ̃ti'nɑ̃], *a.* incontinent, unchaste.
incontinent (2) [ɛ̃kɔ̃ti'nɑ̃], *adv.* at once, immediately, forthwith.
incontrôlable [ɛ̃kɔ̃tro'labl], *a.* that cannot be checked *or* verified.
inconvenance [ɛ̃kɔ̃v'nɑ:s], *n.f.* impropriety, unseemliness; indecorum; ***quelle inconvenance !*** how very improper!
inconvenant [ɛ̃kɔ̃v'nɑ̃], *a.* improper, unbecoming, unseemly.
inconvénient [ɛ̃kɔ̃ve'njɑ̃], *n.m.* inconvenience, harm; drawback, objection.
inconvertible [ɛ̃kɔ̃vɛr'tibl], *a.* unconvertible.
incorporation [ɛ̃kɔrpɔrɑ'sjɔ̃], *n.f.* incorporation.
incorporer [ɛ̃kɔrpɔ're], *v.t.* to incorporate, to embody; to fuse. **s'incorporer**, *v.r.* to be embodied; to unite, to be blended.
incorrect [ɛ̃kɔ'rɛkt], *a.* incorrect, inaccurate.
incorrectement [ɛ̃kɔrɛktə'mɑ̃], *adv.* incorrectly, inaccurately.
incorrection [ɛ̃kɔrɛk'sjɔ̃], *n.f.* incorrectness, inaccuracy.
incorrigible [ɛ̃kɔri'ʒibl], *a.* incorrigible.
incorrigiblement [ɛ̃kɔriʒiblə'mɑ̃], *adv.* incorrigibly.
incorruptible [ɛ̃kɔryp'tibl], *a.* incorruptible, unbribable.
incrédibilité [ɛ̃kredibili'te], *n.f.* incredibility.
incrédule [ɛ̃kre'dyl], *a.* incredulous, unbelieving.—*n.* unbeliever, infidel.
incrédulité [ɛ̃kredyli'te], *n.f.* incredulity, unbelief.
incriminer [ɛ̃krimi'ne], *v.t.* to incriminate, to accuse.
incroyable [ɛ̃krwɑ'jabl], *a.* incredible, past belief.
incroyablement [ɛ̃krwɑjablə'mɑ̃], *adv.* incredibly.
incroyance [ɛ̃krwɑ'jɑ̃:s], *n.f.* unbelief.
incroyant [ɛ̃krwɑ'jɑ̃], *a.* unbelieving.—*n.m.* (*fem.* **-e**) unbeliever.
incruster [ɛ̃krys'te], *v.t.* to encrust, to inlay. **s'incruster**, *v.r.* to become encrusted.
incubateur [ɛ̃kyba'tœ:r], *a.* (*fem.* **-trice**) incubating.—*n.m.* incubator.
incubation [ɛ̃kybɑ'sjɔ̃], *n.f.* incubation, hatching.
incuber [ɛ̃ky'be], *v.t.* to incubate.
inculcation [ɛ̃kylkɑ'sjɔ̃], *n.f.* inculcation.
inculpation [ɛ̃kylpɑ'sjɔ̃], *n.f.* indictment, charge.
inculpé [ɛ̃kyl'pe], *n.m.* (*fem.* **-ée**) defendant, accused.
inculper [ɛ̃kyl'pe], *v.t.* to indict, to inculpate, to charge.
inculquer [ɛ̃kyl'ke], *v.t.* to inculcate, to impress.
inculte [ɛ̃'kylt], *a.* uncultivated; untilled; unpolished; unkempt.
incultivable [ɛ̃kylti'vabl], *a.* untillable, uncultivable.
incultivé [ɛ̃kylti've], *a.* uncultivated; (*fig.*) uncultured.
incurable [ɛ̃ky'rabl], *a.* and *n.* incurable.
incurablement [ɛ̃kyrablə'mɑ̃], *adv.* incurably.
incurie [ɛ̃ky'ri], *n.f.* carelessness, heedlessness; negligence.
incursion [ɛ̃kyr'sjɔ̃], *n.f.* incursion, inroad, irruption; expedition.
incurver [ɛ̃kyr've], *v.t.* to curve (*something*) inwards.
Inde [ɛ̃:d], **l'**, *f.* India; ***les Indes**, the Indies; ***les Indes occidentales***, the West Indies.
indécemment [ɛ̃desa'mɑ̃], *adv.* indecently.
indécence [ɛ̃de'sɑ̃:s], *n.f.* indecency, impropriety.
indécent [ɛ̃de'sɑ̃], *a.* indecent; unseemly.
indéchiffrable [ɛ̃deʃi'frabl], *a.* undecipherable, illegible; obscure, incomprehensible.
indéchirable [ɛ̃deʃi'rabl], *a.* untearable.
indécis [ɛ̃de'si], *a.* undecided, doubtful; irresolute.
indécision [ɛ̃desi'zjɔ̃], *n.f.* indecision, irresolution.
indécrottable [ɛ̃dekrɔ'tabl], *a.* uncleanable; (*fig.*) incorrigible.
indéfendable [ɛ̃defɑ̃'dabl], *a.* indefensible, untenable.
indéfini [ɛ̃defi'ni], *a.* indefinite, unlimited.
indéfiniment [ɛ̃defini'mɑ̃], *adv.* indefinitely.
indéfinissable [ɛ̃defini'sabl], *a.* undefinable; nondescript.
indéfrichable [ɛ̃defri'ʃabl], *a.* unclearable (*of land*).
indéfrisable [ɛ̃defri'zabl], *n.f.* permanent wave.
indélébile [ɛ̃dele'bil], *a.* indelible, ineffaceable.
indélicat [ɛ̃deli'ka], *a.* indelicate; unhandsome.
indélicatement [ɛ̃delikat'mɑ̃], *adv.* indelicately; unhandsomely.
indélicatesse [ɛ̃delika'tɛs], *n.f.* tactlessness; unscrupulousness; objectionable action.
indémaillable [ɛ̃dema'jabl], *a.* ladder-proof (*stocking*).
indemne [ɛ̃'dɛmn], *a.* uninjured.
indemnisation [ɛ̃dɛmnizɑ'sjɔ̃], *n.f.* indemnification, compensation.
indemniser [ɛ̃dɛmni'ze], *v.t.* to indemnify; to make good.

indemnité [ɛ̃dɛmni'te], *n.f.* indemnity; ***indemnité de charges de famille***, family allowance; ***indemnité de chômage***, unemployment benefit; ***indemnité de vie chère***, cost of living bonus.
indéniable [ɛ̃de'njabl], *a.* undeniable; self-evident.
indépendamment [ɛ̃depɑ̃da'mɑ̃], *adv.* independently.
indépendance [ɛ̃depɑ̃'dɑ̃:s], *n.f.* independence.
indépendant [ɛ̃depɑ̃'dɑ̃], *a.* independent.
indescriptible [ɛ̃dɛskrip'tibl], *a.* indescribable.
indésirable [ɛ̃dezi'rabl], *a.* and *n.* undesirable.
indestructible [ɛ̃dɛstryk'tibl], *a.* indestructible.
indéterminable [ɛ̃detɛrmi'nabl], *a.* indeterminable.
indétermination [ɛ̃detɛrminɑ'sjɔ̃], *n.f.* indetermination, irresolution.
indéterminé [ɛ̃detɛrmi'ne], *a.* undetermined, irresolute.
index [ɛ̃'dɛks], *n.m. inv.* fore-finger; index.
indicateur [ɛ̃dika'tœ:r], *a.* (*fem.* **-trice**) indicating, indicatory.—*n.m.* indicator, guide; time-table; (*fem.* **-trice**) (*fig.*) informer.
indicatif [ɛ̃dika'tif], *a.* (*fem.* **-tive**) indicative.—*n.m.* (*Gram.*) indicative mood; call-sign; signature-tune.
indication [ɛ̃dikɑ'sjɔ̃], *n.f.* indication, information; sign, mark.
indice [ɛ̃'dis], *n.m.* indication, sign, mark, clue.
indicible [ɛ̃di'sibl], *a.* inexpressible, unspeakable, indescribable.
indiciblement [ɛ̃disiblə'mɑ̃], *adv.* inexpressibly.
indien [ɛ̃'djɛ̃], *a.* (*fem.* **-enne**) Indian.—*n.m.* (**Indien**, *fem.* **-enne**) Indian (*person*).—*n.f.* (**-enne**) printed calico, printed cotton.
indifféremment [ɛ̃difera'mɑ̃], *adv.* indifferently; alike.
indifférence [ɛ̃dife'rɑ̃:s], *n.f.* indifference, unconcern.
indifférent [ɛ̃dife'rɑ̃], *a.* indifferent, immaterial; unconcerned, heedless.—*n.m.* (*fem.* **-e**) indifferent person.
indigence [ɛ̃di'ʒɑ̃:s], *n.f.* indigence, poverty, need.
indigène [ɛ̃di'ʒɛ:n], *a.* indigenous, native.—*n.* native.
indigent [ɛ̃di'ʒɑ̃], *a.* indigent, needy.—*n.m.* (*fem.* **-e**) pauper, destitute person.
indigéré [ɛ̃diʒe're], *a.* undigested, crude.
indigeste [ɛ̃di'ʒɛst], *a.* indigestible; undigested.
indigestion [ɛ̃diʒɛs'tjɔ̃], *n.f.* indigestion, surfeit.
indignation [ɛ̃diɲɑ'sjɔ̃], *n.f.* indignation.
indigne [ɛ̃'diɲ], *a.* unworthy; infamous, worthless.
indigné [ɛ̃di'ɲe], *a.* indignant; shocked.
indignement [ɛ̃diɲə'mɑ̃], *adv.* unworthily; scandalously.
indigner [ɛ̃di'ɲe], *v.t.* to render indignant; to shock. **s'indigner**, *v.r.* to be indignant; to be shocked.
indignité [ɛ̃diɲi'te], *n.f.* unworthiness, worthlessness; indignity; infamy.
indigo [ɛ̃di'go], *a. inv.* and *n.m.* indigo.
indigotier [ɛ̃digɔ'tje], *n.m.* indigo plant *or* manufacturer.
indiquer [ɛ̃di'ke], *v.t.* to indicate, to point out; to mention; to denote; to appoint, to recommend; to outline.
indirect [ɛ̃di'rɛkt], *a.* indirect; circumstantial (*of evidence*); collateral (*of heirs*).
indirectement [ɛ̃dirɛktə'mɑ̃], *a.* indirectly.
indiscipline [ɛ̃disi'plin], *n.f.* indiscipline, insubordination.
indiscipliné [ɛ̃disipli'ne], *a.* undisciplined.
indiscret [ɛ̃dis'krɛ], *a.* (*fem.* **-ète**) indiscreet, inconsiderate; inquisitive; tell-tale.—*n.m.* (*fem.* **-ète**) babbler.
indiscrètement [ɛ̃diskrɛt'mɑ̃], *adv.* indiscreetly, inconsiderately.
indiscrétion [ɛ̃diskre'sjɔ̃], *n.f.* indiscretion; unwariness.
indiscutable [ɛ̃disky'tabl], *a.* incontestable, indisputable, obvious.
indispensable [ɛ̃dispɑ̃'sabl], *a.* indispensable.
indispensablement [ɛ̃dispɑ̃sablə'mɑ̃], *adv.* indispensably.
indisponible [ɛ̃dispɔ'nibl], *a.* unavailable.
indisposé [ɛ̃dispo'ze], *a.* unwell; unfriendly.
indisposer [ɛ̃dispo'ze], *v.t.* to indispose, to make unwell; to disincline, to set against (***contre***).
indisposition [ɛ̃dispɔzi'sjɔ̃], *n.f.* indisposition; disinclination.
indisputé [ɛ̃dispy'te], *a.* unquestioned.
indissoluble [ɛ̃disɔ'lybl], *a.* indissoluble.
indissolublement [ɛ̃disɔlyblə'mɑ̃], *adv.* indissolubly.
indistinct [ɛ̃dis'tɛ̃:kt], *a.* indistinct.
indistinctement [ɛ̃distɛ̃ktə'mɑ̃], *adv.* indistinctly.
individu [ɛ̃divi'dy], *n.m.* individual; (*colloq.*) fellow.
individualisme [ɛ̃dividɥa'lism], *n.m.* individualism.
individualiste [ɛ̃dividɥa'list], *a.* individualistic.—*n.* individualist.
individualité [ɛ̃dividɥali'te], *n.f.* individuality.
individuel [ɛ̃divi'dɥɛl], *a.* (*fem.* **-elle**) individual.
individuellement [ɛ̃dividɥɛl'mɑ̃], *adv.* individually.
indivisé [ɛ̃divi'ze], *a.* undivided.
indivisément [ɛ̃divize'mɑ̃], *adv.* jointly.
indivisibilité [ɛ̃divizibili'te], *n.f.* indivisibility.
indivisible [ɛ̃divi'zibl], *a.* indivisible.
indivisiblement [ɛ̃diviziblə'mɑ̃], *adv.* indivisibly.
indivision [ɛ̃divi'zjɔ̃], *n.f.* joint-possession.
Indochine [ɛ̃dɔ'ʃin], **l'**, *f.* Indo-China.
indochinois [ɛ̃dɔʃi'nwa], *a.* Indo-Chinese.—*n.m.* (**Indochinois**, *fem.* **-oise**) Indo-Chinese (*person*).
indocile [ɛ̃dɔ'sil], *a.* indocile, unmanageable.
indocilité [ɛ̃dɔsili'te], *n.f.* indocility, intractability.
indolemment [ɛ̃dɔla'mɑ̃], *adv.* indolently.
indolence [ɛ̃dɔ'lɑ̃:s], *n.f.* indolence, sloth.
indolent [ɛ̃dɔ'lɑ̃], *a.* indolent, slothful.—*n.m.* (*fem.* **-e**) sluggard.
indolore [ɛ̃dɔ'lɔ:r], *a.* painless.
indomptable [ɛ̃dɔ̃'tabl], *a.* indomitable, untamable; unmanageable.

indompté [ɛ̃dɔ̃'te], *a.* untamed, wild; unsubdued.
Indonésie [ɛ̃dɔne'zi], **l'**, *f.* Indonesia.
indonésien [ɛ̃dɔne'zjɛ̃], *a.* Indonesian.—*n.m.* Indonesian (*language*); (**Indonésien**, *fem.* **-enne**) Indonesian (*person*).
indou [HINDOU].
indu [ɛ̃'dy], *a.* undue, unseasonable, late.
indubitable [ɛ̃dybi'tabl], *a.* indubitable, certain.
indubitablement [ɛ̃dybitablə'mɑ̃], *adv.* undoubtedly.
inductif [ɛ̃dyk'tif], *a.* (*fem.* **-tive**) inductive.
induction [ɛ̃dyk'sjɔ̃], *n.f.* induction, inference.
induire [ɛ̃'dɥi:r], *v.t. irr.* (*conjug. like* CONDUIRE) to induce, to lead; to infer.
indulgence [ɛ̃dyl'ʒɑ̃:s], *n.f.* indulgence, leniency.
indulgent [ɛ̃dyl'ʒɑ̃], *a.* indulgent, forbearing.
indûment [ɛ̃dy'mɑ̃], *adv.* unduly.
industrialiser [ɛ̃dystriali'ze], *v.t.* to industrialize.
industrialisme [ɛ̃dystria'lism], *n.m.* industrialism.
industrie [ɛ̃dys'tri], *n.f.* skill, ingenuity; business; manufacturing; industry, work; ***chevalier d'industrie***, swindler, sharper; ***industrie de base*** or ***industrie clef***, key industry.
industriel [ɛ̃dystri'ɛl], *a.* (*fem.* **-elle**) industrial, manufacturing.—*n.m.* manufacturer, mill-owner.
industrieusement [ɛ̃dystriøz'mɑ̃], *adv.* ingeniously, skilfully; industriously.
industrieux [ɛ̃dystri'ø], *a.* (*fem.* **-euse**) ingenious, skilful; industrious.
inébranlable [inebrɑ̃'labl], *a.* immovable; firm, resolute.
inébranlablement [inebrɑ̃lablə'mɑ̃], *adv.* immovably, steadily; resolutely.
inédit [ine'di], *a.* unpublished; new.
ineffable [inɛ'fabl], *a.* ineffable, inexpressible, unutterable.
ineffaçable [inɛfa'sabl], *a.* indelible, ineffaceable.
inefficace [inɛfi'kas], *a.* ineffectual, ineffective.
inefficacité [inɛfikasi'te], *n.f.* inefficacy, ineffectiveness.
inégal [ine'gal], *a.* (*m. pl.* **-aux**) unequal; rough; (*fig.*) ill-matched; irregular.
inégalement [inegal'mɑ̃], *adv.* unequally, unevenly.
inégalité [inegali'te], *n.f.* inequality; unevenness; irregularity.
inélégance [inele'gɑ̃:s], *n.f.* inelegance.
inélégant [inele'gɑ̃], *a.* inelegant.
inéligible [ineli'ʒibl], *a.* ineligible.
inéluctable [inelyk'tabl], *a.* unavoidable; unescapable.
inénarrable [inena'rabl], *a.* untellable; incredible.
inepte [i'nɛpt], *a.* foolish, silly, inept, absurd.
ineptie [inɛp'si], *n.f.* ineptitude, foolishness, absurdity.
inépuisable [inepɥi'zabl], *a.* inexhaustible.
inépuisablement [inepɥizablə'mɑ̃], *adv.* inexhaustibly.
inéquitable [ineki'tabl], *a.* unfair.
inerte [i'nɛrt], *a.* inert, sluggish, inactive.
inertie [inɛr'si], *n.f.* inertia; indolence.
inespéré [inɛspe're], *a.* unhoped for, unexpected.
inestimable [inɛsti'mabl], *a.* inestimable.
inévitable [inevi'tabl], *a.* inevitable, unavoidable.
inévitablement [inevitablə'mɑ̃], *adv.* inevitably, unavoidably.
inexact [inɛg'zakt], *a.* inexact, inaccurate, incorrect.
inexactement [inɛgzaktə'mɑ̃], *adv.* inaccurately, incorrectly.
inexactitude [inɛgzakti'tyd], *n.f.* incorrectness; inaccuracy, slip.
inexcusable [inɛksky'zabl], *a.* inexcusable, unwarrantable.
inexécutable [inɛgzeky'tabl], *a.* impracticable.
inexercé [inɛgzɛr'se], *a.* untrained.
inexistant [inɛgzis'tɑ̃], *a.* non-existent.
inexorable [inɛgzɔ'rabl], *a.* inexorable, inflexible; pitiless.
inexorablement [inɛgzɔrablə'mɑ̃], *adv.* inexorably.
inexpérience [inɛkspe'rjɑ̃:s], *n.f.* inexperience.
inexpérimenté [inɛksperimɑ̃'te], *a.* inexperienced; untried (*of things*).
inexplicable [inɛkspli'kabl], *a.* inexplicable, unaccountable.
inexpliqué [inɛkspli'ke], *a.* unexplained.
inexploitable [inɛksplwa'tabl], *a.* unworkable, useless.
inexploité [inɛksplwa'te], *a.* uncultivated (*of land*); unworked (*of mines etc.*); untapped (*resources*).
inexploré [inɛksplɔ're], *a.* unexplored.
inexplosible [inɛksplo'zibl], *a.* unexplosive.
inexpressible [inɛksprɛ'sibl], *a.* inexpressible.
inexpressif [inɛksprɛ'sif], *a.* (*fem.* **-ive**) inexpressive, lacking expression.
inexprimable [inɛkspri'mabl], *a.* inexpressible, unspeakable.
inextinguible [inɛkstɛ̃'gibl], *a.* inextinguishable; unquenchable (*thirst, fire*); irrepressible (*laughter*).
inextricable [inɛkstri'kabl], *a.* inextricable.
inextricablement [inɛkstrikablə'mɑ̃], *adv.* inextricably.
infaillibilité [ɛ̃fajibili'te], *n.f.* infallibility.
infaillible [ɛ̃fa'jibl], *a.* infallible.
infailliblement [ɛ̃fajiblə'mɑ̃], *adv.* infallibly.
infaisable [ɛ̃fə'zabl], *a.* impracticable.
infamant [ɛ̃fa'mɑ̃], *a.* infamous, ignominious.
infâme [ɛ̃'fɑ:m], *a.* infamous; squalid, sordid. —*n.* infamous person, wretch.
infamie [ɛ̃fa'mi], *n.f.* infamy, ignominy; baseness.
infant [ɛ̃'fɑ̃], *n.m.* (*fem.* **-e**) infante, infanta (*Spanish prince* or *princess*).
infanterie [ɛ̃fɑ̃'tri], *n.f.* infantry.
infanticide [ɛ̃fɑ̃ti'sid], *n.m.* infanticide.—*n.* child-murderer.
infantile [ɛ̃fɑ̃'til], *a.* infantile.
infatigable [ɛ̃fati'gabl], *a.* indefatigable, untiring.
infatuation [ɛ̃fatɥa'sjɔ̃], *n.f.* infatuation.
infatuer [ɛ̃fa'tɥe], *v.t.* to infatuate. **s'infatuer**, *v.r.* to become infatuated.
infécond [ɛ̃fe'kɔ̃], *a.* unfruitful, barren, sterile.

infécondité [ɛ̃fekɔ̃di'te], *n.f.* unfruitfulness, barrenness, sterility.
infect [ɛ̃'fɛkt], *a.* infected, foul, noisome, stinking.
infectant [ɛ̃fɛk'tɑ̃], *a.* infecting.
infecter [ɛ̃fɛk'te], *v.t.* to infect, to contaminate; to taint.—*v.i.* to stink.
infectieux [ɛ̃fɛk'sjø], *a.* (*fem.* **-euse**) infectious.
infection [ɛ̃fɛk'sjɔ̃], *n.f.* infection; infectious disease; stench; ***foyer d'infection***, hotbed of disease.
inférence [ɛ̃fe'rɑ̃:s], *n.f.* conclusion, inference.
inférer [ɛ̃fe're], *v.t.* (*conjug. like* CÉDER) to infer, to conclude.
inférieur [ɛ̃fe'rjœ:r], *a.* inferior, lower.—*n.m.* (*fem.* **-e**) inferior; subordinate.
infériorité [ɛ̃ferjɔri'te], *n.f.* inferiority.
infernal [ɛ̃fɛr'nal], *a.* (*m. pl.* **-aux**) infernal, hellish.
infernalement [ɛ̃fɛrnal'mɑ̃], *adv.* infernally.
infertile [ɛ̃fɛr'til], *a.* infertile, unfruitful; sterile, barren.
infertilité [ɛ̃fɛrtili'te], *n.f.* unfruitfulness.
infester [ɛ̃fɛs'te], *v.t.* to infest, to overrun; to haunt.
infidèle [ɛ̃fi'dɛl], *a.* unfaithful, disloyal; unbelieving.—*n.* unfaithful person; infidel.
infidèlement [ɛ̃fidɛl'mɑ̃], *adv.* unfaithfully; inaccurately.
infidélité [ɛ̃fideli'te], *n.f.* infidelity; unbelief; dishonesty.
infiltration [ɛ̃filtrɑ'sjɔ̃], *n.f.* infiltration.
infiltrer (s') [sɛ̃fil'tre], *v.r.* to infiltrate, to percolate.
infime [ɛ̃'fim], *a.* lowest (*of ranks*); tiny.
infini [ɛ̃fi'ni], *a.* infinite, boundless.—*n.m.* infinite, infinity.
infiniment [ɛ̃fini'mɑ̃], *adv.* infinitely, without end; exceedingly, extremely.
infinité [ɛ̃fini'te], *n.f.* infinity, infiniteness; (*fig.*) crowd; no end.
infinitif [ɛ̃fini'tif], *a.* (*fem.* **-tive**) and *n.m.* infinitive (mood).
infirme [ɛ̃'firm], *a.* crippled, invalid; infirm; feeble.—*n.* invalid, cripple.
infirmerie [ɛ̃firm'ri], *n.f.* infirmary, sick-ward; (*sch.*) sanatorium, sick-bay.
infirmier [ɛ̃fir'mje], *n.m.* (*fem.* **-ière**) hospital-attendant; nurse.
infirmité [ɛ̃firmi'te], *n.f.* infirmity, weakness, failing.
inflammable [ɛ̃flɑ'mabl], *a.* inflammable.
inflammation [ɛ̃flɑmɑ'sjɔ̃], *n.f.* inflammation.
inflammatoire [ɛ̃flɑma'twa:r], *a.* inflammatory.
inflation [ɛ̃flɑ'sjɔ̃], *n.f.* inflation, swelling.
inflexible [ɛ̃flɛk'sibl], *a.* inflexible; unyielding, unbending.
inflexiblement [ɛ̃flɛksiblə'mɑ̃], *adv.* inflexibly.
inflexion [ɛ̃flɛk'sjɔ̃], *n.f.* inflexion; modulation, variation.
infliction [ɛ̃flik'sjɔ̃], *n.f.* infliction.
infliger [ɛ̃fli'ʒe], *v.t.* (*conjug. like* MANGER) to inflict, to impose.
influence [ɛ̃fly'ɑ̃:s], *n.f.* influence; sway, power, authority.
influencer [ɛ̃flyɑ̃'se], *v.t.* (*conjug. like* COMMENCER) to influence, to sway, to bias.
influent [ɛ̃fly'ɑ̃], *a.* influential.
influenza [ɛ̃flyɑ̃'za], *n.f.* influenza.
influer [ɛ̃fly'e], *v.i.* to have an influence (***sur***, *on*).
informateur [ɛ̃fɔrma'tœ:r], *n.m.* (*fem.* **-trice**) informant.
information [ɛ̃fɔrmɑ'sjɔ̃], *n.f.* inquiry; information; (*pl.*) news (bulletin).
informe [ɛ̃'fɔrm], *a.* shapeless; misshapen; crude, imperfect.
informer [ɛ̃fɔr'me], *v.t.* to inform, to acquaint, to apprise. **s'informer**, *v.r.* to inquire, to make inquiries, to investigate.
infortune [ɛ̃fɔr'tyn], *n.f.* misfortune, adversity.
infortuné [ɛ̃fɔrty'ne], *a.* unfortunate, unhappy, ill-fated, wretched.—*n.m.* (*fem.* **-ée**) unfortunate, unhappy *or* wretched person.
infraction [ɛ̃frak'sjɔ̃], *n.f.* infringement, breach, violation.
infranchissable [ɛ̃frɑ̃ʃi'sabl], *a.* insurmountable, insuperable.
infra-rouge [ɛ̃fra'ruʒ], *a.* infra-red.
infréquenté [ɛ̃frekɑ̃'te], *a.* unfrequented.
infructueusement [ɛ̃fryktɥøz'mɑ̃], *adv.* fruitlessly, to no purpose, in vain.
infructueux [ɛ̃fryk'tɥø], *a.* (*fem.* **-euse**) unfruitful, vain, unavailing.
infus [ɛ̃'fy] *a.* infused, innate, native (*of knowledge etc.*).
infuser [ɛ̃fy'ze], *v.t.* to infuse, to instil; to steep.
infusion [ɛ̃fy'zjɔ̃], *n.f.* infusion, decoction.
ingambe [ɛ̃'gɑ̃:b], *a.* nimble, brisk, active.
ingénier (s') [sɛ̃ʒe'nje], *v.r.* to tax one's ingenuity, to contrive.
ingénieur [ɛ̃ʒe'njœ:r], *n.m.* engineer.
ingénieusement [ɛ̃ʒenjøz'mɑ̃], *adv.* ingeniously.
ingénieux [ɛ̃ʒe'njø], *a.* (*fem.* **-euse**) ingenious, clever, witty.
ingéniosité [ɛ̃ʒenjɔzi'te], *n.f.* ingenuity; cleverness.
ingénu [ɛ̃ʒe'ny], *a.* ingenuous; guileless, unsophisticated; simple, artless.—*n.m.* (*fem.* **-e**) ingenuous person artless *or* simple-minded person.
ingénuité [ɛ̃ʒenɥi'te], *n.f.* ingenuousness.
ingénument [ɛ̃ʒeny'mɑ̃], *adv.* ingenuously.
ingérence [ɛ̃ʒe'rɑ̃:s], *n.f.* interference, meddling.
ingérer (s') [sɛ̃ʒe're], *v.r.* (*conjug. like* CÉDER) to meddle with, to interfere, to obtrude.
inglorieux [ɛ̃glɔ'rjø], *a.* (*fem.* **-euse**) inglorious.
ingouvernable [ɛ̃guvɛr'nabl], *a.* ungovernable, uncontrollable.
ingrat [ɛ̃'gra], *a.* unthankful, ungrateful; thankless, unprofitable.
ingratitude [ɛ̃grati'tyd], *n.f.* ingratitude, thanklessness.
ingrédient [ɛ̃gre'djɑ̃], *n.m.* ingredient.
inguérissable [ɛ̃geri'sabl], *a.* incurable.
inhabile [ina'bil], *a.* unskilful, unskilled, inexpert.
inhabilement [inabil'mɑ̃], *adv.* unskilfully.
inhabileté [inabil'te], *n.f.* unskilfulness, incompetence, inability.
inhabitable [inabi'tabl], *a.* uninhabitable.
inhabité [inabi'te], *a.* uninhabited.
inhabitué [inabi'tɥe], *a.* unaccustomed, unused.

inhalation [inalɑ'sjɔ̃], *n.f.* inhalation.
inhaler [ina'le], *v.t.* to inhale.
inharmonieux [inarmɔ'njø], *a.* (*fem.* **-euse**) inharmonious, unmusical.
inhérent [ine'rɑ̃], *a.* inherent.
inhospitalier [inɔspita'lje], *a.* (*fem.* **-ière**) inhospitable; (*fig.*) unfriendly, forbidding.
inhumain [iny'mɛ̃], *a.* inhuman, cruel.
inhumainement [inymɛn'mɑ̃], *adv.* inhumanly.
inhumanité [inymani'te], *n.f.* inhumanity, cruelty.
inhumation [inymɑ'sjɔ̃], *n.f.* inhumation, interment.
inhumer [iny'me], *v.t.* to bury, to inter.
inimaginable [inimaʒi'nabl], *a.* unimaginable, inconceivable.
inimitable [inimi'tabl], *a.* inimitable.
inimitié [inimi'tje], *n.f.* enmity, antipathy, aversion.
ininflammable [inɛ̃flɑ'mabl], *a.* non-inflammable, fire-proof.
inintelligemment [inɛ̃tɛliʒa'mɑ̃], *adv.* unintelligently.
inintelligence [inɛ̃tɛli'ʒɑ̃:s], *n.f.* lack of intelligence.
inintelligent [inɛ̃tɛli'ʒɑ̃], *a.* unintelligent.
inintelligible [inɛ̃tɛli'ʒibl], *a.* unintelligible.
inintéressant [inɛ̃terɛ'sɑ̃], *a.* uninteresting.
ininterrompu [inɛ̃tɛrɔ̃'py], *a.* uninterrupted.
inique [i'nik], *a.* iniquitous; unrighteous.
iniquement [inik'mɑ̃], *adv.* iniquitously.
iniquité [iniki'te], *n.f.* iniquity, unrighteousness; injustice.
initial [ini'sjal], *a.* (*m. pl.* **-aux**) initial.
initiale [ini'sjal], *n.f.* initial.
initialement [inisjal'mɑ̃], *adv.* initially.
initiateur [inisja'tœ:r], *n.m.* (*fem.* **-trice**) initiator.
initiation [inisjɑ'sjɔ̃], *n.f.* initiation.
initiative [inisja'ti:v], *n.f.* initiative.
initier [ini'sje], *v.t.* to initiate, to admit.
injecté [ɛ̃ʒɛk'te], *a.* injected; bloodshot; creosoted.
injecter [ɛ̃ʒɛk'te], *v.t.* to inject.
injection [ɛ̃ʒɛk'sjɔ̃], *n.f.* injection.
injonction [ɛ̃ʒɔ̃k'sjɔ̃], *n.f.* injunction, order.
injudicieux [ɛ̃ʒydi'sjø], *a.* (*fem.* **-euse**) injudicious.
injure [ɛ̃'ʒy:r], *n.f.* injury; insult; (*pl.*) abuse, abusive language; slander.
injurier [ɛ̃ʒy'rje], *v.t.* to abuse, to insult.
injurieux [ɛ̃ʒy'rjø], *a.* (*fem.* **-euse**) wrongful; abusive, insulting.
injuste [ɛ̃'ʒyst], *a.* unjust, unfair, wrong.
injustement [ɛ̃ʒystə'mɑ̃], *adv.* unjustly, wrongly.
injustice [ɛ̃ʒys'tis], *n.f.* injustice; wrong.
injustifiable [ɛ̃ʒysti'fjabl], *a.* unjustifiable.
injustifié [ɛ̃ʒysti'fje], *a.* unjustified, groundless.
inlassable [ɛ̃lɑ'sabl], *a.* untirable.
inné [in'ne], *a.* innate, inborn.
innocemment [inɔsa'mɑ̃], *adv.* innocently.
innocence [inɔ'sɑ̃:s], *n.f.* innocence; inoffensiveness; simplicity.
innocent [inɔ'sɑ̃], *a.* innocent; harmless, inoffensive; guileless, simple.—*n.m.* (*fem.* **-e**) simpleton; idiot.
innocenter [inɔsɑ̃'te], *v.t.* to acquit.
innombrable [innɔ̃'brabl], *a.* innumerable, numberless.
innombrablement [inɔ̃brablə'mɑ̃], *adv.* innumerably.
innovateur [innɔva'tœ:r], *n.m.* (*fem.* **-trice**) innovator.
innovation [innɔvɑ'sjɔ̃], *n.f.* innovation.
innover [innɔ've], *v.i.* to make innovations.
inobservable [inɔpsɛr'vabl], *a.* inobservable.
inobservance [inɔpsɛr'vɑ̃:s], **inobservation** [inɔpsɛrvɑ'sjɔ̃], *n.f.* non-observance.
inobservé [inɔpsɛr've], *a.* unobserved, unnoticed.
inoccupé [inɔky'pe], *a.* unoccupied; idle; vacant.
inoculateur [inɔkyla'tœ:r], *n.m.* (*fem.* **-trice**) inoculator.
inoculation [inɔkylɑ'sjɔ̃], *n.f.* inoculation.
inoculer [inɔky'le], *v.t.* to inoculate.
inodore [inɔ'dɔ:r], *a.* odourless.
inoffensif [inɔfɑ̃'sif], *a.* (*fem.* **-sive**) inoffensive; innocuous.
inoffensivement [inɔfɑ̃siv'mɑ̃], *adv.* inoffensively.
inofficiel [inɔfi'sjɛl], *a.* (*fem.* **-elle**) unofficial.
inofficiellement [inɔfisjɛl'mɑ̃], *adv.* unofficially.
inondation [inɔ̃dɑ'sjɔ̃], *n.f.* inundation, flood, deluge.
inonder [inɔ̃'de], *v.t.* to inundate, to overflow; (*fig.*) to overrun.
inopérant [inɔpe'rɑ̃], *a.* inoperative; inefficient.
inopiné [inɔpi'ne], *a.* unforeseen, unexpected, sudden.
inopinément [inɔpine'mɑ̃], *adv.* unawares, unexpectedly, suddenly.
inopportun [inɔpɔr'tœ̃], *a.* inopportune, untimely.
inorganique [inɔrga'nik], *a.* inorganic.
inoubliable [inu'bljabl], *a.* unforgettable.
inoublié [inu'blje], *a.* unforgotten, well-remembered.
inouï [i'nwi], *a.* unheard of, unprecedented.
inoxydable [inɔksi'dabl], *a.* rustless, stainless.
inqualifiable [ɛ̃kali'fjabl], *a.* unspeakable.
inquiet [ɛ̃'kjɛ], *a.* (*fem.* **-ète**) anxious; restless.
inquiétant [ɛ̃kje'tɑ̃], *a.* disquieting, alarming.
inquiéter [ɛ̃kje'te], *v.t.* (*conjug. like* CÉDER) to disquiet; to worry; to disturb. **s'inquiéter**, *v.r.* to be anxious, to be uneasy; to worry.
inquiétude [ɛ̃kje'tyd], *n.f.* anxiety, uneasiness, concern.
inquisiteur [ɛ̃kizi'tœ:r], *a.* inquisitorial; inquisitive.—*n.m.* inquisitor.
inquisitif [ɛ̃kizi'tif], *a.* (*fem.* **-tive**) inquisitive.
inquisition [ɛ̃kizi'sjɔ̃], *n.f.* inquisition.
insaisissable [ɛ̃sɛzi'sabl], *a.* unseizable, imperceptible.
insalubre [ɛ̃sa'lybr], *a.* insalubrious, unhealthy, unwholesome.
insalubrement [ɛ̃salybrə'mɑ̃], *adv.* insalubriously, unhealthily.
insalubrité [ɛ̃salybri'te], *n.f.* insalubrity, unhealthiness.
insanité [ɛ̃sani'te], *n.f.* insanity.
insatiabilité [ɛ̃sasjabili'te], *n.f.* insatiability.
insatiable [ɛ̃sa'sjabl], *a.* insatiable.
insciemment [ɛ̃sja'mɑ̃], *adv.* unwittingly.
inscription [ɛ̃skrip'sjɔ̃], *n.f.* inscription; registration, enrolment; matriculation.

inscrire [ɛ̃s'kriːr], *v.t. irr.* (*conjug. like* ÉCRIRE) to inscribe, to set down, to register. **s'inscrire,** *v.r.* to inscribe oneself; to enter one's name; to register, to enrol.
inscrutable [ɛ̃skry'tabl], *a.* inscrutable, unfathomable.
insecte [ɛ̃'sɛkt], *n.m.* insect.
insecticide [ɛ̃sɛkti'sid], *a.* insecticidal.—*n.m.* insecticide.
insectivore [ɛ̃sɛkti'vɔːr], *a.* insectivorous.
insécurité [ɛ̃sekyri'te], *n.f.* insecurity.
insémination [ɛ̃seminɑ'sjɔ̃], *n.f.* insemination (*cows, ewes etc.*).
inséminer [ɛ̃semi'ne], *v.t.* to inseminate.
insensé [ɛ̃sɑ̃'se], *a.* insane, mad; foolish, senseless.—*n.m.* (*fem.* **-ée**) madman, mad woman, maniac.
insensibiliser [ɛ̃sɑ̃sibili'ze], *v.t.* to anaesthetize.
insensibilité [ɛ̃sɑ̃sibili'te], *n.f.* insensibility; callousness.
insensible [ɛ̃sɑ̃'sibl], *a.* insensible, unconscious; hard-hearted, insensitive.
insensiblement [ɛ̃sɑ̃siblə'mɑ̃], *adv.* insensibly; gradually, imperceptibly.
inséparable [ɛ̃sepa'rabl], *a.* inseparable.—*n.m.* (*pl.*) (*Orn.*) love-birds.
inséparablement [ɛ̃separablə'mɑ̃], *adv.* inseparably.
insérer [ɛ̃se're], *v.t.* (*conjug. like* CÉDER) to insert, to put in.
insertion [ɛ̃sɛr'sjɔ̃], *n.f.* insertion.
insidieusement [ɛ̃sidjøz'mɑ̃], *adv.* insidiously.
insidieux [ɛ̃si'djø], *a.* (*fem.* **-euse**) insidious.
insigne [ɛ̃'siɲ], *a.* distinguished; conspicuous; notorious.—*n.m.* badge, mark; (*pl.*) insignia.
insignifiance [ɛ̃siɲi'fjɑ̃ːs], *n.f.* insignificance.
insignifiant [ɛ̃siɲi'fjɑ̃], *a.* insignificant, trivial.
insincère [ɛ̃sɛ̃'sɛːr], *a.* insincere.
insinuant [ɛ̃si'nɥɑ̃], *a.* insinuating; ingratiating.
insinuation [ɛ̃sinɥɑ'sjɔ̃], *n.f.* insinuation, hint, innuendo.
insinuer [ɛ̃si'nɥe], *v.t.* to insinuate; to hint, to suggest. **s'insinuer,** *v.r.* to insinuate oneself (***dans***), to creep *or* worm one's way (*into*).
insipide [ɛ̃si'pid], *a.* insipid, tasteless; dull.
insipidité [ɛ̃sipidi'te], *n.f.* insipidity.
insistance [ɛ̃sis'tɑ̃ːs], *n.f.* insistence, persistence.
insister [ɛ̃sis'te], *v.i.* to insist, to lay stress (***sur***).
insociable [ɛ̃sɔ'sjabl], *a.* unsociable; difficult to live with.
insolation [ɛ̃sɔlɑ'sjɔ̃], *n.f.* insolation, sunstroke.
insolemment [ɛ̃sɔla'mɑ̃], *adv.* insolently.
insolence [ɛ̃sɔ'lɑ̃ːs], *n.f.* insolence, impertinence.
insolent [ɛ̃sɔ'lɑ̃], *a.* insolent, impudent, rude. —*n.m.* (*fem.* **-e**) insolent person.
insolite [ɛ̃sɔ'lit], *a.* unusual, unwonted.
insolubilité [ɛ̃sɔlybili'te], *n.f.* insolubility.
insoluble [ɛ̃sɔ'lybl], *a.* insoluble.
insolvabilité [ɛ̃sɔlvabili'te], *n.f.* insolvency.
insolvable [ɛ̃sɔl'vabl], *a.* insolvent.
insomnie [ɛ̃sɔm'ni], *n.f.* insomnia.
insondable [ɛ̃sɔ̃'dabl], *a.* unfathomable.
insonore [ɛ̃sɔ'nɔːr], *a.* sound-proof.
insouciance [ɛ̃su'sjɑ̃ːs], *n.f.* carelessness, thoughtlessness.
insouciant [ɛ̃su'sjɑ̃], **insoucieux** [ɛ̃su'sjø] (*fem.* **-euse**), *a.* careless, thoughtless; unconcerned, easy-going.
insoumis [ɛ̃su'mi], *a.* unsubdued; refractory, unruly.—*n.m.* (*Mil.*) defaulter.
insoumission [ɛ̃sumi'sjɔ̃], *n.f.* insubordination.
insoutenable [ɛ̃sut'nabl], *a.* indefensible; unbearable.
inspecter [ɛ̃spɛk'te], *v.t.* to inspect, to survey, to scan.
inspecteur [ɛ̃spɛk'tœːr], *n.m.* (*fem.* **-trice**) inspector, superintendent, surveyor.
inspection [ɛ̃spɛk'sjɔ̃], *n.f.* inspection, survey; superintendence; ***faire l'inspection de,*** to inspect; ***passer à l'inspection,*** to undergo inspection.
inspirateur [ɛ̃spira'tœːr], *a.* (*fem.* **-trice**) inspiring; (*Anat.*) inspiratory.—*n.m.* (*fem.* **-trice**) inspirer.
inspiration [ɛ̃spirɑ'sjɔ̃], *n.f.* inspiration; suggestion; inhaling.
inspiré [ɛ̃spi're], *a.* and *n.m.* (*fem.* **-ée**) inspired (person).
inspirer [ɛ̃spi're], *v.t.* to inspire, to breathe in; (*fig.*) to suggest, to instil. **s'inspirer,** *v.r.* to draw one's inspiration (***de***).
instabilité [ɛ̃stabili'te], *n.f.* instability, fickleness.
instable [ɛ̃'stabl], *a.* unstable; unsteady, wobbly.
installation [ɛ̃stalɑ'sjɔ̃], *n.f.* installation; equipment.
installer [ɛ̃sta'le], *v.t.* to install; to inaugurate, to establish. **s'installer,** *v.r.* to install oneself; to settle.
instamment [ɛ̃sta'mɑ̃], *adv.* earnestly, urgently.
instance [ɛ̃s'tɑ̃ːs], *n.f.* entreaty; urgency, earnestness; (*Law*) instance; (*pl.*) entreaties.
instant (1) [ɛ̃s'tɑ̃], *n.m.* instant, moment; ***à l'instant,*** in an instant, immediately.
instant (2) [ɛ̃s'tɑ̃], *a.* pressing, urgent; imminent.
instantané [ɛ̃stɑ̃ta'ne], *a.* instantaneous.—*n.m.* snapshot.
instantanément [ɛ̃stɑ̃tane'mɑ̃], *adv.* instantaneously.
instar (à l') [alɛ̃s'taːr], *prep. phr.* ***à l'instar de,*** like; in imitation of.
instigateur [ɛ̃stiga'tœːr], *n.m.* (*fem.* **-trice**) instigator.
instigation [ɛ̃stigɑ'sjɔ̃], *n.f.* instigation.
instiller [ɛ̃sti'le], *v.t.* to instil.
instinct [ɛ̃s'tɛ̃], *n.m.* instinct.
instinctif [ɛ̃stɛ̃k'tif], *a.* (*fem.* **-tive**) instinctive.
instinctivement [ɛ̃stɛ̃ktiv'mɑ̃], *adv.* instinctively.
instituer [ɛ̃sti'tɥe], *v.t.* to institute, to establish.
institut [ɛ̃sti'ty], *n.m.* institution; institute; order (*of monks*).
instituteur [ɛ̃stity'tœːr], *n.m.* (*fem.* **-trice**) teacher, schoolmaster, schoolmistress (*in primary schools*); ***institutrice (particulière),*** governess.
institution [ɛ̃stity'sjɔ̃], *n.f.* institution; establishment; (*Law*) appointment.

instructeur [ɛ̃stryk'tœːr], *n.m.* instructor, drill-master.
instructif [ɛ̃stryk'tif], *a.* (*fem.* **-tive**) instructive.
instruction [ɛ̃stryk'sjɔ̃], *n.f.* instruction, tuition, education, learning; (*Law*) inquiry, examination; (*pl.*) directions.
instruire [ɛ̃s'trɥiːr], *v.t. irr.* (*conjug. like* CONDUIRE) to instruct, to teach, to educate; to inform (*de*). **s'instruire**, *v.r.* to instruct, inform *or* improve oneself.
instruit [ɛ̃'strɥi], *a.* instructed, informed; aware; educated.
instrument [ɛ̃stry'mɑ̃], *n.m.* instrument, tool; document.
instrumental [ɛ̃strymɑ̃'tal], *a.* (*m. pl.* **-aux**) instrumental.
instrumentiste [ɛ̃strymɑ̃'tist], *n.* instrumentalist.
insu [ɛ̃'sy], *prep. phr.* ***à l'insu de***, unknown to; ***à mon insu***, unknown to me.
insubmersible [ɛ̃sybmɛr'sibl], *a.* unsinkable.
insubordination [ɛ̃sybɔrdinɑ'sjɔ̃], *n.f.* insubordination.
insubordonné [ɛ̃sybɔrdɔ'ne], *a.* insubordinate.
insuccès [ɛ̃syk'sɛ], *n.m. inv.* failure, lack of success.
insuffisamment [ɛ̃syfiza'mɑ̃], *adv.* insufficiently.
insuffisance [ɛ̃syfi'zɑ̃ːs], *n.f.* insufficiency.
insuffisant [ɛ̃syfi'zɑ̃], *a.* insufficient, inadequate.
insulaire [ɛ̃sy'lɛːr], *a.* insular.—*n.* islander.
insularité [ɛ̃sylari'te], *n.f.* insularity.
insuline [ɛ̃sy'lin], *n.f.* insulin.
insultant [ɛ̃syl'tɑ̃], *a.* insulting.
insulte [ɛ̃'sylt], *n.f.* insult.
insulter [ɛ̃syl'te], *v.t.* to insult, to affront.
insupportable [ɛ̃sypɔr'tabl], *a.* intolerable, unbearable.
insupportablement [ɛ̃sypɔrtablə'mɑ̃], *adv.* intolerably, unbearably.
insurgé [ɛ̃syr'ʒe], *a.* and *n.m.* (*fem.* **-ée**) rebel, insurgent.
insurger **(s')** [sɛ̃syr'ʒe], *v.r.* (*conjug. like* MANGER) to revolt, to rebel.
insurmontable [ɛ̃syrmɔ̃'tabl], *a.* insurmountable, insuperable.
insurrection [ɛ̃syrɛk'sjɔ̃], *n.f.* insurrection, rising.
intact [ɛ̃'takt], *a.* intact, entire, whole.
intangible [ɛ̃tɑ̃'ʒibl], *a.* intangible.
intarissable [ɛ̃tari'sabl], *a.* inexhaustible.
intégral [ɛ̃te'gral], *a.* (*m. pl.* **-aux**) integral, whole, entire.
intégrale [ɛ̃te'gral], *n.f.* (*Math.*) integral.
intégralement [ɛ̃tegral'mɑ̃], *adv.* integrally, entirely, in full.
intègre [ɛ̃'tɛgr], *a.* honest, upright, just.
intègrement [ɛ̃tɛgrə'mɑ̃], *adv.* honestly, uprightly.
intégrer [ɛ̃te'gre], *v.t.* (*conjug. like* CÉDER) to integrate. **s'intégrer**, *v.r.* to combine into; to form an integral part of.
intégrité [ɛ̃tegri'te], *n.f.* integrity, uprightness, probity.
intellect [ɛ̃tɛ'lɛkt], *n.m.* intellect, understanding.
intellectuel [ɛ̃tɛlɛk'tɥɛl], *a.* (*fem.* **-elle**) and *n.m.* (*fem.* **-elle**) intellectual.
intellectuellement [ɛ̃tɛlɛktɥɛl'mɑ̃], *adv.* intellectually.
intelligemment [ɛ̃tɛliʒa'mɑ̃] *adv.* intelligently.
intelligence [ɛ̃tɛli'ʒɑ̃ːs], *n.f.* intelligence, intellect; clear comprehension; cleverness, skill, ability; mutual understanding; ***avec intelligence***, skilfully, cleverly; ***en bonne intelligence avec***, on good terms with; ***être d'intelligence avec***, to be in collusion with.
intelligent [ɛ̃tɛli'ʒɑ̃], *a.* intelligent; bright, clever, sharp.
intelligible [ɛ̃tɛli'ʒibl], *a.* intelligible; distinct, clear.
intelligiblement [ɛ̃tɛliʒiblə'mɑ̃], *adv.* intelligibly, clearly.
intempérance [ɛ̃tɑ̃pe'rɑ̃ːs], *n.f.* intemperance, insobriety.
intempérant [ɛ̃tɑ̃pe'rɑ̃], *a.* intemperate.
intempérie [ɛ̃tɑ̃pe'ri], *n.f.* (*usu. in pl.*) inclemency (*of the weather*).
intempestif [ɛ̃tɑ̃pɛs'tif], *a.* (*fem.* **-tive**) unseasonable, untimely.
intenable [ɛ̃tə'nabl], *a.* untenable, insufferable.
intendance [ɛ̃tɑ̃'dɑ̃ːs], *n.f.* stewardship (*of an estate*); (*Mil.*) commissariat; the Army Service Corps.
intendant [ɛ̃tɑ̃'dɑ̃], *n.m.* intendant, steward; major-domo; (*Mil.*) administrative officer (*having the rank of a general*).
intense [ɛ̃'tɑːs], *a.* intense, violent; severe.
intensité [ɛ̃tɑ̃si'te], *n.f.* intensity, violence, severity.
intensivement [ɛ̃tɑ̃siv'mɑ̃], *adv.* intensively.
intenter [ɛ̃tɑ̃'te], *v.t.* (*Law*) ***intenter une action*** or ***un procès à*** or ***contre quelqu'un***, to enter *or* bring an action against someone.
intention [ɛ̃tɑ̃'sjɔ̃], *n.f.* intention; (*Law*) intent; purpose; ***à l'intention de***, for the sake of; ***avec intention***, on purpose; ***avoir l'intention de***, to intend to; ***sans intention***, unintentionally.
intentionné [ɛ̃tɑ̃sjɔ'ne], *a.* intentioned, disposed, meaning.
intentionnel [ɛ̃tɑ̃sjɔ'nɛl], *a.* (*fem.* **-elle**) intentional.
inter [ɛ̃'tɛr], *n.m.* (*Ftb.*) inside-forward.
interaction [ɛ̃tɛrak'sjɔ̃], *n.f.* interaction.
intercaler [ɛ̃tɛrka'le], *v.t.* to intercalate; to interpolate; (*Elec.*) to switch in.
intercéder [ɛ̃tɛrse'de], *v.i.* (*conjug. like* CÉDER) to intercede, to plead.
intercepter [ɛ̃tɛrsɛp'te], *v.t.* to intercept.
intercession [ɛ̃tɛrsɛ'sjɔ̃], *n.f.* intercession; mediation.
intercontinental [ɛ̃tɛrkɔ̃tinɑ̃'tal], *a.* (*m. pl.* **-aux**) intercontinental.
interdépartemental [ɛ̃tɛrdepartəmɑ̃'tal], *a.* (*m. pl.* **-aux**) interdepartmental.
interdiction [ɛ̃tɛrdik'sjɔ̃], *n.f.* interdiction, prohibition.
interdire [ɛ̃tɛr'diːr], *v.t. irr.* (*conjug. like* MÉDIRE) to interdict, to prohibit; to forbid; to suspend; (*fig.*) to confound, to nonplus.
interdit [ɛ̃tɛr'di], *a.* forbidden, prohibited; (*fig.*) abashed, confused; ***entrée interdite***, no admittance; ***passage interdit***, no thoroughfare.—*n.m.* interdict.—*n.m.* (*fem.* **-e**) person interdicted.

intéressant [ɛ̃terɛ'sɑ̃], *a.* interesting; attractive (*price*).
intéressé [ɛ̃terɛ'se], *a.* interested; selfish.—*n.m.* (*fem.* **-ée**) interested party.
intéresser [ɛ̃terɛ'se], *v.t.* to interest; to concern, to affect. **s'intéresser,** *v.r.* to take an interest in, to be interested (**à**).
intérêt [ɛ̃te'rɛ], *n.m.* interest, concern; share.
interférence [ɛ̃tɛrfe'rɑ̃:s], *n.f.* interference; (*pl.*) (*Rad., Tel.*) interference.
interférer [ɛ̃tɛrfe're], *v.i.* (*conjug. like* CÉDER) to interfere.
intérieur [ɛ̃te'rjœ:r], *a.* inner, inward, internal, interior; inland.—*n.m.* interior; home, private life; ***à l'intérieur***, inside; ***Ministre de l'Intérieur***, Home Secretary.
interlocuteur [ɛ̃tɛrlɔky'tœ:r], *n.m.* (*fem.* **-trice**) speaker (*in a conversation*).
interloquer [ɛ̃tɛrlɔ'ke], *v.t.* to nonplus, to disconcert.
intermède [ɛ̃tɛr'mɛd], *n.m.* interlude.
intermédiaire [ɛ̃tɛrme'djɛ:r], *a.* intermediate, intervening.—*n.m.* medium, agency; intermediary, middleman, agent.
interminable [ɛ̃tɛrmi'nabl], *a.* interminable, endless.
intermission [ɛ̃tɛrmi'sjɔ̃], *n.f.* intermission, pause.
intermittence [ɛ̃tɛrmi'tɑ̃:s], *n.f.* intermission, cessation.
intermittent [ɛ̃tɛrmi'tɑ̃], *a.* intermittent.
internat [ɛ̃tɛr'na], *n.m.* boarding-school; house-surgeonship (*of hospitals*).
international [ɛ̃tɛrnasjɔ'nal], *a.* (*m. pl.* **-aux**) international.
interne [ɛ̃'tɛrn], *a.* internal, inward, resident.—*n.* boarder (*in schools*).
interné [ɛ̃tɛr'ne], *a.* interned.—*n.m.* (*fem.* **-ée**) internee.
interner [ɛ̃tɛr'ne], *v.t.* to intern.
interpellation [ɛ̃tɛrpɛlɑ'sjɔ̃], *n.f.* interpellation.
interpeller [ɛ̃tɛrpə'le], *v.t.* to hail, to call upon, to challenge; (*Polit.*) to interpellate.
interplanétaire [ɛ̃tɛrplane'tɛ:r], *a.* interplanetary.
interpoler [ɛ̃tɛrpɔ'le], *v.t.* to interpolate.
interposer [ɛ̃tɛrpo'ze], *v.t.* to interpose. **s'interposer,** *v.r.* to interpose, to come between.
interprétation [ɛ̃tɛrpretɑ'sjɔ̃], *n.f.* interpretation; rendering (*of a play*).
interprète [ɛ̃tɛr'prɛt], *n.* interpreter, expounder; artist, actor, actress.
interpréter [ɛ̃tɛrpre'te], *v.t.* (*conjug. like* CÉDER) to interpret, to explain; to construe.
interrègne [ɛ̃tɛr'rɛɲ], *n.m.* interregnum.
interrogateur [ɛ̃tɛrɔga'tœr], *n.m.* (*fem.* **-trice**) interrogator questioner, examiner.
interrogatif [ɛ̃tɛrɔga'tif], *a.* (*fem.* **-tive**) interrogative.
interrogation [ɛ̃tɛrɔgɑ'sjɔ̃], *n.f.* interrogation, question; ***point d'interrogation***, question mark.
interrogatoire [ɛ̃tɛrɔga'twa:r], *n.m.* examination.
interroger [ɛ̃tɛrɔ'ʒe], *v.t.* (*conjug. like* MANGER) to interrogate, to question; to examine.
interrompre [ɛ̃tɛ'rɔ̃:pr], *v.t.* (*conjug. like* ROMPRE) to interrupt, to break off; to stop.
interrupteur [ɛ̃tɛryp'tœ:r], *a.* and *n.m.* (*fem.* **-trice**) interrupting; interrupter.—*n.m.* (*Elec.*) switch, cut-out.
interruption [ɛ̃tɛryp'sjɔ̃], *n.f.* interruption; (*Elec.*) disconnection.
interscolaire [ɛ̃tɛrskɔ'lɛ:r], *a.* inter-school (*competition etc.*).
intersection [ɛ̃tɛrsɛk'sjɔ̃], *n.f.* intersection.
interstice [ɛ̃tɛr'stis], *n.m.* interstice, chink, crack.
intervalle [ɛ̃tɛr'val], *n.m.* interval; distance, gap; ***dans l'intervalle***, in the meantime.
intervenir [ɛ̃tɛrvə'ni:r], *v.i. irr.* (*conjug. like* TENIR) to intervene, to interfere; to happen.
intervention [ɛ̃tɛrvɑ̃'sjɔ], *n.f.* intervention, interference.
interversion [ɛ̃tɛrvɛr'sjɔ̃], *n.f.* inversion.
intervertir [ɛ̃tɛrvɛr'ti:r], *v.t.* to invert, to reverse.
intestin [ɛ̃tɛs'tɛ̃], *a.* intestine; internal, domestic, civil.—*n.m.* intestine.
intimation [ɛ̃timɑ'sjɔ̃], *n.f.* notification.
intime [ɛ̃'tim], *a.* intimate, inmost secret; close.—*n.* intimate.
intimement [ɛ̃tim'mɑ̃], *adv.* intimately.
intimider [ɛ̃timi'de], *v.t.* to intimidate, to frighten.
intimité [ɛ̃timi'te], *n.f.* intimacy, closeness.
intitulé [ɛ̃tity'le], *a.* entitled.—*n.m.* title (*of deeds, books etc.*).
intituler [ɛ̃tity'le], *v.t.* to entitle, to call, to name. **s'intituler,** *v.r.* to entitle *or* call oneself.
intolérable [ɛ̃tɔle'rabl], *a.* intolerable, insufferable.
intolérablement [ɛ̃tɔlerablə'mɑ̃], *adv.* unbearably.
intolérance [ɛ̃tɔle'rɑ̃:s], *n.f.* intolerance.
intolérant [ɛ̃tɔle'rɑ̃], *a.* intolerant.
intonation [ɛ̃tonɑ'sjɔ̃], *n.f.* intonation; pitch.
intoxicant [ɛ̃tɔksi'kɑ̃], *a.* poisonous.
intoxication [ɛ̃tɔksikɑ'sjɔ̃], *n.f.* poisoning.
intoxiquer [ɛ̃tɔksi'ke], *v.t.* to poison.
intraduisible [ɛ̃tradɥi'zibl], *a.* untranslatable.
intraitable [ɛ̃trɛ'tabl], *a.* intractable, unmanageable.
intransigeant [ɛ̃trɑ̃zi'ʒɑ̃], *a.* intransigent, uncompromising.—*n.m.* (*fem.* **-e**) intransigent, diehard.
intransitif [ɛ̃trɑ̃zi'tif], *a.* (*fem.* **-tive**) (*Gram.*) intransitive.
intraversable [ɛ̃travɛr'sabl], *a.* impassable.
intrépide [ɛ̃tre'pid], *a.* intrepid, dauntless, fearless.
intrigant [ɛ̃tri'gɑ̃], *a.* intriguing.—*n.m.* (*fem.* **-e**) intriguer, schemer.
intrigue [ɛ̃'trig], *n.f.* intrigue; plot (*of a novel etc.*).
intrigueur [ɛ̃tri'gœ:r], *n.m.* (*fem.* **-euse**) intriguer, plotter.
intrinsèque [ɛ̃trɛ̃'sɛk], *a.* intrinsic.
introduction [ɛ̃trɔdyk'sjɔ̃], *n.f.* introduction; preamble.
introductoire [ɛ̃trɔdyk'twa:r], *a.* introductory, preliminary.
introduire [ɛ̃trɔ'dɥi:r], *v.t. irr.* (*conjug. like* CONDUIRE) to show *or* bring in, to introduce. **s'introduire,** *v.r.* to get in, to find one's way in; to intrude.
introniser [ɛ̃trɔni'ze], *v.t.* to install, to enthrone; (*fig.*) to establish (*a fashion*).
introspectif [ɛ̃trɔspɛk'tif], *a.* (*fem.* **-tive**) introspective.

introuvable [ɛ̃tru'vabl], *a.* not to be found; matchless.
introverti [ɛ̃trɔvɛr'ti], *a.* introverted.—*n.m.* (*fem.* **-e**) introvert.
intrus [ɛ̃'try], *a.* intruding, intruded.—*n.m.* (*fem.* **-e**) intruder.
intrusion [ɛ̃try'zjɔ̃], *n.f.* intrusion.
intuitif [ɛ̃tɥi'tif], *a.* (*fem.* **-tive**) intuitive.
intuition [ɛ̃tɥi'sjɔ̃], *n.f.* intuition.
inusable [iny'zabl], *a.* durable, everlasting.
inusité [inyzi'te], *a.* unused; unusual; obsolete.
inutile [iny'til], *a.* useless, unnecessary.
inutilement [inytil'mɑ̃], *adv.* uselessly, to no purpose, needlessly.
inutilisable [inytili'zabl], *a.* that cannot be utilized, worthless.
inutilité [inytili'te], *n.f.* uselessness; useless thing.
invaincu [ɛ̃vɛ̃'ky], *a.* unvanquished, unconquered.
invalidation [ɛ̃validɑ'sjɔ̃], *n.f.* invalidation.
invalide [ɛ̃va'lid], *a.* disabled, crippled, infirm, invalid; (*Law*) not valid.—*n.* invalid, pensioner; ***Hôtel des Invalides***, the Chelsea Hospital of France.
invalider [ɛ̃vali'de], *v.t.* to invalidate, to annul.
invariable [ɛ̃va'rjabl], *a.* invariable, unchangeable.
invariablement [ɛ̃varjablə'mɑ̃], *adv.* invariably.
invasion [ɛ̃vɑ'zjɔ̃], *n.f.* invasion; inroad.
invective [ɛ̃vɛk'tiːv], *n.f.* invective, (*pl.*) abuse.
invectiver [ɛ̃vɛkti've], *v.t.* to abuse.—*v.i.* to inveigh against, to revile (***contre***).
inventaire [ɛ̃vɑ̃'tɛːr], *n.m.* inventory; stocktaking.
inventer [ɛ̃vɑ̃'te], *v.t.* to invent, to devise; to find out; to imagine; to forge.
inventeur [ɛ̃vɑ̃'tœːr], *n.m.* (*fem.* **-trice**) inventor.
inventif [ɛ̃vɑ̃'tif], *a.* (*fem.* **-tive**) inventive.
invention [ɛ̃vɑ̃'sjɔ̃], *n.f.* invention; inventiveness; device, trick; falsehood; ***brevet d'invention***, patent.
inventorier [ɛ̃vɑ̃tɔ'rje], *v.t.* to draw up an inventory of; to schedule, to catalogue.
inversable [ɛ̃vɛr'sabl], *a.* that cannot be upset.
inverse [ɛ̃'vɛrs], *a.* inverse, inverted.—*n.m.* reverse, contrary.
inversement [ɛ̃vɛrs'mɑ̃], *adv.* inversely.
invertébré [ɛ̃vɛrte'bre], *a.* and *n.m.* (*fem.* **-ée**) invertebrate.
inverti [ɛ̃vɛr'ti], *a.* inverted, reversed.
investigateur [ɛ̃vɛstiga'tœːr], *a.* (*fem.* **-trice**) searching, inquiring.—*n.m.* (*fem.* **-trice**) investigator.
investigation [ɛ̃vɛstigɑ'sjɔ̃], *n.f.* investigation, inquiry.
investir [ɛ̃vɛs'tiːr], *v.t.* to invest; to surround, to lay siege to.
investiture [ɛ̃vɛsti'tyːr], *n.f.* investiture.
invétéré [ɛ̃vete're], *a.* inveterate.
invincibilité [ɛ̃vɛ̃sibili'te], *n.f.* invincibility.
invincible [ɛ̃vɛ̃'sibl], *a.* invincible, unconquerable.
inviolable [ɛ̃vjɔ'labl], *a.* inviolable.
inviolé [ɛ̃vjɔ'le], *a.* inviolate.
invisible [ɛ̃vi'zibl], *a.* invisible.
invisiblement [ɛ̃viziblə'mɑ̃], *adv.* invisibly.
invitation [ɛ̃vitɑ'sjɔ̃], *n.f.* invitation.
invité [ɛ̃vi'te], *n.m.* (*fem.* **-ée**) guest.
inviter [ɛ̃vi'te], *v.t.* to invite, to request; to incite, to tempt.
invocation [ɛ̃vɔkɑ'sjɔ̃], *n.f.* invocation.
involontaire [ɛ̃vɔlɔ̃'tɛːr], *a.* involuntary, unwilling.
involontairement [ɛ̃vɔlɔ̃tɛr'mɑ̃], *adv.* involuntarily.
invoquer [ɛ̃vɔ'ke], *v.t.* to invoke, to call upon; to appeal to.
invraisemblable [ɛ̃vrɛsɑ̃'blabl], *a.* unlikely, improbable.
invraisemblablement [ɛ̃vrɛsɑ̃blablə'mɑ̃], *adv.* improbably.
invraisemblance [ɛ̃vrɛsɑ̃'blɑ̃ːs], *n.f.* unlikelihood, improbability.
invulnérable [ɛ̃vylne'rabl], *a.* invulnerable.
iode [jɔd], *n.m.* iodine.
ion [jɔ̃], *n.m.* (*Phys.*) ion.
ionisation [jɔnizɑ'sjɔ̃], *n.f.* ionization.
ionosphère [jɔnɔs'fɛːr], *n.f.* ionosphere.
iota [jɔ'ta], *n.m.* iota, jot, tittle.
Irak [i'rak], **l'**, *m.* Iraq.
irakien [ira'kjɛ̃], *a.* (*fem.* **-enne**) Iraqi.—*n.m.* (**Irakien**, *fem.* **-enne**) Iraqi (*person*).
Iran [i'rɑ̃], **l'**, *m.* Iran.
iranien [ira'njɛ̃], *a.* (*fem.* **-enne**) Iranian.—*n.m.* (**Iranien**, *fem.* **-enne**) Iranian (*person*).
irascibilite [irasibili'te], *n.f.* irascibility.
irascible [ira'sibl], *a.* irascible, irritable.
iridescence [iridɛ'sɑ̃ːs], *n.f.* iridescence.
iridescent [iridɛ'sɑ̃], *a.* iridescent.
iris [i'riːs], *n.m. inv.* iris; rainbow.
irisé [iri'ze], *a.* rainbow-coloured, iridescent.
irlandais [irlɑ̃'dɛ], *a.* Irish.—*n.m.* Irish (*language*); (**Irlandais**, *fem.* **-aise**) Irishman, Irishwoman.
Irlande [ir'lɑ̃d], **l'**, *f.* Ireland.
ironie [irɔ'ni], *n.f.* irony, mockery, raillery.
ironique [irɔ'nik], *a.* ironical.
irradiation [irradjɑ'sjɔ̃], *n.f.* irradiation.
irradier [irra'dje], *v.t.* to radiate through; (*C*) to broadcast.
irraisonnable [irrɛzɔ'nabl], *a.* irrational.
irraisonnablement [irrɛzɔnablə'mɑ̃], *adv.* irrationally.
irrationnel [irrasjɔ'nɛl], *a.* (*fem.* **-elle**) irrational.
irrationnellement [irrasjɔnɛl'mɑ̃], *adv.* irrationally.
irréalisable [irreali'zabl], *a.* impossible, impracticable.
irréconciliable [irrekɔ̃si'ljabl], *a.* irreconcilable.
irrécusable [irreky'zabl], *a.* unexceptionable, unimpeachable.
irréductible [irredyk'tibl], *a.* irreducible; (*fig.*) unyielding.
irréel [irre'ɛl], *a.* (*fem.* **-éelle**) unreal.—*n.m.* unreality.
irréfléchi [irrefle'ʃi], *a.* thoughtless, inconsiderate.
irréflexion [irreflɛk'sjɔ̃], *n.f.* thoughtlessness, heedlessness.
irréfutable [irrefy'tabl], *a.* irrefutable.
irrégularité [irregylari'te], *n.f.* irregularity.
irrégulier [irregy'lje], *a.* (*fem.* **-ière**) irregular.
irrégulièrement [irregyljɛr'mɑ̃], *adv.* irregularly.

irréligieux [irreli'ʒjø], *a.* (*fem.* **-euse**) irreligious.
irrémédiable [irreme'djabl], *a.* irremediable, irreparable, irretrievable.
irrémédiablement [irremedjablə'mɑ̃], *adv.* irremediably, irreparably.
irrémissible [irremi'sibl], *a.* irremissible, unpardonable.
irremplaçable [irrɑ̃pla'sabl], *a.* irreplaceable.
irréparable [irrepa'rabl], *a.* irreparable.
irrépressible [irreprɛ'sibl], *a.* irrepressible.
irréprochable [irreprɔ'ʃabl], *a.* irreproachable.
irrésistible [irrezis'tibl], *a.* irresistible.
irrésistiblement [irrezistiblə'mɑ̃], *adv.* irresistibly.
irrésolu [irrezɔ'ly], *a.* irresolute, wavering.
irrésolument [irrezɔly'mɑ̃], *adv.* irresolutely.
irrésolution [irrezɔly'sjɔ̃], *n.f.* irresolution, indecision.
irrespectueusement [irrɛspɛktɥøz'mɑ̃], *adv.* disrespectfully.
irrespectueux [irrɛspɛk'tɥø], *a.* (*fem.* **-euse**) disrespectful.
irresponsabilité [irrɛspɔ̃sabili'te], *n.f.* irresponsibility.
irresponsable [irrɛspɔ̃'sabl], *a.* irresponsible.
irrétrécissable [irretresi'sabl], *a.* unshrinkable.
irrévérence [irreve'rɑ̃:s], *n.f.* irreverence, disrespect.
irrévocable [irrevɔ'kabl], *a.* irrevocable.
irrévocablement [irrevɔkablə'mɑ̃], *adv.* irrevocably.
irrigateur [irriga'tœ:r], *n.m.* watering-engine; garden-hose.
irrigation [irrigɑ'sjɔ̃], *n.f.* irrigation.
irriguer [irri'ge], *v.t.* to irrigate, to water.
irritabilité [irritabili'te], *n.f.* irritability.
irritable [irri'tabl], *a.* irritable.
irritant [irri'tɑ̃], *a.* irritating, provoking.
irritation [irritɑ'sjɔ̃], *n.f.* irritation, exasperation.
riter [irri'te], *v.t.* to irritate, to incense, to anger; to provoke, to excite. **s'irriter**, *v.r.* to grow angry; to become irritated.
irruption [irryp'sjɔ̃], *n.f.* irruption, raid; overflow, flood; ***faire irruption dans***, to invade.
Isaïe [iza'i], *m.* Isaiah.
Islam [is'lam], *n.m.* Islam.
islandais [islɑ̃'dɛ], *a.* Icelandic.—*n.m.* Icelandic (*language*); (**Islandais**, *fem.* **-aise**) Icelander.
Islande [is'lɑ̃d], **l'**, *f.* Iceland.
isobare [izɔ'bar], *n.f.* isobar.
isocèle or **isoscèle** [izɔ'sɛl], *a.* (*Geom.*) isosceles.
isolant [izɔ'lɑ̃], *a.* insulating; ***bouteille isolante***, vacuum flask.
isolateur [izɔla'tœ:r], *a.* (*fem.* **-trice**) insulating.—*n.m.* insulator.
isolation [izɔlɑ'sjɔ̃], *n.f.* insulation; isolation.
isolé [izɔ'le], *a.* isolated; lonely, solitary; detached; insulated; apart.
isolement [izɔl'mɑ̃], *n.m.* loneliness, isolation; insulation.
isolément [izɔle'mɑ̃], *adv.* separately.
isoler [izɔ'le], *v.t.* to isolate; to insulate; to detach; to separate.
isotope [izɔ'tɔp], *n.m.* isotope.
Israël [isra'ɛl], **l'**, *m.* Israel.
israélien [israe'ljɛ̃], *a.* (*fem.* **-enne**) Israel(i).—*n.m.* (**Israélien**, *fem.* **-enne**) Israeli (*person*).
issu [i'sy], *a.* born, descended, sprung from.
issue [i'sy], *n.f.* issue, outlet; escape; (*fig.*) end, event.
isthme [ism], *n.m.* isthmus.
Italie [ita'li], **l'**, *f.* Italy.
italien [ita'ljɛ̃], *a.* (*fem.* **-enne**) Italian.—*n.m.* Italian (*language*); (**Italien**, *fem.* **-enne**) Italian (*person*).
italique [ita'lik], *a.* and *n.m.* italic.
itinéraire [itine'rɛ:r], *a.* pertaining to roads etc.—*n.m.* itinerary, route; guide-book.
itinérant [itine'rɑ̃], *a.* itinerant.
ivoire [i'vwa:r], *n.m.* ivory; (*fig.*) whiteness; ***la Côte d'Ivoire***, Ivory Coast.
ivraie [i'vrɛ], *n.f.* darnel, tare.
ivre [i:vr], *a.* drunk; intoxicated; (*fig.*) transported; ***ivre mort***, dead-drunk.
ivresse [i'vrɛs], *n.f.* drunkenness, intoxication; (*fig.*) frenzy, rapture.
ivrogne [i'vrɔɲ], *a.* drunken.—*n.* drunkard.
ivrognerie [ivrɔ'ɲri], *n.f.* habitual drunkenness.

J

J, j [ʒi], *n.m.* the tenth letter of the alphabet.
jabot [ʒa'bo], *n.m.* crop (*of a bird*); frill (*of a shirt* or *blouse*); jabot.
jaboter [ʒabɔ'te], *v.i.* (*colloq.*) to prattle, to chatter.
jacasser [ʒaka'se], *v.i.* to chatter (*of the magpie*); (*fig.*) to chatter, to jabber.
jachère [ʒa'ʃɛ:r], *n.f.* fallow.
jacinthe [ʒa'sɛ̃:t], *n.f.* jacinthe; hyacinth.
Jacques [ʒɑ:k], *m.* James.
jade [ʒad], *n.m.* jade.
jadis [ʒɑ'dis], *adv.* of old, formerly.
jaguar [ʒa'gwa:r], *n.m.* jaguar.
jaillir [ʒa'ji:r], *v.i.* to spout, to gush; to shoot out *or* up.
jaillissant [ʒaji'sɑ̃], *a.* spouting, gushing.
jaillissement [ʒajis'mɑ̃], *n.m.* gushing, spouting, flashing.
jais [ʒɛ], *n.m.* jet.
jalon [ʒa'lɔ̃], *n.m.* levelling-staff, surveying-staff; (*fig.*) landmark, beacon.
jalonnement [ʒalɔn'mɑ̃], *n.m.* (*Land-surveying*) staking-out, marking-out.
jalonner [ʒalɔ'ne], *v.t.* to mark *or* stake out.—*v.i.* to place land marks etc.
jalousement [ʒaluz'mɑ̃], *adv.* jealously.
jalouser [ʒalu'ze], *v.t.* to be jealous of, to envy.
jalousie [ʒalu'zi], *n.f.* jealousy, envy; Venetian blind; (*Bot.*) sweet-william.
jaloux [ʒa'lu], *a.* (*fem.* **-ouse**) jealous; envious; desirous, anxious.—*n.m.* (*fem.* **-ouse**) jealous person.

jamaïquain [ʒamai'kɛ̃], *a.* Jamaican.—*n.m.* (**Jamaïquain**, *fem.* **-aine**) Jamaican (*person*).
Jamaïque [ʒama'ik], **la**, *f.* Jamaica.
jamais [ʒa'mɛ], *adv.* (*neg.*) never, (*affirm.*) ever; ***à jamais***, for ever; ***jamais de la vie***, not on your life!; ***mieux vaut tard que jamais***, better late than never.
jambage [ʒɑ̃'ba:ʒ], *n.m.* jamb (*of a door etc.*); down-stroke, pot-hook (*in writing*).
jambe [ʒɑ̃:b], *n.f.* leg; shank; ***courir à toutes jambes***, to run as fast as one can; ***prendre ses jambes à son cou***, to take to one's heels.
jambière [ʒɑ̃'bjɛ:r], *n.f.* legging, leg-guard.
jambon [ʒɑ̃'bɔ̃], *n.m.* ham.
jamboree [ʒɑ̃bɔ'ri], *n.m.* jamboree.
jante [ʒɑ̃:t], *n.f.* felloe, rim (*of a wheel*).
janvier [ʒɑ̃'vje], *n.m.* January.
Japon [ʒa'pɔ̃], **le**, *m.* Japan.
japonais [ʒapɔ'nɛ], *a.* Japanese.—*n.m.* Japanese (*language*); (**Japonais**, *fem.* **-aise**) Japanese (*person*).
japper [ʒa'pe], *v.i.* to yelp, to yap.
jaquette [ʒa'kɛt], *n.f.* morning coat, tail-coat; woman's jacket; dust-cover (*of book*).
jardin [ʒar'dɛ̃], *n.m.* garden.
jardinage [ʒardi'na:ʒ], *n.m.* gardening; garden-produce.
jardiner [ʒardi'ne], *v.i.* to garden.
jardinier [ʒardi'nje], *a.* (*fem.* **-ière**) (of the) garden.—*n.m.* (*fem.* **-ière**) gardener.—*n.f.* (**-ière**) flower-stand, jardinière.
jardiniste [ʒardi'nist], *n.* landscape-gardener.
jargon [ʒar'gɔ̃], *n.m.* jargon, gibberish; lingo.
jarre [ʒa:r], *n.f.* jar.
jarret [ʒa'rɛ], *n.m.* ham (*of man*); hough, hock (*of horse*).
jarretière [ʒar'tjɛr], *n.f.* garter.
jars (1) [ʒa:r], *n.m.* gander.
jars (2) [ʒa:r], *n.m.* (*another form of* **jargon**) slang.
jaser [ʒɑ'ze], *v.i.* to chatter, to gossip.
jaserie [ʒɑz'ri], *n.f.* chatter; gossip.
jaseur [ʒɑ'zœ:r], *a.* (*fem.* **-euse**) talkative.—*n.m.* (*fem.* **-euse**) chatterer, chatterbox.
jasmin [ʒas'mɛ̃], *n.m.* jasmine.
jaspe [ʒasp], *n.m.* jasper.
jasper [ʒas'pe], *v.t.* to marble, to vein, to variegate.
jaspure [ʒas'py:r], *n.f.* marbling, veining.
jatte [ʒat], *n.f.* bowl, platter; dog's bowl.
jauge [ʒo:ʒ], *n.f.* gauge; (*Naut.*) tonnage.
jaugeage [ʒo'ʒa:ʒ], *n.m.* gauging.
jauger [ʒo'ʒe], *v.t.* (*conjug. like* MANGER) to gauge, to measure the capacity of; (*Naut.*) to draw (*so many feet of water*).
jaunâtre [ʒo'nɑ:tr], *a.* yellowish.
jaune [ʒo:n], *a.* yellow; ***rire jaune***, to give a sickly smile.—*n.m.* yellow; ***jaune d'œuf***, egg-yolk.
jaunir [ʒo'ni:r], *v.t.* to make yellow, to dye yellow.—*v.i.* to grow yellow, to turn yellow.
jaunissant [ʒoni'sɑ̃], *a.* turning yellow, yellowing; ripening.
jaunisse [ʒo'nis], *n.f.* jaundice.
javanais [ʒava'nɛ], *a.* Javanese.—*n.m.* (**Javanais**, *fem.* **-aise**) Javanese (*person*).
javeau [ʒa'vo], *n.m.* (*pl.* **-eaux**) sandbank.
javeline [ʒa'vlin], *n.f.* javelin.
javelle [ʒa'vɛl], *n.f.* swathe, loose sheaf.
javelot [ʒa'vlo], *n.m.* javelin.
jazz [(d)ʒɑ:z], *n.m.* jazz.
je [ʒə], (**j'**, *before a vowel sound*), *pron.* I.
Jean [ʒɑ̃], *m.* John [JEANNOT].
Jeanne [ʒɑ(:)n], *f.* Joan, Jane, Jean.
Jeannot [ʒa'no], *m.* Johnny, Jock.
jeep [(d)ʒip], *n.f.* jeep.
jésuite [ʒe'zɥit], *a.* Jesuit.—*n.m.* (**Jésuite**) Jesuit.
Jésus [ʒe'zy], *m.* Jesus.
jet [ʒɛ], *n.m.* casting, cast, throw; jet, gush, spurt (*of water*); sudden ray (*of light*); casting (*of metal*); shoot, sprout (*of plants*); spout (*of pump etc.*); new swarm (*of bees*); ***arme de jet***, missile weapon.
jetée [ʒə'te], *n.f.* jetty, pier; breakwater.
jeter [ʒə'te], *v.t.* (*conjug. like* APPELER) to throw, to fling, to hurl; to throw up; to throw down, to knock down; to throw out; to mould; to shoot out; to send forth; to empty; to discharge. **se jeter**, *v.r.* to throw oneself, to fling oneself; to fall upon (*attack*); to flow (*of rivers etc.*).
jeton [ʒə'tɔ̃], *n.m.* token, counter; voucher.
jeu [ʒø], *n.m.* (*pl.* **jeux**) play, sport; game; fun; gambling; (*fig.*) stake; manner of playing; performance (*of players*); (*Mach.*) working; clearance; play.
jeudi [ʒø'di], *n.m.* Thursday.
jeun (**à**) [a'ʒœ̃], *adv.* fasting, sober, on an empty stomach.
jeune [ʒœn], *a.* young, youthful; junior; new; early, unripe, green.—*n.* young person *or* animal.
jeûne [ʒø:n], *n.m.* fasting; fast, abstinence.
jeûner [ʒø'ne], *v.i.* to fast.
jeunesse [ʒœ'nɛs], *n.f.* youth, young days; youthfulness; freshness, prime; young people.
jeunet [ʒœ'nɛ], *a.* (*fem.* **-ette**) (*colloq.*) very young.
jiu-jitsu [(d)ʒyʒi'tsy], *n.m.* ju-jitsu.
joaillerie [ʒwɑj'ri], *n.f.* jeweller's trade *or* business; jewellery, jewels.
joaillier [ʒwɑ'je], *n.m.* (*fem.* **-ière**) jeweller.
jobard [ʒɔ'ba:r], *n.m.* (*colloq.*) sucker, mug, fool.
jockey [ʒɔ'kɛ], *n.m.* jockey.
jocrisse [ʒɔ'kris], *n.m.* dolt, simpleton.
joie [ʒwɑ], *n.f.* joy, happiness, joyfulness, gladness; glee, mirth.
joignant [ʒwa'ɲɑ̃], *a.* and *prep.* next to, adjoining.
joindre [ʒwɛ̃:dr], *v.t. irr.* (*conjug. like* CRAINDRE) to join, to put together, to unite, to combine; to add; to meet; to overtake.—*v.i.* to join, to meet. **se joindre**, *v.r.* to join, to be joined, to be united; to be adjoining, to be adjacent; to be added.
joint [ʒwɛ̃], *a.* joined, united; added.—*n.m.* joint; seam, junction.
jointé [ʒwɛ̃'te], *a.* jointed.
jointure [ʒwɛ̃'ty:r], *n.f.* joint, jointing, articulation.
joli [ʒɔ'li], *a.* pretty, pleasing, neat; fine; nice.—*n.m.* what is pretty; ***le joli de la chose c'est que . . .***, the best of the thing is that . . . .
joliment [ʒɔli'mɑ̃], *adv.* prettily; (*iron.*) nicely, finely; (*colloq.*) awfully, jolly, much, very.
jonc [ʒɔ̃], *n.m.* (*Bot.*) rush; cane, Malacca cane; keeper, guard (*ring*).

jonchée [ʒɔ̃'ʃe], *n.f.* strewing (*of flowers*).
joncher [ʒɔ̃'ʃe], *v.t.* to strew; to heap; to scatter.
jonction [ʒɔ̃k'sjɔ̃], *n.f.* junction, joining.
jongler [ʒɔ̃'gle], *v.i.* to juggle.
jonglerie [ʒɔ̃glə'ri], *n.f.* juggling.
jongleur [ʒɔ̃'glœ:r], *n.m.* juggler; (*fig.*) trickster.
jonque [ʒɔ̃:k], *n.f.* junk (*Chinese vessel*).
jonquille [ʒɔ̃'ki:j], *n.f.* jonquil.—*a. inv.* and *n.m.* pale yellow, jonquil (*colour*).
Jordanie [ʒɔrda'ni], **la,** *f.* Jordan.
jordanien [ʒɔrda'njɛ̃], *a.* Jordanian.—*n.m.* (**Jordanien,** *fem.* **-enne**) Jordanian (*person*).
Joseph [ʒo'zef], *m.* Joseph.
jouable [ʒwabl], *a.* playable.
joue [ʒu], *n.f.* cheek; ***coucher*** or ***mettre en joue***, to take aim at.
jouer [ʒwe], *v.t.* to play; to stake; to gamble away; to move (*a piece*); to perform, to act; to pretend to be, to imitate; to ridicule; to deceive.—*v.i.* to play, to amuse oneself; to gambol, to frolic; to gamble, to run the risk; to speculate (*on the funds*); to work, to work loose (*of machinery etc.*); to act, to perform. **se jouer,** *v.r.* to sport, to play; to make game (*of*); to make light of.
jouet [ʒwɛ], *n.m.* plaything, toy; laughing-stock, jest, sport.
joueur [ʒwœ:r], *n.m.* (*fem.* **-euse**) player; gambler; speculator; performer (*on an instrument*).
joufflu [ʒu'fly], *a.* chubby, chubby-cheeked.
joug [ʒu(g)], *n.m.* yoke; bondage, slavery.
jouir [ʒwi:r], *v.i.* to enjoy, to revel; to be in possession (*de*).
jouissance [ʒwi'sɑ̃:s], *n.f.* enjoyment; possession, use; delight; interest payable.
jouissant [ʒwi'sɑ̃], *a.* enjoying, in possession (*de*).
joujou [ʒu'ʒu], *n.m.* (*pl.* **-oux**) plaything, toy.
jour [ʒu:r], *n.m.* day, daylight; light; daybreak; day-time; opening, gap; ***broderie à jours***, open-work embroidery; ***donner le jour à***, to give birth to; ***plat du jour***, today's special; ***se faire jour***, to force one's way through; ***un jour de fête***, a holiday.
Jourdain [ʒur'dɛ̃], **le,** *m.* Jordan (*river*).
journal [ʒur'nal], *n.m.* (*pl.* **-aux**) journal, diary; newspaper; (*Comm.*) day-book.
journalier [ʒurna'lje], *a.* (*fem.* **-ière**) daily, diurnal.—*n.m.* journeyman, day-labourer.
journalisme [ʒurna'lism], *n.m.* journalism.
journaliste [ʒurna'list], *n.* journalist.
journée [ʒur'ne], *n.f.* day (time), day's work *or* wages; day's journey; battle; historic day; ***toute la journée***, all day (long).
journellement [ʒurnɛl'mɑ̃], *adv.* daily, every day.
joute [ʒut], *n.f.* joust, tilting-match; contest; (*C*) game.
jouter [ʒu'te], *v.i.* to joust, to tilt.
jouteur [ʒu'tœ:r], *n.m.* tilter; (*fig.*) antagonist, adversary.
jovial [ʒɔ'vjal], *a.* (*m. pl.* **-aux**) jovial, jolly, merry.
jovialement [ʒɔvjal'mɑ̃], *adv.* jovially.
jovialité [ʒɔvjali'te], *n.f.* joviality, jollity.
joyau [ʒwa'jo], *n.m.* (*pl.* **-aux**) jewel.
joyeusement [ʒwajøz'mɑ̃], *adv.* cheerfully, joyfully.
joyeuseté [ʒwajøz'te], *n.f.* (*fam.*) joke, jest.
joyeux [ʒwa'jø], *a.* (*fem.* **-euse**) joyful, merry; cheerful.
jubilaire [ʒybi'lɛ:r], *a.* jubilee; (*fig.*) of fifty years' standing (*of persons etc.*).
jubilant [ʒybi'lɑ̃], *a.* jubilant, delighted.
jubilation [ʒybilɑ'sjɔ̃], *n.f.* jubilation, rejoicing.
jubilé [ʒybi'le], *n.m.* jubilee; (*fig.*) golden wedding.
jubiler [ʒybi'le], *v.i.* to jubilate, to exult.
jucher [ʒy'ʃe], *v.i.* to roost, to perch; to lodge (*at the top of a house etc.*). **se jucher,** *v.r.* to go to roost; to perch (*oneself*).
juchoir [ʒy'ʃwa:r], *n.m.* roosting-place, perch.
judaïque [ʒyda'ik], *a.* Judaical, Jewish.
judaïsme [ʒyda'ism], *n.m.* Judaism.
judas [ʒy'dɑ], *n.m.* Judas, traitor; peep-hole (*in a door etc.*).
Judée [ʒy'de], **la,** *f.* Judaea.
judicature [ʒydika'ty:r], *n.f.* judicature, magistracy.
judiciaire [ʒydi'sjɛ:r], *a.* judiciary, judicial; legal.
judiciairement [ʒydisjɛr'mɑ̃], *adv.* judicially, by authority of justice.
judicieusement [ʒydisjøz'mɑ̃], *adv.* judiciously, discreetly.
judicieux [ʒydi'sjø], *a.* (*fem.* **-euse**) judicious, wise, discreet.
juge [ʒy:ʒ], *n.m.* judge; magistrate, justice; (*pl.*) bench.
jugé [ʒy'ʒe], *a.* judged.—*n.m.* ***au jugé***, at a guess.
jugement [ʒyʒ'mɑ̃], *n.m.* judgment; opinion, trial; sentence; good sense; ***jugement arbitral***, award; ***jugement provisoire***, decree nisi; ***jugement définitif***, decree absolute.
juger [ʒy'ʒe], *v.t.* (*conjug. like* MANGER) to judge; to try; to pass sentence on; to consider, to think.—*v.i.* to judge (*de*), to give judgment, to deem. **se juger,** *v.r.* to judge oneself; to deem oneself; to be judged.
jugulaire [ʒygy'lɛ:r], *a.* (*Anat.*) jugular.—*n.f.* jugular vein; chin-strap.
juguler [ʒygy'le] *v.t.* to strangle; (*fig.*) to torment; to fleece.
juif [ʒɥif], *a.* (*fem.* **juive**) Jewish.—*n.m.* (**Juif,** *fem.* **Juive**) Jew, Jewess.
juillet [ʒɥi'jɛ], *n.m.* July.
juin [ʒɥɛ̃], *n.m.* June.
juiverie [ʒɥi'vri], *n.f.* Jewry (*Jews' quarter*).
jujube [ʒy'ʒyb] *n.f.* jujube (*fruit*).—*n.m.* or ***pâte de jujube***, jujube (*lozenge*).
julep [ʒy'lɛp], *n.m.* julep.
julienne [ʒy'ljɛn], *n.f.* julienne (*vegetable soup*).
jumeau [ʒy'mo], *a.* (*fem.* **-elle,** *m. pl.* **-eaux**) twin; double (*of fruit etc.*).—*n.m.* twin (brother).
jumelage [ʒym'la:ʒ], *n.m.* twinning (*of towns etc.*).
jumelé [ʒym'le], *a.* twin, in couples; ***maison jumelée***, semi-detached house; (*horse-racing*) ***pari jumelé***, each-way bet.
jumelle [ʒy'mɛl], *n.f.* twin (sister); (*pl.*) binoculars; ***jumelles de campagne***, field-glasses; ***jumelles de théâtre***, opera-glasses; ***jumelles de manchettes***, cuff-links.
jument [ʒy'mɑ̃], *n.f.* mare.
jungle [ʒɔ̃:gl], *n.f.* jungle.
jupe [ʒyp], *n.f.* skirt.

Jupiter [ʒypi'tɛr], *m.* Jupiter, Jove.
jupon [ʒy'pɔ̃], *n.m.* petticoat.
juré [ʒy're], *a.* sworn.—*n.m.* juror, juryman.
jurement [ʒyr'mɑ̃], *n.m.* oath; swearing.
jurer [ʒy're], *v.t.* to swear by; to swear, to vow, to take an oath that; to blaspheme.—*v.i.* to swear, to take an oath; to blaspheme; (*fig.*) to contrast, to jar, to clash (*of colours etc.*).
juridiction [ʒyridik'sjɔ̃], *n.f.* jurisdiction; department, province.
juridique [ʒyri'dik], *a.* juridical, judicial, legal.
juridiquement [ʒyridik'mɑ̃], *adv.* juridically, judicially.
jurisprudence [ʒyrispry'dɑ̃:s], *n.f.* jurisprudence.
juriste [ʒy'rist], *n.m.* jurist.
juron [ʒy'rɔ̃], *n.m.* oath, curse, swear-word.
jury [ʒy'ri], *n.m.* jury; board, committee.
jus [ʒy], *n.m.* juice; gravy.
jusque or ***jusques** [ʒysk], *prep.* even to, as far as; till, until; down to; up to.
juste [ʒyst], *a.* just, equitable; fair, legitimate, lawful; proper, fit; exact; well-fitting; tight; ***au plus juste prix***, at the lowest price; ***un homme juste***, a righteous man.—*n.m.* upright man, virtuous man; what is just.—*adv.* just, exactly, precisely; (*Mus.*) true.
justement [ʒystə'mɑ̃], *adv.* justly, precisely; justifiably.
justesse [ʒys'tɛs], *n.f.* justness, exactness, precision, accuracy; appropriateness.
justice [ʒys'tis], *n.f.* justice; righteousness, probity; fairness, impartiality; reason; courts of justice, judges; ***palais de justice***, law-court.
justifiable [ʒysti'fjabl], *a.* justifiable; warrantable.
justification [ʒystifikɑ'sjɔ̃], *n.f.* justification, vindication, proof.
justifier [ʒysti'fje], *v.t.* to justify, to vindicate, to make good. **se justifier**, *v.r.* to justify, clear *or* vindicate oneself.
jute [ʒyt], *n.m.* jute.
juteux [ʒy'tø], *a.* (*fem.* **-euse**) juicy.
juvénile [ʒyve'nil], *a.* juvenile, youthful.
juvénilement [ʒyvenil'mɑ̃], *adv.* boyishly, in a juvenile manner.
juxtaposer [ʒykstapo'ze], *v.t.* to place side by side. **se juxtaposer**, *v.r.* to be in juxtaposition.
juxtaposition [ʒykstapɔzi'sjɔ̃], *n.f.* juxtaposition.

K

K, k [kɑ], *n.m.* the eleventh letter of the alphabet; ***Échelle K*** (*viz. Kelvin*), absolute scale (*of temperature*).
kakatoès [kakatɔ'ɛs], [CACATOIS].
kaki [ka'ki], *a. inv.* khaki (*colour*).
kaléidoscope [kaleidɔs'kɔp], *n.m.* kaleidoscope.
kangourou [kɑ̃gu'ru], *n.m.* kangaroo.
kaolin [kaɔ'lɛ̃], *n.m.* kaolin, porcelain clay, china-clay.
kapok or **kapoc** [ka'pɔk], *n.m.* kapok.
kascher or **kacher** [ka'ʃɛr], **kachir** [ka'ʃir], *a.* (*Jew. Relig.*) kosher.
kayac [ka'jak], *n.m.* kayak.
Kénia [ke'nja], **le**, *m.* Kenya.
képi [ke'pi], *n.m.* kepi, military cap; peak cap.
kermesse [kɛr'mɛs], *n.f.* kermis (*in the Netherlands*); kermesse; village fair.
kérosène [kero'zɛ:n], *n.m.* kerosene paraffin-oil.
kidnapper [kidna'pe], *v.t.* to kidnap.
kilo [ki'lo], *n.m.* (*abbr.*) kilogramme.
kilocycle [kilɔ'sikl], *n.m.* kilocycle.
kilogramme [kilɔ'gram], *n.m.* kilogramme (*2·2 lb. avoirdupois*).
kilomètre [kilɔ'mɛtr], *n.m.* kilometre (*1093·6 yards*).
kilowatt [kilɔ'wat], *n.m.* kilowatt.
kimono [kimɔ'no], *n.m.* kimono.
kiosque [kjɔsk], *n.m.* kiosk; (*Naut.*) house; ***kiosque à journaux***, newspaper kiosk; ***kiosque à musique***, bandstand.
klakson or **klaxon** [klak'sɔ̃], *n.m.* klaxon, hooter, horn.
kleptomane [klɛptɔ'man], *a.* and *n.* kleptomaniac.
kleptomanie [klɛptɔma'ni], *n.f.* kleptomania.
kola or **cola** [kɔ'la], *n.m.* kola.
Kominform [kɔmɛ̃'fɔrm], *n.m.* Cominform.
Komintern [kɔmɛ̃'tɛrn], *n.m.* Comintern.
Koweit [kɔ'weit], **le**, *m.* Kuwait.
kyrielle [ki'rjɛl], *n.f.* litany; (*fig.*) long string (*of words etc.*), long tedious story.
kyste [kist], *n.m.* (*Path.*) cyst.

L

L, **l** [ɛl], *n.m.* or *f.* the twelfth letter of the alphabet.
l', *art.* and *pron.* (*by elision of* **le** or **la**) the; him, her, it.
la (1) [la], *art* and *pron. f.* the; her, it.
la (2) [lɑ], *n.m.* (*Mus.*) la; the note A.
là [la], *adv.* and *int.* there, thither; then (*of time*); ***çà et là***, here and there; ***là là***, now now! there! there now! ***là où***, where; ***par là***, that way.
là-bas [la'bɑ], *adv.* there, over there.
labbe [lab], *n.m.* (*Orn.*) skua.
label [la'bɛl], *n.m.* (*Ind.*) label; brand, mark.
labeur [la'bœ:r], *n.m.* labour, work, toil.
laboratoire [labɔra'twa:r], *n.m.* laboratory.
laborieusement [labɔrjøz'mɑ̃], *adv.* laboriously; painfully.
laborieux [labɔ'rjø], *a.* (*fem.* **-euse**) laborious, hard-working.
labour [la'bu:r], *n.m.* ploughing, tillage; arable land.
labourable [labu'rabl], *a.* arable.
labourage [labu'ra:ʒ], *n.m.* tillage, ploughing; dressing.
labourer [labu're], *v.t.* to plough, to till; to dig, to turn up; to dress; to toil through.

laboureur [labu'rœːr], *n.m.* husbandman, ploughman.
laboureuse [labu'røːz], *n.f.* tractor plough.
laburne [la'byrn], *n.m.* laburnum.
labyrinthe [labi'rɛ̃ːt], *n.m.* labyrinth, maze.
lac [lak], *n.m.* lake.
laçage [la'saːʒ], *n.m.* lacing.
lacer [la'se], *v.t.* (*conjug. like* COMMENCER) to lace.
lacération [laserɑ'sjɔ̃], *n.f.* laceration.
lacérer [lase're], *v.t.* (*conjug. like* CÉDER) to lacerate, to tear.
lacet [la'sɛ], *n.m.* lace, shoe-lace; noose; bow-string (*for strangling*); winding, hairpin bend (*of road etc.*); (*pl.*) toils.
lâche [lɑːʃ], *a.* loose, slack; faint-hearted, cowardly; base, mean, shameful.—*n.* coward, craven; dastard.—*adv.* loosely.
lâché [lɑ'ʃe], *a.* slovenly, slipshod.
lâchement [lɑʃ'mɑ̃], *adv.* in a dastardly *or* cowardly manner; loosely; shamefully.
lâcher [lɑ'ʃe], *v.t.* to loosen, to slacken; to let go, to release; to unbind; to blurt out; to let fly, to discharge; to let down (*someone*).—*v.i.* to slacken, to become loose; to slip; (*Spt.*) to give up.
lâcheté [lɑʃ'te], *n.f.* cowardice; baseness, meanness.
lacis [la'si], *n.m.* network.
laconique [lakɔ'nik], *a.* laconic.
laconiquement [lakɔnik'mɑ̃], *adv.* laconically.
lacs [la], *n.m. inv.* string; noose; trap; ***lacs d'amour***, love-knot.
lacté [lak'te], *a.* lacteous, milky; ***la voie lactée***, the Milky Way.
lacune [la'kyn], *n.f.* gap, break, hiatus, blank.
là-dedans [ladə'dɑ̃], *adv.* in there.
là-dehors [ladə'ɔːr], *adv.* outside.
là-dessous [la'tsu], *adv.* under there.
là-dessus [la'tsy], *adv.* on that; thereupon.
ladite [la'dit], [LEDIT].
ladre [lɑːdr], *a.* leprous; (*fig.*) mean, sordid, stingy; unfeeling.—*n.m.* (*fem.* **-esse**) leper; (*fig.*) sordid person.
ladrerie [lɑdrə'ri], *n.f.* sordid avarice, stinginess.
lagune [la'gyn], *n.f.* lagoon.
là-haut [la'o], *adv.* up there; upstairs.
lai [lɛ], *n.m.* lay (*poem, song*).
laïc [LAÏQUE].
laid [lɛ], *a.* ugly, unsightly; unseemly, unbecoming.—*n.m.* ugliness; (*fem.* **-e**) ugly person, creature etc.; naughty boy *or* girl.
laidement [lɛd'mɑ̃], *adv.* in an ugly way.
laideron [lɛd'rɔ̃], *n.m.* (*fem.* **-onne**) ugly creature.
laideur [lɛ'dœːr], *n.f.* ugliness, uncomeliness; unseemliness.
laie [lɛ], *n.f.* path (*in a forest*).
lainage [lɛ'naːʒ], *n.m.* woollens, woollen goods.
laine [lɛn], *n.f.* wool; ***laine filée***, yarn; ***laine peignée***, worsted; ***tapis de haute laine***, thick-pile carpet; ***tout laine***, pure wool.
lainerie [lɛn'ri], *n.f.* woollen goods, woollens; wool trade, shop etc.
laineux [lɛ'nø], *a.* (*fem.* **-euse**) woolly, fleecy.
lainier [lɛ'nje], *a.* (*fem.* **-ière**) of wool, woollen.—*n.m.* (*fem.* **-ière**) wool-merchant; wool-worker.
laïque or **laïc** [la'ik], *a.* lay, secular.—*n.* layman, lay person.
laisse [lɛːs], *n.f.* string, leash, lead.
laisser [lɛ'se], *v.t.* to leave, to quit; to leave behind, to part with; to bequeath; to permit, to let, to allow; to let alone; to leave off; to give up. **se laisser**, *v.r.* to allow oneself, to let oneself.
laisser-aller [lɛsea'le], *n.m.* unconstraint, negligence; slovenliness; indolence.
laisser-faire [lɛse'fɛːr], *n.m.* non-interference.
laissez-passer [lɛsepɑ'se], *n.m. inv.* permit, leave, pass.
lait [lɛ], *n.m.* milk; ***au lait***, with milk; ***lait de chaux***, whitewash; ***lait de poule***, egg-flip; ***petit-lait*** or ***lait clair***, whey.
laitage [lɛ'taːʒ], *n.m.* milk puddings; milk products.
laiterie [lɛ'tri], *n.f.* dairy, dairy-farm.
laiteux [lɛ'tø], *a.* (*fem.* **-euse**) lacteous, milky.
laitier [lɛ'tje], *a.* (*fem.* **-ière**) pertaining to milk; having milk, milch (*of cows*).—*n.m.* (*fem.* **-ière**) milkman; milkmaid, dairy-maid.—*n.f.* (**-ière**) milch cow; milk-lorry *or* -cart.
laiton [lɛ'tɔ̃], *n.m.* brass, latten.
laitue [lɛ'ty], *n.f.* lettuce.
lama [la'ma], *n.m.* lama (*priest*); llama.
lambeau [lɑ̃'bo], *n.m.* (*pl.* **-eaux**) shred; rag; fragment, scrap.
lambin [lɑ̃'bɛ̃], *a.* slow, dawdling.—*n.m.* (*fem.* **-e**) dawdler, slowcoach.
lambiner [lɑ̃bi'ne], *v.i.* to dawdle, to dilly-dally.
lambrequin [lɑ̃brə'kɛ̃], *n.m.* valance, cut-out, pelmet.
lambris [lɑ̃'bri] *n.m.* panelling; wainscot; ceiling; (*fig.*) mansion, palace; canopy.
lambrissage [lɑ̃bri'saːʒ], *n.m.* wainscoting, panelling.
lambrisser [lɑ̃bri'se], *v.t.* to panel, to wainscot.
lame [lam], *n.f.* thin plate, leaf of metal; foil; knife (*of mower etc.*), blade; (*fig.*) sword; wave, billow.
lamé [la'me], *a.* spangled with gold *or* silver.
lamentable [lamɑ̃'tabl], *a.* lamentable, sad, distressing; pitiful.
lamentablement [lamɑ̃tablə'mɑ̃], *adv.* woefully.
lamentation [lamɑ̃tɑ'sjɔ̃], *n.f.* lamentation, wailing; lament; whining.
lamenter (se) [səlamɑ̃'te], *v.r.* to lament, to bewail.
laminage [lami'naːʒ], *n.m.* laminating; rolling (*of gold etc.*).
laminer [lami'ne], *v.t.* to laminate, to roll.
laminoir [lami'nwaːr], *n.m.* flattening-mill; rolling-mill.
lampe [lɑ̃ːp], *n.f.* lamp; (*Rad. Tel.*) valve; ***lampe de bord***, (*Motor.*) dashboard light; ***lampe de poche***, electric torch.
lampion [lɑ̃'pjɔ̃], *n.m.* illumination-lamp, fairy-light; Chinese lantern; (*slang*) cocked hat.
lampiste [lɑ̃'pist], *n.m.* lamp-maker; lamp-lighter.
lampisterie [lɑ̃pis'tri], *n.f.* lamp-room.
lamproie [lɑ̃'prwɑ], *n.f.* lamprey.
lance [lɑ̃ːs], *n.f.* lance, spear; staff, flagstaff; nozzle (*of a fire-hose*).

lance-flammes [lɑ̃s'flɑm], *n.m. inv.* flame-thrower.
lancement [lɑ̃s'mɑ̃], *n.m.* throwing, darting; launching, launch.
lance-pierres [lɑ̃s'pjɛ:r], *n.m. inv.* catapult.
lancer [lɑ̃'se], *v.t.* (*conjug. like* COMMENCER) to fling, to hurl, to throw; to launch; to shoot forth, to dart; to issue (*a warrant etc.*). **se lancer**, *v.r.* to dart, to spring; to rush, to fly; to launch out; (*fig.*) to make a start.
lancette [lɑ̃'sɛt], *n.f.* lancet.
lancier [lɑ̃'sje], *n.m.* lancer.
lancinant [lɑ̃si'nɑ̃], *a.* shooting (*of pains*).
lande [lɑ̃:d], *n.f.* waste land, moor, heath.
langage [lɑ̃'ga:ʒ], *n.m.* language; speech, diction.
lange [lɑ̃:ʒ], *n.m.* napkin; swaddling-cloth; (*pl.*) swaddling-clothes.
langoureusement [lɑ̃gurøz'mɑ̃], *adv.* languishingly, languidly.
langoureux [lɑ̃gu'rø], *a.* (*fem.* **-euse**) languishing, languid.
langouste [lɑ̃'gust], *n.f.* spiny lobster.
langoustine [lɑ̃gus'tin], *n.f.* large Brittany prawn; Dublin Bay prawn.
langue [lɑ̃:g] *n.f.* tongue; language; strip (*of land*); ***avoir la langue bien pendue*** or ***bien affilée***, to have the gift of the gab; ***avoir la langue liée***, to be tongue-tied.
languette [lɑ̃'gɛt], *n.f.* small tongue; tongue-like strip; partition; tongue (*of instruments*); index (*of a balance*); tongue (*of shoe*).
langueur [lɑ̃'gœ:r], *n.f.* apathy, languor; weakness, weariness; debility.
languir [lɑ̃'gi:r], *v.i.* to languish, to pine away, to droop; to linger; to flag.
languissant [lɑ̃gi'sɑ̃], *a.* languid, languishing, pining; (*Comm.*) dull, inactive.
lanière [la'njɛ:r], *n.f.* thong, lash.
lanoline [lanɔ'lin], *n.f.* lanoline.
lanterne [lɑ̃'tɛrn], *n.f.* lantern; street-lamp; (*Arch.*) skylight; dawdler; ***lanterne vénitienne***, Chinese lantern.
lanterner [lɑ̃tɛr'ne], *v.i.* to dawdle, to trifle away one's time.
Laos [laɔs], **le**, *m.* Laos.
laotien [laɔ'sjɛ̃], *a.* (*fem.* **-enne**) Laotian.—*n.m.* (**Laotien**, *fem.* **-enne**) Laotian (*person*).
lapement [lap'mɑ̃], *n.m.* lapping.
laper [la'pe], *v.t., v.i.* to lap (up).
lapidaire [lapi'dɛ:r], *a.* and *n.m.* lapidary.
lapidation [lapidɑ'sjɔ̃], *n.f.* lapidation, stoning.
lapider [lapi'de], *v.t.* to lapidate, to stone to death; (*fig.*) to pelt, to abuse.
lapin [la'pɛ̃], *n.m.* rabbit.
lapis [la'pi:s], **lapis lazuli** [lapislazy'li], *n.m. inv.* lapis lazuli.
lapon [la'pɔ̃], *a.* (*fem.* **-onne**) Lapp.—*n.m.* Lappish (*language*); (**Lapon**, *fem.* **-onne**) Laplander.
Laponie [lapɔ'ni], **la**, *f.* Lapland.
laps (1) [laps], *n.m.* lapse (*of time*).
laps (2) [laps], *a.* *lapsed, fallen into heresy.
lapsus [lap'sy:s], *n.m. inv.* slip, mistake.
laquais [la'kɛ], *n.m. inv.* lackey, footman.
laque [lak] *n.f.* lacquer, lac, lake (*paint*).—*n.m.* lacquer.
laquelle [la'kɛl], [LEQUEL].
laquer [la'ke], *v.t.* to lacquer, to japan.
larcin [lar'sɛ̃], *n.m.* larceny, pilfering; petty theft; ***larcin littéraire***, plagiarism.

lard [la:r], *n.m.* fat (*esp. of pigs*); bacon; ***flèche de lard***, flitch of bacon; ***tranche de lard***, rasher of bacon.
larder [lar'de], *v.t.* to lard; to pink, to run through, to pierce.
lardon [lar'dɔ̃], *n.m.* thin slice of bacon; (*fam.*) child, kid, brat.
large [larʒ], *a.* broad, wide; large, great, extensive; generous, liberal; lax, loose.—*n.m.* breadth, width; offing, open sea; ***au large !*** keep off! sheer off! ***au large de Dieppe***, off Dieppe.
largement [larʒ'mɑ̃], *adv.* largely, abundantly; fully; liberally.
largesse [lar'ʒɛs], *n.f.* largess, bounty, munificence.
largeur [lar'ʒœ:r], *n.f.* breadth, width; amplitude.
larme [larm], *n.f.* tear; drop; ***fondre en larmes***, to burst into tears.
larmoiement [larmwa'mɑ̃], *n.m.* watering of the eyes.
larmoyant [larmwa'jɑ̃], *a.* weeping, in tears; tearful, whining.
larmoyer [larmwa'je], *v.i.* (*conjug. like* EMPLOYER) to shed tears; to whine, to snivel; to water (*of the eyes*).
larron [la'rɔ̃], *n.m.* thief.
larve [larv], *n.f.* larva, grub.
laryngite [larɛ̃'ʒit], *n.f.* laryngitis.
larynx [la'rɛ̃:ks], *n.m. inv.* larynx.
las! (1) [lɑ], *int.* alas!
las (2) [lɑ], *a.* (*fem.* **lasse**) tired, weary, fatigued; bored; disgusted.
lascif [la'sif], *a.* (*fem.* **-cive**) lascivious, lewd, wanton.
lascivement [lasiv'mɑ̃], *adv.* lasciviously.
lassant [lɑ'sɑ̃], *a.* tiresome, wearisome, tedious.
lasser [lɑ'se], *v.t.* to tire, to weary, to fatigue, to wear out. **se lasser**, *v.r.* to tire, to grow tired, to be wearied.
lassitude [lɑsi'tyd], *n.f.* lassitude, weariness.
lasso [la'so], *n.m.* lasso.
latent [la'tɑ̃], *a.* latent, concealed, secret.
latéral [late'ral], *a.* (*m. pl.* **-aux**) lateral, side.
latéralement [lateral'mɑ̃], *adv.* laterally.
latin [la'tɛ̃], *a.* Latin.—*n.m.* Latin (*language*); ***latin de cuisine***, dog Latin.—*n.m.* (**Latin**, *fem.* **-ine**) Latin (*person*).
latitude [lati'tyd], *n.f.* latitude; room, space, margin.
latte [lat], *n.f.* lath.
latter [la'te], *v.t.* to lath.
lattis [la'ti], *n.m.* lathing, lath-work; laths.
laudanum [loda'nɔm], *n.m.* laudanum.
laudatif [loda'tif], *a.* (*fem.* **-tive**) laudatory.
lauréat [lɔre'a], *a.* laureate.—*n.m.* (*fem.* **-e**) prize-winner.
laurier [lɔ'rje], *n.m.* laurel, bay-tree; (*fig.*) glory, honour.
lavable [la'vabl], *a.* washable.
lavabo [lava'bo], *n.m.* wash-basin; wash-stand; (*pl.*) conveniences.
lavage [la'va:ʒ], *n.m.* washing; dilution.
lavande [la'vɑ̃:d], *n.f.* lavender.
lavandière [lavɑ̃'djɛ:r], *n.f.* laundress, washerwoman; (*Orn.*) grey wagtail.
lavasse [la'vas], *n.f.* washy soup *or* wine.
lave [la:v], *n.f.* lava.
lavé [la've], *a.* washed out, faint.

lave-dos [lav'do], *n.m. inv.* back-brush.

lavement [lav'mɑ̃], *n.m.* (*Méd.*) enema.

laver [la've], *v.t.* to wash, to cleanse; to purify; to expiate; ***laver à grande eau,*** to swill; ***laver la vaisselle,*** to wash up; ***machine à laver,*** washing machine. **se laver,** *v.r.* to wash, to wash oneself; to clear oneself (*of an accusation*).

lavette [la'vɛt], *n.f.* dish-mop.

laveur [la'vœ:r], *n.m.* (*fem.* **-euse**) washer, scourer; ***laveuse de vaisselle,*** scullery-maid.

lavoir [la'vwa:r], *n.m.* wash-house.

laxatif [laksa'tif], *a.* (*fem.* **-tive**) laxative, opening.—*n.m.* laxative.

layette [lɛ'jɛt], *n.f.* box; baby's trousseau *or* outfit.

le [lə], *art.* and *pron. m.* the; him, it; so; ***je le crois,*** I think so.

lécher [le'ʃe], *v.t.* (*conjug. like* CÉDER) to lick; to lick up; (*fig.*) to labour, to polish, to elaborate, to overdo; ***lécher les vitrines,*** to go window-shopping.

leçon [lə'sɔ̃], *n.f.* lesson; reading (*of a text*).

lecteur [lɛk'tœ:r], *n.m.* (*fem.* **-trice**) reader, lector.

lecture [lɛk'ty:r], *n.f.* reading; perusal.

ledit [lə'di], *a.* (*fem.* **ladite,** *pl.* **lesdit(e)s**) the (afore)said, the same.

légal [le'gal], *a.* (*m. pl.* **-aux**) legal, lawful, legitimate.

légalement [legal'mɑ̃], *adv.* legally, lawfully.

légaliser [legali'ze], *v.t.* to legalize.

légalité [legali'te], *n.f.* legality, lawfulness.

légataire [lega'tɛ:r], *n.* legatee.

légation [legɑ'sjɔ̃], *n.f.* legateship; legation.

légendaire [leʒɑ̃'dɛ:r], *a.* and *n.m.* legendary.

légende [le'ʒɑ̃:d], *n.f.* legend; inscription; caption; key (*to map etc.*).

léger [le'ʒe], *a.* (*fem.* **-ère**) light; slight; buoyant; fleet, fast; nimble; fickle; faint; thoughtless.

légèrement [leʒɛr'mɑ̃], *adv.* lightly, slightly; swiftly; thoughtlessly.

légèreté [leʒɛr'te], *n.f.* lightness; swiftness; fickleness; frivolity; thoughtlessness.

légiférer [leʒife're], *v.i.* (*conjug. like* CÉDER) to legislate.

légion [le'ʒjɔ̃], *n.f.* legion; great number, host.

légionnaire [leʒjɔ'nɛ:r], *n.m.* legionary; member of the Legion of Honour; soldier of the Foreign Legion.

législateur [leʒisla'tœ:r], *a.* (*fem.* **-trice**) legislative, lawgiving.—*n.m.* (*fem.* **-trice**) legislator.

législatif [leʒisla'tif], *a.* (*fem.* **-tive**) legislative.

législation [leʒislɑ'sjɔ̃], *n.f.* legislation.

législature [leʒisla'ty:r], *n.f.* legislature.

légitime [leʒi'tim], *a.* lawful, legitimate, rightful; justifiable.

légitimement [leʒitim'mɑ̃], *adv.* legitimately, lawfully; justifiably.

légitimer [leʒiti'me], *v.t.* to legitimate; to justify; to recognize.

légitimité [leʒitimi'te], *n.f.* legitimacy, lawfulness.

legs [lɛ], *n.m.* legacy, bequest.

léguer [le'ge], *v.t.* (*conjug. like* CÉDER) to leave by will, to bequeath.

légume [le'gym], *n.m.* vegetable.—*n.f. pl.* (*fam.*) ***les grosses légumes,*** the bigwigs.

légumier [legy'mje], *a.* (*fem.* **-ière**) of vegetables.—*n.m.* vegetable-dish.

lendemain [lɑ̃d'mɛ̃], *n.m.* morrow, next day, day after.

lent [lɑ̃], *a.* slow, tardy; backward; sluggish, slack.

lentement [lɑ̃t'mɑ̃], *adv.* slowly, tardily; sluggishly.

lenteur [lɑ̃'tœ:r], *n.f.* slowness; tardiness.

lenticulaire [lɑ̃tiky'lɛ:r], **lenticulé** [lɑ̃tiky'le] *a.* lenticular.

lentille [lɑ̃'ti:j], *n.f.* lentil; lens; (*pl.*) freckles; ***lentille d'eau,*** duckweed.

léonin [leɔ'nɛ̃], *a.* leonine.

léopard [leɔ'pa:r], *n.m.* leopard.

lèpre [lɛpr], *n.f.* leprosy.

lépreux [le'prø], *a.* (*fem.* **-euse**) leprous.—*n.m.* (*fem.* **-euse**) leper.

léproserie [leprо'zri], *n.f.* leper-hospital.

lequel [lə'kɛl], *pron. m.* (*fem.* **laquelle,** *m. pl.* **lesquels,** *f. pl.* **lesquelles**) who, whom, that, which; (*inter.*) which one, which?

les [le], *art.* and *pron. pl.* the; them.

lèse-majesté [lɛzmaʒɛs'te], *n.f.* high treason, lese-majesty.

léser [le'ze], *v.t.* (*conjug. like* CÉDER) to wrong; to injure, to hurt.

lésine [le'zin], *n.f.* niggardliness, stinginess.

lésiner [lezi'ne], *v.i.* to be stingy *or* mean; to haggle.

lésinerie [lezin'ri], *n.f.* stinginess, meanness.

lésion [le'zjɔ̃], *n.f.* (*Law*) wrong, injury; (*Surg.*) lesion.

lessive [lɛ'si:v], *n.f.* wash, linen washed *or* to be washed, washing.

leste [lɛst], *a.* brisk, nimble, active; light; smart; sharp; improper, free.

lestement [lɛst'mɑ̃], *adv.* briskly; cleverly; flippantly; freely.

lester [lɛs'te], *v.t.* to ballast. **se lester,** *v.r.* (*fam.*) to take in ballast; to line one's stomach.

léthargie [letar'ʒi], *n.f.* lethargy.

léthargique [letar'ʒik], *a.* lethargic.

lette [lɛt], **letton** [lɛ'tɔ̃] (*fem.* **-onne**), *a.* Latvian.—*n.m.* Latvian (*language*); (**Lette, Letton,** *fem.* **-onne**) Latvian (*person*).

Lettonie [lɛtɔ'ni], **la,** *f.* Latvia.

lettre [lɛtr], *n.f.* letter, note; (*Print.*) character, type; (*pl.*) literature, letters; ***les belles-lettres,*** humanities; ***lettre de change,*** bill of exchange; ***lettre d'envoi,*** covering letter; ***lettre de voiture,*** way-bill.

lettré [lɛ'tre], *a.* cultured, literate, well-read; literary.—*n.m.* (*fem.* **-ée**) scholar.

leur [lœ:r], *a. poss.* their.—*poss. pron.* ***le leur, la leur*** or ***les leurs,*** theirs.—*pers. pron.* to them, them.

leurre [lœ:r], *n.m.* lure, decoy; bait; snare, trap.

leurrer [lœ're], *v.t.* to lure, to entice, to decoy; to ensnare. **se leurrer,** *v.r.* to delude oneself.

levage [lə'va:ʒ], *n.m.* raising, lifting.

levain [lə'vɛ̃], *n.m.* leaven; (*fig.*) germ.

levant [lə'vɑ̃], *a.* rising.—*n.m.* east; rising sun; Levant.

levantin [ləvɑ̃'tɛ̃], *a.* Levantine.—*n.m.* (**Levantin,** *fem.* **-ine**) Levantine (*person*).

levé [lə've], *a.* lifted up, raised; up, out of bed.

levée [lə've], *n.f.* raising, lifting; levying; gathering (*crop, fruit etc.*); collection (*post-office*); embankment; swell (*of the sea*); (*Cards*) trick.
lever [lə've], *v.t.* (*conjug. like* AMENER) to lift, to lift up, to raise; to heave; to pull up; to weigh (*anchor*); to take away; to take out; to collect; to levy.—*v.i.* to come up; to spring up, to rise. **se lever**, *v.r.* to rise, to get up; to stand up; to heave (*of the sea*); to clear up (*of the weather*).
lever [lə've], *n.m.* rising, getting up; levee (*of king*).
levier [lə'vje], *n.m.* lever; crowbar, hand-spike.
levraut [lə'vro], *n.m.* leveret, young hare.
lèvre [lɛ:vr], *n.f.* lip; rim.
lévrier [levri'e], *n.m.* greyhound.
levure [lə'vy:r], *n.f.* yeast.
lexique [lɛk'sik], *n.m.* lexicon; abridged dictionary.
lézard [le'za:r], *n.m.* lizard.
lézarde [le'zard], *n.f.* crevice, crack, chink.
lézardé [lezar'de], *a.* cracked (*of walls etc.*).
lézarder [lezar'de], *v.t.* to crack (*walls etc.*). **se lézarder**, *v.r.* to crack, to become cracked.
liais [ljɛ], *n.m.* lias; blue limestone.
liaison [ljɛ'zɔ̃], *n.f.* joining; connexion, acquaintance; intimacy; (*Mil.*) liaison.
liane [ljan], *n.f.* liana, tropical creeper.
liant [ljɑ̃], *a.* supple, flexible; affable, sociable. —*n.m.* suppleness; sociability; gentleness.
liard [lja:r], *n.m.* liard (*half-farthing*).
liasse [ljas], *n.f.* bundle, file (*of papers*); wad (*of banknotes*).
Liban [li'bɑ̃], **le**, *m.* Lebanon.
libanais [liba'nɛ], *a.* Lebanese.—*n.m.* (**Libanais**, *fem.* **-aise**) Lebanese (*person*).
libation [libɑ'sjɔ̃], *n.f.* libation; (*fig.*) potation.
libelle [li'bɛl], *n.m.* libel, lampoon.
libellé [libɛl'le], *a.* drawn up, specified.—*n.m.* wording, contents.
libellule [libɛl'lyl], *n.f.* dragon-fly.
libéral [libe'ral], *a.* (*m. pl.* **-aux**) liberal, generous, bountiful; (*Polit.*) Liberal.
libéralement [liberal'mɑ̃], *adv.* liberally, bountifully, generously.
libéralisme [libera'lism], *n.m.* liberalism.
libéralité [liberali'te], *n.f.* generosity, open-handedness.
libérateur [libera'tœ:r], *n.m.* (*fem.* **-trice**) deliverer, liberator, rescuer.
libération [liberɑ'sjɔ̃], *n.f.* liberation, deliverance; rescue, discharge.
libéré [libe're], *a.* liberated, discharged.
libérer [libe're], *v.t.* (*conjug. like* CÉDER) to liberate, to free; to discharge. **se libérer**, *v.r.* to free oneself, to clear oneself (***de***); to pay off one's debts.
Libéria [libe'rja], **le**, *m.* Liberia.
libérien [libe'rjɛ̃], *a.* (*fem.* **-enne**) Liberian. —*n.m.* (**Libérien**, *fem.* **-enne**) Liberian (*person*).
liberté [libɛr'te], *n.f.* liberty, freedom, ease.
libertin [libɛr'tɛ̃], *a.* libertine, licentious; dissolute.—*n.m.* (*fem.* **-e**) libertine, rake.
libertinage [libɛrti'na:ʒ], *n.m.* libertinism, debauchery.
libraire [li'brɛ:r], *n.* bookseller; ***libraire-éditeur***, publisher and bookseller.
librairie [librɛ'ri], *n.f.* book-trade; bookseller's shop.
libre [libr], *a.* free; at liberty; independent; undisciplined, unconfined; bold, broad; exempt; irregular (*of verse*).
libre-échange [libre'ʃɑ̃:ʒ], *n.m.* free trade.
libre-échangiste [libreʃɑ̃'ʒist], *n.m.* (*pl.* **libre-échangistes**) free-trader.
librement [librə'mɑ̃], *adv.* freely, without restraint; boldly.
librettiste [librɛ'tist], *n.m.* librettist.
Libye [li'bi], **la**, *f.* Libya.
libyen [li'bjɛ̃], *a.* (*fem.* **-enne**) Libyan.—*n.m.* (**Libyen**, *fem.* **-enne**) Libyan (*person*).
lice [lis], *n.f.* lists, tilt-yard.
licence [li'sɑ̃:s], *n.f.* licence, leave, permission; licentiousness; licentiate's degree.
licencié [lisɑ̃'sje], *a.* licentiate; (*C*) ***épicier licencié***, licensed grocer.—*n.m.* (*fem.* **-ée**) licenciate.
licenciement [lisɑ̃si'mɑ̃], *n.m.* disbanding.
licencier [lisɑ̃'sje], *v.t.* to disband (*troops*); to declare redundant, to lay off; to dismiss.
licencieusement [lisɑ̃sjøz'mɑ̃], *adv.* licentiously, dissolutely.
licencieux [lisɑ̃'sjø], *a.* (*fem.* **-euse**) licentious, dissolute.
licite [li'sit], *a.* licit, lawful, allowable.
licitement [lisit'mɑ̃], *adv.* lawfully, licitly.
licol [LICOU].
licorne [li'kɔrn], *n.f.* unicorn.
licou [li'ku], **licol** [li'kɔl], *n.m.* halter.
licteur [lik'tœ:r], *n.m.* (*Rom. Ant.*) lictor.
lie [li], *n.f.* lees, dregs; (*fig.*) scum, refuse.
liège [ljɛ:ʒ], *n.m.* cork; cork-tree.
lien [ljɛ̃], *n.m.* bond, tie, link; (*pl.*) bonds, shackles.
lier [lje], *v.t.* to fasten, to tie; to bind, to tie up; to join, to connect (***avec***); to engage in; (*Mus.*) to slur; to thicken (*a sauce etc.*). **se lier**, *v.r.* to become acquainted; to thicken (*of sauce etc.*).
lierre [ljɛ:r], *n.m.* ivy.
lieu [ljø], *n.m.* (*pl.* **lieux**) place, spot; position; cause; (*pl.*) premises, apartments; ***au lieu de***, instead of; ***avoir lieu***, to take place; ***lieu commun***, commonplace.
lieue [ljø], *n.f.* league (*4 kilometres, 2½ miles*).
lieur [ljœ:r], *n.m.* (*fem.* **-euse**) (*Agric.*) binder (*person*).—*n.f.* (**-euse**) binder (*machine*).
lieutenance [ljøt'nɑ̃:s], *n.f.* lieutenancy.
lieutenant [ljøt'nɑ̃], *n.m.* lieutenant; right-hand man.
lièvre [ljɛ:vr], *n.m.* hare.
liftier [lif'tje], *n.m.* (*fem.* **-ière**) lift-boy *or* girl, lift-attendant.
ligament [liga'mɑ̃], *n.m.* ligament.
ligature [liga'ty:r], *n.f.* ligature.
ligaturer [ligaty're], *v.t.* to ligature, to splice.
lignage [li'ɲa:ʒ], *n.m.* lineage.
ligne [liɲ], *n.f.* line; row; path, way; cord; fishing-line; order.
lignée [li'ɲe], *n.f.* issue, progeny, offspring.
ligoter [ligɔ'te], *v.t.* to bind, to tie up.
ligue [lig], *n.f.* league, confederacy.
liguer [li'ge], *v.t.* to unite in a league; **se liguer**, *v.r.* to league, to combine.
ligueur [li'gœ:r], *n.m.* (*fem.* **-euse**) leaguer; plotter.
lilas [li'lɑ], *a. inv.* lilac-coloured.—*n.m.* lilac.
lilliputien [lilipy'sjɛ̃], *a.* (*fem.* **-enne**) Lilliputian.

imace [li'mas], *n.f.* slug; Archimedean screw.
imaçon [lima'sɔ̃], *n.m.* snail.
imbe [lɛ̃:b], *n.m.* (*Math., Bot. etc.*) limb; (*Astron.*) border, halo; (*pl.*) limbo.
ime (1) [lim], *n.f.* file.
ime (2) [lim], *n.f.* lime, citron.
imer [li'me], *v.t.* to file, to smooth.
imeur [li'mœ:r], *n.m.* (*fem.* **-euse**) filer.—*n.f.* (**-euse**) finishing-tool *or* machine.
imier [li'mje], *n.m.* bloodhound; (*fig.*) police-spy, detective.
iminaire [limi'nɛ:r], *a.* prefatory.
imitatif [limita'tif], *a.* (*fem.* **-tive**) limiting, restrictive.
imitation [limitɑ'sjɔ̃], *n.f.* limitation.
imite [li'mit], *n.f.* limit, boundary; border; landmark.
imiter [limi'te], *v.t.* to limit, to bound; to confine.
imitrophe [limi'trɔf], *a.* neighbouring, bordering.
imon [li'mɔ̃], *n.m.* silt, ooze, mud; shaft (*of a carriage*); sour lime (*fruit*).
imonade [limɔ'nad], *n.f.* lemonade.
imonadier [limɔna'dje], *n.m.* (*fem.* **-ière**) seller of lemonade.
imoneux [limɔ'nø], *a.* (*fem.* **-euse**) muddy, turbid, slimy; alluvial.
imonier [limɔ'nje], *n.m.* shaft-horse; lime-tree.
imonière [limɔ'njɛ:r], *n.f.* pair of shafts (*of wagon etc.*); wagon with two shafts.
imousin [limu'zɛ̃], *n.m.* stonemason.
imousine [limu'zin], *n.f.* limousine (*car*); coarse woollen cloak.
impide [lɛ̃'pid], *a.* limpid, clear.
impidité [lɛ̃pidi'te], *n.f.* limpidity.
in [lɛ̃], *n.m.* flax; ***graine de lin***, linseed; ***huile de lin***, linseed oil; ***toile de lin***, linen-cloth.
inceul [lɛ̃'sœl], *n.m.* winding-sheet, shroud.
inéaire [line'ɛ:r], *a.* linear.
inéal [line'al], *a.* (*m. pl.* **-aux**) lineal, in a direct line.
inéament [linea'mɑ̃], *n.m.* lineament, feature; (*fig.*) trace, vestige.
inge [lɛ̃:ʒ], *n.m.* linen; piece, rag.
inger [lɛ̃'ʒe], *n.m.* (*fem.* **-ère**) linen-draper; maker of linen goods; seamstress (*of same*).—*n.f.* (**-ère**) wardrobe woman.
ingerie [lɛ̃'ʒri], *n.f.* linen-trade, linen-drapery; linen goods.
ingot [lɛ̃'go], *n.m.* ingot; bullion.
ingue [lɛ̃:g], *n.f.* (*Ichth.*) ling.
inguiste [lɛ̃'gɥist], *n.* linguist.
inguistique [lɛ̃gɥis'tik], *a.* linguistic.—*n.f.* linguistics.
inier [li'nje], *a.* (*fem.* **-ière**) of flax *or* linen.—*n.f.* (**-ière**) flax-field.
inoléum [linɔle'ɔm], *n.m.* linoleum.
inon [li'nɔ̃], *n.m.* lawn (*fine linen*).
inot [li'no], *n.m.*, **linotte** [li'nɔt], *n.f.* linnet.
inotype [linɔ'tip], *n.f.* linotype.
inotypiste [linɔti'pist], *n.* linotype operator.
inteau [lɛ̃'to], *n.m.* (*pl.* **-eaux**) lintel.
ion [ljɔ̃], *n.m.* (*fem.* **lionne**) lion, lioness; (*fig.*) a bold, brave fellow.
ionceau [ljɔ̃'so], *n.m.* (*pl.* **-eaux**) young lion, lion's cub.
ippe [lip], *n.f.* thick lower lip; pouting lip.
ippu [li'py], *a.* thick-lipped.

liquéfaction [likefak'sjɔ̃], *n.f.* liquefaction.
liquéfiable [like'fjabl], *a.* liquefiable.
liquéfier [like'fje], *v.t.* and **se liquéfier**, *v.r.* to liquefy.
liqueur [li'kœ:r], *n.f.* liquid; liqueur, cordial; (*Chem.*) spirit.
liquidateur [likida'tœ:r], *n.m.* liquidator.
liquidation [likidɑ'sjɔ̃], *n.f.* liquidation; settlement (*of debts etc.*); winding up (*of a business*); clearance sale.
liquide [li'kid], *a.* liquid; clear, net (*of money*).—*n.m.* liquid, fluid; drink.
liquider [liki'de], *v.t.* to liquidate, to settle; to wind up; to sell off; (*fam.*) to get rid of.
liquidité [likidi'te], *n.f.* liquidity, fluidity.
liquoreux [likɔ'rø], *a.* (*fem.* **-euse**) luscious, sweet.
liquoriste [likɔ'rist], *n.m.* wine and spirit merchant.
lire [li:r], *v.t. irr.* to read, to peruse, to study.
lis [lis], *n.m.* lily.
liseré [lizə're], *n.m.* piping; border, edge.
lisérer [lize're], *v.t.* (*conjug. like* CÉDER) to trim (*a dress etc.*) with piping.
liseron [liz'rɔ̃], **liset** [li'zɛ], *n.m.* (*Bot.*) convolvulus.
liseur [li'zœ:r], *n.m.* (*fem.* **-euse**) reader.
lisibilité [lizibili'te], *n.f.* legibility, readableness.
lisible [li'zibl], *a.* legible, readable.
lisiblement [liziblə'mɑ̃], *adv.* legibly.
lisière [li'zjɛ:r], *n.f.* selvedge, edge (*of cloth etc.*), border, verge, outskirts.
lissage [li'sa:ʒ], *n.m.* smoothing, glossing.
lisse (1) [lis], *a.* smooth; sleek; glossy.—*n.m.* smoothness, gloss.
lisse (2) [lis], *n.f.* rail, railing (*of ship*).
lisser [li'se], *v.t.* to smooth, to polish.
lisseur [li'sœ:r], *n.m.* (*fem.* **-euse**) polisher.
liste [list], *n.f.* list, roll; catalogue; schedule.
lit [li], *n.m.* bed; layer (*of clay, mortar*); direction, set (*of tide, current*); (*fig.*) marriage.
litanie [lita'ni], *n.f.* (*fig.*) rigmarole; (*pl.*) litany.
litée [li'te], *n.f.* litter (*of animals*).
literie [li'tri], *n.f.* bedding.
lithographe [litɔ'graf], *n.m.* lithographer.
lithographie [litɔgra'fi], *n.f.* lithography; lithograph.
lithographier [litɔgra'fje], *v.t.* to lithograph.
lithographique [litɔgra'fik] *a.* lithographic.
Lithuanie [LITUANIE].
lithuanien [LITUANIEN].
litière [li'tjɛ:r], *n.f.* stable-litter; litter (*for carrying sick persons etc.*).
litigant [liti'gɑ̃], *a.* litigant.
litige [li'ti:ʒ], *n.m.* litigation, legal dispute; (*fig.*) strife.
litigieux [liti'ʒjø], *a.* (*fem.* **-euse**) litigious, given to lawsuits.
litre [litr], *n.m.* litre (*1·76 pints*).
littéraire [lite'rɛ:r], *a.* literary; ***propriété littéraire***, copyright.
littérairement [literɛr'mɑ̃], *adv.* in a literary manner *or* way.
littéral [lite'ral], *a.* (*m. pl.* **-aux**) literal.
littéralement [literal'mɑ̃], *adv.* literally, word for word.
littérateur [litera'tœ:r], *n.m.* literary man, author, man of letters.
littérature [litera'ty:r], *n.f.* literature.

littoral [litɔ'ral], *a.* (*m. pl.* **-aux**) littoral, coastal.—*n.m.* littoral, seaboard.
Lituanie [litɥa'ni], **la**, *f.* Lithuania.
lituanien [litɥa'njɛ̃], *a.* Lithuanian.—*n.m.* Lithuanian (*language*); (**Lituanien,** *fem.* **-enne**) Lithuanian (*person*).
liturgie [lityr'ʒi], *n.f.* liturgy.
liturgique [lityr'ʒik], *a.* liturgic, liturgical.
liturgiste [lityr'ʒist], *n.* liturgist.
livide [li'vid], *a.* livid, ghastly.
lividité [lividi'te], *n.f.* lividness.
livrable [li'vrabl], *a.* deliverable.
livraison [livrɛ'zɔ̃], *n.f.* delivery (*of goods*); part, number, issue (*of a magazine etc.*).
livre (1) [li:vr], *n.m.* book; register, account-book.
livre (2) [li:vr], *n.f.* pound (*1·1 lb. avoirdupois*); ***livre sterling***, pound sterling.
livrée [li'vre], *n.f.* livery; livery-servants.
livrer [li'vre], *v.t.* to deliver; to give up, to hand over; to betray (*a secret*). **se livrer,** *v.r.* to give oneself up (*à*); to surrender; to devote oneself; to entrust oneself to; to indulge in (*a vice*).
livret [li'vrɛ], *n.m.* little book; memorandum-book; libretto.
livreur [li'vrœ:r], *n.m.* (*fem.* **-euse**) deliverer (*of goods*); delivery-man, van-man.—*n.f.* (**-euse**) delivery-van.
lobe [lɔb], *n.m.* lobe (*of ear, liver etc.*).
lobélie [lɔbe'li], *n.f.* (*Bot.*) lobelia.
local [lɔ'kal], *a.* (*m. pl.* **-aux**) local.—*n.m.* place, premises; quarters.
localement [lɔkal'mɑ̃], *adv.* locally.
localisation [lɔkalizɑ'sjɔ̃], *n.f.* localization.
localiser [lɔkali'ze], *v.t.* to localize. **se localiser,** *v.r.* to become localized.
localité [lɔkali'te], *n.f.* locality.
locataire [lɔka'tɛ:r], *n.* tenant, lodger, occupier.
location [lɔkɑ'sjɔ̃], *n.f.* letting out; hiring, renting; (*Theat.*) booking of seat.
lock-out [lɔ'kaut], *n.m. inv.* lock-out.
lock-outer [lɔkau'te], *v.t.* to lock-out.
locomoteur [lɔkɔmɔ'tœ:r], *a.* (*fem.* **-trice**) locomotor.
locomotif [lɔkɔmɔ'tif], *a.* (*fem.* **-tive**) locomotive.—*n.f.* (**-tive**) locomotive, engine.
locomotion [lɔkɔmɔ'sjɔ̃], *n.f.* locomotion.
locomotive [LOCOMOTIF].
locuste [lɔ'kyst], *n.f.* locust.
locution [lɔky'sjɔ̃], *n.f.* locution, expression, form of speech; term, phrase.
logarithme [lɔga'ritm], *n.m.* logarithm.
loge [lɔ:ʒ], *n.f.* hut; lodge; (*Theat.*) box, dressing-room; stand, stall; kennel; booth.
logeable [lɔ'ʒabl], *a.* tenantable, fit to live in.
logement [lɔʒ'mɑ̃], *n.m.* lodgings; dwelling; house-room, accommodation; quarters.
loger [lɔ'ʒe], *v.t.* (*conjug. like* MANGER) to lodge; to put up, to accommodate, to house; to quarter; to stable.—*v.i.* to lodge, to live; to put up. **se loger,** *v.r.* to lodge, to take up one's abode; to lodge itself.
logette [lɔ'ʒɛt], *n.f.* small lodge.
logeur [lɔ'ʒœ:r], *n.m.* (*fem.* **-euse**) lodging-house keeper.
logicien [lɔʒi'sjɛ̃], *n.m.* (*fem.* **-enne**) logician.
logique [lɔ'ʒik], *a.* logical.—*n.f.* logic.
logiquement [lɔʒik'mɑ̃], *adv.* logically.
logis [lɔ'ʒi], *n.m.* (*rare*) house, dwelling.

loi [lwɑ], *n.f.* law, statute, act; rule.
loin [lwɛ̃], *adv.* far, at a distance; remote distant; ***au loin***, far away, far and wide; ***de loin***, from afar, from a distance; ***de loin en loin***, at long intervals.
lointain [lwɛ̃'tɛ̃], *a.* remote, far off, distant.—*n.m.* distance, distant prospect.
loir [lwa:r], *n.m.* dormouse.
loisible [lwa'zibl], *a.* optional, lawful, allowable.
loisir [lwa'zi:r], *n.m.* leisure, spare time.
lombes [lɔ̃:b], *n.m. pl.* (*Anat.*) lumbar region loins.
londonien [lɔ̃dɔ'njɛ̃], *a.* (*fem.* **-enne**) of or pertaining to London.—*n.m.* (**Londonien**, *fem.* **-enne**) Londoner.
Londres ['lɔ̃drə], *f.* London.
long [lɔ̃], *a.* (*fem.* **longue**) long; slow, tedious diffuse, drawn out.—*n.m.* length; extent (***tout***) ***au long***, in full; ***de long en large*** up and down, to and fro.—*n.f.* ***à la longue*** in the long run.—*adv.* much, great deal.
longanimité [lɔ̃ganimi'te], *n.f.* longanimity forbearance, long-suffering.
long-courrier [lɔ̃ku'rje], *n.m.* (*pl.* **-courriers**) ocean-going ship.
longe (1) [lɔ̃:ʒ], *n.f.* tether, leading-rein thong.
longe (2) [lɔ̃:ʒ], *n.f.* ***longe de veau***, loin of veal.
longer [lɔ̃'ʒe], *v.t.* (*conjug. like* MANGER) to go to run along; to skirt; to extend along.
longévité [lɔ̃ʒevi'te], *n.f.* longevity.
longitude [lɔ̃ʒi'tyd], *n.f.* longitude.
longitudinal [lɔ̃ʒitydi'nal], *a.* (*m. pl.* **-aux** longitudinal.
longitudinalement [lɔ̃ʒitydinal'mɑ̃], *adv* lengthwise.
longtemps [lɔ̃'tɑ̃], *adv.* long, a long while.
longuement [lɔ̃g'mɑ̃], *adv.* long, a long time for a great while.
longueur [lɔ̃'gœ:r], *n.f.* length, extent in time; slowness; prolixity.
longue-vue [lɔ̃g'vy], *n.f.* (*pl.* **longues-vues** telescope, spy-glass.
lopin [lɔ'pɛ̃], *n.m.* small piece *or* share; ***lopin de terre***, plot of ground.
loquace [lɔ'kwas], *a.* loquacious, talkative.
loquacement [lɔkwas'mɑ̃], *adv.* talkatively loquaciously.
loquacité [lɔkwasi'te], *n.f.* loquacity, talkativeness.
loque [lɔk], *n.f.* rag, tatter.
loquet [lɔkɛ], *n.m.* latch; ***fermé au loquet*** on the latch.
loqueteau [lɔk'to], *n.m.* (*pl.* **-eaux**) small latch.
loqueteux [lɔk'tø], *a.* (*fem.* **-euse**) in rags.—*n.m.* (*fem.* **-euse**) ragged person.
lorgner [lɔr'ɲe], *v.t.* to leer at, to ogle.
lorgnette [lɔr'ɲɛt], *n.f.* field *or* opera-glasses
lorgnon [lɔr'ɲɔ̃], *n.m.* (*sometimes pl.*) eye-glasses; lorgnette.
lorry [lɔ'ri], *n.m.* (*Rail.*) lorry, trolley (*of platelayer*).
lors [lɔ:r], *adv.* then; ***depuis*** or ***dès lors*** from that time, since then; ***lors de***, at the time of; ***lors même que***, even though ***pour lors***, then, at the time; so, therefore.
lorsque [lɔrsk, 'lɔrskə], *conj.* when; at the time *or* moment of.

sange [lɔ'zɑ̃:ʒ], *n.m.* diamond-shape, lozenge.
sangé [lɔzɑ̃'ʒe], *a.* in lozenges.
t [lo], *n.m.* lot; portion, share; prize (*in a lottery*); (*fig.*) fate.
terie [lɔ'tri], *n.f.* lottery, raffle.
tion [lo'sjɔ̃], *n.f.* lotion; ablution.
tir [lɔ'ti:r], *v.t.* to divide into lots, to portion off.
tissement [lɔtis'mɑ̃], *n.m.* dividing into lots; building plot.
to [lɔ'to], *n.m.* lotto (*game of chance*); housey-housey, bingo.
tus [lɔ'ty:s], *n.m. inv.* lotus.
uable [lwabl], *a.* laudable, praiseworthy, commendable.
uablement [lwablə'mɑ̃], *adv.* commendably.
uage [lwa:ʒ], *n.m.* letting out, hiring, renting; hire.
uange [lwɑ̃:ʒ], *n.f.* praise, commendation, eulogy.
uanger [lwɑ̃'ʒe], *v.t.* (*conjug. like* MANGER) to praise, to flatter, to extol.
uangeur [lwɑ̃'ʒœ:r], *a.* (*fem.* **-euse**) laudatory, eulogistic.—*n.m.* (*fem.* **-euse**) praiser, flatterer.
uche (1) [luʃ], *n.f.* (*soup*) ladle; scoop; countersink bit.
uche (2) [luʃ], *a.* squint-eyed; dubious, ambiguous; suspicious, shady.
ucher [lu'ʃe], *v.i.* to squint.
ucheur [lu'ʃœ:r], *a.* (*fem.* **-euse**) squinting. —*n.m.* (*fem.* **-euse**) squinter.
uer (1) [lwe], *v.t.* to let *or* hire out; to lease, to rent, to hire; to book. **se louer** (1), *v.r.* to hire oneself out; to be let *or* rented.
uer (2) [lwe], *v.t.* to praise, to commend, to extol. **se louer** (2), *v.r.* to praise oneself; to rejoice.
ueur [lwœ:r], *n.m.* (*fem.* **-euse**) hirer, letter-out.
ugre [lugr], *n.m.* lugger.
ouis [lwi], *m.* Lewis.
uis [lwi], *n.m. inv.* louis (*a French coin worth 20 gold francs*).
up [lu], *n.m.* wolf; black velvet mask.
up-cervier [lusɛr'vje], *n.m.* (*pl.* **loups-cerviers**) lynx; (*fig.*) profiteer.
upe (1) [lup], *n.f.* magnifying-glass.
upe (2) [lup], *n.f.* wen; gnarl (*on trees*).
uper [lu'pe], *v.t.* (*pop.*) to botch (*a piece of work*); (*Exam.*) to fail; to miss (*train*).
upeux [lu'pø], *a.* (*fem.* **-euse**) wenny, knobby.
up-garou [luga'ru], *n.m.* (*pl.* **loups-garous**) wer(e)wolf; bugbear.
urd [lu:r], *a.* heavy, clumsy; stupid; sultry.
urdaud [lur'do], *a.* loutish.—*n.m.* (*fem.* **-e**) blockhead.
urdement [lurdə'mɑ̃], *adv.* heavily; clumsily.
urdeur [lur'dœ:r], *n.f.* heaviness; clumsiness; stupidity; sultriness.
utre [lutr], *n.f.* otter; otter-fur.
uve [lu:v], *n.f.* she-wolf.
uveteau [luv'to], *n.m.* (*pl.* **-eaux**) wolf-cub.
uveterie [luv'tri], *n.f.* wolf-hunting equipage; wolf-hunting.
uvetier [luv'tje], *n.m.* wolf-hunter.
uvoyer [luvwa'je], *v.i.* (*conjug. like* EMPLOYER) to tack, to tack about; (*fig.*) to manœuvre; to dodge.
lover [lɔ've], *v.t.* to coil (*rope etc.*). **se lover**, *v.r.* to coil up (*of snakes*).
loyal [lwa'jal], *a.* (*m. pl.* **-aux**) fair, honest, upright; loyal; (*Comm.*) unadulterated.
loyalement [lwajal'mɑ̃] *adv.* fairly, honestly; loyally.
loyauté [lwajo'te], *n.f.* honesty, fairness; loyalty, faithfulness.
loyer [lwa'je], *n.m.* hire, rent.
lubie [ly'bi] *n.f.* crotchet, whim, fad.
lubrifiant [lybri'fjɑ̃], *a.* lubricating.—*n.m.* lubricant.
lubrification [lybrifikɑ'sjɔ̃], *n.f.* lubrication.
lubrifier [lybri'fje], *v.t.* to lubricate.
Luc [lyk], *m.* Luke.
lucarne [ly'karn], *n.f.* dormer-window, skylight.
lucide [ly'sid], *a.* lucid, clear.
lucidement [lysid'mɑ̃], *adv.* lucidly.
lucidité [lysidi'te], *n.f.* lucidity, clearness.
luciole [ly'sjɔl], *n.f.* (*Ent.*) fire-fly; winged glow-worm.
lucratif [lykra'tif], *a.* (*fem.* **-tive**) lucrative.
lucre [lykr], *n.m.* lucre, gain.
lueur [lɥœ:r], *n.f.* glimmer, gleam; flash.
luffa [ly'fa], *n.m.* or *f.* loofah.
lugubre [ly'gybr], *a.* lugubrious, doleful, dismal.
lugubrement [lygybrə'mɑ̃], *adv.* ominously; dismally.
lui [lɥi], *pers. pron.* he, it, to him, to her, to it.
luire [lɥi:r], *v.i. irr.* to shine; to glitter, to gleam, to glisten; to dawn.
luisant [lɥi'zɑ̃], *a.* glistening, glittering, bright; glossy.—*n.m.* gloss, shine.
lumbago [lœ̃ba'go], *n.m.* lumbago.
lumière [ly'mjɛ:r], *n.f.* light; daylight, day; (*fig.*) enlightenment; knowledge, wisdom.
luminaire [lymi'nɛ:r], *n.m.* luminary, light.
lumineux [lymi'nø], *a.* (*fem.* **-euse**) luminous; bright.
lunaire [ly'nɛ:r], *a.* lunar.
lunatique [lyna'tik], *a.* fantastical, whimsical. —*n.* incalculable *or* whimsical person.
lundi [lœ̃'di], *n.m.* Monday.
lune [lyn], *n.f.* moon.
lunetier [lyn'tje], *n.m.* (*fem.* **-ière**) spectacle-maker; optician.
lunette [ly'nɛt], *n.f.* telescope, field-glass; (*pl.*) spectacles.
lupin [ly'pɛ̃], *n.m.* (*Bot.*) lupin(e).
lupus [ly'py:s], *n.m.* lupus.
luron [ly'rɔ̃], *n.m.* (*fem.* **-onne**) jolly fellow, gay dog; carefree type of girl.
lustrage [lys'tra:ʒ], *n.m.* glossing.
lustral [lys'tral], *a.* (*m. pl.* **-aux**) lustral.
lustration [lystrɑ'sjɔ̃], *n.f.* lustration.
lustre (1) [lystr], *n.m.* lustre, brilliancy, brightness; (*fig.*) distinction; chandelier.
lustre (2) [lystr], *n.m.* (*Rom. Ant.*) lustrum, space of five years.
lustré [lys'tre], *a.* glossy, shiny.
lustrer [lys'tre], *v.t.* to give a lustre *or* gloss to, to glaze.
lustrine [lys'trin], *n.f.* lustring, cotton lustre.
luth [lyt], *n.m.* lute.
luthérien [lyte'rjɛ̃], *a.* Lutheran.—*n.m.* (**Luthérien**, *fem.* **-enne**) Lutheran (*person*)

lutin [ly'tɛ̃], *a.* roguish, sprightly.—*n.m.* goblin, sprite elf, imp.
lutiner [lyti'ne], *v.t.* to plague, to tease, to pester.—*v.i.* to be mischievous, to play the imp.
lutrin [ly'trɛ̃], *n.m.* music-lectern *or* desk; choir.
lutte [lyt], *n.f.* wrestling; struggle, contest, strife; ***de bonne lutte***, by fair play; ***de haute lutte***, by force.
lutter [ly'te], *v.i.* to wrestle; to struggle, to contend.
lutteur [ly'tœ:r], *n.m.* (*fem.* **-euse**) wrestler.
luxation [lyksɑ'sjɔ̃], *n.f.* luxation, dislocation.
luxe [lyks], *n.m.* luxury; profusion; extravagance, excess.
Luxembourg [lyksɑ̃'bu:r], **le**, *m.* Luxembourg.
luxembourgeois [lyksɑ̃bur'ʒwa], *a.* (of) Luxembourg.—*n.m.* (**Luxembourgeois**, *fem.* **-oise**) citizen of Luxembourg.
luxer [lyk'se], *v.t.* to luxate, to dislocate.
luxueusement [lyksɥøz'mɑ̃], *a.* luxuriously, sumptuously, richly.
luxueux [lyk'sɥø], *a.* (*fem.* **-euse**) luxurious; magnificent, rich, sumptuous.
luxure [lyk'sy:r], *n.f.* lust.
luxuriance [lyksy'rjɑ̃:s], *n.f.* luxuriance.
luxuriant [lyksy'rjɑ̃], *a.* luxuriant.
luxurieux [lyksy'rjø], *a.* (*fem.* **-euse**) lustful, lecherous.
lycée [li'se], *n.m.* French grammar- *or* high-school.
lycéen [lise'ɛ̃], *n.m.* (*fem.* **-éenne**) grammar-school pupil.
lymphatique [lɛ̃fa'tik], *a.* lymphatic.
lymphe [lɛ̃:f], *n.f.* lymph; (*Bot.*) sap.
lynchage [lɛ̃'ʃa:ʒ], *n.m.* lynching.
lyncher [lɛ̃'ʃe], *v.t.* to lynch.
lynx [lɛ̃:ks], *n.m. inv.* lynx.
Lyon [ljɔ̃], *m.* Lyons.
lyre [li:r], *n.f.* lyre; (*fig.*) poetry.
lyrique [li'rik], *a.* lyric, lyrical.
lyrisme [li'rism], *n.m.* lyric poetry; poetic fire.

M

M m [ɛm], *n.m.* or *f.* the thirteenth letter of the alphabet; ***M***, 1000; ***M.***, ***MM.***, abbr. of ***Monsieur***, ***Messieurs***.
m' [ME].
ma [ma], *a. poss. f.* [MON].
macabre [ma'kɑ:br], *a.* gruesome, macabre, deathly, ghastly; ***la danse macabre***, the dance of death.
macadam [maka'dam], *n.m.* macadam.
macadamiser [makadami'ze], *v.t.* to macadamize.
macaque [ma'kak], *n.m.* macaco (*monkey*).
macaron [maka'rɔ̃], *n.m.* macaroon.
macaroni [makarɔ'ni], *n.m.* macaroni.
Macédoine [mase'dwan], **la**, *f.* Macedonia.
macédoine [mase'dwan], *n.f.* vegetable hotchpotch; fruit salad; (*fig.*) medley, hotchpotch.
macédonien [masedɔ'njɛ̃], *a.* Macedonian.—*n.m.* (**Macédonien**, *fem.* **-enne**) Macedonian (*person*).
macération [maserɑ'sjɔ̃], *n.f.* maceration.
macérer [mase're], *v.t.* (*conjug. like* CÉDER) to macerate; (*fig.*) to mortify.—*v.i.* to soak. **se macérer**, *v.r.* to macerate one's body; (*fig.*) to mortify oneself.
mâcher [mɑ'ʃe], *v.t.* to chew, to masticate; ***ne pas mâcher ses mots***, not to mince matters.
machiavélique [makjave'lik], *a.* Machiavellian.
machiavélisme [makjave'lism], *n.m.* Machiavellism.
machiavéliste [makjave'list], *n.* Machiavellian.
machinal [maʃi'nal], *a.* (*m. pl.* **-aux**) mechanical automatic, instinctive.
machinalement [maʃinal'mɑ̃], *adv.* mechanically, automatically, instinctively.
machinateur [maʃina'tœ:r], *n.m.* (*fem.* **-trice**) plotter, schemer.
machination [maʃinɑ'sjɔ̃], *n.f.* machination, plot, scheme.
machine [ma'ʃin], *n.f.* machine, engine, piece of machinery; apparatus; scheme, plot; ***machine à coudre***, sewing-machine; ***machine à écrire***, typewriter; ***machine à laver***, washing machine; ***machine pneumatique***, air-pump.
machine-outil [maʃinu'ti], *n.f.* (*pl.* **machines-outils**) machine-tool.
machiner [maʃi'ne], *v.t.* to contrive, to plot.
machiniste [maʃi'nist], *n.m.* machinist, engine-man; (*Theat.*) scene-shifter.
mâchoire [mɑ'ʃwa:r], *n.f.* jaw; jawbone.
mâchonner [mɑʃɔ'ne], *v.t.* to chew with difficulty; to munch; to mumble; to champ (*the bit*).
mâchurer [mɑʃy're], *v.t.* to daub, to smudge; to bruise.
maçon [ma'sɔ̃], *n.m.* mason, bricklayer; freemason.
maçonnage [masɔ'na:ʒ], *n.m.* mason's work, stonework.
maçonner [masɔ'ne], *v.t.* to build; to wall up.
maçonnerie [masɔn'ri], *n.f.* masonry, mason's work, stone-work; freemasonry.
maçonnique [masɔ'nik], *a.* masonic.
macule [ma'kyl], *n.f.* stain, spot.
maculer [maky'le], *v.t.* to blot, to spot.
Madagascar [madagas'ka:r], **le**, *n.m.* Malagasy Republic.
madame [ma'dam], *n.f.* (*pl.* **mesdames**) madam, ma'am; Mrs.; your ladyship.
madécasse [made'kas], *a.* Madagascan.—*n.* (**Madécasse**) Madagascan (*person*).
madeleine [ma'dlɛn], *n.f.* shell-shaped sponge-cake; early pear.
Madelon [ma'dlɔ̃], *f.* Maud.
mademoiselle [madmwa'zɛl], *n.f.* (*pl.* **mesdemoiselles**) Miss; young lady.
Madère [ma'dɛ:r], **la**, *f.* Madeira.
madère [ma'dɛ:r], *n.m.* Madeira wine.
madone [ma'dɔn], *n.f.* Madonna.
madré [mɑ'dre], *a.* veined, mottled; (*fig.*) cunning, sly, sharp.—*n.m.* (*fem.* **-ée**) cunning, sharp *or* sly person.
madrier [madri'e], *n.m.* thick plank.
maestria [maɛs'tria], *n.f.* masterliness; ***avec maestria***, in a masterly manner.

magasin [maga'zɛ̃], *n.m.* warehouse, storehouse; shop, store; magazine (*of fire-arm, camera etc.*).
(*C*) **magasiner** [magazi'ne], *v.i.* to shop.
magasinier [magazi'nje], *n.m.* warehouse-keeper, storeman.
magazine [maga'zin], *n.m.* magazine (*usu. illustrated*).
mage [ma:ʒ], *n.m.* mage, magus; seer; ***les rois mages***, the three wise men.
magicien [maʒi'sjɛ̃], *n.m.* (*fem.* **-enne**) magician, wizard, sorcerer, sorceress.
magie [ma'ʒi], *n.f.* magic.
magique [ma'ʒik], *a.* magic(al).
magister [maʒis'tɛ:r], *n.m.* village schoolmaster; pedant.
magistral [maʒis'tral], *a.* (*m. pl.* **-aux**) magisterial; masterly, authoritative, sovereign.
magistralement [maʒistral'mɑ̃], *adv.* magisterially; in a masterly fashion.
magistrat [maʒis'tra], *n.m.* magistrate, justice; civic officer.
magistrature [maʒistra'ty:r], *n.f.* magistracy; bench.
magnanime [maɲa'nim], *a.* magnanimous, high-minded.
magnanimement [maɲanim'mɑ̃], *adv.* magnanimously.
magnanimité [maɲanimi'te], *n.f.* magnanimity.
magnat [mag'na], *n.m.* magnate.
magnésie [maɲe'zi], *n.f.* magnesia.
magnétique [maɲe'tik], *a.* magnetic.
magnétiser [maɲeti'ze], *v.t.* to magnetize.
magnetiseur [maɲeti'zœ:r], *n.m.* magnetizer.
magnétisme [maɲe'tism], *n.m.* magnetism; (*fig.*) attraction.
magnétophone [maɲetɔ'fɔn], *n.m.* (*Reg. trade mark*) tape-recorder.
magnificence [maɲifi'sɑ̃:s], *n.f.* magnificence, splendour.
magnifier [maɲi'fje], *v.t.* to magnify, to glorify.
magnifique [maɲi'fik], *a.* magnificent, splendid; gorgeous.
magnifiquement [maɲifik'mɑ̃], *adv.* magnificently.
magot [ma'go], *n.m.* magot, ape; grotesque figure (*of china*); (*fig.*) ugly person; (*fam.*) hoard, hidden savings.
Mahomet [maɔ'mɛ], *m.* Mohammed.
mahométan [maɔme'tɑ̃], *a.* Mohammedan. —*n.m.* (**Mahométan**, *fem.* **-ane**) Mohammedan (*person*).
mahométisme [maɔme'tism], *n.m.* Mohammedanism.
mai [mɛ], *n.m.* May; maypole.
maigre [mɛ:gr], *a.* meagre, lean, thin; poor, scanty; barren; fasting; ***repas maigre***, meatless meal; ***maigre repas***, slender meal.
maigrement [mɛgrə'mɑ̃], *adv.* meagrely; poorly; sparingly.
maigreur [mɛ'grœ:r], *n.f.* leanness, meagreness; thinness, poorness, barrenness.
maigrir [mɛ'gri:r], *v.i.* to grow thin, to lose weight.
mail [ma:j], *n.m.* mall (*game, promenade, avenue of trees*).
maille [mɑ:j], *n.f.* mesh; ring of cable; link of mail; stitch.
maillé [mɑ'je], *a.* stitched; mailed.
mailler [mɑ'je], *v.t.* to make with meshes, to lattice; to mail.
maillet [ma'jɛ], *n.m.* mallet.
maillon [mɑ'jɔ̃], *n.m.* link (*of chain*).
maillot [ma'jo], *n.m.* swaddling-band; swaddling-clothes; pair of tights (*for theatre*); bathing costume; (*Spt.*) jersey, vest; ***enfant au maillot***, baby in arms.
main [mɛ̃], *n.f.* hand; handwriting; lead, deal (*at cards*); handle; quire (*of paper*); ***à la main***, in his *or* her hand, by hand; ***à la portée de la main***, within reach; ***à main armée***, by force of arms, armed; ***à pleines mains***, by handfuls, liberally; ***vol à main armée***, armed robbery.
main-d'œuvre [mɛ̃'dœ:vr], *n.f.* (*pl.* **mains-d'œuvre**) man-power, labour; workmanship.
main-forte [mɛ̃'fɔrt], *n.f.* assistance, help.
maint [mɛ̃], *a.* many; ***maintes fois***, many a time.
maintenant [mɛ̃t'nɑ̃], *adv.* now, at this moment, at present, nowadays.
maintenir [mɛ̃t'ni:r], *v.t. irr.* (*conjug. like* TENIR) to uphold, to sustain; to maintain; to enforce. **se maintenir**, *v.r.* to keep up; to subsist; to hold out, to stand one's ground; to remain in force.
maintien [mɛ̃'tjɛ̃], *n.m.* maintenance, keeping up; deportment; attitude.
maire [mɛ:r], *n.m.* mayor.
mairesse [mɛ'rɛs], *n.f.* mayoress.
mairie [mɛ'ri], *n.f.* mayoralty; town hall.
mais [mɛ], *conj.* but; why.
maïs [ma'is], *n.m.* maize, Indian corn.
maison [mɛ'zɔ̃], *n.f.* house; home; housekeeping; family; (*Comm.*) firm; ***à la maison***, at home.
maisonnée [mɛzɔ'ne], *n.f.* (*fam.*) whole house *or* family, household.
maisonnette [mɛzɔ'nɛt], *n.f.* small house, cottage, lodge.
maître [mɛ:tr], *n.m.* master; ruler, lord; proprietor, landlord; teacher, tutor; (*Naut.*) chief petty officer; ***coup de maître***, masterly stroke; ***maître chanteur***, blackmailer.
maître-autel [mɛtro'tɛl], *n.m.* (*pl.* **maîtres-autels**) high altar.
maîtresse [mɛ'trɛs], *a.* chief, leading, main.—*n.f.* mistress; ruler, lady; proprietress; teacher; sweetheart.
maîtrise [mɛ'tri:z], *n.f.* mastery; control; music-school (*in a cathedral*).
maîtriser [mɛtri'ze], *v.t.* to master, to control; to lord (it) over.
majesté [maʒɛs'te], *n.f.* majesty; stateliness.
majestueusement [maʒɛstɥøz'mɑ̃], *adv.* majestically.
majestueux [maʒɛs'tɥø], *a.* (*fem.* **-euse**) majestic.
majeur [ma'ʒœ:r], *a.* major, greater; superior, main, chief, most important; of full age.—*n.m.* (*fem.* **-e**) a male *or* female of full age, major.—*n.m.* middle finger.
majolique [maʒɔ'lik], *n.f.* majolica.
major [ma'ʒɔ:r], *n.m.* major; medical officer.
majordome [maʒɔr'dɔm], *n.m.* major-domo.
majorer [maʒɔ're], *v.t.* to raise (*the price*).
majorité [maʒɔri'te], *n.f.* majority.
majuscule [maʒys'kyl], *a.* capital, large.—*n.f.* capital letter.

mal [mal], *n.m.* (*pl.* **maux**) evil, ill; harm; pain, ache, sickness; hardship, misfortune; trouble; repugnance.—*adv.* wrong, badly; ***mal à propos***, improperly.
malade [ma'lad], *a.* sick, ill; unhealthy.—*n.* sick person, invalid; patient.
maladie [mala'di], *n.f.* illness, sickness, malady.
maladif [mala'dif], *a.* (*fem.* **-dive**) sickly, puny, ailing, unhealthy.
maladivement [maladiv'mɑ̃], *adv.* morbidly.
maladresse [mala'drɛs], *n.f.* awkwardness, clumsiness; blunder.
maladroit [mala'drwɑ], *a.* and *n.m.* (*fem.* **-e**) awkward, clumsy, stupid (person).
maladroitement [maladrwɑt'mɑ̃], *adv.* clumsily.
malais [ma'lɛ], *a.* Malay, Malayan, Malaysian.—*n.m.* Malay (*language*); (**Malais**, *fem.* **-aise**) Malay, Malayan, Malaysian (*person*).
malaise [ma'lɛ:z], *n.m.* uneasiness, discomfort; indisposition.
malaisé [malɛ'ze], *a.* hard, difficult, rough, arduous.
malaisément [malɛze'mɑ̃], *adv.* with difficulty, painfully.
Malaisie [malɛ'zi], **la**, *f.* Malaysia.
malappris [mala'pri], *a.* unmannerly, ill-bred.—*n.m.* (*fem.* **-e**) ill-bred person, lout.
malard [ma'la:r], *n.m.* mallard, wild drake.
malaria [mala'rja], *n.f.* malaria.
malart [MALARD].
malavisé [malavi'ze], *a.* ill-advised, imprudent, unwise, indiscreet.
malaxer [malak'ze], *v.t.* to mix, knead *or* work up; to massage.
malbâti [malbɑ'ti], *a.* ill-shaped, gawky.—*n.m.* (*fem.* **-e**) ill-favoured person.
malchance [mal'ʃɑ̃:s], *n.f.* ill-luck, mishap, mischance.
malchanceux [malʃɑ̃'sø], *a.* (*fem.* **-euse**) unlucky.
mâle [mɑ:l], *a.* male; manly, virile; masculine.—*n.m.* male; cock.
malédiction [maledik'sjɔ̃], *n.f.* malediction, curse.
maléfice [male'fis], *n.m.* evil spell, sorcery.
maléfique [male'fik], *a.* harmful, malefic, baleful.
malencontre [malɑ̃'kɔ̃:tr], *n.f.* mishap, mischance.
malencontreusement [malɑ̃kɔ̃trøz'mɑ̃], *adv.* unluckily, untowardly.
malencontreux [malɑ̃kɔ̃'trø], *a.* (*fem.* **-euse**) unlucky, untoward.
mal-en-point [malɑ̃'pwɛ̃], *adv.* badly off; in a sorry plight.
malentendu [malɑ̃tɑ̃'dy], *n.m.* misunderstanding, misapprehension, mistake.
malfaçon [malfa'sɔ̃], *n.f.* bad work; malpractice, illicit profit.
malfaire [mal'fɛ:r], *v.i.* (*used only in the inf.*) to do evil.
malfaisant [malfə'zɑ̃], *a.* mischievous; spiteful, malevolent.
malfaiteur [malfɛ'tœ:r], *n.m.* (*fem.* **-trice**) malefactor, evil-doer; offender; thief.
malfamé [malfa'me], *a.* ill-famed, of bad repute.
malformation [malfɔrma'sjɔ̃], *n.f.* malformation.
malgache [mal'gaʃ], *a.* Madagascan.—*n* (**Malgache**) Malagasy, Madagascan.
malgracieusement [malgrasjøz'mɑ̃], *adv.* ungraciously, rudely, uncivilly.
malgracieux [malgra'sjø], *a.* (*fem.* **-euse**) rude, ungracious, uncivil.
malgré [mal'gre], *prep.* in spite of, notwithstanding.
malhabile [mala'bil], *a.* unskilled, awkward.
malhabilement [malabil'mɑ̃], *adv.* unskilfully, awkwardly.
malhabileté [malabil'te], *n.f.* unskilfulness, awkwardness, clumsiness.
malheur [ma'lœ:r], *n.m.* unhappiness, misfortune, bad luck; mischance; calamity, disaster; woe, adversity; poverty.
malheureusement [malœrøz'mɑ̃], *adv.* unfortunately.
malheureux [malœ'rø], *a.* (*fem.* **-euse**) unfortunate, unlucky; unsuccessful; unpleasant; unhappy, miserable, wretched.—*n.m.* (*fem.* **-euse**) unhappy person.
malhonnête [malɔ'nɛ:t], *a.* dishonest; uncivil, rude.—*n.* rude person.
malhonnêtement [malɔnɛt'mɑ̃], *adv.* dishonestly; rudely.
malhonnêteté [malɔnɛt'te], *n.f.* rudeness, incivility; dishonesty.
malice [ma'lis], *n.f.* malice, spite; mischievousness; prank, trick.
malicieusement [malisjøz'mɑ̃], *adv.* maliciously; mischievously; slyly.
malicieux [mali'sjø], *a.* (*fem.* **-euse**) malicious, spiteful; mischievous; roguish.
malignement [maliɲ'mɑ̃], *adv.* malignantly; maliciously.
malignité [maliɲi'te], *n.f.* malignity, spite.
malin [ma'lɛ̃], *a.* (*fem.* **maligne**) malicious, mischievous; malignant; waggish, roguish; cunning, clever.—*n.m.* (*fem.* **maligne**) malignant *or* malicious person.—*n.m.* devil, evil spirit, fiend.
maline [ma'lin], *n.f.* spring tide.
malingre [ma'lɛ̃:gr], *a.* sickly, weakly, puny.
malintentionné [malɛ̃tɑ̃sjɔ'ne], *a.* evil-minded, ill-disposed.
malle [mal], *n.f.* trunk, box; mail-coach, mail boat.
malléabilité [maleabili'te], *n.f.* malleability; pliability.
malléable [male'abl], *a.* malleable.
malle-poste [mal'pɔst], *n.f.* (*pl.* **malles-poste**(s)) mail-coach.
mallette [ma'lɛt], *n.f.* small case, suitcase, attaché-case.
malmener [malmə'ne], *v.t.* (*conjug. like* AMENER) to ill-treat, to handle roughly; to abuse.
malodorant [malɔdɔ'rɑ̃], *a.* malodorous, ill-smelling.
malotru [malɔ'try], *a.* coarse, uncouth, vulgar.—*n.m.* (*fem.* **-e**) ill-bred person; lout.
Malouines [ma'lwin], **les Îles**, *f. pl.* the Falkland Islands.
malpeigné [malpɛ'ɲe], *a.* unkempt.—*n.m.* (*fem.* **-ée**) unkempt *or* dirty person.
malplaisant [malplɛ'zɑ̃], *a.* unpleasant, disagreeable.
malpropre [mal'prɔpr], *a.* slovenly, dirty; dishonest; unfit (*à*).
malproprement [malprɔprə'mɑ̃], *adv.* in a slovenly way, dirtily; improperly.

malpropreté [malprɔprə'te], *n.f.* dirtiness.
malsain [mal'sɛ̃], *a.* unhealthy; unwholesome, injurious.
malséant [malse'ɑ̃], *a.* unbecoming, unseemly, improper.
malsonnant [malsɔ'nɑ̃], *a.* ill-sounding; offensive.
malt [malt], *n.m.* malt.
maltais [mal'tɛ], *a.* Maltese.—*n.m.* Maltese (*language*); (**Maltais**, *fem.* **-aise**) Maltese (*person*).
Malte [malt], **la**, *f.* Malta.
maltraiter [maltrɛ'te], *v.t.* to ill-use, to maltreat, to abuse.
malveillamment [malvɛja'mɑ̃], *adv.* malevolently.
malveillance [malvɛ'jɑ̃:s], *n.f.* malevolence, ill-will, malice.
malveillant [malvɛ'jɑ̃], *a.* malevolent, malignant, ill-disposed, spiteful.—*n.m.* (*fem.* **-e**) evil-minded person.
malversation [malvɛrsɑ'sjɔ̃], *n.f.* malversation, peculation, embezzlement.
maman [ma'mɑ̃], *n.f.* mamma, mummy.
mamelle [ma'mɛl], *n.f.* breast; udder.
mamelon [mam'lɔ̃], *n.m.* nipple, teat; dug (*of animals*); pap, hillock, knoll.
mameluk [mam'luk], *n.m.* mameluke.
mammouth [ma'mut], *n.m.* mammoth.
manant [ma'nɑ̃], *n.m.* peasant, clodhopper.
manche (1) [mɑ̃:ʃ], *n.m.* handle; neck (*of violin etc.*).
manche (2) [mɑ̃:ʃ], *n.f.* sleeve; hose(**pipe**); channel; (*Spt.*) rubber, game, heat.
Manche [mɑ̃:ʃ], **la**, *f.* The (English) Channel. ***Les Îles de la Manche***, the Channel Islands.
manchette [mɑ̃'ʃɛt], *n.f.* cuff; ruffle; wristband.
manchon [mɑ̃'ʃɔ̃], *n.m.* muff.
manchot [mɑ̃'ʃo], *a.* one-handed, one-armed.—*n.m.* penguin; (*fem.* **-e**) one-handed, one-armed person.
mandarin [mɑ̃da'rɛ̃], *a.* and *n.m.* (*fem.* **-ine** (1)) mandarin.
mandarine (2) [mɑ̃da'rin], *n.f.* tangerine.
mandat [mɑ̃'da], *n.m.* mandate, authority; warrant, writ; money-order, order.
mandataire [mɑ̃da'tɛ:r], *n.m.* mandatory; proxy, attorney, agent.
mandchou [mɑ̃t'ʃu], *a.* Manchu(rian).—*n.m.* Manchu(rian) (*language*); (**Mandchou**, *fem.* **-oue**) Manchu(rian) (*person*).
Mandchourie [mɑ̃tʃu'ri], **la**, *f.* Manchuria.
mandement [mɑ̃d'mɑ̃], *n.m.* mandate; bishop's letter.
mander [mɑ̃'de], *v.t.* to write, to send word, to inform; to send for.
mandoline [mɑ̃dɔ'lin], *n.f.* mandolin.
mandoliniste [mɑ̃dɔli'nist], *n.* mandolin-player.
manège [ma'nɛ:ʒ], *n.m.* horsemanship; riding-school; merry-go-round; (*fig.*) trick, intrigue.
mânes [mɑ:n], *n.m. pl.* manes, shades.
manette [ma'nɛt], *n.f.* hand-lever, grip; (*Hort.*) trowel.
mangeable [mɑ̃'ʒabl], *a.* eatable, edible.
mangeoire [mɑ̃'ʒwa:r], *n.f.* manger, crib.
manger [mɑ̃'ʒe], *v.t.* (*see Verb Tables*) to eat; (*fig.*) to squander, to run through.—*v.i.* to eat; to feed.—*n.m.* eating; victuals, food.
se manger, *v.r.* to eat each other; to hurt each other; to be edible.
mangeur [mɑ̃'ʒœ:r], *n.m.* (*fem.* **-euse**) eater; spendthrift.
mangouste [mɑ̃'gust], *n.f.* mongoose.
maniable [ma'njabl], *a.* easy to handle; tractable, supple, pliable.
maniaque [ma'njak], *a.* eccentric, having a mania.—*n.* crank, faddist.
manicure [mani'ky:r], [MANUCURE].
manie [ma'ni], *n.f.* mania; fad, hobby; inveterate habit, craze.
maniement [mani'mɑ̃], *n.m.* handling; management, use.
manier [ma'nje], *v.t.* to handle; to touch; to use, to wield; to manage, to govern.
manière [ma'njɛ:r], *n.f.* manner, way, style; sort; affectation; (*pl.*) manners; ***de manière à***, so as to; ***de quelle manière***, how; ***manière d'être***, bearing, attitude.
maniéré [manje're], *a.* affected, unnatural, forced.
maniérisme [manje'rism], *n.m.* mannerism.
manifestation [manifɛstɑ'sjɔ̃], *n.f.* manifestation; (*Polit.*) demonstration.
manifeste [mani'fɛst], *a.* manifest, obvious.—*n.m.* manifesto.
manifestement [manifɛstə'mɑ̃], *adv.* manifestly.
manifester [manifɛs'te], *v.t.* to manifest, to display, to show.—*v.i.* to attend a (*political*) demonstration. **se manifester**, *v.r.* to manifest oneself, to make oneself known.
manigance [mani'gɑ̃:s], *n.f.* (*fam.*) manœuvre, intrigue.
manigancer [manigɑ̃'se], *v.t.* (*conjug. like* COMMENCER) to contrive, to plot.
Manille [ma'ni:j], **la**, *f.* Manila.
manipulateur [manipyla'tœ:r], *n.m.* (*fem.* **-trice**) manipulator.
manipulation [manipylɑ'sjɔ̃], *n.f.* manipulation.
manipuler [manipy'le], *v.t.* to manipulate; (*Teleg.*) to operate.
manivelle [mani'vɛl], *n.f.* crank; handle.
manne (1) [ma:n], *n.f.* manna.
manne (2) [ma:n], *n.f.* hamper, flat basket.
mannequin (1) [man'kɛ̃], *n.m.* small hamper.
mannequin (2) [man'kɛ̃], *n.m.* lay figure; tailor's dummy; model girl; mannequin.
manœuvre [ma'nœ:vr], *n.f.* working; drilling (*of soldiers*); manœuvre; scheme; move; (*Rail.*) marshalling.—*n.m.* unskilled workman, labourer, navvy.
manœuvrer [manœ'vre], *v.t.* to manœuvre; to work (*a machine*); to shunt (*trains*).
manœuvrier [manœvri'e], *a.* (*fem.* **-ière**) highly trained.—*n.m.* expert seaman; tactician.
manoir [ma'nwa:r], *n.m.* manor; country-house.
manouvrier [manuvri'e], *n.m.* (*fem.* **-ière**) day-labourer.
manquant [mɑ̃'kɑ̃], *a.* missing, absent, wanting.—*n.m.* (*fem.* **-e**) absentee, defaulter. —*n.m.* (*pl.*) shortages deficiencies.
manque [mɑ̃:k], *n.m.* want, lack; defect; deficiency.
manqué [mɑ̃'ke], *a.* missed; defective; unsuccessful, abortive.
manquement [mɑ̃kə'mɑ̃], *n.m.* omission, oversight; failure; breach.

manquer [mɑ̃'ke], *v.t.* to miss, to lose; to spoil.—*v.i.* to miss, to fail; to be wanting; to be deficient; to slip; to misfire; to go bankrupt; to miscarry.
mansarde [mɑ̃'sard], *n.f.* roof-window, dormer; garret.
mansardé [mɑ̃sar'de], *a.* with attics.
mansuétude [mɑ̃sɥe'tyd], *n.f.* mildness, gentleness, forbearance.
mante (1) [mɑ̃:t], *n.f.* mantle (*woman's*).
mante (2) [mɑ̃:t], *n.f.* mantis; ***mante religieuse***, praying mantis.
manteau [mɑ̃'to], *n.m.* (*pl.* **-eaux**) cloak, mantle; overcoat; (*fig.*) pretence.
mantille [mɑ̃'ti:j], *n.f.* mantilla.
manucure [many'ky:r], **manicure** [mani'ky:r], *n.* manicure (*person*), manicurist.
manuel [ma'nɥɛl], *a.* (*fem.* **-elle**) manual, portable.—*n.m.* manual, textbook.
manuellement [manɥɛl'mɑ̃], *adv.* by hand, manually.
manufacture [manyfak'ty:r], *n.f.* manufacture, making; factory, mill, works.
manufacturer [manyfakty're], *v.t.* to manufacture.
manufacturier [manyfakty'rje], *a.* (*fem.* **-ière**) manufacturing.—*n.m.* manufacturer.
manuscrit [manys'kri], *a.* handwritten.—*n.m.* manuscript.
manutention [manytɑ̃'sjɔ̃], *n.f.* management, administration; manipulation; handling (*of goods etc.*); army bakery.
mappemonde [map'mɔ̃:d], *n.f.* map of the world, planisphere.
maquereau [ma'kro], *n.m.* (*pl.* **-eaux**) mackerel.
maquette [ma'kɛt], *n.f.* (*Sculp.*) small rough model (*in clay, wax etc.*); (*Paint.*) rough sketch; lay figure; (*Theat., Cine.*) model.
maquignon [maki'ɲɔ̃], *n.m.* (*fem.* **-onne**) horse-dealer, jobber.
maquignonnage [makiɲɔ'na:ʒ], *n.m.* horse-dealing; underhand work, jobbery.
maquignonner [makiɲɔ'ne], *v.t.* to jockey, to bishop (*a horse for sale*); to job.
maquillage [maki'ja:ʒ], *n.m.* make-up.
maquiller [maki'je], *v.t.* to make up; to fake up. **se maquiller**, *v.r.* to make up *or* paint oneself.
maquilleur [maki'jœ:r], *n.m.* (*fem.* **-euse**) (*Theat.*) maker-up; faker (*of paintings etc.*).
maquis [ma'ki], *n.m. inv.* scrub (*in Corsica*); (*1941–44*) underground forces.
maquisard [maki'za:r], *n.m.* free fighter in the maquis.
maraîcher [marɛ'ʃe], *a.* (*fem.* **-ère**) of market-gardening.—*n.m.* market-gardener.
marais [ma'rɛ], *n.m.* marsh, fen, bog, swamp.
marasme [ma'rasm], *n.m.* emaciation; (*fig.*) depression; stagnation, slump.
marâtre [ma'rɑ:tr], *n.f.* stepmother; (*fig.*) harsh mother.
maraudage [maro'da:ʒ], *n.m.* marauding.
maraude [ma'ro:d], *n.f.* pilfering.
marauder [maro'de], *v.i.* to pilfer, to go scrounging.
maraudeur [maro'dœ:r], *n.m.* (*fem.* **-euse**) marauder; plunderer.
marbre [marbr], *n.m.* marble.
marbré [mar'bre], *a.* marbled.
marbrer [mar'bre], *v.t.* to marble, to vein.
marbrerie [marbrə'ri], *n.f.* marble-cutting; marble-works.
marbrier [marbri'e], *a.* (*fem.* **-ière**) of marble.—*n.m.* marble-cutter, marble-polisher; dealer in marble.—*n.f.* (**-ière**) marble-quarry.
marbrure [mar'bry:r], *n.f.* marbling; mottling (*on the skin*).
marc [ma:r], *n.m.* residuum (*of fruit etc. squeezed, boiled* or *strained*); dregs, grounds.
Marc [mark], *m.* Mark.
marchand [mar'ʃɑ̃], *a.* saleable, trading.—*n.m.* (*fem.* **-e**) dealer, tradesman, shopkeeper; merchant; ***marchand des quatre saisons***, costermonger, barrow-boy; ***marchand au détail***, retail merchant; ***marchand en gros***, wholesale dealer.
marchandage [marʃɑ̃'da:ʒ], *n.m.* bargaining, haggling; piece-work.
marchander [marʃɑ̃'de], *v.t.* to bargain for; to haggle over; (*fig.*) to spare; to grudge.—*v.i.* to haggle; to hesitate.
marchandeur [marʃɑ̃'dœ:r], *n.m.* (*fem.* **-euse**) bargainer, haggler; contractor on small scale.
marchandise [marʃɑ̃'di:z], *n.f.* merchandise; goods, wares, commodities.
marche (1) [marʃ], *n.f.* walk; gait; march, journey; procession; movement; conduct; ***marche arrière***, reversing (*of a car*); ***mettre en marche***, to set going.
marche (2) [marʃ], *n.f.* step, stair; treadle.
marché [mar'ʃe], *n.m.* market; market-place; bargain, purchase; price, rate; contract; ***à bon marché***, cheaply; ***bon marché***, cheap, cheapness.
marchepied [marʃə'pje], *n.m.* step (*of a coach, altar etc.*); step-ladder; running-board.
marcher [mar'ʃe], *v.i.* to walk; to progress; to step, to tread; to march; to run, to ply; to work (*of a machine*).
marcheur [mar'ʃœ:r], *n.m.* (*fem.* **-euse**) walker.
mardi [mar'di], *n.m.* Tuesday; ***mardi gras***, Shrove Tuesday.
mare [ma:r], *n.f.* pool, pond.
marécage [mare'ka:ʒ], *n.m.* marsh, bog, fen, swamp.
marécageux [mareka'ʒø], *a.* (*fem.* **-euse**) marshy, swampy, boggy.
maréchal [mare'ʃal], *n.m.* (*pl.* **-aux**) marshal, field-marshal.
maréchalerie [mareʃal'ri], *n.f.* farriery, smithy.
maréchal-ferrant [mareʃalfɛ'rɑ̃], *n.m.* (*pl.* **maréchaux-ferrants**) farrier, shoeing-smith.
marée [ma're], *n.f.* tide, flood; fresh sea-fish.
marelle [ma'rɛl], *n.f.* hopscotch.
mareyeur [marɛ'jœ:r] *n.m.* fish-factor, fish-salesman.
margarine [marga'rin], *n.f.* margarine.
marge [marʒ], *n.f.* margin, border, edge; (*fig.*) freedom, latitude, scope; means.
margelle [mar'ʒɛl], *n.f.* curb, edge (*of a well etc.*).
Marguerite [margə'rit], *f.* Margaret.
marguerite [margə'rit], *n.f.* daisy.
marguillier [margi'je], *n.m.* churchwar[den]
mari [ma'ri], *n.m.* husband.
mariable [ma'rjabl], *a.* marriageable.

mariage [ma'rja:ʒ], *n.m.* marriage; matrimony; wedding; union, blending.
Marie [ma'ri], *f.* Mary, Maria.
marié [ma'rje], *a.* married.—*n.m.* (*fem.* **-ée**) married man; bridegroom; married woman; bride.
marier [ma'rje], *v.t.* to give in marriage, to marry off; to match. **se marier**, *v.r.* to marry, to get married (*avec*).
marieur [ma'rjœ:r], *n.m.* (*fem.* **-euse**) matchmaker.
marin [ma'rɛ̃], *a.* marine; sea-going.—*n.m.* sailor.
marinade [mari'nad], *n.f.* pickle, souse.
marine [ma'rin], *n.f.* sea-service; Admiralty; navy.
mariner [mari'ne], *v.t.* to pickle, to souse.
marinier [mari'nje], *a.* (*fem.* **-ière** (1)) ***officiers mariniers***, petty officers.—*n.m.* bargeman, lighter-man.—*n.f.* (**-ière**) (*Swim.*) side-stroke.
marinière (2) [mari'njɛ:r], *n.f.* (*Cook.*) onion sauce.
marionnette [marjɔ'nɛt], *n.f.* puppet, marionette; (*pl.*) puppet-show.
marital [mari'tal], *a.* (*m. pl.* **-aux**) marital.
maritalement [marital'mɑ̃], *adv.* maritally, as man and wife.
maritime [mari'tim], *a.* maritime, naval.
marmaille [mar'ma:j], *n.f.* (*colloq.*) brats.
marmelade [marmə'lad], *n.f.* compote; (*fig.*) jelly, soup.
marmite [mar'mit], *n.f.* cooking-pot.
marmiteux [marmi'tø], *a.* (*fem.* **-euse**) pitiful, wretched, miserable.—*n.m.* (*fem.* **-euse**) poor devil.
marmiton [marmi'tɔ̃], *n.m.* scullion.
marmonner [marmɔ'ne], *v.t.* to mutter.
marmoréen [marmɔre'ɛ̃], *a.* (*fem.* **-éenne**) marmorean.
marmot [mar'mo], *n.m.* kid, brat, urchin.
marmotte [mar'mɔt], *n.f.* marmot.
marmotter [marmɔ'te], *v.t., v.i.* to mutter, to mumble.
marmouset [marmu'zɛ], *n.m.* grotesque figure; young monkey (*little boy*); fire-dog.
marne [marn], *n.f.* marl, chalk, clay.
marner [mar'ne], *v.t.* to marl.
marneux [mar'nø], *a.* (*fem.* **-euse**) marly.
marnière [mar'njɛ:r], *n.f.* marlpit.
Maroc [ma'rɔk], **le**, *m.* Morocco.
marocain [marɔ'kɛ̃], *a.* Moroccan.—*n.m.* (**Marocain**, *fem.* **-aine**) Moroccan (*person*).
maroquin [marɔ'kɛ̃], *n.m.* morocco leather.
maroquiner [marɔki'ne], *v.t.* to morocco.
maroquinerie [marɔkin'ri], *n.f.* morocco-leather manufacture *or* factory.
maroquinier [marɔki'nje], *n.m.* morocco-leather tanner.
marotte [ma'rɔt], *n.f.* cap and bells; hairdresser's dummy head; (*fig.*) fancy, hobby.
marquant [mar'kɑ̃], *a.* conspicuous, striking.
marque [mark], *n.f.* mark, imprint, stamp; cipher, trade-mark, make; badge, sign, token; proof; distinction.
marqué [mar'ke], *a.* marked, conspicuous, obvious; determined.
marquer [mar'ke], *v.t.* to mark; to stamp; to brand; to indicate; to denote; to testify; to score.—*v.i.* to mark, to be remarkable; to show off.
marqueter [markə'te], *v.t.* (*conjug. like* APPELER) to speckle, to spot; to inlay.
marqueterie [markə'tri], *n.f.* marquetry, inlaid-work, inlaying.
marqueur [mar'kœ:r], *n.m.* (*fem.* **-euse**) marker; scorer.
marquis [mar'ki], *n.m.* marquess, marquis.
marquise [mar'ki:z], *n.f.* marchioness; marquee, glass porch *or* roof.
marraine [ma'rɛn], *n.f.* godmother; sponsor.
marron (1) [ma'rɔ̃], *a. inv.* maroon, chestnut-colour.—*n.m.* chestnut; cracker (*fireworks*); ***marron d'Inde***, horse-chestnut.
marron (2) [ma'rɔ̃], *a.* (*fem.* **-onne**) fugitive, runaway (*of slaves*); (*Comm.*) unlicensed; unqualified (*doctor etc.*).
marronnier [marɔ'nje], *n.m.* chestnut-tree; ***marronnier d'Inde***, horse-chestnut-tree.
mars [mars], *n.m.* March.
Marseillaise [marsɛ'jɛ:z], *n.f.* Marseillaise (*French national anthem*).
marsouin [mar'swɛ̃], *n.m.* porpoise.
marte [MARTRE].
marteau [mar'to], *n.m.* (*pl.* **-eaux**) hammer; ***marteau de porte***, knocker; ***marteau pneumatique***, pneumatic drill.
marteau-pilon [martopi'lɔ̃], *n.m.* (*pl.* **marteaux-pilons**) steam-hammer.
martelage [martə'la:ʒ], *n.m.* hammering; marking (*of trees*).
martelé [martə'le], *a.* hammered; (*Mus.*) brilliant and distinct.
marteler [martə'le], *v.t.* (*conjug. like* AMENER) to hammer; to mark (*trees*).
Marthe [mart], *f.* Martha.
martial [mar'sjal], *a.* (*m. pl.* **-aux**) martial, warlike, soldierly.
martinet (1) [marti'nɛ], *n.m.* (*Orn.*) swift, martlet.
martinet (2) [marti'nɛ], *n.m.* tilt-hammer; cat-o'-nine-tails.
martingale [martɛ̃'gal], *n.f.* martingale; ***jouer la martingale***, to play double or quits.
martin-pêcheur [martɛ̃pɛ'ʃœ:r], *n.m.* (*pl.* **martins-pêcheurs**) kingfisher; ***martin-pêcheur d'Australie***, laughing jackass.
martre [martr], **marte** [mart], *n.f.* marten.
martyr [mar'ti:r], *n.m.* (*fem.* **martyre** (1)) martyr.
martyre (2) [mar'ti:r], *n.m.* martyrdom.
martyriser [martiri'ze], *v.t.* to martyrize; to torment, to torture.
marxisme [mark'sism], *n.m.* Marxism.
marxiste [mark'sist], *a.* and *n.* Marxist.
mascarade [maska'rad], *n.f.* masquerade.
mascotte [mas'kɔt], *n.f.* mascot, charm.
masculin [masky'lɛ̃], *a.* masculine, male.—*n.m.* (*Gram.*) masculine.
masculiniser [maskylini'ze], *v.t.* to make masculine.
masculinité [maskylini'te], *n.f.* masculinity.
masque [mask], *n.m.* mask; (*fig.*) blind, cloak, pretence; masquerader, mummer; (*Fenc.*) face-guard.
masqué [mas'ke], *a.* masked; disguised; concealed; ***virage masqué***, blind corner.
masquer [mas'ke], *v.t.* to mask; to cloak, to disguise; to conceal.
massacrant [masa'krɑ̃], *a. used chiefly in* ***être d'une humeur massacrante***, to be in an awful temper.

massacre [ma'sakr], *n.m.* massacre, butchery, slaughter; (*fig.*) havoc, waste.
massacrer [masa'kre], *v.t.* to massacre, to butcher, to murder, to slaughter; (*fig.*) to bungle.
massacreur [masa'krœ:r], *n.m.* (*fem.* **-euse**) slaughterer, slayer; (*fig.*) bungler.
massage [ma'sa:ʒ], *n.m.* massage.
masse (1) [mas], *n.f.* mass, heap, lump; mob; stock; (*Elec.*) earth.
masse (2) [mas], *n.f.* sledge-hammer.
massepain [mas'pɛ̃], *n.m.* marzipan.
masser [ma'se], *v.t.* to mass (*troops etc.*); to massage.
masseur [ma'sœ:r], *n.m.* (*fem.* **-euse**) masseur, masseuse.
massier [ma'sje], *n.m.* mace-bearer.
massif [ma'sif], *a.* (*fem.* **-ive**) massive, bulky, massy, solid; lumpish, heavy.—*n.m.* clump (*of trees, flowers etc.*); solid mass *or* block (*of masonry*); (*Geog.*) massif.
massivement [masiv'mɑ̃], *adv.* massively, heavily, solidly.
massiveté [masiv'te], *n.f.* massiveness.
massue [ma'sy], *n.f.* club (*weapon*).
mastic [mas'tik], *n.m.* mastic; cement; putty; stopping (*for teeth, tyres*); plastic wood.
masticage [masti'ka:ʒ], *n.m.* cementing, puttying; filling.
mastication [mastikɑ'sjɔ̃], *n.f.* mastication, chewing.
mastiquer (1) [masti'ke], *v.t.* to masticate.
mastiquer (2) [masti'ke], *v.t.* to putty, to cement.
mastodonte [mastɔ'dɔ̃:t], *n.m.* mastodon.
mastoïde [mastɔ'id], *a.* mastoid.
masure [mɑ'zy:r], *n.f.* hovel, tumbledown cottage.
mat (1) [mat], *n.m.* (*Chess*) mate.
mat (2) [mat], *a.* mat, dull, unpolished; dull-sounding; heavy, sodden.
mât [mɑ], *n.m.* mast; pole.
matador [mata'dɔ:r], *n.m.* matador.
matamore [mata'mɔ:r], *n.m.* blusterer, braggart.
match [matʃ], *n.m.* (*pl.* **matches**) (*Spt.*) match; ***match nul***, draw.
matelas [ma'tlɑ], *n.m.* mattress; pad, cushion; ***toile à matelas***, ticking.
matelasser [matla'se], *v.t.* to stuff, to pad.
matelot [ma'tlo], *n.m.* sailor, seaman.
matelote [ma'tlɔt], *n.f.* sailor's wife; fish-stew.
mater (1) [ma'te], *v.t.* to checkmate; to bring down, to subdue.
mater (2) [ma'te], *v.t.* to make mat *or* dull, to deaden.
matérialiser [materjali'ze], *v.t.* to materialize.
matérialisme [materja'lism], *n.m.* materialism.
matérialiste [materja'list], *a.* materialistic.—*n.* materialist.
matériaux [mate'rjo], *n.m. pl.* materials.
matériel [mate'rjɛl], *a.* (*fem.* **-elle**) material; gross, rough; heavy, dull.—*n.m.* material, working-stock, implements, plant.
matériellement [materjɛl'mɑ̃], *adv.* materially; positively; sensually.
maternel [matɛr'nɛl], *a.* (*fem.* **-elle**) maternal, motherly; ***école maternelle***, nursery school.
maternité [matɛrni'te], *n.f.* maternity.
mathématicien [matemati'sjɛ̃], *n.m.* (*fem.* **-enne**) mathematician.
mathématique [matema'tik], *a.* mathematical.—*n.f.* (*usu. in pl.*) mathematics.
mathématiquement [matematik'mɑ̃], *adv.* mathematically.
matière [ma'tjɛ:r], *n.f.* matter; material; subject-matter; cause, motive; contents; ***matière première***, raw material.
matin [ma'tɛ̃], *n.m.* morning, forenoon; prime, dawn.—*adv.* early, early in the morning.
mâtin [mɑ'tɛ̃], *n.m.* mastiff; big mongrel dog.
matinal [mati'nal], *a.* (*m. pl.* **-aux**) morning, early; early-rising.
matinée [mati'ne], *n.f.* morning, forenoon; afternoon performance, matinée.
matines [ma'tin], *n.f. pl.* matins.
matineux [mati'nø], *a.* (*fem.* **-euse**) rising early.
matois [ma'twa], *a.* cunning, artful, sly.—*n.m.* (*fem.* **-e**) cunning person, sly dog.
matoisement [matwaz'mɑ̃], *adv.* cunningly, slyly.
matoiserie [matwaz'ri], *n.f.* cunning; wile.
matou [ma'tu], *n.m.* tom-cat; (*fam.*) curmudgeon.
matraque [ma'trak], *n.f.* bludgeon; truncheon.
matriarcal [matriar'kal], *a.* (*m. pl.* **-aux**) matriarchal.
matriarcat [matriar'ka], *n.m.* matriarchy.
matrice [ma'tris], *n.f.* womb, matrix.
matricide [matri'sid], *a.* matricidal.—*n.* matricide (*person*).—*n.m.* matricide (*crime*).
matricule [matri'kyl], *n.f.* register, roll; matriculation.—*n.m.* regimental number (*of a soldier*); number (*of a rifle etc.*).
matrimonial [matrimɔ'njal], *a.* (*m. pl.* **-aux**) matrimonial.
Matthieu [ma'tjø], *m.* Matthew.
maturation [matyrɑ'sjɔ̃], *n.f.* maturation.
mâture [mɑ'ty:r], *n.f.* masting, masts and spars.
maturité [matyri'te], *n.f.* maturity, ripeness.
maudire [mo'di:r], *v.t. irr.* to curse; to detest.
maudissable [modi'sabl], *a.* execrable, detestable.
maudit [mo'di], *a.* cursed, accursed; wretched.
maugréer [mogre'e], *v.i.* to fret and fume, to curse and swear.
maure [MORE].
Maurice [mɔ'ris], *m.* Maurice; ***l'île Maurice***, Mauritius.
Mauritanie [mɔrita'ni], **la**, *f.* Mauritania.
mauritanien [mɔrita'njɛ̃], *a.* (*fem.* **-enne**) Mauritanian.—*n.m.* (**Mauritanien**, *fem.* **-enne**) Mauritanian (*person*).
mausolée [mozɔ'le], *n.m.* mausoleum.
maussade [mo'sad], *a.* sulky, sullen, cross; disagreeable, dull.
maussadement [mosad'mɑ̃], *adv.* disagreeably, sullenly, peevishly.
maussaderie [mosa'dri], *n.f.* sullenness, sulkiness.
mauvais [mɔ'vɛ], *a.* bad, ill, evil; naughty mischievous; hurtful; wrong; unpleasant; wretched; nasty.—*n.m.* bad.—*adv.* bad, badly, wrong.
mauve [mo:v] *a.* mauve.—*n.f.* (*Bot.*) mallow.

maxillaire [maksi'lɛ:r], *a.* maxillary.—*n.m.* jaw-bone.
maxime [mak'sim], *n.f.* maxim.
maximum [maksi'mɔm], *a.* (*fem.* **maxima**) maximum.—*n.m.* (*pl.* **maxima** or **maximums**) maximum; acme.
mayonnaise [majɔ'nɛ:z], *n.f.* mayonnaise.
mazout [ma'ʒut], *n.m.* fuel oil.
me [mə], *pron. pers.* me; to me.
méandre [me'ɑ̃:dr], *n.m.* meander, winding.
mécanicien [mekani'sjɛ̃], *n.m.* mechanic; engine-driver, (*Am.*) engineer; ***ingénieur mécanicien***, mechanical engineer.
mécanique [meka'nik], *a.* mechanical.—*n.f.* mechanics; mechanism, machinery; machine.
mécaniquement [mekanik'mɑ̃], *adv.* mechanically.
mécanisation [mekanizɑ'sjɔ̃], *n.f.* mechanization.
mécaniser [mekani'ze], *v.t.* to mechanize.
mécanisme [meka'nism], *n.m.* mechanism, machinery.
méchamment [meʃa'mɑ̃], *adv.* wickedly; maliciously.
méchanceté [meʃɑ̃s'te], *n.f.* wickedness; spitefulness; naughtiness.
méchant [me'ʃɑ̃], *a.* wicked, evil, bad; spiteful, malicious; naughty; paltry; vicious (*of an animal*); nasty.—*n.m.* (*fem.* **-e**) wicked person, evil-doer; naughty child.
mèche [mɛ:ʃ], *n.f.* wick (*of candle*); fuse; bit, drill; worm (*of screws*); lock (*of hair*).
mécompte [me'kɔ̃:t], *n.m.* miscalculation; mistake; disappointment.
méconnaissable [mekɔnɛ'sabl], *a.* unrecognizable.
méconnaissance [mekɔnɛ'sɑ̃:s], *n.f.* misappreciation, misreading; ingratitude.
méconnaître [mekɔ'nɛ:tr], *v.t. irr.* (*conjug. like* CONNAÎTRE) not to recognize; to disown; to disregard, to ignore; to misjudge. **se méconnaître**, *v.r.* to forget oneself.
méconnu [mekɔ'ny], *a.* unrecognized, unacknowledged; ignored, disowned.
mécontent [mekɔ̃'tɑ̃], *a.* displeased, dissatisfied.—*n.m.* (*fem.* **-e**) malcontent.
mécontentement [mekɔ̃tɑ̃t'mɑ̃], *n.m.* dissatisfaction, discontent.
mécontenter [mekɔ̃tɑ̃'te], *v.t.* to displease.
Mecque [mɛk], **la**, *f.* Mecca.
mécréant [mekre'ɑ̃], *n.m.* (*fem.* **-e**) unbeliever, infidel.
médaille [me'da:j], *n.f.* medal; (*Arch.*) medallion.
médaillé [meda'je], *a.* with a medal as a reward; having a badge (*of hawker, porter etc.*).—*n.m.* (*fem.* **-ée**) holder of a medal.
médaillon [meda'jɔ̃], *n.m.* medallion; locket.
médecin [med'sɛ̃], *n.m.* physician, doctor; ***faire venir le médecin***, to send for the doctor.
médecine [med'sin], *n.f.* medicine.
médiateur [medja'tœ:r], *a.* (*fem.* **-trice**) mediatory.—*n.m.* (*fem.* **-trice**) mediator.
médiation [medjɑ'sjɔ̃], *n.f.* mediation.
médical [medi'kal], *a.* (*m. pl.* **-aux**) medical.
médicament [medika'mɑ̃], *n.m.* medicine, drug.
médicamenter [medikamɑ̃'te], *v.t.* to physic, to doctor.
médication [medikɑ'sjɔ̃], *n.f.* medication.
médicinal [medisi'nal], *a.* (*m. pl.* **-aux**) medicinal.
médiéval [medje'val], *a.* (*m. pl.* **-aux**) medi(a)eval.
médiocre [me'djɔkr], *a.* mediocre, middling; moderate.—*n.m.* mediocrity.
médiocrement [medjɔkrə'mɑ̃], *adv.* middlingly, indifferently; poorly; barely.
médiocrité [medjɔkri'te], *n.f.* mediocrity.
médire [me'di:r], *v.i. irr.* to slander, to speak ill of, to traduce.
médisance [medi'zɑ̃:s], *n.f.* slander, scandal.
médisant [medi'zɑ̃], *a.* slanderous, scandalous.—*n.m.* (*fem.* **-e**) slanderer, scandalmonger.
méditatif [medita'tif], *a.* (*fem.* **-tive**) meditative, pensive.
méditation [meditɑ'sjɔ̃], *n.f.* meditation.
méditer [medi'te], *v.t.* to meditate, to think over; to plan.—*v.i.* to meditate, to muse.
méditerrané [meditɛra'ne], *a.* inland; ***la (Mer) Méditerranée***, the Mediterranean (Sea).
méditerranéen [meditɛrane'ɛ̃], *a.* (*fem.* **-enne**) Mediterranean.
médium [me'djɔm], *n.m.* medium.
médoc [me'dɔk], *n.m.* or ***vin de Médoc***, Médoc (*claret*).
meeting [mi'tiŋ], *n.m.* (*Polit., Spt.*) meeting.
méfait [me'fɛ], *n.m.* misdeed, crime.
méfiance [me'fjɑ̃:s], *n.f.* mistrust, distrust, suspicion.
méfiant [me'fjɑ̃], *a.* distrustful, suspicious.
méfier (se) [səme'fje], *v.r.* to mistrust, to distrust, to be suspicious of (***de***).
mégaphone [mega'fɔn], *n.m.* megaphone.
mégarde [me'gard], *n.f.* inadvertence; ***par mégarde***, inadvertently.
mégère [me'ʒɛ:r], *n.f.* shrew, vixen.
mégot [me'go], *n.m.* (*pop.*) cigar-stump, cigarette-end.
meilleur [mɛ'jœ:r], *a.* better; preferable; ***le meilleur***, the best; ***meilleur marché***, cheaper; ***de meilleure heure***, earlier.—*n.m.* best.
mélancolie [melɑ̃kɔ'li], *n.f.* melancholy, sadness, gloom, dejection.
mélancolique [melɑ̃kɔ'lik], *a.* melancholy; dismal, gloomy.
mélancoliquement [melɑ̃kɔlik'mɑ̃], *adv.* gloomily.
mélange [me'lɑ̃:ʒ], *n.m.* mixture, mingling; blending (*of tea*); medley, mash (*for brewing*).
mélanger [melɑ̃'ʒe], *v.t.* and **se mélanger**, *v.r.* (*conjug. like* MANGER) to mix, to mingle, to blend.
mélasse [me'las], *n.f.* molasses treacle.
mêlé [mɛ'le], *a.* mixed; miscellaneous.
mêlée [mɛ'le], *n.f.* conflict, fray; scramble, scuffle, free-fight; (*Rugby*) scrum.
mêler [mɛ'le], *v.t.* to mingle, to mix; to blend; to jumble; to entangle, to involve; to shuffle (*cards*). **se mêler**, *v.r.* to mingle to blend, to intermingle; to trouble oneself (***de***); to interfere (***de***); to have a hand in; to get entangled, to get mixed up (***dans***); ***mêlez-vous de vos affaires***, mind your own business.
mélèze [me'lɛ:z], *n.m.* larch.
mélodie [melɔ'di], *n.f.* melody; melodiousness.

mélodieusement [melɔdjøz'mɑ̃], *adv.* tunefully.
mélodieux [melɔ'djø], *a.* (*fem.* **-euse**) melodious, musical, tuneful.
mélodramatique [melɔdrama'tik], *a.* melodramatic.
mélodrame [melɔ'dram], *n.m.* melodrama.
melon [mə'lɔ̃], *n.m.* melon; bowler (hat).
membrane [mɑ̃'bran], *n.f.* membrane; web (*of duck's foot etc.*).
membraneux [mɑ̃bra'nø], *a.* (*fem.* **-euse**) membranous.
membre [mɑ̃:br], *n.m.* limb; member.
membrure [mɑ̃'bry:r], *n.f.* limbs, frame (*of a person etc.*); ribs, timbers (*of a ship*).
même [mɛ:m], *a.* same; self, self-same, very same; ***moi-même***, myself.—*adv.* even, also; ***à même de***, in a position to, able to; ***de même***, likewise; ***quand même***, even though; ***tout de même***, all the same.
mémoire (1) [me'mwa:r], *n.f.* memory; remembrance; commemoration; fame; ***de mémoire***, from memory; ***de mémoire d'homme***, within living memory.
mémoire (2) [me'mwa:r], *n.m.* memorandum, bill, statement of account; (*Sci., Lit.*) treatise; memorial; (*pl.*) memoirs.
mémorable [memɔ'rabl], *a.* memorable.
mémorandum [memɔrɑ̃'dɔm], *n.m.* memorandum; notebook.
mémorial [memɔ'rjal], *n.m.* (*pl.* **-aux**) memorial; memoirs; (*Comm.*) waste-book.
menaçant [məna'sɑ̃], *a.* menacing, threatening.
menace [mə'nas], *n.f.* menace, threat.
menacer [məna'se], *v.t.* (*conjug. like* COMMENCER) to threaten, to menace; to forebode; to impend.
ménage [me'na:ʒ], *n.m.* housekeeping; household, family, married couple; household equipment; economy; ***faire bon ménage***, to live happily together; ***faire des ménages***, to go out charring; ***femme de ménage***, charwoman.
ménagement [menaʒ'mɑ̃], *n.m.* regard, circumspection, caution, discretion.
ménager [mena'ʒe], *v.t.* (*conjug. like* MANGER) to be sparing of, to save; to be careful of, to treat with caution, to humour; to procure; to contrive. **se ménager**, *v.r.* to take care of oneself; to spare oneself.—*a.* (*fem.* **-ère**) thrifty, sparing, frugal; household.—*n.f.* (**-ère**) housewife, housekeeper; cruet-stand; canteen (*of cutlery*).
ménagerie [menaʒ'ri], *n.f.* menagerie.
mendiant [mɑ̃'djɑ̃], *n.m.* (*fem.* **-e**) beggar, mendicant.
mendicité [mɑ̃disi'te], *n.f.* begging, mendicity.
mendier [mɑ̃'dje], *v.t.* to beg for.—*v.i.* to beg.
mener [mə'ne], *v.t.* (*conjug. like* AMENER) to guide, to conduct, to lead; to drive (*a carriage*); to steer (*a boat etc.*); to bring, to take; to manage.—*v.i.* to lead, to conduct, to go.
ménestrel [menɛs'trɛl], *n.m.* minstrel.
meneur [mə'nœ:r], *n.m.* (*fem.* **-euse**) driver, leader; agitator, ringleader.
méningite [menɛ̃'ʒit], *n.f.* meningitis.
menotte [mə'nɔt], *n.f.* (*colloq.*) little hand (*of a child*); (*pl.*) handcuffs.
menotter [mənɔ'te], *v.t.* to handcuff.
mensonge [mɑ̃'sɔ̃:ʒ], *n.m.* lie, falsehood, untruth.
mensonger [mɑ̃sɔ̃'ʒe], *a.* (*fem.* **-ère**) lying, untrue, false.
menstruation [mɑ̃stryɑ'sjɔ̃], *n.f.* menstruation.
menstrues [mɑ̃'stry], *n.f. pl.* menstrua, periods.
mensualité [mɑ̃sɥali'te], *n.f.* monthly payment.
mensuel [mɑ̃'sɥɛl], *a.* (*fem.* **-elle**) monthly.
mensuellement [mɑ̃sɥɛl'mɑ̃], *adv.* monthly.
mensuration [mɑ̃syrɑ'sjɔ̃], *n.f.* measurement.
mental [mɑ̃'tal], *a.* (*m. pl.* **-aux**) mental.
mentalement [mɑ̃tal'mɑ̃], *adv.* mentally.
mentalité [mɑ̃tali'te], *n.f.* mentality.
menteur [mɑ̃'tœ:r], *a.* (*fem.* **-euse**) lying, false, deceitful.—*n.m.* (*fem.* **-euse**) liar, story-teller.
menthe [mɑ̃:t], *n.f.* mint.
mention [mɑ̃'sjɔ̃], *n.f.* mention; (*sch.*) ***reçu avec mention***, passed with distinction.
mentionner [mɑ̃sjɔ'ne], *v.t.* to mention, to name.
mentir [mɑ̃'ti:r], *v.i. irr.* (*conjug. like* SENTIR) to lie, to tell a lie *or* untruth.
menton [mɑ̃'tɔ̃], *n.m.* chin.
mentor [mɑ̃'tɔ:r], *n.m.* mentor, guide, tutor.
menu [mə'ny], *a.* slender, spare, thin, small; petty.—*n.m.* minute detail, particulars; menu, bill of fare; ***par le menu***, in detail.—*adv.* small, fine, minutely, in small pieces; ***hacher menu***, to mince.
menuet [mə'nɥɛ], *n.m.* minuet.
menuiser [mənɥi'ze], *v.t.* to saw, cut etc. (*wood*).—*v.i.* to do joiner's work.
menuiserie [mənɥi'zri], *n.f.* woodwork, joinery, joiner's work.
menuisier [mənɥi'zje], *n.m.* joiner, carpenter.
méprendre (se) [səme'prɑ̃:dr], *v.r. irr.* (*conjug. like* PRENDRE) to mistake, to be mistaken.
mépris [me'pri], *n.m.* contempt, scorn.
méprisable [mepri'zabl], *a.* contemptible, despicable.
méprisant [mepri'zɑ̃], *a.* contemptuous, scornful.
méprise [me'pri:z], *n.f.* mistake, misunderstanding.
mépriser [mepri'ze], *v.t.* to despise, to scorn.
mer [mɛ:r], *n.f.* sea; ***aller au bord de la mer***, to go to the seaside; ***en pleine mer***, on the open sea; ***mal de mer***, seasickness.
mercantile [mɛrkɑ̃'til], *a.* mercantile, commercial; (*fig.*) mercenary.
mercenaire [mɛrsə'nɛ:r], *a.* mercenary, venal.—*n.m.* mercenary, hireling.
mercerie [mɛrsə'ri], *n.f.* haberdashery.
merci [mɛr'si], *n.f.* (*no pl.*) mercy, discretion, will.—*n.m.* thanks.—*int.* thank you, thanks.
mercier [mɛr'sje], *n.m.* (*fem.* **-ière**) haberdasher.
mercredi [mɛrkrə'di], *n.m.* Wednesday; ***mercredi des Cendres***, Ash Wednesday.
mercure [mɛr'ky:r], *n.m.* mercury, quicksilver.
mercuriel [mɛrky'rjɛl], *a.* (*fem.* **-elle**) mercurial.
mère [mɛ:r], *n.f.* mother; dam (*of animals*); (*fig.*) cause, reason.
méridien [meri'djɛ̃], *a.* (*fem.* **-enne**) and *n.m.* meridian.—*n.f.* (**-enne**) siesta.

méridional [meridjɔ'nal], *a.* (*m. pl.* **-aux**) meridional, southern.—*n.m.* (*fem.* **-e**) person of the Midi, southerner.
meringue [mə'rɛ̃:g], *n.f.* meringue (*confection*).
mérinos [meri'nɔ:s], *n.m.* merino sheep; merino wool; merino (*material*).
merise [mə'ri:z], *n.f.* wild cherry.
merisier [məri'zje], *n.m.* wild cherry-tree.
méritant [meri'tɑ̃], *a.* meritorious, worthy.
mérite [me'rit], *n.m.* merit, worth; desert.
mériter [meri'te], *v.t.* to deserve, to merit; to earn.—*v.i.* to be deserving (*de*).
méritoire [meri'twa:r], *a.* meritorious.
méritoirement [meritwar'mɑ̃], *adv.* meritoriously, deservingly.
merlan [mɛr'lɑ̃], *n.m.* whiting.
merle [mɛrl], *n.m.* blackbird.
merluche [mɛr'lyʃ], *n.f.* hake; dried cod.
merveille [mɛr'vɛ:j], *n.f.* wonder, marvel, prodigy; ***à merveille***, wonderfully well.
merveilleusement [mɛrvɛjøz'mɑ̃], *adv.* wonderfully, admirably.
merveilleux [mɛrvɛ'jø], *a.* (*fem.* **-euse**) wonderful, marvellous.—*n.m.* the wonderful, the marvellous part.
mes [me], *pl.* [MON].
mésalliance [meza'ljɑ̃:s], *n.f.* misalliance, bad match.
mésallier [meza'lje], *v.t.* to marry off (*somebody*) badly; (*fig.*) to disparage. **se mésallier**, *v.r.* to marry beneath one.
mésange [me'zɑ̃:ʒ], *n.f.* (*Orn.*) tit.
mésangette [mezɑ̃'ʒɛt], *n.f.* bird-trap.
mésaventure [mezavɑ̃'ty:r], *n.f.* mischance, misadventure, misfortune.
mésentente [mezɑ̃'tɑ̃:t], *n.f.* misunderstanding; disagreement.
mésestime [mezɛs'tim], *n.f.* low esteem.
mésestimer [mezɛsti'me], *v.t.* to underestimate, to underrate.
mésintelligence [mezɛ̃tɛli'ʒɑ̃:s], *n.f.* misunderstanding, variance, disagreement.
mesmérisme [mɛsme'rism], *n.m.* mesmerism.
mesquin [mɛs'kɛ̃], *a.* shabby; paltry; mean.
mesquinement [mɛskin'mɑ̃], *adv.* shabbily, meanly.
mesquinerie [mɛskin'ri], *n.f.* meanness, shabbiness.
mess [mɛs], *n.m. inv.* (*Mil.*) mess.
message [mɛ'sa:ʒ], *n.m.* message.
messager [mɛsa'ʒe], *n.m.* (*fem.* **-ère**) messenger; carrier; (*fig.*) forerunner.
messagerie [mɛsa'ʒri], *n.f.* shipping office; carriage of goods; goods department; parcels office; ***messageries maritimes***, shipping service.
messe [mɛs], *n.f.* (*R.-C. Ch.*) mass.
messéance [mɛse'ɑ̃:s], *n.f.* unseemliness, impropriety.
messéant [mɛse'ɑ̃], *a.* unseemly, unbecoming, improper.
messeigneurs [mɛsɛ'ɲœ:r], *pl.* [MONSEIGNEUR].
Messie [mɛ'si], *m.* Messiah.
messieurs [mɛ'sjø], *pl.* [MONSIEUR].
mesurable [məzy'rabl], *a.* measurable.
mesurage [məzy'ra:ʒ], *n.m.* measurement, measuring.
mesure [mə'zy:r], *n.f.* measure; gauge, standard; measurement, extent, limit; (*fig.*) moderation; dimension; (*Mus.*) bar; (*Pros.*) metre; ***à mesure que***, in proportion as, as; ***outre mesure***, excessively; ***se mettre en mesure de***, to prepare to, to get ready to.
mesuré [məzy're], *a.* measured, regular; cautious.
mesurer [məzy're], *v.t.* to measure; to proportion; to calculate; to compare, to consider. **se mesurer**, *v.r.* to try one's strength; (*fig.*) to vie, to contend, to cope.
mesureur [məzy'rœ:r], *n.m.* measurer; meter.
mésusage [mezy'za:ʒ], *n.m.* misuse, abuse.
mésuser [mezy'ze], *v.i.* to misuse, to abuse (*de*).
métabolisme [metabɔ'lism], *n.m.* metabolism.
métairie [metɛ'ri], *n.f.* land, small farm.
métal [me'tal], *n.m.* (*pl.* **-aux**) metal.
métallique [meta'lik], *a.* metallic.
métallurgie [metalyr'ʒi], *n.f.* metallurgy.
métallurgiste [metalyr'ʒist], *n.m.* metallurgist.
métamorphose [metamɔr'fo:z], *n.f.* metamorphosis, transformation.
métaphore [meta'fɔ:r], *n.f.* metaphor.
métaphorique [metafɔ'rik], *a.* metaphorical.
métaphoriquement [metafɔrik'mɑ̃], *adv.* metaphorically.
métaphysique [metafi'zik], *a.* metaphysical, —*n.f.* metaphysics.
métatarse [meta'tars], *n.m.* (*Anat.*) metatarsus.
métayage [metɛ'ja:ʒ], *n.m.* métayage.
métayer [metɛ'je], *n.m.* (*fem.* **-ère**) small farmer.
météo [mete'o], *n.f.* (*fam.*) meteorology; weather-report; meteorological office.
météore [mete'ɔ:r], *n.m.* meteor.
météorique [meteɔ'rik], *a.* meteoric.
météorite [meteɔ'rit], *n.m.* or *f.* meteorite.
météorologie [meteɔrɔlɔ'ʒi], *n.f.* meteorology.
météorologique [meteɔrɔlɔ'ʒik], *a.* meteorological.
météorologiste [meteɔrɔlɔ'ʒist], **météorologue** [meteɔrɔ'lɔg], *n.* meteorologist.
méthane [me'tan], *n.m.* marsh gas, methane.
méthode [me'tɔd], *n.f.* method, system; way.
méthodique [metɔ'dik], *a.* methodical, systematic.
méthodiquement [metɔdik'mɑ̃], *adv.* methodically.
méthodisme [metɔ'dism], *n.m.* Methodism.
méthodiste [metɔ'dist], *a.* and *n.* Methodist.
méticuleusement [metikyløz'mɑ̃], *adv.* meticulously.
méticuleux [metiky'lø], *a.* (*fem.* **-euse**) meticulous, fastidious.
méticulosité [metikylɔzi'te], *n.f.* meticulousness.
métier [me'tje], *n.m.* trade, business, calling, craft, profession; loom, frame; ***arts et métiers***, arts and crafts; ***corps de métier***, corporation, guild; ***gens de métier***, professionals; ***homme de métier***, craftsman; ***métier manuel***, handicraft.
métis [me'ti:s], *a.* (*fem.* **-isse**) half-caste, cross-bred; hybrid (*plant*); mongrel (*dog*).—*n.m.* (*fem.* **-isse**) half-caste; mongrel (*dog*).
métissage [meti'sa:ʒ], *n.m.* cross-breeding.
métisser [meti'se], *v.t.* to cross-breed.

métrage [me'tra:ʒ], *n.m.* measurement (*in metres*); (*Cine.*) ***court métrage***, short film.
mètre [mɛtr], *n.m.* metre (*1.09 yards*); rule, measure (*of 1 metre*); (*Pros.*) metre.
métrer [me'tre], *v.t.* (*conjug. like* CÉDER) to measure (*by the metre*).
métreur [me'trœ:r], *n.m.* quantity-surveyor.
métrique [me'trik], *a.* metric (*system etc.*); (*Pros.*) metrical.—*n.f.* scansion.
métro [me'tro], *n.m.* (*colloq. abbr. of* ***chemin de fer métropolitain***) the underground (railway), the tube (*in Paris*), (*Am.*) the subway.
métropole [metrɔ'pɔl], *n.f.* mother country; metropolis.
métropolitain [metrɔpɔli'tɛ̃], *a.* metropolitan.—*n.m.* metropolitan, archbishop; underground railway.
mets [mɛ], *n.m.* dish, food, viands.
mettable [mɛ'tabl], *a.* fit to be worn, wearable.
metteur [mɛ'tœ:r], *n.m.* ***metteur en scène***, (*Theat.*) producer, (*Cine.*) director.
mettre [mɛtr], *v.t. irr.* to put, to set, to place; to put on, to wear; to employ; to contribute, to expend; to suppose, to imagine; ***mettre en marche*** or ***en mouvement***, to start up, to set going; ***mettre quelqu'un en état de***, to enable someone to; ***mettre un habit***, to put on a coat. **se mettre**, *v.r.* to put *or* place oneself; to dress; to begin (*à*); to take to; ***se mettre à parler***, to begin to speak; ***se mettre à table***, to sit down to table; ***se mettre bien***, to dress well; ***se mettre en route***, to start.
meuble [mœbl], *a.* movable; ***biens meubles***, (*Law*) personal property.—*n.m.* piece of furniture; (*pl.*) furniture.
meublé [mœ'ble], *a.* furnished.—*n.m.* a furnished room *or* flat.
meubler [mœ'ble], *v.t.* to furnish; to stock, to store. **se meubler**, *v.r.* to furnish one's home.
meule [mø:l], *n.f.* millstone, grindstone; (*Agric.*) stack, rick (*of corn, hay etc.*); (*Hort.*) hotbed.
meunerie [møn'ri], *n.f.* miller's trade; (*collect.*) millers.
meunier [mø'nje], *n.m.* miller; chub (*fish*).
meunière [mø'njɛ:r], *n.f.* miller's wife.
meurtre [mœrtr], *n.m.* murder.
meurtrier [mœrtri'e], *a.* (*fem.* **-ière**) murdering, murderous, deadly; killing.—*n.m.* (*fem.* **-ière** (1)) murderer, murderess.
meurtrière (2) [mœrtri'ɛ:r], *n.f.* (*Fort.*) loophole.
meurtrir [mœr'tri:r], *v.t.* to bruise, to make black and blue.
meurtrissure [mœrtri'sy:r], *n.f.* bruise.
meute [mø:t], *n.f.* pack (*of hounds etc.*).
mévendre [me'vɑ̃:dr], *v.t.* to sell at a loss.
mévente [me'vɑ̃:t], *n.f.* selling at a loss; slump.
mexicain [mɛksi'kɛ̃], *a.* Mexican.—*n.m.* (**Mexicain**, *fem.* **-aine**) Mexican (*person*).
Mexico [mɛksi'ko], *m.* Mexico City.
Mexique [mɛk'sik], **le**, *m.* Mexico.
mi [mi], *n.m.* (*Mus.*) mi; the note E.
mi- [mi], *comb. form.* half, demi-, semi-; mid, middle; ***à mi-chemin***, half-way; ***à mi-corps***, up to the waist; ***à mi-côte***, half-way up the hill; ***à mi-jambe***, half-way up the leg; ***la mi-août***, the middle of August.
miaou [mjau], *n.m. inv.* (*fam.*) mew, miaow; cat.
miaulement [mjol'mɑ̃], *n.m.* mewing.
miauler [mjo'le], *v.i.* to mew; to caterwaul.
mica [mi'ka], *n.m.* mica.
miche [miʃ], *n.f.* round loaf.
Michel [mi'ʃɛl], *m.* Michael; ***la Saint-Michel***, Michaelmas.
Michel-Ange [mikɛl'ɑ̃:ʒ], *m.* Michelangelo.
micheline [miʃ'lin], *n.f.* rail-car.
micro [mi'kro], *n.m.* (*fam. abbr. of* **microphone**) mike.
microbe [mi'krɔb], *n.m.* microbe.
microcosme [mikrɔ'kɔsm], *n.m.* microcosm.
microfilm [mikrɔ'film], *n.m.* microfilm.
micromètre [mikrɔ'mɛtr], *n.m.* micrometer.
micro-organisme [mikroɔrga'nism], *n.m.* micro-organism.
microphone [mikrɔ'fɔn], *n.m.* microphone.
microscope [mikrɔs'kɔp], *n.m.* microscope.
microscopique [mikrɔskɔ'pik], *a.* microscopic.
midi [mi'di], *n.m.* noon, midday, twelve o'clock (*in the day*); meridian; south; ***le Midi (de la France)***, the South of France.
midinette [midi'nɛt], *n.f.* (*fam.*) young dressmaker *or* milliner in Paris.
mie [mi], *n.f.* crumb; soft part of loaf.
miel [mjɛl], *n.m.* honey; ***lune de miel***, honeymoon.
miellé [mjɛ'le], *a.* honeyed; like honey; (*fig.*) sweet, bland.
miellée [mjɛ'le], **miellure** [mjɛ'ly:r], *n.f.* honeydew.
mielleusement [mjɛløz'mɑ̃], *adv.* sweetly, blandly, honey-like.
mielleux [mjɛ'lø], *a.* (*fem.* **-euse**) honeyed; sweet, bland.
mien [mjɛ̃], **a. poss.* and *pron. poss.* (*fem.* **mienne**) mine; ***le mien, la mienne, les miens, les miennes***, mine, my own.
miette [mjɛt], *n.f.* crumb, bit, morsel.
mieux [mjø], *adv.* better; correctly; more agreeably, more comfortably etc.; rather, more; ***faute de mieux***, for want of better; ***mieux vaut tard que jamais***, better late than never; ***tant mieux***, so much the better; ***valoir mieux***, to be better, to be worth more.—*n.m.* best thing; improvement.
mièvre [mjɛ:vr], *a.* finical, affected; delicate (*child*), fragile.
mièvrerie [mjɛvrə'ri], **mièvreté** [mjɛvrə'te], *n.f.* affectation.
mignard [mi'ɲa:r], *a.* delicate, pretty, dainty; mincing, affected.
mignardement [miɲardə'mɑ̃], *adv.* delicately, daintily; mincingly.
mignarder [miɲar'de], *v.t.* to fondle, to pet, to indulge.
mignardise [miɲar'di:z], *n.f.* delicacy, prettiness, daintiness; affectation, mincing ways.
mignon [mi'ɲɔ̃], *a.* (*fem.* **-onne**) delicate, pretty, dainty; sweet; neat, tiny.—*n.m.* (*fem.* **-onne**) darling, pet, favourite.
mignonnement [miɲɔn'mɑ̃], *adv.* daintily, prettily.
migraine [mi'grɛ:n], *n.f.* sick headache; migraine.

migrateur [migra'tœ:r], *a.* (*fem.* **-trice**) migratory.
migration [migrɑ'sjɔ̃], *n.f.* migration.
migratoire [migra'twa:r], *a.* migratory.
mijoter [miʒɔ'te], *v.t., v.i.* to cook slowly to stew; to simmer; (*fig.*) to plot, to brew.
mil (1) [MILLE (2)].
mil (2) [mil], *n.m.* millet.
milan [mi'lɑ̃], *n.m.* kite (*bird*).
milice [mi'lis], *n.f.* militia; (*fig.*) troops, soldiery.
milicien [mili'sjɛ̃], *n.m.* militiaman.
milieu [mi'ljø], *n.m.* (*pl.* **-eux**) middle, midst; heart, centre; mean; environment, surroundings; ***au beau milieu***, in the very middle.
militaire [mili'tɛ:r], *a.* military.—*n.m.* soldier.
militairement [militɛr'mɑ̃], *adv.* in a soldier-like manner.
militant [mili'tɑ̃], *a.* militant.
militer [mili'te], *v.i.* to militate (***pour*** or ***contre***).
(*C*) **millage** [mi'la:ʒ], *n.m.* mileage.
mille (1) [mil], *n.m.* mile (*English mile, 1609·3 metres*).
mille (2) [mil], *a. inv.* and *n.m. inv.* (**mil** *in dates of the Christian era*) thousand, a thousand, one thousand.
millénaire [mille'nɛ:r], *a.* millenary.—*n.m.* millennium.
mille-pattes [mil'pat], *n.m. inv.* centipede.
millésime [mile'zim], *n.m.* date (*on a coin, monument etc.*).
millet [mi'jɛ], *n.m.* millet, millet grass.
milliard [mi'lja:r], *n.m.* one thousand millions, (*Am.*) one billion.
milliardaire [miljar'dɛ:r], *a.* and *n.* multi-millionaire(ss).
millibar [milli'bar], *n.m.* (*Meteor.*) millibar.
millième [mi'ljɛm], *a.* and *n.m.* thousandth.
millier [mi'lje], *n.m.* thousand.
milligramme [milli'gram], *n.m.* milligramme (*·0154 grain*).
millimètre [milli'mɛtr], *n.m.* millimetre (*·03937 in.*).
million [mi'ljɔ̃], *n.m.* million.
millionième [miljɔ'njɛ:m], *a.* and *n.m.* millionth.
millionnaire [miljɔ'nɛ:r], *a.* and *n.* millionaire(ss).
mime [mim], *n.m.* mime; mimic.
mimer [mi'me], *v.t., v.i.* to mimic, to mime.
mimi [mi'mi], *n.m.* (*Childish*) cat, pussy; darling, ducky.
mimique [mi'mik], *a.* mimic, mimetic.—*n.f.* art of mimicry.
mimosa [mimo'za], *n.m.* mimosa.
minable [mi'nabl], *a.* (*colloq.*) seedy, shabby.
minaret [mina'rɛ], *n.m.* minaret.
minauder [mino'de], *v.i.* to smirk, to simper.
minauderie [mino'dri], *n.f.* affected *or* mincing manners, simpering, smirking.
minaudier [mino'dje], *a.* (*fem.* **-ière**) affected, lackadaisical.—*n.m.* (*fem.* **-ière**) affected person.
mince [mɛ̃:s], *a.* thin, slender, slim; puny, slight, trivial; scanty, small.—*int.* (*pop.*) ***ah! mince!*** or ***mince alors!*** my word! well, I never!
minceur [mɛ̃'sœ:r], *n.f.* slenderness, slimness.
mine (1) [min], *n.f.* look, bearing; face, expression; appearance, aspect; (*pl.*) airs.
mine (2) [min], *n.f.* (*Min.*) mine; (*fig.*) source, store.
mine (3) [min], *n.f.* (*Mil., Pyro.*) mine.
miner [mi'ne], *v.t.* to mine, to undermine, to sap; to wear away.
minerai [min'rɛ], *n.m.* ore.
minéral [mine'ral], *a.* (*m. pl.* **-aux**) mineral. —*n.m.* (*pl.* **-aux**) mineral; ore.
minéralogie [mineralɔ'ʒi], *n.f.* mineralogy.
minéralogique [mineralɔ'ʒik], *a.* mineralogical.
minéralogiste [mineralɔ'ʒist], *n.* mineralogist.
Minerve [mi'nɛrv], *f.* Minerva.
minet [mi'nɛ], *n.m.* (*fem.* **-ette**) (*colloq.*) puss, kitten.
mineur (1) [mi'nœ:r], *n.m.* miner, pitman; (*Mil.*) sapper.
mineur (2) [mi'nœ:r], *a.* lesser, minor; under age.—*n.m.* (*fem.* **-e**) minor; (*Law*) infant.
miniature [minja'ty:r], *n.f.* miniature.
miniaturiste [minjaty'rist], *a.* of miniatures. —*n.* miniature-painter.
minier [mi'nje], *a.* (*fem.* **-ière**) pertaining to mines, mining.—*n.f.* (**-ière**) open mine.
minime [mi'nim], *a.* very small, trifling.
minimum [mini'mɔm], *a.* (*usu. inv.*) minimum.—*n.m.* (*pl.* **minimums** *or* **minima**) minimum.
ministère [minis'tɛ:r], *n.m.* ministry; department; minister's office; offices, services; administration.
ministériel [ministe'rjɛl], *a.* (*fem.* **-elle**) ministerial.
ministre [mi'nistr], *n.m.* (*Polit., Ch.*) minister; clergyman.
minois [mi'nwa] *n.m. inv.* pretty face; looks, appearance.
minoritaire [minɔri'tɛ:r], *a.* minority.
minorité [minɔri'te], *n.f.* minority; (*Law*) infancy.
Minorque [mi'nɔrk], *f.* Minorca.
minoterie [minɔ'tri] *n.f.* flour-mill; flour trade.
minotier [minɔ'tje], *n.m.* flour-dealer, corn-factor.
minuit [mi'nɥi], *n.m.* midnight.
minuscule [minys'kyl], *a.* small (*of letters*), minute, tiny.—*n.f.* small letter.
minute [mi'nyt], *n.f.* minute (*of time*), moment, instant; rough draft; minute, record; ***minute!*** (*fam.*) just a moment!
minuter [miny'te], *v.t.* to record; to time.
minuterie [minyt'ri], *n.f.* time-switch.
minutie [miny'si], *n.f.* trifle, (*pl.*) minutiae.
minutieusement [minysjøz'mɑ̃], *adv.* minutely.
minutieux [miny'sjø], *a.* (*fem.* **-euse**) minute; meticulous.
mioche [mjɔʃ], *n.* (*colloq.*) brat, urchin.
mi-parti [mipar'ti], *a.* bipartite, half and half.
mirabelle [mira'bɛl], *n.f.* yellow variety of plum.
miracle [mi'rɑ:kl], *n.m.* miracle; (*fig.*) wonder; ***à miracle***, wonderfully well.
miraculeusement [mirakyløz'mɑ̃], *adv.* miraculously; wonderfully.
miraculeux [miraky'lø], *a.* (*fem.* **-euse**) miraculous; wonderful, marvellous.

mirage [mi'ra:ʒ], *n.m.* mirage; (*Naut.*) looming; (*fig.*) shadow.
mire [mi:r], *n.f.* land-surveyor's pole; (*Artill.*) aim; sight (*of fire-arms*).
mirer [mi're], *v.t.* to aim at; to have in view, to look at; to covet. **se mirer**, *v.r.* to look at oneself; to admire oneself; to be reflected.
mirliton [mirli'tɔ̃], *n.m.* reed-pipe.
mirobolant [mirɔbɔ'lɑ̃], *a.* (*colloq.*) wonderful, prodigious.
miroir [mi'rwa:r], *n.m.* mirror, looking-glass.
miroitant [mirwa'tɑ̃], *a.* reflecting (*like a mirror*), glistening.
miroité [mirwa'te], *a.* shot, shiny; dappled (*of horses*).
miroitement [mirwat'mɑ̃], *n.m.* reflection of the light by polished surfaces; sheen, brilliancy.
miroiter [mirwa'te], *v.i.* to reflect light, to shine, to glisten, to shimmer.
mis [mi], *p.p.* [METTRE] ***bien*** or ***mal mis***, well *or* badly dressed.
misaine [mi'zɛ:n], *n.f.* ***mât de misaine***, foremast; ***voile de misaine***, foresail.
misanthrope [mizɑ̃'trɔp], *n.* misanthrope.
misanthropie [mizɑ̃trɔ'pi], *n.f.* misanthropy.
misanthropique [mizɑ̃trɔ'pik], *a.* misanthropic.
miscellanées [misɛla'ne], *n.f. pl.* miscellanea, miscellany.
mise [mi:z], *n.f.* placing; stake; investment; bidding (*at auctions*); capital; dress; ***mise en marche***, starting; starting-handle; ***mise en marche automatique***, self-starter; ***mise en scène***, (*Theat.*) production, (*Cine.*) direction.
misérable [mize'rabl], *a.* miserable, pitiable; worthless; despicable.—*n.* wretch, miserable person; miscreant.
misérablement [mizerablə'mɑ̃], *adv.* miserably.
misère [mi'zɛ:r], *n.f.* misery, wretchedness, distress; poverty; trouble; trifling thing.
miséreux [mize'rø], *a.* and *n.m.* (*fem.* **-euse**) poor, destitute; seedy looking (person).
miséricorde [mizeri'kɔrd], *n.f.* mercy, pardon, grace.
miséricordieux [mizerikɔr'djø], *a.* (*fem.* **-euse**) merciful, compassionate.
missel [mi'sɛl], *n.m.* missal, mass-book.
mission [mi'sjɔ̃], *n.f.* mission.
missionnaire [misjɔ'nɛ:r], *n.* missionary.
missive [mi'si:v], *a.f.* and *n.f.* missive.
mistral [mis'tral], *n.m.* mistral (*cold north wind in southern France*).
mitaine [mi'tɛn], *n.f.* mitten.
mite [mit], *n.f.* mite; moth; ***mangé des mites***, moth-eaten.
mité [mi'te], *a.* moth-eaten, maggoty.
mi-temps [mi'tɑ̃], *n.f.* (*Ftb.*) half-time.
miteux [mi'tø], *a.* (*fem.* **-euse**) full of mites; (*fig.*) shabby, poverty-stricken.
mitigation [mitigɑ'sjɔ̃], *n.f.* mitigation.
mitiger [miti'ʒe], *v.t.* (*conjug. like* MANGER) to mitigate, to alleviate, to modify.
mitonner [mitɔ'ne], *v.t.* to coddle, to fondle; to nurse.—*v.i.* to let slices of bread simmer in the broth, to simmer.
mitoyen [mitwa'jɛ̃], *a.* (*fem.* **-enne**) middle; intermediate; party, joint; ***mur mitoyen***, party-wall.
mitraille [mi'trɑ:j], *n.f.* grape-shot.
mitrailler [mitrɑ'je], *v.t.*, *v.i.* to machine-gun.
mitraillette [mitrɑ'jɛt], *n.f.* tommy-gun.
mitrailleuse [mitrɑ'jø:z], *n.f.* machine-gun.
mitre [mitr], *n.f.* mitre.
mitré [mi'tre], *a.* mitred.
mitron [mi'trɔ̃], *n.m.* journeyman baker; pastry-cook's boy.
mixte [mikst], *a.* mixed.
mixture [miks'ty:r], *n.f.* mixture.
mobile [mɔ'bil], *a.* mobile, movable; unsteady, variable.—*n.m.* body in motion; mover, motive power.
mobilier [mɔbi'lje], *a.* (*fem.* **-ière**) movable; personal (*of property*).—*n.m.* furniture.
mobilisation [mɔbilizɑ'sjɔ̃], *n.f.* mobilization; liquidation (*of capital*).
mobiliser [mɔbili'ze], *v.t.* (*Law*) to liquidate; (*Mil.*) to mobilize.
mobilité [mɔbili'te], *n.f.* mobility; variability; instability.
mode (1) [mɔd], *n.f.* fashion; manner, way, custom; (*pl.*) millinery.
mode (2) [mɔd], *n.m.* (*Mus. etc.*) mode; (*Gram.*) mood; method; ***mode d'emploi***, directions for use.
modelage [mɔ'dla:ʒ], *n.m.* modelling.
modèle [mɔ'dɛl], *a.* exemplary.—*n.m.* model; pattern, design.
modelé [mɔ'dle], *n.m.* (*Sculp.*, *Paint.*) relief; reproduction.
modeler [mɔ'dle], *v.t.* (*conjug. like* AMENER) to model; to shape; to mould (*clay*). **se modeler**, *v.r.* to model oneself (*sur*).
modeleur [mɔ'dlœ:r], *n.m.* modeller.
modérateur [mɔdera'tœ:r], *a.* (*fem.* **-trice**) moderating.—*n.m.* (*fem.* **-trice**) moderator.—*n.m.* (*Mech.*) regulator.
modération [mɔderɑ'sjɔ̃], *n.f.* moderation; abatement.
modéré [mɔde're], *a.* moderate, reasonable. —*n.m.* (*fem.* **-e**) (*Polit.*) moderate.
modérément [mɔdere'mɑ̃], *adv.* moderately, in moderation.
modérer [mɔde're], *v.t.* (*conjug. like* CÉDER) to moderate, to mitigate; to restrain. **se modérer**, *v.r.* to keep one's temper; to restrain oneself.
moderne [mɔ'dɛrn], *a.* modern, up-to-date. —*n.m.* modern style.
modernisation [mɔdɛrnizɑ'sjɔ̃], *n.f.* modernization.
moderniser [mɔdɛrni'ze], *v.t.* to modernize.
modeste [mɔ'dɛst], *a.* modest, unassuming; quiet; simple.
modestement [mɔdɛstə'mɑ̃], *adv.* modestly, quietly, simply.
modestie [mɔdɛs'ti], *n.f.* modesty, simplicity.
modicité [mɔdisi'te], *n.f.* smallness; modicum.
modification [mɔdifikɑ'sjɔ̃], *n.f.* modification.
modifier [mɔdi'fje], *v.t.* to modify, to change, to alter. **se modifier**, *v.r.* to become modified.
modique [mɔ'dik], *a.* moderate; small.
modiquement [mɔdik'mɑ̃], *adv.* moderately.
modiste [mɔ'dist], *n.* modiste, milliner.
modulation [mɔdylɑ'sjɔ̃], *n.f.* modulation; (*Rad.*) ***modulation de fréquence***, very high frequency, V.H.F.

moduler [mɔdy'le], *v.t.* to modulate.
moelle [mwal], *n.f.* marrow (*of bone*); (*Bot.*) pith.
moelleusement [mwaløz'mɑ̃], *adv.* softly; (*Paint.*) with mellowness.
moelleux [mwa'lø], *a.* (*fem.* **-euse**) full of marrow; pithy; soft; mellow.—*n.m.* softness; mellowness.
moellon [mwa'lɔ̃], *n.m.* rubble; building stone.
mœurs [mœrs], *n.f. pl.* morals; manners, habits, ways, customs; ***certificat de bonne vie et mœurs***, certificate of good character.
Mogol [mɔ'gɔl], *m.* Mogul.
moi [mwa], *pron. pers.* I; me, to me; ***moi-même***, myself.—*n.m.* self, ego.
moignon [mwa'ɲɔ̃], *n.m.* stump (*of limbs, trees etc.*).
moindre [mwɛ̃:dr], *a.* lesser; least.
moine [mwan], *n.m.* monk, friar; bed-warmer.
moineau [mwa'no], *n.m.* (*pl.* **-eaux**) sparrow.
moins [mwɛ̃], *adv.* less; fewer (***de*** or ***que***); not so; ***à moins de*** (or ***que***), unless; ***du moins***, at least, at any rate; ***les moins de seize ans***, the under sixteens.—*prep.* less, minus.—*n.m.* (*Math.*) minus sign; (*Print.*) dash.
moire [mwar], *n.f.* watering; moire, watered silk.
moiré [mwa're], *a.* watered, moiré.—*n.m.* watered effect.
moirer [mwa're], *v.t.* to moire, to give a watered appearance to.
mois [mwɑ], *n.m.* month; monthly allowance, month's pay.
Moïse [mɔ'i:z], *m.* Moses.
moisi [mwa'zi], *a.* mouldy, musty.—*n.m.* mouldiness, mustiness.
moisir [mwa'zi:r], *v.t.* to make mouldy *or* musty.—*v.i.* and **se moisir**, *v.r.* to grow mouldy *or* musty.
moisissure [mwazi'sy:r], *n.f.* mouldiness, mustiness, mildew.
moisson [mwa'sɔ̃], *n.f.* harvest, harvest-time.
moissonner [mwasɔ'ne], *v.t.* to reap, to gather in, to mow.
moissonneur [mwasɔ'nœ:r], *n.m.* (*fem.* **-euse**) reaper, harvester.—*n.f.* (**-euse**) reaping-machine.
moisonneuse-batteuse [mwasɔ'nøzba'tø:z] *n.f.* (*pl.* **moissonneuses-batteuses**) combine harvester.
moite [mwat], *a.* moist, damp; clammy.
moiteur [mwa'tœ:r], *n.f.* moistness, dampness.
moitié [mwa'tje], *n.f.* half; (*colloq.*) better half, wife.—*adv.* half; ***à moitié fait***, half done; ***trop cher de moitié***, too dear by half.
moka [mɔ'ka], *n.m.* mocha (*coffee* or *cake*).
mol [mɔl], [MOU].
molaire [mɔ'lɛ:r], *a.* molar.—*n.f.* molar-tooth.
môle [mo:l], *n.m.* mole, pier.
moléculaire [mɔleky'lɛ:r], *a.* molecular.
molécule [mɔle'kyl], *n.f.* molecule.
molestation [mɔlɛstɑ'sjɔ̃], *n.f.* molestation, annoyance.
molester [mɔlɛs'te], *v.t.* to molest, to trouble.
mollasse [mɔ'las], *a.* flabby; spineless.
molle [mɔl], [MOU].
mollement [mɔl'mɑ̃], *adv.* softly; feebly; indolently.
mollesse [mɔ'lɛs], *n.f.* softness; flabbiness; slackness; indolence.
mollet [mɔ'lɛ], *a.* (*fem.* **-ette**) soft; light (*of bread*).—*n.m.* calf (*of the leg*).
molletière [mɔl'tjɛ:r], *n.f.* legging, puttee.
molleton [mɔl'tɔ̃], *n.m.* thick flannel, duffel.
mollir [mɔ'li:r], *v.i.* to soften; to mellow (*of fruit*); to slacken, to give way.
mollusque [mɔ'lysk], *n.m.* mollusc.
molosse [mɔ'lɔs], *n.m.* mastiff, watch-dog.
môme [mo:m], *n.* (*pop.*) brat, urchin.
moment [mɔ'mɑ̃], *n.m.* moment, instant; favourable occasion; ***au moment de***, just as; ***du moment que***, since.
momentané [mɔmɑ̃ta'ne], *a.* momentary.
momentanément [mɔmɑ̃tane'mɑ̃], *adv.* momentarily.
momie [mɔ'mi], *n.f.* mummy; (*fig.*) old fogy.
momifier [momi'fje], *v.t.* to mummify.
mon [mɔ̃], *a.poss.m.* (*fem.* **ma**, *pl.* **mes**) my.
monarchie [mɔnar'ʃi], *n.f.* monarchy.
monarchique [mɔnar'ʃik], *a.* monarchical.
monarchiste [mɔnar'ʃist], *a.* and *n.* monarchist.
monarque [mɔ'nark], *n.m.* monarch.
monastère [mɔnas'tɛ:r], *n.m.* monastery, convent.
monastique [mɔnas'tik], *a.* monastic.
monceau [mɔ̃'so], *n.m.* (*pl.* **-eaux**) heap, pile.
mondain [mɔ̃'dɛ̃], *a.* worldly, mundane.—*n.m.* (*fem.* **-e**) worldly person.
mondanité [mɔ̃dani'te], *n.f.* worldliness; (*pl.*) social events.
monde [mɔ̃:d], *n.m.* world; universe; mankind; people; society; company, set; men; customers; ***tout le monde***, everybody.
monder [mɔ̃'de], *v.t.* to cleanse; to hull (*barley*), to blanch (*almonds*).
mondial [mɔ̃'djal], *a.* (*m. pl.* **-aux**) world, world-wide.
monétaire [mɔne'tɛ:r], *a.* monetary.
mongol [mɔ̃'gɔl], *a.* Mongolian.—*n.m.* Mongolian (*language*); (**Mongol**, *fem.* **-ole**) Mongol(ian) (*person*).
Mongolie [mɔ̃gɔ'li], **la**, *f.* Mongolia.
Monique [mɔ'nik], *f.* Monica.
moniteur [mɔni'tœ:r], *n.m.* (*fem.* **-trice**) (*sch.*) prefect, monitor; instructor.
monnaie [mɔ'nɛ], *n.f.* coin, money; change; mint; ***monnaie forte***, hard currency; ***monnaie légale***, legal tender.
monnayage [mɔnɛ'ja:ʒ], *n.m.* coining, minting.
monnayer [mɔnɛ'je], *v.t.* (*conjug. like* PAYER) to coin into money, to mint; (*fig.*) to make money out of, to sell.
monnayeur [mɔnɛ'jœ:r], *n.m.* coiner, minter; ***faux monnayeur***, counterfeiter, forger.
monochrome [mɔnɔ'krɔm], *a.* monochrome.
monocle [mɔ'nɔkl], *n.m.* monocle, eyeglass.
monogramme [mɔnɔ'gram], *n.m.* monogram.
monologue [mɔnɔ'lɔg], *n.m.* monologue, soliloquy.
monopole [mɔnɔ'pɔl], *n.m.* monopoly.
monopoliser [mɔnɔpɔli'ze], *v.t.* to monopolize.
monorail [mɔnɔ'ra:j], *a.* and *n.m.* monorail.

monosyllabe [mɔnɔsil'lab], *a.* monosyllabic. —*n.f.* monosyllable.
monosyllabique [mɔnɔsilla'bik], *a.* monosyllabic.
monotone [mɔnɔ'tɔn], *a.* monotonous.
monotonie [mɔnɔtɔ'ni], *n.f.* monotony.
monseigneur [mɔ̃sɛ'ɲœːr], *n.m.* (*pl.* **messeigneurs** or **nosseigneurs**) my lord; your Grace; your Royal *or* Imperial Highness.
monsieur [mə'sjø, msjø], *n.m.* (*pl.* **messieurs**) sir; gentleman; Mr.
monstre [mɔ̃ːstr], *a.* (*fam.*) huge.—*n.m.* monster.
monstrueusement [mɔ̃stryøz'mɑ̃], *adv.* monstrously, prodigiously.
monstrueux [mɔ̃s'tryø], *a.* (*fem.* **-euse**) monstrous, prodigious.
monstruosité [mɔ̃stryɔzi'te], *n.f.* monstrosity.
mont [mɔ̃], *n.m.* hill, mount, mountain.
montage [mɔ̃'taːʒ], *n.m.* carrying up; mounting, setting; assembling; (*Cine.*) editing (*of film*); (*Ind.*) ***chaîne de montage***, assembly line.
montagnard [mɔ̃ta'ɲaːr], *a.* mountain, highland.—*n.m.* (*fem.* **-e**) mountaineer, highlander.
montagne [mɔ̃'taɲ], *n.f.* mountain; hill.
montagneux [mɔ̃ta'ɲø], *a.* (*fem.* **-euse**) mountainous, hilly.
montant (1) [mɔ̃'tɑ̃], *n.m.* upright (*of a ladder etc.*); post (*of door etc.*); (*Naut.*) stanchion; amount, sum total; rising tide; high flavour, pungency; (*Ftb.*) goal-post.
montant (2) [mɔ̃'tɑ̃], *a.* rising; ascending; flowing, coming in; high-necked (*of dresses*).
monte [mɔ̃ːt], *n.f.* mounting, mount (*of a jockey*); serving (*of animals*), covering season.
monte-charge [mɔ̃t'ʃarʒ], *n.m. inv.* hoist, goods lift; (*Am.*) freight elevator.
montée [mɔ̃'te], *n.f.* gradient, slope; ascent; (*Arch. etc.*) height.
monter [mɔ̃'te], *v.t.* to mount, to ascend, to go up; to walk, ride, row etc. up; to get up on, to ride; to raise; to wind up; to equip; to make up; to rouse.—*v.i.* (*with aux.* AVOIR *or* ÊTRE *according as action or condition is meant*) to go (*or* come) up, to mount; to climb; to rise; to increase; to amount. **se monter**, *v.r.* to amount, to rise; to get excited; to supply oneself with (***en***).
monteur [mɔ̃'tœːr], *n.m.* (*fem.* **-euse**) setter, mounter (*of jewels, machinery etc.*); (*Cine.*) (film-)editor.
monticule [mɔ̃ti'kyl], *n.m.* hillock, knoll.
montoir [mɔ̃'twaːr], *n.m.* horse-block; ***côté du montoir***, near side; ***côté hors montoir***, off side.
montre (1) [mɔ̃ːtr], *n.f.* show-case; shop-window; show, display, exhibition.
montre (2) [mɔ̃ːtr], *n.f.* watch.
montre-bracelet [mɔ̃trəbras'lɛ], *n.f.* (*pl.* **montres-bracelets**) wrist-watch.
montrer [mɔ̃'tre], *v.t.* to show, to display; to demonstrate; to teach; to indicate. **se montrer**, *v.r.* to show oneself; to appear; to prove oneself to be, to turn out.
montreur [mɔ̃'trœːr], *n.m.* (*fem* **-euse**) showman, exhibitor.
montueux [mɔ̃'tyø], *a.* (*fem.* **-euse**) hilly.
monture [mɔ̃'tyːr], *n.f.* animal for riding, mount; setting (*of gems etc.*); frame.
monument [mɔny'mɑ̃], *n.m.* monument; memorial.
monumental [mɔnymɑ̃'tal], *a.* (*m. pl.* **-aux**) monumental.
moquer (se) [səmɔ'ke], *v.r.* (***de***) to mock, to jeer, to laugh at; to make fun of.
moquerie [mɔ'kri], *n.f.* mockery, derision; jest.
moquette [mɔ'kɛt], *n.f.* carpet; fitted carpet; velvet pile.
moqueur [mɔ'kœːr], *a.* (*fem.* **-euse**) mocking, jeering, derisive.—*n.m.* (*fem.* **-euse**) mocker, scoffer; wag.
moral [mɔ'ral], *a.* (*m. pl.* **-aux**) moral; mental.—*n.m.* mind, mental faculties, spirit, morale.
morale [mɔ'ral], *n.f.* ethics, moral philosophy; morals, morality; rebuke, lecture; moral (*of a story etc.*).
moralement [mɔral'mɑ̃], *adv.* morally.
moraliste [mɔra'list], *a.* and *n.* moralist.
moralité [mɔrali'te], *n.f.* morality; morals.
morbide [mɔr'bid], *a.* morbid.
morbleu! [mɔr'blø], *int.* the devil! hang it!
morceau [mɔr'so], *n.m.* (*pl.* **-eaux**) bit, piece, morsel, fragment.
morceler [mɔrs'le], *v.t.* (*conjug. like* APPELER) to parcel out, to cut up.
mordant [mɔr'dɑ̃], *a.* biting; cutting, sarcastic.—*n.m.* mordant; pungency, keenness.
mordiller [mɔrdi'je], *v.t.* to nibble, to bite at.
mordoré [mɔrdɔ're], *a.* and *n.m.* reddish brown.
mordre [mɔrdr], *v.t.* to bite; to gnaw; to eat into.—*v.i.* to bite, to nibble; to take hold; to succeed; to criticize. **se mordre**, *v.r.* to bite oneself; ***s'en mordre les doigts***, to repent of a thing.
more [mɔːr], **moresque** [mɔ'rɛsk], *a.* Moorish.—*n.* (**More**) Moor; Negro.
morfondre [mɔr'fɔ̃ːdr], *v.t.* to chill. **se morfondre,** *v.r.* to be chilled, to shiver; to kick one's heels; (*fig.*) to mope.
morfondu [mɔrfɔ̃'dy], *a.* chilled, shivering, benumbed.
morganatique [mɔrgana'tik], *a.* morganatic.
morgue (1) [mɔrg], *n.f.* haughtiness, arrogance.
morgue (2) [mɔrg], *n.f.* morgue, mortuary.
moribond [mɔri'bɔ̃], *a.* moribund, dying.—*n.m.* (*fem.* **-e**) person in a dying state.
moricaud [mɔri'ko], *a.* dark, darkish.—*n.m.* (*fem.* **-e**) (*pej.*) blackamoor, (*pej.*) nigger.
morigéner [mɔriʒe'ne], *v.t.* (*conjug. like* CÉDER) to scold, to reprimand.
mormon [mɔr'mɔ̃], *a.* Mormon.—*n.m.* (**Mormon,** *fem.* **- e**) Mormon (*person*)
morne [mɔrn], *a.* gloomy, dejected, dreary.
morose [mɔ'roːz], *a.* morose, sullen, surly.
morosité [mɔrɔzi'te], *n.f.* moroseness, sullenness, surliness.
Morphée [mɔr'fe], *m.* Morpheus.
morphine [mɔr'fin], *n.f.* morphia.
morphologie [mɔrfɔlɔ'ʒi], *n.f.* morphology.
mors [mɔːr], *n.m. inv.* bit (*of a bridle*); (*fig.*) curb, check.
morse (1) [mɔrs], *n.m.* morse, walrus.
morse (2) [mɔrs], *n.m.* Morse (code).
morsure [mɔr'syːr], *n.f.* bite, biting.

mort [mɔːr], *a.* dead; lifeless, inanimate; dormant; stagnant; out (*of a candle etc.*); ***nature morte***, still life; ***au point mort***, at a standstill, in neutral (gear) (*of a car*).—*n.m.* (*fem.* **-e**) dead person, corpse.—*n.m.* dummy (*at cards*).—*n.f.* death; ***à mort***, mortally, to the death.
mortalité [mɔrtali'te], *n.f.* mortality.
mort-bois [mɔr'bwɑ], *n.m.* (*no pl.*) brushwood, undergrowth.
morte-eau [mɔr'to], *n.f.* (*pl.* **mortes-eaux**) neap tide.
mortel [mɔr'tɛl], *a.* (*fem.* **-elle**) mortal, deadly; grievous.—*n.m.* (*fem.* **-elle**) mortal.
mortellement [mɔrtɛl'mɑ̃], *adv.* fatally, deadly.
morte-saison [mɔrtsɛ'zɔ̃], *n.f.* (*pl.* **mortes-saisons**) slack time, off season.
mortier [mɔr'tje], *n.m.* mortar (*cement, artillery, vessel*).
mortifiant [mɔrti'fjɑ̃], *a.* mortifying, humiliating.
mortification [mɔrtifikɑ'sjɔ̃], *n.f.* mortification, humiliation.
mortifier [mɔrti'fje], *v.t.* to mortify; to humiliate. **se mortifier**, *v.r.* to mortify oneself.
mort-né [mɔr'ne], *a.* and *n.m.* (*fem.* **mort-née**, *pl.* **mort-nés**, **mort-nées**) stillborn (child).
mortuaire [mɔr'tɥɛːr], *a.* mortuary; ***drap mortuaire***, pall.
morue [mɔ'ry], *n.f.* cod, codfish; ***huile de foie de morue***, cod-liver oil.
morveux [mɔr'vø], *a.* (*fem.* **-euse**) snotty; ***qui se sent morveux se mouche***, if the cap fits, wear it.
mosaïque [mɔza'ik], *a.* and *n.f.* mosaic.
Moscou [mɔs'ku], **le**, *m.* Moscow.
mosquée [mɔs'ke], *n.f.* mosque.
mot [mo], *n.m.* word; remark, saying, sentence; motto; note; (*Mil.*) parole, watchword; ***au bas mot***, at the least; ***bon mot***, witticism; ***mots croisés***, crossword.
motel [mɔ'tɛl], *n.m.* motel.
moteur [mɔ'tœːr], *a.* (*fem.* **-trice**) motive, driving.—*n.m.* mover; motor, engine; motive power.
motif [mɔ'tif], *a.* (*fem.* **-tive**) moving, inciting.—*n.m.* motive, incentive; cause; (*Mus. etc.*) motif, design.
motion [mo'sjɔ̃], *n.f.* (*Polit.*) motion.
motiver [mɔti've], *v.t.* to justify; to allege as a motive; to be the cause of, to bring about.
moto [mɔ'to], *n.f.* (*fam.*) motor bike.
motocyclette [mɔtosi'klɛt], *n.f.* motor-cycle.
motte [mɔt], *n.f.* clod; ***motte de beurre***, pat of butter.
motus! [mɔ'tyːs], *int.* (*colloq.*) mum's the word!
mou [mu], *a.* (**mol** before vowel or ***h*** mute, *fem.* **molle**) soft; limp; flabby; weak; slack, sluggish, indolent.—*n.m.* soft part of thing; slack (*of a rope*); lights (*of animals*).
mouchard [mu'ʃaːr], *n.m.* sneak, *esp.* police-spy, nark, informer.
moucharder [muʃar'de], *v.t., v.i.* to inform (*on*), to spy (*on*); to sneak.
mouche [muʃ], *n.f.* fly; patch (*on the face*), beauty-spot; button (*of foil*); bull's-eye (*of a target*); river passenger-steamer.
(*C*) **mouche à feu** [muʃa'fø], *n.f.* firefly.
moucher [mu'ʃe], *v.t.* to wipe the nose of; to snuff. **se moucher**, *v.r.* to blow one's nose.
moucheron [muʃ'rɔ̃], *n.m.* gnat, very small fly.
moucheté [muʃ'te], *a.* spotted, speckled, flecked; capped (*of foils*).
moucheter [muʃ'te], *v.t.* (*conjug. like* APPELER) to spot, to speckle, to fleck; to cap (*foils*).
mouchoir [mu'ʃwaːr], *n.m.* handkerchief.
moudre [mudr], *v.t. irr.* to grind, to crush.
moue [mu], *n.f.* pout; ***faire la moue***, to pout.
mouette [mwɛt], *n.f.* gull, sea-mew.
moufle [mufl], *n.f.* mitten; tackle-block.
mouillage [mu'jaːʒ], *n.m.* soaking, wetting; anchorage.
mouillé [mu'je], *a.* wet, watery; liquid (*of the letter* ***l***); at anchor.
mouiller [mu'je], *v.t.* to wet, to moisten.—*v.i.* to drop anchor; to moor.
moulage [mu'laːʒ], *n.m.* moulding, casting; mould, cast; grinding, milling.
moule (1) [mul], *n.m.* mould, matrix; pattern.
moule (2) [mul], *n.f.* mussel.
moulé [mu'le], *a.* moulded, cast; well-formed; ***lettre moulée***, block letter.
mouler [mu'le], *v.t.* to cast, to mould; to shape. **se mouler**, *v.r.* to model oneself (***sur***).
mouleur [mu'lœːr], *n.m.* moulder.
moulin [mu'lɛ̃], *n.m.* mill; grinder; (*Geol.*) pothole; ***jeter son bonnet par-dessus les moulins***, to throw off all restraint.
moulinet [muli'nɛ], *n.m.* small mill; winch; turnstile; fishing reel.
moulu [mu'ly], *a.* ground; bruised.
moulure [mu'lyːr], *n.f.* (*Arch.*) moulding.
mourant [mu'rɑ̃], *a.* dying, expiring; fading.—*n.m.* (*fem.* **-e**) dying person.
mourir [mu'riːr], *v.i. irr.* (*with aux.* ÊTRE) to die, to expire; to perish; to stop; to go out (*of fire*); to be out (*at play*). **se mourir**, *v.r.* (*Poet., only used in pres. and imp. indic.*) to be dying.
mouron [mu'rɔ̃], *n.m.* (*Bot.*) ***mouron rouge***, scarlet pimpernel; ***mouron des oiseaux***, chickweed.
mousquet [mus'kɛ], *n.m.* musket; ***mousquet à pierre***, flintlock.
mousquetaire [muskə'tɛːr], *n.m.* musketeer.
mousse (1) [mus], *a.* blunt (*of tools*).
mousse (2) [mus], *n.f.* moss; froth, foam; lather; whipped cream.
mousse (3) [mus], *n.m.* ship's boy.
mousseline [mus'lin], *n.f.* muslin.
mousser [mu'se], *v.i.* to froth, to foam; to sparkle (*of wine*).
mousseux [mu'sø], *a.* (*fem.* **-euse**) foaming, frothy; sparkling (*of wine etc.*).
mousson [mu'sɔ̃], *n.f.* monsoon.
moussu [mu'sy], *a.* mossy.
moustache [mus'taʃ], *n.f.* moustache; whiskers (*of animals*).
moustiquaire [musti'kɛːr], *n.f.* mosquito-net.
moustique [mus'tik], *n.m.* mosquito.
moût [mu], *n.m.* must (*wine not fermented*); wort (*of beer*).
moutarde [mu'tard], *n.f.* mustard.

moutardier [mutar'dje], *n.m.* mustard-pot; mustard-maker.
mouton [mu'tɔ̃], *n.m.* sheep; mutton; sheep-skin (*leather*); ram; (*fig.*) ninny; (*slang*) decoy, prison-spy; (*pl.*) white-crested waves; ***revenons à nos moutons***, let us return to the subject.
moutonné [mutɔ'ne], *a.* fleecy, curled; white with foam (*of the sea*).
moutonner [mutɔ'ne], *v.t.* to make woolly *or* fleecy; to curl, to frizzle.—*v.i.* to be ruffled, to foam.
moutonneux [mutɔ'nø], *a.* (*fem.* **-euse**) fleecy; foaming (*of waves*).
moutonnier [mutɔ'nje], *a.* (*fem.* **-ière**) sheep-like.
mouvant [mu'vɑ̃], *a.* moving, shifting; unstable.
mouvement [muv'mɑ̃], *n.m.* movement, motion; march; animation, bustle; emotion, commotion; spirit, impulse; (*Mus.*) time; (*Mil.*) manœuvre.
mouvementé [muvmɑ̃'te], *a.* animated, lively; undulating (*ground*).
mouvoir [mu'vwa:r], *v.t. irr.* to move, to stir; to prompt. **se mouvoir**, *v.r.* to move, to stir.
moyen [mwa'jɛ̃], *a.* (*fem.* **-enne**) mean, middle, medium; average.—*n.m.* means; way, manner, medium; (*pl.*) resources; talents.
moyennant [mwajɛ'nɑ̃], *prep.* by means of; in consideration of.—*conj. phr.* ***moyennant que***, on condition that.
moyenne [mwa'jɛn], *n.f.* average; (*sch.*) pass-mark.
moyeu [mwa'jø], *n.m.* (*pl.* **-eux**) nave (*of cartwheel*); hub (*of bicycle*).
muable [mɥabl], *a.* mutable, changeable.
mucosité [mykozi'te], *n.f.* mucus.
mucus [my'ky:s], *n.m.* mucus.
mue [my], *n.f.* moulting; skin, slough; mew, coop (*cage*).
muer [mɥe], *v.i.* to moult, to cast *or* slough horns etc.; to break (*of the voice*).
muet [mɥɛ], *a.* (*fem.* **muette**) dumb, mute; silent (*of letters*); blank (*of maps*).—*n.m.* (*fem.* **muette** (1)) dumb man *or* woman.
muette (2) [mɥɛt], *n.f.* mews; hunting-lodge.
mufle [myfl], *n.m.* snout, muzzle (*of animals*); (*pop.*) beast, cad.
muflier [myfli'e], *n.m.* (*Bot.*) antirrhinum.
mugir [my'ʒi:r], *v.i.* to bellow, to low; (*fig.*) to roar; to sough (*of the wind*).
mugissement [myʒis'mɑ̃], *n.m.* bellowing, lowing, roaring; soughing (*of the wind*).
muguet [my'gɛ], *n.m.* lily of the valley.
mulâtre [my'lɑ:tr], *a* and *n.m.* (*fem. inv.* or **-esse**) mulatto, half-caste.
mule [myl], *n.f.* mule, slipper; she-mule.
mulet [my'lɛ], *n.m.* he-mule; mullet.
muletier [myl'tje], *a.* (*fem.* **-ière**) pertaining to mules.—*n.m.* muleteer.
mulot [my'lo], *n.m.* field-mouse.
multicolore [myltikɔ'lɔ:r], *a.* many-coloured; motley; variegated.
multiforme [mylti'fɔrm], *a.* multiform.
multilatéral [myltilate'ral], *a.* (*m. pl.* **-aux**) multilateral.
multiple [myl'tipl], *a.* multiple; multifarious. —*n.m.* multiple.
multiplicateur [myltiplika'tœ:r], *a.* (*fem.* **-trice**) multiplying.—*n.m.* (*Arith.*) multiplier, multiplicator.
multiplication [myltiplikɑ'sjɔ̃], *n.f.* multiplication; gearing (-ratio).
multiplicité [myltiplisi'te], *n.f.* multiplicity.
multiplié [myltipli'e], *a.* multiplied; manifold; frequent.
multiplier [myltipli'e], *v.t., v.i.* to multiply; to gear up to. **se multiplier**, *v.r.* to multiply; to be repeated.
multitude [mylti'tyd], *n.f.* multitude; crowd.
muni [my'ni], *a.* supplied, provided (***de***); fortified.
municipal [mynisi'pal], *a.* (*m. pl.* **-aux**) municipal.—*n.m.* soldier of the municipal guard.
municipalité [mynisipali'te], *n.f.* municipality; town council and staff.
munificence [mynifi'sɑ̃:s], *n.f.* bounty, munificence.
munificent [mynifi'sɑ̃], *a.* bountiful.
munir [my'ni:r], *v.t.* to provide, to supply; to arm, to secure. **se munir**, *v.r.* to provide oneself, to be provided (***de***).
munitions [myni'sjɔ̃], *n.f. pl.* ammunition, munitions; military stores.
muqueux [my'kø], *a.* (*fem.* **-euse** (1)) mucous.
muqueuse (2) [my'kø:z], *n.f.* mucous membrane.
mur [my:r], *n.m.* wall; ***le mur du son***, the sound barrier.
mûr [my:r], *a.* ripe, mature, matured.
murage [my'ra:ʒ], *n.m.* walling.
muraille [my'rɑ:j], *n.f.* thick, high wall; (*pl.*) ramparts.
mural [my'ral], *a.* (*m. pl.* **-aux**) mural; ***peinture murale***, mural.
mûre [my:r], *n.f.* mulberry.
mûrement [myr'mɑ̃], *adv.* maturely.
murer [my're], *v.t.* to wall in, to brick up; (*fig.*) to screen.
mûrier [my'rje], *n.m.* mulberry-tree, bramble bush.
mûrir [my'ri:r], *v.t.* to ripen, to mature.—*v.i.* to ripen, to grow ripe, to mature.
murmurant [myrmy'rɑ̃], *a.* murmuring; babbling; grumbling.
murmure [myr'my:r], *n.m.* murmur; grumbling; whispering, babbling; soughing (*of the wind*).
murmurer [myrmy're], *v.t.* to mutter, to whisper.—*v.i.* to murmur, to whisper; to grumble; to gurgle, to prattle, to babble; to sough.
musard [my'za:r], *a.* loitering, dawdling.—*n.m.* (*fem.* **-e**) (*colloq.*) loiterer, dawdler.
musarder [myzar'de], *v.i.* to dawdle.
musarderie [myzar'dri], **musardise** [myzar'di:z], *n.f.* loitering, dawdling, trifling.
musc [mysk], *n.m.* musk-deer, musk.
muscade [mys'kad], *n.f.* nutmeg; juggler's ball.
muscadier [myska'dje], *n.m.* nutmeg-tree.
muscat [mys'ka], *a.* and *n.m.* muscat (grape), muscadine; dried muscatel wine; variety of pear.
muscle [myskl], *n.m.* muscle.
musculaire [mysky'lɛ:r], *a.* muscular.
musculeux [mysky'lø], *a.* (*fem.* **-euse**) muscular, brawny.
muse [my:z], *n.f.* muse.

museau [my'zo], *n.m.* (*pl.* **-eaux**) muzzle, snout, nose.
musée [my'ze], *n.m.* museum, art gallery.
museler [myz'le], *v.t.* (*conjug. like* APPELER) to muzzle; (*fig.*) to gag, to silence.
muselière [myz'ljɛ:r], *n.f.* muzzle.
musellement [myzɛl'mɑ̃], *n.m.* muzzling; (*fig.*) gagging, silencing.
muser [my'ze], *v.i.* to loiter, to moon, to dawdle.
musette [my'zɛt], *n.f.* bagpipe; (*Mil.*) haversack; nosebag (*for horses*).
muséum [myze'ɔm], *n.m.* natural history museum.
musical [myzi'kal], *a.* (*m. pl.* **-aux**) musical.
musicalement [myzikal'mɑ̃], *adv.* musically.
musicien [myzi'sjɛ̃], *n.m.* (*fem.* **-enne**) musician.
musique [my'zik], *n.f.* music; band, musicians.
musoir [my'zwa:r], *n.m.* pier-head, jetty-head.
musqué [mys'ke], *a.* musked, perfumed; (*fig.*) affected (*language etc.*).
musquer [mys'ke], *v.t.* to perfume with musk.
musulman [myzyl'mɑ̃], *a.* Moslem.—*n.m.* (**Musulman**, *fem.* **-ane**) Moslem (*person*).
mutabilité [mytabili'te], *n.f.* mutability, changeableness.
mutation [mytɑ'sjɔ̃], *n.f.* change; (*Biol.*) mutation.
muter [my'te], *v.t.* (*Mil.*, *Adm.*) to transfer.
mutilateur [mytila'tœ:r], *n.m.* (*fem.* **-trice**) mutilator, maimer, defacer.
mutilation [mytilɑ'sjɔ̃], *n.f.* mutilation, maiming.
mutiler [myti'le], *v.t.* to mutilate, to maim; (*fig.*) to disfigure.
mutin [my'tɛ̃], *a.* obstinate; fractious; pert.—*n.m.* (*fem.* **-e**) mutineer, rebel.
mutiné [myti'ne], *a.* mutinous, riotous.
mutiner (se) [səmyti'ne], *v.r.* to mutiny.
mutinerie [mytin'ri], *n.f.* unruliness; mutiny, riot; pertness.
mutisme [my'tism], *n.m.* dumbness; speechlessness.
mutualité [mytɥali'te], *n.f.* mutuality.
mutuel [my'tɥɛl], *a.* (*fem.* **-elle**) mutual, reciprocal; ***société de secours mutuels***, friendly society.
mutuellement [mytɥɛl'mɑ̃], *adv.* mutually.
myope [mjɔp], *a.* myopic, short-sighted.—*n.* short-sighted person.
myopie [mjɔ'pi], *n.f.* myopia, short-sightedness.
myosotis [mjɔzɔ'ti:], *n.m.* myosotis, forget-me-not.
myriade [mi'rjad], *n.f.* myriad.
myrrhe [mi:r], *n.f.* myrrh.
myrte [mirt], *n.m.* myrtle.
myrtille [mir'ti:j], *n.f.* bilberry.
mystère [mis'tɛ:r], *n.m.* mystery; secret; (*fig.*) fuss.
mystérieusement [misterjøz'mɑ̃], *adv.* mysteriously.
mystérieux [miste'rjø], *a.* (*fem.* **-euse**) mysterious.
mysticisme [misti'sism], *n.m.* mysticism.
mystificateur [mistifika'tœ:r], *a.* (*fem.* **-trice**) mystifying, hoaxing.—*n.m.* (*fem.* **-trice**) mystifier, hoaxer.
mystification [mistifikɑ'sjɔ̃], *n.f.* hoax.
mystifier [misti'fje], *v.t.* to mystify; to hoax.
mystique [mis'tik], *a.* mystical, mystic.—*n.* mystic.
mythe [mit], *n.m.* myth; fable, fiction.
mythique [mi'tik], *a.* mythical.
mythologie [mitɔlɔ'ʒi], *n.f.* mythology.
mythologique [mitɔlɔ'ʒik], *a.* mythological.
mythologiste [mitɔlɔ'ʒist], **mythologue** [mitɔ'lɔg], *n.* mythologist.
myxomatose [miksɔma'to:z], *n.f.* myxomatosis.

N

N, n [ɛn], *n.m.* the fourteenth letter of the alphabet.
nabab [na'bab], *n.m.* nabob.
nacelle [na'sɛl], *n.f.* wherry, skiff; gondola (*of airship etc.*).
nacre [nakr], *n.f.* mother-of-pearl.
nacré [na'kre], *a.* nacreous, pearly.
nage [na:ʒ], *n.f.* swimming; rowing, sculling; (*fam.*) ***être en nage***, to be bathed in perspiration.
nageoire [na'ʒwa:r], *n.f.* fin (*of a fish*).
nager [na'ʒe], *v.i.* (*conjug. like* MANGER) to swim; to float; to row.
nageur [na'ʒœ:r], *a.* (*fem.* **-euse**) swimming.—*n.m.* (*fem.* **-euse**) swimmer; rower, oarsman.
naguère [na'gɛ:r], *adv.* lately, not long ago.
naïade [na'jad], *n.f.* naiad, water-nymph.
naïf [na'if], *a.* (*fem.* **naïve**) naïve, artless, ingenuous, unaffected; simple.
nain [nɛ̃], *a.* dwarfish.—*n.m.* (*fem.* **-e**) dwarf.
naissance [nɛ'sɑ̃:s], *n.f.* birth; descent; (*fig.*) beginning, dawn, rise.
naissant [nɛ'sɑ̃], *a.* new-born, in its infancy; beginning, rising.
naître [nɛ:tr], *v.i. irr.* (*with aux.* ÊTRE) to be born, (*fig.*) to originate; to dawn.
naïvement [naiv'mɑ̃], *adv.* naïvely, ingenuously, artlessly.
naïveté [naiv'te], *n.f.* artlessness, simplicity naïvety.
nantir [nɑ̃'ti:r], *v.t.* to give as a pledge, to secure; (*fig.*) to furnish. **se nantir**, *v.r.* to provide oneself (***de***); to take possession (***de***).
nantissement [nɑ̃tis'mɑ̃], *n.m.* security, pledge.
naphte [naft], *n.m.* naphtha.
napolitain [napɔli'tɛ̃], *a.* Neapolitan.—*n.m.* (**Napolitain**, *fem.* **-aine**) Neapolitan (*person*).
nappe [nap], *n.f.* table-cloth, cover; sheet (*of water etc.*).
napperon [na'prɔ̃], *n.m.* tray-cloth; doily.
narcisse [nar'sis], *n.m.* (*Bot.*) narcissus.
narcotique [narkɔ'tik], *a.* and *n.m.* narcotic.
narcotisme [narkɔ'tism], *n.m.* narcotism.
narguer [nar'ge], *v.t.* to defy, to flout.

narine [na'rin], *n.f.* nostril.
narquois [nar'kwa], *a.* cunning, sly; chaffing.
narquoisement [narkwaz'mɑ̃], *adv.* slyly, quizzingly.
narrateur [nara'tœːr], *n.m.* (*fem.* **-trice**) narrator, relater.
narratif [nara'tif], *a.* (*fem.* **-tive**) narrative.
narration [narɑ'sjɔ̃], *n.f.* narration, narrative.
narrer [na're], *v.t.* to narrate, to tell.
nasal [na'zal], *a.* (*m. pl.* **-aux**) nasal.
nasalement [nazal'mɑ̃], *adv.* nasally, with a nasal sound.
naseau [na'zo], *n.m.* (*pl.* **-eaux**) nostril (*of animals*).
nasillant [nazi'jɑ̃], *a.* speaking through the nose.
nasillard [nazi'jaːr], *a.* snuffling, nasal.
nasillement [nazij'mɑ̃], *n.m.* speaking through the nose, snuffling; twang.
nasiller [nazi'je], *v.i.* to speak through the nose, to snuffle.
nasse [nɑːs], *n.f.* bow-net, weir, eel-pot.
natal [na'tal], *a.* (*m. pl.* **-als** (*rare*)) natal, native.
natalité [natali'te], *n.f.* birth-rate.
natation [natɑ'sjɔ̃], *n.f.* swimming.
natif [na'tif], *a.* (*fem.* **-tive**) native; natural. —*n.m.* native.
nation [nɑ'sjɔ̃], *n.f.* nation.
national [nasjɔ'nal], *a.* (*m. pl.* **-aux**) national.
nationalement [nasjɔnal'mɑ̃], *adv.* nationally.
nationalisation [nasjɔnalizɑ'sjɔ̃], *n.f.* nationalization.
nationaliser [nasjɔnali'ze], *v.t.* to nationalize.
nationaliste [nasjɔna'list], *n.* nationalist.
nationalité [nasjɔnali'te], *n.f.* nationality.
nativité [nativi'te], *n.f.* nativity, birth.
natte [nat], *n.f.* mat, matting (*of straw*); plait.
natter [na'te], *v.t.* to mat; to plait, to twist.
naturalisation [natyralizɑ'sjɔ̃], *n.f.* naturalization; taxidermy.
naturaliser [natyrali'ze], *v.t.* to naturalize; to stuff (*animal*).
naturalisme [natyra'lism], *n.m.* naturalness; naturalism.
naturaliste [natyra'list], *a.* naturalistic.—*n.* naturalist; taxidermist.
nature [na'tyːr], *n.f.* nature; kind, sort; temperament; life, life-size; ***de nature à***, likely to; ***dessiner d'après nature***, to draw from life; ***nature morte***, still life; ***payer en nature***, to pay in kind.
naturel [naty'rɛl], *a.* (*fem.* **-elle**) natural; native, innate; artless, plain; ***enfant naturel***, illegitimate child.—*n.m.* (*fem.* **-elle**) native (*of a country*).—*n.m.* disposition, nature; genuineness, simplicity.
naturellement [natyrɛl'mɑ̃], *adv.* naturally. —*int.* of course!
naturiste [naty'rist], *a.* naturistic.—*n.* naturist.
naufrage [no'fraːʒ], *n.m.* shipwreck.
naufragé [nofra'ʒe], *a.* shipwrecked, wrecked. —*n.m.* (*fem.* **-ée**) shipwrecked person, castaway.
nauséabond [nozea'bɔ̃], *a.* nauseating, loathsome, disgusting.
nausée [no'ze], *n.f.* nausea, sickness; (*fig.*) loathing, disgust.
nauséeux [noze'ø], *a.* (*fem.* **-éeuse**) nauseating.
nautique [no'tik], *a.* nautical.
naval [na'val] *a.* (*m. pl.* **-als**) naval, nautical.
navet [na'vɛ], *n.m.* turnip.
navette [na'vɛt], *n.f.* incense-box; weaver's shuttle; (*Bot.*) rape; ***faire la navette***, to run a shuttle-service.
navigabilité [navigabili'te], *n.f.* airworthiness, seaworthiness.
navigable [navi'gabl], *a.* navigable; seaworthy, airworthy.
navigateur [naviga'tœːr], *n.m.* navigator.—*a.m.* seafaring; swimming (*birds etc.*).
navigation [navigɑ'sjɔ̃], *n.f.* navigation; voyage, sailing.
naviguer [navi'ge], *v.i.* to navigate; to row, to sail etc.
navire [na'viːr], *n.m.* vessel, ship.
navrant [nɑ'vrɑ̃], *a.* heartrending, harrowing, distressing.
navrer [nɑ'vre], *v.t.* to distress, to rend (*the heart*).
nazaréen [nazare'ɛ̃], *a.* (*fem.* **-éenne**) of Nazareth.—*n.m.* (**Nazaréen**, *fem.* **-éenne**) Nazarene; Nazarite.
nazi [na'zi], *a.* Nazi.—*n.* (**Nazi**) Nazi.
nazisme [na'zism], *n.m.* Nazism.
ne [nə], *adv.* no, not.
né [ne], *a.* born.
néanmoins [neɑ̃'mwɛ̃], *adv.* nevertheless, however, for all that.
néant [ne'ɑ̃], *n.m.* naught, nothingness; nil.
nébuleux [neby'lø], *a.* (*fem.* **-euse**) cloudy, misty; nebulous; (*fig.*) obscure.—*n.f.* (**-euse**) nebula.
nébulosité [nebylɔzi'te], *n.f.* patch of haze.
nécessaire [nesɛ'sɛːr], *a.* necessary; inevitable.—*n.m.* the needful; necessities (*of life etc.*); dressing-case, work-box.
nécessairement [nesɛsɛr'mɑ̃], *adv.* necessarily; inevitably, of course.
nécessité [nesɛsi'te], *n.f.* necessity; need, want.
nécessiter [nesɛsi'te], *v.t.* to necessitate; to compel, to oblige.
nécessiteux [nesɛsi'tø], *a.* (*fem.* **-euse**) necessitous, needy.—*n.m.* (*fem.* **-euse**) pauper.
nécrologe [nekrɔ'lɔːʒ], *n.m.* obituary list; death roll.
nécrologie [nekrɔlɔ'ʒi], *n.f.* necrology, obituary.
nécrologique [nekrɔlɔ'ʒik], *a.* necrological.
nécromancie [nekrɔmɑ̃'si], *n.f.* necromancy.
nécromancien [nekrɔmɑ̃'sjɛ̃], *n.m.* (*fem.* **-enne**) necromancer.
nécropole [nekrɔ'pɔl], *n.f.* necropolis.
nectar [nɛk'taːr], *n.m.* nectar.
néerlandais [neɛrlɑ̃'dɛ], *a.* Dutch.—*n.m.* Dutch (*language*); (**Néerlandais**, *fem.* **-aise**) Dutchman, Dutchwoman.
nef [nɛf], *n.f.* nave (*of a church*).
néfaste [ne'fast], *a.* inauspicious; disastrous.
nèfle [nɛfl], *n.f.* medlar.
néflier [ne'flje], *n.m.* medlar-tree.
négatif [nega'tif], *a.* (*fem.* **-tive**) negative.—*n.m.* (*Phot.*) negative.—*n.f.* (**-tive**) negative, refusal.
négation [negɑ'sjɔ̃], *n.f.* negation; (*Gram.*) negative.
négativement [negativ'mɑ̃], *adv.* negatively.

négligé [negli'ʒe], *a.* neglected, unnoticed; careless; slovenly.—*n.m.* undress, negligee.

négligeable [negli'ʒabl], *a.* negligible; trifling, unimportant.

négligemment [negliʒa'mɑ̃], *adv.* nonchalantly; negligently.

négligence [negli'ʒɑ̃:s], *n.f.* negligence, neglect, oversight.

négligent [negli'ʒɑ̃], *a.* negligent, careless.—*n.m.* (*fem.* **-e**) negligent person.

négliger [negli'ʒe], *v.t.* (*conjug. like* MANGER) to neglect; to omit. **se négliger**, *v.r.* to neglect oneself; to be careless.

négoce [ne'gɔs], *n.m.* trade, business; trafficking.

négociabilité [negɔsjabili'te], *n.f.* negotiability.

négociable [negɔ'sjabl], *a.* negotiable, transferrable.

négociant [negɔ'sjɑ̃], *n.m.* (*fem.* **-e**) merchant (*wholesale*).

négociateur [negɔsja'tœ:r], *n.m.* (*fem.* **-trice**) negotiator, transactor.

négociation [negɔsjɑ'sjɔ̃], *n.f.* negotiation, transaction.

négocier [negɔ'sje], *v.t.* to negotiate.—*v.i.* to trade.

nègre [nɛ:gr], *a.* and *n.m.* (*fem.* **négresse**) (*pej.*) Negro; (*pl.*) (*pej.*) blacks.

négrier [negri'e], *n.m.* slave-ship, slaver; slave-dealer.

négrillon [negri'jɔ̃], *n.m.* (*fem.* **-onne**) (*pej.*) little Negro, Negro boy *or* girl.

neige [nɛ:ʒ], *n.f.* snow; ***boule de neige***, snowball.

neiger [nɛ'ʒe], *v. impers.* (*conjug. like* MANGER) to snow.

neigeux [nɛ'ʒø], *a.* (*fem.* **-euse**) snowy, snow-covered.

nénuphar [neny'fa:r], *n.m.* water-lily.

néon [ne'ɔ̃], *n.m.* neon.

néo-zélandais [neozelɑ̃'dɛ], *a.* New Zealand (*butter, cheese etc.*).—*n.m.* (**Néo-Zélandais**, *fem.* **-aise**) New Zealander.

Népal [ne'pa:l], **le**, *m.* Nepal.

népalais [nepa'lɛ], *a.* Nepalese.—*n.m.* (**Népalais**, *fem.* **-aise**) Nepalese (*person*).

népotisme [nepɔ'tism], *n.m.* nepotism.

nerf [nɛ:r], *n.m.* nerve; sinew; fortitude, strength.

nerveusement [nɛrvøz'mɑ̃], *adv.* impatiently; nervously.

nerveux [nɛr'vø], *a.* (*fem.* **-euse**) nervous; excitable; muscular.

nervosité [nɛrvɔzi'te], *n.f.* nervousness.

nervure [nɛr'vy:r], *n.f.* (*Bot. etc.*) nervure, nerve; (*Arch.*) moulding; (*Carp.*) rib, fillet; (*Bookb.*) tapes, cording; (*Needlework*) piping.

net [nɛt], *a.* (*fem.* **nette**) clean; pure; clear, distinct; flat, frank, pointblank; net (*of prices*).—*n.m.* fair copy; ***mettre au net***, to make a fair copy.—*adv.* clean off, at once; flatly, point-blank.

nettement [nɛt'mɑ̃], *adv.* cleanly; clearly; plainly, flatly.

netteté [nɛt'te], *n.f.* cleanness; clearness, distinctness.

nettoiement [nɛtwa'mɑ̃], **nettoyage** [nɛtwa'ja:ʒ], *n.m.* cleaning; clearing; wiping.

nettoyer [nɛtwa'je], *v.t.* (*conjug. like* EMPLOYER) to clean; to wipe; to rid (*de*).

neuf (1) [nœf], *a.* and *n.m.* nine, ninth.

neuf (2) [nœf], *a.* (*fem.* **neuve**) new, brand-new; young, raw.—*n.m.* something new.

neurologie [nørɔlɔ'ʒi], *n.f.* neurology.

neutralisation [nøtralizɑ'sjɔ̃], *n.f.* neutralization.

neutraliser [nøtrali'ze], *v.t.* to neutralize. **se neutraliser**, *v.r.* to neutralize each other.

neutralité [nøtrali'te], *n.f.* neutrality.

neutre [nø:tr], *a.* and *n.m.* neuter; neutral.

neutron [nø'trɔ̃], *n.m.* neutron.

neuvième [nœ'vjɛm], *a.* and *n.* ninth.

neveu [nə'vø], *n.m.* (*pl.* **-eux**) nephew; (*pl. poet.*) descendants.

névralgie [nevral'ʒi], *n.f.* neuralgia.

névralgique [nevral'ʒik], *a.* neuralgic.

névrite [ne'vrit], *n.f.* neuritis.

névritique [nevri'tik], *a.* neuritic.

névrose [ne'vro:z], *n.f.* neurosis, nervous disorder.

névrosé [nevro'ze], *a.* and *n.m.* (*fem.* **-ée**) neurotic.

nez [ne], *n.m. inv.* nose; face; scent (*of dogs etc.*).

ni [ni], *conj.* nor, neither . . . nor; (*after* ***sans, sans que***, *etc.*) either . . . or.

niable [njabl], *a.* deniable.

niais [njɛ], *a.* silly, foolish.—*n.m.* (*fem.* **-e**) ninny, simpleton.

niaisement [njɛz'mɑ̃], *adv.* foolishly.

niaiser [njɛ'ze], *v.i.* to play the fool.

niaiserie [njɛz'ri], *n.f.* foolishness; nonsense.

Nicaragua [nikara'gwa], **le**, *m.* Nicaragua.

nicaraguayen [nikaragwa'jɛ̃], *a.* (*fem.* **-enne**) Nicaraguan.—*n.m.* (**Nicaraguayen**, *fem.* **-enne**) Nicaraguan (*person*).

niche [niʃ], *n.f.* niche, nook; recess; kennel; (*fam.*) prank.

nichée [ni'ʃe], *n.f.* nestful (*of young birds*); brood (*of animals, children etc.*).

nicher [ni'ʃe], *v.t.* to lodge, to put.—*v.i.* to build a nest; to nestle. **se nicher**, *v.r.* to nest, to nestle; to hide oneself.

nickel [ni'kɛl], *n.m.* nickel.

nickelage [ni'kla:ʒ], *n.m.* nickel-plating.

nickeler [ni'kle], *v.t.* (*conjug. like* APPELER) to nickel-plate.

Nicolas [nikɔ'lɑ], *m.* Nicholas.

nicotine [nikɔ'tin], *n.f.* nicotine.

nid [ni], *n.m.* nest; berth, post.

nièce [njɛs], *n.f.* niece.

nier [nje], *v.t.* to deny; to repudiate, to disown.

nigaud [ni'go], *a.* (*colloq.*) silly, simple.—*n.m.* (*fem.* **-e**) booby, simpleton.

Nigéria [niʒe'rja], **le**, *m.* Nigeria.

nigérien [niʒe'rjɛ̃], *a.* (*fem.* **-enne**) Nigerian.—*n.m.* (**Nigérien**, *fem.* **-enne**) Nigerian (*person*).

nihilisme [nii'lism], *n.m.* nihilism.

nihiliste [nii'list], *a.* nihilistic.—*n.* nihilist.

Nil [nil], **le**, *m.* the Nile.

nimbe [nɛ̃:b], *n.m.* nimbus, halo.

nippe [nip], *n.f. usu. pl.* (*colloq.*) old clothes, togs.

nipper [ni'pe], *v.t.* (*colloq.*) to fit out, to rig out. **se nipper**, *v.r.* to rig oneself out.

nippon [ni'pɔ̃], *a.* Japanese.—*n.m.* (**Nippon**, *fem.* **-one**) Japanese (*person*).

nitrate [ni'trat], *n.m.* nitrate.

nitre [nitr], *n.m.* nitre, saltpetre.

nitrique [ni'trik], *a.* nitric.

nitrogène [nitrɔ'ʒɛn], *n.m.* nitrogen.
niveau [ni'vo], *n.m.* (*pl.* **-eaux**) level; standard; ***passage à niveau***, level crossing.
niveler [ni'vle], *v.t.* (*conjug. like* APPELER) to level, to flatten (out).
niveleur [ni'vlœ:r], *a.* (*fem.* **-euse**) levelling. —*n.m.* (*fem.* **-euse**) leveller.
nivellement [nivɛl'mɑ̃], *n.m.* levelling.
nobiliaire [nɔbi'ljɛ:r], *a.* of the nobility, nobiliary.
noble [nɔbl], *a.* noble; great, high, exalted.—*n.* noble, nobleman, noblewoman.
noblement [nɔblə'mɑ̃], *adv.* nobly; honourably.
noblesse [nɔ'blɛs], *n.f.* nobility; nobleness, loftiness.
noce [nɔs], *n.f.* wedding; wedding-party; (*colloq.*) jollification.
noceur [nɔ'sœ:r], *n.m.* (*fem.* **-euse**) gay dog, gay woman, rake.
nocif [nɔ'sif], *a.* (*fem.* **-cive**) injurious, noxious.
noctambule [nɔktɑ̃'byl], *a.* noctambulant, noctambulous.—*n.* sleep-walker.
noctambulisme [nɔktɑ̃by'lism], *n.m.* noctambulism, sleep-walking.
nocturne [nɔk'tyrn], *a.* nocturnal, nightly.—*n.m.* (*Mus.*) nocturne.
Noèl [nɔ'ɛl], *n.m.* Christmas, Yule-tide; (**noël**) Christmas carol.
nœud [nø], *n.m.* knot; bow; difficulty, intricacy; (*fig.*) tie; bond.
noir [nwa:r], *a.* black; swarthy; gloomy, dismal; foul; ***bête noire***, pet aversion.—*n.m.* black (*fem.* **-e** (1)); Negro.
noirâtre [nwa'rɑ:tr], *a.* blackish.
noiraud [nwa'ro], *a.* dark, swarthy-looking.
noirceur [nwar'sœ:r], *n.f.* blackness; baseness; foul deed.
noircir [nwar'si:r], *v.t.* to blacken; to sully; to defame; to darken.—*v.i.* and **se noircir**, *v.r.* to blacken, to darken, to grow black *or* dark.
noircissure [nwarsi'sy:r], *n.f.* black spot, smudge.
noire (2) [nwa:r], *n.f.* (*Mus.*) crotchet.
noisetier [nwaz'tje], *n.m.* hazel (*tree* or *bush*).
noisette [nwa'zɛt], *n.f.* hazel-nut.
noix [nwɑ], *n.f. inv.* walnut; nut.
nom [nɔ̃], *n.m.* name; fame, celebrity; noun.
nomade [nɔ'mad], *a.* nomad, nomadic, wandering.—*n.* nomad.
nombre [nɔ̃:br], *n.m.* number; quantity; numbers.
nombrer [nɔ̃'bre], *v.t.* to number, to reckon.
nombreux [nɔ̃'brø], *a.* (*fem.* **-euse**) numerous; harmonious (*prose, style*).
nombril [nɔ̃'bri], *n.m.* navel.
nomenclature [nɔmɑ̃kla'ty:r], *n.f.* nomenclature; list catalogue.
nominal [nɔmi'nal], *a.* (*m. pl.* **-aux**) nominal.
nominalement [nɔminal'mɑ̃], *adv.* nominally.
nominatif [nɔmina'tif], *a.* (*fem.* **-tive**) and *n.m.* nominative.
nomination [nɔminɑ'sjɔ̃], *n.f.* nomination; appointment.
nominativement [nɔminativ'mɑ̃], *adv.* by name.
nommé [nɔ'me], *a.* named, called; appointed.
nommément [nɔme'mɑ̃], *adv.* namely; particularly, especially.
nommer [nɔ'me], *v.t.* to name, to call; to mention; to nominate, to appoint. **se nommer**, *v.r.* to state one's name; to be called.
non [nɔ̃], *adv.* no, not.
non-activité [nɔ̃naktivi'te], *n.f.* state of being unattached *or* unemployed.
nonagénaire [nɔnaʒe'nɛ:r], *a.* ninety years of age.—*n.* nonagenarian.
non-agression [nɔ̃nagrɛ'sjɔ̃], *n.f.* non-aggression.
nonce [nɔ̃:s], *n.m.* nuncio.
nonchalamment [nɔ̃ʃala'mɑ̃], *adv.* nonchalantly, carelessly, heedlessly.
nonchalance [nɔ̃ʃa'lɑ̃:s], *n.f.* carelessness, heedlessness, nonchalance.
nonchalant [nɔ̃ʃa'lɑ̃], *a.* nonchalant, careless; listless.—*n.m.* (*fem.* **-e**) such a person.
non-lieu [nɔ̃'ljø], *n.m.* (*Law*) no true bill.
nonne [nɔn], *n.f.* nun.
nonobstant [nɔnɔps'tɑ̃], *prep.* notwithstanding, in spite of.—*adv.* nevertheless.
nonpareil [nɔ̃pa'rɛ:j], *a.* (*fem.* **-eille**) nonpareil, matchless.
non-sens [nɔ̃'sɑ̃:s], *n.m.* meaningless sentence, translation, *or* action.
nord [nɔ:r], *a. inv.* north, ***Pôle nord***, North Pole.—*n.m.* north; north-wind; ***nord-est***, north-east; ***nord-ouest***, north-west.
nordique [nɔr'dik], *a.* Nordic, Scandinavian. —*n.* (**Nordique**) Nordic, Scandinavian (*person*).
normal [nɔr'mal], *a.* (*m. pl.* **-aux**) normal; (*Geom.*) perpendicular.
normalement [nɔrmal'mɑ̃], *adv.* normally.
normalien [nɔrma'ljɛ̃], *n.m.* (*fem.* **-enne**) training-college student *or* ex-student.
normalité [nɔrmali'te], *n.f.* normality.
normand [nɔr'mɑ̃], *a.* Norman.—*n.m.* (**Normand**, *fem.* **-ande**) Norman (*person*).
Normandie [nɔrmɑ̃'di], **la**, *f.* Normandy.
norme [nɔrm], *n.f.* norm, average.
Norvège [nɔr'vɛ:ʒ], **la**, *f.* Norway.
norvégien [nɔrve'ʒjɛ̃], *a.* (*fem.* **-enne**) Norwegian.—*n.m.* Norwegian (*language*); (**Norvégien**, *fem.* **-enne**) Norwegian (*person*).
nos [no], *pl.* [NOTRE].
nostalgie [nɔstal'ʒi], *n.f.* nostalgia, homesickness.
nostalgique [nɔstal'ʒik], *a.* nostalgic; sad.
notabilité [nɔtabili'te], *n.f.* respectability; person of note.
notable [nɔ'tabl], *a.* notable, of influence.—*n.* notable, person of note.
notablement [nɔtablə'mɑ̃], *adv.* notably.
notaire [nɔ'tɛ:r], *n.m.* notary; solicitor.
notamment [nɔta'mɑ̃], *adv.* specially; more particularly.
notariat [nɔta'rja], *n.m.* profession, business *or* function of notary.
notation [nɔtɑ'sjɔ̃], *n.f.* notation.
note [nɔt], *n.f.* note, memorandum; mark; statement; bill.
noter [nɔ'te], *v.t.* to note; to mark; to note down; to observe, to notice.
notice [nɔ'tis], *n.f.* notice, account; review (*of a book*); notification.
notification [nɔtifikɑ'sjɔ̃], *n.f.* notification, notice, intimation.
notifier [nɔti'fje], *v.t.* to notify; to intimate.
notion [no'sjɔ̃], *n.f.* notion, idea; (*pl.*) elements, rudiments.

notoire [nɔ'twa:r], *a.* notorious; well-known.
notoirement [nɔtwar'mɑ̃], *adv.* notoriously.
notoriété [nɔtɔrje'te], *n.f.* notoriety (*of fact*); repute (*of person*).
notre [nɔtr], *a. poss.* (*pl.* **nos**) our.
nôtre [no:tr], *pron. poss.* (*pl.* **nôtres**) ours; our own; our things, friends, relatives etc.
noué [nwe], *a.* knotty, tied; rickety.
nouer [nwe], *v.t.* to tie, to knot; (*fig.*) to devise; to establish. **se nouer**, *v.r.* to be twisted *or* tied; to fasten oneself.
noueux [nu'ø], *a.* (*fem.* **-euse**) knotty, gnarled.
nougat [nu'gɑ], *n.m.* nougat; almond-cake.
nouilles [nu:j], *n.f. pl.* noodles, spaghetti.
nourri [nu'ri], *a.* nourished, fed; full, rich, copious; brisk (*fire*).
nourrice [nu'ris], *n.f.* nurse; wet-nurse; (*Motor.*, *Av.*) feed-tank.
nourricier [nuri'sje], *a.* (*fem.* **-ière**) life-giving, nourishing; producing food.—*n.m.* (*fem.* **-ière**) foster-parent.
nourrir [nu'ri:r], *v.t.* to nourish, to feed; to keep, to maintain; to nurse; to foster; to rear; to cherish. **se nourrir**, *v.r.* to feed, to live upon.
nourrissage [nuri'sa:ʒ], *n.m.* rearing, feeding (*of cattle*).
nourrissant [nuri'sɑ̃], *a.* nutritious; nourishing; sustaining.
nourrisseur [nuri'sœ:r], *n.m.* cow-keeper; stock-raiser.
nourrisson [nuri'sɔ̃], *n.m.* (*fem.* **-onne**) infant; foster child; nursling.
nourriture [nuri'ty:r], *n.f.* nourishment, food; livelihood.
nous [nu], *pers. pron.* we; us; to us; ourselves; each other.
nouveau [nu'vo] (*before a vowel or unaspirated* h **nouvel**), *a.* (*fem.* **-elle** (1)) new; recent, novel; additional; inexperienced.—*n.m.* (*pl.* **-eaux**) new, something new; ***à nouveau***, afresh; ***de nouveau***, again.
nouveau-né [nuvo'ne], *n.m.* (*fem.* **nouveau-née**, *pl.* **nouveau-né(e)s**) new-born child.
nouveauté [nuvo'te], *n.f.* novelty; change, innovation; (*pl.*) fancy articles; (*fig.*) new book, new play.
nouvelle (2) [nu'vεl], *n.f.* (*often in pl.*) news, tidings; short story, short novel.
nouvellement [nuvεl'mɑ̃], *adv.* newly, lately, recently.
Nouvelle-Zélande [nuvεlze'lɑ̃:d], **la**, *f.* New Zealand.
nouvelliste [nuvε'list], *n.* newswriter; short story writer.
novateur [nɔva'tœ:r], *a.* (*fem.* **-trice**) innovating.—*n.m.* (*fem.* **-trice**) innovator.
novembre [nɔ'vɑ̃:br], *n.m.* November.
novice [nɔ'vis], *a.* novice, inexperienced.—*n.* novice, probationer.
noviciat [nɔvi'sja], *n.m.* noviciate.
noyade [nwa'jad], *n.f.* drowning.
noyau [nwa'jo], *n.m.* (*pl.* **-aux**) stone (*of fruit*), nucleus; core (*of statues, casts etc.*).
noyé [nwa'je], *a.* drowned.—*n.m.* (*fem.* **-ée**) drowned person.
noyer (1) [nwa'je], *n.m.* walnut-tree; walnut (*wood*).
noyer (2) [nwa'je], *v.t.* (*conjug. like* EMPLOYER) to drown; to swamp; to deluge. **se noyer**, *v.r.* to be drowned; to be plunged (***dans***).
nu [ny], *a.* naked, nude, bare; uncovered; unadorned; destitute.—*n.m.* the nude, nudity.
nuage [nɥa:ʒ], *n.m.* cloud; mist; (*fig.*) gloom, dejection.
nuageux [nɥa'ʒø], *a.* (*fem.* **-euse**) cloudy, overcast.
nuance [nɥɑ̃:s], *n.f.* shade, hue; gradation; tinge.
nuancer [nɥɑ̃'se], *v.t.* (*conjug. like* COMMENCER) to shade; to vary slightly.
nubile [ny'bil], *a.* nubile, marriageable.
nubilité [nybili'te], *n.f.* nubility, marriageable age.
nucléaire [nykle'ε:r], *a.* nuclear.
nudité [nydi'te], *n.f.* nudity, nakedness.
nuée [nɥe], *n.f.* cloud; (*fig.*) swarm, host, multitude, flock.
nues [ny], *n.f. pl.* (*Poet.*) skies.
nuire [nɥi:r], *v.i. irr.* to be hurtful, to jeopardize, to harm (***à***).
nuisible [nɥi'zibl], harmful, noxious, prejudicial.
nuit [nɥi], *n.f.* night, night-time; darkness; ***il fait nuit***, it is dark; ***nuit blanche***, sleepless night.
nuitamment [nɥita'mɑ̃], *adv.* by night, in the night.
nul [nyl], *a.* (*fem.* **nulle**) no, not any; void, null.—*pron.* no one, nobody, not one.
nullement [nyl'mɑ̃], *adv.* not at all, by no means.
nullifier [nyli'fje], *v.t.* to nullify.
nullité [nyli'te], *n.f.* nullity; nonentity; (*fig.*) incapacity.
numéraire [nyme'rε:r], *a.* legal (*of coin*).—*n.m.* metallic currency, cash.
numéral [nyme'ral], *a.* (*m. pl.* **-aux**) numeral.
numérateur [nymera'tœ:r], *n.m.* (*Arith.*) numerator.
numération [nymerɑ'sjɔ̃], *n.f.* numeration, notation.
numérique [nyme'rik], *a.* numerical.
numériquement [nymerik'mɑ̃], *adv.* numerically.
numéro [nyme'ro], *n.m.* number.
numérotage [nymerɔ'ta:ʒ], *n.m.*, **numérotation** [nymerɔtɑ'sjɔ̃], *n.f.* numbering.
numéroter [nymerɔ'te], *v.t.* to number.
numismate [nymis'mat], **numismatiste** [nymisma'tist], *n.* numismatist.
numismatique [nymisma'tik], *a.* numismatic.—*n.f.* numismatics.
nuptial [nyp'sjal], *a.* (*m. pl.* **-aux**) nuptial, bridal.
nuque [nyk], *n.f.* nape (*of the neck*).
nutritif [nytri'tif], *a.* (*fem.* **-tive**) nutritious, nourishing.
nutrition [nytri'sjɔ̃], *n.f.* nutrition.
nylon [ni'lɔ̃], *n.m.* nylon; ***des bas nylon***, nylon stockings.
nymphe [nɛ̃:f], *n.f.* nymph.

O

O, o [o], *n.m.* the fifteenth letter of the alphabet.
ô! [o] *int.* oh!

oasis [oa'ziːs], *n.f. inv.* oasis.
obéir [ɔbe'iːr], *v.i.* to obey; to comply, to yield, to submit (*à*).
obéissance [ɔbei'sɑ̃ːs], *n.f.* obedience; allegiance.
obéissant [ɔbei'sɑ̃], *a.* obedient; docile.
obélisque [ɔbe'lisk], *n.m.* obelisk, needle.
obérer [ɔbe're], *v.t.* (*conjug. like* CÉDER) to encumber *or* involve in debt.
obèse [ɔ'bɛːz], *a.* obese, stout.
obésité [ɔbezi'te], *n.f.* obesity, stoutness.
obituaire [ɔbitɥ'ɛːr], *a.* and *n.m.* obituary, register of deaths; mortuary.
objecter [ɔbʒɛk'te], *v.t.* to object; to allege.
objecteur [ɔbʒɛk'tœːr], *n.m.* objector.
objectif [ɔbʒɛk'tif], *a.* (*fem.* **-tive**) objective. —*n.m.* objective, aim; lens; (*Mil.*) target.
objection [ɔbʒɛk'sjɔ̃], *n.f.* objection.
objectivement [ɔbʒɛktiv'mɑ̃], *adv.* objectively.
objectivité [ɔbʒɛktivi'te], *n.f.* objectivity.
objet [ɔb'ʒɛ], *n.m.* object; subject, matter; aim; (*pl.*) articles, goods.
obligation [ɔbliga'sjɔ̃], *n.f.* obligation; (*Law*) bond; (*Comm.*) debenture.
obligatoire [ɔbliga'twaːr], *a.* compulsory, obligatory, incumbent.
obligatoirement [ɔbligatwar'mɑ̃], *adv.* compulsorily.
obligeamment [ɔbliʒa'mɑ̃], *adv.* obligingly.
obligeance [ɔbli'ʒɑ̃ːs], *n.f.* obligingness; kindness.
obligeant [ɔbli'ʒɑ̃], *a.* obliging, kind, helpful.
obliger [ɔbli'ʒe], *v.t.* (*conjug. like* MANGER) to oblige, to bind; to compel; to gratify. **s'obliger**, *v.r.* to put oneself under an obligation.
oblique [ɔ'blik], *a.* oblique, slanting; (*fig.*) indirect, underhand.
obliquement [ɔblik'mɑ̃], *adv.* obliquely, indirectly; unfairly.
obliquer [ɔbli'ke], *v.i.* to slant, to swerve.
obliquité [ɔbliki'te], *n.f.* obliquity.
oblitération [ɔblitera'sjɔ̃], *n.f.* obliteration.
oblitérer [ɔblite're], *v.t.* (*conjug. like* CÉDER) to obliterate; to cancel (*stamps*).
oblong [ɔ'blɔ̃], *a.* (*fem.* **-ue**) oblong.
obole [ɔ'bɔl] *n.f.* obolus; (*fig.*) farthing, mite.
obscène [ɔp'sɛːn], *a.* obscene.
obscénité [ɔpseni'te], *n.f.* obscenity, lewdness.
obscur [ɔps'kyːr], *a.* obscure; dark, gloomy; (*fig.*) humble; mean.
obscurcir [ɔpskyr'siːr], *v.t.* to obscure, to darken, to dim; to tarnish. **s'obscurcir**, *v.r.* to grow dim.
obscurcissement [ɔpskyrsis'mɑ̃], *n.m.* darkening; (*Mil.*) black-out.
obscurément [ɔpskyre'mɑ̃], *adv.* obscurely, dimly.
obscurité [ɔpskyri'te], *n.f.* obscurity, darkness.
obséder [ɔpse'de], *v.t.* (*conjug. like* CÉDER) to beset; to haunt, to importune, to obsess.
obsèques [ɔp'sɛk], *n.f. pl.* obsequies, funeral.
obséquieusement [ɔpsekjøz'mɑ̃], *adv.* obsequiously.
obséquieux [ɔpse'kjø], *a.* (*fem.* **-euse**) obsequious, fawning.
observable [ɔpsɛr'vabl], *a.* observable.
observance [ɔpsɛr'vɑ̃ːs], *n.f.* observance.
observateur [ɔpsɛrva'tœːr], *a.* (*fem.* **-trice**) observant.—*n.m.* (*fem.* **-trice**) observer, onlooker.
observation [ɔpsɛrva'sjɔ̃], *n.f.* observation; observance; remark.
observatoire [ɔpsɛrva'twaːr], *n.m.* observatory; look-out.
observer [ɔpsɛr've], *v.t.* to observe, to notice; to watch; to remark; to perform. **s'observer**, *v.r.* to be circumspect, to be on one's guard; to observe each other.
obsession [ɔpsɛ'sjɔ̃], *n.f.* obsession.
obstacle [ɔps'takl], *n.m.* obstacle, bar, hindrance.
obstination [ɔpstina'sjɔ̃], *n.f.* obstinacy, stubbornness, wilfulness.
obstiné [ɔpsti'ne], *a.* obstinate, self-willed, stubborn; persistent.
obstinément [ɔpstine'mɑ̃], *adv.* obstinately, stubbornly.
obstiner (s') [sɔpsti'ne], *v.r.* to be obstinately resolved (*à*), to insist, to persist.
obstructif [ɔpstryk'tif], *a.* (*fem.* **-tive**) obstructive.
obstruction [ɔpstryk'sjɔ̃], *n.f.* obstruction; stoppage.
obstruer [ɔpstrɥ'e], *v.t.* to obstruct, to block.
obtempérer [ɔptɑ̃pe're], *v.i.* (*conjug. like* CÉDER) to obey, to comply (*à*).
obtenir [ɔptə'niːr], *v.t. irr.* (*conjug. like* TENIR) to obtain, to procure, to get. **s'obtenir**, *v.r.* to be obtained; to be obtainable.
obtention [ɔptɑ̃'sjɔ̃], *n.f.* obtaining, getting.
obturer [ɔpty're], *v.t.* to seal, to obturate; to fill (*gap*), to stop (*a tooth etc.*).
obtus [ɔp'ty], *a.* obtuse; dull, blunt.
obus [o'by], *n.m.* (*Artill.*) shell.
obusier [ɔby'zje], *n.m.* howitzer.
obvier [ɔb'vje], *v.i.* to obviate, to prevent (*à*).
occasion [ɔka'zjɔ̃], *n.f.* opportunity, occasion; cause; bargain, job lot; ***livres d'occasion***, second-hand books.
occasionnel [ɔkazjɔ'nɛl], *a.* (*fem.* **-elle**) occasional.
occasionnellement [ɔkazjɔnɛl'mɑ̃], *adv.* occasionally.
occasionner [ɔkazjɔ'ne], *v.t.* to occasion, to cause.
occident [ɔksi'dɑ̃], *n.m.* west.
occidental [ɔksidɑ̃'tal], *a.* (*m. pl.* **-aux**) occidental, western.
Occidentaux [ɔksidɑ̃'to], *n.m. pl.* natives *or* inhabitants of the western countries, members of the western *bloc*.
occulte [ɔ'kylt], *a.* occult.
occupant [ɔky'pɑ̃], *a.* occupying.—*n.m.* (*fem.* **-e**) occupant, occupier.
occupation [ɔkypa'sjɔ̃], *n.f.* occupation; occupancy; capture.
occupé [ɔky'pe], *a.* occupied, busy, engaged; seized.
occuper [ɔky'pe], *v.t.* to occupy; to employ; to inhabit. **s'occuper**, *v.r.* to occupy oneself; to be busy; to look after; to see to (***de***).
occurrence [ɔky'rɑ̃ːs], *n.f.* occurrence; event; ***en l'occurrence***, under the circumstances.
océan [ɔse'ɑ̃], *n.m.* ocean, high sea.
océanique [ɔsea'nik], *a.* oceanic.
ocre [ɔkr], *n.f.* ochre.
octane [ɔk'tan], *n.m.* octane.
octave [ɔk'taːv], *n.f.* octave.

octavo [ɔkta'vo], *adv.* eighthly.—*n.m.* octavo.
octobre [ɔk'tɔbr], *n.m.* October.
octogénaire [ɔktɔʒe'nɛ:r], *a.* and *n.* octogenarian.
octogone [ɔktɔ'gɔn], *a.* octagonal, eight-sided.—*n.m.* octagon.
octroi [ɔk'trwɑ], *n.m.* grant, concession; town dues, toll; toll-house *or* office.
octroyer [ɔktrwɑ'je], *v.t.* (*conjug. like* EMPLOYER) to grant, to concede.
oculaire [ɔky'lɛ:r], *a.* ocular; ***témoin oculaire***, eyewitness.—*n.m.* eye-piece.
oculiste [ɔky'list], *n.m.* oculist.
odalisque [ɔda'lisk], *n.f.* odalisque.
ode [ɔd], *n.f.* ode.
odeur [o'dœ:r], *n.f.* odour, smell; scent.
odieusement [odjøz'mɑ̃], *adv.* odiously, hatefully.
odieux [o'djø], *a.* (*fem.* **-euse**) odious, hateful, loathsome.—*n.m.* odiousness, hatefulness.
odorant [ɔdɔ'rɑ̃], *a.* fragrant, sweet-smelling.
odorat [ɔdɔ'ra], *n.m.* smell, sense of smell.
odoriférant [ɔdɔrife'rɑ̃], *a.* sweet-smelling.
Odyssée [ɔdi'se], *n.f.* Odyssey.
œil [œ:j], *n.m.* (*pl.* **yeux**) eye; look; lustre; bud; dint, hole (*in bread, cheese*); ***des yeux à fleur de tête***, prominent eyes; ***d'un coup d'œil***, at a glance; ***en un clin d'œil***, in the twinkling of an eye.
œil-de-bœuf [œjdə'bœf], *n.m.* (*pl.* **œils-de-bœuf**) round *or* oval window.
œillade [œ'jad], *n.f.* glance; ogle, leer; wink.
œillère [œ'jɛ:r], *n.f.* blinker; canine tooth; eye-bath.
œillet [œ'jɛ], *n.m.* eyelet; (*Bot.*) dianthus, pink; ***œillet des fleuristes***, carnation; ***œillet de poète***, sweet william; ***petit œillet d'Inde***, French marigold.
œuf [œf], *n.m.* (*pl.* **œufs**) egg; ovum; spawn, roe (*of fish*).
œuvre [œ:vr], *n.f.* work; performance; production; (*pl.*) works (*of an author*).—*n.m.* (*no pl.*) work (*of an author, painter, musician etc.*)
œuvrer [œ'vre], [OUVRER].
offensant [ɔfɑ̃'sɑ̃], *a.* offensive, insulting.
offense [ɔ'fɑ̃:s], *n.f.* offence; injury, wrong, trespass.
offensé [ɔfɑ̃'se], *n.m.* (*fem.* **-ée**) offended party.
offenser [ɔfɑ̃'se], *v.t.* to offend; to sin against; to hurt, to injure (*feelings*); to shock. **s'offenser**, *v.r.* to be offended, to take offence.
offenseur [ɔfɑ̃'sœ:r], *n.m.* offender.
offensif [ɔfɑ̃'sif], *a.* (*fem.* **-sive**) offensive.—*n.f.* (**-sive**) offensive (*attack*).
offensivement [ɔfɑ̃siv'mɑ̃], *adv.* offensively.
office [ɔ'fis], *n.m.* office; duty; employment; service; Divine worship.—*n.f.* servants' hall, pantry, larder.
officiant [ɔfi'sjɑ̃], *a.* officiating.—*n.m.* officiating priest.
officiel [ɔfi'sjɛl], *a.* (*fem.* **-elle**) official, formal.
officiellement [ɔfisjɛl'mɑ̃], *adv.* officially.
officier (1) [ɔfi'sje], *v.i.* to officiate (*at divine service*).
officier (2) [ɔfi'sje], *n.m.* officer.
officieusement [ɔfisjøz'mɑ̃], *adv.* officiously.
officieux [ɔfi'sjø], *a.* (*fem.* **-euse**) officious; semi-official; obliging.—*n.m.* (*fem.* **-euse**) busybody.
offrande [ɔ'frɑ̃:d], *n.f.* offertory; offering.
offre [ɔfr], *n.f.* offer, tender.
offrir [ɔ'fri:r], *v.t.* (*conjug. like* OUVRIR) to offer, to tender; to present, to give. **s'offrir**, *v.r.* to offer oneself; to present itself.
offusquer [ɔfys'ke], *v.t.* to obscure; to dazzle; to offend. **s'offusquer**, *v.r.* (*rare*) to become darkened; (*fig.*) to take offence.
ogival [ɔʒi'val], *a.* (*m. pl.* **-aux**) (*Arch.*) pointed; gothic.
ogive [ɔ'ʒi:v], *n.f.* ogive, pointed arch; nose (*of missile, rocket*).
ogre [ɔgr], *n.m.* (*fem.* **-esse**) ogre, ogress.
oh! [o], *int.* O! ho!
ohm [om], *n.m.* ohm.
oie [wɑ], *n.f.* goose; (*fig.*) simpleton.
oignon [ɔ'ɲɔ̃], *n.m.* onion; bulb; bunion.
oindre [wɛ̃:dr], *v.t. irr.* to anoint.
oiseau [wa'zo], *n.m.* (*pl.* **-eaux**) bird; hod; (*colloq.*) fellow, chap; ***à vol d'oiseau***, as the crow flies.
oiseau-mouche [wazo'muʃ], *n.m.* (*pl.* **oiseaux-mouches**) humming-bird.
oiselet [wa'zlɛ], *n.m.* small bird.
oiseleur [wa'zlœ:r], *n.m.* bird-catcher; fowler.
oiselier [waz'lje], *n.m.* bird-seller; bird-fancier.
oiseux [wa'zø], *a.* (*fem.* **-euse**) idle; useless, trifling.
oisif [wa'zif], *a.* (*fem.* **-sive**) idle, unoccupied; lying dead (*money*).—*n.m.* (*fem.* **-sive**) idler.
oisillon [wazi'jɔ̃], *n.m.* young bird, fledg(e)ling.
oisivement [waziv'mɑ̃], *adv.* idly.
oisiveté [waziv'te], *n.f.* idleness; hours of ease.
oison [wa'zɔ̃], *n.m.* gosling; (*fig.*) simpleton.
oléagineux [ɔleaʒi'nø], *a.* (*fem.* **-euse**) oleaginous, oily.
oléoduc [ɔleo'dyk], *n.m.* pipeline.
oligarchie [ɔligar'ʃi], *n.f.* oligarchy.
oligarchique [ɔligar'ʃik], *a.* oligarchical.
oligarque [ɔli'gark], *n.* oligarch.
olivâtre [ɔli'vɑ:tr], *a.* olivaceous, olive-hued; sallow.
olive [ɔ'li:v], *a. inv.* olive-coloured.—*n.f.* olive.
Olivier [ɔli'vje], *m.* Oliver.
olivier [ɔli'vje], *n.m.* olive-tree; olive-wood.
olographe [ɔlɔ'graf], *a.* holograph(ic) (*will*).
Olympe [ɔ'lɛ̃:p], *n.m.* Olympus; (*fig.*) heaven.
olympien [ɔlɛ̃'pjɛ̃], *a.* (*fem.* **-enne**) Olympian —*n.m.* (**Olympien**, *fem.* **-enne**) Olympian.
olympique [ɔlɛ̃'pik], *a.* Olympic.
ombrage [ɔ̃'bra:ʒ], *n.m.* shade; umbrage, suspicion.
ombrager [ɔ̃bra'ʒe], *v.t.* (*conjug. like* MANGER) to shade; (*fig.*) to protect.
ombrageux [ɔ̃bra'ʒø], *a.* (*fem.* **-euse**) skittish (*of horses*); suspicious, touchy.
ombre [ɔ̃:br], *n.f.* shadow; shade; darkness; ghost; ***à l'ombre***, in the shade.
ombré [ɔ̃'bre], *a.* tinted, shaded.
ombrelle [ɔ̃'brɛl], *n.f.* parasol, sunshade.
ombrer [ɔ̃'bre], *v.t.* to shade; to darken.
ombreux [ɔ̃'brø], *a.* (*fem.* **-euse**) shady.
omelette [ɔm'lɛt], *n.f.* omelet(te).
omettre [ɔ'mɛtr], *v.t. irr.* (*conjug. like* METTRE) to omit.
omission [ɔmi'sjɔ̃], *n.f.* omission.
omnibus [ɔmni'by:s], *a.* suitable for all; ***train omnibus***, slow train, stopping train. —*n.m. inv.* omnibus, bus.

omnipotence [ɔmnipɔ'tɑ̃:s], *n.f.* omnipotence.
omnipotent [ɔmnipɔ'tɑ̃], *a.* omnipotent.
omnivore [ɔmni'vɔ:r], *a.* omnivorous.—*n.m.* omnivore.
omoplate [ɔmɔ'plat], *n.f.* shoulder-blade; scapula.
on [ɔ̃], *indef. pron.* one, they, we, you, people, men, somebody.
once (1) [ɔ̃:s], *n.f.* ounce (*weight*).
once (2) [ɔ̃:s], *n.f.* ounce, snow leopard.
oncle [ɔ̃:kl], *n.m.* uncle.
onction [ɔ̃k'sjɔ̃], *n.f.* unction, anointing; (*fig.*) unctuousness.
onctueusement [ɔ̃ktɥøz'mɑ̃], *adv.* unctuously.
onctueux [ɔ̃k'tɥø], *a.* (*fem.* **-euse**) unctuous, oily.
onctuosité [ɔ̃ktɥɔzi'te], *n.f.* unctuousness; smoothness.
onde [ɔ̃:d], *n.f.* wave, billow; (*fig.*) sea.
ondé [ɔ̃'de], *a.* undulating, wavy; watered (*of silk etc.*).
ondée [ɔ̃'de], *n.f.* shower (*of rain*).
ondoyant [ɔ̃dwa'jɑ̃], *a.* undulating; (*fig.*) changeable.
ondoyer [ɔ̃dwa'je], *v.t.* (*conjug. like* EMPLOYER) to baptize privately.—*v.i.* to undulate; to ripple (*water*).
ondulant [ɔ̃dy'lɑ̃], *a.* undulating; waving, flowing.
ondulation [ɔ̃dylɑ'sjɔ̃], *n.f.* undulation; wave (*of hair*).
ondulé [ɔ̃dy'le], *a.* rolling, undulating; waved (*hair*); corrugated (*iron*).
onduler [ɔ̃dy'le], *v.t.* to wave (*hair*).—*v.i.* to undulate; to ripple.
onduleux [ɔ̃dy'lø], *a.* (*fem.* **-euse**) sinuous, wavy.
onéreux [ɔne'rø], *a.* (*fem.* **-euse**) burdensome, onerous; expensive.
ongle [ɔ̃:gl], *n.m.* nail (*of fingers, claws etc.*); claw, talon; hoof.
onglée [ɔ̃'gle], *n.f.* numbness of the fingers (*from cold*).
onglet [ɔ̃'glɛ], *n.m.* mitre, mitre-joint.
onglier [ɔ̃'glje], *n.m.* manicure-case; (*pl.*) (*curved*) nail-scissors.
onguent [ɔ̃'gɑ̃], *n.m.* ointment, salve.
ongulé [ɔ̃gy'le], *a.* hoofed, ungulate.
onyx [ɔ'niks], *a.* and *n.m. inv.* onyx.
onze [ɔ̃:z], *a.* and *n.m.* eleven, eleventh.
onzième [ɔ̃'zjɛm], *a.* and *n.m.* eleventh.
onzièmement [ɔzjɛm'mɑ̃], *adv.* eleventhly, in the eleventh place.
opacité [ɔpasi'te], *n.f.* opacity; (*fig.*) darkness.
opale [ɔ'pal], *n.f.* opal.
opalescence [ɔpalɛ'sɑ̃:s], *n.f.* opalescence.
opalescent [ɔpalɛ'sɑ̃], *a.* opalescent.
opaque [ɔ'pak], *a.* opaque.
opéra [ɔpe'ra], *n.m.* opera; opera-house.
opéra-bouffe [ɔpera'buf], *n.m.* comic opera; musical comedy.
opérateur [ɔpera'tœ:r], *n.m.* (*fem.* **-trice**) operator; operative.
opératif [ɔpera'tif], *a.* (*fem.* **-tive**) operative.
opération [ɔperɑ'sjɔ̃], *n.f.* operation, working, performance; (*Comm.*) transaction.
opératoire [ɔpera'twa:r], *a.* operative, surgical.
opérer [ɔpe're], *v.t.* (*conjug. like* CÉDER) to operate, to bring about, to perform; to operate upon.—*v.i.* to work, to operate. **s'opérer**, *v.r.* to take place, to be brought about.
opérette [ɔpe'rɛt], *n.f.* operetta, light opera.
ophtalmie [ɔftal'mi], *n.f.* ophthalmia.
ophtalmique [ɔftal'mik], *a.* ophthalmic.
opiner [ɔpi'ne], *v.i.* to opine, to give *or* be of opinion; to speak.
opiniâtre [ɔpi'njɑ:tr], *a.* stubborn, obstinate. —*n.* stubborn person.
opiniâtrement [ɔpinjɑtrə'mɑ̃], *adv.* doggedly.
opiniâtrer (s') [sɔpinjɑ'tre], *v.r.* to be obstinate, to insist.
opiniâtreté [ɔpinjɑtrə'te], *n.f.* obstinacy.
opinion [ɔpi'njɔ̃], *n.f.* opinion; judgment, view; (*pl.*) votes.
opium [ɔ'pjɔm], *n.m.* opium.
opossum [ɔpɔ'sɔm], *n.m.* opossum.
opportun [ɔpɔr'tœ̃], *a.* opportune, timely; expedient.
opportunément [ɔpɔrtyne'mɑ̃], *adv.* seasonably.
opportunisme [ɔpɔrty'nism], *n.m.* opportunism.
opportuniste [ɔpɔrty'nist], *a.* and *n.* opportunist.
opportunité [ɔpɔrtyni'te], *n.f.* opportuneness, expediency.
opposant [ɔpo'zɑ̃], *a.* opposing, adverse.—*n.m.* (*fem.* **-e**) opponent, adversary.
opposé [ɔpo'ze], *a.* opposite, contrary.—*n.m.* the opposite, the reverse, the contrary.
opposer [ɔpo'ze], *v.t.* to oppose; to object; to urge. **s'opposer**, *v.r.* to be opposed *or* contrary (*à*), to set oneself against, to resist.
opposition [ɔpɔzi'sjɔ̃], *n.f.* opposition, resistance; contrast.
oppresser [ɔprɛ'se], *v.t.* (*fig.*) to depress; *to oppress.
oppresseur [ɔprɛ'sœ:r], *a.m.* oppressive.—*n.m.* oppressor.
oppressif [ɔprɛ'sif], *a.* (*fem.* **-ive**) oppressive.
oppression [ɔprɛ'sjɔ̃], *n.f.* oppression.
oppressivement [ɔprɛsiv'mɑ̃], *adv.* tyrannically, oppressively (*person*).
opprimant [ɔpri'mɑ̃], *a.* oppressing.
opprimé [ɔpri'me], *a.* oppressed.—*n.m.* (*fem.* **-ée**) the oppressed.
opprimer [ɔpri'me], *v.t.* to oppress, to crush.
opprobre [ɔ'prɔbr], *n.m.* opprobrium, shame, disgrace.
opter [ɔp'te], *v.i.* to choose, to decide.
opticien [ɔpti'sjɛ̃], *n.m.* optician.
optimisme [ɔpti'mism], *n.m.* optimism.
optimiste [ɔpti'mist], *a.* optimistic.—*n.* optimist.
option [ɔp'sjɔ̃], *n.f.* option, choice.
optique [ɔp'tik], *a.* optic, optical.—*n.f.* optics; perspective.
opulence [ɔpy'lɑ̃:s], *n.f.* opulence, wealth.
opulent [ɔpy'lɑ̃], *a.* opulent, wealthy.
or (1) [ɔ:r], *n.m.* gold; (*Her.*) or.
or (2) [ɔ:r], *conj.* but, now; well.
oracle [ɔ'ra:kl], *n.m.* oracle.
orage [ɔ'ra:ʒ], *n.m.* storm; thunder-storm; (*fig.*) tumult, disorder.
orageusement [ɔraʒøz'mɑ̃], *adv.* tempestuously; boisterously.
orageux [ɔra'ʒø], *a.* (*fem.* **-euse**) stormy, tempestuous; restless.

oraison [ɔrɛ'zɔ̃], *n.f.* speech, oration; prayer.
oral [ɔ'ral], *a.* (*m. pl.* **-aux**) oral, by word of mouth.
oralement [ɔral'mɑ̃], *adv.* orally, by word of mouth.
orange [ɔ'rɑ̃:ʒ], *n.f.* orange (*fruit*).—*a. inv.* and *n.m.* orange (*colour*).
orangé [ɔrɑ̃'ʒe], *a.* orange(-coloured).
orangeade [ɔrɑ̃'ʒad], *n.f.* orangeade, orange squash.
oranger [ɔrɑ̃'ʒe], *n.m.* orange-tree.
orangerie [ɔrɑ̃'ʒri], *n.f.* orange-house; orange-grove, orangery.
orang-outan(g) [ɔrɑ̃u'tɑ̃], *n.m.* (*pl.* **orangs-outans**) orang-utan.
orateur [ɔra'tœːr], *n.m.* (*fem.* **-trice**) orator, speaker.
oratoire [ɔra'twaːr], *a.* oratorical; oratorial.—*n.m.* oratory; private chapel.
orbe [ɔrb], *n.m.* orb, orbit; globe; sphere; coil (*snake*).
orbite [ɔr'bit], *n.f.* orbit; (*Anat.*) socket; (*fig.*) sphere (*of action*).
Orcades [ɔr'kad], **les**, *f. pl.* the Orkneys.
orchestral [ɔrkɛs'tral], *a.* (*m. pl.* **-aux**) orchestral.
orchestration [ɔrkɛstrɑ'sjɔ̃], *n.f.* scoring, orchestration.
orchestre [ɔr'kɛstr], *n.m.* orchestra; band.
orchestrer [ɔrkɛs'tre], *v.t.* to score, to orchestrate.
orchidée [ɔrki'de], *n.f.* orchid; (*pl.*) Orchidaceae.
ordinaire [ɔrdi'nɛːr], *a.* ordinary, common, usual.—*n.m.* ordinary practice; usual fare.
ordinairement [ɔrdinɛr'mɑ̃], *adv.* usually.
ordinal [ɔrdi'nal], *a.* (*m. pl.* **-aux**) ordinal.
ordination [ɔrdinɑ'sjɔ̃], *n.f.* ordination.
ordonnance [ɔrdɔ'nɑ̃:s], *n.f.* order, ordinance, regulation; disposition, arrangement; (*Med.*) prescription.—*n.* (*usu. fem.*) (*Mil.*) batman.
ordonnateur [ɔrdɔna'tœːr], *a.* (*fem.* **-trice**) ordaining, ordering.—*n.m.* (*fem.* **-trice**) organizer, manager; master of ceremonies.
ordonné [ɔrdɔ'ne], *a.* ordered; tidy; ordained (*priest*).
ordonner [ɔrdɔ'ne], *v.t.* to order, to regulate; to direct, to command; to ordain; (*Med.*) to prescribe.
ordre [ɔrdr], *n.m.* order, command; class, tribe; (*pl.*) holy orders.
ordure [ɔr'dyːr], *n.f.* filth, dirt; (*pl.*) sweepings, refuse, garbage.
ordurier [ɔrdy'rje], *a.* (*fem.* **-ière**) filthy, ribald, lewd.
oreille [ɔ'rɛːj], *n.f.* ear; hearing; flange; handle (*of a vase etc.*); ***avoir l'oreille basse***, to be crestfallen; ***avoir mal aux oreilles***, to have ear-ache; ***faire la sourde oreille***, to turn a deaf ear; ***prêter l'oreille à***, to listen to.
oreiller [ɔrɛ'je], *n.m.* pillow.
oreillons [ɔrɛ'jɔ̃], *n.m. pl.* mumps.
orfèvre [ɔr'fɛːvr], *n.m.* goldsmith, silversmith.
orfraie [ɔr'frɛ], *n.f.* osprey.
organdi [ɔrgɑ̃'di], *n.m.* organdie.
organe [ɔr'gan], *n.m.* organ; voice; agent, agency; spokesman.
organique [ɔrga'nik], *a.* organic.
organisateur [ɔrganiza'tœːr], *a.* (*fem.* **-trice**) organizing.—*n.m.* (*fem.* **-trice**) organizer.
organisation [ɔrganizɑ'sjɔ̃], *n.f.* organization; (*fig.*) set-up; constitution.
organisé [ɔrgani'ze], *a.* organized.
organiser [ɔrgani'ze], *v.t.* to organize; to get up, to arrange. **s'organiser**, *v.r.* to become organized.
organisme [ɔrga'nism], *n.m.* organism.
organiste [ɔrga'nist], *n.* organist.
orge [ɔrʒ], *n.f.* barley; (*masc. in* ***orge mondé***, hulled barley, *and* ***orge perlé***, pearl barley).
orgelet [ɔrʒ'lɛ], *n.m.* sty (*in the eye*).
orgie [ɔr'ʒi], *n.f.* orgy; (*fig.*) profusion.
orgue [ɔrg], *n.m.* (*fem. in pl.*) (*Mus.*) organ.
orgueil [ɔr'gœːj], *n.m.* pride; arrogance.
orgueilleusement [ɔrgœjøz'mɑ̃], *adv.* proudly, haughtily.
orgueilleux [ɔrgœ'jø], *a.* (*fem.* **-euse**) proud, haughty, arrogant.—*n.m.* (*fem.* **-euse**) proud and haughty person.
orient [ɔ'rjɑ̃], *n.m.* East, Orient; rise; water (*of pearls*).
oriental [ɔrjɑ̃'tal], *a.* (*m. pl.* **-aux**) oriental, eastern.—*n.m.* (*fem.* **-e**) oriental (*person*).
orientation [ɔrjɑ̃tɑ'sjɔ̃], *n.f.* orientation.
orienter [ɔrjɑ̃'te], *v.t.* to orientate; to set (*a map*) by the compass; (*fig.*) to guide; (*Naut.*) to trim (*sails*). **s'orienter**, *v.r.* to take one's bearings, to ascertain one's position; (*fig.*) to see what one is about.
orifice [ɔri'fis], *n.m.* orifice, aperture, hole.
originaire [ɔriʒi'nɛːr], *a.* originally (*coming*) from; native (*de*); primitive.
originairement [ɔriʒinɛr'mɑ̃], *adv.* originally, primitively.
original [ɔriʒi'nal], *a.* (*m. pl.* **-aux**) original; singular, odd, peculiar, quaint.—*n.m.* original manuscript, drawing etc. (*not a copy*).—*n.m.* (*fem.* **-e**) queer person, character, oddity.
originalement [ɔriʒinal'mɑ̃], *adv.* originally; singularly, oddly.
originalité [ɔriʒinali'te], *n.f.* originality; eccentricity.
origine [ɔri'ʒin], *n.f.* origin, source; descent, derivation, extraction; ***d'origine***, authentic; vintage (*wine*).
originel [ɔriʒi'nɛl], *a.* (*fem.* **-elle**) original, primitive.
originellement [ɔriʒinɛl'mɑ̃], *adv.* originally.
orignal [ɔri'ɲal], *n.m.* elk (*of Canada*), moose.
Orion [ɔ'rjɔ̃], *n.m.* (*Astron.*) Orion.
oripeau [ɔri'po], *n.m.* (*pl.* **-eaux**) tinsel; foil; (*pl.*) tawdry finery; (*more usually*) rags.
orme [ɔrm], *n.m.* elm.
ormeau [ɔr'mo], *n.m.* (*pl.* **-eaux**) young elm.
orné [ɔr'ne], *a.* ornate.
ornement [ɔrnə'mɑ̃], *n.m.* ornament, embellishment.
ornemental [ɔrnəmɑ̃'tal], *a.* (*m. pl.* **-aux**) ornamental.
ornementation [ɔrnəmɑ̃tɑ'sjɔ̃], *n.f.* ornamentation.
orner [ɔr'ne], *v.t.* to adorn, to decorate, to deck, to embellish. **s'orner**, *v.r.* to adorn oneself; to be adorned.
ornière [ɔr'njɛːr], *n.f.* rut.
ornithologie [ɔrnitɔlɔ'ʒi], *n.f.* ornithology.
ornithologiste [ɔrnitɔlɔ'ʒist], **ornithologue** [ɔrnitɔ'lɔg], *n.m.* ornithologist.

Orphée [ɔr'fe], *m.* Orpheus.
orphelin [ɔrfə'lɛ̃], *a.* and *n.m.* (*fem.* **-e**) orphan.
orphelinat [ɔrfəli'na], *n.m.* orphanage.
orphéon [ɔrfe'ɔ̃], *n.m.* male-voice choir.
ort [ɔ:r], *a. inv.* and *adv.* (*Comm.*) gross, gross weight.
orteil [ɔr'tɛ:j], *n.m.* toe, *esp.* the big toe.
orthodoxe [ɔrtɔ'dɔks], *a.* orthodox.
orthodoxie [ɔrtɔdɔk'si], *n.f.* orthodoxy.
orthographe [ɔrtɔ'graf], *n.f.* orthography, spelling.
orthopédie [ɔrtɔpe'di], *n.f.* orthopedics.
ortie [ɔr'ti], *n.f.* nettle.
orvet [ɔr'vɛ], *n.m.* slow-worm.
os [ɔs; *pl.* o], *n.m. inv.* bone.
oscillant [ɔsi'lɑ̃], *a.* oscillating.
oscillation [ɔsilɑ'sjɔ̃], *n.f.* oscillation, vibration.
oscillatoire [ɔsila'twa:r], *a.* oscillatory.
osciller [ɔsi'le], *v.i.* to oscillate, to swing, to vibrate; (*fig.*) to fluctuate.
oscillographe [ɔsilɔ'graf], *n.m.* (*Elec.*) oscillograph.
osé [o'ze], *a.* bold, daring.
oseille [ɔ'zɛ:j], *n.f.* sorrel.
oser [o'ze], *v.t.*, *v.i.* to dare, to venture.
oseraie [oz'rɛ], *n.f.* osier-bed.
osier [o'zje], *n.m.* osier, withy, wicker.
osselet [ɔs'lɛ], *n.m.* knuckle-bone (*of sheep*); ossicle (*of ear*).
ossements [ɔs'mɑ̃], *n.m. pl.* bones (*of the dead*).
osseux [ɔ'sø], *a.* (*fem.* **-euse**) bony, osseous.
ossification [ɔsifikɑ'sjɔ̃], *n.f.* ossification.
ossifier [ɔsi'fje], *v.t.* to ossify. **s'ossifier**, *v.r.* to become ossified.
ossuaire [ɔ'sɥɛ:r], *n.m.* ossuary, charnel-house.
ostensible [ɔstɑ̃'sibl], *a.* open; above-board.
ostensiblement [ɔstɑ̃siblə'mɑ̃], *adv.* openly, publicly.
ostensoir [ɔstɑ̃'swa:r], *n.m.* monstrance.
ostentateur [ɔstɑ̃ta'tœ:r], *a.* (*fem.* **-trice**) ostentatious.
ostentation [ɔstɑ̃tɑ'sjɔ̃], *n.f.* ostentation, show.
ostraciser [ɔstrasi'ze], *v.t.* to ostracize.
ostracisme [ɔstra'sism], *n.m.* ostracism.
ostréiculture [ɔstreikyl'ty:r], *n.f.* oyster-culture.
otage [ɔ'ta:ʒ], *n.m.* hostage; pledge.
ôter [o'te], *v.t.* to take away; to remove; to take off; to deprive of; to deduct; to rid of. **s'ôter**, *v.r.* to remove oneself, to get away; to rid oneself; ***ôtez-vous de mon chemin***, stand aside.
ou [u], *conj.* or, either, else; ***ou bien***, or else; ***ou . . . ou***, either . . . or.
où [u], *adv.* where; whither; at which, in which, to which, through which; when, that; ***par où?*** which way?
ouais! [wɛ], *int.* well now! my word!
ouate [wat], *n.f.* ***l'ouate*** or ***la ouate***, wadding, padding; cotton-wool.
ouater [wa'te], *v.t.* to wad, to pad; to coddle.
oubli [u'bli], *n.m.* forgetfulness; oblivion; oversight, slip; pardon.
oubliable [u'bljabl], *a.* liable *or* deserving to be forgotten.
oublier [u'blje], *v.t.* to forget, to omit, to neglect; to pardon. **s'oublier**, *v.r.* to forget oneself; to be forgotten.
oubliettes [u'bljɛt], *n.f. pl.* oubliette, trap-dungeon.
oublieux [u'bljø], *a.* (*fem.* **-euse**) forgetful, unmindful.
ouest [wɛst], *a. inv.* westerly, western.—*n.m.* west.
ouf! [uf], *int.* oh! (*of relief*).
Ouganda [ugɑ̃'da], **l'**, *m.* Uganda.
oui [wi], *adv.* yes.—*n.m.* yes.
ouï [wi] *p.p.* [OUÏR].
ouï-dire [wi'di:r], *n.m. inv.* hearsay.
ouïe [wi], *n.f.* *hearing; hole (*of a violin etc.*); (*pl.*) gills (*of fish*).
ouïr [wi:r], *v.t. irr.* (*rarely used except in the infinitive and compound tenses*) to hear; ***j'ai ouï dire***, I have heard say.
ouragan [ura'gɑ̃], *n.m.* hurricane; (*fig.*) storm.
ourdir [ur'di:r], *v.t.* to warp (*cloth*); (*fig.*) to weave, to plot, to concoct.
ourdissage [urdi'sa:ʒ], *n.m.* warping.
ourdou [ur'du], *n.m.* Urdu (*language*), Hindustani.
ourler [ur'le], *v.t.* to hem; ***ourler à jour***, to hemstitch.
ourlet [ur'lɛ], *n.m.* hem.
ours [urs], *n.m.* bear.
ourse [urs], *n.f.* she-bear.
oursin [ur'sɛ̃], *n.m.* sea-urchin.
ourson [ur'sɔ̃], *n.m.* bear cub.
outil [u'ti], *n.m.* tool, implement.
outillage [uti'ja:ʒ], *n.m.* stock of tools equipment.
outillé [uti'je], *a.* furnished with tools.
outiller [uti'je], *v.t.* to furnish with tools; to equip.
outrage [u'tra:ʒ], *n.m.* outrage, gross insult; injury, wrong.
outrageant [utra'ʒɑ̃], *a.* outrageous; insulting, abusive.
outrager [utra'ʒe], *v.t.* (*conjug. like* MANGER) to outrage; to insult, to offend.
outrageusement [utraʒøz'mɑ̃], *adv.* insultingly.
outrageux [utra'ʒø], *a.* (*fem.* **-euse**) outrageous.
outrance [u'trɑ̃:s], *n.f.* extreme; excess; ***à outrance***, to the death.
outre (1) [utr], *n.f.* goatskin *or* leather bottle.
outre (2) [utr], *adv.* further, beyond; ***en outre***, besides; ***passer outre***; to go on, to take no notice of a thing.—*prep.* beyond; besides, in addition to; ***outre que***, besides.
outré [u'tre], *a.* exaggerated, strained, excessive; incensed.
outrecuidance [utrəkɥi'dɑ̃:s], *n.f.* presumption.
outrecuidant [utrəkɥi'dɑ̃], *a.* presumptuous, bumptious.
outre-Manche [utrə'mɑ̃:ʃ], *adv.* across the Channel.
outremer [utrə'mɛ:r], *n.m.* ultramarine (*colour*).
outre-mer [utrə'mɛ:r], *adv.* overseas.
outrepasser [utrəpɑ'se], *v.t.* to go beyond, to transgress.
outrer [u'tre], *v.t.* to overdo; to exaggerate.
ouvert [u'vɛ:r], *a.* open; unfortified (*of towns*); (*fig.*) frank.

ouvertement [uvɛrtə'mɑ̃], *adv.* openly, frankly.
ouverture [uvɛr'tyːr], *n.f.* opening; aperture, gap, hole; (*Mus.*) overture; (*Arch.*) span, width (*of a doorway etc.*); (*Av.*) (parachute) drop.
ouvrable [u'vrabl], *a.* working, workable; ***jour ouvrable***, working-day.
ouvrage [u'vraːʒ], *n.m.* work, piece of work; performance, workmanship.
ouvragé [uvra'ʒe], *a.* wrought, figured.
ouvrager [uvra'ʒe], *v.t.* (*conjug. like* MANGER) to work, to figure.
ouvrant [u'vrɑ̃], *a.* opening.
ouvré [u'vre], *a.* wrought; diapered, figured.
ouvre-boîte [uvrə'bwaːt], *n.m.* (*pl.* **-boîtes**) tin-opener.
ouvrer [u'vre], *v.t.* to work (*material*); to diaper (*linen*).—*v.i.* to work.
ouvrier [uvri'e], *a.* (*fem.* **-ière**) operative, working.—*n.m.* (*fem.* **-ière**) workman, (female) worker, hand, operative; labourer.
ouvrir [u'vriːr], *v.t. irr.* to open, to unlock; to sharpen (*the appetite*); to broach (*opinions etc.*).—*v.i.* to open; to expand. **s'ouvrir**, *v.r.* to open; to open for oneself; to open one's mind.
ouvroir [u'vrwaːr], *n.m.* charity workshop; workroom.
ovaire [ɔ'vɛːr], *n.m.* ovary.
ovalaire [ɔva'lɛːr], *a.* (*Anat.*) oval.
ovale [ɔ'val], *a.* and *n.m.* oval.
ovation [ɔvɑ'sjɔ̃], *n.f.* ovation.
ovoïde [ɔvɔ'id], *a.* ovoid, egg-shaped.
ovule [ɔ'vyl], *n.m.* ovule.
oxalique [ɔksa'lik], *a.* oxalic.
oxyacétylénique [ɔksiasetile'nik], *a.* oxyacetylene (*welding etc.*).
oxyde [ɔk'sid], *n.m.* oxide.
oxyder [ɔksi'de], *v.t.* to oxidize.
oxygène [ɔksi'ʒɛːn], *n.m.* oxygen.
oxygéné [ɔksiʒe'ne], *a.* ***eau oxygénée***, peroxide of hydrogen.
ozone [ɔ'zɔn], *n.m.* ozone.

P

P, p [pe], *n.m.* the sixteenth letter of the alphabet.
pacage [pa'kaːʒ], *n.m.* pasture-land; ***droit de pacage***, grazing rights.
pacificateur [pasifika'tœːr], *a.* (*fem.* **-trice**) pacifying, peace-making.—*n.m.* (*fem.* **-trice**) pacifier, peacemaker.
pacification [pasifikɑ'sjɔ̃], *n.f.* pacification.
pacifier [pasi'fje], *v.t.* to pacify, to appease.
pacifique [pasi'fik], *a.* pacific, peaceful.
pacifiquement [pasifik'mɑ̃], *adv.* peaceably, quietly.
pacifisme [pasi'fism], *n.m.* pacifism.
pacifiste [pasi'fist], *a.* and *n.* pacifist.
pacotille [pakɔ'tiːj], *n.f.* goods carried free of charge by passengers *or* seamen; shoddy goods; pack, bale.
pacte [pakt], *n.m.* compact, contract, pact, agreement; ***pacte de préférence***, preference clause.
pactiser [pakti'ze], *v.i.* to covenant, to make a compact (***avec***).
paf! [paf], *int.* slap! bang!
pagaie [pa'gɛ], *n.f.* paddle (*for canoe etc.*).
pagaïe or **pagaille** [pa'gaj], *n.f.* hurry; disorder; ***en pagaïe***, (*pop.*) higgledy-piggledy.
paganisme [paga'nism], *n.m.* paganism.
pagayer [pagɛ'je], *v.t.*, *v.i.* (*conjug. like* PAYER) to paddle.
page (1) [paːʒ], *n.m.* page (boy).
page (2) [paːʒ], *n.f.* page (*of a book*).
pagode [pa'gɔd], *n.f.* pagoda.
paiement [PAYEMENT].
païen [pa'jɛ̃], *a.* and *n.m.* (*fem.* **-enne**) pagan, heathen.
paillard [pɑ'jaːr], *a.* lecherous, lewd.—*n.m.* (*fem.* **-e**) wanton, sensual person, bawd.
paillasse (1) [pɑ'jas], *n.f.* straw mattress.
paillasse (2) [pɑ'jas], *n.m.* clown, buffoon.
paillasson [pɑja'sɔ̃] *n.m.* straw-mat; door-mat.
paille [pɑːj], *a. inv.* straw-coloured.—*n.f.* straw; flaw (*in gems, metals etc.*); ***botte de paille***, bale of straw.
paillé [pɑ'je], *a.* straw-coloured; faulty (*of metals etc.*).
pailler (1) [pɑ'je], *n.m.* farm-yard; heap *or* stack of straw.
pailler (2) [pɑ'je], *v.t.* to mulch (*plants*).
pailleter [pɑj'te], *v.t.* (*conjug. like* APPELER) to spangle.
paillette [pɑ'jɛt], *n.f.* spangle; flaw (*in a gem*); ***savon en paillettes***, soap flakes.
paillis [pɑ'ji], *n.m.* mulch.
paillon [pɑ'jɔ̃], *n.m.* large spangle, tinsel; wisp of straw; straw wrapper (*for bottle*).
pain [pɛ̃], *n.m.* bread; loaf; cake (*of soap etc.*); (*pop.*) blow, punch; ***pain grillé***, toast; ***un pain***, a loaf; ***un petit pain***, a roll.
pair [pɛːr], *a.* equal, even (*of numbers*).—*n.m.* peer; equal; mate (*of birds*); par, equality; ***au pair***, at par, even (*with*), 'au pair'; ***de pair***, on a par; ***hors*** (***de***) ***pair***, beyond comparison.
paire [pɛːr], *n.f.* pair, brace, couple.
pairesse [pɛ'rɛs], *n.f.* peeress.
pairie [pɛ'ri], *n.f.* peerage.
paisible [pɛ'zibl], *a.* peaceful, quiet, calm.
paisiblement [pɛziblə'mɑ̃], *adv.* peacefully.
paître [pɛːtr], *v.t.*, *v.i. irr.* to graze, to feed.
paix [pɛ], *n.f.* peace; quiet; stillness; rest.—*int.* be quiet!
Pakistan [pakis'tɑ̃], **le**, *m.* Pakistan.
pakistanais [pakista'nɛ], *a.* Pakistani.—*n.m.* (**Pakistanais**, *fem.* **-aise**) Pakistani (*person*).
paladin [pala'dɛ̃], *n.m.* paladin, champion.
palais (1) [pa'lɛ], *n.m.* palace; (*fig.*) the Bar; the law; ***palais de justice***, law-courts.
palais (2) [pa'lɛ], *n.m.* palate, roof (*of the mouth*).
palan [pa'lɑ̃], *n.m.* tackle, pulley-block.
pale [pal], *n.f.* blade (*of oar, propeller etc.*); sluice, flood-gate.
pâle [pɑːl], *a.* pale, wan, pallid, ghastly.
palefrenier [palfrə'nje], *n.m.* groom, ostler.
palefroi [pal'frwɑ], *n.m.* palfrey.
Palestine [palɛs'tin], **la**, *f.* Palestine.
palestinien [palɛsti'njɛ̃], *a.* (*fem.* **-enne**) Palestinian.

palet [pa'lɛ], *n.m.* quoit.
palette [pa'lɛt], *n.f.* paddle (*of paddle-wheel*); bat (*ping-pong*); palette (*of painter*).
pâleur [pɑ'lœ:r], *n.f.* pallor, wanness.
pâli [pɑ'li], *a.* grown pale.
palier [pa'lje], *n.m.* landing (*on a staircase*), floor; stage, degree; level stretch; ***vitesse en palier***, speed on the flat.
pâlir [pɑ'li:r], *v.t.* to make pale, to bleach.—*v.i.* to (grow, turn *or* become) pale; to grow dim.
palis [pa'li], *n.m.* stake, pale; paling, enclosure.
palissade [pali'sad], *n.f.* palisade, paling; wooden fence; hedgerow; stockade.
palissader [palisa'de], *v.t.* to palisade; to stockade; to fence in.
pâlissant [pɑli'sɑ̃], *a.* turning pale, fading.
pallier [pa'lje], *v.t.* to palliate, to excuse.
palmarès [palma'rɛ:s], *n.m. inv.* prize-list, list of honours.
palme [palm], *n.f.* palm, palm-branch; palm-tree; (*fig.*) victory, triumph.
palmé [pal'me], *a.* palmate; web-footed.
palmier [pal'mje], *n.m.* palm-tree, palm.
palombe [pa'lɔ̃:b], *n.f.* wood-pigeon, ring-dove.
palonnier [palɔ'nje], *n.m.* pole (*of a coach*); (*Motor.*) compensator (*of brake*); (*Av.*) rudder-bar.
pâlot [pɑ'lo], *a.* (*fem.* **-otte**) palish, rather pale.
palourde [pa'lu:rd], *n.f.* clam.
palpable [pal'pabl], *a.* palpable.
palpablement [palpablə'mɑ̃], *adv.* palpably.
palper [pal'pe], *v.t.* to feel, to touch; (*colloq.*) to pocket.
palpitant [palpi'tɑ̃], *a.* palpitating; thrilling.
palpitation [palpitɑ'sjɔ̃], *n.f.* palpitation; throbbing; thrill, flutter.
palpiter [palpi'te], *v.i.* to palpitate, to throb; to quiver, to flutter.
paludéen [palyde'ɛ̃], *a.* (*fem.* **-éenne**) paludal, marshy.
pâmer [pɑ'me], *v.i.* and **se pâmer**, *v.r.* to swoon.
pâmoison [pɑmwa'zɔ̃], *n.f.* swoon, fainting fit.
pamphlet [pɑ̃'flɛ], *n.m.* satirical booklet, lampoon.
pamphlétaire [pɑ̃fle'tɛ:r], *n.* pamphleteer.
pamplemousse [pɑ̃plə'mus], *n.m.* or *f.* grape-fruit.
pampre [pɑ̃:pr], *n.m.* vine-branch.
pan (1) [pɑ̃], *n.m.* flap, coat-tails, panel (*of dress*); side, section (*of a wall etc.*); ***pan de ciel***, stretch *or* patch of sky; ***pan de mur***, bare wall, piece of wall.
pan! (2) [pɑ̃], *int.* slap! bang! smack!
panacée [pana'se], *n.f.* panacea.
panache [pa'naʃ], *n.m.* plume, bunch of feathers etc.; (*fig.*) show, swagger.
panaché [pana'ʃe], *a.* plumed, tufted; striped; (*colloq.*) variegated, motley; ***glace panachée***, mixed ice-cream.
panacher [pana'ʃe], *v.t.* to plume; to streak, to variegate, to mix.
panais [pa'nɛ], *n.m.* parsnip.
Panama [pana'ma], **le**, *m.* Panama.
panama [pana'ma], *n.m.* panama-hat.
panamien [pana'mjɛ̃], *a.* (*fem.* **-enne**) Panama(nian).—*n.m.* (**Panamien**, *fem.* **-enne**) Panamanian (*person*).
panaris [pana'ri], *n.m.* whitlow.
pancarte [pɑ̃'kart], *n.f.* large placard *or* bill.
pancréas [pɑ̃kre'ɑ:s], *n.m. inv.* pancreas; sweetbread.
panda [pɑ̃'da], *n.m.* panda.
pandémonium [pɑ̃demɔ'njɔm], *n.m.* pandemonium.
pandit [pɑ̃'di], *n.m.* pundit.
Pandore [pɑ̃'dɔ:r], *f.* Pandora.
pané [pa'ne], *a.* covered, *or* fried, in bread-crumbs.
panégyrique [paneʒi'rik], *n.m.* panegyric.
paner [pa'ne], *v.t.* to cover with breadcrumbs.
panier [pa'nje], *n.m.* basket, hamper, pannier; hoop-petticoat; ***le dessus du panier***, the pick of the basket; ***panier à salade***, (*wire*) salad washer; (*slang*) black Maria; ***panier percé***, spendthrift.
panique [pa'nik], *a.* and *n.f.* panic.
panne [pan], *n.f.* plush; fat, lard; purlin; breakdown, mishap; ***panne d'allumage***, (*Motor.*) ignition trouble; ***rester en panne***, (*Motor.*) to have a breakdown.
panneau [pa'no], *n.m.* (*pl.* **-eaux**) panel; snare, trap; (*Naut.*) hatch; (*Hort.*) glass-frame.
panoplie [panɔ'pli], *n.f.* panoply; trophy (*of arms*).
panorama [panɔra'ma], *n.m.* panorama.
panoramique [panɔra'mik], *a.* panoramic.
pansage [pɑ̃'sa:ʒ], *n.m.* grooming (*of horses etc.*).
panse [pɑ̃:s], *n.f.* belly, paunch.
pansement [pɑ̃s'mɑ̃], *n.m.* dressing (*of wounds*); ***pansement sommaire***, first aid; dressing.
panser [pɑ̃'se], *v.t.* to dress (*wounds*); to groom (*a horse*).
pansu [pɑ̃'sy], *a.* and *n.m.* (*fem.* **-e**) pot-bellied (person); bulging.
pantalon [pɑ̃ta'lɔ̃], *n.m.* (pair of) trousers; ***pantalon de femme***, women's knickers, panties.
pantelant [pɑ̃'tlɑ̃], *a.* panting, gasping.
panteler [pɑ̃'tle], *v.i.* (*conjug. like* APPELER) to gasp, to pant.
panthère [pɑ̃'tɛ:r], *n.f.* panther.
pantin [pɑ̃'tɛ̃], *n.m.* nonentity, puppet; (*fig.*) jumping-jack.
pantois [pɑ̃'twa], *a.* (*fig.*) astonished, flabbergasted.
pantomime [pɑ̃tɔ'mim], *a.* pantomimic.—*n.f.* dumb-show, pantomime.—*n.m.* pantomime (*actor*).
pantoufle [pɑ̃'tufl], *n.f.* slipper; ***en pantoufles***, slipshod.
paon [pɑ̃], *n.m.* peacock; emperor-moth; (*fig.*) vain person.
paonne [pan], *n.f.* peahen.
papa [pa'pa], *n.m.* papa, daddy.
papal [pa'pal], *a.* (*m. pl.* **-aux**) papal.
papauté [papo'te], *n.f.* papacy.
pape [pap], *n.m.* pope.
paperasse [pa'pras], *n.f.* useless papers, documents; red-tape; paper-work.
paperasser [papra'se], *v.i.* to rummage among old papers; to scribble.
paperasserie [papras'ri], *n.f.* red-tape.
paperassier [papra'sje], *a.* (*fem.* **-ière**) red-tape, formal.—*n.m.* (*fem.* **-ière**) everlasting scribbler; rummager through old papers.

papeterie [pap'tri], *n.f.* paper-mill, paper-trade; stationery; stationer's shop; stationery case.
papetier [papə'tje], *a.* (*fem.* **-ière**) paper (*industry etc.*).—*n.m.* (*fem.* **-ière**) paper-maker; stationer.
papier [pa'pje], *n.m.* paper; ***papier buvard***, blotting paper; ***papier d'emballage***, brown paper; ***papier de verre***, glass-paper, sand-paper; ***papier hygiénique***, lavatory paper.
papillon [papi'jɔ̃], *n.m.* butterfly.
papillonner [papijɔ'ne], *v.i.* to flutter about, to hover; (*fig.*) to trifle, to flirt.
papillotage [papijɔ'ta:ʒ], *n.m.* blinking (*of the eyes*); dazzle, glitter, tinsel (*of style*).
papillote [papi'jɔt], *n.f.* curl-paper; bonbon; ***fer à papillotes***, curling-irons; ***papillotes à pétard***, Christmas crackers.
papilloter [papijɔ'te], *v.t.* to put (*hair etc.*) in paper.—*v.i.* to blink; to dazzle, to be gaudy.
papisme [pa'pism], *n.m.* papism, popery.
papiste [pa'pist], *a.* popish.—*n.* papist.
papou [pa'pu], *a.* Papuan.—*n.m.* (**Papou**, *fem.* **-oue**) Papuan (*person*).
Papouasie [papwa'zi], **la**, *f.* Papua.
papyrus [papi'ry:s], *n.m.* papyrus.
pâque [pɑ:k], *n.f.* Passover (*among Jews*).
paquebot [pak'bo], *n.m.* packet-boat, steamer, liner.
pâquerette [pɑ'krɛt], *n.f.* daisy.
Pâques [pɑ:k], *n.m.* Easter.
paquet [pa'kɛ], *n.m.* package, bundle, parcel; packet; (*fig.*) clumsy lout.
paqueter [pak'te], *v.t.* (*conjug. like* APPELER) to make into a packet, parcel etc.
par [paɪr], *prep.* by, through, out of, from; about, in, into; for, for the sake of.
parabole [para'bɔl], *n.f.* parabola; parable.
parabolique [parabɔ'lik], *a.* parabolic.
parachutage [paraʃy'ta:ʒ], *n.m.* parachuting; parachute landing.
parachute [para'ʃyt], *n.m.* parachute; ***sauter en parachute***, to bale out.
parachuter [paraʃy'te], *v.t., v.i.* to parachute, to drop (by parachute).
parachutiste [paraʃy'tist], *n.* parachutist, paratrooper.
parade [pa'rad], *n.f.* parade, show, display; pageantry; (*Fenc.*) parry.
parader [para'de], *v.i.* to show off.
paradis [para'di], *n.m.* paradise; (*Theat.*) upper gallery, the gods.
paradoxal [paradɔk'sal], *a.* (*m. pl.* **-aux**) paradoxical.
paradoxe [para'dɔks], *n.m.* paradox.
parafe or **paraphe** [pa'raf], *n.m.* paraph; flourish (*after one's signature*); initials and flourish.
parafer or **parapher** [para'fe], *v.t.* to paraph, to put one's flourish, dash *or* initials to.
paraffine [para'fin], *n.f.* paraffin, paraffin wax; ***huile de paraffine***, liquid paraffin.
parage [pa'ra:ʒ], *n.m.* extraction, descent, lineage; (*usually in pl.*) localities, latitudes, waters; ***dans ces parages***, in these parts.
paragraphe [para'graf], *n.m.* paragraph.
Paraguay [para'gwɛ], **le**, *m.* Paraguay.
paraguayen [paragwɛ'jɛ̃], *a.* (*fem.* **-enne**) Paraguayan.—*n.m.* (**Paraguayen**, *fem.* **-enne**) Paraguayan (*person*).
paraître [pa'rɛ:tr], *v.i. irr.* (*conjug. like* CONNAÎTRE) to appear, to come into sight; to make a show, to seem, to look like; to come out, to be published; ***à ce qu'il paraît***, as it would seem.
parallèle [para'lɛl], *a.* parallel.—*n.f.* parallel line.—*n.m.* parallel, comparison; (*Geog.*) parallel of latitude.
parallèlement [paralɛl'mɑ̃], *adv.* in a parallel way *or* direction.
parallélogramme [paralelɔ'gram], *n.m.* parallelogram.
paralysateur [paraliza'tœ:r] (*fem.* **-trice**), **paralysant** [parali'zɑ̃], *a.* paralysing.
paralyser [parali'ze], *v.t.* to paralyse.
paralysie [parali'zi], *n.f.* paralysis, palsy.
paralytique [parali'tik], *a.* and *n.* paralytic.
parangon [parɑ̃'gɔ̃], *n.m.* model, paragon; comparison; flawless precious stone.
paranoïa [paranɔ'ja], *n.f.* (*Med.*) paranoia.
parapet [para'pɛ], *n.m.* parapet.
paraphrase [para'frɑ:z], *n.f.* paraphrase, amplification.
paraphraser [parafrɑ'ze], *v.t.* to paraphrase; to amplify.
parapluie [para'plɥi], *n.m.* umbrella.
parasite [para'zit], *a.* parasitic; superfluous; extraneous.—*n.m.* parasite; (*fig.*) hanger-on; (*pl.*) (*Rad.*) atmospherics.
parasol [para'sɔl], *n.m.* sunshade.
paratonnerre [paratɔ'nɛ:r], *n.m.* lightning-conductor.
paratyphoïde [paratifɔ'id], *a.* and *n.f.* (*Med.*) paratyphoid (fever).
paravent [para'vɑ̃], *n.m.* folding-screen; (*fig.*) screen.
parbleu! [par'blø], *int.* by Jove! why, of course!
parc [park], *n.m.* park; pen; ***parc à huîtres***, oyster-bed; ***parc d'attractions***, fun fair.
parcage [par'ka:ʒ], *n.m.* folding (*of sheep*); penning (*of cattle*); parking (*of cars*).
parcellaire [parsɛ'lɛ:r], *a.* by small portions, by lots, in detail.
parcelle [par'sɛl], *n.f.* portion; particle; piece (*of land*).
parceller [parsɛ'le], *v.t.* to portion *or* parcel out.
parce que [parsə'kə, pars'kə], *conj.* because, as.—*n.m. inv.* ***les pourquoi et les parce que***, the whys and the wherefores.
parchemin [parʃə'mɛ̃], *n.m.* parchment; (*fam.*) diploma; (*pl.*) titles of nobility.
parcimonie [parsimɔ'ni], *n.f.* parsimony.
parcimonieusement [parsimɔnjøz'mɑ̃], *adv.* parsimoniously.
parcimonieux [parsimɔ'njø], *a.* (*fem.* **-euse**) parsimonious, stingy.
(*C*) **parcomètre** [parko'mɛtr], *n.m.* parking-meter.
parcourir [parku'ri:r], *v.t. irr.* (*conjug. like* COURIR) to travel through; to run over *or* through, to scour; to look over; to peruse, to glance through (*a book*).
parcours [par'ku:r], *n.m.* line, course, road, way; route (*of bus*); distance; course (*golf*).
par-dessous [pardə'su], *prep.* and *adv.* under, beneath, underneath.
par-dessus [pardə'sy], *prep.* and *adv.* over, above.

pardessus [pardə'sy], *n.m.* overcoat.
pardon [par'dɔ̃], *n.m.* pardon, forgiveness; pilgrimage (*in Brittany*); ***pardon !*** excuse me!
pardonnable [pardɔ'nabl] *a.* pardonable, excusable.
pardonner [pardɔ'ne], *v.t.* to pardon, to forgive; to overlook; to excuse.
paré [pa're], *a.* adorned, got up; dressed.
pare-boue [par'bu], *n.m. inv.* mud-guard.
pare-brise [par'bri:z], *n.m. inv.* wind-screen (*of motor-car*).
pare-chocs [par'ʃɔk], *n.m. inv.* bumper (*of car*).
pare-étincelles [paretɛ̃'sɛl], *n.m. inv.* fire-screen, fire-guard.
pareil [pa'rɛ:j], *a.* (*fem.* **-eille**) like, equal, similar; such, like that; same, identical.—*n.m.* (*fem.* **-eille**) similar *or* equal person. —*n.m.* equal, fellow.—*n.f.* (**-eille**) the like, tit for tat.
pareillement [parɛj'mɑ̃], *adv.* in like manner; likewise, also.
parement [par'mɑ̃], *n.m.* ornament; facing (*of dress*); cuff (*of sleeves*); (*Build.*) kerbstone.
parent [pa'rɑ̃], *n.m.* (*fem.* **-e**) relative, kinsman, kinswoman; (*pl.*) parents, relations, relatives; ***être parent***, to be related; ***parents par alliance***, related by marriage.
parenté [parɑ̃'te], *n.f.* relationship, kinship; relatives, kith and kin.
parenthèse [parɑ̃'tɛ:z], *n.f.* parenthesis, digression; (*Print.*) bracket.
parer [pa're], *v.t.* to adorn, to set off, to embellish; to attire, to trim; (*Box.*) to parry; to shelter, to guard.—*v.i.* to fend, to guard (*against*). **se parer**, *v.r.* to adorn oneself; to deck oneself out; to screen *or* guard oneself, to ward off.
pare-soleil [parsɔ'lɛ:j], *n.m. inv.* (*Motor.*) sun-visor.
paresse [pa'rɛs], *n.f.* idleness, sloth, laziness, indolence.
paresser [parɛ'se], *v.i.* to idle, to fritter away one's time.
paresseusement [parɛsøz'mɑ̃], *adv.* lazily, idly.
paresseux [parɛ'sø], *a.* (*fem.* **-euse**) lazy, idle, slothful.—*n.m.* (*fem.* **-euse**) sluggard, lazy person.—*n.m.* (*Zool.*) sloth.
parfaire [par'fɛ:r], *v.t. irr.* (*conjug. like* FAIRE) to complete, to perfect.
parfait [par'fɛ], *a.* perfect, faultless; complete, full.—*n.m.* perfection; (*Gram.*) perfect; ***un parfait au café***, a coffee ice-cream.
parfaitement [parfɛt'mɑ̃], *adv.* perfectly, completely; exactly, just so, decidedly.
parfilage [parfi'la:ʒ], *n.m.* unravelling.
parfois [par'fwa], *adv.* sometimes, occasionally.
parfum [par'fœ̃], *n.m.* perfume, odour, scent.
parfumer [parfy'me], *v.t.* to perfume, to sweeten, to scent; to fumigate. **se parfumer** *v.r.* to use perfume, to scent oneself.
parfumerie [parfym'ri], *n.f.* perfumery.
pari [pa'ri], *n.m.* bet, wager, stake; ***pari mutuel***, totalizator, (*fam.*) tote.
paria [pa'rja], *n.m.* pariah, outcast.
parier [pa'rje], *v.t.* to bet, to stake.
parieur [pa'rjœ:r], *n.m.* (*fem.* **-euse**) punter; backer.
parisien [pari'zjɛ̃], *a.* (*fem.* **-enne**) Parisian.—*n.m.* (**Parisien**, *fem.* **-enne**) Parisian (*person*).
parité [pari'te], *n.f.* parity, likeness, equality; (*Fin.*) par.
parjure [par'ʒy:r], *a.* perjured.—*n.m.* perjury, false oath.—*n.* perjurer.
parjurer (**se**) [səparʒy're], *v.r.* to perjure oneself.
parking [par'kiŋ], *n.m.* parking place, car park.
parlant [par'lɑ̃], *a.* speaking; (*colloq.*) talkative.
parlement [parlə'mɑ̃], *n.m.* parliament.
parlementaire [parləmɑ̃'tɛ:r], *a.* parliamentary.—*n.m.* bearer of a flag of truce; parliamentarian.
parlementer [parləmɑ̃'te], *v.i.* to parley, to come to terms.
parler [par'le], *v.t.* to speak, to talk.—*v.i.* to speak, to talk; to discourse, to converse, to treat (*de*); (*pop.*) ***tu parles !*** you're telling me! **se parler**, *v.r.* to be spoken; to talk to oneself; to talk to each other.—*n.m.* speech.
parleur [par'lœ:r], *n.m.* (*fem.* **-euse**) glib talker.
parloir [par'lwa:r], *n.m.* parlour (*of convent, school, prison*).
parmentier [parmɑ̃'tje], *a.* and *n.m.* ***potage parmentier***, thick potato soup.
parmesan [parmə'zɑ̃], *n.m.* Parmesan (*cheese*).
parmi [par'mi], *prep.* among, amongst, amid, amidst.
parodie [parɔ'di], *n.f.* parody.
parodier [parɔ'dje], *v.t.* to parody, to burlesque.
paroi [pa'rwɑ], *n.f.* wall; partition; inner surface; lining; (*Theat.*) flat.
paroisse [pa'rwɑs], *n.f.* parish; (*collect.*) parishioners.
paroissial [parwɑ'sjal], *a.* (*m. pl.* **-aux**) parochial, parish.
paroissien [parwɑ'sjɛ̃], *n.m.* (*fem.* **-enne**) parishioner.—*n.m.* prayer-book.
parole [pa'rɔl], *n.f.* (spoken) word; speech, utterance, voice; eloquence; promise; parole; ***engager sa parole***, to pledge one's word; ***manquer à sa parole***, to break one's word; ***tenir parole***, to keep one's word.
paroxysme [parɔk'sism], *n.m.* paroxysm; culminating point.
parpaing [par'pɛ̃], *n.m.* (*Build.*) breeze-block.
parquer [par'ke], *v.t.* to fold, to pen; to enclose; (*Motor.*) to park.—*v.i.* to be penned up (*of cattle etc.*). **se parquer**, *v.r.* to be placed in an enclosure.
parquet [par'kɛ], *n.m.* well (*of a court of justice*); prosecuting magistrates; (inlaid) floor.
parquetage [parkə'ta:ʒ], *n.m.* making a floor; flooring.
parqueter [parkə'te], *v.t.* (*conjug. like* APPELER) to floor, to lay a floor.
parqueterie [parkə'tri], *n.f.* floor-making; inlaid flooring.

parrain [pa'rɛ̃], *n.m.* godfather, sponsor; proposer.

parricide [pari'sid], *a.* parricidal.—*n.* parricide (*person*).—*n.m.* parricide *crime*).

parsemer [parsə'me], *v.t.* (*conjug. like* AMENER) to strew, to sprinkle; to be strewn on, to stud, to spangle.

parsi [par'si], *a.* Parsee.—*n.m.* (**Parsi**, *fem.* **-ie**) Parsee (*person*).

part [pa:r], *n.f.* share, part; concern, interest; place (*where*); ***à part***, aside; apart from; ***de part en part***, through and through; ***de toutes parts***, on all sides; ***dites-lui de ma part***, tell him from me; ***nulle part***, nowhere; ***quelque part***, somewhere (or other).

partage [par'ta:ʒ], *n.m.* sharing, share; partition.

partageable [parta'ʒabl], *a.* divisible into shares.

partageant [parta'ʒɑ̃], *n.m.* (*fem.* **-e**) (*Law*) sharer.

partager [parta'ʒe], *v.t.* (*conjug. like* MANGER) to divide, to share out; to participate in; to endow.—*v.i.* to share, to receive a share. **se partager**, *v.r.* to divide, to be divided.

partance [par'tɑ:s], *n.f.* (*Naut.*) sailing, departure; ***en partance pour***, bound for.

partant [par'tɑ̃], *adv.* consequently, hence, therefore.—*n.m.* (*Turf*) starter.

partenaire [partə'nɛ:r], *n.* (*Spt. etc.*) partner.

parterre [par'tɛ:r], *n.m.* flower-bed; (*Theat.*) pit.

parti [par'ti], *n.m.* (*Polit.*) party; part, cause; resolution, course; profit, advantage; match (*marriage*); (*Mil.*) detachment; ***parti pris***, set purpose; rank prejudice; ***le parti conservateur***, the Conservative party; ***le parti travailliste***, the Labour party.

partial [par'sjal], *a.* (*m. pl.* **-aux**) partial, biased.

partialement [parsjal'mɑ̃], *adv.* partially, with partiality.

partialité [parsjali'te], *n.f.* partiality, bias.

participant [partisi'pɑ̃], *a.* participating.—*n.m.* (*fem.* **-e**) participant, sharer.

participation [partisipɑ'sjɔ̃], *n.f.* participation, share.

participe [parti'sip], *n.m.* (*Gram.*) participle.

participer [partisi'pe], *v.i.* to participate in, to share in; to be a party to (***à***); to partake of (*de*).

particularité [partikylari'te], *n.f.* peculiarity; particular circumstance.

particule [parti'kyl], *n.f.* particle.

particulier [partiky'lje], *a.* (*fem.* **-ière**) particular, peculiar; private; special; singular; personal.—*n.m.* (*fem.* **-ière**) private person, individual; (*colloq.*) fellow.

particulièrement [partikyljɛr'mɑ̃], *adv.* particularly, especially.

partie [par'ti] *n.f.* part (*of a whole*); line of business; party, amusement; game, match; client; opponent; (*Law*) party; (*Comm.*) parcel; ***partie nulle***, drawn game.

partiel [par'sjɛl], *a.* (*fem.* **-elle**) partial.

partiellement [parsjɛl'mɑ̃], *adv.* partially, in part.

partir [par'ti:r], *v.i. irr.* (*with aux.* ÊTRE) to set out, to start, to depart, to leave; to rise (*of birds*); to proceed, to emanate (*from*); to go off (*of firearms*); ***à partir d'aujourd'hui***, from this day forward.

partisan [parti'zɑ̃], *n.m.* (*fem.* **-e**) partisan.

partition [parti'sjɔ̃], *n.f.* (*Her.*) partition; (*Mus.*) score.

partout [par'tu], *adv.* everywhere, on all sides.

parure [pa'ry:r], *n.f.* attire, dress, finery, ornament.

parvenir [parvə'ni:r], *v.i. irr.* (*conjug. like* TENIR *but with aux.* ÊTRE) to attain, to reach; to succeed; to get; to arrive; to rise in the world.

parvenu [parvə'ny], *n.m.* (*fem.* **-e**) upstart, self-made person.

parvis [par'vi], *n.m.* parvis, open space (*in front of a church*); (*Poet.*) hall, temple.

pas (1) [pɑ], *n.m. inv.* step, pace; footprint; gait; dance; precedence; threshold; step of stair; strait, pass; thread (*of screw*); ***aller à pas mesurés***, to proceed with circumspection; ***au pas***, at a walking pace; in step; ***faire un faux pas***, to stumble, (*fig.*) to blunder; ***le pas de Calais***, the Straits of Dover; ***pas à pas***, slowly, little by little.

pas (2) [pɑ], *adv.* no; not; ***pas du tout***, not at all.

pascal [pas'kal], *a.* (*m. pl.* **-aux**) paschal.

passable [pɑ'sabl], *a.* passable, tolerable; (*fig.*) middling, so-so.

passablement [pɑsablə'mɑ̃], *adv.* fairly, passably.

passade [pɑ'sad], *n.f.* short stay; (*fig.*) passing fancy.

passage [pɑ'sa:ʒ], *n.m.* passage, transit; thoroughfare; arcade; crossing (*on railway etc.*); ***passage clouté***, pedestrian crossing.

passager [pɑsa'ʒe], *a.* (*fem.* **-ère**) passing, transitory, short-lived; migratory.—*n.m.* (*fem.* **-ère**) passenger (*by sea* or *air*); passer-by.

passagèrement [pɑsaʒɛr'mɑ̃], *adv.* transiently.

passant [pɑ'sɑ̃], *a.* much-frequented.—*n.m.* (*fem.* **-e**) passer-by, wayfarer.

passavant [pɑsa'vɑ̃], *n.m.* pass, permit; (*Naut.*) gangway.

passe [pɑs], *n.f.* passing, passage; permit, pass; situation, state; (*Fenc.*) thrust; channel, narrow passage (*of harbours, rivers etc.*); stake (*at play*); (*Ftb.*) pass; ***être dans une mauvaise passe***, to be in a fix; ***en passe de***, in a fair way to.

passé [pɑ'se], *a.* past, bygone; faded, worn, withered.—*n.m.* past, past life, time past.—*prep.* after, beyond.

passée [pɑ'se], *n.f.* (*Hunt.*) flight, passage (*of woodcock etc.*).

passefiler [pɑsfi'le], *v.t.* to darn.

passement [pɑs'mɑ̃], *n.m.* lace (*of gold, silk etc.*).

passe-partout [pɑspar'tu], *n.m. inv.* master-key; latch-key; passe-partout (*frame*); cross-cut saw.

passeport [pɑs'pɔ:r], *n.m.* passport.

passer [pɑ'se], *v.t.* (*takes the auxiliary* AVOIR *or* ÊTRE *according as action or condition is implied*) to pass; to cross, to go over; to transport; to strain (*liquids*); to sift (*flour*); to put on (*wearing apparel*); to omit; to waive; to allow; to spend (*time*); to take (*an examination*).—*v.i.* to pass to pass on;

to pass away; to die; to pass for; to fade. **se passer**, *v.r.* to pass, to pass away; to fade; to happen; to do without (*de*).
passereau [pɑs'ro], *n.m.* (*pl.* **-eaux**) sparrow.
passerelle [pɑs'rɛl], *n.f.* foot-bridge; (*Naut.*) bridge, gangway.
passe-temps [pɑs'tɑ̃], *n.m. inv.* pastime, hobby.
passeur [pɑ'sœ:r], *n.m.* (*fem.* **-euse**) ferryman, ferrywoman.
passibilité [pɑsibili'te], *n.f.* liability.
passible [pɑ'sibl], *a.* passible; liable (*to*).
passif [pɑ'sif], *a.* (*fem.* **-ive**) passive; (*Comm.*) on debit side.—*n.m.* (*Gram.*) passive; (*Comm.*) liabilities.
passion [pɑ'sjɔ̃], *n.f.* suffering, agony; passion, *esp.* love; (*fig.*) fondness.
passionnant [pɑsjɔ'nɑ̃], *a.* exciting, thrilling.
passionné [pɑsjɔ'ne], *a.* passionate, impassioned, very fond of (*de*).
passionnel [pɑsjɔ'nɛl], *a.* (*fem.* **-elle**) ***crime passionnel***, crime due to jealous love.
passionnément [pɑsjɔne'mɑ̃], *adv.* passionately, fondly.
passionner [pɑsjɔ'ne], *v.t.* to impassion, to interest deeply. **se passionner**, *v.r.* to be passionately fond of; to become enamoured of.
passivement [pɑsiv'mɑ̃], *adv.* passively.
passiveté [pɑsiv'te], **passivité** [pɑsivi'te], *n.f.* passivity.
passoire [pɑ'swa:r], *n.f.* strainer.
pastel [pas'tɛl], *n.m.* pastel, crayon.
pastèque [pas'tɛk], *n.f.* water-melon.
pasteur [pas'tœ:r], *n.m.* pastor, (*Protestant*) minister; clergyman.
pasteurisation [pastœriza'sjɔ̃], *n.f.* pasteurization.
pasteuriser [pastœri'ze], *v.t.* to pasteurize.
pastiche [pas'tiʃ], *n.m.* pastiche; (*Mus.*) medley.
pastille [pas'ti:j], *n.f.* pastille; lozenge; rubber patch (*for tubes of tyre*).
pastoral [pastɔ'ral] *a.* (*m. pl.* **-aux**) pastoral. —*n.f.* (**-e**) pastoral (*play* or *poem*).
patapouf [pata'puf], *int.* ***faire patapouf***, to fall flop.—*n.m.* ***gros patapouf***, fat fellow, fatty.
patate [pa'tat], *n.f.* sweet potato.
patati [pata'ti], *only used in the phrase*, ***et patati et patata***, and so on and so forth.
patatras! [pata'tra], *int.* crack! slap! bang!
pataud [pa'to], *a.* awkward, clumsy.—*n.m.* (*fem.* **-e**) pup with large paws; (*fig.*) lout, clumsy person.
patauger [pato'ʒe], *v.i.* (*conjug. like* MANGER) to splash, to flounder.
pâte [pɑ:t], *n.f.* paste; dough, batter; (*fig.*) kind, sort; (*Print.*) pie.
pâté [pɑ'te], *n.m.* pie, pasty, patty; blot (*of ink*); block (*of buildings*); (*Print.*) pie.
pâtée [pɑ'te], *n.f.* mash (*to fatten poultry*); mess (*for dogs* or *cats*).
patelin [pa'tlɛ̃], *a.* smooth-tongued, wheedling.—*n.m.* (*fem.* **-e**) wheedler.—*n.m.* (*fam.*) village.
patent [pa'tɑ̃], *a.* patent; obvious, manifest.
patenté [patɑ̃'te], *a.* licensed.—*n.m.* (*fem.* **-ée**) licensed dealer.
patenter [patɑ̃'te], *v.t.* to license.
patère [pa'tɛ:r], *n.f.* coat-hook; curtain-hook.
paternel [patɛr'nɛl], *a.* (*fem.* **-elle**) paternal, fatherly.
paternité [patɛrni'te], *n.f.* paternity, fatherhood.
pâteux [pɑ'tø], *a.* (*fem.* **-euse**) pasty, clammy, sticky.
pathétique [pate'tik], *a.* pathetic, moving.—*n.m.* pathos.
pathétiquement [patetik'mɑ̃], *adv.* pathetically.
pathologie [patɔlɔ'ʒi], *n.f.* pathology.
pathologiste [patɔlɔ'ʒist], *n.m.* pathologist.
pathos [pa'tɔ:s], *n.m.* bathos; (*fig.*) bombast.
patiemment [pasja'mɑ̃], *adv.* patiently.
patience [pa'sjɑ̃:s], *n.f.* patience, endurance.
patient [pa'sjɑ̃], *a.* patient, enduring, forbearing.—*n.m.* (*fem.* **-e**) sufferer; (*Med.*) patient.
patienter [pasjɑ̃'te], *v.i.* to be patient.
patin [pa'tɛ̃], *n.m.* skate; flange (*of rail*); skid (*of aeroplane*); shoe (*of brake*); ***patins à roulettes***, roller skates.
patinage [pati'na:ʒ], *n.m.* skating; skidding (*of locomotive, car etc.*).
patine [pa'tin], *n.f.* patina (*of bronze*).
patiner [pati'ne], *v.i.* to skate; to skid (*of wheels*).
patinette [pati'nɛt], *n.f.* scooter.
patineur [pati'nœ:r], *n.m.* (*fem.* **-euse**) skater.
patinoire [pati'nwa:r], *n.f.* skating-rink.
pâtir [pɑ'ti:r], *v.i.* to suffer; to be in distress.
pâtisser [pɑti'se], *v.t.*, to knead (*flour*).—*v.i.* to knead; to make pastry.
pâtisserie [pɑtis'ri], *n.f.* pastry, fancy cake; pastry-cook's shop *or* business.
pâtissier [pɑti'sje], *n.m.* (*fem.* **-ière**) pastry-cook.—*a.f.* (**-ière**) ***crème pâtissière***, custard.
patois [pa'twa], *n.m. inv.* patois, provincial dialect; brogue; jargon.
patouiller [patu'je], [PATAUGER].
patraque [pa'trak], *a.* seedy, broken-down.—*n.f.* old crock.
pâtre [pɑ:tr], *n.m.* herdsman, shepherd.
patriarcal [patriar'kal], *a.* (*m. pl.* **-aux**) patriarchal.
patriarche [patri'arʃ], *n.m.* patriarch.
Patrice [pa'tris], *m.* Patrick.
patrice [pa'tris], *n.m.* patrician.
patricien [patri'sjɛ̃], *a.* and *n.m.* (*fem.* **-enne**) patrician.
patrie [pa'tri], *n.f.* native land, fatherland.
patrimoine [patri'mwan], *n.m.* patrimony, inheritance.
patriote [patri'ɔt], *a.* patriotic (*person*).—*n.* patriot.
patriotique [patriɔ'tik], *a.* patriotic (*song, speech etc.*).
patriotisme [patriɔ'tism], *n.m.* patriotism.
patron (1) [pa'trɔ̃], *n.m.* pattern, model.
patron (2) [pa'trɔ̃], *n.m.* (*fem.* **-onne**) patron; master, mistress, employer; proprietor; (*colloq.*) boss; (*Naut.*) skipper, coxswain.
patronage [patrɔ'na:ʒ], *n.m.* patronage.
patronat [patrɔ'na], *n.m.* management.
patronner [patrɔ'ne], *v.t.* to patronize; to support.
patrouille [pa'tru:j], *n.f.* patrol.
patrouiller [patru'je], *v.i.* to patrol.
patrouilleur [patru'jœ:r], *n.m.* (*Naut.*) patrol-boat.
patte [pat], *n.f.* paw (*of quadruped*); foot (*of bird*); leg (*of insect*); bracket, cramp; flap (*of pocket etc.*); tab, strap (*of clothes*); (*fig.*) claws, clutches.

pâturage [pɑty'ra:ʒ], *n.m.* pasture.
pâture [pɑ'ty:r], *n.f.* food (*for animals*); pasture; fodder.
pâturer [pɑty're], *v.t.* to graze on.—*v.i.* to pasture, to graze, to feed.
pâturon or **paturon** [pɑty'rɔ̃], *n.m.* pastern.
paume [po:m], *n.f.* palm (*of the hand*); ***jeu de paume***, (*court*) tennis, 'real' tennis.
paupérisme [pope'rism], *n.m.* pauperism.
paupière [po'pjɛ:r], *n.f.* eyelid; (*fig.*) eye(s).
pause [po:z], *n.f.* pause, stop; (*Mus.*) rest.
pauser [po'ze], *v.i.* to pause.
pauvre [po:vr], *a.* poor, needy; wretched, paltry, mean.—*n.m.* poor person pauper; beggar.
pauvrement [povrə'mɑ̃], *adv.* poorly, wretchedly.
pauvresse [po'vrɛs], *n.f.* poor woman, beggar-woman.
pauvret [po'vrɛ], *n.m.* (*fem.* **-ette**) poor creature, poor little thing.
pauvreté [povrə'te], *n.f.* poverty; wretchedness; sorry thing.
pavage [pa'va:ʒ], *n.m.* paving; pavement.
pavane [pa'van], *n.f.* pavan (*dance*).
pavaner (se) [səpava'ne], *v.r.* to strut, to stalk proudly.
pavé [pa've], *a.* paved.—*n.m.* paving-stone; paved part of road; (*fig.*) road, street(s).
pavement [pav'mɑ̃], *n.m.* paving; flooring.
paver [pa've], *v.t.* to pave.
paveur [pa'vœ:r], *n.m.* paviour.
pavillon [pavi'jɔ̃], *n.m.* pavilion, tent; summerhouse; detached house; wing (*of a house*), outhouse, lodge; (*Naut.*) flag.
pavoiser [pavwa'ze], *v.t.* to deck with flags, to dress (*ship*).
pavot [pa'vo], *n.m.* poppy.
payable [pɛ'jabl], *a.* payable.
payant [pɛ'jɑ̃], *a.* paying; to be paid for.—*n.m.* (*fem.* **-e**) payer.
paye [pɛ:j], **paie** [pɛ], *n.f.* pay, wages.
payement or **paiement** [pɛ'mɑ̃], *n.m.* payment.
payer [pɛ'je], *v.t.* (*see Verb Tables*) to pay (for); to reward; to expiate, to atone for. **se payer**, *v.r.* to be paid *or* satisfied; to treat oneself to.
payeur [pɛ'jœ:r], *n.m.* (*fem.* **-euse**) payer; pay-clerk; (*Mil.*) pay-master.
pays [pe'i], *n.m. inv.* country, land; region, district; fatherland, home; ***avoir le mal du pays***, to be home-sick; ***pays perdu***, out-of-the-way place.
paysage [pei'za:ʒ], *n.m.* landscape, scenery.
paysagiste [peiza'ʒist], *a.* and *n.m.* landscape (-painter).
paysan [pei'zɑ̃], *a.* (*fem.* **-anne**) rustic.—*n.m.* (*fem.* **-anne**) peasant, countryman, countrywoman; farmer.
paysannerie [peizan'ri], *n.f.* rusticity; peasantry.
Pays-Bas [pei'bɑ], **les**, *m.pl.* the Netherlands.
péage [pe'a:ʒ], *n.m.* toll; toll-house.
péan or **pæan** [pe'ɑ̃], *n.m.* pæan, song of triumph *or* joy.
peau [po] *n.f.* (*pl.* **peaux**) skin; hide; peel, rind.
Peau-Rouge [po'ru:ʒ], *n.* (*pl.* **Peaux-Rouges**) Redskin, Red Indian.
peccadille [pɛka'di:j], *n.f.* peccadillo.
pêche (1) [pɛ:ʃ], *n.f.* peach.
pêche (2) [pɛ:ʃ], *n.f.* fishing, angling.
péché [pe'ʃe], *n.m.* sin, transgression.
pécher [pe'ʃe], *v.i.* (*conjug. like* CÉDER) to sin, to transgress; to offend; to be deficient.
pêcher (1) [pe'ʃe], *n.m.* peach-tree.
pêcher (2) [pe'ʃe], *v.t.* to fish for; to drag out; (*fig.*) to get hold of.—*v.i.* to fish, to angle.
pécheresse [peʃ'rɛs], [PÉCHEUR].
pêcherie [pɛʃ'ri], *n.f.* fishing-ground, fishery.
pécheur [pe'ʃœ:r], *n.m.* (*fem.* **-eresse**) sinner.
pêcheur [pɛ'ʃœ:r], *n.m.* (*fem.* **-euse**) fisher, fisherman, fisherwoman.
pécore [pe'kɔ:r], *n.f.* stupid creature, blockhead; *esp.* silly girl.
pécule [pe'kyl], *n.m.* savings; earnings (*of a prisoner*).
pécuniaire [peky'njɛ:r], *a.* pecuniary.
pédagogie [pedagɔ'ʒi], *n.f.* pedagogy.
pédagogue [peda'gɔg], *n.* pedagogue.
pédale [pe'dal], *n.f.* pedal; treadle.
pédaler [peda'le], *v.i.* to pedal; (*colloq.*) to cycle.
pédant [pe'dɑ̃], *a.* pedantic.—*n.m.* (*fem.* **-e**) pedant.
pédanterie [pedɑ̃'tri], *n.f.* pedantry.
pédantesque [pedɑ̃'tɛsk], *a.* pedantic.
pédantisme [pedɑ̃'tism], *n.m.* pedantry.
pédestre [pe'dɛstr], *a.* pedestrian, on foot.
pédestrement [pedɛstrə'mɑ̃], *adv.* on foot.
pédicure [pedi'ky:r], *n.* chiropodist.
Pégase [pe'gɑ:z], *m.* Pegasus.
peignage [pɛ'ɲa:ʒ], *n.m.* combing, wool-combing.
peigne [pɛɲ], *n.m.* comb.
peigné [pɛ'ɲe], *a.* combed; (*fig.*) arranged.—*n.m.* worsted.
peigner [pɛ'ɲe], *v.t.* to comb; to card; (*fig.*) to polish (*style*). **se peigner**, *v.r.* to comb one's hair.
peignoir [pɛ'ɲwa:r], *n.m.* dressing-gown; (*Am.*) bath-robe.
peindre [pɛ̃:dr], *v.t. irr.* (*conjug. like* CRAINDRE) to paint, to portray; to represent, to express; ***se faire peindre***, to sit for one's portrait. **se peindre**, *v.r.* to paint oneself; to be represented.
peine [pɛn], *n.f.* punishment, penalty; pain, grief, sorrow; anxiety; trouble; difficulty; reluctance; ***à peine***, hardly, scarcely; ***un homme de peine***, an unskilled labourer.
peiné [pɛ'ne], *a.* pained, grieved; laboured; elaborate.
peiner [pɛ'ne], *v.t.* to pain, to trouble, to grieve; (*fig.*) to elaborate.—*v.i.* to labour, to toil; to be reluctant.
peintre [pɛ̃:tr], *n.m.* painter.
peinture [pɛ̃'ty:r], *n.f.* painting; picture; description, appearance; paint, colour.
péjoratif [peʒɔra'tif], *a.* (*fem.* **-tive**) pejorative.
Pékin [pe'kɛ̃], *m.* Peking.
pékinois [peki'nwa], *a.* Pekinese.—*n.m.* Pekinese (*dog*); (**Pékinois**, *fem.* **-oise**) Pekinese (*person*).
pelage [pə'la:ʒ], *n.m.* hair, fur, coat (*of animal*).
pelé [pə'le], *a.* bald; which has lost its hair (*animals*).—*n.m.* (*fem.* **-ée**) bald-headed person.
pêle-mêle [pɛl'mɛl], *adv.* pell-mell, higgledy-piggledy.—*n.m. inv.* disorder, jumble.

peler [pə'le], *v.t.* (*conjug. like* AMENER) to skin, to peel.—*v.i.* to peel off (*of the skin etc.*). **se peler**, *v.r.* to come off, to peel.
pèlerin [pɛl'rɛ̃], *n.m.* (*fem.* **-ine** (1)) pilgrim; peregrine falcon; basking shark.
pèlerinage [pɛlri'na:ʒ], *n.m.* pilgrimage.
pèlerine (2) [pɛl'rin], *n.f.* tippet, cape (*with hood*).
pélican [peli'kɑ̃], *n.m.* pelican.
pelisse [pə'lis], *n.f.* pelisse; fur-lined coat.
pelle [pɛl], *n.f.* shovel, scoop, blade (*of an oar*); (*fam.*) spill, cropper.
pelletée [pɛl'te], *n.f.* shovelful.
pelleter [pɛl'te], *v.t.* (*conjug. like* APPELER) to shovel.
pelletier [pɛl'tje], *n.m.* (*fem.* **-ière**) furrier.
pellicule [pɛli'kyl], *n.f.* pellicle; (*Phot.*) film; (*pl.*) scurf (*of scalp*), dandruff.
pelotage [pəlɔ'ta:ʒ], *n.m.* winding skeins into balls; (*Billiards, Ten.*) knock-up.
pelote [pə'lɔt], *n.f.* ball; ball of thread; pellet; pin-cushion; (*Spt.*) ***pelote basque***, pelota.
peloter [pəlɔ'te], *v.t.* to make *or* wind into a ball.—*v.i.* (*Spt.*) to knock up.
peloton [pəlɔ'tɔ̃], *n.m.* ball; cluster (*of bees*); (*Mil.*) squad; (*Racing*) bunch (*of runners*).
pelotonner [pəlɔtɔ'ne], *v.t.* to wind into balls. **se pelotonner**, *v.r.* to roll oneself up; to curl up.
pelouse [pə'lu:z], *n.f.* lawn, greensward.
peluche [pə'lyʃ], *n.f.* plush.
peluché [pəly'ʃe], *a.* shaggy.
pelucher [pəly'ʃe], *v.i.* to become shaggy, to wear rough.
pelucheux [pəly'ʃø], *a.* (*fem.* **-euse**) shaggy; fluffy.
pelure [pə'ly:r], *n.f.* paring; peel, skin; rind.
pénal [pe'nal], *a.* (*m. pl.* **-aux**) penal.
pénaliser [penali'ze], *v.t.* to penalize.
pénalité [penali'te], *n.f.* penal law; penalty.
pénates [pe'nat], *n.m. pl.* penates, household gods; (*fig.*) home.
penaud [pə'no], *a.* abashed, sheepish, crest-fallen.
penchant [pɑ̃'ʃɑ̃], *a.* inclined, sloping, leaning.—*n.m.* declivity, slope; inclination, bent.
pencher [pɑ̃'ʃe], *v.t.* to incline, to bend.—*v.i.* to lean; to tilt, to slope. **se pencher**, *v.r.* to bend, to stoop; to slope, to be inclined.
pendable [pɑ̃'dabl], *a.* deserving hanging, abominable.
pendaison [pɑ̃dɛ'zɔ̃], *n.f.* hanging (*on the gallows*), death by hanging.
pendant [pɑ̃'dɑ̃], *a.* pendent, hanging; pending; depending.—*n.m.* thing hanging, pendant; counterpart.—*prep.* during; for; ***pendant que***, while, whilst.
pendard [pɑ̃'da:r], *n.m.* (*fem.* **-e**) (*colloq.*) rascal, rogue, jade.
pendeloque [pɑ̃'dlɔk], *n.f.* ear-drop; pendant.
pendiller [pɑ̃di'je], *v.i.* to hang loose, to dangle.
pendre [pɑ̃:dr], *v.t.* to hang, to hang up, to suspend.—*v.i.* to hang; to dangle, to droop. **se pendre**, *v.r.* to hang oneself.
pendu [pɑ̃'dy], *a.* hanging; hanged; hung.—*n.m.* (*fem.* **-e**) one that has been hanged.
pendule [pɑ̃'dyl], *n.f.* clock, time-piece.—*n.m.* pendulum.
pêne [pɛ:n], *n.m.* bolt (*of a lock*).
pénétrabilité [penetrabili'te], *n.f.* penetrability.
pénétrable [pene'trabl], *a.* penetrable.
pénétrant [pene'trɑ̃], *a.* penetrating; piercing, keen; acute; impressive.
pénétration [penetrɑ'sjɔ̃], *n.f.* penetration; acuteness, shrewdness.
pénétré [pene'tre], *a.* penetrated; moved, impressed.
pénétrer [pene'tre], *v.t.* (*conjug. like* CÉDER) to penetrate, to go through; to pierce; to pervade; to fathom; to impress, to affect.—*v.i.* to penetrate (***dans***); to reach (***à***). **se pénétrer**, *v.r.* to penetrate each other; to be impressed.
pénible [pe'nibl], *a.* painful, laborious; troublesome.
péniblement [peniblə'mɑ̃], *adv.* laboriously.
pénicilline [penisi'lin], *n.f.* penicillin.
péninsulaire [penɛ̃sy'lɛ:r], *a.* peninsular.
péninsule [penɛ̃'syl], *n.f.* peninsula.
pénitence [peni'tɑ̃:s], *n.f.* penitence, repentance; penance; punishment.
pénitencier [penitɑ̃'sje], *a.* penitentiary.—*n.m.* penitentiary, reformatory.
pénitent [peni'tɑ̃], *a.* penitent, repentant.—*n.m.* (*fem.* **-e**) penitent.
pénitentiaire [penitɑ̃'sjɛ:r], *a.* penitentiary.
penne [pɛn], *n.f.* tail-feather, wing-feather.
penniforme [pɛni'fɔrm], *a.* penniform.
pennon [pɛ'nɔ̃], *n.m.* pennon.
pénombre [pe'nɔ̃:br], *n.f.* penumbra; semi-darkness, half-light.
pensée [pɑ̃'se], *n.f.* thought; opinion; idea, conception; meaning; (*Bot.*) pansy.
penser [pɑ̃'se], *v.t.* to think, to think of (***à*** or ***de***).—*v.i.* to think, to reflect, to consider; to expect; to take heed, to take care.—*n.m.* (*poet.*) inward reasoning, thought.
penseur [pɑ̃'sœ:r], *a.* (*fem.* **-euse**) thinking, thoughtful.—*n.m.* (*fem.* **-euse**) thinker.
pensif [pɑ̃'sif], *a.* (*fem.* **-sive**) pensive, thoughtful.
pension [pɑ̃'sjɔ̃], *n.f.* board and lodging; boarding-house; boarding-school; pension, allowance, annuity.
pensionnaire [pɑ̃sjɔ'nɛ:r], *n.* boarder; schoolboy *or* -girl; pensioner, resident.
pensionnat [pɑ̃sjɔ'na], *n.m.* private boarding-school.
pensionné [pɑ̃sjɔ'ne], *a.* pensioned.—*n.m.* (*fem.* **-ée**) pensioner.
pensionner [pɑ̃sjɔ'ne], *v.t.* to pension, to grant a pension to.
pensum [pɛ̃'sɔm], *n.m.* imposition, extra task (*at school*).
pente [pɑ̃:t], *n.f.* declivity, slope; acclivity, ascent; gradient; pitch (*of roofs*); (*fig.*) propensity, bent.
Pentecôte [pɑ̃t'ko:t], *n.f.* Pentecost, Whitsuntide.
pénultième [penyl'tjɛm], *a.* last but one, penultimate.
pénurie [peny'ri], *n.f.* scarcity, dearth; penury, want.
pépier [pe'pje], *v.i.* to chirp, to cheep.
pépin [pe'pɛ̃], *n.m.* pip (*of apple etc.*); stone (*of grape*).
pépinière [pepi'njɛ:r], *n.f.* nursery (*of trees*).
pépiniériste [pepinje'rist], *n.m.* nurseryman.
pépite [pe'pit], *n.f.* nugget (*of gold*).
pepsine [pɛp'sin], *n.f.* pepsine.

peptique [pɛp'tik], *a.* peptic.
percale [pɛr'kal], *n.f.* cotton cambric, percale.
percaline [pɛrka'lin], *n.f.* glazed calico *or* lining, percaline.
perçant [pɛr'sɑ̃], *a.* piercing; sharp; shrill, acute.
perce [pɛrs], *n.f.* piercer, borer.
percé [pɛr'se], *a.* pierced, bored, in holes.
percée [pɛr'se], *n.f.* opening, cutting (*in a wood*), vista, glade; (*fig.*) break-through.
percement [pɛrsə'mɑ̃], *n.m.* piercing, boring, perforation.
perce-neige [pɛrs'nɛ:ʒ], *n.f. inv.* snowdrop.
perce-oreille [pɛrsɔ'rɛ:j], *n.m.* (*pl.* **-oreilles**) earwig.
percepteur [pɛrsɛp'tœ:r], *n.m.* collector of taxes.
perceptible [pɛrsɛp'tibl], *a.* collectible; perceptible.
perceptiblement [pɛrsɛptiblə'mɑ̃], *adv.* perceptibly.
perceptif [pɛrsɛp'tif], *a.* (*fem.* **-tive**) perceptive.
perception [pɛrsɛp'sjɔ̃], *n.f.* perception; collecting, receipt; collectorship, collector's office.
percer [pɛr'se], *v.t.* (*conjug. like* COMMENCER) to pierce, to bore, to drill; to make an opening; to tunnel; to wet through (*of rain etc.*).—*v.i.* to pierce through, to come through; to transpire; to manifest itself. **se percer**, *v.r.* to pierce oneself, to be pierced.
perceur [pɛr'sœ:r], *n.m.* (*fem.* **-euse**) borer.—*n.f.* (**-euse**) boring-machine, drill.
percevoir [pɛrsə'vwa:r], *v.t. irr.* (*conjug. like* RECEVOIR) to collect (*taxes etc.*); (*Phil.*) to perceive.
perche [pɛrʃ], *n.f.* perch, pole; (*Ichth.*) perch.
perché [pɛr'ʃe], *a.* perched, perched up, roosting.
percher [pɛr'ʃe], *v.i.* and **se percher**, *v.r.* to perch, to roost.
percheur [pɛr'ʃœ:r], *a.* (*fem.* **-euse**) perching, roosting (*of birds*).
perchoir [pɛr'ʃwa:r], *n.m.* roost.
perclus [pɛr'kly], *a.* crippled, impotent.
percolateur [pɛrkola'tœ:r], *n.m.* percolator.
percussion [pɛrky'sjɔ̃], *n.f.* percussion.
percutant [pɛrky'tɑ̃], *a.* producing percussion; (*colloq.*) fabulous.
percuter [pɛrky'te], *v.t.* to strike; to percuss.—*v.i.* to crash.
perdable [pɛr'dabl], *a.* losable.
perdant [pɛr'dɑ̃], *a.* losing.—*n.m.* (*fem.* **-e**) loser.
perdition [pɛrdi'sjɔ̃], *n.f.* perdition.
perdre [pɛrdr], *v.t.* to lose, to be deprived of; to waste, to ruin, to corrupt, to lead astray.—*v.i.* to lose, to be a loser; to leak. **se perdre**, *v.r.* to be lost; to lose one's way, to be bewildered; to disappear.
perdreau [pɛr'dro], *n.m.* (*pl.* **-eaux**) young partridge.
perdrix [pɛr'dri], *n.f. inv.* partridge.
perdu [pɛr'dy], *a.* lost; ruined; spoilt; stray; obsolete; out of the way; bewildered; ***salle des pas perdus***, waiting hall (*in courts of law*).
père [pɛ:r], *n.m.* father; sire.
pérégrination [peregrinɑ'sjɔ̃], *n.f.* peregrination.
péremptoire [perɑ̃p'twa:r], *a.* peremptory.
péremptoirement [perɑ̃ptwar'mɑ̃], *adv.* peremptorily.
pérennité [perɛni'te], *n.f.* perpetuity.
perfectibilité [pɛrfɛktibili'te], *n.f.* perfectibility.
perfectible [pɛrfɛk'tibl], *a.* perfectible.
perfection [pɛrfɛk'sjɔ̃], *n.f.* perfection; faultlessness; completeness.
perfectionnement [pɛrfɛksjɔn'mɑ̃], *n.m.* improvement, perfecting.
perfectionner [pɛrfɛksjɔ'ne], *v.t.* to perfect; to improve. **se perfectionner**, *v.r.* to perfect oneself; to improve.
perfide [pɛr'fid], *a.* perfidious, treacherous, false.—*n.* perfidious *or* treacherous person.
perfidement [pɛrfid'mɑ̃], *adv.* perfidiously, falsely, treacherously.
perfidie [pɛrfi'di], *n.f.* perfidy, treachery.
perforage [pɛrfɔ'ra:ʒ], *n.m.* boring, perforation.
perforant [pɛrfɔ'rɑ̃], *a.* perforating, penetrating.
perforateur [pɛrfɔra'tœ:r], *a.* (*fem.* **-trice** (1)) perforative.—*n.m.* perforator.
perforation [pɛrfɔrɑ'sjɔ̃], *n.f.* perforation.
perforatrice (2) [pɛrfɔra'tris], *n.f.* drilling-machine.
perforer [pɛrfɔ're], *v.t.* to perforate, to bore, to drill.
péricliter [perikli'te], *v.i.* to be in jeopardy.
péril [pe'ril], *n.m.* peril, danger, hazard, risk.
périlleusement [perijøz'mɑ̃], *adv.* perilously.
périlleux [peri'jø], *a.* (*fem.* **-euse**) perilous, dangerous.
périmé [peri'me], *a.* out-of-date, no longer valid.
période [pe'rjɔd], *n.f.* period of time, era; (*Gram.*) period, sentence; (*Mus.*) phrase.—*n.m.* pitch, summit, degree, acme.
périodicité [perjɔdisi'te], *n.f.* periodicity.
périodique [perjɔ'dik], *a.* periodic, periodical.—*n.m.* periodical.
périodiquement [perjɔdik'mɑ̃], *adv.* periodically.
péripétie [peripe'si], *n.f.* sudden turn of fortune; (*pl.*) vicissitudes.
périr [pe'ri:r], *v.i.* to perish, to die; to be wrecked; to decay.
périscope [peris'kɔp], *n.m.* periscope.
périssable [peri'sabl], *a.* perishable.
péristyle [peris'til], *a.* and *n.m.* peristyle.
péritoine [peri'twan], *n.m.* peritoneum.
péritonite [peritɔ'nit], *n.f.* peritonitis.
perle [pɛrl], *n.f.* pearl; bead, bugle (*for bracelets, necklaces etc.*); (*fig.*) gem, jewel, the best.
perlé [pɛr'le], *a.* pearled, set with pearls; pearly.
perler [pɛr'le], *v.t.* to bead, to form into beads; to pearl.—*v.i.* to form beads (*of sweat etc.*).
perlier [pɛr'lje], *a.* (*fem.* **-ière**) of pearl.
permanence [pɛrma'nɑ̃:s], *n.f.* permanence; headquarters (*of a political party*).
permanent [pɛrma'nɑ̃], *a.* permanent, lasting.
permanente [pɛrma'nɑ̃:t], *n.f.* (*Hairdressing*) permanent wave.

perméabilité [pɛrmeabili'te], *n.f.* permeability.
perméable [pɛrme'abl], *a.* permeable, pervious (*to*).
permettre [pɛr'mɛtr], *v.t. irr.* (*conjug. like* METTRE) to permit, to allow; to enable, to afford room for. **se permettre,** *v.r.* to permit oneself; to indulge, to venture, to take the liberty (***de***).
permis [pɛr'mi], *a.* allowed, permitted, lawful.—*n.m.* permission, leave; permit, licence, pass.
permission [pɛrmi'sjɔ̃], *n.f.* permission, leave, permit.
permutant [pɛrmy'tɑ̃], *n.m.* permuter, exchanger.
permutation [pɛrmytɑ'sjɔ̃], *n.f.* permutation, exchange; (*Mil.*) transfer.
permuter [pɛrmy'te], *v.t.* to exchange, to permute, to transpose.
pernicieusement [pɛrnisjøz'mɑ̃], *adv.* perniciously, mischievously, injuriously.
pernicieux [pɛrni'sjø], *a.* (*fem.* **-euse**) pernicious, mischievous, hurtful.
péronnelle [perɔ'nɛl], *n.f.* pert hussy, saucy baggage.
péroraison [perɔrɛ'zɔ̃], *n.f.* peroration.
pérorer [perɔ're], *v.i.* to hold forth, to speechify.
péroreur [perɔ'rœːr], *n.m.* (*fem.* **-euse**) speechifier, spouter.
Pérou [pe'ru], **le,** *m.* Peru.
perpendiculaire [pɛrpɑ̃diky'lɛːr], *a.* and *n.f.* perpendicular.
perpendiculairement [pɛrpɑ̃dikylɛr'mɑ̃], *adv.* perpendicularly.
perpétration [pɛrpetrɑ'sjɔ̃], *n.f.* perpetration.
perpétrer [pɛrpe'tre], *v.t.* (*conjug. like* CÉDER) to perpetrate, to commit.
perpétuation [pɛrpetɥɑ'sjɔ̃], *n.f.* perpetuation.
perpétuel [pɛrpe'tɥɛl], *a.* (*fem.* **-elle**) perpetual, permanent; for life.
perpétuellement [pɛrpetɥɛl'mɑ̃], *adv.* perpetually; everlastingly.
perpétuer [pɛrpe'tɥe], *v.t.* to perpetuate. **se perpétuer**, *v.r.* to be perpetuated, to continue.
perpétuité [pɛrpetɥi'te], *n.f.* perpetuity; ***à perpétuité,*** for ever, for life.
perplexe [pɛr'plɛks], *a.* perplexed, embarrassed, irresolute; perplexing.
perplexité [pɛrplɛksi'te], *n.f.* perplexity.
perquisition [pɛrkizi'sjɔ̃], *n.f.* perquisition, search; investigation.
perquisitionner [pɛrkizisjɔ'ne], *v.i.* to make a search.
perron [pɛ'rɔ̃], *n.m.* steps (*before a house*).
perroquet [pɛrɔ'kɛ], *n.m.* parrot.
perruche [pɛ'ryʃ], *n.f.* parakeet, budgerigar; (*pop.*) hen-parrot.
perruque [pɛ'ryk], *n.f.* wig, periwig.
perruquier [pɛry'kje], *n.m.* wig-maker; (*obs.*) hair-dresser, barber.
persan [pɛr'sɑ̃], *a.* Persian.—*n.m.* Persian (*language*); (**Persan**, *fem.* **-ane**) Persian (*person*).
Perse [pɛrs], **la**, *f.* Persia.
perse [pɛrs], *n.f.* chintz.
persécuter [pɛrseky'te], *v.t.* to persecute; (*fig.*) to bore, to dun.
persécuteur [pɛrseky'tœːr], *a.* (*fem.* **-trice**) persecuting; troublesome.—*n.m.* (*fem.* **-trice**) persecutor; troublesome person.
persécution [pɛrseky'sjɔ̃], *n.f.* persecution; annoyance, importunity.
persévérance [pɛrseve'rɑ̃ːs], *n.f.* perseverance; firmness, steadiness.
persévérant [pɛrseve'rɑ̃], *a.* persevering; steady, resolute.
persévérer [pɛrseve're], *v.i.* (*conjug. like* CÉDER) to persevere; to be steadfast; to persist.
persienne [pɛr'sjɛn], *n.f.* Venetian shutter.
persiflage [pɛrsi'flaːʒ], *n.m.* banter, chaff, persiflage.
persifler [pɛrsi'fle], *v.t., v.i.* to rally, to banter, to chaff.
persifleur [pɛrsi'flœːr], *a.* (*fem.* **-euse**) bantering, chaffing.—*n.m.* (*fem.* **-euse**) banterer, quiz.
persil [pɛr'si], *n.m.* parsley.
persillé [pɛrsi'je], *a.* spotted; blue-moulded, (*cheese*).
persique [pɛr'sik], *a.* ancient Persian; ***le Golfe Persique***, Persian Gulf.
persistance [pɛrsis'tɑ̃ːs], *n.f.* persistence.
persistant [pɛrsis'tɑ̃], *a.* persistent.
persister [pɛrsis'te], *v.i.* to persist.
personnage [pɛrsɔ'naːʒ], *n.m.* personage, person; (*Theat.*) character, part.
personnalité [pɛrsɔnali'te], *n.f.* personality, personal character; person; selfishness.
personne [pɛr'sɔn], *n.f.* person; own self; appearance.—*pron. indef.* anyone, no one, nobody.
personnel [pɛrsɔ'nɛl], *a.* (*fem.* **-elle**) personal; selfish.—*n.m.* personnel, staff.
personnellement [pɛrsɔnɛl'mɑ̃], *adv.* personally.
personnification [pɛrsɔnifikɑ'sjɔ̃], *n.f.* personification.
personnifier [pɛrsɔni'fje], *v.t.* to personify; to embody.
perspectif [pɛrspɛk'tif], *a.* (*fem.* **-tive**) perspective.—*n.f.* (**-tive**) perspective; view, prospect, distance, vista.
perspicace [pɛrspi'kas], *a.* perspicacious, shrewd.
perspicacité [pɛrspikasi'te], *n.f.* perspicacity, insight.
persuader [pɛrsɥa'de], *v.t.* to persuade; to convince, to satisfy. **se persuader,** *v.r.* to persuade *or* convince oneself; to be persuaded.
persuasible [pɛrsɥa'zibl], *a.* persuadable.
persuasif [pɛrsɥa'zif], *a.* (*fem.* **-sive**) persuasive; convincing.
persuasion [pɛrsɥa'zjɔ̃], *n.f.* persuasion; conviction, belief, opinion.
persuasivement [pɛrsɥaziv'mɑ̃], *adv.* persuasively.
perte [pɛrt], *n.f.* loss; waste; ruin, fall, doom; ***à perte,*** at a loss; ***en pure perte,*** in vain.
pertinemment [pɛrtina'mɑ̃], *adv.* pertinently.
pertinence [pɛrti'nɑ̃ːs], *n.f.* pertinence.
pertinent [pɛrti'nɑ̃], *a.* pertinent, relevant.
pertuis [pɛr'tɥi], *n.m.* opening, sluice; straits.
perturbateur [pɛrtyrba'tœːr], *a.* (*fem.* **-trice**) disturbing.—*n.m.* (*fem.* **-trice**) disturber.
perturbation [pɛrtyrbɑ'sjɔ̃], *n.f.* perturbation, disturbance.

perturber [pɛrtyr'be], *v.t.* to perturb, to disturb.
péruvien [pery'vjɛ̃], *a.* (*fem.* **-enne**) Peruvian.—*n.m.* (**Péruvien**, *fem.* **-enne**) Peruvian (*person*).
pervenche [pɛr'vɑ̃:ʃ], *n.f.* (*Bot.*) periwinkle.
pervers [pɛr'vɛ:r], *a.* perverse, wicked, depraved.—*n.m.* (*fem.* **-e**) perverse person; wrongdoer.
perversion [pɛrvɛr'sjɔ̃], *n.f.* perversion.
perversité [pɛrvɛrsi'te], *n.f.* perverseness.
pervertir [pɛrvɛr'ti:r], *v.t.* to pervert.
pervertissement [pɛrvɛrtis'mɑ̃], *n.m.* perversion.
pervertisseur [pɛrvɛrti'sœ:r], *a.* (*fem.* **-euse**) perverting.—*n.m.* (*fem.* **-euse**) perverter, corrupter.
pesage [pə'za:ʒ], *n.m.* weighing; (*Turf.*) weighing-in room; paddock (*on racecourse*), the enclosure.
pesamment [pəza'mɑ̃], *adv.* heavily, ponderously; clumsily.
pesant [pə'zɑ̃], *a.* heavy, ponderous; unwieldy; sluggish.—*n.m.* weight.—*adv.* in weight.
pesanteur [pəzɑ̃'tœ:r], *n.f.* weight; heaviness; unwieldiness; dullness, ponderousness; (*Phys.*) gravity.
pesée [pə'ze], *n.f.* weighing.
pèse-lettre [pɛz'lɛtr], *n.m.* (*pl.* **-lettres**) letter-scales.
peser [pə'ze], *v.t.* (*conjug. like* AMENER) to weigh; (*fig.*) to ponder, to estimate.—*v.i.* to weigh; to be heavy; to be of importance; to lie heavy; to dwell (*sur*).
peseur [pə'zœ:r], *n.m.* (*fem.* **-euse**) weigher.
pessimisme [pɛsi'mism], *n.m.* pessimism.
pessimiste [pɛsi'mist], *a.* pessimistic.—*n.* pessimist.
peste [pɛst], *n.f.* plague, pestilence; (*fig.*) pest, bore, nuisance.—*int.* the deuce! hang it!
pester [pɛs'te], *v.i.* to inveigh, to storm, to rave.
pestiféré [pɛstife're], *a.* and *n.m.* (*fem.* **-ée**) plague-stricken (person).
pestilence [pɛsti'lɑ̃:s], *n.f.* pestilence.
pestilent [pɛsti'lɑ̃], *a.* pestilent.
pestilentiel [pɛstilɑ̃'sjɛl], *a.* (*fem.* **-elle**) pestilential.
pétale [pe'tal], *n.m.* petal.
pétarade [peta'rad], *n.f.* cracking (*noise*); back-fire (*of car*).
pétard [pe'ta:r], *n.m.* petard; cracker (*firework*); (*Rail.*) detonator, fog-signal.
pétaudière [peto'djɛ:r], *n.f.* bear-garden, noisy *or* disorderly assembly.
pétillant [peti'jɑ̃], *a.* crackling; sparkling.
pétillement [petij'mɑ̃], *n.m.* crackling; sparkling.
pétiller [peti'je], *v.i.* to crackle (*of burning wood*); to sparkle.
petiot [pə'tjo], *a.* (*fam.*) tiny, wee.—*n.m.* (*fem.* **-e**) little one; darling.
petit [pə'ti], *a.* little, small; short; very young; petty, slight; shabby; humble.—*n.m.* (*fem.* **-e**) little child, little one; young one; whelp, pup, kitten, cub.
petite-fille [pətit'fij], *n.f.* (*pl.* **petites-filles**) grand-daughter.
petitement [pətit'mɑ̃], *adv.* in small quantity; not much, poorly, meanly.
petitesse [pəti'tɛs], *n.f.* smallness, littleness; insignificance; meanness; narrowness.
petit-fils [pəti'fis], *n.m.* (*pl.* **petits-fils**) grandson.
pétition [peti'sjɔ̃], *n.f.* petition, request.
pétitionnaire [petisjɔ'nɛ:r], *n.* petitioner.
pétitionnement [petisjɔn'mɑ̃], *n.m.* petitioning.
pétitionner [petisjɔ'ne], *v.i.* to make a request, to petition.
petit-lait [pəti'lɛ], *n.m.* whey.
petits-enfants [pətizɑ̃'fɑ̃], *n.m. pl.* grandchildren.
pétrel [pe'trɛl], *n.m.* petrel.
pétri [pe'tri], *a.* kneaded.
pétrifiant [petri'fjɑ̃], *a.* petrifying.
pétrification [petrifikɑ'sjɔ̃], *n.f.* petrifaction.
pétrifier [petri'fje], *v.t.* to petrify. **se pétrifier**, *v.r.* to turn into stone.
pétrin [pe'trɛ̃], *n.m.* kneading-trough; (*fig.*) scrape.
pétrir [pe'tri:r], *v.t.* to knead; (*fig.*) to mould, to form.
pétrissable [petri'sabl], *a.* that can be kneaded; (*fig.*) yielding, pliant.
pétrissage [petri'sa:ʒ], **pétrissement** [petris'mɑ̃], *n.m.* kneading; (*fig.*) forming.
pétrisseur [petri'sœ:r], *n.m.* (*fem.* **-euse**) kneader.—*n.f.* (**-euse**) kneading-machine.
pétrole [pe'trɔl], *n.m.* petroleum, (mineral) oil; paraffin.
pétrolier [petrɔ'lje], *a.* (*fem.* **-ière**) pertaining to oil.—*n.m.* oil-tanker.
pétulance [pety'lɑ̃:s], *n.f.* liveliness, ebulliency; friskiness.
pétulant [pety'lɑ̃], *a.* lively, ebullient, frisky.
pétunia [pety'nja], *n.m.* petunia.
peu [pø], *adv.* little, not much; few, not many; not very.—*n.m.* little; bit.
peuplade [pœ'plad], *n.f.* clan, tribe, horde.
peuple [pœpl], *a.* plebeian, common, vulgar.—*n.m.* people, nation; the people, the multitude, the lower classes.
peuplé [pœ'ple], *a.* heavily populated, populous.
peuplement [pœplə'mɑ̃], *n.m.* peopling; stocking of a poultry-yard, pond etc.
peupler [pœ'ple], *v.t.* to people; to stock with animals etc.; to populate; to throng.—*v.i.* to multiply, to breed. **se peupler**, *v.r.* to become peopled; to be populated.
peuplier [pœ'plje], *n.m.* poplar.
peur [pœ:r], *n.f.* fear, dread, terror; apprehension; ***avoir peur***, to be afraid; ***de peur de***, for fear of.
peureusement [pœrøz'mɑ̃], *adv.* timorously.
peureux [pœ'rø], *a.* (*fem.* **-euse**) fearful, timid, timorous.—*n.m.* (*fem.* **-euse**) timid person.
peut-être [pø'tɛ:tr], *adv.* perhaps, maybe.
phalange [fa'lɑ̃:ʒ], *n.f.* phalanx; (*poet.*) army, host.
phalène [fa'lɛ:n], *n.f.* moth.
pharaon [fara'ɔ̃], *n.m.* Pharaoh.
phare [fa:r], *n.m.* lighthouse; beacon; (*Motor.*) head-light.
pharisien [fari'zjɛ̃], *n.m.* Pharisee; (*fig.*) hypocrite; self-righteous person.
pharmaceutique [farmasø'tik], *a.* pharmaceutical.—*n.f.* pharmaceutics.

pharmacie [farma'si], *n.f.* pharmacy, chemist and druggist's shop, dispensary; medicine chest.
pharmacien [farma'sjɛ̃], *n.m.* (*fem.* **-enne**) chemist, pharmacist.
phase [fɑːz], *n.f.* phasis (*of planet*); phase; aspect, period.
phénicien [feni'sjɛ̃], *a.* (*fem.* **-enne**) Phoenician.—*n.m.* (**Phénicien**, *fem.* **-enne**) Phoenician (*person*).
phénix [fe'niks], *n.m.* phoenix; paragon.
phénoménal [fenɔme'nal], *a.* (*m. pl.* **-aux**) phenomenal; (*colloq.*) extraordinary.
phénomène [fenɔ'mɛːn], *n.m.* phenomenon; (*colloq.*) remarkable person *or* thing; freak.
philanthrope [filɑ̃'trɔp], *n.* philanthropist.
philanthropie [filɑ̃trɔ'pi], *n.f.* philanthropy.
philanthropique [filɑ̃trɔ'pik], *a.* philanthropic.
philatélie [filate'li], *n.f.* philately, stamp-collecting.
philatéliste [filate'list], *n.* stamp collector.
Philippe [fi'lip], *m.* Philip.
philippine [fili'pin], *a.* Philippine, Filipino. —*n.* (**Philippine**) Filipino (*person*).
Philippines [fili'pin], **les**, *f. pl.* Philippines, Philippine Islands.
Philistin [filis'tɛ̃], *n.m.* (*fem.* **-e**) Philistine, person of vulgar taste.
philosophale [filɔzɔ'fal], *a.* ***la pierre philosophale***, the philosopher's stone.
philosophe [filɔ'zɔf], *a.* philosophical.—*n.* philosopher.
philosopher [filɔzɔ'fe], *v.i.* to philosophize.
philosophie [filɔzɔ'fi], *n.f.* philosophy; class in French school roughly equivalent to English sixth.
philosophique [filɔzɔ'fik], *a.* philosophical.
philosophiquement [filɔzɔfik'mɑ̃], *adv.* philosophically.
philtre or **filtre** [filtr], *n.m.* philtre.
phlébite [fle'bit], *n.f.* phlebitis.
phlegmatique [FLEGMATIQUE].
phobie [fɔ'bi], *n.f.* phobia, morbid dread.
phonétique [fɔne'tik], *a.* phonetic.—*n.f.* phonetics.
phonique [fɔ'nik], *a.* phonic.
phonographe [fɔnɔ'graf], *n.m.* phonograph, gramophone.
phonographie [fɔnɔgra'fi], *n.f.* phonography, sound recording.
phonographique [fɔnɔgra'fik], *a.* phonographic.
phoque [fɔk], *n.m.* (*Zool.*) seal.
phosphate [fɔs'fat], *n.m.* phosphate.
phosphore [fɔs'fɔːr], *n.m.* phosphorus.
phosphorescence [fɔsfɔrɛ'sɑ̃ːs], *n.f.* phosphorescence.
phosphorescent [fɔsfɔrɛ'sɑ̃], *a.* phosphorescent.
phosphoreux [fɔsfɔ'rø], *a.m.* phosphorous.
phosphorique [fɔsfɔ'rik], *a.* phosphoric.
photo [fɔ'to], *n.f. abbr.* [PHOTOGRAPHIE].
photocopie [fɔtɔkɔ'pi], *n.f.* photocopy, photostat.
photogénique [fɔtoʒe'nik], *a.* photogenic.
photographe [fɔtɔ'graf], *n.* photographer.
photographie [fɔtɔgra'fi], *n.f.* photography; photograph.
photographier [fɔtɔgra'fje], *v.t.* to photograph.
photographique [fɔtɔgra'fik], *a.* photographic; ***appareil photographique***, camera.
photogravure [fɔtɔgra'vyːr], *n.f.* photogravure.
phrase [frɑːz], *n.f.* sentence; (*Mus.*) phrase; ***phrase toute faite***, commonplace, stock phrase.
phraséologie [frɑzeɔlɔ'zi], *n.f.* phraseology.
phraser [frɑ'ze], *v.t.* to express in phrases; (*Mus.*) to phrase.—*v.i.* to phrase.
phraseur [frɑ'zœːr], *n.m.* (*fem.* **-euse**) (*fam.*) verbose writer *or* talker.
phtisie [fti'zi], *n.f.* phthisis, consumption.
phtisique [fti'zik], *a.* consumptive.—*n.* consumptive person.
physicien [fizi'sjɛ̃], *n.m.* (*fem.* **-enne**) physicist.
physionomie [fizjɔnɔ'mi], *n.f.* physiognomy, countenance, aspect, look.
physionomiste [fizjɔnɔ'mist], *n.* physiognomist.
physiothérapie [fiziɔtera'pi], *n.f.* (*Med.*) physiotherapy.
physiothérapiste [fiziɔtera'pist], *n.* physiotherapist.
physique [fi'zik], *a.* physical, material bodily.—*n.f.* physics.—*n.m.* physique, natural constitution; outward appearance.
physiquement [fizik'mɑ̃], *adv.* physically.
piaffer [pja'fe], *v.i.* to paw the ground, to prance (*of horses*).
piaffeur [pja'fœːr], *a.* (*fem.* **-euse**) pawing, prancing.—*n.m.* (*fem.* **-euse**) pawer, prancer.
piailler [pja'je], *v.i.* to cheep (*of small birds*); (*fig.*) to squall; to rant.
piaillerie [pjɑj'ri], *n.f.* cheeping; squealing.
piailleur [pjɑ'jœːr], *n.m.* (*fem.* **-euse**) cheeper; squaller.
pianiste [pja'nist], *n.* pianist.
piano [pja'no], *n.m.* piano, pianoforte; ***piano à queue***, grand piano.
piaulement [pjol'mɑ̃], *n.m.* whining, puling; cheeping (*of chickens*).
piauler [pjo'le], *v.i.* to cheep (*of chickens etc.*); (*fig.*) to pule, to whine.
pic [pik], *n.m.* pick, pickaxe; gaff; peak (*of a mountain*); woodpecker.
pick-up [pi'kœp], *n.m. inv.* record player.
picoté [pikɔ'te], *a.* pricked, marked.
picotement [pikɔt'mɑ̃], *n.m.* pricking, tingling.
picoter [pikɔ'te], *v.t.* to cause to tingle; to prick; to peck (*of birds*).
picvert or **pivert** [pi'vɛːr], *n.m.* green woodpecker.
pie [pi], *a. inv.* and *n.* piebald (horse).—*n.f.* magpie.
pièce [pjɛs], *n.f.* piece; patch; cask (*of wine etc.*); head (*of cattle, poultry etc.*); apartment, room; piece of ordnance, cannon; (*Theat.*) play; coin; joint (*of meat*).
pied [pje], *n.m.* foot; footing; footprint, track; leg (*of furniture*); stand, rest; stalk (*of plants*).
pied-à-terre [pjeta'tɛːr], *n.m. inv.* occasional lodging.
pied-de-biche [pjed'biʃ], *n.m.* (*pl.* **pieds-de-biche**) bell-pull; (*Surg.*) forceps; nail-clench.
piédestal [pjedɛs'tal], *n.m.* (*pl.* **-aux**) pedestal.

piège [pjɛːʒ], *n.m.* trap, snare.
piéger [pje'ʒe], *v.t.* (*conjug. like* CÉDER) to trap (*animals*); (*Mil.*) to set a booby trap.
pie-grièche [pigri'ɛʃ], *n.f.* (*pl.* **pies-grièches**) (*Orn.*) shrike; (*fig.*) shrew.
pierraille [pjɛ'rɑːj], *n.f.* rubble, ballast.
Pierre [pjɛːr], *m.* Peter.
pierre [pjɛːr], *n.f.* stone; (*Path.*) calculus.
pierreries [pjɛr'ri], *n.f. pl.* precious stones, gems.
pierreux [pjɛ'rø], *a.* (*fem.* **-euse**) stony, flinty, gritty, gravelly; calculous.
pierrot [pjɛ'ro], *n.m.* pierrot, merry-andrew; house-sparrow.
piété [pje'te], *n.f.* piety, godliness; affection.
piétinement [pjetin'mɑ̃], *n.m.* stamping, trampling.
piétiner [pjeti'ne], *v.t.* to tread *or* trample under foot.—*v.i.* to stamp; to paw the ground (*of horses*).
piéton [pje'tɔ̃], *n.m.* (*fem.* **-onne**) pedestrian.
piètre [pjɛtr], *a.* poor, paltry, pitiful.
piètrement [pjɛtrə'mɑ̃], *adv.* pitifully, wretchedly.
pieu [pjø], *n.m.* (*pl.* **pieux** (1)) stake, pile, post.
pieusement [pjøz'mɑ̃], *adv.* piously, devoutly; obediently; reverently.
pieuvre [pjœːvr], *n.f.* octopus, poulpe.
pieux (2) [pjø], *a.* (*fem.* **pieuse**) pious, godly.
pigeon [pi'ʒɔ̃], *n.m.* pigeon, dove; (*slang*) dupe, gull.
pigeonneau [piʒɔ'no], *n.m.* (*pl.* **-eaux**) young pigeon, squab.
pigeonnier [piʒɔ'nje], *n.m.* pigeon house, dove-cot.
pigment [pig'mɑ̃], *n.m.* (*Anat.*) pigment.
pignon [pi'ɲɔ̃], *n.m.* gable end; pinion; kernel (*of fir-cone*).
pilaire [pi'lɛːr], *a.* pilous, pilose.
pilastre [pi'lastr], *n.m.* (*Arch.*) pilaster.
pilchard [pil'ʃaːr], *n.m.* pilchard.
pile [pil], *n.f.* pile, heap; pier (*of a bridge etc.*); mole (*masonry*); (*Elec.*) battery; reverse (*of coins*); ***pile atomique***, atomic pile.
piler [pi'le], *v.t.* to pound, to crush, to powder.
pileur [pi'lœːr], *n.m.* (*fem.* **-euse** (1)) pounder, beater.
pileux [pi'lø], *a.* (*fem.* **-euse** (2)) pilous, hairy.
pilier [pi'lje], *n.m.* pillar, column, post; (*fig.*) supporter, prop.
pillage [pi'jaːʒ], *n.m.* pillage, plunder; (*fig.*) pilfering.
pillard [pi'jaːr], *a.* plundering; predatory.—*n.m.* (*fem.* **-e**) pillager, plunderer.
piller [pi'je], *v.t.* to pillage, to plunder; to ransack; to pilfer.
pillerie [pij'ri], *n.f.* pillage plunder; extortion.
pilleur [pi'jœːr], *n.m.* (*fem.* **-euse**) pillager, plunderer, pilferer.
pilon [pi'lɔ̃], *n.m.* pestle; rammer, stamper; wooden leg.
pilonnage [pilɔ'naːʒ], *n.m.* ramming, pounding, stamping, milling.
pilonner [pilɔ'ne], *v.t.* to ram, to pound, to mill; to stamp (*ore*).
pilori [pilɔ'ri], *n.m.* pillory.
pilorier [pilɔ'rje], *v.t.* to pillory.
pilotage [pilɔ'taːʒ], *n.m.* (*Civ. Eng.*) pile-driving; (*Naut.*) piloting.
pilote [pi'lɔt], *n.m.* pilot; guide; pilot-fish.
piloter [pilɔ'te], *v.t.* to pile, to drive piles into; (*Naut.*, *Av.*) to pilot; (*fig.*) to guide.
pilotis [pilɔ'ti], *n.m.* pilework.
pilule [pi'lyl], *n.f.* pill.
pimbêche [pɛ̃'bɛʃ], *n.f.* uppish and impertinent woman.
piment [pi'mɑ̃], *n.m.* pimento, allspice.
pimenter [pimɑ̃'te], *v.t.* to flavour with pimento.
pimpant [pɛ̃'pɑ̃], *a.* natty, spruce, smart.
pin [pɛ̃], *n.m.* pine-tree; ***pomme de pin***, fir-cone.
pinacle [pi'nakl], *n.m.* pinnacle.
pince [pɛ̃ːs], *n.f.* pinching, nipping; hold, grip; pincers, pliers, forceps; tongs, clip; crowbar (*lever*); toe (*of a horse's foot*); claw (*of a lobster etc.*).
pincé [pɛ̃'se], *a.* affected, stiff, prim.
pinceau [pɛ̃'so], *n.m.* (*pl.* **-eaux**) paint-brush.
pincée [pɛ̃'se], *n.f.* pinch (*of snuff, salt etc.*).
pince-nez [pɛ̃s'ne], *n.m. inv.* pince-nez, (*folding*) eye-glasses.
pince-notes [pɛ̃s'nɔt], *n.m. inv.* paper-clip.
pincer [pɛ̃'se], *v.t.* (*conjug. like* COMMENCER) to pinch, to nip; to grip; to bite (*of cold etc.*); to pluck (*a musical instrument*); (*Naut.*) to hug (*the wind*).
pince-sans-rire [pɛ̃ssɑ̃'riːr], *n.m. inv.* sly *or* malicious person, dry joker.
pincette(s) [pɛ̃'sɛt], *n.f.* (*pl.*) tongs; tweezers, nippers.
pinçure [pɛ̃'syːr], *n.f.* pinching; crease in cloth.
pingouin [pɛ̃'gwɛ̃], *n.m.* auk.
pingre [pɛ̃ːgr], *a.* avaricious, stingy.—*n.* miser, skinflint.
pinson [pɛ̃'sɔ̃], *n.m.* finch, chaffinch.
pintade [pɛ̃'tad], *n.f.* guinea-fowl.
piochage [pjɔ'ʃaːʒ], *n.m.* digging; (*fig.*) working, fagging.
pioche [pjɔʃ], *n.f.* pickaxe.
piocher [pjɔ'ʃe], *v.t.* to dig.—*v.i.* to dig; (*fig.*) to fag, to work hard, to swot.
piocheur [pjɔ'ʃœːr], *n.m.* (*fem.* **-euse**) digger; (*slang*) hard-working student, swotter.—*n.f.* (**-euse**) (*Civ. Eng.*) excavator.
piolet [pjɔ'lɛ], *n.m.* piolet, ice-axe.
pion [pjɔ̃], *n.m.* pawn (*at chess*); piece (*at draughts*); (*Sch. slang*) usher.
pionnier [pjɔ'nje], *n.m.* pioneer.
pipe [pip], *n.f.* pipe; tobacco-pipe; pipe (*cask*).
pipeau [pi'po], *n.m.* (*pl.* **-eaux**) pipe, reed-pipe; bird-call; limed twig, snare.
pipée [pi'pe], *n.f.* bird-catching (*with a bird-call*); (*fig.*) deceit, trickery.
piper [pi'pe], *v.t.* to catch (*birds*) with a bird-call etc.; (*fig.*) to trick, to decoy.
pipeur [pi'pœːr], *a.* (*fem.* **-euse**) cheating, deceitful.—*n.m.* (*fem.* **-euse**) one who decoys birds; cheat, trickster (*at play*).
piquant [pi'kɑ̃], *a.* prickling, stinging; pungent; biting; cutting, keen; piquant, pointed; smart.—*n.m.* prickle; quill (*of porcupine*); pungency, point, piquancy.
pique [pik], *n.f.* pike (*weapon*); pique, spite, quarrel.—*n.m.* (*Cards*) spade(s).
piqué [pi'ke], *a.* quilted, pinked; worm-eaten; sour (*wine*).—*n.m.* quilting; piqué; nose-dive; ***bombardement en piqué***, dive-bombing.

pique-nique [pik'nik], *n.m.* (*pl.* **-niques**) picnic.
piquer [pi'ke], *v.t.* to prick; to sting; to goad, to spur; to puncture; to bite (*of insects*); to quilt; to lard; to prick off; to excite, to stimulate; to nettle, to rouse; (*Med.*) to inject.—*v.i.* to turn sour (*of wine etc.*). **se piquer**, *v.r.* to prick oneself; to be offended, to be piqued; to pride oneself; to turn sour.
piquet [pi'kɛ], *n.m.* peg, stake; (*Mil.*) picket; piquet (*card game*).
piqueter [pik'te], *v.t.* (*conjug. like* APPELER) to mark out with stakes *or* pegs; to mark with little points.
piquette [pi'kɛt], *n.f.*, **piqueton** [pik'tɔ̃], *n.m.* thin wine.
piqueur (1) [pi'kœːr], *n.m.* outrider; overseer (*of workmen*); stud-groom; huntsman.
piqueur (2) [pi'kœːr], *n.m.* (*fem.* **-euse**) stitcher.
piqûre [pi'kyːr], *n.f.* prick; sting; bite; puncture; (*Needlework*) quilting, stitching; (*Med.*) injection, shot.
pirate [pi'rat], *n.m.* pirate; (*fig.*) extortioner, plagiarist.
pirater [pira'te], *v.i.* to commit piracy.
piraterie [pira'tri], *n.f.* piracy; act of piracy *or* plagiarism.
pire [piːr], *a.* and *n.m.* worse; the worst.
pirogue [pi'rɔg], *n.f.* pirogue, dug-out, canoe.
pirouette [pi'rwɛt], *n.f.* pirouette, whirligig.
pirouetter [pirwɛ'te], *v.i.* to pirouette, to whirl about.
pis (1) [pi], *n.m.* udder, dug (*of cow*).
pis (2) [pi], *adv.* and *n.m.* worse.—*n.m. inv.* ***pis aller***, the worst, last resource, makeshift.
pisciculture [pisikyl'tyːr], *n.f.* fish-culture.
piscine [pi'sin], *n.f.* piscina; swimming-pool.
pissenlit [pisɑ̃'li], *n.m.* dandelion.
pistache [pis'taʃ], *n.f.* pistachio, pistachio-nut.
pistachier [pista'ʃje], *n.m.* pistachio-tree.
piste [pist], *n.f.* track, footprint, trail, scent; course, race-course.
pistolet [pistɔ'lɛ], *n.m.* pistol; spray gun.
piston [pis'tɔ̃], *n.m.* piston; sucker (*of a pump*); press button; (*Mus.*) cornet.
pitance [pi'tɑ̃ːs], *n.f.* pittance; allowance (*of food*), dole.
piteusement [pitøz'mɑ̃], *adv.* piteously, woefully, sadly.
piteux [pi'tø], *a.* (*fem.* **-euse**) piteous, pitiable, woeful.
pitié [pi'tje], *n.f.* pity, compassion; object of pity.
piton [pi'tɔ̃], *n.m.* eye-bolt, screw-ring, ring-bolt; peak (*of mountain*).
pitoyable [pitwa'jabl], *a.* pitiful, piteous; paltry.
pitoyablement [pitwajablə'mɑ̃], *adv.* pitifully.
pittoresque [pitɔ'rɛsk], *a.* picturesque; graphic.—*n.m.* the picturesque, picturesqueness.
pittoresquement [pitɔrɛsk'mɑ̃], *adv.* picturesquely.
pivert [PICVERT].
pivoine [pi'vwan], *n.m.* bullfinch.—*n.f.* peony.
pivot [pi'vo], *n.m.* pivot, pin spindle, hinge.
pivoter [pivɔ'te], *v.i.* to pivot, to turn on a pivot, to revolve, to turn.
placage [pla'kaːʒ], *n.m.* plating (*metal-work*); veneering (*of wood*); (*Lit.*) patchwork.
placard [pla'kaːr], *n.m.* placard, poster, bill; (*Print.*) slip; cupboard (*in a wall*).
placarder [plakar'de], *v.t.* to placard, to post up.
place [plas], *n.f.* place; room; seat; stead; post, job, situation; town; public square; ***faire place***, to make room; ***retenir des places***, to book seats; ***sur place***, on the spot.
placement [plas'mɑ̃], *n.m.* placing; sale; employment; investment.
placer [pla'se], *v.t.* (*conjug. like* COMMENCER) to place, to put; to find a place *or* situation for; to invest; to deposit; to sell. **se placer**, *v.r.* to place oneself; to find a job.
placet [pla'sɛ], *n.m.* petition, address.
placide [pla'sid], *a.* placid, calm.
placidement [plasid'mɑ̃], *adv.* placidly, calmly.
placidité [plasidi'te], *n.f.* placidity.
plafond [pla'fɔ̃], *n.m.* ceiling.
plafonnage [plafɔ'naːʒ], *n.m.* ceiling (*action, work*); (*Av.*) visibility.
plafonner [plafɔ'ne], *v.t.* to ceil, to put a ceiling to.—*v.i.* to reach the highest point (*of prices etc.*); (*Av.*) to fly at the ceiling; (*Motor.*) to travel at maximum speed.
plafonneur [plafɔ'nœːr], *n.m.* plasterer.
plafonnier [plafɔ'nje], *n.m.* ceiling-light.
plage [plaːʒ], *n.f.* beach, shore; sea-side resort.
plagiaire [pla'ʒjɛːr], *a.* and *n.* plagiarist.
plagiat [pla'ʒja], *n.m.* plagiarism.
plagier [pla'ʒje], *v.t.* to plagiarize.
plaid [plɛd], *n.m.* plaid, travelling rug.
plaidant [plɛ'dɑ̃], *a.* pleading, litigant.
plaider [plɛ'de], *v.t.* to defend; to allege.—*v.i.* to go to law, to litigate; to plead, to argue.
plaideur [plɛ'dœːr], *n.m.* (*fem.* **-euse**) litigant, suitor.
plaidoirie [plɛdwa'ri], *n.f.* pleading; counsel's speech.
plaidoyer [plɛdwa'je], *n.m.* speech for the defence, counsel's address.
plaie [plɛ], *n.f.* wound; sore; (*fig.*) plague; evil.
plaignant [plɛ'ɲɑ̃], *a.* complaining; ***la partie plaignante***, the plaintiff.—*n.m.* (*fem.* **-e**) plaintiff, prosecutor.
plain [plɛ̃], *a.* plain, even, flat, level.
plaindre [plɛ̃ːdr], *v.t. irr.* (*conjug. like* CRAINDRE) to pity, to be sorry for. **se plaindre**, *v.r.* to complain; to grumble.
plaine [plɛn], *n.f.* plain; flat country.
plain-pied (de) [dəplɛ̃'pje], *adv. phr.* on a level; (*fig.*) without difficulty.
plainte [plɛ̃ːt], *n.f.* complaint, plaint; lamentation, wail; plaint at law.
plaintif [plɛ̃'tif], *a.* (*fem.* **-tive**) plaintive, complaining; querulous.
plaintivement [plɛtiv'mɑ̃], *adv.* dolefully; querulously.
plaire [plɛːr], *v.i. irr.* to please; to be pleasant *or* agreeable (*à*); ***s'il vous plaît***, please. **se plaire**, *v.r.* to delight, to take pleasure; to like.

plaisamment [plɛza'mɑ̃], *adv.* humorously, amusingly; ludicrously.

plaisance [plɛ'zɑ̃:s], *n.f.* pleasure.

plaisant [plɛ'zɑ̃], *a.* humorous, amusing, funny; (*iron.*) odd, strange.—*n.m.* jester, wag; the funny side; ***un mauvais plaisant***, a practical joker.

plaisanter [plɛzɑ̃'te], *v.t.* to chaff, to banter. —*v.i.* to jest, to joke.

plaisanterie [plɛzɑ̃'tri], *n.f.* jest, joke, witticism; mockery, trifle.

plaisir [plɛ'zi:r], *n.m.* pleasure; delight; diversion, entertainment; favour.

plan [plɑ̃], *a.* even, level, flat.—*n.m.* plane; plan; drawing; scheme, project; (*Paint.*) ground.

planche [plɑ̃:ʃ], *n.f.* board, plank; shelf; (*Engr.*) plate; (*Gard.*) bed, border.

planchéiage [plɑ̃ʃe'ja:ʒ], *n.m.* boarding, planking; flooring.

planchéier [plɑ̃ʃe'je], *v.t.* to board over, to floor.

plancher [plɑ̃'ʃe], *n.m.* floor, deck planking.

planchette [plɑ̃'ʃɛt], *n.f.* small board; (*Math.*) plane-table.

plancton [plɑ̃k'tɔ̃], *n.m.* plankton.

plane [plan], *n.f.* drawing-knife; planisher.

plané [pla'ne], *a.* soaring, gliding; ***un vol plané***, gliding descent.

planer [pla'ne], *v.t.* to make smooth, to plane. —*v.i.* to hover, to soar; to look down (*on*) (***sur***); (*Av.*) to glide.

planétaire [plane'tɛ:r], *a.* planetary.

planète [pla'nɛ:t], *n.f.* planet.

planeur [pla'nœ:r], *n.m.* planisher; glider (*aeroplane*).

planeuse [pla'nø:z], *n.f.* planing-machine.

planification [planifikɑ'sjɔ̃], *n.f.* (*Polit. Econ.*) planning.

planifier [plani'fje], *v.t.* to plan.

plant [plɑ̃], *n.m.* young plant, seedling; slip; sapling; plantation.

plantation [plɑ̃tɑ'sjɔ̃], *n.f.* planting; plantation.

plante [plɑ̃:t], *n.f.* plant; ***la plante du pied***, (*Anat.*) the sole of the foot.

planter [plɑ̃'te], *v.t.* to plant; to set, to drive in; to set up, to erect. **se planter**, *v.r.* to station oneself.

planteur [plɑ̃'tœ:r], *n.m.* planter.

planteuse [plɑ̃'tø:z], *n.f.* potato-planting machine.

plantoir [plɑ̃'twa:r], *n.m.* dibble.

planton [plɑ̃'tɔ̃], *n.m.* (*Mil.*) orderly.

plantureusement [plɑ̃tyrøz'mɑ̃], *adv.* copiously, abundantly, luxuriantly.

plantureux [plɑ̃ty'rø], *a.* (*fem.* **-euse**) plentiful, copious; fertile.

plaquage [pla'ka:ʒ], *n.m.* (*Ftb.*) rugby tackle.

plaque [plak], *n.f.* plate, slab; plaque; badge, star; ***plaque tournante***, (*Rail.*) turn-table.

plaqué [pla'ke], *a.* plated, covered with.

plaquer [pla'ke], *v.t.* to plate (*metal*); to veneer (*wood*); (*Ftb.*) to tackle.

plaquette [pla'kɛt], *n.f.* small thin book; small plate; thin slab.

plasticité [plastisi'te], *n.f.* plasticity.

plastique [plas'tik], *a.* plastic.—*n.m.* plastics. —*n.f.* plastic art; figure.

plastron [plas'trɔ̃], *n.m.* breast-plate; fencing-pad; shirt-front.

plastronner [plastrɔ'ne], *v.i.* to strut, to swagger.

plat (1) [pla], *a.* flat; level; regular, (*fig.*) dull, insipid.—*n.m.* flat part, side; flat racing.

plat (2) [pla], *n.m.* dish (*the vessel and the food*), (*Naut.*) mess; course (*of a meal*).

platane [pla'tan], *n.m.* plane-tree, platan.

plateau [pla'to], *n.m.* (*pl.* **-eaux**) scale (*of a balance*); tray; table-land, plateau; turn-table (*of gramophone*).

plate-bande [plat'bɑ̃:d], *n.f.* (*pl.* **plates-bandes**) border, flower-bed.

plate-forme [plat'fɔrm], *n.f.* (*pl.* **plates-formes**) platform (*of a bus etc.*).

platement [plat'mɑ̃], *adv.* flatly, dully.

platine [pla'tin], *n.f.* lock (*of fire-arms*); plate (*of lock, watch, machine*); platen (*of type-writer*).—*n.m.* platinum.

platiné [plati'ne], *a.* platinum plated; platinum coloured (*of hair*).

platitude [plati'tyd], *n.f.* platitude; flatness, dullness.

Platon [pla'tɔ̃], *m.* Plato.

platonique [platɔ'nik], *a.* Platonic.

platonisme [platɔ'nism], *n.m.* Platonism.

plâtrage [plɑ'tra:ʒ], *n.m.* plaster-work, plastering.

plâtras [plɑ'trɑ], *n.m.* debris of plaster-work; rubbish.

plâtre [plɑ:tr], *n.m.* plaster.

plâtré [plɑ'tre], *a.* plastered.

plâtrer [plɑ'tre], *v.t.* to plaster; (*fig.*) to patch up, to disguise.

plâtreux [plɑ'trø], *a.* (*fem.* **-euse**) chalky.

plâtrier [plɑtri'je], *n.m.* plasterer.

plâtrière [plɑtri'jɛ:r], *n.f.* chalk pit; plaster-kiln.

plâtroir [plɑ'trwa:r], *n.m.* plasterer's trowel.

plausibilité [plozibili'te], *n.f.* plausibility.

plausible [plo'zibl], *a.* plausible (*never of person*).

plausiblement [ploziblə'mɑ̃], *adv.* plausibly.

plèbe [plɛb], *n.f.* common people.

plébéien [plebe'jɛ̃], *a.* and *n.m.* (*fem.* **-enne**) plebeian.

plébiscite [plebi'sit], *n.m.* plebiscite.

plein [plɛ̃], *a.* full; fraught (***de***); filled, replete; entire, whole; thorough; copious; solid; ***en plein air***, in the open air; ***en plein hiver***, in the heart of winter.—*n.m.* full part; plenum.—*adv.* full.

pleinement [plɛn'mɑ̃], *adv.* fully, entirely, thoroughly.

plénier [ple'nje], *a.* (*fem.* **-ière**) plenary; full, complete.

plénipotentiaire [plenipɔtɑ̃'sjɛ:r], *a.* and *n.m.* plenipotentiary.

plénitude [pleni'tyd], *n.f.* plenitude, fullness.

pleur [plœ:r], *n.m.* (*poet.*) tear; lament.

pleurard [plœ'ra:r], *a.* whimpering, tearful.—*n.m.* (*fem.* **-e**) whimperer, blubberer.

pleurer [plœ're], *v.t.* to weep, to bewail, to mourn, to deplore the loss of.—*v.i.* to weep, to cry, to shed tears; to mourn; to run (*of the eyes*); to drip (*of a tap*).

pleurésie [plœre'zi], *n.f.* pleurisy.

pleureur [plœ'rœ:r], *a.* (*fem.* **-euse**) whimpering, tearful; ***saule pleureur***, weeping willow.—*n.m.* (*fem.* **-euse**) whimperer, weeper.—*n.f.* (**-euse**) paid mourner.

pleurnichement [plœrniʃ'mɑ̃], *n.m.* whimpering, snivelling.
pleurnicher [plœrni'ʃe], *v.i.* to whimper, to whine, to snivel.
pleurnicheur [plœrni'ʃœ:r], *a.* (*fem.* **-euse**) whimpering, snivelling.—*n.m.* (*fem.* **-euse**) whimperer, sniveller.
pleutre [plø:tr], *n.m.* contemptible fellow.
pleuvoir [plœ'vwa:r], *v. impers. irr.* to rain; ***il pleut à verse*** or ***à seaux***, it is pouring in buckets; ***pleuvoir des hallebardes***, to rain cats and dogs.
pli [pli], *n.m.* fold; wrinkle; coil; bend; undulation, depression; cover, envelope; habit; (*Cards*) trick; ***mise en pli***, setting (*the hair*); ***sous pli recommandé***, in a registered envelope; ***un faux pli***, a crease.
pliable [pli'jabl], *a.* pliable, flexible, supple.
pliage [pli'ja:ʒ], **pliement** [pli'mɑ̃], *n.m.* folding.
pliant [pli'jɑ̃], *a.* pliant, docile; folding, collapsible.—*n.m.* folding-chair, deck-chair.
plie [pli], *n.f.* plaice.
plier [pli'je], *v.t.* to fold, to fold up; to bend.—*v.i.* to bend, to bow; to give way. **se plier**, *v.r.* to bow, to bend, to yield.
plieur [pli'jœ:r], *n.m.* (*fem.* **-euse**) folder.—*n.f.* (**-euse**) folding-machine.
plinthe [plɛ̃:t], *n.f.* plinth; skirting-board.
plissage [pli'sa:ʒ], *n.m.* pleating, kilting.
plissé [pli'se], *a.* kilted, pleated.—*n.m.* kilting, pleats.
plissement [plis'mɑ̃], *n.m.* folding, doubling over; crumpling.
plisser [pli'se], *v.t.* to fold; to crumple, to wrinkle; to pleat.—*v.i.* and **se plisser**, *v.r.* to be wrinkled, to pucker.
plissure [pli'sy:r], *n.f.* pleating; pleats.
ploiement [plwa'mɑ̃], *n.m.* folding, bending.
plomb [plɔ̃], *n.m.* lead; bullet, shot; plumb-line; sinker; custom-house seal; fuse; ***à plomb***, vertically.
plombage [plɔ̃'ba:ʒ], *n.m.* leading, plumbing; filling (*of teeth*).
plombagine [plɔ̃ba'ʒin], *n.f.* plumbago, blacklead, graphite.
plomber [plɔ̃'be], *v.t.* to cover with lead, to seal; to fill (*a tooth*); to plumb.
plomberie [plɔ̃'bri], *n.f.* plumber's shop; plumbing; lead-making; lead-works.
plombier [plɔ̃'bje], *n.m.* lead-worker; plumber.
plongée [plɔ̃'ʒe], *n.f.* slope; dive.
plongeoir [plɔ̃'ʒwɑ:r], *n.m.* diving-board.
plongeon [plɔ̃'ʒɔ̃], *n.m.* plunge, dive; (*Orn.*) diver.
plonger [plɔ̃'ʒe], *v.t.* (*conjug. like* MANGER) to plunge, to dip, to immerse; to throw, to involve.—*v.i.* to dive, to plunge; to submerge (*of submarine*); to pitch (*of ships*). **se plonger**, *v.r.* to be plunged; to immerse oneself (*in*).
plongeur [plɔ̃'ʒœ:r], *a.* (*fem.* **-euse**) plunging, diving (*bird*).—*n.m.* (*fem.* **-euse**) diver; dish-washer (*in hotels etc.*).
ploutocrate [plutɔ'krat], *n.m.* plutocrat.
ploutocratie [plutɔkra'si], *n.f.* plutocracy.
ploutocratique [plutɔkra'tik], *a.* plutocratic.
ployable [plwa'jabl], *a.* pliable, flexible.
ployer [plwa'je], *v.t.* (*conjug. like* EMPLOYER) to bend; to fold up.—*v.i.* and **se ployer**, *v.r.* to bend, to be folded; to yield, to give way.
pluie [plɥi], *n.f.* rain; (*fig.*) shower.
plumage [ply'ma:ʒ], *n.m.* plumage, feathers.
plumassier [plyma'sje], *n.m.* (*fem.* **-ière**) feather merchant *or* dresser.
plume [plym], *n.f.* feather; plume; quill, pen; nib.
plumeau [ply'mo], *n.m.* (*pl.* **-eaux**) feather-broom; feather-duster.
plumée [ply'me], *n.f.* penful (*of ink*); plucking (*of poultry*).
plumer [ply'me], *v.t.* to pluck, to plume; (*fig.*) to fleece.
plumet [ply'mɛ], *n.m.* plume.
plumetis [plym'ti], *n.m.* feather-stitch.
plumier [ply'mje], *n.m.* pen-box, pen-tray.
plupart [ply'pa:r], *n.f.* ***la plupart***, most, most part, the majority (***de***), most people.
pluralité [plyrali'te], *n.f.* plurality; pluralism.
pluriel [ply'rjɛl], *a.* (*fem.* **-elle**) plural.—*n.m.* plural.
plus [ply], *adv.* more, -er (***que***, than); -est, the most; also, moreover, further, besides; (*with* ***ne***) no more, no longer, never again; ***de plus***, besides, moreover.—*n.m.* the most, the maximum; the more.
plusieurs [ply'zjœ:r], *a. pl.* and *pron. indef.* several, some.
plus-que-parfait [plyskəpar'fɛ], *n.m.* pluperfect.
plutonium [plytɔ'njɔm], *n.m.* plutonium.
plutôt [ply'to], *adv.* rather, sooner (***que***).
pluvial [ply'vjal], *a.* (*m. pl.* **-aux**) pluvial, of rain, rainy.
pluvier [ply'vje], *n.m.* plover.
pluvieux [ply'vjø], *a.* (*fem.* **-euse**) rainy, wet, pluvious.
pluviomètre [plyvjɔ'mɛtr], *n.m.* rain-gauge.
pluviosité [plyvjɔzi'te], *n.f.* rainfall.
pneu [pnø], *n.m.* (*pl.* **pneus**) *fam. abbr.* [PNEUMATIQUE].
pneumatique [pnøma'tik], *a.* pneumatic.—*n.m.* tyre; express letter (*in Paris*).—*n.f.* pneumatics.
pneumonie [pnømɔ'ni], *n.f.* pneumonia.
pochade [pɔ'ʃad], *n.f.* rough sketch; (*fig.*) hurried piece of writing etc.
poche [pɔʃ], *n.f.* pocket; pouch; sack, bag; wrinkle (*in clothes*); crop (*of a bird*).
pocher [pɔ'ʃe], *v.t.* to poach (*eggs*); to give a black eye to; to stencil; to make a rough sketch of.—*v.i.* to become baggy, to bag.
pochet [pɔ'ʃɛ], *n.m.* nosebag (*of horse*).
pochette [pɔ'ʃɛt], *n.f.* small pocket; small net; folder, jacket (*containers*); fancy handkerchief.
pochoir [pɔ'ʃwa:r], *n.m.* stencil.
podagre [pɔ'dagr], *a.* gouty.—*n.f.* gout.—*n.* gouty person.
podomètre [pɔdɔ'mɛtr], *n.m.* pedometer.
poêle [pwɑ:l], *n.f.* frying-pan.—*n.m.* stove; pall (*at a funeral*).
poêlée [pwɑ'le], *n.f.* panful.
poêlon [pwɑ'lɔ̃], *n.m.* small saucepan.
poème [pɔ'ɛ:m], *n.m.* poem.
poésie [pɔe'zi], *n.f.* poetry, verse; poem.
poète [pɔ'ɛ:t], *n.m.* poet.
poétesse [pɔe'tɛs], *n.f.* poetess.
poétique [pɔe'tik], *a.* poetical.—*n.f.* poetics.
poétiquement [pɔetik'mɑ̃], *adv.* poetically.

poétiser [pɔeti'ze], *v.t.* to make poetical, to idealize, to poeticize.
pogrom [pɔ'grɔm], *n.m.* pogrom.
poids [pwɑ], *n.m. inv.* weight; heaviness; gravity; load; (*fig.*) importance, consequence; ***les poids lourds***, heavy vehicles.
poignant [pwa'ɲɑ̃], *a.* poignant; sharp, acute, keen.
poignard [pwa'ɲaːr], *n.m.* dagger.
poignarder [pwaɲar'de], *v.t.* to stab; to knife; (*fig.*) to grieve to the heart.
poigne [pwaɲ], *n.f.* (*colloq.*) grasp, grip; (*fig.*) strength.
poignée [pwa'ɲe], *n.f.* handful; handle, hilt; shake (*of the hand*).
poignet [pwa'ɲɛ], *n.m.* wrist; wristband, cuff.
poil [pwal], *n.m.* hair (*of animals*); hair (*of persons, other than that of the head*); (*fig.*) beard; nap (*of cloth, of hats etc.*); ***à contre-poil***, against the grain.
poilu [pwa'ly], *a.* hairy, shaggy.
poinçon [pwɛ̃'sɔ̃], *n.m.* punch; point, stiletto; awl, stamp, die.
poinçonnage [pwɛ̃sɔ'naːʒ], **poinçonnement** [pwɛ̃sɔn'mɑ̃], *n.m.* stamping, punching.
poinçonner [pwɛ̃sɔ'ne], *v.t.* to punch, to stamp.
poinçonneuse [pwɛ̃sɔ'nøːz], *n.f.* stamping- *or* punching-machine.
poindre [pwɛ̃ːdr], *v.i. irr.* to dawn, to break; (*fig.*) to appear.
poing [pwɛ̃], *n.m.* fist, hand; (*fig.*) force, brute strength; (*fig.*) ***dormir à poings fermés***, to sleep like a log.
point [pwɛ̃], *adv.* (*used with negative*) no, not at all; none (*more emphatic than* **pas**).—*n.m.* point; speck; dot, mark; (*Sch.*) mark; full stop; hole (*of a strap etc.*); (*Needlework*) stitch; matter, question; particular; state, case; degree; place; ***à point***, in the nick of time; well done (*of meat*); ***en tout point***, in every respect; ***sur ce*** or ***en ce point***, on that score.
pointage [pwɛ̃'taːʒ], **pointement** [pwɛ̃t'mɑ̃], *n.m.* pointing, levelling (*of guns*); checking; scrutiny (*of votes*), tally.
pointe [pwɛ̃ːt], *n.f.* point (*sharp end*); tip, head (*of an arrow etc.*); nose (*of a bullet*); cape; peak; etching-needle; nail, tack; (*Print.*) bodkin; (*fig.*) dash, flavour; pungency, sharpness; witticism.
pointement [POINTAGE].
pointer [pwɛ̃'te], *v.t.* to point, to aim (*a gun etc.*); to pierce, to stab, to prick; to mark; to tally, to scrutinize (*votes*); to prick up (*ears etc.*); to sharpen.—*v.i.* to point; to spring, to soar; to rear; to sprout.
pointeur [pwɛ̃'tœːr], *n.m.* (*fem.* **-euse**) pointer, marker, checker; (*Artill.*) gun-layer.
pointillage [pwɛ̃ti'jaːʒ], **pointillement** [pwɛ̃tij'mɑ̃], *n.m.* dotting, stippling; dotted line.
pointillé [pwɛ̃ti'je], *n.m.* stipple drawing *or* engraving; dotted line.
pointiller [pwɛ̃ti'je], *v.t.* to dot, to stipple; (*fig.*) to tease.—*v.i.* to bicker, to cavil.
pointilleux [pwɛ̃ti'jø], *a.* (*fem.* **-euse**) cavilling, captious; fastidious.
pointu [pwɛ̃'ty], *a.* pointed, sharp; (*fig.*) subtle, captious.
pointure [pwɛ̃'tyːr], *n.f.* (*Print.*) point; size, number (*of shoes, gloves etc.*).
poire [pwaːr], *n.f.* pear; bulb (*rubber*).
poiré [pwa're], *n.m.* perry.
poireau [pwa'ro], **porreau** [pɔ'ro], *n.m.* (*pl.* **-eaux**) leek; wart.
poirée [pwa're], *n.f.* white beet.
poirier [pwa'rje], *n.m.* pear-tree.
pois [pwɑ], *n.m. inv.* pea, peas.
poison [pwa'zɔ̃], *n.m.* poison.
poissard [pwa'saːr], *a.* vulgar, low.
poisser [pwa'se], *v.t.* to pitch; to make sticky.
poisseux [pwa'sø], *a.* (*fem.* **-euse**) pitchy, gluey, sticky.
poisson [pwa'sɔ̃], *n.m.* fish; ***poisson d'avril***, April fool.
poissonnerie [pwasɔn'ri], *n.f.* fishmarket; fish-shop.
poissonneux [pwasɔ'nø], *a.* (*fem.* **-euse**) abounding in fish.
poissonnier [pwasɔ'nje], *n.m.* (*fem.* **-ière**) fishmonger, fishwife.—*n.f.* (**-ière**) fishkettle.
poitrail [pwa'traːj], *n.m.* breast (*of a horse*); breast-piece (*of harness*).
poitrinaire [pwatri'nɛːr], *a.* and *n.* consumptive.
poitrine [pwa'trin], *n.f.* chest, breast; breasts; lungs; brisket.
poivrade [pwa'vrad], *n.f.* pepper-sauce.
poivre [pwaːvr], *n.m.* pepper.
poivrer [pwa'vre], *v.t.* to pepper.
poivrier [pwavri'je], *n.m.* pepper-plant; pepper-box.
poivrière [pwavri'jɛːr], *n.f.* pepper-plantation; (*Fort.*) corner turret; pepper-box.
poix [pwɑ], *n.f.* pitch; shoemakers' wax.
polaire [pɔ'lɛːr], *a.* polar.
polariser [pɔlari'ze], *v.t.* to polarize.
pôle [poːl], *n.m.* (*Astron.*, *Geog.*) pole.
polémique [pɔle'mik], *a.* polemical.—*n.f.* polemics, controversy.
poli [pɔ'li], *a.* polished, glossy, sleek; polite, civil; refined.—*n.m.* polish, finish, gloss.
police [pɔ'lis], *n.f.* police; police-regulations; insurance policy; ***agent de police***, police-constable.
policer [pɔli'se], *v.t.* (*conjug. like* COMMENCER) to establish law and order in; to civilize, to polish, to refine.
polichinelle [pɔliʃi'nɛl], *n.m.* Punch; buffoon; Punch and Judy show.
policier [pɔli'sje], *a.* (*fem.* **-ière**) pertaining to the police; ***roman policier***, detective story.—*n.m.* policeman; detective.
policlinique [pɔlikli'nik], *n.f.* out-patients' department.
poliment [pɔli'mɑ̃], *adv.* politely.
poliomyélite [pɔljɔmje'lit], *n.f.* poliomyelitis.
polir [pɔ'liːr], *v.t.* to polish, to burnish; (*fig.*) to civilize, to refine. **se polir**, *v.r.* to become polished; to become refined.
polissage [pɔli'saːʒ], **polissement** [pɔlis'mɑ̃], *n.m.* polishing, finishing.
polisseur [pɔlisœːr], *n.m.* (*fem.* **-euse**) polisher.
polissoir [pɔli'swaːr], *n.m.* polisher (*tool*).
polisson [pɔli'sɔ̃], *a.* (*fem.* **-onne**) loose, naughty, licentious, smutty.—*n.m.* (*fem.* **-onne**) mischievous child, scamp; loose person.

polissonner [pɔlisɔ'ne], *v.i.* to run about the streets (*of children*).
polissonnerie [pɔlisɔn'ri], *n.f.* smutty joke, lewd act.
polissure [pɔli'syːr], *n.f.* polishing.
politesse [pɔli'tɛs], *n.f.* politeness, civility, polite attention; compliment.
politicien [pɔliti'sjɛ̃], *n.m.* (*fem.* **-enne**) (*usu. pej.*) politician.
politique [pɔli'tik], *a.* political; (*fig.*) politic, prudent, wise.—*n.f.* politics; policy, discretion.—*n.m.* politician, statesman.
politiquement [pɔlitik'mɑ̃], *adv.* politically; (*fig.*) shrewdly.
polka [pɔl'ka], *n.f.* polka.
pollen [pɔl'lɛn], *n.m.* pollen.
pollinisation [pɔliniza'sjɔ̃], *n.f.* pollinization.
polluer [pɔl'lɥe], *v.t.* to pollute; to defile; to profane.
pollution [pɔly'sjɔ̃], *n.f.* pollution; profanation.
polo [pɔ'lo], *n.m.* polo.
Pologne [pɔ'lɔɲ], **la**, *f.* Poland.
polonais [pɔlɔ'nɛ], *a.* Polish.—*n.m.* Polish (*language*); (**Polonais**, *fem.* **-aise**) Pole.—*n.f.* (**-aise**) Polonaise (*dress, dance, tune*).
poltron [pɔl'trɔ̃], *a.* (*fem.* **-onne**) cowardly, chicken-hearted. — *n.m.* (*fem.* **-onne**) coward, poltroon.
poltronnerie [pɔltrɔn'ri], *n.f.* cowardice, poltroonery.
polycopier [pɔlikɔ'pje], *v.t.* to cyclostyle.
polygamie [pɔliga'mi], *n.f.* polygamy.
polyglotte [pɔli'glɔt], *a.* and *n.* polyglot.
polytechnique [pɔlitɛk'nik], *a.* polytechnic.
pommade [pɔ'mad], *n.f.* pomade; ointment.
pomme [pɔm], *n.f.* apple; ball, knob; head (*of a cabbage, lettuce, walking-stick etc.*); (*pop.*) head, nut; ***pomme de pin***, fir-cone; ***pomme de terre***, potato.
pommé [pɔ'me], *a.* grown to a round head; (*colloq.*) complete, downright.
pommeau [pɔ'mo], *n.m.* (*pl.* **-eaux**) pommel (*of a saddle, sword etc.*); head, knob.
pommelé [pɔ'mle], *a.* dappled, mottled.
pommeler (se) [səpɔ'mle], *v.r.* (*conjug. like* APPELER) to become dappled.
pommer [pɔ'me], *v.i.* and **se pommer**, *v.r.* to grow to a firm round head (*of cabbage, lettuce etc.*).
pommette [pɔ'mɛt], *n.f.* apple-like ball *or* knob; cheek-bone; (*C*) crab-apple.
pommier [pɔ'mje], *n.m.* apple-tree.
pompe [pɔ̃ːp], *n.f.* pomp, ceremony; display; pump, inflator; ***pompe à incendie***, fire-engine.
pomper [pɔ̃'pe], *v.t.* to pump; (*fig.*) to suck up.—*v.i.* to pump.
pompeusement [pɔ̃pøz'mɑ̃], *adv.* solemnly, with pomp.
pompeux [pɔ̃'pø], *a.* (*fem.* **-euse**) stately, solemn; pompous.
pompier [pɔ̃'pje], *a. inv.* conventional (*art, style*).—*n.m.* fireman.
pompiste [pɔ̃'pist], *n.* pump-attendant (*at petrol-pump etc.*).
pompon [pɔ̃'pɔ̃], *n.m.* pompon, top-knot.
pomponner [pɔ̃pɔ'ne], *v.t.* to ornament with pompons to deck out. **se pomponner**, *v.r.* to dress oneself up.
ponce [pɔ̃ːs] *n.f.* pumice; (*Drawing*) pounce.
ponceau (1) [pɔ̃'so], *n.m.* (*pl.* **-eaux**) small bridge, culvert.
ponceau (2) [pɔ̃'so], *a.* poppy-red.—*n.m.* (*pl.* **-eaux**) corn-poppy.
Ponce Pilate [pɔ̃spi'lat], *m.* Pontius Pilate.
poncer [pɔ̃'se], *v.t.* (*conjug. like* COMMENCER) to pumice; (*Drawing*) to pounce.
poncif [pɔ̃'sif], *n.m.* pounced drawing; (*fig.*) commonplace piece of work.
ponctualité [pɔ̃ktɥali'te], *n.f.* punctuality.
ponctuation [pɔ̃ktɥa'sjɔ̃], *n.f.* punctuation.
ponctué [pɔ̃k'tɥe], *a.* punctuated; dotted; ***ligne ponctuée***, dotted line.
ponctuel [pɔ̃k'tɥɛl], *a.* (*fem.* **-elle**) punctual, exact.
ponctuellement [pɔ̃ktɥɛl'mɑ̃], *adv.* punctually.
ponctuer [pɔ̃k'tɥe], *v.t.* to punctuate; to point.
pondéré [pɔ̃de're], *a.* poised, calm, self-controlled.
pondérer [pɔ̃de're], *v.t.* (*conjug. like* CÉDER) to poise, to balance.
pondeur [pɔ̃'dœːr], *a.* (*fem.* **-euse**) good laying (*of poultry etc.*); (*colloq.*) productive.—*n.f.* (**-euse**) good layer.
pondre [pɔ̃ːdr], *v.t.* to lay (*eggs*).
poney [pɔ'ne], *n.m.* pony.
pont [pɔ̃], *n.m.* bridge; deck; ***Ponts et Chaussées***, (*France*) Department of Bridges and Highways.
ponte (1) [pɔ̃ːt], *n.f.* laying of eggs.
ponte (2) [pɔ̃ːt], *n.m.* punter; (*fam.*) V.I.P.
ponté [pɔ̃'te], *a.* decked (*of ship*); ***non ponté***, open (*boat*).
ponter [pɔ̃'te], *v.i.* to punt, to gamble.
pontet [pɔ̃'tɛ], *n.m.* trigger-guard; saddle-tree.
pontife [pɔ̃'tif], *n.m.* pontiff.
pontifier [pɔ̃ti'fje], *v.i.* (*fam.*) to act *or* speak solemnly *or* pompously; to pontificate, to lay down the law.
pont-levis [pɔ̃l'vi], *n.m.* (*pl.* **ponts-levis**) drawbridge.
ponton [pɔ̃'tɔ̃], *n.m.* bridge of boats; pontoon.
popeline [pɔ'plin], *n.f.* poplin.
populace [pɔpy'las], *n.f.* populace, mob, rabble.
populacier [pɔpyla'sje], *a.* (*fem.* **-ière**) low, vulgar.
populaire [pɔpy'lɛːr], *a.* popular; common.—*n.m.* populace, rabble.
populairement [pɔpylɛr'mɑ̃], *adv.* popularly.
populariser [pɔpylari'ze], *v.t.* to popularize.
popularité [pɔpylari'te], *n.f.* popularity.
population [pɔpyla'sjɔ̃], *n.f.* population.
populeux [pɔpy'lø], *a.* (*fem.* **-euse**) populous.
porc [pɔːr], *n.m.* pig; swine; pork.
porcelaine [pɔrsə'lɛn], *n.f.* porcelain, china, chinaware.
porcelet [pɔrsə'lɛ], *n.m.* young pig, piglet.
porc-épic [pɔrke'pik], *n.m.* (*pl.* **porcs-épics**) porcupine; (*Am.*) hedgehog.
porche [pɔrʃ], *n.m.* porch.
porcher [pɔr'ʃe], *n.m.* (*fem.* **-ère**) swineherd.
porcherie [pɔrʃ'ri], *n.f.* pigsty, piggery.
porcin [pɔr'sɛ̃], *a.* porcine.—*n.m.* (*pl.*) pigs.
pore [pɔːr], *n.m.* pore.
poreux [pɔ'rø], *a.* (*fem.* **-euse**) porous.
pornographie [pɔrnɔgra'fi], *n.f.* pornography.
pornographique [pɔrnɔgra'fik], *a.* pornographic.

porphyre [pɔr'fi:r], *n.m.* porphyry.

porphyriser [pɔrfiri'ze], *v.t.* to porphyrize; to pulverize.

porreau [POIREAU].

port (1) [pɔ:r], *n.m.* haven, harbour, port; seaport town; ***arriver à bon port***, to arrive safely; (*fig.*) to end happily; ***port d'escale***, port of call.

port (2) [pɔ:r], *n.m.* carrying, carriage; postage; bearing, gait; (*Naut.*) tonnage.

portable [pɔr'tabl], *a.* portable; wearable.

portage [pɔr'ta:ʒ], *n.m.* carriage, transport.

portail [pɔr'ta:j], *n.m.* (*pl.* **-s**) portal, front gate (*of a church etc.*).

portant [pɔr'tɑ̃], *a.* bearing, carrying; ***être bien portant***, to be in good health.

portatif [pɔrta'tif], *a.* (*fem.* **-tive**) portable.

porte [pɔrt], *n.f.* doorway, gateway; door; gate; entrance; eye (*of hooks etc.*); defile.

porté [pɔr'te], *a.* carried; inclined, prone, disposed (*à*); projected (*of shadows*).

porte-à-faux [pɔrta'fo], *n.m. inv.* overhang; ***en porte-à-faux***, overhanging; unsteady.

porte-affiches [pɔrta'fiʃ], *n.m. inv.* advertising-board.

porte-avions [pɔrta'vjɔ̃], *n.m. inv.* aircraft carrier.

porte-bagages [pɔrtba'ga:ʒ], *n.m. inv.* luggage-rack.

porte-billets [pɔrtbi'jɛ], *n.m. inv.* note-case; (*Am.*) bill-fold.

porte-bonheur [pɔrtbɔ'nœ:r], *n.m. inv.* good-luck charm; mascot.

porte-bouteilles [pɔrtbu'tɛ:j], *n.m. inv.* bottle-rack, wine-bin.

porte-chapeaux [pɔrtʃa'po], *n.m. inv.* hat-stand.

porte-cigarettes [pɔrtsiga'rɛt], *n.m. inv.* cigarette case.

porte-clefs [pɔrtə'kle], *n.m. inv.* key-ring.

porte-couteau [pɔrtku'to], *n.m. inv.* knife-rest.

porte-crayon [pɔrtəkrɛ'jɔ̃], *n.m. inv.* pencil-case.

porte-documents [pɔrtdɔky'mɑ̃], *n.m. inv.* dispatch-case.

porte-drapeau [pɔrtdra'po], *n.m. inv.* ensign, colour-bearer.

portée [pɔr'te], *n.f.* brood, litter; reach (*of the hand, arm etc.*); hearing; range, shot; scope; capacity; import, significance; bearing; resting-point; (*Mus.*) stave.

porte-étendard [pɔrtetɑ̃'da:r], *n.m. inv.* standard-bearer.

porte-fenêtre [pɔrtfə'nɛ:tr], *n.f.* (*pl.* **portes-fenêtres**) French window.

portefeuille [pɔrtə'fœ:j], *n.m.* wallet; (*fig.*) portfolio; office.

porte-flambeau [pɔrtflɑ̃'bo], *n.m. inv.* torch-bearer, linkman.

porte-jupe [pɔrtə'ʒyp], *n.m. inv.* skirt-hanger.

porte-livres [pɔrtə'li:vr], *n.m. inv.* book-rest.

porte-malheur [pɔrtma'lœ:r], *n.m. inv.* bird of ill-omen, bearer of ill-luck.

portemanteau [pɔrtmɑ̃'to], *n.m.* (*pl.* **-eaux**) coat-stand, coat-rail; peg.

porte-masse [pɔrtə'mas], *n.m. inv.* mace-bearer.

porte-mine(s) [pɔrtə'min], *n.m. inv.* propelling pencil.

porte-monnaie [pɔrtmɔ'nɛ], *n.m. inv.* purse.

porte-musique [pɔrtmy'zik], *n.m. inv.* music-case.

porte-parapluies [pɔrtpara'plɥi], *n.m. inv.* umbrella-stand.

porte-parole [pɔrtpa'rɔl], *n.m. inv.* mouthpiece, spokesman.

porte-plume [pɔrtə'plym], *n.m. inv.* pen-holder.

porte-queue [pɔrtə'kø], *n.m. inv.* train-bearer; swallowtail butterfly.

porter [pɔr'te], *v.t.* to carry, to bear, to support; to endure; to bring, to take; to wear; to deal (*blows etc.*); to turn (*the eyes etc.*); to entertain (*affection etc.*); to incline; to produce; to declare, to show.—*v.i.* to bear; to rest, to lie; to take effect; to hit; to reach; to carry (*of a gun etc.*); (*Naut.*) to stand, to bear off; to be with young (*of animals*). **se porter**, *v.r.* to go, to repair, to move; to resort, to flock; to be inclined *or* disposed, to tend; to be, to do (*of health*); to be worn; to present oneself, to stand forth; to turn, to be directed.

porte-rame [pɔrt'ram], *n.m. inv.* rowlock.

porte-serviette(s) [pɔrtsɛr'vjɛt], *n.m. inv.* towel-rail.

porteur [pɔr'tœ:r], *n.m.* (*fem.* **-euse**) porter, carrier, bearer; holder; sleeper (*on railway track*).

porte-voix [pɔrt'vwa], *n.m. inv.* megaphone.

portier [pɔr'tje], *n.m.* (*fem.* **-ière** (1)) porter, door-keeper.

portière (2) [pɔr'tjɛ:r], *n.f.* door-curtain, door (*of vehicle*).

portion [pɔr'sjɔ̃], *n.f.* portion, part, share, allowance.

portionner [pɔrsjɔ'ne], *v.t.* to share out.

portique [pɔr'tik], *n.m.* portico; porch.

porto [pɔr'to], *n.m.* port (wine).

portrait [pɔr'trɛ], *n.m.* portrait, likeness, picture.

portraitiste [pɔrtrɛ'tist], *n.* portrait painter.

portugais [pɔrty'gɛ], *a.* Portuguese.—*n.m.* Portuguese (*language*); (**Portugais**, *fem.* **-aise**) Portuguese (*person*).

Portugal [pɔrty'gal], **le**, *m.* Portugal.

pose [po:z], *n.f.* laying, setting; pose, posture, attitude; posing, affectation; sitting (*for one's portrait etc.*); hanging (*of bells*); (*Mil.*) posting (*of sentries*); (*Phot.*) (time) exposure.

posé [po'ze], *a.* laid, set, poised; bearing, resting; sedate, staid, sober; ***cela posé***, this being granted.

posément [poze'mɑ̃], *adv.* calmly; sedately.

poser [po'ze], *v.t.* to put, to put in (*a lock, a window-pane*); to place, to lay down; to hang; to suppose, to grant; to post (*sentries etc.*); to lay down, to state; (*Mus.*) to pitch; to sit (*for portrait*); ***poser une question***, to ask a question.—*v.i.* to lie, to rest (***sur***); to stand, to pose, to sit (*for one's portrait*); to show off. **se poser**, *v.r.* to perch (*of birds etc.*); to come down, to land (*plane*); to set up (***en***), to play the part (***en***).

poseur [po'zœ:r], *n.m.* (*Rail.*) plate-layer.—*n.m.* (*fem.* **-euse**) (*colloq.*) poseur, snob, prig.

positif [pɔzi'tif], *a.* (*fem.* **-tive**) positive, certain; practical, actual, matter-of-fact.—*n.m.* positive reality; certainty, fact; (*Phot., Cine., Gram.*) positive.

position [pɔzi'sjɔ̃], *n.f.* position, situation; status, standing; case, state, circumstances.
positivement [pɔzitiv'mɑ̃], *adv.* positively, exactly.
possédé [pose'de], *a.* possessed.—*n.m.* (*fem.* **-ée**) person possessed, madman, maniac.
posséder [pɔse'de], *v.t.* (*conjug. like* CÉDER) to possess, to be possessed of, to own; to be master of; to be conversant with; to dominate (*a person*); (*pop.*) to deceive. **se posséder**, *v.r.* to master one's passions, to contain oneself.
possesseur [pɔsɛ'sœːr], *n.m.* possessor, owner, occupier.
possessif [pɔsɛ'sif], *a.* (*fem.* **-ive**) possessive. —*n.m.* (*Gram.*) possessive adjective *or* pronoun.
possession [pɔsɛ'sjɔ̃], *n.f.* possession; property.
possibilité [pɔsibili'te], *n.f.* possibility; (*pl.*) facilities.
possible [pɔ'sibl], *a.* possible.—*n.m.* possibility; ***au possible***, extremely; ***je ferai tout mon possible***, I'll do the best I can.
postal [pɔs'tal], *a.* (*m. pl.* **-aux**) postal, of the post.
poste (1) [pɔst], *n.m.* post, station; guard-house; place, employment, post; (*Naut.*) berth; (*Teleph.*) extension; entry (*in books*); ***poste de radio***, wireless set; ***poste d'incendie***, fire-station.
poste (2) [pɔst], *n.f.* post (*relay*); post-stage; postal service; post-office, mail; ***bureau de poste***, post-office.
poster [pɔs'te], *v.t.* to station, to post (*sentry* or *letter*).
postérieur [pɔste'rjœːr], *a.* posterior, later; behind.—*n.m.* (*colloq.*) posterior.
postérieurement [pɔsterjœr'mɑ̃], *adv.* subsequently.
postérité [pɔsteri'te], *n.f.* posterity.
posthume [pɔs'tym], *a.* posthumous.
postiche [pɔs'tiʃ], *a.* superadded; false, artificial.—*n.m.* wig.
postier [pɔs'tje], *n.m.* (*fem.* **-ière**) post-office employee.
postillon [pɔsti'jɔ̃], *n.m.* postilion; post-boy.
postscolaire [pɔstskɔ'lɛːr], *a.* continuation (*class*); ***enseignement postscolaire***, adult education.
post-scriptum [pɔstskrip'tɔm] (*abbr.* **P.S.**), *n.m. inv.* postscript.
postulant [pɔsty'lɑ̃], *n.m.* (*fem.* **-e**) candidate, applicant; postulant.
postuler [pɔsty'le], *v.t.* to solicit, to apply for.—*v.i.* (*Law*) to act on behalf of a client.
posture [pɔs'tyːr], *n.f.* posture, attitude; situation.
pot [po], *n.m.* pot; jug, tankard, flagon, can, jar; (*C*) half a gallon.
potable [pɔ'tabl], *a.* drinkable (*water*).
potage [pɔ'taːʒ], *n.m.* soup.
potager (1) [pɔta'ʒe], *n.m.* kitchen-garden; kitchen-stove.
potager (2) [pɔta'ʒe], *a.* (*fem.* **-ère**) culinary; ***jardin potager***, kitchen-garden.
potasse [pɔ'tas], *n.f.* potash.
potassium [pɔta'sjɔm], *n.m.* potassium.
pot-au-feu [pɔto'fø], *n.m. inv.* beef boiled with carrots etc.; broth of this.
pot-de-vin [pod'vɛ̃], *n.m.* (*pl.* **pots-de-vin**) gratuity; bribe; hush-money.
poteau [pɔ'to], *n.m.* (*pl.* **-eaux**) post, stake.
potée [pɔ'te], *n.f.* potful; (*colloq.*) swarm (*of children etc.*); putty; (*Metal.*) moulding.
potelé [pɔ'tle], *a.* plump, chubby.
potence [pɔ'tɑ̃ːs], *n.f.* gallows, gibbet; bracket; crutch; ***gibier de potence***, jail-bird.
potentat [pɔtɑ̃'ta], *n.m.* potentate.
potentiel [pɔtɑ̃'sjɛ], *a.* (*fem.* **-elle**) potential, —*n.m.* potentialities.
potentiellement [pɔtɑ̃sjɛl'mɑ̃], *adv.* potentially.
poterie [pɔ'tri], *n.f.* pottery, earthenware.
poterne [pɔ'tɛrn], *n.f.* postern.
potiche [pɔ'tiʃ], *n.f.* China *or* Japan porcelain vase.
potier [pɔ'tje], *n.m.* potter.
potin [pɔ'tɛ̃], *n.m.* pinchbeck; (*pl.*) gossip.
potion [po'sjɔ̃], *n.f.* potion, draught.
potiron [pɔti'rɔ̃], *n.m.* pumpkin.
pou [pu], *n.m.* (*pl.* **poux**) louse.
pouah! [pwa], *int.* ugh! disgusting!
poubelle [pu'bɛl], *n.f.* dustbin; (*Am.*) ash-can.
pouce [pus], *n.m.* thumb; big toe; inch; ***un morceau sur le pouce***, a snack; (*C*) ***faire du pouce***, to hitch-hike.
poucet [pu'sɛ], *n.m.* ***le petit Poucet***, Tom Thumb.
pouding [pu'diŋ], *n.m.* plum-pudding.
poudre [pudr], *n.f.* powder; gunpowder; dust; ***sucre en poudre***, castor sugar.
poudrer [pu'dre], *v.t.* to powder, to sprinkle with powder.
poudrerie [pudrə'ri], *n.f.* gunpowder-factory; (*C*) blizzard.
poudreux [pu'drø], *a.* (*fem.* **-euse**) dusty, powdery.
poudrier [pudri'e], *n.m.* (powder) compact.
poudrière [pudri'ɛːr], *n.f.* powder-mill, magazine; sand-box.
poudroyer [pudrwɑ'je], *v.i.* (*conjug. like* EMPLOYER) to rise in dust; to be dusty (*of roads etc.*).
pouf! (1) [puf], *int.* plop! flop! phew!
pouf (2) [puf], *n.m.* ottoman (*seat*), pouf; puff (*advertisement*).
pouffer [pu'fe], *v.i.* ***pouffer de rire***, to burst out laughing, to guffaw.
pouilleux [pu'jø], *a.* and *n.m.* (*fem.* **-euse**) lousy; wretched, mean (person).
poulailler [pulɑ'je], *n.m.* hen-house; (*of persons*) poulterer; (*Theat.*) gods.
poulain [pu'lɛ̃], *n.m.* foal, colt.
poularde [pu'lard], *n.f.* fat pullet.
poulbot [pul'bo], *n.m.* Paris street urchin.
poule [pul], *n.f.* hen; fowl; pool (*at games*); eliminating round (*in a competition*).
poulet [pu'lɛ], *n.m.* chicken; love-letter.
poulette [pu'lɛt], *n.f.* pullet.
pouliche [pu'liʃ], *n.f.* filly.
poulie [pu'li], *n.f.* pulley; (*Naut.*) block.
pouliner [puli'ne], *v.i.* to foal (*of mares*).
poulinière [puli'njɛːr], *a.f.* and *n.f.* (***jument***) ***poulinière***, brood mare.
poulpe [pulp], *n.m.* octopus, devil-fish.
pouls [pu], *n.m.* pulse; ***se tâter le pouls***, to feel one's pulse.
poumon [pu'mɔ̃], *n.m.* lung; ***poumon d'acier***, iron lung.

poupard [pu'pa:r], *a.* chubby.—*n.m.* baby; doll.
poupe [pup], *n.f.* stern, poop.
poupée [pu'pe], *n.f.* doll; puppet; tailor's dummy.
poupin [pu'pɛ̃], *a.* fresh-coloured; rosy.
poupon [pu'pɔ̃], *n.m.* (*fem.* **-onne**) baby; plump, chubby-cheeked boy *or* girl.
pouponnière [pupɔ'njɛ:r], *n.f.* (*public*) day-nursery.
pour [pu:r], *prep.* for; on account of; on behalf of; as regards, as for; in order; although.—*n.m.* for, pro.
pourboire [pur'bwa:r], *n.m.* tip, gratuity.
pourceau [pur'so], *n.m.* (*pl.* **-eaux**) hog, pig, swine.
pour-cent [pur'sɑ̃], **pourcentage** [pursɑ̃'ta:ʒ], *n.m.* percentage.
pourchasser [purʃa'se], *v.t.* to pursue, to chase, to badger.
pourfendre [pur'fɑ̃:dr], *v.t.* to cleave asunder.
pourlécher [purle'ʃe], *v.t.* (*conjug. like* CÉDER) to lick all over. **se pourlécher**, *v.r.* to lick one's lips.
pourparler [purpar'le], *n.m.* (*usu. in pl.*) parley, negotiations; talks.
pourpoint [pur'pwɛ̃], *n.m.* doublet.
pourpre [purpr], *a.* purple, dark red.—*n.f.* purple (*stuff*); (*fig.*) sovereign dignity; cardinalate.—*n.m.* purple, crimson (*colour*).
pourpré [pur'pre], *a.* purple.
pourquoi [pur'kwa], *adv.* and *conj.* why, wherefore; ***pourquoi pas?*** why not?—*n.m. inv.* the reason why.
pourri [pu'ri], *a.* rotten; ***temps pourri***, muggy weather.—*n.m.* the rotten part; rottenness.
pourrir [pu'ri:r], *v.t.* to make rotten, to corrupt.—*v.i.* to rot; (*fig.*) to perish. **se pourrir**, *v.r.* to become rotten, to go bad.
pourrissable [puri'sabl], *a.* perishable.
pourrissant [puri'sɑ̃], *a.* rotting, causing rot.
pourriture [puri'ty:r], *n.f.* rot, rottenness, putrefaction; (*fig.*) corruption.
poursuite [pur'sɥit], *n.f.* pursuit, chase; prosecution; (*Law*) suit, proceedings.
poursuivable [pursɥi'vabl], *a.* actionable.
poursuivant [pursɥi'vɑ̃], *a.* suing, prosecuting.—*n.m.* suitor.—*n.m.* (*fem.* **-e**) prosecutor, plaintiff.
poursuivre [pur'sɥi:vr], *v.t. irr.* (*conjug. like* SUIVRE) to pursue; to seek; to persecute; to haunt; to go on with; to follow up; (*Law*) to sue, to prosecute.—*v.i.* to pursue, to go on, to continue. **se poursuivre**, *v.r.* to continue, to follow its course.
pourtant [pur'tɑ̃], *adv.* however, yet, still, nevertheless.
pourtour [pur'tu:r], *n.m.* periphery, circumference; gangway (*in a theatre etc.*); precincts (*of cathedral*).
pourvoi [pur'vwa], *n.m.* (*Law*) appeal.
pourvoir [pur'vwa:r], *v.t. irr.* to invest with, to appoint; to provide, to supply, to endow.—*v.i.* (*followed by* **à**) to see to, to attend to, to provide for; to make an appointment to. **se pourvoir**, *v.r.* to provide oneself; to appeal.
pourvoyeur [purvwa'jœ:r], *n.m.* (*fem.* **-euse**) purveyor, provider, caterer.
pourvu que [pur'vykə], *conj. phr.* provided that, provided.
pousse [pus], *n.f.* shoot, sprout.
pousse-café [puska'fe], *n.m. inv.* (*fam.*) liqueur (*after coffee*).
poussée [pu'se], *n.f.* pushing; shove; thrust (*of arches etc.*); pressure (*of business etc.*).
pousse-pousse [pus'pus], *n.m. inv.* rickshaw (*carriage* or *man*).
pousser [pu'se], *v.t.* to push, to thrust, to shove; to drive on; to carry on, to extend; to grow, to send forth (*of plants etc.*); to urge, to provoke; to assist, to help on; to utter, to heave (*a sigh etc.*); to deal (*a blow etc.*).—*v.i.* to sprout, to shoot (*of plants*); to grow (*of the hair, nails etc.*); to push on, to go on; to bulge; to be broken-winded (*of horses*). **se pousser**, *v.r.* to push forward, to push oneself forward; to push each other, to jostle.
poussette [pu'sɛt], *n.f.* push-chair; movement in dancing.
poussier [pu'sje], *n.m.* coal-dust, screenings.
poussière [pu'sjɛ:r], *n.f.* dust; spray (*of water*).
poussiéreux [pusje'rø], *a.* (*fem.* **-euse**) dusty.
poussif [pu'sif], *a.* (*fem.* **-ive**) shortwinded.
poussin [pu'sɛ̃], *n.m.* chick, chicken just hatched.
poussinière [pusi'njɛ:r], *n.f.* chicken-coop; incubator.
poutre [putr], *n.f.* beam; girder.
poutrelle [pu'trɛl], *n.f.* small beam.
pouvoir [pu'vwa:r], *v.t. irr.* to be able to do.—*v.i.* to be able (*can etc.*), to have power; to be allowed (*may etc.*); (*impers.*) to be possible; ***il peut arriver que***, it may happen that; ***il se peut que***, it is possible that; ***on ne peut plus***, (*followed by adj.*) exceedingly; ***sauve qui peut***, every man for himself.—*n.m.* power; might; authority; command, government.
prairie [prɛ'ri], *n.f.* meadow, grass-land, grass-field; (*U.S.*) prairie.
praline [pra'lin], *n.f.* burnt almond.
praliner [prali'ne], *v.t.* to brown in sugar (*like burnt almonds*).
praticabilité [pratikabili'te], *n.f.* practicability, feasibility.
praticable [prati'kabl], *a.* practicable, feasible; passable (*of roads*); accessible; (*Theat.*) real.
praticien [prati'sjɛ̃], *a.* (*fem.* **-enne**) practising.—*n.m.* (*fem.* **-enne**) practitioner.
pratiquant [prati'kɑ̃], *a.* church-going.—*n.m.* (*fem.* **-e**) church-goer.
pratique [pra'tik], *a.* practical; experienced.—*n.f.* practice; execution; method; experience; usage; custom (*of tradesman*), practice (*of attorneys, physicians etc.*); customer; (*pl.*) dealings.
pratiquement [pratik'mɑ̃], *adv.* in actual fact, practically; in a practical way.
pratiquer [prati'ke], *v.t.* to practise, to exercise; to frequent; to tamper with, to bribe; to obtain; (*Arch.*) to contrive. **se pratiquer**, *v.r.* to be in use, to be practised.
pré [pre], *n.m.* meadow.
préalable [prea'labl], *a.* preliminary; previous.—*n.m.* ***au préalable***, previously, first of all.
préalablement [prealablə'mɑ̃], *adv.* previously, first, to begin with.

préambule [preɑ̃'byl], *n.m.* preamble, preface.
préau [pre'o], *n.m.* (*pl.* **-aux**) courtyard (*of a convent* or *prison*); (*sch.*) covered playground.
préavis [prea'vi], *n.m. inv.* (previous) notice.
précaire [pre'kɛːr], *a.* precarious; uncertain.
précairement [prekɛr'mɑ̃], *adv.* precariously.
précaution [preko'sjɔ̃], *n.f.* precaution; caution, care.
précautionner [prekosjɔ'ne], *v.t.* to warn, to caution. **se précautionner**, *v.r.* to take precautions.
précédemment [preseda'mɑ̃], *adv.* before, previously.
précédent [prese'dɑ̃], *a.* preceding, former.—*n.m.* precedent.
précéder [prese'de], *v.t.* (*conjug. like* CÉDER) to precede, to go before; to take precedence (*of*).
précepte [pre'sɛpt], *n.m.* precept, rule.
précepteur [presɛp'tœːr], *n.m.* (*fem.* **-trice**) tutor, teacher.
prêche [prɛːʃ], *n.m.* sermon (*Protestant*); Protestant church.
prêcher [prɛ'ʃe], *v.t.* to preach; to exhort; to extol, to praise.—*v.i.* to preach.
prêcheur [prɛ'ʃœːr], *n.m.* (*fem.* **-euse**) preacher.
précieusement [presjøz'mɑ̃], *adv.* preciously; carefully; affectedly.
précieux [pre'sjø], *a.* (*fem.* **-euse**) precious, valuable; affected.—*n.m.* affectation.—*n.m.* (*fem.* **-euse**) affected person.
préciosité [presjɔzi'te], *n.f.* affectation.
précipice [presi'pis], *n.m.* precipice.
précipitamment [presipita'mɑ̃], *adv.* precipitately, hurriedly, rashly.
précipitation [presipitɑ'sjɔ̃], *n.f.* haste, hurry; (*Chem.*) precipitation.
précipité [presipi'te], *a.* precipitated, hurled; precipitate, hasty, sudden.—*n.m.* (*Chem.*) precipitate.
précipiter [presipi'te], *v.t.* to precipitate, to hurl; to hasten, to accelerate; (*Chem.*) to precipitate. **se précipiter**, *v.r.* to precipitate, throw *or* hurl oneself; to rush forward, to spring forth, to dart.
précis [pre'si], *a.* fixed, precise, exact; formal, terse, concise.—*n.m.* summary, abstract.
précisément [presize'mɑ̃], *adv.* precisely, exactly; quite; just so.
préciser [presi'ze], *v.t.* to state precisely, to specify.
précision [presi'zjɔ̃], *n.f.* precision, preciseness.
précité [presi'te], *a.* afore-mentioned.
précoce [pre'kɔs], *a.* precocious, early, forward.
précocité [prekɔsi'te], *n.f.* precocity.
préconçu [prekɔ̃'sy], *a.* preconceived.
préconiser [prekɔni'ze], *v.t.* to advocate, to recommend.
préconnaissance [prekɔnɛ'sɑːs], *n.f.* foreknowledge.
précurseur [prekyr'sœːr], *n.m.* forerunner, precursor, harbinger.
prédateur [preda'tœːr], *a.* (*fem.* **-trice**) (*Ent.*) predatory.
prédécéder [predese'de], *v.i.* (*conjug. like* CÉDER) to predecease (*someone*).
prédestination [predɛstinɑ'sjɔ̃], *n.f.* predestination.
prédestiné [predɛsti'ne], *a.* predestined; predetermined.—*n.m.* (*fem.* **-ée**) one of the elect.
prédicateur [predika'tœːr], *n.m.* (*fem.* **-trice**) preacher.
prédiction [predik'sjɔ̃], *n.f.* prediction, forecast.
prédilection [predilɛk'sjɔ̃], *n.f.* predilection, preference.
prédire [pre'diːr], *v.t. irr.* (*conjug. like* MÉDIRE) to predict, to foretell.
prédisposer [predispo'ze], *v.t.* to predispose.
prédisposition [predispozi'sjɔ̃], *n.f.* predisposition.
prédominance [predɔmi'nɑːs], *n.f.* predominance, ascendancy.
prédominant [predɔmi'nɑ̃], *a.* predominant.
prédominer [predɔmi'ne], *v.t.* to prevail over.—*v.i.* to predominate.
prééminence [preemi'nɑːs], *n.f.* pre-eminence.
prééminent [preemi'nɑ̃], *a.* pre-eminent.
préemption [preɑ̃p'sjɔ̃], *n.f.* pre-emption.
préfabriqué [prefabri'ke], *a.* prefabricated.
préface [pre'fas], *n.f.* preface; foreword.
préfecture [prefɛk'tyːr], *n.f.* prefecture; ***préfecture de police***, Paris police headquarters.
préférable [prefe'rabl], *a.* preferable.
préférablement [preferablə'mɑ̃], *adv.* preferably.
préféré [prefe're], *a.* favourite.
préférence [prefe'rɑːs], *n.f.* preference.
préférer [prefe're], *v.t.* (*conjug. like* CÉDER) to prefer.
préfet [pre'fɛ], *n.m.* prefect; chief administrator of a department in France; ***préfet de police***, chief commissioner of Parisian police.
préhensile [preɑ̃'sil], *a.* prehensile.
préhistorique [preistɔ'rik], *a.* prehistoric.
préjudice [preʒy'dis], *n.m.* detriment, injury, damage, prejudice.
préjudiciable [preʒydi'sjabl], *a.* prejudicial, detrimental.
préjudicier [preʒydi'sje], *v.i.* to be prejudicial *or* detrimental.
préjugé [preʒy'ʒe], *n.m.* presumption, prejudice; (*Law*) precedent.
préjuger [preʒy'ʒe], *v.t.* (*conjug. like* MANGER) to prejudge.
prélasser (se) [səprelɑ'se], *v.r.* to strut, to stalk along.
prélat [pre'la], *n.m.* prelate.
prélèvement [prelɛv'mɑ̃], *n.m.* deduction; sample; (*Med.*) swab.
prélever [prelə've], *v.t.* (*conjug. like* AMENER) to deduct; to appropriate.
préliminaire [prelimi'nɛːr], *a.* and *n.m.* preliminary.
prélude [pre'lyd], *n.m.* prelude.
prématuré [prematy're], *a.* premature, untimely.
prématurément [prematyre'mɑ̃], *adv.* prematurely.
préméditation [premeditɑ'sjɔ̃], *n.f.* premeditation.
préméditer [premedi'te], *v.t.* to premeditate.

prémices [pre'mis], *n.f. pl.* first-fruits; (*fig.*) beginning.
premier [prə'mje], *a.* (*fem.* **-ière**) first; foremost, best, chief; former (*of two*); early, pristine, primeval; (*Arith.*) prime; ***au premier abord***, at first sight; ***le premier rang***, the front rank; ***matières premières***, raw materials.—*n.m.* (*fem.* **-ière**) chief, head, leader.—*n.m.* first floor; first of the month etc.—*n.f.* (**-ière**) (*Theat.*) first night; (*Sch.*) sixth form.
premièrement [prəmjɛr'mɑ̃], *adv.* firstly, in the first place.
prémonition [premɔni'sjɔ̃], *n.f.* premonition.
prémunir [premy'niːr], *v.t.* to forewarn, to caution, to secure beforehand. **se prémunir**, *v.r.* to provide (**contre**).
prenant [prə'nɑ̃], taking, prehensile; (*fig.*) fascinating; ***partie prenante***, payee.
prendre [prɑ̃ːdr], *v.t. irr.* to take; to take up; to snatch; to seize; to capture; to contract, to catch (*a cold etc.*); to choose; to fetch; to assume; to collect (*votes etc.*); to help oneself to; to conduct (*an affair etc.*); to entertain (*a feeling etc.*); ***en prendre à son aise***, to take it easy; ***prendre pour dit***, to take for granted; ***que je t'y prenne un peu!*** just let me catch you at it!—*v.i.* to take; to take root; to congeal, to freeze; to curdle (*of milk etc.*); to succeed; to begin to burn. **se prendre**, *v.r.* to be taken, to be caught; to catch; to freeze, to congeal (*of liquids*); to begin.
preneur [prə'nœːr], *n.m.* (*fem.* **-euse**) taker; lessee; purchaser; catcher (*of animals*).
prénom [pre'nɔ̃], *n.m.* Christian name.
prénommé [prenɔ'me], *a.* and *n.m.* (*fem.* **-ée**) (the) above-named, aforesaid; named.
préoccupation [preɔkypɑ'sjɔ̃], *n.f.* preoccupation; anxiety, concern.
préoccupé [preɔky'pe], *a.* preoccupied, absorbed; worried.
préoccuper [preɔky'pe], *v.t.* to engross, to preoccupy; to worry. **se préoccuper**, *v.r.* to see to, to be engaged in (**de**), to be anxious about.
préparateur [prepara'tœːr], *n.m.* (*fem.* **-trice**) preparer, assistant (*in laboratory* or *in a dispensing chemist's*).
préparatif(s) [prepara'tif], *n.m. sing.* or *pl.* preparation.
préparation [preparɑ'sjɔ̃], *n.f.* preparation; ***sans préparation***, extempore.
préparatoire [prepara'twaːr], *a.* preparatory.
préparer [prepa're], *v.t.* to prepare, to make ready; to fit; to make up, to manufacture. **se préparer**, *v.r.* to prepare, to prepare oneself, to get ready.
prépondérance [prepɔ̃de'rɑ̃ːs], *n.f.* preponderance.
prépondérant [prepɔ̃de'rɑ̃], *a.* preponderant; ***voix prépondérante***, casting-vote.
préposé [prepo'ze], *n.m.* (*fem.* **-ée**) officer in charge, superintendent, agent.
préposer [prepo'ze], *v.t.* to set over, to appoint to, to put in charge of.
préposition [prepozi'sjɔ̃], *n.f.* preposition.
prérogative [prerɔga'tiːv], *n.f.* prerogative.
près [prɛ], *adv.* by, near, hard by; nearly, almost, about; on the point of; ***à beaucoup près***, by a great deal; ***à cela près***, with that exception; ***à peu près***, pretty near, nearly so; ***de près***, close, near; ***tout près***, very near.—*prep.* (*usu.* ***près de***) near, close to.
présage [pre'zaːʒ], *n.m.* presage, omen, foreboding.
présager [preza'ʒe], *v.t.* (*conjug. like* MANGER) to presage, to portend.
pré-salé [presa'le], *n.m.* (*pl.* **prés-salés**) salt-marsh sheep *or* mutton.
presbyte [prɛz'bit], *a.* long-sighted.—*n.* long-sighted person.
presbytère [prɛzbi'tɛːr], *n.m.* parsonage, vicarage, rectory; presbytery (*R.-C. Ch.*).
presbytérien [prɛzbite'rjɛ̃], *a.* and *n.m.* (*fem.* **-enne**) Presbyterian.
presbytie [prɛzbi'si], *n.f.* far- *or* long-sightedness.
prescience [pre'sjɑ̃ːs], *n.f.* prescience, foreknowledge.
prescription [prɛskrip'sjɔ̃], *n.f.* prescription; regulation.
prescrire [prɛs'kriːr], *v.t. irr.* (*conjug. like* ÉCRIRE) to prescribe, to stipulate; (*Law*) to bar.
préséance [prese'ɑ̃ːs], *n.f.* precedence.
présence [pre'zɑ̃ːs], *n.f.* presence, attenddance, appearance; ***mettre en présence***, to bring face to face.
présent [pre'zɑ̃], *a.* present; ***présent!*** here! —*n.m.* present, present time; gift; ***dès à présent***, from now on.
présentable [prezɑ̃'tabl], *a.* presentable, fit to be seen.
présentation [prezɑ̃tɑ'sjɔ̃], *n.f.* presentation, introduction.
présentement [prezɑ̃t'mɑ̃], *adv.* now, a present.
présenter [prezɑ̃'te], *v.t.* to present, to offer; to show; to introduce. **se présenter**, *v.r.* to present oneself, to appear.
préservateur [prezɛrva'tœːr], *a.* (*fem.* **-trice**) preservative.
préservatif [prezɛrva'tif], *a.* (*fem.* **-tive**) preservative.
préservation [prezɛrvɑ'sjɔ̃], *n.f.* preservation.
préserver [prezɛr've], *v.t.* to preserve; to defend, to keep safe; ***le ciel m'en préserve!*** heaven forbid! **se préserver**, *v.r.* to preserve oneself, to guard against.
présidence [prezi'dɑ̃ːs], *n.f.* presidency, chairmanship.
président [prezi'dɑ̃], *n.m.* president (*of tribunal*), presiding judge; speaker (*of the House of Commons*), chairman.
présidente [prezi'dɑ̃ːt], *n.f.* lady president; president's wife.
présider [prezi'de], *v.t.* to preside over, to be president *or* chairman of.—*v.i.* to preside, to be president, to be in the chair.
présomptif [prezɔ̃p'tif], *a.* (*fem.* **-tive**) presumptive, apparent, presumed (*of heirs*).
présomption [prezɔ̃p'sjɔ̃], *n.f.* presumption self-conceit.
présomptueusement [prezɔ̃ptɥøz'mɑ̃], *adv.* presumptuously.
présomptueux [prezɔ̃p'tɥø], *a.* (*fem.* **-euse**) presumptuous.
presque [prɛsk], *adv.* almost, nearly, all but; hardly, scarcely; ***presque jamais***, hardly ever; ***presque plus*** (**de**), scarcely any left; ***presque rien***, hardly anything.

presqu'île [prɛs'kil], *n.f.* peninsula.
pressage [prɛ'saːʒ], *n.m.* pressing.
pressant [prɛ'sɑ̃], *a.* pressing, urgent, earnest.
presse [prɛs], *n.f.* throng, crowd; hurry; urgency; (*Navy*) press-gang; press (*newspapers*); printing-press.
pressé [prɛ'se], *a.* pressed; crowded; close, thick; in haste, hurried; urgent; eager; very busy; (*fig.*) condensed, concise.
presse-citron [prɛssi'trɔ̃], *n.m.* (*pl. unchanged* or **-citrons**) lemon-squeezer.
pressée [prɛ'se], *n.f.* pressing, pressure; pressful (*of print etc.*).
pressentiment [prɛsɑ̃ti'mɑ̃], *n.m.* presentiment; foreboding.
pressentir [prɛsɑ̃'tiːr], *v.t. irr.* (*conjug. like* SENTIR) to have a presentiment of; to sound.
presse-papiers [prɛspa'pje], *n.m. inv.* paper-weight.
presse-purée [prɛspy're], *n.m. inv.* potato masher.
presser [prɛ'se], *v.t.* to press, to squeeze; to tread down; to crowd; to hasten; to entreat, to urge.—*v.i.* to be urgent. **se presser**, *v.r.* to press, to squeeze, to crowd; to make haste, to hurry.
pression [prɛ'sjɔ̃], *n.f.* pressure.
pressoir [prɛ'swaːr], *n.m.* press (*wine etc.*).
pressurer [prɛsy're], *v.t.* to press (*grapes, apples etc.*); (*fig.*) to squeeze money etc. out of; to oppress.
pressureur [prɛsy'rœːr], *n.m.* (*fem.* **-euse**) presser (*of fruit etc.*); (*fig.*) squeezer, sponger; oppressor.
prestance [prɛs'tɑ̃ːs], *n.f.* commanding appearance, fine presence.
prestation [prɛsta'sjɔ̃], *n.f.* taking (*of an oath*); prestation (*payment of toll etc.*).
preste [prɛst], *a.* agile, nimble; smart.
prestement [prɛstə'mɑ̃], *adv.* nimbly, quickly.
prestesse [prɛs'tɛs], *n.f.* agility, quickness.
prestidigitateur [prɛstidiʒita'tœːr], *n.m.* conjurer, juggler.
prestidigitation [prɛstidiʒita'sjɔ̃], *n.f.* conjuring, sleight of hand.
prestige [prɛs'tiːʒ], *n.m.* marvel; illusion, magic spell; prestige.
prestigieux [prɛsti'ʒjø], *a.* (*fem.* **-euse**) marvellous, amazing.
(*C*) **presto** [prɛs'to], *n.m.* pressure cooker.
présumer [prezy'me], *v.t.* to presume, to suppose.
présure [pre'zyːr], *n.f.* rennet.
prêt (1) [prɛ], *a.* ready, prepared.
prêt (2) [prɛ], *n.m.* loan; (*Mil.*) pay.
prétantaine [pretɑ̃'tɛn], *n.f.* ***courir la prétantaine***, to gad about.
prêté [prɛ'te], *a.* lent.
prétendant [pretɑ̃'dɑ̃], *n.m.* (*fem.* **-e**) claimant.—*n.m.* suitor; pretender (*to the throne*).
prétendre [pre'tɑ̃ːdr], *v.t.* to claim, to lay claim to; to mean; affirm.—*v.i.* to lay claim (*to*); to aspire (*à*).
prétendu [pretɑ̃'dy], *a.* pretended, supposed, sham, so-called, would-be.—*n.m.* (*fem.* **-e**) future husband *or* wife.
prétentieux [pretɑ̃'sjø], *a.* (*fem.* **-euse**) pretentious, assuming.
prétention [pretɑ̃'sjɔ̃], *n.f.* pretension, claim; intention, wish; expectation.
prêter [prɛ'te], *v.t.* to lend; to impart; to attribute; to bestow.—*v.i.* to give, to stretch; to invite, to give rise to. **se prêter**, *v.r.* to give way; to lend oneself *or* itself; to countenance, to favour.
prêteur [prɛ'tœːr], *n.m.* (*fem.* **-euse**) lender.
prétexte [pre'tɛkst], *n.m.* pretext, pretence; plea.
prétexter [pretɛks'te], *v.t.* to allege (*as pretext*), to pretend, to feign.
prétoire [pre'twaːr], *n.m.* (*Rom. Ant.*) praetorium.
prétorien [pretɔ'rjɛ̃], *a.* (*fem.* **-enne**) praetorian.
prêtre [prɛːtr], *n.m.* priest.
prêtresse [prɛ'trɛs], *n.f.* priestess.
prêtrise [prɛ'triːz], *n.f.* priesthood.
preuve [prœːv], *n.f.* proof; evidence, testimony.
preux [prø], *a. inv.* gallant, doughty, valiant.—*n.m.* valiant knight.
prévaloir [preva'lwaːr], *v.i. irr.* (*conjug. like* VALOIR) to prevail. **se prévaloir**, *v.r.* to take advantage, to avail oneself; to boast.
prévaricateur [prevarika'tœːr], *a.* (*fem.* **-trice**) dishonest, unjust.—*n.m.* (*fem.* **-trice**) betrayer of trust.
prévarication [prevarika'sjɔ̃], *n.f.* betrayal of trust, maladministration of justice.
prévariquer [prevari'ke], *v.i.* to betray one's trust.
prévenance [prev'nɑ̃ːs], *n.f.* (*pl.*) kind attentions.
prévenant [prev'nɑ̃], *a.* obliging, kind; prepossessing, engaging.
prévenir [prev'niːr], *v.t. irr.* (*conjug. like* TENIR) to precede; to forestall; to prevent; to prepossess, to predispose; to warn. **se prévenir**, *v.r.* to be prejudiced.
préventif [prevɑ̃'tif], *a.* (*fem.* **-tive**) preventive.
prévention [prevɑ̃'sjɔ̃], *n.f.* prepossession, prejudice; suspicion; accusation.
préventivement [prevɑ̃tiv'mɑ̃], *adv.* by way of prevention; while awaiting trial.
prévenu [pre'vny], *a.* forestalled, anticipated; prejudiced; accused.—*n.m.* (*fem.* **-e**) the accused.
prévisible [previ'zibl], *a.* foreseeable.
prévision [previ'zjɔ̃], *n.f.* forecast; estimate, expectation.
prévoir [pre'vwaːr], *v.t. irr.* to foresee, to anticipate.
prévôt [pre'vo], *n.m.* provost.
prévôté [prevo'te], *n.f.* provostship; military police.
prévoyance [prevwa'jɑ̃ːs], *n.f.* foresight, forethought, prudence.
prévoyant [prevwa'jɑ̃], *a.* provident, prudent, careful.
prié [pri'je], *a.* invited (*to a feast etc.*).
prie-Dieu [pri'djø], *n.m. inv.* praying-stool.
prier [pri'je], *v.t.* to pray, to beseech; to request; to invite.
prière [pri'jɛːr], *n.f.* prayer; request, entreaty; invitation.
prieur [pri'jœːr], *n.m.* prior (*superior of a convent*).
prieure [pri'jœːr], *n.f.* prioress.
prieuré [prijœ're], *n.m.* priory.
primaire [pri'mɛːr], *a.* primary.

primat [pri'ma], *n.m.* primate, metropolitan.
primauté [primo'te], *n.f.* primacy, priority, pre-eminence; the lead (*at cards, dice etc.*).
prime [prim], *a.* first.—*n.f.* premium; subsidy; (*Mil.*) bounty; bonus, prize; (*Fenc.*) prime; (*Comm.*) free gift; ***certificat de primes***, debenture; ***faire prime***, to be at a premium.
primer [pri'me], *v.t.* to surpass, to excel.—*v.i.* to play first, to lead (*at games*); to excel.
primeur [pri'mœ:r], *n.f.* early vegetables, fruit, flowers, etc.; early sentiment, love etc.; freshness, bloom.
primevère [prim'vɛ:r], *n.f.* (*Bot.*) primula, primrose, cowslip.
primitif [primi'tif], *a.* (*fem.* **-tive**) first, early, primitive, aboriginal; pristine.—*n.m.* (*Gram., Paint.*) primitive.
primitivement [primitiv'mɑ̃], *adv.* primitively, originally.
primo [pri'mo], *adv.* first, in the first place.
primordial [primɔr'djal], *a.* (*m. pl.* **-aux**) primordial.
prince [prɛ̃:s], *n.m.* prince.
princeps [prɛ̃'sɛps], *a. inv.* ***édition princeps***, first edition.
princesse [prɛ̃'sɛs], *n.f.* princess.
princier [prɛ̃'sje], *a.* (*fem.* **-ière**) princely, like a prince.
principal [prɛ̃si'pal], *a.* (*m. pl.* **-aux**) principal, chief, most important.—*n.m.* chief thing, principal point; principal, capital (*money*); headmaster (*of a college*); (*pl.*) chief personages (*of a town etc.*).
principalement [prɛ̃sipal'mɑ̃], *adv.* principally, chiefly.
principauté [prɛ̃sipo'te], *n.f.* principality, princedom.
principe [prɛ̃'sip], *n.m.* beginning, source, basis; principle; (*pl.*) principles, rudiments; ***dès le principe***, from the very first; ***en principe***, as a rule.
printanier [prɛ̃ta'nje], *a.* (*fem.* **-ière**) spring-like, vernal; (*fig.*) youthful, early.
printemps [prɛ̃'tɑ̃], *n.m.* spring, spring-time; (*fig.*) prime, bloom.
priorité [priɔri'te], *n.f.* priority.
pris [pri], *a.* taken, caught, seized; frozen.
prisable [pri'zabl], *a.* estimable, worthy of esteem.
prise [pri:z], *n.f.* taking, capture; prize; hold, purchase; grip; quarrel; dose; pinch (*of snuff etc.*); (*pl.*) fighting.
priser (1) [pri'ze], *v.t., v.i.* to (take) snuff.
priser (2) [pri'ze], *v.t.* to appraise, to estimate; to esteem.
priseur [pri'zœ:r], *n.m.* ***commissaire priseur***, auctioneer, valuer.
prismatique [prisma'tik], *a.* prismatic.
prisme [prism], *n.m.* prism.
prison [pri'zɔ̃], *n.f.* prison, gaol; imprisonment.
prisonnier [prizɔ'nje], *n.m.* (*fem.* **-ière**) prisoner.
privation [privɑ'sjɔ̃], *n.f.* privation; want, need.
privauté [privo'te], *n.f.* extreme familiarity *or* liberty.
privé [pri've], *a.* and *n.m.* (*fem.* **-ée**) private; familiar, intimate; tame (*of animals*).
priver [pri've], *v.t.* to deprive, to bereave; to tame (*animals etc.*). **se priver**, *v.r.* to deprive *or* stint oneself; to abstain (*de*).
privilège [privi'lɛ:ʒ], *n.m.* privilege; licence; prerogative, grant.
privilégié [privile'ʒje], *a.* privileged; licensed; entitled to preference (*of creditors*); preference (*of shares*).—*n.m.* (*fem.* **-ée**) privileged person.
privilégier [privile'ʒje], *v.t.* to privilege; to license.
prix [pri], *n.m. inv.* price, cost, value; rate, return; reward, prize; stakes (*race for prize*); ***à prix d'argent***, for money; ***à vil prix***, dirt-cheap; ***prix coûtant***, cost price; ***prix de gros***, wholesale price; ***remporter le prix***, to carry off the prize.
probabilité [prɔbabili'te], *n.f.* probability, likelihood.
probable [prɔ'babl], *a.* probable, likely, credible.
probablement [prɔbablə'mɑ̃], *adv.* probably.
probant [prɔ'bɑ̃], *a.* convincing, conclusive.
probation [prɔbɑ'sjɔ̃], *n.f.* (*Eccles.*) probation.
probe [prɔb], *a.* honest, upright.
probité [prɔbi'te], *n.f.* probity, honesty, integrity.
problématique [prɔblema'tik], *a.* problematical; questionable, doubtful.
problématiquement [prɔblematik'mɑ̃], *adv.* problematically.
problème [prɔ'blɛm], *n.m.* problem.
procédé [prɔse'de], *n.m.* behaviour, proceeding, conduct; process, operation; (*Billiards*) cue-tip.
procéder [prɔse'de], *v.i.* (*conjug. like* CÉDER) to proceed, to arise, to originate (*de*); to behave.
procédure [prɔse'dy:r], *n.f.* procedure; proceedings.
procès [prɔ'sɛ], *n.m.* lawsuit, action, trial; (*Anat.*) process.
procession [prɔsɛ'sjɔ̃], *n.f.* procession.
processionnel [prɔsɛsjɔ'nɛl], *a.* (*fem.* **-elle**) processional.
procès-verbal [prɔsɛvɛr'bal], *n.m.* (*pl.* **-verbaux**) official report; minute of proceedings; police report.
prochain [prɔ'ʃɛ̃], *a.* near, nearest, next.—*n.m.* neighbour, fellow-creature.
prochainement [prɔʃɛn'mɑ̃], *adv.* shortly, soon.
proche [prɔʃ], *a.* near, neighbouring; nigh, approaching.—*prep.* and *adv.* near, nigh; ***de proche en proche***, gradually.—*n.m.* (*usu. in pl.*) near relation, kin, kindred.
proclamation [prɔklamɑ'sjɔ̃], *n.f.* proclamation.
proclamer [prɔkla'me], *v.t.* to proclaim, to announce, to publish; to disclose.
proclivité [prɔklivi'te], *n.f.* proclivity, slope.
procréateur [prɔkrea'tœ:r], *a.* (*fem.* **-trice**) procreative.—*n.m.* (*fem.* **-trice**) procreator.
procréation [prɔkreɑ'sjɔ̃], *n.f.* procreation.
procréer [prɔkre'e], *v.t.* to procreate, to beget.
procurateur [prɔkyra'tœ:r], *n.m.* (*Hist.*) procurator.
procuration [prɔkyrɑ'sjɔ̃], *n.f.* procuration, power of attorney, proxy (*deed*).

procurer [prɔky're], *v.t.* to procure, to obtain. **se procurer,** *v.r.* to procure, to get for oneself.
procureur [prɔky'rœ:r], *n.m.* (*fem.* **procuratrice**) attorney, procurator, proxy.
prodigalement [prɔdigal'mɑ̃], *adv.* prodigally, extravagantly.
prodigalité [prɔdigali'te], *n.f.* prodigality, lavishness.
prodige [prɔ'di:ʒ], *n.m.* prodigy, marvel.
prodigieusement [prɔdiʒjøz'mɑ̃], *adv.* prodigiously.
prodigieux [prɔdi'ʒjø], *a.* (*fem.* **-euse**) prodigious, wonderful; stupendous.
prodigue [prɔ'dig], *a.* prodigal, lavish; wasteful.—*n.* prodigal, spendthrift.
prodiguer [prɔdi'ge], *v.t.* to be prodigal of; to waste, to squander. **se prodiguer,** *v.r.* to make oneself cheap; not to spare oneself.
prodrome [prɔ'dro:m], *n.m.* introduction, preface, preamble.
producteur [prɔdyk'tœ:r], *a.* (*fem.* **-trice**) productive.—*n.m.* (*fem.* **-trice**) producer.
productif [prɔdyk'tif], *a.* (*fem.* **-tive**) productive.
production [prɔdyk'sjɔ̃], *n.f.* production; produce, product (*of nature*); yield, output.
productivité [prɔdyktivi'te], *n.f.* productivity; productiveness.
produire [prɔ'dɥi:r], *v.t. irr.* (*conjug. like* CONDUIRE) to produce; to bear; to exhibit; to introduce. **se produire,** *v.r.* to put oneself forward; to occur, to happen.
produit [prɔ'dɥi], *n.m.* produce, product, production; proceeds.
proéminence [prɔemi'nɑ̃:s], *n.f.* prominence; protuberance.
proéminent [prɔemi'nɑ̃], *a.* prominent, protuberant.
profanateur [prɔfana'tœ:r], *n.m.* (*fem.* **-trice**) profaner.
profanation [prɔfanɑ'sjɔ̃], *n.f.* profanation.
profane [prɔ'fan], *a.* profane; secular.—*n.* profane person; outsider; layman.
profaner [prɔfa'ne], *v.t.* to profane, to desecrate; to defile.
proférer [prɔfe're], *v.t.* (*conjug. like* CÉDER) to utter, to pronounce.
professer [prɔfɛ'se], *v.t.* to profess; to exercise, to practise; to teach, to lecture on. —*v.i.* to lecture, to teach.
professeur [prɔfɛ'sœ:r], *n.m.* (*fem.* **femme professeur**) professor, lecturer (*at university*); teacher in secondary schools.
profession [prɔfɛ'sjɔ̃], *n.f.* profession, declaration; calling, business.
professionnel [prɔfɛsjɔ'nɛl], *a.* and *n.m.* (*fem.* **-elle**) (*Spt. etc.*) professional.
professoral [prɔfɛsɔ'ral], *a.* (*m. pl.* **-aux**) professorial.
professorat [prɔfɛsɔ'ra], *n.m.* professorship, lectureship; mastership (*of* ***lycée*** or ***collège***).
profil [prɔ'fil], *n.m.* profile, side-view; outline; (*Drawing*) section.
profiler [prɔfi'le], *v.t.* to represent *or* show in profile. **se profiler,** *v.r.* to appear in profile, to be outlined.
profit [prɔ'fi], *n.m.* profit, gain; benefit, utility, use; (*pl.*) perquisites.
profitable [prɔfi'tabl], *a.* profitable, advantageous.
profiter [prɔfi'te], *v.i.* to profit, to gain, to benefit; to take advantage of (*de*).
profiteur [prɔfi'tœ:r], *n.m.* (*fem.* **-euse**) (*pej.*) profiteer.
profond [prɔ'fɔ̃], *a.* deep; profound; vast; sound (*of sleep etc.*); downright; dark (*of night etc.*).—*n.m.* depth, abyss.
profondément [prɔfɔ̃de'mɑ̃], *adv.* deeply, profoundly, greatly; soundly.
profondeur [prɔfɔ̃'dœ:r], *n.f.* depth; profundity; penetration; extent.
profus [prɔ'fy], *a.* profuse.
profusément [prɔfyze'mɑ̃], *adv.* profusely.
profusion [prɔfy'zjɔ̃], *n.f.* profusion.
progéniture [prɔʒeni'ty:r], *n.f.* progeny.
prognostique [prɔgnɔs'tik], *a.* (*Med.*) prognostic.
programmation [prɔgramɑ'sjɔ̃], *n.f.* programming.
programme [prɔ'gram], *n.m.* (*Theat. etc.*) programme; (*sch.*) curriculum, syllabus.
progrès [prɔ'grɛ], *n.m.* progress; advancement, improvement, development.
progresser [prɔgrɛ'se], *v.i.* to progress, to get on.
progressif [prɔgrɛ'sif], *a.* (*fem.* **-ive**) progressive.
progression [prɔgrɛ'sjɔ̃], *n.f.* progression.
progressiste [prɔgrɛ'sist], *a.* progressive.—*n.* progressist, progressive.
progressivement [prɔgrɛsiv'mɑ̃], *adv.* progressively.
prohiber [prɔi'be], *v.t.* to forbid, to prohibit.
prohibitif [prɔibi'tif], *a.* (*fem.* **-tive**) prohibitive, exorbitant.
prohibition [prɔibi'sjɔ̃], *n.f.* prohibition.
proie [prwɑ], *n.f.* prey, prize, booty.
projecteur [prɔʒɛk'tœ:r], *n.m.* searchlight; projector; floodlight.
projectile [prɔʒɛk'til], *a.* and *n.m.* projectile, missile.
projection [prɔʒɛk'sjɔ̃], *n.f.* projection; (*Cine.*) ***appareil de projection***, projector.
projectionniste [prɔʒɛksjɔ'nist], *n.* (*Cine.*) projectionist.
projet [prɔ'ʒɛ], *n.m.* project, plan, idea; rough draft; ***homme à projets***, schemer.
projeter [prɔʒ'te], *v.t.* (*conjug. like* APPELER) to project, to throw; to delineate, to plan, to design; to contemplate, to intend.—*v.i.* to scheme, to form projects. **se projeter,** *v.r.* to project, to stand out.
prolétaire [prɔle'tɛ:r], *a.* and *n.m.* proletarian.
prolétariat [prɔleta'rja], *n.m.* proletariat.
prolifique [prɔli'fik], *a.* prolific.
prolixe [prɔ'liks], *a.* verbose.
prologue [prɔ'lɔg], *n.m.* prologue.
prolongation [prɔlɔ̃gɑ'sjɔ̃], *n.f.* prolongation; extension.
prolongement [prɔlɔ̃ʒ'mɑ̃], *n.m.* prolongation, extension.
prolonger [prɔlɔ̃'ʒe], *v.t.* (*conjug. like* MANGER) to prolong, to lengthen, to protract; to draw out. **se prolonger,** *v.r.* to be protracted; to extend; to continue.
promenade [prɔm'nad], *n.f.* walk; walking; promenade; drive, excursion, pleasure-trip.
promener [prɔm'ne], *v.t.* to take out for a walk, for a drive, for a ride, for an airing; to cast (*one's eyes*) over; to run or pass (*one's hand, fingers*) over. **se promener,** *v.r.* to

walk, to go for a walk, ramble, drive, row, sail etc.; to stroll.
promeneur [prɔm'nœ:r], *n.m.* (*fem.* **-euse**) walker; rider; person taking a drive.
promenoir [prɔm'nwa:r], *n.m.* covered walk; promenade (*in a concert-hall etc.*).
promesse [prɔ'mɛs], *n.f.* promise; promissory note.
promettre [prɔ'mɛtr], *v.t. irr.* (*conjug. like* METTRE) to promise; to forebode.—*v.i.* to be promising. **se promettre**, *v.r.* to promise oneself; to purpose; to promise each other.
promis [prɔ'mi], *a.* promised; intended, engaged.—*n.m.* (*fem.* **-e**) fiancé *or* fiancée.
promiscuité [prɔmiskɥi'te], *n.f.* promiscuity.
promontoire [prɔmɔ̃'twa:r], *n.m.* promontory, headland.
promoteur [prɔmɔ'tœ:r], *n.m.* (*fem.* **-trice**) promoter.
promotion [prɔmo'sjɔ̃], *n.f.* promotion, preferment.
promouvoir [prɔmu'vwa:r], *v.t. irr.* (*conjug. like* MOUVOIR) to promote, to advance.
prompt [prɔ̃], *a.* prompt, quick, active; sudden, swift; hasty.
promptement [prɔ̃t'mɑ̃], *adv.* promptly.
promptitude [prɔ̃ti'ty:d], *n.f.* promptitude, promptness; suddenness; hastiness.
promulgation [prɔmylgɑ'sjɔ̃], *n.f.* promulgation.
promulguer [prɔmyl'ge], *v.t.* to promulgate.
prône [pro:n], *n.m.* sermon (*at Mass*); (*fig.*) lecture, rebuke.
prôner [pro'ne], *v.t.* to lecture, to sermonize; to extol.—*v.i.* to sermonize.
prôneur [pro'nœ:r], *n.m.* (*fem.* **-euse**) long-winded preacher.
pronom [prɔ'nɔ̃], *n.m.* (*Gram.*) pronoun.
prononçable [prɔnɔ̃'sabl], *a.* pronounceable.
prononcé [prɔnɔ̃'se], *a.* pronounced, decided, marked; (*Paint. etc.*) prominent; broad (*of speech*).—*n.m.* judgment delivered, sentence.
prononcer [prɔnɔ̃'se], *v.t.* (*conjug. like* COMMENCER) to pronounce, to utter, to say, to declare; to pass (*a verdict etc.*).—*v.i.* to declare one's sentiments, to decide with authority. **se prononcer**, *v.r.* to declare oneself, to express one's opinion, to give a verdict; to be pronounced.
prononciation [prɔnɔ̃sjɑ'sjɔ̃], *n.f.* pronunciation; utterance.
pronostic [prɔnɔs'tik], *n.m.* prognostic; prognostication; (*Med.*) prognosis; weather forecast; (*racing*) tip.
propagande [prɔpa'gɑ̃:d], *n.f.* propaganda.
propagandiste [prɔpagɑ̃'dist], *n.* propagandist.
propagateur [prɔpaga'tœ:r], *a.* (*fem.* **-trice**) propagating, spreading.—*n.m.* (*fem* **-trice**) propagator.
propagation [prɔpagɑ'sjɔ̃], *n.f.* propagation, spreading, diffusion.
propager [prɔpa'ʒe], *v.t.* (*conjug. like* MANGER) to propagate, to spread abroad, to diffuse. **se propager**, *v.r.* to be propagated, to spread.
propension [prɔpɑ̃'sjɔ̃], *n.f.* propensity, tendency.
prophète [prɔ'fɛ:t], *n.m.* prophet, seer.
prophétesse [prɔfe'tɛs], *n.f.* prophetess.
prophétie [prɔfe'si], *n.f.* prophecy, prophesying.
prophétique [prɔfe'tik], *a.* prophetic.
prophétiser [prɔfeti'ze], *v.t.* to prophesy, to foretell.
propice [prɔ'pis], *a.* propitious, favourable.
propitiation [prɔpisjɑ'sjɔ̃], *n.f.* propitiation.
propitiatoire [prɔpisjɑ'twa:r], *a.* propitiatory.
proportion [prɔpɔr'sjɔ̃], *n.f.* proportion, ratio.
proportionné [prɔpɔrsjɔ'ne], *a.* proportioned, suited.
proportionnel [prɔpɔrsjɔ'nɛl], *a.* (*fem.* **-elle**) proportional.
proportionner [prɔpɔrsj'ɔne], *v.t.* to proportion, to adjust, to adapt.
propos [prɔ'po], *n.m.* talk, words; remark; purpose, resolution; (*pl.*) idle remarks, tittle-tattle; ***à propos***, apt, to the purpose; by the way; ***à propos de***, with respect to; ***à quel propos?*** what about? ***de propos délibéré***, of set purpose; ***mal à propos***, ill-timed; ***propos de table***, table-talk; ***venir fort à propos***, to come in the nick of time.
proposer [prɔpo'ze], *v.t.* to propose; to propound, to move; to designate, to set up. —*v.i.* to propose. **se proposer**, *v.r.* to propose oneself; to intend, to have in view.
proposeur [prɔpo'zœ:r], *n.m.* (*fem.* **-euse**) proposer, propounder.
proposition [prɔpozi'sjɔ̃], *n.f.* proposal; proposition; motion; (*Gram.*) clause.
propre [prɔpr], *a.* own; very, same, selfsame; proper; appropriate, suitable; good, right, correct; clean, neat, tidy; ***le mot propre***, the right word; ***peu propre***, inappropriate; dirty.—*n.m.* characteristic, property; proper sense; (*Law*) real property.
propre à rien [prɔpra'rjɛ̃], *n. inv.* good for nothing.
proprement [prɔprə'mɑ̃], *adv.* properly correctly; cleanly, neatly.
propret [prɔ'prɛ], *a.* (*fem.* **-ette**) spruce, neat, tidy.
propreté [prɔprə'te], *n.f.* cleanliness; neatness.
propriétaire [prɔprie'tɛ:r], *n.* owner, proprietor, proprietress; landlord, householder.
propriété [prɔprie'te], *n.f.* property; estate; characteristic; ***propriété littéraire***, copyright.
propulser [prɔpyl'se], *v.t.* (*Naut.*, *Av.*) to propel.
propulseur [prɔpyl'sœ:r], *n.m.* propeller.
propulsif [prɔpyl'sif], *a.* (*fem.* **-sive**) propelling, propellent.
propulsion [prɔpyl'sjɔ̃], *n.f.* propulsion.
prorogation [prɔrɔgɑ'sjɔ̃], *n.f.* adjournment, prorogation (*of Parliament etc.*); extension.
proroger [prɔrɔ'ʒe], *v.t.* (*conjug. like* MANGER) to prolong the time of; to prorogue (*Parliament etc.*).
prosaïque [prɔza'ik], *a.* prosaic; banal; prosy.
prosaïquement [prɔzaik'mɑ̃], *adv.* prosaically.
prosateur [prɔza'tœ:r], *n.m.* prose-writer.
proscription [prɔskrip'sjɔ̃], *n.f.* proscription.
proscrire [prɔs'kri:r], *v.t. irr.* (*conjug. like* ÉCRIRE) to proscribe, to outlaw; to banish.

proscrit [prɔs'kri], *a.* proscribed, forbidden. —*n.m.* (*fem.* **-e**) proscribed person, outlaw; exile.
prose [pro:z], *n.f.* prose.
prosodie [prɔzɔ'di], *n.f.* prosody.
prospecter [prɔspɛk'te], *v.t.* to prospect (*for oil, minerals*).
prospecteur [prɔspɛk'tœ:r], *n.m.* prospector.
prospectus [prɔspɛk'ty:s], *n.m. inv.* prospectus; handbill.
prospère [prɔs'pɛ:r], *a.* prosperous, thriving.
prospérer [prɔspe're], *v.i.* (*conjug. like* CÉDER) to prosper, to be prosperous, to thrive.
prospérité [prɔsperi'te], *n.f.* prosperity.
prostate [prɔs'tat], *n.f.* (*Anat.*) prostate.
prosternation [prɔstɛrnɑ'sjɔ̃], *n.f.*, **prosternement** [prɔstɛrnə'mɑ̃], *n.m.* prostration, obeisance.
prosterner [prɔstɛr'ne], *v.t.* to prostrate. **se prosterner**, *v.r.* to prostrate oneself, to bow low.
prostituée [prɔsti'tɥe], *n.f.* prostitute.
prostituer [prɔsti'tɥe], *v.t.* to prostitute. **se prostituer**, *v.r.* to prostitute oneself.
prostitution [prɔstity'sjɔ̃], *n.f.* prostitution.
prostration [prɔstrɑ'sjɔ̃], *n.f.* prostration.
protagoniste [prɔtagɔ'nist], *n.m.* protagonist.
protecteur [prɔtɛk'tœ:r], *a.* (*fem.* **-trice**) protective; patronizing.—*n.m.* (*fem.* **-trice**) protector, protectress; patron, patroness.—*n.m.* (*Eng.*) guard (*for machine tool*).
protection [prɔtɛk'sjɔ̃], *n.f.* protection, shelter; support, patronage.
protectorat [prɔtɛktɔ'ra], *n.m.* protectorate.
protégé [prɔte'ʒe], *n.m.* (*fem.* **-ée**) favourite, dependant.
protéger [prɔte'ʒe], *v.t.* (*conjug. like* ASSIÉGER) to protect, to defend; to patronize, to favour.
protège-vue [prɔtɛʒ'vy], *n.m. inv.* eye-shade.
protéine [prɔte'in], *n.f.* protein.
protestant [prɔtɛs'tɑ̃], *a.* and *n.m.* (*fem.* **-e**) Protestant.
protestantisme [prɔtɛstɑ̃'tism], *n.m.* Protestantism.
protestation [prɔtɛstɑ'sjɔ̃], *n.f.* protestation, protest.
protester [prɔtɛs'te], *v.t.* to protest, to affirm.—*v.i.* to protest.
protocole [prɔtɔ'kɔl], *n.m.* protocol.
proton [prɔ'tɔ̃], *n.m.* proton.
protoplasma [prɔtɔplas'ma], **protoplasme** [prɔtɔ'plasm], *n.m.* protoplasm.
prototype [prɔtɔ'tip], *n.m.* prototype.
protubérance [prɔtybe'rɑ̃:s], *n.f.* protuberance.
protubérant [prɔtybe'rɑ̃], *a.* protuberant.
proue [pru], *n.f.* prow, stem, bows (*of ship*).
prouesse [pru'ɛs], *n.f.* prowess, valour; feat.
prouver [pru've], *v.t.* to prove; to substantiate; to show.
provenance [prɔv'nɑ̃:s], *n.f.* origin, source; (*pl.*) produce, commodities.
provençal [prɔvɑ̃'sal], *a.* (*m. pl.* **-aux**) Provençal.—*n.m.* Provençal (*language*); (**Provençal**, *fem.* **-ale**) Provençal (*person*).
provenir [prɔv'ni:r], *v.i. irr.* (*conjug. like* TENIR *but with aux.* ÊTRE) to issue, proceed, spring, originate *or* come from (**de**).
proverbe [prɔ'vɛrb], *n.m.* proverb, saying.
proverbial [prɔvɛr'bjal], *a.* (*m. pl.* **-aux**) proverbial.
providence [prɔvi'dɑ̃:s], *n.f.* providence.
providentiel [prɔvidɑ̃'sjɛl], *a.* (*fem.* **-elle**) providential.
provigner [prɔvi'ɲe], *v.t.* to layer (*vines*).
provin [prɔ'vɛ̃], *n.m.* layer (*of a vine*).
province [prɔ'vɛ̃:s], *n.f.* province, shire; country; ***en province***, in the country, in the provinces.
provincial [prɔvɛ̃'sjal], *a.* (*m. pl.* **-aux**) provincial; countrified.—*n.m.* (*fem.* **-e**) provincial, country person.
proviseur [prɔvi'zœ:r], *n.m.* headmaster (*of a* ***lycée***).
provision [prɔvi'zjɔ̃], *n.f.* provision, stock, store, supply; deposit; (*Comm.*) reserve funds.
provisionnel [prɔvizjɔ'nɛl], *a.* (*fem.* **-elle**) provisional.
provisoire [prɔvi'zwa:r], *a.* provisional, temporary.—*n.m.* provisional nature (*of something*).
provisoirement [prɔvizwar'mɑ̃], *adv.* provisionally, temporarily.
provocant [prɔvɔ'kɑ̃], *a.* provoking, provocative; exciting.
provocateur [prɔvɔka'tœ:r], *a.* (*fem.* **-trice**) provoking, provocative; ***agent provocateur***, agent hired to instigate a riot etc.—*n.m.* (*fem.* **-trice**) provoker; aggressor.
provocation [prɔvɔkɑ'sjɔ̃], *n.f.* provocation.
provoquer [prɔvɔ'ke], *v.t.* to provoke, to incite, to call forth; to instigate.
proximité [prɔksimi'te], *n.f.* proximity, nearness.
prude [pryd], *a.* prudish.—*n.f.* prude.
prudemment [pryda'mɑ̃], *adv.* prudently, discreetly, cautiously.
prudence [pry'dɑ̃:s], *n.f.* carefulness, prudence.
prudent [pry'dɑ̃], prudent, discreet; advisable.
pruderie [pry'dri], *n.f.* prudery, prudishness.
prud'homme [pry'dɔm], *n.m.* upright, honest man; (*Ind.*) arbitrator.
pruine [prɥin], *n.f.* bloom (*on fruits*).
prune [pryn], *n.f.* plum.
pruneau [pry'no], *n.m.* (*pl.* **-eaux**) prune.
prunelle (1) [pry'nɛl], *n.f.* sloe; sloe-gin.
prunelle (2) [pry'nɛl], *n.f.* pupil, apple (*of the eye*), eyeball.
prunellier [prynɛ'lje], *n.m.* sloe-tree, blackthorn.
prunier [pry'nje], *n.m.* plum-tree.
Prusse [prys], **la**, *f.* Prussia.
prussien [pry'sjɛ̃], *a.* (*fem.* **-enne**) Prussian. —*n.m.* (**Prussien**, *fem.* **-enne**) Prussian (*person*).
prussique [pry'sik], *a.* (*Chem.*) prussic.
psalmiste [psal'mist], *n.m.* psalmist.
psalmodie [psalmɔ'di], *n.f.* psalmody, intoning; (*fig.*) sing-song.
psalmodier [psalmɔ'dje], *v.t., v.i.* to recite, to chant (*as the psalms*); to read *or* recite in a sing-song manner.
psaume [pso:m], *n.m.* psalm.
psautier [pso'tje], *n.m.* psalter, psalm-book.
pseudonyme [psødɔ'nim], *a.* pseudonymous. —*n.m.* pseudonym, nom-de-plume.
psychanalyse [psikana'li:z], *n.f.* psychoanalysis.

psychanalyste [psikana'list], *n.m.* psychoanalyst.
psychiatre [psi'kja:tr], *n.m.* psychiatrist.
psychiatrie [psikja'tri], *n.f.* psychiatry.
psychologie [psikɔlɔ'ʒi], *n.f.* psychology.
psychologique [psikɔlɔ'ʒik], *a.* psychological.
psychologue [psikɔ'lɔg], *n.* psychologist.
puant [pɥɑ̃], *a.* stinking; foul.
puanteur [pɥɑ̃'tœ:r], *n.f.* stench, stink.
pubère [py'bɛ:r], *a.* pubescent, puberal.
puberté [pybɛr'te], *n.f.* puberty.
public [py'blik], *a.* (*fem.* **-ique**) public; notorious; ***la chose publique***, the common weal, the State.—*n.m.* public.
publication [pyblikɑ'sjɔ̃], *n.f.* publication; publishing, proclamation.
publiciste [pybli'sist], *n.m.* publicist, journalist.
publicité [pyblisi'te], *n.f.* publicity; advertising.
publier [py'blje], *v.t.* to publish, to make public, to proclaim; to issue.
publiquement [pyblik'mɑ̃], *adv.* in public.
puce (1) [pys], *a. inv.* puce, puce-coloured.
puce (2) [pys], *n.f.* flea.
puceron [pys'rɔ̃], *n.m.* plant-louse, greenfly.
pudeur [py'dœ:r], *n.f.* modesty; bashfulness, shame; reserve.
pudibond [pydi'bɔ̃], *a.* bashful; prudish.
pudicité [pydisi'te], *n.f.* modesty, chastity.
pudique [py'dik], *a.* chaste, modest, bashful.
pudiquement [pydik'mɑ̃], *adv.* modestly.
puer [pɥe], *v.t.* (*fam.*) to smell of, to reek of.—*v.i.* to stink.
puéril [pɥe'ril], *a.* juvenile, childish, puerile.
puérilement [pɥeril'mɑ̃], *adv.* childishly.
puérilité [pɥerili'te], *n.f.* puerility, childishness.
pugilat [pyʒi'la], *n.m.* pugilism, boxing.
pugiliste [pyʒi'list], *n.m.* pugilist, boxer.
pugnace [pyg'nas], *a.* pugnacious.
pugnacité [pygnasi'te], *n.f.* pugnacity.
puîné [pɥi'ne], *a.* (*fem.* **-ée**) younger (*brother or sister*).
puis [pɥi], *adv.* then, afterwards, after that, next; besides.
puisage [pɥi'za:ʒ], **puisement** [pɥiz'mɑ̃], *n.m.* drawing up; drawing water.
puisard [pɥi'za:r], *n.m.* cesspool; sump, water-sump.
puisatier [pɥiza'tje], *n.m.* well-sinker; shaft-sinker (*in mining*).
puisement [PUISAGE].
puiser [pɥi'ze], *v.t.* to draw, to fetch up (*a liquid*); (*fig.*) to imbibe.
puisque [pɥisk], *conj.* since, as, seeing that.
puissamment [pɥisa'mɑ̃], *adv.* powerfully; extremely, very.
puissance [pɥi'sɑ̃:s], *n.f.* power; force; dominion, sway; influence.
puissant [pɥi'sɑ̃], *a.* powerful, mighty; lusty, stout; strong.
puits [pɥi], *n.m. inv.* well; pit, shaft.
pullulation [pylylɑ'sjɔ̃], *n.f.*, **pullulement** [pylyl'mɑ̃], *n.m.* pullulation, swarming.
pulluler [pyly'le], *v.i.* to multiply, to pullulate, to swarm.
pulmonaire [pylmɔ'nɛ:r], *a.* pulmonary; ***phthisie pulmonaire***, consumption.
pulmonique [pylmɔ'nik], *a.* and *n.* consumptive.
pulpe [pylp], *n.f.* pulp.
pulper [pyl'pe], *v.t.* to pulp.
pulpeux [pyl'pø], *a.* (*fem.* **-euse**) pulpous pulpy.
pulsatif [pylsa'tif], *a.* (*fem.* **-tive**) pulsatory, throbbing.
pulsation [pylsɑ'sjɔ̃], *n.f.* beating of the pulse, pulsation, throbbing.
pulvérin [pylve'rɛ̃], *n.m.* spray (*from waterfalls*).
pulvérisateur [pylveriza'tœ:r], *n.m.* pulverizator, vaporizer; spray, atomiser.
pulvérisation [pylverizɑ'sjɔ̃], *n.f.* pulverization.
pulvériser [pylveri'ze], *v.t.* to reduce to powder *or* dust, to pulverize; to atomize; (*fig.*) to annihilate.
pulvérulent [pylvery'lɑ̃], *a.* pulverulent, powdery.
puma [py'ma], *n.m.* puma, cougar.
pumicin [pymi'sɛ̃], *n.m.* palm-oil.
punaise [py'nɛ:z], *n.f.* bug; drawing-pin.
punch [pœ̃:ʃ], *n.m.* (*Box.*) punch; punch (*beverage*).
punique [py'nik], *a.* Punic.
punir [py'ni:r], *v.t.* to punish, to chastise.
punissable [pyni'sabl], *a.* punishable.
punisseur [pyni'sœ:r], *a.* (*fem.* **-euse**) punishing, avenging.—*n.m.* (*fem.* **-euse**) punisher; avenger.
punitif [pyni'tif], *a.* (*fem.* **-tive**) punitive.
punition [pyni'sjɔ̃], *n.f.* punishment.
pupille [py'pil], *n.* ward, minor in charge of guardian.—*n.f.* pupil (*of the eye*).
pupitre [py'pitr], *n.m.* desk; music-stand.
pur [py:r], *a.* pure, unalloyed; unadulterated; unblemished; innocent, chaste; mere, sheer; neat (*of liquor*); ***en pure perte***, to no purpose.
purée [py're], *n.f.* mash, purée, thick soup.
purement [pyr'mɑ̃], *adv.* purely; merely.
pureté [pyr'te], *n.f.* purity, guilelessness, innocence; chastity.
purgatif [pyrga'tif], *a.* (*fem.* **-tive**) purgative, purging.—*n.m.* (*Med.*) purgative.
purgation [pyrgɑ'sjɔ̃], *n.f.* purgation, purge.
purgatoire [pyrga'twa:r], *n.m.* purgatory.
purge [pyrʒ], *n.f.* purge; cleansing; disinfection.
purger [pyr'ʒe], *v.t.* (*conjug. like* MANGER) to purge; to cleanse, to purify. **se purger**, *v.r.* to purge oneself; to clear oneself (*of*).
purificateur [pyrifika'tœ:r], *a.* (*fem.* **-trice**) purifying.—*n.m.* (*fem.* **-trice**) purifier.
purification [pyrifikɑ'sjɔ̃], *n.f.* purification.
purifier [pyri'fje], *v.t.* to purify, to cleanse; to refine (*metals etc.*). **se purifier**, *v.r.* to purify oneself, to become refined.
puritain [pyri'tɛ̃], *a.* and *n.m.* (*fem.* **-e**) Puritan.
puritanisme [pyrita'nism], *n.m.* puritanism.
purpurin [pyrpy'rɛ̃], *a.* purplish.
pur-sang [pyr'sɑ̃], *n.m. inv.* thoroughbred.
pus [py], *n.m.* pus, matter.
pusillanime [pyzila'nim], *a.* pusillanimous, faint-hearted.
pusillanimité [pyzilanimi'te], *n.f.* pusillanimity.
pustule [pys'tyl], *n.f.* pustule, pimple, blotch.
putatif [pyta'tif], *a.* (*fem.* **-tive**) putative reputed, supposed.
putativement [pytativ'mɑ̃], *adv.* reputedly.
putois [py'twa], *n.m.* polecat, skunk.

putréfaction [pytrefak'sjɔ̃], *n.f.* putrefaction; putrescence.
putréfier [pytre'fje], *v.t.* to putrefy; to rot. **se putréfier**, *v.r.* to putrefy; to rot; to decompose.
putride [py'trid], *a.* putrid.
pygmée [pig'me], *n.m.* pygmy.
pyjama [piʒa'ma], *n.m.* pyjamas.
pylône [pi'lo:n], *n.m.* pylon; mast.
pyorrhée [piɔ're], *n.f.* pyorrhœa.
pyramidal [pirami'dal], *a.* (*m. pl.* **-aux**) pyramidal.
pyramide [pira'mid], *n.f.* pyramid.
python [pi'tɔ̃], *n.m.* python (*snake*).

Q

Q, q [ky] *n.m.* the seventeenth letter of the alphabet.
qu' [k], *elision* [QUE].
quadragénaire [kwadraʒe'nɛ:r], *a.* forty years of age.—*n.* person forty years old.
quadrangle [kwa'drɑ̃:gl], *n.m.* quadrangle.
quadrangulaire [kwadrɑ̃gy'lɛ:r], *a.* quadrangular, four-cornered.
quadrillage [kadri'ja:ʒ], *n.m.* chequer-work, pattern in squares; map grid.
quadrille [ka'dri:j], *n.m.* quadrille (*card game*); quadrille (*dance*); check (*in tapestry*).
quadrillé [kadri'je], *a.* chequered (*of cloth*); ruled in squares (*of paper*).
quadriréacteur [kwadrireak'tœ:r], *n.m.* four-engined jet plane.
quadrupède [kwadry'pɛd], *a.* and *n.m.* quadruped.
quadruple [kwa'drypl], *a.* quadruple, four-fold.
quadruplé [kwadry'ple], *n.m.* (*fem.* **-ée**) quadruplet, (*fam.*) quad.
quadrupler [kwadry'ple], *v.t., v.i.* to quadruple, to increase fourfold.
quai [ke], *n.m.* quay, wharf, pier; embankment (*along river*); platform (*railway*).
qualifiable [kali'fjabl], *a.* qualifiable, characterized (*as*).
qualification [kalifikɑ'sjɔ̃], *n.f.* title; designation, qualification.
qualifié [kali'fje], *a.* qualified; named.
qualifier [kali'fje], *v.t.* to qualify; to style. **se qualifier**, *v.r.* to style oneself; to qualify (*for*).
qualité [kali'te], *n.f.* quality; property; excellence; talent; qualification; title; ***en qualité de***, in the capacity of.
quand [kɑ̃], *adv.* when, whenever, what time; while.—*conj.* though; ***quand même***, even though; all the same.
quant [kɑ̃], *adv.* (*followed by* **à**) as for, with regard to.
quant-à-soi [kɑ̃ta'swa], *n.m.* reserve, dignity.
quantième [kɑ̃'tjɛm], *n.m.* which (*day of the month etc.*).
quantité [kɑ̃ti'te], *n.f.* quantity; abundance, plenty; variety.

quarantaine [karɑ̃'tɛn], *n.f.* about forty; age of forty; quarantine.
quarante [ka'rɑ̃t], *a.* and *n.m.* forty.
quarantième [karɑ̃'tjɛm], *a.* and *n.* fortieth.
quart [ka:r], *a.* fourth.—*n.m.* quarter, fourth part; point (*of the compass*); quart (*measure*); (*Mil.*) tin cup; (*Naut.*) watch.
quarte [kart], *n.f.* (*Mus.*) fourth; (*Fenc., Piquet*) carte.
quartier [kar'tje], *n.m.* quarter, fourth part; piece, part; ward, district; gammon; (*Mil.*) quarters, barracks.
quartier-maître [kartje'mɛ:tr], *n.m.* (*pl.* **quartiers-maîtres**) (*Naut.*) leading seaman.
quarto [kwar'to], *adv.* fourthly, in the fourth place.
quartz [kwa:rts], *n.m.* quartz.
quasi [ka'zi], *adv.* almost, as if, quasi.
quasiment [kazi'mɑ̃], *adv.* (*dial.*) almost, nearly, as you might say.
quaternaire [kwatɛr'nɛ:r], *a.* quaternary.
quatorze [ka'tɔrz], *a.* and *n.m.* fourteen; fourteenth.
quatorzième [katɔr'zjɛm], *a.* and *n.* fourteenth.
quatrain [ka'trɛ̃], *n.m.* quatrain.
quatre ['katrə, katr], *a.* and *n.m. inv.* four, fourth.
quatre-temps [katrə'tɑ̃], *n.m. pl.* ember-days.
quatre-vingtième [katrəvɛ̃'tjɛm], *a.* and *n.m.* eightieth.
quatre-vingt(s) [katrə'vɛ̃], *a.* and *n.m.* eighty.
quatrième [kat'rjɛm], *a.* and *n.* fourth.—*n.m.* fourth floor, fourth storey.—*n.f.* third form (*of upper school*); (*Piquet*) quart.
quatrièmement [katrjɛm'mɑ̃], *adv.* fourthly.
quatuor [kwaty'ɔr], *n.m.* (*Mus.*) quartet.
que (1) [kə, k], *pron. rel.* whom, that; which; what? on which; ***qu'est-ce que c'est?*** what is it?
que (2) [kə, k], *conj.* that; than; than that; as, if, whether; when; without; yet; lest; in order that; oh that, may; let; before; so; only, but; ***afin que***, in order that; ***attendez qu'il vienne***, wait till he comes; ***de sorte que***, so that.—*adv.* how, how much, how many; why, wherefore?
quel [kɛl], *a.* (*fem.* **quelle**) what, which, what sort of.
quelconque [kɛl'kɔ̃:k], *a. indef.* any; any whatsoever; mediocre.
quelque ['kɛlkə, kɛlk], *adj.* some, any; a few; whatever, whatsoever.—*adv.* however, howsoever; some, about.
quelquefois [kɛlkə'fwa], *adv.* sometimes.
quelqu'un [kɛl'kœ̃], *pron. indef. m.* someone, somebody; anyone, anybody.—*n.m.* (*fem.* **quelqu'une**, *pl.* **quelques-uns, quelques-unes,** one (or other), some.
quémander [kemɑ̃'de], *v.t. v.i.* to beg, to solicit.
quémandeur [kemɑ̃'dœ:r], *n.m.* (*fem.* **-euse**) importunate beggar.
qu'en-dira-t-on [kɑ̃dira'tɔ̃], *n.m. inv.* public talk, tittle-tattle.
quenelle [kə'nɛl], *n.f.* forcemeat *or* fish ball.
quenotte [kə'nɔt], *n.f.* (*colloq.*) tooth (*of young children*).
quenouille [kə'nu:j], *n.f.* distaff; bed-post.

querelle [kə'rɛl], *n.f.* quarrel; row, brawl; feud; cause of dispute; ***chercher querelle à***, to pick a quarrel with.
quereller [kərɛ'le], *v.t.* to quarrel with; to scold. **se quereller**, *v.r.* to quarrel, to wrangle, to have words.
querelleur [kərɛ'lœ:r], *a.* (*fem.* **-euse**) quarrelsome.—*n.m.* (*fem.* **-euse**) quarreller, wrangler.
quérir [ke'ri:r], *v.t.* to fetch; (*employed only in the infinitive with **aller**, **envoyer**, **venir***).
questeur [kɥɛs'tœ:r], *n.m.* quaestor.
question [kɛs'tjɔ̃], *n.f.* question, interrogation; query, point, issue; rack, torture.
questionnaire [kɛstjɔ'nɛ:r], *n.m.* questionnaire; book of questions.
questionner [kɛstjɔ'ne], *v.t.* to question, to interrogate.
questionneur [kɛstjɔ'nœ:r], *a.* (*fem.* **-euse**) inquisitive.—*n.m.* (*fem.* **-euse**) questioner.
questure [kɥɛs'ty:r], *n.f.* quaestorship; quaestors' office.
quête [kɛ:t], *n.f.* quest, search; collection, offertory; (*Hunt.*) beating about.
quêter [kɛ'te], *v.t.* to look for, to seek, to go in quest of, to gather.—*v.i.* to beg.
quêteur [kɛ'tœ:r], *n.m.* (*fem.* **-euse**) collector; mendicant (friar).
queue [kø], *n.f.* tail; stalk; stem; end; rear; billiard-cue; handle; train (*of robes etc.*); queue.
queue-d'aronde [køda'rɔ̃:d], *n.f.* (*pl.* **queues-d'aronde**) dovetail.
qui [ki], *pron. rel.* and *inter.* who, that, whom, which; whoever, whomsoever, whatever; what; some.
quiconque [ki'kɔ̃:k], *pron. indef.* whoever, whosoever; whomsoever, whichever.
quiétude [kɥie'tyd], *n.f.* quietude.
quignon [ki'ɲɔ̃], *n.m.* hunch, chunk, hunk (*of bread*).
quille [ki:j], *n.f.* keel; skittle, ninepin.
quiller [ki'je], *v.i.* to throw for partners *or* for first play (*at skittles*).
quillier [ki'je], *n.m.* skittle-alley.
quincaillerie [kɛ̃kɑj'ri], *n.f.* ironmongery, hardware.
quincaillier [kɛ̃kɑ'je], *n.m.* ironmonger.
quinconce [kɛ̃'kɔ̃:s], *n.m.* quincunx.
quine [kin], *n.m.* two fives (*at trictrac*); five winning numbers (*in a lottery*).
quinine [ki'nin], *n.f.* quinine.
quinquagénaire [kɥɛ̃kwaʒe'nɛ:r], *a.* fifty years old.—*n.* person of fifty.
quinquennal [kɥɛ̃kɥɛ'nal], *a.* (*m. pl.* **-aux**) quinquennial.
quinquet [kɛ̃'kɛ], *n.m.* argand lamp.
quinquina [kɛ̃ki'na], *n.m.* Peruvian bark.
quintal [kɛ̃'tal], *n.m.* (*pl.* **-aux**) quintal, hundredweight; 100 kilogr.
quinte [kɛ̃:t], *n.f.* (*Mus.*) fifth; (*Piquet*) quint; (*fig.*) freak, whim; (*Fenc.*) quinte; ***quinte de toux***, fit of coughing.
quintessence [kɛ̃tɛ'sɑ̃:s], *n.f.* quintessence; (*fig.*) pith, essential part.
quintette [kɛ̃'tɛt], *n.m.* quintet.
quinteux [kɛ̃'tø], *a.* (*fem.* **-euse**) whimsical, crotchety; jibbing (*of a horse*).
quintuple [kɛ̃'typl], *a.* and *n.m.* quintuple.
quintuplé [kɛ̃ty'ple], *n.m.* quintuplet.
quintupler [kɛ̃ty'ple], *v.t.* to quintuple.
quinzaine [kɛ̃'zɛn], *n.f.* about fifteen; fortnight.
quinze [kɛ̃:z], *a.* and *n.m.* fifteen; fifteenth.
quinzième [kɛ̃'zjɛm], *a.* and *n.* fifteenth.
quinzièmement [kɛ̃zjɛm'mɑ̃], *adv.* fifteenthly, in the fifteenth place.
quiproquo [kiprɔ'ko], *n.m.* mistake; quid pro quo.
quittance [ki'tɑ̃:s], *n.f.* receipt, discharge.
quittancer [kitɑ̃'se], *v.t.* (*conjug. like* COMMENCER) to receipt.
quitte [kit], *a.* discharged (*from debt*); clear, free.
quitter [ki'te], *v.t.* to leave; to discharge; to give up; to leave off, to lay aside; to depart (*life*); ***ne quittez pas !*** (*Teleph.*) hold the line! **se quitter**, *v.r.* to part company, to separate.
qui va là? [kiva'la], *inter. phr.* who goes there?
qui-vive [ki'vi:v], *n.m.* who goes there? (*challenge of a sentry*); ***être sur le qui-vive***, to be on the alert.
quoi [kwa], *pron. rel.* and *inter.* which; what; ***il n'y a pas de quoi***, don't mention it! ***le je ne sais quoi***, the indefinable something; ***quoi que***, whatever.—*int.* what!
quoique ['kwakə], *conj.* although, though.
quolibet [kɔli'bɛ], *n.m.* gibe, jeer.
quote-part [kɔt'pa:r], *n.f.* (*pl.* **quotes-parts**) quota, portion, share.
quotidien [kɔti'djɛ̃], *a.* (*fem.* **-enne**) daily, quotidian.—*n.m.* daily (newspaper).
quotidiennement [kɔtidjɛn'mɑ̃], *adv.* daily.
quotient [kɔ'sjɑ̃], *n.m.* quotient.
quotité [kɔti'te], *n.f.* (*Fin.*) quota, share; proportion.

R

R, r [ɛ:r], *n.m.* the eighteenth letter of the alphabet.
rabâchage [rabɑ'ʃa:ʒ], *n.m.* tiresome repetition; drivel.
rabâcher [rabɑ'ʃe], *v.t., v.i.* to repeat (*the same thing*) over and over again.
rabâcheur [rabɑ'ʃœ:r], *n.m.* (*fem.* **-euse**) eternal repeater, twaddler.
rabais [ra'bɛ], *n.m. inv.* abatement, reduction; discount.
rabaissement [rabɛs'mɑ̃], *n.m.* lowering, depreciation; (*fig.*) humiliation.
rabaisser [rabɛ'se], *v.t.* to lower; to abate, to lessen; to depreciate; to humble, to disparage.
rabat [ra'ba], *n.m.* clerical *or* academic band; beating (*for game*).
rabat-joie [raba'ʒwa], *n.m. inv.* damper, wet blanket, spoil-sport.
rabattage [raba'ta:ʒ], *n.m.* cutting down, diminution; beating (*for game*).
rabattre [ra'batr], *v.t.* (*conjug. like* BATTRE) to beat down, to bring *or* cut down; to smooth down; to humble; (*Hunt.*) to beat up; to abate.—*v.i.* to reduce one's pretensions. **se**

rabattre, *v.r.* to turn off, to change one's road; to come down; to fall back on.
rabbin [ra'bɛ̃], *n.m.* rabbi.
rabbinique [rabi'nik], *a.* rabbinical.
rabique [ra'bik], *a.* rabid, rabic.
râble [rɑːbl], *n.m.* back (*of hare, rabbit etc.*); fire-rake.
râblé [rɑ'ble], *a.* broad-backed; (*fig.*) vigorous, strapping.
rabonnir [rabɔ'niːr], *v.t., v.i.* to improve (*wine*).
rabot [ra'bo], *n.m.* plane.
rabotage [rabɔ'taːʒ], **rabotement** [rabɔt'mɑ̃], *n.m.* planing.
raboter [rabɔ'te], *v.t.* to plane; (*fig.*) to polish; (*slang*) to pilfer, to filch.
raboteur [rabɔ'tœːr], *n.m.* planer.
raboteuse (1) [rabɔ'tøːz], *n.f.* planing-machine.
raboteux [rabɔ'tø], *a.* (*fem.* **-euse** (2)) knotty; rough, rugged, uneven; (*fig.*) harsh (*of style*).
rabougri [rabu'gri], *a.* stunted, dwarfed.
rabougrir [rabu'griːr], *v.t.* to stunt.
raboutir [rabu'tiːr], **rabouter** [rabu'te], *v.t.* to join end to end, to join on.
rabrouer [rabru'e], *v.t.* to snub, to rebuke sharply.
rabroueur [rabru'œːr], *n.m.* (*fem.* **-euse**) snappish person, scold.
racaille [ra'kɑːj], *n.f.* rabble, riffraff; rubbish, trash.
raccommodage [rakɔmɔ'daːʒ], *n.m.* mending, repairing; darning.
raccommodement [rakɔmɔd'mɑ̃], *n.m.* reconciliation.
raccommoder [rakɔmɔ'de], *v.t.* to mend, to repair; to darn; to patch; to set right, to correct; to reconcile. **se raccommoder**, *v.r.* to be reconciled.
raccommodeur [rakɔmɔ'dœːr], *n.m.* (*fem.* **-euse**) mender.
raccompagner [rakɔ̃pa'ɲe], *v.t.* to accompany back.
raccord [ra'kɔːr], *n.m.* joining, fitting; joint, connection.
raccordement [rakɔrdə'mɑ̃], *n.m.* joining, union, junction; levelling; ***voie de raccordement***, loop line.
raccorder [rakɔr'de], *v.t.* to join, to unite, to connect. **se raccorder**, *v.r.* to fit together, to blend.
raccourci [rakur'si], *a.* shortened, abridged. —*n.m.* abridgment, epitome; short cut.
raccourcir [rakur'siːr], *v.t.* to shorten, to curtail, to abridge.—*v.i.* to become shorter; to take a short cut. **se raccourcir**, *v.r.* to grow shorter, to contract, to shrink.
raccourcissement [rakursis'mɑ̃], *n.m.* shortening, abridgment, shrinking.
raccoutrage [raku'traːʒ], **raccoutrement** [rakutrə'mɑ̃], *n.m.* mending (*of clothes etc.*).
raccoutrer [raku'tre], *v.t.* to mend, to repair (*garment*).
raccoutumer (se) [sərakuty'me], *v.r.* to re-accustom oneself, to get used to again.
raccroc [ra'kro], *n.m.* chance, lucky stroke (*esp. at billiards*), fluke.
raccrocher [rakrɔ'ʃe], *v.t.* to hook up again, to hang up again; (*colloq.*) to recover.—*v.i.* to make flukes (*at play*); (*Teleph.*) to ring off. **se raccrocher**, *v.r.* to cling; to retrieve one's losses; to grasp *or* snatch at.
race [ras], *n.f.* race; stock, breed; family, ancestry; generation; ***un cheval de race***, a thoroughbred horse.
rachat [ra'ʃa], *n.m.* repurchase, redemption.
rachetable [raʃ'tabl], *a.* redeemable.
racheter [raʃ'te], *v.t.* (*conjug. like* AMENER) to buy back, to repurchase; to redeem; to ransom; to compensate; to atone for. **se racheter**, *v.r.* to redeem oneself; to be made up for.
rachitique [raʃi'tik], *a.* rachitic, rickety.—*n.* rickety person.
rachitis [raʃi'tis], **rachitisme** [raʃi'tism], *n.m.* rachitis, rickets; (*Bot.*) blight.
racial [ra'sjal], *a.* (*m. pl.* **-aux**) racial.
racine [ra'sin], *n.f.* root; (*fig.*) principle, origin.
racisme [ra'sism], *n.m.* racialism.
raciste [ra'sist], *a.* racial.—*n.* racialist.
raclage [rɑ'klaːʒ], *n.m.* scraping, raking.
racle [rɑːkl], *n.f.* scraper.
raclée [rɑ'kle], *n.f.* (*fam.*) thrashing, hiding.
racler [rɑ'kle], *v.t.* to scrape, to rake; to rasp.
racleur [rɑ'klœːr], *n.m.* (*fem.* **-euse**) scraper; (*fam.*) bad violinist.
racloir [rɑ'klwaːr], *n.m.* scraper, road-scraper.
raclure [rɑ'klyːr], *n.f.* scrapings.
racolage [rakɔ'laːʒ], *n.m.* impressing; recruiting.
racoler [rakɔ'le], *v.t.* to enlist.
racoleur [rakɔ'lœːr], *n.m.* tout.
racontable [rakɔ̃'tabl], *a.* relatable.
racontar [rakɔ̃'taːr], *n.m.* gossip, tittle-tattle.
raconter [rakɔ̃'te], *v.t.* to relate, to tell, to narrate.
raconteur [rakɔ̃'tœːr], *n.m.* (*fem.* **-euse**) story-teller, narrator, raconteur.
racornir [rakɔr'niːr], *v.t.* to harden; to dry up, to shrivel up. **se racornir**, *v.r.* to grow hard; to shrivel up; to grow callous.
racornissement [rakɔrnis'mɑ̃], *n.m.* hardening.
racquit [ra'ki], *n.m.* winning back.
racquitter [raki'te], *v.t.* to indemnify, to recoup. **se racquitter**, *v.r.* to retrieve one's losses.
radar [ra'dar], *n.m.* radar.
radariste [rada'rist], *n.* radar operator.
rade [rad], *n.f.* (*Naut.*) roads, roadstead.
radeau [ra'do], *n.m.* (*pl.* **-eaux**) raft.
radiance [ra'djɑ̃ːs], *n.f.* radiance, lustre.
radiant [ra'djɑ̃], *a.* radiant.
radiateur [radja'tœːr], *a.* (*fem.* **-trice**) radiating.—*n.m.* radiator.
radiation [radjɑ'sjɔ̃], *n.f.* radiation, irradiation; obliteration.
radical [radi'kal], *a.* (*m. pl.* **-aux**) radical; complete.—*n.m.* radical; root.
radicalement [radikal'mɑ̃], *adv.* radically.
radicalisme [radika'lism], *n.m.* radicalism.
radier (1) [ra'dje], *n.m.* floor *or* apron (*of docks, locks, basins etc.*); invert (*of tunnel*).
radier (2) [ra'dje], *v.t.* to strike out, to erase.—*v.i.* to radiate, to beam (*with satisfaction*).
radieux [ra'djø], *a.* (*fem.* **-euse**) radiant, beaming, shining.
radio [ra'djo], *n.f.* broadcasting, radio; wireless set; radiography.—*n.m.* wireless message; wireless-operator.
radio-actif [radjoak'tif], *a.* (*fem.* **-tive**) radio-active.

radio-activité [radjoaktivi'te], *n.f.* radio-activity.
radiodiffuser [radjɔdify'ze], *v.t.* to broadcast.
radiodiffusion [radjɔdify'zjɔ̃], *n.f.* broadcasting.
radiographie [radjɔgra'fi], *n.f.* radiography.
radio-reporter [radjɔrəpɔr'tɛːr], *n.m.* commentator.
radio-thérapie [radjɔtera'pi], *n.f.* X-ray treatment, radio-therapy.
radis [ra'di], *n.m.* radish.
radium [ra'djɔm], *n.m.* radium.
radotage [radɔ'taːʒ], *n.m.* nonsense, drivel; dotage.
radoter [radɔ'te], *v.i.* to talk idly, to talk drivel; to dote.
radoteur [radɔ'tœːr], *n.m.* (*fem.* **-euse**) driveller; dotard.
radoucir [radu'siːr], *v.t.* to soften; to appease, to pacify. **se radoucir**, *v.r.* to grow milder; to soften, to be appeased, to relent, to relax.
radoucissement [radusis'mɑ̃], *n.m.* softening; getting milder (*of the weather*); mitigation, appeasement.
rafale [ra'fal], *n.f.* squall; gust of wind; (*Mil.*) burst of fire.
raffermir [rafɛr'miːr], *v.t.* to make firm, to secure, to strengthen; to confirm. **se raffermir**, *v.r.* to grow stronger; to be established; to improve in strength *or* health.
raffermissement [rafɛrmis'mɑ̃], *n.m.* hardening; securing; strengthening; confirmation.
raffinage [rafi'naːʒ], *n.m.* refining.
raffiné [rafi'ne], *a.* refined, delicate; subtle, clever; polished.—*n.m.* (*fem.* **-ée**) exquisite; sophisticated person.
raffinement [rafin'mɑ̃], *n.m.* refinement, affectation.
raffiner [rafi'ne], *v.t.* to refine.—*v.i.* to split hairs. **se raffiner**, *v.r.* to become refined.
raffinerie [rafin'ri], *n.f.* refinery.
raffineur [rafi'nœːr], *n.m.* (*fem.* **-euse**) refiner.
raffoler [rafɔ'le], *v.i.* to dote, to be passionately fond (***de***).
rafistolage [rafistɔ'laːʒ], *n.m.* (*colloq.*) patching up, mending.
rafistoler [rafistɔ'le], *v.t.* to mend, to patch up.
rafle [rɑːfl], *n.f.* clean sweep (*by thieves*); raid, round-up in the streets by police.
rafler [rɑ'fle], *v.t.* to sweep off, to carry off; to round up (*of police*).
rafraîchir [rafrɛ'ʃiːr], *v.t.* to cool; to refresh, to restore, to renew; to rub up; to trim.—*v.i.* to cool; to freshen. **se rafraîchir**, *v.r.* to cool, to take refreshment; to be refreshed, to rest.
rafraîchissant [rafrɛʃi'sɑ̃], *a.* cooling, refreshing; laxative.
rafraîchissement [rafrɛʃis'mɑ̃], *n.m.* cooling; (*pl.*) cool drinks.
ragaillardir [ragaiar'diːr], *v.t.* to enliven, to cheer up, to buck up.
rage [raːʒ], *n.f.* rabies; hydrophobia; violent pain; rage, fury; passion; mania.
rager [ra'ʒe], *v.i.* (*conjug. like* MANGER) (*colloq.*) to be in a passion; to be angry, to fume.
rageur [ra'ʒœːr], *a.* and *n.m.* (*fem.* **-euse**) ill-tempered (person).
ragot [ra'go], *a.* thick-set.—*n.m.* tittle-tattle.
ragoût [ra'gu], *n.m.* ragout; stew; (*fig.*) relish.
ragoûtant [ragu'tɑ̃], *a.* relishing, savoury, (*fig.*) inviting, tempting.
ragoûter [ragu'te], *v.t.* to restore the appetite of; to stimulate, to stir up.
ragrafer [ragra'fe], *v.t.* to reclasp, to hook again.
ragréer [ragre'e], *v.t.* to give the finishing touch to (*wall, building*); to renovate (*building*).
ragrément or **ragréement** [ragre'mɑ̃], *n.m.* finishing; restoration, renovation.
rai [RAIS].
raid [rɛd], *n.m.* long-distance run *or* flight; raid; ***un raid aérien***, an air-raid.
raide [rɛd], *a.* stiff, rigid; taut; steep; firm; rapid.—*adv.* quickly, swiftly, suddenly.
raideur [rɛ'dœːr], *n.f.* stiffness; inflexibility; steepness; harshness.
raidillon [rɛdi'jɔ̃], *n.m.* stiff ascent.
raidir [rɛ'diːr], *v.t.* to stiffen; to tighten; to make inflexible.—*v.i.* and **se raidir**, *v.r.* to stiffen; to be inflexible; (*fig.*) to harden oneself (***contre***).
raidissement [rɛdis'mɑ̃], *n.m.* stiffening, tautening.
raie [rɛ], *n.f.* line, stroke; stripe; parting (*of hair*); (*Ichth.*) ray, skate.
raifort [rɛ'fɔːr], *n.m.* horse-radish.
rail [rɑːj, raːj], *n.m.* (*Rail.*) rail.
railler [rɑ'je], *v.t.* to chaff; to scoff at.—*v.i.* to banter, to jest. **se railler**, *v.r.* to jest, to mock, to make game (***de***).
raillerie [rɑj'ri], *n.f.* raillery, bantering; jesting.
railleur [rɑ'jœːr], *a.* (*fem.* **-euse**) bantering, joking; jeering, scoffing.—*n.m.* (*fem.* **-euse**) banterer, joker; scoffer.
rainette [rɛ'nɛt], *n.f.* (*Zool.*) tree-frog.
rainure [rɛ'nyːr], *n.f.* groove, rabbet, slot.
rais or **rai** [rɛ], *n.m.* spoke (*of a wheel*); ray (*of light*).
raisin [rɛ'zɛ̃], *n.m.* grapes; ***des raisins secs***, raisins.
raisiné [rɛzi'ne], *n.m.* grape jam.
raison [rɛ'zɔ̃], *n.f.* reason; sense, judgment; satisfaction; justice, right; proof, ground; motive; ***avoir raison***, to be right.
raisonnable [rɛzɔ'nabl], *a.* rational, reasonable, sensible; just, right; adequate, moderate, fair.
raisonnablement [rɛzɔnablə'mɑ̃], *adv.* reasonably, sensibly; fairly, justly; moderately; tolerably.
raisonné [rɛzɔ'ne], *a.* rational, intelligent; systematic; classified, analytical.
raisonnement [rɛzɔn'mɑ̃], *n.m.* reasoning, argument.
raisonner [rɛzɔ'ne], *v.t.* to study; to talk *or* discourse upon.—*v.i.* to reason; to argue; to answer, to murmur. **se raisonner**, *v.r.* to reason with oneself.
raisonneur [rɛzɔ'nœːr], *a.* (*fem.* **-euse**) reasoning; argumentative.—*n.m.* (*fem.* **-euse**) reasoner, logician; argufier, pertinacious answerer.
rajeunir [raʒœ'niːr], *v.t.* to rejuvenate; to make look young *or* younger; to renew; to modernize.—*v.i.* to grow young again. **se**

rajeunir, *v.r.* to make oneself look young again.
rajeunissant [raʒœni'sɑ̃], *a.* that makes one look younger, rejuvenating.
rajeunissement [raʒœnis'mɑ̃], *n.m.* rejuvenation; renewal, renovation.
rajouter [raʒu'te], *v.t.* to add again; to add more of.
rajustement [raʒystə'mɑ̃], *n.m.* readjustment, setting in order; (*fig.*) reconciliation.
rajuster [raʒys'te], *v.t.* to readjust; (*fig.*) to settle, to reconcile. **se rajuster**, *v.r.* to readjust *or* straighten one's dress; to be reconciled.
râle (1) [rɑ:l], **râlement** [rɑ:l'mɑ̃], *n.m.* rattling in the throat; death-rattle.
râle (2) [rɑ:l], *n.m.* (*Orn.*) rail.
ralenti [ralɑ̃'ti], *a.* slower.—*n.m.* (*Cine.*) slow motion; ***tourner au ralenti***, (*Motor.*) to tick over.
ralentir [ralɑ̃'ti:r], *v.t.*, *v.i.* to slow down, to ease up; to lessen, to moderate. **se ralentir**, *v.r.* to slacken, to slow up; to abate, to relax.
ralentissement [ralɑ̃tis'mɑ̃], *n.m.* slackening; decrease; cooling (*of zeal*).
râler [rɑ'le], *v.i.* to be at one's last gasp.
ralliement [rali'mɑ̃], *n.m.* rallying, rally; winning over; ***mot de ralliement***, (*Mil.*) password.
rallier [ra'lje], *v.t.* to rally; to rejoin; to win over. **se rallier**, *v.r.* to rally; to join.
rallonge [ra'lɔ̃:ʒ], *n.f.* lengthening-piece, leaf; ***table à rallonges***, draw-table.
rallongement [ralɔ̃ʒ'mɑ̃], *n.m.* lengthening, extension.
rallonger [ralɔ̃'ʒe], *v.t.* (*conjug. like* MANGER) to lengthen; to let out (*skirt*).
rallumer [raly'me], *v.t.* to relight; to rekindle; to revive. **se rallumer**, *v.r.* to light again; (*fig.*) to rekindle.
rallye [ra'li], *n.m.* (*Motor.*) race meeting, rally.
ramage [ra'ma:ʒ], *n.m.* floral pattern (*on materials*); chirping, warbling (*of birds*); (*fig.*) prattle (*of children*).
ramaigrir [ramɛ'gri:r], *v.t.* to make lean *or* thin again.—*v.i.* to grow thin again.
ramaigrissement [ramɛgris'mɑ̃], *n.m.* emaciation, leanness.
ramas [ra'mɑ], *n.m. inv.* heap, disorderly collection; set, troop, lot, rabble.
ramassé [ramɑ'se], *a.* thick-set, stocky; compact.
ramasser [ramɑ'se], *v.t.* to collect, to gather; to pick up, to take up. **se ramasser**, *v.r.* to assemble, to gather together; to roll itself up (*of an animal*); to crouch; to pick oneself up (*after a spill*).
ramasseur [ramɑ'sœ:r], *n.m.* (*fem.* **-euse**) gatherer, collector.
ramassis [ramɑ'si], [RAMAS].
rame [ram], *n.f.* scull, oar; (*Hort.*) stick, prop; (*Manuf.*) tenter frame; ream (*of paper*); made-up train *or* portion of train; ***une rame de Métro***, an Underground train.
ramé [ra'me], *a.* supported with sticks (*of peas*), staked (*of plants*).
rameau [ra'mo], *n.m.* (*pl.* **-eaux**) bough, small branch (*of a tree*); subdivision.
ramée [ra'me], *n.f.* green boughs, green arbour.
ramener [ram'ne], *v.t.* (*conjug. like* AMENER) to bring back; to take home; to restore; to reclaim; to recall.
ramer (1) [ra'me], *v.t.* to stick (*peas*), to stake (*plants*).
ramer (2) [ra'me], *v.i.* to row, to scull.
rameur [ra'mœ:r], *n.m.* (*fem.* **-euse**) rower.
ramier [ra'mje], *n.m.* wood-pigeon, ring-dove.
ramification [ramifikɑ'sjɔ̃], *n.f.* ramification.
ramifier [rami'fje], *v.t.* to ramify. **se ramifier**, *v.r.* to ramify, to divide.
ramille [ra'mi:j], *n.f.*, **ramillon** [rami'jɔ̃], *n.m.* twig.
ramollir [ramɔ'li:r], *v.t.* to soften, (*fig.*) to enervate, to unman. **se ramollir**, *v.r.* to soften; (*fig.*) to relent.
ramollisant [ramɔli'sɑ̃], *a.* softening, emollient.
ramollissement [ramɔlis'mɑ̃], *n.m.* softening.
ramonage [ramɔ'na:ʒ], *n.m.* chimney sweeping.
ramoner [ramɔ'ne], *v.t.* to sweep (*a chimney*).
ramoneur [ramɔ'nœ:r], *n.m.* chimney-sweeper, sweep.
rampant [rɑ̃'pɑ̃], *a.* creeping, crawling; (*fig.*) cringing, servile.
rampe [rɑ̃:p], *n.f.* banister; flight of stairs; slope, ramp, incline, gradient; (*Theat.*) footlights.
rampement [rɑ̃p'mɑ̃], *n.m.* creeping, crawling.
ramper [rɑ̃'pe], *v.i.* to creep, to crawl; (*fig.*) to crouch, to grovel.
ramure [ra'my:r], *n.f.* branches, boughs; antlers (*of a stag*).
rancart [rɑ̃'ka:r], *n.m.* ***mettre au rancart***, to throw aside, to cast off; to put on the shelf.
rance [rɑ̃:s], *a.* rancid, rank.—*n.m.* rancidness.
ranci [rɑ̃'si], *a.* rancid.
rancidité [rɑ̃sidi'te], **rancissure** [rɑ̃si'sy:r], *n.f.*, **rancissement** [rɑ̃sis'mɑ̃], *n.m.* rancidity.
rancir [rɑ̃'si:r], *v.i.* to grow rancid.
rancœur [rɑ̃'kœ:r], *n.f.* rancour, bitterness.
rançon [rɑ̃'sɔ̃], *n.f.* ransom.
rançonnement [rɑ̃sɔn'mɑ̃], *n.m.* ransoming; (*fig.*) extortion.
rançonner [rɑ̃sɔ'ne], *v.t.* to ransom; (*fig.*) to fleece.
rancune [rɑ̃'kyn], *n.f.* rancour, spite, grudge, malice.
rancunier [rɑ̃ky'nje], *a.* and *n.m.* (*fem.* **-ière**) rancorous, spiteful (person).
randonnée [rɑ̃dɔ'ne], *n.f.* outing, run, ramble, tour.
rang [rɑ̃], *n.m.* row, line; order, class; rank.
rangé [rɑ̃'ʒe], *a.* tidy; steady; ***en bataille rangée***, in a pitched battle.
rangée [rɑ̃'ʒe], *n.f.* row, range, line, tier, set.
rangement [rɑ̃ʒ'mɑ̃], *n.m.* arranging, putting in order.
ranger [rɑ̃'ʒe], *v.t.* (*conjug. like* MANGER) to put in order, to set to rights; to draw up; to arrange; to range; to rank; to reduce, to subdue. **se ranger**, *v.r.* to make room, to make way (*for*); to draw up (*of carriages*,

troops etc.), to pull up (*at kerb*); to fall in (*of soldiers*).
ranimer [rani'me], *v.t.* to restore to life, to revive; to rouse, to enliven; to cheer up. **se ranimer**, *v.r.* to revive, to brighten up, to be enlivened; to cheer up.
Raoul [ra'ul], *m.* Ralph.
rapace [ra'pas], *a.* rapacious; grasping (*of person*).—*n.m.* rapacious bird, bird of prey.
rapacement [rapas'mɑ̃], *adv.* rapaciously.
rapacité [rapasi'te], *n.f.* rapacity; cupidity.
râpage [rɑ'paːʒ], *n.m.* rasping; grating.
rapatriement [rapatri'mɑ̃], *n.m.* repatriation.
rapatrier [rapatri'je], *v.t.* to repatriate; (*dial.*) to reconcile.
râpe [rɑːp], *n.f.* grater; rasp; stalk (*of grapes*).
râpé [rɑ'pe], *a.* grated; rasped; threadbare (*of clothes*).
râper [rɑ'pe], *v.t.* to grate (*cheese*), to rasp; to make threadbare.
rapetassage [rapta'saːʒ], *n.m.* patching up, mending, cobbling.
rapetasser [rapta'se], *v.t.* to patch, to mend, to cobble.
rapetasseur [rapta'sœːr], *n.m.* (*fem.* **-euse**) piecer, patcher; cobbler; (*fig.*) compiler, adapter.
rapetissement [raptis'mɑ̃], *n.m.* shortening, shrinking; (*fig.*) belittling.
rapetisser [rapti'se], *v.t.* to shorten, to make smaller; (*fig.*) to belittle.—*v.i.* to grow less, to shorten, to shrink.
raphia [ra'fja], *n.m.* raffia.
rapide [ra'pid], *a.* rapid, quick, fast; sudden; steep.—*n.m.* rapid; fast train.
rapidement [rapid'mɑ̃], *adv.* rapidly, swiftly; steeply.
rapidité [rapidi'te], *n.f.* rapidity, speed; steepness.
rapiéçage [rapje'saːʒ], **rapiècement** [rapjɛs'mɑ̃], *n.m.* piecing, patching.
rapiécer [rapje'se] (*see Verb Tables*), **rapiéceter** [rapjes'te] (*conjug. like* AMENER), *v.t.* to piece, to patch.
rapière [ra'pjɛːr], *n.f.* rapier.
rapin [ra'pɛ̃], *n.m.* art student; (*fig.*) dauber.
rapine [ra'pin], *n.f.* rapine, robbery; plunder; graft.
rapiner [rapi'ne], *v.t.*, *v.i.* to pillage, to plunder.
rapineur [rapi'nœːr], *n.m.* (*fem.* **-euse**) plunderer, pillager, pilferer.
rappareiller [raparɛ'je], **rapparier** [rapa'rje], *v.t.* to match, to complete.
rappel [ra'pɛl], *n.m.* recall, reminder, call (*to order*); tattoo, assembly; revocation; back pay; (*Theat.*) curtain-call.
rappeler [ra'ple], *v.t.* (*conjug. like* APPELER) to call back, to recall; to restore (*to life etc.*); to muster; to retract; to recall to mind; to remind. **se rappeler**, *v.r.* to recollect, to remember.
rapport [ra'pɔːr], *n.m.* revenue, profit; produce; productiveness; report, account, information, tale; return, statement; resemblance, conformity; agreement; connexion; communication; proportion; reimbursement; ***faire un rapport***, to draw up a report; ***maison de rapport***, tenement house; ***sous tous les rapports***, in every respect.
rapporter [rapɔr'te], *v.t.* to bring back; to bring home; to yield; to retrieve (*of dog*); to refund; to recall; to give an account of; to attribute.—*v.i.* to retrieve (*of dog*); (*sch.*) to tell tales; to be profitable. **se rapporter**, *v.r.* to agree, to correspond, to tally; to be related.
rapporteur [rapɔr'tœːr], *n.m.* (*fem.* **-euse**) tale-bearer; reporter.—*n.m.* (*Geom.*) protractor.
rapprendre [ra'prɑ̃ːdr], *v.t. irr.* (*conjug. like* PRENDRE) to learn anew; to teach again.
rapprochement [raprɔʃ'mɑ̃], *n.m.* drawing closer, bringing together; reconciliation; junction; comparison.
rapprocher [raprɔ'ʃe], *v.t.* to bring near again; to bring together; to reconcile; to compare. **se rapprocher**, *v.r.* to come near again; to draw nearer; to be brought together; to become reconciled; to approximate (*de*).
rapsodie [rapsɔ'di], *n.f.* rhapsody.
rapt [rapt], *n.m.* abduction; kidnapping.
raquette [ra'kɛt], *n.f.* racket, battledore; snow-shoe.
rare [raːr], *a.* rare, uncommon; scarce; thin, scanty.
raréfaction [rarefak'sjɔ̃], *n.f.* rarefaction.
raréfiant [rare'fjɑ̃], *a.* rarefying.
raréfier [rare'fje], *v.t.* to rarefy. **se raréfier** *v.r.* to become rare; to become rarefied.
rarement [rar'mɑ̃], *adv.* rarely, seldom.
rareté [rar'te], *n.f.* rarity; scarcity.
rarissime [rari'sim], *a.* very rare, most rare.
ras [rɑ], *a.* close-shaven, shorn; bare, smooth; open, flat, low; ***faire table rase***, to sweep away all preconceptions; ***rase campagne***, open country.—*n.m.* short-nap cloth; level; raft; race (*of a mill*) [RAZ].
rasade [rɑ'zad], *n.f.* brimful glass (*of wine*).
rasant [rɑ'zɑ̃], *a.* shaving, grazing; sweeping; (*fam.*) boring.
raser [rɑ'ze], *v.t.* to shave; to demolish; to graze, to skim over; (*fam.*) to bore. **se raser**, *v.r.* to shave, to be shaved.
rasoir [rɑ'zwaːr], *n.m.* razor; (*fam.*) bore.
rassasiant [rasa'zjɑ̃], *a.* satiating, filling (*food*).
rassasiement [rasazi'mɑ̃], *n.m.* satiety.
rassasier [rasa'zje], *v.t.* to satisfy, to fill; to satiate; to surfeit. **se rassasier**, *v.r.* to be cloyed; to take one's fill.
rassemblement [rasɑ̃blə'mɑ̃], *n.m.* assembly, muster, crowd, mob; political group.
rassembler [rasɑ̃'ble], *v.t.* to gather together, to collect; to put together; to assemble. **se rassembler**, *v.r.* to assemble, to congregate, to muster.
rasseoir [ra'swaːr], *v.t. irr.* (*conjug. like* ASSEOIR) to seat again, to reseat; to replace; to calm, to compose. **se rasseoir**, *v.r.* to sit down again; to settle (*of liquids*); to become composed again.
rasséréner [rasere'ne], *v.t.* (*conjug. like* CÉDER) to clear up; to restore serenity to. **se rasséréner**, *v.r.* to clear up; to recover one's serenity.
rassis [ra'si], *a.* settled; calm, staid, sedate; stale.
rassortiment [rasɔrti'mɑ̃], **réassortiment** [reasɔrti'mɑ̃], *n.m.* rematching (*of colours, materials etc.*), resorting; restocking.

rassortir [rasɔr'tiːr], **réassortir** [reasɔr'tiːr], *v.t.* to sort *or* match again; to stock (*a shop etc.*).
rassurant [rasy'rɑ̃], *a.* tranquillizing; encouraging, reassuring.
rassurer [rasy're], *v.t.* to make firm; to strengthen; to tranquillize, to reassure. **se rassurer,** *v.r.* to be reassured; to reassure oneself; to clear up (*of the weather*); ***rassurez-vous,*** set your mind at rest.
rat [ra], *n.m.* rat; ***rat des champs,*** field-mouse; ***rat d'hôtel,*** hotel thief.
ratafia [rata'fja], *n.m.* ratafia.
ratatiné [ratati'ne], *a.* shrivelled, shrunken.
ratatiner (se) [səratati'ne], *v.r.* to shrink, to shrivel up.
rate (1) [rat], *n.f.* spleen.
rate (2) [rat], *n.f.* female rat.
râteau [rɑ'to], *n.m.* (*pl.* **-eaux**) rake.
râtelage [rɑt'laːʒ], *n.m.* raking.
râtelée [rɑt'le], *n.f.* rakeful, raking.
râteler [rɑt'le], *v.t.* (*conjug. like* APPELER) to rake.
râteleur [rɑt'lœːr], *n.m.* (*fem.* **-euse**) raker.
râtelier [rɑtə'lje], *n.m.* rack; set of teeth, denture.
rater [ra'te], *v.t.* to miss; (*fig.*) to fail to obtain.—*v.i.* to misfire, to miss (*one's shot*); (*fig.*) to miscarry.
ratière [ra'tjɛːr], *n.f.* rat-trap.
ratification [ratifikɑ'sjɔ̃], *n.f.* ratification.
ratifier [rati'fje], *v.t.* to ratify.
ratine [ra'tin], *n.f.* ratteen, petersham (*cloth*).
ration [rɑ'sjɔ̃], *n.f.* ration, allowance.
rationaliser [rasjɔnali'ze], *v.t.* to rationalize.
rationalisme [rasjɔna'lism], *n.m.* rationalism.
rationaliste [rasjɔna'list], *a.* and *n.* rationalist.
rationalité [rasjɔnali'te], *n.f.* rationality.
rationnel [rasjɔ'nɛl], *a.* (*fem.* **-elle**) rational.
rationnement [rasjɔn'mɑ̃], *n.m.* rationing.
rationner [rasjɔ'ne], *v.t.* to ration.
ratissage [rati'saːʒ], *n.m.* scraping; raking.
ratisser [rati'se], *v.t.* to rake; to scrape.
ratissoire [rati'swaːr], *n.f.* scraper, light rake, hoe.
ratissure [rati'syːr], *n.f.* scrapings.
raton [ra'tɔ̃], *n.m.* little rat; (*fig.*) little pet, darling.
rattacher [rata'ʃe], *v.t.* to refasten; to attach; (*fig.*) to link. **se rattacher,** *v.r.* to be attached *or* connected; to be linked up (*with*).
ratteindre [ra'tɛ̃ːdr], *v.t. irr.* (*conjug. like* CRAINDRE) to retake, to catch again; to overtake.
rattendrir [ratɑ̃'driːr], *v.t.* to soften again.
rattraper [ratra'pe], *v.t.* to catch again, to retake; to overtake; to recover. **se rattraper,** *v.r.* to catch hold (*à*); to be caught again; to make up for one's losses.
rature [ra'tyːr], *n.f.* erasure.
raturer [raty're], *v.t.* to erase.
raucité [rosi'te], *n.f.* raucity, hoarseness.
rauque [roːk], *a.* hoarse, raucous, rough.
ravage [ra'vaːʒ], *n.m.* ravage, havoc.
ravager [rava'ʒe], *v.t.* (*conjug. like* MANGER) to ravage, to lay waste; to spoil, to ruin.
ravageur [rava'ʒœːr], *n.m.* (*fem.* **-euse**) ravager, spoiler.
ravalement [raval'mɑ̃], *n.m.* scraping and pointing (*of a wall*); rough-casting; repainting.
ravaler [rava'le], *v.t.* to swallow again; (*fig.*) to disparage; to point (*stonework*); to rough-cast (*wall*). **se ravaler,** *v.r.* to debase oneself, to lower oneself.
ravaudage [ravo'daːʒ], *n.m.* mending (*of old clothes etc.*).
ravauder [ravo'de], *v.t.* to mend, to darn; (*dial.*) to scold.
ravaudeur [ravo'dœːr], *n.m.* (*fem.* **-euse**) mender (*of stockings, old clothes etc.*).
rave [raːv], *n.f.* (*Bot.*) ***grosse rave,*** French turnip; ***petite rave,*** radish.
ravenelle [rav'nɛl], *n.f.* wallflower.
ravi [ra'vi], *a.* carried away, enraptured, delighted.
ravier [ra'vje], *n.m.* radish-dish.
ravière [ra'vjɛːr], *n.f.* radish-bed.
ravigote [ravi'gɔt], *n.f.* ravigote-sauce.
ravigoter [ravigɔ'te], *v.t.* to revive, to refresh, to buck up. **se ravigoter,** *v.r.* to recover one's spirits, to perk up.
ravilir [ravi'liːr], *v.t.* to degrade, to lower.
ravin [ra'vɛ̃], *n.m.* ravine; gully.
ravine [ra'viːn], *n.f.* mountain torrent; small gully.
ravinement [ravin'mɑ̃], *n.m.* hollowing out *or* furrowing (*by waters*).
raviner [ravi'ne], *v.t.* to channel, to furrow.
ravir [ra'viːr], *v.t.* to carry off, to ravish; (*fig.*) to charm, to enrapture.
raviser (se) [səravi'ze], *v.r.* to change one's mind; to think better of it.
ravissant [ravi'sɑ̃], *a.* ravishing, delightful, charming.
ravissement [ravis'mɑ̃], *n.m.* carrying off; *rape; rapture, delight.
ravisseur [ravi'sœːr], *n.m.* (*fem.* **-euse**) ravisher; kidnapper.
ravitaillement [ravitɑj'mɑ̃], *n.m.* revictualling; supplying; supplies; food.
ravitailler [ravitɑ'je], *v.t.* to provision; to supply.
raviver [ravi've], *v.t.* to revive, to cheer; to freshen up (*colours*).
ravoir [ra'vwaːr], *v.t.* (*usu. in infin.*) to get back again, to recover.
rayé [rɛ'je], *a.* striped (*garment*); rifled (*gun*); scratched (*glass*); struck off (*a list*).
rayer [rɛ'je], *v.t.* (*conjug. like* PAYER) to scratch (*dishes etc.*); to streak, to stripe; to erase; (*Artill.*) to rifle.
rayon [rɛ'jɔ̃], *n.m.* ray; beam, gleam; radius; spoke (*of a wheel*); shelf; department (*of a shop*); ***rayon de miel,*** honeycomb.
rayonnant [rɛjɔ'nɑ̃], *a.* radiant, beaming.
rayonne [rɛ'jɔn], *n.f.* rayon.
rayonnement [rɛjɔn'mɑ̃], *n.m.* radiance; radiation.
rayonner [rɛjɔ'ne], *v.i.* to radiate; to shine, to beam; to sparkle.
rayure [rɛ'jyːr], *n.f.* stripe; streak, scratch; rifling (*of fire-arms*); erasure.
raz or **ras** [rɑ], *n.m. inv.* race (*a violent current*); ***raz de marée,*** tidal wave.
razzia [ra'zja], *n.f.* (*Algerian*) razzia, raid, inroad, foray.
ré [re], *n.m.* (*Mus.*) re, D.
réabonnement [reabɔn'mɑ̃], *n.m.* renewed subscription.

éabonner (se) [səreabɔ'ne], *v.r.* to renew one's subscription.
éacteur [reak'tœ:r], *n.m.* reactor; (*Av.*) jet-engine.
éaction [reak'sjɔ̃], *n.f.* reaction; ***les avions à réaction***, jet-aircraft.
éactionnaire [reaksjɔ'nɛ:r], *a.* and *n.* reactionary.
éactionner [reaksjɔ'ne], *v.t.* to sue again.—*v.i.* (*St. Exch.*) to react against a rise.
éadmettre [read'mɛtr], *v.t. irr.* (*conjug. like* METTRE) to admit again, to readmit.
éadmission [readmi'sjɔ̃], *n.f.* readmission.
éagir [rea'ʒi:r], *v.i.* to react.
éajourner [reaʒur'ne], *v.t.* to readjourn.
éalisable [reali'zabl], *a.* realizable; feasible.
éalisateur [realiza'tœ:r], *n.m.* (*Cine.*) film director.
éalisation [realizɑ'sjɔ̃], *n.f.* realization; achievement; conversion into money; clearance sale.
éaliser [reali'ze], *v.t.* to realize; to achieve; to convert into money. **se réaliser**, *v.r.* to be realized, to come true.
éalisme [rea'lism], *n.m.* realism.
éaliste [rea'list], *a.* realistic.—*n.* realist.
éalité [reali'te], *n.f.* reality.
éapparaître [reapa'rɛ:tr], *v.i. irr.* (*conjug. like* CONNAÎTRE) to reappear.
éapparition [reapari'sjɔ̃], *n.f.* reappearance.
éarmement [rearmə'mɑ̃], *n.m.* rearmament.
éarmer [rear'me], *v.t.* to rearm; (*Navy*) to refit.
éassortiment [RASSORTIMENT].
ebaisser [rəbɛ'se], *v.t.* to lower again.
ébarbatif [rebarba'tif], *a.* (*fem.* **-tive**) stern, surly, forbidding.
ebâtir [rəbɑ'tir], *v.t.* to rebuild.
ebattre [rə'batr], *v.t.* (*conjug. like* BATTRE) to beat again; to repeat; to shuffle (*cards*) again.
ebattu [rəba'ty], *a.* hackneyed, trite.
ebelle [rə'bɛl], *a.* rebellious; disobedient; unyielding; refractory.—*n.* rebel.
ebeller (se) [sərəbɛ'le], *v.r.* to rebel, to revolt.
ébellion [rebɛ'ljɔ̃], *n.f.* rebellion; resistance.
ebiffer (se) [sərəbi'fe], *v.r.* (*fam.*) to bridle up, to kick over the traces.
eblanchir [rəblɑ̃'ʃi:r], *v.t.* to bleach again; to whitewash again.
eboire [rə'bwa:r], *v.t. irr.* (*conjug. like* BOIRE) to drink again.
eboisement [rəbwaz'mɑ̃], *n.m.* retimbering, reafforestation.
eboiser [rəbwa'ze], *v.t.* to retimber, to reafforest.
ebond [rə'bɔ̃], *n.m.* rebound; bounce (*of ball*).
ebondi [rəbɔ̃'di], *a.* plump, chubby.
ebondir [rəbɔ̃'di:r], *v.i.* to rebound; to bounce.
ebondissement [rəbɔ̃dis'mɑ̃], *n.m.* rebounding; bounce.
ebord [rə'bɔ:r], *n.m.* edge, brink; sill (*of window*); border, hem.
eborder [rəbɔr'de], *v.t.* to border again, to re-hem.
ebouillir [rəbu'ji:r], *v.i. irr.* (*conjug. like* BOUILLIR) to boil again.
ebours [rə'bu:r], *a.* cross-grained (*wood*); intractable (*horse*).—*n.m.* wrong side (*of material etc.*); wrong way (*of the grain*); contrary, reverse; ***à rebours*** or ***au rebours*** the wrong way, against the grain, backwards.
reboutage [rəbu'ta:ʒ], *n.m.* bone-setting.
rebouter [rəbu'te], *v.t.* to set (*bones*).
rebouteur [rəbu'tœ:r], **rebouteux** [rəbu'tø], *n.m.* (*fem.* **-euse**) bone-setter.
reboutonner [rəbutɔ'ne], *v.t.* to rebutton. **se reboutonner**, *v.r.* to button up one's clothes again.
rebroussement [rəbrus'mɑ̃], *n.m.* turning back, turning up.
rebrousse-poil (à) [arəbrus'pwal], *adv. phr.* against the grain; the wrong way.
rebrousser [rəbru'se], *v.t.* to turn up (*the hair*); ***rebrousser chemin***, to turn back.
rebuffade [rəby'fad], *n.f.* rebuff, repulse; snub.
rébus [re'by:s], *n.m.* rebus; riddle.
rebut [rə'by], *n.m.* repulse, rebuff; refuse, rubbish; scum.
rebutant [rəby'tɑ̃], *a.* repulsive, disgusting, forbidding.
rebuter [rəby'te], *v.t.* to repulse, to rebuff, to reject, to snub; to disgust. **se rebuter**, *v.r.* to become discouraged.
récalcitrant [rekalsi'trɑ̃], *a.* refractory, recalcitrant; rebellious.
récalcitrer [rekalsi'tre], *v.i.* to kick (*of horses*); (*fig.*) to be refractory.
recaler [rəka'le], *v.t.* to wedge up again, to refix; (*Sch.*) to plough (*at an examination*).
récapitulation [rekapityla'sjɔ̃], *n.f.* recapitulation, summing up; summary.
récapituler [rekapity'le], *v.t.* to recapitulate, to sum up; (*colloq.*) to recap.
recel [rə'sɛl], **recèlement** [rəsɛl'mɑ̃], *n.m.* receiving of stolen goods.
receler [rəs'le] (*conjug. like* AMENER), **recéler** [rəse'le] (*conjug. like* CÉDER), *v.t.* to receive (*stolen goods*); to embezzle; to conceal from justice; to contain.
receleur [rəs'lœ:r], *n.m.* (*fem.* **-euse**) receiver of stolen goods, fence.
récemment [resa'mɑ̃], *adv.* recently, newly.
recensement [rəsɑ̃s'mɑ̃], *n.m.* census; return, inventory; verification.
recenser [rəsɑ̃'se], *v.t.* to take the census of; to record; to verify.
recenseur [rəsɑ̃'sœ:r], *n.m.* (*fem.* **-euse**) census-taker; enumerator.
recension [rəsɑ̃'sjɔ̃], *n.f.* recension; collation (*of books etc.*).
récent [re'sɑ̃], *a.* recent, new, fresh, late.
receper [rəsə'pe] (*conjug. like* AMENER), **recéper** [rəse'pe] (*conjug. like* CÉDER), *v.t.* to cut back; to clear (*a wood*).
récépissé [resepi'se], *n.m.* receipt, acknowledgment (*for documents, papers etc.*).
réceptacle [resɛp'takl], *n.m.* receptacle; repository.
récepteur [resɛp'tœ:r], *a.* (*fem.* **-trice**) receiving; ***poste récepteur***, receiving set. —*n.m.* receiver; reservoir (*in a machine, etc.*); receiving instrument (*of telegraphs*).
réception [resɛp'sjɔ̃], *n.f.* receiving, receipt; admission; (*hotel*) reception desk; reception, party.
réceptionnaire [resɛpsjɔ'nɛ:r], *a.* receiving. —*n.* receiver, receiving clerk; consignee.
réceptionniste [resɛpsjɔ'nist], *n.* receptionist.

recette [rə'sɛt], *n.f.* receipts, returns; takings; (*Cook.*) recipe; receiver's office; ***faire recette***, to be a draw (*of a play*).

recevable [rəsə'vabl], *a.* receivable, admissible.

receveur [rəsə'vœːr], *n.m.* (*fem.* **-euse**) receiver, collector (*of taxes etc.*); (bus-) conductor.

recevoir [rəsə'vwaːr], *v.t. irr.* to receive, to accept, to take, to let in, to admit; to welcome; to entertain.—*v.i.* to receive, to be at home to visitors.

rechange [rə'ʃɑ̃ːʒ], *n.m.* change (*of anything*), replacement; spare things; (*Comm.*) re-exchange; ***roue de rechange***, spare-wheel.

rechanter [rəʃɑ̃'te], *v.t.* to sing again; to retell.

rechaper [rəʃa'pe], *v.t.* to retread (*a tyre*).

réchapper [reʃa'pe], *v.i.* to escape; ***réchapper d'une maladie***, to recover from an illness.

recharge [rə'ʃarʒ], *n.f.* fresh *or* second charge.

rechargement [rəʃarʒə'mɑ̃], *n.m.* reloading, relading; reballasting.

recharger [rəʃar'ʒe], *v.t.* (*conjug. like* MANGER) to load again; to recharge.

réchaud [re'ʃo], *n.m.* small portable stove; chafing-dish; dish-warmer.

réchauffage [reʃo'faːʒ], *n.m.* warming up again, reheating.

réchauffé [reʃo'fe], *n.m.* dish *or* food warmed up again; rehash, stale stuff *or* news.

réchauffer [reʃo'fe], *v.t.* to warm up, to reheat; to reanimate, to stir up. **se réchauffer**, *v.r.* to warm oneself, to get warm.

réchauffoir [reʃo'fwaːr], *n.m.* plate-warmer, hot-plate.

rechausser [rəʃo'se], *v.t.* to put shoes *or* stockings on (*a person*) again; (*Build.*) to underpin.

rêche [rɛːʃ], *a.* rough (*to the taste, touch etc.*); (*fig.*) sour, crabbed (*of persons*).

recherche [rə'ʃɛrʃ], *n.f.* search, pursuit; inquiry, investigation; research; (*fig.*) studied elegance *or* refinement, affectation.

recherché [rəʃɛr'ʃe], *a.* choice, exquisite; affected; far-fetched; in great demand.

rechercher [rəʃɛr'ʃe], *v.t.* to seek again; to seek, to search for; to investigate, to pry into; to desire; to court, to woo.

rechigné [rəʃi'ɲe], *a.* sour-faced, surly, crabbed.

rechignement [rəʃiɲə'mɑ̃], *n.m.* sulking, sullenness.

rechigner [rəʃi'ɲe], *v.i.* to look sulky, sullen, grim etc; to balk (*at something*).

rechute [rə'ʃyt], *n.f.* relapse, set-back.

rechuter [rəʃy'te], *v.i.* to have a relapse; to backslide.

récidive [resi'diːv], *n.f.* recidivism; second offence.

récidiver [residi've], *v.i.* to repeat the offence; to relapse; to recur (*of disease*).

récidiviste [residi'vist], *n.* recidivist, old lag.

récif [re'sif], *n.m.* reef (*of rocks*).

récipé [resi'pe], *n.m.* recipe, prescription.

récipient [resi'pjɑ̃], *n.m.* container, receptacle; reservoir.

réciprocité [resiprɔsi'te], *n.f.* reciprocity, reciprocation.

réciproque [resi'prɔk], *a.* reciprocal, mutual.

réciproquement [resiprɔk'mɑ̃], *adv.* reciprocally, mutually; vice versa.

récit [re'si], *n.m.* recital, account, story narrative, report.

récital [resi'tal], *n.m.* (*pl.* **-als**) musical recital.

récitant [resi'tɑ̃], *a.* (*Mus.*) solo (*instrument voice*).—*n.m.* (*fem.* **-e**) soloist; narrator.

récitateur [resita'tœːr], *n.m.* (*fem.* **-trice**) reciter, repeater.

récitatif [resita'tif], *n.m.* (*Mus.*) recitative.

récitation [resitɑ'sjɔ̃], *n.f.* recitation, reciting repetition.

réciter [resi'te], *v.t.* to recite, to rehearse; to repeat, to say; to tell, to relate, to recount.

réclamant [rekla'mɑ̃], *a.* claiming.—*n.m.* (*fem.* **-e**) claimant.

réclamation [reklamɑ'sjɔ̃], *n.f.* claim request, demand; complaint.

réclame [re'klaːm], *n.f.* advertisement publicity; (*Print.*) catch-word; puff.

réclamer [rekla'me], *v.t.* to crave, to entreat to beseech; to claim.—*v.i.* to object, to complain; to protest (***contre***). **se réclamer** *v.r.* to refer to.

reclus [rə'kly], *a.* shut up, secluded.—*n.m.* (*fem.* **-e**) recluse; monk, nun.

reclusion [rəkly'zjɔ̃], **réclusion** [rekly'zjɔ̃] *n.f.* reclusion, confinement; (*Law*) solitary confinement (*with hard labour*).

recoin [rə'kwɛ̃], *n.m.* corner, nook; ***coins et recoins***, nooks and crannies.

récolte [re'kɔlt], *n.f.* harvest, crop, vintage.

récolter [rekɔl'te], *v.t.* to reap, to gather in to get in.

recommandable [rəkɔmɑ̃'dabl], *a.* respectable; commendable.

recommandation [rəkɔmɑ̃dɑ'sjɔ̃], *n.f.* recommendation; reference; (*fig.*) esteem (*Post*) registration.

recommander [rəkɔmɑ̃'de], *v.t.* to recommend; to enjoin; to request; to commend (*Post*) to register. **se recommander**, *v.r.* to recommend oneself; to refer to.

recommencement [rəkɔmɑ̃s'mɑ̃], *n.m.* recommencement, fresh start.

recommencer [rəkɔmɑ̃'se], *v.t., v.i.* (*conjug. like* COMMENCER) to recommence, to begin again; to do (*it*) again.

récompense [rekɔ̃'pɑ̃ːs], *n.f.* reward, recompense; prize; compensation; ***en récompense de***, in return for.

récompenser [rekɔ̃pɑ̃'se], *v.t.* to reward; to compensate; to repay.

recomposer [rəkɔ̃po'ze], *v.t.* to recompose.

recomposition [rəkɔ̃pozi'sjɔ̃], *n.f.* recomposition.

réconciliable [rekɔ̃si'ljabl], *a.* reconcilable.

réconciliateur [rekɔ̃silja'tœːr], *n.m.* (*fem.* **-trice**) reconciler.

réconciliation [rekɔ̃siljɑ'sjɔ̃], *n.f.* reconciliation.

réconcilier [rekɔ̃si'lje], *v.t.* to reconcile. **se réconcilier**, *v.r.* to be(come) reconciled (*colloq.*) to make it up.

reconduire [rəkɔ̃'dɥiːr], *v.t. irr.* (*conjug. like* CONDUIRE) to lead back, to see home; to show out.

reconduite [rəkɔ̃'dɥit], *n.f.* showing out, seeing out, seeing home.

réconfort [rekɔ̃'fɔːr], *n.m.* comfort, relief.

réconforter [rekɔ̃fɔr'te], *v.t.* to comfort, to cheer up; to fortify.

reconnaissable [rəkɔnɛ'sabl], *a.* recognizable.

reconnaissance [rəkɔnɛ'sɑ̃:s], *n.f.* recognition; discovery; gratitude, thankfulness; survey; acknowledgment, confession; reward; recognizance; pawn-ticket; (*Mil.*) reconnaissance.

reconnaissant [rəkɔnɛ'sɑ̃], *a.* grateful, thankful.

reconnaître [rəkɔ'nɛ:tr], *v.t. irr.* (*conjug. like* CONNAÎTRE) to recognize, to identify; to discover; to acknowledge, to admit; to be grateful for; to reconnoitre. **se reconnaître,** *v.r.* to recognize oneself; to be recognizable; to make out where one is.

reconquérir [rəkɔ̃ke'ri:r], *v.t. irr.* (*conjug. like* ACQUÉRIR) to reconquer; to regain.

reconstituer [rəkɔ̃sti'tɥe], *v.t.* to reconstitute, to restore.

reconstitution [rəkɔ̃stity'sjɔ̃], *n.f.* reconstitution, reorganization; reconstruction (*of a murder*).

reconstruction [rəkɔ̃stryk'sjɔ̃], *n.f.* reconstruction, rebuilding.

reconstruire [rəkɔ̃s'trɥi:r], *v.t. irr.* (*conjug. like* CONDUIRE) to rebuild, to reconstruct; to rehabilitate.

recopier [rəkɔ'pje], *v.t.* to make a copy of.

recoquillement [rəkɔkij'mɑ̃], *n.m.* curling up, dog('s)-earing (*of pages of book*).

recoquiller [rəkɔki'je], *v.t.* to turn up *or* back. **se recoquiller,** *v.r.* to curl up, to shrivel.

record [rə'kɔ:r], *n.m.* record (*in sports etc.*).

recorder [rəkɔr'de], *v.t.* to learn by heart; to tie up again.

recors [rə'kɔ:r], *n.m.* bailiff's man.

recoucher [rəku'ʃe], *v.t.* to put to bed again; to lay down again. **se recoucher,** *v.r.* to go to bed again, to lie down again.

recoudre [rə'kudr], *v.t. irr.* (*conjug. like* COUDRE) to sew again, to sew up.

recoupement [rəkup'mɑ̃], *n.m.* (*Build.*) offset; cross-checking.

recouper [rəku'pe], *v.t.* to cut again; to cross-check.

recourbé [rəkur'be], *a.* curved, bent (back).

recourber [rəkur'be], *v.t.* to bend back, to bend round. **se recourber,** *v.r.* to be curved, to bend.

recourir [rəku'ri:r], *v.i. irr.* (*conjug. like* COURIR) to run again; to resort (*à*); (*Law*) to appeal

recours [rə'kur], *n.m.* recourse; (*fig.*) resource, remedy; (*Law*) appeal.

recousu [rəku'zy], *a.* sewn *or* stitched again.

recouvrement [rəkuvrə'mɑ̃], *n.m.* recovery, regaining; recovering (*of debts etc.*); covering up, overlapping; cap (*of a watch*).

recouvrer [rəku'vre], *v.t.* to recover, to retrieve, to collect.

recouvrir [rəku'vri:r], *v.t. irr.* (*conjug. like* OUVRIR) to cover up, to cover over, to overlay; to hide. **se recouvrir,** *v.r.* to cover oneself again; to cloud over.

recracher [rəkra'ʃe], *v.t.* to spit out again; to disgorge.—*v.i.* to spit again.

récréatif [rekrea'tif], *a.* (*fem.* **-tive**) recreative, entertaining.

récréation [rekreɑ'sjɔ̃], *n.f.* recreation, amusement; (*Sch.*) playtime, break.

recréer [rəkre'e], *v.t.* to re-create, to create again.

récréer [rekre'e], *v.t.* to entertain; to amuse. **se récréer,** *v.r.* to amuse oneself, to take recreation.

recrépir [rəkre'pi:r], *v.t.* to give a fresh coat of plaster to; to repoint (*a wall*); (*fig.* and *fam.*) to paint (*one's face*); to recast.

recrépissement [rəkrepis'mɑ̃], **recrépissage** [rəkrepi'sa:ʒ], *n.m.* replastering; repatching.

récrier (se) [sərekri'je], *v.r.* to exclaim, to cry out; to protest (***contre***); to be amazed.

récrimination [rekriminɑ'sjɔ̃], *n.f.* recrimination.

récriminatoire [rekrimina'twa:r], *a.* recriminatory.

récriminer [rekrimi'ne], *v.i.* to recriminate.

récrire [re'kri:r], *v.t. irr.* (*conjug. like* ÉCRIRE) to rewrite; to write back.

recroqueviller (se) [sərəkrɔkvi'je], *v.r.* to curl up, to shrivel.

recru [rə'kry], *a.* tired out, worn out.

recrudescence [rəkrydɛ'sɑ̃:s], *n.f.* recrudescence.

recrudescent [rəkrydɛ'sɑ̃], *a.* recrudescent.

recrue [rə'kry], *n.f.* recruiting; recruit.

recrutement [rəkryt'mɑ̃], *n.m.* recruiting, recruitment.

recruter [rəkry'te], *v.t.* to recruit; to enrol. **se recruter,** *v.r.* to be recruited.

recruteur [rəkry'tœ:r], *n.m.* recruiter; recruiting officer.

rectangle [rɛk'tɑ̃:gl], *n.m.* rectangle.

rectangulaire [rɛktɑ̃gy'lɛ:r], *a.* rectangular, right-angled.

recteur [rɛk'tœ:r], *n.m.* rector, vice-chancellor (*of a University*); parish priest (*in Brittany*).

rectifiable [rɛkti'fjabl], *a.* rectifiable.

rectification [rɛktifikɑ'sjɔ̃], *n.f.* rectification; adjustment.

rectifier [rɛkti'fje], *v.t.* to rectify; to adjust; to reform.

rectiligne [rɛkti'liɲ], *a.* rectilinear.

rectitude [rɛkti'tyd], *n.f.* rectitude, uprightness.

recto [rɛk'to], *n.m.* first page of a leaf, right-hand page.

rectorat [rɛktɔ'ra], *n.m.* rectorship.

reçu [rə'sy], *a.* received; admitted, recognized; ***être reçu*** (***à un examen***), to pass (an examination).—*n.m.* receipt.

recueil [rə'kœ:j], *n.m.* collection, selection; anthology.

recueillement [rəkœj'mɑ̃], *n.m.* meditation; peaceful contemplation.

recueilli [rəkœ'ji], *a.* meditative, calm, rapt.

recueillir [rəkœ'ji:r], *v.t. irr.* (*conjug. like* CUEILLIR) to gather, to collect; to reap; to receive; to shelter. **se recueillir,** *v.r.* to collect one's thoughts; to be plunged in meditation.

recuire [rə'kɥi:r], *v.t. irr.* (*conjug. like* CONDUIRE) to cook again.

recuit [rə'kɥi], *a.* cooked, baked *or* roasted again.

recul [rə'kyl], *n.m.* recoil (*of cannon*), kick (*of rifle*); backing (*of horse, car*).

reculade [rəky'lad], *n.f.* falling back, retreat.

reculé [rəky'le], *a.* distant, remote.

reculement [rəkyl'mɑ̃], *n.m.* drawing back, backing (*of carriages etc.*); breech (*of saddles*).
reculer [rəky'le], *v.t.* to draw back, to move back, to back; (*fig.*) to put off, to defer.—*v.i.* to go back, to draw back, to retreat; to recoil; to give way. **se reculer**, *v.r.* to draw back, to become more remote.
reculons (à) [arəky'lɔ̃], *adv. phr.* backwards.
récupérage [rekype'ra:ʒ], *n.m.*, **récupération** [rekyperɑ'sjɔ̃], *n.f.* recovery, recuperation.
récupérer [rekype're], *v.t.* (*conjug. like* CÉDER) to recover, to retrieve, to recuperate.
récurer [reky're], *v.t.* to scour, to clean.
récusable [reky'zabl], *a.* (*Law*) exceptionable, doubtful (*of witnesses etc.*).
récusation [rekyzɑ'sjɔ̃], *n.f.* (*Law*) challenge; exception.
récuser [reky'ze], *v.t.* to challenge, to object to (*witnesses, jurors etc.*); to reject. **se récuser**, *v.r.* to excuse oneself, to decline; to decline, to give a decision (*of judges, jurors etc.*).
rédacteur [redak'tœ:r], *n.m.* (*fem.* **-trice**) writer, inditer (*of deed*); clerk (*in public office*); ***rédacteur en chef***, editor.
rédaction [redak'sjɔ̃], *n.f.* drawing up (*deeds etc.*); wording; editing (*periodicals*); essay.
reddition [rɛdi'sjɔ̃], *n.f.* surrender; rendering (*of accounts*).
rédempteur [redɑ̃p'tœ:r], *a.* (*fem.* **-trice**) redeeming, redemptory.—*n.m.* redeemer, saviour.
rédemption [redɑ̃p'sjɔ̃], *n.f.* redemption; redeeming.
redescendre [rədɛ'sɑ̃:dr], *v.t.* (*with aux.* AVOIR) to carry *or* take down again.—*v.i.* (*with aux.* ÊTRE) to come, go *or* step down again.
redevable [rəd'vabl], *a.* indebted, owing.
redevance [rəd'vɑ̃:s], *n.f.* rent, due, tax.
redevenir [rədəv'ni:r], *v.i. irr.* (*conjug. like* TENIR, *but with aux.* ÊTRE) to become again.
redevoir [rəd(ə)'vwa:r], *v.t. irr.* (*conjug. like* DEVOIR) to owe still.
rédiger [redi'ʒe], *v.t.* (*conjug. like* MANGER) to draw up, to draft; to edit.
redingote [rədɛ̃'gɔt], *n.f.* frock-coat.
redire [rə'di:r], *v.t. irr.* (*conjug. like* DIRE) to repeat, to reveal.—*v.i.* to criticize; ***trouver à redire à***, to find fault with.
redondance [rədɔ̃'dɑ̃:s], *n.f.* superfluity of words, redundancy.
redondant [rədɔ̃'dɑ̃], *a.* redundant.
redonner [rədɔ'ne], *v.t.* to give back again, to restore.—*v.i.* to fall again; to begin again; to charge again.
redoublé [rədu'ble], *a.* redoubled, increased.
redoublement [rədublə'mɑ̃], *n.m.* redoubling, increase; (*Med.*) paroxysm.
redoubler [rədu'ble], *v.t.* to redouble, to reiterate; to increase; to reline (*dress*).—*v.i.* to increase, to redouble.
redoutable [rədu'tabl], *a.* formidable, redoubtable.
redoute [rə'dut], *n.f.* redoubt.
redouter [rədu'te], *v.t.* to dread, to fear.
redressement [rədrɛs'mɑ̃], *n.m.* straightening; rectification, redress.
redresser [rədrɛ'se], *v.t.* to make straight; to set up again; to put right; (*colloq.*) to rebuke. **se redresser**, *v.r.* to become straight again; to right itself (*of a ship etc.*); to be redressed; ***redressez-vous***, sit up.
redû [rə'dy], *n.m.* balance due.
réducteur [redyk'tœ:r], *a.* (*fem.* **-trice**) reducing.—*n.m.* (*Chem.*) reducer.
réductible [redyk'tibl], *a.* reducible.
réduction [redyk'sjɔ̃], *n.f.* reduction; subjugation; allowance.
réduire [re'dɥi:r], *v.t. irr.* (*conjug. like* CONDUIRE) to reduce, to diminish; to subdue; to compel, to oblige. **se réduire**, *v.r.* to be reduced, to diminish, to abate, to vanish; to be subdued; to amount to.
réduit [re'dɥi], *a.* reduced; dimmed (*of light*).—*n.m.* retreat, nook; hovel; (*Fort.*) keep.
réédification [reedifikɑ'sjɔ̃], *n.f.* rebuilding.
réédifier [reedi'fje], *v.t.* to rebuild.
rééducatif [reedyka'tif], *a.* (*fem.* **-tive**) ***thérapie rééducative***, occupational therapy.
réel [re'ɛl], *a.* (*fem.* **-elle**) real, actual; genuine.—*n.m.* reality.
réélection [reelɛk'sjɔ̃], *n.f.* re-election.
réélire [ree'li:r], *v.t. irr.* (*conjug. like* LIRE) to re-elect.
réellement [reɛl'mɑ̃], *adv.* really, in reality.
réembobiner [reɑ̃bɔbi'ne], *v.t.* to rewind.
réemploi [reɑ̃'plwa], *n.m.* re-employment.
réexpédier [reɛkspe'dje], *v.t.* to send on, to (re)forward; to send back.
refaçonner [rəfasɔ'ne], *v.t.* to make again, to refashion.
réfaction [refak'sjɔ̃], *n.f.* rebate, allowance.
refaire [rə'fɛ:r], *v.t. irr.* (*conjug. like* FAIRE) to do again, to remake; to recommence; to do up; to deal again (*at cards*); to revive; (*slang*) to diddle. **se refaire**, *v.r.* to recover one's strength; to recoup oneself.
refait [rə'fɛ], *a.* set up, done again; (*slang*) ***j'ai été refait(e)***, I have been had.—*n.m.* drawn game.
réfection [refɛk'sjɔ̃], *n.f.* repairs (*to buildings etc.*).
réfectoire [refɛk'twa:r], *n.m.* refectory, dining-room *or* -hall (*in college, convent etc.*).
refend [rə'fɑ̃], *n.m.* splitting, sawing, dividing; ***mur de refend***, partition wall.
refendre [rə'fɑ̃:dr], *v.t.* to cleave *or* split again; to quarter (*timber*); to saw (*stone*) into slabs.
référence [refe'rɑ̃:s], *n.f.* reference.
referendum [rəferɑ̃'dɔm], **référendum** [referɑ̃'dɔm], *n.m.* referendum.
référer [refe're], *v.t.* (*conjug. like* CÉDER) to refer; to ascribe.—*v.i.* to refer; ***en référer à***, to refer to. **se référer**, *v.r.* to refer, to have reference; to leave it (*à*); to trust (*à*).
refermer [rəfɛr'me], *v.t.* to shut again; to close up. **se refermer**, *v.r.* to shut itself; to close up; to heal up (*of wound*).
réfléchi [refle'ʃi], *a.* reflected; deliberate; reflective, thoughtful; wary; (*Gram.*) reflexive.
réfléchir [refle'ʃi:r], *v.t.* to reflect, to throw back; to reverberate.—*v.i.* to reflect, to consider, to ponder. **se réfléchir**, *v.r.* to be reflected.
réfléchissant [refleʃi'sɑ̃], *a.* reflecting.
réflecteur [reflɛk'tœ:r], *a.* reflecting.—*n.m.* reflector.

eflet [rə'flɛ], *n.m.* reflection, reflex; reflected light.
efléter [rəfle'te], *v.t.* (*conjug. like* CÉDER) to reflect (*light etc.*).—*v.i.* and **se refléter**, *v.r.* to be reflected.
efleurir [rəflœ'ri:r], *v.i.* to blossom again.
éflexe [re'flɛks], *a.* and *n.m.* reflex.
éflexion [reflɛk'sjɔ̃], *n.f.* reflection; thought, consideration.
efluer [rə'flɥe], *v.i.* to reflow, to ebb; (*fig.*) to swing back.
eflux [rə'fly], *n.m.* reflux, ebb; flowing back.
efondre [rə'fɔ̃:dr], *v.t.* to refound (*metal*), to melt down again, to cast again; (*fig.*) to remodel.
efonte [rə'fɔ̃:t], *n.f.* refounding, recasting; recoining; remodelling.
éformateur [refɔrma'tœ:r], *a.* (*fem.* **-trice**) reforming.—*n.m.* (*fem.* **-trice**) reformer.
éformation [refɔrmɑ'sjɔ̃], *n.f.* reformation.
éforme [re'fɔrm], *n.f.* reform, reformation, amendment; (*Mil.*) reduction, discharge.
éformé [refɔr'me], *a.* reformed; (*Mil.*) invalided out of the service.
éformer [refɔr'me], *v.t.* to reform, to improve; (*Mil.*) to invalid. **se réformer**, *v.r.* to reform, to mend one's ways.
eformer [rəfɔr'me], *v.t.* to form again. **se reformer**, *v.r.* to form anew, to re-form (*of troops etc.*).
éformiste [refɔr'mist], *a.* and *n.* reformist.
efoulement [rəful'mɑ̃], *n.m.* driving back; (*Psych.*) inhibition, repression.
efouler [rəfu'le], *v.t.* to drive back; to compress; to suppress; to expel (*aliens*); to stem (*the tide*).—*v.i.* to ebb, to flow back; ***la marée refoule***, the tide is ebbing.
éfractaire [refrak'tɛ:r], *a.* refractory, obstinate, rebellious; ***terre réfractaire***, fire-proof clay.—*n.m.* defaulter.
éfracter [refrak'te], *v.t.* to refract. **se réfracter**, *v.r.* to be refracted.
éfraction [refrak'sjɔ̃], *n.f.* refraction.
efrain [rə'frɛ̃], *n.m.* refrain, chorus; (*fig.*) constant theme.
efréner [rəfre'ne], *v.t.* (*conjug. like* CÉDER) to curb, to control (*passions*); to bridle, to restrain.
éfrigérant [refriʒe'rɑ̃], *a.* refrigerant, cooling.—*n.m.* refrigerator.
éfrigérateur [refriʒera'tœ:r], *n.m.* refrigerating chamber; refrigerator, (*colloq.*) fridge; (*Am.*) icebox.
éfrigération [refriʒerɑ'sjɔ̃], *n.f.* refrigeration.
éfrigérer [refriʒe're], *v.t.* (*conjug. like* CÉDER) to chill, to freeze (*food etc.*).
efroidir [rəfrwɑ'di:r], *v.t.* to cool, to chill.—*v.i.* to cool, to become cold. **se refroidir**, *v.r.* to cool, to grow cold; to catch cold; to slacken, to relax.
efroidissement [rəfrwadis'mɑ̃], *n.m.* cooling, refrigeration; coldness; chill, cold.
efuge [rə'fy:ʒ], *n.m.* refuge, shelter; (street-) island; lay-by.
éfugié [refy'ʒje], *n.m.* (*fem.* **-ée**) refugee.
éfugier (se) [sərefy'ʒje], *v.r.* to take refuge; (*fig.*) to have recourse (*to*) (***dans***).
efus [rə'fy], *n.m. inv.* refusal, denial.
efuser [rəfy'ze], *v.t.* to refuse, to deny, to decline to reject.—*v.i.* to refuse; to decline.
se refuser, *v.r.* to deny oneself; to shun; to resist.
réfuter [refy'te], *v.t.* to refute, to disprove.
regagner [rəgɑ'ɲe], *v.t.* to regain, to recover, to retrieve; to rejoin, to reach.
regain [rə'gɛ̃], *n.m.* aftermath; second crop; (*fig.*) revival, new lease (*of life*).
régal [re'gal], *n.m.* feast, entertainment, treat.
régalade [rega'lad], *n.f.* giving a treat, regaling; blazing fire.
régalant [rega'lɑ̃], *a.* pleasant, entertaining.
régaler [rega'le], *v.t.* to regale, to treat, to entertain. **se régaler**, *v.r.* to regale oneself; to enjoy oneself; to entertain *or* treat each other.
regard [rə'ga:r], *n.m.* look; glance; gaze, notice, attention; inspection-hole; (*pl.*) eyes; ***au regard de***, in comparison with; ***d'un seul regard***, at one glance; ***en regard***, opposite; ***un regard de côté***, a sidelong glance.
regardant [rəgar'dɑ̃], *a.* particular, meticulous; stingy, niggardly.
regarder [rəgar'de], *v.t.* to look at, to behold; to look into, to consider; to face, to be opposite; to concern; ***cela vous regarde***, that concerns you.—*v.i.* to look; to mind, to pay heed. **se regarder**, *v.r.* to look at oneself; to look at each other; to look upon oneself (***comme***); to consider one another (***comme***); to face each other.
regarnir [rəgar'ni:r], *v.t.* to furnish again; to retrim (*dress*); to re-cover (*furniture*) etc.
régate [re'gat], *n.f.* regatta, boat-race.
régence [re'ʒɑ̃:s], *n.f.* regency.
régénérateur [reʒenera'tœ:r], *a.* (*fem.* **-trice**) regenerating.—*n.m.* regenerator.
régénération [reʒenerɑ'sjɔ], *n.f.* regeneration; reclamation (*of land*).
régénérer [reʒene're], *v.t.* (*conjug. like* CÉDER) to regenerate.
régent [re'ʒɑ̃], *a.* and *n.m.* (*fem.* **-e**) regent.
régenter [reʒɑ̃'te], *v.t.* to domineer, to lord it over.
régie [re'ʒi], *n.f.* administration; (*public*) corporation; excise.
regimbement [rəʒɛ̃bə'mɑ̃], *n.m.* kicking (*of horses*); resistance, recalcitrance.
regimber [rəʒɛ̃'be], *v.i.* to kick (*of horses*); (*fig.*) to resist, to jib.
régime [re'ʒim], *n.m.* regimen; diet; form of government; rules, regulations; régime, system; speed (*of motor etc.*); bunch (*of bananas etc.*).
régiment [reʒi'mɑ̃], *n.m.* regiment.
régimentaire [reʒimɑ̃'tɛ:r], *a.* regimental.
région [re'ʒjɔ̃], *n.f.* region; district.
régional [reʒjɔ'nal], *a.* (*m. pl.* **-aux**) local.
régir [re'ʒi:r], *v.t.* to govern, to rule; to administer.
régisseur [reʒi'sœ:r], *n.m.* manager, steward; (*Theat.*) stage manager.
registre [rə'ʒistr], *n.m.* register; account-book; damper (*in chimneys*).
réglable [re'glabl], *a.* adjustable.
réglage [re'gla:ʒ], *n.m.* ruling (*of paper*); regulating, adjusting, tuning.
règle [rɛgl], *n.f.* ruler, rule; order, regularity; model.
réglé [re'gle], *a.* regular, steady; ruled; paid.

règlement [rɛglə'mɑ̃], *n.m.* regulation; settlement (*of accounts*).

réglementaire [regləmɑ̃'tɛːr], *a.* according to regulations, lawful; usual.

réglementer [regləmɑ̃'te], *v.t.* to regulate.—*v.i.* to make regulations.

régler [re'gle], *v.t.* (*conjug. like* CÉDER) to rule (*paper etc.*); to regulate, to order, to adjust, to time (*a watch etc.*); to settle (*an account*). **se régler**, *v.r.* to regulate oneself, to be regulated; to be guided (***sur***).

régleur [re'glœːr], *n.m.* (*fem.* **-euse**) regulator (*of clocks etc.*).

réglisse [re'glis], *n.f.* liquorice.

réglure [re'glyːr], *n.f.* ruling (*of paper*).

régnant [re'ɲɑ̃], *a.* reigning; (*fig.*) prevailing, predominant.

règne [rɛɲ], *n.m.* reign; prevalence, vogue; (*Nat. Hist.*) kingdom.

régner [re'ɲe], *v.i.* (*conjug. like* CÉDER) to reign, to rule; to prevail, to be in fashion.

regonfler [rəgɔ̃'fle], *v.t.* to swell again; to pump up (*tyre*).—*v.i.* to swell again.

regorgeant [rəgɔr'ʒɑ̃], *a.* overflowing; abounding.

regorger [rəgɔr'ʒe], *v.t.* (*conjug. like* MANGER) to regurgitate, to disgorge.—*v.i.* to overflow, to run over; to be crammed (*with*); to be plentiful, to abound.

régressif [regrɛ'sif], *a.* (*fem.* **-ive**) regressive, retrogressive.

régression [regrɛ'sjɔ̃], *n.f.* regression, recession; retrogression; (*fig.*) decline.

regret [rə'grɛ], *n.m.* regret; ***à regret***, with reluctance.

regrettable [rəgrɛ'tabl], *a.* regrettable, deplorable.

regrettablement [rəgrɛtablə'mɑ̃], *adv.* regrettably.

regretter [rəgrɛ'te], *v.t.* to regret; to grieve; to be sorry for, to repent; to miss.

régularisation [regylarizɑ'sjɔ̃], *n.f.* putting in order, regularization.

régulariser [regylari'ze] *v.t.* to put in order, to regularize.

régularité [regylari'te], *n.f.* regularity.

régulateur [regyla'tœːr], *a.* (*fem.* **-trice**) regulating.—*n.m.* regulator; (*Eng. etc.*) governor.

régulier [regy'lje], *a.* (*fem.* **-ière**) regular; steady, exact.—*n.m.* regular (*monk, soldier etc.*).

régulièrement [regyljɛr'mɑ̃], *adv.* regularly.

régurgitation [regyrʒitɑ'sjɔ̃], *n.f.* regurgitation.

régurgiter [regyrʒi'te], *v.t.* to regurgitate.

réhabilitation [reabilitɑ'sjɔ̃], *n.f.* rehabilitation.

réhabiliter [reabili'te], *v.t.* to rehabilitate; to reinstate. **se réhabiliter**, *v.r.* to rehabilitate oneself, to recover one's good name.

rehaussement [rəos'mɑ̃], *n.m.* raising; heightening, enhancing; increase of value (*of coin*).

rehausser [rəo'se], *v.t.* to raise; to heighten, to enhance; to raise the value of; to enrich; to set off.

réimposer [reɛ̃po'ze], *v.t.* to reassess (*tax*); (*Print.*) to reimpose.

réimpression [reɛ̃prɛ'sjɔ̃], *n.f.* reprinting; reprint.

réimprimer [reɛ̃pri'me], *v.t.* to print again, to reprint.

rein [rɛ̃], *n.m.* kidney; (*pl.*) loins, back.

réincarnation [reɛ̃karnɑ'sjɔ̃], *n.f.* reincarnation.

reine [rɛːn], *n.f.* queen.

reine-claude [rɛːn'kloːd], *n.f.* (*pl.* **reines-claude**) greengage.

reine-des-prés [rɛːnde'pre], *n.f.* (*pl.* **reines-des-prés**) meadowsweet.

réinstallation [reɛ̃stalɑ'sjɔ̃], *n.f.* reinstalment, re-establishment.

réinstaller [reɛ̃sta'le], *v.t.* to reinstall.

réintégration [reɛ̃tegrɑ'sjɔ̃], *n.f.* reinstatement.

réintégrer [reɛ̃te'gre], *v.t.* (*conjug. like* CÉDER) to reinstate.

réitératif [reitera'tif], *a.* (*fem.* **-tive**) reiterative.

réitération [reiterɑ'sjɔ], *n.f.* reiteration, repetition.

réitérer [reite're], *v.t.* (*conjug. like* CÉDER) to reiterate, to repeat.

rejaillir [rəʒa'jiːr], *v.i.* to gush, to spurt out; to spring, to spout; (*fig.*) to flash; to reflect; to rebound.

rejaillissement [rəʒajis'mɑ̃], *n.m.* gushing out; spouting, springing; reflection, flashing; rebound.

réjection [reʒɛk'sjɔ̃], *n.f.* rejection.

rejet [rə'ʒɛ], *n.m.* rejection; throwing out; young shoot, sprout.

rejeter [rəʒ'te], *v.t.* (*conjug. like* APPELER) to throw again; to throw back; to tilt back (*one's hat*); to repel; to throw away; to throw up (*of plants*); to reject; to deny.—*v.i.* to shoot (*of plants*). **se rejeter**, *v.r.* to have recourse to; to fall back (*upon*).

rejeton [rəʒ'tɔ̃], *n.m.* shoot, sprout; (*fig.*) scion.

rejoindre [rə'ʒwɛ̃ːdr], *v.t. irr.* (*conjug. like* CRAINDRE) to rejoin, to join; to reunite; to overtake, to catch up. **se rejoindre**, *v.r.* to reunite; to meet; to catch each other up again.

rejouer [rə'ʒwe], *v.t., v.i.* to play again, to replay.

réjoui [re'ʒwi], *a.* and *n.m.* (*fem.* **-e**) jovial, joyous, merry (person).

réjouir [re'ʒwiːr], *v.t.* to rejoice, to delight, to cheer. **se réjouir**, *v.r.* to be *or* to make merry; to rejoice, to be delighted (*de*).

réjouissance [reʒwi'sɑ̃ːs], *n.f.* rejoicing; (*pl.*) merry-making.

réjouissant [reʒwi'sɑ̃], *a.* cheering; diverting, amusing.

relâchant [rəlɑ'ʃɑ̃], *a.* relaxing; laxative, loosening.—*n.m.* (*Med.*) laxative.

relâche (1) [rə'lɑːʃ], *n.m.* intermission, discontinuance, respite; relaxation; (*Theat.*) suspension of performance; ***relâche ce soir***, no performance this evening.

relâche (2) [rə'lɑːʃ], *n.f.* (*Naut.*) putting into a port; port of call.

relâché [rəlɑ'ʃe], *a.* lax, relaxed; loose, remiss.

relâchement [rəlaʃ'mɑ̃], *n.m.* slackening; slackness; laxity (*of morals*); looseness (*of bowels*).

relâcher [rəlɑ'ʃe], *v.t.* to slacken, to loosen, to relax; to release, to unbend (*the mind etc.*); to yield, to abate.—*v.i.* (*Naut.*) to put

into port. **se relâcher,** *v.r.* to grow slack *or* loose; to abate; to relax, to unbend.
relais [rəˈlɛ], *n.m.* relay (*fresh horses*); stage; shift (*of workmen*).
relancer [rəlɑ̃ˈse], *v.t.* (*conjug. like* COMMENCER) to throw back; (*Ten.*) to return (*the ball*); (*Cards*) to raise (*a bid*); (*fig.*) to harry (*someone*).
relaps [rəˈlaps], *a.* relapsed, relapsed into heresy.—*n.m.* (*fem.* **-e**) relapsed heretic.
rélargir [relarˈʒiːr], *v.t.* to widen, to let out (*clothes etc.*).
relater [rəlaˈte], *v.t.* to state, to tell.
relatif [rəlaˈtif], *a.* (*fem.* **-tive**) relative; relating (*à*).
relation [rəlɑˈsjɔ̃], *n.f.* relation, account; statement; respect; connexion; communication, correspondence; (*pl.*) connexions.
relativement [rəlativˈmɑ̃], *adv.* relatively.
relativité [rəlativiˈte], *n.f.* relativity.
relaxation [rəlaksɑˈsjɔ̃], *n.f.* release; relaxation (*of muscles*).
relaxer [rəlakˈse], *v.t.* to release (*a prisoner*); to relax (*muscles*).
relayer [rəlɛˈje] *v.t.* (*conjug. like* PAYER) to take the place of, to relieve; (*Elec. Eng., Rad., Teleg. etc.*) to relay.—*v.i.* to change horses. **se relayer,** *v.r.* to relieve each other; to work in shifts.
relégation [rəlegɑˈsjɔ̃], *n.f.* relegation; transportation (*of convict*).
reléguer [rəleˈge], *v.t.* (*conjug. like* CÉDER) to transport (*for life*), to shut up; to relegate, to consign (*à*). **se reléguer,** *v.r.* to shut oneself up.
relent [rəˈlɑ̃], *a.* mouldy, musty.—*n.m.* mustiness, mouldiness.
relève [rəˈlɛːv], *n.f.* (*Mil.*) relief.
relevé [rəlˈve], *a.* raised, erect; exalted, lofty; refined; highly seasoned.—*n.m.* abstract; statement, return; survey.
relèvement [rəlɛvˈmɑ̃], *n.m.* raising again; recovery (*of business*); relieving (*of sentry*); rise, increase (*of salary*); (*Naut.*) bearing.
relever [rəlˈve], *v.t.* (*conjug. like* AMENER) to raise again, to lift up again; to turn up; to restore; to relieve (*troops*), to change (*sentry*); to raise (*prices, salary*); to set off, to enhance; to extol; to remark; to note, take down (*name, address etc.*); to release (*from vows, oath*); to survey; (*Naut.*) to take the bearings of.—*v.i.* to recover; to turn up; to depend. **se relever,** *v.r.* to rise again; to get up, to pick oneself up; to recover; to be raised; to relieve each other.
relief [rəˈljɛf], *n.m.* relief, embossment; enhancement; (*pl.*) scraps (*from the table*).
relier [rəˈlje], *v.t.* to connect; to hoop (*casks*); to bind (*books*).
relieur [rəˈljœːr], *n.m.* (*fem.* **-euse**) binder, book-binder.
religieusement [rəliʒjøzˈmɑ̃], *adv.* religiously; scrupulously.
religieux [rəliˈʒjø], *a.* (*fem.* **-euse**) religious, strict.—*n.m.* (*fem.* **-euse**) monk, nun.
religion [rəliˈʒjɔ̃], *n.f.* religion.
reliquaire [rəliˈkɛːr], *n.m.* reliquary, shrine.
reliquat [rəliˈka], *n.m.* balance, remainder (*of an account*); after-effects (*of a disease etc.*).
relique [rəˈlik], *n.f.* relic (*of a saint*).
relire [rəˈliːr], *v.t. irr.* (*conjug. like* LIRE) to re-read.
reliure [rəˈljyːr], *n.f.* binding (*of books*).
relouer [rəluˈe], *v.t.* to relet, to sub-let.
reluire [rəlɥiːr], *v.i. irr.* (*conjug. like* LUIRE) to shine, to glitter.
reluisant [rəlɥiˈzɑ̃], *a.* gleaming, shining, glittering.
reluquer [rəlyˈke], *v.t.* (*colloq.*) to ogle, to leer at; (*fig.*) to have an eye on.
remâcher [rəmɑˈʃe], *v.t.* to chew again; (*fig.*) to turn over in one's mind.
remailler [rəmɑˈje], *v.t.* to repair the meshes (*of fishing-nets etc.*); to mend a ladder (*in stocking*).
remaniement or **remanîment** [rəmaniˈmɑ̃], *n.m.* (*Polit.*) reshuffle; handling again, touching up; repairing; changing.
remanier [rəmaˈnje], *v.t.* to handle again; to remodel; to adapt, to revise.
remariage [rəmaˈrjaːʒ], *n.m.* re-marriage.
remarier [rəmaˈrje], *v.t.* to remarry. **se remarier,** *v.r.* to marry again, to remarry.
remarquable [rəmarˈkabl], *a.* remarkable, notable.
remarquablement [rəmarkabləˈmɑ̃], *adv.* remarkably.
remarque [rəˈmark], *n.f.* remark; notice.
remarquer [rəmarˈke], *v.t.* to mark again; to notice; to distinguish; ***faire remarquer,*** to point out. **se remarquer,** *v.r.* to be remarked.
remballer [rɑ̃baˈle], *v.t.* to pack up again.
rembarquement [rɑ̃barkəˈmɑ̃], *n.m.* re-embarkation.
rembarquer [rɑ̃barˈke], *v.t.* to re-embark, to ship again. **se rembarquer,** *v.r.* to go on board again.
rembarrer [rɑ̃baˈre], *v.t.* to repulse; to snub; (*fam.*) to tick someone off.
remblai [rɑ̃ˈblɛ], *n.m.* filling up; embankment.
remblayer [rɑ̃blɛˈje], *v.t.* (*conjug. like* PAYER) to embank, to fill up (*with earth*).
remboîter [rɑ̃bwɑˈte], *v.t.* to fit in again; to reassemble; to reset (*a bone*).
rembourrage [rɑ̃buˈraːʒ], **rembourrement** [rɑ̃burˈmɑ̃], *n.m.* stuffing, padding.
rembourrer [rɑ̃buˈre], *v.t.* to stuff, to pad; to upholster.
remboursable [rɑ̃burˈsabl], *a.* repayable; redeemable.
remboursement [rɑ̃bursəˈmɑ̃], *n.m.* reimbursement, repayment.
rembourser [rɑ̃burˈse], *v.t.* to repay; to reimburse; to redeem (*an annuity etc.*).
rembruni [rɑ̃bryˈni], *a.* dark, gloomy.
rembrunir [rɑ̃bryˈniːr], *v.t.* to darken; to cloud over; (*fig.*) to sadden. **se rembrunir,** *v.r.* to grow darker; to become cloudy *or* gloomy.
remède [rəˈmɛd], *n.m.* remedy, medicine.
remédiable [rəmeˈdjabl], *a.* remediable.
remédier [rəmeˈdje], *v.i.* to remedy, to cure (*à*).
remêler [rəmɛˈle], *v.t.* to mix again, to reshuffle.
remembrement [rəmɑ̃brəˈmɑ̃], *n.m.* consolidation (*of land*).
remémoratif [rəmemɔraˈtif], *a.* (*fem.* **-tive**) commemorative.
remémorer [rəmemɔˈre], *v.t.* to bring (*a thing*) to someone's mind. **se remémorer,** *v.r.* to recollect.

remerciement or **remercîment** [rəmɛrsi'mɑ̃], *n.m.* thanking; (*pl.*) thanks; ***faire des remerciements***, to thank.
remercier [rəmɛr'sje], *v.t.* to thank; to dismiss; ***non, je vous remercie***, no, thank you.
remettre [rə'mɛtr], *v.t. irr.* (*conjug. like* METTRE) to put back; to put on again; to lay down again; to make well again; to deliver; to postpone; to entrust; to forgive; to remember; (*Ten.*) ***(balle) à remettre***, let (ball); ***je vous remets***, I remember your face; ***remettre dans l'esprit***, to remind. **se remettre**, *v.r.* to recover (*oneself*); to resume, to start again; to recollect; to refer; to improve (*of weather*).
réminiscence [remini'sɑ̃:s], *n.f.* reminiscence.
remis [rə'mi], *a.* put back, put off, postponed.
remisage [rəmi'za:ʒ], *n.m.* housing, putting away (*vehicle*).
remise [rə'mi:z], *n.f.* delivery; remittance; discount; commission; delay; coach-house, mews, shed.
remiser [rəmi'ze], *v.t.* to put up, to put away (*vehicle*); to house; (*colloq.*) to put by.
rémissible [remi'si:bl], *a.* remissible, pardonable.
rémission [remi'sjɔ̃], *n.f.* remission, forgiveness.
remmener [rɑ̃m'ne], *v.t.* (*conjug. like* AMENER) to take back, to lead back.
remodeler [rəmɔ'dle], *v.t.* (*conjug. like* AMENER) to remodel.
remontage [rəmɔ̃'ta:ʒ], *n.m.* going up; winding up (*of clock etc.*); assembling; refitting (*of parts of machinery*); restocking (*of shop*).
remonte [rə'mɔ̃:t], *n.f.* remounting, going upstream; run (*of fish*); (*Mil.*) remount.
remonter [rəmɔ̃'te], *v.t.* (*with aux.* AVOIR *or* ÊTRE *according as action or condition is meant*) to go up again; to take up again; to raise; to stock; to wind up (*clock etc.*); to re-string (*instruments*).—*v.i.* to go up again; to go back; to rise *or* increase (*in value etc.*); to date back; to remount (*cavalry*). **se remonter**, *v.r.* to take in a fresh supply (***de***); to be wound up (*of watches etc.*); to recover one's strength *or* spirits.
remontoir [rəmɔ̃'twa:r], *n.m.* winder, key (*of clock, watch*).
remontrance [rəmɔ̃'trɑ̃:s], *n.f.* remonstrance.
remontrer [rəmɔ̃'tre], *v.t.* to show again; to point out; to represent.—*v.i.* ***en remontrer***, (*fig.*) to give advice.
remordre [rə'mɔrdr], *v.t.* to bite again.—*v.i.* to try again.
remords [rə'mɔ:r], *n.m.* remorse.
remorquage [rəmɔr'ka:ʒ], *n.m.* towing, hauling.
remorque [rə'mɔrk], *n.f.* towing; tow; tow-line; trailer (*car*).
remorquer [rəmɔr'ke], *v.t.* to tow, to haul.
remorqueur [rəmɔr'kœ:r], *a.* (*fem.* **-euse**) towing, hauling.—*n.m.* tug-boat, tug.
rémoulade [remu'lad], *n.f.* sharp sauce.
rémouleur [remu'lœ:r], *n.m.* knife-grinder.
remous [rə'mu], *n.m.* eddy; back-wash (*of ship*); slip-stream.
rempailler [rɑ̃pɑ'je], *v.t.* to re-seat (*a straw-bottomed chair*); to re-stuff with straw.
rempailleur [rɑ̃pɑ'jœ:r], *n.m.* (*fem.* **-euse**) chair-mender.
rempaqueter [rɑ̃pak'te], *v.t.* (*conjug. like* APPELER) to pack up again.
rempart [rɑ̃'pa:r], *n.m.* rampart; (*fig.*) bulwark.
remplaçable [rɑ̃pla'sabl], *a.* replaceable.
remplaçant [rɑ̃pla'sɑ̃], *n.m.* (*fem.* **-e**) substitute; locum.
remplacement [rɑ̃plas'mɑ̃], *n.m.* replacing, replacement.
remplacer [rɑ̃pla'se], *v.t.* (*conjug. like* COMMENCER) to take the place of, to replace; to reinvest. **se remplacer**, *v.r.* to be replaced.
rempli [rɑ̃'pli], *a.* filled, full.—*n.m.* tuck, take-up.
remplier [rɑ̃pli'je], *v.t.* to make a tuck in; to turn in.
remplir [rɑ̃'pli:r], *v.t.* to refill, to replenish; to fill, to fill up; to fill in (*form*); to cram; to supply; to occupy (*time etc.*); to fulfil. **se remplir**, *v.r.* to fill oneself; to become full.
remplissage [rɑ̃pli'sa:ʒ], *n.m.* filling, filling up (*of casks etc.*); (*fig.*) rubbish, padding.
remploi [rɑ̃'plwa], *n.m.* reinvestment.
remployer [rɑ̃plwa'je], *v.t.* (*conjug. like* EMPLOYER) to use again; to reinvest.
remplumer [rɑ̃ply'me], *v.t.* to feather again. **se remplumer**, *v.r.* to get new feathers; (*fig.*) to retrieve one's losses; to get plump again.
rempocher [rɑ̃pɔ'ʃe], *v.t.* to put (*something*) back in one's pocket.
remporter [rɑ̃pɔr'te], *v.t.* to carry *or* take back; to carry off, to take away with one; to get; to win.
rempoter [rɑ̃pɔ'te], *v.t.* to repot.
remuant [rə'mɥɑ̃], *a.* restless; bustling; (*fam.*) on the go.
remue-ménage [rəmyme'na:ʒ], *n.m. inv.* stir, disturbance, bustle.
remuement or **remûment** [rəmy'mɑ̃], *n.m.* stir, stirring; removal; disturbance.
remuer [rə'mɥe], *v.t.* to move, to stir; to rouse; to turn up; to shake.—*v.i.* and **se remuer**, *v.r.* to stir, to move; to fidget.
rémunérateur [remynera'tœ:r], *a.* (*fem.* **-trice**) remunerative, profitable.—*n.m.* (*fem.* **-trice**) rewarder.
rémunération [remynerɑ'sjɔ̃], *n.f.* remuneration, reward.
rémunératoire [remynera'twa:r], *a.* remunerative.
rémunérer [remyne're], *v.t.* (*conjug. like* CÉDER) to remunerate; to reward.
renâcler [rənɑ'kle], *v.i.* to snort; (*fam.*) to turn up one's nose; to jib (*at something*).
renaissance [rənɛ'sɑ̃:s], *n.f.* rebirth; renaissance.
renaissant [rənɛ'sɑ̃], *a.* springing up again, reviving.
renaître [rə'nɛ:tr], *v.i. irr.* (*conjug. like* NAÎTRE, *but no p.p.*) to be born again; to grow again; to appear again; to revive.
rénal [re'nal], *a.* (*m. pl.* **-aux**) (*Anat.*) renal.
renard [rə'na:r], *n.m.* fox; (*fig.*) sly fellow; (*pop.*) blackleg.
renarde [rə'nard], *n.f.* vixen.
renardeau [rənar'do], *n.m.* (*pl.* **-eaux**) fox-cub.
Renaud [rə'no], *m.* Reginald.

renchéri [rɑ̃ʃe'ri], *a.* particular, over-nice (*of a person*).—*n.m.* (*fem.* **-e**) fastidious person; ***faire le renchéri***, to put on airs.
renchérir [rɑ̃ʃe'riːr], *v.t.* to raise the price of. —*v.i.* to get dearer, to rise in price; ***renchérir sur***, to improve upon.
renchérissement [rɑ̃ʃeris'mɑ̃], *n.m.* rise in price.
rencogner (se) [sərɑ̃kɔ'ɲe], *v.r.* to retreat, to crouch in a corner.
rencontre [rɑ̃'kɔ̃ːtr], *n.f.* meeting, encounter; duel; accidental meeting, discovery etc.; collision; chance, coincidence.
rencontrer [rɑ̃kɔ̃'tre], *v.t.* to meet, to meet with; to light upon, to encounter. **se rencontrer**, *v.r.* to meet, to meet each other; to be met with; to agree, to coincide.
rendement [rɑ̃d'mɑ̃], *n.m.* produce, yield, output; efficiency (*of a machine etc.*); (*Spt.*) handicap; (*Comm.*) return, profit.
rendez-vous [rɑ̃de'vu], *n.m. inv.* rendezvous, appointment; engagement; place of meeting.
rendormir [rɑ̃dɔr'miːr], *v.t. irr.* (*conjug. like* SENTIR) to send to sleep again. **se rendormir**, *v.r.* to fall asleep again.
rendre [rɑ̃ːdr], *v.t.* to return, to restore, to give back; to repay; to deliver; to give up; to pay; to produce; to reward; to carry; to eject, to emit; to express; to translate; ***rendre visite***, to pay a visit.—*v.i.* to lead (*of roads*); to be lucrative; to function, to work. **se rendre**, *v.r.* to go; to resort; to make oneself, to render oneself; to become; to surrender, to give up; to be worn out.
rendu [rɑ̃'dy], *a.* rendered, delivered; exhausted, tired out; arrived.—*n.m.* return, tit for tat.
rendurcir [rɑ̃dyr'siːr], *v.t.* to make harder. **se rendurcir**, *v.r.* to become harder.
rêne [rɛːn], *n.f.* rein.
renégat [rəne'ga], *a.* and *n.m.* (*fem.* **-e**) renegade, turncoat.
rêner [rɛ'ne], *v.t.* to bridle (*a horse*).
renfermé [rɑ̃fɛr'me], *a.* ***personne renfermée***, close, uncommunicative person.—*n.m.* ***odeur de renfermé***, fustiness; musty smell; ***sentir le renfermé***, to smell close, fusty *or* stuffy.
renfermer [rɑ̃fɛr'me], *v.t.* to shut up; to contain; to include, to comprise; to conceal. **se renfermer**, *v.r.* to shut oneself up; to confine oneself.
renfiler [rɑ̃fi'le], *v.t.* to thread, to string again.
renflammer [rɑ̃flɑ'me], *v.t.* to rekindle. **se renflammer**, *v.r.* to flare up again.
renflé [rɑ̃'fle], *a.* swollen, swelling; (*Bot.*) inflated.
renflement [rɑ̃flə'mɑ̃], *n.m.* swelling, bulge.
renfler [rɑ̃'fle], *v.t.*, *v.i.* to swell.
renflouage [rɑ̃flu'aːʒ], **renflouement** [rɑ̃flu'mɑ̃], *n.m.* refloating (*a ship*).
renflouer [rɑ̃flu'e], *v.t.* to refloat, to raise (*a ship*); (*fig.*) to salvage (*firm, company etc.*).
renfoncement [rɑ̃fɔ̃s'mɑ̃], *n.m.* cavity, hollow, recess.
renfoncer [rɑ̃fɔ̃'se], *v.t.* (*conjug. like* COMMENCER) to drive deeper; to pull (*a hat etc.*) further on.
renforçage [rɑ̃fɔr'saːʒ], *n.m.* strengthening.
renforcé [rɑ̃fɔr'se], *a.* downright, regular; reinforced.
renforcement [rɑ̃fɔrsə'mɑ̃], *n.m.* strengthening; reinforcement.
renforcer [rɑ̃fɔr'se], *v.t.* (*conjug. like* COMMENCER) to strengthen, to reinforce; to increase. **se renforcer**, *v.r.* to gather strength, to grow stronger; (*Mil.*) to be reinforced.
renfort [rɑ̃'fɔːr], *n.m.* reinforcement; (*fig.*) help, aid, relief; strengthening-piece.
renfrogné [rɑ̃frɔ'ɲe], *a.* frowning, scowling, surly.
renfrognement [rɑ̃frɔɲə'mɑ̃], *n.m.* frown, scowl.
renfrogner (se) [sərɑ̃frɔ'ɲe], *v.r.* to frown.
rengagement [rɑ̃gaʒ'mɑ̃], *n.m.* re-engagement; (*Mil.*) re-enlistment.
rengager [rɑ̃ga'ʒe], *v.t.* (*conjug. like* MANGER) to re-engage.—*v.i.* (*Mil.*) to re-enlist. **se rengager**, *v.r.* to re-engage; to begin afresh; to re-enlist.
rengaine [rɑ̃'gɛːn], *n.f.* catch-phrase; (*fam.*) hackneyed story; popular tune.
rengainer [rɑ̃gɛ'ne], *v.t.* to sheathe, to put up (*one's sword*); to withdraw, to put away.
rengorgement [rɑ̃gɔrʒə'mɑ̃], *n.m.* swaggering, puffing out the neck (*of peacock*).
rengorger (se) [sərɑ̃gɔr'ʒe], *v.r.* to carry one's head high; (*fig.*) to give oneself airs.
reniable [rə'njabl], *a.* deniable.
reniement or **renîment** [rəni'mɑ̃], *n.m.* denying, disowning.
renier [rə'nje], *v.t.* to disown (*son, friend etc.*); to deny (*God, doctrine*).
reniflement [rəniflə'mɑ̃], *n.m.* sniffing, snuffing, snivelling.
renifler [rəni'fle], *v.i.* to sniff, to snivel; (*fig.*) to turn up one's nose (***sur***); to hang back.
renne [rɛn], *n.m.* reindeer.
renom [rə'nɔ̃], *n.m.* renown, fame, reputation.
renommé [rənɔ'me], *a.* renowned, famed.
renommée [rənɔ'me], *n.f.* renown, fame, reputation; rumour.
renommer [rənɔ'me], *v.t.* to name again, to re-elect; to make famous, to praise.
renoncement [rənɔ̃s'mɑ̃], *n.m.* renouncement; renunciation.
renoncer [rənɔ̃'se], *v.t.* (*conjug. like* COMMENCER) to renounce, to disclaim, to disown.—*v.i.* to give up, to renounce (***à***).
renonciation [rənɔ̃sjɑ'sjɔ̃], *n.f.* renunciation, self-denial.
renoncule [rənɔ̃'kyl], *n.f.* (*Bot.*) ranunculus, buttercup, crowfoot.
renouer [rənu'e], *v.t.* to tie again, to knot again; to put together; to resume.—*v.i.* to resume relations (***avec***).
renouveau [rənu'vo], *n.m.* (*pl.* **-eaux**) (*poet.*) spring.
renouvelable [rənu'vlabl], *a.* renewable.
renouveler [rənu'vle], *v.t.* (*conjug. like* APPELER) to renew; to renovate; to revive; to recommence, to repeat. **se renouveler**, *v.r.* to be renewed, to be revived, to occur again.
renouvellement [rənuvɛl'mɑ̃], *n.m.* renewal, revival, renovation; increase.
rénovateur [renɔva'tœːr], *a.* (*fem.* **-trice**) renovating.—*n.m.* (*fem.* **-trice**) renovator, restorer.

rénovation [renɔvɑ'sjɔ̃], *n.f.* renovation, renewal.
renseignement [rɑ̃sɛɲ'mɑ̃], *n.m.* (piece of) information, (piece of) intelligence, account; (*pl.*) information; references; ***bureau de renseignements***, information bureau, inquiry-office.
renseigner [rɑ̃sɛ'ɲe], *v.t.* to give information to; to direct. **se renseigner**, *v.r.* to seek information, to make inquiries.
rente [rɑ̃:t], *n.f.* yearly income; revenue; stock, funds.
renté [rɑ̃'te], *a.* of independent means; endowed (*of hospital etc.*).
renter [rɑ̃'te], *v.t.* to allow a yearly income to, to endow (*public services etc.*).
rentier [rɑ̃'tje], *n.m.* (*fem.* **-ière**) stockholder; person of independent means.
rentrant [rɑ̃'trɑ̃], *a.* re-entering, returning; (*Av.*) retractable.—*n.m.* recess (*in a wall*); (*fem.* **-e**) new player.
rentré [rɑ̃'tre], *a.* returned; suppressed; depressed.
rentrée [rɑ̃'tre], *n.f.* re-entrance; return, home-coming; reopening (*of schools etc.*); reappearance; ingathering (*of crops etc.*); receipt, collection.
rentrer [rɑ̃'tre], *v.t.* (*aux.* AVOIR) to take in, to bring in; to suppress.—*v.i.* (*aux.* ÊTRE) to re-enter, to go in again; to return home; to join again; to reopen (*of schools etc.*).
renversable [rɑ̃vɛr'sabl], *a.* liable to be upset; reversible.
renversant [rɑ̃vɛr'sɑ̃], *a.* (*colloq.*) amazing, stunning.
renverse [rɑ̃'vɛrs], *n.f.* ***à la renverse***, backwards.
renversé [rɑ̃vɛr'se], *a.* thrown down, thrown back; upside-down.
renversement [rɑ̃vɛrsə'mɑ̃], *n.m.* reversing; overturning, overthrow; turning upside down; confusion; subversion.
renverser [rɑ̃vɛr'se], *v.t.* to turn upside down, to upset; to reverse; to knock over; to spill (*a liquid*); to destroy; to confuse; to turn (*the brain*); (*fam.*) to astound; to rout; (*Arith.*, *Mus.*) to invert. **se renverser**, *v.r.* to fall back; to fall down; to capsize; to be spilt.
renvoi [rɑ̃'vwa], *n.m.* sending back, return; dismissal; referring (*to a committee etc.*).
renvoyer [rɑ̃vwa'je], *v.t. irr.* (*conjug. like* ENVOYER) to send again; to send back, to return; to dismiss; to refer; to postpone; to throw back; to reflect (*light, heat etc.*); to reverberate (*sound*). **se renvoyer**, *v.r.* to be sent back *or* returned; to send from one to the other.
réoccupation [reɔkypɑ'sjɔ̃], *n.f.* reoccupation.
réoccuper [reɔky'pe], *v.t.* to reoccupy.
réorganisation [reɔrganizɑ'sjɔ̃], *n.f.* reorganization.
réorganiser [reɔrgani'ze], *v.t.* to reorganize.
réouverture [reuvɛr'ty:r], *n.f.* reopening (*of a theatre*).
repaire (1) [rə'pɛ:r], *n.m.* haunt (*of criminals*); den, lair (*of animals*).
repaire (2) [REPÈRE].
repaître [rə'pɛ:tr], *v.t. irr.* (*conjug. like* PAÎTRE) to feed, to nourish. **se repaître**, *v.r.* to feed on, to feast on; to delight in, to indulge in.
répandre [re'pɑ̃:dr], *v.t.* to pour out, to shed; to spill; to scatter; to distribute; to exhale; to spread abroad. **se répandre**, *v.r.* to be poured out, to be shed, to be spilt; to be spread; to be exhaled; to be spread abroad; to be current; to go into society.
répandu [repɑ̃'dy], *a.* spilt, shed; widespread.
réparable [repa'rabl], *a.* reparable; rectifiable.
reparaître [rəpa'rɛ:tr], *v.i. irr.* (*conjug. like* CONNAÎTRE) to reappear.
réparateur [repara'tœ:r], *a.* (*fem.* **-trice**) restorative, refreshing.—*n.m.* (*fem.* **-trice**) repairer, restorer.
réparation [reparɑ'sjɔ̃], *n.f.* repairing, mending; amends; compensation; ***en réparation***, under repair.
réparer [repa're], *v.t.* to repair, to mend; to make amends for, to make up for.
répareur [repa'rœ:r], *n.m.* (*fem.* **-euse**) repairer.
reparler [rəpar'le], *v.i.* to speak again.
repartie [rəpar'ti], *n.f.* repartee, retort.
repartir (1) [rəpar'ti:r], *v.t.*, *v.i.* (*conjug. like* SENTIR) to answer, to retort.
repartir (2) [rəpar'ti:r], *v.i. irr.* (*conjug. like* SENTIR, *but with aux.* ÊTRE) to set out again, to go away again.
répartir [repar'ti:r], *v.t.* to divide, to distribute; to assess.
répartissable [reparti'sabl], *a.* divisible; assessable.
répartiteur [reparti'tœ:r], *n.m.* (*fem.* **-trice**) distributor; assessor (*of taxes etc.*).
répartition [reparti'sjɔ̃], *n.f.* distribution; assessment.
repas [rə'pɑ], *n.m. inv.* meal, repast.
repassage [rəpɑ'sa:ʒ], *n.m.* repassing; grinding, sharpening (*of cutlery*); ironing (*of linen etc.*).
repasser [rəpɑ'se], *v.t.* (*aux.* AVOIR) to pass again; to cross again; to think over; to sharpen, to grind (*tools*); to iron; to repeat; to look over again.—*v.i.* (*aux.* ÊTRE) to pass again; to go, come, call etc., again.
repasseur [rəpɑ'sœ:r], *n.m.* (*fem.* **-euse**) (*Ind.*) examiner; grinder.—*n.f.* (**-euse**), ironer (*person* or *machine*).
repavage [rəpa'va:ʒ], **repavement** [rəpav'mɑ̃], *n.m.* repaving.
repaver [rəpa've], *v.t.* to repave.
repêchage [rəpɛ'ʃa:ʒ], *n.m.* rescuing; (*Spt.*) ***épreuve de repêchage***, supplementary heat; (*Sch.*) second chance (*for candidate who has failed an examination*).
repêcher [rəpɛ'ʃe], *v.t.* to fish up *or* out again; (*fig.*) to recover, to retrieve.
repeindre [rə'pɛ̃:dr], *v.t. irr.* (*conjug. like* CRAINDRE) to repaint.
repenser [rəpɑ̃'se], *v.t.*, *v.i.* to think over; to think again (of).
repentance [rəpɑ̃'tɑ̃:s], *n.f.* repentance, contrition.
repentant [rəpɑ̃'tɑ̃], *a.* repentant.
repenti [rəpɑ̃'ti], *a.* penitent.
repentir [rəpɑ̃'ti:r], *n.m.* repentance, contrition, regret.
repentir (se) [sərəpɑ̃'ti:r], *v.r. irr.* (*conjug. like* SENTIR) to repent; to rue (*de*).

repérage [rəpe'ra:ʒ], *n.m.* locating; (*Cine.*) synchronization; (*Mil.*) spotting.

répercussion [repɛrky'sjɔ̃], *n.f.* repercussion, reverberation.

répercuter [repɛrky'te], *v.t.* to reverberate, to echo; to reflect. **se répercuter**, *v.r.* to be reflected (*light*); to reverberate (*sound*); (*fig.*) to have repercussions.

repère or **repaire** [rə'pɛ:r], *n.m.* mark; benchmark; (*fig.*) landmark.

repérer [rəpe're], *v.t.* (*conjug. like* CÉDER) to locate, to spot; to make a guiding mark upon. **se repérer**, *v.r.* to find one's bearings.

répertoire [repɛr'twa:r], *n.m.* table, list, catalogue; repertory.

répéter [repe'te], *v.t.* (*conjug. like* CÉDER) to repeat, to tell again; to rehearse; to reflect; (*Law*) to demand back. **se répéter**, *v.r.* to be repeated; to repeat oneself.

répétiteur [repeti'tœ:r], *n.m.* (*fem.* **-trice**) private teacher, tutor.

répétition [repeti'sjɔ̃], *n.f.* repetition; recurrence; private lesson; (*Theat.*) rehearsal.

repétrir [rəpe'tri:r], *v.t.* to remould; to refashion.

repeupler [rəpœ'ple], *v.t.* to repeople; to restock. **se repeupler**, *v.r.* to be repeopled; to be restocked.

repiquage [rəpi'ka:ʒ], *n.m.* transplanting, pricking *or* planting out (again); repairing (*of road*).

repiquer [rəpi'ke], *v.t.* to prick again; to prick out, to transplant; to repair (*road*).

répit [re'pi], *n.m.* respite; (*fig.*) rest, breathing space.

replacement [rəplas'mɑ̃], *n.m.* replacing, putting *or* setting again; reinvestment (*of funds*).

replacer [rəpla'se], *v.t.* (*conjug. like* COMMENCER) to replace, to put in place again; to bring back; to reinvest (*funds*). **se replacer**, *v.r.* to find oneself a new situation.

replanir [rəpla'ni:r], *v.t.* to plane down (*wood*).

replanter [rəplɑ̃'te], *v.t.* to replant.

replâtrer [rəplɑ'tre], *v.t.* to replaster; to patch up (*temporarily*).

replet [rə'plɛ], *a.* (*fem.* **-ète**) obese, stout; (*fam.*) podgy.

réplétion [reple'sjɔ̃], *n.f.* stoutness; repletion, surfeit.

repli [rə'pli], *n.m.* fold, crease; (*fig.*) winding, coil, meander (*of river*); (*Mil.*) withdrawal.

repliable [rəpli'jabl], *a.* folding, collapsible.

replier [rəpli'je], *v.t.* to fold again, to fold up; to bend back; to coil (*a rope etc.*). **se replier**, *v.r.* to twist oneself, to writhe, to wind, to coil; (*Mil.*) to retreat.

réplique [re'plik], *n.f.* reply, answer, retort; (*Mus.*) repeat; (*Theat.*) cue.

répliquer [repli'ke], *v.t.*, *v.i.* to reply, to retort.

replonger [rəplɔ̃'ʒe], *v.t.* (*conjug. like* MANGER) to plunge again, to dip again.—*v.i.* and **se replonger**, *v.r.* to plunge again; to dive again.

répondant [repɔ̃'dɑ̃], *n.m.* candidate (*at an examination*); bail, surety.

répondre [re'pɔ̃:dr], *v.t.* to answer, to reply.—*v.i.* to answer, to reply; to write back; to come up (*à*); to correspond; to re-echo; to be answerable (*de*); to pledge oneself (*pour*); ***je vous en réponds***, take my word for it.

répons [re'pɔ̃], *n.m.* response (*in church*).

réponse [re'pɔ̃:s], *n.f.* answer, reply, response.

report [rə'pɔ:r], *n.m.* (*Book-keeping*) carrying forward, bringing forward; amount brought forward.

reportage [rəpɔr'ta:ʒ], *n.m.* (*Journ.*) reporting; feature article.

reporter (1) [rəpɔr'tɛ:r], *n.m.* (*Journ.*) reporter.

reporter (2) [rəpɔr'te], *v.t.* to carry back; to take back; (*Book-keeping*) to carry forward. **se reporter**, *v.r.* to go back; to refer; ***se reporter à***, please refer to.

repos [rə'po], *n.m.* rest, repose; sleep; quiet; resting-place; ***en repos***, at rest; (*Mil.*) ***repos !*** stand at ease!

reposant [rəpo'zɑ̃], *a.* restful, refreshing.

reposé [rəpo'ze], *a.* rested, refreshed; quiet, calm, cool.

reposer [rəpo'ze], *v.t.* to place again, to lay again, to replace; to rest (*on anything*); to refresh.—*v.i.* to rest, to lie down; to sleep; to be at rest. **se reposer**, *v.r.* to rest, to lie down; to settle down; to alight again (*of birds*); ***se reposer sur***, to rely on.

reposoir [rəpo'zwa:r], *n.m.* resting-place; pause.

repoussant [rəpu'sɑ̃], *a.* repulsive, loathsome.

repoussé [rəpu'se], *a.* chased (*silver*), embossed.

repousser [rəpu'se], *v.t.* to push back, to repel; to spurn, to reject; to rebuff; to shoot out (*branches etc.*) again; ***repousser du cuir***, to emboss leather; ***repousser du cuivre***, to chase copper.—*v.i.* to recoil; to spring up again (*of plants etc.*); to grow again (*of hair*); to be repulsive.

repoussoir [rəpu'swa:r], *n.m.* (*Paint.*) foil.

répréhensible [repreɑ̃'sibl], *a.* reprehensible.

répréhension [repreɑ̃'sjɔ̃], *n.f.* reprehension, reproof.

reprendre [rə'prɑ̃:dr], *v.t. irr.* (*conjug. like* PRENDRE) to recover, to recapture; to take up again; to reprove; to repair.—*v.i.* to take root again; to freeze again; to close up again (*of wounds etc.*); to begin again, to return to; to improve; to reply; to resume. **se reprendre**, *v.r.* to correct oneself; to be caught again; to begin again.

représaille [rəpre'zɑ:j], *n.f.* (*usu. pl.*) reprisal; ***user de représailles***, to retaliate.

représentant [rəprezɑ̃'tɑ̃], *n.m.* (*fem.* **-e**) representative.

représentatif [rəprezɑ̃ta'tif], *a.* (*fem.* **-tive**) representative.

représentation [rəprezɑ̃tɑ'sjɔ̃], *n.f.* representation; performance; show; remonstrance; agency.

représenter [rəprezɑ̃'te], *v.t.* to present again; to show, to produce; to represent; to resemble; to act (*a play*); to be the representative of.—*v.i.* to have an imposing appearance; to make a good show. **se représenter**, *v.r.* to present oneself again; to picture to oneself; to occur.

répressible [reprɛ'sibl], *a.* repressible.

répressif [reprɛ'sif], *a.* (*fem.* **-ive**) repressive.

répression [reprɛ'sjɔ̃], *n.f.* repression.

réprimande [repri'mɑ̃:d], *n.f.* reprimand, rebuke.
réprimander [reprimɑ̃'de], *v.t.* to reprimand, to reprove.
réprimant [repri'mɑ̃], *a.* repressive.
réprimer [repri'me], *v.t.* to repress, to restrain.
repris [rə'pri], *a.* retaken, taken up again; reset (*of a bone*).—*n.m.* ***repris de justice***, old offender, (*fam.*) old lag.
reprisage [rəpri'za:ʒ], *n.m.* darn; darning.
reprise [rə'pri:z], *n.f.* resumption; recapture, recovery; revival; darn; (*Mus.*) repetition; refrain (*of a song*); (*Ftb. etc.*) second half; (*Fenc.*) bout; (*Box.*) round; ***à plusieurs reprises***, several times, repeatedly.
repriser [rəpri'ze], *v.t.* to darn.
réprobateur [reprɔba'tœ:r], *a.* (*fem.* **-trice**) reproving.
réprobation [reprɔbɑ'sjɔ̃], *n.f.* reprobation.
reprochable [rəprɔ'ʃabl], *a.* reproachable.
reproche [rə'prɔʃ], *n.m.* reproach.
reprocher [rəprɔ'ʃe], *v.t.* to reproach, to upbraid; to taunt. **se reprocher**, *v.r.* to reproach oneself; to blame oneself.
reproducteur [rəprɔdyk'tœ:r], *a.* (*fem.* **-trice**) reproductive.
reproductif [rəprɔdyk'tif], *a.* (*fem.* **-tive**) reproductive.
reproduction [rəprɔdyk'sjɔ̃], *n.f.* reproduction; copy.
reproduire [rəprɔ'dɥi:r], *v.t. irr.* (*conjug. like* CONDUIRE) to reproduce; to reprint. **se reproduire**, *v.r.* to reproduce; to breed; to recur.
réprouvable [repru'vabl], *a.* censurable, reprehensible.
réprouvé [repru've], *a.* and *n.m.* (*fem.* **-ée**) reprobate.
réprouver [repru've], *v.t.* to disapprove of; (*Theol.*) to condemn.
reps [rɛps], *n.m.* rep (*silk* or *woollen fabric*).
reptile [rɛp'til], *a.* creeping, crawling.—*n.m.* reptile.
repu [rə'py], *a.* and *p.p.* of ***repaître***, full, satiated.
républicain [repybli'kɛ̃], *a.* and *n.m.* (*fem.* **-e**) republican.
republier [rəpybli'je], *v.t.* to republish.
république [repy'blik], *n.f.* republic; commonwealth.
répudiation [repydjɑ'sjɔ̃], *n.f.* repudiation.
répudier [repy'dje], *v.t.* to repudiate.
répugnance [repy'ɲɑ̃:s], *n.f.* repugnance; reluctance.
répugnant [repy'ɲɑ̃], *a.* repugnant.
répugner [repy'ɲe], *v.i.* to be repugnant; to feel repugnance; to clash with.
répulsif [repyl'sif], *a.* (*fem.* **-sive**) repulsive, repellent; (*fig.*) disgusting.
répulsion [repyl'sjɔ̃], *n.f.* repulsion; (*fig.*) aversion, disgust.
réputation [repytɑ'sjɔ̃], *n.f.* reputation, character; fame.
réputé [repy'te], *a.* well-known.
réputer [repy'te], *v.t.* to repute, to consider, to deem.
requérant [rəke'rɑ̃], *n.m.* (*fem.* **-e**) plaintiff, petitioner.
requérir [rəke'ri:r], *v.t. irr.* (*conjug. like* ACQUÉRIR) to request; to require; to claim; to requisition.
requête [rə'kɛ:t], *n.f.* request, petition, demand.
requiem [rekɥi'ɛm], *n.m.* requiem.
requin [rə'kɛ̃], *n.m.* shark.
requis [rə'ki], *a.* required, requisite, necessary.
réquisition [rekizi'sjɔ̃], *n.f.* requisition; summons; levy.
réquisitionner [rekizisjɔ'ne], *v.t.* to requisition, to commandeer.
rescapé [rɛska'pe], *a.* and *n.m.* (*fem.* **-ée**) survivor of a disaster.
rescousse [rɛs'kus], *n.f.* ***venir*** (***aller***) ***à la rescousse***, to come (to go) to the rescue.
réseau [re'zo], *n.m.* (*pl.* **-eaux**) net; network; (*fig.*) web, tangle; (*Rail., Elec. etc.*) network, system.
réséda [reze'da], *n.m.* reseda; mignonette.
réservation [rezɛrvɑ'sjɔ̃], *n.f.* reservation, reserving; booking (*of seats*).
réserve [re'zɛrv], *n.f.* reserve; reservation, caution; modesty; stock, store; preserve (*for game*).
réservé [rezɛr've], *a.* reserved; cautious.
réserver [rezɛr've], *v.t.* to reserve; to keep (***pour***). **se réserver**, *v.r.* to reserve for oneself; to reserve oneself, to wait.
réserviste [rezɛr'vist], *n.m.* (*Mil.*) reservist.
réservoir [rezɛr'vwa:r], *n.m.* reservoir; tank, cistern, well.
résidant [rezi'dɑ̃], *a.* resident.
résidence [rezi'dɑ̃:s], *n.f.* residence, dwelling.
résident [rezi'dɑ̃], *n.m.* (*fem.* **-e**) resident.
résidentiel [rezidɑ̃'sjɛl], *a.* (*fem.* **-elle**) residential.
résider [rezi'de], *v.i.* to reside, to dwell.
résidu [rezi'dy], *n.m.* residue; remainder.
résiduaire [rezi'dɥɛ:r], *a.* waste.
résignation [reziɲɑ'sjɔ̃], *n.f.* resignation.
résigné [rezi'ɲe], *a.* resigned, submissive.
résigner [rezi'ɲe], *v.t.* to resign, to give up. **se résigner**, *v.r.* to resign oneself, to submit.
résiliation [reziljɑ'sjɔ̃], *n.f.*, **résiliement** or **résilîment** [rezili'mɑ̃], *n.m.* cancelling, annulment.
résilience [rezi'ljɑ̃:s], *n.f.* resilience (*in metals*).
résilier [rezi'lje], *v.t.* to cancel, to annul.
résille [re'zi:j], *n.f.* hair-net.
résine [re'zin], *n.f.* resin, rosin.
résineux [rezi'nø], *a.* (*fem.* **-euse**) resinous.
résistance [rezis'tɑ̃:s], *n.f.* resistance, opposition; ***la Résistance***, the Resistance Movement (1940–45).
résistant [rezis'tɑ̃], *a.* unyielding; resistant, tough.—*n.m.* (*fem.* **-e**) member of the Resistance Movement.
résister [rezis'te], *v.i.* to resist, to withstand (***à***).
résistible [rezis'tibl], *a.* resistible.
résistivité [rezistivi'te], *n.f.* (*Elec.*) resistivity.
résolu [rezɔ'ly], *a.* resolved, resolute, determined; solved.
résoluble [rezɔ'lybl], *a.* soluble.
résolument [rezɔly'mɑ̃], *adv.* resolutely, boldly.
résolution [rezɔly'sjɔ̃], *n.f.* resolution, solution; decision, determination; resolve.
résonance [rezɔ'nɑ̃:s], *n.f.* resonance.
résonnant [rezɔ'nɑ̃], *a.* resonant, resounding, sonorous.

résonnement [rezɔn'mɑ̃], *n.m.* resounding, re-echoing.
résonner [rezɔ'ne], *v.i.* to resound, to reverberate, to re-echo.
résoudre [re'zu:dr], *v.t. irr.* to resolve; to dissolve; to solve; to decide upon; to cancel; to persuade. **se résoudre**, *v.r.* to resolve, to determine; to be resolved, to be solved; to dissolve.
respect [rɛs'pɛ], *n.m.* respect, regard, reverence.
respectabilité [rɛspɛktabili'te], *n.f.* respectability.
respectable [rɛspɛk'tabl], *a.* respectable.
respectablement [rɛspɛktablə'mɑ̃], *adv.* respectably.
respecter [rɛspɛk'te], *v.t.* to respect, to revere; to spare.
respectif [rɛspɛk'tif], *a.* (*fem.* **-tive**) respective.
respectivement [rɛspɛktiv'mɑ̃], *adv.* respectively.
respectueusement [rɛspɛktɥøz'mɑ̃], *adv.* respectfully, deferentially.
respectueux [rɛspɛk'tɥø], *a.* (*fem.* **-euse**) respectful, deferential.
respirable [rɛspi'rabl], *a.* respirable, breathable.
respirateur [rɛspira'tœ:r], *a.m.* respiratory. —*n.m.* respirator.
respiration [rɛspirɑ'sjɔ̃], *n.f.* respiration, breathing.
respiratoire [rɛspira'twa:r], *a.* respiratory, breathing.
respirer [rɛspi're], *v.t.* to breathe; (*fig.*) to express; to long for.—*v.i.* to breathe; to take breath, to rest.
resplendir [rɛsplɑ̃'di:r], *v.i.* to shine brightly; to glitter.
resplendissant [rɛsplɑ̃di'sɑ̃], *a.* resplendent, glittering.
resplendissement [rɛsplɑ̃dis'mɑ̃], *n.m.* splendour, refulgence.
responsabilité [rɛspɔ̃sabili'te], *n.f.* responsibility, liability.
responsable [rɛspɔ̃'sabl], *a.* responsible, accountable.
resquillage [rɛski'ja:ʒ], *n.m.*, **resquille** [rɛs'ki:j], *n.f.* (*slang*) gate-crashing; ***entrer à la resquille***, to gate-crash.
resquiller [rɛski'je] *v.i.* to gate-crash; to wangle.
ressac [rə'sak], *n.m.* surf.
ressaisir [rəsɛ'zi:r], *v.t.* to seize again. **se ressaisir**, *v.r.* to regain one's self-control.
ressasser [rəsɑ'se], *v.t.* (*fig.*) to scrutinize; (*fig.*) to repeat tediously, to harp on.
ressaut [rə'so], *n.m.* projection; abrupt fall, dip.
ressauter [rəso'te], *v.t.* to leap over again.—*v.i.* to leap again; (*Arch.*) to project.
ressemblance [rəsɑ̃'blɑ̃:s], *n.f.* resemblance likeness.
ressemblant [rəsɑ̃'blɑ̃], *a.* like, similar.
ressembler [rəsɑ̃'ble], *v.i.* to look like, to resemble (*à*). **se ressembler**, *v.r.* to be like each other; to look alike.
ressemelage [rəsəm'la:ʒ], *n.m.* resoling (*of boots*).
ressemeler [rəsə'mle], *v.t.* (*conjug. like* APPELER) to re-sole (*boots etc.*).
ressenti [rəsɑ̃'ti], *a.* felt; (*Paint.*) strongly expressed.
ressentiment [rəsɑ̃ti'mɑ̃], *n.m.* resentment.
ressentir [resɑ̃'ti:r], *v.t. irr.* (*conjug. like* SENTIR) to feel, to experience; to manifest; to resent. **se ressentir**, *v.r.* to feel the effects (***de***); to be felt.
resserrement [rəsɛr'mɑ̃], *n.m.* contraction, tightening; restriction.
resserrer [rəsɛ're], *v.t.* to tighten; to pen in; to restrain; to abridge; to close up; to lock up again. **se resserrer**, *v.r.* to contract, to be contracted; to confine oneself; to curtail one's expenses.
ressort (1) [rə'sɔ:r], *n.m.* spring; elasticity; energy, activity, strength; means.
ressort (2) [rə'sɔ:r], *n.m.* extent of jurisdiction; (*fig.*) department, line.
ressortir (1) [rəsɔr'ti:r], *v.i. irr.* (*conjug. like* SENTIR, *but with aux.* ÊTRE) to go *or* come out again; (*fig.*) to stand out; to result (***de***); ***faire ressortir***, to throw into relief.
ressortir (2) [rəsɔr'ti:r], *v.i.* to be under the jurisdiction of, to be dependent on.
ressortissant [rəsɔrti'sɑ̃], *n.m.* (*fem.* **-e**) national.
ressource [rə'surs], *n.f.* resource, resort, expedient, shift; (*pl.*) resources; ***il n'y a point de ressource***, there's no help for it; ***ressources personnelles***, private means.
ressouvenir [rəsuv'ni:r], *n.m.* remembrance. recollection, reminiscence.
ressouvenir (se) [sərəsuv'ni:r], *v.r. irr.* (*conjug. like* TENIR, *but with aux.* ÊTRE) to recollect, to remember.
ressuscitation [resysitɑ'sjɔ̃], *n.f.* resuscitation, revival.
ressusciter [resysi'te], *v.t.* to resuscitate; to revive (*a custom etc.*).—*v.i.* to come to life again.
restant [rɛs'tɑ̃], *a.* remaining, left.—*n.m.* remainder, rest.
restaurant [rɛstɔ'rɑ̃], *n.m.* restaurant; restorative.
restaurateur [rɛstɔra'tœ:r], *n.m.* (*fem.* **-trice**) restorer; restaurant keeper.
restauration [rɛstɔrɑ'sjɔ̃], *n.f.* restoration, repair.
restaurer [rɛstɔ're], *v.t.* to restore; to refresh. **se restaurer**, *v.r.* to take refreshment; to build up one's strength (*after illness*).
reste [rɛst], *n.m.* rest, remainder; trace, vestige; (*pl.*) remnants, relics; remains; ***au reste*** or ***du reste***, besides, moreover; ***de reste***, over and above; ***et le reste***, and so on, and so forth; ***être en reste***, to be in arrears; ***les restes***, remnants (*of meal*); mortal remains.
rester [rɛs'te], *v.i.* (*aux.* ÊTRE) to remain; to stay; to last; to pause; ***rester court***, to stop short.
restituable [rɛsti'tɥabl], *a.* repayable returnable.
restituer [rɛsti'tɥe], *v.t.* to restore; to return, to refund.
restitution [rɛstity'sjɔ̃] *n.f.* restitution; restoration.
restreindre [rɛs'trɛ̃:dr], *v.t. irr.* (*conjug. like* CRAINDRE) to restrict; to limit; to restrain. **se restreindre**, *v.r.* to restrain oneself; to curtail one's expenses.
restreint [rɛs'trɛ̃], *a.* restricted, limited.
restrictif [rɛstrik'tif] *a.* (*fem.* **-tive**) restrictive.

restriction [rɛstrik'sjɔ̃], *n.f.* restriction, restraint; ***restriction mentale***, mental reservation.
restringent [rɛstrɛ̃'ʒɑ̃], *a.* and *n.m.* (*Med.*) astringent.
résultant [rezyl'tɑ̃], *a.* resulting.
résultat [rezyl'ta], *n.m.* result.
résulter [rezyl'te], *v.i.* to result.
résumé [rezy'me], *n.m.* recapitulation, summary; ***en résumé***, to sum up.
résumer [rezy'me], *v.t.* to summarize. **se résumer**, *v.r.* to recapitulate, to sum up.
résurrection [rezyrɛk'sjɔ̃], *n.f.* resurrection; revival.
rétablir [reta'bliːr], *v.t.* to re-establish, to restore; to repair; to recover; to retrieve. **se rétablir**, *v.r.* to recover one's health; to be restored.
rétablissement [retablis'mɑ̃], *n.m.* re-establishment, restoration; repair; recovery.
retailler [rətɑ'je], *v.t.* to cut again, to prune again.
rétamer [reta'me], *v.t.* to tin over again; to resilver.
rétameur [reta'mœːr], *n.m.* tinker.
retaper [rəta'pe], *v.t.* (*colloq.*) to do up (*a hat etc.*), to straighten (*bedclothes*). **se retaper**, *v.r.* (*fam.*) to buck up.
retard [rə'taːr], *n.m.* delay; slowness (*of a clock etc.*); ***être en retard***, to be late.
retardataire [rətarda'tɛːr], *a.* in arrears, late; backward.—*n.* late-comer; defaulter.
retardement [rətardə'mɑ̃], *n.m.* delay, retardment.
retarder [rətar'de], *v.t.* to retard, to delay; to defer (*payment*); to put back (*clocks and watches*).—*v.i.* to lose time; to be slow (*of clocks and watches*); to be behind the times.
retenir [rət'niːr] *v.t. irr.* (*conjug. like* TENIR) ber; to reserve; to hold in, to restrain; to to hold back; to retain; to detain; to remem-engage; to prevent; to get hold of again; (*Arith.*) to carry. **se retenir**, *v.r.* to control oneself; to refrain; to catch hold.
retenteur [rətɑ̃'tœːr], *a.* (*fem.* **-trice**) retaining.
rétentif [retɑ̃'tif], *a.* (*fem.* **-tive**) retentive.
rétention [retɑ̃'sjɔ̃], *n.f.* reservation.
etentir [rətɑ̃'tiːr], *v.i.* to resound, to re-echo, to ring.
retentissant [rətɑ̃ti'sɑ̃], *a.* resounding, echoing; ringing, loud; (*fig.*) famous.
retentissement [rətɑ̃tis'mɑ̃], *n.m.* resounding, echo; ringing; (*fig.*) fame, celebrity.
retenu [rət'ny], *a.* reserved, cautious, wary.
retenue [rət'ny], *n.f.* discretion, circumspection, caution; detention; (*Comm.*) deduction; guy-rope.
réticence [reti'sɑ̃ːs], *n.f.* reserve, silence; concealment (*of some particular*).
rétif [re'tif], *a.* (*fem.* **-tive**) restive; stubborn.
rétine [re'tin], *n.f.* retina (*of the eye*).
retirable [rəti'rabl], *a.* withdrawable.
retiré [rəti're], *a.* retired, secluded; in retirement.
retirement [rətir'mɑ̃], *n.m.* contraction; shrinking.
retirer [rəti're], *v.t.* to draw again; to pull back, to withdraw; to take away; to retract; to derive. **se retirer**, *v.r.* to retire, to withdraw; to subside (*of waters*); to contract.
retombée [rətɔ̃'be], *n.f.* fall, fall-out; ***retombée de particules radioactives***, radio-active fall-out.
retomber [rətɔ̃'be], *v.i.* (*aux.* ÊTRE) to fall again; to have a relapse; to subside.
retordre [rə'tɔrdr], *v.t.* to twist again; to twist (*silk, thread etc.*).
rétorquer [retɔr'ke], *v.t.* to retort.
retors [rə'tɔːr], *a.* twisted; artful, cunning, crafty.—*n.m.* twisted thread; crafty person.
retouche [rə'tuʃ], *n.f.* retouching, touching up.
retoucher [rətu'ʃe], *v.t.* to retouch; to touch up.
retour [rə'tuːr], *n.m.* return; repetition, recurrence; sending back; (*fig.*) change; reverse; turning, winding; (*Law*) reversion; ***billet d'aller et retour***, return ticket.
retourne [rə'turn], *n.f.* trump-card.
retourner [rətur'ne], *v.t.* (*aux.* AVOIR) to turn, to turn up, to turn over, round, about etc.; to send back.—*v.i.* (*aux.* ÊTRE) to return, to go again, to go back (again); to recoil upon; to turn up (*cards*). **se retourner**, *v.r.* to turn, to turn round, to look round.
retracer [rətra'se], *v.t.* (*conjug. like* COMMENCER) to trace again, to retrace; to relate. **se retracer**, *v.r.* to recall to mind; to recur, to be retraced (*in mind*).
rétracter [retrak'te], *v.t.* and **se rétracter**, *v.r.* to retract; to recant.
retrait [rə'trɛ], *a.* shrunk (*of grain, wood etc.*).—*n.m.* shrinkage; recess (*in wall*), closet; withdrawal.
retraite [rə'trɛt], *n.f.* retreat, retiring; privacy; refuge; haunt; retirement (*from office*); superannuation; retiring pension; ***battre en retraite***, to beat a retreat.
retraité [rətrɛ'te], *a.* superannuated, retired, pensioned off.
retraiter [rətrɛ'te], *v.t.* to retire, to pension off.
retranchement [rətrɑ̃ʃ'mɑ̃], *n.m.* retrenchment, curtailment; (*Mil.*) entrenchment.
retrancher [rətrɑ̃'ʃe], *v.t.* to retrench, to curtail, to cut short; to cut out; to abridge; (*Arith.*) to subtract; (*Mil.*) to entrench. **se retrancher**, *v.r.* to restrain oneself; to curtail one's expenses; (*Mil.*) to entrench oneself; (*fig.*) to fall back upon.
rétrécir [retre'siːr], *v.t.* to take in, to contract; to narrow, to limit.—*v.i.* and **se rétrécir**, *v.r.* to grow narrower; to shrink, to contract.
rétrécissement [retresis'mɑ̃], *n.m.* narrowing; shrinking.
retremper [rətrɑ̃'pe], *v.t.* to soak again; to temper again; (*fig.*) to strengthen. **se retremper**, *v.r.* to be strengthened *or* invigorated.
rétribuer [retri'bɥe], *v.t.* to remunerate.
rétribution [retriby'sjɔ̃], *n.f.* payment, reward.
rétroactif [retrɔak'tif], *a.* (*fem.* **-tive**) retroactive.
rétroaction [retrɔak'sjɔ̃], *n.f.* retroaction; (*Rad. Teleg.*) feed-back.
rétrograde [retrɔ'grad], *a.* retrograde; backward.
rétrograder [retrɔgra'de], *v.i.* to retrograde; to go back, (*Mil.*) to fall back.
rétrogressif [retrɔgrɛ'sif], *a.* (*fem.* **-ive**) retrogressive.

rétrogression [retrɔgrɛ'sjɔ̃], *n.f.* retrogression.
rétrospectif [retrɔspɛk'tif], *a.* (*fem.* **-tive**) retrospective.
retroussé [rətru'se], *a.* turned up; tucked up; ***nez retroussé***, turned-up nose, snub nose.
retrousser [rətru'se], *v.t.* to turn up, to roll up (*trousers*); to tuck up; to cock (*one's hat*). **se retrousser**, *v.r.* to tuck up one's skirt *or* other garment.
retroussis [rətru'si], *n.m.* cock (*of a hat*); top (*of a boot*); facing (*of a uniform*).
retrouver [rətru've], *v.t.* to find again, to regain, to recover. **se retrouver**, *v.r.* to find each other again; to be oneself again.
rétroviseur [retrɔvi'zœ:r], *n.m.* (*Motor.*) driving mirror.
rets [rɛ], *n.m. inv.* net; (*fig.*) snare, toils.
réunion [rey'njɔ̃], *n.f.* reunion; reconciliation; junction; meeting, assembly, gathering; reception.
réunir [rey'ni:r], *v.t.* to reunite, to join again, to bring together again, to reconcile; to connect; to collect. **se réunir**, *v.r.* to assemble again, to reunite; to meet; to amalgamate.
réussi [rey'si], *a.* successful, brilliant.
réussir [rey'si:r], *v.t.* to carry out well, to accomplish, to perform successfully.—*v.i.* to succeed, to be successful, to prosper, to thrive; to pass (*Exam*).
réussite [rey'sit], *n.f.* success; (*happy*) issue *or* result; (*Cards*) patience.
revaloir [rəva'lwa:r], *v.t. irr.* (*conjug. like* VALOIR) to return like for like, to be even with.
revanche [rə'vɑ̃:ʃ], *n.f.* revenge; return match.
rêvasser [rɛva'se], *v.i.* to day-dream, to muse.
rêvasserie [rɛvas'ri], *n.f.* day-dreams; idle musing.
rêvasseur [rɛva'sœ:r], *n.m.* (*fem.* **-euse**) (*colloq.*) dreamer, muser.
rêve [rɛ:v], *n.m.* dream; day-dream, illusion.
revêche [rə'vɛ:ʃ], *a.* rough; cross, ill-natured, cantankerous.
réveil [re'vɛ:j], *n.m.* waking, awaking; alarm-clock; (*Mil.*) reveille.
réveille-matin [revɛjma'tɛ̃], *n.m. inv.* alarm-clock.
réveiller [revɛ'je], *v.t.* to awake, to arouse; to recall. **se réveiller**, *v.r.* to awake, to wake up; to be roused; to revive.
réveillon [revɛ'jɔ̃], *n.m.* midnight repast, *esp.* Christmas Eve revel.
réveillonner [revɛjɔ'ne], *v.i.* to take part in a ***réveillon.***
révélateur [revela'tœ:r], *a.* (*fem.* **-trice**) revealing, tell-tale.—*n.m.* (*fem.* **-trice**) revealer, informer.—*n.m.* (*Phot.*) developer.
révélation [revelɑ'sjɔ̃], *n.f.* revelation, disclosure.
révéler [reve'le], *v.t.* (*conjug. like* CÉDER) to reveal, to disclose; to betray; (*Phot.*) to develop. **se révéler**, *v.r.* to reveal oneself; to prove (to be).
revenant [rəv'nɑ̃], *a.* pleasing, prepossessing. —*n.m.* ghost.
revendeur [rəvɑ̃'dœ:r], *n.m.* (*fem.* **-euse**) retail dealer, dealer in old clothes etc.
revendicable [rəvɑ̃di'kabl], *a.* claimable.
revendicateur [rəvɑ̃dika'tœ:r], *n.m.* (*fem.* **-trice**) claimant.
revendication [rəvɑ̃dikɑ'sjɔ̃], *n.f.* claim, demand.
revendiquer [rəvɑ̃di'ke], *v.t.* to claim.
revendre [rə'vɑ̃:dr], *v.t.* to sell again, to resell.
revenir [rəv'ni:r], *v.i. irr.* (*conjug. like* TENIR *but with aux.* ÊTRE) to come again, to come back, to return; to reappear, to haunt, to walk (*of ghosts*); to recur; to recover; to amount, to cost; to retract; to please.
revente [rə'vɑ̃:t], *n.f.* resale.
revenu [rəv'ny], *n.m.* revenue, income.
revenue [rəv'ny], *n.f.* young wood, aftergrowth.
rêver [rɛ've], *v.t.* to dream, to dream of.—*v.i.* to dream; to have day-dreams; to muse.
réverbérant [revɛrbe'rɑ̃], *a.* reverberating.
réverbération [revɛrberɑ'sjɔ̃], *n.f.* reverberation; reflection (*of light, heat*).
réverbère [revɛr'bɛ:r], *n.m.* reflector; street lamp.
réverbérer [revɛrbe're], *v.t., v.i.* (*conjug. like* CÉDER) to reverberate; to reflect (*light, heat*).
reverdir [rəvɛr'di:r], *v.t.* to make green again, to revive.—*v.i.* to become green again; (*fig.*) to grow young again.
reverdissement [rəvɛrdis'mɑ̃], *n.m.* growing green again.
révéremment [revera'mɑ̃], *adv.* reverently.
révérence [reve'rɑ̃:s], *n.f.* reverence; bow, curtsy.
révérenciel [reverɑ̃'sjɛl], *a.* (*fem.* **-elle**) reverential.
révérencieusement [reverɑ̃sjøz'mɑ̃], *adv.* reverentially.
révérencieux [reverɑ̃'sjø], *a.* (*fem.* **-euse**) ceremonious, obsequious.
révérend [reve'rɑ̃], *a.* reverend.
révérendissime [reverɑ̃di'sim], *a.* most reverend, right reverend.
révérer [reve're], *v.t.* (*conjug. like* CÉDER) to revere.
rêverie [rɛ'vri], *n.f.* reverie, musing, dreaming.
revers [rə'vɛ:r], *n.m.* back, reverse; facing (*of clothes*); lapel (*of a coat*); turn-up (*of trousers*); top (*of boots*); (*Ten.*) back-hand stroke; misfortune, set back.
reverser [rəvɛr'se], *v.t.* to pour out again; to pour back; to transfer; to pay back.
réversible [revɛr'sibl], *a.* reversible; revertible.
réversion [revɛr'sjɔ̃], *n.f.* reversion.
reversoir [rəvɛr'swa:r], *n.m.* weir.
revêtement [rəvɛt'mɑ̃], *n.m.* facing (*of masonry etc.*); surface (*of road*).
revêtir [rəvɛ'ti:r], *v.t. irr.* (*conjug. like* VÊTIR) to give clothes to, to dress; to put on; to assume; to cover; (*fig.*) to invest *or* endow with. **se revêtir**, *v.r.* to clothe oneself, to array oneself; to put on, to assume.
rêveur [rɛ'vœ:r], *a.* (*fem.* **-euse**) dreaming; (*fig.*) pensive, dreamy.—*n.m.* (*fem.* **-euse**) dreamer; muser.
revient [rə'vjɛ̃], *n.m.* ***prix de revient***, net cost.
revirement [rəvir'mɑ̃], *n.m.* tacking about; (*fig.*) sudden change.
revirer [rəvi're], *v.i.* to tack, to put about; (*fig.*) to change sides.

revisable [rəvi'zabl], **révisable** [revi'zabl], *a.* revisable.
reviser [rəvi'ze], **réviser** [revi'ze], *v.t.* to revise, to review, to examine; to overhaul (*engine*).
reviseur [rəvi'zœːr], **réviseur** [revi'zœːr], *n.m.* reviser, examiner; auditor; proof-reader.
revision [rəvi'zjɔ̃], **révision** [revi'zjɔ̃], *n.f.* revision, review; overhaul (*of engine*).
revivifier [rəvivi'fje], *v.t.* to revivify, to regenerate, to revive.
revivre [rə'viːvr], *v.t. irr.* (*conjug. like* VIVRE) to relive.—*v.i.* to come to life again, to live again.
révocable [revɔ'kabl], *a.* revocable; removable (*of an official*).
révocation [revɔkɑ'sjɔ̃], *n.f.* revocation (*of will*), repeal; dismissal (*of an official*).
revoici [rəvwa'si], **revoilà** [rəvwa'la], *adv.* (*colloq.*) ***me revoici***, here I am again; ***le revoilà***, there he is again.
revoir [rə'vwaːr], *v.t. irr.* (*conjug. like* VOIR) to see again; to meet again; to revise, to review. **se revoir**, *v.r.* to see *or* meet each other again.—*n.m. inv.* ***au revoir***, good-bye (*for the present*).
revoler (1) [rəvɔ'le], *v.t.* to steal again.
revoler (2) [rəvɔ'le], *v.i.* to fly again; to fly back.
révoltant [revɔl'tɑ̃], *a.* revolting, shocking.
révolte [re'vɔlt], *n.f.* revolt, rebellion.
révolté [revɔl'te], *n.m.* (*fem.* **-ée**) rebel, mutineer.
révolter [revɔl'te], *v.t.* to stir up, to rouse; to shock, to disgust. **se révolter**, *v.r.* to revolt, to rebel; to be indignant, to be shocked.
révolu [revɔ'ly], *a.* accomplished, completed; elapsed.
révolution [revɔly'sjɔ̃], *n.f.* revolution.
révolutionnaire [revɔlysjɔ'nɛːr], *a.* revolutionary.—*n.* revolutionary; revolutionist.
révolutionner [revɔlysjɔ'ne], *v.t.* to revolutionize.
revolver [revɔl'vɛːr], *n.m.* revolver.
révoquer [revɔ'ke], *v.t.* to dismiss (*an official etc.*); to recall (*an ambassador etc.*); to repeal, to cancel.
revue [rə'vy], *n.f.* review, survey; revision; magazine; review (*critical article*); (*Mil.*) review; (*Theat.*) revue.
révulsion [revyl'sjɔ̃], *n.f.* revulsion.
rez [re], *prep.* on a level with, even with.
rez-de-chaussée [redʃo'se], *n.m. inv.* ground-level; ground floor.
rhabillage [rabi'jaːʒ], *n.m.* mending, overhaul.
rhabiller [rabi'je], *v.t.* to dress again; to mend.
rhétoricien [retɔri'sjɛ̃], *n.m.* rhetorician.
rhétorique [retɔ'rik], *n.f.* rhetoric.
Rhin [rɛ̃], **le**, *m.* the Rhine.
rhinocéros [rinɔse'rɔs], *n.m. inv.* rhinoceros.
rhododendron [rɔdɔdɛ̃'drɔ̃], *n.m.* rhododendron.
rhombe [rɔ̃ːb], *a.* rhombic.—*n.m.* rhomb; rhombus.
rhubarbe [ry'barb], *n.f.* rhubarb.
rhum [rɔm], *n.m.* rum.
rhumatisant [rymati'zɑ̃], *a.* suffering from rheumatism, rheumatic.—*n.m.* (*fem.* **-e**) sufferer from rheumatism.
rhumatismal [rymatis'mal], *a.* (*m. pl.* **-aux**) rheumatic.
rhumatisme [ryma'tism], *n.m.* rheumatism.
rhume [rym], *n.m.* cold (*illness*).
riant [ri'jɑ̃], *a.* smiling, cheerful, pleasant, pleasing.
ribambelle [ribɑ̃'bɛl], *n.f.* (*colloq.*) swarm, string, lot.
ribaud [ri'bo], *a.* and *n.m.* (*fem.* **-e**) ribald.
ribauderie [ribod'ri], *n.f.* ribaldry.
ricanement [rikan'mɑ̃], *n.m.* sneering, sneer; mocking laughter.
ricaner [rika'ne], *v.i.* to sneer, to snigger.
ricaneur [rika'nœːr], *a.* (*fem.* **-euse**) sneering, derisive.—*n.m.* (*fem.* **-euse**) sneerer.
Richard [ri'ʃaːr], *m.* Richard.
richard [ri'ʃaːr], *n.m.* (*fam.* and *pej.*) moneyed person, capitalist.
riche [riʃ], *a.* rich, wealthy; copious; valuable.—*n.* rich person.
richement [riʃ'mɑ̃], *adv.* richly; splendidly.
richesse [ri'ʃɛs], *n.f.* riches, wealth; copiousness; richness.
richissime [riʃi'sim], *a.* (*colloq.*) rolling in money.
ricin [ri'sɛ̃], *n.m.* castor-oil plant.
ricocher [rikɔ'ʃe], *v.i.* to rebound; to ricochet.
ricochet [rikɔ'ʃɛ], *n.m.* rebound (*on the water*); (*Artill.*) ricochet; (*fig.*) chain (*of events*).
rictus [rik'tyːs], *n.m. inv.* grin; rictus.
ride [rid], *n.f.* wrinkle; ripple.
ridé [ri'de], *a.* wrinkled; rippling; corrugated.
rideau [ri'do], *n.m.* (*pl.* **-eaux**) curtain; screen (*of trees etc.*).
rider [ri'de], *v.t.* to wrinkle; to corrugate; to shrivel; to ruffle (*water*). **se rider**, *v.r.* to be wrinkled; to shrivel up; to ripple (*of water*).
ridicule [ridi'kyl], *a.* ridiculous.—*n.m.* ridicule; ridiculousness.
ridiculement [ridikyl'mɑ̃], *adv.* ridiculously.
ridiculiser [ridikyli'ze], *v.t.* to ridicule, to make fun of.
rien [rjɛ̃], *n.m.* trifle, mere nothing.—*indef. pron.* nothing, nought, not anything; anything.
rieur [ri'jœːr], *a.* (*fem.* **rieuse**) laughing, joking.
rigide [ri'ʒid], *a.* rigid, stiff; strict, severe.
rigidement [riʒid'mɑ̃], *adv.* rigidly, strictly.
rigidité [riʒidi'te], *n.f.* rigidity, stiffness; strictness, severity.
rigole [ri'gɔl], *n.f.* trench, small ditch *or* channel; gutter.
rigoler [rigɔ'le], *v.i.* (*pop.*) to laugh; to have fun; to joke.
rigorisme [rigɔ'rism], *n.m.* rigorism, austerity.
rigoriste [rigɔ'rist], *a.* over-severe.—*n.* rigorist, stickler.
rigoureusement [rigurøz'mɑ̃], *adv.* rigorously, severely, strictly.
rigoureux [rigu'rø], *a.* (*fem.* **-euse**) rigorous, harsh; strict; stern; inclement.
rigueur [ri'gœːr], *n.f.* rigour, strictness; precision; severity; inclemency; ***à la rigueur***, at a pinch; if necessary; ***de rigueur***, indispensable, compulsory.
rimailler [rimɑ'je], *v.i.* to write doggerel.

rimailleur [rima'jœ:r], *n.m.* (*fem.* **-euse**) sorry rhymer, rhymester.
rime [rim], *n.f.* rhyme; (*fig.*) verse.
rimer [ri'me], *v.i.* to rhyme; to write verses.
rimeur [ri'mœ:r], *n.m.* rhymer, versifier.
rinçage [rɛ̃'sa:ʒ], *n.m.* rinsing, washing.
rincer [rɛ̃'se], *v.t.* (*conjug. like* COMMENCER) to rinse, to wash. **se rincer**, *v.r.* to rinse.
ripaille [ri'pɑ:j], *n.f.* feasting, junketing.
riposte [ri'pɔst], *n.f.* (*Fenc.*) ripost, return; (*fig.*) retort, repartee.
riposter [ripɔs'te], *v.i.* (*Fenc.*) to ripost, to parry and thrust; (*fig.*) to make a smart reply.
rire [ri:r], *v.i. irr.* to laugh; to smile; to be favourable; to joke; to mock. **se rire**, *v.r.* to make sport, to scoff (*de*).—*n.m.* laughter, laughing.
ris [ri], *n.m. inv.* laugh, smile, laughter; (*Naut.*) reef (*of sails*); sweetbread.
risée [ri'ze], *n.f.* laugh, laughter; mockery; laughing-stock.
risette [ri'zɛt], *n.f.* pleasant little laugh, smile.
risible [ri'zibl], *a.* comical, laughable; ridiculous.
risiblement [riziblə'mɑ̃], *adv.* laughably, ludicrously.
risque [risk], *n.m.* risk, hazard.
risqué [ris'ke], *a.* risky; ***une plaisanterie risquée***, a doubtful joke.
risquer [ris'ke], *v.t.* to risk, to venture; (*fam.*) to chance. **se risquer**, *v.r.* to risk, to venture.
risque-tout [riskə'tu], *n.m. inv.* (*colloq.*) dare-devil.
rissole [ri'sɔl], *n.f.* rissole.
rissoler [risɔ'le], *v.t.* (*Cook.*) to brown.
ristourne [ris'turn], *n.f.* refund; rebate.
rit or **rite** [rit], *n.m.* rite.
ritournelle [ritur'nɛl], *n.f.* (*Mus.*) ritornello, flourish.
rituel [ri'tɥɛl], *a.* (*fem.* **-elle**) ritual.—*n.m.* ritual (*prayer-book*).
rivage [ri'va:ʒ], *n.m.* shore, strand, beach; bank, waterside.
rival [ri'val], *a.* (*m. pl.* **-aux**) rival, competitive.—*n.m.* (*fem.* **-e**, *m. pl.* **-aux**) rival.
rivaliser [rivali'ze], *v.i.* to rival, to vie, to compete.
rivalité [rivali'te], *n.f.* rivalry, emulation.
rive [ri:v], *n.f.* bank, shore (*of rivers, lakes etc.*); (*fig.*) seashore; border.
rivement [riv'mɑ̃], *n.m.* riveting.
river [ri've], *v.t.* to clinch, to rivet.
riverain [ri'vrɛ̃], *a.* riparian; bordering (*on rivers* or *woods*).—*n.m.* (*fem.* **-e**) riverside resident; borderer.
rivet [ri'vɛ], *n.m.* rivet; clinch.
rivetage [riv'ta:ʒ], *n.m.* riveting.
riveter [riv'te], *v.t.* (*conjug. like* APPELER) to rivet.
riveteur [riv'tœ:r], **riveur** [ri'vœ:r], *n.m.* riveter.
rivière [ri'vjɛ:r], *n.f.* river, stream.
rivoir, *n.m.* or **rivoire** [ri'vwa:r], *n.f.* riveting-hammer *or* machine.
rivure [ri'vy:r], *n.f.* clinching, riveting.
rixe [riks], *n.f.* fight, scuffle; brawl, affray.
riz [ri], *n.m.* rice.
rizière [ri'zjɛ:r], *n.f.* rice-field, paddy-field, rice-plantation; rice-swamp.
robe [rɔb], *n.f.* gown, dress, frock; robe; long robe (*lawyers*), the cloth (*clergy*); coat (*of certain animals*); skin, husk, peel (*of certain fruits etc.*).
robinet [rɔbi'nɛ], *n.m.* tap; cock; ***ouvrir (fermer) le robinet***, to turn on (off) the tap.
robot [rɔ'bo], *a. inv.* ***avion robot***, pilotless plane; ***fusée, satellite robot***, unmanned rocket, satellite.—*n.m.* automaton, robot.
robuste [rɔ'byst], *a.* robust, sturdy; hardy, strong.
robustement [rɔbystə'mɑ̃], *adv.* robustly, athletically.
robustesse [rɔbys'tɛs], *n.f.* robustness, strength, vigour.
roc [rɔk], *n.m.* rock.
rocaille [rɔ'kɑ:j], *n.f.* rock-work, grotto-work.
rocailleux [rɔkɑ'jø], *a.* (*fem.* **-euse**) pebbly, stony; rugged, rough.
roche [rɔʃ], *n.f.* rock; boulder; stony mass.
rocher [rɔ'ʃe], *n.m.* rock, crag.
rochet [rɔ'ʃɛ], *n.m.* rochet (*surplice*); ratchet.
rocheux [rɔ'ʃø], *a.* (*fem.* **-euse**) rocky, stony.
rococo [rɔkɔ'ko], *a. inv.* rococo; antiquated.—*n.m.* rococo, antiquated style.
rodage [rɔ'da:ʒ], *n.m.* grinding in; polishing; ***en rodage***, running in (*engine*).
roder [rɔ'de], *v.t.* to run in (*car*); to grind, to polish.
rôder [ro'de], *v.i.* to prowl.
rôdeur [ro'dœ:r], *a.* (*fem.* **-euse**) prowling.—*n.m.* (*fem.* **-euse**) prowler; vagrant.
rodomontade [rɔdɔmɔ̃'tad], *n.f.* bluster, swagger.
Rodrigue [rɔ'drig], *m.* Roderick.
rogaton [rɔga'tɔ̃], *n.m.* (*pl.*) scraps, odds and ends.
Roger [rɔ'ʒe], *m.* Roger; ***c'est un vrai Roger Bontemps***, he is a happy-go-lucky sort of chap.
rogner [rɔ'ɲe], *v.t.* to cut, to pare, to crop; to clip, to prune.
rogneux [rɔ'ɲø], *a.* (*fem.* **-euse**) mangy, scabby.
rognon [rɔ'ɲɔ̃], *n.m.* kidney (*as food*).
rognure [rɔ'ɲy:r], *n.f.* a paring, a clipping; (*pl.*) scraps, refuse, leavings.
rogue [rɔg], *a.* arrogant, haughty.
roi [rwɑ], *n.m.* king.
roitelet [rwɑ'tlɛ], *n.m.* petty king; wren.
rôle [ro:l], *n.m.* roll; list, roster, catalogue; (*Theat.*) part, character.
romain [rɔ'mɛ̃], *a.* Roman.—*n.m.* (**Romain**, *fem.* **-aine**) Roman (*person*).
roman (1) [rɔ'mɑ̃], *a.* Romance, Romanic.
roman (2) [rɔ'mɑ̃], *n.m.* novel, romance, fiction.
romance [rɔ'mɑ̃:s], *n.f.* (*Mus.*) ballad, sentimental song.
romancier [rɔmɑ̃'sje], *n.m.* (*fem.* **-ière**) novelist.
romanesque [rɔma'nɛsk], *a.* romantic.—*n.m.* the romantic.
roman-feuilleton [rɔmɑ̃fœj'tɔ̃], *n.m.* (*pl.* **romans-feuilletons**) newspaper serial (story).
romantique [rɔmɑ̃'tik], *a.* romantic.—*n.* romanticist.
romantiquement [rɔmɑ̃tik'mɑ̃], *adv.* romantically.
romantisme [rɔmɑ̃'tism], *n.m.* (*Lit. Hist.*) romanticism.

romarin [rɔma'rɛ̃], *n.m.* rosemary.
rompre [rɔ̃:pr], *v.t.* (*see Verb Tables*) to break, to snap; to break off; to rout; to dissolve; to break in; to divert; to interrupt.—*v.i.* to break; to fall out. **se rompre**, *v.r.* to break off, to snap.
rompu [rɔ̃'py], *a.* broken, snapped; broken in.
romsteck [rɔm'stɛk], *n.m.* rump-steak.
ronce [rɔ̃:s], *n.f.* bramble, blackberry-bush.
ronceraie [rɔ̃s'rɛ], *n.f.* brake, brambly ground.
ronchonner [rɔ̃ʃɔ'ne], *v.i.* (*fam.*) to grumble.
rond [rɔ̃], *a.* round; plump, rotund; frank; even (*of money* or *accounts*).—*adv.* normally, true (*of motor*).—*n.m.* round, ring, orb, circle, disk.
ronde [rɔ̃:d], *n.f.* round; patrol; beat; (*Mus.*) semibreve; roundelay; round-hand (*writing*).
rondeau [rɔ̃'do], *n.m.* (*pl.* **-eaux**) rondeau (*French poem*); (*Mus.*) rondo; roller.
rondelet [rɔ̃'dlɛ], *a.* (*fem.* **-ette**) roundish, plump, podgy.
rondelle [rɔ̃'dɛl], *n.f.* rondelle, washer; rundle, ring.
rondement [rɔ̃d'mɑ̃], *adv.* roundly; briskly; frankly, bluntly.
rondeur [rɔ̃'dœ:r], *n.f.* roundness, rotundity; fullness; plain dealing.
rondin [rɔ̃'dɛ̃], *n.m.* round log; cudgel.
rond-point [rɔ̃'pwɛ̃], *n.m.* (*pl.* **ronds-points**) (*Arch.*) apsis; circus (*place where several roads etc. meet*), roundabout.
ronflant [rɔ̃'flɑ̃], *a.* snoring; humming, whirring; sonorous.
ronflement [rɔ̃flə'mɑ̃], *n.m.* snoring; roaring, rumbling; boom; snorting (*of horses*).
ronfler [rɔ̃'fle], *v.i.* to snore; to snort (*of horses*); to roar (*cannon, thunder etc.*); to boom; to peal (*organs*); to hum (*spinning-tops*).
ronfleur [rɔ̃'flœ:r], *n.m.* (*fem.* **-euse**) snorer.
rongeant [rɔ̃'ʒɑ̃], *a.* gnawing, corroding; (*fig.*) tormenting.
ronger [rɔ̃'ʒe], *v.t.* (*conjug. like* MANGER) to gnaw, to nibble; to consume, to corrode; to prey upon (*the mind etc.*); ***ronger son frein***, to champ the bit. **se ronger**, *v.r.* to fret.
rongeur [rɔ̃'ʒœ:r], *a.* (*fem.* **-euse**) gnawing, biting; corroding; consuming.—*n.m.* (*Zool.*) rodent.
ronron [rɔ̃'rɔ̃], *n.m.* purr, purring.
ronronner [rɔ̃rɔ'ne], *v.i.* to purr, to hum.
roquet [rɔ'kɛ], *n.m.* pug-dog; cur, mongrel.
rosace [ro'zas], *n.f.* (*Arch.*) rose; rose-window.
rosage [ro'za:ʒ], *n.m.* rhododendron; azalea.
rosaire [ro'zɛ:r], *n.m.* (*R.-C. Ch.*) rosary.
rosâtre [ro'zɑ:tr], *a.* pinkish.
rosbif [rɔs'bif], *n.m.* roast beef.
rose [ro:z], *a.* rosy; pink, rose-coloured.—*n.f.* rose; rose-window; ***rose trémière***, hollyhock.—*n.m.* rose-colour, pink.
rosé [ro'ze,] *a.* rosy, roseate; ***vin rosé***, light-red wine.
roseau [ro'zo], *n.m.* (*pl.* **-eaux**) reed.
rosée [ro'ze], *n.f.* dew.
roselière [rozə'ljɛ:r], *n.f.* reed-bed.
roséole [roze'ɔl], *n.f.* scarlet rash; German measles.
roser [ro'ze], *v.t.* to make pink.
roseraie [roz'rɛ], *n.f.* rosery, rose garden.
rosette [ro'zɛt], *n.f.* small rose; rosette.
rosier [ro'zje], *n.m.* rose-tree, rose-bush.
rosière [ro'zjɛ:r], *n.f.* rose-queen; queen of the May.
rosiériste [rozje'rist], *n.* rose-grower.
rosse [rɔs], *a.* bad, malicious.—*n.f.* jade, screw; (*fig.* and *fam.*) worthless *or* nasty person.
rossée [rɔ'se], *n.f.* shower of blows, thrashing.
rosser [rɔ'se], *v.t.* (*colloq.*) to thrash, to beat up.
rossignol [rɔsi'ɲɔl], *n.m.* nightingale; pick-lock, skeleton key; (*Carp.*) wedge; (*fig.*) unsaleable article (*in a shop*).
rot [ro], *n.m.* (*pop.*) belch, eructation.
rôt [ro], *n.m.* roast, roast meat.
rotarien [rɔta'rjɛ̃], *n.m.* member of a Rotary Club.
rotateur [rɔta'tœ:r], *a.* (*fem.* **-trice**) (*Anat.*) rotatory.—*n.m.* (*Anat.*) rotator.
rotatif [rɔta'tif], *a.* (*fem.* **-tive**) rotary.
rotation [rɔtɑ'sjɔ̃], *n.f.* rotation.
rotatoire [rɔta'twa:r], *a.* rotatory.
roter [rɔ'te], *v.i.* to belch.
rôti [ro'ti], *n.m.* roast, roast meat.
rôtie [ro'ti], *n.f.* slice of toast.
rôtir [ro'ti:r], *v.t., v.i.* to roast; to broil; to toast (*bread etc.*); (*fig.*) to parch.
rôtissage [roti'sa:ʒ], *n.m.* roasting.
rôtisserie [rotis'ri], *n.f.* cook-shop.
rôtisseur [roti'sœ:r], *n.m.* (*fem.* **-euse**) cook-shop keeper.
rôtissoire [roti'swa:r], *n.f.* roaster, Dutch oven.
rotonde [rɔ'tɔ̃:d], *n.f.* rotunda; long sleeveless cloak.
rotondité [rɔtɔ̃di'te], *n.f.* rotundity; plumpness.
rotor [rɔ'tɔ:r], *n.m.* rotor.
roturier [rɔty'rje], *a.* (*fem.* **-ière**) plebeian; vulgar, mean.—*n.m.* (*fem.* **-ière**) commoner.
rouage [rwa:ʒ], *n.m.* wheelwork; cog-wheel; machinery; (*Horol.*) movement.
rouan [rwɑ̃], *a.* (*fem.* **rouanne**) roan (*of horses, cattle etc.*).—*n.m.* roan horse.
roublard [ru'bla:r], *a.* and *n.m.* (*fem.* **-e**) (*fam.*) wily, crafty (person).
rouble [rubl], *n.m.* rouble (*Russian coin*).
roucoulement [rukul'mɑ̃], *n.m.* cooing; gurgling (*of babies*).
roucouler [ruku'le], *v.t., v.i.* to coo.
roue [ru], *n.f.* wheel; paddle-wheel; ***faire la roue***, to spread (out) its tail (*of peacocks etc.*); to show off; ***mettre*** or ***jeter des bâtons dans les roues***, to put spokes into the wheel (*of*).
roué [rwe], *a.* cunning, sharp, artful; exhausted.—*n.m.* rake, profligate; (*fem.* **-ée**) cunning or unscrupulous person.
rouelle [rwɛl], *n.f.* round slice (*meat*).
rouer [rwe], *v.t.* to break upon the wheel; ***rouer de coups***, to beat unmercifully.
rouerie [ru'ri], *n.f.* piece of knavery, trick, sharp practice.
rouet [rwɛ], *n.m.* spinning-wheel.
rouge [ru:ʒ], *a.* red; red-hot; bloodshot.—*n.m.* rouge; redness.—*n.* (*fam.*) left-winger, communist.
rougeâtre [ru'ʒa:tr], *a.* reddish.
rougeaud [ru'ʒo], *a.* (*colloq.*) red-faced, ruddy.—*n.m.* (*fem.* **-e**) red-faced person.

rouge-gorge [ruʒ'gɔrʒ], *n.m.* (*pl.* **rouges-gorges**) red-breast, robin redbreast.
rougeole [ru'ʒɔl], *n.f.* measles.
rougeoyer [ruʒwɑ'je], *v.i.* (*conjug. like* EMPLOYER) to turn red; to glow.
rouget [ru'ʒɛ], *a.* (*fem.* **-ette**) reddish.—*n.m.* (*Ichth.*) red mullet.
rougeur [ru'ʒœːr], *n.f.* redness; flush, glow, blush.
rougir [ru'ʒiːr], *v.t.* to redden, to tinge with red.—*v.i.* to redden, to grow red, to colour, to blush.
rouille [ruːj], *n.f.* rust, rustiness; (*Agric.*) mildew, blight.
rouillé [ru'je], *a.* rusty; blighted (*of corn*).
rouiller [ru'je], *v.t., v.i.* to rust; to blight; to impair. **se rouiller**, *v.r.* to rust; to grow rusty; to be impaired.
rouilleux [ru'jø], *a.* (*fem.* **-euse**) rust-coloured.
rouillure [ru'jyːr], *n.f.* rustiness; (*Agric.*) rust.
rouir [rwiːr], *v.t.* to steep, to soak, to ret.
rouissage [rwi'saːʒ], *n.m.* steeping, retting.
roulade [ru'lad], *n.f.* roll, rolling down; (*Mus.*) trill.
roulage [ru'laːʒ], *n.m.* rolling; haulage, carriage (*in wagons etc.*); road traffic.
roulant [ru'lɑ̃], *a.* rolling; travelling (*crane*); easy (*of roads*); (*Print.*) at work.
rouleau [ru'lo], *n.m.* (*pl.* **-eaux**) roll; roller; rolling-pin; coil (*rope*).
roulement [rul'mɑ̃], *n.m.* rolling, roll; rumbling, rattle; rotation; ***par roulement***, in rotation; ***roulement à billes***, ball-bearing.
rouler [ru'le], *v.t.* to roll; to roll up; to wind up; to revolve; (*colloq.*) to cheat; (*Golf*) ***coup roulé***, putt.—*v.i.* to roll, to roll along; to revolve; to ride (***en***); to ramble; to keep going. **se rouler**, *v.r.* to roll; to tumble, to wallow.
roulette [ru'lɛt], *n.f.* small wheel; roller, castor, truckle; roulette (*game*).
roulier [ru'lje], *a.* carrying (*trade*).—*n.m.* wagoner, carter, carrier.
roulis [ru'li], *n.m.* rolling, roll (*waves* or *ships*), lurch.
roulotte [ru'lɔt], *n.f.* gipsy-van; (*Motor.*) caravan.
roumain [ru'mɛ̃], *a.* Rumanian.—*n.m.* Rumanian (*language*); (**Roumain**, *fem.* **-aine**) Rumanian (*person*).
Roumanie [ruma'ni], **la**, *f.* Rumania.
roupie [ru'pi], *n.f.* rupee.
roupiller [rupi'je], *v.i.* (*colloq.*) to doze, to snooze.
rouquin [ru'kɛ̃], *a.* (*pop.*) ginger-haired, carroty-haired.
roussâtre [ru'sɑːtr], *a.* reddish, russet.
rousseur [ru'sœːr], *n.f.* redness.
roussi [ru'si], *a.* browned, scorched.—*n.m.* burnt smell; burning.
roussir [ru'siːr], *v.t., v.i.* to redden; to singe, to scorch; ***faire roussir***, to brown (*meat etc.*).
roussissage [rusi'saːʒ], **roussissement** [rusis'mɑ̃], *n.m.* reddening; browning; scorching.
routage [ru'taːʒ], *n.m.* sorting (*of mail*).
route [rut], *n.f.* road, way; route, path, course; track (*of a ship etc.*); highway.
router [ru'te], *v.t.* to sort (*mail*).
routier [ru'tje], *a.* (*fem.* **-ière**) of roads; ***carte routière***, road-map.—*n.m.* lorry-driver; (*fig.*) old hand; road racer (*cyclist*).
routine [ru'tin], *n.f.* routine, habit, practice.
routinier [ruti'nje], *a.* (*fem.* **-ière**) routine, following a routine.—*n.m.* (*fem.* **-ière**) person following a routine; stick-in-the-mud.
rouvrir [ru'vriːr], *v.t., v.i. irr.* (*conjug. like* OUVRIR) to reopen.
roux [ru], *a.* (*fem.* **rousse**) reddish; red-haired, sandy.—*n.m.* (*fem.* **rousse**) red-haired *or* sandy person.—*n.m.* reddish colour.
royal [rwɑ'jal], *a.* (*m. pl.* **-aux**) royal; regal, kingly.
royalement [rwɑjal'mɑ̃], *adv.* royally; regally.
royalisme [rwɑja'lism], *n.m.* royalism.
royaliste [rwɑja'list], *a.* and *n.* royalist.
royaume [rwɑ'joːm], *n.m.* kingdom, realm; ***le Royaume-Uni***, the United Kingdom.
royauté [rwɑjo'te], *n.f.* royalty, kingship, monarchy.
ruade [rɥad], *n.f.* kick (*by horse etc.*); lashing out.
Ruanda [RWANDA].
ruban [ry'bɑ̃], *n.m.* ribbon; (*fig.*) strip; tape.
rubané [ryba'ne], *a.* covered with ribbons.
rubaner [ryba'ne], *v.t.* to trim with ribbons; to cut into ribbons.
rubanerie [ryban'ri], *n.f.* ribbon-weaving; ribbon-trade.
rubéole [rybe'ɔl], *n.f.* rubeola, German measles.
rubescent [rybɛ'sɑ̃], *a.* reddish; growing red.
rubicond [rybi'kɔ̃], *a.* rubicund.
rubis [ry'bi], *n.m. inv.* ruby.
rubrique [ry'brik], *n.f.* red chalk; (*pl.*) rubric; (*fig.*) heading (*of article*).
ruche [ryʃ], *n.f.* hive; (*Needlework*) frilling, ruche.
ruchée [ry'ʃe], *n.f.* hiveful.
rucher (1) [ry'ʃe], *n.m.* stand *or* shed for bee-hives; apiary.
rucher (2) [ry'ʃe], *v.t.* (*Needlework*) to ruche, to frill.
rude [ryd], *a.* harsh, rough, rugged; violent; severe; uncouth; churlish; arduous, difficult.
rudement [ryd'mɑ̃], *adv.* roughly, harshly, severely, violently; (*pop.*) awfully, very.
rudesse [ry'dɛs], *n.f.* roughness, coarseness; ruggedness, uncouthness; harshness; unkindness.
rudiment [rydi'mɑ̃], *n.m.* rudiment; primer.
rudimentaire [rydimɑ̃'tɛːr], *a.* rudimentary.
rudoiement [rydwa'mɑ̃], *n.m.* bullying, brow-beating.
rudoyer [rydwa'je], *v.t.* (*conjug. like* EMPLOYER) to treat roughly; to bully, to ill-treat.
rue [ry], *n.f.* street; rue (*plant*).
ruée [rɥe], *n.f.* rush; onslaught.
ruelle [rɥɛl], *n.f.* lane, alley.
ruer [rɥe], *v.i.* to kick (*of horses etc.*). **se ruer**, *v.r.* to throw oneself, to rush (***sur***).
rugby [ryg'bi], *n.m.* rugby football, rugger.
rugir [ry'ʒiːr], *v.i.* to roar, to bellow.
rugissant [ryʒi'sɑ̃], *a.* roaring.
rugissement [ryʒis'mɑ̃], *n.m.* roaring, roar.
rugosite [rygɔzi'te], *n.f.* rugosity, roughness.
rugueux [ry'gø], *a.* (*fem.* **-euse**) rugose, rough.

ruine [rɥin], *n.f.* ruin; decay, destruction.
ruiner [rɥi'ne], *v.t.* to ruin, to lay waste; to destroy; to spoil. **se ruiner**, *v.r.* to ruin oneself; to fall into decay.
ruineux [rɥi'nø], *a.* (*fem.* **-euse**) ruinous.
ruisseau [rɥi'so], *n.m.* (*pl.* **-eaux**) brook, stream; gutter.
ruisselant [rɥi'slɑ̃], *a.* streaming, dripping.
ruisseler [rɥi'sle], *v.i.* (*conjug. like* APPELER) to run, to be very wet, to stream (with) (*de*).
rumeur [ry'mœ:r], *n.f.* clamour, uproar; (*fig.*) report, rumour.
ruminant [rymi'nɑ̃], *a.* ruminant, ruminating.—*n.m.* ruminant.
rumination [rymina'sjɔ̃], *n.f.* rumination (*chewing the cud*).
ruminer [rymi'ne], *v.t.* to ruminate on; (*fig.*) to think over.—*v.i.* to ruminate, to chew the cud; (*fig.*) to ponder, to muse.
rupture [ryp'ty:r], *n.f.* breaking, rupture; annulment; hernia.
rural [ry'ral], *a.* (*m. pl.* **-aux**) rural, rustic.
ruse [ry:z], *n.f.* guile, cunning; trick, wile ruse.
rusé [ry'ze], *a.* artful, crafty, sly.—*n.m.* (*fem.* **-ée**) artful, crafty *or* sly person.
ruser [ry'ze], *v.i.* to use deceit, craft *or* guile.
russe [rys], *a.* Russian.—*n.m.* Russian (*language*).—*n.* (**Russe**) Russian (*person*).
Russie [ry'si], **la,** *f.* Russia.
rustaud [rys'to], *a.* rustic, boorish, uncouth. —*n.m.* (*fem.* **-e**) rustic, clodhopper.
rusticité [rystisi'te], *n.f.* rusticity, simplicity.
rustique [rys'tik], *a.* rustic, rural; homely, simple.
rustiquement [rystik'mɑ̃], *adv.* rustically; boorishly, uncouthly.
rustre [rystr], *a.* boorish, rude.—*n.m.* boor, lout.
rutabaga [rytaba'ga], *n.m.* swede, Swedish turnip.
rutilant [ryti'lɑ̃], *a.* glowing, gleaming, rutilant.
rutiler [ryti'le], *v.i.* to glow, to gleam (*red*).
Rwanda, Ruanda [rwɑ̃'da], **le,** *m.* Rwanda.
rythme [ritm], *n.m.* rhythm.
rythmique [rit'mik], *a.* rhythmical.

S

S, s [ɛs], *n.m.* the nineteenth letter of the alphabet.
s' [s], *elision*, [SE].
sa [sa], [SON (1)].
sabbat [sa'ba], *n.m.* Sabbath.
sable [sɑ:bl], *n.m.* sand; gravel; (*Zool., Her.*) sable.
sablé [sɑ'ble], *a.* covered with sand *or* gravel.
sabler [sɑ'ble], *v.t.* to sand, to gravel; (*fig.*) to drink off.
sableux [sɑ'blø], *a.* (*fem.* **-euse**) sandy.
sablier [sɑbli'je], *n.m.* sand-glass, hour-glass; egg-timer.
sablière [sɑbli'jɛ:r], *n.f.* sand-pit; gravel-pit.
sablon [sɑ'blɔ̃], *n.m.* fine sand, scouring sand.
sablonner [sɑblɔ'ne], *v.t.* to scour with sand.
sablonneux [sɑblɔ'nø], *a.* (*fem.* **-euse**) sandy, gritty.
sablonnière [sɑblɔ'njɛ:r], *n.f.* sand-pit.
sabord [sa'bɔ:r], *n.m.* (*Naut.*) port-hole.
saborder [sabɔr'de], *v.t.* to scuttle.
sabot [sa'bo], *n.m.* sabot, clog; hoof (*of horse etc.*); drag (*of carriages*); ***dormir comme un sabot***, to sleep like a top.
sabotage [sabɔ'ta:ʒ], *n.m.* sabotage.
saboter [sabɔ'te], *v.t.* (*colloq.*) to bungle; to damage wilfully, to sabotage.
saboteur [sabɔ'tœ:r], *n.m.* (*fem.* **-euse**) bungler; saboteur.
sabotier [sabɔ'tje], *n.m.* (*fem.* **-ière**) sabot maker.
sabre [sɑ:br], *n.m.* sabre; broadsword.
sabrer [sɑ'bre], *v.t.* to strike *or* cut with a sabre, to sabre; (*colloq.*) to hurry over, to botch.
sabreur [sɑ'brœ:r], *n.m.* swashbuckler; (*colloq.*) botcher.
sac (1) [sak], *n.m.* sack, bag; pouch (*of certain animals*).
sac (2) [sak], *n.m.* sack (*plunder*), pillage.
saccade [sa'kad], *n.f.* jerk, jolt.
saccadé [saka'de], *a.* jerky, broken, abrupt; irregular.
saccader [saka'de], *v.t.* to jerk.
saccage [sa'ka:ʒ], *n.m.* upset, confusion; pillage.
saccager [saka'ʒe], *v.t.* (*conjug. like* MANGER) to sack, to plunder; (*fig.*) to play havoc with.
saccharine [saka'rin], *n.f.* saccharine.
sacerdoce [sasɛr'dɔs], *n.m.* priesthood.
sacerdotal [sasɛrdɔ'tal], *a.* (*m. pl.* **-aux**) sacerdotal.
sachée [sa'ʃe], *n.f.* sackful, bagful.
sachet [sa'ʃɛ], *n.m.* small bag, sachet.
sacoche [sa'kɔʃ], *n.f.* (*Mil.*) saddle-bag; money-bag; tool-bag.
sacramental [sakramɑ̃'tal] (*m. pl.* **-aux**), **sacramentel** [sakramɑ̃'tɛl] (*fem.* **-elle**), *a.* sacramental.
sacre [sakr], *n.m.* anointing and coronation of a king; consecration of a bishop.
sacré [sa'kre], *a.* holy, consecrated; sacred, inviolable.
sacrebleu! [sakrə'blø], *int.* confound it! curse it!
sacrement [sakrə'mɑ̃], *n.m.* sacrament, *esp.* matrimony.
sacrer [sa'kre], *v.t.* to anoint, to crown; to consecrate.—*v.i.* to curse and swear.
sacrificateur [sakrifika'tœ:r], *n.m.* (*fem.* **-trice**) sacrificer.
sacrificatoire [sakrifika'twa:r], *a.* sacrificial.
sacrifice [sakri'fis], *n.m.* sacrifice; renunciation.
sacrifier [sakri'fje], *v.t.* to sacrifice; to devote; to give up.—*v.i.* to sacrifice.
sacrilège [sakri'lɛ:ʒ], *a.* sacrilegious.—*n.m.* sacrilege.
sacrilègement [sakrilɛʒ'mɑ̃], *adv.* sacrilegiously.
sacripant [sakri'pɑ̃], *n.m.* rascal, scoundrel.
sacristain [sakris'tɛ̃], *n.m.* sacristan, sexton.
sacristie [sakris'ti], *n.f.* sacristy, vestry; church plate.
sacristine [sakris'tin], *n.f.* vestry-nun, sacristine.

sacro-saint [sakrɔ'sɛ̃], *a.* sacrosanct.
sadique [sa'dik], *a.* sadistic.—*n.* sadist.
sadisme [sa'dism], *n.m.* sadism.
saducéen [sadyse'ɛ̃], *a.* (*fem.* **-éenne**) Sadducean.—*n.m.* (*fem.* **-éenne**) Sadducee.
safran [sa'frɑ̃], *n.m.* saffron; crocus.
safrané [safra'ne], *a.* saffron-coloured.
saga [sa'ga], *n.f.* saga.
sagace [sa'gas], *a.* sagacious, shrewd.
sagacité [sagasi'te], *n.f.* sagacity.
sage [sa:ʒ], *a.* wise; sage, sensible, prudent; sober, well-behaved, good; virtuous, modest; gentle (*of animals*).—*n.m.* wise man, sage.
sage-femme [saʒ'fam], *n.f.* (*pl.* **sages-femmes**) midwife.
sagement [saʒ'mɑ̃] *adv.* wisely; prudently; soberly, steadily.
sagesse [sa'ʒɛs], *n.f.* wisdom; prudence; steadiness; chastity; good behaviour (*of children*); gentleness (*of animals*).
sagittaire [saʒi'tɛ:r], *n.m.* (*Rom. Ant.*) archer; (*Astron.*) Sagittarius.
sagou [sa'gu], *n.m.* sago.
sagouier [sagu'je] or (*preferably*) **sagoutier** [sagu'tje], *n.m.* sago-tree.
sagouin [sa'gwɛ̃], *n.m.* squirrel-monkey; (*fem.* **-e**) (*fig.*) slovenly fellow *or* woman.
Sahara [saa'ra], **le**, *m.* the Sahara.
saignant [sɛ'ɲɑ̃], *a.* bleeding, bloody; underdone (*of meat*).
saignée [sɛ'ɲe] *n.f.* blood-letting, phlebotomy; small of the arm; (*fig.*) drain on the purse.
saignement [sɛɲə'mɑ̃], *n.m.* bleeding.
saigner [sɛ'ɲe], *v.t.* to bleed; to stick (*an animal*); (*fig.*) to drain.—*v.i.* to bleed. **se saigner**, *v.r.* to bleed oneself; to drain oneself *or* one's purse.
saigneux [sɛ'ɲø], *a.* (*fem.* **-euse**) bloody.
saillant [sa'jɑ̃], *a.* jutting out, projecting; (*fig.*) striking, remarkable.—*n.m.* (*Fort.*) salient.
saillie [sa'ji], *n.f.* start, sudden spurt; sally; (*fig.*) witticism; projection.
saillir [sa'ji:r], *v.i.* to gush (*of liquids*); to ripple (*of muscles*).
sain [sɛ̃], *a.* hale, healthy; sound; sane; ***sain et sauf***, safe and sound.
saindoux [sɛ̃'du], *n.m. inv.* lard.
sainement [sɛn'mɑ̃], *adv.* wholesomely; healthily, soundly; judiciously.
sainfoin [sɛ̃'fwɛ̃], *n.m.* sainfoin.
saint [sɛ̃], *a.* holy, sacred; godly, saintly; sanctified, consecrated.—*n.m.* (*fem.* **-e**) saint; patron saint.
saintement [sɛ̃t'mɑ̃], *adv.* sacredly; piously, religiously.
sainteté [sɛ̃tə'te], *n.f.* holiness, sanctity, sacredness, saintliness; ***Sa Sainteté le Pape***, His Holiness the Pope.
saisi [sɛ'zi], *a.* seized, possessed, struck (***de***).
saisie [sɛ'zi], *n.f.* (*Law*) seizure; distraint, execution.
saisir [sɛ'zi:r], *v.t.* to seize, to take hold of; to understand; (*fig.*) to impress, to shock, to startle; to distrain. **se saisir**, *v.r.* to seize, to catch hold (***de***); to take possession (***de***); to arrest.
saisissable [sɛzi'sabl], *a.* distrainable, seizable.
saisissant [sɛzi'sɑ̃], *a.* keen, sharp, piercing (*of cold*); striking, impressive.
saisissement [sɛzis'mɑ̃], *n.m.* shock, violent impression, seizure.
saison [sɛ'zɔ̃], *n.f.* season; ***marchand des quatre saisons***, costermonger, barrow-boy.
saisonnier [sɛzɔ̃'nje], *a.* (*fem.* **-ière**) seasonal.
salade [sa'lad], *n.f.* salad, herb grown for salad; (*fig.*) medley, confusion.
saladier [sala'dje], *n.m.* salad-bowl.
salage [sa'la:ʒ], *n.m.* salting.
salaire [sa'lɛ:r], *n.m.* wages, pay, hire; reward.
salaison [salɛ'zɔ̃], *n.f.* salting; salt provisions; curing (*of bacon etc.*).
salamalec [salama'lɛk], *n.m.* (*used chiefly in pl.*) salaam; (*fig.*) exaggerated politeness.
salamandre [sala'mɑ̃:dr], *n.f.* salamander; slow-combustion stove.
salant [sa'lɑ̃], *a.m.* ***marais salant***, salt-marsh.
salarié [sala'rje], *a.* paid, wage-earning.—*n.m.* (*fem.* **-ée**) wage-earner.
salarier [sala'rje], *v.t.* to pay, to give wages to.
salaud [sa'lo], *n.m.* (*fem.* **-e**) (*pop.* and *rude*) sloven, dirty person, slut; ***quel salaud!*** dirty beast! dirty dog! bastard!
sale [sal], *a.* dirty; nasty, foul; coarse, obscene; squalid.
salé [sa'le], *a.* salted, salt; briny; (*fig.*) keen, biting; coarse; spicy.—*n.m.* salt pork; ***du petit salé***, pickled pork.
salement [sal'mɑ̃], *adv.* dirtily; nastily.
saler [sa'le], *v.t.* to salt; (*fig.*) to overcharge for; to fleece (*customers*).
saleté [sal'te], *n.f.* dirtiness, filthiness; filth, dirt; dirty trick; obscenity.
saleur [sa'lœ:r], *n.m.* (*fem.* **-euse**) salter, curer.
salière [sa'ljɛ:r], *n.f.* salt-cellar; salt-box; eye-pit (*in horses*).
salin [sa'lɛ̃], *a.* salt, saline, briny.—*n.m.* salt-works; salt-marsh.
saline [sa'lin], *n.f.* salt-marsh, salt-mine, salt-pit.
salinier [sali'nje], *n.m.* owner of salt-works; salt-worker *or* -vendor.
salique [sa'lik], *a.* ***loi salique***, Salic law.
salir [sa'li:r], *v.t.* to dirty, to soil; to taint, to sully. **se salir**, *v.r.* to get dirty; to sully one's reputation.
salissant [sali'sɑ̃], *a.* that soils *or* gets dirty easily; dirty (*of job, work etc.*).
salive [sa'li:v], *n.f.* saliva, spittle.
saliver [sali've], *v.i.* to salivate.
salle [sal], *n.f.* hall; large room; gallery (*of museum*); ward (*in hospitals*); (*Theat.*) house; ***salle à manger***, dining-room; ***salle d'attente***, waiting-room; ***salle de bain(s)***, bathroom; ***salle de spectacle***, playhouse.
saloir [sa'lwa:r], *n.m.* salt-box; salting-tub.
salon [sa'lɔ̃], *n.m.* drawing-room, parlour; lounge; saloon; exhibition (*art*); (*pl.*) world of fashion.
salopette [salɔ'pɛt], *n.f.* overall, dungarees.
salpêtrage [salpɛ'tra:ʒ], *n.m.* saltpetre-making; nitrification.
salpêtre [sal'pɛ:tr], *n.m.* saltpetre.
salpêtrer [salpɛ'tre], *v.t.* to cover with saltpetre.
salpêtrerie [salpɛtrə'ri], *n.f.* saltpetre-works.

salpêtreux [salpɛ'trø], *a.* (*fem.* **-euse**) saltpetrous.
salpêtrière [salpɛtri'jɛ:r], *n.f.* saltpetre-works.
salsepareille [salspa'rɛ:j], *n.f.* sarsaparilla.
saltimbanque [saltɛ̃'bɑ̃:k], *n.m.* mountebank, buffoon; (*fig.*) humbug.
salubre [sa'lybr], *a.* salubrious, healthy (*climate*).
salubrité [salybri'te], *n.f.* salubrity, healthfulness, wholesomeness.
saluer [sa'lɥe], *v.t.* to salute, to bow to; to greet; to cheer; to proclaim. **se saluer**, *v.r.* to bow to *or* salute each other.
salure [sa'ly:r], *n.f.* saltness, salinity.
salut [sa'ly], *n.m.* safety; salvation; welfare; escape; salutation, greeting; hail, cheers.
salutaire [saly'tɛ:r], *a.* salutary, advantageous, beneficial.
salutairement [salytɛr'mɑ̃], *adv.* beneficially.
salutation [salytɑ'sjɔ̃], *n.f.* salutation, greeting; (*pl.*) compliments.
Salvador [salva'dɔr], **le**, *m.* El Salvador.
salvadorègne [salvadɔ'rɛɲ], *a.* Salvadorean. —*n.* (**Salvadorègne**) Salvadorean (*person*).
salve [salv], *n.f.* salvo, volley; salute (*of artillery*).
samedi [sam'di], *n.m.* Saturday.
sanatorium [sanatɔ'rjɔm], *n.m.* sanatorium.
sanctifiant [sɑ̃kti'fjɑ̃], *a.* sanctifying.
sanctificateur [sɑ̃ktifika'tœ:r], *a.* (*fem.* **-trice**) sanctifying.—*n.m.* sanctifier.
sanctification [sɑ̃ktifikɑ'sjɔ̃], *n.f.* sanctification.
sanctifier [sɑ̃kti'fje], *v.t.* to sanctify, to hallow.
sanction [sɑ̃k'sjɔ̃], *n.f.* sanction; approbation; penalty.
sanctionner [sɑ̃ksjɔ'ne], *v.t.* to sanction, to approve; to penalize.
sanctuaire [sɑ̃k'tɥɛ:r], *n.m.* sanctuary (*of the temple etc.*), shrine; chancel (*of church*).
sandale [sɑ̃'dal], *n.f.* sandal; fencing-shoe.
sandalier [sɑ̃da'lje], *n.m.* sandal-maker.
sandow [sɑ̃'dɔf], *n.m.* chest-expander; rubber shock-absorber.
sandwich [sɑ̃'dwitʃ], *n.m.* (*pl.* **sandwichs** or **sandwiches**) sandwich.
sang [sɑ̃], *n.m.* blood; race; kindred; ***pur sang***, thoroughbred.
sang-froid [sɑ̃'frwɑ], *n.m.* coolness, composure, sang-froid.
sanglade [sɑ̃'glad], *n.f.* lash, cut (*with a whip*).
sanglant [sɑ̃'glɑ̃], *a.* bloody, bleeding; (*fig.*) biting, outrageous.
sangle [sɑ̃:gl], *n.f.* strap, belt; saddle-girth; ***lit de sangle***, camp-bed.
sangler [sɑ̃'gle], *v.t.* to girth, to strap; to lace too tightly; to deal (*a slashing blow*). **se sangler**, *v.r.* to lace oneself tightly.
sanglier [sɑ̃'glje], *n.m.* wild boar.
sanglot [sɑ̃'glo], *n.m.* sob.
sangloter [sɑ̃glɔ'te], *v.i.* to sob.
sang-mêlé [sɑ̃me'le], *n.m. inv.* half-caste.
sangsue [sɑ̃'sy], *n.f.* leech; (*fig.*) extortioner.
sanguin [sɑ̃'gɛ̃], *a.* of blood; full-blooded; blood-red.
sanguinaire [sɑ̃gi'nɛ:r], *a.* sanguinary bloody, blood-thirsty.
sanitaire [sani'tɛ:r], *a.* sanitary.
sans [sɑ̃], *prep.* without; free from; but for, had it not been for, were it not for; ***cela va sans dire***, of course; ***sans abri, sans gîte, sans logis***, homeless; ***sans cela***, otherwise; ***sans quoi***, otherwise.
sans-atout [sɑ̃za'tu], *n.m.* no trumps.
sans-cœur [sɑ̃'kœ:r], *n. inv.* heartless, unfeeling person.
sanscrit [sɑ̃s'kri], *n.m.* Sanskrit.
sans-façon, [sɑ̃fa'sɔ̃], *n.m.* bluntness; offhandedness.
sans-gêne [sɑ̃'ʒɛ:n], *n.m.* unceremoniousness, coolness; (*fam.*) cheek.
sansonnet [sɑ̃sɔ'nɛ], *n.m.* (*Orn.*) starling.
sans-patrie [sɑ̃pa'tri], *n. inv.* stateless person.
sans-souci [sɑ̃su'si], *a.* carefree, happy-go-lucky.—*n. inv.* (*colloq.*) carefree, easy-going person.—*n.m. inv.* free-and-easy manners.
sans-travail [sɑ̃tra'vaj], *n.m. inv.* ***les sans-travail***, the unemployed.
santal [sɑ̃'tal], *n.m.* (*pl.* **-als**) sandalwood, santal.
santé [sɑ̃'te], *n.f.* health, healthiness; state of health.
saoul [SOUL].
sape [sap], *n.f.* sapping, undermining; mine; trench.
saper [sa'pe], *v.t.* to sap, to undermine.
sapeur [sa'pœ:r], *n.m.* sapper.
sapeur-pompier [sapœrpɔ̃'pje], *n.m.* (*pl.* **sapeurs-pompiers**) fireman.
sapeur-télégraphiste [sapœrtelegra'fist], *n.m.* (*pl.* **sapeurs-télégraphistes**) soldier of the signal corps; (*pl.*) (*fam.*) signals.
saphir [sa'fi:r], *n.m.* sapphire.
sapin [sa'pɛ̃], *n.m.* fir, fir-tree; (***bois de***) ***sapin***, deal.
sapinette [sapi'nɛt], *n.f.* spruce.
sapinière [sapi'njɛ:r], *n.f.* fir wood, fir plantation.
sarabande [sara'bɑ̃:d], *n.f.* saraband (*dance*); (*fam.*) song-and-dance.
sarcasme [sar'kasm], *n.m.* sarcasm, sarcastic remark.
sarcastique [sarkas'tik], *a.* sarcastic.
sarcelle [sar'sɛl], *n.f.* (*Orn.*) teal.
sarclage [sar'kla:ʒ], *n.m.* weeding.
sarcler [sar'kle], *v.t.* to weed; to hoe; (*fig.*) to extirpate.
sarcleur [sar'klœ:r], *n.m.* (*fem.* **-euse**) weeder.
sarcloir [sar'klwa:r], *n.m.* hoe.
sarcophage (1) [sarkɔ'fa:ʒ], *n.m.* sarcophagus.
sarcophage (2) [sarkɔ'fa:ʒ], *n.f.* (*Ent.*) blow-fly.
Sardaigne [sar'dɛɲ], **la**, *f.* Sardinia.
sarde [sard], *a.* Sardinian.—*n.* (**Sarde**) Sardinian (*person*).
sardine [sar'din], *n.f.* sardine.
sardinerie [sardin'ri], *n.f.* sardine packing and curing factory.
sardinier [sardi'nje], *n.m.* (*fem.* **-ière**) sardine fisher; sardine packer *or* curer. —*n.m.* sardine-net; sardine-boat.
sardoine [sar'dwan], *n.f.* sardonyx.
sardonique [sardɔ'nik], *a.* sardonic.
sarigue [sa'rig], *n.* sarigue (*opossum*).
sarment [sar'mɑ̃], *n.m.* vine-shoot, vine-branch.
sarmenteux [sarmɑ̃'tø], *a.* (*fem.* **-euse** branchy, climbing; rambling (*of roses*).
sarrasin [sara'zɛ̃], *n.m.* buckwheat.

sarrau [sa'ro], *n.m.* (*pl.* **-aux**) smock-frock; child's blouse.
sas [sɑ], *n.m. inv.* sieve, screen; (*Naut.*) floating chamber (*of submarine*).
Satan [sa'tɑ̃], *m.* Satan.
satané [sata'ne], *a.* (*colloq.*) devilish, confounded.
satanique [sata'nik], *a.* satanic, diabolical.
sataniquement [satanik'mɑ̃], *adv.* fiendishly, diabolically.
satellite [satɛ'lit], *a.* satellite.—*n.m.* satellite.
satiété [sasje'te], *n.f.* satiety, repletion.
satin [sa'tɛ̃], *n.m.* satin.
satiné [sati'ne], *a.* satin-like, satiny; glazed (*of paper etc.*).
satiner [sati'ne], *v.t.* to satin; to glaze (*paper etc.*).—*v.i.* to look like satin.
satire [sa'ti:r], *n.f.* satire; lampoon.
satirique [sati'rik], *a.* satirical.—*n.m.* satirist.
satiriquement [satirik'mɑ̃], *adv.* satirically.
satiriser [satiri'ze], *v.t.* to satirize.
satisfaction [satisfak'sjɔ̃], *n.f.* satisfaction; gratification; atonement.
satisfaire [satis'fɛ:r], *v.t. irr.* (*conjug. like* FAIRE) to satisfy; to gratify; to answer; to give satisfaction to, to make amends to.—*v.i.* to be satisfactory (*à*); to fulfil (*à*). **se satisfaire**, *v.r.* to satisfy oneself, to indulge oneself.
satisfaisant [satisfə'zɑ̃], *a.* satisfactory.
satisfait [satis'fɛ], *a.* satisfied, contented, pleased.
saturant [saty'rɑ̃], *a.* saturating.
saturation [satyrɑ'sjɔ̃], *n.f.* saturation.
saturer [saty're], *v.t.* to saturate; (*fig.*) to surfeit.
saturnales [satyr'nal], *n.f. pl.* saturnalia.
Saturne [sa'tyrn], *m.* Saturn.
satyre [sa'ti:r], *n.m.* satyr.
sauce [so:s], *n.f.* sauce; ***sauce hollandaise***, egg yolks and melted butter.
saucé [so'se], *a.* soused, wet through.
saucer [so'se], *v.t.* (*conjug. like* COMMENCER) to dip in sauce; to sop, to souse.
saucière [so'sjɛ:r], *n.f.* sauce-boat.
saucisse [so'sis], *n.f.* (*fresh*) sausage.
saucisson [sosi'sɔ̃], *n.m.* large dry sausage; salami.
sauf (1) [sof], *a.* (*fem.* **sauve**) safe; unhurt, unscathed; ***sain et sauf***, safe and sound.
sauf (2) [sof], *prep.* save, except; unless.
sauf-conduit [sofkɔ̃'dɥi], *n.m.* (*pl.* **-conduits**) safe-conduct.
sauge [so:ʒ], *n.f.* sage (*herb*).
saugrenu [sogrə'ny], *a.* absurd, ridiculous, preposterous.
saulaie [so'lɛ], *n.f.* willow-grove.
saule [so:l], *n.m.* willow.
saumâtre [so'mɑ:tr], *a.* brackish, briny.
saumon [so'mɔ̃], *n.m.* salmon.
saumoné [somɔ'ne], *a.* salmon-coloured; ***truite saumonée***, salmon-trout.
saumurage [somy'ra:ʒ], *n.m.* pickling (*in brine*), brining.
saumure [so'my:r], *n.f.* brine, pickle.
saumuré [somy're], *a.* pickled, brined.
saunage [so'na:ʒ], *n.m.*, **saunaison** [sonɛ'zɔ̃], *n.f.* salt-making; salt-trade.
sauner [so'ne], *v.i.* to make salt.
saunerie [son'ri], *n.f.* saltworks.
saunier [so'nje], *n.m.* salt-maker; salt-merchant.
saunière [so'njɛ:r], *n.f.* salt-bin.
saupoudrage [sopu'dra:ʒ], *n.m.* salting; sprinkling, powdering.
saupoudrer [sopu'dre], *v.t.* to sprinkle with salt, pepper etc.; to powder, to sprinkle.
saur or **sor** [sɔ:r], *a.m.* smoked and salted; red (*of herrings*).
saure [sɔr], *a.* yellowish-brown; sorrel (*of horses*); red, smoked (*of herrings*).
saurer [so're], *v.t.* to smoke (*herrings*).
saurin [so'rɛ̃], *n.m.* freshly smoked herring, bloater.
saurisserie [soris'ri], *n.f.* kippering factory.
saut [so], *n.m.* leap, jump, hop, bound; ***de plein saut***, at once, suddenly; ***saut périlleux***, somersault.
sautage [so'ta:ʒ], *n.m.* exploding (*mines*).
saut-de-mouton [sodmu'tɔ̃], *n.m.* (*pl.* **sauts-de-mouton**) fly-over crossing.
saute [sot], *n.f.* (*Naut.*) sudden shift *or* change (*of wind*).
sauté [so'te], *a.* fried, tossed in the pan.
saute-mouton [sotmu'tɔ̃], *n.m.* leap-frog (*game*).
sauter [so'te], *v.t.* to leap over; to leave out, to skip; to toss in the pan.—*v.i.* to leap, to jump; to explode; to spring; to blow out (*of fuse*).
sauterelle [so'trɛl], *n.f.* grasshopper, locust.
sauterie [sot'ri], *n.f.* (*fam.*) informal dance, hop.
saute-ruisseau [sotrɥi'so], *n.m. inv.* messenger-boy (*in offices*).
sauteur [so'tœ:r], *a.* (*fem.* **-euse**) jumping, leaping.—*n.m.* (*fem.* **-euse**) leaper, jumper; vaulter.
sautillant [soti'jɑ̃], *a.* hopping, skipping.
sautiller [soti'je], *v.i.* to hop, to skip, to jump about.
sautoir [so'twa:r], *n.m.* Saint Andrew's cross; watch-guard.
sauvage [so'va:ʒ], *a.* savage, wild; uncivilized; brutal; shy; unsociable.—*n.* savage; unsociable person.
sauvagement [sovaʒ'mɑ̃], *adv.* wildly, savagely; barbarously, fiercely.
sauvageon [sova'ʒɔ̃], *n.m.* (*Agric.*) wild stock (*for grafting*); briar (*of roses*).
sauvagerie [sova'ʒri], *n.f.* unsociableness; shyness; wildness.
sauvagesse [sova'ʒɛs], *n.f.* uncivilized woman; hoyden.
sauvagin [sova'ʒɛ̃], *a.* fishy (*in taste, smell, etc.*).—*n.m.* fishy taste *or* smell.—*n.f.* (**-e**) wild waterfowl.
sauvegarde [sov'gard], *n.f.* safe-keeping, safeguard; safe-conduct; (*Naut.*) life-line.
sauvegarder [sovgar'de], *v.t.* to watch over, to protect, to safeguard.
sauve-qui-peut [sovki'pø], *n.m. inv.* headlong flight, stampede; every man for himself.
sauver [so've], *v.t.* to save, to rescue; to preserve; to exempt; to conceal. **se sauver**, *v.r.* to escape, to make off; (*fam.*) to abscond; to take refuge.
sauvetage [sov'ta:ʒ], *n.m.* salvage; life-saving, rescue; ***appareil de sauvetage***, rescue apparatus, fire-escape; ***bouée de***

sauvetage, life-buoy; ***canot de sauvetage***, life-boat; ***ceinture de sauvetage***, life-belt.
sauveteur [sov'tœ:r], *n.m.* rescuer, lifeboatman.
sauveur [so'vœ:r], *a.* saving, redeeming.—*n.m.* saver, deliverer; Saviour.
savamment [sava'mɑ̃], *adv.* learnedly; knowingly.
savane [sa'van], *n.f.* savanna; (*C*) swamp.
savant [sa'vɑ̃], *a.* learned, expert (***en***); scholarly; clever.—*n.m.* (*fem.* **-e**) scholar, scientist.
savarin [sava'rɛ̃], *n.m.* round, hollow cake.
savate [sa'vat], *n.f.* old shoe; clumsy person.
savetier [sav'tje], *n.m.* cobbler; (*fig.*) bungler.
saveur [sa'vœ:r], *n.f.* savour, flavour, relish.
savoir [sa'vwa:r], *v.t. irr.* to know, to be aware of; to understand; to know how (*can*), to be able. **se savoir**, *v.r.* to get known.—*n.m.* knowledge, learning, scholarship.
savoir-faire [savwar'fɛ:r], *n.m.* tact; savoir-faire; cleverness.
savoir-vivre [savwar'vi:vr], *n.m.* good manners, good breeding.
savon [sa'vɔ̃], *n.m.* soap; (*colloq.*) scolding.
savonnage [savɔ'na:ʒ], *n.m.* soaping, washing with soap.
savonner [savɔ'ne], *v.t.* to soap; to lather; (*colloq.*) to scold. **se savonner**, *v.r.* to be washable, to wash (*of fabrics*); to lather (*oneself*).
savonnerie [savɔn'ri], *n.f.* soap-manufacture; soap-trade; soap-works.
savonnette [savɔ'nɛt], *n.f.* cake of toilet soap.
savonneux [savɔ'nø], *a.* (*fem.* **-euse**) soapy.
savourer [savu're], *v.t.* to savour, to relish; (*fig.*) to enjoy.
savoureusement [savurøz'mɑ̃], *adv.* with relish.
savoureux [savu'rø], *a.* (*fem.* **-euse**) savoury, tasty (*dish*); racy (*story*).
savoyard [savwa'ja:r], *a.* of Savoy.—*n.m.* (**Savoyard**, *fem.* **-arde**) Savoyard (*person*); ***petit Savoyard***, little chimney-sweep.
saxifrage [saksi'fra:ʒ], *a.* saxifragous.—*n.f.* saxifrage.
saxon [sak'sɔ̃], *a.* (*fem.* **-onne**) Saxon.—*n.m.* (**Saxon**, *fem.* **-onne**) Saxon (*person*).
saxophone [saksɔ'fɔn], *n.m.* saxophone.
saynète [sɛ'nɛt], *n.f.* playlet, sketch.
scabieux [ska'bjø], *a.* (*fem.* **-euse**) scabious, scabby.—*n.f.* (**-euse**) scabious (*plant*).
scabreux [ska'brø], *a.* (*fem.* **-euse**) scabrous, rugged, rough; (*fig.*) dangerous, difficult, ticklish; improper.
scalp [skalp], *n.m.* scalp (*of an enemy*).
scalpel [skal'pɛl], *n.m.* scalpel.
scalper [skal'pe], *v.t.* to scalp.
scandale [skɑ̃'dal], *n.m.* scandal; shame, dismay, disgust.
scandaleusement [skɑ̃daløz'mɑ̃], *adv.* scandalously.
scandaleux [skɑ̃da'lø], *a.* (*fem.* **-euse**) scandalous.
scandaliser [skɑ̃dali'ze], *v.t.* to scandalize, to shock. **se scandaliser**, *v.r.* to be shocked.
scander [skɑ̃'de], *v.t.* to scan; to stress (*a phrase*).
scandinave [skɑ̃di'na:v], *a.* Scandinavian.—*n.* (**Scandinave**) Scandinavian (*person*).
Scandinavie [skɑ̃dina'vi], **la**, *f.* Scandinavia.
scansion [skɑ̃'sjɔ̃], *n.f.* scansion.
scaphandre [ska'fɑ̃:dr], *n.m.* diving-suit.
scaphandrier [skafɑ̃dri'je], *n.m.* diver.
scapulaire [skapy'lɛ:r], *a.* and *n.m.* scapular.
scarabée [skara'be], *n.m.* scarabaeus (*beetle*); scarab.
scarlatine [skarla'tin], *a.* and *n.f.* (***fièvre***) ***scarlatine***, scarlet fever.
sceau [so], *n.m.* (*pl.* **sceaux**) seal; (*fig.*) sanction; ***mettre le sceau à***, to seal, (*fig.*) to complete.
scélérat [sele'ra], *a.* wicked, villainous, criminal, vile.—*n.m.* (*fem.* **-e**) scoundrel, villain, miscreant, jade.
scélératesse [selera'tɛs], *n.f.* villainy.
scellé [sɛ'le], *n.m.* seal.
scellement [sɛl'mɑ̃], *n.m.* sealing; fastening.
sceller [se'le], *v.t.* to put an official seal on, to seal; (*Build.*) to fasten; (*fig.*) to ratify.
scénario [sena'rjo], *n.m.* (*pl.* **scénarios** or **scénarii**) scenario (*of ballet etc.*); film script.
scénariste [sena'rist], *n.* script-writer, scenario-writer.
scène [sɛ:n], *n.f.* stage; scenery; (*colloq.*) scene, quarrel.
scénique [se'nik], *a.* scenic, theatrical; ***indications scéniques***, stage directions.
scepticisme [sɛpti'sism], *n.m.* scepticism.
sceptique [sɛp'tik], *a.* sceptical.—*n.* sceptic.
sceptre [sɛptr], *n.m.* sceptre; (*fig.*) sway, dominion.
schah [ʃa], *n.m.* shah (*of Persia*).
scheik or **cheik** [ʃɛk], *n.m.* sheik.
schéma [ʃe'ma], **schème** [ʃɛm], *n.m.* diagram; rough sketch.
schématique [ʃema'tik], *a.* diagrammatic; ***dessin schématique***, draft, diagram.
schibboleth [ʃibɔ'lɛt], *n.m.* catchword, shibboleth.
schisme [ʃism], *n.m.* schism.
schiste [ʃist], *n.m.* schist, slaty rock, shale.
schizophrène [skizɔ'frɛn], *a.* and *n.* schizophrenic.
schizophrénie [skizɔfre'ni], *n.f.* schizophrenia.
schnorkel [ʃnɔr'kɛl], *n.m.* schnorkel, submarine's air-tube.
schooner [sku'nœ:r], *n.m.* schooner.
sciage [sja:ʒ], *n.m.* sawing.
sciatique [sja'tik], *a.* sciatic.—*n.m.* sciatic nerve.—*n.f.* sciatica.
scie [si], *n.f.* saw; (*pop.*) bore, nuisance.
sciemment [sja'mɑ̃], *adv.* wittingly, knowingly.
science [sjɑ̃:s], *n.f.* science, knowledge, learning; skill.
scientifique [sjɑ̃ti'fik], *a.* scientific.
scientifiquement [sjɑ̃tifik'mɑ̃], *adv.* scientifically.
scier [sje], *v.t.* to saw; to cut down.—*v.i.* (*Row.*) to back water.
scierie [si'ri], *n.f.* sawmill.
scieur [sjœ:r], *n.m.* sawyer.
scinder [sɛ̃'de], *v.t.* to divide, to split up.
scintillant [sɛ̃ti'jɑ̃], *a.* scintillating; twinkling.
scintillation [sɛ̃tija'sjɔ̃], *n.f.*, **scintillement** [sɛ̃tij'mɑ̃], *n.m.* scintillation, sparkling; twinkling.
scintiller [sɛ̃ti'je], *v.i.* to scintillate, to sparkle; to twinkle (*of star*); to flicker.

scion [sjø], *n.m.* scion, shoot.

scission [si'sjɔ̃], *n.f.* scission; split, secession.

scissure [si'sy:r], *n.f.* fissure, crack, cleft.

sciure [sjy:r], *n.f.* ***sciure de bois,*** sawdust.

sclérose [skle'ro:z], *n.f.* sclerosis.

scolaire [skɔ'lɛ:r], *a.* of schools; ***année scolaire,*** school year.

scolarité [skɔlari'te], *n.f.* course of study; school attendance.

scolastique [skɔlas'tik], *a.* scholastic.—*n.m.* scholastic; schoolman.—*n.f.* scholasticism.

scolastiquement [skɔlastik'mɑ̃], *adv.* scholastically.

scooter [sku'tɛ:r], *n.m.* motor-scooter; ***autos scooters,*** dodgems.

scorbut [skɔr'byt], *n.m.* scurvy.

scorbutique [skɔrby'tik], *a.* and *n.* scorbutic.

scorie [skɔ'ri], *n.f.* scoria, slag, dross.

scorifier [skɔri'fje], *v.t.* to scorify.

scorpion [skɔr'pjɔ̃], *n.m.* scorpion.

scout [skut], *a.* of scouting.—*n.m.* (boy) scout.

scoutisme [sku'tism], *n.m.* scouting, boy-scout movement.

scratch [skratʃ], *n.m.* (*Spt.*) ***être*** or ***partir scratch,*** to start at scratch.

scratcher [skrat'ʃe], *v.t.* (*Spt.*) to scratch (*horse, competitor etc.*).

scribe [skrib], *n.m.* scribe; copyist.

script [skript], *n.m.* script (*film* or *play*).

scriptural [skripty'ral], *a.* (*m. pl.* **-aux**) scriptural.

scrofule [skrɔ'fyl], *n.f.* scrofula, king's evil.

scrofuleux [skrɔfy'lø], *a.* and *n.m.* (*fem.* **-euse**) scrofulous (person).

scrupule [skry'pyl], *n.m.* scruple, qualm, doubt; scrupulousness.

scrupuleusement [skrypyløz'mɑ̃], *adv.* scrupulously.

scrupuleux [skrypy'lø], *a.* (*fem.* **-euse**) scrupulous, strict, punctilious.

scrutateur [skryta'tœ:r], *a.* (*fem.* **-trice**) searching, scrutinizing.—*n.m.* (*fem.* **-trice**) investigator, scrutinizer; scrutineer, teller (*of a ballot etc.*).

scruter [skry'te], *v.t.* to scrutinize, to investigate.

scrutin [skry'tɛ̃], *n.m.* ballot, balloting, poll.

sculpter [skyl'te], *v.t.* to sculpture, to carve.

sculpteur [skyl'tœ:r], *n.m.* sculptor, carver.

sculptural [skylty'ral], *a.* (*m. pl.* **-aux**) sculptural.

sculpture [skyl'ty:r], *n.f.* sculpture, carving.

se [sə], **s'** [s], *pron. inv.* oneself, himself, herself, itself, themselves; to oneself etc.; one another, each other; ***cela se peut,*** that may be.

séance [se'ɑ̃:s], *n.f.* seat (*right to sit*); session, duration, meeting; sitting (*for one's portrait etc.*); seance; ***être en séance,*** to be in session; ***lever la séance,*** to close the meeting; ***séance tenante,*** there and then, forthwith.

séant [se'ɑ̃], *a.* sitting; fitting, seemly, becoming.—*n.m.* sitting posture; seat.

seau [so], *n.m.* (*pl.* **seaux**) pail, bucket.

sébile [se'bil], *n.f.* small wooden bowl (*used by beggars*); pan (*in gold-mining*).

sec [sɛk], *a.* (*fem.* **sèche**) dry, arid; withered; lean; plain; unfeeling, sharp; ***à pied sec,*** dry-shod; ***coup sec,*** sharp stroke; ***perte sèche,*** dead loss.—*n.m.* dryness.—*adv.* dryly, sharply.

sécateur [seka'tœ:r], *n.m.* (*Gard.*) pruning-shears; secateurs.

seccotine [sɛkɔ'tin], *n.f.* (*reg. trade mark*) Seccotine.

sécession [sesɛ'sjɔ̃], *n.f.* secession.

séchage [se'ʃa:ʒ], *n.m.* drying.

sèchement [sɛʃ'mɑ̃], *adv.* dryly; curtly.

sécher [se'ʃe], *v.t.* (*conjug. like* CÉDER) to dry; to dry up; to cure.—*v.i.* to dry; to wither; to pine away. **se sécher,** *v.r.* to dry oneself; to dry (*of a thing*).

sécheresse [se'ʃrɛs], *n.f.* dryness; drought; (*fig.*) sharpness.

séchoir [se'ʃwa:r], *n.m.* drying-room; clothes-horse; clothes-airer; hair-dryer.

second [sə'gɔ̃, zgɔ̃], *a.* second.—*n.m.* (*fem.* **-e**) second, assistant.—*n.m.* second floor.—*n.f.* (**-e**) second class; (*Sch.*) fifth form; second (*of time*).

secondaire [səgɔ̃'dɛ:r], *a.* secondary; accessory.

secondairement [səgɔ̃dɛr'mɑ̃], *adv.* secondarily.

secondement [səgɔ̃d'mɑ̃], *adv.* secondly.

seconder [səgɔ̃'de], *v.t.* to second, to assist; to back (up), to support; to promote.

secouement [səku'mɑ̃], **secouage** [sə'kwa:ʒ], *n.m.* shaking, jogging, jolting.

secouer [sə'kwe], *v.t.* to shake, to jolt; to shake off; to shock; to rouse. **se secouer,** *v.r.* to shake oneself, to bestir oneself.

secourable [səku'rabl], *a.* helpful, helping; relievable.

secourir [səku'ri:r], *v.t. irr.* (*conjug. like* COURIR) to succour, to assist, to help, to relieve.

secourisme [səku'rism], *n.m.* first-aid.

secouriste [səku'rist], *n.* qualified first-aider.

secours [sə'ku:r], *n.m.* help, assistance, aid, succour; rescue; ***appeler police secours,*** to dial 999; ***au secours !*** help!

secousse [sə'kus], *n.f.* shake, shock; blow, concussion; jerk, jolt.

secret [sə'krɛ], *a.* (*fem.* **-ète**) secret, private, hidden; reserved.—*n.m.* secret; secrecy privacy, mystery.

secrétaire [səkre'tɛ:r], *n.* secretary.—*n.m.* writing-desk.

secrétariat [səkreta'rja], *n.m.* secretaryship; secretary's office; secretariat.

secrètement [səkrɛt'mɑ̃], *adv.* secretly, in secret, inwardly.

sécréter [sekre'te], *v.t.* (*conjug. like* CÉDER) to secrete (*of glands etc.*).

sécréteur [sekre'tœ:r], *a.* (*fem.* **-euse** or **-trice**) secretory.

sécrétion [sekre'sjɔ̃], *n.f.* secretion.

sectaire [sɛk'tɛ:r], *a.* sectarian.—*n.* sectary.

sectateur [sɛkta'tœ:r], *n.m.* (*fem.* **-trice**) follower, votary.

secte [sɛkt], *n.f.* sect.

secteur [sɛk'tœ:r], *n.m.* sector, section; district.

section [sɛk'sjɔ̃], *n.f.* section; division.

sectionnement [sɛksjɔn'mɑ̃], *n.m.* division into parts.

sectionner [sɛksjɔ'ne], *v.t.* to divide into sections; to cut off.

séculaire [seky'lɛ:r], *a.* secular, coming once in a century; ancient; time-honoured.

séculier [seky'lje], *a.* (*fem.* **-ière**) secular, lay; temporal, worldly.—*n.m.* layman.
secundo [səgɔ̃'do], *adv.* secondly.
sécurité [sekyri'te], *n.f.* security, safety.
sédatif [seda'tif], *a.* (*fem.* **-tive**) and *n.m.* sedative.
sédentaire [sedɑ̃'tɛːr], *a.* sedentary; settled, stationary.
sédiment [sedi'mɑ̃], *n.m.* sediment.
sédimentaire [sedimɑ̃'tɛːr], *a.* sedimentary.
séditieusement [sedisjøz'mɑ̃], *adv.* seditiously.
séditieux [sedi'sjø], *a.* (*fem.* **-euse**) seditious; mutinous.—*n.m.* rebel, mutineer.
sédition [sedi'sjɔ̃], *n.f.* sedition, mutiny, riot.
séducteur [sedyk'tœːr], *a.* (*fem.* **-trice**) seductive; enticing, alluring.—*n.m.* (*fem.* **-trice**) seducer, enticer.
séduction [sedyk'sjɔ̃], *n.f.* seduction; allurement; bribing.
séduire [se'dɥiːr], *v.t. irr.* (*conjug. like* CONDUIRE) to seduce; to beguile; to charm; to fascinate; to bribe.
séduisant [sedɥi'zɑ̃], *a.* seductive, alluring; fascinating; tempting.
segment [sɛg'mɑ̃], *n.m.* segment.
ségrégation [segregɑ'sjɔ̃], *n.f.* segregation.
seigle [sɛgl], *n.m.* rye.
seigneur [sɛ'ɲœːr], *n.m.* lord; lord of the manor, squire; nobleman; ***le Seigneur***, the Lord.
seigneurial [sɛɲœ'rjal], *a.* (*m. pl.* **-aux**) manorial; lordly.
seigneurie [sɛɲœ'ri], *n.f.* lordship; manor.
sein [sɛ̃], *n.m.* breast, bosom; (*fig.*) heart, midst; womb.
seine [sɛːn], *n.f.* seine, (fishing-) net.
séisme [se'ism], *n.m.* earthquake.
seize [sɛːz], *a.* and *n.m.* sixteen, sixteenth.
seizième [sɛ'zjɛm], *a.* and *n.* sixteenth.
séjour [se'ʒuːr], *n.m.* stay, abode, sojourn; place where one sojourns.
séjourner [seʒur'ne], *v.i.* to stay, to sojourn.
sel [sɛl], *n.m.* salt; (*fig.*) wit, pungency; (*pl.*) smelling-salts.
sélecteur [selɛk'tœːr], *a.* (*fem.* **-trice**) selecting; selective.
sélection [selɛk'sjɔ̃], *n.f.* selection.
sélectivité [selɛktivi'te], *n.f.* selectivity.
sellage [sɛ'laːʒ], *n.m.* saddling.
selle [sɛl], *n.f.* saddle; motion of the bowels.
seller [sɛ'le], *v.t.* to saddle.
sellerie [sɛl'ri], *n.f.* saddlery; harness-room.
sellette [sɛ'lɛt], *n.f.* stool of repentance; shoeblack's box; (*Naut.*) slung cradle.
sellier [sɛ'lje], *n.m.* saddler.
selon [sə'lɔ̃], *prep.* according to; ***c'est selon***, that depends; ***selon moi***, in my opinion; ***selon que***, according as.
semailles [sə'mɑːj], *n.f. pl.* seeds; sowing; sowing-time.
semaine [sə'mɛn], *n.f.* week; week's work; week's money.
semainier [səmɛ'nje], *n.m.* (*fem.* **-ière**) person on duty for the week.—*n.m.* (*Ind.*) time-sheet; weekly output.
sémaphore [sema'fɔːr], *n.m.* semaphore, signal-post.
semblable [sɑ̃'blabl], *a.* like, similar, alike.—*n.* like; fellow, match, equal.—*n.m.* fellow-creature.
semblablement [sɑ̃blablə'mɑ̃], *adv.* likewise, also.
semblant [sɑ̃'blɑ̃], *n.m.* appearance, semblance, look; pretence; ***faire semblant***, to pretend.
sembler [sɑ̃'ble], *v.i.* to seem, to appear.
semé [sə'me], *a.* sowed, sown; strewn (***de***).
semelle [sə'mɛl], *n.f.* sole (*of boots, shoes etc.*); foot (*of stockings*); length of a foot.
semence [sə'mɑ̃ːs], *n.f.* seed; semen; (*fig.*) cause.
semer [sə'me], *v.t.* (*conjug. like* AMENER) to sow; to scatter, to strew, to sprinkle.
semestre [sə'mɛstr], *n.m.* half-year, six months.
semestriel [səmɛstri'ɛl], *a.* (*fem.* **-elle**) half-yearly.
semeur [sə'mœːr], *n.m.* (*fem.* **-euse**) sower; (*fig.*) disseminator.
semi-circulaire [səmisirky'lɛːr], *a.* semi-circular.
sémillance [semi'jɑ̃ːs], *n.f.* sprightliness, liveliness.
sémillant [semi'jɑ̃], *a.* brisk, lively, sprightly.
semi-mensuel [səmimɑ̃'sɥɛl], *a.* (*fem.* **-elle**) fortnightly.
séminaire [semi'nɛːr], *n.m.* seminary, theological college; specialized course.
semis [sə'mi], *n.m.* sowing; seed-bed; seedlings.
sémitique [semi'tik], *a.* Semitic.
sémitisme [semi'tism], *n.m.* Semitism.
semi-ton [səmi'tɔ̃], *n.m.* (*pl.* **-tons**) semitone.
semoir [sə'mwaːr], *n.m.* seed-bag; seed-drill.
semonce [sə'mɔ̃ːs], *n.f.* rebuke, reprimand, lecture.
semoncer [səmɔ̃'se], *v.t.* (*conjug. like* COMMENCER) to reprimand, to lecture.
semoule [sə'mul], *n.f.* semolina.
sempiternel [sɛ̃pitɛr'nɛl], *a.* (*fem.* **-elle**) sempiternal, everlasting.
sénat [se'na], *n.m.* senate; senate-house.
sénateur [sena'tœːr], *n.m.* senator.
sénatorial [senatɔ'rjal], *a.* (*m. pl.* **-aux**) senatorial.
séné [se'ne], *n.m.* senna.
seneçon [sən'sɔ̃], *n.m.* groundsel.
Sénégal [sene'gal], **le**, *m.* Senegal.
sénégalais [senega'lɛ], *a.* Senegalese.—*n.m.* (**Sénégalais**, *fem.* **-aise**) Senegalese (*person*).
Sénèque [se'nɛk], *m.* Seneca.
***sénestre** [se'nɛstr], **senestre** [sə'nɛstr], *a.* left, (*Her.*) sinister.
sénile [se'nil], *a.* senile.
sénilité [senili'te], *n.f.* senility, old age.
senne [sɛn], [SEINE].
sens [sɑ̃ːs], *n.m. inv.* sense; senses, feelings; intelligence; consciousness; meaning; opinion; way, direction; ***à contre-sens***, in a wrong sense; ***à double sens***, with double meaning; ***sens dessus dessous***, upside down; ***sens interdit***, no entry.
sensation [sɑ̃sɑ'sjɔ̃], *n.f.* sensation, feeling.
sensationnel [sɑ̃sasjɔ'nɛl], *a.* (*fem.* **-elle**) sensational.
sensé [sɑ̃'se], *a.* sensible, intelligent.
sensément [sɑ̃se'mɑ̃], *adv.* sensibly, judiciously.
sensibilité [sɑ̃sibili'te], *n.f.* sensibility, sensitiveness, feeling; compassion.

sensible [sɑ̃'sibl], *a.* sensitive, susceptible, sympathetic; tender, sore (*skin etc.*); perceptible, noticeable, tangible.
sensiblement [sɑ̃siblə'mɑ̃], *adv.* appreciably; feelingly, deeply; obviously; considerably.
sensiblerie [sɑ̃siblə'ri], *n.f.* sentimentality; (*fam.*) sob-stuff.
sensitif [sɑ̃si'tif], *a.* (*fem.* **-tive**) sensitive; sensory.—*n.f.* (**-tive**) sensitive plant.
sensitivité [sɑ̃sitivi'te], *n.f.* sensitivity.
sensualiste [sɑ̃sɥa'list], *a.* sensual.—*n.* sensualist.
sensualité [sɑ̃sɥali'te], *n.f.* sensuality.
sensuel [sɑ̃'sɥɛl], *a.* (*fem.* **-elle**) sensual.—*n.m.* (*fem.* **-elle**) sensualist.
sensuellement [sɑ̃sɥɛl'mɑ̃], *adv.* sensually.
sentence [sɑ̃'tɑ̃:s], *n.f.* maxim; sentence, judgment, verdict.
sentencieusement [sɑ̃tɑ̃sjøz'mɑ̃], *adv.* sententiously.
sentencieux [sɑ̃tɑ̃'sjø], *a.* (*fem.* **-euse**) sententious.
senteur [sɑ̃'tœ:r], *n.f.* smell; scent, perfume; ***pois de senteur***, sweet pea.
senti [sɑ̃'ti], *a.* felt, experienced.
sentier [sɑ̃'tje], *n.m.* path, footpath; ***sentier battu***, beaten track.
sentiment [sɑ̃ti'mɑ̃], *n.m.* feeling; sensation; sentiment; affection, *esp.* love; perception, sense; opinion.
sentimental [sɑ̃timɑ̃'tal], *a.* (*m. pl.* **-aux**) sentimental.
sentimentalement [sɑ̃timɑ̃tal'mɑ̃], *adv.* sentimentally.
sentimentaliste [sɑ̃timɑ̃ta'list], *n.* sentimentalist.
sentimentalité [sɑ̃timɑ̃tali'te], *n.f.* sentimentality.
sentinelle [sɑ̃ti'nɛl], *n.f.* sentinel, sentry.
sentir [sɑ̃'ti:r], *v.t. irr.* to feel; to guess; to perceive; to smell; to savour of; to seem.—*v.i.* to smell. **se sentir**, *v.r.* to feel oneself, to feel; to be conscious; to feel the effects (*de*); to be perceived, felt etc.
seoir (1) [swa:r], *v.i. irr.* (*only used in pres. p.* **séant** *and p.p.* **sis**) to sit, to be sitting.
seoir (2) [swa:r], *v.i. irr.* (*pres. p.* **seyant**, *no p.p.*) to suit, to become.
Séoudite [seu'dit], [ARABIE].
séparable [sepa'rabl], *a.* separable.
séparation [separɑ'sjɔ̃], *n.f.* separation, parting.
séparé [sepa're], *a.* separate; distinct.
séparément [separe'mɑ̃], *adv.* separately; apart.
séparer [sepa're], *v.t.* to separate, to part; to sever. se **séparer**, *v.r.* to separate, to part; to divide.
sépia [se'pja], *n.f.* sepia.
sept [sɛt], *a.* and *n.m. inv.* seven; seventh.
septembre [sɛp'tɑ̃:br], *n.m.* September.
septénaire [sɛpte'nɛ:r], *a.* and *n.m.* septenary.
septennal [sɛptɛ'nal], *a.* (*m. pl.* **-aux**) septennial.
septentrion [sɛptɑ̃tri'ɔ̃], *n.m.* north.
septentrional [sɛptɑ̃triɔ'nal], *a.* (*m. pl.* **-aux**) north, northern.
septicémie [sɛptise'mi], *n.f.* (*Med.*) septicaemia, blood poisoning.
septième [sɛ'tjɛm], *a.* and *n.* seventh.
septique [sɛp'tik], *a.* septic.
septuagénaire [sɛptɥaʒe'nɛ:r], *a.* and *n.* septuagenarian.
sépulcral [sepyl'kral], *a.* (*m. pl.* **-aux**) sepulchral.
sépulcre [se'pylkr], *n.m.* sepulchre.
sépulture [sepyl'ty:r], *n.f.* burial, interment; burial place, tomb.
séquelle [se'kɛl], *n.f.* (*pl.*) after-effects (*of illness*).
séquence [se'kɑ̃:s], *n.f.* sequence.
séquestration [sekɛstrɑ'sjɔ̃], *n.f.* sequestration.
séquestre [se'kɛstr], *n.m.* sequestration; sequestrator; depository.
séquestrer [sekɛs'tre], *v.t.* to sequester, to sequestrate; to shut up illegally. **se séquestrer**, *v.r.* to sequester oneself.
sequin [sə'kɛ̃], *n.m.* sequin (*gold coin*).
sérail [se'ra:j], *n.m.* seraglio.
séraphin [sera'fɛ̃], *n.m.* seraph.
séraphique [sera'fik], *a.* seraphic.
serbe [sɛrb], *a.* Serbian.—*n.* (**Serbe**) Serb.
Serbie [sɛr'bi], **la**, *f.* Serbia.
serein [sə'rɛ̃], *a.* serene, placid, calm.—*n.m.* (*poet.*) night-dew.
sérénade [sere'nad], *n.f.* serenade.
sérénité [sereni'te], *n.f.* serenity, calmness; equanimity.
séreux [se'rø], *a.* (*fem.* **-euse**) serous, watery.
serf [sɛrf], *a.* (*fem.* **serve**) in bondage, servile.—*n.m.* (*fem.* **serve**) serf, bondsman, bondswoman.
serge [sɛrʒ], *n.f.* serge.
sergent [sɛr'ʒɑ̃], *n.m.* sergeant; ***sergent de ville***, police constable.
séricicole [serisi'kɔl], *a.* silk-producing.
sériciculteur [serisikyl'tœ:r], *n.m.* silk-grower.
sériciculture [serisikyl'ty:r], *n.f.* silk-culture.
série [se'ri], *n.f.* series; succession; run; (*Spt.*) heat; ***fabrication en série***, mass-production.
sérieusement [serjøz'mɑ̃], *adv.* seriously, gravely.
sérieux [se'rjø], *a.* (*fem.* **-euse**) serious, grave; earnest; real, true.—*n.m.* seriousness, importance, gravity.
serin [sə'rɛ̃], *n.m.* canary; (*fig.*) duffer, fool.
seriner [səri'ne], *v.t.* to din (*something*) into someone.
seringue [sə'rɛ̃:g], *n.f.* syringe, squirt.
seringuer [sərɛ̃'ge], *v.t.* to syringe, to squirt; to inject.
serment [sɛr'mɑ̃], *n.m.* oath, promise, solemn declaration; (*pl.*) swearing.
sermon [sɛr'mɔ̃], *n.m.* sermon; lecture.
sermonner [sɛrmɔ'ne], *v.t.*, *v.i.* to sermonize, to lecture, to reprimand.
sermonneur [sɛrmɔ'nœ:r], *n.m.* (*fem.* **-euse**) sermonizer, preacher, fault-finder.
sérosité [serozi'te], *n.f.* serosity, wateriness.
serpe [sɛrp], *n.f.* bill-hook.
serpent [sɛr'pɑ̃], *n.m.* serpent, snake; ***serpent à sonnettes***, rattlesnake.
serpenter [sɛrpɑ̃'te], *v.i.* to meander, to wind.
serpentin [sɛrpɑ̃'tɛ̃], *a.* serpentine.—*n.m.* paper streamer.
serpette [sɛr'pɛt], *n.f.* pruning-knife.
serpolet [sɛrpɔ'lɛ], *n.m.* wild thyme.
serrage [sɛ'ra:ʒ], *n.m.* tightening, pressing.

serre [sɛːr], *n.f.* squeeze, pressure; talon, claw (*of birds*); clip; hot-house, greenhouse, conservatory.
serré [sɛ're], *a.* close; compact; tight; clenched; (*fam.*) close-fisted.
serre-frein(s) [sɛr'frɛ̃], *n.m. inv.* (*Rail.*) brakesman.
serre-livres [sɛːr'livr], *n.m. inv.* book-ends.
serrement [sɛr'mɑ̃], *n.m.* pressing, squeezing; ***serrement de cœur***, pang (*of grief*); ***serrement de main***, handshake.
serre-papiers [sɛrpa'pje], *n.m. inv.* paper-clip; file (*for papers*); set of pigeon-holes (*for papers*).
serrer [sɛ're], *v.t.* to press, to squeeze; to fasten, to lock; to grip; to condense, to put close together; to press; to close (*the ranks*); to clench (*one's fist, teeth etc.*). **se serrer,** *v.r.* to press each other close; to sit, lie *or* stand close together; to stint oneself.
serre-tête [sɛr'tɛːt], *n.m. inv.* headband; crash-helmet.
serrure [sɛ'ryːr], *n.f.* lock.
serrurier [sɛry'rje], *n.m.* locksmith.
sérum [se'rɔm], *n.m.* serum.
servage [sɛr'vaːʒ], *n.m.* servitude, bondage.
servant [sɛr'vɑ̃], *a.m.* serving; in waiting.—*n.m.* (*Artill.*) gunner.
servante [sɛr'vɑ̃ːt], *n.f.* maid-servant; servant-girl; dinner-wagon.
serveur [sɛr'vœːr], *n.m.* (*fem.* **-euse**) (*Ten.*) server; waiter, barman; (*Cards*) dealer.
serviable [sɛr'vjabl], *a.* willing, obliging.
service [sɛr'vis], *n.m.* service; attendance; duty; function; divine service.
serviette [sɛr'vjɛt], *n.f.* napkin, serviette; towel; briefcase.
servile [sɛr'vil], *a.* servile, menial; slavish.
servilement [sɛrvil'mɑ̃], *adv.* servilely, slavishly.
servir [sɛr'viːr], *v.t. irr.* (*conjug. like* SENTIR) to serve, to attend; to serve up; to be of service to; to assist.—*v.i.* to serve, to be of use; to serve up a meal. **se servir,** *v.r.* **to** serve oneself; to be served up (*of dishes*); ***servez-vous***, help yourself.
serviteur [sɛrvi'tœːr], *n.m.* servant, man-servant.
servitude [sɛrvi'tyd], *n.f.* servitude, slavery.
ses [sɛ], [SON].
session [sɛ'sjɔ̃], *n.f.* session, sitting; term (*of law courts etc.*).
seuil [sœːj], *n.m.* threshold; door-step; shelf (*of ocean bed*).
seul [sœl], *a.* alone; single, only, sole; mere, bare.—*n.m.* one only, the only one.
seulement [sœl'mɑ̃], *adv.* only; but; solely, merely.
sève [sɛːv], *n.f.* sap; (*fig.*) pith, vigour, strength.
sévère [se'vɛːr], *a.* severe, stern, austere; strict.
sévèrement [sevɛr'mɑ̃], *adv.* severely, sternly; strictly.
sévérité [severi'te], *n.f.* severity; strictness; purity.
séveux [se'vø], *a.* (*fem.* **-euse**) (*Bot.*) sappy; (*fig.*) vigorous.
sévices [se'vis], *n.m. pl.* (*Law*) cruelty, ill-treatment.
sévir [se'viːr], *v.i.* to deal severely (***contre***); to rage (*of war etc.*).
sevrage [sə'vraːʒ], *n.m.* weaning.
sevrer [sə'vre], *v.t.* (*conjug. like* AMENER) to wean; (*fig.*) to deprive (***de***).
sexagénaire [sɛkzaʒe'nɛːr], *a.* and *n.* sexagenarian.
sexe [sɛks], *n.m.* sex.
sextant [sɛks'tɑ̃], *n.m.* sextant.
sextuple [sɛks'typl], *a.* and *n.m.* sextuple, six-fold.
sexualité [sɛksɥali'te], *n.f.* sexuality.
sexuel [sɛk'sɥɛl], *a.* (*fem.* **-elle**) sexual.
shampooing [ʃɑ̃'pwɛ̃], *n.m.* shampoo, hair-wash.
shérif [ʃe'rif], *n.m.* sheriff.
short [ʃɔrt], *n.m.* (*Cost.*) shorts.
shunt [ʃœːt], *n.m.* (*Elec.*) shunt.
shunter [ʃœː'te], *v.t.* to shunt.
si (1) [si], *conj.* if; whether; supposing, what if.
si (2) [si], *adv.* so, so much, however much; yes.
si (3) [si], *n.m. inv.* (*Mus.*) si; the note B.
Siam [sjam], **le**, *m.* Thailand, Siam.
siamois [sja'mwa], *a.* Siamese.—*n.m.* Siamese (*language*); (**Siamois**, *fem.* **-oise**) Siamese (*person*).
Sibérie [sibe'ri], **la**, *f.* Siberia.
sibérien [sibe'rjɛ̃], *a.* (*fem.* **-enne**) Siberian.—*n.m.* (**Sibérien**, *fem.* **-enne**) Siberian (*person*).
sibilant [sibi'lɑ̃], *a.* sibilant, hissing.
siccatif [sika'tif], *a.* (*fem.* **-tive**) siccative, drying.
Sicile [si'sil], **la**, *f.* Sicily.
sicilien [sisi'ljɛ̃], *a.* (*fem.* **-enne**) Sicilian.—*n.m.* (**Sicilien**, *fem.* **-enne**) Sicilian (*person*).
sidérurgie [sideryr'ʒi], *n.f.* iron and steel industry.
siècle [sjɛkl], *n.m.* century; age, period.
siège [sjɛːʒ], *n.m.* seat; bench (*of a court of justice*); headquarters (*of society etc.*); (*Eccles.*) see; siege.
siéger [sje'ʒe], *v.i.* (*conjug. like* ASSIÉGER) to sit (*of assemblies, courts etc.*); to hold one's see (*of bishops*); to be seated; (*fig.*) to lie (*of a thing*); to have one's headquarters (*of business, society*).
sien [sjɛ̃], *pron. poss. 3rd pers. sing.* (*fem.* **sienne**) his, hers, its, one's.—*n.m.* one's own (*property, work etc.*).
Sienne [sjɛn], *f.* Sienna.
Sierra-Leone [sjɛrale'ɔn], **le**, *m.* Sierra Leone.
sieste [sjɛst], *n.f.* siesta.
sifflant [si'flɑ̃], *a.* hissing; whistling; wheezing.
sifflement [siflə'mɑ̃], *n.m.* hissing, hiss; whistling, whistle; whizzing; wheezing.
siffler [si'fle], *v.t.* to whistle; to hiss.—*v.i.* to hiss; to whistle; to whizz; to wheeze.
sifflet [si'flɛ], *n.m.* whistle (*instrument and sound*); catcall; hiss; (*colloq.*) windpipe.
siffleur [si'flœːr], *a.* (*fem.* **-euse**) whistling, piping (*of birds*); wheezing (*of horses*).—*n.m.* (*fem.* **-euse**) whistler; hisser.
sigle [sigl], *n.m.* initial letter; group of initial letters used as abbreviation of phrase (*U.N. etc.*).
signal [si'ɲal], *n.m.* (*pl.* **-aux**) signal.
signalé [siɲa'le], *a.* signal, remarkable, conspicuous.
signalement [siɲal'mɑ̃], *n.m.* description (*of a man etc.*), particulars.

signaler [siɲa'le], *v.t.* to signal; to give the description of; to point out, to mark out; to signalize. **se signaler**, *v.r.* to signalize *or* distinguish oneself.
signaleur [siɲa'lœ:r], *n.m.* signalman; (*Mil.*) signaller.
signalisateur [siɲaliza'tœ:r], *n.m.* traffic indicator, trafficator.
signataire [siɲa'tɛ:r], *n.* signer, subscriber, signatory.
signature [siɲa'ty:r], *n.f.* signature; signing.
signe [siɲ], *n.m.* sign; mark, indication; badge; omen; ***faire signe de la main***, to beckon; ***signe de la tête***, nod.
signer [si'ɲe], *v.t., v.i.* to sign, to subscribe. **se signer**, *v.r.* to cross oneself.
signet [si'ɲɛ], *n.m.* signet; book-mark; signet-ring.
significatif [siɲifika'tif], *a.* (*fem.* **-tive**) significant.
signification [siɲifikɑ'sjɔ̃], *n.f.* signification, meaning; (*Law*) legal notice.
significativement [siɲifikativ'mɑ̃], *adv.* significantly.
signifier [siɲi'fje], *v.t.* to signify, to mean; to notify, to intimate; (*Law*) to serve.
silence [si'lɑ̃:s], *n.m.* silence; stillness; secrecy; (*Mus.*) rest.
silencieusement [silɑ̃sjøz'mɑ̃], *adv.* silently.
silencieux [silɑ̃'sjø], *a.* (*fem.* **-euse**) silent; still.—*n.m.* (*Motor.*) silencer.
silex [si'lɛks], *n.m.* silex, flint.
silhouette [si'lwɛt], *n.f.* silhouette; outline, profile.
silice [si'lis], *n.f.* (*Chem.*) silica, flint.
sillage [si'ja:ʒ], *n.m.* wake, wash; slip-stream.
sillon [si'jɔ̃], *n.m.* furrow made by plough; seed-drill; (*fig.*) track, wake (*of a ship etc.*); wrinkle.
sillonner [sijɔ'ne], *v.t.* to furrow; to streak.
silo [si'lo], *n.m.* silo (*pit* or *tower for preserving fodder*).
silotage [silɔ'ta:ʒ], *n.m.* silage.
simagrée [sima'gre], *n.f.* pretence, affectation; (*pl.*) fuss.
simiesque [si'mjɛsk], *a.* ape-like, apish (*face*).
similaire [simi'lɛ:r], *a.* similar.
similarité [similari'te], *n.f.* similarity, likeness.
similitude [simili'tyd], *n.f.* similitude, resemblance; simile.
simoun [si'mu:n], *n.m.* simoom, simoon.
simple [sɛ̃:pl], *a.* simple, single; easy; only, mere; common, plain; private (*soldier*); simple-minded, silly; natural.—*n.m.* that which is simple; (*Ten.*) singles; ***simple dames***, women's singles.
simplement [sɛ̃plə'mɑ̃], *adv.* simply.
simplet [sɛ̃'plɛ], *a.* (*fem.* **-ette**) naïve, simple; (*fam.*) a bit daft; (*Am.*) green.—*n.m.* (*fem.* **-ette**) simpleton, silly.
simplicité [sɛ̃plisi'te], *n.f.* simplicity; artlessness; silliness.
simplification [sɛ̃plifikɑ'sjɔ̃], *n.f.* simplification.
simplifier [sɛ̃pli'fje], *v.t.* to simplify.
simulacre [simy'lakr], *n.m.* image; phantom; semblance, sham.
simulé [simy'le], *a.* feigned, sham.
simuler [simy'le], *v.t.* to feign, to sham.
simultané [simylta'ne], *a.* simultaneous.
simultanément [simyltane'mɑ̃], *adv.* simultaneously.
sincère [sɛ̃'sɛ:r], *a.* sincere, frank; honest.
sincèrement [sɛ̃sɛr'mɑ̃], *adv.* sincerely, honestly.
sincérité [sɛ̃seri'te], *n.f.* sincerity.
sinécure [sine'ky:r], *n.f.* sinecure.
Singapour [sɛ̃ga'pu:r], *m.* Singapore.
singe [sɛ̃:ʒ], *n.m.* ape, monkey; hoist; (*Mil. slang*) bully beef.
singer [sɛ̃'ʒe], *v.t.* (*conjug. like* MANGER) to ape, to mimic.
singerie [sɛ̃'ʒri], *n.f.* monkey-house; grimace; antic; mimicry.
singeur [sɛ̃'ʒœ:r], *a.* (*fem.* **-euse**) aping, mimicking.—*n.m.* (*fem.* **-euse**) ape, mimic.
singulariser [sɛ̃gylari'ze], *v.t.* to singularize; to make conspicuous. **se singulariser**, *v.r.* to make oneself conspicuous.
singularité [sɛ̃gylari'te], *n.f.* singularity; peculiarity.
singulier [sɛ̃gy'lje], *a.* (*fem.* **-ière**) singular; peculiar; odd.—*n.m.* (*Gram.*) singular.
singulièrement [sɛ̃gyljɛr'mɑ̃], *adv.* singularly, oddly.
sinistre [si'nistr], *a.* sinister; dismal; evil.—*n.m.* disaster, calamity.
sinistré [sinis'tre], *a.* affected by disaster (*shipwreck, fire etc.*).—*n.m.* (*fem.* **-ée**) victim of disaster; casualty.
sinon [si'nɔ̃], *conj.* otherwise, if not, else; except, unless; ***sinon que***, except that.
sinueux [si'nɥø], *a.* (*fem.* **-euse**) sinuous, winding.
sinuosité [sinɥɔzi'te], *n.f.* sinuosity, winding.
sinus [si'ny:s], *n.m. inv.* sine; (*Anat.*) sinus.
sinusite [siny'zit], *n.f.* sinusitis.
siphon [si'fɔ̃], *n.m.* siphon; (*Naut.*) water-spout.
sire [si:r], *n.m.* sire (*title of kings and emperors*).
sirène [si'rɛn], *n.f.* siren, mermaid; hooter, fog-horn.
sirocco [sirɔ'ko], *n.m.* sirocco.
sirop [si'ro], *n.m.* syrup.
siroter [sirɔ'te], *v.t.* to sip; (*pop.*) to tipple.
sirupeux [siry'pø], *a.* (*fem.* **-euse**) syrupy.
sis [si], *a.* seated, situated [SEOIR (I)].
Sisyphe [si'zif], *m.* Sisyphus.
site [sit], *n.m.* site (*situation with regard to scenery etc.*); ***un beau site***, a beauty spot.
sitôt [si'to], *adv.* so soon, as soon; ***sitôt dit, sitôt fait***, no sooner said than done; ***sitôt que***, as soon as.
situation [sitɥɑ'sjɔ̃], *n.f.* situation, site, position; state of affairs, predicament.
situé [si'tɥe], *a.* situated, lying.
situer [si'tɥe], *v.t.* to place.
six [si *before a consonant*, siz *before a vowel* sis *at the end of a sentence*], *a.* six; sixth.—[sis], *n.m.* six; sixth; sixth day.
sixième [si'zjɛm], *a.* and *n.* sixth.—*n.m.* sixth (part); sixth floor.—*n.f.* (*in France*) sixth class, (*in England*) first form (*of upper school*).
ski [ski], *n.m.* ski; ***faire du ski***, to go in for ski-ing; ***ski nautique***, water-ski-ing.
slave [slav], *a.* Slav, Slavonic.—*n.* (**Slave**) Slav (*person*).
slip [slip], *n.m.* (*Cost.*) trunks, briefs; ***slip de bain***, (swimming) trunks.

slovène [slɔ'vɛn], *a.* Slovenian.—*n.* (**Slovène**) Slovene.
smoking [smɔ'kiŋ], *n.m.* dinner-jacket.
snob [snɔb], *a.* (*fam.*) swanky.—*n.m.* person who tries to be always in the swim.
snobisme [snɔ'bism], *n.m.* affected up-to-dateness.
sobre [sɔbr], *a.* (*of persons*) abstemious, temperate, moderate; (*of colours, style etc.*) sober, quiet, unadorned.
sobrement [sɔbrə'mɑ̃], *adv.* soberly, moderately.
sobriété [sɔbrie'te], *n.f.* sobriety; abstemiousness (*in food and drink*).
sobriquet [sɔbri'kɛ], *n.m.* nickname.
soc [sɔk], *n.m.* ploughshare.
sociabilité [sɔsjabili'te], *n.f.* sociability, good fellowship.
sociable [sɔ'sjabl], *a.* sociable, companionable.
sociablement [sɔsjablə'mɑ̃], *adv.* sociably.
social [sɔ'sjal], *a.* (*m. pl.* **-aux**) social; ***siège social***, registered office; head office.
socialement [sɔsjal'mɑ̃], *adv.* socially.
socialisme [sɔsja'lism], *n.m.* socialism.
socialiste [sɔsja'list], *a.* and *n.* socialist.
sociétaire [sɔsje'tɛːr], *n.* associate, member; partner; shareholder.
société [sɔsje'te], *n.f.* society, association; community; firm; partnership; ***société anonyme***, private company.
sociologie [sɔsjɔlɔ'ʒi], *n.f.* sociology.
sociologiste [sɔsjɔlɔ'ʒist], **sociologue** [sɔsjɔ'lɔg], *n.* sociologist.
socle [sɔkl], *n.m.* socle, pedestal, stand, base.
socque [sɔk], *n.m.* clog, patten.
Socrate [sɔ'krat], *m.* Socrates.
sœur [sœːr], *n.f.* sister; nun.
sœurette [sœ'rɛt], *n.f.* (*colloq.*) little sister, sis(s).
sofa [sɔ'fa], *n.m.* sofa, settee.
soi [swa], **soi-même** [swa'mɛm], *impers. pron. 3rd pers. sing.* oneself, itself; self.
soi-disant [swadi'zɑ̃], *a. inv.* self-styled, would-be, so-called.
soie [swɑ], *n.f.* silk; silken hair; bristle (*of hogs*); ***papier de soie***, tissue paper.
soierie [swɑ'ri], *n.f.* silks, silk goods; silk-trade; silk-factory.
soif [swaf], *n.f.* thirst; ***avoir soif***, to be thirsty.
soigné [swa'ɲe], *a.* carefully done; neat, smart; (*colloq.*) first-rate.
soigner [swa'ɲe], *v.t.* to take care of, to look after; to nurse. **se soigner**, *v.r.* to take care of oneself.
soigneusement [swaɲøz'mɑ̃], *adv.* carefully.
soigneux [swa'ɲø], *a.* (*fem.* **-euse**) careful; solicitous.
soi-même [SOI].
soin [swɛ̃], *n.m.* care; attendance; (*pl.*) attentions, pains, trouble.
soir [swaːr], *n.m.* evening; night.
soirée [swa're], *n.f.* evening (*duration*); evening party.
soit [swat, swa], *adv.* be it so, well and good, granted; let us say.—*conj.* either, or; whether.
soixantaine [swasɑ̃'tɛn], *n.f.* about sixty.
soixante [swa'sɑ̃ːt], *a.* and *n.m.* sixty.
soixantième [swasɑ̃'tjɛːm], *a.* and *n.* sixtieth.
sol [sɔl], *n.m.* ground; soil; earth.
solaire [sɔ'lɛːr], *a.* solar.
soldat [sɔl'da], *n.m.* soldier; ***simple soldat***, private; ***les simples soldats***, the rank and file.
soldatesque [sɔlda'tɛsk], *n.f.* (*usu. pej.*) soldiery.
solde (1) [sɔld], *n.f.* (*Mil.*) pay.
solde (2) [sɔld], *n.m.* balance (*between debit and credit*); clearance sale; (*pl.*) sale bargains, reductions.
solder (1) [sɔl'de], *v.t.* to pay (*soldiers*); to have in one's pay.
solder (2) [sɔl'de], *v.t.* to settle (*an account*); to sell off, to clear.
sole [sɔl], *n.f.* sole (*of animal's foot*); sole (*fish*).
solécisme [sɔle'sism], *n.m.* solecism.
soleil [sɔ'lɛːj], *n.m.* sun; sunshine; (*fig.*) star; catherine-wheel (*firework*); sunflower.
solennel [sɔla'nɛl], *a.* (*fem.* **-elle**) solemn.
solennellement [sɔlanɛl'mɑ̃], *adv.* solemnly.
solenniser [sɔlani'ze], *v.t.* to solemnize.
solennité [sɔlani'te], *n.f.* solemnity.
solénoïde [sɔlenɔ'id], *n.m.* solenoid.
solidaire [sɔli'dɛːr], *a.* jointly and separately liable.
solidairement [sɔlidɛr'mɑ̃], *adv.* jointly and severally.
solidariser [sɔlidari'ze], *v.t.* to render jointly liable.
solidarité [sɔlidari'te], *n.f.* joint and separate liability; solidarity, fellowship.
solide [sɔ'lid], *a.* solid; strong; substantial, sound; reliable.—*n.m.* solid, solid body.
solidement [sɔlid'mɑ̃], *adv.* solidly; firmly; soundly.
solidification [sɔlidifikɑ'sjɔ̃], *n.f.* solidification.
solidifier [sɔlidi'fje], *v.t.* and **se solidifier,** *v.r.* to solidify.
solidité [sɔlidi'te], *n.f.* solidity; strength; stability; soundness.
soliloque [sɔli'lɔk], *n.m.* soliloquy.
soliste [sɔ'list], *a.* solo.—*n.* soloist.
solitaire [sɔli'tɛːr], *a.* solitary, single, alone; lonely, desert.—*n.m.* lonely person, recluse; solitaire (*diamond* or *game*).
solitairement [sɔlitɛr'mɑ̃], *adv.* solitarily, alone.
solitude [sɔli'tyd], *n.f.* solitude, loneliness; desert.
solive [sɔ'liːv], *n.f.* joist.
soliveau [sɔli'vo], *n.m.* (*pl.* **-eaux**) small joist.
sollicitation [sɔlisitɑ'sjɔ̃], *n.f.* solicitation; pull (*of magnet*).
solliciter [sɔlisi'te], *v.t.* to incite; to solicit, to entreat; to call into action; to attract (*of magnet*).
sollicitude [sɔlisi'tyd], *n.f.* solicitude, care; concern.
solo [sɔ'lo], *a. inv.* solo.—*n.m.* (*pl.* **solos** or **soli**) solo.
solstice [sɔls'tis], *n.m.* solstice.
solubilité [sɔlybili'te], *n.f.* solubility.
soluble [sɔ'lybl], *a.* soluble.
solution [sɔly'sjɔ̃], *n.f.* solution; resolution; (*Law*) discharge; ***solution de continuité,*** interruption, break, fault.
solvabilité [sɔlvabili'te], *n.f.* solvency.
solvable [sɔl'vabl], *a.* solvent.
solvant [sɔl'vɑ̃], *n.m.* solvent.

somali [sɔma'li], *a.* Somali.—*n.m.* Somali (*language*).—*n.* (**Somali**) Somali (*person*); ***Côte Française des Somalis***, French Somaliland.
Somalie [sɔma'li], **la**, *f.* Somalia, Somaliland.
sombre [sɔ̃:br], *a.* dark, sombre, gloomy; dim; overcast; melancholy.
sombrer [sɔ̃'bre], *v.i.* (*Naut.*) to founder.
sombrero [sɔ̃bre'ro], *n.m.* sombrero.
sommaire [sɔ'mɛ:r], *a.* summary, concise; scanty.—*n.m.* summary, abstract.
sommairement [sɔmɛr'mɑ̃], *adv.* summarily; hastily.
sommation [sɔmɑ'sjɔ̃], *n.f.* summons, demand; (*Mil.*) challenge.
somme [sɔm], *n.f.* sum, total; amount; summary; burden.—*n.m.* nap; ***faire un somme***, to have forty winks.
sommeil [sɔ'mɛ:j], *n.m.* sleep; ***avoir sommeil***, to be sleepy.
sommeiller [sɔmɛ'je], *v.i.* to slumber; to doze.
sommelier [sɔmə'lje], *n.m.* butler, cellarman, wine-waiter.
sommellerie [sɔmɛl'ri], *n.f.* butler's pantry.
sommer [sɔ'me], *v.t.* to summon, to call upon; to sum up.
sommet [sɔ'mɛ], *n.m.* top, summit; acme; crown (*of the head etc.*).
sommier (1) [sɔ'mje], *n.m.* pack-horse; box-mattress; wind-chest (*of organ*); (*Arch.*) cross-beam.
sommier (2) [sɔ'mje], *n.m.* cash-book, register.
sommité [sɔmi'te], *n.f.* summit, top; head, principal; chief point; prominent person.
somnambule [sɔmnɑ̃'byl], *a.* somnambulistic.—*n.* sleepwalker.
somnambulisme [sɔmnɑ̃by'lism], *n.m.* somnambulism, sleep-walking.
somnolence [sɔmnɔ'lɑ̃:s], *n.f.* somnolence.
somnolent [sɔmnɔ'lɑ̃], *a.* somnolent, sleepy.
somptuaire [sɔ̃p'tɥɛ:r], *a.* sumptuary.
somptueusement [sɔ̃ptɥøz'mɑ̃], *adv.* sumptuously.
somptueux [sɔ̃p'tɥø], *a.* (*fem.* **-euse**) sumptuous; magnificent.
somptuosité [sɔ̃ptɥozi'te], *n.f.* sumptuousness.
son (1) [sɔ̃], *a.* (*fem.* **sa**, *pl.* **ses**) his, her, its; one's.
son (2) [sɔ̃], *n.m.* sound.
son (3) [sɔ̃], *n.m.* bran; ***tache de son***, freckle.
sonate [sɔ'nat], *n.f.* sonata.
sondage [sɔ̃'da:ʒ], *n.m.* sounding; (*Mining*) boring.
sonde [sɔ̃:d], *n.f.* sounding-line, lead; (*Surg. etc.*) probe; (*Mining*) drill, boring machine.
sonder [sɔ̃'de], *v.t.* to sound; to taste; to search, to fathom, to investigate.
sondeur [sɔ̃'dœ:r], *n.m.* (*Naut.*) leadsman; (*Mining*) driller, borer.
songe [sɔ̃:ʒ], *n.m.* dream; dreaming.
songe-creux [sɔ̃ʒ'krø], *n.m. inv.* dreamer, visionary.
songer [sɔ̃'ʒe], *v.t.* (*conjug. like* MANGER) to dream; (*fig.*) to imagine; to think of.—*v.i.* to dream; (*fig.*) to day-dream; to think; to mean, to intend, to propose.
songerie [sɔ̃'ʒri], *n.f.* dreaming; musing; day-dreaming.
songeur [sɔ̃'ʒœ:r], *a.* (*fem.* **-euse**) thoughtful, dreamy.—*n.m.* (*fem.* **-euse**) dreamer.
sonique [sɔ'nik], *a.* sonic.
sonnant [sɔ'nɑ̃], *a.* sounding; sonorous.
sonner [sɔ'ne], *v.t., v.i.* to sound; to ring, to toll, to strike (*of clocks etc.*).
sonnerie [sɔn'ri], *n.f.* ring, ringing (*of bells*); bells, chimes; striking part (*of a clock etc.*); (*Mil.*) bugle-call.
sonnet [sɔ'nɛ], *n.m.* sonnet.
sonnette [sɔ'nɛt], *n.f.* small bell; hand-bell.
sonneur [sɔ'nœ:r], *n.m.* bell-ringer.
sonore [sɔ'nɔ:r], *a.* resonant; clear; ***ondes sonores***, sound waves.
sonorité [sɔnɔri'te], *n.f.* resonance.
sophisme [sɔ'fism], *n.m.* sophism, fallacy.
sophiste [sɔ'fist], *a.* sophistical.—*n.* sophist.
sophistiqué [sɔfisti'ke], *a.* sophisticated; affected.
soporifique [sɔpɔri'fik], *a.* soporific; (*fig.*) tedious.—*n.m.* soporific.
soprano [sɔpra'no], *n.* (*pl.* **soprani** or **sopranos**) soprano, treble.
sorbet [sɔr'bɛ], *n.m.* sherbet.
sorbier [sɔr'bje], *n.m.* mountain-ash, rowan tree.
sorcellerie [sɔrsɛl'ri], *n.f.* sorcery, witchcraft.
sorcier [sɔr'sje], *n.m.* (*fem.* **-ière**) sorcerer, wizard, sorceress, witch.
sordide [sɔr'did], *a.* sordid, filthy; mean, vile.
sordidement [sɔrdid'mɑ̃], *adv.* sordidly.
Sorlingues [sɔr'lɛ̃:g], **les**, *f. pl.* the Scilly Isles.
sornette [sɔr'nɛt], *n.f.* (*usu. in pl.*) idle talk, small talk.
sort [sɔ:r], *n.m.* fate, destiny; lot; condition; fortune; chance; spell, charm; ***au sort***, by lot; ***le sort en est jeté***, the die is cast; ***tirer au sort***, to draw lots; to toss.
sortable [sɔr'tabl], *a.* suitable.
sortablement [sɔrtablə'mɑ̃], *adv.* suitably.
sortant [sɔr'tɑ̃], *a.* outgoing, retiring, leaving (*office etc.*); drawn (*of numbers in lotteries*).—*n.m.* person going out; person leaving office etc.; ***les entrants et les sortants***, the incomers and outgoers.
sorte [sɔrt], *n.f.* sort, kind, species; manner, way; ***de la sorte***, thus, in that way; ***de sorte que*** or ***en sorte que***, so that.
sortie [sɔr'ti], *n.f.* going *or* coming out; exit, way out; outing, trip; exportation; sortie; (*colloq.*) outburst, attack; ***droit de sortie***, export duty; ***jour de sortie***, day out.
sortilège [sɔrti'lɛ:ʒ], *n.m.* sorcery, magic; spell, charm.
sortir [sɔr'ti:r], *v.t. irr.* (*conjug. like* SENTIR *with aux.* AVOIR) to bring out, to take out; to pull out, to extricate.—*v.i.* (*with aux.* ÊTRE) to go out, to come out, to come forth, to emerge; to make one's exit; to leave, to depart; to swerve; to wander (*from a subject*); to proceed, to result; to spring, to come up; to sally forth; to burst forth; to escape; (*Paint. etc.*) to stand out; to be in relief.—*n.m.* going out, leaving; rising.
sosie [sɔ'zi], *n.m.* double, counterpart.
sot [so], *a.* (*fem.* **sotte**) stupid, silly, foolish; (*fig.*) embarrassed, sheepish.—*n.m.* (*fem.* **sotte**) fool, ass, idiot.
sottement [sɔt'mɑ̃], *adv.* stupidly; foolishly.

sottise [sɔ'ti:z], *n.f.* silliness, folly; foolish trick, nonsense; insult; (*pl.*) abusive language.
sou [su], *n.m.* sou (*copper coin worth 5 centimes*); copper, halfpenny.
soubresaut [subrə'so], *n.m.* sudden leap *or* bound; plunge (*of a horse*); start; jolt.
soubresauter [subrə'sote], *v.i.* to start, to jump, to plunge.
soubrette [su'brɛt], *n.f.* lady's maid, waiting-woman.
souche [suʃ], *n.f.* stump, stock, stub, stem; (*fig.*) blockhead; founder (*of a family etc.*); origin; chimney-stack; counterfoil; tally; ***faire souche***, to found a family.
souci (1) [su'si], *n.m.* care, anxiety.
souci (2) [su'si], *n.m.* (*Bot.*) marigold.
soucier (se) [səsu'sje], *v.r.* to care, to mind, to be concerned, to be anxious (***de***).
soucieux [su'sjø], *a.* (*fem.* **-euse**) anxious, full of care; pensive, thoughtful.
soucoupe [su'kup], *n.f.* saucer.
soudage [su'da:ʒ], *n.m.* soldering, welding; (*fig.*) reconciliation.
soudain [su'dɛ̃], *a.* sudden, unexpected.—*adv.* suddenly.
soudainement [sudɛn'mɑ̃], *adv.* suddenly, all of a sudden.
soudaineté [sudɛn'te], *n.f.* suddenness.
Soudan [su'dɑ̃], **le**, *n.m.* the Sudan.
soudanais [suda'nɛ], *a.* Sudanese.—*n.m.* (**Soudanais**, *fem.* **-aise**) Sudanese (*person*).
soude [sud], *n.f.* soda.
souder [su'de], *v.t.* to solder, to braze, to weld; (*fig.*) to unite. **se souder**, *v.r.* to be soldered *or* welded; to knit (*of bones*).
soudeur [su'dœ:r], *n.m.* welder.
soudoyer [sudwa'je], *v.t.* (*conjug. like* EMPLOYER) to keep in one's pay; to hire; to bribe.
soudure [su'dy:r], *n.f.* solder; soldering, welding; ***soudure autogène***, oxyacetylene welding.
soue [su], *n.f.* pigsty.
soufflage [su'fla:ʒ], *n.m.* glass-blowing.
soufflant [su'flɑ̃], *a.* blowing.
souffle [sufl], *n.m.* breath, breathing; puff (*of wind etc.*); (*fig.*) inspiration, influence.
soufflé [su'fle], *a.* soufflé (*of pastry etc.*); exaggerated (*reputation*).—*n.m.* soufflé (*light dish*).
soufflement [suflə'mɑ̃], *n.m.* blowing.
souffler [su'fle], *v.t.* to blow, to blow out; to inflate; to whisper; (*Theat.*) to prompt; to huff (*at draughts*); (*Naut.*) to sheathe.—*v.i.* to blow, to breathe; to pant, to puff; (*fig.*) to breathe a word etc.; ***souffler aux oreilles de quelqu'un***, to whisper in someone's ear.
soufflerie [suflə'ri], *n.f.* bellows (*of an organ*); wind-tunnel.
soufflet [su'flɛ], *n.m.* pair of bellows; box on the ear, slap in the face; affront.
souffleter [suflə'te], *v.t.* (*conjug. like* APPELER) to slap in the face, to box the ears of; (*fig.*) to insult.
souffleur [su'flœ:r], *a.* (*fem.* **-euse**) blowing, puffing.—*n.m.* (*fem.* **-euse**) blower; (*Theat.*) prompter.—(*C*) *n.f.* (**-euse**) snow blower.
souffrance [su'frɑ̃:s], *n.f.* suffering, pain; suspense; (*Law*) sufferance; ***en souffrance***, awaiting delivery; in abeyance.
souffrant [su'frɑ̃], *a.* suffering; unwell; long-suffering.
souffre-douleur [sufrədu'lœ:r], *n.m. inv.* drudge; butt, laughing-stock.
souffreteux [sufrə'tø], *a.* (*fem.* **-euse**) needy; poorly, sickly, weakly.
souffrir [su'fri:r], *v.t. irr.* (*conjug. like* OUVRIR) to suffer; to bear, to endure, to undergo, to sustain; to stand, to tolerate; to admit of; ***faire souffrir***, to pain, to grieve.—*v.i.* to suffer, to be in pain; to be pained; to be injured.
soufre [sufr], *n.m.* sulphur, brimstone.
souhait [swɛ], *n.m.* wish, desire; ***à souhait***, to one's heart's content, as one would have it.
souhaitable [swɛ'tabl], *a.* desirable.
souhaiter [swɛ'te], *v.t.* to desire, to wish for.
souiller [su'je], *v.t.* to soil, to dirty; to stain, to blemish, to sully; to defile. **se souiller**, *v.r.* to soil oneself, to get dirty; to tarnish one's good name.
souillon [su'jɔ̃], *n.* sloven, slut; scullion.
souillure [su'jy:r], *n.f.* spot, stain; blot, blemish; contamination.
soûl or **saoul** [su], *a.* glutted, surfeited (***de***); drunk; satiated, heartily sick (***de***).—*n.m.* fill, bellyful; ***tout son soûl***, to one's heart's content.
soulagement [sulaʒ'mɑ̃], *n.m.* relief, alleviation; solace, help.
soulager [sula'ʒe], *v.t.* (*conjug. like* MANGER) to relieve, to ease; to alleviate, to allay; to soothe, to comfort. **se soulager**, *v.r.* to relieve oneself; to help each other.
soûlard [su'la:r], *a.* drunken.—*n.m.* (*fem.* **-e**) drunkard, sot.
soûler [su'le], *v.t.* to fill, to glut; to make drunk. **se soûler**, *v.r.* to gorge; to get drunk.
soûlerie [sul'ri], *n.f.* drinking bout, 'binge'.
soulèvement [sulɛv'mɑ̃], *n.m.* heaving; swelling (*of sea waves etc.*); rising (*of the stomach*); (*fig.*) insurrection, revolt.
soulever [sul've], *v.t.* (*conjug. like* AMENER) to raise, to lift up; to heave; to take up; (*fig.*) to excite, to stir up; to sicken; to rouse the indignation of. **se soulever**, *v.r.* to raise oneself, to rise; to heave, to swell; to rise in insurrection.
soulier [su'lje], *n.m.* shoe; ***être dans ses petits souliers***, to be ill at ease; ***souliers ferrés***, hobnailed boots.
soulignement [suliɲ'mɑ̃], *n.m.* underlining.
souligner [suli'ɲe], *v.t.* to underline; (*fig.*) to emphasize.
soumettre [su'mɛtr], *v.t. irr.* (*conjug. like* METTRE) to subdue, to subject; to submit, to refer; to subordinate. **se soumettre**, *v.r.* to submit, to yield; to comply, to assent (***à***).
soumis [su'mi], *a.* submissive.
soumission [sumi'sjɔ̃], *n.f.* submission, compliance, obedience; subjection; mark of respect; tender for a contract etc.
soumissionner [sumisjɔ'ne], *v.t.* to tender for.
soupape [su'pap], *n.f.* valve; ***soupape de sûreté***, safety-valve.
soupçon [sup'sɔ̃], *n.m.* suspicion; surmise, conjecture; (*fig.*) slight taste, dash, touch.
soupçonner [supsɔ'ne], *v.t.* to suspect; to surmise.

soupçonneux [supsɔ'nø], *a.* (*fem.* **-euse**) suspicious.

soupe [sup], *n.f.* soup; sop; ***c'est une soupe au lait***, he has a quick temper; ***trempé comme une soupe***, drenched to the skin.

soupente [su'pɑ̃:t], *n.f.* straps (*of a horse*); loft, garret.

souper [su'pe], *v.i.* to sup, to have supper.—*n.m.* supper.

soupeser [supə'ze], *v.t.* (*conjug. like* AMENER) to weigh in one's hand, to try the weight of.

soupière [su'pjɛ:r], *n.f.* soup-tureen.

soupir [su'pi:r], *n.m.* sigh; breath, gasp; (*Mus.*) crotchet-rest.

soupirail [supi'ra:j], *n.m.* (*pl.* **-aux**) air-hole, ventilator.

soupirant [supi'rɑ̃], *a.* sighing.—*n.m.* wooer, lover.

soupirer [supi're], *v.t.* to breathe forth, to sigh out.—*v.i.* to sigh; to gasp; to long.

souple [supl], *a.* supple, pliant, flexible, yielding; docile.

souplesse [su'plɛs], *n.f.* suppleness, flexibility; compliance, pliancy; versatility; toughness.

souquenille [suk'ni:j], *n.f.* smock-frock; (shabby) old garment.

source [surs], *n.f.* spring, source, fountain.

sourcier [sur'sje], *n.m.* (*fem.* **-ière**) water-diviner.

sourcil [sur'si], *n.m.* eyebrow, brow; ***froncer le sourcil***, to frown.

sourciller [sursi'je], *v.i.* to knit one's brows, to frown; to wince.

sourcilleux [sursi'jø], *a.* (*fem.* **-euse**) haughty, proud, supercilious; frowning; uneasy.

sourd [su:r], *a.* deaf; (*fig.*) dull; insensible; hollow, muffled (*of sound*); underhand.—*n.m.* (*fem.* **-e**) deaf person.

sourdement [surdə'mɑ̃], *adv.* indistinctly; with a hollow voice; in an underhand manner.

sourdine [sur'din], *n.f.* sordine (*of a musical instrument*); damper (*of a piano etc.*); ***en sourdine***, secretly, on the sly.

sourd-muet [sur'mɥɛ], *a.* and *n.m.* (*fem.* **sourde-muette**) deaf-and-dumb (person), deaf-mute.

sourdre [surdr], *v.i.* to spring, to gush, to well; (*fig.*) to result.

souriant [su'rjɑ̃], *a.* smiling.

souricière [suri'sjɛ:r], *n.f.* mouse-trap.

sourire [su'ri:r], *v.i. irr.* (*conjug. like* RIRE) to smile; to be agreeable, to delight, to please; to be propitious.—*n.m.* smile; ***large sourire***, grin; ***sourire affecté***, smirk.

souris [su'ri], *a. inv.* mouse-coloured.—*n.f.* mouse; mouse-colour; knuckle (*of a leg of mutton*).

sournois [sur'nwa], *a.* artful, cunning, sly.—*n.m.* (*fem.* **-e**) sneak.

sournoisement [surnwaz'mɑ̃], *adv.* cunningly, slyly.

sournoiserie [surnwaz'ri], *n.f.* slyness, cunning; underhand trick.

sous [su], *prep.* under, beneath, below; on, upon; with; in; by; ***affirmer sous serment***, to swear on oath; ***sous dix jours***, within ten days; ***sous peu***, in a short time.

sous-alimentation [suzalimɑ̃tɑ'sjɔ̃], *n.f.* malnutrition.

sous-alimenté [suzalimɑ̃'te], *a.* underfed.

sous-chef [su'ʃɛf], *n.m.* deputy head-clerk; assistant manager.

souscripteur [suskrip'tœ:r], *n.m.* subscriber; (*Comm.*) underwriter.

souscription [suskrip'sjɔ̃], *n.f.* subscription; signature.

souscrire [sus'kri:r], *v.t. irr.* (*conjug. like* ÉCRIRE) to subscribe, to sign.—*v.i.* to consent, to agree (*à*).

sous-développé [sudevlɔ'pe], *a.* underdeveloped (*country*).

sous-dit [su'di], *a.* undermentioned.

sous-entendre [suzɑ̃'tɑ̃:dr], *v.t.* not to express fully, to hint, to imply.

sous-entendu [suzɑ̃tɑ̃'dy], *n.m.* thing understood, implication.

sous-entente [suzɑ̃'tɑ̃:t], *n.f.* mental reservation.

sous-lieutenant [suljøt'nɑ̃], *n.m.* second-lieutenant; ***sous-lieutenant aviateur***, pilot officer.

sous-louer [su'lwe], *v.t.* to sub-let.

sous-main [su'mɛ̃], *n.m. inv.* writing-pad; ***en sous-main***, behind the scenes.

sous-marin [suma'rɛ̃], *a.* and *n.m.* submarine.

sous-off [su'zɔf], *abbr. fam. of* **sous-officier** [suzɔfi'sje], *n.m.* non-commissioned officer, N.C.O.

sous-ordre [su'zɔrdr], *n.m. inv.* subordinate.

sous-préfet [supre'fɛ], *n.m.* subprefect, under-sheriff.

sous-produit [suprɔ'dɥi], *n.m.* by-product.

sous-secrétaire [susəkre'tɛ:r], *n.* under-secretary.

soussigné [susi'ɲe], *a.* undersigned; ***nous soussignés certifions***, we, the undersigned, certify.

sous-sol [su'sɔl], *n.m.* subsoil; basement.

sous-titre [su'titr], *n.m.* sub-title.

soustraction [sustrak'sjɔ̃], *n.f.* taking away, subtraction.

soustraire [sus'trɛ:r], *v.t. irr.* (*conjug. like* TRAIRE) to take away, to withdraw, to screen; (*Arith.*) to subtract. **se soustraire**, *v.r.* to escape, to flee, to avoid; to withdraw oneself; to be subtracted.

sous-traitant [sutrɛ'tɑ̃], *n.m.* subcontractor.

soutache [su'taʃ], *n.f.* braid.

soutane [su'tan], *n.f.* cassock; (*fig.*) the cloth.

soute [sut], *n.f.* (*Naut.*) store-room; (*Av.*) luggage-bay, bomb-bay.

soutenable [sut'nabl], *a.* sustainable; tenable.

soutènement [sutɛn'mɑ̃], *n.m.* (*Arch.*) support.

soutenir [sut'ni:r], *v.t. irr.* (*conjug. like* TENIR) to hold up, to support, to sustain, to keep up, to prop up; (*fig.*) to maintain, to uphold; to countenance; to afford (*an expense*); to endure. **se soutenir**, *v.r.* to support oneself; to hold oneself up; to bear up, to hold out; to stand firm; to succeed; to continue; to sustain one another.

soutenu [sut'ny], *a.* sustained; unremitting, unceasing, constant; lofty, elevated.

souterrain [sutɛ'rɛ̃], *a.* underground; (*fig.*) underhand.—*n.m.* underground vault, cavern; (*Rail.*) tunnel; subway.

soutien [su'tjɛ̃], *n.m.* support, prop, stay, staff.
soutien-gorge [sutjɛ̃'gɔrʒ], *n.m. inv.* brassière.
soutirer [suti're], *v.t.* to draw off, to rack (*liquors*); (*fig.*) to worm out (*à*), to extract (*money, information*).
souvenir [suv'ni:r], *n.m.* recollection; reminder, souvenir, keepsake.—*v. impers. irr.* (*conjug. like* TENIR *but with aux.* ÊTRE) to occur to the mind; ***il m'en souvient***, I remember it. **se souvenir**, *v.r.* to remember, to call to mind, to recollect.
souvent [su'vɑ̃], *adv.* often, frequently.
souverain [su'vrɛ̃], *a.* sovereign, supreme; highest, extreme; infallible.—*n.m.* (*fem.* **-e**) sovereign (*monarch*).—*n.m.* sovereign (*coin*).
souverainement [suvrɛn'mɑ̃], *adv.* in the extreme; supremely.
souveraineté [suvrɛn'te], *n.f.* sovereignty, dominion.
soviet [sɔ'vjɛt], *n.m.* Soviet.
soviétique [sɔvje'tik], *a.* ***l'Union des Républiques socialistes soviétiques*** (*U.R.S.S.*), the Union of Soviet Socialist Republics (*U.S.S.R.*).—*n.* (**Soviétique**) Soviet citizen.
soyeux [swɑ'jø], *a.* (*fem.* **-euse**) silky, silken.
spacieusement [spasjøz'mɑ̃], *adv.* spaciously.
spacieux [spa'sjø], *a.* (*fem.* **-euse**) spacious, wide, roomy.
spahi [spa'i], *n.m.* spahi (*Algerian native trooper*).
sparadrap [spara'dra], *n.m.* sticking plaster.
Sparte [spart], **la**, *f.* Sparta.
spartiate [spar'sjat], *a.* Spartan.—*n.* (**Spartiate**) Spartan (*person*).
spasme [spasm], *n.m.* spasm.
spasmodique [spasmɔ'dik], *a.* spasmodic.
spasmodiquement [spasmɔdik'mɑ̃], *adv.* spasmodically.
spatule [spa'tyl], *n.f.* spatula.
speaker [spi'kœ:r], *n.m.* (*fem.* **speakerine**) (*Rad.*) announcer.
spécial [spe'sjal], *a.* (*m. pl.* **-aux**) special, especial, particular; professional.
spécialement [spesjal'mɑ̃], *adv.* especially, particularly.
spécialisation [spesjalizɑ'sjɔ̃], *n.f.* specialization.
spécialiser [spesjali'ze], *v.t.* to specialize.
spécialiste [spesja'list], *n.* specialist, expert.
spécialité [spesjali'te], *n.f.* peculiarity, speciality; patent medicine.
spécieux [spe'sjø], *a.* (*fem.* **-euse**) specious, plausible.
spécification [spesifikɑ'sjɔ̃], *n.f.* specification.
spécifier [spesi'fje], *v.t.* to specify.
spécifique [spesi'fik], *a.* and *n.m.* specific.
spécifiquement [spesifik'mɑ̃], *adv.* specifically.
spécimen [spesi'mɛn], *n.m.* specimen.
spectacle [spɛk'takl], *n.m.* spectacle, scene, sight; theatre; play, performance; show; ***se donner en spectacle***, to make an exhibition of oneself.
spectaculaire [spɛktaky'lɛ:r], *a.* spectacular.
spectateur [spɛkta'tœ:r], *n.m.* (*fem.* **-trice**) spectator, looker-on.
spectral [spɛk'tral], *a.* (*m. pl.* **-aux**) spectral.
spectre [spɛktr], *n.m.* spectre, ghost; spectrum.
spéculateur [spekyla'tœ:r], *n.m.* (*fem.* **-trice**) speculator.
spéculatif [spekyla'tif], *a.* (*fem.* **-tive**) speculative.
spéculation [spekylɑ'sjɔ̃], *n.f.* speculation.
spéculativement [spekylativ'mɑ̃], *adv.* in a speculative manner.
spéculer [speky'le], *v.i.* to speculate.
sperme [spɛrm], *n.m.* sperm, seed.
sphaigne [sfɛ:ɲ], *n.f.* sphagnum moss.
sphère [sfɛ:r], *n.f.* sphere, orb, globe; (*fig.*) circle.
sphérique [sfe'rik], *a.* spherical.
sphinx [sfɛ̃:ks], *n.m.* sphinx.
spinal [spi'nal], *a.* (*m. pl.* **-aux**) spinal.
spiral [spi'ral], *a.* (*m. pl.* **-aux**) spiral.—*n.m.* hair-spring (*of watch*).
spirale [spi'ral], *n.f.* spiral.
spirite [spi'rit], *a.* spiritualistic.—*n.* spiritualist.
spiritisme [spiri'tism], *n.m.* spiritualism.
spiritualisme [spiritɥa'lism], *n.m.* spiritualism.
spiritualiste [spiritɥa'list], *a.* and *n.* spiritualist.
spirituel [spiri'tɥɛl], *a.* (*fem.* **-elle**) spiritual; intellectual; witty, shrewd, lively, intelligent.
spirituellement [spiritɥɛl'mɑ̃], *adv.* spiritually; wittily, cleverly.
spiritueux [spiri'tɥø], *a.* (*fem.* **-euse**) spirituous.—*n.m.* spirit, spirituous liquor.
spleen [splin], *n.m.* spleen; (*fam.*) ***avoir le spleen***, to be in the dumps.
splendeur [splɑ̃'dœ:r], *n.f.* splendour, brilliance; magnificence.
splendide [splɑ̃'did], *a.* sumptuous, magnificent.
splendidement [splɑ̃did'mɑ̃], *adv.* splendidly.
spoliateur [spɔlja'tœ:r], *a.* (*fem.* **-trice**) despoiling.—*n.m.* (*fem.* **-trice**) spoiler, despoiler.
spoliation [spɔljɑ'sjɔ̃], *n.f.* spoliation.
spolier [spɔ'lje], *v.t.* to despoil, to plunder.
spongieux [spɔ̃'ʒjø], *a.* (*fem.* **-euse**) spongy.
spontané [spɔ̃ta'ne], *a.* spontaneous.
spontanéité [spɔ̃tanei'te], *n.f.* spontaneity.
spontanément [spɔ̃tane'mɑ̃], *adv.* spontaneously.
sporadique [spɔra'dik], *a.* sporadic.
spore [spɔ:r], *n.f.* spore.
sport [spɔ:r], *n.m.* games, outdoor games; ***faire du sport***, to play games.
sportif [spɔr'tif], *a.* (*fem.* **-tive**) sporting; ***réunion sportive***, athletics meeting.—*n.m.* (*fem.* **-tive**) athlete; devotee of out-door games; sportsman, sportswoman.
spumeux [spy'mø], *a.* (*fem.* **-euse**) spumy.
square [skwa:r], *n.m.* residential square with enclosed garden.
squelette [skə'lɛt], *n.m.* skeleton; carcass, frame (*of a ship*).
squelettique [skəlɛ'tik], *a.* lanky.
stabilisateur [stabiliza'tœ:r], *a.* (*fem.* **-trice**) stabilizing.—*n.m.* (*Av., Naut.*) stabilizer.
stabiliser [stabili'ze], *v.t.* to stabilize.
stabilité [stabili'te], *n.f.* stability, durability.
stable [sta:bl], *a.* stable, firm; durable, lasting, permanent.
stade [stad], *n.m.* sports ground, stadium; (*fig.*) stage, period.

stage [sta:ʒ], *n.m.* term of probation, study, residence etc.; training course; (*fig.*) probation.

stagiaire [sta'ʒjɛ:r], *n.* probationer, trainee.

stagnant [stag'nɑ̃], *a.* stagnant, at a standstill.

stagnation [stagnɑ'sjɔ̃], *n.f.* stagnation.

stagner [stag'ne], *v.i.* to stagnate.

stalactite [stalak'tit], *n.f.* stalactite.

stalagmite [stalag'mit], *n.f.* stalagmite.

stalle [stal], *n.f.* stall; box (*for horses*) (*Theat.*) stall, seat.

stance [stɑ̃:s], *n.f.* stanza.

stand [stɑ̃:d], *n.m.* rifle-range; shooting-gallery; stall, stand (*at exhibitions etc.*).

standard [stɑ̃'da:r], *n.m.* (*in house* or *office*) switchboard; standard (*of living*).

standardiser [stɑ̃dardi'ze], *v.t.* to standardize.

standardiste [stɑ̃dar'dist], *n.* switchboard operator.

star [sta:r], *n.f.* (*Cine.*) star.

starlette [star'lɛt], *n.f.* starlet.

starter [star'tɛ:r], *n.m.* (*Motor.*) choke; (*Racing*) starter.

station [stɑ'sjɔ̃], *n.f.* station, standing; stage (*of bus, trams*), taxi-rank; resort.

stationnaire [stasjɔ'nɛ:r], *a.* stationary.

stationnement [stasjɔn'mɑ̃], *n.m.* stationing, standing; parking; ***stationnement interdit***, no parking, no waiting.

stationner [stasjɔ'ne], *v.i.* to stop, to stand, to park (*of cars*).

statique [sta'tik], *a.* static.—*n.f.* statics.

statisticien [statisti'sjɛ̃], *n.m.* statistician.

statistique [statis'tik], *a.* statistical.—*n.f.* statistics.

statuaire [sta'tɥɛ:r], *a.* statuary.—*n.* sculptor. —*n.f.* statuary (*art*).

statue [sta'ty], *n.f.* statue.

statuer [sta'tɥe], *v.t.* to decree, to resolve, to ordain.—*v.i.* to give a ruling.

statuette [sta'tɥɛt], *n.f.* statuette.

stature [sta'ty:r], *n.f.* stature, height.

statut [sta'ty], *n.m.* statute, ordinance, by-law; status.

statutaire [staty'tɛ:r], *a.* statutory.

stellaire [stɛl'lɛ:r], *a.* stellar, starry.

stencil [stɛn'sil], *n.m.* stencil.

sténo [ste'no], *abbr. of* **sténographe** or **sténographie.**

sténo-dactylo(graphe) [stenodakti'lo('graf)], *n.* shorthand typist.

sténographe [stenɔ'graf], *n.* stenographer, shorthand writer.

sténographie [stenɔgra'fi], *n.f.* stenography, shorthand.

sténographier [stenɔgra'fje], *v.t.* to take down in shorthand.

stentor [stɑ̃'tɔ:r], *n.m.* Stentor; ***d'une voix de stentor***, in a stentorian voice.

steppe [stɛp], *n.f.* steppe.

stéréoscope [stereɔs'kɔp], *n.m.* stereoscope.

stéréotypé [stereɔti'pe], *a.* stereotyped, hackneyed.

stérile [ste'ril], *a.* sterile, barren; (*fig.*) fruitless, vain.

stérilisant [sterili'zɑ̃], *a.* sterilizing.—*n.m.* sterilizing agent.

stérilisation [sterilizɑ'sjɔ̃], *n.f.* sterilization.

stériliser [sterili'ze], *v.t.* to sterilize.

stérilité [sterili'te], *n.f.* sterility, barrenness.

sterling [stɛr'liŋ], *a. inv.* and *n.m.* sterling.

stéthoscope [stetɔs'kɔp], *n.m.* stethoscope.

stigmate [stig'mat], *n.m.* scar, stigma, stain; brand.

stigmatiser [stigmati'ze], *v.t.* to stigmatize, to brand.

stimulant [stimy'lɑ̃], *a.* stimulating.—*n.m.* stimulant; stimulus; incentive.

stimulation [stimylɑ'sjɔ̃], *n.f.* stimulation.

stimuler [stimy'le], *v.t.* to stimulate; to excite, to rouse.

stipendiaire [stipɑ̃'djɛ:r], *a.* and *n.m.* stipendiary, mercenary.

stipendié [stipɑ̃'dje], *a.* hired.—*n.m.* stipendiary, hireling.

stipendier [stipɑ̃'dje], *v.t.* to hire, to keep in pay.

stipulation [stipylɑ'sjɔ̃], *n.f.* stipulation.

stipuler [stipy'le], *v.t.* to stipulate; to contract.

stock [stɔk], *n.m.* (*Comm.*) stock.

stocker [stɔ'ke], *v.t.* to stock; to stockpile.

stockiste [stɔ'kist], *n.m.* warehouseman; stockist; agent (*for a certain make of car*); service-station (*with spare parts*).

stoïcien [stɔi'sjɛ̃], *a.* Stoic, stoical.—*n.m.* (*fem.* **-enne**) Stoic.

stoïcisme [stɔi'sism], *n.m.* stoicism.

stoïque [stɔ'ik], *a.* Stoic, stoical.—*n.* Stoic.

stoïquement [stɔik'mɑ̃], *adv.* stoically.

stop [stɔp], *int.* stop!—*n.m.* (*Motor.*) stop-light.

stoppage [stɔ'pa:ʒ], *n.m.* invisible mending; stoppage (*of motion, current*).

stopper [stɔ'pe], *v.t.* to mend invisibly; to stop.—*v.i.* to stop (*of a train, steamboat etc.*).

store [stɔ:r], *n.m.* (*spring-roller*) blind.

strabisme [stra'bism], *n.m.* squinting.

strangulation [strɑ̃gylɑ'sjɔ̃], *n.f.* strangulation.

strapontin [strapɔ̃'tɛ̃], *n.m.* folding-seat, tip-up seat.

strass or **stras** [stras], *n.m.* strass, paste jewels.

stratagème [strata'ʒɛm], *n.m.* stratagem.

strate [strat], *n.f.* stratum.

stratégie [strate'ʒi], *n.f.* strategy.

stratégique [strate'ʒik], *a.* strategic.

stratégiquement [strateʒik'mɑ̃], *adv.* strategically.

stratégiste [strate'ʒist], *n.m.* strategist.

stratosphère [stratɔs'fɛ:r], *n.f.* stratosphere.

strict [strikt], *a.* strict, precise; severe.

strictement [striktə'mɑ̃], *adv.* strictly; severely.

strident [stri'dɑ̃], *a.* strident, jarring.

strié [stri'e], *a.* striate, streaked; corrugated; scored.

strontium [strɔ̃'sjɔm], *n.m.* strontium.

strophe [strɔf], *n.f.* strophe; stanza.

structural [strykty'ral], *a.* (*m. pl.* **-aux**) structural.

structure [stryk'ty:r], *n.f.* structure; form, make.

strychnine [strik'nin], *n.f.* strychnin(e).

stuc [styk], *n.m.* stucco.

stucage [sty'ka:ʒ], *n.m.* stucco-work.

studieusement [stydjøz'mɑ̃], *adv.* studiously.

studieux [stu'djø], *a.* (*fem.* **-euse**) studious.

studio [sty'djo], *n.m.* (*Cine.*) film-studio; (*Rad., Tel.*) broadcasting studio; **one-**roomed flat.

stupéfaction [stypefak'sjɔ̃], *n.f.* stupefaction, amazement.
stupéfait [stype'fɛ], *a.* amazed, dumbfounded.
stupéfiant [stype'fjɑ̃], *a.* stupefactive; amazing, astounding.—*n.m.* narcotic.
stupéfier [stype'fje], *v.t.* to stupefy, to astound, to dumbfound.
stupeur [sty'pœ:r], *n.f.* stupor; amazement.
stupide [sty'pid], *a.* stunned; stupid, foolish, dull.
stupidement [stypid'mɑ̃], *adv.* stupidly.
stupidité [stypidi'te], *n.f.* stupidity.
style (1) [stil], *n.m.* style.
style (2) [stil], *n.m.* stylus.
stylé [sti'le], *a.* stylate; (*colloq.*) trained, taught, clever.
styler [sti'le], *v.t.* to train, to form, to school.
stylet [sti'lɛ], *n.m.* stiletto; (*Surg.*) probe.
stylo [sti'lo], *abbr. of* **stylographe** [stilɔ'graf], *n.m.* fountain-pen; ***stylo à bille***, ball-point pen.
stylomine [stilo'min], *n.m.* propelling pencil.
styptique [stip'tik], *a.* and *n.m.* styptic.
su (1) [sy], *n.m.* knowledge; ***au vu et au su de tout le monde***, as everybody knows.
su (2) [sy], *p.p.* [SAVOIR].
suaire [sɥɛ:r], *n.m.* winding-sheet, shroud.
suant [sɥɑ̃], *a.* sweating, in a sweat.
suave [sɥa:v], *a.* sweet, agreeable; suave, bland; soft.
suavement [sɥav'mɑ̃], *adv.* suavely; sweetly.
suavité [sɥavi'te], *n.f.* suavity; sweetness.
subalterne [sybal'tɛrn], *a.* and *n.* subaltern, subordinate; inferior.
subdiviser [sybdivi'ze], *v.t.* to subdivide. **se subdiviser**, *v.r.* to be subdivided.
subdivision [sybdivi'zjɔ̃], *n.f.* subdivision.
subir [sy'bi:r], *v.t.* to support; to go through, to undergo, to suffer; to submit to.
subit [sy'bit], *a.* sudden, unexpected.
subitement [sybit'mɑ̃], *adv.* suddenly, all of a sudden.
subjectif [sybʒɛk'tif], *a.* (*fem.* **-tive**) subjective.
subjection [sybʒɛk'sjɔ̃], *n.f.* subjection.
subjectivement [sybʒɛktiv'mɑ̃], *adv.* subjectively.
subjonctif [sybʒɔ̃k'tif], *a.* (*fem.* **-tive**) and *n.m.* subjunctive.
subjugation [sybʒyga'sjɔ̃], *n.f.* subjugation.
subjuguer [sybʒy'ge], *v.t.* to subjugate, to subdue.
sublimation [syblima'sjɔ̃], *n.f.* sublimation.
sublime [sy'blim], *a.* lofty, sublime, splendid. —*n.m.* the sublime.
sublimement [syblim'mɑ̃], *adv.* sublimely.
submerger [sybmɛr'ʒe], *v.t.* (*conjug. like* MANGER) to submerge, to swamp, to flood; (*fig.*) to overwhelm.
submersible [sybmɛr'sibl], *a.* submersible. —*n.m.* submarine (*boat*).
submersion [sybmɛr'sjɔ̃], *n.f.* submersion.
subordination [sybɔrdina'sjɔ̃], *n.f.* subordination.
subordonné [sybɔrdɔ'ne], *a.* and *n.m.* (*fem.* **-ée**) subordinate, dependent.
subordonner [sybɔrdɔ'ne], *v.t.* to subordinate.
suborner [sybɔr'ne], *v.t.* to suborn, to bribe.
suborneur [sybɔr'nœ:r], *a.* (*fem.* **-euse**) suborning, bribing.—*n.m.* (*fem.* **-euse**) suborner, briber.
subreptice [sybrɛp'tis], *a.* surreptitious.
subrepticement [sybrɛptis'mɑ̃], *adv.* surreptitiously.
subséquemment [sybseka'mɑ̃], *adv.* subsequently.
subséquent [sybse'kɑ̃], *a.* subsequent.
subside [syb'sid], *n.m.* subsidy; (*colloq.*) aid.
subsidiaire [sybsi'djɛ:r], *a.* subsidiary, auxiliary.
subsidiairement [sybsidjɛr'mɑ̃], *adv.* further, also, additionally.
subsistance [sybzis'tɑ̃:s], *n.f.* subsistence, sustenance, maintenance; (*pl.*) provisions.
subsistant [sybzis'tɑ̃], *a.* subsisting, existing.
subsister [sybzis'te], *v.i.* to subsist, to stand; to hold good; to exist, to live.
substance [sybs'tɑ̃:s], *n.f.* substance.
substantiel [sybstɑ̃'sjɛl], *a.* (*fem.* **-elle**) substantial.
substantiellement [sybstɑ̃sjɛl'mɑ̃], *adv.* substantially.
substantif [sybstɑ̃'tif], *a.* (*fem.* **-tive**) substantive.—*n.m.* (*Gram.*) noun.
substituer [sybsti'tɥe], *v.t.* to substitute; (*Law*) to entail.
substitut [sybsti'ty], *n.m.* substitute, deputy (*to someone*).
substitution [sybstity'sjɔ̃], *n.f.* substitution; (*Law*) entail.
subterfuge [sybtɛr'fy:ʒ], *n.m.* subterfuge, evasion, shift.
subtil [syb'til], *a.* subtile, tenuous; penetrating; acute, keen, sharp; cunning; fine-spun, subtle.
subtilement [sybtil'mɑ̃], *adv.* subtly, craftily.
subtiliser [sybtili'ze], *v.t.* to subtilize, to refine; (*colloq.*) to sneak, to steal.
subtilité [sybtili'te], *n.f.* subtlety, fineness; acuteness; shrewdness.
suburbain [sybyr'bɛ̃], *a.* suburban.
subvenir [sybvə'ni:r], *v.i. irr.* (*conjug. like* TENIR) to be helpful; to supply, to provide.
subvention [sybvɑ̃'sjɔ̃], *n.f.* subsidy, aid.
subventionner [sybvɑ̃sjɔ'ne], *v.t.* to subsidize, to make a grant to.
subversif [sybvɛr'sif], *a.* (*fem.* **-sive**) subversive.
subversion [sybvɛr'sjɔ̃], *n.f.* subversion, overthrow.
suc [syk], *n.m.* juice; (*fig.*) essence, quintessence.
succéder [sykse'de], *v.i.* (*conjug. like* CÉDER) to succeed, to follow after (*à*). **se succéder**, *v.r.* to succeed each other.
succès [syk'sɛ], *n.m.* success.
successeur [syksɛ'sœ:r], *n.m.* successor.
successif [syksɛ'sif], *a.* (*fem.* **-ive**) successive, in succession.
succession [syksɛ'sjɔ̃], *n.f.* succession; inheritance; heritage, estate.
successivement [syksɛsiv'mɑ̃], *adv.* successively, in succession.
succinct [syk'sɛ̃], *a.* succinct, concise.
succinctement [syksɛ̃t'mɑ̃], *adv.* succinctly, briefly.
succion [syk'sjɔ̃], *n.f.* suction.
succomber [sykɔ̃'be], *v.i.* to sink, to faint; to yield, to succumb; to fail; to die.
succulence [syky'lɑ̃:s], *n.f.* succulence.
succulent [syky'lɑ̃], *a.* succulent, juicy; rich.

succursale [sykyr'sal], *n.f.* branch (*of a bank etc.*).
sucement [sys'mɑ̃], *n.m.* sucking, suck.
sucer [sy'se], *v.t.* (*conjug. like* COMMENCER) to suck, to suck in; to imbibe.
sucette [sy'sɛt], *n.f.* lollipop; comforter (*for baby*).
suceur [sy'sœ:r], *a.* (*fem.* **-euse**) sucking.—*n.m.* sucker; nozzle (*of a vacuum cleaner*).
suçoir [sy'swa:r], *n.m.* sucker.
sucre [sykr], *n.m.* sugar; ***sucre cristallisé***, granulated sugar; ***sucre d'orge***, barley-sugar; ***sucre en poudre***, castor-sugar.
sucré [sy'kre], *a.* sugared, sweet, sugary; (*fig.*) demure, prim.
sucrer [sy'kre], *v.t.* to sugar, to sweeten.
sucrerie [sykrə'ri], *n.f.* sugar-refinery; (*pl.*) sweets.
sucrier [sykri'e], *n.m.* sugar-basin; sugar-maker.
sud [syd], *a. inv.* south, southerly (*of the wind*).—*n.m.* south; south wind.
sud-est [sy'dɛst], *a. inv.* and *n.m.* south-east.
Sudètes [sy'dɛt], **les**, *m. pl.* Sudetenland.
sud-ouest [sy'dwɛst], *a. inv.* and *n.m.* south-west.
Suède [sɥɛd], **la**, *f.* Sweden.
suède [sɥɛd], *n.m.* suède (*glove leather*).
suédois [sɥe'dwa], *a.* Swedish.—*n.m.* Swedish (*language*); (**Suédois**, *fem.* **-oise**) Swede.
suée [sɥe], *n.f.* sweating.
suer [sɥe], *v.t.* to sweat.—*v.i.* to sweat, to perspire; (*fig.*) to toil, to drudge; to ooze (*of walls*).
sueur [sɥœ:r], *n.f.* sweat, perspiration; (*pl.*) labour, toil.
suffire [sy'fi:r], *v.i. irr.* to suffice, to be sufficient; to be adequate; ***cela suffit***, that's enough. **se suffire**, *v.r.* to provide for oneself.
suffisamment [syfiza'mɑ̃], *adv.* sufficiently.
suffisance [syfi'zɑ̃:s], *n.f.* sufficiency, adequacy; conceit, self-sufficiency.
suffisant [syfi'zɑ̃], *a.* sufficient; conceited.—*n.m.* (*fem.* **-e**) conceited person.
suffixe [sy'fiks], *n.m.* suffix.
suffocant [syfɔ'kɑ̃], *a.* suffocating, choking.
suffocation [syfɔkɑ'sjɔ̃], *n.f.* suffocation.
suffoquer [syfɔ'ke], *v.t.* to suffocate, to choke.—*v.i.* to choke.
suffrage [sy'fra:ʒ], *n.m.* suffrage, vote; approbation, commendation.
suggérer [sygʒe're], *v.t.* (*conjug. like* CÉDER) to suggest.
suggestif [sygʒɛs'tif], *a.* (*fem.* **-tive**) suggestive; erotic.
suggestion [sygʒɛs'tjɔ̃], *n.f.* suggestion, hint, instigation.
suicide [sɥi'sid], *n.m.* suicide.
suicidé [sɥisi'de], *n.m.* (*fem.* **-ée**) suicide.
suicider (se) [səsɥisi'de], *v.r.* to commit suicide.
suie [sɥi], *n.f.* soot.
suif [sɥif], *n.m.* tallow.
suintement [sɥɛ̃t'mɑ̃], *n.m.* oozing, sweating.
suinter [sɥɛ̃'te], *v.i.* to ooze, to sweat (*of walls etc.*); to leak, to run (*of vessels*).
Suisse [sɥis], **la**, *f.* Switzerland.
suisse [sɥis], *a.* Swiss.—*n.m.* porter (*of a mansion*); church officer; (**Suisse**, *fem.* **Suissesse**) Swiss (*person*).
suite [sɥit], *n.f.* the rest; retinue, attendants; sequel, continuation; series; set; connexion; result; ***à la suite***, after, behind; ***de suite***, consecutively; ***et ainsi de suite***, and so on; ***tout de suite***, immediately.
suivant [sɥi'vɑ̃], *prep.* according to; in the direction of; ***suivant que***, as, according as.—*a.* next, following, subsequent.—*n.m.* (*fem.* **-e**) follower, attendant.—*n.f.* (**-e**) lady's maid.
suivi [sɥi'vi], *a.* followed; connected; consistent; popular.
suivre [sɥi:vr], *v.t. irr.* to follow; to be next to; to attend; to observe; to pursue; to practise (*a profession etc.*).—*v.i.* to follow; to come after; to result, to ensue; ***à faire suivre***, to be forwarded; ***à suivre***, to be continued. **se suivre**, *v.r.* to follow each other, to be continuous.
sujet [sy'ʒɛ], *a.* (*fem.* **-ette**) subject, subjected, liable, exposed; apt, addicted, inclined (*à*).—*n.m.* subject; topic; cause.
sujétion [syʒe'sjɔ̃], *n.f.* subjection, servitude; constraint.
sulfate [syl'fat], *n.m.* sulphate.
sulfureux [sylfy'rø], *a.* (*fem.* **-euse**) sulphurous, sulphureous.
sulfurique [sylfy'rik], *a.* sulphuric (*acid*).
sultan [syl'tɑ̃], *n.m.* sultan.
sultane [syl'tan], *n.f.* sultana, sultaness.
sumac [sy'mak], *n.m.* sumac.
superbe [sy'pɛrb], *a.* proud, arrogant; superb; stately; lofty; vainglorious.—*n.* proud person.—*n.f.* arrogance; vainglory.
superbement [sypɛrbə'mɑ̃], *adv.* haughtily, superbly.
supercarburant [sypɛrkarby'rɑ̃], *n.m.* high-octane petrol.
supercherie [sypɛrʃə'ri], *n.f.* deceit, fraud.
superficie [sypɛrfi'si], *n.f.* area, surface; (*fig.*) superficiality.
superficiel [sypɛrfi'sjɛl], *a.* (*fem.* **-elle**) superficial; shallow.
superficiellement [sypɛrfisjɛl'mɑ̃], *adv.* superficially.
superfin [sypɛr'fɛ̃], *a.* superfine, of superior quality.
superflu [sypɛr'fly], *a.* superfluous; unnecessary.—*n.m.* superfluity, excess.
superfluité [sypɛrflɥi'te], *n.f.* superfluity.
supérieur [sype'rjœ:r], *a.* superior; upper, higher.—*n.m.* (*fem.* **-e**) superior.
supérieurement [syperjœr'mɑ̃], *adv.* in a superior manner; superlatively.
supériorité [syperjɔri'te], *n.f.* superiority.
superlatif [sypɛrla'tif], *a.* (*fem.* **-tive**) superlative.—*n.m.* (*Gram.*) superlative.
superlativement [sypɛrlativ'mɑ̃], *adv.* superlatively.
superposer [sypɛrpo'ze], *v.t.* to superpose; to superimpose.
superposition [sypɛrpozi'sjɔ̃], *n.f.* superposition; superimposition.
supersonique [sypɛrsɔ'nik], *a.* supersonic.
superstitieusement [sypɛrstisjøz'mɑ̃], *adv.* superstitiously.
superstitieux [sypɛrsti'sjø], *a.* (*fem.* **-euse**) superstitious.
superstition [sypɛrsti'sjɔ̃], *n.f.* superstition.
superstructure [sypɛrstryk'ty:r], *n.f.* superstructure; permanent way (*of railway*).
supin [sy'pɛ̃], *n.m.* (*Gram.*) supine.

supplantation [syplɑ̃tɑ'sjɔ̃], *n.f.* supplantation; supersession.
supplanter [syplɑ̃'te], *v.t.* to supplant, to oust, to supersede.
suppléance [syple'ɑ̃:s], *n.f.* substitution, deputyship.
suppléant [syple'ɑ̃], *a.* and *n.m.* (*fem.* **-e**) substitute, assistant, deputy, understudy.
suppléer [syple'e], *v.t.* to supply, to fill up; to take the place of.—*v.i.* to make up the deficiency, to compensate for (*à*).
supplément [syple'mɑ̃], *n.m.* supplement; additional price, excess fare.
supplémentaire [syplemɑ̃'tɛ:r], *a.* supplementary, supplemental, additional, extra.
suppliant [sypli'ɑ̃], *a.* suppliant, beseeching. —*n.m.* (*fem.* **-e**) suppliant, supplicant, petitioner.
supplication [syplikɑ'sjɔ̃], *n.f.* supplication, entreaty.
supplice [sy'plis], *n.m.* corporal punishment; torture; (*fig.*) torment, ordeal; ***être au supplice***, to be upon the rack.
supplicié [sypli'sje], *n.m.* (*fem.* **-ée**) executed criminal.
supplicier [sypli'sje], *v.t.* to put to death, to execute.
supplier [sypli'e], *v.t.* to beseech, to entreat, to beg.
supplique [sy'plik], *n.f.* petition, entreaty.
support [sy'pɔ:r], *n.m.* support, prop; rest, stand, bracket.
supportable [sypɔr'tabl], *a.* supportable, bearable, tolerable.
supportablement [sypɔrtablə'mɑ̃], *adv.* tolerably.
supporter (1) [sypɔr'tœ:r], *n.m.* (*Spt.*) supporter, partisan.
supporter (2) [sypɔr'te], *v.t.* to support, to uphold; to endure, to suffer; to stand. **se supporter**, *v.r.* to be borne; to bear with each other.
supposable [sypo'zabl], *a.* supposable.
supposé [sypo'ze], *a.* pretended, forged, assumed; reputed.
supposer [sypo'ze], *v.t.* to suppose; to admit, to imply; to conjecture; to forge (*a will*).
supposition [sypozi'sjɔ̃], *n.f.* supposition; substitution; forgery.
suppôt [sy'po], *n.m.* agent, tool, abettor.
suppressif [syprɛ'sif], *a.* (*fem.* **-ive**) suppressive.
suppression [syprɛ'sjɔ̃], *n.f.* suppression; cancelling (*of passage*); concealment.
supprimer [sypri'me], *v.t.* to suppress; to omit; to abolish, to cancel.
suppuration [sypyrɑ'sjɔ̃], *n.f.* suppuration.
suppurer [sypy're], *v.i.* to suppurate, to run.
supputation [sypytɑ'sjɔ̃], *n.f.* computation, calculation.
supputer [sypy'te], *v.t.* to calculate, to compute, to reckon.
suprématie [syprema'si], *n.f.* supremacy.
suprême [sy'prɛ:m], *a.* supreme, highest; last.
suprêmement [syprɛmə'mɑ̃], *adv.* supremely.
sur (1) [syr], *prep.* on, upon; over; in; towards; about; concerning; out of.
sur (2) [sy:r], *a.* sour, tart.
sûr [sy:r], *a.* sure, certain; safe, secure; firm, steady; trustworthy; ***à coup sûr***, for certain; ***en lieu sûr***, in a place of safety; ***je suis sûr de vous***, I can depend on you; ***sûr et certain***, positive.
surabondamment [syrabɔ̃da'mɑ̃], *adv.* superabundantly.
surabondance [syrabɔ̃'dɑ̃:s], *n.f.* superabundance; glut.
surabondant [syrabɔ̃'dɑ̃], *a.* superabundant.
surabonder [syrabɔ̃'de], *v.i.* to superabound; to be glutted (***de***).
suraigu [syre'gy], *a.* (*fem.* **-ë**) overshrill; very acute (*inflammation*).
suralimenté [syralimɑ̃'te], *a.* overfed.
suralimenter [syralimɑ̃'te], *v.t.* to overfeed, to feed up; (*Motor.*) to supercharge.
suranné [syra'ne], *a.* expired; superannuated, antiquated.
surcharge [syr'ʃarʒ], *n.f.* overloading; (*stamp*) surcharge; excess.
surcharger [syrʃar'ʒe], *v.t.* (*conjug. like* MANGER) to overload, to overtax; (*fig.*) to overwhelm; to oppress; ***surcharger d'impôts***, to overtax.
surchauffer [syrʃo'fe], *v.t.* to overheat.
surclasser [syrklɑ'se], *v.t.* to outclass.
surcompresseur [syrkɔ̃prɛ'sœ:r], *n.m.* supercharger.
surcompression [syrkɔ̃prɛ'sjɔ̃], *n.f.* supercharging.
surcomprimé [syrkɔ̃pri'me], *a.* supercharged.
surcroît [syr'krwɑ], *n.m.* addition, increase; surplus, excess.
surcuit [syr'kɥi], *a.* overdone.
surdité [syrdi'te], *n.f.* deafness.
sureau [sy'ro], *n.m.* (*pl.* **-eaux**) elder(-tree).
surélever [syrel've], *v.t.* (*conjug. like* AMENER) to raise higher; (*Golf*) to tee.
sûrement [syr'mɑ̃], *adv.* surely, certainly, to be sure; safely.
surenchère [syrɑ̃'ʃɛ:r], *n.f.* higher bid, outbidding.
surenchérir [syrɑ̃ʃe'ri:r], *v.i.* to overbid, to bid higher.
surestimation [syrɛstimɑ'sjɔ̃], *n.f.* overestimate, overvaluation.
surestimer [syrɛsti'me], *v.t.* to overestimate; to overrate.
sûreté [syr'te], *n.f.* safety, security; warranty; ***la Sûreté***, Criminal Investigation Department.
surexcitation [syrɛksitɑ'sjɔ̃], *n.f.* excitement, overexcitement.
surexciter [syrɛksi'te], *v.t.* to overexcite.
surexposer [syrɛkspo'ze], *v.t.* (*Phot.*) to overexpose.
surexposition [syrɛkspozi'sjɔ̃], *n.f.* (*Phot.*) overexposure.
surface [syr'fas], *n.f.* surface; outside.
surfaire [syr'fɛ:r], *v.t. irr.* (*conjug. like* FAIRE) to ask too much for; to overrate, to overpraise.
surfin [syr'fɛ̃], *a.* (*Comm.*) superfine.
surgir [syr'ʒi:r], *v.i.* to rise, to surge; to loom up.
surgissement [syrʒis'mɑ̃], *n.m.* upheaval.
surhomme [sy'rɔm], *n.m.* superman.
surhumain [syry'mɛ̃], *a.* superhuman.
surintendant [syrɛ̃tɑ̃'dɑ̃], *n.m.* superintendent, overseer; steward (*of large estate*).
surintendante [syrɛ̃tɑ̃'dɑ̃:t], *n.f.* woman superintendent; superintendent's wife.
surir [sy'ri:r], *v.i.* to turn sour.
sur-le-champ [syrlə'ʃɑ̃], *adv.* at once.

surlendemain [syrlɑ̃d'mɛ̃], *n.m.* two days after.

surmenage [syrmə'na:ʒ], *n.m.* excess fatigue; overworking.

surmener [syrmə'ne], *v.t.* (*conjug. like* AMENER) to overwork, to overtire. **se surmener**, *v.r.* to overwork.

surmontable [syrmɔ̃'tabl], *a.* surmountable, superable.

surmonter [syrmɔ̃'te], *v.t.* to surmount; to overcome, to surpass.

surmultiplication [syrmyltiplikɑ'sjɔ̃], *n.f.* (*Motor.*) overdrive.

surnager [syrna'ʒe], *v.i.* (*conjug. like* MANGER) to float on the surface; (*fig.*) to survive.

surnaturel [syrnaty'rɛl], *a.* (*fem.* **-elle**) supernatural.—*n.m.* supernatural.

surnaturellement [syrnatyrɛl'mɑ̃], *adv.* supernaturally.

surnom [syr'nɔ̃], *n.m.* nickname.

surnommer [syrnɔ'me], *v.t.* to nickname.

surnuméraire [syrnyme'rɛ:r], *a.* and *n.m.* supernumerary.

surpasser [syrpɑ'se], *v.t.* to surpass, to excel, to outdo, to exceed.

surpeuplé [syrpœ'ple], *a.* overpopulated.

surpeuplement [syrpœplə'mɑ̃], *n.m.* overpopulation, overcrowding.

surplis [syr'pli], *n.m. inv.* surplice.

surplomb [syr'plɔ̃], *n.m.* overhang (*of buildings*); ***en surplomb***, overhanging.

surplomber [syrplɔ̃'be], *v.t.*, *v.i.* to overhang.

surplus [syr'ply], *n.m. inv.* surplus, remainder, excess.

surpoids [syr'pwɑ], *n.m.* overweight, excess weight.

surprenant [syrprə'nɑ̃], *a.* surprising, astonishing.

surprendre [syr'prɑ̃:dr], *v.t. irr.* (*conjug. like* PRENDRE) to surprise, to catch; to overhear; to entrap; to intercept. **se surprendre**, *v.r.* to surprise oneself; to catch oneself (*napping etc.*).

surprise [syr'pri:z], *n.f.* surprise; amazement.

surproduction [syrprɔdyk'sjɔ̃], *n.f.* overproduction.

surréalisme [syrrea'lism], *n.m.* surrealism.

surréaliste [syrrea'list], *a.* and *n.* surrealist.

sursaut [syr'so], *n.m.* start, jump.

sursauter [syrso'te], *v.i.* to start up; ***faire sursauter (quelqu'un)***, to startle (someone).

surseoir [syr'swa:r], *v.t.*, *v.i. irr.* to suspend, to delay, to postpone.

sursis [syr'si], *n.m.* delay, respite, reprieve.

surtaxe [syr'taks], *n.f.* surtax; surcharge.

surtaxer [syrtak'se], *v.t.* to overtax.

surtout [syr'tu], *adv.* above all, chiefly.—*n.m.* overcoat; centrepiece (*for table*).

surveillance [syrvɛ'jɑ̃:s], *n.f.* supervision; surveillance.

surveillant [syrvɛ'jɑ̃], *n.m.* (*fem.* **-e**) inspector, superintendent; supervisor.

surveiller [syrvɛ'je], *v.t.* to superintend, to inspect; to watch, to supervise.

survenir [syrvə'ni:r], *v.i. irr.* (*conjug. like* TENIR, *but with aux.* ÊTRE) to arrive *or* happen unexpectedly; to drop in.

survêtement [syrvɛt'mɑ̃], *n.m.* (*Spt.*) tracksuit.

survivant [syrvi'vɑ̃], *a.* surviving.—*n.m.* (*fem.* **-e**) survivor.

survivre [syr'vi:vr], *v.i. irr.* (*conjug. like* VIVRE) to survive, to outlive someone (*à*). **se survivre**, *v.r.* to live *or* exist again.

survoler [syrvɔ'le], *v.t.* to fly over (*of aircraft*).

sus [sys], *prep.* upon; ***en sus***, over and above.—*int.* courage! come on!

susceptibilité [sysɛptibili'te], *n.f.* susceptibility; irritability.

susceptible [sysɛp'tibl], *a.* susceptible, capable; likely to; touchy; irascible.

susciter [sysi'te], *v.t.* to raise up, to set up; to create; to arouse, to instigate.

suscription [syskrip'sjɔ̃], *n.f.* superscription, address.

susdit [sys'di], *a.* and *n.m.* (*fem.* **-e**) aforesaid.

suspect [sys'pɛkt, sys'pɛ], *a.* suspected, suspicious, suspect, doubtful.—*n.m.* suspect.

suspecter [syspɛk'te], *v.t.* to suspect.

suspendre [sys'pɑ̃:dr], *v.t.* to suspend, to hang up; to delay, to defer.

suspendu [syspɑ̃'dy], *a.* suspended, hung up; in suspense.

suspens [sys'pɑ̃], *adv. phr.* ***en suspens***, in suspense; (*person*) in doubt; (*thing*) in abeyance.

suspension [syspɑ̃'sjɔ̃], *n.f.* suspension, interruption; hanging-lamp.

suspicion [syspi'sjɔ̃], *n.f.* suspicion.

susurration [sysyrɑ'sjɔ̃], *n.f.*, **susurrement** [sysyr'mɑ̃], *n.m.* susurration, whispering, murmur; rustling.

suttee [sy'te], **suttie** [sy'ti], *n.f.* suttee.

suture [sy'ty:r], *n.f.* suture; joint; stitching.

Suzanne [sy'zan], *f.* Susan.

suzerain [syz'rɛ̃], *a.* paramount, suzerain.—*n.m.* (*fem.* **-e**) suzerain, lord *or* lady paramount.

suzeraineté [syzrɛn'te], *n.f.* suzerainty.

svastika [zvasti'ka], *n.m.* swastika.

svelte [zvɛlt], *a.* slender, slim.

sveltesse [zvɛl'tɛs], *n.f.* slenderness, slimness.

sybarite [siba'rit], *a.* sybaritic.—*n.* sybarite, voluptuary.

sycomore [sikɔ'mɔ:r], *n.m.* sycamore.

sycophante [sikɔ'fɑ̃:t], *a.* sycophantic.—*n.m.* informer; hypocrite, impostor; sycophant, (*fam.*) toady.

syllabe [sil'lab], *n.f.* syllable.

syllabique [silla'bik], *a.* syllabic.

syllogisme [sillɔ'ʒism], *n.m.* syllogism.

sylphe [silf], *n.m.*, **sylphide** [sil'fid], *n.f.* sylph.

sylvain [sil'vɛ̃], *n.m.* sylvan.

sylvestre [sil'vɛstr], *a.* sylvan, growing in woods.

Sylvie [sil'vi], *f.* Sylvia.

symbole [sɛ̃'bɔl], *n.m.* symbol, sign, emblem; creed.

symbolique [sɛ̃bɔ'lik], *a.* symbolic, symbolical.

symboliser [sɛ̃bɔli'ze], *v.t.* to symbolize.

symbolisme [sɛ̃bɔ'lism], *n.m.* symbolism.

symétrie [sime'tri], *n.f.* symmetry.

symétrique [sime'trik], *a.* symmetrical.

symétriquement [simetrik'mɑ̃], *adv.* symmetrically.

sympathie [sɛ̃pa'ti], *n.f.* liking, fellow-feeling.

sympathique [sɛ̃pa'tik], *a.* congenial, likeable.

sympathisant [sɛ̃pati'zɑ̃], *a.* sympathizing.—*n.m.* (*Pol.*) fellow-traveller.
sympathiser [sɛ̃pati'ze], *v.i.* to get on well together.
symphonie [sɛ̃fɔ'ni], *n.f.* symphony.
symptomatique [sɛ̃ptɔma'tik], *a.* symptomatic.
symptôme [sɛ̃p'to:m], *n.m.* symptom; indication, sign; token.
synagogue [sina'gɔg], *n.f.* synagogue.
synchronisation [sɛ̃krɔnizɑ'sjɔ̃], *n.f.* synchronization.
synchroniser [sɛ̃krɔni'ze], *v.t.* to synchronize.
syncope [sɛ̃'kɔp], *n.f.* syncope, swoon, fainting fit; (*Mus.*) syncopation.
syndic [sɛ̃'dik], *n.m.* syndic, trustee; assignee (*in bankruptcy*).
syndicalisme [sɛ̃dika'lism], *n.m.* ***syndicalisme ouvrier***, trade-unionism.
syndicaliste [sɛ̃dika'list], *a.* and *n.* trade-unionist.
syndicat [sɛ̃di'ka], *n.m.* syndicate, trusteeship; ***syndicat d'initiative***, tourists' information bureau; ***syndicat ouvrier***, trade-union.
synonyme [sinɔ'nim], *a.* synonymous.—*n.m.* synonym.
syntaxe [sɛ̃'taks], *n.f.* syntax.
synthétique [sɛ̃te'tik], *a.* synthetic.
syriaque [si'rjak], *a.* Syriac.—*n.m.* Syriac (*language*).
Syrie [si'ri], **la**, *f.* Syria.
syrien [si'rjɛ̃], *a.* Syrian.—*n.m.* Syrian (*language*); (**Syrien**, *fem.* **-enne**) Syrian (*person*).
systématique [sistema'tik], *a.* systematic(al).
systématiquement [sistematik'mɑ̃], *adv.* systematically.
système [sis'tɛm], *n.m.* system, scheme, plan; device.

T

T, t [te], *n.m.* the twentieth letter of the alphabet.
t' [t], *elision* [TE].
ta [ta], [TON (1)].
tabac [ta'ba], *n.m.* tobacco; snuff.
tabatière [taba'tjɛ:r], *n.f.* snuff-box.
tabernacle [tabɛr'nakl], *n.m.* tent; tabernacle.
table [tabl], *n.f.* table; board (*food, fare*); mess (*of officers etc.*); slab; face (*of anvil etc.*); table of contents etc.; ***faire table rase***, to make a clean sweep; ***mettre*** or ***dresser la table***, to lay the table.
tableau [ta'blo], *n.m.* (*pl.* **-eaux**) picture, painting, tableau; scene; description; list; blackboard.
tablée [ta'ble], *n.f.* company at table.
tablette [ta'blɛt], *n.f.* shelf; tablet; slab, bar (*of chocolate*); (*Pharm.*) lozenge; note-book.
tablier [ta'blje], *n.m.* apron (*in all senses*); chess- *or* draught-board.
tabou [ta'bu], *a.* and *n.m.* taboo.
tabouret [tabu'rɛ], *n.m.* stool, foot-stool.
tabourin [tabu'rɛ̃], *n.m.* chimney-cowl.
tabulateur [tabyla'tœ:r], *n.m.* tabulator; (*Teleph.*) dial.
tachant [ta'ʃɑ̃], *a.* easily soiled.
tache [taʃ], *n.f.* spot, stain; (*fig.*) blot.
tâche [tɑ:ʃ], *n.f.* task, job.
tacher [ta'ʃe], *v.t.* to stain, to spot; (*fig.*) to taint.
tâcher [tɑ'ʃe], *v.i.* to try, to endeavour, to strive.
tacheter [taʃ'te], *v.t.* (*conjug. like* APPELER) to fleck, to speckle, to mottle.
tacite [ta'sit], *a.* tacit, implied.
tacitement [tasit'mɑ̃], *adv.* tacitly.
taciturne [tasi'tyrn], *a.* taciturn.
taciturnité [tasityrni'te], *n.f.* taciturnity.
tact [takt], *n.m.* feeling, touch; tact.
tacticien [takti'sjɛ̃], *n.m.* tactician.
tactile [tak'til], *a.* tactile.
tactilité [taktili'te], *n.f.* tactility.
tactique [tak'tik], *a.* tactical.—*n.f.* tactics; (*fig.*) stratagem, move.
taffetas [taf'tɑ], *n.m.* taffeta.
taie (1) [tɛ], *n.f.* ***taie d'oreiller***, pillow-case.
taie (2) [tɛ], *n.f.* film, speck (*in the eye*).
taillade [tɑ'jad], *n.f.* slash, gash, cut.
taillader [tɑja'de], *v.t.* to slash, to cut, to gash.
taillant [tɑ'jɑ̃], *n.m.* edge (*of a knife etc.*).
taille [tɑ:j], *n.f.* cutting, cut, fashion; edge (*of a sword*); height, stature; waist, figure; (*Hort.*) pruning; ***de taille à***, quite capable of.
taillé [tɑ'je], *a.* cut, carved; well-built (*person*).
taille-crayon [tɑjkrɛ'jɔ̃], *n.m.* (*pl.* **-crayons**) pencil-sharpener.
taille-ongles [tɑj'ɔ̃:gl], *n.m. inv.* nail-clippers.
tailler [tɑ'je], *v.t.* to cut, to cut out; to carve; to hew; to prune; to sharpen; to shape; to deal (*cards*).
tailleur [tɑ'jœ:r], *n.m.* tailor; cutter; hewer; (*woman's two-piece*) suit.
tailleuse [tɑ'jø:z], *n.f.* tailoress.
taillis [tɑ'ji], *n.m. inv.* copse; brushwood.
tain [tɛ̃], *n.m.* foil; silvering (*for mirrors*).
taire [tɛ:r], *v.t. irr.* to say nothing of, to pass over in silence, to suppress, to keep dark. **se taire**, *v.r.* to be silent; to remain unsaid.
talc [talk], *n.m.* talc, talcum powder.
talent [ta'lɑ̃], *n.m.* talent; (*fig.*) ability.
talion [ta'ljɔ̃], *n.m.* talion, retaliation.
talisman [talis'mɑ̃], *n.m.* talisman.
taloche [ta'lɔʃ], *n.f.* cuff, thump, buffet.
talocher [talɔ'ʃe], *v.t.* to cuff, to box (*someone's*) ears.
talon [ta'lɔ̃], *n.m.* heel; counterfoil.
talonner [talɔ'ne], *v.t.* to be close on the heels of; to press hard, to spur.—*v.i.* (*Naut.*) to ground; (*Ftb.*) to heel out (*of the scrum*).
talonneur [talɔ'nœ:r], *n.m.* (*Ftb.*) hooker.
talus [ta'ly], *n.m.* slope, ramp; embankment.
talutage [taly'ta:ʒ], *n.m.* sloping, embanking.
tamarin [tama'rɛ̃], *n.m.* tamarind.
tamaris [tama'ris], **tamarisc** [tama'risk], *n.m.* tamarisk.
tambour [tɑ̃'bu:r], *n.m.* drum; drummer; embroidery frame; (*Anat.*) tympanum; ***tambour de ville***, town crier.
tambourin [tɑ̃bu'rɛ̃], *n.m.* Provençal tabor.
tambourinage [tɑ̃buri'na:ʒ], *n.m.* drumming.
tambouriner [tɑ̃buri'ne] *v.t.* to advertise.—*v.i.* to drum, to tattoo.

tambour-major [tɑ̃burma'ʒɔ:r], *n.m.* (*pl.* **tambours-majors**) drum-major.
tamis [ta'mi], *n.m. inv.* sieve, sifter, strainer.
tamisage [tami'za:ʒ], *n.m.* sifting, straining.
Tamise [ta'mi:z], **la**, *f.* the Thames.
tamiser [tami'ze], *v.t.* to sift, to strain; to filter.
tamiseur [tami'zœ:r], *n.m.* (*fem.* **-euse**) sifter.
tampon [tɑ̃'pɔ̃], *n.m.* stopper; plug; bung; buffer; pad (*used in engraving etc.*).
tamponnement [tɑ̃pɔn'mɑ̃], *n.m.* plugging, stopping; (*Rail.*) head-on collision.
tamponner [tɑ̃pɔ'ne], *v.t.* to plug, to stop up; to run into (*another train etc.*). **se tamponner**, *v.r.* to collide.
tan [tɑ̃], *a. inv.* tan(-coloured).—*n.m.* tan; tanner's bark.
tancer [tɑ̃'se], *v.t.* (*conjug. like* COMMENCER) to rate, to lecture, to scold.
tanche [tɑ̃:ʃ], *n.f.* tench.
tandem [tɑ̃'dɛm], *n.m.* tandem.
tandis [tɑ̃'di] **que**, *conj. phr.* while; whereas.
tangage [tɑ̃'ga:ʒ], *n.m.* pitching (*of ship, aeroplane*).
tangent [tɑ̃'ʒɑ̃], *a.* tangential.—*n.f.* (**-e**) tangent.
tangible [tɑ̃'ʒibl], *a.* tangible.
tangiblement [tɑ̃ʒiblə'mɑ̃], *adv.* tangibly.
tangue [tɑ̃:g], *n.f.* slimy sand (*used as manure*).
tanguer [tɑ̃'ge], *v.i.* (*Naut.*) to pitch.
tanière [ta'njɛ:r], *n.f.* den, hole, lair (*of beasts*).
tank [tɑ̃k], *n.m.* (*Mil.*) tank.
tannage [ta'na:ʒ], *n.m.* tanning.
tannant [ta'nɑ̃], *a.* tanning; (*pop.*) tiresome, annoying.
tanné [ta'ne], *a.* tanned, sunburnt (*skin*); tawny.—*n.m.* tan (*colour*).
tanner [ta'ne], *v.t.* to tan; (*pop.*) to tease; to beat.
tannerie [tan'ri], *n.f.* tan-yard, tannery.
tanneur [ta'nœ:r], *n.m.* tanner.
tant [tɑ̃], *adv.* so much, such; so many; as much, as many; to such a degree, so; so far; so long, as long; ***tant bien que mal***, somehow or other, after a fashion; ***tant pis***, too bad, never mind.
tantaliser [tɑ̃tali'ze], *v.t.* to tantalize.
tante [tɑ̃:t], *n.f.* aunt; (*pop.*) pawn-broker, 'uncle'.
tantôt [tɑ̃'to], *adv.* presently, by and by, anon; soon; a little while ago, just now; sometimes.
Tanzanie [tɑ̃za'ni], **la**, *f.* Tanzania.
taon [tɑ̃], *n.m.* ox-fly, gadfly, cleg.
tapage [ta'pa:ʒ], *n.m.* noise, uproar, row; (*colloq.*) show.
tapageur [tapa'ʒœ:r], *a.* (*fem.* **-euse**) rackety, boisterous, noisy; flashy.—*n.m.* (*fem.* **-euse**) noisy person, blusterer.
tape [tap], *n.f.* rap, slap, tap, thump.
taper [ta'pe], *v.t.* to hit, to slap; to smack, to tap.—*v.i.* to hit, to stamp; to strum; to beat down (*of sun*).
tapinois [tapi'nwa], *only in* ***en tapinois***, *adv. phr.* stealthily, slyly.
tapioca [tapjɔ'ka], *n.m.* tapioca.
tapir [ta'pi:r], *n.m.* tapir (*animal*).
tapir (se) [səta'pi:r], *v.r.* to squat, to crouch, to cower, to lurk.
tapis [ta'pi], *n.m.* carpet, rug; cover-cloth (*for tables etc.*).
tapis-brosse [tapi'brɔs], *n.m.* (*pl.* **-brosses**) door-mat.
tapisser [tapi'se], *v.t.* to hang with tapestry; to cover; to deck, to adorn; to paper; to carpet.
tapisserie [tapis'ri], *n.f.* tapestry, hangings; wallpaper; upholstery.
tapissier [tapi'sje], *n.m.* (*fem.* **-ière**) upholsterer; tapestry-worker.
tapoter [tapɔ'te], *v.t.* to pat, to tap; to strum.
taquin [ta'kɛ̃], *a.* teasing.—*n.m.* (*fem.* **-e**) tease, teasing person.
taquiner [taki'ne], *v.t.* to tease, to plague.
taquinerie [takin'ri], *n.f.* teasing; teasing disposition.
tard [ta:r], *adv.* late.—*n.m.* late hour.
tarder [tar'de], *v.i.* to delay; to tarry, to loiter; to be long; (*impers.*) to long (*de*).
tardif [tar'dif], *a.* (*fem.* **-dive**) tardy, late; slow, belated; backward.
tardivement [tardiv'mɑ̃], *adv.* tardily, slowly, belatedly.
tare [ta:r], *n.f.* tare; (*Comm.*) waste, damage; (*fig.*) blemish, defect.
taré [ta're], *a.* damaged, spoiled; disreputable.
tarentule [tarɑ̃'tyl], *n.f.* tarantula.
tarer [ta're], *v.t.* to injure, to damage, to spoil; (*Comm.*) to tare. **se tarer**, *v.r.* to spoil, to deteriorate.
targuer (se) [sətar'ge], *v.r.* to boast, to brag.
tarif [ta'rif], *n.m.* tariff, rate, scale of prices.
tarifer [tari'fe], *v.t.* to tariff, to price, to rate.
tarir [ta'ri:r], *v.t.* to dry up; to exhaust.—*v.i.* to dry up; to be exhausted; to cease. **se tarir**, *v.r.* to dry up.
tarissable [tari'sabl], *a.* exhaustible.
tarissement [taris'mɑ̃], *n.m.* exhausting, drying up.
tartan [tar'tɑ̃], *n.m.* tartan, plaid.
tarte [tart], *n.f.* tart, flan.
tartelette [tar'tlɛt], *n.f.* tartlet.
tartine [tar'tin], *n.f.* slice of bread (*with butter, jam etc.*).
tartufe [tar'tyf], *n.m.* hypocrite.
tas [tɑ], *n.m. inv.* heap, pile; (*fig.*) lot, set (*of persons etc.*).
Tasmanie [tasma'ni], **la**, *f.* Tasmania.
tasmanien [tasma'njɛ̃], *a.* Tasmanian.—*n.m.* (**Tasmanien**, *fem.* **-enne**) Tasmanian (*person*).
tasse [tɑ:s], *n.f.* cup.
tassement [tɑs'mɑ̃], *n.m.* settling, sinking, subsidence.
tasser [tɑ'se], *v.t.* to heap *or* pile up; to compress, to squeeze, to cram.—*v.i.* to grow thick. **se tasser**, *v.r.* to sink, to settle, to subside; to huddle together (*of persons*).
tâter [tɑ'te], *v.t.* to feel; to try, to taste; to sound, to test.—*v.i.* to taste, to try (*de* or *à*). **se tâter**, *v.r.* to examine oneself.
tatillon [tati'jɔ̃], *a.* (*fem.* **-onne**) niggling, finical.
tâtonnement [tɑtɔn'mɑ̃], *n.m.* groping.
tâtonner [tɑtɔ'ne], *v.i.* to feel one's way, to grope.
tâtons (à) [atɑ'tɔ̃], *adv. phr.* gropingly.
tatouage [ta'twa:ʒ], *n.m.* tattooing.
tatouer [ta'twe], *v.t.* to tattoo.
taudis [to'di], *n.m.* hovel, slum, hole.
taupe [to:p], *n.f.* mole; moleskin.

taupier [to'pje], *n.m.* mole-catcher.
taupière [to'pjɛ:r], *n.f.* mole-trap.
taupinière [topi'njɛ:r], **taupinée** [topi'ne], *n.f.* mole-hill; hillock, knoll.
taure [to:r], *n.f.* heifer.
taureau [tɔ'ro], *n.m.* (*pl.* **-eaux**) bull; (*Astron.*) Taurus.
taux [to], *n.m. inv.* price, rate; rate of interest.
taverne [ta'vɛrn], *n.f.* tavern, café, restaurant.
tavernier [tavɛr'nje], *n.m.* (*fem.* **-ière**) innkeeper.
taxation [taksɑ'sjɔ̃], *n.f.* taxation; fixing of prices.
taxe [taks], *n.f.* tax; duty, rate; fixing of prices; controlled price.
taxer [tak'se], *v.t.* to tax; to rate, to fix the price of; to accuse (*de*).
taxi [tak'si], *n.m.* taxi (-cab).
taxiphone [taksi'fɔn], *n.m.* public telephone (*box*).
Tchécoslovaquie [tʃekɔslɔva'ki], **la**, *f.* Czechoslovakia.
tchèque [tʃɛk], *a.* Czech.—*n.m.* Czech (*language*).—*n.* (**Tchèque**) Czech (*person*).
te [tə, t], *pron. obj.* *thee, you.
technicien [tɛkni'sjɛ̃], *n.m.* (*fem.* **-enne**) technician.
technique [tɛk'nik], *a.* technical.—*n.f.* technique.
techniquement [tɛknik'mɑ̃], *adv.* technically.
technologie [tɛknɔlɔ'ʒi], *n.f.* technology.
technologique [tɛknɔlɔ'ʒik], *a.* technological.
technologue [tɛknɔ'lɔg], *n.* technologist.
teck or **tek** [tɛk], *n.m.* teak, teak-wood.
teigne [tɛɲ], *n.f.* tinea (*moth*); tinea (*skin-disease, such as ringworm*).
teigneux [tɛ'ɲø], *a.* (*fem.* **-euse**) scurvy.—*n.m.* (*fem.* **-euse**) scurfy person.
teindre [tɛ̃:dr], *v.t. irr.* (*conjug. like* CRAINDRE) to dye, to stain.
teint [tɛ̃], *n.m.* dye, colour; complexion; hue.
teinte [tɛ̃:t], *n.f.* tint, colour, shade, hue; (*fig.*) smack, touch.
teinter [tɛ̃'te], *v.t.* to tint; to give a colour to.
teinture [tɛ̃'ty:r], *n.f.* dye; dyeing; colour, hue; (*Pharm.*) tincture.
teinturerie [tɛ̃tyr'ri], *n.f.* dyeing; dye-works; dry-cleaning.
teinturier [tɛ̃ty'rje], *n.m.* (*fem.* **-ière**) dyer; dry-cleaner.
tek [TECK].
tel [tɛl], *a.* (*fem.* **telle**) such; like, similar.—*pron. indef.* such a one; ***M. un tel***, Mr. So-and-so.
télécommande [telekɔ'mɑ̃:d], *n.f.* remote control.
télécommunications [telekɔmynikɑ'sjɔ̃], *n.f. pl.* telecommunications.
télégramme [tele'gram], *n.m.* telegram.
télégraphe [tele'graf], *n.m.* telegraph.
télégraphie [telegra'fi], *n.f.* telegraphy; ***télégraphie sans fil***, wireless telegraphy.
télégraphier [telegra'fje], *v.t., v.i.* to telegraph; to wire, to cable.
télégraphique [telegra'fik], *a.* telegraphic.
télégraphiste [telegra'fist], *n.* telegraphist.
téléguidé [telegi'de], *a.* guided; ***engin téléguidé***, guided missile.
téléimprimeur [teleɛ̃pri'mœ:r], **téléscripteur** [teleskrip'teur], *n.m.* teleprinter.
télémètre [tele'mɛtr], *n.m.* rangefinder.
télépathie [telepa'ti], *n.f.* telepathy.
télépathique [telepa'tik], *a.* telepathic.
téléphérique [telefe'rik], *a.* and *n.m.* teleferic.
téléphone [tele'fɔn], *n.m.* telephone; ***un coup de téléphone***, a telephone call.
téléphoner [telefɔ'ne], *v.t., v.i.* to telephone, to ring up.
téléphonique [telefɔ'nik], *a.* ***cabine téléphonique***, call-box.
téléphoniste [telefɔ'nist], *n.* telephone operator.
télescope [telɛs'kɔp], *n.m.* telescope.
télescopique [telɛskɔ'pik], *a.* telescopic.
téléscripteur [teleskrip'tœ:r], [TÉLÉIMPRIMEUR].
téléspectateur [telespɛkta'tœ:r], *n.m.* (*fem.* **-trice**) televiewer.
téléviser [televi'ze], *v.t.* to televise.
téléviseur [televi'zœ:r], *n.m.* television (receiving-)set.
télévision [televi'zjɔ̃], *n.f.* television.
tellement [tɛl'mɑ̃], *adv.* so, in such a manner; so much, so far.
téméraire [teme'rɛ:r], *a.* rash, reckless.—*n.* reckless person, daredevil.
témérairement [temerɛr'mɑ̃], *adv.* rashly, recklessly.
témérité [temeri'te], *n.f.* temerity.
témoignage [temwa'ɲa:ʒ], *n.m.* testimony, evidence, witness; testimonial; (*fig.*) token, mark, proof.
témoigner [temwa'ɲe], *v.t.* to testify; to show, to prove, to be the sign of.—*v.i.* to testify, to give evidence (*de*).
témoin [te'mwɛ̃], *n.m.* witness, evidence, proof, mark; second (*in duels*).
tempe [tɑ̃:p], *n.f.* (*Anat.*) temple.
tempérament [tɑ̃pera'mɑ̃], *n.m.* constitution, temperament; temper; (*fig.*) moderation, compromise; ***à tempérament***, by instalments.
tempérance [tɑ̃pe'rɑ̃:s], *n.f.* temperance.
température [tɑ̃pera'ty:r], *n.f.* temperature.
tempéré [tɑ̃pe're], *a.* temperate (*of climate*); limited, constitutional (*of governments*); restrained, sober (*of style*).
tempérer [tɑ̃pe're], *v.t.* (*conjug. like* CÉDER) to temper, to moderate, to allay, to assuage, to check. **se tempérer**, *v.r.* to become mild (*of the weather*).
tempête [tɑ̃'pɛ:t], *n.f.* storm, tempest.
tempêter [tɑ̃pe'te], *v.i.* to storm, to bluster, to fume.
tempétueusement [tɑ̃petɥøz'mɑ̃], *adv.* tempestuously, violently.
tempétueux [tɑ̃pe'tɥø], *a.* (*fem.* **-euse**) tempestuous, boisterous, stormy.
temple [tɑ̃:pl], *n.m.* temple; French Protestant church.
templier [tɑ̃pli'e], *n.m.* Knight-Templar.
temporaire [tɑ̃pɔ'rɛ:r], *a.* temporary.
temporairement [tɑ̃pɔrɛr'mɑ̃], *adv.* temporarily, provisionally.
temporel [tɑ̃pɔ'rɛl], *a.* (*fem.* **-elle**) temporal.
temporisateur [tɑ̃pɔriza'tœ:r], *a.* (*fem.* **-trice**) procrastinating, temporizing.—*n.m.* (*fem.* **-trice**) temporizer, procrastinator.
temporisation [tɑ̃pɔrizɑ'sjɔ̃], *n.f.* temporizing, procrastination.
temporiser [tɑ̃pɔri'ze], *v.i.* to temporize, to delay.

temps [tɑ̃], *n.m. inv.* time, while, period, term; occasion; season; weather; (*Gram.*) tense; ***à temps***, in time; ***avec le temps***, in course of time; ***dans le temps***, formerly; ***en temps et lieu***, in proper time and place.
tenable [tə'nabl], *a.* tenable; bearable.
tenace [tə'nas], *a.* tenacious, adhesive, sticky.
ténacité [tenasi'te], *n.f.* tenacity, toughness; retentiveness (*of memory*).
tenaille [tə'nɑ:j], *n.f.* (*usu. in pl.*) pincers, nippers, pliers.
tenailler [tənɑ'je], *v.t.* to torture with red-hot pincers; (*fig.*) to torture.
tenant [tə'nɑ̃], *a.* ***séance tenante***, during the sitting; forthwith, then and there.—*n.m.* holder (*at a tournament*); (*fig.*) champion, defender.
tendance [tɑ̃'dɑ̃:s], *n.f.* tendency; leaning, bent, inclination.
tendancieux [tɑ̃dɑ̃'sjø], *a.* (*fem.* **-euse**) tendentious; insinuating, suggestive.
tendeur [tɑ̃'dœ:r], *n.m.* (*fem* **-euse**) spreader, layer, setter (*of snares*); wire-strainer.
tendoir [tɑ̃'dwɑ:r], *n.m.* clothes-line.
tendon [tɑ̃'dɔ̃], *n.m.* tendon, sinew.
tendre (1) [tɑ̃:dr], *a.* tender, soft; delicate, sensitive; affectionate; moving; early, young, new.
tendre (2) [tɑ̃:dr], *v.t.* to stretch, to strain; to bend (*a bow etc.*); to spread, to lay, to set; to hold out; to pitch (*tents*); to hang (*tapestry etc.*).—*v.i.* to lead; to tend, to conduce.
tendrement [tɑ̃drə'mɑ̃], *adv.* tenderly, affectionately.
tendresse [tɑ̃'drɛs], *n.f.* tenderness, fondness; (*pl.*) endearments.
tendron [tɑ̃'drɔ̃], *n.m.* shoot (*of plants*).
tendu [tɑ̃'dy], *a.* stretched, held out; tight, tense; strained.
ténèbres [te'nɛ:br], *n.f.* (*used only in pl.*) darkness, night, gloom.
ténébreusement [tenebrøz'mɑ̃], *adv.* darkly gloomily; secretly.
ténébreux [tene'brø], *a.* (*fem.* **-euse**) dark, gloomy, overcast; obscure, mysterious.
teneur (1) [tə'nœ:r], *n.f.* tenor, terms, text; purport.
teneur (2) [tə'nœ:r], *n.m.* (*fem.* **-euse**) holder; ***teneur de livres***, book-keeper.
ténia [te'nja], *n.m.* tapeworm.
tenir [tə'ni:r], *v.t. irr.* to hold, to have hold of; to have, to possess; to seize; to occupy; to keep, to follow; to retain; to perform; to consider.—*v.i.* to hold; to adhere, to stick; to hold together; to cling; to prize (***à***); to be attached *or* related (***à***); to be contiguous; to depend, to result (***de***); to be held (*of fairs, markets, assemblies etc.*); to take after; to savour; to persist; to resist; to be anxious (***à***). **se tenir**, *v.r.* to hold fast, to remain; to adhere; to consider oneself; to contain oneself, to refrain.
tennis [te'nis], *n.m.* lawn-tennis.
tenon [tə'nɔ̃], *n.m.* tenon; bolt (*of fire-arms*).
ténor [te'nɔ:r], *n.m.* (*Mus.*) tenor.
tension [tɑ̃'sjɔ̃], *n.f.* tension, strain; tenseness; (*Elec.*) voltage.
tentacule [tɑ̃tɑ'kyl], *n.m.* tentacle, feeler.
tentant [tɑ̃'tɑ̃], *a.* tempting.
tentateur [tɑ̃tɑ'tœ:r], *a.* (*fem.* **-trice**) tempting.—*n.m.* (*fem.* **-trice**) tempter, temptress.
tentation [tɑ̃tɑ'sjɔ̃], *n.f.* temptation.
tentative [tɑ̃tɑ'ti:v], *n.f.* attempt, trial, endeavour.
tente [tɑ̃:t], *n.f.* tent, pavilion; (*Naut.*) awning.
tenter [tɑ̃'te], *v.t.* to attempt, to try; to tempt.
tenture [tɑ̃'ty:r], *n.f.* hangings, tapestry; wall-paper; paper-hanging.
ténu [te'ny], *a.* tenuous, thin, slender.
tenue [tə'ny], *n.f.* holding (*of assemblies etc.*); session; attitude (*of a person*); behaviour, bearing; dress; keeping (*of books*); ***grande tenue***, (*Mil.*) full dress; ***petite tenue***, undress.
ténuité [tenɥi'te], *n.f.* tenuity, thinness; (*fig.*) insignificance.
tenure [tə'ny:r], *n.f.* tenure.
ter [tɛ:r], *adv.* thrice; for the third time.
térébenthine [terebɑ̃'tin], *n.f.* turpentine.
térébinthe [tere'bɛ̃:t], *n.m.* turpentine-tree, terebinth.
tergiversation [tɛrʒivɛrsɑ'sjɔ̃], *n.f.* tergiversation, evasion.
tergiverser [tɛrʒivɛr'se], *v.i.* to waver, to beat about the bush.
terme [tɛrm], *n.m.* term; termination, end; limit, boundary; time; three months; quarter's rent; expression; (*pl.*) state, conditions, terms; ***avant terme***, prematurely.
terminaison [tɛrminɛ'zɔ̃], *n.f.* termination, ending.
terminer [tɛrmi'ne], *v.t.* to bound, to limit; to terminate, to conclude. **se terminer**, *v.r.* to terminate, to be bounded.
terminus [tɛrmi'nys], *n.m.* terminus (*of railway*).
terne [tɛrn], *a.* dull, dim; wan; spiritless.
ternir [tɛr'ni:r], *v.t.* to dull, to deaden; to tarnish. **se ternir**, *v.r.* to tarnish, to grow dull; to fade (*of colours*).
ternissure [tɛrni'sy:r], *n.f.* tarnishing, fading; stain.
terrain [tɛ'rɛ̃], *n.m.* piece of ground; soil, earth; site; field, course.
terrassant [tɛra'sɑ̃], *a.* crushing (*news etc.*).
terrasse [tɛ'ras], *n.f.* terrace; flat roof, balcony.
terrassement [tɛras'mɑ̃], *n.m.* earthwork, embankment; ballasting.
terrasser [tɛra'se], *v.t.* to embank; to throw to the ground; to beat; to confound, to dismay.
terrassier [tɛra'sje], *n.m.* digger, excavator, navvy; earthwork contractor.
terre [tɛ:r], *n.f.* earth; land; ground, soil; dominion, territory; grounds, estate, property; (*C*) farm.
terreau [tɛ'ro], *n.m.* (*pl.* **-eaux**) compost.
Terre-Neuve [tɛr'nœ:v], *f.* Newfoundland.
terre-neuve [tɛr'nœ:v], *n.m. inv.* Newfoundland (*dog*).
terrer [tɛ're], *v.t.* to earth up (*a tree etc.*). *v.i.* to burrow. **se terrer**, *v.r.* to go to ground.
terrestre [tɛ'rɛstr], *a.* terrestrial, earthly.
terreur [tɛ'rœ:r], *n.f.* terror; awe, dread.
terreux [tɛ'rø], *a.* (*fem.* **-euse**) terreous, earthy; dirty; dull (*of colours*); ashen (*of the face*).
terrible [tɛ'ribl], *a.* terrible, dreadful; unmanageable (*of children*).

terriblement [tɛriblə'mɑ̃], *adv.* terribly; (*colloq.*) with a vengeance.
terrier [tɛ'rje], *n.m.* burrow, hole; earth (*of fox*); terrier (*dog*).
terrifier [tɛri'fje], *v.t.* to terrify, to dismay.
terrine [tɛ'rin], *n.f.* earthen pan, dish; potted meat.
territoire [tɛri'twa:r], *n.m.* territory, district
territorial [tɛritɔ'rjal], *a.* (*m. pl.* **-aux**) territorial.
terroir [tɛ'rwa:r], *n.m.* soil, ground; ***goût de terroir***, raciness (*of style*); native tang (*of wine*).
terroriser [tɛrɔri'ze], *v.t.* to terrorize.
terrorisme [tɛrɔ'rism], *n.m.* terrorism.
terroriste [tɛrɔ'rist], *n.m.* terrorist.
tertiaire [tɛr'sjɛ:r], *a.* tertiary.
tertre [tɛrtr], *n.m.*, knoll, hillock.
tes [te], [TON (1)].
tesson [tɛ'sɔ̃], *n.m.* potsherd, fragment of broken glass etc.
test [tɛst], *n.m.* shell; trial, test.
testacé [tɛsta'se], *a.* testaceous.—*n.m.* testacean.
testament [tɛsta'mɑ̃], *n.m.* will.
tester [tɛs'te], *v.t.* to test.—*v.i.* to make one's will.
testimonial [tɛstimɔ'njal], *a.* (*m. pl.* **-aux**) testifying, testimonial.
tétanos [teta'nɔs], *n.m.* tetanus, lock-jaw.
têtard [tɛ'ta:r], *n.m.* tadpole.
tête [tɛ:t], *n.f.* head; head-piece; face; beginning; top; van, vanguard; (*fig*). brains, sense, judgment; presence of mind; ***en tête***, in one's head; in front, ahead; ***mal de tête***, headache; ***tête de mort***, skull.
tête-à-tête [tɛta'tɛ:t], *n.m. inv.* tête-à-tête, private interview *or* conversation; settee (*for two*).
téter [te'te], *v.t.* (*conjug. like* CÉDER) to suck.
têtière [tɛ'tjɛ:r], *n.f.* infant's cap; head-stall (*of a bridle*); antimacassar.
tétin [te'tɛ̃], *n.m.* nipple, teat; breast.
téton [te'tɔ̃], *n.m.* teat; (*fam.*) breast.
tétrarque [te'trark], *n.m.* tetrarch.
tétras [te'trɑ], *n.m. inv.* (*Orn.*) grouse.
têtu [te'ty], *a.* headstrong, stubborn, obstinate.
teutonique [tøtɔ'nik], *a.* teutonic.
texte [tɛkst], *n.m.* text; theme, matter, subject; passage (*of Scripture*).
textile [tɛks'til], *a.* and *n.m.* textile.
textuel [tɛks'tɥɛl], *a.* (*fem.* **-elle**) textual, word for word.
textuellement [tɛkstɥɛl'mɑ̃], *adv.* textually.
texture [tɛks'ty:r], *n.f.* texture; disposition.
thaïlandais [tailɑ̃'dɛ], *a.* Thai.—*n.m.* Thai (*language*); (**Thaïlandais**, *fem.* **-aise**) Thai (*person*).
Thaïlande [tai'lɑ̃:d], **la**, *f.* Thailand, Siam.
thé [te], *n.m.* tea; tea-party.
théâtral [teɑ'tral], *a.* (*m. pl.* **-aux**) theatrical.
théâtre [te'ɑ:tr], *n.m.* theatre, playhouse; stage; plays (*collection*), scene; ***coup de théâtre***, striking event.
théerie [te'ri], *n.f.* tea-plantation.
théière [te'jɛ:r], *n.f.* teapot.
théisme [te'ism], *n.m.* theism.
thème [tɛ:m], *n.m.* topic, subject, theme; (*sch.*) prose, composition.
théodolite [teɔdɔ'lit], *n.m.* theodolite.
théologie [teɔdɔ'ʒi], *n.f.* theology; divinity.
théologien [teɔlɔ'ʒjɛ̃], *n.m.* theologian.
théorème [teɔ'rɛm], *n.m.* theorem.
théorie [teɔ'ri], *n.f.* theory, speculation.
théorique [teɔ'rik], *a.* theoretical.
théoriquement [teɔrik'mɑ̃], *adv.* theoretically.
théoriser [teɔri'ze], *v.t.*, *v.i.* to theorize.
théoriste [teɔ'rist], *n.* theorist.
thérapie [tera'pi], *n.f.* therapy.
Thérèse [te'rɛ:z], *f.* Theresa.
thermal [tɛr'mal], *a.* (*m. pl.* **-aux**) thermal; ***eaux thermales***, hot springs.
thermomètre [tɛrmɔ'mɛtr], *n.m.* thermometer.
thermos [tɛr'mɔs], *n.m.* thermos (flask).
thermostat [tɛrmo'sta], *n.m.* thermostat.
thésauriser [tezɔri'ze], *v.t.* to treasure.—*v.i.* to hoard treasure.
thèse [tɛ:z], *n.f.* thesis, proposition.
thibaude [ti'bo:d], *n.f.* hair-cloth, coarse drugget.
Thomas [tɔ'mɑ], *m.* Thomas.
thon [tɔ̃], *n.m.* tunny-fish.
thoracique [tɔra'sik], *a.* thoracic.
thorax [tɔ'raks], *n.m.* thorax, chest.
thrombose [trɔ̃'bo:z], *n.f.* thrombosis.
thym [tɛ̃], *n.m.* thyme.
thyroïde [tirɔ'id], *a.* thyroid.
tiare [tja:r], *n.f.* tiara.
Tibet [ti'bɛ], **le** *m.* Tibet.
tibétain [tibe'tɛ̃], *a.* Tibetan.—*n.m.* Tibetan (*language*); (**Tibétain**, *fem.* **-aine**) Tibetan (*person*).
tibia [ti'bja], *n.m.* (*Anat.*) tibia, shin-bone.
tic [tik], *n.m.* tic, twitching; bad habit.
ticket [ti'kɛ], *n.m.* ticket (*for bus, underground etc., but not railways*).
tiède [tjɛd], *a.* lukewarm, tepid, mild; (*fig.*) indifferent.
tièdement [tjɛd'mɑ̃], *adv.* with indifference.
tiédeur [tje'dœ:r], *n.f.* lukewarmness; (*fig.*) indifference.
tiédir [tje'dir], *v.t.* to take the chill off, to tepefy.—*v.i.* to cool, to grow lukewarm.
tien [tjɛ̃], *pron. poss. m.* (*fem.* **tienne**) *thine, yours.—*n.* (*pl.*) ***les tiens***, your relations and friends.
tiens! [tjɛ̃], *imperative* [TENIR], *int.* well, hello! look here! here! really? you don't say so!
tierce (1) [tjɛrs], *n.f.* a third (*of time*); tierce (*at cards etc.*).
tiers [tj:ɛr], *a.* (*fem.* **tierce** (2)) third.—*n.m.* third person, third party; (*fig.*) stranger; third part.
tige [ti:ʒ], *n.f.* stem, stalk; trunk (*of tree*); straw (*of corn*); shank (*of a key, anchor etc.*); stock (*of a family*).
tignasse [ti'ɲas], *n.f.* old wig; (*pop.*) mop, shock (*of hair*).
tigre [tigr], *n.m.* (*fem.* **-esse**) tiger, tigress.
tigrer [ti'gre], *v.t.* to stripe, to spot, to speckle.
tillac [ti'jak], *n.m.* deck.
tilleul [ti'jœl], *n.m.* lime-tree, linden-tree.
timbale [tɛ̃'bal], *n.f.* kettledrum, timbal; metal cup *or* mug; kitchen-mould.
timbre [tɛ̃:br], *n.m.* bell, clock-chime; sound, tone; stamp; stamp-duty; postmark.
timbré [tɛ̃:bre], *a.* stamped; (*fam.*) cracked.
timbre-poste [tɛ̃brə'pɔst], *n.m.* (*pl.* **timbres-poste**) postage-stamp.

imbrer [tɛ̃'bre], *v.t.* to stamp; to stick a stamp on (*a letter*).
imide [ti'mid], *a.* shy, bashful, self-conscious; timid.
imidement [timid'mɑ̃], *adv.* shyly; timidly.
imidité [timidi'te], *n.f.* shyness, bashfulness; timidity.
imon [ti'mɔ̃], *n.m.* pole (*of a carriage, cart etc.*); shaft; beam (*of a plough*); (*Naut.*) helm, tiller; (*fig.*) direction, government.
imonerie [timɔn'ri], *n.f.* steerage, steering.
imonier [timɔ'nje], *n.m.* steersman, helmsman; wheel-horse.
imoré [timɔ're], *a.* timorous, fearful.
imothée [timɔ'te], *m.* Timothy.
ine [tin], *n.f.* tub, water-cask.
intamarre [tɛ̃ta'maːr], *n.m.* hubbub, uproar, hurly-burly, din.
intement [tɛ̃t'mɑ̃], *n.m.* ringing sound, tinkling; tolling; singing *or* buzzing (*in the ears etc.*).
inter [tɛ̃'te], *v.t.* to ring, to toll; to sound (*a knell etc.*); (*Naut.*) to prop, to support.—*v.i.* to ring, to toll; to tinkle, to jingle; to tingle.
intouin [tɛ̃'twɛ̃], *n.m.* (*fam.*) anxiety, trouble.
ique [tik], *n.f.* cattle-tick, dog-tick.
iquer [ti'ke], *v.i.* to have a tic, to twitch.
iqueté [tik'te], *a.* speckled, spotted.
iqueture [tik'tyːr], *n.f.* mottling, speckles.
ir [tiːr], *n.m.* shooting; firing, fire; shooting-gallery, rifle-range.
irade [ti'rad], *n.f.* passage (*of prose* or *verse*); tirade.
irage [ti'raːʒ], *n.m.* drawing, hauling, towing; tow-path; (*fig.*) difficulties; working off; printing, circulation (*of newspaper*); drawing (*of a lottery*); focal length (*of camera*).
iraillement [tirɑj'mɑ̃], *n.m.* pulling, hauling about; twinge, pain; (*fig.*) jarring, wrangling, vexation.
irailler [tirɑ'je], *v.t.* to pull about; to tease, to pester.—*v.i.* to shoot wildly; to skirmish. **se tirailler,** *v.r.* to pull each other about.
irailleur [tirɑ'jœːr], *n.m.* sharpshooter; skirmisher.
irant [ti'rɑ̃], *n.m.* purse-string; boot-strap; (*Carp. etc.*) tie-beam; brace (*of a drum*); ***tirant d'eau,*** ship's draught.
ire [tiːr], *n.f.* pull.
iré [ti're], *a.* drawn; fatigued.—*n.m.* (*Comm.*) drawee (*of a bill*).
ire-bouchon [tirbu'ʃɔ̃], *n.m.* (*pl.* **-bouchons**) corkscrew; ringlet (*of hair*).
ire-bouton [tirbu'tɔ̃], *n.m.* (*pl.* **-boutons**) button-hook.
ire-d'aile (à) [atir'dɛl], *adv. phr.* at full speed (*of a bird flying*).
ire-larigot (à) [atirlari'go], *adv. phr.* (*fam.*) to one's heart's content.
tirelire [tir'liːr], *n.f.* money-box.
tirer [ti're], *v.t.* to draw, to pull; to take out, to extract; to tap (*liquors*); to stretch, to tighten; to receive, to reap; to infer; to put on; to get; to shoot, to fire; (*Print.*) to print.—*v.i.* to draw, to pull; to fire; to tend, to border, to verge (***sur***). **se tirer,** *v.r.* to extricate oneself; to get out; to recover (*from illness*).
tiret [ti'rɛ], *n.m.* hyphen, dash.
tiretaine [tir'tɛːn], *n.f.* linsey-woolsey.
tireur [ti'rœːr], *n.m.* (*fem.* **-euse**) one who draws; marksman, sharpshooter.
tiroir [ti'rwaːr], *n.m.* drawer (*in a table etc.*); slide, slide-valve (*steam engine*).
tisane [ti'zan], *n.f.* infusion of herbs etc.
tison [ti'zɔ̃], *n.m.* brand, fire-brand; (*fig.*) embers.
tisonner [tizɔ'ne], *v.t., v.i.* to poke (*the fire*).
tisonnier [tizɔ'nje], *n.m.* poker, fire-iron.
tissage [ti'saːʒ], *n.m.* weaving; cloth mill.
tisser [ti'se], *v.t.* to weave; ***métier à tisser*** weaving-loom.
tisserand [tis'rɑ̃], *n.m.* (*fem.* **-e**) weaver.
tissu [ti'sy], *a.* woven.—*n.m.* material, fabric; tissue.
tissure [ti'syːr], *n.f.* tissue, texture.
titan [ti'tɑ̃], *n.m.* Titan.
titanesque [tita'nɛsk], **titanique** [tita'nik], *a.* titanic.
titillant [titil'lɑ̃], *a.* titillating, tickling.
titillation [titillɑ'sjɔ̃], *n.f.* titillation, tickling.
titiller [titil'le], *v.t., v.i.* to titillate, to tickle.
titre [titr], *n.m.* title, style, denomination; title-page; head, heading; right, claim, reason; voucher; title-deed; ***titre de circulation,*** (railway) ticket *or* pass; ***à bon titre*** or ***à juste titre,*** deservedly, justly.
titrer [ti'tre], *v.t.* to give a title to.
titubant [tity'bɑ̃], *a.* staggering.
titubation [titybɑ'sjɔ̃], *n.f.* reeling, staggering.
tituber [tity'be], *v.i.* to stagger, to reel.
titulaire [tity'lɛːr], *a.* titular.—*n.* titular incumbent, holder, chief.
toast [tost], *n.m.* toast, health; toast(ed bread); ***porter un toast*** (*à quelqu'un*), to toast (*someone*).
toboggan [tɔbɔ'gɑ̃], *n.m.* toboggan.
toc [tɔk], *int.* tap, rap.—*n.m.* rap, knock (*at a door etc.*).
tocsin [tɔk'sɛ̃], *n.m.* tocsin, alarm-bell.
toge [tɔːʒ], *n.f.* toga; (*fig.*) robe, gown (*of a judge etc.*).
Togo [tɔ'go], **le,** *m.* Togo.
togolais [tɔgɔ'lɛ], *a.* of Togo.—*n.m.* (**Togolais,** *fem.* **-aise**) native of Togo.
tohu-bohu [tɔybɔ'y], *n.m.* chaos; (*fig.*) confusion; jumble, hubbub.
toi [twa], *pron. pers.* *thou, *thee, you.
toile [twal], *n.f.* linen, cloth; canvas; sail; painting, picture; web; ***toile cirée,*** oilcloth; ***toile d'araignée,*** cobweb, spider's web.
toilette [twa'lɛt], *n.f.* doily; toilet-set; dressing-table, wash-stand; dress, attire; ***cabinet de toilette,*** dressing-room; ***grande toilette,*** full dress; ***les toilettes,*** toilets.
toise [twaːz], *n.f.* fathom; fathom-measure; (*fig.*) measure, standard.
toiser [twa'ze], *v.t.* to measure; to survey; (*fig.*) to eye from head to foot.
toiseur [twa'zœːr], *n.m.* measurer; quantity surveyor.
toison [twa'zɔ̃], *n.f.* fleece; (*fig.*) mop, thick head of hair.
toit [twɑ], *n.m.* roof, house-top; top, roof (*of a mine*); (*fig.*) house, home; ***toit à cochons*** pigsty.
toiture [twɑ'tyːr], *n.f.* roofing, roof.
tôle [toːl], *n.f.* sheet-iron; plate of steel; ***tôle ondulée,*** corrugated iron.

tolérable [tɔle'rabl], *a.* tolerable, bearable; middling.
tolérablement [tɔlerablə'mɑ̃], *adv.* tolerably.
tolérance [tɔle'rɑ̃:s], *n.f.* tolerance, toleration; endurance, forbearance; indulgence; deduction (*in coins*).
tolérant [tɔle'rɑ̃], *a.* tolerant.
tolérer [tɔle're], *v.t.* (*conjug. like* CÉDER) to tolerate, to allow; to endure, to bear; to wink at.
tomate [tɔ'mat], *n.f.* tomato.
tombal [tɔ̃'bal], *a.* (*m. pl.* **-aux**) pertaining to a tomb; ***pierre tombale***, tombstone.
tombe [tɔ̃:b], *n.f.* tomb, grave; tombstone.
tombeau [tɔ̃'bo], *n.m.* (*pl.* **-eaux**) tomb, grave; (*fig.*) sepulchre, death.
tombée [tɔ̃'be], *n.f.* fall (*of night etc.*).
tomber [tɔ̃'be], *v.i.* (*with aux.* ÊTRE) to fall, to fall down; to sink; to decay, to droop; to abate; to sag; to fall into; to meet, to light (upon) (***sur***); ***laisser tomber***, to drop; ***tomber amoureux*** (***de***), to fall in love (with); ***tomber bien*** or ***mal***, to come at the right *or* wrong moment; ***tomber d'accord***, to agree; ***tomber malade***, to fall ill.
tombereau [tɔ̃'bro], *n.m.* (*pl.* **-eaux**) tip-cart.
tombola [tɔ̃bɔ'la], *n.f.* tombola; raffle.
tome [to:m], *n.m.* volume, tome.
ton (1) [tɔ̃], *a. poss. m.* (*fem.* **ta**, *pl.* **tes**) *thy, your.
ton (2) [tɔ̃], *n.m.* tone; intonation, accent; tint; (*fig.*) manner, style; breeding; (*Mus.*) pitch, key.
tondaison [TONTE].
tondeur [tɔ̃'dœ:r], *n.m.* (*fem.* **-euse**) shearer, clipper.—*n.f.* (**-euse**) shearing-machine, clipper; ***tondeuse*** (***de gazon***), lawn-mower.
tondre [tɔ̃:dr], *v.t.* to shear, to clip, to crop; to cut, to mow, to trim.
tondu [tɔ̃'dy], *a.* shorn.
tonique [tɔ'nik], *a.* tonic; stressed.—*n.m.* (*Med.*) tonic.—*n.f.* (*Mus.*) keynote.
tonnage [tɔ'na:ʒ], *n.m.* tonnage; displacement.
tonne [tɔn], *n.f.* tun (*wooden vessel*); ton (*20 cwt., approx. 1000 kil.*).
tonneau [tɔ'no], *n.m.* (*pl.* **-eaux**) tun (*cask*); tun (*measure*); ton [TONNE]; (*colloq.*) drunkard; ***mettre un tonneau en perce***, to broach a cask; ***tonneau percé***, (*fig.*) spendthrift.
tonnelier [tɔnə'lje], *n.m.* cooper.
tonnelle [tɔ'nɛl], *n.f.* arbour, bower.
tonnellerie [tɔnɛl'ri], *n.f.* cooperage.
tonner [tɔ'ne], *v.i.* to thunder; (*fig.*) to inveigh.
tonnerre [tɔ'nɛ:r], *n.m.* thunder, thunderbolt; ***coup*** or ***éclat de tonnerre***, clap of thunder.
tonsure [tɔ̃'sy:r], *n.f.* tonsure.
tonsuré [tɔ̃sy're], *a.m.* tonsured, shaven.—*n.m.* cleric, priest.
tonte [tɔ̃:t], **tondaison** [tɔ̃dɛ'zɔ̃], *n.f.* sheep-shearing, clipping.
tonture [tɔ̃'ty:r], *n.f.* shearings, clippings; flock (*of cloth*); (*Naut.*) sheer.
top [tɔp], *n.m.* time signal; ***les tops***, the pips.
topaze [tɔ'pɑ:z], *n.f.* topaz.
toper [tɔ'pe], *v.i.* to agree; ***tope là!*** done! agreed!
topinambour [tɔpinɑ̃'bu:r], *n.m.* Jerusalem artichoke.
topographe [tɔpɔ'graf], *n.m.* topographer.
topographie [tɔpɔgra'fi], *n.f.* topography.
topographique [tɔpɔgra'fik], *a.* topographical.
toquade or **tocade** [tɔ'kad], *n.f.* (*colloq.*) infatuation, whim, fad, craze.
toque [tɔk], *n.f.* toque; jockey's cap; magistrate's cap.
toqué [tɔ'ke], *a.* (*fam.*) cracked, touched; infatuated.
torche [tɔrʃ], *n.f.* torch, link; twist (*of straw etc.*); pad (*on head*).
torcher [tɔr'ʃe], *v.t.* to wipe, to clean; (*fig.*) to polish off. **se torcher**, *v.r.* to wipe oneself.
torchère [tɔr'ʃɛ:r], *n.f.* torch-holder, tall candelabrum, hall-lamp.
torchis [tɔr'ʃi], *n.m.* cob, loam; ***mur de torchis***, mud-wall.
torchon [tɔr'ʃɔ̃], *n.m.* duster, house-cloth, dish-cloth.
tordage [tɔr'da:ʒ], *n.m.* twisting, twist.
tordeur [tɔr'dœ:r], *n.m.* (*fem.* **-euse**) twister (*of wool etc.*); throwster (*of silk*).
tordoir [tɔr'dwa:r], *n.m.* mangle, wringer.
tordre [tɔrdr], *v.t.* to twist, to wring; to contort, to disfigure. **se tordre**, *v.r.* to twist; to writhe.
tordu [tɔr'dy], *a.* twisted, distorted.
toréador [tɔrea'dɔ:r], *n.m.* toreador, bull-fighter.
tornade [tɔr'nad], *n.f.* tornado.
torpédo [tɔrpe'do], *n.f.* (*Motor.*) open tourer.
torpeur [tɔr'pœ:r], *n.f.* torpor.
torpide [tɔr'pid], *a.* torpid.
torpille [tɔr'pi:j], *n.f.* torpedo (*numb-fish*); (*Navy, Av.*) torpedo.
torpiller [tɔrpi'je], *v.t.* to torpedo.
torpilleur [tɔrpi'jœ:r], *n.m.* torpedo-boat.
torréfier [tɔre'fje], *v.t.* to torrefy, to roast (*coffee*).
torrent [tɔ'rɑ̃], *n.m.* torrent, stream; flood (*of tears etc.*); flow (*of words etc.*).
torrentiel [tɔrɑ̃'sjɛl], **torrentueux** [tɔrɑ̃'tɥø], *a.* (*fem.* **-elle, -euse**) torrential; impetuous.
torride [tɔ'rid], *a.* torrid.
tors [tɔr], *a.* (*fem.* **torse** (1) or **torte**) twisted, wreathed, contorted; wry, crooked.—*n.m.* twisting (*of ropes etc.*); torsion.
torsade [tɔr'sad], *n.f.* twisted fringe *or* cord; bullion (*on epaulets etc.*).
torse (2) [tɔrs], *n.m.* torso, trunk, bust.
torsion [tɔr'sjɔ̃], *n.f.* torsion, twisting.
tort [tɔ:r], *n.m.* wrong, injustice; harm, injury, mischief, offence; prejudice, detriment; ***à tort ou à raison***, rightly or wrongly; ***avoir tort***, to be wrong.
torticolis [tɔrtikɔ'li], *n.m.* wryneck, stiff-neck; crick (*in the neck*).
tortiller [tɔrti'je], *v.t.* to twist.—*v.i.* to wriggle, to shuffle; to prevaricate. **se tortiller**, *v.r.* to wriggle, to writhe.
tortionnaire [tɔrsjɔ'nɛ:r], *n.m.* executioner, torturer.
tortu [tɔr'ty], *a.* crooked, tortuous; ***jambes tortues***, bandy legs.
tortue [tɔr'ty], *n.f.* tortoise; ***tortue de mer***, turtle.

tortueux [tɔr'tɥø], *a.* (*fem.* **-euse**) tortuous, winding, crooked; (*fig.*) artful, crafty.

torture [tɔr'tyːr], *n.f.* torture; the rack.

torturer [tɔrty're], *v.t.* to torture, to put on the rack.

tôt [to], *adv.* soon, quickly; early; ***au plus tôt*** or ***le plus tôt possible***, as soon as possible; ***tôt ou tard***, sooner or later.

total [tɔ'tal], *a.* (*m. pl.* **-aux**) total, whole, entire; utter.—*n.m.* whole, total, sum-total.

totalement [tɔtal'mɑ̃], *adv.* totally, wholly; utterly, completely.

totalisateur [tɔtaliza'tœːr], *n.m.* calculating-machine; totalisator.

totaliser [tɔtali'ze], *v.t.* to tot up, to total up.

totalitaire [tɔtali'tɛːr], *a.* totalitarian.

totalitarisme [tɔtalita'rism], *n.m.* totalitarianism.

totalité [tɔtali'te], *n.f.* totality, whole.

touage [twaːʒ], *n.m.* towage, towing, warping.

toucan [tu'kɑ̃], *n.m.* toucan.

touchant [tu'ʃɑ̃], *a.* touching, moving, affecting.—*n.m.* the moving, affecting *or* impressive part.—*prep.* concerning, with regard to.

touche [tuʃ], *n.f.* touch; assay, trial; (*Paint. etc.*) manner, style; key (*of piano, typewriter etc.*); stop (*of organ*); (*Fishing*) nibble, bite; (*Fenc. etc.*) hit; drove of cattle; ***pierre de touche***, touchstone.

touche-à-tout [tuʃa'tu], *a. inv.* meddling.—*n. inv.* meddler; Jack of all trades.

toucher [tu'ʃe], *v.t.* to touch; to handle, to feel, to finger; to assay, to try (*precious metals etc.*); to receive (*money*); to hit; to offend; to move, to affect; to whip, to drive (*animals*); to play on (*a musical instrument*); to express, to describe; to allude to; to concern, to regard; ***toucher un chèque***, to cash a cheque.—*v.i.* to touch, to meddle (*à*); to reach; to play (*on a musical instrument*); to draw near, to be related, to be like; to concern; (*Naut.*) to go aground. **se toucher**, *v.r.* to touch, to touch each other; to be adjoining.—*n.m.* touch, feeling.

toue [tu], *n.f.* barge.

touée [tu'e], *n.f.* towing, warping; towline.

touer [tu'e], *v.t.* to tow, to warp.

toueur [tu'œːr], *n.m.* tower; tow-boat, tug.

touffe [tuf], *n.f.* tuft, clump, bunch, wisp.

touffer [tu'fe], *v.t.* to arrange in tufts.—*v.i.* to grow in a tuft *or* tufts.

touffu [tu'fy], *a.* tufted, bushy; leafy; full, thick; laboured (*of style*).

toujours [tu'ʒuːr], *adv.* always, ever, for ever; still; all the same, nevertheless, at least; ***toujours est-il que . . .***, still, the fact remains that . . . .

toupet [tu'pɛ], *n.m.* tuft of hair; forelock; front, foretop (*on a horse*); (*colloq.*) effrontery, cheek, impudence.

toupie [tu'pi], *n.f.* top, spinning-top.

toupiller [tupi'je], *v.i.* to spin, to whirl round and round.

tour (1) [tuːr], *n.f.* tower; (*Chess*) rook, castle.

tour (2) [tuːr], *n.m.* turn, winding; revolution; circumference, circuit; twist, strain; tour, trip; trick; feat; ***à tour de rôle***, in turn; ***tour de force***, feat of strength; ***tour de reins***, sprain in the back.

tour (3) [tuːr], *n.m.* lathe.

tourangeau [turɑ̃'ʒo], *a.* (*fem.* **-elle**, *m. pl.* **-eaux**) of Touraine.—*n.m.* (**Tourangeau**, *fem.* **-elle**) native of Touraine.

tourbe [turb], *n.f.* mob, rabble; peat, turf.

tourbeux [tur'bø], *a.* (*fem.* **-euse**) peaty.

tourbillon [turbi'jɔ̃], *n.m.* whirlwind; whirlpool, eddy; (*fig.*) hurly-burly, bustle.

tourbillonner [turbijɔ'ne], *v.i.* to whirl, to eddy; to swirl.

tourelle [tu'rɛl], *n.f.* turret; gun-turret; ***tourelle de veille***, conning-tower.

touret [tu'rɛ], *n.m.* wheel (*of a lathe etc.*); angler's reel.

tourie [tu'ri], *n.f.* carboy.

tourillon [turi'jɔ̃], *n.m.* axle; axle-tree, arbor; spindle, pivot.

tourisme [tu'rism], *n.m.* touring, tourism.

touriste [tu'rist], *n.* tourist, tripper.

tourment [tur'mɑ̃], *n.m.* torment, torture; anguish, pain; agony of mind.

tourmente [tur'mɑ̃ːt], *n.f.* tempest, storm; (*fig.*) disturbance, turmoil.

tourmenter [turmɑ̃'te], *v.t.* to torment, to torture, to rack; to distress, to harass; to worry; to jolt; to toss. **se tourmenter**, *v.r.* to be uneasy, to fret; to warp (*of wood*); to labour hard (*of a ship*).

tourmenteur [turmɑ̃'tœːr], *a.* (*fem.* **-euse**) torturing, tormenting.—*n.m.* (*fem.* **-euse**) torturer, tormentor.

tournailler [turnɑ'je], *v.i.* (*colloq.*) to prowl round.

tournant [tur'nɑ̃], *a.* turning, winding; ***plaque tournante***, turn-table, ***pont tournant***, swing-bridge.—*n.m.* turn, turning, bend; street corner; (*fig.*) indirect means; turning-point.

tourné [tur'ne], *a.* turned, shaped; expressed; sour, spoilt; ***avoir l'esprit mal tourné***, to be cross-grained.

tournebroche [turnə'brɔʃ], *n.m.* roasting-jack; turnspit.

tourne-disques [turnə'disk], *n.m. inv.* record-player.

tournedos [turnə'do], *n.m. inv.* fillet steak.

tournée [tur'ne], *n.f.* round, turn, visit, journey; circuit.

tournemain (en un) [ɑ̃nœturnə'mɛ̃], *adv. phr.* in a trice.

tourner [tur'ne], *v.t.* to turn; to turn round, to revolve, to twirl; to wind; (*Cine.*) to shoot (*a film*); to convert; to interpret; to shape.—*v.i.* to turn, to turn round, to revolve; to turn out; to change; to ripen; to spoil, to curdle (*of liquids*). **se tourner**, *v.r.* to turn round; to turn; to change.

tournesol [turnə'sɔl], *n.m.* turnsole, sunflower; (*Chem.*) litmus.

tourneur [tur'nœːr], *n.m.* turner.

tournevent [turnə'vɑ̃], *n.m.* cowl (*for chimney*).

tournevis [turnə'vis], *n.m.* screwdriver.

tourniole [tur'njɔl], *n.f.* whitlow.

tourniquet [turni'kɛ], *n.m.* turnstile; swivel; (*Surg.*) tourniquet.

tournoi [tur'nwa], *n.m.* tournament.

tournoiement [turnwa'mɑ̃], *n.m.* turning round, whirling, swirling; dizziness.

tournoyer [turnwa'je], *v.i.* (*conjug. like* EMPLOYER) to turn round and round, to wind; to eddy; (*fig.*) to beat about the bush, to shilly-shally.

tournure [tur'ny:r], *n.f.* turn, direction, course; figure, shape; (*fig.*) cast (*of mind, style etc.*); phrase, construction (*of language*); ***les choses commencent à prendre une mauvaise tournure,*** things are beginning to look bad.
tourte [turt], *n.f.* raised pie; big round loaf.
tourtereau [turtə'ro], *n.m.* (*pl.* **-eaux**) young turtle-dove; (*pl.*) (*fam.*) lovers.
tourterelle [turtə'rɛl], *n.f.* turtle-dove.
Toussaint [tu'sɛ̃], **la**, *f.* All Saints' Day.
tousser [tu'se], *v.i.* to cough.
tout [tu; *liaison-form*, tut], *a.* (*m. pl.* **tous**) all; whole, the whole of; every; each; any; ***tous les jours***, every day; ***toutes les fois que***, as often as, every time that; ***tout le monde***, all the world, everybody.—*pron. indef.* (*m. pl. pronounced* tu:s) all, everything; (*pl.*) all men; ***à tout prendre***, on the whole; ***comme tout***, exceedingly, extremely; ***du tout***, not at all; ***en tout***, in all, on the whole.—*n.m.* whole, the whole; the chief point, only thing.—*adv.* wholly, entirely, quite, thoroughly; all, altogether; although, however, for all; ***parler tout haut***, to speak aloud; ***tout à coup***, suddenly; ***tout à fait***, quite, entirely; ***tout à l'heure***, just now; presently; ***tout à vous***, sincerely yours; ***tout beau*** or ***tout doux***, softly, gently, not so fast; ***tout de bon***, in earnest; ***tout de suite***, immediately; ***tout nu***, stark naked.
toutefois [tut'fwa], *adv.* yet, nevertheless, however, still.
toute-puissance [tutpɥi'sɑ̃:s], *n.f.* omnipotence, almighty power.
tout-puissant [tupɥi'sɑ̃], *a.* (*fem.* **toute-puissante**) almighty. — *n.m.* (**Tout-Puissant**) the Almighty.
toux [tu], *n.f. inv.* cough.
toxémie [tɔkse'mi], *n.f.* (*Med.*) toxaemia, blood poisoning.
toxique [tɔk'sik], *a.* toxic, poisonous.—*n.m.* poison.
tracas [tra'kɑ], *n.m.* bustle, turmoil, disturbance; worry, annoyance.
tracassement [trakas'mɑ̃], *n.m.* worrying.
tracasser [traka'se], *v.t.* to worry, to pester. **se tracasser**, *v.r.* to worry.
tracasserie [trakas'ri], *n.f.* worry, pestering, annoyance, vexation; (*pl.*) bickering.
tracassier [traka'sje], *a.* (*fem.* **-ière**) pestering, worrying, annoying; fussy; mischief-making.—*n.m.* (*fem.* **-ière**) pesterer, busybody; troublesome person, mischief-maker.
trace [tras], *n.f.* trace, track, footprint; spoor, trail; mark, impression, vestige; outline, sketch.
tracé [tra'se], *n.m.* outline, sketch (*of figure*); marking out; laying out (*of grounds etc.*); direction.
tracement [tras'mɑ̃], *n.m.* tracing, laying out (*of grounds, roads etc.*).
tracer [tra'se], *v.t.* (*conjug. like* COMMENCER) to trace, to draw, to trace out; to sketch; to portray; to lay out (*grounds, roads etc.*); (*fig.*) to set forth, to mark out.—*v.i.* to spread roots (*of trees*); to burrow (*of moles*).
trachée [tra'ʃe], *n.f.* trachea, air-vessel.
trachée-artère [traʃear'tɛ:r], *n.f.* (*pl.* **trachées-artères**) trachea, windpipe.
tract [trakt], *n.m.* tract, leaflet (*for propaganda*).
tracteur [trak'tœ:r], *n.m.* tractor, traction-engine.
traction [trak'sjɔ̃], *n.f.* traction; pulling; draught; ***traction avant***, front-wheel drive.
tradition [tradi'sjɔ̃], *n.f.* tradition; (*Law*) delivery.
traditionnel [tradisjɔ'nɛl], *a.* (*fem.* **-elle**) traditional.
traducteur [tradyk'tœ:r], *n.m.* (*fem.* **-trice**) translator.
traduction [tradyk'sjɔ̃], *n.f.* translation, (*sch.*) crib.
traduire [tra'dɥi:r], *v.t. irr.* (*conjug. like* CONDUIRE) to translate; to interpret, to construe; to convey, to express; to indicate, to denote.
traduisible [tradɥi'zibl], *a.* translatable.
trafic [tra'fik], *n.m.* traffic; trading, trade; dealings.
trafiquant [trafi'kɑ̃], *n.m.* (*fem.* **-e**) trafficker.
trafiquer [trafi'ke], *v.i.* to traffic, to trade, to deal (***de***).
tragédie [traʒe'di], *n.f.* tragedy.
tragédien [traʒe'djɛ̃], *n.m.* (*fem.* **-enne**) tragedian.
tragique [tra'ʒik], *a.* tragic, tragical.—*n.m.* tragedy, tragic art; tragic writer.
trahir [tra'i:r], *v.t.* to betray; to deceive; to divulge, to reveal. **se trahir**, *v.r.* to betray oneself; to betray each other.
trahison [trai'zɔ̃], *n.f.* treachery, treason, perfidy; breach of faith.
train [trɛ̃], *n.m.* pace, rate; train, suite, attendants; way, manner; noise, clatter, dust; carriage; quarters (*of a horse etc.*); (*Rail.*) train; ***à fond de train***, at full speed; ***être en train de faire quelque chose***, to be (in the act of) doing something; ***train de maison***, style of living; ***train de marchandises***, goods train; ***train omnibus***, slow *or* stopping train.
traînage [trɛ'na:ʒ], *n.m.* dragging, drawing; sledging, sleighing.
traînant [trɛ'nɑ̃], *a.* dragging, trailing (*dress*); drawling (*voice*); shuffling (*gait*).
traînard [trɛ'na:r], *n.m.* straggler, laggard; slow-coach.
traîne [trɛ:n], *n.f.* dragging, being dragged *or* drawn; train (*of a dress etc.*).
traîneau [trɛ'no], *n.m.* (*pl.* **-eaux**) sledge, sleigh; drag-net.
traînée [trɛ'ne], *n.f.* train (*of gunpowder etc.*); trail, track.
traîner [trɛ'ne], *v.t.* to drag, to draw; to track; to spin out, to drag out, to protract; to drawl; to put off.—*v.i.* to trail, to draggle, to lag; to droop; to languish, to flag; to lie about; to loiter, to linger, to be protracted. **se traîner**, *v.r.* to crawl along, to creep; to lag, to drag oneself along.
train-train [trɛ̃'trɛ̃], *n.m.* (*colloq.*) routine, regular course.
traire [trɛ:r], *v.t. irr.* to milk; to draw (*milk*).
trait [trɛ], *n.m.* arrow, dart, bolt, shaft; thunderbolt; stroke, hit; trace (*of harness*); leash (*for dogs*); turn (*of the scale*); draught, gulp; dash (*of the pen etc.*); flash (*of light*); stroke, touch; trait, feature, lineament; act,

deed; prime move (*at chess, draughts etc.*); ***avoir trait à***, to have reference to; ***boire à longs traits***, to drink long draughts of; ***d'un seul trait***, at one gulp; ***trait de génie***, stroke of genius, (*fam.*) brain-wave; ***trait d'union***, hyphen.
traite [trɛt], *n.f.* stage, journey, stretch; milking; (*Comm.*) draft, bill; ***traite des nègres***, slave-trade.
traité [trɛ'te], *n.m.* treatise, tract, dissertation; treaty; agreement.
traitement [trɛt'mɑ̃], *n.m.* treatment; (*Ind.*) processing; reception; salary, pay.
traiter [trɛ'te], *v.t.* to treat; (*Ind.*) to process; to entertain; to use, to behave to; to discuss, to handle; to call, to style; to negotiate; to execute, to do.—*v.i.* to treat, to negotiate.
traiteur [trɛ'tœ:r], *n.m.* restaurant-keeper; caterer.
traître [trɛ:tr], *a.* (*fem.* **-esse**) treacherous, perfidious.—*n.m.* (*fem.* **-esse**) treacherous person, traitor, traitress.
traîtreusement [trɛtrøz'mɑ̃], *adv.* treacherously.
traîtrise [trɛ'tri:z], *n.f.* treachery.
trajectoire [traʒɛk'twa:r], *a.* and *n.f.* trajectory.
trajet [tra'ʒɛ], *n.m.* passage, journey, crossing, voyage; (*Med.*) course.
trame [tram], *n.f.* weft, woof; plot, conspiracy; course, progress, thread.
tramer [tra'me], *v.t.* to weave; (*fig.*) to plot, to contrive, to hatch.
tramontane [tramɔ̃'tan], *n.f.* tramontane, north wind; north; North Star.
tramway [tra'mwe], *n.m.* tramcar.
tranchant [trɑ̃'ʃɑ̃], *a.* sharp, cutting; (*fig.*) trenchant, decisive; salient, prominent.—*n.m.* edge.
tranche [trɑ̃:ʃ], *n.f.* slice, chop; slab; edge (*of a book*); ***doré sur tranche***, gilt-edged (*of a book*); ***tranche de lard***, rasher of bacon.
tranchée [trɑ̃'ʃe], *n.f.* trench, cutting; (*pl.*) colic.
trancher [trɑ̃'ʃe], *v.t.* to cut; to cut off; to slice; to decide, to determine, to settle.—*v.i.* to cut; to decide; to set up for; to affect; to be glaring (*of colours*).
tranchoir [trɑ̃'ʃwa:r], *n.m.* trencher, cutting-board.
tranquille [trɑ̃'kil], *a.* quiet, calm, tranquil, placid, peaceful; undisturbed (*in mind etc.*); ***soyez tranquille***, set your mind at ease.
tranquillement [trɑ̃kil'mɑ̃], *adv.* peacefully, quietly.
tranquillisant [trɑ̃kili'zɑ̃], *a.* tranquillizing.—*n.m.* tranquillizer.
tranquilliser [trɑ̃kili'ze], *v.t.* to tranquillize, to make easy, to soothe. **se tranquilliser**, *v.r.* to become tranquil, to calm down.
tranquillité [trɑ̃kili'te], *n.f.* tranquillity, quiet, peace.
transaction [trɑ̃zak'sjɔ̃], *n.f.* transaction, arrangement.
transalpin [trɑ̃zal'pɛ̃], *a.* transalpine.
transatlantique [trɑ̃zatlɑ̃'tik], *a.* transatlantic.—*n.m.* liner; deck-chair.
transborder [trɑ̃sbɔr'de], *v.t.* to tranship.
transbordeur [trɑ̃sbɔr'dœ:r], *n.m.* transporter; ***pont transbordeur***, transporter bridge.
transcendant [trɑ̃sɑ̃'dɑ̃], *a.* transcendent.
transcription [trɑ̃skrip'sjɔ̃], *n.f.* transcription, transcript, copy.
transcrire [trɑ̃'skri:r], *v.t. irr.* (*conjug. like* ÉCRIRE) to transcribe, to copy out.
transe [trɑ̃:s], *n.f.* fright, apprehension; trance.
transférable [trɑ̃sfe'rabl], *a.* transferable.
transférer [trɑ̃sfe're], *v.t.* (*conjug. like* CÉDER) to transfer, to transport, to convey, to move.
transfert [trɑ̃s'fɛ:r], *n.m.* transfer.
transfiguration [trɑ̃sfigyra'sjɔ̃], *n.f.* transfiguration.
transfigurer [trɑ̃sfigy're], *v.t.* to transfigure. **se transfigurer**, *v.r.* to be transfigured.
transformateur [trɑ̃sfɔrma'tœ:r], *n.m.* (*Elec.*) transformer.
transformation [trɑ̃sfɔrma'sjɔ̃], *n.f.* transformation.
transformer [trɑ̃sfɔr'me], *v.t.* to transform; to change, to convert. **se transformer**, *v.r.* to be transformed.
transfuge [trɑ̃s'fy:ʒ], *n.m.* deserter; fugitive; turncoat.
transgresser [trɑ̃sgrɛ'se], *v.t.* to transgress, to infringe, to contravene.
transgression [trɑ̃sgrɛ'sjɔ̃], *n.f.* transgression.
transhumance [trɑ̃zy'mɑ̃:s], *n.f.* transhumance.
transi [trɑ̃'zi], *a.* chilled, benumbed.
transiger [trɑ̃zi'ʒe], *v.i.* (*conjug. like* MANGER) to compound, to compromise, to come to terms (***avec***).
transir [trɑ̃'zi:r], *v.t.* to chill, to benumb; to paralyse.—*v.i.* to be chilled; to be paralysed (*with fear etc.*).
transissement [trɑ̃zis'mɑ̃], *n.m.* chill, numbness; shivering (*with terror etc.*).
transistor [trɑ̃zis'tɔr], *n.m.* transistor.
transit [trɑ̃'zit], *n.m.* transit.
transitaire [trɑ̃zi'tɛ:r], *a.* pertaining to the transit of goods.
transitif [trɑ̃zi'tif], *a.* (*fem.* **-tive**) transitive.
transition [trɑ̃zi'sjɔ̃], *n.f.* transition.
transitoire [trɑ̃zi'twa:r], *a.* transitory.
translation [trɑ̃sla'sjɔ̃], *n.f.* transfer(ring), relaying.
translucide [trɑ̃sly'sid], *a.* translucent.
translucidité [trɑ̃slysidi'te], *n.f.* translucence.
transmarin [trɑ̃sma'rɛ̃], *a.* transmarine, oversea.
transmetteur [trɑ̃smɛ'tœ:r], *n.m.* (*Rad.*) transmitter.
transmettre [trɑ̃s'mɛtr], *v.t. irr.* (*conjug. like* METTRE) to transmit, to convey, to send on; to transfer.
transmigration [trɑ̃smigra'sjɔ̃], *n.f.* transmigration.
transmigrer [trɑ̃smi'gre], *v.i.* to transmigrate.
transparence [trɑ̃spa'rɑ̃:s], *n.f.* transparency.
transparent [trɑ̃spa'rɑ̃], *a.* transparent.—*n.m.* paper ruled with black lines; transparency.
transpercer [trɑ̃spɛr'se], *v.t.* (*conjug. like* COMMENCER) to pierce through; to run through (*with a sword etc.*), to transfix.
transpiration [trɑ̃spira'sjɔ̃], *n.f.* perspiration, perspiring.
transpirer [trɑ̃spi're], *v.i.* to perspire; to ooze out; to transpire.

transplanter [trɑ̃splɑ̃'te], *v.t.* to transplant.
transport [trɑ̃s'pɔːr], *n.m.* carriage, conveyance; transport, removal; transfer, assignment; (*fig.*) rapture, ecstasy; transport-ship; ***transport au cerveau***, stroke, fit of delirium.
transportation [trɑ̃spɔrtɑ'sjɔ̃], *n.f.* transportation.
transporté [trɑ̃spɔr'te], *n.m.* (*fem.* **-ée**) transported person, convict.
transporter [trɑ̃spɔr'te], *v.t.* to convey, to transport; to transfer; to banish; to enrapture. **se transporter**, *v.r.* to transport oneself, to go.
transporteur [trɑ̃spɔr'tœːr], *n.m.* carrier, conveyor.
transposer [trɑ̃spo'ze], *v.t.* to transpose.
transposition [trɑ̃spozi'sjɔ̃], *n.f.* transposition.
transrhénan [trɑ̃sre'nɑ̃], *a.* from beyond the Rhine.
transsubstantiation [trɑ̃ssybstɑ̃sjɑ'sjɔ̃], *n.f.* transubstantiation.
transvaser [trɑ̃svɑ'ze], *v.t.* to decant.
transversal [trɑ̃zvɛr'sal], *a.* (*m.pl.* **-aux**) transversal, transverse.
trapèze [tra'pɛːz], *n.m.* trapezium; trapeze.
trappe [trap], *n.f.* trap-door; trap, pitfall; curtain, register (*of chimney*).
trappeur [tra'pœːr], *n.m.* trapper.
trappiste [tra'pist], *a.* and *n.m.* Trappist.
trapu [tra'py], *a.* squat, dumpy, thick-set, stocky.
traquer [tra'ke], *v.t.* (*Hunt.*) to beat for game; to enclose, to encircle; to track down.
travail [tra'vaːj], *n.m.* (*pl.* **-aux**) labour, work; toil; travail; piece of work; workmanship; occupation; study; ***cabinet de travail***, study (*room*); ***travaux forcés***, hard labour.
travaillé [travɑ'je], *a.* worked, wrought; laboured, elaborate; labouring (*under*).
travailler [travɑ'je], *v.t.* to work, to work at; to do with care; to fashion; to till (*the ground*).—*v.i.* to labour, to work; to study; to strive; to ferment (*of wines*); to warp (*of wood*). **se travailler**, *v.r.* to torment oneself; to be overwrought.
travailleur [travɑ'jœːr], *a.* (*fem.* **-euse**) industrious, hard-working; painstaking.—*n.m.* (*fem.* **-euse**) workman, labourer; hard-working person.
travailliste [travɑ'jist], *a.* Labour, Socialist. —*n.* member of the Labour Party.
travée [tra've], *n.f.* (*Arch.*) bay; truss (*of bridges*); (*Av.*) rib (*of wing*).
travers [tra'vɛːr], *n.m.* breadth; fault, failing; oddity; (*Naut.*) side, broadside; ***à travers***, across; ***au travers de***, through; ***de travers***, obliquely, awry, askew; ***en travers***, across, crosswise; ***à tort et à travers***, at random.
traverse [tra'vɛrs], *n.f.* cross-bar, cross-piece; cross-road, short cut; (*Rail.*) sleeper; (*pl.*) (*fig.*) setbacks.
traversée [travɛr'se], *n.f.* passage, crossing.
traverser [travɛr'se], *v.t.* to cross, to go over *or* through, to traverse, to get through *or* across; to run through (*with a sword etc.*); to lie across, to span; to intersect; to penetrate; to thwart.
traversier [travɛr'sje], *a.* (*fem.* **-ière**) cross-; that plies across.
traversin [travɛr'sɛ̃], *n.m.* bolster; (*Carp. etc.*) cross-beam; (*Naut.*) stretcher (*in boats*).
travesti [travɛs'ti], *a.* disguised; travestied, parodied.
travestir [travɛs'tiːr], *v.t.* to disguise, to travesty; (*fig.*) to misrepresent.
travestissement [travɛstis'mɑ̃], *n.m.* disguise; travesty.
trébuchant [treby'ʃɑ̃], *a.* of full weight (*of coins*); stumbling.
trébucher [treby'ʃe], *v.i.* to stumble, to slip; to err; (*fig.*) to turn the scale.
trébuchet [treby'ʃɛ], *n.m.* bird-trap; assay-balance.
tréfiler [trefi'le], *v.t.* to wire-draw.
trèfle [trɛfl], *n.m.* trefoil, clover; (*Cards*) clubs; ***trèfle blanc***, shamrock.
tréfonds [tre'fɔ̃], *n.m.* subsoil; (*fig.*) bottom; heart.
treillage [trɛ'jaːʒ], *n.m.* trellis(-work), lattice-work.
treille [trɛːj], *n.f.* vine-trellis; shrimp-net.
treillis [trɛ'ji], *n.m.* trellis, lattice; coarse canvas etc., sackcloth.
treizaine [trɛ'zɛn], *n.f.* baker's dozen.
treize [trɛːz], *a.* and *n.m.* thirteen; thirteenth.
treizième [trɛ'zjɛm], *a.* and *n.* thirteenth (part).
tréma [tre'ma], *n.m.* diaeresis.
tremblant [trɑ̃'blɑ̃], *a.* trembling, quivering; flickering (*of light etc.*).
tremble [trɑ̃ːbl], *n.m.* aspen.
tremblé [trɑ̃'ble], *a.* wavy (*of lines*); shaky (*of writing*).
tremblement [trɑ̃blə'mɑ̃], *n.m.* trembling, shaking, quaking, trepidation, tremor; flickering (*of light*); (*Mus.*) tremolo; ***tremblement de terre***, earthquake.
trembler [trɑ̃'ble], *v.i.* to tremble, to shake, to shiver; to quake, to fear; to flutter (*of wings*).
tremblotant [trɑ̃blɔ'tɑ̃], *a.* trembling, tremulous (*of sound etc.*); shivering, quivering, fluttering.
tremblotement [trɑ̃blɔt'mɑ̃], *n.m.* trembling, shivering.
trembloter [trɑ̃blɔ'te], *v.i.* to tremble (*of sound*); to quiver, to shiver; to flutter (*of wings*); to flicker (*of light*).
trémousser [tremu'se], *v.t.* to bestir, to move about, to flutter.—*v.i.* to shake, to stir. **se trémousser**, *v.r.* to flutter *or* frisk about; to bestir oneself.
trempage [trɑ̃'paːʒ], *n.m.* steeping, soaking; (*Print.*) wetting.
trempe [trɑ̃ːp], *n.f.* temper (*of steel etc.*); (*fig.*) character, stamp, quality.
tremper [trɑ̃'pe], *v.t.* to soak, to steep, to wet, to drench; to temper (*iron, steel etc.*); to dilute (*wine etc.*).—*v.i.* to soak, to be steeped; to be implicated (*in a crime*).
tremplin [trɑ̃'plɛ̃], *n.m.* spring-board, diving board; trampoline.
trentaine [trɑ̃'tɛn], *n.f.* about thirty; age of thirty.
trente [trɑ̃ːt], *a.* and *n.m.* thirty; thirtieth.
trentième [trɑ̃'tjɛm], *a.* and *n.* thirtieth (part).

trépan [tre'pã], *n.m.* trepan (*instrument*); trepanning.
trépaner [trepa'ne], *v.t.* to trepan.
trépas [tre'pɑ], *n.m. inv.* (*poet.*) decease, death.
trépassé [trepɑ'se], *n.m.* (*fem.* **-ée**) dead person.
trépasser [trepɑ'se], *v.i.* to depart this life, to pass away.
trépidant [trepi'dɑ̃], *a.* vibrating; (*fig.*) agitated, hectic.
trépidation [trepidɑ'sjɔ̃], *n.f.* trepidation, trembling; agitation.
trépied [tre'pje], *n.m.* trivet; tripod.
trépignement [trepiɲ'mɑ̃], *n.m.* stamping (*of feet*).
trépigner [trepi'ɲe], *v.i.* to stamp, to stamp one's foot.
très [trɛ], *adv.* very; most; very much.
trésor [tre'zɔːr], *n.m.* treasure; treasury; exchequer; thesaurus.
trésorerie [trezɔr'ri], *n.f.* treasury; treasurer-ship.
trésorier [trezɔ'rje], *n.m.* treasurer; (*Mil.*) paymaster.
tressage [trɛ'saːʒ], *n.m.* plaiting, braiding.
tressaillement [trɛsɑj'mɑ̃], *n.m.* start, bound, thrill, shudder; flutter.
tressaillir [trɛsɑ'jir], *v.i. irr.* (*conjug. like* ASSAILLIR) to start, to thrill; to quake, to tremble, to shudder.
tresse [trɛs], *n.f.* tress, plait (*of hair*); braid.
tresser [trɛ'se], *v.t.* to weave, to plait, to braid; to wreathe.
tréteau [tre'to], *n.m.* (*pl.* **-eaux**) trestle; (*pl.*) stage.
treuil [trœːj], *n.m.* windlass; winch.
trêve [trɛːv], *n.f.* truce.
tri [tri], *n.m.* sorting (*of letters etc.*).
triage [tri'jaːʒ], *n.m.* picking, sorting; choice, selection.
triangle [tri'jɑ̃ːgl], *n.m.* triangle.
triangulaire [trijɑ̃gy'lɛːr], *a.* triangular.
tribord [tri'bɔːr], *n.m.* (*Naut.*) starboard.
tribu [tri'by], *n.f.* tribe.
tribulation [tribylɑ'sjɔ̃], *n.f.* tribulation.
tribun [tri'bœ̃], *n.m.* tribune; (*fig.*) democratic leader.
tribunal [triby'nal], *n.m.* (*pl.* **-aux**) tribunal, bench; court of justice.
tribune [tri'byn], *n.f.* tribune (*rostrum*); hustings; gallery.
tribut [tri'by], *n.m.* tribute; grant, contribution; *duty; (*fig.*) debt.
tributaire [triby'tɛːr], *a.* dependent (*upon*).—*n.m.* tributary.
tricher [tri'ʃe], *v.t., v.i.* to cheat, to trick.
tricherie [triʃ'ri], *n.f.* cheating, trick, trickery.
tricheur [tri'ʃœːr], *n.m.* (*fem.* **-euse**) cheat, trickster.
tricolore [trikɔ'lɔːr], *a.* tricoloured.
tricorne [tri'kɔrn], *a.* three-cornered.—*n.m.* three-cornered hat.
tricot [tri'ko], *n.m.* knitting; jersey, jumper, (*fam.*) woolly; ***tricot de corps***, vest.
tricotage [trikɔ'taːʒ], *n.m.* knitting.
tricoter [trikɔ'te], *v.t., v.i.* to knit.
trictrac [trik'trak], *n.m.* tric-trac (*form of backgammon*).
tricycle [tri'sikl], *n.m.* three-wheeled vehicle; tricycle.
trident [tri'dɑ̃], *n.m.* trident.
triennal [triɛ'nal], *a.* (*m. pl.* **-aux**) triennial.
trier [tri'je], *v.t.* to pick, to choose, to sort, to select; to marshal (*trucks*).
trieur [tri'jœːr], *n.m.* (*fem.* **-euse**) sorter, picker.
trigonométrie [trigɔnɔme'tri], *n.f.* trigonometry.
trille [triːj], *n.m.* quaver, trill.
triller [tri'je], *v.t.* to trill, to quaver.
trillion [tri'ljɔ̃], *n.m.* (*since 1948 = 1 followed by 18 ciphers*) trillion, one million billion(s); (*Am.*) quintillion.
trilogie [trilɔ'ʒi], *n.f.* trilogy.
trimbaler [trɛ̃ba'le], *v.t.* (*fam.*) to drag *or* lug about (*parcels*); to trail (*children*) about. **se trimbaler**, *v.r.* (*pop.*) to traipse round.
trimer [tri'me], *v.i.* (*pop.*) to drudge, to wear oneself out.
trimestre [tri'mɛstr], *n.m.* quarter (*three months*); quarter's pay; (*Sch.*) term.
trimestriel [trimɛstri'ɛl], *a.* (*fem.* **-elle**) quarterly.
tringle [trɛ̃ːgl], *n.f.* rod.
Trinité [trini'te], *n.f.* Trinity; ***la Trinité***, Trinity Sunday; ***l'Île de la Trinité***, Trinidad.
trinquer [trɛ̃'ke], *v.i.* to clink glasses (*before drinking*); to drink to one another's health; (*pop.*) to suffer, to be hurt.
trio [tri'o], *n.m.* trio.
triomphal [triɔ̃'fal], *a.* (*m. pl.* **-aux**) triumphal.
triomphalement [triɔ̃fal'mɑ̃], *adv.* triumphantly.
triomphant [triɔ̃'fɑ̃], *a.* triumphant.
triomphe [tri'ɔ̃ːf], *n.m.* triumph.
triompher [triɔ̃'fe], *v.i.* to triumph; to overcome; to exult; to excel.
triparti [tripar'ti], **tripartite** [tripar'tit], *a.* tripartite.
tripe [trip], *n.f.* tripe; imitation velvet, velveteen (*also called* ***tripe de velours***).
triperie [trip'ri], *n.f.* tripe-shop.
triple [tripl], *a.* and *n.m.* treble, triple, three-fold.
tripler [tri'ple], *v.t., v.i.* to treble, to triple.
triplicata [triplika'ta], *n.m. inv.* triplicate.
tripode [tri'pɔd], *a.* and *n.m.* tripod.
tripot [tri'po], *n.m.* gambling-den; house of ill-fame.
tripotage [tripɔ'taːʒ], *n.m.* mess; underhand dealing; chore.
tripoter [tripɔ'te], *v.t.* to meddle with; to speculate in.—*v.i.* to make mischief, to mess about; to act in an underhand way.
tripoteur [tripɔ'tœːr], *n.m.* (*fem.* **-euse**) mischief-maker, shady speculator.
trique [trik], *n.f.* (*fam.*) cudgel, stick, bludgeon.
trisaïeul [triza'jœl], *n.m.* (*pl.* **-aïeuls**) great-great-grandfather.
trisaïeule [triza'jœl], *n.f.* great-great-grand-mother.
triste [trist], *a.* sorrowful, mournful, sad, melancholy, dejected; dull, dreary, dismal; poor, sorry (*of persons*); mean, paltry.
tristement [tristə'mɑ̃], *adv.* sadly.
tristesse [tris'tɛs], *n.f.* sadness; melancholy; dreariness.
triton [tri'tɔ̃], *n.m.* triton, newt.
trivial [tri'vjal], *a.* (*m. pl.* **-aux**) vulgar, trifling; trite, hackneyed.—*n.m.* vulgarity.

trivialité [trivjali'te], *n.f.* vulgarity; triteness.
troc [trɔk], *n.m.* truck; barter; swop.
troène [trɔ'ɛn], *n.m.* privet.
troglodyte [trɔglɔ'dit], *n.m.* troglodyte.
trogne [trɔɲ], *n.f.* reddish *or* bloated face.
trognon [trɔ'ɲɔ̃], *n.m.* core (*of a pear* or *apple*); stump (*of a cabbage*); runt.
Troie [trwɑ], *f.* Troy.
trois [trwɑ], *a.* and *n.m. inv.* three; third.
troisième [trwɑ'zjɛm], *a.* third.—*n.* third.—*n.m.* third floor.
troisièmement [trwɑzjɛm'mɑ̃], *adv.* thirdly.
trombe [trɔ̃:b], *n.f.* waterspout.
tromblon [trɔ̃'blɔ̃], *n.m.* blunderbuss.
trombone [trɔ̃'bɔn], *n.m.* trombone; paper-clip (*of wire*).
trompe [trɔ̃:p], *n.f.* *trump, horn; proboscis, trunk (*of elephants*).
tromper [trɔ̃'pe], *v.t.* to deceive, to impose upon; to delude; to cheat, to take in; to betray, to be unfaithful to (*wife, husband*). **se tromper**, *v.r.* to be mistaken, to make a mistake, to deceive oneself.
tromperie [trɔ̃'pri], *n.f.* cheat, fraud; illusion, delusion.
trompeter [trɔ̃pə'te], *v.t.* (*conjug. like* APPELER) to trumpet abroad.
trompette [trɔ̃'pɛt], *n.f.* trumpet.—*n.m.* trumpeter.
trompeur [trɔ̃'pœ:r], *a.* (*fem.* **-euse**) deceitful; false, misleading.—*n.m.* (*fem.* **-euse**) deceiver, cheat, impostor; betrayer.
trompeusement [trɔ̃pøz'mɑ̃], *adv.* deceitfully, deceptively.
tronc [trɔ̃], *n.m.* trunk, bole (*of tree*); stock; poor-box.
tronçon [trɔ̃'sɔ̃], *n.m.* broken piece, fragment, stump.
tronçonner [trɔ̃sɔ'ne], *v.t.* to cut into pieces.
trône [tro:n], *n.m.* throne.
trôner [tro'ne], *v.i.* to sit on a throne; (*fig.*) to lord it.
tronquer [trɔ̃'ke], *v.t.* to mutilate, to truncate; (*fig.*) to garble, to mangle.
trop [tro], *adv.* too much, too, over, too many; ***de trop***, too much, too many; ***être de trop***, to be in the way, not to be wanted; ***par trop***, excessively.—*n.m.* excess, superfluity.
trophée [trɔ'fe], *n.m.* trophy.
tropical [trɔpi'kal], *a.* (*m. pl.* **-aux**) tropical.
tropique [trɔ'pik], *n.m.* tropic.
trop-plein [trɔ'plɛ̃], *n.m.* (*pl.* **-pleins**) overflow, waste; surplus, excess.
troquer [trɔ'ke], *v.t.* to truck, to barter, to exchange.
trot [tro], *n.m.* trot.
trotte-menu [trɔtmə'ny] *a. inv.* running with little steps, pitter-pattering.
trotter [trɔ'te], *v.i.* to trot; to run about, to toddle (*children*).
trotteur [trɔ'tœ:r], *n.m.* (*fem.* **-euse**) trotter. —*n.f.* (**-euse**) second(s) hand (*of watch*).
trottin [trɔ'tɛ̃], *n.m.* errand girl.
trottiner [trɔti'ne], *v.i.* to go at a jog-trot; to toddle along.
trottinette [trɔti'nɛt], *n.f.* (*child's*) scooter.
trottoir [trɔ'twa:r], *n.m.* foot-path, pavement, (*Am.*) sidewalk; ***le bord du trottoir***, the kerb.
trou [tru], *n.m.* hole; gap; orifice, mouth; ***boucher un trou***, to stop a gap, to pay a debt; ***trou d'air***, air pocket; ***trou de la serrure***, keyhole; ***trou du souffleur***, (*Theat.*) prompter's box.
troubadour [truba'du:r], *n.m.* troubadour.
troublant [tru'blɑ̃], *a.* disturbing, troubling.
trouble [trubl], *a.* thick, muddy, turbid, cloudy; dull.—*adv.* dimly, confusedly.—*n.m.* confusion, disorder, disturbance; perplexity, uneasiness; dispute, quarrel; (*pl.*) disturbances, dissensions.
trouble-fête [trublə'fɛ:t], *n.m. inv.* kill-joy.
troubler [tru'ble], *v.t.* to disturb, to make thick, to make muddy; to muddle, to turn; to confuse, to agitate; to perplex, to disconcert; to trouble; to interrupt; to ruffle, to annoy; to dim, to dull. **se troubler**, *v.r.* to grow thick, to become muddy; to be confused, to be disconcerted; to become cloudy; to become confused.
trouée [tru'e], *n.f.* opening, gap, breach; pass.
trouer [tru'e], *v.t.* to bore, to make a hole in. **se trouer**, *v.r.* to get holes in it.
trouille [tru:j], *n.f.* (*vulg.*) fear, funk.
troupe [tru:p], *n.f.* troop, band; crew, gang, set; company (*of actors*); flock, crowd; (*pl.*) troops, forces.
troupeau [tru'po], *n.m.* (*pl.* **-eaux**) flock, herd, drove.
troupier [tru'pje], *n.m.* soldier.
trousse [tru:s], *n.f.* bundle, truss; (*Surg.*) case of instruments; case for razors, toilet articles etc; ***je suis à ses trousses***, I am after him.
troussé [tru'se], *a.* tucked up; ***bien troussé***, well set up, neat, dapper.
trousseau [tru'so], *n.m.* (*pl.* **-eaux**) bunch (*of keys*); trousseau; outfit, kit.
trousser [tru'se], *v.t.* to tuck up, to turn up, to pin up; to truss; to dispatch (*business etc.*). **se trousser**, *v.r.* to tuck up one's clothes.
trouvaille [tru'vɑ:j], *n.f.* godsend, windfall; find.
trouvé [tru've], *a.* found; ***bien trouvé***, felicitous; ***enfant trouvé***, foundling.
trouver [tru've], *v.t.* to find, to discover, to meet with, to hit upon; to detect; to find out; to deem, to judge; ***trouver à dire*** or ***à redire à***, to find fault with; ***trouver bon***, to think fit; ***trouver mauvais***, to blame, to be displeased with; ***vous trouvez?*** you think so, do you? **se trouver**, *v.r.* to find oneself; to be, to exist; to feel; to prove, to turn out; ***se trouver mal***, to faint.
truand [try'ɑ̃], *a.* vagrant.—*n.m.* (*fem.* **-e**) vagrant, beggar, tramp; crook.
truc (1) [tryk], *n.m.* knack, dodge, trick; (*Theat.*) machinery; (*pop.*) thing, thingummy, gadget.
truc (2) or **truck** [tryk], *n.m.* truck, bogie, (*Rail.*) open wagon.
trucheman or **truchement** [tryʃ'mɑ̃], *n.m.* interpreter; go-between.
truculent [tryky'lɑ̃], *a.* truculent.
truelle [try'ɛl], *n.f.* trowel; ***truelle à poisson***, fish-slice.
truffe [tryf], *n.f.* truffle.
truie [trɥi], *n.f.* sow.
truite [trɥit], *n.f.* trout.
truité [trɥi'te], *a.* spotted, speckled.
trumeau [try'mo], *n.m.* (*pl.* **-eaux**) pier; pier-glass; leg of beef.

tsar [tsa:r], *n.m.* Tsar.
tsigane [TZIGANE].
tu [ty], *pron.* *thou, you.
tuant [ty'ɑ̃], *a.* killing, tiresome, laborious.
tube [tyb], *n.m.* tube, pipe; (*Anat.*) duct.
tuberculeux [tybɛrky'lø], *a.* (*fem.* **-euse**) tuberculous.
tuberculose [tybɛrky'lo:z], *n.f.* tuberculosis.
tubulaire [tyby'lɛ:r], *a.* tubular.
tuer [tɥe], *v.t.* to kill, to slay; to slaughter, to butcher; to tire to death; to while away. **se tuer**, *v.r.* to kill oneself, to be killed; (*fig.*) to wear oneself out.
tuerie [ty'ri], *n.f.* slaughter, butchery; slaughter-house.
tue-tête (à) [aty'tɛ:t], *adv. phr.* at the top of one's voice.
tueur [tɥœ:r], *n.m.* (*fem.* **-euse**) killer, thug.
tuile [tɥil], *n.f.* tile.
tuilerie [tɥil'ri], *n.f.* tile-works; ***les Tuileries***, the Tuileries (*before 1871 a Royal palace, now a garden in Paris*).
tulipe [ty'lip], *n.f.* tulip.
tulle [tyl], *n.m.* tulle, net.
tumeur [ty'mœ:r], *n.f.* tumour, swelling.
tumulte [ty'mylt], *n.m.* tumult, uproar; hubbub.
tumultueux [tymyl'tɥø], *a.* (*fem.* **-euse**) tumultuous, riotous.
tunique [ty'nik], *n.f.* tunic; envelope, film.
Tunisie [tyni'zi], **la**, *f.* Tunisia.
tunisien [tyniz'jɛ̃], *a.* Tunisian.—*n.m.* (**Tunisien**, *fem.* **-enne**) Tunisian (*person*).
tunnel [ty'nɛl], *n.m.* tunnel.
turban [tyr'bɑ̃], *n.m.* turban.
turbine [tyr'bin], *n.f.* turbine.
turbopropulseur [tyrbɔprɔpyl'sœ:r], *n.m.* turbo-prop(ulsor).
turboréacteur [tyrboreak'tœ:r], *n.m.* jet-engine; turbo-jet.
turbot [tyr'bo], *n.m.* turbot.
turbulence [tyrby'lɑ̃:s], *n.f.* turbulence.
turbulent [tyrby'lɑ̃], *a.* turbulent, boisterous; rowdy.
turc [tyrk], *a.* (*fem.* **turque**) Turkish.—*n.m.* Turkish (*language*); (**Turc**, *fem.* **Turque**) Turk.
turelure [tyr'ly:r], *n.f.* fol-de-rol (*burden of a song*).
turf [tyrf], *n.m.* the turf, horse-racing.
turpitude [tyrpi'tyd], *n.f.* turpitude, baseness, ignominy.
turque [TURC].
Turquie [tyr'ki], **la**, *f.* Turkey.
turquoise [tyr'kwa:z], *a.* and *n.f.* turquoise.
tussor [ty'sɔ:r], *n.m.* tussore (*silk*).
tutelle [ty'tɛl], *n.f.* tutelage, guardianship; (*Polit.*) trusteeship.
tuteur [ty'tœ:r], *n.m.* (*fem.* **tutrice**) guardian, trustee, protector.—*n.m.* (*Hort.*) stake.
tutoiement or **tutoîment** [tytwa'mɑ̃], *n.m.* addressing a person as 'tu', 'theeing and thouing'.
tutoyer [tytwa'je], *v.t.* (*conjug. like* EMPLOYER) to be on intimate terms with. **se tutoyer**, *v.r.* to be on familiar terms.
tutrice [ty'tris], [TUTEUR].
tuyau [tɥi'jo], *n.m.* (*pl.* **-aux**) pipe; tube; (chimney-)flue; shaft, funnel; stalk (*of corn*); nozzle (*of bellows etc.*); stem (*of a tobacco-pipe*); ***tuyau d'arrosage***, garden-hose; ***tuyau d'incendie***, fire-hose; ***tuyau de poêle***, stove-pipe.
tuyautage [tɥijo'ta:ʒ], *n.m.* frilling, fluting; tubing.
tuyauter [tɥijo'te], *v.t.* to goffer, to frill.
tuyauterie [tɥijo'tri], *n.f.* system of pipes; plumbing; pipe-trade.
tympan [tɛ̃'pɑ̃], *n.m.* ear-drum, tympanum; tympan; spandrel.
type [tip], *n.m.* type; model, pattern; symbol, emblem; standard; (*Astron.*) plan, drawing; (*colloq.*) bloke, chap, fellow.
typhoïde [tifɔ'id], *a.* typhoid.
typhon [ti'fɔ̃], *n.m.* typhoon.
typhus [ti'fy:s], *n.m.* typhus.
typique [ti'pik], *a.* typical; characteristic.
typographe [tipɔ'graf], *n.m.* typographer.
typographie [tipɔgra'fi], *n.f.* typography.
tyran [ti'rɑ̃], *n.m.* tyrant.
tyrannie [tira'ni], *n.f.* tyranny.
tyrannique [tira'nik], *a.* tyrannical.
tyranniser [tirani'ze], *v.t.* to tyrannize, to oppress.
tzar [TSAR].
tzigane or **tsigane** [tsi'gan], *a.* and *n.* gipsy.

U

U, u [y], *n.m.* the twenty-first letter of the alphabet.
ubiquité [ybikɥi'te], *n.f.* ubiquity.
Ukraine [y'krɛn], **l'**, *f.* the Ukraine.
ukrainien [ykrɛ'njɛ̃], *a.* Ukrainian.—*n.m.* (**Ukrainien**, *fem.* **-enne**) Ukrainian (*person*).
ulcère [yl'sɛ:r], *n.m.* ulcer.
ulcéré [ylse're], *a.* ulcerated; (*fig.*) embittered.
ulcérer [ylse're], *v.t.* (*conjug. like* CÉDER) to ulcerate; (*fig.*) to embitter, to incense.
ultérieur [ylte'rjœ:r], *a.* ulterior, further, later, subsequent.
ultérieurement [ylterjœr'mɑ̃], *adv.* later on.
ultimatum [yltima'tɔm], *n.m.* ultimatum.
ultime [yl'tim], *a.* last, final, ultimate.
ultra-sonore [yltrasɔ'nɔ:r], *a.* supersonic.
ultra-violet [yltraviɔ'lɛ], *a.* (*fem.* **-ette**) ultra-violet.
ululer [yly'le], *v.i.* to ululate, to hoot.
Ulysse [y'lis], *m.* Ulysses.
umbre [ɔ̃:br], **omble** [ɔ̃:bl], **ombre** [ɔ̃:br], *n.m.* grayling.
un [œ̃], *a.* and *art. indef.* (*fem.* **une**) one, the first; single; a, an; any, a certain.—*pron. indef.* one thing; one; ***c'est tout un***, it is all one; ***les uns disent oui, les autres disent non***, some say yes, others say no; ***les uns et les autres***, all, all together; ***l'un et l'autre***, both; ***l'un ou l'autre***, the one or the other; ***l'un vaut l'autre***, one is as good as the other; ***un à un***, one by one.—*n.m.* one.
unanime [yna'nim], *a.* unanimous.
unanimement [ynanim'mɑ̃], *adv.* unanimously.
unanimité [ynanimi'te], *n.f.* unanimity.

uni [y'ni], *a.* united; smooth, even, level; uniform; plain, unaffected.
unicorne [yni'kɔrn], *n.m.* unicorn.
unième [y'njɛm], *a.* (*in compounds only*) first; ***vingt et unième***, 21st.
unification [ynifikɑ'sjɔ̃], *n.f.* unification.
unifier [yni'fje], *v.t.* to unify, to unite; to amalgamate.
uniforme [yni'fɔrm], *a.* uniform.—*n.m.* uniform, regimentals.
uniformément [ynifɔrme'mɑ̃], *adv.* uniformly.
uniformité [ynifɔrmi'te], *n.f.* uniformity.
unilatéral [ynilate'ral], *a.* (*m. pl.* **-aux**) unilateral.
uniment [yni'mɑ̃], *adv.* evenly, smoothly; plainly.
union [y'njɔ̃], *n.f.* union; concord, agreement; mixture; marriage.
unique [y'nik], *a.* only, sole; single, unique, unparalleled; odd, singular; ***fils unique***, only son; ***sens unique***, one way (*street*).
uniquement [ynik'mɑ̃], *adv.* solely.
unir [y'ni:r], *v.t.* to unite, to join; to smooth, to level; to pair. **s'unir**, *v.r.* to unite, to join together.
unisson [yni'sɔ̃], *n.m.* unison; (*fig.*) harmony, concert.
unité [yni'te], *n.f.* unity; unit; (*fig.*) concord, agreement.
univers [yni'vɛ:r], *n.m. inv.* universe.
universalité [ynivɛrsali'te], *n.f.* universality; sum total, whole.
universel [ynivɛr'sɛl], *a.* (*fem.* **-elle**) universal; residuary (*of legacies*).
universellement [ynivɛrsɛl'mɑ̃], *adv.* universally.
universitaire [ynivɛrsi'tɛ:r], *a.* of the university, academic.—*n.* teacher, professor.
université [ynivɛrsi'te], *n.f.* university.
uranium [yra'njɔm], *n.m.* uranium.
urbain [yr'bɛ̃], *a.* urban.
urbanisme [yrba'nism], *n.m.* town-planning.
urbaniste [yrba'nist], *n.m.* town-planner.
urbanité [yrbani'te], *n.f.* urbanity.
urgence [yr'ʒɑ̃:s], *n.f.* urgency; emergency; ***d'urgence***, urgently, immediately.
urgent [yr'ʒɑ̃], *a.* urgent, pressing.
urinaire [yri'nɛ:r], *a.* urinary.
urine [y'rin], *n.f.* urine.
uriner [yri'ne], *v.i.* to urinate, to make water.
urinoir [yri'nwa:r], *n.m.* (public) urinal.
urne [yrn], *n.f.* urn; ***urne électorale***, ballot-box.
Ursule [yr'syl], *f.* Ursula.
urticaire [yrti'kɛ:r], *n.f.* nettle-rash; urticaria.
Uruguay [yry'gɛ], **l'**, *m.* Uruguay.
uruguayen [yrygɛ'jɛ̃], *a.* Uruguayan.—*n.m.* (**Uruguayen**, *fem.* **-enne**) Uruguayan (*person*).
us [ys, yz], *n.m. pl.* ***les us et coutumes***, the ways and customs.
usage [y'za:ʒ], *n.m.* custom, practice, usage; use; wear (*of clothes etc.*); ***avoir de l'usage***, to have breeding; ***hors d'usage***, out of use; ***faire de l'usage*** or ***faire un bon usage***, to last *or* wear a long time.
usagé [yza'ʒe], *a.* used, worn, second-hand.
usager [yza'ʒe], *n.m.* user; ***les usagers de la route***, road-users.
usé [y'ze], *a.* worn-out, threadbare; stale, trite, hackneyed.
user [y'ze], *v.t.* to use up, to consume; to wear out; to spend, to waste.—*v.i.* to make use of. **s'user**, *v.r.* to wear oneself out; to wear away.
usine [y'zin], *n.f.* works, mills, factory.
usinier [yzi'nje], *n.m.* manufacturer, mill-owner.
usité [yzi'te], *a.* used, usual, in common use.
ustensile [ystɑ̃'sil], *n.m.* utensil; tool, implement.
usuel [y'zɥɛl], *a.* (*fem.* **-elle**) usual, customary, ordinary.
usuellement [ysɥɛl'mɑ̃], *adv.* habitually, ordinarily.
usure [y'zy:r], *n.f.* usury, excessive interest; wear and tear.
usurier [yzy'rje], *a.* (*fem.* **-ière**) usurious.—*n.m.* (*fem.* **-ière**) usurer.
usurpateur [yzyrpa'tœ:r], *a.* (*fem.* **-trice**) usurping.—*n.m.* (*fem.* **-trice**) usurper.
usurpation [yzyrpɑ'sjɔ̃], *n.f.* usurpation; encroachment.
usurper [yzyr'pe], *v.t.* to usurp; to encroach upon.
ut [yt], *n.m.* (*Mus.*) ut, do, the note C.
utérus [yte'rys], *n.m.* uterus, womb.
utile [y'til], *a.* useful, serviceable; advantageous, expedient, beneficial; ***en temps utile***, in due *or* good time.—*n.m.* utility, usefulness.
utilement [ytil'mɑ̃], *adv.* usefully.
utilisation [ytilizɑ'sjɔ̃], *n.f.* use, utilization.
utiliser [ytili'ze], *v.t.* to use, to find use for, to employ.
utilité [ytili'te], *n.f.* utility, usefulness; benefit, profit, service, avail.
utopie [ytɔ'pi], *n.f.* utopia.
utopique [ytɔ'pik], *a.* utopian.

V

V, v [ve], *n.m.* the twenty-second letter of the alphabet.
vacance [va'kɑ̃:s], *n.f.* vacancy; (*pl.*) vacation, holiday; recess (*of parliament etc.*).
vacant [va'kɑ̃], *a.* vacant; unoccupied, empty.
vacarme [va'karm], *n.m.* hubbub, uproar, fuss.
vacation [vakɑ'sjɔ̃], *n.f.* attendance, sitting (*of public officers etc.*); day's sale (*at auctions*); vacation (*of courts*).
vaccin [vak'sɛ̃], *n.m.* vaccine.
vaccination [vaksinɑ'sjɔ̃], *n.f.* inoculation, vaccination.
vacciner [vaksi'ne], *v.t.* to inoculate, to vaccinate; to immunize.
vache [vaʃ], *n.f.* cow; cow-hide.
vacher [va'ʃe], *n.m.* (*fem.* **-ère**) cow-herd.
vacherie [va'ʃri], *n.f.* cow-house, byre.
vacillant [vasi'jɑ̃], *a.* vacillating, wavering, flickering; shaky, uncertain, unsteady.
vacillation [vasijɑ'sjɔ̃], *n.f.* wobbling, flickering.

vaciller [vasi'je], *v.i.* to vacillate; to waver, to stagger; to flicker (*of light etc.*).
vacuité [vakɥi'te], *n.f.* vacuity, emptiness.
vacuum [va'kɥɔm], *n.m.* vacuum.
va-et-vient [vae'vjɛ̃], *n.m. inv.* reciprocating motion, swing, see-saw motion, oscillation; (*fig.*) coming and going.
vagabond [vaga'bɔ̃], *a.* and *n.m.* (*fem.* **-e**) vagabond, vagrant.
vagabondage [vagabɔ̃'da:ʒ], *n.m.* vagrancy.
vagabonder [vagabɔ̃'de], *v.i.* to be a vagabond; to roam; (*fig.*) to flit from one thing to another.
vagin [va'ʒɛ̃], *n.m.* (*Anat.*) vagina.
vagir [va'ʒi:r], *v.i.* to wail, to pule (*of infants*).
vague (1) [vag], *n.f.* wave, billow.
vague (2) [vag], *a.* vague, indeterminate, uncertain; faint, indistinct, hazy; empty, vacant; ***terres vagues***, waste-land; ***terrain vague***, vacant site, piece of waste ground.—*n.m.* vagueness, looseness, uncertainty; empty space.
vaguement [vag'mɑ̃], *adv.* vaguely, dimly.
vaguer [va'ge], *v.i.* to ramble, to wander, to stray.
vaillamment [vaja'mɑ̃], *adv.* valiantly.
vaillance [va'jɑ̃:s], *n.f.* valour, bravery.
vaillant [va'jɑ̃], *a.* valiant, brave, gallant; stout (*heart*); ***n'avoir pas un sou vaillant***, to be penniless.
vain [vɛ̃], *a.* vain, fruitless, ineffectual; empty, hollow; trifling; vainglorious; conceited; ***en vain***, vainly, in vain.
vaincre [vɛ̃:kr], *v.t. irr.* to vanquish, to conquer, to overcome, to defeat; to outdo, to surpass; ***se laisser vaincre***, to give way to, to yield.
vaincu [vɛ̃'ky], *a.* conquered, vanquished.—*n.m.* (*fem.* **-e**) conquered person, loser.
vainement [vɛn'mɑ̃], *adv.* vainly, in vain.
vainqueur [vɛ̃'kœ:r], *a.* conquering, victorious.—*n.m.* vanquisher, conqueror, victor; prize-winner.
vairon [vɛ'rɔ̃], *n.m.* minnow.
vaisseau [vɛ'so], *n.m.* (*pl.* **-eaux**) vessel, receptacle; ship; large covered space (*of a building*); (*Anat.*, *Bot.*) vessel, tube, duct; (*pl.*) shipping.
vaisselle [vɛ'sɛl], *n.f.* plates and dishes; plate (*of gold* or *silver*); ***faire la vaisselle***, to wash up.
val [val], *n.m.* (*pl.* **vals** or **vaux**) narrow valley, vale, dale.
valable [va'labl], *a.* valid, good.
valet [va'lɛ], *n.m.* footman, valet, manservant; knave (*at cards*); door-weight; holdfast; ***valet de chambre***, valet; ***valet de chiens***, whipper-in; ***valet de ferme***, farm-worker.
valeter [val'te], *v.i.* (*conjug. like* APPELER) to cringe, to dance attendance.
valétudinaire [valetydi'nɛ:r], *a.* valetudinary.—*n.* valetudinarian, invalid.
valeur [va'lœ:r], *n.f.* value, worth, price; consideration; import, meaning; valour, bravery; (*pl.*) bills, paper, stocks, shares, securities.
valeureusement [valœrøz'mɑ̃], *adv.* bravely, courageously.
valeureux [valœ'rø], *a.* (*fem.* **-euse**) brave, courageous, gallant.
valide [va'lid], *a.* valid, good; healthy, able-bodied.—*n.* person in good health.
valider [vali'de], *v.t.* to make valid; to ratify, to validate.
validité [validi'te], *n.f.* validity; availability (*of a ticket*).
valise [va'li:z], *n.f.* suit-case; valise, portmanteau.
vallée [va'le], *n.f.* valley.
vallon [va'lɔ̃], *n.m.* small valley, vale, dale.
valoir [va'lwa:r], *v.t. irr.* to yield, to bring in; to procure, to furnish.—*v.i.* to be worth, to be as good as, to be equal to; to deserve to merit; ***autant vaut***, to all intents and purposes; ***à valoir***, on account; ***faire valoir son droit***, to assert one's right; ***se faire valoir***, to boast; ***vaille que vaille***, for better or worse; ***valoir mieux***, to be better.
valse [vals], *n.f.* waltz.
valser [val'se], *v.i.* to waltz.
valve [valv], *n.f.* valve, clack, trap-door.
vampire [vɑ̃'pi:r], *n.m.* vampire.
van [vɑ̃], *n.m.* (*Agric.*) winnowing-basket.
vandale [vɑ̃'dal], *n.* vandal.
vandalisme [vɑ̃da'lism], *n.m.* vandalism.
vanille [va'ni:j], *n.f.* vanilla.
vanité [vani'te], *n.f.* vanity, conceit.
vaniteux [vani'tø], *a.* (*fem.* **-euse**) vainglorious, vain.
vannage [va'na:ʒ], *n.m.* winnowing.
vanne [van], *n.f.* sluice, sluice-gate.
vanneau [va'no], *n.m.* (*pl.* **-eaux**) lapwing, peewit.
vanner [va'ne], *v.t.* to winnow, to fan, to sift; (*pop.*) to tire out.
vannerie [van'ri], *n.f.* basket-making, basket-trade.
vanneur [va'nœ:r], *a.* (*fem.* **-euse**) winnowing.—*n.m.* (*fem.* **-euse**) winnower.—*n.f.* (**-euse**) winnowing-machine.
vannier [va'nje], *n.m.* (*fem.* **-iere**) basket-maker.
vannure [va'ny:r], *n.f.* chaff.
vantard [vɑ̃'ta:r], *a.* boasting, boastful, bragging.—*n.m.* (*fem.* **-e**) boaster, braggart.
vantardise [vɑ̃tar'di:z], *n.f.* boasting, bragging.
vanter [vɑ̃'te], *v.t.* to praise, to commend, to extol. **se vanter**, *v.r.* to boast, to pride oneself on (*de*).
vanterie [vɑ̃'tri], *n.f.* boasting, bragging.
va-nu-pieds [vany'pje], *n. inv.* ragamuffin.
vapeur [va'pœ:r], *n.f.* vapour; steam; haze, mist; ***à la vapeur*** or ***à toute vapeur***, at full speed.—*n.m.* steamer, steamship.
vaporeux [vapɔ'rø], *a.* (*fem.* **-euse**) vaporous; steamy, hazy.
vaquer [va'ke], *v.i.* to be vacant; to attend, to devote oneself (***à***).
varech or **varec** [va'rɛk], *n.m.* sea-wrack, seaweed.
variabilité [varjabili'te], *n.f.* variability, changeableness.
variable [va'rjabl], *a.* variable, fickle, unsettled.—*n.f.* (*Math.*) variable.
variant [va'rjɑ̃], *a.* variable, fickle.—*n.f.* (**-e**) variant (*reading* or *interpretation*).
variation [varjɑ'sjɔ̃], *n.f.* variation.
varice [va'ris], *n.f.* varix varicose vein.
varier [va'rje], *v.t.* to vary, to change; to variegate.—*v.i.* to vary to be changeable; to disagree.

variété [varje'te], *n.f.* variety, diversity, change; (*pl.*) miscellanea.
variole [va'rjɔl], *n.f.* smallpox.
Varsovie [varsɔ'vi], *f.* Warsaw.
vase (1) [vɑ:z], *n.m.* vase, vessel.
vase (2) [vɑ:z], *n.f.* slime, mud, mire, ooze.
vaseline [vaz'lin], *n.f.* petroleum jelly, Vaseline (*reg. trade mark*).
vaseux [va'zø], *a.* (*fem.* **-euse**) slimy, muddy, miry.
vasistas [vazis'tɑ:s], *n.m. inv.* opening, fan-light (*over a door* or *a window*).
vassal [va'sal], *n.m.* (*fem.* **-e**, *m. pl.* **-aux**) vassal.
vaste [vast], *a.* vast, wide, spacious.
vastement [vastə'mɑ̃], *adv.* vastly, widely.
Vatican [vati'kɑ̃], **le**, *m.* the Vatican.
va-tout [va'tu], *n.m. inv.* one's all (*at cards*); ***jouer son va-tout***, to stake one's all.
vaudeville [vod'vil], *n.m.* vaudeville; light form of comedy.
vau-l'eau (**à**) [avo'lo], *adv. phr.* with the current, down-stream; to rack and ruin.
vaurien [vo'rjɛ̃], *n.m.* (*fem.* **-enne**) good-for-nothing, scamp; rogue.
vautour [vo'tu:r], *n.m.* vulture.
vautre [vo:tr], *n.m.* boar-hound.
vautrer (**se**) [səvo'tre], *v.r.* to wallow; to sprawl.
veau [vo], *n.m.* (*pl.* **veaux**) calf; (*Cook.*) veal; calf-skin, calf-leather; (*fig.*) slow-witted fellow; ***veau marin***, seal, seal-skin.
vedette [və'dɛt], *n.f.* vedette, mounted sentinel; scout; observation post, watch-tower; (*Theat.*) star.
végétal [veʒe'tal], *a.* (*m. pl.* **-aux**) vegetable.—*n.m.* (*pl.* **-aux**) vegetable, plant.
végétarien [veʒeta'rjɛ̃], *a.* and *n.m.* (*fem.* **-enne**) vegetarian.
végétation [veʒetɑ'sjɔ̃], *n.f.* vegetation; (*pl.*) adenoids.
végéter [veʒe'te], *v.i.* (*conjug. like* CÉDER) to vegetate.
véhémence [vee'mɑ̃:s], *n.f.* vehemence.
véhément [vee'mɑ̃], *a.* vehement, impetuous, hot, passionate.
véhiculaire [veiky'lɛ:r], *a.* vehicular.
véhicule [vei'kyl], *n.m.* vehicle; medium.
veille [vɛ:j], *n.f.* sleeplessness, watching; being awake; vigil; eve, day before; point, verge; (*pl.*) midnight work; ***être à la veille de***, to be on the point of; ***la veille de Noël***, Christmas Eve.
veillée [vɛ'je], *n.f.* time from supper to bed-time, evening (*in company*); sitting up to work etc. in company; night attendance (*upon a sick person*).
veiller [vɛ'je], *v.t.* to watch by, to nurse, to look after, to sit up with.—*v.i.* to sit up, to watch; to attend, to take care, to have an eye (*à*).
veilleur [vɛ'jœ:r], *n.m.* (*fem.* **-euse**) watcher; ***veilleur de nuit***, night-watchman.—*n.f.* (**-euse**) night-light.
veinard [vɛ'na:r], *a.* and *n.m.* (*fem.* **-e**) (*pop.*) lucky (person), lucky dog.
veine [vɛ:n], *n.f.* vein; (*Geol. etc.*) seam; (*pop.*) good luck; ***avoir de la veine***, to be in luck; ***en veine de***, in the mood for; ***un coup de veine***, a fluke.
veiné [vɛ'ne], *a.* veined, veiny.
veineux [vɛ'nø], *a.* (*fem.* **-euse**) veined, veiny; venous (*system, blood*).
vélin [ve'lɛ̃], *n.m.* vellum.
velléité [vɛlei'te], *n.f.* passing fancy, mind, whim.
vélo [ve'lo], *n.m.* (*fam.*) bike.
vélocité [velɔsi'te], *n.f.* velocity.
vélodrome [velɔ'drɔm], *n.m.* cycle racing-track.
vélomoteur [velɔmɔ'tœ:r], *n.m.* moped.
velours [və'lu:r], *n.m.* velvet; ***velours à côtes***, corduroy; ***velours de coton***, velveteen.
velouté [vəlu'te], *a.* velvet, velvety, velvet-like; soft and smooth to the palate (*of wines*).—*n.m.* velvet-pile; softness; bloom (*of fruit*); smooth rich soup *or* sauce; ***velouté de laine***, velours cloth.
velu [və'ly], *a.* hairy, shaggy, rough.—*n.m.* shagginess.
vélum [ve'lɔm], *n.m.* awning.
venaison [vənɛ'zɔ̃], *n.f.* venison.
vénal [ve'nal], *a.* (*m. pl.* **-aux**) venal, mercenary.
vénalité [venali'te], *n.f.* venality.
venant [və'nɑ̃], *a.* coming, thriving.—*n.m.* comer; ***tout-venant***, unsorted (*of produce*).
vendable [vɑ̃'dabl], *a.* saleable, marketable.
vendange [vɑ̃'dɑ̃:ʒ], *n.f.* vintage, grape-gathering.
vendanger [vɑ̃dɑ̃'ʒe], *v.t.* (*conjug. like* MANGER) to gather in the grapes from; (*fig.*) to ravage, to spoil.—*v.i.* to pick (*the grapes*); (*fig.*) to make illicit profits.
vendangeur [vɑ̃dɑ̃'ʒœ:r], *n.m.* (*fem.* **-euse**) vintager, grape-gatherer.
vendéen [vɑ̃de'ɛ̃], *a.* (*fem.* **-éenne**) Vendean.
vendetta [vɛ̃dɛ'ta], *n.f.* vendetta.
vendeur [vɑ̃'dœ:r], *n.m.* (*fem.* **-euse**) vendor, seller, dealer; salesman, shop assistant.
vendre [vɑ̃:dr], *v.t.* to sell; (*fig.*) to betray; ***à vendre***, for sale. **se vendre**, *v.r.* to sell oneself; to be sold; to go off (*well etc.*).
vendredi [vɑ̃drə'di], *n.m.* Friday; ***le Vendredi saint***, Good Friday.
vené [və'ne], *a.* high (*of meat*).
vénéneux [vene'nø], *a.* (*fem.* **-euse**) poisonous (*when eaten*).
vénérable [vene'rabl], *a.* venerable.
vénération [venerɑ'sjɔ̃], *n.f.* veneration.
vénérer [vene're], *v.t.* (*conjug. like* CÉDER) to venerate, to hold in reverence.
vénerie [ven'ri], *n.f.* venery, hunting.
veneur [və'nœ:r], *n.m.* huntsman.
Vénézuéla [venezɥe'la], **le**, *m.* Venezuela.
vénézuélien [venezɥe'ljɛ̃], *a.* (*fem.* **-enne**) Venezuelan.—*n.m.* (**Vénézuélien**, *fem.* **-enne**) Venezuelan (*person*).
vengeance [vɑ̃'ʒɑ̃:s], *n.f.* vengeance, revenge.
venger [vɑ̃'ʒe], *v.t.* (*conjug. like* MANGER) to revenge, to avenge. **se venger**, *v.r.* ***se venger de quelqu'un***, to revenge oneself on someone.
vengeur [vɑ̃'ʒœ:r], *a.* (*fem.* **-eresse**) revengeful, avenging.—*n.m.* (*fem.* **-eresse**) avenger, revenger.
véniel [ve'njɛl], *a.* (*fem.* **-elle**) venial.
venimeux [vəni'mø], *a.* (*fem.* **-euse**) communicating poison (*from outside*), venomous (*snake etc.*); (*fig.*) malignant, harmful.

venin [və'nɛ̃], *n.m.* venom, poison; (*fig.*) spite, malice.
venir [və'ni:r], *v.i. irr.* (*conjug. like* TENIR, *but with aux.* ÊTRE) to come, to be coming; to arrive; to reach; to occur, to happen; to grow, to grow up; to thrive; to issue, to arise; to be descended; ***d'où vient cela?*** what is the cause of that? ***en venir aux mains***, to come to blows; ***faire venir le médecin***, to send for the doctor; ***il va et vient***, he goes in and out; ***je ne ferai qu'aller et venir***, I will not stay, I shall come straight back; ***le voilà qui vient***, here he comes; ***où voulez-vous en venir?*** what are you getting at? ***s'en venir***, to come away; ***si ma lettre venait à se perdre***, if my letter should happen to go astray; ***venir à bout de***, to master; ***venir de***, to come from, (*followed by an infinitive*, to have just—***je viens de le voir***, I have just seen him; ***je venais de le quitter***, I had just left him).
Venise [və'ni:z], *f.* Venice.
vent [vɑ̃], *n.m.* wind; breeze; breath, breathing; (*Med.*) (*pl.*) flatulence; (*Hunt.*) scent; (*fig.*) vanity, emptiness; ***autant en emporte le vent***, all that is idle talk; ***avoir vent de***, to get wind of; ***coup de vent***, gust of wind; (*colloq.*) ***dans le vent***, 'with it'; ***en plein vent***, in the open air; ***il fait du vent***, it is windy.
vente [vɑ̃:t], *n.f.* sale; selling, auction; felling *or* cutting (*of timber*); ***en vente***, for sale, on sale; ***vente aux enchères***, sale by auction.
venter [vɑ̃'te], *v.i.* (*usu. impers.*) to blow, to be windy.
venteux [vɑ̃'tø], *a.* (*fem.* **-euse**) windy, gusty.
ventilateur [vɑ̃tila'tœ:r], *n.m.* ventilator, fan, blower.
ventilation [vɑ̃tilɑ'sjɔ̃], *n.f.* ventilation, airing.
ventiler [vɑ̃ti'le], *v.t.* to ventilate, to air; (*fig.*) to discuss.
ventosité [vɑ̃tozi'te], *n.f.* flatulence.
ventouse [vɑ̃'tu:z], *n.f.* cupping-glass; vent, air-hole; sucker (*of leech*); nozzle (*of vacuum-cleaner*).
ventre [vɑ̃:tr], *n.m.* belly, abdomen; stomach; womb; bowels, one's inside; bulge; ***à plat ventre***, flat on one's face; ***ventre à terre***, at full speed; ***j'ai mal au ventre***, I have a stomach-ache.
ventrière [vɑ̃tri'ɛ:r], *n.f.* abdominal belt; sling, brace; girth (*of horse*).
ventriloque [vɑ̃tri'lɔk], *n.* ventriloquist.
ventriloquie [vɑ̃trilɔ'ki], *n.f.* ventriloquy.
ventru [vɑ̃'try], *a.* big-bellied, corpulent; bulging.—*n.m.* (*fem.* **-e**) pot-bellied person.
venu [və'ny], *a.* come; done; come up, grown; ***bien venu*** [BIENVENU]; ***enfant bien venu***, well-grown child; ***mal venu***, unwelcome; open to censure.—*n.m.* (*fem.* **-e**) ***le dernier venu***, the last arrival; ***le premier venu*** or ***la première venue***, the first comer, anyone.—*n.f.* (**-e**) coming, arrival, advent; growth.
Vénus [ve'nys], *f.* Venus.
vêpres [vɛ:pr], *n.f. pl.* vespers.
ver [vɛ:r], *n.m.* worm; maggot, mite; moth; ***mangé*** or ***rongé des vers***, worm-eaten; ***nu comme un ver***, stark naked; ***ver blanc***, grub; ***ver à soie***, silkworm; ***ver luisant***, glow-worm; ***ver solitaire***, tapeworm.
véracité [verasi'te], *n.f.* veracity.
véranda [verɑ̃'da], *n.f.* veranda.
verbal [vɛr'bal], *a.* (*m. pl.* **-aux**) verbal.
verbalement [vɛrbal'mɑ̃], *adv.* verbally; (*colloq.*) by word of mouth.
verbaliser [vɛrbali'ze], *v.i.* to draw up a written statement.
verbe [vɛrb], *n.m.* verb; (*Theol.*) ***le Verbe***, the Word.
verbeux [vɛr'bø], *a.* (*fem.* **-euse**) verbose.
verbiage [vɛr'bja:ʒ], *n.m.* verbiage.
verbosité [vɛrbɔzi'te], *n.f.* verbosity.
verdâtre [vɛr'dɑ:tr], *a.* greenish.
verdelet [vɛr'dlɛ], *a.* (*fem.* **-ette**) greenish; tart (*of wine*); hale (*of old people*).
verdeur [vɛr'dœ:r], *n.f.* greenness, sap (*of wood*); tartness, harshness (*of wine*); vigour; spryness (*of old people*); (*fig.*) crudeness (*of language*).
verdict [vɛr'dikt], *n.m.* verdict, finding.
verdier [vɛr'dje], *n.m.* greenfinch; verderer, ranger.
verdir [vɛr'di:r], *v.t.* to make *or* paint green. —*v.i.* to turn green.
verdoyant [vɛrdwa'jɑ̃], *a.* verdant, green.
verdoyer [vɛrdwa'je], *v.i.* (*conjug. like* EMPLOYER) to become green.
verdure [vɛr'dy:r], *n.f.* verdure; greenery; pot-herbs.
verdurier [vɛrdy'rje], *n.m.* (*fem.* **-ière**) greengrocer.
véreux [ve'rø], *a.* (*fem.* **-euse**) worm-eaten, maggoty; rotten; (*fig.*) suspect; insecure (*of bills etc.*).
verge [vɛ:rʒ], *n.f.* rod, wand; shaft, pin; shank (*of an anchor etc.*); (*C*) yard (*measure*).
verger [vɛr'ʒe], *n.m.* orchard.
vergeté [vɛrʒə'te], *a.* streaky.
vergette [vɛr'ʒɛt], *n.f.* clothes-brush; bundle of rods, switch.
verglacé [vɛrgla'se], *a.* covered with glazed frost; icy.
verglas [vɛr'glɑ], *n.m.* thin coating of ice, frost after a thaw *or* rain; glazed frost.
vergne [vɛrɲ], **verne** [vɛrn], *n.m.* alder(-tree).
vergogne [vɛr'gɔɲ], *n.f.* shame; ***sans vergogne***, shameless(ly).
vergue [vɛrg], *n.f.* yard (*for sail*).
véridicité [veridisi'te], *n.f.* veracity, truthfulness.
véridique [veri'dik], *a.* veracious, truthful.
vérificateur [verifika'tœ:r], *n.m.* verifier, examiner, inspector; (*Eng.*) calipers, gauge; ***vérificateur des comptes***, auditor.
vérification [verifikɑ'sjɔ̃], *n.f.* verification, auditing, probate.
vérifier [veri'fje], *v.t.* to verify, to inspect, to examine, to audit; to prove.
vérin [ve'rɛ̃], *n.m.* (*Eng.*) jack.
véritable [veri'tabl], *a.* true, genuine, real; staunch, downright, thorough.
véritablement [veritablə'mɑ̃], *adv.* truly, in reality, indeed.
vérité [veri'te], *n.f.* truth, verity, truthfulness; ***à la vérité***, indeed, it is true, I admit; ***dire la vérité***, to speak the truth; ***en vérité***, indeed, truly.
verjus [vɛr'ʒy], *n.m.* verjuice; sour grapes.
verjuté [vɛrʒy'te], *a.* sharp, tart, acid.

vermeil [vɛr'mɛːj], *a.* (*fem.* **-eille**) vermilion, ruddy, rosy.—*n.m.* vermeil, silver-gilt.
vermicelle [vɛrmi'sɛl], *n.m.* vermicelli.
vermiculaire [vɛrmiky'lɛːr], *a.* vermicular, worm-shaped.
vermillon [vɛrmi'jɔ̃], *a. inv.* and *n.m.* vermilion.
vermine [vɛr'min], *n.f.* vermin (*only insects such as fleas, lice etc.*); (*fig.*) rabble.
vermoulu [vɛrmu'ly], *a.* worm-eaten.
vermoulure [vɛrmu'lyːr], *n.f.* worm-hole, rottenness caused by worms (*in wood*).
vermout(h) [vɛr'mut], *n.m.* vermouth.
vernaculaire [vɛrnaky'lɛːr], *a.* and *n.m.* vernacular.
vernal [vɛr'nal], *a.* (*m. pl.* **-aux**) vernal, spring-like.
vernier [vɛr'nje], *n.m.* vernier, sliding-scale.
vernir [vɛr'niːr], *v.t.* to varnish; to glaze, to polish.
vernis [vɛr'ni], *n.m.* varnish, polish, glaze.
vernissage [vɛrni'saːʒ], *n.m.* varnishing; private view (*of art exhibition*).
vernisser [vɛrni'se], *v.t.* to glaze (*pottery etc.*).
vérole [ve'rɔl], *n.f.* ***petite vérole***, smallpox; ***petite vérole volante***, chicken-pox.
véronal [verɔ'nal], *n.m.* (*Chem.*) veronal, barbitone.
Véronique [verɔ'nik], *f.* Veronica.
véronique [verɔ'nik], *n.f.* veronica, speedwell.
verrat [vɛ'ra], *n.m.* boar.
verre [vɛːr], *n.m.* glass; ***verre à eau*** or ***verre gobelet***, tumbler; ***verre à vin***, wine-glass; ***verre de vin***, glass of wine.
verrerie [vɛr'ri], *n.f.* glass-works; glass-ware.
verrier [vɛ'rje], *n.m.* glass-maker.
verrière [vɛ'rjɛːr], *n.f.* stained-glass window.
verroterie [vɛrɔ'tri], *n.f.* small glass-ware, glass beads.
verrou [vɛ'ru], *n.m.* bolt.
verrouiller [vɛru'je], *v.t.* to bolt. **se verrouiller**, *v.r.* to bolt oneself in.
verrue [vɛ'ry], *n.f.* wart; ***verrue plantaire***, verruca.
vers (1) [vɛːr], *n.m. inv.* verse, line (*of poetry*).
vers (2) [vɛːr], *prep.* towards, to; about; ***vers (les) quatre heures***, about four o'clock.
versable [vɛr'sabl], *a.* apt to overturn, liable to upset.
versage [vɛr'saːʒ], *n.m.* emptying, tipping; (*Agric.*) first ploughing (*of fallow land*).
versant (1) [vɛr'sɑ̃], *a.* liable to be overturned.
versant (2) [vɛr'sɑ̃], *n.m.* declivity, side, slope; watershed.
versatile [vɛrsa'til], *a.* inconstant, changeable.
versatilité [versatili'te], *n.f.* inconstancy.
verse (à) [a'vɛrs], *adv.* abundantly; ***il pleut à verse***, it is pouring with rain.
versé [vɛr'se], *a.* spilt; well versed, conversant.
versement [vɛrsə'mɑ̃], *n.m.* payment; deposit.
verser [vɛr'se], *v.t.* to pour, to pour out; to discharge, to empty; to shed, to spill; to pay in, to deposit; to overturn, to upset; to lay (*corn*).—*v.i.* to overturn, to upset (*of vehicles*); to be laid (*of standing corn*).
verset [vɛr'sɛ], *n.m.* (*Bibl. etc.*) verse.
versificateur [vɛrsifika'tœːr], *n.m.* (*fem.* **-trice**) versifier.
versification [vɛrsifikɑ'sjɔ̃], *n.f.* versification.
versifier [vɛrsi'fje], *v.t., v.i.* to versify.
version [vɛr'sjɔ̃], *n.f.* version; (*Sch.*) translation.
verso [vɛr'so], *n.m.* verso, back, left-hand page.
vert [vɛːr], *a.* green; sharp, harsh (*of things*); tart (*of wine*); raw; sour; (*fig.*) vigorous, robust; spicy (*of stories*).—*n.m.* green, green colour; green food; sharpness (*of wine etc.*); (*Golf*) (putting-)green.
vert-de-gris [vɛrdə'gri], *n.m.* verdigris.
vertèbre [vɛr'tɛːbr], *n.f.* vertebra.
vertébré [vɛrte'bre], *a.* and *n.m.* vertebrate.
vertement [vɛrtə'mɑ̃], *adv.* sharply; harshly, severely.
vertical [vɛrti'kal], *a.* (*m. pl.* **-aux**) vertical.
verticalement [vɛrtikal'mɑ̃], *adv.* vertically.
vertige [vɛr'tiːʒ], *n.m.* dizziness, giddiness, vertigo; (*fig.*) madness, intoxication.
vertigineux [vɛrtiʒi'nø], *a.* (*fem.* **-euse**) dizzy, giddy; (*fig.*) breath-taking.
vertigo [vɛrti'go], *n.m.* staggers; (*fig.*) whim.
vertu [vɛr'ty], *n.f.* virtue, chastity; property, faculty, quality; efficacy, force.
vertueusement [vɛrtɥøz'mɑ̃], *adv.* virtuously.
vertueux [vɛr'tɥø], *a.* (*fem.* **-euse**) virtuous, chaste.
verve [vɛrv], *n.f.* warmth, animation, verve, spirit, zest.
verveine [vɛr'vɛːn], *n.f.* vervain, verbena.
vésicule [vezi'kyl], *n.f.* vesicle, bladder; ***vésicule biliaire***, gall-bladder.
vespasienne [vɛspa'zjɛn], *n.f.* public urinal; public convenience.
vessie [vɛ'si], *n.f.* bladder.
veste [vɛst], *n.f.* jacket.
vestiaire [vɛs'tjɛːr], *n.m.* cloakroom; changing-room; robing-room (*for judges*); hat-and-coat rack.
vestibule [vɛsti'byːl], *n.m.* vestibule, lobby, hall.
vestige [vɛs'tiːʒ], *n.m.* footprint, vestige, sign, mark; trace, remains.
veston [vɛs'tɔ̃], *n.m.* jacket, lounge-coat; ***complet veston***, lounge-suit.
Vésuve [ve'zyːv], **le**, *m.* Vesuvius.
vêtement [vɛt'mɑ̃], *n.m.* garment; (*pl.*) dress, clothes; (*poet.*) raiment; ***vêtements de dessous***, underwear.
vétéran [vete'rɑ̃], *n.m.* veteran; (*Sch.*) boy who stays in a form a second year.
vétérinaire [veteri'nɛːr], *a.* veterinary.—*n.m.* veterinary surgeon, vet.
vétille [ve'tiːj], *n.f.* trifle, bagatelle.
vétiller [veti'je], *v.i.* to trifle; to split hairs.
vétilleux [veti'jø], *a.* (*fem.* **-euse**) particular, finicky.
vêtir [vɛ'tiːr], *v.t. irr.* to clothe; to array, to dress; to put on. **se vêtir**, *v.r.* to dress oneself.
véto [ve'to], *n.m.* veto.
vêtu [vɛ'ty], *a.* dressed, clothed, arrayed.
vétuste [ve'tyst], *a.* old, antiquated; dilapidated, worn out.
vétusté [vetys'te], *n.f.* antiquity, old age, decay.

veuf [vœf], *a.* (*fem.* **veuve**) widowed.—*n.m.* widower.—*n.f.* (**veuve**) widow.
veule [vœ:l], *a.* feckless, weak, feeble.
veuvage [vœ'va:ʒ], *n.m.* widowhood, widowerhood.
vexant [vɛk'sɑ̃], *a.* vexing, provoking.
vexer [vɛk'se], *v.t.* to vex, to plague, to annoy.
viable [vjabl], *a.* likely to live, viable; fit for traffic.
viaduc [vja'dyk], *n.m.* viaduct.
viager [vja'ʒe], *a.* (*fem.* **-ère**) for life, during life; ***rente viagère***, life-annuity.
viande [vjɑ̃:d], *n.f.* meat; ***menue viande***, fowl and game; ***grosse viande***, butcher's meat.
vibrant [vi'brɑ̃], *a.* vibrating; vibrant, resonant.
vibration [vibrɑ'sjɔ̃], *n.f.* vibration.
vibrer [vi'bre], *v.i.* to vibrate.
vicaire [vi'kɛ:r], *n.m.* curate (*of a parish*).
vicariat [vika'rja], *n.m.*, **vicairie** [vikɛ'ri], *n.f.* curacy, chapel of ease.
vice [vis], *n.m.* fault, defect, flaw, blemish; vice, viciousness.
vice-amiral [visami'ral], *n.m.* (*pl.* **-aux**) vice-admiral; second ship of a fleet.
vice-roi [vis'rwɑ], *n.m.* (*pl.* **vice-rois**) viceroy.
vicié [vi'sje], *a.* vitiated, depraved, corrupted; foul (*of air etc.*).
vicier [vi'sje], *v.t.* to vitiate, to taint, to corrupt.
vicieusement [visjøz'mɑ̃], *adv.* viciously.
vicieux [vi'sjø], *a.* (*fem.* **-euse**) vicious; faulty, defective.
vicinal [visi'nal], *a.* (*m. pl.* **-aux**) local, connecting (*of roads*); ***chemin vicinal***, by-road.
vicissitude [visisi'tyd], *n.f.* vicissitude, change.
vicomte [vi'kɔ̃:t], *n.m.* viscount.
vicomtesse [vikɔ̃'tɛs], *n.f.* viscountess.
victime [vik'tim], *n.f.* victim; sufferer; casualty.
Victoire [vik'twa:r], **Victoria** [viktɔ'rja], *f.* Victoria.
victoire [vik'twa:r], *n.f.* victory.
victorieux [viktɔ'rjø], *a.* (*fem.* **-euse**) victorious.
victuaille [vik'tɥɑ:j], *n.f.* (*colloq.*) provisions.
vidange [vi'dɑ̃:ʒ], *n.f.* emptying; draining off; night-soil; ***tonneau en vidange***, broached cask.
vidanger [vidɑ̃'ʒe], *v.t.* (*conjug. like* MANGER) to empty, to clean out, to drain, to blow off.
vidangeur [vidɑ̃'ʒœ:r], *n.m.* scavenger.
vide [vid], *a.* empty; void, vacant, blank; destitute.—*n.m.* empty space, blank; vacuum; gap, hole; emptiness.—*adv. phr.* ***à vide***, empty.
vidé [vi'de], *a.* emptied, exhausted.
vider [vi'de], *v.t.* to empty; to drain; to hollow out; to draw (*poultry*); to gut (*fish*); to vacate; to decide, to settle.
vie [vi], *n.f.* life; lifetime; existence, days; vitality: livelihood, living; food, subsistence; spirit, animation; noise; ***être en vie***, to be alive; ***le coût de la vie***, the cost of living; ***niveau de vie***, standard of living.
vieil [vjɛj], [VIEUX].
vieillard [vjɛ'ja:r], *n.m.* old man.
vieille [vjɛj], [VIEUX].
vieillerie [vjɛj'ri], *n.f.* (*usu. pl.*) old things old clothes, old lumber, rubbish; obsolete ideas.
vieillesse [vjɛ'jɛs], *n.f.* old age; oldness.
vieillir [vjɛ'ji:r], *v.t.* to make old; to make look old.—*v.i.* to grow old; to become obsolete.
vieillissant [vjɛji'sɑ̃], *a.* growing old.
vieillot [vjɛ'jo], *a.* (*fem.* **-otte**) oldish.
vielle [vjɛl], *n.f.* *hurdy-gurdy.
Vienne [vjɛn], *f.* Vienna.
viennois [vjɛ'nwa], *a.* Viennese.—*n.m.* (**Viennois**, *fem.* **-oise**) Viennese (*person*).
vierge [vjɛrʒ], *a.* virgin, virginal, maiden; pure, untrodden; unwrought; free (*from*).—*n.f.* virgin, maid; (*Astron.*) Virgo.
Viet-Nam [vjɛt'nam], **le**, *m.* Vietnam.
vietnamien [vjɛtna'mjɛ̃], *a.* (*fem.* **-enne**) Vietnamese.—*n.m.* Vietnamese (*language*); (**Vietnamien**, *fem.* **-enne**) Vietnamese (*person*).
vieux [vjø], *a.* (*before a vowel or* h *mute*, **vieil**, *fem.* **vieille**) old, aged, advanced in years; ancient, venerable; ***vieux jeu***, old-fashioned.—*n.m.* (*fem.* **vieille**) old man, old woman; ***la retraite des vieux***, old-age pension; ***mon vieux***, (*a term of endearment*) old friend, old chap.
vif [vif], *a.* (*fem.* **vive**) alive, live, living; quick; lively, brisk, sprightly, animated, fiery, mettlesome, ardent, eager; hasty; keen; sharp, violent (*of pain etc.*); bracing (*of air etc.*); vivid, bright (*of colours*).—*n.m.* the quick (*live flesh*); living person; ***être pris sur le vif***, to be very lifelike; ***piquer au vif***, to sting to the quick.
vif-argent [vifar'ʒɑ̃], *n.m.* quicksilver.
vigie [vi'ʒi], *n.f.* look-out man; look-out (*station* or *ship*); (*Rail.*) seat on the top of guard's van.
vigilance [viʒi'lɑ̃:s], *n.f.* vigilance.
vigilant [viʒi'lɑ̃], *a.* vigilant, watchful.
vigile [vi'ʒil], *n.f.* vigil, eve.
vigne [viɲ], *n.f.* vine; vineyard; ***vigne vierge***, wild-grape, virginia-creeper.
vigneron [viɲə'rɔ̃], *n.m.* (*fem.* **-onne**) vine-dresser, wine-grower.
vignette [vi'ɲɛt], *n.f.* vignette; (*pop.*) meadow-sweet.
vignoble [vi'ɲɔbl], *n.m.* vineyard.
vigoureusement [vigurøz'mɑ̃], *adv.* vigorously, energetically.
vigoureux [vigu'rø], *a.* (*fem.* **-euse**) vigorous, energetic; stout, stalwart.
vigueur [vi'gœ:r], *n.f.* vigour, strength; force, power, energy; ***entrer en vigueur***, to come into force (*of laws etc.*).
vil [vil], *a.* vile, base, mean; abject, low; worthless; ***à vil prix***, dirt cheap.
vilain [vi'lɛ̃], *a.* ugly; unsightly; pitiful; nasty; sordid, wretched; naughty (*of a child*); ***un vilain tour***, a dirty trick; ***vilain temps***, vile weather.—*n.m.* (*fem.* **-e**) *villein (*bondman*); nasty fellow; (*childish*) naughty boy *or* girl.
vilainement [vilɛn'mɑ̃], *adv.* uglily; basely shamefully, deplorably.
vilebrequin [vilbrə'kɛ̃], *n.m.* brace, wimble; (*Mech.*) crankshaft.
vilement [vil'mɑ̃], *adv.* vilely, basely.

vilenie [vil'ni], *n.f.* nastiness, foulness; vile action; stinginess, meanness; (*pl.*) offensive words.
vileté [vil'te], *n.f.* cheapness, low price; vileness; mean action.
vilipender [vilipɑ̃'de], *v.t.* to vilify; to disparage.
villa [vil'la], *n.f.* villa.
village [vi'la:ʒ], *n.m.* village.
villageois [vila'ʒwa], *a.* rustic.—*n.m.* (*fem.* **-e**) villager.
ville [vil], *n.f.* town, city; ***être en ville***, to be out (*not at home*); ***hôtel de ville***, town hall; ***ville d'eaux***, spa.
villégiature [vileʒja'ty:r], *n.f.* sojourn in the country; ***en villégiature***, staying in the country.
vin [vɛ̃], *n.m.* wine; ***à bon vin point d'e-n seigne***, good wine needs no bush; ***vin de Bordeaux rouge***, claret; ***vin de marque***, vintage wine; ***vin mousseux***, sparkling wine; ***vin ordinaire***, dinner wine.
vinaigre [vi'nɛ:gr], *n.m.* vinegar.
vinaigrer [vinɛ'gre] *v.t.* to season with vinegar.
vindicatif [vɛ̃dika'tif], *a.* (*fem.* **-tive**) vindictive, revengeful.
vingt [vɛ̃], *a.* and *n.m. inv.* twenty, score; twentieth.
vingtaine [vɛ̃'tɛ:n], *n.f.* a score, about twenty.
vingt-et-un [vɛ̃te'œ̃], *n.m.* vingt-et-un (*card game*).
vingtième [vɛ̃'tjɛ:m], *a.* and *n.* twentieth.
vinicole [vini'kɔl], *a.* wine-growing, wine-producing.
viol [vjɔl], *n.m.* rape.
violateur [vjɔla'tœ:r], *a.* (*fem.* **-trice**) violating, transgressing, infringing.—*n.m.* (*fem.* **-trice**) violator, infringer, breaker.
violation [vjɔlɑ'sjɔ̃], *n.f.* violation, breach, infringement.
violâtre [vjɔ'lɑ:tr], *a.* purplish.
viole [vjɔl], *n.f.* viol.
violemment [vjɔla'mɑ̃], *adv.* violently.
violence [vjɔ'lɑ̃:s], *n.f.* violence; (*Law*) duress; (*fig.*) stress, fury.
violent [vjɔ'lɑ̃], *a.* violent; strong (*of suspicion etc.*); (*colloq.*) excessive; ***c'est par trop violent***, it really is too bad.
violenter [vjɔlɑ̃'te], *v.t.* to offer *or* do violence to, to force; to constrain; to violate.
violer [vjɔ'le], *v.t.* to violate; to outrage, to transgress.
violet [vjɔ'lɛ], *a.* (*fem.* **-ette**) violet-coloured, purple.—*n.m.* violet(-colour).—*n.f.* (**-ette**) (*Bot.*) violet.
violier [vjɔ'lje], *n.m.* wallflower, gillyflower.
violon [vjɔ'lɔ̃], *n.m.* violin, fiddle; violinist, fiddler; (*pop.*) lock-up, cells (*prison*).
violoncelle [vjɔlɔ̃'sɛl], *n.m.* violoncello, 'cello.
violoncelliste [vjɔlɔ̃sɛ'list], *n.* violoncellist, 'cellist.
violoniste [vjɔlɔ'nist], *n.* violinist.
viorne [vjɔrn], *n.f.* viburnum.
vipère [vi'pɛ:r], *n.f.* viper, adder.
virage [vi'ra:ʒ], *n.m.* turning, cornering; turn, bend, corner; (*Naut.*) tacking; ***virage incliné***, bank; ***virage en épingle à cheveux***, hair-pin bend.
virago [vira'go], *n.f.* virago, termagant.
virée [vi're], *n.f.* turning; winding.
virement [vir'mɑ̃], *n.m.* turning; (*Naut.*) veering about, tacking; (*Book-keeping*) clearing, transfer; ***banque de virement***, clearing-bank.
virer [vi're], *v.t.* to transfer, to clear (*a sum of money*).—*v.i.* to turn, to turn about; (*Naut.*) to tack, to veer about.
vireux [vi'rø], *a.* (*fem.* **-euse**) poisonous, noxious, nauseous.
virginal [virʒi'nal], *a.* (*m. pl.* **-aux**) virginal, maidenly.
Virginie [virʒi'ni], *f.* Virginia; (*Geog.*) ***La Virginie***, Virginia.
virginité [virʒini'te], *n.f.* virginity, maidenhood.
virgule [vir'gyl], *n.f.* comma; ***point et virgule***, semi-colon.
viril [vi'ril], *a.* virile, male; manly.
virilement [viril'mɑ̃], *adv.* like a man; in a manly way.
virilité [virili'te], *n.f.* virility; manhood.
virole [vi'rɔl], *n.f.* ferrule.
virtuel [vir'tɥɛl], *a.* (*fem.* **-elle**) virtual.
virtuellement [virtɥɛl'mɑ̃], *adv.* virtually; potentially.
virtuose [vir'tɥo:z], *n.* virtuoso.
virtuosité [virtɥɔzi'te], *n.f.* virtuosity.
virulence [viry'lɑ̃:s], *n.f.* virulence.
virulent [viry'lɑ̃], *a.* virulent.
virus [vi'ry:s], *n.m.* virus.
vis [vis], *n.f. inv.* screw; ***escalier à vis***, spiral staircase.
visa [vi'za], *n.m.* visa, signature, endorsement (*on passports etc.*).
visage [vi'za:ʒ], *n.m.* face, visage, countenance; aspect, look, air; ***à deux visages***, double-faced; ***à visage découvert***, openly, barefacedly; ***avoir bon visage***, to look well.
vis-à-vis [viza'vi], *prep. phr.* opposite, over against; towards, in relation to; ***vis-à-vis de l'église***, opposite the church.—*adv. phr.* opposite.—*n.m. inv.* vis-à-vis (*in dancing etc.*); person opposite (*at table etc.*).
viscère [vi'sɛ:r], *n.m.* any of the viscera *or* vital organs.
viscosité [viskozi'te], *n.f.* viscosity, viscidity, stickiness.
visée [vi'ze], *n.f.* aim, end; design, plan.
viser [vi'ze], *v.t.* to aim at; to allude to; to pursue; to endorse.—*v.i.* to aim, to take aim; to aspire (*à*).
viseur [vi'zœ:r], *n.m.* (*Phot.*) view-finder.
visibilité [vizibili'te], *n.f.* visibility.
visible [vi'zibl], *a.* visible; evident, manifest, obvious.
visiblement [viziblə'mɑ̃], *adv.* visibly, obviously.
visière [vi'zjɛ:r], *n.f.* visor (*of a helmet*); peak (*of caps etc.*), eye-shade; sight (*on fire-arms*).
vision [vi'zjɔ̃], *n.f.* vision, sight; dream, phantom, fancy.
visionnaire [vizjɔ'nɛ:r], *a.* visionary, fanciful.—*n.* seer; dreamer, visionary.
visite [vi'zit], *n.f.* visit; call; visitation (*of a bishop etc.*); examination, inspection; search; ***droit de visite***, right of search; ***faire la visite des bagages***, to examine luggage; ***faire une visite*** or ***rendre visite***, to pay a visit.

visiter [vizi'te], *v.t.* to visit (*patients, clients etc.*); to go over (*cathedral etc.*); to search, to examine, to inspect.
visiteur [vizi'tœ:r], *n.m.* (*fem.* **-euse**) visitor, caller; inspector, searcher.
vison [vi'zɔ̃], *n.m.* mink (*animal*).
visqueux [vis'kø], *a.* (*fem.* **-euse**) viscous, sticky; slimy; clammy.
visser [vi'se], *v.t.* to screw, to screw on, up *or* down. **se visser**, *v.r.* to fix *or* attach oneself firmly.
visserie [vi'sri], *n.f.* screws, nuts and bolts.
Vistule [vis'tyl], **la**, *f.* the Vistula.
visuel [vi'zɥɛl], *a.* (*fem.* **-elle**) visual.
vital [vi'tal], *a.* (*m. pl.* **-aux**) vital; (*fig.*) essential.
vitalement [vital'mɑ̃], *adv.* vitally.
vitalité [vitali'te], *n.f.* vitality.
vitamine [vita'min], *n.f.* vitamin.
vite [vit], *a.* swift, quick, speedy, rapid.—*adv.* quick, quickly, fast, rapidly, expeditiously; ***vite !*** quick! look sharp!
vitesse [vi'tɛs], *n.f.* quickness, rapidity, celerity, swiftness, speed; (*Motor.*) gear; ***à grande*** or ***à toute vitesse***, at full speed; ***boîte de vitesse***, gear-box; ***changement de vitesse***, change of gear; ***gagner (quelqu'un) de vitesse***, to outrun (someone).
Viti [vi'ti], **les Îles**, *f.pl.* the Fiji Islands.
viticole [viti'kɔl], *a.* pertaining to vine culture, viticultural.
viticulture [vitikyl'ty:r], *n.f.* vine-growing.
vitrage [vi'tra:ʒ], *n.m.* glazing; glass windows.
vitrail [vi'tra:j], *n.m.* (*pl.* **-aux**) stained-glass window.
vitre [vitr], *n.f.* pane of glass; window.
vitré [vi'tre], *a.* glazed, of glass; (*Anat. etc.*) vitreous; ***porte vitrée***, glass door.
vitrer [vi'tre], *v.t.* to furnish with glass windows, to glaze.
vitreux [vi'trø], *a.* (*fem.* **-euse**) vitreous, glassy.
vitrier [vitri'e], *n.m.* glass-maker; glazier.
vitrine [vi'trin], *n.f.* shop-window; show-case.
vitriol [vitri'ɔl], *n.m.* vitriol.
vitupération [vitypera'sjɔ̃], *n.f.* vituperation.
vitupérer [vitype're], *v.t.* (*conjug. like* CÉDER) to vituperate, to reprimand.
vivace [vi'vas], *a.* long-lived, perennial (*of plants*); inveterate, deep-rooted.
vivacité [vivasi'te], *n.f.* vivacity, liveliness, sprightliness; spirit, life, ardour.
vivant [vi'vɑ̃], *a.* living, alive; lively, animated; ***langue vivante***, modern language; ***portrait vivant***, lifelike portrait.—*n.m.* life, lifetime; ***de son vivant***, in his lifetime. —*n.m.* (*fem.* **-e**) living person.
vivat! [vi'vat], *int.* and *n.m.* hurrah! huzza!
vivement [viv'mɑ̃] *adv.* quickly, briskly, sharply, vigorously; eagerly; keenly, acutely; smartly, angrily; spiritedly.
viveur [vi'vœ:r], *n.m.* (*fem.* **-euse**) rake, gay dog, person who leads a fast life.
vivier [vi'vje], *n.m.* fish-pond.
vivifiant [vivi'fjɑ̃], *a.* vivifying, quickening; refreshing, invigorating.
vivifier [vivi'fje], *v.t.* to vivify, to quicken, to give life to; to enliven, to revive.
vivisection [vivisɛk'sjɔ̃], *n.f.* vivisection.
C) **vivoir [vi'vwa:r]**, *n.m.* **living-room.**
vivoter [vivɔ'te], *v.i.* to live poorly, to rub along.
vivre [vi:vr], *v.i. irr.* to live, to be alive; to subsist, to live on, to be maintained; to board, to take one's meals; to behave; to last; ***vive la France !*** long live France! ***qui vive?*** who goes there? ***il ne sait pas vivre***, he has no manners.—*n.m.* living, board, food; (*pl.*) provisions, victuals, rations.
vocable [vɔ'kabl], *n.m.* vocable, word, name.
vocabulaire [vokaby'lɛ:r], *n.m.* vocabulary.
vocal [vɔ'kal], *a.* (*m. pl.* **-aux**) vocal.
vocation [vɔkɑ'sjɔ̃], *n.f.* vocation, calling, call; inclination; bent, talent.
vociférant [vɔsife'rɑ̃], *a.* vociferous.
vociférer [vɔsife're], *v.t.* (*conjug. like* CÉDER) to vociferate, to bawl.
vœu [vø], *n.m.* (*pl.* **vœux**) vow; prayer, wish, desire; vote, suffrage.
vogue [vɔg], *n.f.* vogue, fashion; credit, craze; ***avoir de la vogue***, to be in fashion.
voguer [vɔ'ge], *v.i.* to move forward by rowing (*of a galley etc.*); to sail, to float, to move along.
voici [vwa'si], *prep.* see here, behold; here is, here are, this is, these are; ago, past; ***le voilà, me voici***, there he is, here I am; ***monsieur que voici***, this gentleman; ***voici trois mois que je suis à l'hôpital***, I have been in hospital for the past three months.
voie [vwɑ], *n.f.* way, road; line, path, track; (*fig.*) organ, medium, channel, course; conveyance; gauge, breadth (*between the wheels of carriages*); load; (*Chem.*) process; ***être en voie de***, to be in a fair way to; ***voie d'eau***, (*Naut.*) leak; ***voie ferrée***, railway track; ***voie libre***, line clear.
voilà [vwa'la], *prep.* there, behold, there now, there is, there are, that is; ***ah ! vous voilà***, oh! there you are! ***voilà une heure qu'il parle***, he has been speaking for an hour.
voile (1) [vwal], *n.m.* veil; (*fig.*) cover, mask, disguise, show, pretence.
voile (2) [vwal], *n.f.* sail; canvas; (*fig.*) ship; ***faire voile***, to sail, to set sail.
voilé [vwa'le], *a.* rigged; veiled; clouded, dull, dim; (*wheel*) buckled, out of true.
voiler [vwa'le], *v.t.* to veil; to cover, to cloak, to blind, to disguise, to conceal; to buckle (*wheel*).—*v.i.* and **se voiler**, *v.r.* to wear a veil; to cloud over (*of the sky*); to buckle (*of a wheel*).
voilier [vwa'lje], *n.m.* sail-maker; sailing-ship.
voir [vwa:r], *v.t. irr.* to see; to behold; to witness; to look at, to observe, to view; to inspect, to superintend; to overlook; to visit; to frequent; ***faire voir***, to show, to let see; ***voyons !*** let us see! now then!—*v.i.* to see, to look, to watch; to have one's sight; ***voir à*** or ***voir à ce que***, to see to it that. **se voir**, *v.r.* to see oneself; to see each other; to visit each other; to be obvious.
voire [vwa:r], *adv.* and even, and indeed.
voirie [vwa'ri], *n.f.* roads, system of roads; commission of public streets and highways; refuse-dump.
voisin [vwa'zɛ̃], *a.* bordering, adjacent, next; next door, neighbouring.—*n.m.* (*fem.* **-e**) neighbour.

voisinage [vwazi'na:ʒ], *n.m.* neighbourhood; vicinity, proximity, nearness; neighbours.
voiturage [vwaty'ra:ʒ], *n.m.* carriage, cartage (*of goods etc.*).
voiture [vwa ty:r], *n.f.* vehicle, conveyance; carriage; coach; cart, car; cart-load; ***descendre de voiture***, to alight from a carriage; ***en voiture !*** take your seats! ***se promener en voiture*** or ***aller en voiture***, to drive; ***voiture d'enfant***, perambulator, baby-carriage, (*fam.*) pram.
voiturer [vwaty're], *v.t.* to carry, to convey, to cart.
voiturier [vwaty'rje], *n.m.* carrier, carter.
voix [vwa], *n.f. inv.* voice; tone, sound; vote, suffrage; opinion, judgment; singer; ***à demi-voix***, in a low voice; ***à haute voix***, aloud; in a loud voice, loudly; ***de vive voix***, by word of mouth.
vol (1) [vɔl], *n.m.* flying, soaring; flight; flock (*of birds*); spread (*of wings*); ***au vol***, on the wing; ***à vol d'oiseau***, as the crow flies.
vol (2) [vɔl], *n.m.* theft, robbery, stealing, larceny; stolen goods; ***vol à l'étalage***, shoplifting; ***vol avec effraction***, burglary.
volage [vɔ'la:ʒ], *a.* fickle, inconstant, flighty.
volaille [vɔ'lɑ:j], *n.f.* poultry, fowls; ***marchand de volaille***, poulterer.
volant [vɔ'lɑ̃], *a.* flying; loose, floating; movable, portable.—*n.m.* shuttlecock; flounce (*of a dress*); flywheel (*of machinery*); steering-wheel (*of a car*); sail (*of a windmill*).
volatil [vɔla'til], *a.* (*Chem.*) volatile; (*fig.*) volatile (*of temperament*).
volatile [vɔla'til], *a.* winged.—*n.m.* winged creature, bird.
vol-au-vent [vɔlo'vɑ̃], *n.m. inv.* vol-au-vent, puff-pie.
volcan [vɔl'kɑ̃], *n.m.* volcano.
volcanique [vɔlka'nik], *a.* volcanic, fiery.
volée [vɔ'le], *n.f.* flight (*of birds etc.*); flock, covey; brood; bevy; volley (*of guns*); shower (*of blows*); thrashing; peal (*of bells*); ***à la volée***, flying, as it flies, in the air; (*fig.*) rashly, at random; ***sonner à toute volée***, to ring a full peal; ***volée d'escalier***, flight of stairs.
voler (1) [vɔ'le], *v.i.* to fly; to take wing, to soar; ***entendre voler une mouche***, to hear a pin drop.
voler (2) [vɔ'le], *v.t.* to steal, to rob; to fleece, to plunder; (*fig.*) to embezzle, to usurp.—*v.i.* to steal.
volerie [vɔl'ri], *n.f.* robbery; pilfering.
volet [vɔ'lɛ], *n.m.* (window-)shutter; dove-cot; (*Av.*) flap.
voleter [vɔl'te], *v.i.* (*conjug. like* APPELER) to flutter.
voleur [vɔ'lœ:r], *n.m.* (*fem.* **-euse**) thief, robber; plunderer, extortioner; stealer; ***au voleur !*** stop thief!
volière [vɔ'ljɛ:r], *n.f.* aviary, large bird-cage.
volontaire [vɔlɔ̃'tɛ:r], *a.* voluntary, willing; intended, intentional; spontaneous; obstinate, wilful.—*n.* volunteer.
volontairement [vɔlɔ̃tɛr'mɑ̃], *adv.* voluntarily; wilfully.
volonté [vɔlɔ̃'te], *n.f.* will; (*pl.*) whims, caprices; ***avoir de la bonne volonté***, to be willing; ***à volonté***, at pleasure, at will; ***dernières volontés***, last will and testament; ***faire ses quatre volontés***, (*colloq.*) to do as one pleases; ***mauvaise volonté***, illwill; unwillingness.
volontiers [vɔlɔ̃'tje], *adv.* willingly, gladly, with pleasure.
volt [vɔlt], *n.m.* (*Elec.*) volt.
voltage [vɔl'ta:ʒ], *n.m.* voltage.
volte-face [vɔlt'fas], *n.f. inv.* turning round; ***faire volte-face***, to face about; (*fig.*) to reverse one's opinions completely.
voltige [vɔl'ti:ʒ], *n.f.* slack-rope gymnastics, flying-trapeze exercises.
voltigeant [vɔlti'ʒɑ̃], *a.* fluttering, hovering.
voltigement [vɔltiʒ'mɑ̃], *n.m.* tumbling; fluttering.
voltiger [vɔlti'ʒe], *v.i.* (*conjug. like* MANGER) to flutter, to fly about, to hover.
voltigeur [vɔlti'ʒœ:r], *n.m.* vaulter; light-infantry soldier, rifleman.
voltmètre [vɔlt'mɛtr], *n.m.* voltmeter.
volubilis [vɔlybi'lis], *n.m.* convolvulus.
volubilité [vɔlybili'te], *n.f.* volubility, fluency, glibness.
volume [vɔ'lym], *n.m.* volume; bulk, size mass.
volumineux [vɔlymi'nø], *a.* (*fem.* **-euse**) voluminous, bulky.
volupté [vɔlyp'te], *n.f.* voluptuousness, sensual pleasure.
voluptueux [vɔlyp'tyø], *a.* (*fem.* **-euse**) voluptuous, sensual.—*n.m.* (*fem.* **-euse**) voluptuary
volute [vɔ'ly:t], *n.f.* volute; scroll.
vomir [vɔ'mi:r], *v.t.* to vomit, to throw up, (*fig.*) to belch forth.—*v.i.* to vomit, to be sick.
vomissement [vɔmis'mɑ̃], *n.m.* vomit(ing).
vorace [vɔ'ras], *a.* voracious, ravenous.
voracité [vɔrasi'te], *n.f.* voracity.
vos [vo], [VOTRE].
votant [vɔ'tɑ̃], *n.m.* (*fem.* **-e**) voter.
vote [vɔt], *n.m.* vote; division, voting, poll.
voter [vɔ'te], *v.t., v.i.* to vote; to pass (*a bill*).
votif [vɔ'tif], *a.* (*fem.* **-tive**) votive.
votre [vɔtr], *a. poss.* (*pl.* **vos**) your.
vôtre [vo:tr], *pron.poss.* (*m. sing.* **le vôtre**, *fem. sing.* **la vôtre**, *pl.* **les vôtres**) yours.—*n.* your own, your own property; (*pl.*) your relations, friends etc.; your pranks, tricks.
vouer [vwe], *v.t.* to devote, to dedicate; to vow, to swear. **se vouer**, *v.r.* to devote oneself.
vouloir [vu'lwa:r], *v.t. irr.* to want; to desire, to wish, to require; to consent; to please; to choose; to determine; to try, to attempt; to admit, to grant; to mean; ***en vouloir à quelqu'un***, to bear someone a grudge; ***oui, je (le) veux bien***, yes, I am willing; ***que veut dire cela?*** what does that mean? ***que voulez-vous?*** what do you want? what can I do for you? what can you expect? ***veuillez me dire***, please tell me.—*n.m.* will; ***bon vouloir***, goodwill, ***mauvais vouloir***, illwill.
voulu [vu'ly], *a.* wished, desired, required, requisite; due. received; deliberate, studied,
vous [vu], *pron. pers.* you; to you.
voûte [vut], *n.f.* arch, vault; (*fig.*) roof, canopy; ***clef de voûte***, keystone.
voûté [vu'te], *a.* vaulted, curved.
voûter [vu'te], *v.t.* to vault, to arch over; to bend. **se voûter**, *v.r.* to arch, to vault; to be bent, to stoop.

vouvoyer [vuvwa'je], *v.t.* (*conjug. like* EMPLOYER) to say ***vous*** instead of ***tu*** when addressing somebody.
voyage [vwa'ja:ʒ], *n.m.* travel; journey, voyage, trip; visit; (*pl.*) travels; ***bon voyage !*** pleasant journey to you! ***être en voyage***, to be travelling.
voyager [vwaja'ʒe], *v.i.* (*conjug. like* MANGER) to travel, to journey.
voyageur [vwaja'ʒœ:r], *a.* (*fem.* **-euse**) travelling; migrating; ***commis voyageur***, commercial traveller; ***oiseau voyageur***, migratory bird; ***pigeon voyageur***, carrier pigeon.—*n.m.* (*fem.* **-euse**) traveller, passenger.
voyant [vwa'jɑ̃], *a.* gaudy, showy (*of colours*). —*n.m.* (*fem.* **-e**) seer, clairvoyant.
voyelle [vwa'jɛl], *n.f.* vowel.
voyou [vwa'ju], *n.m.* (*fam.*) guttersnipe, hooligan; loafer.
vrac (en) [ɑ̃'vrak], *adv. phr.* in bulk, loose, pell-mell.
vrai [vrɛ], *a.* true, real, genuine; right, proper, fit; downright, arrant.—*int.* truly, really, in truth!—*n.m.* truth; ***à vrai dire***, to tell the truth, as a matter of fact.
vraiment [vrɛ'mɑ̃], *adv.* truly, in truth; indeed, really!
vraisemblable [vrɛsɑ̃'blabl], *a.* likely, probable.—*n.m.* probability, likelihood.
vraisemblance [vrɛsɑ̃'blɑ̃:s], *n.f.* probability, likelihood, verisimilitude.
vrille [vri:j], *n.f.* gimlet, borer, piercer; (*Bot.*) tendril; (*Av.*) tail-spin.
vriller [vri'je], *v.t.* to bore.—*v.i.* to ascend spirally.
vrillette [vri'jɛt], *n.f.* death-watch beetle.
vrombir [vrɔ̃'bi:r], *v.i.* to buzz, to hum, to whirr, to purr, to throb.
vu [vy], *a.* considered, regarded; seen, observed.—*prep.* considering, in view of.—*n.m.* sight, examination, inspection; (*Law*) preamble.—*conj. phr.* ***vu que***, seeing that whereas.
vue [vy], *n.f.* sight, eyesight; eyes; view, survey, inspection; prospect; appearance; light, window; design; ***à perte de vue***, as far as the eye can reach, out of sight; ***à vue d'œil***, visibly.
Vulcain [vyl'kɛ̃], *m.* Vulcan.
vulcaniser [vylkani'ze], *v.t.* to vulcanize.
vulgaire [vyl'gɛ:r], *a.* vulgar, common.—*n.m.* the common herd.
vulgairement [vylgɛr'mɑ̃], *adv.* vulgarly, commonly.
vulgariser [vylgari'ze], *v.t.* to popularize.
vulgarité [vylgari'te], *n.f.* vulgarity.
vulnérabilité [vylnerabili'te], *n.f.* vulnerability.
vulnérable [vylne'rabl], *a.* vulnerable.

W

W, w [dublə've], *n.m.* this twenty-third letter of the alphabet is used only in borrowed words.
wagon [va'gɔ̃], *n.m.* (*Rail.*) carriage, truck, van.
wagon-lit [vagɔ̃'li], *n.m.* (*pl.* **wagons-lits**) sleeping-car, sleeper.
wagonnet [vagɔ'nɛ], *n.m.* tip-truck.
wallon [wa'lɔ̃], *a.* (*fem.* **-onne**) Walloon.—*n.m.* Walloon (*language*); (**Wallon,** *fem.* **-onne**) Walloon (*person*).
warrant [va'rɑ̃], *n.m.* warrant.
warranter [varɑ̃'te], *v.t.* to warrant, to guarantee, to certify.
water [wa'tɛr], **les W.C.** [lɛve'se], *n.m. pl.* water-closet, lavatory, W.C.
watt [wat], *n.m.* (*Elec.*) watt.
wattman [wat'man], *n.m.* (*pl.* **-men**) tram-driver.
week-end [wik'ɛnd], *n.m.* (*pl.* **week-ends**) week-end.
whisky [wis'ki], *n.m.* whisky.
whist [wist], *n.m.* whist.
wigwam [wig'wam], *n.m.* wigwam.
wolfram [vɔl'fram], *n.m.* wolfram (*tungsten-ore*).

X

X, x [iks], *n.m.* the twenty-fourth letter of the alphabet; ***rayons X***, X-rays.
xénophobe [ksenɔ'fɔb], *a.* and *n.* xenophobe.
xérès [kse'rɛs], *n.m.* sherry (*wine*).
xylophone [ksilɔ'fɔn], *n.m.* (*Mus.*) xylophone.

Y

Y, y [i grɛk], *n.m.* the twenty-fifth letter of the alphabet.
y [i], *adv.* there; thither; within, at home; ***ça y est !*** that's it! ***il y a***, there is, there are; ***je l'y ai vu***, I saw him there; ***j'y suis***, I follow you, I get you; ***y compris***, included.—*pron.* by, for, in, at *or* to him, her, it *or* them.
yacht [jɔt, jak], *n.m.* yacht.
Yémen [je'mɛn], **le**, *m.* Yemen.
yéménite [jemə'nit], *a.* Yemeni.—*n.* (**Yéménite**) Yemeni (*person*).
yeuse [jø:z], *n.f.* ilex, holm-oak.
yeux [jø:], [ŒIL].
yodler [jɔ'dle], *v.i.* (*Mus.*) to yodel.
yogi or **yogui** [jo'gi], *n.m.* yogi.
yole [jɔl], *n.f.* yawl, gig.
yougoslave [jugɔs'lav], *a.* Yugoslav.—*n.m.* Yugoslav (*language*).—*n.* (**Yougoslave**) Yugoslav (*person*).
Yougoslavie [jugɔsla'vi], **la**, *f.* Yugoslavia.
youyou [ju'ju], *n.m.* dinghy.

Z

Z, z [zed], *n.m.* the twenty-sixth letter of the alphabet.
Zambie [zɑ̃'bi], **la**, *f.* Zambia.
zèbre [zɛbr], *n.m.* zebra.
zébré [ze'bre], *a.* striped like the zebra.
zèle [zɛ:l], *n.m.* zeal, warmth, ardour, enthusiasm.
zélé [ze'le], *a.* zealous.
zélote [ze'lɔt], *n.m.* zealot.
zénith [ze'nit], *n.m.* zenith.
zéphire, zéphyr or **zéphyre** [ze'fi:r], *n.m.* zephyr, gentle breeze.
zéro [ze'ro], *n.m.* nought; zero (*of the thermometer*); (*fig.*) a mere cipher, nonentity.
zeste [zɛst], *n.m.* woody skin dividing sections of a walnut; peel (*of orange, lemon etc.*), rind; (*fig.*) straw, fig, nothing.
zézaiement or **zézayement** [zezɛ(j)'mɑ̃] *n.m.* lisping, lisp (*incorrect pronunciation of* [z] *instead of* [ʒ]).
zézayer [zezɛ'je], *v.i.* (*conjug. like* PAYER) to lisp.
zibeline [zi'blin], *n.f.* sable.
zigzag [zig'zag], *n.m.* zigzag; ***éclair en zigzag***, forked lightning.
zinc [zɛ̃:g], *n.m.* zinc; (*slang*) bar *or* counter of public-house.
zingaro [zɛ̃ga'ro], *n.m.* (*pl.* **zingari**) gipsy.
zinguer [zɛ̃'ge], *v.t.* to cover with zinc; to zinc.
zizanie [ziza'ni], *n.f.* tare, *darnel; (*fig.*) discord, bickering.
zodiaque [zɔ'djak], *n.m.* zodiac.
zone [zo:n], *n.f.* zone, belt, area.
zoo [zɔ'o], *n.m.* (*fam.*) zoo.
zoologie [zɔɔlɔ'ʒi], *n.f.* zoology.
zoologique [zɔɔlɔ'ʒik], *a.* zoological.
zoologiste [zɔɔlɔ'ʒist], *n.* zoologist.
zouave [zwa:v], *n.m.* Zouave (*soldier*).
zut! [zyt], *int.* (*fam.*) (*to convey anger, scorn, disappointment, flat refusal*); ***zut! zut alors! non, zut!*** be blowed! no go! never! bother! dash it!

A, a (1) [ei], première lettre de l'alphabet; (*Mus.*) la, *m.*; ***a.m.***, du matin.
a (2) [ei, ə], **an** [æn, ən] (*before vowel*), *indef. art.* un, *m.*, une, *f.*; ***a shilling a pound***, un shilling la livre; ***three a day***, trois par jour.
aback [ə'bæk], *adv.* en arrière; (*fig.*) à l'improviste, au dépourvu.
abacus ['æbəkəs], *n.* (*pl.* **abaci** ['æbəkai]) (*Arch., Math.*) abaque, *m.*
abaft [ə'bɑːft], *adv.* sur l'arrière, en arrière.—*prep.* en arrière de, à l'arrière de.
abandon [ə'bændən], *v.t.* abandonner; délaisser, quitter; renoncer à, se désister de.—*n.* abandon, *m.*; désinvolture, *f.*
abandoned [ə'bændənd], *a.* abandonné; dépravé.
abandonment [ə'bændənmənt], *n.* abandonnement; délaissement; abandon, *m.*
abase [ə'beis], *v.t.* abaisser; ravaler.
abasement [ə'beismənt], *n.* abaissement; ravalement, *m.*; humiliation, *f.*
abash [ə'bæʃ], *v.t.* déconcerter, décontenancer; interdire, confondre.
abate [ə'beit], *v.t.* diminuer; rabattre; affaiblir, atténuer; amortir; calmer, apaiser.—*v.i.* diminuer; s'affaiblir; se calmer, s'apaiser (*temps etc.*); tomber, baisser, s'abattre (*vent etc.*).
abatement [ə'beitmənt], *n.* diminution, réduction, *f.*, rabais; affaiblissement, adoucissement; apaisement, *m.*
abbacy ['æbəsi], *n.* dignité d'abbé, *f.*
abbess ['æbes], *n.* abbesse, *f.*
abbey ['æbi], *n.* abbaye, *f.*
abbot ['æbət], *n.* abbé, supérieur (*d'abbaye*), *m.*
abbreviate [ə'briːvieit], *v.t.* abréger; raccourcir.
abbreviation [əbriːvi'eiʃən], *n.* abréviation, *f.*
abdicate ['æbdikeit], *v.t., v.i.* abdiquer.
abdication [æbdi'keiʃən], *n.* abdication, *f.*
abdomen [æb'doumən, 'æbdəmən], *n.* abdomen, bas-ventre, *m.*
abdominal [æb'dɔminəl], *a.* abdominal.
abduct [æb'dʌkt], *v.t.* détourner, enlever (*clandestinement* ou *par force*).
abduction [æb'dʌkʃən], *n.* abduction, *f.*, enlèvement (*de mineur etc.*), détournement, *m.*
abductor [æb'dʌktə], *n.* (*Anat.*) abducteur; (*Law*) ravisseur, *m.*
abed [ə'bed], *adv.* au lit, couché.
aberration [æbə'reiʃən], *n.* aberration, *f.*; éloignement, écart, égarement, *m.*; erreur (*de jugement*), *f.*
abet [ə'bet], *v.t.* soutenir, encourager (*à un crime*); ***to aid and abet***, être le complice.
abetment [ə'betmənt], **abetting** [ə'betiŋ], *n.* encouragement (*à un crime*), *m.*
abettor [ə'betə], *n.* instigateur (*d'un crime*), *m.*; complice, *m., f.*
abeyance [ə'beiəns], *n.* vacance; suspension, *f.*; ***in abeyance***, en suspens; ***to fall into abeyance***, tomber en désuétude.
abhor [əb'hɔː], *v.t.* abhorrer, détester.
abhorrence [əb'hɔrəns], *n.* horreur, *f.*
abhorrent [əb'hɔrənt], *a.* odieux, répugnant (*à*).
abide [ə'baid], *v.t. irr.* attendre; supporter; subir, souffrir.—*v.i.* demeurer, rester; séjourner; durer; ***to abide by*** (*a decision etc.*), rester fidèle à; ***to abide by*** (*the laws etc.*), se conformer à.
abiding [ə'baidiŋ], *a.* constant, immuable.
ability [ə'biliti], *n.* capacité, *f.*; pouvoir; talent, *m.*; habileté, *f.*
abject ['æbdʒekt], *a.* abject, bas, vil.
abjection [æb'dʒekʃən], **abjectness** ['æbdʒektnis], *n.* abjection, misère, *f.*
abjectly ['æbdʒektli], *adv.* d'une manière abjecte.
abjure [æb'dʒuə], *v.t.* abjurer; renoncer à, renier.
ablative ['æblətiv], *a.* and *n.* (*Gram.*) ablatif, *m.*
ablaze [ə'bleiz], *a.* en feu, en flammes; (*fig.*) enflammé.
able [eibl], *a.* capable (*de*), à même (*de*); habile; ***to be able to***, pouvoir.
able-bodied ['eiblbɔdid], *a.* fort, robuste, vigoureux.
ablution [ə'bluːʃən], *n.* ablution, *f.*
ably ['eibli], *adv.* habilement, avec talent.
abnegation [æbni'geiʃən], *n.* abnégation, renonciation, *f.*; désaveu, *m.*
abnormal [æb'nɔːməl], *a.* anormal.
abnormality [æbnɔː'mæliti], *n.* anomalie; difformité, *f.*
abnormally [æb'nɔːməli], *adv.* anormalement.
aboard [ə'bɔːd], *adv.* à bord (*de*).
abode (1) [ə'boud], *n.* demeure, habitation, *f.*; séjour, *m.*
abode (2) [ə'boud], *past* and *p.p.* [ABIDE].
abolish [ə'bɔliʃ], *v.t.* abolir; supprimer.
abolishment [ə'bɔliʃmənt], **abolition** [æbə'liʃən], *n.* abolition, suppression, *f.*; abolissement, *m.*
abominable [ə'bɔminəbl], *a.* abominable, infâme, détestable.
abominably [ə'bɔminəbli], *adv.* abominablement.
abominate [ə'bɔmineit], *v.t.* abominer, détester.
abomination [əbɔmi'neiʃən], *n.* abomination, horreur, *f.*
aboriginal [æbə'ridʒinəl], *a.* aborigène, primitif.—*n.* aborigène, *m., f.*
aborigine [æbə'ridʒini], *n.* aborigène, *m., f.*
abortion [ə'bɔːʃən], *n.* avortement (*acte*); avorton (*embryon*), *m.*
abortive [ə'bɔːtiv], *a.* abortif, manqué; avorté.
abortively [ə'bɔːtivli], *adv.* avant terme; (*fig.*) sans résultat, sans succès.
abortiveness [ə'bɔːtivnis], *n.* (*fig.*) insuccès, *m.*
abound [ə'baund], *v.i.* abonder (*de* ou *en*), regorger (*de*).

abounding [ə'baundiŋ], *a.* abondant.
about [ə'baut], *prep.* autour de; auprès de; sur; vers; environ; touchant, au sujet de, à l'égard de; à peu près; sur le point de; dans, par; ***about that***, là-dessus, à ce sujet; ***about two o'clock***, vers (les) deux heures; ***what is it all about?*** de quoi s'agit-il?—*adv.* tout autour, à l'entour, à la ronde; çà et là; ***to be about to***, être sur le point de.
above [ə'bʌv], *prep.* au-dessus de, par-dessus; en amont de; plus de; au delà de; ***above all***, surtout, par-dessus tout; ***above board***, ouvertement, franchement.—*adv.* en haut; là-haut; au-dessus; ci-dessus.
abrasion [ə'breiʒən], *n.* abrasion, écorchure, *f.*
abrasive [ə'breisiv], *a.* and *n.* abrasif, *m.*
abreast [ə'brest], *adv.* de front, à côté l'un de l'autre; (*fig.*) de pair avec.
abridge [ə'bridʒ], *v.t.* abréger, raccourcir; restreindre, priver; ***abridged edition*** (*of book*), édition réduite, *f.*
abridgment [ə'bridʒmənt], *n.* abrégé, précis, *m.*; réduction, diminution, *f.*
abroad [ə'brɔ:d], *adv.* à l'étranger; au loin, de tous côtés; ***to get abroad***, se répandre (*nouvelles*).
abrogate ['æbrogeit], *v.t.* abroger.
abrogation [æbro'geiʃən], *n.* abrogation, *f.*
abrupt [ə'brʌpt], *a.* brusque; brisé, saccadé; précipité, soudain; abrupt, escarpé, à pic.
abruptly [ə'brʌptli], *adv.* brusquement, tout à coup.
abruptness [ə'brʌptnis], *n.* précipitation; (*fig.*) brusquerie, rudesse, *f.*; escarpement, *m.*
abscess ['æbses], *n.* abcès, dépôt, *m.*
abscond [əb'skɔnd], *v.i.* se soustraire (*furtivement*) aux poursuites de la justice; disparaître; (*fam.*) décamper.
absconder [əb'skɔndə], *n.* fugitif, *m.*; (*Law*) contumace, *m., f.*
absence ['æbsəns], *n.* absence, *f.*; éloignement, *m.*; absence d'esprit, distraction, *f.*; manque, *m.*
absent ['æbsənt], *a.* absent.—[æb'sent], *v.r.* ***to absent oneself***, s'absenter.
absentee [æbsən'ti:], *n.* absent, manquant, *m.*
absenteeism [æbsən'ti:izm], *n.* absentéisme, *m.*
absent-minded ['æbsənt'maindid], *a.* distrait.
absinthe ['æbsinθ], *n.* absinthe, *f.*
absolute ['æbsəlu:t], *a.* absolu, illimité; irrévocable (*décret*); véritable.
absolutely [æbsə'lu:tli], *adv.* absolument.
absolution [æbsə'lu:ʃən], *n.* absolution; (*R.-C. Ch.*) absoute, *f.*
absolve [əb'zɔlv], *v.t.* absoudre (*de*); délier, décharger, dégager, affranchir.
absorb [əb'sɔ:b], *v.t.* absorber; amortir (*un choc*).
absorbent [əb'sɔ:bənt], *a.* and *n.* absorbant, *m.*
absorption [əb'sɔ:pʃən], *n.* absorption, *f.*; absorbement, amortissement, *m.*
abstain [əb'stein], *v.i.* s'abstenir (*de*).
abstainer [əb'steinə], *n.* buveur d'eau, *m.*, abstème, *m., f.*; ***total abstainer***, personne qui ne boit jamais d'alcool, *f.*
abstemious [əb'sti:miəs], *a.* tempérant, sobre.
abstemiously [əb'sti:miəsli], *adv.* sobrement, avec modération.
abstemiousness [əb'sti:miəsnis], *n.* abstinence; modération, sobriété, *f.*
abstention [əb'stenʃən], *n.* abstention, *f.*
abstinence ['æbstinəns], *n.* abstinence, *f.*
abstinent ['æbstinənt], *a.* abstinent, sobre.
abstract (1) [æb'strækt], *v.t.* soustraire, dérober, détourner; faire abstraction de; résumer, abréger.
abstract (2) ['æbstrækt], *a.* abstrait.—*n.* abrégé, résumé, précis, *m.*; analyse, *f.*; (*Comm.*) relevé, *m.*
abstracted [æb'stræktid], *a.* séparé; distrait, rêveur, pensif; soustrait, dérobé.
abstractedness [æb'stræktidnis], *n.* caractère abstrait, *m.*; préoccupation, *f.*
abstraction [æb'strækʃən], *n.* soustraction, distraction; abstraction; préoccupation, *f.*
abstractly ['æbstræktli], *adv.* abstractivement, d'une manière abstraite.
abstruse [æb'stru:s], *a.* caché; abstrus, obscur.
absurd [əb'sə:d], *a.* absurde.
absurdity [əb'sə:diti], *n.* absurdité, *f.*
absurdly [əb'sə:dli], *adv.* absurdement.
abundance [ə'bʌndəns], *n.* abondance, grande quantité, *f.*; grand nombre, *m.*; (*fig.*) prospérité, *f.*
abundant [ə'bʌndənt], *a.* abondant.
abundantly [ə'bʌndəntli], *adv.* abondamment, en abondance, à foison.
abuse (1) [ə'bju:z], *v.t.* abuser de; maltraiter; médire de; injurier, dire des injures à; séduire.
abuse (2) [ə'bju:s], *n.* abus, *m.*; insultes injures, *f. pl.*
abuser [ə'bju:zə], *n.* détracteur; séducteur; trompeur, *m.*
abusive [ə'bju:siv], *a.* abusif; injurieux.
abusively [ə'bju:sivli], *adv.* abusivement; injurieusement.
abusiveness [ə'bju:sivnis], *n.* langage injurieux *ou* grossier, *m.*
abut [ə'bʌt], *v.i.* aboutir (*à*); (*Build.*) s'appuyer (*contre*).
abysmal [ə'bizməl], *a.* sans fond; (*ignorance*) profonde.
abyss [ə'bis], *n.* abîme, gouffre, *m.*
Abyssinia [æbi'sinjə]. l'Abyssinie, l'Éthiopie, *f.*
Abyssinian [æbi'sinjən], *a.* abyssinien.—*n.* Abyssinien (*personne*), *m.*
acacia [ə'keiʃə], *n.* acacia, *m.*
academic [ækə'demik], **academical** [ækə'demikəl], *a.* académique, universitaire, classique, scolaire.
academician [əkædə'miʃən], *n.* académicien, *m.*
academy [ə'kædəmi], *n.* académie (*société savante*); école libre, *f.*, pensionnat, *m.*, institution, *f.*
acanthus [ə'kænθəs], *n.* acanthe, *f.*
accede [æk'si:d], *v.i.* accéder consentir (*à*); monter (*sur le trône*).
accelerate [æk'seləreit], *v.t.* accélérer; hâter.—*v.i.* s'accélérer.
acceleration [æksələ'reiʃən], *n.* accélération, *f.*
accelerator [æk'seləreitə], *n.* accélérateur, *m.*
accent (1) [æk'sent], *v.t.* accentuer.
accent (2) ['æksənt], *n.* accent, *m.*
accentuate [æk'sentjueit], *v.t.* accentuer.

accept [ək sept], *v.t.* accepter, agréer, admettre.
acceptability [əkseptə'biliti], **acceptableness** [ək'septəblnis], *n.* acceptabilité, *f.*; droit au bon accueil, *m.*
acceptable [ək'septəbl], *a.* acceptable; agréable.
acceptance [ək'septəns], *n.* acceptation, *f.*; accueil favorable, *m.*
acceptation [æksep'teiʃən], *n.* acception, *f.*, sens (*d'un mot*), *m.*
access ['ækses], *n.* accès, abord, *m.*; entrée, admission, *f.*
accessible [æk'sesibl], *a.* accessible, abordable.
accession [æk'seʃən], *n.* acquisition; augmentation, addition, *f.*, accroissement; avènement (*au trône etc.*), *m.*
accessory [æk'sesəri], *a.* accessoire.—*n.* accessoire (*chose*), *m.*; complice (*personne*), *m.*, *f.*
accidence ['æksidəns], *n.* morphologie, *f.*; rudiments (*de grammaire*), *m. pl.*
accident ['æksidənt], *n.* accident, *m.*, avarie, *f.*, hasard; incident; malheur, *m.*
accidental [æksi'dentəl], *a.* accidentel, fortuit.
accidentally [æksi'dentəli], *adv.* accidentellement; par hasard.
acclaim [ə'kleim], *v.t.* acclamer, applaudir à; proclamer.—*n.* acclamation, *f.*
acclamation [æklə'meiʃən], *n.* acclamation, *f.*
acclimatation [əklaimə'teiʃən], **acclimation** [æklai'meiʃən], *n.* acclimatement, *m.*; acclimatation, *f.*
acclimatization [əklaimətai'zeiʃən], *n.* acclimatation, *f.*
acclimatize [ə'klaimətaiz], *v.t.* acclimater; ***to become acclimatized***, s'acclimater; s'accoutumer.
acclivity [ə'kliviti], *n.* montée, côte, rampe, *f.*
accolade [æko'leid], *n.* accolade, *f.*
accommodate [ə'kɔmədeit], *v.t.* accommoder, ajuster; loger, recevoir; fournir; obliger (*par*), servir (*de*).
accommodating [ə'kɔmədeitiŋ], *a.* accommodant, obligeant; complaisant.
accommodation [əkɔmə'deiʃən], *n.* ajustement accommodement, *m.*; complaisance; convenance, *f.*; logement, *m.*; facilités, *f.pl.*
accompaniment [ə'kʌmpnimənt], *n.* accompagnement, *m.*
accompanist [ə'kʌmpənist], *n.* (*Mus.*) accompagnateur, *m.*, accompagnatrice, *f.*
accompany [ə'kʌmpəni], *v.t.* accompagner; reconduire (*à sa voiture etc.*).
accomplice [ə'kʌmplis], *n.* complice, *m.*, *f.*, compère, *m.*
accomplish [ə'kʌmpliʃ], *v.t.* accomplir, achever; effectuer; réaliser (*une prédiction etc.*).
accomplished [ə'kʌmpliʃt], *a.* accompli, achevé; parfait.
accomplishment [ə'kʌmpliʃmənt], *n.* accomplissement, *m.*; exécution, *f.*; (*usu. pl.*) arts d'agrément, talents, *m.pl.*
accord [ə'kɔ:d], *v.t.* accorder, concéder.—*v.i.* s'accorder, être d'accord.—*n.* accord, consentement, *m.*; ***of one's own accord***, de son propre gré, spontanément; ***with one accord***, d'un commun accord.
accordance [ə'kɔ:dəns], *n.* accord, rapport, *m.*; conformité, *f.*
according [ə'kɔ:diŋ], *a.* conforme (*à*); ***according as***, selon que, suivant que; ***according to***, selon, suivant, conformément à, d'après.
accordingly [ə'kɔ:diŋli], *adv.* en conséquence; donc, aussi.
accordion [ə'kɔ:diən], *n.* accordéon, *m.*
accost [ə'kɔst], *v.t.* accoster, aborder.
account [ə'kaunt], *n.* compte; mémoire, rapport, exposé, compte rendu, *m.*; relation, *f.*, récit, *m.*; raison; cause; (*fig.*) considération, valeur, *f.*; cas, poids, *m.*; ***by all accounts***, au dire de tout le monde; ***current account***, compte courant; ***on account of***, à cause de; ***to keep accounts***, tenir les livres.—*v.t.* compter; estimer (*de*), regarder (*comme*), tenir (*pour*).—*v.i.* ***to account for***, rendre compte de, expliquer; répondre de, rendre raison de.
accountable [ə'kauntəbl], *a.* responsable; comptable.
accountancy [ə'kauntənsi], *n.* comptabilité, *f.*
accountant [ə'kauntənt], *n.* comptable, agent comptable, *m.*; ***chartered accountant***, expert comptable, *m.*
account-book [ə'kauntbuk], *n.* livre de comptes, *m.*
accoutre [ə'ku:tə], *v.t.* habiller, équiper; accoutrer (*un chevalier etc.*).
accoutrement [ə'ku:təmənt], *n.* harnachement; équipement (*du soldat*), *m.*
accredit [ə'kredit], *v.t.* accréditer.
accretion [ə'kri:ʃən], *n.* accroissement, *m.*
accrue [ə'kru:], *v.i.* provenir, résulter (*de*); s'accumuler.
accumulate [ə'kju:mjuleit], *v.t.* accumuler, entasser; amonceler.—*v.i.* s'accumuler, s'amonceler.
accumulation [əkju:mju'leiʃən], *n.* accumulation, *f.*; amoncellement, amas, entassement, *m.*
accumulative [ə'kju:mjulətiv], *a.* (*chose*) qui s'accumule; (*personne*) qui accumule, thésauriseur.
accumulator [ə'kju:mjuleitə], *n.* accumulateur, *m.*
accuracy ['ækjurisi], **accurateness** ['ækjuritnis], *n.* exactitude, justesse; précision, *f.*; soin, *m.*
accurate ['ækjurit], *a.* exact, juste, correct, précis.
accurately ['ækjuritli], *adv.* exactement, avec justesse.
accurateness [ACCURACY].
accursed [ə'kə:sid], *a.* maudit; détestable, exécrable.
accusation [ækju'zeiʃən], *n.* accusation, *f.*
accusative [ə'kju:zətiv], *a.* and *n.* (*Gram.*), accusatif, *m.*
accusatory [ə'kju:zətri], *a.* accusateur.
accuse [ə'kju:z], *v.t.* accuser.
accuser [ə'kju:zə], *n.* accusateur, *m.*
accustom [ə'kʌstəm], *v.t.* accoutumer, habituer.
ace [eis], *n.* as; (*fig.*) point, iota, *m.*; ***within an ace of***, à deux doigts de.
acerb [ə'sə:b], *a.* acerbe, aigre.
acerbity [ə'sə:biti], *n.* acerbité, aigreur; (*fig.*) âpreté, sévérité, *f.*
acetic [ə'si:tik, ə'setik], *a.* acétique.

acetylene [ə'setili:n], *n.* acétylène, *m.*
ache [eik], *n.* mal, *m.*; douleur, *f.*; ***headache***, mal de tête; ***toothache***, mal de dents.—*v.i.* faire mal; (*fig.*) souffrir (*de*); ***my head aches***, j'ai mal à la tête.
achieve [ə'tʃi:v], *v.t.* exécuter, accomplir; remporter (*une victoire*); atteindre (*à*).
achievement [ə'tʃi:vmənt], *n.* exploit, fait d'armes; accomplissement, succès, *m.*; réalisation, *f.*
aching ['eikiŋ], *a.* endolori, douloureux; ***an aching heart***, un cœur dolent.
acid ['æsid], *a.* and *n.* acide, *m.*; ***acid drops***, bonbons acidulés, *m.pl.*
acidity [ə'siditi], *n.* acidité, *f.*
acknowledge [æk'nɔlidʒ], *v.t.* reconnaître; avouer, confesser; accuser réception de (*lettre*); répondre à.
acknowledgment [æk'nɔlidʒmənt], *n.* reconnaissance, *f.*; aveu; accusé de réception, *m.*; remerciements, *m.pl.*
acme ['ækmi], *n.* comble, faîte; apogée, *m.*
acolyte ['ækolait], *n.* acolyte, *m.*
aconite ['ækonait], *n.* (*Bot.*) aconit, *m.*
acorn ['eikɔ:n], *n.* gland, *m.*
acoustic [ə'ku:stik], *a.* acoustique.—*n.* (*pl.*) acoustique, *f.*
acquaint [ə'kweint], *v.t.* informer (*de*); faire savoir à, faire part à; ***to be acquainted with***, connaître, savoir.
acquaintance [ə'kweintəns], *n.* connaissance (*de*); personne de ma (sa *etc.*) connaissance, *f.*
acquainted [ə'kweintid], *a.* connu; instruit (*de*), familier (*avec*).
acquiesce [ækwi'es], *v.i.* acquiescer (*à*); accéder (*à*).
acquiescence [ækwi'esəns], *n.* acquiescement; consentement, *m.*
acquiescent [ækwi'esənt], *a.* résigné, soumis; consentant.
acquire [ə'kwaiə], *v.t.* acquérir, obtenir, gagner.
acquirement [ə'kwaiəmənt], *n.* acquisition; connaissance, *f.*
acquisition [ækwi'ziʃən], *n.* acquisition, *f.*
acquisitive [ə'kwizitiv], *a.* âpre au gain.
acquit [ə'kwit], *v.t.* régler (*une dette*); absoudre, acquitter (*un accusé*); s'acquitter (*d'un devoir*); ***to acquit oneself well***, faire son devoir.
acquittal [ə'kwitəl], *n.* acquittement, *m.*
acre ['eikə], *n.* arpent, *m.*, acre, *f.*
acreage ['eikəridʒ], *n.* superficie, *f.*
acrid ['ækrid], *a.* âcre; (*fig.*) acerbe.
acridity [æ'kriditi], *n.* âcreté, *f.*
acrimonious [ækri'mouniəs], *a.* acrimonieux.
acrimoniously [ækri'mouniəsli], *adv.* avec aigreur, avec acrimonie.
acrimony ['ækriməni], *n.* acrimonie, aigreur, *f.*
acrobat ['ækrəbæt], *n.* acrobate, *m.*, *f.*
acrobatic [ækro'bætik], *a.* acrobatique.—*n.* (*pl.*) acrobatie, *f.*
acropolis [ə'krɔpəlis], *n.* acropole, *f.*
across [ə'krɔs, ə'krɔ:s], *prep.* à travers, sur; ***to come across***, rencontrer.—*adv.* à travers, en travers; de l'autre côté; ***across the street***, de l'autre côté de la rue.
acrostic [ə'krɔstik], *n.* acrostiche, *m.*
act [ækt], *n.* acte, *m.*, loi; action, *f.*; ***in the act***, sur le fait; ***in the act of doing it***, en train de le faire; ***in the very act***, en flagrant délit.—*v.t.* jouer, représenter; feindre, contrefaire.—*v.i.* agir (*en, sur etc.*); se conduire; se comporter; opérer.
acting ['æktiŋ], *a.* qui agit; suppléant; (*Comm.*) gérant; ***acting manager***, directeur gérant, *m.*—*n.* (*Theat.*) jeu, *m.*; (*fig.*) feinte, *f.*
action ['ækʃən], *n.* action, *f.*, fait; (*Law*) procès, *m.*; bataille, *f.*
actionable ['ækʃənəbl], *a.* actionnable, sujet à procès.
activate ['æktiveit], *v.t.* activer; rendre radioactif.
active ['æktiv], *a.* actif, agile, alerte.
actively ['æktivli], *adv.* activement.
activity [æk'tiviti], *n.* activité, *f.*
actor ['æktə], *n.* acteur, comédien, *m.*
actress ['æktris], *n.* actrice, comédienne, *f.*
actual ['æktjuəl], *a.* réel, véritable, effectif.
actuality [æktju'æliti], *n.* réalité, *f.*
actually ['æktjuəli], *adv.* réellement, en effet, positivement, véritablement; à vrai dire.
actuarial [æktju'ɛəriəl], *a.* actuariel.
actuary ['æktjuəri], *n.* actuaire, *m.*
actuate ['æktjueit], *v.t.* mettre en action; pousser, animer.
acuity [ə'kjuiti], *n.* acuité, *f.*
acumen [ə'kju:mən], *n.* finesse, pénétration, *f.*
acute [ə'kju:t], *a.* aigu, pointu, fin; (*fig.*) violent, poignant; perçant, pénétrant.
acutely [ə'kju:tli], *adv.* vivement; avec finesse.
acuteness [ə'kju:tnis], *n.* acuité; intensité; finesse, pénétration, *f.*
adage ['ædidʒ], *n.* adage, proverbe, *m.*
adamant ['ædəmənt], *a.* inflexible, intransigeant.—*n.* diamant, *m.*
adamantine [ædə'mæntain], *a.* adamantin, inflexible.
adapt [ə'dæpt], *v.t.* adapter, approprier, ajuster (*à*).
adaptability [ədæptə'biliti], *n.* faculté d'adaptation, souplesse, *f.*
adaptable [ə'dæptəbl], *a.* adaptable, qui peut s'adapter.
adapter [ə'dæptə], *n.* (*Elec.*) raccord, *m.*
add [æd], *v.t.* ajouter, joindre; additionner.
adder ['ædə], *n.* vipère, *f.*
addict ['ædikt], *n.* personne adonnée à (*stupéfiants etc.*), *f.*—[ə'dikt], *v.i.* s'adonner, se livrer (*à*).
addictedness [ə'diktidnis], **addiction** [ə'dikʃən], *n.* attachement, goût (*pour*), penchant (*à*), *m.*
addition [ə'diʃən], *n.* addition, *f.*; surcroît, supplément, accroissement, *m.*
additional [ə'diʃənəl], *a.* additionnel, supplémentaire, de plus.
additionally [ə'diʃənəli], *adv.* par addition, en sus, de plus, en outre.
addle [ædl], *v.t.* rendre couvi, corrompre; (*fig.*) brouiller (*le cerveau*).—*a.* or **addled** [ædld], couvi (*œuf*); pourri; (*fig.*) stérile.
addle-headed ['ædl'hedid], *a.* à cerveau vide, écervelé, à l'esprit brouillon.
address [ə'dres], *n.* adresse; habileté, dextérité; allocution, *f.*, discours; (*fig.*) abord, *m.*—*v.t.* adresser (*une lettre*); adresser la parole à, aborder (*quelqu'un*); (*Golf*) ***to address the ball***, viser la balle.
addressee [ædre'si:], *n.* destinataire, *m.*, *f.*

adduce [ə'dju:s], *v.t.* alléguer; apporter, avancer, produire.
Adela ['ædilə]. Adèle, *f.*
Adelaide ['ædəleid]. Adélaïde, *f.*
adenoid ['ædinɔid], *a.* adénoïde.—*n.* (*pl.*) adénite, *f.*; végétations, *f. pl.*
adept [æ'dept], *a.* adepte, habile, versé (*dans*).—*n.* adepte, *m., f.*
adequacy ['ædikwəsi], **adequateness** ['ædikwitnis], *n.* juste proportion, suffisance, *f.*
adequate ['ædikwit], *a.* proportionné, suffisant (*à*), compétent.
adequately ['ædikwitli], *adv.* en juste proportion, suffisamment, convenablement.
adequateness [ADEQUACY].
adhere [əd'hiə], *v.i.* adhérer, s'attacher, s'en tenir (*à*).
adherence [əd'hiərəns], *n.* adhérence, *f.*, attachement, *m.*
adherent [əd'hiərənt], *n.* adhérent, *m.*
adhesion [əd'hi:ʒən], *n.* adhésion, *f.*
adhesive [əd'hi:siv], *a.* adhésif, tenace; gommé, agglutinant.
adieu [ə'dju:], *adv.* and *n.* adieu, *m.*; ***to bid someone adieu***, faire ses adieux à quelqu'un.
adipose ['ædipous], *a.* adipeux.
adjacency [ə'dʒeisənsi], *n.* contiguïté, *f.*, voisinage, *m.*
adjacent [ə'dʒeisənt], *a.* adjacent, contigu (*à*), avoisinant.
adjectival [ædʒək'taivəl], *a.* comme adjectif.
adjectivally [ædʒək'taivəli], *adv.* adjectivement.
adjective ['ædʒəktiv], *a.* and *n.* adjectif, *m.*
adjoin [ə'dʒɔin], *v.t.* adjoindre, joindre; toucher, se joindre à.—*v.i.* se toucher, être contigu.
adjoining [ə'dʒɔiniŋ], *a.* adjacent, avoisinant contigu (*à*).
adjourn [ə'dʒə:n], *v.t.* ajourner, différer, remettre.—*v.i.* s'ajourner, lever la séance.
adjournment [ə'dʒə:nmənt], *n.* ajournement, *m*; remise, *f.*
adjudge [ə'dʒʌdʒ], *v.t.* adjuger; juger, condamner; (*fig.*) estimer.
adjudicate [ə'dʒu:dikeit], *v.t.* adjuger; prononcer.
adjudication [ədʒu:di'keiʃən], *n.* jugement, *m.*; décision, *f.*, arrêt, *m.*
adjudicator [ə'dʒu:dikeitə], *n.* juge, arbitre, *m.*, *f.*
adjunct ['ædʒʌŋkt], *a.* adjoint, accessoire.—*n.* accessoire; adjoint, *m.*
adjure [ə'dʒuə], *v.t.* adjurer.
adjust [ə'dʒʌst], *v.t.* ajuster, régler, arranger.
adjustable [ə'dʒʌstəbl], *a.* réglable.
adjustment [ə'dʒʌstmənt], *n.* ajustement, arrangement, accord, *m.*; mise au point, *f.*, réglage, *m.*
adjutant ['ædʒutənt], *n.* capitaine adjudant major; major de la garnison, *m.*
administer [əd'ministə], *v.t.* administrer, gérer, régir; faire prêter (*un serment*).
administrate [əd'ministreit], *v.t.* administrer; régir.
administration [ədminis'treiʃən], *n.* administration, *f.*, gouvernement, *m.*
administrative [əd'ministrətiv], *a.* administratif.
administrator [əd'ministreitə], *n.* administrateur; (*Law*) curateur, *m.*
admirable ['ædmərəbl], *a.* admirable.
admirably ['ædmərəbli], *adv.* admirablement, à ravir, à merveille.
admiral ['ædmərəl], *n.* amiral, *m.*; ***rear-admiral***, contre-amiral, *m.*; ***vice-admiral***, vice-amiral, *m.*
admiralty ['ædmərəlti], *n.* amirauté, *f.*; Ministère de la Marine (*en France*), *m.*; ***Board of Admiralty***, conseil d'amirauté, *m.*; ***First Lord of the Admiralty***, ministre de la marine, *m.*
admiration [ædmə'reiʃən], *n.* admiration, *f.*; étonnement, *m.*
admire [əd'maiə], *v.t.* admirer; aimer; s'étonner de.—*v.i.* s'étonner.
admirer [əd'maiərə], *n.* admirateur, *m.*, admiratrice, *f.*
admissible [əd'misibl], *a.* admissible.
admission [əd'miʃən], *n.* admission, entrée, *f.*; accès; aveu, *m.*, concession, *f.*
admit [əd'mit], *v.t.* admettre, laisser entrer; avouer, reconnaître; tolérer.—*v.i.* ***to admit of***, comporter, permettre; souffrir.
admittance [əd'mitəns], *n.* accès, *m.*; admission, entrée, *f.*; ***no admittance***, défense d'entrer.
admittedly [əd'mitidli], *adv.* de l'aveu général; il est vrai que.
admixture [əd'mikstʃə], *n.* mélange, *m.*
admonish [əd'mɔniʃ], *v.t.* avertir, exhorter; reprendre, réprimander.
admonishment [əd'mɔniʃmənt], **admonition** [ædmə'niʃən], *n.* admonition, *f.*, avertissement, *m.*; remontrance, réprimande, *f.*
ado [ə'du:], *n.* bruit, fracas, *m.*, façons, cérémonies, *f.pl.*, embarras, *m.*, peine, difficulté, *f.*; ***much ado about nothing***, beaucoup de bruit pour rien; ***without any more ado***, sans plus de façons.
adolescence [ædo'lesəns], *n.* adolescence, *f.*
adolescent [ædo'lesənt], *a.* and *n.* adolescent, *m.*
Adolphus [ə'dɔlfəs]. Adolphe, *m.*
adopt [ə'dɔpt], *v.t.* adopter.
adopted [ə'dɔptid], **adoptive** [ə'dɔptiv], *a.* adoptif, adopté, d'adoption.
adoption [ə'dɔpʃən], *n.* adoption, *f.*
adoptive [ADOPTED].
adorable [ə'dɔ:rəbl], *a.* adorable.
adorably [ə'dɔ:rəbli], *adv.* d'une manière adorable, adorablement.
adoration [ædo'reiʃən], *n.* adoration, *f.*
adore [ə'dɔ:], *v.t.* adorer.
adorer [ə'dɔ:rə], *n.* adorateur, *m.*
adoringly [ə'dɔ:riŋli], *adv.* avec adoration.
adorn [ə'dɔ:n], *v.t.* orner; parer, embellir; (*fig.*) faire l'ornement de.
adornment [ə'dɔ:nmənt], *n.* ornement, *m.*, parure; ornementation, *f.*
Adrian ['eidriən]. Adrien, *m.*
Adriatic Sea [eidri'ætik'si:]. la mer Adriatique, l'Adriatique, *f.*
adrift [ə'drift], *adv.* en *ou* à la dérive; à l'abandon.
adroit [ə'drɔit], *a.* adroit, habile.
adroitly [ə'drɔitli], *adv.* adroitement.
adroitness [ə'drɔitnis], *n.* adresse, dextérité, *f.*
adulate ['ædjuleit], *v.t.* aduler.
adulation [ædju'leiʃən], *n.* adulation, *f.*
adulatory ['ædjuleitəri], *a.* adulateur.
adult [ə'dʌlt, 'ædʌlt], *a.* and *n.* adulte, *m.*, *f.*

adulterate [ə'dʌltəreit], *v.t.* adultérer, frelater, falsifier, sophistiquer; (*fig.*) corrompre.
adulteration [ədʌltə'reiʃən], *n.* falsification, sophistication, *f.*, frelatage, *m.*
adulterator [ə'dʌltəreitə], *n.* frelateur, falsificateur, *m.*
adulterer [ə'dʌltərə], *n.* adultère, *m.*
adulteress [ə'dʌltəris], *n.* (femme) adultère, *f.*
adulterous [ə'dʌltərəs], *a.* adultère; (*fig.*) altéré, faux.
adultery [ə'dʌltəri], *n.* adultère, *m.*
advance [əd'vɑ:ns], *v.t.* avancer, faire avancer; élever, hausser, augmenter.—*v.i.* avancer, s'avancer, se porter en avant.—*n.* mouvement en avant, *m.*; avance (*de fonds*), *f.*; avancement, progrès, *m.*; ***in advance***, d'avance.
advance-guard [əd'vɑ:nsgɑ:d], *n.* avant-garde, *f.*
advancement [əd'vɑ:nsmənt], *n.* avancement, progrès, *m.*; (*Comm.*) avance, *f.*
advantage [əd'vɑ:ntidʒ], *n.* avantage; profit, intérêt, *m.*; ***to have the advantage***, avoir le dessus; ***to take advantage of***, profiter de; ***to take advantage of someone's kindness***, abuser de la bonté de quelqu'un.
advantageous [ædvən'teidʒəs], *a.* avantageux (*à* ou *de*).
advantageously [ædvən'teidʒəsli], *adv.* avantageusement.
Advent ['ædvənt]. (*Eccles.*) l'Avent, *m.*
advent ['ædvənt], *n.* venue, *f.*
adventitious [ædven'tiʃəs], *a.* adventice, fortuit.
adventure [əd'ventʃə], *n.* aventure, entreprise hasardeuse, *f.*—*v.t.* aventurer, hasarder.—*v.i.* s'aventurer, se hasarder.
adventurer [əd'ventʃərə], *n.* aventurier, *m.*
adventuress [əd'ventʃəris], *n.* aventurière, *f.*
adventurous [əd'ventʃərəs], *a.* aventureux, hardi.
adventurously [əd'ventʃərəsli], *adv.* aventureusement.
adverb ['ædvə:b], *n.* adverbe, *m.*
adverbial [əd'və:bjəl], *a.* adverbial.
adverbially [əd'və:bjəli], *adv.* adverbialement.
adversary ['ædvəsəri], *n.* adversaire, *m., f.*
adverse ['ædvə:s], *a.* adverse, contraire (*à*); défavorable.
adversely ['ædvə:sli], *adv.* d'une manière hostile, malheureusement.
adversity [əd'və:siti], *n.* adversité, *f.*
advert [əd'və:t], *v.i.* faire allusion (*à*); parler (*de*).
advertise ['ædvətaiz], *v.t.* annoncer, faire annoncer, afficher, faire de la publicité pour.
advertisement [əd'və:tizmənt], *n.* annonce (*journal*), publicité, réclame, *f.*; avis, *m.*; ***classified advertisements***, petites annonces, *f.pl.*
advertiser ['ædvətaizə], *n.* personne qui fait des annonces, *f.*; journal d'annonces, *m.*
advertising ['ædvətaiziŋ], *n.* publicité, réclame, *f.*; ***advertising agency***, agence de publicité, *f.*
advice [əd'vais], *n.* avis, conseil, *m.*; ***if you take my advice***, si vous m'en croyez; ***to take advice***, prendre conseil (*de*), consulter (*un médecin etc.*).
advisable [əd'vaizəbl], *a.* judicieux, convenable (*pour* ou *de*); opportun.
advisability [ədvaizə'biliti], *n.* convenance, utilité, opportunité, *f.*
advise [əd'vaiz], *v.t.* conseiller; donner avis (*de*); prévenir (*de*); annoncer.—*v.i.* délibérer, prendre conseil, consulter.
advisedly [əd'vaizidli], *adv.* avec réflexion, de propos délibéré.
adviser [əd'vaizə], *n.* conseiller, *m.*
advisory [əd'vaizəri], *a.* consultatif.
advocacy ['ædvəkəsi], *n.* profession d'avocat; défense, *f.*, plaidoyer, *m.*
advocate ['ædvəkit], *n.* avocat, défenseur; intercesseur, *m.*—['ædvəkeit], *v.t.* défendre, plaider; soutenir, appuyer, préconiser.
adze [ædz], *n.* herminette, doloire; aissette, *f.* —*v.t.* entailler à l'herminette, doler.
Aegean Sea [i:'dʒi:ənsi:]. la mer Égée, *f.*
aegis ['i:dʒis], *n.* égide, *f.*
Aeneas [i:'ni:əs]. Énée, *m.*
Aeneid [i:'ni:id]. l'Énéide, *f.*
aeon ['i:ən], *n.* éternité, *f.*, éon, *m.*
aerate ['εəreit], *v.t.* aérer; gazéifier.
aeration [εə'reiʃən], *n.* aération, *f.*
aerial ['εəriəl], *a.* aérien.—*n.* antenne, *f.*
aerie, aery, eyrie, eyry ['εəri, 'iəri], *n.* aire, *f.*
aerobatics [εəro'bætiks], *n.pl.* acrobaties aériennes, *f.pl.*
aerodrome ['εərodroum], *n.* aérodrome, *m.*
aerodynamic ['εərodai'næmik], *a.* aérodynamique.—*n.* (*pl.*) aérodynamique, *f.*
aerolite ['εərolait], **aerolith** ['εəroliθ], *n.* aérolithe, bolide, *m.*
aeronaut ['εərono:t], *n.* aéronaute, *m., f.*
aeronautic [εəro'no:tik], *a.* aéronautique.
aeroplane ['εəroplein], *n.* aéroplane, avion, *m.*
aerostat ['εərostæt], *n.* aérostat, *m.*
Aeschylus ['i:skiləs]. Eschyle, *m.*
Aesop ['i:səp]. Ésope, *m.*
aesthete ['i:sθi:t], *n.* esthète, *m., f.*
aesthetic [i:s'θetik], **aesthetical** [i:s'θetikəl], *a.* esthétique.
aesthetically [i:s'θetikəli], *adv.* esthétiquement.
aestival [i:s'taivəl], *a.* estival.
aether [ETHER].
afar [ə'fɑ:], *adv.* loin, de loin, au loin.
affability [æfə'biliti], **affableness** ['æfəblnis], *n.* affabilité, *f.*
affable ['æfəbl], *a.* affable, doux, gracieux.
affably ['æfəbli], *adv.* affablement, avec affabilité.
affair [ə'fεə], *n.* affaire, *f.*
affect [ə'fekt], *v.t.* affecter; intéresser, toucher, émouvoir.
affectation [æfek'teiʃən], **affectedness** [ə'fektidnis], *n.* affectation, *f.*
affected [ə'fektid], *a.* disposé (*pour etc.*); affecté, précieux; maniéré, prétentieux (*style*).
affecting [ə'fektiŋ], *a.* touchant, émouvant, attendrissant.
affection [ə'fekʃən], *n.* affection, *f.*, amour; goût, attachement, penchant, *m.*; maladie, *f.*
affectionate [ə'fekʃənit], *a.* affectueux, affectionné.
affectionately [ə'fekʃənitli], *adv.* affectueusement.
affiance [ə'faiəns], *v.t.* fiancer.—*n.* fiançailles, *f.pl.*

affianced [ə'faiənst], *a.* fiancé.
affidavit [æfi'deivit], *n.* déclaration par écrit sous serment, attestation, *f.*
affiliate [ə'filieit], *v.t.* affilier; attribuer, rattacher (*à*).
affiliation [əfili'eiʃən], *n.* affiliation, *f.*
affinity [ə'finiti], *n.* affinité, *f.*
affirm [ə'fə:m], *v.t.* affirmer.
affirmation [æfə'meiʃən], *n.* affirmation, *f.*
affirmative [ə'fə:mətiv], *a.* affirmatif.—*n.* affirmative, *f.*
affirmatively [ə'fə:mətivli], *adv.* affirmativement.
affix [ə'fiks], *v.t.* apposer, attacher (*à*).
afflatus [ə'fleitəs], *n.* souffle, *m.*, inspiration, *f.*
afflict [ə'flikt], *v.t.* affliger (*de*); tourmenter.
afflicting [ə'fliktiŋ], *a.* affligeant.
affliction [ə'flikʃən], *n.* affliction; calamité, *f.*, malheur, *m.*
affluence ['æfluəns], *n.* opulence, affluence; abondance, *f.*, concours (*de personnes*), *m.*
affluent ['æfluənt], *a.* opulent, riche; affluent.
afford [ə'fɔ:d], *v.t.* donner, fournir, accorder; avoir les moyens de, pouvoir.
afforestation [əfɔris'teiʃən], *n.* boisement; reboisement, *m.*
affranchise [ə'fræntʃaiz], *v.t.* affranchir.
affray [ə'frei], *n.* bagarre, échauffourée, *f.*
affright [ə'frait], *v.t.* effrayer.
affront [ə'frʌnt], *n.* affront, *m.*, insulte, injure, *f.*, outrage, *m.*—*v.t.* affronter, offenser, insulter.
afield [ə'fi:ld], *adv.* aux champs, à la campagne; ***to go far afield***, aller très loin.
afire [ə'faiə], *adv.* en feu.
aflame [ə'fleim], *adv.* en flammes.
afloat [ə'flout], *adv.* à flot; (*fig.*) en circulation.
afoot [ə'fut], *adv.* à pied; en marche, en route; (*fig.*) sur pied; en train.
afore [ə'fɔ:], *adv.* précédemment, auparavant; par devant.
aforementioned [ə'fɔ:menʃənd], *a.* mentionné plus haut, susdit, précité.
aforesaid [ə'fɔ:sed], *a.* susdit, ledit, susnommé.
aforethought [ə'fɔ:θɔ:t], *a.* ***with malice aforethought***, avec intention criminelle.
afraid [ə'freid], *a.* effrayé, pris de peur; ***I am afraid not***, je crains que non; ***I am afraid she's gone***, je crains bien qu'elle ne soit partie; ***to be afraid of***, avoir peur de.
afresh [ə'freʃ], *adv.* de nouveau, de plus belle.
Africa ['æfrikə]. l'Afrique, *f.*
African ['æfrikən], *a.* africain.—*n.* Africain (*personne*), *m.*
aft [ɑ:ft], *a.* arrière, de l'arrière.—*adv.* (*Naut.*) à l'arrière.
after ['ɑ:ftə], *a.* subséquent, ultérieur, futur; arrière.—*prep.* après; sur, à la suite de; selon, d'après.—*adv.* après, d'après, ensuite. —*conj.* après que.
aftercrop ['ɑ:ftəkrɔp], *n.* seconde récolte, *f.*; regain, *m.*
after-effects ['ɑ:ftərifekts], *n. pl.* suites, *f. pl.*, répercussion, *f.*
after-life ['ɑ:ftəlaif], *n.* suite de la vie, *f.*; au-delà, *m.*
aftermath ['ɑ:ftəmæθ], *n.* regain, *m.*; (*fig.*) suites, *f.pl.*
afternoon [ɑ:ftə'nu:n], *n.* après-midi, *m.* ou *f.*
afterthought ['ɑ:ftəθɔ:t], *n.* réflexion après coup, *f.*
afterward ['ɑ:ftəwəd], **afterwards** ['ɑ:ftəwədz], *adv.* après, ensuite, plus tard.
again [ə'gein], *adv.* encore; encore une fois, de nouveau; ***again and again***, à plusieurs reprises; ***as much again***, encore autant; ***never again***, jamais plus.
against [ə'geinst], *prep.* contre; vis-à-vis; vers; pour.
agape [ə'geip], *adv.* bouche bée.
agate ['ægeit], *n.* agate, *f.*
Agatha ['ægəθə]. Agathe, *f.*
age [eidʒ], *n.* âge, *m.*; époque, *f.*; ***of age***, majeur; ***under age***, mineur; ***Middle Ages***, moyen âge.—*v.t.*, *v.i.* vieillir.
aged ['eidʒid, (*after prefix*) eidʒd], *a.* vieux, âgé; ***middle-aged***, entre deux âges.
ageless ['eidʒlis], *a.* toujours jeune.
agency ['eidʒənsi], *n.* action, entremise; (*Comm.*) agence, *f.*
agenda [ə'dʒendə], *n.* ordre du jour; programme, *m.*
agent ['eidʒənt], *n.* représentant, agent, mandataire, *m.*
agglomerate [ə'glɔməreit], *v.t.* agglomérer.—*v.i.* s'agglomérer.—*a.* aggloméré.
agglomeration [əglɔmə'reiʃən], *n.* agglomération, *f.*
aggrandize [ə'grændaiz], *v.t.* agrandir.
aggrandizement [ə'grændizmənt], *n.* agrandissement, *m.*
aggravate ['ægrəveit], *v.t.* aggraver; exagérer; (*colloq.*) agacer, pousser à bout, exaspérer.
aggravation [ægrə'veiʃən], *n.* aggravation; circonstance aggravante, *f.*, agacement, *m.*
aggregate ['ægrigit], *a.* collectif, global, réuni. —*n.* masse, *f.*; ensemble, *m.*, somme totale, *f.*—['ægrigeit], *v.t.* rassembler.
aggregation [ægri'geiʃən], *n.* agrégation, *f.*, assemblage, *m.*
aggression [ə'greʃən], *n.* agression, *f.*
aggressive [ə'gresiv], *a.* agressif.
aggressiveness [ə'gresivnis], *n.* caractère agressif, *m.*
aggressor [ə'gresə], *n.* agresseur, *m.*
aggrieve [ə'gri:v], *v.t.* chagriner, affliger; blesser, léser.
aghast [ə'gɑ:st], *a.* consterné, ébahi, médusé, tout pantois.
agile ['ædʒail], *a.* agile, leste.
agility [ə'dʒiliti], *n.* agilité, *f.*
agio ['ædʒiou], *n.* prix du change, agio, *m.*
agiotage ['ædʒətidʒ], *n.* agiotage, *m.*
agitate ['ædʒiteit], *v.t.* agiter, exciter; remuer, troubler.
agitation [ædʒi'teiʃən], *n.* agitation; discussion, *f.*, examen, *m.*
agitator ['ædʒiteitə], *n.* agitateur; meneur, *m.*
aglow [ə'glou], *a.* enflammé, resplendissant.
agnostic [æg'nɔstik], *a.* and *n.* agnosticiste, agnostique, *m.*, *f.*
agnosticism [æg'nɔstisizm], *n.* agnosticisme, *m.*
ago [ə'gou], *adv.* passé, il y a; ***two days ago***, il y a deux jours.
agog [ə'gɔg], *adv.* excité, impatient, empressé; en train, en l'air; ***to be all agog***, avoir la tête montée.
agonize ['ægənaiz], *v.t.* torturer, mettre au supplice.—*v.i.* souffrir l'agonie, être au supplice.

agonizing ['ægənaiziŋ], *a.* atroce, déchirant.
agony ['ægəni], *n.* douleur, angoisse, *f.*, paroxysme, *m.*
agrarian [ə'grɛəriən], *a.* agraire.
agree [ə'gri:], *v.i.* s'accorder (*à* ou *avec*); être d'accord; consentir (*à*); convenir (*de*); être conforme (*à*).
agreeable [ə'gri:əbl], *a.* agréable, aimable; conforme (*à*); consentant.
agreeably [ə'gri:əbli], *adv.* agréablement; conformément (*à*).
agreed [ə'gri:d], *a.* convenu, d'accord; ***it's agreed***, c'est entendu.
agreement [ə'gri:mənt], *n.* accord, *m.*; convention, *f.*, contrat, pacte, marché, *m.*; conformité, *f.*
agricultural [ægri'kʌltʃərəl], *a.* agricole, d'agriculture.
agriculture ['ægrikʌltʃə], *n.* agriculture, *f.*
agriculturist [ægri'kʌltʃərist], *n.* agriculteur, agronome, *m.*
aground [ə'graund], *adv.* échoué; à terre.
ague ['eigju:], *n.* fièvre intermittente, *f.*
ahead [ə'hed], *adv.* en avant; (*fig.*) en tête; ***go ahead!*** en avant! vas-y! ***straight ahead***, tout droit; ***ahead of time***, en avance.
aid [eid], *v.t.* aider, assister; secourir; ***to aid each other***, s'entr'aider.—*n.* aide, assistance, *f.*; secours, concours, subside, *m.*; ***with the aid of***, à l'aide de.
aide-de-camp [eiddə'kɑ̃], *n.* aide de camp, *m.*
aigrette ['eigret], *n.* aigrette, *f.*
ail [eil], *v.t.* faire mal à; chagriner; ***what ails him?*** qu'est-ce qu'il a ?—*v.i.* être souffrant.
aileron ['eilerən], *n.* aileron, *m.*
ailing ['eiliŋ], *a.* souffrant, indisposé, mal portant.
ailment ['eilmənt], *n.* mal, malaise, *m.*, indisposition, *f.*
aim [eim], *v.t.* viser; diriger, lancer (*un coup etc.*).—*v.i.* viser (*à*); aspirer (*à*); avoir pour but (*de*).—*n.* point de mire, but, objet, dessein, *m.*; visée, *f.*; ***to take aim at***, viser, coucher en joue.
aimless ['eimlis], *a.* sans but, sans objet.
air [ɛə], *n.* air; vent, *m.*, brise; (*fig.*) mine, expression, *f.*; ***in the air***, en l'air; ***in the open air***, en plein air.—*v.t.* aérer, donner de l'air à, mettre à l'air; sécher.
air-balloon ['ɛəbəlu:n], *n.* ballon aérostatique, *m.*
airborne ['ɛəbɔ:n], *a.* (*Av.*) aéroporté.
air-conditioned ['ɛəkəndiʃənd], *a.* climatisé.
air-conditioning ['ɛəkəndiʃəniŋ], *n.* climatisation, *f.*
air-cooling ['ɛəku:liŋ], *n.* refroidissement par air, *m.*
aircraft ['ɛəkrɑ:ft], *n.* avion, *m.*; les avions, *m.pl.*
air-crew ['ɛəkru:], *n.* équipage (d'avion), *m.*
airfield ['ɛəfi:ld], *n.* terrain d'aviation, *m.*
air-hostess ['ɛəhoustis], *n.* hôtesse de l'air, *f.*
airily ['ɛərili], *adv.* allègrement, légèrement.
airiness ['ɛərinis], *n.* situation aérée; (*fig.*) légèreté, vivacité, désinvolture, *f.*
airing ['ɛəriŋ], *n.* aérage, *m.*, exposition à l'air, *f.*, éventage, *m.*; promenade, *f.*
airlift ['ɛəlift], *n.* pont aérien, *m.*
air-line ['ɛəlain], *n.* ligne aérienne, *f.*
air-liner ['ɛəlainə], *n.* avion de ligne, *m.*
air-mail ['ɛəmeil], *n.* poste aérienne, *f.*
airman ['ɛəmən], *n.* aviateur, *m.*
air-mattress ['ɛəmætris], *n.* matelas à air, *m.*
air-pocket ['ɛəpɔkit], *n.* (*Av.*) trou d'air, *m.*
airport ['ɛəpɔ:t], *n.* aéroport, *m.*
airship ['ɛəʃip], *n.* dirigeable, *m.*
airsickness ['ɛəsiknis], *n.* mal de l'air, *m.*
airstrip ['ɛəstrip], *n.* piste d'atterrissage, *f.*
airtight ['ɛətait], *a.* imperméable à l'air, hermétique.
airworthy ['ɛəwə:ði], *a.* navigable.
airy ['ɛəri], *a.* ouvert à l'air; aérien, aéré; (*fig.*) léger, dégagé, gai, enjoué, insouciant; ***airy words***, paroles en l'air, *f.pl.*
aisle [ail], *n.* bas-côté, *m.*, nef latérale, *f.*
ajar [ə'dʒɑ:], *a.* entr'ouvert, entrebâillé.
akimbo [ə'kimbou], *adv.* appuyé sur la hanche; ***with one's arms akimbo***, les poings sur les hanches.
akin [ə'kin], *a.* allié (*à*); parent (*de*); (*fig.*) qui a rapport (*avec*).
alabaster ['æləbɑ:stə], *a.* d'albâtre.—*n.* albâtre, *m.*
alack! [ə'læk], *int.* hélas!
alacrity [ə'lækriti], *n.* alacrité, *f.*, empressement, *m.*, promptitude, *f.*
Alan, Allan, Allen ['ælən]. Alain, *m.*
alarm [ə'lɑ:m], *n.* alarme, alerte, *f.*; réveil (*réveille-matin*), *m.*—*v.t.* alarmer; effrayer, faire peur à.
alarm-bell [ə'lɑ:mbel], *n.* cloche d'alarme, *f.*, tocsin, *m.*
alarm-clock [ə'lɑ:mklɔk], *n.* réveille-matin, *m.*
alarming [ə'lɑ:miŋ], *a.* alarmant.
alarmingly [ə'lɑ:miŋli], *adv.* d'une manière alarmante.
alarmist [ə'lɑ:mist], *n.* alarmiste, *m.*, *f.*
alas! [ə'læs], *int.* hélas!
Albania [æl'beinjə]. l'Albanie, *f.*
Albanian [æl'beinjən], *a.* albanais.—*n.* Albanais (*personne*), *m.*
albatross ['ælbətrɔs], *n.* albatros, *m.*
***albeit** [ɔ:l'bi:it], *conj.* quoique, bien que (*with subj.*).
albino [æl'bi:nou], *a.* and *n.* albinos, *m.*, *f.*
album ['ælbəm], *n.* album, *m.*
albumen [æl'bju:min], *n.* albumen; blanc d'œuf, *m.*; albumine, *f.*
albuminous [æl'bju:minəs], *a.* albumineux.
alburnum [æl'bə:nəm], *n.* aubier, *m.*
alchemic [æl'kemik], **alchemical** [æl'kemikəl], *a.* alchimique.
alchemist ['ælkimist], *n.* alchimiste, *m.*
alchemistic [ælki'mistik], **alchemistical** [ælki'mistikəl], *a.* d'alchimiste, alchimique.
alchemy ['ælkimi], *n.* alchimie, *f.*
alcohol ['ælkəhɔl], *n.* alcool, *m.*
alcoholic [ælkə'hɔlik], *a.* and *n.* alcoolique, *m.*, *f.*
alcoholism ['ælkəhɔlizm], *n.* alcoolisme, *m.*
Alcoran [ælkɔ'rɑ:n]. le Coran, le Koran.
alcove ['ælkouv], *n.* alcôve; niche, *f.*, enfoncement, *m.*
alder ['ɔ:ldə], *n.* aune, vergne, *m.*
alder-grove ['ɔ:ldəgrouv], *n.* aunaie, *f.*
alderman ['ɔ:ldəmən], *n.* (*pl.* **-men** [men]) conseiller municipal, alderman, échevin, *m.*
ale [eil], *n.* ale, bière, *f.*
ale-house ['eilhaus], *n.* taverne, *f.*
alembic [ə'lembik], *n.* alambic, *m.*
alert [ə'lə:t], *a.* alerte, vigilant, éveillé.—*n.* alerte, *f.*; ***on the alert***, sur le qui-vive.

alertness [ə'lə:tnis], *n.* vigilance, promptitude, prestesse, *f.*

Alexander [ælig'zɑ:ndə]. Alexandre, *m.*

alexandrine [ælig'zɑ:ndrin], *n.* (*Pros.*) alexandrin, *m.*

alfresco [æl'freskou], *adv.* en plein air.

algebra ['ældʒəbrə], *n.* algèbre, *f.*

algebraic [ældʒə'breiik], **algebraical** [ældʒə'breiikəl], *a.* algébrique.

Algeria [æl'dʒiəriə]. l'Algérie, *f.*

Algerian [æl'dʒiəriən], *a.* algérien.—*n.* Algérien (*personne*), *m.*

Algiers [æl'dʒiəz]. Alger, *m.*

alias ['eiliəs], *n.* nom d'emprunt *ou* de rechange, *m.*—*adv.* dit, autrement nommé, alias.

alibi ['ælibai], *n.* alibi, *m.*

alien ['eiljən], *a.* étranger (*à*); éloigné (*de*).—*n.* étranger, *m.*

alienate ['eiljəneit], *v.t.* aliéner (*de*).

alienation [eiljə'neiʃən], *n.* aliénation, *f.*

alienist ['eiljənist], *n.* aliéniste, *m.*, *f.*

alight [ə'lait], *a.* allumé, embrasé.—*v.i.* descendre; mettre pied à terre; s'abattre (*oiseau etc.*); atterrir (*aviateur*), amerrir (*sur l'eau*).

align [ALINE].

alike [ə'laik], *adv.* également; de même, de la même manière; à la fois.—*a.* semblable, pareil; ***to be alike***, se ressembler.

aliment ['ælimənt], *n.* aliment, *m.*

alimentary [æli'mentəri], *a.* alimentaire.

alimony ['æliməni], *n.* pension alimentaire, *f.*

aline, align [ə'lain], *v.t.* aligner; dresser.—*v.i.* s'aligner.

alinement, alignment [ə'lainmənt], *n.* alignment, *m.*

alive [ə'laiv], *a.* en vie, vivant; vif, éveillé; au monde; animé, sensible (*à*); ***dead or alive***, mort ou vif; ***to be alive with***, grouiller de, fourmiller de; ***alive to***, sensible à; ***while alive***, de son vivant.

alkali ['ælkəlai], *n.* alcali, *m.*

Alkoran [ALCORAN].

all [ɔ:l], *a.* tout, tous; ***all of you***, vous tous; ***for all that***, malgré cela; ***it is all the same to me***, cela m'est égal; ***with all speed***, au plus vite, à toute vitesse.—*adv.* tout, entièrement; ***all at once***, tout à coup, tout d'un coup; ***all the better***, tant mieux; ***not at all***, point du tout.—*n.* and *pron.* tout, *m.*; ***above all***, surtout; ***all but***, presque.

allay [ə'lei], *v.t.* apaiser, adoucir, calmer.

allegation [ælə'geiʃən], *n.* allégation, *f.*

allege [ə'ledʒ], *v.t.* alléguer, prétendre (***that***, *que*).

allegiance [ə'li:dʒəns], *n.* fidélité; obéissance, *f.*

allegorical [ælə'gɔrikəl], *a.* allégorique.

allegorically [ælə'gɔrikəli], *adv.* allégoriquement.

allegory ['æləgəri], *n.* allégorie, *f.*

allelujah [æli'lu:jə], *n.* and *int.* alléluia, *m.*

allergic [ə'lə:dʒik], *a.* (*Med.*) allergique.

allergy ['ælədʒi], *n.* allergie, *f.*

alleviate [ə'li:vieit], *v.t.* alléger, soulager, adoucir.

alleviation [əli:vi'eiʃən], *n.* allégement, adoucissement, soulagement, *m.*

alley ['æli], *n.* ruelle (*d'une ville*); allée (*jardin*), *f.*; ***blind alley***, impasse, *f.*, cul de sac, *m.*

All Fools' Day [ɔ:l'fu:lzdei]. le Ier avril.

alliance [ə'laiəns], *n.* alliance, *f.*

allied ['ælaid, ə'laid], *a.* allié; parent, voisin (*de*).

alligator ['æligeitə], *n.* alligator, caïman, *m.*

alliteration [əlitə'reiʃən], *n.* allitération, *f.*

alliterative [ə'litərətiv], *a.* allitératif.

allocate ['ælokeit], *v.t.* allouer, assigner.

allocation [ælo'keiʃən], *n.* allocation, *f.*

allot [ə'lɔt], *v.t.* assigner, donner en partage; répartir.

allotment [ə'lɔtmənt], *n.* partage, lot, lotissement, *m.*, portion; distribution, *f.*; lopin de terre, jardin ouvrier, *m.*

allow [ə'lau], *v.t.* permettre, autoriser; accorder, allouer; admettre, reconnaître; ***to allow someone to do something***, permettre à quelqu'un de faire quelque chose.

allowable [ə'lauəbl], *a.* permis, admissible, légitime.

allowance [ə'lauəns], *n.* pension, rente; allocation; ration; remise, réduction; indulgence, indemnité, *f.*; ***to make allowance for***, tenir compte de; ***to put on short allowance***, rationner.

alloy [ə'lɔi], *n.* alliage, mélange, *m.*—*v.t.* allier; (*fig.*) altérer, diminuer, corrompre.

All Saints' Day [ɔ:l'seintsdei]. la Toussaint, *f.*

All Souls' Day [ɔ:l'soulzdei]. Jour des Morts, *m.*

allude [ə'lju:d], *v.i.* faire allusion (*à*).

allure [ə'ljuə], *v.t.* amorcer, attirer, séduire, inviter (*à*).

allurement [ə'ljuəmənt], *n.* amorce, *f.*, appât, charme, attrait, *m.*

alluring [ə'ljuəriŋ], *a.* attrayant, séduisant.

alluringly [ə'ljuəriŋli], *adv.* d'une manière séduisante.

allusion [ə'lju:ʒən], *n.* allusion, *f.*

allusive [ə'lju:siv], *a.* allusif, plein d'allusions.

allusively [ə'lju:sivli], *adv.* par allusion.

alluvia [ə'lju:viə], *n.pl.* terres d'alluvion, *f.pl.*, alluvion, *f.*

alluvial [ə'lju:viəl], *a.* alluvial, d'alluvion.

alluvium [ə'lju:viəm], *n.* alluvion, *f.*

ally [ə'lai], *v.t.* allier.—*v.i.* s'allier (*à* ou *avec*).—['ælai, ə'lai], *n.* allié, confédéré, *m.*

almanac ['ɔ:lmənæk], *n.* almanach, *m.*

almighty [ɔ:l'maiti], *a.* tout-puissant; ***the Almighty***, le Tout-Puissant.

almond ['ɑ:mənd], *n.* amande, *f.*; ***burnt almond***, praline, *f.*

almond-tree ['ɑ:məndtri:], *n.* amandier, *m.*

almost ['ɔ:lmoust], *adv.* presque, à peu près; ***I almost fell***, j'ai failli tomber.

alms [ɑ:mz], *n.* aumône, *f.*; ***to give alms***, faire l'aumône.

alms-house ['ɑ:mzhaus], *n.* maison de retraite, *f.*, asile, *m.*

aloe ['ælou], *n.* aloès, *m.*; ***bitter aloes***, amer d'aloès, *m.*

aloft [ə'lɔft], *adv.* en haut, en l'air; (*Naut.*) dans la mâture.

alone [ə'loun], *a.* seul, solitaire; ***leave me alone***, laissez-moi tranquille.

along [ə'lɔŋ], *adv.* and *prep.* le long de; ***all along*** (*time*), tout le temps; (*place*) tout le long du chemin; ***along with***, avec; ***come along***, venez donc; ***get along with you***, allez-vous en, allez-vous promener.

alongside [ə'lɔŋsaid], *adv.* bord à bord; bord à quai.—*prep.* à côté de.
aloof [ə'lu:f], *a.* distant.—*adv.* au loin, (*Naut.*) au large; éloigné, à l'écart; ***to keep aloof***, se tenir à l'écart.
aloofness [ə'lu:fnis], *n.* attitude distante, *f.*
aloud [ə'laud], *adv.* à haute voix, haut.
alpaca [æl'pækə], *n.* alpaga (*tissu*); alpaca (*animal*), *m.*
alphabet ['ælfəbet], *n.* alphabet; abécédaire (*livre d'enfant*), *m.*
alphabetic [ælfə'betik], **alphabetical** [ælfə'betikəl], *a.* alphabétique.
alphabetically [ælfə'betikəli], *adv.* alphabétiquement.
alpine ['ælpain], *a.* alpin; des Alpes, alpestre.
alpinist ['ælpinist], *n.* alpiniste, *m., f.*
Alps [ælps]. les Alpes, *f. pl.*
already [ɔ:l'redi], *adv.* déjà.
Alsatian [æl'seiʃən], *a.* alsacien.—*n.* (*chien*) chien-loup; (*personne*) Alsacien, *m.*
also ['ɔ:lsou], *adv.* aussi, également.
altar ['ɔ:ltə], *n.* autel, *m.*; ***high altar***, maître-autel, *m.*
altar-cloth ['ɔ:ltəklɔθ], *n.* nappe d'autel, *f.*
altar-screen ['ɔ:ltəskri:n], *n.* retable, *m.*
alter ['ɔ:ltə], *v.t.* changer, modifier; retoucher, corriger.—*v.i.* changer, se changer.
alteration [ɔ:ltə'reiʃən], *n.* changement, *m.*, modification, *f.*
altercation [ɔ:ltə'keiʃən], *n.* altercation, dispute, *f.*
alternate ['ɔ:ltəneit], *v.t.* alterner, faire alternativement.—*v.i.* alterner; se succéder; ***alternating current***, courant alternatif, *m.*—[ɔ:l'tə:nit], *a.* alternatif; alternant; ***alternate rhymes***, rimes croisées, *f.pl.*
alternately [ɔ:l'tə:nitli], *adv.* alternativement, tour à tour.
alternative [ɔ:l'tə:nətiv], *a.* alternatif.—*n.* alternative; autre solution, *f.*
alternatively [ɔ:l'tə:nətivli], *adv.* alternativement, tour à tour.
alternator ['ɔ:ltəneitə], *n.* (*Elec.*) alternateur, *m.*
although [ɔ:l'ðou], *conj.* quoique, bien que (*with subj.*).
altimeter [ælti'mi:tə], *n.* altimètre, *m.*
altitude ['æltitju:d], *n.* altitude, élévation, hauteur, *f.*
alto ['æltou], *n.* alto, *m.*
altogether [ɔ:ltə'geðə], *adv.* tout à fait, entièrement.
altruistic [æltru'istik], *a.* altruiste.
alum ['æləm], *n.* alun, *m.*
aluminium [ælju'minjəm], *n.* aluminium, *m.*
always ['ɔ:lweiz], *adv.* toujours.
***amain** [ə'mein], *adv.* avec force, de toutes ses forces.
amalgam [ə'mælgəm], *n.* amalgame, *m.*
amalgamate [ə'mælgəmeit], *v.t.* amalgamer; (*Comm.*) fusionner.—*v.i.* s'amalgamer; (*Comm.*) fusionner.
amalgamation [əmælgə'meiʃən], *n.* amalgamation, *f.*; (*fig.*) amalgame, fusionnement, *m.*
amanuensis [əmænju'ensis], *n.* (*pl.* **amanuenses** [əmænju'ensi:z]) secrétaire, *m., f.*
amaranth ['æmərænθ], *n.* amarante, *f.*
amass [ə'mæs], *v.t.* amasser.
amateur ['æmətə:, 'æmətjuə], *n.* amateur, *m.*
amateurish [æmə'tə:riʃ, 'æmətjuəriʃ], *a.* d'amateur.
amateurism ['æmətə:rizm, 'æmətjuərizm], *n.* (*Spt.*) amateurisme, *m.*
amatory ['æmətəri], *a.* d'amour, amoureux.
amaze [ə'meiz], *v.t.* étonner, confondre, stupéfier; ***to be amazed***, s'étonner.
amazement [ə'meizmənt], **amazedness** [ə'meizidnis], *n.* étonnement, *m.*, stupeur, stupéfaction, *f.*
amazing [ə'meiziŋ], *a.* étonnant.
Amazon ['æməzən], **the.** l'Amazone, *m.*
amazon ['æməzən], *n.* amazone, *f.*
ambassador [æm'bæsədə], *n.* ambassadeur, *m.*
ambassadress [æm'bæsədris], *n.* ambassadrice, *f.*
amber ['æmbə], *a.* d'ambre; ***amber light*** (*traffic*), feu orange, *m.*—*n.* ambre, *m.*
amber-coloured ['æmbəkʌləd], *a.* ambré.
ambergris ['æmbəgris], *n.* ambre gris, *m.*
ambidexter [æmbi'dekstə], *a.* and *n.* ambidextre, *m., f.*
ambidextrous [æmbi'dekstrəs], *a.* ambidextre.
ambient ['æmbiənt], *a.* ambiant.
ambiguity [æmbi'gju:iti], **ambiguousness** [æm'bigjuəsnis], *n.* ambiguïté; équivoque, *f.*
ambiguous [æm'bigjuəs], *a.* ambigu; équivoque; douteux.
ambiguously [æm'bigjuəsli], *adv.* ambigument, d'une manière équivoque.
ambit ['æmbit], *n.* tour, circuit, *m.*; (*fig.*) étendue, portée, *f.*
ambition [æm'biʃən], *n.* ambition, *f.*
ambitious [æm'biʃəs], *a.* ambitieux.
ambitiously [æm'biʃəsli], *adv.* ambitieusement.
amble [æmbl], *v.i.* aller (à) l'amble (*cheval*); (*fig.*) trottiner, aller son chemin, déambuler.—*n.* amble, *m.*
Ambrose ['æmbrouz]. Ambroise, *m.*
ambrosia [æm'brouziə], *n.* ambroisie, *f.*
ambulance ['æmbjuləns], *n.* ambulance, *f.*; hôpital militaire, *m.*
ambulant ['æmbjulənt], *a.* ambulant.
ambulatory ['æmbjulətri], *a.* ambulatoire.
ambuscade [æmbəs'keid], *n.* embuscade, *f.*; ***to lay an ambuscade for***, dresser une embuscade à.—*v.t.* embusquer; mettre en embuscade.
ambush ['æmbuʃ], *n.* embuscade, *f.*, guet-apens, *m.*—*v.t.* embusquer.
Amelia [ə'mi:liə]. Amélie, *f.*
ameliorate [ə'mi:ljəreit], *v.t.* améliorer.—*v.i.* s'améliorer.
amelioration [əmi:ljə'rəiʃən], *n.* amélioration, *f.*
amen [ɑ:'men], *int.* amen, ainsi soit-il.
amenable [ə'mi:nəbl], *a.* responsable, comptable; docile, soumis, sujet (*à*).
amend [ə'mend], *v.t.* amender, corriger; réformer.—*v.i.* s'amender, se corriger.
amendment [ə'mendmənt], *n.* modification, *f.*, amendement, *m.*, amélioration, *f.*
amends [ə'mɛndz], *n.pl.* dédommagement, *m.*, compensation, réparation, *f.*; ***to make amends for***, dédommager de, faire réparation de.
amenity [ə'mi:niti, ə'meniti], *n.* aménité, *f.* agrément, *m.*
America [ə'merikə]. l'Amérique, *f.*

American [ə'merikən], *a.* américain.—*n.* Américain (*personne*), *m.*
amethyst ['æməθist], *n.* améthyste, *f.*
amiability [eimjə'biliti], **amiableness** ['eimjəblnis], *n.* amabilité, *f.*
amiable ['eimjəbl], *a.* aimable.
amiably ['eimjəbli], *adv.* aimablement, avec amabilité.
amicable ['æmikəbl], *a.* amical; ***amicable settlement***, arrangement à l'amiable, *m.*
amicably ['æmikəbli], *adv.* amicalement; à l'amiable.
amid [ə'mid], *prep.* au milieu de; parmi.
amidships [ə'midʃips], *adv.* (*Naut.*) par le travers.
amidst [ə'midst], [AMID].
amiss [ə'mis], *adv.* mal, en mauvaise part; (*unseasonably*) mal à propos.
amity ['æmiti], *n.* amitié, *f.*
ammeter ['æmitə], *n.* ampèremètre, *m.*
ammonia [ə'mouniə], *n.* ammoniaque, *f.*
ammunition [æmju'niʃən], *n.* munitions de guerre; cartouches, *f.pl.*
amnesia [æm'ni:ziə], *n.* amnésie, *f.*
amnesty ['æmnəsti], *n.* amnistie, *f.*—*v.t.* amnistier.
amoeba [ə'mi:bə], *n.* (*pl.* **amoebae** [ə'mi: bai], **amoebas** [ə'mi:bəz]) amibe, *f.*
amok [AMUCK].
among [ə'mʌŋ], **amongst** [ə'mʌŋst], *prep.* entre, parmi; au milieu de, chez, avec; ***among other things***, entre autres choses; ***from among***, d'entre.
amorous ['æmərəs], *a.* amoureux; porté à l'amour.
amorously ['æmərəsli], *adv.* amoureusement.
amorousness ['æmərəsnis], *n.* tempérament amoureux, *m.*, tendance à l'amour, *f.*
amorphous [ə'mɔ:fəs], *a.* amorphe.
amount [ə'maunt], *n.* montant, total, *m.*, somme; quantité; (*fig.*) valeur, *f.*, résultat, *m.*; ***to the amount of***, jusqu'à concurrence de.—*v.i.* s'élever, se monter (*à*); revenir (*à*), se réduire (*à*); ***that amounts to the same thing***, cela revient au même.
amour [ə'muə], *n.* intrigue amoureuse, *f.*
ampere ['æmpɛə], *n.* (*Elec.*) ampère, *m.*
amphibian [æm'fibiən], *n.* amphibie, *m.*
amphibious [æm'fibiəs], *a.* amphibie.
amphitheatre [æmfi'θiətə], *n.* amphithéâtre, *m.*
amphitheatrical [æmfiθi'ætrikəl], *a.* amphithéâtral, d'amphithéâtre.
amphora ['æmfərə], *n.* amphore, *f.*
ample [æmpl], *a.* ample, large, abondant, copieux; très suffisant.
ampleness ['æmplnis], *n.* ampleur; grandeur, *f.*
amplification [æmplifi'keiʃən], *n.* amplification, *f.*
amplifier ['æmplifaiə], *n.* (*Rad., Tel.*) amplificateur, *m.*
amplify ['æmplifai], *v.t.* amplifier; exagérer.
amplitude ['æmplitju:d], *n.* amplitude, étendue, largeur, *f.*
amply ['æmpli], *adv.* amplement.
amputate ['æmpjuteit], *v.t.* amputer.
amputation [æmpju'teiʃən], *n.* amputation, *f.*
amuck [ə'mʌk], **amock, amok** [ə'mɔk], *adv.* ***to run amuck***, devenir fou furieux.
amulet ['æmjulit], *n.* amulette, *f.*
amuse [ə'mju:z], *v.t.* amuser, divertir; ***to be amused at***, s'amuser *ou* se divertir de.
amusement [ə'mju:zmənt], *n.* amusement, divertissement, *m.*
amusing [ə'mju:ziŋ], *a.* amusant, divertissant.
amusingly [ə'mju:ziŋli], *adv.* d'une manière amusante.
Amy ['eimi]. Aimée, *f.*
an [A (2)].
anachronism [ə'nækrənizm], *n.* anachronisme, *m.*
anachronistic [ənækrə'nistik], *a.* anachronique.
anaconda [ænə'kɔndə], *n.* anaconda, eunecte, *m.*
anaemia [ə'ni:miə], *n.* anémie, *f.*
anaemic [ə'ni:mik], *a.* anémique.
anaesthesia [ænəs'θi:ziə], *n.* anesthésie, *f.*
anaesthetic [ænəs'θetik], *a.* and *n.* anesthésique, *m.*
anaesthetist [ə'ni:sθətist], *n.* anesthésiste, *m., f.*
anaesthetize [ə'ni:sθətaiz], *v.t.* anesthésier.
anagram ['ænəgræm], *n.* anagramme, *f.*
analgesia [ænæl'dʒi:ziə], *n.* analgésie, analgie, *f.*
analogical [ænə'lɔdʒikəl], *a.* analogique.
analogism [ə'nælədʒizm], *n.* (*Phil.*) analogisme, *m.*
analogous [ə'næləgəs], *a.* analogue.
analogy [ə'nælədʒi], *n.* analogie, *f.*
analyse ['ænəlaiz], *v.t.* analyser, faire l'analyse de.
analysis [ə'nælisis], *n.* analyse, *f.*
analyst ['ænəlist], *n.* analyste, *m., f.*
analytic [ænə'litik], **analytical** [ænə'litikəl], *a.* analytique.
analytically [ænə'litikəli], *adv.* analytiquement.
anarchism ['ænəkizm], *n.* anarchisme, *m.*
anarchist ['ænəkist], *a.* and *n.* anarchiste, *m., f.*
anarchy ['ænəki], *n.* anarchie, *f.*
anathema [ə'næθimə], *n.* anathème, *m.*
anathematize [ə'næθimətaiz], *v.t.* anathématiser, frapper d'anathème; maudire.
anatomical [ænə'tɔmikəl], *a.* anatomique.
anatomically [ænə'tɔmikəli], *adv.* anatomiquement.
anatomist [ə'nætəmist], *n.* anatomiste, *m., f.*
anatomize [ə'nætəmaiz], *v.t.* anatomiser.
anatomy [ə'nætəmi], *n.* anatomie, *f.*
ancestor ['ænsəstə], *n.* aïeul, *m.*
ancestors ['ænsəstəz], *n.pl.* ancêtres, pères, aïeux, *m.pl.*
ancestral [æn'sestrəl], *a.* ancestral, d'ancêtres, de ses ancêtres; héréditaire.
ancestry ['ænsəstri], *n.* ancêtres, *m.pl.*; race, origine, naissance, *f.*, lignage, *m.*
anchor ['æŋkə], *n.* ancre, *f.*; ***sheet-anchor***, maîtresse ancre, (*fig.*) ancre de miséricorde; ***to ride at anchor***, être à l'ancre; ***to weigh anchor***, lever l'ancre.—*v.t.* mouiller, ancrer.—*v.i.* ancrer, s'ancrer, jeter l'ancre, mouiller; (*fig.*) se fixer.
anchorage ['æŋkəridʒ], *n.* mouillage, ancrage *m.*; retraite (*d'anachorète*), .
anchoret ['æŋkəret], **anchorite** ['æŋkərait], *n.* anachorète, ermite, *m., f.*
anchovy [æn'tʃouvi, 'æntʃəvi], *n.* anchois, *m.*

ancient ['einʃənt], *a.* ancien; antique.—*n.* ancien, *m.*; ***the Ancient of Days***, l'Éternel, *m.*
anciently ['einʃəntli], *adv.* anciennement.
ancillary [æn'siləri], *a.* ancillaire, subordonné, auxiliare.
and [ænd], *conj.* et; ***and so on***, et ainsi de suite; ***better and better***, de mieux en mieux; ***carriage and pair***, voiture à deux chevaux, *f.*; ***go and see***, allez voir.
Andes ['ændi:z], **the.** les Andes, *f.pl.*
andiron ['ændaiən], *n.* landier; chenet, *m.*
Andrew ['ændru:]. André, *m.*
anecdote ['ænikdout], *n.* anecdote, *f.*
anecdotal [ænik'doutl], *a.* anecdotique.
anemone [ə'neməni], *n.* anémone, *f.*
***anent** [ə'nent], *prep.* touchant, sur, à propos de.
aneroid ['ænərɔid], *a.* and *n.* anéroïde, *m.*
aneurism ['ænjurizm], *n.* anévrisme, *m.*
anew [ə'nju:], *adv.* de nouveau.
angel ['eindʒəl], *n.* ange, *m.*
Angela ['ændʒələ]. Angèle, *f.*
angelic [æn'dʒelik], **angelical** [æn'dʒelikəl], *a.* angélique.
angelica [æn'dʒelikə], *n.* angélique, *f.*
angelus ['ændʒələs], *n.* angélus, *m.*
anger ['æŋgə], *n.* colère, *f.*; emportement; courroux, *m.*—*v.t.* fâcher, irriter, mettre en colère.
angina [æn'dʒainə], *n.* (*Path.*) angine, *f.*
angle (1) [æŋgl], *n.* angle; coin, *m.*
angle (2) [æŋgl], *v.i.* pêcher à la ligne.
angled [æŋgld], *a.* à angles; ***right-angled***, rectangulaire.
angler ['æŋglə], *n.* pêcheur à la ligne, *m.*; (*Ichth.*) baudroie, *f.*; crapaud de mer, *m.*
Anglican ['æŋglikən], *a.* anglican.—*n.* Anglican, *m.*
anglicism ['æŋglisizm], *n.* anglicisme, *m.*
anglicize ['æŋglisaiz], *v.t.* angliciser.
angling ['æŋgliŋ], *n.* pêche à la ligne, *f.*
anglophil(e) ['æŋglof(a)il], *n.* anglophile, *m.,f.*
Anglo-Saxon ['æŋglo'sæksən], *a.* anglo-saxon.—*n.* Anglo-Saxon, *m.*
angrily ['æŋgrili], *adv.* en colère, avec colère.
angry ['æŋgri], *a.* en colère, fâché, irrité (*contre* ou *de*), courroucé; ***to be angry with***, être en colère contre, en vouloir à.
anguish ['æŋgwiʃ], *n.* angoisse, douleur, *f.*—*v.t.* angoisser, navrer de douleur.
angular ['æŋgjulə], *a.* angulaire, angulé; anguleux; maigre, décharné.
angularity [æŋgju'læriti], *n.* angularité, *f.*
angularly ['æŋgjuləli], *adv.* angulairement.
anile ['einail], *a.* de vieille femme, débile.
aniline ['ænilain], *n.* (*Chem.*) aniline, *f.*
anility [ə'niliti], *n.* seconde enfance, *f.*, radotage, *m.*
animadversion [ænimæd'və:ʃən], *n.* animadversion, censure, critique, *f.*
animadvert [ænimæd'və:t], *v.i.* ***to animadvert upon***, critiquer, censurer.
animal ['æniməl], *a.* and *n.* animal, *m.*
animalism ['æniməlizm], **animality** [æni'mæliti], *n.* animalité, *f.*
animalize ['æniməlaiz], *v.t.* animaliser.
animate ['ænimeit], *v.t.* animer (*de*).—['ænimit], *a.* animé.
animated ['ænimeitid], *a.* animé, vif.
animatedly ['ænimeitidli], *adv.* vivement.
animating ['ænimeitiŋ], *a.* qui anime, qui ranime.
animation [æni'meiʃən], *n.* animation vivacité, vie, *f.*
animator ['ænimeitə], *n.* animateur, *m.*
animosity [æni'mɔsiti], *n.* animosité, *f.*
animus ['æniməs], *n.* animosité, hostilité, *f.* esprit (*de*), *m.*
anise ['ænis], *n.* anis, *m.*
aniseed ['ænisi:d], *n.* graine d'anis, *f.*
ankle [æŋkl], *n.* cheville du pied, *f.*
ankle-bone ['æŋklboun], *n.* astragale, *m.*
ankle-deep ['æŋkldi:p], *adv.* jusqu'aux chevilles.
Anna ['ænə]. Anne, *f.*
annalist ['ænəlist], *n.* annaliste, *m.*, *f.*
annals ['ænəlz], *n.pl.* annales, *f.pl.*
Ann(e) [æn]. Anne, *f.*
anneal [ə'ni:l], *v.t.* détremper; adoucir (*acier etc.*), recuire (*verre*).
annealing [ə'ni:liŋ], *n.* recuite, *f.*
annex [ə'neks], *v.t.* annexer, joindre (*à*).—['æneks], *n.* annexe, *f.*
annexation [ænek'seiʃən], *n.* annexation, *f.*
annexed [ə'nekst], *a.* ci-joint, annexé.
annihilate [ə'naiileit], *v.t.* anéantir, annihiler.
annihilation [ənaii'leiʃən], *n.* anéantissement, *m.*, annihilation, *f.*
annihilator [ə'naiileitə], *n.* annihilateur, *m.*
anniversary [æni'və:səri], *a.* and *n.* anniversaire, *m.*
Anno Domini ['ænou'dɔminai], (*abbr.* **A.D.** [ei'di:]). l'an du Seigneur; l'an de grâce; ap. J.-C.
annotate ['ænoteit], *v.t.* annoter.
annotation [æno'teiʃən], *n.* annotation, *f.*
annotator ['ænoteitə], *n.* annotateur, *m.*
announce [ə'nauns], *v.t.* annoncer, proclamer.
announcement [ə'naunsmənt], *n.* annonce, *f.*, avis, *m.*; lettre de faire-part, *f.*
announcer [ə'naunsə], *n.* annonciateur; (*Theat.*) compère, *m.*, commère, *f.*; (*Rad.*, *Tel.*) speaker, *m.*, speakerine, *f.*
annoy [ə'nɔi], *v.t.* gêner; incommoder, ennuyer, importuner; contrarier, tracasser.
annoyance [ə'nɔiəns], *n.* ennui, désagrément, chagrin, *m.*; contrariété, *f.*
annoying [ə'nɔiiŋ], *a.* ennuyeux, contrariant, vexant.
annoyingly [ə'nɔiiŋli], *adv.* ennuyeusement.
annual ['ænjuəl], *a.* annuel.—*n.* annuaire, *m.*
annually ['ænjuəli], *adv.* annuellement, tous les ans.
annuitant [ə'nju:itənt], *n.* bénéficiaire d'une pension *ou* d'une rente viagère, *m.*, *f.*
annuity [ə'nju:iti], *n.* annuité, rente annuelle, pension, *f.*; ***life annuity***, rente viagère, *f.*
annul [ə'nʌl], *v.t.* annuler.
annular ['ænjulə], *a.* annulaire.
annulet ['ænjulit], *n.* annelet, filet, *m.*
annulment [ə'nʌlmənt], *n.* annulation, *f.*; ***decree of annulment***, décret abolitif, *m.*
Annunciation [ənʌnsi'eiʃən], **the.** (*Eccles.*) l'Annonciation, *f.*
annunciation [ənʌnsi'eiʃən], *n.* annonce, proclamation, *f.*, avis, *m.*
anode ['ænoud], *n.* (*Elec.*) anode, *f.*
anodyne ['ænədain], *a.* anodin, calmant.—*n.* anodin (*remède*), *m.*
anoint [ə'nɔint], *v.t.* oindre.

anointed [ə'nɔintid], *a.* oint; ***the Lord's Anointed***, l'Oint du Seigneur, *m.*
anomalous [ə'nɔmələs], *a.* anomal, irrégulier.
anomaly [ə'nɔməli], *n.* anomalie, *f.*
anon [ə'nɔn], *adv.* tout à l'heure, bientôt; à l'instant.
anonymity [æno'nimiti], *n.* anonymat, *m.*
anonymous [ə'nɔniməs], *a.* anonyme.
anonymously [ə'nɔniməsli], *adv.* anonymement.
another [ə'nʌðə], *a.* and *pron.* autre, un autre; encore un; ***one another***, l'un l'autre, les uns les autres.
answer ['ɑ:nsə], *v.t.* répondre; répondre à; satisfaire, suffire à.—*v.i.* faire réponse; répondre (*de* ou *pour*); raisonner; réussir.—*n.* réponse; solution (*d'un problème*), *f.*
answerable ['ɑ:nsərəbl], *a.* susceptible de réponse; responsable (*for, de*).
ant [ænt], *n.* fourmi, *f.*
antagonism [æn'tægənizm], *n.* antagonisme, *m.*, opposition, *f.*
antagonist [æn'tægənist], *n.* antagoniste, *m.,f.*
antagonistic [æntægə'nistik], *a.* opposé (*à*); antagonique.
antagonize [æn'tægənaiz], *v.t.* eveiller l'antagonisme (*de*).
Antarctic [ænt'ɑ:ktik], *a.* antarctique.—*n.* Antarctique, *m.*
ant-eater ['ænti:tə], *n.* fourmilier, *m.*
antecedence [ænti'si:dəns], *n.* antériorité, *f.*
antecedent [ænti'si:dənt], *a.* and *n.* antécédent, *m.*
ante-chamber ['æntitʃeimbə], *n.* antichambre, *f.*
antediluvian [æntidi'lu:viən], *a.* and *n.* antédiluvien, *m.*
antelope ['æntiloup], *n.* antilope, *f.*
ante-meridiem [æntimə'ridiəm], (*abbr.* **a.m.** [ei'em]), *adv.* avant midi; ***at* 11 *a.m.***, à onze heures du matin.
ante-natal ['ænti'neitəl], *a.* prénatal.
antenna [æn'tenə], *n.* (*pl.* **antennae** [æn'teni:]) antenne, *f.*
antepenult [æntipi'nʌlt], **antepenultimate** [æntipi'nʌltimit], *a.* and *n.* antépénultième, *f.*
anterior [æn'tiəriə], *a.* antérieur.
anteroom ['æntiru:m], *n.* antichambre, *f.*
anthem ['ænθəm], *n.* hymne (national), *m.*; antienne, *f.*
ant-hill ['ænthil], *n.* fourmilière, *f.*
anthology [æn'θɔlədʒi], *n.* anthologie, chrestomathie, *f.*
Anthony ['æntəni]. Antoine, *m.*
anthracite ['ænθrəsait], *n.* anthracite, *m.*
anthrax ['ænθræks], *n.* (*Med.*) anthrax, *m.*
anthropoid ['ænθrəpɔid], *a.* and *n.* anthropoïde, *m.*
anthropological [ænθrəpə'lɔdʒikəl], *a.* anthropologique.
anthropologist [ænθrə'pɔlədʒist], *n.* anthropologiste, anthropologue, *m.,f.*
anthropology [ænθrə'pɔlədʒi], *n.* anthropologie, *f.*
anti-aircraft [ænti'ɛəkrɑ:ft], *a.* contre-avion, antiaérien.
antibiotic ['æntibai'ɔtik], *a.* and *n.* antibiotique, *m.*
antic ['æntik], *n.* bouffonnerie, farce, *f.*
Antichrist ['æntikraist], *n.* antéchrist, *m.*
antichristian ['ænti'kristjən], *a.* and *n.* antichrétien, *m.*
anticipate [æn'tisipeit], *v.t.* anticiper; prévenir, devancer; s'attendre à, prévoir, envisager; jouir d'avance de; se promettre.
anticipation [æntisi'peiʃən], *n.* anticipation, *f.*; avant-goût, *m.*; attente, *f.*
anticipatory [æn'tisipətri], *a.* par anticipation.
anticlerical [ænti'klerikəl], *a.* and *n.* anticlérical, *m.*
anticlericalism [ænti'klerikəlizm], *n.* anticléricalisme, *m.*
anti-climax [ænti'klaimæks], *n.* anticlimax, *m.*
anti-clockwise [COUNTER-CLOCKWISE].
anticyclone [ænti'saikloun], *n.* anticyclone, *m.*
anti-dazzle ['ænti'dæzl], *a.* anti-aveuglant; (***Motor***) ***anti-dazzle head lights***, pharescode, *m.pl.*
antidote ['æntidout], *n.* antidote, contrepoison, *m.*
anti-freeze ['æntifri:z], *n.* anti-gel, *m.*
Antilles [æn'tili:z], **the**. les Antilles, *f.pl.*
antimacassar [æntimə'kæsə], *n.* têtière, *f.*
antimony ['æntiməni], *n.* antimoine, *m.*
antinomy [æn'tinəmi], *n.* antinomie, *f.*
antipathetic [æntipə'θetik], **antipathetical** [æntipə'θetikəl], *a.* antipathique.
antipathy [æn'tipəθi], *n.* antipathie, aversion, *f.*
antiphony [æn'tifəni], *n.* contre-chant, *m.*
antiphrasis [æn'tifrəsis], *n.* antiphrase, *f.*
antipodal [æn'tipədəl], *a.* antipodal.
antipodes [æn'tipədi:z], *n. pl.* antipodes, *m.pl.*
anti-pope ['æntipoup], *n.* antipape *m.*
antiquarian [ænti'kwɛəriən], *a.* d'antiquaire; archéologique.—*n.* antiquaire, *m.*
antiquary ['æntikwəri], *n.* archéologue; antiquaire, *m.*
antiquated ['æntikweitid], *a.* vieilli, vétuste; suranné, démodé.
antique [æn'ti:k], *a.* antique, ancien.—*n.* ***the antique***, l'antique, *m.*; ***an antique***, un objet antique, une antiquité.
antiquity [æn'tikwiti], *n.* antiquité; ancienneté, *f.*
antirrhinum [ænti'rainəm], *n.* antirrhine, *f.*
anti-Semitism [ænti'semitizm], *n.* antisémitisme, *m.*
antiseptic [ænti'septik], *a.* and *n.* antiseptique, *m.*
anti-tank [ænti'tæŋk], *a.* anti-chars.
antithesis [æn'tiθisis], *n.* antithèse, *f.*
antithetic [ænti'θetik], **antithetical** [ænti'θetikəl], *a.* antithétique.
antler ['æntlə], *n.* andouiller, bois (*de cerf*), *m.*
Antony ['æntəni]. Antoine, *m.*
Antwerp ['æntwə:p]. Anvers, *m.*
anvil ['ænvil], *n.* enclume, *f.*; (*fig.*) ***on the anvil***, sur le métier, en préparation.
anxiety [æŋ'zaiəti], *n.* anxiété, inquiétude, sollicitude, *f.*; désir, *m.*
anxious ['æŋkʃəs], *a.* inquiet, soucieux, plein de sollicitude (*pour*); désireux (*de*); ***to be anxious to***, désirer vivement (*de*), tenir à.
anxiously ['æŋkʃəsli], *adv.* anxieusement, avec anxiété, avec inquiétude.

any ['eni], *a.* and *pron.* du, de la, etc.; en; aucun; quelque; n'importe lequel; ***any man***, tout homme; ***any others***, d'autres; ***at any rate***, en tout cas; ***I haven't any***, je n'en ai pas; ***scarcely any***, presque pas.
anybody ['enibɔdi], **anyone** ['eniwʌn], *pron.* quelqu'un, chacun, qui que ce soit, n'importe qui, tout le monde; ***I didn't see anybody***, je n'ai vu personne.
anyhow ['enihau], **anyway** ['eniwei], *adv.* de toute façon, de quelque manière que ce soit, en tout cas, quand même.
anyone [ANYBODY].
anything ['eniθiŋ], *pron.* quelque chose, *m.*, quoi que ce soit, n'importe quoi; ***not to say anything***, ne rien dire.
anyway [ANYHOW].
anywhere ['eniwɛə], *adv.* quelque part, dans quelque endroit que ce soit, n'importe où; ***not anywhere***, nulle part.
apace [ə'peis], *adv.* vite, à grands pas.
apanage, appanage ['æpənidʒ], *n.* apanage, *m.*
apart [ə'pɑ:t], *adv.* à part; de côté, séparément.
apartheid [ə'pɑ:theit], *n.* (*en Afrique du Sud*) ségrégation, *f.*
apartment [ə'pɑ:tmənt], *n.* chambre; pièce (*d'un appartement*), *f.*; logement; (*Am.*) appartement; (*pl.*) appartement, *m.*
apathetic [æpə'θetik], *a.* apathique.
apathy ['æpəθi], *n.* apathie, *f.*
ape [eip], *n.* singe, *m.*, guenon, *f.*—*v.t.* singer.
aperient [ə'piəriənt], **aperitive** [ə'peritiv], *a.* and *n.* laxatif, *m.*
aperture ['æpətjuə], *n.* ouverture, *f.*; orifice, *m.*
apex ['eipeks], *n.* (*pl.* **apices** ['eipisi:z], **apexes** ['eipeksiz]) sommet, *m.*, pointe, *f.*
aphorism ['æfərizm], *n.* aphorisme, *m.*
apiary ['eipiəri], *n.* rucher, *m.*
apiece [ə'pi:s], *adv.* la pièce; par tête, par personne, chacun.
apish ['eipiʃ], *a.* de singe, simiesque; ***apish trick***, singerie, *f.*
apocalypse [ə'pɔkəlips], *n.* apocalypse, *f.*
apocalyptic [əpɔkə'liptik], **apocalyptical** [əpɔkə'liptikəl], *a.* apocalyptique.
Apocrypha [ə'pɔkrifə], *n.pl.* les Apocryphes, *m.pl.*
apocryphal [ə'pɔkrifəl], *a.* apocryphe.
apogee ['æpədʒi:], *n.* apogée, *m.*
apologetic [əpɔlə'dʒetik], **apologetical** [əpɔlə'dʒetikəl], *a.* qui s'excuse, qui regrette; ***he was quite apologetic about it***, il s'en excusa vivement.
apologetically [əpɔlə'dʒetikəli], *adv.* pour s'excuser, en s'excusant.
apologia [æpə'loudʒiə], *n.* apologie; justification, *f.*
apologist [ə'pɔlədʒist], *n.* apologiste, *m.*, *f.*
apologize [ə'pɔlədʒaiz], *v.i.* s'excuser, faire des excuses (*de* ou *auprès de*).
apologue ['æpəlɔg], *n.* apologue, *m.*
apology [ə'pɔlədʒi], *n.* excuses, *f.pl.*, apologie, *f.*
apoplectic [æpə'plektik], *a.* apoplectique; ***apoplectic stroke***, coup de sang, *m.*
apoplexy ['æpəpleksi], *n.* apoplexie, *f.*; ***a fit of apoplexy***, congestion cérébrale, *f.*
apostasy [ə'pɔstəsi], *n.* apostasie, *f.*
apostate [ə'pɔsteit], *a.* and *n.* apostat, *m.*
apostle [ə'pɔsl], *n.* apôtre, *m.*; ***the Acts of the Apostles***, les actes des apôtres, *m.pl.*
apostolic [æpəs'tɔlik], **apostolical** [æpəs'tɔlikəl], *a.* apostolique.
apostrophe [ə'pɔstrəfi], *n.* apostrophe, *f.*
apostrophize [ə'pɔstrəfaiz], *v.t.* apostropher.
apothecary [ə'pɔθikəri], *n.* apothicaire; pharmacien, *m.*
apotheosis [əpɔθi'ousis], *n.* apothéose, *f.*
appal [ə'pɔ:l], *v.t.* épouvanter, consterner.
appalling [ə'pɔ:liŋ], *a.* épouvantable, effrayant.
appallingly [ə'pɔ:liŋli], *adv.* épouvantablement.
appanage [APANAGE].
apparatus [æpə'reitəs], *n.* appareil, dispositif, *m.*
apparel [ə'pærəl], *v.t.* vêtir; parer.—*n.* habillement, vêtement, *m.*
apparent [ə'pærənt], *a.* évident, manifeste, apparent; ***heir apparent***, héritier présomptif, *m.*
apparently [ə'pærəntli], *adv.* en apparence, apparemment.
apparition [æpə'riʃən], *n.* apparition, *f.*
appeal [ə'pi:l], *v.i.* appeler, en appeler (*de*), faire appel (*à*); (*Law*) se pourvoir en cassation, réclamer (*contre* ou *à*); (*fig.*) attirer, séduire.—*n.* appel, attrait, *m.*; ***Court of Appeal***, cour de cassation, *f.*
appealing [ə'pi:liŋ], *a.* suppliant, attrayant, séduisant.
appear [ə'piə], *v.i.* paraître, apparaître; se montrer, se présenter (*à*).
appearance [ə'piərəns], *n.* apparition; apparence, figure, mine, *f.*, air, aspect, *m.*; (*Law*) comparution, *f.*; ***at first appearance***, au premier abord, au premier coup d'œil.
appeasable [ə'pi:zəbl], *a.* qu'on peut apaiser.
appease [ə'pi:z], *v.t.* apaiser, pacifier.
appeasement [ə'pi:zmənt], *n.* apaisement, adoucissement, *m.*; conciliation, *f.*
appellant [ə'pelənt], *a.* and *n.* (*Law*) appelant, *m.*
appellation [æpə'leiʃən], *n.* nom, *m.*, appellation, dénomination, *f.*
append [ə'pend], *v.t.* apposer, attacher (*à*).
appendage [ə'pendidʒ], *n.* accessoire, apanage, *m.*
appendant [ə'pendənt], *a.* accessoire, attaché, annexé (*à*).
appendicitis [əpendi'saitis], *n.* appendicite, *f.*
appendix [ə'pendiks], *n.* (*pl.* **appendixes** [ə'pendiksiz], **appendices** [ə'pendisi:z]) appendice, *m.*
appertain [æpə'tein], *v.i.* appartenir (*à*).
appetite ['æpitait], *n.* appétit; (*fig.*) désir, *m.*, soif, *f.*
appetize ['æpitaiz], *v.t.* mettre en appétit.
appetizer ['æpitaizə], *n.* apéritif, *m.*
appetizing ['æpitaiziŋ], *a.* appétissant.
applaud [ə'plɔ:d], *v.t.*, *v.i.* applaudir (*à*).
applause [ə'plɔ:z], *n.* applaudissements, *m.pl.*
apple [æpl], *n.* pomme, *f.*; ***apple of the eye***, prunelle, *f.*
apple-pie ['æpl'pai], *n.* tourte aux pommes, *f.*
apple-sauce ['æpl'sɔ:s], *n.* compote de pommes, *f.*
apple-tart ['æpl'tɑ:t], *n.* tarte aux pommes, *f.*
apple-tree ['æpltri:], *n.* pommier, *m.*

appliance [ə'plaiəns], *n.* instrument, appareil, dispositif, *m.*

applicability [æplikə'biliti], **applicableness** ['æplikəblnis], *n.* applicabilité, *f.*

applicable ['æplikəbl], *a.* applicable.

applicant ['æplikənt], *n.* postulant, candidat; (*Law*) demandeur, *m.*

application [æpli'keiʃən], *n.* application; sollicitation, demande, *f.*; usage, *m.*; ***for external application***, usage externe; ***on application***, sur demande; ***to make application to***, s'adresser à, faire une demande à.

apply [ə'plai], *v.t.* appliquer (*à*); ***to apply the brake***, freiner; serrer le frein.—*v.i.* s'adresser (*à*); s'appliquer, être applicable; ***to apply for (a job)***, faire une demande (d'emploi); ***to apply to***, s'adresser à *ou* chez.

appoint [ə'pɔint], *v.t.* arrêter, désigner, fixer; nommer; installer, équiper; ***at the appointed hour***, à l'heure convenue; ***a well-appointed house***, une maison bien installée.

appointment [ə'pɔintmənt], *n.* nomination, *f.*; décret, arrêt; établissement; emploi; rendez-vous, *m.*; convocation, *f.*

apportion [ə'pɔ:ʃən], *v.t.* partager, répartir, assigner.

apportionment [ə'pɔ:ʃənmənt], *n.* répartition, *f.*, partage, *m.*

apposite ['æpəzait], *a.* juste; à propos; approprié, convenable (*à*).

appositely ['æpəzaitli], *adv.* convenablement, justement, à propos.

appositeness ['æpəzaitnis], *n.* à-propos, *m.*, opportunité, *f.*

appraisal [APPRAISMENT].

appraise [ə'preiz], *v.t.* priser, évaluer, estimer.

appraisement [ə'preizmənt], **appraisal** [ə'preizəl], *n.* évaluation, estimation; expertise, *f.*

appraiser [ə'preizə], *n.* commissaire-priseur, expert, *m.*

appreciable [ə'pri:ʃəbl], *a.* appréciable, sensible.

appreciably [ə'pri:ʃəbli], *adv.* sensiblement.

appreciate [ə'pri:ʃieit], *v.t.* apprécier, estimer.—*v.i.* (*Comm. etc.*) augmenter de valeur.

appreciation [əpri:ʃi'eiʃən], *n.* appréciation; hausse de valeur, *f.*

appreciative [ə'pri:ʃjətiv], *a.* appréciateur.

apprehend [æpri'hend], *v.t.* comprendre; prendre, saisir, arrêter, appréhender; craindre.

apprehension [æpri'henʃən], *n.* appréhension; arrestation, prise de corps; crainte, inquiétude, *f.*

apprehensive [æpri'hensiv], *a.* intelligent, prompt à saisir; appréhensif, inquiet.

apprentice [ə'prentis], *n.* apprenti, *m.*—*v.t.* mettre en apprentissage.

apprenticeship [ə'prentisʃip], *n.* apprentissage, *m.*

apprise [ə'praiz], *v.t.* prévenir; informer, instruire.

approach [ə'proutʃ], *n.* approche, *f.*; abord, accès; rapprochement, *m.*; (*Math.*) approximation, *f.*—*v.t.* approcher de, s'approcher de, aborder; (*fig.*) pressentir, tâter (*quelqu'un*).—*v.i.* approcher, s'approcher.

approachable [ə'proutʃəbl], *a.* abordable, accessible.

approbation [æpro'beiʃən], *n.* approbation, *f.*; ***on approbation***, à condition, à l'essai.

appropriate [ə'prouprieit], *v.t.* approprier, affecter (*à*); s'approprier; s'emparer de.—[ə'proupriət], *a.* approprié; propre, convenable (*à*).

appropriately [ə'proupriətli], *adv.* à juste titre; convenablement.

appropriateness [ə'proupriətnis], *n.* convenance, *f.*, à-propos, *m.*, justesse, *f.*

appropriation [əproupri'eiʃən], *n.* application, destination, appropriation, *f.*; crédit (*budgétaire*), *m.*

approval [ə'pru:vəl], *n.* approbation, *f.*; ***on approval***, à condition.

approve [ə'pru:v], *v.t.* approuver; trouver bon (*que, with subj.*).

approver [ə'pru:və], *n.* approbateur, *m.*

approving [ə'pru:viŋ], *a.* approbateur, approbatif.

approvingly [ə'pru:viŋli], *adv.* avec approbation, d'un air approbateur.

approximate [ə'prɔksimeit], *v.t.* rapprocher.—*v.i.* se rapprocher (*de*).—[ə'prɔksimit], *a.* approximatif.

approximately [ə'prɔksimitli], *adv.* approximativement, à peu près.

approximation [əprɔksi'meiʃən], *n.* approximation, *f.*; rapprochement, *m.*

appulse [ə'pʌls], *n.* choc, *m.*

appurtenance [ə'pə:tinəns], *n.* appartenance, dépendance, *f.*; (*pl.*) accessoires, *m.pl.*

appurtenant [ə'pə:tinənt], *a.* appartenant (*à*), dépendant (*de*).

apricot ['eiprikɔt], *n.* abricot, *m.*

apricot-tree ['eiprikɔttri:], *n.* abricotier, *m.*

April ['eipril]. avril, *m.*; ***to make an April fool of***, donner un poisson d'avril à.

apron ['eiprən], *n.* tablier, *m.*; (*Av.*) aire de manœuvre *ou* d'atterrissage, *f.*

apron-stage ['eiprənsteidʒ], *n.* avant-scène, *f.*

apse [æps], **apsis** ['æpsis], *n.* (*pl.* **apses** ['æpsi:z], **apsides** [æp'saidi:z]) abside; (*Astron.*) apside, *f.*

apt [æpt], *a.* sujet, enclin, porté (*à*); propre, convenable (*à*); capable; juste (*mot*).

aptitude ['æptitju:d], **aptness** ['æptnis], *n.* aptitude, disposition, *f.*

aptly ['æptli], *adv.* à propos; convenablement.

aqua-fortis [ækwə'fɔ:tis], *n.* eau-forte, *f.*

aquamarine [ækwəmə'ri:n], *n.* aigue-marine, *f.*

aqua-regia [ækwə'ri:dʒiə], *n.* eau régale, *f.*

aquarium [ə'kwɛəriəm], *n.* aquarium, *m.*

aquatic [ə'kwɔtik, ə'kwætik], *a.* aquatique.

aquatics [ə'kwætiks], **aquatic sports** [ə'kwætikspɔ:ts], *n.pl.* sports nautiques, *m.pl.*

aquavitae [ækwə'vaiti:], *n.* eau de vie, *f.*

aqueduct ['ækwidʌkt], *n.* aqueduc, *m.*

aqueous ['eikwiəs], *a.* aqueux.

aquiline ['ækwilain], *a.* aquilin, d'aigle.

Arab ['ærəb], *a.* arabe.—*n.* Arabe, *m.*, *f.*

arabesque [ærə'besk], *a.* and *n.* arabesque, *f.*

Arabia [ə'reibjə]. l'Arabie, *f.*; ***Saudi Arabia***, l'Arabie Séoudite.

Arabian [ə'reibiən], *a.* arabe.

Arabic [ˈærəbik], *a.* arabe, arabique; ***Arabic figures***, chiffres arabes, *m.pl.*—*n.* arabe (*langue*), *m.*
arable [ˈærəbl], *a.* arable, labourable.
arbalest [ˈɑːbəlest], *n.* arbalète, *f.*
arbiter [ˈɑːbitə], *n.* arbitre, *m.*, *f.*
arbitrament [ɑːˈbitrəmənt], *n.* arbitrage, *m.*, arbitration, *f.*; jugement, *m.*
arbitrarily [ˈɑːbitrərəli], *adv.* arbitrairement.
arbitrary [ˈɑːbitrəri], *a.* arbitraire.
arbitrate [ˈɑːbitreit], *v.t.*, *v.i.* arbitrer, décider.
arbitration [ɑːbiˈtreiʃən], *n.* arbitrage, *m.*
arbitrator [ˈɑːbitreitə], *n.* arbitre, *m.*, *f.*
arbour [ˈɑːbə], *n.* berceau, *m.*, tonnelle, *f.*
arbutus [ɑːˈbjuːtəs], *n.* arbousier, *m.*
arc [ɑːk], *n.* arc, *m.*
arcade [ɑːˈkeid], *n.* arcade, *f.*; passage, *m.*
arch [ɑːtʃ], *a.* moqueur, malin, espiègle; grand, maître, archi-, insigne, fieffé.—*n.* arche, *f.*; arc, cintre, *m.*, voûte, *f.*; ***pointed arch***, ogive, *f.*; ***triumphal arch***, arc de triomphe.—*v.t.* voûter, cintrer, arquer.
archaeological [ɑːkiəˈlɔdʒikəl], *a.* archéologique.
archaeologist [ɑːkiˈɔlədʒist], *n.* archéologue, *m.*, *f.*
archaeology [ɑːkiˈɔlədʒi], *n.* archéologie, *f.*
archaic [ɑːˈkeiik], *a.* archaïque.
archaism [ˈɑːkeiizm], *n.* archaïsme, *m.*
archangel [ˈɑːkeindʒəl], *n.* archange, *m.*
archbishop [ɑːtʃˈbiʃəp], *n.* archevêque, *m.*
archbishopric [ɑːtʃˈbiʃəprik], *n.* archevêché, *m.*
archdeacon [ɑːtʃˈdiːkən], *n.* archidiacre, *m.*
archduchess [ɑːtʃˈdʌtʃis], *n.* archiduchesse, *f.*
archduchy [ɑːtʃˈdʌtʃi], *n.* archiduché, *m.*
archduke [ɑːtʃˈdjuːk], *n.* archiduc, *m.*
archer [ˈɑːtʃə], *n.* archer, *m.*; (*Astron.*) ***the Archer***, Sagittaire, *m.*
archery [ˈɑːtʃəri], *n.* tir à l'arc, *m.*
archetype [ˈɑːkitaip], *n.* archétype; étalon (*mesure*), *m.*
archiepiscopal [ɑːkiəˈpiskəpəl], *a.* archiépiscopal.
archipelago [ɑːkiˈpeləgou], *n.* archipel, *m.*
architect [ˈɑːkitekt], *n.* architecte; (*fig.*) artisan, *m.*
architectural [ɑːkiˈtektʃərəl], *a.* architectural.
architecture [ˈɑːkitektʃə], *n.* architecture, *f.*
archives [ˈɑːkaivz], *n. pl.* archives, *f.pl.*
archivist [ˈɑːkivist], *n.* archiviste, *m.*, *f.*
archly [ˈɑːtʃli], *adv.* avec espièglerie, d'un air malin.
archness [ˈɑːtʃnis], *n.* malice, espièglerie, *f.*
arc-lamp [ˈɑːklæmp], *n.* lampe à arc, *f.*
Arctic [ˈɑːktik], *a.* arctique.
ardent [ˈɑːdənt], *a.* ardent; ***ardent spirits***, spiritueux, *m.pl.*
ardently [ˈɑːdəntli], *adv.* ardemment, avec ardeur.
ardour [ˈɑːdə], *n.* ardeur, *f.*
arduous [ˈɑːdjuəs], *a.* ardu, rude, pénible, difficile.
arduously [ˈɑːdjuəsli], *adv.* difficilement, péniblement.
arduousness [ˈɑːdjuəsnis], *n.* difficulté, *f.*
area [ˈɛəriə], *n.* étendue; aire, surface, superficie; région, zone; courette d'entrée (*devant la maison*), *f.*; ***area steps***, escalier de service, *m.*; ***postal area***, zone postale, *f.*

arena [əˈriːnə], *n.* arène, *f.*
argent [ˈɑːdʒənt], *a.* argenté.—*n.* (*Her.*) argent, *m.*
Argentina [ɑːdʒənˈtiːnə]. l'Argentine, la République Argentine, *f.*
Argentine [ˈɑːdʒəntain], *a.* argentin.—*n.* Argentin, *m.*; ***the Argentine*** [ARGENTINA].
Argentinian [ɑːdʒənˈtinjən], *a.* argentin.—*n.* Argentin (*personne*), *m.*
argil [ˈɑːdʒil], *n.* argile, *f.*
argonaut [ˈɑːgənɔːt], *n.* argonaute, *m.*
argosy [ˈɑːgəsi], *n.* caraque, *f.*
argue [ˈɑːgjuː], *v.t.* discuter; soutenir; (*fig.*) dénoter, indiquer, accuser.—*v.i.* argumenter (*contre*), raisonner (*sur*), discuter (*avec*); (*Law*) plaider.
argument [ˈɑːgjumənt], *n.* argument, raisonnement, *m.*; discussion, dispute; thèse, *f.*; ***for argument's sake***, à titre d'exemple.
argumentative [ɑːgjuˈmentətiv], *a.* raisonneur; disposé à argumenter.
aria [ˈɑːriə], *n.* aria, *f.*
arid [ˈærid], *a.* aride.
aridity [əˈriditi], **aridness** [ˈæridnis], *n.* aridité, *f.*
aright [əˈrait], *adv.* correctement; bien.
arise [əˈraiz], *v.i. irr.* (*conjug. like* RISE) se lever; s'élever; survenir, se présenter; provenir, résulter (*de*); ***if the question arises***, le cas échéant.
aristocracy [ærisˈtɔkrəsi], *n.* aristocratie, *f.*
aristocrat [ˈæristəkræt], *n.* aristocrate, *m.*, *f.*
aristocratic [æristəˈkrætik], *a.* aristocratique.
arithmetic [əˈriθmətik], *n.* arithmétique, *f.*, calcul, *m.*
arithmetical [æriθˈmetikəl], *a.* arithmétique.
arithmetically [æriθˈmetikəli], *adv.* arithmétiquement.
arithmetician [æriθməˈtiʃən], *n.* arithméticien, *m.*
ark [ɑːk], *n.* arche, *f.*; ***Noah's ark***, l'arche de Noé.
arm [ɑːm], *n.* bras, *m.*; arme (*à feu*), *f.*; (*pl.*) (*Her.*) armes, armoiries, *f.pl.*; ***arm in arm***, bras dessus bras dessous; ***with arms folded***, les bras croisés; ***with open arms***, à bras ouverts.—*v.t.* armer; donner des armes à.—*v.i.* armer; s'armer (*de*); prendre les armes.
armada [ɑːˈmɑːdə], *n.* armada, *f.*
armadillo [ɑːməˈdilou], *n.* tatou, *m.*
armament [ˈɑːməmənt], *n.* armement, *m.*, armée, flotte, *f.*; ***armaments race***, course aux armements, *f.*
armature [ˈɑːmətjuə], *n.* armature, *f.*, induit, *m.*
arm-band [ˈɑːmbænd], *n.* brassard, *m.*
arm-chair [ˈɑːmtʃɛə], *n.* fauteuil, *m.*
Armenia [ɑːˈmiːniə]. l'Arménie, *f.*
Armenian [ɑːˈmiːniən], *a.* arménien.—*n.* arménien (*langue*); Arménien (*personne*), *m.*
armful [ˈɑːmful], *n.* brassée, *f.*
arm-hole [ˈɑːmhoul], *n.* emmanchure, entournure, *f.*
armistice [ˈɑːmistis], *n.* armistice, *m.*
armless [ˈɑːmlis], *a.* sans bras.
armlet [ˈɑːmlit], *n.* brassard; bracelet; petit bras (*de mer*), *m.*
armorial [ɑːˈmɔːriəl], *a.* armorial; ***armorial bearings***, armoiries, *f.pl.*
armour [ˈɑːmə], *n.* armure, *f.*; blindés, *m.pl.* —*v.t.* cuirasser, blinder.

armoured [ˈɑːməd], *a.* cuirassé, blindé.
armourer [ˈɑːmərə], *n.* armurier, *m.*
armour-plate [ˈɑːməˈpleit], *n.* plaque de blindage, *f.*
armour-plated [ˈɑːməˈpleitid], *a.* cuirassé, blindé.
armoury [ˈɑːməri], *n.* arsenal, *m.*; salle d'armes; armurerie, *f.*
armpit [ˈɑːmpit], *n.* aisselle, *f.*
army [ˈɑːmi], *n.* armée; (*fig.*) foule, multitude, *f.*; ***the Salvation Army***, l'Armée du Salut.
Arnold [ˈɑːnəld]. Arnaud, *m.*
aroma [əˈroumə], *n.* arome *ou* arôme; bouquet (*de vin*), *m.*
aromatic [ærəˈmætik], *a.* aromatique.
around [əˈraund], *prep.* autour de; (*colloq.*) environ, vers, à peu près.—*adv.* autour, à l'entour, aux alentours.
arouse [əˈrauz], *v.t.* réveiller, éveiller; exciter, provoquer.
arraign [əˈrein], *v.t.* accuser, poursuivre en justice, attaquer.
arraignment [əˈreinmənt], *n.* mise en accusation, *f.*
arrange [əˈreindʒ], *v.t.* arranger, régler, disposer, distribuer; organiser.
arrangement [əˈreindʒmənt], *n.* arrangement, *m.*, disposition, organisation, *f.*, dispositif, *m.*
arrant [ˈærənt], *a.* insigne, achevé, fieffé.
arrantly [ˈærəntli], *adv.* notoirement, impudemment.
array [əˈrei], *v.t.* ranger, déployer; revêtir, parer.—*n.* ordre, rang; étalage; appareil, *m.*
arrear [əˈriə], *n.* arriéré, *m.*; (*pl.*) arrérages, *m.pl.*; ***to be in arrears***, être en retard, avoir de l'arriéré.
arrest [əˈrest], *v.t.* arrêter; fixer; suspendre. —*n.* arrestation, prise de corps, *f.*; arrêt, *m.*, suspension, *f.*
arresting [əˈrestiŋ], *a.* frappant, qui arrête l'attention.
arrival [əˈraivəl], *n.* arrivée, *f.*; arrivage (*de marchandises etc.*), *m.*; ***arrival platform***, quai d'arrivée, débarcadère, *m.*
arrive [əˈraiv], *v.i.* arriver (*à*); parvenir (*à*).
arrogance [ˈærəgəns], *n.* arrogance, *f.*
arrogant [ˈærəgənt], *a.* arrogant.
arrogantly [ˈærəgəntli], *adv.* arrogamment.
arrogate [ˈærogeit], *v.t.* attribuer injustement; ***to arrogate to oneself***, s'arroger.
arrogation [æroˈgeiʃən], *n.* prétention, usurpation, *f.*
arrow [ˈærou], *n.* flèche, *f.*; (*fig.*) trait, *m.*— *v.t.* indiquer par des flèches.
arrow-root [ˈærouruːt], *n.* arrow-root, *m.*
arsenal [ˈɑːsənəl], *n.* arsenal, *m.*
arsenic [ɑːˈsenik], *a.* arsénique.—[ˈɑːsənik], *n.* arsenic, *m.*
arson [ˈɑːsən], *n.* incendie volontaire, *m.*
art [ɑːt], *n.* art, *m.*; adresse, habileté, *f.*; ***faculty of arts***, faculté des lettres, *f.*; ***fine arts***, beaux-arts, *m.pl.*; ***school of art***, école de dessin, académie, *f.*
arterial [ɑːˈtiəriəl], *a.* artériel; ***arterial road***, route à grande circulation, *f.*
artery [ˈɑːtəri], *n.* artère, *f.*
artesian [ɑːˈtiːʒən], *a.* artésien.
artful [ˈɑːtful], *a.* rusé, fin, artificieux.
artfully [ˈɑːtfuli], *adv.* avec artifice, artificieusement, adroitement.
artfulness [ˈɑːtfulnis], *n.* ruse, finesse, *f.*, artifice, *m.*
arthritic [ɑːˈθritik], *a.* arthritique.
arthritis [ɑːˈθraitis], *n.* arthrite, *f.*
artichoke [ˈɑːtitʃouk], *n.* ***Chinese artichoke***, crosne (du Japon), *m.*; ***globe artichoke***, artichaut, *m.*; ***Jerusalem artichoke***, topinambour, *m.*
article [ˈɑːtikl], *n.* article; objet; statut, *m.*— *v.t.* engager par contrat; placer (*chez un avoué*) comme clerc; ***articled clerk***, clerc d'avoué, *m.*
articulate [ɑːˈtikjuleit], *v.t.*, *v.i.* articuler; énoncer, parler distinctement.—[ɑːˈtikjulit], *a.* articulé.
artifice [ˈɑːtifis], *n.* artifice, *m.*, ruse, finesse, *f.*
artificer [ɑːˈtifisə], *n.* artisan, ouvrier; mécanicien, *m.*
artificial [ɑːtiˈfiʃəl], *a.* artificiel; factice.
artificiality [ɑːtifiʃiˈæliti], *n.* nature artificielle, *f.*
artificially [ɑːtiˈfiʃəli], *adv.* artificiellement.
artillery [ɑːˈtiləri], *n.* artillerie, *f.*
artilleryman [ɑːˈtilərimən], *n.* (*pl.* **-men** [men]) artilleur, *m.*
artisan [ɑːtiˈzæn], *n.* artisan, ouvrier, *m.*
artist [ˈɑːtist], *n.* artiste, *m.*,*f.*
artistic [ɑːˈtistik], *a.* artistique.
artistically [ɑːˈtistikli], *adv.* artistement, avec art.
artless [ˈɑːtlis], *a.* ingénu, naïf; sans art, naturel.
artlessly [ˈɑːtlisli], *adv.* ingénument, naïvement; sans art.
artlessness [ˈɑːtlisnis], *n.* naïveté; simplicité, *f.*
as [æz], *conj.* comme; tel que; à titre de; aussi . . . que; à mesure que; en, pour; parce que; ***as big as***, aussi gros que; ***as cold as charity***, froid comme le marbre; ***as for***, quant à, pour; ***as he advanced***, à mesure qu'il avançait; ***as he was walking***, comme il marchait; ***as if***, comme si; ***as it were***, pour ainsi dire; ***as much as***, autant que, tant que; ***as yet***, jusqu'à présent, encore; ***as you were***, (*Mil.*) au temps! ***be that as it may***, quoi qu'il en soit; ***do as you wish***, faites comme vous voudrez; ***rich as she is***, toute riche qu'elle est; ***she was dressed as a page***, elle était habillée en page; ***that's as may be***, c'est selon; ***to act as***, agir en.
asbestos [æzˈbestəs], *n.* asbeste, amiante, *m.*
ascend [əˈsend], *v.t.* monter; gravir, faire l'ascension de; remonter (*un fleuve*).—*v.i.* monter (*à* ou *sur*); remonter; s'élever (*montagne etc.*).
ascendancy [əˈsendənsi], *n.* ascendant, *m.*; supériorité, influence, *f.*
ascendant [əˈsendənt], *a.* ascendant; supérieur.—*n.* ascendant, *m.*; supériorité, *f.*, dessus, *m.*
Ascension [əˈsenʃən], *n.* (*Eccles.*) Ascension, *f.*; ***Ascension Day***, jour de l'Ascension, *m.*
ascent [əˈsent], *n.* ascension; élévation, montée, pente, *f.*
ascertain [æsəˈtein], *v.t.* s'assurer, s'informer de, constater, vérifier.
ascetic [əˈsetik], *a.* ascétique.—*n.* ascète, ascétique, *m.*,*f.*
asceticism [əˈsetisizm], *n.* ascétisme, *m.*

ascribable [ə'skraibəbl], *a.* attribuable, imputable.
ascribe [ə'skraib], *v.t.* attribuer, imputer (*à*).
aseptic [æ'septik], *a.* and *n.* aseptique, *m.*
asexual [æ'seksjuəl], *a.* asexué, asexuel.
ash (1) [æʃ], *a.* de frêne.—*n.* frêne (*arbre*); bâton, *m.*; ***mountain-ash***, sorbier, *m.*
ash (2) [æʃ], *n.* cendre, *f.*; cendres, *f.pl.*
ashamed [ə'ʃeimd], *a.* honteux, confus; ***to be ashamed of***, avoir honte de.
ash-bin, -pit ['æʃbin, -pit], *n.* cendrier, *m.*
ashcan ['æʃkæn], *n.* (*Am.*) boîte à ordures, *f.*
ashen (1) [æʃn], *a.* de frêne.
ashen (2) [æʃn], *a.* cendré; gris pâle.
ashore [ə'ʃɔ:], *adv.* à terre; échoué (*navire*); ***to go ashore***, débarquer.
ash-pit [ASH-BIN].
ashtray ['æʃtrei], *n.* cendrier, *m.*
Ash Wednesday [æʃ'wenzdi]. mercredi des Cendres, *m.*
ashy ['æʃi], *a.* cendré; gris pâle.
Asia ['eiʃə]. l'Asie, *f.*
Asia Minor ['eiʃə'mainə]. l'Asie-Mineure, *f.*
Asiatic [eiʃi'ætik], **Asian** ['eiʃən], *a.* asiatique. —*n.* Asiatique (*personne*), *m.,f.*
aside [ə'said], *adv.* de côté; (*Theat.*) à part; à l'écart.—*n.* (*Theat.*) aparté, *m.*
asinine ['æsinain], *a.* d'âne; sot.
ask [ɑ:sk], *v.t.* demander, prier (*de*); inviter (*à*); s'informer, se renseigner; poser (*une question*); ***to ask in***, prier d'entrer; ***to ask someone to do something***, demander à quelqu'un de faire quelque chose; ***to ask to see***, demander à voir.
askance [ə'skɑ:ns], *adv.* de travers, obliquement.
askew [ə'skju:], *adv.* de côté, de biais.
aslant [ə'slɑ:nt], *adv.* obliquement, de biais, de côté, en travers.
asleep [ə'sli:p], *a.* endormi; ***to be asleep***, dormir; ***to fall asleep***, s'endormir.
asp (1) [æsp], **aspic** ['æspik], *n.* aspic, *m.*
asp (2) [æsp], **aspen** ['æspən], *n.* tremble, *m.*
asparagus [əs'pærəgəs], *n.* asperges, *f.pl.*
aspect ['æspekt], *n.* aspect, *m.*; exposition, *f.*; ***to have a southern aspect***, être exposé au midi.
aspen ['æspən], *a.* de tremble.—*n.* [ASP (2)].
asperity [æs'periti], *n.* aspérité, âpreté, rudesse, *f.*
aspersion [æs'pə:ʃən], *n.* calomnie, *f.*; ***to cast aspersions on***, répandre des calomnies sur.
asphalt ['æsfælt], *a.* d'asphalte.—*n.* asphalte, *m.*
asphyxia [æs'fiksiə], *n.* asphyxie, *f.*
asphyxiate [æs'fiksieit], *v.t.* asphyxier.
aspic [ASP (1)].
aspirant [ə'spaiərənt], *n.* aspirant, candidat, *m.*
aspirate ['æspireit], *v.t.* aspirer.—['æspirit] *a.* aspiré.
aspiration [æspi'reiʃən], *n.* aspiration, *f.*
aspire [ə'spaiə], *v.i.* aspirer (*à*), ambitionner.
aspirin ['æspirin], *n.* aspirine, *f.*
asquint [ə'skwint], *adv.* de travers, en louchant.
ass [æs], *n.* âne, *m.*; ***he is a silly ass***, il est bête à manger du foin; ***she-ass***, ânesse, *f.*; ***to make an ass of oneself***, agir sottement; ***young ass***, ânon, *m.*
assail [ə'seil], *v.t.* assaillir, attaquer.
assailant [ə'seilənt], *n.* assaillant, *m.*
assassin [ə'sæsin], *n.* assassin (*politique*), *m.*
assassinate [ə'sæsineit], *v.t.* assassiner.
assassination [əsæsi'neiʃən], *n.* assassinat, *m.*
assault [ə'sɔ:lt], *n.* assaut, *m.*, attaque brusquée; (*Law*) tentative de voie de fait, *f.*; ***assault and battery***, voies de fait, *f.pl.*; ***indecent assault***, outrage aux mœurs, *m.* —*v.t.* assaillir, attaquer.
assay [ə'sei], *n.* épreuve, vérification, *f.*; essai, *m.*—*v.t.* essayer.
assemble [ə'sembl], *v.t.* assembler, réunir.—*v.i.* s'assembler, se réunir.
assembly [ə'sembli], *n.* assemblée, réunion, *f.*; assemblage (*d'une machine*), *m.*; ***assembly line***, chaîne de montage, *f.*
assent [ə'sent], *v.i.* donner son assentiment (*à*), admettre.—*n.* assentiment, consentement, *m.*
assert [ə'sə:t], *v.t.* affirmer, prétendre, soutenir; revendiquer, faire valoir (*ses droits etc.*).
assertion [ə'sə:ʃən], *n.* assertion, revendication, *f.*
assertive [ə'sə:tiv], *a.* assertif.
assertively [ə'sə:tivli], *adv.* d'un ton péremptoire.
assess [ə'ses], *v.t.* répartir, fixer; imposer; évaluer.
assessment [ə'sesmənt], *n.* imposition, répartition, assiette; évaluation, *f.*
assessor [ə'sesə], *n.* assesseur; répartiteur, *m.*
asset ['æset], *n.* avoir; avantage, *m.*
assets ['æsets], *n.pl.* actif, *m*; ***assets and liabilities***, actif et passif, *m.*; ***personal assets***, biens meubles, *m.pl.*; ***real assets***, biens immobiliers, *m.pl.*
asseverate [ə'sevəreit], *v.t.* affirmer solennellement.
assiduity [æsi'dju:iti], *n.* assiduité, *f.*
assiduous [ə'sidjuəs], *a.* assidu.
assiduously [ə'sidjuəsli], *adv.* assidûment.
assign [ə'sain], *v.t.* assigner, attribuer; transférer (*à*).—*n.* (*Law*) ayant droit, *m.*
assignation [æsig'neiʃən], *n.* attribution, assignation, cession, *f.*; rendez-vous, *m.*
assignee [æsi'ni:], *n.* cessionnaire, *m.,f.*; syndic (*de faillite*), *m.*
assimilate [ə'simileit], *v.t.* assimiler.—*v.i.* s'assimiler.
assimilation [əsimi'leiʃən], *n.* assimilation, *f.*
assist [ə'sist], *v.t.* aider; ***to assist each other***, s'entr'aider.
assistance [ə'sistəns], *n.* assistance, aide, *f.*; secours, concours, *m.*
assistant [ə'sistənt], *a.* qui aide, auxiliaire.—*n.* aide; adjoint; commis (*dans une boutique*), *m.*; ***assistant examiner***, examinateur adjoint, *m.*; ***assistant manager***, sous-directeur, *m.*
assizes [ə'saiziz], *n. pl.* assises, *f.pl.*
associate [ə'souʃieit], *v.t.* associer (*avec* ou *à*). —*v.i.* s'associer (*avec* ou *à*); ***to associate with***, fréquenter.—[ə'souʃiit], *a.* associé.—*n.* associé, *m.*; complice, *m., f.*
association [əsousi'eiʃən], *n.* association, *f.*; souvenir, *m.*
assort [ə'sɔ:t], *v.t.* assortir.
assorted [ə'sɔ:tid], *a.* assorti.
assortment [ə'sɔ:tmənt], *n.* assortiment, *m.*; classification, *f.*

assuage [ə'sweidʒ], *v.t.* adoucir, apaiser calmer, soulager.—*v.i.* s'apaiser, se calmer.
assume [ə'sju:m], *v.t.* prendre sur soi, s'arroger, s'attribuer; assumer (*une responsabilité*); supposer, présumer; se donner; affecter.
assuming [ə'sju:miŋ], *a.* arrogant, présomptueux, prétentieux; ***assuming that***, en supposant que.
assumption [ə'sʌmpʃən], *n.* supposition; prétention, *f.*; (*Eccles.*) ***the Assumption***, l'Assomption (*de la Sainte Vierge*), *f.*
assurance [ə'ʃuərəns], *n.* assurance, *f.*
assure [ə'ʃuə], *v.t.* assurer.
assuredly [ə'ʃuəridli], *adv.* assurément, à coup sûr.
Assyria [ə'siriə]. l'Assyrie, *f.*
Assyrian [ə'siriən], *a.* assyrien.—*n.* assyrien (*langue*); Assyrien (*personne*), *m.*
aster ['æstə], *n.* (*Bot.*, *Biol.*) aster, *m.*
asterisk ['æstərisk], *n.* astérisque, *m.*
astern [ə'stə:n], *adv.* (*Naut.*) à l'arrière, sur l'arrière; ***to go astern***, culer.
asteroid ['æstərɔid], *n.* astéroïde, *m.*
asthma ['æsθmə], *n.* asthme, *m.*
asthmatic [æsθ'mætik], *a.* asthmatique.
astigmatism [ə'stigmətizm], *n.* astigmatisme, *m.*
astir [ə'stə:], *a.* en mouvement, agité, en émoi; debout.
astonish [ə'stɔniʃ], *v.t.* étonner.
astonishing [ə'stɔniʃiŋ], *a.* étonnant.
astonishment [ə'stɔniʃmənt], *n.* étonnement, *m.*
astound [ə'staund], *v.t.* étonner, ébahir, étourdir.
astounding [ə'staundiŋ], *a.* renversant, abasourdissant.
astray [ə'strei], *adv.* égaré, (*fig.*) dévoyé; ***to go astray***, s'égarer.
astride [ə'straid], *adv.* à califourchon; ***astride upon***, à cheval sur.
astringent [ə'strindʒənt], *a.* and *n.* astringent, *m.*
astrologer [ə'strɔlədʒə], *n.* astrologue, *m.,f.*
astrology [ə'strɔlədʒi], *n.* astrologie, *f.*
astronaut ['æstrənɔ:t], *n.* astronaute, *m.,f.*
astronomer [ə'strɔnəmə], *n.* astronome, *m.,f.*
astronomic [æstrə'nɔmik], **astronomical** [æstrə'nɔmikəl], *a.* astronomique.
astronomy [ə'strɔnəmi], *n.* astronomie, *f.*
astute [ə'stju:t], *a.* fin, avisé; rusé, astucieux.
astuteness [ə'stju:tnis], *n.* astuce, sagacité, *f.*
asunder [ə'sʌndə], *adv.* en deux.
asylum [ə'sailəm], *n.* asile, refuge; hospice, *m.*
at [æt], *prep.* à, en, dans; après; ***at first*** d'abord; ***at hand***, sous la main; ***at home***, chez soi; ***at last***, enfin; ***at least***, (*quantity*) au moins; (*fig.*) du moins; ***at once***, tout de suite; à la fois; ***at school***, à l'école; ***at the same time***, en même temps; ***at work***, à l'ouvrage.
atheism ['eiθiizm], *n.* athéisme, *m.*
atheist ['eiθiist], *n.* athée, *m.*, *f.*
atheistic [eiθi'istik], *a.* athée, athéistique.
Athens ['æθənz]. Athènes, *f.*
athirst [ə'θə:st], *a.* altéré, assoiffé.
athlete ['æθli:t], *n.* athlète, *m.*, *f.*
athletic [æθ'letik], *a.* athlétique.
athletics [æθ'letiks], *n. pl.* l'athlétisme, *m.*
Atlantic [ət'læntik], *a.* atlantique.—*n.* l'(Océan) Atlantique, *m.*
atlas ['ætləs], *n.* atlas, *m.*
atmosphere ['ætməsfiə], *n.* atmosphère, *f.*
atmospheric [ætməs'ferik], **atmospherical** [ætməs'ferikəl], *a.* atmosphérique.
atmospherics [ætməs'feriks], *n.pl.* (*Rad.*) parasites, *m.pl.*
atoll ['ætɔl], *n.* atoll, attoll, *m.*
atom ['ætəm], *n.* atome, *m.*; ***atom bomb***, bombe atomique, *f.*
atomic [ə'tɔmik], *a.* atomique.
atomize ['ætəmaiz], *v.t.* pulvériser, vaporiser.
atomizer ['ætəmaizə], *n.* pulvérisateur, *m.*
atone [ə'toun], *v.t.*, *v.i.* expier; racheter.
atonement [ə'tounmənt], *n.* expiation, *f.*
atop [ə'tɔp], *adv.* au sommet, en haut.
atrocious [ə'trouʃəs], *a.* atroce.
atrociously [ə'trouʃəsli], *adv.* atrocement.
atrocity [ə'trɔsiti], *n.* atrocité, *f.*
atrophy ['ætrəfi], *n.* atrophie, *f.*—*v.t.* atrophier.—*v.i.* s'atrophier.
attach [ə'tætʃ], *v.t.* attacher, lier (*à*).
attachable [ə'tætʃəbl], *a.* qu'on peut attacher.
attaché-case [ə'tæʃikeis], *n.* mallette, *f.*
attachment [ə'tætʃmənt], *n.* attachement, *m.*
attack [ə'tæk], *v.t.* attaquer.—*n.* attaque, *f.*, accès, assaut, *m.*
attacker [ə'tækə], *n.* agresseur, *m.*
attain [ə'tein], *v.t.* atteindre, parvenir à.
attainable [ə'teinəbl], *a.* qu'on peut atteindre.
attainment [ə'teinmənt], *n.* acquisition, *f.*; talent, *m.*; (*pl.*) connaissances, *f.pl.*
attaint [ə'teint], *v.t.* accuser; condamner; flétrir, dégrader.
attempt [ə'tempt], *v.t.* tenter, essayer tâcher (*de*).—*n.* tentative, *f.*, essai, effort; attentat, *m.*
attend [ə'tend], *v.t.* s'occuper de; soigner (*un malade*); servir; assister (*à*).—*v.i.* faire attention, écouter; assister (*à*); servir; s'appliquer (*à*).
attendance [ə'tendəns], *n.* service, *m.*; assistance (*à une réunion*); présence; fréquentation (*scolaire*), *f.*; soins (*pour un malade*), *m.pl.*
attendant [ə'tendənt], *a.* qui suit.—*n.* assistant, aide; serviteur, *m.*
attention [ə'tenʃən], *n.* attention, *f.*; (*pl.*) soins, *m.pl.*
attentive [ə'tentiv], *a.* attentif (*à*), assidu (*auprès de*).
attentively [ə'tentivli], *adv.* attentivement.
attest [ə'test], *v.t.* attester.
attic ['ætik], *n.* mansarde, *f.*, grenier, *m.*
attire [ə'taiə], *v.t.* vêtir, parer.—*n.* vêtements *m.pl.*, costume, *m.*; parure, *f.*, atours, *m.pl.*
attitude ['ætitju:d], *n.* attitude, pose, *f.*
attorney [ə'tə:ni], *n.* (*Am.*) avoué; mandataire, *m.*; ***power of attorney***, procuration, *f.*
attorney-general [ə'tə:ni'dʒenərəl], *n.* procureur-général, *m.*
attract [ə'trækt], *v.t.* attirer.
attraction [ə'trækʃən], *n.* attraction, *f.*; (*pl.*) attraits, appas, *m.pl.*
attractive [ə'træktiv], *a.* attrayant, séduisant; attractif (*de l'aimant etc.*).
attractiveness [ə'træktivnis], *n.* attrait, charme, *m.*
attributable [ə'tribjutəbl], *a.* attribuable.
attribute [ə'tribju:t], *v.t.* attribuer, imputer (*à*).—['ætribju:t], *n.* attribut, *m.*, qualité, *f.*

attrition [ə'triʃən], *n.* attrition, *f.*; ***war of attrition***, guerre d'usure, *f.*
attune [ə'tju:n], *v.t.* accorder.
auburn ['ɔ:bən], *a.* châtain roux.
auction ['ɔ:kʃən], *n.* enchère, *f.*—*v.t.* vendre aux enchères.
auctioneer [ɔ:kʃə'niə], *n.* commissaire-priseur, *m.*
auction-room ['ɔ:kʃənru:m], *n.* salle des ventes, *f.*
audacious [ɔ:'deiʃəs], *a.* audacieux.
audaciously [ɔ:'deiʃəsli], *adv.* audacieusement.
audacity [ɔ:'dæsiti], *n.* audace, *f.*
audible ['ɔ:dibl], *a.* qu'on peut entendre, audible; distinct, intelligible.
audibly ['ɔ:dibli], *adv.* de manière à être entendu.
audience ['ɔ:djəns], *n.* auditoire, *m.*, assistance, audience, *f.*
audio-visual ['ɔ:djo'vizjuəl], *a.* audio-visuel.
audit ['ɔ:dit], *v.t.* apurer, vérifier (*des comptes*).—*n.* apurement, *m.*, vérification de comptes, *f.*; ***audit office***, cour des comptes, *f.*
audition [ɔ:'diʃən], *n.* audition, *f.*—*v.t.* (*fam.*) auditionner.
auditor ['ɔ:ditə], *n.* vérificateur; expert comptable, *m.*
auger ['ɔ:gə], *n.* tarière, *f.*
aught [ɔ:t], *n.* quelque chose; quoi que ce soit, *m.*; ***for aught I know***, pour autant que je sache.
augment [ɔ:g'ment], *v.t.* augmenter, accroître.
augur ['ɔ:gə], *v.t.*, *v.i.* augurer, présager.—*n.* augure, *m.*
augury ['ɔ:gjuri], *n.* augure, *m.*
August ['ɔ:gəst]. août, *m.*; ***in August***, en août.
august [ɔ:'gʌst], *a.* auguste, imposant.
auk [ɔ:k], *n.* (*Orn.*) pingouin, *m.*
aunt [ɑ:nt], *n.* tante, *f.*
auntie ['ɑ:nti], *n.* (*colloq.*) tata, *f.*
aura ['ɔ:rə], *n.* exhalaison, *f.*, effluve, *m.*
aural ['ɔ:rəl], *a.* de l'oreille.
Aurora [ɔ:'rɔ:rə], *n.* aurore, *f.*; ***Aurora Borealis***, aurore boréale.
auspice ['ɔ:spis], *n.* (*usu. in pl.*) auspice, *m.*
auspicious [ɔ:'spiʃəs], *a.* de bon augure, propice.
auspiciously [ɔ:'spiʃəsli], *adv.* sous d'heureux auspices.
austere [ɔ:s'tiə], *a.* austère; âpre.
austerity [ɔ:s'teriti], *n.* austérité, *f.*
Australasia [ɔstrə'leiʃiə]. l'Australasie, *f.*
Australia [ɔs'treiliə]. l'Australie, *f.*
Australian [ɔs'treiliən], *a.* australien.—*n.* Australien (*personne*), *m.*
Austria ['ɔstriə]. l'Autriche, *f.*
Austrian ['ɔstriən], *a.* autrichien.—*n.* Autrichien (*personne*), *m.*
authentic [ɔ:'θentik], *a.* authentique.
authentically [ɔ:'θentikli], *adv.* authentiquement.
authenticate [ɔ:'θentikeit], *v.t.* authentiquer, constater.
authenticated [ɔ:'θentikeitid], *a.* authentique, avéré.
authenticity [ɔ:θen'tisiti], *n.* authenticité, *f.*
author ['ɔ:θə], *n.* auteur, *m.*
authoress ['ɔ:θəris], *n.* femme auteur, femme écrivain, *f.*
authoritative [ɔ:'θɔritətiv], *a.* d'autorité; autorisé; autoritaire, impérieux.
authority [ɔ:'θɔriti], *n.* autorité; autorisation, *f.*, mandat, *m.*
authorization [ɔ:θərai'zeiʃən], *n.* autorisation, *f.*
authorize ['ɔ:θəraiz], *v.t.* autoriser.
authorship ['ɔ:θəʃip], *n.* qualité d'auteur; (*colloq.*) paternité, *f.*
autobiographer [ɔ:təbai'ɔgrəfə], *n.* autobiographe, *m.*, *f.*
autobiography [ɔ:təbai'ɔgrəfi], *n.* autobiographie, *f.*
autocracy [ɔ:'tɔkrəsi], *n.* autocratie, *f.*
autocrat ['ɔ:təkræt], *n.* autocrate, *m.*, *f.*
auto-cycle ['ɔ:tosaikl], *n.* cyclomoteur, *m.*
autograph ['ɔ:təgrɑ:f], *n.* autographe, *m.*—*v.t.* signer, autographier.
autogyro [ɔ:to'dʒairou], *n.* autogyre, *m.*
automatic [ɔ:tə'mætik], *a.* automatique.
automatically [ɔ:tə'mætikli], *adv.* automatiquement; machinalement.
automation [ɔ:tə'meiʃən], *n.* automation, *f.*
automaton [ɔ:'tɔmətən], *n.* (*pl.* **automata** [ɔ:'tɔmətə]) automate, *m.*
automobile ['ɔ:təməbi:l], *n.* (*Am.*) automobile, auto, voiture, *f.*
autonomous [ɔ:'tɔnəməs], *a.* autonome.
autonomy [ɔ:'tɔnəmi], *n.* autonomie, *f.*
autopsy ['ɔ:tɔpsi, ɔ:'tɔpsi], *n.* autopsie, *f.*
autumn ['ɔ:təm], *n.* automne, *m.* ou *f.*
autumnal [ɔ:'tʌmnəl], *a.* automnal, d'automne.
auxiliary [ɔ:g'ziljəri], *a.* and *n.* auxiliaire, *m.*
avail [ə'veil], *v.t.*, *v.i.* profiter, servir; ***to avail oneself of***, se servir de.—*n.* service, avantage, *m.*, utilité, *f.*; ***of what avail is it?*** à quoi bon?
available [ə'veiləbl], *a.* disponible; valable.
avalanche ['ævəlɑ:nʃ], *n.* avalanche, *f.*
avarice ['ævəris], *n.* avarice, *f.*
avaricious [ævə'riʃəs], *a.* avare, avaricieux.
avenge [ə'vendʒ], *v.t.* venger; ***to avenge oneself***, se venger (*de* ou *sur*).
avenger [ə'vendʒə], *n.* vengeur, *m.*
avenging [ə'vendʒiŋ], *a.* vengeur.—*n.* vengeance, *f.*
avenue ['ævənju:], *n.* avenue, *f.*
aver [ə'və:], *v.t.* affirmer.
average ['ævəridʒ], *a.* commun, moyen.—*n.* moyenne, *f.*, prix moyen, terme moyen, *m.*; (*Naut*). avarie, *f.*; ***on an average***, en moyenne.—*v.t.* établir la moyenne de; atteindre une moyenne de.
averse [ə'və:s], *a.* opposé (*à*), ennemi (*de*).
aversely [ə'və:sli], *adv.* à contre-cœur.
aversion [ə'və:ʃən], *n.* répugnance, aversion, *f.*; ***it is his pet aversion***, c'est sa bête noire.
avert [ə'və:t], *v.t.* détourner, écarter.
aviary ['eiviəri], *n.* volière, *f.*
aviation [eivi'eiʃən], *n.* aviation, *f.*
aviator ['eivieitə], *n.* aviateur, *m.*
avid ['ævid], *a.* avide.
avidly ['ævidli], *adv.* avec avidité, avidement.
avoid [ə'vɔid], *v.t.* éviter.
avoidable [ə'vɔidəbl], *a.* évitable.
avoidance [ə'vɔidəns], *n.* action d'éviter, *f.*
avoirdupois [ævədə'pɔiz], *n.* poids du commerce, *m.*
avow [ə'vau], *v.t.* avouer, confesser, déclarer.

avowal [ə'vauəl], *n.* aveu, *m.*
avowedly [ə'vauidli], *adv.* de son propre aveu.
await [ə'weit], *v.t.* attendre.
awake [ə'weik], *v.t. irr.* éveiller, réveiller.—*v.i.* s'éveiller, se réveiller.—*a.* éveillé; attentif.
awaken [ə'weikən], *v.t.* éveiller, réveiller.
awakening [ə'weikniŋ], *n.* réveil, *m.*
award [ə'wɔ:d], *v.t.* décerner, adjuger.—*n.* décision, *f.*, jugement, *m.*, sentence; (*Sch.*) récompense, *f.*
aware [ə'wɛə], *a.* qui sait; instruit; ***to be aware of***, savoir, avoir connaissance de; ***not to be aware of***, ignorer.
awareness [ə'wɛənis], *n.* conscience, *f.*
away [ə'wei], *adv.* absent; loin, au loin; ***away with you!*** allez-vous en! ***far away***, au loin; ***right away***, immédiatement.
awe [ɔ:], *n.* crainte, terreur, *f.*, respect, *m.*
awe-inspiring ['ɔ:inspaiəriŋ], *a.* terrifiant.
awestruck ['ɔ:strʌk], *a.* frappé de terreur.
awful ['ɔ:ful], *a.* terrible, redoutable, effroyable; solennel; ***what awful weather!*** quel temps affreux!
awfully ['ɔ:fuli], *adv.* horriblement, terriblement; (*fam.*) diablement.
awhile [ə'wail], *adv.* un instant, un peu.
awkward ['ɔ:kwəd], *a.* gauche, maladroit; embarrassant.
awkwardly ['ɔ:kwədli], *adv.* gauchement, maladroitement.
awkwardness ['ɔ:kwədnis], *n.* gaucherie, maladresse, *f.*
awl [ɔ:l], *n.* alène, *f.*; poinçon, *m.*
awning ['ɔ:niŋ], *n.* tente, banne, bâche, *f.*
awry [ə'rai], *a.* and *adv.* de travers.
axe [æks], *n.* hache, cognée, *f.*
axiom ['æksiəm], *n.* axiome, *m.*
axiomatic [æksiə'mætik], *a.* axiomatique.
axis ['æksis], *n.* (*pl.* **axes** ['æksi:z]) axe, *m.*
axle [æksl], *n.* arbre, essieu, *m.*; (*Motor.*) ***rear axle***, pont arrière, *m.*
ay, aye [ai], *adv.* oui, c'est vrai; ***aye, aye!*** (*Naut.*) bon quart!—*n.* ***ayes and noes***, voix pour et contre, *f.pl.*
azalea [ə'zeiliə], *n.* (*Bot.*) azalée, *f.*
Azores [ə'zɔ:z], **the.** les Açores, *f.pl.*
azote [ə'zout], *n.* (*Chem.*) azote, *m.*
azure ['æʒuə, 'eiʒə], *a.* d'azur.—*n.* azur, *m.*

B

B, b [bi:]. deuxième lettre de l'alphabet; (*Mus.*) si, *m.*
baa [bɑ:], *v.i.* bêler.—*n.* bêlement, *m.*
babble [bæbl], *v.i.* babiller; gazouiller jaser; (*fig.*) murmurer (*ruisseau*).—*n.* babil, caquet; (*fig.*) murmure, *m.*, jaserie, *f.*
babbler ['bæblə], *n.* babillard, *m.*
babbling ['bæbliŋ], *a.* babillard, bavard.
babe [beib], *n.* enfant nouveau-né, petit enfant, *m.*
Babel ['beibəl]. Babel, *f.*
baboon [bə'bu:n], *n.* babouin, *m.*
baby ['beibi], *n.* bébé, *m.*; ***baby grand (piano)***, piano à demi-queue, *m.*; ***baby linen***, layette, *f.*
babyhood ['beibihud], *n.* première enfance, *f.*
babyish ['beibiiʃ], *a.* enfantin.
bacchanalia [bækə'neiliə], *n.pl.* bacchanales, *f.pl.*
bacchanalian [bækə'neiliən], *a.* bachique.—*n.* ivrogne, *m.*
bachelor ['bætʃələ], *n.* célibataire, vieux garçon; bachelier (*ès lettres*), *m.*
back [bæk], *a.* arrière, de derrière; ***a back street***, une petite rue.—*n.* dos, *m.*, reins, *m.pl.*; envers (*d'un tissu*); verso (*d'une page etc.*); fond (*d'une salle etc.*); (*Ftb.*) arrière; revers (*d'une colline etc.*); derrière (*d'une maison etc.*); dossier (*d'une chaise*), *m.*; ***at the back of***, derrière; ***back to back***, dos à dos; ***on the back of*** (*a letter etc.*), au verso.—*adv.* en arrière; de retour, rentré; ***a few years back***, il y a quelques années; ***to be back***, être de retour; ***to call back***, rappeler; ***to come back***, revenir.—*v.t.* soutenir; (*Betting*) jouer (*un cheval*); faire reculer.—*v.i.* reculer.
backbite ['bækbait], *v.t.* médire de, calomnier.
backbiting ['bækbaitiŋ], *n.* médisance, *f.*
backbone ['bækboun], *n.* épine dorsale, *f.*
back-door ['bæk'dɔ:], *n.* porte de derrière, *f.*
backer ['bækə], *n.* partisan, second; parieur pour, *m.*
back-fire [bæk'faiə], *v.i.* (*Motor.*) pétarader.
backgammon [bæk'gæmən], *n.* trictrac, *m.*
back-garden ['bæk'gɑ:dn], *n.* jardin de derrière, *m.*
background ['bækgraund], *n.* arrière-plan, fond, *m.*
back-room ['bæk'ru:m], *n.* chambre de derrière, *f.*
backside ['bæk'said], *n.* (*pop.*) derrière, *m.*
backslide ['bæk'slaid], *v.i.* retomber dans le vice *ou* le pêché.
backstage ['bæk'steidʒ], *adv.* derrière la scène; dans les coulisses.
backstairs [bæk'stɛəz], *n.* escalier de service, *m.*
backward ['bækwəd], *a.* arriéré; en retard; en arrière; lent, tardif.
backward(s) ['bækwəd(z)], *adv.* à reculons; en arrière; à la renverse.
backwoodsman ['bækwudzmən], *n.* (*pl.* **-men** [men]) défricheur de forêts, *m.*
back-yard ['bæk'jɑ:d], *n.* cour de derrière, *f.*
bacon ['beikən], *n.* lard, *m.*
bacterium [bæk'tiəriəm], *n.* (*pl.* **bacteria** [bæk'tiəriə]) bactérie, *f.*
bad [bæd], *a.* mauvais; méchant (*enfant etc.*); gâté (*aliment etc.*); malade; ***that is too bad***, c'est trop fort.
badge [bædʒ], *n.* insigne, *m.*; plaque, *f.*; (*Mil.*) écusson; brassard, *m.*
badger ['bædʒə], *n.* blaireau, *m.*—*v.t.* harceler.
badly ['bædli], *adv.* mal; grièvement, fort, beaucoup.
badness ['bædnis], *n.* méchanceté, *f.*; mauvais état, *m.*
baffle [bæfl], *v.t.* déjouer; confondre.

bag [bæg], *n.* sac; cornet (*papier*), *m.*; ***game-bag***, gibecière, *f.*; ***with bag and baggage***, avec armes et bagages.—*v.t.* mettre en sac; abattre (*du gibier*); (*colloq.*) s'emparer de; (*slang*) chiper.—*v.i.* bouffer (*pantalon*).
baggage ['bægidʒ], *n.* (*chiefly Am.*) bagages, *m.pl.*
bagpipes ['bægpaips], *n. pl.* cornemuse, *f.*
bail (1) [beil], *n.* caution, *f.*; ***on bail***, sous caution.
bail (2), **bale** (1) [beil], *v.t.* écoper.
bailiff ['beilif], *n.* huissier, *m.*; ***farm bailiff***, régisseur, *m.*
bait [beit], *v.t.* amorcer (*un hameçon*); (*fig.*) harceler, tourmenter.—*n.* amorce, *f.*; appât, leurre, *m.*
baize [beiz], *n.* serge, *f.*; ***green baize***, tapis vert, *m.*
bake [beik], *v.t.*, *v.i.* cuire au four.
bakehouse ['beikhaus], *n.* fournil, *m.*, boulangerie, *f.*
Bakelite ['beikəlait], *n.* bakélite (*reg. trade mark*), *f.*
baker ['beikə], *n.* boulanger, *m.*
bakery ['beikəri], *n.* boulangerie, *f.*
baking ['beikiŋ], *n.* cuisson; fournée, *f.*
balance ['bæləns], *n.* balance, *f.*; équilibre; balancier (*d'une pendule*), *m.*—*v.t.* équilibrer, balancer; ***to balance up***, arrêter.
balance-sheet ['bælənsʃi:t], *n.* bilan, *m.*
balance-weight ['bælənsweit], *n.* contrepoids, *m.*
balcony ['bælkəni], *n.* balcon, *m.*
bald [bɔ:ld], *a.* chauve; (*fig.*) plat, sec (*style*).
baldly ['bɔ:ldli], *adv.* pauvrement, platement, sèchement.
baldness ['bɔ:ldnis], *n.* calvitie; (*fig.*) platitude, *f.*
bale (1) [BAIL (2)].
bale (2) [beil], *n.* balle, *f.*, ballot, *m.*—*v.t.* emballer.—*v.i.* ***to bale out***, (*Av.*) sauter en parachute.
baleful ['beilful], *a.* sinistre, funeste.
balefully ['beilfuli], *adv.* d'une manière funeste.
balk, baulk [bɔ:k], *n.* poutre, bille; (*Billiards*) ligne de départ, *f.*—*v.t.* frustrer, contrarier, déjouer.
Balkan ['bɔ:lkən], *a.* balkanique.
Balkans ['bɔ:lkənz], **the.** les Balkans, les États Balkaniques, *m.pl.*
ball (1) [bɔ:l], *n.* balle; boule (*de neige*); pelote, *f.*, peloton (*de laine, de ficelle*); boulet (*de canon*), *m.*; (*Billiards*) bille; (*Cook.*) boulette, *f.*; ballon (*plein d'air*), *m.*; prunelle (*d'œil*), *f.*; ***ball-point pen***, stylo à bille, *m.*
ball (2) [bɔ:l], *n.* bal, *m.*; ***fancy-dress ball***, bal masqué.
ballad ['bæləd], *n.* (*Mus.*) romance; ballade, *f.*
ballast ['bæləst], *n.* lest; (*Rail.*) ballast, *m.*; ***in ballast***, sur lest.—*v.t.* lester; (*Rail.*) ensabler.
ballerina [bælə'ri:nə], *n.* ballerine, *f.*
ballet ['bælei], *n.* ballet, *m.*
balloon [bə'lu:n], *n.* ballon, aérostat, *m.*—*v.i.* se ballonner.
ballot ['bælət], *n.* boule, *f.*; bulletin, scrutin, *m.*; ***by ballot***, au scrutin.—*v.i.* voter au scrutin.
ballot-box ['bælətbɔks], *n.* urne électorale, *f.*
ballot-paper ['bælətpeipə], *n.* bulletin de vote, *m.*
balm [bɑ:m], *n.* baume, *m.*; mélisse, *f.*—*v.t.* parfumer.
balmy ['bɑ:mi], *a.* embaumé, parfumé.
balsam ['bɔ:lsəm], *n.* baume, *m.*
Baltic ['bɔ:ltik], **the.** la Baltique, *f.*
balustrade [bæləs'treid], *n.* balustrade, *f.*
bamboo [bæm'bu:], *n.* bambou, *m.*
bamboozle [bæm'bu:zl], *v.t.* (*colloq.*) tromper, duper, enjôler.
ban [bæn], *n.* ban, *m.*; interdiction, *f.*; (*Eccles.*) interdit, *m.*—*v.t.* interdire, proscrire.
banal [bə'næl, 'beinəl], *a.* banal.
banality [bə'næliti], *n.* banalité, *f.*
banana [bə'nɑ:nə], *n.* banane, *f.*
banana-tree [bə'nɑ:nətri:], *n.* bananier, *m.*
band (1) [bænd], *n.* bande, *f.*, lien; ruban, *m.*; raie, *f.*—*v.t.* bander.
band (2) [bænd], *n.* bande, troupe; (*Mil.*) musique, *f.*; orchestre, *m.*; ***brass band***, fanfare, *f.*—*v.t.* liguer, réunir en troupe.—*v.i.* se liguer.
bandage ['bændidʒ], *n.* bandeau; (*Surg.*) bandage, pansement, *m.*
bandbox ['bændbɔks], *n.* carton (*de modiste*), *m.*
bandit ['bændit], *n.* bandit, *m.*
bandmaster ['bændmɑ:stə], *n.* chef de musique, *m.*
bandoleer, bandolier [bændə'liə], *n.* bandoulière, *f.*
bandsman ['bændzmən], *n.* (*pl.* **-men** [men]) musicien, *m.*
bandstand ['bændstænd], *n.* kiosque à musique, *m.*
bandy ['bændi], *v.t.* renvoyer; échanger; se renvoyer; ***to bandy words***, se renvoyer des paroles.—*v.i.* se disputer.
bandy-legged ['bændilegd], *a.* bancal.
bane [bein], *n.* poison; (*fig.*) fléau, *m.*
baneful ['beinful], *a.* pernicieux, funeste, nuisible.
bang [bæŋ], *n.* coup, grand bruit, *m.*, détonation, *f.*—*v.t.* frapper violemment, taper; ***to bang a door***, claquer une porte.—*int.* pan! paf! boum!
bangle [bæŋgl], *n.* porte-bonheur, bracelet, *m.*
banish ['bæniʃ], *v.t.* bannir, exiler.
banishment ['bæniʃmənt], *n.* bannissement, exil, *m.*
bank (1) [bæŋk], *n.* rivage, bord, *m.*; berge, rive; terrasse, *f.*, remblai, talus; banc (*de sable, de gazon etc.*), *m.*; digue, *f.*; carreau (*de mine*), *m.*—*v.t.* terrasser, remblayer.
bank (2) [bæŋk], *n.* (*Comm.*) banque, *f.*; ***savings-bank***, caisse d'épargne, *f.*—*v.t.* encaisser (*de l'argent*).
banker ['bæŋkə], *n.* banquier, *m.*
banking ['bæŋkiŋ], *n.* banque, *f.*
bank-note ['bæŋknout], *n.* billet de banque, *m.*
bankrupt ['bæŋkrʌpt], *a.* failli, en faillite; (*fig.*) ruiné.—*v.t.* mettre en faillite, ruiner.—*n.* banqueroutier, failli, *m.*; ***to go bankrupt***, faire faillite.
bankruptcy ['bæŋkrʌptsi], *n.* banqueroute, faillite, *f.*
banner ['bænə], *n.* bannière, *f.*
bannock ['bænək], *n.* (*grosse*) galette d'avoine *f.*
banns [bænz], *n.pl.* ***banns of marriage***, bans de mariage, *m.pl.*

banquet ['bæŋkwit], *n.* banquet; *festin, *m.*
banter ['bæntə], *v.t.* railler, badiner.—*n.* badinage, *m.*, raillerie, *f.*
baptism ['bæptizm], *n.* baptême, *m.*
baptismal [bæp'tizməl], *a.* baptismal.
baptist ['bæptist], *n.* baptiste, *m., f.*
baptize [bæp'taiz], *v.t.* baptiser.
bar (1) [bɑ:], *n.* barre, *f.*; (*Law etc.*) barreau, parquet, *m.*; (*fig.*) barrière; buvette, *f.*, comptoir, bar (*de café, hôtel etc.*); (*Law*) banc des accusés, *m.*; (*Mus.*) mesure; tablette (*de chocolat*), *f.*; ***to be called to the bar***, être reçu avocat.—*v.t.* barrer, empêcher; exclure.
bar (2) [BARRING].
barb [bɑ:b], *n.* barbillon, dardillon (*hameçon*), *m.*; pointe (*flèche*); barbe, arête (*blé*), *f.*
Barbados [bɑ:'beidɔs]. la Barbade, *f.*
barbarian [bɑ:'bɛəriən], *a.* and *n.* barbare, *m., f.*
barbaric [bɑ:'bærik], *a.* barbare.
barbarism ['bɑ:bərizm], *n.* barbarie, *f.*; (*Gram.*) barbarisme, *m.*
barbarity [bɑ:'bæriti], *n.* barbarie, cruauté, *f.*
barbarous ['bɑ:bərəs], *a.* barbare.
barbecue ['bɑ:bəkju:], *n.* grand gril; grand pique-nique (en plein air), *m.*—*v.t.* rôtir à la broche.
barbed [bɑ:bd], *a.* barbelé; (*fig.*) acére; ***barbed wire***, fil de fer barbelé, *m.*
barbel ['bɑ:bəl], *n.* (*Ichth.*) barbeau, *m.*
barber ['bɑ:bə], *n.* coiffeur, *m.*
Barcelona [bɑ:sə'lounə]. Barcelone, *f.*
bard [bɑ:d], *n.* barde, trouvère, *m.*
bare [bɛə], *a.* nu, découvert; (*fig.*) seul, simple; pauvre.—*v.t.* découvrir, dépouiller; mettre à nu.
bareback ['bɛəbæk], *adv.* à dos nu.
barefaced ['bɛəfeist], *a.* à visage découvert; éhonté, sans déguisement.
barefoot ['bɛəfut], *a.* nu-pieds, les pieds nus.
bareheaded ['bɛə'hedid], *a.* nu-tête, la tête nue.
barely ['bɛəli], *adv.* à peine; tout juste, simplement, seulement; pauvrement.
bareness ['bɛənis], *n.* nudité; misère, *f.*
bargain ['bɑ:gin], *n.* marché, *m.*, affaire; occasion, *f.*; ***into the bargain***, par-dessus le marché; ***it is a bargain***, c'est convenu; ***to strike a bargain***, conclure un marché. —*v.i.* marchander, faire marché.
barge [bɑ:dʒ], *n.* chaland, *m.*; péniche, *f.*—*v.i.* ***to barge into***, se heurter contre, bousculer.
bargee [bɑ:'dʒi:], **bargeman** ['bɑ:dʒmən] (*pl.* **-men** [men]), *n.* batelier, *m.*
baritone ['bæritoun], *a.* de baryton.—*n.* baryton, *m.*
bark (1) [bɑ:k], *n.* écorce, *f.*; tan, *m.*
bark (2) [bɑ:k], *n.* aboiement, *m.*—*v.i.* aboyer.
bark (3), **barque** [bɑ:k], *n.* trois-mâts, *m.*
barking ['bɑ:kiŋ], *n.* aboiement, *m.*
barley ['bɑ:li], *n.* orge, *f.*
barmaid ['bɑ:meid], *n.* barmaid, *f.*
barman ['bɑ:mən], *n.* (*pl.* **-men** [men]) barman, *m.*
barmy ['bɑ:mi], *a.* (*colloq.*) fou, toqué.
barn [bɑ:n], *n.* grange; (*Am.*) étable, *f.*
barnacle ['bɑ:nəkl], *n.* barnache (*oie*), *f.*; balane, anatife (*crustacé*), *m.*
barometer [bə'rɔmitə], *n.* baromètre, *m.*
barometric [bæro'metrik], *a.* barométrique.
baron ['bærən], *n.* baron, *m.*; ***baron of beef***, double aloyau, *m.*
baroness ['bærənis], *n.* baronne, *f.*
baronet ['bærənet], *n.* baronnet, *m.*
baronial [bə'rouniəl], *a.* baronnial, seigneurial.
barony ['bærəni], *n.* baronnie, *f.*
barouche [bə'ru:ʃ], *n.* calèche, *f.*
barque [BARK (3)].
barrack ['bærək], *n.* (*usu. in pl.*) caserne, *f.*; quartier (*pour la cavalerie*), *m.*
barrage ['bæridʒ, 'bærɑ:ʒ], *n.* barrage, *m.*
barrel ['bærəl], *n.* baril, *m.*; gonne, caque (*de poissons etc.*), *f.*; corps (*de pompe*); cylindre, tambour (*de machine*); canon (*de fusil*), *m.* —*v.t.* embariller, entonner, mettre en baril, encaquer.
barrel-organ ['bærəlɔ:gən], *n.* orgue de Barbarie, *m.*
barren ['bærən], *a.* stérile; infertile (*terre*).
barrenness ['bærənnis], *n.* stérilité, *f.*
barricade [bæri'keid], *n.* barricade, *f.*—*v.t.* barricader.
barrier ['bæriə], *n.* barrière, *f.*
barring ['bɑ:riŋ], **bar** (2) [bɑ:], *prep.* excepté, hormis, sauf.
barrister ['bæristə], *n.* avocat, *m.*
barrow ['bærou], *n.* brouette, *f.*
barrow-boy ['bæroubɔi], *n.* (*fam.*) marchand des quatre saisons, *m.*
barter ['bɑ:tə], *n.* échange, troc; trafic, *m.*—*v.t.* troquer, échanger.—*v.i.* échanger, faire échange.
basalt [bə'sɔ:lt], *n.* basalte, *m.*
base (1) [beis], *a.* bas, vil, indigne, méprisable; illégitime (*enfant*); de mauvais aloi; non précieux, faux (*monnaie*).
base (2) [beis], *n.* base, *f.*, fondement; fond, *m.*—*v.t.* fonder (*sur*); asseoir (*l'impôt*).
baseball ['beisbɔ:l], *n.* (*Spt.*) base-ball, *m.*
baseless ['beislis], *a.* sans fondement.
basely ['beisli], *adv.* bassement, lâchement.
basement ['beismənt], *n.* sous-sol, *m.*
baseness ['beisnis], *n.* bassesse, lâcheté, *f.*
bashful ['bæʃful], *a.* timide, intimidé.
bashfully ['bæʃfuli], *adv.* timidement, en rougissant.
bashfulness ['bæʃfulnis], *n.* timidité, fausse honte, *f.*
basic ['beisik], *a.* (*Chem.*) basique; de base.
basilica [bə'zilikə], *n.* basilique, *f.*
basilisk ['bæzilisk], *n.* basilic, *m.*
basin ['beisən], *n.* bassin; bol, *m.*; cuvette, *f.*
basis ['beisis], *n.* (*pl.* **bases** ['beisi:z]) base, *f.* fondement, *m.*
bask [bɑ:sk], *v.i.* se chauffer.
basket ['bɑ:skit], *n.* panier, *m.*, corbeille, *f.*
basket-ball ['bɑ:skitbɔ:l], *n.* (*Spt.*) basket-ball, (*fam.*) basket, *m.*
Basle [bɑ:l]. Bâle, *f.*
bas-relief [bɑ:rə'li:f], *n.* bas-relief, *m.*
bass (1) [beis], *n.* (*Mus.*) basse; basse-taille, *f.*; ***double bass***, contre-basse, *f.*
bass (2) [bæs], *n.* (*Ichth.*) bar, *m.*; perche, *f.*
bassinet [bæsi'net], *n.* bercelonnette, *f.*, moïse, *m.*
bassoon [bə'su:n], *n.* basson, *m.*
bastard ['bæstəd], *a.* bâtard; (*fig.*) faux.—*n.* bâtard, *m.*, bâtarde, *f.*; (*pop.*) salaud, *m.*
baste [beist], *v.t.* arroser (*viande*); (*fig.*) bâtonner; (*Needlework*) bâtir.

bastion ['bæstiən], *n.* bastion, *m.*
bat (1) [bæt], *n.* (*Cricket*) batte, *f.*; ***off his own bat***, de sa propre initiative.—*v.i.* être au guichet.
bat (2) [bæt], *n.* (*Zool.*) chauve-souris, *f.*
Batavian [bə'teiviən], *a.* batave.—*n.* Batave (*personne*), *m., f.*
batch [bætʃ], *n.* fournée (*pain*); (*fig.*) troupe, bande, *f.*; tas; lot, *m.*
bate [beit], *v.t.* rabattre, rabaisser.
bath [bɑ:θ], *n.* bain, *m.*; baignoire, *f.*; ***shower-bath***, douche, *f.*—*v.t.* donner un bain à, baigner.—*v.i.* prendre un bain.
bathe [beið], *v.t.* baigner; tremper, mouiller.—*v.i.* se baigner.—*n.* baignade, *f.*
bather ['beiðə], *n.* baigneur, *m.*, baigneuse, *f.*
bathing ['beiðiŋ], *n.* baignade, *f.*; bains, *m.pl.*
bathing-costume ['beiðiŋkɔstjum], *n.* costume de bain, maillot, *m.*
bathos ['beiθɔs], *n.* pathos, *m.*, enflure, *f.*
bath-room ['bɑ:θrum], *n.* salle de bain(s), *f.*
batman ['bætmən], *n.* (*pl.* **-men** [men]) ordonnance, brosseur, *m.*
baton ['bætən], *n.* bâton, *m.*; baguette, *f.*
batsman ['bætsmən], *n.* (*Cricket*) batteur, *m.*
battalion [bə'tæliən], *n.* bataillon, *m.*
batten ['bætən], *n.* volige, latte, *f.*—*v.t.* fermer; (*Carp.*) voliger.—*v.i.* s'engraisser.
batter ['bætə], *v.t.* battre en brèche; battre; délabrer, ébranler, démolir.—*n.* pâte, *f.*
battered ['bætəd], *a.* délabré.
battering-ram ['bætəriŋræm], *n.* bélier, *m.*
battery ['bætəri], *n.* batterie; (*Elec.*) pile, batterie, *f.*, accumulateur, *m.*; action de battre en brèche, *f.*; (*Law*) voies de fait, *f.pl.*
battle [bætl], *n.* bataille, *f.*, combat, *m.*; ***pitched battle***, bataille rangée; ***to give battle***, livrer bataille.—*v.i.* lutter, combattre; (*colloq.*) batailler.
battle-axe ['bætlæks], *n.* hache d'armes, *f.*
battledore ['bætldɔ:], *n.* raquette, *f.*
battle-dress ['bætldres], *n.* tenue de campagne, *f.*
battle-field ['bætlfi:ld], *n.* champ de bataille, *m.*
battlement ['bætlmənt], *n.* créneau, *m.*
battleship ['bætlʃip], *n.* cuirassé, *m.*
bauble [bɔ:bl], *n.* babiole, fanfreluche, *f.*; ***fool's bauble***, marotte, *f.*
baulk [BALK].
bauxite ['bɔ:ksait, 'bouzait], *n.* bauxite, *f.*
Bavaria [bə'vɛəriə]. la Bavière, *f.*
Bavarian [bə'vɛəriən], *a.* bavarois.—*n.* Bavarois (*personne*).
bawdy ['bɔ:di], *a.* obscène, paillard.
bawl [bɔ:l], *v.i.* crier, brailler.
bay (1) [bei], *a.* bai (*cheval*).
bay (2) [bei], *n.* baie, *f.*, golfe, *m.*; (*Arch.*) baie, *f.*
bay (3) [bei], *n.* (*Bot.*) baie, *f.*; laurier, *m.*
bay (4) [bei], *n.* abois, *m.pl.*; ***at bay***, aux abois.—*v.i.* aboyer.
bayonet ['beiənit], *n.* baïonnette, *f.*—*v.t.* tuer *ou* percer à coups de baïonnette.
bay-window ['beiwindou], *n.* fenêtre en saillie *ou* à baie, *f.*
bazaar [bə'zɑ:], *n.* bazar, *m.*; vente de charité, *f.*
bazooka [bə'zu:kə], *n.* bazooka, *m.*
be [bi:], *v.i. irr.* être; exister; subsister; y avoir, se trouver; avoir; faire; devoir, falloir; ***be it so***, soit; ***be that as it may***, quoi qu'il en soit; ***how is it that . . .?*** comment se fait-il que . . .? ***I was to***, je devais; ***to be better***, valoir mieux; se porter mieux; ***to be mistaken***, se tromper; ***to be right***, avoir raison.
beach [bi:tʃ], *n.* plage, grève, *f.*, rivage, *m.*—*v.t.* échouer.
beacon ['bi:kən], *n.* phare, fanal, *m.*; balise, *f.*—*v.t.* baliser, éclairer.
bead [bi:d], *n.* grain (*de chapelet, de bracelet, de collier*); globule, *m.*; ***string of beads***, collier, chapelet, *m.*; ***to tell one's beads***, égrener son chapelet.
beadle [bi:dl], *n.* bedeau; appariteur, *m.*
beagle [bi:gl], *n.* chien briquet, bigle, *m.*
beak [bi:k], *n.* bec, *m.*; bigorne (*enclume*), *f.*; (*Naut.*) éperon, *m.*
beaker ['bi:kə], *n.* gobelet, *m.*, coupe, *f.*
beakful ['bi:kful], *n.* becquée, *f.*
beam [bi:m], *n.* poutre, *f.*; timon (*charrue, voiture etc.*); rayon (*lumière*); large sourire (*de joie etc.*), *m.*—*v.t.* lancer, darder (*des rayons*).—*v.i.* rayonner.
beaming ['bi:miŋ], *a.* rayonnant, radieux.—*n.* rayonnement, *m.*
bean [bi:n], *n.* fève, *f.*; haricot; grain (*de café*), *m.*; ***French beans***, haricots verts; ***kidney beans***, haricots blancs.
bear (1) [bɛə], *n.* ours; (*St. Exch.*) joueur à la baisse, baissier, *m.*; ***polar bear***, ours blanc.
bear (2) [bɛə], *v.t. irr.* porter, soutenir; endurer, supporter, souffrir, subir; avoir produire (*fruits etc.*); enfanter; donner naissance à; y tenir; remporter.—*v.i.* endurer, souffrir; porter, peser; avoir rapport (*à*); appuyer; porter (*sur*); rapporter.
bearable ['bɛərəbl], *a.* supportable.
beard [biəd], *n.* barbe, *f.*—*v.t.* braver, défier.
bearded ['biədid], *a.* barbu.
beardless ['biədlis], *a.* imberbe.
bearer ['bɛərə], *n.* porteur; (*Arch.*) support, *m.*
bearing ['bɛəriŋ], *n.* rapport; maintien, port *m.*, conduite, relation, *f.*, aspect, *m.*, portée; face, *f.*; (*Arch.*) support; (*Mech.*) coussinet, *m.*; ***ball-bearings***, roulement à billes, *m.*; ***to take one's bearings***, s'orienter.
bearskin ['bɛəskin], *n.* (*Mil.*) bonnet d'oursin, *m.*
beast [bi:st], *n.* bête, *f.*; (*fig.*) animal, cochon, *m.*
beastliness ['bi:stlinis], *n.* saleté, saloperie, *f.*
beastly ['bi:stli], *a.* bestial; sale, malpropre, dégoûtant.
beat [bi:t], *v.t. irr.* battre; frapper; piler, broyer; l'emporter sur; fouetter (*pluie, neige etc.*); se frapper (*la poitrine etc.*); ***beat it!*** fiche-moi le camp! ***that beats all***, cela dépasse tout; ***to beat a retreat***, battre en retraite.—*v.i.* battre; être agité.—*n.* coup, battement; son; itinéraire, *m.*; ronde (*d'un agent de police*), *f.*, parcours (*facteurs etc.*), *m.*; (*Hunt.*) battue; (*Mus.*) mesure, *f.*, temps, *m.*; ***beat of the drum***, batterie de tambour, *f.*
beaten [bi:tn], *a.* battu.
beater ['bi:tə], *n.* batteur; (*Spt.*) rabatteur, *m.*; batte (*instrument*), *f.*
beating ['bi:tiŋ], *n.* battement, *m.*; rossée, *f.*; coups, *m.pl.*; batterie, *f.*; roulement (*tambour etc.*), *m.*

beau [bou], *n.* (*pl.* **beaux** [bouz]) petit-maître; prétendant (*amant*), *m.*

beauteous ['bju:tiəs], *a.* (*Poet.*) beau.

beauteously ['bju:tiəsli], *adv.* avec beauté.

beautiful ['bju:tiful], *a.* très beau; (*colloq.*) magnifique.

beautifully ['bju:tifuli], *adv.* admirablement.

beautify ['bju:tifai], *v.t.* embellir, orner.—*v.i.* s'embellir.

beauty ['bju:ti], *n.* beauté (*personne et qualité*), *f.*

beauty-spot ['bju:tispɔt], *n.* mouche, *f.*, grain de beauté; site pittoresque, *m.*

beaver ['bi:və], *n.* castor; chapeau de castor, *m.*

becalm [bi'kɑ:m], *v.t.* *apaiser, calmer; abriter (*navire*).

because [bi'kɔz], *conj.* parce que; ***because of***, à cause de.

beck (1) [bek], *n.* signe (*du doigt etc.*), *m.*—*v.i.* faire signe (*du doigt etc.*).

beck (2) [bek], *n.* ruisseau, *m.*

beckon ['bekən], *v.t.* faire signe à, appeler.—*v.i.* faire signe (*à*).

become [bi'kʌm], *v.t. irr.* (*conjug. like* COME) aller bien à, convenir à, être propre à.—*v.i.* devenir, commencer à être.

becoming [bi'kʌmiŋ], *a.* bienséant, convenable, qui va bien, attrayant.

becomingly [bi'kʌmiŋli], *adv.* avec bienséance.

bed [bed], *n.* lit, *m.*; couche; (*Geol.*) assise, *f.*; encaissement (*rue*); parterre, *m.*, plate-bande (*fleurs*), *f.*; carré, *m.*—*v.t.* coucher, mettre au lit; loger, fixer, enfoncer; parquer (*huîtres*).—*v.i.* coucher, se coucher.

bedaub [bi'dɔ:b], *v.t.* barbouiller.

bedazzle [bi'dæzl], *v.t.* éblouir.

***bed-chamber** [BEDROOM].

bedclothes ['bedklouðz], *n.pl.* les draps et les couvertures, *m.pl.*

bedding ['bediŋ], *n.* literie; litière (*pour animaux*), *f.*

bedeck [bi'dek], *v.t.* parer (*de*).

bedfellow ['bedfelou], *n.* camarade de lit, *m.*

***bedizen** [bi'daizn], *v.t.* attifer, parer.

bedraggle [bi'drægl], *v.t.* crotter, traîner dans la boue.

bedridden ['bedridn], *a.* alité.

bedroom ['bedru:m], ***bed-chamber** [bed tʃeimbə], *n.* chambre (à coucher), *f.*

bedside ['bedsaid], *n.* ruelle, *f.*, chevet, bord du lit, *m.*

bed-spread ['bedspred], *n.* couvrelit, dessus de lit, *m.*

bedstead ['bedsted], *n.* lit, bois de lit, *m.*; couchette, *f.*

bee [bi:], *n.* abeille, *f.*; ***to have a bee in one's bonnet***, avoir une araignée dans le plafond.

beech [bi:tʃ], *n.* hêtre, *m.*

beef [bi:f], *n.* bœuf (*viande*); *(*pl.* **beeves** [bi:vz]) bœuf (*animal*), *m.*

beef-steak ['bi:f'steik], *n.* bifteck, *m.*

beehive ['bi:haiv], *n.* ruche, *f.*

bee-line ['bi:lain], *n.* ligne droite, *f.*; ***in a bee-line***, à vol d'oiseau; ***to make a bee-line for***, se diriger tout droit vers.

Beelzebub [bi'elzəbʌb]. Belzébuth, *m.*

beer [biə], *n.* bière, *f.*; ***glass of beer***, bock, *m.*

beet [bi:t], *n.* betterave, *f.*

beetle (1) [bi:tl], *n.* coléoptère, scarabée, escarbot, *m.*

beetle (2) [bi:tl], *n.* maillet, *m.*, mailloche; batte, *f.*, battoir (*de laveuse*), *m.*; hie, demoiselle (*d'un paveur*), *f.*; mouton (*à enfoncer les pieux*), *m.*

beetle (3) [bi:tl], *v.i.* surplomber.—*a.* en surplomb.

beetroot ['bi:tru:t], *n.* betterave rouge, *f.*

beet-sugar ['bi:tʃugə], *n.* sucre de betterave, *m.*

befall [bi'fɔ:l], *v.t.*, *v.i. irr.* (*conjug. like* FALL) arriver, survenir (*à*).

befit [bi'fit], *v.t.* convenir à.

befitting [bi'fitiŋ], *a.* convenable à.

before [bi'fɔ:], *adv.* avant (*temps, ordre etc.*); auparavant, en avant; plus haut; jusqu'alors, naguère, jusqu'ici.—*prep.* devant (*endroit*); avant (*temps etc.*); ***before going there***, avant d'y aller.—*conj.* avant que (*with subj.*).

beforehand [bi'fɔ:hænd], *adv.* à l'avance, d'avance.

befriend [bi'frend], *v.t.* seconder, aider, secourir; devenir l'ami de (*quelqu'un*).

beg [beg], *v.t.* mendier (*demander l'aumône*); demander, prier (*de*).—*v.i.* mendier.

beget [bi'get], *v.t. irr.* engendrer; (*fig.*) produire, causer.

beggar ['begə], *n.* mendiant, *m.*, mendiante, *f.*; gueux, *m.*, gueuse, *f.*—*v.t.* appauvrir, ruiner; (*fig.*) épuiser.

beggarly ['begəli], *a.* chétif, pauvre, misérable.

beggary ['begəri], *n.* mendicité, misère, *f.*

begging ['begiŋ], *n.* mendicité, *f.*

begin [bi'gin], *v.t. irr.* commencer; entamer, débuter; se mettre à.—*v.i.* commencer (***by, with***, *par*); ***begin afresh***, recommencez.

beginner [bi'ginə], *n.* commençant; débutant, *m.*

beginning [bi'giniŋ], *n.* commencement, début, *m.*, origine, *f.*

begone! [bi'gɔn], *int.* va-t'en! allez-vous-en!

begonia [bi'gounjə], *n.* (*Bot.*) bégonia, *m.*

begrudge [bi'grʌdʒ], *v.t.* envier; refuser (*à*).

begrudgingly [bi'grʌdʒiŋli], *adv.* à contre-cœur.

beguile [bi'gail], *v.t.* tromper, séduire; (*fig.*) passer (*le temps*).

behalf [bi'hɑ:f], *n.* faveur, part, *f.*; ***on behalf of***, au nom de.

behave [bi'heiv], *v.i.* se comporter, se conduire; ***well-behaved***, sage.

behaviour [bi'heivjə], *n.* conduite, tenue, *f.*; comportement, *m.*; manières, *f.pl.*

behead [bi'hed], *v.t.* décapiter.

behest [bi'hest], *n.* commandement, ordre, *m.*

behind [bi'haind], *adv.* derrière, par derrière, en arrière.—*prep.* derrière, en arrière de; après, en retard de.—*n.* (*colloq.*) derrière, *m.*

behindhand [bi'haindhænd], *a.* and *adv.* en arrière, en retard.

***behold** [bi'hould], *v.t. irr.* (*conjug. like* HOLD) voir, regarder.—*int.* voyez! voici! voilà!

beholden [bi'houldən], *a.* redevable (*à*).

behove [bi'houv], *v.i. impers.* incomber à; ***it behoves***, il faut, il convient.

beige [beiʒ], *a.* and *n.* beige, *m.*

being ['bi:iŋ], *n.* être, *m.*; existence, *f.*; ***in being***, existant, vivant.—*pres.p.* [BE] étant; ***for the time being***, pour le moment.

Beirut [bei'ru:t]. Beyrouth, *m.*

belated [bi'leitid], *a.* attardé; tardif.

belch [beltʃ], *v.t., v.i.* roter, éructer; ***to belch forth***, vomir; ***to belch out flames***, vomir des flammes.—*n.* rot, *m.*, éructation, *f.*
beleaguer [bi'li:gə], *v.t.* assiéger, investir.
belfry ['belfri], *n.* clocher, beffroi, *m.*
Belgian ['beldʒən], *a.* belge.—*n.* Belge (*personne*), *m., f.*
Belgium ['beldʒəm]. la Belgique, *f.*
belie [bi'lai], *v.t.* démentir.
belief [bi'li:f], *n.* croyance, *f.*; credo, *m.*
believable [bi'li:vəbl], *a.* croyable.
believe [bi'li:v], *v.t.* croire.—*v.i.* croire (*en* ou *à*); ***I believe not***, je crois que non, je ne le crois pas; ***I believe so***, je crois que oui, je le crois.
believer [bi'li:və], *n.* croyant, *m.*
bell [bel], *n.* cloche, clochette, *f.*; grelot (*de chevaux etc.*), *m.*; sonnette (*de maison*), *f.*; timbre (*horloge, bicyclette*); (*Arch.*) vase, *m.*
belle [bel], *n.* belle, beauté, *f.*
bellicose ['belikous], *a.* belliqueux.
belligerent [bi'lidʒərənt], *a.* and *n.* belligérant, *m.*
bellow ['belou], *v.i.* beugler; mugir (*mer*); gronder (*tonnerre*).—*n.* beuglement, *m.*
bellows ['belouz], *n.pl.* soufflet, *m.*
bell-ringer ['belriŋə], *n.* sonneur, *m.*
bell-rope ['belroup], *n.* corde de cloche, *f.*
bell-tower ['beltauə], *n.* campanile; clocher, *m.*
belly ['beli], *n.* ventre, *m.*—*v.i.* bomber, s'enfler, se gonfler.
belong [bi'lɔŋ], *v.i.* appartenir, être (*à*).
belongings [bi'lɔŋiŋz], *n.pl.* effets, *m.pl.*, affaires, *f.pl.*
beloved [bi'lʌvd, bi'lʌvid], *a.* cher, chéri, bien-aimé.
below [bi'lou], *prep.* sous au-dessous de; en aval de.—*adv.* au-dessous, dessous, en bas; ***here below***, ici-bas.
belt [belt], *n.* ceinture, *f.*; ceinturon; baudrier, *m.*; (*Mach.*) courroie, *f.*; ***green belt***, zone verte, *f.*—*v.t.* ceindre, entourer.
bemoan [bi'moun], *v.t.* pleurer, déplorer.—*v.i.* gémir (*sur*).
bemuse [bi'mju:z], *v.t.* stupéfier.
bench [bentʃ], *n.* banc; gradin, *m.*; banquette, *f.*; établi (*de menuisier*); siège, tribunal, *m.*
bend [bend], *v.t. irr.* plier; courber, faire plier; incliner, tendre (*un arc*); fléchir (*le genou*); (*fig.*) appliquer.—*v.i.* plier, ployer; se courber, se pencher, s'incliner; s'appliquer (*à*); tourner; fléchir.—*n.* courbure, *f.*; coude; (*Motor.*) tournant, virage, *m.*
beneath [bi'ni:θ], *prep.* sous, au-dessous de.—*adv.* au-dessous, en bas.
Benedict ['benidikt]. Benoît, *m.*
benediction [beni'dikʃən], *n.* bénédiction, *f.*
benefaction [beni'fækʃən], *n.* bienfait, *m.*
benefactor ['benifæktə], *n.* bienfaiteur, *m.*
benefactress ['benifæktris], *n.* bienfaitrice, *f.*
benefice ['benifis], *n.* bénéfice, *m.*
beneficence [bə'nefisəns], *n.* bienfaisance, *f.*
beneficial [beni'fiʃəl], *a.* salutaire, avantageux.
beneficiary [beni'fiʃəri], *a.* and *n.* bénéficiaire, *m., f.*
benefit ['benifit], *n.* bienfait, profit; bénéfice, *m.*; indemnité (*de chômage etc.*), *f.*—*v.t.* faire du bien à.—*v.i.* profiter.
Benelux ['benilʌks]. Bénélux, *m.*
benevolence [bə'nevələns], *n.* bienveillance, *f.*
benevolent [bə'nevələnt], *a.* bienveillant, bienfaisant.
benighted [bi'naitid], *a.* anuité, surpris par la nuit.
benign [bi'nain], *a.* bénin, *m.*, bénigne (*maladie, médecine etc.*), *f.*; bienfaisant (*personne*); doux, affable.
benignant [bi'nignənt], *a.* bon, bienveillant.
bent (1) [bent], *past* and *p.p.* [BEND].
bent (2) [bent], *a.* courbé, plié; ***bent on***, résolu à.—*n.* penchant, *m.*, disposition, tendance, *f.*
benumb [bi'nʌm], *v.t.* engourdir.
benzene ['benzi:n], *n.* benzène, benzol, *m.*
benzine ['benzi:n], *n.* benzine, *f.*
bequeath [bi'kwi:ð], *v.t.* léguer.
bequest [bi'kwest], *n.* legs, *m.*
bereave [bi'ri:v], *v.t. irr.* priver (*de*).
bereavement [bi'ri:vmənt], *n.* privation, perte, *f.*; deuil, *m.*
beret ['berei], *n.* béret, *m.*
Bermuda(s) [bə:'mju:də(z)], **(the).** les (Îles) Bermudes, *f.pl.*
berry ['beri], *n.* baie, *f.*; grain, *m.*
berth [bə:θ], *n.* mouillage; lit, *m.*, couchette, *f.*; poste, *m.*, place, *f.*, emploi, *m.*—*v.t.* amarrer à quai.—*v.i.* mouiller.
Bertha ['bə:θə]. Berthe, *f.*
beseech [bi'si:tʃ], *v.t. irr.* supplier, implorer.
beset [bi'set], *v.t. irr.* (*conjug. like* SET) obséder, entourer, assaillir.
besetting [bi'setiŋ], *a.* habituel, obsesseur.
beside [bi'said], *prep.* à côté de, auprès de; hors, hormis, excepté.
besides [bi'saidz], *prep.* outre, hors, hormis, excepté.—*adv.* d'ailleurs, du reste, en outre, de plus.
besiege [bi'si:dʒ], *v.t.* assiéger.
besmear [bi'smiə], *v.t.* barbouiller; souiller.
besmirch [bi'smə:tʃ], *v.t.* tacher, salir.
besom ['bi:zəm], *n.* balai, *m.*
bespatter [bi'spætə], *v.t.* éclabousser, couvrir de boue.
bespeak [bi'spi:k], *v.t. irr.* (*conjug. like* SPEAK) commander; retenir; annoncer, dénoter, accuser.
best [best], *a.* and *n.* le meilleur, la meilleure, le mieux; ***at best***, au mieux, tout au plus; ***best man*** (*at weddings*), garçon d'honneur, *m.*; ***to do one's best***, faire de son mieux; ***to have the best of it***, avoir le dessus; ***to make the best of it***, tirer le meilleur parti; ***to the best of my belief***, autant que je sache.—*adv.* le mieux.
bestial ['bestiəl], *a.* bestial, de bête.
bestir [bi'stə:], *v.t.* remuer, mettre en mouvement.
bestow [bi'stou], *v.t.* donner, accorder.
bestrew [bi'stru:], *v.t. irr.* (*conjug. like* STREW) joncher (*de*), parsemer (*de*).
bestride [bi'straid], *v.t. irr.* (*conjug. like* STRIDE) enjamber, enfourcher (*un cheval*); être à cheval sur.
bet [bet], *n.* pari, *m.*, gageure, *f.*—*v.t., v.i.* parier.
betake [bi'teik], *v.r. irr.* (*conjug. like* TAKE) ***to betake oneself to***, se mettre à, s'en aller à, avoir recours à.
bethink [bi'θiŋk], *v.t. irr.* (*conjug. like* THINK) s'aviser (*de*); ***to bethink oneself of***, se rappeler.

Bethlehem ['beθlihem, 'beθliəm]. Bethléem, *m.*
betide [bi'taid], *v.t.* ***woe betide you***, malheur à vous.—*v.i.* arriver, advenir.
***betimes** [bi'taimz], *adv.* de bonne heure.
betoken [bi'toukn], *v.t.* annoncer, présager.
betray [bi'trei], *v.t.* trahir; tromper; révéler; faire tomber, entraîner.
betrayal [bi'treiəl], *n.* trahison, perfidie, *f.*
betrayer [bi'treiə], *n.* traître, *m.*
betroth [bi'trouð], *v.t.* fiancer.
betrothal [bi'trouðəl], *n.* fiançailles, *f.pl.*
betrothed [bi'trouðd], *a.* and *n.* fiancé, *m.* fiancée, *f.*
better ['betə], *a.* meilleur; ***to get the better of***, l'emporter sur.—*adv.* mieux; ***better late than never***, mieux vaut tard que jamais; ***better and better***, de mieux en mieux; ***for better for worse***, vaille que vaille; ***I had better***, je ferais mieux; ***so much the better !*** tant mieux!—*n.* meilleur; supérieur, *m.*—*v.t.* améliorer, avancer.
betterment ['betəmənt], *n.* amélioration, *f.*
betting ['betiŋ], *n.* paris, *m.pl.*
Betty ['beti]. Babette, *f.*
between [bi'twi:n], *prep.* entre.
betwixt** [bi'twikst], *prep.* entre; ***betwixt and between, entre les deux.
bevel ['bevəl], *a.* de biais, en biseau.—*n.* fausse équerre (*outil*), *f.*—*v.t.* tailler en biseau.—*v.i.* biaiser.
beverage ['bevəridʒ], *n.* boisson, *f.*; *breuvage, *m.*
bevy ['bevi], *n.* volée; troupe, compagnie, *f.*
bewail [bi'weil], *v.t.* pleurer, lamenter.
bewailing [bi'weiliŋ], *n.* lamentation, *f.*
beware [bi'wεə], *v.i.* se garder (*de*), prendre garde (*à*); se méfier (*de*).
bewilder [bi'wildə], *v.t.* égarer, embarrasser.
bewildering [bi'wildəriŋ], *a.* déroutant, ahurissant.
bewilderment [bi'wildəmənt], *n.* égarement, *m.*
bewitch [bi'witʃ], *v.t.* ensorceler.
bewitching [bi'witʃiŋ], *a.* enchanteur, séduisant.
beyond [bi'jɔnd], *prep.* par delà, au delà de; au-dessus de; outre, hors de.—*adv.* là-bas.—*n.* au-delà, *m.*
bias ['baiəs], *a.* and *adv.* de biais, de travers.—*n.* biais, *m.*, pente, *f.*; penchant, parti pris, préjugé, *m.*—*v.t.* décentrer (*boule*); faire pencher; prévenir; influencer.
biased ['baiəst], *a.* décentré; partial, prédisposé.
bib (1) [bib], *n.* bavette, *f.*
bib (2) [bib], *n.* tacaud (*poisson*), *m.*
Bible [baibl], *n.* Bible, *f.*
biblical ['biblikəl], *a.* biblique.
biceps ['baiseps], *n.* (*Anat.*) biceps, *m.*
bicker ['bikə], *v.i.* se quereller, se chamailler.
bickering ['bikəriŋ], *n.* bisbille, *f.*, querelles, *f.pl.*
bicycle ['baisikl], *n.* bicyclette, *f.*; (*pop.*) vélo, *m.*, bécane, *f.*
bid [bid], *v.t. irr.* ordonner, dire, commander (*de*); inviter (*à*); offrir, enchérir; ***to bid good-bye to***, dire adieu à.—*n.* enchère, *f.*
bidder ['bidə], *n.* enchérisseur, acheteur, *m.*
bidding ['bidiŋ], *n.* commandement, ordre, *m.*; invitation, prière, *f.*; enchères, *f.pl.*
bide [baid], *v.t. irr. archaic except in* ***to bide one's time***, attendre le bon moment.
biennial [bai'eniəl], *a.* biennal; (*Bot.*) bisannuel.
biennially [bai'eniəli], *adv.* tous les deux ans.
bier [biə], *n.* civière, *f.*, corbillard, *m.*
big [big], *a.* gros; grand, vaste; enceinte, grosse (*d'enfant*), pleine (*bête*); (*fig.*) fier, hautain.
bigamist ['bigəmist], *n.* bigame, *m.*, *f.*
bigamy ['bigəmi], *n.* bigamie, *f.*
bigness ['bignis], *n.* grosseur, grandeur, *f.*
bigot ['bigət], *n.* bigot, cagot, *m.*, fanatique, *m.*, *f.*
bigoted ['bigətid], *a.* bigot.
bigotry ['bigətri], *n.* bigoterie, *f.*, sectarisme, fanatisme, *m.*
bigwig ['bigwig], *n.* (*fam.*) gros bonnet, *m.*
bike [baik], *n.* (*colloq.*) vélo, *m.*, bécane, *f.*
bikini [bi'ki:ni], *n.* (*Cost.*) bikini, *m.*
bile [bail], *n.* bile, *f.*
bilge [bildʒ], *n.* (*Naut.*) sentine, *f.*; (*colloq.*) bêtises, *f.pl.*
bilge-water ['bildʒwɔ:tə], *n.* eau de la cale, *f.*
bilingual [bai'liŋgwəl], *a.* bilingue.
bilious ['biljəs], *a.* bilieux.
bill (1) [bil], *n.* bec (*d'oiseau*), *m.*
bill (2) [bil], *n.* hallebarde, *f.*
bill (3) [bil], *n.* mémoire, compte, *m.*; facture (*invoice*), note (*hôtels etc.*), addition (*restaurants*); (*Comm.*) note, *f.*; billet, effet, *m.*; (*Banking*) lettre de change, *f.*; (*Parl.*) projet de loi, *m.*; affiche, *f.*, placard, *m.*; ***bill of fare***, menu, *m.*, carte, *f.*, ***bill of health***, patente de santé, *f.*; ***stick no bills !*** défense d'afficher!
billet ['bilit], *n.* bûche, *f.*; (*Mil.*) billet de logement, *m.*—*v.t.*, *v.i.* loger chez l'habitant.
bill-hook ['bilhuk], *n.* serpe, *f.*, vouge, *m.*
billiard ['biljəd], *a.* de billard.
billiard-ball ['biljədbɔ:l], *n.* bille, *f.*
billiards ['biljədz], *n.pl.* billard, *m.*; ***to play a game of billiards***, faire une partie de billard.
billiard-table ['biljədteibl], *n.* billard, *m.*
billion ['biliən], *n.* (*since 1948*) billion; (*Am.*) milliard, *m.*
billow ['bilou], *n.* grande vague, lame, *f.*—*v.i.* s'élever en vagues, rouler.
billowy ['biloui], *a.* houleux.
bill-sticker ['bilstikə], *n.* afficheur, colleur d'affiches, *m.*
billy-goat ['biligout], *n.* bouc, *m.*
bin [bin], *n.* huche, *f.*, bac; coffre, *m.*
binary ['bainəri], *a.* binaire.
bind [baind], *v.t. irr.* lier; obliger; resserrer; border (*chaussures etc.*); garrotter, serrer; rendre constipé; relier (*livres*); ***to be bound to***, être tenu de.—*n.* (*pop.*) ***that's a bind***, quelle scie!
binder ['baində], *n.* lieur; relieur, *m.*; bande, attache, *f.*
binding ['baindiŋ], *a.* obligatoire; (*Med.*) astringent.—*n.* reliure, *f.*; bandeau, galon, *m.*, bordure, *f.*
bindweed ['baindwi:d], *n.* liseron, *m.*
binge [bindʒ], *n.* (*pop.*) bombe, *f.*; ***to be on the binge***, faire la bombe.
binoculars [bi'nɔkjuləz], *n.pl.* jumelles, *f.pl.*
binomial [bai'noumiəl], *a.* (*Alg.*) binôme.
biochemist [baio'kemist], *n.* biochimiste, *m.*
biochemistry [baio'kemistri], *n.* biochimie, *f.*

biographer [bai'ɔgrəfə], *n.* biographe, *m.*
biography [bai'ɔgrəfi], *n.* biographie, *f.*
biologist [bai'ɔlədʒist], *n.* biologiste, biologue, *m.*
biology [bai'ɔlədʒi], *n.* biologie, *f.*
biped ['baiped], *n.* bipède, *m.*
birch [bə:tʃ], *n.* bouleau, *m.*; verges, *f.pl.*; ***silver birch***, bouleau blanc.—*v.t.* fouetter.
bird [bə:d], *n.* oiseau; (*fig.*) type, *m.*; (*pop.*) femme, fille, poule, *f.*; ***little bird***, oiselet, *m.*
bird-cage ['bə:dkeidʒ], *n.* cage d'oiseau, *f.*
bird-lime ['bə:dlaim], *n.* glu, *f.*
bird's-eye view ['bə:dzai'vju:], *n.* vue à vol d'oiseau, *f.*
bird's-nest ['bə:dznest], *n.* nid d'oiseau, *m.*
birth [bə:θ], *n.* naissance, *f.*; enfantement, *m.*; (*fig.*) origine, source, *f.*
birth-control ['bə:θkəntroul], *n.* limitation des naissances, *f.*
birthday ['bə:θdei], *n.* anniversaire, *m.*
birthplace ['bə:θpleis], *n.* lieu de naissance, pays natal, *m.*
birth-rate ['bə:θreit], *n.* natalité, *f.*
birthright ['bə:θrait], *n.* droit d'aînesse, *m.*
Biscay ['biskei]. la Biscaye, *f.*; ***the Bay of Biscay***, le Golfe de Gascogne, *m.*
biscuit ['biskit], *n.* biscuit, *m.*
bisect [bai'sekt], *v.t.* couper en deux.
bishop ['biʃəp], *n.* évêque; (*Chess*) fou, *m.*
bishopric ['biʃəprik], *n.* évêché, *m.*
bit (1) [bit], *n.* morceau, *m.*; pièce (*de monnaie*), *f.*; (*colloq.*) brin, bout, peu, *m.*; mèche (*outil*); (*Naut.*) bitte, *f.*; mors (*de bride*), *m.*
bit (2) [bit], *past* [BITE].
bitch [bitʃ], *n.* chienne; femelle (*in compounds*), *f.*
bite [bait], *n.* morsure; piqûre, *f.*; coup de dent, *m.*, bouchée; (*Fishing*) touche, *f.*—*v.t. irr.* mordre; piquer; ronger; (*fig.*) attraper, pincer, couper (*vent*).—*v.i.* mordre.
biting ['baitiŋ], *a.* mordant, piquant; coupant (*vent*).
bitter ['bitə], *a.* amer, acerbe; (*fig.*) acharné, mordant, aigre.—*n.* amer, *m.*
bitterly ['bitəli], *adv.* avec amertume; amèrement.
bittern ['bitə:n], *n.* butor, *m.*
bitterness ['bitənis], *n.* amertume, aigreur, âpreté, *f.*
bitumen [bi'tju:mən], *n.* bitume, *m.*
bivouac ['bivuæk], *n.* bivouac, *m.*—*v.i.* bivouaquer.
blab [blæb], *v.i.* jaser, bavarder.—*n.* bavard, *m.*
black [blæk], *a.* noir; (*fig.*) obscur, sombre, triste.—*v.t.* noircir; cirer (*chaussures*).—*n.* noir, *m.*
black-ball ['blækbɔ:l] *n.* boule noire, *f.*—*v.t.* rejeter au scrutin.
black-beetle ['blæk'bi:tl], *n.* cafard, *m.*, blatte, *f.*
blackberry ['blækbəri], *n.* mûre (sauvage), *f.*
blackbird ['blækbə:d], *n.* merle, *m.*
blackboard ['blækbɔ:d], *n.* tableau noir, *m.*
black-currant ['blæk'kʌrənt], *n.* cassis, *m.*
blacken ['blækən], *v.t.*, *v.i.* noircir.
blackguard ['blægɑ:d], *n.* polisson, gredin, vaurien, *m.*
blacking ['blækiŋ], *n.* cirage (*chaussures*); noircissement, *m.*
blackish ['blækiʃ], *a.* noirâtre.
blacklead [blæk'led], *n.* mine de plomb, *f.*
blackleg ['blækleg], *n.* (*Gambling*) escroc; (*Strikes*) renard, jaune, *m.*
blackmail ['blækmeil], *n.* chantage, *m.*—*v.t.* faire chanter.
blackmailer ['blækmeilə], *n.* maître-chanteur, *m.*
black-market [blæk'mɑ:kit], *n.* marché noir, *m.*
blackness ['blæknis], *n.* noirceur, *f.*
black-out ['blækaut], *n.* extinction des lumières, *f.*; black-out, *m.*
blacksmith ['blæksmiθ], *n.* forgeron, *m.*
bladder ['blædə], *n.* vessie; (*Bot.*) vésicule, *f.*
blade [bleid], *n.* lame (*de couteau etc.*), *f.*; brin (*d'herbe*), *m.*; pelle (*d'un aviron*); pale (*d'hélice*), *f.*; (*fig.*) gaillard (*personne*), *m.*
blain [blein], *n.* pustule, *f.*
blame [bleim], *n.* blâme, *m.*; faute, *f.*—*v.t.* blâmer, s'en prendre à; censurer, reprocher.
blameless ['bleimlis], *a.* innocent, sans tache.
blanch [blɑ:ntʃ], *v.t.* blanchir; pâlir; faire pâlir; monder (*amandes*).—*v.i.* blanchir; pâlir.
blancmange [blə'mɔnʒ], *n.* blanc-manger, *m.*
bland [blænd], *a.* doux, aimable, affable.
blandish ['blændiʃ], *v.t.* caresser, flatter, cajoler.
blandishment ['blændiʃmənt], *n.* flatterie, *f.*
blank [blæŋk], *a.* blanc, en blanc; (*fig.*) vide, confus, déconcerté.—*n.* blanc; (*Lotteries*) billet blanc; (*fig.*) vide, *m.*, lacune, *f.*
blanket ['blæŋkit], *n.* couverture, *f.*
blare [blɛə], *v.t.* faire retentir.—*v.i.* sonner (*comme une trompette*), cuivrer.—*n.* sonnerie, *f.*
blaspheme [blæs'fi:m], *v.t.*, *v.i.* blasphémer.
blasphemer [blæs'fi:mə], *n.* blasphémateur, *m.*
blasphemous ['blæsfəməs], *a.* blasphématoire.
blasphemy ['blæsfəmi], *n.* blasphème, *m.*
blast [blɑ:st], *n.* vent, coup de vent; son (*d'un instrument à vent*), *m.*; explosion, *f.*—*v.t.* flétrir, brûler; détruire, ruiner; faire sauter.—*int.* sacrebleu!
blast-furnace ['blɑ:stfə:nis], *n.* haut fourneau, *m.*
blasting ['blɑ:stiŋ], *a.* destructeur.—*n.* coup de mine, *m.*, explosion, *f.*
blatant ['bleitənt], *a.* bruyant, criard.
blatantly ['bleitəntli], *adv.* avec une vulgarité criarde.
blaze (1) [bleiz], *n.* flamme; flambée, *f.*; feu; (*fig.*) éclat, *m.*; étoile (*de cheval*), *f.*—*v.t.* ***to blaze a trail***, se frayer un chemin.—*v.i.* être en flammes; flamber, brûler.
blaze (2) [bleiz], **blazon** (1) ['bleizən], *v.t.* proclamer; ***to blaze abroad***, répandre, crier par-dessus les toits.
blazing ['bleiziŋ], *a.* flambant; enflammé, embrasé; (*fig.*) brillant.
blazon (2) ['bleizən], *n.* blason, *m.*—*v.t.* blasonner.
bleach [bli:tʃ], *v.t.*, *v.i.* blanchir; (*Hairdressing*) oxygéner.—*n.* agent de blanchiment, *m.*, eau de javel; (*Hairdressing*) oxygénée, *f.*
bleak [bli:k], *a.* ouvert, sans abri; froid; désert; triste, morne.
bleakness ['bli:knis], *n.* exposition découverte, *f.*; froid, *m.*; tristesse, *f.*; aspect morne, *m.*
blear [bliə], **bleary** ['bliəri], *a.* larmoyant.
bleat [bli:t], *v.i.* bêler.—*n.* bêlement, *m.*

bleed [bli:d], *v.t. irr.* saigner; (*colloq.*) débourser.—*v.i.* saigner; pleurer (*vignes etc.*).
bleeding ['bli:diŋ], *a.* saignant.—*n.* saignement, *m.*; (*Surg.*) saignée, *f.*
blemish ['blemiʃ], *v.t.* tacher, flétrir.—*n.* tache, flétrissure, *f.*, défaut, *m.*
blend [blend], *v.t.* mêler, mélanger; fondre.—*v.i.* se fondre, se marier (*à* ou *avec*).—*n.* mélange, *m.*
bless [bles], *v.t.* bénir; rendre heureux, réjouir.
blessed [blest, 'blesid], *a.* béni, saint; bienheureux.
blessedness ['blesidnis], *n.* béatitude, félicité, *f.*, bonheur, *m.*
blessing ['blesiŋ], *n.* bénédiction, *f.*; bonheur, bien, *m.*
blight [blait], *v.t.* flétrir (*vent*); brouir (*soleil*); (*fig.*) frustrer, détruire.—*n.* brouissure (*des fleurs et des fruits*); rouille (*du blé etc.*); (*fig.*) flétrissure, *f.*
blind [blaind], *a.* aveugle; obscur; ***blind alley***, impasse, *f.*; ***blind in one eye***, borgne; ***blind side***, côté faible, *m.*—*n.* store (*fenêtre*); abat-jour, *m.*; banne (*de boutique*); persienne (*à l'extérieur*), *f.*; (*fig.*) voile, *m.*; ***Venetian blind***, jalousie, *f.*—*v.t.* aveugler; (*fig.*) éblouir.
blindfold ['blaindfould], *v.t.* bander les yeux à.—*a.* les yeux bandés.
blindly ['blaindli], *adv.* aveuglément.
blind-man's buff ['blaindmænz'bʌf], *n.* colin-maillard, *m.*
blindness ['blaindnis], *n.* cécité, *f.*; aveuglement, *m.*
blink [bliŋk], *v.i.* clignoter, cligner des yeux; vaciller (*lumière*).—*n.* clignotement, *m.*
blinker ['bliŋkə], *n.* œillère (*de cheval*), *f.*
bliss [blis], *n.* félicité, béatitude, *f.*
blissful ['blisful], *a.* bienheureux.
blister ['blistə], *n.* ampoule, bulle; cloque (*peinture*), *f.*—*v.t.* faire venir des ampoules à.—*v.i.* se couvrir d'ampoules; se cloquer (*peinture*).
blithe [blaið], **blithesome** ['blaiðsəm], *a.* gai, joyeux.
blitz [blits], *n.* bombardement aérien (*2me guerre mondiale*), *m.*
blizzard ['blizəd], *n.* tempête de neige, *f.*
bloat [blout], *v.t.* gonfler, bouffir, enfler.
bloater ['bloutə], *n.* hareng saur, *m.*
blob [blɔb], *n.* goutte (*d'eau*), *f.*; pâté (*d'encre*), *m.*; (*fam.*) bévue, *f.*
block [blɔk], *n.* bloc, *m.*, bille, *f.*; billot; (*fig.*) obstacle, *m.*; ***block of houses***, pâté de maisons, *m.*; ***block of flats***, immeuble, *m.*—*v.t.* bloquer; ***to block up***, fermer, boucher.
blockade [blɔ'keid], *n.* blocus, *m.*—*v.t.* bloquer.
blockhead ['blɔkhed], *n.* imbécile, sot, *m.*
bloke [blouk], *n.* (*pop.*) type, *m.*
blond(e) [blɔnd], *a.* and *n.* blond, *m.*
blood [blʌd], *n.* sang, *m.*; (*fig.*) parenté, *f.*; tempérament, *m.*; race (*de cheval*), *f.*
blood-group ['blʌdgru:p], *n.* groupe sanguin, *m.*
bloodhound ['blʌdhaund], *n.* limier, *m.*
bloodless ['blʌdlis], *a.* exsangue; pâle.
bloodshed ['blʌdʃed], *n.* effusion de sang, *f.*
bloodshot ['blʌdʃɔt], *a.* injecté de sang.
bloodthirsty ['blʌdθə:sti], *a.* sanguinaire.
bloody ['blʌdi], *a.* sanglant, ensanglanté, sanguinaire.
bloom [blu:m], *n.* fleur, *f.*; duvet, velouté (*de fruit*), *m.*; (*Metal.*) loupe, *f.*—*v.i.* fleurir; (*fig.*) être éclatant.
blooming ['blu:miŋ], *a.* fleurissant; (*pop.*) sacré, satané.—*n.* floraison, *f.*
blossom ['blɔsəm], *n.* fleur, *f.*—*v.i.* fleurir; être en fleur; ***to blossom out***, s'épanouir.
blossoming ['blɔsəmiŋ], *n.* floraison, *f.*
blot [blɔt], *n.* tache, *f.*; pâté (*d'encre*), *m.*—*v.t.* tacher, salir; faire un pâté sur; sécher (*avec papier buvard*); ***to blot out***, rayer, effacer.—*v.i.* boire (*papier*).
blotch [blɔtʃ], *n.* pustule, tache, *f.*
blotchy ['blɔtʃi], *a.* tacheté.
blotting-paper ['blɔtiŋpeipə], *n.* papier buvard, *m.*
blouse [blauz], *n.* blouse; chemisette, *f.*; corsage, chemisier, *m.*
blow (1) [blou], *n.* coup, *m.*; ***to come to blows***, en venir aux mains.
blow (2) [blou], *v.t. irr.* souffler; sonner (*un instrument à vent*); faire sauter (*plomb*); ***to blow away***, chasser; ***to blow out***, éteindre (*une lumière*); faire sauter (*la cervelle*); ***to blow up***, faire sauter; gonfler (*un pneu*).—*v.i.* souffler; faire du vent; sauter (*plomb*); claquer (*ampoule électrique*); ***to blow up***, sauter, éclater.
blow (3) [blou], *v.i.* s'épanouir (*fleurs*).
blower ['blouə], *n.* souffleur; rideau de cheminée, *m.*; (*pop.*) téléphone, *f.*
blow-lamp ['bloulæmp], *n.* lampe à souder, *f.*
blubber ['blʌbə], *n.* graisse de baleine, *f.*
bludgeon ['blʌdʒən], *n.* gourdin, *m.*; trique, *f.*
blue [blu:], *a.* bleu.—*n.* bleu; azur, *m.*—*v.t.* bleuir; (*slang*) gaspiller (*argent*).
blue-bell ['blu:bel], *n.* jacinthe des prés, *f.*
blueness ['blu:nis], *n.* couleur bleue, *f.*
blue-print ['blu:print], *n.* dessin négatif; (*fam.*) bleu, projet, *m.*
bluestocking ['blu:stɔkiŋ], *n.* bas bleu, *m.*
bluff (1) [blʌf], *a.* escarpé, accore; brusque (*personne*).—*n.* à-pic, *m.*, falaise, *f.*, escarpement, *m.*
bluff (2) [blʌf], *n.* bluff (*feinte*), *m.*—*v.t.* bluffer.
bluffness ['blʌfnis], *n.* rudesse, brusquerie, *f.*
bluish ['blu:iʃ], *a.* bleuâtre.
blunder ['blʌndə], *n.* bévue, étourderie, balourdise, *f.*—*v.t.* embrouiller.—*v.i.* faire une bévue.
blunderbuss ['blʌndəbʌs], *n.* tromblon, *m.*
blunderer ['blʌndərə], *n.* maladroit, étourdi, *m.*
blundering ['blʌndəriŋ], *a.* maladroit.
blunt [blʌnt], *a.* émoussé; (*fig.*) brusque, bourru.—*v.t.* émousser, épointer; (*fig.*) amortir.
bluntly ['blʌntli], *adv.* brusquement, carrément.
bluntness ['blʌntnis], *n.* état émoussé, *m.*; brusquerie, *f.*
blur [blə:], *v.t.* tacher, barbouiller; (*fig.*) brouiller.
blurt [blə:t], *v.t.* ***to blurt out***, laisser échapper.
blush [blʌʃ], *v.i.* rougir.—*n.* rougeur, *f.*; ***at the first blush***, au premier abord.
blushing ['blʌʃiŋ], *a.* rougissant.

bluster ['blʌstə], *v.i.* tempêter, crier (*contre*), fanfaronner.—*n.* fracas, tapage, *m.*, fanfaronnade, fureur (*d'une tempête*), *f.*
blusterer ['blʌstərə], *n.* fanfaron, *m.*, bravache, *m.*, *f.*
blustering ['blʌstəriŋ], *a.* orageux; bruyant; bravache.
boa ['bouə], *n.* boa, *m.*
boar [bɔ:], *n.* verrat, *m.*; ***wild boar***, sanglier, *m.*
board [bɔ:d], *n.* planche, *f.*; écriteau, *m.*; table, pension, *f.*; conseil, *m.*, administration, *f.*; (*Bookb.*) carton; (*Tailors*) établi; (*Naut.*) bord; (*Chess*) échiquier, *m.*; ***Board of Trade***, ministère du commerce, *m.*; ***on board***, à bord.—*v.t.* planchéier; nourrir; (*Naut.*) aborder; ***to board out***, mettre en pension.—*v.i.* se mettre en pension.
boarder ['bɔ:də], *n.* pensionnaire; interne, *m.*, *f.*
boarding ['bɔ:diŋ], *n.* planchéiage, plancher, *m.*; table, pension, *f.*; (*Naut.*) abordage, *m.*
boarding-house ['bɔ:diŋhaus], *n.* pension de famille, *f.*
boarding-school ['bɔ:diŋsku:l], *n.* pensionnat, internat, *m.*
boast [boust], *v.i.* se vanter, se glorifier.—*n.* vanterie, *f.*
boaster ['boustə], *n.* vantard, *m.*
boastful ['boustful], *a.* vantard.
boat [bout], *n.* bateau, canot, *m.*, barque, *f.*
boating ['boutiŋ], *n.* canotage, *m.*
boatman ['boutmən], *n.* batelier, *m.*
boatswain, bosun [bousn], *n.* maître d'équipage, *m.*
bob [bɔb], *n.* (*Hairdressing*) perruque ronde; lentille (*d'un pendule*); secousse, *f.*; coup, *m.*, tape; petite révérence, *f.*—*v.t.* écourter (*la queue*); secouer, ballotter, balancer.—*v.i.* pendiller, osciller, s'agiter; ***to bob up***, revenir à la surface.
bobbin ['bɔbin], *n.* bobine, *f.*
bode [boud], *v.t.*, *v.i.* présager; ***to bode well*** (***ill***), être de bon (mauvais) augure.
bodice ['bɔdis], *n.* corsage, *m.*
bodiless ['bɔdilis], *a.* sans corps.
bodily ['bɔdili], *a.* corporel, matériel.—*adv.* corporellement; entièrement, en masse.
boding ['boudiŋ], *n.* présage, pressentiment, *m.*
bodkin ['bɔdkin], *n.* poinçon; passe-lacet, *m.*
body ['bɔdi], *n.* corps; fond; cœur, centre; gros (*d'une armée*), *m.*; bande, troupe; nef (*d'une église*); personne; sève (*de vin*), carrosserie (*d'un véhicule*), *f.*; corsage (*d'une robe*), *m.*
body-guard ['bɔdigɑ:d], *n.* garde du corps, *m.*
body-work ['bɔdiwə:k], *n.* carrosserie, *f.*
boffin ['bɔfin], *n.* (*fam.*) savant, inventeur, *m.*
bog [bɔg], *n.* marécage, *m.*, fondrière, *f.*; ***to get bogged down***, s'embourber.
boggle [bɔgl], *v.i.* hésiter (*à*); reculer (*devant*).
boggy ['bɔgi], *a.* marécageux.
bogie ['bougi], *n.* (*Rail.*) bogie, *m.*
bogus ['bougəs], *a.* faux, simulé.
boil (1) [bɔil], *v.t.* faire bouillir; faire cuire à l'eau.—*v.i.* bouillir; bouillonner; ***to boil over***, déborder.
boil (2) [bɔil], *n.* (*Med.*) furoncle, clou, *m.*
boiled [bɔild], *a.* bouilli, cuit à l'eau; ***a boiled egg***, un œuf à la coque.
boiler ['bɔilə], *n.* chaudière, *f.*; réservoir à eau chaude, *m.*
boiler-house ['bɔiləhaus], *n.* salle des chaudières, *f.*
boiler-maker ['bɔiləmeikə], *n.* chaudronnier, *m.*
boiler-suit ['bɔiləsju:t], *n.* bleus, *m.pl.*
boiling ['bɔiliŋ], *a.* en ébullition.—*n.* bouillonnement, *m.*
boisterous ['bɔistərəs], *a.* orageux, violent; bruyant, turbulent.
boisterously ['bɔistərəsli], *adv.* impétueusement; violemment; bruyamment.
boisterousness ['bɔistərəsnis], *n.* impétuosité, turbulence; violence, *f.*
bold [bould], *a.* hardi; audacieux, téméraire; impudent, effronté; saillant, net.
bold-faced ['bouldfeist], *a.* impudent, effronté.
boldly ['bouldli], *adv.* hardiment, intrépidement; impudemment.
boldness ['bouldnis], *n.* hardiesse, audace; assurance, effronterie, *f.*
bole [boul], *n.* tronc, fût (*d'un arbre*), *m.*
Bolivia [bə'liviə]. la Bolivie, *f.*
Bolivian [bə'liviən], *a.* bolivien.—*n.* Bolivien (*personne*), *m.*
bollard ['bɔləd], *n.* (*Naut.*) pieu d'amarrage, *m.*
Bolshevik ['bɔlʃivik], *a.* bolchevik.—*n.* Bolchevik, *m.*
Bolshevism ['bɔlʃivizm], *n.* bolchevisme, *m.*
bolster ['boulstə], *n.* traversin; coussin, *m.*—*v.t.* mettre un traversin sous; (*fig.*) appuyer, soutenir.
bolt [boult], *n.* verrou; pêne; (*Tech.*) boulon, *m.*, cheville, *f.*; (*fig.*) trait, *m.*, flèche; fuite, *f.*; ***thunder-bolt***, éclair, *m.*—*v.t.* verrouiller; fermer au verrou; gober, avaler (*to swallow*).—*v.i.* décamper, filer; s'emporter, s'emballer (*cheval*).
bomb [bɔm], *n.* bombe, *f.*—*v.t.* bombarder.
bombard [bɔm'bɑ:d], *v.t.* bombarder.
bombardier [bɔmbə'diə], *n.* bombardier, *m.*
bombardment [bɔm'bɑ:dmənt], *n.* bombardement, *m.*
bombast ['bɔmbæst], *n.* emphase, enflure, *f.*, boursouflage, *m.*
bombastic [bɔm'bæstik], *a.* enflé, ampoulé.
bomber ['bɔmə], *n.* avion de bombardement, *m.*
bombing ['bɔmiŋ], *n.* bombardement, *m.*
bona fide [bounə'faidi], *a.* sérieux, de bonne foi.
bond [bɔnd], *n.* lien, *m.*; liaison, *f.*; engagement, *m.*; obligation, *f.*; (*Fin.*) bon, *m.*; ***in bonds***, dans les fers.—*v.t.* entreposer; ***bonded goods***, marchandises entreposées, *f.pl.*
bondage ['bɔndidʒ], *n.* esclavage, *m.*, servitude, *f.*
bond-holder ['bɔndhouldə], *n.* obligataire, *m.*, *f.*, porteur d'obligation, *m.*
bondman ['bɔndmən], **bondsman** ['bɔndzmən], *n.* (*pl.* **-men** [men]) serf, esclave, *m.*
bondwoman ['bɔndwumən], **bondswoman** ['bɔndzwumən], *n.* (*pl.* **-women** [wimin]) esclave, *f.*
bone [boun], *n.* os, *m.*; arête (*de poisson*); baleine (*whale bone*); ivoire (*des dents*), *f.*; (*pl.*) ossements, *m.pl.*; ***bone of contention***, pomme de discorde, *f.*—*v.t.* désosser.

bonfire ['bɔnfaiə], *n.* feu de joie *ou* de jardin, *m.*
bonnet ['bɔnit], *n.* chapeau (*de femme*); bonnet (*d'un Écossais*); (*Motor.*) capot, *m.*
bonny ['bɔni], *a.* gentil, joli, joyeux, gai.
bonus ['bounəs], *n.* boni, *m.*; prime, *f.*
bony ['bouni], *a.* osseux; plein d'arêtes (*poisson*).
boo [bu:], *v.t.*, *v.i.* huer.—*n.* huée, *f.*—*int.* hou!
booby ['bu:bi], *n.* nigaud, benêt, *m.*
booby-trap ['bu:bitræp], *n.* attrape-nigaud, *m.*; (*Mil.*) mine-piège, *f.*
book [buk], *n.* livre, livret; registre; bouquin (*vieux livre*), *m.*; ***exercise-book***, cahier, *m.* —*v.t.* retenir, réserver; enregistrer, inscrire.
bookbinder ['bukbaində], *n.* relieur, *m.*
bookbinding ['bukbaindiŋ], *n.* reliure, *f.*
book-case ['bukkeis], *n.* bibliothèque, *f.*
booking-office ['bukiŋɔfis], *n.* bureau d'enregistrement; guichet (*de gare etc.*), *m.*
bookish ['bukiʃ], *a.* studieux; livresque (*style*).
book-keeper ['bukki:pə], *n.* teneur de livres, *m.*
book-keeping ['bukki:piŋ], *n.* comptabilité, *f.*
booklover ['buklʌvə], *n.* bibliophile, *m.*, *f.*
bookseller ['bukselə], *n.* libraire, *m.*, *f.*
bookshelf ['bukʃelf], *n.* rayon (*de bibliothèque*), *m.*
book-shop ['bukʃɔp], (*Am.*) **book-store** ['buksto:], *n.* librairie, *f.*
book-stall ['buksto:l], *n.* (*Rail.*) bibliothèque, *f.*, étalage de livres, *m.*
boom [bu:m], *n.* (*Naut.*) bout-dehors, *m.*; chaîne (*des ports etc.*); (*Cine.*) perche, *f.*; grondement, retentissement, *m.*; (*fig.*, *Comm.*) grande (et rapide) hausse, *f.*—*v.i.* gronder, retentir; (*Comm.*) être en hausse, prospérer.
boomerang ['bu:məræŋ], *n.* boumerang, *m.*
boon (1) [bu:n], *n.* bienfait, *m.*, faveur, *f.*; bien, avantage, *m.*
boon (2) [bu:n], *a.* gai, joyeux.
boor [buə], *n.* rustre, *m.*
boorish ['buəriʃ], *a.* rustre, grossier.
boost [bu:st], *v.t.* (*Am.*) pousser (*par derrière*); lancer; (*Elec.*) survolter.
boot (1) [bu:t], *n.* chaussure, bottine, botte, *f.*; coffre (*d'auto*), *m.*
boot (2) [bu:t], *n.* (*used only in*) ***to boot***, en sus, par-dessus le marché.
booth [bu:ð], *n.* baraque, tente; cabine, *f.*
booty ['bu:ti], *n.* butin, *m.*
borax ['bo:ræks], *n.* borax, *m.*
border ['bo:də], *n.* bord, *m.*; bordure (*de vêtement etc.*); frontière (*d'un pays*), *f.*; (*Gard.*) parterre, *m.*, platebande, *f.*—*v.t.* border.—*v.i.* aboutir, toucher (*à*); avoisiner.
bordering ['bo:dəriŋ], *a.* contigu, voisin.
border-line ['bo:dəlain], *a.* indéterminé.—*n.* ligne de démarcation, *f.*
bore (1) [bo:], *v.t.* percer, forer; sonder, creuser; (*fig.*) ennuyer, embêter.—*v.i.* percer.—*n.* trou; calibre; (*fig.*) fâcheux (*personne*); ennui (*chose*); mascaret (*d'un fleuve*), *m.*
bore (2) [bo:], *past* [BEAR].
boredom ['bo:dəm], *n.* ennui, *m.*
born [bo:n], *a.* né; ***to be born***, naître.
borough ['bʌrə], *n.* bourg, *m.*, ville, *f.*
borrow ['bɔrou], *v.t.* emprunter (*à*).
borrower ['bɔrouə], *n.* emprunteur, *m.*
bosh [bɔʃ], *n.* blague, farce, *f.*, bêtises, *f.pl.* galimatias, *m.*
bosom ['buzəm], *n.* sein; (*fig.*) cœur, *m.*
boss (1) [bɔs], *n.* bosse, *f.*; moyeu (*d'une roue*), *m.*
boss (2) [bɔs], *n.* patron, chef, contremaître, *m.*—*v.t.* diriger, contrôler; régenter.
bosun [BOATSWAIN].
botanic [bə'tænik], **botanical** [bə'tænikəl], *a.* botanique.
botanist ['bɔtənist], *n.* botaniste, *m.*, *f.*
botany ['bɔtəni], *n.* botanique, *f.*
botch [bɔtʃ], *n.* pustule, *f.*; (*fig.*) ravaudage, replâtrage, travail mal fait, *m.*—*v.t.* ravauder, replâtrer, saboter.
both [bouθ], *a.* and *pron.* tous les deux, tous deux, l'un et l'autre.—*conj.* tant, à la fois.
bother ['bɔðə], *v.t.* ennuyer, tracasser; (*colloq.*) embêter.—*n.* ennui, tracas, embêtement, *m.*
bottle [bɔtl], *n.* bouteille, *f.*; flacon; biberon (*d'enfant*), *m.*; botte (*de foin*), *f.*; ***hot water bottle***, bouillotte, *f.*—*v.t.* mettre en bouteille.
bottle-neck ['bɔtlnek], *n.* goulot; embouteillage (*de circulation routière*), *m.*
bottling ['bɔtliŋ], *n.* mise en bouteilles, *f.*
bottom ['bɔtəm], *n.* fond; bas; dessous, pied; derrière, *m.*; base; (*Naut.*) carène, *f.*
bottomless ['bɔtəmlis], *a.* sans fond.
boudoir ['bu:dwa:], *n.* boudoir, *m.*
bough [bau], *n.* branche, *f.*, rameau, *m.*
boulder ['bouldə], *n.* grosse pierre, *f.* bloc, *m.*
bounce [bauns], *v.i.* sauter, (re)bondir; se vanter, poser.—*n.* saut, (re)bond, *m.*; vanterie, *f.*
bouncer ['baunsə], *n.* fanfaron, hâbleur, vantard, *m.*
bound (1) [baund], *n.* bond, saut *m.*—*v.i.* bondir, sauter.
bound (2) [baund], *n.* borne, limite, *f.*—*v.t.* borner, limiter.
bound (3) [baund], *a.* (*Naut.*) allant (*à*), en partance (*pour*).
bound (4) [baund], *past* and *p.p.* [BIND].
boundary ['baundri], *n.* limite, borne, frontière, *f.*
bounden ['baundən], *a.* obligatoire, impérieux.
boundless ['baundlis], *a.* sans bornes; illimité.
bounteous ['bauntiəs], **bountiful** ['bauntiful], *a.* libéral, généreux; abondant.
bounty ['baunti], *n.* bonté, générosité, libéralité, *f.*; don, *m.*
bouquet [bu'kei], *n.* bouquet, *m.*
bourne, bourn [bo:n], *n.* borne, frontière, limite, *f.*; terme, but, *m.*
bout [baut], *n.* tour, *m.*, partie, *f.*; accès, *m.*, crise, *f.*
bovine ['bouvain], *a.* bovin.
bow (1) [bau], *v.t.* courber, plier, fléchir, incliner.—*v.i.* se courber, s'incliner; saluer; se soumettre (*à*).—*n.* salut, *m.*, révérence, *f.*
bow (2) [bau], *n.* (*Naut.*) avant, bossoir, *m.*
bow (3) [bou], *n.* arc; archet (*de violon*); nœud (*rubans*), *m.*
bowels ['bauəlz], *n.pl.* entrailles, *f.pl.*, intestins, boyaux, *m.pl.*; (*fig.*); compassion, *f.*
bower ['bauə], *n.* berceau de verdure, *m.*, tonnelle, *f.*

bowl [boul], *n.* bol, vase, *m.*, coupe; jatte, *f.*; fourneau (*d'une pipe*), *m.*; boule (*sphère*), *f.*; (*pl.*) boules, *f.pl.*; ***to play (at) bowls***, jouer aux boules.—*v.t.* rouler, faire rouler; (*Cricket*) lancer, bôler.
bow-legged ['bouleg(i)d], *a.* à jambes arquées, bancal.
bowler(-hat) ['boulə(hæt)], *n.* chapeau melon, *m.*
bowsprit ['bousprit], *n.* (*Naut.*) beaupré, *m.*
bow-tie ['bou'tai], *n.* nœud carré, *m.*
bow-window ['bou'windou], *n.* fenêtre en saillie, *f.*
box (1) [bɔks], *n.* boîte, *f.*; coffret (*petit*); coffre (*grand*), *m.*, caisse; malle; (*Theat.*) loge, *f.*; buis (*arbre*), *m.*—*v.t.* enfermer dans une boîte, emboîter, encaisser.
box (2) [bɔks], *v.t.* souffleter, gifler.—*v.i.* boxer.—*n.* soufflet, *m.*, gifle, *f.*
boxer ['bɔksə], *n.* boxeur, pugiliste, *m.*
boxing ['bɔksiŋ], *n.* la boxe, *f.*
box-office ['bɔksɔfis], *n.* (*Theat.*) bureau de location, *m.*
boy [bɔi], *n.* garçon, petit garçon; fils, *m.*
boycott ['bɔikɔt], *v.t.* boycotter.
boycotting ['bɔikɔtiŋ], *n.* boycottage, *m.*
boyhood ['bɔihud], *n.* enfance, adolescence, *f.*
boyish ['bɔiiʃ], *a.* puéril; d'enfant, enfantin.
boy scout ['bɔi'skaut], *n.* (jeune) éclaireur, scout, *m.*
bra [brɑ:], (*pop.*) [BRASSIÈRE].
brace [breis], *n.* couple (*gibier*); paire (*pistolets*), *f.*; vilebrequin (*outil*), *m.*; (*pl.*) bretelles, *f.pl.*—*v.t.* lier, serrer, attacher; (*fig.*) fortifier.
bracelet ['breislit], *n.* bracelet, *m.*
bracing ['breisiŋ], *a.* fortifiant, tonifiant.
bracken ['brækən], *n.* fougère, *f.*
bracket ['brækit], *n.* console, applique, *f.*, tasseau, *m.*; accolade, *f.*; bras (*pour une lampe etc.*), *m.*; (*Print.*) parenthèse, *f.*
brackish ['brækiʃ], *a.* saumâtre.
bradawl ['brædɔ:l], *n.* poinçon, *m.*
brag [bræg], *v.i.* se vanter.—*n.* fanfaronnade, vanterie, *f.*
braggart ['brægət], *n.* fanfaron, *m.*
braid [breid], *n.* tresse; soutache, ganse, *f.*; lacet; galon, *m.*—*v.t.* tresser, natter, soutacher.
braille [breil], *n.* braille, *m.*
brain [brein], *n.* cerveau (*organe*), *m.*; cervelle (*substance*), *f.*; (*fig.*) jugement, esprit, *m.*; tête, *f.*
brainless ['breinlis], *a.* sans cervelle; stupide.
brainy ['breini], *a.* intelligent.
braise [breiz], *v.t.* braiser.
brake (1) [breik], *n.* fourré, hallier, *m.*, fougère (*thicket*), *f.*
brake (2) [breik], *n.* frein; *m.*; ***to put on the brake***, serrer le frein.—*v.t.*, *v.i.* freiner.
braking ['breikiŋ], *n.* freinage, *m.*
bramble [bræmbl], *n.* ronce, *f.*
bran [bræn], *n.* son, *m.*
branch [brɑ:ntʃ], *n.* branche, *f.*, rameau, *m.*; succursale (*d'une banque etc.*), *f.*—*v.i.* ***to branch off***, s'embrancher, bifurquer; ***to branch out***, se ramifier.
brand [brænd], *n.* brandon, tison; fer chaud, stigmate, *m.*; flétrissure (*d' infamie*); (*Comm.*) marque, *f.*—*v.t.* marquer au fer chaud; flétrir; (*fig.*) stigmatiser (*de*).
brandish ['brændiʃ], *v.t.* brandir.
brand-new ['brænd'nju:], *a.* tout (flambant) neuf.
brandy ['brændi], *n.* eau-de-vie, *f.*, cognac, *m.*
brash [bræʃ], *a.* effronté, présomptueux.
brass [brɑ:s], *n.* cuivre jaune, laiton; (*fig.*) toupet, *m.*, effronterie, *f.*
brassière ['bræsjɛə], *n.* soutien-gorge, *m.*
brat [bræt], *n.* marmot, bambin, *m.*
bravado [brə'vɑ:dou], *n.* bravade, *f.*
brave [breiv], *a.* courageux, brave, vaillant; (*fig.*) fameux, excellent.—*v.t.* braver, défier.
bravely ['breivli], *adv.* courageusement, bravement.
bravery ['breivəri], *n.* bravoure, *f.*, courage, *m.*
brawl [brɔ:l], *n.* dispute, rixe, querelle, *f.*; bruit, tapage, *m.*—*v.i.* brailler, disputer.
brawler ['brɔ:lə], *n.* tapageur; braillard, querelleur, *m.*
brawn [brɔ:n], *n.* pâté de cochon, fromage de tête, *m.*; (*fig.*) muscles, *m.pl.*
brawny ['brɔ:ni], *a.* charnu, musculeux.
bray (1) [brei], *v.t.* broyer, piler.
bray (2) [brei], *v.i.* braire (*ânes etc.*); (*fig.*) résonner.—*n.* braiment, *m.*
brazen ['breizən], *a.* d'airain; (*fig.*) effronté, impudent.—*v.t.* ***to brazen it out***, payer d'effronterie.
brazen-faced ['breizənfeist], *a.* à front d'airain; effronté.
brazier ['breiziə], *n.* chaudronnier, *m.*
Brazil [brə'zil]. le Brésil, *m.*
Brazilian [brə'ziljən], *a.* brésilien.—*n.* Brésilien (*personne*), *m.*
brazil-nut [brə'zilnʌt], *n.* noix du Brésil, *f.*
breach [bri:tʃ], *n.* brèche, rupture; (*fig.*) violation, infraction, *f.*—*v.t.* battre en brèche.
bread [bred], *n.* pain, *m.*; ***brown bread***, pain bis; ***stale bread***, pain rassis.
breadcrumb ['bredkrʌm], *n.* miette, *f.*; (*pl.*) (*Cook.*) chapelure, *f.*, gratin, *m.*
breadth [bredθ], *n.* largeur, *f.*
bread-winner ['bredwinə], *n.* soutien de famille, *m.*
break [breik], *v.t. irr.* casser; briser; rompre; violer, enfreindre; ruiner; défricher (*terrain inculte*); (*fig.*) faire part de, communiquer (*une nouvelle*); amortir (*un choc*); ***to break through the sound barrier***, franchir le mur du son.—*v.i.* se casser, se briser, se rompre, casser, rompre; éclater (*tempête etc.*); (*Comm.*) faire faillite; poindre (*jour*); changer (*temps*); ***to break away***, se détacher; (*Mil.*) rompre les rangs; (*Box.*) cesser le corps-à-corps; ***to break down***, s'abattre, se délabrer, s'effondrer, s'écrouler; (*Motor.*) tomber en panne; défaillir, s'altérer (*santé*); fondre en larmes; ***to break in***, envahir, pénétrer, entrer dans; ***to break into***, entamer; éclater en; ***to break loose***, s'échapper, s'évader, (*fig.*) s'émanciper; ***to break off***, rompre, s'arrêter; ***to break out***, éclater, se déclarer (*maladie*), jaillir, paraître, s'échapper; ***to break up***, se disperser; entrer en vacances; ***to break with***, rompre avec.—*n.* rupture, brisure, fracture; trouée, fente; (*fig.*) interruption, *f.*; changement (*de temps*); arrêt (*dans un voyage*), *m.*; (*Sch.*) récréation, *f.*; ***break of day***, point du jour *m.*

breakage ['breikidʒ], *n.* rupture, cassure; (*Comm.*) casse, *f.*

breakdown ['breikdaun], *n.* (*Motor., Mech.*) panne; (*fig.*) débâcle, *f.*; ***nervous breakdown***, dépression nerveuse, *f.*

breaker ['breikə], *n.* infracteur, briseur; violateur; brisant (*mer*), *m.*

breakfast ['brekfəst], *n.* petit déjeuner, *m.*—*v.i.* prendre le petit déjeuner.

breakwater ['breikwɔːtə], *n.* brise-lames, *m.*, digue, jetée, *f.*

bream [briːm], *n.* (*Ichth.*) brème, *f.*

breast [brest], *n.* sein, *m.*, poitrine, *f.*; (*fig.*) cœur, *m.*, âme, conscience, *f.*; poitrail (*d'un cheval*), *m.*

breastplate ['brestpleit], *n.* cuirasse, *f.*

breath [breθ], *n.* haleine, respiration, *f.*, souffle, *m.*; (*fig.*) vie, existence, *f.*; ***to be out of breath***, être hors d'haleine *ou* tout essoufflé.

breathe [briːð], *v.t.* respirer, souffler; ***to breathe in***, aspirer; ***to breathe one's last***, rendre le dernier soupir; ***to breathe out***, exhaler.—*v.i.* respirer; souffler, reprendre haleine.

breathing-space ['briːðiŋ'speis], *n.* temps de respirer, relâche, répit, *m.*

breathless ['breθlis], *a.* hors d'haleine, essoufflé, haletant.

breech [briːtʃ], *n.* culasse (*fusil*), *f.*—*v.t.* culotter.

breeches ['britʃiz], *n.pl.* culotte, *f.*

breed [briːd], *v.t. irr.* élever; faire naître.—*v.i.* multiplier, se reproduire.—*n.* race, *f.*

breeder ['briːdə], *n.* éleveur, *m.*

breeding ['briːdiŋ], *n.* élevage (*de bestiaux etc.*), *m.*; reproduction; éducation, *f.*; ***good breeding***, politesse, *f.*, savoir-vivre, *m.*

breeze [briːz], *n.* (forte) brise, *f.*, vent assez fort, *m.*

breezy ['briːzi], *a.* frais; jovial.

brevity ['breviti], *n.* brièveté, concision, *f.*

brew [bruː], *v.t.* brasser; faire une infusion; (*fig.*) tramer, machiner.—*v.i.* faire de la bière; (*fig.*) se préparer, se tramer, couver.

brewer ['bruːə], *n.* brasseur, *m.*

brewery ['bruːəri], *n.* brasserie, *f.*

bribe [braib], *n.* présent (*dans le but de corrompre*); pot-de-vin, *m.*—*v.t.* gagner, corrompre, acheter.

bribery ['braibəri], *n.* corruption, *f.*

brick [brik], *a.* de briques, en briques.—*n.* brique, *f.*; (*fig.*) brave garçon, bon enfant, *m.*

brickbat ['brikbæt], *n.* briqueton, *m.*

brick-kiln ['brikkiln], *n.* four à briques, *m.*

bricklayer ['brikleiə], *n.* maçon, *m.*

bridal [braidl], *a.* nuptial, de noces.—*n.* fête nuptiale, noce, *f.*

bride [braid], *n.* nouvelle mariée, mariée, *f.*

bridegroom ['braidgruːm], *n.* nouveau marié, *m.*

bridesmaid ['braidzmeid], *n.* demoiselle d'honneur, *f.*

bridge [bridʒ], *n.* pont, *m.*; passerelle (*de navire etc.*), *f.*; chevalet (*d'instrument à cordes*); dos (*du nez*); (*Cards*) bridge, *m.*—*v.t.* jeter un pont sur; (*fig.*) combler (*une lacune*).

bridge-head ['bridʒhed], *n.* tête de pont, *f.*, point d'appui, *m.*

Bridget ['bridʒit]. Brigitte, *f.*

bridle [braidl], *n.* bride, *f.*; (*fig.*) frein, *m.*—*v.t.* brider; (*fig.*) mettre un frein à.—*v.i.* redresser la tête, se rebiffer.

brief [briːf], *a.* bref, court; (*fig.*) concis.—*n.* abrégé; dossier, *m.*—*v.t.* confier une cause à; donner des instructions à.

brief-case ['briːfkeis], *n.* serviette, *f.*

briefly ['briːfli], *adv.* brièvement, en peu de mots.

brier ['braiə], *n.* bruyère, *f.*; églantier, *m.*; (*pl.*) ronces, *f.pl.*

brig [brig], *n.* (*Naut.*) brick, *m.*

brigade [bri'geid], *n.* brigade, *f.*

brigadier [brigə'diə], *n.* général de brigade, *m.*

brigand ['brigənd], *n.* brigand, *m.*

brigantine ['brigəntiːn], *n.* brigantin, *m.*

bright [brait], *a.* brillant; poli; clair, lumineux; éclatant, vif; (*fig.*) joyeux, intelligent.

brighten [braitn], *v.t.* faire briller; éclaircir, égayer; polir; (*fig.*) illustrer, embellir; dégourdir.—*v.i.* s'éclaircir; briller, étinceler.

brightly ['braitli], *adv.* brillamment, avec éclat.

brightness ['braitnis], *n.* brillant, *m.*; clarté, *f.*; éclat, *m.*; (*fig.*) joie, vivacité; intelligence, *f.*

brill [bril], *n.* (*Ichth.*) barbue, *f.*

brilliance ['briljəns], **brilliancy** ['briljənsi], *n.* lustre, éclat, *m.*

brilliant ['briljənt], *a.* brillant, éclatant.—*n.* brillant (*diamant*), *m.*

brilliantly ['briljəntli], *adv.* brillamment, avec éclat.

brim [brim], *n.* bord, *m.*—*v.i.* être plein jusqu'au bord; ***brimming over***, débordant.

brimful ['brimful], *a.* rempli jusqu'au bord, tout plein.

brimstone ['brimstən], *n.* soufre, *m.*

brindle(d) [brindl(d)], *a.* tacheté, bringé.

brine [brain], *n.* saumure, *f.*

bring [briŋ], *v.t. irr.* apporter (*choses*); amener (*personnes et animaux*); conduire; porter (*to carry*); transporter; réduire (*to reduce*); (*fig.*) mettre; ***to bring about***, amener, causer, opérer, provoquer; ***to bring down***, descendre, abattre; ***to bring forth***, produire, mettre au monde, mettre bas; ***to bring forward***, amener, avancer; ***to bring in***, faire entrer, rapporter; ***to bring into play***, mettre en œuvre; ***to bring off***, tirer d'affaire, sauver; conduire à bien, réussir; ***to bring on***, amener, occasionner; ***to bring to again***, faire reprendre connaissance **à**; ***to bring together***, réunir, assembler, réconcilier; ***to bring up***, nourrir, élever.

brink [briŋk], *n.* bord, *m.*

briny ['braini], *a.* saumâtre, salé; (*fig.*) amer.

brisk [brisk], *a.* vif; (*fig.*) animé, actif, gai, frais, dispos.

briskly ['briskli], *adv.* vivement.

briskness ['brisknis], *n.* vivacité; activité, *f.*

bristle [brisl], *n.* soie, *f.*; poil raide, *m.*—*v.i.* se hérisser (*de*); se raidir (*contre*).

bristling ['brisliŋ], **bristly** ['brisli], *a.* hérissé (*de*); (*Bot.*) poilu.

Britain ['britən]. la Grande-Bretagne, *f.*

Britannic [bri'tænik], *a.* (*rare*) britannique.

British ['britiʃ], *a.* britannique; ***the British***, les Anglais, les Britanniques, *m.pl.*

Brittany ['britəni]. la Bretagne, *f.*
brittle [britl], *a.* fragile, cassant.
brittleness ['britlnis], *n.* fragilité, *f.*
broach [broutʃ], *n.* broche, *f.*—*v.t.* embrocher; mettre (*un tonneau*) en perce; introduire, entamer (*un sujet*).
broad [brɔ:d], *a.* large, grand, gros, vaste; (*fig.*) libre, grossier, hardi; peu voilé (*allusion*); prononcé (*accent*).
broadcast ['brɔ:dkɑ:st], *a.* à la volée; radiodiffusé.—*v.t. irr.* semer (*du grain*) à la volée; répandre (*une nouvelle*); radiodiffuser.—*n.* émission, *f.*
broadcaster ['brɔ:dkɑ:stə], *n.* speaker, *m.*
broadcasting ['brɔ:dkɑ:stiŋ], *n.* radiodiffusion, *f.*; ***broadcasting station***, poste émetteur, *m.*
broaden [brɔ:dn], *v.t.* élargir.—*v.i.* s'élargir, s'étendre.
broadly ['brɔ:dli], *adv.* largement.
broad-minded ['brɔ:d'maindid], *a.* tolérant, à l'esprit large.
broadness ['brɔ:dnis], *n.* largeur; (*fig.*) grossièreté, *f.*
broadside ['brɔ:dsaid], *n.* (*Naut.*) côté, flanc, *m.*; bordée, *f.*
brocade [bro'keid], *n.* brocart, *m.*
brogue (1) [broug], *n.* accent irlandais, *m.*
brogue (2) [broug], *n.* brogue (*chaussure*), *f.*
broil (1) [brɔil], *n.* querelle, *f.*, tumulte, *m.*
broil (2) [brɔil], *v.t.* griller.—*v.i.* se griller.
broken ['broukən], *a.* cassé, brisé, rompu; (*fig.*) navré; entrecoupé, décousu (*discours etc.*); accidenté (*terrain*); interrompu (*sommeil*); délabré (*santé*).
broker ['broukə], *n.* courtier; brocanteur (*articles d'occasion*), *m.*; ***ship-broker***, courtier maritime; ***stockbroker***, agent de change, *m.*
brokerage ['broukəridʒ], *n.* courtage, *m.*
bromide ['broumaid], *n.* bromure, *m.*
bromine ['broumi:n, 'broumain], *n.* brome, *m.*
bronchia ['brɔŋkiə], *n.pl.* bronches, *f.pl.*
bronchial ['brɔŋkiəl], *a.* bronchial.
bronchitis [brɔŋ'kaitis], *n.* bronchite, *f.*
bronze [brɔnz], *n.* bronze, *m.*
bronzed [brɔnzd], *a.* bronzé, basané.
brooch [broutʃ], *n.* broche, *f.*
brood [bru:d], *v.i.* couver; ***to brood over***, rêver à, ruminer.—*n.* couvée, *f.*
broody ['bru:di], *a.* couveuse (*poule*); distrait (*personne*).
brook (1) [bruk], *n.* ruisseau, *m.*
brook (2) [bruk], *v.t.* (*always neg.*) souffrir; avaler, digérer.
broom [bru:m], *n.* balai; genêt (*plante*), *m.*
broth [brɔθ], *n.* bouillon, potage, *m.*
brother ['brʌðə], *n.* (*pl.* **brothers** ['brʌðəz], *rhet.* **brethren** ['breðrin]) frère, *m.*; ***brother in arms***, frère d'armes; ***foster-brother***, frère de lait.
brotherhood ['brʌðəhud], *n.* fraternité; confrérie, confraternité, *f.*
brother-in-law ['brʌðərinlɔ:], *n.* beau-frère, *m.*
brotherly ['brʌðəli], *a.* fraternel.
brow [brau], *n.* front; sourcil; (*fig.*) sommet, *m.*
browbeat ['braubi:t], *v.t. irr.* (*conjug. like* BEAT) intimider, rudoyer.
brown [braun], *a.* brun; sombre, rembruni; châtain (*chevelure*); (*Cook.*) rissolé; ***brown bread***, pain bis, *m.*; ***brown study***, rêverie, *f.*; ***brown sugar***, sucre brut, *m.*—*n.* brun, *m.*—*v.t.* brunir; (*Cook.*) rissoler, faire dorer.
brownie ['brauni], *n.* jeannette, *f.*
brownish ['brauniʃ], *a.* brunâtre.
browse [brauz], *v.i.* brouter.
bruise [bru:z], *v.t.* meurtrir, contusionner; écraser, froisser.—*n.* meurtrissure, contusion, *f.*
brunette [bru:'net], *a.* and *n.* brune, *f.*
brunt [brʌnt], *n.* choc, *m.*, violence, fureur, *f.*; ***to bear the brunt of***, faire tous les frais de.
brush [brʌʃ], *n.* brosse, *f.*; balai; pinceau, *m.*; (*fig.*) escarmouche; queue (*d'un renard*), *f.*—*v.t.* brosser; balayer; (*fig.*) effleurer, raser.
brush-maker ['brʌʃmeikə], *n.* brossier, *m.*
brushwood ['brʌʃwud], *n.* broussailles, *f.pl.*, fourré, *m.*
brusque [brusk], *a.* brusque.
Brussels [brʌslz]. Bruxelles, *f*; ***Brussels sprouts***, choux de Bruxelles, *m.pl.*
brutal [bru:tl], *a.* brutal, cruel, inhumain.
brutality [bru:'tæliti], *n.* brutalité, cruauté, *f.*
brutally ['bru:təli], *adv.* brutalement.
brute [bru:t], *a.* brut, insensible; sauvage; brutal (*animaux*).—*n.* animal, *m.*, brute, bête, *f.*, brutal, *m.*
bubble [bʌbl], *n.* bulle; (*fig.*) chimère, illusion; duperie, *f.*—*v.i.* bouillonner; pétiller (*vin*).
bubonic [bju:'bɔnik], *a.* bubonique.
buccaneer [bʌkə'niə], *n.* boucanier, flibustier, *m.*
buck [bʌk], *n.* daim; chevreuil; mâle (*lièvre* ou *lapin*); (*fig.*) gaillard, beau, élégant, *m.*
bucket ['bʌkit], *n.* seau; baquet, *m.*
buckle [bʌkl], *n.* boucle, agrafe, *f.*—*v.t.* boucler, agrafer.—*v.i.* se boucler; se courber.
buckler ['bʌklə], *n.* bouclier, *m.*
buckram ['bʌkrəm], *n.* bougran, *m.*
buckwheat ['bʌkwi:t], *n.* sarrasin, blé noir, *m.*
bucolic [bju:'kɔlik], *a.* bucolique.—*n.* poème bucolique, *m.*
bud [bʌd], *n.* bourgeon, bouton; (*fig.*) germe, *m.*—*v.t.* écussonner.—*v.i.* bourgeonner.
Buddha ['budə]. Bouddha, *m.*
Buddhism ['budizm], *n.* bouddhisme, *m.*
Buddhist ['budist], *n.* bouddhiste, *m., f.*
budge [bʌdʒ], *v.t.* bouger.—*v.i.* bouger, se remuer.
budgerigar [bʌdʒəri'gɑ:], *n.* (*Orn.*) perruche inséparable, *f.*
budget ['bʌdʒit], *n.* sac; (*Fin.*) budget, *m.*
buff [bʌf], *a.* de couleur chamois.—*n.* buffle, *m.*, peau de buffle; couleur chamois, *f.*—*v.t.* polir au buffle.
buffalo ['bʌfəlou], *n.* buffle, *m.*
buffer ['bʌfə], *n.* tampon, amortisseur, *m.*
buffet (1) ['bʌfit], *n.* buffet (*sideboard*); ['bufei], buffet, *m.*
buffet (2) ['bʌfit], *v.t.* frapper à coups de poing, souffleter.—*v.i.* se battre à coups de poing.—*n.* soufflet, coup de poing, *m.*
buffoon [bʌ'fu:n], *n.* bouffon, *m.*
buffoonery [bʌ'fu:nəri], *n.* bouffonnerie, *f.*
bug [bʌg], *n.* punaise, *f.*
bugle [bju:gl], *n.* cor de chasse; (*Mil.*) clairon, *m.*
bugler ['bju:glə], *n.* clairon, *m.*
build [bild], *v.t. irr.* bâtir, faire bâtir, construire; (*fig.*) édifier, fonder, baser.—*n.* construction; forme, carrure, taille, *f.*

builder ['bildə], *n.* constructeur, entrepreneur de maçonnerie, *m.*
building ['bildiŋ], *n.* construction, *f.*; édifice, bâtiment, *m.*; ***building society***, société immobilière, *f.*
bulb [bʌlb], *n.* bulbe, oignon, *m.*; cuvette (*de thermomètre*); poire (*en caoutchouc*); (*Elec.*) ampoule, lampe, *f.*
bulbous ['bʌlbəs], *a.* bulbeux.
Bulgaria [bʌl'gɛəriə]. la Bulgarie, *f.*
Bulgarian [bʌl'gɛəriən], *a.* bulgare.—*n.* bulgare (*langue*), *m.*; Bulgare (*personne*), *m.*, *f.*
bulge [bʌldʒ], *n.* bombement, *m.*, bosse, *f.*—*v.t.*, *v.i.* faire saillie, bomber.
bulging ['bʌldʒiŋ], *a.* bombé.
bulk [bʌlk], *n.* volume, *m.*, grosseur; masse, *f.*, gros, *m.*; (*Naut.*) charge, *f.*; ***in bulk***, en bloc, en gros.
bulkhead ['bʌlkhed], *n.* cloison étanche, *f.*
bulky ['bʌlki], *a.* gros, encombrant.
bull (1) [bul], *n.* taureau; (*St. Exch.*) haussier, *m.*
bull (2) [bul], *n.* bulle (*du Pape*), *f.*
bulldog ['buldɔg], *n.* bouledogue, *m.*
bulldozer ['buldouzə], *n.* bulldozer, *m.*
bullet ['bulit], *n.* balle, *f.*
bulletin ['bulətin], *n.* bulletin, communiqué, *m.*
bullet-proof ['bulitpru:f], *a.* à l'épreuve des balles.
bullfinch ['bulfintʃ], *n.* (*Orn.*) bouvreuil, *m.*
bullion ['buljən], *n.* or *ou* argent en lingots, *m.*
bullock ['bulək], *n.* bœuf, bouvillon, *m.*
bull's-eye ['bulzai], *n.* centre, noir (*d'une cible*); œil-de-bœuf (*fenêtre*), *m.*
bully ['buli], *n.* matamore, bravache, *m.*; brute, *f.*—*v.t.* malmener, intimider.—*v.i.* faire le matamore.
bulrush ['bulrʌʃ], *n.* (*Bot.*) jonc, *m.*
bulwark ['bulwək], *n.* rempart; (*Naut.*) pavois, *m.*
bumble-bee ['bʌmblbi:], *n.* bourdon, *m.*
bump [bʌmp], *n.* bosse, *f.*; heurt, cahot, coup, choc, *m.*—*v.t.* frapper, cogner.—*v.i.* se cogner, se heurter.
bumper ['bʌmpə], *n.* rasade, *f.*, rouge-bord; (*Motor.*) pare-choc, *m.*
bumpkin ['bʌmpkin], *n.* rustre, lourdaud, *m.*
bumpy ['bʌmpi], *a.* cahoteux (*route*).
bun [bʌn], *n.* petit pain rond au lait; chignon (*coiffure*), *m.*
bunch [bʌntʃ], *n.* botte, *f.*; bouquet, *m.*, gerbe (*de fleurs*); grappe (*de raisins*), *f.*; régime (*de bananes*); trousseau (*de clefs*), *m.*
bundle [bʌndl], *n.* paquet; ballot; faisceau; fagot (*de bois etc.*), *m.*; liasse (*de papiers*), *f.*—*v.t.* empaqueter.
bung [bʌŋ], *n.* bondon, tampon, *m.*—*v.t.* boucher.
bungalow ['bʌŋgəlou], *n.* maison sans étage, *f.*
bung-hole ['bʌŋhoul], *n.* bonde, *f.*
bungle [bʌŋgl], *v.t.* bousiller, gâcher, rater.—*v.i.* s'y prendre gauchement, faire de la mauvaise besogne.—*n.* bousillage; gâchis, *m.*
bungler ['bʌŋglə], *n.* maladroit, savetier, bousilleur, *m.*
bungling ['bʌŋgliŋ], *a.* maladroit, gauche.
bunion ['bʌnjən], *n.* oignon (*de pied*), *m.*
bunk [bʌŋk], *n.* (*Naut.*) couchette, *f.*
bunker ['bʌŋkə], *n.* soute (*à charbon*); (*Golf*) banquette, *f.*
bunting ['bʌntiŋ], *n.* étamine, *f.*; (*Orn.*) bruant, *m.*; (*fig.*) drapeaux, pavillons, *m.pl.*
buoy [bɔi], *n.* bouée, *f.*; ***life-buoy***, bouée de sauvetage; ***mooring buoy***, coffre d'amarrage, *m.*—*v.t.* ***to buoy up***, soutenir sur l'eau; (*fig.*) encourager.
buoyancy ['bɔiənsi], *n.* légèreté, *f.*; élan, *m.*; vivacité, animation, *f.*
buoyant ['bɔiənt], *a.* léger, flottant; animé, vif.
burble [bə:bl], *v.i.* murmurer, bafouiller.—*n.* murmure, *m.*
burden [bə:dn], *n.* fardeau, *m.*; charge, *f.*; poids; refrain (*d'une chanson*), *m.*—*v.t.* charger.
burdensome ['bə:dnsəm], *a.* pesant, lourd; ennuyeux.
bureau [bjuə'rou], *n.* bureau, *m.*
bureaucracy [bjuə'rɔkrəsi], *n.* bureaucratie, *f.*
bureaucrat ['bjuərokræt], *n.* bureaucrate, *m.*, *f.*
bureaucratic [bjuəro'krætik], *a.* bureaucratique.
burgess ['bə:dʒis], *n.* bourgeois, citoyen, électeur, *m.*
burgh ['bʌrə], *n.* (*Sc.*) bourg, *m.*
burglar ['bə:glə], *n.* cambrioleur, *m.*
burglary ['bə:gləri], *n.* vol avec effraction; cambriolage, *m.*
burgle [bə:gl], *v.t.*, *v.i.* cambrioler.
burgomaster ['bə:goma:stə], *n.* bourgmestre, *m.*
burial ['beriəl], *n.* enterrement, *m.*, obsèques, *f.pl.*; inhumation, *f.*
burlesque [bə:'lesk], *a.* and *n.* burlesque, *m.*—*v.t.* parodier, travestir.
burliness ['bə:linis], *n.* grosseur, corpulence, *f.*
burly ['bə:li], *a.* de forte carrure.
Burma(h) ['bə:mə]. la Birmanie, *f.*
Burmese [bə:'mi:z], *a.* birman.—*n.* birman (*langue*); Birman (*personne*), *m.*
burn [bə:n], *v.t. irr.* brûler; cuire (*briques etc.*); incendier.—*v.i.* brûler; (*fig.*) brûler, être impatient de.—*n.* brûlure, *f.*
burner ['bə:nə], *n.* brûleur; bec (*de gaz etc.*), *m.*
burning ['bə:niŋ], *a.* en feu; brûlant, ardent.—*n.* brûlure, *f.*; incendie, *m.*
burnish ['bə:niʃ], *v.t.* brunir, polir.
burrow ['bʌrou], *n.* terrier, trou, *m.*—*v.t.* creuser.—*v.i.* se terrer; (*fig.*) se cacher.
bursar ['bə:sə], *n.* économe, intendant; trésorier; boursier, *m.*
bursary ['bə:səri], *n.* bourse (*d'études*), *f.*
burst [bə:st], *v.t. irr.* crever; faire éclater; fendre; rompre.—*v.i.* crever, éclater; sauter; jaillir; s'élancer; éclore (*bourgeon*); ***to burst into tears***, fondre en larmes; ***to burst out laughing***, éclater de rire.—*n.* éclat, éclatement, *m.*, explosion; rupture, hernie, *f.*
bury ['beri], *v.t.* enterrer, ensevelir; (*fig.*) enfoncer; cacher.
bus [bʌs], *n.* autobus, *m.*
bus-conductor ['bʌskəndʌktə], *n.* receveur (d'autobus), *m.*
bush [buʃ], *n.* buisson; fourré, *m.*
bushel [buʃl], *n.* boisseau, *m.*
bushy ['buʃi], *a.* buissonneux; touffu.

busily ['bizili], *adv.* activement; avec empressement.
business ['biznis], *n.* affaire, occupation, *f.*, devoir; état, métier, *m.*; affaires, *f.pl.*, commerce, *m.*; ***what business is that of yours?*** est-ce que cela vous regarde? ***you have no business here,*** vous n'avez que faire ici.
businesslike ['biznislaik], *a.* pratique, régulier, méthodique; franc, droit, sérieux.
buskin ['bʌskin], *n.* brodequin; (*fig.*) cothurne, *m.*
bust [bʌst], *n.* (*Sculp.*) buste, *m.*; gorge (*de femme*); (*Art*) bosse, *f.*
bustard ['bʌstəd], *n.* (*Orn.*) outarde, *f.*
bustle [bʌsl], *n.* mouvement; bruit, *m.*, confusion, activité, agitation, *f.*—*v.i.* se remuer, s'empresser.
bustling ['bʌsliŋ], *a.* empressé, affairé, remuant; bruyant.
busy ['bizi], *a.* affairé, occupé, empressé, diligent.—*v.r.* ***to busy oneself,*** s'occuper.
busybody ['bizibədi], *n.* officieux, *m.*
but [bʌt], *conj.* mais, que; sauf que; qui ne; ***but that,*** sans que.—*adv.* ne . . . que; seulement; ***all but,*** presque.—*prep.* sans, excepté, à part.
butcher ['butʃə], *n.* boucher, *m.*; ***butcher's shop,*** boucherie, *f.*—*v.t.* égorger, massacrer.
butchery ['butʃəri], *n.* boucherie; tuerie, *f.*, massacre, carnage, *m.*
butler ['bʌtlə], *n.* maître d'hôtel, *m.*
butt (1) [bʌt], *n.* bout, *m.*; crosse (*d'un fusil*); masse (*d'une queue de billard*), *f.*
butt (2) [bʌt], *n.* cible, *f.*; (*fig.*) point de mire; plastron (*personne*), *m.*
butt (3) [bʌt], *n.* coup de tête, *m.*—*v.t.* cosser, frapper de la tête (*animal*).
butt (4) [bʌt], *n.* barrique, *f.*
butter ['bʌtə], *n.* beurre, *m.*—*v.t.* beurrer.
buttercup ['bʌtəkʌp], *n.* bouton d'or, *m.*
butter-dish ['bʌtədiʃ], *n.* beurrier, *m.*
butterfly ['bʌtəflai], *n.* papillon, *m.*
buttermilk ['bʌtəmilk], *n.* petit-lait, *m.*
buttery ['bʌtəri], *a.* de beurre, graisseux.—*n.* dépense, *f.*
buttock ['bʌtək], *n.* fesse; croupe (*de cheval*); culotte (*de bœuf*), *f.*
button [bʌtn], *n.* bouton, *m.*—*v.t.* boutonner. —*v.i.* se boutonner.
buttonhole ['bʌtnhoul], *n.* boutonnière, *f.*—*v.t.* accrocher (*quelqu'un*).
button-hook ['bʌtnhuk], *n.* tire-bouton, *m.*
buttress ['bʌtris], *n.* contrefort, éperon, *m.*; ***flying-buttress,*** arc-boutant, *m.*—*v.t.* arc-bouter.
buxom ['bʌksəm], *a.* plein de santé et d'entrain; rondelette et fraîche (*femme*).
buy [bai], *v.t. irr.* acheter; prendre (*billet*); corrompre, acheter (*quelqu'un*); ***to buy up,*** accaparer.
buyer ['baiə], *n.* acheteur, acquéreur, *m.*
buying ['baiiŋ], *n.* achat, *m.*
buzz [bʌz], *v.i.* bourdonner.—*n.* bourdonnement; brouhaha (*de conversation*), *m.*
buzzard ['bʌzəd], *n.* (*Orn.*) buse, *f.*
buzzer ['bʌzə], *n.* trompe, *f.*; vibreur, appel vibré, *m.*
by [bai], *prep.* par; de; à; sur; près de, auprès de, à côté de; en (*with participles*); ***by far,*** de beaucoup; ***by no means,*** nullement; ***by sight,*** de vue.—*adv.* près; passé.
by-election ['baiilekʃən], *n.* élection partielle, *f.*
bygone ['baigɔn], *a.* passé, d'autrefois.
by-law ['bailɔ:], *n.* règlement local, *m.*
by-pass ['baipɑ:s], *n.* route d'évitement, déviation, *f.*—*v.t.* contourner, éviter (*une ville*).
by-play ['baiplei], *n.* jeu de scène, jeu muet, *m.*
by-product ['baiprɔdʌkt], *n.* sous-produit, *m.*
byre ['baiə], *n.* étable à vaches, *f.*
bystander ['baistændə], *n.* spectateur, assistant, *m.*
byword ['baiwə:d], *n.* dicton, proverbe, *m.*, (*fig.*) risée, *f.*

C

C, c [si:]. troisième lettre de l'alphabet; (*Mus.*) ut, do, *m.*
cab [kæb], *n.* fiacre, taxi, *m.*
cabal [kə'bæl], *n.* cabale, *f.*—*v.i.* cabaler.
cabbage ['kæbidʒ], *n.* chou, *m.*
cabin ['kæbin], *n.* cabine, chambre (*pour officiers etc.*); (*Av.*) carlingue; cabane, case, hutte, *f.*
cabin-boy ['kæbinbɔi], *n.* mousse, *m.*
cabinet ['kæbinit], *n.* meuble à tiroirs, classeur; cabinet; ministère, *m.*
cabinet-maker ['kæbinit'meikə], *n.* ébéniste, *m.*, *f.*
cable [keibl], *n.* câble; câblogramme, *m.*—*v.t.* câbler, télégraphier.
cablegram ['keiblgræm], *n.* câblogramme, *m.*
caboose [kə'bu:s], *n.* (*Naut.*) cuisine, cambuse, *f.*; (*Am. Rail.*) fourgon, *m.*
cackle [kækl], *n.* caquet, *m.*—*v.i.* caqueter, (*fig.*) ricaner, glousser; cacarder (*oie*).
cackling ['kækliŋ], *n.* caquetage, *m.*
cactus ['kæktəs], *n.* cactus, *m.*
cad [kæd], *n.* goujat, *m.*; canaille, *f.*
cadaverous [kə'dævərəs], *a.* cadavéreux.
caddie ['kædi], *n.* (*Golf*) cadet, *m.*—*v.i.* servir de cadet.
caddy ['kædi], *n.* boîte à thé, *f.*
cadet [kə'det], *n.* cadet; élève-officier (d'une école militaire *ou* d'une école navale), *m.*
cadge [kædʒ], *v.t.*, *v.i.* colporter; quémander, écornifler.
cage [keidʒ], *n.* cage, *f.*—*v.t.* mettre en cage.
Cairo ['kaiərou]. le Caire, *m.*
cajole [kə'dʒoul], *v.t.* cajoler, enjôler.
cake [keik], *n.* gâteau, *m.*; masse, croûte (*matière solidifiée*), *f.*; ***cake of soap,*** savonnette, *f.*—*v.i.* se cailler, se prendre, se coller.
calamitous [kə'læmitəs], *a.* calamiteux, désastreux, funeste.
calamity [kə'læmiti], *n.* calamité, *f.*, désastre, malheur, *m.*
calculate ['kælkjuleit], *v.t.* calculer; adapter; (*Am.*) penser, croire.
calculation [kælkju'leiʃən], *n.* calcul, compte, *m.*

calculus ['kælkjuləs], *n.* (*Med.*) calcul; (*Math.*) calcul infinitésimal, *m.*
Caledonia [kæli'douniə]. la Calédonie, *f.*
calendar ['kæləndə], *n.* calendrier, *m.*; (*Law*) liste, *f.*
calender ['kæləndə], *n.* calandre, *f.*
calends ['kæləndz], *n.pl.* calendes, *f.pl.*
calf [kɑ:f], *n.* (*pl.* **calves** [kɑ:vz]) veau; mollet (*de la jambe*), *m.*
calibre ['kælibə], *n.* calibre; (*Tech.*) compas, *m.*
calibrate ['kælibreit], *v.t.* calibrer, graduer.
calico ['kælikou], *n.* calicot, *m.*; ***printed calico***, indienne, *f.*
California [kæli'fɔ:niə]. la Californie, *f.*
caliph ['keilif], *n.* calife, *m.*
calk [kɔ:k], *v.t.* ferrer à glace (*cheval etc.*).
call [kɔ:l], *n.* appel, cri, *m.*; voix, *f.*; (*Naut.*) sifflet, *m.*; (*fig.*) obligation, *f.*, devoir, *m.*; demande, invitation; visite, *f.*; coup de téléphone, *m.*; ***within call***, à portée de voix.—*v.t.* appeler; nommer, qualifier (*de*); convoquer; rappeler; ***to be called Peter***, s'appeler Pierre; ***to call for***, demander, exiger; aller chercher; ***to call in***, faire rentrer; ***to call in a doctor***, faire venir un médecin; ***to call off***, rappeler, rompre, décommander; ***to call out***, appeler, crier; ***to call to mind***, se rappeler; ***to call up***, faire monter; réveiller; appeler sous les drapeaux, mobiliser.—*v.i.* appeler, crier; venir *ou* aller (*chez*), rendre visite (*à*); (*Naut.*) toucher (*à*); ***to call at***, passer par, s'arrêter à; ***to call on***, inviter, prier; rendre visite à; ***to call upon***, faire appel (*à quelqu'un*).
call-box ['kɔ:lbɔks], *n.* cabine téléphonique, *f.*
call-boy ['kɔ:lbɔi], *n.* (*Theat.*) avertisseur, *m.*
caller ['kɔ:lə], *n.* visiteur, *m.*; (*Teleph.*) celui *ou* celle qui appelle, *m.*, *f.*
calling ['kɔ:liŋ], *n.* appel, *m.*; profession, vocation, *f.*, métier, état, *m.*
callipers ['kælipəz], *n.* compas de calibre, *m.*
callous ['kæləs], *a.* calleux, endurci; insensible.
callously ['kæləsli], *adv.* durement, impitoyablement.
callousness ['kæləsnis], *n.* insensibilité, *f.*, endurcissement, *m.*
callow ['kælou], *a.* sans plume; (*fig.*) jeune, novice.
call-up ['kɔ:lʌp], *n.* (*Mil.*) appel sous les drapeaux, *m.*
calm [kɑ:m], *a.* and *n.* calme, *m.*—*v.t.* calmer, apaiser.
calmly ['kɑ:mli], *adv.* avec calme, tranquillement.
calorie ['kæləri], *n.* calorie, *f.*
calumniate [kə'lʌmnieit], *v.t.* calomnier.
calumnious [kə'lʌmniəs], *a.* calomnieux.
calumny ['kæləmni], *n.* calomnie, *f.*
calvary ['kælvəri], *n.* calvaire; chemin de la croix, *m.*
calve [kɑ:v], *v.i.* vêler.
calves [CALF].
calyx ['keiliks, 'kæliks], *n.* calice, *m.*
cam [kæm], *n.* (*Mech.*) came, *f.*
camber ['kæmbə], *n.* cambrure, *f.*
Cambodia [kæm'boudiə]. le Cambodge, *m.*
Cambodian [kæm'boudiən], *a.* cambodgien. —*n.* cambodgien (*langue*); Cambodgien (*personne*), *m.*
cambric ['keimbrik], *n.* batiste, *f.*
camel ['kæməl], *n.* chameau, *m.*
camellia [kə'mi:ljə], *n.* camélia, *m.*
camel-hair ['kæməlhεə], *n.* poil de chameau, *m.*
cameo ['kæmiou], *n.* camée, *m.*
camera ['kæmərə], *n.* appareil (photographique), *m.*; ***cine-camera***, (ciné)caméra, *f.*
cameraman ['kæmərəmæn], *n.* (*pl.* **cameramen** ['kæmərəmen]) photographe (*de presse*); (*Cine. Tel.*) opérateur, cameraman, *m.*
camouflage ['kæmuflɑ:ʒ], *n.* camouflage, *m.* —*v.t.* camoufler.
camp [kæmp], *n.* camp, *m.*; ***to break up a camp***, lever un camp; ***to pitch a camp***, établir un camp.—*v.i.* camper.
campaign [kæm'pein], *n.* campagne, *f.*—*v.i.* faire campagne.
campaigner [kæm'peinə], *n.* vieux soldat, *m.*
campanile [kæmpə'ni:li], *n.* campanile, *m.*
campanula [kæm'pænjulə], *n.* (*Bot.*) campanule, *f.*
camp-bed ['kæmpbed], *n.* lit de camp, *m.*
camper ['kæmpə], *n.* campeur, *m.*
camphor ['kæmfə], *n.* camphre, *m.*
camping ['kæmpiŋ], *n.* (*Mil.*) campement; camping, *m.*; ***to go camping***, faire du camping.
can (1) [kæn], *n.* pot, broc, bidon, *m.*; boîte en fer blanc, *f.*—*v.t.* mettre en boîte.
can (2) [kæn], *v. aux. irr.* (*inf.* **to be able**) pouvoir (*to be able*); savoir (*to know how to*); ***he can read***, il sait lire; ***I can do it***, je peux *ou* je sais le faire.
Canada ['kænədə]. le Canada, *m.*
Canadian [kə'neidiən], *a.* canadien.—*n.* Canadien (*personne*), *m.*
canal [kə'næl], *n.* canal, *m.*
canary [kə'nεəri], *n.* (*Orn.*) serin, *m.*
cancel ['kænsəl], *v.t.* annuler; effacer, biffer, rayer; oblitérer (*un timbre*); décommander; (*Comm.*) résilier.
cancellation [kænsə'leiʃən], *n.* annulation; résiliation, oblitération, *f.*
cancer ['kænsə], *n.* cancer, *m.*
cancerous ['kænsərəs], *a.* cancéreux.
candelabrum [kændi'lɑ:brəm], **candelabra** [kændi'lɑ:brə], *n.* candélabre, *m.*
candid ['kændid], *a.* sincère, franc.
candidate ['kændidit], *n.* aspirant, candidat, *m.*
candidature ['kændiditʃə], *n.* candidature, *f.*
candidly ['kændidli], *adv.* franchement, de bonne foi.
candle [kændl], *n.* chandelle; bougie; (*fig.*) lumière, *f.*; (*Ch.*) cierge, *m.*
candle-grease ['kændlgri:s], *n.* suif, *m.*
Candlemas ['kændlməs]. la Chandeleur, *f.*
candlestick ['kændlstik], *n.* chandelier; bougeoir, *m.*
candour ['kændə], *n.* franchise, sincérité, bonne foi, *f.*
candy ['kændi], *n.* candi, *m.*; (*Am.*) bonbons, *m.pl.*
cane [kein], *n.* canne, *f.*; (*Agric.*) cep *m.*—*v.t.* donner des coups de canne à.
canine ['kænain, 'keinain], *a.* canin, de chien.
caning ['keiniŋ], *n.* coups de canne, *m.pl.*, râclée, *f.*

canister ['kænistə], *n.* boîte en fer blanc; boîte à thé, *f.*
canker ['kæŋkə], *n.* chancre; (*fig.*) ver rongeur; fléau, *m.*—*v.t.* ronger; (*fig.*) corrompre, empoisonner.—*v.i.* se ronger; (*fig.*) se gangrener, se corrompre.
canned [kænd], *a.* (*Am.*) conservé en boîtes (*fruits etc.*); (*fam.*) enregistré (*musique*).
cannibal ['kænibəl], *n.* cannibale, anthropophage, *m., f.*
cannibalism ['kænibəlizm], *n.* cannibalisme, *m.*
cannon ['kænən], *n.* canon; (*Billiards*) carambolage, *m.*—*v.i.* caramboler.
cannonade [kænə'neid], *n.* canonnade, *f.*
cannon-ball ['kænənbɔ:l], *n.* boulet de canon, *m.*
canoe [kə'nu:], *n.* canoë, *m.*; périssoire; pirogue, *f.*
canoeist [kə'nu:ist], *n.* canoëiste, *m., f.*
canon ['kænən], *n.* chanoine; canon (*règle*), *m.*
canonical [kə'nɔnikl], *a.* canonique.
canonization [kænənai'zeiʃən], *n.* canonisation, *f.*
canonize ['kænənaiz], *v.t.* canoniser.
can-opener ['kænoupənə], *n.* (*Am.*) ouvre-boîte, *m.*
canopy ['kænəpi], *n.* dais; (*Arch.*) baldaquin, *m.*; voûte (*du ciel*), *f.*
cant (1) [kænt], *n.* cant, langage hypocrite, *m.*; afféterie; hypocrisie, *f.*—*v.i.* parler avec afféterie *ou* avec affectation.
cant (2) [kænt], *n.* (*Arch.*) pan coupé, *m.*—*v.t.* pousser, jeter de côté, incliner.
cantankerous [kæn'tæŋkərəs], *a.* acariâtre, revêche, bourru.
cantankerousness [kæn'tæŋkərəsnis], *n.* humeur acariâtre, *f.*
cantata [kæn'tɑ:tə], *n.* cantate, *f.*
canteen [kæn'ti:n], *n.* cantine, *f.*, restaurant; bidon (*boîte*), *m.*; ***canteen of cutlery***, ménagère, *f.*
canter ['kæntə], *n.* petit galop, *m.*—*v.i.* aller au petit galop.
canticle ['kæntikl], *n.* cantique, *m.*
cantilever ['kæntili:və], *n.* (*Arch.*) encorbellement, modillon, *m.*
canto ['kæntou], *n.* chant, *m.*
canton ['kæntən], *n.* canton, *m.*
cantonment [kæn'tu:nmənt], *n.* cantonnement, *m.*
canvas ['kænvəs], *n.* toile, *f.*; tableau, *m.*, peinture; voile, toile à voiles, *f.*; ***under canvas***, sous la tente.
canvass ['kænvəs], *n.* débat, *m.*, discussion; sollicitation de suffrages, *f.*—*v.t.* agiter, discuter; solliciter.—*v.i.* solliciter des suffrages; faire la place.
canvasser ['kænvəsə], *n.* agent électoral; (*Comm.*) représentant, *m.*
canvassing ['kænvəsiŋ], *n.* propagande électorale; (*Comm.*) prospection, *f.*
canyon ['kænjən], *n.* gorge, *f.*, défilé, *m.*
cap [kæp], *n.* bonnet (*de femme*), *m.*; casquette (*d'homme*); barrette (*d'un cardinal*); capsule, amorce (*d'armes à feu*), *f.*; (*Phot.*) chapeau (*d'un objectif etc.*); capuchon (*d'un stylo*), *m.* —*v.t.* coiffer, couvrir; (*fig.*) couronner, surpasser.
capability [keipə'biliti], *n.* capacité, *f.*
capable ['keipəbl], *a.* capable; susceptible (*de*); compétent.
capacious [kə'peiʃəs], *a.* ample, vaste, spacieux.
capaciousness [kə'peiʃəsnis], *n.* capacité, étendue, *f.*
capacitate [kə'pæsiteit], *v.t.* rendre capable de.
capacity [kə'pæsiti], *n.* capacité, *f.*; ***in the capacity of***, en qualité de.
cap-à-pie [kæpə'pi:], *adv.* de pied en cap.
caparison [kə'pærizn], *n.* caparaçon, *m.*—*v.t.* caparaçonner.
cape (1) [keip], *n.* cap, promontoire, *m.*
cape (2) [keip], *n.* pèlerine, cape (*manteau*), *f.*
caper (1) ['keipə], *n.* bond, entrechat, *m.*—*v.i.* cabrioler; bondir, sauter.
caper (2) ['keipə], *n.* (*Bot.*) câpre, *f.*
capillary [kə'piləri], *a.* capillaire.
capital ['kæpitl], *a.* capital; (*colloq.*) excellent; (*Print.*) majuscule.—*n.* capital, *m.*, capitaux, *m.pl.*; capitale (*ville*), *f.*; (*Comm.*) fonds; (*Arch.*) chapiteau, *m.*; (*Print.*) majuscule, *f.*
capitalism ['kæpitəlizm], *n.* capitalisme, *m.*
capitalist ['kæpitəlist], *n.* capitaliste, *m., f.*
capitalize ['kæpitəlaiz], *v.t.* capitaliser.
capitally ['kæpitəli], *adv.* principalement; admirablement, à merveille.
capitulate [kə'pitjuleit], *v.i.* capituler.
capitulation [kəpitju'leiʃən], *n.* capitulation, *f.*
capon ['keipən], *n.* chapon, *m.*
caprice [kə'pri:s], *n.* caprice, *m.*
capricious [kə'priʃəs], *a.* capricieux.
capriciously [kə'priʃəsli], *adv.* capricieusement.
capsize [kæp'saiz], *v.t.* faire chavirer.—*v.i.* chavirer (*bateau*).
capstan ['kæpstən], *n.* cabestan, *m.*
capsule ['kæpsju:l], *n.* capsule, *f.*
captain ['kæptin], *n.* capitaine, *m.*
caption ['kæpʃən], *n.* arrestation; saisie (*choses*), *f.*; en-tête (*d'un chapitre etc.*), *m.*, légende (*d'une photographie etc.*), *f.*; (*Cine.*) sous-titre, *m.*
captious ['kæpʃəs], *a.* insidieux, chicaneur.
captiousness ['kæpʃəsnis], *n.* esprit de chicane; sophisme, *m.*
captivate ['kæptiveit], *v.t.* captiver; charmer, séduire.
captivating ['kæptiveitiŋ], *a.* enchanteur, séduisant.
captive ['kæptiv], *a.* captif.—*n.* captif, prisonnier, *m.*
captivity [kæp'tiviti], *n.* captivité, *f.*
capture ['kæptʃə], *n.* capture; prise, arrestation, *f.*—*v.t.* capturer, prendre, arrêter.
car [kɑ:], *n.* (*Motor.*) auto, voiture, *f.*; (*Rail.*) wagon; (*Lit.*) char, chariot, *m.*; nacelle (*d'un ballon*), *f.*; ***dining-car***, wagon-restaurant, *m.*; ***sleeping-car***, wagon-lit, *m.*
caramel ['kærəmel], *n.* caramel, *m.*
carat ['kærət], *n.* carat, *m.*
caravan [kærə'væn, 'kærəvæn], *n.* caravane; roulotte, *f.*
caravanserai [kærə'vænsərai], *n.* caravansérail, *m.*
caraway ['kærəwei], *n.* (*Bot.*) carvi, cumin des prés, *m.*
carbide ['kɑ:baid], *n.* carbure, *m.*
carbine ['kɑ:bain], *n.* carabine, *f.*
carbohydrate [kɑ:bou'haidreit], *n.* hydrate de carbone, *m.*

carbolic [kɑː'bɔlik], *a.* phénique.
carbon ['kɑːbən], *n.* (*Chem.*) carbone; (*Elec.*) charbon, *m.*
carbonic [kɑː'bɔnik], *a.* carbonique.
carboniferous [kɑːbə'nifərəs], *a.* carbonifère.
carboy ['kɑːbɔi], *n.* tourie, bonbonne, *f.*
carbuncle ['kɑːbʌŋkl], *n.* escarboucle, *f.*; (*Med.*) charbon, furoncle, *m.*
carburation [kɑːbju'reiʃən], *n.* carburation, *f.*
carburettor [kɑːbju'retə], *n.* carburateur, *m.*
carcase, carcass ['kɑːkəs], *n.* carcasse, *f.*; cadavre, *m.*
card [kɑːd], *n.* carte à jouer; fiche, carte; (*Manuf.*) carde, *f.*—*v.t.* carder.
cardboard ['kɑːdbɔːd], *n.* carton, *m.*
cardiac ['kɑːdiæk], *a.* cardiaque.
cardigan ['kɑːdigən], *n.* gilet de tricot, *m.*
cardinal ['kɑːdinl], *a.* cardinal, fondamental. —*n.* cardinal, *m.*
card-index ['kɑːdindeks], *n.* fichier, *m.*—*v.t.* encarter.
cardiograph ['kɑːdiogræf, -grɑːf], *n.* cardiographe, *m.*
card-sharper ['kɑːdʃɑːpə], *n.* grec, fileur de cartes, *m.*
card-table ['kɑːdteibl], *n.* table de jeu, *f.*
care [kɛə], *n.* soin; souci, *m.*, sollicitude; précaution, attention, *f.*; ***care of*** (*abbr.* **c/o**), aux bons soins de, chez; ***to take care of***, avoir soin de, s'occuper de.—*v.i.* se soucier, s'inquiéter (*de*); ***I dont care!*** cela m'est égal! je m'en moque!
career [kə'riə], *n.* carrière, course, *f.*—*v.i.* courir rapidement.
careerist [kə'riərist], *n.* arriviste, *m.*, *f.*
carefree ['kɛəfriː], *a.* libre de soucis; insouciant.
careful ['kɛəful], *a.* soigneux, attentif; prudent, économe; soucieux.
carefully ['kɛəfuli], *adv.* soigneusement, avec soin.
carefulness ['kɛəfulnis], *n.* attention, *f.*; soin, *m.*
careless ['kɛəlis], *a.* insouciant, nonchalant; négligent (*de*).
carelessly ['kɛəlisli], *adv.* nonchalamment, négligemment.
carelessness ['kɛəlisnis], *n.* insouciance, nonchalance; négligence, *f.*
caress [kə'res], *n.* caresse, *f.*—*v.t.* caresser.
caretaker ['kɛəteikə], *n.* gardien, *m.*, concierge, *m.*, *f.*
cargo ['kɑːgou], *n.* cargaison, *f.*, chargement, *m.*
cargo-boat ['kɑːgoubout], *n.* cargo, *m.*
Caribbean [kæri'biːən], *a.* antillais; ***Caribbean Sea***, la mer des Antilles, *f.*—*n.* ***the Caribbean***, les Antilles, *f.pl.*
caribou [kæri'buː], *n.* caribou, *m.*
caricature [kærikə'tjuə], *n.* caricature, charge, *f.*—*v.t.* caricaturer, faire la charge de.
carking ['kɑːkiŋ], *a.* cuisant (*souci*); rongeur.
carmine ['kɑːmain], *a.* and *n.* carmin, *m.*
carnage ['kɑːnidʒ], *n.* carnage, *m.*
carnal [kɑːnl], *a.* charnel.
carnally ['kɑːnəli], *adv.* charnellement.
carnation [kɑː'neiʃən], *n.* (*Bot.*) œillet; incarnat, *m.*, carnation (*couleur*), *f.*
carnival ['kɑːnivl], *n.* carnaval, *m.*
carnivorous [kɑː'nivərəs], *a.* carnivore, carnassier.
carol ['kærəl], *n.* chanson, *f.*, chant, *m.*; ***Christmas carol***, noël, *m.*—*v.i.* chanter.
carousal [kə'rauzəl], *n.* orgie, débauche, ripaille, *f.*; festin, *m.*
carouse [kə'rauz], *v.i.* boire, faire la fête.
carp (1) [kɑːp], *n.* (*Ichth.*) carpe, *f.*
carp (2) [kɑːp], *v.i.* critiquer, chicaner (*sur*), censurer.
car-park ['kɑːpɑːk], *n.* parc de stationnement, *m.*
carpenter ['kɑːpintə], *n.* menuisier, charpentier, *m.*
carpentry ['kɑːpintri], *n.* grosse menuiserie, charpenterie, *f.*
carpet ['kɑːpit], *n.* tapis, *m.*; ***fitted carpet***, moquette, *f.*—*v.t.* garnir de tapis, tapisser.
carpet-sweeper ['kɑːpitswiːpə], *n.* balai mécanique, *m.*
carping ['kɑːpiŋ], *a.* chicanier, pointilleux.
carpingly ['kɑːpiŋli], *adv.* en glosant; malignement.
carriage ['kæridʒ], *n.* voiture, *f.*; équipage; (*Rail.*) wagon, *m.*, voiture, *f.*; port, factage (*de paquets etc.*); affût (*de canon*), *m.*; (*Comm.*) frais de transport, *m.pl.*; (*fig.*) maintien, *m.*, tenue, démarche, *f.*
carriageway ['kæridʒwei], *n.* ***dual carriageway***, route à double circulation, *f.*
carrier ['kæriə], *n.* camionneur; porteur, messager; (*Cycl.*) porte-bagages, *m.*; ***aircraft-carrier***, porte-avions, *m.inv.*; ***carrier pigeon***, pigeon voyageur, *m.*
carrion ['kæriən], *n.* charogne, *f.*
carrion-crow ['kæriən'krou], *n.* corbeau, *m.*, corbine, *f.*
carrot ['kærət], *n.* carotte, *f.*
carry ['kæri], *v.t.* porter; emporter; rapporter (*chien*); mener, conduire, entraîner; faire voter, adopter; (*Arith.*) retenir; ***to carry away***, emporter, enlever, emmener; ***to carry off***, emporter, enlever, remporter; ***to carry on***, poursuivre, continuer; ***to carry out***, porter dehors; mettre à exécution; ***to carry through***, mener à bonne fin. —*v.i.* porter (*sons*).
cart [kɑːt], *n.* charrette, *f.*; (*Mil.*) fourgon, *m.*; carriole (*de paysan*), *f.*—*v.t.* charrier, transporter, voiturer.
cartage ['kɑːtidʒ], *n.* charriage, transport, *m.*
carte [kɑːt], *n.* carte, *f.*; menu, *m.*
carter ['kɑːtə], *n.* charretier, roulier, voiturier, *m.*
cart-horse ['kɑːthɔːs], *n.* cheval de trait, *m.*
cartilage ['kɑːtilidʒ], *n.* cartilage, *m.*
cart-load ['kɑːtloud], *n.* charretée, *f.*
carton ['kɑːtən], *n.* carton, *m.*; petite boîte en carton, *f.*
cartoon [kɑː'tuːn], *n.* carton, *m.*; (*Polit.*) caricature, *f.*; dessin humoristique; (*Cine.*) dessin animé, *m.*
cartoonist [kɑː'tuːnist], *n.* caricaturiste, *m.*, *f.*
cartridge ['kɑːtridʒ], *n.* cartouche, *f.*
cartridge-paper ['kɑːtridʒpeipə], *n.* (*Ind.*) papier à cartouche, *m.*
cartridge-pouch ['kɑːtridʒpautʃ], *n.* cartouchière, giberne, *f.*
cart-shed ['kɑːtʃed], *n.* hangar, *m.*
cartwright ['kɑːtrait], *n.* charron, *m.*
carve [kɑːv], *v.t.* sculpter, tailler; graver, ciseler; découper (*viande etc.*).

carver ['kɑːvə], *n.* découpeur; (*Art.*) sculpteur, graveur, ciseleur, *m.*
carving ['kɑːviŋ], *n.* découpage (*de viande*), *m.*; (*Art*) sculpture, gravure, ciselure, *f.*
cascade [kæs'keid], *n.* cascade, *f.*—*v.i.* tomber en cascade, cascader.
case (1) [keis], *n.* cas, état, *m.*; question; (*Law*) cause, affaire, *f.*; (*Med.*) malade, blessé, *m.*; ***in any case***, en tout cas; ***in case***, dans le cas où.
case (2) [keis], *n.* étui, fourreau, *m.*; caisse (*d'emballage*), *f.*; écrin (*à bijoux*), *m.*—*v.t.* enfermer; emballer; encaisser.
casemate ['keismeit], *n.* casemate, *f.*—*v.t.* casemater.
casement ['keismənt], *n.* châssis de fenêtre, *m.*
cash [kæʃ], *n.* argent, numéraire, *m.*; espèces (*argent*), *f.pl.*; ***cash down***, argent comptant; ***cash on delivery***, contre remboursement; ***to pay cash***, payer en espèces; ***to sell for cash***, vendre au comptant.—*v.t.* toucher, encaisser (*chèque*, *mandat-poste*); changer (*billet*); ***to cash in on***, tirer profit de, tirer parti de.
cash-book ['kæʃbuk], *n.* livre de caisse, *m.*
cash-box ['kæʃbɔks], *n.* caisse, *f.*
cash-desk ['kæʃdesk], *n.* caisse, *f.*
cashier (1) [kæ'ʃiə], *n.* caissier, *m.*
cashier (2) [kæ'ʃiə], *v.t.* (*Mil.*) casser, dégrader.
cashmere ['kæʃmiə], *n.* cachemire, *m.*
cash-register ['kæʃredʒistə], *n.* caisse enregistreuse, *f.*
cask [kɑːsk], *n.* fût, baril, *m.*, barrique, *f.*, tonneau, *m.*
casket ['kɑːskit], *n.* écrin, *m.*, cassette, *f.*
Caspian (Sea) ['kæspiən(siː)], **the.** la mer Caspienne, *f.*
cassock ['kæsək], *n.* soutane, *f.*
cast [kɑːst], *v.t. irr.* jeter; se dépouiller de (*arbre*, *animal*); (*Metal.*) couler, fondre; (*Theat.*) distribuer les rôles; ***to cast a glance at***, jeter un regard sur; ***to cast aside***, mettre de côté, rejeter; ***to cast down***, jeter par terre, abattre, décourager; ***to cast its slough***, faire peau neuve; ***to cast off***, rejeter, repousser, abandonner.—*v.i.* se jeter; se déjeter (*arbre*).—*a.* fondu.—*n.* coup, jet; moule, *m.*; (*Metal.*) fonte; (*Theat.*) distribution des rôles, *f.*; rôles, acteurs, *m.pl.*; (*fig.*) nuance, tournure, *f.*, air, caractère, *m.*; (*Sculp.*) statuette, figure, *f.*, plâtre, *m.*
castanet [kæstə'net], *n.* castagnette, *f.*
castaway ['kɑːstəwei], *a.* rejeté.—*n.* naufragé, *m.*
caste [kɑːst], *n.* caste, *f.*
castigate ['kæstigeit], *v.t.* châtier, punir; critiquer sévèrement.
castigation [kæsti'geiʃən], *n.* châtiment, *m.*, correction, discipline, *f.*
casting ['kɑːstiŋ], *n.* (*Metal.*) coulée, fonte, *f.*, moulage, *m.*; (*Theat.*) distribution des rôles, *f.*
cast-iron ['kɑːst'aiən], *a.* en fonte; (*fig.*) de fer, rigide.—*n.* fonte, *f.*
castle [kɑːsl], *n.* château, château fort, *m.*; (*Chess*) tour, *f.*; ***castles in the air***, châteaux en Espagne.
castor ['kɑːstə], *n.* roulette (*de meuble*); poivrière, *f.*; ***(pair of) castors***, huilier, *m.*
castor-oil ['kɑːstər'ɔil], *n.* huile de ricin, *f.*
castrate [kæs'treit], *v.t.* châtrer.
casual ['kæʒjuəl], *a.* fortuit, accidentel, casuel, de passage; insouciant.
casually ['kæʒjuəli], *adv.* fortuitement, par hasard; négligemment.
casualty ['kæʒjuəlti], *n.* accident; accidenté (*personne*), *m.*; (*pl.*) (*Mil.*) pertes, *f.pl.*
cat [kæt], *n.* chat; (*Mil.*, *Navy*) fouet, martinet (à neuf queues), *m.*; ***tom-cat***, matou, *m.*
catacombs ['kætəkuːmz], *n.pl.* catacombes *f.pl.*
catalepsy ['kætəlepsi], *n.* catalepsie, *f.*
catalogue ['kætəlɔg], *n.* catalogue, *m.*, liste, *f.*
catamaran [kætəmə'ræn], *n.* catamaran, *m.*
catapult ['kætəpult], *n.* catapulte, *f.*; lance-pierre (*jouet*), *m.*
cataract ['kætərækt], *n.* cataracte, *f.*
catarrh [kə'tɑː], *n.* catarrhe, *m.*
catastrophe [kə'tæstrəfi], *n.* catastrophe, *f.*, désastre, *m.*
catch [kætʃ], *v.t. irr.* attraper, prendre, saisir; (*colloq.*) pincer; frapper (*l'œil etc.*); ***to catch a cold***, s'enrhumer; ***to catch on***, avoir du succès, réussir; ***to catch up***, atteindre, rattraper.—*v.i.* s'accrocher (*à*), se prendre (*à*).—*n.* prise; attrape; (*fig.*) aubaine, belle affaire, *f.*; cliquet (*d'une roue*); crampon (*d'une porte*); mentonnet (*d'un loquet*), *m.*
catching ['kætʃiŋ], *a.* contagieux; communicatif (*rire*); facile à retenir (*air*).—*n.* prise, capture, *f.*
catechism ['kætəkizm], *n.* catéchisme, *m.*
categorical [kætə'gɔrikəl], *a.* catégorique.
categorically [kætə'gɔrikəli], *adv.* catégoriquement.
category ['kætəgəri], *n.* catégorie, *f.*
cater ['keitə], *v.i.* pourvoir (*à*).
caterer ['keitərə], *n.* pourvoyeur, fournisseur, *m.*
caterpillar ['kætəpilə], *n.* chenille, *f.*; ***caterpillar tractor***, tracteur à chenilles, *m.*
cathedral [kə'θiːdrəl], *n.* cathédrale, *f.*
catholic ['kæθəlik], *a.* universel; éclectique; catholique.
catkin ['kætkin], *n.* (*Bot.*) chaton, *m.*
cattiness ['kætinis], **cattishness** ['kætiʃnis], *n.* méchanceté, sournoiserie, *f.*
cattish ['kætiʃ], **catty** ['kæti], *a.* méchant, sournois, rosse.
cattle [kætl], *n.* bétail, *m.*, bestiaux, *m.pl.*
Caucasus ['kɔːkəsəs], **the.** le Caucase, *m.*
cauldron ['kɔːldrən], *n.* chaudron, *m.*, chaudière, *f.*
cauliflower ['kɔliflauə], *n.* chou-fleur, *m.*
caulk [kɔːk], *v.t.* calfater (*navire*).
cause [kɔːz], *n.* raison, cause, *f.*, motif, sujet, *m.*—*v.t.* causer, être cause de; occasionner, provoquer (*un accident*).
causeway ['kɔːzwei], *n.* chaussée, *f.*
caustic ['kɔːstik], *a.* caustique, corrosif; (*fig.*) mordant.
cauterize ['kɔːtəraiz], *v.t.* cautériser.
cautery ['kɔːtəri], *n.* cautère, *m.*
caution ['kɔːʃən], *n.* avis (*avertissement*), *m.*; précaution, prévoyance, prudence; caution, garantie, *f.*—*v.t.* avertir, aviser (*de*); réprimander.
cautious ['kɔːʃəs], *a.* circonspect, prudent, en garde.

cautiously ['kɔːʃəsli], *adv.* avec précaution, prudemment.
cavalcade [kævəl'keid], *n.* cavalcade, *f.*
cavalier [kævə'liə], *a.* cavalier, désinvolte.—*n.* cavalier, *m.*
cavalry ['kævəlri], *n.* cavalerie, *f.*
cave [keiv], *n.* caverne, *f.*, antre, souterrain, *m.* —*v.t.* creuser.—*v.i.* ***to cave in***, céder, s'affaisser, s'effondrer (*édifice*).
cavern ['kævən], *n.* caverne, *f.*
cavernous ['kævənəs], *a.* caverneux.
caviare [kævi'ɑː], *n.* caviar, *m.*
cavil ['kævil], *v.i.* chicaner (*sur*).
cavilling ['kæviliŋ], *a.* chicaneur.—*n.* chicanerie, *f.*
cavity ['kæviti], *n.* cavité, *f.*
cavort [kə'vɔːt], *v.i.* cabrioler.
caw [kɔː], *v.i.* croasser.
cawing ['kɔːiŋ], *n.* croassement, *m.*
cease [siːs], *v.t.* cesser; faire cesser.—*v.i.* cesser, discontinuer.
ceaseless ['siːslis], *a.* incessant, continuel.
ceaselessly ['siːslisli], *adv.* sans cesse.
Cecilia [sə'siliə]. Cécile, *f.*
cedar ['siːdə], *n.* cèdre, *m.*
cede [siːd], *v.t.*, *v.i.* (*Law*) céder.
cedilla [sə'dilə], *n.* (*Gram.*) cédille, *f.*
ceiling ['siːliŋ], *n.* plafond, *m.*
celebrate ['selibreit], *v.t.* célébrer, fêter.
celebrated ['selibreitid], *a.* célèbre, fameux.
celebration [seli'breiʃən], *n.* célébration, *f.*
celebrity [sə'lebriti], *n.* célébrité, *f.*
celerity [sə'leriti], *n.* célérité, vitesse, *f.*
celery ['seləri], *n.* céleri, *m.*
celestial [sə'lestjəl], *a.* céleste.
celibacy ['selibəsi], *n.* célibat, *m.*
celibate ['selibit], *a.* and *n.* célibataire, *m.*, *f.*
cell [sel], *n.* cellule, case; alvéole (*d'abeilles*), *f.*; compartiment; cachot; (*Elec.*) élément, *m.*, pile, *f.*
cellar ['selə], *n.* cave, *f.*; cellier, caveau, *m.*
'cello ['tʃelou], *n.* (*abbr.* of **violoncello**) violoncelle, *m.*
cellophane ['seləfein], *n.* cellophane, *f.*
celluloid ['seljulɔid], *n.* celluloïd, celluloïde, *m.*
Celt [kelt, selt], *n.* Celte, *m.*, *f.*
Celtic ['keltik, 'seltik], *a.* celtique.
cement [si'ment], *n.* ciment, *m.*—*v.t.* cimenter; (*fig.*) consolider, fortifier.
cement-mixer [si'mentmiksə], *n.* bétonnière, *f.*
cemetery ['semətri], *n.* cimetière, *m.*
cenotaph ['senotæf, -tɑːf], *n.* cénotaphe, *m.*
censer ['sensə], *n.* encensoir, *m.*
censor ['sensə], *n.* censeur, *m.*—*v.t.* soumettre à des coupures; censurer.
censorious [sen'sɔːriəs], *a.* critique, hargneux.
censorship ['sensəʃip], *n.* censure, *f.*; fonctions de censeur, *f.pl.*
censure ['senʃə], *n.* censure, critique, *f.*, blâme, *m.*—*v.t.* censurer, critiquer, blâmer.
census ['sensəs], *n.* recensement, *m.*
cent [sent], *n.* cent; sou (*pièce de monnaie*), *m.*; ***ten per cent***, dix pour cent.
centaur ['sentɔː], *n.* centaure, *m.*
centenarian [senti'nɛəriən], *n.* centenaire, *m.*, *f.*
centenary [sen'tiːnəri], *a.* and *n.* centenaire, *m.*
centennial [sen'teniəl], *a.* de cent ans, séculaire.
centesimal [sen'tesiməl], *a.* centésimal.—*n.* centième, *m.*
centigrade ['sentigreid], *a.* centigrade.
centipede ['sentipiːd], *n.* scolopendre, *f.*, mille-pattes, *m.*
central ['sentrəl], *a.* central; ***central heating***, chauffage central, *m.*
centralization [sentrəlai'zeiʃən], *n.* centralisation, *f.*
centralize ['sentrəlaiz], *v.t.* centraliser.
centre ['sentə], *n.* centre; milieu; (*fig.*) foyer, *m.*—*v.t.* placer au centre; concentrer.—*v.i.* se concentrer.
centrifugal [sen'trifjugəl], *a.* centrifuge.
centripetal [sen'tripitl], *a.* centripète.
centuple ['sentjupl], *a.* and *n.* centuple, *m.*—*v.t.* centupler.
centurion [sen'tjuəriən], *n.* centurion, (*Bibl.*) centenier, *m.*
century ['sentʃuri], *n.* siècle, *m.*
ceramic [sə'ræmik], *a.* céramique.
ceramics [sə'ræmiks], *n.pl.* céramique, *f.*
cereal ['siəriəl], *a.* and *n.* céréale, *f.*
cerebral ['serəbrəl], *a.* cérébral.
ceremonial [seri'mouniəl], *a.* de cérémonie.—*n.* cérémonie, étiquette, *f.*, cérémonial, *m.*
ceremonially [seri'mouniəli], *adv.* rituellement.
ceremonious [seri'mouniəs], *a.* cérémonieux.
ceremoniously [seri'mouniəsli], *adv.* cérémonieusement.
ceremony ['seriməni], *n.* cérémonie, solennité, *f.*; ***without ceremony***, sans façon.
cerise [sə'riːs], *a.* and *n.* cerise (*couler*), *m.*
certain ['səːtin], *a.* certain, sûr; ***he is certain to do it***, il le fera certainement; ***to make certain of something***, s'assurer de quelque chose.
certainly ['səːtinli], *adv.* certainement.
certainty ['səːtinti], *n.* certitude; chose certaine, *f.*
certificate [sə'tifikit], *n.* certificat; diplôme, brevet; concordat (*de faillite*); acte (*de naissance, de mariage* ou *de mort*), *m.*
certify ['səːtifai], *v.t.* certifier; notifier, donner avis à.
certitude ['səːtitjuːd], *n.* certitude, *f.*
cessation [se'seiʃən], *n.* cessation, suspension, *f.*
cession ['seʃən], *n.* cession, *f.*
cesspit ['sespit], **cesspool** ['sespuːl], *n.* puisard, *m.*, fosse d'aisances; (*fig.*) sentine, *f.*
Ceylon [si'lɔn]. le Ceylan, *m.*
Ceylonese [silɔ'niːz], *a.* cingalais.—*n.* Cingalais (*personne*), *m.*
chafe [tʃeif], *v.t.* échauffer, irriter; érailler (*un câble*).—*v.i.* frotter; s'user, s'érailler (*un câble*); s'irriter; s'enflammer.
chafer (1) ['tʃeifə], *n.* hanneton (*insecte*), *m.*
chafer (2) [tʃeifə], *n.* réchaud (*plat*), *m.*
chafing-dish ['tʃeifiŋdiʃ], *n.* réchaud (*de table*), *m.*
chaff [tʃɑːf], *n.* menue paille; (*colloq.*) plaisanterie, raillerie, blague, *f.*—*v.t.* blaguer, taquiner, se moquer de.
chaffinch ['tʃæfintʃ], *n.* (*Orn.*) pinson, *m.*
chagrin [ʃæ'griːn], *n.* chagrin; dépit, *m.*—*v.t.* chagriner, vexer.
chain [tʃein], *n.* chaîne; chaînée, *f.*—*v.t.* enchaîner.

chair [tʃɛə], *n.* chaise, *f.*; siège, *m.*; chaire (*à l'université*), *f.*; fauteuil (*d'un président*), *m.*; ***arm-chair***, fauteuil; ***deck-chair***, chaise longue, transat(lantique), *m.*; ***rocking-chair***, fauteuil à bascule; ***wheel-chair***, fauteuil roulant; ***to be in the chair***, présider.
chairman ['tʃɛəmən], *n.* président, *m.*
chalice ['tʃælis], *n.* calice, *m.*, coupe, *f.*
chalk [tʃɔ:k], *n.* craie, *f.*, calcaire; crayon (*pour dessiner*), *m.*—*v.t.* blanchir avec de la craie; marquer *ou* écrire à la craie.
chalk-pit ['tʃɔ:kpit], *n.* carrière de craie, *f.*
chalky ['tʃɔ:ki], *a.* crayeux, crétacé, calcaire.
challenge ['tʃælindʒ], *n.* défi, cartel, *m.*; (*fig.*) provocation, demande; (*Law*) récusation, *f.*; (*Mil.*) qui-vive; (*Spt.*) challenge, *m.*—*v.t.* défier; contester; (*Law*) récuser.
challenger ['tʃælindʒə], *n.* auteur d'un cartel; provacateur, agresseur, champion; (*Spt.*) challenger, *m.*
chamber ['tʃeimbə], *n.* chambre; salle, pièce, *f.*, cabinet, *m.*; (*Artill.*) âme, *f.*; (*pl.*) bureaux, *m.pl.*, étude, *f.*
chamberlain ['tʃeimbəlin], *n.* chambellan; camérier (*du Pape*), *m.*
chamber-maid ['tʃeimbəmeid], *n.* femme de chambre, *f.*
chamber-music ['tʃeimbəmju:zik], *n.* musique de chambre, *f.*
chameleon [kə'mi:ljən], *n.* caméléon, *m.*
chamfer ['tʃæmfə], *n.* chanfrein, *m.*—*v.t.* chanfreiner, biseauter.
chamois ['ʃæmwɑ:], *n.* chamois, *m.*
chamois-leather ['ʃæmi'leðə], *n.* chamois, *m.*, peau de chamois, *f.*
champ [tʃæmp], *v.t.* ronger, mâcher.—*v.i.* ronger son frein.
champagne [ʃæm'pein], *n.* champagne, vin de Champagne, *m.*
champion ['tʃæmpiən], *n.* champion, *m.*—*v.t.* soutenir, défendre.
championship ['tʃæmpiənʃip], *n.* championnat, *m.*
chance [tʃɑ:ns], *a.* accidentel, de hasard.—*n.* chance, *f.*, hasard, sort, *m.*; ***by chance***, par hasard; ***to stand a chance of***, avoir des chances de.—*v.t.* risquer.—*v.i.* arriver par hasard, venir à.
chancel ['tʃɑ:nsəl], *n.* sanctuaire, chœur, *m.*
chancellery ['tʃɑ:nsələri], *n.* chancellerie, *f.*
chancellor ['tʃɑ:nsələ], *n.* chancelier, *m.*
chancery ['tʃɑ:nsəri], *n.* cour de la chancellerie, *f.*
chandelier [ʃændi'liə], *n.* lustre, *m.*
chandler ['tʃɑ:ndlə], *n.* marchand *ou* fabricant de chandelles, *m.*; ***corn-chandler***, marchand de blé; ***ship-chandler***, approvisionneur de navires, *m.*
change [tʃeindʒ], *n.* changement, *m.*; phase (*de la lune*); monnaie (*espèces*), *f.*; ***change of life***, retour d'âge, *m.*; ***changes of life***, vicissitudes, *f.pl.*; ***for a change***, pour changer.—*v.t.* changer; modifier; donner la monnaie de.—*v.i.* changer (*de*); se renouveler (*la lune*); ***to change for the better***, s'améliorer.
changeable ['tʃeindʒəbl], *a.* changeant, variable, inconstant.
changer ['tʃeindʒə], *n.* changeur, *m.*
channel [tʃænl], *n.* canal; lit (*de rivière*), *m.*; passe (*de port*), *f.*; (*Naut.*) détroit, *m.*; (*fig.*) voie, *f.*, moyen, *m.*, entremise, *f.*; ***the Channel Islands***, les îles Anglo-normandes, *f.pl.*; ***the English Channel***, la Manche, *f.*—*v.t.* creuser.
chant [tʃɑ:nt], *n.* chant, plain-chant, *m.*—*v.t.*, *v.i.* chanter.
chaos ['keiɔs], *n.* chaos, *m.*
chaotic [kei'ɔtik], *a.* chaotique.
chap (1) [tʃæp], *v.t.* gercer.—*v.i.* gercer, se gercer.—*n.* gerçure, crevasse (*dans la peau etc.*), *f.*
chap (2) [tʃæp], *n.* garçon, gaillard, type, *m.*; ***old chap***, (*colloq.*) mon vieux.
chap (3) [tʃæp], **chop** (1) [tʃɔp], *n.* mâchoire, bouche; bajoue (*de cochon*), *f.*
chapel [tʃæpl], *n.* chapelle, *f.*
chaperon ['ʃæpəroun], *n.* chaperon, *m.*—*v.t.* chaperonner.
chap-fallen ['tʃæpfɔ:lən], *a.* (*fam.*) penaud, abattu, consterné.
chaplain ['tʃæplin], *n.* aumônier, *m.*
chaplet ['tʃæplit], *n.* chapelet, *m.*, guirlande, *f.*
chapter ['tʃæptə], *n.* chapitre, *m.*
chapter-house ['tʃæptəhaus], *n.* chapitre, *m.*
char (1) [tʃɑ:], *v.t.* carboniser.—*v.i.* se carboniser.
char (2) [tʃɑ:], *v.i.* faire des ménages.—*n.* (*pop. abbr. of* CHARWOMAN) femme de ménage, *f.*
character ['kæriktə], *n.* caractère; (*Theat.*) rôle, personnage; genre, *m.*, nature, qualité, réputation, *f.*; certificat (*de mœurs*); (*fig.*) personnage, type, *m.*; ***a bad character***, un mauvais sujet; ***he is quite a character***, c'est un vrai original; ***out of character***, déplacé.
characteristic [kæriktə'ristik], *a.* caractéristique.—*n.* trait caractéristique, *m.*
charade [ʃə'rɑ:d], *n.* charade, *f.*
charcoal ['tʃɑ:koul], *n.* charbon de bois, *m.*
charge [tʃɑ:dʒ], *v.t.* charger, accuser (*de*); faire payer; (*fig.*) adjurer; ordonner à.—*v.i.* (*Mil.*) charger.—*n.* charge, *f.*; prix, *m.*; garde, *f.*; soin; ordre, commandement; (*Law*) acte d'accusation, *m.*, accusation, *f.*; mandement (*d'un évêque*); résumé (*d'un juge*), *m.*; (*pl.*) frais, dépens, *m.pl.*; ***free of charge***, gratis; ***the officer in charge***, l'officier commandant, *m.*; ***to take charge of***, se charger de.
chargeable ['tʃɑ:dʒəbl], *a.* à charge (*à*); accusable (*de*).
charger ['tʃɑ:dʒə], *n.* grand plat; cheval de bataille; (*Elec.*) chargeur, *m.*
charily ['tʃɛərili], *adv.* avec précaution; frugalement.
chariot ['tʃæriət], *n.* char, chariot, *m.*
charioteer [tʃæriə'tiə], *n.* conducteur de chariot, *m.*
charitable ['tʃæritəbl], *a.* de charité; charitable.
charitably ['tʃæritəbli], *adv.* charitablement.
charity ['tʃæriti], *n.* charité, bienveillance; aumône, *f.*
charlatan ['ʃɑ:lətən], *n.* charlatan, *m.*
charm [tʃɑ:m], *n.* charme, *m.*; breloque (*trinket*), *f.*, porte-bonheur, *m. inv.*; (*pl.*) attraits, *m.pl.*—*v.t.* charmer, enchanter.
charmer ['tʃɑ:mə], *n.* enchanteur, charmeur, *m.*
charming ['tʃɑ:miŋ], *a.* enchanteur, charmant; ravissant.

charnel ['tʃɑːnəl], *a.* de charnier.
charnel-house ['tʃɑːnəlhaus], *n.* charnier, ossuaire, *m.*
chart [tʃɑːt], *n.* carte marine, *f.*—*v.t.* porter sur une carte.
charter ['tʃɑːtə], *n.* charte, *f.*, acte, *m.*; ***on charter***, loué, affrété.—*v.t.* établir par un acte; (*Comm.*) fréter, affréter; ***chartered accountant***, expert comptable, *m.*; ***charter plane***, avion-taxi, *m.*
charwoman ['tʃɑːwumən], *n.* (*pl.* **-women** [wimin]) femme de journée, femme de ménage, *f.*
chary ['tʃɛəri], *a.* prudent, économe.
chase (1) [tʃeis], *n.* chasse; poursuite, *f.*—*v.t.* chasser, poursuivre; ***to chase away***, chasser.
chase (2) [tʃeis], *v.t.* (*Metal.*) ciseler.
chasm [kæzm], *n.* abîme; chasme; vide énorme, *m.*, brèche, fissure, *f.*
chassis ['ʃæsi], *n.* (*Motor.*) châssis, *m.*
chaste [tʃeist], *a.* chaste, pudique; pur (*langage*); de bon goût.
chasten [tʃeisn], *v.t.* châtier; purifier.
chastise [tʃæs'taiz], *v.t.* châtier.
chastisement ['tʃæstizmənt], *n.* châtiment, *m.*
chastity ['tʃæstiti], *n.* chasteté, pureté, *f.*
chasuble ['tʃæzjubl], *n.* chasuble, *f.*
chat [tʃæt], *n.* causerie; (*colloq.*) causette, *f.*, entretien, *m.*—*v.i.* causer, bavarder; (*colloq.*) faire la causette.
chattel [tʃætl], *n.* bien meuble, *m.*; ***goods and chattels***, biens et effets, *m.pl.*
chatter ['tʃætə], *v.i.* jaser, bavarder; jacasser (*singes etc.*); babiller; claquer (*dents*).—*n.* caquetage, *m.*, jaserie, *f.*
chatterbox ['tʃætəbɔks], *n.* moulin à paroles, jaseur, babillard, *m.*
chattering ['tʃætəriŋ], *n.* jaserie, *f.*; claquement (*des dents*), *m.*
chatty ['tʃæti], *a.* causeur, bavard.
chauffeur ['ʃoufə, ʃou'fəː], *n.* chauffeur, *m.*
cheap [tʃiːp], *a.* (à) bon marché; peu coûteux; de peu de valeur; ***dirt cheap***, pour rien, à vil prix.
cheapen ['tʃiːpən], *v.t.* faire baisser le prix de; ***to cheapen oneself***, se déprécier.
cheaper ['tʃiːpə], *a.* (à) meilleur marché.
cheaply ['tʃiːpli], *adv.* à bon marché, à bon compte.
cheapness ['tʃiːpnis], *n.* bon marché, bas prix, *m.*
cheat [tʃiːt], *n.* fourberie, tromperie, *f.*; trompeur; (*Cards etc.*) tricheur, *m.*—*v.t.* tromper; (*Cards etc.*) tricher.
cheating ['tʃiːtiŋ], *n.* tromperie; (*Cards etc.*) tricherie, *f.*
check [tʃek], *v.t.* réprimer; arrêter; contenir; (*Comm.*) vérifier; enregistrer (*bagages etc.*); contrôler (*comptes*); (*Chess*) faire échec à.—*n.* échec, obstacle; (*Comm.*) bon; (*Am.*) [CHEQUE]; carreau, damier (*dessin*); (*Chess*) échec, *m.*
checking ['tʃekiŋ], *n.* répression, *f.*; contrôle, *m.*
checkmate ['tʃekmeit], *n.* échec et mat, *m.*—*v.t.* mettre échec et mat, mater.
cheek [tʃiːk], *n.* joue; bajoue (*cochon*); (*fig.*) impudence, *f.*, front, toupet, *m.*; ***cheek by jowl***, côte à côte.—*v.t.* narguer.
cheek-bone ['tʃiːkboun], *n.* pommette, *f.*
cheeky ['tʃiːki], *a.* impudent, effronté.
cheep [tʃiːp], *n.* piaulement, *m.*—*v.i.* piauler.
cheer [tʃiə], *n.* chère (*aliment etc.*); gaieté, *f.*, courage, *m.*; acclamation, *f.*, applaudissement, hourra, vivat, *m.*—*v.t.* égayer, réjouir, animer; applaudir, acclamer.—*v.i.* se réjouir; applaudir.
cheerful ['tʃiəful], *a.* joyeux, gai; riant (*paysage etc.*).
cheerfully ['tʃiəfuli], *adv.* gaiement, joyeusement.
cheerfulness ['tʃiəfulnis], *n.* gaieté, allégresse, bonne humeur, *f.*
cheerily ['tʃiərili], *adv.* gaiement.
cheering ['tʃiəriŋ], *a.* consolant, encourageant.—*n.* applaudissements, *m.pl.*
cheerio! ['tʃiəriou], *int.* (*fam.*) (*good-bye*) à bientôt! (*when drinking*) à votre santé!
cheerless ['tʃiəlis], *a.* triste, morne.
cheery ['tʃiəri], *a.* gai, joyeux, réjoui.
cheese [tʃiːz], *n.* fromage, *m.*
cheese-paring ['tʃiːzpɛəriŋ], *n.* (*fig.*) économie de bouts de chandelle, *f.*
cheetah, chetah ['tʃiːtə], *n.* guépard, *m.*
chef [ʃef], *n.* chef (cuisinier), *m.*
chemical ['kemikəl], *a.* chimique.
chemically ['kemikli], *adv.* chimiquement.
chemicals ['kemikəlz], *n.pl.* produits chimiques, *m.pl.*
chemise [ʃi'miːz], *n.* chemise de femme, *f.*
chemist ['kemist], *n.* (*scientist*) chimiste, *m., f.*; (*druggist*) pharmacien, *m.*; ***chemist's shop***, pharmacie, *f.*
chemistry ['kemistri], *n.* chimie, *f.*
cheque [tʃek], *n.* chèque, *m.*; ***crossed*** or ***open cheque***, chèque barré *ou* non barré.
cheque-book ['tʃekbuk], *n.* carnet de chèques, *m.*
cherish ['tʃeriʃ], *v.t.* chérir; soigner; nourrir, entretenir (*de l'espoir etc.*).
cherry ['tʃeri], *n.* cerise, *f.*
cherry-tree ['tʃeritriː], *n.* cerisier, *m.*
cherub ['tʃerəb], *n.* (*pl.* **cherubs** ['tʃerəbz], **cherubim** ['tʃerəbim]), chérubin, *m.*
cherubic [tʃə'ruːbik], *a.* de chérubin, angélique.
chess [tʃes], *n.* échecs, *m.pl.*
chess-board ['tʃesbɔːd], *n.* échiquier, *m.*
chessman ['tʃesmən], *n.* (*pl.* **chessmen** ['tʃesmen]) pièce, *f.*; ***a set of chessmen***, un jeu d'échecs.
chest [tʃest], *n.* coffre, *m.*, caisse; (*Anat.*) poitrine, *f.*; poitrail (*de cheval*), *m.*; ***chest of drawers***, commode, *f.*
chestnut ['tʃesnʌt], *a.* châtain, marron (*couleur*); alezan (*cheval*).—*n.* marron, *m.*; châtaigne, *f.*
chestnut-tree ['tʃesnʌttriː], *n.* châtaignier (*Spanish chestnut*); marronnier (d'Inde) (*horse-chestnut*), *m.*
chevalier [ʃevə'liə], *n.* chevalier, *m.*
chevron ['ʃevrən], *n.* chevron, *m.*
chew [tʃuː], *v.t.* mâcher; (*fig.*) ***to chew over***, ruminer.
chick [tʃik], *n.* poussin; (*fig.*) poulet, *m.*
chicken ['tʃikin], *n.* poussin; poulet, *m.*
chicken-hearted ['tʃikin'hɑːtid], *a.* peureux, poltron.
chicken-pox ['tʃikinpɔks], *n.* varicelle, *f.*
chickweed ['tʃikwiːd], *n.* mouron des oiseaux, *m.*

chicory [ˈtʃikəri], *n.* chicorée (*assaisonnement* ou *pour remplacer le café*); endive (*légume*), *f.*
chide [tʃaid], *v.t.* gronder, blâmer.
chief [tʃi:f], *a.* principal.—*n.* chef, *m.*; partie principale, *f.*; (*fam.*) ***the chief***, le patron, *m.*
chiefly [ˈtʃi:fli], *adv.* surtout, principalement.
chieftain [ˈtʃi:ftən], *n.* chef de clan, *m.*
chiffon [ˈʃifɔn], *n.* chiffon, *m.*
chiffonier [ʃifəˈniə], *n.* chiffonnier, *m.*
chilblain [ˈtʃilblein], *n.* engelure, *f.*
child [tʃaild], *n.* (*pl.* **children** [ˈtʃildrən]) enfant, *m.,f.*; ***with child***, enceinte.
child-bed [ˈtʃaildbed], *n.* couches, *f.pl.*
child-birth [ˈtʃaildbə:θ], *n.* enfantement, *m.*
childhood [ˈtʃaildhud], *n.* enfance, *f.*
childish [ˈtʃaildiʃ], *a.* enfantin; puéril.
childishness [ˈtʃaildiʃnis], *n.* puérilité, *f.*; enfantillage, *m.*
Chile [ˈtʃili]. le Chili, *m.*
Chilean [ˈtʃiliən], *a.* chilien.—*n.* Chilien (*personne*), *m.*
chill [tʃil], *a.* froid; glacé.—*n.* froid; refroidissement, frisson, *m.*; ***to catch a chill***, prendre froid.—*v.t.* refroidir; (*fig.*) glacer; décourager.
chilli [ˈtʃili], *n.* piment, *m.*
chilliness [ˈtʃilinis], *n.* froid, frisson, *m.*; froideur, *f.*
chilly [ˈtʃili], *a.* un peu froid (*chose*); frileux (*personne* ou *temps*).
chime [tʃaim], *n.* carillon, *m.*—*v.t.*, *v.i.* carillonner.
chimera [kaiˈmiərə], *n.* chimère, *f.*
chimney [ˈtʃimni], *n.* cheminée, *f.*
chimney-corner [ˈtʃimniˈkɔ:nə], *n.* coin du feu, *m.*
chimney-piece [ˈtʃimnipi:s], *n.* chambranle *ou* manteau de cheminée, *m.*; (*colloq.*) cheminée, *f.*
chimney-pot [ˈtʃimnipɔt], *n.* tuyau de cheminée, *m.*
chimney-sweep [ˈtʃimniswi:p], *n.* ramoneur, *m.*
chimpanzee [tʃimpænˈzi:], *n.* chimpanzé, *m.*
chin [tʃin], *n.* menton, *m.*
China [ˈtʃainə]. la Chine, *f.*
china [ˈtʃainə], *n.* porcelaine, *f.*
Chinese [tʃaiˈni:z], *a.* chinois, de Chine.—*n.* chinois (*langue*); Chinois (*personne*), *m.*
chink [tʃiŋk], *n.* crevasse, fente, lézarde, *f.*; son, tintement; (*slang*) argent, *m.*—*v.t.* crevasser; faire sonner.—*v.i.* se fendiller; sonner.
chintz [tʃints], *n.* (*Tex.*) indienne, *f.*
chip [tʃip], *n.* copeau, fragment, éclat (*de bois*); (*Cards*) jeton, *m.*; (*pl.*, *Cook.*) (pommes de terre) frites, *f.pl.*—*v.t.* tailler; railler.—*v.i.* s'écorner; s'écailler (*porcelaine etc.*).
chiropodist [kiˈrɔpədist], *n.* pédicure, *m.,f.*
chirp [tʃə:p], *v.i.* pépier, gazouiller; crier (*insectes*).—*n.* gazouillement, pépiement; cri (*insectes*), *m.*
chirpy [ˈtʃə:pi], *a.* (*colloq.*) gai, réjoui.
chirrup [ˈtʃirəp], [CHIRP].
chisel [tʃizl], *n.* ciseau, *m.*—*v.t.* ciseler.
chit [tʃit], *n.* marmot, bambin; billet (*lettre*), *m.*
chitchat [ˈtʃittʃæt], *n.* caquet, babillage, *m.*
chivalrous [ˈʃivəlrəs], *a.* chevaleresque.
chivalry [ˈʃivəlri], *n.* chevalerie, *f.*
chives [tʃaivz], *n.pl.* ciboulette, *f.*
chlorate [ˈklɔ:reit], *n.* (*Chem.*) chlorate, *m.*
chlorinate [ˈklɔ:rineit], *v.t.* verdunise (*eau potable*).
chlorine [ˈklɔ:ri:n], *n.* chlore, *m.*
chloroform [ˈklɔrəfɔ:m], *n.* chloroforme, *m*—*v.t.* chloroformer.
chlorophyll [ˈklɔrəfil], *n.* chlorophylle, *f.*
choc-ice [ˈtʃɔkais], *n.* chocolat glacé, *m.*
chock-full [tʃɔkˈful], (*fam.*) **chock-a-bloc** [ˈtʃɔkəˈblɔk], *a.* plein comme un œuf comble.
chocolate [ˈtʃɔkəlit], *n.* chocolat, *m.*
choice [tʃɔis], *a.* choisi; de choix; recherché fin (*vin*).—*n.* choix, *m.*; élite, *f.*; assortiment *m.*
choir [ˈkwaiə], *n.* chœur, *m.*
choke [tʃouk], *v.t.* étouffer, suffoquer; engorger.—*v.i.* s'engorger.—*n.* étranglemen (*de voix*); (*Motor.*) starter, *m.*
choking [ˈtʃoukiŋ], *a.* étouffant.—*n.* étouffement, *m.*, suffocation, *f.*
choky [ˈtʃouki], *a.* étouffant, suffoquant.
choler [ˈkɔlə], *n.* colère, bile, *f.*
cholera [ˈkɔlərə], *n.* choléra, *m.*
choleric [ˈkɔlərik], *a.* colérique, irascible.
choose [tʃu:z], *v.t. irr.* choisir; élire; préférer vouloir.
chop (1) [CHAP].
chop (2) [tʃɔp], *v.t.* couper en morceaux hacher; trafiquer, troquer; ***to chop down*** abattre.—*v.i.* trafiquer, troquer; (*Naut.* tourner (*vent*); clapoter (*mer*); ***to chop and change***, (*fig.*) girouetter.—*n.* tranche côtelette (*de mouton*); (*colloq.*, *pl.*) gueule, *f*
chopper [ˈtʃɔpə], *n.* couperet, *m.*
chopping [ˈtʃɔpiŋ], *n.* coupe, action d couper, *f.*
choppy [ˈtʃɔpi], *a.* crevassé, haché; clapoteux (*mer*).
choral [ˈkɔ:rəl], *a.* choral, en *ou* de chœur.
chord [kɔ:d], *n.* corde, *f.*; (*Mus.*) accord, *m.*
chores [tʃɔ:z], *n.pl.* corvées domestiques, *f.pl*
chorister [ˈkɔristə], *n.* choriste, *m.*; enfant de chœur, *m.,f.*
chorus [ˈkɔ:rəs], *n.* chœur; refrain, *m.*
Christ [kraist]. le Christ, *m.*
christen [krisn], *v.t.* baptiser.
Christendom [ˈkrisndəm]. chrétienté, *f.*
christening [ˈkrisniŋ], *n.* baptême, *m.*
Christian [ˈkristjən], *a.* and *n.* chrétien, *m.* ***Christian name***, prénom, *m.*
Christianity [kristiˈæniti], *n.* christianisme *m.*
Christmas [ˈkrisməs]. Noël, *m.*, la fête de Noël, *f.*; ***Christmas carol***, chant de Noël *m.*; ***Christmas Eve***, la veille de Noël, *f.*
Christmas-box [ˈkrisməsbɔks], *n.* étrennes *f.pl.*
Christopher [ˈkristəfə]. Christophe, *m.*
chrome [kroum], *n.* bichromate de potasse *m.*; ***chrome leather***, cuir chromé, *m.*
chromium [ˈkroumiəm], *n.* chrome, *m.*
chronic [ˈkrɔnik], *a.* chronique.
chronicle [ˈkrɔnikl], *n.* chronique, *f.*
chronicler [ˈkrɔniklə], *n.* chroniqueur, *m.*
chronological [krɔnəˈlɔdʒikəl], *a.* chronologique.
chrysalis [ˈkrisəlis], *n.* chrysalide, *f.*
chrysanthemum [kriˈsænθəmʌm], *n.* chrysanthème, *m.*
chub [tʃʌb], *n.* (*Ichth.*) chabot, chevesne, *m.*
chubby [ˈtʃʌbi], *a.* joufflu; potelé (*mains*).

chuck (1) [tʃʌk], *n.* gloussement, *m.*—*v.i.* glousser.
chuck (2) [tʃʌk], *n.* petite tape sous le menton, *f.*
chuckle [tʃʌkl], *v.i.* rire tout bas, rire sous cape (*de*).—*n.* rire étouffé, gloussement, *m.*
chum [tʃʌm], *n.* copain, *m.*
chummy ['tʃʌmi], *a.* intime.
chump [tʃʌmp], *n.* tronçon (*de bois*); (*colloq.*) idiot, *m.*; ***chump chop***, côtelette de gigot, *f.*
chunk [tʃʌŋk], *n.* gros morceau, *m.*
church [tʃə:tʃ], *n.* église, *f.*; (*Protestant*) temple, *m.*
churchwarden ['tʃə:tʃ'wɔ:dn], *n.* marguillier, *m.*
churchyard ['tʃə:tʃjɑ:d], *n.* cimetière, *m.*
churl [tʃə:l], *n.* rustre, manant, ladre, *m.*
churlish ['tʃə:liʃ], *a.* grossier, rude, ladre.
churlishly ['tʃə:liʃli], *adv.* grossièrement.
churlishness ['tʃə:liʃnis], *n.* grossièreté, *f.*
churn [tʃə:n], *n.* baratte, *f.*; (*Rail.*) ***milk churn***, bidon à lait, *m.*—*v.t.* baratter.
chute [ʃu:t], *n.* chute (*d'eau*); glissière, piste (*de luges*), *f.*
Cicero ['sisərou]. Cicéron, *m.*
cider ['saidə], *n.* cidre, *m.*
cigar [si'gɑ:], *n.* cigare, *m.*
cigarette [sigə'ret], *n.* cigarette, *f.*
cinder ['sində], *n.* cendre, *f.*; (*pl.*) escarbilles (*de charbon*), *f.pl.*
Cinderella [sində'relə]. Cendrillon, *f.*
cine-camera ['sinikæmərə], *n.* (ciné)caméra, *f.*
cinema ['sinimə], *n.* cinéma, *m.*
cinnamon ['sinəmən], *n.* cannelle, *f.*
cipher ['saifə], *n.* zéro; chiffre, *m.*—*v.t.*, *v.i.* chiffrer; calculer.
circle [sə:kl], *n.* cercle, *m.*; (*fig.*) coterie, *f.*—*v.t.* entourer (*de*).—*v.i.* tournoyer.
circlet ['sə:klit], *n.* petit cercle, anneau, *m.*
circuit ['sə:kit], *n.* rotation, révolution, *f.*, tour; circuit, *m.*, circonférence; tournée (*de juge etc.*), *f.*
circuitous [sə:'kju:itəs], *a.* détourné, sinueux.
circular ['sə:kjulə], *a.* circulaire.—*n.* circulaire, *f.*, bulletin, *m.*
circulate ['sə:kjuleit], *v.t.* mettre en circulation, faire circuler, répandre.—*v.i.* circuler.
circulating ['sə:kjuleitiŋ], *a.* circulant.
circulation [sə:kju'leiʃən], *n.* circulation, *f.*; tirage (*d'un journal etc.*), *m.*
circumference [sə:'kʌmfərəns], *n.* circonférence, périphérie, *f.*
circumflex ['sə:kəmfleks], *a.* (*Gram.*) circonflexe.
circumlocution [sə:kəmlə'kju:ʃən], *n.* circonlocution, *f.*
circumscribe ['sə:kəmskraib], *v.t.* circonscrire.
circumspect ['sə:kəmspekt], *a.* circonspect.
circumstance ['sə:kəmstæns], *n.* circonstance, *f.*; état, *m.*; (*pl.*) moyens, *m.pl.*; ***in straitened circumstances***, dans la gêne; ***in easy circumstances***, dans l'aisance; ***under no circumstances***, en aucun cas.
circumstantial [sə:kəm'stænʃəl], *a.* circonstancié, minutieux; indirect (*témoignage*).
circumvent [sə:kəm'vent], *v.t.* circonvenir.
circumvention [sə:kəm'venʃən], *n.* circonvention, *f.*
circus ['sə:kəs], *n.* cirque; rond-point (*de rues*), *m.*
cistern ['sistən], *n.* citerne, *f.*, réservoir, *m.*
citadel ['sitədl], *n.* citadelle, *f.*
citation [sai'teiʃən], *n.* citation, *f.*
cite [sait], *v.t.* citer; sommer (*de*).
citizen ['sitizn], *n.* citoyen, bourgeois; habitant, *m.*
citron ['sitrən], *n.* cédrat, *m.*
city ['siti], *n.* ville; cité, *f.*
civet ['sivit], *n.* civette, *f.*
civic ['sivik], *a.* civique.
civil [sivl], *a.* civil; municipal; honnête, poli; ***civil servant***, fonctionnaire, *m.*; ***in the Civil Service***, dans l'administration.
civilian [si'viljən], *n.* bourgeois, civil, *m.*
civility [si'viliti], *n.* civilité, politesse, *f.*
civilization [sivilai'zeiʃən], *n.* civilisation, *f.*
civilize ['sivilaiz], *v.t.* civiliser.
claim [kleim], *v.t.* demander, prétendre (*à*), réclamer, revendiquer.—*n.* demande, *f.*; titre, droit, *m.*
claimant ['kleimənt], *n.* réclamateur, prétendant, *m.*
clam [klæm], *n.* peigne (*bivalve*), *m.*, palourde, *f.*
clamber ['klæmbə], *v.i.* grimper (*sur* ou *à*).
clammy ['klæmi], *a.* visqueux, pâteux; moite (*mains*).
clamorous ['klæmərəs], *a.* bruyant; criard.
clamour ['klæmə], *n.* clameur, *f.*, bruit, *m.*—*v.i.* crier, vociférer.
clamp [klæmp], *n.* crampon; (*Carp.*) serre-joints, *m.*—*v.t.* cramponner; serrer; entasser.
clan [klæn], *n.* clan, *m.*; clique, coterie, *f.*
clandestine [klæn'destin], *a.* clandestin.
clang [klæŋ], **clank** [klæŋk], *n.* cliquetis, son métallique, *m.*—*v.t.* faire résonner.—*v.i.* résonner.
clap [klæp], *n.* coup, *m.*; claque, *f.*; battement de mains; coup (*de tonnerre*), *m.*—*v.t.* claquer, frapper, battre (*mains*, *ailes etc.*); applaudir.—*v.i.* claquer *ou* battre des mains; applaudir.
clapper ['klæpə], *n.* applaudisseur; battant (*d'une cloche*); claquet (*d'un moulin*), *m.*
clapping ['klæpiŋ], *n.* battement des mains, *m.*, applaudissements, *m.pl.*
Clara ['klɛərə], **Clare** [klɛə]. Claire, *f.*
claret ['klærət], *n.* vin de Bordeaux rouge, *m.*
clarify ['klærifai], *v.t.* clarifier.—*v.i.* se clarifier.
clarinet [klæri'net], *n.* clarinette, *f.*
clarion ['klæriən], *n.* clairon, *m.*
clarity ['klæriti], *n.* clarté, *f.*
clash [klæʃ], *v.t.* faire résonner (*en frappant*); choquer, heurter.—*v.i.* résonner, se heurter; (*fig.*) être aux prises (*avec*), s'opposer.—*n.* fracas, choc, conflit; cliquetis (*d'armes etc.*), *m.*
clasp [klɑ:sp], *n.* fermoir, *m.*; agrafe, *f.*; (*fig.*) embrassement, *m.*, étreinte, *f.*—*v.t.* agrafer; serrer, presser.
clasp-knife ['klɑ:spnaif], *n.* couteau de poche, *m.*
class [klɑ:s], *n.* classe, *f.*; (*Sch.*) cours; genre, *m.*, catégorie, *f.*—*v.t.* classer.
classic ['klæsik], *a.* and *n.* classique, *m*; ***to study classics***, faire ses humanités *f.pl.*
classical ['klæsikəl], *a.* classique.
classification [klæsifi'keiʃən], *n.* classification, *f.*

classify ['klæsifai], *v.t.* classifier.
classroom ['klɑ:sru:m], *n.* salle de classe, classe, *f.*
clatter ['klætə], *n.* bruit, tapage, fracas (*de ferraille etc.*), tintamarre, *m.*—*v.i.* faire du bruit, claquer.
clause [klɔ:z], *n.* clause; proposition, *f.*
clavicle ['klævikl], *n.* (*Anat.*) clavicule, *f.*
claw [klɔ:], *n.* griffe; (*Zool.*) serre; pince (*de crabes*), *f.*—*v.t.* griffer; déchirer; égratigner; (*fig.*) railler, gronder.
clay [klei], *n.* argile, terre glaise, glaise, *f.*—*v.t.* (*Agric.*) glaiser; terrer (*sucre*).
clayey ['kleii], *a.* argileux.
clean [kli:n], *a.* propre; blanc (*linge*); ciré (*chaussures*); (*fig.*) net, droit.—*adv.* entièrement, tout à fait, droit, raide.—*v.t.* nettoyer; décrotter, cirer (*chaussures*); écurer (*égouts, canaux etc.*).
cleaner ['kli:nə], *n.* nettoyeur (*personne*), *m.*
cleaning ['kli:niŋ], *n.* nettoyage, nettoiement, *m.*; ***dry cleaning***, nettoyage à sec.
cleanliness ['klenlinis], **cleanness** ['kli:nnis], *n.* propreté; netteté, *f.*
cleanly ['klenli], *a.* propre; (*fig.*) pur.—['kli:nli], *adv.* proprement, nettement.
cleanness [CLEANLINESS].
cleanse [klenz], *v.t.* nettoyer; curer (*égouts etc.*); (*fig.*) purifier.
cleansing ['klenziŋ], *n.* nettoiement, nettoyage, *m.*; (*fig.*) purification, *f.*
clear [kliə], *a.* clair; net, évident; sûr; innocent, sans tache.—*adv.* clair.—*v.t.* éclaircir; clarifier (*liquides*); faire évacuer (*salle etc.*); déblayer (*débris etc.*); gagner (*profit etc.*); (*Agric.*) défricher; (*fig.*) acquitter; (*Customs*) passer.—*v.i.* s'éclaircir; ***to clear off***, s'en aller, filer; ***to clear out***, se retirer; ***to clear up***, élucider (*problème, mystère*); s'éclaircir, se rasséréner (*temps*).
clearance ['kliərəns], *n.* dégagement; déblaiement (*débris*), *m.*; levée (*du courrier*), *f.*; (*Naut.*) congé; (*Customs*) dédouanement, *m.*; ***clearance sale***, solde, *m.*; liquidation, *f.*
clear-cut ['kliəkʌt], *a.* net, d'une grande netteté.
clear-headed ['kliə'hedid], *a.* à l'esprit clair.
clearing ['kliəriŋ], *n.* éclaircissement; débrouillement; acquittement; (*Customs*) dédouanement; défrichement (*de terrain*), *m.*; éclaircie (*de forêt*), *f.*; déblaiement (*débris*), *m.*
clearing-house ['kliəriŋhaus], *n.* (*Rail.*) bureau de liquidation, *m.*; (*Banking*) banque de virement, *f.*
clearly ['kliəli], *adv.* nettement, clairement, évidemment.
clearness ['kliənis], *n.* clarté, netteté, pureté, *f.*
cleavage ['kli:vidʒ], *n.* clivage, *m.*; fissure, scission, *f.*
cleave [kli:v], *v.t. irr.* fendre, se fendre; ***in a cleft stick***, (*fig.*) dans une impasse.
clef [klef], *n.* (*Mus.*) clef, *f.*
cleft [kleft], *n.* fente, fissure, crevasse, *f.*
clemency ['klemənsi], *n.* clémence; douceur (*du temps*), *f.*
clement ['klemənt], *a.* doux, clément.
clench [klentʃ], *v.t.* river (*clous etc.*); serrer (*poing*).
Cleopatra [kliə'pætrə]. Cléopâtre, *f.*
clergy ['klə:dʒi], *n.* clergé, *m.*
clergyman ['klə:dʒimən], *n.* (*pl.* **-men** [men]) ecclésiastique; (*R.-C. Ch.*) prêtre, abbé, curé; (*Protestant*) ministre, pasteur, *m.*
cleric ['klerik], *n.* ecclésiastique, prêtre, *m.*
clerical ['klerikəl], *a.* clérical; ***clerical error***, faute de copiste, *f.*
clerk [klɑ:k], *n.* (*Law*) clerc; (*Eccles.*) ecclésiastique; (*Comm.*) commis; (*Civil Service*) employé, *m.*
clerkship ['klɑ:kʃip], *n.* place de clerc, place de commis, *f.*
clever ['klevə], *a.* adroit, habile, (*colloq.*) malin; intelligent; bien fait; (*Am.*) aimable; ***to be clever at***, être fort en.
cleverly ['klevəli], *adv.* habilement, adroitement, avec adresse.
cleverness ['klevənis], *n.* habileté, dextérité, adresse; intelligence, *f.*
click [klik], *v.i.* faire tic-tac, cliqueter.—*n.* bruit sec, clic; cliquetis; déclic, *m.*
client ['klaiənt], *n.* client, *m.*
clientele [kli:ɑ̃'tel], *n.* clientèle, *f.*
cliff [klif], *n.* falaise, *f.*; rocher escarpé, *m.*
climate ['klaimit], *n.* climat, *m.*
climatic [klai'mætic], *a.* climatique.
climax ['klaimæks], *n.* gradation, *f.*; (*fig.*) comble, apogée, *m.*
climb [klaim], *v.t.* escalader, gravir, monter.—*v.i.* grimper; monter (*sur*); (*fig.*) s'élever.—*n.* ascension, montée, *f.*
climber ['klaimə], *n.* grimpeur, *m.*; alpiniste, *m., f.*; ***social climber***, arriviste, *m., f.*
clime [klaim], *n.* (*poet.*) climat; pays, *m.*
clinch [klintʃ], *v.t.* river (*clous*); ***to clinch an argument***, confirmer un argument.—*n.* (*Box.*) corps à corps, *m.*
cling [kliŋ], *v.i. irr.* se cramponner, s'attacher, s'accrocher (*à*); coller (*à*) (*robe*).
clinic ['klinik], *a.* and *n.* clinique, *f.*
clinical ['klinikəl], *a.* clinique.
clink [kliŋk], *n.* tintement, cliquetis, *m.*—*v.t.* faire tinter.—*v.i.* tinter.
clinker ['kliŋkə], *n.* mâchefer, *m.*
clip [klip], *v.t.* couper (*à ciseaux*); tondre (*chiens, chevaux*); écorcher, estropier (*paroles*); contrôler (*billets*).—*n.* tonte, *f.*; pince-notes, *m.*
clipper ['klipə], *n.* rogneur; (*Naut.*) fin voilier, *m.*
clippers ['klipəz], *n.pl.* tondeuse, *f.*
clique [kli:k], *n.* coterie, *f.*
cloak [klouk], *n.* manteau; (*fig.*) voile, masque, prétexte, *m.*—*v.t.* couvrir d'un manteau, (*fig.*) masquer, voiler, cacher.
cloak-room ['kloukru:m], *n.* (*Rail.*) consigne, *f.*, (*Theat.*) vestiaire, *m.*
clock [klɔk], *n.* horloge (*grand*); pendule (*petit*), *f.*; ***alarm clock***, réveille-matin, *m.*—*v.i.* (*Ind.*) ***to clock in*** or ***out***, pointer à l'arrivée *ou* au départ.
clock-maker ['klɔkmeikə], *n.* horloger, *m.*
clockwise ['klɔkwaiz], *adv.* dans le sens des aiguilles d'une montre.
clockwork ['klɔkwə:k], *a.* mécanique.—*n.* mouvement, mécanisme d'horlogerie; (*fig.*) travail régulier, *m.*
clod [klɔd], *n.* motte de terre, *f.*
clodhopper ['klɔdhɔpə], *n.* rustre; manant, *m.*
clog [klɔg], *n.* sabot, *m.*—*v.t.* obstruer.—*v.i.* se boucher, s'obstruer.

cloister ['klɔistə], *n.* cloître, *m.*
close (1) [klouz], *v.t.* fermer; clore, terminer.—*v.i.* se fermer; clore, se terminer, conclure, finir.—*n.* fin, conclusion, clôture, *f.*
close (2) [klous], *a.* clos, bien fermé; serré; lourd (*temps*); (*fig.*) mystérieux.—*adv.* près; de près; ***close by***, tout près; ***close to***, près de.
close-fisted ['klous'fistid], *a.* avare.
closely ['klousli], *adv.* de près; étroitement; secrètement.
closeness ['klousnis], *n.* proximité; exactitude; lourdeur (*temps*); intimité, *f.*
closet ['klɔzit], *n.* cabinet; boudoir, *m.*; garde-robe, armoire, *f.*—*v.t.* ***to be closeted with***, être en tête-à-tête avec.
close-up ['klousʌp], *n.* (*Cine.*) gros plan, *m.*
closing ['klouziŋ], *a.* dernier, final.—*n.* clôture, fermeture (*de magasin*); fin, conclusion, *f.*
closure ['klouʒə], *n.* clôture, fermeture, *f.*
clot [klɔt], *n.* grumeau, caillot, *m.*—*v.i.* se cailler, se figer.
cloth [klɔ:θ], *n.* drap (*de laine* ou *tissu d'or* ou *d'argent*), *m.*; toile (*de lin*), *f.*; ***table-cloth***, nappe, *f.*, tapis (*de laine*), *m.*
clothe [klouð], *v.t.* habiller, (re)vêtir.
clothes [klouðz], *n.pl.* habits, vêtements, *m.pl.*, hardes, *f.pl.*; ***bed-clothes***, draps et couvertures, *m.pl.*
clothing ['klouðiŋ], *n.* vêtement, habillement, *m.*; vêtements, *m.pl.*
cloud [klaud], *n.* nuage, *m.*; (*poet.*) nue; (*fig.*) nuée, *f.*; ***every cloud has a silver lining***, après la pluie le beau temps; ***to be under a cloud***, être mal vu du monde.—*v.t.* couvrir de nuages; obscurcir; (*fig.*) assombrir.—*v.i.* se couvrir (de nuages).
cloudburst ['klaudbə:st], *n.* trombe, rafale de pluie, *f.*
cloudless ['klaudlis], *a.* sans nuage.
cloudy ['klaudi], *a.* nuageux, couvert; trouble (*liquides*); (*fig.*) ténébreux.
clout [klaut], *n.* torchon, linge, *m.*; gifle, tape, *f.*—*v.t.* rapetasser; taper, souffleter.
clove [klouv], *n.* clou de girofle, *m.*; ***clove of garlic***, gousse d'ail, *f.*
cloven [klouvn], *a.* fendu; fourchu; ***to show the cloven foot***, laisser voir le bout de l'oreille.
clover ['klouvə], *n.* trèfle, *m.*
clown [klaun], *n.* rustre, manant; (*Theat.*) bouffon, clown, *m.*
cloy [klɔi], *v.t.* écœurer, rassasier.
club [klʌb], *n.* massue, *f.*; (*Golf*) club (*instrument*), *m.*; crosse, *f.*; cercle, club, *m.*, association, *f.*; (*Cards*) trèfle, *m.*—*v.t.* frapper avec une massue.—*v.i.* se cotiser, s'associer.
club-foot ['klʌbfut], *n.* pied bot, *m.*
club-house ['klʌbhaus], *n.* cercle; pavillon (*de golf etc.*), *m.*
cluck [klʌk], *v.i.* glousser.
clucking ['klʌkiŋ], *n.* gloussement, *m.*
clue [klu:], *n.* fil, indice, signe, *m.*; idée, *f.*
clueless ['klu:lis], *a.* (*fam.*) ***to be clueless***, ne savoir rien de rien.
clump [klʌmp], *n.* masse, *f.*, gros bloc; (*fig.*) groupe, *m.*; ***clump of trees***, bouquet d'arbres, *m.*
clumsily ['klʌmzili], *adv.* gauchement, maladroitement.
clumsiness ['klʌmzinis], *n.* gaucherie, maladresse, *f.*
clumsy ['klʌmzi], *a.* gauche, maladroit; mal fait (*chose*).
cluster ['klʌstə], *n.* grappe (*de raisin*), *f.*; bouquet (*de fleurs*); régime (*de bananes*); nœud (*de diamants*), *m.*—*v.i.* se former en grappes; se grouper.
clutch [klʌtʃ], *v.t.* saisir, empoigner.—*n.* griffe, serre, étreinte, *f.*; (*Motor.*) embrayage, *m.*; couvée (*d'œufs*), *f.*
clutter ['klʌtə], *n.* fracas, vacarme; encombrement, désordre, *m.*—*v.t.* ***to clutter up***, encombrer.
coach [koutʃ], *n.* voiture, *f.*, carrosse, *m.*; (*Rail.*) voiture, *f.*, wagon; autocar, car; (*Sch.*) répétiteur; (*Spt.*) entraîneur, *m.*—*v.t.* entraîner; préparer aux examens.
coaching ['koutʃiŋ], *n.* (*Spt.*) entraînement (*d'équipe*), *m.*; (*Sch.*) répétitions, *f.pl.*
coachman ['koutʃmən], *n.* (*pl.* **-men** [men]) cocher, *m.*
coachwork ['koutʃwə:k], *n.* carrosserie, *f.*
coagulate [kou'ægjuleit], *v.t.* coaguler.—*v.i.* se coaguler.
coal [koul], *n.* charbon, *m.*; houille, *f.*; ***live coal***, charbon ardent.—*v.t.* charbonner.—*v.i.* s'approvisionner de charbon (*navire*).
coal-cellar ['koulselə], *n.* cave à charbon, *f.*
coalesce [kouə'les], *v.i.* s'unir, se fondre, fusionner.
coal-field ['koulfi:ld], *n.* bassin houiller, *m.*
coalition [kouə'liʃən], *n.* coalition, *f.*
coal-mine ['koulmain], *n.* mine de charbon, houillère, *f.*
coal-miner ['koulmainə], *n.* mineur, *m.*
coal-scuttle ['koulskʌtl], *n.* seau à charbon, *m.*
coarse [kɔ:s], *a.* gros, grossier.
coarseness ['kɔ:snis], *n.* grossièreté, *f.*
coast [koust], *n.* côte, plage, *f.*, rivage, littoral, *m.*—*v.t.* côtoyer.—*v.i.* côtoyer, suivre la côte; caboter; planer (*oiseau*); (*Motor.*) rouler au débrayé.
coastal ['koustəl], *a.* côtier.
coaster ['koustə], *n.* caboteur, *m.*
coast-guard ['koustgɑ:d], *n.* garde-côte, *m.*
coast-line ['koustlain], *n.* littoral, *m.*
coat [kout], *n.* habit; enduit (*de goudron etc.*), *m.*; robe (*de certains animaux*); (*Mil.*) tunique; (*Paint.*) couche, *f.*; ***coat of mail***, cotte de mailles, *f.*; ***double breasted coat***, veston croisé, *m.*—*v.t.* revêtir; enduire (*de*).
coat-hanger ['kouthæŋə], *n.* cintre, *m.*; porte-vêtements, *m. inv.*
coax [kouks], *v.t.* amadouer, cajoler, flatter.
co-axial [kou'æksiəl], *a.* coaxial.
coaxing ['kouksiŋ], *n.* cajolerie, *f.*, enjôlement, *m.*
cob [kɔb], *n.* bidet, goussant (*cheval*); épi (*de maïs*), *m.*
cobalt ['koubɔ:lt], *n.* cobalt, *m.*
cobble [kɔbl], *v.t.* saveter, raccommoder; paver en cailloutis.—*n.* galet rond, pavé *m.*
cobbler ['kɔblə], *n.* cordonnier, *m.*
cobnut ['kɔbnʌt], *n.* aveline, *f.*
cobra ['koubrə], *n.* cobra, *m.*
cobweb ['kɔbweb], *n.* toile d'araignée, *f.*
cocaine [ko'kein], *n.* cocaïne, *f.*
cochineal ['kɔtʃini:l], *n.* cochenille, *f.*

cock [kɔk], *n.* coq; mâle (*de petits oiseaux*); robinet (*tap*); chien (*de fusil*); tas, meulon (*de foin*), *m.*; ***black-cock***, coq de bruyère; ***cock-and-bull story***, coq-à-l'âne, *m.*—*v.t.* relever; retrousser; armer (*fusil*); ***cocked hat***, chapeau à cornes, *m.*
cockade [kɔ'keid], *n.* cocarde, *f.*
cock-a-doodle-doo ['kɔkədu:dl'du:], *n.* coquerico, cocorico, *m.*
cockatoo [kɔkə'tu:], *n.* kakatoès, cacatois, *m.*
cockatrice ['kɔkətri:s], *n.* basilic, *m.*
cockchafer ['kɔktʃeifə], *n.* hanneton, *m.*
cock-crow ['kɔkkrou], *n.* chant du coq; (*fig.*) point du jour, *m.*
cockerel ['kɔkərəl], *n.* jeune coq, *m.*
cock-eyed ['kɔkaid], *a.* de biais, de travers.
cockle [kɔkl], *n.* bucarde, *f.*
cock-pit ['kɔkpit], *n.* arène des combats de coqs; (*Av.*) carlingue, *f.*
cockroach ['kɔkroutʃ], *n.* blatte, *f.*
cockscomb ['kɔkskoum], *n.* crête de coq, *f.*; [COXCOMB].
cocksure ['kɔkʃuə], *a.* sûr et certain, outrecuidant.
cocktail ['kɔkteil], *n.* cocktail, *m.*; ***cocktail party***, cocktail.
cocky ['kɔki], *a.* effronté, suffisant.
coco ['koukou], *n.* coco, *m.*
cocoa ['koukou], *n.* cacao, *m.*
coconut, cocoa-nut ['koukənʌt], *n.* coco, *m.*, noix de coco, *f.*
cocoon [kə'ku:n], *n.* cocon, *m.*
cod [kɔd], *n.* morue, *f.*; cabillaud (*morue fraîche*), *m.*
coddle [kɔdl], *v.t.* mitonner; dorloter, choyer.
code [koud], *n.* code, *m.*—*v.t.* coder; chiffrer.
codicil ['kɔdisil], *n.* codicille, *m.*
codify ['koudifai], *v.t.* codifier.
cod-liver oil ['kɔdlivər'ɔil], *n.* huile de foie de morue, *f.*
co-education ['kouedju'keiʃən], *n.* enseignement mixte, *m.*
co-educational ['kouedju'keiʃənəl], *a.* (*Sch.*) mixte.
coefficient [koui'fiʃənt], *n.* coefficient, *m.*
coerce [kou'ə:s], *v.t.* forcer, contraindre.
coercion [kou'ə:ʃən], *n.* coercition, contrainte, *f.*
coexist [kouig'zist], *v.i.* coexister.
coexistence [kouig'zistəns], *n.* coexistence, *f.*
coffee ['kɔfi], *n.* café, *m.*; ***white coffee***, café au lait.
coffee-bean ['kɔfibi:n], *n.* grain de café, *m.*
coffee-house ['kɔfihaus], *n.* café, *m.*
coffee-mill ['kɔfimil], **coffee-grinder** ['kɔfi graində], *n.* moulin à café, *m.*
coffee-pot ['kɔfipɔt], *n.* cafetière, *f.*
coffer ['kɔfə], *n.* coffre; caisson; sas, *m.*
coffin ['kɔfin], *n.* cercueil, *m.*, bière, *f.*
cog [kɔg], *n.* dent, *f.*
cogency ['koudʒənsi], *n.* force, puissance, *f.*
cogent ['koudʒənt], *a.* puissant, fort.
cogged [kɔgd], *a.* denté, à dents.
cogitate ['kɔdʒiteit], *v.t.* penser (à.)—*v.i.* méditer, penser.
cogitation [kɔdʒi'teiʃən], *n.* réflexion, pensée, méditation, *f.*
cognate ['kɔgneit], *a.* de la même famille; analogue.
cognizance ['kɔgnizəns], *n.* connaissance, *f.*; (*Her.*) insigne, *m.*
cognomen [kɔg'noumən], *n.* surnom; nom de guerre, sobriquet, *m.*
cog-wheel ['kɔgwi:l], *n.* roue d'engrenage, *f.*
cohabit [kou'hæbit], *v.i.* cohabiter.
cohabitation [kouhæbi'teiʃən], *n.* cohabitation, *f.*
coherence [kou'hiərəns], *n.* cohésion, cohérence, *f.*
coherent [kou'hiərənt], *a.* cohérent; conséquent.
coherently [kou'hiərəntli], *adv.* d'une manière cohérente.
cohesion [kou'hi:ʒən], *n.* cohésion, *f.*
cohesive [kou'hi:siv], *a.* cohésif.
cohort ['kouhɔ:t], *n.* cohorte, *f.*
coil [kɔil], *n.* rouleau (*de cheveux etc.*); repli (*de serpents*), *m.*; (*Elec.*) bobine, *f.*—*v.t.* replier, enrouler.—*v.i.* se replier, s'enrouler.
coin [kɔin], *n.* pièce de monnaie, *f.*—*v.t.* monnayer; forger, fabriquer, inventer.
coinage ['kɔinidʒ], *n.* monnayage, *m.*, monnaie; (*fig.*) fabrication, *f.*
coincide [kouin'said], *v.i.* s'accorder, coïncider (*avec*).
coincidence [kou'insidəns], *n.* coïncidence, *f.*
coincidental [kouinsi'dentl], *a.* de coïncidence.
coiner ['kɔinə], *n.* monnayeur; faux monnayeur, *m.*
coition [kou'iʃən], *n.* coït, *m.*
coke [kouk], *n.* coke, *m.*
colander ['kʌləndə], *n.* passoire, *f.*
cold [kould], *a.* froid; ***it is cold***, il fait froid; ***to be cold*** (*of people*), avoir froid.—*n.* froid; rhume (*maladie*), refroidissement; frisson (*sensation*), *m.*; ***to catch cold***, s'enrhumer.
coldly ['kouldli], *adv.* froidement.
cole [koul], *n.* chou marin, *m.*
colic ['kɔlik], *n.* colique, *f.*
collaborate [kə'læbəreit], *v.i.* collaborer.
collaboration [kəlæbə'reiʃən], *n.* collaboration, *f.*
collaborator [kə'læbəreitə] *n.* collaborateur, *m.*
collapse [kə'læps], *v.i.* s'affaisser, s'écrouler, s'effondrer.—*n.* affaissement, *m.*, débâcle, *f.*
collapsible [kə'læpsibl], *a.* pliant, démontable.
collar ['kɔlə], *n.* collier (*de chien, de cheval, de décoration*); col (*de chemise*); collet (*de pardessus*), *m.*; collerette (*de dames*), *f.*—*v.t.* colleter, prendre au collet.
collar-bone ['kɔləboun], *n.* clavicule, *f.*
collar-stud ['kɔləstʌd], *n.* bouton de col, *m.*
collate [kə'leit], *v.t.* collationner, comparer.
collateral [kə'lætərəl], *a.* collatéral.
collation [kə'leiʃən], *n.* collation, *f.*; don, présent; repas froid, *m.*
colleague ['kɔli:g], *n.* collègue, confrère, *m.*
collect (1) [kə'lekt], *v.t.* recueillir; ramasser; collectionner; percevoir, encaisser (*impôts*); recouvrer (*dettes*); quêter; faire la levée (*du courrier*).—*v.i.* s'amasser.
collect (2) ['kɔlikt], *n.* collecte; (courte) prière, *f.*
collected [kə'lektid], *a.* rassemblé; (*fig.*) recueilli, calme, tranquille.
collection [kə'lekʃən], *n.* collection, *f.*; assemblage, rassemblement, *m.*; collecte, quête; levée (*du courrier*), *f.*
collective [kə'lektiv], *a.* collectif.

collector [kə'lektə], *n.* collecteur; collectionneur; percepteur (*impôts*); quêteur (*aumône*); receveur (*douane*), *m.*

college ['kɔlidʒ], *n.* collège (d'Université), *m.*; école, *f.*

collide [kə'laid], *v.i.* se heurter.

collier ['kɔliə], *n.* mineur; (*Naut.*) (bateau) charbonnier, *m.*

colliery ['kɔljəri], *n.* houillère, mine de charbon, *f.*

collision [kə'li:ʒən], *n.* collision, *f.*, choc, *m.*

colloquial [kə'loukwiəl], *a.* de la conversation, familier; ***colloquial French***, français parlé, *m.*

colloquialism [kə'loukwiəlizm], *n.* expression familière, *f.*

colloquy ['kɔləkwi], *n.* colloque, entretien, *m.*

collusion [kə'lu:ʒən], *n.* collusion, connivence, *f.*

Colombia [kə'lʌmbiə]. la Colombie, *f.*

colon (1) ['koulən], *n.* (*Anat.*) colon, *m.*

colon (2) ['koulən], *n.* (*Gram.*) deux points, *m.pl.*

colonel [kə:nl], *n.* colonel, *m.*

colonial [kə'lounjəl], *a.* colonial.

colonist ['kɔlənist], *n.* colon, *m.*

colonization [kɔlənai'zeiʃən], *n.* colonisation, *f.*

colonize ['kɔlənaiz], *v.t.* coloniser.

colony ['kɔləni], *n.* colonie, *f.*

Colorado-beetle ['kɔlərɑ:dou'bi:tl], *n.* doryphore, *m.*

colossal [kə'lɔsl], *a.* colossal.

Colosseum [kɔlə'si:əm]. Colisée, *m.*

colossus [kə'lɔsəs], *n.* (*pl.* **colossi** [kə'lɔsai], **colossuses** [kə'lɔsəsiz]) colosse, *m.*

colour ['kʌlə], *n.* couleur, *f.*; (*fig.*) prétexte, *m.*, apparence, *f.*; (*pl.*) (*Mil.*) drapeau; (*Navy*) pavillon, *m.*; ***to be off colour***, être pâle, n'être pas bien en train; ***with the colours***, sous les drapeaux.—*v.t.* colorer; colorier, enluminer (*gravure etc.*).—*v.i.* rougir (*personne*); se colorer (*chose*).

colour-blind ['kʌləblaind], *a.* daltonien.

colour-blindness ['kʌləblaindnis], *n.* daltonisme, *m.*

coloured ['kʌləd], *a.* coloré; colorié; de couleur.

colourful ['kʌləful], *a.* coloré, pittoresque.

colouring ['kʌləriŋ], *n.* coloris, *m.*; couleur, *f.*

colourless ['kʌləlis], *a.* sans couleur.

colt [koult], *n.* poulain; (*fig.*) novice, *m.*

Columbus [kə'lʌmbəs]. Colomb, *m.*

column ['kɔləm], *n.* colonne, *f.*

coma ['koumə], *n.* coma; assoupissement, *m.*

comb [koum], *n.* peigne, *m.*; étrille (*chevaux*); crête (*coq*), *f.*; rayon (*miel*) *m.*—*v.t.* peigner; étriller (*cheval*).

combat ['kɔmbæt], *n.* combat, *m.*—*v.t.*, *v.i.* combattre.

combatant ['kɔmbətənt], *n.* combattant, *m.*

combination [kɔmbi'neiʃən], *n.* combinaison; association, coalition, *f.*; concours (*de circonstances*), *m.*

combine [kəm'bain], *v.t.* combiner; réunir; allier.—*v.i.* se combiner; se coaliser (*avec*); s'unir (*à*); se syndiquer.—['kɔmbain], *n.* (*Comm.*) cartel, *m.*

combine-harvester ['kɔmbain'hɑ:vistə], *n.* moissonneuse-batteuse, *f.*

combustion [kəm'bʌstʃən], *n.* combustion, *f.*

come [kʌm], *v.i. irr.* venir; arriver, parvenir; se présenter, advenir, se faire; devenir; ***come in!*** entrez! ***come on!*** allons! ***to come back***, revenir; ***to come down***, descendre; ***to come for***, venir chercher; ***to come forward***, s'avancer; ***to come home***, rentrer; ***to come in***, entrer; ***to come off***, se détacher; ***to come out***, sortir; ***to come up***, monter.

comedian [kə'mi:diən], *n.* comédien, *m.*

comedy ['kɔmidi], *n.* comédie, *f.*

comeliness ['kʌmlinis], *n.* aspect gracieux, *m.*; agréments, *m.pl.*

comely ['kʌmli], *a.* avenant.

comer ['kʌmə], *n.* venant; venu, *m.*; ***first comer***, premier venu; ***newcomer***, nouveau venu.

comet ['kɔmit], *n.* comète, *f.*

comfort ['kʌmfət], *n.* réconfort; bien-être, agrément, confort, *m.*; aise(s); aisance, *f.*; ***to take comfort***, se consoler.—*v.t.* réconforter, soulager; consoler.

comfortable ['kʌmfətəbl], *a.* à son aise; agréable, confortable.

comfortably ['kʌmfətəbli], *adv.* à son aise, confortablement.

comforter ['kʌmfətə], *n.* consolateur (*le Saint Esprit*); cache-nez (*foulard*), *m.*; tétine (*de bébé*), *f.*

comfortless ['kʌmfətlis], *a.* sans consolation; désolé, triste.

comic ['kɔmik], **comical** ['kɔmikəl], *a.* comique, drôle.

comically ['kɔmikli], *adv.* comiquement.

coming ['kʌmiŋ], *n.* venue; arrivée; approche, *f.*

comma ['kɔmə], *n.* virgule, *f.*; ***inverted commas***, guillemets, *m.pl.*

command [kə'mɑ:nd], *n.* ordre, commandement; pouvoir, *m.*; autorité, *f.*—*v.t.* commander; posséder; inspirer (*respect*).

commandant ['kɔməndænt], *n.* commandant, *m.*

commandeer [kɔmən'diə], *v.t.* réquisitionner.

commander [kə'mɑ:ndə], *n.* commandant; commandeur (*décoration*); (*Navy*) capitaine (*de frégate etc.*), *m.*

commander-in-chief [kəmɑ:ndərin'tʃi:f], *n.* généralissime, commandant en chef, *m.*

commanding [kə'mɑ:ndiŋ], *a.* commandant; imposant (*important*); qui domine (*surplombant*); impérieux (*de commandement*).

commandment [kə'mɑ:ndmənt], *n.* commandement (*de Dieu*), *m.*

commando [kə'mɑ:ndou], *n.* (*Mil.*) corps franc, commando, *m.*

commemorate [kə'meməreit], *v.t.* célébrer, solenniser; commémorer.

commemoration [kəmemə'reiʃən], *n.* célébration, commémoration, *f.*; souvenir, *m.*

commence [kə'mens], *v.t.*, *v.i.* commencer.

commencement [kə'mensmənt], *n.* commencement, début, *m.*

commend [kə'mend], *v.t.* confier (*à*); recommander; louer.

commendable [kə'mendəbl], *a.* louable.

commendation [kɔmen'deiʃən], *n.* éloge, *m.*, louange, *f.*

comment ['kɔment], *n.* commentaire, *m.*—*v.i.* commenter.

commentary ['kɔmәntәri], *n.* commentaire, *m.*; ***running commentary***, radio-reportage (*d'un match*), *m.*
commerce ['kɔmә:s], *n.* commerce, *m.*
commercial [kә'mә:ʃәl], *a.* commercial, de commerce; commerçant (*ville etc.*); ***commercial traveller***, commis voyageur, *m.*—*n.* (*Tel.*) film publicitaire, *m.*
commingle [kɔ'miŋgl], *v.t.* mêler ensemble, mêler.—*v.i.* se mêler ensemble *ou* avec; se fondre (*dans* ou *en*).
commissariat [kɔmi'sɛәriәt], *n.* commissariat, *m.*, intendance, *f.*
commission [kә'miʃәn], *n.* commission, *f.*; (*Mil.*) brevet; (*Law*) mandat, *m.*—*v.t.* charger, commissionner.
commissionaire [kәmiʃә'nɛә], *n.* portier (*de magasin*); chasseur (*d'hôtel*); commissionnaire, *m.*
commissioner [kә'miʃәnә], *n.* commissaire, *m.*
commit [kә'mit], *v.t.* commettre; confier, livrer, consigner; engager.
committee [kә'miti], *n.* comité, *m.*; (*Parl.*) commission, *f.*
commode [kә'moud], *n.* commode, *f.*
commodious [kә'moudjәs], *a.* spacieux.
commodity [kә'mɔditi], *n.* marchandise, denrée, *f.*, produit, *m.*
commodore ['kɔmәdɔ:], *n.* (*Navy*) chef de division, *m.*; ***air-commodore***, général de brigade, *m.*
common ['kɔmәn], *a.* commun; ordinaire; vulgaire; (*fig.*) trivial; (*Mil.*) simple.—*n.* commune, *f.*; communal, *m.*; bruyère, lande, *f.*; ***House of Commons***, Chambre des Communes, *f.*
commoner ['kɔmәnә], *n.* bourgeois, roturier, *m.*
commonly ['kɔmәnli], *adv.* ordinairement.
commonplace ['kɔmәnpleis], *a.* banal, commun, trivial.—*n.* lieu commun, *m.*, banalité, *f.*
commonweal ['kɔmәn'wi:l], *n.* le bien public, *m.*
commonwealth ['kɔmәnwelθ], *n.* la chose publique, *f.*, l'État, *m.*; ***the (British) Commonwealth***, le Commonwealth (britannique).
commotion [kә'mouʃәn], *n.* secousse, agitation, *f.*, tumulte, *m.*
communal ['kɔmjunәl], *a.* communal.
commune (1) [kә'mju:n], *v.i.* parler, converser, s'entretenir (*avec*).
commune (2) ['kɔmju:n], *n.* commune, *f.*
communicate [kә'mju:nikeit], *v.t.* communiquer.—*v.i.* se communiquer.
communication [kәmju:ni'keiʃәn], *n.* communication, *f.*
communion [kә'mju:njәn], *n.* (*Eccles.*) communion, *f.*; commerce, *m.*
communiqué [kә'mju:nikei], *n.* communiqué, *m.*
Communism ['kɔmjunizm], *n.* communisme, *m.*
Communist ['kɔmjunist], *a.* and *n.* communiste, *m.*, *f.*
community [kә'mju:niti], *n.* communauté, société, *f.*
commutator ['kɔmjuteitә], *n.* commutateur, *m.*

compact (1) ['kɔmpækt], *n.* pacte, contrat; poudrier (*de dame*), *m.*
compact (2) [kәm'pækt], *a.* compact, serré, bien lié; concis.—*v.t.* rendre compact, unir.
companion [kәm'pænjәn], *n.* compagnon, *m.*, compagne; dame *ou* demoiselle de compagnie (*to a lady*), *f.*; pendant (*mobilier*), *m.*
companionship [kәm'pænjәnʃip], *n.* camaraderie; compagnie, *f.*
company ['kʌmpәni], *n.* compagnie; société, corporation; troupe (*acteurs*), *f.*; (*Naut.*) équipage, *m.*; ***we have company today***, nous avons du monde aujourd'hui.
comparable ['kɔmpәrәbl], *a.* comparable.
comparative [kәm'pærәtiv], *a.* comparatif.
comparatively [kәm'pærәtivli], *adv.* relativement, comparativement.
compare [kәm'pɛә], *v.t.* comparer.—*v.i.* être comparable à, rivaliser.
comparison [kәm'pærisәn], *n.* comparaison, *f.*
compartment [kәm'pɑ:tmәnt], *n.* compartiment, *m.*
compass ['kʌmpәs], *n.* compas; circuit, cercle, *m.*; boussole; portée (*atteinte*); étendue (*de la voix*), *f.*; ***a pair of compasses***, un compas.—*v.t.* faire le tour de, entourer; accomplir; ***to compass about***, environner.
compassion [kәm'pæʃәn], *n.* compassion, pitié, *f.*
compassionate [kәm'pæʃәnit], *a.* compatissant.
compatible [kәm'pætәbl], *a.* compatible (*avec*).
compatriot [kәm'pætriәt], *n.* compatriote, *m.*, *f.*
compel [kәm'pel], *v.t.* contraindre, forcer (*de*), obliger (*à* ou *de*).
compelling [kәm'peliŋ], *a.* compulsif, irrésistible.
compensate ['kɔmpәnseit], *v.t.* dédommager (*de*); compenser.—*v.i.* ***to compensate for***, remplacer, racheter.
compensation [kɔmpәn'seiʃәn], *n.* dédommagement, *m.*; compensation, *f.*
compete [kәm'pi:t], *v.i.* concourir (*pour*), faire concurrence (*à*); disputer, rivaliser.
competence ['kɔmpitәns], *n.* capacité, aptitude; (*fig.*) aisance (*fortune*), *f.*
competent ['kɔmpitәnt], *a.* compétent (*pour*), capable (*de*).
competently ['kɔmpitәntli], *adv.* avec compétence; suffisamment.
competition [kɔmpi'tiʃәn], *n.* (*Comm.*) concurrence, *f.*; concours, *m.*
competitive [kәm'petitiv], *a.* compétitif, de concurrence; ***competitive examination***, concours, *m.*
competitor [kәm'petitә], *n.* compétiteur; (*Comm.*) concurrent, *m.*
compile [kәm'pail], *v.t.* compiler, composer.
complacent [kәm'pleisәnt], *a.* suffisant, de suffisance.
complacently [kәm'pleisәntli], *adv.* avec un air *ou* ton suffisant.
complain [kәm'plein], *v.i.* se plaindre (*de*).
complaint [kәm'pleint], *n.* plainte; maladie, *f.*, mal (*illness*), *m.*; réclamation, *f.*; ***to lodge a complaint***, porter plainte.
complaisance [kәm'pleisәns], *n.* complaisance, *f.*
complement ['kɔmplimәnt], *n.* complément, *m.*

complementary [kɔmpli'mentəri], *a.* complémentaire.
complete [kəm'pli:t], *a.* complet, entier; achevé.—*v.t.* compléter, achever; (*fig.*) accomplir; remplir (*une fiche*).
completely [kəm'pli:tli], *adv.* complètement.
completion [kəm'pli:ʃən], *n.* achèvement, accomplissement, *m.*, perfection, *f.*
complex ['kɔmpleks], *a.* and *n.* complexe, *m.*
complexion [kəm'plekʃən], *n.* teint, *m.*, couleur, *f.*; caractère, *m.*; ***to put a different complexion on***, présenter sous un autre jour.
complexity [kəm'pleksiti], *n.* complexité, *f.*
compliance [kəm'plaiəns], *n.* acquiescement, *m.*; obéissance, *f.*; ***in compliance with***, conformément à.
complicate ['kɔmplikeit], *v.t.* compliquer; embrouiller.
complicated ['kɔmplikeitid], *a.* compliqué.
complication [kɔmpli'keiʃən], *n.* complication, *f.*
compliment ['kɔmplimənt], *n.* compliment, *m.*; (*pl.*) salutations, *f.pl.*, hommages (*à une dame*), *m.pl.*—[kɔmpli'ment], *v.t.* complimenter, féliciter.
complimentary [kɔmpli'mentəri], *a.* flatteur; en hommage; ***complimentary ticket***, billet de faveur, *m.*
comply [kəm'plai], *v.i.* se soumettre, se conformer; accéder (*à*).
component [kəm'pounənt], *a.* constituant, composant.—*n.* (*Mech.*) composant, *m.*
compose [kəm'pouz], *v.t.* composer; écrire; rédiger, arranger; calmer.
composed [kəm'pouzd], *a.* composé; calme.
composer [kəm'pouzə], *n.* auteur; (*Mus.*) compositeur, *m.*
composite ['kɔmpəzit] *a.* composé; (*Arch.*) composite.
composition [kɔmpə'ziʃən], *n.* composition; (*Sch.*) rédaction, *f.*; ***French composition***, thème français, *m.*
compositor [kəm'pɔzitə], *n.* (*Print.*) compositeur, *m.*
compost ['kɔmpɔst], *n.* compost, terreau, *m.*
composure [kəm'pouʒə], *n.* calme, *m.*
compound ['kɔmpaund], *a.* and *n.* composé, *m.*; ***compound interest***, intérêts composés, *m.pl.*—[kəm'paund], *v.t.* composer; mêler, combiner; (*Comm.*) atermoyer.—*v.i.* s'arranger.
comprehend [kɔmpri'hend], *v.t.* comprendre.
comprehensible [kɔmpri'hensibl], *a.* compréhensible.
comprehension [kɔmpri'henʃən], *n.* compréhension, *f.*
comprehensive [kɔmpri'hensiv], *a.* étendu, compréhensif; ***comprehensive study***, étude d'ensemble, *f.*
compress ['kɔmpres], *n.* compresse, *f.*—[kəm'pres], *v.t.* comprimer; (*fig.*) resserrer.
comprise [kəm'praiz], *v.t.* contenir, renfermer, comporter.
compromise ['kɔmprəmaiz], *n.* compromis, arrangement, *m.*—*v.t.* compromettre.—*v.i.* transiger.
compromising ['kɔmprəmaiziŋ], *a.* compromettant.
compulsion [kəm'pʌlʃən], *n.* contrainte, *f.*
compulsorily [kəm'pʌlsərili], *adv.* par force, forcément.
compulsory [kəm'pʌlsəri], *a.* forcé, obligatoire.
compute [kəm'pju:t], *v.t.* calculer, supputer.
computer [kəm'pju:tə], *n.* machine à calculer, *f.*; ordinateur, *m.*
comrade ['kɔmrid], *n.* camarade, compagnon, *m.*
comradeship ['kɔmridʃip], *n.* camaraderie, *f.*
concave ['kɔnkeiv], *a.* concave, creux.
conceal [kən'si:l], *v.t.* cacher; (*fig.*) dissimuler; celer *ou* céler (*à*).
concealment [kən'si:lmənt], *n.* dissimulation, *f.*; secret, mystère, *m.*; retraite, cachette, *f.*
concede [kən'si:d], *v.t.* concéder, accorder, admettre.—*v.i.* faire des concessions.
conceit [kən'si:t], *n.* suffisance, vanité, *f.*
conceited [kən'si:tid], *a.* suffisant, vaniteux.
conceivable [kən'si:vəbl], *a.* concevable, imaginable.
conceive [kən'si:v], *v.t.* concevoir; imaginer.—*v.i.* concevoir, devenir enceinte (*femme*).
concentrate ['kɔnsəntreit], *v.t.* concentrer.—*v.i.* se concentrer.
concentration [kɔnsən'treiʃən], *n.* concentration, *f.*
conception [kən'sepʃən], *n.* conception, idée, *f.*
concern [kən'sə:n], *n.* intérêt; soin, souci, *m.*, anxiété; (*Comm.*) entreprise; (*fig.*) affaire, *f.*—*v.t.* concerner, regarder; intéresser; inquiéter.
concerning [kən'sə:niŋ], *prep.* touchant, concernant, en ce qui concerne, à l'égard de.
concert [kən'sə:t], *v.t.* concerter.—*v.i.* se concerter.—['kɔnsət], *n.* concert; accord, *m.*
concerto [kən'tʃə:tou], *n.* (*Mus.*) concerto, *m.*
concession [kən'seʃən], *n.* concession, *f.*
concessionary [kən'seʃənəri], *a.* concessionnaire.
conch [kɔŋk], *n.* conque, *f.*
conciliate [kən'silieit], *v.t.* concilier.
conciliation [kənsili'eiʃən], *n.* conciliation, *f.*
conciliator [kən'silieitə], *n.* conciliateur, *m.*
conciliatory [kən'siljətri], *a.* conciliant, conciliatoire.
concise [kən'sais], *a.* concis.
concisely [kən'saisli], *adv.* succinctement.
conclude [kən'klu:d], *v.t.* conclure; terminer, achever; estimer.
concluding [kən'klu:diŋ], *a.* final, dernier.
conclusion [kən'klu:ʒən], *n.* conclusion, fin; décision, *f.*
conclusive [kən'klu:siv], *a.* concluant; conclusif.
concoct [kən'kɔkt], *v.t.* confectionner; inventer, préparer; machiner (*un plan*), tramer.
concoction [kən'kɔkʃən], *n.* confection (*d'un plat*); potion; (*fig.*) machination (*complot*), *f.*
concord ['kɔŋkɔ:d], *n.* concorde, harmonie, *f.*; (*Mus.*) accord, *m.*
concourse ['kɔŋkɔ:s], *n.* concours, *m.*, affluence, foule; réunion, *f.*
concrete ['kɔŋkri:t], *a.* concret.—*n.* béton; bétonnage, *m.*; ***reinforced concrete***, béton armé.—*v.t.* bétonner.
concubine ['kɔŋkjubain], *n.* concubine, *f.*
concur [kən'kə:], *v.i.* s'accorder, être d'accord (*avec*).
concurrence [kən'kʌrəns], *n.* assentiment; concours, *m.*

concurrent [kən'kʌrənt], *a.* qui concourt, qui s'accorde, concourant.
concurrently [kən'kʌrəntli], *adv.* concurremment.
concussion [kən'kʌʃən], *n.* secousse, *f.*; choc, *m.*; (*Med.*) commotion, *f.*
condemn [kən'dem], *v.t.* condamner (*à*); déclarer coupable; blâmer.
condemnation [kɔndem'neiʃən], *n.* condamnation, censure, *f.*, blâme, *m.*
condensation [kɔnden'seiʃən], *n.* condensation, *f.*
condense [kən'dens], *v.t.* condenser; (*fig.*) resserrer, abréger.
condenser [kən'densə], *n.* condenseur; (*Phys.*) condensateur, *m.*
condescend [kɔndə'send], *v.i.* condescendre, daigner (*à*).
condescension [kɔndə'senʃən], *n.* condescendance, *f.*; acte de condescendance, *m.*
condiment ['kɔndimənt], *n.* assaisonnement, condiment, *m.*
condition [kən'diʃən], *n.* condition, *f.*, état, *m.*—*v.t.* conditionner.
conditional [kən'diʃənəl], *a.* conditionnel.
conditionally [kən'diʃənəli], *adv.* conditionnellement.
condole [kən'doul], *v.i.* prendre part à la douleur (*de*), exprimer ses condoléances.
condolence [kən'douləns], *n.* condoléance, *f.*
condone [kən'doun], *v.t.* excuser, pardonner.
condor ['kɔndə], *n.* condor, *m.*
conduce [kən'dju:s], *v.i.* contribuer (*à*).
conducive [kən'dju:siv], *a.* qui contribue (*à*).
conduct ['kɔndəkt], *n.* conduite; direction, *f.*; ***safeconduct***, sauf-conduit, *m.*—[kən'dʌkt], *v.t.* conduire (*à*); diriger, mener.
conductor [kən'dʌktə], *n.* receveur (d'autobus); (*Am.*) (*Rail.*) chef de train; (*Mus.*) chef d'orchestre; (*Phys.*) conducteur, *m.*; ***lightning-conductor***, paratonnerre, *m.*
conductress [kən'dʌktris], *n.* receveuse (d'autobus), *f.*
conduit ['kʌndit, 'kɔndit], *n.* conduit; tuyau, *m.*
cone [koun], *n.* cône; (*Bot.*) strobile, *m.*, pomme de pin, *f.*; ***ice-cream cone***, cornet de glace, *m.*
confection [kən'fekʃən], *n.* bonbon, *m.*, friandise, *f.*
confectioner [kən'fekʃənə], *n.* confiseur, *m.*
confectionery [kən'fekʃənəri], *n.* confiserie, *f.*, bonbons, *m.pl.*
confederacy [kən'fedərəsi], *n.* confédération (*d'États*); ligue (*de conspirateurs*), *f.*
confederate [kən'fedərit], *a.* confédéré.—*n.* confédéré, *m.*, complice, *m.*, *f.*
confederation [kənfedə'reiʃən], *n.* confédération, *f.*
confer [kən'fə:], *v.t.* conférer, accorder.—*v.i.* conférer (*de*).
conference ['kɔnfərəns], *n.* conférence, *f.*, congrès, *m.*
confess [kən'fes], *v.t.* confesser, avouer.—*v.i.* se confesser.
confessed [kən'fest], *a.* reconnu, confessé, avoué.
confessedly [kən'fesidli], *adv.* de son propre aveu.
confession [kən'feʃən], *n.* confession, *f.*, aveu, *m.*
confessor [kən'fesə], *n.* confesseur, *m.*

confidant ['kɔnfidænt], *n.* confident, *m.*
confide [kən'faid], *v.t.* confier (*à*).—*v.i.* se confier, se fier (*à*).
confidence ['kɔnfidəns], *n.* confiance; hardiesse; assurance; confidence (*secret*), *f.*
confident ['kɔnfidənt], *a.* confiant, certain, sûr; assuré.
confidential [kɔnfi'denʃəl], *a.* de confiance (*personne*); confidentiel (*chose*).
confidentially [kɔnfi'denʃəli], *adv.* de confiance; confidentiellement.
confidently ['kɔnfidəntli], *adv.* avec confiance.
confine [kən'fain], *v.t.* confiner, enfermer; retenir; limiter; ***to be confined*** (*of woman*), faire ses couches, accoucher.—['kɔnfain], *n.* (*usu. in pl.*) confins, *m.pl.*; (*fig.*) limite, borne, *f.*
confinement [kən'fainmənt], *n.* emprisonnement, *m.*; (*Mil.*) arrêts, *m.pl.*; accouchement, *m.*, couches (*de femme*), *f.pl.*
confirm [kən'fə:m], *v.t.* confirmer; affermir.
confirmation [kɔnfə'meiʃən], *n.* confirmation, *f.*, affermissement, *m.*
confirmed [kən'fə:md], *a.* invétéré, fieffé, incorrigible.
confiscate ['kɔnfiskeit], *v.t.* confisquer.
confiscation [kɔnfis'keiʃən], *n.* confiscation, *f.*
conflagration [kɔnflə'greiʃən], *n.* conflagration, *f.*, incendie, *m.*
conflict ['kɔnflikt], *n.* conflit, *m.*; (*fig.*) lutte, contradiction, *f.*—[kən'flikt], *v.i.* s'entrechoquer, lutter (*contre*); être en conflit (*avec*).
conflicting [kən'fliktiŋ], *a.* en conflit, contradictoire.
confluence ['kɔnfluəns], *n.* confluent; concours, *m.*; (*Path.*) confluence, *f.*
conform [kən'fɔ:m], *v.t.* conformer.—*v.i.* se conformer.
conformity [kən'fɔ:miti], *n.* conformité, *f.*; ***in conformity with***, conformément (*à*).
confound [kən'faund], *v.t.* confondre; (*fig.*) bouleverser; embarrasser; ***confound it!*** zut!
confounded [kən'faundid], *a.* maudit, sacré.
confoundedly [kən'faundidli], *adv.* terriblement, furieusement, diablement.
confront [kən'frʌnt], *v.t.* confronter; affronter, faire face à.
confuse [kən'fju:z], *v.t.* rendre confus, embrouiller; (*fig.*) déconcerter.
confused [kən'fju:zd], *a.* confus; embrouillé.
confusedly [kən'fju:zidli], *adv.* confusément.
confusion [kən'fju:ʒən], *n.* confusion, *f.*, désordre; (*fig.*) embarras, *m.*
confute [kən'fju:t], *v.t.* réfuter.
congeal [kən'dʒi:l], *v.t.* congeler, glacer, geler, figer.—*v.i.* se congeler, se geler, se figer.
congenial [kən'dʒi:niəl], *a.* de la même nature; sympathique (*à* ou *avec*); qui convient (*à*); ***a congenial task***, une tâche agréable.
conger ['kɔŋgə], *n.* (*Ichth.*) congre, *m.*, anguille de mer, *f.*
congest [kən'dʒest], *v.t.* entasser; engorger; ***to become congested***, se congestionner; s'embouteiller (*rues*).
congestion [kən'dʒestʃən], *n.* amoncellement, *m.*; (*Path.*) congestion, *f.*; encombrement (*des rues*), *m.*

conglomerate [kən'glɔməreit], *v.t.* conglomérer.—*v.i.* se conglomérer.—[kən'glɔ mərit], *n.* (*Geol.*) conglomérat, *m.*
conglomeration [kɔnglɔmə'reiʃən], *n.* conglomération, *f.*
Congo ['kɔŋgou]. le Congo, *m.*
Congolese [kɔŋgo'li:z], *a.* congolais.—*n.* Congolais (*personne*).
congratulate [kən'grætjuleit], *v.t.* féliciter.
congratulation [kəngrætju'leiʃən], *n.* félicitation, *f.*
congregate ['kɔŋgrigeit], *v.t.* rassembler.—*v.i.* se rassembler.
congregation [kɔŋgri'geiʃən], *n.* (*Eccles.*) congrégation, *f.*, fidèles, *m.pl.*; assemblée, *f.*, auditoire, *m.*, assistance, *f.*
congress ['kɔŋgres], *n.* congrès, *m.*
congressional [kən'greʃənl], *a.* congressionnel.
congressman ['kɔŋgresmən], *n.* (*pl.* **-men** [men]) (*U.S.*) membre du Congrès, *m.*
conic ['kɔnik], **conical** ['kɔnikəl], *a.* conique.
conifer ['kounifə], *n.* conifère, *m.*
coniferous [ko'nifərəs], *a.* conifère.
conjecture [kən'dʒektʃə], *v.t.*, *v.i.* conjecturer.—*n.* conjecture, *f.*
conjugal ['kɔndʒugəl], *a.* conjugal.
conjugate ['kɔndʒugeit], *v.t.* conjuguer.
conjugation [kɔndʒu'geiʃən], *n.* conjugaison, *f.*
conjunction [kən'dʒʌŋkʃən], *n.* conjonction, *f.*
conjure ['kʌndʒə], *v.t.* ensorceler; escamoter; ***to conjure up***, évoquer.
conjurer, conjuror ['kʌndʒərə], *n.* escamoteur, prestidigitateur, illusionniste, *m.*
conjuring ['kʌndʒəriŋ], *n.* prestidigitation, *f.*, escamotage, *m.*
connect [kə'nekt], *v.t.* lier, joindre, rattacher, unir (*à*); accoupler.—*v.i.* se lier; faire correspondance (*trains*).
connected [kə'nektid], *a.* joint, uni, lié; cohérent; en relations.
connection, connexion [kə'nekʃən], *n.* connexion, liaison, suite, *f.*; rapport, *m.*; (*Rail.*) correspondance, *f.*; (*Elec.*) contact, *m.*; (*Comm.*) clientèle, *f.*; (*pl.*) parents, *m.pl.*; ***in connexion with***, à propos de.
connivance [kə'naivəns], *n.* connivence, *f.*
connive [kə'naiv], *v.i.* ***to connive at***, fermer les yeux sur, être de connivence dans.
connoisseur [kɔnə'sə:], *n.* connaisseur, *m.*
connubial [kə'nju:biəl], *a.* conjugal.
conquer ['kɔŋkə], *v.t.* vaincre, dompter; conquérir.—*v.i.* vaincre, remporter la victoire.
conqueror ['kɔŋkərə], *n.* vainqueur, conquérant, *m.*
conquest ['kɔŋkwest], *n.* conquête, *f.*
conscience ['kɔnʃəns], *n.* conscience, *f.*; ***conscience money***, restitution anonyme, *f.*
conscientious [kɔnʃi'enʃəs], *a.* consciencieux; de conscience; ***conscientious objector***, objecteur de conscience, *m.*
conscientiously [kɔnʃi'enʃəsli], *adv.* consciencieusement.
conscious ['kɔnʃəs], *a.* conscient; ***to be conscious***, avoir sa connaissance; ***to be conscious of***, avoir conscience de.
consciously ['kɔnʃəsli], *adv.* sciemment, en connaissance de cause.
consciousness ['kɔnʃəsnis], *n.* conscience; connaissance, *f.*
conscript ['kɔnskript], *a.* and *n.* conscrit, *m.* —[kən'skript], *v.t.* enrôler (par la conscription).
conscription [kən'skripʃən], *n.* conscription, *f.*
consecrate ['kɔnsikreit], *v.t.* consacrer (*une église*); bénir (*pain*); sacrer (*évêque, roi*); ***consecrated ground***, terre sainte, *f.*
consecration [kɔnsi'kreiʃən], *n.* consécration; canonisation, *f.*; sacre (*d'évêque, de roi etc.*), *m.*
consecutive [kən'sekjutiv], *a.* consécutif.
consent [kən'sent], *v.i.* consentir (*à*).—*n.* consentement; accord, *m.*
consequence ['kɔnsikwəns], *n.* conséquence, suite, *f.*, effet, *m.*; importance, *f.*
consequent ['kɔnsikwənt], *a.* résultant; (*Log.*) conséquent.—*n.* conséquent, *m.*
consequential [kɔnsi'kwenʃəl], *a.* conséquent, logique; (*fig.*) suffisant, important.
consequently ['kɔnsikwəntli], *adv.* and *conj.* par conséquent.
conservative [kən'sə:vətiv], *a.* and *n.* conservateur, *m.*
conservatory [kən'sə:vətri], *n.* conservatoire (*théâtre, musique*), *m.*; (*Hort.*) serre, *f.*
consider [kən'sidə], *v.t.* considérer, examiner; estimer.—*v.i.* considérer, réfléchir (*à*).
considerable [kən'sidərəbl], *a.* considérable, grand, important.
considerably [kən'sidərəbli], *adv.* considérablement.
considerate [kən'sidərit], *a.* modéré, indulgent; attentif, plein d'égards; prévenant.
consideration [kənsidə'reiʃən], *n.* considération, *f.*, examen, *m.*; égards, *m.pl.*; récompense, *f.*, dédommagement, *m.*; ***to take into consideration***, tenir compte de.
considering [kən'sidəriŋ], *prep.* eu égard à, étant donné, vu.—*conj.* vu que, attendu que, étant donné que.
consign [kən'sain], *v.t.* consigner, livrer, confier (*à*); (*Comm.*) expédier.
consignment [kən'sainmənt], *n.* expédition, *f.*, envoi, *m.*
consist [kən'sist], *v.i.* consister (*en*); ***to consist of***, se composer (*de*).
consistency [kən'sistənsi], *n.* consistance, suite, *f.*, esprit de suite; accord, *m.*, harmonie; stabilité, *f.*
consistent [kən'sistənt], *a.* consistant; compatible (*avec*), conséquent.
consistently [kən'sistəntli], *adv.* d'une manière conséquente, conséquemment.
consolation [kɔnsə'leiʃən], *n.* consolation, *f.*
console [kən'soul], *v.t.* consoler (*de*).
consolidate [kən'sɔlideit], *v.t.* consolider.—*v.i.* se consolider; ***consolidated annuities***, (*abbr.*) ***consols***, consolidés, *m.pl.*
consolidation [kənsɔli'deiʃən], *n.* consolidation, *f.*
consoling [kən'souliŋ], *a.* consolant, consolateur.
consonant ['kɔnsənənt], *a.* consonant, conforme (*à*).—*n.* (*Phon.*) consonne, *f.*
consort ['kɔnsɔ:t], *n.* compagnon, *m.*, compagne, *f.*; époux, *m.*, épouse, *f.*—[kən'sɔ:t], *v.i.* s'associer (*à*); ***to consort with***, fréquenter.

conspicuous [kən'spikjuəs], *a.* bien visible, en évidence; remarquable, éminent.
conspicuously [kən'spikjuəsli], *adv.* visiblement, manifestement, éminemment.
conspiracy [kən'spirəsi], *n.* conspiration, conjuration, *f.*
conspirator [kən'spirətə], *n.* conspirateur; conjuré, *m.*
conspire [kən'spaiə], *v.i.* conspirer, comploter (*contre*); (*fig.*) se réunir (*pour*).
constable ['kʌnstəbl], *n.* gouverneur (*de château*); agent de police, *m.*; ***chief constable,*** commissaire de police, *m.*
constabulary [kən'stæbjuləri], *n.* police; gendarmerie, *f.*
constancy ['kɔnstənsi], *n.* constance, fermeté, fidélité; régularité, *f.*
constant ['kɔnstənt], *a.* stable, constant, fidèle; continu.
constantly ['kɔnstəntli], *adv.* constamment, invariablement.
constellation [kɔnstə'leiʃən], *n.* constellation, *f.*
consternation [kɔnstə'neiʃən], *n.* consternation, *f.*, atterrement, *m.*
constipation [kɔnsti'peiʃən], *n.* constipation, *f.*
constituency [kən'stitjuənsi], *n.* circonscription électorale, *f.*, électeurs, *m.pl.*
constituent [kən'stitjuənt], *a.* constituant.—*n.* constituant; (*Polit.*) commettant, électeur, *m.*
constitute ['kɔnstitju:t], *v.t.* constituer, faire.
constitution [kɔnsti'tju:ʃən], *n.* constitution, *f.*, tempérament, *m.*
constitutional [kɔnsti'tju:ʃənəl], *a.* constitutionnel.—*n.* promenade de santé, *f.*
constrain [kən'strein], *v.t.* contraindre, forcer; retenir; gêner.
constraint [kən'streint], *n.* contrainte, gêne, *f.*
constrict [kən'strikt], *v.t.* resserrer, étrangler; brider.
construct [kən'strʌkt], *v.t.* construire, bâtir.
construction [kən'strʌkʃən], *n.* construction, *f.*; bâtiment, *m.*; (*fig.*) interprétation, *f.*, sens, *m.*
constructive [kən'strʌktiv], *a.* constructif; implicite.
construe [kən'stru:], *v.t.* traduire mot-à-mot; (*fig.*) expliquer, interpréter.
consul ['kɔnsəl], *n.* consul, *m.*
consular ['kɔnsjulə], *a.* consulaire.
consulate ['kɔnsjulit], **consulship** ['kɔnsəl ʃip], *n.* consulat, *m.*
consult [kən'sʌlt], *v.t.* consulter.—*v.i.* délibérer.
consultation [kɔnsəl'teiʃən], *n.* consultation, délibération, *f.*
consume [kən'sju:m], *v.t.* consumer, dissiper, dévorer; gaspiller; consommer (*to use*).
consumer [kən'sju:mə], *n.* consommateur; abonné (*de gaz etc.*), *m.*; ***consumer goods,*** biens de consommation, *m.pl.*
consummate ['kɔnsəmeit], *v.t.* consommer, achever, accomplir.—[kən'sʌmit], *a.* consommé, complet, achevé, fieffé.
consummation [kɔnsə'meiʃən], *n.* consommation, fin, *f.*; (*fig.*) comble, *m.*
consumption [kən'sʌmpʃən], *n.* consommation; phtisie, consomption (*maladie*), *f.*
consumptive [kən'sʌmptiv], *a.* poitrinaire, phtisique, tuberculeux.

contact ['kɔntækt], *n.* contact, rapport, *m.*—*v.t.* contacter, se mettre en relation avec, entrer en contact avec.
contagion [kən'teidʒən], *n.* contagion, *f.*
contagious [kən'teidʒəs], *a.* contagieux.
contain [kən'tein], *v.t.* contenir; retenir, renfermer.
container [kən'teinə], *n.* récipient, réservoir, *m.*; (*Comm.*) boîte, *f.*
contaminate [kən'tæmineit], *v.t.* souiller, contaminer.
contamination [kəntæmi'neiʃən], *n.* souillure, contamination, *f.*
contemplate ['kɔntəmpleit], *v.t.* contempler; méditer, projeter.—*v.i.* songer, méditer.
contemplation [kɔntəm'pleiʃən], *n.* contemplation; méditation, *f.*; projet, *m.*
contemplative [kən'templətiv], *a.* contemplatif; pensif.
contemporaneous [kəntempə'reinjəs], *a.* contemporain.
contemporary [kən'tempərəri], *a.* and *n.* contemporain, *m.*
contempt [kən'tempt], *n.* mépris, dédain, *m.*
contemptible [kən'temptəbl], *a.* méprisable, à dédaigner.
contemptuous [kən'temptjuəs], *a.* méprisant, dédaigneux.
contend [kən'tend], *v.i.* lutter, combattre; contester; prétendre (*que*).
contender [kən'tendə], *n.* compétiteur, concurrent, *m.*
content (1) [kən'tent], *a.* content, satisfait; ***to be content with,*** se contenter de.—*n.* contentement, *m.*—*v.t.* contenter, satisfaire.
content (2) ['kɔntent], *n.* contenu, *m.*; ***table of contents,*** table des matières, *f.*
contented [kən'tentid], *a.* satisfait, content (*de*).
contentedly [kən'tentidli], *adv.* avec contentement.
contention [kən'tenʃən], *n.* dispute, lutte, *f.*, débat, *m.*; prétention, *f.*; ***bone of contention,*** pomme de discorde, *f.*
contentious [kən'tenʃəs], *a.* contentieux, litigieux, querelleur.
contentiousness [kən'tenʃəsnis], *n.* humeur querelleuse, *f.*
contentment [kən'tentmənt], *n.* contentement, *m.*
conterminous [kən'tə:minəs], *a.* limitrophe, voisin (*de*); attenant (*à*).
contest ['kɔntest], *n.* lutte, *f.*, combat; concours, *m.*—[kən'test], *v.t.*, *v.i.* contester, disputer.
contestant [kən'testənt], *n.* contestant, concurrent, *m.*
context ['kɔntekst], *n.* contexte, *m.*; ***in this context,*** à ce sujet.
contiguity [kɔnti'gju:iti], *n.* contiguïté, *f.*
contiguous [kən'tigjuəs], *a.* contigu, attenant (*à*).
continence ['kɔntinəns], *n.* continence, chasteté; (*fig.*) retenue, *f.*
continent (1) ['kɔntinənt], *a.* continent, chaste; (*fig.*) modéré, retenu.
continent (2) ['kɔntinənt], *n.* continent, *m.*
continental [kɔnti'nentl], *a.* and *n.* continental, *m.*
contingence [kən'tindʒəns], **contingency** [kən'tindʒənsi], *n.* éventualité, *f.* cas imprévu, *m.*

contingent [kən'tindʒənt], *a.* contingent, fortuit, imprévu.—*n.* (*Mil.*) contingent, *m.*

contingently [kən'tindʒəntli], *adv.* éventuellement, fortuitement.

continual [kən'tinjuəl], *a.* continuel.

continually [kən'tinjuəli], *adv.* continuellement.

continuance [kən'tinjuəns], *n.* continuation; durée, *f.*

continuation [kəntinju'eiʃən], *n.* continuation, durée, *f.*

continue [kən'tinju:], *v.t.* continuer; prolonger; reprendre; perpétuer.—*v.i.* continuer; demeurer; durer.

continued [kən'tinju:d], *a.* continu, suivi; à suivre (*feuilleton*); ***to be continued***, à suivre.

continuity [kənti'nju:iti], *n.* continuité, *f.*

continuous [kən'tinjuəs], *a.* continu.

continuously [kən'tinjuəsli], *adv.* continûment, sans interruption.

contort [kən'tɔ:t], *v.t.* tordre, contourner, défigurer.

contorted [kən'tɔ:tid], *a.* tordu, contourné, défiguré.

contortion [kən'tɔ:ʃən], *n.* contorsion; (*Anat.*) luxation, *f.*

contortionist [kən'tɔ:ʃənist], *n.* contorsionniste, *m, f.*

contour ['kəntuə], *n.* contour, tracé (*de niveau*), *m.*

contra ['kəntrə], *prep.* contre; (*Comm.*) d'autre part.

contraband ['kəntrəbænd], *a.* de contrebande.—*n.* contrebande, *f.*

contraception [kəntrə'sepʃən], *n.* procédés anticonceptionnels, *m.pl.*

contraceptive [kəntrə'septiv], *a.* anticonceptionnel.—*n.* procédé *ou* appareil anticonceptionnel, *m.*

contract [kən'trækt], *v.t.* contracter (*dans tous les sens*); abréger; (*fig.*) resserrer; rider, froncer (*les sourcils etc.*); prendre (*habitude*).—*v.i.* se contracter, se resserrer, se rétrécir; (*Comm.*) traiter (*pour*), contracter, entreprendre, soumissionner; ***to contract out of something***, renoncer à *ou* se dégager de quelquechose par contrat.—['kəntrækt], *n.* contrat; pacte, *m.*, convention; adjudication, *f.*

contractible [kən'træktəbl], *a.* contractile.

contraction [kən'trækʃən], *n.* contraction, *f.*, rétrécissement; raccourcissement; retrait (*métaux*), *m.*; (*Math.*) abréviation, *f.*

contractor [kən'træktə], *n.* contractant; entrepreneur (*constructeur*); fournisseur (*aux forces armées*); adjudicataire (*concesseur*), *m.*

contradict [kəntrə'dikt], *v.t.* contredire, démentir.

contradiction [kəntrə'dikʃən], *n.* contradiction, incompatibilité, *f.*, démenti (*négation*), *m.*

contradictory [kəntrə'diktəri], *a.* contradictoire.

contralto [kən'træltou], *n.* (*Mus.*) contralto, contralte, *m.*

contrariety [kəntrə'raiəti], *n.* contrariété, opposition, *f.*

contrarily ['kəntrərili], *adv.* contrairement, en sens contraire.

contrary ['kəntrəri], *a.* contraire, opposé; (*fam.*) [kən'trɛəri], contrariant (*personne*).—*n.* contraire, *m.*; ***on the contrary***, au contraire.—*adv.* contrairement (*à*); à l'encontre (*de*).

contrast ['kəntrɑ:st], *n.* contraste, *m.*—[kən'trɑ:st], *v.t.* faire contraster; mettre en contraste.—*v.i.* contraster, faire contraste.

contravene [kəntrə'vi:n], *v.t.* contrevenir à, enfreindre.

contravention [kəntrə'venʃən], *n.* contravention, infraction, *f.*

contribute [kən'tribju:t], *v.t.* contribuer, payer.—*v.i.* contribuer (*à*).

contribution [kəntri'bju:ʃən], *n.* contribution, *f.*

contributor [kən'tribjutə], *n.* contribuant; (*Journ.*) collaborateur, *m.*

contributory [kən'tribjutəri], *a.* contribuant.

contrite ['kəntrait], *a.* contrit, pénitent.

contritely ['kəntraitli], *adv.* avec contrition.

contriteness ['kəntraitnis], **contrition** [kən'triʃən], *n.* contrition, pénitence, *f.*

contrivance [kən'traivəns], *n.* invention; combinaison, idée, *f.*; artifice, *m.*

contrive [kən'traiv], *v.t.* inventer, imaginer; pratiquer, ménager.—*v.i.* s'arranger (*pour*), trouver moyen (*de*); parvenir (*à*).

contriver [kən'traivə], *n.* inventeur, *m.*, inventrice, *f.*

contriving [kən'traiviŋ], *a.* ingénieux.

control [kən'troul], *n.* autorité (*supérieure*); surveillance; (*Tech.*) commande, *f.*; ***out of control***, désemparé; ***remote control***, télécommande, *f.*—*v.t.* diriger, régler; gouverner, commander; ***to control oneself***, se dominer, se retenir.

controller [kən'troulə], *n.* contrôleur, *m.*

controversial [kəntrə'və:ʃəl], *a.* sujet à controverse, polémique.

controversy ['kəntrəvə:si], *n.* controverse, polémique, *f.*; différend, *m.*

controvert ['kəntrəvə:t], *v.t.* controverser, disputer.

contumacious [kəntju'meiʃəs], *a.* obstiné, récalcitrant, opiniâtre; (*Law*) contumace.

contumaciousness [kəntju'meiʃəsnis], **contumacy** ['kəntjuməsi], *n.* obstination, opiniâtreté; (*Law*) contumace, *f.*

contumelious [kəntju'mi:liəs], *a.* injurieux, outrageant.

contumely ['kəntjuməli], *n.* injure, *f.*, outrage, *m.*, honte, *f.*

contuse [kən'tju:z], *v.t.* contusionner.

contusion [kən'tju:ʃən], *n.* contusion, meurtrissure, *f.*

conundrum [kə'nʌndrəm], *n.* énigme, devinette, *f.*

convalesce [kənvə'les], *v.i.* être en convalescence.

convalescence [kənvə'lesəns], *n.* convalescence, *f.*

convalescent [kənvə'lesənt], *a.* and *n.* convalescent, *m.*, convalescente, *f.*

convection [kən'vekʃən], *n.* convection, *f.*

convene [kən'vi:n], *v.t.* convoquer, réunir, assembler.—*v.i.* s'assembler, se réunir.

convenience [kən'vi:niəns], *n.* commodité, convenance, *f.*

convenient [kən'vi:niənt], *a.* commode, convenable.

conveniently [kən'vi:niəntli], *adv.* commodément, convenablement, sans inconvénient.
convent ['kɔnvənt], *n.* couvent, *m.*
conventicle [kən'ventikl], *n.* conventicule, *m.*
convention [kən'venʃən], *n.* convention; assemblée, *f.*; (*pl.*) convenances, *f.pl.*
conventional [kən'venʃənəl], *a.* conventionnel, de convention.
conventual [kən'ventjuəl], *a.* conventuel.—*n.* conventuel, religieux, *m.*, religieuse, *f.*
converge [kən'və:dʒ], *v.i.* converger.
conversant [kən'və:sənt], *a.* versé (*dans*); familier (*avec*), au courant de.
conversation [kɔnvə'seiʃən], *n.* conversation, *f.*, entretien, *m.*
conversational [kɔnvə'seiʃənəl], *a.* de conversation.
conversationalist [kɔnvə'seiʃənəlist], *n.* causeur, *m.*
converse [kən'və:s], *v.i.* causer, converser, s'entretenir.—['kɔnvə:s], *n.* entretien, *m.*, conversation; (*Math.*) réciproque, *f.*
conversely ['kɔnvə:sli], *adv.* réciproquement.
conversion [kən'və:ʃən], *n.* conversion, *f.*
convert [kən'və:t], *v.t.* convertir, transformer; faire servir.—['kɔnvə:t], *n.* converti, *m.*, convertie, *f.*
converter [kən'və:tə], *n.* convertisseur, *m.*
convertible [kən'və:tibl], *a.* convertible (*chose*); convertissable (*personne*); (*Motor.*) décapotable.
convex ['kɔnveks], *a.* convexe.
convey [kən'vei], *v.t.* transporter (*marchandises etc.*); porter, conduire, amener; transmettre (*son etc.*); présenter (*remerciements etc.*); donner (*idée etc.*); communiquer (*nouvelle etc.*); céder (*propriété etc.*).
conveyable [kən'veiəbl], *a.* transportable; exprimable.
conveyance [kən'veiəns], *n.* transport, *m.*; transmission, *f.*; véhicule, *m.*; (*Law*) cession, *f.*
conveyor [kən'veiə], *n.* porteur, voiturier; (appareil) transporteur; conducteur (électrique), *m.*; ***conveyor belt***, chaîne de montage, *f.*
convict [kən'vikt], *v.t.* condamner, déclarer coupable; convaincre (*quelqu'un de son erreur etc.*).—['kɔnvikt], *n.* forçat, *m.*
conviction [kən'vikʃən], *n.* conviction, persuasion; (*Law*) condamnation, *f.*
convince [kən'vins], *v.t.* convaincre, persuader.
convincing [kən'vinsiŋ], *a.* convaincant; persuasif.
convincingly [kən'vinsiŋli], *adv.* d'une manière convaincante.
convivial [kən'viviəl], *a.* joyeux, jovial.
conviviality [kənvivi'æliti], *n.* franche gaieté, *f.*; (*pl.*) joyeux repas, *m.pl.*
convocation [kɔnvə'keiʃən], *n.* convocation; (*Eccles.*) assemblée, *f.*, synode, *m.*
convoke [kən'vouk], *v.t.* convoquer, assembler.
convolvulus [kən'vɔlvjuləs], *n.* (*pl.* **convolvuli** [kən'vɔlvjulai]) volubilis, liseron, *m.*, belle-de-jour, *f.*
convoy ['kɔnvɔi], *n.* convoi, *m.*, escorte, *f.*
convulse [kən'vʌls], *v.t.* convulser; (*fig.*) ébranler, bouleverser.
convulsion [kən'vʌlʃən], *n.* convulsion; (*fig.*) commotion, *f.*
convulsive [kən'vʌlsiv], *a.* convulsif.
cony, coney ['kouni], *n.* lapin, *m.*
coo [ku:], *v.i.* roucouler.
cooing ['ku:iŋ], *n.* roucoulement, *m.*
cook [kuk], *n.* cuisinier, *m.*, cuisinière, *f.*; (*Naut.*) coq, *m.*; ***head cook***, chef, *m.*—*v.t.* cuire, faire cuire.—*v.i.* cuire; faire la cuisine, cuisiner.
cooker ['kukə], *n.* cuisinière (*appareil*), *f.*; fruit à cuire, *m.*; ***pressure cooker***, cocotte-minute, *f.*
cookery ['kukəri], *n.* cuisine (*art*), *f.*
cooking ['kukiŋ], *n.* cuisine; cuisson, *f.*
cool [ku:l], *a.* frais, (*fig.*) calme, tranquille; peu gêné.—*n.* frais, *m.*, fraîcheur, *f.*—*v.t.* rafraîchir; refroidir; (*fig.*) calmer.—*v.i.* se refroidir; refroidir; ***to cool down***, se calmer, s'apaiser.
cooling ['ku:liŋ], *a.* rafraîchissant, calmant; ***cooling tower***, refroidisseur, *m.*
coolly ['ku:lli], *adv.* fraîchement; (*fig.*) de sangfroid, tranquillement.
coolness ['ku:lnis], *n.* fraîcheur, *f.*, frais, *m.*; (*fig.*) froideur (*indifférence*), *f.*; sang-froid, sans-gêne (*insolence*), *m.*
coop [ku:p], *n.* cage à poules, mue, *f.*—*v.t.* mettre en mue; ***to coop up***, enfermer étroitement, claquemurer.
cooper ['ku:pə], *n.* tonnelier, *m.*
co-operate [kou'ɔpəreit], *v.i.* coopérer, concourir (*à*).
co-operation [kouɔpə'reiʃən], *n.* coopération, *f.*; concours, *m.*
co-operative [kou'ɔpərətiv], *a.* coopérant, coopératif.
co-opt [kou'ɔpt], *v.t.* coopter.
co-ordinate [kou'ɔ:dineit], *v.t.* coordonner.—[kou'ɔ:dinit], *a.* du même rang, égal; (*Math.*) coordonné.
coot [ku:t], *n.* (*Orn.*) foulque, *f.*
cop [kɔp], *n.* cime, *f.*, sommet, *m.*; huppe, aigrette (*d'oiseau*), *f.*; (*slang*) flic (*agent de police*), *m.*
copartner [kou'pɑ:tnə], *n.* associé, *m.*
copartnership [kou'pɑ:tnəʃip], *n.* société en nom collectif, *f.*
cope (1) [koup], *n.* chaperon, *m.*, chape (*vêtement sacerdotal*), *f.*—*v.t.* couvrir, chaperonner.
cope (2) [koup], *v.i.* se débrouiller; ***to cope with***, tenir tête à; venir à bout de.
Copenhagen [koupən'heigən]. Copenhague, *f.*
copier ['kɔpiə], **copyist** ['kɔpiist], *n.* copiste, *m.*, *f.*; (*fig.*) imitateur, *m.*
coping ['koupiŋ], *n.* faîte (*d'un édifice*), couronnement (*d'un mur*), *m.*
copious ['koupiəs], *a.* abondant, copieux.
copiously ['koupiəsli], *adv.* copieusement, abondamment.
copiousness ['koupiəsnis], *n.* abondance, *f.*
copper ['kɔpə], *a.* de cuivre, en cuivre.—*n.* cuivre (rouge), *m.*; chaudière (*boiler*), *f.*; (*slang*) flic (*agent de police*), *m.*; (*pl.*) petite monnaie, *f.*—*v.t.* cuivrer; (*Naut.*) doubler en cuivre.
copper-beech ['kɔpə'bi:tʃ], *n.* hêtre rouge, *m.*
copper-smith ['kɔpəsmiθ], *n.* chaudronnier, *m.*
coppice ['kɔpis], **copse** [kɔps], *n.* taillis, *m.*

copy ['kɔpi], *n.* copie, *f.*; exemple (*d'écriture*); exemplaire (*livre*); numéro (*journal*); modèle (*de dessin*), *m.*; ***rough copy***, brouillon, *m.*—*v.t.* copier; imiter; ***to copy out***, transcrire.
copy-book ['kɔpibuk], *n.* cahier d'écriture, *m.*
copyist [COPIER].
copyright ['kɔpirait], *n.* droits d'auteur, *m.pl.*; propriété littéraire, *f.*
coquet [ko'ket], *v.i.* faire des coquetteries (*à*); faire la coquette (*avec*).
coquette [ko'ket], *n.* coquette, *f.*
coquetry ['koukətri], *n.* coquetterie, *f.*
coquettish [ko'ketiʃ], *a.* coquet, en coquette; provocant (*sourire*).
coquettishly [ko'ketiʃli], *adv.* d'un air provocant.
coral ['kɔrəl], *a.* de corail.—*n.* corail, *m.*
cord [kɔ:d], *n.* corde, *f.*, cordon; cordage, *m.*, ganse, *f.*; (*fig.*) lien, *m.*—*v.t.* corder.
cordial ['kɔ:diəl], *a.* cordial.—*n.* cordial, *m.*, liqueur, *f.*
cordiality [kɔ:di'æliti], *n.* cordialité, *f.*
cordially ['kɔ:diəli], *adv.* cordialement.
cordon ['kɔ:dən], *n.* cordon, *m.*—*v.t.* ***to cordon off***, isoler par un cordon (*de police*).
corduroy ['kɔ:djurɔi], *n.* velours à côtes, *m.*
core [kɔ:], *n.* cœur; noyau (*d'un moule*); (*fig.*) milieu, centre, *m.*; (*Naut.*) âme (*de corde*), *f.*; trognon (*de pomme*), *m.*—*v.t.* vider (*une pomme*); creuser, évider (*un moule*).
co-respondent [kouris'pɔndənt], *n.* complice, *m.*, *f.*, co-défendeur (*en adultère*), *m.*
corgi, corgy ['kɔ:gi], *n.* basset gallois, *m.*
cork [kɔ:k], *n.* liège; bouchon (*à bouteille etc.*), *m.*—*v.t.* boucher.
corkscrew ['kɔ:kskru], *n.* tire-bouchon, *m.*; ***corkscrew staircase***, escalier en colimaçon, *m.*
cork-tipped ['kɔ:k'tipt], *a.* à bouts de liège (*cigarettes*).
corm [kɔ:m], *n.* (*Bot.*) bulbe, *m.*
cormorant ['kɔ:mərənt], *n.* cormoran; (*fig.*) rapace, affameur, *m.*
corn (1) [kɔ:n], *n.* grain, *m.*; céréales, *f.pl.*; blé, *m.*; ***Indian corn***, maïs, *m.*—*v.t.* saler (*bœuf*).
corn (2) [kɔ:n], *n.* cor (au pied), *m.*
corn-chandler ['kɔ:ntʃɑ:ndlə], *n.* blatier, marchand de blé, *m.*
corn-crake ['kɔ:nkreik], *n.* râle de genêt, *m.*
cornea ['kɔ:niə], *n.* (*Anat.*) cornée, *f.*
corned beef ['kɔ:nd'bi:f], *n.* bœuf salé, bœuf de conserve, *m.*
corner ['kɔ:nə], *n.* coin, angle, *m.*; encoignure, *f.*; (*fig.*) monopole, accaparement, *m.*; ***blind corner***, tournant (*ou* virage) masqué, *m.*—*v.t.* (*Comm.*) accaparer; (*fig.*) pousser dans un coin, acculer.—*v.i.* prendre un virage, virer.
corner-stone ['kɔ:nəstoun], *n.* pierre angulaire, *f.*
cornet ['kɔ:nit], *n.* cornet (*à pistons*), *m.*
cornfield ['kɔ:nfi:ld], *n.* champ de blé, *m.*
cornflakes ['kɔ:nfleiks], *n.pl.* paillettes de maïs, *f.pl.*
corn-flour ['kɔ:nflauə], *n.* farine de maïs, *f.*
corn-flower ['kɔ:nflauə], *n.* bluet, *m.*
cornice ['kɔ:nis], *n.* corniche, *f.*
corn-poppy ['kɔ:npɔpi], *n.* coquelicot, *m.*
corollary [kə'rɔləri], *n.* corollaire, *m.*
coronation [kɔrə'neiʃən], *n.* couronnement, sacre, *m.*
coroner ['kɔrənə], *n.* coroner, *m.*
coronet ['kɔrənit], *n.* (petite) couronne, *f.*
corporal ['kɔ:pərəl], *a.* corporel.—*n.* caporal (*infanterie*); brigadier (*cavalerie*), *m.*
corporate ['kɔ:pərit], *a.* érigé en corporation; de corporation.
corporately ['kɔ:pəritli], *adv.* collectivement.
corporation [kɔ:pə'reiʃən], *n.* corporation, *f.*; conseil municipal, *m.*, municipalité (*d'une ville*), *f.*
corporeal [kɔ:'pɔ:riəl], *a.* corporel, matériel.
corps [kɔ:], *n.inv.* corps, *m.*, formation, *f.*
corpse [kɔ:ps], *n.* cadavre, *m.*
corpulence ['kɔ:pjuləns], **corpulency** ['kɔ:pjulənsi], *n.* corpulence, *f.*, embonpoint, *m.*
corpulent ['kɔ:pjulənt], *a.* corpulent, gros, gras.
corpuscle ['kɔ:pʌsl], *n.* corpuscule, globule, *m.*
correct [kə'rekt], *a.* correct, exact, juste; (*fig.*) convenable, en règle; pur, bon (*style*); bien élevé (*personne*); comme il faut.—*v.t.* corriger, rectifier, reprendre; punir.
correction [kə'rekʃən], *n.* correction; punition, *f.*
correctly [kə'rektli], *adv.* correctement, exactement, justement.
correctness [kə'rektnis], *n.* exactitude, justesse; pureté (*de style*), *f.*
correlate ['kɔrileit], *v.t.* mettre en corrélation.—*v.i.* correspondre.
correlation [kɔri'leiʃən], *n.* corrélation, *f.*
correspond [kɔris'pɔnd], *v.i.* correspondre (*à ou avec*), répondre (*à*); s'accorder (*avec*); être conforme (*à*).
correspondence [kɔris'pɔndəns], *n.* correspondance, *f.*, rapport, *m.*
correspondent [kɔris'pɔndənt], *a.* conforme, qui se rapporte (*à*).—*n.* correspondant, *m.*
corridor ['kɔridɔ:], *n.* corridor; couloir, *m.*
corroborate [kə'rɔbəreit], *v.t.* corroborer, confirmer.
corroboration [kərɔbə'reiʃən], *n.* corroboration, confirmation, *f.*; ***in corroboration of***, à l'appui de.
corrode [kə'roud], *v.t.* corroder, ronger; (*fig.*) détruire.—*v.i.* se corroder.
corrosion [kə'rouʒən], *n.* corrosion; (*fig.*) destruction, *f.*
corrosive [kə'rouziv], *a.* corrosif; (*fig.*) rongeur.—*n.* corrosif, *m.*
corrugate ['kɔrugeit], *v.t.* rider, plisser, froncer; onduler; ***corrugated iron***, tôle ondulée, *f.*—*v.i.* se plisser, se froncer.
corrupt [kə'rʌpt], *v.t.* corrompre.—*v.i.* se corrompre.—*a.* corrompu, dépravé, vicié.
corruption [kə'rʌpʃən], *n.* corruption; (*fig.*) altération (*d'un texte etc.*), *f.*
corruptive [kə'rʌptiv], *a.* corruptif.
corruptly [kə'rʌptli], *adv.* par corruption.
corsair ['kɔ:sɛə], *n.* corsaire, *m.*
corset ['kɔ:sit], *n.* corset, *m.*
corset-maker ['kɔ:sitmeikə], *n.* corsetier, *m.* corsetière, *f.*
Corsica ['kɔ:sikə]. la Corse, *f.*
Corsican ['kɔ:sikən], *a.* corse.—*n.* Corse (*personne*), *m.*, *f.*

corslet ['kɔːslit], *n.* corselet, *m.*
cortège [kɔː'teiʒ], *n.* cortège (*funèbre*), *m.*, procession; suite, *f.*
cortisone ['kɔːtizoun], *n.* cortisone, *f.*
coruscate ['kɔrəskeit], *v.i.* scintiller, briller.
corvette [kɔː'vet], *n.* (*Naut.*) corvette, *f.*
cosh [kɔʃ], *n.* matraque, *f.*—*v.t.* matraquer.
cosily ['kouzili], *adv.* à l'aise, bien au chaud, douillettement.
cosmetic [kɔz'metik], *a.* and *n.* cosmétique, *m.*
cosmic ['kɔzmik], **cosmical** ['kɔzmikəl], *a.* cosmique.
cosmopolitan [kɔzmo'pɔlitən], *a.* and *n.* cosmopolite, *m., f.*
cosmos ['kɔzmɔs], *n.* cosmos, *m.*
cosset ['kɔsit], *v.t.* dorloter, choyer.
cost [kɔst], *n.* prix; frais, *m.*, dépense, *f.*; (*Comm.*) coût, *m.*; (*Law, pl.*) dépens, *m.pl.*; ***at any cost, at all costs***, à tout prix; ***cost of living***, coût de la vie.—*v.i. irr.* coûter; ***cost what it may***, coûte que coûte.
coster ['kɔstə], **costermonger** ['kɔstəmʌŋgə], *n.* marchand des quatre saisons, *m.*
costive ['kɔstiv], *a.* constipé.
costliness ['kɔstlinis], *n.* haut prix, prix élevé, *m.*
costly ['kɔstli], *a.* coûteux, de prix; somptueux.
costume ['kɔstjuːm], *n.* costume, *m.*
cosy ['kouzi], *a.* chaud, confortable, douillet; commode et petit (*appartement*).—*n.* (***tea***) ***cosy***, couvre-théière, *m.*
cot [kɔt], *n.* cabane, chaumière, *f.*; bercail, parc (*à moutons*); petit lit, lit d'enfant, *m.*
coterie ['koutəri], *n.* coterie, clique, *f.*
cottage ['kɔtidʒ], *n.* chaumière; petite maison, villa, *f.*
cotton [kɔtn], *n.* coton, *m.*
cotton-mill ['kɔtnmil], *n.* filature de coton, *f.*
cotton-plant ['kɔtnplɑːnt], *n.* cotonnier, *m.*
cotton-spinning ['kɔtnspiniŋ], *n.* filage du coton, *m.*
cotton-tree ['kɔtntriː], *n.* bombax, *m.*
cotton-wool ['kɔtn'wul], *n.* ouate, *f.*
couch [kautʃ], *n.* canapé, divan, *m.*—*v.t.* coucher; (*fig.*) rédiger, exprimer.—*v.i.* se coucher; se tapir.
cougar ['kuːgə], *n.* couguar, puma, *m.*
cough [kɔf], *n.* toux, *f.*; ***whooping-cough***, coqueluche, *f.*—*v.i.* tousser.
coughing ['kɔfiŋ], *n.* toux, *f.*; ***fit of coughing***, quinte de toux, *f.*
council ['kaunsil], *n.* conseil; (*Eccles.*) concile, *m.*
councillor ['kaunsilə], *n.* conseiller, *m.*
counsel ['kaunsəl], *n.* conseil, avis; dessein; avocat, *m.*—*v.t.* conseiller.
counsellor ['kaunsələ], *n.* conseiller; avocat, *m.*
count (1) [kaunt], *n.* comte (*titre*), *m.*
count (2) [kaunt], *n.* calcul, compte, total, *m.* —*v.t.* compter; (*fig.*) regarder, considérer; ***to count on*** or ***upon***, compter sur.
countenance ['kauntinəns], *n.* figure, mine, *f.*, air, *m.*; (*fig.*) approbation, *f.*, appui, *m.*; ***to give countenance to***, favoriser, encourager; ***to keep one's countenance***, garder son sérieux; ***to put out of countenance***, décontenancer.—*v.t.* appuyer, encourager, favoriser; être en faveur de.
counter ['kauntə], *n.* calculateur; compteur (*instrument*); (*Cards etc.*) jeton; comptoir (*de magasin*), *m.*—*adv.* contre, contrairement (*à*), à l'encontre (*de*).—*v.t., v.i.* parer; contrer.
counteract [kauntə'rækt], *v.t.* contrecarrer, contre-balancer, neutraliser.
counteraction [kauntə'rækʃən], *n.* action contraire, opposition, résistance, *f.*
counter-clockwise ['kauntə'klɔkwaiz], **anti-clockwise** ['ænti'klɔkwaiz], *adv.* dans le sens contraire des aiguilles d'une montre.
counter-espionage ['kauntər'espiənɑːʒ], *n.* contre-espionnage, *m.*
counterfeit ['kauntəfiːt], *a.* contrefait, imité; faux.—*n.* contrefaçon; fausse pièce, fausse monnaie; imitation, *f.*—*v.t.* contrefaire, imiter; feindre.—*v.i.* feindre.
counterfoil ['kauntəfɔil], *n.* talon (*de registre*), *m.*, souche, *f.*
countermand [kauntə'mɑːnd], *v.t.* contremander.—*n.* contremandement, *m.*
counterpane ['kauntəpein], *n.* couvre-pied, couvre-lit, *m.*
counterpart ['kauntəpɑːt], *n.* contre-partie, *f.*; pendant, *m.*
countess ['kauntis], *n.* comtesse, *f.*
counting ['kauntiŋ], *n.* compte; dépouillement (*élections*), *m.*
counting-house ['kauntiŋhaus], *n.* bureau, comptoir, *m.*, caisse, *f.*
countless ['kauntlis], *a.* innombrable, sans nombre.
countrified ['kʌntrifaid], *a.* (devenu) campagnard *ou* provincial.
country ['kʌntri], *n.* pays, *m.*; contrée; région; campagne (*opposée à la ville*); province (*opposée à la capitale*); patrie (*fatherland*), *f.*; ***across country***, à travers champs; ***in open country***, en rase campagne; ***in the country***, à la campagne.
countryman ['kʌntrimən], *n.* (*pl.* **-men** [men]) paysan, campagnard, *m.*; ***fellow-countryman***, compatriote, *m.*
countryside ['kʌntrisaid], *n.* campagne, *f.*; paysage, *m.*
country-woman ['kʌntriwumən], *n.* (*pl.* **-women** [wimin]) paysanne, *f.*
county ['kaunti], *n.* comté, *m.*; ***county council***, conseil général, *m.*; ***county town***, chef-lieu, *m.*
couple [kʌpl], *n.* couple, *f.*; couple (*mâle et femelle*), *m.*—*v.t.* coupler, accoupler; atteler; joindre.—*v.i.* s'accoupler.
couplet ['kʌplit], *n.* couplet, distique, *m.*
coupling ['kʌpliŋ], *n.* accouplement, *m.*
coupon ['kuːpɔn] *n.* coupon; bon, *m.*
courage ['kʌridʒ], *n.* courage, *m.*
courageous [kə'reidʒəs], *a.* courageux.
courageously [kə'reidʒəsli], *adv.* courageusement.
courier ['kuriə], *n.* courrier, *m.*
course [kɔːs], *n.* cours, *m.*; carrière, voie, suite, *f.*; lit (*d'une rivière*); genre (*de vie*); service (*de repas*); courant (*durée*); (*Racing*) terrain de course; hippodrome, *m.*; (*Naut.*) route, *f.*; (*Med., pl.*) règles, *f.pl.*; ***in due course***, en temps voulu; ***of course***, naturellement, bien entendu—*v.t.* courir; faire courir; chasser (*le lièvre*).—*v.i.* courir; circuler (*sang*).
courser ['kɔːsə], *n.* coureur, coursier, *m.*

court [kɔ:t], *n.* cour, *f.*; tribunal, *m.*; impasse, *f.*, passage (*petite rue*); (*Ten.*) court, *m.*—*v.t.* faire sa cour à, courtiser; rechercher; briguer.
courteous ['kə:tiəs], *a.* courtois, poli.
courteously ['kə:tiəsli], *adv.* courtoisement, poliment.
courtesan [kɔ:ti'zæn], *n.* courtisane, *f.*
courtesy ['kə:təsi], *n.* courtoisie, politesse, *f.*
court-house ['kɔ:thaus], *n.* palais de justice, *m.*
courtier ['kɔ:tiə], *n.* courtisan, homme de cour, *m.*
courtliness ['kɔ:tlinis], *n.* élégance, politesse, *f.*
courtly ['kɔ:tli], *a.* poli, élégant, courtois.
court-martial ['kɔ:t'mɑ:ʃəl], *n.* conseil de guerre, *m.*—*v.t.* faire passer en conseil de guerre.
courtship ['kɔ:tʃip], *n.* cour, *f.*
courtyard ['kɔ:tjɑ:d], *n.* cour (*de maison*), *f.*
cousin [kʌzn], *n.* cousin, *m.*
cove [kouv], *n.* anse, crique, *f.*
covenant ['kʌvənənt], *n.* convention, *f.*, pacte, contrat, *m.*—*v.t.* stipuler par contrat. —*v.i.* convenir (*de*), s'engager (*à*).
Coventry ['kɔvəntri, 'kʌvəntri]. (*colloq.*) ***to send to Coventry***, mettre en quarantaine.
cover ['kʌvə], *v.t.* couvrir; voiler, déguiser; cacher.—*n.* couverture; cloche (*d'un plat etc.*); enveloppe (*d'une lettre etc.*); housse (*d'une chaise*), *f.*; couvercle (*d'une casserole etc.*); couvert (*gibier*); (*fig.*) voile, abri, *m.*; ***under cover of***, sous la protection de, à la faveur de.
covering ['kʌvəriŋ], *n.* couverture; enveloppe; housse (*de chaise*), *f.*; habits (*vêtements*), *m.pl.*; ***covering letter***, lettre d'envoi, *f.*
coverlet ['kʌvəlit], *n.* couvre-pied, couvre-lit, *m.*
covert ['kʌvə:t], *a.* couvert, caché, secret.—*n.* couvert, abri; gîte, *m.*, tanière, *f.*
covertly ['kʌvə:tli], *adv.* secrètement, en cachette.
covet ['kʌvit], *v.t.* convoiter, désirer ardemment.
covetous ['kʌvitəs], *a.* avide, avaricieux, cupide.
covetously ['kʌvitəsli], *adv.* avec convoitise, avidement.
covetousness ['kʌvitəsnis], *n.* convoitise, cupidité, *f.*
covey ['kʌvi], *n.* compagnie (*de perdrix*), *f.*
cow (1) [kau], *n.* vache, *f.*
cow (2) [kau], *v.t.* intimider, dompter.
coward ['kauəd], *n.* lâche, poltron, *m.*, poltronne, *f.*
cowardice ['kauədis], **cowardliness** ['kauədlinis], *n.* couardise, poltronnerie, lâcheté, *f.*
cowardly ['kauədli], *a.* couard, lâche, poltron. —*adv.* lâchement.
cowboy ['kaubɔi], *n.* jeune vacher; (*Am.*) cowboy, *m.*
cower ['kauə], *v.i.* s'accroupir, se blottir, se tapir.
cowherd ['kauhə:d], *n.* vacher, *m.*
cowhide ['kauhaid], *n.* peau de vache, *f.*
cowl [kaul], *n.* capuchon; (*Naut.*, *Av.*) capot; tabourin (*de cheminée*), *m.*
cow-shed ['kauʃed], *n.* vacherie, étable à vaches, *f.*
cowslip ['kauslip], *n.* primevère, *f.*, coucou, *m.*
coxcomb, cockscomb ['kɔkskoum], *n.* petit-maître, freluquet, fat, *m.*
coxswain [kɔksn], *n.* patron de chaloupe; (*Row.*) barreur, *m.*
coy [kɔi], *a.* timide, réservé.
coyly ['kɔili], *adv.* timidement, avec réserve.
coyness ['kɔinis], *n.* timidité, réserve, *f.*
coyote [kɔi'jouti], *n.* loup de prairie, coyote, *m.*
cozen [kʌzn], *v.t.* duper, tromper.
crab [kræb], *n.* crabe, cancre; (*Astron.*) cancer, *m.*
crab-apple ['kræbæpl], *n.* pomme sauvage, *f.*
crabbed [kræbd], *a.* acariâtre, revêche, bourru.
crab-tree ['kræbtri:], *n.* pommier sauvage, *m.*
crabwise ['kræbwaiz], *adv.* comme un crabe, de biais.
crack [kræk], *v.t.* fendre; fêler (*porcelaine etc.*); gercer (*la peau etc.*); casser (*noix etc.*); faire claquer (*fouet*); faire sauter (*bouteille de vin*); faire, lâcher (*plaisanterie*); (*fig.*) rompre, briser.—*v.i.* se fendre, se lézarder; se gercer (*la peau etc.*); claquer (*fouet*); se fêler (*verre etc.*); muer (*la voix*).—*a.* fameux, d'élite; ***to be a crack shot***, être un fin tireur.—*n.* fente, crevasse, fissure; détonation (*de fusil*); lézarde, fêlure (*verre*), *f.*; craquement (*bruit*); claquement (*d'un fouet*), *m.*; mue (*de la voix*); hâblerie (*boast*), *f.*
crack-brained ['krækbreind], *a.* (*fam.*) timbré, fou.
cracked [krækd], *a.* fendu, fêlé; (*fig.*) timbré.
cracker ['krækə], *n.* vantard; pétard (*feu d'artifice*); (*Am.*) biscuit, *m.*; ***nut-crackers***, casse-noix, *m.inv.*
crackle [krækl], *v.i.* pétiller, craqueter, crépiter.
crackling ['krækliŋ], *n.* pétillement, crépitement; (*fig.*) rissolé (*de rôti de porc*), *m.*
cracknel ['kræknəl], *n.* craquelin, *m.*, croquignole, *f.*
cradle [kreidl], *n.* berceau; (*Naut.*) ber, *m.*—*v.t.* bercer; endormir (*en berçant*).
cradle-song ['kreidlsɔŋ], *n.* berceuse, *f.*
craft [krɑ:ft], *n.* métier (*trade*), *m.*; ruse, astuce (*cunning*); (*Naut.*) embarcation, *f.*, bâtiment, *m.*
craftily ['krɑ:ftili], *adv.* sournoisement, avec ruse.
craftiness ['krɑ:ftinis], *n.* artifice, *m.*, ruse, astuce, *f.*
craftsman ['krɑ:ftsmən], *n.* (*pl.* **-men** [men]) artisan; artiste dans son métier, *m.*
craftsmanship ['krɑ:ftsmənʃip], *n.* habileté technique, exécution, *f.*
crafty ['krɑ:fti], *a.* rusé, astucieux.
crag [kræg], *n.* rocher escarpé, rocher à pic, *m.*
craggy ['krægi], *a.* rocailleux, escarpé, abrupt.
crake [kreik], *n.* (*Orn.*) râle, *m.*
cram [kræm], *v.t.* fourrer, remplir, bourrer; préparer, chauffer (*étudiants*).—*v.i.* se bourrer, s'empiffrer; (*fig.*) en conter, blaguer.
crammer ['kræmə], *n.* préparateur; (*colloq.*) colleur, *m.*
cramp [kræmp], *n.* crampe, *f.*; (*Tech.*) crampon, *m.*; (*fig.*) gêne, entrave, *f.*—*v.t.* cramponner; resserrer; (*fig.*) gêner, entraver, restreindre.
cramped [kræmpt], *a.* gêné; ***to be cramped (for space)***, être très à l'étroit.

cranberry ['krænbəri], *n.* (*Bot.*) canneberge, *f.*
crane [krein], *n.* (*Orn.*, *Tech.*) grue, *f.*—*v.t.* allonger, tendre (*le cou*).
cranial ['kreiniəl], *a.* crânien.
cranium ['kreiniəm], *n.* crâne, *m.*
crank [kræŋk], *n.* manivelle, *f.*; coude, *m.*; (*fig.*) maniaque, excentrique, *m.*, *f.*, original (*personne*), *m.*
crankshaft ['kræŋkʃɑ:ft], *n.* arbre de manivelle; (*Motor.*) vilebrequin, *m.*
cranky ['kræŋki], *a.* capricieux, fantasque; impatient.
crannied ['krænid], *a.* crevassé, lézardé.
cranny ['kræni], *n.* crevasse, fente, lézarde, fissure, *f.*
crape [kreip], *n.* crêpe, *m.*
crash [kræʃ], *v.t.* fracasser, briser.—*v.i.* éclater, retentir; se tamponner (*deux autos etc.*).—*n.* fracas, grand bruit, *m.*; (*Motor.*) collision; (*fig.*) débâcle, ruine; faillite, *f.*
crash-helmet ['kræʃhelmit], *n.* casque, *m.*
crash-landing ['kræʃ'lændiŋ], *n.* (*Av.*) atterrissage brutal; crash, *m.*
crass [kræs], *a.* crasse, grossier, stupide.
crate [kreit], *n.* caisse à claire-voie, *f.*—*v.t.* emballer.
crater ['kreitə], *n.* cratère, *m.*
cravat [krə'væt], *n.* cravate, *f.*
crave [kreiv], *v.t.* implorer, solliciter; (*fig.*) soupirer après.
craven [kreivn], *a.* and *n.* lâche, poltron, *m.*
craving ['kreiviŋ], *n.* désir ardent, besoin impérieux, *m.*
crawfish [CRAYFISH].
crawl [krɔ:l], *v.i.* ramper, se traîner; ***to crawl with***, grouiller de.—*n.* mouvement traînant; (*Swim.*) crawl, *m.*
crawling ['krɔ:liŋ], *a.* rampant; grouillant, fourmillant (*de*).
crayfish ['kreifiʃ], **crawfish** ['krɔ:fiʃ], *n.* écrevisse (*d'eau douce*), *f.*; ***sea crayfish***, langouste, *f.*
crayon ['kreiən], *n.* crayon, pastel, fusain, *m.* —*v.t.* crayonner, dessiner au pastel.
craze [kreiz], *v.t.* craqueler (*porcelaine*); frapper de folie, rendre fou.—*n.* folie; (*fig.*) passion folle; toquade, *f.*
crazed [kreizd], *a.* craquelé (*porcelaine*); fou, dément.
crazily ['kreizili], *adv.* follement.
craziness ['kreizinis], *n.* délabrement, *m.*; démence, folie, *f.*
crazy ['kreizi], *a.* délabré; (*fam.*) fou, toqué.
creak [kri:k], *v.i.* crier, craquer, grincer.—*n.* cri, grincement, *m.*
creaking ['kri:kiŋ], *a.* qui crie, qui craque.—*n.* cri, grincement, *m.*
cream [kri:m], *n.* crème, *f.*—*v.i.* crémer, mousser.
cream-colour(ed) ['kri:mkʌlə(d)], *a.* crème.
creamery ['kri:məri], *n.* crémerie, *f.*
cream-jug ['kri:mdʒʌg], *n.* pot à crème, *m.*
creamy ['kri:mi], *a.* crémeux; de crème.
crease [kri:s], *n.* pli, faux pli, *m.*—*v.t.* faire des plis à, plisser, chiffonner, friper.—*v.i.* se plisser; se friper.
create [kri:'eit], *v.t.* créer, faire naître; produire, engendrer, occasionner; faire.
creation [kri:'eiʃən], *n.* création; nature, *f.*, univers, *m.*; dernière mode, *f.*
creative [kri:'eitiv], *a.* créateur.
creator [kri:'eitə], *n.* créateur, *m.*
creature ['kri:tʃə], *n.* créature, personne, *f.*, être; animal, *m.*
crèche [kreiʃ], *n.* crèche, *f.*
credence ['kri:dəns], *n.* créance, croyance, foi, *f.*; ***to give credence to***, ajouter foi à.
credentials [kri'denʃəlz], *n.pl.* lettres de créance, *f.pl.*
credibility [kredi'biliti], *n.* crédibilité, *f.*
credible ['kredibl], *a.* croyable, digne de foi.
credibly ['kredibli], *adv.* d'une manière digne de foi; ***to be credibly informed***, tenir de bonne source.
credit ['kredit], *n.* croyance, foi; (*fig.*) influence; réputation, *f.*; mérite, honneur; (*Comm.*) crédit, *m.*; ***on credit***, à crédit; ***to do credit to***, faire honneur à.—*v.t.* ajouter foi à, croire à; faire honneur à; (*Comm.*) faire crédit à.
creditable ['kreditəbl], *a.* honorable, estimable.
creditably ['kreditəbli], *adv.* honorablement.
creditor ['kreditə], *n.* créancier; (*Book-keeping*) créditeur, avoir, *m.*
credulity [kre'dju:liti], **credulousness** ['kredjuləsnis], *n.* crédulité, *f.*
credulous ['kredjuləs], *a.* crédule.
creed [kri:d], *n.* credo, *m.*; (*fig.*) profession de foi; croyance, foi, *f.*
creek [kri:k], *n.* crique, anse, *f.*
creel [kri:l], *n.* panier de pêche, *m.*
creep [kri:p], *v.i. irr.* se traîner, ramper, se glisser.
creeper ['kri:pə], *n.* reptile, *m.*; plante grimpante, *f.*; ***tree creeper***, (*Orn.*) grimpereau, *m.*
creeping ['kri:piŋ], *a.* rampant, grimpant; qui fait frissonner.—*n.* fourmillement (*sensation*), *m.*
creepy ['kri:pi], *a.* horrifique, qui donne la chair de poule; rampant.
cremate [kri'meit], *v.t.* incinérer.
cremation [kri'meiʃən], *n.* crémation, incinération, *f.*
crematorium [kremə'tɔ:riəm], *n.* crématorium, *m.*
Creole ['kri:oul], *a.* créole.—*n.* Créole, *m.*, *f.*
creosote ['kri:əsout], *n.* créosote, *f.*
crêpe [kreip], *n.* crêpe blanc (*ou* clair), *m.*
crescent ['kresənt], *a.* croissant.—*n.* croissant, *m.*, demi-lune; rue en demi-cercle, *f.*
cress [kres], *n.* cresson, *m.*
crest [krest], *n.* cimier, *m.*; crête (*d'un coq* ou *d'une montagne*), huppe (*d'un oiseau*); aigrette (*de paon*), *f.*; (*Her.*) écusson, *m.*; armoiries, *f.pl.*
crestfallen ['krestfɔ:lən], *a.* abattu, découragé, l'oreille basse.
Cretan ['kri:tən], *a.* crétois.—*n.* Crétois, *m.*
Crete [kri:t]. la Crète, la Candie, *f.*
crevasse [krə'væs], *n.* crevasse (*d'un glacier*), *f.*—*v.i.* se crevasser.
crevice ['krevis], *n.* crevasse, lézarde, fente (*mur*); fissure (*rocher*), *f.*—*v.t.* crevasser, lézarder, fissurer.
crew (1) [kru:], *n.* bande, troupe, *f.*; (*Naut.*) équipage, *m.*
crew (2) [kru:], *past* [CROW (2)].
crib [krib], *n.* lit d'enfant, *m.*; crèche, mangeoire, *f.*; (*colloq.*) livre de corrigés, *m.*—*v.t.* chiper; copier (*sur*).

crick [krik], *n.* crampe, *f.*, effort, torticolis, *m.* —*v.t.* ***to crick one's neck***, se donner le torticolis.
cricket (1) ['krikit], *n.* (*Ent.*) grillon, *m.*
cricket (2) ['krikit], *n.* cricket (*jeu*), *m.*; (*colloq.*) ***that's not cricket***, ça ne se fait pas, ce n'est pas loyal.
crier ['kraiə], *n.* crieur; huissier (*d'une cour*), *m.*
crime [kraim], *n.* crime, *m.*
Crimea [krai'mi:ə]. la Crimée, *f.*
criminal ['kriminl], *a.* and *n.* criminel, *m.*
criminologist [krimi'nɔlədʒist], *n.* criminaliste, *m*, *f.*
criminology [krimi'nɔlədʒi], *n.* criminologie, *f.*
crimp [krimp], *v.t.* gaufrer; friser, boucler (*les cheveux*).
crimson [krimzn], *a.* and *n.* cramoisi; pourpre, *m.*—*v.t.* teindre en cramoisi.—*v.i.* devenir cramoisi.
cringe [krindʒ], *v.i.* faire des courbettes; s'humilier, ramper.
cringing ['krindʒiŋ], *a.* craintif; obséquieux. —*n.* basse servilité, *f.*
crinkle [kriŋkl], *v.t.* froisser; former en zigzag.—*v.i.* serpenter, aller en zigzag.—*n.* sinuosité, *f.*; pli, *m.*; fronce, *f.*
crinkly ['kriŋkli], *a.* ratatiné.
cripple [kripl], *n.* boiteux; estropié, *m.*—*v.t.* estropier; (*fig.*) paralyser.
crisis ['kraisis], *n.* (*pl.* **crises** ['kraisi:z]) crise, *f.*; dénouement, *m.*
crisp [krisp], *a.* croquant, croustillant (*pâtisserie etc.*); crépu, frisé (*cheveux*).—*v.t.* friser (*cheveux etc.*); crêper (*tissu*).—*v.i.* se crêper.
crispness ['krispnis], *n.* qualité de ce qui est croquant *ou* cassant; frisure; netteté (*style etc.*), *f.*
criss-cross ['kriskrɔs], *a.* entrecroisé, croisé, en croix.—*n.* entrecroisement, *m.*—*v.t.* entrecroiser.—*v.i.* s'entrecroiser.
criterion [krai'tiəriən], *n.* critérium, *m.*
critic ['kritik], *n.* critique; censeur, *m.*; ***dramatic critic***, critique de théâtre.
critical ['kritikl], *a.* critique, (*fig.*) difficile, délicat.
critically ['kritikli], *adv.* d'une manière critique; avec soin; ***critically ill***, dangereusement malade.
criticism ['kritisizm], *n.* critique, appréciation, censure, *f.*
criticize ['kritisaiz], *v.t.* critiquer, faire la critique de, censurer.—*v.i.* faire de la critique.
croak [krouk], *v.i.* coasser (*grenouille*); croasser (*freux*); (*fig.*) gronder, grogner.—*n.* coassement (*grenouille*); croassement (*freux*); (*fig.*) grognement, *m.*
croaker ['kroukə], *n.* grognon, *m.*; (*fig.*) pessimiste, *m.*, *f.*
croaky ['krouki], *a.* enroué, rauque.
crochet ['krouʃei], *n.* ouvrage au crochet, *m.* —*v.t.*, *v.i.* broder au crochet.
crock [krɔk], *n.* cruche, *f.*; pot de terre, *m.*; (*fam.*) ***old crock***, vieux clou, tacot (*bicyclette, auto etc.*); vieux débris, croulant (*personne*), *m.*
crockery ['krɔkəri], *n.* faïence, vaisselle, *f.*
crocodile ['krɔkədail], *n.* crocodile, *m.*; (*fig.*) procession, *f.*
crocus ['kroukəs], *n.* safran, crocus, *m.*
croft [krɔft], *n.* petit clos, *m.*, petite ferme, *f.*
crofter ['krɔftə], *n.* petit cultivateur, *m.*
crone [kroun], *n.* vieille femme, vieille, *f.*
crony ['krouni], *n.* vieux camarade; copain, compère, *m.*
crook [kruk], *n.* courbure; houlette (*de berger*); crosse (*d'evêque*), *f.*; (*fig.*) escroc (*personne*), *m.*; ***by hook or by crook***, coûte que coûte, par un moyen ou par un autre.—*v.t.* courber; (*fig.*) pervertir.—*v.i.* se courber.
crook-backed ['krukbækt], *a.* bossu, voûté.
crooked ['krukid], *a.* courbé, crochu, tortueux; tortu; (*fig.*) malhonnête.
crookedly ['krukidli], *adv.* tortueusement, de travers.
crookedness ['krukidnis], *n.* nature tortueuse; difformité, *f.*; (*fig.*) travers, *m.*, perversité, *f.*
croon [kru:n], *v.i.* chantonner, fredonner.
crooner ['kru:nə], *n.* fredonneur, chanteur de charme, *m.*
crop [krɔp], *n.* récolte, moisson; cueillette (*de fruits*), *f.*; jabot (*d'un oiseau*), *m.*; coupe (*cheveux*), *f.*; ***hunting-crop***, fouet (de chasse), *m.*; ***second crop***, regain, *m.*—*v.t.* tondre; couper; écourter (*chevaux*); brouter (*l'herbe*).
crosier, crozier ['krouziə], *n.* crosse (*d'évêque*), *f.*
cross [krɔs], *a.* en travers, de travers; fâcheux, contraire; maussade, de mauvaise humeur, fâché.—*n.* croix, *f.*; (*fig.*) malheur, *m.*, traverse, *f.*; croisement (*dans la reproduction*), *m.*; ***criss-cross***, croisé, en croix.—*v.t.* croiser; marquer d'une croix, barrer (*un chèque*); (*fig.*) franchir; contrarier; ***to cross off*** or ***out***, effacer, rayer, biffer; ***to cross oneself***, faire le signe de la croix.—*v.i.* être mis en travers; faire la traversée; se croiser (*lettres*).
crossbow ['krɔsbou], *n.* arbalète, *f.*
cross-breed ['krɔsbri:d], *n.* race croisée, *f.*; métis, *m.*—*v.t.* croiser.
cross-country ['krɔs'kʌntri], *a.* à travers champs; (*Racing*) ***cross-country running***, cross, *m.*
cross-examination ['krɔsigzæmi'neiʃən], *n.* contre-interrogatoire, *m.*
cross-examine ['krɔsig'zæmin], *v.t.* interroger; (*Law*) contre-interroger.
crossing ['krɔsiŋ], *n.* traversée (*de la mer*), *f.*; passage; carrefour, croisement (*de routes*); croisement (*animaux*), *m.*; ***pedestrian crossing***, passage clouté.
crossly ['krɔsli], *adv.* de travers; avec mauvaise humeur.
crossness ['krɔsnis], *n.* mauvaise humeur, méchanceté, *f.*
cross-roads ['krɔsroudz], *n.pl.* carrefour, *m.*
crossword ['krɔswə:d], *n.* ***crossword*** (***puzzle***), mots croisés, *m.pl.*
crotchet ['krɔtʃit], *n.* lubie, *f.*, caprice, *m.*, marotte; (*Mus.*) noire, *f.*
crotchety ['krɔtʃiti], *a.* capricieux, d'humeur difficile.
crouch [krautʃ], *v.i.* se tapir, se blottir.
crouching ['krautʃiŋ], *a.* accroupi, tapi.
croup [kru:p], *n.* croupe (*animaux*), *f.*; croupion (*oiseaux*); (*Path.*) croup, *m.*

crow (1) [krou], *n.* corneille, *f.*; ***as the crow flies***, à vol d'oiseau; ***crow's nest***, (*Naut.*) hune, *f.*
crow (2) [krou], *v.i. irr.* chanter (*coq*).—*n.* chant du coq, *m.*
crow-bar ['krouba:], *n.* pince, *f.*; levier, *m.*
crowd [kraud], *n.* foule, cohue, *f.*—*v.t.* serrer, encombrer; presser.—*v.i.* se presser en foule, se serrer.
crown [kraun], *n.* couronne; crête, *f.*, sommet; écu (*pièce de monnaie*); fond (*d'un chapeau*), *m.*—*v.t.* couronner; combler.
crozier [CROSIER].
crucial ['kru:ʃəl], *a.* crucial; (*fig.*) définitif, décisif.
crucible ['kru:sibl], *n.* creuset, *m.*
crucifix ['kru:sifiks], *n.* crucifix, *m.*
crucifixion [kru:si'fikʃən], *n.* crucifiement, *m.*, crucifixion, *f.*
crucify ['kru:sifai], *v.t.* crucifier.
crude [kru:d], *a.* cru; (*fig.*) informe, indigeste; grossier; brut.
crudely ['kru:dli], *adv.* crûment.
crudeness ['kru:dnis], **crudity** ['kru:diti], *n.* crudité, nature informe, *f.*
cruel ['kru:əl], *a.* cruel.
cruelly ['kru:əli], *adv.* cruellement.
cruelty ['kru:əlti], *n.* cruauté, inhumanité, *f.*
cruet ['kru:it], *n.* burette, *f.*
cruet-stand ['kru:itstænd], *n.* huilier, *m.*
cruise ['kru:z], *n.* croisière, course, *f.*—*v.i.* croiser, faire la course; marauder (*taxi*).
cruiser ['kru:zə], *n.* croiseur, *m.*
crumb [krʌm], *n.* mie; miette, *f.*—*v.t.* émietter.
crumble [krʌmbl], *v.t.* émietter; (*fig.*) pulvériser, broyer.—*v.i.* s'émietter; tomber en poussière; ***to crumble down***, tomber en ruine, s'écrouler.
crump [krʌmp], *n.* coup violent, *m.*; chute, *f.*
crumpet ['krʌmpit], *n.* sorte de petite crêpe, crêpe bretonne (*pour le thé*), *f.*
crumple [krʌmpl], *v.t.* chiffonner, froisser.—*v.i.* se rider, se chiffonner.
crunch [krʌntʃ], *v.t.* croquer; broyer, écraser.—*v.i.* crisser, s'écraser.—*n.* coup de dent; grincement; crissement, *m.*
crupper ['krʌpə], *n.* croupe; croupière, *f.*
crusade [kru:'seid], *n.* croisade, *f.*
crusader [kru:'seidə], *n.* croisé, *m.*
crush [krʌʃ], *n.* écrasement, choc, *m.*; foule, cohue, *f.*—*v.t.* écraser, broyer; froisser (*une robe*); (*fig.*) accabler, anéantir.—*v.i.* s'écraser.
crushing ['krʌʃiŋ], *a.* écrasant; (*fig.*) foudroyant.—*n.* broiement, écrasement, *m.*
crust [krʌst], *n.* croûte, *f.*, croûton, *m.*—*v.i.* s'encroûter.
crustily ['krʌstili], *adv.* d'une manière morose.
crusty ['krʌsti], *a.* couvert d'une croûte; (*fig.*) bourru, hargneux.
crutch [krʌtʃ], *n.* béquille, *f.*
crux [krʌks], *n.* nœud (*d'une question*), *m.*; crise, *f.*
cry [krai], *n.* cri, *m.*—*v.t.* crier.—*v.i.* pleurer; crier; s'écrier.
crying ['kraiiŋ], *n.* larmes, *f.pl.*, pleurs, *m.pl.*; cri, *m.*, cris, *m.pl.*
crypt [kript], *n.* crypte, *f.*
cryptic ['kriptik], *a.* secret; énigmatique.
crystal [kristl], *a.* de cristal.—*n.* cristal, *m.*
crystallize ['kristəlaiz], *v.t.* cristalliser.—*v.i.* se cristalliser; ***crystallized fruits***, fruits glacés, *m.pl.*
cub [kʌb], *n.* petit (*d'une bête sauvage*); ourson (*ours*); lionceau (*lion*); louveteau (*loup*); renardeau (*renard*), *m.*
Cuba ['kju:bə]. le Cuba, *m.*
Cuban ['kju:bən], *a.* cubain.—*n.* Cubain, *m.*
cubby-hole ['kʌbihoul], *n.* retraite, *f.*; placard, *m.*; niche, *f.*
cube [kju:b], *n.* cube, *m.*
cubicle ['kju:bikl], *n.* compartiment, *m.* cabine, *f.*
cubit ['kju:bit], *n.* coudée, *f.*
cuckoo ['kuku:], *n.* coucou, *m.*
cucumber ['kju:kʌmbə], *n.* concombre, *m.*
cud [kʌd], *n.* bol alimentaire, *m.*; ***to chew the cud***, ruminer.
cuddle [kʌdl], *v.t.* serrer (tendrement) dans ses bras; étreindre.—*v.i.* s'étreindre (amoureusement); se blottir; se peloter.
cudgel ['kʌdʒəl], *n.* bâton, gourdin, *m.*—*v.t.* bâtonner.
cue [kju:], *n.* queue de billard; (*Theat.*) réplique, *f.*; (*fig.*) avis, mot, indice, *m.*
cuff (1) [kʌf], *v.t.* souffleter, calotter, battre.—*n.* calotte, taloche, *f.*
cuff (2) [kʌf], *n.* manchette (*d'une manche*), *f.*; parement (*d'un pardessus*); poignet (*d'une robe*), *m.*
cuff-link ['kʌfliŋk], *n.* bouton de manchette, *m.*
cuirass [kwi'ræs], *n.* cuirasse, *f.*
cuirassier [kwi'ræsiə], *n.* cuirassier, *m.*
culinary ['kʌlinəri], *a.* de cuisine, culinaire.
cull [kʌl], *v.t.* recueillir, cueillir; (*fig.*) choisir.
culminate ['kʌlmineit], *v.i.* se terminer (*en*), finir (*par*); (*Astron.*) culminer.
culmination [kʌlmi'neiʃən], *n.* point culminant, apogée, *m.*; (*Astron.*) culmination, *f.*
culpable ['kʌlpəbl], *a.* coupable.
culprit ['kʌlprit], *n.* accusé; inculpé, *m.*; coupable, *m.*, *f.*
cult [kʌlt], *n.* culte, *m.*
cultivate ['kʌltiveit], *v.t.* cultiver.
cultivation [kʌlti'veiʃən], *n.* culture, *f.*
cultivator ['kʌltiveitə], *n.* cultivateur, *m.*
cultural ['kʌltʃərəl], *a.* agricole, cultural; culturel.
culture ['kʌltʃə], *n.* culture; (*fig.*) instruction, éducation, *f.*
cultured ['kʌltʃəd], *a.* cultivé.
culvert ['kʌlvə:t], *n.* ponceau, petit aqueduc, *m.*
cumber ['kʌmbə], *v.t.* embarrasser, encombrer (*de*).—*n.* embarras, obstacle, *m.*
cumbersome ['kʌmbəsəm], **cumbrous** ['kʌmbrəs], *a.* embarrassant, gênant.
cumulate ['kju:mjuleit], *v.t.* accumuler, cumuler.
cunning ['kʌniŋ], *a.* fin, rusé, adroit, astucieux.—*n.* finesse, ruse, astuce, *f.*
cunningly ['kʌniŋli], *adv.* avec finesse, adroitement; par ruse.
cup [kʌp], *n.* tasse, coupe, *f.*; gobelet; (*Bot. etc.*) calice, *m.*; (*Med.*) ventouse, *f.*—*v.t.* (*Med.*) appliquer des ventouses à.
cupbearer ['kʌpbɛərə], *n.* échanson, *m.*
cupboard ['kʌbəd], *n.* armoire (*pour vêtements etc.*), *f.*; placard (*dans un mur*), *m.*
cupidity [kju:'piditi], *n.* cupidité, *f.*
cupola ['kju:pələ], *n.* coupole, *f.*

cur [kəː], *n.* chien bâtard; roquet; (*fig.*) malotru, *m.*, vilaine bête, *f.*
curable ['kjuərəbl], *a.* guérissable.
curate ['kjuərit], *n.* vicaire, desservant, *m.*
curator [kjuə'reitə], *n.* administrateur; conservateur (*de musée*), *m.*
curb [kəːb], *n.* gourmette, *f.*; (*fig.*) frein, *m.*; [KERB].—*v.t.* gourmer; (*fig.*) réprimer, contenir, brider; freiner.
curd [kəːd], *n.* caillé, lait caillé, *m.*—*v.t.* cailler, figer.
curdle [kəːdl], *v.t.* cailler, figer.—*v.i.* se cailler, se figer.
cure [kjuə], *n.* guérison, *f.*; remède, *m.*; (*Eccles.*) cure, *f.*—*v.t.* guérir; sécher (*foin etc.*); mariner (*poisson etc.*); saler (*viande etc.*); (*fig.*) corriger.
curfew ['kəːfjuː], *n.* couvre-feu, *m.*
curio ['kjuəriou], *n.* curiosité, *f.*; bibelot, *m.*
curiosity [kjuəri'ɔsiti], *n.* curiosité, *f.*
curious ['kjuəriəs], *a.* curieux; (*fig.*) remarquable, singulier.
curiously ['kjuəriəsli], *adv.* curieusement.
curl [kəːl], *n.* boucle (*de cheveux*); moue (*de lèvres*); spirale (*de fumée*); ondulation, *f.*—*v.t.* boucler, friser, (*fig.*) faire onduler.—*v.i.* friser; se replier (*serpent etc.*); s'entrelacer (*vignes etc.*); tourbillonner (*fumée*); onduler (*vagues*); ***to curl up***, s'enrouler, se pelotonner (*chat*).
curled [kəːld], *a.* frisé.
curlew ['kəːljuː], *n.* (*Orn.*) courlis, *m.*
curly ['kəːli], *a.* frisé, bouclé.
curmudgeon [kəː'mʌdʒən], *n.* ladre, pingre; bourru, *m.*
currant ['kʌrənt], *n.* groseille (*à grappes*), *f.*; ***black currant***, cassis, *m.*; ***(dried) currants***, raisins de Corinthe, *m.pl.*
currant-bush ['kʌrəntbuʃ], *n.* groseillier, *m.*
currency ['kʌrənsi], *n.* circulation (*d'argent etc.*); monnaie, *f.*; cours; crédit, *m.*, vogue, *f.*
current ['kʌrənt], *a.* courant; actuel; admis, reçu; ***current events***, actualités, *f.pl.*—*n.* courant; cours d'eau, *m.*
currently ['kʌrəntli], *adv.* couramment; généralement.
curriculum [kə'rikjuləm], *n.* (*Sch.*) programme, plan d'études, *m.*
currier ['kʌriə], *n.* corroyeur, *m.*
curry (1) ['kʌri], *v.t.* corroyer (*cuir*); étriller (*un cheval*); (*fig.*) rosser.
curry (2) ['kʌri], *v.t.* (*Cook.*) apprêter au cari. —*n.* cari, *m.*
curry-comb ['kʌrikoum], *n.* étrille, *f.*
curse [kəːs], *n.* malédiction, *f.*; (*fig.*) fléau, malheur, *m.*—*v.t.* maudire; (*fig.*) affliger.—*v.i.* jurer; (*colloq.*) sacrer.
cursed ['kəːsid], *a.* maudit, exécrable.
cursorily ['kəːsərili], *adv.* rapidement, superficiellement.
cursory ['kəːsəri], *a.* rapide, superficiel; général.
curt [kəːt], *a.* brusque, bref, sec.
curtail [kəː'teil], *v.t.* retrancher, raccourcir, abréger.
curtailment [kəː'teilmənt], *n.* raccourcissement, *m.*, réduction, *f.*
curtain [kəːtn], *n.* rideau, *m.*; toile, *f.*—*v.t.* garnir de rideaux; (*fig.*) voiler.
curtly ['kəːtli], *adv.* brusquement, sèchement.
curtsy, or **curtsey** ['kəːtsi], *n.* révérence, *f.*—*v.i.* faire la révérence.
curve [kəːv], *n.* courbe, *f.*—*v.t.* courber; cintrer.—*v.i.* se courber.
curvet [kəː'vet], *v.i.* faire des courbettes; sauter, gambader.—*n.* courbette, *f.*
cushion ['kuʃən], *n.* coussin, *m.*; (*Billiards*) bande, *f.*—*v.t.* garnir de coussins; amortir.
custard ['kʌstəd], *n.* crème (au lait), *f.*; flan, *m.*
custodian [kʌs'toudiən], *n.* gardien; conservateur, *m.*
custody ['kʌstədi], *n.* garde; prison, détention, *f.*
custom ['kʌstəm], *n.* coutume, habitude, *f.*, usage, *m.*; pratique (*d'une boutique*), *f.*; achalandage (*d'un magasin*), *m.*; (*pl.*) douane, *f.*; droits (*taxes*), *m.pl.*
customarily ['kʌstəmərili], *adv.* ordinairement, d'habitude.
customary ['kʌstəməri], *a.* ordinaire, d'usage.
customer ['kʌstəmə], *n.* chaland, client, *m.*; pratique, *f.*; (*colloq.*) individu, *m.*
customs-officer ['kʌstəmzɔfisə], *n.* douanier, *m.*
cut [kʌt], *n.* coup, *m.*; coupure (*place cut open*); coupe (*de vêtements, cheveux, cartes à jouer*); taille (*forme*), façon, tournure (*silhouette*); (*Engr.*) gravure, planche, *f.*; chemin de traverse (*raccourci*); (*Ten. etc.*) coup tranchant, *m.*—*v.t. irr.* couper, trancher; fendre; rogner; se rogner (*les ongles*); piquer, percer; faire (*une dent*); ***to cut down***, abattre; réduire; ***to cut out***, tailler, découper; ***to cut short***, abréger; interrompre, couper la parole à; ***to be cut up***, être blessé; avoir de la peine.—*v.i.* couper; se couper; percer (*dent*).
cute [kjuːt], *a.* rusé, fin; (*Am.*) attirant (*enfant, fille*); amusant (*chose, truc*).
cuticle ['kjuːtikl], *n.* cuticule, *f.*
cutler ['kʌtlə], *n.* coutelier, *m.*
cutlery ['kʌtləri], *n.* coutellerie, *f.*
cutlet ['kʌtlit], *n.* côtelette; escalope, *f.*
cut-price ['kʌtprais], *n.* prix réduit, *m.*
cutter ['kʌtə], *n.* coupeur; coupoir (*outil*); (*Naut.*) cutter, cotre, *m.*
cutting ['kʌtiŋ], *a.* incisif; (*fig.*) piquant, tranchant, mordant.—*n.* incision; rognure (*morceau*); coupe (*bois, cartes, cheveux etc.*); (*Hort.*) bouture, *f.*
cyanide ['saiənaid], *n.* cyanure, *m.*
cycle [saikl], *n.* cycle, *m.*; bicyclette, *f.*, vélo, *m.*—*v.i.* aller à bicyclette.
cyclone ['saikloun], *n.* cyclone, *m.*
cygnet ['signit], *n.* jeune cygne, *m.*
cylinder ['silində], *n.* cylindre, *m.*
cymbal ['simbəl], *n.* cymbale, *f.*
cynic ['sinik], *n.* cynique; sceptique, *m., f.*
cynical ['sinikl], *a.* cynique.
cynically ['sinikli], *adv.* cyniquement.
cynicism ['sinisizm], *n.* cynisme, *m.*
cynosure ['sainəʃuə], *n.* (*fig.*) point de mire, *m.*
cypress ['saiprəs], *n.* cyprès, *m.*
Cyprian ['siprion], *a.* cypriote.—*n.* Cypriote, *m., f.*
Cypriot ['sipriət], *n.* Cypriote, *m., f.*
Cyprus ['saiprəs]. la Chypre, *f.*
cyst [sist], *n.* (*Anat. etc.*) kyste, *m.*
czar [TSAR].

Czech [tʃek], *a.* tchèque.—*n.* tchèque (*langue*), *m.*; Tchèque (*personne*), *m., f.*
Chechoslovak [tʃeko'slouvæk], *a.* tchécoslovaque.—*n.* tchécoslovaque (*langue*), *m.*; Tchécoslovaque (*personne*), *m., f.*
Czechoslovakia [tʃekoslo'vækiə]. la Tchécoslovaquie, *f.*

D

D, d [di:]. quatrième lettre de l'alphabet; (*Mus.*) ré, *m.*
dab [dæb], *n.* coup léger, *m.*, tape; éclaboussure, tache, *f.*; (*slang*) adepte, *m.*; (*Ichth.*) limande, *f.*—*v.t.* toucher légèrement; éponger à petits coups.
dabble [dæbl], *v.t.* humecter; éclabousser.—*v.i.* barboter, patauger; ***to dabble in,*** se mêler de.
dace [deis], *n.* (*Ichth.*) vandoise, *f.*, dard, *m.*
dachshund ['dækshund], *n.* basset allemand, *m.*
dad [dæd], **daddy** ['dædi], *n.* papa, *m.*
dado ['deidou], *n.* lambris (*de mur*), *m.*
daffodil ['dæfədil], *n.* jonquille, *f.*, narcisse des prés, *m.*
daft [dɑ:ft], *a.* niais, sot, à moitié fou.
dagger ['dægə], *n.* poignard, *m.*, dague, *f.*
dahlia ['deiliə], *n.* (*Bot.*) dahlia, *m.*
daily ['deili], *a.* journalier, quotidien.—*n.* (journal) quotidien, *m.*; femme de ménage, *f.*—*adv.* journellement, tous les jours.
daintily ['deintili], *adv.* délicatement; avec délicatesse.
daintiness ['deintinis], *n.* délicatesse, *f.*, goût difficile, *m.*
dainty ['deinti], *a.* friand; délicat, difficile.—*n.* friandise, *f.*
dairy ['dɛəri], *n.* laiterie, *f.*
dairy-farm ['dɛərifɑ:m], *n.* ferme laitière, *f.*
dairy-man ['dɛərimən], *n.* (*pl.* **-men** [men]) nourrisseur; crémier, *m.*
dais [deis, 'deiis], *n.* estrade, *f.*
daisy ['deizi], *n.* marguerite, pâquerette, *f.*
dale [deil], *n.* vallon, *m.*; vallée, *f.*
dalliance ['dæliəns], *n.* folâtrerie, *f.*; badinage, *m.*; caresses, *f.pl.*
dally ['dæli], *v.i.* folâtrer, perdre son temps; tarder; (*fig.*) badiner (*avec*).
dam (1) [dæm], *n.* mère (*animaux*), *f.*
dam (2) [dæm], *n.* digue (*d'un canal*), *f.*; barrage (*d'une rivière*), *m.*—*v.t.* diguer, barrer.
damage ['dæmidʒ], *n.* dommage; tort, dégât; (*fig.*) préjudice, détriment, *m.*; (*pl.*) (*Law*) dommages-intérêts, *m.pl.*—*v.t.* endommager; avarier (*en transportant*); (*fig.*) faire tort à, nuire à.—*v.i.* s'endommager.
damask ['dæməsk], *n.* damas; damassé, *m.*
dame [deim], *n.* (*poet.*) dame, *f.*
damn [dæm], *v.t.* damner; (*fig.*) condamner, désapprouver.
damnation [dæm'neiʃən], *n.* damnation, *f.*
damnatory ['dæmnətəri], *a.* condamnatoire.
damned [dæmd], *a.* damné, maudit, exécrable.
damning ['dæmiŋ], *a.* écrasant (*témoignage*).
damp [dæmp], *a.* humide; moite; (*fig.*) triste, abattu.—*n.* or **dampness** ['dæmpnis], humidité; (*fig.*) tristesse, *f.*—*v.t.* rendre humide; (*fig.*) décourager.
damper ['dæmpə], *n.* éteignoir; (*Piano*) étouffoir; (*fig.*) rabat-joie, *m.*
***damsel** ['dæmzəl], *n.* jeune fille, demoiselle, *f.*
damson ['dæmzən], *n.* prune de Damas, *f.*
dance [dɑ:ns], *n.* danse, *f.*; bal, *m.*—*v.t.* danser; faire danser.—*v.i.* danser.
dancer ['dɑ:nsə], *n.* danseur, *m.*, danseuse, *f.*
dandelion ['dændilaiən], *n.* (*Bot.*) pissenlit, *m.*
dandle [dændl], *v.t.* dorloter, bercer.
dandruff ['dændrʌf], *n.* pellicules, *f.pl.*
dandy ['dændi], *n.* dandy, élégant, petit-maître, *m.*
Dane [dein], *n.* Danois (*personne*), *m.*
danger ['deindʒə], *n.* danger, péril, *m.*
dangerous ['deindʒərəs], *a.* dangereux.
dangerously ['deindʒərəsli], *adv.* dangereusement.
dangle [dæŋgl], *v.t.* laisser pendre, balancer.—*v.i.* pendiller, baller.
Danish ['deiniʃ], *a.* danois.—*n.* danois (*langue*), *m.*
dank [dæŋk], *a.* humide et froid.
Danube ['dænju:b], **the.** le Danube, *m.*
dapper ['dæpə], *a.* petit et vif, pimpant; soigné (*homme*).
dapple [dæpl], *v.t.* tacheter, pommeler.—*v.i.* se pommeler, se tacheter.—*a.* or **dappled** [dæpld], pommelé, truité, miroité.
dare [dɛə], *v.t.* défier, braver; provoquer.—*v.i.* oser; ***I dare say!*** sans doute; je le crois bien.
dare-devil ['dɛədevəl], *a.* and *n.* cassecou, *m.*
daring ['dɛəriŋ], *a.* audacieux, hardi, cassecou.—*n.* hardiesse, audace, *f.*
dark [dɑ:k], *a.* obscur, sombre, noir; foncé (*couleur*); brun, basané (*teint*); (*fig.*) secret, mystérieux.—*n.* ténèbres, *f.pl.*, obscurité, *f.*; ***after dark,*** à la nuit close.
darken ['dɑ:kən], *v.t.* obscurcir; brunir (*teint*); (*Paint.*) assombrir (*couleurs*).—*v.i.* s'obscurcir; s'assombrir.
darkening ['dɑ:kniŋ], *n.* obscurcissement, assombrissement, *m.*
darkness ['dɑ:knis], *n.* obscurité, *f.*, ténèbres, *f.pl.*, teint brun (*du visage*), *m.*
darling ['dɑ:liŋ], *a.* and *n.* chéri, mignon, bien-aimé, *m.*; ***my darling,*** (*colloq.*) mon ange, mon chou, *m.*, ma chérie, *f.*
darn [dɑ:n], *n.* reprise, *f.*—*v.t.* repriser.
darning ['dɑ:niŋ], *n.* reprise, *f.*
dart [dɑ:t], *n.* dard, trait, *m.*; fléchette, *f.*; élan soudain, *m.*—*v.t.* darder, lancer (*contre*).—*v.i.* se lancer, s'élancer (*sur*)
dash [dæʃ], *n.* choc, coup, *m.*; impétuosité, *f.*, entrain, cran; élan soudain; tiret; trait (*de plume*); (*fig.*) soupçon (*petite quantité*), *m.*—*v.t.* jeter; heurter, briser; abattre.—*v.i.* se briser; se précipiter.—*int.* zut!
dash-board ['dæʃbɔ:d], *n.* (*Motor.*) tableau de bord, *m.*
dashing ['dæʃiŋ], *a.* fougueux, brillant; pimpant, élégant.
dastard ['dæstəd], *n.* lâche ignoble, *m.*
dastardly ['dæstədli] *a.* lâche.

date (1) [deit], *n.* date, échéance, *f.*, millésime (*de pièce de monnaie*); (*Am. pop.*) rendez-vous, *m.*; ***up to date***, à la page, à jour.—*v.t.* dater.—*v.i.* dater (*de*).
date (2) [deit], *n.* datte (*fruit*), *f.*
date-palm ['deitpɑ:m], *n.* dattier, *m.*
dative ['deitiv], *a.* and *n.* datif, *m.*
datum ['deitəm], *n.* (*pl.* **data** ['deitə]) donnée, *f.*
daub [dɔ:b], *v.t.* barbouiller, enduire; (*fig.*) déguiser (*de*).—*n.* barbouillage, *m.*; (*Paint.*) croûte, *f.*
daughter ['dɔ:tə], *n.* fille, *f.*
daughter-in-law ['dɔ:tərinlɔ:], *n.* belle-fille, bru, *f.*
daunt [dɔ:nt], *v.t.* effrayer, intimider, décourager.
dauntless ['dɔ:ntlis], *a.* intrépide.
dauphin ['dɔ:fin], *n.* dauphin, *m.*
David ['deivid]. David, *m.*
davit ['dævit], *n.* (*Naut.*) bossoir, *m.*
dawdle [dɔ:dl], *v.i.* flâner, muser.
dawdler ['dɔ:dlə], *n.* flâneur, musard, *m.*
dawn [dɔ:n], *v.i.* poindre, paraître; (*fig.*) naître, percer.—*n.* aube, *f.*, point du jour, *m.*; aurore, *f.*
day [dei], *n.* jour, *m.*; journée (*de travail etc.*); (*fig.*) bataille, victoire, *f.*; ***at the present day***, de nos jours; ***every day***, tous les jours; ***the day after***, le lendemain; ***the day before***, la veille; ***today***, aujourd'hui.
day-boarder ['deibɔ:də], *n.* demi-pensionnaire, *m.*, *f.*
day-book ['deibuk], *n.* journal, *m.*
day-boy ['deibɔi], **day girl** ['deigə:l], *n.* externe, *m.*, *f.*
day-break ['deibreik], *n.* [DAWN].
daylight ['deilait], *n.* lumière du jour, *f.*
daze [deiz], *v.t.* éblouir; hébéter.—*n.* stupéfaction, *f.*; ***in a daze***, hébété.
dazzle [dæzl], *v.t.* éblouir, aveugler.
dazzling ['dæzliŋ], *a.* éblouissant.
deacon ['di:kən], *n.* diacre, *m.*
dead [ded], *a.* mort; inanimé; inerte, insensible; éventé (*boisson alcoolique*); mat (*couleur*); au rebut (*lettres*); ***dead drunk***, ivre-mort; ***dead loss***, perte sèche, *f.*; (*fig.*) crétin (*personne*), *m.*; ***dead march***, marche funèbre, *f.*; ***dead stop***, halte subite, *f.* ***dead weight***, poids mort, *m.*; ***for a dead certainty***, à coup sûr.—*n.* cœur (*de l'hiver*), fort, *m.*; ***at dead of night***, au plus profond de la nuit.
dead-beat ['ded'bi:t], *a.* éreinté, épuisé.
deaden [dedn], *v.t.* amortir; émousser (*les sens*); éventer (*boisson alcoolique*); assourdir (*son*).
dead-end ['ded'end], *n.* cul-de-sac, *m.*; impasse, *f.*
deadlock ['dedlɔk], *n.* situation sans issue; impasse, *f.*
deadly ['dedli], *a.* mortel, à mort; meurtrier.—*adv.* mortellement.
deadness ['dednis], *n.* mort, *f.*; (*fig.*) engourdissement, *m.*, froideur, *f.*
deaf [def], *a.* sourd; (*fig.*) insensible.
deafen [defn], *v.t.* rendre sourd, assourdir.
deafening ['defniŋ], *a.* assourdissant.
deaf-mute ['def'mju:t], *n.* sourd-muet, *m.*
deafness ['defnis], *n.* surdité, *f.*
deal (1) [di:l], *n.* quantité; (*Cards*) donne; affaire, *f.*, marché, *m.*; ***a great*** or ***good deal***, beaucoup (*de*); ***by a good deal***, à beaucoup près.—*v.t. irr.* distribuer; répartir; (*Cards*) donner; porter, asséner (*coups*).—*v.i.* agir, traiter, en user (*avec*).
deal (2) [di:l], *n.* bois blanc, bois (de sapin), *m.*
dealer ['di:lə], *n.* marchand; (*Cards*) donneur, *m.*
dealing ['di:liŋ], *n.* conduite, *f.*; procédé, *m.*, affaire, *f.*; (*pl.*) relations, *f.pl.*, rapports, *m.pl.*
dean [di:n], *n.* doyen, *m.*
dear [diə], *a.* cher; précieux; (*fig.*) joli, gentil, charmant.—*adv.* cher; chèrement, beaucoup.—*n.* cher; cher ami, *m.*—*int.* ***oh dear!*** mon Dieu!
dearth [də:θ], *n.* disette, *f.*
death [deθ], *n.* mort, *f.*; (*poet.*) trépas; (*Law*) décès, *m.*
death-duties ['deθdju:tiz], *n.pl.* droits de succession, *m.pl.*
death-rate ['deθreit], *n.* taux de mortalité, *m.*
death-rattle ['deθrætl], *n.* râle, *m.*
death-throes ['deθθrouz], *n.* agonie, *f.*
debar [di'bɑ:], *v.t.* exclure, priver (*de*).
debase [di'beis], *v.t.* avilir, abaisser; abâtardir; (*Chem.*) adultérer; (*Coin.*) altérer.
debasement [di'beismənt], *n.* abaissement, avilissement, *m.*; (*Coin.*) altération, dépréciation, *f.*
debasing [di'beisiŋ], *a.* avilissant.
debatable [di'beitəbl], *a.* contestable.
debate [di'beit], *n.* débat, *m.*; discussion, *f.*—*v.t.* débattre, discuter, disputer.—*v.i.* délibérer (*sur*), contester (*avec*).
debauch [di'bɔ:tʃ], *n.* débauche, *f.*—*v.t.* débaucher, corrompre, pervertir.
debauchery [di'bɔ:tʃəri], *n.* débauche, *f.*
debenture [di'bentʃə], *n.* obligation, *f.*
debilitate [di'biliteit], *v.t.* débiliter, affaiblir, anémier.
debilitation [dibili'teiʃən], *n.* débilitation, *f.*, affaiblissement, *m.*
debility [di'biliti], *n.* débilité, faiblesse, *f.*
debit ['debit], *n.* débit, *m.*—*v.t.* débiter (*de*).
debonair [debə'nεə], *a.* jovial; de caractère enjoué; élégant.
debouch [di'bu:ʃ], *v.i.* déboucher.
débris, debris ['debri:], *n.* débris, *m.pl.*
debt [det], *n.* dette, *f.*; dettes, *f.pl.*; créance, *f.*
debtor ['detə], *n.* débiteur, *m.*
debutante ['deibjutɑ̃:t], *n.* débutante (*à la cour*), *f.*
decade ['dekeid], *n.* décade; décennie, *f.*
decadence ['dekədəns], *n.* décadence, *f.*
decadent ['dekədənt], *a.* décadent.
decamp [di'kæmp], *v.i.* décamper; lever le camp.
decant [di'kænt], *v.t.* décanter, verser.
decanter [di'kæntə], *n.* carafe, *f.*
decapitate [di'kæpiteit], *v.t.* décapiter.
decapitation [dikæpi'teiʃən], *n.* décapitation, *f.*
decay [di'kei], *n.* décadence; pourriture; ruine; carie (*de dent*), *f.*—*v.i.* tomber en décadence; dépérir (*plante*); se carier (*dent*).
decease [di'si:s], *n.* (*Law*) décès, *m.*—*v.i.* décéder.
deceased [di'si:st], *a.* décédé, feu.—*n.* défunt, *m.*
deceit [di'si:t], *n.* supercherie, fourberie, tromperie, ruse, *f.*

deceitful [di'si:tful], *a.* trompeur; décevant (*choses*).
deceive [di'si:v], *v.t.* tromper, abuser.
deceiver [di'si:və], *n.* imposteur, trompeur, *m.*
decelerate [di:'seləreit], *v.t.*, *v.i.* ralentir.
December [di'sembə]. décembre, *m.*
decency ['di:sənsi], *n.* bienséance, *f.*, convenances, *f.pl.*; décence (*modestie*), *f.*
decennial [di'senjəl], *a.* décennal.
decent ['di:sənt], *a.* bienséant, décent; propre, convenable; gentil.
decently ['di:səntli], *adv.* décemment; convenablement.
decentralization ['di:sentrəlai'zeiʃən], *n.* décentralisation, *f.*, régionalisme, *m.*
decentralize [di:'sentrəlaiz], *v.t.* décentraliser.
deception [di'sepʃən], *n.* tromperie, fraude, duperie, *f.*
deceptive [di'septiv], *a.* trompeur.
decibel ['desibel], *n.* décibel, *m.*
decide [di'said], *v.t.* décider; décider de.—*v.i.* se décider.
decided [di'saidid], *a.* décidé, prononcé; positif; résolu.
decidedly [di'saididli], *adv.* décidément; positivement.
decimal ['desiməl], *a.* décimal; ***decimal point***, virgule, *f.*—*n.* (fraction) décimale, *f.*
decimate ['desimeit], *v.t.* décimer.
decipher [di'saifə], *v.t.* déchiffrer.
decision [di'siʒən], *n.* décision; (*fig.*) résolution, fermeté, *f.*
decisive [di'saisiv], *a.* décisif; concluant.
decisively [di'saisivli], *adv.* décisivement.
deck [dek], *n.* (*Naut.*) pont; tillac (*navire marchand*); plan (*avion*), *m.*—*v.t.* parer (*de*); orner.
deck-chair ['dek'tʃɛə], *n.* transat(lantique), *m.*
declaim [di'kleim], *v.t.*, *v.i.* déclamer (*contre*).
declamatory [di'klæmətəri], *a.* déclamatoire.
declaration [deklə'reiʃən], *n.* déclaration; proclamation, *f.*
declare [di'klɛə], *v.t.* déclarer; (*fig.*) annoncer, affirmer.—*v.i.* se déclarer, se prononcer (*pour*).
decline [di'klain], *v.t.* pencher, incliner; refuser.—*v.i.* pencher; décliner; baisser (*prix*).—*n.* déclin, *m.*, décadence; (*Path.*) maladie de langueur, *f.*
declutch [di:'klʌtʃ], *v.i.* débrayer.
decode [di:'koud], *v.t.* déchiffrer.
decompose [di:kəm'pouz], *v.t.* décomposer.—*v.i.* se décomposer.
decompression [di:kəm'preʃən], *n.* décompression, *f.*
decontaminate [di:kən'tæmineit], *v.t.* désinfecter.
decontrol [di:kən'troul], *v.t.* rendre libre de nouveau, libérer (*prix, loyers etc.*).—*n.* libération (*prix, loyers etc.*), *f.*
decorate ['dekəreit], *v.t.* décorer, orner.
decoration [dekə'reiʃən], *n.* décoration, *f.*; ornement, *m.*
decorator ['dekəreitə], *n.* décorateur, *m.*
decorous ['dekərəs, di'kɔ:rəs], *a.* bienséant, convenable.
decorously ['dekərəsli, di'kɔ:rəsli], *adv.* convenablement.
decorum [di'kɔ:rəm], *n.* bienséance, *f.*, décorum, *m.*
decoy [di'kɔi], *v.t.* leurrer, amorcer.—*n.* leurre; piège, *m.*
decrease ['di:kri:s], *n.* décroissement, *m.*; diminution; décrue (*eau*), *f.*—[di'kri:s], *v.t.* faire décroître.—*v.i.* diminuer; décroître.
decree [di'kri:], *n.* décret; (*Law*) arrêt, *m.*—*v.t.* arrêter, décréter.
decrepit [di'krepit], *a.* décrépit, caduc.
decry [di'krai], *v.t.* décrier, dénigrer.
dedicate ['dedikeit], *v.t.* dédier (*à*); consacrer (*à*).
dedication [dedi'keiʃən], *n.* dédicace, *f.*
deduce [di'dju:s], *v.t.* déduire, inférer (*de*).
deduct [di'dʌkt], *v.t.* déduire, rabattre.
deduction [di'dʌkʃən], *n.* déduction, *f.*
deed [di:d], *n.* action, *f.*; fait, exploit; (*Law*) titre, *m.*
deem [di:m], *v.t.* juger; penser, estimer.
deep [di:p], *a.* profond, extrême; foncé (*couleur*); grave (*son*); (*fig.*) rusé.—*n.* (*poet.*) océan, *m.*
deepen ['di:pən], *v.t.* approfondir; assombrir.—*v.i.* devenir plus profond *ou* plus foncé.
deep-freeze ['di:p'fri:z], *n.* réfrigérateur à basse température, *m.*
deeply ['di:pli], *adv.* profondément; extrêmement.
deep-rooted ['di:p'ru:tid], **deep-seated** ['di:p'si:tid], *a.* profond, enraciné.
deer [diə], *n.* cervidé, *m.*; ***fallow deer***, daim, *m.*, daine, *f.*; ***red deer***, cerf, *m.*
deface [di'feis], *v.t.* défigurer; mutiler.
defamation [defə'meiʃən], *n.* diffamation, *f.*
defame [di'feim], *v.t.* diffamer.
default [di'fɔ:lt], *n.* défaut, manque, *m.*; (*Law*) contumace, *f.*
defaulter [di'fɔ:ltə], *n.* délinquant; (*Mil.*) réfractaire; (*Law*) défaillant, *m.*
defeat [di'fi:t], *n.* défaite, déroute, *f.*—*v.t.* battre, vaincre; (*fig.*) annuler, déjouer.
defeatism [di'fi:tizm], *n.* défaitisme, *m.*
defeatist [di'fi:tist], *a.* and *n.* défaitiste, *m., f.*
defect [di'fekt], *n.* défaut, *m.*; imperfection, *f.*
defective [di'fektiv], *a.* défectueux, imparfait.
defence [di'fens], *n.* défense, *f.*
defend [di'fend], *v.t.* défendre (*de*), protéger (*contre*).
defender [di'fendə], *n.* défenseur, *m.*
defensible [di'fensəbl], *a.* défendable; (*fig.*) soutenable.
defensive [di'fensiv], *a.* défensif.—*n.* défensive, *f.*
defer [di'fə:], *v.t.* différer, remettre.—*v.i.* différer; déférer (*à*).
deference ['defərəns], *n.* déférence, *f.*
deferential [defə'renʃəl] *a.* de déférence, respectueux.
deferment [di'fə:mənt], *n.* (*Mil.*) sursis, *m.*
defiance [di'faiəns], *n.* défi, *m.*
defiant [di'faiənt], *a.* défiant.
deficiency [di'fiʃənsi], *n.* défaut, *m.*; insuffisance, *f.*
deficient [di'fiʃənt], *a.* défectueux; insuffisant.
deficit ['defisit], *n.* déficit, *m.*
defile (1) [di:'fail], *n.* défilé, *m.*
defile (2) [di'fail], *v.t.* souiller; déshonorer.
define [di'fain], *v.t.* définir; déterminer.
definite ['definit], *a.* déterminé; (*Gram.*) défini.

definitely [ˈdefinitli], *adv.* absolument, nettement, d'une manière déterminée.
definition [defiˈniʃən], *n.* définition, *f.*
deflate [diˈfleit], *v.t.* dégonfler.
deflation [diˈfleiʃən], *n.* dégonflement, *m.*; déflation monétaire, *f.*
deflect [diˈflekt], *v.t.* faire dévier, détourner.—*v.i.* dévier.
deforestation [di:fɔrisˈteiʃən], *n.* déboisement, *m.*
deform [diˈfɔ:m], *v.t.* déformer, défigurer.
deformation [di:fɔ:ˈmeiʃən], *n.* déformation, *f.*
deformed [diˈfɔ:md], *a.* difforme.
deformity [diˈfɔ:miti], *n.* difformité; laideur, *f.*
defraud [diˈfrɔ:d], *v.t.* frauder.
defray [diˈfrei], *v.t.* défrayer; payer.
deft [deft], *a.* adroit, habile.
deftly [ˈdeftli], *adv.* adroitement, lestement.
defunct [diˈfʌŋkt], *a.* défunt, trépassé, décédé.—*n.* défunt, *m.*
defy [diˈfai], *v.t.* défier, braver.
degeneracy [diˈdʒenərəsi], **degeneration** [didʒenəˈreiʃən], *n.* dégénérescence, *f.*
degenerate [diˈdʒenərit], *a.* and *n.* dégénéré, *m.*—[diˈdʒenəreit], *v.i.* dégénérer, s'abâtardir (*dans* ou *en*).
degradation [degrəˈdeiʃən], *n.* dégradation, *f.*; (*fig.*) avilissement, *m.*
degrade [diˈgreid], *v.t.* dégrader; (*fig.*) avilir.
degrading [diˈgreidiŋ], *a.* dégradant, avilissant.
degree [diˈgri:], *n.* degré; rang, ordre, *m.*, qualité, *f.*; ***university degree***, grade universitaire, *m.*
de-ice [di:ˈais], *v.t.*, *v.i.* dégivrer.
deify [ˈdi:ifai], *v.t.* déifier.
deign [dein], *v.t.*, *v.i.* daigner.
deity [ˈdi:iti], *n.* divinité; (*Myth.*) déité, *f.*
dejected [diˈdʒektid], *a.* abattu, triste.
dejection [diˈdʒekʃən], *n.* abattement, *m.*
delay [diˈlei], *n.* délai, retard, *m.*—*v.t.* différer; remettre.—*v.i.* tarder.
delegacy [ˈdeligəsi], *n.* délégation, *f.*
delegate [ˈdeligit], *n.* délégué, *m.*—[ˈdeligeit], *v.t.* déléguer.
delegation [deliˈgeiʃən], *n.* délégation, *f.*
delete [diˈli:t], *v.t.* effacer, rayer, biffer.
deletion [diˈli:ʃən], *n.* rature, *f.*, grattage, *m.*
deliberate [diˈlibərit], *a.* délibéré, prémédité; réfléchi.—[diˈlibəreit], *v.i.* délibérer.
deliberately [diˈlibəritli], *adv.* à dessein; lentement.
deliberation [dilibəˈreiʃən], *n.* délibération, *f.*
delicacy [ˈdelikəsi], *n.* délicatesse; friandise (*a titbit*), *f.*
delicate [ˈdelikit], *a.* délicat.
delicious [diˈliʃəs], *a.* délicieux.
deliciously [diˈliʃəsli], *adv.* délicieusement.
delight [diˈlait], *n.* délices, *f.pl.*, plaisir, *m.*—*v.t.* plaire à, réjouir, enchanter; ***to be delighted to***, être enchanté de.—*v.i.* se plaire à.
delightful [diˈlaitful], *a.* délicieux; charmant (*personne*).
delineate [diˈlinieit], *v.t.* esquisser, dessiner; (*fig.*) décrire.
delinquency [diˈliŋkwənsi], *n.* délit, *m.*; ***juvenile delinquency***, délinquance juvénile, *f.*
delinquent [diˈliŋkwənt], *n.* délinquant, *m.*; ***juvenile delinquent***, jeune délinquant.
delirious [diˈliriəs], *a.* en délire; délirant.
delirium [diˈliriəm], *n.* délire; (*fig.*) transport de joie, *m.*
deliver [diˈlivə], *v.t.* délivrer, sauver; distribuer (*lettres etc.*); remettre (*lettre, paquet etc.*); livrer (*marchandises*), prononcer (*un discours*); (faire) accoucher (*femme*).
deliverance [diˈlivərəns], *n.* délivrance, *f.*
deliverer [diˈlivərə], *n.* libérateur, sauveur, *m.*
delivery [diˈlivəri], *n.* délivrance, remise, *f.*; débit, *m.*, diction (*d'un discours*); livraison (*de marchandises*); distribution (*du courrier*), *f.*; (*Med.*) accouchement, *m.*; ***payment on delivery***, livraison contre remboursement.
delivery-van [dəˈlivərivæn], *n.* camion de livraison, *m.*; camionnette, *f.*
dell [del], *n.* vallon, *m.*
delta [ˈdeltə], *n.* delta, *m.*
delude [diˈlju:d], *v.t.* tromper, abuser.
deluge [ˈdelju:dʒ], *n.* déluge, *m.*—*v.t.* inonder.
delusion [diˈlju:ʒən], *n.* illusion, erreur, *f.*
delve [delv], *v.t.*, *v.i.* bêcher, creuser; (*fig.*) sonder.
demagnetize [di:ˈmægnitaiz], *v.t.* démagnétiser.
demagogue [ˈdeməgɔg], *n.* démagogue, *m.*, *f.*
demand [diˈmɑ:nd], *n.* exigence; réclamation; demande, requête, *f.*; ***in great demand***, très demandé, très recherché; ***on demand***, sur demande; ***supply and demand***, l'offre et la demande, *f.*—*v.t.* exiger; réclamer; demander.
demarcation [di:mɑ:ˈkeiʃən], *n.* démarcation, *f.*; ***line of demarcation***, ligne de démarcation, *f.*
demean [diˈmi:n], *v.i.* se comporter, se conduire; (*colloq.*) s'abaisser, se dégrader.
demeanour [diˈmi:nə], *n.* conduite, *f.*, maintien, *m.*; tenue, *f.*
demented [diˈmentid], *a.* fou, dément.
demi [ˈdemi], *prep.* demi, à demi.
demigod [ˈdemigɔd], *n.* demi-dieu, *m.*
demise [diˈmaiz], *n.* décès, *m.*, mort, *f.*—*v.t.* léguer; céder à bail.
demi-semiquaver [ˈdemiˈsemikweivə], *n.* (*Mus.*) triple croche, *f.*
demister [di:ˈmistə], *n.* (*Motor.*) appareil antibuée, *m.*
demobilization [di:moubilaiˈzeiʃən], *n.* démobilisation, *f.*
demobilize [di:ˈmoubilaiz], *v.t.* démobiliser.
democracy [diˈmɔkrəsi], *n.* démocratie, *f.*
democrat [ˈdeməkræt], *n.* démocrate, *m.*, *f.*
democratic [deməˈkrætik], *a.* démocratique.
democratically [deməˈkrætikəli], *adv.* démocratiquement.
demolish [diˈmɔliʃ], *v.t.* démolir.
demolition [deməˈliʃən], *n.* démolition, *f.*
demon [ˈdi:mən], *n.* démon, diable, *m.*
demonstrate [ˈdemənstreit], *v.t.* démontrer.—*v.i.* (*Polit.*) manifester.
demonstration [demənˈstreiʃən], *n.* démonstration; (*Polit.*) manifestation, *f.*
demonstrative [diˈmɔnstrətiv], *a.* démonstratif.
demoralize [di:ˈmɔrəlaiz], *v.t.* démoraliser.
demote [diˈmout], *v.t.* (*Mil.*) réduire à un grade inférieur, rétrograder.
demur [diˈmə:], *n.* hésitation, objection, *f.*—*v.i.* hésiter, temporiser.

demure [di'mjuə], *a.* réservé, posé; d'une modestie affectée.
demurely [di'mjuəli], *adv.* d'un air posé; avec une modestie affectée.
den [den], *n.* antre; repaire (*de voleurs etc.*), *m.*; loge (*de ménagerie*), *f.*; (*fig.*) bouge, taudis; (*colloq.*) cabinet de travail, *m.*
denationalize [di:'næʃnəlaiz], *v.t.* dénationaliser.
denial [di'naiəl], *n.* déni, *m.*, dénégation, *f.*
denier ['deniə], *n.* (*Hosiery*) denier, *m.*; ***a 15-denier stocking***, un bas 15 deniers.
denigrate ['denigreit], *v.t.* noircir, dénigrer.
Denis [DENNIS].
denizen ['denizn], *n.* citoyen, habitant, *m.*
Denmark ['denma:k]. le Danemark, *m.*
Dennis ['denis]. Denis, *m.*
denomination [dinəmi'neiʃən], *n.* dénomination, *f.*; culte, *m.*, secte, *f.*
denominational [dinəmi'neiʃənl], *a.* confessionnel (*école*).
denote [di'nout], *v.t.* dénoter, marquer, indiquer; signifier.
denounce [di'nauns], *v.t.* dénoncer.
dense [dens], *a.* dense, épais; compact; stupide.
densely ['densli], *adv.* en masse.
density ['densiti], *n.* densité, épaisseur, *f.*
dent [dent], *n.* renfoncement, *m.*, bosselure; coche, *f.*—*v.t.* bosseler, cabosser.
dental [dentl], *a.* dentaire; (*Phon.*) dental; ***dental surgeon***, chirurgien dentiste, *m.*
dentifrice ['dentifris], *n.* dentrifrice, *m.*
dentist ['dentist], *n.* dentiste, *m.*, *f.*
dentistry ['dentistri], *n.* dentisterie, *f.*
denture ['dentʃə], *n.* dentier; (*fam.*) râtelier, *m.*
denude [di'nju:d], *v.t.* dénuder; (*fig.*) dénuer.
denunciation [dinʌnsi'eiʃən], *n.* dénonciation, *f.*
deny [di'nai], *v.t.* nier, démentir; (*Law*) dénier, renier; refuser.
deodorant [di:'oudərənt], **deodorizer** [di:'oudəraizə], *n.* désinfectant, désinfecteur, désodorisant, *m.*
depart [di'pa:t], *v.t.* quitter.—*v.i.* partir, s'en aller, se retirer, s'éloigner; (*fig.*) mourir.
departed [di'pa:tid], *a.* mort, défunt; passé, évanoui.—*n.* ***the departed***, le défunt, *m.*, les trépassés, *m.pl.*
department [di'pa:tmənt], *n.* département, service; (*Polit.*) bureau; comptoir, rayon (*de boutique*), *m.*; ***department store***, grand magasin, *m.*
departmental [di:pa:t'mentl], *a.* départemental.
departure [di'pa:tʃə], *n.* départ; éloignement, *m.*; déviation; (*fig.*) mort, *f.*
depend [di'pend], *v.i.* dépendre (*de*); compter (*sur*), se reposer (*sur*).
dependable [di'pendəbl], *a.* digne de confiance; sûr.
dependent [di'pendənt], *a.* dépendant; (*Law*) à la charge de; (*Gram.*) subordonné; ***dependent relatives***, parents à charge, *m.pl.*
depict [di'pikt], *v.t.* peindre, dépeindre.
deplete [di'pli:t], *v.t.* amoindrir, épuiser.
deplorable [di'plɔ:rəbl], *a.* déplorable; pitoyable (*lamentable*).
deplore [di'plɔ:], *v.t.* déplorer.
deploy [di'plɔi], *v.t.* (*Mil.*) déployer.—*v.i.* se déployer.
depopulate [di:'pɔpjuleit], *v.t.* dépeupler.—*v.i.* se dépeupler.
deport [di'pɔ:t], *v.t.* déporter, expulser; ***to deport oneself***, se comporter.
deportment [di'pɔ:tmənt], *n.* tenue, conduite, *f.*, manières, *f.pl.*
depose [di'pouz], *v.t.*, *v.i.* déposer (*de*).
deposit [di'pɔzit], *n.* dépôt; (*Banking*) versement; gage, nantissement, *m.*, arrhes, *f.pl.*, caution, *f.*; (*Geol.*) gisement, gîte, *m.*; ***deposit account***, compte de dépôt, *m.*—*v.t.* déposer; verser.
deposition [depə'ziʃən, di:pə'ziʃən], *n.* déposition, *f.*; dépôt, *m.*
depositor [di'pɔzitə], *n.* (*Comm.*) déposant, *m.*
depository [di'pɔzitri], *n.* dépôt; garde-meubles, *m.*
depot ['depou], *n.* dépôt, *m.*; (*Am.*) ['di:pou], gare, *f.*
deprave [di'preiv], *v.t.* dépraver, corrompre.
depraved [di'preivd], *a.* dépravé, corrompu.
depravity [di'præviti], *n.* dépravation, *f.*
deprecate ['deprikeit], *v.t.* désapprouver, désavouer, s'opposer à.
deprecatingly ['deprikeitiŋli], *adv.* avec désapprobation.
deprecative ['deprikeitiv], **deprecatory** ['deprikeitəri], *a.* de déprécation.
depreciate [di'pri:ʃieit], *v.t.* déprécier.—*v.i.* se déprécier.
depreciation [dipri:ʃi'eiʃən], *n.* dépréciation, *f.*
depress [di'pres], *v.t.* baisser, abaisser; abattre; accabler, décourager.
depressed [di'prest], *a.* abattu; bas.
depression [di'preʃən], *n.* abaissement, *m.*; dépression; (*Comm.*) crise, *f.*
deprivation [depri'veiʃən], *n.* privation; perte, *f.*
deprive [di'praiv], *v.t.* priver (*de*); déposséder.
depth [depθ], *n.* profondeur, *f.*; enfoncement (*recoin*); fort (*des saisons*), *m.*; ***in the depth of winter***, au cœur *ou* au plus fort de l'hiver, *m.*; ***to get out of one's depth***, perdre pied.
depth-charge ['depθtʃa:dʒ], *n.* grenade sous-marine, *f.*
deputation [depju'teiʃən], *n.* députation, délégation, *f.*
depute [di'pju:t], *v.t.* députer, déléguer.
deputize ['depjutaiz], *v.i.* remplacer quelqu'un.
deputy ['depjuti], *n.* député, délégué; adjoint, *m.*
derail [di:'reil], *v.t.* (*Rail.*) dérailler.
derailment [di:'reilmənt], *n.* déraillement, *m.*
derange [di'reindʒ], *v.t.* déranger.
derangement [di'reindʒmənt], *n.* dérangement, *m.*
derelict ['derilikt], *a.* délaissé, abandonné.
deride [di'raid], *v.t.* tourner en dérision, se moquer de.
derision [di'riʒən], *n.* dérision, moquerie, *f.*
derisive [di'raisiv], *a.* dérisoire.
derivation [deri'veiʃən], *n.* dérivation; origine, *f.*
derivative [di'rivətiv], *n.* (*Gram.*) dérivé, *m.*
derive [di'raiv], *v.t.* dériver.—*v.i.* venir, dériver (*de*).

derogatory [di'rɔgətəri], *a.* péjoratif, dérogatoire, dérogeant (*à*).
derrick ['derik], *n.* grue, *f.*; derrick, *m.*
dervish ['də:viʃ], *n.* derviche, *m.*
descend [di'send], *v.i.* descendre, tomber; s'abaisser; ***to be descended from***, descendre de; ***to descend upon***, tomber sur.
descendant [di'sendənt], *n.* descendant, *m.*
descendent [di'sendənt], *a.* descendant, qui descend, provenant (*de*).
descent [di'sent], *n.* descente; chute, pente; descendance, naissance, origine (*lignée*), *f.*
describe [dis'kraib], *v.t.* décrire, dépeindre, peindre.
description [dis'kripʃən], *n.* description; désignation (*d'une personne*), *f.*; (*Law*) signalement, *m.*; (*colloq.*) qualité, sorte, espèce, *f.*
descriptive [dis'kriptiv], *a.* descriptif.
descry [dis'krai], *v.t.* découvrir, apercevoir; aviser; reconnaître.
desecrate ['desəkreit], *v.t.* profaner.
desecration [desə'kreiʃən], *n.* profanation, *f.*
desert (1) [di'zə:t], *n.* mérite, *m.*; mérites, *m.pl.*
desert (2) ['dezət], *a.* désert; solitaire.—*n.* désert, *m.*; solitude, *f.*
desert (3) [di'zə:t], *v.t.* abandonner, déserter.
deserted [di'zə:tid], *a.* abandonné, désert.
deserter [di'zə:tə], *n.* déserteur, *m.*
desertion [di'zə:ʃən], *n.* désertion, *f.*, abandon, *m.*
deserve [di'zə:v], *v.t.* mériter, être digne de.
deservedly [di'zə:vidli], *adv.* à bon droit, justement.
deserving [di'zə:viŋ], *a.* de mérite, méritoire.
desiccated ['desikeitid], *a.* desséché.
design [di'zain], *n.* dessein, projet; dessin (*drawing*); (*Manuf.*) modèle, *m.*; ***by design***, à dessein.—*v.t.* projeter, se proposer de; dessiner.
designedly [di'zainidli], *adv.* à dessein.
designer [di'zainə], *n.* inventeur; auteur; architecte; dessinateur (*draughtsman*), *m.*
designing [di'zainiŋ], *a.* artificieux, intrigant.
designate ['dezigneit], *v.t.* désigner, nommer.—['dezignit], *a.* désigné, nommé.
desirable [di'zaiərəbl], *a.* désirable, à souhaiter.
desire [di'zaiə], *n.* désir, *m.*; prière, demande, *f.*—*v.t.* désirer, souhaiter; prier.
desirous [di'zaiərəs], *a.* désireux (*de*), empressé (*à*); ***to be desirous of***, avoir envie de.
desist [di'zist], *v.i.* se désister, cesser (*de*).
desk [desk], *n.* pupitre (*école*); bureau (*meuble*), *m.*; caisse (*boutique*); chaire (*de professeur*), *f.*
desolate ['desəlit], *a.* désolé, inhabité, solitaire, dévasté.
desolation [desə'leiʃən], *n.* désolation, *f.*
despair [dis'pεə], *n.* désespoir, *m.*—*v.i.* désespérer (*de*).
despatch [DISPATCH].
desperado [despə'reidou, despə'rɑ:dou], *n.* désespéré, *m.*
desperate ['despərit], *a.* désespéré; furieux, forcené; acharné, terrible.
desperately ['despəritli], *adv.* désespérément; (*fig.*) excessivement.
desperation [despə'reiʃən], *n.* désespoir, *m.*; fureur, *f.*, acharnement, *m.*
despicable ['dispikəbl], *a.* méprisable.
despise [dis'paiz], *v.t.* mépriser, dédaigner.
despite [dis'pait], *n.* (*Lit.*) dépit, *m.*—*prep.* en dépit de, malgré.
despoil [dis'pɔil], *v.t.* dépouiller.
despondency [dis'pɔndənsi], *n.* abattement, désespoir, *m.*
despondent [dis'pɔndənt], *a.* découragé, abattu.
despot ['despɔt], *n.* despote, *m.*, *f.*
despotic [des'pɔtik], *a.* despotique.
despotism ['despətizm], *n.* despotisme, *m.*
dessert [di'zə:t], *n.* dessert, *m.*
destination [desti'neiʃən], *n.* destination, *f.*
destine ['destin], *v.t.* destiner, désigner.
destiny ['destini], *n.* destin, *m.*, destinée, *f.*
destitute ['destitju:t], *a.* dépourvu, destitué; indigent.
destitution [desti'tju:ʃən], *n.* dénuement, abandon, *m.*, indigence, *f.*
destroy [dis'trɔi], *v.t.* détruire, ruiner.
destroyer [dis'trɔiə], *n.* (*Naut.*) contre-torpilleur, *m.*
destroying [dis'trɔiiŋ], *a.* destructeur, destructif.
destruction [dis'trʌkʃən], *n.* destruction, *f.*, anéantissement, *m.*; ruine, *f.*
destructive [dis'trʌktiv], *a.* destructeur; funeste, fatal (*à*).
desultorily ['desəltərili], *adv.* à bâtons rompus, sans suite.
desultory ['desəltəri], *a.* à bâtons rompus, décousu, sans suite.
detach [di'tætʃ], *v.t.* détacher (*de*); isoler; ***to become detached***, se détacher.
detachable [di'tætʃəbl], *a.* démontable, détachable.
detached [di'tætʃt], *a.* détaché, isolé.
detachment [di'tætʃmənt], *n.* détachement, *m.*
detail ['di:teil], *n.* détail, *m.*—[di'teil], *v.t.* détailler; (*Mil.*) désigner (*pour*).
detain [di'tein], *v.t.* retenir; détenir; (*Law*) empêcher.
detect [di'tekt], *v.t.* découvrir; détecter.
detection [di'tekʃən], *n.* découverte, *f.*
detective [di'tektiv], *n.* agent de la (police de) sûreté, policier, détective, *m.*; ***a detective story***, un roman policier.
detention [di'tenʃən], *n.* action de retenir; (*Law*) détention; (*Sch.*) consigne, *f.*
deter [di'tə:], *v.t.* détourner, empêcher (*de*); dissuader (*de*).
detergent [di'tə:dʒənt], *a.* and *n.* détersif, détergent, *m.*
deteriorate [di'tiəriəreit], *v.i.* se détériorer.
deterioration [ditiəriə'reiʃən], *n.* détérioration, *f.*; dépérissement, *m.*
determination [ditə:mi'neiʃən], *n.* détermination, décision, *f.*
determine [di'tə:min], *v.t.* déterminer, décider.—*v.i.* se déterminer, se décider, résoudre.
determined [di'tə:mind], *a.* résolu, obstiné.
deterrent [di'terənt], *a.* préventif.—*n.* arme préventive, *f.*
detest [di'test], *v.t.* détester.
detestable [di'testəbl], *a.* détestable; (*fig.*) odieux.
detestation [di:tes'teiʃən], *n.* détestation, *f.*

dethrone [di'θroun], *v.t.* détrôner.
detonation [detə'neiʃən], *n.* détonation, *f.*
detonator ['detəneitə], *n.* détonateur, *m.*
detract [di'trækt], *v.t.* enlever, ôter (*à*); dénigrer.—*v.i.* déroger (*à*).
detriment ['detrimənt], *n.* détriment, préjudice, *m.*
detrimental [detri'mentl], *a.* préjudiciable, nuisible (*à*).
deuce [dju:s], *n.* (*Cards*) deux; (*Ten.*) à deux; à égalité; (*colloq.*) diable, diantre, *m.*
Deuteronomy [dju:tə'ronəmi]. Deutéronome, *m.*
devaluation [di:vælju'eiʃən], *n.* dévaluation, *f.*
devalue [di:'vælju], **devaluate** [di:'væljueit] *v.t.* dévaluer, déprécier.
devastate ['devəsteit], *v.t.* dévaster.
devastation [devəs'teiʃən], *n.* dévastation, *f.*
develop [di'veləp], *v.t.* développer.
developer [di'veləpə], *n.* (*Phot.*) révélateur, *m.*
development [di'veləpmənt], *n.* développement, *m.*
deviate ['di:vieit], *v.i.* dévier, se dévier; s'écarter (*de*).
deviation [di:vi'eiʃən], *n.* déviation, *f.*, écart, *m.*
device [di'vais], *n.* dessein, moyen, stratagème; dispositif, mécanisme, *m.*; devise (*motto*), *f.*
devil [devl], *n.* diable, démon, *m.*; ***dare-devil***, téméraire, *m.*, *f.*—*v.t.* griller et poivrer; ***devil-may-care***, étourdi, *m.*
devilish ['deviliʃ], *a.* maudit, diabolique.
devilment ['devilmənt], **devilry** ['devilri], *n.* diablerie, *f.*
devious ['di:viəs], *a.* détourné, écarté; (*fig.*) errant.
devise [di'vaiz], *v.t.* imaginer, inventer; tramer, machiner.
devitalize [di:'vaitəlaiz], *v.t.* dévitaliser.
devoid [di'vɔid], *a.* exempt, dénué (*de*).
devote [di'vout], *v.t.* dévouer, consacrer (*à*).
devoted [di'voutid], *a.* dévoué, consacré.
devotee [devo'ti:], *n.* dévot; passionné, *m.*, fanatique, *m.*, *f.*
devotion [di'vouʃən], *n.* dévotion, *f.*; dévouement, *m.*
devour [di'vauə], *v.t.* dévorer.
devout [di'vaut], *a.* dévot, pieux, fervent.
devoutly [di'vautli], *adv.* dévotement.
dew [dju:], *n.* rosée, *f.*
dewdrop ['dju:drɔp], *n.* goutte de rosée, *f.*
dewlap ['dju:læp], *n.* fanon, *m.*
dewy ['dju:i], *a.* (couvert) de rosée.
dexterity [deks'teriti], *n.* dextérité, adresse, *f.*
dexterous ['dekstrəs], *a.* adroit; habile.
diabetes [daiə'bi:ti:z], *n.* diabète, *m.*
diabetic [daiə'betik], *a.* and *n.* diabétique, *m.*, *f.*
diabolic [daiə'bɔlik], **diabolical** [daiə'bɔlikl], *a.* diabolique.
diadem ['daiədem], *n.* diadème, *m.*
diæresis [dai'iərəsis], *n.* (*pl.* **diæreses** [dai'iərəsi:z]) tréma, *m.*
diagnose [daiəg'nouz], *v.t.* diagnostiquer.
diagnosis [daiəg'nousis], *n.* (*pl.* **diagnoses** [daiəg'nousi:z]) diagnose, *f.*; diagnostic, *m.*
diagonal [dai'ægənəl], *a.* diagonal.—*n.* diagonale, *f.*
diagram ['daiəgræm], *n.* diagramme, schéma, *m.*, épure, *f.*
diagrammatic [daiəgrə'mætik], *a.* schématique.
dial ['daiəl], *n.* cadran, *m.*; ***sun-dial***, cadran solaire.—*v.t.* (*Teleph.*) composer (*un numéro*).
dialect ['daiəlekt], *n.* dialecte, patois; (*fig.*) langage, *m.*
dialogue ['daiəlɔg], *n.* dialogue; entretien, *m.*
diameter [dai'æmitə], *n.* diamètre, *m.*
diamond ['daiəmənd], *n.* diamant; (*Cards*) carreau, *m.*
diamond-cutter ['daiəməndkʌtə], *n.* lapidaire, *m.*
diamond-shaped ['daiəməndʃeipt], *a.* en losange.
Diana [dai'ænə]. (*Myth.*) Diane, *f.*
diaper ['daiəpə], *n.* linge ouvré, *m.*; (*Am.*) serviette hygiénique, couche (*d'enfant*), *f.*
diarrhoea [daiə'ri:ə], *n.* diarrhée, *f.*
diary ['daiəri], *n.* journal (particulier); agenda, *m.*
diatribe ['daiətraib], *n.* diatribe, *f.*
dice [dais], *n.pl.* dés, *m.pl.*—*v.i.* jouer aux dés.
dicky ['diki], *a.* (*fam.*) défectueux.
dictate [dik'teit], *v.t.* dicter.—*v.i.* commander (*à*).—['dikteit], *n.* précepte, ordre, *m.*
dictation [dik'teiʃən], *n.* dictée, *f.*
dictator [dik'teitə], *n.* dictateur, *m.*
dictatorial [diktə'tɔ:riəl], *a.* dictatorial; impérieux.
dictatorship [dik'teitəʃip], *n.* dictature, *f.*
diction ['dikʃən], *n.* diction, *f.*; débit, *m.*
dictionary ['dikʃənri], *n.* dictionnaire, *m.*
dictum ['diktəm], *n.* (*pl.* **dicta** ['diktə]) dicton, *m.*
diddle [didl], *v.t.* (*colloq.*) duper, rouler.
die (1) [dai], *n.* (*pl.* **dies** [daiz]) coin (*pour estamper*).
die (2) [dai], *n.* (*pl.* **dice** [dais]) dé (*à jouer*), *m.*; (*fig.*) chance, *f.*
die (3) [dai], *v.i.* mourir; (*fig.*) s'éteindre; ***to die down***, s'apaiser, se calmer; ***to die of***, mourir de; ***to die out***, s'éteindre, disparaître, s'oublier.
die-hard ['daihɑ:d], *n.* intransigeant, *m.*
diet ['daiət], *n.* diète, *f.*, régime, *m.*; diète (*assemblée*), *f.*—*v.t.* mettre à la diète, mettre au régime.—*v.i.* faire diète, être au régime.
dietetics [daiə'tetiks], *n.pl.* diététique, *f.*
differ ['difə], *v.i.* différer (*de*); se quereller (*avec*).
difference ['difrəns], *n.* différence; dispute, *f.*; différend (*de valeur*), *m.*; ***to split the difference***, partager le différend.
different ['difrənt], *a.* différent.
differentiate [difə'renʃieit], *v.t.* différencier, distinguer.
differently ['difrəntli], *adv.* différemment, autrement.
difficult ['difikəlt], *a.* difficile; malaisé.
difficulty ['difikəlti], *n.* difficulté; peine, *f.*, embarras; (*pl.*) embarras pécuniaire, *m.*
diffidence ['difidəns], *n.* défiance (*de soi*), modestie, timidité, *f.*
diffident ['difidənt], *a.* timide, hésitant.
diffidently ['difidəntli], *adv.* avec hésitation, timidement.
diffuse [di'fju:s], *a.* répandu, étendu; diffus, verbeux (*style*).—[di'fju:z], *v.t.* répandre.
diffusely [di'fju:sli], *adv.* diffusément.

dig [dig], *v.t. irr.* creuser; bêcher; piocher.—*v.i.* bêcher, piocher; faire des fouilles.—*n.* coup (*de coude*); (*colloq.*) coup de patte, *m.*
digest [di'dʒest], *v.t.* digérer (*aliment etc.*); résumer.—*v.i.* digérer.—['daidʒest], *n.* sommaire, abrégé, *m.*
digestion [di'dʒestʃən], *n.* digestion, *f.*
digestive [di'dʒestiv], *a.* and *n.* digestif, *m.*
digger ['digə], *n.* terrassier; mineur; fouilleur (*archéologue*); (*pop.*) Australien, *m.*
digging ['digiŋ], *n.* fouille, *f.*, creusement, *m.*; (*pl.*) (*pop.*) (*abbr.* **digs** [digz]) logement, *m.*
dignified ['dignifaid], *a.* plein de dignité, digne; noble.
dignify ['dignifai], *v.t.* honorer, élever, illustrer.
dignitary ['dignitri], *n.* dignitaire, *m.*, *f.*
dignity ['digniti], *n.* dignité, *f.*
digress [dai'gres], *v.i.* faire une digression; s'écarter (*de*).
digression [dai'greʃən], *n.* digression, *f.*
dike or **dyke** [daik], *n.* digue, *f.*, fossé, *m.*
dilapidated [di'læpideitid], *a.* délabré.
dilapidation [dilæpi'deiʃən], *n.* délabrement, *m.*
dilate [dai'leit], *v.t.* dilater, élargir, étendre.—*v.i.* se dilater.
dilatory ['dilətəri], *a.* négligent, lent.
dilemma [di'lemə, dai'lemə], *n.* dilemme; (*fig.*) embarras, *m.*; ***on the horns of a dilemma***, enfermé dans un dilemme.
diligence ['dilidʒəns], *n.* diligence, assiduité, *f.*
diligent ['dilidʒənt], *a.* diligent, appliqué.
dilute [dai'lju:t, di'lju:t], *v.t.* délayer; diluer; couper (*vin*); (*fig.*) affaiblir.—*a.* dilué, mitigé.
dilution [dai'lju:ʃən, di'lju:ʃən], *n.* dilution (*liquides*), *f.*; délayement; (*fig.*) affaiblissement, *m.*
dim [dim], *a.* obscur, trouble; blafard; terne (*lumière*); indécis.—*v.t.* obscurcir; ternir.
dimension [di'menʃən, dai'menʃən], *n.* dimension, étendue, *f.*
dimensional [di'menʃənəl, dai'menʃənəl], *a.* dimensionnel; (*Cine.*) ***three-dimensional (3-D) film***, film en relief, *m.*
diminish [di'miniʃ], *v.t.* diminuer; abaisser. —*v.i.* diminuer.
diminutive [di'minjutiv], *a.* diminutif, minuscule.
dimly ['dimli], *adv.* obscurément, indistinctement, faiblement, à peine; sans éclat.
dimness ['dimnis], *n.* obscurcissement, *m.*; obscurité; faiblesse (*de vue*), *f.*
dimple [dimpl], *n.* fossette, *f.*—*v.i.* (*fig.*) se rider (*eau etc.*).
din [din], *n.* vacarme, tapage, fracas; cliquetis (*d'armes etc.*), *m.*
dine [dain], *v.i.* dîner (*de*).
diner ['dainə], *n.* dîneur, *m.*
dinghy ['diŋgi], *n.* (*Naut.*) youyou, canot, *m.*
dinginess ['dindʒinis], *n.* couleur terne, *f.*; aspect sale, *m.*
dingy ['dindʒi], *a.* terne; sale; défraîchi.
dining-car ['dainiŋka:], *n.* wagon-restaurant, *m.*
dining-room ['dainiŋrum], *n.* salle à manger, *f.*
dinner ['dinə], *n.* dîner, *m.*
dinner-jacket ['dinədʒækit], *n.* smoking, *m.*
dint (1) [dint], *n.* force, *f.*, pouvoir, *m.*; ***by dint of***, à force de.
dint (2) [dint], [DENT].
diocese ['daiəsis], *n.* diocèse, *m.*
dioxide [dai'ɔksaid], *n.* (*Chem.*) bioxyde, *m.*
dip [dip], *v.t.* plonger (*dans*); tremper, mouiller; (*Motor.*) mettre en code (*phares*).—*v.i.* plonger; ***to dip into***, s'engager dans, feuilleter (*un livre*).—*n.* plongeon, *m.*, baignade, *f.*
diphtheria [dif'θiəriə], *n.* diphtérie, *f.*
diphthong ['difθɔŋ], *n.* diphtongue, *f.*
diploma [di'ploumə], *n.* diplôme, *m.*
diplomacy [di'plouməsi], *n.* diplomatie, *f.*
diplomat ['diplomæt], **diplomatist** [di'ploumətist], *n.* diplomate, *m.*, *f.*
diplomatic [diplo'mætik], *a.* diplomatique.
dip-stick ['dipstik], *n.* (*Motor.*) réglette-jauge, *f.*
dire ['daiə], *a.* terrible, affreux; cruel.
direct [di'rekt, dai'rekt], *a.* direct, droit; exprès, clair.—*adv.* (*colloq.*) directement.—*v.t.* diriger; ordonner, charger (*de*); indiquer, donner des renseignements à; ***to direct a letter***, adresser une lettre.
direction [di'rekʃən], *n.* direction, *f.*; ordre, *m.*, instruction, *f.*; sens, côté, *m.*; adresse (*d'une lettre*), *f.*
directly [di'rektli], *adv.* directement, immédiatement; (*colloq.*) tout de suite; aussitôt que (*as soon as*).
director [di'rektə], *n.* directeur, administrateur, gérant; (*Cine.*) réalisateur, *m.*
directory [di'rektəri], *n.* directoire; (*Postal, Teleph.*) annuaire, *m.*
direful ['daiəful], *a.* terrible, affreux.
dirge [də:dʒ], *n.* chant funèbre, *m.*
dirt [də:t], *n.* saleté; crasse; boue, fange; ordure, *f.*
dirtily ['də:tili], *adv.* salement; (*fig.*) vilainement.
dirtiness ['də:tinis], *n.* saleté; (*fig.*) bassesse, *f.*
dirty ['də:ti], *a.* sale, malpropre, crasseux; (*fig.*) bas, vilain.—*v.t.* salir, crotter; (*fig.*) souiller.
disability [disə'biliti], *n.* incapacité, *f.*
disable [dis'eibl], *v.t.* rendre incapable, mettre hors d'état (*de*).
disabled [dis'eibld], *a.* hors de service; (*Mil.*) hors de combat; ***disabled ex-service men***, mutilés de guerre, *m.pl.*
disadvantage [disəd'va:ntidʒ], *n.* désavantage, inconvénient, *m.*; perte, *f.*
disagree [disə'gri:], *v.i.* différer, ne pas s'accorder; ***my dinner disagreed with me***, mon dîner m'a fait mal.
disagreeable [disə'gri:əbl], *a.* désagréable; fâcheux.
disagreeableness [disə'gri:əblnis], *n.* désagrément, *m.*, nature désagréable, *f.*
disagreeably [disə'gri:əbli], *adv.* désagréablement.
disagreement [disə'gri:mənt], *n.* différence, *f.*, désaccord; différend, *m.*; brouille, *f.*
disallow [disə'lau], *v.t.* désapprouver; refuser, défendre.
disappear [disə'piə], *v.i.* disparaître.
disappearance [disə'piərəns], *n.* disparition, *f.*
disappoint [disə'pɔint], *v.t.* désappointer, décevoir.
disappointing [disə'pɔintiŋ], *a.* décevant.

disappointment [disə'pɔintmənt], *n.* désappointement, *m.*; déception, *f.*; contretemps, *m.*
disapprobation [disæpro'beiʃən], **disapproval** [disə'pruːvəl], *n.* désapprobation, *f.*
disapprove [disə'pruːv], *v.t.* désapprouver.—*v.i.* *to* ***disapprove of***, désapprouver.
disarm [dis'ɑːm], *v.t.* désarmer.
disarmament [dis'ɑːməmənt], *n.* désarmement, *m.*
disarrange [disə reindʒ], *v.t.* déranger.
disarray [disə'rei], *v.i.* mettre en désarroi *ou* en désordre.—*n.* désarroi, désordre, *m.*
disaster [di'zɑːstə], *n.* désastre, malheur, *m.*
disastrous [di'zɑːstrəs], *a.* désastreux.
disavow [disə'vau], *v.t.* désavouer.
disband [dis'bænd], *v.t.* licencier, congédier; disperser.—*v.i.* se disperser.
disbelief [disbi'liːf], *n.* incrédulité, *f.*
disbelieve [disbi'liːv], *v.t.* ne pas croire, refuser de croire.
disbeliever [disbi'liːvə], *n.* incrédule, *m.*, *f.*
disc [DISK].
discard [dis'kɑːd], *v.t.* mettre de côté; congédier; écarter; éliminer; (*Cards*) faire son écart.—['diskɑːd], *n.* (*Cards*) écart, *m.*
discern [di'səːn, di'zəːn], *v.t.* discerner, distinguer.
discerning [di'səːniŋ, di'zəːniŋ], *a.* judicieux, éclairé, attentif.
discernment [di'səːnmənt, di'zəːnmənt], *n.* discernement, jugement, *m.*
discharge [dis'tʃɑːdʒ], *n.* déchargement, *m.*; décharge (*arme à feu etc.*); mise en liberté (*d'un prisonnier*), *f.*; accomplissement (*d'un devoir*), *m.*; réhabilitation (*d'un failli*); quittance (*récépissé*), *f.*; congé (*d'employé*); (*Mil.*) congé définitif; (*Med.*) écoulement, *m.*—*v.t.* décharger; congédier (*employé*); libérer (*de prison*); acquitter (*dette*); décharger (*arme à feu*); remplir (*devoir*); (*Mil.*, *Navy*) congédier; (*Law*) quitter.—*v.i.* suppurer (*blessure etc.*).
disciple [di'saipl], *n.* disciple, *m.*
disciplinarian [disipli'nεəriən], *a.* disciplinaire.—*n.* personne rigide pour la discipline, *f.*
disciplinary ['disiplinəri], *a.* disciplinaire.
discipline ['disiplin], *n.* discipline, *f.*—*v.t.* discipliner.
disclaim [dis'kleim], *v.t.* désavouer, renier, nier.
disclose [dis'klouz], *v.t.* découvrir, révéler.
disclosure [dis'klouʒə], *n.* révélation, découverte, *f.*
discolour [dis'kʌlə], *v.t.* décolorer.
discomfort [dis'kʌmfət], *n.* incommodité, *f.*, inconfort, malaise, *m.*; gêne, *f.*
discompose [diskəm'pouz], *v.t.* déranger, troubler.
discomposure [diskəm'pouʒə], *n.* trouble, désordre, *m.*, agitation, *f.*
disconcert [diskən'səːt], *v.t.* déconcerter.
disconnect [diskə'nekt], *v.t.* désunir, séparer; (*Elec.*) débrancher; (*Mach.*) désembrayer.
disconnected [diskə'nektid], *a.* débrayé; déconnecté; (*fig.*) décousu.
disconsolate [dis'kɔnsəlit], *a.* inconsolable, désolé.
discontent [diskən'tent], *n.* mécontentement, *m.*
discontented [diskən'tentid], *a.* mécontent (*de*).
discontinue [diskən'tinjuː], *v.t.*, *v.i.* discontinuer; cesser de.
discord ['diskɔːd], *n.* discorde; (*Mus.*) dissonance, *f.*
discordant [dis'kɔːdənt], *a.* discordant; (*fig.*) en désaccord.
discount ['diskaunt], *n.* escompte; rabais, *m.* ***at a discount***, au rabais, en baisse.—[dis'kaunt], *v.t.* escompter; (*fig.*) décompter, rabattre.—*v.i.* faire l'escompte.
discourage [dis'kʌridʒ], *v.t.* décourager, détourner.
discouragement [dis'kʌridʒmənt], *n.* découragement, *m.*
discouraging [dis'kʌridʒiŋ], *a.* décourageant.
discourse (I) ['diskɔːs], *n.* discours, entretien; (*fig.*) langage, propos, *m.*—[dis'kɔːs], *v.i.* discourir, s'entretenir, traiter (*de*).
discourteous [dis'kəːtiəs], *a.* impoli.
discourtesy [dis'kəːtisi], *n.* impolitesse, *f.*
discover [dis'kʌvə], *v.t.* découvrir; révéler, montrer.
discovery [dis'kʌvəri], *n.* découverte, *f.*
discredit [dis'kredit], *n.* discrédit, *m.*; honte, *f.*—*v.t.* ne pas croire; déshonorer.
discreditable [dis'kreditəbl], *a.* peu honorable; honteux.
discreet [dis'kriːt], *a.* discret, prudent, circonspect, sage.
discreetly [dis'kriːtli], *adv.* discrètement, sagement, prudemment.
discrepancy [dis'krepənsi], *n.* désaccord, *m.*
discretion [dis'kreʃən], *n.* discrétion, prudence, sagesse, *f.*; jugement, discernement, *m.*
discriminate [dis'krimineit], *v.t.* discriminer, distinguer.—*v.i.* faire des distinctions.
discriminating [dis'krimineitiŋ], *a.* discriminatoire, distinctif.
discrimination [diskrimi'neiʃən], *n.* discrimination, *f.*, discernement, *m.*
discuss [dis'kʌs], *v.t.* discuter, débattre.
discussion [dis'kʌʃən], *n.* discussion, *f.*, débat, *m.*
disdain [dis'dein], *n.* dédain, mépris, *m.*—*v.t.* dédaigner, mépriser.
disdainful [dis'deinful], *a.* dédaigneux, méprisant.
disease [di'ziːz], *n.* maladie, *f.*, mal; (*fig.*) vice, *m.*
diseased [di'ziːzd], *a.* malade; (*fig.*) dérangé.
disembark [disim'bɑːk], *v.t.*, *v.i.* débarquer.
disembarkation [disembɑː'keiʃən], *n.* débarquement, *m.*
disembodied [disim'bɔdid], *a.* désincarné.
disembowel [disim'bauəl], *v.t.* éventrer.
disengage [disin'geidʒ], *v.t.* dégager; (*Tech.*) débrayer.—*v.i.* se dégager.
disengaged [disin'geidʒd], *a.* dégagé; libre.
disentangle [disin'tæŋgl], *v.t.* démêler, débrouiller.
disentanglement [disin'tæŋglmənt], *n.* débrouillement, *m.*
disestablish [disis'tæbliʃ], *v.t.* séparer (*l'Église de l'État*).
disestablishment [disis'tæbliʃmənt], *n.* séparation de l'Église et de l'État, *f.*
disfavour [dis'feivə], *n.* défaveur, *f.*
disfigure [dis'figə], *v.t.* défigurer, enlaidir.

disfigurement [dis'figəmənt], *n.* action de défigurer; difformité, *f.*
disfranchisement [dis'fræntʃizmənt], *n.* privation *ou* perte de privilèges électoraux, *f.*
disgorge [dis'gɔ:dʒ], *v.t.* dégorger, rendre, vomir.—*v.i.* rendre gorge.
disgrace [dis'greis], *n.* disgrâce, honte, *f.*, déshonneur, *m.*—*v.t.* disgracier; déshonorer.
disgraceful [dis'greisful], *a.* honteux; déshonorant, ignoble.
disgracefully [dis'greisfuli], *adv.* honteusement.
disgruntled [dis'grʌntld], *a.* mécontent; de mauvaise humeur.
disguise [dis'gaiz], *n.* déguisement, travestissement; (*fig.*) masque, voile, *m.*—*v.t.* déguiser; (*fig.*) cacher, voiler.
disguised [dis'gaizd], *a.* déguisé.
disgust [dis'gʌst], *n.* dégoût, *m.*, aversion, *f.*; ennui, *m.*—*v.t.* dégoûter (*de*); écœurer.
disgusting [dis'gʌstiŋ], *a.* dégoûtant.
dish [diʃ], *n.* (*pl.* **dishes** ['diʃiz]) plat (*vaisselle*); mets (*aliment*), *m.*; (*pl.*) vaisselle, *f.*—*v.t.* dresser, servir, apprêter; (*colloq.*) enfoncer.
dish-cloth ['diʃkləθ], *n.* torchon, *m.*
dishearten [dis'hɑ:tn], *v.t.* décourager.
disheartening [dis'hɑ:tniŋ], *a.* décourageant.
dishevel [di'ʃevəl], *v.t.* ébouriffer.
dishevelled [di'ʃevəld], *a.* dépeigné, ébouriffé.
dishonest [dis'ɔnist], *a.* malhonnête.
dishonestly [dis'ɔnistli], *adv.* malhonnêtement.
dishonesty [dis'ɔnisti], *n.* improbité, malhonnêteté, *f.*
dishonour [dis'ɔnə], *n.* déshonneur, *m.*—*v.t.* déshonorer; avilir; (*Comm.*) ***dishonoured cheque***, chèque impayé, *m.*
dishonourable [dis'ɔnərəbl], *a.* sans honneur; honteux (*chose*).
dishonourably [dis'ɔnərəbli], *adv.* malhonnêtement.
disillusion [disi'lju:ʒən], *v.t.* désillusionner. —*n.*, *also* **disillusionment** [disi'lju:ʒənmənt], désillusionnement, *m.*
disinclination [disinkli'neiʃən], *n.* éloignement, *m.*; aversion, *f.*
disinclined [disin'klaind], *a.* peu disposé.
disinfect [disin'fekt], *v.t.* désinfecter.
disinfectant [disin'fektənt], *n.* désinfectant, *m.*
disingenuous [disin'dʒenjuəs], *a.* sans franchise, de mauvaise foi, dissimulé.
disingenuously [disin'dʒenjuəsli], *adv.* de mauvaise foi.
disingenuousness [disin'dʒenjuəsnis], *n.* dissimulation, mauvaise foi, fausseté, *f.*
disinherit [disin'herit], *v.t.* déshériter.
disinheritance [disin'heritəns], *n.* déshéritement, *m.*
disintegrate [dis'intigreit], *v.t.* désagréger; désintégrer.—*v.i.* se désagréger, se désintégrer.
disintegration [disinti'greiʃən], *n.* désagrégation; désintégration, *f.*
disinter [disin'tə:], *v.t.* déterrer, exhumer.
disinterested [dis'intrəstid], *a.* désintéressé.
disjointed [dis'dʒɔintid], *a.* désarticulé, disloqué; (*fig.*) décousu, sans suite (*style etc.*).
disjointedly [dis'dʒɔintidli], *adv.* d'une manière décousue *ou* incohérente.
disk [disk], *n.* disque, *m.*; (*Med.*) ***slipped disk***, hernie discale, *f.*
dislike [dis'laik], *v.t.* ne pas aimer; avoir du dégoût pour.—*n.* aversion, *f.*; dégoût, *m.*
dislocate ['dislokeit], *v.t.* disloquer, démettre; déboîter (*os etc.*).
dislodge [dis'lɔdʒ], *v.t.* déloger; déplacer.
disloyal [dis'lɔiəl], *a.* perfide, déloyal.
disloyalty [dis'lɔiəlti], *n.* défection (*de*), déloyauté, perfidie, *f.*
dismal ['dizməl], *a.* sombre, morne, triste.
dismally ['dizməli], *adv.* lugubrement, tristement.
dismantle [dis'mæntl], *v.t.* dévêtir; démonter (*machine*).
dismay [dis'mei], *n.* effroi, *m.*, terreur, épouvante, *f.*—*v.t.* effarer, épouvanter, consterner.
dismiss [dis'mis], *v.t.* renvoyer (*de*); congédier; quitter (*sujet etc.*); rejeter (*appel etc.*); chasser (*pensées etc.*).
dismissal [dis'misəl], *n.* renvoi; congé; (*Law*) acquittement, *m.*
dismount [dis'maunt], *v.t.* démonter.—*v.i.* descendre de cheval.
disobedience [diso'bi:diəns], *n.* désobéissance, *f.*
disobedient [diso'bi:diənt], *a.* désobéissant.
disobey [diso'bei], *v.t.* désobéir à.
disobliging [diso'blaidʒiŋ], *a.* désobligeant.
disorder [dis'ɔ:də], *n.* désordre, dérèglement, *m.*; maladie (*Med.*), *f.*—*v.t.* déranger, troubler.
disordered [dis'ɔ:dəd], *a.* en désordre, dérangé; malade.
disorderly [dis'ɔ:dəli], *a.* en désordre, déréglé; vicieux; tumultueux.
disorganization [disɔ:gəni'zeiʃən], *n.* désorganisation, *f.*
disorganize [dis'ɔ:gənaiz], *v.t.* désorganiser.
disown [dis'oun], *v.t.* désavouer, nier.
disparage [dis'pæridʒ], *v.t.* déprécier, ravaler, dénigrer.
disparagement [dis'pæridʒmənt], *n.* dénigrement, déshonneur, reproche, *m.*; honte, *f.*, tort, *m.*
disparaging [dis'pæridʒiŋ], *a.* dénigrant, injurieux.
disparagingly [dis'pæridʒiŋli], *adv.* avec mépris.
dispassionate [dis'pæʃənit], *a.* calme; impartial.
dispatch, despatch [dis'pætʃ], *v.t.* dépêcher, expédier; achever.—*n.* dépêche, *f.*, envoi, *m.*; promptitude, *f.*; ***mentioned in dispatches***, cité à l'ordre du jour.
dispel [dis'pel], *v.t.* dissiper, chasser.
dispensary [dis'pensəri], *n.* dispensaire, *m.*; pharmacie, *f.*
dispensation [dispən'seiʃən], *n.* dispensation, *f.*; (*fig.*) bienfait, don, *m.*
dispense [dis'pens], *v.t.* distribuer, dispenser, administrer; (*Pharm.*) préparer (*médecine*); ***to dispense with***, se passer de.
dispenser [dis'pensə], *n.* dispensateur, pharmacien, *m.*
dispersal [dis'pə:səl], *n.* dispersion, *f.*
disperse [dis'pə:s], *v.t.* disperser; dissiper.—*v.i.* se disperser.
dispirited [dis'piritid], *a.* découragé, abattu.

displace [dis'pleis], *v.t.* déplacer; destituer (*d'un emploi*).
displacement [dis'pleismənt], *n.* déplacement, *m.*
display [dis'plei], *n.* exposition, parade, *f.*; (*fig.*) étalage, *m.*—*v.t.* montrer, exposer, étaler.
displease [dis'pli:z], *v.t.* déplaire à; fâcher.
displeased [dis'pli:zd], *a.* mécontent, offensé (*de*).
displeasing [dis'pli:ziŋ], *a.* désagréable.
displeasure [dis'pleʒə], *n.* déplaisir; courroux, *m.*
disport [dis'pɔ:t], *v.t.* ***to disport oneself***, s'amuser, se divertir.
disposal [dis'pouzəl], *n.* disposition; vente, cession (*sale*), *f.*
dispose [dis'pouz], *v.t.* disposer; porter (*à croire*); ***to dispose of***, céder, vendre, se défaire de, se débarrasser de.
disposition [dispə'ziʃən], *n.* disposition, *f.*; caractère, naturel, *m.*
dispossess [dispə'zes], *v.t.* déposséder (*de*).
disproportionate [disprə'pɔ:ʃənit], *a.* disproportionné.
disprove [dis'pru:v], *v.t.* réfuter.
dispute [dis'pju:t], *n.* différend; conflit, *m.*; ***beyond dispute***, sans contredit.—*v.t.* disputer, discuter.
disqualification [diskwɔlifi'keiʃən], *n.* incapacité, *f.*
disqualify [dis'kwɔlifai], *v.t.* rendre incapable (*de*).
disquiet [dis'kwaiət], *n.* inquiétude, *f.*
disregard [disri'gɑ:d], *n.* insouciance, indifférence, *f.*—*v.t.* négliger, faire peu de cas de.
disrepair [disri'pɛə], *n.* délabrement, *m.*
disreputable [dis'repjutəbl], *a.* de mauvaise réputation; compromettant, déshonorant (*chose*).
disrepute [disri'pju:t], *n.* discrédit, déshonneur, *m.*; mauvaise réputation, *f.*
disrespect [disris'pekt], *n.* manque de respect, irrespect, *m.*
disrespectful [disris'pektful], *a.* irrespectueux.
disrobe [dis'roub], *v.t.* déshabiller, dévêtir. —*v.i.* se déshabiller.
disrupt [dis'rʌpt], *v.t.* rompre.
dissatisfaction [dissætis'fækʃən], *n.* mécontentement, *m.*
dissatisfied [dis'sætisfaid], *a.* mécontent (*de*).
dissect [di'sekt], *v.t.* disséquer.
dissection [di'sekʃən], *n.* dissection, *f.*
dissemble [di'sembl], *v.t.* dissimuler, déguiser, cacher.—*v.i.* dissimuler, feindre.
disseminate [di'semineit], *v.t.* disséminer, répandre, propager.
dissension [di'senʃən], *n.* dissension, *f.*; ***to sow dissension***, semer la zizanie.
dissent [di'sent], *n.* dissentiment, *m.*; (*Relig.*) dissidence, *f.*—*v.i.* différer (*de*); différer de sentiment (*avec*).
dissenter [di'sentə], *n.* dissident, *m.*, nonconformiste, *m.*, *f.*
disservice [di'sə:vis], *n.* mauvais service, *m.*
dissever [di'sevə], *v.t.* séparer (*de*).
dissimilar [di'similə], *a.* dissemblable (*à*); différent (*de*).
dissimulate [di'simjuleit], *v.t.* dissimuler.
dissipate ['disipeit], *v.t.* dissiper.—*v.i.* se dissiper.
dissociate [di'souʃieit], *v.t.* désassocier, dissocier.
dissolute ['disəlu:t], *a.* dissolu.
dissolve [di'zɔlv], *v.t.* dissoudre; désunir; supprimer; résoudre (*doute etc.*).—*v.i.* se dissoudre.
dissonance ['disənəns], *n.* dissonance; discordance, *f.*
dissuade [di'sweid], *v.t.* dissuader (*de*).
distaff ['distɑ:f], *n.* quenouille, *f.*; ***the distaff side***, le côté maternel.
distance ['distəns], *n.* distance, *f.*; éloignement, lointain, *m.*; (*fig.*) réserve, *f.*
distant ['distənt], *a.* éloigné, lointain; (*fig.*) réservé, froid.
distaste [dis'teist], *n.* dégoût, *m.*, aversion (*pour*), *f.*
distasteful [dis'teistful], *a.* désagréable, offensant.
distemper [dis'tempə], *n.* maladie (*de chien*); (*Paint.*) détrempe, *f.*—*v.t.* peindre en détrempe.
distend [dis'tend], *v.t.* étendre; dilater, enfler. —*v.i.* se détendre.
distil [dis'til], *v.t.*, *v.i.* distiller.
distillation [disti'leiʃən], *n.* distillation, *f.*
distiller [dis'tilə], *n.* distillateur, *m.*
distillery [dis'tiləri], *n.* distillerie, *f.*
distinct [dis'tiŋkt], *a.* distinct; exprès, clair, net.
distinction [dis'tiŋkʃən], *n.* distinction; (*Sch.*) mention, *f.*
distinctive [dis'tiŋktiv], *a.* distinctif.
distinctly [dis'tiŋktli], *adv.* distinctement, clairement; (*fig.*) indéniablement.
distinguish [dis'tiŋgwiʃ], *v.t.* distinguer (*de*).
distinguished [dis'tiŋgwiʃt], *a.* distingué; ***a distinguished man***, un homme éminent.
distort [dis'tɔ:t], *v.t.* tordre, contourner; décomposer (*les traits*); (*fig.*) torturer, défigurer.
distorted [dis'tɔ:tid], *a.* tordu, décomposé; (*fig.*) torturé.
distortion [dis'tɔ:ʃən], *n.* contorsion, déformation, *f.*
distract [dis'trækt], *v.t.* distraire, détourner (*de*); tourmenter.
distracted [dis'træktid], *a.* bouleversé, fou, hors de soi.
distracting [dis'træktiŋ], *a.* atroce, déchirant, affolant.
distraction [dis'trækʃən], *n.* distraction, *f.*, trouble, *m.*, confusion; démence, folie, *f.*; ***to drive to distraction***, mettre hors de soi.
distraught [dis'trɔ:t], *a.* affolé, éperdu.
distress [dis'tres], *n.* détresse, affliction, peine, *f.*, chagrin, *m.*; misère (*pauvreté*), *f.*—*v.t.* affliger, désoler.
distressed [dis'trest], *a.* affligé, malheureux; dans la misère (*pauvre*).
distressing [dis'tresiŋ], *a.* affligeant, désolant; pénible.
distribute [dis'tribju:t], *v.t.* distribuer.
distribution [distri'bju:ʃən], *n.* distribution, répartition, *f.*
district ['distrikt], *n.* contrée, région, *f.*, arrondissement, district; quartier (*de ville*); (*Postal*) secteur, *m.*
distrust [dis'trʌst], *n.* méfiance, *f.*—*v.t.* se méfier de.

distrustful [dis'trʌstful], *a.* défiant; méfiant, soupçonneux.
disturb [dis'tə:b], *v.t.* troubler; déranger.
disturbance [dis'tə:bəns], *n.* trouble, *m.*; confusion, émeute, *f.*; bruit, tapage; désordre, *m.*
disuse [dis'ju:s], *n.* désuétude, *f.*
disused [dis'ju:zd], *a.* hors d'usage.
ditch [ditʃ], *n.* fossé, *m.*—*v.t.* (*pop.*) abandonner.—*v.i.* creuser un fossé.
dither ['diðə], *n.* ***to be all of a dither***, être tout agité.—*v.i.* trembler, trembloter, hésiter.
ditto ['ditou], *adv.* idem; (*Comm.*) dito.
ditty ['diti], *n.* chanson, chansonnette, *f.*
diurnal [dai'ə:nəl], *a.* journalier, du jour; (*Med.*) quotidien.
divan [di'væn], *n.* divan, *m.*
dive [daiv], *v.i.* plonger.—*n.* plongeon, *m.*; (*pop.*) boîte de nuit, *f.*
diver ['daivə], *n.* plongeur; plongeon (*oiseau*), *m.*
diverge [dai'və:dʒ], *v.i.* diverger (*de*).
divergent [dai'və:dʒənt], *a.* divergent.
diverse [dai'və:s], *a.* divers, varié.
diversify [dai'və:sifai], *v.t.* diversifier; varier (*couleurs*).
diversion [dai'və:ʃən], *n.* divertissement, amusement, *m.*; diversion, distraction, *f.*
diversity [dai'və:siti], *n.* diversité, variété, *f.*
divert [dai'və:t], *v.t.* divertir, réjouir; distraire; dévier, détourner (*de*).
diverting [dai'və:tiŋ], *a.* divertissant, amusant.
divest [di'vest, dai'vest], *v.t.* dépouiller (*de*).
divide [di'vaid], *v.t.* diviser; partager.—*v.i.* se diviser.
dividend ['dividend], *n.* dividende, *m.*
dividers [di'vaidəz], *n. pl.* compas à pointes sèches, *m.*
divine [di'vain], *a.* divin; (*fam.*) adorable.—*n.* théologien, ecclésiastique, *m.*—*v.t.* deviner, pressentir.
diving ['daiviŋ], *n.* plongement, plongeon, *m.*
diving-board ['daiviŋbɔ:d], *n.* plongeoir, *m.*
divinity [di'viniti], *n.* divinité; théologie, *f.*
divisible [di'vizibl], *a.* divisible.
division [di'viʒən], *n.* division, *f.*, partage, *m.*; scission, *f.*; vote, *m.*
divorce [di'vɔ:s], *n.* divorce, *m.*; séparation, *f.* —*v.t.* séparer, divorcer avec.—*v.i.* se séparer (*de*).
divorcee [divɔ:'si:], *n.* divorcé, *m.*, divorcée, *f.*
divulge [dai'vʌldʒ, di'vʌldʒ], *v.t.* divulguer, publier.
dizziness ['dizinis], *n.* vertige, étourdissement, *m.*
dizzy ['dizi], *a.* étourdi; vertigineux (*élévation*).
do [du:], *v.t. irr.* faire; rendre (*service, justice etc.*); finir (*achever*); (*Cook.*) cuire; (*colloq.*) duper; ***done!*** c'est entendu! ***done to a turn***, cuit à point; ***he is done for***, c'en est fait de lui; ***it can't be done***, pas moyen; ***overdone***, trop cuit (*viande*); ***to be doing well***, faire de bonnes affaires, réussir; ***to do over***, enduire (*de*), couvrir (*de*); ***to do up***, empaqueter, emballer, remettre en état, remettre à neuf; ***underdone***, saignant (*viande*); ***well done!*** bravo! ***what is to be done?*** que faire?—*v.i.* se porter, se conduire; aller, convenir (*faire l'affaire*); suffire (*répondre à un besoin*); finir (*terminer*); ***how do you do?*** comment allez-vous? ***to do away with***, supprimer, se défaire de, faire disparaître; ***to do by***, agir envers; ***to do without***, se passer de.—*n.* duperie; soirée, réception, *f.*
docile ['dousail], *a.* docile.
docility [dou'siliti], *n.* docilité, *f.*
dock [dɔk], *v.t.* écourter; rogner (*comptes etc.*); (*Naut.*) mettre dans le bassin.—*v.i.* entrer aux docks.—*n.* bassin, dock, *m.*; (*Bot.*) patience, *f.*; (*Law*) banc des accusés, *m.*
docker ['dɔkə], *n.* déchargeur, docker, *m.*
docket ['dɔkit], *n.* étiquette, fiche, *f.*—*v.t.* étiqueter; enregistrer.
doctor ['dɔktə], *n.* docteur, médecin, *m.*—*v.t.* soigner, droguer; (*fig.*) altérer; frelater (*vin*).
doctrinaire [dɔktri'nεə], *a.* doctrinaire.
doctrinal [dɔk'trainəl], *a.* doctrinal.
doctrine ['dɔktrin], *n.* doctrine, *f.*
document ['dɔkjumənt], *n.* document, titre, *m.*—*v.t.* munir de documents.
documentary [dɔkju'mentəri], *a.* justificatif, authentique.—*n.* (*Cine.*) documentaire, *m.*
documentation [dɔkjumen'teiʃən], *n.* documentation, *f.*
dodge [dɔdʒ], *v.t.* éviter; esquiver.—*v.i.* s'esquiver; (*fig.*) ruser, faire des détours.—*n.* tour, détour, *m.*; (*fig.*) ruse, ficelle, *f.*
dodger ['dɔdʒə], *n.* rusé, malin, finaud, *m.*
doe [dou], *n.* daine, *f.*
doer ['du:ə], *n.* faiseur; auteur, *m.*
doff [dɔf], *v.t.* tirer, enlever, ôter.
dog [dɔg], *n.* chien; (*facet.*) coquin, gaillard, *m.*; ***lucky dog!*** quel veinard!—*v.t.* suivre à la piste; harceler, épier.
dog-days ['dɔgdeiz], *n.pl.* canicule, *f.*
dogged ['dɔgid], *a.* obstiné; acharné.
doggedly ['dɔgidli], *adv.* avec acharnement.
doggedness ['dɔgidnis], *n.* obstination, *f.* acharnement, *m.*
doggerel ['dɔgərəl], *n.* vers burlesques, vers de mirliton, *m.pl.*
doggie ['dɔgi], *n.* (*Childish*) tou-tou, *m.*
doggo ['dɔgou], *adv.* ***to lie doggo***, se tenir coi.
dogma ['dɔgmə], *n.* dogme, *m.*
dogmatic [dɔg'mætik], *a.* dogmatique.
dogmatism ['dɔgmətizm], *n.* dogmatisme, *m.*
doily ['dɔili], *n.* serviette de dessert, *f.* napperon, *m.*
doing ['du:iŋ], *n.* (*usu. in pl.*) faits, *m.pl.*; actions, *f.pl.*, exploits, *m.pl.*
dole [doul], *n.* aumône, *f.*, partage, *m.*; allocation de chômage, *f.*—*v.t.* ***to dole out***, distribuer, répartir avec parcimonie.
doleful ['doulful], *a.* plaintif, lugubre.
doll [dɔl], *n.* poupée, *f.*—*v.r.* ***to doll oneself up***, se pomponner.
dollar ['dɔlə], *n.* dollar, *m.*
dolphin ['dɔlfin], *n.* dauphin, *m.*
dolt [doult], *n.* lourdaud, sot, butor, *m.*
domain [do'mein], *n.* domaine, *m.*
dome [doum], *n.* dôme, *m.*
domestic [də'mestik], *a.* de famille; domestique (*animaux*).—*n.* domestique, *m. f.*, servante, *f.*
domesticate [də'mestikeit], *v.t.* domestiquer, apprivoiser; *fig.*) rendre casanier.

domesticated [də'mestikeited], *a.* casanier (*personnes*); apprivoisé (*animaux*).
domicile ['dəmisail, 'dəmisil], *n.* domicile, *m.*
dominance ['dəminəns], *n.* dominance, *f.*
dominant ['dəminənt], *a.* dominant.
dominate ['dəmineit], *v.t.* dominer sur.—*v.i.* dominer; prévaloir, prédominer.
domination [dəmi'neiʃən], *n.* domination, *f.*
domineer [dəmi'niə], *v.i.* dominer (*sur*).
domineering [dəmi'niəriŋ], *a.* impérieux, autoritaire.
Dominican [do'minikən], *a.* dominicain.—*n.* Dominicain (*personne*), *m.*; ***Dominican nun***, Dominicaine, *f.*
dominie ['dəmini], *n.* (*Sc.*) maître d'école, *m.*
dominion [do'miniən], *n.* domination, autorité, *f.*; empire, *m.*; (*pl.*) états, *m.pl.*
domino ['dəminou], *n.* domino (*capuchon, jeu*), *m.*
don [dən], *n.* don (*titre*); (*fig.*) grand seigneur; (*Univ.*) professeur d'université, *m.*—*v.t.* mettre, endosser.
donate [do'neit], *v.t.* faire un don de.
donation [do'neiʃən], *n.* donation, *f.*, don, *m.*
donkey ['dəŋki], *n.* âne, baudet, *m.*
donor ['dounə], *n.* donateur, *m.*
doodle [du:dl], *v.i.* griffonner.—*n.* griffonnage, *m.*
doom [du:m], *v.t.* condamner (*à*); (*fig.*) destiner (*à*).—*n.* jugement; destin funeste, *m.*; perte, ruine, *f.*
doomsday ['du:mzdei], *n.* jour du jugement dernier, *m.*
door [dɔ:], *n.* porte; portière (*d'une voiture*), *f.*; ***folding-doors***, porte à deux battants; ***next door***, à côté; ***indoors***, à la maison; ***out of doors***, dehors; ***behind closed doors***, à huis clos.
door-bell ['dɔ:bel], *n.* sonnette, *f.*
door-keeper ['dɔ:ki:pə] *n.* concierge, portier (*d'une maison*); gardien (*des monuments publics*), *m.*
doorman ['dɔ:mən], *n.* portier, *m.*
door-mat ['dɔ:mæt], *n.* paillasson, *m.*
door-step ['dɔ:step], *n.* seuil de la porte, pas de (la) porte, *m.*
door-way ['dɔ:wei], *n.* entrée, porte, *f.*
dope [doup], *n.* drogue, *f.*, narcotique, *m.*—*v.t.* droguer.
dormant ['dɔ:mənt], *a.* dormant; assoupi.
dormer-window ['dɔ:məwindou], *n.* lucarne, *f.*
dormitory ['dɔ:mitri], *n.* dortoir, *m.*
dormouse ['dɔ:maus], *n.* (*pl.* **dormice** ['dɔ:mais]) loir, *m.*
Dorothy ['dərəθi]. Dorothée, *f.*
dose [dous], *n.* dose, *f.*—*v.t.* médicamenter; doser.
dossier ['dəsjei], *n.* dossier, *m.*
dot [dət], *n.* point, *m.*—*v.t.* marquer d'un point, marquer avec des points; (*Paint.*) pointiller.
dotage ['doutidʒ], *n.* seconde enfance, *f.*, radotage, *m.*
dote [dout], *v.i.* radoter; raffoler (*de*).
double [dʌbl], *a.* double, en deux; ***bent double***, voûté.—*n.* double, pendant, sosie; (*Mil.*) pas de course, *m.*—*adv.* double; au double; ***to fold double***, plier en deux.—*v.t.* doubler; serrer (*poings*).—*v.i.* doubler; user de ruse; ***to double back***, revenir sur ses pas.
double-bed ['dʌbl'bed], *n.* lit à deux places, *m.*
double-breasted ['dʌblbrestid], *a.* croisé.
double-cross ['dʌbl'krəs], *v.t.* duper, tromper.
double-dealing ['dʌbl'di:liŋ], *n.* duplicité, *f.*
double-decker ['dʌbl'dekə], *n.* autobus à impériale, *m.*
double-room ['dʌbl'ru:m], *n.* chambre pour deux personnes, *f.*
doubt [daut], *n.* doute, *m.*; hésitation, *f.*; ***beyond a doubt***, sans aucun doute.—*v.t.* douter de.—*v.i.* douter; soupçonner.
doubtful ['dautful], *a.* douteux, incertain.
doubtless ['dautlis], *adv.* sans doute.
dough [dou], *n.* pâte, *f.*
dough-nut ['dounʌt], *n.* pet de nonne, *m.*
doughty ['dauti], *a.* vaillant, preux.
dour ['duə], *a.* (*Sc.*) austère et froid.
douse [daus], *v.t.* plonger dans l'eau; éteindre.
dove [dʌv], *n.* colombe, *f.*; pigeon, *m.*
dove-cot(e) ['dʌvkət, 'dʌvkout], *n.* colombier, *m.*
Dover ['douvə]. Douvres, *m.*; ***the Straits of Dover***, le Pas-de-Calais, *m.*
dowager ['dauədʒə], *n.* douairière, *f.*
dowdy ['daudi], *a.f.* gauche et mal mise, mal fagotée.
dowel ['dauəl], *n.* (*Carp.*) goujon, *m.*
down (1) [daun], *n.* duvet (*poil follet*), *m.*; dune (*colline*), *f.*
down (2) [daun], *adv.* en bas; à bas; bas, à terre; tombé, apaisé (*vent*); couché (*soleil*); à plat (*pneu*); en baisse (*prix*); (*fig.*) sur le déclin; ***to go down***, descendre.—*prep.* en bas de; vers le bas de.
downcast ['daunkɑ:st], *a.* abattu.
downfall ['daunfɔ:l], *n.* chute; (*fig.*) débâcle, *f.*
downhill ['daunhil], *a.* incliné; en pente.—[daun'hil], *adv.* en descendant.
downpour ['daunpɔ:], *n.* averse, *f.*
downright ['daunrait], *a.* direct; franc.—*adv.* net, tout à fait.
downstairs [daun'stɛəz], *adv.* en bas (de l'escalier).
downtrodden ['dauntrədn], *a.* opprimé.
downward ['daunwəd], *a.* de haut en bas, qui descend, descendant.—*adv.* (*also* **downwards** ['daunwədz]) en bas, en descendant; en aval.
downy ['dauni], *a.* de duvet, duveteux.
dowry ['dauri], *n.* dot, *f.*
doze [douz], *v.i.* s'assoupir, sommeiller, être assoupi.—*n.* petit somme, *m.*
dozen [dʌzn], *n.* douzaine, *f.*
drab [dræb], *a.* gris sale, brun terne; (*fig.*) terne, décoloré.—*n.* (*fig.*) traînée (*femme*), *f.*
draft [drɑ:ft], *v.t.* dessiner, rédiger; (*Mil.*) detacher.—*n.* dessin (*esquisse*); brouillon (*projet*), *m.*; (*Comm.*) traite, *f.*; (*Mil.*) détachement, *m.*
drag [dræg], *v.t.* traîner, tirer; (*Naut.*) draguer; ***to drag away from***, entraîner, arracher de; ***to drag on***, entraîner; (*fig.*) traîner en longueur; ***to drag out***, faire sortir de force.—*v.i.* se traîner; traîner; chasser (*ancre*).
draggle [drægl], *v.t.* traîner dans la boue.
drag-net ['drægnet], *n.* seine, *f.*, chalut, *m.*
dragoman ['drægomən], *n.* drogman, *m.*
dragon ['drægən], *n.* dragon, *m.*

dragon-fly ['drægənflai], *n.* demoiselle, libellule, *f.*, agrion, *m.*
dragoon [drə'gu:n], *n.* (*Mil.*) dragon, *m.*—*v.t.* (*fig.*) forcer par des mesures violentes.
drain [drein], *v.t.* faire écouler; dessécher; drainer; (*fig.*) épuiser; vider (*verre etc.*).—*v.i.* s'écouler.—*n.* tranchée, *f.*, égout, *m.*
drainage ['dreinidʒ], **draining** ['dreiniŋ] *n.* écoulement; (*Agric.*) drainage, *m.*
draining-board ['dreiniŋbɔ:d], *n.* égouttoir, *m.*
drake [dreik], *n.* canard, *m.*
dram [dræm], *n.* (*Pharm.*) drachme, *f.*
drama ['drɑ:mə], *n.* drame; (*fig.*) théâtre, *m.*
dramatic [drə'mætik], **dramatical** [drə'mætikəl], *a.* dramatique.
dramatist ['drɑ:mətist, 'dræmətist], *n.* auteur dramatique, *m.*, dramaturge, *m.*, *f.*
dramatize ['drɑ:mətaiz, 'dræmətaiz], *v.t.* dramatiser.
drape [dreip], *v.t.* draper, tendre (*de*).—*n.* (*Am.*) rideau, *m.*
draper ['dreipə], *n.* drapier; marchand de drap *m.*
drapery ['dreipəri], *n.* draperie, *f.*
drastic ['dræstik], *a.* énergique, radical, brutal.
draught [drɑ:ft], *n.* tirage; trait; courant d'air; coup (*boisson*); dessin (*esquisse*); coup de filet (*de pêcheur*); tirant (*d'un navire*), *m.*; (*Med.*) potion, *f.*; (*pl.*) jeu de dames, *m.*
draught-board ['drɑ:ftbɔ:d], *n.* damier, *m.*
draught-horse ['drɑ:fthɔ:s], *n.* cheval de trait, *m.*
draughtsman ['drɑ:ftsmən], *n.* (*pl.* **-men** [men]) dessinateur, *m.*
draughty ['drɑ:fti], *a.* plein de courants d'air.
draw [drɔ:], *v.t. irr.* tirer; traîner; dessiner (*tableau etc.*); toucher (*rations, appointements etc.*); arracher (*dent*); puiser (*eau etc.*); (*fig.*) attirer (*à* ou *sur*); ***to draw lots for***, tirer au sort.—*v.i.* tirer; dégainer; dessiner (*au crayon*); (*Spt.*) faire partie nulle *ou* match nul.—*n.* tirage (*au sort*), *m.*; attraction; (*Spt.*) partie nulle, *f.*
drawback ['drɔ:bæk], *n.* mécompte, désavantage, inconvénient, *m.*
drawbridge ['drɔ:bridʒ], *n.* pont-levis, *m.*
drawer ['drɔ:ə], *n.* tireur (*d'un chèque*); puiseur (*d'eau*); tiroir (*meuble*); (*pl.*) caleçon (*vêtement*), *m.*; ***chest of drawers***, commode, *f.*
drawing ['drɔ:iŋ], *n.* tirage; dessin (*croquis*), *m.*
drawing-board ['drɔ:iŋbɔ:d], *n.* planche à dessin, *f.*
drawing-pin ['drɔ:iŋpin], *n.* punaise (*pour le dessin*), *f.*
drawing-room ['drɔ:iŋru:m], *n.* salon, *m.*; (*Court*) réception, *f.*
drawl [drɔ:l], *v.i.* parler d'une voix traînante.—*n.* voix traînante *f.*
drawling ['drɔ:liŋ], *a.* traînant.
drawn [drɔ:n], *a.* indécis, égal (*bataille etc.*); tiré, nu (*épée*); ***drawn game***, partie nulle, *f.*
dray [drei], *n.* camion, haquet, *m.*
dread [dred], *a.* redoutable, terrible; auguste.—*n.* terreur, crainte, *f.*—*v.t.* craindre, redouter.
dreadful ['dredful], *a.* affreux, terrible, épouvantable.
dreadfully ['dredfuli], *adv.* terriblement, affreusement.
dream [dri:m], *n.* songe, rêve, *m.*; ***day-dream***, rêverie, *f.*—*v.t. irr.* rêver.—*v.i.* rêver; (*fig.*) s'imaginer.
dreamer ['dri:mə], *n.* rêveur, *m.*; (*fig.*) visionnaire, *m.*, *f.*
dreamy ['dri:mi], *a.* rêveur; chimérique, visionnaire.
drear [driə], **dreary** ['driəri], *a.* triste, morne, lugubre.
drearily ['driərili], *adv.* tristement, lugubrement.
dreariness ['driərinis], *n.* tristesse, *f.*, aspect morne, *m.*
dredge (1) [dredʒ], *n.* drague, *f.*—*v.t.*, *v.i.* draguer.
dredge (2) [dredʒ], *v.t.* saupoudrer (*de farine etc.*).
dredger (1) ['dredʒə], *n.* dragueur (*bateau*), *m.*
dredger (2) ['dredʒə], *n.* saupoudreuse, *f.*
dregs [dregz], *n.pl.* lie, *f.*
drench [drentʃ], *v.t.* tremper, mouiller (*de*); noyer (*de*).
dress [dres], *v.t.* habiller, vêtir, parer, orner; panser (*blessure etc.*); apprêter (*aliments etc.*); (*Mil.*) aligner; (*Navy*) pavoiser.—*v.i.* s'habiller; faire sa toilette; (*Mil.*) s'aligner.—*n.* habillement, *m.*; robe (*de femme*); mise, toilette; (*Mil.*) tenue, *f.*; ***dress rehearsal***, répétition générale, *f.*; ***evening dress***, tenue de soirée, *f.*
dress-circle ['dressə:kl], *n.* (*Theat.*) fauteuils de balcon, *m.pl.*
dresser ['dresə], *n.* habilleur (*personne*); dressoir (*de cuisine*), *m.*
dressing ['dresiŋ], *n.* toilette, *f.*, habillement; pansement (*de blessure etc.*); (*Cook.*) assaisonnement, *m.*; (*Agric.*) fumure, *f.*, engrais, *m.*
dressing-case ['dresiŋkeis], *n.* mallette de toilette, *f.*
dressing-gown ['dresiŋgaun], *n.* robe de chambre, *f.*, peignoir, *m.*
dressing-room ['dresiŋru:m], *n.* cabinet de toilette, *m.*
dressing-table ['dresiŋteibl], *n.* coiffeuse, table de toilette, *f.*
dressmaker ['dresmeikə], *n.* couturière, *f.*
dressmaking ['dresmeikiŋ], *n.* confections pour dames, *f.pl.*, couture, *f.*
dressy ['dresi], *a.* élégant, chic, coquet (*personne*); habillé (*robe*).
dribble [dribl], *v.t.* laisser dégoutter, laisser tomber goutte à goutte; (*Ftb.*) dribbler.—*v.i.* tomber goutte à goutte, dégoutter; baver; (*Ftb.*) dribbler.
drier ['draiə], *comp. a.* [DRY].—*n.* [DRYER].
drift [drift], *n.* monceau; tourbillon, *m.*, rafale, *f.*; objet flottant, *m.*; (*fig.*) tendance; (*Naut.*) dérive, *f.*—*v.t.* chasser, pousser; amonceler.—*v.i.* dériver, aller à la dérive, flotter; s'amonceler, s'amasser.
drifter ['driftə], *n.* (*Naut.*) chalutier, *m.*
drill [dril], *n.* foret, *m.*, mèche, *f.*; (*Agric.*) sillon; (*Mil.*) exercice, *m.*, manœuvre, *f.*—*v.t.* forer, percer; (*Mil.*) exercer.—*v.i.* (*Mil.*) faire l'exercice.

drilling ['driliŋ], *n.* forage; (*Dent.*) fraisage; (*Mil.*) exercice, *m.*
drink [driŋk], *n.* boisson; (*fig.*) ivresse (*drunkenness*), *f.*—*v.t.*, *v.i. irr.* boire.
drinker ['driŋkə], *n.* buveur; ivrogne, *m.*
drinking ['driŋkiŋ], *a.* potable; à boire.—*n.* boire, *m.*; ivrognerie, *f.*, alcoolisme, *m.*
drinking-fountain ['driŋkiŋfauntin], *n.* fontaine publique, *f.*
drip [drip], *v.t.* faire dégoutter.—*v.i.* dégoutter, tomber goutte à goutte.—*n.* goutte, *f.*; égout, *m.*
dripping ['dripiŋ], *n.* graisse de rôti, *f.*; (*pl.*) gouttes, *f.pl.*
drive [draiv], *v.t. irr.* pousser; chasser; enfoncer (*clou etc.*); mener, conduire (*voiture, cheval etc.*); forcer, réduire (*à*); ***to drive away***, chasser, éloigner; ***to drive back***, repousser; ***to drive in***, faire entrer, enfoncer; ***to drive out*** faire sortir, chasser.—*v.i.* conduire; aller en voiture; ***to drive at***, tendre à, vouloir en venir à; ***to drive up***, arriver (en voiture).—*n.* promenade *ou* course en voiture; grande avenue *ou* allée, *f.*
drivel [drivl], *n.* bave, *f.*—*v.i.* baver; (*fig.*) radoter.
driver ['draivə], *n.* cocher (*d'un carrosse*); voiturier (*d'une charrette*); (*Rail.*) mécanicien; (*Motor. etc.*) chauffeur, conducteur, *m.*
driving ['draiviŋ], *n.* action de conduire, *f.*; percement (*d'un tunnel*), *m.*
driving-licence ['draiviŋlaisəns], *n.* permis de conduire, *m.*
driving-test ['draiviŋtest], *n.* examen pour permis de conduire, *m.*
drizzle [drizl], *v.i.* bruiner.—*n.* bruine, pluie fine, *f.*
droll [droul], *a.* plaisant, drôle.
drollery ['drouləri], *n.* plaisanterie, drôlerie, farce, *f.*
dromedary ['drʌmədəri, 'drɔmədəri], *n.* dromadaire, *m.*
drone [droun], *n.* (*Ent., Mus.*) faux-bourdon; (*fig.*) frelon; fainéant (*personne*); bourdonnement (*son*), *m.*—*v.i.* bourdonner.
droning ['drouniŋ], *a.* bourdonnant.—*n.* bourdonnement, *m.*
droop [dru:p], *v.t.* laisser tomber, laisser pendre.—*v.i.* languir, se pencher, tomber, pencher; (*fig.*) s'affaiblir.
drooping ['dru:piŋ], *a.* languissant, abattu; penché.—*n.* abattement, *m.*, langueur, *f.*
drop [drɔp], *n.* goutte; chute (*descente*), *f.*; pendant (*bijou*), *m.*—*v.t.* laisser tomber; jeter (*l'ancre*); sauter (*une maille*); déposer (*quelqu'un*) quelque part; laisser échapper (*prononcer*); abandonner (*lâcher*).—*v.i.* tomber goutte à goutte; dégoutter (*de*); échapper (*glisser*); ***to drop behind***, se laisser dépasser, rester en arrière; ***to drop in***, entrer en passant; ***to drop out***, se retirer.
dropsy ['drɔpsi], *n.* hydropisie, *f.*
dross [drɔs], *n.* scorie, crasse, *f.*; (*fig.*) rebut, *m.*
drought [draut], *n.* sécheresse, *f.*
drove (1) [drouv], *n.* troupeau (*en marche*), *m.*; (*fig.*) foule (*en marche*), *f.*
drove (2) [drouv], *past* [DRIVE].
drover ['drouvə], *n.* conducteur de bestiaux, bouvier, *m.*
drown [draun], *v.t.* noyer; (*fig.*) submerger; étouffer (*bruit*).—*v.i.* se noyer.
drowsily ['drauzili], *adv.* comme endormi; (*fig.*) avec indolence.
drowsiness ['drauzinis], *n.* assoupissement, *m.*
drowsy ['drauzi], *a.* assoupi; somnolent; lourd, stupide.
drub [drʌb], *v.t.* rosser, battre.
drubbing ['drʌbiŋ], *n.* volée (de coups), *f.*
drudge [drʌdʒ], *n.* homme (*ou* femme) de peine, souffre-douleur, *m., f.*—*v.i.* travailler sans relâche, peiner.
drudgery ['drʌdʒəri], *n.* travail pénible, *m.*; corvée, vile besogne, *f.*
drug [drʌg], *n.* drogue, *f.*—*v.t.* droguer; (*fig.*) empoisonner.
drug-addict ['drʌgædikt], *n.* toxicomane, *m., f.*
druggist ['drʌgist], *n.* (*Am.*) pharmacien, *m.*
drug-store ['drʌgstɔ:], *n.* (*Am.*) pharmacie, *f.*
druid ['dru:id], *n.* druide, *m.*
drum [drʌm], *n.* tambour, *m.*; caisse, *f.*; tympan (*de l'oreille*), *m.*—*v.t.* (*Mil.*) ***to drum out***, dégrader.—*v.i.* battre du tambour (*sur*); (*fig.*) tinter.
drum-major ['drʌmmeidʒə], *n.* tambour-major, *m.*
drummer ['drʌmə], *n.* tambour (*homme*), *m.*
drum-stick ['drʌmstik], *n.* baguette de tambour, *f.*
drunk [drʌŋk], *a.* ivre, gris, soûl.
drunkard ['drʌŋkəd], *n.* ivrogne, *m.*
drunkenness ['drʌŋkənnis], *n.* ivresse; ivrognerie, *f.*
dry [drai], *a.* sec, desséché; aride; altéré; (*fig.*) caustique; ennuyeux.—*v.t.* sécher; dessécher.—*v.i.* sécher; ***to dry up***, tarir; se taire.
dry-dock ['draidɔk], *n.* bassin de radoub, *m.*, cale sèche, *f.*
dryer, drier ['draiə], *n.* (*Ind. etc.*) séchoir; (*Paint.*) siccatif, dessiccatif, *m.*; ***spin dryer***, essoreuse (rotative), *f.*
dryness ['drainis], *n.* sécheresse, aridité, *f.*
dry-shod ['draiʃɔd], *a.* and *adv.* à pied sec.
dual ['dju:əl], *a.* double; ***dual carriage-way***, route à double circulation, *f.*—*n.* (*Gram.*) duel, *m.*
dub [dʌb], *v.t.* armer chevalier; (*colloq.*) qualifier, baptiser; (*Cine.*) doubler (*film*).
dubiety [dju'baiəti], **dubiousness** ['dju:biəsnis], *n.* doute, *m.*, incertitude, *f.*
dubious ['dju:biəs], *a.* douteux, incertain.
dubiously ['dju:biəsli], *adv.* douteusement.
duchess ['dʌtʃis], *n.* duchesse, *f.*
duchy ['dʌtʃi], *n.* duché, *m.*
duck (1) [dʌk], *n.* cane, *f.*; canard; (*colloq.*) chou (*mot tendre*), *m.*
duck (2) [dʌk], *n.* (*Box.*) esquive, *f.*—*v.t.* plonger dans l'eau.—*v.i.* plonger; baisser la tête subitement; (*Box.*) esquiver.
duck (3) [dʌk], *n.* toile à voile, *f.*; (*pl.*) pantalon blanc, *m.*
ducking ['dʌkiŋ], *n.* plongeon; (*Naut.*) baptême de la ligne, *m.*
duckling ['dʌkliŋ], *n.* caneton, *m.*
duck-weed ['dʌkwi:d], *n.* lentille d'eau, *f.*
duct [dʌkt], *n.* conduit; (*Anat.*) canal, *m.*
dudgeon ['dʌdʒən], *n.* colère, *f.*; ***in high dudgeon***, fort en colère.

due [dju:], *a.* dû; convenable, propre, juste; (*Comm.*) échu; (*fig.*) requis, voulu; ***to fall due***, échoir.—*n.* dû; (*pl.*) droit, impôt, *m.*, redevance, *f.*—*adv.* droit, directement.
duel ['dju:əl], *n.* duel, *m.*, (*fig.*) lutte, *f.*
duellist ['dju:əlist], *n.* duelliste, *m.*
duenna [dju:'enə], *n.* duègne, *f.*
duet [dju:'et], *n.* duo, *m.*
duke [dju:k], *n.* duc, *m.*
dukedom ['dju:kdəm], *n.* duché, *m.*; dignité de duc, *f.*
dull [dʌl], *a.* lourd, hébété, stupide (*personne*); lourd, gris, sombre (*temps*); sourd (*son*); triste (*morne*); émoussé (*moins aigu*); terne (*couleur*); ennuyeux.—*v.t.* hébéter; émousser (*rendre moins aigu*); ternir (*ôter l'éclat de*); engourdir (*de froid*).—*v.i.* s'hébéter; s'engourdir; s'émousser.
dullard ['dʌləd], *n.* âne, lourdaud (*personne*), *m.*
dullness ['dʌlnis], *n.* lenteur, *f.*; assoupissement, ennui; manque d'éclat, *m.*, faiblesse (*de son*), *f.*
dully ['dʌlli], *adv.* lourdement, tristement.
duly ['dju:li], *adv.* dûment, justement.
dumb [dʌm], *a.* muet, réduit au silence; (*Am.*) stupide.
dumb-bells ['dʌmbelz], *n.pl.* haltères, *m.pl.*
dumbfound [dʌm'faund], *v.t.* confondre, abasourdir, interdire.
dumbly ['dʌmli], *adv.* en silence.
dumbness ['dʌmnis], *n.* mutisme; (*fig.*) silence, *m.*
dumb-show ['dʌmʃou], *n.* pantomime, *f.*, jeu muet, *m.*
dummy ['dʌmi], *n.* muet, *m.*, muette, *f.*; mannequin, objet imité; (*fig.*) homme de paille; (*Cards*) mort, *m.*
dump [dʌmp], *v.t.* déposer, décharger, déverser.—*n.* tas; dépotoir, *m.*
dumpling ['dʌmpliŋ], *n.* pâte cuite, *f.*
dumpy ['dʌmpi], *a.* trapu, gros et court.
dun (1) [dʌn], *a.* brun foncé; bai (*cheval*).
dun (2) [dʌn], *n.* créancier importun, *m.*—*v.t.* importuner.
dunce [dʌns], *n.* ignorant, âne, sot, *m.*
dune [dju:n], *n.* dune, *f.*
dung [dʌŋ], *n.* crotte, *f.*; crottin; (*Agric.*) fumier, *m.*
dung-cart ['dʌŋkɑ:t], *n.* tombereau à fumier, *m.*
dungeon ['dʌndʒən], *n.* cachot, *m.*
dunghill ['dʌŋhil], *n.* fumier, *m.*
duodenal [dju:o'di:nl], *a.* (*Anat.*) duodénal; ***duodenal ulcer***, ulcère au duodénum, *m.*
dupe [dju:p], *n.* dupe, *f.*—*v.t.* duper, tromper.
duplicate ['dju:plikit], *a.* double.—*n.* double, duplicata, *m.*—['dju:plikeit], *v.t.* doubler; copier.
duplicity [dju:'plisiti], *n.* duplicité, mauvaise foi, *f.*
durability [djuərə'biliti], **durableness** ['djuərəblnis], *n.* solidité, durabilité, *f.*
durable ['djuərəbl], *a.* durable.
duration [djuə'reiʃən], *n.* durée, *f.*
during ['djuəriŋ], *prep.* pendant, durant.
dusk [dʌsk], *n.* crépuscule, *m.*; obscurité, *f.*
duskiness ['dʌskinis], *n.* obscurité, teinte sombre, *f.*
dusky ['dʌski], *a.* foncé, sombre; noiraud, noirâtre.
dust [dʌst], *n.* poussière; poudre, *f.*; (*fig.*) cendres (des morts), *f.pl.*; ***sawdust***, sciure, *f.*—*v.t.* épousseter.
dust-bin ['dʌstbin], *n.* boîte à ordures, poubelle, *f.*
dust-cart ['dʌstkɑ:t], *n.* tombereau, *m.*
duster ['dʌstə], *n.* torchon, chiffon, *m.*
dustman ['dʌstmən], *n.* (*pl.* **-men** [men]) boueur, *m.*
dusty ['dʌsti], *a.* poussiéreux, couvert de poussière; poudreux.
Dutch [dʌtʃ], *a.* hollandais, de Hollande.—*n.* hollandais (*langue*), *m.*; ***the Dutch***, les Hollandais, *m.pl.*
Dutchman ['dʌtʃmən], *n.* (*pl.* **-men** [men]) Hollandais, *m.*
Dutchwoman ['dʌtʃwumən], *n.* (*pl.* **-women** [wimin]) Hollandaise, *f.*
duteous ['dju:tiəs], **dutiful** ['dju:tiful], *a.* obéissant, soumis.
dutifully ['dju:tifuli], *adv.* avec soumission, respectueusement.
duty ['dju:ti], *n.* (*pl.* **duties** ['dju:tiz]) devoir; (*Customs*) droit; (*Mil. etc.*) service, *m.*; ***on duty***, de service, de garde, en faction.
dwarf [dwɔ:f], *a.* and *n.* nain, *m.*, naine, *f.*—*v.t.* rapetisser; (*Hort.*) rabougrir.
dwell [dwel], *v.i. irr.* demeurer, habiter, rester; ***to dwell on***, insister sur.
dweller ['dwelə], *n.* habitant, *m.*, habitante, *f.*
dwelling ['dweliŋ], *n.* habitation, demeure, *f.*
dwindle [dwindl], *v.i.* diminuer, s'amoindrir; dépérir.
dye [dai], *v.t.* teindre.—*v.i.* teindre, se teindre.—*n.* teinture, teinte; couleur, nuance, *f.*; (*fig.*) caractère, *m.*
dyeing ['daiiŋ], *n.* teinture, *f.*
dyer ['daiə], *n.* teinturier, *m.*, teinturière, *f.*
dye-works ['daiwə:ks], *n.pl.* teinturerie, *f.*
dying ['daiiŋ], *a.* mourant, moribond; suprême, dernier.
dyke [DIKE].
dynamic [dai'næmik], **dynamical** [dai'næmikəl], *a.* dynamique.
dynamics [dai'næmiks], *n.pl.* dynamique, *f.*
dynamite ['dainəmait], *n.* dynamite, *f.*—*v.t.* dynamiter.
dynamo ['dainəmou], *n.* dynamo, *f.*
dynasty ['dinəsti], *n.* dynastie, *f.*
dysentery ['disəntri], *n.* dysenterie, *f.*
dyspepsia [dis'pepsiə], *n.* dyspepsie, *f.*
dyspeptic [dis'peptik], *a.* dyspepsique, dyspeptique.

E

E, e [i:]. cinquième lettre de l'alphabet; (*Mus.*) mi, *m.*
each [i:tʃ], *a.* chaque.—*pron.* chacun, *m.*, chacune, *f.*; ***each other***, l'un l'autre, les uns les autres.
eager ['i:gə], *a.* vif, ardent (*à*); impatient (*de*); désireux; empressé (*à* ou *de*).
eagerly ['i:gəli], *adv.* ardemment; impatiemment.

eagerness ['i:gənis], *n.* ardeur, *f.*; empressement, *m.*
eagle [i:gl], *n.* aigle, *m.*, *f.*
eaglet ['i:glit], *n.* aiglon, *m.*
ear [iə], *n.* oreille, *f.*; épi (*de blé*), *m.*—*v.i.* monter en épi.
ear-ache ['iəreik], *n.* mal d'oreille, *m.*
ear-drum ['iədrʌm], *n.* tympan, tambour de l'oreille, *m.*
earl [ə:l], *n.* comte, *m.*
earldom ['ə:ldəm], *n.* comté, *m.*
earliness ['ə:linis], *n.* heure peu avancée; précocité (*de fruits*), *f.*
early ['ə:li], *a.* matinal; matineux (*personne*); ancien; précoce, hâtif (*fruit etc.*).—*adv.* de bonne heure, de bon matin, de grand matin; tôt.
ear-mark ['iəma:k], *v.t.* (*fig.*) réserver, mettre de côté.
earn [ə:n], *v.t.* gagner, acquérir; (*fig.*) mériter.
earnest (1) ['ə:nist], *a.* sérieux, empressé, sincère.
earnest (2) ['ə:nist], *n.* gage, *m.*, garantie, *f.*, arrhes, *f.pl.*
earnestly ['ə:nistli], *adv.* sérieusement, avec empressement.
earnestness ['ə:nistnis], *n.* ardeur, *f.*, empressement; sérieux, *m.*
earnings ['ə:niŋz], *n.pl.* gain, *m.*; gages, *m.pl.*
ear-phones ['iəfounz], *n.pl.* casque, *m.*
ear-ring ['iəriŋ], *n.* boucle d'oreille, *f.*
earth [ə:θ], *n.* terre, *f.*; terrier (*de renard etc.*), *m.*—*v.t.* enterrer, enfouir, couvrir de terre; (*Elec.*) joindre à la terre.
earthen ['ə:θən], *a.* de terre.
earthenware ['ə:θənwɛə], *n.* poterie, vaisselle de terre, faïence, *f.*
earthly ['ə:θli], *a.* terrestre.
earthquake ['ə:θkweik], *n.* tremblement de terre, *m.*
earthy ['ə:θi], *a.* de terre, terreux.
earwig ['iəwig], *n.* perce-oreille, *m.*
ease [i:z], *n.* aisance, aise; facilité; tranquillité, *f.*, repos; (*fig.*) abandon; soulagement (*de douleur*), *m.*—*v.t.* soulager, mettre à l'aise; (*fig.*) tranquilliser, calmer.
easel [i:zl], *n.* chevalet, *m.*
easily ['i:zili], *adv.* facilement, sans peine; aisément.
east [i:st], *a.* d'est, d'orient; oriental.—*n.* est, orient; levant, *m.*
Easter ['i:stə]. Pâques, *m.*; (*Jewish*) Pâque, *f.*
easterly ['i:stəli], *a.* d'est.—*adv.* vers l'orient, vers l'est.
eastern ['i:stən], *a.* d'est, d'orient, oriental.
eastward ['i:stwəd], *adv.* vers l'est, vers l'orient.
easy ['i:zi], *a.* facile; aisé; confortable; tranquille; naturel (*style*); à l'aise; ***easy chair***, fauteuil, *m.*—*adv.* doucement.
easy-going ['i:zigouiŋ], *a.* accommodant, peu exigeant.
eat [i:t], *v.t.*, *v.i. irr.* manger; ronger (*corroder*); ***to eat away***, consumer, ronger; ***to eat up***, manger, achever de manger.
eatable ['i:təbl], *a.* mangeable, comestible.—*n.* comestible, *m.*; (*pl.*) vivres, *m.pl.*
eating ['i:tiŋ], *n.* action de manger, *f.*; manger, *m.*
eaves [i:vz], *n.* avance du toit, *f.*; gouttières, *f.pl.*
eavesdrop ['i:vzdrɔp], *v.i.* écouter aux portes.
eavesdropper ['i:vzdrɔpə], *n.* écouteur aux portes, *m.*
ebb [eb], *v.i.* baisser; décliner, refluer, se retirer.—*n.* reflux; (*fig.*) déclin, *m.*, décadence, *f.*
ebb-tide ['ebtaid], *n.* jusant, *m.*
ebony ['ebəni], *a.* d'ébène.—*n.* ébène, *f.*, bois d'ébène, *m.*
ebony-tree ['ebənitri:], *n.* ébénier, *m.*
ebullience [i'bʌliəns], **ebulliency** [i'bʌliənsi], *n.* ébullition, effervescence, *f.*
ebullient [i'bʌliənt], *a.* en ébullition, bouillonnant; (*fig.*) exubérant, pétulant.
ebullition [ebə'liʃən], *n.* ébullition; (*fig.*) effervescence, *f.*, transport, *m.*
eccentric [ek'sentrik], *a.* excentrique; désaxé; (*fig.*) singulier.
eccentricity [eksen'trisiti], *n.* excentricité, *f.*
ecclesiastic [ikli:zi'æstik], *a.* and *n.* ecclésiastique, *m.*
echo ['ekou], *n.* écho, *m.*—*v.t.* répercuter; (*fig.*) répéter.—*v.i.* faire écho; retentir, résonner (*de*).
eclipse [i'klips], *n.* éclipse, *f.*—*v.t.* éclipser; (*fig.*) surpasser.—*v.i.* s'éclipser.
economic [i:kə'nɔmik], **economical** [i:kə'nɔmikəl], *a.* économique (*chose*); économe, ménager (*personne*).
economically [i:kə'nɔmikəli], *adv.* économiquement.
economics [i:kə'nɔmiks], *n.pl.* économie politique, *f.*
economist [i'kɔnəmist], *n.* économiste, *m.*, *f.*
economize [i'kɔnəmaiz], *v.t.* économiser.—*v.i.* user d'économie.
economy [i'kɔnəmi], *n.* économie, *f.*; système, *m.*; ***planned economy***, économie planifiée.
ecstasy ['ekstəsi], *n.* extase, *f.*, transport, *m.*
ecstatic [eks'tætik], **ecstatical** [eks'tætikəl], *a.* extatique, d'extase.
Ecuador [ekwə'dɔ:]. (la République de) l'Équateur, *f.*
Ecuadorean [ekwə'dɔ:riən], *a.* équatorien.—*n.* Équatorien (*personne*), *m.*
eczema ['eksimə], *n.* eczéma, *m.*
eddy ['edi], *n.* remous (*eau*); tourbillon (*vent*), *m.*—*v.i.* tourbillonner.
Eden ['i:dən]. Éden, *m.*
edge [edʒ], *n.* bord (*marge*); fil, tranchant (*de couteau etc.*), *m.*; lisière (*d'une forêt etc.*), *f.*; cordon (*d'une pièce de monnaie*), *m.*; tranche (*d'un livre*), *f.*—*v.t.* affiler, aiguiser; border (*entourer*).—*v.i.* ***to edge away***, s'éloigner graduellement.
edged [edʒd], *a.* tranchant; bordé.
edgeways ['edʒweiz], **edgewise** ['edʒwaiz], *adv.* de côté, de champ.
edging ['edʒiŋ], *n.* bordure, *f.*
edible ['edibl], *a.* comestible, bon à manger.
edict ['i:dikt], *n.* édit, *m.*
edifice ['edifis], *n.* édifice, *m.*
edify ['edifai], *v.t.* édifier.
Edinburgh ['edinbrə]. Édimbourg, *m.*
edit ['edit], *v.t.* éditer, rédiger.
edition [i'diʃən], *n.* édition, *f.*
editor ['editə], *n.* compilateur, annotateur; (*Journ.*) rédacteur en chef, directeur, *m.*
editorial [edi'tɔ:riəl], *a.* de rédacteur.—*n.* article de fond, éditorial, *m.*

Edmund ['edmənd]. Edmond, *m.*

educate ['edjukeit], *v.t.* élever; instruire.

education [edju'keiʃən], *n.* éducation, *f.*; enseignement, *m.*; instruction, *f.*

Edward ['edwəd]. Édouard, *m.*

eel [i:l], *n.* anguille, *f.*

eerie ['iəri], *a.* étrange, mystérieux.

eeriness ['iərinis], *n.* étrangeté surnaturelle, *f.*

efface [i'feis], *v.t.* effacer.

effect [i'fekt], *n.* effet, *m.*; (*pl.*) effets, biens, *m.pl.*; ***in effect***, en effet; ***to carry into effect***, accomplir, exécuter, mettre à effet; ***to no effect***, en vain, sans résultat; ***to take effect***, faire son effet, opérer; (*Law*) entrer en vigueur.—*v.t.* effectuer, exécuter, accomplir.

effective [i'fektiv], *a.* effectif; efficace.

effectively [i'fektivli], *adv.* effectivement; efficacement.

effeminacy [i'feminəsi], *n.* mollesse, nature efféminée, *f.*

effeminate [i'feminit], *a.* efféminé.

effervesce [efə'ves], *v.i.* être en effervescence; mousser (*boisson*).

effervescence [efə'vesəns], *n.* effervescence, *f.*

effervescent [efə'vesənt], **effervescing** [efə'vesiŋ], *a.* effervescent; mousseux; gazeux (*eau minérale*).

effete [i'fi:t], *a.* usé; stérile, épuisé, caduc.

efficacious [efi'keiʃəs], *a.* efficace.

efficacy ['efikəsi], *n.* efficacité, *f.*

efficiency [i'fiʃənsi], *n.* efficacité; bonne condition, *f.*; (*Mach.*) rendement, *m.*

efficient [i'fiʃənt], *a.* efficace (*remède*); capable, compétent (*personne*).

efficiently [i'fiʃəntli], *adv.* efficacement.

effigy ['efidʒi], *n.* effigie, *f.*

effloresce [eflɔ'res], *v.i.* s'effleurir.

efflorescence [eflɔ'resəns], *n.* efflorescence; (*Bot.*) floraison, *f.*

efflorescent [eflɔ'resənt], *a.* efflorescent; (*Bot.*) fleurissant.

effluvium [i'flu:viəm], *n.* (*pl.* **effluvia** [i'flu:viə]) exhalaison, *f.*, effluve, *m.*

effort ['efət], *n.* effort, *m.*

effortless ['efətlis], *a.* sans effort.

effrontery [i'frʌntəri], *n.* effronterie, *f.*

effulgence [i'fʌldʒəns], *n.* splendeur, *f.*, éclat, *m.*

effulgent [i'fʌldʒənt], *a.* resplendissant, éclatant.

effusion [i'fju:ʒən], *n.* effusion, *f.*, épanchement, *m.*

effusive [i'fju:siv], *a.* expansif; (*fig.*) excessif, exubérant.

egg [eg], *n.* œuf, *m.*; ***boiled egg***, œuf à la coque; ***fried egg***, œuf sur le plat; ***hard-boiled egg***, œuf dur; ***new-laid egg***, œuf frais.—*v.t.* pousser (*à*).

egg-cup ['egkʌp], *n.* coquetier, *m.*

egg-shell ['egʃel], *n.* coquille d'œuf, *f.*

eglantine ['egləntain], *n.* églantier, *m.*; églantine (*fleur*), *f.*

egoism ['egouizm], *n.* égoïsme, *m.*

egoist ['egouist], *n.* égoïste, *m.*, *f.*

egotism ['egətizm], *n.* égotisme, culte du moi, *m.*

egotist ['egətist], *n.* égotiste, *m.*, *f.*

egregious [i'gri:dʒəs], *a.* insigne, énorme; fameux.

egress ['i:gres], *n.* sortie, issue, *f.*

Egypt ['i:dʒipt]. l'Égypte, *f.*

Egyptian [i'dʒipʃən], *a.* égyptien.—*n.* Égyptien (*personne*), *m.*

eider ['aidə], **eider-duck** ['aidədʌk], *n.* eider, *m.*

eiderdown ['aidədaun], *n.* édredon, *m.*

eight [eit], *a.* huit.

eighteen ['eiti:n], *a.* dix-huit.

eighteenth ['eiti:nθ], *a.* dix-huitième; dix-huit (*roi etc.*).—*n.* dix-huitième (*fraction*), *m.*

eighth [eitθ], *a.* huitième; huit (*roi etc.*).—*n.* huitième (*fraction*), *m.*; (*Mus.*) octave, *f.*

eightieth ['eitiiθ], *a.* quatre-vingtième.—*n.* quatre-vingtième (*fraction*), *m.*

eighty ['eiti], *a.* quatre-vingts.

Eire ['ɛərə]. l'Irlande, *f.*

either ['aiðə, 'i:ðə], *pron.* l'un ou l'autre, *m.*, l'une ou l'autre, *f.*; l'un d'eux, *m.*, l'une d'elles, *f.*; (*used negatively*) ni l'un ni l'autre, *m.*, ni l'une ni l'autre, *f.*—*conj.* ou, soit.—*adv.* non plus.

ejaculate [i'dʒækjuleit], *v.t.* pousser (*un cri*).—*v.i.* s'écrier; éjaculer.

ejaculation [idʒækju'leiʃən], *n.* cri, *m.* exclamation; éjaculation, *f.*

eject [i'dʒekt], *v.t.* rejeter; émettre (*flammes*); chasser, expulser.

ejection [i'dʒekʃən], **ejectment** [i'dʒektmənt], *n.* expulsion, éjection; (*Law*) éviction, *f.*

eke [i:k], *v.t.* ***to eke out***, allonger; suppléer à, augmenter; ménager; ***to eke out a living***, se faire une maigre pitance.

elaborate [i'læbərit], *a.* élaboré, soigné; compliqué.—[i'læbəreit], *v.t.* élaborer.

elaboration [ilæbə'reiʃən], *n.* élaboration, *f.*

elapse [i'læps], *v.i.* s'écouler.

elastic [i'læstik], *a.* and *n.* élastique, *m.*

elasticity [elæs'tisiti], *n.* élasticité, *f.*

elate [i'leit], *v.t.* élever, exalter, transporter.

elation [i'leiʃən], *n.* transport de joie, *m.*, exaltation, ivresse, *f.*

elbow ['elbou], *n.* coude, *m.*—*v.t.* coudoyer, pousser du coude.

elder (1) ['eldə], *n.* sureau (*arbre*), *m.*

elder (2) ['eldə], *a.* aîné, plus âgé; plus ancien.—*n.* aîné; ancien, *m.*

elderly ['eldəli], *a.* d'un certain âge.

eldest ['eldist], *a.* le plus âgé, l'aîné.

Eleanor ['elinə]. Éléonore, *f.*

elect [i'lekt], *a.* élu, choisi, nommé.—*n.* élu, *m.*—*v.t.* élire, nommer, choisir; (*fig.*) se décider à.

election [i'lekʃən], *n.* élection, *f.*

electioneer [ilekʃə'niə], *v.i.* solliciter des votes, travailler les électeurs.

electioneering [ilekʃə'niəriŋ], *n.* manœuvres électorales, *f.pl.*

elective [i'lektiv], *a.* électif; électoral.

elector [i'lektə], *n.* électeur, votant, *m.*

electric [i'lektrik], **electrical** [i'lektrikəl], *a.* électrique; ***electric shock***, secousse électrique, *f.*

electrician [elek'triʃən, ilek'triʃən], *n.* électricien, *m.*

electricity [elek'trisiti, ilek'trisiti], *n.* électricité, *f.*

electrify [i'lektrifai], *v.t.* électriser; électrifier.

electrocute [i'lektrokju:t], *v.t.* électrocuter.

electron [i'lektrən] *n.* électron *m.*

electronic [elek'trɔnik, ilek'trɔnik], *a.* électronique.
electronics [elek'trɔniks, ilek'trɔniks], *n.* électronique, *f.*
electro-plate [i'lektroupleit], *n.* argenture électrique, *f.*—*v.t.* plaquer, argenter.
elegance ['eligəns], *n.* élégance, *f.*
elegant ['eligənt], *a.* élégant, chic.—*n.* élégant, beau, *m.*
elegantly ['eligəntli], *adv.* élégamment.
elegiac [eli'dʒaiək], *a.* élégiaque.—*n.* vers élégiaque, *m.*
elegist ['elidʒist], *n.* poète élégiaque, *m.*
elegy ['elidʒi], *n.* élégie, *f.*
element ['elimənt], *n.* élément, *m.*; (*pl.*) rudiments, *m.pl.*
elemental [eli'mentl], **elementary** [eli'mentri], *a.* élémentaire.
elephant ['elifənt], *n.* éléphant, *m.*
elephantine [eli'fæntain], *a.* éléphantin.
elevate ['eliveit], *v.t.* élever; hausser, exalter, exciter.
elevation [eli'veiʃən], *n.* élévation; hauteur, altitude, *f.*
elevator [eli'veitə], *n.* (*Anat. etc.*) élévateur; (*Am.*) [LIFT].
eleven [i'levn], *a.* onze; ***the eleven***, les apôtres, *m.pl.*; (*Spt.*) le onze, *m.*
eleventh [i'levnθ], *a.* onzième; onze (*roi etc.*). —*n.* onzième (*fraction*), *m.*
elf [elf], *n.* (*pl.* **elves** [elvz]) esprit follet, lutin, elfe, *m.*
elfin ['elfin], *a.* des lutins, des elfes.—*n.* gamin, bambin, *m.*
elicit [i'lisit], *v.t.* faire sortir, tirer (*de*); déduire, découvrir, faire avouer (*à*).
elide [i'laid], *v.t.* (*Gram.*) élider.—*v.i.* s'élider.
eligible ['elidʒibl], *a.* éligible; convenable (*pour*); acceptable.
eliminate [i'limineit], *v.t.* éliminer, supprimer.
eliminating [i'limineitiŋ], *a.* éliminateur, éliminatoire.
elimination [ilimi'neiʃən], *n.* élimination, *f.*
elision [i'liʒən], *n.* élision, *f.*
elixir [i'liksə], *n.* élixir, *m.*
Elizabeth [i'lizəbəθ]. Élisabeth, *f.*
elk [elk], *n.* (*Zool.*) élan, *m.*
ell [el], *n.* aune, *f.*
Ellen ['elin]. Hélène, *f.*
ellipse [i'lips], *n.* ellipse, *f.*
elliptic [i'liptik], **elliptical** [i'liptikəl], *a.* elliptique.
elm [elm], *n.* orme, *m.*
elocution [elo'kju:ʃən], *n.* élocution, diction, *f.*
elocutionist [elo'kju:ʃənist], *n.* déclamateur, *m.*
elongate ['i:lɔŋgeit], *v.t.* allonger, prolonger.
elongation [i:lɔŋ'geiʃən], *n.* allongement, prolongement, *m.*; (*Surg.*) élongation, *f.*
elope [i'loup], *v.i.* s'enfuir (*avec un amant*).
elopement [i'loupmənt], *n.* fuite, *f.*, enlèvement, *m.*
eloquence ['eləkwəns], *n.* éloquence, *f.*
eloquent ['eləkwənt], *a.* éloquent.
eloquently ['eləkwəntli], *adv.* éloquemment.
else [els], *adv.* autrement, ou bien, ailleurs.—*a.* autre; ***anywhere else***, n'importe où ailleurs; ***everything else***, tout le reste; ***nobody else***, personne d'autre; ***nothing else***, rien d'autre; ***someone*** (***somebody***) ***else***, quelqu'un d'autre.
elsewhere ['elswɛə], *adv.* ailleurs, autre part.
Elsie ['elsi]. Élise, *f.*
elucidate [i'lju:sideit], *v.t.* expliquer, éclaircir, élucider.
elucidation [ilju:si'deiʃən], *n.* éclaircissement, *m.*, élucidation, explication, *f.*
elude [i'lju:d], *v.t.* éluder, éviter, échapper à.
elusion [i'lju:ʒən], *n.* subterfuge, *m.*, réponse évasive, *f.*
elusive [i'lju:siv], *a.* artificieux (*réponse*); fuyant, insaisissable (*personne*).
elves [ELF].
emaciate [i'meiʃieit], *v.t.* amaigrir.—*v.i.* maigrir, s'amaigrir.
emaciated [i'meiʃieitid], *a.* amaigri, maigre, décharné.
emaciation [imeiʃi'eiʃən], *n.* amaigrissement, *m.*, maigreur, *f.*
emanate ['eməneit], *v.i.* émaner.
emancipate [i'mænsipeit], *v.t.* affranchir, émanciper (*de*).
emancipation [imænsi'peiʃən], *n.* affranchissement, *m.*, émancipation, *f.*
emasculate [i'mæskjuleit], *v.t.* châtrer; (*fig.*) affaiblir, efféminer.
embalm [im'bɑ:m], *v.t.* embaumer.
embalmer [im'bɑ:mə], *n.* embaumeur, *m.*
embalming [im'bɑ:miŋ], *n.* embaumement, *m.*
embank [im'bæŋk], *v.t.* endiguer, remblayer; encaisser (*canal etc.*).
embankment [im'bæŋkmənt], *n.* levée, *f.*; terrassement, talus; (*Rail.*) remblai; quai (*rivière, canal*), *m.*
embarcation [EMBARKATION].
embargo [im'bɑ:gou], *n.* embargo, *m.*—*v.t.* mettre l'embargo sur; défendre, interdire.
embark [im'bɑ:k], *v.t.* embarquer.—*v.i.* s'embarquer (*sur*); (*fig.*) s'engager (*dans*).
embarkation or **embarcation** [embɑ:'keiʃən], *n.* embarquement, *m.*
embarrass [im'bærəs], *v.t.* embarrasser; gêner.
embarrassment [im'bærəsmənt], *n.* embarras, *m.*; (*fig.*) perplexité; gêne (*manque d'argent*), *f.*
embassy ['embəsi], *n.* ambassade, *f.*
embellish [im'beliʃ], *v.t.* embellir, orner (*avec*).
embellishment [im'beliʃmənt] *n.* embellissement, ornement, *m.*
ember ['embə], *n.* braise, cendre ardente, *f.*
embezzle [im'bezl], *v.t.* détourner; s'approprier frauduleusement (*des fonds*).
embezzlement [im'bezlmənt], *n.* détournement, *m.*
embezzler [im'bezlə], *n.* détourneur (*de fonds*), *m.*
embitter [im'bitə], *v.t.* rendre amer; (*fig.*) empoisonner; aigrir.
emblazon [im'bleizn], *v.t.* blasonner (*de*); (*fig.*) publier, proclamer.
emblem ['embləm], *n.* emblème, *m.*; (*Her.*) devise, *f.*
embodiment [im'bɔdimənt], *n.* incarnation; personnification; (*Mil.*) incorporation, *f.*
embody [im'bɔdi], *v.t.* incarner; (*Mil. etc.*) incorporer (*dans*); (*fig.*) personnifier.
embolden [im'bouldn], *v.t.* enhardir.
emboss [im'bɔs], *v.t.* bosseler, relever en bosse; gaufrer (*papier*).

embossing [im'bɔsiŋ], *n.* bosselage; gaufrage, *m.*
embrace [im'breis], *n.* embrassement, *m.*, étreinte, *f.*—*v.t.* embrasser, étreindre; (*fig.*) accepter; comprendre.
embrocation [embrə'keiʃən], *n.* embrocation, *f.*
embroider [im'brɔidə], *v.t.* broder.
embroidery [im'brɔidəri], *n.* broderie, *f.*
embroil [im'brɔil], *v.t.* brouiller, embrouiller.
embryo ['embriou], *n.* embryon, germe, *m.*
emend [i'mend], *v.t.* corriger; (*Law*) émender.
emendation [i:men'deiʃən], *n.* correction, émendation, *f.*
emerald ['emərəld], *n.* émeraude, *f.*
emerge [i'mə:dʒ], *v.i.* surgir; sortir (*de*); ressortir.
emergency [i'mə:dʒənsi], *n.* circonstance critique; crise, *f.*, cas imprévu, *m.*; ***in case of emergency***, en cas d'urgence; ***emergency exit***, sortie de secours, *f.*
emery ['eməri], *n.* émeri, *m.*; ***emery cloth***, toile d'émeri, *f.*
emetic [i'metik], *n.* émétique, *m.*
emigrant ['emigrənt], *n.* émigrant; (*Fr. Hist.*) émigré, *m.*
emigrate ['emigreit], *v.i.* émigrer.
emigration [emi'greiʃən], *n.* émigration, *f.*
Emily ['emili]. Émilie, *f.*
eminence ['eminəns], *n.* éminence, colline; (*fig.*) grandeur, distinction, *f.*
eminent ['eminənt], *a.* éminent; distingué, illustre.
eminently ['eminəntli], *adv.* éminemment, par excellence.
emissary ['emisəri], *n.* émissaire, messager, *m.*
emission [i'miʃən], *n.* émission, *f.*
emit [i'mit], *v.t.* jeter; exhaler, dégager; (*Fin.*) émettre.
emolument [i'mɔljumənt], *n.* (*usu. pl.*) émoluments, *m.pl.*, rémunération, *f.*; (*fig.*) profit, *m.*
emotion [i'mouʃən], *n.* émotion, *f.*
emotional [i'mouʃənəl], *a.* porté à l'émotion, émotif.
emperor ['empərə], *n.* empereur, *m.*
emphasis ['emfəsis], *n.* (*pl.* **emphases** ['emfəsi:z]) force, énergie, emphase, *f.*; accent, *m.*
emphasize ['emfəsaiz], *v.t.* appuyer sur; accentuer, souligner.
emphatic [im'fætik], *a.* fort, énergique; expressif; accentué, emphatique; (*fig.*) positif.
emphatically [im'fætikəli], *adv.* avec force, énergiquement; positivement.
empire ['empaiə], *n.* empire, *m.*
empiric [em'pirik], *n.* empirique; charlatan, *m.*—*a.* (*also* **empirical** [em'pirikəl]) empirique, guidé par l'expérience.
employ [im'plɔi], *v.t.* employer; se servir de. —*n.* emploi, *m.*; occupation, *f.*
employee [im'plɔii:], *n.* employé, *m.*
employer [im'plɔiə], *n.* patron; employeur, *m.*
employment [im'plɔimənt], *n.* emploi, *m.*, occupation, *f.*
emporium [em'pɔ:riəm], *n.* entrepôt; (*fam.*) grand magasin, *m.*
empower [em'pauə], *v.t.* autoriser (*à*), mettre à même (*de*).
empress ['empris], *n.* impératrice, *f.*
emptiness ['emptinis], *n.* vide, *m.*; (*fig.*) vanité, *f.*, néant, *m.*
empty ['empti], *a.* vide, à vide; désert (*rues etc.*); (*fig.*) vain, stérile.—*v.t.* vider, décharger.—*v.i.* se vider.
emu ['i:mju:], *n.* (*Orn.*) émeu, *m.*
emulate ['emjuleit], *v.t.* rivaliser avec; imiter.
emulation [emju'leiʃən], *n.* émulation, rivalité, *f.*
emulsion [i'mʌlʃən], *n.* émulsion, *f.*
enable [i'neibl], *v.t.* mettre à même (*de*); mettre en état (*de*); permettre (*de*).
enact [i'nækt], *v.t.* ordonner, arrêter; rendre (*loi*); jouer, faire (*un rôle*).
enactment [i'næktmənt], *n.* loi, ordonnance, *f.*, décret, *m.*
enamel [i'næml], *n.* émail, *m.*—*v.t.* émailler (*de*).—*v.i.* peindre en émail.
enamelling [i'næməliŋ], *n.* émaillure, *f.*; émaillage, *m.*
enamour [i'næmə], *v.t.* (*used now only in p.p.*) ***to be enamoured of***, être épris de.
encamp [in'kæmp], *v.t.*, *v.i.* camper.
encase [in'keis], *v.t.* encaisser, enfermer.
enchain [in'tʃein], *v.t.* enchaîner.
enchant [in'tʃɑ:nt], *v.t.* enchanter; (*fig.*) charmer, ravir (*de*).
enchanter [in'tʃɑ:ntə], *n.* enchanteur, *m.*
enchanting [in'tʃɑ:ntiŋ], *a.* enchanteur, ravissant, charmant.
enchantment [in'tʃɑ:ntmənt], *n.* enchantement, charme, *m.*, fascination, *f.*
enchantress [in'tʃɑ:ntris], *n.* enchanteresse, *f.*
encircle [in'sə:kl], *v.t.* ceindre, entourer (*de*), encercler.
enclose [in'klouz], *v.t.* enclore; entourer, environner; renfermer; envoyer sous le même pli (*lettre etc.*).
enclosed [in'klouzd], *a.* entouré, environné; inclus, ci-inclus, sous ce pli (*paquet, lettre etc.*).
enclosure [in'klouʒə], *n.* clôture; enceinte (*espace clos*), *f.*; contenu (*objet renfermé*), *m.*
encomium [en'koumjəm], *n.* éloge, *m.*, louange, *f.*
encompass [in'kʌmpəs], *v.t.* entourer, environner; renfermer.
encore [ɔŋ'kɔ:], *n.* and *int.* bis.—*v.t.* bisser.
encounter [in'kauntə], *n.* rencontre, *f.*; combat, *m.*, lutte, *f.*—*v.t.* rencontrer, aborder; (*fig.*) éprouver, essuyer.
encourage [in'kʌridʒ], *v.t.* encourager.
encouragement [in'kʌridʒmənt], *n.* encouragement, *m.*
encroach [in'kroutʃ], *v.i.* empiéter (*sur*); abuser (*de*).
encroachment [in'kroutʃmənt], *n.* empiétement, *m.*, usurpation, *f.*
encumber [in'kʌmbə], *v.t.* encombrer, accabler, embarrasser (*de*); grever (*un héritage*).
encumbrance [in'kʌmbrəns], *n.* encombrement, embarras, *m.*; (*Law*) hypothèque, *f.*
encyclopaedia [insaiklə'pi:diə], *n.* encyclopédie, *f.*
encyclopaedic [insaiklə'pi:dik], *a.* encyclopédique.

end [end], *n.* fin; extrémité, *f.*, bout; but, objet; (*fig.*) dessein, *m.*, issue, *f.*; ***at an end***, fini, terminé; ***big end***, (*Motor.*) tête de bielle, *f.*; ***from end to end***, d'un bout à l'autre; ***in the end***, à la fin; ***three days on end***, trois jours de suite; ***to be at a loose end***, être désœuvré, se trouver sans avoir rien à faire; ***to draw to an end***, tirer *ou* toucher à sa fin; ***to make an end of***, en finir avec; ***to make both ends meet***, joindre les deux bouts.—*v.t.* finir, terminer, achever.—*v.i.* finir, se terminer (*en*); cesser (*de*); aboutir (*à*).
endanger [in'deindʒə], *v.t.* mettre en danger, compromettre, risquer.
endear [in'diə], *v.t.* rendre cher (*à*).
endearing [in'diəriŋ], *a.* tendre, affectueux.
endearment [in'diəmənt], *n.* charme, *m.*; (*pl.*) caresses, *f.pl.*
endeavour [in'devə], *n.* effort, *m.*, tentative, *f.* —*v.i.* tâcher, essayer, tenter (*de*), chercher (*à*).
ending ['endiŋ], *n.* fin, conclusion; (*Gram.*) terminaison, *f.*
endive ['endiv], *n.* chicorée, *f.*
endless ['endlis], *a.* sans fin; éternel, perpétuel, interminable.
endlessly ['endlisli], *adv.* à l'infini, sans cesse.
endorse [in'dɔ:s], *v.t.* endosser; viser (*passeport*); (*fig.*) sanctionner, approuver.
endorsement [in'dɔ:smənt], *n.* suscription, *f.*; (*Comm.*) endossement (*signature au dos*); visa (*de passeport*), *m.*; (*fig.*) sanction, *f.*
endow [in'dau], *v.t.* doter (*de*); (*fig.*) douer (*de*).
endowment [in'daumənt], *n.* dotation, *f.*
endurable [in'djuərəbl], *a.* supportable, endurable.
endurance [in'djuərəns], *n.* endurance; souffrance, patience, *f.*
endure [in'djuə], *v.t.* supporter, souffrir, endurer.—*v.i.* durer; endurer, souffrir.
enduring [in'djuəriŋ], *a.* endurant, qui endure, patient; durable, qui dure (*permanent*).
endways ['endweiz], **endwise** ['endwaiz], *adv.* debout, de champ; bout à bout (*horizontalement*).
enema ['enimə, i'ni:mə], *n.* lavement, *m.*
enemy ['enəmi], *n.* ennemi, *m.*
energetic [enə'dʒetik], *a.* énergique.
energy ['enədʒi], *n.* énergie, *f.*
enervate ['enəveit], *v.t.* affaiblir, énerver.
enfeeble [in'fi:bl], *v.t.* affaiblir.
enfold [in'fould], *v.t.* envelopper.
enforce [in'fɔ:s], *v.t.* donner de la force à; faire respecter; faire exécuter; forcer.
enforcement [in'fɔ:smənt], *n.* mise en vigueur, exécution, *f.*
enfranchise [in'fræntʃaiz], *v.t.* affranchir (*un esclave*); donner le droit de vote à.
enfranchisement [in'fræntʃizmənt], *n.* affranchissement, *m.*; admission au suffrage, *f.*
engage [in'geidʒ], *v.t.* engager; retenir, prendre (*réserver*); louer (*prendre à louage*); arrêter (*un marché*); occuper (*attention etc.*); (*fig.*) en venir aux mains avec.—*v.i.* s'engager (*à*); livrer combat.
engaged [in'geidʒd], *a.* fiancé (*futur époux*); occupé (*pris par le travail*); pas libre (*téléphone, cabinets*); aux prises (*combat*).
engagement [in'geidʒmənt], *n.* engagement, *m.*; occupation, *f.*; fiançailles, *f.pl.*; combat, *m.*
engaging [in'geidʒiŋ], *a.* engageant, attrayant.
engender [in'dʒendə], *v.t.* engendrer, faire naître, causer.
engine ['endʒin], *n.* machine, *f.*, moteur, *m.*; (*Rail.*) locomotive, *f.*; ***fire-engine***, pompe à incendie, *f.*; ***steam-engine***, machine à vapeur.
engine-driver ['endʒindraivə], *n.* (*Rail.*) mécanicien, *m.*
engineer [endʒi'niə], *n.* ingénieur; (*Manuf.*) constructeur-mécanicien; (*Mil.*) soldat du génie; (*pl.*) le génie, *m.*
engineering [endʒi'niəriŋ], *n.* art de l'ingénieur, *m.*; ***civil engineering***, génie civil, *m.*; ***electrical engineering***, technique électrique, *f.*
England ['iŋglənd]. l'Angleterre, *f.*
English ['iŋgliʃ], *a.* anglais; de l'Angleterre; ***the English Channel***, la Manche, *f.*—*n.* anglais (*langue*), *m.*; ***the English***, les Anglais, *m.pl.*
Englishman ['iŋgliʃmən], *n.* (*pl.* **-men** [men]) Anglais, *m.*
Englishwoman ['iŋgliʃwumən], *n.* (*pl.* **-women** [wimin]) Anglaise, *f.*
engrave [in'greiv], *v.t.* graver.
engraver [in'greivə], *n.* graveur, *m.*
engraving [in'greiviŋ], *n.* gravure; ***copperplate engraving***, taille-douce, *f.*
engross [in'grous], *v.t.* grossoyer (*copier*); accaparer (*monopoliser*); absorber, occuper (*l'esprit*).
engulf [in'gʌlf], *v.t.* engouffrer; (*fig.*) engloutir.
enhance [in'hɑ:ns], *v.t.* enchérir, renchérir; (*fig.*) rehausser.
enhancement [in'hɑ:nsmənt], *n.* hausse, *f.*; (*fig.*) rehaussement, *m.*
enigma [i'nigmə], *n.* énigme, *f.*
enigmatic [enig'mætik], **enigmatical** [enig'mætikəl], *a.* énigmatique, obscur.
enjoin [in'dʒɔin], *v.t.* enjoindre; prescrire (*à*).
enjoy [in'dʒɔi], *v.t.* jouir de, posséder; goûter; ***to enjoy oneself***, s'amuser.
enjoyable [in'dʒɔiəbl], *a.* agréable.
enjoyment [in'dʒɔimənt], *n.* jouissance (*de*) *f.*; plaisir, *m.*
enkindle [in'kindl], *v.t.* enflammer; (*fig.*) exciter.
enlace [in'leis], *v.t.* enlacer.
enlarge [in'lɑ:dʒ], *v.t.* agrandir, étendre, dilater.—*v.i.* grandir, s'agrandir.
enlargement [in'lɑ:dʒmənt], *n.* agrandissement (*also Phot.*), *m.*; augmentation, *f.*
enlighten [in'laitn], *v.t.* éclairer; (*fig.*) éclaircir.
enlightenment [in'laitnmənt], *n.* éclaircissement, *m.*; lumières, *f.pl.*
enlist [in'list], *v.t.* enrôler, engager.—*v.i.* s'engager.
enlistment [in'listmənt], *n.* engagement, enrôlement, *m.*
enliven [in'laivn], *v.t.* égayer, animer.
enmity ['enmiti], *n.* inimitié; animosité, haine, hostilité, *f.*
ennoble [i'noubl], *v.t.* anoblir; (*fig.*) ennoblir.

ennoblement [i'noublmənt], *n.* anoblissement; (*fig.*) ennoblissement, *m.*
enormity [i'nɔ:miti], **enormousness** [i'nɔ:məsnis], *n.* énormité, *f.*
enormous [i'nɔ:məs], *a.* énorme; (*fig.*) atroce, monstrueux.
enormously [i'nɔ:məsli], *adv.* énormément.
enough [i'nʌf], *a.* and *adv.* assez; ***large enough***, assez grand; ***more than enough***, plus qu'il n'en faut.
enquire [INQUIRE].
enrage [in'reidʒ], *v.t.* faire enrager; exaspérer.
enrapture [in'ræptʃə], *v.t.* transporter, ravir.
enrich [in'ritʃ], *v.t.* enrichir.
enrichment [in'ritʃmənt], *n.* enrichissement, *m.*
enrol [in'roul], *v.t.* enrôler, enregistrer, inscrire.—*v.i.* s'enrôler, se faire inscrire.
enrolment [in'roulmənt], *n.* enrôlement, *m.*, inscription, *f.*
ensconce [in'skɔns], *v.t.* cacher; ***to ensconce oneself***, se cacher (*dans*), se blottir.
enshrine [in'ʃrain], *v.t.* enchâsser (*dans*).
enshroud [in'ʃraud], *v.t.* mettre dans un linceul; (*fig.*) couvrir.
ensign ['ensain, (*R. Navy*) 'ensin], *n.* enseigne, *f.*, drapeau; (*Mil.*) porte-drapeau (*personne*), *m.*
enslave [in'sleiv], *v.t.* asservir; (*fig.*) captiver.
ensnare [in'snɛə], *v.t.* prendre au piège; (*fig.*) attraper séduire.
ensue [in'sju:], *v.i.* s'ensuivre.
ensuing [in'sju:iŋ], *a.* suivant; prochain.
ensure [in'ʃuə], *v.t.* assurer, garantir.
entail [en'teil], *v.t.* substituer (*à*); (*fig.*) entraîner; impliquer.
entangle [in'tæŋgl], *v.t.* emmêler; enchevêtrer; empêtrer (*les pieds*); (*fig.*) embrouiller.
entanglement [in'tæŋglmənt], *n.* embrouillement, embarras, *m.*
enter ['entə], *v.t.* entrer dans, pénétrer; inscrire (*nom etc.*); enregistrer (*paquet*).—*v.i.* entrer; s'engager (*dans*).
enteritis [entə'raitis], *n.* entérite, *f.*
enterprise ['entəpraiz], *n.* entreprise, hardiesse, *f.*; esprit d'entreprise, *m.*
entertain [entə'tein], *v.t.* recevoir (*des invités*); divertir, amuser (*distraire*); concevoir (*idée etc.*); accepter (*proposition*).—*v.i.* recevoir (*invités*).
entertainer [entə'teinə], *n.* (*Theat. etc.*) diseur, *m.*, diseuse, *f.*, comique, *m.*, *f.*; hôte, *m.*, hôtesse, *f.*
entertainment [entə'teinmənt], *n.* hospitalité, *f.*; accueil (*reception*); festin, *m.*, fête, *f.*; divertissement, spectacle (*amusement*), *m.*
enthrall [in'θrɔ:l], *v.t.* asservir, assujettir; (*fig.*) ravir.
enthuse [in'θju:z], *v.i.* s'enthousiasmer de *ou* pour.
enthusiasm [in'θju:ziæzm], *n.* enthousiasme, *m.*
enthusiast [in'θju:ziæst], *n.* enthousiaste, *m.*, *f.*
enthusiastic [inθju:zi'æstik], *a.* enthousiaste.
entice [in'tais], *v.t.* attirer; entraîner (*dans*); séduire (*à*).
enticement [in'taismənt], *n.* appât, charme, *m.*; tentation, *f.*
enticer [in'taisə], *n.* tentateur, séducteur, *m.*
enticing [in'taisiŋ], *a.* séduisant, attrayant, tentant.
entire [in'taiə], *a.* entier, complet.
entirely [in'taiəli], *adv.* entièrement, complètement, tout entier.
entirety [in'taiəti], *n.* totalité; intégrité, *f.*
entitle [in'taitl], *v.t.* intituler, appeler; donner droit à.
entity ['entiti], *n.* entité, *f.*, être de raison, *m.*
entomb [in'tu:m], *v.t.* ensevelir.
entrails ['entreilz], *n.pl.* entrailles, *f.pl.*
entrance (1) ['entrəns], *n.* entrée, *f.*; commencement, début (*de carrière*), *m.*; (*fig.*) initiation, *f.*
entrance (2) [in'trɑ:ns], *v.t.* extasier, ravir.
entrancing [in'trɑ:nsiŋ], *a.* prenant; ravissant.
entrant ['entrənt], *n.* inscrit (*de concours*), *m.*; inscrite, *f.*; débutant (*dans une profession nouvelle*), *m.*, débutante, *f.*
entrap [in'træp], *v.t.* prendre au piège, attraper (*dans*).
entreat [in'tri:t], *v.t.* supplier, prier instamment (*de*).
entreaty [in'tri:ti], *n.* prière; supplication; (*pl.*) sollicitation, *f.*, instances, *f.pl.*
entrust [in'trʌst], *v.t.* charger (*de*).
entry ['entri], *n.* entrée; inscription (*enregistrement*); (*Book-keeping*) écriture, *f.*, article, *m.*; (*Customs*) déclaration d'entrée, *f.*; ***no entry***, sens interdit, passage interdit.
entwine [in'twain], *v.t.* enlacer, entortiller.—*v.i.* s'enlacer, s'entortiller.
enumerate [i'nju:məreit], *v.t.* énumérer, dénombrer.
enunciate [i'nʌnsieit], *v.t.* énoncer; prononcer.—*v.i.* articuler.
envelop [in'veləp], *v.t.* envelopper (*de ou dans*).
envelope ['enviloup, 'ɔnviloup], *n.* enveloppe, *f.*
envenom [in'venəm], *v.t.* envenimer; exaspérer (*aigrir*).
envious ['enviəs], *a.* envieux (*de*).
environ [in'vaiərən], *v.t.* environner (*de*).
environment [in'vaiərənmənt], *n.* milieu, entourage, environnement, *m.*
environs [in'vaiərənz], *n.pl.* environs, *m.pl.*
envisage [in'vizidʒ], *v.t.* envisager.
envoy ['envɔi], *n.* envoyé, *m.*
envy ['envi], *n.* envie, *f.*—*v.t.* envier, porter envie à.
epaulet(te) ['epɔ:let], *n.* épaulette, *f.*
ephemeral [i'femərəl], *a.* éphémère.
epic ['epik], *a.* épique; (*fig.*) légendaire.—*n.* épopée, *f.*, poème épique, *m.*
epicure ['epikjuə], *n.* gourmet, *m.*, gastronome, *m.*, *f.*
epidemic [epi'demik], *a.* épidémique.—*n.* épidémie, *f.*
epigram ['epigræm], *n.* épigramme, *f.*
epilepsy ['epilepsi], *n.* épilepsie, *f.*
epileptic [epi'leptik], *a.* and *n.* épileptique, *m.*, *f.*
epilogue ['epilɔg], *n.* épilogue, *m.*
episcopacy [i'piskəpəsi], *n.* épiscopat, *m.*
episcopal [i'piskəpəl], *a.* épiscopal.
episode ['episoud], *n.* épisode, *m.*
epistle [i'pisl], *n.* épître, *f.*
epitaph ['epitɑ:f], *n.* épitaphe, *f.*
epithet ['epiθet], *n.* épithète, *f.*

epitome [i'pitəmi], *n.* épitomé, abrégé, précis, *m.*
epitomize [i'pitəmaiz], *v.t.* faire un abrégé de; être une image en petit de.
epoch ['i:pɔk], *n.* époque, *f.*
equable ['ekwəbl], *a.* uniforme, égal.
equal ['i:kwəl], *a.* égal; (*fig.*) impartial, juste; ***equal to***, de force à, à la hauteur de.—*n.* égal, *m.*, égale, *f.*; (*pl.*) pareils, égaux, *m.pl.* —*v.t.* égaler, être égal à.
equality [i'kwɔliti], *n.* égalité, *f.*
equalize ['i:kwəlaiz], *v.t.* égaliser; compenser.
equally ['i:kwəli], *adv.* également, pareillement.
equanimity [i:kwə'nimiti], *n.* égalité d'âme, équanimité, *f.*
equation [i'kweiʃən], *n.* équation, *f.*
equator [i'kweitə], *n.* équateur, *m.*
equatorial [ekwə'tɔ:riəl], *a.* équatorial, de l'équateur.
equerry ['ekwəri], *n.* écuyer, *m.*
equestrian [i'kwestriən], *a.* équestre.—*n.* cavalier; (*Circus*) écuyer, *m.*
equilibrium [i:kwi'libriəm], *n.* équilibre, *m.*
equine ['i:kwain, 'ekwain], *a.* du cheval, équin.
equinox ['i:kwinɔks], *n.* équinoxe, *m.*
equip [i'kwip], *v.t.* équiper; (*Tech.*) outiller.
equipment [i'kwipmənt], *n.* équipement, matériel outillage, *m.*
equitable ['ekwitəbl], *a.* équitable, juste.
equity ['ekwiti], *n.* équité, justice, *f.*
equivalent [i'kwivələnt], *a.* équivalent (*à*); ***to be equivalent to***, être équivalent à, équivaloir à.—*n.* équivalent, *m.*
equivocal [i'kwivəkl], *a.* équivoque, ambigu.
equivocate [i'kwivəkeit], *v.i.* user d'équivoque, équivoquer.
era ['iərə], *n.* ère, *f.*
eradicate [i'rædikeit], *v.t.* déraciner; (*fig.*) exterminer.
erase [i'reiz], *v.t.* raturer, effacer, rayer.
eraser [i'reizə], *n.* grattoir, *m.*, gomme à effacer, *f.*
erasure [i'reiʒə], *n.* grattage, *m.*, rature, *f.*
***ere** [ɛə], *conj.* avant que; plutôt que.—*prep.* avant.
erect [i'rekt], *a.* debout, droit, élevé.—*v.t.* ériger, dresser; (*fig.*) établir.
erection [i'rekʃən], *n.* construction, érection, élévation; (*fig.*) fondation, *f.*
ermine ['ə:min], *a.* d'hermine.—*n.* hermine, *f.*
erode [i'roud], *v.t.* éroder, ronger.
erosion [i'rouʒən], *n.* érosion, *f.*
erotic [i'rɔtik], *a.* érotique.
err [ə:], *v.i.* s'écarter, s'égarer (*de*); (*fig.*) se tromper.
errand ['erənd], *n.* message, *m.*, commission, course, *f.*
errand-boy ['erəndbɔi], *n.* petit commissionnaire; saute-ruisseau (*de bureau*), chasseur (*dans un restaurant*), *m.*
erratic [i'rætik], *a.* erratique; errant, excentrique; irrégulier; inégal.
erroneous [i'rouniəs], *a.* erroné, faux.
erroneously [i'rouniəsli], *adv.* à faux, à tort.
error ['erə], *n.* erreur, faute, *f.*, écart, *m.*
erudite ['erudait], *a.* érudit, savant.
erudition [eru'diʃən], *n.* érudition, *f.*
erupt [i'rʌpt], *v.i.* faire éruption (*volcan*); percer (*dent*).
eruption [i'rʌpʃən], *n.* éruption, *f.*
erysipelas [eri'sipiləs], *n.* érysipèle, *m.*
escalade [eskə'leid], *n.* escalade, *f.*—*v.t.* escalader.
escalate ['eskəleit], *v.i.* escalader.
escalation [eskə'leiʃən], *n.* escalade, *f.*
escalator ['eskəleitə], *n.* escalier roulant, *m.*
escapade [eskə'peid], *n.* escapade, *f.*
escape [is'keip], *n.* évasion; fuite (*gaz*); (*fig.*) délivrance, *f.*; ***fire-escape***, échelle de sauvetage, *f.*; ***to have a narrow escape***, l'échapper belle.—*v.t.* échapper à; éviter.—*v.i.* (s')échapper; s'évader (*de prison*).
escarpment [is'ka:pmənt], *n.* escarpement, talus, *m.*
eschew [is'tʃu:], *v.t.* éviter; renoncer à.
escort [is'kɔ:t], *v.t.* escorter.—['eskɔ:t], *n.* escorte, *f.*; cavalier, *m.*
escutcheon [is'kʌtʃən], *n.* écusson, *m.*
Eskimo ['eskimou], *a.* esquimau.—*n.* Esquimau (*personne*), *m.*
especial [is'peʃəl], *a.* spécial, particulier.
especially [is'peʃəli], *adv.* spécialement, surtout.
esplanade [esplə'neid], *n.* esplanade, promenade, *f.*
espouse [is'pauz], *v.t.* épouser; (*fig.*) adopter.
espy [is'pai], *v.t.* apercevoir, aviser, épier.
essay ['esei], *n.* essai; effort, *m.*; (*Sch.*) composition, dissertation, *f.*—[e'sei], *v.t.* essayer (*de*).
essence ['esəns], *n.* essence, *f.*
essential [i'senʃəl], *a.* essentiel.—*n.* (*also pl.*) essentiel, *m.*
essentially [i'senʃəli], *adv.* essentiellement.
establish [is'tæbliʃ], *v.t.* établir, fonder; (*fig.*) confirmer; prouver.
establishment [is'tæbliʃmənt], *n.* établissement, *m.*; maison; (*fig.*) confirmation, *f.*
estate [is'teit], *n.* état, rang (*condition*), *m.*; propriété, *f.*, bien (*immeuble*), *m.*
estate-agent [is'teiteidʒənt], *n.* agent immobilier, *m.*
estate duty [is'teitdju:ti], *n.* droits de succession, *m.pl.*
esteem [is'ti:m], *n.* estime, considération, *f.* —*v.t.* estimer, regarder comme.
estimate ['estimit], *n.* évaluation, *f.*, calcul, devis, *m.*; (*fig.*) appréciation, *f.*—['estimeit] *v.t.* estimer, apprécier; évaluer, calculer.
Estonia [es'touniə]. l'Esthonie, *f.*
Estonian [es'touniən], *a.* esthonien.—*n.* esthonien (*langue*); Esthonien (*personne*), *m.*
estrange [is'treindʒ], *v.t.* aliéner, éloigner (*de*).
estrangement [is'treindʒmənt], *n.* aliénation, *f.*, éloignement, *m.*, brouille, *f.*
estuary ['estjuəri], *n.* estuaire, *m.*
etching ['etʃiŋ], *n.* gravure à l'eau-forte, *f.*
eternal [i'tə:nl], *a.* and *n.* éternel, *m.*
eternity [i'tə:niti], *n.* éternité, *f.*
ether ['i:θə], *n.* éther, *m.*
ethereal [i'θiəriəl], *a.* éthéré; céleste.
ethic ['eθik], **ethical** ['eθikəl], *a.* éthique; moral.
ethics ['eθiks], *n.pl.* morale, éthique, *f.*
Ethiopia [i:θi'oupiə]. l'Éthiopie, *f.*
Ethiopian [i:θi'oupiən], *a.* éthiopien.—*n.* Éthiopien (*personne*), *m.*
etiquette ['etiket], *n.* étiquette, *f.*, convenances, *f.pl.*
Etruria [i'truəriə]. **l'Étrurie,** *f.*

Etruscan [i'trʌskən], *a.* étrusque.—*n.* étrusque (*langue*); Étrusque (*personne*), *m., f.*
etymology [eti'mɔlədʒi], *n.* étymologie, *f.*
eucharist ['ju:kərist], *n.* eucharistie, *f.*
eulogium [ju:'loudʒiəm], **eulogy** ['ju:lədʒi], *n.* éloge, panégyrique, *m.*
eulogize ['ju:lədʒaiz], *v.t.* louer, faire l'éloge de.
eunuch ['ju:nək], *n.* eunuque, *m.*
euphemism ['ju:fimizm], *n.* euphémisme, *m.*
euphony ['ju:fəni], *n.* euphonie, *f.*
Eurasian [juə'reiʒən], *a.* eurasien.—*n.* Eurasien (*personne*), *m.*
Europe ['juərəp]. l'Europe, *f.*
European [juərə'pi:ən], *a.* européen.—*n.* Européen (*personne*), *m.*
euthanasia [ju:θə'neiziə], *n.* euthanasie, *f.*
evacuate [i'vækjueit], *v.t.* évacuer.
evacuation [ivækju'eiʃən], *n.* évacuation, *f.*
evade [i'veid], *v.t.* éluder, esquiver, éviter, se soustraire à; échapper à, déjouer (*la loi*).
evaluate [i'væljueit], *v.t.* évaluer.
evaporate [i'væpəreit], *v.t.* faire évaporer.—*v.i.* s'évaporer.
evaporation [ivæpə'reiʃən], *n.* évaporation, *f.*
evasion [i'veiʒən], *n.* subterfuge, *m.*; échappatoire, défaite, *f.*
eve [i:v], *n.* veille, *f.*; ***on the eve of***, à la veille de.
even (1) [i:vn], *n.* (*Poet.*) soir, *m.*
even (2) [i:vn], *a.* égal; régulier (*respiration, pouls*); uni (*lisse*); de niveau (*avec*); pair (*numéro*).—*adv.* même, aussi bien; précisément.—*v.t.* égaler, égaliser; niveler.
evening ['i:vniŋ], *a.* du soir; ***evening dress***, tenue de soirée, *f.*—*n.* soir, *m.*; soirée, *f.*; (*fig.*) déclin, *m.*
evenly ['i:vnli], *adv.* également; de niveau; (*fig.*) impartialement.
evenness ['i:vnnis], *n.* égalité; régularité; sérénité, *f.*
evensong ['i:vnsɔŋ], *n.* chant du soir, *m.*, vêpres, *m.pl.*
event [i'vent], *n.* événement, *m.*; issue, *f.*; ***at all events***, en tout cas, dans tous les cas; ***in the event of***, au cas où.
even-tempered ['i:vntempəd], *a.* calme, placide, égal.
eventful [i'ventful], *a.* mouvementé.
eventual [i'ventjuəl], *a.* éventuel, aléatoire; final, définitif.
eventually [i'ventjuəli], *adv.* finalement, à la fin, par la suite.
ever ['evə], *adv.* toujours; jamais; ***ever since***, depuis; ***for ever***, à jamais.
evergreen ['evəgri:n], *a.* toujours vert.—*n.* arbre toujours vert, *m.*
everlasting [evə'lɑ:stiŋ], *a.* éternel, perpétuel.—*n.* éternité, *f.*; éternel, *m.*
everlastingly [evə'lɑ:stiŋli], *adv.* éternellement.
evermore ['evəmɔ:], *adv.* toujours; éternellement.
every ['evri], *a.* chaque, tout, tous les; ***every one***, chacun, *m.*, chacune, *f.*, tous, *pl.*
everybody [EVERYONE].
everyday ['evridei], *a.* quotidien; ordinaire; de tous les jours.
everyone ['evriwʌn], **everybody** ['evribɔdi], *n.* tout le monde, *m.*
everything ['evriθiŋ], *n.* tout, *m.*
everywhere ['evriwεə], *adv.* partout.
evict [i'vikt], *v.t.* évincer, expulser.
eviction [i'vikʃən], *n.* éviction, expulsion, *f.*
evidence ['evidəns], *n.* évidence; preuve, *f.*, témoignage; témoin (*personne*), *m.*—*v.t.* montrer, prouver, démontrer.
evident ['evidənt], *a.* évident, visible.
evidently ['evidəntli], *adv.* évidemment.
evil [i:vl], *a.* mauvais; malheureux, malfaisant, méchant (*esprit etc.*).—*n.* mal; malheur, *m.*, calamité, *f.*—*adv.* mal.
evil-doer ['i:vlduə], *n.* malfaiteur, méchant, *m.*
evil-speaking ['i:vl'spi:kiŋ], *n.* médisance, *f.*
evince [i'vins], *v.t.* montrer, manifester, démontrer.
evoke [i'vouk], *v.t.* évoquer; susciter.
evolution [i:və'lu:ʃən], *n.* évolution, *f.*
evolve [i'vɔlv], *v.t.* dérouler; développer.—*v.i.* se dérouler; se développer.
ewe [ju:], *n.* brebis, *f.*
ewer ['juə], *n.* aiguière, *f.*, broc, *m.*
exact [ig'zækt], *v.t.* exiger, extorquer.—*a.* exact, précis.
exaction [ig'zækʃən], *n.* exaction, *f.*
exactitude [ig'zæktitju:d], **exactness** [ig'zæktnis], *n.* exactitude, *f.*
exactly [ig'zæktli], *adv.* exactement, précisément, au juste; juste.
exaggerate [ig'zædʒəreit], *v.t.* exagérer.
exaggeration [igzædʒə'reiʃən], *n.* exagération, *f.*
exalt [ig'zɔ:lt], *v.t.* exalter, élever; (*fig.*) louer.
exaltation [egzɔ:l'teiʃən], *n.* exaltation, élévation, *f.*
examination [igzæmi'neiʃən], *n.* examen, *m.*; inspection, vérification, *f.*; (*Law*) interrogatoire (*de prisonniers*), *m.*; audition (*de témoins*), *f.*; ***to pass an examination***, réussir à un examen; ***to sit (for) an examination***, passer un examen.
examine [ig'zæmin], *v.t.* examiner; visiter; (*Law*) interroger.
examiner [ig'zæminə], *n.* examinateur; (*Law*) juge d'instruction, *m.*
example [ig'zɑ:mpl], *n.* exemple, *m.*; ***for example***, par exemple.
exasperate [ig'zɑ:spəreit], *v.t.* exaspérer; irriter, aigrir.
exasperation [igzɑ:spə'reiʃən], *n.* exaspération, irritation, *f.*
excavate ['ekskəveit], *v.t.* creuser, excaver.
excavation [ekskə'veiʃən], *n.* excavation, *f.*; fouilles, *f.pl.*
excavator ['ekskəveitə], *n.* piocheuse-défonceuse, *f.*
exceed [ik'si:d], *v.t.* excéder, dépasser; (*fig.*) surpasser.
exceeding [ik'si:diŋ], *a.* grand, extrême.
exceedingly [ik'si:diŋli], *adv.* très, fort, extrêmement.
excel [ik'sel], *v.t.* surpasser, l'emporter sur.—*v.i.* exceller, se distinguer (*à*).
excellence ['eksələns], *n.* excellence, supériorité, *f.*
excellent ['eksələnt], *a.* excellent.
excellently ['eksələntli], *adv.* excellemment, parfaitement.
except [ik'sept], *v.t.* excepter; exclure (*de*).—*prep.* excepté, à l'exception de, hors, sauf.—*conj.* à moins que, à moins de.
excepting [ik'septiŋ], *prep.* excepté, hormis.

exception [ik'sepʃən], *n.* exception; objection, *f.*; ***to take exception to,*** se formaliser de.
exceptionable [ik'sepʃənəbl], *a.* blâmable, à critiquer.
exceptional [ik'sepʃənəl], *a.* exceptionnel.
exceptionally [ik'sepʃənəli], *adv.* exceptionnellement.
excerpt ['eksə:pt], *n.* extrait, *m.*, citation, *f.*
excess [ik'ses], *n.* excès; excédent (*poids*), *m.*
excessive [ik'sesiv], *a.* excessif, extrême; immodéré.
excessively [ik'sesivli], *adv.* excessivement, à l'excès.
exchange [iks'tʃeindʒ], *n.* échange; (*Comm.*) change, *m.*; Bourse (*édifice*), *f.*; ***bill of exchange,*** lettre de change, *f.*; ***rate of exchange,*** taux du change, *m.*; ***telephone exchange,*** central téléphonique, *m.*—*v.t.* échanger, changer (*contre* ou *pour*).
exchequer [iks'tʃekə], *n.* trésor; Ministère des Finances, *m.*
excisable [ek'saizəbl], *a.* imposable; sujet aux droits de l'accise.
excise ['eksaiz], *n.* (*England*) excise, *f.*; (*France*) contributions indirectes, *f.pl.*, régie, *f.*
excise-man ['eksaizmən], *n.* (*pl.* **-men** [men]) préposé *ou* employé de la régie, *m.*
excitable [ik'saitəbl], *a.* excitable, impressionnable.
excite [ik'sait], *v.t.* exciter; irriter; émouvoir; (*fig.*) provoquer.
excitement [ik'saitmənt], *n.* émoi, *m.*, surexcitation; émotion, agitation, *f.*
exciting [ik'saitiŋ], *a.* émouvant, passionnant, palpitant.
exclaim [iks'kleim], *v.i.* s'écrier, se récrier, s'exclamer.
exclamation [ekskləˈmeiʃən], *n.* exclamation, *f.*, cri, *m.*
exclude [iks'klu:d], *v.t.* exclure (*de*); proscrire.
excluding [iks'klu:diŋ], *prep.* sans compter.
exclusion [iks'klu:ʒən], *n.* exclusion, *f.*
exclusive [iks'klu:siv], *a.* exclusif.
excommunicate [ekskə'mju:nikeit], *v.t.* excommunier.
excrement ['ekskrimənt], *n.* excrément, *m.*
excrescence [iks'kresəns], *n.* excroissance, *f.*
excruciate [iks'kru:ʃieit], *v.t.* tourmenter, torturer.
excruciating [iks'kru:ʃieitiŋ], *a.* atroce, affreux, horrible.
exculpate ['ekskʌlpeit], *v.t.* disculper, justifier.
excursion [iks'kə:ʃən], *n.* excursion, randonnée; (*fig.*) digression, *f.*
excusable [iks'kju:zəbl], *a.* excusable.
excuse [iks'kju:s], *n.* excuse, *f.*; prétexte, *m.*; ***to find an excuse,*** chercher des excuses; ***to make excuses,*** s'excuser.—[eks'kju:z], *v.t.* excuser, pardonner; ***excuse me!*** pardon! ***to be excused from duty,*** être exempt de service.
execrable ['eksikrəbl], *a.* exécrable.
execrate ['eksikreit], *v.t.* exécrer, maudire.
execute ['eksikju:t], *v.t.* exécuter, accomplir; remplir (*un ordre*); ***to execute a deed,*** signer un contrat.
execution [eksi'kju:ʃən], *n.* exécution, *f.*; accomplissement, supplice, *m.*
executioner [eksi'kju:ʃənə], *n.* bourreau, *m.*
executive [ig'zekjutiv], *a.* exécutif.—*n.* pouvoir exécutif; (*Comm.*) directeur, *m.*
executor [ig'zekjutə], *n.* exécuteur testamentaire, *m.*
exemplar [ig'zemplə], *n.* modèle, exemplaire, *m.*
exemplary [ig'zempləri], *a.* exemplaire; modèle.
exemplify [ig'zemplifai], *v.t.* démontrer par des exemples, illustrer; donner un exemple de.
exempt [ig'zempt, eg'zemt], *v.t.* exempter (*de*).—*a.* exempt.
exemption [ig'zempʃən], *n.* exemption, *f.*
exercise ['eksəsaiz], *n.* exercice; (*Sch.*) thème, devoir, *m.*—*v.t.* exercer; promener (*un chien*).—*v.i.* s'exercer; (*Mil.*) faire l'exercice.
exercise-book ['eksəsaizbuk], *n.* cahier (*de devoirs*), *m.*
exert [ig'zə:t], *v.t.* déployer; mettre en œuvre; exercer (*influence, pression etc.*); ***to exert oneself,*** faire des efforts (*pour*).
exertion [ig'zə:ʃən], *n.* effort, *m.*
exhale [eks'heil], *v.t.* exhaler, émettre.
exhaust [ig'zɔ:st], *v.t.* épuiser.—*n.* échappement, *m.*
exhausted [ig'zɔ:stid], *a.* épuisé.
exhaustion [ig'zɔ:stʃən], *n.* épuisement, *m.*
exhaustive [ig'zɔ:stiv], *a.* qui épuise; (*fig.*) complet.
exhaust-pipe [ig'zɔ:stpaip], *n.* (*Motor.*) tuyau d'échappement, *m.*
exhibit [ig'zibit], *v.t.* montrer; exposer; (*fig.*) exhiber.—*n.* objet exposé, *m.*
exhibition [eksi'biʃən], *n.* exposition; représentation, *f.*, spectacle, *m.*; (*Univ.*) bourse, *f.*
exhibitioner [eksi'biʃənə], *n.* (*Univ.*) boursier, *m.*
exhibitor [ig'zibitə], *n.* exposant, *m.*
exhilarate [ig'ziləreit], *v.t.* réjouir, égayer.
exhilarating [ig'ziləreitiŋ], *a.* qui égaye, réjouissant.
exhilaration [igziləˈreiʃən], *n.* réjouissance, gaieté, joie de vivre, *f.*
exhort [ig'zɔ:t], *v.t.* exhorter (*à*).
exhortation [egzɔ:'teiʃən], *n.* exhortation, *f.*
exhume [eks'hju:m], *v.t.* exhumer, déterrer.
exile ['eksail], *n.* exil; exilé (*personne*), *m.*—*v.t.* exiler.
exist [ig'zist], *v.i.* exister.
existence [ig'zistəns], *n.* existence, *f.*; être, *m.*
exit ['eksit], *n.* sortie, *f.*—*v.i.* (*Theat.*) il (elle) sort.
exodus ['eksədəs], *n.* exode, *m.*
exonerate [ig'zɔnəreit], *v.t.* décharger, exempter, exonérer, justifier.
exorbitant [ig'zɔ:bitənt], *a.* exorbitant, excessif, exagéré.
exotic [eg'zɔtik], *a.* exotique.
expand [iks'pænd], *v.t.* étendre, faire épanouir; amplifier; dilater (*gaz*).—*v.i.* se dilater; s'épanouir; se développer.
expanse [iks'pæns], *n.* étendue, *f.*
expansion [iks'pænʃən], *n.* expansion, *f.*
expatiate [eks'peiʃieit], *v.i.* s'étendre (*sur*).
expatriate [eks'peitrieit], *v.t.* expatrier, bannir.
expect [iks'pekt], *v.t.* attendre; s'attendre à, compter sur (*choses*); espérer; ***she is expecting,*** elle attend un bébé; ***to know what to expect,*** savoir à quoi s'en tenir.

expectant [iks'pektənt], *a.* expectant.
expectation [ekspek'teiʃən], *n.* attente, espérance; expectative; probabilité, *f.*
expedience [iks'pi:diəns], **expediency** [iks'pi:diənsi], *n.* convenance, utilité, opportunité, *f.*
expedient [iks'pi:diənt], *a.* convenable, à propos, utile, opportun.—*n.* expédient, *m.*
expedite ['ekspədait], *v.t.* expédier, hâter, accélerer.
expedition [ekspə'diʃən], *n.* expédition; promptitude, *f.*
expeditious [ekspi'diʃəs], *a.* expéditif, prompt.
expel [iks'pel], *v.t.* expulser, chasser; (*Sch.*) renvoyer.
expend [iks'pend], *v.t.* dépenser; (*fig.*) employer.
expenditure [iks'penditʃə], *n.* dépense, *f.*, dépenses, *f.pl.*; (*fig.*) sacrifice, *m.*
expense [iks'pens], *n.* dépense, *f.*; dépens; frais, *m.pl.*; ***at any expense***, à tout prix; ***incidental expenses***, faux frais; ***to clear one's expenses***, faire ses frais.
expensive [iks'pensiv], *a.* coûteux, cher (*chose*); dépensier (*personne*).
expensively [iks'pensivli], *adv.* à grands frais.
experience [iks'piəriəns], *n.* expérience, *f.*; sentiment, *m.*—*v.t.* éprouver, faire l'expérience de.
experienced [iks'piəriənst], *a.* éprouvé, expérimenté.
experiment [eks'perimənt], *n.* expérience, *f.* —*v.i.* expérimenter.
experimental [eksperi'mentl], *a.* expérimental.
expert ['ekspə:t], *a.* expert, habile.—*n.* expert, *m.*
expiate ['ekspieit], *v.t.* expier.
expiation [ekspi'eiʃən], *n.* expiation, *f.*
expiration [ekspi'reiʃən], **expiry** [iks'paiəri], *n.* expiration; fin, *f.*, terme, *m.*
expire [iks'paiə], *v.i.* expirer, mourir.
explain [iks'plein], *v.t.* expliquer.—*v.i.* s'expliquer.
explanation [eksplə'neiʃən], *n.* explication, *f.*
explanatory [iks'plænətri], *a.* explicatif.
explicit [iks'plisit], *a.* explicite, formel; franc.
explode [iks'ploud], *v.t.* faire éclater; faire sauter (*mine*); (*fig.*) discréditer; ***exploded theory***, théorie abandonnée, *f.*—*v.i.* éclater, sauter, faire explosion.
exploit ['eksplɔit], *n.* exploit, haut fait, *m.* —[iks'plɔit], *v.t.* exploiter.
exploitation [eksplɔi'teiʃən], *n.* exploitation, *f.*
exploration [eksplɔ:'reiʃən], *n.* exploration, *f.*; (*fig.*) examen, *m.*
explore [iks'plɔ:], *v.t.* explorer; (*fig.*) examiner.
explorer [iks'plɔ:rə], *n.* explorateur, *m.*
explosion [iks'plouʒən], *n.* explosion, *f.*
explosive [iks'plousiv], *a.* and *n.* explosif, *m.*
exponent [eks'pounənt], *n.* (*Math.*) exposant; (*fig.*) représentant, *m.*
export ['ekspɔ:t], *n.* exportation; marchandise exportée, *f.*—[eks'pɔ:t], *v.t.* exporter, *f.*
expose [iks'pouz] *v.t.* exposer; (*fig.*) révéler, découvrir démasquer.
expostulate [iks'pɔstjuleit], *v.i.* faire des remontrances (*à*).
exposure [iks'pouʒə], *n.* exposition (*aux intempéries, à un danger*), *f.*; étalage (*de marchandises*); esclandre, *m.*; (*Phot.*) pose, *f.*; ***to die of exposure***, mourir de froid.
expound [iks'paund], *v.t.* expliquer, exposer.
express [iks'pres], *a.* exprès; formel, explicite; ***by express delivery***, par exprès.—*n.* exprès (*messager*); train express, *m.*—*v.t.* exprimer.
expression [iks'preʃən], *n.* expression, *f.*
expressive [iks'presiv], *a.* expressif.
expressly [iks'presli], *adv.* expressément, formellement.
expropriate [eks'prouprieit], *v.t.* exproprier.
expulsion [iks'pʌlʃən], *n.* expulsion, *f.*
expurgate ['ekspə:geit], *v.t.* corriger, expurger (*livre*).
exquisite ['ekskwizit], *a.* exquis; vif, extrême (*douleur*); raffiné, délicat.
exquisitely ['ekskwizitli], *adv.* d'une manière exquise; parfaitement.
ex-service man [eks'sə:vismən], *n.* (*pl.* **-men** [men]) ancien combattant, *m.*
extant [ek'stænt], *a.* qui existe encore.
extempore [eks'tempəri], *a.* improvisé.—*adv.* impromptu, sans préparation.
extemporize [eks'tempəraiz], *v.t.* improviser.
extend [iks'tend], *v.t.* étendre; prolonger; tendre (*la main*); ***to extend a welcome***, souhaiter la bienvenue.—*v.i.* s'étendre; se prolonger (*temps*).
extension [iks'tenʃən], *n.* extension; étendue, prolongation (*de temps*), *f.*; (*Teleph.*) poste, *m.*
extensive [iks'tensiv], *a.* étendu, vaste; ample.
extensively [iks'tensivli], *adv.* d'une manière étendue; bien, très au loin.
extent [iks'tent], *n.* étendue, *f.*; (*fig.*) degré, point, *m.*; ***to a certain extent***, jusqu'à un certain point; ***to the extent of***, jusqu'à.
extenuate [eks'tenjueit], *v.t.* atténuer, amoindrir.
extenuating [eks'tenjueitiŋ], *a.* (*Law*) atténuant.
exterior [eks'tiəriə], *a.* extérieur, en dehors.—*n.* extérieur, *m.*
exterminate [iks'tə:mineit], *v.t.* exterminer; extirper.
extermination [ikstə:mi'neiʃən], *n.* extermination, *f.*
external [eks'tə:nl], *a.* extérieur; externe (*étudiant etc.*).
extinct [iks'tiŋkt], *a.* éteint; qui n'existe plus (*espèce etc.*); aboli.
extinguish [iks'tiŋgwiʃ], *v.t.* éteindre; (*fig.*) éclipser.
extinguisher [iks'tiŋgwiʃə], *n.* extincteur (*appareil*), *m.*
extirpate ['ekstə:peit], *v.t.* extirper.
extol [iks'toul], *v.t.* exalter, vanter.
extort [iks'tɔ:t], *v.t.* extorquer, arracher.
extortion [iks'tɔ:ʃən], *n.* extorsion, *f.*
extortionate [iks'tɔ:ʃənit], *a.* extorsionnaire, exorbitant.
extra ['ekstrə], *a.* en sus; supplémentaire; ***extra charge***, prix en sus, supplément, *m.* —*n.* supplément; (*Cine.*) figurant, *m.*—*adv.* en sus, de plus; ***extra strong***, extra-solide.
extract ['ekstrækt], *n.* extrait; concentré (*de viande etc.*), *m.*—[iks'trækt], *v.t.* extraire tirer (*de*); arracher (*dent*) à.

extraction [iks'trækʃən], *n.* extraction; origine, *f.*
extraneous [eks'treinjəs], *a.* étranger (*à*); non-essentiel.
extraordinarily [iks'trɔ:dnrili], *a.* extraordinairement.
extraordinary [iks'trɔ:dnri], *a.* extraordinaire, rare.
extravagance [iks'trævəgəns], *n.* extravagance; prodigalité, *f.*, gaspillage, *m.*
extravagant [iks'trævəgənt], *a.* extravagant (*immodéré*); prodigue, dépensier; exorbitant (*prix*).
extravagantly [iks'trævəgəntli], *adv.* d'une manière extravagante.
extreme [iks'tri:m], *a.* extrême.—*n.* extrémité, *f.*; extrême, *m.*
extremely [iks'tri:mli], *adv.* extrêmement, au dernier degré.
extremist [iks'tri:mist], *n.* extrémiste, *m., f.*; ultra, *m.*
extremity [iks'tremiti], *n.* extrémité, *f.*, extrême; bout, comble, *m.*
extricate ['ekstrikeit], *v.t.* débarrasser, dégager; ***to extricate oneself***, se tirer d'affaire.
extrovert ['ekstrəvə:t], *n.* extroverti, *m.*
exuberance [ig'zju:bərəns], *n.* exubérance, surabondance, *f.*
exuberant [ig'zju:bərənt], *a.* exubérant, surabondant.
exude [ek'sju:d], *v.t.* faire exsuder.—*v.i.* exsuder.
exult [ig'zʌlt], *v.i.* se réjouir, exulter (*de*).
exultant [ig'zʌltənt], *a.* joyeux, triomphant.
exultation [egzʌl'teiʃən], *n.* triomphe, *m.*, exultation, *f.*
eye [ai], *n.* œil; trou (*d'une aiguille*); (*Bot.*) œil, bouton, *m.*; (*Needlework*) porte; (*fig.*) vue, *f.*; ***black eye***, œil poché; ***blind in one eye***, borgne; ***in the twinkling of an eye***, en un clin d'œil; ***to keep an eye on***, surveiller.—*v.t.* regarder; lorgner.
eyeball ['aibɔ:l], *n.* bulbe de l'œil, *m.*
eyebrow ['aibrau], *n.* sourcil, *m.*
eyed [aid], *a.* ***blue-eyed***, aux yeux bleus.
eyeglass ['aiglɑ:s], *n.* monocle (*un seul verre*); lorgnon, pince-nez (*double*), *m.*
eye-hole ['aihoul], *n.* orbite; petit judas, *m.*
eyelash ['ailæʃ], *n.* cil, *m.*
eyelet ['ailit], *n.* œillet, *m.*
eyelid ['ailid], *n.* paupière, *f.*
eyesight ['aisait], *n.* vue, *f.*
eyesore ['aisɔ:], *n.* chose qui blesse l'œil, *f.*, objet d'aversion, *m.*
eye-witness ['aiwitnis], *n.* témoin oculaire, *m.*
eyrie, eyry [AERIE].

F

F, f [ef]. sixième lettre de l'alphabet; (*Mus.*) fa, *m.*
fable [feibl], *n.* fable, *f.*, conte, *m.*
fabric ['fæbrik], *n.* construction *f.*; édifice, ouvrage, *m.*; étoffe, *f.*; (*fig.*) système, *m.*
fabricate ['fæbrikeit], *v.t.* fabriquer, inventer, contrefaire.
fabrication [fæbri'keiʃən], *n.* fabrication, *f.*
fabulous ['fæbjuləs], *a.* fabuleux.
face [feis], *n.* figure, *f.*; visage, *m.*; face, surface (*des choses*); (*fig.*) apparence, *f.*, état, *m.*; mine, physionomie, *f.*; front (*insolence*), *m.*; façade, *f.*, devant (*front*), *m.*; facette (*d'un diamant*), *f.*; cadran (*de pendule*), *m.*; ***face to face***, vis-à-vis; ***to make faces at***, faire des grimaces à.—*v.t.* faire face à, affronter; mettre un revers à, parer (*vêtements*); revêtir (*mur etc.*); donner sur (*maison etc.*).—*v.i.* prendre un faux dehors; (*Mil.*) faire front; ***face about!*** volte-face!
facet ['fæsit], *n.* facette, *f.*—*v.t.* facetter.
facetious [fə'si:ʃəs], *a.* facétieux.
facetiously [fə'si:ʃəsli], *adv.* facétieusement.
facetiousness [fə'si:ʃəsnis], *n.* plaisanterie, *f.*
facial ['feiʃəl], *a.* facial.
facile ['fæsail], *a.* facile; complaisant.
facility [fə'siliti], *n.* facilité, *f.*
facilitate [fə'siliteit], *v.t.* faciliter.
facing ['feisiŋ], *n.* parement (*de vêtements*); revers, *m.*
facsimile [fæk'simili], *n.* fac-similé, *m.*
fact [fækt], *n.* fait, *m.*; ***as a matter of fact, in fact***, en effet; ***in point of fact***, au fait; ***matter-of-fact man***, homme positif, *m.*
faction ['fækʃən], *n.* faction; (*fig.*) discorde, dissension, *f.*
factor ['fæktə], *n.* agent; facteur, *m.*
factory ['fæktri], *n.* usine, fabrique, *f.*; (*obs.*), comptoir (*d'outre-mer*) *m.*
faculty ['fækəlti], *n.* faculté, *f.*, pouvoir, talent, *m.*
fad [fæd], *n.* marotte, manie, *f.*
fade [feid], *v.t.* flétrir, faire flétrir.—*v.i.* se faner, se flétrir; disparaître, périr.
fag [fæg], *v.t.* forcer à piocher; fatiguer, éreinter; ***fagged out***, éreinté.—*v.i.* travailler dur, piocher (*à*).—*n.* fatigue, peine, corvée, *f.*; (*pop.*) cigarette, *f.*
fag-end ['fægend], *n.* (*pop.*) mégot (*de cigarette*), *m.*
faggot ['fægət], *n.* fagot, *m.*
fail [feil], *v.t.* manquer à, abandonner.—*v.i.* faillir; manquer (*to miss*); échouer (*ne pas réussir*); (*Comm.*) faire faillite.—*n.* manque, insuccès, *m.*
failing ['feiliŋ], *n.* défaut, *m.*, faute; (*Comm.*) faillite, *f.*—*prep.* à défaut de.
failure ['feiljə], *n.* manque, défaut (*want*); échec; insuccès, *m.*, affaire manquée, *f.*, fiasco, *m.*; chute (*d'une pièce etc.*); (*Comm.*) faillite, *f.*; ***he is a failure***, c'est un raté.
***fain** [fein], *adv.* avec plaisir, volontiers.
faint [feint], *a.* faible; affaibli; languissant; découragé; timide.—*v.i.* s'évanouir, défaillir.—*n.* évanouissement, *m.*
faint-hearted ['feinthɑ:tid], *a.* timide, sans courage, découragé.
fainting ['feintiŋ], *n.* évanouissement, *m.*, défaillance, *f.*
faintly ['feintli], *adv.* faiblement; mollement.
faintness ['feintnis], *n.* faiblesse, *f.*
fair [fɛə], *a.* beau; favorable (*vent*); clai (*teint*); blond (*cheveux etc.*); juste, équitable

(*fig.*) assez bon, passable; ***fair play***, franc jeu, *m.*; ***fair price***, juste prix, *m.*; ***that is not fair*** (*at games*), cela n'est pas de jeu.—*adv.* bien; de bonne foi, honorablement.—*n.* foire (*marché*), *f.*
fairly ['fɛəli], *adv.* bien; loyalement; doucement; avec justesse; de bonne foi; passablement, assez.
fairness ['fɛənis], *n.* beauté; couleur blonde (*des cheveux*); blancheur (*du teint*); équité, impartialité, *f.*
fairy ['fɛəri], *a.* des fées, féerique.—*n.* fée, *f.*
fairy-tale ['fɛəriteil], *n.* conte de fées, *m.*
faith [feiθ], *n.* foi, croyance; (*fig.*) fidélité, *f.*—*int.* ma foi! en vérité!
faithful ['feiθful], *a.* fidèle.
faithfully ['feiθfuli], *adv.* fidèlement; ***yours faithfully*** (*lettre d'affaires*), veuillez agréer mes salutations distinguées.
faithfulness ['feiθfulnis], *n.* fidélité, *f.*
faithless ['feiθlis], *a.* sans foi, infidèle.
faithlessness ['feiθlisnis], *n.* infidélité; déloyauté, *f.*
fake [feik], *v.t., v.i.* truquer, maquiller.
falcon ['fɔːlkən], *n.* faucon, *m.*
fall [fɔːl], *v.i. irr.* tomber; s'abaisser; baisser, diminuer; ***to fall away from***, abandonner, quitter; ***to fall back*** tomber en arrière; (*Mil.*) reculer; ***to fall down***, tomber par terre; ***to fall for***, tomber amoureux de; ***to fall for it***, s'y laisser prendre; ***to fall in***, s'écrouler; (*Mil.*) se mettre en rangs, s'aligner; ***to fall off***, tomber; diminuer; ***to fall out***, tomber; se brouiller; (*Mil.*) ***fall out!*** rompez vos rangs! ***to fall through***, échouer; ***to fall to***, se mettre à; ***to fall under***, être compris sous; tomber sous; ***to fall upon***, tomber sur, attaquer; incomber à.—*n.* chute, *f.*; (*Am.*) automne, *m.* ou *f.*; tombée (*de la nuit*); baisse (*de prix*), *f.*; éboulement (*de terre*), *m.*; chute, cascade (*de rivières etc.*); décrue (*des eaux*); diminution (*de quantité*), *f.*
fallacy ['fæləsi], *n.* erreur, fausseté, illusion, *f.*
fallible ['fæləbl], *a.* faillible.
fall-out ['fɔːlaut], *n.* retombées radioactives, *f.pl.*
fallow ['fælou], *a.* en jachère; (*fig.*) inculte; fauve (*daim etc.*).—*n.* jachère, friche, *f.*
false [fɔːls], *a.* faux, perfide, déloyal; infidèle; prétendu; illégal (*détention*).
falsehood ['fɔːlshud], *n.* mensonge, *m.*
falsely ['fɔːlsli], *adv.* faussement.
falseness ['fɔlsnis], *n.* fausseté; perfidie, *f.*
falsetto [fɔːl'setou], *n.* (*Mus.*) voix de fausset, *f.*
falsify ['fɔːlsifai], *v.t.* falsifier; fausser.
falter ['fɔːltə], *v.i.* hésiter; bégayer; chanceler.
faltering ['fɔːltəriŋ], *n.* hésitation, *f.*
fame [feim], *n.* gloire, renommée, *f.*
famed [feimd], *a.* renommé.
familiar [fə'miljə], *a.* familier, intime; de la famille; ***to be familiar with***, être familier avec, connaître.—*n.* ami intime; esprit familier, *m.*
familiarity [fəmili'æriti], *n.* familiarité, *f.*
familiarly [fə'miliəli], *adv.* familièrement, sans cérémonie.
family ['fæmili], *a.* de famille, de la famille.—*n.* famille, *f.*
famine ['fæmin], *n.* famine, disette, *f.*
famished ['fæmiʃt], *a.* affamé.
famous ['feiməs], *a.* fameux, célèbre.
famously ['feiməsli], *adv.* fameusement; (*fig.*) prodigieusement.
fan [fæn], *n.* éventail; ventilateur; (*colloq.*) admirateur enthousiaste (*d'un artiste* ou *d'un sport*), *m.*—*v.t.* éventer; souffler (*feu*); (*Agric.*) vanner; (*fig.*) exciter, activer.
fanatic [fə'nætik], *a.* and *n.* fanatique, *m., f.*
fanatical [fə'nætikəl], *a.* fanatique.
fanaticism [fə'nætisizm], *n.* fanatisme, *m.*
fancied ['fænsid], *a.* imaginaire, imaginé; (*Turf*) bien coté (*cheval*).
fancier ['fænsiə], *n.* amateur (*de*), *m.*
fanciful ['fænsiful], *a.* fantasque, capricieux.
fancy ['fænsi], *a.* de fantaisie.—*n.* fantaisie, imagination; idée, *f.*, caprice, goût (*pour*), *m.*, envie (*de*), *f.*—*v.t.* s'imaginer, se figurer; avoir du goût pour.—*v.i.* s'imaginer, se figurer; ***just fancy!*** figurez-vous!
fancy-dress ['fænsidres], *n.* travesti, *m.*; ***fancy-dress ball***, bal costumé, *m.*
fane [fein], *n.* temple, édifice sacré, *m.*
fanfare ['fænfɛə], *n.* fanfare, *f.*
fang [fæŋ], *n.* croc (*de chien*), *m.*; racine (*d'une dent*); défense (*de sanglier*); (*fig.*) griffe, *f.*
fantastic [fæn'tæstik], *a.* fantastique; fantasque (*personne*).
fantasy ['fæntəsi], *n.* fantaisie, *f.*
far [fɑː], *a.* (*comp.* **farther**, **further**; *superl.* **farthest**, **furthest**) lointain, éloigné, reculé; ***the Far East***, l'extrême Orient, *m.*—*adv.* loin, au loin; bien, fort, beaucoup; ***as far as***, aussi loin que, jusqu'à; ***by far***, de beaucoup; ***far and wide***, de tous côtés; ***how far?*** jusqu'où?
far-away ['fɑːrəwei], *a.* rêveur (*regard*); lointain.
farce [fɑːs], *n.* farce, *f.*
farcical ['fɑːsikl], *a.* burlesque; (*fig.*) drôle.
fare [fɛə], *v.i.* aller; se porter; se nourrir, vivre.—*n.* prix de la course; prix de la place, *m.*, place, *f.*; voyageur (*personne*), *m.*; chère (*aliment*), *f.*; ***bill of fare***, menu, *m.*, carte du jour, *f.*; ***return fare***, aller et retour, *m.*; ***single fare***, billet simple, *m.*
farewell ['fɛəwel, fɛə'wel], *a.* d'adieu.—*n.* adieu, *m.*
far-fetched [fɑː'fetʃt], *a.* recherché; tiré par les cheveux.
farm [fɑːm], *n.* ferme, *f.*—*v.t.* affermer, prendre à ferme; exploiter.
farmer ['fɑːmə], *n.* fermier, métayer; cultivateur, *m.*
farm-house ['fɑːmhaus], *n.* ferme, *f.*
farming ['fɑːmiŋ], *n.* agriculture, exploitation agricole, *f.*
farm-yard ['fɑːmjɑːd], *n.* basse-cour, *f.*
Faroe ['fɛərou] **Islands.** les îles Féroé, *f.pl.*
far-reaching ['fɑː'riːtʃiŋ], *a.* d'une grande portée.
farrier ['færiə] *n.* maréchal ferrant, *m.*
farther [FURTHER].
farthest [FURTHERMOST].
fascinate ['fæsineit], *v.t.* fasciner; charmer, séduire.
fascinating ['fæsineitiŋ], *a.* fascinateur, enchanteur, séduisant.
fascination [fæsi'neiʃən], *n.* fascination, *f.*, charme, *m.*
fascism ['fæʃizm], *n.* fascisme, *m.*
fascist ['fæʃist], *a.* and *n.* fasciste, *m., f.*

fashion ['fæʃən], *n.* façon, forme; mode, *f.*; le grand monde, *m.*; ***after a fashion***, tant bien que mal; ***in fashion***, à la mode; ***to set the fashion***, donner le ton.—*v.t.* façonner, former.
fashionable ['fæʃnəbl], *a.* à la mode, élégant, de bon ton, (*fam.*) chic.
fashionably ['fæʃnəbli], *adv.* à la mode, élégamment.
fast (1) [fɑːst], *n.* jeûne, *m.*—*v.i.* jeûner.
fast (2) [fɑːst], *a.* ferme, fixe (*solide*); fidèle (*constant*); bon teint (*couleur*); serré (*nœud*); (*Naut.*) amarré (*fixé*); bien fermé (*porte*); vite, rapide; en avance (*horloge etc.*); (*fig.*) dissolu; ***to make fast***, assujettir, fermer (*porte, fenêtre*); (*Naut.*) amarrer.—*adv.* ferme (*stable*); vite, rapidement (*avec célérité*); fort (*pluie*); ***to hold fast***, tenir bon; ***to stand fast***, ne pas broncher.
fasten [fɑːsn], *v.t.* attacher, fixer; lier; fermer (*fenêtre, porte etc.*).—*v.i.* s'attacher (*à*); se fermer.
fastener ['fɑːsnə], **fastening** ['fɑːsniŋ], *n.* attache; agrafe (*de robe*); fermeture, *f.*
fastidious [fæs'tidiəs], *a.* difficile; dédaigneux; délicat; exigeant.
fastness ['fɑːstnis], *n.* fermeté; vitesse; place forte (*forteresse*); légèreté de conduite, *f.*
fat [fæt], *a.* gras; gros (*personne*); (*fig.*) riche, fertile.—*n.* gras, *m.*; graisse; (*fig.*) substance, *f.*; (*pl.*) matières grasses, *f.pl.*
fatal [feitl], *a.* fatal, funeste; mortel.
fatality [fə'tæliti], *n.* fatalité, *f.*; accident mortel, *m.*
fatally ['feitəli], *adv.* fatalement, mortellement.
fate [feit], *n.* destin, sort, *m.*
fated ['feitid], *a.* destiné.
fateful ['feitful], *a.* fatal; décisif.
fat-head ['fæthed], *n.* (*colloq.*) nigaud, *m.*
father ['fɑːðə], *n.* père, *m.*; (*pl.*) pères, ancêtres, aïeux, *m.pl.*; ***godfather***, parrain, *m.*; ***grandfather***, grand-père, *m.*; ***stepfather***, beau-père, *m.*
father-in-law ['fɑːðərinlɔː], *n.* beau-père, *m.*
fatherland ['fɑːðəlænd], *n.* pays natal, *m.*, patrie, *f.*
fatherly ['fɑːðəli], *a.* paternel, de père.
fathom ['fæðəm], *n.* toise; (*Naut.*) brasse (=6 pieds=1 m. 829); (*fig.*) portée, profondeur, *f.*—*v.t.* sonder; (*fig.*) approfondir.
fatigue [fə'tiːg], *n.* fatigue; (*Mil.*) corvée, *f.*—*v.t.* fatiguer, lasser.
fatiguing [fə'tiːgiŋ], *a.* fatigant.—*pres.p.* fatiguant.
fatten [fætn], *v.t.* engraisser; (*fig.*) enrichir.
fattening ['fætniŋ], *a.* engraissant.—*n.* engraissement, *m.*
fatty ['fæti], *a.* graisseux.
fatuous ['fætjuəs], *a.* sot; béat.
fatuousness ['fætjuəsnis], *n.* fatuité, *f.*
fault [fɔːlt], *n.* faute, *f.*; défaut, vice, *m.*; (*Geol.*) faille, *f.*
faultless ['fɔːltlis], *a.* sans défaut, sans faute, impeccable.
faultlessly ['fɔːltlisli], *adv.* irréprochablement.
faultlessness ['fɔːltlisnis], *n.* perfection, *f.*
faulty ['fɔːlti], *a.* fautif, blâmable, défectueux.
favour ['feivə], *n.* faveur, *f.*, bonnes grâces, *f.pl.*; bienfait, *m.*; grâce (*permission*), *f.*; couleurs, faveurs (*rubans*), *f.pl.*; (*Comm.* honorée, *f.*—*v.t.* favoriser, honorer (*de*).
favourable ['feivərəbl], *a.* favorable.
favourably ['feivərəbli], *adv.* favorablement.
favourite ['feivərit], *a.* favori, préféré.—*n.* favori, *m.*
fawn [fɔːn], *n.* faon, *m.*—*v.i.* ***to fawn upon***, caresser, flatter.
fawning ['fɔːniŋ], *a.* flatteur, servile.—*n.* caresse, flatterie, *f.*
fear [fiə], *n.* crainte, peur; inquiétude, *f.*; ***for fear of***, de peur de.—*v.t.* craindre, redouter, avoir peur de.—*v.i.* craindre, avoir peur.
fearful ['fiəful], *a.* craintif, timide; terrible, affreux, effrayant.
fearless ['fiəlis], *a.* sans peur, intrépide.
fearlessly ['fiəlisli], *adv.* sans crainte, avec intrépidité.
feasible ['fiːzəbl], *a.* faisable, praticable.
feast [fiːst], *n.* festin, *m.*; fête, *f.*; régal, *m.*—*v.t.* fêter, régaler.—*v.i.* faire festin, se régaler.
feat [fiːt], *n.* exploit, fait, haut fait, *m.*
feather ['feðə], *n.* plume; penne (*aile et queue d'oiseau*), *f.*; (*Mil.*) plumet, *m.*—*v.t.* orner d'une plume; ***to feather one's nest***, faire sa pelote.
feature ['fiːtʃə], *n.* trait; (*pl.*) visage, *m.* figure; (*fig.*) spécialité, *f.*
February ['februəri]. février, *m.*
feckless ['feklis], *a.* faible, veule.
fecundity [fə'kʌnditi], *n.* fécondité, *f.*
federal ['fedərəl], *a.* fédéral.
federate ['fedərit], *a.* fédéré.—['fedəreit], *v.t.* fédérer.—*v.i.* se fédérer.
federation [fedə'reiʃən], *n.* fédération, *f.*
fee [fiː], *n.* honoraires, *m.pl.*, cachet, salaire; (*Eccles. etc.*) droit, *m.*
feeble [fiːbl], *a.* faible; débile.
feebleness ['fiːblnis], *n.* faiblesse, *f.*
feebly ['fiːbli], *adv.* faiblement.
feed [fiːd], *n.* nourriture; pâture, *f.*, pâturage (*pour bestiaux*), *m.*—*v.t. irr.* nourrir; donner à manger à; paître, faire paître (*bestiaux*); (*pop.*) ***to be fed up***, en avoir marre.—*v.i.* se nourrir; paître (*animaux*).
feed-back ['fiːdbæk], *n.* (*Rad.*) rétro-action, *f.*
feeding ['fiːdiŋ], *n.* nourriture; pâture (*pour bestiaux*), *f.*
feeding bottle ['fiːdiŋbɔtl], *n.* biberon, *m.*
feel [fiːl], *v.t. irr.* tâter, toucher, sentir; éprouver; ***to feel one's way***, avancer à tâtons.—*v.i.* sentir, se sentir; se trouver; ***to feel cold***, avoir froid; ***to feel like doing something***, avoir envie de faire quelque chose.—*n.* toucher; attouchement; tact, *m.*
feeler ['fiːlə], *n.* antenne (*d'insecte*), *f.*; (*fig.*) ballon d'essai, *m.*
feeling ['fiːliŋ], *a.* tendre, touchant.—*n.* toucher; sentiment, *m.*, sensibilité, émotion, *f.*
feet [FOOT].
feign [fein], *v.t.* feindre, simuler.—*v.i.* feindre, faire semblant (*de*).
feigned [feind], *a.* feint, simulé.
feint [feint], *n.* feinte, *f.*—*v.i.* feinter.
felicitate [fi'lisiteit], *v.t.* féliciter.
felicitation [filisi'teiʃən], *n.* félicitation, *f.*
felicity [fi'lisiti], *n.* félicité, *f.*, bonheur, *m.*
fell (1) [fel], *v.t.* abattre, assommer, terrasser.

fell (2) [fel], *past* [FALL].
fellow ['felou], *n.* compagnon, camarade, confrère; associé, membre; pendant, pareil (*choses*); (*colloq.*) garçon; individu, type, *m.*; ***good fellow***, brave type.
fellow-citizen ['felou'sitizn], *n.* concitoyen, *m.*
fellow-countryman ['felou'kʌntrimən], *n.* (*pl.* **-men** [men]) compatriote, *m.*
fellow-feeling ['felou'fi:liŋ], *n.* sympathie, *f.*
fellowship ['felouʃip], *n.* société, association; camaraderie, *f.*
fellow-traveller ['felou'trævlə], *n.* compagnon de voyage; (*Polit.*) sympathisant communiste, communisant, *m.*
felon ['felən], *a.* félon, traître.—*n.* criminel, *m.*
felony ['feləni], *n.* crime, *m.*
felt (1) [felt], *n.* feutre, chapeau de feutre, *m.*; ***roofing felt***, carton bitumé, *m.*
felt (2) [felt], *past* [FEEL].
female ['fi:meil], *a.* féminin, de femme; femelle (*animaux*); ***a female friend***, une amie.—*n.* femme; jeune personne; femelle (*animaux*), *f.*
feminine ['feminin], *a.* féminin.
fen [fen], *n.* marais, marécage, *m.*
fence [fens], *n.* clôture, enceinte; palissade, barrière; (*Turf*) haie; (*Spt.*) escrime (*à l'épée*); (*fig.*) défense, *f.*; (*slang*) receleur (*d'objets volés*), *m.*; ***to sit on the fence***, (*fig.*) ne pas s'engager, ménager la chèvre et le chou.—*v.t.* enclore, mettre une clôture à, palissader; (*fig.*) protéger.—*v.i.* faire des armes.
fencing ['fensiŋ], *n.* (*Spt.*) escrime; enceinte, clôture, *f.*
fencing-master ['fensiŋmɑ:stə], *n.* maître d'armes, *m.*
fend [fend], *v.t.* ***to fend off***, parer.—*v.i.* ***to fend for oneself***, se débrouiller, veiller à ses intérêts.
fender ['fendə], *n.* garde-feu, *m.*; (*Naut.*) défense, *f.*; (*Am. Motor.*) pare-boue, *m.*
ferment ['fə:mənt], *n.* ferment, *m.*; fermentation, *f.*—[fə:'ment], *v.t.* faire fermenter.—*v.i.* fermenter.
fermentation [fə:mən'teiʃən], *n.* fermentation, *f.*
fern [fə:n], *n.* fougère, *f.*
ferocious [fə'rouʃəs], *a.* féroce.
ferociously [fə'rouʃəsli], *adv.* avec férocité.
ferocity [fə'rɔsiti], *n.* férocité, *f.*
ferret ['ferit], *n.* furet, *m.*—*v.t.* fureter; ***to ferret out***, dépister, dénicher.
ferrule ['feru:l], *n.* virole (*anneau*), *f.*
ferry ['feri], *v.t.* passer en bac.—*n.* bac, passage, *m.*; ***air-ferry***, avion transbordeur, *m.*
ferry-boat ['feribout], *n.* bac, bateau transbordeur de trains, *m.*
fertile ['fə:tail], *a.* fertile, fécond.
fertility [fə'tiliti], *n.* fertilité, fécondité, *f.*
fertilize ['fə:tilaiz], *v.t.* fertiliser.
fertilizer ['fə:tilaizə], *n.* fertilisant, engrais, *m.*
fervent ['fə:vənt], *a.* ardent, fervent, vif.
fervently ['fə:vəntli], *adv.* ardemment, avec ferveur.
fester ['festə], *v.i.* s'ulcérer; (*fig.*) se corrompre.—*n.* abcès, *m.*, pustule, *f.*
festival ['festivl], *a.* de fête, joyeux.—*n.* fête, *f.*; (*Mus., Theat.*) festival, *m.*
festive ['festiv], *a.* de fête, joyeux.
festivity [fes'tiviti], *n.* fête, *f.*; réjouissances, *f.pl.*
festoon [fes'tu:n], *n.* feston, *m.*—*v.t.* festonner (*de*).
fetch [fetʃ], *v.t.* chercher, aller chercher; apporter (*choses*); amener (*personnes etc.*); rapporter (*prix*).—*n.* ruse, *f.*; tour, *m.*
fête [feit], *n.* fête, *f.*—*v.t.* fêter.
fetlock ['fetlɔk], *n.* fanon (de cheval), *m.*
fetter ['fetə], *v.t.* entraver, enchaîner.
fetters ['fetəz], *n.pl.* (*fig.*) fers, *m.pl.*, chaînes; entraves (*de cheval*), *f.pl.*
fettle [fetl], *v.t.* arranger, préparer.—*n.* bon état, *m.*
feud [fju:d], *n.* querelle; vendetta, *f.*
feudal [fju:dl], *a.* féodal.
feudalism ['fju:dlizm], *n.* féodalité, *f.*
fever ['fi:və], *n.* fièvre, *f.*
feverish ['fi:vəriʃ], *a.* fiévreux; (*fig.*) fébrile.
few [fju:], *a.* peu de; ***a few***, quelques.—*n.* peu de gens, *m.pl.*; ***a few***, quelques-uns, *m.pl.*, quelques-unes, *f.pl.*
fewer ['fju:ə], *a.* moins (*de*); moins nombreux.
fiasco [fi'æskou], *n.* fiasco, four, *m.*
fib [fib], *n.* petit mensonge, *m.*—*v.i.* mentir.
fibber ['fibə], *n.* menteur, *m.*
fibre ['faibə], *n.* fibre, *f.*
fibrositis [faibrə'saitis], *n.* (*Med.*) cellulite, *f.*
fibrous ['faibrəs], *a.* fibreux.
fickle [fikl], *a.* volage, inconstant.
fickleness ['fiklnis], *n.* inconstance, légèreté, *f.*
fiction ['fikʃən], *n.* fiction, *f.*; ***works of fiction***, romans, *m.pl.*
fictitious [fik'tiʃəs], *a.* fictif, imaginaire; (*fig.*) faux, factice.
fiddle [fidl], *n.* violon; (*pej.*) crincrin, *m.*; (*pop.*) resquille, combine, *f.*—*v.i.* jouer du violon; (*fig.*) niaiser (*baguenauder*); (*pop.*) resquiller.
fiddler ['fidlə], *n.* joueur de violon; ménétrier, *m.*
fiddlesticks! ['fidlstiks], *int.* bah! quelle blague!
fidelity [fi'deliti], *n.* fidélité, *f.*
fidget ['fidʒit], *n.* agitation, *f.*; être remuant (*personne*), *m.*—*v.i.* se remuer, s'agiter.
fidgety ['fidʒiti], *a.* remuant, agité; ennuyeux (*gênant*).
field [fi:ld], *n.* champ; pré, *m.*, prairie; (*Mil.*) campagne, *f.*; champ de bataille, *m.*; (*Turf etc.*) courants, *m.pl.*; ***in the scientific field***, dans le domaine des sciences.—*v.t.* (*Cricket*) arrêter (*une balle*); réunir (*équipe*).—*v.i.* (*Cricket*) tenir le champ.
field-day ['fi:lddei], *n.* (*Mil.*) jour de manœuvres; (*fig.*) jour de grand succès, *m.*
field-marshal ['fi:ldmɑ:ʃl], *n.* maréchal, *m.*
fiend [fi:nd], *n.* démon, *m.*
fiendish ['fi:ndiʃ], *a.* diabolique, infernal.
fierce [fiəs], *a.* féroce, farouche, furieux.
fiercely ['fiəsli], *adv.* férocement, furieusement.
fierceness ['fiəsnis], *n.* violence, fureur, brutalité, *f.*; (*fig.*) acharnement, *m.*
fieriness ['faiərinis], *n.* fougue, ardeur, *f.*
fiery ['faiəri], *a.* de feu; (*fig.*) ardent, fougueux.
fife [faif], *n.* fifre, *m.*
fifteen [fif'ti:n], *a.* and *n.* quinze, *m.*
fifteenth [fif'ti:nθ], *a.* quinze (*jour du mois, roi etc.*).—*n.* quinzième (*fraction*), *m.*

fifth [fifθ], *a.* cinquième; cinq (*jour du mois, roi etc.*); ***Charles the Fifth***, Charles-Quint.—*n.* cinquième (*fraction*), *m.*; (*Mus.*) quinte, *f.*
fiftieth [ˈfiftiəθ], *a.* cinquantième.—*n.* cinquantième (*fraction*), *m.*
fifty [ˈfifti], *a.* and *n.* cinquante, *m.*; ***about fifty***, une cinquantaine.
fig [fig], *n.* figue, *f.*; figuier (*arbre*), *m.*
fight [fait], *v.t. irr.* se battre avec, combattre; livrer (*une bataille*).—*v.i.* se battre; combattre (*avec*).—*n.* combat, *m.*, bataille; (*fig.*) lutte, *f.*
fighter [ˈfaitə], *n.* combattant; (*pej.*) batailleur; (*Av.*) chasseur, *m.*
fighting [ˈfaitiŋ], *n.* combat, *m.*; lutte, *f.*
figment [ˈfigmənt], *n.* fiction, invention, *f.*
figurative [ˈfigjuərətiv], *a.* figuré; figuratif.
figuratively [ˈfigjuərətivli], *adv.* au figuré; figurativement.
figure [ˈfigə], *n.* figure; taille, tournure (*d'une personne*), *f.*; dessin (*sur un tissu*); (*Arith.*) chiffre, *m.*; ***figure of speech***, figure de rhétorique, métaphore; (*fam.*) façon de parler, *f.*; ***to cut a figure***, faire figure.—*v.t.* figurer, former; façonner; (*fig.*) imaginer; ***to figure out***, calculer.—*v.i.* figurer.
figure-head [ˈfigəhed], *n.* (*Naut.*) figure de proue, *f.*; (*fig.*) homme de paille; prête-nom, *m.*
Fiji [ˈfiːdʒiː], **the Fiji Islands.** les îles Fidji *ou* Viti, *f.pl.*
filament [ˈfiləmənt], *n.* filament, *m.*
filbert [ˈfilbət], *n.* aveline, grosse noisette, *f.*
filch [filtʃ], *v.t.* escamoter, filouter, chiper.
file [fail], *n.* lime (*outil*); liasse, *f.*, dossier, classeur (*de papiers*), *m.*; liste; collection (*de journaux*); (*Mil.*) file; (*Theat. etc.*) queue, *f.*; ***card-index file***, fichier, *m.*—*v.t.* limer, affiler; mettre en liasse; (*Law*) déposer (*une requête etc.*); ***to file away***, classer.—*v.i.* (*Mil.*) marcher à la file; ***to file off*** or ***past***, défiler.
filial [ˈfiliəl], *a.* filial.
filibuster [ˈfilibʌstə], *n.* flibustier, *m.*
filing [ˈfailiŋ], *n.* limage, *m.*; mise en liasse, *f.*, classement, *m.*; (*pl.*) limaille, *f.*
filing-cabinet [ˈfailiŋkæbinit], *n.* cartonnier, classeur, *m.*
fill [fil], *v.t.* emplir, remplir; combler (*jusqu'au bord*); occuper; rassasier; ***to fill a tooth***, plomber une dent.—*v.i.* se remplir, s'emplir.—*n.* suffisance, *f.*; (*colloq.*) ***one's fill***, tout son soûl.
fillet [ˈfilit], *n.* bandeau; filet (*de poisson*), *m.*
filling [ˈfiliŋ], *a.* qui remplit; rassasiant.
filling-station [ˈfiliŋˈsteiʃən], *n.* poste d'essence, *m.*
filly [ˈfili], *n.* pouliche, *f.*
film [film], *n.* taie (*devant les yeux*), pellicule; (*Anat.*) tunique, *f.*; (*fig.*) nuage, voile, *m.*; (*Phot.*) pellicule, couche sensible, *f.*; (*Cine.*) film, *m.*; ***film script***, scénario, script, *m.*; ***film star***, vedette de cinéma, *f.*—*v.t.* couvrir d'une tunique, d'une pellicule etc.; filmer, mettre à l'écran.—*v.i.* tourner un film.
film-strip [ˈfilmstrip], *n.* film fixe, *m.*
filter [ˈfiltə], *n.* filtre, *m.*—*v.t.* filtrer.
filter-tip [ˈfiltəˈtip], *n.* bout filtrant, *m.*
filth [filθ], *n.* ordure saleté; (*fig.*) corruption, *f.*
filthy [ˈfilθi], *a.* sale, immonde; (*fig.*) obscène, infect.
fin [fin], *n.* nageoire, *f.*; aileron (*de requin*), *m.*; (*Naut.*, *Av.*) dérive; (*Motor.*) ailette (*de radiateur*), *f.*
final [fainl], *a.* final, dernier; décisif.—*n.* (*Spt.*) finale, *f.*
finally [ˈfainəli], *adv.* enfin, finalement; définitivement.
finance [fiˈnæns, faiˈnæns], *n.* finance, *f.*
financial [fiˈnænʃəl], *a.* financier.
financier [fiˈnænsiə], *n.* financier, *m.*
finch [fintʃ], *n.* (*Orn.*) pinson, *m.*
find [faind], *v.t. irr.* trouver; estimer; (*Law*) déclarer (*coupable*); prononcer (*un verdict*); (*fig.*) pourvoir; ***to find out***, trouver, découvrir, inventer, résoudre; démasquer; ***to find out about***, se renseigner sur; découvrir la vérité de.—*n.* découverte, trouvaille, *f.*
finding [ˈfaindiŋ], *n.* (*Law*) verdict, *m.*
fine (1) [fain], *n.* amende, *f.*—*v.t.* mettre à l'amende.
fine (2) [fain], *a.* fin; raffiné; subtil; beau (*à voir*); (*fig.*) bon, accompli; (*colloq.*) fameux; ***it is fine***, il fait beau (*temps*).
fine arts [fainˈɑːts], *n.pl.* beaux arts, *m.pl.*
finely [ˈfainli], *adv.* fin, délicatement; élégamment; (*colloq.*) bien; (*iron.*) joliment.
fineness [ˈfainnis], *n.* finesse, délicatesse, *f.*
finery [ˈfainəri], *n.* parure, *f.*, beaux habits, *m.pl.*
finesse [fiˈnes], *n.* finesse, *f.*
finger [ˈfiŋgə], *n.* doigt, *m.*; (*fig.*) main, *f.*—*v.t.* toucher, manier.—*v.i.* (*Mus.*) doigter.
fingering [ˈfiŋgəriŋ], *n.* maniement; (*Mus.*) doigté, *m.*
finger-nail [ˈfiŋgəneil], *n.* ongle de la main, *m.*
finger-print [ˈfiŋgəprint], *n.* empreinte digitale, *f.*
finger-stall [ˈfiŋgəstɔːl], *n.* doigtier, *m.*
finical [ˈfinikl], **finicking** [ˈfinikiŋ], (*colloq.*) **finicky** [ˈfiniki], *a.* précieux, méticuleux, vétilleux.
finish [ˈfiniʃ], *v.t.* finir, terminer; achever; (*Tech.*) usiner.—*v.i.* cesser, finir, prendre fin.—*n.* fini, *m.*; (*fig.*) fin; (*Spt.*) arrivée, *f.*
finished [ˈfiniʃt], *a.* fini; (*fig.*) parfait.
finishing [ˈfiniʃiŋ], *a.* dernier; (*Spt.*) ***finishing line***, ligne d'arrivée, *f.*
finite [ˈfainait], *a.* fini; borné.
Finland [ˈfinlənd]. la Finlande, *f.*
Finn [fin], *n.* Finlandais, Finnois, *m.*
Finnish [ˈfiniʃ], *a.* finlandais.—*n.* finnois (*langue*), *m.*
fir [fəː], *n.* sapin; bois de sapin, *m.*
fir-cone [ˈfəːkoun], *n.* pomme de pin, *f.*
fire [faiə], *n.* feu; incendie (*accidentel*), *m.*; (*fig.*) ardeur, *f.*; ***fire !*** au feu! ***to be on fire***, être en feu; ***to catch fire***, prendre feu; ***to hang fire***, faire long feu; ***to miss fire***, rater; ***to set on fire, to set fire to***, mettre le feu à.—*v.t.* mettre le feu à; embraser, incendier; tirer (*fusil*); (*pop.*) renvoyer.—*v.i.* prendre feu; tirer; (*Motor.*) donner; ***fire !*** (*Mil.*) feu!
fire-alarm [ˈfaiərəlɑːm], *n.* avertisseur d'incendie, *m.*
fire-arms [ˈfaiərɑːmz], *n.pl.* armes à feu, *f.pl.*

fire-brigade ['faiəbrigeid], *n.* (corps de) sapeurs pompiers, *m.*
fire-engine ['faiərendʒin], *n.* pompe à incendie, *f.*
fire-escape ['faiəriskeip], *n.* échelle de sauvetage, *f.*
fire-extinguisher ['faiərikstiŋgwiʃə], *n.* extincteur, *m.*
fire-fly ['faiəflai], *n.* luciole, *f.*
fire-guard ['faiəgɑːd], *n.* garde-feu, *m.*
fireman ['faiəmən], *n.* (*pl.* **-men** [men]) pompier, *m.*
fireplace ['faiəpleis], *n.* cheminée, *f.*, foyer, âtre, *m.*
fireproof ['faiəpruːf], *a.* incombustible, ignifuge.
fireside ['faiəsaid], *n.* coin du feu; (*fig.*) foyer domestique, *m.*
fire-station ['faiəsteiʃən], *n.* caserne de pompiers, *f.*
fireworks ['faiəwəːks], *n.pl.* feu d'artifice, *m.*
firing ['faiəriŋ], *n.* action d'incendier, *f.*; chauffage (*heating*), *m.*; cuisson (*de poterie etc.*), *f.*; combustible (*fuel*); (*Mil.*) feu, tir, *m.*, fusillade, *f.*
firm [fəːm], *a.* ferme, solide; constant.—*n.* maison de commerce, raison sociale, firme, *f.*
firmament ['fəːməmənt], *n.* firmament, *m.*
firmly ['fəːmli], *adv.* fermement, solidement.
firmness ['fəːmnis], *n.* fermeté, solidité, *f.*
first [fəːst], *a.* premier; (*in compounds*) unième; ***twenty-first***, vingt et unième.—*n.* (le) premier, *m.*, (la) première, *f.*—*adv.* premièrement; ***at first***, d'abord.
first-aid ['fəːst'eid], *n.* premiers secours, *m.pl.*; ***first-aid post***, poste de secours, *m.*
first-born ['fəːstbɔːn], *a.* premier-né, aîné.
first-class ['fəːst'klɑːs], **first-rate** ['fəːst'reit], *a.* de premier ordre; de premier choix; (*colloq.*) de première force; ***first-class compartment***, compartiment de première classe, *m.*
firth [fəːθ], *n.* (*Sc.*) estuaire, *m.*
fiscal ['fiskəl], *a.* fiscal.
fiscally ['fiskəli], *adv.* fiscalement.
fish [fiʃ], *n.* poisson, *m.*; ***a pretty kettle of fish***, un beau gâchis; ***a queer fish***, un drôle de type.—*v.t.* pêcher.—*v.i.* pêcher; ***to fish for***, pêcher; (*fig.*) rechercher, quêter.
fish-bone ['fiʃboun], *n.* arête, *f.*
fisher ['fiʃə], **fisherman** ['fiʃəmən] (*pl.* **-men** [men]), *n.* pêcheur, *m.*
fishery ['fiʃəri], *n.* pêche; pêcherie, *f.*
fish-hook ['fiʃhuk], *n.* hameçon.
fishing ['fiʃiŋ], *n.* pêche, *f.*; ***to go fishing***, aller à la pêche.
fishing-boat ['fiʃiŋbout], *n.* bateau de pêche, *m.*
fishing-rod ['fiʃiŋrɔd], *n.* canne à pêche, *f.*
fish-knife ['fiʃnaif], *n.* couteau à poisson, *m.*
fishmonger ['fiʃmʌŋgə], *n.* marchand de poisson, *m.*
fish-slice ['fiʃslais], *n.* truelle à poisson, *f.*
fishy ['fiʃi], *a.* de poisson, poissonneux; qui sent le poisson; (*slang*) louche, véreux.
fission ['fiʃən], *n.* (*Biol.*) fissiparité; (*Phys*). fission, désintégration, *f.*; ***nuclear fission***, fission nucléaire.
fissure ['fiʃə], *n.* fissure, fente, *f.*
fist [fist], *n.* poing, *m.*
fisted ['fistid], *a.* ***close-fisted***, avare, dur à la détente.
fisticuffs ['fistikʌfs], *n.pl.* coups de poing, *m.pl.*
fit (1) [fit], *n.* accès (*de colère etc.*), *m.*; attaque (*de maladie*); convulsion, *f.*; ***by fits and starts***, à bâtons rompus, par accès.
fit (2) [fit], *a.* propre, bon, convenable (*à*); juste, à propos; capable (*de*); en bonne santé, en forme; ***to think fit***, juger convenable, juger bon.—*n.* ajustement (*de vêtements*), *m.*; (*fig.*) coupe, forme, *f.*—*v.t.* convenir à; aller à (*vêtements*); habiller; adapter, ajuster; ***to fit out***, équiper, monter, armer (*un navire*).—*v.i.* convenir; s'adapter (*à*), aller bien (*vêtements*); ***to fit in with***, s'accorder avec.
fitful ['fitful], *a.* agité; capricieux; irrégulier.
fitfully ['fitfuli], *adv.* par boutades; irrégulièrement.
fitly ['fitli], *adv.* à propos, convenablement.
fitness ['fitnis], *n.* convenance, *f.*; à-propos, *m.*; ***physical fitness***, bonne forme, *f.*
fitter ['fitə], *n.* ajusteur; (*Dress.*) essayeur, *m.*
fitting ['fitiŋ], *a.* convenable, à propos, juste. —*n.* ajustement, essayage, *m.*, (*pl.*) garniture, *f.*
five [faiv], *a.* and *n.* cinq, *m.*
fix [fiks], *v.t.* fixer, attacher, arrêter, établir; (*colloq.*) réparer.—*v.i.* se fixer.—*n.* difficulté, impasse, *f.*, embarras, *m.*
fixation [fik'seiʃən], *n.* fixation, *f.*
fixed [fikst], *a.* fixe, fixé.
fixedly ['fiksidli], *adv.* fixement.
fixture ['fikstʃə], *n.* meuble à demeure, *m.*, agencements fixes, *m.pl.*; match, engagement (*prévu, annoncé*), *m.*
fizzy ['fizi], *a.* gazeux (*limonade etc.*), mousseux (*vin*).
flabby ['flæbi], *a.* flasque; mollasse (*personne*).
flag (1) [flæg], *v.i.* pendre mollement; se relâcher, faiblir; s'affaisser.
flag (2) [flæg], *n.* drapeau; (*Naut.*) pavillon; iris (*plante*); carreau, *m.*, dalle (*pierre*), *f.*—*v.t.* paver, daller; pavoiser.
flag-day ['flægdei], *n.* jour de quête, *m.*
flag-officer ['flægɔfisə], *n.* chef d'escadre, *m.*
flagon ['flægən], *n.* flacon, *m.*; burette (*d'église*), *f.*
flagrancy ['fleigrənsi], *n.* énormité, notoriété, *f.*
flagrant ['fleigrənt], *a.* flagrant, notoire, énorme.
flag-ship ['flægʃip], *n.* vaisseau amiral, *m.*
flagstaff ['flægstɑːf], *n.* mât de pavillon, *m.*
flagstone ['flægstoun], *n.* dalle, *f.*
flail [fleil], *n.* fléau, *m.*
flair [flɛə], *n.* perspicacité, *f.*, flair, *m.*; aptitude (*à*), *f.*
flake [fleik], *n.* flocon, *m.*; écaille; étincelle, *f.* —*v.t.* former en flocons, écailler.—*v.i.* s'écailler.
flaky ['fleiki], *a.* floconneux; écaillé; feuilleté (*pâtisserie*).
flame [fleim], *n.* flamme, *f.*; feu, *m.*—*v.i.* flamber.
flaming ['fleimiŋ], *a.* flamboyant, flambant; (*fig.*) violent, ardent; (*pop.*) sacré.
flamingo [flə'miŋgou], *n.* (*Orn.*) flamant, *m.*
flan [flæn], *n.* flan, *m.*
Flanders ['flɑːndəz]. la Flandre, *f.*

flange [flændʒ], *n.* bride, *f.*, rebord (*d'un tube etc.*); (*Tech.*) boudin (*de roue*), *m.*; (*Motor.*) ailette, collerette, *f.*
flank [flæŋk], *n.* flanc; côté, *m.*—*v.t.* flanquer (*de*); (*Mil.*) prendre en flanc.—*v.i.* border.
flannel [flænl], *a.* de flanelle.—*n.* flanelle, *f.*; (*pl.*) pantalon de flanelle, *m.*
flap [flæp], *v.t.* frapper légèrement; battre, agiter.—*v.i.* battre légèrement; (*fig.*, *pop.*) s'affoler.—*n.* battement (*d'aile*); claquement (*de voile*); petit coup (*de la main*), *m.*, tape, *f.*; battant (*d'une table etc.*), *m.*; patte (*d'une poche*), *f.*, pan (*d'un habit*); rabat (*d'une enveloppe*); (*fig.*, *pop.*) affolement, *m.*
flare [flɛə], *v.i.* flamboyer; s'évaser (*jupe*); ***to flare up***, flamber; (*fig.*) se mettre en colère.—*n.* flamme, *f.*; (*Av.*) brûlot, *m.*
flash [flæʃ], *n.* éclair, éclat, jet de lumière; (*fig.*) trait; (*Mil.*) écusson, *m.*—*v.t.* faire jaillir, lancer.—*v.i.* luire, éclater, étinceler.
flashy ['flæʃi], *a.* voyant, clinquant; superficiel.
flask [flɑːsk], *n.* flacon, *m.*, gourde, *f.*
flat [flæt], *a.* plat; étendu (*à terre*); éventé (*vin etc.*); (*Comm.*) languissant; (*Mus.*) bémol; grave (*son*); (*fig.*) net, clair; fade, insipide (*goût*).—*n.* surface plane, *f.*; étage (*d'une maison*), appartement; (*Mus.*) bémol; (*Theat.*) châssis, *m.*
flat-iron ['flætaiən], *n.* fer à repasser, *m.*
flatly ['flætli], *adv.* à plat; (*fig.*) nettement, clairement.
flatten [flætn], *v.t.* aplatir, aplanir; éventer (*boisson alcoolique*); (*fig.*) abattre, attrister; (*Mus.*) rendre grave.—*v.i.* s'aplatir; s'éventer (*boisson alcoolique*).
flatter ['flætə], *v.t.* flatter.
flatterer ['flætərə], *n.* flatteur, *m.*
flattering ['flætəriŋ], *a.* flatteur.
flattery ['flætəri], *n.* flatterie, *f.*
flatulence ['flætjuləns], *n.* flatuosité; flatulence, *f.*
flatulent ['flætjulənt], *a.* flatueux.
flaunt [flɔːnt], *v.t.* faire parade de, étaler, déployer.—*v.i.* se pavaner, parader, flotter.—*n.* étalage, *m.*, parade, *f.*
flavour ['fleivə], *n.* saveur, *f.*; goût, fumet (*de viande*); arome (*de thé, café etc.*); bouquet (*de vin*), *m.*—*v.t.* donner du goût, un arome etc. à, assaisonner (*de*).
flavouring ['fleivəriŋ], *n.* assaisonnement, *m.*
flaw [flɔː], *n.* défaut, *m.*; fêlure; brèche, fente; paille (*de pierres précieuses*), *f.*
flawless ['flɔːlis], *a.* parfait, sans défaut.
flax [flæks], *a.* de lin.—*n.* lin, *m.*
flaxen ['flæksən], *a.* de lin; blond filasse (*cheveux*).
flay [flei], *v.t.* écorcher.
flaying ['fleiiŋ], *n.* écorchement, *m.*
flea [fliː], *n.* puce, *f.*
fleck [flek], *n.* tache, moucheture, marque, *f.*—*v.t.* moucheter, tacheter (*de*).
fledg(e)ling ['fledʒliŋ], *n.* oisillon, *m.*
flee [fliː], *v.t. irr.* fuir, éviter.—*v.i.* s'enfuir, se réfugier.
fleece [fliːs], *n.* toison, *f.*—*v.t.* tondre; (*fig.*) écorcher, plumer.
fleecy ['fliːsi], *a.* laineux, (*fig.*) floconneux.
fleet (1) [fliːt], *n.* flotte, *f.*; ***the Home Fleet***, la flotte métropolitaine.
fleet (2) [fliːt], *a.* vite, rapide, leste.
fleeting ['fliːtiŋ], *a.* fugitif, passager.
Fleming ['flemiŋ], *n.* Flamand, *m.*
Flemish ['flemiʃ], *a.* flammand.—*n.* flamand (*langue*), *m.*
flesh [fleʃ], *n.* chair; viande (*meat*), *f.*; ***in the flesh***, en chair et en os; ***to put on flesh***, s'empâter, prendre de l'embonpoint.—*v.t.* (*Hunt.*) acharner; écharner (*peaux*).
fleshy ['fleʃi], *a.* charnu.
flex (1) [fleks], *n.* fil électrique, *m.*
flex (2) [fleks], *v.t.* fléchir.
flexibility [fleksi'biliti], *n.* flexibilité, souplesse, *f.*
flexible ['fleksibl], *a.* flexible, souple.
flick [flik], *n.* petit coup (*de fouet, de torchon*), *m.*; chiquenaude, *f.*; (*pl.*) (*pop.*) ciné, *m.*—*v.t.* effleurer; donner une chiquenaude à.
flicker ['flikə], *v.i.* trembloter, vaciller (*lumière*); ciller (*paupières*).
flickering ['flikəriŋ], *a.* vacillant, clignotant.—*n.* trémoussement; clignement, *m.*; vacillation, *f.*
flight [flait], *n.* vol, *m.*, volée (*d'oiseaux etc.*); fuite, *f.*; (*fig.*) élan, *m.*; (*Av.*) escadrille, *f.*; ***flight of stairs***, escalier, *m.*; ***flight of steps***, perron, *m.*; ***in flight***, en déroute.
flightiness ['flaitinis], *n.* légèreté, étourderie, *f.*
flighty ['flaiti], *a.* étourdi, léger; volage.
flimsiness ['flimzinis], *n.* légèreté; (*fig.*) mesquinerie, *f.*
flimsy ['flimzi], *a.* mollasse, léger, sans consistance.
flinch [flintʃ], *v.i.* reculer, céder.
fling [fliŋ], *v.t. irr.* jeter, lancer.—*n.* coup (*lancé*), *m.*; ruade (*de cheval*), *f.*; pas seul (*danse écossaise*); (*fig.*) essai; trait, coup de patte, *m.*, raillerie, *f.*
flint [flint], *n.* silex, *m.*, pierre à briquet; (*fig.*) roche, dureté, *f.*
flip [flip], *n.* petit coup, *m.*, chiquenaude, *f.*; flip (*boisson*), *m.*
flippancy ['flipənsi], *n.* ton léger; bavardage, *m.*
flippant ['flipənt], *a.* léger; désinvolte; cavalier (*manières, mine*).
flipper ['flipə], *n.* nageoire, *f.*
flirt [fləːt], *v.i.* faire la coquette, flirter (*femme*); conter fleurette (*homme*).—*n.* coquette, *f.*
flirtation [fləː'teiʃən], *n.* coquetterie, *f.*; flirt, *m.*
flit [flit], *v.i.* fuir, voltiger; (*Sc.*) déménager.—*n.* ***to do a moonlight flit***, déménager à la cloche de bois.
float [flout], *v.t.* faire flotter, (*fig.*) lancer.—*v.i.* flotter, surnager; ***to float on one's back***, faire la planche.—*n.* train (*bois*); flotteur; char (*carnaval*), *m.*
floating ['floutiŋ], *a.* flottant; ***floating capital***, fonds de roulement, *m.*; ***floating dock***, bassin à flot, *m.*
flock [flɔk], *n.* troupeau, *m.*; bande, troupe, *f.*; ouailles (*paroissiens*), *f.pl.*; flocon, *m.*, bourre (*de laine etc.*), *f.*—*v.i.* s'attrouper, s'assembler.
floe [flou], *n.* nappe de glaçons flottants; banquise, *f.*
flog [flɔg], *v.t.* fouetter, flageller; (*pop.*) bazarder.
flogging ['flɔgiŋ], *n.* fouet, *m.*; flagellation, *f.*

flood [flʌd], *n.* déluge, *m.*; inondation, crue, *f.*; (*fig.*) cours d'eau, torrent, *m.*; marée, *f.*—*v.t.* inonder, submerger, noyer.
flood-light ['flʌdlait], *n.* projecteur, *m.*—*v.t.* illuminer (*un monument*) avec des projecteurs.
flood-tide ['flʌdtaid], *n.* marée montante, *f.*
floor [flɔ:], *n.* plancher; carreau, parquet (*pavage*); étage (*storey*), *m.*—*v.t.* planchéier, parqueter; (*fig.*) terrasser, réduire au silence.
flooring ['flɔ:riŋ], *n.* plancher, parquet, *m.*
flop [flɔp], *int.* plouf!—*n.* (*Theat.*) four, *m.*
floral ['flɔrəl, 'flɔ:rəl], *a.* floral; ***floral games***, jeux floraux, *m.pl.*
Florence ['flɔrəns]. Florence, *f.*
florid ['flɔrid], *a.* fleuri.
Florida ['flɔridə]. la Floride, *f.*
florist ['flɔrist], *n.* fleuriste, *m., f.*
floss [flɔs], *n.* bourre (*de soie*), *f.*; (*Metal.*) floss; (*Bot.*) duvet, *m.*
flotilla [flo'tilə], *n.* flottille, *f.*
flounder (1) ['flaundə], *n.* (*Ichth.*) flet, petit flétan, *m.*
flounder (2) ['flaundə], *v.i.* se débattre; patauger.
flour ['flauə], *n.* farine; fécule (*des pommes de terre etc.*), *f.*
flourish ['flʌriʃ], *n.* éclat, *m.*; fleur de rhétorique, *f.*; panache (*manières, geste*); moulinet, tour, *m.*; (*Mus.*) fioriture; fanfare (*trompettes*), *f.*—*v.t.* fleurir; parafer; brandir (*épée etc.*).—*v.i.* fleurir; venir bien (*plantes*); prospérer.
flourishing ['flʌriʃiŋ], *a.* florissant.
flout [flaut], *v.t.* railler; se moquer de.—*n.* moquerie, raillerie, *f.*
flow [flou], *v.i.* s'écouler, couler; monter (*marée*); (*fig.*) découler (*de*).—*n.* écoulement; flux; (*fig.*) épanchement, *m.*
flower ['flauə], *n.* fleur; (*fig.*) élite, *f.*—*v.i.* fleurir, être en fleur.
flower-bed ['flauəbed], *n.* plate-bande, *f.*, parterre, *m.*
flowered ['flauəd], *a.* figuré; fleuri; ***double flowered***, à fleurs doubles.
flower-garden ['flauəgɑ:dn], *n.* jardin d'agrément, *m.*
flower-pot ['flauəpɔt], *n.* pot à fleurs, *m.*
flowing ['flouiŋ], *a.* coulant; (*fig.*) naturel.—*n.* cours, écoulement, *m.*
flown [floun], *a.* envolé; ***high-flown***, gonflé, outré (*style*).
flu [flu:], (*colloq.*) [INFLUENZA].
fluctuate ['flʌktjueit], *v.i.* balancer, flotter, varier.
fluctuating ['flʌktjueitiŋ], *a.* flottant; incertain; variable.
fluctuation [flʌktju'eiʃən], *n.* fluctuation, *f.*; (*fig.*) balancement, doute, *m.*
flue [flu:], *n.* tuyau de cheminée; carneau (*d'un fourneau*), *m.*
fluency ['flu:ənsi], *n.* facilité (*de parole*), *f.*
fluent ['flu:ənt], *a.* coulant, courant; facile.
fluently ['flu:əntli], *adv.* couramment, avec facilité.
fluff [flʌf], *n.* duvet, *m.*, peluches, *f.pl.*
fluid ['flu:id], *a.* and *n.* fluide, liquide, *m.*
fluke [flu:k], *n.* patte (*d'ancre*), *f.*; carrelet (*poisson*); (*fig.*) coup de raccroc, *m.*
flunkey ['flʌŋki], *n.* laquais; (*colloq.*) sycophante, *m.*
flurry ['flʌri], *n.* agitation, *f.*, désordre, émoi, *m.*—*v.t.* agiter, ahurir.
flush [flʌʃ], *a.* frais, plein de vigueur; à fleur, au ras (*de niveau*); ***flush with the ground***, à ras de terre.—*n.* rougeur, *f.*; transport, *m.*; chasse d'eau, *f.*; (*Cards*), flush, *m.*—*v.t.* faire rougir; laver à grande eau; (*Hunt.*) lever; (*fig.*) animer.—*v.i.* rougir; partir tout à coup.
fluster ['flʌstə], *v.t.* déconcerter, agiter, ahurir.—*n.* agitation, *f.*
flute [flu:t], *n.* flûte, *f.*
fluted ['flu:tid], *a.* cannelé.
flutter ['flʌtə], *n.* trémoussement, émoi, *m.*; agitation, *f.*; battement d'ailes, *m.*—*v.t.* mettre en désordre, agiter, ahurir.—*v.i.* battre des ailes; s'agiter; palpiter.
flux [flʌks], *n.* flux, courant; (*Metal.*) fondant, *m.*
fly (1) [flai], *n.* (*pl.* **flies** [flaiz]) (*Ent.*) mouche, *f.*
fly (2) [flai], *v.t. irr.* faire voler; fuir, éviter.—*v.i.* voler, s'envoler, se sauver, prendre la fuite, fuir, s'enfuir; ***to fly into a passion***, s'emporter, se mettre en colère; ***to fly over***, survoler.—*a.* (*pop.*) malin.
flyer ['flaiə], *n.* aviateur, *m.*
flying ['flaiiŋ], *a.* volant; ***flying squad***, brigade mobile, *f.*
flying-boat ['flaiiŋbout], *n.* hydravion, *m.*
flying-buttress ['flaiiŋ'bʌtris], *n.* arc-boutant, *m.*
fly-over ['flaiouvə], *n.* enjambement, *m.*
fly-paper ['flaipeipə], *n.* papier tue-mouches, *m.*
fly-past ['flaipɑ:st], *n.* défilé aérien, *m.*
foal [foul], *n.* poulain, *m.*, pouliche, *f.*—*v.i.* pouliner, mettre bas.
foam [foum], *n.* écume; bave; mousse, *f.*—*v.i.* écumer; moutonner (*mer*); baver (*animaux*).
foaming ['foumiŋ], *a.* écumant.
fob [fɔb], *n.* gousset (*de pantalon*), *m.*—*v.t.* (*fam.*) ***to fob someone off with something***, refiler quelque chose à quelqu'un.
fo'c'sle [fouksl], [FORECASTLE].
focus ['foukəs], *n.* (*pl.* **foci** ['fousai], **focuses** ['foukəsiz]) foyer, *m.*—*v.t.* mettre au point.
fodder ['fɔdə], *n.* fourrage, *m.*, pâture, *f.*; ***cannon-fodder***, chair à canon, *f.*
foe [fou], *n.* ennemi, adversaire, *m.*
fog [fɔg], *n.* brouillard, *m.*; (*fig.*) perplexité, *f.*; ***sea fog***, brume, *f.*
fog-bound ['fɔgbaund], *a.* enveloppé de brouillard; arrêté par le brouillard.
foggy ['fɔgi], *a.* brumeux; (*fig.*) sombre; ***it is foggy***, il fait du brouillard.
fogy, fogey ['fougi], *n.* ganache, vieille perruque, *f.*
foil [fɔil], *n.* feuille de métal, *f.*; tain (*de miroir*), *m.*; défaite, *f.*, échec (*check*); contraste, repoussoir (*set off*); (*Fenc.*) fleuret, *m.*—*v.t.* déjouer, faire échouer; frustrer.
fold (1) [fould], *v.t.* plier, ployer; envelopper; serrer; ***to fold one's arms***, croiser les bras.—*n.* pli, repli, *m.*; ***threefold***, triple; ***twofold***, double.
fold (2) [fould], *n.* parc (*à moutons*), *m.*, bergerie, *f.*—*v.t.* ***to fold sheep***, parquer des moutons.
folder ['fouldə], *n.* chemise (*à documents*), *f.*; dépliant, prospectus, *m.*

folding ['fouldiŋ], *a.* pliant; brisé, à deux battants (*porte*).
foliage ['fouliidʒ], *n.* feuillage, *m.*
folio ['fouliou], *n.* in-folio, *m.*; page, *f.*, folio, *m.*
folk(s) [fouk(s)], *n.* (*pl.*) gens, *m.pl.*, *f.pl.*, personnes, *f.pl.*
folklore ['fouklɔ:], *n.* folklore, *m.*, légendes, traditions populaires, *f.pl.*
folk-song ['fouksɔŋ], *n.* chanson populaire, *f.*
follow ['fɔlou], *v.t.* suivre; poursuivre; observer, imiter; exercer (*une profession*).—*v.i.* s'ensuivre, résulter; ***as follows***, comme suit.
follower ['fɔlouə], *n.* suivant; partisan; compagnon; (*colloq.*) amoureux, *m.*
following ['fɔlouiŋ], *a.* suivant.—*n.* suite, *f.*, parti, *m.*
folly ['fɔli], *n.* folie, sottise, bêtise, *f.*
foment [fo'ment], *v.t.* fomenter.
fond [fɔnd], *a.* passionné (*pour*); fou (*de*); indulgent (*pour*); doux, cher (*espoir*); vain, sot; ***to be (passionately) fond of***, aimer (à la folie).
fondle [fɔndl], *v.t.* câliner, caresser.
fondly ['fɔndli], *adv.* tendrement.
fondness ['fɔndnis], *n.* tendresse; affection, *f.*; penchant, goût, *m.*
font [fɔnt], *n.* fonts baptismaux, *m.pl.*
food [fu:d], *n.* nourriture, *f.*, aliment. *m.*; vivres, *m.pl.*; denrées, *f.pl.*; pâture (*pour animaux*), *f.*
food-stuffs ['fu:dstʌfs], *n.pl.* comestibles, *m.pl.*
fool [fu:l], *n.* sot; insensé, imbécile, niais, *m.*; dupe, *f.*, fou (*bouffon*), *m.*; ***to make a fool of***, se moquer de; ***to make a fool of oneself***, se rendre ridicule, se faire moquer de soi.—*v.t.* duper; (*colloq.*) se moquer de.—*v.i.* faire la bête; ***you are fooling***, vous plaisantez; vous blaguez.
foolery ['fu:ləri], *n.* folie, sottise; niaiserie, *f.*
foolhardy ['fu:lha:di], *a.* téméraire.
foolish ['fu:liʃ], *a.* sot, insensé, bête, ridicule.
foolishly ['fu:liʃli], *adv.* follement, sottement.
foolishness ['fu:liʃnis], *n.* folie, sottise, *f.*
foolproof ['fu:lpru:f], *a.* indéréglable.
foot [fut], *n.* (*pl.* **feet** [fi:t]) pied, *m.*; patte (*d'insectes etc.*); base (*de colonne*), *f.*; bas (*d'une page*), *m.*; (*Mil.*) infanterie, *f.*; ***on foot***, à pied.
football ['futbɔ:l], *n.* ballon; football (*jeu*), *m.*
foot-bridge ['futbridʒ], *n.* passerelle, *f.*
footfall ['futfɔ:l], *n.* pas, bruit de pas, *m.*
foothold ['futhould], *n.* prise pour le pied, *f.*; (*fig.*) point d'appui, *m.*
footing ['futiŋ], *n.* pied, point d'appui; établissement, *m.*; position, *f.*; ***on an equal footing***, sur un pied d'égalité.
footlights ['futlaits], *n.pl.* (*Theat.*) rampe, *f.*
footman ['futmən], *n.* (*pl.* **-men** [men]) laquais, valet de pied, *m.*
footnote ['futnout], *n.* note au bas de la page, apostille, *f.*
foot-path ['futpa:θ], *n.* sentier; trottoir (*de rue*), *m.*
foot-print ['futprint], *n.* empreinte du pied, *f.*
foot-soldier ['futsouldʒə], *n.* fantassin, *m.*
footstep ['futstep], *n.* pas, *m.*; trace, *f.*; vestige, *m.*
footstool ['futstu:l], *n.* tabouret, *m.*
footwear ['futwɛə], *n.* chaussures, *f.pl.*

fop [fɔp], *n.* fat, *m.*
foppery ['fɔpəri], *n.* affectation, fatuité, *f.*
foppish ['fɔpiʃ], *a.* affecté, sot, fat.
for [fɔ:], *prep.* pour, par; de, à, vers, pendant; depuis; en place de, en lieu de; en faveur de; à cause de, pour le compte de; malgré; pour avoir; pour que (*with subj.*).—*conj.* car.
forage ['fɔridʒ], *n.* fourrage, *m.*—*v.i.* fourrager.
forasmuch** [fɔrəz'mʌtʃ], *conj.* ***forasmuch as, d'autant que, vu que.
foray ['fɔrei], *n.* incursion, razzia, *f.*, raid, *m.*
forbear (1) [FOREBEAR].
forbear (2) [fɔ:'bɛə], *v.t. irr.* cesser; épargner, supporter.—*v.i.* s'abstenir, se garder (*de*).
forbearance [fɔ:'bɛərəns], *n.* patience; indulgence, *f.*
forbid [fə'bid], *v.t. irr.* défendre, interdire (*de*); empêcher (*de*); ***God forbid!*** à Dieu ne plaise!
forbidding [fə'bidiŋ], *a.* rebutant, repoussant.
force [fɔ:s], *n.* force; violence; efficacité; valeur, *f.*; (*Mil.*, *pl.*) forces, *f.pl.*, armée, *f.*; ***in force***, (*Law*) en vigueur.—*v.t.* forcer, contraindre (*à* ou *de*); violenter.
forced [fɔ:st], *a.* forcé, contraint; guindé (*style*).
forcedly ['fɔ:sidli], *adv.* de force.
forceps ['fɔ:seps], *n.pl.* (*Surg.*) pince, *f.*, forceps, *m.*
forcible ['fɔ:sibl], **forceful** ['fɔ:sful], *a.* fort; énergique.
forcibly ['fɔ:sibli], *adv.* par force; fortement.
ford [fɔ:d], *n.* gué, *m.*—*v.t.* passer à gué, guéer.
fore! (1) [fɔ:], *int.* (*Golf*) gare devant!
fore (2) [fɔ:], *a.* antérieur; de devant; (*Naut.*) de misaine; ***fore and aft***, (*Naut.*) de l'avant à l'arrière.—*adv.* d'avance; (*Naut.*) de l'avant.
forearm (1) [fɔ:r'a:m], *v.t.* prémunir.
forearm (2) ['fɔ:ra:m], *n.* avant-bras, *m.*
forebear ['fɔ:bɛə], *n.* aïeul, ancêtre, *m.*
forebode [fɔ:'boud], *v.t.* présager, prédire; pressentir.
foreboding [fɔ:'boudiŋ], *n.* présage, pressentiment, *m.*
forecast ['fɔ:ka:st], *n.* prévoyance, prévision, *f.*; pronostic, *m.*; ***weather forecast***, prévisions météorologiques, *f.pl.*—*v.t.* prévoir; pronostiquer.
forecastle [fouksl, 'fɔ:ka:sl], *n.* gaillard d'avant, *m.*
fore-court ['fɔ:kɔ:t], *n.* avant-cour, *f.*
forefather ['fɔ:fa:ðə], *n.* aïeul, ancêtre, *m.*
forefinger ['fɔ:fiŋgə], *n.* index, *m.*
forego [fɔ:'gou], *v.t.* précéder, aller devant.
foregone [fɔ:'gɔ:n], *a.* prévu, résolu, décidé d'avance.
foreground ['fɔ:graund], *n.* premier plan, *m.*
forehead ['fɔrid], *n.* front, *m.*
foreign ['fɔrin], *a.* étranger; ***Foreign Office***, Ministère des Affaires Étrangères, *m.*
foreigner ['fɔrinə], *n.* étranger, *m.*
foreland ['fɔ:lənd], *n.* promontoire, cap, *m.*
foreleg ['fɔ:leg], *n.* patte de devant, *f.*
forelock ['fɔ:lɔk], *n.* goupille, *f.*; toupet, *m.*
foreman ['fɔ:mən], *n.* (*pl.* **-men** [men]) chef (*d'un jury*); contremaître; chef d'atelier *ou* d'équipe; brigadier, *m.*
foremast ['fɔ:ma:st], *n.* mât de misaine, *m.*

foremost ['fɔːmoust], *a.* premier; en tête, au premier rang; ***first and foremost,*** tout d'abord.

forenoon ['fɔːnuːn], *n.* matin, *m.*, matinée, *f.*

forensic [fə'rensik], *a.* ***forensic medicine,*** médecine légale, *f.*

forerunner ['fɔːrʌnə], *n.* précurseur, *m.*

foresee [fɔː'siː], *v.t. irr.* (*conjug. like* SEE) prévoir.

foreseeable [fɔː'siːəbl], *a.* prévisible.

foreshore ['fɔːʃɔː], *n.* plage, *f.*

foreshorten [fɔː'ʃɔːtn], *v.t.* (*Paint.*) dessiner en raccourci.

foreshortening [fɔː'ʃɔːtniŋ], *n.* raccourci, *m.*

foresight ['fɔːsait], *n.* prévoyance, *f.*; guidon (*d'arme à feu*), *m.*; ***lack of foresight,*** imprévoyance, *f.*

forest ['fɔrist], *a.* de forêt, forestier.—*n.* forêt, *f.*

forestall [fɔː'stɔːl], *v.t.* anticiper, devancer.

forester ['fɔristə], *n.* garde forestier; habitant d'une forêt, *m.*

forestry ['fɔristri], *n.* sylviculture, *f.*

foretaste ['fɔːteist], *n.* avant-goût, *m.*; anticipation, *f.*

foretell [fɔː'tel], *v.t. irr.* (*conjug. like* TELL) prédire.

forethought ['fɔːθɔːt], *n.* prévoyance, prescience, *f.*

forewarn [fɔː'wɔːn], *v.t.* prévenir, avertir.

foreword ['fɔːwəːd], *n.* préface, *f.*; avant-propos, *m.*

forfeit ['fɔːfit], *a.* confisqué; (*fig.*) perdu.—*n.* amende (*à payer*); forfaiture, confiscation, *f.*; (*Games*) gage, *m.*—*v.t.* forfaire (*à*); confisquer; perdre.

forfeiture ['fɔːfitʃə], *n.* forfaiture, confiscation; perte, déchéance, *f.*

forgather [fɔː'gæðə], *v.i.* s'assembler, se réunir.

forge [fɔːdʒ], *n.* forge, *f.*—*v.t.* forger; contrefaire (*monnaie etc.*), fabriquer (*document etc.*).—*v.i.* commettre un faux; ***to forge ahead,*** pousser de l'avant.

forger ['fɔːdʒə], *n.* faussaire; faux-monnayeur, *m.*

forgery ['fɔːdʒəri], *n.* falsification; contrefaçon, *f.*; faux, *m.*

forget [fə'get], *v.t., v.i. irr.* oublier.

forgetful [fə'getful], *a.* oublieux.

forgetfulness [fə'getfulnis], *n.* oubli, manque de mémoire, *m.*; négligence, *f.*

forget-me-not [fə'getminɔt], *n.* myosotis, *m.*

forgive [fə'giv], *v.t. irr.* (*conjug. like* GIVE) pardonner, faire grâce de; pardonner à.

forgiveness [fə'givnis], *n.* pardon, *m.*; clémence, grâce, *f.*

forgiving [fə'giviŋ], *a.* clément, miséricordieux.

forgo [fɔː'gou], *v.t. irr.* (*conjug. like* GO) renoncer à, s'abstenir de, se refuser à.

fork [fɔːk], *n.* fourchette; fourche; bifurcation (*de rues*); pointe (*d'une flèche etc.*), *f.*; zigzag (*d'éclair*), *m.*—*v.t.* enlever avec une fourche.—*v.i.* fourcher; bifurquer.

forked [fɔːkt], *a.* fourchu; (*Bot.*) bifurqué.

forlorn [fə'lɔːn], *a.* abandonné, désespéré, délaissé.

forlornness [fə'lɔːnnis], *n.* délaissement, abandon; état désespéré, *m.*

form [fɔːm], *n.* forme, figure; formalité, *f.*; banc (*siège*), *m.*; (*Sch.*) classe, *f.*; gîte (*de lièvre*); imprimé (*fiche*), *m.*—*v.t.* former, faire; façonner.—*v.i.* se former; se gîter (*lièvres*).

formal ['fɔːməl], *a.* formel; pointilleux; affecté, cérémonieux, formaliste.

formality [fɔː'mæliti], *n.* formalité, cérémonie, *f.*

formally ['fɔːməli], *adv.* avec formalité, en forme, formellement.

formation [fɔː'meiʃən], *n.* formation, *f.*; ordre, *m.*

formative ['fɔːmətiv], *a.* formatif, formateur, plastique.

former ['fɔːmə], *a.* précédent, passé; ancien; premier (*de deux*).—*pron.* celui-là, celle-là.—*n.* moule, *m.*

formerly ['fɔːməli], *adv.* autrefois, auparavant; jadis.

formidable ['fɔːmidəbl], *a.* formidable, redoutable.

formless ['fɔːmlis], *a.* informe, sans forme.

Formosa [fɔː'mouzə]. Formose, *f.*

formula ['fɔːmjulə], *n.* (*pl.* **formulæ** ['fɔːmjul(a)i]) formule, *f.*

forsake [fə'seik], *v.t. irr.* délaisser, abandonner.

forsaking [fə'seikiŋ], *n.* délaissement, abandon, *m.*

***forsooth** [fə'suːθ], *adv.* en vérité, ma foi.

forswear [fɔː'swɛə], *v.t. irr.* (*conjug. like* SWEAR) abjurer, répudier.—*v.i.* se parjurer.

fort [fɔːt], *n.* fort, *m.*, forteresse, *f.*

forth [fɔːθ], *adv.* en avant; au dehors; ***and so forth,*** et ainsi de suite.

forthcoming [fɔːθ'kʌmiŋ], *a.* tout prêt, prêt à paraître; prochain, à venir.

forthright ['fɔːθrait], *a.* franc, carré, brutal.

forthwith [fɔːθ'wið], *adv.* incontinent, aussitôt, sur-le-champ, tout de suite.

fortieth ['fɔːtiəθ], *a.* quarantième.—*n.* quarantième (*fraction*), *m.*

fortification [fɔːtifi'keiʃən], *n.* fortification, *f.*

fortify ['fɔːtifai], *v.t.* fortifier; munir (*de*).

fortifying ['fɔːtifaiiŋ], *a.* (*fig.*) réconfortant, fortifiant.

fortitude ['fɔːtitjuːd], *n.* force d'âme, *f.*, courage, *m.*

fortnight ['fɔːtnait], *n.* quinze jours, *m.pl.*, quinzaine, *f.*

fortnightly ['fɔːtnaitli], *a.* bimensuel.—*adv.* tous les quinze jours.

fortress ['fɔːtris], *n.* forteresse, place forte, *f.*

fortuitous [fɔː'tjuːitəs], *a.* fortuit.

fortuitously [fɔː'tjuːitəsli], *adv.* fortuitement, par hasard.

fortunate ['fɔːtʃənit, 'fɔːtjunit], *a.* heureux, fortuné.

fortunately ['fɔːtʃənitli], *adv.* heureusement.

fortune ['fɔːtʃən], *n.* fortune, *f.*, sort (*lot*), destin, *m.*; ***by good fortune,*** par bonheur.

fortune-hunter ['fɔːtʃənhʌntə], *n.* aventurier, coureur de dots, *m.*

fortune-teller ['fɔːtʃəntelə], *n.* diseur de bonne aventure, *m.*

forty ['fɔːti], *a.* quarante; ***she must be nearly forty,*** elle doit friser la quarantaine.

forward ['fɔːwəd], *a.* avancé; (*fig.*) empressé (*de*), ardent (*à*); précoce (*fruits etc.*); présomptueux.—*n.* (*Ftb.*) avant, *m.*—*adv.* en avant; en évidence.—*v.t.* avancer, hâter; (*Comm.*) envoyer, expédier; faire suivre (*lettre*).

forwardness ['fɔ:wədnis], *n.* empressement; progrès, *m.*; précocité (*fruits etc.*); hardiesse; effronterie, *f.*
fossil ['fɔsil], *a.* and *n.* fossile, *m.*
foster ['fɔstə], *v.t.* élever, nourrir; (*fig.*) encourager.
foster-brother ['fɔstəbrʌðə], *n.* frère de lait, *m.*
foster-child ['fɔstətʃaild], *n.* nourrisson, *m.*
foster-father ['fɔstəfɑ:ðə], *n.* père nourricier, *m.*
foster-mother ['fɔstəmʌðə], *n.* mère nourricière, *f.*
foster-sister ['fɔstəsistə], *n.* sœur de lait, *f.*
foul [faul], *a.* sale, malpropre, immonde, trouble, bourbeux (*eau*); grossier (*langage*); ***by fair means or foul***, de gré ou de force; ***foul air***, air vicié, *m.*; ***foul play***, trahison, *f.*—*n.* (*Spt.*) coup-bas, *m.*—*v.t.* salir, souiller, troubler; encrasser (*arme à feu*); (*Naut.*) aborder; s'engager (*cordes*).
foully ['faulli], *adv.* salement, honteusement.
foul-mouthed ['faulmauðd], *a.* grossier.
foulness ['faulnis], *n.* saleté, impureté; turpitude, noirceur, *f.*
found (1) [faund], *past* and *p.p.* [FIND].
found (2) [faund], *v.t.* fonder, établir; fondre (*to cast*).
foundation [faun'deiʃən], *n.* fondement, *m.*, fondation; (*fig.*) base, source, *f.*
founder (1) ['faundə], *n.* fondateur, auteur; (*Metal.*) fondeur, *m.*
founder (2) ['faundə], *v.t.* surmener (*un cheval*).—*v.i.* (*Naut.*) sombrer, couler bas; broncher (*un cheval*); (*fig.*) échouer.
foundered ['faundəd], *a.* courbatu (*cheval*); sombré (*navire*).
foundling ['faundliŋ], *n.* enfant trouvé, *m.*
foundry ['faundri], *n.* fonderie, *f.*
fount [faunt], *n.* fontaine, (*fig.*) cause, source, *f.*
fountain ['fauntin], *n.* fontaine, source, *f.*; jet d'eau, *m.*
fountain-head ['fauntinhed], *n.* source, origine, *f.*
fountain-pen ['fauntinpen], *n.* stylo, *m.*
four [fɔ:], *a.* and *n.* quatre, *m.*; ***carriage and four***, voiture à quatre chevaux, *f.*; ***on all fours***, à quatre pattes.
four-engined ['fɔ:rendʒind], *a.* (*Av.*) quadrimoteur.
four-fold ['fɔ:fould], *a.* quatre fois, quatre fois autant, quadruple.
four-footed ['fɔ:futid], *a.* quadrupède, à quatre pieds.
fourteen ['fɔ:ti:n], *a.* and *n.* quatorze, *m.*
fourteenth ['fɔ:ti:nθ], *a.* quatorzième; quatorze (*date*; *rois etc.*).—*n.* quatorzième (*fraction*), *m.*
fourth [fɔ:θ], *a.* quatrième; quatre (*date, roi etc.*).—*n.* quart (*fraction*), *m.*; (*Mus.*) quarte, *f.*
fowl [faul], *n.* oiseau, *m.*, poule (*hen*); (*Cook.*) volaille, *f.*
fowler ['faulə], *n.* oiseleur, *m.*
fowl-house ['faulhaus], *n.* poulailler, *m.*
fowling-piece ['fauliŋpi:s], *n.* fusil de chasse, *m.*
fox [fɔks], *n.* (*pl.* **foxes** ['fɔksiz]) renard; (*fig.*) rusé, *m.*
foxglove ['fɔksglʌv], *n.* digitale, *f.*
foxy ['fɔksi], *a.* de renard, rusé; roux (*red*).
fraction ['frækʃən], *n.* fraction, *f.*
fractious ['frækʃəs], *a.* revêche, maussade, hargneux, de mauvaise humeur.
fracture ['fræktʃə], *n.* fracture, cassure, *f.*—*v.t.* casser, rompre; (*Surg.*) fracturer.
fragile ['frædʒail], *a.* fragile.
fragility [frə'dʒiliti], *n.* fragilité, *f.*
fragment ['frægmənt], *n.* fragment, éclat, *m.*
fragrance ['freigrəns], *n.* odeur suave, *f.* parfum, *m.*
fragrant ['freigrənt], *a.* odoriférant, parfumé.
frail [freil], *a.* frêle, fragile, faible.—*n.* cabas, panier d'emballage, *m.*
frailty ['freilti], *n.* faiblesse, fragilité, *f.*
frame [freim], *n.* charpente, *f.*; châssis (*de fenêtre etc.*), chambranle (*de porte*), *m.*; (*fig.*) forme, *f.*; cadre (*de tableau etc.*), *m.*; disposition (*d'esprit*), *f.*—*v.t.* former, construire; encadrer; inventer.
framer ['freimə], *n.* encadreur; (*fig.*) auteur (*d'un projet*), *m.*
France [frɑ:ns]. la France, *f.*
Frances ['frɑ:nsis]. Françoise, *f.*
franchise ['fræntʃaiz], *n.* franchise, *f.*, droit de vote, *m.*
Francis ['frɑ:nsis]. François, Francis, *m.*
Franciscan [fræn'siskən], *a.* and *n.* Franciscain, *m.*
frank [fræŋk], *a.* franc, sincère, libéral; libre.—*v.t.* affranchir.
frankincense ['fræŋkinsens], *n.* encens, *m.*
frankly ['fræŋkli], *adv.* franchement.
frankness ['fræŋknis], *n.* franchise, sincérité, *f.*
frantic ['fræntik], *a.* frénétique, forcené, furieux.
frantically ['fræntikəli], *adv.* follement, avec frénésie.
fraternal [frə'tə:nəl], *a.* fraternel.
fraternity [frə'tə:niti], *n.* fraternité, confrérie, *f.*
fraud [frɔ:d], *n.* imposteur (*personne*), *m.*; (*also* **fraudulence** ['frɔ:djuləns]) fraude, supercherie, *f.*, dol, *m.*
fraudulent ['frɔ:djulənt], *a.* frauduleux, de mauvaise foi.
fraught [frɔ:t], *a.* rempli, plein (*de*); riche fertile (*en*).
fray (1) [frei], *n.* échauffourée, mêlée, bagarre, *f.*
fray (2) [frei], *v.t.* érailler, effilocher.—*v.i.* s'érailler.
fraying ['freiiŋ], *n.* éraillure, *f.*
freak [fri:k], *n.* caprice, *m.*; bizarrerie, *f.*; monstre, *m.*; bigarrure, *f.*—*v.t.* bigarrer, tacheter (*de*).
freakish ['fri:kiʃ], *a.* bizarre, fantasque, capricieux.
freckle [frekl], *n.* tache de rousseur, tache de son, *f.*—*v.t.* tacheter.
Frederick ['fredrik]. Frédéric, *m.*
free [fri:], *a.* libre; exempt; sincère, franc; gratuit; aisé, dégagé; ***delivered free***, rendu franco à domicile; ***free and easy***, sans façon.—*adv.* gratis.—*v.t.* délivrer, libérer.
freebooter ['fri:bu:tə], *n.* maraudeur; flibustier, *m.*
freedman ['fri:dmən], *n.* (*pl.* **-men** [men]) affranchi, *m.*
freedom ['fri:dəm], *n.* liberté; indépendance; aisance; bourgeoisie (*d'une ville*), *f.*

freehold ['fri:hould], *n.* propriété foncière libre, *f.*
free-holder ['fri:houldə], *n.* propriétaire foncier, *m.*
freely ['fri:li], *adv.* librement, sans contrainte, gratuitement; libéralement.
freeman ['fri:mən], *n.* (*pl.* **-men** [men]) citoyen, homme libre, *m.*
freemason ['fri:meisn], *n.* franc-maçon, *m.*
freemasonry ['fri:meisnri], *n.* franc-maçonnerie, *f.*
freestone ['fri:stoun], *n.* pierre de taille, *f.*
freestyle ['fri:stail], *n.* nage libre, *f.*
freethinker ['fri:'θiŋkə], *n.* esprit fort, libre penseur, *m.*
free-trade ['fri:'treid], *n.* libre-échange, *m.*; ***free-trade area***, zone de libre-échange, *f.*
free-trader ['fri:'treidə], *n.* libre-échangiste, *m., f.*
freeze [fri:z], *v.t. irr.* geler; (*Fin.*) bloquer (*prix, salaires*).—*v.i.* se geler, se glacer.
freezing ['fri:ziŋ], *a.* glacial.—*n.* congélation, *f.*; (*Fin.*) blocage, *m.*
freight [freit], *n.* cargaison, *f.*, chargement; fret (*cost*), *m.*—*v.t.* fréter.
French [frentʃ], *a.* français; ***French window***, porte-fenêtre, *f.*—*n.* français (*langue*), *m.*; ***the French***, les Français, *m.pl.*
Frenchman ['frentʃmən], *n.* (*pl.* **-men** [men]) Français, *m.*
Frenchwoman ['frentʃwumən], *n.* (*pl.* **-women** [wimin]) Française, *f.*
frenzy ['frenzi], *n.* frénésie, *f.*; délire, *m.*
frequence ['fri:kwəns], **frequency** ['fri:kwənsi], *n.* fréquence; répétition fréquente, *f.*; ***V.H.F.***, modulation de fréquence, *f.*
frequent ['fri:kwənt], *a.* fréquent, très répandu; rapide (*pouls*).—[fri'kwent], *v.t.* fréquenter; hanter.
frequently ['fri:kwəntli], *adv.* fréquemment, souvent.
fresco ['freskou], *n.* fresque, *f.*
fresh [freʃ], *a.* frais; récent, nouveau; (*fig.*) vigoureux; novice, vert; ***fresh water***, eau douce, *f.*
freshen ['freʃən], *v.t.* rafraîchir.—*v.i.* se rafraîchir.
freshly ['freʃli], *adv.* fraîchement; récemment, depuis peu.
freshman ['freʃmən], *n.* (*pl.* **-men** [men]) étudiant de première année, bizuth, *m.*
freshness ['freʃnis], *n.* fraîcheur; (*fig.*) nouveauté, *f.*
freshwater ['freʃwɔ:tə], *a.* d'eau douce *ou* de rivière.
fret [fret], *n.* fermentation; (*fig.*) agitation de l'âme, *f.*—*v.t.* frotter (*contre*); ronger, écorcher (*excorier*); chagriner, irriter; découper.—*v.i.* se chagriner, s'inquiéter; s'user, s'érailler.
fretful ['fretful], *a.* chagrin, maussade; agité, inquiet.
fretfulness ['fretfulnis], *n.* mauvaise humeur, irritation, *f.*
fretsaw ['fretsɔ:], *n.* scie à découper, *f.*
fretwork ['fretwə:k], *n.* ouvrage à claire-voie; découpage, *m.*
friable ['fraiəbl], *a.* friable.
friar ['fraiə], *n.* moine, *m.*
friction ['frikʃən], *n.* frottement, *m.*; (*Med.*) friction, *f.*
Friday ['fraid(e)i]. vendredi, *m.*; ***Good Friday***, vendredi saint.
friend [frend], *n.* ami, *m.*, amie, *f.*
friendless ['frendlis], *a.* sans ami, délaissé.
friendliness [frendlinis], *n.* bienveillance, *f.*
friendly ['frendli], *a.* d'ami, amical; bienveillant (*pour*).
friendship ['frendʃip], *n.* amitié, *f.*
frieze [fri:z], *a.* de frise.—*n.* frise, *f.*
frigate ['frigit], *n.* frégate, *f.*
fright [frait], *n.* effroi, *m.*, épouvante, frayeur, *f.*
frighten [fraitn], *v.t.* épouvanter, effrayer, faire peur à.
frightful ['fraitful], *a.* épouvantable, effroyable, affreux.
frightfulness ['fraitfulnis], *n.* horreur, frayeur, *f.*
frigid ['fridʒid], *a.* froid, glacial.
frigidity [fri'dʒiditi], **frigidness** ['fridʒidnis], *n.* frigidité, froideur, *f.*
frill [fril], *n.* volant, *m.*, ruche, *f.*, jabot (*de chemise*), *m.*; ***without frills***, sans façons.—*v.t.* plisser, froncer; rucher.
fringe [frindʒ], *n.* frange; crépine, *f.*; bord, *m.*; bordure, *f.*; effilé, *m.*—*v.t.* franger, border.
frippery ['fripəri], *n.* parure sans valeur, *f.*; clinquant, *m.*
frisk [frisk], *n.* gambade, *f.*—*v.i.* sautiller, gambader, frétiller.
friskiness ['friskinis], *n.* folâtrerie, gaieté, vivacité, *f.*
frisky ['friski], *a.* vif, enjoué, folâtre; fringant (*cheval*).
fritter ['fritə], *n.* (*Cook.*) beignet, *m.*—*v.t.* couper en morceaux, morceler; ***to fritter away*** (***one's time*** or ***money***), gaspiller *ou* dissiper (son temps *ou* son argent).
frivolity [fri'vɔliti], *n.* frivolité, *f.*
frivolous ['frivələs], *a.* frivole.
frivolousness ['frivələsnis], *n.* frivolité, *f.*
frizz [friz], **frizzle** [frizl], *v.t.* friser, crêper.—*v.i.* frisotter (*cheveux*).—*n.* frisure, *f.*
frizzy ['frizi], *a.* frisottant, crêpé.
fro [frou], *adv.* en s'éloignant; ***to go to and fro***, aller et venir.
frock [frɔk], *n.* robe d'enfant, robe, *f.*; froc (*de moine*), *m.*
frock-coat ['frɔkkout], *n.* redingote, *f.*
frog [frɔg], *n.* grenouille, *f.*
frogman ['frɔgmən], *n.* (*pl.* **-men** [men]) homme-grenouille, *m.*
frolic ['frɔlik], *n.* espièglerie, *f.*, ébats, *m.pl.*, gambades, *f.pl.*—*v.i.* folâtrer, gambader.
frolicsome ['frɔliksəm], *a.* folâtre, espiègle.
from [frɔm], *prep.* de; depuis, dès, à partir de; par (*à cause de*); d'après (*selon*); par suite de, en conséquence de (*en raison de*); de la part de (*comme représentant de*); ***as from***, à partir de (*telle ou telle date*); ***from above***, d'en haut; ***from afar***, de loin; ***from behind***, de derrière; ***from hence***, d'ici; ***from thence***, de là; ***from . . . till***, depuis . . . jusqu'à; ***from you***, de votre part.
front [frʌnt], *n.* devant, *m.*; face, façade (*d'un édifice*); audace, *f.*, front, *m.*—*v.t.* faire face à; s'opposer à; donner sur.
frontage ['frʌntidʒ], *n.* façade, devanture (*de magasin*), *f.*
front-door ['frʌnt'dɔ:], *n.* porte d'entrée, *f.*

frontier ['frʌntiə], *a.* and *n.* frontière, *f.*
frontispiece ['frʌntispi:s], *n.* frontispice, *m.*
frost [frɔst], *n.* gelée, *f.*, gel, *m.*; ***glazed frost***, verglas, *m.*; ***ground frost***, gelée blanche; ***hoar-frost***, givre, *m.*—*v.t.* glacer; damasquiner.
frost-bite ['frɔstbait], *n.* gelure, froidure, *f.*
frosted ['frɔstid], *a.* givré; dépoli (*verre*).
frosty ['frɔsti], *a.* de gelée; glacé; (*fig.*) froid.
froth [frɔθ], *n.* écume; mousse (*de boisson*), *f.* —*v.i.* écumer; mousser.
frothy ['frɔθi], *a.* écumeux; écumant; mousseux; (*fig.*) vain, frivole.
frown [fraun], *n.* froncement de sourcil, *m.*—*v.i.* froncer les sourcils; être contraire (*à*); (*fig.*) ***to frown upon***, désapprouver.
frowning ['fraunin], *a.* rechigné, renfrogné; (*fig.*) menaçant.
frowzy ['frauzi], *a.* sale, malpropre.
frozen [frouzn], *a.* glacé, gelé; (*Fin.*) bloqué.
fructify ['frʌktifai], *v.t.* fertiliser, féconder.—*v.i.* fructifier.
frugal [fru:gl], *a.* frugal, économe, ménager.
frugality [fru:'gæliti], *n.* économie, frugalité, *f.*
fruit [fru:t], *a.* à fruit, fruitier.—*n.* fruit, *m.*; fruits, *m.pl.*; (*fig.*) avantage, profit, *m.*; ***first fruits***, prémices, *f.pl.*
fruiterer ['fru:tərə], *n.* fruitier, *m.*
fruitful ['fru:tful], *a.* fertile; (*fig.*) fécond.
fruitfully ['fru:tfuli], *adv.* fertilement, abondamment.
fruitfulness ['fru:tfulnis], *n.* fertilité; (*fig.*) fécondité, *f.*
fruition [fru:'iʃən], *n.* jouissance, réalisation, *f.*
fruitless ['fru:tlis], *a.* stérile; (*fig.*) infructueux, inutile.
frump [frʌmp], *n.* femme désagréable et mal habillée, *f.*
frustrate [frʌs'treit], *v.t.* frustrer, rendre inutile, déjouer.
frustration [frʌs'treiʃən], *n.* frustration, *f.*, insuccès, *m.*
fry (1) [frai], *n.* fretin, frai (*petits poissons*), *m.*
fry (2) [frai], *n.* (*Cook.*) friture, *f.*—*v.t.* frire, faire frire, sauter; ***fried eggs***, œufs au plat, *m.pl.*—*v.i.* frire.
frying-pan ['fraiiŋpæn], *n.* poêle à frire, *f.*
fuchsia ['fju:ʃə], *n.* fuchsia, *m.*
fuddle [fʌdl], *v.t.* griser; hébéter.—*v.i.* se griser.
fudge [fʌdʒ], *int.* bah!—*n.* blague, faribole, *f.*; fondant américain (*bonbon*), *m.*
fuel ['fjuəl], *n.* combustible; (*fig.*) aliment, *m.*
fuel-oil ['fjuəlɔil], *n.* mazout, *m.*
fugitive ['fju:dʒitiv], *a.* fugitif; fuyard, passager.—*n.* fugitif, transfuge, déserteur; (*Mil.*) fuyard, *m.*
fugue [fju:g], *n.* (*Mus.*) fugue, *f.*
fulcrum ['fʌlkrəm], *n.* (*pl.* **fulcra** ['fʌlkrə]) point d'appui, *m.*
fulfil [ful'fil], *v.t.* accomplir, réaliser; satisfaire.
fulfilment [ful'filmənt], *n.* exécution, *f.*, accomplissement, *m.*
full [ful], *a.* plein, rempli; comble, replet, gras; entier, complet; ample; (*fig.*) repu; (*Gram.*) ***full stop***, point, *m.*; ***full up!*** (*autobus etc.*) complet!—*adv.* tout à fait, entièrement; parfaitement.—*n.* plein; comble, *m.*, satiété, *f.*; soûl, *m.*
full-back ['fulbæk], *n.* (*Ftb. etc.*) arrière, *m.*
full-blown ['fulbloun], *a.* épanoui; (*fig.*) dans tout son éclat.
full-bodied ['fulbɔdid], *a.* gros, replet; corsé (*vin*).
fuller ['fulə], *n.* foulon, *m.*
full-faced ['ful'feist], *a.* au visage plein.
full-length ['ful'leŋθ], *a.* en pied (*portrait*).
fullness ['fulnis], *n.* plénitude, abondance; ampleur, *f.*
fully ['fuli], *adv.* pleinement, entièrement, tout à fait; parfaitement.
fulmar ['fulmə], *n.* (*Orn.*) fulmar, *m.*
fulminate ['fʌlmineit], *v.t.*, *v.i.* fulminer.
fulsome ['fulsəm], *a.* excessif, écœurant, servile; gonflé (*style*).
fumble [fʌmbl], *v.t.* manier maladroitement. —*v.i.* farfouiller; tâtonner.
fumbler ['fʌmblə], *n.* maladroit, *m.*
fume [fju:m], *n.* fumée, vapeur; (*fig.*) colère, *f.*—*v.t.* fumer.—*v.i.* fumer, s'exhaler; (*fig.*) être en colère.
fumigate ['fju:migeit], *v.t.* fumiger; désinfecter.
fun [fʌn], *n.* amusement, *m.*, plaisanterie, drôlerie, *f.*
function ['fʌŋkʃən], *n.* fonction, *f.*, métier, *m.*; cérémonie, réception, *f.*—*v.i.* fonctionner, marcher.
fund [fʌnd], *n.* fonds, *m.*; caisse, *f.*
fundamental [fʌndə'mentl], *a.* fondamental. —*n.*(*pl.*) principe fondamental, *m.*
funeral ['fju:nərəl], *a.* funèbre, funéraire.—*n.* enterrement, convoi funèbre, *m.*; funérailles, obsèques, *f.pl.*
funereal [fju'niəriəl], *a.* funèbre; lugubre.
fungus ['fʌŋgəs], *n.* (*pl.* **fungi** ['fʌndʒai]) champignon; (*Med.*) fongus, *m.*
funk [fʌŋk], *n.* peur, *f.*—*v.t.* éviter, avoir peur de.
funnel [fʌnl], *n.* entonnoir; tuyau, *m.*; cheminée (*de bateau à vapeur*), *f.*
funny ['fʌni], *a.* amusant, drôle, comique; bizarre.
fur [fə:], *n.* fourrure, *f.*; gibier à poil; (*fig.*) dépôt, *m.*, incrustation, *f.*—*v.t.* fourrer, garnir de fourrure.—*v.i.* s'incruster, s'encrasser (*la langue*).
furbish ['fə:biʃ], *v.t.* fourbir.
furious ['fjuəriəs], *a.* furieux, acharné.
furiously ['fjuəriəsli], *adv.* avec fureur, avec acharnement.
furl [fə:l], *v.t.* (*Naut.*) ferler, serrer.
furlong ['fə:lɔŋ], *n.* furlong (*le huitième d'un mille anglais, 201 mètres*), *m.*
furlough ['fə:lou], *n.* (*Mil.*) congé, *m.*
furnace ['fə:nis], *n.* fournaise, *f.*; fourneau (*d'une forge*); foyer (*de locomotive*), *m.*; ***blast-furnace***, haut fourneau.
furnish ['fə:niʃ], *v.t.* fournir, garnir, pourvoir (*de*); meubler.
furnisher ['fə:niʃə], *n.* fournisseur, marchand de meubles, *m.*
furnishing ['fə:niʃiŋ], *n.* ameublement, *m.*, garniture, *f.*
furniture ['fə:nitʃə], *n.* meubles, *m.pl.* mobilier, ameublement; équipage, *m.*; ***a piece of furniture***, un meuble.
furrier ['fʌriə], *n.* fourreur, pelletier, *m.*
furrow ['fʌrou], *n.* sillon, *m.*; ride; rainure, *f.* —*v.t.* sillonner, rider (*la figure*).
furry ['fə:ri], *a.* fourré.

further ['fəːðə], *v.t.* avancer; faciliter, favoriser, seconder.—*a.* (*also* **farther** ['fɑːðə]) plus éloigné, ultérieur; autre, nouveau; ***further end***, extrémité, *f.*—*adv.* (*also* **farther** ['fɑːðə]) plus loin; de plus, en outre, davantage, encore; ultérieurement; au delà.
furtherance ['fəːðərəns], *n.* avancement; progrès, *m.*
furthermore ['fəːðəmɔː], *adv.* de plus, en outre, d'ailleurs.
furthermost ['fəːðəmoust], **furthest** ['fəːðist], **farthest** ['fɑːðist], *a.* le plus éloigné; le plus reculé.—*adv.* and *n.* le plus loin.
furtive ['fəːtiv], *a.* furtif.
furtively ['fəːtivli], *adv.* furtivement, à la dérobée.
fury ['fjuəri], *n.* furie, fureur, *f.*; acharnement, *m.*
furze [fəːz], *n.* ajonc, genêt épineux, *m.*
fuse [fjuːz], *v.t.* fondre, liquéfier.—*v.i.* se fondre.—*n.* mèche, fusée, *f.*; (*Elec.*) fusible, plomb, *m.*; ***the fuse has gone***, le plomb a sauté.
fuselage ['fjuːzilɑːʒ, 'fjuːzilidʒ], *n.* fuselage, *m.*
fuse-wire ['fjuːzwaiə], *n.* fil fusible, *m.*
fusible ['fjuːzibl], *a.* fusible.
fusilier [fjuːzi'liə], *n.* fusilier, *m.*
fusillade [fjuːzi'leid], *n.* fusillade, *f.*
fusion ['fjuːʒən], *n.* fusion, *f.*
fuss [fʌs], *n.* fracas, embarras, *m.*, façons, *f.pl.*
fussily ['fʌsili], *adv.* avec embarras.
fussy ['fʌsi], *a.* qui fait des embarras; affairé.
fustian ['fʌstjən], *n.* futaine, *f.*; (*fig.*) galimatias, *m.*
fusty ['fʌsti], *a.* qui sent le renfermé *ou* le moisi.
futile ['fjuːtail], *a.* futile, vain, frivole.
futility [fju'tiliti], *n.* futilité, *f.*
future ['fjuːtʃə], *a.* futur, à venir.—*n.* avenir; (*Gram.*) futur, *m.*
fuzz [fʌz], *n.* bourre, *f.*, duvet (*de couverture*); flou (*de photographie*), *m.*
fuzzy ['fʌzi], *a.* duveteux, floconneux; bouffant, moutonné (*cheveux*); flou (*photographie*).

G

G, g [dʒiː]. septième lettre de l'alphabet; (*Mus.*) sol, *m.*
gab [gæb], *n.* faconde, *f.*, bagout, *m.*; ***to have the gift of the gab***, (*colloq.*) avoir la langue bien pendue.
gabardine [GABERDINE].
gabble [gæbl], *v.i.* parler très vite, bredouiller; caqueter, jacasser.—*n.* bredouillement; caquet, *m.*
gaberdine, gabardine [gæbə'diːn], *n.* gabardine, *f.*
gable [geibl], *n.* pignon, gable, *m.*
gadfly ['gædflai], *n.* taon, *m.*
gadget ['gædʒit], *n.* instrument, accessoire; truc, machin, *m.*
gaff [gæf], *n.* gaffe, *f.*—*v.t.* gaffer (*poisson*).
gag [gæg], *n.* bâillon, *m.*; (*Theat.*) plaisanterie, *f.*; (*Cine.*) gag, *m.*—*v.t.* bâillonner.
gage [geidʒ], *n.* gage, *m.*, assurance, *f.*
gaggle [gægl], *n.* troupeau d'oies, *m.*
gaiety ['geiəti], *n.* gaieté, *f.*; éclat, *m.*
gaily ['geili], *adv.* gaiement, joyeusement.
gain [gein], *n.* gain, profit, avantage, *m.*—*v.t.* gagner, acquérir; remporter (*victoire*); atteindre.—*v.i.* avancer (*montre etc.*).
gainings ['geiniŋz], *n.pl.* gains, profits, *m.pl.*
gainsay ['geinsei, gein'sei], *v.t.* contredire.
gait [geit], *n.* démarche, allure, *f.*
gaiter ['geitə], *n.* guêtre, *f.*
gala ['geilə, 'gɑːlə], *n.* gala, *m.*; fête, *f.*
galaxy ['gæləksi], *n.* voie lactée, galaxie, *f.*; (*fig.*) assemblage brillant, *m.*
gale [geil], *n.* coup de vent, *m.*, tempête, *f.*
Galilee ['gælilіː]. la Galilée, *f.*
gall [gɔːl], *n.* fiel, *m.*; écorchure (*plaie*); noix de galle, galle (*d'arbres etc.*); (*fig.*) rancune, *f.*, chagrin, *m.*—*v.t.* écorcher; (*fig.*) fâcher.
gallant ['gælənt], *a.* brave, intrépide; [gə'lænt] gallant.—*n.* brave; preux; [gə'lænt] galant; amant, *m.*
gallantry ['gæləntri], *n.* vaillance; galanterie, *f.*
gall-bladder ['gɔːlblædə], *n.* vésicule bilaire, *f.*
galleon ['gæliən], *n.* galion, *m.*
gallery ['gæləri], *n.* galerie, *f.*; (*Theat.*) balcon, *m.*; (*Parl.*) tribune publique, *f.*
galley ['gæli], *n.* galère; (*Naut.*) cuisine, *f.*
galley-slave ['gælisleiv], *n.* galérien, *m.*
Gallic ['gælik], *a.* gaulois.
galling ['gɔːliŋ], *a.* irritant, vexant.
gallon ['gælən], *n.* gallon (*quatre litres et demi*), *m.*
gallop ['gæləp], *n.* galop, *m.*—*v.i.* galoper, aller au galop.
gallows ['gælouz], *n.* potence, *f.*
galvanize ['gælvənaiz], *v.t.* galvaniser.
Gambia ['gæmbiə]. la Gambie, *f.*
gamble [gæmbl], *v.i.* jouer de l'argent.
gambler ['gæmblə], *n.* joueur, *m.*
gambling ['gæmbliŋ], *n.* jeu, *m.*
gambol [gæmbl], *n.* gambade, *f.*; ébats, *m.pl.*—*v.i.* gambader, folâtrer.
game (1) [geim], *a.* estropié (*jambe, bras etc.*).
game (2) [geim], *a.* courageux.—*n.* jeu, *m.*, partie, *f.*; ***drawn game***, partie nulle; ***to make game of***, se moquer de.—*v.i.* jouer de l'argent.
game (3) [geim], *n.* gibier, *m.*
game-bag ['geimbæg], *n.* carnassière, *f.*
game-keeper ['geimkiːpə], *n.* garde-chasse, *m.*
gamester ['geimstə], *n.* joueur, *m.*
gammon ['gæmən], *n.* quartier de lard fumé, *m.*—*v.t.* saler et fumer (*jambon*).
gamut ['gæmət], *n.* (*Mus.*) gamme, *f.*
gander ['gændə], *n.* jars, *m.*
gang [gæŋ], *n.* bande, troupe, brigade, équipe (*d'ouvriers*), *f.*
ganger ['gæŋə], *n.* chef d'équipe; cantonnier, *m.*
Ganges ['gændʒiːz]. le Gange, *m.*
gangrene ['gæŋgriːn], *n.* gangrène, *f.*
gangster ['gæŋstə], *n.* (*Am.*) bandit, gangster, *m.*
gangway ['gæŋwei], *n.* passage, *m.*; (*Naut.*) passerelle (*pour débarquer*), coupée, *f.*
gannet ['gænit], *n.* (*Orn.*) fou, *m.*

gaol [JAIL].
gap [gæp], *n.* brèche, ouverture, *f.*, trou, *m.*; (*fig.*) lacune; trouée (*dans une forêt*), *f.*
gape [geip], *v.i.* bâiller; s'entr'ouvrir (*porte etc.*); (*fig.*) bayer; ***to gape at***, regarder bouche bée.—*n.* bâillement, *m.*
gaping ['geipiŋ], *a.* béant.—*n.* bâillement, *m.*
garage ['gærɑ:ʒ], *n.* garage, *m.*—*v.t.* garer.
garb [gɑ:b], *n.* costume, habit, habillement, *m.*
garbage ['gɑ:bidʒ], *n.* entrailles, issues; (*Am.*) ordures, *f.pl.*
garble [gɑ:bl], *v.t.* mutiler, tronquer (*citation etc.*), altérer.
garden [gɑ:dn], *n.* jardin, *m.*—*v.i.* jardiner.
garden-city ['gɑ:dn'siti], *n.* cité-jardin, *f.*
gardener ['gɑ:dnə], *n.* jardinier, *m.*
gardenia [gɑ:'di:njə], *n.* gardenia, *m.*
gardening ['gɑ:dniŋ], *n.* jardinage, *m.*
gargle [gɑ:gl], *v.i.* se gargariser.—*n.* gargarisme, *m.*
gargoyle ['gɑ:gɔil], *n.* gargouille, *f.*
garish ['gɛəriʃ], *a.* éclatant, voyant.
garland ['gɑ:lənd], *n.* guirlande, *f.*—*v.t.* enguirlander.
garlic ['gɑ:lik], *n.* ail, *m.*
garment ['gɑ:mənt], *n.* vêtement, *m.*
garner ['gɑ:nə], *n.* grenier, *m.*—*v.t.* mettre en grenier, engranger; (*fig.*) amasser.
garnet ['gɑ:nit], *n.* grenat, *m.*
garnish ['gɑ:niʃ], *v.t.* garnir, orner de.—*n.* garniture, *f.*
garret ['gærət], *n.* galetas, *m.*, mansarde, soupente, *f.*
garrison ['gærisən], *n.* garnison, *f.*—*v.t.* mettre garnison dans; mettre en garnison.
garrotte [gə'rɔt], *n.* garrotte, *f.*—*v.t.* garrotter.
garrulity [gə'ru:liti], *n.* garrulité, loquacité, *f.*
garrulous ['gæruləs], *a.* babillard, loquace.
garter ['gɑ:tə], *n.* jarretière, *f.*; (*Am.*) support-chaussette, *m.*
gas [gæs], *n.* (*pl.* **gases** ['gæsiz]) gaz, *m.*; ***laughing gas***, gaz hilarant.—*v.t.* gazer; intoxiquer par un gaz.
gas-cooker ['gæs'kukə], *n.* réchaud à gaz, four à gaz, *m.*
gaseous ['geisiəs], *a.* gazeux.
gash [gæʃ], *n.* balafre, estafilade, entaille, *f.*—*v.t.* balafrer, taillader.
gas-holder ['gæshouldə], **gasometer** [gæ'sɔmitə], *n.* gazomètre, *m.*
gas-mask ['gæsmɑ:sk], *n.* masque à gaz, *m.*
gasometer [GAS-HOLDER].
gasp [gɑ:sp], *v.i.* respirer avec peine.—*n.* respiration haletante, *f.*; sursaut (*de surprise*), soupir convulsif, *m.*
gasping ['gɑ:spiŋ], *a.* haletant.—*n.* respiration haletante, *f.*
gas-stove ['gæsstouv], *n.* fourneau à gaz, *m.*
gastric ['gæstrik], *a.* gastrique.
gastronomy [gæs'trɔnəmi], *n.* gastronomie, *f.*
gate [geit], *n.* porte; barrière (*de péage*); grille (*en fer forgé*), *f.*
gate-keeper ['geitki:pə], *n.* portier; (*Rail.*) garde-barrière, *m.*
gate-post ['geitpoust], *n.* montant de porte, *m.*
gateway ['geitwei], *n.* porte, porte cochère, *f.*; portail (*grand*); guichet (*petit*), *m.*
gather ['gæðə], *v.t.* ramasser; assembler; recueillir (*réunir*); cueillir (*fruits etc.*); (*fig.*) conclure; (*Dress.*) froncer.—*v.i.* se rassembler, se réunir, s'assembler; s'amasser.—*n.* pli, froncis, *m.*
gatherer ['gæðərə], *n.* cueilleur; percepteur (*des contributions directes*); vendangeur (*de raisins*), *m.*
gathering ['gæðəriŋ], *n.* rassemblement, *m.*; assemblée, réunion; perception (*des contributions directes*); récolte (*de fruits etc.*), *f.*; (*Dress.*) froncis; (*Med.*) abcès, *m.*
gaudiness ['gɔ:dinis], *n.* faste, faux brillant, *m.*
gaudy ['gɔ:di], *a.* éclatant; criard, fastueux, de mauvais goût.
gauge [geidʒ], *v.t.* jauger, mesurer; (*fig.*) juger.—*n.* jauge, mesure, *f.*; calibre, *m.*; (*Rail.*) voie, *f.*
Gaul [gɔ:l]. la Gaule, *f.*
Gauls [gɔ:lz], **the.** les Gaulois, *m.pl.*
gaunt [gɔ:nt], *a.* maigre, décharné.
gauntlet ['gɔ:ntlit], *n.* gantelet, *m.*
gauze [gɔ:z], *n.* gaze, *f.*
gawk [gɔ:k], *n.* sot, maladroit, *m.*
gawky ['gɔ:ki], *a.* dégingandé.
gay [gei], *a.* gai, réjoui, joyeux; pimpant.
gayety [GAIETY].
gayly [GAILY].
gaze [geiz], *v.i.* regarder fixement.—*n.* regard fixe *ou* attentif, *m.*
gazelle [gə'zel], *n.* gazelle, *f.*
gazette [gə'zet], *n.* gazette, *f.*; bulletin officiel, *m.*—*v.t.* publier *ou* annoncer dans le journal officiel.
gazetteer [gæzi'tiə], *n.* dictionnaire géographique; gazetier, *m.*
gear [giə], *n.* appareil, attirail; harnais (*d'un cheval*), *m.*; (*colloq.*) vêtements; (*Naut.*) apparaux, *m.pl.*; (*Mach.*) engrenage, *m.*; (*Motor.*) vitesse, *f.*; (*Motor.*) ***bottom, first*** or ***low gear***, première, *f.*; ***neutral gear***, point mort, *m.*; ***in top gear***, en prise.
gear-box ['giəbɔks], *n.* boîte de changement de vitesse, *f.*
geese [GOOSE].
gelatine ['dʒeləti:n], *n.* gélatine, *f.*
gelatinous [dʒe'lætinəs], *a.* gélatineux.
gelding ['geldiŋ], *n.* cheval hongre, *m.*
gem [dʒem], *n.* pierre précieuse, *f.*, joyau, *m.*
gender ['dʒendə], *n.* genre, *m.*
genealogical [dʒi:niə'lɔdʒikl], *a.* généalogique.
genealogist [dʒi:ni'ælədʒist], *n.* généalogiste, *m., f.*
genealogy [dʒi:ni'ælədʒi], *n.* généalogie, *f.*
general ['dʒenərəl], *a.* général, commun.—*n.* général, *m.*
generalize ['dʒenrəlaiz], *v.t.* généraliser.
generally ['dʒenrəli], *adv.* en général, ordinairement, généralement.
generate ['dʒenəreit], *v.t.* produire, engendrer.
generation [dʒenə'reiʃən], *n.* génération, famille; production, *f.*; âge, *m.*
generator ['dʒenəreitə], *n.* générateur, *m.*; ***electricity generator***, génératrice, *f.*
generic [dʒə'nerik], **generical** [dʒe'nerikəl], *a.* générique.
generosity [dʒenə'rɔsiti], *n.* générosité, magnanimité, libéralité, *f.*
generous ['dʒenərəs], *a.* généreux; (*fig.*) abondant, riche (*en*).

generously [ˈdʒenərəsli], *adv.* généreusement.
genesis [ˈdʒenəsis], *n.* genèse, *f.*
genetics [dʒəˈnetiks], *n.* génétique, *f.*
Geneva [dʒəˈniːvə]. Genève, *f.*
genial [ˈdʒiːniəl], *a.* bon; affable; cordial, joyeux.
geniality [dʒiːniˈæliti], *n.* bonne humeur, nature sympathique, gaieté, *f.*, entrain, *m.*
genially [ˈdʒiːniəli], *adv.* avec bonté, d'un air affable.
genie [ˈdʒiːni], *n.* (*Myth.*) génie, djinn, *m.*
genitive [ˈdʒenitiv], *n.* (*Gram.*) génitif, *m.*
genius [ˈdʒiːniəs], *n.* génie, *m.*
Genoa [ˈdʒenouə]. Gênes, *f.*
genteel [dʒenˈtiːl], *a.* (*now often iron.*) de bon ton, comme il faut, distingué.
gentility [dʒenˈtiliti], *n.* bon ton, *m.*, distinction, *f.*
gentle [dʒentl], *a.* doux, aimable; paisible; modéré (*pente etc.*).
gentlefolk [ˈdʒentlfouk], *n.pl.* personnes de bon ton, *f.pl.*, gens comme il faut, *m.pl.*
gentleman [ˈdʒentlmən], *n.* (*pl.* **gentlemen** [-men]) monsieur; homme comme il faut, galant homme, homme bien né, *m.*
gentlemanly [ˈdʒentlmənli], *a.* distingué, de bon ton, comme il faut.
gentleness [ˈdʒentlnis], *n.* douceur, bonté, *f.*
gentlewoman [ˈdʒentlwumən], *n.* (*pl.* **-women** [wimin]) dame *ou* jeune fille de bonne famille, *f.*
gently [ˈdʒentli], *adv.* doucement.
genuine [ˈdʒenjuin], *a.* pur, vrai, véritable, authentique, naturel; sincère.
genuinely [ˈdʒenjuinli], *adv.* purement, sincèrement, authentiquement.
genuineness [ˈdʒenjuinnis], *n.* authenticité; sincérité, *f.*
genus [ˈdʒiːnəs], *n.* (*pl.* **genera** [ˈdʒenərə]) genre, *m.*
Geoffrey [ˈdʒefri]. Geoffroi, *m.*
geographer [dʒiˈɔgrəfə], *n.* géographe, *m., f.*
geographical [dʒiəˈgræfikl], *a.* géographique.
geography [dʒiˈɔgrəfi], *n.* géographie, *f.*
geology [dʒiˈɔlədʒi], *n.* géologie, *f.*
geometry [dʒiˈɔmitri], *n.* géométrie, *f.*
George [dʒɔːdʒ]. Georges, *m.*
geranium [dʒəˈreiniəm], *n.* (*Bot.*) géranium, *m.*
germ [dʒəːm], *n.* germe, *m.*
German [ˈdʒəːmən], *a.* allemand.—*n.* allemand (*langue*); Allemand (*personne*), *m.*
Germany [ˈdʒəːməni]. l'Allemagne, *f.*
germinate [ˈdʒəːmineit], *v.t.* germer; pousser.
gesticulate [dʒesˈtikjuleit], *v.i.* gesticuler.
gesticulation [dʒestikjuˈleiʃən], *n.* gesticulation, *f.*
gesture [ˈdʒestʃə], *n.* geste, *m.*, action, *f.*—*v.i.* gesticuler.
get [get], *v.t. irr.* (se) procurer, acquérir, obtenir; recevoir; remporter (*to gain*); gagner (*to earn*); avoir; acheter (*to buy*); arriver à, atteindre (*to reach*); aller chercher (*to fetch*); trouver (*to find*); faire, se faire (*to induce, make, cause etc.*); attraper, s'attirer (*to catch etc.*); ***to get hold of***, s'emparer de, saisir, obtenir.—*v.i.* se mettre (*en*); devenir, se faire (*to become*); aller (*to go*); ***to get about***, sortir, prendre de l'exercice; ***to get at***, arriver à; attaquer; atteindre; ***to get away***, s'en aller, se sauver, échapper (*à*); ***to get back***, revenir, regagner; recouvrer; ***to get in***, entrer, faire entrer, rentrer; ***to get off***, s'en tirer, s'échapper; descendre; ôter, enlever; ***to get on***, avancer, réussir, faire des progrès; monter sur; ***to get out***, sortir, s'en tirer, faire sortir; ***to get over***, passer, surmonter, vaincre; se consoler de; ***to get rid of***, se débarrasser de; ***to get through***, passer par, parcourir; réussir (*à un examen*); ***to get up***, se lever, monter, faire monter, lever; préparer.
gewgaw [ˈgjuːgɔː], *n.* babiole, bagatelle, *f.*, colifichet, *m.*
geyser [ˈgiːzə], *n.* chauffe-bain; (*Geol.*) geyser, *m.*
Ghana [ˈgɑːnə]. le Ghana, *m.*
Ghanaian [gɑːˈneiən], *a.* du Ghana.—*n.* citoyen(ne) du Ghana, *m., f.*
ghastliness [ˈgɑːstlinis], *n.* pâleur, *f.*; aspect effrayant, *m.*
ghastly [ˈgɑːstli], *a.* pâle, pâle comme la mort; horrible, affreux.
gherkin [ˈgəːkin], *n.* cornichon, *m.*
ghetto [ˈgetou], *n.* ghetto, *m.*
ghost [goust], *n.* revenant, fantôme, spectre, *m.*; ombre, *f.*; ***the Holy Ghost***, le Saint-Esprit.
ghostly [ˈgoustli], *a.* spirituel; de spectre.
ghoul [guːl], *n.* goule, *f.*
ghoulish [ˈguːliʃ], *a.* de goule.
ghyll [GILL (2)].
giant [ˈdʒaiənt], *a.* de géant.—*n.* géant, *m.*
gibber [ˈdʒibə], *v.i.* baragouiner.
gibberish [ˈdʒibəriʃ], *n.* baragouin, charabia, *m.*
gibbet [ˈdʒibit], *n.* potence, *f.*, gibet, *m.*
gibe [dʒaib], *v.t., v.i.* railler, se moquer (*de*).—*n.* sarcasme, *m.*; raillerie, moquerie, *f.*
giblets [ˈdʒiblits], *n.pl.* abatis, *m.pl.*
giddily [ˈgidili], *adv.* étourdiment, à l'étourdie.
giddiness [ˈgidinis], *n.* vertige, *m.*; (*fig.*) étourderie, *f.*
giddy [ˈgidi], *a.* étourdi; (*fig.*) volage; vertigineux; ***I feel giddy***, la tête me tourne; ***that makes me feel giddy***, cela me donne le vertige.
gift [gift], *n.* don, présent, cadeau; (*fig.*) talent, *m.*; ***Christmas gifts***, étrennes, *f.pl.*—*v.t.* douer, doter (*de*).
gifted [ˈgiftid], *a.* doué, de talent.
gigantic [dʒaiˈgæntik], *a.* gigantesque, de géant.
giggle [gigl], *v.i.* rire nerveusement, rire un peu bêtement.—*n.* ricanement, petit rire bête, *m.*
gild [gild], *v.t.* dorer; (*fig.*) embellir.
gilding [ˈgildiŋ], *n.* dorure, *f.*
Giles [dʒailz]. Gilles, *m.*
gill (1) [gil], *n.* (*usu. pl.*) ouïe (*de poisson*), *f.*
gill (2), **ghyll** [gil], *n.* ravin boisé; ruisseau (*du ravin*), *m.*
gill (3) [dzil], *n.* treize centilitres, *m.pl.*
***gillyflower** [ˈdʒiliflauə], *n.* giroflée, *f.*
gilt [gilt], *a.* doré.—*n.* dorure, *f.*
gilt-edged [ˈgiltedʒd], *a.* ***gilt-edged securities***, valeurs de tout repos, *f.pl.*
gimcrack [ˈdʒimkræk], *n.* pacotille, camelote, *f.*
gimlet [ˈgimlit], *n.* vrille, *f.*
gimmick [ˈgimik], *n.* machin; tour (*artifice*), *m.*

gin (1) [dʒin], *n.* trébuchet, piège, *m.*
gin (2) [dʒin], *n.* genièvre, gin (*liquor*), *m.*
ginger [ˈdʒindʒə], *n.* gingembre; (*fam.*) poil de carotte (*personne aux cheveux roux*), *m.*
gingerbread [ˈdʒindʒəbred], *n.* pain d'épice, *m.*
gingerly [ˈdʒindʒəli], *adv.* tout doucement, délicatement.
gipsy, gypsy [ˈdʒipsi], *n.* bohémien, tzigane, *m.*, bohémienne, *f.*
giraffe [dʒiˈrɑ:f], *n.* girafe, *f.*
gird (1) [gə:d], *v.t. irr.* ceindre (*de*); entourer (*de*).
gird (2) [gə:d], *v.i.* ***to gird at***, railler.
girder [ˈgə:də], *n.* poutre, solive, traverse, *f.*
girdle [gə:dl], *n.* ceinture, *f.*; ceinturon, *m.*; gaine, *f.*—*v.t.* ceinturer.
girl [gə:l], *n.* fille, jeune fille; jeune personne *f.*
girlish [ˈgə:liʃ], *a.* de jeune fille.
girth [gə:θ], *n.* sangle, *f.*; tour, *m.*, circonférence, *f.*
gist [dʒist], *n.* fond, fin mot; point principal, *m.*, substance (*d'un discours*), *f.*
give [giv], *v.t. irr.* donner; livrer, rendre, accorder; faire (*réponse, crédit, compliment, amitiés etc.*); remettre; porter (*un coup etc.*); pousser (*un gémissement etc.*); émettre (*un son*); ***to give away***, donner; trahir; ***to give up***, abandonner, renoncer à.—*v.i.* ceder; plier (*se courber*); prêter (*s'allonger*); ***give and take***, donnant donnant; ***to give in***, céder; ***to give oneself up***, se rendre; ***to give way***, céder, se relâcher.
given [givn], *a.* adonné, porté (*à*); donné; ***given these difficulties***, étant donné ces difficultés.
giver [ˈgivə], *n.* donneur, *m.*
gizzard [ˈgizəd], *n.* gésier, *m.*
glacial [ˈgleiʃəl], *a.* glacial, glaciaire.
glacier [ˈglæsiə], *n.* glacier, *m.*
glad [glæd], *a.* content, aise, bien aise; heureux (*de*).
gladden [glædn], *v.t.* réjouir.
glade [gleid], *n.* clairière, percée, *f.*
gladiator [ˈglædieitə], *n.* gladiateur, *m.*
gladiolus [glædiˈouləs], *n.* (*pl.* **gladioli** [glædiˈoulai]) glaïeul, *m.*
gladly [ˈglædli], *adv.* volontiers, avec plaisir.
glamorous [ˈglæmərəs], *a.* charmeur, ensorcelant.
glamour [ˈglæmə], *n.* charme, prestige, éclat, *m.*
glance [glɑ:ns], *n.* ricochet, coup en biais; regard, coup d'œil, *m.*—*v.i.* jeter un coup d'œil (*sur*); étinceler; ***to glance off***, ricocher.
gland [glænd], *n.* (*Anat.*) glande, *f.*
glare [glɛə], *n.* éclat, *m.*, lueur, *f.*; regard irrité *ou* farouche, *m.*—*v.i.* éblouir; luire; regarder d'un air furieux.
glaring [ˈglɛəriŋ], *a.* voyant, éblouissant; choquant; manifeste.
glass [glɑ:s], *a.* de verre.—*n.* (*pl.* **glasses** [ˈglɑ:siz]) verre, *m.*; vitre (*de fenêtre*), *f.*; (*pl.*) lunettes, *f. pl.*; ***cut glass***, cristal taillé, *m.*; ***field-glasses***, jumelles, *f.pl.*; ***looking-glass***, miroir, *m.*; ***magnifying glass***, loupe, *f.*; ***stained glass***, vitraux, *m.pl.*; (***weather-***)***glass***, baromètre, *m.*
glass-maker [ˈglɑ:smeikə], *n.* verrier, *m.*
glass-ware [ˈglɑ:swɛə], *n.* verrerie, *f.*
glassy [ˈglɑ:si], *a.* vitreux, transparent.
glaze [gleiz], *v.t.* vitrer; vernir.
glazier [ˈgleizjə], *n.* vitrier, *m.*
glazing [ˈgleiziŋ], *n.* vitrage (*de fenêtres*); vernissage (*de peintures*), *m.*
gleam [gli:m], *n.* rayon, *m.*, lueur, *f.*—*v.i.* briller, luire (*de*).
gleaming [ˈgli:miŋ], *a.* miroitant, luisant.
glean [gli:n], *v.t.* glaner.
gleaner [ˈgli:nə], *n.* glaneur, *m.*
glebe [gli:b], *n.* glèbe, terre, *f.*, sol, *m.*
glee [gli:], *n.* joie, gaieté, *f.*
gleeful [ˈgli:ful], *a.* joyeux, gai.
glen [glen], *n.* vallon, ravin, *m.*
glib [glib], *a.* coulant, délié, volubile.
glibly [ˈglibli], *adv.* avec volubilité; doucereusement.
glide [glaid], *v.i.* couler, glisser; se glisser (*dans*).—*n.* glissade, *f.*; (*Av.*) vol plané, *m.*
glider [ˈglaidə], *n.* (*Av.*) planeur, *m.*
glimmer [ˈglimə], *n.* lueur, *f.*, faible rayon, *m.*—*v.i.* entre-luire, luire faiblement; poindre (*l'aube*).
glimpse [glimps], *n.* coup d'œil, *m.*, vue rapide, *f.*; ***to catch a glimpse of***, entrevoir.
glint [glint], *n.* trait de lumière, *m.*, lueur, *f.*—*v.i.* luire par moments.
glisten [glisn], **glister** [ˈglistə], **glitter** [ˈglitə], *v.i.* reluire, scintiller, chatoyer.—*n.* éclat, lustre, *m.*
gloaming [ˈgloumiŋ], *n.* crépuscule, *m.*
gloat [glout], *v.i.* dévorer *ou* couver des yeux; (*fig.*) se régaler de.
global [gloubl], *a.* global; ***global war***, conflit mondial, *m.*
globe [gloub], *n.* globe, *m.*
globule [ˈglɔbju:l], *n.* globule, *m.*
gloom [glu:m], **gloominess** [ˈglu:minis], *n.* obscurité, *f.*, ténèbres, *f.pl.*; (*fig.*) tristesse, *f.*
gloomily [ˈglu:mili], *adv.* obscurément; d'un air triste, lugubrement.
gloomy [ˈglu:mi], *a.* sombre, obscur; morne; triste.
glorify [ˈglɔ:rifai], *v.t.* glorifier.
glorious [ˈglɔ:riəs], *a.* glorieux; illustre, superbe.
glory [ˈglɔ:ri], *n.* gloire; (*Paint.*) auréole, *f.*—*v.i.* se glorifier (*de*).
gloss [glɔs], *n.* lustre; apprêt, *m.*; (*fig.*) glose, *f.*, commentaire, *m.*—*v.i.* gloser, interpréter; lustrer; ***to gloss over***, glisser sur.
glossary [ˈglɔsəri], *n.* glossaire, *m.*
glossiness [ˈglɔsinis], *n.* lustre, brillant, glacé, *m.*
glossy [ˈglɔsi], *a.* lustré, brillant, luisant.
glove [glʌv], *n.* gant, *m.*
glover [ˈglʌvə], *n.* gantier, *m.*
glow [glou], *v.i.* brûler (*de*); briller; (*fig.*) s'échauffer.—*n.* lueur rouge, *f.*; (*fig.*) feu, éclat, *m.*, splendeur, *f.*
glowing [ˈglouiŋ], *a.* embrasé; ardent, chaleureux.
glow-worm [ˈglouwə:m], *n.* ver luisant, *m.*
glue [glu:], *n.* colle-forte, *f.*—*v.t.* coller.
glum [glʌm], *a.* maussade, de mauvaise humeur, morne.
glut [glʌt], *v.t.* gorger, rassasier; engorger (*le marché*).—*n.* surabondance, *f.*, excès, *m.*
glutton [glʌtn], *n.* gourmand, goinfre, *m.*

gluttonous ['glʌtənəs], *a.* gourmand, glouton, vorace.
gluttony ['glʌtəni], *n.* gloutonnerie, *f.*
glycerine ['glisəri:n], *n.* glycérine, *f.*
gnarled [nɑ:ld], *a.* noueux.
gnash [næʃ], *v.t.* grincer.—*v.i.* grincer des dents.
gnashing ['næʃiŋ], *n.* grincement, *m.*
gnat [næt], *n.* cousin, moucheron, *m.*
gnaw [nɔ:], *v.t.* ronger.
gnawing ['nɔ:iŋ], *a.* rongeant, rongeur.—*n.* rongement, *m.*
gnome [noum], *n.* gnome, *m.*
gnu [nu:], *n.* gnou, *m.*
go [gou], *v.i. irr.* aller, se rendre; marcher, passer; s'en aller, partir (*to leave*); disparaître; devenir (*to become*); ***to go astray***, s'égarer; ***to go away***, s'en aller, partir; ***to go back***, retourner, s'en retourner, reculer; ***to go backward***, aller à reculons, reculer; ***to go down***, descendre; se coucher (*soleil*); tomber; ***to go off***, partir (*fusil*); s'en aller; ***to go on***, aller, avancer, continuer; se passer; ***to go through***, passer par, traverser; subir, souffrir; ***to go to sleep***, s'endormir; ***to go without***, se passer de; ***to let go***, lâcher prise.—*n.* mode, vogue, *f.*; (*fig.*) entrain, coup, essai, *m.*
goad [goud], *n.* aiguillon, *m.*—*v.t.* aiguillonner; (*fig.*) stimuler.
goal [goul], *n.* but; terme, *m.*
goal-keeper ['goulki:pə], *n.* (*Ftb.*) gardien de but, *m.*
goat [gout], *n.* chèvre, *f.*; ***he goat***, bouc, *m.*
gobble [gɔbl], *v.t.* gober, avaler.—*v.i.* glouglouter (*dindon*).
goblet ['gɔblit], *n.* gobelet, *m.*
goblin ['gɔblin], *n.* lutin, *m.*
God [gɔd]. Dieu, *m.*
god [gɔd], *n.* dieu, *m.*
godchild ['gɔdtʃaild], *n.* filleul, *m.*, filleule, *f.*
goddaughter ['gɔddɔ:tə], *n.* filleule, *f.*
goddess ['gɔdis], *n.* déesse, *f.*
godfather ['gɔdfɑ:ðə], *n.* parrain, *m.*
Godfrey ['gɔdfri]. Godefroi, *m.*
godless ['gɔdlis], *a.* athée, impie.
godliness ['gɔdlinis], *n.* piété, *f.*
godly ['gɔdli], *a.* pieux, dévot.
godmother ['gɔdmʌðə], *n.* marraine, *f.*
godsend ['gɔdsend], *n.* aubaine, trouvaille, *f.*
godson ['gɔdsʌn], *n.* filleul, *m.*
godspeed ['gɔd'spi:d], *n.* succès, *m.*
goffer ['gɔfə], *v.t.* gaufrer.
goggle [gɔgl], *v.i.* rouler de gros yeux; ***goggle eyes***, des yeux en boules de loto, *m.pl.*
goggles [gɔglz], *n.pl.* lunettes (protectrices), *f.pl.*
going ['gouiŋ], *n.* marche, démarche, allée, *f.*, départ, *m.*
goitre ['gɔitə], *n.* (*Med.*) goitre, *m.*
gold [gould], *a.* d'or, en or.—*n.* or, *m.*
golden [gouldn], *a.* d'or.
goldfinch ['gouldfintʃ], *n.* chardonneret, *m.*
goldfish ['gouldfiʃ], *n.* poisson rouge, *m.*
goldsmith ['gouldsmiθ], *n.* orfèvre, *m.*
golf [gɔlf, gɔf], *n.* golf, *m.*
golf-club ['gɔlfklʌb], *n.* club de golf (*société* ou *instrument*), *m.*
golf-course ['gɔlfkɔ:s], *n.* terrain de golf, *m.*
gondola ['gɔndələ], *n.* gondole; nacelle (*de ballon*), *f.*
gondolier [gɔndə'liə], *n.* gondolier, *m.*
gone [gɔ:n, gɔn], *a.* allé, parti; perdu, disparu; passé, écoulé; adjugé (*aux enchères*).
gong [gɔŋ], *n.* gong; timbre (*d'une horloge*), *m.*
good [gud], *a.* bon; de bien, honnête; convenable, avantageux; valide, solide; (*colloq.*) sage; ***good luck***, bonheur, *m.*, bonne chance, *f.*; ***to make good***, exécuter; compenser, indemniser; assurer.—*n.* bien, bon, avantage, profit, *m.*; ***for good (and all)***, pour (tout) de bon; ***what's the good of?*** à quoi bon? (*pl.*) effets, biens, *m.pl.*, marchandises, *f.pl.*—*adv.* bien.—*int.* bon! bien! c'est très bien!
good-bye! [gud'bai], *int.* adieu! ***good-bye for the present***, au revoir.
good-for-nothing [gudfə'nʌθiŋ], *n.* vaurien, *m.*
Good Friday [gud'fraid(e)i]. vendredi saint, *m.*
good-humoured ['gud'hju:məd], *a.* de bonne humeur, enjoué, gai.
good-natured ['gud'neitʃəd], *a.* d'un bon naturel, bon, bienveillant.
goodness ['gudnis], *n.* bonté; probité, *f.*; ***thank goodness!*** Dieu merci!
goodwill [gud'wil], *n.* bienveillance, bonne volonté, bonté; (*Comm.*) clientèle, *f.*
goose [gu:s], *n.* (*pl.* **geese** [gi:s]) oie, *f.*; (*fig.*) imbécile, nigaud, *m.*
gooseberry ['guzbri], *n.* groseille à maquereau, *f.*
gooseberry-bush ['guzbribuʃ], *n.* groseillier, *m.*
goose-flesh ['gu:sfleʃ], *n.* chair de poule, *f.*
gore [gɔ:], *n.* sang, sang caillé, *m.*—*v.t.* donner un coup de corne à.
gorge [gɔ:dʒ], *n.* gorge, *f.*; gosier, *m.*—*v.t.* gorger, avaler, rassasier.—*v.i.* se gorger (*de*).
gorgeous ['gɔ:dʒəs], *a.* magnifique, splendide, fastueux.
gorilla [gə'rilə], *n.* gorille, *m.*
gorse [gɔ:s], *n.* ajonc, *m.*
gory ['gɔ:ri], *a.* sanglant, couvert de sang.
gosling ['gɔzliŋ], *n.* oison, *m.*
gospel ['gɔspəl], *n.* évangile, *m.*
gossamer ['gɔsəmə], *n.* fil de la Vierge, *m.*
gossip ['gɔsip], *n.* commère, *f.*, causeur (*personne*), *m.*; causerie, *f.*, commérage, *m.*—*v.i.* bavarder, faire des commérages.
gossip-writer ['gɔsipraitə], *n.* (*Journ.*) échotier, *m.*
Goth [gɔθ], *n.* Goth; (*fig.*) barbare, *m.*
Gothic ['gɔθik], *a.* gothique, ogival.
gouge [gaudʒ], *n.* gouge, *f.*—*v.t.* gouger; ***to gouge out***, arracher (*l'œil etc.*).
gourd [guəd], *n.* gourde, calebasse, *f.*
gout [gaut], *n.* goutte, *f.*
gouty ['gauti], *a.* goutteux.
govern ['gʌvən], *v.t.* gouverner, régir, diriger.
governess ['gʌvənis], *n.* institutrice, gouvernante, *f.*
government ['gʌvənmənt], *n.* gouvernement, *m.*, administration, *f.*, régime, *m.*
governor ['gʌvənə], *n.* gouverneur, gouvernant; directeur (*d'une institution*); (*Mech.*) régulateur, *m.*
gown [gaun], *n.* robe, *f.*; ***dressing-gown***, peignoir, *m.*, robe de chambre, *f.*; ***night-gown***, chemise de nuit, *f.*
grab [græb], *v.t.* empoigner, saisir (d'un geste brusque).

grace [greis], *n.* grâce; faveur, *f.*; pardon; (*Mus.*) agrément; bénédicité (*avant le repas*) *m.*; grâces (*après le repas*), *f.pl.*—*v.t.* orner, embellir; illustrer, honorer (*de*).
graceful ['greisful], *a.* gracieux, bien fait, élégant.
gracefully ['greisfuli], *adv.* gracieusement, élégamment.
gracefulness ['greisfulnis], *n.* grâce, *f.*
graceless ['greislis], *a.* sans grâce; dépravé.
gracious ['greiʃəs], *a.* gracieux, clément, bon, favorable, bénin.
graciously ['greiʃəsli], *adv.* gracieusement, avec bonté, favorablement.
graciousness ['greiʃəsnis], *n.* bonté, grâce, *f.*
grade [greid], *n.* grade; degré, rang, *m.*—*v.t.* classer; calibrer; graduer.
grading ['greidiŋ], *n.* classement; calibrage, *m.*; graduation, *f.*
gradient ['greidiənt], *n.* (*Rail.*) rampe, inclinaison, *f.*
gradual ['grædjuəl], *a.* graduel, par degrés, gradué.
gradually ['grædjuəli], *adv.* graduellement, par degrés, peu à peu.
graduate ['grædjueit], *v.t.* graduer.—*v.i.* être reçu à un examen d'enseignement supérieur.—['grædjuit], *n.* gradué, *m.*
graduation [grædju'eiʃən], *n.* graduation; (*Univ.*) remise d'un diplôme, *f.*
graft (1) [grɑːft], *v.t.* greffer, enter (*sur*).—*n.* greffe, *f.*
graft (2) [grɑːft], *n.* (*colloq.*) corruption, *f.*
grafting ['grɑːftiŋ], *n.* greffe, *f.*
grafting-knife ['grɑːftiŋnaif], *n.* greffoir, *m.*
grain [grein], *n.* grain, *m.*; céréales; fibres (*de bois*), *f.pl.*; ***against the grain***, contre le fil, (*fig.*) à contre-cœur, à rebrousse-poil.
gram, gramme [græm], *n.* gramme, *m.*
grammar ['græmə], *n.* grammaire, *f.*
grammar-school ['græməskuːl], *n.* lycée, collège, *m.*
grammatical [grə'mætikəl], *a.* grammatical; de grammaire.
gramophone ['græməfoun], *n.* gramophone; phonographe, *m.*
grampus ['græmpəs], *n.* épaulard, *m.*
granary ['grænəri], *n.* grenier, *m.*
grand [grænd], *a.* grand, magnifique, sublime, grandiose; ***grand (piano)***, piano à queue, *m.*
grandchild ['græntʃaild], *n.* (*pl.* **grandchildren** ['græntʃildrən]) petit-fils, *m.*, petite-fille, *f.*
granddaughter ['grændɔːtə], *n.* petite-fille, *f.*
grandee [græn'diː], *n.* grand d'Espagne, *m.*
grandeur ['grændjə], *n.* grandeur, *f.*, éclat, *m.*
grandfather ['grænfɑːðə], *n.* grand-père, *m.*
grandiloquence [græn'diləkwəns], *n.* langage pompeux, *m.*; emphase, grandiloquence, *f.*
grandiloquent [græn'diləkwənt], *a.* pompeux, enflé, grandiloquent.
grandly ['grændli], *adv.* grandement, avec éclat.
grandmother ['grænmʌðə], *n.* grand-mère, *f.*
grandson ['grænsʌn], *n.* petit-fils, *m.*
grandstand ['grændstænd], *n.* tribune, *f.*
grange [greindʒ], *n.* manoir (avec ferme), *m.*
granite ['grænit], *n.* granit, *m.*
grant [grɑːnt], *v.t.* accorder, concéder; convenir, avouer, admettre.—*n.* aide, bourse; concession, *f.*

granulate ['grænjuleit], *v.t.* grener, granuler —*v.i.* se granuler.
granule ['grænjuːl], *n.* granule, *m.*
grape [greip], *n.* grain de raisin, *m.*; (*pl.* raisins, *m.pl.*; ***a bunch of grapes***, une grappe de raisin.
grape-fruit ['greipfruːt], *n.* pamplemousse *m.*
grape-shot ['greipʃɔt], *n.* mitraille, *f.*
graph [grɑːf], *n.* (*Math.*) courbe, *f.*; graphique, *m.*—*v.t.* graphiquer.
graphic ['græfik], *a.* graphique, pittoresque
graph-paper ['grɑːfpeipə], *n.* papier quadrillé *m.*
graphite ['græfait], *n.* graphite, *m.*
grapnel ['græpnəl], *n.* grappin, *m.*
grapple [græpl], *n.* grappin, *m.*; lutte, *f.*—*v.t.* accrocher; grappiner.—*v.i.* en venir aux prises; lutter (*contre*).
grasp [grɑːsp], *v.t.* empoigner, saisir, serrer; embrasser; vouloir se saisir de.—*n.* prise, étreinte, poignée; (*fig.*) portée; compréhension, *f.*; ***within one's grasp***, à la portée de la main.
grasping ['grɑːspiŋ], *a.* avide, cupide, avare.
grass [grɑːs], *n.* herbe, *f.*; gazon, herbage, *m.*
grasshopper ['grɑːshɔpə], *n.* sauterelle, *f.*
grassy ['grɑːsi], *a.* herbeux, couvert de gazon, verdoyant.
grate [greit], *n.* grille, *f.*; foyer (*âtre*), *m.*—*v.t.* râper; frotter.—*v.i.* crisser (*sur* ou *contre*).
grateful ['greitful], *a.* reconnaissant; (*fig.*) agréable.
gratefully ['greitfuli], *adv.* avec reconnaissance; (*fig.*) agréablement.
grater ['greitə], *n.* râpe, *f.*
gratification [grætifi'keiʃən], *n.* satisfaction, *f.*; plaisir, *m.*; gratification, récompense, *f.*
gratify ['grætifai], *v.t.* satisfaire, faire plaisir à; récompenser.
gratifying ['grætifaiiŋ], *a.* agréable; (*fig.*) flatteur.
grating ['greitiŋ], *a.* grinçant, discordant, choquant, désagréable.—*n.* grille, *f.*, grillage; grincement (*bruit*), *m.*
gratis ['greitis], *adv.* gratuitement, gratis pour rien.
gratitude ['grætitjuːd], *n.* gratitude, reconnaissance, *f.*
gratuitous [grə'tjuːitəs], *a.* gratuit; (*fig.*) volontaire; bénévole.
gratuitously [grə'tjuːitəsli], *adv.* gratuitement; (*fig.*) sans motif.
gratuity [grə'tjuːiti], *n.* don, présent, *m.* gratification, *f.*; pourboire, *m.*
grave (1) [greiv], *n.* tombe, fosse, *f.*; tombeau, *m.*
grave (2) [greiv], *a.* grave, sérieux.
grave (3) [greiv], *v.t.* graver, tailler, ciseler.
grave-digger ['greivdigə], *n.* fossoyeur, *m.*
gravel [grævl], *n.* gravier, sable, *m.*—*v.t.* sabler.
gravely ['greivli], *adv.* gravement, sérieusement.
graven [greivn], *a.* gravé, taillé, ciselé.
graver ['greivə], *n.* graveur; burin (*instrument*), *m.*
gravity ['græviti], *n.* gravité, *f.*, air sérieux, *m.*; pesanteur, *f.*
gravy ['greivi], *n.* jus (*de viande*), *m.*; sauce, *f.*
gray (*Am.*) [GREY].

grayling ['greiliŋ], *n.* (*Ichth.*) ombre, *m.*

graze [greiz], *v.t.* effleurer, raser, frôler; érafler, écorcher (*la peau*).—*v.i.* paître, brouter.—*n.* écorchure, éraflure, *f.*

grease [gri:s], *n.* graisse, *f.*—*v.t.* graisser.

greasiness ['gri:sinis, 'gri:zinis], *n.* état graisseux, *m.*; (*fig.*) onctuosité, *f.*

greasy ['gri:si, 'gri:zi], *a.* gras, graisseux; (*fig.*) onctueux.

great [greit], *a.* grand; considérable; important, principal; gros (*de*); ***a great deal*** (***of***), ***a great many*** (***of***), beaucoup (de).

great-coat ['greitkout], *n.* pardessus, *m.*; (*Mil.*) capote, *f.*

great-grandparents ['greitgrændpɛərənts], *n.pl.* arrière-grands-parents, *m.pl.*

greatly ['greitli], *adv.* grandement, fort, beaucoup, de beaucoup.

greatness ['greitnis], *n.* grandeur; sublimité; force, *f.*

Grecian ['gri:ʃən], *a.* grec, de Grèce.—*n.* Helléniste, *m., f.*

Greece [gri:s]. la Grèce, *f.*

greed [gri:d], **greediness** ['gri:dinis], *n.* cupidité, avidité; gourmandise, *f.*

greedily ['gri:dili], *adv.* avidement.

greedy ['gri:di], *a.* cupide, avide; glouton.

Greek [gri:k], *a.* grec, de Grèce.—*n.* grec (*langue*); Grec (*personne*), *m.*

green [gri:n], *a.* vert; (*fig.*) frais, nouveau; novice.—*n.* vert, *m.*; verdure, *f.*; gazon, *m.*; (*pl.*) légumes verts, *m.pl.*

greenfinch ['gri:nfintʃ], *n.* verdier, *m.*

greengage ['gri:ngeidʒ], *n.* reine-claude, *f.*

greengrocer ['gri:ngrousə], *n.* fruitier, marchand de légumes, *m.*

greenhorn ['gri:nhɔ:n], *n.* blanc-bec, niais, *m.*

greenhouse ['gri:nhaus], *n.* serre, *f.*

greenish ['gri:niʃ], *a.* verdâtre.

Greenland ['gri:nlənd]. le Groenland, *m.*

greet [gri:t], *v.t.* saluer, accueillir.

greeting ['gri:tiŋ], *n.* salutation, *f.*, salut, *m.*; (*pl.*) compliments, *m.pl.*

gregarious [gri'gɛəriəs], *a.* grégaire.

Gregory ['gregəri]. Grégoire, *m.*

grenade [grə'neid], *n.* grenade, *f.*

grenadier [grenə'diə], *n.* grenadier, *m.*

grey [grei], *a.* gris.

greyhound ['greihaund], *n.* lévrier, *m.*

greyish ['greiiʃ], *a.* grisâtre.

grid [grid], **gridiron** ['gridaiən], *n.* gril, *m.*

grief [gri:f], *n.* douleur, tristesse, peine, *f.*; chagrin, *m.*

grievance ['gri:vəns], *n.* grief, *m.*; injustice, *f.*

grieve [gri:v], *v.t.* chagriner, attrister, faire de la peine à.—*v.i.* se chagriner, s'affliger.

grievous ['gri:vəs], *a.* lourd, douloureux, grave, affligeant; atroce.

grievously ['gri:vəsli], *adv.* grièvement, cruellement.

grill [gril], *v.t.* griller, faire griller.—*n.* gril, *m.*; grillade; viande grillée, *f.*

grim [grim], *a.* farouche, féroce; lugubre, effrayant; sinistre.

grimace [gri'meis], *n.* grimace; (*pl.*) grimacerie, *f.*—*v.i.* grimacer.

grime [graim], *n.* saleté, noirceur, *f.*

grimly ['grimli], *adv.* d'un air farouche *ou* sinistre.

grimness ['grimnis], *n.* air renfrogné, air farouche, *m.*

grimy ['graimi], *a.* sale, noirci, encrassé.

grin [grin], *n.* grimace, *f.*, ricanement, *m.*—*v.i.* ricaner, grimacer.

grind [graind], *v.t. irr.* moudre; broyer; aiguiser, repasser (*couteau etc.*); grincer (*dents*); (*fig.*) opprimer.

grinder ['graində], *n.* repasseur, émouleur; broyeur, *m.*; dent molaire, *f.*

grinding ['graindiŋ], *n.* broiement, grincement (*des dents etc.*); repassage (*de couteaux*), *m.*; (*fig.*) oppression, *f.*

grindstone ['graindstoun], *n.* meule, *f.*

grip [grip], *n.* prise, étreinte, *f.*, serrement, *m.*—*v.t.* empoigner, saisir, serrer.

gripe [graip], *v.t.* saisir; opprimer; donner la colique à.—*v.i.* avoir la colique.—*n.* saisine; (*pl.*) colique, *f.*

griping ['graipiŋ], *a.* (*fig.*) cuisant, affreux; avare (*pingre*).—*n.* colique, *f.*

grisly ['grizli], *a.* hideux, affreux, horrible.

grist [grist], *n.* blé à moudre, *m.*, mouture, *f.*; (*fig.*) gain, profit, *m.*

gristle [grisl], *n.* cartilage, *m.*

grit [grit], *n.* grès, sable; (*fig.*) courage, *m.*

gritty ['griti], *a.* graveleux.

grizzled [grizld], *a.* grison, grisâtre.

grizzly ['grizli], *a.* grisâtre; ***grizzly bear***, ours gris d'Amérique, *m.*

groan [groun], *n.* gémissement, grognement, *m.*—*v.i.* gémir, grogner.

grocer ['grousə], *n.* épicier, *m.*

grocery ['grousəri], *n.* épicerie, *f.*

groggy ['grɔgi], *a.* gris, pochard; titubant; aux jambes faibles (*cheval*).

groin [grɔin], *n.* aine; (*Arch.*) arête, *f.*

groom [gru:m], *n.* palefrenier, valet d'écurie, *m.*—*v.t.* panser; ***well-groomed***, bien soigné, *m.*

groove [gru:v], *n.* rainure, rayure, cannelure; (*fig.*) ornière (*rut*), *f.*—*v.t.* creuser, canneler.

grope [group], *v.i.* tâtonner.

gropingly ['groupiŋli], *adv.* à tâtons.

gross [grous], *a.* gros; grossier, rude; (*Comm.*) brut; (*fig.*) flagrant, énorme.—*n.* gros, *m.*, grosse; masse, *f.*

grossly ['grousli], *adv.* grossièrement; d'une manière flagrante.

grossness ['grousnis], *n.* grossièreté; énormité, *f.*

grotto ['grɔtou], *n.* grotte, *f.*

grotesque [gro'tesk], *a.* grotesque.

ground (1) [graund], *past* and *p.p.* [GRIND] and *a.* broyé, moulu; aiguisé (*affilé*).

ground (2) [graund], *n.* terre, *f.*; terrain (*plot*); sol (*soil*), *m.*; fond (*de tableau, de dessin textile etc.*); (*fig.*) fondement, sujet, motif, *m.*, cause, *f.*; (*pl.*) terrains, *m.pl.*, sédiment, marc de café, *m.*—*v.t.* fonder, baser, établir, appuyer (*sur*).—*v.i.* échouer.

grounded ['graundid], *a.* fondé, établi; ***well-grounded***, bien fondé.

ground-floor ['graund'flɔ:], *n.* rez-de-chaussée, *m.*

groundless ['graundlis], *a.* sans fondement.

groundlessly ['graundlisli], *adv.* sans fondement.

group [gru:p], *n.* groupe, peloton, *m.*—*v.t.* grouper.

grouping ['gru:piŋ], *n.* groupement, *m.*

grouse (1) [graus], *n.* (*Orn.*) tétras; coq de bruyère, *m.*

grouse (2) [graus], *v.i.* grogner, grincher.

grove [grouv], *n.* bocage, bosquet, *m.*
grovel [grɔvl], *v.i.* ramper, se vautrer.
grovelling ['grɔvliŋ], *a.* rampant, abject, vil.—*n.* bassesse, *f.*
grow [grou], *v.t. irr.* cultiver.—*v.i.* croître, pousser; s'accroître; devenir, se faire (*to become*); ***to grow up***, croître, grandir, arriver à maturité.
grower ['grouə], *n.* cultivateur, producteur, *m.*
growing ['grouiŋ], *a.* croissant.—*n.* croissance; culture, *f.*
growl [graul], *v.i.* grogner, gronder.—*n.* grognement, grondement, *m.*
grown-up ['grounʌp], *a.* fait, grand.—*n.* adulte, *m.*, *f.*
growth [grouθ], *n.* croissance, *f.*; produit cru, *m.*, récolte (*produce*), *f.*; (*fig.*) progrès, *m.*
grub [grʌb], *n.* larve, *f.*, ver blanc, *m.*—*v.t.* défricher, fouiller.—*v.i.* bêcher, creuser.
grubby ['grʌbi], *a.* véreux; (*fig.*) sale.
grudge [grʌdʒ], *n.* rancune, animosité, *f.*; ***to bear a grudge against***, en vouloir à.—*v.t.* donner à contre-cœur.
grudgingly ['grʌdʒiŋli], *adv.* à contre-cœur; de mauvaise grâce.
gruel ['gru:əl], *n.* gruau, *m.*
gruesome ['gru:səm], *a.* macabre, horrible, lugubre.
gruff [grʌf], *a.* bourru, rude, rébarbatif.
grumble [grʌmbl], *v.i.* se plaindre, grogner grommeler (*contre* ou *de*).
grumbler ['grʌmblə], *n.* grondeur, grogneur *m.*
grumbling ['grʌmbliŋ], *n.* grognement, *m.*
grunt [grʌnt], *v.i.* grogner.—*n.* grognement, *m.*
guarantee [gærən'ti:], *n.* garant, *m.*, caution, garantie, *f.*—*v.t.* garantir.
guard [gɑ:d], *n.* garde; défense, protection, *f.*; garde (*personne*); (*Rail.*) conducteur, chef de train, *m.*—*v.t.* garder, défendre, protéger, veiller sur.—*v.i.* se garder, se prémunir (*contre*).
guarded ['gɑ:did], *a.* prudent, circonspect; réservé.
guardedly ['gɑ:didli], *adv.* avec circonspection, avec réserve.
guardian ['gɑ:djən], *a.* gardien, tutélaire.—*n.* gardien; tuteur (*de jeunes*), *m.*
guardianship ['gɑ:djənʃip], *n.* tutelle, protection, *f.*
guard-room ['gɑ:drum], *n.* corps de garde, *m.*, salle de police, *f.*
Guatemala [gwætə'mɑ:lə]. le Guatemala, *m.*
gudgeon ['gʌdʒən], *n.* goujon; (*Mech.*) tourillon, *m.*; (*fig.*) dupe, *f.*
guess [ges], *v.t.*, *v.i.* deviner, conjecturer.—*n.* conjecture, *f.*
guest [gest], *n.* invité, *m.*, convive, *m.*, *f.*; hôte, *m.*
guffaw [gə'fɔ:], *n.* gros rire, *m.*—*v.i.* pouffer de rire.
guidance ['gaidəns], *n.* conduite, direction, *f.*
guide [gaid], *n.* guide, conducteur, *m.*; ***Girl Guide***, éclaireuse, *f.*—*v.t.* conduire, guider; diriger; ***guided missile***, (*Mil.*) engin téléguidé, *m.*
guild [gild], *n.* corporation, guilde, *f.*
guildhall ['gildhɔ:l], *n.* hôtel de ville, *m.*
guile [gail], *n.* astuce, *f.*, artifice, *m.*
guilt [gilt], *n.* culpabilité, *f.*
guiltily ['giltili], *adv.* criminellement.
guiltless ['giltlis], *a.* innocent.
guilty ['gilti], *a.* coupable; ***the guilty party***, le coupable; ***to find guilty***, (*Law*) déclarer coupable; ***to plead guilty***, s'avouer coupable.
Guinea ['gini]. la Guinée, *f.*
guinea ['gini], *n.* guinée, *f.*
guinea-fowl ['ginifaul], *n.* pintade, *f.*
guinea-pig ['ginipig], *n.* cochon d'Inde, *m.*
guise [gaiz], *n.* guise, façon, apparence, *f.*; costume, *m.*, dehors, *m.pl.*
guitar [gi'tɑ:], *n.* guitare, *f.*
gulf [gʌlf], *n.* golfe; (*fig.*) gouffre, *m.*
gull [gʌl], *n.* mouette, *f.*, goéland; (*fig.*) jobard, *m.*—*v.t.* duper, flouer.
gullet ['gʌlit], *n.* gosier, *m.*
gullible ['gʌlibl], *a.* crédule.
gully ['gʌli], *n.* ravin, *m.*
gulp [gʌlp], *v.t.* avaler, gober.—*n.* goulée, gorgée, *f.*, trait, *m.*; ***at a gulp***, d'un trait.
gum [gʌm], *n.* gomme; (*Anat.*) gencive, *f.*
gumboil ['gʌmbɔil], *n.* abcès aux gencives, *m.*
gumption ['gʌmpʃən], *n.* (*colloq.*) sens pratique, *m.*, jugeotte, *f.*
gum-tree ['gʌmtri:], *n.* gommier, *m.*; (*fig.*) ***up a gum-tree***, dans le pétrin.
gun [gʌn], *n.* canon, *m.*; pièce d'artillerie, bouche à feu, *f.*; fusil (non rayé); (*Am.*) revolver, *m.*; ***machine-gun***, mitrailleuse *f.*
gunboat ['gʌnbout], *n.* canonnière, *f.*
guncarriage ['gʌnkæridʒ], *n.* affût (de canon), *m.*
gunnel [GUNWALE].
gunner ['gʌnə], *n.* canonnier, servant, artilleur, *m.*
gunnery ['gʌnəri], *n.* artillerie, *f.*; tir au canon, *m.*
gunpowder ['gʌnpaudə], *n.* poudre à canon, *f.*
gunshot ['gʌnʃɔt], *n.* portée de fusil (*distance*), *f.*; coup de canon (*décharge*); coup de feu (*blessure*), *m.*
gunwale [gʌnl], *n.* (*Naut.*) plat-bord, *m.*
gurgle [gə:gl], *v.i.* faire glouglou; gargouiller.
gush [gʌʃ], *n.* jaillissement, *m.*; effusion, *f.*, jet; débordement (*de sentiments*), *m.*—*v.i.* jaillir; (*fig.*) être sentimental à l'excès.
gusher ['gʌʃə], *n.* (*Min.*) puits jaillissant, *m.*
gushing ['gʌʃiŋ], *a.* jaillissant; bouillonnant; (*fig.*) expansif, empressé.
gusset ['gʌsit], *n.* gousset, *m.*
gust [gʌst], *n.* coup de vent, *m.*, bouffée, rafale, *f.*
gusty ['gʌsti], *a.* orageux, venteux.
gut [gʌt], *n.* boyau, intestin, *m.*; corde à boyau (*fabriqué*), *f.*; (*pl.*) (*fam.*) intestins, *m.pl.*, ventre; courage, cran, *m.*—*v.t.* éventrer, vider; (*fig.*) détruire.
gutter ['gʌtə], *n.* gouttière (*d'une maison*), *f.*; ruisseau, caniveau (*dans la rue*), *m.*—*v.i.* couler.
guttersnipe ['gʌtəsnaip], *n.* gamin, voyou, *m.*
guttural ['gʌtərəl], *a.* guttural.
guy [gai], *n.* épouvantail, *m.*; (*Naut.*) corde soutien, *f.*, guide; (*Am.*) type, individu, *m.*
Guyana [gi'ɑ:nə, gai'ɑ:nə]. la Guyane, *f.*
guzzle [gʌzl], *v.t.*, *v.i.* bouffer (*aliment*), lamper (*boisson*).
gym [dʒim], [GYMNASIUM].
gymkhana [dʒim'kɑ:nə], *n.* gymkhana, *m.*
gymnasium [dʒim'neiziəm], *n.* gymnase, *m.*

gymnast ['dʒimnæst], *n.* gymnaste, *m., f.*
gymnastic [dʒim'næstik], *a.* gymnastique.—*n.(pl.)* gymnastique, *f.*
gypsum ['dʒipsəm], *n.* gypse, *m.*
gypsy [GIPSY].
gyrate [dʒai'reit], *v.i.* tournoyer.
gyration [dʒai'reiʃən], *n.* mouvement giratoire, *m.*

H

H, h [eitʃ]. huitième lettre de l'alphabet, *m.* ou *f.*; ***H-bomb***, [HYDROGEN].
haberdasher ['hæbədæʃə], *n.* mercier, *m.*
haberdashery ['hæbədæʃəri], *n.* mercerie, *f.*
habit ['hæbit], *n.* habitude, coutume, *f.*; (*pl.*) mœurs, *f.pl.*; ***riding-habit***, amazone, *f.*; ***to be in the habit of***, avoir coutume de.—*v.t.* vêtir.
habitable ['hæbitəbl], *a.* habitable.
habitation [hæbi'teiʃən], *n.* habitation, demeure, *f.*
habitual [hə'bitjuəl], *a.* habituel.
habitually [hə'bitjuəli], *adv.* habituellement, d'habitude.
habituate [hə'bitjueit], *v.t.* habituer, accoutumer.
hack (1) [hæk], *v.t.* hacher, couper; ébrécher; (*fig.*) massacrer, écorcher.
hack (2) [hæk], *n.* cheval de louage, *m.*; rosse (*cheval sans force*), *f.*; (*fig.*) écrivassier à gages, *m.*
hackney ['hækni], *n.* ***hackney-carriage***, fiacre, *m.*
hackneyed ['hæknid], *a.* banal, rebattu; ***hackneyed phrase***, cliché, *m.*
haddock ['hædək], *n.* (*Ichth.*) aiglefin, *m.*
Hades ['heidi:z]. les Enfers, *m.pl.*
haemoglobin [hi:mə'gloubin], *n.* hémoglobine, *f.*
haemorrhage ['hemərid ʒ], *n.* hémorrhagie, *f.*
haft [ha:ft], *n.* manche, *m.*, poignée, *f.*
hag [hæg], *n.* vieille sorcière; (*pop.*) vieille fée, *f.*
haggard ['hægəd], *a.* hagard, farouche, égaré.
haggle [hægl], *v.i.* marchander.
Hague [heig], **The.** La Haye, *f.*
hail (1) [heil], *n.* grêle, *f.*—*v.i.* grêler.
hail (2) [heil], *n.* salut, appel, *m.*—*int.* salut! —*v.t.* saluer; (*Naut.*) héler; ***to hail a taxi***, héler *ou* appeler un taxi; ***to hail from***, venir de.
hailstone ['heilstoun], *n.* grêlon, *m.*
hailstorm ['heilstɔ:m], *n.* tempête de grêle, *f.*
hair [hɛə], *n.* cheveu (*a single hair*), *m.*; cheveux, *m.pl.*, chevelure (*head of hair*), *f.*; poil (*on the body, on animals etc.*), crin (*horsehair*), *m.*; soies (*bristles*), *f.pl.*; ***to do one's hair***, se coiffer; ***to split hairs***, chicaner sur les mots.
hair-brush ['hɛəbrʌʃ], *n.* brosse à cheveux, *f.*
hair-cut ['hɛəkʌt], *n.* coupe de cheveux, *f.*
hairdresser ['hɛədresə], *n.* coiffeur, *m.*
hairless ['hɛəlis], *a.* chauve, sans cheveux; sans poil (*animal*).
hair-net ['hɛənet], *n.* résille, *f.*
hairy ['hɛəri], *a.* velu, chevelu, poilu.
Haiti [hai'i:ti]. Haïti, *m.* ou *f.*
Haitian [hai'i:ʃən], *a.* haïtien.—*n.* Haïtien (*personne*), *m.*
hake [heik], *n.* (*Ichth.*) merluche, *f.*, (*fam.*) colin, *m.*
halberd ['hælbəd], *n.* hallebarde, *f.*
hale [heil], *a.* robuste, sain, bien portant; ***to be hale and hearty***, avoir bon pied, bon œil.
half [ha:f], *a.* demi.—*n.* (*pl.* **halves** [ha:vz]) moitié, *f.*, demi, *m.*, ***half an hour***, une demi-heure, *f.*; (*pop.*) ***not half!*** tu parles! —*adv.* à demi, à moitié.
half-back ['ha:fbæk], *n.* (*Ftb.*) demi, *m.*
half-brother ['ha:fbrʌðə], *n.* demi-frère, frère utérin, frère consanguin, *m.*
half-caste ['ha:fka:st], *n.* métis, *m.*
half-fare ['ha:f'fɛə], *n.* demi-place, *f.*, demi-tarif, *m.*
half-holiday ['ha:f'hɔlidi], *n.* demi-congé, *m.*
half-pay ['ha:f'pei], *n.* demi-solde, *f.*
half-time ['ha:f'taim], *n.* (*Spt.*) la mi-temps, *f.*
half-way ['ha:f'wei], *adv.* à mi-chemin; ***half-way up the hill***, à mi-côte.
half-witted ['ha:f'witid], *a.* niais, sot, idiot.
half-year ['ha:f'jiə], *n.* semestre, *m.*
halibut ['hælibət], *n.* (*Ichth.*) flétan, *m.*
hall [hɔ:l], *n.* salle, *f.*; vestibule (*entrance-hall*); château, manoir (*seat*); réfectoire (*dining-hall*); hôtel de ville (*town hall*), *m.*; ***hall porter***, concierge, *m.*
hall-mark ['hɔ:lma:k], *n.* poinçon de contrôle, *m.*—*v.t.* contrôler.
hallo! [hə'lou], *int.* holà! hé!
hallow ['hælou], *v.t.* sanctifier, consacrer.
hallucinate [hə'lju:sineit], *v.t.* halluciner.
hallucination [həlju:si'neiʃən], *n.* hallucination; (*fig.*) déception, illusion, *f.*
halo ['heilou], *n.* (*Astron.*) halo, *m.*; (*Paint. etc.*) auréole, *f.*
halt (1) [hɔ:lt], *n.* halte, *f.*; arrêt; clochement, *m.*—*v.i.* faire halte.—*int.* halte-là!
***halt** (2) [hɔ:lt], *a.* boiteux, estropié.
halter ['hɔ:ltə], *n.* licou, *m.*, longe (*à cheval*); corde (*du gibet*), *f.*
halve [ha:v], *v.t.* diviser en deux.
ham [hæm], *n.* jambon; *jarret (*humain*), *m.*
hamlet ['hæmlit], *n.* hameau, *m.*
hammer ['hæmə], *n.* marteau; chien (*de fusil*), *m.*; ***to bring under the hammer***, mettre aux enchères.—*v.t.* marteler, forger. —*v.i.* marteler.
hammock ['hæmək], *n.* hamac, *m.*
hamper (1) ['hæmpə], *n.* panier, *m.*, manne, *f.*
hamper (2) ['hæmpə], *v.t.* empêtrer, embarrasser, gêner.
hamstring ['hæmstriŋ], *n.* tendon du jarret, *m.*—*v.t. irr.* (*conjug. like* STRING) couper le jarret à; (*fig.*) couper les moyens à.
hand [hænd], *n.* main; palme (*mesure de 4 pouces*); signature; écriture (*calligraphie*), *f.*; (*Cards*) jeu, *m.*; aiguille (*d'une montre etc.*), *f.*; ouvrier, employé, *m.*; ***at hand***, sous la main; ***off-hand***, sur-le-champ; ***second-hand***, d'occasion.—*v.t.* passer, donner, remettre; donner la main à; conduire, guider; ***to hand about*** or ***round***, faire passer de main en main, faire circuler; ***to hand down***, transmettre; ***to hand over***, remettre, céder.

handbag ['hændbæg], *n.* sac à main, *m.*
hand-bell ['hændbel], *n.* sonnette, clochette, *f.*
handbook ['hændbuk], *n.* manuel; guide, *m.*
handcuff ['hændkʌf], *n.* menotte, *f.*—*v.t.* mettres les menottes à.
handful ['hændful], *n.* poignée, *f.*; (*fig.*) petit nombre, peu, *m.*
handicap ['hændikæp], *n.* handicap, *m.*—*v.t.* handicaper.
handicraft ['hændikrɑːft], *n.* métier, travail manuel, *m.*
handiwork ['hændiwəːk], *n.* ouvrage, travail manuel, *m.*
handkerchief ['hæŋkətʃif], *n.* mouchoir, *m.*
handle [hændl], *n.* manche, *m.*; poignée (*d'une epée etc.*), *f.*; bouton (*d'une porte*), *m.*; anse (*d'une cruche*); queue (*d'une poêle*), *f.*; ***starting handle***, (*Motor.*) manivelle (de mise en marche), *f.*—*v.t.* manier; toucher à, manipuler.
handle-bar ['hændlbɑː], *n.* guidon (*de bicyclette*), *m.*
handling ['hændliŋ], *n.* maniement, traitement, *m.*
handmaid ['hændmeid], *n.* servante, *f.*
handrail ['hændreil], *n.* garde-fou, *m.*, rampe, main courante, *f.*
handshake ['hændʃeik], *n.* poignée de main, *f.*, serrement de main, *m.*
handsome ['hænsəm], *a.* beau, élégant; (*fig.*) gracieux.
handsomely ['hænsəmli], *adv.* joliment, élégamment; généreusement.
handwriting ['hændraitiŋ], *n.* écriture, *f.*
handy ['hændi], *a.* adroit (*personne*); commode; à portée de la main.
hang [hæŋ], *v.t. irr.* pendre, suspendre; accrocher (*à*); tendre, tapisser (*de*); laisser pendre, pencher, baisser (*la tête etc.*); poser (*portes etc.*); ***hang it!*** fichtre! ***go and be hanged***, va-t'en au diable! ***to hang fire***, faire long feu; (*fig.*) vaciller.—*v.i.* pendre, être suspendu; s'accrocher, se pendre; baisser, se pencher (*à*); ***to hang about***, rôder autour de; ***to hang over***, être suspendu sur, surplomber.
hangar ['hæŋə], *n.* (*Av.*) hangar, *m.*
hang-dog ['hæŋdɔg], *n.* ***hang-dog look***, mine patibulaire, *f.*
hanger-on ['hæŋə'rɔn], *n.* dépendant, parasite, *m.*
hanging ['hæŋiŋ], *a.* suspendu.—*n.* suspension, pendaison; pose (*papier de tenture*), *f.*; collage, *m.*; (*pl.*) tapisserie, tenture, *f.*
hangman ['hæŋmən], *n.* (*pl.* **-men** [men]) bourreau, *m.*
hank [hæŋk], *n.* poignée, *f.*, écheveau, *m.*
hanker ['hæŋkə], *v.i.* ***to hanker after***, désirer ardemment.
hankering ['hæŋkəriŋ], *n.* grande envie, *f.*, vif désir, *m.*
haphazard [hæp'hæzəd], *a.* au petit bonheur, fortuit.—*n.* hasard, sort, *m.*
haply ['hæpli], *adv.* par hasard; peut-être.
happen [hæpn], *v.i.* arriver, advenir, se passer; se trouver par hasard.
happily ['hæpili], *adv.* heureusement, par bonheur.
happiness ['hæpinis], *n.* bonheur, *m.*
happy ['hæpi], *a.* heureux, content.
harass ['hærəs], *v.t.* harasser, harceler.
harbinger ['hɑːbindʒə], *n.* avant-coureur, précurseur, *m.*
harbour ['hɑːbə], *n.* port, havre; (*fig.*) refuge, asile, gîte, *m.*—*v.t.* héberger, recéler, donner asile à; (*fig.*) entretenir, nourrir.—*v.i.* se réfugier.
hard [hɑːd], *a.* dur, ferme; (*fig.*) malaisé, difficile; pénible, rude, rigoureux; dur à la détente (*pingre*); ***hard frost***, forte gelée, *f.*; ***hard labour***, travaux forcés, *m.pl.*; ***hard up***, à court (d'argent).—*adv.* dur, rudement, péniblement; fort, ferme.
harden [hɑːdn], *v.t.* durcir; (*fig.*) endurcir (*à*).—*v.i.* s'endurcir, devenir dur.
hardening ['hɑːdniŋ], *n.* durcissement; (*fig.*) endurcissement, *m.*; trempe (*d'acier*), *f.*
hardihood ['hɑːdihud], *n.* hardiesse, audace, intrépidité, *f.*
hardily ['hɑːdili], *adv.* durement, hardiment.
hardiness ['hɑːdinis], *n.* hardiesse, *f.*; tempérament robuste, *m.*; (*fig.*) effronterie, assurance, *f.*
hardly ['hɑːdli], *adv.* durement, rudement, mal; à peine, guère (*presque pas*); ***hardly ever***, presque jamais.
hardness ['hɑːdnis], *n.* dureté, solidité; difficulté; crudité (*d'eau*), *f.*
hardship ['hɑːdʃip], *n.* fatigue, peine, privation, *f.*; (*pl.*) épreuves, souffrances, *f.pl.*
hardware ['hɑːdwɛə], *n.* quincaillerie, *f.*
hardy ['hɑːdi], *a.* hardi, courageux; fort; de pleine terre (*plantes*).
hare [hɛə], *n.* lièvre, *m.*
hare-brained ['hɛəbreind], *a.* écervelé, étourdi.
hare-lip ['hɛəlip], *n.* bec-de-lièvre, *m.*
hark [hɑːk], *v.i.* écouter, prêter l'oreille.—*int.* écoutez!
harlequin ['hɑːlikwin], *n.* arlequin *m.*
harm [hɑːm], *n.* tort, dommage, mal, *m.*—*v.t.* nuire à, faire du mal à.
harmful ['hɑːmful], *a.* nuisible, malfaisant, nocif.
harmless ['hɑːmlis], *a.* innocent, inoffensif.
harmonic [hɑː'mɔnik], *a.* harmonique; harmonieux.—*n.*(*pl.*) harmonique, *f.*
harmonious [hɑː'mouniəs], *a.* harmonieux; mélodieux.
harmonize ['hɑːmənaiz], *v.t.* rendre harmonieux, accorder, harmoniser.—*v.i.* s'harmoniser; (*fig.*) s'accorder.
harmony ['hɑːməni], *n.* harmonie, *f.*; accord, *m.*
harness ['hɑːnis], *n.* harnais, harnachement, *m.*—*v.t.* harnacher; atteler (*à une voiture*).
harp [hɑːp], *n.* harpe, *f.*; ***Jew's harp***, guimbarde, *f.*—*v.i.* jouer de la harpe; ***to harp on one string***, rabâcher toujours la même chose.
harpist ['hɑːpist], *n.* harpiste, *m.*, *f.*
harpoon [hɑː'puːn], *n.* harpon, *m.*—*v.t.* harponner.
harpsichord ['hɑːpsikɔːd], *n.* clavecin, *m.*
harridan ['hæridən], *n.* chipie, mégère, *f.*
harrow ['hærou], *n.* herse, *f.*—*v.t.* herser; (*fig.*) torturer.
harrowing ['hærouiŋ], *a.* navrant.—*n.* hersage; (*fig.*) déchirement, *m.*
Harry ['hæri]. Henri, *m.*
harry ['hæri], *v.t.* harceler; piller.
harsh [hɑːʃ], *a.* âpre, rude, dur; discordant.
harshly ['hɑːʃli], *adv.* durement, sévèrement.

harshness ['hɑːʃnis], *n.* âpreté; discordance, *f.*
hart [hɑːt], *n.* cerf, *m.*
harum-scarum ['hɛərəm'skɛərəm], *a.* écervelé, étourdi.
harvest ['hɑːvist], *n.* moisson (*de blé*); récolte (*de fruits etc.*); vendange (*de raisins*), *f.*—*v.t.* moissonner; récolter; vendanger.
hash [hæʃ], *n.* hachis, *m.*—*v.t.* hacher, hacher menu; (*fig.*) plagier.
hasp [hæsp, hɑːsp], *n.* loquet, *m.*
hassock ['hæsək], *n.* coussin (*pour les genoux* ou *les pieds*), *m.*
haste [heist], *n.* hâte, précipitation, *f.*, emportement, *m.*; diligence, *f.*; ***in haste***, à la hâte; ***to make haste***, se hâter, se dépêcher. —*v.i.* or **hasten** [heisn], se hâter, se dépêcher, s'empresser.
hasten [heisn], *v.t.* hâter, dépêcher.
hastily ['heistili], *adv.* à la hâte; brusquement.
hastiness ['heistinis], *n.* hâte, précipitation, *f.*; emportement, *m.*
hasty ['heisti], *a.* rapide, précipité; inconsidéré, emporté.
hat [hæt], *n.* chapeau, *m.*; ***bowler-hat***, chapeau melon; ***felt hat***, feutre, *m.*; ***soft felt hat***, chapeau mou; ***straw hat***, chapeau de paille; ***top hat***, chapeau haut de forme.
hatch (1) [hætʃ], *n.* (*pl.* **hatches** ['hætʃiz]) couvée (*de poulets*); éclosion (*d'œufs*); porte coupée (*dans le mur*); (*Naut.*) écoutille, *f.*; (*pl.*) panneaux des écoutilles, *m.pl.*—*v.t.* couver (*incuber*); faire éclore; (*fig.*) tramer, produire.—*v.i.* éclore.
hatch (2) [hætʃ], *v.t.* hacher (*un dessin*).
hatchet ['hætʃit], *n.* cognée, hachette, hache, *f.*
hate [heit], *n.* haine, *f.*—*v.t.* haïr, détester.
hateful ['heitful], *a.* odieux, détestable.
hatred ['heitrid], *n.* haine, *f.*
hat-stand ['hætstænd], *n.* porte-chapeaux, *m. inv.*
hatter ['hætə], *n.* chapelier, *m.*
haughtily ['hɔːtili], *adv.* hautainement avec arrogance.
haughtiness ['hɔːtinis], *n.* arrogance, *f.*
haughty ['hɔːti], *a.* hautain, arrogant.
haul [hɔːl], *n.* tirage, remorquage; coup de filet, *m.*—*v.t.* tirer, remorquer, haler; charrier, transporter.
haulage ['hɔːlidʒ], *n.* camionnage, roulage; remorquage, *m.*
haulier ['hɔːljə], *n.* camionneur, *m.*
haunch [hɔːntʃ], *n.* hanche (*d'un animal*), *f.*, cuissot (*de venaison*), *m.*
haunt [hɔːnt], *n.* retraite, *f.*; repaire (*de voleur, etc.*), *m.*—*v.t.* hanter, fréquenter; (*fig.*) obséder.
Havana [hə'vænə]. la Havane, *f.*
have [hæv], *v.t.* and *aux. irr.* avoir; tenir, posséder; contenir; prendre; faire; ***I had rather***, j'aimerais mieux; ***I have it***, j'y suis; ***to have to***, devoir, falloir, avoir à.
haven [heivn], *n.* havre, port; (*fig.*) asile, *m.*
haversack ['hævəsæk], *n.* (*Mil.*) musette, *f.*; havresac, *m.*
havoc ['hævək], *n.* dégât, ravage, *m.*
hawk [hɔːk], *n.* faucon, *m.*—*v.t.* chasser au faucon; colporter (*vendre*).
hawker ['hɔːkə], *n.* colporteur, *m.*
hawser ['hɔːzə], *n.* haussière, *f.*, grelin, *m.*
hawthorn ['hɔːθɔːn], *n.* aubépine, *f.*
hay [hei], *n.* foin, *m.*
hay-fever ['hei'fiːvə], *n.* rhume des foins, *m.*
hay-making ['heimeikiŋ], *n.* fenaison, *f.*
hayrick ['heirik], **haystack** ['heistæk], *n.* meule de foin, *f.*
hazard ['hæzəd], *n.* hasard, danger, risque, *m.* —*v.t.* hasarder, risquer.—*v.i.* se hasarder, s'aventurer.
hazardous ['hæzədəs], *a.* hasardeux, risqué, dangereux.
haze [heiz], *n.* petite brume; (*fig.*) obscurité, *f.*
hazel [heizl], *a.* noisette.—*n.* noisetier, coudrier, *m.*
hazel-nut ['heizlnʌt], *n.* noisette, *f.*
hazily ['heizili], *adv.* indistinctement.
hazy ['heizi], *a.* brumeux; ***to have hazy notions***, avoir des idées vagues.
he [hiː], *pron.* il, celui, lui; ***he and I***, lui et moi; ***he that*** or ***he who***, celui qui.
he- [hiː], *pref.* mâle.
head [hed], *a.* premier, principal, en chef.—*n.* tête, *f.*; chef, avant, *m.*; proue (*de navire*), *f.*; haut bout (*d'une table*); chevet (*d'un lit*), *m.*; chute (*d'eau*), *f.*; pièces (*de gibier*), *f.pl.*; source (*d'une rivière*), *f.*; (*fig.*) sujet, chapitre, *m.*—*v.t.* conduire, diriger.—*v.i.* ***to head for***, (*Naut.*) mettre le cap sur; se diriger vers, s'avancer vers.
headache ['hedeik], *n.* mal de tête, *m.*, migraine, *f.*
head-dress ['heddres], *n.* coiffure, *f.*
heading ['hediŋ], *n.* titre, en-tête, *m.*
headland ['hedlənd], *n.* cap, promontoire, *m.*
head-light ['hedlait], *n.* (*Motor.*) phare, *m.*
headline ['hedlain], *n.* (*Journ.*) titre, sous-titre, *m.*
headlong ['hedlɔŋ], *adv.* la tête la première (*fig.*) tête baissée.—*a.* précipité, irréfléchi.
headmaster ['hed'mɑːstə], *n.* principal, directeur, proviseur, *m.*
head-mistress ['hed'mistris], *n.* directrice, *f.*
head-phone ['hedfoun], *n.* (*Teleph.*) écouteur, *m.*
head-quarters ['hed'kwɔːtəz], *n.pl.* quartier général, *m.*
headstone ['hedstoun], *n.* pierre tombale, *f.*
headstrong ['hedstrɔŋ], *a.* opiniâtre, obstiné, entêté.
headway ['hedwei], *n.* progrès, *m.*; ***to make headway***, avancer, progresser.
heady ['hedi], *a.* capiteux (*boisson*).
heal [hiːl], *v.t.* guérir; (*fig.*) apaiser.—*v.i.* guérir, se guérir; se cicatriser.
healing ['hiːliŋ], *a.* curatif; (*fig.*) salutaire.—*n.* guérison, *f.*
health [helθ], *n.* santé, *f.*; toast, *m.*; ***National Health Service***, sécurité sociale, *f.*; ***bill of health***, patente de santé, *f.*
healthily ['helθili], *adv.* en santé; sainement.
healthy ['helθi], *a.* bien portant, en bonne santé; sain, salubre.
heap [hiːp], *n.* tas, monceau, amas, *m.*—*v.t.* entasser, amonceler.
hear [hiə], *v.t. irr.* entendre; entendre dire; écouter (*faire attention à*); (*fig.*) apprendre; ***to hear it said***, entendre dire.—*v.i.* entendre; entendre parler; écouter; recevoir des nouvelles, avoir des nouvelles (*de*) ***hear! hear!*** très bien! bravo!

hearing ['hiəriŋ], *n.* ouïe (*sens auditif*); audition (*de témoins*), *f.*; ***hard of hearing***, dur d'oreille; ***within hearing***, à portée de la voix.
hearken [hɑ:kn], *v.i.* écouter.
hearsay ['hiəsei], *n.* ouï-dire, *m.*
hearse [hə:s], *n.* corbillard, *m.*
heart [hɑ:t], *n.* cœur; (*fig.*) courage; centre, *m.*
heart-attack ['hɑ:tətæk], *n.* crise cardiaque, *f.*
heart-breaking ['hɑ:tbreikiŋ], *a.* qui fend le cœur, navrant.
heart-broken ['hɑ:tbroukən], *a.* qui a le cœur brisé.
heartburn ['hɑ:tbə:n], *n.* brûlures d'estomac, aigreurs, *f.pl.*
hearten [hɑ:tn], *v.t.* encourager, animer.
heart-failure ['hɑ:tfeiljə], *n.* arrêt du cœur *m.*
heartfelt ['hɑ:tfelt], *a.* qui vient du cœur.
hearth [hɑ:θ], *n.* âtre, foyer, *m.*
heartily ['hɑ:tili], *adv.* cordialement, de bon cœur; de bon appétit (*manger*).
heartiness ['hɑ:tinis], *n.* cordialité; vigueur (*de l'appétit*), *f.*
heartless ['hɑ:tlis], *a.* sans cœur, sans pitié.
hearty ['hɑ:ti], *a.* sincère, cordial; abondant, bon (*repas*).
heat [hi:t], *n.* chaleur; (*fig.*) ardeur; colère (*courroux*); (*Racing*) épreuve, *f.*—*v.t.* chauffer, échauffer.—*v.i.* s'échauffer.
heated ['hi:tid], *a.* chaud; échauffé; animé.
heath [hi:θ], *n.* bruyère, lande; brande (*plante*), *f.*
heathen [hi:ðn], *a.* and *n.* païen, *m.*
heather ['heðə], *n.* bruyère, brande, *f.*
heating ['hi:tiŋ], *n.* chauffage, *m.*
heave [hi:v], *n.* effort (*pour soulever*), *m.*, secousse, *f.*; soulèvement, *m.*—*v.t. irr.* lever; élever; soulever; pousser (*un soupir*). —*v.i.* se soulever; palpiter, battre (*sein, cœur etc.*).
heaven [hevn], *n.* ciel, *m.*, cieux, *m.pl.*
heavenly ['hevnli], *a.* céleste, divin.
heavily ['hevili], *adv.* pesamment, lourdement; fortement.
heaviness ['hevinis], *n.* pesanteur, lourdeur; (*fig.*) tristesse, *f.*
heavy ['hevi], *a.* lourd, pesant; (*fig.*) gros; triste.
Hebrew ['hi:bru:], *a.* hébreu, *m.*; hébraïque, *f.*—*n.* hébreu (*langue*); Hébreu, Juif (*personne*), *m.*
heckle [hekl], *v.t.* embarrasser de questions, harasser (*en public*).
hectic ['hektik], *a.* hectique; agité, fiévreux.
hedge [hedʒ], *n.* haie, *f.*—*v.t.* entourer d'une haie.—*v.i.* (*fig.*) éviter de se compromettre.
hedgehog ['hedʒhɔg], *n.* hérisson, *m.*
hedge-sparrow ['hedʒspærou], *n.* mouchet, *m.*, fauvette d'hiver, *f.*
heed [hi:d], *n.* attention, *f.*, soin, *m.*—*v.t.* faire attention à, prendre garde à, écouter.
heedless ['hi:dlis], *a.* étourdi, inattentif, insouciant.
heedlessly ['hi:dlisli], *adv.* négligemment; étourdiment.
heel [hi:l], *n.* talon, *m.*; ***to be down at heel***, traîner la savate; ***to cool one's heels***, faire antichambre.—*v.i.* ***to heel over***, (*Naut.*) donner de la bande.
hefty ['hefti], *a.* (*fam.*) solide, costaud,
heifer ['hefə], *n.* génisse, *f.*
height [hait], *n.* hauteur, élévation; taille, *f.*; (*fig.*) comble, faîte, *m.*; ***the height of summer***, le cœur *ou* le fort de l'été.
heighten [haitn], *v.t.* rehausser, relever.
heinous ['heinəs], *a.* atroce.
heir [ɛə], *n.* héritier, *m.*
heiress ['ɛəris], *n.* héritière, *f.*
heirloom ['ɛəlu:m], *n.* meuble *ou* bijou (de famille), *m.*
Helen ['helin]. (*Myth.*) Hélène, *f.*
helicopter ['helikɔptə], *n.* hélicoptère, *m.*
helium ['hi:liəm], *n.* (*Chem.*) hélium, *m.*
hell [hel], *n.* enfer, *m.*
hellish ['heliʃ], *a.* infernal, d'enfer.
hello! [he'lou], **hullo!** [hʌ'lou], *int.* holà! allô! (*au téléphone*); tiens! (*surprise*).
helm (1) [helm], *n.* (*Naut.*) gouvernail, timon, *m.*, barre, *f.*
helm (2) [helm], *n.* (*poet.*) heaume (*casque*), *m.*
helmet ['helmit], *n.* casque, *m.*
helmsman ['helmzmən], *n.* (*pl.* **-men** [men]) timonier, *m.*
help [help], *n.* secours, *m.*; aide, assistance, *f.*; remède (*recours*), *m.*; ***help !*** au secours!—*v.t.* aider, secourir, assister; servir (*à table*); empêcher (*prevent*); éviter (*avoid*); ***help yourself*** (*at table*), servez-vous; ***how can I help it?*** que voulez-vous que j'y fasse? ***how can it be helped?*** qu'y faire? ***I can't help it***, je n'y puis rien; ***I cannot help saying***, je ne puis m'empêcher de dire.—*v.i.* aider, servir, contribuer.
helper ['helpə], *n.* aide, *m., f.*
helpful ['helpful], *a.* utile; secourable.
helpless ['helplis], *a.* faible, impuissant; sans appui.
helplessly ['helplisli], *adv.* faiblement; sans ressource.
helter-skelter ['heltə'skeltə], *adv.* pêle-mêle; en pagaille.
helve [helv], *n.* manche, *m.*
hem [hem], *n.* ourlet, bord, *m.*—*v.t.* ourler, border; ***to hem in***, entourer.
hemisphere ['hemisfiə], *n.* hémisphère, *m.*
hemlock ['hemlɔk], *n.* ciguë, *f.*
hemorrhage [HAEMORRHAGE].
hemp [hemp], *n.* (*Bot.*) chanvre, *m.*; (*fig.*) corde, *f.*
hen [hen], *n.* poule; femelle (*d'oiseau*), *f.*
hence [hens], *adv.* d'ici; de là, ainsi (*pour cela*); désormais (*temps*).
henceforth ['hensfɔ:θ], **henceforward** [hens'fɔ:wəd], *adv.* désormais, dorénavant, à l'avenir.
henchman ['hentʃmən], *n.* (*pl.* **-men** [men]) écuyer, valet; (*fig.*) partisan, *m.*
hen-house ['henhaus], *n.* poulailler, *m.*
hen-pecked ['henpekt], *a.* gouverné par sa femme.
Henry ['henri]. Henri, *m.*
her [hə:], *pers. pron.* elle, la, lui.—*poss. a.* son, sa, ses.—*dem. pron.* celle, *f.*
herald ['herəld], *n.* héraut; (*fig.*) avant-coureur, précurseur, *m.*—*v.t.* annoncer.
heraldry ['herəldri], *n.* science héraldique, *f.*, blason, *m.*
herb [hə:b], *n.* herbe, *f.*; ***pot-herbs***, herbes potagères, *f.pl.*; ***sweet herbs***, fines herbes, *f.pl.*
herbaceous [hə:'beiʃəs], *a.* herbacé.
herbage ['hə:bidʒ], *n.* herbage, *m.*

herbalist ['hə:bəlist], *n.* herboriste, *m., f.*
Hercules ['hə:kjuli:z]. Hercule, *m.*
herd [hə:d], *n.* troupeau, *m.*, troupe, *f.*—*v.t.* garder.—*v.i.* vivre en troupeau.
herdsman ['hə:dzmən], *n.* (*pl.* **-men** [men]) bouvier, *m.*
here [hiə], *adv.* ici; voici, que voici; ***here!*** présent! ***here and there***, çà et là; ***here they are***, les voici; ***I am here***, me voici; ***this one here***, celui-ci.
hereafter [hiər'ɑ:ftə], *adv.* désormais; dans la vie à venir.—*n.* l'au-delà, *m.*
hereby [hiə'bai], *adv.* par ce moyen, par là.
hereditary [hi'reditəri], *a.* héréditaire.
heredity [hi'rediti], *n.* hérédité, *f.*
heresy ['herisi], *n.* hérésie, *f.*
heretic ['heritik], *n.* hérétique, *m., f.*
heretical [hi'retikəl], *a.* hérétique.
heretofore ['hiətufɔ:], *adv.* jadis, jusqu'ici.
hereupon [hiərə'pɔn], *adv.* là-dessus.
herewith [hiə'wið], *adv.* ci-joint.
heritage ['heritidʒ], *n.* héritage, *m.*
hermetic [hə:'metik], *a.* hermétique.
hermetically [hə:'metikli], *adv.* hermétiquement.
hermit ['hə:mit], *n.* ermite, *m.*
hero ['hiərou], *n.* (*pl.* **heroes** ['hiərouz]) héros, *m.*
heroic [hi'rouik], **heroical** [-əl], *a.* héroïque.
heroine ['herouin], *n.* héroïne, *f.*
heroism ['herouizm], *n.* héroïsme, *m.*
heron ['herən], *n.* héron, *m.*
herring ['heriŋ], *n.* hareng, *m.*; ***red herring***, hareng saur; (*fig.*) diversion, *f.*
hers [hə:z], *pron.* le sien, *m.*, la sienne, *f.*, les siens, *m.pl.*, les siennes, *f.pl.*; ***a friend of hers***, une de ses amies, *f.*
herself [hə:'self], *pron.* elle-même, elle; (*reflexive*) se; ***by herself***, toute seule.
hesitant ['hezitənt], *a.* hésitant.
hesitate ['heziteit], *v.i.* hésiter.
hesitation [hezi'teiʃən], *n.* hésitation, *f.*
heterodox ['hetərədɔks], *a.* hétérodoxe.
heterogeneous [hetəro'dʒi:niəs], *a.* hétérogène.
hew [hju:], *v.t. irr.* tailler, couper.
hewer ['hjuə], *n.* tailleur (*de pierre*); piqueur (*de charbon*); fendeur (*de bois*), *m.*
hexagon ['heksəgən], *n.* hexagone, *m.*
heyday ['heidei], *n.* beaux jours, *m.pl.*
hiatus [hai'eitəs], *n.* hiatus, *m.*; (*fig.*) lacune, *f.*
hibernate ['haibəneit], *v.i.* hiverner, hiberner.
hiccough, hiccup ['hikʌp], *n.* hoquet, *m.*—*v.i.* avoir le hoquet.
hidden [hidn], *a.* caché, secret; (*fig.*) occulte.
hide (1) [haid], *n.* peau, *f.*, cuir, *m.*
hide (2) [haid], *v.t. irr.* cacher; enfouir (*en terre*); ***hide-and-seek***, cache-cache, *m.*—*v.i.* se cacher, se tenir caché.
hideous ['hidiəs], *a.* hideux, affreux.
hiding (1) ['haidiŋ], *n.* (*colloq.*) rossée, raclée, *f.*; ***to give someone a good hiding***, tanner le cuir à quelqu'un.
hiding (2) ['haidiŋ], *n.* ***in hiding***, caché; ***hiding-place***, cachette, *f.*
hie [hai], *v.i.* se hâter, se rendre (*à*).
hierarchy ['haiərɑ:ki], *n.* hiérarchie, *f.*
high [hai], *a.* haut, élevé; (*fig.*) grand; sublime; fier, altier; faisandé (*gibier*); avancé (*viande*); ***from on high***, d'en haut; ***high road***, grand-route, *f.*; ***high street***, grand-rue, *f.*; ***it is high time***, il est grand temps.—*adv.* haut, hautement; grandement; fort; ***to run high***, s'échauffer (*sentiments*).
highbrow ['haibrau], *a.* and *n.* (*fam.*) intellectuel, *m.*
higher ['haiə], *comp. a.* plus haut, plus élevé; supérieur.
highest ['haiist], *superl. a.* le plus haut, le plus élevé; ***at the highest***, au comble.
high-flown ['haifloun], *a.* enflé; ampoulé (*style*).
high-handed ['hai'hændid], *a.* arbitraire, tyrannique.
Highland ['hailənd], *a.* de la Haute Écosse.
highland ['hailənd], *a.* des montagnes.
Highlander ['hailəndə], *n.* montagnard de l'Écosse, *m.*
Highlands ['hailəndz], **the.** les hautes terres d'Écosse, *f.pl.*, la haute Écosse, *f.*
highlands ['hailəndz], *n.pl.* pays montagneux, *m.*
highlight ['hailait], *n.* point culminant, (*fam.*) clou, *m.*
highly ['haili], *adv.* hautement; fortement.
Highness ['hainis], *n.* Altesse (*titre*), *f.*
highness ['hainis], *n.* hauteur, *f.*
high-pitched ['haipitʃt], *a.* aigu (*son*).
high-sounding ['haisaundiŋ], *a.* pompeux; ronflant (*style*).
high-spirited ['haispiritid], *a.* fougueux, plein de cœur.
highway ['haiwei], *n.* grand chemin, *m.*, grand-route, *f.*
highwayman ['haiweimən], *n.* (*pl.* **-men** [men]) voleur de grand chemin, *m.*
hike [haik], *n.* excursion à pied, *f.*—*v.i.* aller à pied, vagabonder; faire des excursions à pied.
hiker ['haikə], *n.* touriste à pied, *m., f.*
hilarious [hi'lɛəriəs], *a.* gai, joyeux.
hilarity [hi'læriti], *n.* hilarité, *f.*
hill [hil], *n.* colline, montagne, *f.*, coteau, *m.*, butte; côte, *f.*
hillock ['hilək], *n.* monticule, *m.*, butte, *f.*
hilly ['hili], *a.* montagneux, accidenté.
hilt [hilt], *n.* poignée, garde, *f.*
him [him], *pers. pron.* le, lui.—*dem. pron.* celui.
himself [him'self], *pron.* lui-même, lui; (*reflexive*) se; ***by himself***, tout seul.
hind (1) [haind], *n.* (*Zool.*) biche, *f.*
hind (2) [haind], *a.* de derrière, postérieur, arrière.
hinder ['hində], *v.t.* empêcher; gêner, embarrasser, retarder.
hindrance ['hindrəns], *n.* empêchement, obstacle, *m.*
Hindu [hin'du:], *a.* hindou.—*n.* Hindou, *m.*
hinge [hindʒ], *n.* gond, *m.*; paumelle; charnière (*butt-hinge*), *f.*; (*fig.*) pivot, *m.*
hint [hint], *n.* insinuation, allusion, *f.*; (*fig.*) soupçon, *m.*; conseils, *m.pl.*; ***broad hint***, allusion évidente; ***to take the hint***, comprendre à demi-mot.—*v.i.* donner à entendre (*à*), insinuer, suggérer.
hip [hip], *n.* hanche, *f.*
hippopotamus [hipə'pɔtəməs], *n.* (*pl.* **hippopotami** [hipə'pɔtəmai], **hippopotamuses** [hipə'pɔtəməsəz]) hippopotame, *m.*
hire ['haiə], *n.* louage, prix de louage; salaire *m.*, gages, *m.pl.*; ***for hire***, à louer, libre (*taxi*).—*v.t.* louer; engager, employer.
hireling ['haiəliŋ], *a.* and *n.* mercenaire, *m.*

hire-purchase ['haiə'pə:tʃəs], *n.* vente à tempérament, location-vente, *f.*
hirsute ['hə:sju:t], *a.* velu, hirsute.
his [hiz], *a.* son, sa, ses.—*pron.* le sien, *m.*, la sienne, *f.*, les siens, *m.pl.*, les siennes, *f.pl.*; ***a friend of his***, un de ses amis; ***it is his***, c'est à lui.
hiss [his], *v.t.*, *v.i.* siffler.—*n.* sifflement; sifflet, *m.*
hissing ['hisiŋ], *a.* sifflant.—*n.* sifflement, *m.*
historian [his'tɔ:riən], *n.* historien, *m.*
historic [his'tɔrik], **historical** [his'tɔrikəl], *a.* historique.
history ['histəri], *n.* histoire, *f.*
hit [hit], *v.t. irr.* frapper, heurter; atteindre (*le but*); donner (*un coup*); toucher.—*v.i.* frapper, heurter (*contre*).—*n.* coup, *m.*; chance, trouvaille; (*fig.*) invention, *f.*; (*Theat.*) succès, *m.*
hitch [hitʃ], *v.t.* accrocher, attacher; (*Naut.*) nouer, amarrer.—*n.* accroc, *m.*; entrave, *f.*; empêchement; (*Naut.*) nœud, *m.*
hitch-hike ['hitʃhaik], *v.i.* faire de l'auto-stop.
hither ['hiðə], *adv.* ici; ***hither and thither***, çà et là.
hitherto [hiðə'tu:], *adv.* jusqu'ici.
hive [haiv], *n.* ruche, *f.*; (*fig.*) essaim (*swarm*), *m.*
hoard [hɔ:d], *n.* monceau, amas (*secret*); trésor, *m.*—*v.t.* amasser, accumuler.—*v.i.* thésauriser.
hoarding ['hɔ:diŋ], *n.* accumulation, *f.*; panneau-réclame, *m.*
hoar-frost ['hɔ:frɔst], *n.* gelée blanche, *f.*, givre, *m.*
hoarse [hɔ:s], *a.* enroué, rauque.
hoary ['hɔ:ri], *a.* blanc; aux cheveux gris *ou* blancs.
hoax [houks], *n.* mystification, *f.*; mauvais tour (*brimade*); canard (*fausse nouvelle*), *m.* —*v.t.* mystifier; attraper.
hob [hɔb], *n.* plaque (*de l'âtre*), *f.*
hobble [hɔbl], *v.t.* entraver.—*v.i.* clocher, clopiner; aller clopin clopant.—*n.* clochement, *m.*, difficulté, *f.*, embarras, *m.*; entrave, *f.*
hobby ['hɔbi], *n.* marotte (*manie*), distraction, *f.*, passe-temps, *m.*
hobby-horse ['hɔbihɔ:s], *n.* cheval de bois, dada, *m.*
hobgoblin [hɔb'gɔblin], *n.* lutin, *m.*
hobnob ['hɔb'nɔb], *v.i.* trinquer ensemble.
hobo ['houbou], *n.* (*Am.*) chemineau, *m.*
hock [hɔk], *n.* jarret (*d'un cheval*); vin du Rhin, *m.*
hockey ['hɔki], *n.* hockey, *m.*
hockey-stick ['hɔkistik], *n.* crosse de hockey, *f.*
hoe [hou], *n.* houe, binette, *f.*; ***Dutch hoe***, sarcloir, *m.*—*v.t.*, *v.i.* houer; biner, sarcler.
hog [hɔg], *n.* cochon; goret; (*Comm.*) porc, pourceau; (*fam.*) glouton, *m.*
hogshead ['hɔgzhed], *n.* muid, *m.*; barrique de 240 litres (*tonneau*), *f.*
hoist [hɔist], *v.t.* hisser; guinder (*avec un treuil*); lever; arborer (*un drapeau*).—*n.* grue, *f.*, palan, *m.*
hold [hould], *n.* prise, *f.*; soutien (*appui*), *m.*; garde (*custody*); place forte (*forteresse*); (*Naut.*) cale, *f.*; ***to take hold of***, prendre, saisir; ***to let go one's hold***, lâcher prise.—*v.t. irr.* tenir, retenir; arrêter; garder, maintenir; occuper, avoir; contenir (*to contain*); regarder comme; célébrer; ***to hold back***, retenir, cacher; ***to hold fast***, tenir ferme, tenir bon; ***to hold off***, tenir à distance; ***to hold over***, remettre, ajourner; ***to hold up***, lever, soulever, soutenir; arrêter, retarder. —*v.i.* tenir; se maintenir, durer; supporter; adhérer (*à*); rester; s'arrêter; être vrai; ***hold on***, arrêtez! (*Teleph.*) ne quittez pas! ***hold tight!*** ne lâchez pas! ***to hold back***, se tenir en arrière, hésiter; ***to hold fast***, tenir ferme; ***to hold forth***, haranguer, pérorer; ***to hold on***, s'accrocher à; persévérer, poursuivre.
hold-all ['houldɔ:l], *n.* enveloppe de voyage, *f.*
holder ['houldə], *n.* personne qui tient, *f.*; (*Spt.*) tenant, locataire, *m.*; poignée, anse, *f.*, manche, *m.*, (*in compound words*) porte-; (*Fin.*) titulaire, *m.*
holding ['houldiŋ], *n.* possession, tenure; ferme, *f.*
hold-up ['houldʌp], *n.* arrêt de la circulation, *m.*; panne, *f.*; hold-up, *m.*
hole [houl], *n.* trou; antre, *m.*, caverne, *f.*; orifice, *m.*, ouverture, *f.*
holiday ['hɔlidei], *a.* de fête, de congé; de vacances.—*n.* fête, *f.*, jour de fête, jour férié, (*Sch. etc.*) congé, *m.*, (*pl.*) vacances, *f.pl.*; ***bank-holiday***, fête légale; ***on holiday***, en vacance(s).
holiness ['houlinis], *n.* sainteté, *f.*
Holland ['hɔlənd]. la Hollande, *f.*
hollow ['hɔlou], *a.* creux; vide; sourd (*son*).—*n.* creux, *m.*, cavité, *f.*; bas-fond, *m.*—*v.t.* creuser, évider.
holly ['hɔli], *n.* houx, *m.*
hollyhock ['hɔlihɔk], *n.* rose trémière, *f.*
holster ['houlstə], *n.* fonte (*de selle*), *f.*; étui (de revolver), *m.*
holy ['houli], *a.* saint, sacré; bénit; ***Holy Ghost***, le Saint-Esprit; ***Holy Land***, la Terre Sainte; ***holy water***, eau bénite, *f.*; ***Holy Week***, la semaine sainte, *f.*
homage ['hɔmidʒ], *n.* hommage, *m.*
home [houm], *a.* de la maison, domestique; (*fig.*) qui porte (*coup*).—*n.* foyer domestique, chez-soi; logis, *m.*, maison, *f.*, intérieur, *m.*; (*fig.*) demeure, *f.*; pays, *m.*, patrie (*pays natal*), *f.*; ***at home***, chez soi, à la maison; ***Home Office***, Ministère de l'Intérieur, *m.*; ***to make oneself at home***, faire comme chez soi.—*adv.* chez soi, au logis, à la maison; dans son pays; (*fig.*) directement; ***to bring home to***, faire admettre à; ***homing pigeon***, pigeon voyageur, *m.*
home-coming ['houmkʌmiŋ], *n.* retour au foyer, *m.*
homeland ['houmlænd], *n.* patrie, *f.*; pays natal, *m.*
homeliness ['houmlinis], *n.* caractère domestique, *m.*; simplicité; rusticité, *f.*
homely ['houmli], *a.* du ménage; simple, sans façon; (*Am.*) laid.
Homer ['houmə]. Homère, *m.*
home-sick ['houmsik], *a.* qui a le mal du pays, nostalgique.
home-sickness ['houmsiknis], *n.* mal du pays, *m.*, nostalgie, *f.*
homestead ['houmsted], *n.* manoir, *m.*, ferme, *f.*
homeward(s) ['houmwəd(z)], *adv.* vers la maison; vers son pays.

homework ['houmwəːk], *n.* devoirs, *m.pl.*
homicide ['hɔmisaid], *n.* homicide, *m.*
homogeneous [hɔmə'dʒiːniəs], *a.* homogène.
homosexual [houmo'seksjuəl], *a.* and *n.* homosexuel, *m.*
Honduran [hɔn'djuərən], *a.* hondurien.—*n.* Hondurien (*personne*), *m.*
Honduras [hɔn'djuərəs]. l'Honduras, *m.*
hone [houn], *n.* pierre à aiguiser *f.*—*v.t.* aiguiser.
honest ['ɔnist], *a.* honnête, loyal, probe, de bonne foi, sincère; ***honest man***, homme de bien, honnête homme, *m.*
honestly ['ɔnistli], *adv.* honnêtement, sincèrement.
honesty ['ɔnisti], *n.* honnêteté, probité, bonne foi, sincérité, *f.*
honey ['hʌni], *n.* miel, *m.*; (*fig.*) (*Am.*) chérie, *f.*, ange, *m.*
honeycomb ['hʌnikoum], *n.* rayon de miel, *m.*
honeymoon ['hʌnimuːn], *n.* lune de miel, *f.*
honeysuckle ['hʌnisʌkl], *n.* chèvrefeuille, *m.*
honorary ['ɔnərəri], *a.* honoraire.
honour ['ɔnə], *n.* honneur, *m.*; (*fig.*) dignité, estime, *f.*—*v.t.* honorer (*de*); faire honneur à, faire bon accueil à (*une facture*).
honourable ['ɔnərəbl], *a.* honorable, d'honneur.
hood [hud], *n.* capuchon, *m.*; coiffe; capote (*de voiture*), *f.*; (*Am. Motor.*) [BONNET].
hoodwink ['hudwiŋk], *v.t.* bander les yeux à; (*fig.*) tromper.
hoof [huːf, huf], *n.* (*pl.* **hooves** [huːvz]) sabot, *m.*
hook [huk], *n.* crochet, croc; hameçon (*pour pêcher*), *m.*; faucille (*sickle*), *f.*; ***hook and eye***, agrafe et porte, *f.*—*v.t.* accrocher; agrafer; attraper.
hooked [hukt], *a.* crochu, recourbé; aquilin (*nez*).
hooligan ['huːligən], *n.* voyou, *m.*
hooliganism ['huːligənizm], *n.* voyouterie, *f.*
hoop [huːp], *n.* cercle; cerceau, *m.*; huppe (*d'oiseau*); jante (*de roue*), *f.*; panier (*de robe*); (*Croquet*) arceau, *m.*—*v.t.* cercler; (*fig.*) entourer.
hoot [huːt], *v.t.*, *v.i.* hululer (*hibou*); huer; (*Motor.*) klaxonner.
hooter ['huːtə], *n.* (*colloq.*) sirène d'usine, *f.* klaxon, *m.*
hop (1) [hɔp], *n.* saut, sautillement; bal populaire, *m.*—*v.i.* sauter, sautiller; (*pop.*) ***to hop it***, ficher le camp.
hop (2) [hɔp], *n.* (*Bot.*) houblon, *m.*
hop-field ['hɔpfiːld], *n.* houblonnière, *f.*
hopscotch ['hɔpskɔtʃ], *n.* marelle, *f.*
hope [houp], *n.* espérance, *f.*, espoir, *m.*, attente, *f.*—*v.t.* espérer, s'attendre à.—*v.i.* espérer.
hopeful ['houpful], *a.* plein d'espérance; qui promet beaucoup; encourageant.
hopefully ['houpfuli], *adv.* avec espoir, avec confiance; si tout va bien.
hopeless ['houplis], *a.* vain (*effort*); non valable (*excuse*); inextricable (*difficulté*); inconsolable (*douleur*); irrémédiable (*mal*); inutile (*négociation*); incorrigible (*personne*); désespéré (*situation*).
hopelessly ['houplisli], *adv.* sans espoir.
hopper ['hɔpə], *n.* trémie (*d'un moulin*), *f.*; (*Agric.*) semoir, *m.*
horizon [hə'raizən], *n.* horizon, *m.*
horizontal [hɔri'zɔntl], *a.* horizontal.
hormone ['hɔːmoun], *n.* hormone, *f.*
horn [hɔːn], *a.* de corne.—*n.* corne, *f.*; bois (*de cerf*), *m.*; coupe (*à boire*); (*Ent.*) antenne *f.*; (*Mus.*) cor, cornet, *m.*
hornet ['hɔːnit], *n.* frelon, *m.*
horrible ['hɔribl], *a.* horrible, affreux.
horribly ['hɔribli], *adv.* horriblement, affreusement.
horrid ['hɔrid], *a.* affreux, horrible.
horrific [hɔ'rifik], *a.* horrifique.
horrify ['hɔrifai], *v.t.* horrifier.
horror ['hɔrə], *n.* horreur, *f.*
horse [hɔːs], *n.* cheval, *m.*, chevaux, *m.pl.*; (*Mil.*) cavalerie, *f.*; chevalet (*pour scier*), séchoir (*pour le linge*), *m.*
horseback ['hɔːsbæk], *n.* dos de cheval, *m.*; ***on horseback***, à cheval.
horseblock ['hɔːsblɔk], *n.* montoir, *m.*
horse-chestnut ['hɔːs'tʃesnʌt], *n.* marron d'Inde; marronnier d'Inde (*arbre*), *m.*
horse-dealer ['hɔːsdiːlə], *n.* maquignon, *m.*
horse-doctor ['hɔːsdɔktə], *n.* vétérinaire, *m.*
horse-fly ['hɔːsflai], *n.* taon, *m.*
horseman ['hɔːsmən], *n.* (*pl.* **-men** [men]) cavalier; écuyer, *m.*
horsemanship ['hɔːsmənʃip], *n.* équitation, *f.*; manège, *m.*
horse-play ['hɔːsplei], *n.* jeu de mains, *m.*
horse-power ['hɔːspauə], *n.* cheval-vapeur, *m.*
horseshoe ['hɔːʃʃuː], *a.* en fer à cheval.—*n.* fer de cheval; fer à cheval, *m.*
horsewhip ['hɔːswip], *n.* cravache, *f.*—*v.t.* cravacher.
horticulture ['hɔːtikʌltʃə], *n.* horticulture, *f.*
hose [houz], *n.* bas, *m.pl.*; tuyau d'arrosage, boyau, *m.*
hosiery ['houʒəri], *n.* bonneterie, *f.*
hospitable ['hɔspitəbl], *a.* hospitalier.
hospital ['hɔspitl], *n.* hôpital, *m.*, infirmerie, *f.*; hospice, *m.*
hospitality [hɔspi'tæliti], *n.* hospitalité, *f.*
host [houst], *n.* hôte; hôtelier, aubergiste, *m.*; armée, foule; (*R.-C. Ch.*) hostie, *f.*
hostage ['hɔstidʒ], *n.* otage, *m.*
hostel ['hɔstəl], *n.* hôtel *ou* foyer pour les étudiants etc., *m.*; ***youth hostel***, auberge de la jeunesse, *f.*
hostess ['houstis, 'houstes], *n.* hôtesse, *f.*
hostile ['hɔstail], *a.* hostile, ennemi; (*fig.*) opposé (*à*).
hostility [hɔs'tiliti], *n.* hostilité, *f.*
hot [hɔt], *a.* chaud, ardent; brûlant, piquant, épicé (*plat, sauce*); (*fig.*) vif, violent, échauffé; ***boiling hot***, tout bouillant; ***to be hot***, avoir chaud (*personne*), faire chaud (*temps*), être chaud (*chose*).
hotbed ['hɔtbed], *n.* couche, *f.*
hotel [ho'tel], *n.* hôtel, *m.*
hot-headed ['hɔt'hedid], *a.* violent, fougueux.
hot-house ['hɔthaus], *n.* serre, *f.*
hotly ['hɔtli], *adv.* avec chaleur, avec acharnement.
hotness ['hɔtnis], *n.* chaleur; (*fig.*) passion, violence, *f.*
hot-water-bottle [hɔt'wɔːtəbɔtl], *n.* bouillotte, *f.*
hough [hɔk], *n.* jarret (*d'animal*), *m.*
hound [haund], *n.* chien de chasse, *m.*—*v.t.* chasser; (*fig.*) traquer; exciter.

hour ['auə], *n.* heure, *f.*; ***an hour ago***, il y a une heure; ***an hour and a half***, une heure et demie; ***a quarter of an hour***, un quart d'heure; ***half an hour***, une demi-heure.
hourly ['auəli], *a.* continuel, d'heure en heure, à l'heure.—*adv.* d'heure en heure.
house [haus], *n.* maison, *f.*, logis, *m.*, demeure, habitation, *f.*; ménage (*household*), *m.*; famille; (*Parl.*) chambre; (*Theat.*) salle, *f.*; ***a country-house***, une maison de campagne; ***a nobleman's house***, un hôtel; ***house full***, (*Theat.*) salle comble; ***public house***, café, *m.*, brasserie, *f.*—[hauz], *v.t.* loger, héberger; garer (*une voiture*); rentrer (*blé etc.*); faire rentrer (*bestiaux etc.*).
house-agent ['hauseidʒənt], *n.* agent de location, agent immobilier, *m.*
house-breaker ['hausbreikə], *n.* cambrioleur (*voleur*); démolisseur (*ouvrier*), *m.*
house-breaking ['hausbreikiŋ], *n.* vol avec effraction, *m.*
household ['haushould], *a.* de ménage, domestique.—*n.* maison, *f.*, ménage, *m.*, famille, *f.*
householder ['haushouldə], *n.* chef de famille, chef de maison, *m.*
housekeeper ['hauski:pə], *n.* femme de charge, ménagère, *f.*; concierge, *m.*, *f.*
housekeeping ['hauski:piŋ], *n.* ménage, *m.*
housemaid ['hausmeid], *n.* bonne à tout faire, *f.*
house-surgeon ['haussə:dʒən], *n.* interne (en chirurgie), *m.*
housewife ['hauswaif], *n.* ménagère, *f.*
housework ['hauswə:k], *n.* travaux ménagers, *m.pl.*; ***to do the housework***, faire le ménage.
housing ['hauziŋ], *n.* logement, *m.*; rentrée, *f.*, rentrage, *m.*; (*Tech.*) enchâssure, *f.*
hovel [hɔvl], *n.* appentis, *m.*, bicoque, *f.*, taudis, *m.*, masure, *f.*
hover ['hɔvə], *v.i.* planer; hésiter.
how [hau], *adv.* comment, de quelle façon; combien; comme, que; ***how are you?*** comment allez-vous? ***how far***, jusqu'où; ***how many, how much***, combien de; ***how old are you?*** quel âge avez-vous?
however [hau'evə], *conj.* cependant, pourtant, du reste, d'ailleurs, toutefois.—*adv.* de quelque manière que; quelque . . . que; ***however rich he may be***, quelque riche qu'il soit, tout riche qu'il est; ***however that may be***, quoi qu'il en soit.
howl [haul], *n.* hurlement, cri; mugissement, *m.*—*v.i.* hurler, crier; mugir.
howler ['haulə], *n.* faute grossière, bévue, *f.*
howling ['hauliŋ], *a.* hurlant; ***a howling success***, un succès fou.—*n.* hurlement, *m.*
hoyden [hɔidn], *n.* garçon manqué (*se dit d'une jeune fille*), *m.*
hub [hʌb], *n.* moyeu; (*fig.*) centre, *m.*
hubbub ['hʌbʌb], *n.* vacarme, brouhaha, tintamarre, *m.*
hub-cap ['hʌbkæp], *n.* (*Motor.*) enjoliveur, *m.*
huddle [hʌdl], *v.t.* entasser pêle-mêle, (*fig.*) brouiller, confondre ensemble.—*v.i.* se mêler, se presser les uns contre les autres; (*fig.*) se confondre.—*n.* tas confus, fouillis, méli-mélo, ramassis, *m.*
hue [hju:], *n.* couleur, teinte, nuance; huée, clameur, *f.*; ***to raise a hue and cry after***, crier haro sur, élever un tollé contre.
huff [hʌf], *n.* emportement, accès de colère, *m.* —*v.t.* froisser; (*Draughts*) souffler.—*v.i.* se gonfler, se mettre en colère.
hug [hʌg], *v.t.* embrasser, étreindre; étouffer (*en serrant*).—*n.* embrassement, *m.*, étreinte, *f.*
huge [hju:dʒ], *a.* vaste, immense, énorme.
hulk [hʌlk], *n.* carcasse (*d'un navire*), *f.*, ponton; (*pl.*) bagne, *m.*
hulking ['hʌlkiŋ], *a.* gros, lourd.
hull [hʌl], *n.* coque (*d'un navire*); cosse, gousse (*de pois, fèves etc.*); écale (*de noix*), *f.*—*v.t.* écaler (*noix*); écosser (*fèves*).
hullo [HELLO].
hum [hʌm], *v.t.*, *v.i.* fredonner (*personne*), bourdonner (*abeilles*); ***to hum and ha(w)***, bredouiller.—*n.* bourdonnement; brouhaha (*de conversation*), *m.*
human ['hju:mən], *a.* humain.
humane [hju:'mein], *a.* humain, compatissant.
humanist ['hju:mənist], *n.* humaniste, *m.*, *f.*
humanity [hju:'mæniti], *n.* humanité, *f.*
humanly ['hju:mənli], *adv.* humainement.
humble [hʌmbl], *a.* humble; modeste.—*v.t.* humilier, abaisser, mortifier.
humble-bee ['hʌmblbi:], *n.* bourdon, *m.*
humbly ['hʌmbli], *adv.* humblement, avec humilité; modestement.
humbug ['hʌmbʌg], *n.* blague, farce, *f.*, charlatanisme; blagueur, farceur, charlatan, *m.*
humdrum ['hʌmdrʌm], *a.* monotone, assommant.
humid ['hju:mid], *a.* humide.
humidity [hju:'miditi], *n.* humidité, *f.*
humiliate [hju:'milieit], *v.t.* humilier, abaisser.
humiliating [hju:'milieitiŋ], *a.* humiliant.
humiliation [hju:mili'eiʃən], *n.* humiliation, *f.*
humility [hju:'militi], *n.* humilité, *f.*
humming ['hʌmiŋ], *n.* bourdonnement, fredonnement; (*fig.*) murmure, *m.*
humming-bird ['hʌmiŋbə:d], *n.* oiseau-mouche, colibri, *m.*
humorist ['hju:mərist], *n.* humoriste, *m.*, *f.* personne spirituelle, *f.*
humorous ['hju:mərəs], *a.* humoristique; plaisant, drôle, comique.
humour ['hju:mə], *n.* humeur, disposition, *f.*; humour, *m.*—*v.t.* complaire à, laisser faire.
hump [hʌmp], *n.* bosse, *f.*; ***to have the hump***, (*slang*) être maussade.
humpbacked ['hʌmpbækt], *a.* bossu.
hunch [hʌntʃ], *n.* gros morceau (*de pain, de fromage*) *m.*; bosse (*du dos*); (*fig.*, *fam.*) idée, *f.*, soupçon, *m.*; ***to have a hunch that***, soupçonner que.
hunchback ['hʌntʃbæk], *n.* bossu, *m.*
hundred ['hʌndrəd], *a.* cent.—*n.* cent, *m.*; centaine, *f.*; canton, district, *m.*
hundredth ['hʌndrətθ], *a.* centième.—*n.* centième (*fraction*), *m.*
hundredweight ['hʌndrədweit], *n.* quintal, *m.*
Hungarian [hʌŋ'gɛəriən], *a.* hongrois.—*n.* hongrois (*langue*); Hongrois (*personne*), *m.*
Hungary ['hʌŋgəri]. la Hongrie, *f.*
hunger ['hʌŋgə], *n.* faim, *f.*—*v.i.* avoir faim; être affamé (*de*).
hungrily ['hʌŋgrili], *adv.* avidement.

hungry ['hʌŋgri], *a.* affamé, qui a faim; maigre (*terre etc.*); ***to be hungry***, avoir faim.
hunk [hʌŋk], *n.* gros morceau (*de gâteau, de fromage*), *m.*
hunt [hʌnt], *v.t.* chasser à courre; (*fig.*) poursuivre, chercher.—*v.i.* chasser, aller à la chasse.—*n.* chasse à courre, *f.*
hunter ['hʌntə], *n.* chasseur; cheval de chasse, *m.*
hunting ['hʌntiŋ], *n.* chasse; (*fig.*) recherche, *f.*
huntress ['hʌntris], *n.* chasseuse; (*poet.*) chasseresse, *f.*
huntsman ['hʌntsmən], *n.* (*pl.* **-men** [men]) veneur, piqueur, *m.*
hurdle [hə:dl], *n.* claie, *f.*; (*Spt.*) obstacle, *m.*, haie, *f.*; ***hurdle-race***, course de haies, *f.*
hurdy-gurdy ['hə:di'gə:di], *n.* vielle, *f.*
hurl [hə:l], *v.t.* lancer (avec force), précipiter, jeter.
hurly-burly ['hə:li'bə:li], *n.* tintamarre, brouhaha, tohu-bohu, *m.*
hurrah [hu'rɑ:], **hurray** [hu'rei], *n.* hourra, *m.*
hurricane ['hʌrikən], *n.* ouragan, *m.*
hurried ['hʌrid], *a.* précipité, pressé; fait à la hâte.
hurriedly ['hʌridli], *adv.* précipitamment, à la hâte.
hurry ['hʌri], *n.* hâte, précipitation, *f.*; (*fig.*) tumulte, *m.*, confusion, *f.*; ***to be in a hurry***; être pressé.—*v.t.* hâter, presser, précipiter.—*v.i.* se hâter, se dépêcher, se presser.
hurt [hə:t], *n.* mal, *m.*, blessure, *f.*; (*fig.*) tort, *m.*—*v.t. irr.* faire mal à, (*fig.*) nuire à, offenser, blesser; ***to hurt oneself***, se faire du mal.—*v.i.* faire du mal; faire mal.
hurtful ['hə:tful], *a.* nuisible (*à*).
hurtle [hə:tl], *v.t.* lancer.—*v.i.* se précipiter; se heurter.
husband ['hʌzbənd], *n.* mari, époux, *m.*—*v.t.* ménager, économiser.
husbandman ['hʌzbəndmən], *n.* (*pl.* **-men** [men]) laboureur, cultivateur, *m.*
husbandry ['hʌzbəndri], *n.* agriculture, industrie agricole; économie, *f.*
hush [hʌʃ], *n.* silence, calme, *m.*—*int.* chut! paix!—*v.t.* taire, faire taire; (*fig.*) calmer.—*v.i.* se taire, faire silence.
husk [hʌsk], *n.* cosse, gousse (*de pois etc.*), *f.*; brou, *m.*, écale (*de noix*); balle, pellicule (*de grain*), *f.*
huskiness ['hʌskinis], *n.* enrouement (*de la voix*), *m.*
husky ['hʌski], *a.* cossu; rauque, enroué (*voix*); (*colloq.*) costaud, fort.—*n.* chien esquimau, *m.*
hussar [hu'zɑ:] *n.* hussard, *m.*
hussy ['hʌsi], *n.* friponne, coquine, *f.*
hustle [hʌsl], *v.t.* bousculer, presser, pousser. —*v.i.* se presser, se dépêcher.
hut [hʌt], *n.* hutte, cabane; (*Mil.*) baraque, *f.*
hutch [hʌtʃ], *n.* huche, *f.*; clapier (*de lapin*), *m.*
hyacinth ['haiəsinθ], *n.* (*Bot.*) jacinthe, *f.*
hybrid ['haibrid], *a.* and *n.* hybride, *m.*
hydrangea [hai'drændʒə, hai'dreindʒə], *n.* (*Bot.*) hortensia, *m.*
hydrant ['haidrənt], *n.* prise d'eau, *f.*; ***fire hydrant***, bouche d'incendie, *f.*
hydraulic [hai'drɔ:lik], *a.* hydraulique.
hydrochloric [haidrə'klɔrik], *a.* (*acide*) chlorhydrique.
hydrogen ['haidridʒən], *n.* hydrogène, *m.*; ***hydrogen bomb*** or (*fam.*) ***H-bomb***, bombe à hydrogène, bombe H, *f.*
hydrophobia [haidro'foubiə], *n.* hydrophobie, rage, *f.*
hyena [hai'i:nə], *n.* hyène, *f.*
hygiene ['haidʒi:n], *n.* hygiène, *f.*
hygienic [hai'dʒi:nik], *a.* hygiénique.
hymn [him], *n.* (*Eccles.*) hymne, *m.* ou *f.*, cantique, *m.*
hymn-book ['himbuk], **hymnal** [himnl], *n.* hymnaire, *m.*
hyperbola [hai'pə:bələ], *n.* (*Geom.*) hyperbole, *f.*
hyperbole [hai'pə:bəli], *n.* (*Gram.*) hyperbole, *f.*
hyphen ['haifən], *n.* trait d'union, *m.*
hypnosis [hip'nousis], *n.* hypnose, *f.*
hypnotism ['hipnətizm], *n.* hypnotisme, *m.*
hypnotist ['hipnətist], *n.* hypnotiste, *m.*, *f.*
hypocrisy [hi'pɔkrisi], *n.* hypocrisie, *f.*
hypocrite ['hipəkrit], *n.* hypocrite, *m.*, *f.*
hypocritical [hipə'kritikl], *a.* hypocrite.
hypothesis [hai'pɔθisis], *n.* (*pl.* **hypotheses** [hai'pɔθisi:z]) hypothèse, *f.*
hysteria [his'tiəriə], *n.*, **hysterics** [his'teriks], *n.pl.* crise de nerfs, attaque de nerfs, *f.*
hysterical [his'terikəl], *a.* hystérique.

I

I (1), **i** [ai]. neuvième lettre de l'alphabet, *m.*
I (2) [ai], *pron.* je; moi.
ibex ['aibeks], *n.* bouquetin, *m.*
ibis ['aibis], *n.* (*Orn.*) ibis, *m.*
ice [ais], *n.* glace, *f.*—*v.t.* glacer (*gâteau*); frapper (*vin*).—*v.i.* (*Av.*) ***to ice up***, givrer.
ice-axe ['aisæks], *n.* piolet, *m.*
iceberg ['aisbə:g], *n.* iceberg, *m.*
ice-bound ['aisbaund], *a.* pris dans *ou* bloqué par les glaces.
ice-box ['aisbɔks], *n.* glacière, *f.*
ice-breaker ['aisbreikə], *n.* brise-glace, *m.*
ice-cream ['ais'kri:m], *n.* glace, *f.*
iced [aist], *a.* glacé; frappé (*vin etc.*); ***iced lolly***, sucette, *f.*
ice-floe ['aisflou], *n.* banc de glace, *m.*
Iceland ['aislənd]. l'Islande, *f.*
Icelander ['aisləndə], *n.* Islandais, *m.*
Icelandic [ais'lændik], *a.* islandais, d'Islande.
icicle ['aisikl], *n.* petit glaçon, *m.*
icing ['aisiŋ], *n.* glacé; frappage (*de vin*), *m.*
icon ['aikɔn], *n.* icone, *f.*
icy ['aisi], *a.* glacé, glacial; ***icy road***, route verglacée, *f.*
idea [ai'diə], *n.* idée, *f.*
ideal [ai'diəl], *a.* and *n.* idéal, *m.*
idealism [ai'diəlizm], *n.* idéalisme, *m.*
idealist [ai'diəlist], *n.* idéaliste, *m.*, *f.*
ideally [ai'diəli], *adv.* idéalement.
identical [ai'dentikl], *a.* identique.
identification [aidentifi'keiʃən], *n.* identification, *f.*

identify [ai'dentifai], *v.t.* identifier (*avec*); reconnaître.
identity [ai'dentiti], *n.* identité, *f.*
idiocy ['idiəsi], *n.* idiotie, *f.*
idiom ['idiəm], *n.* idiome; idiotisme, *m.*
idiomatic [idiə'mætik], *a.* idiomatique.
idiot ['idiət], *n.* idiot, *m.*; imbécile, *m., f.*
idiotic [idi'ɔtik], *a.* idiot, d'imbécile.
idle [aidl], *a.* oisif, paresseux (*indolent*); désœuvré (*inactif*); en chômage (*personne sans travail*), en repos (*machine*); (*fig.*) inutile, frivole; ***idle fellow***, fainéant, paresseux, *m.*; ***idle talk***, balivernes, *f.pl.*—*v.t.* ***to idle away***, perdre, gaspiller.—*v.i.* ne rien faire, faire le paresseux, fainéanter; (*Motor.*) tourner au ralenti.
idleness ['aidlnis], *n.* paresse; oisiveté; (*fig.*) inutilité, *f.*; désœuvrement, *m.*
idler ['aidlə], *n.* oisif, fainéant, paresseux, *m.*
idly ['aidli], *adv.* dans l'oisiveté, en paresseux; inutilement.
idol [aidl], *n.* idole, *f.*
idolater [ai'dɔlətə], **idolatress** [ai'dɔlətris], *n.* idolâtre, *m., f.*
idolatry [ai'dɔlətri], *n.* idolâtrie, *f.*
idolize ['aidəlaiz], *v.t.* idolâtrer.
idyllic [ai'dilik, i'dilik], *a.* idyllique.
if [if], *conj.* si, quand, quand même; ***even if***, même si, quand même; ***if necessary***, s'il le faut, au besoin; ***if not***, sinon, si ce n'est.
igloo ['iglu:], *n.* hutte de neige, *f.*; igloo (*des Esquimaux*), *m.*
ignite [ig'nait], *v.t.* allumer.—*v.i.* prendre feu.
ignition [ig'niʃən], *n.* ignition, *f.*; (*Motor.*) allumage, *m.*; ***ignition key***, clé de contact, *f.*
ignoble [ig'noubl], *a.* roturier; ignoble.
ignominious [ignə'miniəs], *a.* ignominieux.
ignominy ['ignəmini], *n.* ignominie, *f.*
ignoramus [ignə'reiməs], *n.* ignorant, (*fam.*) âne bâté, *m.*
ignorance ['ignərəns], *n.* ignorance, *f.*
ignorant ['ignərənt], *a.* ignorant.
ignore [ig'nɔ:], *v.t.* feindre d'ignorer; ne tenir aucun compte de.
ill [il], *a.*; malade (*santé*); mauvais, méchant.—*n.* mal, *m.*—*adv.* mal; peu; ***it ill becomes you***, il vous sied mal.
ill-bred ['il'bred], *a.* mal élevé.
illegal [i'li:gəl], *a.* illégal; illicite.
illegible [i'ledʒibl], *a.* illisible.
illegitimate [ilə'dʒitimit], *a.* illégitime; naturel (*enfant*).
ill-fated ['il'feitid], *a.* infortuné, malheureux.
ill-feeling ['il'fi:liŋ], *n.* ressentiment, *m.*
ill-gotten ['il'gɔtn], *a.* mal acquis.
ill-health ['il'helθ], *n.* mauvaise santé, *f.*
illicit [i'lisit], *a.* illicite.
ill-informed ['ilin'fɔ:md], *a.* mal renseigné.
illiteracy [i'litərəsi], *n.* analphabétisme, *m.*
illiterate [i'litərit], *a.* and *n.* illettré, *m.*
ill-mannered ['il'mænəd], *a.* malappris.
ill-natured ['il'neitʃəd], *a.* méchant, d'un mauvais naturel.
illness ['ilnis], *n.* maladie, indisposition, *f.*
illogical [i'lɔdʒikl], *a.* illogique peu logique.
ill-tempered ['il'tempəd], *a.* maussade, de mauvaise humeur.
ill-treat ['il'tri:t], *v.t.* maltraiter.
illuminate [i'lju:mineit], *v.t.* illuminer, éclairer; enluminer (*un livre*).
illumination [ilju:mi'neiʃən], *n.* illumination; enluminure (*de livres etc.*), *f.*
illusion [i'lu:ʒən, i'lju:ʒən], *n.* illusion, *f.*
illustrate ['iləstreit], *v.t.* illustrer; (*fig* expliquer; orner, embellir.
illustration [iləs'treiʃən], *n.* illustratio explication, *f.*; éclaircissement, *m.*
illustrative [i'lʌstrətiv], *a.* explicatif.
illustrious [i'lʌstriəs], *a.* illustre, célèbre
ill-will ['il'wil], *n.* mauvais vouloir, *m* rancune, *f.*
I'm [aim] (=**I am**) [BE].
image ['imidʒ], *n.* image, *f.*; (*fig.*) portrait, *n*
imagery ['imidʒri], *n.* images, *f.pl.*; langag figuré, *m.*
imaginable [i'mædʒinəbl], *a.* imaginable.
imaginary [i'mædʒinri], *a.* imaginaire.
imagination [imædʒi'neiʃən], *n.* imagina tion; conception, idée, *f.*
imagine [i'mædʒin], *v.t.* imaginer; s'ima giner, se figurer.
imbecile ['imbisi:l], *a.* and *n.* faible d'espri *m., f.*
imbecility [imbi'siliti], *n.* faiblesse d'esprit,
imbibe [im'baib], *v.t.* imbiber, absorber (*fig.*) puiser.
imbue [im'bju:], *v.t.* imprégner, teindre (*fig.*) pénétrer, douer (*de*).
imbued [im'bju:d], *a.* imbu, pénétré (*de*).
imitate ['imiteit], *v.t.* imiter.
imitation [imi'teiʃən], *n.* imitation; (*Comm.* contrefaçon, *f.*
imitative ['imitətiv], *a.* imitatif, imitateur.
immaculate [i'mækjulit], *a.* sans tache, im maculé.
immaterial [imə'tiəriəl], *a.* immatériel; pe important.
immature [imə'tjuə], *a.* pas mûr; prématuré
immeasurable [i'meʒərəbl], *a.* infini; in commensurable.
immeasurably [i'meʒərəbli], *adv.* outr mesure, infiniment.
immediate [i'mi:djit], *a.* immédiat; urgent très pressé (*sur enveloppe*).
immediately [i'mi:djitli], *adv.* immédiate ment, tout de suite, sur-le-champ.—*conj* aussitôt que, dès que.
immense [i'mens], *a.* immense.
immensely [i'mensli], *adv.* immensément.
immensity [i'mensiti], *n.* immensité, *f.*
immerse [i'mə:s], *v.t.* plonger, immerger.
immigrant ['imigrənt], *a.* and *n.* immigrant *m.*
immigrate ['imigreit], *v.i.* immigrer.
immigration [imi'greiʃən], *n.* immigration *f.*
imminent ['iminənt], *a.* imminent.
immobilize [i'moubilaiz], *v.t.* immobiliser.
immodest [i'mɔdist], *a.* immodeste, peu modeste, impudique.
immoral [i'mɔrl], *a.* immoral; dissolu.
immorality [imə'ræliti], *n.* immoralité, *f.*
immortal [i'mɔ:tl], *a.* immortel.
immortality [imɔ:'tæliti], *n.* immortalité, *f.*
immortalize [i'mɔ:təlaiz], *v.t.* immortaliser, rendre immortel.
immovable [i'mu:vəbl], *a.* fixe, immuable, inébranlable.
immutable [i'mju:təbl], *a.* immuable.
imp [imp], *n.* diablotin, petit démon; petit diable (*gamin*), *m.*
impact ['impækt], *n.* choc, impact, *m.*—[im'pækt], *v.t.* serrer, encastrer.
impair [im'pɛə], *v.t.* altérer, affaiblir.

impale [im'peil], *v.t.* empaler.
impalpable [im'pælpəbl], *a.* impalpable; intangible.
impart [im'pɑːt], *v.t.* accorder, donner; communiquer.
impartial [im'pɑːʃl], *a.* impartial, désintéressé.
impartially [im'pɑːʃəli], *adv.* impartialement.
impassable [im'pɑːsəbl], *a.* impraticable, infranchissable.
impassioned [im'pæʃənd], *a.* passionné.
impassive [im'pæsiv], *a.* impassible, insensible.
impatience [im'peiʃəns], *n.* impatience, *f.*
impatient [im'peiʃənt], *a.* impatient; (*fig.*) emporté.
impatiently [im'peiʃəntli], *adv.* impatiemment.
impeach [im'piːtʃ], *v.t.* accuser; attaquer.
impeachment [im'piːtʃmənt], *n.* mise en accusation; accusation, *f.*
impeccable [im'pekəbl], *a.* impeccable.
impecunious [impi'kjuːniəs], *a.* besogneux.
impede [im'piːd], *v.t.* empêcher; retarder, gêner.
impediment [im'pedimənt], *n.* empêchement, obstacle, *m.*; (*fig.*) difficulté, *f.*
impel [im'pell], *v.t.* pousser (*à*); forcer (*de*).
impelling [im'peliŋ], *a.* impulsif, moteur.
impend [im'pend], *v.i.* être suspendu sur, menacer; être imminent.
impending [im'pendiŋ], *a.* imminent, menaçant.
impenetrable [im'penitrəbl], *a.* impénétrable; (*fig.*) insensible.
impenitent [im'penitənt], *a.* impénitent.
imperative [im'perətiv], *a.* impératif; (*fig.*) obligatoire.—*n.* (*Gram.*) impératif, *m.*
imperceptible [impə'septibl], *a.* imperceptible, insensible.
imperceptibly [impə'septibli], *adv.* imperceptiblement.
imperfect [im'pəːfikt], *a.* imparfait; incomplet; (*Gram.*) imparfait.—*n.* (*Gram.*) imparfait, *m.*
imperfection [impə'fekʃən], *n.* imperfection, *f.*
imperfectly [im'pəːfiktli], *adv.* imparfaitement.
imperial [im'piəriəl], *a.* impérial; (*fig.*) princier.
imperil [im'peril], *v.t.* mettre en danger, hasarder.
imperious [im'piəriəs], *a.* impérieux.
imperishable [im'periʃəbl], *a.* impérissable.
impersonal [im'pəːsənəl], *a.* impersonnel.
impersonate [im'pəːsəneit], *v.t.* personnifier; (*Theat.*) représenter, jouer le rôle de.
impertinence [im'pəːtinəns], *n.* impertinence, insolence, *f.*
impertinent [im'pəːtinənt], *a.* impertinent, insolent; hors de propos.
impertinently [im'pəːtinəntli], *adv.* d'un ton insolent; mal à propos.
imperturbable [impə'təːbəbl], *a.* imperturbable.
impervious [im'pəːviəs], *a.* imperméable, impénétrable; (*fig.*) inaccessible.
impetuous [im'petjuəs], *a.* impétueux.
impetus ['impitəs], *n.* impulsion, *f.*; élan, essor, *m.*
impinge [im'pindʒ], *v.i.* se heurter (*à* ou *contre*); empiéter (*sur*).
impious ['impiəs], *a.* impie.
impiously ['impiəsli], *adv.* en impie, avec impiété.
impish ['impiʃ], *a.* espiègle, malicieux.
implacable [im'plækəbl], *a.* implacable, acharné.
implant [im'plɑːnt], *v.t.* implanter; (*fig.*) imprimer, inculquer.
implement ['implimənt], *n.* outil; instrument; ustensile, *m.*—['impliment], *v.t.* exécuter; accomplir.
implicate ['implikeit], *v.t.* impliquer.
implication [impli'keiʃən], *n.* implication, *f.*; ***by implication***, implicitement.
implicit [im'plisit], *a.* implicite; (*fig.*) aveugle.
implied [im'plaid], *a.* implicite, tacite.
implore [im'plɔː], *v.t.* implorer, conjurer, supplier (*de*).
imply [im'plai], *v.t.* impliquer, signifier, vouloir dire; donner à entendre (*suggérer*).
impolite [impə'lait], *a.* impoli.
impoliteness [impə'laitnis], *n.* impolitesse, *f.*
import ['impɔːt], *n.* portée, signification, *f.*, sens, *m.*; importance; (*Comm.*) importation, *f.*—[im'pɔːt], *v.t.* importer; introduire; signifier.
importance [im'pɔːtəns], *n.* importance, *f.*
important [im'pɔːtənt], *a.* important.
importer [im'pɔːtə], *n.* importateur, *m.*
importunate [im'pɔːtjunit], *a.* importun; pressant.
importune [impɔː'tjuːn], *v.t.* importuner.
impose [im'pouz], *v.t.* imposer.—*v.i.* en imposer (*à*).
imposing [im'pouziŋ], *a.* imposant.
imposition [impə'ziʃən], *n.* impôt (*taxe*), *m.*; imposture (*tromperie*), *f.*; (*Sch.*) pensum, *m.*
impossibility [impɔsi'biliti], *n.* impossibilité, *f.*
impossible [im'pɔsibl], *a.* impossible.
impostor [im'pɔstə], *n.* imposteur, *m.*
imposture [im'pɔstʃə], *n.* imposture, tromperie, *f.*
impotence ['impətəns], **impotency** ['impətənsi], *n.* impuissance, *f.*
impotent ['impətənt], *a.* impuissant, faible.
impound [im'paund], *v.t.* mettre en fourrière; (*fig.*) enfermer, confisquer.
impoverish [im'pɔvəriʃ], *v.t.* appauvrir.
impracticable [im'præktikəbl], *a.* impossible, impraticable; intraitable (*personne*).
imprecation [imprə'keiʃən], *n.* imprécation, *f.*
impregnable [im'pregnəbl], *a.* imprenable; (*fig.*) inébranlable.
impregnate [im'pregneit], *v.t.* imprégner (*de*); féconder.
impress [im'pres], *v.t.* imprimer (*à*); faire bien comprendre (*quelque chose à quelqu'un*); pénétrer (*de*); impressionner.
impression [im'preʃən], *n.* impression, empreinte; (*fig.*) idée, *f.*
impressive [im'presiv], *a.* impressionnant, frappant, touchant, émouvant.
impressiveness [im'presivnis], *n.* force, puissance, grandeur, *f.*
imprint [im'print], *v.t.* imprimer, empreindre.—['imprint], *n.* empreinte, *f.*

imprison [im'prizn], *v.t.* emprisonner, enfermer.
imprisonment [im'priznmənt] *n.* emprisonnement, *m.*, détention, *f.*
improbability [imprɔbə'biliti], *n.* improbabilité; invraisemblance, *f.*
improbable [im'prɔbəbl], *a.* improbable, invraisemblable.
impromptu [im'prɔmptju:], *a.* impromptu, improvisé.—*adv.* par improvisation, impromptu.
improper [im'prɔpə], *a.* inconvenant; peu propre (*à*), impropre (*langage*).
improperly [im'prɔpəli], *adv.* d'une manière peu convenable; à tort, mal à propos.
impropriety [imprə'praiəti], *n.* inconvenance (*de conduite*); impropriété (*de langage*), *f.*
improve [im'pru:v], *v.t.* améliorer, perfectionner (*invention etc.*); faire avancer; utiliser; bonifier (*terre etc.*); embellir (*rendre plus beau*); exploiter (*cultiver*).—*v.i.* s'améliorer; se perfectionner; se bonifier (*vin etc.*); faire des progrès; (*Comm.*) hausser; augmenter de prix; ***to improve upon***, améliorer, perfectionner, surpasser.
improvement [im'pru:vmənt], *n.* amélioration, *f.*; perfectionnement; progrès, avancement (*en connaissances*), *m.*
improvident [im'prɔvidənt], *a.* imprévoyant.
improvisation [imprəvai'zeiʃən], *n.* improvisation, *f.*
improvise ['imprəvaiz], *v.t.* improviser.
imprudence [im'pru:dəns], *n.* imprudence, *f.*
imprudent [im'pru:dənt], *a.* imprudent.
imprudently [im'pru:dəntli], *adv.* imprudemment.
impudence ['impjudəns], *n.* impudence, effronterie, *f.*
impudent ['impjudənt], *a.* impudent, effronté.
impudently ['impjudəntli], *adv.* impudemment, effrontément.
impugn [im'pju:n], *v.t.* attaquer, contester; (*fig.*) mettre en doute.
impulse ['impʌls], **impulsion** [im'pʌlʃən], *n.* impulsion, *f.*, mouvement; (*fig.*) élan, *m.*; ***sudden impulse***, coup de tête, *m.*
impulsive [im'pʌlsiv], *a.* impulsif, primesautier.
impulsively [im'pʌlsivli], *adv.* par impulsion, par un mouvement involontaire.
impunity [im'pju:niti], *n.* impunité, *f.*; ***with impunity***, impunément.
impure [im'pjuə], *a.* impur; impudique.
impurity [im'pjuəriti], *n.* impureté; impudicité, *f.*
imputation [impju'teiʃən], *n.* imputation, accusation, *f.*
impute [im'pju:t], *v.t.* imputer, attribuer (*à*).
in [in], *prep.* en, dans; à; par; pour; sur; avec, chez, parmi (*en compagnie de*); ***he will do it in one hour***, il fera cela en une heure; ***he will start in one hour***, il partira dans une heure; ***in bed***, au lit; ***in England***, en Angleterre; ***in Japan***, au Japon; ***in Paris***; à Paris; ***in spite of***, malgré; ***in spring***, au printemps; ***in summer*** (***autumn, winter***), en été (automne, hiver); ***in the morning***, le matin; ***in the U.S.A.***, aux États-Unis; ***one in ten***, un sur dix; ***to be clothed in***, être vêtu de.—*adv.* dedans, au dedans, rentré; chez soi, à la maison, y (*at home*); élu (*vainqueur aux élections*); au pouvoir (*parti politique*); ***all in***, tout compris. —*n.* ***to know all the ins and outs of a matter***, connaître les tenants et les aboutissants d'une affaire.
inability [inə'biliti], *n.* impuissance, incapacité, *f.*
inaccessible [inæk'sesibl], *a.* inaccessible; inabordable (*à*).
inaccuracy [in'ækjurəsi], *n.* inexactitude, *f.*
inaccurate [in'ækjurit], *a.* inexact.
inaction [in'ækʃən], *n.* inaction, inertie, *f.*
inactive [in'æktiv], *a.* inactif; inerte (*choses*).
inactivity [inæk'tiviti], *n.* inactivité, *f.*
inadequacy [in'ædikwəsi], *n.* insuffisance, imperfection, *f.*
inadequate [in'ædikwit], *a.* insuffisant; imparfait, défectueux, incomplet.
inadequately [in'ædikwitli], *adv.* insuffisamment.
inadmissible [inəd'misibl], *a.* inadmissible.
inadvertence [inəd'və:təns], **inadvertency** [inəd'və:tənsi], *n.* inadvertance, *f.*
inadvertent [inəd'və:tənt], *a.* négligent, inattentif.
inadvertently [inəd'və:təntli], *adv.* par inadvertance.
inalienable [in'eiliənəbl], *a.* inaliénable; inséparable.
inane [i'nein], *a.* vide; (*fig.*) inepte, absurde.
inanimate [in'ænimit], *a.* inanimé; mort.
inanition [inə'niʃən], *n.* inanition, *f.*
inanity [i'næniti], *n.* inanité, *f.*
inapplicable [in'æplikəbl], *a.* inapplicable.
inappreciable [inə'pri:ʃiəbl], *a.* inappréciable, insensible.
inappropriate [inə'proupriit], *a.* peu propre, qui ne convient pas.
inapt [in'æpt], *a.* inapte, impropre, peu propre (*à*).
inarticulate [inɑ:'tikjulit], *a.* inarticulé, qui s'exprime peu clairement.
inartistic [inɑ:'tistik], *a.* peu artistique.
inasmuch [inəz'mʌtʃ], *adv.* vu que, attendu que, d'autant que.
inattention [inə'tenʃən], *n.* inattention; distraction, *f.*
inattentive [inə'tentiv], *a.* inattentif, distrait; négligent.
inattentively [inə'tentivli], *adv.* sans attention, négligemment.
inaudible [in'ɔ:dibl], *a.* imperceptible, qu'on ne peut entendre.
inaudibly [in'ɔ:dibli], *adv.* à ne pouvoir être entendu.
inaugural [in'ɔ:gjurəl], *a.* inaugural.
inaugurate [in'ɔ:gjureit], *v.t.* inaugurer.
inauspicious [inɔ:'spiʃəs], *a.* malheureux, peu propice.
inauspiciously [inɔ:'spiʃəsli], *adv.* sous de mauvais auspices.
inborn ['inbɔ:n], **inbred** ['inbred], *a.* inné, naturel.
incalculable [in'kælkjuləbl], *a.* incalculable.
incapable [in'keipəbl], *a.* incapable (*de*).
incapacitate [inkə'pæsiteit], *v.i.* rendre incapable (*de*).
incarcerate [in'kɑ:səreit], *v.t.* incarcérer, mettre en prison.
incarnate [in'kɑ:nit], *a.* incarné.
incautious [in'kɔ:ʃəs], *a.* inconsidéré, imprudent.

incendiarism [in'sendjərizm] *n.* crime d'incendie, *m.*
incendiary [in'sendjəri], *a.* and *n.* incendiaire, *m.*, *f.*
incense ['insens], *n.* encens, *m.*—[in'sens], *v.t.* irriter, exaspérer (*contre*).
incentive [in'sentiv], *a.* excitant, stimulant.—*n.* motif, stimulant, encouragement, *m.*
inception [in'sepʃən], *n.* commencement, *m.*
incessant [in'sesənt], *a.* incessant; continuel.
incest ['insest], *n.* inceste, *m.*
inch [intʃ], *n.* pouce (*2·539 centimètres*), *m.*
incident ['insidənt], *a.* qui arrive; particulier.—*n.* incident, événement, *m.*
incidental [insi'dentl], *a.* fortuit, accidentel; accessoire; ***incidental expenses***, faux frais, *m.pl.*
incidentally [insi'dentli], *adv.* fortuitement, par hasard; soit dit en passant.
incinerate [in'sinəreit], *v.t.* incinérer.
incipient [in'sipiənt], *a.* naissant, qui commence.
incise [in'saiz], *v.t.* inciser, graver.
incision [in'siʒən], *n.* incision, *f.*
incisive [in'saisiv], *a.* incisif.
incite [in'sait], *v.t.* inciter, stimuler; encourager (*à*).
incitement [in'saitmənt], *n.* encouragement, motif, stimulant, *m.*
incivility [insi'viliti], *n.* incivilité, impolitesse, *f.*
inclemency [in'klemənsi], *n.* inclémence, *f.*; intempéries, *f.pl.*, rigueur (*du temps etc.*), *f.*
inclement [in'klemənt], *a.* inclément; rigoureux.
inclination [inkli'neiʃən], *n.* inclinaison, pente; inclination (*de la tête* ou *du corps*), *f.*; penchant, goût (*disposition*), *m.*
incline ['inklain], *n.* pente; (*Rail.*) rampe, *f.*—[in'klain], *v.t.* incliner, (faire) pencher; (*fig.*) porter, disposer (*à*).—*v.i.* incliner, s'incliner, pencher; (*fig.*) être porté (*à*).
inclined [in'klaind], *a.* incliné; enclin (*à*); porté, disposé (*à*).
include [in'klu:d], *v.t.* comprendre, renfermer.
included [in'klu:did], *a.* compris, y compris.
including [in'klu:diŋ], *prep.* comprenant, y compris.
inclusion [in'klu:ʒən], *n.* inclusion, *f.*
inclusive [in'klu:siv], *a.* inclusif; qui renferme, qui comprend; ***inclusive of***, y compris.
incoherence [inko'hiərəns], *n.* incohérence, *f.*
incoherent [inko'hiərənt], *a.* incohérent.
incombustible [inkəm'bʌstibl], *a.* incombustible.
income ['inkəm], *n.* revenu, *m.*; ***private income***, rente, *f.*, rentes, *f.pl.*
income-tax ['inkəmtæks], *n.* impôt sur le revenu, *m.*
incommode [inkə'moud], *v.t.* incommoder gêner, déranger.
incommodious [inkə'moudjəs], *a.* incommode.
incomparable [in'kəmprəbl], *a.* incomparable.
incompatible [inkəm'pætibl], *a.* incompatible.
incompetence [in'kəmpitəns], *n.* incompétence, insuffisance; incapacité *f.*
incompetent [in'kəmpitənt], *a.* incompétent, incapable.
incompetently [in'kəmpitəntli], *adv.* avec incompétence.
incomplete [inkəm'pli:t], *a.* imparfait, inachevé, incomplet.
incompletely [inkəm'pli:tli], *adv.* incomplètement, imparfaitement.
incomprehensibility [inkəmprihensi'biliti], *n.* incompréhensibilité, *f.*
incomprehensible [inkəmpri'hensibl], *a.* incompréhensible.
inconceivable [inkən'si:vəbl], *a.* inconcevable.
inconclusive [inkən'klu:siv], *a.* qui n'est pas concluant.
incongruity [inkəŋ'gru:iti], *n.* désaccord, *m.*, incongruité; inconvenance, *f.*
incongruous [in'kəŋgruəs], *a.* incongru, inconvenant, (*fig.*) disparate.
inconsequence [in'kənsikwəns], *n.* inconséquence; fausse déduction, *f.*
inconsequent [in'kənsikwənt], *a.* inconséquent.
inconsiderable [inkən'sidərəbl], *a.* petit, insignifiant; de peu d'importance.
inconsiderate [inkən'sidərit], *a.* inconsidéré, irréfléchi; sans égards pour les autres.
inconsistency [inkən'sistənsi], *n.* inconséquence; contradiction, *f.*
inconsistent [inkən'sistənt], *a.* incompatible (*avec*), contradictoire (*à*); inconséquent.
inconsistently [inkən'sistəntli], *adv.* avec un manque de continuité.
inconspicuous [inkən'spikjuəs], *a.* peu apparent, peu remarquable; discret.
inconstancy [in'kənstənsi], *n.* inconstance, *f.*; caractère changeant, *m.*
inconstant [in'kənstənt], *a.* inconstant, volage, changeant.
incontestable [inkən'testəbl], *a.* incontestable, irrécusable.
incontrovertible [inkəntrə'və:tibl], *a.* incontestable, indisputable.
inconvenience [inkən'vi:niəns], *n.* inconvénient; embarras, dérangement, *m.*—*v.t.* déranger, incommoder, gêner.
inconvenient [inkən'vi:niənt], *a.* incommode, gênant.
inconveniently [inkən'vi:niəntli], *adv.* incommodément mal.
incorporate [in'kə:pəreit], *v.t.* incorporer, former en société.—*v.i.* s'incorporer.
incorrect [inkə'rekt], *a.* incorrect, inexact.
incorrectly [inkə'rektli], *adv.* incorrectement; inexactement.
incorrectness [inkə'rektnis], *n.* incorrection; inexactitude, *f.*
incorrigible [in'kəridʒibl], *a.* incorrigible.
incorrupt [inkə'rʌpt], *a.* incorrompu, pur, intègre.
incorruptible [inkə'rʌptibl], *a.* incorruptible.
increase [in'kri:s], *v.t.* augmenter, agrandir, accroître.—*v.i.* croître, s'accroître; augmenter.—['inkri:s], *n.* augmentation (*de prix*), *f.*, accroissement (*de vitesse*); (*fig.*) produit, *m.*; crue (*de rivière*), *f.*
increasing [in'kri:siŋ], *a.* croissant.
increasingly [in'kri:siŋli], *adv.* de plus en plus.
incredible [in'kredibl], *a.* incroyable.

incredibly [in'kredibli], *adv.* incroyablement, d'une manière incroyable.
incredulity [inkrə'dju:liti], *n.* incrédulité, *f.*
incredulous [in'kredjuləs], *a.* incrédule.
increment ['inkrimənt], *n.* augmentation, *f.*; produit, *m.*
incriminate [in'krimineit], *v.t.* incriminer.
incubate ['inkjubeit], *v.t.* couver.
incubation [inkju'beiʃən], *n.* incubation, *f.*
incubator ['inkjubeitə], *n.* couveuse artificielle, *f.*
incubus ['inkjubəs], *n.* incube, cauchemar; (*fig.*) grand poids, *m.*
inculcate ['inkʌlkeit], *v.t.* inculquer (*à*).
incumbent [in'kʌmbənt], *a.* couché (*sur*); imposé, obligatoire; ***to be incumbent on***, incomber à; ***to feel it incumbent on one to do***, se faire un devoir de.—*n.* titulaire, bénéficier, *m.*
incur [in'kə:], *v.t.* encourir (*blâme*), s'attirer (*colère*); faire (*dettes*).
incurable [in'kjuərəbl], *a.* incurable, inguérissable.—*n.* incurable, *m.*, *f.*
incursion [in'kə:ʃən], *n.* incursion, irruption, *f.*
indebted [in'detid], *a.* endetté; redevable (*de*).
indebtedness [in'detidnis], *n.* dette, obligation, *f.*
indecency [in'di:sənsi], *n.* indécence, *f.*
indecent [in'di:sənt], *a.* indécent.
indecently [in'di:səntli], *adv.* indécemment.
indecision [indi'siʒən], *n.* irrésolution, *f.*
indecisive [indi'saisiv], *a.* peu décisif, indécis.
indecorous [in'dekərəs], *a.* inconvenant.
indecorousness [in'dekərəsnis], **indecorum** [indi'kɔ:rəm], *n.* manque de décorum, *m.*, inconvenance, *f.*
indeed [in'di:d], *adv.* en effet, en vérité; vraiment; à dire vrai, à la vérité.—*int.* vraiment! allons donc!
indefatigable [indi'fætigəbl], *a.* infatigable.
indefensible [indi'fensibl], *a.* indéfendable, inexcusable.
indefinable [indi'fainəbl], *a.* indéfinissable.
indefinite [in'definit], *a.* indéfini, vague.
indefinitely [in'definitli], *adv.* indéfiniment, vaguement.
indelible [in'delibl], *a.* indélébile, ineffaçable.
indelibly [in'delibli], *adv.* d'une manière indélébile, ineffaçablement.
indelicacy [in'delikəsi], *n.* indélicatesse, grossièreté, inconvenance, *f.*
indelicate [in'delikit], *a.* indélicat, grossier, inconvenant.
indemnify [in'demnifai], *v.t.* dédommager, indemniser (*de*).
indemnity [in'demniti], *n.* dédommagement, *m.*; indemnité, *f.*
indent [in'dent], *v.t.* denteler; ébrécher, échancrer.—*v.i.* ***to indent for***, réquisitionner.—*n.* dentelure, bosselure, *f.*
indented [in'dentid], *a.* dentelé; échancré.
indenture [in'dentʃə], *n.* titre; (*esp. pl.*) contrat d'apprentissage, *m.*—*v.t.* mettre en apprentissage.
independence [indi'pendəns], **independency** [indi'pendənsi], *n.* indépendance, *f.*
independent [indi'pendənt], *a.* indépendant; libre.
independently [indi'pendəntli], *adv.* indépendamment; dans l'indépendance.
indescribable [indi'skraibəbl], *a.* indicible, indescriptible.
indestructible [indi'strʌktibl], *a.* indestructible.
index ['indeks], *n.* (*pl.* **indexes** ['indeksiz] **indices** ['indisi:z]) indice, signe, indicateur; index (*d'un livre*), *m.*; aiguille (*d'une montre etc.*), *f.*; (*Anat.*) index, doigt indicateur; (*Math.*) exposant, *m.*
India ['indjə]. l'Inde, *f.*
Indian ['indjən], *a.* indien; des Indiens; de l'Inde, des Indes; ***Indian corn***, maïs, *m.*—*n.* Indien (*personne*), *m.*; ***Red Indian*** Peau-Rouge, *m.*, *f.*
india-rubber ['indjə'rʌbə], *n.* caoutchouc, *m*
indicate ['indikeit], *v.t.* indiquer.
indication [indi'keiʃən], *n.* indication, *f.* signe, indice, *m.*
indicative [in'dikətiv], *a.* and *n.* indicatif, *m*
indicator ['indikeitə], *n.* indicateur, *m.*
indict [in'dait], *v.t.* inculper, mettre en accusation.
indictment [in'daitmənt], *n.* accusation mise en accusation, *f.*
Indies ['indiz], **the.** les Indes, *f.pl.*; ***the West Indies***, les Antilles, *f.pl.*
indifference [in'difrəns], *n.* indifférence apathie, *f.*
indifferent [in'difrənt], *a.* indifférent; impartial; passable, médiocre.
indifferently [in'difrəntli], *adv.* indifféremment; médiocrement.
indigence ['indidʒəns], *n.* indigence, *f.*
indigent ['indidʒənt], *a.* nécessiteux, indigent.
indigenous [in'didʒinəs], *a.* du pays, indigène.
indigestible [indi'dʒestibl], *a.* indigeste.
indigestion [indi'dʒestʃən], *n.* indigestion dyspepsie, *f.*
indignant [in'dignənt], *a.* indigné (*de*); plein d'indignation.
indignantly [in'dignəntli], *adv.* avec indignation.
indignation [indig'neiʃən], *n.* indignation, *f.*
indignity [in'digniti], *n.* indignité, *f.*; outrage, affront, *m.*
indigo ['indigou], *n.* indigo, *m.*
indirect [indi'rekt], *a.* indirect; (*fig.*) oblique insidieux.
indiscreet [indis'kri:t], *a.* indiscret, irréfléchi, imprudent.
indiscreetly [indis'kri:tli], *adv.* indiscrètement.
indiscretion [indis'kreʃən], *n.* indiscrétion imprudence, *f.*
indiscriminate [indis'kriminit], *a.* confus sans distinction; aveugle.
indiscriminately [indis'kriminitli], *adv.* sans distinction, à tort et à travers, aveuglément
indispensable [indis'pensəbl], *a.* indispensable, nécessaire.
indispose [indis'pouz], *v.t.* indisposer (*contre*), déranger, détourner (*de*).
indisposed [indis'pouzd], *a.* souffrant.
indisposition [indispə'ziʃən], *n.* indisposition, *f.*; malaise, *m.*
indisputable [indis'pju:təbl], *a.* incontestable, indiscutable.
indisputably [indis'pju:təbli], *adv.* incontestablement.
indissoluble [indi'sɔljubl], *a.* indissoluble.
indistinct [indis'tiŋkt], *a.* indistinct, confus, imprécis, vague.

indistinctly [indis'tiŋktli], *adv.* indistinctement, confusément, vaguement.
indistinguishable [indis'tiŋgwiʃəbl], *a.* indistinct, imperceptible.
indite [in'dait], *v.t.* rédiger.
individual [indi'vidjuəl], *a.* individuel; seul, unique.—*n.* individu, particulier, *m.*
individuality [individju'æliti], *n.* individualité, personnalité, *f.*
individually [indi'viduəli], *adv.* individuellement.
indivisible [indi'vizibl], *a.* indivisible.
indoctrinate [in'dɔktrineit], *v.t.* instruire; endoctriner.
indolence ['indələns], *n.* indolence, paresse, *f.*
indolent ['indələnt], *a.* indolent, paresseux.
indolently ['indələntli], *adv.* indolemment, nonchalamment.
indomitable [in'dɔmitəbl], *a.* indomptable.
Indonesia [indo'ni:ziə]. l'Indonésie, *f.*
Indonesian [indo'ni:ziən], *a.* indonésien.—*n.* indonésien (*langue*); Indonésien (*personne*), *m.*
indoors [in'dɔ:z], *adv.* à la maison, au dedans.
indubitable [in'dju:bitəbl], *a.* indubitable, incontestable.
induce [in'dju:s], *v.t.* porter, persuader, induire, pousser (*à*); amener, causer, produire.
inducement [in'dju:smənt], *n.* raison, tentation, *f.*, motif, mobile, *m.*
induction [in'dʌkʃən], *n.* installation; induction, *f.*
indulge [in'dʌldʒ], *v.t.* satisfaire; avoir trop d'indulgence pour; (*fig.*) flatter, caresser (*une espérance etc.*).—*v.i.* se laisser aller, se livrer à, s'abandonner (*à*).
indulgence [in'dʌldʒəns], *n.* faveur, *f.*, plaisir, agrément, *m.*; (*R.-C. Ch.*) indulgence, *f.*
indulgent [in'dʌldʒənt], *a.* indulgent, facile, complaisant.
industrial [in'dʌstriəl], *a.* industriel, de l'industrie.
industrialist [in'dʌstriəlist], *n.* industriel, *m.*
industrious [in'dʌstriəs], *a.* travailleur; diligent, laborieux.
industriously [in'dʌstriəsli], *adv.* assidûment, diligemment.
industry ['indəstri], *n.* travail, *m.*, diligence, assiduité, *f.*; (*fig.*) empressement, *m.*; industrie (*production*), *f.*
inebriate [i'ni:brieit], *v.t.* enivrer.—[i'ni:briit], *a.* enivré.—*n.* ivrogne, *m., f.*
inebriation [ini:bri'eiʃən], **inebriety** [ini'braiəti], *n.* ivresse, ébriété, *f.*
inedible [in'edibl], *a.* immangeable; non comestible.
ineffable [in'efəbl], *a.* ineffable.
ineffaceable [ini'feisəbl], *a.* ineffaçable, indélébile.
ineffective [ini'fektiv], *a.* inefficace, sans effet.
ineffectual [ini'fektjuəl], *a.* inefficace, inutile, vain; incapable.
ineffectually [ini'fektjuəli], *adv.* inutilement, sans effet.
inefficacious [inefi'keiʃəs], *a.* inefficace.
inefficiency [ini'fiʃənsi], *n.* inefficacité, incapacité, incompétence, *f.*
inefficient [ini'fiʃənt], *a.* inefficace; incapable.
ineligible [in'elidʒibl], *a.* inéligible; peu propre (*à*).
inept [in'ept], *a.* inepte, sot, absurde, peu propre (*à*).
inequality [ini'kwɔliti], *n.* inégalité, disparité, *f.*
inert [i'nə:t], *a.* inerte.
inertia [i'nə:ʃə], *n.* inertie, inactivité, *f.*
inestimable [in'estiməbl], *a.* inestimable; incalculable.
inevitable [in'evitəbl], *a.* inévitable; fatal.
inevitably [in'evitəbli], *adv.* inévitablement.
inexact [inig'zækt], *a.* inexact.
inexcusable [iniks'kju:zəbl], *a.* inexcusable, sans excuse.
inexhaustible [inig'zɔ:stibl], *a.* inépuisable.
inexorable [in'eksərəbl], *a.* inexorable, inflexible.
inexpedient [iniks'pi:dʒənt], *a.* inopportun, mal à propos.
inexpensive [iniks'pensiv], *a.* peu coûteux, bon marché.
inexperience [iniks'piəriəns], *n.* inexpérience, *f.*
inexperienced [iniks'piəriənst], *a.* inexpérimenté, sans expérience.
inexplicable [in'eksplikəbl], *a.* inexplicable.
inexpressible [iniks'presibl], *a.* inexprimable, indicible.
inextricable [in'ekstrikəbl], *a.* inextricable.
infallible [in'fælibl], *a.* infaillible, immanquable.
infamous ['infəməs], *a.* infâme.
infamy ['infəmi], *n.* infamie, *f.*
infancy ['infənsi], *n.* première enfance, *f.*, bas âge, *m.*
infant ['infənt], *a.* en bas âge, dans l'enfance, petit; (*fig.*) naissant, qui commence.—*n.* enfant en bas âge, nourrisson, bébé; (*Law*) mineur, *m.*
infantile ['infəntail], *a.* enfantin, d'enfant.
infantry ['infəntri], *n.* infanterie, *f.*
infant-school ['infənt'sku:l], *n.* école maternelle, *f.*
infatuate [in'fætjueit], *v.t.* infatuer, entêter, affoler; ***to become infatuated with***, s'engouer de, s'amouracher de.
infatuation [infætju'eiʃən], *n.* engouement, *m.*; infatuation; (*fam.*) toquade, *f.*
infect [in'fekt], *v.t.* infecter (*de*).
infection [in'fekʃən], *n.* infection, contagion, *f.*
infectious [in'fekʃəs], *a.* infect; contagieux, infectieux.
infectiousness [in'fekʃəsnis], *n.* nature contagieuse, contagion, *f.*
infer [in'fə:], *v.t.* inférer; (*fig.*) supposer.
inference ['infərəns], *n.* conséquence, conclusion, déduction, *f.*
inferior [in'fiəriə], *a.* inférieur; subordonné.—*n.* inférieur, *m.*
inferiority [infiəri'ɔriti], *n.* infériorité, *f.*
infernal [in'fə:nəl], *a.* infernal, d'enfer; (*fig.*) diabolique.
inferno [in'fə:nou], *n.* enfer; brasier, *m.*
infest [in'fest], *v.t.* infester.
infidel ['infidəl], *a.* and *n.* infidèle; incrédule, *m., f.*
infidelity [infi'deliti], *n.* infidélité; déloyauté (*d'un serviteur*), *f.*
infiltrate ['infiltreit], *v.i.* s'infiltrer (*dans*); pénétrer.

infinite ['infinit], *a.* and *n.* infini, *m.*
infinitely ['infinitli], *adv.* infiniment, à l'infini; fort.
infinitive [in'finitiv], *a.* and *n.* infinitif, *m.*
infinity [in'finiti], *n.* infinité; immensité, *f.*
infirm [in'fə:m], *a.* infirme, faible; (*fig.*) inconstant, irrésolu.
infirmary [in'fə:məri], *n.* hôpital, *m.*, infirmerie, *f.*
infirmity [in'fə:miti], *n.* infirmité, faiblesse, *f.*
inflame [in'fleim], *v.t.* enflammer; (*fig.*) exciter.—*v.i.* s'enflammer.
inflammable [in'flæməbl], *a.* inflammable.
inflammation [inflə'meiʃən], *n.* inflammation, fluxion, *f.*
inflammatory [in'flæmətri], *a.* inflammatoire; (*fig.*) incendiaire.
inflate [in'fleit], *v.t.* enfler, gonfler.
inflated [in'fleitid], *a.* enflé, gonflé; exagéré; boursouflé (*style*).
inflation [in'fleiʃən], *n.* enflure, *f.*, gonflement, *m.*; inflation (monétaire), *f.*
inflect [in'flekt], *v.t.* fléchir; varier, moduler (*la voix*).
inflection [in'flekʃən], *n.* inflexion, modulation, *f.*
inflexible [in'fleksibl], *a.* inflexible.
inflict [in'flikt], *v.t.* infliger, faire (*une peine*).
infliction [in'flikʃən], *n.* infliction; (*fig.*) peine, *f.*
influence ['influəns], *n.* influence (*sur*), *f.*, empire, *m.*—*v.t.* influencer; influer (*sur*).
influential [influ'enʃəl], *a.* influent, qui a de l'influence.
influenza [influ'enzə], *n.* influenza, grippe, *f.*
influx ['inflʌks], *n.* affluence; invasion; embouchure, *f.*
inform [in'fɔ:m], *v.t.* informer, instruire, renseigner, avertir; faire savoir à; ***to inform against***, dénoncer.
informal [in'fɔ:məl], *a.* sans cérémonie, simple.
informality [infɔ:'mæliti], *n.* manque de cérémonie, *m.*; simplicité, *f.*
informally [in'fɔ:məli], *adv.* sans cérémonie; sans façon.
informant [in'fɔ:mənt], *n.* correspondant; informateur, *m.*
information [infə'meiʃən], *n.* renseignements, *m.pl.*; ***piece of information***, renseignement, avis, *m.*, nouvelle, *f.*; savoir, *m.*; (*Law*) dénonciation, *f.*
informative [in'fɔ:mətiv], *a.* instructif; éducatif.
informer [in'fɔ:mə], *n.* délateur, dénonciateur, *m.*
infraction [in'frækʃən], *n.* infraction, contravention, *f.*
infra-red [infrə'red], *a.* infra-rouge.
infrequent [in'fri:kwənt], *a.* rare.
infringe [in'frindʒ], *v.t.* enfreindre, violer, transgresser.
infringement [in'frindʒmənt], *n.* infraction, violation; contrefaçon (*d'un brevet*), *f.*
infuriate [in'fjuərieit], *v.t.* rendre furieux.
infuriated [in'fjuərieitid], *a.* furieux, en fureur.
infuse [in'fju:z], *v.t.* infuser; faire infuser; macérer; (*fig.*) inspirer (*à*).
infusion [in'fju:ʒən], *n.* infusion, *f.*
ingenious [in'dʒi:niəs], *a.* ingénieux, habile.
ingeniously [in'dʒi:niəsli], *adv.* ingénieusement; spirituellement.
ingeniousness [in'dʒi:niəsnis], **ingenuity** [indʒi'nju:iti], *n.* ingéniosité, habileté, *f.*
ingenuous [in'dʒenjuəs], *a.* ingénu; naïf; candide.
ingenuously [in'dʒenjuəsli], *adv.* ingénument, naïvement.
ingenuousness [in'dʒenjuəsnis], *n.* ingénuité, naïveté, *f.*
inglorious [in'glɔ:riəs], *a.* obscur; inconnu; honteux.
ingloriously [in'glɔ:riəsli], *adv.* sans gloire; honteusement.
ingoing ['ingouiŋ], *a.* entrant, nouveau.—*n.* entrée, *f.*
ingot ['iŋgət], *n.* lingot, *m.*
ingrained [in'greind], *a.* encrassé; (*fig.*) enraciné, invétéré.
ingratiate [in'greiʃieit], *v.t.* insinuer (*dans*); ***to ingratiate oneself with***, s'insinuer dans les bonnes grâces de.
ingratitude [in'grætitju:d], *n.* ingratitude, *f.*
ingredient [in'gri:diənt], *n.* ingrédient; élément, *m.*
ingrowing ['ingrouiŋ], *a.* incarné (*ongle*).
inhabit [in'hæbit], *v.t.* habiter; habiter (*dans*).
inhabitable [in'hæbitəbl], *a.* habitable.
inhabitant [in'hæbitənt], *n.* habitant, *m.*
inhabited [in'hæbitid], *a.* habité.
inhalation [inhə'leiʃən], *n.* inhalation; inspiration, *f.*
inhale [in'heil], *v.t.* aspirer; respirer, humer.
inherent [in'hiərənt], *a.* inhérent, naturel (*à*).
inherit [in'herit], *v.t.* hériter (*de*).—*v.i.* hériter.
inheritance [in'heritəns], *n.* héritage, patrimoine, *m.*
inhibit [in'hibit], *v.t.* arrêter, empêcher interdire.
inhibition [inhi'biʃən], *n.* interdiction; (*Psych.*) inhibition, *f.*
inhospitable [in'hɔspitəbl], *a.* inhospitalier.
inhuman [in'hju:mən], *a.* inhumain; dénaturé; cruel.
inhumanity [inhju'mæniti], *n.* inhumanité; brutalité, *f.*
inhumation [inhju'meiʃən], *n.* inhumation, *f.*, enterrement, *m.*
inimical [i'nimikl], *a.* hostile, ennemi; contraire (*à*).
inimitable [i'nimitəbl], *a.* inimitable.
iniquitous [i'nikwitəs], *a.* inique, injuste.
iniquity [i'nikwiti], *n.* iniquité, *f.*
initial [i'niʃəl], *a.* initial; premier.—*n.* initiale, *f.*—*v.t.* mettre ses initiales à; parafer.
initially [i'niʃəli], *adv.* au commencement.
initiate [i'niʃieit], *v.t.* initier (*à* ou *dans*); amorcer, commencer.
initiation [iniʃi'eiʃən], *n.* initiation, *f.*
initiative [i'niʃiətiv], *n.* initiative, *f.*
inject [in'dʒekt], *v.t.* injecter; faire une piqûre.
injection [in'dʒekʃən], *n.* injection; (*Med.*) piqûre, *f.*
injudicious [indʒu'diʃəs], *a.* peu judicieux malavisé, imprudent.
injudiciously [indʒu'diʃəsli], *adv.* peu judicieusement, imprudemment.
injunction [in'dʒʌŋkʃən], *n.* injonction; recommandation, *f.*

injure ['indʒə], *v.t.* nuire à, faire tort à, léser; endommager (*to damage*); faire mal à, blesser.
injured ['indʒəd], *a.* offensé; blessé; ***the injured***, les blessés, les accidentés, *m.pl.*
injurious [in'dʒuəriəs], *a.* nuisible, préjudiciable (*à*).
injuriously [in'dʒuəriəsli], *adv.* à tort.
injury ['indʒəri], *n.* tort, mal; dégât, dommage (*à des marchandises*), *m.*; (*Med.*) lésion, blessure, *f.*
injustice [in'dʒʌstis], *n.* injustice, *f.*
ink [iŋk], *n.* encre, *f.*; ***Indian ink***, encre de Chine.—*v.t.* tacher *ou* barbouiller d'encre.
inkling ['iŋkliŋ], *n.* soupçon, vent (*d'une affaire*), *m.*
inkstand ['iŋkstænd], *n.* encrier de bureau, *m.*
ink-well ['iŋkwel], *n.* encrier, *m.*
inky ['iŋki], *a.* d'encre; taché d'encre.
inlaid [in'leid], *a.* incrusté, marqueté.
inland ['inlənd], *a.* intérieur, de l'intérieur.—*n.* intérieur (*d'un pays*), *m.*
inlay ['inlei], *n.* marqueterie, incrustation, *f.* —[in'lei], *v.t. irr.* (*conjug. like* LAY) marqueter, incruster.
inlet ['inlit], *n.* entrée, *f.*, passage, *m.*, voie, *f.*; petit bras de mer, *m.*
inmate ['inmeit], *n.* habitant, *m.*, locataire (*dans une maison*); interne, pensionnaire (*dans une maison de santé*), *m.*, *f.*
inmost ['inmoust], *a.* le plus profond, le plus secret.
inn [in], *n.* auberge, *f.*; hôtel, *m.*; hôtellerie, *f.*; ***to put up at an inn***, descendre à une auberge.
innate [i'neit], *a.* inné; foncier.
innavigable [i'nævigəbl], *a.* innavigable.
inner ['inə], *a.* intérieur, de l'intérieur; (*fig.*) interne, secret.
innermost ['inəmoust], *a.* le plus intérieur, le plus reculé.
innkeeper ['inki:pə], *n.* aubergiste, *m.*, *f.*, hôtelier, *m.*
innocence ['inəsəns], *n.* innocence, *f.*
innocent ['inəsənt], *a.* innocent; permis, légitime.
innocently ['inəsəntli], *adv.* innocemment.
innocuous [i'nɔkjuəs], *a.* innocent, inoffensif.
innovate ['inoveit], *v.i.* innover.
innovation [ino'veiʃən], *n.* innovation, *f.*, changement, *m.*
innuendo [inju'endou], *n.* insinuation, allusion malveillante, *f.*
innumerable [i'nju:mərəbl], *a.* innombrable, sans nombre.
inoculate [i'nɔkjuleit], *v.t.* inoculer, vacciner.
inoculation [inɔkju'leiʃən], *n.* inoculation, *f.*, vaccin, *m.*
inodorous [in'oudərəs], *a.* inodore.
inoffensive [ino'fensiv], *a.* inoffensif.
inopportune [in'ɔpətju:n], *a.* inopportun, intempestif, mal à propos.
inopportunely [in'ɔpətju:nli], *adv.* inopportunément, mal à propos.
inordinate [i'nɔ:dinit], *a.* démesuré, immodéré.
inordinately [i'nɔ:dinitli], *adv.* démesurément, immodérément.
inorganic [inɔ:'gænik], *a.* inorganique.
inquest ['inkwest], *n.* enquête (*après une mort subite*), *f.*
inquire [in'kwaiə], *v.t.* demander.—*v.i.* s'enquérir, s'informer (*de*); s'adresser (*à* ou *chez*).
inquiring [in'kwaiəriŋ], *a.* investigateur, curieux.
inquiry [in'kwaiəri], *n.* demande, investigation, recherche, *f.*; (*pl.*) informations, *f.pl.* renseignements, *m.pl.*, (*Law*) enquête, *f.*
inquisition [inkwi'ziʃən], *n.* recherche, investigation; (*R.-C. Ch.*) inquisition, *f.*
inquisitive [in'kwizitiv], *a.* curieux.
inroad ['inroud], *n.* incursion, invasion, *f.*; (*fig.*) empiétement (*sur*), *m.*
insalubrious [insə'lju:briəs], *a.* insalubre.
insane [in'sein], *a.* fou, aliéné; dérangé; (*fig.*) insensé.
insanitary [in'sænitəri], *a.* insalubre, malsain.
insanity [in'sæniti], *n.* folie, démence, *f.*
insatiable [in'seiʃəbl], *a.* insatiable.
insatiate [in'seiʃiit], *a.* insatiable; inassouvi.
inscribe [in'skraib], *v.t.* inscrire; dédier (*à*).
inscription [in'skripʃən], *n.* inscription, *f.*; titre (*title*), *m.*; dédicace (*dedication*), *f.*
inscrutable [in'skru:təbl], *a.* inscrutable, impénétrable.
insect ['insekt], *n.* insecte, *m.*
insecticidal [in'sektisaidl], *a.* insecticide.
insecticide [in'sektisaid], *n.* insecticide, *m.*
insecure [insi'kjuə], *a.* en danger; chanceux, hasardeux; peu sûr, mal assuré.
insecurely [insi'kjuəli], *adv.* sans sûreté, en danger.
insecurity [insi'kjuəriti], *n.* manque de sûreté; danger, péril, *m.*; incertitude, *f.*
insensible [in'sensibl], *a.* imperceptible; insignifiant; inconscient (*unconscious*); sans connaissance.
insensibly [in'sensibli], *adv.* insensiblement, peu à peu.
insensitive [in'sensitiv], *a.* insensible.
inseparable [in'sepərəbl], *a.* inséparable.
insert [in'sə:t], *v.t.* insérer, faire insérer (*dans*).
insertion [in'sə:ʃən], *n.* insertion; interpolation, *f.*
inshore [in'ʃɔ:], *a.* and *adv.* près du rivage.
inside ['insaid], *a.* intérieur, d'intérieur.—*n.* dedans, intérieur, *m.*; ***inside out***, à l'envers; [in'said] entrailles, *f.pl.*—[in'said], *adv.* à l'intérieur, en dedans.—[in'said], *prep.* en, dans, à l'intérieur de.
insidious [in'sidiəs], *a.* insidieux, captieux, perfide.
insight ['insait], *n.* perspicacité, pénétration, *f.*
insignia [in'signiə], *n.pl.* insignes, *m.pl.*
insignificance [insig'nifikəns], *n.* insignifiance, *f.*, peu d'importance, *m.*
insignificant [insig'nifikənt], *a.* insignifiant.
insincere [insin'siə], *a.* peu sincère, faux, hypocrite.
insincerely [insin'siəli], *adv.* de mauvaise foi, hypocritement.
insincerity [insin'seriti], *n.* manque de sincérité, *m.*, fausseté, *f.*
insinuate [in'sinjueit], *v.t.* insinuer, glisser (*dans*); donner à entendre.—*v.i.* s'insinuer, se glisser (*dans*).
insinuation [insinju'eiʃən], *n.* insinuation, *f.*
insipid [in'sipid], *a.* insipide, fade.
insipidity [insi'piditi], *n.* insipidité, fadeur, *f.*
insist [in'sist], *v.i.* insister (*sur* ou *à*); persister; vouloir absolument.
insistence [in'sistəns], *n.* insistance, *f.*

insistent [in'sistənt], *a.* insistant.
insobriety [inso'braiəti], *n.* intempérance, *f.*
insolence ['insələns], *n.* insolence; effronterie, *f.*
insolent ['insələnt], *a.* insolent.
insolently ['insələntli], *adv.* insolemment.
insoluble [in'sɔljubl], *a.* insoluble.
insolvency [in'sɔlvənsi], *n.* insolvabilité, faillite, *f.*
insolvent [in'sɔlvənt], *a.* insolvable, en faillite.
insomnia [in'sɔmniə], *n.* insomnie, *f.*
insomuch [inso'mʌtʃ], *adv.* au point (*que*), à un tel point (*que*), tellement (*que*).
inspect [in'spekt], *v.t.* inspecter, examiner, visiter.
inspection [in'spekʃən], *n.* inspection, revue, *f.*, contrôle, examen, *m.*; surveillance, *f.*
inspector [in'spektə], *n.* inspecteur, *m.*
inspiration [inspi'reiʃən], *n.* inspiration, *f.*; encouragement, *m.*
inspire [in'spaiə], *v.t.* inspirer, souffler (*dans*); animer (*de*).—*v.i.* aspirer.
inspiring [in'spaiəriŋ], *a.* inspirateur; qui donne du courage; qui élève l'esprit.
inspirit [in'spirit], *v.t.* animer, encourager.
instability [instə'biliti], *n.* instabilité, *f.*
install [in'stɔ:l], *v.t.* installer; monter (*appareil, machine*).
installation [instə'leiʃən], *n.* installation, *f.*; montage (*de machine, équipement*), *m.*
instalment [in'stɔ:lmənt], *n.* installation, *f.*; (*Comm.*) accompte, versement (*partiel*); épisode (*de feuilleton*), *m.*
instance ['instəns], *n.* requête, demande, *f.*; exemple, *m.*, occasion, *f.*, cas, *m.*; ***for instance***, par exemple; ***in the first instance***, en premier lieu.—*v.t.* citer comme exemple.
instant ['instənt], *a.* instant, pressant, immédiat; courant (*mois*).—*n.* instant, moment, *m.*
instantaneous [instən'teiniəs], *a.* instantané.
instantaneously [instən'teiniəsli], *adv.* instantanément.
instantly ['instəntli], *adv.* à l'instant; tout de suite; sur-le-champ.
instead [in'sted], *adv.* à la place; ***instead of***, au lieu de.
instep ['instep], *n.* cou-de-pied, *m.*
instigate ['instigeit], *v.t.* exciter, inciter, pousser (*à*).
instigation [insti'geiʃən], *n.* instigation, *f.*
instil [in'stil], *v.t.* instiller; (*fig.*) inspirer (*à*).
instillation [insti'leiʃən], *n.* instillation; (*fig.*) inspiration, *f.*
instinct ['instiŋkt], *n.* instinct, *m.*
instinctive [in'stiŋktiv], *a.* instinctif; (*fig.*) spontané.
instinctively [in'stiŋktivli], *adv.* d'instinct, instinctivement.
institute ['institju:t], *n.* institut, *m.*—*v.t.* instituer, établir; intenter (*un procès*).
institution [insti'tju:ʃən], *n.* institution, *f.*, établissement, *m.*
instruct [in'strʌkt], *v.t.* instruire, enseigner; charger (*de*).
instruction [in'strʌkʃən], *n.* instruction, *f.*, enseignement, *m.*
instructive [in'strʌktiv], *a.* instructif.
instructor [in'strʌktə], *n.* (*Mil.*) instructeur; précepteur, *m.*
instructress [in'strʌktris], *n.* préceptrice, monitrice, *f.*
instrument ['instrumənt], *n.* instrument; (*fig.*) agent, *m.*
instrumental [instru'mentl], *a.* instrumental; ***to be instrumental in***, contribuer à.
insubordinate [insə'bɔ:dinit], *a.* insubordonné; indocile.
insubordination [insəbɔ:di'neiʃən], *n.* insubordination; insoumission, *f.*
insufferable [in'sʌfərəbl], *a.* insupportable intolérable.
insufficiency [insə'fiʃənsi], *n.* insuffisance, *f.*
insufficient [insə'fiʃənt], *a.* insuffisant.
insufficiently [insə'fiʃəntli], *adv.* insuffisamment.
insular ['insjulə], *a.* insulaire; (*fig.*) borné, rétréci.
insularity [insju'læriti], *n.* insularité, *f.*
insulate ['insjuleit], *v.t.* isoler; calorifuger.
insulation [insju'leiʃən], *n.* isolement, *m.*; (*Phys.*) isolation, *f.*
insulator ['insjuleitə], *n.* isolateur, isoloir, *m.*
insulin ['insjulin], *n.* insuline, *f.*
insult [in'sʌlt], *v.t.* insulter, faire insulte à, injurier.—['insʌlt], *n.* insulte, injure, *f.*, affront, *m.*
insulting [in'sʌltiŋ], *a.* insultant, outrageux, injurieux.
insultingly [in'sʌltiŋli], *adv.* insolemment, injurieusement.
insuperable [in'sju:pərəbl], *a.* insurmontable, invincible.
insupportable [insə'pɔ:təbl], *a.* insupportable, intolérable.
insuppressible [insə'presibl], *a.* irrépressible, irrésistible, inextinguible (*rire*).
insurance [in'ʃuərəns], *n.* assurance, *f.*; ***fire-insurance***, assurance contre l'incendie; ***life-insurance***, assurance sur la vie.
insure [in'ʃuə], *v.t.* assurer, faire assurer; (*fig.*) garantir.
insurgent [in'sə:dʒənt], *a.* and *n.* insurgé, *m.*
insurmountable [insə'mauntəbl], *a.* insurmontable, infranchissable.
insurrection [insə'rekʃən], *n.* insurrection, *f.* soulèvement, *m.*
intact [in'tækt], *a.* intact, indemne.
intangible [in'tændʒibl], *a.* intangible.
integer ['intədʒə], *n.* entier, nombre entier, *m.*
integral ['intəgrəl], *a.* intégral; ***an integral part***, une partie intégrante.—*n.* totalité, *f.*, tout, *m.*
integrate ['intigreit], *v.t.* compléter, rendre entier.
integrity [in'tegriti], *n.* intégrité, probité, *f.*
intellect ['intilekt], *n.* intelligence, *f.*, esprit, *m.*
intellectual [inti'lektjuəl], *a.* intellectuel; intelligent.—*n.* intellectuel, *m.*
intellectually [inti'lektjuəli], *adv.* intellectuellement.
intelligence [in'telidʒəns], *n.* intelligence, *f.*, esprit; renseignement, avis, *m.*; nouvelle, *f.*
intelligent [in'telidʒənt], *a.* intelligent.
intelligently [in'telidʒəntli], *adv.* intelligemment, avec intelligence.
intelligibility [intelidʒi'biliti], *n.* intelligibilité, clarté, *f.*
intelligible [in'telidʒibl], *a.* intelligible.

intemperance [in'tempərəns], *n.* intempérance, *f.*
intemperate [in'tempərit], *a.* démesuré, immodéré; intempérant; violent, emporté (*langage*).
intend [in'tend], *v.t.* se proposer de, avoir l'intention de, compter, vouloir; destiner (*à*); vouloir dire.
intended [in'tendid], *a.* projeté; intentionnel; ***to be intended for***, être destiné à.
intense [in'tens], *a.* intense, véhément; (*fig.*) opiniâtre, très sérieux; vif, fort, aigu (*douleur etc.*).
intensely [in'tensli], *adv.* avec intensité, vivement, fortement.
intenseness [in'tensnis], **intensity** [in'tensiti], *n.* intensité; force, violence, *f.*
intensify [in'tensifai], *v.t.* rendre plus vif, intensifier.
intensive [in'tensiv], *a.* intensif.
intent [in'tent], *a.* attentif, absorbé (*par*); déterminé (*à*); fixe (*regard*).—*n.* dessein, but; sens, *m.*, intention, portée, *f.*; ***to all intents and purposes***, à tous égards.
intention [in'tenʃən], *n.* intention, *f.*; dessein, but, *m.*
intentional [in'tenʃənəl], *a.* intentionnel, fait à dessein.
intentionally [in'tenʃənəli], *adv.* avec intention, à dessein, exprès.
intently [in'tentli], *adv.* attentivement.
intentness [in'tentnis], *n.* attention, force d'application, *f.*
inter [in'tə:], *v.t.* enterrer, inhumer, ensevelir.
intercede [intə'si:d], *v.i.* intercéder (*auprès de*).
intercept [intə'sept], *v.t.* intercepter; arrêter; (*fig.*) surprendre.
interchange [intə'tʃeindʒ], *v.t.* échanger.—['intətʃeindʒ], *n.* échange, *m.*, succession; (*fig.*) variété, *f.*
intercourse ['intəkɔ:s], *n.* commerce, *m.*, relations, *f.pl.*, rapports, *m.pl.*
interdict [intə'dikt], *v.t.* interdire, interdire à, défendre à.—['intədikt], *n.* or **interdiction** [intə'dikʃən], interdit, *m.*, défense, interdiction, *f.*
interest ['intrəst], *v.t.* intéresser; ***to be interested in***, s'intéresser à.—*n.* intérêt, *m.*; protection, *f.*, crédit, *m.*
interested ['intrəstid], *a.* intéressé.
interesting ['intrəstiŋ], *a.* intéressant.
interfere [intə'fiə], *v.i.* intervenir, se mêler (*de*); ***to interfere with***, se mêler de, gêner, contrarier, déranger.
interference [intə'fiərəns], *n.* intervention, *f.*; (*Rad.*) brouillage, *m.*
interim ['intərim], *a.* provisoire.—*n.* intérim, intervalle, *m.*; ***in the interim***, en attendant.
interior [in'tiəriə], *a.* and *n.* intérieur, *m.*; ***interior angle***, angle interne, *m.*
interject [intə'dʒekt], *v.t.* interjecter; s'écrier (*en conversation*).
interjection [intə'dʒekʃən], *n.* interjection, *f.*
interlace [intə'leis], *v.t.* entrelacer.
interlacing [intə'leisiŋ], *n.* entrelacement, *m.*
interleave [intə'li:v], *v.t.* interfolier (*de*).
interloper ['intəloupə], *n.* intrus, *m.*
interlude ['intəlu:d], *n.* intermède, *m.*
intermediary [intə'mi:diəri], *a.* and *n.* intermédiaire, *m.*
intermediate [intə'mi:djit], *a.* intermédiaire, moyen.
interment [in'tə:mənt], *n.* enterrement, *m.*, inhumation, *f.*
interminable [in'tə:minəbl], *a.* interminable.
intermingle [intə'miŋgl], *v.t.* entremêler.—*v.i.* s'entremêler.
intermission [intə'miʃən], *n.* interruption momentanée, *f.*; relâche, intervalle; (*Cine.*) entr'acte, *m.*
intermittent [intə'mitənt], *a.* intermittent.
intermittently [intə'mitəntli], *adv.* par intervalles.
intern [in'tə:n], *v.t.* interner.
internal [in'tə:nl], *a.* interne, intérieur.
international [intə'næʃənl], *a.* international.—*n.* (joueur) international, *m.*
internecine [intə'ni:sain], *a.* meurtrier.
internee [intə:'ni:], *n.* interné, *m.*
internment [in'tə:nmənt], *n.* internement, *m.*; ***internment camp***, camp de concentration, camp de prisonniers, *m.*
interplanetary [intə'plænətəri], *a.* interplanétaire.
interpolate [in'tə:poleit], *v.t.* interpoler; intercaler.
interpose [intə'pouz], *v.t.* interposer.—*v.i.* s'interposer, intervenir.
interpret [in'tə:prit], *v.t.* interpréter; expliquer.
interpretation [intə:pri'teiʃən], *n.* interprétation, *f.*
interpreter [in'tə:pritə], *n.* interprète, *m.*, *f.*
interracial [intə'reiʃəl], *a.* interracial.
interrogate [in'terəgeit], *v.t.* interroger questionner.
interrogation [interə'geiʃən], *n.* interrogation, question, *f.*
interrogative [intə'rɔgətiv], *a.* interrogatif interrogateur.
interrupt [intə'rʌpt], *v.t.* interrompre.
interruption [intə'rʌpʃən], *n.* interruption, *f.*; (*fig.*) obstacle, *m.*
intersect [intə'sekt], *v.t.* entrecouper; (*Geom.*) couper.—*v.i.* (*Geom.*) se couper, se croiser.
intersection [intə'sekʃən], *n.* intersection, *f.*
intersperse [intə'spə:s], *v.t.* entremêler (*de*); parsemer (*de*).
interstice [in'tə:stis], *n.* interstice; intervalle, *m.*
intertwine [intə'twain], *v.t.* entrelacer.—*v.i.* s'entrelacer.
interval ['intəvəl], *n.* intervalle; (*Theat.*) entr'acte, *m.*; (*Ftb.*) mi-temps, *f.*
intervene [intə'vi:n], *v.i.* intervenir, s'interposer; survenir, arriver (*événements*); s'écouler (*temps*).
intervening [intə'vi:niŋ], *a.* intervenant (*personnes*); intermédiaire (*espace, endroits, temps etc.*).
intervention [intə'venʃən], *n.* intervention, *f.*
interview ['intəvju:], *n.* entrevue; (*Journ.*) interview, *f.*—*v.t.* avoir une entrevue avec; (*Journ.*) interviewer.
interviewer ['intəvju:ə], *n.* interviewer, *m.*
interweave [intə'wi:v], *v.t. irr.* (*conjug. like* WEAVE) entrelacer; entremêler.
intestate [in'testit], *a.* intestat.
intestine [in'testin], *a.* and *n.* intestin, *m.*
intimacy ['intiməsi], *n.* intimité, *f.*
intimate ['intimit], *a.* intime, lié.—['intimeit], *v.t.* donner à entendre; intimer (*à*).

intimately [ˈintimitli], *adv.* intimement.
intimation [intiˈmeiʃən], *n.* avis, *m.*, indication, *f.*
intimidate [inˈtimideit], *v.t.* intimider.
intimidation [intimiˈdeiʃən], *n.* intimidation, *f.*
into [ˈintu], *prep.* dans, en, à, entre.
intolerable [inˈtɔlərəbl], *a.* intolérable, insupportable.
intolerance [inˈtɔlərəns], *n.* intolérance, *f.*
intolerant [inˈtɔlərənt], *a.* intolérant.
intonation [intoˈneiʃən], *n.* intonation, *f.*
intone [inˈtoun], *v.t.*, *v.i.* psalmodier; entonner.
intoxicant [inˈtɔksikənt], *n.* boisson alcoolique, *f.*
intoxicate [inˈtɔksikeit], *v.t.* enivrer (*de*).
intoxicated [inˈtɔksikeitid], *a.* ivre; (*fig.*) enivré (*de*).
intoxicating [inˈtɔksikeitiŋ], *a.* enivrant.
intoxication [intɔksiˈkeiʃən], *n.* ivresse, *f.*; (*fig.*) enivrement, *m.*
intractability [intræktəˈbiliti], *n.* naturel intraitable, *m.*, indocilité, *f.*
intractable [inˈtræktəbl], *a.* intraitable, indocile.
intransigence [inˈtrænsidʒəns, inˈtrɑːnsidʒəns], *n.* intransigeance, *f.*
intransigent [inˈtrænsidʒənt, inˈtrɑːnsidʒənt], *a.* intransigeant.
intransitive [inˈtrænsitiv, inˈtrɑːnsitiv], *a.* intransitif.
intrepid [inˈtrepid], *a.* intrépide.
intricacy [ˈintrikəsi], *n.* embrouillement, *m.*; complication, *f.*, dédale, *m.*
intricate [ˈintrikit], *a.* embrouillé; embarrassé; obscur; compliqué.
intrigue [inˈtriːg], *n.* intrigue, *f.*—*v.t.* intriguer.—*v.i.* intriguer, s'intriguer.
intriguing [inˈtriːgiŋ], *a.* intrigant, qui excite la curiosité.
intrinsic [inˈtrinsik], **intrinsical** [inˈtrinsikəl], *a.* intrinsèque.
introduce [intrəˈdjuːs], *v.t.* introduire, faire entrer; présenter (*personnes*), faire connaître (*à*).
introduction [intrəˈdʌkʃən], *n.* introduction; présentation; recommandation (*par lettre*), *f.*; avant-propos (*de livre*), *m.*
introductory [intrəˈdʌktəri], *a.* introductoire, préliminaire.
introspection [introˈspekʃən], *n.* introspection, *f.*
introspective [introˈspektiv], *a.* introspectif; qui s'analyse.
introvert [ˈintrovəːt], *n.* introverti, *m.*
intrude [inˈtruːd], *v.i.* s'introduire, se faufiler, se fourrer; ***to intrude on***, importuner, déranger.
intruder [inˈtruːdə], *n.* intrus, *m.*
intrusion [inˈtruːʒən], *n.* intrusion, importunité; (*fig.*) usurpation, *f.*, empiètement, *m.*
intuition [intjuˈiʃən], *n.* intuition, *f.*
intuitive [inˈtjuːitiv], *a.* intuitif, d'intuition.
inundate [ˈinʌndeit], *v.t.* inonder (*de*).
inundation [inʌnˈdeiʃən], *n.* inondation, *f.*, débordement, *m.*
inure [iˈnjuə], *v.t.* habituer, endurcir, rompre.
invade [inˈveid], *v.t.* envahir.
invader [inˈveidə], *n.* envahisseur, *m.*
invading [inˈveidiŋ], *a.* envahissant; d'invasion.
invalid [ˈinvəliːd], *a.* malade, infirme; [inˈvælid], (*Law*) invalide, de nul effet.—*n.* malade, *m.*, *f.*, personne malade, *f.*—*v.t.* ***to invalid out*** (*of the army*), réformer.
invalidate [inˈvælideit], *v.t.* invalider, casser.
invaluable [inˈvæljuəbl], *a.* inestimable, sans prix.
invariable [inˈvɛəriəbl], *a.* invariable, constant, uniforme.
invariably [inˈvɛəriəbli], *adv.* invariablement; constamment.
invasion [inˈveiʒən], *n.* invasion, *f.*, envahissement, *m.*; (*fig.*) violation, *f.*
invective [inˈvektiv], *n.* invective, *f.*
inveigh [inˈvei], *v.i.* invectiver (*contre*).
inveigle [inˈviːgl, inˈveigl], *v.t.* séduire, attirer, entraîner.
invent [inˈvent], *v.t.* inventer.
invention [inˈvenʃən], *n.* invention, *f.*
inventive [inˈventiv], *a.* inventif.
inventor [inˈventə], *n.* inventeur, *m.*
inventory [ˈinvəntri], *n.* inventaire, *m.*
inverse [inˈvəːs], *a.* inverse.
inversely [inˈvəːsli], *adv.* en sens inverse, inversement.
inversion [inˈvəːʃən], *n.* inversion, *f.*
invert [inˈvəːt], *v.t.* tourner sens dessus dessous, renverser.
invertebrate [inˈvəːtibrit], *a.* and *n.* invertébré, *m.*
invest [inˈvest], *v.t.* vêtir, revêtir (*de*); (*Mil.*) investir, bloquer; placer (*argent*).
investigate [inˈvestigeit], *v.t.* rechercher, examiner; enquêter sur.
investigation [investiˈgeiʃən], *n.* investigation, recherche, enquête, *f.*
investigator [inˈvestigeitə], *n.* investigateur, *m.*; ***private investigator***, détective privé, *m.*
investment [inˈvestmənt], *n.* placement (*d'argent*); (*Mil.*) investissement, *m.*
investor [inˈvestə], *n.* actionnaire, *m.*, *f.*, personne qui place ses fonds, *f.*
inveterate [inˈvetərit], *a.* invétéré, enraciné; acharné.
invidious [inˈvidiəs], *a.* odieux; désagréable, ingrat (*tâche*).
invigorate [inˈvigəreit], *v.t.* fortifier; donner de la vigueur à.
invigorating [inˈvigəreitiŋ], *a.* fortifiant, vivifiant, tonifiant.
invincible [inˈvinsibl], *a.* invincible.
inviolable [inˈvaiələbl], *a.* inviolable.
inviolate [inˈvaiəlit], *a.* inviolé, pur, intact.
invisible [inˈvizibl], *a.* invisible.
invitation [inviˈteiʃən], *n.* invitation, *f.*
invite [inˈvait], *v.t.* inviter, engager (*à*); (*fig.*) appeler, provoquer.
inviting [inˈvaitiŋ], *a.* attrayant, appétissant, tentant.
invoice [ˈinvɔis], *n.* facture, *f.*—*v.t.* facturer.
invoke [inˈvouk], *v.t.* invoquer.
involuntarily [inˈvɔləntərili], *adv.* involontairement.
involuntary [inˈvɔləntəri], *a.* involontaire.
involve [inˈvɔlv], *v.t.* envelopper (*to envelop*); compromettre, impliquer, entraîner (*to entail*); comprendre, renfermer (*to comprise*); embarrasser, entortiller (*to entangle*).
involved [inˈvɔlvd], *a.* embrouillé, entortillé, compliqué.
invulnerable [inˈvʌlnərəbl], *a.* invulnérable.

inward ['inwəd], *a.* intérieur, interne.—*adv.* (*also* **inwards** ['inwədz]) en dedans, intérieurement.
inwardly ['inwədli], *adv.* intérieurement, intimement.
iodine ['aiədi:n, 'aiədain], *n.* iode, *m.*
ion ['aiən], *n.* ion, *m.*
ionosphere [ai'ɔnəsfiə], *n.* ionosphère, *f.*
iota [ai'outə], *n.* iota; rien, *m.*
Iran [i'rɑ:n]. l'Iran, *m.*
Iranian [i'reiniən, ai'reiniən], *a.* iranien, *m.*—*n.* Iranien (*personne*), *m.*
Iraq, Irak [i'rɑ:k]. l'Irak, *m.*
Iraqi [i'rɑ:ki], *a.* irakien.—*n.* Irakien (*personne*), *m.*
irascible [i'ræsibl], *a.* irascible.
irate [ai'reit], *a.* courroucé, irrité.
ire ['aiə], *n.* colère, *f.*, courroux, *m.*
Ireland ['aiələnd]. l'Irlande, *f.*
Irene [ai'ri:ni, ai'ri:n]. Irène, *f.*
iridescent [iri'desənt], *a.* iridescent, irisé; chatoyant.
iris ['aiəris], *n.* (*pl.* **irises** ['aiərisiz]) iris, *m.*
Irish ['aiəriʃ], *a.* irlandais.—*n.* irlandais (*langue*), *m.*; ***the Irish***, les Irlandais, *m.pl.*
Irishman ['aiəriʃmən], *n.* (*pl.* **-men** [men]) Irlandais, *m.*
Irishwoman ['aiəriʃwumən], *n.* (*pl.* **-women** [wimin]) Irlandaise, *f.*
irk [ə:k], *v.t.* peiner, affliger; ennuyer.
irksome ['ə:ksəm], *a.* pénible, ennuyeux, ingrat.
iron ['aiən], *a.* de fer, en fer.—*n.* fer, *m.*; ***cast iron***, fonte, *f.*; ***corrugated iron***, tôle ondulée, *f.*; ***sheet iron***, tôle, *f.*, ***wrought iron***, fer forgé.—*v.t.* repasser (*linge etc.*).
ironic [aiə'rɔnik], **ironical** [aiə'rɔnikəl], *a.* ironique.
ironing ['aiəniŋ], *a.* à repasser.—*n.* repassage, *m.*
ironing-board ['aiəniŋbɔ:d], *n.* planche à repasser, *f.*
ironmonger ['aiənmʌŋgə], *n.* quincaillier, *m.*
ironmongery ['aiənmʌŋgəri], *n.* quincaillerie, *f.*
iron-ore ['aiən'ɔ:], *n.* minerai de fer, *m.*
iron-works ['aiənwə:ks], *n.pl.* forges, *f.pl.*; usine métallurgique, *f.*
irony ['aiərəni], *n.* ironie, *f.*
irradiate [i'reidieit], *v.t.* rayonner sur; éclairer.—*v.i.* rayonner.
irrational [i'ræʃənl], *a.* irraisonnable, déraisonnable; (*Math.*) irrationnel.
irreclaimable [iri'kleiməbl], *a.* incorrigible, invétéré.
irreconcilable [irekən'sailəbl], *a.* irréconciliable (*avec*); incompatible (*avec*); implacable.
irrecoverable [iri'kʌvərəbl], *a.* irrécouvrable; irréparable.
irredeemable [iri'di:məbl], *a.* irrachetable; irrémédiable.
irreducible [iri'dju:sibl], *a.* irréductible.
irreformable [iri'fɔ:məbl], *a.* inaltérable, irréformable.
irrefutable [i'refjutəbl], *a.* irréfutable.
irregular [i'regjulə], *a.* irrégulier, anormal; déréglé.
irregularity [iregju'læriti], *n.* irrégularité, *f.*, dérèglement, *m.*
irregularly [i'regjuləli], *adv.* irrégulièrement.
irrelevant [i'reləvənt], *a.* hors de propos, non pertinent; inapplicable (*à*).
irreligious [iri'lidʒəs], *a.* irréligieux.
irremediable [iri'mi:diəbl], *a.* irrémédiable, sans remède.
irremovable [iri'mu:vəbl], *a.* inébranlable, immuable; inamovible.
irreparable [i'repərəbl], *a.* irréparable.
irreplaceable [iri'pleisəbl], *a.* irremplaçable.
irrepressible [iri'presibl], *a.* irrépressible; inextinguible (*rire*).
irreproachable [iri'proutʃəbl], *a.* irréprochable, sans tache.
irresistible [iri'zistibl], *a.* irrésistible.
irresolute [i'rezolju:t], *a.* irrésolu, indécis.
irresolutely [i'rezolju:tli], *adv.* irrésolument, avec hésitation.
irresolution [irezo'lju:ʃən], **irresoluteness** [i'rezolju:tnis], *n.* irrésolution, indécision, *f.*
irrespective [iris'pektiv], *a.* indépendant (*de*), sans égard (*pour*); ***irrespective of*** indépendamment de.
irrespectively [iris'pektivli], *adv.* indépendamment (*de*), sans égard (*pour*).
irresponsibility [irispɔnsi'biliti], *n.* irresponsabilité, étourderie, *f.*
irresponsible [iris'pɔnsibl], *a.* irresponsable; irréfléchi, étourdi.
irretrievable [iri'tri:vəbl], *a.* irréparable, irrémédiable.
irreverence [i'revərəns], *n.* irrévérence, *f.*, manque de respect, *m.*
irreverent [i'revərənt], *a.* irrévérencieux.
irrevocable [i'revəkəbl], *a.* irrévocable.
irrigate ['irigeit], *v.t.* arroser, irriguer.
irrigation [iri'geiʃən], *n.* arrosement, *m.* irrigation, *f.*
irritability [iritə'biliti], *n.* irritabilité, *f.*
irritable ['iritəbl], *a.* irritable.
irritate ['iriteit], *v.t.* irriter; ***to be irritated***, s'irriter.
irritation [iri'teiʃən], *n.* irritation, *f.*
irruption [i'rʌpʃən], *n.* irruption, *f.*
Isabel ['izəbel], **Isabella** [izə'belə]. Isabelle, *f.*
island ['ailənd], *n.* île, *f.*; refuge (*au centre de la rue*), *m.*
islander ['ailəndə], *n.* insulaire, *m.*, *f.*
isle [ail], *n.* île, *f.*
islet ['ailit], *n.* îlot, *m.*
isobar ['aisobɑ:], *n.* isobare, *f.*
isolate ['aisəleit], *v.t.* isoler.
isolated ['aisəleitid], *a.* isolé, seul.
isolation [aisə'leiʃən], *n.* isolement, *m.*
isosceles [ai'sɔsəli:z], *a.* isocèle, isoscèle.
Israel ['izreil]. l'Israel, *m.*
Israeli [iz'reili], *a.* israélien.—*n.* Israélien (*personne*), *m.*
issue ['isju:, 'iʃju:], *n.* issue, sortie (*egress*), *f.*; écoulement (*d'eau etc.*), *m.*; distribution (*envoi*); émission (*de billets de banque, timbres-poste*); publication (*de livres etc.*), *f.*; résultat (*conséquence*), *m.*; enfants, *m.pl.*; (*Law*) question, *f.*; ***at issue***, en question.—*v.t.* publier; expédier, distribuer; émettre (*billets de banque*).—*v.i.* sortir, jaillir (*de*); (*fig.*) provenir.
isthmus ['isməs], *n.* isthme, *m.*
it [it], *pron.* il, *m.*, elle, *f.*; (*accusatif*) le, *m.*, la, *f.*; (*datif*) lui; (*impersonnel*) il, ce, cela.
Italian [i'tæliən], *a.* italien.—*n.* italien (*langue*); Italien (*personne*), *m.*

italic [i'tælik], *a.* italique.—*n.* (*pl.*) italiques, *m.pl.*
italicize [i'tælisaiz], *v.t.* mettre *ou* imprimer en italiques.
Italy ['itəli]. l'Italie, *f.*
itch [itʃ], *n.* démangeaison; gale (*maladie*), *f.*—*v.i.* démanger.
item ['aitəm], *n.* article; détail, *m.*, rubrique, *f.*; ***item of news***, nouvelle, *f.*—*adv.* item, de plus.
itinerant [i'tinərənt], *a.* ambulant.
itinerary [i'tinərəri], *n.* itinéraire, *m.*
its [its], *poss. a.* son, *m.*, sa, *f.*; ses, *m.pl.*
itself [it'self], *pron.* lui, *m.*, elle, *f.*, soi, lui-même, *m.*, elle-même, *f.*, soi-même, *m.*; (*reflexive*) se.
ivory ['aivəri], *a.* d'ivoire.—*n.* ivoire, *m.*
ivy ['aivi], *n.* lierre, *m.*

J

J, j [dʒei]. dixième lettre de l'alphabet, *m.*
jabber ['dʒæbə], *v.i.* jaboter, baragouiner.—*n.* bavardage, baragouinage, *m.*
jack [dʒæk], *n.* chevalet (*de scieur*); cric (*pour auto*); (*Cards*) valet; (*Bowls*) cochonnet, *m.*—*v.t.* ***to jack up***, soulever avec un cric.
jackal ['dʒækɔ:l], *n.* chacal, *m.*
jackanapes ['dʒækəneips], *n.* singe; fat, *m.*
jackass ['dʒækæs], *n.* âne, baudet, bourriquet; (*fig.*) idiot, *m.*
jackdaw ['dʒækdɔ:], *n.* choucas, *m.*
jacket ['dʒækit], *n.* veste, *f.*; veston, *m.*; (*Tech.*) chemise, enveloppe, jaquette, *f.*
jack-in-the-box ['dʒækinðəbɔks], *n.* boîte à surprise, *f.*
jack-tar ['dʒæk'tɑ:], *n.* marin, *m.*
jade (1) [dʒeid], *n.* rosse; haridelle; (*fig.*) coquine (*femme*), *f.*—*v.t.* surmener, harasser, éreinter.
jade (2) [dʒeid], *n.* (*Min.*) jade, *m.*
jaded ['dʒeidid], *a.* surmené, éreinté.
jagged ['dʒægid], **jaggy** ['dʒægi], *a.* dentelé, ébréché.
jaguar ['dʒægjuə], *n.* jaguar, *m.*
jail [dʒeil], *n.* prison, geôle, *f.*
jailer ['dʒeilə], *n.* geôlier, *m.*
jam [dʒæm], *n.* confitures, *f.pl.*; encombrement, embouteillage (*de circulation*), *m.*—*v.t.* serrer, presser, bloquer; (*Rad.*) brouiller. —*v.i.* se coincer.
jamming ['dʒæmiŋ], *n.* coincement; (*Rad.*) brouillage, *m.*
Jamaica [dʒə'meikə]. la Jamaïque, *f.*
Jamaican [dʒə'meikən], *a.* jamaïquain.—*n.* Jamaïquain (*personne*), *m.*
James [dʒeimz]. Jacques, *m.*
Jane [dʒein]. Jeanne, *f.*
jangle [dʒæŋgl], *v.t.* choquer avec bruit; (*fig.*) agacer (*nerfs*).—*v.i.* faire un bruit de ferraille.
janitor ['dʒænitə], *n.* portier, concierge, *m.*
January ['dʒænjuəri]. janvier, *m.*
Japan [dʒə'pæn]. le Japon, *m.*
japan [dʒə'pæn], *n.* laque, vernis, *m.*—*v.t.* laquer; vernir.
Japanese [dʒæpə'ni:z], *a.* japonais.—*n.* japonais (*langue*); Japonais (*personne*), *m.*
jar (1) [dʒɑ:], *v.t.* remuer, secouer; ébranler —*v.i.* être discordant (*instrument de musique*); heurter, s'entrechoquer (*être en conflit*); jurer (*couleurs*); (*fig.*) se disputer.—*n.* son discordant, choc, *m.*; querelle, *f.*
jar (2) [dʒɑ:], *n.* jarre, cruche (*faïence*), *f.* bocal (*verre*), *m.*
jargon ['dʒɑ:gən], *n.* jargon, *m.*
jarring ['dʒɑ:riŋ], *a.* discordant; en conflit.—*n.* son discordant, *m.*; querelles, *f.pl.*
jasmine ['dʒæzmin], *n.* jasmin, *m.*
jasper ['dʒæspə], *n.* jaspe, *m.*
jaundice ['dʒɔ:ndis], *n.* jaunisse, *f.*
jaundiced ['dʒɔ:ndist], *a.* qui a la jaunisse (*fig.*) prévenu (*contre*).
jaunt [dʒɔ:nt], *n.* petite promenade *ou* excursion, *f.*—*v.i.* faire une petite promenade *ou* excursion.
jauntily ['dʒɔ:ntili], *adv.* avec insouciance, légèrement.
jauntiness ['dʒɔ:ntinis], *n.* légèreté, *f.*, enjouement, *m.*
jaunty ['dʒɔ:nti], *a.* léger, enjoué, sémillant.
javelin ['dʒævəlin], *n.* javeline, *f.*, javelot, *m.*
jaw [dʒɔ:], *n.* mâchoire, *f.*; (*fig.*, *pl.*) portes, *f.pl.*; bras, *m.pl.*, étreintes, *f.pl.*
jawbone ['dʒɔ:boun], *n.* mâchoire, *f.*
jay [dʒei], *n.* geai, *m.*
jay-walker ['dʒeiwɔ:kə], *n.* piéton distrait, *m*
jazz [dʒæz], *n.* jazz, *m.*
jealous ['dʒeləs], *a.* jaloux.
jealously ['dʒeləsli], *adv.* jalousement; par jalousie.
jealousy ['dʒeləsi], *n.* jalousie, *f.*
jean [dʒi:n], *n.* coutil, treillis; (*pl.*) pantalon (de coutil), *m.*
jeep [dʒi:p], *n.* jeep, *f.*
jeer [dʒiə], *n.* raillerie, moquerie, *f.*—*v.t* railler, huer, se moquer de.—*v.i.* railler, se moquer, goguenarder.
jeering ['dʒiəriŋ], *a.* railleur, moqueur goguenard.—*n.* raillerie, moquerie, *f.*
jeeringly ['dʒiəriŋli], *adv.* en raillant, d'un ton moqueur.
jelly ['dʒeli], *n.* gelée, *f.*
jelly-fish ['dʒelifiʃ], *n.* méduse, *f.*
jennet ['dʒenit], *n.* genet (*d'Espagne*), *m.*
jeopardize ['dʒepədaiz], *v.t.* hasarder, risquer, mettre en danger.
jeopardy ['dʒepədi], *n.* danger, hasard, *m.*
jerk [dʒə:k], *n.* saccade, secousse, *f.*—*v.t* donner une poussée à; jeter.
jerkily ['dʒə:kili], *adv.* par saccades.
jerkin ['dʒə:kin], *n.* pourpoint; paletot (de cuir), *m.*
jerky ['dʒə:ki], *a.* saccadé; irrégulier.
jersey ['dʒə:zi], *n.* vareuse de laine, *f.*, maillot tricot, *m.*
jest [dʒest], *n.* plaisanterie, facétie, *f.*, bon mot, *m.*; risée (*objet de rire*), *f.*—*v.i* plaisanter (*de* ou *avec*), badiner (*sur*).
jester ['dʒestə], *n.* plaisant, railleur; bouffon fou, *m.*
jesting ['dʒestiŋ], *a.* pour rire, badin.—*n* raillerie, plaisanterie, *f.*, badinage, *m.*
jestingly ['dʒestiŋli], *adv.* en plaisantant, pour rire.
Jesuit ['dʒezjuit], *n.* Jésuite, *m.*

Jesus ['dʒi:zəs]. Jésus, *m.*

jet [dʒet], *n.* jet, jet d'eau; (*Min.*) jais, *m.*; ***jet engine***, turbo-réacteur, *m.*; ***jet plane***, avion à réaction, *m.*—*v.i.* s'élancer; gicler.

jet-black ['dʒet'blæk], *a.* noir comme du jais.

jetsam ['dʒetsəm], *n.* marchandise jetée à la mer, *f.*, épaves, *f.pl.*

jettison ['dʒetisən], *n.* jet à la mer, *m.*—*v.t.* jeter par-dessus bord.

jetty ['dʒeti], *n.* jetée, *f.*

Jew [dʒu:], *n.* Juif, *m.*

jewel ['dʒu:əl], *n.* joyau, bijou, *m.*, pierre précieuse, *f.*; (*pl.*) pierreries, *f.pl.*; rubis (*de montre*), *m.pl.*—*v.t.* orner de bijoux.

jeweller ['dʒu:ələ], *n.* joaillier, bijoutier, *m.*

jewellery ['dʒu:əlri], *n.* joaillerie, bijouterie, *f.*

Jewess ['dʒu:is], *n.* Juive, *f.*

Jewish ['dʒu:iʃ], *a.* juif, des Juifs.

Jewry ['dʒu:ri], *n.* Juiverie, *f.*

jib [dʒib], *n.* (*Naut.*) foc, *m.*—*v.i.* reculer; regimber.

jiffy ['dʒifi], *n.* ***in a jiffy***, en un clin d'œil.

jig [dʒig], *n.* gigue (*danse*), *f.*, gabarit, *m.*—*v.i.* danser la gigue.

jilt [dʒilt], *n.* coquette, *f.*—*v.t.* planter là; abandonner, (*fam.*) plaquer (*un amoureux*).

jingle [dʒiŋgl], *n.* tintement (*de cloches*); cliquetis (*de verres, métaux etc.*), *m.*—*v.t.* faire tinter, faire cliqueter.—*v.i.* tinter (*grelots etc.*); s'entrechoquer (*verres etc.*).

jingo ['dʒiŋgou], *n.* chauvin, *m.*; ***by jingo!*** par exemple!

jingoism ['dʒiŋgouizm], *n.* chauvinisme, *m.*

jinx [dʒiŋks], *n.* porte-guigne, *m.*

Joan [dʒoun]. Jeanne, *f.*; ***Joan of Arc***, Jeanne d'Arc.

job [dʒɔb], *n.* travail, ouvrage, *m.*; tâche, pièce; besogne, affaire, *f.*; emploi, *m.*; ***job lot***, solde, *m.*, occasion, *f.*; ***that's just the job***, cela fait juste l'affaire.—*v.t.* louer; tripoter.—*v.i.* travailler à la tâche; (*Comm.*) agioter, spéculer.

jobber ['dʒɔbə], *n.* ouvrier à la tâche; (*Comm.*) agioteur, coulissier; exploiteur, *m.*

jobbing ['dʒɔbiŋ], *a.* ***jobbing gardener***, jardinier à la journée, *m.*—*n.* ouvrage à la tâche; (*Comm.*) agiotage; tripotage, *m.*

jockey ['dʒɔki], *n.* jockey, *m.*

jocose [dʒo'kous], *a.* plaisant, jovial.

jocular ['dʒɔkjulə], *a.* plaisant, facétieux.

jocularly ['dʒɔkjuləli], *adv.* facétieusement.

jocund ['dʒɔkənd], *a.* joyeux, enjoué, gai.

jog [dʒɔg], *v.t.* pousser d'un coup de coude; secouer, cahoter; (*fig.*) rafraîchir (*la mémoire*).—*v.i.* se mouvoir; marcher lentement; ***to jog along***, aller doucement.—*n.* secousse légère, *f.*, cahot; coup de coude, *m.*; ***jog trot***, petit trot, *m.*

John [dʒɔn]. Jean, *m.*; ***Johnnie***, (*colloq.*) Jeannot, *m.*

join [dʒɔin], *v.t.* joindre, unir; associer (*à*); rejoindre (*rattraper*); relier (*rues etc.*); ***will you join us?*** voulez-vous être des nôtres? —*v.i.* se joindre, s'unir; s'inscrire; s'associer; prendre part (*à*).

joiner ['dʒɔinə], *n.* menuisier, *m.*

joinery ['dʒɔinəri], *n.* menuiserie, *f.*

joint [dʒɔint], *a.* commun, ensemble, réuni.—*n.* jointure, *f.*, joint, *m.*; pièce, *f.*; rôti (*de viande*), *m.*; phalange (*du doigt*); charnière (*de porte*); soudure; (*Anat.*) articulation, *f.*; (*Bot.*) nœud, *m.*; (*slang*) boîte, *f.*; ***out of joint***, disloqué, (*fig.*) dérangé; ***to put one's arm out of joint***, se démettre le bras.—*v.t.* couper aux jointures; joindre.

jointed ['dʒɔintid], *a.* articulé, jointé; séparé.

jointly ['dʒɔintli], *adv.* conjointement.

joint-stock ['dʒɔintstɔk], *n.* capital, fonds commun, *m.*; ***joint-stock bank***, banque par actions, *f.*; ***joint-stock company***, société anonyme, *f.*

joist [dʒɔist], *n.* solive, poutre, poutrelle, *f.*

joke [dʒouk], *n.* bon mot, mot pour rire, *m.*, plaisanterie, (*fam.*) blague, *f.*; ***a practical joke***, une farce, un mauvais tour; ***to crack a joke***, dire un bon mot.—*v.t.* plaisanter sur, railler de.—*v.i.* plaisanter, badiner; rire de.

joker ['dʒoukə], *n.* plaisant, farceur; (*Cards*) joker, *m.*

joking ['dʒoukiŋ], *n.* plaisanterie, farce, *f.*

jokingly ['dʒoukiŋli], *adv.* en plaisantant, pour rire.

jollification [dʒɔlifi'keiʃən], *n.* partie de plaisir, *f.*

jollity ['dʒɔliti], *n.* joie, gaieté, *f.*

jolly ['dʒɔli], *a.* gai, joyeux, gaillard, réjoui.

jolt [dʒoult], *n.* cahot, choc, *m.*—*v.t.* cahoter. —*v.i.* faire des cahots.

Jonah ['dʒounə]. Jonas, *m.*—*n.* porte-malheur, *m.*

jonquil ['dʒɔŋkwil], *n.* (*Bot.*) jonquille, *f.*

Jordan ['dʒɔ:dən]. le Jourdain (*rivière*), *m.*; la Jordanie (*pays*), *f.*

Jordanian [dʒɔ:'deiniən], *a.* jordanien.—*n.* Jordanien (*personne*), *m.*

jostle [dʒɔsl], *v.t.* pousser, bousculer; (*Spt.*) gêner (*un concurrent*).—*v.i.* jouer des coudes.

jot [dʒɔt], *n.* iota, brin, *m.*—*v.t.* ***to jot down***, noter, prendre note de.

journal ['dʒə:nəl], *n.* journal, *m.*; revue, *f.*

journalism ['dʒə:nəlizm], *n.* journalisme, *m.*

journalist ['dʒə:nəlist], *n.* journaliste, *m.*, *f.*

journey ['dʒə:ni], *n.* voyage; trajet (*distance*), *m.*; ***a pleasant journey to you!*** bon voyage! ***on the journey***, en route; ***to go on a journey***, faire un voyage.—*v.i.* voyager.

journeyman ['dʒə:nimən], *n.* (*pl.* **-men** [men]) garçon, ouvrier, *m.*

joust [dʒaust, dʒu:st], *n.* joute, *f.*—*v.t.* jouter.

Jove [dʒouv]. Jupiter, *m.*; ***by Jove!*** bigre! mâtin!

jovial ['dʒouviəl], *a.* joyeux, gai.

joviality [dʒouvi'æliti], *n.* humeur joviale, jovialité, *f.*

jowl [dʒaul], *n.* joue; hure (*de saumon*), *f.*; ***cheek by jowl***, côte à côte.

joy [dʒɔi], *n.* joie, *f.*; ***to wish someone joy***, féliciter quelqu'un.—*v.i.* se réjouir (*de* ou *avec*).

joyful ['dʒɔiful], *a.* joyeux.

joyfully ['dʒɔifuli], *adv.* joyeusement.

joyfulness ['dʒɔifulnis], *n.* allégresse, joie, *f.*

joyous ['dʒɔiəs], *a.* joyeux.

jubilant ['dʒu:bilənt], *a.* réjoui; jubilant.

jubilation [dʒu:bi'leiʃən], *n.* réjouissances de triomphe, *f.pl.*, jubilation, *f.*

jubilee ['dʒu:bili:], *n.* jubilé, *m.*

Judaea [dʒu'diə]. la Judée, *f.*

Judaism ['dʒu:deiizm], *n.* judaïsme, *m.*

judge [dʒʌdʒ], *n.* juge; (*fig.*) connaisseur, *m.*; ***to be a judge of***, se connaître à *ou* en.—*v.t.* juger; discerner, considérer.
judgment ['dʒʌdʒmənt], *n.* jugement; arrêt, *m.*, sentence, *f.*; (*fig.*) avis, sens, *m.*, opinion, *f.*
judicature ['dʒu:dikətʃə], *n.* judicature, justice; cour de justice, *f.*
judicial [dʒu:'diʃl], *a.* judiciaire, juridique.
judicious [dʒu:'diʃəs], *a.* judicieux, prudent.
judiciously [dʒu:'diʃəsli], *adv.* judicieusement.
judo ['dʒu:dou], *n.* jiu-jitsu, (*fam.*) judo, *m.*
jug [dʒʌg], *n.* broc, *m.*; cruche, *f.*; ***water jug***, pot à eau, *m.*—*v.t.* faire un civet de (*lièvre*); ***jugged hare***, civet de lièvre, *m.*
juggle [dʒʌgl], *v.t.* jouer, duper, escamoter.—*v.i.* faire des tours de passe-passe; (*fig.*) escamoter.—*n.* jonglerie, *f.*; escamotage, tour de passe-passe, *m.*
juggler ['dʒʌglə], *n.* jongleur; escamoteur; (*fig.*) charlatan, *m.*
juggling ['dʒʌgliŋ], *n.* jonglerie, *f.*, escamotage, *m.*
jugular ['dʒʌgjulə], *a.* and *n.* jugulaire, *f.*
juice [dʒu:s], *n.* jus; suc, *m.*
juicy ['dʒu:si], *a.* juteux; succulent.
ju-jitsu [dʒu:'dʒitsu], *n.* jiu-jitsu, *m.*
jukebox ['dʒu:kbɔks], *n.* phonographe à sous, jukebox, *m.*
Julian ['dʒu:liən]. Julien, *m.*
Juliet ['dʒu:liət]. Juliette, *f.*
July [dʒu'lai]. juillet, *m.*
jumble [dʒʌmbl], *v.t.* jeter pêle-mêle, mêler ensemble, confondre.—*n.* pêle-mêle, méli-mélo, *m.*, confusion, *f.*; ***jumble-sale***, vente de charité, *f.*
jump [dʒʌmp], *n.* saut, bond; sursaut; obstacle (à sauter), *m.*; ***high jump***, saut en hauteur; ***long jump***, saut en longueur.—*v.t* sauter, franchir d'un bond; sauter de; faire sauter; (*fam.*) ***to jump the queue***, resquiller (dans une queue).—*v.i.* sauter; se jeter, se précipiter (*sur*); ***to jump at***, accepter avec empressement.
jumper (1) ['dʒʌmpə], *n.* sauteur, *m.*
jumper (2) ['dʒʌmpə], *n.* chandail, jersey, jumper, *m.*
jumpy ['dʒʌmpi], *a.* nerveux.
junction ['dʒʌŋkʃən], *n.* jonction, *f.*; (*Rail.*) embranchement, *m.*
juncture ['dʒʌŋktʃə], *n.* jointure, *f.*; moment critique, *m.*
June [dʒu:n]. juin, *m.*
jungle [dʒʌŋgl], *n.* jungle, *f.*; fourré, *m.*
junior ['dʒu:niə], *a.* jeune, cadet.—*n.* cadet, inférieur en âge, *m.*
juniper ['dʒu:nipə], *n.* genièvre, *m.*
junk (1) [dʒʌŋk], *n.* jonque (*navire*), *f.*
junk (2) [dʒʌŋk], *n.* objets de rebut, *m.pl.*
junket ['dʒʌŋkit], *n.* lait caillé, *m.*; jonchée (*fromage*), talmouse (*gâteau*), *f.*—*v.t.* régaler.—*v.i.* se régaler.
jurisdiction [dʒuəris'dikʃən], *n.* juridiction, *f.*
jurisprudence [dʒuəris'pru:dəns], *n.* jurisprudence, *f.*
jurist ['dʒuərist], *n.* juriste, *m.*, *f.*
juror ['dʒuərə], *n.* juré, *m.*
jury ['dʒuəri], *n.* jury, *m.*
juryman ['dʒuərimən], *n.* (*pl.* **-men** [men]) juré, *m.*
just [dʒʌst], *a.* juste, équitable.—*adv.* juste, justement, précisément; tout, tout juste, seulement, un peu; ***he has just gone out***, il vient de sortir; ***just now***, à l'instant, tout à l'heure; ***just so***, précisément.
justice ['dʒʌstis], *n.* justice, *f.*; juge (*magistrat*), *m.*; ***Justice of the Peace***, juge de paix; ***to do justice to***, (*fig.*) faire honneur à (*un repas etc.*).
justifiable [dʒʌsti'faiəbl], *a.* justifiable, légitime.
justification [dʒʌstifi'keiʃən], *n.* justification, *f.*
justify ['dʒʌstifai], *v.t.* justifier, autoriser, permettre; ***to feel justified in***, se croire autorisé à, croire devoir.
justly ['dʒʌstli], *adv.* exactement, justement; à bon droit.
jut [dʒʌt], *v.i.* avancer, faire saillie.
jute [dʒu:t], *n.* jute, *m.*
jutting ['dʒʌtiŋ], *a.* en saillie, saillant.
juvenile ['dʒu:vənail], *a.* jeune; juvénile, de jeunesse; ***juvenile delinquent***, jeune délinquant, *m.*—*n.* jeune, *m.*, *f.*; adolescent, *m.*
juxtaposition [dʒʌkstəpə'ziʃən], *n.* juxtaposition, *f.*; ***in juxtaposition***, juxtaposé.

K

K, k [kei]. onzième lettre de l'alphabet, *m.*
kale, kail [keil], *n.* (*Sc.*) chou, *m.*; ***sea-kale***, chou marin.
kaleidoscope [kə'laidəskoup], *n.* kaléidoscope, *m.*
kangaroo [kæŋgə'ru:], *n.* kangourou, *m.*
Katharine, Katherine ['kæθərin]. Catherine, *f.*
keel [ki:l], *n.* quille; carène, *f.*
keen [ki:n], *a.* affilé, aigu, aiguisé; (*fig.*) vif, ardent; amer, mordant (*acerbe*); pénétrant, perçant (*brisant la surface de*); dévorant (*appétit*).
keenly ['ki:nli], *adv.* vivement, ardemment, âprement.
keenness ['ki:nnis], *n.* finesse (*de tranchant*); (*fig.*) subtilité; vivacité, ardeur, *f.*, empressement; mordant (*de troupes*), *m.*, âpreté (*du froid*), *f.*
keep [ki:p], *v.t. irr.* tenir, retenir, garder; maintenir, conserver (*ne pas perdre*); avoir (*volaille etc.*); entretenir (*subvenir aux besoins de*); nourrir (*avoir en pension*); avoir à son service; (*fig.*) observer; célébrer, fêter; garantir, protéger; remplir; continuer; ***keep it up!*** continuez! ***to keep away***, éloigner, tenir éloigné; ***to keep back***, retenir, garder, tenir en réserve; retarder; ***to keep from***, préserver de, empêcher de; ***to keep in***, tenir enfermé, retenir; ***to keep on***, continuer; ***to keep out***, ne pas admettre, écarter, éloigner; ***to keep to***, s'en tenir à; ***to keep up***, tenir levé, soutenir; continuer; entretenir.—*v.i.* se tenir; rester, demeurer (*ne pas cesser d'être*); se garder, se

conserver (*durer*); (*fig.*) se garder, s'abstenir; ***to keep away***, se tenir éloigné; ***to keep back***, se tenir en arrière; ***to keep*** (*doing, saying, telling etc.*), ne pas cesser de; ***to keep silent***, se taire; ***to keep up with***, aller de pair avec.—*n.* donjon, réduit (*forteresse*), *m.*; nourriture, *f.*, entretien (*subsistance*), *m.*

keeper ['ki:pə], *n.* garde; gardien; surveillant, *m.*

keeping ['ki:piŋ], *n.* garde, surveillance; conservation; (*fig.*) harmonie, *f.*

keepsake ['ki:pseik], *n.* souvenir, *m.*

keg [keg], *n.* caque (*de hareng*), *f.*, petit baril, *m.*

ken [ken], *n.* vue; portée, *f.*

kennel [kenl], *n.* chenil, *m.*; niche, *f.*

Kenya ['kenjə]. le Kénya, *m.*

kept [kept], *a.* entretenu.—*p.p.* [KEEP].

kerb [kə:b], *n.* bordure (*de trottoir*), margelle (*de puits*), *f.*

kerb-stone ['kə:bstoun], *n.* bordure (*de trottoir*), *f.*, parement, *m.*

***kerchief** ['kə:tʃif], *n.* fichu, *m.*

kernel [kə:nl], *n.* graine, amande, *f.*, pignon (*de pomme de pin*); noyau (*de drupe*); (*fig.*) fond, essentiel, *m.*

kerosene ['kerosi:n], *n.* kérosène; pétrole lampant, *m.*

kestrel ['kestrəl], *n.* crécerelle, *f.*

ketch [ketʃ], *n.* (*Naut.*) quaiche, *f.*, ketch, *m.*

kettle [ketl], *n.* bouilloire, *f.*; chaudron (*bassine à confitures*), *m.*; ***a pretty kettle of fish***, un beau gâchis.

kettledrum ['ketldrʌm], *n.* timbale, *f.*

key [ki:], *n.* clef, clé, *f.*; (*Arith. etc.*) corrigé; (*Mus.*) ton, *m.*; touche (*sur le piano etc.*), *f.*; ***under lock and key***, sous clef.

key-board ['ki:bɔ:d], *n.* clavier, *m.*

keyhole ['ki:houl], *n.* trou de la serrure, *m.*

key-note ['ki:nout], *n.* tonique; (*fig.*) idée maîtresse, *f.*

key-stone ['ki:stoun], *n.* clef de voûte, *f.*

khaki ['kɑ:ki], *n.* kaki, *m.*

khan [kɑ:n], *n.* kan, khan, *m.*

kick [kik], *n.* coup de pied; recul (*d'un fusil*), *m.*; ruade (*d'animal*), *f.*; (*Ftb.*) ***free kick***, coup franc, *m.*—*v.t.* donner un coup de pied à; frapper *ou* pousser du pied; (*Ftb.*) botter; ***to kick out***, chasser à coups de pied; ***to kick up a row***, faire du tapage.—*v.i.* donner des coups de pied; ruer, regimber (*animal*); reculer (*fusil*).

kick-off ['kikɔf], *n.* (*Ftb.*) coup d'envoi, *m.*

kid [kid], *a.* de chevreau; ***kid gloves***, gants de chevreau, *m.pl.*—*n.* chevreau; (*colloq.*) enfant, gosse, *m.*—*v.t.* (*fam.*) en conter à; ***no kidding!*** sans blague!

kidnap ['kidnæp], *v.t.* enlever.

kidney ['kidni], *n.* rein; rognon (*d'animal*), *m.*

kidney-bean ['kidni'bi:n], *n.* haricot, *m.*

kill [kil], *v.t.* tuer; faire mourir; abattre (*assassiner*).

killer ['kilə], *n.* tueur, *m.*

killing ['kiliŋ], *a.* mortel; assommant (*travail*). —*n.* tuerie, boucherie, *f.*, massacre, *m.*

kiln [kiln], *n.* four, *m.*

kilogramme ['kilogræm], *n.* kilogramme, *m.*

kilometre ['kiləmi:tə], *n.* kilomètre, *m.*

kilowatt ['kilowɔt], *n.* kilowatt, *m.*

kin [kin], *n.* parenté, *f.*; parent, allié, *m.*; ***next of kin***, le plus proche parent.

kind [kaind], *a.* bon, bienveillant, bienfaisant; obligeant, complaisant (*accommodant*); ***my kind regards to him***, faites-lui toutes mes amitiés; ***will you be so kind as to***, voulez-vous avoir la bonté de.—*n.* genre, *m.*, sorte, espèce, *f.*; ***in kind***, en nature.

kindergarten ['kindəgɑ:tn], *n.* école maternelle, *f.*

kindhearted ['kaind'hɑ:tid], *a.* bon, bienveillant.

kindle [kindl], *v.t.* allumer, enflammer; (*fig.*) éveiller, exciter.—*v.i.* s'allumer, s'enflammer.

kindliness ['kaindlinis], *n.* bienveillance, bonté, *f.*

kindly ['kaindli], *a.* bon, bienveillant, favorable.—*adv.* avec bienveillance.

kindness ['kaindnis], *n.* bienveillance, bonté, *f.*; bienfait, *m.*

kindred ['kindrid], *a.* de même nature.—*n.* parenté, *f.*; parents, *m.pl.*

kinema ['kinimə], [CINEMA].

king [kiŋ], *n.* roi, *m.*; (*Draughts*) dame, *f.*

kingdom ['kiŋdəm], *n.* royaume; (*fig.*) empire; (*Nat. Hist.*) règne, *m.*; ***the United Kingdom***, le Royaume-Uni.

kingfisher ['kiŋfiʃə], *n.* (*Orn.*) martin-pêcheur, *m.*

kingly ['kiŋli], *a.* de roi, royal.

kink [kiŋk], *n.* nœud; (*colloq.*) point faible, défaut, *m.*

kinsman ['kinzmən], *n.* (*pl.* **-men** [men]) parent, allié, *m.*

kiosk ['ki:ɔsk], *n.* kiosque, *m.*; ***telephone kiosk***, cabine téléphonique, *f.*

kirk [kə:k], *n.* église d'Écosse, *f.*

kiss [kis], *n.* baiser, *m.*—*v.t.*, *v.i.* embrasser; ***to kiss*** (***each other***), s'embrasser.

kit [kit], *n.* petit équipement, *m.*, effets, *m.pl.*; trousse, *f.*; outils (*d'un ouvrier*), *m.pl.*

kit-bag ['kitbæg], *n.* sac, *m.*

kitchen ['kitʃin], *n.* cuisine, *f.*

kitchen-garden ['kitʃingɑ:dn], *n.* jardin potager, *m.*

kitchen-utensils ['kitʃinju:tenslz], *n.pl.* batterie de cuisine, *f.*

kite [kait], *n.* milan (*oiseau*); cerf-volant (*jouet*), *m.*

kith [kiθ], *n.* ***kith and kin***, parents et amis, *m.pl.*

kitten [kitn], *n.* chaton, petit chat, *m.*

knack [næk], *n.* adresse, *f.*, tour de main, *m.*

knapsack ['næpsæk], *n.* havresac, *m.*

knave [neiv], *n.* fripon, coquin; (*Cards*) valet, *m.*

knavery ['neivəri], *n.* friponnerie, coquinerie, *f.*

knavish ['neiviʃ], *a.* fripon; malin.

knead [ni:d], *v.t.* pétrir.

knee [ni:], *n.* genou, *m.*

knee-breeches ['ni:britʃiz], *n.pl.* culotte courte, *f.*

knee-cap ['ni:kæp], *n.* genouillère; (*Anat.*) rotule, *f.*

kneel [ni:l], *v.i. irr.* s'agenouiller.

knell [nel], *n.* glas, *m.*

knickers ['nikəz], *n.* culotte (de femme), *f.*

knick-knack ['niknæk], *n.* brimborion, *m.*, babiole, *f.*; colifichet, bibelot, *m.*

knife [naif], *n.* (*pl.* **knives** [naivz]) couteau; (*Tech.*) coupoir; (*Surg.*) scalpel, bistouri, *m.*; ***carving-knife***, couteau à découper; ***pen-knife***, canif, *m.*—*v.t.* poignarder.

knife-grinder ['naifgraində], *n.* rémouleur, *m.*
knight [nait], *n.* chevalier; (*Chess*) cavalier, *m.*—*v.t.* créer chevalier.
knighthood ['naithud], *n.* chevalerie, *f.*
knightly ['naitli], *a.* chevaleresque, de chevalier.
knit [nit], *v.t.* tricoter; froncer (*les sourcils*); (*fig.*) joindre, attacher, lier.
knitting ['nitiŋ], *n.* tricot, *m.*
knitting-needle ['nitiŋni:dl], *n.* aiguille à tricoter, *f.*
knives [KNIFE].
knob [nɔb], *n.* bosse, *f.*; bouton (*de porte*), *m.*
knock [nɔk], *v.t.* frapper, heurter, cogner; ***to knock about***, bousculer, malmener; ***to knock down***, renverser, assommer; adjuger (*aux enchères*).—*v.i.* ***to knock about***, rouler sa bosse, aller de par le monde; ***to knock off***, cesser le travail.—*n.* coup, choc; cognement, *m.*
knocker ['nɔkə], *n.* marteau (*de porte*), *m.*
knocking ['nɔkiŋ], *n.* coups, *m.pl.*
knoll [noul], *n.* monticule, tertre, *m.*, butte, *f.*
knot [nɔt], *n.* nœud; groupe (*de personnes etc.*), *m.*; (*fig.*) difficulté, *f.*, embarras, *m.*—*v.t.* nouer; lier; (*fig.*) embrouiller.—*v.i.* faire des nœuds; se nouer.
knotted ['nɔtid], *a.* noueux.
knotty ['nɔti], *a.* noueux; (*fig.*) dur (*difficile*); embrouillé, compliqué.
know [nou], *v.t. irr.* savoir, apprendre (*to learn*); connaître (*to be acquainted with*); reconnaître (*to recognize*); ***to know by heart***, savoir par cœur; ***to know by sight***, connaître de vue; ***to know someone***, connaître quelqu'un; ***to know something***, savoir quelque chose.—*n.* ***to be in the know***, être dans le secret.
know-how ['nouhau], *n.* savoir-faire, *m.*
knowing ['nouiŋ], *a.* intelligent, instruit; fin, malin.
knowingly ['nouiŋli], *adv.* sciemment; avec ruse.
knowledge ['nɔlidʒ], *n.* connaissance, science, *f.*; savoir, *m.*; ***not to my knowledge***, pas que je sache; ***without my knowledge***, à mon insu.
knowledgeable ['nɔlidʒəbl], *a.* bien informé.
knuckle [nʌkl], *n.* jointure, articulation du doigt, *f.*; jarret (*de viande*), *m.*—*v.i.* ***to knuckle under***, se soumettre, mettre les pouces.
knuckle-bone ['nʌklboun], *n.* osselet, *m.*
Korea [kə'ri:ə]. la Corée, *f.*
Korean [kə'ri:ən], *a.* coréen.—*n.* coréen (*langue*); Coréen (*personne*), *m.*
Kuwait [ku'weit]. le Koweït, *m.*

L

L, l [el]. douzième lettre de l'alphabet *m.*
la [lɑ:], *n.* (*Mus.*) la, *m.*
lab [læb], *n.* (*fam.*) labo, *m.*
label [leibl], *n.* étiquette, *f.*; (*Ind.*) label, *m.*—*v.t.* étiqueter; (*fig.*) désigner sous le nom de
laboratory [lə'bɔrətəri, 'læbrətəri], *n.* laboratoire, *m.*
laborious [lə'bɔ:riəs], *a.* laborieux, pénible.
laboriously [lə'bɔ:riəsli], *adv.* laborieusement péniblement.
labour ['leibə], *n.* travail, labeur, *m.*, peine, *f.* ouvrage (*piece of work*); travail d'enfan (*accouchement*), *m.*; ***hard labour***, travaux forcés, *m.pl.*; ***manual labour***, main-d'œuvre, *f.*; ***the Labour Party***, le part travailliste.—*v.t.* travailler; (*fig.*) élaborer.—*v.i.* travailler; souffrir, peiner; chercher (*à*) s'efforcer (*de*); ***to labour under a delusion***, être dans l'erreur.
labourer ['leibərə], *n.* manœuvre, homme de peine, *m.*
labour-exchange ['leibəriks'tʃeindʒ], *n* bureau de placement (*municipal* ou *d'état*) *m.*
labour-saving ['leibəseiviŋ], *a.* ***labour-saving device***, économiseur de travail, *m.*
Labrador ['læbrədɔ:]. le Labrador, *m.*
labrador ['læbrədɔ:], *n.* chien de Labrador, *m.*
laburnum [lə'bə:nəm], *n.* faux ébénier cytise, *m.*
labyrinth ['læbirinθ], *n.* labyrinthe, *m.*
lace [leis], *n.* dentelle, *f.*, point, galon; lace (*cordon*); ruban (*bande*), *m.*; ***boot-lace***, lace de bottine.—*v.t.* lacer (*ses souliers*); garnir de dentelle, galonner (*orner de dentelle*); (*fig.*) orner.
lacerate ['læsəreit], *v.t.* déchirer, lacérer.
laceration [læsə'reiʃən], *n.* déchirure, lacération, *f.*
lachrymose ['lækrimous], *a.* larmoyant.
lacing ['leisiŋ], *n.* lacement, *m.*
lack [læk], *n.* manque, besoin, défaut, *m.*; ***for lack of***, faute de.—*v.t.* manquer de.—*v.i.* manquer.
lackey ['læki], *n.* laquais, *m.*
lacking ['lækiŋ], *a.* manquant (*de*), dépourvu (*de*).
laconic [lə'kɔnik], *a.* laconique.
lacquer ['lækə], *n.* laque, *m.*
lad [læd], *n.* garçon, jeune homme; gaillard, *m.*
ladder ['lædə], *n.* échelle, *f.*; démaillage (*d'un bas*) *m.*; ***ladder-proof***, indémaillable (*bas*). —*v.t.* démailler (*un bas*).
lade [kid], *v.t.* (*Naut.*) charger.
laden [leidn], *a.* chargé.
lading ['leidiŋ], *n.* chargement, *m.*; ***bill of lading***, connaissement, *m.*
ladle [leidl], *n.* louche, cuiller à pot, *f.*
lady ['leidi], *n.* (*pl.* **ladies** ['leidiz]) dame, *f.*; ***young lady***, demoiselle, *f.*
lady-bird ['leidibə:d], *n.* coccinelle, bête à bon Dieu, *f.*
lady-killer ['leidikilə], *n.* bourreau des cœurs, *m.*
lady-like ['leidilaik], *a.* de dame, comme il faut, qui a l'air distingué.
lag [læg], *v.i.* se traîner; traîner (*choses*).—*n.* retard, *m.*
laggard ['lægəd], *n.* traînard, lambin, *m.*
lager ['lɑ:gə], *n.* bière blonde (allemande), *f.*
lagoon [lə'gu:n], *n.* lagune, *f.*
lair [lɛə], *n.* repaire, antre, *m.*
laird [lɛəd], *n.* (*Sc.*) propriétaire, châtelain, *m.*
laity ['leiiti], *n.* laïques, *m.pl.*

lake [leik], *n.* lac, *m.*; laque (*couleur*), *f.*
lamb [læm], *n.* agneau, *m.*—*v.i.* agneler.
lambkin ['læmkin], *n.* agnelet, petit agneau, *m.*
lame [leim], *a.* boiteux, estropié (*infirme*); (*fig.*) défectueux, imparfait; ***a lame excuse***, une piètre excuse; ***a lame man***, un boiteux.—*v.t.* estropier.
lamely ['leimli], *adv.* en boitant; (*fig.*) imparfaitement, mal.
lameness ['leimnis], *n.* claudication, *f.*; clochement, boitement, *m.*; (*fig.*) faiblesse (*d'une excuse*), *f.*
lament [lə'ment], *v.t.* se lamenter sur, pleurer; s'affliger de.—*v.i.* se lamenter, pleurer.—*n.* lamentation, complainte, plainte, *f.*
lamentable ['læməntəbl], *a.* lamentable, pitoyable.
lamentation [læmən'teiʃən], *n.* lamentation, plainte, jérémiade, *f.*
lamented [lə'mentid], *a.* regretté (*feu*).
lamp [læmp], *n.* lampe; lanterne (*carrosse etc.*); (*fig.*) lumière, *f.*; ***street-lamp***, réverbère, *m.*
lampoon [læm'pu:n], *n.* satire, *f.*, libelle, *m.*
lamp-post ['læmppoust], *n.* lampadaire, *m.*
lamp-shade ['læmpʃeid], *n.* abat-jour, *m.*
lance [lɑ:ns], *n.* lance, *f.*—*v.t.* percer d'un coup de lance; (*Surg.*) donner un coup de lancette à, percer.
lance-corporal ['lɑ:ns'kɔ:pərəl], *n.* soldat de première classe, *m.*
lancer ['lɑ:nsə], *n.* lancier, *m.*
lancet ['lɑ:nsit], *n.* lancette; (*Arch.*) ogive, *f.*
land [lænd], *n.* terre, *f.*; pays (*territoire*); (*Law*) bien-fonds, *m.*; ***Holy Land***, la Terre Sainte.—*v.t.* mettre à terre, prendre (*poisson*); débarquer.—*v.i.* débarquer (*à* ou *sur*), aborder; (*fig.*) arriver; (*Av.*) atterrir.
landed ['lændid], *a.* foncier; territorial.
landing ['lændiŋ], *n.* palier (*d'escalier*); (*Naut.*) débarquement; (*Av.*) atterrissage, *m.*
landing-ground ['lændiŋgraund], *n.* terrain d'atterrissage, *m.*
landing-stage ['lændiŋsteidʒ], *n.* débarcadère, *m.*
landing-strip ['lændiŋstrip], *n.* piste d'atterrissage, *f.*
landlady ['lændleidi], *n.* propriétaire (*d'une maison*), logeuse (*d'un meuble*); aubergiste, hôtesse (*d'une auberge*), *f.*
landlord ['lændlɔ:d], *n.* propriétaire; hôte, hôtelier, aubergiste (*d'une auberge*), *m.*
landlubber ['lændlʌbə], *n.* marin d'eau douce, *m.*
landmark ['lændmɑ:k], *n.* borne, limite, *f.*; point de repère, *m.*
landowner ['lændounə], *n.* propriétaire foncier, *m.*
landscape ['lændskeip], *n.* paysage, *m.*; vue, *f.*
landscape-garden ['lændskeip'gɑ:dən], *n.* jardin paysager, *m.*
land-tax ['lændtæks], *n.* impôt foncier, *m.*
lane [lein], *n.* ruelle, *f.*, passage, *m.*; voie (*d'autoroute*), *f.*; chemin vicinal (*de campagne*), *m.*
language ['læŋgwidʒ], *n.* langage, *m.*, langue, expression, *f.*; ***modern languages***, langues vivantes, *f.pl.*
languid ['læŋgwid], *a.* languissant.
languish ['læŋgwiʃ], *v.i.* languir.
languishing ['læŋgwiʃiŋ], *a.* languissant, langoureux.
languor ['læŋgə], *n.* langueur, *f.*
laniard [LANYARD].
lank [læŋk], *a.* efflanqué; maigre; décharné; fluet, grêle.
lanky ['læŋki], *a.* grand et maigre; ***lanky fellow***, grand flandrin, *m.*
lantern ['læntən], *n.* lanterne, *f.*; (*Mil.*) falot; (*Naut.*) fanal, phare, *m.*; ***Chinese lantern***, lanterne vénitienne; ***dark lantern***, lanterne sourde; ***lantern-jaws***, joues creuses, *f.pl.*
lanyard ['lænjəd], *n.* (*Naut.*) ride, *f.*; (*Artill.*) (cordon) tire-feu, *m.*
Laos [laus]. le Laos, *m.*
Laotian ['lauʃən], *a.* laotien.—*n.* laotien (*langue*); Laotien (*personne*), *m.*
lap (1) [læp], *n.* pan (*de manteau etc.*); giron, *m.*; (*fig.*) genoux, *m.pl.*; sein; (*Racing*) tour de piste, *m.*; ***in the lap of***, au sein de.—*v.i.* se replier.
lap (2) [læp], *v.t.* (*Racing*) prendre un tour (*à*).
lap (3) [læp], *v.t.* laper (*boire*).—*v.i.* laper; clapoter (*vagues*).
lap-dog ['læpdɔg], *n.* bichon, petit chien, *m.*
lapel [lə'pel], *n.* revers (*d'habit*), *m.*
lapidary ['læpidəri], *a.* and *n.* lapidaire, *m.*—*v.t.* lapider.
lapidation [læpi'deiʃən], *n.* lapidation, *f.*
Lapland ['læplənd]. la Laponie, *f.*
Laplander ['læpləndə], *n.* Lapon, *m.*
Lapp [læp], *a.* lapon.—*n.* lapon (*langue*); Lapon (*personne*), *m.*
lapse [læps], *n.* cours, laps (*temps*), *m.*; faute, erreur, *f.*; manquement, écart, manque (*divergence*), *m.*—*v.i.* s'écouler; tomber, faillir, manquer (*à*).
lapsed [læpst], *a.* périmé; caduc (*contrat, testament*).
lapwing ['læpwiŋ], *n.* vanneau, *m.*
larceny ['lɑ:səni], *n.* larcin, vol, *m.*
larch [lɑ:tʃ], *n.* (*Bot.*) mélèze, *m.*
lard [lɑ:d], *n.* saindoux, *m.*—*v.t.* larder (*de*).
larder ['lɑ:də], *n.* garde-manger, *m.*
large [lɑ:dʒ], *a.* grand, gros; étendu, considérable; fort; ***as large as life***, grandeur nature; ***at large***, en liberté, libre; en général.
largely ['lɑ:dʒli], *adv.* amplement, largement; au long, en grande partie.
largeness ['lɑ:dʒnis], *n.* grandeur, étendue, ampleur, *f.*
largess(e) ['lɑ:dʒes], *n.* largesse, libéralité, *f.*
lark [lɑ:k], *n.* alouette; (*fig.*) escapade, *f.*
larkspur ['lɑ:kspə:], *n.* pied-d'alouette, *m.*
larva ['lɑ:və], *n.* (*pl.* **larvae** ['lɑ:vi]) larve, *f.*
laryngitis [lærin'dʒaitis], *n.* laryngite, *f.*
larynx ['læriŋks], *n.* (*pl.* **larynges** ['lærindjiz]) larynx, *m.*
lascar ['læskə], *n.* matelot indien, *m.*
lascivious [lə'siviəs], *a.* lascif.
lash [læʃ], *n.* coup de fouet; (*fig.*) coup, trait, *m.*; ***eyelash*** [EYE].—*v.t.* cingler, fouetter; châtier; lier, attacher (*to tie*).
lashing ['læʃiŋ], *a.* cinglant, fouettant.—*n.* coups de fouet, *m.pl.*; (*Naut.*) ligne d'amarrage, *f.*
lass [læs], *n.* (*Sc.*) jeune fille, *f.*
lassitude ['læsitju:d], *n.* lassitude, *f.*

last (1) [lɑ:st], *a.* dernier, passé; ***last but one,*** avant-dernier; ***last night,*** hier soir; ***last week,*** la semaine dernière; ***the last time,*** la dernière fois; ***this day last week,*** il y a aujourd'hui huit jours.—*n.* bout, *m.*, fin, *f.*; ***at last,*** à la fin, enfin; ***to the last,*** jusqu'au bout, jusqu'à la fin.—*v.i.* durer.
last (2) [lɑ:st], *n.* forme (*pour chaussures*), *f.*
lasting ['lɑ:stiŋ], *a.* durable, permanent.
lastly ['lɑ:stli], *adv.* en dernier lieu, enfin.
latch [lætʃ], *n.* loquet, *m.*—*v.t.* fermer au loquet.
latchkey ['lætʃki:], *n.* passe-partout, *m.* clef de la maison, *f.*
late [leit], *a.* tard; en retard; tardif (*fruits, légumes etc.*); avancé (*heure*); ancien, ex- (*autrefois*); feu (*décédé*); récent, dernier (*depuis peu*); ***the late king,*** feu le roi; ***to be late,*** être en retard.—*adv.* tard; sur la fin; récemment, depuis peu; ***at latest,*** au plus tard; ***better late than never,*** mieux vaut tard que jamais; ***of late,*** récemment; ***to be getting late,*** (*impers.*) se faire tard.
lately ['leitli], *adv.* dernièrement, récemment.
lateness ['leitnis], *n.* retard, *m.*; heure avancée, *f.*, temps avancé, *m.*; tardiveté, *f.*
latent ['leitənt], *a.* caché, secret, latent.
later ['leitə], *a.* postérieur, ultérieur.—*adv.* plus tard.
lateral ['lætərəl] *a.* de côté, latéral.
latest ['leitist], *a.* dernier; ***at the latest,*** au plus tard.
lath [lɑ:θ], *n.* latte, *f.*
lathe [leið], *n.* tour, *m.*
lather ['læðə, lɑ:ðə], *n.* mousse; (*fig.*) écume, *f.*—*v.t.* savonner; (*colloq.*) rosser.
Latin ['lætin], *a.* latin.—*n.* latin (*langue*), *m.*
Latin-American [lætinə'merikən], *a.* latino-américain.—*n.* Latino-Américain (*personne*), *m.*
latish ['leitiʃ], *a.* un peu tard, un peu en retard.—*adv.* un peu tard.
latitude ['lætitju:d], *n.* latitude; étendue (*breadth*), *f.*
latter ['lætə], *a.* dernier; moderne, récent; ***the latter,*** ce dernier, celui-ci, *m.*
lattice ('lætis], *n.* trellis, treillage, *m.*
Latvia ['lætviə]. la Lettonie, *f.*
Latvian ['lætviən], *a.* lette, letton.—*n.* lette, letton (*langue*), *m.*; Lette, *m.*, *f.*, Letton, *m.* (*personne*).
laud [lɔ:d], *v.t.* louer, célébrer.
laudable ['lɔ:dəbl], *a.* louable, digne de louanges.
laugh [lɑ:f], *n.* rire, *m.*, risée (*moquerie*), *f.*; ***loud laugh,*** gros rire, éclat de rire, *m.*—*v.i.* rire; ***to burst out laughing,*** éclater de rire; ***to laugh at,*** se moquer de.
laughable ['lɑ:fəbl], *a.* risible.
laughing ['lɑ:fiŋ], *a.* rieur, enjoué; ***it is no laughing matter,*** il n'y a pas de quoi rire.
laughing-stock ['lɑ:fiŋstɔk], *n.* risée, *f.*
laughingly ['lɑ:fiŋli], *adv.* en riant.
laughter ['lɑ:ftə], *n.* rire, *m.*, rires, *m.pl.*; risée, moquerie, *f.*; ***burst of laughter,*** éclat de rire, *m.*
launch [lɔ:ntʃ], *v.t.* lancer; mettre à la mer.—*v.i.* se lancer, se jeter.—*n.* lancement, *m.*; chaloupe (*bateau*), vedette, *f.*
launching ['lɔ:ntʃiŋ], *n.* (*Naut.*) mise à l'eau, *f.*, lancement, *m.*; ***launching pad,*** piste de lancement, *f.*
launder ['lɔ:ndə] *v.t.* blanchir; lessiver (*linge*).
launderette [lɔ:ndə'ret], *n.* laverie automatique. *f.*
laundress ['lɔ:ndris], *n.* blanchisseuse, *f.*
laundromat ['lɔ:ndromæt], (*Am.*) [LAUNDERETTE].
laundry ['lɔ:ndri], *n.* buanderie; blanchisserie, *f.*; linge à blanchir, *m.*
laurel ['lerəl], *n.* laurier, *m.*
lava ['lɑ:və], *n.* lave, *f.*
lavatory ['lævət(ə)ri], *n.* water-clo et, *m.*, les lavabos, les water, *m.pl.*
lavender ['lævində], *n.* lavande, *f.*
lavish ['læviʃ], *a.* prodigue.—*v.t.* prodiguer.
lavishly ['læviʃli], *adv.* prodigalement.
lavishness ['læviʃnis], *n.* prodigalité, *f.*
law [lɔ:], *n.* loi, *f.*; droit, *m.*; ***Law Courts,*** Palais de Justice, *m.*
lawful ['lɔ:ful], *a.* légitime, licite, permis.
lawfully ['lɔ:fuli], *adv.* légitimement.
lawless ['lɔ:lis], *a.* sans loi; (*fig.*) sans trein, déréglé.
lawlessness ['le:lisnis], *n.* désordre, *m.*, licence, *f.*
lawn (1) [lɔ:n], *n.* pelouse, *f.*
lawn (2) [lɔ:n] *n.* linon (*tissu*), *m.*
lawn-mower ['le:nmouə], *n.* tondeuse de gazon, *f.*
lawsuit ['lɔ:sju:t], *n.* procès, *m.*
lawyer ['lɔ:jə], *n.* homme de loi; avocat; avoué (*solicitor*); notaire (*notary*), *m.*
lax [læks], *a.* lâche, mou, flasque; (*fig.*) relâché, négligent.
laxative ['læksətiv], *a.* and *n.* laxatif, *m.*
laxity ['læksiti], **laxness** ['læksnis], *n.* relâchement, *m.*; flaccidité, *f.*; manque d'exactitude, *m.*
lay (1) [lei], *past* [LIE (2)].
lay (2) [lei], *v.t. irr.* placer, mettre, poser; coucher, étendre (*de tout son long*); faire; parier (*pari*); pondre (*œuf*); tendre, dresser (*piège*); abattre (*poussière*); calmer, apaiser (*rendre tranquille*); ***to lay aside,*** mettre de côté; ***to lay claim to,*** prétendre à; ***to lay down,*** mettre bas, poser (*principe*); ***to lay down one's life for,*** donner sa vie pour; ***to lay hold of,*** s'emparer de; ***to lay in,*** faire provision de; ***to lay on,*** appliquer, (*fam.*) arranger; ***to lay out,*** arranger; ensevelir (*cadavre*); disposer (*jardin etc.*); ***to lay siege to,*** assiéger; ***to lay up,*** mettre do côté, faire garder la chambre à; ***to lay waste,*** dévaster.—*v.i.* pondre (*œufs*).
lay (3) [lei], *n.* lai, *m.*, chanson, *f.*, chant, *m.*
lay (4) [lei], *a.* lai, laïque.
layer ['leiə], *n.* couche, *f.*, lit (*strate*), *m.*; (*Geol.*) assise; (*Hort.*) marcotte, *f.*; provin (*de vigne*), *m.*; pondeuse (*poule*), *f.*
laying ['leiiŋ], *n.* mise, pose; ponte (*d'œufs*), *f.*
layman ['leimən], *n.* (*pl.* **-men** [men]) laïque, profane, séculier, *m.*
lay-out ['leiaut], *n.* dessin, tracé, *m.*; disposition, *f.*
Lazarus ['læzərəs]. Lazare, *m.*
laze [leiz], *v.i.* ***to laze about,*** baguenauder.
lazily ['leizili], *adv.* lentement; en paresseux.
laziness ['leizinis], *n.* paresse, oisiveté, *f.*
lazy ['leizi], *a.* paresseux, indolent; ***lazy fellow,*** fainéant, *m.*

lea [li:], *n.* (*poet.*) prairie, *f.*

lead (1) [led], *n.* plomb (*métal*), *m.*; (*Naut.*) sonde; (*Print.*) interligne; mine de plomb (*pour des crayons*), *f.*; ***blacklead***, mine de plomb.

lead (2) [li:d], *v.t. irr.* mener, guider, conduire; porter, faire, induire (*à*); entraîner (*à* ou *dans*); ***to lead astray***, égarer; ***to lead back***, ramener, reconduire; ***to lead in***, introduire; ***to lead out***, emmener; ***to lead someone to believe***, faire croire à quelqu'un; ***to lead up to***, amener.—*v.i.* conduire, mener; (*Spt.*) jouer le premier. —*n.* conduite, direction, *f.*, commandement, *m.*; laisse (*chien*), *f.*; (*Spt.*) début; (*Theat.*) premier rôle, *m.*, vedette, *f.*; (*Elec.*) conducteur, *m.*

leader ['li:də], *n.* conducteur, guide, chef, meneur; (*Journ.*) article de fond, éditorial; (*Polit.*) chef de parti, leader, *m.*

leadership ['li:dəʃip], *n.* conduite, direction, *f.*; qualités de chef, *f.pl.*

leading ['li:diŋ], *a.* premier, principal; ***leading article***, article de fond, *m.*—*n.* conduite, direction, *f.*

leaf [li:f], *n.* (*pl.* **leaves** [li:vz]) feuille, *f.*; feuillet (*livre etc.*); battant (*porte*), *m.*; rallonge (*table*), *f.*; ***to turn over a new leaf***, (*fig.*) changer de conduite; ***to turn over the leaves of***, feuilleter.

leaflet ['li:flit], *n.* feuillet, imprimé, prospectus, *m.*

leafy ['li:fi], *a.* feuillu, couvert de feuilles.

league [li:g], *n.* ligue; lieue (*3 miles*), *f.*

leak [li:k], *n.* fuite, perte d'eau; (*Naut.*) voie d'eau, *f.*; ***to spring a leak***, (*Naut.*) faire eau.—*v.i.* fuir, couler, faire eau; prendre l'eau (*chaussures*); ***to leak out***, s'éventer.

leakage ['li:kidʒ], *n.* coulage, *m.*; fuite, *f.*

leaky ['li:ki], *a.* qui coule; (*Naut.*) qui fait eau.

lean (1) [li:n], *a.* and *n.* maigre, *m.*

lean (2) [li:n], *v.t. irr.* appuyer, faire pencher, incliner.—*v.i.* s'appuyer, s'incliner, se pencher; ***to lean back against***, s'adosser à; ***to lean out***, se pencher au dehors.

leaning ['li:niŋ], *a.* penché.—*n.* penchant, *m.*; (*fig.*) tendance, *f.*

leanness ['li:nnis], *n.* maigreur, *f.*

lean-to ['li:ntu:], *n.* appentis, *m.*

leap [li:p], *n.* saut, bond, *m.*—*v.t. irr.* sauter, franchir.—*v.i.* sauter, bondir; s'élancer, se précipiter.

leap-frog ['li:pfrɔg], *n.* saute-mouton, *m.*

leap-year ['li:pjiə], *n.* année bissextile, *f.*

learn [lə:n], *v.t. irr.* apprendre.—*v.i.* apprendre, s'instruire.

learned ['lə:nid], *a.* savant, instruit, érudit; ***learned man***, savant, *m.*; ***learned profession***, profession libérale, *f.*

learner ['lə:nə], *n.* élève, commençant, apprenti, *m.*; ***learner driver***, élève chauffeur.

learning ['lə:niŋ], *n.* science, instruction, *f.*, savoir, *m.*, connaissances, *f.pl.*; érudition, *f.*

lease [li:s], *n.* bail, *m.*—*v.t.* louer, donner à bail; prendre à bail.

leasehold ['li:should], *a.* à bail.—*n.* tenure par bail, *f.*

leash [li:ʃ], *n.* laisse, *f.*—*v.t.* mener en laisse, attacher.

least [li:st], *a.* le moindre, le plus petit.—*adv.* le moins; ***at least***, au moins, du moins; ***not in the least***, point du tout, nullement.

leather ['leðə], *a.* de cuir.—*n.* cuir, *m.*; ***upper leather***, empeigne, *f.*—*v.t.* (*colloq.*) étriller, rosser.

leave [li:v], *n.* permission, *f.*, congé; adieu, *m.*; ***on leave***, en congé (*un mois ou plus*), en permission (*moins d'un mois*); ***with your leave***, avec votre permission.—*v.t. irr.* laisser; quitter, partir de (*s'en aller de*); cesser (*de*); ***he left the house***, il quitta la maison, il partit de la maison; ***he left the pen on the table***, il laissa le stylo sur la table; ***to be left***, rester; ***to leave about***, laisser traîner; ***to leave alone***, laisser tranquille; ***to leave off***, cesser (*de*); ***to leave out***, supprimer, omettre, oublier. —*v.i.* partir, quitter; cesser.

leaven [levn], *n.* levain, *m.*—*v.t.* faire lever.

leaves [LEAF].

leave-taking ['li:vteikiŋ], *n.* adieux, *m.pl.*

leavings ['li:viŋz], *n.pl.* restes, *m.pl.*

Lebanese ['lebəni:z], *a.* libanais.—*n.* Libanais (*personne*), *m.*

Lebanon ['lebənən]. le Liban, *m.*

lecherous ['letʃərəs], *a.* lascif, libertin, lubrique.

lecherousness ['letʃərəsnis], **lechery** ['letʃəri], *n.* lasciveté, *f.*

lectern ['lektə:n], *n.* lutrin, *m.*

lecture ['lektʃə], *n.* conférence (*sur*), leçon (*de*), *f.*; (*fig.*) sermon, *m.*, semonce, *f.*—*v.t.* faire un cours à; (*fig.*) sermonner, semoncer. —*v.i.* faire un cours (*de*), faire une conférence (*sur*).

lecturer ['lektʃərə], *n.* conférencier; maître de conférences, *m.*

lecture-room ['lektʃəru:m], *n.* salle de conférences, *f.*

ledge [ledʒ], *n.* rebord, bord, *m.*; (*Arch.*) saillie, *f.*

ledger ['ledʒə], *n.* grand livre, *m.*

lee [li:], *a.* sous le vent.—*n.* (*Naut.*) côté sous le vent, *m.*

leech [li:tʃ], *n.* sangsue, *f.*

leek [li:k], *n.* poireau, *m.*

leer [liə], *n.* œillade, *f.*; regard de côté, *m.*—*v.i.* lorgner.

lees [li:z], *n.pl.* lie, *f.*

leeward ['lu:əd], *a.* and *adv.* (*Naut.*) sous le vent.

lee-way ['li:wei], *n.* dérive; (*fig.*) marge, *f.*

left (1) [left], *past* and *p.p.* [LEAVE].

left (2) [left], *a.* and *n.* gauche, *f.*; ***on the left***, à gauche.

left-handed ['left'hændid], *a.* gaucher; à gauche (*vis*); (*fig.*) gauche.

left-overs ['leftouvəz], *n.pl.* restes (*d'un repas*), *m.pl.*

leg [leg], *n.* jambe; patte (*d'oiseau, d'insecte etc.*); tige (*bottines*); cuisse (*volaille*), *f.*; pied (*meuble*); gigot (*mouton*); trumeau (*bœuf*), *m.*; branche (*compas*), *f.*; ***to pull someone's leg***, se moquer de quelqu'un.

legacy ['legəsi], *n.* legs, *m.*

legal [li:gl], *a.* légal, judiciaire, juridique.

legality [li'gæliti], *n.* légalité, *f.*

legalize ['li:gəlaiz], *v.t.* légaliser, (*fig.*) autoriser.

legally ['li:gəli], *adv.* légalement.

legation [li'geiʃən], *n.* légation, *f.*

legend ['ledʒənd], *n.* légende, *f.*

legendary ['ledʒəndri], *a.* légendaire, fabuleux.

legged [legd, 'legid], *a.* à jambes, à pieds;

four-legged, à quatre pattes; ***two-legged***, à deux jambes, bipède.
leggings [ˈleginz], *n.pl.* jambières, guêtres, *f.pl.*
legibility [ledʒiˈbiliti], *n.* lisibilité, netteté d'écriture, *f.*
legible [ˈledʒibl], *a.* lisible.
legion [ˈli:dʒən], *n.* légion, *f.*; ***the Foreign Legion***, la Légion (étrangère).
legislate [ˈledʒisleit], *v.t.* légiférer, faire des lois.
legislation [ledʒisˈleiʃən], *n.* législation, *f.*
legislative [ˈledʒislətiv], *a.* législatif.
legitimate [ləˈdʒitimit], *a.* légitime; juste, correct.
leisure [ˈleʒə], *n.* loisir, *m.*; ***at leisure***, de loisir; ***at one's leisure***, à loisir; ***you are at leisure to come or not***, il vous est loisible de venir ou non.
leisurely [ˈleʒəli], *a.* sans hâte, mesuré.—*adv.* à loisir.
lemon [ˈlemən], *n.* citron, limon, *m.*
lemonade [leməˈneid], *n.* limonade, *f.*
lemon squash [ˈlemənˈskwɔʃ], *n.* citronnade, *f.*
lemon-squeezer [ˈlemənˈskwi:zə], *n.* presse-citrons, *m.inv.*
lemon-tree [ˈlemәntri:], *n.* citronnier, *m.*
lend [lend], *v.t. irr.* prêter; (*fig.*) donner.
lender [ˈlendə], *n.* prêteur, *m.*
lending [ˈlendiŋ], *n.* prêt, *m.*; ***lending library***, bibliothèque de prêt, *f.*
length [leŋθ], *n.* longueur; étendue, *f.*; degré, point (*extrémité*), *m.*; durée (*temps*), *f.*; ***at full length***, tout au long (*non abrégé*); en toutes lettres (*mots*); de tout son; long (*personnes*); ***at great length***, longuement; ***at length***, enfin; ***full length***, de grandeur nature; ***two feet in length***, deux pieds de longueur *ou* de long.
lengthen [leŋθn], *v.t.* allonger, étendre; prolonger (*temps*).—*v.i.* s'allonger, s'étendre; se prolonger (*temps*); (*colloq.*) rallonger (*journées etc.*).
lengthening [ˈleŋθniŋ], *n.* allongement, *m.*; prolongation (*de temps*), *f.*; accroissement (*des journées*), *m.*
lengthways [ˈleŋθweiz], **lengthwise** [ˈleŋθ waiz], *adv.* en longueur, en long.
lengthy [ˈleŋθi], *a.* un peu long, ennuyeux.
leniency [ˈli:niənsi], *n.* douceur, clémence, indulgence (*pour*), *f.*
lenient [ˈli:niənt], *a.* doux, indulgent (*à*, *envers* ou *pour*).
leniently [ˈli:niəntli], *adv.* avec douceur, avec indulgence.
lens [lenz], *n.* (*pl.* **lenses** [ˈlenziz]) (*Opt.*) lentille, loupe, *f.*
Lent [lent]. le carême, *m.*
lentil [ˈlentil], *n.* lentille, *f.*
leonine [ˈli:ənain], *a.* de lion, léonin.
leopard [ˈlepəd], *n.* léopard, *m.*
leper [ˈlepə], *n.* lépreux, *m.*
leprosy [ˈleprəsi], *n.* lèpre, *f.*
leprous [ˈleprəs], *a.* lépreux.
less [les], *a.* moindre, plus petit, inférieur; ***to grow less***, diminuer.—*adv.* moins; ***less and less***, de moins en moins; ***no less***, rien moins, pas moins; ***so much the less***, d'autant moins; ***the less . . . the more . . .***, moins . . . plus. . . .—*n.* moins; moindre, *m.*
essee [leˈsi:], *n.* locataire à bail, *m.*, *f.*
lessen [lesn], *v.t.* diminuer, amoindrir, rape tisser, rabaisser (*to lower*); ralentir (*l vitesse*).—*v.i.* diminuer, s'amoindrir.
lesser [ˈlesə], *a.* moindre, plus petit.
lesson [lesn], *n.* leçon, *f.*
lest [lest], *conj.* de peur que, de crainte qu (*followed by* ne *with subj.*).
let (1) [let], *v.t. irr.* laisser, permettre à (*donne la permission à*); souffrir que (*with subjunc tive*); faire (*causer*); louer (*maison*); ***let hir come***, qu'il vienne; ***let me see***, voyons; ***le us go***, allons; ***to let alone***, laisser trar quille; ***to let down***, descendre, fair descendre, baisser, rabattre; ***to let fal*** laisser tomber; ***to let go***, lâcher; ***to let i*** faire entrer; ***to let know***, faire savoir à; ***let off***, laisser échapper; tirer (*arme à feu*, ***to let out***, faire sortir, laisser sortir; élarg (*vêtements*).
let (2) [let], *n.* empêchement; obstacle, déla *m.*; (*Tennis*) (balle) à remettre.
lethal [li:θl], *a.* mortel, fatal.
lethargic [ləˈθɑ:dʒik], *a.* léthargique.
lethargy [ˈleθədʒi], *n.* léthargie, *f.*
letter [ˈletə], *n.* lettre, *f.*; (*pl.*, *fig.*) belles lettres, *f.pl.*; ***registered letter***, lettr recommandée.
letter-box [ˈletəbɔks], *n.* boîte aux lettres,
letter-card [ˈletəkɑ:d], *n.* carte-lettre, *f.*
lettered [ˈletəd], *a.* lettré, savant.
lettering [ˈletəriŋ], *n.* titre, *m.*
letting [ˈletiŋ], *n.* louage, *m.*; ***letting ou*** location, *f.*; agrandissement (*de vêtement*), *m*
lettuce [ˈletis], *n.* laitue, *f.*
let-up [ˈletʌp], *n.* diminution, *f.*
Levant [ləˈvænt], **the.** le Levant, *m.*
Levantine [liˈvæntain], *a.* du Levant, levan tin.—*n.* Levantin (*personne*), *m.*; levantin (*soie*), *f.*
level [levl], *a.* de niveau (*avec*), au niveau (*de*) uni (*surface*); égal (*à*); ***level crossing*** passage à niveau, *m.*—*n.* niveau, *m.*, surfac unie, *f.*; ***at ministerial level***, à l'échelo ministériel.—*v.t.* aplanir, niveler, mettre d niveau; braquer, pointer (*arme à feu*); porte (*coup*).—*v.i.* viser, mettre en joue, pointer.
level-headed [ˈlevlhedid], *a.* équilibré, d sens rassis.
levelling [ˈlevliŋ], *n.* nivellement; pointag (*de fusil*), *m.*
lever [ˈli:və], *n.* levier, *m.*; ***hand-lever*** manette, *f.*
leveret [ˈlevərit], *n.* levraut, *m.*
levity [ˈleviti], *n.* légèreté, *f.*; manque d sérieux, *m.*
levy [ˈlevi], *n.* levée; perception (*d'impôts*), —*v.t.* lever; imposer (*amende etc.*).
lewd [lju:d], *a.* impudique, lascif.
lexicon [ˈleksikn], *n.* lexique, dictionnaire, *m.*
liability [laiəˈbiliti], *n.* responsabilité; ten dance, *f.*; danger, *m.*; (*Comm.*) (*pl.*) engage ments, *m.pl.*, passif, *m.*; ***assets and liabilities***, actif et passif, *m.*
liable [ˈlaiəbl], *a.* sujet (*à*), exposé (*à*), responsable (*de*).
liar [ˈlaiə], *n.* menteur, *m.*
libel [laibl], *n.* libelle, écrit diffamatoire, *m.*—*v.t.* diffamer.
libellous [ˈlaibələs], *a.* diffamatoire.
liberal [ˈlibərəl], *a.* libéral, généreux; prodigue, abondant.—*n.* (*Polit.*) Libéral, *m.*
liberality [libəˈræliti], *n.* libéralité, *f.*

liberate ['libəreit], *v.t.* libérer, rendre libre; délivrer (*de*).
liberation [libə'reiʃən], *n.* mise en liberté, *f.*, élargissement (*de prisonniers*); affranchissement, *m.*; libération, délivrance, *f.*
liberator ['libəreitə], *n.* libérateur, *m.*
Liberia [lai'biəriə]. le Libéria, *m.*
Liberian [lai'biəriən], *a.* libérien.—*n.* Libérien (*personne*), *m.*
liberty ['libəti], *n.* liberté, *f.*; privilèges, *m.pl.*, franchises, *f.pl.*
librarian [lai'brɛəriən], *n.* bibliothécaire, *m.*,*f.*
library ['laibrəri], *n.* bibliothèque, *f.*; ***film library***, cinémathèque, *f.*; ***record library***, discothèque, *f.*
Libya ['libiə]. la Lybie, *f.*
Libyan ['libiən], *a.* libyen.—*n.* Libyen (*personne*), *m.*
lice [LOUSE].
licence ['laisəns], *n.* licence, liberté; permission, *f.*, permis; certificat; (*fig.*) dérèglement, *m.*; autorisation (*de prédicateur*), *f.*; brevet (*de libraire*), *m.*; (*Comm.*) patente, *f.*; ***driving licence***, permis de conduire; ***gun-licence***, permis de port d'armes; permis de chasse; ***marriage-licence***, dispense de bans, *f.*
license ['laisəns], *v.t.* autoriser, accorder un permis à.
licensed ['laisənst], *a.* autorisé; breveté; (*Comm.*) patenté.
licentious [lai'senʃəs], *a.* licencieux.
lichen ['laikən], *n.* lichen, *m.*
lick [lik], *v.t.* lécher; laper (*boire*); (*slang*) rosser (*battre*).—*n.* coup de langue, *m.*
licking ['likiŋ], *n.* (*slang*) coups, *m.pl.*, raclée, *f.*
licorice [LIQUORICE].
lid [lid], *n.* couvercle, *m.*; paupière (*d'œil*), *f.*
lie (1) [lai], *n.* mensonge; démenti, *m.*; ***to give the lie to***, donner un démenti à; ***white lie***, mensonge pieux.—*v.i.* mentir.
lie (2) [lai], *v.i. irr.* être couché, se coucher; reposer, être, être situé, se trouver; s'appuyer (*se soutenir*); rester (*to remain*); consister; ***here lies***, ci-gît; ***lie down!*** (*à un chien*) couchez! ***to lie about*** (*objets*), traîner çà et là; ***to lie down***, se coucher, se reposer.—*n.* gisement, *m.*, position, situation, *f.*
lieutenant [lef'tenənt], *n.* lieutenant, *m.*
life [laif], *n.* (*pl.* **lives** [laivz]) vie, *f.*; homme vivant, *m.*; personne; (*fig.*) vie, âme, vivacité, *f.*, entrain; mouvement; (*Paint. etc.*) naturel, *m.*; ***a double life***, une vie double; ***for life***, à vie, à perpétuité; ***from life***, d'après nature; ***high life***, le grand monde, *m.*; ***never in my life***, jamais de ma vie; ***pension for life***, pension viagère, *f.*; ***prime of life***, fleur de l'âge, *f.*; ***single life***, célibat, *m.*; ***to come to life***, s'animer.
life-belt ['laifbelt], *n.* ceinture de sauvetage, *f.*
life-boat ['laifbout], *n.* canot de sauvetage, *m.*
life-buoy ['laifbɔi], *n.* bouée de sauvetage, *f.*
lifeguard ['laifgɑ:d], *n.* garde du corps, *m.*; (*pl.*) les Gardes du corps, *m.pl.*; sauveteur, *m.*
life-insurance ['laifinʃuərəns], *n.* assurance sur la vie, *f.*
lifeless ['laiflis], *a.* sans vie, inanimé.
lifelike ['laiflaik], *a.* comme un être vivant, d'après nature, vivant.
lifelong ['laiflɔŋ], *a.* de toute la vie.
life-size ['laifsaiz], *a.* de grandeur nature.
lifetime ['laiftaim], *n.* vie, *f.*, vivant, *m.*; ***in his*** or ***her lifetime***, de son vivant.
lift [lift], *n.* action de lever, élévation, *f.*, effort; coup de main (*aide*); monte-charge (*machine*); ascenseur, *m.*—*v.t.* lever, soulever, hausser, soupeser (*évaluer le poids de*); (*fig.*) élever, relever.
lift-man ['liftmən], *n.* (*pl.* **-men** [men]) liftier, *m.*
light (1) [lait], *n.* lumière, *f.*, jour (*du soleil*); clair (*de la lune etc.*), *m.*; clarté (*de l'œil etc.*); lueur, *f.*; (*fig.*) aspect, point de vue, *m.*; ***electric light***, éclairage à l'électricité, *m.*; ***it is light***, il fait jour; ***light and shade***, clair-obscur, *m.*; ***traffic lights***, feux de circulation, *m.pl.*; ***will you give me a light?*** voulez-vous me donner du feu?—*v.t. irr.* allumer; illuminer, éclairer (*fenêtres etc.*).—*v.i.* ***to light up***, briller, s'enflammer.
light (2) [lait], *v.i.* ***to light upon***, descendre *ou* tomber sur.
light (3) [lait], *a.* léger; (*fig.*) gai, frivole; clair (*couleur etc.*); blond (*teint*).
lighten (1) [laitn], *v.t.* éclairer, illuminer.—*v.i.* éclairer; faire des éclairs.
lighten (2) [laitn], *v.t.* soulager, alléger (*adoucir*).
lightening ['laitniŋ], *n.* éclaircissement; allègement; soulagement, *m.*
lighter ['laitə], *n.* allumeur; briquet (*pour cigarettes*), *m.*; (*Naut.*) allège, gabare, *f.*, chaland, *m.*
light-hearted [lait'hɑ:tid], *a.* gai, réjoui.
light-heartedness [lait'hɑ:tidnis], *n.* enjouement, *m.*, gaieté, *f.*
lighthouse ['laithaus], *n.* phare, *m.*
lighting ['laitiŋ], *n.* éclairage, *m.*; ***lighting-up time***, heure d'éclairage, *f.*
lightly ['laitli], *adv.* légèrement, à la légère; lestement, facilement, aisément; gaiement.
lightness ['laitnis], *n.* légèreté, *f.*
lightning ['laitniŋ], *n.* éclair, *m.*, les éclairs, *m.pl.*; foudre, *f.*; ***flash of lightning***, éclair.
lightning-conductor ['laitniŋkən'dʌktə], *n.* paratonnerre, *m.*
lights [laits], *n.pl.* mou (*d'animal*), *m.*
lightship ['laitʃip], *n.* bateau-feu, *m.*
like (1) [laik], *a.* semblable, tel, pareil; même, égal, *vraisemblable; ***as like as not***, probablement; ***that is something like!*** à la bonne heure! ***to be like***, ressembler à; ***to feel like doing something***, avoir envie de faire quelque chose; ***what is he like?*** comment est-il?—*prep.* comme, semblable à, pareil à.—*n.* chose pareille, *f.*, pareil, *m.*; même chose, *f.*; ***the likes of you***, les gens de votre sorte, *m.pl.*, *f.pl.*
like (2) [laik], *v.t.* aimer, aimer bien, trouver bon, trouver bien; vouloir (bien), désirer, être bien aise (*de*); ***as you like***, comme il vous plaira, comme vous voudrez.—*n.* goût, *m.*; préférence, *f.*; ***everyone has his likes and dislikes***, chacun son goût.
likeable ['laikəbl], *a.* sympathique, aimable.
likelihood ['laiklihud], *n.* probabilité, vraisemblance, *f.*
likely ['laikli], *a.* probable, vraisemblable.—*adv.* probablement, vraisemblablement.

liken [laikn], *v.t.* comparer (*à* ou *avec*).
likeness ['laiknis], *n.* ressemblance, *f.*; portrait, *m.*
likewise ['laikwaiz], *adv.* également, pareillement, de même, aussi.
liking ['laikiŋ], *n.* gré, goût, penchant, *m.*, inclination; amitié, *f.*
lilac ['lailək], *n.* lilas, *m.*
lily ['lili], *n.* lis, *m.*; ***lily of the valley***, muguet, *m.*
limb [lim], *n.* membre (*du corps*); (*colloq.*) enfant terrible, *m.*; grosse branche (*d'arbre*), *f.*
limber (1) ['limbə], *a.* souple, flexible; (*fig.*) agile.—*v.i.* ***to limber up***, se chauffer les muscles.
limber (2) ['limbə], *n.* avant-train, *m.*
limbo ['limbou], *n.* limbes, *m.pl.*
lime (1) [laim], *n.* (*Bot.*) lime, limette, *f.*; ***lime-juice***, jus de limette, *m.*; ***lime-tree***, tilleul (*linden*); limettier, *m.*
lime (2) [laim], *n.* chaux; glu (*pour prendre des oiseaux*), *f.*
limelight ['laimlait], *n.* (*Theat.*) les feux de la lampe, *m.pl.*; ***to be in the limelight***, être en évidence.
limestone ['laimstoun], *n.* pierre à chaux, *f.*; (*Geol.*) calcaire, *m.*
limit ['limit], *n.* limite, borne, *f.*; (*fam.*) ***that's the limit!*** ça c'est le comble!—*v.t.* limiter, borner, restreindre.
limitation [limi'teiʃən], *n.* limitation, restriction, *f.*
limited ['limitid], *a.* limité, borné; (*Comm.*) anonyme.
limitless ['limitlis], *a.* sans limite.
limp [limp], *a.* mou, flasque, sans consistance. —*v.i.* boiter.
limpet ['limpit], *n.* lépas, *m.*, patelle, *f.*
limpid ['limpid], *a.* limpide.
linden [lindn], *n.* (*Bot.*) tilleul, *m.*
line (1) [lain], *n.* ligne; corde, *f.*, cordeau (*ficelle*), *m.*; file, *f.*, alignement (*rang*); trait (*écrit*), *m.*; raie (*bande*), *f.*; contour (*profil*), *m.*; ride (*pli du visage*); (*Rail.*) voie; lignée, race (*descendance*), *f.*; (*fig.*) genre (*d'affaires etc.*); (*Pros.*) vers; mot, petit mot (*lettre brève*), *m.*; limite (*de territoire*), *f.*; ***air-line***, ligne aérienne; (*Teleph.*) ***hold the line!*** ne quittez pas! ***it is hard lines***, c'est dur; ***not in my line***, pas de mon ressort.—*v.t.* ligner, régler; ***to line up***, aligner.
line (2) [lain], *v.t.* doubler (*vêtement*); garnir (*de*); border (*de*).
lineage ['liniidʒ], *n.* lignée, race, famille, *f.*
lineal ['liniəl], *a.* linéaire.
lineally ['liniəli], *adv.* en ligne directe.
linear ['liniə], *a.* linéaire.
linen ['linin], *a.* de toile.—*n.* toile, toile de lin, *f.*, lin; linge (*habits*), *m.*
liner ['lainə], *n.* (*Naut.*) paquebot de ligne, transatlantique, *m.*
linesman ['lainzmən], *n.* (*pl.* **-men** [men]) (*Ftb.*) arbitre de touche, *m.*
linger ['liŋgə], *v.i.* traîner, tarder; hésiter.
lingering ['liŋgəriŋ], *a.* qui traîne, lent; languissant.—*n.* retard, *m.*, lenteur; hésitation, *f.*
lingo ['liŋgou], *n.* (*slang*) jargon, *m.*; langue, *f.*
linguist ['liŋgwist], *n.* linguiste, *m.*, *f.*
liniment ['linimənt], *n.* liniment, *m.*
lining ['lainiŋ], *n.* doublure; garniture (*de vêtement*); coiffe (*de chapeau*), *f.*; (*Build.*) revêtement, *m.*
link [liŋk], *n.* chaînon, anneau; (*fig.*) lien; trait d'union, *m.*; ***cuff-links***, boutons de manchettes, *m.pl.*—*v.t.* lier, relier (*avec.*); enchaîner (*dans*); unir.—*v.i.* s'allier (*à*).
links [liŋks], *n.pl.* ***golf-links***, terrain de golf, *m.*
linnet ['linit], *n.* linotte, *f.*
linoleum [li'nouljəm], *n.* linoléum, *m.*
linotype ['lainotaip], *n.* linotype, *f.*
linseed ['linsi:d], *n.* graine de lin, *f.*; ***linseed-oil***, huile de lin, *f.*
lint [lint], *n.* charpie, *f.*
lintel [lintl], *n.* linteau, *m.*
lion ['laiən], *n.* lion, *m.*; (*fig.*) célébrité, *f.*; ***lion's cub***, lionceau, *m.*
lioness ['laiənes], *n.* lionne, *f.*
lion-tamer ['laiənteimə], *n.* dompteur de lions, *m.*
lip [lip], *n.* lèvre; babine (*de certains animaux*), *f.*; bord (*de choses*), *m.*; (*fig.*) impertinence, *f.*
lipstick ['lipstik], *n.* bâton de rouge, *m.*
liquefy ['likwifai], *v.t.* liquéfier.—*v.i.* se liquéfier.
liqueur [li'kjuə], *n.* liqueur, *f.*
liquid ['likwid], *a.* liquide; doux, coulant.—*n.* liquide, *m.*
liquidate ['likwideit], *v.t.* liquider.
liquidation [likwi'deiʃən], *n.* liquidation, *f.*, acquittement (*d'une dette*), *m.*
liquor ['likə], *n.* (*Chem.*) liqueur, solution; (*Am.*) boisson alcoolique, *f.*; (*Am.*) ***hard liquor***, alcool, *m.*
liquorice ['likəris], *n.* réglisse, *f.*
Lisbon ['lizbən]. Lisbonne, *f.*
lisp [lisp], *v.t.*, *v.i.* dire (θ, ð) au lieu de (s, z); (*colloq.*) susurrer, zozoter.
lissom [lism], *a.* souple, leste.
list (1) [list], *n.* liste, *f.*, rôle, *m.*; ***Army List***, annuaire de l'armée, *m.*—*v.t.* enrôler, enregistrer.
list (2) [list], *v.i.* (*Naut.*) donner de la bande. —*n.* (*Naut.*) bande, *f.*
listen [lisn], *v.i.* écouter.
listener ['lisnə], *n.* auditeur, *m.*
listless ['listlis], *a.* apathique.
listlessness ['listlisnis], *n.* apathie, *f.*
lists [lists], *n. pl.* lice, arène (*arena*), *f.*
litany ['litəni], *n.* litanie, *f.*
literal ['litərəl], *a.* littéral.
literally ['litərəli], *adv.* littéralement, à la lettre.
literary ['litərəri], *a.* littéraire; lettré (*personne*).
literature ['litəritʃə], *n.* littérature, *f.*
lithe [laið], *a.* pliant, flexible, souple.
lithograph ['liθogrɑ:f], *n.* lithographie, *f.*
lithographer [li'θɔgrəfə], *n.* lithographe, *m.*,*f.*
Lithuania [liθju'einiə]. la Lituanie, la Lithuanie, *f.*
Lithuanian [liθju'einiən], *a.* lituanien, lithuanien.—*n.* lituanien, lithuanien (*langue*); Lituanien, Lithuanien (*personne*), *m.*
litigant ['litigənt], *n.* plaideur, *m.*
litigate ['litigeit], *v.t.* plaider, disputer.—*v.i.* être en procès.
litigation [liti'geiʃən], *n.* litige; procès, *m.*
litre ['li:tə], *n.* litre, *m.*
litter ['litə], *n.* litière, civière (*véhicule*), *f.*; ordures, *f.pl.*, détritus, *m.pl.*; (*fig.*) fouillis, désordre, *m.*; portée (*d'animal*), *f.*—*v.t.*

joncher; jeter çà et là; (*fig.*) mettre en désordre; mettre bas (*animal*); salir; ***to litter down*** (*of horse*), faire la litière à.

litter-bin ['litəbin], *n.* boîte à ordures, *f.*

little [litl], *a.* petit; minime, exigu; mesquin; ***little one***, enfant, *m.*, *f.*, petit, *m.*—*n.* peu, *m.*; ***to think little of***, faire peu de cas de.—*adv.* peu, un peu, pas beaucoup, peu de chose, peu de; ***a little***, un peu; ***as little as possible***, le moins possible; ***little by little***, petit à petit, peu à peu; ***little or none***, peu ou point.

littleness ['litlnis], *n.* petitesse, *f.*

liturgy ['litədʒi], *n.* liturgie, *f.*

live (1) [liv], *v.t.* mener (une vie).—*v.i.* vivre; résider, demeurer, habiter; ***long live the Queen!*** vive la Reine! ***to live by***, vivre de; ***to live down a scandal***, faire oublier un scandale avec le temps; ***to live on***, se nourrir de.

live (2) [laiv], *a.* en vie, vivant; ardent, vif (*charbons*); ***live rail***, rail conducteur, *m.*; ***livestock***, bétail, *m.*; ***live wire***, fil sous tension, *m.*

lived [livd], *a.* de vie; ***long-lived***, qui vit longtemps, de longue vie.

livelihood ['laivlihud], *n.* vie, subsistance, *f.*; gagne-pain, *m.*

liveliness ['laivlinis], *n.* vivacité, gaieté, *f.*

livelong ['livlɔŋ], *a.* durable, long, sans fin; ***the livelong day***, toute la sainte journée.

lively ['laivli], *a.* vif, gai, enjoué, animé; vivant (*endroit*).

liven [laivn], *v.t.* ***to liven up***, animer.

liver (1) ['livə], *n.* ***fast liver***, viveur, noceur, *m.*

liver (2) ['livə], *n.* (*Anat.*) foie, *m.*

livery ['livəri], *n.* livrée; pension (*de chevaux*), *f.*

lives [LIFE].

livestock ['laivstɔk], [LIVE (2)].

livid ['livid], *a.* livide, blême.

living ['liviŋ], *a.* en vie, vivant; vif.—*n.* vie, subsistance, existence, *f.*; genre de vie, *m.*, chère, *f.*; (*Eccles.*) bénéfice, *m.*, cure, *f.*

living-room ['liviŋrum], *n.* salle de séjour, *f.*

lizard ['lizəd], *n.* lézard, *m.*

llama ['lɑːmə], *n.* lama, *m.*

lo! [lou], *int.* voici! voilà! voyez! regardez!

load [loud], *n.* charge, *f.*, fardeau; (*fig.*) chargement, *m.*; charretée (*cartful*), *f.*—*v.t.* charger; (*fig.*) combler, accabler (*de*).

loaf [louf], *n.* (*pl.* **loaves** [louvz]) pain (*long*), *m.*; miche (*rond*), *f.*—*v.i.* flâner, fainéanter; ***to loaf about town***, battre le pavé.

loafer ['loufə], *n.* fainéant, batteur de pavé, *m.*

loam [loum], *n.* terre grasse, *f.*

loamy ['loumi], *a.* glaiseux.

loan [loun], *n.* emprunt; prêt, *m.*; ***to raise a loan***, faire un emprunt.—*v.t.* prêter.

loath [louθ], *a.* fâché, peiné; ***to be loath to***, faire à contre-cœur.

loathe [louð], *v.t.* détester.

loathing ['louðiŋ], *n.* dégoût, *m.*, aversion, *f.*

loathsome ['louðsəm], *a.* dégoûtant, odieux.

loaves [LOAF].

lobby ['lɔbi], *n.* couloir, *m.*; salle d'attente (*vestibule*); (*Theat.*) entrée, *f.*—*v.t.*, *v.i.* (*Polit.*) faire les couloirs.

lobe [loub], *n.* lobe, *m.*

lobelia [lo'biːliə], *n.* lobélie, *f.*

lobster ['lɔbstə], *n.* homard, *m.*

local ['loukəl], *a.* local; topographique.

locality [lo'kæliti], *n.* localité, *f.*

localize ['loukəlaiz], *v.t.* localiser.

locally ['loukəli], *adv.* localement.

locate [lo'keit], *v.t.* placer, localiser; repérer.

location [lo'keiʃən], *n.* situation, *f.*, emplacement, *m.*; location, *f.*; (*Cine.*) extérieurs, *m.pl.*

loch [lɔx], *n.* (*Sc.*) lac, *m.*

lock [lɔk], *n.* serrure; écluse (*de canal*); platine (*de fusil*); mèche, boucle (*de cheveux*), *f.*; flocon (*de laine*), *m.*; (*pl.*) cheveux, *m.pl.*; ***dead-lock***, impasse, *f.*; ***padlock***, cadenas, *m.*—*v.t.* fermer à clef; accrocher (*roues etc.*); ***to lock in***, enfermer; ***to lock up***, serrer, enfermer, mettre en prison.—*v.i.* fermer à clef.

locker ['lɔkə], *n.* armoire, *f.*; coffre, *m.*

locket ['lɔkit], *n.* médaillon, *m.*

lock-jaw ['lɔkdʒɔː], *n.* trisme, tétanos, *m.*

locksmith ['lɔksmiθ], *n.* serrurier, *m.*

locomotion [loukə'mouʃən], *n.* locomotion, *f.*

locomotive ['loukəmoutiv], *a.* locomotif.—*n.* locomotive, *f.*

locust (1) ['loukəst], *n.* sauterelle d'Orient, *f.*, criquet, *m.*

locust (2) ['loukəst], *n.* caroubier (*plante*), *m.*; ***locust-tree***, robinier, *m.*

lodge [lɔdʒ], *n.* loge (*de concierge*), *f.*; pavillon, *m.*; maisonnette (*de garde*), *f.*—*v.t.* loger; abriter; enfoncer (*mettre dans*); déposer (*placer*); implanter (*dans le cœur*); interjeter (*appel*); ***to lodge a complaint***, porter plainte.—*v.i.* loger, se loger; s'arrêter, se fixer.

lodger ['lɔdʒə], *n.* locataire; pensionnaire, *m.*, *f.*

lodging ['lɔdʒiŋ], *n.* logement; appartement, *m.*; ***to live in furnished lodgings***, loger en garni *ou* en meublé.

lodging-house ['lɔdʒiŋhaus], *n.* hôtel garni, hôtel meublé, *m.*

loft [lɔft], *n.* grenier, *m.*; tribune, *f.*; pigeonnier, *m.*

loftily ['lɔftili], *adv.* haut, avec hauteur, pompeusement.

loftiness ['lɔftinis], *n.* élévation; hauteur, fierté, pompe; sublimité, *f.*

lofty ['lɔfti], *a.* haut, élevé; altier; sublime (*style*).

log [lɔg], *n.* bûche, *f.*; (*Naut.*) loch, *m.*; ***to sleep like a log***, dormir comme une souche.

loganberry ['lougənberi], *n.* ronce-framboise, *f.*

logarithm ['lɔgəriðm], *n.* logarithme, *m.*

log-book ['lɔgbuk], *n.* journal *ou* livre de bord; (*Motor.*) carnet de route, *m.*

loggerhead ['lɔgəhed], *n.* lourdaud, *m.*; ***to be at loggerheads***, être aux prises *ou* à couteaux tirés.

logic ['lɔdʒik], *n.* logique, *f.*

logical ['lɔdʒikəl], *a.* logique, de la logique.

loin [lɔin], *n.* longe (*de veau*), *f.*; filet (*de mouton*), *m.*; (*pl.*) reins, lombes, *m.pl.*

loiter ['lɔitə], *v.t.* perdre, gaspiller.—*v.i.* flâner, traîner, s'amuser en chemin.

loiterer ['lɔitərə], *n.* musard, flâneur, *m.*

loitering ['lɔitəriŋ], *n.* flânerie, *f.*

loll [lɔl], *v.t.* laisser pendre (*la langue*).—*v.i.* s'étaler, se pencher; pendre (*la langue*).

lolling ['lɔliŋ], *a.* étendu, étalé.
lollipop ['lɔlipɔp], *n.* sucre d'orge, *m.*, sucette, *f.*
lolly ['lɔli], *n.* (*fam.*) sucette; (*slang*) galette (*argent*), *f.*
London ['lʌndən]. Londres, *m.* ou *f.*
Londoner ['lʌndənə], *n.* Londonien, *m.*
lone [loun], *a.* isolé, solitaire; délaissé.
loneliness ['lounlinis], *n.* solitude, *f.*; isolement, *m.*
lonely ['lounli], *a.* isolé; délaissé.
long (1) [lɔŋ], *v.i.* avoir bien envie, brûler (*de*); (*impers.*) tarder (*de*).
long (2) [lɔŋ], *a.* long; étendu, prolongé, allongé; ***a long time***, longtemps, depuis longtemps, pendant longtemps; ***in the long run***, à la longue; ***to be three feet long***, avoir trois pieds de long, être long de trois pieds.—*n.* ***the long and the short of***, le fort et le faible de.—*adv.* fort; longtemps, longuement; depuis longtemps; pendant longtemps; durant; ***all night long***, tout le long de la nuit; ***before long***, bientôt, avant peu, sous peu; ***how long have you been here?*** combien de temps y a-t-il que vous êtes ici ? ***long ago***, il y a longtemps, depuis longtemps; ***not long after***, peu de temps après; ***so long as***, tant que.
longer ['lɔŋgə], *a.* plus long.—*adv.* plus longtemps; de plus.
longing ['lɔŋiŋ], *n.* désir ardent, *m.*, envie, *f.*
longitude ['lɔndʒitju:d], *n.* longitude, *f.*
long-sighted ['lɔŋsaitid], *a.* presbyte; (*fig.*) clairvoyant; ***I am long-sighted***, j'ai la vue longue.
look [luk], *v.i.* regarder (*d'une fenêtre*); sembler, avoir l'air, paraître; donner sur (*maison etc.*); ***look out !*** attention! gare! ***to look after***, soigner, s'occuper de; ***to look away***, détourner ses regards; ***to look back***, regarder en arrière; ***to look down upon***, mépriser; ***to look for***, chercher; ***to look forward to***, attendre avec impatience; ***to look in***, faire une petite visite, dire un petit bonjour à; ***to look into***, examiner; ***to look like***, ressembler à; ***to look on***, regarder, considérer; ***to look over***, jeter un coup d'œil sur, examiner.—*n.* regard, air, *m.*, apparence, mine, *f.*; coup d'œil, *m.*
looker-on ['lukərɔn], *n.* spectateur, *m.*
looking ['lukiŋ], *a.* à l'air . . .; à la mine . . .; ***good-looking***, beau.
looking-glass ['lukiŋglɑ:s], *n.* miroir, *m.*, glace, *f.*
look-out ['lukaut], *n.* guet, *m.*, vigilance, vue, *f.*; (*Mil.*) guetteur, *m.*; (*Naut.*) vigie, *f.*; ***to keep a look-out***, avoir l'œil au guet.
loom [lu:m], *n.* métier à tisser, *m.*—*v.i.* apparaître indistinctement, surgir.
looming ['lu:miŋ], *a.* vague, estompé.
loop [lu:p], *n.* boucle; bride (*pour bouton*), *f.*; (*Av.*) looping, *m.*
loop-hole ['lu:phoul], *n.* meurtrière (*pour bouton*); (*fig.*) échappatoire, *f.*, faux-fuyant, *m.*
loose [lu:s], *a.* délié, défait; branlant; (*fig.*) relâché, lâche (*mœurs*); vague; licencieux; libre; ***loose cash***, menue monnaie, *f.*—*n.* ***on the loose***, dissolu, dissipé.—*v.t.* délier, lâcher, (*fig.*) déchaîner.
loosely ['lu:sli], *adv.* librement, négligemment; licencieusement.
loosen [lu:sn], *v.t.* délier, détacher, défaire; desserrer; ébranler.—*v.i.* se délier; se défaire; se desserrer.
looseness ['lu:snis], *n.* état desserré, relâchement; caractère vague, *m.*
loot [lu:t], *n.* butin; pillage, *m.*—*v.t.* piller.
looter ['lu:tə], *n.* pillard, *m.*
lop [lɔp], *v.t.* élaguer, ébrancher.
lopsided ['lɔpsaidid], *a.* qui penche trop d'un côté, déjeté.
loquacious [lo'kweiʃəs], *a.* loquace.
lord [lɔ:d], *n.* seigneur; (*fig.*) maître; lord (*titre anglais*); Monseigneur (*à un prince, noble, évêque etc.*), *m.*; ***Our Lord***, notre Seigneur; ***the Lord's Prayer***, l'oraison dominicale, *f.*; ***the year of our Lord***, l'an de grâce, *m.*—*v.t.* ***to lord it over***, dominer, faire le maître.
lordliness ['lɔ:dlinis], *n.* hauteur, *f.*, orgueil, *m.*
lordling ['lɔ:dliŋ], *n.* petit seigneur; hobereau, *m.*
lordly ['lɔ:dli], *a.* de seigneur, noble; hautain, fier.
lore [lɔ:], *n.* savoir, *m.*; science, *f.*
lorry ['lɔri], *n.* camion, *m.*
lose [lu:z], *v.t. irr.* perdre; égarer; ***to lose one's temper***, s'emporter; ***to lose one's way***, s'égarer; ***to lose sight of***, perdre de vue.—*v.i.* perdre (*de valeur*); retarder (*horloge etc.*).
loss [lɔs], *n.* perte, *f.*; (*Hunt.*) défaut, *m.*; extinction (*de voix*), *f.*; ***at a loss***, dans l'embarras; ***dead loss***, perte sèche.
lost [lɔst], *a.* perdu; égaré (*fourvoyé*); abîmé (*endommagé*).
lot [lɔt], *n.* sort, destin, *m.*, part; quantité, *f.*; tas (*de personnes*); lot (*à une vente*), *m.*; ***a lot of***, beaucoup de; ***to draw*** or ***cast lots***, tirer au sort.
lotion ['louʃən], *n.* lotion, *f.*
lottery ['lɔtəri], *n.* loterie, *f.*
loud [laud], *a.* haut; fort, grand; bruyant, retentissant; tapageur (*tumultueux*); criard (*couleurs*).
loudly ['laudli], *adv.* haut, fort, à haute voix; avec grand bruit, à grands cris.
loudness ['laudnis], *n.* force, *f.*, grand bruit, éclat, *m.*
loud-speaker [laud'spi:kə], *n.* (*Rad.*) haut-parleur, *m.*
Louisa [lu'i:zə], **Louise** [lu'i:z]. Louise, *f.*
lounge [laundʒ], *v.i.* flâner; être couché *ou* étendu *ou* appuyé paresseusement (*sur*).—*n.* promenoir; sofa (*canapé*); petit salon; hall (*d'hôtel*), *m.*; ***lounge jacket***, veston, *m.*; ***lounge suit***, complet veston, *m.*
lounger ['laundʒə], *n.* flâneur, *m.*
lour, lower (1) ['lauə], *v.i.* froncer les sourcils; s'assombrir, s'obscurcir (*du temps*); ***the sky lours***, le temps se couvre.
louring, lowering (1) ['lauəriŋ], *a.* couvert, sombre; (*fig.*) menaçant.
louse [laus], *n.* (*pl.* **lice** [lais]) pou, *m.*
lousy ['lauzi], *a.* pouilleux; (*fig.*) bas, vil, sale.
lout [laut], *n.* rustre, butor, *m.*
loutish ['lautiʃ], *a.* rustre.
lovable ['lʌvəbl], *a.* digne d'être aimé; aimable.
love [lʌv], *v.t.* aimer, adorer.—*n.* amour, *m.*, affection; amitié, *f.*; ami (*mot tendre*), *m.*; (*Ten.*) zéro, rien, *m.*; ***my love to all***, mes

amitiés à tous; ***to be in love with***, être amoureux de.
love-affair ['lʌvəfɛə], *n.* amourette, *f.*
love-letter ['lʌvletə], *n.* billet doux, *m.*
loveliness ['lʌvlinis], *n.* amabilité; beauté, *f.*, charme, *m.*
lovely ['lʌvli], *a.* charmant, ravissant, séduisant, gracieux.
lover ['lʌvə], *n.* amant, amoureux; amateur (*de*), *m.*
lovesick ['lʌvsik], *a.* en mal d'amour.
loving ['lʌviŋ], *a.* aimant, affectueux, affectionné, tendre; d'amour (*choses*); ***loving kindness***, bonté, miséricorde, *f.*
low (1) [lou], *a.* bas; petit; peu élevé, vulgaire; profond (*révérence*); (*fig.*) lent (*fièvre*); abattu (*humeur*); ***at low water***, à marée basse; ***in a low voice***, d'une voix basse. —*adv.* bas, en bas; à voix basse; profondément (*révérence*).
low (2) [lou], *v.i.* beugler.
low-brow ['loubrau], *a.* peu intellectuel.—*n.* philistin, *m.*
lower (1) [LOUR].
lower (2) ['louə], *a.* plus bas, inférieur; bas.—*v.t.* baisser, abaisser; descendre; rabaisser humilier; diminuer, affaiblir.
lower-class ['louəklɑːs], *n.* peuple, *m.*
lowering (1) [LOURING].
lowering (2) ['louəriŋ], *n.* abaissement, *m.*, diminution, *f.*
lowest ['louist], *a.* le plus bas, le dernier.
lowing ['louiŋ], *n.* mugissement, beuglement, *m.*
lowliness ['loulinis], *n.* humilité, *f.*
lowly ['louli], *a.* humble.—*adv.* humblement.
lowness ['lounis], *n.* situation basse, petitesse; faiblesse (*santé*); dépression (*prix*), *f.*; abaissement (*température*); abattement (*humeur*), découragement, *m.*; vulgarité, *f.*
loyal ['lɔiəl], *a.* fidèle, loyal.
loyalty ['lɔiəlti], *n.* fidélité, *f.*
lozenge ['lɔzindʒ], *n.* pastille, *f.*; (*Geom., Her. etc.*) losange, *m.*
lubber ['lʌbə], *n.* lourdaud, *m.*; ***land-lubber***, marin d'eau douce, *m.*
lubricant ['luːbrikənt] *n.* lubrifiant, *m.*
lubricate ['luːbrikeit], *v.t.* lubrifier.
lubrication [luːbri'keiʃən], *n.* lubrication, *f.*
lucid ['luːsid], *a.* lucide; limpide, transparent.
lucidity [luː'siditi], **lucidness** ['luːsidnis], *n.* transparence, limpidité, lucidité, *f.*
luck [lʌk], *n.* chance, fortune, *f.*, bonheur, *m.*; ***by good luck***, par bonheur; ***by ill luck***, par malheur; ***good luck***, bonne chance.
luckily ['lʌkili], *adv.* heureusement, par bonheur.
lucky ['lʌki], *a.* heureux; ***to be lucky***, avoir de la chance; porter bonheur (*chose*).
lucrative ['luːkrətiv], *a.* lucratif.
lucre ['luːkə], *n.* lucre, *m.*
Lucy ['luːsi]. Lucie, *f.*
ludicrous ['luːdikrəs], *a.* risible, comique, ridicule.
luggage ['lʌgidʒ], *n.* bagage, *m.*, bagages *m.pl.*; ***left-luggage office***, consigne, *f.*
lugubrious [lu'gjuːbriəs], *a.* lugubre.
lukewarm ['luːkwɔːm], *a.* tiède; (*fig.*) peu zélé.
lull [lʌl], *v.t.* bercer, endormir; calmer.—*v.i.* se calmer, s'apaiser.—*n.* moment de calme, *m.*; (*Naut.*) accalmie, *f.*
lullaby ['lʌləbai], *n.* berceuse, *f.*
lumbago [lʌm'beigou], *n.* lumbago, *m.*
lumber ['lʌmbə], *n.* vieilleries, *f.pl.*; (*Am.*) bois de charpente, *m.*—*v.t.* entasser sans ordre; remplir de fatras.—*v.i.* se traîner lourdement.
lumbering ['lʌmbəriŋ], *a.* lourd, encombrant.
lumberjack ['lʌmbədʒæk], *n.* bûcheron, *m.*
luminous ['ljuːminəs], *a.* lumineux.
lump [lʌmp], *n.* masse, *f.*; morceau, bloc (*pièce*), *m.*—*v.t.* prendre en bloc; réunir ensemble.
lumpish ['lʌmpiʃ], *a.* gros, lourd, pesant.
lumpy ['lʌmpi], *a.* grumeleux.
lunacy ['luːnəsi], *n.* aliénation mentale, *f.*
lunar ['luːnə], *a.* lunaire.
lunatic ['luːnətik], *a.* de fou, d'aliéné.—*n.* aliéné; fou, *m.*, folle, *f.*
lunatic-asylum ['luːnətikəsailəm], *n.* asile d'aliénés, *m.*
lunch [lʌntʃ], *n.* déjeuner (*vers midi*), *m.*—*v.i.* déjeuner.
lung [lʌŋ], *n.* (*usu. in pl.*) poumon; mou (*de veau*), *m.*; ***iron lung***, poumon d'acier.
lunge [lʌndʒ], *n.* (*Fenc.*) botte, *f.*, coup droit, *m.*—*v.i.* porter une botte.
lupin ['ljuːpin], *n.* (*Bot.*) lupin, *m.*
lurch [ləːtʃ], *n.* embardée, *f.*, cahot; (*fig.*) embarras, *m.*; ***to leave in the lurch***, planter là.—*v.i.* faire une embardée (*navire*).
lure [ljuə], *n.* leurre, appât, piège; (*fig.*) attrait, *m.*—*v.t.* leurrer, attirer, séduire.
lurid ['ljuərid], *a.* sombre, blafard; sensationnel.
lurk [ləːk], *v.i.* être aux aguets; se tenir caché.
luscious ['lʌʃəs], *a.* délicieux, savoureux; liquoreux (*vin*).
lusciousness ['lʌʃəsnis], *n.* nature succulente, douceur extrême; volupté, *f.*
lush [lʌʃ], *a.* luxuriant.
lust [lʌst], *n.* luxure, *f.*; désir lascif, *m.*; (*fig.*) convoitise, *f.*—*v.i.* désirer immodérément; ***to lust after***, convoiter.
lustily ['lʌstili], *adv.* vigoureusement.
lustre ['lʌstə], *n.* brillant, lustre; (*fig.*) éclat, *m.*, splendeur, *f.*
lustrous ['lʌstrəs], *a.* brillant, lustré.
lusty ['lʌsti], *a.* vigoureux, robuste, fort.
lute [ljuːt], *n.* luth, *m.*
Luxembourg ['lʌksəmbəːg]. le Luxembourg (*Duché*), *m.*
luxuriance [lʌg'zjuəriəns], *n.* exubérance, surabondance, luxuriance, *f.*
luxuriant [lʌg'zjuəriənt], *a.* exubérant, surabondant, luxuriant.
luxurious [lʌg'zjuəriəs], *a.* de luxe, somptueux, luxueux.
luxuriously [lʌg'zjuəriəsli], *adv.* avec luxe, somptueusement.
luxuriousness [lʌg'zjuəriəsnis], *n.* somptuosité, *f.*
luxury ['lʌkʃəri], *n.* luxe, *m.*, exubérance, *f.*; fin morceau; objet de luxe, *m.*
lying ['laiiŋ], *a.* menteur; mensonger (*choses*). —*n.* mensonge, *m.*
lymph [limf], *n.* lymphe, *f.*; vaccin, *m.*
lynch [lintʃ], *v.t.* lyncher (*exécuter sommairement*).
lynx [liŋks], *n.* lynx, *m.*

lyre ['laiə], *n.* lyre, *f.*
lyric ['lirik], *a.* lyrique.—*n.* poème lyrique, *m.*; (*pl.*) paroles (*d'une chanson*), *f.pl.*
lyrical ['lirikəl], *a.* lyrique.

M

M, m [em]. treizième lettre de l'alphabet, *m.*
macadam [mə'kædəm], *n.* macadam, *m.*
macaroni [mækə'rouni], *n.* macaroni, *m.*
macaroon [mækə'ru:n], *n.* macaron, *m.*
mace [meis], *n.* masse (*de cérémonie*), *f.*
mace-bearer ['meisbɛərə], *n.* massier, *m.*
Macedonia [mæsə'douniə]. la Macédoine, *f.*
Macedonian [mæsə'douniən], *a.* macédonien. —*n.* Macédonien (*personne*), *m.*
macerate ['mæsəreit], *v.t.* macérer.
machine [mə'ʃi:n], *n.* machine, *f.*; (*fig.*) instrument; appareil (*avion*), *m.*
machine-gun [mə'ʃi:ngʌn], *n.* mitrailleuse, *f.*
machinery [mə'ʃi:nəri], *n.* mécanique, *f.*, mécanisme, *m.*; machines, *f.pl.*
machine-tool [mə'ʃi:ntu:l], *n.* machine-outil, *f.*
mackerel ['mækərəl], *n.* maquereau, *m.*
mackintosh ['mækintɔʃ], *n.* imperméable, *m.*
mad [mæd], *a.* fou, aliéné, insensé; affolé; furieux (*déchaîné*); enragé (*animal*).
Madagascan [mædə'gæskən], *a.* malgache.—*n.* Malgache (*personne*), *m.*, *f.*
Madagascar [mædə'gæskə]. Madagascar, *m.*
madam ['mædəm], *n.* madame, *f.*
madcap ['mædkæp], *a.* étourdi, fou.—*n.* fou, *m.*
madden [mædn], *v.t.* rendre fou; faire enrager.
maddening ['mædniŋ], *a.* à rendre fou, enrageant.
madder ['mædə], *n.* garance, *f.*
made [meid], *a.* fait, confectionné; ***self-made man***, fils de ses œuvres, *m.*; ***made up***, inventé (*histoire*); maquillé (*visage*).
Madeira [mə'diərə]. Madère, *f.*—*n.* madère (*vin*), *m.*
madly ['mædli], *adv.* follement, furieusement.
madman ['mædmən], *n.* (*pl.* **-men** [men]) aliéné, fou, *m.*
madness ['mædnis], *n.* démence, fureur, folie; rage (*d'animal*), *f.*
Madonna [mə'dɔnə]. la Madone, *f.*
maelstrom ['meilstroum, 'meilstrəm], *n.* (*Geog.*) malstrom; (*fig.*) tourbillon, *m.*
magazine [mægə'zi:n], *n.* magasin (*boutique; aussi chargeur d'arme à feu*); magazine, *m.*, revue (*périodique*), *f.*
magenta [mə'dʒentə], *a.* and *n.* magenta (*couleur*), *m.*
maggot ['mægət], *n.* larve, *f.*, ver, asticot, *m.*
magic ['mædʒik], *a.* magique.—*n.* magie, *f.*
magical ['mædʒikəl], *a.* magique.
magician [mə'dʒiʃən], *n.* magicien, *m.*
magisterial [mædʒis'tiəriəl], *a.* de maître; magistral.
magistrate ['mædʒistreit], *n.* magistrat, *m.*; ***examining magistrate***, juge d'instruction, *m.*; ***police court magistrate***, juge de paix, *m.*
magnanimity [mægnə'nimiti], *n.* magnanimité, *f.*
magnanimous [mæg'næniməs], *a.* magnanime.
magnate ['mægneit], *n.* magnat; grand; (*colloq.*) gros bonnet, *m.*
magnesia [mæg'ni:ʃə], *n.* magnésie, *f.*
magnesium [mæg'ni:ziəm], *n.* magnésium, *m.*
magnet ['mægnit], *n.* aimant, *m.*
magnetic [mæg'netik], *a.* aimanté; magnétique; (*fig.*) attirant.
magnetism ['mægnitizm], *n.* magntéisme, *m.*; (*Elec.*) aimantation, *f.*
magnetize ['mægnitaiz], *v.t.* aimanter; (*fig.* magnétiser.
magneto [mæg'ni:tou], *n.* magnéto, *f.*
magnificence [mæg'nifisəns], *n.* magnificence, *f.*
magnificent [mæg'nifisənt], *a.* magnifique, superbe.
magnify ['mægnifai], *v.t.* magnifier, augmenter, grossir; (*fig.*) exalter.
magnifying ['mægnifaiiŋ], *a.* qui grossit; ***magnifying-glass***, loupe, *f.*
magnitude ['mægnitju:d], *n.* grandeur; importance, *f.*
magnolia [mæg'nouliə], *n.* (*Bot.*) magnolia, magnolier, *m.*
magpie ['mægpai], *n.* pie, *f.*
mahogany [mə'hɔgəni], *n.* acajou, bois d'acajou, *m.*
maid [meid], *n.* fille, jeune fille; vierge (*virgin*); bonne, servante, domestique, *f.*; ***chambermaid***, fille de chambre; ***kitchen-maid***, fille de cuisine; ***maid of all work***, bonne à tout faire; ***maid of honour***, demoiselle d'honneur, *f.*
maiden [meidn], *a.* de fille, de jeune fille; virginal; (*fig.*) pur, neuf; ***maiden aunt***, tante non mariée, *f.*; ***maiden name***, nom de jeune fille, *m.*; ***maiden speech***, premier discours (*d'un nouveau membre du Parlement*), *m.*; ***maiden voyage***, premier voyage, *m.*—*n.* jeune fille, fille, *f.*
maidenly ['meidnli], *a.* de jeune fille; modeste, chaste.
mail (1) [meil], *n.* mailles (*armure*), *f.pl.*
mail (2) [meil], *n.* courrier, *m.*, dépêches (*lettres*), *f.pl.*—*v.t.* (*Am.*) mettre à la poste.
mail-bag ['meilbæg], *n.* sac postal, *m.*
mail-train ['meiltrein], *n.* train-postal, *m.*
maim [meim], *v.t.* mutiler, estropier.
main (1) [mein], *a.* principal, premier; grand; important, essentiel.—*n.* gros, *m.*, plus grande partie, *f.*; principal océan, *m.*; ***in the main***, pour la plupart, en général.
main (2) [mein], *n.* force, *f.*
main-deck ['meindek], *n.* premier pont, *m.*
mainland ['meinlənd], *n.* continent, *m.*
mainly ['meinli], *adv.* principalement, surtout.
mainmast ['meinmɑ:st], *n.* grand mât, *m.*
mainstay ['meinstei], *n.* soutien, *m.*
maintain [mein'tein], *v.t.* maintenir; soutenir, alléguer; conserver; entretenir, nourrir (*subvenir aux besoins de*).
maintenance ['meintənəns], *n.* maintien, soutien; entretien, *m.*
maize [meiz], *n.* maïs, *m.*

majestic [mə'dʒestik], *a.* majestueux.

majesty ['mædʒəsti], *n.* majesté, *f.*; ***His** or **Her Majesty***, Sa Majesté.

major ['meidʒə], *a.* plus grand, majeur.—*n.* commandant, *m.*; (*Law*) personne majeure, *f.*; ***drum-major***, tambour-major, *m.*; ***sergeant-major***, adjudant, *m.*

Majorca [mə'jɔ:kə]. Majorque, *f.*

majority [mə'dʒɔriti], *n.* majorité, *f.*

make [meik], *v.t. irr.* faire; créer, façonner, fabriquer, confectionner; rendre (*faire devenir*); forcer, contraindre (*obliger*); amasser, gagner (*argent*); ***to make a mistake***, se tromper; ***to make a noise***, faire du bruit; ***to make believe***, faire accroire à; ***to make fun of***, se moquer de; ***to make good***, soutenir; réparer; dédommager de; ***to make it up***, se raccommoder; ***to make known***, faire connaître, faire savoir à; ***to make out***, comprendre, déchiffrer, distinguer; ***to make over to***, céder à; ***to make sure of***, s'assurer de; ***to make up***, compléter, inventer (*histoire*); arranger (*querelle*); régler (*comptes*); ***to make up for***, suppléer à; rattraper (*temps*); ***to make up one's mind***, se décider.—*v.i.* se diriger (*vers*); contribuer (*à*); faire (*comme si*); ***to make believe***, faire semblant; ***to make of***, comprendre; ***to make off***, se sauver; ***to make up***, se maquiller; ***to make up for***, suppléer à; dédommager de, compenser.—*n.* façon, forme, tournure; fabrication, *f.*

make-believe ['meikbili:v], *n.* feinte, *f.*, semblant, *m.*

maker ['meikə], *n.* créateur, auteur; faiseur; (*Comm.*) fabricant, *m.*

makeshift ['meikʃift], *n.* pis aller, expédient, *m.*

make-up ['meikʌp], *n.* contexture, *f.*; maquillage (*du visage*), *m.*

make-weight ['meikweit], *n.* supplément; (*fig.*) remplissage, *m.*

making ['meikiŋ], *n.* création; façon, fabrication, construction; confection (*de vêtements*), *f.*

maladjusted [mælə'dʒʌstid], *a.* inadapté.

maladjustment [mælə'dʒʌstmənt], *n.* inadaptation, *f.*

maladministration [mælədminis'treiʃən], *n.* mauvaise administration, *f.*

malady ['mælədi], *n.* maladie, *f.*

malaria [mə'lɛəriə], *n.* malaria, *f.*, paludisme, *m.*

Malay [mə'lei], *a.* malais.—*n.* malais (*langue*); Malais (*personne*), *m.*

Malaysia [mə'leiziə]. la Malaisie, *f.*

Malaysian [mə'leiziən], *a.* malais.—*n.* Malais (*personne*), *m.*

malcontent ['mælkəntent], *a.* and *n.* mécontent, *m.*

male [meil], *a.* mâle; masculin.—*n.* mâle, *m.*

malediction [mæli'dikʃən], *n.* malédiction, *f.*

malefactor ['mælifæktə], *n.* malfaiteur, *m.*

malevolence [mə'levələns], *n.* malveillance, *f.*

malevolent [mə'levələnt], *a.* malveillant.

Mali ['mɑ:li]. le Mali, *m.*

malice ['mælis], *n.* malice; malveillance, méchanceté; rancune, *f.*; ***to bear malice***, vouloir du mal à, garder rancune à.

malicious [mə'liʃəs], *a.* malicieux, méchant.

maliciously [mə'liʃəsli], *adv.* méchamment.

maliciousness [mə'liʃəsnis], *n.* malice, malveillance, *f.*

malign [mə'lain], *a.* malin; méchant.—*v.t.* diffamer, noircir.

malignant [mə'lignənt], *a.* malin, méchant.

malignantly [mə'lignəntli], *adv.* malignement, méchamment.

malignity [mə'ligniti], *n.* malignité, malveillance, *f.*

malinger [mə'liŋgə], *v.i.* (*Mil.*) faire le malade; tirer au flanc.

mall (1) [mɔ:l], *n.* gros maillet, *m.*

mall (2) [mæl], *n.* mail (*rue*), *m.*

mallard ['mæləd], *n.* (*Orn.*) canard sauvage, *m.*

malleability [mæliə'biliti], *n.* malléabilité, *f.*

malleable ['mæliəbl], *a.* malléable.

mallet ['mælit], *n.* maillet, *m.*; tapette, *f.*

mallow ['mælou], *n.* (*Bot.*) mauve, *f.*

malmsey ['mɑ:mzi], *n.* malvoisie, *f.*

malnutrition [mælnju'triʃən], *n.* sous-alimentation, *f.*

malpractice [mæl'præktis], *n.* malversation *f.*, méfait, *m.*

malt [mɔ:lt], *n.* malt, *m.*—*v.t.* malter.

Malta ['mɔ:ltə]. Malte, *f.*

Maltese [mɔ:l'ti:z], *a.* maltais.—*n.* Maltais (*personne*), *m.*

maltreat [mæl'tri:t], *v.t.* maltraiter.

maltreatment [mæl'tri:tmənt], *n.* mauvais traitement, *m.*

mammal ['mæməl], *n.* mammifère, *m.*

mammoth ['mæməθ], *n.* mammouth, *m.*

man [mæn], *n.* (*pl.* **men** [men]) homme; domestique, valet (*servant*), *m.*; (*Chess*) pièce, *f.*; (*Draughts*) pion, *m.*; ***the man in the street***, l'homme de la rue, le grand public; ***well, my man!*** eh bien! mon brave!—*v.t.* garnir d'hommes; armer (*pompe, bateau*).

manacle ['mænəkl], *v.t.* mettre les menottes à.—*n.* (*pl.*) menottes, *f.pl.*

manage ['mænidʒ], *v.t.* diriger, mener, conduire; arranger (*choses*); gouverner, administrer, gérer; ménager (*habilement*); manier, dompter (*cheval*).—*v.i.* s'arranger (*pour*), parvenir à; venir à bout (*de*).

manageable ['mænidʒəbl], *a.* traitable, maniable.

management ['mænidʒmənt], *n.* conduite, administration; (*Comm.*) gestion (*direction*), *f.*; artifice, savoir-faire (*manège*), *m.*

manager ['mænidʒə], *n.* directeur, administrateur; (*Comm.*) gérant; (*Theat.*) régisseur; (*Spt.*) manager, *m.*

manageress [mænidʒə'res], *n.* directrice, gérante, *f.*

Manchuria [mæn'tʃuəriə]. la Mandchourie, *f.*

Manchu(rian) [mæn'tʃu(əriən)], *a.* mandchou.—*n.* mandchou (*langue*); Mandchou (*personne*), *m.*

mandarin ['mændərin], *n.* mandarin, *m.*; mandarine (*orange*), *f.*

mandate ['mændeit], *n.* commandement, mandat; ordre, *m.*

mandatory ['mændətəri], *a.* and *n.* mandataire, *m.*

mandolin ['mændəlin], *n.* mandoline, *f.*

mane [mein], *n.* crinière, *f.*

manfully ['mænfuli], *adv.* en homme, virilement, vaillamment.

manganese ['mæŋgəni:z], *n.* manganèse, *m.*

mange [meindʒ], *n.* gale (*d'animaux*), *f.*
manger ['meindʒə], *n.* mangeoire, crèche, *f.*
mangle [mæŋgl], *v.t.* déchirer, mutiler; calandrer (*linge*).—*n.* calandre, *f.*
mango ['mæŋgou], *n.* (*Bot.*) mangue, *f.*; manguier (*arbre*), *m.*
mangrove ['mæŋgrouv], *n.* (*Bot.*) mangle, *f.*; manglier, manguier (*arbre*), *m.*
mangy ['meindʒi], *a.* galeux.
man-handle ['mænhændl], *v.t.* manutentionner; (*fig.*) maltraiter.
man-hole ['mænhoul], *n.* bouche d'égout, *f.*
manhood ['mænhud], *n.* virilité, *f.*; âge viril, *m.*; nature humaine, *f.*
mania ['meiniə], *n.* folie, rage, manie, *f.*
maniac ['meiniæk], *a.* furieux, fou.—*n.* fou furieux, fou, *m.*; (*fig.*) maniaque, *m.*, *f.*
maniacal [mə'naiəkl], *a.* furieux, fou.
manicure ['mænikjuə], *n.* soin des ongles, *m.* —*v.t.* soigner les ongles.
manicurist ['mænikjuərist], *n.* manucure, *m.*, *f.*
manifest ['mænifest], *v.t.* manifester, témoigner, montrer; ***to manifest a cargo***, déclarer une cargaison.—*a.* manifeste, évident.—*n.* manifeste, *m.*
manifestation [mænifes'teiʃən], *n.* manifestation, *f.*
manifesto [mæni'festou], *n.* manifeste, *m.*
manifold ['mænifould], *a.* divers, multiple; varié.
manikin ['mænikin], *n.* bout d'homme, mannequin, homuncule, *m.*
Manila [mə'nilə]. Manille, *f.*
manipulate [mə'nipjuleit], *v.t.* manipuler.
mankind [mæn'kaind], *n.* genre humain, *m.*, l'humanité, *f.*
manlike ['mænlaik], *a.* d'homme, viril; mâle; hommasse (*femme*).
manliness ['mænlinis], *n.* caractère viril, *m.*
manly ['mænli], *a.* d'homme, viril, mâle.
manna ['mænə], *n.* manne, *f.*
mannequin ['mænikin], *n.* (*Dress.*) mannequin, *m.*; ***mannequin parade***, défilé de mannequins, *m.*
manner ['mænə], *n.* manière, *f.*, air; genre, *m.*, sorte, façon, espèce; coutume, habitude, *f.*; (*pl.*) mœurs, *f.pl.*, politesse, *f.*; ***after the manner of***, à la manière de, d'après; ***all manner of things***, toutes sortes de choses, *f.pl.*; ***in the same manner as***, de même que.
mannerism ['mænərizm], *n.* air maniéré, maniérisme; tic, *m.*
mannerly ['mænəli], *a.* poli.
manning ['mæniŋ], *n.* armement, équipement, *m.*
mannish ['mæniʃ], *a.* hommasse.
manœuvre [mə'nu:və], *n.* manœuvre, *f.*—*v.t.*, *v.i.* manœuvrer.
manor ['mænə], *n.* seigneurie, *f.*; manoir, château seigneurial, *m.*
manorial [mə'nɔ:riəl], *a.* seigneurial.
man-power ['mænpauə], *n.* main d'œuvre, *f.*
manse [mæns], *n.* presbytère, *m.*
mansion ['mænʃən], *n.* château (*à la campagne*); hôtel particulier (*en ville*), *m.*
manslaughter ['mænslɔ:tə], *n.* (*Law*) homicide involontaire, *m.*
mantel [mæntl], **mantelpiece** ['mæntlpi:s], *n.* manteau *ou* dessus de cheminée, *m.*, cheminée, *f.*
mantilla [mæn'tilə], *n.* mantille, *f.*
mantis ['mæntis], *n.* (*Ent.*) mante, *f.*; ***praying mantis***, mante religieuse.
mantle [mæntl], *n.* manteau, *m.*—*v.t.* couvrir, voiler.
manual ['mænjuel], *a.* manuel, de la main.—*n.* manuel (*livre*); (*Organ*) clavier, *m.*
manufacture [mænju'fæktʃə], *n.* manufacture, confection, fabrication, *f.*; (*pl.*) produits manufacturés, *m.pl.*—*v.t.* manufacturer, fabriquer.
manufacturer [mænju'fæktʃərə], *n.* fabricant, industriel, *m.*
manure [mə'njuə], *n.* engrais, fumier, *m.*—*v.t.* engraisser, fumer.
manuscript ['mænjuskript], *a.* and *n.* manuscrit, *m.*
Manx [mæŋks], *a.* de l'île de Man, mannois; ***Manx cat***, chat sans queue, *m.*
many ['meni], *a.* beaucoup (*de*), bien (*des*); nombreux; plusieurs, maint; ***as many as***, autant que, jusqu'à (*devant un numéro*); ***how many?*** combien? ***many a time***, maintes fois; ***so many***, tant, tant de; ***too many***, trop, trop de.—*n.* ***the many***, la multitude, la foule, *f.*
many-coloured ['menikʌləd], *a.* multicolore.
many-sided ['menisaidid], *a.* polygone; (*fig.*) complexe.
map [mæp], *n.* carte, carte géographique, *f.*; ***map of a town***, plan d'une ville, *m.*; ***map of the world***, mappemonde, *f.*—*v.t.* faire une carte *ou* un plan de, tracer.
maple [meipl], *n.* érable, *m.*
mar [mɑ:], *v.t.* gâter, défigurer; (*fig.*) troubler.
marathon ['mærəθən], *n.* marathon, *m.*
marauder [mə'rɔ:də], *n.* maraudeur, malandrin, *m.*
marauding [mə'rɔ:diŋ], *n.* maraude, *f.* maraudage, *m.*
marble [mɑ:bl], *a.* de marbre.—*n.* marbre, *m.*; bille (*jouet*), *f.*
marbled [mɑ:bld], *a.* marbré.
marbling ['mɑ:bliŋ], *n.* marbrure, *f.*
March [mɑ:tʃ]. mars (*mois*), *m.*
march (1) [mɑ:tʃ], *n.* (*Mil.*) marche, *f.*; (*fig.*) progrès, *m.*; ***march past***, défilé, *m.*—*v.t.* mettre en marche; emmener.—*v.i.* marcher, se mettre en marche; (*fig.*) avancer; ***to march past***, défiler devant.
march (2) [mɑ:tʃ], *n.* frontière, *f.*
marching ['mɑ:tʃiŋ], *a.* de marche.—*n.* marche, *f.*
marchioness [mɑ:ʃə'nes], *n.* marquise, *f.*
mare [mɛə], *n.* jument, *f.*
Margaret ['mɑ:gərit]. Marguerite, *f.*
margarine ['mɑ:gəri:n, 'mɑ:dʒəri:n], *n.* margarine, *f.*
margin ['mɑ:dʒin], *n.* marge (*de papier etc.*), *f.*; bord (*de rivière, de lac*), *m.*—*v.t.* border.
marginal ['mɑ:dʒinəl], *a.* en marge; marginal.
marigold ['mærigould], *n.* (*Bot.*) souci, *m.*
marine [mə'ri:n], *a.* marin, de mer; naval.—*n.* fusilier marin, *m.*; ***tell that to the marines***, allez conter cela à d'autres.
mariner ['mærinə], *n.* marin, *m.*
maritime ['mæritaim], *a.* maritime.
Mark [mɑ:k]. Marc, *m.*
mark (1) [mɑ:k], *n.* marque, *f.*, signe, *m.*; em-

preinte; (*fig.*) distinction, importance, *f.*; témoignage (*d'estime*), *m.*; (*Sch.*) note, *f.*, point, *m.*; cible (*but*); croix (*signature*), *f.* —*v.t.* marquer, remarquer; (*Sch.*) noter; (*fig.*) observer, faire attention à.
mark (2) [mɑːk], *n.* marc (*pièce de monnaie*), *m.*
marked [mɑːkt], *a.* marqué évident; prononcé (*accent*).
marker [ˈmɑːkə], *n.* marqueur; jeton (*au jeu*); signet (*de livre*), *m.*
market [ˈmɑːkit], *n.* marché, *m.*; halle, *f.*; débit (*vente*); cours (*prix*); (*Comm.*) débouché, *m.*—*v.t.* acheter au marché vendre au marché.
market-garden [ˈmɑːkitˈgɑːdn], *n.* jardin maraîcher, *m.*
market-gardener [ˈmɑːkitˈgɑːdnə], *n.* maraîcher, *m.*
marking [ˈmɑːkiŋ], *n.* marquage, *m.*
marking-ink [ˈmɑːkiŋiŋk], *n.* encre à marquer, *f.*
marksman [ˈmɑːksmən], *n.* (*pl.* **-men** [men]) bon tireur, *m.*
marksmanship [ˈmɑːksmənʃip], *n.* adresse au tir, *f.*
marl [mɑːl], *n.* marne, *f.*—*v.t.* marner.
marline-spike [ˈmɑːlinspaik], *n.* épissoir, *m.*
marmalade [ˈmɑːməleid], *n.* confiture d'oranges, *f.*
marmoset [ˈmɑːməzet], *n.* ouistiti, *m.*
marmot [ˈmɑːmət], *n.* marmotte, *f.*
maroon (1) [məˈruːn], *n.* nègre marron, *m.*—*v.t.* abandonner dans une île déserte.
maroon (2) [məˈruːn], *a.* and *n.* marron pourpré (*couleur*), *m.*
marquee [mɑːˈkiː], *n.* grande tente, *f.*
marquess, **marquis** [ˈmɑːkwis], *n.* marquis, *m.*
marquetry [ˈmɑːkətri], *n.* marqueterie, *f.*
marquis [MARQUESS].
marriage [ˈmæridʒ], *n.* mariage, *m.*; noces (*fêtes*), *f.pl.*
marriageable [ˈmæridʒəbl], *a.* mariable, nubile.
married [ˈmærid], *a.* marié; conjugal.
marrow [ˈmærou], *n.* moelle; (*fig.*) essence, *f.*; ***vegetable marrow***, courgette, *f.*
marry [ˈmæri], *v.t.* marier (*donner* ou *unir en mariage*); se marier avec, épouser (*prendre pour époux*).—*v.i.* se marier.
Marseilles [mɑːˈseilz]. Marseille, *f.*
marsh [mɑːʃ], *n.* marais, *m.*
marshal [mɑːʃl], *n.* maréchal.—*v.t.* ranger; mettre en ordre; classer.
marsh-mallow [ˈmɑːʃˈmælou], *n.* (*Bot.*) guimauve, *f.*; bonbon à la guimauve, *m.*
marshy [ˈmɑːʃi], *a.* marécageux.
mart [mɑːt], *n.* marché, entrepôt, *m.*
marten [mɑːtn], *n.* martre, *f.*; ***beech marten***, fouine, *f.*
Martha [ˈmɑːθə]. Marthe, *f.*
martial [mɑːʃl], *a.* martial; de guerre, de bataille; guerrier, belliqueux.
martin [ˈmɑːtin], *n.* martin, martinet, *m.*
martinet [mɑːtiˈnet], *n.* officier strict sur la discipline, *m.*
Martinmas [ˈmɑːtinmæs]. la Saint-Martin, *f.*
martyr [ˈmɑːtə], *n.* martyr, *m.*—*v.t.* martyriser.
martyrdom [ˈmɑːtədəm], *n.* martyre, *m.*
martyrize [ˈmɑːtəraiz], *v.t.* (*fam.*) faire souffrir, martyriser.
marvel [mɑːvl], *n.* merveille, *f.*—*v.i.* s'émerveiller, s'étonner.
marvellous [ˈmɑːv(i)ləs], *a.* merveilleux, étonnant.
marvellously [ˈmɑːv(i)ləsli], *adv.* à merveille.
Marxism [ˈmɑːksizm], *n.* Marxisme, *m.*
Marxist [ˈmɑːksist], *a.* marxiste.—*n.* Marxiste, *m.*, *f.*
Mary [ˈmɛəri]. Marie, *f.*
marzipan [mɑːziˈpæn], *n.* massepain, *m.*
mascot [ˈmæskət], *n.* mascotte, *f.*
masculine [ˈmæskjulin], *a.* mâle, d'homme; (*Gram.*) masculin; hommasse (*femme*).—*n.* masculin, *m.*
mash [mæʃ], *n.* mélange, *m.*, pâte, bouillie; mâche (*pour bestiaux*); pâtée (*pour chien, volaille*), *f.*—*v.t.* broyer; mélanger; (*Brewing*) brasser; ***mashed potatoes***, purée de pommes de terre, *f.*
mask [mɑːsk], *n.* masque; loup (*de soie, de velours*), *m.*—*v.t.* masquer; déguiser.—*v.i.* se masquer.
mason [meisn], *n.* maçon, *m.*; ***freemason***, franc-maçon, *m.*
masonic [məˈsɔnik], *a.* maçonnique.
masonry [ˈmeisənri], *n.* maçonnerie, *f.*; ***freemasonry***, franc-maçonnerie, *f.*
masquerade [mæskəˈreid], *n.* mascarade *f.* —*v.i.* se masquer; ***to masquerade as***, se faire passer pour.
mass (1) [mæs], *n.* masse, *f.*; amas, gros, *m.*; multitude, foule (*de gens*), *f.*—*v.i.* se masser; s'amonceler (*nuages*).
mass (2) [mæs, mɑːs], *n.* (*R.-C. Ch.*) messe, *f.*
massacre [ˈmæsəkə], *n.* massacre, *m.*—*v.t.* massacrer.
massive [ˈmæsiv], *a.* massif.
mass-meeting [ˈmæsˈmiːtiŋ], *n.* assemblée en masse, *f.*, grand meeting, *m.*
mast [mɑːst], *n.* mât, *m.*; (*pl.*) mâts, *m.pl.*, mâture, *f.*; ***half-mast***, à mi-mât, en berne.
master [ˈmɑːstə], *n.* maître, directeur, chef; (*Naut.*) patron, maître (*d'un navire*); patron (*d'ouvriers*); (*Sch. etc.*) maître d'école, professeur; (*fig.*) possesseur, *m.*—*v.t.* maîtriser, surmonter, dompter, vaincre; se rendre maître de; l'emporter sur.
masterful [ˈmɑːstəful], *a.* de maître, impérieux, dominateur.
master-key [ˈmɑːstəkiː], *n.* passe-partout, *m.*
masterly [ˈmɑːstəli], *a.* de maître; magistral.
master-mind [ˈmɑːstəmaind], *n.* esprit supérieur, *m.*
masterpiece [ˈmɑːstəpiːs], *n.* chef-d'œuvre, *m.*
master-stroke [ˈmɑːstəstrouk], **master-touch** [ˈmɑːstətʌtʃ], *n.* coup de maître, *m.*
mastery [ˈmɑːstəri], *n.* empire, pouvoir, *m.*; supériorité, maîtrise, *f.*
masticate [ˈmæstikeit], *v.t.* mâcher.
mastication [mæstiˈkeiʃən], *n.* mastication, *f.*
mastiff [ˈmæstif], *n.* mâtin, *m.*
mastitis [mæsˈtaitis], *n.* mastite, *f.*
mastodon [ˈmæstodɔn], *n.* mastodonte, *m.*
mastoid [ˈmæstɔid], *a.* mastoïde.
mat [mæt], *n.* natte, *f.*; dessous de lampe, *m.*; ***door-mat***, paillasson, *m.*; ***table-mat***, dessous de plat, *m.*—*v.t.* natter, tresser.

match (1) [mætʃ], *n.* pareil, pendant, égal (*semblable*); mariage; parti (*futur époux*), *m.*; lutte (*concours*), *f.*; (*Spt.*) match, *m.*, partie; course, *f.*; ***to be a bad match***, aller mal ensemble (*choses*); ***to be more than a match for***, être trop fort pour; ***to make a good match***, faire un bon mariage.—*v.t.* assortir, appareiller, égaler, apparier (*deux choses*); se mesurer avec (*opposer*).—*v.i.* s'assortir, être pareil.
match (2) [mætʃ], *n.* allumette, *f.*
match-box ['mætʃbɔks], *n.* boîte d'allumettes *ou* à allumettes, *f.*
matchless ['mætʃlis], *a.* incomparable, sans pareil.
match-maker (1) ['mætʃmeikə], *n.* marieur, *m.*
match-maker (2) ['mætʃmeikə], *n.* fabricant d'allumettes, *m.*
mate (1) [meit], *n.* camarade, compagnon, *m.*, compagne, *f.*; second (*de marine marchande*), *m.*—*v.t.* égaler, assortir, apparier; tenir compagnie avec; accoupler (*oiseaux*).—*v.i.* s'accoupler (*animaux*).
mate (2) [meit], *n.* (*Chess*) mat, *m.*—*v.t.* mater.
material [mə'tiəriəl], *a.* matériel; important. —*n.* matière; étoffe, *f.*, tissu (*textile*); matériel (*réserves*), *m.*; (*pl.*) matériaux, *m.pl.*; ***raw material***, matière première.
materialism [mə'tiəriəlizm], *n.* matérialisme, *m.*
materialist [mə'tiəriəlist], *n.* matérialiste, *m.*, *f.*
materialistic [mətiəriə'listik], *a.* matérialiste.
materialize [mə'tiəriəlaiz], *v.t.* matérialiser. —*v.i.* se réaliser; se concrétiser.
materially [mə'tiəriəli], *adv.* matériellement; essentiellement.
maternal [mə'tə:nl], *a.* maternel.
maternity [mə'tə:niti], *n.* maternité, *f.*
mathematics [mæθə'mætiks], *n.pl.* mathématiques, *f.pl.*
Matilda [mə'tildə]. Mathilde, *f.*
matins ['mætinz], *n.pl.* matines, *f.pl.*
matriarch ['meitriɑ:k], *n.* matriarche, *f.*
matricide ['mætrisaid], *n.* matricide (*crime*), *m.*; matricide (*criminel*), *m.*, *f.*
matrimonial [mætri'mouniəl], *a.* conjugal.
matrimony ['mætriməni], *n.* mariage, *m.*, vie conjugale, *f.*
matron ['meitrən], *n.* matrone, mère de famille; infirmière en chef, *f.*
matronly ['meitrənli], *a.* de matrone; d'un certain âge; respectable.
matt [mæt], *a.* mat.
matter ['mætə], *n.* matière; chose, affaire, *f.*; fond; sujet; (*Med.*) pus, *m.*; (*fig.*) importance, *f.*; ***as a matter of fact***, le fait est que; ***what is the matter? Nothing***, qu'y a-t-il? Il n'y a rien; ***what is the matter with you? Nothing***, qu'avez-vous? Je n'ai rien.—*v.imp.* importer; ***it doesn't matter***, n'importe; ***it doesn't matter very much***, ce n'est pas grand'chose; ***it matters little***, peu importe; ***what matter?*** qu'importe?
matter-of-fact ['mætərəvfækt], *a.* pratique, positif.
Matthew ['mæθju]. Mathieu, *m.*
mattock ['mætək], *n.* pioche, *f.*
mattress ['mætris], *n.* matelas, *m.*
mature [mə'tjuə], *a.* mûr, mûri.—*v.t.* mûrir, faire mûrir.—*v.i.* mûrir; (*Comm.*) échoir.
maturity [mə'tjuəriti], *n.* maturité; (*Comm.*) échéance, *f.*
matutinal [mætju'tainl], *a.* matutinal, du matin.
Maud [mɔ:d]. Madelon, *f.*
maudlin ['mɔ:dlin], *a.* pleurard, pleurnichard.
maul [mɔ:l], *n.* maillet, *m.*—*v.t.* rosser, rouer de coups.
maul-stick ['mɔ:lstik], *n.* (*Paint.*) appuimain, *m.*
Mauritania [mɔri'teiniə]. la Mauritanie, *f.*
Mauritanian [mɔri'teiniən], *a.* mauritanien. —*n.* Mauritanien (*personne*), *m.*
Mauritian [mə'riʃən], *a.* mauritien.—*n.* Mauritien (*personne*), *m.*
Mauritius [mə'riʃəs]. l'Île Maurice, *f.*
mausoleum [mɔ:sə'li:əm], *n.* mausolée, *m.*
mauve [mouv], *a.* mauve.
maw [mɔ:], *n.* jabot (*d'oiseau*), *m.*; caillette (*de ruminant*), *f.*
mawkish ['mɔ:kiʃ], *a.* fade, insipide; sottement sentimental.
maxim ['mæksim], *n.* maxime, *f.*
maximum ['mæksiməm], *n.* (*pl.* **maxima** ['mæksimə]) maximum, *m.*
May [mei]. mai (*mois*), *m.*
may [mei], *v.aux. irr.* pouvoir, être autorisé à; ***he may go***, il peut sortir; ***it may be that***, il se peut que (*with subj.*); ***it might be***, cela se pourrait; ***maybe***, peut-être; ***may I?*** puis-je? ***one might as well***, autant vaudrait; ***that may be***, cela se peut; ***that might be***, cela pourrait être; ***you might have gone there***, vous auriez pu y aller.
may-blossom ['meiblɔsəm], *n.* aubépine, *f.*
May-day ['meidei], *n.* premier mai, *m.*
mayor [mɛə], *n.* maire, *m.*
maze [meiz], *n.* labyrinthe, dédale; (*fig.*) embarras, *m.*
mazy ['meizi], *a.* sinueux; (*fig.*) compliqué.
mazurka [mə'zə:kə], *n.* mazurka, *f.*
me [mi:], *pron.* me, moi.
mead [mi:d], *n.* hydromel; (*poet.*) pré (*champ*), *m.*
meadow ['medou], *n.* pré, *m.*, prairie, *f.*
meagre ['mi:gə], *a.* maigre; pauvre.
meagreness ['mi:gənis], *n.* maigreur; pauvreté, *f.*
meal (1) [mi:l], *n.* repas, *m.*
meal (2) [mi:l], *n.* farine, *f.*
mealy ['mi:li], *a.* farineux, poudreux.
mealy-mouthed ['mi:limauðd], *a.* doucereux.
mean (1) [mi:n], *a.* bas, méprisable, vil, abject; médiocre (*de peu de valeur*); mesquin; pauvre, humble; sordide; avare; ***a mean trick***, un vilain tour.
mean (2) [mi:n], *a.* moyen.—*n.* milieu, moyen terme, *m.*; (*Math.*) moyenne, *f.*; ***golden mean***, le juste milieu.
mean (3) [mi:n], *v.t. irr.* signifier, vouloir dire, entendre; se proposer de, avoir l'intention de, vouloir (*to intend*); destiner (*pour* ou *de*); ***do you mean it?*** êtes-vous sérieux? ***what does that word mean?*** que veut dire ce mot? ***what do you mean?*** que voulez-vous dire?—*v.i.* vouloir, entendre; ***to mean well***, avoir de bonnes intentions.

meander [mi'ændə], *n.* détour, méandre, *m.*, sinuosité, *f.*—*v.i.* serpenter.
meandering [mi'ændəriŋ], *a.* onduleux, sinueux, tortueux.
meaning ['mi:niŋ], *a.* significatif; à intentions; ***well-meaning***, bien intentionné.—*n.* signification, *f.*, sens, *m.*; intention, *f.*, dessein, *m.*; pensée (*idée*), *f.*; ***double meaning***, double sens.
meaningless ['mi:niŋlis], *a.* qui n'a pas de sens, dénué de sens.
meanly ['mi:nli], *adv.* bassement; vilement, abjectement; pauvrement; médiocrement.
meanness ['mi:nnis], *n.* bassesse; pauvreté, mesquinerie; médiocrité, *f.*
means [mi:nz], *n.* moyen, *m.*, voie, *f.*; moyens, *m.pl.*, fortune, *f.*, ressources, *f.pl.*
meantime ['mi:ntaim], **meanwhile** ['mi:n wail], *n.* and *adv.* ***in the meantime***, dans l'intervalle, en attendant, cependant, sur ces entrefaites.
measles [mi:zlz], *n.pl.* rougeole, *f.*; ***German measles***, rubéole, *f.*
measurable ['meʒərəbl], *a.* mesurable.
measure ['meʒə], *n.* mesure; (*fig.*) capacité, portée, *f.*; (*Parl.*) projet de loi, *m.*; assise (*de charbon*), *f.*—*v.t.* mesurer; arpenter (*terre*); prendre mesure à (*une personne pour vêtements*); (*fig.*) considérer, toiser, métrer; ***this measures ten feet***, ceci a dix pieds de longueur.
measured ['meʒəd], *a.* mesuré; égal, cadencé.
measurement ['meʒəmənt], *n.* mesurage; arpentage (*de terre*), *m.*; mesure, dimension, *f.*
meat [mi:t], *n.* viande; nourriture, *f.*, aliment (*manger*), *m.*
meat-safe ['mi:tseif], *n.* garde-manger, *m.*
meaty ['mi:ti], *a.* charnu; (*fig.*) bien rempli.
Mecca ['mekə]. la Mecque, *f.*
mechanic [mi'kænik], *n.* artisan, ouvrier mécanicien, *m.*; ***garage mechanic***, garagiste, *m.*
mechanical [mi'kænikəl], *a.* mécanique; d'ouvrier; machinal (*fait sans intelligence*).
mechanically [mi'kænikli], *adv.* mécaniquement; machinalement (*sans intelligence*).
mechanics [mi'kæniks], *n.pl.* mécanique, *f.*
mechanism ['mekənizm], *n.* mécanisme, *m.*
mechanization [mekənai'zeiʃən], *n.* mécanisation, *f.*
mechanize ['mekənaiz], *v.t.* mécaniser; ***mechanized farming***, motoculture, *f.*; ***mechanized army***, armée motorisée, *f.*
medal [medl], *n.* médaille, *f.*
medallion [mi'dæljən], *n.* médaillon, *m.*
medallist ['medlist], *n.* médaillé (*honoré*), *m.*
meddle [medl], *v.i.* se mêler (*de*), toucher (*à*), s'immiscer (*dans*).
meddler ['medlə], *n.* intrigant; officieux, *m.*
meddlesome ['medlsəm], **meddling** ['medliŋ], *a.* intrigant; officieux.
mediaeval [medi'i:vəl], *a.* du moyen âge.
medial ['mi:diəl], *a.* moyen; (*Gram.*) médial.
mediate ['mi:dieit], *v.i.* s'entremettre; s'interposer (*dans*).
mediation [mi:di'eiʃən], *n.* médiation, entremise, *f.*
mediator ['mi:dieitə], *n.* médiateur, *m.*
medical ['medikəl], *a.* médical; de médecine (*école*); en médecine (*étudiant*); ***medical officer***, officier sanitaire, *m.*; ***to take medical advice***, consulter un médecin.
medicament [me'dikəmənt], *n.* médicament, *m.*
medicinal [mə'disinl], *a.* médicinal.
medicine ['medsin], *n.* médecine, *f.*, médicament; (*fig.*) remède, *m.*
medicine-chest ['medsintʃest], *n.* pharmacie, *f.*
medicine-man ['medsinmæn], *n.* sorcier, *m.*
mediocre ['mi:dioukə], *a.* médiocre.
mediocrity [mi:di'ɔkriti], *n.* médiocrité, *f.*
meditate ['mediteit], *v.t.* se proposer de, projeter.—*v.i.* méditer (*sur.*).
meditation [medi'teiʃən], *n.* méditation, *f.*
Mediterranean [meditə'reiniən], *a.* méditerrané; méditerranéen.—*n.* la Méditerranée, *f.*
medium ['mi:djəm], *a.* moyen.—*n.* (*pl.* **media** ['mi:diə], **mediums** ['mi:djəmz]) milieu, moyen, *m.*; voie, entremise; (*Math.*) moyenne proportionnelle, *f.*; agent intermédiaire; (*Spiritualism*) médium, *m.*
medlar ['medlə], *n.* nèfle (*fruit*), *f.*; néflier (*arbre*), *m.*
medley ['medli], *a.* mêlé, hétéroclite.—*n.* mélange, *m.*; confusion, *f.*; (*Mus.*) pot pourri, *m.*
medulla [mi'dʌlə], *n.* médulle, moelle, *f.*
meed [mi:d], *n.* récompense; part (*portion*), *f.*
meek [mi:k], *a.* doux, humble, soumis.
meekly ['mi:kli], *adv.* avec douceur; humblement.
meekness ['mi:knis], *n.* douceur; humilité, *f.*
meet (1) [mi:t], *v.t. irr.* rencontrer, aller à la rencontre de; trouver, recevoir (*atteindre*); faire la connaissance de; faire face à, affronter (*braver*); se présenter devant (*paraître devant*); faire honneur à (*dette*); (*fig.*) satisfaire, remplir (*demande*).—*v.i.* se rencontrer; se voir; se réunir, s'assembler; se joindre (*s'unir*); ***to meet half-way***, se faire des concessions mutuelles.—*n.* rendez-vous de chasse, *m.*
meet (2) [mi:t], *a.* propre, convenable.
meeting ['mi:tiŋ], *n.* rencontre; entrevue; assemblée, réunion, *f.*, meeting, *m.*; séance (*session*), *f.*; confluent (*rivières*), *m.*; jonction (*routes*), *f.*
megaton ['megətʌn], *n.* mégatonne, *f.*
melancholy ['melənkəli], *a.* mélancolique, triste, affligeant.—*n.* mélancolie, tristesse, *f.*
mellifluous [mə'lifluəs], *a.* mielleux, doucereux.
mellow ['melou], *a.* mûr, fondant (*fruit*); moelleux, doux; gris (*à moitié ivre*); meuble (*terre*).—*v.t.* mûrir, faire mûrir; ameublir (*terre*); (*fig.*) adoucir.—*v.i.* mûrir; devenir meuble (*terre*); (*fig.*) s'adoucir.
mellowness ['melounis], *n.* maturité, *f.*; moelleux, *m.*; (*fig.*) douceur, *f.*
melodious [mə'loudiəs], *a.* mélodieux.
melodiously [mə'loudiəsli], *adv.* mélodieusement.
melodrama ['melədrɑ:mə], *n.* mélodrame, *m.*
melodramatic [melədrə'mætik], *a.* mélodramatique.
melody ['melədi], *n.* mélodie, *f.*, air, *m.*
melon ['melən], *n.* melon, *m.*
melt [melt], *v.t.* fondre, faire fondre; (*fig.*) attendrir.—*v.i.* fondre, se fondre; (*fig.*) s'attendrir.

melting ['meltiŋ], *a.* qui fond; fondant (*fruit*); (*fig.*) attendrissant.—*n.* fusion, fonte, *f.*; attendrissement, *m.*
melting-pot ['meltiŋpɔt], *n.* creuset, *m.*
member ['membə], *n.* membre; (*Parl.*) député, *m.*
membered ['membəd], *a.* membré; qui a des membres; ***large-membered***, membru.
membership ['membəʃip], *n.* les membres d'une société etc., *m.pl.*
membrane ['membrein], *n.* membrane, *f.*
memento [mə'mentou], *n.* souvenir, mémento, *m.*
memoir ['memwɑː], *n.* mémoire, *m.*
memorable ['memərəbl], *a.* mémorable.
memorandum [memə'rændəm], *n.* (*pl.* **memoranda** [memə'rændə]) note, *f.*, mémorandum; (*Comm.*) bordereau, *m.*
memorial [mi'mɔːriəl], *a.* commémoratif.—*n.* souvenir, mémoire; monument commémoratif, *m.*; requête, pétition, *f.*
memorize ['meməraiz], *v.t.* apprendre par cœur.
memory ['meməri], *n.* mémoire, *f.*; (*colloq.*) souvenir, *m.*; ***in memory of***, en souvenir de; ***to the best of my memory***, autant qu'il m'en souvient.
men [MAN].
menace ['menəs], *n.* menace, *f.*—*v.t.* menacer.
menagerie [mə'nædʒəri], *n.* ménagerie, *f.*
mend [mend], *v.t.* raccommoder, réparer; corriger, améliorer; ***to mend one's ways***, rentrer dans le bon chemin.—*v.i.* s'améliorer, se corriger; se rétablir (*santé*); se remettre au beau (*temps*).
mendacious [men'deiʃəs], *a.* mensonger.
mendacity [men'dæsiti], *n.* mensonge, *m.*; duplicité, *f.*
mendicant ['mendikənt], *a.* and *n.* mendiant, *m.*
mendicity [men'disiti], *n.* mendicité, *f.*
mending ['mendiŋ], *n.* raccommodage; reprisage (*des bas*), *m.*; réparation, *f.*
menial ['miːniəl], *a.* de domestique; (*fig.*) servile.—*n.* domestique, *m.*, *f.*; (*fig.*) valet, laquais, *m.*
meningitis [menin'dʒaitis], *n.* méningite, *f.*
mental [mentl], *a.* mental; ***a mental case***, un aliéné.
mentality [men'tæliti], *n.* mentalité, *f.*; esprit, *m.*
mention ['menʃən], *n.* mention, indication, *f.*—*v.t.* dire, faire mention de, mentionner, parler de; citer; ***don't mention it!*** il n'y a pas de quoi! ***not to mention***, sans compter.
menu ['menju], *n.* menu, *m.*, carte, *f.*
mercantile ['məːkəntail], *a.* marchand, de commerce, commerçant; ***mercantile marine***, marine marchande, *f.*
mercenary ['məːsənri], *a.* mercenaire, vénal.—*n.* mercenaire, *m.*
merchandise ['məːtʃəndaiz], *n.* marchandise, *f.*
merchant ['məːtʃənt], *a.* marchand; commercial.—*n.* négociant, commerçant; marchand en gros, *m.*
merchantman ['məːtʃəntmən] (*pl.* **-men** [men]), **merchant-ship** ['məːtʃəntʃip], *n.* navire marchand, *m.*
merchant-service ['məːtʃənt'səːvis], *n.* marine marchande, *f.*
merciful ['məːsiful], *a.* miséricordieux.
merciless ['məːsilis], *a.* sans pitié, impitoyable.
mercurial [məː'kjuəriəl], *a.* de Mercure; de mercure; (*fig.*) mercuriel, vif.
mercury ['məːkjuəri], *n.* mercure, *m.*
mercy ['məːsi], *n.* miséricorde; pitié; grâce, indulgence (*pardon*), *f.*; ***for mercy's sake***, par grâce; ***recommendation to mercy***, recours en grâce, *m.*; ***sisters of mercy***, sœurs de charité, *f.pl.*
mere (1) [miə], *n.* lac, étang, *m.*
mere (2) [miə], *a.* pur, simple, seul, rien que.
merely ['miəli], *adv.* simplement, seulement, rien que.
meretricious [meri'triʃəs], *a.* d'un éclat factice (*style*).
merge [məːdʒ], *v.t.* fondre, amalgamer, absorber.—*v.i.* se perdre (*dans*).
merger ['məːdʒə], *n.* fusion, *f.*
meridian [mə'ridiən], *a.* méridien; de midi.—*n.* méridien; (*fig.*) apogée, *m.*
merino [mə'riːnou], *n.* mérinos, *m.*
merit ['merit], *n.* mérite, *m.*—*v.t.* mériter.
meritorious [meri'tɔːriəs], *a.* méritoire (*choses*); méritant (*personnes*).
meritoriously [meri'tɔːriəsli], *adv.* d'une manière méritoire.
mermaid ['məːmeid], *n.* sirène, *f.*
merrily ['merili], *adv.* joyeusement, gaiement.
merriment ['merimənt], *n.* gaieté, réjouissance, *f.*
merry ['meri], *a.* joyeux, gai, plaisant; un peu gris; ***to make merry***, se réjouir, se divertir.
merry-go-round ['merigouraund], *n.* chevaux de bois, *m.pl.*; manège, *m.*
merry-making ['merimeikiŋ], *n.* réjouissance, fête, *f.*, divertissement, *m.*
mesh [meʃ], *n.* maille, *f.*; engrenage, *m.*
mesmerism ['mezmərizm], *n.* mesmérisme, magnétisme animal, *m.*
mesmerize ['mezməraiz], *v.t.* magnétiser; hypnotiser.
mess (1) [mes], *n.* gâchis, *m.*; saleté, *f.*; ***to be in a fine mess***, être dans de beaux draps; ***what a mess!*** quel gâchis!—*v.t.* salir.—*v.i.* faire du gâchis.
mess (2) [mes], *n.* mets, plat; (*Mil.*) mess, *m.*; ***mess tin***, gamelle (individuelle), *f.*—*v.t.* donner à manger à.—*v.i.* manger; manger ensemble.
message ['mesidʒ], *n.* message, *m.*, commission, *f.*
messenger ['mesəndʒə], *n.* messager; commissionnaire; coursier (*dans un bureau*); (*fig.*) avant-coureur, *m.*
Messiah [mə'saiə], *n.* Messie, *m.*
messmate ['mesmeit], *n.* camarade de table, *m.*
messy ['mesi], *a.* sale; graisseux, salissant.
metabolism [mə'tæbolizm], *n.* métabolisme, *m.*
metal [metl], *n.* métal; cailloutis, empierrement (*pour routes*); (*Rail.*) rail, *m.*
metalled [metld], *a.* empierré.
metallic [mə'tælik], *a.* métallique.
metallurgy [me'tælədʒi], *n.* métallurgie, *f.*
metamorphosis [metə'mɔːfəsis], *n.* métamorphose, *f.*
metaphor ['metəfə], *n.* métaphore, *f.*
metaphysical [metə'fizikl], *a.* métaphysique.

metaphysics [metə'fiziks], *n.pl.* métaphysique, *f.*
mete [mi:t], *v.t.* mesurer; ***to mete out***, distribuer, décerner (*prix*); assigner (*punitions*).
meteor ['mi:tiə], *n.* météore, *m.*
meteoric [mi:ti'ɔrik], *a.* météorique.
meteorite ['mi:tiərait], *n.* météorite, *m.* ou *f.*
meteorological [mi:tiərə'lɔdʒikl], *a.* météorologique.
meteorologist [mi:tiə'rɔlədʒist], *n.* météorologiste, *m., f.*
meteorology [mi:tiə'rɔlədʒi], *n.* météorologie, *f.*
meter ['mi:tə], *n.* mesureur; compteur (*de gaz*), *m.*
method ['meθəd], *n.* méthode, *f.*; procédé, *m.*; modalité; (*fig.*) manière, *f.*, ordre, *m.*
methodical [mə'θɔdikəl], *a.* méthodique.
methylate ['meθileit], *v.t.* méthyler; ***methylated spirit***, alcool à brûler, *m.*
meticulous [mə'tikjuləs], *a.* méticuleux.
meticulousness [mə'tikjuləsnis], *n.* méticulosité, *f.*
metre ['mi:tə], *n.* mètre; (*Pros.*) vers, *m.*, mesure, *f.*
metric ['metrik], *a.* métrique.
metrical ['metrikl], *a.* métrique; en vers.
metropolis [mə'trɔpəlis], *n.* capitale, métropole, *f.*
metropolitan [metrə'pɔlitən], *a.* de la capitale, métropolitain.
mettle [metl], *n.* courage, cœur, *m.*; fougue, ardeur, vivacité, *f.*; caractère, *m.*; ***to put someone on his mettle***, piquer quelqu'un d'honneur.
mettled [metld], **mettlesome** ['metlsəm], *a.* fougueux, ardent, vif.
mew (1) [mju:], *n.* mue, cage, *f.*; (*pl.*) écuries, *f.pl.*; impasse, ruelle (*derrière les grandes maisons de ville*), *f.*—*v.t.* enfermer (*emprisonner*).—*v.i.* changer.
mew (2) [mju:], *v.i.* miauler (*chat*).
mew (3) [mju:], *n.* (*Orn.*) mouette, *f.*
mewing ['mju:iŋ], *n.* miaulement (*de chat*), *m.*
Mexican ['meksikn], *a.* mexicain.—*n.* Mexicain (*personne*), *m.*
Mexico ['meksikou]. le Mexique (*pays*); ***Mexico City***, Mexico, *m.*
miasma [mi'æzmə], *n.* (*pl.* **miasmata** [mi'æzmətə]) miasme, *m.*
mica ['maikə], *n.* mica, *m.*
mice [MOUSE].
Michael [maikl]. Michel, *m.*
Michaelmas ['miklməs]. la Saint-Michel, *f.*
microbe ['maikroub], *n.* microbe, *m.*
microphone ['maikrəfoun], *n.* microphone, *m.*
microscope ['maikrəskoup], *n.* microscope, *m.*
microscopic [maikrə'skɔpik], *a.* microscopique.
mid [mid], *a.* du milieu, moyen.—*prep.* au milieu de.
mid-air [mid'ɛə], *n.* milieu de l'air, haut des airs, *m.*; ***in mid-air***, entre ciel et terre.
midday ['middei], *a.* de midi.—*n.* midi, *m.*
middle [midl], *a.* du milieu, central; moyen; ***Middle Ages***, Moyen Âge, *m.*; ***middle class***, bourgeoisie, *f.*; ***middle course***, moyen terme, *m.*—*n.* milieu, centre, *m.*; ceinture, *f.*
middle-aged ['midleidʒd], *a.* entre deux âges.
middle-man ['midlmæn], *n.* (*pl.* **-men** [men]) intermédiaire, tiers, *m.*
middling ['midliŋ], *a.* médiocre, passable, assez bien (*santé*); (*Comm.*) bon, ordinaire.
midget ['midʒit], *n.* nain, nabot, *m.*
midland ['midlənd], *a.* de l'intérieur, du centre.
Mid-Lent ['mid'lent], mi-carême, *f.*
midnight ['midnait], *a.* de minuit.—*n.* minuit, *m.*
midriff ['midrif], *n.* diaphragme, *m.*
midshipman ['midʃipmən], *n.* (*pl.* **-men** [men]) aspirant de marine, *m.*
midships ['midʃips], [AMIDSHIPS].
midst [midst], *n.* milieu; (*fig.*) fort, sein, cœur, *m.*—*prep.* au milieu de, parmi.
midstream ['midstri:m], *n.* milieu du courant; milieu du fleuve, *m.*
midsummer ['midsʌmə], *n.* milieu de l'été, cœur de l'été, *m.*; ***Midsummer Day***, la Saint-Jean, *f.*
midway ['midwei], *a.* and *adv.* à mi-chemin; à mi-côte (*d'une colline*).
midwife ['midwaif], *n.* (*pl.* **midwives** ['midwaivz]) sage-femme, accoucheuse, *f.*
midwifery ['midwifri], *n.* obstétrique, *f.*
midwinter ['midwintə], *n.* fort de l'hiver, *m.*
mien [mi:n], *n.* mine, *f.*, air, *m.*
might (1) [mait], *past* [MAY].
might (2) [mait], *n.* force, puissance, *f.*
mightily ['maitili], *adv.* fortement, vigoureusement; extrêmement.
mighty ['maiti], *a.* fort, puissant; grand, important.—*adv.* fort, très, extrêmement.
mignonette [minjə'net], *n.* réséda, *m.*
migraine ['mi:grein], *n.* (*Med.*) migraine, *f.*
migrate [mai'greit], *v.i.* émigrer.
migration [mai'greiʃən], *n.* migration, *f.*
migratory ['maigrətəri], *a.* migratoire; migrateur.
milch [miltʃ], *a.* à lait, laitière.
mild [maild], *a.* doux; léger (*boisson, tabac etc.*); bénin.
mildew ['mildju:], *n.* rouille, moisissure, *f.*, taches d'humidité, *f.pl.*—*v.t.* gâter par l'humidité; souiller, tacher.
mildly ['maildli], *adv.* doucement, avec douceur; modérément.
mildness ['maildnis], *n.* douceur, *f.*
mile [mail], *n.* mille, *m.*
mileage ['mailidʒ], *n.* distance en milles, *f.*; prix par mille, *m.*
milestone ['mailstoun], *n.* borne milliaire, borne kilométrique, *f.*
militant ['militənt], *a.* militant.—*n.* activiste, *m., f.*
militarism ['militərizm], *n.* militarisme, *m.*
military ['militəri], *a.* militaire.—*n.* ***the military***, les militaires, *m.pl.*, la troupe, *f.*
militate ['militeit], *v.i.* militer (*contre*).
militia [mi'liʃə], *n.* milice, *f.*
milk [milk], *n.* lait, *m.*; ***milk and water***, lait coupé; (*fig.*) fade, insipide, sans caractère; ***skim milk***, lait écrémé; ***to come home with the milk***, rentrer à la première heure.—*v.t.* traire.
milk-can ['milkkæn], *n.* pot au lait, *m.*
milkiness ['milkinis], *n.* nature laiteuse; (*fig.*) douceur, *f.*
milkmaid ['milkmeid], *n.* laitière, *f.*

milkman ['milkmən], *n.* (*pl.* **-men** [men]) laitier, *m.*
milk-pail ['milkpeil], *n.* seau à lait, *m.*
milksop ['milksɔp], *n.* (*colloq.*) poule mouillée, *f.*
milky ['milki], *a.* laiteux; ***Milky Way***, voie lactée, *f.*
mill [mil], *n.* moulin, *m.*; filature, fabrique (*usine*), *f.*—*v.t.* moudre; (*Coin.*) estamper.—*v.i.* fourmiller (*foule*).
millenary ['milənəri], *a.* millénaire.
millennium [mi'leniəm], *n.* millénaire, *m.*, mille ans; les temps messianiques, *m.pl.*
miller ['milə], *n.* meunier, *m.*
millet ['milit], *n.* millet, mil, *m.*
millimetre ['milimi:tə], *n.* millimètre, *m.*
milliner ['milinə], *n.* marchande de modes; modiste, *f.*
millinery ['milinri], *n.* modes, *f.pl.*
million ['miljən], *n.* million, *m.*
millionaire [miljə'nɛə], *n.* millionnaire, *m.*, *f.*
millstone ['milstoun], *n.* meule de moulin, *f.*
mime [maim], *n.* mime, *m.*—*v.t.* mimer (*une scène*).—*v.i.* jouer par gestes.
mimic ['mimik], *a.* imitateur, mimique; imitatif (*animaux*).—*n.* mime, imitateur, *m.*—*v.t.* contrefaire, imiter.
mimicry ['mimikri], *n.* mimique, imitation, *f.*
minatory ['minətəri], *a.* menaçant.
mince [mins], *v.t.* hacher menu.—*v.i.* marcher à petits pas; minauder (*parler d'une façon affectée*).—*n.* hachis, haché, *m.*
mincemeat ['minsmi:t], *n.* hachis, *m.*; pâte d'épices, *f.*, mincemeat, *m.*
mince-pie ['mins'pai], *n.* tartelette au mincemeat, *f.*
mincing ['minsiŋ], *a.* affecté, minaudier.
mind [maind], *n.* esprit, *m.*, intelligence; envie, *f.*, désir (*inclination*), *m.*; pensée, *f.*, avis (*opinion*); souvenir (*mémoire*), *m.*—*v.t.* songer à, faire attention à; regarder à (*s'occuper de*); se défier de (*se douter de*); obéir à, écouter (*se soumettre à*); soigner, garder (*veiller sur*); surveiller, observer (*étudier*); ***mind your own business***, mêlez-vous de ce qui vous regarde; ***never mind***, peu importe, tant pis.
minded ['maindid], *a.* disposé, enclin.
mindful ['maindful], *a.* attentif (*à*), soigneux (*de*); qui se souvient (*de*).
mindfulness ['maindfulnis], *n.* attention, *f.*
mindless ['maindlis], *a.* inattentif (*à*); sans esprit.
mine (1) [main], *pron.poss.* le mien, *m.*, la mienne, *f.*; les miens, *m.pl.*, les miennes, *f.pl.*—*a.* à moi; ***a friend of mine***, un de mes amis.
mine (2) [main], *n.* mine, *f.*—*v.t.* miner, saper.
mine-layer ['mainleiə], *n.* (*Navy*) mouilleur de mines, *m.*
miner ['mainə], *n.* mineur, *m.*
mineral ['minərəl], *a.* and *n.* minéral, *m.*
mineralogy [minə'rælədʒi], *n.* minéralogie, *f.*
mine-sweeper ['mainswi:pə], *n.* (*Navy*) dragueur de mines, *m.*
mingle [miŋgl], *v.t.* mélanger, mêler.—*v.i.* se mêler, se mélanger (*avec*, *dans* ou *en*).
mingling ['miŋgliŋ], *n.* mélange, *m.*
miniature ['mini(ə)tʃə], *a.* en miniature.—*n.* miniature, *f.*
minim ['minim], *n.* goutte; (*Mus.*) blanche, *f.*
minimum ['minimәm], *n.* (*pl.* **minima** ['minimə]) minimum, *m.*
mining ['mainiŋ], *a.* des mines; de mineur, minier.—*n.* travail dans les mines, *m.*
minion ['minjən], *n.* favori, *m.*, favorite, *f.*
minister ['ministə], *n.* ministre; (*Eccles.*) pasteur, *m.*—*v.t.* administrer; fournir.—*v.i.* servir (*à*); (*Eccles.*) officier à.
ministerial [minis'tiəriəl], *a.* de ministère, ministériel.
ministration [minis'treiʃən], *n.* ministère; service, *m.*
ministry ['ministri], *n.* ministère, département, *m.*
mink [miŋk], *n.* vison, *m.*
minnow ['minou], *n.* vairon, *m.*
minor ['mainə], *a.* moindre; secondaire; (*Mus.*, *Geog. etc.*) mineur.—*n.* mineur, *m.*
Minorca [mi'nɔ:kə]. Minorque, *f.*
minority [mai'nɔriti], *n.* minorité, *f.*
minster ['minstə], *n.* cathédrale, église abbatiale, *f.*
minstrel ['minstrəl], *n.* ménestrel; (*fam.*) poète, musicien, chanteur, *m.*
mint (1) [mint], *n.* menthe, *f.*; ***peppermint***, menthe poivrée.
mint (2) [mint], *n.* ***The Mint***, la Monnaie, *f.*—*v.t.* monnayer, frapper; (*fig.*) forger.
mintage ['mintidʒ], *n.* objet monnayé, *m.*
minting ['mintiŋ], *n.* monnayage, *m.*
minuet [minju'et], *n.* menuet, *m.*
minus ['mainəs], *prep.* moins; sans (*n'ayant pas de*).—*n.* moins, *m.*
minute (1) [mai'nju:t], *a.* menu, minuscule, très petit; minutieux.
minute (2) ['minit], *n.* minute, *f.*; instant; moment, *m.*; note, *f.*; (*pl.*) procès-verbal, compte-rendu (*d'une réunion*), *m.*—*v.t.* minuter, prendre note de.
minute-book ['minitbuk], *n.* journal, *m.*
minute-hand ['minithænd], *n.* grande aiguille, *f.*
minutely [mai'nju:tli], *adv.* minutieusement; exactement; en détail.
minuteness [mai'nju:tnis], *n.* petitesse; exactitude, *f.*; détails minutieux, *m.pl.*
minx [miŋks], *n.* coquine, friponne, *f.*
miracle ['mirəkl], *n.* miracle, *m.*
miraculous [mi'rækjuləs], *a.* miraculeux.
mirage [mi'rɑ:ʒ], *n.* mirage, *m.*
mire ['maiə], *n.* boue, bourbe, fange, vase, *f.*
miry ['maiəri], *a.* fangeux, bourbeux.
mirror ['mirə], *n.* miroir, *m.*, glace, *f.*; ***driving-mirror***, rétroviseur, *m.*—*v.t.* refléter.
mirth [mə:θ], *n.* gaieté, hilarité, *f.*, rire, *m.*
mirthful ['mə:θful], *a.* gai, joyeux.
misadventure [misəd'ventʃə], *n.* mésaventure, *f.*, contretemps, *m.*
misanthropist [mi'sænθrəpist], *n.* misanthrope, *m.*, *f.*
misanthropy [mi'sænθrəpi], *n.* misanthropie, *f.*
misapplication [misæpli'keiʃən], *n.* mauvaise application, *f.*
misapply [misə'plai], *v.t.* mal appliquer, détourner (*fonds etc.*).
misapprehend [misæpri'hend], *v.t.* comprendre mal.
misapprehension [misæpri'henʃən], *n.* malentendu, *m.*, méprise, *f.*

misappropriate [misə'prouprieit], *v.t.* détourner.
misappropriation [misəproupri'eiʃən], *n.* détournement, mauvais emploi, *m.*
misbehave [misbi'heiv], *v.i.* se conduire mal.
misbehaviour [misbi'heivjə], *n.* mauvaise conduite, *f.*
miscalculate [mis'kælkjuleit], *v.t.* calculer mal.
miscalculation [miskælkju'leiʃən], *n.* calcul erroné; mécompte, *m.*
miscarriage [mis'kæridʒ], *n.* insuccès, coup manqué, *m.*; fausse couche (*de femme*), *f.*
miscarry [mis'kæri], *v.i.* manquer, échouer; faire une fausse couche (*femme*).
miscellaneous [misi'leinjəs], *a.* varié, divers; général; ***miscellaneous news***, faits divers, *m.pl.*
miscellany [mi'seləni], *n.* (*pl.* **miscellanies** [mi'seləniz]) mélange, *m.*; mélanges (*livre*), *m.pl.*
mischance [mis'tʃɑ:ns], *n.* malheur, accident, *m.*, mésaventure, infortune, *f.*
mischief ['mistʃif], *n.* mal, dommage, dégât, tort, *m.*
mischief-maker ['mistʃifmeikə], *n.* brouillon, *m.*
mischievous ['mistʃivəs], *a.* méchant, malicieux; malfaisant, mauvais, nuisible (*chose*); espiègle (*enfant*).
mischievously ['mistʃivəsli], *adv.* méchamment.
mischievousness ['mistʃivəsnis], *n.* méchanceté; espièglerie (*d'enfant*), *f.*
misconceive [miskən'si:v], *v.t.*, *v.i.* mal concevoir, jugcr mal.
misconception [miskən'sepʃən], *n.* malentendu, *m.*
misconduct [mis'kɔndʌkt], *n.* mauvaise conduite, *f.*—[miskən'dʌkt], *v.t.* conduire mal; ***to misconduct oneself***, se conduire mal.
misconstruction [miskən'strʌkʃən], *n.* fausse interprétation, *f.*, contresens, *m.*
misconstrue [miskən'stru:], *v.t.* mal interpréter.
miscount [mis'kaunt], *v.t.* compter mal.—*v.i.* faire une erreur de compte.—*n.* mécompte, *m.*
miscreant ['miskriənt], *n.* mécréant, *m*; (*fig.*) misérable, *m.*, *f.*
misdeal [mis'di:l], *v.t.* maldonner.—*n.* maldonne, *f.*
misdeed [mis'di:d], *n.* méfait, *m.*
misdemean [misdə'mi:n], *v.r.* ***to misdemean oneself***, se comporter mal.
misdemeanour [misdə'mi:nə], *n.* délit, crime, *m.*, offense, *f.*
misdirect [misdi'rekt], *v.t.* mal diriger, renseigner mal; mettre une fausse adresse à (*lettre*).
misdoing [mis'du:iŋ], *n.* méfait, *m.*
miser ['maizə], *n.* avare, *m.*, *f.*
miserable ['mizərəbl], *a.* misérable, pitoyable, malheureux; mesquin (*piètre*).
miserliness ['maizəlinis], *n.* avarice, *f.*
miserly ['maizəli], *a.* d'avare, avare, sordide.
misery ['mizəri], *n.* misère, *f.*; (*fig.*) tourment; supplice, *m.*; ***to put out of misery***, mettre fin aux souffrances (*de*).
misfire [mis'faiə], *v.i.* rater; (*Motor.*) avoir des ratés.—*n.* raté d'allumage, *m.*
misfit ['misfit], *n.* vêtement manqué; inadapté (*personne*), *m.*
misfortune [mis'fɔ:tʃən], *n.* malheur, *m.*, infortune, *f.*
misgiving [mis'giviŋ], *n.* pressentiment, soupçon, doute, *m.*; inquiétude, *f.*
misgovern [mis'gʌvən], *v.t.* gouverner mal.
misgovernment [mis'gʌvənmənt], *n.* mauvais gouvernement, *m.*
misguided [mis'gaidid], *a.* malencontreux; peu judicieux; dévoyé.
mishandle [mis'hændl], *v.t.* manier mal, malmener.
mishap [mis'hæp], *n.* contretemps, malheur, *m.*, mésaventure, *f.*
misinform [misin'fɔ:m], *v.t.* mal renseigner.
misinterpret [misin'tə:prit], *v.t.* interpréter mal.
misjudge [mis'dʒʌdʒ], *v.t.* juger mal, méjuger.
mislay [mis'lei], *v.t. irr.* (*conjug. like* LAY) égarer.
mislead [mis'li:d], *v.t. irr.* (*conjug. like* LEAD) égarer; induire en erreur, fourvoyer; tromper.
misleading [mis'li:diŋ], *a.* trompeur.
mismanage [mis'mænidʒ], *v.t.* diriger mal. —*v.i.* s'y prendre mal, s'arranger mal (*pour*).
mismanagement [mis'mænidʒmənt], *n.* mauvaise administration, *f.*
misnomer [mis'noumə], *n.* faux nom, *m.*
misogynist [mi'sɔdʒinist], *n.* misogyne, *m.*
misogyny [mi'sɔdʒini], *n.* misogynie, *f.*
misplace [mis'pleis], *v.t.* mal placer; déplacer.
misprint ['misprint], *n.* faute d'impression, *f.* —[mis'print], *v.t.* imprimer incorrectement.
mispronounce [misprə'nauns], *v.t.* prononcer mal.
mispronunciation [misprənʌnsi'eiʃən], *n.* prononciation incorrecte, *f.*
misquote [mis'kwout], *v.t.* citer à faux.
misread [mis'ri:d], *v.t. irr.* (*conjug. like* READ) mal lire, mal interpréter.
misrepresent [misrepri'zent], *v.t.* représenter mal, dénaturer.
misrepresentation [misreprizen'teiʃən], *n.* faux rapport, *m.*
misrule [mis'ru:l], *n.* désordre; mauvais gouvernement, *m.*
miss (1) [mis], *n.* mademoiselle, demoiselle, *f.*
miss (2) [mis], *n.* manque, *m.*; perte (*privation*); erreur (*méprise*), *f.*; coup manqué, *m.* —*v.t.* manquer; omettre; s'apercevoir de l'absence de, regretter vivement, ne plus trouver; ***I miss my friend very much***, mon ami me manque beaucoup.—*v.i.* manquer; ne pas réussir, échouer, se tromper; ***to be missing***, être absent, manquer.
missal [misl], *n.* missel, *m.*
misshapen [mis'ʃeipən], *a.* difforme.
missile ['misail], *a.* de jet, de trait.—*n.* projectile, *m.*; ***guided missile***, engin téléguidé, *m.*
missing ['misiŋ], *a.* absent, perdu, disparu.
mission ['miʃən], *n.* mission, *f.*
missionary ['miʃənəri], *a.* des missions.—*n.* missionnaire, *m.*, *f.*
missive ['misiv], *a.* missive.—*n.* missive, lettre, *f.*
misspell [mis'spel], *v.t. irr.* (*conjug. like* SPELL) épeler mal.

misspelling [mis'speliŋ], *n.* faute d'orthographe, *f.*
misspend [mis'spend], *v.t. irr.* (*conjug. like* SPEND) employer mal; gaspiller.
misstate [mis'steit], *v.t.* rapporter incorrectement.
misstatement [mis'steitmənt], *n.* rapport erroné, *m.*
mist [mist], *n.* brume; buée (*sur une glace*), *f.*; ***Scotch mist***, bruine, *f.*—*v.t.* couvrir (*une glace*) de buée.—*v.i.* se couvrir de buée.
mistake [mis'teik], *v.t. irr.* (*conjug. like* TAKE) se tromper de *ou* sur, se méprendre à *ou* sur; prendre (*pour*).—*v.i.* se tromper, se méprendre, s'abuser.—*n.* erreur, méprise, faute; bévue (*erreur grossière*), *f.*; ***to make a mistake***, se tromper.
mistaken [mis'teikən] *a.* qui se trompe; faux, erroné (*chose*).
mistimed [mis'taimd], *a.* inopportun.
mistletoe ['misltou], *n.* gui, *m.*
mistress ['mistris], *n.* maîtresse; patronne; institutrice (*d'école primaire*), *f.*; ***headmistress***, directrice, *f.*
mistrust [mis'trʌst], *n.* méfiance, *f.*, soupçon, *m.*—*v.t.* se méfier de, soupçonner.
mistrustful [mis'trʌstful], *a.* méfiant.
misty ['misti], *a.* brumeux; vaporeux (*lumière*); (*fig.*) confus.
misunderstand [misʌndə'stænd], *v.t. irr.* (*conjug. like* STAND) mal comprendre, entendre mal, se méprendre sur.
misunderstanding [misʌndə'stændiŋ], *n.* malentendu (*manque de compréhension*), *m.*; mésintelligence (*querelle*), *f.*
misuse [mis'ju:s], *n.* abus, *m.*—[mis'ju:z], *v.t.* mésuser de; maltraiter (*faire du mal à*).
mite (1) [mait], *n.* (*Zool.*) mite, *f.*
mite (2) [mait], *n.* denier (*argent*); (*fig.*) rien, *m.*, obole, *f.*; (*fam.*) petit gosse, *m.*
mitigate ['mitigeit], *v.t.* mitiger, adoucir, modérer.
mitigating ['mitigeitiŋ], *a.* adoucissant, atténuant.
mitigation [miti'geiʃən], *n.* mitigation, *f.*, adoucissement, *m.*
mitre ['maitə], *n.* mitre, *f.*
mitten [mitn], *n.* mitaine, *f.*
mix [miks], *v.t.* mêler, mélanger; couper (*boissons*); ***to mix up***, mêler, embrouiller, confondre.—*v.i.* se mélanger, se mêler (*de*); s'associer (*à*).
mixed [mikst], *a.* mélangé, mêlé (*de*); mixte.
mixture ['mikstʃə], *n.* mélange, *m.*; (*Pharm.*) potion, mixture, *f.*
mix-up ['miksʌp], *n.* confusion, *f.*, embrouillement, *m.*; (*pop.*) pagaïe, *f.*
mizzen [mizn], *n.* artimon, *m.*
mizzen-mast ['miznmɑ:st], *n.* mât d'artimon, *m.*
moan [moun], *n.* gémissement, *m.*, plainte; (*fig.*) lamentation, *f.*—*v.t.* gémir de *ou* sur; se lamenter sur.—*v.i.* gémir; (*fig.*) se lamenter; (*pop.*) grognonner.
moat [mout], *n.* fossé, *m.*, douve, *f.*
mob [mɔb], *n.* foule; populace, canaille, *f.*—*v.t.* houspiller, malmener; assiéger.
mobile ['moubail], *a* mobile.
mobility [mou'biliti], *n.* mobilité; légèreté (*inconstance*), *f.*
mobilization [moubilai'zeiʃən], *n.* mobilisation, *f.*
mobilize ['moubilaiz], *v.t.* mobiliser.
mock [mɔk], *v.t.* se moquer de; narguer.—*v.i.* railler.—*a.* dérisoire; faux, simulé (*false*).
mocker ['mɔkə], *n.* moqueur, *m.*
mockery ['mɔkəri], *n.* moquerie, *f.*
mocking-bird ['mɔkiŋbə:d], *n.* oiseau moqueur, *m.*
mode [moud], *n.* mode, façon, manière, *f.*
model [mɔdl], *n.* modèle; mannequin, *m.*—*v.t.* modeler; (*Cloth.*) présenter des vêtements (*défilé de mannequins*).
moderate ['mɔdərit], *a.* modéré; modique ordinaire, passable, médiocre.—['mɔdəreit] *v.t.* modérer, adoucir, tempérer.—*v.i.* se modérer.
moderately ['mɔdəritli], *adv.* modérément passablement.
moderation [mɔdə'reiʃən], *n.* modération, *f*
moderator ['mɔdəreitə], *n.* modérateur, *m.*
modern ['mɔdən], *a.* and *n.* moderne, *m., f.*; ***modern languages***, langues vivantes, *f.pl.*
modernize ['mɔdənaiz], *v.t.* moderniser.
modest ['mɔdist], *a.* modeste; pudique; modéré (*demandes etc.*).
modesty ['mɔdisti], *n.* modestie, *f.*
modicum ['mɔdikəm], *n.* petite portion, *f.*
modification [mɔdifi'keiʃən], *n.* modification, *f.*
modify ['mɔdifai], *v.t.* modifier.
modulate ['mɔdjuleit], *v.t.* moduler.
modulation [mɔdju'leiʃən], *n.* modulation, *f.*
Mohair ['mouhɛə], *n.* poil de chèvre angora, mohair, *m.*
Mohammed [mo'hæməd]. Mahomet, *m.*
Mohammedan [mo'hæmədən], *a.* mahométan.—*n.* Mahométan, *m.*
mohammedanism [mo'hæmədənizm], *n.* mahométisme, *m.*
moist [mɔist], *a.* moite, humide.
moisten [mɔisn], *v.t.* humecter; mouiller.
moisture ['mɔistʃə], **moistness** ['mɔistnis], *n.* moiteur, humidité, *f.*
molasses [mo'læsiz], *n.pl.* mélasse, *f.*
mole (1) [moul], *n.* taupe (*animal*), *f.*
mole (2) [moul], *n.* tache, *f.*, grain de beauté (*sur la peau*), *m.*
mole (3) [moul], *n.* môle (*jetée*), *m.*
molecular [mo'lekjulə], *a.* moléculaire.
molecule ['mɔlikju:l], *n.* molécule *f.*
mole-hill ['moulhil], *n.* taupinière, *f.*
moleskin ['moulskin], *n.* peau de taupe, molesquine, *f.*, velours de coton, *m.*
molest [mo'lest], *v.t.* molester; vexer.
mollify ['mɔlifai], *v.t.* amollir; adoucir.
molten ['moultən], *a.* fondu.
moment ['moumənt], *n.* moment, instant, *m.*; (*fig.*) importance, *f.*; ***at the present moment***, actuellement; ***at this moment***, en ce moment; ***not for a moment***, pour rien au monde; ***of no moment***, d'aucune importance; ***the moment that***, dès que, aussitôt que.
momentarily ['mouməntərili], *adv.* momentanément.
momentary ['mouməntəri], *a.* momentané.
momentous [mo'mentəs], *a.* important, d'une importance capitale.
momentum [mo'mentəm], *n.* (*Phys.*) force vive; vitesse acquise, *f.*; élan, *m.*
monarch ['mɔnək], *n.* monarque, *m.*

monarchy ['mɔnəki], *n.* monarchie, *f.*
monastery ['mɔnəstri], *n.* monastère, *m.*
monastic [mə'næstik], *a.* monastique.
monasticism [mə'næstisizm], *n.* monachisme, *m.*
Monday ['mʌndi], lundi, *m.*
monetary ['mʌnətəri], *a.* monétaire.
money ['mʌni], *n.* argent, *m.*; monnaie, *f.*, espèces (*pièces*), *f.pl.*; ***made of money***, cousu d'or; ***ready money***, argent comptant; ***to make money***, gagner de l'argent.
money-box ['mʌnibɔks], *n.* tirelire, *f.*
money-changer ['mʌnitʃeindʒə], *n.* changeur, *m.*
moneyed ['mʌnid], *a.* riche.
money-grubber ['mʌnigrʌbə], *n.* grippe-sou, *m.*
money-lender ['mʌnilendə], *n.* prêteur d'argent, *m.*
money-market ['mʌnimɑ:kit], *n.* bourse, *f.*
money-order ['mʌniɔ:də], *n.* mandat, *m.*
Mongol ['mɔŋgəl], *a.* mongol.—*n.* Mongol (*personne*), *m.*
Mongolia [mɔŋ'gouliə]. la Mongolie, *f.*
Mongolian [mɔŋ'gouliən], *a.* mongol.—*n.* mongol (*langue*); Mongol (*personne*), *m.*
mongrel ['mʌŋgrəl], *a.* métis.—*n.* métis, *m.* métisse, *f.*
monitor ['mɔnitə], *n.* moniteur, *m.*
monk [mʌŋk], *n.* moine, *m.*
monkey ['mʌŋki], *n.* singe, *m.*; guenon, *f.*
monkey-wrench ['mʌŋkirentʃ], *n.* clé anglaise, *f.*
monocle ['mɔnəkl], *n.* monocle, *m.*
monogram ['mɔnəgræm], *n.* monogramme, *m.*
monologue ['mɔnəlɔg], *n.* monologue, *m.*
monoplane ['mɔnəplein], *n.* monoplan, *m.*
monopoly [mə'nɔpəli], *n.* monopole, accaparement, *m.*
monorail ['mɔnəreil], *n.* monorail, *m.*
monotonous [mə'nɔtənəs], *a.* monotone.
monotonously [mə'nɔtənəsli], *adv.* avec monotonie.
monotony [mə'nɔtəni], *n.* monotonie, *f.*
monsoon [mɔn'su:n], *n.* mousson, *f.*
monster ['mɔnstə], *n.* monstre, *m.*
monstrosity [mɔn'strɔsiti], *n.* monstruosité, *f.*
monstrous ['mɔnstrəs], *a.* monstrueux; prodigieux.
month [mʌnθ], *n.* mois, *m.*; ***calendar month***, mois civil; ***the day of the month***, le quantième du mois, *m.*
monthly ['mʌnθli], *a.* mensuel, de tous les mois.—*n.* (*fam.*) revue mensuelle, *f.*—*adv.* tous les mois, par mois.
monument ['mɔnjumənt], *n.* monument, *m.*
monumental [mɔnju'mentl], *a.* monumental.
moo [mu:], *v.i.* meugler, beugler.—*n.* meuglement, *m.*
mood [mu:d], *n.* humeur, *f.*; (*Gram. etc.*) mode, *m.*
moody ['mu:di], *a.* de mauvaise humeur, triste.
moon [mu:n], *n.* lune, *f.*; ***by the light of the moon***, au clair de la lune.—*v.i.* muser; ***to moon about***, flâner.
moonbeam ['mu:nbi:m], *n.* rayon de lune, *m.*
moonlight ['mu:nlait], *n.* clair de lune, *m.*
moonlit ['mu:nlit], *a.* éclairé par la lune.
moonshine ['mu:nʃain], *n.* clair de lune, *m.*; (*fig.*) chimères, *f.pl.*
moonstrike ['mu:nstraik], *n.* alunissage, *m.*
moonstruck ['mu:nstrʌk], *a.* lunatique.
Moor [muə], *n.* Maure, *m.*, *f.*
moor (1) [muə], *n.* lande, bruyère, *f.*; marais, *m.*
moor (2) [muə], *v.t.* amarrer.—*v.i.* s'amarrer.
moor-hen ['muəhen], *n.* poule d'eau, *f.*
moorings ['muəriŋz], *n.* amarres, *f.pl.*, mouillage, *m.*
moorland ['muələnd], *n.* lande, bruyère, *f.*, marais, *m.*
moose [mu:s], *n.* élan du Canada, *m.*
moot [mu:t], *v.t.* discuter, débattre, controverser.—*a.* ***moot point***, question discutable, *f.*
mop [mɔp], *n.* balai à laver, *m.*—*v.t.* nettoyer avec un balai, éponger; ***to mop one's face***, s'éponger la figure.
mope [moup], *v.i.* s'ennuyer; être hébété.
moping ['moupiŋ], *a.* triste, hébété.
moral ['mɔrəl], *a.* moral.—*n.* morale; moralité, *f.*; (*pl.*) mœurs, *f.pl.*
morale [mɔ'rɑ:l], *n.* moral (*de militaires etc.*), *m.*
morality [mə'ræliti], *n.* morale; moralité, *f.*
moralize ['mɔrəlaiz], *v.i.* moraliser.
morally ['mɔrəli], *adv.* moralement.
morass [mə'ræs], *n.* marais, *m.*, fondrière, *f.*
morbid ['mɔ:bid], *a.* maladif, malsain, morbide.
morbidly ['mɔ:bidli], *adv.* morbidement.
morbidity [mɔ:'biditi], **morbidness** ['mɔ:bidnis], *n.* état maladif, état morbide, *m.*
more [mɔ:], *a.* and *adv.* plus; plus de; plus nombreux; encore; davantage; ***more and more***, de plus en plus; ***more than***, plus que, plus de (*suivi d'un nombre*); ***no more***, pas davantage; ***no more of that!*** arrêtez cela! ***once more***, encore une fois; ***some more***, encore un peu, davantage.
moreover [mɔ:'rouvə], *adv.* de plus, d'ailleurs, en outre.
moribund ['mɔribʌnd], *a.* moribond.
Mormon ['mɔ:mən], *a.* mormon.—*n.* Mormon (*personne*), *m.*
morn [mɔ:n], *n.* (*poet.*) matin, *m.*, aurore, *f.*
morning ['mɔ:niŋ], *a.* du matin.—*n.* matin, *m.*, matinée, *f.*; ***good morning***, bonjour; ***in the morning***, le matin; ***the next morning***, le lendemain matin.
Moroccan [mə'rɔkən], *a.* marocain.—*n.* Marocain (*personne*), *m.*
Morocco [mə'rɔkou]. le Maroc, *m.*
morocco-leather [mə'rɔkou'leðə], *n.* maroquin, *m.*
moron ['mɔ:rɔn], *n.* crétin, idiot, *m.*
morose [mə'rous], *a.* morose.
morphia ['mɔ:fiə], **morphine** ['mɔ:fi:n], *n.* morphine, *f.*
morrow ['mɔrou], *n.* (*poet.*) demain, lendemain, *m.*; ***tomorrow***, demain.
morsel [mɔ:sl], *n.* morceau, *m.*
mortal [mɔ:tl], *a.* mortel, funeste (*fatal*); des mortels, humain (*terrestre*); à outrance, à mort (*combat*); ***any mortal thing***, n'importe quoi.—*n.* mortel, *m.*
mortality [mɔ:'tæliti], *n.* mortalité; humanité, *f.*
mortally ['mɔ:təli], *adv.* mortellement, à mort.
mortar ['mɔ:tə], *n.* mortier, *m.*

mortgage [ˈmɔːgidʒ], *n.* hypothèque, *f.*—*v.t.* hypothéquer.
mortician [mɔːˈtiʃən], *n.* (*Am.*) entrepreneur de pompes funèbres, *m.*
mortification [mɔːtifiˈkeiʃən], *n.* mortification; (*Path.*) gangrène, *f.*
mortify [ˈmɔːtifai], *v.t.* mortifier; (*Path.*) faire gangrener.—*v.i.* se gangrener.
mortise [ˈmɔːtis], *n.* mortaise, *f.*—*v.t.* mortaiser.
mortuary [ˈmɔːtjuəri], *a.* mortuaire.—*n.* morgue, *f.*, dépôt mortuaire, *m.*
mosaic [moˈzeiik], *a.* and *n.* mosaïque, *f.*
Moscow [ˈmɔskou]. Moscou, *m.*
Moses [ˈmouziz]. Moïse, *m.*
Moslem [ˈmʌzlim, ˈmɔzləm], *a.* musulman.—*n.* Musulman (*personne*), *m.*
mosque [mɔsk], *n.* mosquée, *f.*
mosquito [mɔsˈkiːtou], *n.* moustique, *m.*
mosquito-net [mɔsˈkiːtounet], *n.* moustiquaire, *f.*
moss [ˈmɔs], *n.* mousse, *f.*; marais, *m.*; ***peat-moss***, tourbière, *f.*
moss-grown [ˈmɔsgroun], **mossy** [ˈmɔsi], *a.* couvert de mousse, moussu.
moss-rose [ˈmɔsrouz], *n.* rose moussue, *f.*
most [moust], *a.* le plus; le plus grand; ***most men***, la plupart des hommes; ***the most part***, la plus grande partie.—*adv.* le plus, plus; très, fort; ***a most valuable book***, un livre des plus précieux; ***most likely***, très probablement.—*n.* la plupart, *f.*; le plus grand nombre, *m.*
mostly [ˈmoustli], *adv.* pour la plupart; le plus souvent; principalement.
mote [mout], *n.* grain de poussière, *m.*; paille (*dans l'œil*), *f.*
motel [ˈmoutel], *n.* motel, *m.*
motet [mouˈtet], *n.* (*Mus.*) motet, *m.*
moth [mɔθ], *n.* (*Ent.*) lépidoptère; papillon de nuit, *m.*; phalène; mite (*de vêtements*), *f.*
moth-eaten [ˈmɔθiːtn], *a.* mité.
mother [ˈmʌðə], *a.* mère; maternel; métropolitain (*église*); ***mother tongue***, langue maternelle, *f.*—*n.* mère; bonne mère, bonne femme (*terme familier*), *f.*; ***stepmother***, belle-mère, *f.*—*v.t.* servir de mère à; adopter; enfanter (*quelque chose*).
mother-country [ˈmʌðəkʌntri], *n.* mère patrie, *f.*
mother-in-law [ˈmʌðərinlɔː], *n.* belle-mère, *f.*
motherly [ˈmʌðəli], *a.* maternel, de mère.—*adv.* maternellement, en mère.
mother-of-pearl [mʌðərəvˈpəːl], *n.* nacre, *f.*
motion [ˈmouʃən], *n.* mouvement; signe (*signal*), *m.*; motion, proposition (*à une réunion*); (*Med.*) selle, *f.*—*v.t.* faire signe (*à*).
motionless [ˈmouʃənlis], *a.* immobile.
motivate [ˈmoutiveit], *v.t.* motiver (*une action*).
motive [ˈmoutiv], *a.* moteur, qui fait mouvoir; ***motive power***, force motrice, *f.*—*n.* motif, mobile, *m.*
motley [ˈmɔtli], *a.* bigarré, mélangé.
motor [ˈmoutə], *n.* moteur, *m.*—*v.i.* aller *ou* voyager en auto.
motor-boat [ˈmoutəbout], *n.* canot automobile, *m.*
motor-car [ˈmoutəkɑː], *n.* automobile, auto, voiture, *f.*
motor-cycle [ˈmoutəsaikl], *n.* motocyclette, *f.*
motoring [ˈmoutəriŋ], *n.* automobilisme, *m.*
motorist [ˈmoutərist], *n.* automobiliste, *m., f.*
motorway [ˈmoutəwei], *n.* autoroute, *f.*
mottle [mɔtl], *v.t.* madrer; marbrer.
motto [ˈmɔtou], *n.* (*pl.* **mottoes** [ˈmɔtouz]) devise, *f.*
mould (1) [mould], *n.* moisi (*mousse*); terreau (*humus*), *m.*—*v.i.* se moisir.
mould (2) [mould], *n.* moule, *m.*, forme, *f.*—*v.t.* mouler; (*fig.*) petrir.
moulder [ˈmouldə], *v.i.* se réduire en poudre *ou* en poussière.
mouldiness [ˈmouldinis], *n.* moisissure, *f.*
moulding [ˈmouldiŋ], *n.* moulure, *f.*
mouldy [ˈmouldi], *a.* moisi.
moult [moult], *v.i.* muer.
moulting [ˈmoultiŋ], *n.* mue, *f.*
mound [maund], *n.* butte, *f.*, tertre, *m.*; (*Fort.*) remparts, *m.pl.*
mount [maunt], *n.* mont, *m.*, montagne; monture (*cheval*); (*Turf*) monte, *f.*; (*Phot.*) carton, *m.*—*v.t.* monter, monter sur.—*v.i.* monter, s'élever; monter à cheval.
mountain [ˈmauntin], *a.* de montagne, des montagnes, montagnard, montagneux (*paysage*).—*n.* montagne, *f.*
mountaineer [mauntiˈniə], *n.* montagnard, *m.*; alpiniste, *m., f.*
mountaineering [mauntiˈniəriŋ], *n.* alpinisme, *m.*
mountainous [ˈmauntinəs], *a.* montagneux, de montagnes; (*fig.*) énorme.
mountebank [ˈmauntibæŋk], *n.* charlatan, *m.*
mounted [ˈmauntid], *a.* monté, à cheval; (*Phot.*) collé.
mounting [ˈmauntiŋ], *n.* montage, *m.*, monture, *f.*; (*Phot.*) collage, *m.*
mourn [mɔːn], *v.t.* pleurer, déplorer.—*v.i.* pleurer, se lamenter.
mourner [ˈmɔːnə], *n.* personne affligée, *f.*; pleureur (*professionnel*), *m.*, personne qui suit le convoi, *f.*
mournful [ˈmɔːnful], *a.* triste, lugubre.
mourning [ˈmɔːniŋ], *a.* affligé, triste; de deuil.—*n.* affliction, lamentation, *f.*; deuil (*vêtements*), *m.*
mouse [maus], *n.* (*pl.* **mice** [mais]) souris, *f.*; ***field-mouse***, mulot, *m.*
mouse-trap [ˈmaustræp], *n.* souricière, *f.*
moustache [məˈstɑːʃ], *n.* moustache, *f.*
mousy [ˈmausi], *a.* gris (*couleur*); timide.
mouth [mauθ], *n.* (*pl.* **mouths** [mauðz]) bouche; gueule (*de bête sauvage*); embouchure (*de rivière*); ouverture, entrée, *f.*, orifice (*donnant accès*); goulot (*d'une bouteille*), *m.*; ***by word of mouth***, de vive voix.—[mauð], *v.t., v.i.* crier.
mouthed [mauðd], *a.* ***foul-mouthed***, mal embouché; ***mealy-mouthed***, doucereux.
mouthful [ˈmauθful], *n.* bouchée; gorgée (*de vin*), *f.*
mouthpiece [ˈmauθpiːs], *n.* embouchure, *f.*; (*fig.*) interprète, porte-parole, *m.*
movable [ˈmuːvəbl], *a.* mobile.—*n.* meuble, *m.*
move [muːv], *v.t.* remuer; déplacer; mouvoir, faire mouvoir, mettre en mouvement, faire marcher, faire aller; transporter (*marchandises etc.*); (*fig.*) émouvoir, toucher; exciter, pousser (*à*); proposer (*que*); (*Chess*) jouer; ***to move forward***, avancer; ***to move out***, déloger, sortir.—*v.i.* bouger, se remuer, se

mouvoir, se déplacer; se mettre en mouvement, aller, partir, marcher, s'avancer; s'ébranler (*armée*); déménager (*changer de résidence*); (*Chess*) jouer; ***move on!*** circulez! ***to move aside***, s'écarter; ***to move away***, s'éloigner; ***to move back***, reculer, se reculer; ***to move in***, emménager; ***to move off***, s'éloigner, s'en aller; ***to move on***, avancer; ***to move out***, sortir, déménager.—*n.* mouvement; coup; (*Chess*) trait, *m.*; ***masterly move***, coup de maître; ***to be on the move***, être en mouvement, se remuer; ***to get a move on***, se presser; ***to make a move***, se préparer à partir.

movement ['mu:vmənt], *n.* mouvement, *m.*

mover ['mu:və], *n.* moteur; mobile, *m.*; force motrice, *f.*; auteur d'une proposition, *m.*

movie ['mu:vi], *n.* (*Am.*) film, *m.*; ***the movies***, le cinéma, *m.*

moving ['mu:viŋ], *a.* mouvant, mobile; (*fig.*) émouvant.—*n.* mouvement; déménagement (*de mobilier*); déplacement (*changement de place*), *m.*

movingly ['mu:viŋli], *adv.* d'une manière émouvante.

mow [mou], *v.t. irr.* faucher; tondre.

mower ['mouə], *n.* faucheur (*personne*), *m.*; faucheuse, tondeuse (*machine*), *f.*

Mr. ['mistə]. Monsieur (*abbr.* M.).

Mrs. ['misiz]. Madame (*abbr.* Mme.).

much [mʌtʃ], *adv.* beaucoup, bien, fort, très; ***as much***, autant; ***how much?*** combien (*de*)? ***much more***, bien plus; ***nothing much***, pas grand'chose; ***pretty much***, à peu près; ***so much***, tant; ***so much more***, d'autant plus; ***so much the better***, tant mieux; ***to make much of***, faire grand cas de; ***too much***, trop (*de*).

muck [mʌk], *n.* fumier (*engrais*), *m.*; fange (*boue*); (*fig.*) saleté, *f.*—*v.t.* fumer; salir.

muckiness ['mʌkinis], *n.* saleté, ordure, *f.*

mucky ['mʌki], *a.* sale, malpropre.

mucous ['mju:kəs], *a.* muqueux; ***mucous membrane***, muqueuse, *f.*

mucus ['mju:kəs], *n.* mucus, *m.*; mucosité, *f.*

mud [mʌd], *n.* boue, bourbe, vase, *f.*, limon, *m.*

mudguard ['mʌdgɑ:d], *n.* garde-boue, *m.*

muddle [mʌdl], *v.t.* brouiller; troubler; gâcher.—*v.i.* faire du gâchis.—*n.* confusion, *f.*, désordre, gâchis, *m.*

muddled [mʌdld], *a.* troublé; hébété.

muddler ['mʌdlə], *n.* brouillon, *m.*

muddy ['mʌdi], *a.* boueux, bourbeux; crotté.

muff [mʌf], *n.* manchon, *m.*

muffle [mʌfl], *v.t.* emmitoufler, affubler; assourdir (*cloche*); voiler (*tambour*).—*n.* moufle, *f.*

muffler ['mʌflə], *n.* cache-nez, *m.*

mug [mʌg], *n.* pot, *m.*, tasse; (*slang*) gueule, binette, *f.*; (*colloq.*) imbécile, *m.*, *f.*

muggy ['mʌgi], *a.* humide, lourd.

mulberry ['mʌlbəri], *n.* mûre, *f.*; ***mulberry-tree***, mûrier, *m.*

mulch [mʌltʃ], *n.* paillis, *m.*—*v.t.* pailler, fumer.

mule [mju:l], *n.* mulet, *m.*, mule, *f.*

mulish ['mju:liʃ], *a.* de mulet; (*fig.*) têtu.

mull [mʌl], *n.* gâchis, *m.*—*v.t.* faire chauffer et épicer; ***mulled wine***, vin chaud épicé.

multicoloured ['mʌltikʌləd], *a.* multicolore.

multifarious [mʌlti'fɛəriəs], *a.* varié, divers, multiplié.

multi-millionaire ['mʌltimiljə'nɛə], *n.* milliardaire, *m.*, *f.*

multiple ['mʌltipl], *a.* and *n.* multiple, *m.*; ***multiple store***, maison à succursales, *f.*

multiplication [mʌltipli'keiʃən], *n.* multiplication, *f.*

multiplicity [mʌlti'plisiti], *n.* multiplicité, *f.*

multiply ['mʌltiplai], *v.t.* multiplier.—*v.i.* multiplier, se multiplier.

multitude ['mʌltitju:d], *n.* multitude, *f.*

multitudinous [mʌlti'tju:dinəs], *a.* très nombreux, innombrable.

mum (1) [mʌm], *a.* muet.—*int.* bouche close! chut!

mum (2) [mʌm], *n.* (*fam.*) maman, *f.*

mumble [mʌmbl], *v.i.* marmotter.

mumbler ['mʌmblə], *n.* marmotteur, *m.*

mummer ['mʌmə], *n.* mime (*acteur*), *m.*

mummify ['mʌmifai], *v.t.* momifier.

mummy (1) ['mʌmi], *n.* momie, *f.*

mummy (2), **mummie** ['mʌmi], *n.* (*fam.*) maman, *f.*

mumps [mʌmps], *n.pl.* (*Med.*) oreillons, *m.pl.*

munch [mʌntʃ], *v.t.*, *v.i.* mâcher, croquer.

mundane ['mʌndein], *a.* mondain.

municipal [mju'nisipl], *a.* municipal.

municipality [mjunisi'pæliti], *n.* municipalité, *f.*

munificence [mju'nifisəns], *n.* munificence, *f.*

munificent [mju'nifisənt], *a.* libéral, généreux.

munition [mju'niʃən], *n.* munitions (de guerre), *f.pl.* —*v.t.* approvisionner.

mural ['mjuərəl], *a.* mural.—*n.* peinture murale, *f.*

murder ['mə:də], *n.* meurtre, homicide, *m.*; ***wilful murder***, meurtre avec préméditation, assassinat, *m.*—*v.t.* assassiner, tuer; (*fig.*) écorcher (*une langue etc.*).

murderer ['mə:dərə], *n.* meurtrier, assassin, *m.*

murderess ['mə:dəris], *n.* meurtrière, *f.*

murdering ['mə:dəriŋ], **murderous** ['mə:dərəs], *a.* meurtrier, assassin.

murkiness ['mə:kinis], *n.* obscurité, *f.*

murky ['mə:ki], *a.* sombre, obscur, ténébreux.

murmur ['mə:mə], *n.* murmure, *m.*—*v.i.* murmurer.

murmuring ['mə:məriŋ], *a.* murmurant, murmurateur.—*n.* murmure, *m.*, murmures, *m.pl.*

muscle [mʌsl], *n.* muscle, *m.*

muscular ['mʌskjulə], *a.* musculaire (*force*); musculeux (*membres*).

Muse [mju:z], *n.* muse, *f.*

muse [mju:z], *v.i.* méditer (*sur*) rêver (*à*).—*n.* muse, rêverie, méditation, *f.*

museum [mju'zi:əm], *n.* musée, *m.*

mushroom ['mʌʃrum], *n.* champignon, *m.*

music ['mju:zik], *n.* musique, *f.*

musical ['mju:zikəl], *a.* musical; (*fig.*) harmonieux, mélodieux; qui aime la musique.

musician [mju:'ziʃən], *n.* musicien, *m.*

music-stand ['mju:zikstænd], *n.* pupitre à musique, *m.*

music-stool ['mju:zikstu:l], *n.* tabouret de piano, *m.*

musing ['mju:ziŋ], *n.* méditation; (*pl.*) rêverie, *f.*

musk [mʌsk], *n.* musc, *m.*
musket ['mʌskit], *n.* fusil, mousquet, *m.*
musketeer [mʌski'tiə], *n.* mousquetaire, *m.*
musketry ['mʌskitri], *n.* mousqueterie, *f.*, tir, *m.*
musky ['mʌski], *a.* musqué, parfumé de musc.
Muslim ['mʌzlim], [MOSLEM].
muslin ['mʌzlin], *a.* de mousseline.—*n.* mousseline, *f.*
mussel [mʌsl], *n.* moule, *f.*
must (1) [mʌst], *v. aux.* falloir; devoir; ***I must do it***, il faut que je le fasse; ***you must know***, vous devez savoir.
must (2) [mʌst], *n.* moût (*de vin*), *m.*
mustard ['mʌstəd], *n.* moutarde, *f.*
muster ['mʌstə], *n.* appel, *m.*, revue, *f.*; rassemblement, *m.*; troupe, bande, *f.*; contrôles (*liste*), *m.pl.*—*v.t.* faire l'appel de; passer en revue; réunir, rassembler; se procurer; ***to muster up courage***, prendre son courage à deux mains.—*v.i.* s'assembler, se réunir.
mustiness ['mʌstinis], *n.* moisi, *m.*
musty ['mʌsti], *a.* moisi; qui sent le renfermé.
mutability [mju:tə'biliti], *n.* mutabilité, *f.*
mutation [mju:'teiʃən], *n.* mutation, *f.*
mute [mju:t], *a.* and *n.* muet, *m.*—*v.t.* amortir (*les cordes d'un violon etc.*).
mutely ['mju:tli], *adv.* en silence.
mutilate ['mju:tileit], *v.t.* mutiler, estropier.
mutilated ['mju:tileitid], *a.* mutilé.
mutilation [mju:ti'leiʃən], *n.* mutilation, *f.*
mutineer [mju:ti'niə], *n.* révolté, rebelle, mutin, *m.*
mutinous ['mju:tinəs], *a.* rebelle, mutiné, mutin.
mutinously ['mju:tinəsli], *adv.* séditieusement.
mutiny ['mju:tini], *n.* mutinerie, sédition, révolte, *f.*—*v.i.* se mutiner, s'insurger.
mutter ['mʌtə], *v.t.*, *v.i.* marmotter.—*n.* marmottement, *m.*
muttering ['mʌtəriŋ], *a.* marmotteur, murmurant.—*n.* murmure, marmottement, marmottage, *m.*
mutton [mʌtn], *n.* mouton (*viande*), *m.*; ***leg of mutton***, gigot, *m.*
mutton-chop ['mʌtn'tʃɔp], *n.* côtelette de mouton, *f.*
mutual ['mju:tjuəl], *a.* mutuel, réciproque; ***mutual friend***, ami commun, *m.*
mutually ['mju:tjuəli], *adv.* mutuellement.
muzzle [mʌzl], *n.* museau (*d'animal*), *m.*; bouche, gueule (*de canon*), *f.*; bout (*de fusil etc.*), *m.*; muselière (*pour chien*), *f.*—*v.t.* museler.
muzzy ['mʌzi], *a.* brouillé, confus.
my [mai], *poss. a.* mon, *m.*, ma, *f.*, mes, *pl.*
myopic [mai'ɔpik], *a.* myope.
myriad ['miriəd], *a.* (*poet.*) innombrable.—*n.* myriade, *f.*
myrrh [mə:], *n.* myrrhe, *f.*
myrtle [mə:tl], *n.* myrte, *m.*
myself [mai'self], *pron.* me; moi-même; moi; ***I consider myself***, je me crois.
mysterious [mis'tiəriəs], *a.* mystérieux.
mysteriously [mis'tiəriəsli], *adv.* mystérieusement.
mystery ['mistəri], *n.* mystère, *m.*
mystic ['mistik], *a.* and *n.* (*Theol.*) mystique, *m.*, *f.*
mysticism ['mistisizm], *n.* mysticisme, *m.*
mystify ['mistifai], *v.t.* envelopper de mystère, mystifier.
mystique [mis'ti:k], *n.* mystique, *f.*
myth [miθ], *n.* mythe, *m.*
mythical ['miθikl], *a.* mythique.
mythology [mi'θɔlədʒi], *n.* mythologie, *f.*

N

N, n [en]. quatorzième lettre de l'alphabet, *m.* ou *f.*
nab [næb], *v.t.* happer, saisir, pincer.
nag (1) [næg], *n.* bidet, petit cheval, *m.*
nag (2) [næg], *v.t.*, *v.i.* gronder, chamailler, criailler.
nagging ['nægiŋ], *a.* querelleur (*personne*); agaçant (*sensation*).
nail [neil], *n.* clou; ongle (*de griffes, de doigts*), *m.*—*v.t.* clouer; clouter.
nail-brush ['neilbrʌʃ], *n.* brosse à ongles, *f.*
naïve [nai'i:v], *a.* naïf, ingénu.
naked ['neikid], *a.* nu, à nu; à découvert, ouvert (*sans protection*); dégarni (*sans meubles*); ***stark naked***, tout nu.
nakedness ['neikidnis], *n.* nudité, *f.*
name [neim], *n.* nom; (*fig.*) renom, *m.*, renommée, réputation, *f.*; ***Christian name***, nom de baptême, prénom, *m.*; ***maiden name***, nom de jeune fille; ***what is your name?*** comment vous appelez-vous?—*v.t.* nommer, appeler; désigner; ***to be named***, s'appeler, se nommer.
named [neimd], *a.* nommé, désigné.
nameless ['neimlis], *a.* sans nom, anonyme; inconnu.
namely ['neimli], *adv.* à savoir, c'est-à-dire.
namesake ['neimseik], *n.* homonyme, *m.*
nanny ['næni], *n.* bonne d'enfant; (*childish*) nounou, *f.*
nap (1) [næp], *n.* somme (*sommeil*), *m.*; ***afternoon nap***, sieste, *f.*; ***to take a nap***, faire un somme; ***to catch napping***, prendre au dépourvu.
nap (2) [næp], *n.* poil (*de tissu etc*), *m.*
nap (3) [næp], *n.* napoléon (*jeu*); tuyau certain (*courses de chevaux*), *m.*
nape [neip], *n.* nuque, *f.*
napkin ['næpkin], *n.* serviette; couche (*de bébé*), *f.*
Napoleon [nə'pouljən]. Napoléon, *m.*
narcissus [nɑ:'sisəs], *n.* narcisse, *m.*
narcotic [nɑ:'kɔtik], *a.* and *n.* narcotique, *m.*
narrate [nə'reit], *v.t.* raconter, narrer.
narration [nə'reiʃən], *n.* narration, *f.*, récit, *m.*
narrative ['nærətiv], *a.* narratif.—*n.* récit, narré, *m.*
narrator [nə'reitə], *n.* narrateur, *m.*
narrow ['nærou], *a.* étroit, resserré; à l'étroit, gêné; rétréci, limité, borné (*esprit*); ***to have a narrow escape***, l'échapper belle.—*n.* (*pl.*) détroit, pas, *m.*—*v.t.* rétrécir, resserrer, limiter, borner.—*v.i.* se rétrécir, se resserrer.
narrowly ['nærouli], *adv.* étroitement, à l'étroit; de près.

narrow-minded ['nærou'maindid], *a.* à l'esprit étroit.
narrowness ['nærounis], *n.* étroitesse, *f.*
nasal [neizl], *a.* nasal, du nez.
nascent ['næsənt], *a.* naissant.
nastily ['nɑ:stili], *adv.* salement, malproprement.
nastiness ['nɑ:stinis], *n.* saleté; grossièreté, *f.*
nasturtium [nəs'tə:ʃəm], *n.* capucine, *f.*
nasty ['nɑ:sti], *a.* sale, malpropre; (*fig.*) méchant, vilain; dégoûtant.
natal [neitl], *a.* natal, de naissance.
nation ['neiʃən], *n.* nation, *f.*
national ['næʃənl], *a.* national; ***national anthem***, hymne national, *m.*; ***national debt***, dette publique, *f.*; ***national insurance***, assurances sociales, *f.pl.*
nationalism ['næʃnəlizm], *n.* nationalisme, *m.*
nationality [næʃə'næliti], *n.* nationalité, *f.*
nationalization [næʃnəlai'zeiʃən], *n.* nationalisation (*d'une industrie*); (*Am.*) naturalisation (*d'une personne*), *f.*
nationalize ['næʃnəlaiz], *v.t.* nationaliser.
native ['neitiv], *a.* natif, naturel; indigène (*personne* ou *plante*); maternel (*langue etc.*); ***native land***, patrie, *f.*—*n.* natif (*d'une ville*); habitant (*d'une île*); naturel (*de tribu sauvage*); indigène (*des pays d'outremer*), *m.*; ***a native of England***, Anglais de naissance, *m.*; ***a native of Paris***, natif de Paris.
nativity [nə'tiviti], *n.* nativité; naissance, *f.*
natty ['næti], *a.* pimpant, propret, coquet.
natural ['nætʃərəl], *a.* naturel; réel; naïf, simple; (*Mus.*) bécarre.
naturalist ['nætʃərəlist], *n.* naturaliste, *m.*, *f.*
naturalization [nætʃərəlai'zeiʃən], *n.* naturalisation, *f.*
naturally ['nætʃərəli], *adv.* naturellement.
nature ['neitʃə], *n.* nature, *f.*; naturel (*disposition*), *m.*
naught [nɔ:t], *n.* néant, rien; (*Arith.*) zéro, *m.*; ***to come to naught***, échouer.
naughtily ['nɔ:tili], *adv.* par méchanceté.
naughtiness ['nɔ:tinis], *n.* méchanceté, *f.*
naughty ['nɔ:ti], *a.* méchant, vilain.
nausea ['nɔ:ziə], *n.* nausée, *f.*
nauseating ['nɔ:zieitiŋ], *a.* nauséabond, dégoûtant, écœurant.
nautical ['nɔ:tikl], *a.* nautique; marin (*milles etc.*).
naval [neivl], *a.* naval; maritime; de la marine (de guerre); ***naval officer***, officier de marine, *m.*
nave (1) [neiv], *n.* nef (*d'église*), *f.*
nave (2) [neiv], *n.* moyeu (*de roue*), *m.*
navel [neivl], *n.* nombril, *m.*
navigable ['nævigəbl], *a.* navigable.
navigate ['nævigeit], *v.t.* gouverner.—*v.i.* naviguer.
navigation [nævi'geiʃən], *n.* navigation, *f.*
navigator ['nævigeitə], *n.* navigateur, *m.*
navvy ['nævi], *n.* terrassier, *m.*
navy ['neivi], *n.* marine de guerre, *f.*; ***Merchant Navy***, marine marchande.
navy blue ['neivi'blu:], *a.* and *n.* bleu marine, *m.inv.*
nay** [nei], *adv.* non; bien plus; et même, qui plus est; ***to say nay, refuser.
Neapolitan [niə'pɔlitən], *a.* napolitain, de Naples.—*n.* Napolitain (*personne*), *m.*
neap tide ['ni:p'taid], *n.* marée de morte eau, *f.*
near [niə], *a.* proche, rapproché; chiche (*parcimonieux*); cher (*bien-aimé*); fidèle (*intime*); de gauche (*left*).—*adv.* près, près de, de près; presque.—*prep.* près de, auprès de.—*v.t.*, *v.i.* s'approcher de.
nearby ['niəbai], *a.*, [niə'bai], *adv.* tout près, tout proche.
nearly ['niəli], *adv.* de près; à peu près; presque; ***he was nearly drowned***, il faillit se noyer.
nearness ['niənis], *n.* proximité; parcimonie (*avarice*), *f.*
neat [ni:t], *a.* propre, soigné, net; simple et élégant; pur, sec (*sans mélange*).
neatly ['ni:tli], *adv.* proprement; nettement; adroitement (*habilement*).
neatness ['ni:tnis], *n.* propreté, netteté, *f.*
nebula ['nebjulə], *n.* (*Astron.*) nébuleuse, *f.*
nebulous ['nebjuləs], *a.* nébuleux.
necessaries ['nesəsəriz], *n.pl.* nécessaire, *m.*
necessarily ['nesəsərili], *adv.* nécessairement, forcément.
necessary ['nesəsri], *a.* nécessaire.
necessitate [ni'sesiteit], *v.t.* nécessiter.
necessitous [ni'sesitəs], *a.* nécessiteux, dans le besoin.
necessity [ni'sesiti], *n.* nécessité, *f.*; besoin (*indigence*), *m.*; ***of necessity***, nécessairement, forcément.
neck [nek], *n.* cou; goulot (*de bouteille etc.*); manche (*de violon*); collet (*de viande*), *m.*; encolure (*d'une robe*), langue (*de terre*), *f.*; ***stiff neck***, torticolis, *m.*
neckerchief ['nekətʃif], *n.* foulard (*d'homme*), fichu (*de femme*), *m.*
necklace ['neklis], *n.* collier, *m.*
neck-tie ['nektai], *n.* cravate, *f.*
necromancy ['nekrəmænsi], *n.* nécromancie, *f.*
necropolis [ni'krɔpəlis], *n.* nécropole, *f.*
nectar ['nektə], *n.* nectar, *m.*
nectarine ['nektərin], *n.* brugnon, *m.*
need [ni:d], *n.* besoin, *m.*; nécessité; indigence, *f.*; ***if need be***, le cas échéant; ***in case of need***, au besoin; ***to be in need***, être dans la misère; ***to be in need of*** or ***to have need of***, avoir besoin de.—*v.t.* avoir besoin de; exiger.—*v.i.* avoir besoin; devoir, avoir (*à*); (*impers.*) falloir, être nécessaire.
needful ['ni:dful], *a.* nécessaire; ***the needful***, le nécessaire, *m.*
needle [ni:dl], *n.* aiguille, *f.*
needless ['ni:dlis], *a.* inutile.
needlework ['ni:dlwə:k], *n.* ouvrage à l'aiguille, *m.*; (*Sch.*) couture, *f.*
needs** [ni:dz], *adv.* (*used only with* must) nécessairement, absolument; ***I must needs, il faut absolument que je (*with subj.*).
needy ['ni:di], *a.* indigent, nécessiteux.
ne'er [nɛə], (*poet.*) [NEVER].
nefarious [ni'fɛəriəs], *a.* abominable, infâme.
negation [ni'geiʃən], *n.* négation, *f.*
negative ['negətiv], *a.* négatif.—*n.* négative, *f.*; (*Phot.*) cliché, négatif, *m.*—*v.t.* rejeter.
neglect [ni'glekt], *n.* négligence, *f.*; oubli, *m.*—*v.t.* négliger.
neglected [ni'glektid], *a.* négligé.
neglectful [ni'glektful], *a.* négligent.
negligence ['neglidʒəns], *n.* négligence, *f.*
negligent ['neglidʒənt], *a.* négligent.

negligible [ˈneglidʒibl], *a.* négligeable.
negotiable [niˈgouʃiəbl], *a.* négociable.
negotiate [niˈgouʃieit], *v.t., v.i.* négocier.
negotiation [nigouʃiˈeiʃən], *n.* négociation, *f.*
negotiator [niˈgouʃieitə], *n.* négociateur, *m.*
Negress [ˈni:gres], *n.* (*sometimes pej.*) noire, *f.*
Negro [ˈni:grou], *n.* noir, *m.*
neigh [nei], *v.i.* hennir.—*n.* hennissement, *m.*
neighbour [ˈneibə], *n.* voisin; (*Bibl.*) prochain, *m.*
neighbourhood [ˈneibəhud], *n.* voisinage, *m.*; alentours, environs, *m.pl.*; quartier, *m.*
neighbouring [ˈneibəriŋ], *a.* voisin.
neighbourly [ˈneibəli], *a.* de voisin, de bon voisin.
neighing [ˈneiiŋ], *n.* hennissement, *m.*
neither [ˈnaiðə, ˈni:ðə], *a.* and *pron.* ni l'un ni l'autre, *m.*—*conj.* ni; non plus; ***neither . . . nor***, ni . . . ni.—*adv.* du reste, d'ailleurs.
Nemesis [ˈnemisis]. némésis, *f.*
neolithic [ni:əˈliθik], *a.* néolithique.
neon [ˈni:ɔn], *a.* ***neon light***, lampe au néon, *f.*—*n.* (*Chem.*) néon, *m.*
Nepal [nəˈpɔ:l]. le Népal, *m.*
Nepalese [nepəˈli:z], *a.* népalais.—*n.* Népalais (*personne*), *m.*
nephew [ˈnefju, ˈnevju], *n.* neveu, *m.*
nepotism [ˈnepətizm], *n.* népotisme, *m.*
Nero [ˈniərou]. Néron, *m.*
nerve [nə:v], *n.* nerf; (*fig.*) courage, *m.*; audace, *f.*; (*pop.*) toupet, *m.*
nerve-cell [ˈnə:vsel], *n.* cellule nerveuse, *f.*
nerveless [ˈnə:vlis], *a.* sans nerf; (*fig.*) sans vigueur.
nerve-racking [ˈnə:vrækiŋ], *a.* horripilant, énervant.
nervous [ˈnə:vəs], *a.* nerveux (*physiquement*); timide, craintif (*moralement*); ***nervous breakdown***, dépression nerveuse, *f.*
nervousness [ˈnə:vəsnis], *n.* inquiétude, timidité; nervosité, *f.*
nest [nest], *n.* nid, *m.*; nichée (*couvée d'oiseaux*), *f.*; (*fig.*) repaire, *m.*; ***nest of tables***, table gigogne, *f.*—*v.i.* nicher, faire un nid.
nestle [nesl], *v.i.* nicher, se nicher.
nestling [ˈnesliŋ], *n.* petit oiseau encore au nid, béjaune, *m.*
net [net], *a.* net; pur.—*n.* filet, rets, *m.*; résille (*à cheveux*), *f.*; tulle (*tissu*), *m.*—*v.t.* prendre dans un filet; (*Comm.*) rapporter net.
nether [ˈneðə], *a.* bas, inférieur.
Netherlands [ˈneðələnds], **the.** les Pays-Bas, *m.pl.*
nethermost [ˈneðəmoust], *a.* le plus bas.
netting [ˈnetiŋ], *n.* filet, réseau; grillage (*de fil de fer*), *m.*
nettle [netl], *n.* ortie, *f.*—*v.t.* piquer, agacer, irriter.
nettlerash [ˈnetlræʃ], *n.* urticaire, *f.*
network [ˈnetwə:k], *n.* réseau, enchevêtrement, *m.*
neuralgia [njuˈrældʒə], *n.* névralgie, *f.*
neuritis [njuˈraitis], *n.* névrite, *f.*
neurosis [njuˈrousis], *n.* névrose, *f.*
neurotic [njuˈrɔtik], *a.* and *n.* névrosé, *m.*, neurotique, *m.*, *f.*
neuter [ˈnju:tə], *a.* and *n.* neutre, *m.*
neutral [ˈnju:trəl], *a.* neutre; indifférent.—*n.* (*Motor.*) point-mort, *m.*
neutrality [njuˈtræliti], *n.* neutralité; indifférence, *f.*
neutralize [ˈnju:trəlaiz], *v.t.* neutraliser.
neutron [ˈnju:trɔn], *n.* neutron, *m.*
never [ˈnevə], *adv.* jamais; ne . . . jamais; ***never mind!*** peu importe!
nevermore [nevəˈmɔ:], *adv.* ne . . . jamais plus, ne . . . plus jamais.
nevertheless [nevəðəˈles], *conj.* néanmoins, cependant, pourtant.
new [nju:], *a.* neuf (*qui n'a pas servi*); nouveau (*récemment acquis, différent*); frais, récent (*arrivé depuis peu*); ***brand-new***, flambant neuf, tout battant neuf; ***New Year's Day***, le jour de l'an, *m.*
new-born [ˈnju:bɔ:n], *a.* nouveau-né; ***new-born daughters***, filles nouveau-nées, *f.pl.*
new-comer [ˈnju:kʌmə], *n.* nouveau venu, *m.*
Newfoundland [ˈnju:fəndlænd, nju:ˈfaundlənd]. la Terre-Neuve, *f.*—*n.* terre-neuve (*chien*), *m.*
New Guinea [nju:ˈgini]. la Nouvelle-Guinée, *f.*
new-laid [ˈnju:leid], *a.* frais (*œuf*).
newly [ˈnju:li], *adv.* nouvellement, fraîchement, récemment, de nouveau.
newness [ˈnju:nis], *n.* nouveauté, *f.*
New Orleans [nju:ˈɔ:liənz]. la Nouvelle-Orléans, *f.*
news [nju:z], *n.* nouvelle, *f.*, nouvelles, *f.pl.*; (*Rad.*, *Tel.*) bulletin d'informations, *m.*
news-agent [ˈnju:zeidʒənt], *n.* marchand de journaux, *m.*
newspaper [ˈnju:speipə], *n.* journal, *m.*
newt [nju:t], *n.* triton, *m.*, salamandre, *f.*
New Zealand [nju:ˈzi:lənd]. la Nouvelle-Zélande, *f.*—*a.* néo-zélandais.
New Zealander [nju:ˈzi:ləndə], *n.* Néo-Zélandais, *m.*
next [nekst], *a.* voisin, le plus voisin; le plus près; de côté; prochain (*dans l'avenir*); suivant (*dans le passé*); premier (*à la suite de*).—*adv.* après, ensuite, puis; ***what next?*** et après ? ensuite ?—*prep.* ***next to***, à côté de.
nib [nib], *n.* bec (*de stylo*), *m.*; pointe (*d'outil*), *f.*
nibble [nibl], *v.t.* mordiller, grignoter; mordre à (*l'hameçon*); brouter (*l'herbe etc.*).—*n.* grignotement, *m.*; touche (*du poisson*), *f.*
Nicaragua [nikəˈrægjuə]. le Nicaragua, *m.*
Nicaraguan [nikəˈrægjuən], *a.* nicaraguayen.—*n.* Nicaraguayen (*personne*), *m.*
nice [nais], *a.* bon, agréable, friand; (*colloq.*) délicat, gentil, aimable, charmant, propre; exact, difficile, exigeant (*délicat*); ***a nice child***, un enfant gentil, *m.*
nicely [ˈnaisli], *adv.* bien, agréablement; délicatement; gentiment, aimablement; joliment; d'une manière recherchée.
nicety [ˈnaisəti], *n.* (*pl.* **niceties** [ˈnaisətiz]) délicatesse, finesse, *f.*; soin scrupuleux, *m.*; précision; exactitude, *f.*; (*pl.*) subtilités, finesses, *f.pl.*
niche [nitʃ], *n.* niche, *f.*
Nicholas [ˈnikələs]. Nicolas, *m.*
nick [nik], *n.* moment précis, *m.*; encoche, entaille (*coupure*), *f.*; (*Print.*) cran, *m.*; ***in the nick of time***, fort à propos, à point nommé.
nickel [nikl], *n.* nickel, *m.*; (*Am.*) pièce de cinq cents, *f.*
nickname [ˈnikneim], *n.* sobriquet, surnom, *m.*—*v.t.* donner un sobriquet à.
nicotine [ˈnikəti:n], *n.* nicotine, *f.*

niece [niːs], *n.* nièce, *f.*
nifty ['nifti], *a.* (*fam.*) pimpant.
Niger ['naidʒə], **the.** le Niger, *m.*
Nigeria [nai'dʒiəriə]. le Nigéria, *m.*
Nigerian [nai'dʒiəriən], *a.* nigérien.—*n.* Nigérien (*personne*), *m.*
niggard ['nigəd], *a.* and *n.* avare, ladre, *m.*
niggardliness ['nigədlinis], *n.* mesquinerie, ladrerie, *f.*
niggardly ['nigədli], *a.* mesquin, ladre, chiche.—*adv.* avec avarice, en avare.
niggle [nigl], *v.i.* tatillonner; fignoler.
nigh [nai], *adv.* près; presque; ***to draw nigh***, approcher, s'approcher (*de*).
night [nait], *n.* nuit, *f.*; soir, *m.*; ***first night*** première, *f.*
night-club ['naitklʌb], *n.* boîte de nuit, *f.*
night-dress ['naitdres], *n.* chemise de nuit, *f.*
night-fall ['naitfɔːl], *n.* tombée de la nuit, *f.*
nightie ['naiti], *colloq. abbr.* [NIGHT-DRESS].
nightingale ['naitiŋgeil], *n.* rossignol, *m.*
night-light ['naitlait], *n.* veilleuse, *f.*
nightly ['naitli], *a.* nocturne, de nuit.—*adv.* chaque nuit, toutes les nuits; tous les soirs.
nightmare ['naitmɛə], *n.* cauchemar, *m.*
night-time ['naittaim], *n.* nuit, *f.*; ***in the night-time***, pendant la nuit.
night-watchman ['nait'wɔtʃmən], *n.* (*pl.* **-men** [men]) veilleur de nuit, *m.*
nihilism ['naiilizm], *n.* nihilisme, *m.*
nil [nil], *n.* rien, néant, zéro, *m.*
Nile [nail], **the.** le Nil, *m.*
nimble [nimbl], *a.* agile, léger, leste.
nimbly ['nimbli], *adv.* agilement, lestement.
nine [nain], *a.* and *n.* neuf, *m.*
ninefold ['nainfould], *a.* neuf fois autant.
ninepins ['nainpinz], *n.pl.* quilles, *f.pl.*; jeu de quilles, *m.*
nineteen [nain'tiːn], *a.* and *n.* dix-neuf, *m.*
nineteenth [nain'tiːnθ], *a.* dix-neuvième; dix-neuf (*du mois* ou *souverains*).—*n.* dix-neuvième (*fraction*), *m.*
ninetieth ['naintiiθ], *a.* quatre-vingt-dixième. —*n.* quatre-vingt-dixième (*fraction*), *m.*
ninety ['nainti], *a.* and *n.* quatre-vingt-dix, *m.*
ninny ['nini], *n.* nigaud, niais, *m.*
ninth [nainθ], *a.* neuvième; neuf (*du mois* ou *souverains*).—*n.* neuvième (*fraction*), *m.*
nip [nip], *n.* pincement, *m.*, pince, *f.*, serrement, *m.*; morsure; (*Hort.*) brûlure (par le froid), *f.*—*v.t.* pincer; mordre; (*Hort.*) brûler (par le froid); ***to nip off***, couper, enlever le bout de.
nipper ['nipə], *n.* pince, *f.*; (*colloq.*) gamin, gosse, *m.*; (*pl.*) pincettes, pinces, *f.pl.*
nipple [nipl], *n.* mamelon, bout de sein, *m.*
nippy ['nipi], *a.* preste, rapide; perçant (*froid*).
nit [nit], *n.* lente, *f.*
nitrate ['naitreit], *n.* nitrate, *m.*
nitre ['naitə], *n.* nitre, *m.*
nitric ['naitrik], *a.* nitrique, azotique.
nitrogen ['naitrədʒən], *n.* azote, *m.*
nitwit ['nitwit], *n.* imbécile, *m., f.*
no [nou], *a.* and *adv.* non, pas, ne . . . pas de ne . . . point de; pas un, nul, aucun.—*n.* non, *m.*
Noah ['nouə]. Noé, *m.*
nob [nɔb], *n.* (*colloq.*) caboche, *f.*; gros bonnet, *m.*
nobility [no'biliti], *n.* noblesse, *f.*
noble [noubl], *a.* noble; illustre, grand; généreux.—*n.* noble, *m.*
nobleman ['noublmən], *n.* (*pl.* **-men** [men] noble, gentilhomme, *m.*
nobly ['noubli], *adv.* noblement; superbement.
nobody ['noubədi], *pron.* personne, *m.*; ***I know nobody***, je ne connais personne; ***nobody else***, personne d'autre.—*n.* zéro, inconnu, *m.*
nocturnal [nɔk'təːnl], *a.* nocturne, de nuit.
nod [nɔd], *n.* signe de tête, *m.*; inclination de tête, *f.*—*v.i.* faire un signe de tête; s'incliner; sommeiller (*s'assoupir*).
noggin ['nɔgin], *n.* petit pot (*en étain*), *m.*
noise [nɔiz], *n.* bruit; tapage, fracas, vacarme; tintement (*de cloche*), bourdonnement (*d'insectes etc.*); (*fig.*) éclat, *m.*—*v.t.* ébruiter, publier, répandre.
noiseless ['nɔizlis], *a.* sans bruit; silencieux.
noiselessly ['nɔizlisli], *adv.* sans bruit.
noisily ['nɔizili], *adv.* bruyamment.
noisome ['nɔisəm], *a.* malsain, infect, nuisible.
noisy ['nɔizi], *a.* bruyant; turbulent (*enfants*).
nomad ['noumæd], *n.* nomade, *m.*
nomadic [no'mædik], *a.* nomade.
nominal ['nɔminl], *a.* nominal; de nom; ***nominal roll***, état nominatif, *m.*
nominally ['nɔminəli], *adv.* de nom; nominalement.
nominate ['nɔmineit], *v.t.* nommer; désigner; présenter, proposer (*un candidat etc.*).
nomination [nɔmi'neiʃən], *n.* nomination; présentation, *f.*
nominative ['nɔminətiv], *a.* au nominatif, nominatif.—*n.* (*Gram.*) nominatif, *m.*
nominee [nɔmi'niː], *n.* personne nommée, *f.*
nonagenarian [nounədʒi'nɛəriən], *a.* and *n.* nonagénaire, *m., f.*
non-aggression [nɔnə'greʃən], *n.* non-agression, *f.*
non-alcoholic [nɔnælkə'hɔlik], *a.* non-alcoolique.
non-attendance [nɔnə'tendəns], *n.* absence, *f.*
nonchalance ['nɔnʃələns], *n.* nonchalance, *f.*
non-combatant [nɔn'kʌmbətənt, nɔn'kɔmbətənt], *a.* and *n.* non-combattant, *m.*
non-commissioned [nɔnkə'miʃənd], *a.* sans brevet; ***non-commissioned officer***, sous-officier, *m.*
non-committal [nɔnkə'mitl], *a.* qui n'engage à rien, diplomatique.
nonconformist [nɔnkən'fɔːmist], *a.* and *n.* dissident, *m.*, nonconformiste, *m., f.*
nondescript ['nɔndiskript], *a.* indéfinissable, quelconque.—*n.* chose sans nom, chose indéfinissable, *f.*
none [nʌn], *a.* and *pron.* nul, *m.*, nulle, *f.*, aucun, *m.*, aucune, *f.*, pas un, *m.*, pas une, *f.*, personne, *m.*—*adv.* pas, point; néant (*sur des bordereaux*).
nonentity [nɔ'nentiti], *n.* néant, *m.*; (*fig.*) nullité, *f.*, zéro, *m.*
nonesuch ['nʌnsʌtʃ], *a.* sans pareil, nonpareil.
non-existent ['nɔnig'zistənt], *a.* qui n'existe pas.
non-intervention ['nɔnintə'venʃən], *n.* non-intervention, *f.*
non-observance ['nɔnəb'zəːvəns], *n.* inobservation, *f.*
non-payment ['nɔn'peimənt], *n.* non-payement, *m.*

nonplussed ['nɔn'plʌst], *a.* embarrassé, dérouté.
nonsense ['nɔnsəns], *n.* non-sens, *m.*; sottise, absurdité, *f.*; ***nonsense!*** allons donc! quelle sottise!
nonsensical [nɔn'sensikl], *a.* vide de sens, absurde.
non-skid ['nɔn'skid], *a.* antidérapant.
non-stop ['nɔn'stɔp], *a.* and *adv.* sans arrêt.
noodle [nu:dl], *n.* nigaud, benêt, sot, *m.*; (*pl.*) (*Cook.*) nouilles, *f.pl.*
nook [nuk], *n.* recoin, réduit, *m.*
noon [nu:n], *n.* midi, *m.*
noonday ['nu:ndei], *a.* de midi.—*n.* midi, *m.*
noontide ['nu:ntaid], *n.* heure de midi, *f.*, midi, *m.*
noose [nu:s], *n.* nœud coulant, lacet, *m.*
nor [nɔ:], *conj.* ni; ni . . . ne.
norm [nɔ:m], *n.* norme, *f.*
normal [nɔ:ml], *a.* normal.
normally ['nɔ:məli], *adv.* normalement.
Norman ['nɔ:mən], *a.* normand.—*n.* Normand (*personne*), *m.*
Normandy ['nɔ:məndi]. la Normandie, *f.*
north [nɔ:θ], *a.* du nord, septentrional.—*n.* nord, septentrion, *m.*—*adv.* au nord.
north-east [nɔ:θ'i:st], *n.* nord-est, *m.*
northerly ['nɔ:ðəli], *a.* septentrional, du nord. —*adv.* au nord, vers le nord.
northern ['nɔ:ðən], *a.* du nord; ***northern lights***, aurore boréale, *f.*
northerner ['nɔ:ðənə], *n.* habitant du nord, *m.*
north-west [nɔ:θ'west], *n.* nord-ouest, *m.*
Norway ['nɔ:wei]. la Norvège, *f.*
Norwegian ['nɔ:'wi:dʒən], *a.* norvégien.—*n.* norvégien (*langue*); Norvégien (*personne*), *m.*
nose [nouz], *n.* nez; museau (*d'animal*); odorat (*flair*), *m.*; ***Roman nose***, nez aquilin; ***to blow one's nose***, se moucher; ***to put someone's nose out of joint***, supplanter quelqu'un; ***to turn up one's nose at***, faire fi de; ***turned-up nose***, nez retroussé.—*v.t.* flairer.—*v.i.* ***to nose about***, fureter.
nose-bag ['nouzbæg], *n.* musette (*de cheval etc.*), *f.*
nose-dive ['nouzdaiv], *v.i.* (*Av.*) piquer du nez.—*n.* piqué, *m.*
nosegay ['nouzgei], *n.* bouquet, *m.*
nostalgia [nɔs'tældʒiə], *n.* nostalgie, *f.*, mal du pays, *m.*
nostril ['nɔstril], *n.* narine, *f.*; naseau (*de cheval etc.*), *m.*
nosy ['nouzi], *a.* (*pop.*) fouinard.
not [nɔt], *adv.* non; ne . . . pas, ne . . . point, pas, non pas; ***not at all***, point du tout; ***why not?*** pourquoi pas?
notability [noutə'biliti], *n.* notabilité, *f.*
notable ['noutəbl], *a.* notable, insigne; remarquable.—*n.* notable, *m.*, *f.*
notably ['noutəbli], *adv.* notamment (*particulièrement*).
notary ['noutəri], *n.* notaire, *m.*
notation [no'teiʃən], *n.* notation, *f.*
notch [nɔtʃ], *n.* encoche, entaille, brèche, *f.*—*v.t.* entailler, ébrècher.
note [nout], *n.* note, marque, *f.*, signe, *m.*; lettre, *f.*, billet, *m.*; marque (*distinction*), *f.*; ***bank-note***, billet de banque; ***to take a note of***, prendre note de.—*v.t.* noter; remarquer.
notebook ['noutbuk], *n.* carnet, *m.*
noted ['noutid], *a.* distingué (*personne*); célèbre (*chose*).
notepaper ['noutpeipə], *n.* papier à lettres, *m.*
noteworthy ['noutwə:ði], *a.* remarquable.
nothing ['nʌθiŋ], *n.* rien, néant, *m.*; ***a mere nothing***, (*fig.*) un zéro.—*pron.* (ne) . . . rien; ***good-for-nothing***, bon à rien, *m.*; ***nothing at all***, rien du tout; ***to do nothing but***, ne faire que.—*adv.* en rien, nullement, aucunement.
nothingness ['nʌθiŋnis], *n.* néant, rien, *m.*
notice ['noutis], *n.* connaissance; attention, *f.*; préavis, *m.*; notice (*article dans un journal*); (*Law*) notification; annonce (*dans un journal*); affiche (*avis placardé*), *f.*; ***a week's notice***, un préavis de huit jours; ***at short notice***, à court délai; ***to give notice***, avertir, donner congé; ***to take notice of***, faire attention à, remarquer; ***until further notice***, jusqu'à nouvel ordre.—*v.t.* prendre connaissance de, remarquer, s'apercevoir de.
noticeable ['noutisəbl], *a.* perceptible.
noticeably ['noutisəbli], *adv.* perceptiblement, sensiblement.
notice-board ['noutisbɔ:d], *n.* écriteau, *m.*
notification [noutifi'keiʃən], *n.* notification, *f.*, avis, avertissement, *m.*
notify ['noutifai], *v.t.* faire savoir, notifier.
notion ['nouʃən], *n.* notion, idée, *f.*
notoriety [noutə'raiəti], *n.* notoriété, *f.*
notorious [no'tɔ:riəs], *a.* notoire.
notwithstanding [nɔtwið'stændiŋ], *prep.* malgré, nonobstant.—*adv.* néanmoins.
noun [naun], *n.* nom, substantif, *m.*
nourish ['nʌriʃ], *v.t.* nourrir; (*fig.*) entretenir.
nourishing ['nʌriʃiŋ], *a.* nourrissant, nutritif.
nourishment ['nʌriʃmənt], *n.* nourriture, alimentation, *f.*
Nova Scotia ['nouvə'skouʃə]. la Nouvelle-Écosse, *f.*
novel [nɔvl], *a.* nouveau, original.—*n.* roman, *m.*
novelist ['nɔvəlist], *n.* romancier, *m.*
novelty ['nɔvəlti], *n.* nouveauté, *f.*
November [no'vembə]. novembre, *m.*
novercal [no'və:kl], *a.* de marâtre.
novice ['nɔvis], *n.* novice, *m.*, *f.*
novitiate [nə'viʃiit], *n.* noviciat, *m.*
now [nau], *adv.* maintenant, à présent, actuellement; alors, or, donc (*raisonnement*); ***now and then***, de temps en temps; ***now . . . now***, tantôt . . . tantôt; ***now then!*** eh bien!
nowadays ['nauədeiz], *adv.* aujourd'hui, de nos jours.
nowhere ['nouwɛə], *adv.* nulle part.
nowise ['nouwaiz], *adv.* en aucune manière.
noxious ['nɔkʃəs], *a.* nuisible.
nozzle [nɔzl], *n.* nez; bec, bout; (*Motor. etc.*) ajutage, *m.*; lance (*de tuyau*), *f.*
nuclear ['nju:kliə], *a.* nucléaire; ***nuclear fission***, fission de l'atome, *f.*; ***nuclear war***, guerre atomique, *f.*
nucleus ['nju:kliəs], *n.* noyau, *m.*
nude [nju:d], *a.* and *n.* nu, *m.*
nudge [nʌdʒ], *n.* coup de coude, *m.*—*v.t.* donner un coup de coude à, pousser du coude.
nugget ['nʌgit], *n.* pépite (*d'or*), *f.*
nuisance ['nju:səns], *n.* peste, plaie, *f.*, fléau; (*Law*) dommage, *m.*

null [nʌl], *a.* nul; ***null and void***, nul et non avenu.
nullify ['nʌlifai], *v.t.* annuler.
nullity ['nʌliti], *n.* nullité, *f.*
numb [nʌm], *a.* engourdi, transi.—*v.t.* engourdir (*par*).
number ['nʌmbə], *n.* nombre; chiffre (*de 0 à 9*); numéro (*d'une série*), *m.*; livraison (*de publications*), *f.*; (*fig., pl.*) nombres, *m.pl.*; ***a number of***, plusieurs, une foule de (*gens*); ***cardinal, ordinal, odd,*** or ***even number***, nombre cardinal, ordinal, impair *ou* pair.—*v.t.* compter; numéroter (*en série*).
numberless ['nʌmbəlis], *a.* innombrable.
number-plate ['nʌmbəpleit], *n.* (*Motor.*) plaque d'immatriculation, *f.*
numbness ['nʌmnis], *n.* engourdissement, *m.*
numeral ['nju:mərəl], *a.* numéral.—*n.* lettre numérale, *f.*, chiffre, *m.*
numerical [nju'merikl], *a.* numérique.
numerous ['nju:mərəs], *a.* nombreux.
numskull ['nʌmskʌl], *n.* benêt, idiot, *m.*
nun [nʌn], *n.* religieuse, (*fam.*) nonne, *f.*
nunnery ['nʌnəri], *n.* couvent (de religieuses), *m.*
nuptial ['nʌpʃəl], *a.* nuptial, de noces.
nuptials ['nʌpʃəlz], *n.pl.* noces, *f.pl.*
nurse [nə:s], *n.* bonne d'enfant, *f.*; garde-malade, *m., f.*; infirmier, *m.*, infirmière, *f.* (*à l'hôpital*); ***wet nurse***, nourrice, *f.*—*v.t.* nourrir, élever; soigner, garder (*les malades*).
nurse-maid ['nə:smeid], *n.* bonne d'enfant, *f.*
nursery ['nə:səri], *n.* chambre d'enfants; (*Hort.*) pépinière, *f.*; ***nursery rhyme***, chanson d'enfants, *f.*
nursery-man ['nə:sərimən], *n.* (*pl.* **-men** [men]) pépiniériste, *m.*
nursery-school ['nə:sərisku:l], *n.* école maternelle, *f.*
nursing-home ['nə:siŋhoum], *n.* clinique, maison de santé, *f.*
nurture ['nə:tʃə], *n.* nourriture; éducation, *f.*—*v.t.* nourrir; élever.
nut [nʌt], *n.* noix (*du noyer etc.*); noisette (*du noisetier*), *f.*; (*Tech.*) écrou, *m.*
nut-brown ['nʌtbraun], *a.* châtain.
nut-cracker ['nʌtkrækə], *n.* casse-noix (*oiseau*), *m.*; (*pl.*) casse-noisettes, *m.pl.*
nutmeg ['nʌtmeg], *n.* muscade, *f.*
nutrient ['nju:triənt], *a.* nourrissant.
nutrition [nju'triʃən], *n.* nutrition; alimentation, *f.*
nutritious [nju'triʃəs], *a.* nourrissant, nutritif.
nutshell ['nʌtʃel], *n.* coquille de noix, *f.*
nut-tree ['nʌttri:], *n.* noisetier, *m.*
nutty ['nʌti], *a.* qui a un goût de noisette; (*pop.*) fêlé, toqué.
nylon ['nailən], *n.* nylon, *m.*
nymph [nimf], *n.* nymphe, *f.*

O

O, o [ou]. quinzième lettre de l'alphabet, *m.*
oaf [ouf], *n.* idiot, *m.*
oafish ['oufiʃ], *a.* stupide, idiot.
oak [ouk], *n.* chêne; bois de chêne, *m.*
oak-apple ['oukæpl], *n.* pomme de chêne, *f.*
oak-tree ['ouktri:], *n.* chêne, *m.*
oar [ɔ:], *n.* aviron, *m.*, rame, *f.*
oarsman ['ɔ:zmən], *n.* (*pl.* **-men** [men]) rameur, *m.*
oasis [ou'eisis], *n.* (*pl.* **oases** [ou'eisi:z]) oasis, *f.*
oat [out], [OATS].
oatcake ['outkeik], *n.* galette d'avoine, *f.*
oaten [outn], *a.* d'avoine.
oath [ouθ], *n.* serment; juron, *m.*; ***on oath***, sous serment; ***to take an oath***, prêter serment.
oatmeal ['outmi:l], *n.* farine d'avoine, *f.*
oats [outs], *n.pl.* avoine, *f.*
obduracy ['ɔbdjurəsi], *n.* endurcissement, entêtement, *m.*
obdurate ['ɔbdjurit], *a.* endurci; obstiné, opiniâtre; impénitent.
obedience [o'bi:djəns], *n.* obéissance, soumission, *f.*
obedient [o'bi:djənt], *a.* obéissant, soumis.
obediently [o'bi:djəntli], *adv.* avec obéissance.
obeisance [o'beisəns], *n.* révérence, *f.*
obelisk ['ɔbəlisk], *n.* obélisque, *m.*
obese [o'bi:s], *a.* obèse.
obesity [o'bi:siti], *n.* obésité, *f.*
obey [o'bei], *v.t.* obéir à.—*v.i.* obéir.
obfuscate ['ɔbfʌskeit], *v.t.* offusquer, obscurcir.
obituary [ɔ'bitjuəri], *a.* obituaire; nécrologique.—*n.* nécrologie, *f.*
object (1) ['ɔbdʒikt], *n.* objet; but (*fin*), *m.*; considération, *f.*; (*Gram.*) régime, *m.*
object (2) [əb'dʒckt], *v.t.* objecter.—*v.i.* s'opposer (*à*).
objection [əb'dʒekʃən], *n.* objection, *f.*; obstacle, *m.*; (*Racing*) contestation, *f.*
objectionable [əb'dʒekʃənəbl], *a.* déplaisant; inadmissible.
objective [əb'dʒektiv], *a.* objectif.—*n.* objectif, but, *m.*
objectively [əb'dʒektivli], *adv.* objectivement.
oblation [o'bleiʃən], *n.* oblation, offrande, *f.*
obligation [ɔbli'geiʃən], *n.* obligation, *f.*; engagement, *m.*
obligatory [ə'bligətəri], *a.* obligatoire.
oblige [ə'blaidʒ], *v.t.* obliger; faire plaisir à.
obliging [ə'blaidʒiŋ], *a.* obligeant.
oblique [o'bli:k], *a.* oblique; indirect.
obliterate [ə'blitəreit], *v.t.* effacer, oblitérer.
obliteration [əblitə'reiʃən], *n.* oblitération, *f.*
oblivion [ə'bliviən], *n.* oubli, *m.*; ***act of oblivion***, loi d'amnistie, *f.*
oblivious [ə'bliviəs], *a.* oublieux (*de*).
oblong ['ɔblɔŋ], *a.* oblong.—*n.* rectangle, *m.*
obnoxious [əb'nɔkʃəs], *a.* odieux, désagréable, déplaisant.
oboe ['oubou], *n.* hautbois, *m.*
obscene [əb'si:n], *a.* obscène, sale.
obscenity [əb'seniti], *n.* obscénité, *f.*
obscure [əb'skjuə], *a.* obscur; (*fig.*) caché.—*v.t.* obscurcir; voiler (*lumière*).
obscurely [əb'skjuəli], *adv.* obscurément.
obscurity [əb'skjuəriti], *n.* obscurité, *f.*
obsequies ['ɔbsikwiz], *n.pl.* obsèques, *f.pl.*
obsequious [əb'si:kwiəs], *a.* obséquieux.
obsequiousness [əb'si:kwiəsnis], *n.* soumission obséquieuse, *f.*

observance [əb'zə:vəns], *n.* observance; pratique, observation, *f.*
observant [əb'zə:vənt], *a.* observateur.
observation [əbzə'veiʃən], *n.* observation, *f.*
observatory [əb'zə:vətri], *n.* observatoire, *m.*
observe [əb'zə:v], *v.t.* observer; remarquer; faire remarquer.
observer [əb'zə:və], *n.* observateur, *m.*
obsess [əb'ses], *v.t.* obséder.
obsessed [əb'sest], *a.* obsédé.
obsession [əb'seʃən], *n.* obsession, *f.*
obsolete ['ɔbsəli:t], *a.* vieilli, suranné; tombé en désuétude.
obstacle ['ɔbstəkl], *n.* obstacle, *m.*
obstetrics [əb'stetriks], *n.pl.* obstétrique, *f.*
obstinacy ['ɔbstinəsi], *n.* obstination, opiniâtreté, *f.*; entêtement (*de caractère*), *m.*
obstinate ['ɔbstinit], *a.* obstiné, opiniâtre, entêté; têtu (*enfant*).
obstinately ['ɔbstinitli], *adv.* obstinément.
obstreperous [əb'strepərəs], *a.* turbulent, tapageur; récalcitrant.
obstruct [əb'strʌkt], *v.t.* empêcher, retarder; obstruer, encombrer, boucher.
obstruction [əb'strʌkʃən], *n.* empêchement, obstacle, *m.*; (*Med.*, *Polit.*) obstruction, *f.*; encombrement (*circulation*), *m.*
obstructive [əb'strʌktiv], *a.* qui empêche; (*Med.*) obstructif.
obtain [əb'tein], *v.t.* obtenir, gagner; se procurer.—*v.i.* prévaloir.
obtainable [əb'teinəbl], *a.* qu'on peut obtenir, procurable.
obtrude [əb'tru:d], *v.t.* imposer.—*v.i.* s'introduire de force; être importun.
obtrusive [əb'tru:siv], *a.* importun.
obtuse [əb'tju:s], *a.* obtus; émoussé; stupide.
obtuseness [əb'tju:snis], *n.* (*fig.*) stupidité, *f.*
obverse ['ɔbvə:s], *n.* face, *f.*, avers, obvers (*de médaille etc.*), *m.*
obviate ['ɔbvieit], *v.t.* éviter, obvier à.
obvious ['ɔbviəs], *a.* évident, clair.
obviously ['ɔbviəsli], *adv.* évidemment.
occasion [ə'keiʒən], *n.* occasion, rencontre; raison, cause, *f.*; besoin (*nécessité*), *m.*—*v.t.* occasionner, causer.
occasional [ə'keiʒənəl], *a.* occasionnel, fortuit.
occasionally [ə'keiʒənəli], *adv.* quelquefois, de temps en temps.
occident ['ɔksidənt], *n.* occident, *m.*
occidental [ɔksi'dentl], *a.* occidental.
occult [ə'kʌlt], *a.* occulte.
occupant ['ɔkjupənt], *n.* occupant, *m.*; locataire (*de chambre louée*); titulaire (*d'un poste*), *m.*, *f.*
occupation [ɔkju'peiʃən], *n.* occupation, *f.*; emploi, métier, *m.*; possession, *f.*
occupier ['ɔkjupaiə], *n.* occupant, *m.*; locataire (*de chambre louée*), *m.*, *f.*, habitant, *m.*
occupy ['ɔkjupai], *v.t.* occuper; employer; habiter (*une maison*).
occur [ə'kə:], *v.i.* arriver, avoir lieu, se produire; venir à l'esprit; ***it occurred to me that***, l'idée m'est venue que.
occurrence [ə'kʌrəns], *n.* occurrence, rencontre, *f.*, événement, *m.*
ocean ['ouʃən], *a.* de l'océan.—*n.* océan, *m.*
oceanic [ousi'ænik], *a.* océanique.
ochre ['oukə], *n.* ocre, *f.*
o'clock [ə'klɔk], [CLOCK].
octagon ['ɔktəgən], *n.* octogone, *m.*
octagonal [ɔk'tægənəl], *a.* octogone, octogonal.
octane ['ɔktein], *n.* octane, *m.*; ***high-octane fuel***, supercarburant, *m.*
octave ['ɔktiv], *n.* (*Mus.*, *Eccles.*) octave, *f.*
octavo [ɔk'teivou], *n.* in-octavo, *m.*
octet(te) [ɔk'tet], *n.* (*Mus.*) octuor, *m.*
October [ɔk'toubə]. octobre, *m.*
octogenarian [ɔktoudʒi'nɛəriən], *a.* and *n.* octogénaire, *m.*, *f.*
octopus ['ɔktəpəs], *n.* pieuvre, *f.*
ocular ['ɔkjulə], *a.* oculaire.
oculist ['ɔkjulist], *n.* oculiste, *m.*
odd [ɔd], *a.* impair; de surplus; d'appoint (*argent*); dépareillé (*article isolé d'une collection*); étrange, singulier, bizarre; ***odd moments***, moments perdus, *m.pl.*; ***odd number***, nombre impair, *m.*
oddity ['ɔditi], *n.* bizarrerie, *f.*; original (*personne*), *m.*
odd-looking ['ɔdlukiŋ], *a.* à la mine bizarre.
oddly ['ɔdli], *adv.* étrangement; bizarrement.
oddments ['ɔdmənts], *n.pl.* bric-à-brac, *m.*, fins de séries, *f.pl.*
odds [ɔdz], *n.pl.* inégalité, *f.*; (*fig.*) avantage, *m.*, supériorité, *f.*; chances, *f.pl.*; ***it makes no odds***, cela ne fait rien; ***odds and ends***, petits bouts, *m.pl.*; ***to be at odds with***, être mal avec.
ode [oud], *n.* ode, *f.*
odious ['oudiəs], *a.* odieux.
odium ['oudiəm], *n.* détestation, *f.*
odorous ['oudərəs], *a.* odorant.
odour ['oudə], *n.* odeur, *f.*, parfum, *m.*; ***in bad odour***, en mauvaise odeur.
odourless ['oudəlis], *a.* sans odeur.
o'er ['ɔ:ə], (*poet.*) [OVER].
of [ɔv], *prep.* de; d'entre.
off [ɔf, ɔ:f], *adv.* au loin, à distance; d'ici; rompu, enlevé; fini; fermé (*électricité etc.*); qui n'est plus frais (*aliments*); ***day off***, jour de congé, *m.*; ***fifty yards off***, à cinquante pas; ***I am off***, je m'en vais; ***off and on***, de temps à autre; ***time off***, temps libre, *m.*; ***to be well off***, être dans l'aisance.—*a.* ***off day***, jour de congé, *m.*; ***off side***, côté droit, hors montoir; (*Ftb.*) hors-jeu; ***off white***, blanc teinté.—*prep.* de, de dessus; éloigné de; (*Naut.*) au large de.
offal [ɔfl], *n.* issues, *f.pl.*; abats, *m.pl.*; rebut, *m.*
offence [ə'fens], *n.* agression; offense; injure; violation (*d'une loi etc.*), *f.*, délit, crime, *m.*
offend [ə'fend], *v.t.* offenser, outrager, blesser; violer (*transgresser*).—*v.i.* déplaire (*à*); commettre une offense.
offender [ə'fendə], *n.* offenseur; (*Law*) délinquant, *m.*
offensive [ə'fensiv], *a.* offensant, désagréable; choquant; offensif (*attaquant*).—*n.* offensive, *f.*
offensively [ə'fensivli], *adv.* d'une manière offensante; offensivement.
offensiveness [ə'fensivnis], *n.* nature offensante, *f.*
offer ['ɔfə], *v.t.* offrir, présenter, proposer à.—*v.i.* s'offrir, se présenter à; essayer de.—*n.* offre, *f.*
offering ['ɔfəriŋ], *n.* offrande, *f.*; sacrifice, *m.*
off-hand ['ɔf'hænd], *adv.* au premier abord; sans réflexion, sur-le-champ; cavalière-

ment.—*a.* brusque, cavalier; impromptu, improvisé.
off-handed ['ɔf'hændid], *a.* sans façon, sans gêne.
off-handedness ['ɔf'hændidnis], *n.* sans-façon, sans-gêne, *m.*
office ['ɔfis], *n.* bureau (*immeuble*), *m.*, agence, *f.*; cabinet (*du directeur*), *m.*; étude (*d'avoué etc.*), *f.*; office, emploi; ministère, *m.*, charge, *f.*, fonctions, *f.pl.*; (*pl.*) devoirs (*services*), *m.pl.*; place, *f.*; office (*d'une maison*), *m.*
officer ['ɔfisə], *n.* officier; fonctionnaire (*du gouvernement*); agent (*de police*), *m.*; ***non-commissioned officer***, sous-officier, *m.*—*v.t.* fournir des officiers à; encadrer.
official [ə'fiʃəl], *a.* officiel.—*n.* fonctionnaire; employé, *m.*
officialdom [ə'fiʃəldəm], *n.* bureaucratie, *f.*
officially [ə'fiʃəli], *adv.* officiellement.
officiate [ə'fiʃieit], *v.i.* officier, desservir.
officious [ə'fiʃəs], *a.* officieux; importun.
officiousness [ə'fiʃəsnis], *n.* zèle officieux, *m.*
offing ['ɔfiŋ], *n.* (*Naut.*) ***in the offing***, au large; (*fig.*) en perspective.
offset ['ɔfset], *v.t.* (*Comm.*) compenser; (*Tech.*) désaxer, décaler.
offshoot ['ɔfʃu:t], *n.* rejeton, *m.*
offspring ['ɔfspriŋ], *n.* enfants, descendants, *m.pl.*; (*fig.*) fruit, produit, *m.*
often [ɔfn], ***oft** [ɔft], ***oftentimes** ['ɔfn taimz], ***oft-times** ['ɔfttaimz], *adv.* souvent, maintes fois.
ogle [ougl], *v.t.* lorgner; lancer des œillades à.—*n.* œillade, *f.*
ogler ['ouglə], *n.* lorgneur, *m.*
ogling ['ougliŋ], *n.* lorgnerie, *f.*, œillades, *f.pl.*
ogre ['ougə], *n.* ogre, *m.*
ogress ['ougris], *n.* ogresse, *f.*
oh! [ou], *int.* oh! hélas!
ohm [oum], *n.* (*Elec.*) ohm, *m.*
oil [ɔil], *n.* huile, *f.*; ***(crude) oil***, pétrole (brut), *m.*; ***fuel oil***, mazout, *m.*; ***paraffin oil***, pétrole (lampant), *m.*—*v.t.* huiler; graisser; (*fig.*) délier (*la langue*).
oilcake ['ɔilkeik], *n.* tourteau, *m.*
oil-can ['ɔilkæn], *n.* burette, *f.*
oil-cloth ['ɔilklɔθ], *n.* toile cirée, *f.*
oil-field ['ɔilfi:ld], *n.* gisement pétrolifère, *m.*
oiliness ['ɔilinis], *n.* onctuosité, nature huileuse, *f.*
oil-lamp ['ɔillæmp], *n.* lampe à huile *ou* à pétrole, *f.*
oil-painting ['ɔilpeintiŋ], *n.* peinture à l'huile, *f.*
oilskin ['ɔilskin], *n.* toile cirée vernie, *f.*
oil-stove ['ɔilstouv], *n.* réchaud à pétrole, *m.*
oil-tanker ['ɔiltæŋkə], *n.* (*Naut.*) pétrolier; (*Motor.*) camion-citerne, *m.*
oil-well ['ɔilwel], *n.* puits de pétrole, *m.*
oily ['ɔili], *a.* huileux; (*fig.*) oléagineux, onctueux.
ointment ['ɔintmənt], *n.* onguent, *m.*, pommade, *f.*
old [ould], *a.* vieux; âgé; ancien, antique; ***how old are you?*** quel âge avez-vous? ***old man (chap, boy)***, mon vieux, mon brave; ***to grow old***, vieillir.
olden ['ouldən], *a.* vieux, ancien; ***in olden times***, au temps jadis.
old-fashioned [ould'fæʃənd] *a.* démodé, suranné.
oldish ['ouldiʃ], *a.* un peu vieux, vieillot.
old-maid ['ouldmeid], *n.* vieille fille, *f.*
oleaginous [ouli'ædʒinəs], *a.* oléagineux.
oleander [ouli'ændə], *n.* (*Bot.*) laurier-rose, oléandre, *m.*
oligarchy ['ɔligɑ:ki], *n.* oligarchie, *f.*
olive ['ɔliv], *n.* olive, *f.*, olivier (*arbre*), *m.*
Oliver ['ɔlivə]. Olivier, *m.*
Olympian [o'limpiən], *a.* olympien.
Olympic [o'limpik], *a.* olympique; ***the Olympic Games***, les jeux olympiques, *m.pl.*
Olympus [o'limpəs]. Olympe, *m.*
omega ['oumigə], *n.* oméga, *m.*
omelet(te) ['ɔməlit], *n.* omelette, *f.*
omen ['oumən], *n.* augure, *m.*
ominous ['ɔminəs], *a.* de mauvais augure, sinistre; menaçant.
ominously ['ɔminəsli], *adv.* de mauvais augure.
omission [o'miʃən], *n.* omission, *f.*
omit [o'mit], *v.t.* omettre; oublier.
omnipotence [ɔm'nipətəns], *n.* omnipotence, toute-puissance, *f.*
omnipotent [ɔm'nipətənt], *a.* tout-puissant, omnipotent.
omniscient [ɔm'nisiənt], *a.* omniscient.
omnivorous [ɔm'nivərəs], *a.* omnivore.
on [ɔn], *prep.* sur, dessus; à; de; en, dans; lors de, après; ***on foot***, à pied; ***on Monday***, lundi; ***on purpose***, à dessein, exprès; ***on the whole***, en somme.—*adv.* dessus; en avant, avant, avancé; toujours (*continuation*); de suite (*succession*); ***and so on***, et ainsi de suite; ***on and on***, sans cesse, interminablement; ***play on***, continuez de jouer; ***read on***, lisez toujours.
once [wʌns], *adv.* une fois, une seule fois; autrefois, jadis (*anciennement*); ***at once***, sur-le-champ, tout de suite; ***once upon a time there was***, il était une fois.
one [wʌn], *a.* un; seul, unique; un certain.—*n.* un, *m.*, une, *f.*—*pron.* on, l'on; vous (*accusatif*); celui, *m.*, celle, *f.*; quelqu'un; un homme, *m.*, une femme, *f.*
one-armed ['wʌnɑ:md], *a.* manchot.
one-eyed ['wʌnaid], *a.* borgne.
onerous ['ɔnərəs], *a.* onéreux.
onerousness ['ɔnərəsnis], *n.* poids, *m.*, charge, *f.*
oneself [wʌn'self], *pron.* soi, soi-même; (*reflexive*) se.
one-sided ['wʌn'saidid], *a.* à un côté, à une face; (*fig.*) partial, unilatéral.
one-sidedness ['wʌn'saididnis], *n.* partialité, *f.*
one-way ['wʌnwei], *a.* ***one-way street***, rue à sens unique, *f.*; ***one-way ticket***, billet simple, *m.*
onion ['ʌnjən], *n.* oignon, *m.*; ***spring onion***, ciboule, *f.*
onion-bed ['ʌnjənbed], *n.* oignonnière, *f.*
onlooker ['ɔnlukə], *n.* spectateur, *m.*
only ['ounli], *a.* seul; unique; ***only child***, enfant unique, *m.*, *f.*—*adv.* seulement; rien que; uniquement; ne . . . que.—*conj.* mais.
onset ['ɔnset], *n.* assaut, *m.*, attaque, charge, *f.*
onslaught ['ɔnslɔ:t], *n.* attaque, *f.*; assaut, *m.*
onus ['ounəs], *n.* charge, responsabilité, obligation, *f.*

onward ['ɔnwəd], *a.* en avant; avancé, progressif.—*adv.* or **onwards** ['ɔnwədz], en avant.
onyx ['ɔniks], *n.* onyx, *m.*
ooze [u:z], *n.* limon, *m.*—*v.i.* suinter, filtrer; (*fig.*) s'ébruiter.
oozing ['u:ziŋ], *n.* suintement; (*fig.*) ébruitement, *m.*
oozy ['u:zi], *a.* vaseux, limoneux.
opal [oupl], *n.* opale, *f.*
opaque [o'peik], *a.* opaque; (*fig.*) épais.
opaqueness [o'peiknis], *n.* opacité, *f.*
open ['oupən], *v.t.* ouvrir; déboucher (*une bouteille*); (*fig.*) expliquer; commencer, entamer; révéler; décacheter (*une lettre*); défaire (*un colis*); inaugurer.—*v.i.* s'ouvrir; commencer.—*a.* ouvert, découvert, à découvert, nu, à nu; franc, sincère; libre; (*fig.*) clair; ***in the open (air)***, en plein air; ***on the open sea***, en pleine mer.
opener ['oupnə], *n.* ouvreur, *m.*; ***tin-opener***, ouvre-boîte, *m.*
open-handed ['oupən'hændid], *a.* libéral, généreux.
open-hearted ['oupən'hɑ:tid], *a.* franc.
opening ['oupniŋ], *a.* qui commence, d'inauguration; ***the opening chapter***, le premier chapitre.—*n.* ouverture, embrasure, *f.*; commencement, début, *m.*; chance; éclaircie (*dans une forêt etc.*), *f.*
openly ['oupənli], *adv.* ouvertement; franchement.
open-minded ['oupən'maindid], *a.* sans parti pris, libéral, à l'esprit ouvert.
open-mouthed ['oupən'mauðd], *a.* bouche béante, bouche bée.
openness ['oupənnis], *n.* franchise, sincérité, candeur, *f.*
opera ['ɔpərə], *n.* opéra, *m.*
opera-glass ['ɔprəglɑ:s], *n.* lorgnette, *f.*; (*pl.*) jumelles, *f.pl.*
opera-hat ['ɔprəhæt], *n.* claque, *m.*
opera-house ['ɔprəhaus], *n.* opéra, *m.*
operate ['ɔpəreit], *v.t.* opérer, effectuer.—*v.i.* opérer, agir; (*Fin.*) spéculer; ***to operate on someone for appendicitis***, opérer quelqu'un de l'appendicite.
operatic [ɔpə'rætik], *a.* d'opéra.
operation [ɔpə'reiʃən], *n.* opération, action, *f.*
operative ['ɔpərətiv], *a.* actif, efficace; des ouvriers.—*n.* artisan, ouvrier, *m.*
operator ['ɔpəreitə], *n.* opérateur, *m.* ***telephone operator***, téléphoniste, *m.*, *f.*; ***wireless operator***, radio, *m.*
operetta [ɔpə'retə], *n.* opérette, *f.*
opiate ['oupiit], *a.* opiacé.—*n.* opiat, *m.*
opinion [ə'pinjən], *n.* opinion, *f.*, avis, sentiment, *m.*; idée, pensée; (*Law*) consultation, *f.*; ***in my opinion***, à mon avis.
opinionated [ə'pinjəneitid], *a.* opiniâtre; têtu, imbu de ses opinions.
opium ['oupjəm], *n.* opium, *m.*
opossum [o'pɔsəm], *n.* opossum, *m.*; sarigue, *f.*
opponent [ə'pounənt], *n.* opposant, *m.*, adversaire, *m.*, *f.*
opportune ['ɔpətju:n], *a.* opportun, à propos.
opportunely ['ɔpətju:nli], *adv.* à propos.
opportunity [ɔpə'tju:niti], *n.* occasion, *f.*
oppose [ə'pouz], *v.t.* opposer; s'opposer à.
opposite ['ɔpəzit], *a.* opposé; vis-à-vis, contraire (*à*), en face.—*n.* opposé, contre-pied, *m.*—*adv.* vis-à-vis, en face.—*prep.* en face de, vis-à-vis de.
opposition [ɔpə'ziʃən], *n.* opposition, résistance; concurrence (*rivalité*), *f.*; obstacle, *m.*
oppress [ə'pres], *v.t.* opprimer; accabler.
oppression [ə'preʃən], *n.* oppression, *f.*
oppressive [ə'presiv], *a.* accablant, oppressif; lourd.
oppressiveness [ə'presivnis], *n.* caractère oppressif, *m.*, lourdeur, *f.*
oppressor [ə'presə], *n.* oppresseur, *m.*
opprobrious [ə'proubriəs], *a.* infamant; injurieux.
opprobrium [ə'proubriəm], *n.* opprobre, *m.*
opt [ɔpt], *v.i.* opter.
optic ['ɔptik], **optical** ['ɔptikəl], *a.* optique; d'optique.
optician [ɔp'tiʃən], *n.* opticien, *m.*
optimism ['ɔptimizm], *n.* optimisme, *m.*
optimist ['ɔptimist], *n.* optimiste, *m.*, *f.*
optimistic [ɔpti'mistik], *a.* optimiste.
option ['ɔpʃən], *n.* option, *f.*, choix, *m.*
optional ['ɔpʃənəl], *a.* facultatif.
opulence ['ɔpjuləns], *n.* opulence, *f.*
opulent ['ɔpjulənt], *a.* opulent.
or [ɔ:], *conj.* ou; (*negatively*) ni; ***or else***, ou bien, autrement.
oracle ['ɔrəkl], *n.* oracle, *m.*
oracular [ɔ'rækjulə], *a.* d'oracle; (*fig.*) dogmatique.
oral ['ɔ:rəl], *a.* oral.
orally ['ɔ:rəli], *adv.* oralement; par la bouche.
orange ['ɔrindʒ], *n.* orange; couleur orange, *f.*
orangery ['ɔrindʒəri], *n.* orangerie, *f.*
orange-tree ['ɔrindʒtri:], *n.* oranger, *m.*
orang-outang [o'ræŋu'tæŋ], *n.* orang-outang, *m.*
oration [o'reiʃən], *n.* allocution, *f.*, discours, *m.*; ***funeral oration***, oraison funèbre, *f.*
orator ['ɔrətə], *n.* orateur, *m.*
oratorical [ɔrə'tɔrikəl], *a.* oratoire.
oratorio [ɔrə'tɔ:riou], *n.* oratorio, *m.*
oratory ['ɔrətri], *n.* art oratoire, *m.*, éloquence, *f.*; oratoire (*chapelle*), *m.*
orb [ɔ:b], *n.* globe; corps sphérique; orbe, *m.*
orbit ['ɔ:bit], *n.* orbe, *m.*; (*Anat.*, *Astron.*) orbite, *f.*
orchard ['ɔ:tʃəd], *n.* verger, *m.*
orchestra ['ɔ:kistrə], *n.* orchestre, *m.*
orchestral [ɔ:'kestrəl], *a.* d'orchestre, orchestral.
orchid ['ɔ:kid], *n.* orchidée, *f.*
ordain [ɔ:'dein], *v.t.* ordonner, décréter.
ordeal [ɔ:'di:əl], *n.* dure épreuve, *f.*
order ['ɔ:də], *n.* ordre; règlement, *m.*; décoration (*insigne*); (*Mil.*) consigne; classe, *f.*, rang, *m.*; commande (*de marchandises*), *f.*; mandat (*de payer*), *m.*; ***in order that***, afin que; ***in order to***, afin de; ***postal order***, mandat-poste, *m.*—*v.t.* ordonner; régler; diriger (*administrer*); commander; prescrire (*médecine*).
ordering ['ɔ:dəriŋ], *n.* disposition, *f.*, arrangement, *m.*
orderliness ['ɔ:dəlinis], *n.* bon ordre, *m.*, méthode, *f.*
orderly ['ɔ:dəli], *a.* en bon ordre, méthodique, rangé.—*n.* (*Mil.*) planton, *m.*
ordinal ['ɔ:dinl], *a.* ordinal.
ordinance ['ɔ:dinəns], *n.* ordonnance, *f.*

ordinarily ['ɔ:dinrili], *adv.* ordinairement, d'ordinaire.
ordinary ['ɔ:dinri], *a.* ordinaire; moyen.—*n.* ordinaire, *m.*; table d'hôte, *f.*
ordination [ɔ:di'neiʃən], *n.* ordination, *f.*
ordnance ['ɔ:dnəns], *n.* artillerie, *f.*; ***ordnance map***, carte d'état major, *f.*
ore [ɔ:], *n.* minerai, *m.*
organ ['ɔ:gən], *n.* (*Anat. etc.*) organe; (*Mus.*) orgue, *m.*
organic [ɔ:'gænik], *a.* organique; des organes.
organism ['ɔ:gənizm], *n.* organisme, *m.*
organist ['ɔ:gənist], *n.* organiste, *m.*, *f.*
organization [ɔ:gənai'zeiʃən], *n.* organisation; œuvre, *f.*
organize ['ɔ:gənaiz], *v.t.* organiser; aménager.
organizer ['ɔ:gənaizə], *n.* organisateur, *m.*
orgy ['ɔ:dʒi], *n.* orgie, *f.*
orient ['ɔ:riənt], *n.* orient, *m.*
Oriental [ɔ:ri'entl], *a.* oriental, d'Orient.—*n.* natif de l'Orient, oriental, *m.*
orifice ['ɔrifis], *n.* orifice, *m.*, ouverture, *f.*
origin ['ɔridʒin], *n.* origine, source; provenance, *f.*
original [ə'ridʒinl], *a.* original, inédit (*nouveau*); primitif (*sens des mots etc.*).—*n.* original, *m.*
originality [əridʒi'næliti], *n.* originalité, *f.*
originally [ə'ridʒinəli], *adv.* originairement; originalement.
originate [ə'ridʒineit], *v.t.* faire naître, produire; (*fig.*) inventer.—*v.i.* tirer son origine (*de*), provenir de.
originator [ə'ridʒineitə], *n.* initiateur, auteur, *m.*
oriole ['ɔ:rioul], *n.* (*Orn.*) loriot, *m.*
orison ['ɔrizn], *n.* oraison, prière, *f.*
Orkneys ['ɔ:kniz], **the.** les Orcades, *f.pl.*
ornament ['ɔ:nəmənt], *n.* ornement, *m.*—*v.t.* orner, décorer (*de*).
ornamental [ɔ:nə'mentl], *a.* ornemental, d'ornement; d'agrément.
ornate [ɔ:'neit], *a.* orné, élégant, paré.
ornately [ɔ:'neitli], *adv.* avec ornement.
ornithologist [ɔ:ni'θɔlədʒist], *n.* ornithologiste, ornithologue, *m.*, *f.*
ornithology [ɔ:ni'θɔlədʒi], *n.* ornithologie, *f.*
orphan ['ɔ:fən], *a.* and *n.* orphelin, *m.*
orphanage ['ɔ:fənidʒ], *n.* état d'orphelin; orphelinat, *m.*
orthodox ['ɔ:θədɔks], *a.* orthodoxe.
orthodoxy ['ɔ:θədɔksi], *n.* orthodoxie, *f.*
orthographic [ɔ:θə'græfik], *a.* orthographique.
orthography [ɔ:'θɔgrəfi], *n.* orthographe, orthographie, *f.*
orthop(a)edic [ɔ:θə'pi:dik], *a.* orthopédique.
orthop(a)edist [ɔ:θə'pi:dist], *n.* orthopédiste, *m.*
orthop(a)edy ['ɔ:θəpi:di], *n.* orthopédie, *f.*
oscillate ['ɔsileit], *v.i.* osciller; (*fig.*) balancer, vaciller.
oscillation [ɔsi'leiʃən], *n.* oscillation, *f.*
oscillatory ['ɔsileitəri], *a.* oscillatoire.
osier ['ouʒiə], *n.* osier, *m.*
osier-bed ['ouʒiəbed], *n.* oseraie, *f.*
osprey ['ɔsprei], *n.* (*Orn.*) orfraie, *f.*
osseous ['ɔsiəs], *a.* osseux.
ossicle ['ɔsikl], *n.* ossicule, osselet, *m.*
ossification [ɔsifi'keiʃən], *n.* ossification, *f.*
ossify ['ɔsifai], *v.t.* ossifier.—*v.i.* s'ossifier.
ostensible [ɔs'tensibl], *a.* prétendu.
ostensibly [ɔs'tensibli], *adv.* en apparence.
ostentation [ɔsten'teiʃən], *n.* ostentation, *f.*, faste, *m.*
ostentatious [ɔsten'teiʃəs], *a.* pompeux, fastueux.
osteopath ['ɔstiopæθ], *n.* ostéopathe, *m.*
ostler ['ɔslə], *n.* garçon d'écurie, *m.*
ostracism ['ɔstrəsizm], *n.* ostracisme, *m.*
ostracize ['ɔstrəsaiz], *v.t.* frapper d'ostracisme, exiler.
ostrich ['ɔstritʃ], *n.* autruche, *f.*
other ['ʌðə], *a.* autre; ***every other day***, tous les deux jours; ***other people***, d'autres, autrui.—*pron.* autre; autrui; ***all the others***, tous les autres.
otherwise ['ʌðəwaiz], *adv.* autrement; sans quoi.
otter ['ɔtə], *n.* loutre, *f.*
ought [ɔ:t], *v.aux.* devoir; falloir; ***you ought to do it***, vous devriez le faire; ***you ought to have seen***, il aurait fallu voir.
ounce (1) [auns], *n.* once (*poids*), *f.*
ounce (2) [auns], *n.* (*Zool.*) once, *f.*
our ['auə], *a.poss.* notre, *sing.*, nos, *pl.*
ours ['auəz], *pron.* le nôtre, *m.*, la nôtre, *f.*, les nôtres, *pl.*; à nous.
ourselves [auə'selvz], *pron.* nous-mêmes; nous.
oust [aust], *v.t.* évincer, déloger.
out [aut], *adv.* hors, dehors; sorti (*pas chez soi*); découvert, exposé (*dévoilé*); éteint (*feu etc.*); épuisé, fini (*tout vendu* ou *tout consumé*), jusqu'au bout; haut, à haute voix (*parler*); dans l'erreur (*pas exact*); publié, paru (*livre*); épanoui (*fleur*).—*a.* externe.
outbid [aut'bid], *v.t. irr.* (*conjug. like* BID) enchérir sur, surenchérir.
outboard ['autbɔ:d], *a.* ***outboard motor-boat***, hors-bord, *m.*
outbreak ['autbreik], *n.* éruption, explosion; épidémie, *f.*
outburst ['autbə:st], *n.* explosion, *f.*, transport, éclat, *m.*
outcast ['autkɑ:st], *a.* expulsé, proscrit, rejeté.—*n.* proscrit, banni, paria, *m.*
outcome ['autkʌm], *n.* résultat, *m.*
outcry ['autkrai], *n.* clameur, *f.*, tollé, *m.*
outdated [aut'deitid], *a.* démodé.
outdo [aut'du], *v.t. irr.* (*conjug. like* DO) surpasser, exceller.
outdoor ['autdɔ:], *a.* en plein air; externe.
outdoors [aut'dɔ:z], *adv.* en plein air; hors de la maison.
outer ['autə], *a.* extérieur, du dehors, externe.
outermost ['autəmoust], *a.* le plus extérieur.
outfit ['autfit], *n.* attirail, équipement; trousseau, *m.*
outfitter ['autfitə], *n.* confectionneur et chemisier, *m.*
outflank [aut'flæŋk], *v.t.* déborder, tourner.
outgoing ['autgouiŋ], *a.* sortant, qui sort.—*n.* (*pl.*) dépenses, *f.pl.*
outgrow [aut'grou], *v.t. irr.* (*conjug. like* GROW) dépasser, surpasser.
outgrowth ['autgrouθ], *n.* excroissance; conséquence, *f.*
outhouse ['authaus], *n.* hangar, *m.*; dépendance, *f.*
outing ['autiŋ], *n.* excursion, promenade, *f.*
outlandish [aut'lændiʃ], *a.* étranger; bizarre; retiré.
outlast [aut'lɑ:st], *v.t.* survivre à.

outlaw ['autlɔ:], *n.* proscrit, *m.*—*v.t.* mettre hors la loi, proscrire.
outlay ['autlei], *n.* dépense, *f.*, débours, *m.pl.*
outlet ['autlit], *n.* issue, sortie, *f.*; (*Comm.*) débouché, *m.*
outline ['autlain], *n.* contour; profil, *m.*, ébauche, *f.*—*v.t.* esquisser.
outlive [aut'liv], *v.t.* survivre à.
outlook ['autluk], *n.* vue, perspective, *f.*
outlying ['autlaiiŋ], *a.* éloigné, détaché.
outnumber [aut'nʌmbə], *v.t.* surpasser en nombre.
out-of-date [autəv'deit], *a.* démodé, dépassé.
outpost ['autpoust], *n.* avant-poste, *m.*
outpour [aut'pɔ:], *v.t.* épancher, verser à flots.
outpouring ['autpɔ:riŋ], *n.* effusion, *f.*, épanchement, *m.*
outrage ['autreidʒ], *n.* outrage, *m.*—*v.t.* outrager.
outrageous [aut'reidʒəs], *a.* outrageux, outrageant.
outrageousness [aut'reidʒəsnis], *n.* nature outrageante, énormité, *f.*
outright ['autrait], *adv.* complètement; carrément (*à cœur ouvert*).
outrun [aut'rʌn], *v.t. irr.* (*conjug. like* RUN) dépasser à la course, gagner de vitesse.
outset ['autset], *n.* début, commencement, *m.*; ***at the very outset***, dès l'origine.
outshine [aut'ʃain], *v.t. irr.* (*conjug. like* SHINE) surpasser en éclat, éclipser.
outside ['autsaid], *a.* extérieur, externe, du dehors.—*n.* dehors, extérieur, *m.*—[aut 'said], *adv.* en dehors, à l'extérieur.—[aut'said], *prep.* hors de, à l'extérieur de.
outsider [aut'saidə], *n.* étranger; (*Racing*) outsider, *m.*
outsize ['autsaiz], *a.* de grande taille, hors série.
outskirts ['autskə:ts], *n.pl.* bords, *m.pl.*; lisière (*d'un bois*), banlieue, *f.*, faubourg (*d'une ville*), *m.*
outspoken [aut'spoukən], *a.* franc, clair, carré.
outstanding [aut'stændiŋ], *a.* saillant, remarquable, excellent; non payé; en suspens (*affaires*).
outstretched [aut'stretʃt], *a.* étendu, déployé, tendu.
outstrip [aut'strip], *v.t.* devancer, distancer.
outward ['autwəd], *a.* extérieur, du dehors, externe; superficiel.—*adv.* or **outwards** ['autwədz], à l'extérieur; au dehors, extérieurement; ***outward bound***, en partance.
outwardly ['autwədli], *adv.* extérieurement, à l'extérieur; (*fig.*) en apparence.
outweigh [aut'wei], *v.t.* peser plus que; l'emporter sur.
outwit [aut'wit], *v.t.* surpasser en finesse, duper.
oval [ouvl], *a.* and *n.* ovale, *m.*
ovary ['ouvəri], *n.* ovaire, *m.*
ovation [o'veiʃən], *n.* ovation, *f.*
oven [ʌvn], *n.* four, *m.*
over ['ouvə], *prep.* sur; par-dessus; au-dessus de; de l'autre côté de (*en face*); pendant (*au cours de*); ***over there***, là-bas. —*adv.* d'un côté à l'autre; par-dessus, au-dessus; trop (*à l'excès*); plus de (*excédant*); de reste (*surplus inemployé*); fini, terminé, fait; passé.
overact [ouvər'ækt], *v.t.* outrer, exagérer.
overall ['ouvərɔ:l], *a.* total.—*n.* blouse, *f.*; tablier, *m.*; (*pl.*) salopette, combinaison, *f.*
overawe [ouvər'ɔ:], *v.t.* intimider, imposer à.
overbalance [ouvə'bæləns], *v.t.* l'emporter sur.—*v.i.* perdre l'équilibre.
overbearing [ouvə'bɛəriŋ], *a.* impérieux, autoritaire.
overboard ['ouvəbɔ:d], *adv.* par-dessus bord.
overburden [ouvə'bə:dn], *v.t.* surcharger; accabler (*de*).
overcast ['ouvəkɑ:st], *a.* couvert, nuageux.
overcharge [ouvə'tʃɑ:dʒ], *v.t.* surcharger; faire payer trop cher.—*n.* prix excessif, *m.*
overcoat ['ouvəkout], *n.* pardessus, *m.*
overcome [ouvə'kʌm], *v.t. irr.* (*conjug. like* COME) surmonter, vaincre, accabler.—*v.i.* l'emporter.
over-confident ['ouvə'kɔnfidənt], *a.* trop confiant; présomptueux, téméraire.
overcrowd [ouvə'kraud], *v.t.* encombrer à l'excès, trop remplir.
overcrowding [ouvə'kraudiŋ], *n.* surpeuplement, *m.*
overdo [ouvə'du:], *v.t. irr.* (*conjug. like* DO) exagérer, outrer; faire trop cuire; harasser.
overdone [ouvə'dʌn], *a.* trop cuit; (*fig.*) exagéré.
overdose ['ouvədous], *n.* dose trop forte, *f.*
overdraw [ouvə'drɔ:], *v.t. irr.* (*conjug. like* DRAW) excéder; ***to overdraw one's account***, tirer à découvert; tirer un chèque sans provision.
overdue [ouvə'dju:], *a.* en retard.
overestimate [ouvər'estimeit], *v.t.* évaluer trop haut.
overflow [ouvə'flou], *v.t.* inonder.—*v.i.* déborder, se déborder.—['ouvəflou], *n.* inondation, *f.*, débordement, *m.*
overflowing [ouvə'flouiŋ], *a.* qui déborde, trop plein.—*n.* débordement, *m.*
overgrown [ouvə'groun], *a.* couvert (*d'herbes, ronces*); trop grand, énorme.
overhang ['ouvəhæŋ], *n.* surplomb, *m.*—[ouvə'hæŋ], *v.t. irr.* (*conjug. like* HANG) pencher sur, surplomber; faire saillie.
overhanging ['ouvəhæŋiŋ], *a.* en surplomb.
overhaul [ouvə'hɔ:l], *v.t.* examiner, revoir; réviser, vérifier, démonter.—['ouvəhɔ:l], *n.* examen détaillé, *m.*
overhead [ouvə'hed], *adv.* par-dessus la tête, en haut.—*a.* aérien (*fil etc.*).—['ouvə hedz], *n.* (*pl.*) (*Comm.*) frais généraux, *m.pl.*
overhear [ouvə'hiə], *v.t. irr.* (*conjug. like* HEAR) entendre par hasard.
overheat [ouvə'hi:t], *v.t.* surchauffer.
overjoyed [ouvə'dʒɔid], *a.* transporté de joie, ravi.
overland ['ouvəlænd], *a.* and *adv.* par voie de terre.
overlap [ouvə'læp], *v.t.* recouvrir.—['ouvə læp], *n.* recouvrement, *m.*
overlapping [ouvə'læpiŋ], *n.* recouvrement, chevauchement, *m.*
overload [ouvə'loud], *v.t.* surcharger, surmener.
overlook [ouvə'luk], *v.t.* donner sur, dominer; surveiller (*diriger*); fermer les yeux sur (*passer sur*); oublier, négliger.

overlooking [ouvə'lukiŋ], *a.* donnant (*sur*).
overmuch ['ouvəmʌtʃ], *a.* excessif.—*n.* trop, *m.*—*adv.* par trop, excessivement.
overnight [ouvə'nait], *adv.* durant la nuit; hier soir; du jour au lendemain.
overpay [ouvə'pei], *v.t. irr.* (*conjug. like* PAY) payer trop.
overpower [ouvə'pauə], *v.t.* vaincre; accabler (*de*).
overpowering [ouvə'pauəriŋ], *a.* accablant, écrasant.
overproduction [ouvəprə'dʌkʃən], *n.* surproduction, *f.*
overrate [ouvə'reit], *v.t.* estimer trop haut.
overreach [ouvə'ri:tʃ], *v.t.* tromper.—*v.i.* forger (*chevaux*); ***to overreach oneself,*** trop présumer de ses forces.
override [ouvə'raid], *v.t. irr.* (*conjug. like* RIDE) surmener, outrepasser.
overrule [ouvə'ru:l], *v.t.* dominer; (*Law*) rejeter.
overrun [ouvə'rʌn], *v.t. irr.* (*conjug. like* RUN) envahir, faire une irruption dans; infester (*de*).—*v.i.* déborder.
oversea ['ouvəsi:], **overseas** ['ouvəsi:z, ouvə'si:z], *a.* and *adv.* d'outre-mer.
oversee [ouvə'si:], *v.t. irr.* (*conjug. like* SEE) surveiller.
overseer ['ouvəsiə], *n.* surveillant; contremaître (*d'usine etc.*), *m.*
overshadow [ouvə'ʃædou], *v.t.* ombrager; éclipser.
overshoes ['ouvəʃu:z], *n.pl.* caoutchoucs, *m.pl.*
overshoot [ouvə'ʃu:t], *v.t. irr.* (*conjug. like* SHOOT) dépasser.
oversight ['ouvəsait], *n.* inadvertance, *f.*, oubli, *m.*
oversleep [ouvə'sli:p], *v.i. irr.* (*conjug. like* SLEEP) dormir au delà de son heure.
overstate [ouvə'steit], *v.t.* exagérer.
overstatement [ouvə'steitmənt], *n.* exagération, *f.*
overstep [ouvə'step], *v.t.* dépasser.
overt ['ouvə:t], *a.* ouvert, manifeste.
overtake [ouvə'teik], *v.t. irr.* (*conjug. like* TAKE) rattraper; doubler, dépasser.
overtax [ouvə'tæks], *v.t.* surtaxer, surcharger.
overthrow [ouvə'θrou], *v.t. irr.* (*conjug. like* THROW) renverser; défaire, détruire.—['ouvəθrou], *n.* renversement, *m.*, défaite; destruction, *f.*
overtime ['ouvətaim], *n.* heures supplémentaires, *f.pl.*
overtop [ouvə'tɔp], *v.t.* s'élever au-dessus de, dépasser.
overture ['ouvətjuə], *n.* ouverture; offre, *f.*
overturn [ouvə'tə:n], *v.t.* renverser; bouleverser.—*v.i.* verser.
overweening [ouvə'wi:niŋ], *a.* présomptueux, outrecuidant.
overweight ['ouvəweit], *n.* excédent, *m.*
overwhelm [ouvə'welm], *v.t.* accabler (*de*); combler (*de*) (*bontés etc.*).
overwhelming [ouvə'welmiŋ], *a.* accablant, écrasant.
overwork [ouvə'wə:k], *v.t.* surcharger de travail, surmener.—*n.* travail excessif; surmenage, *m.*
ovoid ['ouvɔid], *a.* ovoïde.
owe [ou], *v.t.* devoir; être redevable à . . . de.
owing ['ouiŋ], *a.* dû (*à*); ***owing to,*** à cause de grâce à.
owl [aul], *n.* hibou, *m.*; chouette, *f.*
owlet ['aulit], *n.* jeune hibou, *m.*
own (1) [oun], *a.* propre (*à soi*); ***my own money,*** mon propre argent; ***to hold one's own,*** se maintenir.—*v.t.* posséder, être propriétaire de (*avoir*).
own (2) [oun], *v.t.* avouer, confesser.
owner ['ounə], *n.* possesseur, *m.*, propriétaire, *m., f.*
ownership ['ounəʃip], *n.* propriété, *f.*
ox [ɔks], *n.* (*pl.* **oxen** ['ɔksən]) bœuf, *m.*
oxalic [ɔk'sælik], *a.* oxalique.
ox-fly ['ɔksflai], *n.* taon, *m.*
oxide ['ɔksaid], *n.* oxyde, *m.*
oxidization [ɔksidai'zeiʃən], *n.* oxydation, calcination, *f.*
oxidize ['ɔksidaiz], *v.t.* oxyder; calciner.
oxyacetylene [ɔksiə'setili:n], *a.* oxyacétylénique.
oxygen ['ɔksidʒən], *n.* oxygène, *m.*
oxygenate ['ɔksidjəneit], *v.t.* oxygéner.
oxygenous [ɔk'sidʒənəs], *a.* d'oxygène.
oyster ['ɔistə], *n.* huître, *f.*
oyster-bed ['ɔistəbed], *n.* banc d'huîtres, *m.*
ozone [ou'zoun], *n.* ozone, *m.*

P

P, p [pi:]. seizième lettre de l'alphabet, *m.*
pabulum ['pæbjuləm], *n.* aliment, *m.*, nourriture, *f.*
pace [peis], *n.* pas, *m.*; allure (*de cheval*), *f.*; train, *m.*; vitesse, *f.*; ***to put someone through his paces,*** mettre quelqu'un à l'épreuve.—*v.t.* arpenter; (*Spt.*) entraîner. —*v.i.* aller au pas, marcher.
pacific [pə'sifik], *a.* pacifique, paisible.—*n.* ***the Pacific (Ocean),*** le Pacifique, l'océan Pacifique, *m.*
pacification [pæsifi'keiʃən], *n.* pacification, *f.*
pacifier ['pæsifaiə], *n.* pacificateur, *m.*
pacifism ['pæsifizm], *n.* pacifisme, *m.*
pacifist ['pæsifist], *n.* pacifiste, *m., f.*
pacify ['pæsifai], *v.t.* pacifier, apaiser.
pack [pæk], *n.* paquet, ballot, *m.*; meute (*chiens de chasse*), *f.*; jeu (*de cartes*), *m.*—*v.t.* emballer, empaqueter.—*v.i.* s'assembler; se grouper; faire sa malle.
package ['pækidʒ], *n.* colis, paquet, *m.*
packer ['pækə], *n.* emballeur, *m.*
packet ['pækit], *n.* paquet; paquebot (*bateau*), *m.*
pack-horse ['pækhɔ:s], *n.* cheval de bât, *m.*
pack-ice ['pækais], *n.* glace de banquise, *f.*, pack, *m.*
packing ['pækiŋ], *n.* emballage, *m.*
pact [pækt], *n.* pacte, *m.*
pad [pæd], *n.* tampon; coussinet, *m.*; ***writing-pad,*** sous-main, bloc de papier, *m.*—*v.t.* ouater; rembourrer.—*v.i.* aller à pied.
padding ['pædiŋ], *n.* ouate, bourre, *f.*

paddle [pædl], *n.* pagaie; aube (*de roue*), *f.* —*v.t.* pagayer.—*v.i.* patauger.
paddle-boat ['pædlbout], *n.* bateau à aubes, *m.*
paddock ['pædək], *n.* enclos, pré, pâturage, *m.*
padlock ['pædlək], *n.* cadenas, *m.*—*v.t.* cadenasser, fermer au cadenas.
paean ['pi:ən], *n.* péan, *m.*
pagan ['peigən], *a.* and *n.* païen, *m.*
paganism ['peigənizm], *n.* paganisme, *m.*
page (1) [peidʒ], *n.* page (*garçon*), *m.*
page (2) [peidʒ], *n.* page (*de livre*), *f.*
pageant ['pædʒənt], *n.* spectacle pompeux, cortège *ou* spectacle historique, *m.*
pageantry ['pædʒəntri], *n.* pompe, *f.*, faste, apparat, *m.*
pagoda [pə'goudə], *n.* pagode, *f.*
paid [peid], *a.* payé, acquitté; affranchi (*lettres*).
pail [peil], *n.* seau, *m.*
pailful ['peilful], *n.* (plein) seau, *m.*
pain [pein], *n.* douleur; peine (*effort*), *f.*; ***on pain of***, sous peine de; ***to take pains***, se donner de la peine.—*v.t.* faire mal à; (*fig.*) faire de la peine à; affliger.
painful ['peinful], *a.* douloureux, pénible.
painless ['peinlis], *a.* sans douleur, indolore.
painstaking ['peinzteikiŋ], *a.* soigneux, assidu.
paint [peint], *n.* couleur; peinture, *f.*; fard (*pour le visage*), *m.*—*v.t.* peindre; farder (*le visage*).—*v.i.* peindre; se farder.
painter (1) ['peintə], *n.* peintre, *m.*
painter (2) ['peintə], *n.* (*Naut.*) amarre, *f.*
painting ['peintiŋ], *n.* peinture, *f.*; tableau (*picture*), *m.*
pair [pɛə], *n.* paire, *f.*; couple (*époux etc.*), *m.* —*v.t.* accoupler.—*v.i.* s'accoupler.
Pakistan [pɑ:ki'stɑ:n]. le Pakistan, *m.*
Pakistani [pɑ:ki'stɑ:ni], *a.* pakistanais.—*n.* Pakistanais (*personne*), *m.*
pal [pæl], *n.* (*colloq.*) camarade, copain, *m.*
palace ['pælis], *n.* palais, *m.*; ***archbishop's palace***, archevêché, *m.*; ***bishop's palace***, évêché, *m.*
palatable ['pælətəbl], *a.* agréable au goût, bon.
palate ['pælit], *n.* palais; (*fig.*) goût, *m.*
palatial [pə'leiʃl], *a.* du palais, palatial; grandiose.
palaver [pə'lɑ:və], *n.* palabre (*chez certains peuples primitifs*), *f.*; verbiage, *m.*; flagornerie, *f.*—*v.i.* palabrer, faire des phrases.
pale (1) [peil], *a.* pâle, blême; (*fig.*) blafard (*lumière*).—*v.i.* pâlir; (*fig.*) s'éclipser.
pale (2) [peil], *n.* pieu, palis, *m.*; limites (*bornes*), *f.pl.*; ***beyond the pale***, au ban de la société.
pale-faced ['peilfeist], *a.* au teint pâle.
paleness ['peilnis], *n.* pâleur, *f.*
Palestine ['pælistain]. la Palestine, *f.*
Palestinian [pælis'tiniən], *a.* palestinien.
palette ['pælit], *n.* palette, *f.*
palfrey ['pɔ:lfri], *n.* palefroi, *m.*
paling ['peiliŋ], *n.* palissade, *f.*
palisade [pæli'seid], *n.* palissade, *f.*—*v.t.* palissader.
palish ['peiliʃ], *a.* un peu pâle, pâlot.
pall [pɔ:l], *n.* poêle; (*fig.*) drap mortuaire; voile (*de fumée etc.*), *m.*—*v.i.* devenir fade, s'affadir.
pallet ['pælit], *n.* grabat, *m.*, paillasse, *f.*
palliate ['pælieit], *v.t.* pallier.
palliation [pæli'eiʃən], *n.* palliation, *f.*
palliative ['pæliətiv], *a.* and *n.* palliatif, *m.*
pallid ['pælid], *a.* pâle, blême, blafard.
pallor ['pælə], *n.* pâleur, *f.*
palm (1) [pɑ:m], *n.* paume (*de main*), *f.*—*v.t.* ***to palm off*** (*something on someone*), passer refiler (*quelque chose à quelqu'un*).
palm (2) [pɑ:m], *n.* palmier (*arbre*), *m.*; palme (*rameau*), *f.*; ***Palm Sunday***, dimanche des Rameaux, *m.*
palmist ['pɑ:mist], *n.* chiromancien, *m.*
palmistry ['pɑ:mistri], *n.* chiromancie, *f.*
palmy ['pɑ:mi], *a.* beau, glorieux, heureux.
palpable ['pælpəbl], *a.* palpable; manifeste.
palpitate ['pælpiteit], *v.i.* palpiter.
palpitation [pælpi'teiʃən], *n.* palpitation, *f.*
palsied ['pɔ:lzid], *a.* frappé de paralysie, paralytique.
palsy ['pɔ:lzi], *n.* paralysie, *f.*
palter ['pɔ:ltə], *v.i.* tergiverser, biaiser.
paltriness ['pɔ:ltrinis], *n.* mesquinerie, *f.*
paltry ['pɔ:ltri], *a.* mesquin, misérable.
pamper ['pæmpə], *v.t.* choyer, dorloter.
pamphlet ['pæmflit], *n.* brochure, *f.*; (*pej.*) pamphlet, *m.*
pamphleteer [pæmfli'tiə], *n.* auteur de brochures, *m.*; (*pej.*) pamphlétaire, *m.*, *f.*
pan [pæn], *n.* casserole, *f.*; poêlon, *m.*; ***frying-pan***, poêle, *f.*
panacea [pænə'si:ə], *n.* panacée, *f.*
Panama ['pænəmɑ:]. le Panama, *m.*
Panamanian [pænə'meiniən], *a.* panamanien. —*n.* Panamanien (*personne*), *m.*
pancake ['pænkeik], *n.* crêpe, *f.*
pancreas ['pænkriəs], *n.* (*Anat.*) pancréas, *m.*
pandemonium [pændi'mouniəm], *n.* pandémonium, *m.*
pander ['pændə], *v.i.* se prêter à, se faire complaisant pour.
pane [pein], *n.* carreau, *m.*, vitre, *f.*
panegyric [pæni'dʒirik], *a.* de panégyrique.—*n.* panégyrique, *m.*
panegyrist [pæni'dʒirist], *n.* panégyriste, *m.*, *f.*
panel [pænl], *n.* panneau, *m.*; liste (*de juré etc.*), *f.*; ***instrument panel***, tableau de manœuvre, *m.*—*v.t.* diviser en panneaux; lambrisser.
panelling ['pænliŋ], *n.* panneaux, *m.pl.*, lambrissage, *m.*
pang [pæŋ], *n.* angoisse, vive douleur, *f.*, serrement de cœur, *m.*
panic ['pænik], *a.* panique.—*n.* panique; terreur panique, *f.*—*v.i.* s'affoler.
pannier ['pæniə], *n.* panier, *m.*, hotte, *f.*
panoply ['pænəpli], *n.* panoplie, armure complète, *f.*
panorama [pænə'rɑ:mə], *n.* panorama, *m.*
panoramic [pænə'ræmik], *a.* panoramique.
pansy ['pænzi], *n.* (*Bot.*) pensée, *f.*
pant [pænt], *n.* palpitation, *f.*, halètement, *m.* —*v.i.* haleter, palpiter, panteler.
pantechnicon [pæn'teknikn], *n.* garde-meuble, *m.*; voiture de déménagement, *f.*
pantheism ['pænθi:izm], *n.* panthéisme, *m.*
pantheist ['pænθi:ist], *n.* panthéiste, *m.*, *f.*
pantheistic [pænθi:'istik], *a.* panthéistique.
panther ['pænθə], *n.* panthère, *f.*

pantile ['pæntail], *n.* tuile faîtière *ou* flamande, *f.*
pantomime ['pæntəmaim], *n.* pantomime, *f.*
pantomimic [pæntə'mimik], *a.* pantomime.
pantry ['pæntri], *n.* office, *f.*, garde-manger, *m.*
pants [pænts], *n.pl.* (*colloq.*) caleçon; (*Am.*) pantalon, *m.*
pap [pæp], *n.* mamelle; bouillie (*aliment*), *f.*
papacy ['peipəsi], *n.* papauté, *f.*
papal ['peipəl], *a.* papal, du pape.
paper ['peipə], *a.* de papier.—*n.* papier, *m.*; feuille de papier, *f.*; journal; papier-monnaie, *m.*; billets, *m.pl.*; mémoire, *m.*, étude (*article*); composition (*d'examen*), *f.*; (*pl.*) papiers, *m.pl.*; dossier, *m.*; ***blotting-paper***, papier buvard; ***brown paper***, papier gris.—*v.t.* tapisser (de papier).
paper-back ['peipəbæk], *n.* livre broché, *m.*
paper-clip ['peipəklip], *n.* attache, *f.*, trombone (*de fil*), *m.*
paper-hanger ['peipəhæŋə], *n.* colleur de papier, *m.*
paper-knife ['peipənaif], *n.* coupe-papier, *m.*
paper-maker ['peipəmeikə], *n.* fabricant de papier, *m.*
paper-mill ['peipəmil], *n.* papeterie, *f.*
paper-trade ['peipətreid], *n.* papeterie, *f.*
papism ['peipizm], *n.* papisme, *m.*
papist ['peipist], *n.* papiste, *m.*, *f.*
Papua [pə'puə]. la Papouasie, *f.*
Papuan [pə'puən], *a.* papou.—*n.* Papou (*personne*), *m.*
papyrus [pə'paiərəs], *n.* (*pl.* **papyri** [pə'paiərai]) papyrus, *m.*
par [pɑ:], *n.* pair, *m.*, égalité, (*Golf*) normale, *f.*; ***at par***, au pair.
parable ['pærəbl], *n.* parabole, *f.*
parabola [pə'ræbələ], *n.* (*Math.*) parabole, *f.*
parachute [pærə'ʃu:t], *n.* parachute, *m.*—*v.t.*, *v.i.* parachuter.
parachutist [pærə'ʃu:tist], *n.* parachutiste, *m.*, *f.*
parade [pə'reid], *n.* parade, *f.*; étalage, *m.*; esplanade, *f.*; (*Mil.*) rassemblement, *m.*; procession, *f.*—*v.t.* faire parade de.—*v.i.* faire de la parade; (*Mil.*) parader.
paradise ['pærədais], *n.* paradis, *m.*
paradox ['pærədɔks], *n.* paradoxe, *m.*
paradoxical [pærə'dɔksikl], *a.* paradoxal.
paraffin ['pærəfin], *n.* (*Chem.*) paraffine, *f.*; ***paraffin*** (*oil*), pétrole (lampant), *m.*
paragon ['pærəgən], *n.* parangon; modèle, *m.*
paragraph ['pærəgrɑ:f], *n.* paragraphe; alinéa, *m.*—*v.t.* diviser en paragraphes.
Paraguay ['pærəgwai]. le Paraguay, *m.*
Paraguayan [pærə'gwaiən], *a.* paraguayen.—*n.* Paraguayen (*personne*), *m.*
parakeet ['pærəki:t], *n.* (*Orn.*) perruche, *f.*
parallel ['pærəlel], *a.* parallèle; (*fig.*) semblable, pareil.—*n.* ligne parallèle, *f.*, parallèle, *m.*; (*fig.*) comparaison, *f.*—*v.t.* mettre en parallèle; (*fig.*) comparer (*à*); être pareil (*à*).
parallelism ['pærəlelizm], *n.* parallélisme, *m.*; (*fig.*) comparaison, *f.*
parallelogram [pærə'leləgræm], *n.* parallélogramme, *m.*
paralyse ['pærəlaiz], *v.t.* paralyser.
paralysis [pə'rælisis], *n.* paralysie, *f.*
paralytic [pærə'litik], *a.* and *n.* paralytique, *m.*, *f.*
paramount ['pærəmaunt], *a.* souverain, suprême; ***of paramount importance***, d'une importance capitale.—*n.* souverain, seigneur, *m.*
paramour ['pærəmuə], *n.* amant, *m.*, maîtresse, *f.*
parapet ['pærəpit], *n.* (*Fort.*) parapet; garde-fou (*sur un pont etc.*), *m.*
paraphernalia [pærəfə'neiliə], *n.pl.* (*Law*) biens paraphernaux, *m.pl.*; équipage, attirail, *m.*
paraphrase ['pærəfreiz], *n.* paraphrase, *f.*—*v.t.* paraphraser.
parasite ['pærəsait], *n.* parasite, *m.*
parasitic [pærə'sitik], **parasitical** [pærə'sitikəl], *a.* parasite, parasitique.
parasol [pærə'sɔl], *n.* ombrelle, *f.*, parasol, *m.*
paratrooper ['pærətru:pə], *n.* (soldat) parachutiste, *m.*
parcel [pɑ:sl], *n.* colis, paquet; lot, *m.*—*v.t.* morceler, diviser, partager; empaqueter.
parch [pɑ:tʃ], *v.t.* brûler, dessécher (*par la chaleur*).—*v.i.* se brûler; se dessécher.
parchment ['pɑ:tʃmənt], *n.* parchemin, *m.*
pardon [pɑ:dn], *n.* pardon, *m.*; (*Law*) grâce, *f.*; ***I beg your pardon?*** plaît-il? pardon? comment?—*v.t.* pardonner (*quelque chose à quelqu'un*); ***pardon me!*** pardon! permettez!
pardonable ['pɑ:dnəbl], *a.* excusable, pardonnable (*acte*); digne de pardon (*personne*).
pare [pɛə], *v.t.* peler (*fruits etc.*); éplucher; rogner (*ongles etc.*).
parent ['pɛərənt], *a.* mère.—*n.* père, *m.*, mère, *f.*; (*pl.*) parents, les père et mère, *m.pl.*
parentage ['pɛərəntidʒ], *n.* parentage, *m.*; extraction, *f.*
parental [pə'rentl], *a.* des parents, du père, de la mère; paternel, maternel.
parenthesis [pə'renθisis], *n.* (*pl.* **parentheses** [pə'renθisi:z]) parenthèse, *f.*
parenthetic [pærən'θetik], **parenthetical** [pærən'θetikəl], *a.* entre parenthèses.
pariah ['pæriə], *n.* paria, *m.*
paring ['pɛəriŋ], *n.* rognage; épluchage, *m.*
paring-knife ['pɛəriŋ'naif], *n.* tranchet, *m.*
parish ['pæriʃ], *a.* de la commune; communal, vicinal (*routes, impôts etc.*); (*Eccles.*) de la paroisse, paroissial.—*n.* (*Eccles.*) paroisse; (*civil*) commune, *f.*
parishioner [pə'riʃənə], *n.* paroissien, *m.*
Parisian [pə'riziən], *a.* de Paris, parisien.—*n.* Parisien (*personne*), *m.*
parity ['pæriti], *n.* parité; égalité (*de rang etc.*), *f.*
park [pɑ:k], *n.* parc, *m.*—*v.t.* parquer, garer.—*v.i.* stationner.
parking ['pɑ:kiŋ], *n.* stationnement, parcage, *m.*
parlance ['pɑ:ləns], *n.* parler, langage, *m.*; ***in common parlance***, dans le langage ordinaire.
parley ['pɑ:li], *n.* pourparlers, *m.pl.*—*v.i.* être *ou* entrer en pourparlers (*avec*); (*Mil.*) parlementer.
parliament ['pɑ:ləmənt], *n.* parlement, *m.*; (*France*) les Chambres, *f.pl.*
parliamentary [pɑ:lə'mentəri], *a.* parlementaire, du parlement.
parlour ['pɑ:lə], *n.* petit salon; parloir (*de couvent* ou *école*), *m.*
parlous ['pɑ:ləs], *a.* alarmant, précaire.

parochial [pə'roukiəl], *a.* communal; (*Eccles.*) paroissial.
parody ['pærədi], *n.* parodie, *f.*—*v.t.* parodier.
parole [pə'roul], *n.* parole (d'honneur), *f.*
paroxysm ['pærəksizm], *n.* paroxysme, accès, *m.*
parquet ['pɑ:kei, pɑ:'ket], *n.* parquet, *m.*—*v.t.* parqueter.
parquetry ['pɑ:kitri], *n.* parqueterie, *f.*
parricidal [pæri'saidl], *a.* parricide.
parricide ['pærisaid], *n.* parricide (*crime*), *m.*; parricide (*personne*), *m., f.*
parrot ['pærət], *n.* (*Orn.*) perroquet, *m.*
parry ['pæri], *v.t.* parer, détourner; (*fig.*) éviter.
parse [pɑ:z], *v.t.* analyser (grammaticalement).
parsimonious [pɑ:si'mouniəs], *a.* parcimonieux; pingre.
parsimony ['pɑ:siməni], *n.* parcimonie, épargne, *f.*
parsley ['pɑ:sli], *n.* (*Bot.*) persil, *m.*
parsnip ['pɑ:snip], *n.* (*Bot.*) panais, *m.*
parson [pɑ:sn], *n.* curé; (*Protestant*) pasteur, *m.*
parsonage ['pɑ:snidʒ], *n.* presbytère, *m.*, cure, *f.*
part [pɑ:t], *n.* partie; part, portion, *f.*; (*Theat.*) rôle; parti (*dans une dispute etc.*), *m.*; région (*de ville, pays etc.*), *f.*, quartier (*de ville*); (*pl.*) talent, *m.*; ***spare parts***, pièces de rechange, *f.pl.*—*v.t.* partager; séparer (*de*). —*v.i.* se séparer (*de*); se quitter; se rompre (*câble*).
partake [pɑ:'teik], *v.t.*, *v.i. irr.* (*conjug. like* TAKE) prendre part à, participer à.
partaker [pɑ:'teikə], *n.* participant, *m.*
partial [pɑ:ʃl], *a.* partial (*prévenu*), injuste; partiel (*en partie*).
partiality [pɑ:ʃi'æliti], *n.* partialité (*favoritisme*), *f.*; (*fig.*) goût, *m.*
partially ['pɑ:ʃəli], *adv.* partialement (*injustement*); en partie.
participant [pɑ:'tisipənt], *a.* and *n.* participant, *m.*
participate [pɑ:'tisipeit], *v.i.* participer (*à*).
participation [pɑ:tisi'peiʃən], *n.* participation, *f.*
participle ['pɑ:tisipl], *n.* participe, *m.*
particle ['pɑ:tikl], *n.* particule, molécule, parcelle, *f.*; atome, *m.*
particular [pə'tikjulə], *a.* particulier, spécial; méticuleux, pointilleux; exigeant (*difficile*), —*n.* particularité, *f.*, détail, *m.*; (*pl.*) renseignements, *m.pl.*; signalement, *m.*
particularity [pətikju'læriti], *n.* particularité, *f.*; détail, *m.*
particularize [pə'tikjuləraiz], *v.t.* particulariser.—*v.i.* préciser.
particularly [pə'tikjuləli], *adv.* particulièrement; principalement, surtout.
parting ['pɑ:tiŋ], *a.* de séparation; d'adieu; dernier.—*n.* séparation; raie (*cheveux*), *f.*
partisan [pɑ:ti'zæn], *n.* partisan, *m.*
partition [pɑ:'tiʃən], *n.* partage (*division*), *m.*; cloison (*dans une pièce etc.*), *f.*—*v.t.* partager, diviser.
partitive ['pɑ:titiv], *a.* and *n.* partitif, *m.*
partly ['pɑ:tli], *adv.* en partie, partiellement.
partner ['pɑ:tnə], *n.* (*Comm.*) associé; (*Dancing*) danseur, cavalier, *m.*; (*Cards, Spt.*) partenaire, *m., f.*—*v.t.* s'associer à; (*Spt.*) être le partenaire de; mener (*une femme en dansant*).
partnership ['pɑ:tnəʃip], *n.* association, *f.*
partridge ['pɑ:tridʒ], *n.* (*Orn.*) perdrix, *f.*; ***young partridge***, perdreau, *m.*
part-time ['pɑ:ttaim], *a.* and *n.* (emploi) à temps partiel, *m.*; ***to be on part-time***, être en chômage partiel.
party ['pɑ:ti], *n.* parti (*politique*), *m.*; partie (*de plaisir*), *f.*; (*fig.*) réunion; réception, *f.*, groupe, *m.*; ***to give a party***, recevoir du monde, donner une soirée.
party-wall ['pɑ:tiwɔ:l], *n.* mur mitoyen, *m.*
pasha ['pɑ:ʃə], *n.* pacha, *m.*
pass [pɑ:s], *v.t.* passer; passer par, passer devant; dépasser; devancer; faire passer; prononcer (*sur*); voter (*un projet de loi etc.*); ***to pass an examination***, être reçu *ou* réussir à un examen.—*v.i.* passer, se passer, s'écouler (*temps*); mourir; (*Exam.*) être reçu; (*Ftb.*) faire une passe; (*fig.*) arriver; ***to pass away***, disparaître, mourir; ***to pass out***, sortir; (*fig.*) s'évanouir.—*n.* passage, défilé, *m.*; gorge, *f.*, col; permis; laissez-passer, *m.*, permission; (*Ftb.*) passe, *f.*; (*fig.*) point, état, *m.*, extrémité, *f.*
passable ['pɑ:səbl], *a.* praticable; navigable (*fleuve etc.*); passable.
passage ['pæsidʒ], *n.* passage, *m.*, traversée, *f.*; (*Arch.*) couloir, corridor, *m.*
pass-book ['pɑ:sbuk], *n.* livre de compte, carnet de banque, *m.*
passenger ['pæsindʒə], *n.* voyageur; passager (*par mer* ou *avion*), *m.*
passer-by ['pɑ:sə'bai], *n.* (*pl.* **passers-by** ['pɑ:səz'bai]) passant, *m.*
passing ['pɑ:siŋ], *a.* passager, éphémère, fugitif.—*adv.* extrêmement, éminemment. —*n.* passage; écoulement (*de temps*); (*fig.*) trépas (*mort*), *m.*
passion ['pæʃən], *n.* passion; colère, *f.*, emportement, *m.*
passionate ['pæʃənit], *a.* passionné, ardent; irascible.
passionately ['pæʃənitli], *adv.* à la passion; à la folie, passionnément.
passion-flower ['pæʃənflauə], *n.* passiflore, fleur de la passion, *f.*
passion-play ['pæʃənplei], *n.* mystère (de la Passion), *m.*
Passion Week ['pæʃənwi:k]. semaine de la Passion, *f.*
passive ['pæsiv], *a.* and *n.* passif, *m.*
passiveness ['pæsivnis], *n.* passivité, inertie, *f.*
pass-key ['pɑ:ski:], *n.* passe-partout, *m.*
Passover ['pɑ:souvə]. la Pâque, *f.*
passport ['pɑ:spɔ:t], *n.* passeport, *m.*
password ['pɑ:swə:d], *n.* mot de passe; mot d'ordre, *m.*
past [pɑ:st], *a.* passé; ancien; dernier (*récent*). —*prep.* au-delà de; près de; sans, hors de; plus de (*âge*); ***past three o'clock***, trois heures passées.—*n.* passé, *m.*
paste [peist], *n.* colle (*glu*); pâte (*pour pâtisseries*), *f.*; stras (*faux diamant*), *m.*—*v.t.* coller; ***to paste up***, afficher.
pastel ['pæstəl], *n.* pastel, *m.*
pastern ['pæstə:n], *n.* paturon, *m.*
pasteurize ['pɑ:stjuəraiz], *v.t.* pasteuriser (*lait*).
pastille [pæs'ti:l], *n.* pastille, *f.*

pastime ['pɑ:staim], *n.* passe-temps, amusement, *m.*, distraction, *f.*
pastor ['pɑ:stə], *n.* (*literal and fig.*) pasteur; (*literal*) berger, *m.*
pastoral ['pɑ:stərəl], *a.* pastoral.—*n.* pastorale, églogue, *f.*
pastry ['peistri], *n.* pâtisserie, *f.*
pastry-cook ['peistrikuk], *n.* pâtissier, *m.*
pasture ['pɑ:stʃə], *n.* pâture, *f.*, herbage; pâturage (*champ etc.*), *m.*—*v.t.* faire paître. —*v.i.* paître.
pasty ['peisti], *a.* pâteux.—['pɑ:sti], *n.* pâté, *m.*
pat [pæt], *a.* and *adv.* à propos, tout juste.—*n.* petite tape; caresse, *f.*; rond de beurre, *m.*—*v.t.* taper, tapoter, caresser.
patch [pætʃ], *n.* pièce; mouche (*pour le visage*), *f.*; morceau (*de terre*); pan (*de ciel*), *m.*; tache (*de couleur*), *f.*—*v.t.* rapiécer, raccommoder; arranger.
patching ['pætʃiŋ], *n.* rapiéçage, ravaudage, *m.*
patchwork ['pætʃwə:k], *n.* mélange, *m.*, mosaïque, *f.*
patchy ['pætʃi], *a.* inégal.
pate [peit], *n.* (*colloq.*) caboche, tête, *f.*
patent ['peitənt, 'pætənt], *a.* breveté; (*fig.*) patent, apparent, évident.—*n.* lettres patentes, *f.pl.*, brevet d'invention, *m.*—*v.t.* breveter.
patentee [peitən'ti:], *n.* breveté, *m.*
paternal [pə'tə:nl], *a.* paternel.
paternally [pə'tə:nəli], *adv.* paternellement.
paternity [pə'tə:niti], *n.* paternité, *f.*
paternoster ['pætə'nɔstə], *n.* patenôtre, *f.*, pater, *m.*
path [pɑ:θ], *n.* sentier, chemin, *m.*; allée (*dans un jardin*), *f.*
pathless ['pɑ:θlis], *a.* sans chemin frayé; (*fig.*) inconnu.
pathetic [pə'θetik], *a.* and *n.* pathétique, *m.*
pathfinder ['pɑ:θfaində], *n.* pionnier, éclaireur, *m.*
pathological [pæθə'lɔdʒikl], *a.* pathologique.
pathologist [pə'θɔlədʒist], *n.* pathologiste, *m.*, *f.*
pathology [pə'θɔlədʒi], *n.* pathologie, *f.*
pathos ['peiθɔs], *n.* pathétique, *m.*
pathway ['pɑ:θwei], *n.* sentier; trottoir (*de rue*); accotement (*de route*), *m.*
patience ['peiʃəns], *n.* patience; (*Cards*) réussite, *f.*
patient ['peiʃənt], *a.* patient, endurant.—*n.* malade, *m.*, *f.*; patient; client (*de médecin*), *m.*
patiently ['peiʃəntli], *adv.* patiemment.
patriarch ['peitriɑ:k], *n.* patriarche, *m.*
patriarchal [peitri'ɑ:kl], *a.* patriarcal.
Patrick ['pætrik]. Patrice, *m.*
patrimony ['pætriməni], *n.* patrimoine, *m.*
patriot ['peitriət, 'pætriət], *n.* patriote, *m.*, *f.*
patriotic [peitri'ɔtik], *a.* patriotique (*chose*); patriote (*personne*).
patriotism ['peitriətizm], *n.* patriotisme, *m.*
patrol [pə'troul], *n.* patrouille, ronde, *f.*—*v.t.* faire la patrouille dans.—*v.i.* patrouiller; faire une ronde.
patron ['peitrən], *n.* patron; protecteur; (*Comm.*) client, *m.*; pratique, *f.*
patronage ['pætrənidʒ], *n.* patronage, *m.*, protection, *f.*
patroness ['peitrənes], *n.* patronne, protectrice; dame patronnesse (*d'œuvre de bienfaisance*), *f.*
patronize ['pætrənaiz], *v.t.* protéger, patronner; fréquenter (*un magasin*); traiter avec condescendance.
patronizing ['pætrənaiziŋ], *a.* protecteur; ***patronizing tone***, ton de condescendance, *m.*
patronymic [pætrə'nimik], *a.* patronymique. —*n.* nom patronymique, *m.*
patten ['pætən], *n.* patin, socque; (*Arch.*) soubassement, *m.*
patter ['pætə], *v.i.* frapper à petits coups, crépiter; trottiner.
pattering ['pætəriŋ], *n.* grésillement; bruit de petits coups, *m.*
pattern ['pætən], *n.* modèle (*pour*); patron (*à couper*); échantillon (*morceau de tissu etc.*); dessin (*de décoration*); exemple, *m.*
patty ['pæti], *n.* petit pâté, *m.*; bouchée (à la reine), *f.*
paucity ['pɔ:siti], *n.* petit nombre, *m.*, disette (*de*), *f.*
Paul [pɔ:l]. Paul, *m.*
Paula ['pɔ:lə]. Paule, *f.*
paunch [pɔ:ntʃ], *n.* panse, *f.*, ventre, *m.*
paunchy ['pɔ:ntʃi], *a.* pansu.
pauper ['pɔ:pə], *n.* indigent, *m.*
pauperism ['pɔ:pərizm], *n.* paupérisme, *m.*
pauperize ['pɔ:pəraiz], *v.t.* réduire à l'indigence.
pause [pɔ:z], *n.* pause, *f.*; moment de silence; intervalle, *m.*—*v.i.* faire une pause, s'arrêter.
pave [peiv], *v.t.* paver (*de*); ***to pave the way for***, frayer le chemin à *ou* pour.
pavement ['peivmənt], *n.* trottoir (*bord de rue*); dallage; pavé (*de marbre etc.*), *m.*
paver ['peivə], **paviour** ['peivjə], *n.* paveur, *m.*
pavilion [pə'viliən], *n.* pavillon, *m.*, tente, *f.*
paving ['peiviŋ], *n.* pavage, *m.*
paw [pɔ:], *n.* patte; (*facet.*) main, *f.*—*v.t.* manier, tripoter (*manier*); ***to paw the ground***, piaffer.
pawn (1) [pɔ:n], *n.* (*Chess*) pion, *m.*
pawn (2) [pɔ:n], *v.t.* engager, mettre en gage. —*n.* gage, *m.*
pawnbroker ['pɔ:nbroukə], *n.* prêteur sur gage, *m.*
pawnshop ['pɔ:nʃɔp], *n.* mont-de-piété, *m.*
pay [pei], *n.* paie, *f.*, salaire (*ouvrier*), traitement (*fonctionnaire*), *m.*, gages (*domestique*), *m.pl.*; (*Mil.*) solde (*officier*), *f.*, prêt (*soldat*), *m.*—*v.t. irr.* payer, acquitter, s'acquitter de; faire (*compliments etc.*); rendre (*honneur*); ***carriage paid***, port payé; ***to pay a visit to***, faire une visite à.—*v.i.* payer; rapporter.
payable ['peiəbl], *a.* payable; ***payable to bearer***, au porteur; ***payable to order***, à l'ordre de.
payee [pei'i:], *n.* porteur, *m.*, bénéficiaire, *m.*, *f.*
payer ['peiə], *n.* payeur, *m.*
pay-load ['peiloud], *n.* (*Av.*) poids utile, *m.*
paymaster ['peimɑ:stə], *n.* payeur; trésorier, *m.*
payment ['peimənt], *n.* payement, paiement, versement, *m.*
pea [pi:], *n.* pois, *m.*; ***green peas***, petits pois, *m.pl.*; ***sweet pea***, pois de senteur.
peace [pi:s], *n.* paix, *f.*

peaceable ['pi:səbl], *a.* pacifique.
peaceably ['pi:səbli], *adv.* en paix; avec calme.
peaceful ['pi:sful], *a.* paisible; tranquille, calme.
peacefully ['pi:sfuli], *adv.* paisiblement, tranquillement.
peacefulness ['pi:sfulnis], *n.* tranquillité, *f.*, calme, *m.*
peaceless ['pi:slis], *a.* sans paix, agité.
peacemaker ['pi:smeikə], *n.* pacificateur, *m.*
peach [pi:tʃ], *n.* pêche, *f.*
peach-tree ['pi:tʃtri:], *n.* pêcher, *m.*
peacock ['pi:kɔk], *n.* paon, *m.*
pea-green ['pi:gri:n], *a.* and *n.* vert pois.
pea-hen ['pi:hen], *n.* paonne, *f.*
peak [pi:k], *n.* cime (*de montagne*), *f.*; pic, sommet, *m.*; visière (*d'une casquette*), *f.*
peaked [pi:kt], *a.* à pic, à pointe; à visière.
peal [pi:l], *n.* carillon (*de cloches*); coup, bruit, grondement (*de tonnerre etc.*); éclat (*de rire*), *m.*—*v.i.* carillonner; retentir, résonner; gronder.
peanut ['pi:nʌt], *n.* arachide, cacahuète, *f.*
pea-pod ['pi:pɔd], *n.* cosse de pois, *f.*
pear [pɛə], *n.* poire, *f.*
pearl [pə:l], *n.* perle, *f.*; ***mother-of-pearl***, nacre, *f.*—*v.t.*, *v.i.* perler.
pearl-oyster ['pə:l'ɔistə], *n.* huître perlière, *f.*
pearly ['pə:li], *a.* de perle, perlé.
pear-tree ['pɛətri:], *n.* poirier, *m.*
peasant ['pezənt], *n.* paysan, *m.*
peasantry ['pezəntri], *n.* paysans, *m.pl.*
pea-soup ['pi:'su:p], *n.* purée de pois, *f.*
peat [pi:t], *n.* tourbe, *f.*
peat-bog ['pi:tbɔg], **peat-moss** ['pi:tmɔs], *n.* tourbière, *f.*
pebble [pebl], *n.* caillou, galet (*de plage*), *m.*
pebbly ['pebli], *a.* caillouteux.
peccadillo [pekə'dilou], *n.* peccadille, *f.*
peck (1) [pek], *n.* picotin (*d'avoine etc.*), *m.*
peck (2) [pek], *n.* coup de bec (*d'oiseau*), *m.*—*v.t.* becqueter; ***a hen-pecked husband***, un mari mené par sa femme.
pectoral ['pektərəl], *a.* and *n.* pectoral, *m.*
peculation [pekju'leiʃən], *n.* péculat, *m.*
peculator ['pekjuleitə], *n.* concussionnaire, *m.*, *f.*
peculiar [pi'kju:liə], *a.* particulier, propre; singulier, bizarre.
peculiarity [pikjuli'æriti], *n.* singularité, particularité, *f.*
peculiarly [pi'kju:liəli], *adv.* particulièrement, singulièrement.
pecuniary [pi'kju:niəri], *a.* pécuniaire.
pedagogic(al) [pedə'gɔdʒik(l)], *a.* pédagogique.
pedagogue ['pedəgɔg], *n.* pédagogue, *m.*, *f.*
pedal [pedl], *n.* pédale, *f.*—*v.i.* pédaler.
pedant ['pedənt], *n.* pédant, *m.*
pedantic [pi'dæntik], *a.* pédant (*personne*), pédantesque (*choses*).
pedantry ['pedəntri], *n.* pédantisme, *m.*, pédanterie, *f.*
peddle [pedl], *v.t.* colporter.—*v.i.* faire le colportage.
peddler [PEDLAR].
pedestal ['pedistl], *n.* piédestal, socle, *m.*
pedestrian [pə'destriən], *a.* à pied, pédestre; (*fig.*) prosaïque.—*n.* piéton, marcheur, *m.*
pedigree ['pedigri:], *n.* généalogie; origine, *f.*; arbre généalogique, *m.*
pediment ['pedimənt], *n.* (*Arch.*) fronton, *m.*
pedlar ['pedlə], *n.* colporteur, *m.*
pedometer [pə'dɔmitə], *n.* podomètre, *m.*
peel [pi:l], *n.* pelure; écorce (*d'orange etc.*), *f.*—*v.t.* peler; éplucher.—*v.i.* se peler; s'écailler.
peep [pi:p], *n.* coup d'œil furtif, *m.*; pointe (*du jour*), *f.*—*v.i.* regarder à la dérobée, paraître, poindre.
peeper ['pi:pə], *n.* curieux, *m.*
peep-hole ['pi:phoul], *n.* judas, *m.*
peeping-Tom ['pi:piŋ'tɔm], *n.* voyeur, *m.*
peer (1) [piə], *v.i.* scruter du regard.
peer (2) [piə], *n.* pair; (*fig.*) égal, pareil, *m.*
peerage ['piəridʒ], *n.* pairie, *f.*; les pairs, *m.pl.*
peeress ['piəris], *n.* pairesse, *f.*
peerless ['piəlis], *a.* incomparable; sans pareil.
peerlessly ['piəlisli], *adv.* incomparablement.
peerlessness ['piəlisnis], *n.* supériorité incomparable, *f.*
peevish ['pi:viʃ], *a.* irritable, maussade.
peevishly ['pi:viʃli], *adv.* maussadement, avec mauvaise humeur.
peevishness ['pi:viʃnis], *n.* maussaderie, humeur acariâtre, *f.*
peewit [PEWIT].
peg [peg], *n.* cheville; patère (*à chapeau etc.*), *f.*; fausset (*de tonneaux*), piquet (*de tente*), *m.*; ***clothes-peg***, pince à linge, *f.*—*v.t.*, *v.i.* cheviller.
pejorative [pə'dʒɔrətiv, 'pi:dʒərətiv], *a.* péjoratif.
Pekinese [pi:ki'ni:z], *a.* pékinois.—*n.* (épagneul) pékinois; Pékinois (*personne*), *m.*
Peking [pi:'kiŋ]. Pékin, *m.*
Pekingese [pi:kiŋ'i:z], [PEKINESE].
pelican ['pelikən], *n.* pélican, *m.*
pellet ['pelit], *n.* boulette, *f.*; grain de plomb, *m.*
pellicle ['pelikl], *n.* pellicule, *f.*
pell-mell ['pel'mel], *adv.* pêle-mêle.
pellucid [pə'lju:sid], *a.* transparent, clair, pellucide.
pelmet ['pelmit], *n.* lambrequin, *m.*
pelt (1) [pelt], *v.t.* assaillir, battre.
pelt (2) [pelt], *n.* peau, *f.*—*v.t.* écorcher.
pelting ['peltiŋ], *a.* battant (*pluie*).—*n.* attaque, *f.*, assaut, *m.*; grêle (*de pierres*), *f.*
pelvic ['pelvik], *a.* pelvien.
pelvis ['pelvis], *n.* bassin, *m.*
pemmican ['pemikən], *n.* conserve de viande, *f.*; pemmican, *m.*
pen [pen], *n.* plume, *f.*; parc, enclos (*bestiaux etc.*); poulailler (*pour volaille*), *m.*; ***fountain-pen***, stylo, *m.*—*v.t.* écrire; rédiger; parquer, enfermer (*bétail*).
penal [pi:nl], *a.* pénal, passible d'une amende; ***penal servitude***, travaux forcés, *m.pl.*
penalize ['pi:nəlaiz], *v.t.* infliger une peine à (*quelqu'un*); (*Spt.*) pénaliser.
penalty ['penəlti], *n.* peine; pénalité, amende, *f.*; (*Ftb.*) penalty, *m.*
penance ['penəns], *n.* pénitence, *f.*
pence [PENNY].
pencil [pensl], *n.* crayon, *m.*—*v.t.* dessiner ou écrire au crayon.
pencil-case ['penslkeis], *n.* porte-crayon, *m.*
pencil-sharpener ['pensl'ʃɑ:pnə], *n.* taille-crayon, *m.*
pendant ['pendənt], *n.* pendant, *m.*; pendeloque, *f.*; pendentif, *m.*

pendent ['pendənt], *a.* pendant; suspendu.

pending ['pendiŋ], *a.* pendant, non décidé; en cours.—*prep.* en attendant.

pendulum ['pendjuləm], *n.* pendule, balancier, *m.*

penetrable ['penitrəbl], *a.* pénétrable, sensible.

penetrate ['penitreit], *v.t.*, *v.i.* pénétrer (*dans*).

penetrating ['penitreitiŋ], *a.* pénétrant, perçant; clairvoyant, perspicace.

penetration [peni'treiʃən], *n.* pénétration, *f.*

penguin ['peŋgwin], *n.* manchot, *m.*

pen-holder ['penhouldə], *n.* porte-plume, *m.*

penicillin [peni'silin], *n.* pénicilline, *f.*

peninsula [pi'ninsjulə], *n.* péninsule, presqu'île, *f.*

peninsular [pi'ninsjulə], *a.* péninsulaire.

penitence ['penitəns], *n.* pénitence, *f.*, repentir, *m.*

penitent ['penitənt], *a.* pénitent, repentant.

penitentiary [peni'tenʃəri], *a.* pénitentiaire. —*n.* pénitencier, *m.*; (*Am.*) prison, *f.*

penknife ['pennaif], *n.* canif, *m.*

pennant ['penənt], *n.* (*Naut.*) flamme, *f.*

penniless ['penilis], *a.* sans le sou, sans ressources.

penny ['peni], *n.* (*pl.* **pence** [pens], *of a sum*, or **pennies** ['peniz], *of a number of coins*) penny, *m.*

pension ['penʃən], *n.* pension; pension de retraite, retraite (*d'officiers etc.*), *f.*—*v.t. to* ***pension off***, mettre à la retraite.

pensioner ['penʃənə], *n.* pensionnaire, *m.*, *f.*; (*Mil.*) invalide, *m.*

pensive ['pensiv], *a.* pensif, préoccupé, rêveur.

pensively ['pensivli], *adv.* d'un air pensif.

pensiveness ['pensivnis], *n.* air pensif, air préoccupé, *m.*

pent [pent], *a.* ***pent up***, enfermé, (*fig.*) étouffé, refoulé.

pentagon ['pentəgən], *n.* pentagone, *m.*

Pentecost ['pentikɔst]. Pentecôte, *f.*

penthouse ['penthaus], *n.* appartement sur toit; appentis, *m.*

penultimate [pe'nʌltimit], *a.* pénultième, avant-dernier.

penurious [pi'njuəriəs], *a.* avare; ladre; pauvre (*choses*).

penury ['penjuəri], *n.* pénurie, *f.*

peony ['pi:əni], *n.* pivoine, *f.*

people [pi:pl], *n.* peuple, *m.*, nation, *f.*, gens, *m.pl.*; on, monde, *m.*, personnes (*en général*), *f.pl.*—*v.t.* peupler (*de*).

pepper ['pepə], *n.* poivre, *m.*—*v.t.* poivrer; (*fig.*) cribler de coups.

pepper-caster ['pepə'kɑ:stə], *n.* poivrière, *f.*

peppercorn ['pepəkɔ:n], *n.* grain de poivre, *m.*

peppermint ['pepəmint], *n.* menthe poivrée, *f.*

peppery ['pepəri], *a.* poivré; (*fig.*) irritable.

per [pə:], *prep.* par; le, *m.*, la, *f.*, les, *pl.*; ***three francs per pound***, trois francs la livre.

perambulate [pə'ræmbjuleit], *v.t.* parcourir.

perambulation [pəræmbju'leiʃən], *n.* parcours, *m.*; promenade, *f.*

perambulator [pə'ræmbjuleitə], *n.* voiture d'enfant, *f.*

perceive [pə'si:v], *v.t.* apercevoir (*visuellement*), s'apercevoir de (*se rendre compte de*).

percentage [pə'sentidʒ], *n.* pourcentage, *m.*

perceptibility [pəsepti'biliti], *n.* perceptibilité, *f.*

perceptible [pə'septibl], *a.* perceptible, sensible.

perceptibly [pə'septibli], *adv.* perceptiblement, sensiblement.

perception [pə'sepʃən], *n.* perception, sensibilité; découverte, *f.*

perceptive [pə'septiv], *a.* perceptif.

perch (1) [pə:tʃ], *n.* perche (*poisson*), *f.*

perch (2) [pə:tʃ], *n.* perchoir (*à poules etc.*) *m.* —*v.t.*, *v.i.* percher.

percolate ['pə:kəleit], *v.t.*, *v.i.* filtrer, passer.

percolation [pə:kə'leiʃən], *n.* filtration, infiltration, *f.*

percolator ['pə:kəleitə], filtre (à café), *m.*

percussion [pə'kʌʃən], *n.* percussion, *f.*

percussion-cap [pə'kʌʃənkæp], *n.* capsule, *f.*

perdition [pə'diʃən], *n.* perdition, ruine, *f.*

peregrinate ['perigrineit], *v.i.* voyager.

peregrination [perigri'neiʃən], *n.* pérégrination, *f.*, voyage à l'étranger, *m.*

peremptorily [pə'remptərili], *adv.* péremptoirement, absolument, formellement.

peremptory [pə'remptəri], *a.* péremptoire, absolu.

perennial [pə'reniəl], *a.* vivace (*plantes*); (*fig.*) éternel.—*n.* plante vivace, *f.*

perfect (1) ['pə:fikt], *a.* parfait; achevé.— [pə'fekt], *v.t.* rendre parfait, perfectionner; achever.

perfect (2) ['pə:fikt], *n.* (*Gram.*) parfait, *m.*

perfection [pə'fekʃən], *n.* perfection, *f.*

perfectly ['pə:fiktli], *adv.* parfaitement.

perfidious [pə'fidiəs], *a.* perfide.

perfidiousness [pə'fidiəsnis], **perfidy** ['pə:fidi], *n.* perfidie, *f.*

perforate ['pə:fəreit], *v.t.* perforer, percer.

perforation [pə:fə'reiʃən], *n.* percement, *m.*, perforation; dentelure (*de timbre-poste*), *f.*

perforce [pə'fɔ:s], *adv.* forcément, de force.

perform [pə'fɔ:m], *v.t.* exécuter, accomplir; (*Theat.*) jouer.—*v.i.* jouer un rôle.

performance [pə'fɔ:məns], *n.* accomplissement; ouvrage, *m.*, œuvre (*chose achevée*), *f.*; (*Mach.*) fonctionnement, *m.*; (*Theat.*) représentation; (*Mus.*) exécution; (*Spt.*) performance, *f.*

performer [pə'fɔ:mə], *n.* (*Theat.*) acteur, *m.*, actrice, *f.*; (*Mus.*) artiste, *m.*, *f.*

perfume ['pə:fjum], *n.* parfum, *m.*—[pə 'fju:m], *v.t.* parfumer (*de*).

perfumery [pə'fju:məri], *n.* parfumerie, *f.*

perfunctorily [pə'fʌŋktərili], *adv.* par manière d'acquit; tant bien que mal.

perfunctory [pə'fʌŋktəri], *a.* de pure forme; négligent.

perhaps [pə'hæps], *adv.* peut-être; ***perhaps not***, peut-être que non; ***perhaps so***, peut-être que oui.

peril ['peril], *n.* péril, danger, *m.*

perilous ['periləs], *a.* périlleux, dangereux.

perilously ['periləsli], *adv.* périlleusement.

perimeter [pə'rimitə], *n.* périmètre, *m.*

period ['piəriəd], *n.* période, *f.*, temps, *m.*, durée; époque; fin, *f.*, terme (*conclusion*); (*Am.*) point (*ponctuation*), *m.*; (*Rhet. etc.*) phrase, *f.*; (*pl.*) (*Physiol.*) règles, *f.pl.*

periodic [piəri'ɔdik], *a.* périodique.

periodical [piəri'ɔdikl], *a.* and *n.* périodique, *m.*

periodically [piəri'ɔdikli], *adv.* périodiquement.
peripatetic [peripə'tetik], *a.* péripatéticien.
periphery [pə'rifəri], *n.* périphérie, *f.*
periphrasis [pə'rifrəsis], *n.* (*pl.* **periphrases** [pə'rifrəsi:z]) périphrase, *f.*
periscope ['periskoup], *n.* périscope, *m.*
perish ['periʃ], *v.i.* périr (*de*), mourir; dépérir.
perishable ['periʃəbl], *a.* périssable.
peritonitis [peritə'naitis], *n.* péritonite, *f.*
***periwig** ['periwig], *n.* perruque, *f.*
periwinkle ['periwiŋkl], *n.* (*Bot.*) pervenche, *f.*; bigorneau (*mollusque*), *m.*
perjure ['pə:dʒə], *v.t.* ***to perjure oneself,*** se parjurer.
perjurer ['pə:dʒərə], *n.* parjure, *m., f.*
perjury ['pə:dʒəri], *n.* parjure; (*Law*) faux témoignage, faux serment, *m.*; ***wilful perjury,*** parjure prémédité.
perk [pə:k], *v.i.* ***to perk up,*** se ranimer, se raviver.—*n.* (*pl.*) (*fam.*) [PERQUISITE].
perky ['pə:ki], *a.* déluré; outrecuidant.
permanency ['pə:mənənsi], **permanence** ['pə:mənəns], *n.* permanence, *f.*
permanent ['pə:mənənt], *a.* permanent; en permanence.
permanently ['pə:mənəntli], *adv.* en permanence.
permeable ['pə:miəbl], *a.* perméable.
permeate ['pə:mieit], *v.t.* pénétrer.
permissible [pə'misibl], *a.* permis.
permission [pə'miʃən], *n.* permission, *f.*, permis, *m.*
permissive [pə'misiv], *a.* qui permet; toléré.
permit [pə'mit], *v.t.* permettre (*à quelqu'un de . . .*).—['pə:mit], *n.* permis, *m.*
permutation [pə:mju'teiʃən], *n.* permutation, *f.*
pernicious [pə'niʃəs], *a.* pernicieux.
perniciously [pə'niʃəsli], *adv.* pernicieusement.
peroration [perə'reiʃən], *n.* péroraison, *f.*
peroxide [pə'rɔksaid], *n.* peroxyde, *m.*—*v.t.* oxygéner (*cheveux*).
perpendicular [pə:pən'dikjulə], *a.* and *n.* perpendiculaire, *f.*
perpendicularly [pə:pən'dikjuləli], *adv.* perpendiculairement.
perpetrate ['pə:pitreit], *v.t.* commettre; (*Law*) perpétrer.
perpetration [pə:pi'treiʃən], *n.* exécution; (*Law*) perpétration, *f.*
perpetrator ['pə:pitreitə], *n.* auteur (*d'un crime*), *m.*
perpetual [pə'petjuəl], *a.* perpétuel.
perpetually [pə'petjuəli], *adv.* perpétuellement.
perpetuate [pə'petjueit], *v.t.* perpétuer.
perpetuation [pəpetju'eiʃən], *n.* perpétuation, *f.*
perpetuity [pə:pi'tju:iti], *n.* perpétuité, *f.*
perplex [pə'pleks], *v.t.* embarrasser.
perplexed [pə'plekst], *a.* perplexe, embarrassé.
perplexing [pə'pleksiŋ], *a.* embarrassant.
perplexity [pə'pleksiti], *n.* perplexité, *f.*
perquisite ['pə:kwizit], *n.* émolument casuel, *m.*
perry ['peri], *n.* poiré, *m.*
persecute ['pə:sikju:t], *v.t.* persécuter.
persecuting ['pə:sikju:tiŋ], *a.* persécuteur.
persecution [pə:si'kju:ʃən], *n.* persécution, *f.*
persecutor ['pə:sikjutə], *n.* persécuteur, *m.*
perseverance [pə:si'viərəns], *n.* persévérance *f.*
persevere [pə:si'viə], *v.i.* persévérer (*à* ou *dans*).
persevering [pə:si'viəriŋ], *a.* persévérant.
perseveringly [pə:si'viəriŋli], *adv.* avec persévérance.
Persia ['pə:ʃə]. la Perse, *f.*
Persian ['pə:ʃən], *a.* de Perse, persan.—*n.* perse (*langue*); Persan (*personne*), *m.*; ***the Persian Gulf,*** le Golfe Persique.
persist [pə'sist], *v.i.* persister (*dans* ou *à*) continuer.
persistence [pə'sistəns], *n.* persistance, *f.*
persistent [pə'sistənt], *a.* persistant; opiniâtre
person ['pə:sən], *n.* personne, *f.*; personnage caractère, *m.*; (*pl.*) personnes, *f.pl.*, gens *m.pl., f.pl.*; ***young persons,*** les jeunes gens
personage ['pə:sənidʒ], *n.* personnage, *m.*
personal ['pə:sənl], *a.* personnel.
personality [pə:sə'næliti], *n.* personnalité, *f.*
personally ['pə:sənli], *adv.* personnellement.
personate ['pə:səneit], *v.t.* se faire passer pour; représenter, contrefaire.
personification [pəsɔnifi'keiʃən], *n.* personnification, *f.*
personify [pə'sɔnifai], *v.t.* personnifier.
personnel [pə:sə'nel], *n.* personnel, *m.*
perspective [pə'spektiv], *a.* perspectif.—*n.* perspective, *f.*
perspicacious [pə:spi'keiʃəs], *a.* pénétrant, perspicace; perçant (*la vision*).
perspicacity [pə:spi'kæsiti], *n.* perspicacité, *f.*
perspicuity [pə:spi'kju:iti], *n.* clarté, *f.*
perspicuous [pə'spikjuəs], *a.* clair, net.
perspiration [pə:spi'reiʃən], *n.* transpiration, sueur, *f.*
perspire [pə'spaiə], *v.i.* transpirer, suer.
persuade [pə'sweid], *v.t.* persuader; ***to persuade from,*** dissuader de.
persuasion [pə'sweiʒən], *n.* persuasion, *f.*
persuasive [pə'sweisiv], *a.* persuasif.
persuasiveness [pə'sweisivnis], *n.* force persuasive, *f.*
pert [pə:t], *a.* mutin, hardi; impertinent, insolent (*effronté*).
pertain [pə'tein], *v.i.* appartenir.
pertinacious [pə:ti'neiʃəs], *a.* obstiné, opiniâtre.
pertinacity [pə:ti'næsiti], *n.* obstination, *f.*
pertinence ['pə:tinəns], *n.* convenance, *f.*
pertinent ['pə:tinənt], *a.* pertinent, convenable.
pertly ['pə:tli], *adv.* impertinemment, insolemment.
pertness ['pə:tnis], *n.* impertinence, *f.*
perturb [pə'tə:b], *v.t.* agiter, troubler.
perturbation [pə:tə'beiʃən], *n.* agitation, *f.*
perturbed [pə'tə:bd], *a.* troublé, inquiet.
Peru [pə'ru:]. le Pérou, *m.*
perusal [pə'ru:zl], *n.* lecture, *f.*
peruse [pə'ru:z], *v.t.* lire attentivement.
Peruvian [pə'ru:viən], *a.* péruvien, du Pérou.—*n.* Péruvien (*personne*), *m.*
pervade [pə'veid], *v.t.* pénétrer dans; se répandre dans, remplir.
pervading [pə'veidiŋ], *a.* ***all-pervading,*** dominant.
perverse [pə'və:s], *a.* pervers.

perversely [pə'və:sli], *adv.* avec perversité.
perverseness [pə'və:snis], **perversity** [pə'və:siti], *n.* perversité, *f.*
perversion [pə'və:ʃən], *n.* perversion, *f.*
pervert [pə'və:t], *v.t.* pervertir; fausser, dénaturer.—['pə:və:t], *n.* perverti, *m.*
perverted [pə'və:tid], *a.* perverti.
pervious ['pə:viəs], *a.* perméable, pénétrable.
pessimism ['pesimizm], *n.* pessimisme, *m.*
pessimist ['pesimist], *n.* pessimiste, *m., f.*
pessimistic [pesi'mistik], *a.* pessimiste.
pest [pest], *n.* peste, *f.*
pester ['pestə], *v.t.* tourmenter, ennuyer.
pestilence ['pestiləns], *n.* peste, pestilence, *f.*
pestilent ['pestilənt], *a.* pestilentiel, contagieux.
pestilential [pesti'lenʃl], *a.* pestilentiel.
pet (1) [pet], *a.* favori; ***pet aversion***, bête noire, *f.*—*n.* chéri, *m.*, chérie, *f.*, favori, *m.*, favorite, *f.*; animal familier; enfant gaté, *m.* —*v.t.* choyer, dorloter; (*Am.*) caresser.
pet (2) [pet], *n.* accès d'humeur, *m.*
petal [petl], *n.* pétale, *m.*
Peter ['pi:tə]. Pierre, *m.*
peter out [pi:tə'raut], *v.i.* (*colloq.*) s'épuiser; tomber à l'eau (*projet*), flancher (*machine*).
petition [pi'tiʃən], *n.* pétition, *f.*—*v.t.* pétitioner.
petitioner [pi'tiʃənə], *n.* (*Law*) requérant, *m.*; pétitionnaire, *m., f.*
petrel ['petrəl], *n.* (*Orn.*) pétrel, *m.*
petrifaction [petri'fækʃən], *n.* pétrification, *f.*
petrify ['petrifai], *v.t.* pétrifier.—*v.i.* se pétrifier.
petrol ['petrəl], *n.* essence, *f.*; ***petrol station***, poste d'essence, *m.*
petrol-can ['petrəlkæn], *n.* bidon d'essence, *m.*
petroleum [pi'trouliəm], *n.* pétrole, *m.*, huile de pétrole, *f.*
petticoat ['petikout], *n.* jupon, *m.*
pettifogging ['petifɔgiŋ], *a.* avocassier, chicaneur; chicanier (*méthodes etc.*).
pettiness ['petinis], *n.* petitesse, mesquinerie, *f.*
petty ['peti], *a.* petit; mesquin, chétif; (*Law*) inférieur.
petty-officer ['peti'ɔfisə], *n.* (*Navy*) officier marinier, *m.*
petulance ['petjuləns], *n.* irritabilité, *f.*
petulant ['petjulənt], *a.* irritable.
pew [pju:], *n.* banc d'église, *m.*
pewit ['pi:wit], *n.* (*Orn.*) vanneau, *m.*
pewter ['pju:tə], *n.* étain, potin, *m.*; vaisselle d'étain, *f.*
phalanx ['fælæŋks], *n.* (*pl.* **phalanges** [fə'lændʒi:z]) phalange, *f.*
phantom ['fæntəm], *n.* fantôme, *m.*
Pharaoh ['fɛərou], *n.* Pharaon, *m.*
Pharisee ['færisi:], *n.* Pharisien, *m.*
pharmaceutical [fɑ:mə'sju:tikəl], *a.* pharmaceutique.
pharmacy ['fɑ:məsi], *n.* pharmacie, *f.*
phase [feiz], *n.* phase, *f.*
pheasant ['fezənt], *n.* faisan, *m.*
phenomenal [fi'nɔmənəl], *a.* phénoménal.
phenomenon [fi'nɔmənən], *n.* (*pl.* **phenomena** [fi'nɔmənə]) phénomène, *m.*
phew! [fju:], *int.* pouf!
phial ['faiəl], *n.* fiole, *f.*
philanthropic [filən'θrɔpik], *a.* philanthropique.
philanthropist [fi'lænθrəpist], *n.* philanthrope, *m., f.*
philanthropy [fi'lænθrəpi], *n.* philanthropie, *f.*
philatelist [fi'lætəlist], *n.* philatéliste, *m., f.*
philharmonic [filhɑ:'mɔnik], *a.* philharmonique.
Philip ['filip]. Philippe, *m.*
Philippine ['filipi:n], *a.* philippine.
Philippines ['filipi:nz], **the**, les Philippines, *f.pl.*
Philistine ['filistain], *a.* philistin.—*n.* Philistin (*personne*), *m.*
philologist [fi'lɔlədʒist], *n.* philologue, *m., f.*
philology [fi'lɔlədʒi], *n.* philologie, *f.*
philosopher [fi'lɔsəfə], *n.* philosophe, *m., f.*
philosophical [filə'sɔfikl], *a.* philosophique; philosophe (*personnes*).
philosophize [fi'lɔsəfaiz], *v.i.* philosopher.
philosophy [fi'lɔsəfi], *n.* philosophie, *f.*; ***natural philosophy***, la physique, *f.*
philter, philtre ['filtə], *n.* philtre, *m.*
phlegm [flem], *n.* flegme, *m.*
phlegmatic [fleg'mætik], *a.* flegmatique.
phobia ['foubiə], *n.* phobie, *f.*
Phoebe ['fi:bi]. Phébé, *f.*
Phoenician [fi'ni:ʃən], *a.* phénicien.—*n.* Phénicien (*personne*), *m.*
phoenix ['fi:niks], *n.* phénix, *m.*
phone [foun], (*colloq.*) [TELEPHONE].
phonetic [fə'netik], *a.* phonétique.
phonetics [fə'netiks], *n.pl.* phonétique, *f.*
phoney ['founi], *a.* (*colloq.*) faux, factice.—*n.* charlatan, *m.*
phonic ['fɔnik], *a.* phonique.
phosphate ['fɔsfeit], *n.* phosphate, *m.*
phosphor ['fɔsfə], *n.* phosphore, *m.*
phosphoric [fɔs'fɔrik], *a.* phosphorique.
phosphorus ['fɔsfərəs], *n.* phosphore, *m.*
photo ['foutou], (*colloq.*) [PHOTOGRAPH].
photogenic [foutə'dʒenik], *a.* photogénique.
photograph ['foutəgrɑ:f, 'foutəgræf], *n.* photographie, (*colloq.*) photo, *f.*—*v.t.* photographier.
photographer [fə'tɔgrəfə], *n.* photographe, *m., f.*
photographic [foutə'græfik], *a.* photographique.
photography [fə'tɔgrəfi], *n.* photographie, *f.*
photostat ['foutəstæt], *n.* appareil photostat, *m.*
phrase [freiz], *n.* phrase, locution, *f.*—*v.t.* exprimer, nommer; (*Mus.*) phraser.
phraseology [freizi'ɔlədʒi], *n.* phraséologie, *f.*
phrenetic [fre'netik], *a.* fou, frénétique.
phrenologist [fre'nɔlədʒist], *n.* phrénologiste, phrénologue, *m., f.*
phrenology [fre'nɔlədʒi], *n.* phrénologie, *f.*
physic ['fizik], *n.* médecine, *f.*—*v.t.* médicamenter; purger.
physical ['fizikəl], *a.* physique; ***physical training***, éducation physique, *f.*
physically ['fizikəli], *adv.* physiquement.
physician [fi'ziʃən], *n.* médecin, *m.*
physicist ['fizisist], *n.* physicien, *m.*
physics ['fiziks], *n.pl.* physique, *f.*
physiognomy [fizi'ɔnəmi, fizi'ɔgnəmi], *n.* physionomie, *f.*
physiological [fiziə'lɔdʒikl], *a.* physiologique.
physiology [fizi'ɔlədʒi], *n.* physiologie, *f.*

physiotherapy [fizio'θerəpi], *n.* physiothérapie, *f.*
physique [fi'zi:k], *n.* physique, *m.*
pianist ['piənist], *n.* pianiste, *m., f.*
piano ['pjænou, 'pjɑ:nou], **pianoforte** [-'fɔ:ti], *n.* piano, *m*; ***grand piano***, piano à queue; ***to play (on) the piano***, jouer du piano.
pick [pik], *n.* pic, *m.*, pioche (*outil*), *f.*; choix, *m.*—*v.t.* piquer; cueillir; choisir, trier; ronger (*un os*); chercher (*querelle*); voler à la tire (*dans une poche*); crocheter (*une serrure*); ***to pick up***, ramasser, relever.
pickaback ['pikəbæk], *adv.* sur le dos.
pickaxe ['pikæks], *n.* pioche, *f.*
picked [pikt], *a.* d'élite, choisi.
picker ['pikə], *n.* cueilleur, *m.*
picket ['pikit], *n.* piquet, jalon; petit poste, *m.* —*v.t.* former en piquet; guetter (*grévistes etc.*).
pickle [pikl], *n.* saumure, marinade, *f.*; (*pl.*) conserves au vinaigre, *f.pl.*—*v.t.* conserver au vinaigre, mariner; saler.
pickled [pikld], *a.* mariné, conservé au vinaigre; (*pop.*) ivre.
pickpocket ['pikpɔkit], *n.* voleur à la tire, *m.*
pick-up ['pikʌp], *n.* ramassage, *m.*; reprise (*de machine, des affaires*), *f.*; pick-up (*tourne-disque*), *m.*
picnic ['piknik], *n.* pique-nique, *m.*—*v.i.* faire un pique-nique.
pictorial [pik'tɔ:riəl], *a.* illustré; de peintre.
pictorially [pik'tɔ:riəli], *adv.* avec illustrations.
picture ['piktʃə], *n.* tableau, *m.*; peinture; (*fig.*) image, *f.*; ***the pictures***, le cinéma.—*v.t.* peindre; (*fig.*) dépeindre, représenter.
picturesque [piktʃə'resk], *a.* pittoresque.
pie [pai], *n.* pâté (*de viande*), *m.*; tourte (*de fruit*), *f.*; (*colloq.*) ***as easy as pie***, simple comme bonjour; ***to eat humble pie***, avaler des couleuvres.
piebald ['paibɔ:ld], *a.* pie (*cheval*).
piece [pi:s], *n.* pièce (*grand*), *f.*; morceau (*petit*); fragment, bout, *m.*; ***a piece of furniture***, un meuble; ***a piece of news***, une nouvelle; ***to break to pieces***, mettre en pièces; ***to take to pieces***, démonter.—*v.t.* rapiécer.
piecemeal ['pi:smi:l], *adv.* par morceaux, peu à peu.
pied [paid], *a.* bariolé, bigarré; pie (*cheval*).
pie-dish ['paidiʃ], *n.* tourtière, terrine, *f.*
pier [piə], *n.* jetée, *f.*; ponton (*de rivière*), *m.*; pile (*d'un pont*), *f.*
pierce [piəs], *v.t.* percer, pénétrer.
pierced [piəst], *a.* à jour (*ouvrage*), *m.*
piercing ['piəsiŋ], *a.* perçant; pénétrant.
pier-glass ['piəglɑ:s], *n.* trumeau, *m.*
piety ['paiəti], *n.* piété, *f.*
pig [pig], *n.* cochon, porc, pourceau, *m.*; ***to buy a pig in a poke***, acheter chat en poche.
pigeon ['pidʒin], *a.* timide, craintif.—*n.* pigeon, *m.*; ***carrier-pigeon***, pigeon voyageur.
pigeon-hole ['pidʒinhoul], *n.* boulin, *m.*; case (*à papiers etc.*), *f.*; ***set of pigeon-holes***, casier, *m.*—*v.t.* classer.
piggery ['pigəri], *n.* étable à cochons, *f.*
piggy ['pigi], **piglet** ['piglit], *n.* porcelet, goret, *m.*
pigheaded ['pighedid], *a.* têtu, stupide.
pig-iron ['pigaiən], *n.* gueuse, *f.*
pigment ['pigmənt], *n.* couleur, *f.*, pigment, *m.*
pigmy [PYGMY].
pigsty ['pigstai], *n.* porcherie, *f.*
pigtail ['pigteil], *n.* queue (de cheveux), *f.*
pigtailed ['pigteild], *a.* à queue.
pike [paik], *n.* pique (*arme*), *f.*; brochet (*poisson*), *m.*
pilchard ['piltʃəd], *n.* (*Ichth.*) pilchard, *m.*
pile [pail], *n.* tas, monceau; (*fig.*) (*Build.*) édifice, bâtiment; pieu (*poteau*); poil (*de tissu*), *m.*; ***atomic pile***, pile atomique, *f.*; ***funeral pile***, bûcher, *m.*—*v.t.* entasser, empiler, amonceler.—*v.i.* ***to pile up***, s'empiler, s'entasser.
piles [pailz], *n.pl.* (*Path.*) hémorroïdes, *f.pl.*
pilfer ['pilfə], *v.t.* dérober, chiper.—*v.i.* dérober.
pilferer ['pilfərə], *n.* chapardeur, chipeur, *m.*
pilfering ['pilfəriŋ], *n.* petit vol, larcin, *m.*
pilgrim ['pilgrim], *n.* pèlerin, *m.*
pilgrimage ['pilgrimidʒ], *n.* pèlerinage, *m.*
pill [pil], *n.* pilule, *f.*
pillage ['pilidʒ], *n.* pillage, saccagement, *m.*—*v.t.* saccager, piller.
pillar ['pilə], *n.* pilier, *m.*, colonne, *f.*; (*fig.*) soutien, *m.*
pillar-box ['piləbɔks], *n.* boîte aux lettres, *f.*
pillion ['piljən], *n.* coussinet (de cheval), *m.*; siège, *m.* (*ou* selle, *f.*) arrière (*de motocyclette*); ***to ride pillion***, monter en croupe, monter derrière.
pillory ['piləri], *n.* pilori, *m.*—*v.t.* pilorier, mettre au pilori.
pillow ['pilou], *n.* oreiller, *m.*—*v.t.* reposer, coucher.
pillow-case ['piloukeis], **pillow-slip** ['pilou slip], *n.* taie d'oreiller, *f.*
pilot ['pailət], *n.* pilote, *m.*; ***test pilot***, pilote d'essais.—*v.t.* piloter, servir de pilote à.
pilotage ['pailətidʒ], *n.* pilotage, *m.*
pimpernel ['pimpənel], *n.* pimprenelle, *f.*, mouron, *m.*
pimple [pimpl], *n.* bouton, *m.*
pimply ['pimpli], *a.* bourgeonné, pustuleux.
pin [pin], *n.* épingle; cheville (*de bois*), *f.*; (*fig.*) rien, *m.*—*v.t.* épingler, attacher; cheviller.
pinafore ['pinəfɔ:], *n.* tablier (d'enfant), *m.*
pincers ['pinsəz], *n.pl.* pince, *f.*, tenailles, *f.pl.*
pinch [pintʃ], *n.* pincée (*de sel etc.*); prise (*de tabac*), *f.*; (*fig.*) embarras, *m.*; ***at a pinch***, à la rigueur, au besoin.—*v.t.* pincer; serrer, gêner (*habits*); (*pop.*) chiper (*voler*); pincer (*arrêter*).—*v.i.* pincer; se gêner.
pinching ['pintʃiŋ], *a.* pressant, piquant (*froid*).—*n.* pincement, *m.*
pin-cushion ['pinkuʃən], *n.* pelote, *f.*
pine (1) [pain], *n.* pin (*arbre*); bois de pin, *m.*
pine (2) [pain], *v.i.* languir; ***to pine after***, soupirer après.
pineapple ['painæpl], *n.* ananas, *m.*
ping [piŋ], *n.* sifflement (*de balle de fusil*), *m.*—*v.i.* siffler.
ping-pong ['piŋpɔŋ], *n.* ping-pong, *m.*
pinion ['pinjən], *n.* aileron, bout d'aile, *m.*—*v.t.* couper le bout de l'aile à; lier.
pink (1) [piŋk], *a.* couleur de rose, rose.—*n.* œillet (*fleur*); rose (*couleur*), *m.*; ***in the pink of condition***, en excellente condition;

(*colloq.*) ***to be in the pink,*** se porter à merveille.

pink (2) [piŋk], *v.i.* cliqueter (*moteur*).

pinnace ['pinəs], *n.* pinasse, *f.*

pinnacle ['pinəkl], *n.* pinacle, *m.*

pin-point ['pinpɔint], *v.t.* indiquer exactement.

pin-pricks ['pinpriks], *n.pl.* coups d'épingles, *m.pl.*

pint [paint], *n.* pinte (*un demi-litre*), *f.*

pintail ['pinteil], *n.* (*Orn.*) pilet, *m.*

pioneer [paiə'niə], *n.* pionnier, *m.*

pious ['paiəs], *a.* pieux.

piously ['paiəsli], *adv.* pieusement.

pip [pip], *n.* pépin (*de fruit*); (*Rad.*) top, *m.*—*v.i.* piauler (*oiseaux*).

pipe [paip], *n.* tuyau, conduit, *m.*; pipe (*à fumer, à vin etc.*), *f.*; (*Mus.*) pipeau, chalumeau, *m.*—*v.i.* jouer du chalumeau, siffler; (*pop.*) ***pipe down!*** boucle-la!

pipe-line ['paiplain], *n.* canalisation, *f.*, oléoduc, pipe-line, *m.*

piper ['paipə], *n.* joueur de flûte etc., *m.*

piping ['paipiŋ], *a.* qui joue du chalumeau, sifflant; flûté (*la voix*).—*n.* tubulure, *f.*, tuyautage, *m.*

pipit ['pipit], *n.* (*Orn.*) pipit, *m.*

pippin ['pipin], *n.* reinette, *f.*

piquancy ['pi:kənsi], *n.* goût piquant, *m.*

piquant ['pi:kənt], *a.* piquant.

pique [pi:k], *n.* pique, brouillerie, *f.*

piquet [pi'ket], *n.* (*Cards*) piquet, *m.*

piracy ['pairəsi], *n.* piraterie; (*fig.*) contrefaçon, *f.*, plagiat, *m.*

pirate ['pairit], *n.* pirate; (*fig.*) contrefacteur, *m.*

piratical [pai'rætikl], *a.* de pirate; (*fig.*) de contrefaçon.

pirouette [piru'et], *n.* pirouette, *f.*

pish! [piʃ], *int.* bah!

piss [pis], *v.i.* (*vulg.*) pisser.—*n.* urine, *f.*

pistol [pistl], *n.* pistolet, *m.*

piston ['pistən], *n.* piston, *m.*

piston-ring ['pistənriŋ], *n.* segment de piston, *m.*

piston-rod ['pistənrɔd], *n.* tige de piston, *f.*

pit [pit], *n.* fosse; (*fig.*) cavité, *f.*; (*Theat.*) parterre; (*Mining*) puits; creux (*de l'estomac*), *m.*; aisselle (*du bras*), *f.*—*v.t.* creuser; marquer de petits creux.

pitch (1) [pitʃ], *n.* jet, lancement (*de caillou, balle*); (*Naut.*) tangage; point, degré, *m.*; pente (*de toit etc.*), *f.*; (*Mus.*) ton, diapason, *m.*; ***to play pitch-and-toss,*** jouer à pile ou face.—*v.t.* jeter, lancer; établir (*fixer*); dresser (*une tente*).—*v.i.* (*Naut.*) tanguer, plonger; tomber, se jeter.

pitch (2) [pitʃ], *n.* poix, *f.*; ***pitch dark,*** noir comme dans un four.

pitched [pitʃt], *a.* rangé; ***pitched battle,*** bataille rangée, *f.*

pitcher ['pitʃə], *n.* cruche, *f.*

pitchfork ['pitʃfɔ:k], *n.* fourche, *f.*

pitching ['pitʃiŋ], *n.* plongement (*de véhicules*); (*Naut.*) tangage, *m.*

pitch-pine ['pitʃpain], *n.* pin à trochets, pitchpin, *m.*

piteous ['pitiəs], *a.* piteux; pitoyable (*digne de pitié*).

piteously ['pitiəsli], *adv.* piteusement.

piteousness ['pitiəsnis], *n.* état piteux, *m.*; tristesse, *f.*

pitfall ['pitfɔ:l], *n.* trappe, *f.*, piège, *m.*

pith [piθ], *n.* moelle; vigueur, énergie, *f.*; essentiel, *m.*

pithily ['piθili], *adv.* fortement, vigoureusement.

pithy ['piθi], *a.* plein de moelle; (*fig.*) substantiel, concis.

pitiable ['pitiəbl], *a.* pitoyable, à faire pitié.

pitiful ['pitiful], *a.* pitoyable.

pitifully ['pitifuli], *adv.* pitoyablement.

pitiless ['pitilis], *a.* impitoyable, sans pitié.

pitilessly ['pitilisli], *adv.* impitoyablement, sans pitié.

pitman ['pitmən], *n.* (*pl.* **-men** [men]) mineur, *m.*

pittance ['pitəns], *n.* pitance, *f.*

pitted ['pitid], *a.* grêlé (*de petite vérole*).

pity ['piti], *n.* pitié, *f.*; dommage (*regret*), *m.*; ***what a pity!*** quel dommage!—*v.t.* avoir pitié de, plaindre.

pityingly ['pitiiŋli], *adv.* avec pitié.

pivot ['pivət], *n.* pivot, *m.*

placable ['plækəbl], *a.* facile à apaiser.

placard ['plækɑ:d], *n.* placard, *m.*, affiche, pancarte, *f.*—*v.t.* afficher, placarder (*de*).

placate [plə'keit], *v.t.* apaiser.

place [pleis], *n.* lieu, endroit, *m.*, localité; place (*siège etc.*); position, *f.*, rang (*classe*), *m.*; demeure, résidence (*chez soi*), *f.*; emploi (*profession*), *m.*; ***come to my place,*** venez chez moi; ***to take place,*** avoir lieu; ***out of place,*** déplacé, inopportun.—*v.t.* placer, mettre.

placid ['plæsid], *a.* placide, tranquille, calme.

plagiarism ['pleidʒiərizm], *n.* plagiat, *m.*

plagiarist ['pleidʒiərist], *n.* plagiaire, *m.*, *f.*

plagiarize ['pleidʒiəraiz], *v.t.* plagier.

plague [pleig], *n.* peste; (*fig.*) plaie, *f.*, fléau, *m.*—*v.t.* (*fig.*) tourmenter.

plaice [pleis], *n.* carrelet, *m.*; plie franche, *f.*

plaid [plæd], *n.* (*Sc.*) plaid; tartan, *m.*

plain [plein], *a.* uni, plat; simple, sans façon; ordinaire; sans attraits (*mine*); évident (*qui saute aux yeux*); franc (*sincère*); ***in plain clothes,*** en civil; ***plain cooking,*** cuisine bourgeoise *ou* au naturel, *f.*—*n.* plaine, *f.*—*adv.* simplement; franchement.

plainly ['pleinli], *adv.* bonnement; distinctement; franchement.

plainness ['pleinnis], *n.* simplicité; clarté; sincérité, *f.*

plain-speaking ['plein'spi:kiŋ], *n.* franchise, *f.*

plain-spoken ['plein'spoukn], *a.* franc, clair, explicite.

plaint [pleint], *n.* plainte, *f.*

plaintiff ['pleintif], *n.* plaignant, *m.*

plaintive ['pleintiv], *a.* plaintif.

plaintively ['pleintivli], *adv.* d'une voix plaintive.

plaintiveness ['pleintivnis], *n.* ton plaintif, *m.*

plait [plæt], *n.* natte, tresse (*de cheveux*), *f.*; pli, *m.*—*v.t.* tresser, natter (*cheveux*); plisser.

plaited ['plætid], *a.* tressé (*cheveux*); plissé.

plan [plæn], *n.* plan; dessein, projet; système, *m.*—*v.t.* tracer un plan de; (*fig.*) projeter.

plane (1) [plein], *n.* (*Geom.*) plan; (*Carp.*) rabot; (*colloq.*) avion, *m.*—*v.t.* raboter, aplanir.

plane (2) [plein], **plane-tree** ['pleintri:], *n.* platane, *m.*

planet ['plænit], *n.* planète, *f.*

planetarium [plæni'tɛəriəm], *n.* planétarium, *m.*
planetary ['plænitəri], *a.* planétaire.
planing ['pleiniŋ], *n.* rabotage, *m.*
plank [plæŋk], *n.* planche, *f.*, madrier; (*Naut.*) bordage, *m.*—*v.t.* planchéier; (*Naut.*) border.
plankton ['plæŋktən], *n.* plancton, *m.*
planner ['plænə], *n.* auteur d'un plan, *m.*; ***town-planner***, urbaniste, *m.*
planning ['plæniŋ], *n.* tracé d'un plan, *m.*; planification; (*fig.*) invention, *f.*; ***town-planning***, urbanisme, *m.*
plant [plɑ:nt], *n.* plante, *f.*; (*Tech.*) matériel, *m.*—*v.t.* planter; (*fig.*) poser.
plantain ['plæntin], *n.* plantain, *m.*
plantation [plɑ:n'teiʃən], *n.* plantation, *f.*
planter ['plɑ:ntə], *n.* planteur, colon, *m.*
planting ['plɑ:ntiŋ], *n.* plantage, *m.*, plantation, *f.*
plasma ['plæzmə], *n.* plasma (du sang), *m.*
plaster ['plɑ:stə], *n.* plâtre; (*Pharm.*) emplâtre, *m.*; ***sticking plaster***, sparadrap, *m.* —*v.t.* plâtrer.
plasterer ['plɑ:stərə], *n.* plâtrier, *m.*
plastering ['plɑ:stəriŋ], *n.* plâtrage, *m.*
plastic ['plæstik], *a.* plastique.—*n.* (*pl.*) plastiques, *m.pl.*
plat [PLAIT].
Plate [pleit], **the River**. le Rio de la Plata, *m.*
plate [pleit], *n.* assiette; (*Metal.*, *Phot.*) plaque, *f.*—*v.t.* plaquer (*de*); laminer; étamer (*une glace*).
plateau ['plætou, plə'tou], *n.* plateau, *m.*
plated ['pleitid], *a.* plaqué.
plateful ['pleitful], *n.* assiettée, *f.*
plate-glass ['pleitglɑ:s], *n.* glace sans tain, *f.*
plate-layer ['pleitleiə], *n.* (*Rail.*) poseur de rails, *m.*
plate-rack ['pleitræk], *n.* porte-assiettes, *m.*
platform ['plætfɔ:m], *n.* plateforme; estrade, *f.*; (*Rail.*) quai, *m.*
plating ['pleitiŋ], *n.* placage, *m.*; ***armour-plating***, blindage, *m.*
platinum ['plætinəm], *n.* platine, *m.*
platitude ['plætitju:d], *n.* platitude, *f.*
Plato ['pleitou]. Platon, *m.*
platoon [plə'tu:n], *n.* (*Mil.*) section, *f.*
platter ['plætə], *n.* écuelle, *f.*; (*Am.*) plat, *m.*
platypus ['plætipəs], *n.* ornithor(h)ynque, *m.*
plaudit ['plɔ:dit], *n.* applaudissement, *m.*
plausible ['plɔ:zibl], *a.* plausible; spécieux.
play [plei], *n.* jeu, *m.*; récréation (*d'enfants*), *f.*; essor (*champ libre*); badinage, *m.*; (*Mus.*) exécution; (*Theat.*) comédie, pièce, *f.*; ***fair play***, franc jeu.—*v.t.* jouer, jouer à; faire jouer (*une machine etc.*); représenter, faire (*une pièce, un rôle etc.*); (*Mus.*) jouer de.—*v.i.* jouer; folâtrer (*s'amuser*).
play-bill ['pleibil], *n.* affiche de théâtre, *f.*
player ['pleiə], *n.* joueur; (*Theat.*) acteur, *m.*, actrice, *f.*; artiste, *m.*, *f.*
playfellow ['pleifelou], **playmate** ['plei meit], *n.* camarade de jeu, *m.*, *f.*
playful ['pleiful], *a.* folâtre, badin.
playfully ['pleifuli], *adv.* en badinant.
playfulness ['pleifulnis], *n.* badinage, enjouement, *m.*
playground ['pleigraund], *n.* cour de récréation, *f.*
playhouse ['pleihaus], *n.* théâtre, *m.*
plaything ['pleiθiŋ], *n.* jouet, joujou, *m.*
playtime ['pleitaim], *n.* récréation, *f.*
playwright ['pleirait], *n.* auteur dramatique, *m.*, dramaturge, *m.*, *f.*
plea [pli:], *n.* procès, *m.*, cause, *f.*; prétexte, *m.*, excuse, *f.*
plead [pli:d], *v.t.*, *v.i.* plaider.
pleasant ['plezənt], *a.* agréable, charmant.
pleasantly ['plezəntli], *adv.* agréablement.
pleasantness ['plezəntnis], *n.* agrément, charme, *m.*
pleasantry ['plezəntri], *n.* plaisanterie, *f.*
please [pli:z], *v.t.* plaire à; ***to be pleased***, être content.—*v.i.* plaire (*à*); (*impers.*) il plaît; ***as you please***, comme vous voudrez; ***if I please***, si cela me plaît; (***if you***) ***please***, s'il vous plaît.
pleased [pli:zd], *a.* charmé, content (*de*); satisfait (*de choses*).
pleasing ['pli:ziŋ], *a.* agréable, charmant.
pleasurable ['pleʒərəbl], *a.* agréable.
pleasure ['pleʒə], *n.* plaisir; gré (*will*), *m.*
pleasure-ground ['pleʒəgraund], *n.* parc, jardin d'agrément, *m.*
pleat [pli:t], *n.* plissé, *m.*—*v.t.* plisser.
plebeian [plə'bi:ən], *a.* and *n.* plébéien, *m.*
pledge [pledʒ], *n.* gage; nantissement, *m.*; (*Law*) caution, *f.*—*v.t.* engager; garantir.
plenary ['pli:nəri], *a.* plein, complet, entier.
plenipotentiary [plenipo'tenʃəri], *a.* and *n.* plénipotentiaire, *m.*, *f.*
plenitude ['plenitju:d], *n.* plénitude, *f.*
plenteous ['plentiəs], *a.* abondant.
plenteously ['plentiəsli], *adv.* abondamment.
plentiful ['plentiful], *a.* abondant.
plenty ['plenti], *n.* abondance, *f.*; ***plenty of***, beaucoup de.
plethora ['pleθərə], *n.* pléthore, *f.*
pleurisy ['pluərəsi], *n.* pleurésie, *f.*
pliable ['plaiəbl], *a.* pliable, flexible.
pliancy ['plaiənsi], *n.* flexibilité, *f.*
pliant ['plaiənt], *a.* pliant, flexible.
pliers ['plaiəz], *n.pl.* pinces, *f.pl.*
plight [plait], *n.* état, *m.*, condition; situation difficile, *f.*—*v.t.* engager.
plinth [plinθ], *n.* plinthe, *f.*
plod [plɔd], *v.i.* marcher péniblement; (*fig.*) peiner, travailler assidûment.
plodder ['plɔdə], *n.* piocheur, *m.*
plodding ['plɔdiŋ], *a.* laborieux, piocheur.—*n.* travail pénible, *m.*
plop [plɔp], *adv.*, *n.* and *int.* plouf, flac, pouf, *m.*
plot [plɔt], *n.* complot; petit terrain, *m.*; intrigue (*d'une pièce etc.*), *f.*; ***building-plot***, lotissement, *m.*—*v.t.* comploter; (*Surv.*) faire le plan de.—*v.i.* comploter.
plotter ['plɔtə], *n.* conspirateur, comploteur, *m.*
plotting ['plɔtiŋ], *n.* complots, *m.pl.*; (*Surv.*) action de rapporter, *f.*
plough [plau], *n.* charrue, *f.*; ***the Plough***, le Chariot, *m.*, la Grande-Ourse, *f.*—*v.t.* labourer; (*fig.*) sillonner.—*v.i.* labourer.
ploughing ['plauiŋ], *n.* labourage, *m.*
ploughman ['plaumən], *n.* (*pl.* **-men** [men]) laboureur, *m.*
ploughshare ['plauʃɛə], *n.* soc de charrue, *m.*
plover ['plʌvə], *n.* (*Orn.*) pluvier, vanneau, *m.*
pluck [plʌk], *v.t.* cueillir (*fleurs, fruits etc.*); plumer (*volaille*); épiler (*sourcils*).—*n.* cœur, courage, *m.*
pluckily ['plʌkili], *adv.* courageusement.

plucky ['plʌki], *a.* courageux.

plug [plʌg], *n.* tampon, bouchon, *m.*; bonde (*de tonneau*); (*Elec.*) prise de courant; (*Teleph.*) fiche, *f.*; ***sparking plug***, bougie (d'allumage), *f.*—*v.t.* tamponner, boucher.

plum [plʌm], *n.* prune, *f.*

plumage ['plu:midʒ], *n.* plumage, *m.*

plumb [plʌm], *a.* droit, vertical.—*adv.* à plomb; (*Am.*, *colloq.*) complètement.—*v.t.* plomber; (*Naut.*) sonder.—*n.* plomb, *m.*

plumber ['plʌmə], *n.* plombier, *m.*

plumbing ['plʌmiŋ], *n.* plomberie; tuyauterie, *f.*

plumb-line ['plʌmlain], *n.* fil à plomb, *m.*

plume [plu:m], *n.* plume, *f.*; plumet, *m.*—*v.t.* plumer.

plummet ['plʌmit], *n.* plomb, *m.*

plump (1) [plʌmp], *a.* dodu, potelé, gras.

plump (2) [plʌmp], *adv.* tout d'un coup; droit.—*v.i.* ***to plump for***, donner tous ses votes pour.

plumpness ['plʌmpnis], *n.* embonpoint, *m.*, rondeur, *f.*

plum-tree ['plʌmtri:], *n.* prunier, *m.*

plunder ['plʌndə], *v.t.* piller, dépouiller.—*n.* butin (*chose pillée*); pillage (*acte de piller*), *m.*

plunderer ['plʌndərə], *n.* pillard, *m.*

plunge [plʌndʒ], *v.t.* plonger, précipiter.—*v.i.* plonger; se précipiter.—*n.* plongeon, *m.*

plural ['pluərəl], *a.* and *n.* pluriel, *m.*

plus [plʌs], *prep.* (*Math.*) plus.—*a.* positif.—*n.* plus, *m.*—*adv.* et davantage.

plush [plʌʃ], *n.* peluche, *f.*

plutocrat ['plu:tokræt], *n.* ploutocrate, *m.*, *f.*

plutocratic [plu:to'krætik], *a.* ploutocratique.

plutonium [plu'tounjəm], *n.* plutonium, *m.*

pluvial ['plu:viəl], *a.* pluvial.

ply (1) [plai], *v.t.* manier (*fortement*); exercer, employer; presser (*quelqu'un de prendre quelque chose*).—*v.i.* travailler; faire le service.

ply (2) [plai], *n.* pli (*de tissu*); fil (*de laine*); toron (*de corde*), *m.*

plywood ['plaiwud], *n.* contre-plaqué, *m.*

pneumatic [nju'mætik], *a.* pneumatique.

pneumonia [nju'mouniə], *n.* pneumonie, *f.*

poach (1) [poutʃ], *v.t.* braconner, voler.—*v.i.* braconner.

poach (2) [poutʃ], *v.t.* pocher (*œufs*).

poacher ['poutʃə], *n.* braconnier, *m.*

poaching ['poutʃiŋ], *n.* braconnage, *m.*

pock [pɔk], *n.* pustule (*de petite vérole*), *f.*

pocket ['pɔkit], *n.* poche, *f.*; gousset (*du gilet*), *m.*; blouse (*de billard*), *f.*—*v.t.* empocher, mettre en poche.

pocket-book ['pɔkitbuk], *n.* portefeuille (*pour l'argent*); livre de poche; calepin (*carnet*), *m.*

pocketful ['pɔkitful], *n.* pleine poche, *f.*

pocket-knife ['pɔkitnaif], *n.* couteau de poche, canif, *m.*

pocket-money ['pɔkitmʌni], *n.* argent de poche, *m.*

pod [pɔd], *n.* cosse, gousse, *f.*—*v.t.* écosser.

podgy ['pɔdʒi], *a.* gras, potelé.

poem ['pouim], *n.* poème, *m.*

***poesy** ['pouizi], *n.* poésie, *f.*

poet ['pouit], *n.* poète, *m.*

poetaster [poui'tæstə], *n.* rimailleur, *m.*

poetess [poui'tes], *n.* poétesse, *f.*

poetic [pou'etik], **poetical** [pou'etikəl], *a.* poétique.

poetry ['pouitri], *n.* poésie, *f.*

poignancy ['pɔinjənsi], *n.* piquant, *m.*; nature poignante, *f.*

poignant ['pɔinjənt], *a.* piquant, vif, poignant.

poignantly ['pɔinjəntli], *adv.* d'une manière piquante.

point [pɔint], *n.* point (*endroit*), *m.*; pointe (*bout aiguisé etc.*), *f.*; (*Compass*) quart de vent; (*Spt.*) point; (*fig.*) but; (*pl.*) (*Rail.*) aiguillage, *m.*; ***decimal point***, virgule, *f.*; ***in point of fact***, en effet; ***not to the point***, hors de propos; ***that is not the point***, ce n'est pas là la question; ***to make a point of***, se faire un devoir de; ***to the point***, à propos.—*v.t.* aiguiser, tailler (*affiler*); indiquer; pointer (*fusils etc.*); (*Build.*) jointoyer; ***to point out***, signaler; faire remarquer.—*v.i.* se tourner (*vers*); tomber en arrêt (*chiens*); ***to point at***, montrer du doigt, indiquer.

point-blank ['pɔint'blæŋk], *adv.* à bout portant; à brûle-pourpoint, carrément.

pointed ['pɔintid], *a.* pointu; (*fig.*) mordant.

pointedly ['pɔintidli], *adv.* d'une manière piquante.

pointer ['pɔintə], *n.* index; chien d'arrêt, *m.*

pointing ['pɔintiŋ], *n.* (*Build.*) jointoiement, *m.*

pointless ['pɔintlis], *a.* sans pointe; (*fig.*) inutile, plat.

pointsman ['pɔintsmən], *n.* (*pl.* **-men** [men]) (*Rail.*) aiguilleur, *m.*

poise [pɔiz], *n.* poids, équilibre, *m.*—*v.t.* balancer, tenir en équilibre.

poison ['pɔizn], *n.* poison, *m.*—*v.t.* empoisonner.

poisoner ['pɔiznə], *n.* empoisonneur, *m.*

poisoning ['pɔizniŋ], *n.* empoisonnement, *m.*

poisonous ['pɔiznəs], *a.* vénéneux (*plante*); venimeux (*serpent etc.*); toxique (*gaz*).

poke (1) [pouk], *n.* coup de coude *ou* de poing, *m.*—*v.t.* fourrer; pousser (*des doigts*); remuer, fourgonner (*le feu*); ***to poke fun at***, se moquer de.—*v.i.* ***to poke about***, tâtonner.

poke (2) [pouk], *n.* *sac, *m.*; poche, *f.*

poker ['poukə], *n.* tisonnier, *m.*

poky ['pouki], *a.* (*colloq.*) petit, mesquin.

Poland ['poulənd]. la Pologne, *f.*

polar ['poulə], *a.* polaire.

Pole [poul], *n.* Polonais (*personne*), *m.*

pole (1) [poul], *n.* perche, *f.*; bâton (*de rideau*); timon (*d'une voiture*); échalas (*de vignes etc.*); mât (*de drapeau etc.*); poteau (*télégraphique*), *m.*

pole (2) [poul], *n.* (*Astron.*, *Geog.*) pôle, *m.*

poleaxe ['poulæks], *n.* hache d'armes, *f.*; assommoir, merlin, *m.*—*v.t.* assommer.

polecat ['poulkæt], *n.* putois, *m.*

polemics [pə'lemiks], *n.pl.* polémique, *f.*

pole-star ['poulstɑ:], *n.* étoile polaire, *f.*

pole-vault ['poulvɔ:lt], *n.* saut à la perche, *m.*

police [pə'li:s], *n.* police, *f.*; ***county police***, gendarmerie, *f.*; ***police-court***, tribunal de simple police, *m.*; ***police-station***, commissariat *ou* poste de police, *m.*—*v.t.* policer.

policeman [pə'li:smən], *n.* (*pl.* **-men** [men]) agent de police, gardien de la paix, *m.*

policewoman [pə'li:swumən], *n.* (*pl.* **-women** [wimin]) femme agent, *f.*

policy ['pɔlisi], *n.* politique, *f.*; plan, *m.*; ***insurance policy***, police d'assurance, *f.*

poliomyelitis ['pouliomaiə'laitis], (*fam.*) **polio** ['pouliou], *n.* poliomyélite, *f.*
Polish ['pouliʃ], *a.* polonais.—*n.* polonais (*langue*), *m.*
polish ['pɔliʃ], *v.t.* polir; vernir (*meubles*); cirer (*chaussures*).—*v.i.* se polir.—*n.* poli, *m.*; (*fig.*) élégance, *f.*; ***floor polish***, cire à parquet, *f.* ***shoe polish***, cirage, *m.*
polished ['pɔliʃt], *a.* poli.
polisher ['pɔliʃə], *n.* polisseur; polissoir (*outil*), *m.*; ***floor polisher***, cireur de parquet, *m.*
polite [pə'lait], *a.* poli, élégant, complaisant (*pour*).
politely [pə'laitli], *adv.* poliment.
politeness [pə'laitnis], *n.* politesse, *f.*
politic ['pɔlitik], *a.* politique.
political [pə'litikl], *a.* politique.
politically [pə'litikli], *adv.* politiquement.
politician [pɔli'tiʃən], *n.* homme politique; (*pej.*) politicien, *m.*
politics ['pɔlitiks], *n.pl.* politique, *f.*
poll [poul], *n.* (*Anat.*) *tête; liste électorale; élection, *f.*, scrutin; sondage (*de l'opinion publique*), *m.*—*v.t.* étêter (*arbres*); voter; obtenir (*un certain nombre de votes*).
pollen ['pɔlən], *n.* pollen, *m.*
pollination [pɔli'neiʃən], *n.* pollination, *f.*
polling ['pouliŋ], *n.* élection, *f.*; ***polling-booth***, bureau de scrutin, *m.*
pollute [pə'lju:t], *v.t.* polluer, souiller (*de*).
pollution [pə'lju:ʃən], *n.* pollution, souillure, *f.*
polo ['poulou], *n.* polo, *m.*
polygamist [pə'ligəmist], *n.* polygame, *m., f.*
polygamy [pə'ligəmi], *n.* polygamie, *f.*
polyglot ['pɔliglɔt], *a.* and *n.* polyglotte, *m., f.*
polygon ['pɔligən], *n.* polygone, *m.*
Polynesia [pɔli'ni:ziə]. la Polynésie, *f.*
polypus ['pɔlipəs], *n.* polype, *m.*
polytechnic [pɔli'teknik], *a.* polytechnique. —*n.* école d'arts et métiers, *f.*
pomade [pə'meid], *n.* pommade, *f.*
pomegranate ['pɔmgrænit], *n.* grenade, *f.*; ***pomegranate tree***, grenadier, *m.*
pommel [pʌml], *v.t.* battre, rosser.—*n.* pommeau (*d'une selle, d'une epée etc.*), *m.*
pomp [pɔmp], *n.* pompe, *f.*, éclat, faste, *m.*
Pompey ['pɔmpi]. Pompée, *m.*
pompon ['pɔmpɔn], *n.* pompon, *m.*
pomposity [pɔm'pɔsiti], *n.* pompe, *f.*
pompous ['pɔmpəs], *a.* pompeux, fastueux.
pompously ['pɔmpəsli], *adv.* pompeusement.
pond [pɔnd], *n.* étang, vivier, *m.*; mare (*pool*), *f.*
ponder ['pɔndə], *v.t.* peser, considérer, réfléchir à.—*v.i.* méditer.
ponderous ['pɔndərəs], *a.* lourd, pesant.
ponderously ['pɔndərəsli], *adv.* pesamment.
pontiff ['pɔntif], *n.* pontife, *m.*
pontificate [pɔn'tifikeit], *n.* pontificat, *m.*—*v.i.* pontifier.
Pontius Pilate ['pɔntʃəs'pailət]. Ponce Pilate, *m.*
pontoon [pɔn'tu:n], *n.* ponton; (*Cards*) vingt-et-un, *m.*
pony ['pouni], *n.* poney, petit cheval, *m.*
poodle [pu:dl], *n.* caniche, *m.*
pooh! [pu:], *int.* bah! allons donc!
pooh-pooh ['pu:'pu:] *v.t.* tourner en ridicule.
pool [pu:l], *n.* étang, *m.*, mare; piscine (*pour nager*); (*Cards, Billiards etc.*) poule; mise en commun, *f.*—*v.t.* mettre en commun.
poop [pu:p], *n.* dunette, poupe, *f.*
poor [puə], *a.* pauvre, indigent; malheureux (*sans joie*); triste (*de pauvre qualité*); mauvais (*pas bon*).
poor-box ['puəbɔks], *n.* tronc des pauvres, *m.*
***poor-house** ['puəhaus], *n.* asile des indigents, *m.*
***poor-law** ['puəlɔ:], *n.* loi sur l'assistance publique, *f.*
poorly ['puəli], *a.* indisposé, souffrant.—*adv.* pauvrement, mal, tristement.
poorness ['puənis], *n.* pauvreté; médiocrité, *f.*
pop (1) [pɔp], *n.* petit bruit vif et sec, *m.*; (*colloq.*) boisson pétillante, *f.*—*v.t.* pousser, fourrer *ou* mettre subitement.—*v.i.* entrer *ou* sortir subitement.—*int.* crac! pan!
pop (2) [pɔp], *n.* (*Am., colloq.*) papa, *m.*
pop (3) [pɔp], *a.* and *n.* (*colloq.*) (musique) populaire, *f.*; ***the pops***, les chansons en vogue, *f.pl.*
Pope [Poup], *n.* Pape, *m.*
popedom ['poupdəm], *n.* papauté, *f.*
popery ['poupəri], *n.* papisme, *m.*
popish ['poupiʃ], *a.* papiste; de papiste (*choses*).
poplar ['pɔplə], *n.* (*Bot.*) peuplier, *m.*
poplin ['pɔplin], *n.* popeline, *f.*
poppet ['pɔpit], *n.* poupée, marionnette, *f.*
poppy ['pɔpi], *n.* pavot (*cultivé*); coquelicot (*sauvage*), *m.*
populace ['pɔpjuləs], *n.* populace, *f.*
popular ['pɔpjulə], *a.* populaire; en vogue.
popularity [pɔpju'læriti], *n.* popularité, *f.*
popularize ['pɔpjuləraiz], *v.t.* populariser.
popularly ['pɔpjuləli], *adv.* populairement.
populate ['pɔpjuleit], *v.t.* peupler.
population [pɔpju'leiʃən], *n.* population, *f.*
populous ['pɔpjuləs], *a.* populeux.
porcelain ['pɔ:slin], *n.* porcelaine, *f.*
porch [pɔ:tʃ], *n.* porche, *m.*
porcupine ['pɔ:kjupain], *n.* porc-épic, *m.*
pore (1) [pɔ:], *n.* pore, *m.*
pore (2) [pɔ:], *v.i.* regarder avec grande attention; ***to pore over***, dévorer (*un livre*).
pork [pɔ:k], *n.* porc, *m.*
pork-butcher ['pɔ:kbutʃə], *n.* charcutier, *m.*; ***pork-butcher's shop***, charcuterie, *f.*
porker ['pɔ:kə], *n.* porc d'engrais, cochon, *m.*
pork-pie ['pɔ:k'pai], *n.* pâté de porc, *m.*
pornography [pɔ:'nɔgrəfi], *n.* pornographie, *f.*
porous ['pɔ:rəs], *a.* poreux.
porphyry ['pɔ:firi], *n.* porphyre, *m.*
porpoise ['pɔ:pəs], *n.* marsouin, *m.*
porridge ['pɔridʒ], *n.* bouillie, *f.*
porringer ['pɔrindʒə], *n.* bol à bouillie, *m.*
port (1) [pɔ:t], *n.* port (*ville maritime*), *m.*
port (2) [pɔ:t], *n.* (*Naut.*) bâbord, *m.*
port (3) [pɔ:t], *n.* porto (*vin*), *m.*
portable ['pɔ:təbl], *a.* portatif, transportable.
portal [pɔ:tl], *n.* portail, *m.*
portcullis [pɔ:t'kʌlis], *n.* herse, *f.*
portend [pɔ:'tend], *v.t.* présager, augurer.
portent ['pɔ:tənt], *n.* mauvais augure, *m.*
portentous [pɔ:'tentəs], *a.* de mauvais augure.
porter ['pɔ:tə], *n.* commissionnaire; concierge (*de maison*); porteur (*de rue*); (*Rail.*) porteur, *m.*
porterage ['pɔ:təridʒ], *n.* port; factage, *m.*

portfolio [pɔ:t'fouliou], *n.* carton, *m.*; serviette, *f.*; (*Polit.*) portefeuille, *m.*
port-hole ['pɔ:thoul], *n.* sabord, *m.*
portico ['pɔ:tikou], *n.* portique, *m.*
portion ['pɔ:ʃən], *n.* partie, part; dot (*de mariage*), *f.*—*v.t.* partager; doter (*pour le mariage*).
portliness ['pɔ:tlinis], *n.* corpulence, *f.*
portly ['pɔ:tli], *a.* d'un port majestueux; corpulent.
portmanteau [pɔ:t'mæntou], *n.* valise, *f.*
portrait ['pɔ:trit], *n.* portrait, *m.*
portray [pɔ:'trei], *v.t.* peindre; (*fig.*) dépeindre, décrire.
Portugal ['pɔ:tʃug(ə)l]. le Portugal, *m.*
Portuguese [pɔ:tʃu'gi:z], *a.* portugais.—*n.* portugais (*langue*); Portugais (*personne*), *m.*
pose [pouz], *v.t.* embarrasser, confondre; poser (*une question*).—*v.i.* poser (*avec affectation*).—*n.* pose, *f.*
poser ['pouzə], *n.* question embarrassante, *f.*
poseur [pou'zə:], *n.* poseur, *m.*
position [pə'ziʃən], *n.* situation, position, *f.*
positive ['pɔzitiv], *a.* positif; absolu, sûr; décisif.—*n.* positif, *m.*
positively ['pɔzitivli], *adv.* positivement; absolument.
positiveness ['pɔzitivnis], *n.* nature positive, *f.*
***posse** ['pɔsi], *n.* détachement (d'agents de police), *m.*; foule (*de civils*), *f.*
possess [pə'zes], *v.t.* posséder; avoir; jouir de.
possession [pə'zeʃən], *n.* possession, *f.*
possessive [pə'zesiv], *a.* possessif.
possessor [pə'zesə], *n.* possesseur, *m.*
***posset** ['pɔsit], *n.* lait caillé au vin, *m.*
possibility [pɔsi'biliti], *n.* possibilité, *f.*; moyen (*façon*), *m.*
possible ['pɔsibl], *a.* possible.
possibly ['pɔsibli], *adv.* peut-être.
post (1) [poust], *n.* emploi; (*Mil.*) poste; courrier (*livraison de lettres*), *m.*; (*Post-office*) poste, *f.*—*v.t.* mettre à la poste; (*Mil. etc.*) poster, affecter.
post (2) [poust], *n.* poteau (*en bois*); montant (*de porte*), *m.*—*v.t.* afficher.
postage ['poustidʒ], *n.* port de lettre, port, affranchissement, *m.*
postage-stamp ['poustidʒstæmp], *n.* timbre-poste, *m.*
postal ['poustəl], *a.* postal; ***postal order***, mandat-poste, *m.*
postcard ['poustkɑ:d], *n.* carte postale, *f.*
postdate [poust'deit], *v.t.* postdater.
poster ['poustə], *n.* affiche, *f.*, placard, *m.*
posterior [pɔs'tiəriə], *a.* postérieur.
posterity [pɔs'teriti], *n.* postérité, *f.*
postern ['poustə:n], *a.* de derrière.—*n.* poterne, *f.*
post-haste ['poust'heist], *adv.* en grande hâte.
posthumous ['pɔstjuməs], *a.* posthume.
posthumously ['pɔstjuməsli], *adv.* après décès.
postillion [pɔs'tiliən], *n.* postillon, *m.*
postman ['poustmən], *n.* (*pl.* **-men** [men]) facteur, *m.*
postmark ['poustmɑ:k], *n.* cachet de la poste, *m.*
postmaster ['poustmɑ:stə], *n.* receveur des postes, *m.*
post meridiem ['poustmə'ridiəm], (*abbr.* **p.m.** ['pi:'em]) *adv.* de l'après-midi, du soir.
post-mortem [poust'mɔ:təm], *adv.* après décès.—*n.* autopsie, *f.*
post-office ['poustɔfis], *n.* bureau de poste, *m.*, poste, *f.*
postpone [poust'poun], *v.t.* ajourner, différer, remettre.
postponement [poust'pounmənt], *n.* ajournement, *m.*, remise, *f.*
postscript ['poustskript], (*abbr.* **P.S.** ['pi:'es]) *n.* post-scriptum, *m.*
postulate ['pɔstjuleit], *v.t.* postuler.
posture ['pɔstʃə], *n.* posture, pose, *f.*
post-war [poust'wɔ:], *a.* d'après guerre.
posy ['pouzi], *n.* petit bouquet, *m.*
pot [pɔt], *n.* pot, *m.*; marmite, *f.*; ***pots and pans***, batterie de cuisine, *f.*—*v.t.* empoter, mettre en pot.
potable ['poutəbl], *a.* potable.
potash ['pɔtæʃ], *n.* potasse, *f.*
potassium [pə'tæsiəm], *n.* potassium, *m.*
potato [pə'teitou], *n.* (*pl.* **potatoes** [pə'teitouz]) pomme de terre, *f.*
pot-bellied ['pɔtbelid], *a.* pansu, ventru.
potency ['poutənsi], *n.* puissance, force, *f.*
potent ['poutənt], *a.* puissant, fort; (*fig.*) efficace.
potentate ['poutənteit], *n.* potentat, *m.*
potential [pə'tenʃəl], *a.* potentiel, latent.—*n.* (*Elec. etc.*) potentiel, *m.*
potful ['pɔtful], *n.* potée, *f.*
***pother** ['pɔðə], *n.* tumulte; bruit, *m.*
pot-hole ['pɔthoul], *n.* (*Geol.*) marmite torrentielle; (*Motor.*) flache, *f.*
pot-holer ['pɔthoulə], *n.* spéléologue, *m.*, *f.*
pot-holing ['pɔthouliŋ], *n.* spéléologie, *f.*
pothook ['pɔthuk], *n.* crémaillère, *f.*
potion ['pouʃən], *n.* potion, *f.*; breuvage, *m.*
pot-luck ['pɔt'lʌk], *n.* fortune du pot, *f.*
pot-shot ['pɔtʃɔt], *n.* coup tiré au petit bonheur, *m.*
***pottage** ['pɔtidʒ], *n.* potage (épais), *m.*
potted ['pɔtid], *a.* en pot, en terrine; ***potted meat***, conserve de viande, *f.*
potter ['pɔtə], *n.* potier, *m.*—*v.i.* ***to potter about***, s'amuser à des riens.
pottery ['pɔtəri], *n.* poterie, *f.*
potting ['pɔtiŋ], *a.* ***potting shed***, serre, resserre, *f.*—*n.* (*Hort.*) mise en pot, *f.*
pouch [pautʃ], *n.* poche, *f.*, petit sac, *m.*; blague (*à tabac*), *f.*
poulterer ['poultərə], *n.* marchand de volailles, *m.*
poultice ['poultis], *n.* cataplasme, *m.*—*v.t.* mettre un cataplasme à.
poultry ['poultri], *n.* volaille, *f.*
pounce [pauns], *v.i.* fondre (*sur*).
pound [paund], *n.* livre; livre sterling; fourrière (*clôture*), *f.*—*v.t.* broyer; (*Metal.*) bocarder.
poundage ['paundidʒ], *n.* commission de tant par livre, *f.*
pounding ['paundiŋ], *n.* broiement; (*Metal.*) bocardage, *m.*
pour [pɔ:], *v.t.* verser.—*v.i.* couler; pleuvoir à verse (*pluie*).
pouring ['pɔ:riŋ], *a.* torrentiel (*pluie*).
pout [paut], *v.i.* bouder, faire la moue.—*n.* bouderie, moue, *f.*
pouting ['pautiŋ], *a.* qui fait la moue; boudeur.

poverty ['pɔvəti], *n.* pauvreté, misère, indigence, *f.*
poverty-stricken ['pɔvətistrikn], *a.* réduit à la misère, indigent.
powder ['paudə], *n.* poudre, *f.*; ***face-powder***, poudre de riz; ***gunpowder***, poudre à canon; ***tooth-powder***, poudre dentifrice.—*v.t.* réduire en poudre; poudrer (*les cheveux*); (*Cook.*) saupoudrer; ***to powder one's face***, se poudrer.
powder-compact ['paudəkɔmpækt], *n.* poudrier (*de dame*), *m.*
powdered ['paudəd], *a.* pulvérisé; poudré (*cheveux*).
powder-puff ['paudəpʌf], *n.* houppe, *f.*, pompon, *m.*
powdery ['paudəri], *a.* poudreux; friable.
power ['pauə], *n.* pouvoir, *m.*; force (*physique*); autorité, puissance (*morale*), *f.*; ***the Great Powers***, les grandes puissances, *f.pl.*; ***to be in power***, être au pouvoir.
powerful ['pauəful], *a.* puissant, fort.
powerfully ['pauəfuli], *adv.* puissamment, fortement.
powerless ['pauəlis], *a.* impuissant, faible.
power-station ['pauəsteiʃən], *n.* usine génératrice, centrale électrique, *f.*
pox [pɔks], *n.* vérole, *f.*; ***chicken-pox***, varicelle, *f.*; ***small-pox***, petite vérole, variole, *f.*
practicability [præktikə'biliti], *n.* possibilité, praticabilité, *f.*
practicable ['præktikəbl], *a.* praticable.
practical ['præktikl], *a.* pratique; ***practical joke***, mauvaise farce, *f.*
practically ['præktikli], *adv.* en pratique; à peu près.
practice ['præktis], *n.* pratique, habitude, *f.*, usage, exercice, *m.*; clientèle (*de médecin, d'avocat etc.*); intrigue, *f.*
practise ['præktis], *v.t.* pratiquer, mettre en pratique; exercer, pratiquer (*une profession etc.*); (*Mus.*) étudier.—*v.i.* (*Mus.*) étudier; s'exercer (*à*); exercer, faire de la clientèle (*médecin*).
practised ['præktist], *a.* exercé (*à*); versé (*dans*); habile.
practising ['præktisiŋ], *a.* praticien, exerçant.
practitioner [præk'tiʃənə], *n.* praticien, *m.*; ***general practitioner***, médecin ordinaire, *m.*; ***medical practitioner***, médecin, *m.*
pragmatic [præg'mætik], **pragmatical** [præg'mætikəl], *a.* pragmatique; officieux; infatué de soi.
pragmatism ['prægmətizm], *n.* pragmatisme, *m.*
prairie ['prɛəri], *n.* prairie, savane, *f.*
praise [preiz], *n.* louange, *f.*, éloge, *m.*—*v.t.* louer, faire l'éloge de; vanter.
praiseworthy ['preizwəːði], *a.* louable, digne d'éloges.
pram [præm], *n.* voiture d'enfant, *f.*
prance [prɑːns], *v.i.* fringuer (*cheval*).
prancing ['prɑːnsiŋ], *a.* fringant.
prank [præŋk], *n.* escapade, niche, *f.*, tour, *m.*
prate [preit], *v.i.* jaser, babiller, bavarder (*de*).
prating ['preitiŋ], *a.* bavard, babillard.
pratingly ['preitiŋli], *adv.* en bavard, en babillard.
prattle [prætl], *v.i.* babiller, jaser, caqueter.—*n.* babil, caquetage, bavardage, *m.*
prattler ['prætlə], *n.* bavard, babillard, *m.*
prattling ['prætliŋ], *n.* bavardage, caquet, *m.*
prawn [prɔːn], *n.* crevette rouge; salicoque, *f.*
pray [prei], *v.t.* prier, supplier.—*v.i.* prier.
prayer [prɛə], *n.* prière, supplication; (*Law*) demande, *f.*; ***the Lord's Prayer***, l'oraison dominicale, *f.*
prayer-book ['prɛəbuk], *n.* livre de prières, *m.*; liturgie, *f.*
preach [priːtʃ], *v.t.*, *v.i.* prêcher.
preacher ['priːtʃə], *n.* prédicateur, *m.*
preaching ['priːtʃiŋ], *n.* prédication, *f.*
preamble [priː'æmbl], *n.* préambule, *m.*
prearrange [priːə'reindʒ], *v.t.* arranger d'avance.
prebendary ['prebəndəri], *n.* chanoine, prébendier, *m.*
precarious [pri'kɛəriəs], *a.* précaire.
precariously [pri'kɛəriəsli], *adv.* précairement.
precariousness [pri'kɛəriəsnis], *n.* nature précaire; incertitude, *f.*
precaution [pri'kɔːʃən], *n.* précaution, *f.*
precautionary [pri'kɔːʃənri], *a.* de précaution.
precede [pri'siːd], *v.t.* précéder.
precedence ['presidəns], *n.* préséance, *f.*; ***to have*** or ***take precedence over***, avoir le pas sur.
precedent (1) [pri'siːdənt], **preceding** [pri'siːdiŋ], *a.* précédent.
precedent (2) ['presidənt], *n.* précédent, *m.*
precept ['priːsept], *n.* précepte, *m.*
precinct ['priːsiŋkt], *n.* limite, borne, enceinte, *f.*
precious ['preʃəs], *a.* précieux; affecté; (*fam.*) fameux, fichu.
preciously ['preʃəsli], *adv.* précieusement; (*fam.*) fameusement, diablement.
preciousness ['preʃəsnis], *n.* haute valeur, *f.*
precipice ['presipis], *n.* précipice, *m.*
precipitate (1) [pri'sipitit], *a.* précipité.—*n.* (*Chem.*) précipité, *m.*
precipitate (2) [pri'sipiteit], *v.t.* précipiter.—*v.i.* se précipiter.
precipitation [prisipi'teiʃən], *n.* précipitation, *f.*
precipitous [pri'sipitəs], *a.* escarpé, abrupt.
precipitously [pri'sipitəsli], *adv.* à pic, en précipice; (*fig.*) précipitamment.
precise [pri'sais], *a.* précis, exact; formaliste, pointilleux, scrupuleux.
precisely [pri'saisli], *adv.* précisément.
precision [pri'siʒən], *n.* précision, exactitude, *f.*
preclude [pri'kluːd], *v.t.* exclure; empêcher (*mettre obstacle à*).
preclusion [pri'kluːʒən], *n.* exclusion, *f.*
precocious [pri'kouʃəs], *a.* précoce.
precociousness [pri'kouʃəsnis], *n.* précocité, *f.*
preconceived ['priːkən'siːvd], *a.* formé d'avance; ***preconceived idea***, idée préconçue, *f.*
precursor [pri'kəːsə], *n.* précurseur, avant-coureur, *m.*
predatory ['predətəri], *a.* de rapine, de proie, pillard, rapace.
predecease ['priːdi'siːs], *v.t.* prédécéder.
predestinate [priː'destineit], **predestine** [priː'destin], *v.t.* prédestiner.

predestination [pri:desti'neiʃən], *n.* prédestination, *f.*
predetermine [pri:di'tə:min], *v.t.* prédéterminer, arrêter d'avance.
predicament [pri'dikəmənt], *n.* état, *m.*, position difficile, situation fâcheuse; catégorie, *f.*, ordre, *m.*
predicate ['predikit], *n.* prédicat, attribut, *m.*
predict [pri'dikt], *v.t.* prédire.
prediction [pri'dikʃən], *n.* prédiction, prévision, *f.*
predilection [pri:di'lekʃən], *n.* prédilection, *f.*
predispose [pri:dis'pouz], *v.t.* prédisposer.
predisposition [pri:dispə'ziʃən], *n.* prédisposition, *f.*
predominance [pri'dɔminəns], *n.* prédominance, *f.*, ascendant, *m.*
predominant [pri'dɔminənt], *a.* prédominant.
predominantly [pri'dɔminəntli], *adv.* d'une manière prédominante.
predominate [pri'dɔmineit], *v.i.* prédominer, prévaloir.
pre-eminence [pri:'eminəns], *n.* prééminence, supériorité, *f.*
pre-eminent [pri:'eminənt], *a.* prééminent.
pre-eminently [pri:'eminəntli], *adv.* par excellence.
preen [pri:n], *v.t* lisser, nettoyer (ses plumes); ***to preen oneself***, se piquer.
pre-engage [pri:in'geidʒ], *v.t.* engager d'avance.
pre-exist [pri:ig'zist], *v.i.* préexister.
pre-existence [pri:ig'zistəns], *n.* préexistence, *f.*
prefabricate [pri:'fæbrikeit], *v.t.* préfabriquer.
preface ['prefis], *n.* préface, *f.*; avant-propos, *m.*—*v.t.* faire une préface à.
prefect ['pri:fekt], *n.* préfet; (*Sch.*) surveillant, *m.*
prefer [pri'fə:], *v.t.* préférer, aimer mieux; avancer, élever (*aux honneurs*); porter (*une accusation*).
preferable ['prefərəbl], *a.* préférable (*à*).
preferably ['prefərəbli], *adv.* préférablement, de préférence.
preference ['prefərəns], *n.* préférence, *f.*
preferential [prefə'renʃl], *a.* préférentiel.
preferment [pri'fə:mənt], *n.* avancement, *m.*, promotion, *f.*
prefix ['pri:fiks], *n.* (*Gram.*) préfixe, *m.*
pregnancy ['pregnənsi], *n.* grossesse, *f.*
pregnant ['pregnənt], *a.* enceinte, grosse; (*fig.*) gros, plein (*de*); fertile, fécond (*en*).
prehensile [pri'hensail], *a.* préhensile.
prehistoric [pri:his'tɔrik], *a.* préhistorique.
prejudge [pri:'dʒʌdʒ], *v.t.* juger d'avance.
prejudice ['predʒudis], *v.t.* prévenir, nuire à (*faire du tort à*).—*n.* prévention, *f.*, préjugé; préjudice, tort (*détriment*), *m.*
prejudiced ['predʒudist], *a.* prévenu.
prejudicial [predʒu'diʃl], *a.* préjudiciable, nuisible (*à*).
prelate ['prelit], *n.* prélat, *m.*
preliminary [pri'liminəri], *a.* and *n.* préliminaire, *m.*
prelude ['prelju:d], *n.* prélude, *m.*
premature ['prematjuə], *a.* prématuré.
prematurely [premə'tjuəli], *adv.* prématurément.
premeditate [pri'mediteit], *v.t.* préméditer.
premeditated [pri'mediteitid], *a.* prémédité.
premeditation [primedi'teiʃən], *n.* préméditation, *f.*
premier ['pri:miə, 'premiə], *a.* premier (*de rang*).—*n.* premier ministre, *m.*
premise ['premis], *n.* (*Log.*) prémisse, *f.*
premises ['premisiz], *n.pl.* lieux, *m.pl.*; établissement, local, *m.*
premium ['pri:miəm], *n.* prime, *f.*; prix, *m.*
premonition [pri:mə'niʃən], *n.* avertissement; pressentiment, *m.*
prenatal [pri:'neitl], *a.* prénatal.
preoccupied [pri:'ɔkjupaid], *a.* préoccupé.
preordain [pri:ɔ:'dein], *v.t.* ordonner *ou* arranger d'avance.
prep [prep], *n.* (*Sch. fam. abbr.* **preparation**) étude, *f.*; devoirs, *m.pl.*
prepaid [pri:'peid], *a.* affranchi, franc de port. —*adv.* franco.
preparation [prepə'reiʃən], *n.* préparation, *f.*; préparatifs, apprêts (*de voyage etc.*), *m.pl.*
preparatory [pri'pærətri], *a.* préparatoire.
prepare [pri'pɛə], *v.t.* préparer.—*v.i.* se préparer, s'apprêter (*à*).
preparedness [pri'pɛə(ri)dnis], *n.* état de préparation, *m.*
prepay [pri:'pei], *v.t. irr* (*conjug. like* PAY) payer d'avance; affranchir (*lettres*).
prepayment [pri:'peimənt], *n.* payement d'avance; affranchissement (*de lettres*), *m.*
preponderance [pri'pɔndərəns], *n.* prépondérance, *f.*
preponderant [pri'pɔndərənt], *a.* prépondérant.
preponderate [pri'pɔndəreit], *v.i.* avoir la prépondérance, l'emporter (*sur*).
preposition [prepə'ziʃən], *n.* préposition, *f.*
prepossessing [pri:pə'zesiŋ], *a.* prévenant, engageant.
preposterous [pri'pɔstərəs], *a.* absurde, déraisonnable.
preposterously [pri'pɔstərəsli], *adv.* absurdement, déraisonnablement.
prerogative [pri'rɔgətiv], *n.* prérogative, *f.*
Presbyterian [prezbi'tiəriən], *a.* and *n.* presbytérien, *m.*
Presbyterianism [prezbi'tiəriənizm], *n.* presbytérianisme, *m.*
presbytery ['prezbitəri], *n.* presbytère, *m.*
prescience ['preʃiəns], *n.* prescience, *f.*
prescribe [pri'skraib], *v.t.* prescrire; (*Med.*) ordonner.—*v.i.* (*Med.*) faire une ordonnance.
prescription [pri'skripʃən], *n.* (*Law*) prescription; (*Med.*) ordonnance, *f.*
presence ['prezəns], *n.* présence, *f.*; air, maintien, *m.*, mine (*aspect*), *f.*; personnage supérieur, *m.*; ***presence of mind***, présence d'esprit.
present ['prezənt], *a.* présent; actuel; ***at the present moment***, à présent, actuellement; ***to be present at***, assister à.—*n.* présent; cadeau, don, *m.*; ***for the present***, pour le moment.—[pri'zent], *v.t.* présenter, offrir (*à*).
presentable [pri'zentəbl], *a.* présentable.
presentation [prezən'teiʃən], *n.* présentation, *f.*; don, *m.*

presentiment [pri'zentimənt], *n.* pressentiment, *m.*
presently ['prezəntli], *adv.* tout à l'heure, bientôt.
preservation [prezə'veiʃən], *n.* salut, *m.*, conservation; préservation (*de*), *f.*
preservative [pri'zə:vətiv], *a.* and *n.* préservateur, préservatif, *m.*
preserve [pri'zə:v], *n.* confiture, *f.*, conserves, *f.pl.*; réserve, chasse réservée, *f.*—*v.t.* préserver (*de*); conserver; confire (*fruits etc.*); ***preserved fruits***, fruits confits, *m.pl.*; ***preserved meat***, conserves de viande, *f.pl.*
preserver [pri'zə:və], *n.* sauveur; conservateur, *m.*; ***life preserver***, porte-respect, *m.*
preside [pri'zaid], *v.i.* présider (*à*).
presidency ['prezidənsi], *n.* présidence, *f.*
president ['prezidənt], *n.* président, *m.*; ***vice-president***, vice-président, *m.*
presidential [prezi'denʃəl], *a.* présidentiel; de président.
presiding [pri'zaidiŋ], *a.* présidant.
press (1) [pres], *v.t.* presser; serrer, étreindre; satiner (*papier*); pressurer (*fruits*); repasser (*vêtements*); (*fig.*) insister sur.—*v.i.* presser, pousser; avancer, se presser.—*n.* presse, pression, *f.*; pressoir (*à fruits etc.*), *m.*; armoire à linge, *f.*; ***the press***, la presse.
press (2) [pres], *v.t.* enrôler (*marins*) de force.
press-agency ['preseidʒənsi], *n.* agence de presse, *f.*
press-cutting ['preskʌtiŋ], *n.* coupure de journal, *f.*
pressed [prest], *a.* satiné; ***hard pressed***, serré de près; aux abois; ***pressed for time***, très pressé.
***press-gang** ['presgæŋ], *n.* (*Naut.*) presse, *f.*
pressing ['presiŋ], *a.* urgent, pressant.
pressman ['presmən], *n.* (*pl.* **-men** [men]) journaliste, reporter, *m.*
pressure ['preʃə], *n.* pression; tension; urgence, *f.*; poids (*lourdeur*), *m.*; ***blood pressure***, tension artérielle.
pressure-cooker ['preʃəkukə], *n.* autoclave; auto-cuiseur, *m.*, cocotte-minute, *f.*
pressure-gauge ['preʃəgeidʒ], *n.* manomètre *m.*
pressurize ['preʃəraiz], *v.t.* pressuriser.
prestige [pres'ti:ʒ], *n.* prestige, *m.*
presumably [pri'zju:məbli], *adv.* probablement.
presume [pri'zju:m], *v.t.* présumer; supposer.—*v.i.* présumer se permettre, avoir l'audace (*de*), prendre la liberté (*de*); ***to presume upon***, présumer trop de.
presuming [pri'zju:miŋ], *a.* présomptueux, indiscret.
presumption [pri'zʌmpʃən], *n.* présomption, *f.*
presumptive [pri'zʌmptiv], *a.* présumé; (*Law*) présomptif.
presumptuous [pri'zʌmptjuəs], *a.* présomptueux.
presumptuousness [pri'zʌmptjuəsnis], *n.* présomption, *f.*
presuppose [pri:sə'pouz], *v.t.* présupposer.
pretence [pri'tens], *n.* prétexte, *m.*, simulation; prétention, *f.*; ***to make a pretence of***, faire semblant de; ***under false pretences***, par des moyens frauduleux.
pretend [pri'tend], *v.t.* prétexter; feindre.—*v.i.* prétendre (*à*); feindre (*de*), faire semblant (*de*).
pretended [pri'tendid], *a.* prétendu, soi-disant.
pretender [pri'tendə], *n.* prétendant, *m.*
pretension [pri'tenʃən], *n.* prétention, *f.*
pretentious [pri'tenʃəs], *a.* prétentieux, ambitieux.
pretentiousness [pri'tenʃəsnis], *n.* air prétentieux, *m.*, prétention, *f.*
preternatural [pri:tə'nætʃərəl], *a.* surnaturel, contre nature.
pretext ['pri:tekst], *n.* prétexte, faux semblant, *m.*; ***under the pretext of***, sous prétexte de.
prettily ['pritili], *adv.* joliment, gentiment.
prettiness ['pritinis], *n.* gentillesse, *f.*, agrément, *m.*
pretty ['priti], *a.* joli, gentil.—*adv.* assez; passablement; ***pretty much***, presque, à peu près.
prevail [pri'veil], *v.i.* prévaloir, l'emporter (*sur*); réussir (*avoir du succès*); dominer.
prevailing [pri'veiliŋ], *a.* dominant, régnant; général.
prevalence ['prevələns], *n.* influence, prédominance; fréquence, durée (*de temps, maladie etc.*), *f.*
prevalent ['prevələnt], *a.* régnant, dominant; général.
prevaricate [pri'værikeit], *v.i.* équivoquer; tergiverser, mentir.
prevarication [priværi'keiʃən], *n.* tergiversation, *f.*
prevaricator [pri'værikeitə], *n.* chicaneur, menteur, *m.*
prevent [pri'vent], *v.t.* empêcher, détourner (*de*); prévenir.
preventable [pri'ventəbl], *a.* évitable.
prevention [pri'venʃən], *n.* empêchement, *m.*
preventive [pri'ventiv], *a.* préventif.—*n.* préservatif, *m.*
preview ['pri:vju:], *n.* avant-première, *f.*
previous ['pri:viəs], *a.* antérieur, préalable.
previously ['pri:viəsli], *adv.* antérieurement, auparavant.
previousness ['pri:viəsnis], *n.* antériorité, priorité; (*colloq.*) anticipation, *f.*
prey [prei], *n.* proie, *f.*; ***to be a prey to***, être en proie à.—*v.i.* ***to prey on***, faire sa proie de; tourmenter, obséder (*l'esprit*).
price [prais], *n.* prix, *m.*; ***at any price***, à tout prix; ***cost price***, prix coûtant; ***market price***, prix courant.—*v.t.* tarifer, mettre un prix à.
priceless ['praislis], *a.* sans prix, inappréciable; impayable (*plaisanterie etc.*).
price-list ['praislist], *n.* tarif, *m.*
prick [prik], *n.* piqûre; pointe, *f.*; (*fig.*) aiguillon (*stimulant*); remords, *m.*—*v.t.* piquer; dresser (*les oreilles*); aiguillonner (*stimuler*); (*fig.*) exciter, tourmenter de remords.
pricker ['prikə], *n.* poinçon, *m.*, pointe, *f.*
pricking ['prikiŋ], *a.* qui pique, piquant.—*n.* piqûre, *f.*; picotement (*sensation*), *m.*
prickle [prikl], *n.* aiguillon, piquant, *m.*; épine, *f.*—*v.t.* piquer.
prickly ['prikli], *a.* piquant, épineux, hérissé.
pride [praid], *n.* orgueil, *m.*, fierté; bande (*de lions*), *f.*—*v.r.* ***to pride oneself on***, se piquer de, s'enorgueillir de.
prier ['praiə], *n.* curieux, *m.*

priest [pri:st], *n.* prêtre, *m.*

priestess ['pri:stes], *n.* prêtresse, *f.*

priesthood ['pri:sthu:d], *n.* prêtrise, *f.*, sacerdoce, clergé, *m.*

priestly ['pri:stli], *a.* de prêtre, sacerdotal.

prig [prig], *n.* faquin, fat; pédant, *m.*

priggish ['prigiʃ], *a.* suffisant, pédant.

priggishly ['prigiʃli], *adv.* avec suffisance.

prim [prim], *a.* affecté, précieux, collet monté.

primacy ['praiməsi], *n.* primauté, *f.*

primal ['praiməl], *a.* primitif; principal.

primarily ['praimərili], *adv.* dans le principe.

primary ['praiməri], *a.* primitif, premier; principal; (*Sch.*) primaire, élémentaire.

primate ['praimit], *n.* primat, *m.*

prime [praim], *a.* premier, principal; de premier rang, de première qualité; ***prime minister***, premier ministre, *m.*—*n.* aube, *f.*; commencement; printemps, *m.*; fleur, élite, *f.*, choix (*mieux*), *m.*; première jeunesse, *f.*; ***prime of life***, fleur de l'âge, *f.* —*v.t.* amorcer (*fusils*); (*Paint.*) imprimer.

primer ['praimə], *n.* premier livre (*de lecture etc.*); (*R.-C. Ch.*) livre d'heures, *m.*

primeval [prai'mi:vəl], *a.* primitif, primordial.

priming ['praimiŋ], *n.* amorçage, *m.*; amorce (*d'un fusil*); (*Paint.*) impression, *f.*

primitive ['primitiv], *a.* and *n.* primitif, *m.*

primitiveness ['primitivnis], *n.* caractère primitif, *m.*

primly ['primli], *adv.* d'un air collet monté.

primness ['primnis], *n.* afféterie, *f.*

primogeniture [praimou'dʒenitjuə], *n.* primogéniture, *f.*

primordial [prai'mɔ:diəl], *a.* primordial.

primrose ['primrouz], *n.* primevère, *f.*

prince [prins], *n.* prince, *m.*

princeliness ['prinslinis], *n.* caractère de prince, *m.*

princely ['prinsli], *a.* de prince, princier; magnifique.—*adv.* en prince, en princesse, magnifiquement.

princess [prin'ses], *n.* princesse, *f.*

principal ['prinsipl], *a.* principal, premier, en chef.—*n.* partie principale, *f.*, chef; directeur, patron; proviseur (*d'un lycée*), *m.*; directrice, *f.*

principality [prinsi'pæliti], *n.* principauté, *f.*

principally ['prinsipli], *adv.* principalement, surtout.

principle ['prinsipl], *n.* principe, *m.*

principled ['prinsipld], *a.* qui a des principes.

print [print], *v.t.* imprimer; faire une empreinte sur; (*Phot. etc.*) tirer; ***printed matter***, imprimé(s), *m.* (*pl.*).—*n.* empreinte (*de pas etc.*), impression; estampe, gravure; indienne (*tissu*); (*Phot.*) épreuve, *f.*; (*Print.*) caractère, *m.*

printer ['printə], *n.* imprimeur, typographe, *m.*

printing ['printiŋ], *n.* impression (*tirage*); imprimerie (*art etc.*), *f.*

printing-machine ['printiŋmə'ʃi:n], *n.* presse mécanique, *f.*

printing-press ['printiŋpres], *n.* presse à imprimer, *f.*

prior ['praiə], *a.* antérieur.—*adv.* antérieurement (*à*), avant.—*n.* prieur, *m.*

prioress ['praiəris], *n.* prieure, *f.*

priority [prai'ɔriti], *n.* priorité, *f.*

priory ['praiəri], *n.* prieuré, *m.*

prise [praiz], *n.* levier, *m.*—*v.t.* ***to prise open***, ouvrir avec un levier.

prism [prizm], *n.* prisme, *m.*

prismatic [priz'mætik], **prismatical** [priz'mætikəl], *a.* prismatique.

prison [prizn], *n.* prison, *f.*

prisoner ['priznə], *n.* prisonnier, *m.*; (*Law*) ***prisoner (at the bar)***, accusé, prévenu, *m.*

prison-van ['priznvæn], *n.* voiture cellulaire, *f.*

pristine ['pristain], *a.* primitif, premier.

privacy ['praivəsi, 'privəsi], *n.* retraite, solitude, intimité, *f.*

private ['praivit], *a.* particulier, personnel, privé; confidentiel, secret; (*Law*) à huis clos.—*n.* (*Mil.*) simple soldat, *m.*

privateer [praivə'tiə], *n.* corsaire, *m.*

privately ['praivitli], *adv.* en particulier; en secret; (*Law*) à huis clos.

privation [prai'veiʃən], *n.* privation, *f.*

privet ['privit], *n.* (*Bot.*) troène, *m.*

privilege ['privilidʒ], *n.* privilège, *m.*, (*Law*) immunité, *f.*—*v.t.* privilégier.

privileged ['privilidʒd], *a.* privilégié.

privily ['privili], *adv.* secrètement, en secret.

privy ['privi], *a.* privé, secret; caché; ***Privy Council***, conseil privé, *m.*

prize [praiz], *n.* prise (*ce qu'on prend*), *f.*; prix (*récompense*); lot (*dans une loterie*), *m.*—*v.t.* priser, estimer.

prize-giving ['praizgiviŋ], *n.* distribution des prix, *f.*

prize-winner ['praizwinə], *n.* lauréat, gagnant, *m.*

pro [prou], *prep.* pour; ***pros and cons***, le pour et le contre.

probability [prɔbə'biliti], *n.* probabilité, vraisemblance, *f.*

probable ['prɔbəbl], *a.* probable; vraisemblable.

probably ['prɔbəbli], *adv.* probablement.

probate ['proubeit], *n.* vérification (*d'un testament*), *f.*

probation [prə'beiʃən], *n.* probation, épreuve; *f.*; (*Univ. etc.*) examen, stage, *m.*; ***on probation***, (*Law*) sous surveillance de la police.

probationary [prə'beiʃənəri], *a.* d'épreuve; de probation.

probationer [prə'beiʃənə], *n.* aspirant, *m.*, stagiaire; novice, *m.*, *f.*

probe [proub], *n.* sonde, *f.*, stylet, *m.*—*v.t.* sonder; (*fig.*) examiner à fond.

probing ['proubiŋ], *a.* pénétrant (*question*).

probity ['proubiti], *n.* probité, *f.*

problem ['prɔbləm], *n.* problème, *m.*

problematic [prɔbli'mætik], **problematical** [prɔbli'mætikəl], *a.* problématique.

proboscis [prə'bɔsis], *n.* (*pl.* **probosces** [prə'bɔsi:z]) trompe, *f.*, (*facet.*) nez, *m.*

procedure [prə'si:dʒə], *n.* procédé, *m.*, procédure, *f.*

proceed [prə'si:d], *v.i.* procéder, avancer, continuer son chemin; provenir (*de*); se mettre (*à*).

proceeding [prə'si:diŋ], *n.* procédé, *m.*; manière d'agir, *f.*; (*pl.*) démarches, *f.pl.*, faits, actes, *m.pl.*

proceeds ['prousi:dz], *n.pl.* produit, montant, *m.*

process ['prouses], *n.* procédé; processus; cours, *m.*, marche, suite (*du temps*), *f.*—*v.t.* (*Ind.*) traiter.
procession [prə'seʃən], *n.* procession, *f.*, cortège, *m.*
processional [prə'seʃənəl], *a.* processionnel. —*n.* hymne processionnel, *m.*
proclaim [prə'kleim], *v.t.* proclamer, déclarer, publier.
proclamation [prɔklə'meiʃən], *n.* proclamation, publication, déclaration; ordonnance, *f.*
proclivity [prə'kliviti], *n.* penchant, *m.*, inclination (*à*), *f.*
procrastinate [pro'kræstineit], *v.t.* remettre. —*v.i.* retarder.
procrastination [prokræsti'neiʃən], *n.* retardement, délai, *m.*
procrastinator [pro'kræstineitə], *n.* temporiseur, *m.*
procreate ['proukrieit], *v.t.* procréer.
procreation [proukri'eiʃən], *n.* procréation, *f.*
procreative ['proukrieitiv], *a.* procréateur, productif.
proctor ['prɔktə], *n.* (*Univ.*) censeur; (*Law*) procureur, *m.*
procurable [prə'kjuərəbl], *a.* qu'on peut se procurer.
procuration [prɔkju'reiʃən], *n.* gestion des affaires d'autrui; (*Law*) procuration, *f.*
procurator ['prɔkjureitə], *n.* agent d'affaires; (*Law*) procurateur, *m.*
procure [prə'kjuə], *v.t.* procurer, faire avoir, se procurer.
prod [prɔd], *v.t.* pousser du doigt *ou* du bout d'un bâton; piquer; (*fig.*) aiguillonner.—*n.* coup de pointe, *m.*
prodigal ['prɔdigl], *a.* and *n.* prodigue, *m.*, *f.*
prodigality [prɔdi'gæliti], *n.* prodigalité, *f.*
prodigious [prə'didʒəs], *a.* prodigieux.
prodigy ['prɔdidʒi], *n.* prodige, *m.*, *f.*
produce ['prɔdju:s], *n.* produit, *m.*—[prə'dju:s], *v.t.* produire; exhiber, montrer; (*Geom.*) prolonger; (*Theat.*) mettre en scène.
producer [prə'dju:sə], *n.* producteur; (*Theat.*) metteur en scène, *m.*
producible [prə'dju:sibl], *a.* productible.
product ['prɔdʌkt], *n.* produit, *m.*; ***by-product***, sous-produit, *m.*
production [prə'dʌkʃən], *n.* production, *f.*; (*Chem. etc.*) produit, *m.*; (*Theat.*) mise en scène, *f.*
productive [prə'dʌktiv], *a.* productif; fécond.
productivity [prɔdʌk'tiviti], *n.* productivité, *f.*
profanation [prɔfə'neiʃən], *n.* profanation, *f.*
profane [prə'fein], *a.* profane.—*v.t.* profaner.
profanely [prə'feinli], *adv.* d'une manière profane.
profaner [prə'feinə], *n.* profanateur, *m.*
profanity [prə'fæniti], *n.* conduite profane, impiété, *f.*; langage profane, *m.*
profess [prə'fes], *v.t.* professer, faire profession de, déclarer.
professed [prə'fest], *a.* déclaré, de profession.
professedly [prə'fesidli], *adv.* ouvertement; de profession.
profession [prə'feʃən], *n.* profession, *f.*; état, métier (*emploi*), *m.*
professional [prə'feʃənəl], *a.* de sa profession, professionnel; ***professional man***, homme qui exerce une carrière libérale, *m.*—*n.* homme du métier, homme de l'art; (*Spt.*) professionnel, *m.*
professionalism [prə'feʃənəlizm], *n.* caractère professionnel; (*Spt.*) professionnalisme, *m.*
professionally [prə'feʃənəli], *adv.* par profession; en homme du métier.
professor [prə'fesə], *n.* professeur (d'université), *m.*
professorial [prɔfe'sɔ:riəl], *a.* de professeur, professoral.
professorship [prə'fesəʃip], *n.* professorat, *m.*, chaire, *f.*
proffer ['prɔfə], *n.* offre, *f.*—*v.t.* offrir, proposer.
proficiency [prə'fiʃənsi], *n.* capacité, *f.*; talent, *m.*, compétence, *f.*
proficient [prə'fiʃənt], *a.* versé, fort, compétent.
profile ['proufail], *n.* profil, *m.*; ***in profile***, de profil.
profit ['prɔfit], *n.* profit, bénéfice, rapport; (*fig.*) avantage, *m.*—*v.t.* profiter à, faire du bien à; avantager.—*v.i.* profiter (*de*).
profitable ['prɔfitəbl], *a.* profitable, avantageux.
profitably ['prɔfitəbli], *adv.* avantageusement, avec profit.
profiteer [prɔfi'tiə], *n.* profiteur, *m.*—*v.i.* faire des bénéfices excessifs.
profitless ['prɔfitlis], *a.* sans profit, inutile.
profligacy ['prɔfligəsi], *n.* dérèglement, *m.*, dissolution, *f.*, libertinage, *m.*
profligate ['prɔfligit], *a.* débauché, dissolu, libertin.—*n.* libertin, mauvais sujet, *m.*
profound [prə'faund], *a.* profond; approfondi.
profoundly [prə'faundli], *adv.* profondément.
profundity [prə'fʌnditi], *n.* profondeur, *f.*
profuse [prə'fju:s], *a.* prodigue; abondant, excessif (*choses*).
profusely [prə'fju:sli], *adv.* profusément, à profusion.
profuseness [prə'fju:snis], **profusion** [prə'fju:ʒən], *n.* profusion, prodigalité, abondance, *f.*
progenitor [prou'dʒenitə], *n.* aïeul, ancêtre, *m.*
progeny ['prɔdʒəni], *n.* postérité, *f.*, descendants, *m.pl.*
prognostic [prɔg'nɔstik], *a.* pronostique.—*n.* pronostic, *m.*
prognosticate [prɔg'nɔstikeit], *v.t.* pronostiquer.
prognostication [prɔgnɔsti'keiʃən], *n.* pronostic, *m.*
programme ['prougræm], *n.* programme, *m.*
progress ['prougres], *n.* progrès, avancement, cours, *m.*; marche, *f.*; voyage (*de cérémonie*), *m.*—[prə'gres], *v.i.* s'avancer, faire des progrès, avancer.
progression [prə'greʃən], *n.* progression, *f.*
progressive [prə'gresiv], *a.* and *n.* progressif, *m.*; (*Polit.*) progressiste, *m.*, *f.*
progressiveness [prə'gresivnis], *n.* marche progressive, *f.*
prohibit [prə'hibit], *v.t.* prohiber, défendre, interdire (*à*); ***smoking prohibited***, défense de fumer.
prohibition [prouhi'biʃən], *n.* prohibition, défense, *f.*

prohibitive [prə'hibitiv], **prohibitory** [prə'hibitri], *a.* prohibitif (*mœurs*); ***prohibitive price***, prix exorbitant, *m.*
project ['prɔdʒekt], *n.* projet, dessein, *m.*—[prə'dʒekt], *v.t.* projeter.—*v.i.* avancer, faire saillie.
projectile [prə'dʒektail], *n.* projectile, *m.*
projecting [prə'dʒektiŋ], *a.* saillant, en saillie.
projection [prə'dʒekʃən], *n.* projection, saillie, *f.*; (*Arch.*) ressaut, *m.*
projector [prə'dʒektə], *n.* homme à projets, projeteur; projecteur (*lumière*); (*Cine.*) appareil de projection, *m.*
proletarian [prouli'tɛəriən], *a.* and *n.* prolétaire, *m., f.*
proletariat [prouli'tɛəriət], *n.* prolétariat, *m.*
prolific [prə'lifik], *a.* prolifique; fécond, fertile.
prolix ['prouliks], *a.* prolixe.
prolixity [prə'liksiti], **prolixness** ['prouliks nis], *n.* prolixité, *f.*
prologue ['proulɔg], *n.* prologue, *m.*
prolong [prə'lɔŋ], *v.t.* prolonger; retarder, différer (*remettre*); ***to be prolonged***, se prolonger.
prolongation [proulɔŋ'geiʃən], *n.* prolongement, *m.*; prolongation (*du temps etc.*), *f.*
promenade [prɔmə'nɑːd], *n.* promenade; esplanade (*au bord de la mer*), *f.*—*v.i.* se promener, se faire voir.
promenader [prɔmə'nɑːdə], *n.* promeneur, *m.*
prominence ['prɔminəns], *n.* proéminence; (*fig.*) distinction, *f.*
prominent ['prɔminənt], *a.* proéminent, saillant; prononcé (*remarquable*); (*fig.*) éminent, distingué.
prominently ['prɔminəntli], *adv.* en saillie; d'une manière frappante.
promiscuity [prɔmis'kjuːiti], **promiscuousness** [prə'miskjuəsnis], *n.* mélange confus, *m.*; promiscuité, *f.*
promiscuous [prə'miskjuəs], *a.* sans distinction de sexe, promiscu; mêlé, confus, sans ordre.
promiscuously [prə'miskjuəsli], *adv.* confusément; en commun, en promiscuité.
promise ['prɔmis], *n.* promesse; (*fig.*) espérance, *f.*—*v.t., v.i.* promettre.
promising ['prɔmisiŋ], *a.* prometteur, qui promet; qui donne des espérances.
promissory ['prɔmisəri], *a.* qui contient une promesse; ***promissory note***, billet à ordre, *m.*
promontory ['prɔməntri], *n.* promontoire, *m.*
promote [prə'mout], *v.t.* servir, avancer; promouvoir; encourager; ***to promote a company***, lancer une société anonyme.
promoter [prə'moutə], *n.* promoteur, protecteur, instigateur; (*Comm.*) lanceur d'affaires, *m.*
promotion [prə'mouʃən], *n.* promotion, *f.*, avancement, *m.*
prompt [prɔmpt], *v.t.* exciter, porter, pousser; inspirer, suggérer; (*Theat.*) souffler.—*a.* prompt, empressé.
prompter ['prɔmptə], *n.* souffleur, *m.*; ***prompter's box***, trou du souffleur, *m.*
promptitude, ['prɔmptitjuːd], **promptness** ['prɔmptnis], *n.* promptitude, *f.*, empressement, *m.*
promptly ['prɔmptli], *adv.* promptement, avec empressement.
promptness [PROMPTITUDE].
promulgate ['prɔməlgeit], *v.t.* promulguer.
promulgation [prɔməl'geiʃən], *n.* promulgation, *f.*
promulgator ['prɔməlgeitə], *n.* promulgateur, *m.*
prone [proun], *a.* penché, incliné; couché, étendu; (*fig.*) disposé, porté (*à*).
proneness ['prounnis], *n.* disposition, inclination, *f.*, penchant, *m.*
prong [prɔŋ], *n.* fourchon, *m.*, dent, *f.*
pronged [prɔŋd], *a.* à fourchons, à dents.
pronoun ['prounaun], *n.* pronom, *m.*
pronounce [prə'nauns], *v.t.* prononcer; déclarer, annoncer, dire.
pronounceable [prə'naunsəbl], *a.* prononçable.
pronouncement [prə'naunsmənt], *n.* prononcement, *m.*, déclaration, *f.*
pronunciation [prənʌnsi'eiʃən], *n.* prononciation, *f.*, accent, *m.*
proof [pruːf], *a.* ***proof against***, résistant à, à l'épreuve de; ***waterproof***, imperméable.—*n.* preuve; épreuve, *f.*
proofless ['pruːflis], *a.* sans preuve.
proof-sheet ['pruːfʃiːt], *n.* (*Print.*) épreuve, *f.*
prop [prɔp], *n.* étai, étançon; (*Hort.*) tuteur, échalas; (*fig.*) appui, soutien; (*Theat.*) (*fam.*) accessoire, *m.*—*v.t.* étayer; appuyer, soutenir; (*Hort.*) échalasser.
propaganda [prɔpə'gændə], *n.* propagande, *f.*
propagandist [prɔpə'gændist], *n.* propagandiste, *m., f.*
propagate ['prɔpəgeit], *v.t.* propager; (*fig.*) répandre; créer, enfanter (*des êtres*).—*v.i.* se propager.
propagation [prɔpə'geiʃən], *n.* propagation, *f.*
propagator ['prɔpəgeitə], *n.* propagateur, *m.*
propel [prə'pel], *v.t.* pousser en avant, faire marcher, propulser.
propeller [prə'pelə], *n.* hélice, *f.*; propulseur, moteur, *m.*
propelling [prə'peliŋ], *a.* propulseur, moteur; ***propelling force***, force motrice, *f.*
propensity [prə'pensiti], *n.* penchant, *m.*, tendance, *f.*
proper ['prɔpə], *a.* propre, particulier; convenable, à propos (*comme il faut*); juste, exact (*correct*).
properly ['prɔpəli], *adv.* proprement, comme il faut.
property ['prɔpəti], *n.* propriété, *f.*; bien, *m.*, biens, *m.pl.*; qualité, *f.*; (*Theat., Cine.*) accessoire, *m.*
property-tax ['prɔpətitæks], *n.* impôt foncier, *m.*
prophecy ['prɔfəsi], *n.* prophétie, *f.*
prophesy ['prɔfəsai], *v.t.* prophétiser, prédire.
prophet ['prɔfit], *n.* prophète, *m.*
prophetess ['prɔfites], *n.* prophétesse, *f.*
prophetic [prə'fetik], **prophetical** [prə'feti kəl], *a.* prophétique.
propinquity [prə'piŋkwiti], *n.* proximité; parenté (*de personnes*), *f.*
propitiate [prə'piʃieit], *v.t.* rendre propice.
propitiation [prəpiʃi'eiʃən], *n.* propitiation, *f.*
propitiator [prə'piʃieitə], *n.* propitiateur, *m.*
propitiatory [prə'piʃiətri], *a.* and *n.* propitiatoire, *m.*
propitious [prə'piʃəs], *a.* propice, favorable.

propitiousness [prə'piʃəsnis], *n.* nature propice, *f.*
proportion [prə'pɔ:ʃən], *n.* proportion; partie; portion, *f.*; ***in proportion as***, à mesure que.—*v.t.* proportionner.
proportional [prə'pɔ:ʃənəl], *a.* en proportion; proportionnel.
proportionate [prə'pɔ:ʃənit], *a.* proportionné.
proposal [prə'pouzl], *n.* proposition; demande en mariage, *f.*
propose [prə'pouz], *v.t.* proposer; offrir; ***to propose a toast***, porter un toast.—*v.i.* se proposer; faire une demande en mariage.
proposer [prə'pouzə], *n.* auteur d'une proposition, *m.*
proposition [prɔpə'ziʃən], *n.* proposition; affaire, *f.*
propound [prə'paund], *v.t.* proposer, exposer, mettre en avant.
proprietary [prə'praiətri], *a.* de propriété.—*n.* actionnaires, *m.pl.*
proprietor [prə'praiətə], *n.* propriétaire, *m.*
proprietress [prə'praiətris], *n.* propriétaire, maîtresse, *f.*
propriety [prə'praiəti], *n.* convenance, propriété, *f.*
propulsion [prə'pʌlʃən], *n.* propulsion, *f.*; ***jet propulsion***, propulsion à réaction.
prorogation [prourə'geiʃən], *n.* prorogation, *f.*
prorogue [prə'roug], *v.t.* proroger.
prosaic [pro'zeiik], *a.* prosaïque.
proscenium [prə'si:niəm], *n.* proscenium, *m.*, avant-scène, *f.*
proscribe [pro'skraib], *v.t.* proscrire.
proscription [pro'skripʃən], *n.* proscription, *f.*
prose [prouz], *n.* prose, *f.*, (*Sch.*) thème, *m.*
prosecute ['prɔsikju:t], *v.t.* poursuivre; revendiquer (*ses droits etc.*).
prosecution [prɔsi'kju:ʃən], *n.* poursuite, *f.*, procès criminel, *m.*; ***witness for the prosecution***, témoin à charge, *m.*
prosecutor ['prɔsikju:tə], *n.* poursuivant, plaignant, *m.*; ***public prosecutor***, procureur de la république, *m.*
prosecutrix ['prɔsikju:triks], *n.* poursuivante, plaignante, *f.*
proselyte ['prɔsəlait], *n.* prosélyte, *m.*, *f.*
proselytism ['prɔsəlitizm], *n.* prosélytisme, *m.*
proselytize ['prɔsəlitaiz], *v.t.* convertir.—*v.i.* faire des prosélytes.
prose-writer ['prouzraitə], *n.* prosateur, *m.*
prosily ['prouzili], *adv.* prosaïquement, ennuyeusement.
prosiness ['prouzinis], *n.* prosaïsme, *m.*; verbosité, *f.*
prosody ['prɔsədi], *n.* prosodie, *f.*
prospect ['prɔspekt], *n.* vue; perspective, *f.*; (*fig.*) espoir; avenir, *m.*—[prə'spekt], *v.i.* faire des recherches (*minerai, pétrole etc.*), prospecter.
prospective [prə'spektiv], *a.* en perspective; à venir.
prospectively [prə'spektivli], *adv.* pour l'avenir.
prospector [prə'spektə], *n.* explorateur; *orpailleur, *m.*
prospectus [prə'spektəs], *n.* prospectus, *m.*
prosper ['prɔspə], *v.t.* faire prospérer, favoriser.—*v.i.* prospérer, réussir.
prosperity [prɔs'periti], *n.* prospérité, *f.*
prosperous ['prɔspərəs], *a.* prospère; florissant (*affaires*); (*fig.*) heureux; favorable.
prostitute ['prɔstitju:t], *n.* prostituée, *f.*—*v.t.* prostituer.
prostitution [prɔsti'tju:ʃən], *n.* prostitution, *f.*
prostrate [prɔs'treit], *v.t.* coucher, prosterner; (*fig.*) renverser; ***to prostrate oneself before***, se prosterner devant.—['prɔstrit], *a.* prosterné; (*fig.*) abattu.
prostration [prɔs'treiʃən], *n.* prosternation, *f.*; (*fig.*) abattement, *m.*
prosy ['prouzi], *a.* ennuyeux, fastidieux.
protagonist [prou'tægənist], *n.* protagoniste, *m.*
protect [prə'tekt], *v.t.* protéger, défendre; garantir, abriter (*contre le temps etc.*); sauvegarder (*intérêts*).
protection [prə'tekʃən], *n.* protection, défense; garantie, *f.*, abri (*contre le temps etc.*), *m.*; (*Law*) sauvegarde, *f.*
protectionism [prə'tekʃənizm], *n.* protectionnisme, *m.*
protectionist [prə'tekʃənist], *a.* and *n.* protectionniste, *m.*, *f.*
protective [prə'tektiv], *a.* protecteur.
protector [prə'tektə], *n.* protecteur, *m.*
protectorate [prə'tektərit], *n.* protectorat, *m.*
protectress [prə'tektris], *n.* protectrice, *f.*
protein ['prouti:n], *n.* protéine, *f.*
protest ['proutest], *n.* protestation, *f.*; (*Comm.*) protêt, *m.*—[prə'test], *v.t.*, *v.i.* protester.
Protestant ['prɔtistənt], *a.* and *n.* protestant, *m.*
Protestantism ['prɔtistəntizm], *n.* protestantisme, *m.*
protestation [prɔtes'teiʃən], *n.* protestation, *f.*
protester [prə'testə], *n.* personne qui fait faire un protêt, *f.*
protocol ['proutəkɔl], *n.* protocole, *m.*
proton ['proutɔn], *n.* proton, *m.*
prototype ['proutətaip], *n.* prototype, *m.*
protract [prə'trækt], *v.t.* prolonger, traîner en longueur.
protraction [prə'trækʃən], *n.* prolongation, *f.*
protractor [prə'træktə], *n.* rapporteur (*instrument*), *m.*
protrude [prə'tru:d], *v.t.* pousser en avant, faire sortir.—*v.i.* s'avancer, faire saillie.
protruding [prə'tru:diŋ], *a.* en saillie, saillant.
protrusion [prə'tru:ʒən], *n.* saillie, *f.*
protuberance [prə'tju:bərəns], *n.* protubérance, *f.*
protuberant [prə'tju:bərənt], *a.* protubérant.
proud [praud], *a.* fier (*de*); orgueilleux.
proudly ['praudli], *adv.* fièrement, orgueilleusement.
provable ['pru:vəbl], *a.* prouvable, démontrable.
prove [pru:v], *v.t.* prouver, démontrer; mettre à l'épreuve, éprouver (*la qualité de*); vérifier (*testament etc.*).—*v.i.* se montrer, se révéler.
proved [pru:vd], *a.* prouvé, démontré, reconnu.
provender ['prɔvəndə], *n.* fourrage, *m.*, nourriture (*d'animaux*), *f.*

proverb ['prɔvə:b], *n.* proverbe, *m.*
proverbial [prə'və:biəl], *a.* proverbial.
provide [prə'vaid], *v.t.* pourvoir, fournir, munir; préparer (*à*); stipuler.—*v.i.* pourvoir.
provided [prə'vaidid], *a.* pourvu.—*conj.* ***provided that***, pourvu que (*with subj.*).
providence ['prɔvidəns], *n.* providence (*divine*); prévoyance (*humaine*), *f.*
provident ['prɔvidənt], *a.* prévoyant; économe.
providential [prɔvi'denʃəl], *a.* providentiel, de la providence.
providently ['prɔvidəntli], *adv.* avec prévoyance.
provider [prə'vaidə], *n.* pourvoyeur, fournisseur, *m.*
province ['prɔvins], *n.* province, *f.*; (*fig.*) département, ressort, *m.*
provincial [prə'vinʃəl], *a.* provincial, de province.—*n.* provincial, *m.*
provincialism [prə'vinʃəlizm], *n.* provincialisme, *m.*
proving ['pru:viŋ], *n.* vérification, mise à l'épreuve, *f.*
provision [prə'viʒən], *n.* action de pourvoir; stipulation; (*Law*) disposition (*d'un projet de loi etc.*), *f.*; (*pl.*) vivres, comestibles, *m.pl.*—*v.t.* approvisionner.
provisional [prə'viʒənəl], *a.* provisoire.
provision-dealer [prə'viʒəndi:lə], *n.* marchand de comestibles, *m.*
proviso [prə'vaizou], *n.* condition, clause conditionnelle, *f.*
provisory [prə'vaizəri], *a.* provisoire, conditionnel.
provocation [prɔvə'keiʃən], *n.* provocation, *f.*
provocative [prə'vɔkətiv], *a.* provocant, provocateur.
provoke [prə'vouk], *v.t.* provoquer; inciter; fâcher, irriter.
provoker [prə'voukə], *n.* provocateur, *m.*
provoking [prə'voukiŋ], *a.* provocant; ennuyeux, fâcheux, agaçant.
provokingly [prə'voukiŋli], *adv.* d'une manière provocante *ou* contrariante.
provost ['prɔvəst], *n.* prévôt; (*Univ.*) principal; (*Sc.*) maire, *m.*
prow [prau], *n.* proue, *f.*
prowess ['prauis], *n.* bravoure, prouesse, *f.*
prowl [praul], *n.* action de rôder, *f.*—*v.i.* rôder.
prowler ['praulə], *n.* rôdeur, *m.*
proximate ['prɔksimit], *a.* proche, immédiat.
proximity [prɔk'simiti], *n.* proximité, *f.*
proximo ['prɔksimou], *adv.* du mois prochain.
proxy ['prɔksi], *n.* mandataire, *m.*, *f.*, délégué, *m.*; procuration (*chose*), *f.*; ***by proxy***, par procuration.
prude [pru:d], *n.* prude, mijaurée, *f.*
prudence ['pru:dəns], *n.* prudence, *f.*
prudent ['pru:dənt], *a.* prudent, sage.
prudential [pru'denʃəl], *a.* de prudence, dicté par la prudence.
prudently ['pru:dəntli], *adv.* prudemment, sagement.
prudery ['pru:dəri], *n.* pruderie, *f.*
prudish ['pru:diʃ], *a.* prude, de prude.
prudishly ['pru:diʃli], *adv.* avec pruderie.
prune [pru:n], *n.* pruneau, *m.*—*v.t.* élaguer, tailler, émonder.
prunella [pru'nelə], *n.* prunelle, *f.*
pruning ['pru:niŋ], *n.* taille, *f.*, élagage, *m.*
pruning-shears ['pru:niŋʃiəz], *n.pl.* sécateur, *m.*, cisailles, *f.pl.*
prurience ['pruəriəns], **pruriency** ['pruəriənsi], *n.* démangeaison, *f.*
prurient ['pruəriənt], *a.* qui démange.
Prussia ['prʌʃə]. la Prusse, *f.*
Prussian ['prʌʃən], *a.* prussien.—*n.* Prussien (*personne*), *m.*
prussic ['prʌsik], *a.* prussique.
pry [prai], *v.t.* soulever avec un levier.—*v.i.* fureter; fouiller (*dans*); ***to pry into***, se mêler de.—*n.* regard scrutateur, regard indiscret, *m.*
prying ['praiiŋ], *a.* scrutateur, curieux.—*n.* curiosité, *f.*
psalm [sɑ:m], *n.* psaume, *m.*
psalmist ['sɑ:mist], *n.* psalmiste, *m.*
psalmody ['sɑ:mədi], *n.* psalmodie, *f.*
psalter ['sɔ:ltə], *n.* psautier, *m.*
pseudonym ['sju:dənim], *n.* pseudonyme, *m.*
pshaw! [pʃɔ:], *int.* bah! fi donc!
psychiatric [saiki'ætrik], *a.* psychiatrique.
psychiatrist [sai'kaiətrist], *n.* psychiatre, *m.*, *f.*
psychiatry [sai'kaiətri], *n.* psychiatrie, *f.*
psychic(al) ['saikik(l)], *a.* psychique.
psycho-analyse [saikou'ænəlaiz], *v.t.* psychanalyser.
psycho-analysis [saikouə'næləsis], *n.* psychanalyse, *f.*
psycho-analyst [saikou'ænəlist], *n.* psychanalyste, *m.*, *f.*
psychological [saikə'lɔdʒikl], *a.* psychologique.
psychologist [sai'kɔlədʒist], *n.* psychologiste, psychologue, *m.*
psychology [sai'kɔlədʒi], *n.* psychologie, *f.*
psychopath ['saikopæθ], *n.* psychopathe, *m.*, *f.*
psychosis [sai'kousis], *n.* psychose, *f.*
ptarmigan ['tɑ:migən], *n.* lagopède, *m.*
ptomaine ['toumein], *n.* ptomaïne, *f.*; ***ptomaine poisoning***, intoxication alimentaire, *f.*
puberty ['pju:bəti], *n.* puberté, *f.*
pubescence [pju'besəns], *n.* pubescence, *f.*
pubescent [pju'besənt], *a.* pubescent.
public ['pʌblik], *a.* and *n.* public, *m.*
publican ['pʌblikən], *n.* cafetier, patron de bistro(t); (*Bibl.*) publicain, *m.*
publication [pʌbli'keiʃən], *n.* publication, *f.*
public-house ['pʌblik'haus], *n.* café, *m.*, brasserie, *f.*, bistro(t), *m.*
publicist ['pʌblisist], *n.* publiciste, journaliste; publicitaire, *m.*, *f.*
publicity [pʌb'lisiti], *n.* publicité; réclame, *f.*
publicize ['pʌblisaiz], *v.t.* faire connaître au public.
publicly ['pʌblikli], *adv.* publiquement; en public.
publish ['pʌbliʃ], *v.t.* publier; éditer.
publisher ['pʌbliʃə], *n.* éditeur, *m.*; ***bookseller and publisher***, libraire-éditeur, *m.*
puce [pju:s], *a.* puce.
puck (1) [pʌk], *n.* lutin, *m.*
puck (2) [pʌk], *n.* (*Spt.*) palet de hockey (sur glace), *m.*
pucker ['pʌkə], *v.t.* rider, plisser; (*Dress.*) faire goder.—*v.i.* goder.—*n.* ride; (*Dress.*) poche, *f.*; mauvais pli, *m.*
puckering ['pʌkəriŋ], *n.* froncement, *m.*
puckish ['pʌkiʃ], *a.* malicieux; de lutin.

pudding ['pudiŋ], *n.* pudding, pouding, *m.*; ***black pudding***, boudin (noir), *m.*
puddle [pʌdl], *n.* flaque (d'eau), mare, *f.*—*v.t.* troubler, rendre bourbeux.
puerile ['pjuərail], *a.* puéril.
puerility [pjuə'riliti], *n.* puérilité, *f.*
puff [pʌf], *n.* souffle (*d'haleine*), *m.*; bouffée (*de vent, fumée etc.*), *f.*; feuilleté (*pâtisserie*), *m.*; houppe à poudrer (*de dames*), *f.*; bouillon (*de robes*); puff, *m.*, réclame tapageuse, *f.*—*v.t.* souffler, bouffir (*les joues*), gonfler; (*fig.*) faire mousser (*publicité*).—*v.i.* souffler, boursoufler, bouffir, bouffer, se gonfler; haleter.
puffin ['pʌfin], *n.* (*Orn.*) macareux, *m.*
puffiness ['pʌfinis], *n.* boursouflure, enflure, *f.*
puff-pastry ['pʌfpeistri], *n.* pâte feuilletée, *f.*
puffy ['pʌfi], *a.* bouffi, gonflé.
pug [pʌg], *n.* carlin (*chien*), *m.*
pugilism ['pju:dʒilizm], *n.* pugilat, *m.*, boxe, *f.*
pugilist ['pju:dʒilist], *n.* boxeur, pugiliste, *m.*
pugilistic [pjudʒi'listik], *a.* de pugilat.
pugnacious [pʌg'neiʃəs], *a.* querelleur; batailleur.
pugnaciously [pʌg'neiʃəsli], *adv.* d'un air batailleur.
pugnacity [pʌg'næsiti], *n.* pugnacité, *f.*
pug-nose ['pʌgnouz], *n.* nez épaté, *m.*
puke [pju:k], *v.i.* vomir.
pule [pju:l], *v.i.* piauler.
puling ['pju:liŋ], *n.* cri; piaulement, *m.*
pull [pul], *v.t.* tirer; arracher; presser (*la détente*); ***to pull a wry face***, faire la grimace; ***to pull down***, abattre, démolir; ***to pull off***, arracher, enlever; ***to pull up***, hisser; déraciner; arrêter.—*v.i.* ramer (*tirer la rame*); ***to pull in***, s'arrêter; ***to pull round***, se remettre; ***to pull through***, guérir, s'en tirer; ***to pull up***, s'arrêter.—*n.* action de tirer, traction, *f.*; coup (d'aviron), effort, *m.*; secousse, *f.*; (*fig.*) avantage, *m.*; ***hard pull***, rude effort.
pullet ['pulit], *n.* poulette, *f.*
pulley ['puli], *n.* poulie, *f.*
pullover ['pulouvə], *n.* pull-over, *m.*
pulmonary ['pʌlmənəri], *a.* pulmonaire.
pulp [pʌlp], *n.* pulpe; pâte (*papier*), *f.*—*v.t.* réduire en pâte.
pulpiness ['pʌlpinis], *n.* nature pulpeuse, *f.*
pulpit ['pulpit], *n.* chaire, *f.*
pulpous ['pʌlpəs], **pulpy** ['pʌlpi], *a.* pulpeux.
pulsate [pʌl'seit], *v.i.* battre; palpiter.
pulsation [pʌl'seiʃən], *n.* pulsation, *f.*
pulsatory ['pʌlsətri], *a.* pulsatoire.
pulse [pʌls], *n.* pouls, *m.*; pulsation, *f.*; plantes légumineuses, *f.pl.*
pulverization [pʌlvərai'zeiʃən], *n.* pulvérisation, *f.*
pulverize ['pʌlvəraiz], *v.t.* pulvériser.
puma ['pju:mə], *n.* puma, couguar, *m.*
pumice ['pʌmis], *n.* pierre ponce, *f.*
pump [pʌmp], *n.* pompe, *f.*; escarpin (*chaussure*), *m.*—*v.t.* pomper; (*fig.*) sonder; ***to pump up***, gonfler (*pneu*).—*v.i.* pomper.
pumpkin ['pʌmpkin], *n.* citrouille, courge, *f.*, potiron, *m.*
pump-room ['pʌmpru:m], *n.* buvette, *f.*
pun [pʌn], *n.* calembour, jeu de mots, *m.*—*v.i.* faire des calembours.
punch (1) [pʌntʃ], *n.* emporte-pièce; (*Print.*) poinçon, *m.*—*v.t.* percer, poinçonner.
punch (2) [pʌntʃ], *n.* coup de poing, *m.*—*v.t.* donner un coup de poing à.
punch (3) [pʌntʃ], *n.* punch (*boisson*), *m.*
punch-bowl ['pʌntʃboul], *n.* bol à punch, *m.*
puncheon ['pʌntʃən], *n.* poinçon, *m.*, pièce (de vin), *f.*
punctilio [pʌŋk'tiliou], *n.* exactitude scrupuleuse, *f.*, point d'étiquette, *m.*
punctilious [pʌŋk'tiliəs], *a.* pointilleux.
punctiliousness [pʌŋk'tiliəsnis], *n.* exactitude scrupuleuse, pointillerie, *f.*
punctual ['pʌŋktjuəl], *a.* ponctuel, exact.
punctuality [pʌŋktju'æliti], *n.* ponctualité, exactitude, *f.*
punctually ['pʌŋktjuəli], *adv.* ponctuellement, exactement.
punctuate ['pʌŋktjueit], *v.t.* ponctuer.
punctuation [pʌŋktju'eiʃən], *n.* ponctuation, *f.*
puncture ['pʌŋktʃə], *n.* piqûre; crevaison (*d'un pneu*), *f.*—*v.t.* piquer; crever (*pneu*).
pundit ['pʌndit], *n.* pandit, *m.*
pungency ['pʌndʒənsi], *n.* âcreté; aigreur, *f.*
pungent ['pʌndʒənt], *a.* âcre; piquant, mordant.
pungently ['pʌndʒəntli], *adv.* avec causticité.
puniness ['pju:ninis], *n.* petitesse, nature chétive, *f.*
punish ['pʌniʃ], *v.t.* punir, corriger; malmener.
punishable ['pʌniʃəbl], *a.* punissable.
punishment ['pʌniʃmənt], *n.* punition; peine, *f.*, châtiment, *m.*; ***capital punishment***, peine capitale.
punitive ['pju:nitiv], *a.* punitif.
punnet ['pʌnit], *n.* maniveau, *m.*
punt [pʌnt], *n.* bachot, *m.*—*v.i.* conduire un bachot (*à la perche*).
puny ['pju:ni], *a.* petit, chétif.
pup [pʌp], *n.* petit chien, petit; (*pej.*) freluquet, fat, *m.*
pupil (1) ['pju:pil], *n.* élève, *m., f.*
pupil (2) ['pju:pil], *n.* pupille (*de l'œil*), *f.*
pupilary ['pju:piləri], *a.* pupillaire.
puppet ['pʌpit], *n.* marionnette, *f.*; ***glove puppet***, marionnette à gaine; ***puppet government***, gouvernement fantoche, *m.*
puppet-show ['pʌpitʃou], *n.* (spectacle de) marionnettes, *f.pl.*
puppy ['pʌpi], *n.* petit chien; (*fig.*) fat, freluquet, *m.*
purblind ['pə:blaind], *a.* myope.
purchase ['pə:tʃis], *n.* achat, *m.*, acquisition, emplette; (*Mech.*) prise, *f.*—*v.t.* acheter, acquérir.
purchase-deed ['pə:tʃisdi:d], *n.* contrat d'achat, *m.*
purchaser ['pə:tʃisə], *n.* acquéreur, acheteur, *m.*
purchasing ['pə:tʃisiŋ], *n.* achat, *m.*; ***purchasing power***, pouvoir d'achat, *m.*
pure [pjuə], *a.* pur; ***pure-bred***, de race.
purely ['pjuəli], *adv.* purement.
pureness ['pjuənis], *n.* pureté, *f.*
purgation [pə'geiʃən], *n.* purgation, *f.*
purgative ['pə:gətiv], *a.* and *n.* purgatif, *m.*
purgatorial [pə:gə'tə:riəl], *a.* du purgatoire.
Purgatory ['pə:gətəri], *n.* purgatoire, *m.*
purge [pə:dʒ], *v.t.* purger; purifier, épurer.—*n.* purgation, purge, *f.*; (*Polit.*) nettoyage, *m.*

purification [pjuərifi'keiʃən], *n.* purification; épuration, *f.*
purifier ['pjuərifaiə], *n.* purificateur, *m.*
purify ['pjuərifai], *v.t.* purifier.—*v.i.* se purifier.
purist ['pjuərist], *n.* puriste, *m., f.*
Puritan ['pjuəritən], *n.* puritain, *m.*
puritan ['pjuəritən], *a.* puritain.
puritanical [pjuəri'tænikl], *a.* de puritain, puritain.
Puritanism ['pjuəritənizm], *n.* puritanisme, *m.*
purity ['pjuəriti], *n.* pureté, *f.*
purl [pəːl], *v.t.* engrêler (*dentelle*).—*v.i.* murmurer, gazouiller.—*n.* engrêlure (*de dentelle*), *f.*; doux murmure; gazouillement, *m.*
purlieu ['pəːljuː], *n.* alentours, environs, *m.pl.*
purloin [pə'lɔin], *v.t.* dérober, voler.
purple [pəːpl], *a.* violet, mauve; pourpre.—*n.* pourpre, mauve (*couleur*), *m.*; pourpre (*teinture etc.*), *f.*—*v.t.* teindre en pourpre, empourprer, rougir.
purport ['pəːpət], *n.* sens, *m.*, teneur, portée, *f.*—[pə'pɔːt], *v.t.* tendre à montrer, signifier, vouloir dire.
purpose ['pəːpəs], *n.* but, objet, *m.*, fin, *f.*, dessein, *m.*, intention, *f.*; ***on purpose***, exprès, à dessein; ***to answer one's purpose***, faire son affaire.—*v.t., v.i.* se proposer, avoir l'intention (*de*).
purposely ['pəːpəsli], *adv.* à dessein, exprès.
purr [pəː], *v.i.* ronronner.
purring ['pəːriŋ], *a.* qui fait ronron.—*n.* ronron, *m.*
purse [pəːs], *n.* porte-monnaie, *m.*; bourse, *f.*; (*Am.*) sac à main, *m.*—*v.t.* plisser, froncer (*les sourcils etc.*).
purser ['pəːsə], *n.* commissaire (*de navire*); (*Mining*) agent comptable, *m.*
pursuance [pə'sjuːəns], *n.* poursuite, conséquence, *f.*; ***in pursuance of***, conformément à.
pursuant [pə'sjuːənt], *a.* en conséquence (*de*), conforme (*à*).
pursue [pə'sjuː], *v.t.* poursuivre; suivre, chercher.
pursuer [pə'sjuːə], *n.* poursuivant, *m.*
pursuit [pə'sjuːt], *n.* poursuite, recherche; occupation, *f.*; (*pl.*) travaux, *m.pl.*
purulence ['pjuərulәns], **purulency** ['pjuərulənsi], *n.* purulence, *f.*
purulent ['pjuərulənt], *a.* purulent.
purvey [pə'vei], *v.t.* fournir, approvisionner; procurer.
purveyor [pə'veiə], *n.* pourvoyeur, fournisseur, *m.*
pus [pʌs], *n.* pus, *m.*
push [puʃ], *v.t.* pousser; (*fig.*) presser, importuner; ***to push back***, repousser, faire reculer; ***to push down***, faire tomber, renverser.—*v.i.* pousser; faire un effort; ***to push off***, pousser au large; ***to push on***, pousser en avant.—*n.* impulsion, poussée, *f.*; effort, *m.*; extrémité, *f.*
pushing ['puʃiŋ], *a.* entreprenant.
pusillanimity [pjuːsilə'nimiti], *n.* pusillanimité, *f.*
pusillanimous [pjuːsi'læniməs], *a.* pusillanime.
puss [pus], *n.* (*colloq.*) minet, *m.*, minette, *f.*
pustule ['pʌstjuːl], *n.* pustule, *f.*
put [put], *v.t. irr.* mettre, poser, placer; proposer (*solution etc.*); lancer (*poids etc.*); ***to put about***, gêner; ***to put aside***, mettre de côté; ***to put back***, replacer, remettre; ***to put by***, mettre de côté; ***to put forward***, mettre en avant; ***to put off***, ôter; remettre; ***to put on***, mettre (*vêtements*); ***to put on the light***, allumer; ***to put out***, mettre dehors; éteindre (*feu etc.*); ***to put up***, installer; loger, caser (*dans un hôtel etc.*).—*v.i.* aller; germer, pousser; (*Naut.*) se mettre; ***to put in***, entrer au port; ***to put up***, loger (*à* ou *chez*), descendre (*à*); ***to put up with***, supporter.
putrefaction [pjuːtri'fækʃən], *n.* putréfaction, *f.*
putrefy ['pjuːtrifai], *v.t.* putréfier.—*v.i.* se putréfier.
putrid ['pjuːtrid], *a.* putride.
putridity [pju'triditi], *n.* putridité, *f.*
putt [pʌt], *v.t.* (*Golf*) poter.
putter ['pʌtə], *n.* (*Golf*) poteur, *m.*
putting ['putiŋ], *n.* action du mettre, mise, *f.*
putty ['pʌti], *n.* mastic, *m.*
puzzle [pʌzl], *n.* (*fig.*) énigme, *f.*; jeu de patience, casse-tête (*jouet*), *m.*; ***crossword puzzle***, mots croisés, *m.pl.*—*v.t.* intriguer, embarrasser; ***to puzzle one's brains***, se creuser la tête.
pygmean [pig'miən], *a.* de pygmée.
pygmy ['pigmi], *n.* pygmée, *m., f.*
pyjamas [pi'dʒɑːməz], *n.pl.* pyjama, *m.*
pylon ['pailən], *n.* pylône, *m.*
pyramid ['pirəmid], *n.* pyramide, *f.*
pyramidal [pi'ræmidl], *a.* pyramidal.
pyre ['paiə], *n.* bûcher, *m.*
Pyrenees [pirə'niːz], **the.** les Pyrénées, *f.pl.*
pyrethrum [pai'riːθrəm], *n.* (*Bot.*) pyrèthre, *m.*
pyrotechnic [paiərou'teknik], **pyrotechnical** [paiərou'teknikəl], *a.* pyrotechnique, pyrique.
pyrotechnics [paiərou'tekniks], *n.pl.* pyrotechnie, *f.*
pyrotechnist [paiərou'teknist], *n.* artificier, *m.*
python ['paiθən], *n.* python, *m.*
pyx [piks], *n.* ciboire, *m.*

Q

Q, q [kjuː]. dix-septième lettre de l'alphabet, *m.*
quack [kwæk], *a.* de charlatan.—*n.* charlatan; couac, cri du canard, *m.*—*v.i.* crier (comme les canards *etc.*).
quackery ['kwækəri], *n.* charlatanisme, *m.*
Quadragesima [kwɔdrə'dʒesimə]. Quadragésime, *f.*
quadrangle ['kwɔdræŋgl], *n.* quadrilatère carré, *m.*; (*Univ.*) cour d'honneur, *f.*
quadrant ['kwɔdrənt], *n.* quart de cercle, *m.*
quadratic [kwɔd'rætik], *a.* du second degré.
quadrennial [kwɔd'reniəl], *a.* quadriennal.
quadrennially [kwɔd'reniəli], *adv.* tous les quatre ans.

quadrilateral [kwɔdri'lætərəl], *a.* quadrilatéral.—*n.* quadrilatère, *m.*
quadrille [kwə'dril], *n.* quadrille, *m.*; contredanse, *f.*
quadroon [kwə'druːn], *n.* quarteron, *m.*
quadruped ['kwɔdruped], *n.* quadrupède, *m.*
quadruple ['kwɔdrupl], *a.* and *n.* quadruple, *m.*—*v.t.* quadrupler.
quadruplet ['kwɔdruplit], *n.* quadruplette, *f.*; (*pl.*) (*colloq.*) **quads** [kwɔdz], quadruplés, *m.pl.*
quaff [kwæf], *v.t.* boire à grands traits.
quaffer ['kwæfə], *n.* buveur, *m.*
quagmire ['kwægmaiə], *n.* fondrière, *f.*
quail (1) [kweil], *v.i.* perdre courage, fléchir.
quail (2) [kweil], *n.* (*Orn.*) caille, *f.*
quaint [kweint], *a.* singulier, bizarre; pittoresque.
quaintly ['kweintli], *adv.* singulièrement, bizarrement.
quaintness ['kweintnis], *n.* bizarrerie, originalité, *f.*
quake [kweik], *v.i.* trembler; branler.—*n.* tremblement, *m.*
Quaker ['kweikə], *n.* Quaker, *m.*
Quakerism ['kweikərizm], *n.* Quakerisme, *m.*
quaking ['kweikiŋ], *a.* tremblant.—*n.* tremblement, *m.*; terreur, *f.*
qualifiable ['kwɔlifaiəbl], *a.* qualifiable.
qualification [kwɔlifi'keiʃən], *n.* qualification, qualité; aptitude, *f.*, talent, *m.*; réserve, restriction, *f.*; (*pl.*) qualités, *f.pl.*, titres, *m.pl.*
qualified ['kwɔlifaid], *a.* qui a les qualités requises (*pour*), propre (*à*); ***qualified teacher***, professeur diplômé, *m.*
qualify ['kwɔlifai], *v.t.* rendre capable (*de*); autoriser (*à*); modérer.—*v.i.* se préparer (*à*).
qualifying ['kwɔlifaiiŋ], *a.* qualificatif.
quality ['kwɔliti], *n.* qualité, *f.*; (*colloq.*) talent, *m.*
qualm [kwɑːm], *n.* nausée, *f.*; (*fig.*) scrupule, *m.*
qualmish ['kwɑːmiʃ], *a.* qui a mal au cœur.
quandary ['kwɔndəri], *n.* embarras, *m.*, impasse, *f.*
quantitative ['kwɔntitətiv], *a.* quantitatif.
quantity ['kwɔntiti], *n.* quantité, *f.*; grand nombre, *m.*
quantum ['kwɔntəm], *n.* montant, quantum, *m.*
quarantine ['kwɔrəntiːn], *n.* quarantaine, *f.* —*v.t.* mettre en quarantaine.
quarrel ['kwɔrəl], *n.* querelle, dispute, brouille, *f.*—*v.i.* se quereller, se brouiller.
quarreller ['kwɔrələ], *n.* querelleur, *m.*
quarrelling ['kwɔrəliŋ], *n.* querelle; dispute, *f.*
quarrelsome ['kwɔrəlsəm], *a.* querelleur.
quarrelsomeness ['kwɔrəlsəmnis], *n.* humeur querelleuse, *f.*
quarry (1) ['kwɔri], *n.* carrière, *f.*—*v.t.* tirer d'une carrière.
quarry (2) ['kwɔri], *n.* (*Hunt.*) curée; proie, *f.*
quarrying ['kwɔriiŋ], *n.* extraction d'une carrière, *f.*
quarryman ['kwɔrimən], *n.* (*pl.* **-men** [men]) carrier, *m.*
quart [kwɔːt], *n.* quart de gallon (*1·14 litre*), *m.*
quarter ['kwɔːtə], *n.* quart; quart de quintal (*12·70 kg.*); quartier (*de ville, de la lune, de mouton etc.*), *m.*; partie, région (*d'un pays*), *f.*; côté (*direction*); trimestre (*de l'année*), *m.*; hanche (*de navire*), *f.*; (*pl.*) logement; (*Mil.*) quartier, *m.*; ***to come to close quarters*** en venir aux mains.—*v.t.* diviser en quatre; (*Mil.*) caserner; loger (*dans une maison*); (*Her.*) écarteler.
quarter-day ['kwɔːtədei], *n.* jour du terme, *m.*
quarter-deck ['kwɔːtədek], *n.* gaillard d'arrière, *m.*
quartering ['kwɔːtəriŋ], *n.* division en quatre parties, *f.*; (*Mil.*) logement; (*Her.*) écartèlement, *m.*
quarterly ['kwɔːtəli], *a.* trimestriel.—*adv.* par trimestre, tous les trois mois.
quartermaster ['kwɔːtəmɑːstə], *n.* (*Navy*) maître timonier; (*Mil.*) officier d'approvisionnement, *m.*
quartet [kwɔː'tet], *n.* quatuor, *m.*
quarto ['kwɔːtou], *a.* and *n.* in-quarto, *m.*
quartz [kwɔːts], *n.* quartz, *m.*
quash [kwɔʃ], *v.t.* écraser; (*fig.*) dompter; (*Law*) annuler, casser.
quasi ['kweisai], *adv.* quasi.
quatrain ['kwɔtrein], *n.* quatrain, *m.*
quaver ['kweivə], *n.* tremblement de la voix, trille, *m.*; (*Mus.*) croche, *f.*—*v.i.* trembler; (*Mus.*) faire des trilles.
quavering ['kweivəriŋ], *a.* tremblant, chevrotant.—*n.* trille, tremolo; tremblement de voix, *m.*
quay [kiː], *n.* quai, *m.*
quayage ['kiːidʒ], *n.* quayage, *m.*
queen [kwiːn], *n.* reine; (*Cards etc.*) dame, *f.*
queen-bee ['kwiːnbiː], *n.* reine-abeille, *f.*
queen-like ['kwiːnlaik], **queenly** ['kwiːnli], *adv.* de reine, digne d'une reine.
queen-mother [kwiːn'mʌðə], *n.* reine-mère, *f.*
queer [kwiə], *a.* bizarre, étrange, drôle.
queerly ['kwiəli], *adv.* étrangement, bizarrement.
queerness ['kwiənis], *n.* étrangeté, bizarrerie, *f.*; malaise, *m.*
quell [kwel], *v.t.* réprimer, dompter.
quench [kwentʃ], *v.t.* éteindre; étancher; étouffer (*élan etc.*); ***to quench one's thirst***, étancher sa soif, se désaltérer.
quenchable ['kwentʃəbl], *a.* extinguible.
quenchless ['kwentʃlis], *a.* inextinguible.
querulous ['kweruləs], *a.* plaintif, maussade.
querulousness ['kweruləsnis], *n.* humeur chagrine, *f.*
query ['kwiəri], *n.* question, *f.*; point d'interrogation, *m.*—*v.t.* mettre en doute.—*v.i.* questionner.
quest [kwest], *n.* enquête; recherche, *f.*; ***in quest of***, à la recherche de.
question ['kwestʃən], *n.* question, interrogation, demande, *f.*; sujet (*problème*), *m.*; (*Parl.*) interpellation, *f.*; ***out of the question*** absolument impossible; ***that is not the question***, il ne s'agit pas de cela; ***to ask a question***, poser une question.—*v.t.* questionner, interroger; mettre en doute.—*v.i.* se demander (*si*).
questionable ['kwestʃənəbl], *a.* contestable, douteux, incertain; suspect, équivoque.
questioner ['kwestʃənə], *n.* questionneur, *m.*
questioning ['kwestʃəniŋ], *n.* questions, *f.pl.*, interrogation, *f.*

question-master ['kwestʃənmɑːstə], *n.* (*Rad., Tel.*) meneur de débats, *m.*
questionnaire [kwestʃə'nɛə], *n.* questionnaire, *m.*
queue [kjuː], *n.* queue, *f.*—*v.i.* faire la queue.
quibble [kwibl], *n.* argutie, chicane, *f.*—*v.i.* ergoter, chicaner.
quibbler ['kwiblə], *n.* ergoteur, chicaneur, *m.*
quick [kwik], *a.* vite, rapide, prompt; agile, leste; vif (*vivant*); (*fig.*) fin.—*adv.* vite, promptement, lestement.—*n.* vif, *m.*; chair vive, *f.*; ***stung to the quick***, piqué au vif; (*collect.*) ***the quick***, les vivants, *m.pl.*
quicken ['kwikən], *v.t.* animer, vivifier; raviver, accélérer, hâter.—*v.i.* prendre vie, s'animer.
quickening ['kwikəniŋ], *a.* vivifiant, qui ranime.
quicklime ['kwiklaim], *n.* chaux vive, *f.*
quickly ['kwikli], *adv.* vite; promptement; bientôt.
quickness ['kwiknis], *n.* vitesse; promptitude; activité; pénétration; fréquence (*du pouls*), *f.*
quicksand ['kwiksænd], *n.* sable mouvant, *m.*
quickset ['kwikset], *a.* vive; ***quickset hedge***, haie vive, *f.*—*n.* plante vive, *f.*
quicksilver ['kwiksilvə], *n.* vif-argent, mercure, *m.*
quicksilvered ['kwiksilvəd], *a.* étamé.
quicksilvering ['kwiksilvəriŋ], *n.* étamage, *m.*
quick-tempered ['kwik'tempəd], *a.* emporté, vif, colérique.
quick-witted ['kwik'witid], *a.* à l'esprit vif.
quid [kwid], *n.* chique; (*slang*) livre sterling, *f.*
quidnunc ['kwidnʌŋk], *n.* curieux, colporteur de nouvelles, *m.*
quiescence [kwi'esəns], *n.* quiétude, tranquillité, *f.*, repos, *m.*
quiescent [kwi'esənt], *a.* paisible, en repos, tranquille.
quiet ['kwaiət], *a.* tranquille, calme; paisible, silencieux; (*fig.*) modeste; ***be quiet!*** silence! taisez-vous! ***to keep quiet***, se tenir tranquille, rester tranquille.—*n.* tranquillité, quiétude, *f.*; repos, calme, *m.*—*v.t.* (*also* **quieten** ['kwaiətn]) tranquilliser, apaiser, calmer.—*v.i.* ***to quiet(en) down***, s'apaiser, se calmer.
quieten, *v.t.*, *v.i.* [QUIET].
quieting ['kwaiətiŋ], *a.* calmant, tranquillisant.
quietly ['kwaiətli], *adv.* tranquillement; doucement; en silence, sans bruit, discrètement, sans éclat.
quietness ['kwaiətnis], *n.* tranquillité, *f.*; calme, repos, *m.*
quietude ['kwaiitjuːd], *n.* quiétude, tranquillité, *f.*
quietus [kwai'iːtəs], *n.* repos, *m.*; mort, *f.*; (*fig.*) coup de grâce, *m.*; décharge, quittance, *f.*
quill [kwil], *n.* (tuyau de) plume; plume d'oie (*pour écrire*), *f.*; piquant (*de porc-épic*), *m.*—*v.t.* tuyauter, rucher.
quilling ['kwiliŋ], *n.* tuyautage, *m.*, ruche, *f.*
quilt [kwilt], *n.* édredon, *m.*, courtepointe, *f.*—*v.t.* piquer.
quilting ['kwiltiŋ], *n.* piqué; piquage, *m.*
quince [kwins], *n.* coing; cognassier (*arbre*), *m.*
quinine [kwi'niːn], *n.* quinine, *f.*
Quinquagesima [kwiŋkwə'dʒesimə]. Quinquagésime, *f.*
quinquennial [kwiŋ'kweniəl], *a.* quinquennial.
quinquina [kiŋ'kiːnə], *n.* quinquina, *m.*
quinsy ['kwinzi], *n.* angine, *f.*
quint [kwint], *n.* quinte, *f.*
quintal [kwintl], *n.* quintal, *m.*
quintessence [kwin'tesəns], *n.* quintessence, *f.*
quintet [kwin'tet], *n.* quintette, *m.*
quintuple ['kwintjupl], *a.* quintuple.—*v.t.* quintupler.
quintuplets ['kwintjuplits], (*colloq.*) **quins** [kwinz], *n.pl.* quintuplés, *m.pl.*
quip [kwip], *n.* mot piquant, sarcasme, *m.*—*v.t.* railler.
quire ['kwaiə], *n.* main (*de papier*), *f.*
quirk [kwəːk], *n.* sarcasme, *m.*, pointe; subtilité (*chicane*), *f.*
quit [kwit], *v.t. irr.* quitter, abandonner; ***notice to quit***, congé, *m.*—*a.* quitte; ***to get quit of***, se débarrasser de.
quite [kwait], *adv.* tout à fait, entièrement, complètement, tout; bien, parfaitement; assez.
quits [kwits], *a.* quitte.
quiver ['kwivə], *n.* carquois, *m.*—*v.i.* trembler, frissonner; palpiter (*la chair*); frémir.
quivering ['kwivəriŋ], *n.* tremblement, frissonnement; battement des paupières, *m.*
Quixote ['kwiksət], **Don.** Don Quichotte, *m.*
quixotic [kwik'sɔtik], *a.* de Don Quichotte; extravagant, exalté.
quiz [kwiz], *n.* plaisanterie, devinette, *f.*; persifleur, railleur, *m.*; ***radio quiz***, jeu radiophonique, *m.*—*v.t.* railler, persifler; lorgner (*to stare at*).
quizzical ['kwizikəl], *a.* railleur; risible.
quizzing ['kwiziŋ], *n.* raillerie, *f.*, persiflage, *m.*; lorgnerie, *f.*
quodlibet ['kwɔdlibet], *n.* quolibet, *m.*, subtilité, *f.*
quoin [kɔin], *n.* coin, *m.*
quoit [kɔit], *n.* palet, *m.*
quondam ['kwɔndəm], *a.* ci-devant, ancien.
quorum ['kwɔːrəm], *n.* nombre suffisant, quorum, *m.*
quota ['kwoutə], *n.* quote-part, *f.*
quotable ['kwoutəbl], *a.* citable.
quotation [kwo'teiʃən], *n.* citation; (*Comm.*) cote, *f.*; (*St. Exch.*) cours, *m.*
quote [kwout], *v.t.* citer; alléguer; (*Comm.*) coter.
quotidian [kwo'tidiən], *a.* quotidien, journalier.
quotient ['kwouʃənt], *n.* quotient, *m.*

R

R, r [ɑː]. dix-huitième lettre de l'alphabet, *m.*
rabbet ['ræbət], *n.* feuillure, rainure, *f.*—*v.t.* faire une rainure à.
rabbet-plane ['ræbətplein], *n.* guillaume, *m.*

rabbi ['ræbai], *n.* rabbin, *m.*; ***chief rabbi***, grand rabbin.
rabbit ['ræbit], *n.* lapin, *m.*; ***young rabbit***, lapereau, *m.*
rabble [ræbl], *n.* foule; populace, canaille, *f.*
rabid ['ræbid], *a.* féroce, furieux; enragé (*chien*).
rabies ['reibi:z], *n.* rage, hydrophobie, *f.*
raccoon [RACOON].
race (1) [reis], *n.* (*Biol.*) race, *f.*
race (2) [reis], *n.* (*Spt.*) course, *f.*; raz, raz de marée (*courant*), *m.*—*v.i.* courir vite, courir, lutter de vitesse; ***to go racing***, aller aux courses.
race-course ['reiskɔ:s], *n.* champ de courses, hippodrome, *m.*
race-horse ['reishɔ:s], *n.* cheval de course, *m.*
racer ['reisə], *n.* coureur; cheval de course, *m.*
race-track ['reistræk], *n.* piste, *f.*
racial ['reiʃəl], *a.* de (la) race, ethnique.
raciness ['reisinis], *n.* piquant, *m.*, verve, *f.*
racing ['reisiŋ], *a.* de course.—*n.* les courses, *f.pl.*
racing-car ['reisiŋkɑ:], *n.* automobile de course, *f.*
racism ['reisizm], *n.* racisme, *m.*
rack [ræk], *n.* râtelier (*dans une écurie etc.*); chevalet (*instrument de tension*), *m.*; roue (*instrument de supplice*); (*Tech.*) crémaillère, *f.*; ***luggage-rack***, (*Rail.*) filet, *m.*—*v.t.* mettre à la torture; (*fig.*) tourmenter; ***to rack one's brains***, se creuser la cervelle.
racket ['rækit], *n.* fracas, tapage, tintamarre, caquet, *m.*; (*Ten.*) raquette; escroquerie, supercherie, combine, *f.*
rackety ['rækiti], *a.* tapageur.
racking ['rækiŋ], *a.* de torture; atroce (*douleur*).
racoon [rə'ku:n], *n.* raton laveur, *m.*
racy ['reisi], *a.* (*fig.*) vif, piquant, plein de verve (*style etc.*).
radar ['reidɑ:], *n.* radar, *m.*
radiance ['reidiəns], **radiancy** ['reidiənsi], *n.* rayonnement, éclat, *m.*, splendeur, *f.*
radiant ['reidiənt], *a.* rayonnant (*de*); radieux, éclatant.
radiantly ['reidiəntli], *adv.* en rayonnant, splendidement.
radiate ['reidieit], *v.t.* émettre comme des rayons.—*v.i.* rayonner (*de*).
radiation [reidi'eiʃən], *n.* rayonnement, *m.*, radiation, *f.*
radiator ['reidieitə], *n.* radiateur, *m.*
radical ['rædikəl], *a.* radical; fondamental.—*n.* radical, *m.*
radicalism ['rædikəlizm], *n.* radicalisme, *m.*
radically ['rædikəli], *adv.* radicalement, essentiellement.
radio ['reidiou], *n.* radio, la T.S.F., *f.*
radioactive [reidiou'æktiv], *a.* radio-actif.
radioactivity ['reidiouæk'tiviti], *n.* radioactivité, *f.*
radio-control ['reidioukən'troul], *n.* téléguidage, *m.*—*v.t.* téléguider.
radiogram ['reidiougræm], *n.* combiné radio-électrophone, *m.*
radiography [reidi'ɔgrəfi], *n.* radiographie, *f.*
radish ['rædiʃ], *n.* radis, *m.*; ***horse-radish***, raifort, *m.*
radium ['reidiəm], *n.* radium, *m.*
radius ['reidiəs], *n.* rayon, *m.*
radix ['reidiks], *n.* (*pl.* **radices** ['reidisi:z]) racine; base, *f.*
raffle [ræfl], *n.* loterie, tombola, *f.*—*v.t.* mettre en tombola.
raft [rɑ:ft], *n.* radeau; train de bois, *m.*
rafter ['rɑ:ftə], *n.* chevron, *m.*
raftered ['rɑ:ftəd], *a.* à chevrons.
rafting ['rɑ:ftiŋ], *n.* flottage en train, *m.*
raftsman ['rɑ:ftsmən], *n.* flotteur, *m.*
rag [ræg], *n.* chiffon (*nettoyage etc.*); haillon, *m.*, guenille, loque (*de vêtement*), *f.*; (*Sch.*) chahut, *m.*; brimade, *f.*—*v.t.* (*Sch.*) chahuter, brimer.
ragamuffin ['rægəmʌfin], *n.* gueux, polisson, va-nu-pieds, *m.*
rage [reidʒ], *n.* rage, fureur, *f.*, emportement, *m.*; furie, manie, *f.*; ***it's all the rage***, cela fait fureur.—*v.i.* être furieux, être en fureur, s'emporter; (*fig.*) sévir.
ragged ['rægid], *a.* en haillons, déguenillé (*personnes*); en lambeaux, déchiré (*choses*).
raggedness ['rægidnis], *n.* délabrement, déguenillement, *m.*; guenilles, *f.pl.*
raging ['reidʒiŋ], *a.* furieux, en fureur; déchaîné, acharné, violent (*tempête, guerre etc.*).—*n.* fureur, violence, *f.*
ragman ['rægmən], *n.* (*pl.* **-men** [men]) chiffonnier, *m.*
rag-time ['rægtaim], *n.* (*Mus.*) musique syncopée, *f.*
raid [reid], *n.* incursion, *f.*; raid, coup de main, *m.*; ***air raid***, raid aérien.—*v.t.* faire une incursion dans; piller; bombarder.
raider ['reidə], *n.* maraudeur; commando, *m.*
rail (1) [reil], *n.* barre, *f.*, barreau (*bois, métal etc.*), *m.*; rampe (*d'escalier*), *f.*; parapet (*de pont etc.*); (*Rail.*) rail, *m.*—*v.t.* enclore, griller.
rail (2) [reil], *v.i.* ***to rail at***, criailler, invectiver.
railer ['reilə], *n.* criailleur, médisant, *m.*
railing (1) ['reiliŋ], *n.* grille, *f.*, garde-fou, *m.*
railing (2) ['reiliŋ], *n.* injures, invectives, *f.pl.*
raillery ['reiləri], *n.* raillerie, *f.*
railway ['reilwei], *n.* chemin de fer, *m.*, voie ferrée, *f.*
railwayman ['reilweimən], *n.* (*pl.* **-men** [men]) employé des chemins de fer, cheminot, *m.*
raiment ['reimənt], *n.* vêtement, *m.*
rain [rein], *n.* pluie, *f.*—*v.t.* faire pleuvoir.—*v.i.* pleuvoir; ***it is pouring with rain***, il pleut à verse.
rainbow ['reinbou], *n.* arc-en-ciel, *m.*
raincoat ['reinkout], *n.* imperméable, *m.*
rainfall ['reinfɔ:l], *n.* pluie annuelle, pluie tombée, *f.*
rain-gauge ['reingeidʒ], *n.* pluviomètre, *m.*
rainy ['reini], *a.* pluvieux.
raise [reiz], *v.t.* lever; élever; hausser (*prix etc.*); soulever (*élever à une petite hauteur etc.*); cultiver (*légumes*); augmenter, accroître (*ajouter à*); faire naître (*soupçons*); pousser (*un cri*); faire lever (*pâte*); se procurer (*argent*); faire (*un emprunt etc.*).
raised [reizd], *a.* levé; en relief.
raisin [reizn], *n.* raisin sec, *m.*
raising ['reiziŋ], *n.* augmentation, *f.*, accroissement, *m.*; levée (*d'impôts, de troupes, de sièges etc.*), *f.*; élevage (*de bestiaux*), *m.*; culture (*de plantes etc.*), *f.*

rake (1) [reik], *n.* (*Hort.*) râteau.—*v.t.* (*Agric.*) râteler; (*Hort.*) ratisser; ramasser (*rassembler*); (*Mil.*) enfiler.
rake (2) [reik], *n.* roué (*libertin*), *m.*
raking ['reikiŋ], *a.* d'enfilade.—*n.* (*Hort.*) ratissage; (*Agric.*) râtelage, *m.*
rakish ['reikiʃ], *a.* dissolu; élancé (*navire*).
rakishness ['reikiʃnis], *n.* libertinage; air crâne, *m.*
rally ['ræli], *v.t.* rallier, rassembler.—*v.i.* se rallier, se rassembler; (*fig.*) se remettre.—*n.* ralliement, *m.*
Ralph [reif, rælf]. Raoul, *m.*
ram [ræm], *n.* bélier; mouton, *m.*—*v.t.* enfoncer; pilonner, tasser (*terre etc.*); bourrer (*dans un canon*).
ramble [ræmbl], *n.* excursion à pied, grande promenade; (*fig.*) divagation, *f.*—*v.i.* errer, se promener; errer çà et là; (*fig.*) divaguer.
rambler ['ræmblə], *n.* excursionniste (à pied), *m.*, *f.*; (*Hort.*) rosier grimpant, *m.*
rambling ['ræmbliŋ], *a.* errant, vagabond; (*fig.*) décousu, incohérent.—*n.* excursions, promenades à l'aventure; (*fig.*) divagations, *f.pl.*
ramification [ræmifi'keiʃən], *n.* ramification, *f.*
ramify ['ræmifai], *v.i.* se ramifier.
rammer ['ræmə], *n.* pilon, *m.*
ramp [ræmp], *n.* rampe, montée; (*fam.*) escroquerie, *f.*
rampant ['ræmpənt], *a.* dominant, violent; effréné; (*Her.*) rampant.
rampart ['ræmpɑ:t], *n.* rempart, *m.*
ramrod ['ræmrɔd], *n.* baguette (*de fusil*), *f.*; écouvillon (*de canon*), *m.*; ***stiff as a ramrod***, droit comme un piquet.
ramshackle ['ræmʃækl], *a.* qui tombe en ruines, délabré.
rancid ['rænsid], *a.* rance.
rancidity [ræn'siditi], **rancidness** ['rænsidnis], *n.* rancidité, *f.*
rancorous ['ræŋkərəs], *a.* rancunier, haineux.
rancour ['ræŋkə], *n.* haine, rancune, *f.*
Randolph ['rændɔlf]. Rodolphe, *m.*
random ['rændəm], *a.* fait au hasard.—*n.* hasard, *m.*; ***at random***, au hasard.
range [reindʒ], *n.* rangée, *f.*, rang (*file*), *m.*; chaîne (*de montagnes etc.*); étendue, portée, *f.*, fourneau; tir (*armes à feu*), *m.*; gamme (*de couleurs*), *f.*—*v.t.* ranger, arranger; aligner (*avec*); parcourir.—*v.i.* s'aligner; être rangé.
range-finder ['reindʒfaində], *n.* télémètre, *m.*
ranger ['reindʒə], *n.* garde-forestier, *m.*
rank (1) [ræŋk], *n.* rang, ordre, *m.*, classe, *f.*; (*Mil.*) grade; (*fig.*) haut rang, *m.*; station de taxis, *f.*—*v.t.* ranger, classer.—*v.i.* se ranger, être classé; occuper un rang.
rank (2) [ræŋk], *a.* luxuriant; (*fig.*) rude; extrême; fétide (*odeur*).
rankle [ræŋkl], *v.i.* s'envenimer, s'enflammer.
rankness ['ræŋknis], *n.* surabondance; grossièreté; rancidité, *f.*
ransack ['rænsæk], *v.t.* saccager, piller; fouiller.
ransacking ['rænsækiŋ], *n.* pillage, *m.*
ransom ['rænsəm], *n.* rançon, *f.*—*v.t.* rançonner.
rant [rænt], *n.* déclamation extravagante, *f.*—*v.i.* extravaguer; tempêter.
ranter ['ræntə], *n.* déclamateur, énergumène, *m.*
ranting ['ræntiŋ], *a.* d'énergumène, extravagant.
ranunculus [rə'nʌŋkjuləs], *n.* (*Bot.*) renoncule, *f.*
rap [ræp], *n.* tape, *f.*, petit coup sec, *m.*—*v.t.* *v.i.* frapper.
rapacious [rə'peiʃəs], *a.* rapace.
rapaciously [rə'peiʃəsli], *adv.* avec rapacité.
rapaciousness [rə'peiʃəsnis], **rapacity** [rə'pæsiti], *n.* rapacité, *f.*
rape (1) [reip], *n.* (*Poet.*) rapt, enlèvement; (*Law*) viol, *m.*—*v.t.* enlever de force; violer.
rape (2) [reip], *n.* (*Agric.*) colza, *m.*, navette, *f.*
rapid ['ræpid], *a.* and *n.* rapide, *m.*
rapidity [rə'piditi], **rapidness** ['ræpidnis], *n.* rapidité, *f.*
rapidly ['ræpidli], *adv.* rapidement.
rapier ['reipiə], *n.* rapière, *f.*
rapine ['ræpain], *n.* rapine, *f.*
rapt [ræpt], *a.* ravi, extasié; profond (*attention*).
rapture ['ræptʃə], *n.* ravissement, transport, *m.*, extase, *f.*
rapturous ['ræptʃərəs], *a.* ravissant; joyeux.
rapturously ['ræptʃərəsli], *adv.* avec transport.
rare [rɛə], *a.* rare; clairsemé; à moitié cru (*viande*).
rarefaction [rɛəri'fækʃən], *n.* raréfaction, *f.*
rarefy ['rɛərifai], *v.t.* raréfier.—*v.i.* se raréfier.
rarely ['rɛəli], *adv.* rarement.
rareness ['rɛənis], **rarity** ['rɛəriti], *n.* rareté, *f.*
rascal [rɑ:skl], *n.* coquin, fripon, gredin, *m.*
rascality [rɑ:s'kæliti], *n.* friponnerie, gredinerie, coquinerie, *f.*
rascally ['rɑ:skəli], *a.* coquin, fripon.
rase [RAZE].
rash (1) [ræʃ], *a.* téméraire; irréfléchi, imprudent.
rash (2) [ræʃ], *n.* éruption, *f.*
rasher ['ræʃə], *n.* tranche, *f.*
rashly ['ræʃli], *adv.* témérairement; imprudemment.
rashness ['ræʃnis], *n.* témérité; précipitation, imprudence, *f.*
rasp [rɑ:sp], *n.* râpe, *f.*—*v.t.* râper; râcler, écorcher (*surface, peau*).—*v.i.* grincer, crisser.
raspberry ['rɑ:zbəri], *n.* framboise, *f.*
raspberry-bush ['rɑ:zbəribuʃ], *n.* framboisier, *m.*
rasping ['rɑ:spiŋ], *a.* grinçant, âpre, rauque (*voix*).—*n.* râpage; crissement, *m.*
rat [ræt], *n.* rat, *m.*; ***to smell a rat***, se douter de quelque chose.
ratchet ['rætʃit], *n.* cliquet, *m.*, dent d'engrenage, *f.*
ratchet-brace ['rætʃitbreis], **ratchet-jack** ['rætʃitdʒæk], *n.* vilbrequin à cliquet, *m.*
rate (1) [reit], *n.* prix, *m.*; raison, proportion, *f.*; taux (*argent, population*); cours (*de change*); degré, rang, ordre, *m.*; vitesse; taxe, *f.*, impôt (*taxe municipale*), *m.*; ***at any rate***, en tout cas; ***first-rate***, de première classe.—*v.t.* évaluer; classer; taxer; faire une estimation; regarder (*comme*).—*v.i.* ***to rate as***, être classé comme.
rate (2) [reit], *v.t.* gronder.

rateable ['reitəbl], *a.* imposable; ***rateable value***, valeur locative imposable (*d'un immeuble*), *f.*
rate-payer ['reitpeiə], *n.* contribuable, *m., f.*
rather ['rɑːðə], *adv.* plutôt; un peu, quelque peu (*légèrement*); assez, passablement (*suffisamment*).
ratification [rætifi'keiʃən], *n.* ratification, *f.*
ratify ['rætifai], *v.t.* ratifier, approuver.
ratifying ['rætifaiiŋ], *a.* ratificatif.
rating (1) ['reitiŋ], *n.* estimation, évaluation; répartition d'impôt, *f.*; (*Navy*) matelot, *m.*
rating (2) ['reitiŋ], *n.* gronderie, *f.*
ratio ['reiʃiou], *n.* proportion, raison, *f.*, rapport, *m.*
ration ['ræʃən], *n.* ration, *f.*—*v.t.* rationner.
ration-book ['ræʃənbuk], *n.* carte d'alimentation, *f.*
rationing ['ræʃəniŋ], *n.* rationnement, *m.*
rational ['ræʃənl], *a.* raisonnable, rationnel.
rationalism ['ræʃnəlizm], *n.* rationalisme, *m.*
rationalist ['ræʃnəlist], *n.* rationaliste, *m., f.*
rationalize ['ræʃnəlaiz], *v.t.* rationaliser.
rationally ['ræʃnəli], *adv.* raisonnablement, rationnellement.
rattan [rə'tæn], *n.* rotin, *m.*
ratten [rætn], *v.t.* intimider; saboter.
rattle [rætl], *v.t.* faire claquer, faire sonner; secouer (*chaînes etc.*).—*v.i.* faire un bruit sec, cliqueter, crépiter.—*n.* bruit; cliquetis (*de métaux*); râle (*à la gorge*); hochet (*jouet*), *m.*; crécelle. *f.*
rattlesnake ['rætlsneik], *n.* serpent à sonnettes, crotale, *m.*
rattling ['rætliŋ], *a.* bruyant; (*fig.*) excellent. —*n.* bruit, cliquetis, *m.*
rat-trap ['rættræp], *n.* ratière, *f.*
raucous ['rɔːkəs], *a.* rauque.
ravage ['rævidʒ], *n.* ravage, *m.*—*v.t.* ravager.
ravager ['rævidʒə], *n.* ravageur, dévastateur, *m.*
rave [reiv], *v.i.* être en délire; (*fig.*) extravaguer.
ravel [rævl], *v.t.* embrouiller, entortiller.—*v.i.* s'embrouiller, s'entortiller.
raven (1) [reivn], *n.* (*Orn.*) corbeau, *m.*
raven (2) [rævn], *v.t.* dévorer.
ravenous ['rævənəs], *a.* dévorant, vorace.
ravenously ['rævənəsli], *adv.* avec voracité.
ravenousness ['rævənəsnis], *n.* voracité, rapacité, *f.*
ravine [rə'viːn], *n.* ravin, *m.*
raving ['reiviŋ], *a.* en délire, délirant; furieux, fou.—*n.* délire, *m.*
ravish ['ræviʃ], *v.t.* ravir; enlever; (*fig.*) transporter.
ravisher ['ræviʃə], *n.* ravisseur, *m.*
ravishing ['ræviʃiŋ], *a.* ravissant.
raw [rɔː], *a.* cru; vif, écorché (*égratigné etc.*); (*fig.*) sans expérience, novice; pur (*alcool*); brut (*cuir etc.*); froid et humide (*temps*); ***raw materials***, matières premières, *f.pl.*
raw-boned ['rɔːbound], *a.* maigre, décharné.
rawness ['rɔːnis], *n.* crudité, *f.*; froid humide (*du temps*), *m.*; (*fig.*) inexpérience, *f.*
ray (1) [rei], *n.* rayon, *m.*
ray (2) [rei], *n.* (*Ichth.*) raie, *f.*
rayless ['reilis], *a.* sans rayon, sans lumière.
Raymond ['reimənd]. Raymond, *m.*
rayon ['reiən], *n.* rayonne, *f.*
raze [reiz], *v.t.* raser, effleurer; rayer, effacer (*supprimer*); abattre, détruire (*édifice*).

razor ['reizə], *n.* rasoir, *m.*; ***safety razor***, rasoir de sûreté.
razor-bill ['reizəbil], *n.* petit pingouin, *m.*
re [riː, rei], *prep.* au sujet de, à propos de.
reach [riːtʃ], *n.* portée, atteinte; étendue (*capacité*), *f.*; bief (*de canal*), *m.*—*v.t.* atteindre, toucher; passer, donner (*rendre*); arriver à, parvenir à (*accomplir*).—*v.i.* s'étendre de . . . à.
reachable ['riːtʃəbl], *a.* qu'on peut atteindre.
react [riː'ækt], *v.i.* réagir (*sur*).
reaction [riː'ækʃən], *n.* réaction, *f.*
reactionary [riː'ækʃənəri], *a.* and *n.* réactionnaire, *m., f.*
reactor [riː'æktə], *n.* réacteur, *m.*
read [riːd], *v.t. irr.* lire; faire la lecture de; (*fig.*) étudier.—*v.i.* lire; faire la lecture; se lire.
readable ['riːdəbl], *a.* lisible; qui se lit avec plaisir.
readableness ['riːdəblnis], *n.* lisibilité, *f.*
readdress [riːə'dres], *v.t.* faire suivre (*lettre*).
reader ['riːdə], *n.* lecteur; (*Print.*) correcteur; liseur (*amateur de lecture*); (*Sch.*) livre de lecture, *m.*
readily ['redili], *adv.* tout de suite, promptement; volontiers (*de bon gré*), avec plaisir.
readiness ['redinis], *n.* empressement, *m.*, promptitude; facilité; bonne volonté (*complaisance*), *f.*
reading ['riːdiŋ], *n.* lecture; variante (*textuelle*), leçon; hauteur (*de baromètre*), *f.*
reading-book ['riːdiŋbuk], *n.* livre de lecture, *m.*
reading-desk ['riːdiŋdesk], *n.* pupitre, *m.*
reading-lamp ['riːdiŋlæmp], *n.* lampe de travail, *f.*
reading-room ['riːdiŋruːm], *n.* salle de lecture, *f.*
readjust [riːə'dʒʌst], *v.t.* rajuster, rectifier.
readjustment [riːə'dʒʌstmənt], *n.* rajustement, *m.*
ready ['redi], *a.* prêt, prompt; facile; vif (*qui comprend vite*); ***ready money***, argent comptant, *m.*
ready-made ['redimeid], *a.* tout fait, confectionné.
ready-reckoner ['redi'reknə], *n.* barême, *m.*
ready-witted ['redi'witid], *a.* à l'esprit vif.
reaffirm [riːə'fəːm], *v.t.* réaffirmer.
reafforestation [riːəfɔris'teiʃən], *n.* reboisement, *m.*
real ['riːəl], *a.* réel; vrai, véritable; effectif; (*Law*) immeuble, immobilier.
realism ['riːəlizm], *n.* réalisme, *m.*
realist ['riːəlist], *n.* réaliste, *m., f.*
realistic [riːə'listik], *a.* réaliste.
reality [riː'æliti], *n.* réalité, *f.*; réel, *m.*
realizable ['riːəlaizəbl], *a.* réalisable.
realization [riːəlai'zeiʃən], *n.* réalisation; conception nette, *f.*
realize ['riːəlaiz], *v.t.* réaliser; effectuer; se rendre compte de, bien comprendre; se figurer; rapporter (*somme*).
really ['riːəli], *adv.* réellement, en effet, effectivement; vraiment.—*int.* en vérité! à vrai dire!
realm [relm], *n.* royaume, (*fig.*) domaine, *m.*
realty ['riːəlti], *n.* biens immeubles, *m.pl.*
ream [riːm], *n.* rame (*de papier*), *f.*

reap [ri:p], *v.t.*, *v.i.* moissonner; (*fig.*) recueillir.
reaper ['ri:pə], *n.* moissonneur, *m.*
reaping ['ri:piŋ], *n.* moisson, *f.*
reaping machine ['ri:piŋməʃi:n], *n.* moissonneuse, *f.*
reappear [ri:ə'piə], *v.i.* reparaître, réapparaître.
reappearance [ri:ə'piərəns], *n.* réapparition; rentrée (*d'acteur*), *f.*
reappoint [ri:ə'pɔint], *v.t.* réintégrer; renommer.
reappointment [ri:ə'pɔintmənt], *n.* réintégration, *f.*
rear (1) [riə], *a.* situé à l'arrière; postérieur; ***rear wheel***, roue arrière, *f.*—*n.* dernier rang, *m.*; arrière-garde, *f.*; derrière (*d'édifice etc.*), *m.*; ***to bring up the rear***, fermer la marche.
rear (2) [riə], *v.t.* élever.—*v.i.* se cabrer.
rear-admiral ['riərædmərəl], *n.* contre-amiral, *m.*
re-arm [ri:'ɑ:m], *v.t.*, *v.i.* réarmer.
re-armament [ri:'ɑ:məmənt], *n.* réarmement, *m.*
rearwards ['riəwədz], *adv.* à l'arrière.
reascend [ri:ə'send], *v.t.*, *v.i.* remonter.
reason [ri:zn], *n.* raison, *f.*; raisonnement, *m.*; ***the reason why***, la raison pour laquelle; ***that stands to reason***, cela va sans dire; ***to have reason to believe***, avoir lieu de croire.—*v.t.*, *v.i.* raisonner.
reasonable ['ri:znəbl], *a.* raisonnable; modéré.
reasonableness ['ri:znəblnis], *n.* raison, modération, *f.*
reasonably ['ri:znəbli], *adv.* raisonnablement.
reasoner ['ri:zənə], *n.* raisonneur, logicien, *m.*
reasoning ['ri:zəniŋ], *n.* raisonnement, *m.*
reassemble [ri:ə'sembl], *v.t.* rassembler.—*v.i.* se rassembler.
reassert [ri:ə'sə:t], *v.t.* affirmer de nouveau.
reassess [ri:ə'ses], *v.t.* réévaluer.
reassessment [ri:ə'sesmənt], *n.* réimposition; réévaluation, *f.*
reassign [ri:ə'sain], *v.t.* réassigner.
reassignment [ri:ə'sainmənt], *n.* réassignation, *f.*
reassume [ri:ə'sju:m], *v.t.* réassumer; reprendre (*position*).
reassurance [ri:ə'ʃuərəns], *n.* action de rassurer; (*Comm.*) réassurance, *f.*
reassure [ri:ə'ʃuə], *v.t.* rassurer; (*Comm.*) réassurer.
rebate ['ri:beit], *n.* rabais, *m.*, remise, *f.*—[ri'beit], *v.t.* diminuer, rabattre.
rebel [rebl], *n.* rebelle, *m.*, *f.*, révolté, *m.*—[ri'bel], *v.i.* se révolter, se soulever (*contre*).
rebellion [ri'beljən], *n.* rébellion, *f.*
rebellious [ri'beljəs], *a.* rebelle.
rebelliously [ri'beljəsli], *adv.* en rebelle.
rebelliousness [ri'beljəsnis], *n.* rébellion, *f.*
rebirth [ri:'bə:θ], *n.* renaissance, *f.*
reborn [ri:'bɔ:n], *a.* né de nouveau; réincarné.
rebound ['ri:baund], *n.* rebondissement, contre-coup, *m.*—[ri'baund], *v.i.* rebondir.
rebuff [ri'bʌf], *n.* rebuffade, *f.*, échec, *m.*—*v.t.* rebuter, repousser.
rebuild [ri:'bild], *v.t. irr.* (*conjug. like* BUILD) rebâtir, reconstruire.
rebuke [ri'bju:k], *n.* réprimande, *f.*, reproche, *m.*—*v.t.* réprimander, reprendre, censurer.
rebus ['ri:bəs], *n.* rébus, *m.*
rebut [ri'bʌt], *v.t.* rebuter, repousser, réfuter.
recalcitrant [ri'kælsitrənt], *a.* récalcitrant, insoumis, réfractaire.
recall [ri'kɔ:l], *n.* rappel, *m.*; révocation, *f.*; ***beyond recall***, irrévocablement.—*v.t.* rappeler; se rappeler (*se souvenir de*).
recant [ri'kænt], *v.t.* rétracter, désavouer, abjurer.—*v.i.* se rétracter.
recantation [ri:kæn'teiʃən], *n.* rétractation, palinodie, *f.*
recapitulate [ri:kə'pitjuleit], *v.t.* récapituler.
recapitulation [ri:kəpitju'leiʃən], *n.* récapitulation, *f.*
recapture [ri:'kæptʃə], *n.* reprise, *f.*—*v.t* reprendre.
recast [ri:'kɑ:st], *v.t. irr.* (*conjug. like* CAST) refondre; (*Theat.*) faire une nouvelle distribution des rôles.
recede [ri'si:d], *v.i.* se retirer (*de*); s'éloigner.
receding [ri'si:diŋ], *a.* fuyant (*le front*), effacé (*menton*).
receipt [ri'si:t], *n.* reçu, *m.*, quittance, *f.*, acquit, *m.*; réception (*le fait de recevoir*); (*pl.*) recette, *f.*, recettes, *f.pl.*; récépissé, *m.* —*v.t.* acquitter.
receive [ri'si:v], *v.t.* recevoir, accepter; accueillir; recéler (*biens volés*).
receiver [ri'si:və], *n.* receveur; receleur (*d'objets volés*); liquidateur (*faillite*); (*Teleph.*) récepteur, *m.*
receiving [ri'si:viŋ], *n.* réception, *f.*; recel (*d'objets volés*), *m.*
recent ['ri:sənt], *a.* récent, frais, nouveau.
recently ['ri:səntli], *adv.* récemment, depuis peu.
receptacle [ri'septəkl], *n.* réceptacle; récipient, *m.*
reception [ri'sepʃən], *n.* réception, *f.*; accueil, *m.*
receptionist [ri'sepʃənist], *n.* réceptionniste, *m.*, *f.*
receptive [ri'septiv], *a.* réceptif (*esprit*).
recess [ri'ses], *n.* enfoncement, *m.*, niche, *f.*; recoin, *m.*; vacances, *f.pl.*
recession [ri'seʃən], *n.* retraite, *f.*; désistement (*d'une revendication*), *m.*; (*St. Exch.*) baisse, *f.*
recidivist [ri'sidivist], *n.* récidiviste, *m.*, *f.*
recipe ['resipi], *n.* (*Cook.*) recette, *f.*
recipient [ri'sipiənt], *n.* personne qui reçoit, *f.*, destinataire (*de lettre*), *m.*, *f.*; (*Chem.*) récipient, *m.*
reciprocal [ri'siprəkl], *a.* réciproque.
reciprocate [ri'siprəkeit], *v.t.* échanger; répondre à.—*v.i.* alterner, se succéder.
reciprocation [risiprə'keiʃən], **reciprocity** [resi'prɔsiti], *n.* réciprocité, *f.*
recital [ri'saitl], *n.* récit, *m.*; narration, énumération, *f.*; (*Mus.*) récital, *m.*
recitation [resi'teiʃən], *n.* récitation, *f.*
recitative [resitə'ti:v], *n.* récitatif, *m.*
recite [ri'sait], *v.t.* réciter, faire le récit de; raconter.
reciter [ri'saitə], *n.* récitateur; diseur, narrateur, *m.*
reck [rek], *v.i.* se soucier de.
reckless ['reklis], *a.* insouciant (*de*); téméraire, insensé.

recklessly ['reklisli], *adv.* témérairement, avec insouciance.
recklessness ['reklisnis], *n.* insouciance, témérité, *f.*
reckon [rekn], *v.t.* compter, calculer; regarder, évaluer (*comme*).—*v.i.* compter; ***to reckon on***, compter sur; ***to reckon with***, tenir compte de.
reckoner ['reknə], *n.* calculateur, chiffreur, *m.*; ***ready-reckoner***, barême, *m.*
reckoning ['rekniŋ], *n.* compte, calcul; écot, *m.*, note (*dans un hôtel*); addition (*dans un restaurant*); (*Naut.*) estime, *f.*
reclaim [ri:'kleim], *v.t.* réformer, corriger; ramener (*de*); réclamer, revendiquer (*ses droits*); défricher (*terre*).
reclaimable [ri:'kleiməbl], *a.* corrigible; cultivable, défrichable (*terre*).
reclaiming [ri:'kleimiŋ], **reclamation** [reklə'meiʃən], *n.* défrichement (*de terre*), *m.*; réforme, correction (*de criminels*), *f.*
recline [ri'klain], *v.i.* s'appuyer, se reposer, se coucher.
reclining [ri'klainiŋ], *a.* incliné, appuyé, couché.
reclothe [ri:'klouð], *v.t.* rhabiller.
recluse [ri'klu:s], *a.* reclus; solitaire, retiré.—*n.* reclus, *m.*
reclusion [ri'klu:ʒən], *n.* réclusion, *f.*
recognition [rekəg'niʃən], *n.* reconnaissance, *f.*
recognizable [rekəg'naizəbl], *a.* reconnaissable.
recognizance [ri'kɔgnizəns], *n.* reconnaissance; (*Law*) obligation contractée, *f.*
recognize ['rekəgnaiz], *v.t.* reconnaître.
recoil [ri'kɔil], *n.* recul; contre-coup, *m.*; (*fig.*) répugnance, *f.*—*v.i.* reculer; retomber.
recollect [rekə'lekt], *v.t.* se souvenir de, se rappeler.
recollection [rekə'lekʃən], *n.* souvenir, *m.*; mémoire, *f.*
recommence [ri:kə'mens], *v.t.*, *v.i.* recommencer.
recommend [rekə'mend], *v.t.* recommander.
recommendation [rekəmen'deiʃən], *n.* recommandation; apostille (*d'une pétition*), *f.*
recompense ['rekəmpens], *n.* récompense, *f.*; dédommagement, *m.*—*v.t.* récompenser (*de*); dédommager (*de*); compenser, réparer.
reconcilable [rekən'sailəbl], *a.* réconciliable; conciliable (*avec*) (*choses*).
reconcile ['rekənsail], *v.t.* réconcilier (*avec*); habituer, accoutumer (*familiariser*); ***to reconcile oneself to***, se résigner à.
reconciliation [rekənsili'eiʃən], *n.* réconciliation; conciliation (*de choses*); (*Bibl.*) expiation, *f.*
recondite [ri'kɔndait, 'rekəndait], *a.* secret, abstrus, profond, mystérieux.
recondition [ri:kən'diʃən], *v.t.* remettre à neuf, refaire.
reconnaissance [ri'kɔnisəns], *n.* reconnaissance, *f.*
reconnoitre [rekə'nɔitə], *v.t.* reconnaître.—*v.i.* faire une reconnaissance.
reconsider [ri:kən'sidə], *v.t.* considérer de nouveau; revenir sur (*une décision*).
reconsideration [ri:kənsidə'reiʃən], *n.* reconsidération, *f.*
reconstitute [ri:'kɔnstitju:t], *v.t.* reconstituer.
reconstruct [ri:kən'strʌkt], *v.t.* reconstruire.
reconstruction [ri:kən'strʌkʃən], *n.* reconstruction, *f.*
record ['rekɔ:d], *n.* registre, *m.*, archives, *f.pl.*; disque (*de phonographe*); (*Spt.*) record; dossier, *m.*; ***keeper of the records***, archiviste, *m.*, *f.*; ***long-playing record***, disque longue durée, *m*; ***public records***, archives, *f.pl.*; ***record library***, discothèque, *f.*; greffe, *m.*—[ri'kɔ:d], *v.t.* enregistrer; graver, imprimer (*dans l'esprit etc.*); mentionner (*fait historique*).
recorder [ri'kɔ:də], *n.* enregistreur, archiviste; greffier; (*Law*) officier judiciaire d'une ville; (*Mus.*) flageolet, *m.*; ***tape recorder***, magnétophone, *m.*
recording [ri'kɔ:diŋ], *n.* enregistrement, *m.*
recount (1) [ri'kaunt], *v.t.* raconter.
recount (2) [ri:'kaunt], *v.t.* recompter.—['ri:kaunt], *n.* nouvelle addition des voix (*aux élections*), *f.*
recoup [ri'ku:p], *v.t.* rembourser, dédommager (*de*).
recourse [ri'kɔ:s], *n.* recours, *m.*
recover (1) [ri'kʌvə], *v.t.* recouvrer, retrouver; réparer (*perte*).—*v.i.* se rétablir, guérir; se remettre (*d'une maladie*); se relever (*d'une perte*).
recover (2) [ri:'kʌvə], *v.t.* recouvrir; regarnir.
recovery [ri'kʌvəri], *n.* recouvrement, *m.*; guérison, *f.*; rétablissement, *m.*; (*Econ.*) reprise, *f.*; ***past recovery***, incurable, sans remède.
recreant ['rekriənt], *a.* and *n.* lâche, infidèle, *m.*, *f.*, apostat, *m.*
re-create [ri:kri'eit], *v.t.* recréer.
recreation [rekri'eiʃən], *n.* récréation, *f.*, divertissement, *m.*
recriminate [ri'krimineit], *v.i.* récriminer (*contre*).
recrimination [rikrimi'neiʃən], *n.* récrimination, *f.*
recriminatory [ri'kriminətri], *a.* récriminatoire.
recrudescence [ri:kru'desəns], *n.* recrudescence, *f.*
recruit [ri'kru:t], *n.* recrue, *f.*, conscrit, *m.*—*v.t.* rétablir, réparer (*restaurer*); (*Mil.*) recruter.—*v.i.* se recruter, se remettre.
recruiting [ri'kru:tiŋ], **recruitment** [ri'kru:tmənt], *n.* recrutement, *m.*; ***recruiting-officer***, officier de recrutement, *m.*
rectangle ['rektæŋgl], *n.* rectangle, *m.*
rectangular [rek'tæŋgjulə], *a.* rectangulaire, rectangle, à angle droit.
rectifiable ['rektifaiəbl], *a.* rectifiable.
rectification [rektifi'keiʃən], *n.* rectification, *f.*
rectifier ['rektifaiə], *n.* rectificateur; (*Elec.*) redresseur, *m.*
rectify ['rektifai], *v.t.* rectifier; redresser.
rectilineal [rekti'liniəl], *a.* rectiligne.
rectitude ['rektitju:d], *n.* rectitude, droiture, *f.*
rector ['rektə], *n.* (*Ch. of England*) prêtre; (*R.-C.*) curé; (*Univ. etc.*) recteur, principal, *m.*
rectorial [rek'tɔ:riəl], *a.* rectoral.
rectorship ['rektəʃip], *n.* rectorat, *m.*
rectory ['rektəri], *n.* cure, *f.*, presbytère, *m.*
recumbent [ri'kʌmbənt], *a.* couché, étendu; appuyé (*sur*).

recuperate [ri'ku:pəreit], *v.t.* recouvrer, récupérer.—*v.i.* se rétablir, se remettre, reprendre ses forces.
recuperation [riku:pə'reiʃən], *n.* recouvrement; rétablissement (*personne*), *m.*
recur [ri'kə:], *v.i.* revenir; se reproduire.
recurrence [ri'kʌrəns], *n.* retour, *m.*
recurrent [ri'kʌrənt], **recurring** [ri'kə:riŋ], *a.* périodique; (*Anat. etc.*) récurrent.
red [red], *a.* rouge; roux (*cheveux*); vermeil (*lèvres etc.*); ***red lead***, minium, *m.*; ***red-letter day***, jour de fête, *m.*—*n.* rouge, *m.*
redbreast ['redbrest], *n.* rouge-gorge, *m.*
redden [redn], *v.t.*, *v.i.* rougir.
reddish ['rediʃ], *a.* rougeâtre, roussâtre.
redeem [ri'di:m], *v.t.* racheter; (*Fin.*) rembourser, amortir; retirer (*objets mis en gage*); (*fig.*) réparer.
redeemable [ri'di:məbl], *a.* rachetable.
redeemer [ri'di:mə], *n.* rédempteur, *m.*
redeeming [ri'di:miŋ], *a.* qui rachète.
redemption [ri'dempʃən], *n.* rédemption, *f.*; (*Fin.*) amortissement; rachat (*de billets*), *m.*
red-hot ['redhɔt], *a.* tout rouge, chauffé au rouge, ardent (*charbon*).
redirect [ri:di'rekt], *v.t.* faire suivre (*lettre*).
rediscover [ri:dis'kʌvə], *v.t.* redécouvrir.
redistribution [ri:distri'bju:ʃən], *n.* nouvelle distribution, répartition, *f.*
redness ['rednis], *n.* rougeur; rousseur (*de cheveux*), *f.*
redolence ['redoləns], *n.* parfum, *m.*; senteur, *f.*
redolent ['redolənt], *a.* qui a un parfum de; ***redolent of . . .***, qui sent le . . . .
redouble [ri:'dʌbl], *v.t.*, *v.i.* redoubler.
redoubt [ri'daut], *n.* redoute, *f.*
redoubtable [ri'dautəbl], *a.* redoutable.
redound [ri'daund], *v.t.* contribuer (*à*, *en*), résulter (*pour*), rejaillir (*sur*).
redpole, redpoll ['redpoul], *n.* (*pop.*) linotte, *f.*
redraft [ri:'drɑ:ft], *n.* nouveau dessin, *m.*; (*Comm.*) retraite, *f.*—*v.t.* rédiger de nouveau.
redress [ri'dres], *v.t.* redresser, corriger, réparer.—*n.* redressement, *m.*, réparation, *f.*, remède, *m.*
redshank ['redʃæŋk], *n.* (*Orn.*) chevalier, *m.*, gambette, *f.*
Redskin ['redskin], *n.* Peau-Rouge, *m.*, *f.*
red-tape ['red'teip], *n.* bolduc, *m.*; (*fig.*) routine administrative, *f.*
reduce [ri'dju:s], *v.t.* réduire (*à* ou *en*); maigrir (*chair*); dégrader (*abaisser*); ***a person in reduced circumstances***, une personne tombée dans la gêne.—*v.i.* maigrir.
reduction [ri'dʌkʃən], *n.* réduction, *f.*; ***a reduction in prices***, une baisse des prix, *f.*; ***reduction to the ranks***, cassation, *f.*
redundance [ri'dʌndəns], **redundancy** [ri'dʌndənsi], *n.* redondance, *f.*
redundant [ri'dʌndənt], *a.* redondant, superflu.
re-echo [ri:'ekou], *v.t.* répéter.—*v.i.* retentir.—*n.* écho répété, *m.*
reed [ri:d], *n.* roseau; chalumeau, *m.*; (*Mus.*) anche, *f.*
reed-pipe ['ri:dpaip], *n.* chalumeau, pipeau, *m.*
reedy ['ri:di], *a.* couvert de roseaux; flûtée (*voix*).
reef (1) [ri:f], *n.* récif, écueil, *m.*
reef (2) [ri:f], *n.* ris (*de voile*), *m.*—*v.t.* prendre un ris dans.
reef-knot ['ri:fnɔt], *n.* nœud plat, *m.*
reek [ri:k], *n.* fumée, *f.*, relent, *m.*—*v.i.* fumer; exhaler; ***reeking with***, tout fumant de; ***to reek of***, puer, empester.
reel (1) [ri:l], *n.* dévidoir, *m.*; bobine (*de coton*), *f.*; (*Angling*) moulinet, *m.*; (*Cine.*) bobine, bande, *f.*; ***newsreel***, les actualités, *f.pl.*—*v.t.* ***to reel off***, dévider, débiter.—*v.i.* tournoyer, chanceler, trébucher.
reel (2) [ri:l], *n.* branle écossais (*danse*), *m.*
re-elect [ri:i'lekt], *v.t.* réélire.
re-election [ri:i'lekʃən], *n.* réélection, *f.*
re-embark [ri:əm'bɑ:k], *v.t.* rembarquer.—*v.i.* se rembarquer.
re-embarkation [ri:embɑ:'keiʃən], *n.* rembarquement, *m.*
re-embody [ri:əm'bɔdi], *v.t.* réincorporer.
re-enact [ri:i'nækt], *v.t.* remettre en vigueur (*une loi*); reconstituer (*un crime*).
re-enactment [ri:i'næktmənt], *n.* remise en vigueur; reconstitution, *f.*
re-engage [ri:in'geidʒ], *v.t.* rengager.
re-enlist [ri:in'list], *v.t.*, *v.i.* (se) rengager.
re-enter [ri:'entə], *v.t.*, *v.i.* rentrer.
re-entrant [ri:'entrənt], *a.* and *n.* rentrant, *m.*
re-establish [[ri:is'tæbliʃ], *v.t.* rétablir.
re-establishment [ri:is'tæbliʃmənt], *n.* rétablissement, *m.*
re-examine [ri:ig'zæmin], *v.t.* examiner de nouveau, revoir.
re-export [ri:iks'pɔ:t], *v.t.* réexporter.
refashion [ri:'fæʃən], *v.t.* refaçonner.
refasten [ri:'fɑ:sn], *v.t.* rattacher; ragrafer.
refection [ri'fekʃən], *n.* repas, *m.*, collation, *f.*
refectory [ri'fektəri], *n.* réfectoire, *m.*
refer [ri'fə:], *v.t.* renvoyer, rapporter; adresser (*à*); remettre à la décision de.—*v.i.* se référer, se rapporter, avoir rapport (*à*); s'en rapporter, se référer (*personnes*); s'adresser (*à*).
referee [refə'ri:], *n.* arbitre, *m.*, *f.*—*v.t.*, *v.i.* (*Spt.*) arbitrer.
reference ['refərəns], *n.* renvoi; rapport (*respect*), *m.*; allusion, *f.*; renseignements, *m.pl.*, références (*de bonne vie et mœurs*), *f.pl.*; (*Comm.*) référence, *f.*; ***book of reference***, ouvrage à consulter, *m.*; ***with reference to***, au sujet de; ***to make reference to***, faire allusion à.
referendum [refə'rendəm], *n.* référendum, *m.*
refill [ri:'fil], *v.t.* remplir.—*v.i.* (*Motor.*) faire le plein (d'essence).—['ri:fil], *n.* objet (*feuilles, pile, ampoule*) de rechange; (*Motor.*) plein (d'essence), *m.*
refine [ri'fain], *v.t.* épurer (*liquides*); (*Metal.*) affiner; raffiner (*sucre etc.*); (*fig.*) purifier.
refined [ri'faind], *a.* raffiné; pur, délicat (*goût*).
refinement [ri'fainmənt], *n.* raffinage (*de sucre*); (*Metal.*) affinage, *m.*; épuration (*de liquides*); (*fig.*) délicatesse, *f.*
refinery [ri'fainəri], *n.* raffinerie (*de sucre*); (*Metal.*) affinerie, *f.*
refit [ri:'fit], *v.t.* réparer; (*Naut.*) radouber.—['ri:fit], *n.* réparation; (*Naut.*) refonte, *f.*
reflect [ri'flekt], *v.t.* réfléchir; faire rejaillir sur; refléter.—*v.i.* réfléchir; ***to reflect upon***, réfléchir à, méditer sur.
reflected [ri'flektid], *a.* réfléchi.

reflection [REFLEXION].
reflective [ri'flektiv], *a.* réfléchissant; méditatif.
reflector [ri'flektə], *n.* réflecteur; (*Cycl., Motor.*) catadioptre, *m.*
reflex ['ri:fleks], *a.* réfléchi; (*Paint.*) reflété; (*Physiol. etc.*) réflexe.—*n.* (*Paint.*) reflet; (*Physiol.*) réflexe, *m.*
reflexion [ri'flekʃən], *n.* réflexion, *f.*; reflet (*lumière etc.*), *m.*; censure, *f.*; blâme, *m.*
reflexive [ri'fleksiv], *a.* réfléchi.
reform [ri'fɔ:m], *n.* réforme, *f.*—*v.t.* réformer; corriger.—*v.i.* se réformer, se corriger.
re-form [ri:'fɔ:m], *v.t.* reformer.—*v.i.* se reformer.
reformation [refɔ:'meiʃən], *n.* réformation; réforme, *f.*; ***the Reformation***, (*Hist.*) la Réforme.
re-formation [ri:fɔ:'meiʃən], *n.* formation nouvelle, *f.*
reformer [ri'fɔ:mə], *n.* réformateur, *m.*
refract [ri'frækt], *v.t.* réfracter.
refraction [ri'frækʃən], *n.* réfraction, *f.*
refractive [ri'fræktiv], *a.* réfractif; refringent.
refractory [ri'fræktri], *a.* indocile, récalcitrant, intraitable, rebelle; (*Chem. etc.*) réfractaire; rétif (*cheval*).
refrain [ri'frein], *v.i.* se retenir, s'abstenir (*de*).—*n.* refrain, *m.*
refresh [ri'freʃ], *v.t.* rafraîchir; délasser, restaurer; ***to refresh oneself***, se rafraîchir.
refreshing [ri'freʃiŋ], *a.* rafraîchissant; réparateur, qui repose.
refreshment [ri'freʃmənt], *n.* rafraîchissement, *m.*; ***refreshment-bar***, buvette, *f.*; ***refreshment-car***, wagon-restaurant, *m.*; ***refreshment-room***, buffet, *m.*
refrigerate [ri'fridʒəreit], *v.t.* réfrigérer, frigorifier.
refrigeration [rifridʒə'reiʃən], *n.* réfrigération, *f.*
refrigerator [ri'fridʒəreitə], *n.* réfrigérateur; (*fam.*) Frigidaire (*marque déposée*), *m.*
refuel [ri:'fjuəl], *v.i.* (*Av.*) faire le plein (d'essence).
refuge ['refju:dʒ], *n.* refuge (*contre*), *m.*; ***to take refuge***, se réfugier.
refugee [refju'dʒi:], *n.* réfugié, *m.*
refulgence [ri'fʌldʒəns], *n.* éclat, *m.*, splendeur, *f.*
refulgent [ri'fʌldʒənt], *a.* éclatant.
refund [ri'fʌnd], *v.t.* rembourser, rendre.—['ri:fʌnd], *n.* remboursement, *m.*
refurnish [ri:'fə:niʃ], *v.t.* remeubler.
refusal [ri'fju:zl], *n.* refus, *m.*
refuse ['refju:s], *n.* rebut, *m.*, ordures (*ménagères, de marché*), *f.pl.*; ***refuse dump***, voirie, *f.*—[ri'fju:z], *v.t.* refuser; rejeter.—*v.i.* refuser.
refute [ri'fju:t], *v.t.* réfuter.
regain [ri'gein], *v.t.* regagner, reprendre.
regal [ri:gl], *a.* royal.
regale [ri'geil], *v.t.* régaler.—*v.i.* se régaler.
regally ['ri:gəli], *adv.* royalement, en roi.
regard [ri'gɑ:d], *n.* égard, *m.*; considération, *f.*; respect (*estime*), *m.*; (*pl.*) amitiés, *f.pl.*, compliments, *m.pl.*; ***out of regard for***, par égard pour; ***with regard to***, quant à.—*v.t.* regarder; considérer; ***as regards***, quant à.
regarding [ri'gɑ:diŋ], *prep.* quant à, concernant.
regardless [ri'gɑ:dlis], *a.* peu soigneux (*de*) sans égard (*pour*); ***regardless of***, sans se soucier de.
regatta [ri'gætə], *n.* régate(s), *f.*(*pl.*).
regency ['ri:dʒənsi], *n.* régence, *f.*
regenerate [ri'dʒenərət], *a.* régénéré.—[ri:'dʒenəreit], *v.t.* régénérer.
regenerating [ri'dʒenəreitiŋ], *a.* régénérateur.
regeneration [ri:dʒenə'reiʃən], *n.* régénération, *f.*
regent ['ri:dʒənt], *n.* régent, *m.*
regicide ['redʒisaid], *n.* régicide (*crime*), *m.*; régicide (*personne*), *m., f.*
régime [rei'ʒi:m], *n.* (*Polit.*) régime, *m.*
regimen ['redʒimən], *n.* (*Gram., Med.*) régime, *m.*
regiment ['redʒimənt], *n.* régiment, *m.*
regimental [redʒi'mentl], *a.* du régiment, de régiment.
regimentation [redʒimen'teiʃən], *n.* enrégimentation, *f.*
Reginald ['redʒinəld]. Renaud, *m.*
region ['ri:dʒən], *n.* région, *f.*
regional ['ri:dʒənl], *a.* régional.
register ['redʒistə], *n.* registre, *m.*; liste électorale (*de votants*), *f.*—*v.t.* enregistrer recommander (*lettre, paquet*); déclarer (*naissance*); immatriculer (*voiture*); déposer (*marque de fabrique etc.*).
registrar ['redʒistrɑ:], *n.* (*Law*) greffier (*Univ.*) secrétaire et archiviste; officier de l'état civil (*de naissances etc.*), *m.*
registration [redʒis'treiʃən], *n.* enregistrement; chargement (*de lettres*); dépôt (*d'une marque de fabrique etc.*), *m.*; immatriculation (*de véhicule*); inscription (*des bagages*) *f.*; ***registration number***, (*Motor.*) numéro minéralogique, *m.*
registry ['redʒistri], *n.* enregistrement; (*Law*) greffe, *m.*
registry-office ['redʒistri'ɔfis], *n.* bureau de l'état civil, *m.*
regret [ri'gret], *n.* regret, *m.*—*v.t.* regretter (*de*), avoir du regret (*à*).
regretful [ri'gretful], *a.* plein de regrets, regrettable.
regretfully [ri'gretfuli], *adv.* avec regret, à regret.
regrettable [ri'gretəbl], *a.* fâcheux, regrettable.
regular ['regjulə], *a.* régulier; réglé; en règle; ordinaire (*normal*); (*fig.*) franc, fieffé
regularity [regju'læriti], *n.* régularité, *f.*
regularly ['regjuləli], *adv.* régulièrement.
regulate ['regjuleit], *v.t.* régler; diriger.
regulation [regju'leiʃən], *a.* réglementaire.—*n.* règlement, *m.*
regulator ['regjuleitə], *n.* régulateur, *m.*
rehabilitate [ri:hə'biliteit], *v.t.* réhabiliter.
rehabilitation [ri:həbili'teiʃən], *n.* réhabilitation, *f.*
rehearsal [ri'hə:sl], *n.* récit, *m.*; (*Theat.*) répétition, *f.*; ***dress rehearsal***, répétition générale.
rehearse [ri'hə:s], *v.t.* (*Theat.*) répéter; (*fig.*) raconter (*narrer*).
rehouse [ri:'hauz], *v.t.* reloger.
reign [rein], *n.* règne, *m.*—*v.i.* régner.

reigning [ˈreiniŋ], *a.* régnant; (*fig.*) dominant (*prevailing*).
reimburse [ri:imˈbə:s], *v.t.* rembourser.
reimbursement [ri:imˈbə:smənt], *n.* remboursement, *m.*
rein [rein], *n.* rêne, *f.*—*v.t.* conduire à la bride, gouverner, brider; contenir.
reincarnation [ri:inkɑ:ˈneiʃən], *n.* réincarnation, *f.*
reindeer [ˈreindiə], *n.* renne, *m.*
reinforce [ri:inˈfɔ:s], *v.t.* renforcer; ***reinforced concrete***, béton armé, *m.*
reinforcement [ri:inˈfɔ:smənt], *n.* renforcement; (*Mil.*) renfort, *m.*
reinstall [ri:inˈstɔ:l], *v.t.* réinstaller.
reinstate [ri:inˈsteit], *v.t.* rétablir.
reinstatement [ri:inˈsteitmənt], *n.* rétablissement, *m.*
reintroduce [ri:intrəˈdju:s], *v.t.* introduire de nouveau, réintroduire.
reinvest [ri:inˈvest], *v.t.* replacer.
reinvigorate [ri:inˈvigəreit], *v.t.* ranimer.
reissue [ri:ˈisju:], *v.t.* émettre de nouveau; rééditer (*livre*).—*n.* nouvelle émission; nouvelle édition, *f.*
reiterate [ri:ˈitəreit], *v.t.* réitérer.
reiteration [ri:itəˈreiʃən], *n.* réitération, *f.*
reiterative [ri:ˈitərətiv], *a.* réitératif.
reject [riˈdʒekt], *v.t.* rejeter.—[ˈri:dʒekt], *n.* pièce de rebut, *f.*
rejection [riˈdʒekʃən], *n.* rejet, *m.*
rejoice [riˈdʒɔis], *v.t.* réjouir.—*v.i.* se réjouir (*de*).
rejoicing [riˈdʒɔisiŋ], *n.* réjouissance, joie, *f.*
rejoin [ri:ˈdʒɔin], *v.t.* rejoindre.—[riˈdʒɔin], *v.i.* répliquer, répondre.
rejoinder [riˈdʒɔində], *n.* repartie; (*Law*) réplique, *f.*
rejuvenate [riˈdʒu:vəneit], *v.t.* rajeunir.
rejuvenation [ridʒu:vəˈneiʃən], *n.* rajeunissement, *m.*
rekindle [ri:ˈkindl], *v.t.* rallumer.
relapse [riˈlæps], *n.* rechute, *f.*—*v.i.* retomber (*dans*); récidiver (*criminel*).
relate [riˈleit], *v.t.* raconter; rapporter.—*v.i.* se rapporter, avoir rapport (*à*).
related [riˈleitid], *a.* ayant rapport; parent (*de*); allié (*à*) (*par mariage etc.*).
relating [riˈleitiŋ], *a.* relatif, qui se rapporte (*à*).
relation [riˈleiʃən], *n.* relation, *f.*, rapport; récit (*narration*); parent (*de la famille*); allié (*par mariage*), *m.*; (*pl.*) relations, *f.pl.*, rapports (*contact*), *m.pl.*
relationship [riˈleiʃənʃip], *n.* parenté, *f.*; rapport, *m.*
relative [ˈrelətiv], *a.* relatif (*à*).—*n.* parent; (*Gram.*) relatif, *m.*
relatively [ˈrelətivli], *adv.* relativement.
relativity [reləˈtiviti], *n.* relativité, *f.*
relax [riˈlæks], *v.t.* relâcher, détendre.—*v.i.* se relâcher; se détendre; se délasser.
relaxation [ri:lækˈseiʃən], *n.* relâchement, relâche, *m.*, détente, *f.*; (*Med.*) repos, *m.*
relaxing [riˈlæksiŋ], *a.* relâchant; énervant, débilitant (*climat*).
relay [ˈri:lei], *n.* relais, *m.*—*v.t.* relayer.
re-lay [ri:ˈlei], *v.t.* poser de nouveau.
release [riˈli:s], *v.t.* relâcher, élargir (*un prisonnier*); décharger (*de*); déclencher.—*n.* élargissement, *m.*; délivrance; décharge (*d'une obligation*); (*Cine.*) sortie (*d'un film*), *f.*; déclenchement (*de ressort etc.*), *m.*
relegate [ˈreləgeit], *v.t.* reléguer.
relegation [reləˈgeiʃən], *n.* relégation, *f.*
relent [riˈlent], *v.i.* s'amollir, s'attendrir; se repentir (*regretter*).
relenting [riˈlentiŋ], *n.* attendrissement, *m.*
relentless [riˈlentlis], *a.* inflexible, impitoyable.
relentlessly [riˈlentlisli], *adv.* impitoyablement.
relentlessness [riˈlentlisnis], *n.* rigueur, dureté, *f.*
relevance [ˈreləvəns], **relevancy** [ˈreləvənsi], *n.* relation, *f.*, rapport, *m.*; pertinence, convenance, *f.*, à-propos, *m.*
relevant [ˈreləvənt], *a.* relatif, applicable (*à*); à propos, pertinent.
reliable [riˈlaiəbl], *a.* digne de confiance; sûr, exact, bien fondé (*renseignement*).
reliability [rilaiəˈbiliti], *n.* crédibilité, véracité; sûreté, *f.*
reliance [riˈlaiəns], *n.* confiance, *f.*
relic [ˈrelik], *n.* relique (*de saint* ou *martyr*), *f.*; (*pl.*) restes (*d'un être*); vestiges (*du passé*), *m.pl.*
relief [riˈli:f], *n.* soulagement (*de douleur etc.*); secours (*aide*), *m.*; (*Mil.*) relève, *f.*; (*Sculp. etc.*) relief, *m.*; ***relief train***, train supplémentaire, *m.*
relieve [riˈli:v], *v.t.* soulager, adoucir; délivrer (*de*); secourir, aider (*assister*); (*Mil.*) relever (*sentinelle*).
religion [riˈlidʒən], *n.* religion, *f.*
religious [riˈlidʒəs], *a.* religieux; de religion.
religiously [riˈlidʒəsli], *adv.* religieusement.
relinquish [riˈliŋkwiʃ], *v.t.* abandonner; renoncer à.
relinquishment [riˈliŋkwiʃmənt], *n.* abandon, *m.*; renonciation, *f.*
reliquary [ˈrelikwəri], *n.* reliquaire, *m.*
relish [ˈreliʃ], *n.* goût, *m.*, saveur, *f.*; (*Cook.*) assaisonnement; (*fig.*) charme; appétit, *m.*—*v.t.* goûter, savourer; relever le goût de.
relive [ri:ˈliv], *v.t.* revivre.
reload [ri:ˈloud], *v.t.* recharger.
reluctance [riˈlʌktəns], *n.* répugnance, *f.*
reluctant [riˈlʌktənt], *a.* qui a de la répugnance,à, qui agit à contre-cœur; peu disposé (*à*).
reluctantly [riˈlʌktəntli], *adv.* à contre-cœur.
rely [riˈlai], *v.i.* compter (*sur*), avoir confiance (*en*).
remain [riˈmein], *v.i.* rester, demeurer.
remainder [riˈmeində], *n.* reste, *m.*
remaining [riˈmeiniŋ], *a.* de reste, restant.
remains [riˈmeinz], *n.pl.* restes; débris, *m.pl.*; ***mortal remains***, dépouille mortelle, *f.*
remake [ri:ˈmeik], *v.t. irr.* (*conjug. like* MAKE) refaire.
remand [riˈmɑ:nd], *v.t.* renvoyer à une autre audience.—*n.* renvoi à une autre audience, *m.*
remark [riˈmɑ:k], *n.* remarque, *f.*—*v.t.* remarquer, observer; faire remarquer, faire observer (*à une personne*).
remarkable [riˈmɑ:kəbl], *a.* remarquable.
remarkably [riˈmɑ:kəbli], *adv.* remarquablement.
remarriage [ri:ˈmæridʒ], *n.* remariage, *m.*
remarry [ri:ˈmæri], *v.t.* épouser de nouveau.—*v.i.* se remarier.

remedial [ri'mi:djəl], *a.* réparateur; (*Med.*) curatif.
remedy ['remədi], *n.* remède; (*Law*) recours, *m.*—*v.t.* remédier à, porter remède à.
remember [ri'membə], *v.t.* se souvenir de, se rappeler; reconnaître (*de vue*).
remembrance [ri'membrəns], *n.* souvenir, *m.*, mémoire, *f.*
remind [ri'maind], *v.t.* rappeler à, faire souvenir (*à . . . de*), faire penser à.
reminder [ri'maində], *n.* mémento, *m.*
reminisce [remi'nis], *v.i.* raconter ses souvenirs.
reminiscence [remi'nisəns], *n.* réminiscence, *f.*
reminiscent [remi'nisənt], *a.* qui rappelle.
remiss [ri'mis], *a.* négligent.
remission [ri'miʃən], *n.* rémission, *f.*, pardon; relâchement (*détente*), *m.*; remise (*de dette, peine*), *f.*
remit [ri'mit], *v.t.* relâcher (*détendre*); remettre (*amende etc.*).—*v.i.* se relâcher, se calmer; diminuer.
remittance [ri'mitəns], *n.* remise, *f.*; envoi de fonds, *m.*
remittent [ri'mitənt], *a.* (*Path.*) rémittent.
remnant ['remnənt], *n.* reste; coupon, bout (*de tissu*), *m.*; (*pl.*) restes, débris, *m.pl.*
remodel [ri:'mɔdl], *v.t.* remodeler.
remonstrance [ri'mɔnstrəns], *n.* remontrance, *f.*
remonstrate ['remənstreit], *v.i.* remontrer.
remorse [ri'mɔ:s], *n.* remords, *m.*
remorseful [ri'mɔ:sful], *a.* rempli de remords.
remorseless [ri'mɔ:slis], *a.* sans remords, impitoyable.
remorselessness [ri'mɔ:slisnis], *n.* cruauté, inhumanité, *f.*
remote [ri'mout], *a.* éloigné, lointain; reculé (*époque*); distant (*personne*).
remotely [ri'moutli], *adv.* de loin; faiblement.
remoteness [ri'moutnis], *n.* éloignement, *m.*; réserve (*attitude*), *f.*
remould [ri:'mould], *v.t.* mouler de nouveau.
remount [ri:'maunt], *v.t., v.i.* remonter.—*n.* remonte, *f.*
removable [ri'mu:vəbl], *a.* transportable; (*fig.*) amovible (*fonctionnaire etc.*).
removal [ri'mu:vl], *n.* éloignement, départ; transport; déménagement (*de meubles*); déplacement, *m.*; révocation (*de ses fonctions*), *f.*
remove [ri'mu:v], *n.* degré (*parenté*), *m.*; distance, *f.*—*v.t.* éloigner; déplacer (*bouger*); transporter; déménager (*meubles*); ôter, enlever (*emporter*); renvoyer (*de ses fonctions*).—*v.i.* s'éloigner, se déplacer; déménager (*changer de domicile*).
removed [ri'mu:vd], *a.* éloigné; ***first cousin once removed***, cousin issu de germains, *m.*
remover [ri'mu:və], *n.* déménageur, *m.*; ***nail-varnish remover***, dissolvant (pour ongles), *m.*
remunerate [ri'mju:nəreit], *v.t.* rémunérer.
remuneration [rimju:nə'reiʃən], *n.* rétribution, rémunération, *f.*
remunerative [ri'mju:nərətiv], *a.* rémunérateur; (*Law*) rémunératoire.
rename [ri:'neim], *v.t.* renommer.
rend [rend], *v.t. irr.* déchirer; (*fig.*) fendre.
render ['rendə], *v.t.* rendre; interpréter, traduire; (*Cook.*) fondre (*graisse etc.*).
rendering ['rendəriŋ], *n.* traduction, interprétation, *f.*
renegade ['renigeid], *n.* renégat, *m.*
renew [ri'nju:], *v.t.* renouveler; renouer (*connaissance*).
renewal [ri'nju:əl], *n.* renouvellement, *m.*; ***renewal of subscription***, réabonnement, *m*
renounce [ri'nauns], *v.t.* renoncer (*à*); renier
renouncement [ri'naunsmənt], *n.* renoncement, *m.*, renonciation, *f.*
renovate ['renəveit], *v.t.* renouveler; rajeunir
renovation [renə'veiʃən], *n.* rénovation, *f.*
renovator ['renəveitə], *n.* rénovateur, *m.*
renown [ri'naun], *n.* renommée, *f.*, renom, *m.*
renowned [ri'naund], *a.* renommé.
rent (1) [rent], *n.* déchirure, fente, *f.*; accroc (*de vêtements*), *m.*
rent (2) [rent], *n.* loyer (*de maison* ou *d'appartement*); fermage (*de ferme*), *m.*; (*pl.*) rentes, *f.pl.*, revenu, *m.*; ***ground-rent***, rente foncière, *f.*—*v.t.* louer, prendre à ferme, donner à ferme.—*v.i.* se louer.
rent (3) [rent], *past* and *p.p.* [REND].
rental [rentl], *n.* valeur locative, *f.*
rent-free ['rentfri:], *a.* exempt de loyer.
renunciation [rinʌnsi'eiʃən], *n.* renonciation, *f.*, renoncement, *m.*
reoccupation [ri:ɔkju'peiʃən], *n.* réoccupation, *f.*
reoccupy [ri:'ɔkjupai], *v.t.* réoccuper.
reopen [ri:'oupən], *v.t.* rouvrir.—*v.i.* rentrer (*écoles, tribunaux etc.*).
reopening [ri:'oupniŋ], *n.* réouverture; rentrée (*d'écoles etc.*), *f.*
reorganization [ri:ɔ:gənai'zeiʃən], *n.* réorganisation, *f.*
reorganize [ri:'ɔ:gənaiz], *v.t.* réorganiser.
rep (1) [rep], *a.* de reps.—*n.* reps (*tissu*), *m.*
rep (2) [rep], [REPERTORY].
rep (3) [rep], [REPRESENTATIVE].
repaint [ri:'peint], *v.t.* repeindre.
repair (1) [ri'pɛə], *v.t.* réparer; raccommoder (*vêtements etc.*); (*fig.*) rétablir.—*n.* réparation, *f.*; raccommodage (*de vêtements etc.*); ***to keep in repair***, entretenir.
repair (2) [ri'pɛə], *n.* séjour (*retraite*), *m.*—*v.i.* aller; se rendre (*à*).
repairer [ri'pɛərer], *n.* réparateur; raccommodeur (*de vêtements*), *m.*
reparable ['repərəbl], *a.* réparable.
reparation [repə'reiʃən], *n.* réparation (*d'une offense*), *f.*
repartee [repɑ:'ti:], *n.* repartie, riposte, *f.*
repast [ri'pɑ:st], *n.* repas, *m.*
repatriate [ri:'pætrieit], *v.t.* rapatrier.
repay [ri'pei], *v.t. irr.* (*conjug. like* PAY) rembourser; (*fig.*) valoir la peine (*de*).
repayment [ri:'peimənt], *n.* remboursement, *m.*
repeal [ri'pi:l], *v.t.* révoquer; abroger (*loi etc.*).—*n.* révocation; abrogation (*de loi*), *f.*
repeat [ri'pi:t], *v.t.* répéter, réitérer; réciter (*par cœur*); bis (*après vers de chanson etc.*).—*n.* répétition; (*Mus.*) reprise, *f.*
repeated [ri'pi:tid], *a.* répété, réitéré.
repeatedly [ri'pi:tidli], *adv.* à plusieurs reprises; souvent, bien des fois.
repeating [ri'pi:tiŋ], *a.* qui répète; à répétition.

repel [ri'pel], *v.t.* repousser; combattre.

repellent [ri'pelənt], *a.* répulsif, répugnant.—*n.* répulsif; (*Med.*) révulsif, *m.*

repent [ri'pent], *v.t.* se repentir de.—*v.i.* se repentir.

repentance [ri'pentəns], *n.* repentir, *m.*

repentant [ri'pentənt], *a.* répentant.

repercussion [ri:pə'kʌʃən], *n.* répercussion, *f.*

repertory ['repətri], *n.* répertoire, *m.*; ***repertory theatre***, (*fam.*) ***rep***, troupe à demeure, *f.*

repetition [repi'tiʃən], *n.* répétition; (*Mus.*) reprise, *f.*

repetitive [ri'petitiv], *a.* qui se répète.

repine [ri'pain], *v.i.* murmurer (*contre*); se plaindre (*de*).

repining [ri'painiŋ], *a.* disposé à se plaindre, mécontent.—*n.* plainte, *f.*, regret, *m.*

replace [ri:'pleis], *v.t.* replacer; remplacer (*substituer*).

replacement [ri:'pleismənt], *n.* remplacement, *m.*

replant [ri:'plɑ:nt], *v.t.* replanter.

replay ['ri:plei], *n.* match rejoué *m.*—[ri:'plei], *v.t.*, *v.i.* rejouer.

replenish [ripleniʃ], *v.t.* remplir (*de*).—*v.i.* se remplir.

replenishment [ri'pleniʃmənt], *n.* remplissage, *m.*

replete [ri'pli:t], *a.* plein, rempli (*de*).

repletion [ri'pli:ʃən], *n.* plénitude; (*Med.*) réplétion, *f.*

replica ['replikə], *n.* double, *m.*, copie, *f.*

reply [ri'plai], *n.* réponse; (*Law*) réplique, *f.*—*v.t.*, *v.i.* répondre, répliquer.

repopulate [ri:'pɔpjuleit], *v.t.* repeupler.

report [ri'pɔ:t], *v.t.* rapporter, raconter, dire; rendre compte de; signaler; dénoncer (*à la police*); ***to report oneself***, se présenter à.—*n.* rapport; bruit, ouï-dire (*rumeur*); compte rendu, procès-verbal (*de réunion etc.*); (*Sch.*) bulletin; coup (*de fusil*), *m.*; réputation (*renom*), *f.*

reporter [ri'pɔ:tə], *n.* rapporteur; reporter (*journaliste*), *m.*

reporting [ri'pɔ:tiŋ], *n.* reportage, *m.*

repose [ri'pouz], *v.t.* reposer.—*v.i.* se reposer.—*n.* repos, *m.*

repository [ri'pɔzitri], *n.* dépôt, *m.*

repossess [ri:pə'zes], *v.t.* rentrer en possession de.

reprehend [repri'hend], *v.t.* réprimander, censurer, blâmer (*de*).

reprehensible [repri'hensibl], *a.* répréhensible, blâmable.

represent [repri'zent], *v.t.* représenter.

representation [reprizen'teiʃən], *n.* représentation, *f.*

representative [repri'zentətiv], *a.* représentatif, qui représente.—*n.* représentant; (*Comm.*) (*fam. abbr.* ***rep***) agent, *m.*

repress [ri'pres], *v.t.* réprimer.

repression [ri'preʃən], *n.* répression, *f.*

repressive [ri'presiv], *a.* répressif.

reprieve [ri'pri:v], *n.* sursis; répit, *m.*—*v.t.* accorder un sursis à; commuer (*une peine*), grâcier.

reprimand ['reprimɑ:nd], *n.* réprimande, *f.*—[repri'mɑ:nd], *v.t.* réprimander.

reprint ['ri:print], *n.* réimpression, *f.*—[ri:'print], *v.t.* réimprimer.

reprisal [ri'praizl], *n.* représailles, *f.pl.*

reproach [ri'proutʃ], *n.* reproche; opprobre (*honte*), *m.*; ***above reproach***, irréprochable.—*v.t.* reprocher.

reprobate ['reprəbit], *n.* vaurien, *m.*

reprobation [reprə'beiʃən], *n.* réprobation, *f.*

reproduce [ri:prə'dju:s], *v.t.* reproduire.—*v.i.* se reproduire.

reproduction [ri:prə'dʌkʃən], *n.* reproduction, *f.*

reproductive [ri:prə'dʌktiv], *a.* reproducteur.

reproof [ri'pru:f], *n.* reproche, *m.*, réprimande, *f.*

reprove [ri'pru:v], *v.t.* blâmer; censurer.

reproving [ri'pru:viŋ], *a.* réprobateur.

reprovingly [ri'pru:viŋli], *adv.* d'un air *ou* ton réprobateur.

reptile ['reptail], *a.* reptile; (*fig.*) rampant, vil.—*n.* reptile, *m.*

reptilian [rep'tiliən], *a.* reptilien.

republic [ri'pʌblik], *n.* république, *f.*

republican [ri'pʌblikən], *a.* and *n.* républicain, *m.*

republication [ri:pʌbli'keiʃən], *n.* nouvelle edition, réimpression (*de livre*), *f.*

republish [ri:pʌbliʃ], *v.t.* republier, rééditer.

repudiate [ri'pju:dieit], *v.t.* répudier.

repudiation [ripju:di'eiʃən], *n.* répudiation, *f.*

repugnance [ri'pʌgnəns], *n.* répugnance, *f.*

repugnant [ri'pʌgnənt], *a.* répugnant.

repulse [ri'pʌls], *v.t.* repousser, rebuter.—*n.* échec, refus, *m.*, rebuffade, *f.*; ***to meet with a repulse***, essuyer un échec.

repulsion [ri'pʌlʃən], *n.* répulsion, *f.*

repulsive [ri'pʌlsiv], *a.* rebutant, repoussant (*forbidding*).

repulsiveness [ri'pʌlsivnis], *n.* caractère repoussant, *m.*

repurchase [ri:'pɔ:tʃis], *v.t.* racheter.—*n.* rachat; (*Law*) réméré, *m.*

reputable ['repjutəbl], *a.* honourable, de bonne réputation, considéré.

reputably ['repjutəbli], *adv.* honorablement.

reputation [repju'teiʃən], *n.* réputation, *f.*

repute [ri'pju:t], *v.t.* (*usu. pass.*) réputer, estimer.—*n.* réputation, *f.*, renom, *m.*

reputed [ri'pju:tid], *a.* réputé, censé, qui passe pour.

request [ri'kwest], *n.* demande, prière; (*Law*) requête, *f.*; ***request stop***, arrêt facultatif (*autobus*), *m.*—*v.t.* demander; prier.

requiem ['rekwiem], *n.* requiem, *m.*

require [ri'kwaiə], *v.t.* exiger, requérir; avoir besoin de (*manquer de*); (*impers.*) falloir.

requirement [ri'kwaiəmənt], *n.* exigence, nécessité, *f.*, besoin, *m.*; condition requise, *f.*

requisite ['rekwizit], *a.* requis, exigé, nécessaire.—*n.* qualité *ou* condition requise; chose requise, *f.*

requisition [rekwi'ziʃən], *n.* réquisition, *f.*—*v.t.* réquisitionner.

requital [ri'kwaitl], *n.* récompense, *f.*

requite [ri'kwait], *v.t.* récompenser; rendre la pareille à; payer de retour.

reredos ['riədɔs], *n.* retable, *m.*

rescind [ri'sind], *v.t.* rescinder, annuler.

rescue ['reskju:], *n.* délivrance, *f.*; sauvetage, *m.*; ***to the rescue***, au secours!—*v.t.* sauver, délivrer (*de*).

rescuer ['reskju:ə], *n.* sauveteur, libérateur, *m.*

research [ri'sə:tʃ], *n.* recherche, *f.*—*v.i.* faire des recherches.

reseat [riː'siːt], *v.t.* rasseoir.
resemblance [ri'zembləns], *n.* ressemblance, *f.*; (*fig.*) rapport, *m.*
resemble [ri'zembl], *v.t.* ressembler (*à*); ***to resemble each other***, se ressembler.
resent [ri'zent], *v.t.* ressentir, se ressentir de; s'offenser de; prendre en mauvaise part.
resentful [ri'zentful], *a.* rancunier.
resentfully [ri'zentfuli], *adv.* avec ressentiment.
resentment [ri'zentmənt], *n.* ressentiment, *m.*, rancœur, *f.*
reservation [rezə'veiʃən], *n.* réserve, restriction, arrière-pensée, *f.*; (*Am.*) terrain réservé, *m.*; réservation, location (*place assise*), *f.*
reserve [ri'zəːv], *n.* réserve; retenue, prudence; arrière-pensée, *f.*—*v.t.* réserver.
reserved [ri'zəːvd], *a.* réservé.
reservedly [ri'zəːvidli], *adv.* avec réserve.
reservist [ri'zəːvist], *n.* réserviste, *m.*, *f.*
reservoir ['rezəvwɑː], *n.* réservoir, *m.*
reset [riː'set], *v.t. irr.* (*conjug. like* SET) poser *ou* fixer de nouveau; (*Print.*) composer de nouveau; (*Surg.*) remettre.
resetting [riː'setiŋ], *n.* remontage (*de pierre précieuse*), *m.*; (*Print.*) recomposition, *f.*
resettle [riː'setl], *v.t.* rétablir.—*v.i.* s'établir de nouveau.
resettlement [riː'setlmənt], *n.* rétablissement, *m.*
reshape [riː'ʃeip], *v.t.* reformer; remanier.
reside [ri'zaid], *v.i.* résider, demeurer.
residence ['rezidəns], *n.* résidence, demeure, *f.*; ***board (and) residence***, la table et le logement.
resident ['rezidənt], *a.* résidant; interne (*de la maison*).—*n.* habitant; résident, *m.*
residential [rezi'denʃl], *a.* résidentiel.
residual [ri'zidjuəl], *a.* résiduel.
residuary [ri'zidjuəri], *a.* de résidu, de reste; universel (*légataire*).
residue ['rezidjuː], *n.* reste, (*Chem.*) résidu; reliquat (*de dette*), *m.*
resign [ri'zain], *v.t.* donner sa démission de; renoncer à; ***to be resigned to*** or ***resign oneself to***, se résigner à.—*v.i.* donner sa démission, démissionner (*de*).
resignation [rezig'neiʃən], *n.* résignation; cession; démission (*de ses fonctions*), *f.*
resigned [ri'zaind], *a.* résigné; démissionnaire (*d'un poste*).
resilience [ri'ziliəns], **resiliency** [ri'ziliənsi], *n.* rebondissement, *m.*; élasticité, *f.*
resilient [ri'ziliənt], *a.* rebondissant.
resin ['rezin], *n.* résine; colophane (*pour violons*), *f.*
resist [ri'zist], *v.t.* résister à.—*v.i.* résister.
resistance [ri'zistəns], *n.* résistance, *f.*
resistant [ri'zistənt], *a.* résistant.
re-sole [riː'soul], *v.t.* ressemeler.
resolute ['rezəljuːt], *a.* déterminé, résolu.
resolutely ['rezəljuːtli], *adv.* résolument.
resoluteness ['rezəljuːtnis], *n.* résolution, fermeté, *f.*
resolution [rezə'ljuːʃən], *n.* résolution; décision (*d'assemblée*), *f.*
resolve [ri'zɔlv], *n.* résolution, *f.*—*v.t.* résoudre; fondre (*liquéfier*); éclaircir, dissiper (*doutes etc.*); déterminer, décider (*assemblée*). —*v.i.* se résoudre, se décider; se fondre (*se dissoudre*).
resolved [ri'zɔlvd], *a.* résolu.
resolvent [ri'zɔlvənt], *n.* (*Med.*) résolvant, *m.*
resonance ['rezənəns], *n.* résonance, *f.*
resonant ['rezənənt], *a.* résonnant, sonore.
resort [ri'zɔːt], *n.* ressource, *f.*, recours, séjour, rendezvous (*endroit*); (*Law*) ressort, *m.*; ***seaside resort***, station balnéaire, plage, *f.*—*v.i.* recourir, avoir recours (*à*); se rendre, aller (*à*).
resound [ri'zaund], *v.i.* résonner, retentir.
resounding [ri'zaundiŋ], *a.* retentissant.—*n.* retentissement, *m.*
resource [ri'sɔːs], *n.* ressource, *f.*
resourceful [ri'sɔːsful], *a.* plein de ressources.
respect [ri'spekt], *n.* respect, *m.*, estime, *f.*; égard, *m.*; (*pl.*) respects, hommages, *m.pl.* ***in every respect***, sous tous les rapports; ***in respect of***, à l'égard de.—*v.t.* respecter, considérer, avoir égard à.
respectability [rispektə'biliti], *n.* honorabilité, *f*; convenances, *f.pl.*; bienséance, *f.*
respectable [ri'spektəbl], *a.* respectable, honorable; comme il faut, convenable.
respectably [ri'spektəbli], *adv.* comme il faut, très bien.
respectful [ri'spektful], *a.* respectueux.
respectfully [ri'spektfuli], *adv.* avec respect; ***yours respectfully*** (*à un supérieur hiérarchique*), veuillez agréer, Monsieur, l'assurance de mes sentiments respectueux.
respecting [ri'spektiŋ], *prep.* à l'égard de, quant à, touchant.
respective [ri'spektiv], *a.* respectif, relatif.
respectively [ri'spektivli], *adv.* respectivement.
respiration [respi'reiʃən], *n.* respiration, *f.*
respirator ['respireitə], *n.* respirateur, *m.*
respiratory ['respirətri], *a.* respiratoire.
respire [ri'spaiə], *v.t., v.i.* respirer.
respite ['respit] *n.* répit, relâche; (*Law*) sursis, *m.*
resplendence [ri'splendəns], *n.* éclat, *m.*, splendeur, *f.*
resplendent [ri'splendənt], *a.* resplendissant (*de*).
respond [ri'spɔnd], *v.i.* répondre (*à*).
respondent [ri'spɔndənt], *n.* répondant; (*Law*) défendeur, *m.*
response [ri'spɔns], *n.* réponse, *f.*; (*fig*). écho; (*Eccles.*) répons, *m.*
responsibility [rispɔnsi'biliti], *n.* responsabilité, *f.*
responsible [ri'spɔnsibl], *a.* chargé (*de*), responsable (*de*); digne de confiance.
responsive [ri'spɔnsiv], *a.* sensible, facile à émouvoir.
rest (1) [rest], *n.* repos, *m.*; (*Mus.*) pause, *f.*; appui (*soutien*), *m.*; ***at rest***, en repos.—*v.t.* reposer; faire reposer; (*fig.*) fonder.—*v.i.* se reposer; s'appuyer; ***it rests with me to . . .***, c'est à moi de . . .; ***to rest assured***, être assuré.
rest (2) [rest], *n.* reste, restant, *m.*; les autres, *m.pl.*—*v.i.* demeurer, rester.
restart [riː'stɑːt], *v.t., v.i.* recommencer.
restaurant ['restərɑ̃ː], *n.* restaurant, *m.*
restful ['restful], *a.* qui donne du repos, paisible.
resting ['restiŋ], *a.* couché, se reposant; appuyé, s'appuyant.—*n.* repos, *m.*
resting-place ['restiŋpleis], *n.* lieu de repos, gîte, *m.*

restitution [resti'tju:ʃən], *n.* restitution, *f.*
restive ['restiv], *a.* rétif; inquiet.
restiveness ['restivnis], *n.* naturel rétif, *m.*; nervosité, *f.*
restless ['restlis], *a.* sans repos; inquiet; agité.
restlessly ['restlisli], *adv.* sans repos.
restlessness ['restlisnis], *n.* agitation; insomnie, *f.*
restock [ri:'stɔk], *v.t.* repeupler (*chasse réservée*); regarnir (*boutique*), réassortir.
restoration [restə'reiʃən], *n.* restauration, *f.*; rétablissement, *m.*; restitution (*après une perte injuste*), *f.*
restorative [ri'stɔ:rətiv], *a.* and *n.* fortifiant, *m.*
restore [ri'stɔ:], *v.t.* restituer, rendre (*redonner*); ramener (*personne*); restaurer (*bâtiment etc.*); remettre (*replacer*); rétablir.
restorer [ri'stɔ:rə], *n.* restaurateur, *m.*
restrain [ri'strein], *v.t.* retenir, contenir; ***to restrain from,*** empêcher de; ***to restrain oneself,*** se contraindre, se contenir.
restraining [ri'streiniŋ], *a.* qui restreint, restrictif.
restraint [ri'streint], *n.* contrainte; gêne, *f.*
restrict [ri'strikt], *v.t.* restreindre.
restriction [ri'strikʃən], *n.* restriction, *f.*
restrictive [ri'striktiv], *a.* restrictif.
result [ri'zʌlt], *n.* résultat, *m.*; ***as a result of,*** par suite de.—*v.i.* résulter; ***to result in,*** aboutir à.
resultant [ri'zʌltənt], *a.* résultant.—*n.* résultante, *f.*
resume [ri'zju:m], *v.t.* reprendre, renouer, continuer.
resumption [ri'zʌmpʃən], *n.* reprise, *f.*
resurface [ri:'sə:fis], *v.t.* remettre en état (*route*).—*v.i.* remonter à la surface.
resurgence [ri:'sə:dʒəns], *n.* résurrection, *f.*
resurrect [rezə'rekt], *v.t.* ranimer, ressusciter.
resurrection [rezə'rekʃən], *n.* résurrection, *f.*
resuscitate [ri'sʌsiteit], *v.t.* ressusciter.
resuscitation [risʌsi'teiʃən], *n.* résurrection; renaissance (*des arts etc.*); (*Med.*) ressuscitation, *f.*
retail ['ri:teil], *a.* en détail; ***retail price,*** prix de détail *m.*—*n.* détail, *m.*, vente au détail, *f.* —[ri'teil], *v.t.* vendre en détail, détailler; (*fig.*) débiter; colporter (*nouvelles*).
retailer [ri'teilə], *n.* détaillant; colporteur (*de nouvelles*), *m.*
retain [ri'tein], *v.t.* retenir; engager (*en payant des arrhes*).
retainer [ri'teinə], *n.* serviteur, dépendant, *m.*; honoraires donnés d'avance (*acompte*), *m.pl.*
retaining [ri'teiniŋ], *a.* qui retient; ***retaining wall,*** mur de soutènement, *m.*
retake [ri:'teik], *v.t. irr.* (*conjug. like* TAKE) reprendre; (*Cine.*) retourner (*un plan*).
retaking [ri:'teikiŋ], *n.* reprise, *f.*
retaliate [ri'tælieit], *v.i.* rendre la pareille à.
retaliation [ritæli'eiʃən], *n.* représailles, *f.pl.*
retaliatory [ri'tæliətəri], *a.* de représailles.
retard [ri'tɑ:d], *v.t.* retarder.
retch [ri:tʃ], *v.i.* avoir des haut-le-cœur.
retching ['ri:tʃiŋ], *n.* haut-le-cœur, *m.*
retell [ri:'tel], *v.t. irr.* (*conjug. like* TELL) redire, répéter.
retention [ri'tenʃən], *n.* conservation; (*Med.*) rétention, *f.*
retentive [ri'tentiv], *a.* qui retient; tenace, fidèle (*la mémoire*).
retentiveness [ri'tentivnis], *n.* pouvoir de rétention, *m.*; fidélité (*de la mémoire*), *f.*
reticence ['retisəns], *n.* réticence, *f.*
reticent ['retisənt], *a.* réservé, taciturne.
reticular [re'tikjulə], *a.* réticulaire.
reticulate [re'tikjulit], *a.* réticulé.
retina ['retinə], *n.* rétine, *f.*
retinue ['retinju:], *n.* suite, *f.*; cortège, *m.*
retire [ri'taiə], *v.t.* retirer.—*v.i.* se retirer, prendre sa retraite.
retired [ri'taiəd], *a.* retiré, retraité (*qui a pris sa retraite*); ancien (*qui n'exerce plus cette profession*); ***on the retired list,*** en retraite.
retirement [ri'taiəmənt], *n.* retraite; (*fig.*) solitude, *f.*
retiring [ri'taiəriŋ], *a.* réservé, timide, modeste; sortant (*d'un emploi*).
retort (1) [ri'tɔ:t], *n.* réplique, riposte, *f.*—*v.i.* riposter, répliquer.
retort (2) [ri'tɔ:t], *n.* (*Chem.*) cornue, *f.*
retouch [ri:'tʌtʃ], *v.t.* retoucher.
retrace [ri'treis], *v.t.* (*Paint.*) retracer; ***to retrace one's steps,*** revenir sur ses pas, rebrousser chemin.
retract [ri'trækt], *v.t.* rétracter.—*v.i.* se rétracter, se dédire.
retractable [ri'træktəbl], *a.* (*Av.*) escamotable.
retransmit [ri:trɑ:ns'mit], *v.t.* retransmettre.
retread [ri:'tred], *v.t.* (*Motor.*) rechaper (*pneu*).—['ri:tred], *n.* pneu rechapé, *m.*
retreat [ri'tri:t], *n.* retraite, *f.*—*v.i.* se retirer (*à* ou *dans*); (*Mil.*) battre en retraite.
retreating [ri'tri:tiŋ], *a.* qui bat en retraite; fuyant (*le front*).
retrench [ri'trentʃ], *v.t.* retrancher.—*v.i.* se retrancher.
retrenchment [ri'trentʃmənt], *n.* retranchement, *m.*
retribution [retri'bju:ʃən], *n.* récompense, rétribution, *f.*; (*fig.*) châtiment, *m.*, vengeance, *f.*
retrievable [ri'tri:vəbl], *a.* recouvrable (*argent*); réparable (*perte*).
retrieve [ri'tri:v], *v.t.* rétablir; réparer (*chose brisée*); recouvrer (*chose perdue*); rapporter (*chien*).
retriever [ri'tri:və], *n.* chien rapporteur, *m.*
retroaction [ri:trou'ækʃən], *n.* rétroaction, *f.*
retroactive [ri:trou'æktiv], *a.* rétroactif.
retrograde ['retrogreid], *a.* rétrograde.
retrogression [retro'greʃən], *n.* rétrogression, rétrogradation, *f.*
retrogressive [retro'gresiv], *a.* rétrogressif.
retrospect ['retrospekt], *n.* regard jeté en arrière, *m.*; revue, *f.*; ***in retrospect,*** en rétrospective.
retrospective [retro'spektiv], *a.* rétrospectif; (*Law*) rétroactif.
retrospectively [retro'spektivli], *adv.* rétrospectivement; (*Law*) rétroactivement.
retroversion [retro'və:ʃən], *n.* renversement, *m.*
retrovert [retro'və:t], *v.t.* renverser.
return [ri'tə:n], *v.t.* rendre; renvoyer; rembourser (*argent etc.*); rapporter (*intérêt*); (*Comm.*) rendre compte; élire (*candidat*); ***he was returned,*** il fut élu.—*v.i.* revenir; retourner; rentrer.—*n.* retour, *m.*; rentrée, *f.*; renvoi, *m.*; remise en place (*chose déplacée*), *f.*; profit, *m.*; restitution, *f.*; remboursement,

m.; élection, *f.*; rapport, relevé, état (*impôts etc.*); bilan (*de banque*); (*pl.*) produit, *m.*; ***by return of post***, par retour du courrier; ***in return for***, en retour de; ***nil return***, état néant; ***on sale or return***, en dépôt; ***return journey***, retour; ***return match***, revanche, *f.*; ***return ticket***, billet d'aller et retour, *m.*
returnable [ri'tə:nəbl], *a.* restituable.
reunion [ri:'ju:niən], *n.* réunion, *f.*
reunite [ri:ju'nait], *v.t.* réunir.—*v.i.* se réunir.
rev [rev], *n.* (*colloq., Motor.*) tour, *m.*—*v.t.* ***to rev the engine***, faire s'emballer le moteur. —*v.i.* s'emballer.
reveal [ri'vi:l], *v.t.* révéler.
reveille [ri'væli], *n.* réveil, *m.*
revel [revl], *n.* (*pl.*) divertissements, *m.pl.*—*v.i.* se réjouir, se divertir; ***to revel in***, se délecter à.
revelation [revə'leiʃən], *n.* révélation, *f.*; ***Book of Revelation***, Apocalypse, *f.*
reveller ['revələ], *n.* joyeux convive, *m.*
revelry ['revəlri], *n.* réjouissances, *f.pl.*, joyeux ébats, *m.pl.*
revenge [ri'vendʒ], *n.* vengeance; (*Spt.*) revanche, *f.*—*v.t.* venger; se venger de; ***to revenge oneself on***, se venger de.
revengeful [ri'vendʒful], *a.* vindicatif.
revengefully [ri'vendʒfuli], *adv.* par vengeance.
revenue ['revənju:], *n.* revenu; (*State*) fisc, trésor, *m.*; ***revenue-officer***, officier de la douane, *m.*
reverberate [ri'və:bəreit], *v.t.* réverbérer; renvoyer (*son, chaleur etc.*).—*v.i.* se répercuter.
reverberation [rivə:bə'reiʃən], *n.* réverbération (*de chaleur*); répercussion, *f.*
revere [ri'viə], *v.t.* révérer, vénérer.
reverence ['revərəns], *n.* révérence, *f.*
reverend ['revərənd], *a.* révérend (*titre ecclésiastique*).
reverent ['revərənt], *a.* révérencieux.
reverently ['revərəntli], *adv.* avec révérence.
reverie ['revəri], *n.* rêverie, *f.*
reversal [ri'və:sl], *n.* annulation; cassation, *f.*
reverse [ri'və:s], *a.* contraire, opposé.—*n.* revers, *m.*; défaite, *f.*; ***quite the reverse***, tout le contraire (*de*); ***the reverse way***, en sens inverse.—*v.t.* renverser; appliquer en sens inverse; (*Law*) infirmer, casser.—*v.i.* (*Motor.*) faire marche *ou* machine en arrière.
reversed [ri'və:st], *a.* renversé; inverse.
reversible [ri'və:sibl], *a.* révocable, réversible, à double face (*tissu*).
reversion [ri'və:ʃən], *n.* réversion, *f.*
revert [ri'və:t], *v.i.* revenir (*sur*).
revertible [ri'və:tibl], *a.* réversible.
revetment [ri'vetmənt], *n.* revêtement, *m.*
revictual [ri:'vitl], *v.t.* ravitailler.
revictualling [ri:'vitliŋ], *n.* ravitaillement, *m.*
review [ri'vju:], *n.* revue, revision; critique; revue, *f.*, périodique, *m.*—*v.t.* revoir, reviser; passer en revue; analyser, critiquer (*livre etc.*).
reviewer [ri'vju:ə], *n.* critique, *m.*, *f.*
revile [ri'vail], *v.t.* injurier, insulter, outrager.
revilement [ri'vailmənt], *n.* injure, insulte, *f.*
reviling [ri'vailiŋ], *a.* diffamatoire, outrageant. —*n.* insultes, injures, *f.pl.*
revisal [ri'vaizl], *n.* revision, *f.*
revise [ri'vaiz], *v.t.* revoir, reviser, réviser.
reviser [ri'vaizə], *n.* personne qui revoit, *f.*, reviseur, *m.*
revision [ri'viʒən], *n.* revision, révision, *f.*
revisit [ri:'vizit], *v.t.* revisiter, retourner voir.
revitalize [ri:'vaitəlaiz], *v.t.* revivifier.
revival [ri'vaivl], *n.* rétablissement, *m.*; renaissance (*des arts*); reprise (*d'une pièce*), *f.*; réveil (*religieux*), *m.*
revive [ri'vaiv], *v.t.* ressusciter; raviver.—*v.i.* se ranimer; renaître (*arts etc.*).
revivify [ri'vivifai], *v.t.* revivifier.
revocable ['revəkəbl], *a.* révocable.
revocation [revə'keiʃən], *n.* révocation, *f.*
revoke [ri'vouk], *v.t.* révoquer.—*v.i.* (*Cards*) renoncer.—*n.* (*Cards*) renonce, *f.*
revolt [ri'voult], *n.* révolte, *f.*—*v.i.* se révolter, se soulever.
revolting [ri'voultiŋ], *a.* révoltant.
revolution [revə'lju:ʃən], *n.* révolution, *f.*; tour (*de roue*), *m.*
revolutionary [revə'lju:ʃənəri], *a.* and *n.* révolutionnaire, *m.*, *f.*
revolve [ri'vɔlv], *v.t.* tourner; retourner, repasser, rouler (*dans l'esprit*).—*v.i.* tourner; (*fig.*) retourner, revenir.
revolver [ri'vɔlvə], *n.* revolver, *m.*
revolving [ri'vɔlviŋ], *a.* tournant.
revue [ri'vju:], *n.* (*Theat.*) revue, *f.*
revulsion [ri'vʌlʃən], *n.* révulsion, *f.*
reward [ri'wɔ:d], *n.* récompense, *f.*; prix, *m.* —*v.t.* récompenser (*de*).
rewind [ri:'waind], *v.t. irr.* (*conjug. like* WIND) rebobiner (*soie etc.*); remonter (*montre, horloge*); rembobiner (*film*).
rewrite [ri:'rait], *v.t. irr.* (*conjug. like* WRITE) récrire.
rhapsody ['ræpsədi], *n.* rapsodie, *f.*
Rheims [ri:mz]. Reims, *m.*
Rhenish ['reniʃ], *a.* du Rhin.—*n.* vin du Rhin, *m.*
rheostat ['ri:ostæt], *n.* rhéostat, *m.*
rhesus ['ri:səs], *a.* (*Med.*) rhésus.
rhetoric ['retərik], *n.* rhétorique, *f.*
rhetorical [ri'tɔrikl], *a.* de rhétorique; ***rhetorical question***, question de pure forme, *f.*
rheum [ru:m], *n.* rhume, catarrhe, *m.*
rheumatic [ru:'mætik], *a.* rhumatismal; ***rheumatic fever***, rhumatisme articulaire aigu, *m.*
rheumatism ['ru:mətizm], *n.* rhumatisme, *m.*
rheumatoid ['ru:mətɔid], *a.* rhumatoïde; ***rheumatoid arthritis***, rhumatisme articulaire, *m.*
Rhine [rain], **the**. le Rhin, *m.*
Rhineland ['rainlænd]. la Rhénanie, *f.*
Rhinelander ['rainlændə], *n.* Rhénan, *m.*
rhinoceros [rai'nɔsərəs], *n.* rhinocéros, *m.*
Rhodesia [rou'di:ziə]. la Rhodésie, *f.*
Rhodesian [rou'di:ziən], *a.* rhodésien.—*n.* Rhodésien (*personne*), *m.*
rhododendron [roudə'dendrən], *n.* rhododendron, *m.*
rhombus ['rɔmbəs], *n.* losange, *m.*
Rhone [roun]. le Rhône, *m.*
rhubarb ['ru:bɑ:b], *n.* rhubarbe, *f.*
rhyme [raim], *n.* rime, *f.*; (*pl.*) vers, *m.pl.*—*v.t., v.i.* rimer; rimailler.
rhythm [riðm], *n.* rythme, *m.*; cadence, *f.*
rhythmical ['riðmikl], *a.* rythmique.
rhythmically ['riðmikli], *adv.* avec rythme.
rib [rib], *n.* côte; baleine (*de parapluie*), *f.*

ribald ['ribəld], *a.* grossier, obscène.

ribaldry ['ribəldri], *n.* obscénités, *f.pl.*

ribbed [ribd], *a.* à côtes.

ribbon ['ribən], *n.* ruban; cordon (*de médaille*); lambeau (*morceau de tissu déchiré*), *m.*

rice [rais], *n.* riz, *m.*; ***rice-field***, rizière, *f.*

rich [ritʃ], *a.* riche; fertile, fécond (*terre*); de haut goût (*fort assaisonné*); voyant (*couleur*); (*fig.*) délicieux, généreux (*vin*); ***the rich***, les riches, *m.pl.*; ***to grow rich***, s'enrichir.

riches ['ritʃiz], *n.pl.* richesse, *f.*

richly ['ritʃli], *adv.* richement; grandement; (*fam.*) joliment.

richness ['ritʃnis], *n.* richesse; fécondité, *f.*; haut goût, *m.*

rick [rik], *n.* meule, *f.*

rickets ['rikits], *n.pl.* rachitis, rachitisme, *m.*

rickety ['rikiti], *a.* (*fig.*) boiteux (*meuble*).

rickshaw ['rikʃɔː], *n.* pousse-pousse, *m.*

ricochet ['rikəʃei], *n.* ricochet, *m.*—*v.i.* ricocher.

rid [rid], *v.t. irr.* délivrer, débarrasser; ***to get rid of***, se débarrasser de.

riddance ['ridəns], *n.* débarras, *m.*

riddle (1) [ridl], *n.* énigme, *f.*

riddle (2) [ridl], *v.t.* cribler.—*n.* crible, *m.*

ride [raid], *v.t. irr.* monter, être monté sur; mener, conduire; faire (*une distance précise*). —*v.i.* monter (*à cheval, à bicyclette etc.*), aller, venir, être *ou* se promener (*à cheval, à bicyclette, en voiture etc.*); être monté (*sur*); flotter, voguer (*sur*); être (à l'ancre); ***to ride away***, partir, s'en aller; ***to ride back***, revenir, s'en retourner.—*n.* promenade, course (*à cheval, en voiture, à bicyclette etc.*), *f.*; trajet, *m.*; allée cavalière (*sentier dans un bois etc.*), *f.*

rider ['raidə], *n.* cavalier, *m.*, cavalière, *f.*; écuyer, *m.*, écuyère (*de cirque*), *f.*; jockey; codicille (*document*), *m.*

riderless ['raidəlis], *a.* sans cavalier.

ridge [ridʒ], *n.* sommet (*pic*), *m.*, cime; chaîne (*de montagnes*); arête, crête (*d'une montagne*) *f.*; faîte (*de toit*); (*Agric.*) sillon, billon, *m.*—*v.t.* sillonner.

ridicule ['ridikjuːl], *n.* ridicule, *m.*—*v.t.* tourner en ridicule, ridiculiser.

ridiculous [ri'dikjuləs], *a.* ridicule.

ridiculously [ri'dikjuləsli], *adv.* ridiculement.

riding (1) ['raidiŋ], *n.* promenade à cheval, *f.*, exercice à cheval, *m.*, équitation, *f.*; (*Naut.*) mouillage, *m.*

riding (2) ['raidiŋ], *n.* (*Yorkshire*) arrondissement, *m.*

riding-habit ['raidiŋhæbit], *n.* amazone, *f.*

riding-hood ['raidiŋhud], *n.* capuchon, *m.*; ***Little Red RidingHood***, le petit Chaperon rouge.

rife [raif], *a.* abondant, répandu; ***to be rife***, régner (*tumulte etc.*), courir (*bruit*).

riff-raff ['rifræf], *n.* racaille, canaille, *f.*

rifle (1) [raifl], *v.t.* piller, dévaliser.

rifle (2) [raifl], *v.t.* rayer (*armes à feu*).—*n.* fusil (rayé), *m.*, carabine, *f.*; ***rifle-gallery*** or ***-range***, tir, *m.*; ***rifle-practice*** or ***-shooting***, tir au fusil, tir à la carabine, *m.*; ***rifle-shot***, coup de fusil, *m.*

rifleman ['raiflmən], *n.* (*pl.* **-men** [men]) carabinier, *m.*

rifling (1) ['raifliŋ], *n.* pillage.

rifling (2) ['raifliŋ], *n.* rayage (*de fusils*), *m.*

rift [rift], *n.* fente; éclaircie (*aux nuages*), *f.*

rig [rig], *n.* gréement; accoutrement (*vêtements*), *m.*—*v.t.* équiper, gréer; (*fig.*) accoutrer, attifer.

rigged [rigd], *a.* gréé.

rigging ['rigiŋ], *n.* gréement, *m.*, agrès, *m.pl.*

right [rait], *a.* droit; direct, en ligne droite; vrai, véritable; bon, propre, convenable; juste, correct; en règle; ***all right!*** c'est bien! ***that is right***, c'est cela; ***the right man***, l'homme qu'il faut; ***the right road***, le bon chemin; ***to be right***, avoir raison; être juste (*compte*); ***to put right***, mettre en bon ordre, arranger.—*adv.* droit, tout droit; justement (*avec justice*); comme il faut, bien (*correctement*); tout à fait (*entièrement*); fort (*beaucoup*); très.—*n.* droit, *m.*, justice, raison, *f.*; côté droit, *m.*, droite, *f.*; ***on*** or ***to the right***, à droite; ***right of way***, droit de passage; ***to put*** or ***set to rights***, arranger, mettre en ordre.—*v.t.* redresser, corriger (*choses*).—*v.i.* se redresser se relever.

righteous ['raitʃəs], *a.* juste, droit.

righteously ['raitʃəsli], *adv.* justement.

righteousness ['raitʃəsnis], *n.* droiture, vertu, *f.*

rightful ['raitful], *a.* légitime, véritable.

right-handed ['raithændid], *a.* droitier.

rightly ['raitli], *adv.* bien; à juste titre; comme il faut (*convenablement*); juste (*exactement*).

rightness ['raitnis], *n.* rectitude; droiture; justesse, *f.*

rigid ['ridʒid], *a.* rigide, raide.

rigidity [ri'dʒiditi], *n.* rigidité; raideur, *f.*

rigidly ['ridʒidli], *adv.* rigidement; avec raideur.

rigmarole ['rigməroul], *n.* galimatias, *m.*

rigor ['rigə, 'raigə], *n.* (*Path.*) rigidité, *f.*

rigorous ['rigərəs], *a.* rigoureux.

rigorously ['rigərəsli], *adv.* rigoureusement, avec rigueur, à la rigueur.

rigour ['rigə], *n.* rigueur, *f.*

rile [rail], *v.t.* (*colloq.*) faire enrager, agacer.

rill [ril], *n.* petit ruisseau, *m.*

rim [rim], *n.* bord, rebord, *m.*; jante (*de roue*), *f.*

rime [raim], *n.* givre, *m.*; gelée blanche, *f.*

rimless ['rimlis], *a.* sans monture (*lunettes*).

rind [raind], *n.* écorce, peau, pelure; croûte (*de fromage*); couenne (*de lard*), *f.*

ring (1) [riŋ], *n.* anneau, *m.*, bague (*pour le doigt etc.*), *f.*; cercle, rond, *m.*; arène (*pour se battre*), *f.*; ring (*pour la boxe*), *m.*; (*fig.*) bande, clique, *f.*; (*Comm.*) syndicat, *m.*—*v.t.* mettre un anneau à; entourer.

ring (2) [riŋ], *v.t. irr.* sonner, faire sonner; ***to ring someone up***, téléphoner à quelqu'un. —*v.i.* sonner; retentir (*de*), tinter (*aux oreilles*).—*n.* son, tintement, coup de sonnette, *m.*; sonnerie, *f.*; ***there's a ring at the door***, on sonne.

ring-dove ['riŋdʌv], *n.* pigeon ramier, *m.*

ringer ['riŋə], *n.* sonneur, *m.*

ringing ['riŋiŋ], *n.* son (*de cloche*), *m.*; sonnerie, *f.*, tintement, retentissement, *m.*

ringleader ['riŋliːdə], *n.* meneur, chef de bande, *m.*

ringlet ['riŋlit], *n.* boucle (*de cheveux*), *f.*

ring-road ['riŋroud], *n.* route de ceinture, *f.*

ringworm ['riŋwəːm], *n.* herpès tonsurant, *m.*

rink [riŋk], *n.* patinoire (*de glace*), *f.*; skating (*pour patinage à roulettes*), *m.*
rinse [rins], *v.t.* rincer.
riot ['raiət], *n.* émeute, *f.*; vacarme, tumulte (*bruit*), *m.*; (*fig.*) festins, *m.pl.*—*v.i.* faire une émeute.
rioter ['raiətə], *n.* émeutier; tapageur, *m.*
riotous ['raiətəs], *a.* séditieux, tumultueux.
rip (1) [rip], *v.t.* fendre, déchirer; ***to rip open***, ouvrir.—*n.* déchirure, *f.*
rip (2) [rip], *n.* (*slang*) vaurien, polisson, *m.*
ripe [raip], *a.* mûr.
ripen ['raipən], *v.t.* mûrir, faire mûrir.—*v.i.* mûrir, venir à maturité.
ripeness ['raipnis], *n.* maturité, *f.*
ripening ['raipniŋ], *n.* maturation, *f.*
ripple [ripl], *v.t.* rider.—*v.i.* se rider; onduler. —*n.* ride (*d'eau*), *f.*
rippling ['ripliŋ], *n.* clapotis, murmure, *m.*
rip-roaring ['riprɔ:riŋ], *a.* tumultueux; robuste; épatant.
rise [raiz], *v.i. irr.* se lever, se relever (*après une chute, un malheur etc.*); s'élever, monter; se dresser (*montagne etc.*); s'augmenter, hausser (*prix*); aller en montant (*rue*); se soulever (*rébellion*); ressusciter (*les morts*); prendre sa source (*en* ou *dans*).—*n.* lever, *m.*; montée (*de colline etc.*); crue (*des eaux*); hausse (*de prix*), augmentation; source, origine, *f.*
riser ['raizə], *n.* marche (*d'escalier*), *f.*; ***early riser***, personne matinale, *f.*
risible ['rizibl], *a.* rieur.
rising ['raiziŋ], *a.* levant; montant (*marée*); (*fig.*) naissant; qui a de l'avenir (*qui promet*). —*n.* lever (*du lit, du soleil*), *m.*; montée (*de colline*); crue (*des eaux*); clôture (*d'assemblée*); résurrection, *f.*; soulèvement, *m.*, insurrection, *f.*
risk [risk], *n.* risque, *m.*—*v.t.* risquer.
risky ['riski], *a.* risqué, hasardeux.
rite [rait], *n.* rite, *m.*, cérémonie, *f.*
ritual ['ritjuəl], *a.* du rite.—*n.* rituel, *m.*
rival [raivl], *a.* and *n.* rival, *m.*—*v.t.* rivaliser avec.
rivalry ['raivlri], *n.* rivalité, *f.*
rive [raiv], *v.t. irr.* fendre.—*v.i.* se fendre.
river ['rivə], *a.* de rivière, fluvial.—*n.* fleuve (*qui débouche dans la mer*), *m.*; (*autrement*) rivière, *f.*; ***down the river***, en aval; ***up the river***, en amont.
riverside ['rivəsaid], *a.* au bord de l'eau.—*n.* bord de l'eau, *m.*
rivet ['rivit], *n.* rivet, *m.*; attache (*de porcelaine*), *f.*—*v.t.* river, riveter; (*fig.*) fixer.
riveting ['rivitiŋ], *n.* rivetage, *m.*
rivulet ['rivjulit], *n.* ruisseau, *m.*
roach [routʃ], *n.* (*Ichth.*) gardon, *m.*
road [roud], *n.* route, *f.*, chemin, *m.*; chaussée; rue (*en ville*); (*Naut.*) rade, *f.*; ***by-road***, chemin détourné; ***carriage-road***, route carrossable; ***cross-roads***, carrefour, *m.*; ***high road***, grand-route, *f.*; ***roads and bridges***, ponts et chaussées, *m.pl.*
road-hog ['roudhɔg], *n.* (*Motor.*) chauffard, *m.*
road-house ['roudhaus], *n.* auberge, hôtellerie, *f.*
road-map ['roudmæp], *n.* carte routière, *f.*
road-mender ['roudmendə], *n.* cantonnier, *m.*
road-metal ['roudmetl], *n.* cailloutis, empierrement, *m.*
roadside ['roudsaid], *n.* bord de la route, *m.*; ***by the roadside***, au bord de la route.
roadstead ['roudsted], *n.* rade, *f.*
roadway ['roudwei], *n.* chaussée; voie (*de pont*), *f.*
roadworthy ['roudwə:ði], *a.* (*Motor.*) en état de marche.
roam [roum], *v.t.* rôder dans *ou* parmi.—*v.i.* errer, rôder.
roan [roun], *a.* rouan.
roar [rɔ:], *n.* rugissement (*de lion etc.*); mugissement (*de la mer etc.*); éclat (*de rire*); grondement (*de tonnerre etc.*), *m.*—*v.i.* rugir (*lion etc.*); mugir (*mer etc.*); gronder (*tonnerre, canon etc.*); (*colloq.*) vociférer; ***to roar with laughter***, rire aux éclats.
roaring ['rɔ:riŋ], *a.* rugissant, mugissant; ***to do a roaring trade***, faire des affaires d'or.
roast [roust], *v.t.* rôtir; faire rôtir; torréfier (*café*); (*Metal.*) griller.—*v.i.* rôtir; griller. —*a.* rôti; ***roast beef***, rosbif, *m.*; ***roast pork***, rôti de porc, *m.*
roaster ['roustə], *n.* rôtisseur (*personne*), *m.*; rôtissoire (*chose*), *f.*
roasting ['roustiŋ], *a.* brûlant.—*n.* (*Metal.*) grillage, *m.*; torréfaction (*de café*), *f.*
rob [rɔb], *v.t.* voler; piller; priver (*de*).
robber ['rɔbə], *n.* voleur, *m.*
robbery ['rɔbəri], *n.* vol, *m.*
robe [roub], *n.* robe, *f.*—*v.t.* vêtir (d'une robe); revêtir (*de*).
robin ['rɔbin], **robin-redbreast** [rɔbin'redbrest], *n.* (*Orn.*) rouge-gorge, *m.*
robot ['roubɔt], *n.* automate, robot, *m.*
robust [ro'bʌst], *a.* robuste, vigoureux.
robustness [ro'bʌstnis], *n.* robustesse, vigueur, *f.*
rock (1) [rɔk], *n.* rocher, roc, *m.*; (*Geol.*) roche, *f.*; sucre d'orge (*bonbon*), *m.*
rock (2) [rɔk], *v.t.* balancer; bercer, remuer.—*v.i.* se balancer; branler, trembler.
rockery ['rɔkəri], *n.* jardin de rocaille, *m.*
rocket ['rɔkit], *n.* fusée, *f.*; ***rocket-launcher***, lance-fusée, *m.*—*v.i.* monter en flèche (*prix*).
rockiness ['rɔkinis], *n.* nature rocailleuse, *f.*
rocking ['rɔkiŋ], *n.* balancement; bercement, *m.*
rocking-chair ['rɔkiŋtʃɛə], *n.* chaise à bascule, *f.*
rocking-horse ['rɔkiŋhɔ:s], *n.* cheval à bascule, *m.*
rock-salt ['rɔksɔ:lt], *n.* sel gemme, *m.*
rocky ['rɔki], *a.* rocailleux, rocheux.
rod [rɔd], *n.* verge; baguette; tringle (*à rideaux etc.*); canne à pêche; perche (= *5·0291 metres*); bielle (*de piston*), *f.*
rodent ['roudənt], *n.* (*Zool.*) rongeur, *m.*
rodeo [ro'deiou], *n.* rodéo, *m.*
roe (1) [rou], *n.* œufs (de poisson), *m.pl.*
roe (2) [rou], *n.* chevreuil, *m.*, chevrette, *f.*
roebuck ['roubʌk], *n.* chevreuil, *m.*
Roger ['rɔdʒə]. Roger, *m.*
rogue [roug], *n.* coquin, fripon, fourbe, *m.*
roguery ['rougəri], *n.* coquinerie, friponnerie, fourberie, *f.*
roguish ['rougiʃ], *a.* coquin, fripon; (*facet.*) espiègle.
roguishly ['rougiʃli], *adv.* en fripon, en fourbe; (*facet.*) avec espièglerie.

roister [ˈrɔistə], *v.i.* faire du tapage.
roisterer [ˈrɔistərə], *n.* tapageur, *m.*
roistering [ˈrɔistəriŋ], *a.* tapageur, bruyant. —*n.* tapage, *m.*
role [roul], *n.* rôle, *m.*
roll [roul], *n.* rouleau; roulement (*acte de rouler quelque chose*); roulis (*de navire*); petit pain; roulement (*de tambour*); rôle (*liste*), *m.*; (*pl.*) rôles, *m.pl.*; annales, archives, *f.pl.*—*v.t.* rouler; passer au rouleau (*gazon, gravier etc.*); (*Metal.*) laminer.—*v.i.* rouler, se rouler; tourner; (*Naut.*) avoir du roulis.
roll-call [ˈroulkɔːl], *n.* appel, *m.*
roller [ˈroulə], *n.* rouleau; cylindre, *m.*
roller-skate [ˈrouləskeit], *n.* patin à roulettes, *m.*
rollicking [ˈrɔlikiŋ], *a.* folâtre, joyeux.
rolling [ˈrouliŋ], *n.* roulement; roulis (*de navire*); (*Metal.*) laminage, *m.*; ***rolling stock***, matériel roulant, *m.*
rolling-pin [ˈrouliŋpin], *n.* rouleau, *m.*
Roman [ˈroumən], *a.* romain; aquilin (*nez*).—*n.* Romain (*personne*), *m.*
Romance [roˈmæns], *a.* roman; ***Romance languages***, langues romanes, *f.pl.*
romance [roˈmæns], *n.* roman de chevalerie, *m.*; histoire romanesque; (*Mus.*) romance; (*fam.*) amourette, aventure, *f.*—*v.i.* inventer à plaisir, exagérer, broder.
romanesque [rouməˈnesk], *a.* (*Arch.*) roman.
Romania [roˈmeiniə], [RUMANIA].
romantic [roˈmæntik], *a.* romanesque; romantique (*paysage, style etc.*).
romanticism [roˈmæntisizm], *n.* romantisme, *m.*
romanticist [roˈmæntisist], *n.* romantique, *m., f.*
Rome [roum]. Rome, *f.*
romp [rɔmp], *n.* gamine, garçonnière (*jeune fille*), *f.*; jeu violent, tapage, *m.*—*v.i.* jouer rudement, folâtrer.
rompers [ˈrɔmpəz], *n.pl.* barboteuse, *f.*
romping [ˈrɔmpiŋ], *n.* jeux rudes, *m.pl.*
roof [ruːf], *n.* toit; palais (*de la bouche*), *m.*—*v.t.* couvrir d'un toit; couvrir.
roofing [ˈruːfiŋ], *n.* toiture, *f.*
roof-rack [ˈruːfræk], *n.* (*Motor.*) galerie, *f.*
rook (1) [ruk], *n.* freux, *m.*, (*pop.*) corneille, *f.*; (*slang*) tricheur, *m.*—*v.t.*, *v.i.* (*slang*) friponner, filouter.
rook (2) [ruk], *n.* (*Chess*) tour, *f.*
rookery [ˈrukəri], *n.* colonie de freux, *f.*
rookie [ˈruki], *n.* (*Mil. slang*) bleu, *m.*
room [ruːm], *n.* place, *f.*, espace, *m.*; chambre, salle, pièce (*d'appartement*), *f.*
roomful [ˈruːmful], *n.* chambrée, *f.*
roominess [ˈruːminis], *n.* nature spacieuse, grandeur, *f.*
roomy [ˈruːmi], *a.* spacieux, vaste.
roost [ruːst], *n.* juchoir, perchoir, *m.*—*v.i.* se jucher.
rooster [ˈruːstə], *n.* coq, *m.*
root [ruːt], *n.* racine; (*fig.*) source, *f.*—*v.t.* ***to root out***, déraciner, extirper.
rooted [ˈruːtid], *a.* enraciné; (*fig.*) invétéré.
rooting [ˈruːtiŋ], *n.* enracinement, *m.*; ***rooting out***, arrachement, *m.*, extirpation, *f.*
rope [roup], *n.* corde, *f.*; (*Naut.*) cordage, *m.*; (*Mount.*) cordée, *f.*; ***a piece of rope***, un bout de filin.—*v.t.* attacher avec une corde; lier.—*v.i.* filer (*vin etc.*); (*Mount.*) s'encorder.
rope-walker [ˈroupwɔːkə], *n.* funambule, *m., f.*
ropiness [ˈroupinis], *n.* viscosité, *f.*
ropy [ˈroupi], *a.* qui file, filant, visqueux.
rosary [ˈrouzəri], *n.* chapelet, *m.*
rose (1) [rouz], *n.* rose; (*Tech.*) pomme d'arrosoir; (*Arch.*) rosace, *f.*
rose (2) [rouz], *past* [RISE].
roseate [ˈrouziit], *a.* rosé.
rose-bed [ˈrouzbed], *n.* massif de rosiers, *m.*
rosebud [ˈrouzbʌd], *n.* bouton de rose, *m.*
rose-bush [ˈrouzbuʃ], *n.* rosier, *m.*
rose-garden [ˈrouzgɑːdn], *n.* roseraie, *f.*
rosemary [ˈrouzməri], *n.* romarin, *m.*
rosette [roˈzet], *n.* rosette, *f.*
rose-window [ˈrouzwindou], *n.* rosace, *f.*
rosin [ˈrɔzin], *n.* colophane, *f.*
rosiness [ˈrouzinis], *n.* couleur rose, *f.*
rostrum [ˈrɔstrəm], *n.* (*Rom. Hist.*) rostres, *m.pl.*; tribune (*estrade*), *f.*
rosy [ˈrouzi], *a.* de rose, rose, rosé, vermeil.
rot [rɔt], *n.* pourriture; (*colloq.*) blague, *f.*—*v.t.* pourrir, faire pourrir; carier (*dent*).—*v.i.* pourrir, se pourrir; se carier (*dent*).
rota [ˈroutə], *n.* ***by rota***, à tour de rôle.
rotary [ˈroutəri], *a.* rotatif, rotatoire.
rotate [roˈteit], *v.t.*, *v.i.* tourner.
rotation [roˈteiʃən], *n.* rotation, succession, *f.*; ***rotation of crops***, assolement, *m.*
rote [rout], *n.* routine, *f.*; ***by rote***, par cœur.
rotten [rɔtn], *a.* pourri; carié (*dent*); gâté (*œuf*).
rottenness [ˈrɔtnnis], *n.* pourriture; carie (*des dents*), *f.*
rotter [ˈrɔtə], *n.* (*fam.*) sale type, *m.*
rotting [ˈrɔtiŋ], *a.* qui pourrit; qui se carie.—*n.* putréfaction, *f.*
rotund [roˈtʌnd], *a.* rond, arrondi.
rotundity [roˈtʌnditi], *n.* rondeur, rotondité, *f.*
rouble [ruːbl], *n.* rouble, *m.*
rouge [ruːʒ], *n.* rouge, fard, *m.*
rough [rʌf], *a.* rude; hérissé; raboteux (*chemin*); grosse, houleuse (*mer*); orageux (*temps*); âpre (*goût*); dépoli (*verre*); grossier (*manières*); approximatif (*pas exact*); ***rough-and-ready***, fait à la va-vite; ***rough copy*** or ***draft***, brouillon, *m.*; ***rough estimate***, appréciation en gros, *f.*—*adv.* brutalement, rudement.—*n.* voyou, polisson, *m.*; ***rough-and-tumble***, mêlée, bousculade, *f.*
roughcast [ˈrʌfkɑːst], *v.t.* ébaucher; (*Build.*) crépir.—*n.* ébauche, *f.*; (*Build.*) crépi, *m.*
roughen [rʌfn], *v.t.* rendre rude.
rough-hewn [ˈrʌfhjuːn], *a.* ébauché.
rough-house [ˈrʌfhaus], *n.* (*fam.*) chahut, *m.*
roughly [ˈrʌfli], *adv.* rudement; grossièrement; à peu près.
roughness [ˈrʌfnis], *n.* aspérité, rudesse; apreté (*au goût*); agitation (*de la mer*); grossièreté (*de manières*), *f.*; mauvais état (*de rue*), *m.*
round [raund], *a.* rond; circulaire; en rond.—*adv.* en rond; à la ronde; tout autour, à l'entour; ***to go round***, faire le tour de.—*prep.* autour de.—*n.* rond, cercle; tour (*petite promenade*), *m.*; rouelle (*de bœuf etc.*); salve (*d'applaudissements*), *f.*; (*Artill.*) coup de canon, *m.*; ronde (*de veilleurs, police etc.*); (*Golf*) tournée, *f.*; (*Box.*) round, *m.*; ***round***

of ammunition, cartouche, *f.*—*v.t.* arrondir; entourer, faire le tour de (*faire un cercle*); doubler (*cap*); ***to round off***, arrondir, finir, compléter; ***to round up***, rassembler (*bestiaux etc.*); faire une rafle.—*v.i.* s'arrondir.

roundabout ['raundəbaut], *a.* détourné; indirect.—*n.* manège; (*Motor.*) rondpoint, *m.*

rounded ['raundid], *a.* arrondi.

***roundelay** ['raundəlei], *n.* rondeau, *m.*

rounders ['raundəz], *n.pl.* balle au camp, *f.*

roundish ['raundiʃ], *a.* arrondi; rondelet (*personne*).

roundly ['raundli], *adv.* en rond; (*fig.*) rondement.

roundness ['raundnis], *n.* rondeur; (*fig.*) franchise, *f.*

roundsman ['raundzmən], *n.* (*pl.* **-men** [men]); (*Comm.*) livreur, *m.*

round-up ['raundʌp], *n.* rassemblement (*de bétail*), *m.*; rafle (*de criminels*), *f.*

roup [ru:p], *n.* pépie (*maladie de volaille*), *f.*

rouse [rauz], *v.t.* éveiller, (*fig.*) réveiller, exciter.

rout [raut], *n.* cohue; déroute (*d'une armée*), *f.* —*v.t.* mettre en déroute.

route [ru:t], *n.* itinéraire, parcours, *m.*—*v.t.* router (*circulation, colis etc.*).

route-map ['ru:tmæp], *n.* carte routière, *f.*

routine [ru:'ti:n], *n.* routine, *f.*

rove [rouv], *v.i.* rôder, courir.

rover ['rouvə], *n.* rôdeur, vagabond; pirate; (*Scouting*) éclaireur chevalier, *m.*

roving ['rouviŋ], *a.* errant, vagabond.

row (1) [rau], *n.* tapage, vacarme, *m.*; querelle, scène, *f.*

row (2) [rou], *n.* rang, *m.*, rangée, file; colonne (*de chiffres*), *f.*

row (3) [rou], *n.* promenade en bateau, *f.*—*v.t.* (*Naut.*) faire aller à la rame.—*v.i.* ramer; (*Naut.*) nager.

rowan ['rauən], *n.* (*Sc.*) sorbier des oiseaux, *m.*

rowdy ['raudi], *a.* tapageur.—*n.* voyou, gredin, *m.*

rowdyism ['raudiizm], **rowdiness** ['raudinis], *n.* tapage, *m.*

rower ['rouə], *n.* rameur; (*Naut.*) nageur, *m.*

rowing ['rouiŋ], *n.* canotage, *m.*

rowing-boat ['rouiŋbout], *n.* bateau à rames, *m.*

rowlock ['rʌlək], *n.* tolet, *m.*, dame, *f.*

royal ['rɔiəl], *a.* royal, de roi.

royalist ['rɔiəlist], *a.* and *n.* royaliste, *m.*, *f.*

royally ['rɔiəli], *adv.* royalement, en roi.

royalty ['rɔiəlti], *n.* royauté; (*usu. pl.*) commission, *f.*, droit d'auteur, *m.*

rub [rʌb], *v.t.*, *v.i.* frotter; (*Med.*) frictionner. —*n.* frottement; coup de brosse, *m.*; (*fig.*) difficulté, *f.*, obstacle, *m.*

rubber (1) ['rʌbə], *n.* frotteur; frottoir (*chose*), *m.*; (*pl.*) (*Am.*) caoutchoucs (*chaussures*), *m.pl.*; ***indiarubber***, caoutchouc, *m.*, gomme (à effacer), *f.*

rubber (2) ['rʌbə], *n.* (*Cards*) rob, *m.*

rubber-stamp ['rʌbəstæmp], *n.* tampon; (*fig.*) béni-oui-oui, *m.*—*v.t.* ratifier.

rubbing ['rʌbiŋ], *n.* frottement; frottage, *m.*; (*Med.*) friction, *f.*

rubbish ['rʌbiʃ], *n.* débris, *m.pl.*; ordures, *f.pl.*; fatras (*sottises*), *m.*

rubbish-bin ['rʌbiʃbin], *n.* poubelle, *f.*

rubbish-cart ['rʌbiʃkɑ:t], *n.* tombereau, *m.*

rubbish-dump ['rʌbiʃdʌmp], *n.* dépotoir, *m.*

rubbishy ['rʌbiʃi], *a.* de rebut, sans valeur.

rubble [rʌbl], *n.* blocaille, *f.*, moellons; décombres, *m.pl.*

rubicund ['ru:bikənd], *a.* rubicond.

rubric ['ru:brik], *n.* rubrique, *f.*

ruby ['ru:bi], *a.* de rubis, vermeil.—*n.* rubis, *m.*; teinte rouge, *f.*, incarnat, *m.*

ruck [rʌk], *n.* peloton (*de coureurs, cyclistes*), *m.*

rucksack ['rʌksæk], *n.* sac à dos, *m.*

ruction ['rʌkʃən], *n.* (*colloq.*) bagarre, dispute, *f.*

rudder ['rʌdə], *n.* gouvernail, *m.*

ruddiness ['rʌdinis], *n.* rougeur, *f.*

ruddy ['rʌdi], *a.* rouge, au teint vermeil; (*slang*) sacré.

rude [ru:d], *a.* grossier, impoli; (*fig.*) rude, violent.

rudely ['ru:dli], *adv.* grossièrement; rudement.

rudeness ['ru:dnis], *n.* rudesse; grossièreté; insolence; violence, *f.*

rudiment ['ru:dimənt], *n.* rudiment, *m.*

rudimentary [ru:di'mentri], *a.* rudimentaire.

rue [ru:], *v.t.* se repentir de, regretter.

rueful ['ru:ful], *a.* triste; lamentable.

ruefully ['ru:fuli], *adv.* tristement, déplorablement.

ruff [rʌf], *n.* fraise, collerette, *f.*

ruffian ['rʌfiən], *n.* bandit, *m.*; brute, *f.*

ruffianism ['rʌfiənizm], *n.* brutalité, *f.*

ruffianly ['rʌfiənli], *a.* de brigand, brutal.

ruffle [rʌfl], *n.* manchette, ruche, *f.*—*v.t.* froncer (*le front etc.*); froisser (*sentiments*); ébouriffer (*les cheveux*).

rug [rʌg], *n.* couverture, *f.*; tapis, *m.*

rugby ['rʌgbi], *n.* (*Spt.*) rugby, *m.*

rugged ['rʌgid], *a.* rude; raboteux; âpre; bourru (*personne*).

ruggedness ['rʌgidnis], *n.* rudesse, âpreté, *f.*

ruin ['ru:in], *n.* ruine; perte, *f.*—*v.t.* ruiner.

ruination [ru:i'neiʃən], *n.* perte, *f.*

ruinous ['ru:inəs], *a.* ruineux; en ruine.

ruinously ['ru:inəsli], *adv.* ruineusement.

rule [ru:l], *n.* règle, *f.*; règlement; gouvernement, empire (*domination*), *m.*; (*Law*) ordonnance, *f.*; ***as a rule***, en général, d'ordinaire.—*v.t.* régler, diriger; gouverner, régir; (*Law*) décider.—*v.i.* gouverner; (*Law*) décider; ***to rule over***, régner sur.

ruler ['ru:lə], *n.* gouvernant, souverain, *m.*; règle (*instrument*), *f.*

ruling ['ru:liŋ], *a.* dominant, régnant, dirigeant.—*n.* (*Law*) ordonnance de juge, décision, *f.*

rum (1) [rʌm], *a.* drôle; (*colloq.*) cocasse.

rum (2) [rʌm], *n.* rhum, *m.*

Rumania [ru:'meinjə]. la Roumanie, *f.*

Rumanian [ru:'meinjən], *a.* roumain.—*n.* roumain (*langue*); Roumain (*personne*), *m.*

rumba ['rʌmbə], *n.* rumba, *f.*

rumble [rʌmbl], *v.i.* gronder, gargouiller.

rumbling ['rʌmbliŋ], *a.* qui gronde; qui gargouille.—*n.* grondement; gargouillement, *m.*

rumbustious [rʌm'bʌstʃəs], *a.* (*fam.*) turbulent, tapageur.

ruminant ['ru:minənt], *a.* and *n.* ruminant, *m.*

ruminate ['ru:mineit], *v.i.* ruminer.

rumination [ru:mi'neiʃən], *n.* rumination, *f.*

rummage [ˈrʌmidʒ], *v.t., v.i.* fouiller.—*n.* remue-ménage, *m.*

rummage-sale [ˈrʌmidʒseil], *n.* vente d'objets usagés, *f.*

rumour [ˈru:mə], *n.* rumeur, *f.*; bruit, *m.*—*v.t.* faire courir le bruit de.

rump [rʌmp], *n.* croupe; culotte (*de viande*), *f.*; croupion (*de volaille*), *m.*

rumple [rʌmpl], *v.t.* chiffonner, froisser.—*n.* pli, *m.*, froissure, *f.*

rumpus [ˈrʌmpəs], *n.* (*colloq.*) boucan, tapage, *m.*

run [rʌn], *v.t. irr.* courir; encourir; faire courir, faire marcher, conduire (*machines*); pousser, enfoncer; diriger, exploiter, tenir; ***to run down***, dénigrer (*décrier*); (*Hunt.*) forcer; ***to run for***, courir chercher; ***to run in***, enfoncer; arrêter, coffrer; (*Motor.*) roder; ***to run out***, faire sortir; épuiser; ***to run over***, (*Motor.*) écraser (*personne, animal*); ***to run up***, monter en courant.—*v.i.* courir; accourir (*s'approcher*); se sauver (*s'échapper*); s'étendre; fuir (*bateau*); couler (*liquide*); se fondre (*couleurs*); fondre (*se dissoudre*); être (*exister*); courir, circuler; faire le service (*autobus etc.*); marcher, être en marche (*mécanisme*); s'écouler (*temps*); pleurer (*les yeux*); rouler (*avancer en tournant*); devenir; filer (*navire etc.*); suppurer (*ulcère etc.*); monter (*somme*); (*Am.*) se présenter (*aux élections*); ***to run about***, courir çà et là; ***to run after***, chercher; ***to run against***, courir contre; ***to run aground***, échouer; ***to run at***, attaquer; ***to run away***, se sauver, s'emballer (*cheval*); s'écouler (*liquide etc.*); ***to run down***, descendre en courant, aller, venir, couler (*liquide*); s'arrêter (*mécanisme*); ***to run from***, s'enfuir de; ***to run in***, entrer, entrer précipitamment; ***to run out***, courir dehors; couler, fuir; se terminer, expirer, tirer à sa fin; descendre (*marée*); ***to run over***, déborder (*liquide etc.*); ***to run through***, passer à travers de, parcourir; gaspiller; ***to run up***, courir en haut, monter; ***to run up to***, s'élever à, monter à.—*n.* course (*action de courir*), *f.*; cours (*série*); trajet, voyage, *m.*; durée, *f.*, succès (*vogue*), *m.*; irruption (*dans une banque etc.*), *f.*; commun (*généralité*), *m.*; ***in the long run***, à la longue, à la fin.

runaway [ˈrʌnəwei], *a.* emballé (*cheval*).—*n.* fuyard; fugitif, déserteur, *m.*

rung (1) [rʌŋ], *n.* échelon (*d'échelle*); bâton (*de chaise etc.*), *m.*

rung (2) [rʌŋ], *p.p.* [RING (2)].

runner [ˈrʌnə], *n.* coureur; messager, courrier; (*Bot.*) rejeton, *m.*; ***scarlet runner***, haricot d'Espagne, *m.*

running [ˈrʌniŋ], *a.* courant; de suite (*consécutivement*).—*n.* course, *f.*; écoulement (*d'eau*), *m.*

runt [rʌnt], *n.* bétail petit *ou* chétif; (*fig.*) avorton, nain, *m.*

runway [ˈrʌnwei], *n.* (*Av.*) piste d'envol, *f.*

rupee [ru:ˈpi:], *n.* roupie, *f.*

rupture [ˈrʌptʃə], *n.* rupture; (*Med.*) hernie, *f.*—*v.t.* rompre.—*v.i.* se rompre.

rural [ˈruərəl], *a.* champêtre, rural, rustique.

ruse [ru:z], *n.* ruse, *f.*, stratagème, *m.*

rush (1) [rʌʃ], *n.* (*Bot.*) jonc, *m.*

rush (2) [rʌʃ], *n.* ruée, *f.*, mouvement précipité, *m.*; foule, presse (*gens*), *f.*—*v.t.* entraîner brusquement; dépêcher; envahir.—*v.i.* se jeter, se ruer, se précipiter (*sur*).

rushing [ˈrʌʃiŋ], *a.* impétueux.—*n.* élan, *m.*, précipitation, *f.*

rusk [rʌsk], *n.* biscotte, *f.*

russet [ˈrʌsit], *a.* roussâtre.—*n.* roux, *m.*; reinette grise (*pomme*), *f.*

Russia [ˈrʌʃə]. la Russie, *f.*

Russian [ˈrʌʃən], *a.* russe, de Russie.—*n.* russe (*langue*), *m.*; Russe (*personne*), *m., f.*

rust [rʌst], *n.* rouille, *f.*—*v.i.* se rouiller.

rustic [ˈrʌstik], *a.* rustique, champêtre.—*n.* rustre, paysan, *m.*

rusticate [ˈrʌstikeit], *v.t.* reléguer à la campagne; (*Univ.*) renvoyer temporairement.—*v.i.* se retirer à *ou* habiter la campagne.

rustication [rʌstiˈkeiʃən], *n.* villégiature, *f.*; (*Univ.*) renvoi temporaire, *m.*

rusticity [rʌsˈtisiti], *n.* simplicité, rusticité, *f.*

rustiness [ˈrʌstinis], *n.* rouille, *f.*

rustle [rʌsl], *v.t.* (*Am.*) voler (du bétail).—*v.i.* bruire, frémir; faire frou-frou (*robe*); ***to rustle against***, frôler.—*n.* frôlement; bruissement; frou-frou (*de robe*), *m.*

rustler [ˈrʌslə], *n.* (*Am.*) voleur de bétail, *m.*

rustless [ˈrʌstlis], *a.* inoxydable.

rustling [ˈrʌsliŋ], *a.* qui fait frou-frou, frémissant.—*n.* (*Am.*) vol de bétail, *m.*

rusty [ˈrʌsti], *a.* rouillé; roux (*couleur*).

rut [rʌt], *n.* ornière (*de route*), *f.*—*v.t.* sillonner d'ornières.

ruthless [ˈru:θlis], *a.* impitoyable, insensible.

ruthlessly [ˈru:θlisli], *adv.* sans pitié, sans merci.

ruthlessness [ˈru:θlisnis], *n.* cruauté, inhumanité, *f.*

Rwanda [ˈrwʌndə]. le Rwanda, le Ruanda, *m.*

rye [rai], *n.* seigle, *m.*

rye-grass [ˈraigrɑ:s], *n.* ivraie, *f.*, ray-grass, *m.*

S

S, s [es]. dix-neuvième lettre de l'alphabet, *m.*

Saar [sɑ:]. la Sarre, *f.*

Sabbath [ˈsæbəθ], *n.* (*Jews*) sabbat; dimanche; (*fig.*) repos, *m.*

sabbatic [səˈbætik], **sabbatical** [səˈbætikəl], *a.* sabbatique, du sabbat.

sable [seibl], *a.* de zibeline, de martre; (*Her.*) de sable.—*n.* martre, zibeline, *f.*; (*Her.*) sable, *m.*

sabot [ˈsæbou], *n.* sabot, *m.*

sabotage [ˈsæbətɑ:ʒ], *n.* sabotage, *m.*—*v.t.* saboter.

saboteur [sæbəˈtə:], *n.* saboteur, *m.*

sabre [ˈseibə], *n.* sabre, *m.*—*v.t.* sabrer.

sac [sæk], *n.* (*Anat.*) sac, *m.*; bourse, *f.*

saccharine [ˈsækərin], *n.* saccharine, *f.*

sacerdotal [sæsəˈdoutl], *a.* sacerdotal.

sack (1) [sæk], *n.* sac, *m.*; ***to get the sack***, (*colloq.*) être renvoyé; ***to give the sack to***, renvoyer, congédier.—*v.t.* (*colloq.*) congédier.

sack (2) [sæk], *n.* sac, saccagement (*d'une ville*), *m.*—*v.t.* saccager, mettre à sac.

sackcloth ['sækklɔθ], *n.* toile à sac, *f.*
sackful ['sækful], *n.* sac plein, *m.*, sachée, *f.*
sacking (1) ['sækiŋ], *n.* toile à sac, *f.*
sacking (2) ['sækiŋ], *n.* sac, saccagement (*de ville*), *m.*
sacrament ['sækrəmənt], *n.* sacrement, *m.*
sacramental [sækrə'mentl], *a.* sacramentel.
sacred ['seikrid], *a.* sacré; saint (*histoire etc.*); (*fig.*) inviolable.
sacredly ['seikridli], *adv.* saintement; religieusement.
sacredness ['seikridnis], *n.* sainteté, *f.*, caractère sacré, *m.*
sacrifice ['sækrifais], *v.t., v.i.* sacrifier.—*n.* sacrifice, *m.*; victime, *f.*
sacrificer ['sækrifaisə], *n.* sacrificateur, *m.*
sacrificial [sækri'fiʃl], *a.* des sacrifices, sacrificatoire.
sacrilege ['sækrilidʒ], *n.* sacrilège, *m.*
sacrilegious [sækri'lidʒəs], *a.* sacrilège.
sacrilegiously [sækri'lidʒəsli], *adv.* d'une manière sacrilège.
sacrilegiousness [sækri'lidʒəsnis], *n.* caractère sacrilège, *m.*
sacristy ['sækristi], *n.* sacristie, *f.*
sacrosanct ['sækrosæŋkt], *a.* sacro-saint.
sad [sæd], *a.* triste; pitoyable, déplorable; cruel (*perte*)
sadden [sædn], *v.t.* attrister.—*v.i.* s'attrister.
saddle [sædl], *n.* selle, *f.*; ***pack-saddle***, bât, *m.*; ***side-saddle***, selle d'amazone.—*v.t.* seller; charger, accabler.
saddle-bag ['sædlbæg], *n.* sacoche, *f.*
saddle-bow ['sædlbou], *n.* arçon, *m.*
saddler ['sædlə], *n.* sellier, *m.*
saddle-room ['sædlru:m], *n.* sellerie, *f.*
saddlery ['sædləri], *n.* sellerie, *f.*
sadism ['seidizm], *n.* sadisme, *m.*
sadist ['seidist], *n.* sadique, *m., f.*
sadistic [sə'distik], *a.* sadique.
sadly ['sædli], *adv.* tristement; mal, beaucoup, grandement.
sadness ['sædnis], *n.* tristesse, *f.*
safe [seif], *a.* sauf, en sûreté; à l'abri (*de*); sûr; ***safe and sound***, sain et sauf.—*n.* coffre-fort (*pour l'argent*); garde-manger (*pour aliments*), *m.*
safe-conduct ['seif'kɔndʌkt], *n.* sauf-conduit, *m.*
safeguard ['seifgɑ:d], *n.* sauvegarde, *f.*—*v.t.* sauvegarder.
safe-keeping ['seif'ki:piŋ], *n.* bonne garde, sûreté, *f.*
safely ['seifli], *adv.* sain et sauf; en sûreté.
safety ['seifti], *a.* de sûreté.—*n.* sûreté, *f.*, salut, *m.*
safety-catch ['seiftikætʃ], *n.* cran de sûreté, cran d'arrêt, *m.*
safety-lamp ['seiftilæmp], *n.* lampe de sûreté, *f.*
safety-match ['seiftimætʃ], *n.* allumette suédoise, *f.*
safety-pin ['seiftipin], *n.* épingle de sûreté, *f.*
safety-valve ['seiftivælv], *n.* soupape de sûreté, *f.*
saffron ['sæfrən], *a.* couleur safran; de safran. —*n.* safran, *m.*
saffrony ['sæfrəni], *a.* safrané.
sag [sæg], *v.i.* plier, ployer, s'affaisser; se relâcher (*câble*).
saga ['sɑ:gə], *n.* saga, *f.*
sagacious [sə'geiʃəs], *a.* sagace; intelligent (*animal*).
sagaciously [sə'geiʃəsli], *adv.* avec sagacité.
sagaciousness [sə'geiʃəsnis], **sagacity** [sə'gæsiti], *n.* sagacité, *f.*
sage (1) [seidʒ], *a.* sage, prudent.—*n.* sage, *m.*
sage (2) [seidʒ], *n.* sauge (*herbes*), *f.*
sagely ['seidʒli], *adv.* sagement, prudemment.
sagging ['sægiŋ], *a.* affaissé, fléchi, ployé.—*n.* courbure, *f.*, affaissement, *m.*; baisse (*de prix*), *f.*
sago ['seigou], *n.* sagou; sagouier, sagoutier (*arbre*), *m.*
sagy ['seidʒi], *a.* qui a un goût de sauge.
Sahara [sə'hɑ:rə], **the.** le Sahara, *m.*
said [sed], *a.* dit, susdit [SAY].
sail [seil], *n.* voile, *f.*; (*collect.*) voiles, *f.pl.*, voilure; aile (*de moulin à vent*); course ou promenade à la voile (*sur l'eau*), *f.*—*v.t.* naviguer (*sur*), voguer (*sur* ou *dans*).—*v.i.* faire voile; cingler, naviguer; mettre à la voile, appareiller.
sailable ['seiləbl], *a.* navigable.
sail-cloth ['seilklɔθ], *n.* toile à voiles, *f.*
sailing ['seiliŋ], *a.* à voiles.—*n.* navigation, *f.*; appareillage, *m.*; partance (*départ*), *f.*
sailing-boat ['seiliŋbout], *n.* bateau à voiles, *m.*
sailing-ship ['seiliŋʃip], *n.* bâtiment à voiles voilier, *m.*
sail-maker ['seilmeikə], *n.* voilier, *m.*
sailor ['seilə], *n.* marin, matelot, *m.*
saint [seint] *strong form*, [sənt] *weak form*, *n.* saint, *m.*, sainte, *f.*; ***All Saints' Day***, la Toussaint, *f.*
saintliness ['seintlinis], *n.* sainteté, *f.*
saintly ['seintli], *a.* saint; de saint, vénérable.
sake [seik], *n.* (*used only with* FOR); ***art for art's sake***, l'art pour l'art; ***for God's sake***, pour l'amour de Dieu; ***for the sake of appearances***, pour sauver les apparences; ***for the sake of health***, pour cause de santé; ***for your sake***, par égard pour vous.
sal [sæl], *n.* sel, *m*
salaam [sə'lɑ:m], *n.* salamalec, *m.*
salad ['sæləd], *n.* salade, *f.*
salad-bowl ['sælədboul], *n.* saladier, *m.*
salad-oil ['sælədɔil], *n.* huile de table, *f.*
salamander ['sæləmændə], *n.* salamandre, *f.*
salaried ['sælərid], *a.* qui touche des appointements.
salary ['sæləri], *n.* appointements, *m.pl.*; traitement (*de fonctionnaire*), *m.*
sale [seil], *n.* vente; mise en vente, *f.*; ***for sale***, à vendre; ***on sale***, en vente; ***private sale***, vente à l'amiable; ***sale by auction***, vente aux enchères; ***to put up for sale***, mettre en vente.
saleable ['seiləbl], *a.* vendable; de bonne vente.
sale-room ['seilru:m], *n.* salle des ventes, *f.*
salesman ['seilzmən], *n.* (*pl.* **-men** [men]) vendeur, marchand; courtier de commerce, *m.*
Salic ['sælik], *a.* salique.
salient ['seiliənt], *a.* and *n.* saillant, *m.*
saliently ['seiliəntli], *adv.* d'une manière saillante.
salify ['sælifai], *v.t.* salifier.
saline ['seilain], *a.* salin.
saliva [sə'laivə], *n.* salive, *f.*

salivate ['sæliveit], *v.t.* faire saliver.
sallow ['sælou], *a.* jaunâtre, jaune, blême.
sallowness ['sælounis], *n.* teint blême, *m.*
sally ['sæli], *n.* sortie; (*fig.*) excursion; saillie (*d'esprit*), *f.*—*v.i.* sortir, faire une sortie.
salmon ['sæmən], *n.* saumon, *m.*
salmon-trout ['sæməntraut], *n.* truite saumonée, *f.*
saloon [sə'lu:n], *n.* (grand) salon, *m.*, salle; (*Am.*) buvette, *f.*, bar, *m.*; conduite-intérieure (*voiture*), *f.*
salsify ['sælsifi], *n.* (*Bot.*) salsifis, *m.*
salt [sɔ:lt], *a.* salé; de sel.—*n.* sel, *m.*; ***Epsom salts***, sels anglais, *m.pl.*—*v.t.* saler.
salt-cellar ['sɔ:ltselə], *n.* salière, *f.*
salted ['sɔ:ltid], *a.* salé; (*fig.*) aguerri.
salter ['sɔ:ltə], *n.* saunier; saleur, *m.*
salting ['sɔ:ltiŋ], *n.* salaison, *f.*, salage, *m.*
saltish ['sɔ:ltiʃ], *a.* un peu salé, saumâtre.
saltless ['sɔ:ltlis], *a.* sans sel; (*fig.*) insipide.
salt-marsh ['sɔ:ltmɑ:ʃ], *n.* marais salant, *m.*
salt-mine ['sɔ:ltmain], *n.* mine de sel, *f.*
saltness ['sɔ:ltnis], *n.* salure, *f.*
saltpetre [sɔ:lt'pi:tə], *n.* salpêtre, *m.*
saltpetre-works [sɔ:lt'pi:təwə:ks], *n.pl.* salpêtrière, *f.*
saltpetrous [sɔ:lt'petrəs], *a.* salpêtreux.
salt-water ['sɔ:ltwɔ:tə], *n.* eau de mer, *f.*
salty ['sɔ:lti], *a.* salé; qui a un goût de sel.
salubrious [sə'lju:briəs], *a.* salubre, sain.
salubriously [sə'lju:briəsli], *adv.* d'une manière salubre.
salubrity [sə'lju:briti], *n.* salubrité, *f.*
salutary ['sæljutəri], *a.* salutaire.
salutation [sælju'teiʃən], *n.* salut, *m.*, salutation, *f.*
salute [sə'lju:t], *n.* salut, *m.*, salutation, salve (*de fusils*), *f.*—*v.t.* saluer.
Salvador ['sælvədɔ:], **El.** le Salvador, *m.*
Salvadorean [sælvə'dɔ:riən], *a.* salvadorègne. —*n.* Salvadorègne (*personne*) *m.*, *f.*
salvage ['sælvidʒ], *n.* sauvetage, *m.*, objets sauvés, *m.pl.*; (*Ind.*) récupération, *f.*—*v.t.* récupérer; relever (*navire*).
salvage-money ['sælvidʒmʌni], *n.* prix *ou* droit de sauvetage, *m.*
salvage-vessel ['sælvidʒvesl], *n.* navire de relevage, *m.*
salvation [sæl'veiʃən], *n.* salut, *m.*; ***Salvation Army***, Armée du Salut, *f.*
salve [sælv, sɑ:v], *n.* onguent; (*fig.*) remède, baume, *m.*—[sælv], *v.t.* remédier à; (*Naut.*) sauver, sauveter.
salver ['sælvə], *n.* plateau, *m.*
salvo ['sælvou], *n.* réserve, restriction; salve (*d'artillerie*), *f.*
Samaritan [sə'mæritən], *a.* samaritain.—*n.* Samaritain (*personne*), *m.*
same [seim], *a.* même.—*n.* le même, *m.*, la même; même chose, *f.*; ledit, *m.*, ladite, *f.*, lesdits, *m.pl.*, lesdites, *f.pl.*; ***all the same***, néanmoins, quand même; ***it is all the same***, c'est égal; ***just the same***, tout de même; ***much about the same***, à peu près de même; ***the same to you***, et vous de même.
sameness ['seimnis], *n.* identité; uniformité, *f.*
sample [sɑ:mpl], *n.* échantillon, *m.*—*v.t.* échantillonner; déguster (*vin*).
sampler ['sɑ:mplə], *n.* modèle; (*Needlework*) canevas, *m.*
sampling ['sɑ:mpliŋ], *n.* échantillonnage, *m.*; gustation (*des mets*), *f.*
sanatorium [sænə'tɔ:riəm], *n.* sanatorium, *m.*
sanctification [sæŋktifi'keiʃən], *n.* sanctification, *f.*
sanctified ['sæŋktifaid], *a.* sanctifié, saint.
sanctify ['sæŋktifai], *v.t.* sanctifier.
sanctimonious [sæŋkti'mouniəs], *a.* papelard, béat, hypocrite.
sanctimoniously [sæŋkti'mouniəsli], *adv.* d'un air béat.
sanctimoniousness [sæŋkti'mouniəsnis], *n.* dévotion affectée; cagoterie, *f.*
sanction ['sæŋkʃən], *n.* sanction, autorité, *f.*—*v.t.* sanctionner, autoriser.
sanctity ['sæŋktiti], *n.* sainteté, *f.*
sanctuary ['sæŋktjuəri], *n.* sanctuaire, asile, refuge, *m.*
sanctum ['sæŋktəm], *n.* sanctuaire; (*colloq.*) cabinet de travail, *m.*, retraite, *f.*
sand [sænd], *n.* sable; sablon (*sable fin*), *m.*; (*pl.*) plage, *f.*, bord de la mer, *m.*—*v.t.* sabler.
sandal [sændl], *n.* sandale, *f.*; santal, *m.*
sandbag ['sændbæg], *n.* sac de terre, *m.*
sand-bank ['sændbæŋk], *n.* banc de sable, *m.*
sand-drift ['sænddrift], *n.* amas de sable, *m.*
sand-eel ['sændi:l], *n.* lançon, *m.*, équille, *f.*
sand-glass ['sændglɑ:s], *n.* sablier, *m.*
sand-martin ['sændmɑ:tin], *n.* hirondelle de rivage, *f.*
sand-paper ['sændpeipə], *n.* papier de verre, *m.*—*v.t.* passer au papier de verre.
sand-pit ['sændpit], *n.* sablière, sablonnière, *f.*
sand-shoes ['sændʃu:z], *n.pl.* espadrilles, *f.pl.*
sandstone ['sændstoun], *n.* grès, *m.*
sand-storm ['sændstɔ:m], *n.* ouragan de sable, *m.*
sandwich ['sændwitʃ], *n.* sandwich, *m.*
sandwich-man ['sændwitʃmən], *n.* (*pl.* **-men** [men]) homme-sandwich, homme-affiche, *m.*
sandy ['sændi], *a.* sablonneux, de sable; d'un blond ardent, roux (*couleur*).
sane [sein], *a.* sain, sain d'esprit.
sanguinary ['sæŋgwinəri], *a.* sanguinaire.
sanguine ['sæŋgwin], *a.* sanguin; plein de confiance, confiant.
sanguineness ['sæŋgwinnis], *n.* confiance, assurance, *f.*
sanitary ['sænitəri], *a.* sanitaire, hygiénique; ***sanitary towel***, serviette hygiénique, *f.*
sanitation [sæni'teiʃən], *n.* assainissement, *m.*
sanity ['sæniti], *n.* état sain, jugement sain, *m.*
Sanskrit ['sænskrit], *a.* and *n.* sanscrit, *m.*
Santa Claus ['sæntə'klɔ:z]. Père Noël, *m.*
sap (1) [sæp], *n.* sève, *f.*
sap (2) [sæp], *n.* (*Mil.*) sapé, *f.*—*v.t.* saper.
sapience ['seipiəns], *n.* sagesse, *f.*
sapient ['seipiənt], *a.* sage.
sapless ['sæplis], *a.* sans sève; sec, desséché.
sapling ['sæpliŋ], *n.* jeune arbre, baliveau, *m.*
saponaceous [sæpə'neiʃəs], *a.* saponacé.
saponify [sə'pɔnifai], *v.t.* saponifier.—*v.i.* se saponifier.
sapper ['sæpə], *n.* sapeur, *m.*
sapphic ['sæfik], *a.* and *n.* (*Pros.*) saphique, *m.*
sapphire ['sæfaiə], *n.* saphir, *m.*
sappiness ['sæpinis], *n.* abondance de sève, *f.*
sappy ['sæpi], *a.* plein de sève.
saraband ['særəbænd], *n.* sarabande, *f.*

Saracen ['særəsn], *a.* sarrasin.—*n.* Sarrasin, *m.*
sarcasm ['sɑːkæzm], *n.* sarcasme, *m.*
sarcastic [sɑː'kæstik], *a.* sarcastique.
sarcastically [sɑː'kæstikəli], *adv.* d'une manière *ou* d'un ton sarcastique.
sarcophagus [sɑː'kɔfəgəs], *n.* sarcophage, *m.*
sardine [sɑː'diːn], *n.* sardine, *f.*
Sardinia [sɑː'dinjə]. la Sardaigne, *f.*
Sardinian [sɑː'dinjən], *a.* sarde.—*n.* Sarde (*personne*), *m., f.*
sardonic [sɑː'dɔnik], *a.* sardonique.
sarong [sə'rɔŋ], *n.* pagne, *m.*, jupe (*malaisien*), *f.*
sarsaparilla [sɑːsəpə'rilə], *n.* salsepareille, *f.*
sash (1) [sæʃ], *n.* ceinture; écharpe (*décoration*), *f.*
sash (2) [sæʃ], *n.* châssis (*de fenêtre*), *m.*
sash-window ['sæʃwindou], *n.* fenêtre à guillotine, *f.*
sassafras ['sæsəfræs], *n.* (*Bot.*) sassafras, *m.*
Satan ['seitən]. Satan, *m.*
satanic [sə'tænik], **satanical** [sə'tænikəl], *a.* satanique.
satchel [sætʃl], *n.* sacoche, *f.*; sac d'écolier, cartable, *m.*
sate [seit], *v.t.* rassasier (*de*), assouvir.
satellite ['sætəlait], *n.* satellite, *m.*
satiate ['seiʃieit], *v.t.* rassasier (*de*).
satiated ['seiʃieitid], *a.* rassasié (*de*); gorgé.
satiety [sə'taiəti], *n.* satiété, *f.*
satin ['sætin], *a.* de satin.—*n.* satin, *m.*
satin-wood ['sætinwuːd], *n.* bois de citronnier, *m.*
satire ['sætaiə], *n.* satire, *f.*
satiric [sə'tirik], **satirical** [sə'tirikəl], *a.* satirique.
satirist ['sætirist], *n.* satirique, *m., f.*
satirize ['sætiraiz], *v.t.* satiriser.
satisfaction [sætis'fækʃən], *n.* satisfaction; réparation (*récompense*), *f.*
satisfactorily [sætis'fæktərili], *adv.* d'une manière satisfaisante.
satisfactory [sætis'fæktri], *a.* satisfaisant.
satisfy ['sætisfai], *v.t.* satisfaire; satisfaire à; acquitter (*dette*); assouvir (*passion*); rassasier (*de*) (*appétit*); ***to be satisfied that***, être persuadé, être convaincu que; ***to be satisfied with***, être satisfait de, être content de.—*v.i.* satisfaire, donner satisfaction.
satisfying ['sætisfaiiŋ], *a.* satisfaisant; nourrissant (*nourriture*).
saturate ['sætʃureit], *v.t.* saturer.
saturation [sætʃu'reiʃən], *n.* saturation, *f.*
Saturday ['sætədei]. samedi, *m.*
Saturn ['sætən]. Saturne, *m.*
Saturnalia [sætə'neiliə]. saturnales, *f.pl.*
saturnine ['sætənain], *a.* sombre, taciturne.
satyr ['sætə], *n.* satyre, *m.*
sauce [sɔːs], *n.* sauce; (*fig.*) insolence, impertinence, *f.*—*v.t.* assaisonner; flatter (*le goût*); (*fig.*) dire des impertinences à.
sauce-boat ['sɔːsbout], *n.* saucière, *f.*
saucer ['sɔːsə], *n.* soucoupe, *f.*; ***flying saucer***, soucoupe volante.
saucepan ['sɔːspən], *n.* casserole, *f.*
saucily ['sɔːsili], *adv.* insolemment.
sauciness ['sɔːsinis], *n.* insolence, impertinence, *f.*
saucy ['sɔːsi], *a.* insolent, impertinent.
Saudi Arabia ['saudiə'reibiə]. l'Arabie Séoudite, *f.*
sauerkraut ['sauəkraut], *n.* choucroute, *f.*
saunter ['sɔːntə], *v.i.* flâner.—*n.* flânerie, *f.*
saunterer ['sɔːntərə], *n.* flâneur, *m.*
sauntering ['sɔːntəriŋ], *a.* de flâneur.—*n.* flânerie, *f.*
sausage ['sɔsidʒ], *n.* saucisse (*à cuire*), *f.* saucisson (*salami etc.*), *m.*
sausage-meat ['sɔsidʒmiːt], *n.* chair à saucisse, *f.*
sausage-roll ['sɔsidʒ'roul], *n.* friand, *m.*
savage ['sævidʒ], *a.* sauvage; féroce.—*n.* sauvage, *m., f.*—*v.t.* attaquer, mordre (*bête*).
savagely ['sævidʒli], *adv.* sauvagement, en sauvage; d'une manière féroce.
savageness ['sævidʒnis], *n.* férocité, brutalité, sauvagerie, *f.*
savagery ['sævidʒəri], *n.* férocité, barbarie, *f.*
savannah [sə'vænə], *n.* savane, prairie, *f.*
save [seiv], *v.t.* sauver (*de*); épargner (*argent etc.*); mettre de côté, économiser.—*v.i.* économiser, faire des économies.—*n.* (*Spt.*) arrêt, *m.*—*prep.* hormis, excepté, sauf.
saver ['seivə], *n.* sauveur, libérateur, *m.*, économe (*ménager*), *m., f.*
saving ['seiviŋ], *a.* économe, ménager.—*n.* épargne; économie, *f.*; salut, *m.*
savings-bank ['seiviŋzbæŋk], *n.* caisse d'épargne, *f.*
saviour ['seivjə], *n.* sauveur, *m.*
savour ['seivə], *n.* saveur, *f.*; goût, *m.*, odeur, *f.*—*v.t.* goûter, savourer.—*v.i.* avoir du goût; sentir.
savouriness ['seivərinis], *n.* goût agréable, *m.*, saveur, *f.*
savoury ['seivəri], *a.* savoureux, appétissant.—*n.* plat épicé, *m.*
saw (1) [sɔː], *past* [SEE].
saw (2) [sɔː], *n.* scie, *f.*—*v.t.*, *v.i. irr.* scier.
saw (3) [sɔː], *n.* adage, dicton (*proverbe*), *m.*
sawdust ['sɔːdʌst], *n.* sciure (de bois), *f.*
saw-mill ['sɔːmil], *n.* scierie, *f.*
sawyer ['sɔːjə], *n.* scieur, scieur de long, *m.*
saxifrage ['sæksifreidʒ], *n.* (*Bot.*) saxifrage, *f.*
Saxon ['sæksən], *a.* saxon, de Saxe.—*n.* saxon (*langue*); Saxon (*personne*), *m.*
saxophone ['sæksəfoun], *n.* saxophone, *m.*
say [sei], *v.t. irr.* dire; parler, répéter, réciter; ***I say!*** dites donc! ***that is to say***, c'est-à-dire; ***they say***, on dit.—*n.* dire, mot, ce qu'on a à dire, *m.*
saying ['seiiŋ], *n.* mot, proverbe, dicton, *m.*; sentence, maxime, *f.*
scab [skæb], *n.* croûte (*sur blessure etc.*); gale (*de mouton etc.*), *f.*
scabbard ['skæbəd], *n.* fourreau, *m.*
scabbiness ['skæbinis], *n.* état galeux, *m.*
scabby ['skæbi], *a.* couvert de croûtes; galeux.
scabious ['skeibiəs], *a.* scabieux.—*n.* scabieuse (*plante*), *f.*
scaffold ['skæfəld], *n.* échafaud, *m.*—*v.t.* échafauder.
scaffolding ['skæfəldiŋ], *n.* échafaudage, *m.*
scald [skɔːld], *n.* brûlure, *f.*—*v.t.* échauder, ébouillanter.
scalding ['skɔːldiŋ], *n.* échaudage, *m.*
scalding-hot ['skɔːldiŋ'hɔt], *a.* tout bouillant.
scale (1) [skeil], *n.* échelle; (*Mus.*) gamme, *f.*—*v.t.* escalader.
scale (2) [skeil], *n.* écaille (*de poisson*), *f.*
scale (3) [skeil], *n.* bassin, plateau (*balance*), *m.*; ***scales*** or ***pair of scales***, balance, *f.*

scale-maker ['skeilmeikə], *n.* balancier, *m.*
scalene ['skeili:n], *a.* scalène.
scaliness ['skeilinis], *n.* nature écailleuse, *f.*
scaling (1) ['skeiliŋ], *n.* escalade (*montagnes*), *f.*
scaling (2) ['skeiliŋ], *n.* écaillage (*peintures*), *m.*
scallop ['skɔləp], *n.* coquille Saint-Jacques; coquille; dentelure, *f.*, feston, *m.*—*v.t.* denteler; (*Needlework*) festonner.
scalp [skælp], *n.* cuir chevelu, *m.*, chevelure, *f.*, scalpe; (*fig.*) front, *m.*, tête, *f.*—*v.t.* scalper.
scalpel ['skælpəl], *n.* (*Surg.*) scalpel, *m.*
scaly ['skeili], *a.* écaillé; (*Bot.*) écailleux.
scamp [skæmp], *n.* chenapan, vaurien, *m.*; ***young scamp***, petit polisson, *m.*—*v.t.* bâcler.
scamper ['skæmpə], *v.i.* courir, s'enfuir.—*n.* course rapide, *f.*
scampi ['skæmpi], *n.pl.* langoustine, *f.*
scan [skæn], *v.t.* scruter; (*Pros.*) scander; (*Rad.*) balayer.
scandal [skændl], *n.* scandale, *m.*; honte; médisance, *f.*
scandalize ['skændəlaiz], *v.t.* scandaliser, choquer; calomnier.
scandal-monger ['skændlmʌŋgə], *n.* médisant, *m.*
scandalous ['skændələs], *a.* scandaleux; honteux.
Scandinavia [skændi'neivjə]. la Scandinavie, *f.*
Scandinavian [skændi'neivjən], *a.* scandinave.—*n.* Scandinave (*personne*), *m.*, *f.*
scanner ['skænə], *n.* scrutateur, *m.*; ***radar scanner***, déchiffreur de radar, *m.*
scanning ['skæniŋ], *n.* examen minutieux, *m.*; (*Pros.*) scansion, *f.*; (*Rad.*) balayage, *m.*
scansion ['skænʃən], *n.* scansion, *f.*
scant [skænt], *a.* rare; rétréci; faible; peu de.
scantily ['skæntili], *adv.* faiblement, d'une manière insuffisante.
scantiness ['skæntinis], *n.* insuffisance (*de vivres etc.*); faiblesse (*de poids*), *f.*
scantling ['skæntliŋ], *n.* échantillon, *m.*; (*Carp.*) volige, *f.*, équarrissage, *m.*
scanty ['skænti], *a.* rétréci, faible, peu abondant, insuffisant; clairsemé (*cheveux*).
scapegoat ['skeipgout], *n.* bouc émissaire; (*fig.*) souffre-douleur, *m.*
scapegrace ['skeipgreis], *n.* vaurien, mauvais sujet, *m.*
scapement ['skeipmənt], *n.* échappement, *m.*
scapula ['skæpjulə], *n.* (*Anat.*) omoplate, *f.*
scapular ['skæpjulə], *a.* scapulaire.
scapulary ['skæpjuləri], *n.* (*R.-C. Ch.*) scapulaire, *m.*
scar [skɑ:], *n.* cicatrice, balafre, *f.*—*v.t.* cicatriser; balafrer.
scarab ['skærəb], **scarabaeus** [skærə'bi:əs], *n.* scarabée, *m.*
scaramouch ['skærəmu:ʃ], *n.* scaramouche, *m.*
scarce [skεəs], *a.* rare; ***to make oneself scarce***, disparaître, décamper, filer.
scarcely ['skεəsli], *adv.* à peine, presque pas, guère.
scarcity ['skεəsiti], *n.* rareté; disette (*famine*), *f.*
scare [skεə], *n.* panique, frayeur subite, *f.*—*v.t.* effrayer, épouvanter, effaroucher.
scarecrow ['skεəkrou], *n.* épouvantail, *m.*
scarf [skɑ:f], *n.* (*pl.* **scarfs** [skɑ:fs], **scarves** [skɑ:vz]) écharpe, *f.*; cache-nez, *m.inv.*; foulard, *m.*
scarifier ['skærifaiə], *n.* scarificateur, *m.*
scarify ['skærifai], *v.t.* scarifier (*peau*), ameublir (*terre*).
scarlatina [skɑ:lə'ti:nə], *n.* (fièvre) scarlatine, *f.*
scarlet ['skɑ:lit], *a.* and *n.* écarlate, *f.*; ***scarlet fever***, fièvre scarlatine, *f.*; ***scarlet runner***, haricot d'Espagne, *m.*
scarp [skɑ:p], *n.* (*Fort.*) escarpe, *f.*—*v.t.* escarper.
scarves [SCARF].
scatheless ['skeiðlis], *a.* sans dommage, sain et sauf.
scathing ['skeiðiŋ], *a.* acerbe, cinglant, cassant.
scatter ['skætə], *v.t.* disperser, dissiper; répandre, éparpiller.—*v.i.* se disperser, se répandre.
scattered ['skætəd], *a.* dispersé, éparpillé, épars.
scattering ['skætəriŋ], *n.* éparpillement; petit nombre, *m.*
scavenge ['skævindʒ], *v.t.* ébouer, balayer.
scavenger ['skævindʒə], *n.* boueur; balayeur, *m.*
scavenging ['skævindʒiŋ], *n.* ébouage, balayage, *m.*
scene [si:n], *n.* scène; (*Theat.*) scène, décoration, *f.*; décor; (*fig.*) théâtre, *m.*; ***behind the scenes***, dans la coulisse; ***scene-shifter***, machiniste, *m.*,
scenery ['si:nəri], *n.* scène; (*fig.*) vue, perspective, *f.*, paysage, *m.*; (*Theat.*) décors, *m.pl.*
scenic ['si:nik], *a.* scénique.
scent [sent], *n.* odeur, senteur, *f.*, parfum; odorat; flair, nez (*de chien*), *m.*; voie (*de cerf*); (*fig.*) piste (*traces*), *f.*—*v.t.* parfumer (*de*); sentir, flairer (*animal*).
scent-bottle ['sentbɔtl], *n.* flacon de parfum, *m.*
scentless ['sentlis], *a.* sans odeur, inodore.
scent-spray ['sentsprei], *n.* vaporisateur, *m.*
sceptic ['skeptik], *n.* sceptique, *m.*, *f.*
sceptical ['skeptikl], *a.* sceptique.
scepticism ['skeptisizm], *n.* scepticisme, *m.*
sceptre ['septə], *n.* sceptre, *m.*
sceptred ['septəd], *a.* portant le sceptre.
schedule ['ʃedju:l, (*Am.*) 'skedju:l], *n.* liste, *f.*, inventaire; (*Comm.*) bilan; (*Law*) bordereau, *m.*—*v.t.* enregistrer, inventorier.
scheme [ski:m], *n.* arrangement, *m.*, combinaison, *f.*; projet, système, *m.*—*v.t.* projeter, combiner.—*v.i.* faire des projets; (*fig.*) intriguer.
schemer ['ski:mə], *n.* faiseur de projets; (*fig.*) intrigant, *m.*
scheming ['ski:miŋ], *a.* à projets; intrigant.—*n.* projets *m.pl.*, intrigues, *f.pl.*
schism [sizm], *n.* schisme, *m.*
schismatic [siz'mætik], *n.* schismatique, *m.*, *f.*
schizophrenia [skitso'fri:niə], *n.* (*Med.*) schizophrénie, *f.*
schizophrenic [skitso'fri:nik], *a.* and *n.* schizophrène, *m.*, *f.*
scholar ['skɔlə], *n.* écolier; érudit, savant (*learned person*), *m.*; ***day scholar***, externe, *m.*, *f.*

scholarly ['skɔləli], *a.* d'érudit, savant.
scholarship ['skɔləʃip], *n.* érudition, *f.*, savoir, *m.*; (*Univ. etc.*) bourse, *f.*
scholastic [sko'læstik], *a.* and *n.* scolastique, *m.*, *f.*
scholasticism [sko'læstisizm], *n.* scolastique, *f.*
school [sku:l], *n.* école; bande, troupe (*de baleines etc.*), *f.*; *at school*, en classe, à l'école; *boarding-school*, pension, *f.*, pensionnat, *m.*; *primary school*, école primaire; *grammar school*, collège, lycée, *m.*; *infant-school*, école maternelle.—*v.t.* instruire, enseigner; réprimander.
schooled [sku:ld], *a.* formé, entraîné, dressé.
schooling ['sku:liŋ], *n.* instruction; réprimande, *f.*
schoolmaster ['sku:lmɑ:stə], *n.* instituteur, professeur, *m.*
schoolmistress ['sku:lmistris], *n.* maîtresse d'école, institutrice, *f.*
schooner ['sku:nə], *n.* (*Naut.*) goélette, *f.*
sciatic [sai'ætik], *a.* sciatique.
sciatica [sai'ætikə], *n.* sciatique, *f.*
science ['saiəns], *n.* science, *f.*
scientific [saiən'tifik], *a.* scientifique.
scientist ['saiəntist], *n.* homme de science, savant, *m.*
Scilly Isles ['siliailz], *the*, les Sorlingues, *f.pl.*
scimitar ['simitə], *n.* cimeterre, *m.*
scintillant ['sintilənt], *a.* scintillant.
scintillate ['sintileit], *v.i.* scintiller.
scintillation [sinti'leiʃən], *n.* scintillation, *f.*, scintillement, *m.*
scion ['saiən], *n.* (*Bot.*) scion; (*fig.*) rejeton, *m.*
scission ['siʃən], *n.* scission, *f.*
scissors ['sizəz], *n.pl.* ciseaux, *m.pl.*
scoff [skɔf], *n.* moquerie, *f.*, sarcasme, *m.*—*v.t.* se moquer de, bafouer.—*v.i.* railler.
scoffer ['skɔfə], *n.* moqueur, railleur, *m.*
scoffing ['skɔfiŋ], *a.* moqueur.—*n.* moquerie, dérision, *f.*
scoffingly ['skɔfiŋli], *adv.* par moquerie, en dérision.
scold [skould], *v.t.* gronder, criailler (*après*).—*v.i.* gronder.
scolding ['skouldiŋ], *a.* bougon.—*n.* semonce, *f.*
sconce [skɔns], *n.* candélabre (*fixé au mur*), *m.*; bobèche (*de bougeoir*), *f.*
scone [skɔn, skoun], *n.* petite galette (ronde), *f.*
scoop [sku:p], *n.* grande cuiller; (*Naut.*) écope; (*Journ. slang*) nouvelle à sensation, *f.*—*v.t.* vider, creuser; (*Naut.*) écoper.
scooter ['sku:tə], *n.* patinette, *f.*; scooter, *m.*
scope [skoup], *n.* portée, étendue; visée; liberté, *f.*
scorch [skɔ:tʃ], *v.t.* brûler, roussir, griller.—*v.i.* se brûler.
scorching ['skɔ:tʃiŋ], *a.* brûlant, très chaud.
score [skɔ:], *n.* entaille, coche, *f.*; compte; vingt, *m.*, vingtaine, *f.*; (*Games*) nombre de points; (*fig.*) motif, *m.*, raison, cause; (*Mus.*) partition, *f.*; *on what score?* à quel titre ?—*v.t.* entailler, marquer; rayer; (*Mus.*) orchestrer; *to score out*, rayer, biffer (*texte*).—*v.i.* marquer des points.
scorer ['skɔ:rə], *n.* marqueur, *m.*
scoring ['skɔ:riŋ], *n.* (*Games etc.*) marque; (*Mus.*) orchestration, *f.*
scorn [skɔ:n], *v.t.* mépriser; dédaigner.—*v.i.* mépriser; dédaigner (*de*); *to scorn to fly*, dédaigner de fuir.—*n.* mépris, dédain, *m.*; dérision, *f.*
scornful ['skɔ:nful], *a.* méprisant, dédaigneux.
scornfully ['skɔ:nfuli], *adv.* dédaigneusement, avec dédain.
scornfulness ['skɔ:nfulnis], *n.* caractère dédaigneux, *m.*
scorpion ['skɔ:pjən], *n.* scorpion, *m.*
Scot [skɔt], *n.* Écossais, *m.*
Scotch [skɔtʃ], *a.* écossais (*but used* ONLY *in certain fixed expressions, which include the following*) *Scotch terrier*, terrier griffon, *m.*; *Scotch* (*whisky*), whisky écossais, *m.*; [SCOTS].
scotch [skɔtʃ], *v.t.* entailler; enrayer (*roue*); (*fig.*) annuler.
scot-free [skɔt'fri:], *a.* sans frais; (*fig.*) sain et sauf, indemne.
Scotland ['skɔtlənd]. l'Écosse, *f.*
Scots [skɔts], **Scottish** ['skɔtiʃ], *a.* écossais; *Scots Law*, droit écossais, *m.*
Scotsman ['skɔtsmən], *n.* (*pl.* **-men** [men]) Écossais, *m.*
Scotswoman ['skɔtswumən], *n.* (*pl.* **-women** [wimin]) Écossaise, *f.*
Scottish [SCOTS].
scoundrel ['skaundrəl], *n.* gredin, coquin, scélérat, *m.*
scour (1) ['skauə], *v.t.* nettoyer, récurer, purger, écurer.—*v.i.* écurer; nettoyer.
scour (2) ['skauə], *v.t.* parcourir.—*v.i.* courir.
scourer ['skauərə], *n.* récureur, nettoyeur, *m.*
scourge [skə:dʒ], *n.* fouet; (*fig.*) fléau, *m.*—*v.t.* fouetter, flageller; (*fig.*) châtier.
scourger ['skə:dʒə], *n.* châtieur; (*Eccles. Hist.*) flagellant, *m.*
scourging ['skə:dʒiŋ], *n.* flagellation, *f.*
scouring ['skauəriŋ], *n.* récurage; nettoyage, *m.*
scout [skaut], *n.* éclaireur; scout, *m.*; (*Naut.*) vedette, *f.*; (*Av.*) avion de chasse, *m.*—*v.t.* repousser avec mépris.—*v.i.* aller en éclaireur.
scowl [skaul], *v.i.* se re(n)frogner, froncer le sourcil.—*n.* re(n)frognement, froncement de sourcil, *m.*
scowling ['skauliŋ], *a.* re(n)frogné, menaçant.
scrag [skræg], *n.* corps décharné, squelette, *m.*; *scrag-end*, bout saigneux (*de viande*), *m.*
scragginess ['skræginis], *n.* état raboteux, *m.*; maigreur, *f.*
scraggy ['skrægi], *a.* noueux, rugueux; rabougri.
scramble [skræmbl], *v.t.* (*Teleg.*) brouiller (*message*); *scrambled eggs*, œufs brouillés, *m.pl.*—*v.i.* grimper; se battre, se disputer.—*n.* mêlée, lutte, *f.*
scrap (1) [skræp], *n.* morceau, fragment, bout, *m.*; (*pl.*) bribes, *f.pl.*; restes, *m.pl.*—*v.t.* mettre au rebut.
scrap (2) [skræp], *n.* (*slang*) bagarre, rixe, *f.*
scrap-book ['skræpbuk], *n.* album, *m.*
scrape [skreip], *v.t.* gratter, érafler, râcler; décrotter (*bottes etc.*); (*Cook.*) ratisser; *to scrape together*, amasser petit à petit.—*v.i.* gratter; (*fam.*) râcler (*jouer du violon*); *to scrape through*, passer de justesse; *to bow and scrape*, faire des salamalecs.—*n.* grattage, *m.*; (*fig.*) difficulté, mauvaise affaire, *f.*

scraper ['skreipə], *n.* grattoir; râcloir, *m.*; (*Agric.*) ratissoire, *f.*; décrottoir (*pour chaussures*), *m.*

scrap-heap ['skræphi:p], *n.* tas de ferraille, *m.*

scraping ['skreipiŋ], *n.* grattage, *m.*; ratissure (*de légumes*), *f.*; ***with much bowing and scraping***, avec force révérences.

scrap-iron ['skræpaiən], *n.* ferraille, *f.*

scratch [skrætʃ], *n.* égratignure, *f.*; coup de griffe *ou* d'ongle, *m.*; raie, rayure (*sur une surface polie*), *f.*—*v.t.* gratter; rayer (*surface polie*).—*v.i.* gratter; (*Spt.*) renoncer à concourir.

scratcher ['skrætʃə], *n.* égratigneur; grattoir (*instrument*), *m.*

scratching ['skrætʃiŋ], *n.* grattage, *m.*; égratignure; rayure, *f.*

scrawl [skrɔ:l], *n.* griffonnage, *m.*, pattes de mouche, *f.pl.*—*v.t.*, *v.i.* griffonner.

scrawler ['skrɔ:lə], *n.* griffonneur, *m.*

scrawny ['skrɔ:ni], *a.* décharné, émacié.

scream [skri:m], *n.* cri perçant, *m.*—*v.i.* crier, pousser des cris.

screamer ['skri:mə], *n.* crieur, *m.*

screaming ['skri:miŋ], *a.* perçant; qui crie.—*n.* cris, *m.pl.*

screech [skri:tʃ], *n.* cri perçant, *m.*—*v.i.* crier.

screech-owl ['skri:tʃaul], *n.* effraie, chouette, *f.*

screen [skri:n], *n.* écran; paravent (*pliant*); rideau (*d'arbres etc.*), *m.*; (*fig.*) voile, *f.*, abri, *m.*; défense, *f.*—*v.t.* mettre à couvert; abriter (*contre*).

screw [skru:], *a.* à hélice.—*n.* vis; hélice (*de navire etc.*), *f.*—*v.t.* visser; (*fig.*) serrer (*presser*); pressurer (*opprimer*).—*v.i.* se visser.

screw-bolt ['skru:boult], *n.* boulon à vis, *m.*

screw-cap ['skru:kæp], *n.* couvercle à vis, *m.*

screw-driver ['skru:draivə], *n.* tournevis, *m.*

screw-nail ['skru:neil], *n.* vis à bois, *f.*

screw-nut ['skru:nʌt], *n.* écrou, *m.*

screw-wrench ['skru:rentʃ], *n.* clef anglaise, *f.*

scribble [skribl], *n.* griffonnage; barbouillage, *m.*—*v.t.*, *v.i.* griffonner.

scribbler ['skriblə], *n.* griffonneur; gratte-papier, *m.*

scribe [skraib], *n.* scribe; écrivain, *m.*—*v.t.* (*Carp.*) tracer.

scrimmage ['skrimidʒ], *n.* lutte, rixe; (*Ftb.*) mêlée, *f.*

scrip [skrip], *n.* petit sac; (*Comm.*) titre *ou* certificat provisoire, *m.*

script [skript], *n.* manuscrit; (*Cine.*) scénario, *m.*

scriptural ['skriptʃuərəl], *a.* de l'Écriture Sainte, biblique, scriptural.

Scripture ['skriptʃə], *n.* l'Écriture Sainte, *f.*

script-writer ['skriptraitə], *n.* (*Cine.*) scénariste, *m.*, *f.*

scrofula ['skrɔfjulə], *n.* scrofule, *f.*

scrofulous ['skrɔfjuləs], *a.* scrofuleux.

scroll [skroul], *n.* rouleau, *m.*

scrounge [skraundʒ], *v.t.*, *v.i.* (*slang*) chiper, chaparder, grapiller; ***to scrounge on someone***, vivre aux crochets de quelqu'un.

scrounger ['skraundʒə], *n.* chapardeur, *m.*

scrub [skrʌb], *v.t.*, *v.i.* frotter fort; laver, récurer.—*n.* broussailles, *f.pl.*; maquis, *m.*

scrubbing ['skrʌbiŋ], *n.* frottage, récurage, *m.*

scrubbing-brush ['skrʌbiŋbrʌʃ], *n.* brosse de cuisine, *f.*

scrubby ['skrʌbi], *a.* rabougri, chétif, mal rasé.

scruff [skrʌf], *n.* nuque, *f.*

scruple [skru:pl], *n.* scrupule, *m.*—*v.i.* se faire scrupule (*de*), hésiter (*à*).

scrupulous ['skru:pjuləs], *a.* scrupuleux.

scrupulously ['skru:pjuləsli], *adv.* scrupuleusement.

scrupulousness ['skru:pjuləsnis], *n.* scrupule, doute, *m.*

scrutator [skru:'teitə], *n.* scrutateur, *m.*

scrutineer [skru:ti'niə], *n.* pointeur (*de votes*); scrutateur, *m.*

scrutinize ['skru:tinaiz], *v.t.* scruter, examiner à fond.

scrutinizing ['skru:tinaiziŋ], *a.* scrutateur, inquisiteur.

scrutiny ['skru:tini], *n.* enquête rigoureuse, vérification, *f.*

scud [skʌd], *n.* léger nuage, *m.*; course rapide, *f.*—*v.i.* s'enfuir; courir (*nuages*).

scuffle [skʌfl], *n.* bagarre, rixe, mêlée, *f.*—*v.i.* se battre; traîner les pieds.

scull [skʌl], *n.* rame; godille, *f.*—*v.i.* ramer.

scullery ['skʌləri], *n.* arrière-cuisine, laverie, *f.*; ***scullery maid***, laveuse de vaisselle, *f.*

sculptor ['skʌlptə], *n.* sculpteur, *m.*

sculpture ['skʌlptʃə], *n.* sculpture, *f.*—*v.t.* sculpter.

scum [skʌm], *n.* écume, *f.*; (*fig.*) rebut (*ordures*), *m.*; lie, *f.*—*v.t.* écumer.

scupper ['skʌ́pə], *n.* (*Naut.*) dalot, *m.*—*v.t.* saborder.

scurf [skə:f], *n.* pellicules (*des cheveux*), *f.pl.*

scurfy ['skə:fi], *a.* pelliculeux (*cheveux*).

scurrility [skʌ'riliti], **scurrilousness** ['skʌriləsnis], *n.* grossièreté, *f.*

scurrilous ['skʌriləs], *a.* grossier, ordurier.

scurry ['skʌri], *n.* débandade, *f.*; tourbillon (*de poussière, de neige etc.*), *m.*—*v.i.* se hâter.

scurvily ['skə:vili], *adv.* bassement, vilement.

scurviness ['skə:vinis], *n.* état scorbutique, *m.*; (*fig.*) bassesse; mesquinerie (*avarice*), *f.*

scurvy ['skə:vi], *a.* scorbutique; (*fig.*) vil, vilain.—*n.* scorbut, *m.*

scut [skʌt], *n.* couette (*de lièvre etc.*), *f.*

scutcheon ['skʌtʃən], [ESCUTCHEON].

scuttle (1) [skʌtl], *n.* panier; seau à charbon, *m.*

scuttle (2) [skʌtl], *n.* (*Naut.*) hublot, *m.*; écoutille, *f.*—*v.t.* saborder.

scuttle (3) [skʌtl], *v.i.* aller à pas précipités.

scuttling ['skʌtliŋ], *a.* en fuite, qui détale.—*n.* sabordage, *m.*

scythe [saið], *n.* faux, *f.*—*v.t.* faucher.

sea [si:], *a.* de mer, marin, maritime.—*n.* mer; lame; (*fig.*) multitude, *f.*, déluge, *m.*; ***at sea***, en mer; ***heavy sea***, mer houleuse; ***in the open sea***, en pleine mer, au grand large.

seaboard ['si:bɔ:d], *n.* littoral, rivage, *m.*, côte, *f.*

sea-borne ['si:bɔ:n], *a.* transporté par mer.

sea-calf ['si:kɑ:f], *n.* veau marin, *m.*

sea-cow ['si:kau], *n.* lamantin, *m.*

sea-dog ['si:dɔg], *n.* loup de mer (*marin*), *m.*

seafarer ['si:fɛərə], *n.* homme de mer, marin, *m.*

seafaring ['si:fɛəriŋ], *a.* marin; ***seafaring man***, marin, *m.*

sea-front ['si:frʌnt], *n.* esplanade, *f.*, bord de mer, *m.*

sea-gauge ['si:geidʒ], *n.* tirant d'eau, *m.*
sea-going ['si:gouiŋ], *a.* de haute mer.
sea-gull ['si:gʌl], *n.* mouette, *f.*, goéland, *m.*
sea-horse ['si:hɔ:s], *n.* morse, *m.*
sea-kale ['si:keil], *n.* chou marin, *m.*
seal (1) [si:l], *n.* cachet; sceau (*officiel*), *m.*; (*Law*) scellés, *m.pl.*; ***Privy Seal***, petit sceau.—*v.t.* cacheter; (*Law*) sceller; (*Customs*) plomber.
seal (2) [si:l], *n.* phoque, *m.*
sea-legs ['si:legz], *n.pl.* pied marin, *m.*
sea-level ['si:levəl], *n.* niveau de la mer, *m.*
sealing ['si:liŋ], *n.* action de sceller, *f.*
sealing-wax ['si:liŋwæks], *n.* cire à cacheter, *f.*
sea-lion ['si:laiən], *n.* lion de mer, *m.*, otarie, *f.*
seam [si:m], *n.* (*Dress.*) couture; (*Mining*) couche; (*Geol.*) veine, *f.*—*v.t.* coudre; couturer.
seaman ['si:mən], *n.* (*pl.* **-men** [men]) marin, matelot, homme de mer, *m.*
seamanship ['si:mənʃip], *n.* matelotage, *m.*
seamless ['si:mlis], *a.* sans couture.
seamstress ['si:mstris], [SEMPSTRESS].
seamy ['si:mi], *a.* plein de coutures; ***the seamy side of life***, les dessous de la vie, *m.pl.*
sea-nymph ['si:nimf], *n.* néréide, *f.*
seaplane ['si:plein], *n.* hydravion, *m.*
seaport ['si:pɔ:t], *n.* port de mer, *m.*
sear [siə], *a.* séché, fané, flétri.—*v.t.* brûler; cautériser; faner.
search [sə:tʃ], *n.* recherche; (*Law*) perquisition; (*Customs*) visite, *f.*—*v.t.* chercher, examiner; fouiller; (*Law*) faire une perquisition chez; (*Customs*) visiter.—*v.i.* chercher; fouiller.
searcher ['sə:tʃə], *n.* chercheur, *m.*
searching ['sə:tʃiŋ], *a.* scrutateur, pénétrant; vif, perçant (*vent*).
searchingly ['sə:tʃiŋli], *adv.* minutieusement.
searchlight ['sə:tʃlait], *n.* projecteur, *m.*
search-party ['sə:tʃpɑ:ti], *n.* expédition de secours, *f.*
search-warrant ['sə:tʃwɔrənt], *n.* mandat de perquisition, *m.*
sea-route ['si:ru:t], *n.* voie de mer, *f.*
seascape ['si:skeip], *n.* (*Paint.*) marine, *f.*
sea-scout ['si:skaut], *n.* (boy-)scout marin, *m.*
sea-shell ['si:ʃel], *n.* coquillage, *m.*
seashore ['si:ʃɔ:], *n.* bord de la mer, rivage, *m.*, côte, *f.*
sea-sick ['si:sik], *a.* qui a le mal de mer.
sea-sickness ['si:siknis], *n.* mal de mer, *m.*
seaside ['si:said], *n.* bord de la mer, *m.*
season [si:zn], *n.* saison, *f.*; (*fig.*) temps, moment opportun, *m.*—*v.t.* assaisonner (*de*); sécher (*bois*); (*fig.*) accoutumer (*à*).—*v.i.* s'acclimater; se sécher (*bois*).
seasonable ['si:znəbl], *a.* de saison; (*fig.*) à propos, opportun, convenable.
seasonably ['si:znəbli], *adv.* à propos.
seasonal ['si:znəl], *a.* des saisons; saisonnier.
seasoned [si:znd], *a.* assaisonné (*viande*); (*fig.*) endurci, aguerri, acclimaté.
seasoning ['si:zniŋ], *n.* assaisonnement; séchage (*du bois*), *m.*
season-ticket ['si:zn'tikit], *n.* carte d'abonnement, *f.*
seat [si:t], *n.* siège; banc, *m.*; banquette (*dans un véhicule*); (*fig.*) place; demeure (*château*), *f.*; théâtre (*de guerre*); fond (*de pantalon*), *m.*; ***take your seats, please!*** en voiture!—*v.t.* asseoir; faire asseoir; placer.
seated ['si:tid], *a.* assis, placé.
sea-wall ['si:wɔ:l], *n.* digue, chaussée, *f.*
seaward ['si:wəd], *a.* tourné vers la mer.—*adv.* vers la mer.
seaweed ['si:wi:d], *n.* algue, *f.*, goémon, varech, *m.*
seaworthiness ['si:wə:ðinis], *n.* navigabilité (*navire*), *f.*
seaworthy ['si:wə:ði], *a.* en bon état (de navigation).
secant ['si:kənt], *a.* sécant.—*n.* sécante, *f.*
secede [si'si:d], *v.i.* se séparer (*de*).
seceder [si'si:də], *n.* scissionnaire, *m.*, *f.*; dissident, *m.*
secession [si'seʃən], *n.* sécession, séparation, *f.*
seclude [si'klu:d], *v.t.* séparer; éloigner.
secluded [si'klu:did], *a.* retiré, isolé, solitaire.
seclusion [si'klu:ʒən], *n.* retraite, solitude, *f.*
second ['sekənd], *a.* second, deuxième; deux (*du mois*); inférieur; ***on second thoughts***, à la réflexion.—*n.* témoin, second (*dans un duel*), *m.*; seconde (*temps*), *f.*—*v.t.* seconder, aider; appuyer (*une motion*); [si'kɔnd] détacher (*fonctionnaire*).
secondary ['sekəndri], *a.* secondaire; accessoire.
seconder ['sekəndə], *n.* personne qui appuie, *f.*
second-hand ['sekənd'hænd], *a.* and *adv.* d'occasion.
secondly ['sekəndli], *adv.* secondement; en second lieu.
second-rate ['sekəndreit], *a.* de second ordre.
secrecy ['si:krəsi], *n.* secret, *m.*; discrétion, *f.*
secret ['si:krit], *a.* secret; retiré (*maison etc.*).—*n.* secret, *m.*
secretarial [sekrə'tɛəriəl], *a.* de secrétaire.
secretariat [sekrə'tɛəriæt], *n.* secrétariat, *m.*
secretary ['sekrətri], *n.* secrétaire, *m.*, *f.*
secretaryship ['sekrətriʃip], *n.* secrétariat, *m.*
secrete [si'kri:t], *v.t.* cacher; (*Physiol.*) sécréter.
secretion [si'kri:ʃən], *n.* sécrétion, *f.*
secretive ['si:krətiv], *a.* réservé; dissimulé.
secretiveness ['si:krətivnis], *n.* caractère cachottier, *m.*
secretly ['si:krətli], *adv.* en secret; intérieurement.
sect [sekt], *n.* secte, *f.*
sectarian [sek'tɛəriən], *a.* de sectaire.—*n.* sectaire, *m.*, *f.*
sectarianism [sek'tɛəriənizm], *n.* esprit de secte, sectarisme, *m.*
section ['sekʃən], *n.* section; coupe, *f.*, profil; (*Mil.*) groupe de combat, *m.*
sectional ['sekʃənəl], *a.* en coupe; en sections.
sector ['sektə], *n.* secteur, *m.*
secular ['sekjulə], *a.* temporel; laïque; séculaire (*année*).
secularity [sekju'læriti], **secularness** ['sekjulənis], *n.* sécularité, mondanité, *f.*
secularization [sekjulərai'zeiʃən], *n.* sécularisation, *f.*
secularize ['sekjuləraiz], *v.t.* séculariser.
secure [si'kjuə], *a.* dans la sécurité, en sûreté; sûr, assuré (*chose*); bien fermé.—*v.t.* mettre en sûreté; assurer (*garantir*); s'assurer de; fermer; barrer (*attacher fortement*); (*fig.*) affermir.
securely [si'kjuəli], *adv.* en sûreté; sûrement; fortement.

secureness [si'kjuənis], *n.* sécurité, *f.*

security [si'kjuəriti], *n.* sécurité, sûreté; garantie, *f.*; (*pl.*) titres, *m.pl.*, valeurs, *f.pl.*; (*Law*) caution, *f.*

sedan-chair [si'dæn'tʃɛə], *n.* chaise à porteurs, *f.*

sedate [si'deit], *a.* posé, calme, rassis.

sedately [si'deitli], *adv.* posément, avec calme.

sedateness [si'deitnis], *n.* calme, *m.*

sedative ['sedətiv], *a.* and *n.* sédatif, *m.*

sedentary ['sedntri], *a.* sédentaire; inactif.

sedge [sedʒ], *n.* laîche, *f.*, jonc, *m.*

sediment ['sedimənt], *n.* sédiment, dépôt, *m.*

sedition [si'diʃən], *n.* sédition, *f.*

seditious [si'diʃəs], *a.* séditieux.

seditiousness [si'diʃəsnis], *n.* esprit séditieux, *m.*

seduce [si'dju:s], *v.t.* séduire.

seducer [si'dju:sə], *n.* séducteur, *m.*

seducing [si'dju:siŋ], *a.* séduisant.

seduction [si'dʌkʃən], *n.* séduction, *f.*

seductive [si'dʌktiv], *a.* séducteur, séduisant.

sedulity [si'dju:liti], **sedulousness** ['sedjuləsnis], *n.* assiduité, diligence, *f.*

sedulous ['sedjuləs], *a.* assidu, diligent, zélé.

sedulously ['sedjuləsli], *adv.* assidûment, diligemment, avec application.

sedulousness [SEDULITY].

see (1) [si:], *n.* siège épiscopal, évêché; archevêché (*d'un archevêque*), *m.*; ***the Holy See***, le Saint-Siège, *m.*

see (2) [si:], *v.t. irr.* voir; comprendre; accompagner, conduire.—*v.i.* voir; s'occuper (*de*); ***I will see to it***, j'y veillerai.

seed [si:d], *n.* semence; graine (*de légumes*); (*fig.*) race, *f.*; ***to run to seed***, monter en graine.—*v.t.* ensemencer; (*Spt.*) trier.—*v.i.* grener.

seed-bed ['si:dbed], *n.* semis, *m.*

seed-cake ['si:dkeik], *n.* gâteau à l'anis, *m.*

seedling ['si:dliŋ], *n.* semis, sauvageon, *m.*

seedsman ['si:dzmən], *n.* (*pl.* **-men** [men]) grainetier, *m.*

seed-time ['si:dtaim], *n.* semailles, *f.pl.*

seedy ['si:di], *a.* râpé, usé (*vêtement*); souffrant; miteux.

seeing ['si:iŋ], *n.* vue; vision, *f.*—*conj. phr.* ***seeing that***, vu que, puisque.

seek [si:k], *v.t. irr.* chercher; poursuivre, en vouloir à (*la vie etc.*).—*v.i.* chercher.

seeker ['si:kə], *n.* chercheur, *m.*

seeking ['si:kiŋ], *n.* recherche, poursuite, *f.*

seem [si:m], *v.i.* sembler, paraître, avoir l'air (*de*).

seeming ['si:miŋ], *a.* apparent, spécieux.—*n.* semblant, *m.*, apparence, *f.*, dehors, *m.*

seemingly ['si:miŋli], *adv.* en apparence, apparemment.

seemliness ['si:mlinis], *n.* bienséance; convenance, *f.*

seemly ['si:mli], *a.* bienséant, convenable; joli.—*adv.* convenablement.

seep [si:p], *v.i.* s'infiltrer, suinter.

seer ['si:ə], *n.* prophète, voyant, *m.*

seesaw ['si:sɔ:], *n.* bascule, balançoire, *f.*, va-et-vient, *m.*—*v.i.* faire la bascule.

seethe [si:ð], *v.t.* faire bouillir.—*v.i.* bouillir, bouillonner.

segment ['segmənt], *n.* segment, *m.*

segregate ['segrigeit], *v.t.* séparer.—*v.i.* se diviser.

segregation [segri'geiʃən], *n.* séparation, ségrégation, *f.*

seize [si:z], *v.t.* saisir; se saisir de, s'emparer de; (*Naut.*) amarrer.—*v.i.* (*Mech.*) gripper, caler; se coincer.

seizure ['si:ʒə], *n.* saisie, prise de possession; (*Path.*) attaque, *f.*

seldom ['seldəm], *adv.* rarement.

select [si'lekt], *a.* choisi; d'élite.—*v.t.* choisir.

selection [si'lekʃən], *n.* choix, *m.*

selectness [si'lektnis], *n.* excellence, *f.*

selector [si'lektə], *n.* (*Spt.*) sélectionneur, *m.*

self [self], *pron.* (*pl.* **selves** [selvz]) même, soi-même; (*reflexively*) se.—*n.* le moi, individu, *m.*, personne, *f.*

self-assertion ['selfə'sə:ʃən], *n.* caractère impérieux, *m.*, outrecuidance, *f.*

self-assertive ['selfə'sə:tiv], *a.* autoritaire, outrecuidant.

self-centred ['self'sentəd], *a.* égocentrique.

self-confidence ['self'kɔnfidəns], *n.* confiance en soi-même, assurance, *f.*

self-confident ['self'kɔnfidənt], *a.* sûr de soi-même.

self-conscious ['self'kɔnʃəs], *a.* embarrassé, intimidé; gêné.

self-consciousness ['self'kɔnʃəsnis], *n.* embarras, *m.*, gêne, *f.*

self-contained ['selfkən'teind], *a.* indépendant; avec entrée particulière (*appartement*).

self-control ['selfkən'troul], *n.* sang-froid, *m.*; maîtrise de soi, *f.*

self-defence ['selfdi'fens], *n.* défense personnelle; légitime défense, *f.*

self-denial ['selfdi'naiəl], *n.* abnégation, *f.*; désintéressement, *m.*

self-denying ['selfdi'naiiŋ], *a.* qui fait abnégation de soi.

self-educated ['self'edjukeitid], *a.* autodidacte.

self-esteem ['selfi'sti:m], *n.* amour-propre, *m.*

self-evident ['self'evidənt], *a.* évident en soi, qui saute aux yeux.

self-governed ['self'gʌvənd], *a.* indépendant autonome.

self-government ['self'gʌvənmənt], *n.* autonomie, *f.*

self-help ['self'help], *n.* efforts personnels, *m.pl.*

self-importance ['selfim'pɔ:təns], *n.* suffisance, vanité, *f.*

self-important ['selfim'pɔ:tənt], *a.* plein de soi, suffisant.

self-inflicted ['selfin'fliktid], *a.* volontaire.

selfish ['selfiʃ], *a.* égoïste.

selfishly ['selfiʃli], *adv.* en égoïste, d'une manière égoïste.

selfishness ['selfiʃnis], *n.* égoïsme, *m.*

selfless ['selflis], *a.* désintéressé.

self-made ['self'meid], *a.* qui s'est fait ce qu'il est; ***he is a self-made man***, il est fils de ses œuvres.

self-opinioned ['selfə'pinjənd], **self-opinionated** ['selfə'pinjəneitid], *a.* entêté.

self-possessed ['selfpə'zest], *a.* calme; maître de soi.

self-possession ['selfpə'zeʃən], *n.* sang-froid, aplomb, *m.*

self-praise ['self'preiz], *n.* éloge de soi-même, *m.*

self-preservation ['selfprezə'veiʃən], *n.* conservation de soi-même, *f.*

self-propelled ['selfprə'peld], *a.* autopropulsé.
self-registering ['self'redʒistriŋ], *a.* à registre, enregistreur.
self-reliance ['selfri'laiəns], *n.* confiance en soi, indépendance, *f.*
self-respect ['selfris'pekt], *n.* respect de soi-même, amour-propre, *m.*; dignité, *f.*
self-righteous ['self'raitʃəs], *a.* pharisaïque.
self-sacrifice ['self'sækrifais], *n.* sacrifice de soi-même, *m.*, abnégation, *f.*
self-same ['selfseim], *a.* absolument le même.
self-satisfied ['self'sætisfaid], *a.* content de soi.
self-seeking ['self'si:kiŋ], *a.* égoïste.
self-service ['self'sə:vis], *n.* libre service, self-service, *m.*
self-starter ['self'stɑ:tə], *n.* démarreur automatique, *m.*
self-styled ['self'staild], *a.* soi-disant, prétendu.
self-sufficiency ['selfsə'fiʃənsi], *n.* suffisance; indépendance, *f.*
self-sufficient ['selfsə'fiʃənt], *a.* suffisant; indépendant.
self-supporting ['selfsə'pɔ:tiŋ], *a.* qui subsiste par ses propres moyens.
self-taught ['self'tɔ:t], *a.* autodidacte.
self-will ['self'wil], *n.* obstination, opiniâtreté, *f.*
self-willed ['self'wild], *a.* obstiné, opiniâtre.
sell [sel], *v.t. irr.* vendre.—*v.i.* se vendre; ***to be sold out of an article***, avoir tout vendu, ne plus avoir d'un article.—*n.* attrape, *f.*
seller ['selə], *n.* vendeur, *m.*, vendeuse, *f.*
selling ['seliŋ], *n.* vente, *f.*; ***selling off***, liquidation, *f.*
seltzer ['seltsə], **seltzer water** ['seltsə'wɔ:tə], *n.* eau de Seltz, *f.*
selvedge ['selvidʒ], *n.* lisière, *f.*
selves [SELF].
semaphore ['seməfɔ:], *n.* sémaphore, *m.*
semblance ['sembləns], *n.* semblant, *m.*, apparence, *f.*
semi ['semi], *pref.* semi, demi, à demi, à moitié.
semibreve ['semibri:v], *n.* (*Mus.*) ronde, *f.*
semi-circle ['semisə:kl], *n.* demi-cercle, *m.*
semicolon ['semi'koulən], *n.* point-virgule, *m.*
semi-detached ['semidi'tætʃt], *a.* ***semi-detached houses***, maisons jumelles, *f.pl.*
semi-final ['semifainl], *n.* demi-finale, *f.*
seminary ['seminəri], *n.* séminaire, *m.*; institution (*école*), *f.*
semi-official ['semiə'fiʃl], *a.* demi-officiel, officieux.
semiquaver ['semikweivə], *n.* (*Mus.*) double croche, *f.*
semitone ['semitoun], *n.* (*Mus.*) demi-ton, semi-ton, *m.*
semolina [semə'li:nə], *n.* semoule, *f.*
sempstress ['sempstris, 'semstris], *n.* couturière, *f.*
senate ['senit], *n.* sénat, *m.*
senator ['senitə], *n.* sénateur, *m.*
senatorial [seni'tɔ:riəl], *a.* sénatorial.
send [send], *v.t. irr.* envoyer, faire parvenir; expédier (*marchandises*); ***to send away***, renvoyer, congédier; ***to send back***, renvoyer; ***to send for***, envoyer chercher, faire venir; ***to send forth***, lancer, émettre; ***to send in***, faire entrer; ***to send on***, faire suivre (*lettres etc.*).—*v.i.* envoyer.
sender ['sendə], *n.* envoyeur; (*Comm.*) expéditeur, *m.*
Senegal ['senigɔ:l]. le Sénégal, *m.*
Senegalese [senigə'li:z], *a.* sénégalais.—*n.* Sénégalais (*personne*), *m.*
senile ['si:nail], *a.* de vieillard, sénile.
senility [sə'niliti], *n.* sénilité, *f.*
senior ['si:njə], *a.* aîné; ancien; plus ancien, supérieur.—*n.* aîné; ancien; doyen, *m.*
seniority [si:ni'ɔriti], *n.* priorité d'âge; ancienneté, *f.*
senna ['senə], *n.* séné, *m.*
sensation [sen'seiʃən], *n.* sensation, *f.*
sensational [sen'seiʃənl], *a.* à sensation, à effet.
sensationalism [sen'seiʃənlizm], *n.* recherche du sensationnel, *f.*
sense [sens], *n.* sens; bon sens, sens commun; sentiment, *m.*; signification, *f.*
senseless ['senslis], *a.* sans connaissance, insensible; insensé, absurde (*pas raisonnable*).
senselessly ['senslisli], *adv.* d'une manière insensée; sottement.
senselessness ['senslisnis], *n.* sottise, absurdité, *f.*
sensibility [sensi'biliti], *n.* sensibilité, *f.*; sentiment, *m.*
sensible ['sensibl], *a.* sensé, raisonnable (*intelligent*); sensible (*de*); en pleine connaissance.
sensibly ['sensibli], *adv.* sensiblement; sensément, sagement (*avec intelligence*).
sensitive ['sensitiv], *a.* sensible (*à*); sensitif, impressionnable; susceptible (*ombrageux*).
sensitiveness ['sensitivnis], **sensitivity** [sensi'tiviti], *n.* sensibilité; susceptibilité (*facilité à se vexer etc.*), *f.*
sensitized ['sensitaizd], *a.* (*Phot.*) sensible (*papier*).
sensory ['sensəri], *a.* sensoriel, des sens.
sensual ['sensjuəl], *a.* sensuel; des sens.
sensualist ['sensjuəlist], *n.* sensualiste, *m.*, *f.*, sensuel, *m.*
sensuality [sensju'æliti], *n.* sensualité, *f.*
sentence ['sentəns], *n.* phrase; maxime, *f.*; jugement, arrêt, *m.*, sentence, *f.*—*v.t.* prononcer une sentence *ou* un jugement (*contre*), condamner.
sententious [sen'tenʃəs], *a.* sentencieux.
sententiousness [sen'tenʃəsnis], *n.* caractère sentencieux, *m.*
sentient ['senʃənt], *a.* sensible.
sentiment ['sentimənt], *n.* sentiment; avis, *m.*, pensée, *f.*
sentimental [senti'mentl], *a.* sentimental.
sentimentality [sentimen'tæliti], *n.* sensiblerie, sentimentalité, *f.*
sentinel ['sentinl], **sentry** ['sentri], *n.* sentinelle, *f.*, factionnaire, *m.*
sentry-box ['sentribɔks], *n.* guérite, *f.*
separable ['sepərəbl], *a.* séparable, divisible.
separate ['sepərit], *a.* séparé; disjoint, désuni.—['sepəreit], *v.t.* séparer; disjoindre, désunir.—*v.i.* se séparer; se disjoindre.
separately ['sepəritli], *adv.* séparément, à part.
separation [sepə'reiʃən], *n.* séparation; désunion, *f.*
sepia ['si:pjə], *n.* sépia (*couleur*); seiche (*poisson*), *f.*

sepoy ['si:pɔi], *n.* cipaye, *m.*
September [sep'tembə]. septembre, *m.*
septennial [sep'teniəl], *a.* septennal.
septennially [sep'teniəli], *adv.* tous les sept ans.
septic ['septik], *a.* septique; infecté (*blessure*).
septuagenarian [septjuədʒə'nɛəriən], *a.* and *n.* septuagénaire, *m., f.*
Septuagesima [septjuə'dʒesimə]. Septuagésime, *f.*
sepulchral [si'pʌlkrəl], *a.* sépulcral.
sepulchre ['sepəlkə], *n.* sépulcre, *m.*
sepulture ['sepəltʃə], *n.* sépulture; inhumation, *f.*
sequel ['si:kwəl], *n.* suite, conséquence, *f.*
sequence ['si:kwəns], *n.* suite, série; succession; (*Cine.*) séquence, *f.*
sequester [si'kwestə], *v.t.* séquestrer.
sequestered [si'kwestəd], *a.* retiré, écarté; (*Law*) en séquestre.
sequestrate ['si:kwəstreit, si'kwestreit], *v.t.* séquestrer.
sequestration [si:kwəs'treiʃən], *n.* séquestre, *m.*; retraite, *f.*, isolement (*personne*), *m.*
sequestrator ['si:kwəstreitə], *n.* (*Law*) séquestre, *m.*
sequin ['si:kwin], *n.* sequin, *m.*
seraglio [se'rɑ:ljou], *n.* sérail, *m.*
seraph ['serəf], *n.* (*pl.* **seraphim** ['serəfim]) séraphin, *m.*
seraphic [sə'ræfik], *a.* séraphique.
Serbia ['sə:biə]. la Serbie, *f.*
Serbian ['sə:biən], *a.* serbe.—*n.* serbe (*langue*), *m.*; Serbe (*personne*), *m., f.*
sere [SEAR].
serenade [serə'neid], *n.* sérénade, *f.*—*v.t.* donner une sérénade à.
serene [si'ri:n], *a.* serein, calme; sérénissime (*titre*).
serenely [si'ri:nli], *adv.* avec sérénité.
sereneness [si'ri:nnis], **serenity** [si'reniti], *n.* sérénité, *f.*, calme, *m.*
serf [sə:f], *n.* serf, *m.*
serfdom ['sə:fdəm], *n.* servage, *m.*
serge [sə:dʒ], *n.* serge, *f.*
sergeant, serjeant ['sɑ:dʒənt], *n.* sergent (*infanterie*); maréchal des logis (*cavalerie, artillerie*); brigadier (*police*), *m.*
sergeant-major ['sɑ:dʒənt'meidʒə], *n.* adjudant, *m.*
serial ['siəriəl], *a.* paraissant par numéros *ou* par livraisons; ***serial (story)***, (roman-) feuilleton, *m.*
serially ['siəriəli], *adv.* par numéros.
seriatim [siəri'eitim], *adv.* par série; successivement.
series ['siəri:z], *n.* série, suite, succession, *f.*
serious ['siəriəs], *a.* sérieux; grave.
seriously ['siəriəsli], *adv.* sérieusement; gravement.
seriousness ['siəriəsnis], *n.* sérieux, *m.*; gravité, *f.*
serjeant [SERGEANT].
sermon ['sə:mən], *n.* sermon, *m.*
sermonize ['sə:mənaiz], *v.t.* prêcher; sermonner.
sermonizer ['sə:mənaizə], *n.* sermonneur, *m.*
serpent ['sə:pənt], *n.* serpent, *m.*
serpentine ['sə:pəntain], *a.* serpentin, sinueux.—*n.* (*Min.*) serpentine, *f.*
serrate ['sereit], *a.* en scie, dentelé; serraté.
serration [se'reiʃən], *n.* dentelure, *f.*
serried ['serid], *a.* compact, serré.
serum ['siərəm], *n.* sérum, *m.*
servant ['sə:vənt], *n.* serviteur, *m.*, servante, *f.*; employé (*de compagnies etc.*), *m.*; domestique, *m.*; ordonnance (*d'officier*), *m., f.*; ***civil servant***, fonctionnaire, *m., f.*
serve [sə:v], *v.t.* servir; servir à, être bon à; faire (*apprentissage*); desservir (*localité*); signifier (*une assignation*); ***it serves him right***, c'est bien fait.—*v.i.* servir; être au service; suffire.—*n.* (*fam.*) (*Ten.*) service, *m.*
server ['sə:və], *n.* servant; (*Ten.*) serveur; (*Eccles.*) acolyte, *m.*
service ['sə:vis], *n.* service; (*fig.*) avantage, *m.*; utilité; signification (*d'assignation*); (*Mil.*) arme, *f.*—*v.t.* (*Motor.*) entretenir, réparer.
serviceable ['sə:visəbl], *a.* utile (*à*), avantageux, de bon usage.
serviceableness ['sə:visəblnis], *n.* utilité, *f.*
service-station ['sə:vissteiʃən], *n.* station-service, *f.*
serviette [sə:vi'et], *n.* serviette de table, *f.*
servile ['sə:vail], *a.* servile; asservi.
servility [sə'viliti], *n.* servilité, bassesse, *f.*
serving ['sə:viŋ], *a.* servant, qui sert.
servitude ['sə:vitju:d], *n.* servitude, *f.*, asservissement, *m.*; ***penal servitude***, travaux forcés, *m.pl.*
sesame ['sesəmi], *n.* sésame, *m.*
session ['seʃən], *n.* session, séance, *f.*; (*pl.*) assises, *f.pl.*
set [set], *v.t. irr.* poser, opposer (*sceau, signature*), mettre, placer, poster; planter (*fleurs*), fixer; ajuster, arranger (*régler*); affûter (*outil*); donner (*exemple*); (*Mus.*) mettre en musique; remettre (*os*); sertir (*pierre précieuse*); dresser, tendre (*piège*); déployer (*voiles*); (*Print.*) composer; ***to set aside***, mettre de côté; ***to set at ease***, mettre à l'aise; ***to set back***, reculer; ***to set forth***, énoncer; ***to set forward***, avancer; ***to set off***, faire ressortir (*faire valoir*); ***to set up***, ériger, établir (*fonder*).—*v.i.* se fixer; diriger, porter (*vers* ou *à*); se coucher (*soleil*); prendre (*confitures etc.*); ***to set about***, commencer, se mettre à; ***to set out***, partir, se mettre en route; ***to set up*** (*dans un commerce etc.*), s'établir.—*a.* mis, posé, placé; serti (*pierre précieuse*); prêt; arrêté, fixe; réglé; d'apparat, préparé (*discours*); ***all set?*** ça y est?—*n.* collection, *f.*, ensemble, assortiment, *m.*, série, *f.*, jeu; service (*de porcelaine etc.*), *m.*; parure (*de pierres précieuses*); mise en plis (*cheveux*), *f.*; (*Theat.*) décor; groupe, *m.*
set-back ['setbæk], *n.* recul, échec, *m.*
set-square ['setskwɛə], *n.* équerre, *f.*
settee [se'ti:], *n.* canapé, *m.*, causeuse, *f.*
setter ['setə], *n.* chien d'arrêt, *m.*; ***bonesetter***, rebouteur, rebouteux, *m.*
setting ['setiŋ], *n.* mise, pose, *f.*; coucher (*du soleil etc.*); décor (*naturel* ou *de théâtre*), *m.* (*Mus.*) mise en musique, *f.*; remboîtement (*d'os*), *m.*; monture (*de pierre précieuse*), *f.*
settle (1) [setl], *v.t.* fixer; établir; décider, arrêter; assigner (*des biens à*); coloniser (*un pays*); accommoder; payer, régler (*dettes*).—*v.i.* s'établir, se fixer; se marier; se calmer (*devenir tranquille*); se poser (*oiseau*); s'ar-

ranger (*avec*); ***to settle down***, se fixer, s'établir; ***to settle down to***, s'appliquer à.
settle (2) [setl], *n.* banc (à dossier), *m.*
settled [setld], *a.* établi; calme, tranquille.
settlement ['setlmənt], **settling** ['setliŋ], *n.* établissement, arrangement; dépôt (*au fond des liquides*); accord, contrat, *m.*; colonisation; colonie, *f.*; règlement, solde (*des comptes*); (*Build.*) tassement, *m.*
settler ['setlə], *n.* colon, immigrant, *m.*
set-up ['setʌp], *n.* organisation, *f.*
seven ['sevən], *a.* and *n.* sept, *m.*
sevenfold ['sevənfould], *a.* septuple.—*adv.* sept fois.
seventeen [sevən'ti:n], *a.* and *n.* dix-sept, *m.*
seventeenth ['sevənti:nθ], *a.* dix-septième; dix-sept (*des rois etc.*).—*n.* dix-septième (*fraction*), *m.*
seventh ['sevənθ], *a.* septième; sept (*des rois etc.*).—*n.* septième (*fraction*), *m.*; (*Mus.*) septième, *f.*
seventieth ['sevəntiiθ], *a.* soixante-dixième. —*n.* soixante-dixième (*fraction*), *m.*
seventy ['sevənti], *a.* and *n.* soixante-dix, *m.*
sever ['sevə], *v.t.* séparer, diviser (*de*); disjoindre; couper.—*v.i.* se séparer (*de*).
several ['sevrəl], *a.* plusieurs, divers; distinct, respectif.
severally ['sevrəli], *adv.* séparément, individuellement.
severance ['sevərəns], *n.* séparation, disjonction; rupture, *f.*
severe [si'viə], *a.* sévère; rigoureux, rude (*temps etc.*); violent, aigu, vif (*douleur etc.*).
severity [si'veriti], *n.* sévérité; rigueur, *f.*
sew [sou], *v.t. irr.* coudre; brocher (*livre*).
sewage ['sju:idʒ], *n.* eaux d'égout, *f.pl.*
sewer (1) ['souə], *n.* couseur, *m.*
sewer (2) ['sju:ə], *n.* égout, *m.*
sewerage ['sju:əridʒ], *n.* système d'égouts, *m.*, égouts, *m.pl.*
sewing ['souiŋ], *n.* couture, *f.*; ***sewing-machine***, machine à coudre, *f.*
sex [seks], *n.* sexe, *m.*
sexagenarian [seksədʒə'nɛəriən], *a.* and *n.* sexagénaire, *m.*, *f.*
Sexagesima [seksə'dʒesimə]. Sexagésime, *f.*
sexennial [sek'seniəl], *a.* sexennal.
sexennially [sek'seniəli], *adv.* tous les six ans.
sextant ['sekstənt], *n.* sextant, *m.*
sextet [seks'tet], *n.* (*Mus.*) sextuor, *m.*
sexton ['sekstən], *n.* sacristain; fossoyeur, *m.*
sextuple ['sekstjupl], *a.* and *n.* sextuple, *m.*
sexual ['seksjuəl], *a.* sexuel.
sexuality [seksju'æliti], *n.* sexualité, *f.*
shabbily ['ʃæbili], *adv.* mal, pauvrement (*mis ou vêtu*); (*fig.*) mesquinement.
shabbiness ['ʃæbinis], *n.* état râpé (*de vêtements*), *m.*; (*fig.*) mesquinerie, *f.*
shabby ['ʃæbi], *a.* râpé; mal vêtu, mal mis; (*fig.*) mesquin, ignoble.
shackle [ʃækl], *v.t.* enchaîner; (*fig.*) entraver.
shackles [ʃæklz], *n.pl.* fers, *m.pl.*, chaînes; (*fig.*) entraves, *f.pl.*
shad [ʃæd], *n.* alose (*poisson*), *f.*
shade [ʃeid], *n.* ombre, *f.*; ombrage (*d'arbre etc.*); abat-jour (*de lampe etc.*); garde-vue (*pour les yeux*), *m.*; nuance (*couleur*), *f.*; (*pl.*) enfers (*où vivent les immortels*), *m.pl.*; ***in the shade***, à l'ombre.—*v.t.* ombrager (*de*); obscurcir; abriter (*protéger*); (*Paint.*) ombrer, nuancer; hachurer (*une carte*).
shaded ['ʃeidid], *a.* à l'ombre; ombragé (*de*), (*Paint.*) ombré.
shadiness ['ʃeidinis], *n.* ombrage, *m.*, ombre, (*fig.*) nature suspecte, *f.*
shading ['ʃeidiŋ], *n.* ombres, nuances, hachures, *f.pl.*
shadow ['ʃædou], *n.* ombre, *f.*—*v.t.* ombrager; filer, espionner (*suivre de près*).
shadowing ['ʃædouiŋ], *n.* espionnage, *m.*, filature, *f.*
shadowy ['ʃædoui], *a.* ombragé; sombre (*morne*); vague, chimérique (*irréel*).
shady ['ʃeidi], *a.* ombragé, ombreux; sombre (*noir*); (*colloq.*) louche (*malhonnête*).
shaft [ʃɑ:ft], *n.* flèche, *f.*, dard, trait; brancard (*de charette*); manche (*d'outil, d'arme*); puits (*de mine*); (*Mach.*) arbre, *m.*
shag [ʃæg], *n.* poil rude; caporal (*tabac*); cormoran huppé (*oiseau*), *m.*
shagginess ['ʃæginis], *n.* état poilu, état hérissé, *m.*
shaggy ['ʃægi], *a.* poilu, velu; raboteux (*pays*).
shagreen [ʃə'gri:n], *a.* de peau de chagrin.—*n.* peau de chagrin, *f.*
shah [ʃɑ:], *n.* shah, *m.*
shake [ʃeik], *n.* secousse, *f.*; serrement, *m.*; poignée (de main), *f.*; hochement (de tête), *m.*—*v.t. irr.* secouer, branler, agiter; ébranler, faire trembler; ***to shake hands with***, serrer la main à.—*v.i.* trembler (*de*); s'agiter, branler; chanceler (*sur ses jambes*).
shakedown ['ʃeikdaun], *n.* lit improvisé, *m.*
shakily ['ʃeikili], *adv.* en branlant; à pas chancelants.
shaking ['ʃeikiŋ], *n.* secousse, *f.*, ébranlement, tremblement; ballottement (*à cheval*), *m.*
shako ['ʃækou], *n.* shako, *m.*
shaky ['ʃeiki], *a.* branlant; (*fig.*) peu solide; faible, chancelant (*personne*).
shale [ʃeil], *n.* argile schisteuse, *f.*
shall [ʃæl], *v.aux. irr.* (*used as sign of the future*) ***I shall go***, j'irai; devoir; vouloir; ***shall I go?*** dois-je aller ? voulez-vous que j'aille ? ***but he shall***, mais je l'y forcerai; ***but I shall not***, mais je n'en ferai rien.
shallop ['ʃæləp], *n.* chaloupe, péniche, pinasse, *f.*
shallot [ʃə'lɔt], *n.* échalote, *f.*
shallow ['ʃælou], *a.* peu profond; (*fig.*) superficiel, léger, borné.
shallowness ['ʃælounis], *n.* peu de profondeur; esprit borné, *m.*
sham [ʃæm], *a.* feint, simulé; faux, factice.—*n.* feinte, *f.*, prétexte, *m.*; imposture, frime, *f.*—*v.t.* feindre, simuler; faire le, la *ou* les.—*v.i.* feindre, faire semblant; jouer la comédie.
shamble [ʃæmbl], *v.i.* marcher en traînant les pieds.
shambles [ʃæmblz], *n.pl.* abattoir, *m.*; (*fig.*) scène de carnage; une belle pagaille, *f.*
shambling ['ʃæmbliŋ], *a.* traînant.
shame [ʃeim], *n.* honte; ignominie (*déshonneur*), *f.*; opprobre, *m.*; ***what a shame!*** quel dommage!—*v.t.* faire honte à.
shamefaced ['ʃeimfeist], *a.* honteux, confus.
shamefacedly ['ʃeim'feisidli], *adv.* d'un air penaud.
shamefacedness ['ʃeimfeistnis], *n.* mauvaise honte; timidité, *f.*
shameful ['ʃeimful], *a.* honteux; déshonnête.

hamefulness ['ʃeimfulnis], *n.* honte, ignominie, *f.*

hameless ['ʃeimlis], *a.* éhonté, effronté, impudent.

hamelessly ['ʃeimlisli], *adv.* sans honte, effrontément.

hamelessness ['ʃeimlisnis], *n.* effronterie, impudence, *f.*

hammer ['ʃæmə], *n.* simulateur, *m.*

hampoo [ʃæm'pu:], *v.t.* frictionner; nettoyer (*la tête*).—*n.* shampooing, *m.*

hamrock ['ʃæmrɔk], *n.* trèfle (d'Irlande), *m.*

hank [ʃæŋk], *n.* jambe, *f.*

hanty ['ʃænti], *n.* cabane, bicoque, hutte, *f.*

hanty-town ['ʃæntitaun], *n.* bidonville, *m.*

hape [ʃeip], *n.* forme, figure; tournure, taille (*de personne*); façon, coupe (*de vêtement*), *f.* —*v.t.* former, façonner; modeler (*sur*).

hapeless ['ʃeiplis], *a.* informe, sans forme.

hapelessness ['ʃeiplisnis], *n.* absence de forme, difformité, *f.*

hapeliness ['ʃeiplinis], *n.* beauté de forme, *f.*, galbe, *m.*

hapely ['ʃeipli], *a.* bien fait, beau.

hare (1) [ʃɛə], *n.* soc (*de charrue*), *m.*

hare (2) [ʃɛə], *n.* part, portion; (*St. Exch.*) action, *f.*; ***preference share***, action privilégiée.—*v.t.*, *v.i.* partager; prendre part à; avoir part à.

shareholder ['ʃɛəhouldə], *n.* actionnaire, *m.*, *f.*

sharer ['ʃɛərə], *n.* participant; (*Law*) partageant, *m.*

sharing ['ʃɛəriŋ], *n.* partage, *m.*

shark [ʃɑ:k], *n.* requin; (*fig.*) escroc, filou (*personne*), *m.*

sharp [ʃɑ:p], *a.* tranchant, affilé, qui coupe bien; pointu, aigu; saillant (*angle*); (*fig.*) vif, intelligent, pénétrant, perçant; anguleux (*traits*); piquant, aigre (*goût etc.*); rusé (*astucieux*); (*Mus.*) dièse; ***sharp practice***, filouterie, rouerie, *f.*—*adv.* précise (*l'heure*); ***at four o'clock sharp***, à quatre heures précises; ***look sharp!*** faites vite!—*n.* (*Mus.*) dièse, *m.*

sharpen ['ʃɑ:pən], *v.t.* affiler, aiguiser; tailler en pointe, tailler (*crayon etc.*); (*fig.*) rendre vif.

sharper ['ʃɑ:pə], *n.* aigrefin, escroc, chevalier d'industrie, *m.*

sharply ['ʃɑ:pli], *adv.* rudement, vivement; nettement.

sharpness ['ʃɑ:pnis], *n.* tranchant (*d'une lame*), *m.*; pointe (*acuité*); acidité (*de fruit*); violence (*de douleur etc.*); âpreté (*de langage etc.*); netteté (*de contour etc.*), *f.*; esprit éveillé (*d'enfants etc.*), *m.*

sharp-sighted ['ʃɑ:p'saitid], *a.* à la vue perçante.

sharp-witted ['ʃɑ:p'witid], *a.* à l'esprit délié.

shatter ['ʃætə], *v.t.* fracasser, briser en pièces. —*v.i.* se briser, se fracasser.

shave [ʃeiv], *v.t.* raser; faire la barbe à; effleurer (*friser*); (*Tech.*) planer.—*v.i.* se raser, se faire la barbe; ***to have a close shave***, l'échapper belle; ***to have a shave***, se raser, se faire raser.

shaving ['ʃeiviŋ], *n.* action de raser, *f.*; copeau (*de bois*), *m.*

shaving-brush ['ʃeiviŋbrʌʃ], *n.* blaireau, *m.*

shaving-cream ['ʃeiviŋkri:m], *n.* crème à raser, *f.*

shaving-soap ['ʃeiviŋsoup], *n.* savon pour la barbe, *m.*

shawl [ʃɔ:l], *n.* châle, *m.*

she [ʃi:], *pron.* elle; femelle (*de certains animaux*), *f.*

sheaf [ʃi:f], *n.* (*pl.* **sheaves** [ʃi:vz]) gerbe, *f.*; faisceau (*de flèches*), *m.*—*v.t.* engerber, mettre en gerbe.

shear [ʃiə], *v.t. irr.* tondre.

shearer ['ʃiərə], *n.* tondeur, *m.*; tondeuse (*machine*), *f.*

shearing ['ʃiəriŋ], *n.* tonte, tondaison, *f.*

shears [ʃiəz], *n.pl.* grands ciseaux, *m.pl.*; cisailles (*pour haie, pour métal*), *f.pl.*

she-ass ['ʃi:æs], *n.* ânesse, *f.*

sheath [ʃi:θ], *n.* (*pl.* **sheaths** [ʃi:ðz]) gaine, *f.*; fourreau (*à épée*); étui (*à ciseaux etc.*); (*Ent.*) élytre, *m.*

sheathe [ʃi:ð], *v.t.* mettre dans le fourreau, rengainer; envelopper; revêtir (*de*).

sheaves [SHEAF].

she-cat ['ʃi:kæt], *n.* chatte, *f.*

shed (1) [ʃed], *n.* hangar; (*Build.*) atelier, *m.*; ***cow-shed***, étable (à vaches), *f.*; ***lean-to shed***, appentis, *m.*

shed (2) [ʃed], *v.t. irr.* répandre, verser; se dépouiller de, perdre (*feuilles etc.*); jeter (*animal*).

shedding ['ʃediŋ], *n.* effusion (*de sang*); perte (*feuilles etc.*), *f.*

sheen [ʃi:n], *n.* éclat, lustre, brillant, *m.*

sheep [ʃi:p], *n.inv.* mouton, *m.*; (*fig.*) brebis, *f.*; ***black sheep***, brebis galeuse; ***lost sheep***, brebis égarée.

sheep-dip ['ʃi:pdip], *n.* bain parasiticide, *m.*

sheep-dog ['ʃi:pdɔg], *n.* chien de berger, *m.*

sheep-fold ['ʃi:pfould], *n.* bergerie, *f.*, bercail, *m.*

sheepish ['ʃi:piʃ], *a.* penaud, bête, niais.

sheepishly ['ʃi:piʃli], *adv.* d'un air penaud.

sheep-pen ['ʃi:ppen], *n.* parc à moutons, *m.*

sheep-shearing ['ʃi:pʃiəriŋ], *n.* tonte, *f.*

sheepskin ['ʃi:pskin], *n.* peau de mouton; basane (*cuir*), *f.*

sheer (1) [ʃiə], *a.* pur; escarpé, à pic (*rocher*); ***sheer force***, pure force, *f.*; ***sheer nonsense***, pure sottise, *f.*—*adv.* tout droit; tout à fait.

sheer (2) [ʃiə], *n.* (*Naut.*) tonture; embardée, *f.*—*v.i.* faire des embardées; ***to sheer off***, pousser au large, s'esquiver.

sheet [ʃi:t], *n.* drap, *m.*; feuille (*de papier* ou *métal*); nappe (*d'eau etc.*); (*Naut.*) écoute (*corde*), *f.*; ***winding-sheet***, linceul, *m.*

sheet-anchor ['ʃi:tæŋkə], *n.* ancre de miséricorde; (*fig.*) ancre de salut, *f.*

sheet-iron ['ʃi:taiən], *n.* tôle, *f.*

sheet-lightning ['ʃi:t'laitniŋ], *n.* éclair en nappe, *m.*

sheikh [ʃeik], *n.* cheik, *m.*

shelf [ʃelf], *n.* (*pl.* **shelves** [ʃelvz]) planche, *f.*; rayon (*de bibliothèque*), *m.*; tablette, *f.*; écueil (*dans la mer*), *m.*; ***set of shelves***, étagères, *f.pl.*

shell [ʃel], *n.* coque (*d'œuf, fruits etc.*); coquille (*œuf vide*); cosse (*de petits pois etc.*); écaille (*d'huître, de tortue*); carapace (*de homard*), *f.*; (*Artill.*) obus; (*fig.*) extérieur, *m.* —*v.t.* écaler (*noisette etc.*); écosser (*petits pois etc.*); égrener (*graine*); (*Mil.*) bombarder.

shell-fish ['ʃelfiʃ], *n.* coquillage, mollusque, *m.*, crustacés, *m.pl.*

shelling ['ʃeliŋ], *n.* écossage; égrenage; (*Mil.*) bombardement, *m.*
shell-proof ['ʃelpru:f], *a.* blindé.
shelter ['ʃeltə], *n.* abri, couvert; (*fig.*) asile, *m.*; ***to take shelter***, s'abriter.—*v.t.* abriter; protéger.—*v.i.* s'abriter.
sheltered ['ʃeltəd], *a.* abrité.
shelve [ʃelv], *v.t.* mettre sur un rayon; (*fig.*) enterrer.—*v.i.* aller en pente.
shelves [SHELF].
shelving ['ʃelviŋ], *a.* en pente, incliné.
shepherd ['ʃepəd], *n.* berger, pâtre; (*fig.*) pasteur, *m.*—*v.t.* piloter, guider.
shepherdess ['ʃepədes], *n.* bergère, *f.*
sherbet ['ʃə:bət], *n.* sorbet, *m.*
sheriff ['ʃerif], *n.* shérif; (*Am.*) chef de l'administration de la justice (d'un comté), *m.*
sherry ['ʃeri], *n.* vin de Xérès, *m.*
shield [ʃi:ld], *n.* bouclier; écran protecteur; (*Her.*) écu, écusson, *m.*—*v.t.* défendre de, protéger contre.
shift [ʃift], *n.* changement; expédient, *m.*, ressource, *f.*; détour, faux-fuyant (*artifice*), *m.*; *chemise de femme; équipe, journée (*d'ouvriers*), *f.*—*v.t.*, *v.i.* changer; changer de place; (*fig.*) trouver des expédients; ***to shift for oneself***, se débrouiller.
shiftiness ['ʃiftinis], *n.* manque de franchise, *m.*
shifting ['ʃiftiŋ], *a.* changeant; ***shifting sand***, sable mouvant, *m.*—*n.* changement; déplacement (*de cargaison etc.*), *m.*
shiftless ['ʃiftlis], *a.* sans initiative; sans énergie; paresseux.
shifty ['ʃifti], *a.* plein d'expédients; ***he is a shifty customer***, c'est un roublard.
shilling ['ʃiliŋ], *n.* shilling, *m.*
shilly-shally ['ʃili'ʃæli], *n.* irrésolution, *f.*—*v.i.* hésiter, être irrésolu.
shimmer ['ʃimə], *n.* lueur, *f.*—*v.i.* miroiter.
shin [ʃin], *n.* devant de la jambe; jarret (*de bœuf*), *m.*
shin-bone ['ʃinboun], *n.* tibia, *m.*
shindy ['ʃindi], *n.* tapage, *m.*
shine [ʃain], *v.i. irr.* luire; reluire; briller.—*n.* brillant, éclat, lustre, *m.*
shingle (1) [ʃiŋgl], *n.* bardeau (*pour toiture*), *m.*; coiffure à la garçonne, *f.*
shingle (2) [ʃiŋgl], *n.* galets, cailloux (*au bord de la mer*), *m.*
shingles [ʃiŋglz], *n.pl.* (*Med.*) zona, *m.*
shingly ['ʃiŋgli], *a.* couvert de galets.
shining ['ʃainiŋ], *a.* luisant, brillant.
shiny ['ʃaini], *a.* luisant, reluisant.
ship [ʃip], *n.* navire; vaisseau, bâtiment, *m.*—*v.t.* embarquer; expédier (*marchandises*); armer (*avirons*).—*v.i.* s'embarquer.
shipboard ['ʃipbɔ:d], *n.* bord de navire, *m.*
shipbuilder ['ʃipbildə], *n.* constructeur de navires, *m.*
shipbuilding ['ʃipbildiŋ], *n.* construction navale, *f.*
ship-chandler ['ʃip'tʃɑ:ndlə], *n.* fournisseur de navires, *m.*
shipmate ['ʃipmeit], *n.* camarade de bord, *m.*
shipment ['ʃipmənt], *n.* chargement, *m.*
shipowner ['ʃipounə], *n.* armateur, *m.*
shipper ['ʃipə], *n.* expéditeur, *m.*
shipping ['ʃipiŋ], *a.* maritime.—*n.* vaisseaux, navires, *m.pl.*; navigation; marine marchande; mise à bord (*chargement*), *f.*
ship's-boat ['ʃips'bout], *n.* chaloupe, *f.*
ship's-carpenter ['ʃips'kɑ:pintə], *n.* charpentier du bord, *m.*
shipshape ['ʃipʃeip], *a.* en ordre, bien arrangé.
shipwreck ['ʃiprek], *n.* naufrage, *m.*—*v.t.* faire faire naufrage à; ***to be shipwrecked***, faire naufrage.
shipwrecked ['ʃiprekt], *a.* naufragé.
shipwright ['ʃiprait], *n.* constructeur de navires, *m.*
shipyard ['ʃipjɑ:d], *n.* chantier naval, *m.*
shire ['ʃaiə], *n.* comté, *m.*
shirk [ʃə:k], *v.t.* éviter, éluder.—*v.i.* finasser, tirer au flanc.
shirker ['ʃə:kə], *n.* carottier; flanchard, *m.*
shirt [ʃə:t], *n.* chemise (*d'homme*), *f.*; ***shirt-collar***, col de chemise, *m.*; ***shirt-front***, devant de chemise, plastron, *m.*
shiver (1) ['ʃivə], *v.t.* briser en morceaux, fracasser.—*v.i.* se briser en morceaux.—*n.* fragment, morceau, éclat, *m.*
shiver (2) ['ʃivə], *v.i.* grelotter (*de froid*); frissonner (*de peur*).—*n.* frisson, tremblement, *m.*
shivering ['ʃivəriŋ], *a.* frissonnant.—*n.* frissonnement, frisson, *m.*
shoal [ʃoul], *n.* banc (*de poissons*), *m.*; (*fig.*) foule, *f.*; bas-fond, haut-fond (*de la mer*), *m.*; ***in shoals***, en foule.
shock (1) [ʃɔk], *n.* choc, *m.*; (*Elec.*) secousse, *f.*—*v.t.* choquer, heurter; scandaliser.
shock (2) [ʃɔk], *n.* moyette (*de blé*); tignasse (*de cheveux*), *f.*
shock-absorber ['ʃɔkəbsɔ:bə], *n.* (*Motor.*) amortisseur, *m.*
shocking ['ʃɔkiŋ], *a.* choquant, affreux, dégoûtant.
shockingly ['ʃɔkiŋli], *adv.* affreusement.
shod [ʃɔd], *a.* ferré (*cheval*); chaussé (*personne*).
shoddy ['ʃɔdi], *a.* d'effilochage; de pacotille.—*n.* drap de laine d'effilochage, *m.*
shoe [ʃu:], *n.* soulier, *m.*; chaussure, *f.*; fer (*à cheval*); sabot (*en bois*), *m.*—*v.t. irr.* chausser; ferrer (*cheval etc.*).
shoe-black ['ʃu:blæk], *n.* cireur, *m.*
shoe-horn ['ʃu:hɔ:n], *n.* chausse-pied, *m.*
shoeing ['ʃu:iŋ], *n.* ferrage, *m.*
shoeing-smith ['ʃu:iŋsmiθ], *n.* maréchal ferrant, *m.*
shoe-lace ['ʃu:leis], *n.* lacet de chaussure, *m.*
shoemaker ['ʃu:meikə], *n.* cordonnier, *m.*
shoe-making ['ʃu:meikiŋ], *n.* cordonnerie, *f.*
shoe-polish ['ʃu:pɔliʃ], *n.* cirage, *m.*
shoot [ʃu:t], *v.t. irr.* tirer, lancer, darder; décharger, tirer un coup (*de fusil etc.*); atteindre (*une cible*); tuer (*faire mourir*); fusiller; descendre (*rapides etc.*); ***to shoot a film***, tourner un film; ***to shoot oneself***, se tuer.—*v.i.* tirer; chasser (*gibier*); (*fig.*) s'élancer; filer (*étoile etc.*); pousser (*plante etc.*).—*n.* rejeton, *m.*, pousse (*plante*), *f.*; sarment (*de vigne*); dépôt de décombres (*ordures*), *m.*
shooter ['ʃu:tə], *n.* tireur, *m.*
shooting ['ʃu:tiŋ], *a.* lancinant (*douleur*); ***shooting star***, étoile filante, *f.*—*n.* tir (*de fusil*), *m.*; chasseau fusil, *f.*; élancement (*de douleur*), *m.*; pousse (*de plante*); décharge (*des ordures*), *f.*; (*Cine.*) tournage (*de film*), *m.*
shooting-brake ['ʃu:tiŋbreik], *n.* (*Motor.*) canadienne, *f.*

shooting-gallery ['ʃu:tiŋgæləri], *n.* tir, stand, *m.*
shop [ʃɔp], *n.* boutique (*petit*), *f.*, magasin (*grand*); atelier (*de fabrication*), *m.*—*v.i.* faire des emplettes; ***to go shopping***, aller faire des courses.
shop-assistant ['ʃɔpəsistənt], *n.* vendeur, *m.*, vendeuse, commise, *f.*
shopkeeper ['ʃɔpki:pə], *n.* marchand, *m.*
shoplifter ['ʃɔpliftə], *n.* voleur à l'étalage, *m.*
shoplifting ['ʃɔpliftiŋ], *n.* vol à l'étalage, *m.*
shopper ['ʃɔpə], *n.* acheteur, client, *m.*
shopping-centre ['ʃɔpiŋsentə], *n.* quartier commerçant, *m.*
shop-soiled ['ʃɔpsɔild], *a.* défraîchi.
shop-steward ['ʃɔpstjuəd], *n.* responsable syndical, délégué ouvrier, *m.*
shop-walker ['ʃɔpwɔ:kə], *n.* chef de rayon; inspecteur de magasin, *m.*
shop-window ['ʃɔp'windou], *n.* devanture, vitrine, *f.*, étalage, *m.*
shore [ʃɔ:], *n.* rivage, bord, *m.*, plage, côte, *f.* —*v.t.* étayer, étançonner.
short [ʃɔ:t], *a.* court; bref; passager (*temps*); petit (*taille*); insuffisant; croquant (*pâte*); brusque (*bourru*); ***short circuit***, court-circuit, *m.*; ***short story***, conte, *m.*, nouvelle, *f.*; ***to cut the matter short***, pour en finir. —*adv.* court, vivement, brusquement; ***it falls far short of it***, il s'en faut de beaucoup.
shortbread ['ʃɔ:tbred], *n.* (gâteau) sablé, *m.*
short-circuit ['ʃɔ:t'sə:kit], *v.t.* mettre en court-circuit.
shortcoming ['ʃɔ:tkʌmiŋ], *n.* défaut, *m.*, insuffisance, *f.*
shorten [ʃɔ:tn], *v.t.* raccourcir; abréger.—*v.i.* (se) raccourcir.
shortening ['ʃɔ:tniŋ], *n.* raccourcissement, *m.*
shorthand ['ʃɔ:thænd], *n.* sténographie, *f.*
short-handed ['ʃɔ:t'hændid], *a.* à court de personnel.
shorthand-typist ['ʃɔ:thænd'taipist], *n.* sténodactylographe, (*fam.*) sténodactylo, *f.*
short-lived ['ʃɔ:t'livd], *a.* qui vit peu de temps, éphémère.
shortly ['ʃɔ:tli], *adv.* bientôt, sous peu; brièvement.
shortness ['ʃɔ:tnis], *n.* courte durée, *f.*; peu d'étendue, *m.*; petitesse (*de taille*), *f.*
shorts ['ʃɔ:ts], *n.pl.* culotte courte, *f.*, caleçon court, slip; short, *m.*
short-sighted ['ʃɔ:t'saitid], *a.* myope; (*fig.*) peu prévoyant.
short-sightedness ['ʃɔ:t'saitidnis], *n.* myopie, *f.*; (*fig.*) manque de prévoyance, *m.*
short-tempered ['ʃɔ:t'tempəd], *a.* vif, pétulant, brusque.
short-winded ['ʃɔ:t'windid], *a.* à l'haleine courte; poussif (*cheval*).
shot (1) [ʃɔt], *past* and *p.p.* [SHOOT].
shot (2) [ʃɔt], *a.* chatoyant; ***shot silk***, soie gorge-de-pigeon, *f.*—*n.* coup de fusil, coup; trait (*d'arc*), *m.*; balle (*de fusil*), *f.*, boulet (*de canon*); plomb (*de fusil de chasse*), *m.*; (*Artill.*) charge; portée (*étendue*), *f.*; tireur (*personne*); (*Ftb.*) coup au but, *m.*; (*Med.*) injection; (*Cine.*) prise, *f.*; ***at a shot***, d'un seul coup; ***like a shot***, comme un trait; ***to be a good shot***, être bon tireur; ***to fire a shot***, tirer un coup de feu.
shot-gun ['ʃɔtgʌn], *n.* fusil de chasse, *m.*
should [ʃud], *v.aux.* (*past of* **shall**, *used as sign of the conditional*) ***I should speak***, je parlerais; (=***ought to***, *conditional tense of* **devoir**) ***you should see it***, vous devriez le voir.
shoulder ['ʃouldə], *n.* épaule; (*Tech.*) languette, *f.*; ***round shoulders***, dos rond, *m.*—*v.t.* charger sur les épaules; se charger de; porter (*armes*).
shoulder-blade ['ʃouldəbleid], *n.* omoplate, *f.*
shout [ʃaut], *v.t.*, *v.i.* crier, huer, pousser des cris; vociférer.—*n.* cri, *m.*; acclamations, *f.pl.*; éclat (*de rire*), *m.*
shouting ['ʃautiŋ], *n.* acclamation, *f.*, cris, *m.pl.*
shove [ʃʌv], *v.t.* pousser; ***to shove away***, repousser, éloigner.—*v.i.* pousser.—*n.* coup, *m.*, poussée, *f.*
shovel [ʃʌvl], *n.* pelle, *f.*—*v.t.* ramasser avec la pelle, pelleter.
shovelful ['ʃʌvlful], *n.* pelletée, *f.*
show [ʃou], *v.t. irr.* montrer, faire voir, exposer à la vue; manifester, témoigner, démontrer; indiquer; expliquer; ***to show in***, faire entrer; ***to show off***, faire valoir.—*v.i.* paraître, se montrer; se faire remarquer; ***to show off***, poser, se donner des airs.—*n.* apparence, *f.*; étalage, *m.*, parade, *f.*; spectacle, concours, *m.*; exposition, *f.*
show-case ['ʃoukeis], *n.* montre, vitrine, *f.*
shower ['ʃauə], *n.* ondée (*légère*); averse (*grosse*); pluie, grêle (*de coups, pierres etc.*); douche, *f.*—*v.t.* inonder (de pluie); (*fig.*) verser.
shower-bath ['ʃauəbɑ:θ], *n.* douche, *f.*, bain-douche, *m.*
showery ['ʃauəri], *a.* pluvieux.
show-ring ['ʃouriŋ], *n.* arène de vente, *f.*
show-room ['ʃouru:m], *n.* salle d'exposition, *f.*
showy ['ʃoui], *a.* voyant, prétentieux, criard.
shrapnel ['ʃræpnəl], *n.* éclats d'obus, *m.pl.*
shred [ʃred], *n.* lambeau, bout, brin, *m.*; ***to tear to shreds***, déchirer en lambeaux.—*v.t.* déchiqueter; râper grossièrement.
shrew [ʃru:], *n.* mégère, femme acariâtre, *f.*
shrewd [ʃru:d], *a.* sagace, fin, perspicace.
shrewdly ['ʃru:dli], *adv.* avec sagacité, avec pénétration, finement.
shrewdness ['ʃru:dnis], *n.* sagacité, pénétration, finesse, *f.*
shrewish ['ʃru:iʃ], *a.* acariâtre.
shrewishly ['ʃru:iʃli], *adv.* en mégère.
shrewishness ['ʃru:iʃnis], *n.* humeur acariâtre, *f.*
shriek [ʃri:k], *n.* cri perçant, *m.*—*v.t.* crier.—*v.i.* jeter un cri aigu.
shrieking ['ʃri:kiŋ], *n.* cris stridents, *m.pl.*
shrift [ʃrift], *n.* confession, *f.*; (*fig.*) ***short shrift***, très court délai, *m.*
shrill [ʃril], *a.* aigu, perçant; aigre (*voix*).
shrillness ['ʃrilnis], *n.* son aigu, ton aigu, *m.*
shrilly ['ʃrilli], *adv.* d'un ton aigu.
shrimp [ʃrimp], *n.* crevette (*grise*), *f.*
shrine [ʃrain], *n.* châsse, *f.*; tombeau, *m.*; chapelle (*d'un saint*), *f.*
shrink [ʃriŋk], *v.t. irr.* rétrécir, faire rétrécir. —*v.i.* rétrécir, se rétrécir; se retirer; reculer; se ratatiner; se tasser (*en vieillissant*).
shrinkage ['ʃriŋkidʒ], *n.* rétrécissement, *m.*, contraction, *f.*

shrinking ['ʃriŋkiŋ], *n.* rétrécissement, *m.*; action de reculer, *f.*
***shrive** [ʃraiv], *v.t. irr.* confesser.
shrivel [ʃrivl], *v.t.* faire ratatiner, faire recroqueviller, rider, racornir.—*v.i.* se ratatiner, se recroqueviller.
shroud [ʃraud], *n.* linceul, suaire, *m.*; (*Naut., pl.*) haubans, *m.pl.*—*v.t.* (*fig.*) abriter, couvrir.
Shrovetide ['ʃrouvtaid]. les jours gras, *m.pl.*; ***Shrove Tuesday***, mardi-gras, *m.*
shrub [ʃrʌb], *n.* arbuste, arbrisseau, *m.*
shrubbery ['ʃrʌbəri], *n.* plantation d'arbrisseaux, *f.*
shrubby ['ʃrʌbi], *a.* plein d'arbrisseaux, touffu.
shrug [ʃrʌg], *n.* haussement d'épaules, *m.*—*v.t.* hausser; ***to shrug one's shoulders***, hausser les épaules.
shudder ['ʃʌdə], *v.i.* frissonner, frémir (*de*).—*n.* frissonnement, frémissement, *m.*
shuffle [ʃʌfl], *v.t.* mêler; (*Cards*) battre.—*v.i.* traîner les pieds; battre les cartes; tergiverser (*équivoquer*).
shuffling ['ʃʌfliŋ], *a.* chicaneur, biaiseur; traînant (*allure*).—*n.* marche traînante, *f.*; (*Cards*) battement des cartes, *m.*; (*fig.*) chicane, *f.*
shun [ʃʌn], *v.t.* éviter, fuir.
shunt [ʃʌnt], *v.t.* garer (*train*); détourner.
shunting ['ʃʌntiŋ], *n.* changement de voie, garage, *m.*
shut [ʃʌt], *v.t. irr.* fermer; enfermer; ***to shut off***, intercepter, couper (*vapeur etc.*); ***to shut out***, exclure; ***to shut up***, fermer, enfermer; condamner (*porte etc.*); faire taire.—*v.i.* fermer, se fermer; ***shut up!*** taisez-vous!
shutter ['ʃʌtə], *n.* volet, contrevent (*à l'extérieur de la fenêtre*), *m.*
shuttle [ʃʌtl], *n.* navette; vanne, *f.*
shuttle-cock ['ʃʌtlkɔk], *n.* volant, *m.*
shuttle-service ['ʃʌtlsə:vis], *n.* navette, *f.*
shy (1) [ʃai], *a.* réservé, timide, honteux.—*v.i.* être ombrageux, faire un écart (*cheval*).
shy (2) [ʃai], *v.t.* jeter, lancer.—*n.* coup (de pierre *etc.*); essai, *m.*; ***to have a shy at***, s'essayer à (*faire quelque chose*).
shyly ['ʃaili], *adv.* timidement, avec réserve.
shyness ['ʃainis], *n.* timidité, retenue, réserve; fausse honte, *f.*
Siam [sai'æm]. le Siam, *m.*
Siamese [saiə'mi:z], *a.* siamois.—*n.* siamois (*langue*); Siamois (*personne*), *m.*
Siberia [sai'biəriə]. la Sibérie, *f.*
Siberian [sai'biəriən], *a.* sibérien.—*n.* Sibérien (*personne*), *m.*
sibilant ['sibilənt], *a.* sifflant.—*n.* lettre sifflante, *f.*
siccative ['sikətiv], *a.* and *n.* siccatif, *m.*
Sicilian [si'siliən], *a.* sicilien.—*n.* Sicilien (*personne*), *m.*
Sicily ['sisili]. la Sicile, *f.*
sick [sik], *a.* malade; qui a des nausées, qui a mal au cœur; ***sick headache***, migraine, *f.*; ***sick man*** or ***woman***, malade, *m., f.*; ***sick of***, dégoûté de; ***to be sea-sick***, avoir le mal de mer; ***to be sick***, vomir.
sick-bed ['sikbed], *n.* lit de douleur, *m.*
sicken [sikn], *v.t.* rendre malade; (*fig.*) lasser, dégoûter.—*v.i.* tomber malade.
sickening ['sikniŋ], *a.* écœurant; (*fig.*) dégoûtant.
sickle [sikl], *n.* faucille, *f.*
sick-leave ['sikli:v], *n.* congé de convalescence, *m.*
sickliness ['siklinis], *n.* mauvaise santé, *f.*
sick-list ['siklist], *n.* rôle des malades, *m.*
sickly ['sikli], *a.* maladif; affadissant, affadi (*goût etc.*).
sickness ['siknis], *n.* maladie, *f.*; nausées, *f.pl.*
sick-nurse ['siknə:s], *n.* garde-malade, *f.*
sick-room ['sikru:m], *n.* chambre de malade, *f.*
side [said], *a.* de côté; latéral; indirect.—*n.* côté; flanc; bord; versant (*de montagne*); parti; (*Spt.*) camp, *m.*; ***by his side***, à côté de lui; ***side by side***, côte à côte; ***this side up*** (*caisses*), dessus; ***to take sides***, prendre parti; ***wrong side out***, à l'envers.—*v.i.* ***to side with***, se ranger du côté de.
sideboard ['saidbɔ:d], *n.* buffet, *m.*
sided ['saidid], *a.* à côtés, à faces; ***two-sided***, à deux faces.
side-door ['saiddɔ:], *n.* porte latérale, *f.*
side-line ['saidlain], *n.* occupation secondaire, *f.*
sidelong ['saidlɔŋ], *a.* and *adv.* de côté.
side-show ['saidʃou], *n.* spectacle forain, *m.*
sidesman ['saidzmən], *n.* (*pl.* **-men** [men]) (*Eccles.*) marguillier, *m.*
side-track ['saidtræk], *v.t.* garer (*train*); (*fig.*) semer (*quelqu'un*).
sidewalk ['saidwɔ:k], *n.* (*Am.*) trottoir (*de rue*), *m.*
sideways ['saidweiz], *adv.* de côté; obliquement.
siding ['saidiŋ], *n.* voie d'évitement, voie de garage, *f.*
sidle [saidl], *v.i.* marcher de côté; s'insinuer.
siege [si:dʒ], *n.* siège, *m.*; ***to lay siege to***, mettre le siège devant, faire le siège de, assiéger.
Sienna [si'enə]. Sienne, *f.*
sierra [si'ɛərə], *n.* sierra, *f.*
Sierra Leone [si'ɛərəli'oun]. le Sierra-Leone, *m.*
siesta [si'estə], *n.* sieste, *f.*
sieve [siv], *n.* tamis (*fin*); crible (*grand*), *m.*
sift [sift], *v.t.* tamiser; cribler; sasser (*farine*); (*fig.*) examiner.
sifting ['siftiŋ], *n.* tamisage; (*fig.*) examen minutieux, *m.*
sigh [sai], *n.* soupir, *m.*—*v.i.* soupirer; ***to sigh after***, soupirer après; ***to sigh over***, gémir sur.
sighing ['saiiŋ], *n.* soupirs, *m.pl.*
sight [sait], *n.* vue, vision, *f.*; regard, *m.*, yeux, *m.pl.*; guidon, *m.*, hausse (*armes à feu*), *f.*; spectacle, *m.*; ***a sight better***, beaucoup mieux; ***at first sight***, à première vue; ***by sight***, de vue; ***in sight***, en vue; ***out of sight***, hors de vue; ***second sight***, clairvoyance, *f.*; ***to catch sight of***, apercevoir; ***to come in sight***, apparaître.—*v.t.* apercevoir.
sighted ['saitid], *a.* en vue; qui voit, voyant; ***long-sighted***, presbyte; ***short-sighted***, myope; (*fig.*) peu clairvoyant.
sightliness ['saitlinis], *n.* beauté, *f.*
sight-reading ['saitri:diŋ], *n.* (*Mus.*) déchiffrement, *m.*

sight-seeing ['saitsiːiŋ], *n.* ***to go sight-seeing***, aller voir les curiosités.

sight-seer ['saitsiːə], *n.* touriste, *m.*, *f.*, visiteur (*d'une ville*), *m.*

sign [sain], *n.* signe; indice, *m.*; enseigne (*panneau*), *f.*—*v.t.*, *v.i.* signer.

signal ['signəl], *a.* signalé, insigne.—*n.* signal; signe; (*Rail.*) sémaphore, *m.*; (*pl.*) (*Mil.*) les transmissions, *f.pl.*—*v.t.* signaler, faire signe à.—*v.i.* signaler; donner un signal.

signal-box ['signəlbɔks], *n.* poste à signaux, *m.*

signalman ['signəlmən], *n.* (*pl.* **-men** [men]) (*Rail.*) signaleur, *m.*

signaller ['signələ], *n.* signaleur, *m.*

signally ['signəli], *adv.* remarquablement.

signatory ['signətəri], *a.* and *n.* signataire, *m.*, *f.*

signature ['signətʃə], *n.* signature, *f.*

sign-board ['sainbɔːd], *n.* enseigne, *f.*

signet ['signit], *n.* sceau; cachet, *m.*

signet-ring ['signitriŋ], *n.* chevalière, *f.*

significance [sig'nifikəns], *n.* signification, *f.*, sens, *m.*; importance, *f.*

significant [sig'nifikənt], *a.* significatif.

signification [signifi'keiʃən], *n.* signification, *f.*

signify ['signifai], *v.t.* vouloir dire, signifier; faire connaître; importer.

sign-post ['sainpoust], *n.* poteau indicateur, *m.*

silence ['sailəns], *n.* silence, *m.*; ***silence!*** (*notice*), défense de parler.—*v.t.* réduire au silence, faire taire.

silent ['sailənt], *a.* silencieux; peu loquace (*qui ne parle pas beaucoup*); muet (*lettre, film*).

silently ['sailəntli], *adv.* silencieusement, en silence; sans bruit.

Silesia [sai'liːʃə, sai'liːsiə]. la Silésie, *f.*

silex ['saileks], *n.* silex, *m.*

silhouette [silu'et], *n.* silhouette, *f.*

silica ['silikə], *n.* silice, *f.*

silicon ['silikən], *n.* silicium, *m.*

silicosis [sili'kousis], *n.* (*Med.*) silicose, *f.*

silk [silk], *a.* de soie, en soie.—*n.* soie, *f.*; (*pl.*) soieries, *f.pl.*

silken ['silkən], *a.* de soie; soyeux.

silkiness ['silkinis], *n.* nature soyeuse, *f.*

silkworm ['silkwəːm], *n.* ver à soie, *m.*

silky ['silki], *a.* de soie, soyeux.

sill [sil], *n.* seuil (*d'une porte*); rebord (*d'une fenêtre*), *m.*

silliness ['silinis], *n.* sottise, niaiserie, *f.*

silly ['sili], *a.* and *n.* sot, nigaud, niais, *m.*; ***silly ass***, imbécile, *m.*; ***silly thing***, sottise, *f.*; nigaud (*personne*).

silt [silt], *v.t.* envaser.—*v.i.* s'envaser.—*n.* vase, *f.*, limon, *m.*

silting ['siltiŋ], *n.* envasement, *m.*

silver ['silvə], *a.* d'argent; argenté (*couleur*); argentin (*son*).—*n.* argent, *m.*; monnaie d'argent; argenterie (*vaisselle*), *f.*—*v.t.* argenter; étamer (*miroir*).

silver-gilt ['silvəgilt], *n.* argent doré, vermeil, *m.*

silvering ['silvəriŋ], *n.* argenture, *f.*; étamage (*de miroirs*), *m.*

silver-plated ['silvə'pleitid], *a.* argenté, en plaqué.

silversmith ['silvəsmiθ], *n.* orfèvre, *m.*

silvery ['silvəri], *a.* d'argent; argenté (*couleur*); argentin (*son*).

similar ['similə], *a.* semblable, pareil; similaire (*de nature*).

similarity [simi'læriti], *n.* ressemblance, similitude; similarité (*de nature*), *f.*

similarly ['similəli], *adv.* pareillement, d'une manière semblable.

simile ['simili], *n.* comparaison, *f.*

similitude [si'militjuːd], *n.* similitude, *f.*

simmer ['simə], *v.i.* bouillir lentement, mijoter.

simmering ['simərin], *n.* mijotement, *m.*

simnel ['simnəl], *n.* gâteau de Pâques *ou* de la mi-carême, *m.*

simper ['simpə], *n.* sourire niais, *m.*—*v.i.* sourire niaisement, minauder.

simpering ['simpəriŋ], *a.* minaudier.—*n.* minauderie, *f.*

simperingly ['simpəriŋli], *adv.* en minaudant.

simple [simpl], *a.* simple; ***as simple as ABC***, simple comme bonjour.—*n.* simple, *m.*

simple-hearted ['simpl'hɑːtid], **simple-minded** ['simplmaindid], *a.* simple, ingénu, naïf.

simpleness ['simplnis], *n.* simplicité, *f.*

simpleton ['simpltən], *n.* niais, nigaud, *m.*

simplicity [sim'plisiti], *n.* simplicité, *f.*

simplification ['simplifi'keiʃən], *n.* simplification, *f.*

simplify ['simplifai], *v.t.* simplifier.

simply ['simpli], *adv.* simplement (*sans complexité*); tout bonnement (*et rien de plus*).

simulate ['simjuleit], *v.t.* feindre, simuler.

simulation [simju'leiʃən], *n.* simulation, *f.*

simulator ['simjuleitə], *n.* simulateur, *m.*

simultaneous [siməl'teinjəs], *a.* simultané.

simultaneously [siməl'teinjəsli], *adv.* simultanément.

sin [sin], *n.* péché, *m.*; (*fig.*) offense, *f.*—*v.i.* pécher.

since [sins], *conj.* puisque (*parce que*); depuis que (*temps*).—*prep.* depuis; ***since then***, depuis lors.—*adv.* depuis; ***ever since***, depuis ce temps-là; ***long since***, il y a longtemps.

sincere [sin'siə], *a.* sincère.

sincerely [sin'siəli], *adv.* sincèrement; ***yours sincerely*** (*lettre amicale mais sans intimité*), veuillez croire, cher Monsieur, à mes sentiments les meilleurs.

sincerity [sin'seriti], *n.* sincérité, bonne foi, *f.*

sine [sain], *n.* (*Trig.*) sinus, *m.*

sinecure ['sainəkjuə], *n.* sinécure, *f.*

sinew ['sinjuː], *n.* tendon, (*colloq.*) nerf, *m.*

sinewy ['sinjuːi], *a.* tendineux; (*fig.*) nerveux, vigoureux.

sinful ['sinful], *a.* pécheur, coupable.

sinfully ['sinfuli], *adv.* d'une manière coupable, en pécheur.

sinfulness ['sinfulnis], *n.* culpabilité, iniquité, *f.*

sing [siŋ], *v.t.*, *v.i. irr.* chanter; célébrer (*louer*); siffler (*vent*); ***to make someone sing small***, rabattre le caquet à quelqu'un.

Singapore [siŋə'pɔː]. Singapour, *m.*

singe [sindʒ], *v.t.* flamber; roussir (*vêtements etc.*); (*Tech.*) griller.—*n.* légère brûlure, *f.*

singeing ['sindʒiŋ], *n.* flambage; (*Tech.*) grillage, *m.*

singer ['siŋə], *n.* chanteur, *m.*; cantatrice (*professionnelle*), *f.*

singing ['siŋiŋ], *a.* qui chante; chanteur (*oiseau*).—*n.* chant; bourdonnement (*dans les oreilles*), *m.*
single [siŋgl], *a.* seul, simple, unique; particulier (*individuel*); singulier (*combat*); non marié, célibataire; ***single bedroom***, chambre à un lit, *f.*; ***single man***, célibataire, garçon, *m.*; ***single (ticket)***, billet simple, *m.*; ***single woman***, femme non mariée, fille, *f.*—*n.* (*pl.*) (*Ten.*) partie simple, *f.*—*v.t.* choisir; ***to single out***, choisir, distinguer de la foule.
single-handed ['siŋgl'hændid], *adv.* tout seul, sans aide.
single-hearted ['siŋgl'hɑ:tid], *a.* sincère, honnête.
singleness ['siŋglnis], *n.* sincérité, simplicité, *f.*
singlet ['siŋglit], *n.* maillot fin, *m.*
single-track ['siŋgltræk], *a.* (*Rail.*) à voie unique; (*Cine.*) à simple piste.
singly ['siŋgli], *adv.* seulement; séparément; individuellement, un à un.
singsong ['siŋsɔŋ], *n.* chant monotone, *m.*
singular ['siŋgjulə], *a.* singulier; étrange (*bizarre*); simple (*pas complexe*), (*Gram.*)—*n.* singulier, *m.*
singularity [siŋgju'læriti], *n.* singularité, *f.*
singularly ['siŋgjuləli], *adv.* singulièrement.
sinister ['sinistə], *a.* sinistre; (*Her.*) sénestre.
sink [siŋk], *n.* évier (*de cuisine*); égout (*conduit*), *m.*; ***a sink of iniquity***, un cloaque d'iniquité.—*v.t. irr.* faire tomber au fond, enfoncer; couler (*navire*); creuser (*puits etc.*); placer (*argent*) à fonds perdu; amortir (*dette*).—*v.i.* aller au fond, tomber au fond; s'enfoncer; sombrer, couler (*navire*); décliner, s'affaiblir (*santé etc.*); baisser (*prix etc.*); être abattu (*âme, cœur etc.*); descendre, se coucher (*soleil etc.*); dégénérer (*en*).
sinker ['siŋkə], *n.* plomb (*de ligne de pêche*), *m.*
sinking ['siŋkiŋ], *a.* qui coule (*navire*).—*n.* foncement (*de puits etc.*); tassement (*de fondements*); affaissement (*santé*); placement à fonds perdu (*d'argent*); amortissement (*d'une dette*); engloutissement (*de navire*), *m.*
sinking-fund ['siŋkiŋfʌnd], *n.* fonds, *m.*, *ou* caisse d'amortissement (*d'une dette publique*), *f.*
sinless ['sinlis], *a.* sans péché, innocent; pur.
sinner ['sinə], *n.* pécheur, *m.*, pécheresse, *f.*
sinuous ['sinjuəs], *a.* sinueux.
sinus ['sainəs], *n.* (*Anat.*) sinus, *m.*
sip [sip], *n.* petit coup, *m.*, petite gorgée, *f.*—*v.t.*, *v.i.* boire à petit coups, siroter.
siphon ['saifən], *n.* siphon, *m.*—*v.t.* siphonner.
sir [sə:], *n.* monsieur, *m.*
sire ['saiə], *n.* père; sire (*à un roi*), *m.*; (*pl.*) pères, aïeux, *m.pl.*; ***grand-sire***, grand-père, *m.*
siren ['saiərən], *n.* sirène, *f.*
Sirius ['siriəs]. (*Astron.*) Sirius, *m.*
sirloin ['sə:lɔin], *n.* aloyau; faux-filet, *m.*
sirocco [si'rɔkou], *n.* siroco, *m.*
siskin ['siskin], *n.* (*Orn.*) tarin, *m.*
sissy ['sisi], *n.* (*colloq.*) poule mouillée, *f.*
sister ['sistə], *a.* sœur; du même gabarit (*navire*).—*n.* sœur; (*Med.*) infirmière-major, *f.*
sisterhood ['sistəhud], *n.* communauté de sœurs, *f.*, sœurs, *f.pl.*
sister-in-law ['sistərinlɔ:], *n.* belle-sœur, *f.*
sisterly ['sistəli], *a.* de sœur, en sœur.

sit [sit], *v.t. irr.* asseoir; se tenir sur (*cheval*).—*v.i.* s'asseoir (*acte*); être assis (*attitude*) siéger. tenir séance, se réunir (*assemblée cour, juge etc.*); couver (*poule etc.*), perche (*oiseau*); poser (*pour un portrait*); ***to sit down***, s'asseoir; ***to sit up***, se tenir droit veiller (*s'abstenir du sommeil*).
sit-down strike ['sitdaunstraik], *n.* grève sur le tas, *f.*
site [sait], *n.* situation, *f.*, emplacement (*de bâtiment*); site (*paysage*), *m.*—*v.t.* placer.
sitfast ['sitfɑ:st], *n.* (*Vet.*) cor, durillon, *m.*
sitter ['sitə], *n.* personne assise, *f.*; (*Paint.*) modèle, *m.*
sitting ['sitiŋ], *a.* assis; en séance (*cour etc.*); perché (*oiseau*); qui couve (*poule*).—*n.* séance; audience (*d'une cour*); couvaison (*des œufs*); place (*réservée*); (*Paint.*) séance, *f.*
sitting-room ['sitiŋru:m], *n.* petit salon, *m.*
situate (1) ['sitjueit], *v.t.* situer.
situate (2) ['sitjuit], **situated** ['sitjueitid], *a.* situé; (*Law*) sis.
situation [sitju'eiʃən], *n.* situation, position, *f.*, état, *m.*; place, *f.*, emploi, *m.*
six [siks], *a.* and *n.* six, *m.*
sixteen ['siks'ti:n], *a.* and *n.* seize, *m.*
sixteenth [siks'ti:nθ], *a.* seizième; seize (*rois etc.*).—*n.* seizième (*fraction*), *m.*
sixth [siksθ], *a.* sixième; six (*rois etc.*).—*n.* sixième (*fraction*), *m.*; (*Mus.*) sixte, *f.*; ***sixth form***, (*Sch.*) la classe de première, *f.*
sixthly ['siksθli], *adv.* sixièmement.
sixtieth ['sikstiiθ], *a.* soixantième.—*n.* soixantième (*fraction*), *m.*
sixty ['siksti], *a.* and *n.* soixante, *m.*; ***about sixty***, une soixantaine (*de*), *f.*
sizable ['saizəbl], *a.* d'une bonne grosseur.
size (1) [saiz], *n.* grandeur, dimension, taille (*physique*); grosseur, *f.*, volume (*espace occupé*); calibre (*de cartouche*); format (*de livre* ou *de papier*), *m.*; encolure (*de chemise*); pointure (*de gant, de chaussure etc.*), *f.*; effectif (*d'école, de classe etc.*); (*Comm.*) numéro, *m.*—*v.t.* classer, ranger (*par grosseur, par taille*); ***to size up***, juger.
size (2) [saiz], *n.* colle, *f.*, encollage, *m.*—*v.t.* coller, encoller.
sized [saizd], *a.* de grosseur; de taille.
sizzle [sizl], *n.* grésillement, *m.*—*v.i.* grésiller.
skate (1) [skeit], *n.* (*Ichth.*) raie, *f.*
skate (2) [skeit], *n.* patin, *m.*; ***roller skate***, patin à roulettes.—*v.i.* patiner.
skater ['skeitə], *n.* patineur, *m.*
skating ['skeitiŋ], *n.* patinage, *m.*
skating-rink ['skeitiŋriŋk], *n.* patinoire, *f.*
skein [skein], *n.* écheveau, *m.*
skeleton ['skelətən], *n.* squelette, *m.*; (*Tech.*) charpente, carcasse, *f.*
skeleton-key ['skelətən'ki:], *n.* passe-partout, *m.inv.*, crochet, *m.*
sketch [sketʃ], *n.* esquisse, *f.*, croquis, *m.*, ébauche; (*Theat.*) saynète, *f.*; (*fig.*) aperçu, *m.*—*v.t.* esquisser, ébaucher.
sketch-book ['sketʃbuk], *n.* cahier de croquis, *m.*
sketchily ['sketʃili], *adv.* incomplètement.
sketchy ['sketʃi], *a.* d'esquisse, ébauché; rudimentaire.
skew [skju:], *a.* oblique, en biais.
skewer ['skju:ə], *n.* brochette, *f.*—*v.t.* embrocher.
ski [ski:], *n.* ski, *m.*—*v.i.* faire du ski.

skid [skid], *n.* (*Motor.*) dérapage (*de*), *m.*, embardée, *f.*; (*Av.*) patin, *m.*—*v.i.* déraper (*bicyclette* ou *véhicule*).
skier ['ski:ə], *n.* skieur, *m.*
skiff [skif], *n.* esquif, *m.*
ski-ing ['ski:iŋ], *n.* le ski, *m.*
skilful ['skilful], *a.* adroit, habile.
skilfully ['skilfuli], *adv.* adroitement, habilement.
ski-lift ['ski:lift], *n.* remonte-pentes, *m.inv.*
skill [skil], *n.* habileté, dextérité, adresse, *f.*
skilled [skild], *a.* habile, adroit; ***skilled labour***, main-d'œuvre spécialisée, *f.*; ***skilled workman***, ouvrier qualifié, *m.*
skim [skim], *v.t.* écumer; écrémer (*lait*); (*fig.*) raser, effleurer.
skimp [skimp], *v.t.* lésiner; bâcler (*travail*).
skimpy ['skimpi], *a.* mesquin, chiche; étriqué.
skin [skin], *n.* peau, *f.*; ***banana skin***, pelure de banane, *f.*; ***to escape by the skin of one's teeth***, l'échapper belle; ***wet to the skin***, trempé jusqu'aux os.—*v.t.* écorcher (*personne* ou *animal*); peler, éplucher (*fruits etc.*); (*fig.*) écorcher, plumer.
skin-deep ['skindi:p], *a.* superficiel, peu profond.
skinflint ['skinflint], *n.* pince-maille, grigou, ladre, *m.*
skinless ['skinlis], *a.* sans peau.
skinner ['skinə], *n.* écorcheur; pelletier (*marchand*), *m.*
skinny ['skini], *a.* maigre, décharné.
skip [skip], *n.* saut, bond, *m.*—*v.t.* sauter; passer (*en lisant*).—*v.i.* sauter, sautiller, gambader.
skipper ['skipə], *n.* patron (*de navire marchand*); (*Spt.*) chef d'équipe, *m.*
skipping ['skipiŋ], *n.* action de sauter, *f.*; saut à la corde, *m.*
skipping-rope ['skipiŋroup], *n.* corde à sauter, *f.*
skirmish ['skə:miʃ], *n.* escarmouche, *f.*—*v.i.* escarmoucher.
skirmisher ['skə:miʃə], *n.* tirailleur, *m.*
skirmishing ['skə:miʃiŋ], *n.* escarmouches, *f.pl.*
skirt [skə:t], *n.* pan (*d'un habit*), *m.*; jupe (*de robe*); (*pl.*) lisière, extrémité, *f.*, bord (*de forêt etc.*), *m.*; ***outskirts***, bords, faubourgs, *m.pl.*—*v.t.* border; longer (*rivière etc.*).
skirting ['skə:tiŋ], **skirting-board** ['skə:tiŋ bɔ:d], *n.* bord, *m.*, bordure; (*Arch.*) plinthe, *f.*
skit [skit], *n.* parodie, *f.*
skittish ['skitiʃ], *a.* capricieux, volage.
skittishly ['skitiʃli], *adv.* capricieusement.
skittishness ['skitiʃnis], *n.* légèreté, inconstance, *f.*
skittle [skitl], *n.* quille, *f.*
skittle-alley ['skitl'æli], *n.* jeu de quilles, *m.*
skulk [skʌlk], *v.i.* se cacher; rôder (*autour de*).
skull [skʌl], *n.* crâne, *m.*
skull-cap ['skʌlkæp], *n.* calotte, *f.*
skunk [skʌŋk], *n.* putois d'Amérique, *m.*
sky [skai], *n.* ciel, *m.*
sky-blue ['skaiblu:], *a.* bleu ciel, azuré.
sky-high ['skai'hai], *a.* qui touche aux cieux; ***to blow up sky-high***, faire sauter jusqu'aux cieux; (*fig.*) tancer vertement.
skylark ['skailɑ:k], *n.* alouette (des champs), *f.* —*v.i.* (*fig.*) faire des farces.
skylarking ['skailɑ:kiŋ], *n.* farces, *f.pl.*
skylight ['skailait], *n.* châssis vitré, *m.* lucarne faîtière, *f.*
sky-line ['skailain], *n.* horizon, *m.*
sky-scraper ['skaiskreipə], *n.* gratte-ciel, *m.*
slab [slæb], *n.* dalle, plaque, table; tablette (*de chocolat*); dosse, *f.*
slack [slæk], *a.* lâche; faible, mou; détendu (*corde*); négligent; ***business is slack***, les affaires ne vont pas; ***the slack season***, la morte-saison, *f.*—*n.* menu charbon; mou (*de corde*); (*Eng.*) jeu; (*pl.*) pantalon, *m.*
slacken ['slækən], *v.t.* relâcher, détendre; affaiblir (*la rigueur*); ralentir (*vitesse*).—*v.i.* se relâcher, se détendre; se ralentir; diminuer; tomber.
slackening ['slækniŋ], *n.* relâchement, *m.*
slacker ['slækə], *n.* paresseux, *m.*
slacking ['slækiŋ], *n.* paresse, *f.*
slackly ['slækli], *adv.* mollement, lâchement; négligemment.
slackness ['slæknis], *n.* relâchement, *m.*; négligence, nonchalance (*morale*), *f.*
slag [slæg], *n.* scorie, *f.*; mâchefer, *m.*
slag-heap ['slæghi:p], *n.* crassier, *m.*
slake [sleik], *v.t.* éteindre (*chaux*); ***to slake one's thirst***, se désaltérer.
slam [slæm], *v.t.* fermer avec violence, claquer.—*v.i.* se fermer avec bruit.—*n.* (*Cards*) vole, *f.*, chelem, *m.*
slander ['slɑ:ndə], *n.* calomnie; (*Law*) diffamation, *f.*—*v.t.* calomnier; (*Law*) diffamer.
slanderer ['slɑ:ndərə], *n.* calomniateur; (*Law*) diffamateur, *m.*
slanderous ['slɑ:ndərəs], *a.* calomnieux; (*Law*) diffamatoire.
slang [slæŋ], *n.* argot, *m.*, langue verte, *f.*
slangy ['slæŋi], *a.* d'argot, argotique.
slant [slɑ:nt], *v.t.* incliner.—*v.i.* incliner; être de biais, biaiser.—*n.* inclinaison, pente, *f.*; ***on the slant***, en écharpe, en biais.
slanting ['slɑ:ntiŋ], *a.* oblique; en écharpe (*coup d'épée etc.*).
slantingly ['slɑ:ntiŋli], **slantwise** ['slɑ:nt waiz], *adv.* obliquement, en biais.
slap [slæp], *n.* tape, *f.*; soufflet (*sur la figure*), *m.*—*v.t.* souffleter, donner une fessée à (*un enfant*).—*adv.* tout droit, en plein.
slapdash ['slæpdæʃ], *adv.* à la six-quatre-deux, n'importe comment.—*a.* fait à la hâte.
slap-happy ['slæp'hæpi], *a.* toqué.
slapstick ['slæpstik], *n.* (*Theat.*, *Cine.*) ***slapstick comedy*** (*fam.*), tarte à la crème, *f.*
slash [slæʃ], *n.* taillade; balafre (*sur la figure*), *f.*—*v.t.* taillader; balafrer (*la figure*).—*v.i.* frapper.
slashing ['slæʃiŋ], *a.* mordant, cinglant.
slate [sleit], *n.* ardoise, *f.*—*v.t.* couvrir d'ardoises; (*colloq.*) tancer.
slate-coloured ['sleitkʌləd], *a.* ardoisé, gris d'ardoise.
slate-pencil ['sleitpensl], *n.* crayon d'ardoise, *m.*
slater ['sleitə], *n.* couvreur en ardoise, *m.*
slating ['sleitiŋ], *n.* toiture en ardoise; (*colloq.*) semonce, *f.*
slattern ['slætən], *n.* femme malpropre, souillon, *f.*
slatternly ['slætənli], *a.* négligent, malpropre, mal soigné.

slaty ['sleiti], *a.* schisteux, d'ardoise; ardoisé (*couleur*).
slaughter ['slɔ:tə], *n.* tuerie, boucherie, *f.*, massacre; abattage (*des animaux*), *m.*—*v.t.* massacrer; abattre (*animaux*).
slaughterer ['slɔ:tərə], *n.* abatteur, *m.*
slaughter-house ['slɔ:təhaus], *n.* abattoir, *m.*
Slav [slɑ:v], *a.* slave.—*n.* Slave (*personne*), *m.*, *f.*
slave [sleiv], *n.* esclave, *m.*, *f.*—*v.i.* travailler comme un esclave, peiner.
slave-driver ['sleivdraivə], *n.* (*fig.*) maître sévère et cruel, *m.*
slaver (1) ['sleivə], *n.* négrier, bâtiment négrier, *m.*
slaver (2) ['slævə], *v.i.* baver (*sur*).—*n.* bave, salive, *f.*
slavery ['sleivəri], *n.* esclavage, *m.*
slave-trade ['sleivtreid], *n.* traite des noirs, *f.*
slavish ['sleiviʃ], *a.* d'esclave; servile (*imitation etc.*).
slavishly ['sleiviʃli], *adv.* en esclave; servilement.
slavishness ['sleiviʃnis], *n.* servilité, *f.*
Slavonic [slə'vɔnik], *a.* slave.—*n.* slave (*langues*), *m.*
slay [slei], *v.t. irr.* tuer.
slayer ['sleiə], *n.* tueur (*de*), meurtrier, *m.*
slaying ['sleiiŋ], *n.* tuerie, *f.*
sledge [sledʒ], *n.* traîneau, *m.*—*v.i.* (*also* ***to go sledging***) se promener en traîneau.
sledge-hammer ['sledʒhæmə], *n.* marteau à deux mains, *m.*
sleek [sli:k], *a.* lisse, luisant, poli; (*fig.*) doucereux, onctueux.
sleekness ['sli:knis], *n.* luisant, *m.*; (*fig.*) douceur, onctuosité, *f.*
sleep [sli:p], *n.* sommeil, *m.*; ***beauty sleep***, sommeil avant minuit; ***sound sleep***, profond sommeil; ***to go to sleep***, s'endormir; ***to put a dog to sleep***, tuer un chien.—*v.t. irr.* dormir.—*v.i.* dormir, coucher (*à*, *chez* ou *dans*).
sleeper ['sli:pə], *n.* dormeur, *m.*; (*Rail.*) traverse, *f.*; (*colloq.*) wagon-lit, *m.*
sleepily ['sli:pili], *adv.* d'un air endormi.
sleepiness ['sli:pinis], *n.* assoupissement, *m.*
sleeping ['sli:piŋ], *a.* endormi; dormant.—*n.* sommeil, repos, *m.*; ***sleeping pills*** or ***tablets***, somnifère, *m.*
sleeping-bag ['sli:piŋbæg], *n.* sac de couchage, *m.*
sleeping-berth ['sli:piŋbə:θ], *n.* couchette, *f.*
sleeping-car ['sli:piŋkɑ:], *n.* wagon-lit, *m.*
sleeping-draught ['sli:piŋdrɑ:ft], *n.* somnifère, *m.*
sleeping-partner ['sli:piŋ'pɑ:tnə], *n.* associé commanditaire, *m.*
sleepless ['sli:plis], *a.* sans sommeil.
sleeplessness ['sli:plisnis], *n.* insomnie, *f.*
sleep-walker ['sli:pwɔ:kə], *n.* somnambule, *m.*, *f.*
sleepy ['sli:pi], *a.* qui a envie de dormir; soporifique (*somnifère*); ***to feel sleepy***, avoir sommeil.
sleepy-head ['sli:pihed], *n.* paresseux, *m.*
sleet [sli:t], *n.* neige fondue, *f.*; grésil, *m.*
sleeve [sli:v], *n.* manche, *f.*
sleeveless ['sli:vlis], *a.* sans manches.
sleigh [slei], *n.* traîneau, *m.*
sleight [slait], *n.* habileté, *f.*, escamotage, *m.*; ***sleight of hand***, tour de passe-passe, *m.*
slender ['slendə], *a.* mince; élancé; svelt (*taille*); (*fig.*) léger; chétif, maigre.
slenderness ['slendənis], *n.* minceur, légè reté; modicité, *f.*
sleuth(-hound) ['slu:θ(haund)], *n.* (chien limier; (*fig.*) détective, *m.*
slice [slais], *n.* tranche; écumoire (*ustensile*), *f.* ***fish-slice***, truelle, *f.*; ***slice of bread an jam***, tartine de confiture, *f.*—*v.t.* couper e tranches.
slick [slik], *a.* adroit.
slickness ['sliknis], *n.* adresse, habileté, *f.*
slide [slaid], *n.* glissoire, glissade, *f.*; ***lantern slide***, diapositive, vue fixe, *f.*—*v.t. ir* glisser; tirer (*de*).—*v.i.* glisser; couler.
slide-rule ['slaidru:l], *n.* règle à calcul, *f.*
sliding ['slaidiŋ], *a.* glissant; à coulisse.—*n* glissade, *f.*, glissement, *m.*
sliding-door ['slaidiŋ'dɔ:], *n.* porte à coulisse *f.*
sliding-scale ['slaidiŋ'skeil], *n.* (*Econ.*) échell mobile, *f.*
slight [slait], *a.* mince, léger; insignifiant ***not in the slightest***, pas le moins du monde.—*n.* manque d'égards; affront, *m.* insulte, *f.*—*v.t.* traiter sans égards; mépriser
slightingly ['slaitiŋli], *adv.* avec mépris, avec dédain.
slightly ['slaitli], *adv.* légèrement, un peu.
slightness ['slaitnis], *n.* minceur; légèreté, *f.*
slim [slim], *a.* svelte, mince; (*colloq.*) rusé.—*v.i.* s'amincir.
slime [slaim], *n.* vase, *f.*, limon, *m.*, bave (*de colimaçon*), *f.*
sliminess ['slaiminis], *n.* viscosité, *f.*
slimness ['slimnis], *n.* sveltesse, taille mince, *f.*
slimy ['slaimi], *a.* vaseux, limoneux; visqueux, gluant; (*fam.*) obséquieux.
sling [sliŋ], *n.* fronde; bretelle (*de fusil*); écharpe (*pour un membre cassé*), *f.*—*v.t. irr.* lancer (*avec une fronde*); suspendre (*fusil etc.*).
slinger ['sliŋə], *n.* frondeur, *m.*
slink [sliŋk], *v.i. irr.* s'esquiver, se dérober.
slip [slip], *v.t.* glisser, couler; perdre; lâcher; filer (*câble*); pousser (*verrou*); ***to slip in***, introduire; ***to slip off***, enlever, ôter; ***to slip on***, passer, mettre.—*v.i.* glisser, couler (*nœud*); patiner (*roues*); (*fig.*) faire un faux pas; ***to slip away***, s'esquiver; ***to slip down***, tomber; ***to slip in***, se faufiler, entrer furtivement; ***to slip up***, (*fam.*) se tromper.—*n.* glissade; combinaison (*sous-vêtement*); laisse (*à chien*), *f.*; engobe (*céramique*); (*Hort.*) scion, *m.*; cale (*de port etc.*); faute d'étourderie, *f.*, lapsus, *m.*; ***pillow-slip***, taie d'oreiller, *f.*; ***slip of paper***, bout de papier, *m.*; ***slip of the pen***, erreur de plume, *f.*; ***to give someone the slip***, planter quelqu'un là; ***to make a slip***, faire un faux pas.
slip-knot ['slipnɔt], *n.* nœud coulant, *m.*
slipper ['slipə], *n.* pantoufle, *f.*
slippered ['slipəd], *a.* en pantoufles.
slipperiness ['slipərinis], *n.* nature glissante; volubilité (*de la langue*), *f.*
slippery ['slipəri], *a.* glissant; incertain, peu sûr; peu stable; matois, rusé; ***slippery customer***, rusé compère, *m.*
slipshod ['slipʃɔd], *a.* (*fig.*) négligé; décousu (*style*).

lipstream ['slipstri:m], *n.* sillage, *m.*
lipway ['slipwei], *n.* cale, *f.*
lit [slit], *v.t. irr.* fendre.—*v.i.* se fendre.—*n.* fente, fissure, *f.*
lither ['sliðə], *v.i.* glisser; ramper (*reptile*).
liver ['slivə, 'slaivə], *n.* éclat, *m.*, tranche, *f.*, ruban, *m.*
lobber ['slɔbə], *v.i.* baver.
loe [slou], *n.* (*Bot.*) prunelle, *f.*
loe-tree ['sloutri:], *n.* prunellier, *m.*
logan ['slougən], *n.* mot d'ordre, *m.*, devise, *f.*, slogan, *m.*
loop [slu:p], *n.* sloop, aviso, *m.*
lop [slɔp], *n.* (*usu. in pl.*) rinçures, *f.pl.*—*v.t.* répandre, renverser.
lop-basin ['slɔpbeisn], **slop-bowl** ['slɔp boul], *n.* bol à rinçures (*de thé*), *m.*
lope [sloup], *n.* pente, *f.*; talus, versant, *m.*—*v.t.* couper en biais; taluter.—*v.i.* pencher, aller en pente, incliner.
sloping ['sloupiŋ], *a.* de biais, en pente.
sloppiness ['slɔpinis], *n.* état détrempé, *m.*; mollesse (*personne*), *f.*
sloppy ['slɔpi], *a.* bourbeux, humide; (*fig.*) mou.
slot [slɔt], *n.* rainure, mortaise, fente; barre de bois, *f.*
sloth (1) [slouθ], *n.* paresse, fainéantise, *f.*
sloth (2) [slouθ], *n.* (*Zool.*) paresseux, aï, *m.*
slothful ['slouθful], *a.* paresseux, fainéant.
slot-machine ['slɔtməʃi:n], *n.* distributeur automatique, *m.*
slouch [slautʃ], *n.* démarche molle *ou* lourde, *f.*; lourdaud (*personne*), *m.*—*v.i.* marcher lourdement; ***to slouch along***, marcher d'un pas traînant.
slouching ['slautʃiŋ], *a.* lourd et gauche.
slough [slau], *n.* bourbier, *m.*, fondrière; dépouille (*de serpent*), *f.*
Slovak ['slouvæk], *a.* slovaque.—*n.* Slovaque (*personne*), *m.*, *f.*
sloven [slʌvn], *n.* sans-soin, mal-soigné, *m.*
Slovene ['slouvi:n], *n.* Slovène (*personne*), *m.*, *f.*
Slovenian [slo'vi:niən], *a.* slovène.
slovenliness ['slʌvnlinis], *n.* malpropreté, saleté, négligence, *f.*
slovenly ['slʌvnli], *a.* mal soigné, mal peigné, débraillé.
slow [slou], *a.* lent, tardif; lourd (*pesant*); en retard (*montre etc.*).—*adv.* lentement.—*v.t.* ralentir.—*v.i.* se ralentir.
slowly ['slouli], *adv.* lentement, tardivement.
slowness ['slounis], *n.* lenteur; paresse; lourdeur (*pesanteur*), *f.*; retard (*de montre etc.*), *m.*
slow-worm ['slouwə:m], *n.* orvet, *m.*
sludge [slʌdʒ], *n.* boue, vase, *f.*; cambouis, *m.*
slug [slʌg], *n.* limace, *f.*; lingot (*de fusil*), *m.*
sluggard ['slʌgəd], *n.* paresseux, *m.*
sluggish ['slʌgiʃ], *a.* paresseux, indolent, lourd; lent (*ruisseau*).
sluggishly ['slʌgiʃli], *adv.* paresseusement, lourdement.
sluggishness ['slʌgiʃnis], *n.* paresse; lenteur (*de ruisseau*), *f.*
sluice [slu:s], *n.* écluse; bonde (*dans un étang*), *f.*—*v.t.* lâcher par une écluse; inonder d'eau.
sluice-gate ['slu:sgeit], *n.* vanne, *f.*
slum [slʌm], *n.* taudis, *m.*, (*pl.*) bas quartiers, *m.pl.*; ***slum-clearance***, lutte contre les taudis, *f.*

slumber ['slʌmbə], *n.* sommeil, *m.*—*v.i.* sommeiller, dormir.
slumberer ['slʌmbərə], *n.* dormeur, *m.*
slumbering ['slʌmbəriŋ], *a.* endormi, assoupi.—*n.* sommeil, assoupissement, *m.*
slump [slʌmp], *v.i.* s'enfoncer soudainement.—*n.* baisse subite; crise, *f.*
slur [slə:], *n.* tache; (*Mus.*) liaison, *f.*; ***to cast a slur upon***, flétrir, dénigrer.—*v.t.* tacher, salir; (*Mus.*) lier; ***to slur over***, glisser sur.
slurred [slə:d], *a.* (*Mus.*) coulé; brouillé (*paroles*).
slurring ['slə:riŋ], *n.* (*Mus.*) liaison, *f.*
slush [slʌʃ], *n.* boue, fange; neige à moitié fondue, *f.*
slut [slʌt], *n.* saligaude, souillon, *f.*
sly [slai], *a.* sournois, rusé; ***on the sly***, en sourdine; ***sly dog***, fin matois, *m.*
slyly ['slaili], *adv.* avec ruse, sournoisement.
slyness ['slainis], *n.* ruse, finesse, nature sournoise, *f.*
smack (1) [smæk], *n.* claquement (*de fouet*), *m.*; claque (*de la main*); gifle (*sur la figure*), *f.*; gros baiser, *m.*—*adv.* ***smack in the middle***, en plein milieu.—*v.t.* faire claquer (*fouet, les lèvres*); donner une claque à.
smack (2) [smæk], *n.* (*fig.*) saveur, *f.*—*v.i.* ***to smack of***, sentir (*le, la etc.*).
smack (3) [smæk], *n.* bateau de pêche, *m.*
smacking ['smækiŋ], *n.* claquement, *m.*; fessée, *f.*
small [smɔ:l], *a.* petit; fin, menu; (*fig.*) chétif, mince, pauvre; modeste, peu considérable; ***small arms***, armes portatives, *f.pl.*; ***small fry***, menu fretin, *m.*; ***small letters***, minuscules, *f.pl.*—*n.* partie mince, *f.*; ***small of the back***, chute des reins, *f.*
smallish ['smɔ:liʃ], *a.* un peu petit, un peu menu.
smallness ['smɔ:lnis], *n.* petitesse, *f.*; peu d'importance, *m.*
smallpox ['smɔ:lpɔks], *n.* petite vérole, *f.*
smarmy ['smɑ:mi], *a.* (*pop.*) mielleux.
smart [smɑ:t], *a.* piquant, cuisant, vif; vigoureux, rude; intelligent, éveillé; beau, élégant, pimpant, chic; ***look smart!*** dépêchez-vous! ***smart Aleck***, finaud, *m.*—*n.* douleur aiguë, vive douleur, cuisson, *f.*—*v.i.* cuire, éprouver une vive douleur.
smarten [smɑ:tn] (**up**), *v.t.* animer; ***to smarten oneself up***, se faire beau, s'attifer.
smarting ['smɑ:tiŋ], *a.* cuisant, poignant.—*n.* douleur cuisante, *f.*
smartly ['smɑ:tli], *adv.* lestement, vivement; habilement; vigoureusement, rudement; élégamment.
smartness ['smɑ:tnis], *n.* force, vigueur; élégance, *f.*, éclat (*de vêtements*), *m.*; finesse (*astuce*), *f.*
smash [smæʃ], *v.t.* briser, écraser; (*fig.*) ruiner.—*v.i.* se briser.—*n.* fracas, *m.*; (*Fin.*) déconfiture, faillite, banqueroute; (*Rail.*) catastrophe, *f.*—*adv.* ***to go smash***, faire faillite.
smashing ['smæʃiŋ], *a.* (*pop.*) formidable, épatant.
smattering ['smætəriŋ], *n.* connaissances superficielles, *f.pl.*
smear [smiə], *v.t.* enduire; (*fig.*) salir.—*n.* tache, *f.*; (*fig.*) calomnie, atteinte à la réputation, *f.*

smell [smel], *n.* odeur, *f.*; odorat (*sens*); flair (*de chien*), *m.*—*v.t.*, *v.i. irr.* sentir; flairer (*chien*).

smelly ['smeli], *a.* malodorant.

smelt (1) [smelt], *n.* (*Ichth.*) éperlan, *m.*

smelt (2) [smelt], *v.t.* fondre.

smelting ['smeltiŋ], *n.* fonte, *f.*

smile [smail], *n.* sourire, *m.*—*v.i.* sourire.

smiling ['smailiŋ], *a.* souriant; riant (*paysage etc.*).

smilingly ['smailiŋli], *adv.* en souriant.

smirch [smə:tʃ], *v.t.* souiller, salir.—*n.* tache, *f.*

smirk [smə:k], *v.i.* minauder.—*n.* sourire affecté, *m.*

smirking ['smə:kiŋ], *a.* affecté, minaudier.

smite [smait], *v.t. irr.* frapper; détruire; châtier; (*fig.*) charmer.

smith [smiθ], *n.* forgeron, *m.*

smithereens [smiðə'ri:nz], *n.pl.* ***to smash to smithereens***, mettre en miettes.

smithy ['smiði], *n.* forge, *f.*

smock [smɔk], *n.* blouse, *f.*

smog [smɔg], *n.* brouillard épais et enfumé, *m.*

smoke [smouk], *n.* fumée, *f.*—*v.t.*, *v.i.* fumer.

smokeless ['smouklis], *a.* sans fumée.

smoker ['smoukə], *n.* fumeur (*personne*), *m.*

smoke-stack ['smoukstæk], *n.* cheminée, *f.*

smokiness ['smoukinis], *n.* état enfumé, *m.*

smoking ['smoukiŋ], *a.* fumant.—*n.* habitude de fumer, *f.*; ***no smoking***, défense de fumer.

smoky ['smouki], *a.* qui fume, plein de fumée.

smooth [smu:ð], *a.* uni; égal (*régulier*); doux (*non âpre*); poli, lisse (*verni*); plat (*mer*); doucereux (*personne*).—*v.t.* polir; adoucir; aplanir, unir; dérider (*le front*); lisser (*les cheveux*).

smooth-faced ['smu:ðfeist], *a.* imberbe.

smoothing-iron ['smu:ðiŋaiən], *n.* fer à repasser, *m.*

smoothly ['smu:ðli], *adv.* uniment; sans difficulté; doucement.

smoothness ['smu:ðnis], *n.* égalité; douceur, *f.*; calme (*de la mer*), *m.*

smooth-tongued ['smu:ð'tʌŋd], *a.* mielleux, doucereux.

smother ['smʌðə], *v.t.* suffoquer, étouffer.

smothering ['smʌðəriŋ], *a.* étouffant, suffocant.—*n.* étouffement, *m.*

smoulder ['smouldə], *v.i.* brûler sans fumée ni flamme; (*fig.*) couver.

smouldering ['smouldəriŋ], *a.* qui couve.

smudge [smʌdʒ], *v.t.* barbouiller, noircir.—*n.* barbouillage, *m.*, tache, *f.*

smudgy ['smʌdʒi], *a.* barbouillé; taché.

smug [smʌg], *a.* suffisant, content de soi.

smuggle [smʌgl], *v.t.* passer en contrebande.—*v.i.* faire la contrebande.

smuggled [smʌgld], *a.* de contrebande.

smuggler ['smʌglə], *n.* contrebandier, *m.*

smuggling ['smʌgliŋ], *n.* contrebande, fraude, *f.*

smugness ['smʌgnis], *n.* suffisance, *f.*

smut [smʌt], *n.* tache de suie; (*fig.*) saleté (*grivoiserie*), *f.*—*v.t.* noircir.

smuttiness ['smʌtinis], *n.* noirceur; (*fig.*) saleté, *f.*

smutty ['smʌti], *a.* noir; (*fig.*) obscène, grivois.

snack [snæk], *n.* morceau; casse-croûte, *m.*

snack-bar ['snækbɑ:], *n.* snack-bar, *m.*

snaffle [snæfl], *n.* mors de bridon, filet, *m.*-

snag [snæg], *n.* (*fig.*) obstacle caché, *m.*

snail [sneil], *n.* escargot, limaçon, colimaço *m.*

snail's-pace ['sneilzpeis], *n.* pas de tortue, *m*

snake [sneik], *n.* serpent, *m.*—*v.i.* (*Naut* serpenter.

snap [snæp], *v.t.* saisir, happer; casse rompre, éclater; faire claquer (*fouet etc.* fermer avec un bruit sec; dire d'un ton se —*v.i.* tâcher de mordre *ou* de happer; s casser, se rompre; craquer; ***to snap a*** (*fam.*) brusquer.—*a.* imprévu.—*n.* coup d dent, *m.*; cassure, *f.*; claquement (*de fou etc.*); bruit sec; fermoir (*de sac à main*) biscuit craquant, *m.*; vivacité, *f.*

snapdragon ['snæpdrægn], *n.* muflier, *m.*

snappy ['snæpi], *a.* vif; ***make it snappy*** dépêchez-vous!

snapshot ['snæpʃɔt], *n.* (*colloq.* **snap** [snæp] instantané, *m.*

snare [snɛə], *n.* lacet, collet; (*fig.*) piège, *m.*—*v.t.* prendre (au piège).

snarl [snɑ:l], *v.i.* grogner; montrer les dents —*n.* grognement, *m.*

snarling ['snɑ:liŋ], *a.* hargneux.—*n.* grognement, *m.*

snatch [snætʃ], *v.t.* saisir; ***to snatch a*** chercher à saisir; ***to snatch from***, arrache à; ***to snatch up***, empoigner.—*n.* ***b snatches***, à bâtons rompus; ***snatches o conversation***, des bribes de conversation *f.pl.*

sneak [sni:k], *v.t.* chiper.—*v.i.* s'en alle furtivement; (*Sch.*) cafarder, moucharder.—*n.* pleutre, pied-plat; cafard, *m.*

sneaking ['sni:kiŋ], *a.* rampant, servile furtif, inavoué.

sneer [sniə], *n.* rire *ou* sourire moqueur sarcasme, ricanement, *m.*—*v.i.* ricaner, s moquer (*de*).

sneering ['sniəriŋ], *a.* ricaneur, moqueur.—*n.* ricanement, *m.*

sneeringly ['sniəriŋli], *adv.* en ricanant.

sneeze [sni:z], *n.* éternuement, *m.*—*v.i.* éternuer.

sneezing ['sni:ziŋ], *n.* éternuement, *m.*

sniff [snif], *v.t.* flairer.—*v.i.* renifler.—*n.* reniflement, *m.*

snigger ['snigə], *v.i.* rire du bout des lèvres, ricaner.—*n.* rire en dessous, *m.*

snip [snip], *n.* coup de ciseaux, *m.*; (*pop.*) certitude, *f.*—*v.t.* couper (*d'un coup de ciseaux*).

snipe [snaip], *n.* bécassine, *f.*—*v.i.* (*Shooting*) canarder.

sniper ['snaipə], *n.* tireur embusqué, franc-tireur, *m.*

snippet ['snipit], *n.* petit morceau, *m.*

snivel [snivl], *v.i.* être morveux; (*fig.*) pleurnicher.

sniveller ['snivlə], *n.* pleurnicheur, *m.*

snivelling ['snivliŋ], *a.* morveux; (*fig.*) pleurnicheur.—*n.* pleurnicherie, *f.*

snob [snɔb], *n.* poseur; fat, snob, *m.*

snobbery ['snɔbəri], *n.* snobisme, *m.*

snobbish ['snɔbiʃ], *a.* affecté, poseur, prétentieux.

snobbishness ['snɔbiʃnis], *n.* snobisme, *m.*

snoop [snu:p], *v.i.* fureter.

snooper ['snu:pə], *n.* fureteur, *m.*

snooze [snu:z], *n.* somme, *m.*—*v.i.* sommeiller.
snore [snɔ:], *v.i.* ronfler.—*n.* ronflement, *m.*
snoring ['snɔ:riŋ], *n.* ronflement, *m.*
snort [snɔ:t], *v.i.* renâcler, s'ébrouer (*cheval*); ronfler.
snorting ['snɔ:tiŋ], *n.* ronflement, *m.*
snot [snɔt], *n.* (*vulg.*) morve, *f.*
snotty ['snɔti], *a.* (*vulg.*) morveux.
snout [snaut], *n.* museau; mufle (*de taureau*); groin (*de cochon*), *m.*
snow [snou], *n.* neige, *f.*—*v.i.* neiger, tomber de la neige.
snowball ['snoubɔ:l], *n.* boule de neige, *f.*
snow-capped ['snoukæpt], *a.* couronné de neige.
snow-drift ['snoudrift], *n.* congère, *f.*, amas de neige, *m.*
snowdrop ['snoudrɔp], *n.* perce-neige, *m.*
snowflake ['snoufleik], *n.* flocon de neige, *m.*
snow-man ['snoumæn], *n.* (*pl.* **-men** [men]) bonhomme de neige, *m.*
snow-plough ['snouplau], *n.* chasse-neige, *m.*
snow-shoe ['snouʃu:], *n.* raquette, *f.*
snow-storm ['snoustɔ:m], *n.* tempête de neige, *f.*
Snow White ['snou'wait]. Blanche-Neige, *f.*
snow-white ['snouwait], *a.* blanc comme la neige.
snowy ['snoui], *a.* de neige; neigeux.
snub [snʌb], *n.* rebuffade, *f.*; affront, *m.*—*v.t.* rabrouer, rembarrer.
snub-nosed ['snʌbnouzd], *a.* au nez camus.
snuff (1) [snʌf], *n.* tabac (à priser), *m.*; ***pinch of snuff***, prise de tabac, *f.*
snuff (2) [snʌf], *n.* lumignon (*de mèche*), *m.*—*v.t.* moucher (*chandelle*).
snuff-box ['snʌfbɔks], *n.* tabatière, *f.*
snuffle [snʌfl], *n.* reniflement, *m.*—*v.i.* nasiller, renifler.
snuffling ['snʌfliŋ], *a.* nasillard.—*n.* nasillement, *m.*
snug [snʌg], *a.* confortable, commode et agréable, où l'on est bien; gentil; serré, compact; ***we are very snug here***, nous sommes on ne peut mieux ici.
snuggery ['snʌgəri], *n.* endroit petit et commode (*où l'on se sent chez soi*), *m.*
snuggle [snʌgl], *v.t.* serrer.—*v.i.* se serrer.
snugly ['snʌgli], *adv.* commodément, à son aise.
snugness ['snʌgnis], *n.* confort, bien-être, *m.*
so [sou], *adv.* and *conj.* ainsi, de cette manière, comme cela, comme ça (*de cette façon*); de même, de la même manière, tel (*pareillement*); si, tellement, tant (*à tel point*); aussi, donc (*alors*); ***and so on***, et ainsi de suite; ***be it so***, soit! ***how so?*** comment cela? ***is that so?*** vraiment? ***just so!*** parfaitement! ***Mr. So-and-So***, Monsieur un tel; ***or so***, environ, à peu près; ***so as to***, de manière à; ***so that***, de sorte que.
soak [souk], *v.t.* tremper; (*colloq.*) estamper. —*v.i.* tremper, s'infiltrer.
soaking ['soukiŋ], *a.* qui trempe.—*n.* trempée (*de pluie*), *f.*
soap [soup], *n.* savon, *m.*—*v.t.* savonner.
soap-bubble ['soupbʌbl], *n.* bulle de savon, *f.*
soap-flakes ['soupfleiks], *n.pl.* savon en paillettes, *m.*
soap-suds ['soupsʌdz], *n.pl.* eau de savon, *f.*
soar [sɔ:], *v.i.* prendre l'essor, s'élever; ***to soar over***, planer sur.
soaring ['sɔ:riŋ], *a.* qui s'élève; (*fig.*) élevé.—*n.* essor, élan, *m.*
sob [sɔb], *v.i.* sangloter.—*n.* sanglot, *m.*
sobbing ['sɔbiŋ], *n.* sanglots, *m.pl.*
sober ['soubə], *a.* qui n'a pas bu, qui n'est pas ivre; sobre, tempéré; grave, sérieux; sensé; calme, posé, rassis.—*v.t.* dégriser; (*fig.*) calmer.—*v.i.* ***to sober up***, se désenivrer.
soberly ['soubəli], *adv.* sobrement; raisonnablement.
soberness ['soubənis], **sobriety** [sə'braiəti], *n.* sobriété, tempérance; gravité, *f.*
so-called ['soukɔ:ld], *a.* soi-disant, prétendu.
soccer ['sɔkə], *n.* (*fam.*) football, *m.*
sociability [souʃə'biliti], *n.* sociabilité, *f.*
sociable ['souʃəbl], *a.* sociable.
social ['souʃəl], *a.* social.
socialism ['souʃəlizm], *n.* socialisme, *m.*
socialist ['souʃəlist], *a.* and *n.* socialiste, *m., f.*
socially ['souʃəli], *adv.* socialement.
society [sə'saiəti], *n.* société; la société, *f.*; le monde, *m.*
sociology [sousi'ɔlədʒi], *n.* sociologie, *f.*
sock [sɔk] *n.* chaussette; semelle (*intérieure*), *f.*
socket ['sɔkit], *n.* emboîture; orbite (*de l'œil*), *f.*; trou, *m.*, cavité; douille (*d'outil etc.*), *f.*
Socrates ['sɔkrəti:z]. Socrate, *m.*
sod [sɔd], *n.* gazon, *m.*; motte de gazon, *f.*
soda ['soudə], *n.* soude, *f.*; ***baking soda***, bicarbonate de soude, *m.*
soda-water ['soudəwɔ:tə], *n.* eau de Seltz, *f.*, soda, *m.*
sodden [sɔdn], *a.* imprégné d'eau, détrempé; pâteux (*pain*); abruti (*d'alcool*).
sodium ['soudiəm], *n.* (*Chem.*) sodium, *m.*
sodomy ['sɔdəmi], *n.* sodomie, *f.*
sofa ['soufə], *n.* canapé, *m.*
soft [sɔft], *a.* mou, mol, mollet; délicat, doux, facile, pas résistant; tendre; efféminé; faible; sot, niais; (*Gram.*) doux; ***soft fruits***, fruits rouges, *m.pl.*—*adv.* mollement, doucement.—*int.* doucement! tout doux!
soften [sɔfn], *v.t.* amollir, ramollir; adoucir, apaiser; affaiblir; attendrir (*cœur*).—*v.i.* s'amollir, se ramollir; s'affaiblir; s'attendrir (*cœur*).
softener ['sɔfnə], *n.* chose qui amollit, *f.*
softening ['sɔfniŋ], *n.* amollissement; affaiblissement; attendrissement (*du cœur*), *m.*
soft-headed ['sɔft'hedid], *a.* niais; sot.
soft-hearted ['sɔft'hɑ:tid], *a.* tendre, compatissant.
softly ['sɔftli], *adv.* mollement; doucement; tendrement.
softness ['sɔftnis], *n.* mollesse; faiblesse; niaiserie; douceur, *f.*
soggy ['sɔgi], *a.* détrempé; pâteux (*pain*).
soil (1) [sɔil], *n.* sol, terrain, terroir, *m.*, terre, *f.*
soil (2) [sɔil], *n.* tache, souillure, *f.*—*v.t.* salir, souiller.
sojourn ['sɔdʒən], *n.* séjour, *m.*—*v.i.* séjourner.
sojourning ['sɔdʒəniŋ], *n.* séjour, *m.*
solace ['sɔlis], *n.* consolation, *f.*, soulagement, *m.*—*v.t.* consoler (*de*).
solar ['soulə], *a.* solaire, du soleil.
solder ['sɔ(l)də], *n.* soudure, *f.*—*v.t.* souder.
soldering ['sɔ(l)dəriŋ], *n.* soudure, *f.*; soudage (*action*), *m.*; ***soldering-iron***, fer à souder, *m.*

soldier ['souldʒə], *n.* soldat, militaire, *m.*; ***foot-soldier***, fantassin, *m.*; ***private soldier***, simple soldat.—*v.i.* servir comme soldat.
soldierly ['souldʒəli], *a.* de soldat, militaire, martial.
soldiery ['souldʒəri], *n.* troupes, *f.pl.*, soldats, *m.pl.*
sole (1) [soul], *a.* seul, unique.
sole (2) [soul], *n.* plante (*du pied*); semelle (*de soulier, d'outil etc.*), *f.*—*v.t.* ressemeler.
sole (3) [soul], *n.* (*Ichth.*) sole, *f.*
solecism ['sɔlisizm], *n.* solécisme, *m.*
solely ['soulli], *adv.* seulement, uniquement.
solemn ['sɔləm], *a.* solennel.
solemnity [sə'lemniti], *n.* solennité, *f.*
solemnization [sɔləmnai'zeiʃən], *n.* solennisation; célébration solennelle, *f.*
solemnize ['sɔləmnaiz], *v.t.* solenniser, célébrer.
solemnly ['sɔləmli], *adv.* solennellement.
solenoid ['sɔlinɔid], *n.* (*Elec.*) solénoïde, *m.*
solicit [sə'lisit], *v.t.* solliciter.
solicitation [səlisi'teiʃən], *n.* sollicitation, *f.*
solicitor [sə'lisitə], *n.* (*Law*) avoué et notaire, *m.*
solicitous [sə'lisitəs], *a.* désireux; ***solicitous about***, soigneux, attentif à.
solicitude [sə'lisitju:d], *n.* sollicitude, *f.*
solid ['sɔlid], *a.* solide, massif.—*n.* solide, *m.*
solidarity [sɔli'dæriti], *n.* solidarité, *f.*
solidification [səlidifi'keiʃən], *n.* solidification, *f.*
solidify [sə'lidifai], *v.t.* solidifier.—*v.i.* se solidifier.
solidity [sə'liditi], **solidness** ['sɔlidnis], *n.* solidité, *f.*
solidly ['sɔlidli], *adv.* solidement.
soliloquize [sə'liləkwaiz], *v.i.* faire un soliloque.
soliloquy [sə'liləkwi], *n.* soliloque, *m.*
soling ['souliŋ], *n.* ressemelage, *m.*
solitary ['sɔlitəri], *a.* solitaire, retiré, isolé; seul.
solitude ['sɔlitju:d], *n.* solitude, *f.*
solo ['soulou], *n.* solo, *m.*
soloist ['soulouist], *n.* soliste, *m.*, *f.*
Solomon ['sɔləmən]. Salomon, *m.*
solstice ['sɔlstis], *n.* solstice, *m.*
solubility [sɔlju'biliti], *n.* solubilité, *f.*
soluble ['sɔljubl], *a.* soluble.
solution [sə'lju:ʃən], *n.* solution, *f.*
solvable ['sɔlvəbl], *a.* soluble.
solve [sɔlv], *v.t.* résoudre, expliquer, éclaircir.
solvency ['sɔlvənsi], *n.* (*Fin.*) solvabilité, *f.*
solvent ['sɔlvənt], *a.* dissolvant; (*Comm.*) solvable.—*n.* dissolvant, *m.*
Somali [so'mɑ:li], *a.* somali.—*n.* somali (*langue*); Somali (*personne*), *m.*
Somalia [so'mɑ:liə]. la Somalie, *f.*
Somaliland [so'mɑ:lilænd]. la Somalie, *f.*
sombre ['sɔmbə], *a.* sombre.
sombrely ['sɔmbəli], *adv.* sombrement.
some [sʌm], *a.* quelque, *m.*, *f.*, quelques, *pl.*; un certain, *m.*, certains, *m.pl.*, plusieurs, *pl.*; du, *m.*, de la, *f.*, de l', *m.*, *f.*, des, *pl.*, de; quelconque; un certain nombre de, un peu de, une partie de.—*adv.* à peu près, environ, quelque.—*pron.* quelques-uns, *m.pl.*, quelques-unes, *f.pl.*; les uns, *m.pl.*, les unes, *f.pl.*, . . . les autres, *pl.*; en.
somebody ['sʌmbədi], **someone** ['sʌmwʌn], *pron.* quelqu'un, *m.*, quelqu'une, *f.*, on; ***somebody else***, quelqu'un d'autre, quelque autre, un autre.
somehow ['sʌmhau], *adv.* d'une manière ou d'une autre, de façon ou d'autre.
someone [SOMEBODY].
somersault ['sʌməsɔ:lt], *n.* saut périlleux, *m.*, culbute, *f.*
something ['sʌmθiŋ], *n.* and *pron.* quelque chose (*de*), *m.*; ***something else***, autre chose, *f.*—*adv.* un peu, quelque peu, tant soit peu.
sometime ['sʌmtaim], *adv.* autrefois, jadis; ***sometime or other***, tôt ou tard.—*a.* ancien.
sometimes ['sʌmtaimz], *adv.* quelquefois, parfois; tantôt.
somewhat ['sʌmwɔt], *adv.* quelque peu, un peu; assez.—*n.* un peu, quelque peu, tant soit peu, *m.*
somewhere ['sʌmwɛə], *adv.* quelque part; ***somewhere else***, ailleurs.
somnambulist [sɔm'næmbjulist], *n.* somnambule, *m.*, *f.*
somniferous [sɔm'nifərəs], *a.* somnifère.
somnolence ['sɔmnələns], *n.* somnolence, *f.*
somnolent ['sɔmnələnt], *a.* somnolent.
son [sʌn], *n.* fils; (*fig.*) descendant, *m.*
sonata [sə'nɑ:tə], *n.* sonate, *f.*
song [sɔŋ], *n.* chanson, *f.*; chant, *m.*; (*fig.*) ballade, *f.*; ***a mere song***, un rien, *m.*, une bagatelle, *f.*
songster ['sɔŋstə], *n.* chanteur; oiseau chanteur, *m.*
songstress ['sɔŋstris], *n.* chanteuse, *f.*
song-thrush ['sɔŋθrʌʃ], *n.* grive chanteuse, *f.*
song-writer ['sɔŋraitə], *n.* chansonnier, *m.*
son-in-law ['sʌninlɔ:], *n.* gendre, *m.*
sonnet ['sɔnit], *n.* sonnet, *m.*
sonny ['sʌni], *n.* (*fam.*) mon petit, mon fiston, *m.*
sonorous ['sɔnərəs], *a.* sonore.
soon [su:n], *adv.* bientôt; tôt (*de bonne heure*); ***as soon as***, aussitôt que, dès que; ***how soon?*** quand ? ***see you soon!*** à bientôt; ***so soon***, si tôt; ***too soon***, trop tôt.
sooner ['su:nə], *adv.* plus tôt (*de meilleure heure*); plutôt (*mieux*); ***no sooner said than done***, aussitôt dit, aussitôt fait; ***sooner or later***, tôt ou tard; ***sooner than***, plutôt que.
soonest ['su:nist], *adv.* le plus tôt.
soot [sut], *n.* suie, *f.*
soothe [su:ð], *v.t.* apaiser, calmer; (*fig.*) charmer.
soothing ['su:ðiŋ], *a.* calmant, consolant; flatteur.
soothingly ['su:ðiŋli], *adv.* d'un ton doux.
soothsay ['su:θsei], *v.i.* prophétiser, prédire.
soothsayer ['su:θseiə], *n.* devin, *m.*, devineresse, *f.*, prophète, *m.*
sooty ['suti], *a.* de suie, fuligineux; plein *ou* couvert de suie.
sop [sɔp], *n.* morceau (de pain) trempé; (*fig.*) pot-de-vin (*pourboire*), *m.*—*v.t.* tremper.
Sophia [sə'faiə]. Sophie, *f.*
sophism ['sɔfizm], *n.* sophisme, *m.*
sophist ['sɔfist], *n.* sophiste, *m.*, *f.*
sophisticate [sə'fistikeit], *v.t.* sophistiquer, falsifier.

sophisticated [sə'fistikeitid], *a.* falsifié; blasé (*personne*).
sophistication [səfisti'keiʃən], *n.* sophistication, falsification, *f.*
sophistry ['sɔfistri], *n.* sophismes, *m.pl.*
Sophocles ['sɔfəkli:z]. Sophocle, *m.*
soporific [sɔpə'rifik], *a.* and *n.* soporifique, *m.*
sopping ['sɔpiŋ] (**wet**), *a.* trempé.
soprano [sə'prɑ:nou], *n.* soprano, *m., f.*
sorcerer ['sɔ:sərə], *n.* sorcier, magicien, *m.*
sorceress ['sɔ:səris], *n.* sorcière, magicienne, *f.*
sorcery ['sɔ:səri], *n.* sorcellerie, magie, *f.*
sordid ['sɔ:did], *a.* sordide, sale; bas, vil.
sordidly ['sɔ:didli], *adv.* sordidement.
sordidness ['sɔ:didnis], *n.* sordidité, *f.*
sore [sɔ:], *a.* douloureux, endolori, sensible; (*fig.*) rude; fâché; ***sore throat***, mal à la gorge, *m.*—*n.* plaie, *f.*
sorely ['sɔ:li], *adv.* gravement, fortement, cruellement, rudement.
soreness ['sɔ:nis], *n.* douleur; sensation pénible, *f.*
sorrel ['sɔrəl], *a.* saure; alezan.—*n.* oseille, *f.*; alezan (*cheval*), *m.*
sorrily ['sɔrili], *adv.* misérablement, pauvrement.
sorrow ['sɔrou], *n.* chagrin, *m.*, douleur; peine, tristesse, *f.*—*v.i.* être affligé.
sorrowful ['sɔroful], *a.* triste, affligé.
sorrowfully ['sɔrofuli], *adv.* tristement.
sorrowing ['sɔrouiŋ], *a.* affligé.
sorry ['sɔri], *a.* fâché, désolé (*de*); triste, pauvre, méchant, pitoyable; ***I am sorry for you***, je vous plains; ***I am sorry to say that*** . . ., je regrette d'avoir à dire que . . .; ***sorry !*** pardon!
sort (1) [sɔ:t], *n.* sorte, *f.*, genre, *m.*, espèce; manière, façon, *f.*; ***nothing of the sort***, pas du tout.
sort (2) [sɔ:t], *v.t.* assortir, classer, distribuer; trier (*lettres etc.*).
sorted ['sɔ:tid], *a.* assorti; trié, arrangé, séparé.
sorter ['sɔ:tə], *n.* trieur, *m.*
sortie ['sɔ:ti], *n.* (*Mil.*) sortie, *f.*; (*Av.*) vol, *m.*
sorting ['sɔ:tiŋ], *n.* triage, tri; assortiment (*classement*), *m.*
so-so ['sou'sou], *a.* comme ci comme ça, (*fam.*) couci-couça.
sot [sɔt], *n.* ivrogne, *m., f.*
sottish ['sɔtiʃ], *a.* hébété, abruti.
sough [sau, sʌf], *v.i.* murmurer, soupirer (*vent*).
soughing ['sauiŋ], *n.* bruissement, murmure, *m.*
soul [soul], *n.* âme, *f.*; (*fig.*) être; principe (*essence*), *m.*; ***All Souls' Day***, le jour des morts, *m.*
soulful ['soulful], *a.* sentimental.
soulfully ['soulfuli], *adv.* avec expression; avec sentiment.
soulless ['soullis], *a.* sans âme; abrutissant.
sound (1) [saund], *n.* détroit (*goulet*), *m.*; (*Surg.*) sonde, *f.*—*v.t.* sonder (*les profondeurs etc.*); (*Surg.*) ausculter.
sound (2) [saund], *a.* en bon état, sain; (*fig.*) solide; profond (*sommeil*); valide, bien fondé; ***safe and sound***, sain et sauf.
sound (3) [saund], *v.t.* faire sonner; proclamer.—*v.i.* sonner; retentir, résonner (*de*); sembler.—*n.* son, bruit, *m.*; ***to break the sound barrier***, (*Av.*) franchir le mur du son.
sounding (1) ['saundiŋ], *n.* sondage, *m.*; (*Surg.*) auscultation, *f.*
sounding (2) ['saundiŋ], *a.* résonnant, retentissant; (*fig.*) pompeux.—*n.* retentissement, résonnement, *m.*
sounding-balloon ['saundiŋbə'lu:n], *n.* (*Meteor.*) ballon sonde, *m.*
sounding-lead ['saundiŋled], *n.* plomb de sonde, *m.*
sounding-line ['saundiŋlain], *n.* ligne de sonde, *f.*
soundless ['saundlis], *a.* sans bruit, muet.
soundly ['saundli], *adv.* vigoureusement, rudement, ferme, bien; sainement, solidement; profondément (*sommeil*).
soundness ['saundnis], *n.* bon état, *m.*; force, vigueur (*physique*); droiture (*morale*), *f.*
sound-proof ['saundpru:f], *a.* insonore.
sound-track ['saundtræk], *n.* (*Cine.*) piste sonore, *f.*
sound-wave ['saundweiv], *n.* onde sonore, *f.*
soup [su:p], *n.* potage, *m.*, soupe, *f.*; (*colloq.*) ***to be in the soup***, être dans le pétrin.
soup-ladle ['su:pleidl], *n.* louche, *f.*
soup-tureen ['su:ptju'ri:n], *n.* soupière, *f.*
sour ['sauə], *a.* aigre, acide; tourné (*lait*); (*fig.*) âpre.—*v.t.* aigrir; (*fig.*) empoisonner.—*v.i.* s'aigrir.
source [sɔ:s], *n.* source, *f.*
souring ['sauəriŋ], *n.* aigrissement, *m.*
sourish ['sauəriʃ], *a.* suret, aigrelet.
sourly ['sauəli], *adv.* avec aigreur; (*fig.*) aigrement, âprement.
sourness ['sauənis], *n.* aigreur, acidité; (*fig.*) âpreté, *f.*
souse [saus], *v.t.* tremper; faire mariner.—*n.* marinade, *f.*
south [sauθ], *a.* sud, du sud, du midi, méridional.—*n.* sud, midi, *m.*—*adv.* vers le midi, vers le sud, au sud; ***South Africa***, l'Afrique du Sud, *f.*; ***South America***, l'Amérique du Sud, *f.*
south-east [sauθ'i:st], *a.* sud-est, du sud-est.—*n.* sud-est, *m.*—*adv.* vers le sud-est.
south-easter [sauθ'i:stə], *n.* vent du sud-est, *m.*
south-easterly [sauθ'i:stəli], **south-eastern** [sauθ'i:stn], *a.* du sud-est.
southerly ['sʌðəli], **southern** ['sʌðən], *a.* du sud, du midi, méridional.
southerner ['sʌðənə], *n.* méridional, *m.*; (*Am.*) sudiste, *m., f.*
southernmost ['sʌðənmost], *a.* à l'extrême sud.
southward ['sauθwəd], *adv.* vers le sud, au sud.
south-west ['sauθ'west], *a.* sud-ouest, du sud-ouest.—*n.* sud-ouest, *m.*—*adv.* vers le sud-ouest.
southwester [sau'westə], [SOU'WESTER].
south-westerly ['sauθ'westəli], **south-western** ['sauθ'westən], *a.* du sud-ouest, sud-ouest.
souvenir ['su:vəniə], *n.* souvenir, *m.*
sou'wester, southwester [sau'westə], *n.* vent du sud-ouest; suroît (*coiffure*), *m.*
sovereign ['sɔvrin], *a.* and *n.* souverain, *m.*
sovereignty ['sɔvrinti], *n.* souveraineté, *f.*
Soviet ['souviet], *n.* Soviet, *m.*; ***the Soviet Union***, l'Union Soviétique, *f.*

sow (1) [sau], *n.* truie; gueuse (*de fer*), *f.*
sow (2) [sou], *v.t. irr.* semer.—*v.i.* semer, faire les semailles.
sower ['souə], *n.* semeur, *m.*
sowing ['souiŋ], *n.* semailles, *f.pl.*, ensemencement, *m.*
soya-bean ['sɔiə'bi:n], *n.* soya, soja, *m.*
spa [spɑ:], *n.* source minérale; ville d'eaux, *f.*
space [speis], *n.* espace, *m.*, étendue; place, *f.*; intervalle, *m.*—*v.t.* (*Print.*) espacer.
space-ship ['speisʃip], *n.* astronef, *m.*
space-suit ['speissju:t], *n.* combinaison spatiale, *f.*
space-travel ['speistrævl], *n.* astronautique, *f.*, voyages interplanétaires, *m.pl.*
space-traveller ['speistrævlə], *n.* astronaute, cosmonaute, *m., f.*
spacing ['speisiŋ], *n.* espacement; (*Print.*) interligne, *m.*
spacious ['speiʃəs], *a.* spacieux, vaste.
spaciously ['speiʃəsli], *adv.* spacieusement; amplement.
spaciousness ['speiʃəsnis], *n.* vaste étendue, *f.*
spade [speid], *n.* bêche, pelle (*d'enfant*), *f.*; (*Cards*) pique, *m.*
spadeful ['speidful], *n.* pelletée, *f.*
Spain [spein]. l'Espagne, *f.*
span [spæn], *n.* empan, *m.*; envergure (*d'ailes*), *f.*; moment, instant, *m.*—*v.t.* mesurer; embrasser; traverser.
spangle [spæŋgl], *n.* paillette, *f.*—*v.t.* pailleter (*de*).
Spaniard ['spænjəd], *n.* Espagnol, *m.*
spaniel ['spænjəl], *n.* épagneul, *m.*
Spanish ['spæniʃ], *a.* espagnol, d'Espagne.—*n.* espagnol (*langue*), *m.*
spank [spæŋk], *v.t.* fesser.—*n.* (*also* **spanking** (1) ['spæŋkiŋ]) fessée, *f.*
spanking (2) ['spæŋkiŋ], *a.* vigoureux; rapide (*pas*).
spanner ['spænə], *n.* clef à écrous, *f.*; ***adjustable spanner***, clef anglaise, *f.*
spar [spɑ:], *n.* perche, *f.*, poteau; (*Naut.*) espar; (*Box.*) combat d'entraînement, *m.*—*v.i.* faire un assaut amical (*de boxe* ou *de paroles*); se disputer.
spare [spεə], *v.t.* épargner; ménager, économiser (*dépenser avec précaution*); se passer de (*se priver de*); donner, céder; prêter.—*a.* disponible, de reste (*superflu*); libre (*temps*); (*Motor. etc.*) de rechange; modique, faible, pauvre; maigre, sec (*taille*).
spareness ['spεənis], *n.* maigreur, *f.*
spare-rib ['spεə'rib], *n.* côte de porc, *f.*
sparing ['spεəriŋ], *a.* économe, ménager, frugal, sobre (*de*); parcimonieux.
sparingly ['spεəriŋli], *adv.* frugalement, avec parcimonie; économiquement.
sparingness ['spεəriŋnis], *n.* frugalité, épargne, parcimonie, *f.*
spark [spɑ:k], *n.* étincelle; (*fig.*) lueur, *f.*—*v.i.* produire des étincelles.
sparking-plug ['spɑ:kiŋplʌg], *n.* (*Motor.*) bougie (d'allumage), *f.*
sparkle [spɑ:kl], *n.* étincellement, éclat, *m.*; vivacité (*d'esprit*), *f.*—*v.i.* étinceler, scintiller; pétiller (*boisson*).
sparkling ['spɑ:kliŋ], *a.* étincelant; mousseux (*boisson*).
sparling ['spɑ:liŋ], *n.* (*Ichth.*) éperlan, *m.*
sparrow ['spærou], *n.* moineau, passereau, *m.*
sparrow-hawk ['spærouhɔ:k], *n.* épervier, *m.*
sparse [spɑ:s], *a.* épars; éparpillé, clairsemé.
sparsely ['spɑ:sli], *adv.* d'une manière éparse, de loin en loin.
sparseness ['spɑ:snis], *n.* rareté, *f.*; éparpillement, *m.*
Sparta ['spɑ:tə]. Sparte, *f.*
Spartan ['spɑ:tən], *a.* spartiate.—*n.* Spartiate (*personne*), *m., f.*
spasm [spæzm], *n.* spasme, accès, *m.*
spasmodic [spæz'mɔdik], **spasmodical** [spæz'mɔdikəl], *a.* spasmodique.
spasmodically [spæz'mɔdikəli], *adv.* par à-coups.
spastic ['spæstik], *a.* spasmodique.—*n.* paraplégique, *m., f.*
spat (1) [spæt], *past* and *p.p.* [SPIT].
spat (2) [spæt], *n.* guêtre de ville, *f.*
spate [speit], *n.* crue (*de rivière*); (*fig.*) affluence, *f.*
spatter ['spætə], *v.t.* éclabousser (*de*).
spatula ['spætjulə], *n.* spatule, *f.*
spavin ['spævin], *n.* éparvin, *m.*
spawn [spɔ:n], *n.* frai, *m.*; (*fig.*) race, engeance, *f.*—*v.t.* (*fig.*) engendrer.—*v.i.* frayer; (*fig.*) naître.
spawning-ground ['spɔ:niŋgraund], *n.* frayère, *f.*
speak [spi:k], *v.t. irr.* parler; dire; (*Naut.*) héler; ***to speak one's mind***, dire sa pensée.—*v.i.* parler; causer (*avec*); faire un discours (*en public*); dire; ***so to speak***, pour ainsi dire; ***to speak out***, parler à haute voix; ***to speak up***, parler plus fort.
speaker ['spi:kə], *n.* personne qui parle, *f.*; orateur; (*Parl.*) président; (*Rad.* = ***loud-speaker***) haut-parleur, *m.*
speaking ['spi:kiŋ], *a.* parlant, qui parle.—*n.* parole, *f.*, langage, discours, *m.*
speaking-tube ['spi:kiŋtju:b], *n.* tuyau *ou* tube acoustique, *m.*
spear [spiə], *n.* lance, *f.*—*v.t.* percer d'un coup de lance; harponner (*poisson etc.*).
spear-head ['spiəhed], *n.* fer de lance, *m.*; (*Mil.*) avancée, pointe, *f.*
spearman ['spiəmən], *n.* (*pl.* **-men** [men]) lancier, *m.*
spearmint ['spiəmint], *n.* menthe verte, *f.*
special [speʃl], *a.* spécial, exprès; extraordinaire.
specialist ['speʃəlist], *n.* spécialiste, *m., f.*
speciality [speʃi'æliti], **specialty** ['speʃəlti], *n.* spécialité, *f.*
specialization [speʃəlai'zeiʃən], *n.* spécialisation, *f.*
specialize ['speʃəlaiz], *v.i.* se spécialiser.
specially ['speʃəli], *adv.* particulièrement, surtout.
specie ['spi:ʃi:], *n.* espèces, *f.pl.*, numéraire, *m.*
species ['spi:ʃi:z], *n.* espèce, *f.*; (*fig.*) genre, *m.*, sorte, *f.*
specific [spi'sifik], *a.* spécifique; précis.
specification [spesifi'keiʃən], *n.* spécification; description précise (*de brevet d'invention*), *f.*
specify ['spesifai], *v.t.* spécifier, déterminer; fixer d'avance (*une heure*).
specimen ['spesimən], *n.* spécimen, modèle, échantillon, *m.*
specious ['spi:ʃəs], *a.* spécieux, captieux.
speciousness ['spi:ʃəsnis], *n.* spéciosité, apparence plausible, *f.*

speck [spek], *n.* petite tache, marque, *f.*, point; grain (*de poussière*), *m.*—*v.t.* tacher, marquer.
speckle [spekl], *v.t.* tacheter, marqueter, moucheter (*de*).—*n.* moucheture (*peau d'animal*), *f.*
speckled [spekld], *a.* tacheté, marqueté, moucheté.
spectacle ['spektəkl], *n.* spectacle, *m.*; (*pl.*) lunettes, *f.pl.*
spectacle-case ['spektəklkeis], *n.* étui à lunettes, *m.*
spectacle-maker ['spektəklmeikə], *n.* lunetier, *m.*
spectacular [spek'tækjulə], *a.* théâtral, impressionnant.
spectator [spek'teitə], *n.* spectateur, *m.*; (*pl.*) assistants, *m.pl.*
spectral ['spektrəl], *a.* de spectre, spectral.
spectre ['spektə], *n.* spectre, fantôme, *m.*
spectroscope ['spektrəskoup], *n.* spectroscope, *m.*
spectrum ['spektrəm], *n.* (*pl.* **spectra** ['spektrə]) spectre, *m.*
speculate ['spekjuleit], *v.i.* spéculer (*sur*), méditer (*sur*).
speculation [spekju'leiʃən], *n.* spéculation, méditation, *f.*
speculative ['spekjulətiv], *a.* spéculatif, contemplatif; (*Comm.*) spéculateur.
speculatively ['spekjulətivli], *adv.* en théorie.
speculator ['spekjuleitə], *n.* spéculateur, *m.*
speech [spi:tʃ], *n.* parole, *f.*; discours, *m.*, allocution (*public*); langue (*parler*), *f.*; ***extempore speech***, improvisation, *f.*; (*Parl.*) ***maiden speech***, discours de début.
speech-day ['spi:tʃdei], *n.* (*Sch.*) distribution des prix, *f.*
speechless ['spi:tʃlis], *a.* sans voix; muet, interdit.
speechlessness ['spi:tʃlisnis], *n.* mutisme, *m.*
speed [spi:d], *n.* vitesse, rapidité, célérité; hâte, diligence, promptitude, *f.*; (*fig.*) succès, *m.*; ***God-speed!*** bon succès! bonne chance!—*v.t. irr.* expédier, hâter; faire réussir (*faciliter*).—*v.i.* se hâter, se dépêcher.
speed-boat ['spi:dbout], *n.* motoglisseur, *m.*; hors-bord, *m.inv.*
speedily ['spi:dili], *adv.* vite, en toute hâte.
speediness ['spi:dinis], *n.* célérité, hâte, *f.*
speed-limit ['spi:dlimit], *n.* limitation de vitesse, *f.*
speedometer [spi:'dɔmitə], *n.* indicateur de vitesse, tachymètre, *m.*
speedwell ['spi:dwel], *n.* (*Bot.*) véronique, *f.*
speedy ['spi:di], *a.* rapide, vite, prompt.
spell (1) [spel], *n.* temps, *m.*, période, *f.*; tour (*de service*), *m.*
spell (2) [spel], *n.* charme, *m.*—*v.t.*, *v.i. irr.* épeler (*nommer les lettres*); orthographier (*écrire correctement*); signifier.
spell-bound ['spelbaund], *a.* charmé, fasciné.
speller ['spelə], *n.* personne qui orthographie *ou* qui épèle, *f.*
spelling ['speliŋ], *n.* orthographe; épellation, *f.*
spelling-bee ['speliŋbi:], *n.* concours orthographique, *m.*
spelling-book ['speliŋbuk], *n.* abécédaire, syllabaire, *m.*
spelter ['speltə], *n.* zinc, *m.*
spend [spend], *v.t. irr.* dépenser; gaspiller, perdre (*prodiguer*); passer (*temps*).—*v.i.* dépenser; se perdre (*se dissiper*); se consumer.
spending ['spendiŋ], *n.* action de dépenser, dépense, *f.*
spendthrift ['spendθrift], *n.* prodigue, *m.*, *f.*, dissipateur, *m.*
spent [spent], *a.* épuisé; mort (*balle etc.*).
sperm [spə:m], *n.* sperme; frai (*poisson etc.*); blanc de baleine, *m.*
spew [spju:], *v.t.*, *v.i.* vomir.
spewing ['spju:iŋ], *n.* vomissement, *m.*
sphere ['sfiə], *n.* sphère, *f.*
spherical ['sferikl], *a.* sphérique.
spherics ['sferiks], *n.pl.* théorie de la sphère, *f.*
spheroid ['sfiərɔid], *n.* sphéroïde, *m.*
sphinx [sfiŋks], *n.* (*pl.* **sphinxes** ['sfiŋksiz]) sphinx, *m.*
spice [spais], *n.* épice, *f.*—*v.t.* épicer (*de*).
spiciness ['spaisinis], *n.* goût épicé, *m.*
spick-and-span ['spikənd'spæn], *a.* tiré à quatre épingles; bien astiqué.
spicy ['spaisi], *a.* épicé, aromatique, parfumé.
spider ['spaidə], *n.* araignée, *f.*
spigot ['spigət], *n.* fausset; (*Am.*, *Sc.*) robinet, *m.*
spike [spaik], *n.* pointe, *f.*; clou à grosse tête (*de métal*), *m.*; cheville (*de bois*), *f.*; ***marline-spike***, épissoir, *m.*—*v.t.* clouer; hérisser.
spiked [spaikt], *a.* à pointes, barbelé.
spikenard ['spaiknɑ:d], *n.* nard indien, *m.*
spiky ['spaiki], *a.* à pointe aiguë; armé de pointes.
spill (1) [spil], *v.t. irr.* répandre, verser; renverser.—*v.i.* se verser, se répandre.—*n.* culbute (*renversement*), *f.*
spill (2) [spil], *n.* allumette de papier, allumette en copeau, *f.*
spin [spin], *v.t. irr.* filer; faire tourner.—*v.i.* filer (*aller vite*); tourner.—*n.* tournoiement, *m.*; (*Av.*) vrille, *f.*; (*Motor.*) tour, *m.*; promenade, *f.*
spinach ['spinidʒ], *n.* épinards, *m.pl.*
spinal [spainl], *a.* spinal; ***spinal column***, colonne vertébrale, *f.*
spindle [spindl], *n.* fuseau; pivot; (*Mach.*) essieu; (*Tech.*) axe, *m.*
spindleful ['spindlful], *n.* fusée, *f.*
spindle-legs ['spindllegz], **spindle-shanks** ['spindlʃæŋks], *n.pl.* jambes de fuseau, *f.pl.*
spindrift ['spindrift], *n.* embrun, *m.*
spine [spain], *n.* épine dorsale; (*Bot.*) épine, *f.*
spineless ['spainlis], *a.* sans épines; (*fig.*) mou, flasque, invertébré.
spinet ['spinit, spi'net], *n.* épinette, *f.*
spinner ['spinə], *n.* fileur, *m.*
spinney ['spini], *n.* petit bois, bosquet, *m.*
spinning ['spiniŋ], *a.* tournoyant, tournant.—*n.* filage (*processus*), *m.*; filature (*art*), *f.*; tournoiement, *m.*
spinning-machine ['spiniŋmə'ʃi:n], *n.* machine à filer, *f.*
spinning-mill ['spiniŋmil], *n.* filature, *f.*
spinning-top ['spiniŋtɔp], *n.* toupie, *f.*
spinning-wheel ['spiniŋwi:l], *n.* rouet, *m.*
spinous ['spainəs], *a.* épineux.
spinster ['spinstə], *n.* fille non mariée, célibataire, *f.*
spinsterhood ['spinstəhud], *n.* célibat, *m.*
spiny ['spaini], *a.* épineux, couvert d'épines; (*fig.*) difficile.

spiraea [spai'ri:ə], *n.* (*Bot.*) spirée, *f.*
spiral ['spaiərəl], *a.* spiral; en colimaçon (*escalier*).—*n.* spirale, *f.*—*v.i.* monter en spirale.
spirally ['spaiərəli], *adv.* en spirale.
spire ['spaiə], *n.* aiguille, flèche, *f.*
spirit (1) ['spirit], *n.* esprit, *m.*, âme, *f.*, fantôme, spectre (*apparition*), *m.*—*v.t.* ***to spirit away***, faire disparaître.
spirit (2) ['spirit], **spiritedness** ['spiritidnis], *n.* (*fig.*) ardeur, force, vigueur, *f.*, feu, élan, entrain, *m.*; fougue (*d'un cheval*); verve, bonne humeur, *f.*, entrain, courage, *m.*—*v.t.* animer, encourager.
spirit (3) ['spirit], *n.* (*sing.* or *pl.*) spiritueux, *m. inv.*; liqueur spiritueuse *ou* alcoolique, *f.*; esprit (*de vin etc.*), *m.*; ***methylated spirit***, alcool à brûler, *m.*
spirited ['spiritid], *a.* animé, plein de cœur, plein de vivacité; vif, plein de verve; fougueux (*cheval*).
spiritedly ['spiritidli], *adv.* avec ardeur, chaleureusement, avec force, avec entrain.
spiritedness [SPIRIT (2)].
spirit-lamp ['spiritlæmp], *n.* lampe à alcool, *f.*
spiritless ['spiritlis], *a.* sans vigueur, mou, énervé; sans courage; abattu (*découragé*).
spirit-level ['spiritlevl], *n.* niveau à bulle d'air, *m.*
spiritual ['spiritjuəl], *a.* spirituel.—*n.* chant religieux (des Noirs), *m.*
spiritualism ['spiritjuəlizm], *n.* spiritisme (*communication avec les esprits*), *m.*
spiritualist ['spiritjuəlist], *n.* spirite (*adepte du spiritisme*), *m.*, *f.*
spiritualize ['spiritjuəlaiz], *v.t.* spiritualiser.
spirituous ['spiritjuəs], *a.* spiritueux.
spiry ['spaiəri], *a.* en flèche, élancé.
spit (1) [spit], *n.* broche; profondeur de bêche (*plongée dans la terre*), *f.*—*v.t.* embrocher, mettre à la broche.
spit (2) [spit], *n.* crachat, *m.*, salive, *f.*—*v.t. irr.* cracher.—*v.i.* cracher (*sur* ou *à*).
spite [spait], **spitefulness** ['spaitfulnis], *n.* dépit, *m.*; rancune, malveillance, *f.*; ***in spite of***, en dépit de, malgré; ***out of spite***, par dépit; ***to have a spite against***, en vouloir à.—*v.t.* vexer, blesser, contrarier.
spiteful ['spaitful], *a.* rancunier, malveillant, vindicatif.
spitefully ['spaitfuli], *adv.* par dépit, par rancune.
spitefulness [SPITE].
spitfire ['spitfaiə], *n.* rageur, *m.*
spitter ['spitə], *n.* cracheur, *m.*
spitting ['spitiŋ], *n.* crachement, *m.*
spittle [spitl], *n.* salive, *f.*; (*colloq.*) crachat, *m.*
splash [splæʃ], *v.t.* éclabousser.—*v.i.* éclabousser; clapoter (*vagues*); patauger.—*n.* éclaboussure, *f.*; clapotement, clapotis (*des vagues*); flac (*bruit*), *m.*
splashing ['splæʃiŋ], *n.* éclaboussement (*acte*), *m.*; éclaboussure (*ce qui rejaillit*), *f.*
splashy ['splæʃi], *a.* éclaboussé, bourbeux.
splay [splei], *v.t.* évaser; (*Arch.*) ébraser; épauler (*cheval*).—*n.* écartement; (*Arch.*) ébrasement, *m.*
splay-footed ['spleifutid], *a.* aux pieds plats et tournés en dehors.
spleen [spli:n], *n.* rate, *f.*; (*fig.*) fiel, *m.*, animosité, *f.*; spleen, *m.*, mélancolie, *f.*

splendid ['splendid], *a.* resplendissan somptueux, magnifique.
splendidly ['splendidli], *adv.* avec écla magnifiquement.
splendour ['splendə], *n.* splendeur, *f.*, écla *m.*
splenetic [splə'netik], *a.* splénétique, atrabi laire.
splice [splais], *n.* épissure, *f.*, raccordemen *m.*—*v.t.* épisser; (*Carp.*) joindre.
splint [splint], *n.* éclisse, attelle, *f.*—*v.* éclisser.
splinter ['splintə], *n.* éclat, éclat de bois, *m.*—*v.t.* briser en éclats.—*v.i.* voler en éclats.
splintery ['splintəri], *a.* plein d'éclats, esqui leux.
split [split], *a.* fendu; ***split personalit*** dédoublement de la personnalité, *m.*; ***spli pin***, goupille, *f.*—*n.* fente; (*fig.*) scission, —*v.t. irr.* fendre; diviser, partager.—*v.i.* s fendre; se quereller.
split-second ['splitsekənd], *a.* ultra-rapide.
splitting ['splitiŋ], *n.* fendage, *m.*; ***splittin of the atom***, fission de l'atome, *f.*
splotch [splɔtʃ], *n.* grosse tache, *f.*, barbouillage, *m.*
splutter ['splʌtə], *v.i.* bredouiller, crache (*plume* ou *graisse*).—*n.* or **splutterin** ['splʌtəriŋ], bredouillement, crachage, *m.*
spoil [spɔil], *v.t. irr.* gâter, abîmer; dépouille (*de*); ravager (*piller*).—*v.i.* se gâter, s'abîmer —*n.* butin, *m.*, dépouille, *f.*, pillage, *m.*
spoiled [spɔild], *a.* gâté.
spoiler ['spɔilə], *n.* personne qui gâte, *f.*; spoliateur (*pilleur*), *m.*
spoiling ['spɔiliŋ], *n.* action de gâter; avarie, *f*
spoil-sport ['spɔilspɔ:t], *n.* trouble-fête, *m.*
spoke [spouk], *n.* rais, rayon, *m.*
spoke-shave ['spoukʃeiv], *n.* (*Carp.*) plane, *f.*
spokesman ['spouksmən] (*pl.* **-men** [men]), **spokeswoman** ['spoukswumən] (*pl.* **-women** [wimin]), *n.* porte-parole, *m.inv.*
spoliate ['spoulieit], *v.t.* spolier, piller.
spoliation [spouli'eiʃən], *n.* spoliation, *f.*
sponge [spʌndʒ], *n.* éponge, *f.*; (*Artill.*) écouvillon, *m.*—*v.t.* éponger; (*Artill.*) écouvillonner.—*v.i.* ***to sponge on***, vivre aux dépens de.
sponge-cake ['spʌndʒkeik], *n.* gâteau de Savoie, *m.*
sponger ['spʌndʒə], *n.* pique-assiette, parasite, *m.*
sponginess ['spʌndʒinis], *n.* nature spongieuse, *f.*
sponging ['spʌndʒiŋ], *n.* épongement, *m.*; (*fig.*) écorniflerie, *f.*
spongy ['spʌndʒi], *a.* spongieux.
sponsor ['spɔnsə], *n.* parrain, *m.*, marraine, *f.*; garant (*qui cautionne*), *m.*—*v.t.* répondre pour; parrainer.
sponsorship ['spɔnsəʃip], *n.* parrainage, *m.*
spontaneity [spɔntə'ni:iti], *n.* spontanéité, *f.*
spontaneous [spɔn'teiniəs], *a.* spontané.
spontaneously [spɔn'teiniəsli], *adv.* spontanément.
spool [spu:l], *n.* bobine, *f.*
spoon [spu:n], *n.* cuiller, cuillère, *f.*
spoonbill ['spu:nbil], *n.* (*Orn.*) palette, *f.*
spoonful ['spu:nful], *n.* cuillerée, *f.*
spoor [spuə], *n.* trace, *f.*, empreintes, *f.pl.*
sporadic [spə'rædik], *a.* sporadique.
spore [spɔ:], *n.* spore, *f.*

sport [spɔ:t], *n.* jeu, divertissement, amusement, *m.*; moquerie, raillerie, *f.*; jouet; sport, *m.*—*v.t.* faire parade de.—*v.i.* se divertir, s'amuser.
sporting ['spɔ:tiŋ], *a.* de sport; sportif.
sportive ['spɔ:tiv], *a.* badin, folâtre.
sportively ['spɔ:tivli], *adv.* en badinant.
sportiveness ['spɔ:tivnis], *n.* folâtrerie, *f.*
sportsman ['spɔ:tsmən], *n.* (*pl.* **-men** [men]) sportif, sportsman, *m.*
sportsmanship ['spɔ:tsmənʃip], *n.* sportivité, *f.*
spot [spɔt], *n.* tache, *f.*; endroit, lieu, *m.*; ***on the spot***, sur place, sur-le-champ.—*v.t.* tacheter, moucheter; tacher; (*fam.*) repérer; (*colloq.*) observer.
spot-check ['spɔt'tʃek], *n.* contrôle-surprise, *m.*
spotless ['spɔtlis], *a.* sans tache; (*fig.*) immaculé, pur, irréprochable.
spotlessness ['spɔtlisnis], *n.* pureté, *f.*
spotted ['spɔtid], *a.* tacheté, moucheté; truité.
spotter ['spɔtə], *n.* (*Mil. Av.*) observateur, *m.*
spotty ['spɔti], *a.* couvert de taches, moucheté, tacheté.
spouse [spauz], *n.* époux, *m.*, épouse, *f.*; mari, *m.*, femme, *f.*
spout [spaut], *n.* tuyau, *m.*; gouttière (*de maison*), *f.*; bec (*de cruche etc.*), *m.*—*v.i.* jaillir; (*fam.*) déclamer.
spouter ['spautə], *n.* (*fam.*) déclamateur, *m.*
spouting ['spautiŋ], *n.* jaillissement, *m.*; déclamation, *f.*
sprain [sprein], *n.* entorse, foulure, *f.*—*v.t.* fouler; se faire une entorse à.
sprat [spræt], *n.* esprot, sprat, *m.*
sprawl [sprɔ:l], *v.i.* s'étendre, s'étaler.
spray [sprei], *n.* branche, ramille (*d'arbrisseau etc.*), *f.*; embrun, *m.*; poussière (*d'eau*), *f.*; vaporisateur, *m.*—*v.t.* pulvériser, vaporiser, asperger.
spread [spred], *v.t. irr.* étendre, déployer; répandre; couvrir (*table*); mettre (*nappe*); tendre (*voiles etc.*).—*v.i.* s'étendre, se déployer; se répandre, se propager.—*n.* étendue; envergure (*ailes*), *f.*; (*fam.*) festin (*banquet*), *m.*
spreading ['sprediŋ], *a.* étendu, qui se répand.
spree [spri:], *n.* (*colloq.*) bamboche, bombe, *f.*
sprig [sprig], *n.* brin, *m.*, brindille; pointe (*clou*), *f.*
sprightliness ['spraitlinis], *n.* vivacité, *f.*, entrain, *m.*
sprightly ['spraitli], *a.* enjoué, vif, animé, gai.
spring [spriŋ], *v.t. irr.* (*Naut.*) ***to spring a leak***, faire une voie d'eau; ***to spring upon***, présenter à l'improviste . . . à.—*v.i.* bondir, s'élancer; jaillir (*sourdre*); pousser, naître (*se développer*); paraître, poindre (*jour*); provenir, découler, descendre (*avoir pour ancêtres*).—*n.* saut, bond, élan; ressort (*élasticité*), *m.*; source; cause, origine, *f.*; printemps, *m.*; (*pl.*) suspension (*de voiture*), *f.*
spring-board ['spriŋbɔ:d], *n.* tremplin, *m.*
springiness ['spriŋinis], *n.* élasticité, *f.*
springlike ['spriŋlaik], *a.* printanier.
spring-tide ['spriŋtaid], *n.* grande marée, *f.*
springy ['spriŋi], *a.* élastique.
sprinkle [spriŋkl], *v.t.* répandre; arroser (*de*), asperger (*de*) (*eau bénite*); saupoudrer (*de*).
sprinkler ['spriŋklə], *n.* (*Eccles.*) aspersoir, *m.*; (*Hort.*) arroseuse à jet tournant, *f.*
sprinkling ['spriŋkliŋ], *n.* arrosage, *m.*; (*Eccles.*) aspersion, *f.*; (*fig.*) petit nombre, *m.*
sprint [sprint], *n.* sprint, *m.*—*v.i.* courir à toute vitesse.
sprinter ['sprintə], *n.* coureur de vitesse, sprinter, *m.*
sprite [sprait], *n.* esprit follet, lutin, *m.*
sprout [spraut], *n.* pousse, *f.*, jet, rejeton, *m.*; ***Brussels sprouts***, choux de Bruxelles, *m.pl.*—*v.i.* pousser, bourgeonner (*plantes*).
sprouting ['sprautiŋ], *n.* germination, *f.*
spruce (1) [spru:s], *a.* paré, bien mis, pimpant.—*v.t.* attifer.
spruce (2) [spru:s], *n.* sapin (*arbre*), *m.*
spry [sprai], *a.* alerte, plein d'entrain.
spunk [spʌŋk], *n.* amadou; (*colloq.*) cœur, courage, *m.*
spur [spə:], *n.* éperon; ergot (*de coq etc.*); (*fig.*) aiguillon, stimulant, *m.*—*v.t.* éperonner; stimuler.
spurious ['spjuəriəs], *a.* faux, falsifié.
spuriousness ['spjuəriəsnis], *n.* fausseté, *f.*
spurn [spə:n], *v.t.* repousser, écarter (*du pied*); mépriser.—*n.* mépris, dédain, *m.*
spurred [spə:d], *a.* éperonné.
spurt [spə:t], *v.t.* faire jaillir.—*v.i.* s'élancer; (*Spt.*) démarrer.—*n.* jaillissement; (*fig.*) effort soudain; (*Spt.*) démarrage, *m.*
sputnik ['spʌtnik, 'sputnik], *n.* spoutnik, *m.*
sputter ['spʌtə], *v.i.* cracher; bredouiller.—*n.* salive, *f.*
sputtering ['spʌtəriŋ], *n.* bredouillement, *m.*
sputum ['spju:təm], *n.* crachat, *m.*
spy [spai], *n.* espion, *m.*—*v.t.* scruter; apercevoir.—*v.i.* épier, espionner.
spy-glass ['spaiglɑ:s], *n.* longue-vue, *f.*
spying ['spaiiŋ], *n.* espionnage, *m.*
spy-ring ['spairiŋ], **spy-system** ['spaisistəm], *n.* espionnage, *m.*
squabble [skwɔbl], *n.* dispute, querelle, *f.*—*v.i.* se chamailler.
squabbler ['skwɔblə], *n.* querelleur, *m.*
squad [skwɔd], *n.* (*Mil.*) peloton, *m.*; (*Rail.*) brigade; équipe (*de sauvetage etc.*), *f.*
squadron ['skwɔdrən], *n.* (*Mil.*) escadron, *m.*; (*Av.*) escadrille; (*Naut.*) escadre, *f.*
squadron-leader ['skwɔdrənli:də], *n.* (*Av.*) commandant, *m.*
squalid ['skwɔlid], *a.* malpropre, sale.
squalidness [SQUALOR].
squall [skwɔ:l], *n.* cri; coup de vent, *m.*, bourrasque, rafale (*de vent*), *f.*—*v.i.* crier, brailler.
squalling ['skwɔ:liŋ], *a.* criard, braillard.—*n.* criaillerie, *f.*
squally ['skwɔ:li], *a.* à grains, à rafales.
squalor ['skwɔlə], **squalidness** ['skwɔlidnis], *n.* malpropreté, *f.*
squamous ['skweiməs], *a.* squameux; écailleux.
squander ['skwɔndə], *v.t.* dissiper, gaspiller.
squanderer ['skwɔndərə], *n.* gaspilleur, *m.*, prodigue, *m.*, *f.*
squandering ['skwɔndəriŋ], *n.* gaspillage, *m.*
square [skwɛə], *a.* carré; soldé (*comptes etc.*); (*fig.*) équitable, juste; de superficie (*mesure*).—*n.* carré; carreau (*de verre etc.*), *m.*; case (*d'échiquier*); place (*dans une ville*); place d'armes (*de ville de garnison*), *f.*, parvis (*devant une église*), *m.*—*v.t.* carrer; (*Carp.*)

équarrir; balancer (*comptes*); (*fig.*) régler, ajuster.—*v.i.* cadrer, s'accorder (*avec*).
square-built ['skwɛəbilt], *a.* aux épaules carrées.
squarely ['skwɛəli], *adv.* carrément; (*fig.*) justement.
squareness ['skwɛənis], *n.* forme carrée, *f.*
squaring ['skwɛəriŋ], *n.* équarrissage, *m.*; ***squaring of the circle***, quadrature du cercle, *f.*
squarish ['skwɛəriʃ], *a.* à peu près carré.
squash [skwɔʃ], *v.t.* écraser, aplatir; (*fig.*) rembarrer (*personne*).—*n.* écrasement (*aplatissement*), *m.*; foule serrée (*de gens*), *f.*; ***lemon squash***, citronnade, *f.*
squashy ['skwɔʃi], *a.* mou et humide.
squat [skwɔt], *a.* accroupi, blotti; trapu, ramassé (*courtaud*).—*v.i.* s'accroupir; se blottir; (*Am.*) s'établir (sans droit).
squatter ['skwɔtə], *n.* personne accroupie, *f.*; colon (*sans droit*), *m.*
squatting ['skwɔtiŋ], *n.* accroupissement, *m.*
squaw [skwɔ:], *n.* femme peau-rouge, *f.*
squawk [skwɔ:k], *n.* cri rauque; couac, *m.*—*v.i.* pousser des cris rauques.
squeak [skwi:k], *n.* petit cri aigu, *m.*—*v.i.* pousser des cris aigus; jurer (*instrument de musique*).
squeaking ['skwi:kiŋ], *a.* criard; qui jure (*instrument de musique*).
squeal [skwi:l], *v.i.* pousser des cris perçants. —*n.* cri perçant, *m.*
squeamish ['skwi:miʃ], *a.* qui se soulève (*l'estomac*); trop délicat, difficile (*scrupuleux*).
squeamishly ['skwi:miʃli], *adv.* avec dégoût.
squeamishness ['skwi:miʃnis], *n.* délicatesse exagérée, *f.*, goût difficile, *m.*
squeeze [skwi:z], *n.* compression; cohue, *f.*—*v.t.* serrer, presser; ***to squeeze money out of***, extorquer de l'argent à; ***to squeeze out***, exprimer; ***to squeeze through***, forcer à travers.—*v.i.* ***to squeeze through***, se forcer à travers.
squeezing ['skwi:ziŋ], *n.* étreinte, compression, *f.*; serrement (*de la main*), *m.*
squelch [skweltʃ], *v.t.* écraser, aplatir.
squib [skwib], *n.* pétard, *m.*; (*fig.*) satire, *f.*
squill [skwil], *n.* scille (*plante*), *f.*
squint [skwint], *a.* louche.—*n.* regard louche, *m.*—*v.i.* loucher.
squinting ['skwintiŋ], *a.* louche.—*n.* action de loucher, *f.*, strabisme, *m.*
squire ['skwaiə], *n.* écuyer; châtelain; cavalier servant (*d'une dame*), *m.*—*v.t.* escorter (*une dame*).
squireen [skwaiə'ri:n], *n.* hobereau, *m.*
squirm [skwə:m], *v.i.* se tortiller, se tordre (*de douleur* ou *d'embarras*).
squirrel ['skwirəl], *n.* écureuil, *m.*
squirt [skwə:t], *n.* seringue, *f.*—*v.t.* seringuer, faire jaillir.—*v.i.* jaillir.
stab [stæb], *n.* coup de poignard, de couteau etc., *m.*—*v.t.* poignarder.
stabbing ['stæbiŋ], *a.* lancinant.—*n.* coup de poignard, *m.*
stability [stə'biliti], *n.* stabilité, solidité; (*fig.*) fermeté, *f.*
stabilization [steibilai'zeiʃən], *n.* stabilisation, *f.*
stabilize ['steibilaiz], *v.t.* stabiliser.
stable (1) [steibl], *a.* stable, fixe, solide; (*fig.*) constant.
stable (2) [steibl], *n.* écurie, *f.*—*v.t.* loger (*chevaux*); établer (*bétail*).
stable-boy ['steiblbɔi], **stableman** ['steibl mən] (*pl.* **-men** [men]), *n.* garçon d'écurie, *m.*
stabling ['steibliŋ], *n.* écuries (*pour chevaux*) étables (*pour bétail*), *f.pl.*
staccato [stə'kɑ:tou], *a.* saccadé.—*adv.* en staccato.
stack [stæk], *n.* souche (*d'une cheminée*); pile *f.*, tas (*de charbon, de bois*), *m.*; meule (*de foin etc.*), *f.*—*v.t.* empiler (*bois*); emmeuler (*foin etc.*).
stacking ['stækiŋ], *n.* emmeulage, empilage entassement, *m.*
stack-yard ['stækjɑ:d], *n.* cour de ferme, *f.*
stadium ['steidiəm], *n.* stade, *m.*
staff [stɑ:f], *n.* (*pl.* **staves** [steivz]) bâton, bourdon (*de pèlerin*), *m.*; hampe (*à drapeau*), *f.*; (*pl.* **staffs**) corps, personnel; (*Mil.*) état-major, *m.*; ***to be on the staff***, être attaché à, faire partie du personnel de.—*v.t.* fournir le personnel de.
staff-officer ['stɑ:fɔfisə], *n.* officier d'état-major, *m.*
stag [stæg], *n.* cerf, *m.*
stag-beetle ['stægbi:tl], *n.* (*Ent.*) cerf-volant lucane, *m.*
stage [steidʒ], *n.* estrade (*dans une salle*); (*Theat.*) scène, *f.*; (*fig.*) théâtre, *m.*; étape (*voyage*), *f.*; (*fig.*) degré, *m.*, phase, période, *f.*—*v.t.* ***to stage a play***, monter une pièce.
stage-coach ['steidʒkoutʃ], *n.* diligence, *f.*
stage-door ['steidʒ'dɔ:], *n.* entrée des artistes, *f.*
stage-effect ['steidʒifekt], *n.* effet scénique, *m.*
stage-hand ['steidʒhænd], *n.* machiniste, *m.*
stage-manager ['steidʒ'mænidʒə], *n.* régisseur, *m.*
stage-properties ['steidʒ'prɔpətiz], *n.pl.* accessoires de théâtre, *m.pl.*
stage-set ['steidʒset], *n.* décor, *m.*
stagger ['stægə], *v.t.* faire chanceler; (*fig.*) étonner; échelonner (*heures, vacances etc.*). —*v.i.* chanceler.
staggering ['stægəriŋ], *a.* chancelant; incertain.—*n.* chancellement; échelonnage, *m.*
stagnancy ['stægnənsi], **stagnation** [stæg 'neiʃən], *n.* stagnation, *f.*
stagnant ['stægnənt], *a.* stagnant: (*fig.*) inactif, mort.
stagnate [stæg'neit], *v.i.* être stagnant.
stagnation [STAGNANCY].
staid [steid], *a.* posé, sérieux, grave.
staidness ['steidnis], *n.* gravité, *f.*
stain [stein], *n.* tache; (*Paint.*) teinte; (*fig.*) honte, *f.*, opprobre (*disgrâce*), *m.*—*v.t.* tacher (*de*); (*fig.*) souiller; (*Dyeing*) teindre. —*v.i.* se tacher.
stained [steind], *a.* taché; (*fig.*) souillé; (*Dyeing*) teint; ***stained glass***, vitrail, *m.*
stainer ['steinə], *n.* teinturier, *m.*
staining ['steiniŋ], *n.* teinture, *f.*
stainless ['steinlis], *a.* sans tache; inoxydable (*acier*).
stair [stɛə], *n.* marche, *f.*; degré; (*pl.*) escalier, *m.*
staircase ['stɛəkeis], *n.* escalier, *m.*; cage d'escalier, *f.*; ***back-staircase***, escalier de service; ***moving staircase***, escalier roulant.

stair-rod ['stɛərɔd], *n.* tringle (de tapis) d'escalier, *f.*
stake [steik], *n.* pieu, poteau, bûcher (*de martyre*); (*Cards etc.*) enjeu, *m.* mise, *f.* —*v.t.* parier, gager; hasarder (*risquer*); ***to stake out***, jalonner.
stalactite ['stæləktait], *n.* stalactite, *f.*
stalagmite ['stæləgmait], *n.* stalagmite, *f.*
stale [steil], *a.* vieux, rassis (*pain*); (*fig.*) suranné, passé, usé.
stalemate ['steilmeit], *v.t.* (*Chess*) faire pat.—*n.* pat, *m.*; (*fig.*) impasse, *f.*
staleness ['steilnis], *n.* vieillesse, *f.*; état rassis (*pain*), *m.*; banalité, *f.*
stalk [stɔ:k], *n.* tige; queue (*de fleur*), *f.* trognon (*de chou*), *m.*; démarche fière (*allure*), *f.*—*v.t.* chasser à l'affût.—*v.i.* marcher fièrement.
stalker ['stɔ:kə], *n.* chasseur à l'affût, *m.*
stalking ['stɔ:kiŋ], *n.* (*Hunt.*) chasse à l'affût, *f.*
stall (1) [stɔ:l], *n.* stalle (*d'église* ou *d'écurie*), étable (*à bétail*); écurie (*à chevaux*); échoppe, boutique, *f.*, étalage; (*Theat.*) fauteuil d'orchestre, *m.*
stall (2) [stɔ:l], *v.t.*, *v.i.* caler (*machine*).
stallion ['stæljən], *n.* étalon, *m.*
stalwart ['stɔ:lwət], *a.* vigoureux, robuste; vaillant.
stamen ['steimen], *n.* (*Bot.*) étamine, *f.*
stamina ['stæminə], *n.* vigueur, résistance, *f.*
stammer ['stæmə], *v.t.*, *v.i.* bégayer, balbutier.—*n.* bégaiement, *m.*
stammerer ['stæmərə], *n.* bègue, *m.*, *f.*
stammering ['stæməriŋ], *a.* bègue.—*n.* bégaiement, *m.*
stamp [stæmp], *v.t.* frapper du pied; piétiner; empreindre, imprimer; contrôler (*garantir*); estamper (*pièce de monnaie*); timbrer (*documents, lettres etc.*); (*Metal.*) bocarder; estampiller (*marchandises*); affranchir (*payer d'avance*); poinçonner (*billet*).—*v.i.* trépigner, frapper du pied.—*n.* estampe (*outil*), *f.*; coin, poinçon, *m.*; empreinte, marque (*impression*), *f.*; poinçon de contrôle (*sur l'or*); timbre (*sur documents*); (*Metal.*) bocard, *m.*; (*Comm.*) estampille (*sur marchandises*), *f.*; (*fig.*) caractère, *m.*, trempe, *f.*; coup de pied, trépignement; timbre-poste, *m.*; ***rubber stamp***, tampon, *m.*
stamp-collecting ['stæmpkəlektiŋ], *n.* philatélie, *f.*
stamp-collector ['stæmpkə'lektə], *n.* philatéliste, *m.*, *f.*
stamp-duty ['stæmp'dju:ti], *n.* droit de timbre, *m.*
stampede [stæm'pi:d], *n.* débandade, panique, *f.*—*v.i.* fuir en désordre.
stamping ['stæmpiŋ], *n.* contrôlage (*garantie*); timbrage; (*Metal.*) bocardage; piétinement, trépignement (*des pieds*), *m.*
stamp-machine ['stæmpmə'ʃi:n], *n.* distributeur automatique de timbres-poste, *m.*
stanch [stɑ:ntʃ], **staunch** [stɔ:ntʃ], *a.* solide, ferme; (*fig.*) sûr, dévoué.—*v.t.* étancher.
stanchion ['stɑ:nʃən], *n.* étançon, étai, *m.*
stanchness ['stɑ:ntʃnis], **staunchness** ['stɔ:ntʃnis], *n.* fermeté; constance, dévotion, *f.*
stand [stænd], *v.t. irr.* mettre debout, placer, poser; endurer, souffrir, supporter, soutenir; subir; résister à; payer (*à boire*).—*v.i.* se tenir; rester debout; se soutenir (*difficilement*); se placer, se mettre (*prendre place*); être debout; se trouver, être (*bâtiment*); se maintenir (*ne pas lâcher pied*); se présenter (*comme candidat*); ***stand by!*** attention! ***to stand aside***, se tenir à l'écart; ***to stand by***, assister à (*être présent*); défendre, s'en tenir à (*un avis etc.*); se tenir prêt; ***to stand down***, se retirer; ***to stand firm***, tenir ferme, tenir bon; ***to stand for***, soutenir; signifier; ***to stand in for someone***, remplacer quelqu'un; ***to stand out***, se dessiner (*être en relief*); résister; ***to stand still***, s'arrêter, se tenir tranquille; ***to stand up***, se lever.—*n.* arrêt, *m.*, halte, pause, *f.*; stand, étalage (*exposition etc.*); socle (*à vases etc.*), *m.*; (*fig.*) cessation, résistance, *f.*
standard ['stændəd], *a.* type, standard, normal; étalon; au titre (*argent*); classique (*livre*); (*Hort.*) en plein vent (*arbre*), sur tige (*roses*); régulateur (*prix*).—*n.* étendard, (*Naut.*) pavillon; étalon (*de poids et mesures*); titre (*d'or et d'argent*); (*fig.*) type, modèle; (*Hort.*) arbre en plein vent, *m.*
standard-bearer ['stændədbɛərə], *n.* porte-étendard, *m.*
standardization [stændədai'zeiʃən], *n.* étalonnage, *m.*; (*Comm.*) standardisation, *f.*
standardize ['stændədaiz], *v.t.* étalonner, standardiser.
stand-by ['stændbai], *n.* appui, soutien, *m.*, ressource, *f.*
stand-in ['stændin], *n.* remplaçant, *m.*
standing ['stændiŋ], *a.* stagnant; fixe; debout, sur pied (*non abattu*); (*fig.*) invariable.—*n.* position, *f.*; rang, *m.*; durée, date, *f.*, service, *m.*
stand-offish ['stænd'ɔfiʃ], *a.* réservé, distant.
stand-point ['stændpɔint], *n.* point de vue, *m.*
standstill ['stændstil], *n.* arrêt, *m.*
stand-to ['stænd'tu:], *n.* (*Mil.*) alerte, *f.*
stanza ['stænzə], *n.* stance, strophe, *f.*
staple (1) [steipl], *a.* établi; principal.—*n.* denrée principale (*marchandises*), *f.*; (*fig.*) fond, *m.*
staple (2) [steipl], *n.* agrafe; gâche (*de serrure*) *f.*—*v.t.* agrafer.
stapler ['steiplə], *n.* agrafeuse (*machine*), *f.*
star [stɑ:], *n.* étoile, *f.*, astre, *m.*; (*Theat. Cine.*) vedette, *f.*—*v.t.* étoiler, parsemer d'étoiles; avoir comme vedettes.—*v.i.* tenir le premier rôle.
starboard ['stɑ:bəd], *n.* tribord, *m.*
starch [stɑ:tʃ], *n.* amidon, *m.*; fécule (*aliment*); (*fig.*) raideur, *f.*—*v.t.* empeser.
starchiness ['stɑ:tʃinis], *n.* raideur, *f.*
starchy ['stɑ:tʃi], *a.* féculent; empesé; (*fig.*) guindé.
stare [stɛə], *v.t.* dévisager.—*v.i.* regarder fixement; ouvrir de grands yeux (*être ébahi*).—*n.* regard fixe; regard ébahi, *m.*
starfish ['stɑ:fiʃ], *n.* étoile de mer, *f.*
star-gazer ['stɑ:geizə], *n.* astrologue, *m.*, *f.*; rêveur, *m.*
staring ['stɛəriŋ], *a.* voyant, tranchant (*couleur etc.*).
stark [stɑ:k], *adv.* tout, tout à fait.—*a.* raide; stérile (*paysage*).
starless ['stɑ:lis], *a.* sans étoiles.
starling ['stɑ:liŋ], *n.* étourneau, sansonnet, *m.*
starlit ['stɑ:lit], *a.* étoilé.
starry ['stɑ:ri], *a.* étoilé; (*fig.*) étincelant; ***starry-eyed***, peu pratique.

start [stɑ:t], *v.t.* commencer; faire lever (*gibier*); faire partir; mettre en marche (*machine*).—*v.i.* tressaillir (*de* ou *à*); partir (*s'en aller*); commencer, débuter; sursauter (*faire un bond*).—*n.* tressaillement; saut, bond; commencement, début; départ, *m.*; ***to wake with a start***, se réveiller en sursaut.
starter ['stɑ:tə], *n.* starter (*de course*); (*Motor.*) démarreur, *m.*
starting ['stɑ:tiŋ], *n.* tressaillement; départ; commencement, début, *m.*; mise en marche (*de moteur etc.*), *f.*
starting-handle ['stɑ:tiŋhændl], *n.* (*Motor.*) manivelle, *f.*
starting-point ['stɑ:tiŋpɔint], *n.* point de départ, *m.*
starting-post ['stɑ:tiŋpoust], *n.* poteau de départ, *m.*
startle [stɑ:tl], *v.t.* faire tressaillir, effrayer.
startling ['stɑ:tliŋ], *a.* étonnant, saisissant.
starvation [stɑ:'veiʃən], *n.* inanition, faim, *f.*
starve [stɑ:v], *v.t.* faire mourir de faim; affamer.—*v.i.* mourir de faim.
starveling ['stɑ:vliŋ], *n.* affamé, meurt-de-faim, *m.*
starving ['stɑ:viŋ], *a.* affamé, mourant de faim.
state [steit], *n.* état, *m.*, condition, *f.*; état (*organisme politique*); rang (*classe*), *m.*; pompe, *f.*, apparat (*pompe*), *m.*; ***the (United) States***, les États-Unis, *m.pl.*—*v.t.* énoncer, déclarer.
state-controlled ['steitkən'trould], *a.* étatisé.
statecraft ['steitkrɑ:ft], *n.* politique, *f.*
stated ['steitid], *a.* réglé, fixe.
stateless ['steitlis], *a.* ***stateless person***, apatride, *m.*, *f.*
stateliness ['steitlinis], *n.* majesté, grandeur, *f.*
stately ['steitli], *a.* imposant, majestueux, noble.—*adv.* majestueusement, avec dignité.
statement ['steitmənt], *n.* exposé, énoncé, rapport, *m.*; déclaration, *f.*
statesman ['steitsmən], *n.* (*pl.* **-men** [men]) homme d'État, *m.*
statesmanlike ['steitsmənlaik], *a.* d'homme d'État.
statesmanship ['steitsmənʃip], *n.* science du gouvernement, politique, *f.*
static ['stætik], **statical** ['stætikəl], *a.* statique.
station ['steiʃən], *n.* station, *f.*; rang (*classe*), *m.*; position; (*Rail.*) gare, *f.*; (*Mil.*) poste, *m.*, garnison, *f.*—*v.t.* placer; (*Mil.*) poster.
stationary ['steiʃənəri], *a.* stationnaire; fixe.
stationer ['steiʃənə], *n.* papetier, *m.*
stationery ['steiʃənəri], *n.* papeterie, *f.*
station-master ['steiʃənmɑ:stə], *n.* chef de gare, *m.*
statistic [stə'tistik], **statistical** [stə'tistikəl], *a.* statistique.
statistician [stætis'tiʃən], *n.* statisticien, *m.*
statistics [stə'tistiks], *n.pl.* statistique, *f.*
statuary ['stætjuəri], *n.* statuaire, *f.*
statue ['stætju:], *n.* statue, *f.*
statuesque [stætju:'esk], *a.* plastique.
stature ['stætʃə], *n.* stature, taille, *f.*
status ['steitəs], *n.* statut légal, *m.*; condition, *f.*, rang, *m.*
statute ['stætju:t], *n.* statut, *m.*, loi, *f.*
statutory ['stætjutəri], *a.* réglementaire, statutaire.
staunch [STANCH].
stave [steiv], *n.* douve (*de baril*); (*Mus.*) portée, *f.*; verset (*de psaume*), *m.*—*v.t. irr.* crever; défoncer (*baril*); ***to stave off***, chasser, repousser, éloigner, écarter, prévenir (*danger*).
staves [STAFF].
stay [stei], *v.t.* arrêter; apaiser (*sa faim*); étayer, accoter (*appuyer*).—*v.i.* rester; demeurer (*séjourner*); descendre; attendre. —*n.* séjour; (*Law*) sursis; soutien, appui (*aide*), *m.*
stay-at-home ['steiəthoum], *a.* and *n.* casanier, *m.*
stead [sted], *n.* lieu, *m.*, place, *f.*
steadfast ['stedfəst], *a.* ferme, constant, stable.
steadfastly ['stedfəstli], *adv.* fermement, avec constance.
steadfastness ['stedfəstnis], *n.* fermeté, constance, *f.*
steadily ['stedili], *adv.* fermement, avec persistance.
steadiness ['stedinis], *n.* fermeté; assurance, *f.*
steady ['stedi], *a.* ferme, assuré; posé (*sérieux*); régulier.—*adv.* doucement.—*v.t.* affermir; assujettir (*fixer*); calmer.
steak [steik], *n.* tranche (*de viande*), *f.*; entrecôte, *m.*; ***fillet steak***, bifteck dans le filet, *m.*
steal [sti:l], *v.t. irr.* voler, dérober.—*v.i.* se dérober, se glisser furtivement, aller *ou* venir à la dérobée.
stealer ['sti:lə], *n.* voleur, *m.*
stealing ['sti:liŋ], *n.* vol, *m.*
stealth [stelθ], *n.* ***by stealth***, à la dérobée, furtivement.
stealthily ['stelθili], *adv.* à la dérobée, furtivement, à pas de loup.
stealthy ['stelθi], *a.* dérobé, furtif.
steam [sti:m], *n.* vapeur, *f.*—*v.t.* (*Cook.*) cuire à la vapeur.—*v.i.* jeter de la vapeur; fumer.
steamboat ['sti:mbout], *n.* bateau à vapeur, *m.*
steam-engine ['sti:mendʒin], *n.* machine à vapeur, *f.*
steamer ['sti:mə], *n.* vapeur, steamer, *m.*
steam-gauge ['sti:mgeidʒ], *n.* manomètre *m.*
steaming ['sti:miŋ], *a.* fumant.
steam-pipe ['sti:mpaip], *n.* tuyau de vapeur, *m.*
steam-roller ['sti:mroulə], *n.* rouleau compresseur, *m.*—*v.t.* (*fig.*) écraser.
steamship ['sti:mʃip], *n.* vapeur, *m.*
steam-whistle ['sti:mwisl], *n.* sifflet à vapeur, *m.*
steamy ['sti:mi], *a.* humide.
steed [sti:d], *n.* (*poet*) coursier, *m.*
steel [sti:l], *a.* d'acier, en acier.—*n.* acier; fusil (*pour aiguiser un couteau*); (*fig.*) fer, *m.* —*v.t.* acérer, garnir d'acier; (*fig.*) fortifier.
steel-clad ['sti:lklæd], *a.* revêtu d'acier, bardé de fer.
steeliness ['sti:linis], *n.* dureté d'acier; (*fig.*) dureté, *f.*
steel-plated ['sti:lpleitid], *a.* cuirassé.
steel-works ['sti:lwə:ks], *n.pl.* aciérie, *f.*
steely ['sti:li], *a.* d'acier; (*fig.*) dur, de fer.

steelyard ['sti:ljɑ:d], *n.* romaine, *f.*
steep (1) [sti:p], *a.* escarpé, à pic; raide (*escalier*).—*n.* pente rapide, *f.*; escarpement, *m.*
steep (2) [sti:p], *v.t.* tremper; (*fig.*) saturer (*de*).
steeping ['sti:piŋ], *n.* trempage, *m.*
steeple [sti:pl], *n.* clocher, *m.*
steeplechase [sti:pltʃeis], *n.* course au clocher, *f.*, steeplechase, *m.*
steepled [sti:pld], *a.* à clocher.
steeple-jack ['sti:pldʒæk], *n.* réparateur de clochers *ou* de cheminées, *m.*
steeply ['sti:pli], *adv.* en pente rapide.
steepness ['sti:pnis], *n.* raideur, pente rapide, *f.*
steer [stiə], *n.* bouvillon, jeune bœuf, *m.*—*v.t.* gouverner; diriger; (*Motor. etc.*) conduire.—*v.i.* se diriger.
steerage ['stiəridʒ], *n.* timonerie, *f.*; l'avant; logement des passagers de troisième classe, *m.*
steering ['stiəriŋ], *n.* direction; (*Motor.*) conduite, *f.*
steering-wheel ['stiəriŋwi:l], *n.* volant, *m.*
steersman ['stiəzmən], *n.* (*pl.* **-men** [men]) timonier, *m.*
stellar ['stelə], *a.* stellaire.
stem [stem], *n.* tige; queue (*d'une fleur etc.*); (*fig.*) souche (*d'une famille*), *f.*—*v.t.* refouler (*courant*); (*fig.*) résister à.—*v.i.* ***to stem from***, être issu de.
stench [stentʃ], *n.* puanteur, *f.*
stencil ['stensil], *n.* patron, pochoir, stencil *m.*—*v.t.* tracer au patron, tirer au stencil.
sten-gun ['stengʌn], *n.* fusil mitrailleur, *m.*
stenographer [ste'nɔgrəfə], *n.* sténographe *m., f.*
stenography [ste'nɔgrəfi], *n.* sténographie, *f.*
stentorian [sten'tɔ:riən], *a.* de stentor.
step [step], *v.t.* mesurer en comptant les pas, arpenter.—*v.i.* faire un pas, marcher pas à pas; marcher, aller; monter (*dans*); descendre (*de*); ***to step aside***, s'écarter; ***to step back***, reculer; ***to step forward***, s'avancer; ***to step on***, fouler; ***to step over***, enjamber.—*n.* pas; degré, *m.*, marche (*d'escalier*), *f.*; échelon (*d'échelle*); marchepied (*de voiture* ou *de bicyclette*), *m.*; (*fig.*) démarche; (*pl.*) échelle, *f.*
stepbrother ['stepbrʌðə], *n.* beau-frère, *m.*
stepchild ['steptʃaild], *n.* beau-fils, *m.*, belle-fille, *f.*
stepfather ['stepfɑ:ðə], *n.* beau-père, *m.*
Stephen [sti:vn]. Étienne, *m.*
stepmother ['stepmʌðə], *n.* belle-mère; marâtre, *f.*
steppe [step], *n.* steppe (*plaine*), *f.*
stepping ['stepiŋ], *n.* marche, allure, *f.*
stepping-stone ['stepiŋstoun], *n.* (*pl.*) pierres de gué, *f.pl.*; (*fig.*) introduction, *f.*
stepsister ['stepsistə], *n.* belle-sœur, *f.*
stereoscopic [stiəriə'skɔpik], *a.* stéréoscopique.
stereotype ['stiəriətaip], *a.* stéréotypé; cliché.—*n.* stéréotypage; (*fig.*) cliché, *m.*—*v.t.* clicher; stéréotyper.
stereotyped ['stiəriətaipt], *a.* (*usu. fig.*) stéréotypé.
sterile ['sterail], *a.* stérile.
sterility [stə'riliti], *n.* stérilité, *f.*
sterilization [sterilai'zeiʃən], *n.* stérilisation, *f.*
sterilize ['sterilaiz], *v.t.* stériliser.
sterling ['stə:liŋ], *a.* sterling; (*fig.*) vrai, de bon aloi.
stern (1) [stə:n], *a.* sévère, dur; rigoureux.
stern (2) [stə:n], *n.* (*Naut.*) arrière, *m.*
sternly ['stə:nli], *adv.* sévèrement, durement.
sternmost ['stə:nmoust], *a.* le dernier.
sternness ['stə:nnis], *n.* sévérité, austérité, *f.*
stethoscope ['steθəskoup], *n.* stéthoscope, *m.*
stevedore ['sti:vədɔ:], *n.* arrimeur; déchargeur, *m.*
stew [stju:], *n.* étuvée, *f.*, ragoût (*de viande*); (*fig.*) embarras, *m.*, confusion, *f.*; ***Irish stew***, ragoût de mouton.—*v.t.* étuver; mettre en ragoût, faire un ragoût de.—*v.i.* cuire à l'étuvée; (*fig.*) cuire dans sa peau.
steward ['stju:əd], *n.* intendant, régisseur (*d'une propriété*); économe (*de collège*); commissaire (*de bal etc.*); (*Naut.*) steward, *m.*; ***steward's room***, cambuse, *f.*
stewardess ['stju:ədis], *n.* femme de chambre (de bord), stewardesse, *f.*
stewardship ['stju:ədʃip], *n.* intendance; (*fig.*) administration, *f.*
stewed [stju:d], *a.* étuvé, en ragoût; en compote.
stew-pan ['stju:pæn], *n.* casserole, *f.*
stew-pot ['stju:pɔt], *n.* cocotte, *f.*, faitout, *m.*
stick (1) [stik], *n.* bâton, *m.*; canne (*pour marcher*), *f.*; (*Av.*) manche; chapelet (*de bombes*), *m.*
stick (2) [stik], *v.t. irr.* percer, piquer; enfoncer; coller; ***stick no bills***, défense d'afficher.—*v.i.* se coller, s'attacher; rester (*demeurer*); ***to stick close***, ne pas quitter; ***to stick out***, faire saillie; persister; ***to stick to***, s'en tenir à; ***to stick up***, se dresser.
stickiness ['stikinis], *n.* viscosité, *f.*
sticking-plaster ['stikiŋ'plɑ:stə], *n.* taffetas d'Angleterre, *m.*
stickle [stikl], *v.i.* tenir beaucoup (*à*); se disputer.
stickleback ['stiklbæk], *n.* épinoche, *f.*
stickler ['stiklə], *n.* partisan, *m.*; rigoriste, *m., f.*
sticky ['stiki], *a.* gluant, collant; (*fig.*) difficile (*personne*).
stiff [stif], *a.* raide, rigide, tenace; dur, ferme (*non fluide*); opiniâtre (*entêté*); gêné (*contraint*); courbatu (*muscles*); affecté, guindé (*style*).
stiffen [stifn], *v.t.* raidir; (*fig.*) endurcir.—*v.i.* se raidir; (*fig.*) s'endurcir.
stiffening ['stifniŋ], *n.* raidissement; soutien (*appui*), *m.*
stiffly ['stifli], *adv.* avec raideur; obstinément.
stiff-neck ['stifnek], *n.* torticolis, *m.*
stiff-necked ['stifnekt], *a.* opiniâtre, entêté.
stiffness ['stifnis], *n.* raideur; gêne (*contrainte*); opiniâtreté (*entêtement*), *f.*; (*fig.*) air guindé, *m.*
stifle [staifl], *v.t., v.i.* étouffer, suffoquer.—*n.* (*Vet.*) grasset, *m.*
stifling ['staifliŋ], *a.* étouffant, suffocant.—*n.* suffocation, *f.*
stigma ['stigmə], *n.* stigmate, *m.*, flétrissure, *f.*
stigmatize ['stigmətaiz], *v.t.* stigmatiser, flétrir.

stile [stail], *n.* échallier, échalis, *m.*
stiletto [sti'letou], *n.* stylet, *m.*; ***stiletto heels***, talons aiguille, *m.pl.*
still (1) [stil], *a.* silencieux; tranquille, calme, paisible, en repos; immobile; non mousseux (*vin*).—*adv.* encore, toujours; cependant, néanmoins (*malgré tout*).—*v.t.* calmer, apaiser.
still (2) [stil], *n.* alambic, *m.*
still-born ['stilbɔːn], *a.* mort-né.
stillness ['stilnis], *n.* tranquillité, *f.*, calme, *m.*
still-room ['stilruːm], *n.* distillerie, *f.*, laboratoire, *m.*
stilt [stilt], *n.* échasse, *f.*; pilotis, pieu (*de pont etc.*), *m.*
stilted ['stiltid], *a.* guindé, pompeux.
stimulant ['stimjulənt], *n.* stimulant, *m.*
stimulate ['stimjuleit], *v.t.* stimuler; (*fig.*) exciter.
stimulating ['stimjuleitiŋ], *a.* stimulant.
stimulation [stimju'leiʃən], *n.* stimulation, *f.*
stimulus ['stimjuləs], *n.* stimulant, aiguillon, stimulus, *m.*
sting [stiŋ], *n.* aiguillon; dard (*d'ortie etc.*), *m.*; piqûre; (*fig.*) pointe, *f.*—*v.t. irr.* piquer; (*fig.*) irriter.
stingily ['stindʒili], *adv.* chichement, mesquinement.
stinginess ['stindʒinis], *n.* mesquinerie, ladrerie, *f.*
stinging ['stiŋiŋ], *a.* piquant; cinglant.—*n.* piqûre, *f.*
stingy ['stindʒi], *a.* avare, mesquin, ladre, chiche.
stink [stiŋk], *n.* puanteur, mauvaise odeur, *f.*—*v.i. irr.* puer; sentir mauvais.
stinking ['stiŋkiŋ], *a.* puant.
stint [stint], *v.t.* limiter, restreindre; ***to stint oneself***, se priver (*de*).—*n.* limite, borne; portion; besogne, *f.*
stipend ['staipend], *n.* traitement (*d'ecclésiastique* ou *de magistrat*), *m.*
stipendiary [sti'pendiəri], *a.* appointé.
stipple [stipl], *v.t.* pointiller.
stippling ['stipliŋ], *n.* pointillage (*processus*); pointillé (*résultat*), *m.*
stipulate ['stipjuleit], *v.i.* stipuler (*de* ou *que*).
stipulation [stipju'leiʃən], *n.* stipulation, condition, *f.*
stipulator ['stipjuleitə], *n.* partie stipulante, *f.*
stir [stəː], *v.t.* remuer; (*fig.*) agiter; ***to stir the fire***, attiser le feu.—*v.i.* remuer, se remuer, bouger.—*n.* remuement, bruit, *m.*; agitation, *f.*
stirring ['stəːriŋ], *a.* remuant; émouvant (*histoire etc.*).—*n.* agitation, *f.*
stirrup ['stirəp], *n.* étrier, *m.*
stirrup-cup ['stirəpkʌp], *n.* coup de l'étrier, *m.*
stirrup-leather ['stirəp'leðə], *n.* étrivière, *f.*
stitch [stitʃ], *n.* point, *m.*; maille (*en tricot*), *f.*; (*Med.*) point de suture, *m.*; ***a stitch in time saves nine***, un point à temps en épargne cent.—*v.t.* piquer, coudre; brocher (*livres*); (*Med.*) suturer.
stitched [stitʃt], *a.* piqué, broché (*livre*).
stitching ['stitʃiŋ], *n.* couture, *f.*; brochage (*de livre*), *m.*; (*Med.*) suture, *f.*
stoat [stout], *n.* hermine d'été, *f.*
stock (1) [stɔk], *a.* courant, habituel.—*n.* souche (*d'arbre, famille etc.*), *f.*; cep (*de vigne*); bloc (*de bois etc.*), *m.*; monture (*de fusil*); (*Hort.*) ente (*pour greffer*), *f.*; (*Cook.*) consommé, *m.*; (*fig.*) race, famille, *f.*; approvisionnement, stock (*réserve*), assortiment (*sélection*), *m.*; (*pl.*) fonds, fonds publics, *m.pl.*, rentes, actions, *f.pl.*; (*Shipbuilding*) chantier, *m.*, cale de construction, *f.*; ceps (*punition*), *m.pl.*; ***rolling stock***, matériel roulant, *m.*; ***to take stock of***, faire l'inventaire de.—*v.t.* pourvoir (*de*); stocker (*magasin*); meubler (*ferme*); empoissonner (*vivier*).
stock (2) [stɔk], *n.* (*Bot.*) giroflée, *f.*
stockade [stɔ'keid], *n.* palissade, *f.*—*v.t.* palissader.
stock-book ['stɔkbuk], *n.* livre de magasin magasinier, *m.*
stock-breeder ['stɔkbriːdə], *n.* éleveur, *m.*
stock-breeding ['stɔkbriːdiŋ], *n.* élevage, *m.*
stockbroker ['stɔkbroukə], *n.* agent de change, *m.*
stock-exchange ['stɔkikstʃeindʒ], *n.* bourse; compagnie des agents de change, *f.*
stockholder ['stɔkhouldə], *n.* actionnaire, *m., f.*, rentier, *m.*
stocking ['stɔkiŋ], *n.* bas, *m.*
stockpile ['stɔkpail], *n.* stocks de réserve, *m.pl.*—*v.t., v.i.* stocker.
stock-still ['stɔk'stil], *a.* immobile.—*adv.* sans bouger.
stock-taking ['stɔkteikiŋ], *n.* inventaire, *m.*
stocky ['stɔki], *a.* trapu.
stodgy ['stɔdʒi], *a.* pâteux, lourd.
stoic ['stouik], *n.* stoïcien, *m.*
stoic ['stouik], **stoical** ['stouikəl], *a.* stoïcien; (*fig.*) stoïque.
stoicism ['stouisizm], *n.* stoïcisme, *m.*
stoke [stouk], *v.t.* chauffer; tisonner (*le feu*).
stoker ['stoukə], *n.* chauffeur, *m.*
stoking ['stoukiŋ], *n.* chauffage, *m.*, chauffe, *f.*
stole (1) [stoul], *n.* étole; (*Cost.*) écharpe, *f.*
stole (2) [stoul], *past* [STEAL].
stolen ['stoulən], *a.* volé, dérobé.
stolid ['stɔlid], *a.* lourd, impassible.
stolidity [stə'liditi], **stolidness** ['stɔlidnis], *n.* flegme, *m.*
stomach ['stʌmək], *n.* estomac; (*euph.*) ventre; appétit, *m.*—*v.t.* avaler; endurer.
stomach-ache ['stʌməkeik], *n.* mal à l'estomac, *m.*, colique, *f.*
stone [stoun], *a.* de pierre, en pierre; de grès (*céramique*).—*n.* pierre, *f.*; caillou (*galet*); noyau (*de fruits*); pépin (*de raisins*); (*Path.*) calcul; (*Weight*) stone (*kg. 6·348*), *m.*—*v.t.* lapider; ôter les noyaux de (*fruits*).
stone-blind ['stounblaind], *a.* complètement aveugle.
stone-cold ['stounkould], *a.* complètement froid.—*adv.* complètement.
stone-dead ['stoun'ded], *a.* raide mort.
stone-deaf ['stoundef], *a.* complètement sourd.
stone-fruit ['stounfruːt], *n.* fruit à noyau, *m.*
stone-mason ['stounmeisən], *n.* maçon, marbrier (*pour tombes*), *m.*
stone's-throw ['stounzθrou], *n.* jet de pierre, *m.*
stoneware ['stounwɛə], *n.* grès, *m.*, poterie de grès, *f.*
stonework ['stounwəːk], *n.* maçonnerie, *f.*
stoniness ['stouninis], *n.* nature pierreuse; (*fig.*) dureté, *f.*
stoning ['stouniŋ], *n.* lapidation, *f.*

stony ['stouni], *a.* de pierre; pierreux (*plein de pierres*); (*fig.*) insensible; ***stony-hearted***, au cœur de pierre.
stook [stu:k], *n.* tas de gerbes, *m.*—*v.t.* mettre en gerbes.
stool [stu:l], *n.* tabouret; escabeau, *m.*
stoop [stu:p], *v.i.* se pencher, se baisser; se voûter; (*fig.*) s'abaisser.—*n.* inclination, *f.*; (*fig.*) abaissement, *m.*
stooping ['stu:piŋ], *a.* penché, courbé.
stop [stɔp], *n.* halte; pause, *f.*; obstacle; (*Organ*) jeu, registre; arrêt (*de trains etc.*), *m.*; (*Gram.*) ***full stop***, point, *m.*—*v.t.* arrêter, empêcher; couper (*le souffle*); suspendre (*paiement etc.*); retenir (*la paye*); (*Mus.*) presser; (*Gram.*) ponctuer; boucher (*trou etc.*); stopper (*machine*); plomber (*dent*).—*v.i.* s'arrêter; stopper.
stopcock ['stɔpkɔk], *n.* robinet d'arrêt, *m.*
stop-gap ['stɔpgæp], *n.* bouche-trou, *m.*
stoppage ['stɔpidʒ], *n.* interruption, halte, *f.*; arrêt (*d'un train etc.*), *m.*; obstruction; retenue (*de salaire*), *f.*; chômage (*arrêt de travail*); plombage (*de dent*), *m.*
stopper ['stɔpə], *n.* bouchon (*en verre*), *m.*—*v.t.* boucher.
stopping ['stɔpiŋ], *n.* arrêt; plombage (*de dent*), *m.*; matière à plomber, *f.*
stop-watch ['stɔpwɔtʃ], *n.* chronomètre, *m.*
storage ['stɔ:ridʒ], *n.* emmagasinage, *m.*, accumulation, *f.*
store [stɔ:], *n.* provision, *f.*; approvisionnement, *m.*, réserve, *f.*; magasin, *m.*, boutique, *f.*; (*fig.*) fonds, trésor, *m.*; ***in store***, en réserve; ***to lay in a store of***, faire une provision de.—*v.t.* pourvoir, munir, approvisionner (*de*); enrichir (*l'esprit*).
store-house ['stɔ:haus], *n.* magasin, entrepôt, dépôt, *m.*
store-keeper ['stɔ:ki:pə], *n.* garde-magasin; marchand (*boutiquier*), *m.*
store-room ['stɔ:ru:m], *n.* dépôt, office, *m.*; réserve, *f.*
storey, story (1) ['stɔ:ri], *n.* étage, *m.*
storied (1) ['stɔ:rid], *a.* à étage.
storied (2) ['stɔ:rid], *a.* orné d'inscriptions etc.
stork [stɔ:k], *n.* cigogne, *f.*
storm [stɔ:m], *n.* orage, *m.*, tempête, *f.*—*v.t.* donner l'assaut à, prendre d'assaut.—*v.i.* faire de l'orage; (*fig.*) tempêter, s'emporter.
storm-bell ['stɔ:mbel], *n.* tocsin, *m.*
storm-cloud ['stɔ:mklaud], *n.* nuée, *f.*
storminess ['stɔ:minis], *n.* état orageux, *m.*
storming ['stɔ:miŋ], *n.* assaut, *m.*, prise d'assaut; (*fig.*) rage, *f.*
stormy ['stɔ:mi], *a.* orageux, à l'orage; ***stormy petrel***, pétrel, *m.*
story (1) [STOREY].
story (2) ['stɔ:ri], *n.* histoire, *f.*, récit; conte (*littéraire*); mensonge (*tromperie*), *m.*
story-book ['stɔ:ribuk], *n.* livre de contes, *m.*
story-teller ['stɔ:ritelə], *n.* conteur (*narrateur*); menteur (*trompeur*), *m.*
stout [staut], *a.* fort; gros, corpulent; (*fig.*) brave, courageux.—*n.* stout, *m.*, bière brune forte (*boisson*), *f.*
stoutly ['stautli], *adv.* vigoureusement, fort et ferme.
stoutness ['stautnis], *n.* embonpoint, *m.*, corpulence; (*fig.*) fermeté, *f.*
stove (1) [stouv], *past* and *p.p.* [STAVE].
stove (2) [stouv], *n.* poêle; fourneau (*de cuisine*), *m.*
stow [stou], *v.t.* mettre en place; (*Naut.*) arrimer; ***to stow away***, emmagasiner.
stowage ['stouidʒ], *n.* mise en place, *f.*, (*Naut.*) arrimage, *m.*
stowaway ['stouəwei], *n.* passager clandestin *m.*—*v.i.* s'embarquer clandestinement.
straddle [strædl], *v.t.* enfourcher.—*v.i.* écarter les jambes, marcher les jambes écartées.
strafe [strɑ:f], *v.t.* mitrailler, bombarder.
straggle [strægl], *v.i.* s'écarter; marcher à la débandade.
straggler ['stræglə], *n.* rôdeur; (*Mil.*) traînard, *m.*
straggling ['stræglıŋ], *a.* séparé; éparpillé (*disséminé*).
straight [streit], *a.* droit; (*fig.*) équitable, juste.—*adv.* droit, tout droit, directement; ***straight away***, sur-le-champ, tout de suite.
straight-edge ['streitedʒ], *n.* règle à araser, *f.*
straighten [streitn], *v.t.* rendre droit, redresser; ajuster (*habits*); mettre en ordre (*affaires, maison*).
straight-faced ['streit'feisd], *a.* imperturbable.
straightforward [streit'fɔ:wəd], *a.* droit, direct; (*fig.*) franc; simple (*problème*).
straightforwardly [streit'fɔ:wədli], *adv.* avec droiture; (*colloq.*) carrément.
straightforwardness [streit'fɔ:wədnis], *n.* droiture, franchise, *f.*
straightness ['streitnis], *n.* ligne directe; droiture, *f.*
straightway ['streitwei], *adv.* sur-le-champ, à l'instant.
strain (1) [strein], *v.t.* tendre; forcer (*contraindre*); se fouler (*muscles*); filtrer, passer (*liquide*).—*v.i.* s'efforcer; se filtrer (*liquide*).—*n.* grand effort, *m.*, tension; entorse, foulure (*de muscles*), *f.*; ton; chant, *m.*
strain (2) [strein], *n.* race, lignée, *f.*
strained [streind], *a.* forcé, pas naturel (*langage etc.*); tendu.
strainer ['streinə], *n.* passoire, *f.*
straining ['streiniŋ], *n.* tension, *f.*, grand effort, *m.*, exagération, *f.*; filtrage (*d'un liquide*), *m.*
strait [streit], *a.* étroit, serré; strict.—*n.* (*usu. pl.*) (*Geog.*) détroit, *m.*; (*pl.*) gêne, difficulté, *f.*, embarras, *m.*
straiten [streitn], *v.t.* rétrécir (*resserrer*); (*fig.*) gêner.
strait-laced ['streitleist], *a.* lacé étroitement; (*fig.*) sévère, prude.
straitness ['streitnis], *n.* étroitesse, *f.*
strait-waistcoat ['streitweiskout], **strait-jacket** ['streitdʒækit], *n.* camisole de force, *f.*
strand (1) [strænd], *n.* plage, grève, *f.*—*v.t.* jeter à la côte, échouer.—*v.i.* échouer.
strand (2) [strænd], *n.* cordon (*de corde*), *m.*
stranded ['strændid], *a.* échoué; (*fig.*) dans l'embarras.
stranding ['strændiŋ], *n.* échouement, échouage, *m.*
strange [streindʒ], *a.* étrange, singulier, bizarre.
strangely ['streindʒli], *adv.* étrangement, singulièrement.

strangeness ['streindʒnis], *n.* étrangeté, bizarrerie, *f.*
stranger ['streindʒə], *n.* étranger, inconnu, *m.*
strangle [stræŋgl], *v.t.* étrangler.
strangler ['stræŋglə], *n.* étrangleur, *m.*
strangling ['stræŋgliŋ], *n.* étranglement, *m.*
strangulation [strængju'leiʃən], *n.* strangulation, *f.*
strap [stræp], *n.* courroie, *f.*; lien, *m.*, bande (*de fer*), *f.*—*v.t.* attacher avec une courroie; lier.
strapper ['stræpə], *n.* grand gaillard, *m.*
strapping ['stræpiŋ], *a.* bien découplé, bien bâti.
stratagem ['strætədʒəm], *n.* stratagème, *m.*
strategic [strə'ti:dʒik], **strategical** [strə'ti:dʒikəl], *a.* stratégique.
strategist ['strætədʒist], *n.* stratégiste, *m.*, *f.*
strategy ['strætədʒi], *n.* stratégie, *f.*
stratify ['strætifai], *v.t.* stratifier.
stratocruiser ['stræto'kru:zə], *n.* avion stratosphérique, *m.*
stratosphere ['strætəsfiə], *n.* stratosphère, *f.*
stratum ['strɑ:təm], *n.* (*pl.* **strata** ['strɑ:tə]) couche, *f.*
straw [strɔ:], *a.* de paille.—*n.* paille, *f.*; ***it's the last straw***, c'est le comble.—*v.t.* rempailler (*chaise*).
strawberry ['strɔ:bəri], *n.* fraise, *f.*; fraisier (*plante*), *m.*
straw-coloured ['strɔ:kʌləd], *a.* jaune-paille.
straw-mat ['strɔ:'mæt], *n.* paillasson, *m.*
stray [strei], *v.i.* s'égarer, errer, vaguer; s'écarter (*de*).—*a.* égaré; (*fig.*) fortuit.—*n.* épave, *f.*; ***waifs and strays***, des épaves, *f.pl.*
straying ['streiiŋ], *n.* égarement, *m.*
streak [stri:k], *n.* raie, bande, *f.*; ***streak of lightning***, éclair, *m.*—*v.t.* rayer, strier; barioler, bigarrer.—*v.i.* filer.
streaked [stri:kt], *a.* rayé (*de*); bariolé, bigarré.
streaky ['stri:ki], *a.* rayé; veiné (*marbre*); entrelardé (*viande*).
stream [stri:m], *n.* courant; cours d'eau, *m.*, rivière, *f.*; ruisseau; (*fig.*) cours; jet (*de lumière etc.*); torrent (*de paroles etc.*), *m.*; ***to go down stream***, aller en aval; ***to go up stream***, aller en amont.—*v.i.* couler; ruisseler (*sang etc.*); rayonner (*lumière*).
streamer ['stri:mə], *n.* banderole; (*Naut.*) flamme, *f.*; (*pl.*) serpentins (*de papier*), *m.pl.*
streamlet ['stri:mlit], *n.* petit ruisseau; ru, *m.*
stream-line ['stri:mlain], *n.* fil de l'eau, *m.* —*v.t.* caréner; (*fig.*) moderniser.
stream-lined ['stri:mlaind], *a.* ***stream-lined body***, carrosserie carénée, *f.*; ***stream-lined car***, voiture aérodynamique, *f.*
street [stri:t], *n.* rue, *f.*
street-door ['stri:t'dɔ:], *n.* porte sur la rue, *f.*
street-lamp ['stri:tlæmp], *n.* réverbère, *m.*
street-sweeper ['stri:tswi:pə], *n.* balayeur de rue (*personne*), *m.*; balayeuse (*machine*), *f.*
strength [streŋθ], *n.* force, *f.*, forces, *f.pl.*; (*Build.*) solidité, *f.*; (*Mil.*) effectif, *m.*
strengthen [streŋθn], *v.t.* fortifier, affermir, raffermir; (*Mil.*) renforcer.—*v.i.* se fortifier, s'affermir, se raffermir.
strengthener ['streŋθnə], *n.* (*Med.*) fortifiant, *m.*
strengthening ['streŋθniŋ], *a.* fortifiant.

strenuous ['strenjuəs], *a.* énergique, vif ardent, vigoureux.
strenuously ['strenjuəsli], *adv.* avec zèle ardemment; vigoureusement.
strenuousness ['strenjuəsnis], *n.* zèle, *m.*, ardeur; vigueur, *f.*
streptococcus [strepto'kɔkəs], *n.* streptocoque, *m.*
streptomycin [strepto'maisin], *n.* streptomycine, *f.*
stress [stres], *n.* force, emphase, *f.*, poids; (*Gram.*) accent, *m.*; violence (*du temps*); (*Mech.*) tension, *f.*—*v.t.* appuyer sur, accentuer.
stretch [stretʃ], *v.t.* tendre (*un élastique*); étendre; déployer (*ailes*); élargir; forcer (*faire violence à*); (*fig.*) exagérer.—*v.i.* s'étendre; s'étirer; se déployer; s'élargir; prêter (*gants, tissu*).—*n.* étendue, tension, extension; section (*de route*), *f.*; (*fig.*) effort, *m.*; ***at a stretch***, d'un trait.
stretcher ['stretʃə], *n.* brancard, *m.*, civière; baguette (*à gants*), *f.*, tendeur (*à chaussures*), *m.*
stretcher-bearer ['stretʃəbɛərə], *n.* brancardier, *m.*
stretching ['stretʃiŋ], *n.* élargissement, *m.*; tension, *f.*
strew [stru:], *v.t. irr.* répandre, parsemer, semer.
strewing ['stru:iŋ], *n.* jonchée, *f.*
striate ['straiit], **striated** [strai'eitid], *a.* strié.
striation [strai'eiʃən], *n.* striure, *f.*
stricken [strikn], *p.p.* [STRIKE].—*a.* affligé; (*Med.*) atteint (*de*).
strict [strikt], *a.* exact, strict, précis; rigide; sévère.
strictly ['striktli], *adv.* strictement, formellement; ***strictly speaking***, rigoureusement parlant.
strictness ['striktnis], *n.* exactitude, rigueur; sévérité, *f.*
stricture ['striktʃə], *n.* censure, critique, *f.*; (*Med.*) étranglement, *m.*
stride [straid], *n.* grand pas, *m.*, enjambée, *f.* —*v.i. irr.* marcher à grands pas *ou* à grandes enjambées.
strident ['straidənt], *a.* strident.
strife [straif], *n.* lutte, querelle, dispute, *f.*
strike [straik], *v.t. irr.* frapper; battre, cogner; asséner, porter (*un coup*); sonner (*l'heure*); rendre (*muet etc.*); établir (*l'équilibre*); allumer (*allumette*); faire (*marché etc.*); amener (*drapeau*); plier (*tente*); ***to strike down***, abattre; ***to strike off***, retrancher, effacer.—*v.i.* frapper; toucher; échouer (*heurter un écueil etc.*); heurter, donner (*contre*); sonner (*pendule etc.*); (*Hort.*) prendre racine; faire grève, se mettre en grève (*ouvriers*); ***to strike out***, se lancer; (*Mus.*) ***to strike up***, commencer à jouer.—*n.* grève (*d'ouvriers*), *f.*; ***sit-down strike***, débrayage, *m.*; ***stay-in-strike***, grève sur le tas.
striker ['straikə], *n.* frappeur, *m.*; gréviste (*ouvrier en grève*), *m.*, *f.*; percuteur (*de fusil*), *m.*
striking ['straikiŋ], *a.* frappant, saisissant; remarquable.—*n.* frappement, *m.*; frappe; sonnerie (*de pendule*), *f.*
strikingly ['straikiŋli], *adv.* d'une manière frappante.

string [striŋ], *n.* ficelle, corde, *f.*, fil; cordon, lacet (*de chaussures etc.*); chapelet (*d'oignons etc.*), *m.*; corde (*de violon*); bride (*de bonnet etc.*); (*fig.*) suite, série, *f.*; ***the strings***, les instruments à cordes (*d'un orchestre*), *m.pl.*—*v.t. irr.* garnir de cordes; enfiler (*grains etc.*); (*Mus.*) accorder.
stringed [striŋd], *a.* à cordes (*instrument de musique*).
stringency ['strindʒənsi], *n.* rigueur, *f.*
stringent ['strindʒənt], *a.* rigoureux, strict.
stringy ['striŋi], *a.* fibreux; filandreux (*viande*).
strip [strip], *n.* bande, *f.*, ruban; lambeau, *m.*, langue (*de terre*), *f.*—*v.t.* dépouiller (*de*); dévaliser (*voler*); déshabiller (*dévêtir*); ***to strip off***, se dépouiller de.—*v.i.* se déshabiller.
stripe [straip], *n.* raie; barre, bande; marque (*cicatrice*), *f.*; (*Mil.*) chevron, galon, *m.*—*v.t.* rayer, barrer.
striped [straipt], **stripy** ['straipi], *a.* rayé, à raies, zébré.
stripling ['stripliŋ], *n.* adolescent, *m.*
strive [straiv], *v.i. irr.* s'efforcer (*de*), faire des efforts (*pour*), se débattre; se disputer (*rivaliser*).
striving ['straiviŋ], *n.* lutte, *f.*, efforts, *m.pl.*
stroke [strouk], *n.* coup; trait; trait de plume; coup d'aviron, *m.*; brassée (*de la nage*), course (*de piston*), *f.*; (*Med.*) coup de sang, *m.*, attaque, *f.*; chef de nage (*de bateau à rames*), *m.*; ***at a stroke***, d'un coup, d'un trait.—*v.t.* caresser.
stroking ['stroukiŋ], *n.* caresses, *f.pl.*
stroll [stroul], *n.* (courte) promenade, *f.*, tour, *m.*, flânerie, *f.*—*v.i.* errer, flâner.
stroller ['stroulə], *n.* flâneur, *m.*
strong [strɔŋ], *a.* fort, solide; (*fig.*) vigoureux, résolu; ***strong light***, vive lumière, *f.*
strong-box ['strɔŋbɔks], *n.* coffre-fort, *m.*
stronghold ['strɔŋhould], *n.* forteresse, *f.*, fort, *m.*
strongly ['strɔŋli], *adv.* fortement, fermement.
strong-room ['strɔŋru:m], *n.* cave aux coffres-forts, *f.*
strontium ['strɔnʃiəm], *n.* strontium, *m.*
strop [strɔp], *n.* cuir à rasoir, *m.*—*v.t.* repasser, affiler.
strophe ['stroufi, 'strɔfi], *n.* stance, strophe, *f.*
structural ['strʌktʃərəl], *a.* de structure, structural.
structure ['strʌktʃə], *n.* construction, structure, *f.*; édifice, *m.*; facture (*de pièce, de poème*), *f.*
struggle [strʌgl], *n.* lutte, *f.*, effort, *m.*—*v.i.* lutter, se débattre.
struggling ['strʌgliŋ], *n.* lutte, *f.*; effort, *m.*
strum [strʌm], *v.i.* tapoter, taper (*sur*).
strumming ['strʌmiŋ], *n.* tapotage, *m.*
strut [strʌt], *n.* démarche fière, *f.*; (*Carp. etc*). étai, *m.*—*v.i.* se pavaner, se carrer.
strychnine ['strikni:n], *n.* strychnine, *f.*
stub [stʌb], *n.* souche, *f.*; bout, *m.*
stubble [stʌbl], *n.* chaume, *m.*
stubborn ['stʌbən], *a.* obstiné, opiniâtre.
stubbornness ['stʌbənnis], *n.* opiniâtreté, *f.*
stubby ['stʌbi], *a.* trapu (*taille*).
stucco ['stʌkou], *n.* stuc, *m.*
stud (1) [stʌd], *n.* bouton de chemise; clou, *m.*—*v.t.* clouter; parsemer (*de*).
stud (2) [stʌd], *n.* écurie, *f.*; ***stud-farm***, haras, *m.*
student ['stju:dənt], *n.* étudiant, *m.*, élève, *m., f.*
studied ['stʌdid], *a.* étudié (*style etc.*); prémédité (*calculé*).
studio ['stju:diou], *n.* atelier; (*Cine.*, *Rad.*) studio, *m.*
studious ['stju:diəs], *a.* studieux; diligent.
studiously ['stju:diəsli], *adv.* studieusement.
studiousness ['stju:diəsnis], *n.* application, *f.*
study ['stʌdi], *n.* étude, *f.*; soin, *m.*, application (*attention*), *f.*; cabinet d'étude (*pièce*), *m.*; ***to be in a brown study***, être dans la lune.—*v.t.* étudier, s'occuper de.—*v.i.* étudier, travailler.
stuff [stʌf], *n.* étoffe, *f.*, tissu, *m.*; (*fig.*) matière, *f.*; fatras (*bêtises*), *m.*—*v.t.* rembourrer; bourrer (*remplir*); boucher (*trou*); (*Taxidermy*) empailler; (*Cook.*) farcir.—*v.i.* se bourrer; se gorger.
stuffing ['stʌfiŋ], *n.* bourre (*substances*), *f.*; rembourrage (*opération*), *m.*; (*Cook.*) farce, *f.*; (*Taxidermy*) empaillage, *m.*
stuffy ['stʌfi], *a.* privé d'air, renfermé; ***to be stuffy***, sentir le renfermé; (*fig.*) avoir des préjugés.
stultify ['stʌltifai], *v.t.* rendre nul; contredire (*démentir*); ***to stultify oneself***, se rendre ridicule.
stumble [stʌmbl], *v.i.* trébucher, broncher; (*fig.*) faire un faux pas, faillir.—*n.* faux pas, *m.*
stumbling ['stʌmbliŋ], *a.* trébuchant.—*n.* trébuchement, *m.*
stumbling-block ['stʌmbliŋblɔk], *n.* pierre d'achoppement, *f.*
stump [stʌmp], *n.* tronçon, *m.*, souche, *f.*; chicot (*de dent*); trognon (*de chou*); moignon (*de membre*), *m.*; (*Drawing*) estompe, *f.*
stumpy ['stʌmpi], *a.* trapu (*personne*).
stun [stʌn], *v.t.* étourdir.
stunning ['stʌniŋ], *a.* étourdissant; (*slang*) épatant.
stunt (1) [stʌnt], *v.t.* rabougrir.
stunt (2) [stʌnt], *n.* tour de force, *m.*; réclame, *f.*
stunted ['stʌntid], *a.* rabougri.
stupefaction [stju:pi'fækʃən], *n.* stupéfaction, *f.*
stupefy ['stju:pifai], *v.t.* hébéter, abrutir; stupéfier.
stupefying ['stju:pifaiiŋ], *a.* stupéfiant.
stupendous [stju'pendəs], *a.* prodigieux, foudroyant.
stupid ['stju:pid], *a.* stupide, sot, bête.
stupidity [stju'piditi], *n.* stupidité, bêtise, *f.*
stupidly ['stju:pidli], *adv.* stupidement.
stupor ['stju:pə], *n.* stupeur, *f.*
sturdy ['stə:di], *a.* vigoureux, fort, robuste; hardi.
sturgeon ['stə:dʒən], *n.* esturgeon, *m.*
stutter ['stʌtə], *v.t., v.i.* bégayer.
stutterer ['stʌtərə], *n.* bègue, *m., f.*
stuttering ['stʌtəriŋ], *n.* bégaiement, *m.*
sty (1) [stai], *n.* étable (*à cochons*), *f.*
sty (2), **stye** [stai], *n.* orgelet (*à l'œil*), *m.*
Stygian ['stidʒiən], *a.* stygien.
style [stail], *n.* style; (*fig.*) genre, *m.*, manière, *f.*; titre, *m.*; raison sociale (*d'une compagnie*), *f.*; ***to live in style***, avoir un train de maison.—*v.t.* appeler, qualifier de.

stylish ['stailiʃ], *a.* élégant, de bon ton.
stylus ['stailəs], *n.* style, *m.*
styptic ['stiptik], *a.* and *n.* (*Med.*) styptique, *m.*
suave [swɑːv], *a.* suave.
suavity ['swɑːviti], *n.* suavité, *f.*
subaltern ['sʌbəltən], *a.* subalterne.—*n.* (sous-)lieutenant, *m.*
subconscious [sʌb'kɔnʃəs], *a.* and *n.* (*Psych.*) subconscient, *m.*
subconsciously [sʌb'kɔnʃəsli]. *adv.* inconsciemment.
subdivide [sʌbdi'vaid], *v.t.* subdiviser.
subdue [səb'djuː], *v.t.* subjuguer; dompter, étouffer; ***subdued light***, demi-jour, *m.*
sub-editor [sʌb'editə], *n.* secrétaire de la rédaction, *m., f.*
subject ['sʌbdʒikt], *a.* assujetti, soumis; sujet (*à*), exposé (*à*).—*n.* sujet, *m.*; (*Sch.*) matière, *f.*; particulier, *m.*, personne, *f.*—[səb'dʒekt], *v.t.* assujettir, soumettre; rendre sujet (*à*), exposer (*à*).
subjection [səb'dʒekʃən], *n.* sujétion, *f.*
subjective [səb'dʒektiv], *a.* subjectif.
subjectively [səb'dʒektivli], *adv.* subjectivement.
subject-matter ['sʌbdʒiktmætə], *n.* sujet, *m.* matière, *f.*
subjugate ['sʌbdʒugeit], *v.t.* subjuguer.
subjunctive [səb'dʒʌŋktiv], *a.* and *n.* (*Gram.*) subjonctif, *m.*
sublet [sʌb'let], *v.t. irr.* (*conjug. like* LET) sous-louer.
sub-lieutenant [sʌblef'tenənt], *n.* (*Navy*) enseigne, *m.*
sublimate ['sʌblimeit], *v.t.* sublimer.
sublime [sə'blaim], *a.* and *n.* sublime, *m.*
sublimeness [sə'blaimnis], *n.* sublimité, *f.*; sublime, *m.*
sub-machine-gun [sʌbmə'ʃiːngʌn], *n.* mitraillette, *f.*
submarine ['sʌbməriːn], *a.* and *n.* sous-marin, *m.*
submerge [səb'məːdʒ], *v.t.* submerger.—*v.i.* plonger.
submission [səb'miʃən], *n.* soumission; résignation, déférence, *f.*
submissive [səb'misiv], *a.* soumis (*à*); docile.
submit [səb'mit], *v.t.* soumettre (*à*).—*v.i.* se soumettre (*à*).
subnormal [sʌb'nɔːml], *a.* sous-normal.
subordinate [sə'bɔːdinit], *a.* subordonné (*à*).—*n.* subordonné, *m.*—[sə'bɔːdineit], *v.t.* subordonner (*à*).
subordination [səbɔːdi'neiʃən], *n.* subordination, *f.*; rang inférieur, *m.*
suborn [sə'bɔːn], *v.t.* suborner.
subpoena [sʌb'piːnə], *n.* (*Law*) citation, assignation, *f.*—*v.t.* citer, assigner.
subscribe [səb'skraib], *v.t.* souscrire.—*v.i.* souscrire (*à* ou *pour*); s'abonner (*à un journal*).
subscriber [səb'skraibə], *n.* abonné (*à un journal*), *m.*
subscription [səb'skripʃən], *n.* souscription, *f.*; abonnement (*à un journal etc.*), *m.*
subsection ['sʌbsekʃən], *n.* subdivision, *f.*
subsequent ['sʌbsikwənt], *a.* subséquent, postérieur.
subsequently ['sʌbsikwəntli], *adv.* ensuite, après.

subservient [səb'səːvjənt], *a.* subordonné (*à*) qui contribue à; obséquieux.
subserviently [səb'səːviəntli], *adv.* en sous ordre, utilement; servilement.
subside [səb'said], *v.i.* s'affaisser (*êtr accablé*); baisser, s'abaisser, se calme s'apaiser (*s'adoucir*); se taire (*personne*); *t* ***subside into***, se changer en.
subsidence ['sʌbsidəns, səb'saidəns], *n* affaissement, *m.*; (*fig.*) baisse (*rivière*), *f.*
subsidiary [səb'sidjəri], *a.* subsidiaire (*à*).—*n.* auxiliaire, *m.*; filiale (*compagnie*), *f.*
subsidize ['sʌbsidaiz], *v.t.* subventionner.
subsidy ['sʌbsidi], *n.* subvention, *f.*
subsist [səb'sist], *v.i.* subsister, exister.
subsistence [səb'sistəns], *n.* subsistance, *f.* entretien, *m.*; existence, *f.*
subsistent [səb'sistənt], *a.* existant, qui existe
subsoil ['sʌbsɔil], *n.* sous-sol, *m.*
sub-species ['sʌbspiːʃiːz], *n.* sous-espèce, *f.*
substance ['sʌbstəns], *n.* substance, *f.*; fon (*l'essentiel*), *m.*; biens (*richesses*), *m.pl.*
substantial [səb'stænʃl], *a.* substantiel, rée solide; aisé (*riche*).
substantially [səb'stænʃəli], *adv.* solidement fortement, considérablement.
substantiate [səb'stænʃieit], *v.t.* établir, con firmer.
substantive ['sʌbstəntiv], *a.* indépendant (*Gram.*) substantif.—*n.* (*Gram.*) substantif *m.*
substitute ['sʌbstitjuːt], *v.t.* substituer (*à*).—*n.* substitut, remplaçant, *m.*
substitution [sʌbsti'tjuːʃən], *n.* substitution *f.*
substratum [sʌb'strɑːtəm], *n.* (*pl.* **substrat** [sʌb'strɑːtə]) substratum, substrat, *m.* couche inférieure, *f.*; (*Agric.*) sous-sol, *m.*
subtenant ['sʌbtenənt], *n.* sous-locataire, *m. f.*
subterfuge ['sʌbtəfjuːdʒ], *n.* subterfuge faux-fuyant, *m.*
subterranean [sʌbtə'reiniən], *a.* souterrain.
sub-title ['sʌbtaitl], *n.* sous-titre, *m.*
subtle [sʌtl], *a.* subtil, rusé; fin.
subtlety ['sʌtlti], *n.* subtilité, finesse, *f.*
subtly ['sʌtli], *adv.* subtilement.
subtract [səb'trækt], *v.t.* défalquer; (*Arith.* soustraire.
subtraction [səb'trækʃən], *n.* (*Arith.*) soustraction, *f.*
suburb ['sʌbəːb], *n.* faubourg, *m.*, (*pl.*) alentours, environs, *m.pl.*, banlieue, *f.*; ***garden suburb***, cité-jardin, *f.*
suburban [sə'bəːbən], *a.* de la banlieue, suburbain.
subvention [səb'venʃən], *n.* subvention, *f.*
subversive [səb'vəːsiv], *a.* subversif.
subway ['sʌbwei], *n.* passage souterrain; (*Am.*) métro, *m.*
succeed [sək'siːd], *v.t.* succéder à, suivre; ***to succeed each other***, se succéder.—*v.i.* succéder (*à*); hériter (*une propriété*); parvenir (*à*), réussir (*avoir du succès*).
succeeding [sək'siːdiŋ], *a.* suivant (*dans le passé*); à venir, futur (*à l'avenir*); successif (*consécutif*).
success [sək'ses], *n.* succès, *m.*; ***I wish you success!*** bonne chance!
successful [sək'sesful], *a.* heureux; couronné de succès, réussi, victorieux; ***to be successful***, réussir.

uccessfully [sək'sesfuli], *adv.* heureusement, avec succès.
uccession [sək'seʃən], *n.* succession, suite, *f.*; avènement (*au trône etc.*), *m.*; postérité (*descendance*), *f.*; ***in succession***, successivement, de suite.
uccessive [sək'sesiv], *a.* successif, consécutif.
uccessor [sək'sesə], *n.* successeur, *m.*
uccinct [sək'siŋkt], *a.* succinct, concis.
uccinctly [sək'siŋktli], *adv.* avec concision.
uccinctness [sək'siŋktnis], *n.* concision, brièveté, *f.*
uccour ['sʌkə], *v.t.* secourir, aider.—*n.* secours, *m.*, aide, *f.*
ucculent ['sʌkjulənt], *a.* succulent, plein de jus.
uccumb [sə'kʌm], *v.i.* succomber (*à*).
uch [sʌtʃ], *a.* tel, pareil, semblable; ***he is such a bore***, il est si ennuyeux; ***such a one***, un tel, *m.*, une telle, *f.*; ***such a one as***, tel que; ***such as it is***, tel quel, *m.*, telle quelle, *f.*; ***such as you***, tel que vous.
uchlike ['sʌtʃlaik], *a.* semblable, pareil; de ce genre.
uck [sʌk], *v.t.*, *v.i.* sucer; têter (*à la mamelle*); aspirer.
ucker ['sʌkə], *n.* suceur; (*fig.*) gobeur, *m.*
ucking ['sʌkiŋ], *a.* qui suce, aspirant.—*n.* sucement, *m.*, succion, *f.*
ucking-pig ['sʌkiŋpig], *n.* cochon de lait, *m.*
uckle [sʌkl], *v.t.* allaiter, nourrir.
uction ['sʌkʃən], *n.* succion, aspiration, *f.*
udan [su'dæn, su'dɑ:n]. le Soudan, *m.*
udanese [sudə'ni:z], *a.* soudanais.—*n.* Soudanais (*personne*), *m.*
udden [sʌdn], *a.* subit, soudain; (*fam.*) ***all of a sudden***, tout à coup.
uddenly ['sʌdnli], *adv.* subitement, soudain, tout à coup.
uddenness ['sʌdnnis], *n.* soudaineté, *f.*
udetenland [su'deitnlænd]. les Sudètes, *m.pl.*
uds [sʌdz], **soap-suds** ['soupsʌdz], *n.pl.* eau de savon, lessive, *f.*
ue [sju:], *v.t.* poursuivre (en justice).—*v.i.* implorer.
uède [sweid], *n.* daim (*chaussures*); suède (*gants*), *m.*
uet ['sju:it], *n.* graisse de bœuf, *f.*
uffer ['sʌfə], *v.t.* souffrir; supporter, endurer, subir (*éprouver*); laisser, permettre (*autoriser*).—*v.i.* souffrir (*de*); ***to suffer for***, porter la peine de.
ufferable ['sʌfərəbl], *a.* supportable, tolérable.
ufferance ['sʌfərəns], *n.* tolérance, *f.*
ufferer ['sʌfərə], *n.* victime (*de*), *f.*; patient, *m.*
uffering ['sʌfəriŋ], *a.* souffrant.—*n.* souffrance, douleur, *f.*
uffice [sə'fais], *v.t.* suffire à, satisfaire.—*v.i.* suffire.
ufficiency [sə'fiʃənsi], *n.* suffisance; aisance (*financière*), *f.*
ufficient [sə'fiʃənt], *a.* suffisant, assez.
ufficiently [sə'fiʃəntli], *adv.* suffisamment, assez.
uffix ['sʌfiks], *n.* suffixe, *m.*
uffocate ['sʌfəkeit], *v.t.*, *v.i.* suffoquer, étouffer, asphyxier.
uffocating ['sʌfəkeitiŋ], *a.* suffocant, étouffant, asphyxiant.
suffocation [sʌfə'keiʃən], *n.* suffocation, asphyxie, *f.*
suffrage ['sʌfridʒ], *n.* suffrage, *m.*
suffuse [sə'fju:z], *v.t.* répandre, couvrir (*de*); répandre sur; se répandre sur.
suffusion [sə'fju:ʒən], *n.* épanchement, *m.*, suffusion, *f.*
sugar ['ʃugə], *n.* sucre, *m.*; ***barley sugar***, sucre d'orge; ***brown sugar*** or ***moist sugar***, cassonade, *f.*; ***castor sugar***, sucre en poudre; ***granulated sugar***, sucre cristallisé; ***lump sugar***, sucre cassé.—*v.t.* sucrer; (*fig.*) adoucir.
sugar-basin ['ʃugəbeisn], *n.* sucrier, *m.*
sugar-beet ['ʃugəbi:t], *n.* betterave à sucre, *f.*
sugar-cane ['ʃugəkein], *n.* canne à sucre, *f.*
sugared ['ʃugəd], *a.* sucré; (*fig.*) doux.
sugar-loaf ['ʃugəlouf], *n.* pain de sucre, *m.*
sugar-refinery ['ʃugəri'fainəri], *n.* raffinerie de sucre, *f.*
sugary ['ʃugəri], *a.* sucré; trop sucré.
suggest [sə'dʒest], *v.t.* suggérer; inspirer.
suggestion [sə'dʒestʃən], *n.* suggestion; proposition, idée; nuance, *f.*
suggestive [sə'dʒestiv], *a.* suggestif.
suicidal [sju:i'saidl], *a.* de suicide; fatal.
suicide ['sju:isaid], *n.* suicide (*acte*); suicidé (*personne*), *m.*; ***to commit suicide***, se suicider.
suit [sju:t], *n.* suite, collection complète, *f.*, assortiment, *m.*; (*Cards*) couleur; sollicitation, prière; recherche en mariage; (*Law*) instance, *f.*, procès, *m.*; ***suit (of clothes)***, complet (*d'homme*), tailleur (*de femme*), *m.*—*v.t.* adapter; convenir à, aller à; plaire à—*v.i.* s'accorder (*à*).
suitability [sju:tə'biliti], *n.* convenance, *f.*
suitable ['sju:təbl], *a.* convenable (*à*); à propos.
suitably ['sju:təbli], *adv.* convenablement.
suite [swi:t], *n.* suite, *f.*, ensemble, *m.*; ***suite of rooms***, appartement, *m.*; ***suite of furniture***, ameublement complet, *m.*
suitor ['sju:tə], *n.* prétendant (*amoureux*); (*Law*) plaideur, *m.*
sulk [sʌlk], *v.i.* bouder, faire la mine.
sulkily ['sʌlkili], *adv.* en boudant, en faisant la mine.
sulkiness ['sʌlkinis], **sulking** ['sʌlkiŋ], *n.* bouderie, *f.*
sulks [sʌlks], *n.pl.* mauvaise humeur, bouderie, *f.*
sulky ['sʌlki], *a.* boudeur.
sullen ['sʌlən], *a.* maussade, morose, renfrogné.
sullenly ['sʌlənli], *adv.* maussadement, d'un air renfrogné.
sullenness ['sʌlənnis], *n.* air maussade, *m.*
sully ['sʌli], *v.t.* souiller, ternir (*de*).
sulphate ['sʌlfeit], *n.* sulfate, *m.*
sulphide ['sʌlfaid], *n.* sulfure, *m.*
sulphite ['sʌlfait], *n.* sulfite, *m.*
sulphonamide [sʌl'founəmaid], *n.* sulfamide, *f.*
sulphur ['sʌlfə], *n.* soufre, *m.*
sulphuric [sʌl'fjuərik], *a.* sulfurique.
sulphurous ['sʌlfjurəs], *a.* sulfureux.
sultan ['sʌltən], *n.* sultan, *m.*
sultana [sʌl'tɑ:nə], *n.* sultane, *f.*; (*pl.*) raisins de Smyrne, *m.pl.*
sultriness ['sʌltrinis], *n.* chaleur étouffante, *f.*

sultry ['sʌltri], *a.* d'une chaleur étouffante, étouffant, suffocant; (*fam.*) épicé, salé (*histoire etc.*); ***it is very sultry***, il fait très lourd.

sum [sʌm], *n.* somme (*d'argent*), *f.*; (*Arith.*) problème, calcul, *m.*; ***the four sums***, les quatre opérations, *f.pl.*—*v.t.* ***to sum up***, additionner, faire l'addition de; (*fig.*) récapituler.

summarily ['sʌmərili], *adv.* sommairement.

summarize ['sʌməraiz], *v.t.* résumer sommairement.

summary ['sʌməri], *a.* sommaire, prompt.—*n.* sommaire, résumé, *m.*

summer ['sʌmə], *a.* d'été, estival—*n.* été, *m.*; ***in summer***, en été.

summer-house ['sʌməhaus], *n.* pavillon, *m.*

summing-up ['sʌmiŋ'ʌp], *n.* résumé, *m.*

summit ['sʌmit], *n.* sommet, *m.*, cime, *f.*; (*fig.*) comble, *m.*

summon ['sʌmən], *v.t.* convoquer (*un rassemblement etc.*); sommer (*ordonner*); (*Law*) citer en justice; assigner (*témoins*).

summons ['sʌmənz], *n.* sommation (*commandement*); convocation, *f.*; appel (*invitation*), *m.*; (*Law*) citation, *f.*, mandat de comparution, *m.*—*v.t.* assigner, citer (en justice), appeler à comparaître.

sump [sʌmp], *n.* (*Mining*) puisard; (fond de) carter (*de voiture*), *m.*

sumptuous ['sʌmptjuəs], *a.* somptueux.

sumptuously ['sʌmptjuəsli], *adv.* somptueusement.

sun [sʌn], *n.* soleil, *m.*—*v.t.* exposer au soleil.

sun-bath ['sʌnbɑːθ], *n.* bain de soleil, *m.*

sun-bathe ['sʌnbeið], *v.i.* prendre des bains de soleil.

sunbeam ['sʌnbiːm], *n.* rayon de soleil, *m.*

sun-blind ['sʌnblaind], *n.* store, *m.*

sunburn ['sʌnbəːn], *n.* hâle; coup de soleil, *m.*

sunburnt ['sʌnbəːnt], *a.* hâlé; basané.

Sunday ['sʌndi], *n.* dimanche, *m.*

sunder ['sʌndə], *v.t.* séparer; couper en deux.

sundial ['sʌndaiəl], *n.* cadran solaire, *m.*

sundries ['sʌndriz], *n.pl.* choses diverses, *f.pl.*

sundry ['sʌndri], *a.* divers.

sun-flower ['sʌnflauə], *n.* tournesol, *m.*

sunken ['sʌŋkən], *a.* enfoncé; cave (*joues*); creux (*yeux*).

sunless ['sʌnlis], *a.* sans soleil.

sunlight ['sʌnlait], *n.* lumière du soleil, *f.*

sunlit ['sʌnlit], *a.* ensoleillé.

sunny ['sʌni], *a.* ensoleillé; (*fig.*) heureux; ***it is sunny***, il fait du soleil.

sunrise ['sʌnraiz], *n.* lever du soleil, *m.*

sunset ['sʌnset], *n.* coucher du soleil, *m.*

sunshade ['sʌnʃeid], *n.* parasol, *m.*, ombrelle *f.*

sunshine ['sʌnʃain], *n.* soleil, *m.*, clarté du soleil, *f.*

sunstroke ['sʌnstrouk], *n.* coup de soleil, *m.* insolation, *f.*

sup [sʌp], *n.* (*Sc.*) petit coup, *m.*, gorgée, *f.*—*v.t.* boire à petits coups.—*v.i.* souper.

super ['sjuːpə], *a.* (*slang*) ***it is super***, c'est sensass (sensationnel).

superable ['sjuːpərəbl], *a.* surmontable.

superabundance [sjuːpərə'bʌndəns], *n.* surabondance, *f.*

superannuate [sjuːpər'ænjueit], *v.t.* mettre à la retraite.

superannuated [sjuːpər'ænjueitid], *a.* mis à la retraite, en retraite (*personne*); démodé.

superannuation [sjuːpərænju'eiʃən], *n.* mise à la retraite, retraite, *f.*; ***superannuation fund***, caisse de retraites, *f.*

superb [sju'pəːb], *a.* superbe.

superbly [sju'pəːbli], *adv.* superbement.

supercilious [sjuːpə'siliəs], *a.* hautain, arrogant.

superciliously [sjuːpə'siliəsli], *adv.* avec hauteur.

superciliousness [sjuːpə'siliəsnis], *n.* hauteur; arrogance, *f.*

superficial [sjuːpə'fiʃl], *a.* superficiel; de superficie (*mesure*).

superficiality [sjuːpəfiʃi'æliti], *n.* caractère superficiel, *m.*

superficially [sjuːpə'fiʃəli], *adv.* superficiellement.

superfine ['sjuːpəfain], *a.* superfin; (*Comm.*) surfin.

superfluity [sjuːpə'fluːiti], *n.* superfluité, *f.*; superflu, *m.*

superfluous [sju'pəːfluəs], *a.* superflu, inutile.

superhuman [sjuːpə'hjuːmən], *a.* surhumain.

superimpose [sjuːpərim'pouz], *v.t.* superposer, surimposer.

superintend [sjuːpərin'tend], *v.t.* surveiller.

superintendent [sjuːpərin'tendənt], *n.* chef; directeur, inspecteur, surintendant; commissaire de police, *m.*

superior [sju'piəriə], *a.* and *n.* supérieur, *m.*

superiority [sjupiəri'ɔriti], *n.* supériorité, *f.*

superlative [sju'pəːlətiv], *a.* suprême; (*Gram.*) superlatif.—*n.* (*Gram.*) superlatif, *m.*

superman ['sjuːpəmæn], *n.* (*pl.* **-men** [men]) surhomme, *m.*

supernatural [sjuːpə'nætʃərəl], *a.* and *n.* surnaturel, *m.*

supernumerary [sjuːpə'njuːmərəri], *a.* surnuméraire.—*n.* surnuméraire; (*Theat.*) figurant, *m.*

superscribe [sjuːpə'skraib], *v.t.* mettre une adresse, une suscription *ou* une inscription à.

superscription [sjuːpə'skripʃən], *n.* suscription; inscription; (*Coin.*) légende, *f.*; entête (*de lettre*), *m.*

supersede [sjuːpə'siːd], *v.t.* remplacer.

superseded [sjuːpə'siːdid], *a.* démodé, périmé.

supersonic [sjuːpə'sɔnik], *a.* (*onde*) ultrasonore; (*Av.*) supersonique.

superstition [sjuːpə'stiʃən], *n.* superstition, *f.*

superstitious [sjuːpə'stiʃəs], *a.* superstitieux.

superstructure ['sjuːpəstrʌktʃə], *n.* superstructure, *f.*

super-tax ['sjuːpətæks], *n.* surtaxe, *f.*

supervene [sjuːpə'viːn], *v.i.* survenir.

supervention [sjuːpə'venʃən], *n.* survenance, *f.*

supervise ['sjuːpəvaiz], *v.t.* surveiller.

supervision [sjuːpə'viʒən], *n.* surveillance; inspection, *f.*

supervisor ['sjuːpəvaizə], *n.* surveillant, *m.*

supine [sju'pain], *a.* couché sur le dos; (*fig.*) nonchalant.—['sjuːpain], *n.* (*Gram.*) supin, *m.*

supper ['sʌpə], *n.* souper, *m.*; ***supper-time***, heure du souper, *f.*

supplant [sə'plɑːnt], *v.t.* supplanter.

supple [sʌpl], *a.* souple, flexible.

supplement [sʌpli'ment], *v.t.* suppléer à; compléter.—['sʌplimənt], *n.* supplément, *m.*

supplementary [sʌpli'mentəri], *a.* supplémentaire.

suppleness ['sʌplnis], *n.* souplesse, *f.*

suppliant ['sʌpliənt], *a.* and *n.* suppliant, *m.*

supplicate ['sʌplikeit], *v.t.* supplier, implorer.

supplication [sʌpli'keiʃən], *n.* supplication, prière, *f.*

supplier [sə'plaiə], *n.* pourvoyeur; fournisseur, *m.*

supply [sə'plai], *n.* fourniture; provision, *f.* approvisionnement (*réserve*), *m.*; (*Elec.*) alimentation, *f.*; (*Mil.*, *pl.*) vivres (*ravitaillement*); (*Parl.*) subsides, *m.pl.*—*v.t.* fournir; pourvoir à, subvenir à (*besoins*), ravitailler.

support [sə'pɔ:t], *v.t.* soutenir, supporter; entretenir (*faire vivre*); appuyer (*aider*).—*n.* appui, soutien; support (*physique*); entretien (*des dépendants*), *m.*

supportable [sə'pɔ:təbl], *a.* supportable.

supporter [sə'pɔ:tə], *n.* adhérent, partisan; appui, soutien; (*Spt.*) supporter; (*Her.*) support, *m.*

suppose [sə'pouz], *v.t.* supposer, s'imaginer; ***to be supposed to*** (***know***), être censé (savoir); ***suppose we go***, si nous y allions.

supposed [sə'pouzd], *a.* présumé; prétendu, soi-disant; censé.

supposedly [sə'pouzidli], *adv.* censément.

supposing [sə'pouziŋ], *conj.* supposons, supposé (*que*).

supposition [sʌpə'ziʃən], *n.* supposition, *f.*

suppress [sə'pres], *v.t.* supprimer; réprimer (*révolte etc.*); étouffer; ***a suppressed laugh***, un rire étouffé.

suppression [sə'preʃən], *n.* suppression; répression; dissimulation (*de la vérité*), *f.*

suppressor [sə'presə], *n.* (*Rad.*, *Tel.*) dispositif anti-parasites, *m.*

suppurate ['sʌpjureit], *v.i.* suppurer.

suppuration [sʌpju'reiʃən], *n.* suppuration, *f.*

supremacy [sju'preməsi], *n.* suprématie, *f.*

supreme [sju'pri:m], *a.* suprême.

supremely [sju'pri:mli], *adv.* suprêmement.

surcharge ['sə:tʃɑ:dʒ], *n.* surcharge, surtaxe, *f.*

sure [ʃuə], *a.* sûr, certain; assuré; ***to be sure!*** certainement! bien sûr! ***to be sure to***, ne pas manquer de.—*adv.* sûrement, à coup sûr.

sure-footed [ʃuə'futid], *a.* au pied sûr.

surely ['ʃuəli], *adv.* sûrement, assurément, à coup sûr.

sureness ['ʃuənis], *n.* certitude, sûreté, *f.*

surety ['ʃuəti], *n.* certitude (*véracité*); sûreté, sécurité (*garantie*), *f.*; (*Law*) garant, *m.*

surf [sə:f], *n.* ressac, *m.*, brisants sur la plage, *m.pl.*

surface ['sə:fis], *n.* surface, *f.*

surfeit ['sə:fit], *n.* rassasiement, *m.*; ***to have a surfeit of***, être rassasié de.

surf-riding ['sə:fraidiŋ], *n.* sport de l'aquaplane, planking, surf, *m.*

surge [sə:dʒ], *n.* houle, lame de fond, *f.*—*v.i.* s'enfler, s'élever.

surgeon ['sə:dʒən], *n.* chirurgien, *m.*

surgery ['sə:dʒəri], *n.* chirurgie (*art*), *f.*; dispensaire; cabinet (*de consultations*), *m.*

surgical ['sə:dʒikl], *a.* chirurgical.

surliness ['sə:linis], *n.* morosité, *f.*

surly ['sə:li], *a.* morose; hargneux (*chien*).

surmise ['sə:maiz], *n.* soupçon, *m.*, conjecture, *f.*—[sə'maiz], *v.t.* soupçonner, conjecturer.

surmount [sə'maunt], *v.t.* surmonter.

surmountable [sə'mauntəbl], *a.* surmontable.

surname ['sə:neim], *n.* nom de famille, *m.*

surpass [sə'pɑ:s], *v.t.* surpasser, l'emporter sur.

surpassable [sə'pɑ:səbl], *a.* qu'on peut surpasser.

surpassing [sə'pɑ:siŋ], *a.* éminent, supérieur, rare.

surplice ['sə:plis], *n.* surplis, *m.*

surplus ['sə:pləs], *a.* de surplus.—*n.* surplus, *m.*; ***surplus stock***, solde, *m.*

surprise [sə'praiz], *n.* surprise, *f.*; étonnement, *m.*—*v.t.* surprendre, étonner.

surprising [sə'praiziŋ], *a.* surprenant, étonnant.

surrealism [sə'ri:əlizm], *n.* surréalisme, *m.*

surrender [sə'rendə], *n.* reddition, capitulation, *f.*; abandon (*d'un titre, d'un droit*), *m.*; (*Law*) cession, *f.*—*v.t.* rendre; (*fig.*) abandonner, livrer (*personne etc.*); (*Law*) céder. —*v.i.* se rendre.

surreptitious [sʌrəp'tiʃəs], *a.* subreptice, clandestin; frauduleux.

surreptitiously [sʌrəp'tiʃəsli], *adv.* subrepticement.

surround [sə'raund], *n.* encadrement (*de porte, de fenêtre*), *m.*—*v.t.* entourer, environner (*de*), (*Mil.*) cerner.

surrounding [sə'raundiŋ], *a.* environnant, d'alentour.—*n.* (*pl.*) alentours, environs, *m.pl.*, entourage, milieu, *m.*

surtax ['sə:tæks], *n.* surtaxe, *f.*

survey ['sə:vei], *n.* vue, *f.*, coup d'œil, *m.*; inspection (*examen*); expertise (*évaluation*), *f.*; arpentage (*de terrain etc.*); (*Ordnance*) levé topographique, *m*; ***aerial survey***, levé aérophotogrammétrique, *m.*—[sə'vei], *v.t.* arpenter (*terrain*); (*Ordnance*) lever le plan de; (*fig.*) examiner, contempler.

surveying [sə'veiiŋ], *n.* arpentage, levé de plans, *m.*

surveyor [sə'veiə], *n.* inspecteur; arpenteur (*de terrain*); agent voyer (*ponts et chaussées*), *m.*

survival [sə'vaivl], *n.* survivance; survie, *f.*

survive [sə'vaiv], *v.t.* survivre à.—*v.i.* survivre.

surviving [sə'vaiviŋ], *a.* survivant.

survivor [sə'vaivə], *n.* survivant, *m.*

Susan [su:zn]. Suzanne, *f.*

susceptibility [səsepti'biliti], *n.* susceptibilité; sensibilité, *f.*

susceptible [sə'septibl], *a.* susceptible (*de*).

suspect ['sʌspekt], *a.* and *n.* suspect, *m.*—[sə'spekt], *v.t.*, *v.i.* soupçonner.

suspend [sə'spend], *v.t.* suspendre; cesser (*payements*).

suspender [sə'spendə], *n.* (*pl.*) jarretelles (*pour bas*); (*Am.*) bretelles (*pour pantalon*), *f.pl.*

suspense [sə'spens], *n.* suspens, doute, *m.*

suspension [sə'spenʃən], *n.* suspension, *f.*

suspicion [sə'spiʃən], *n.* soupçon, *m.*

suspicious [sə'spiʃəs], *a.* soupçonneux; suspect, louche (*équivoque*).

suspiciously [sə'spiʃəsli], *adv.* avec méfiance; d'une manière suspecte.

suspiciousness [sə'spiʃəsnis], *n.* caractère soupçonneux, *m.*, défiance, méfiance, *f.*
sustain [sə'stein], *v.t.* soutenir, supporter; éprouver, essuyer (*perte*).
sustaining [sə'steiniŋ], *a.* fortifiant, nourrissant.
sustenance ['sʌstinəns], *n.* nourriture, *f.*, aliments, *m.pl.*; entretien, *m.*, subsistance, *f.*
suzerain ['sju:zərein], *a.* and *n.* suzerain, *m.*
suzerainty ['sju:zəreinti], *n.* suzeraineté, *f.*
swab [swɔb], *n.* torchon; (*Naut.*) faubert; tampon (*de coton hydrophile*) *m.*—*v.t.* fauberter; nettoyer.
swaddle [swɔdl], *v.t.* emmailloter.
swaddling ['swɔdliŋ], *n.* emmaillotement, *m.*; ***swaddling-clothes***, maillot, *m.*
swag [swæg], *n.* (*slang*) butin; (*Australia*) baluchon, *m.*
swagger ['swægə], *v.i.* faire le rodomont; se donner des airs, se vanter.
swaggerer ['swægərə], *n.* fanfaron, *m.*
swaggering ['swægəriŋ], *a.* de fanfaron.—*n.* fanfaronnade, *f.*
swagman ['swægmən], *n.* (*pl.* **-men** [men]) (*Australia*) chemineau, *m.*
swain [swein], *n.* (*poet.*) berger, jeune paysan, *m.*
swallow (1) ['swɔlou], *v.t.* avaler; engloutir (*faire disparaître*); consumer; (*fig.*) gober. —*n.* (*pop.*) avaloir, gosier (*gorge*), *m.*; gorgée (*ce qu'on avale*), *f.*
swallow (2) ['swɔlou], *n.* hirondelle (*oiseau*), *f.*
swallow-dive ['swɔloudaiv], *n.* (*Swim.*) saut de l'ange, *m.*
swallower ['swɔlouə], *n.* avaleur, *m.*
swallow-tail ['swɔlouteil], *a.* en queue d'aronde.—*n.* habit à queue de morue, *m.*
swamp [swɔmp], *n.* marais, marécage, *m.*—*v.t.* submerger; faire couler (*bateau*).
swampy ['swɔmpi], *a.* marécageux.
swan [swɔn], *n.* cygne, *m.*
swank [swæŋk], *n.* pose; (*pop.*) épate, *f.*—*v.i.* (*pop.*) crâner, poser; faire du chiqué.
swanky ['swæŋki], *a.* chic, rupin.
swap [swɔp], *v.t.* (*colloq.*) échanger, troquer. —*n.* troc, échange, *m.*
sward [swɔ:d], *n.* (*poet.*) gazon, *m.*, pelouse, *f.*
swarm [swɔ:m], *n.* essaim (*d'abeilles*), *m.*—*v.i.* essaimer; (*fig.*) accourir en foule.
swarming ['swɔ:miŋ], *n.* essaimage, *m.*
swarthiness ['swɔ:ðinis], *n.* teint basané, *m.*
swarthy ['swɔ:ði], *a.* basané, hâlé.
swashbuckler ['swɔʃbʌklə], *n.* fanfaron, matamore, *m.*
swastika ['swɔstikə], *n.* croix gammée, *f.*
swat [swɔt], *v.t.* écraser, tuer (*mouche*).
swath [swɔ:θ], *n.* andain, *m.*, fauchée, *f.*
swathe [sweið], *v.t.* emmailloter.
sway [swei], *v.t.* manier, porter; balancer (*agiter*); (*fig.*) diriger (*gouverner*); influencer (*l'opinion*).—*v.i.* se balancer.—*n.* empire, *m.*; domination (*règne*), *f.*
swaying ['sweiiŋ], *n.* balancement, *m.*; oscillation, *f.*
swear [swɛə], *v.t.* **irr.** faire prêter serment à (*témoins etc.*); prêter (*serment*); ***to swear at***, injurier.—*v.i.* jurer; prêter serment.
swearer ['swɛərə], *n.* jureur, *m.*
swearing ['swɛəriŋ], *n.* serments; jurons (*gros mots*), *m.pl.*; ***swearing in***, prestation de serment, assermentation (*de juges etc.*), *f.*
swear-word ['swɛəwə:d], *n.* juron, gros mot, *m.*
sweat [swet], *n.* sueur, transpiration, *f.*—*v.t.* faire suer.—*v.i.* suer, transpirer.
sweater ['swetə], *n.* chandail, tricot, pullover (*vêtement*), *m.*
sweatiness ['swetinis], *n.* sueur, *f.*, état de sueur, *m.*
sweating ['swetiŋ], *a.* en sueur; tout en sueur. —*n.* moiteur; fatigue, *f.*
sweaty ['sweti], *a.* en sueur.
Swede [swi:d], *n.* Suédois (*personne*), *m.*
swede [swi:d], *n.* (*Bot.*) rutabaga, *m.*
Sweden [swi:dn]. la Suède, *f.*
Swedish ['swi:diʃ], *a.* suédois, de Suède,—*n.* suédois (*langue*), *m.*
sweep [swi:p], *v.t.* **irr.** balayer; ramoner (*cheminée*); draguer (*rivière*).—*v.i.* passer rapidement.—*n.* coup de balai; ramoneur (*de cheminées*), *m.*; étendue, portée (*distance*), courbe, *f.*; (*fig.*) sweepstake, *m.*; ***to make a clean sweep of***, faire table rase de.
sweeper ['swi:pə], *n.* balayeur; ramoneur (*de cheminées*), *m.*
sweeping ['swi:piŋ], *a.* rapide, irrésistible; (*fig.*) général.—*n.* balayage; ramonage (*de cheminées*), *m.*; (*pl.*) balayures, ordures, *f.pl.*
sweepstake ['swi:psteik], *n.* poule, *f.*; sweepstake, *m.*
sweet [swi:t], *a.* doux, sucré; parfumé (*odeur*); (*Mus.*) suave, mélodieux; frais (*poisson etc.*); (*fig.*) joli, charmant.—*n.* chose douce, *f.*; (*pl.*) entremets, sucreries, *f.pl.*; chéri, *m.*
sweetbread ['swi:tbred], *n.* ris de veau *ou* d'agneau, *m.*
sweeten [swi:tn], *v.t.* sucrer; purifier (*salle, l'air etc.*); (*fig.*) adoucir.
sweetener ['swi:tnə], *n.* adoucissant, *m.*
sweetening ['swi:tniŋ], *n.* adoucissement, *m.*
sweetheart ['swi:thɑ:t], *n.* amoureux; amant; bon ami, *m.*
sweetly ['swi:tli], *adv.* doucement, gentiment; mélodieusement.
sweetmeat ['swi:tmi:t], *n.* sucrerie, *f.*, bonbon, *m.*
sweetness ['swi:tnis], *n.* douceur; fraîcheur; mélodie, *f.*; (*fig.*) charme, *m.*
sweet-pea ['swi:t'pi:], *n.* pois de senteur, *m.*
sweet-shop ['swi:tʃɔp], *n.* confiserie, *f.*
sweet-william ['swi:t'wiljəm], *n.* œillet de poète, *m.*
swell [swel], *v.t.* **irr.** enfler, gonfler; aggraver; augmenter (*ajouter à*).—*v.i.* enfler, s'enfler, se gonfler; grossir, croître (*multiplier*); (*fig.*) bouffir (*d'orgueil, de colère etc.*).—*a.* (*colloq.*) à la mode, chic; épatant.—*n.* élévation, montée, *f.*; renflement (*de son*), *m.*; houle (*de mer*), *f.*; (*colloq.*) rupin, élégant, *m.*
swelling ['sweliŋ], *a.* grandissant (*qui augmente*).—*n.* enflure; bouffissure (*pathologique*), *f.*; gonflement (*protubérance*), *m.*, crue (*de rivière*), *f.*; soulèvement (*des vagues*); (*fig.*) mouvement, transport (*de colère etc.*), *m.*
swelter ['sweltə], *v.i.* étouffer de chaleur; ***it is sweltering hot***, il fait une chaleur étouffante.
swerve [swə:v], *v.i.* s'écarter, se détourner, faire un écart (*cheval*), faire une embardée (*voiture*).
swerving ['swə:viŋ], *n.* écart, *m.*, déviation, embardée (*de voiture*), *f.*

swift [swift], *a.* vite; rapide, prompt.—*n.* (*Orn.*) martinet, *m.*
swift-footed ['swift'futid], *a.* rapide à la course; au pied léger.
swiftly ['swiftli], *adv.* vite, rapidement.
swiftness ['swiftnis], *n.* rapidité, vitesse, *f.*
swig [swig], *v.t.*, *v.i.* (*pop.*) boire à longs traits. —*n.* long trait (*d'alcool*), *m.*
swill [swil], *v.t.* laver, rincer; boire avidement.—*v.i.* boire; (*colloq.*) s'enivrer.—*n.* lavure de vaisselle, lavure, *f.*; grand coup (*d'alcool*), *m.*
swim [swim], *v.t. irr.* traverser à la nage.—*v.i.* nager; flotter, surnager; (*fam.*) tourner (*la tête*); être inondé (de) (*être submergé*).—*n.* nage, *f.*; ***in the swim***, à la page.
swimmer ['swimə], *n.* nageur, *m.*
swimming ['swimiŋ], *n.* natation (*sport*); nage (*action*), *f.*; (*fam.*) étourdissement (*de tête*), *m.*; ***by swimming***, à la nage.
swimming-baths ['swimiŋbɑ:θz], **swimming-pool** ['swimiŋpu:l], *n.* piscine, *f.*
swimmingly ['swimiŋli], *adv.* à merveille.
swim-suit ['swimsju:t], *n.* maillot de bain, *m.*
swindle [swindl], *v.t.* escroquer.—*n.* escroquerie, *f.*
swindler ['swindlə], *n.* escroc, filou, *m.*
swindling ['swindliŋ], *n.* escroquerie, *f.*
swine [swain], *n.inv.* cochon, pourceau, porc; (*pop.*) salaud, *m.*
swing [swiŋ], *v.t. irr.* balancer; brandir (*une arme etc.*).—*v.i.* se balancer; osciller; pendiller, être suspendu.—*n.* oscillation (*mouvement*), *f.*; balancement, *m.*; balançoire (*siège*), *f.*; (*Mus.*) swing, *m.*; ***in full swing***, en pleine activité.
swing-door ['swiŋ'dɔ:], *n.* porte battante, *f.*
swinging ['swiŋiŋ], *n.* balancement, *m.*, oscillation, *f.*
swipe [swaip], *n.* taloche, *f.*—*v.t.* donner une taloche à; (*fam.*) chiper.
swirl [swə:l], *v.i.* tourbillonner.—*n.* remous, *m.*
swish [swiʃ], *v.t.* cingler, fouetter.—*v.i.* siffler, bruire.
Swiss [swis], *a.* helvétique, suisse.—*n.* Suisse (*personne*), *m.*, Suissesse, *f.*
switch [switʃ], *n.* badine, houssine, gaule; (*Rail.*) aiguille, *f.*; (*Elec.*) commutateur, interrupteur, *m.*—*v.t.* houspiller, cingler; (*Rail.*) aiguiller; changer (*de*); ***to switch off***, couper; ***to switch on***, ouvrir.—*v.i.* ***to switch off***, couper le courant; ***to switch on***, mettre le courant.
switchboard ['switʃbɔ:d], *n.* standard (téléphonique), *m.*; ***switchboard operator***, standardiste, *m.*, *f.*
Switzerland ['switsələnd]. la Suisse, *f.*
swivel [swivl], *n.* émerillon; pivot, *m.*—*v.i.* pivoter.
swoon [swu:n], *v.i.* s'évanouir.—*n.* évanouissement, *m.*
swoop [swu:p], *v.i.* fondre (*sur*).—*n.* ***at one (fell) swoop***, d'un seul coup (*fatal*).
sword [sɔ:d], *n.* épée, *f.*
sword-bearer ['sɔ:dbɛərə], *n.* porte-épée, *m.*
sword-fish ['sɔ:dfiʃ], *n.* espadon, *m.*
swordsman ['sɔ:dzmən], *n.* (*pl.* **-men** [men]) tireur, homme d'épée, *m.*
swordstick ['sɔ:dstik], *n.* canne à épée, *f.*
sworn [swɔ:n], *a.* juré; (*Law*) assermenté; acharné (*ennemi*).
swot [swɔt], *v.i.* (*Sch. slang*) piocher, bûcher.—*n.* bûcheur, *m.*
sycamore ['sikəmɔ:], *n.* sycomore, *m.*
sycophancy ['sikəfənsi], *n.* adulation, *f.*
sycophant ['sikəfənt], *n.* adulateur, *m.*
sycophantic [sikə'fæntik], *a.* adulateur.
syllabic [si'læbik], *a.* syllabique.
syllable ['siləbl], *n.* syllabe, *f.*
syllabus ['siləbəs], *n.* résumé; sommaire, programme (*surtout d'études scolaires*), *m.*
syllogism ['silədʒizm], *n.* syllogisme, *m.*
sylph [silf], *n.* sylphe, *m.*
sylvan ['silvən], *a.* sylvestre, des bois, champêtre, agreste.
symbol [simbl], *n.* symbole, *m.*
symbolic [sim'bɔlik], **symbolical** [sim'bɔlikl], *a.* symbolique.
symbolism ['simbəlizm], *n.* symbolisme, *m.*
symbolize ['simbəlaiz], *v.t.*, *v.i.* symboliser.
symmetrical [si'metrikl], *a.* symétrique.
symmetry ['simitri], *n.* symétrie, *f.*
sympathetic [simpə'θetik], *a.* sympathique (*nerf*); compatissant.
sympathize ['simpəθaiz], *v.i.* sympathiser (*avec*); compatir (*à*).
sympathizer ['simpəθaizə], *n.* sympathisant, *m.*
sympathy ['simpəθi], *n.* sympathie; compréhension, *f.*; condoléances, *f.pl.*
symphony ['simfəni], *n.* symphonie, *f.*
symposium [sim'pouzjəm], *n.* (*fig.*) recueil d'articles (*sur un seul sujet*), *m.*
symptom ['simptəm], *n.* symptôme, *m.*
symptomatic [simptə'mætik], *a.* symptomatique.
synagogue ['sinəgɔg], *n.* synagogue, *f.*
synchromesh ['siŋkromeʃ], *a.* and *n.* synchromesh, *m.*
synchronise ['siŋkrənaiz], *v.i.* synchroniser (*avec*).
syncopate ['siŋkəpeit], *v.t.* syncoper.
syndic ['sindik], *n.* syndic, *m.*
syndicate ['sindikit], *n.* syndicat, *m.*—['sindikeit], *v.t.* syndiquer.—*v.i.* se syndiquer.
synod ['sinəd], *n.* synode, *m.*
synonym ['sinənim], *n.* synonyme, *m.*
synonymous [si'nɔniməs], *a.* synonyme.
synopsis [si'nɔpsis], *n.* (*pl.* **synopses** [si'nɔpsi:z]) sommaire, *m.*
syntax ['sintæks], *n.* syntaxe, *f.*
synthesis ['sinθisis], *n.* (*pl.* **syntheses** ['sinθisi:z]) synthèse, *f.*
synthesize ['sinθisaiz], *v.t.* synthétiser.
synthetic [sin'θetik], *a.* synthétique.
synthetically [sin'θetikli], *adv.* synthétiquement.
Syria ['siriə]. la Syrie, *f.*
Syriac ['siriæk], *a.* syriaque.—*n.* syriaque (*langue*), *m.*
Syrian ['siriən], *a.* syrien.—*n.* syrien (*langue*); Syrien (*personne*), *m.*
syringe ['sirindʒ], *n.* seringue, *f.*—*v.t.* seringuer.
syrup ['sirəp], *n.* sirop, *m.*
syrupy ['sirəpi], *a.* sirupeux.
system ['sistəm], *n.* système, régime; réseau (*ferroviaire*), *m.*

systematic [sistə'mætik], *a.* systématique.
systematically [sistə'mætikli], *adv.* systématiquement.
systematize ['sistəmətaiz], *v.t.* systématiser.

T

T, t [ti:]. vingtième lettre de l'alphabet, *m.*; ***T-square***, té à dessin, *m.*
tab [tæb], *n.* étiquette; patte, *f.*, écusson, *m.*
tabby ['tæbi], *a.* tacheté, moucheté.—*n.* chat moucheté, rayé *ou* tigré, *m.*
tabernacle ['tæbənækl], *n.* tabernacle, *m.*
table [teibl], *n.* table, *f.*; ***to be seated at table***, être attablé; ***to clear the table***, desservir; ***to lay the table***, mettre le couvert; ***to sit down to table***, se mettre à table.—*v.t.* déposer (*un projet de loi*).
table-cloth ['teiblklɔθ], *n.* nappe, *f.*
table-linen ['teibllinin], *n.* linge de table, *m.*
tablespoon ['teiblspu:n], *n.* cuiller à soupe, *f.*
tablespoonful ['teiblspu:nful], *n.* grande cuillerée, *f.*
tablet ['tæblit], *n.* tablette, *f.*; (*Med.*) comprimé, *m.*
taboo [tə'bu:], *a.* and *n.* tabou, *m.*
tabulate ['tæbjuleit], *v.t.* cataloguer.
tacit ['tæsit], *a.* tacite, implicite.
tacitly ['tæsitli], *adv.* tacitement, implicitement.
taciturn ['tæsitə:n], *a.* taciturne.
Tacitus ['tæsitəs]. (*L. Lit.*) Tacite, *m.*
tack [tæk], *n.* petit clou, *m.*, broquette; (*Naut.*) amure, *f.*—*v.t.* clouer; (*Needlework*) bâtir, faufiler.—*v.i.* (*Naut.*) virer vent devant.
tackiness ['tækinis], *n.* viscosité, *f.*
tacking ['tækiŋ], *n.* cloutage, *m.*; (*Needlework*) faufilure, *f.*; (*Naut.*) virement de bord, louvoyage, *m.*
tackle [tækl], *n.* attirail; (*Naut.*) palan; (*Spt.*) plaquage, *m.*; (*fig.*) ustensiles, *m.pl.*; ***fishing-tackle***, articles de pêche, *m.pl.*—*v.t.* empoigner; (*Ftb.*) plaquer; (*fig.*) attaquer (*travail etc.*).
tacky ['tæki], *a.* collant, visqueux, gluant.
tact [tækt], *n.* toucher; (*fig.*) tact, savoir-faire, *m.*
tactful ['tæktful], *a.* plein de tact.
tactical ['tæktikl], *a.* tactique.
tactician [tæk'tiʃən], *n.* tacticien, *m.*
tactics ['tæktiks], *n.pl.* tactique, *f.*
tactile ['tæktail], *a.* tactile.
tactless ['tæktlis], *a.* sans tact, sans savoir-faire.
tadpole ['tædpoul], *n.* têtard, *m.*
taffeta ['tæfitə], *n.* taffetas, *m.*
taffrail ['tæfreil], *n.* couronnement (*de la poupe*), *m.*
tag [tæg], *n.* ferret, fer, bout ferré, *m.*; étiquette (*fiche*), *f.*; dicton, *m.*—*v.t.* ferrer (*cordon*); (*fig.*) coudre (*à*).
tail [teil], *n.* queue; (*fig.*) extrémité, *f.*; bout; pan (*d'habit*), *m.*; pile (*de pièce de monnaie*), *f.*; empennage (*d'avion*), *m.*—*v.t.* couper la queue (*d'un animal*); ôter les queues (*d*… *fruits*); (*fam.*) filer (*criminels etc.*).
tail-coat ['teilkout], *n.* habit, *m.*
tailed [teild], *a.* à queue.
tailless ['teillis], *a.* sans queue, anoure.
tail-light ['teillait], *n.* feu arrière, *m.*
tailor ['teilə], *n.* tailleur, *m.*
tailor-made ['teilə'meid], *a.* and *n.* tailleu… *m.*
tail-plane ['teilplein], *n.* (*Av.*) stabilisateur, *n*…
taint [teint], *v.t.* corrompre, gâter.—*v.i.* s… corrompre; se gâter (*viande*).—*n.* souillur… corruption; tache (*du péché*), *f.*
take [teik], *v.t. irr.* prendre; mener (*que… qu'un*); conduire (*personne en voiture*… porter (*chose*); emmener (*quelqu'un*); enleve… (*voler*); soustraire (*retrancher*); saisir; ac… cepter; (*fig.*) supposer; profiter de (*un… occasion*); contenir (*avoir de la place pour*… faire (*une promenade etc.*); avoir (*vengean… etc.*); retenir (*chambre etc.*); suivre (*un… route etc.*); mettre (*temps*); ***to take advan… tage of***, profiter de; ***to take away***, em… mener (*personne*), emporter (*choses*), ôte… (*retirer*); desservir (*le couvert etc.*); dérobe… (*voler*); ***to take back***, reprendre, rem… porter; ***to take down***, descendre; rabattr… (*humilier*); démolir (*maison*); prendre not… de (*inscrire*); ***to take heed***, prendre gard… (*à*); ***to take in***, faire entrer; comprendr… (*consister en*); recevoir, recevoir chez s… (*loger*); tromper, duper; faire sa provision d… (*vivres etc.*); ***to take off***, enlever, ôte… retirer (*vêtement*); caricaturer (*imiter*); ***t… take out***, faire sortir, sortir (*chose*); pro… mener (*personne*); arracher (*dents*); ôte… enlever (*taches etc.*); ***to take over***, s… charger de, prendre la succession d… (*affaires*); ***to take up***, monter, faire monte… soulever (*lever*); ramasser (*relever*); com… mencer, entamer, aborder (*des études etc.*… occuper (*temps*).—*v.i.* réussir (*avoir d… succès*); prendre (*feu etc.*); ***to take after*** ressembler à; (*Av.*) ***to take off***, décoller (*fam.*) ***to take on***, se lamenter, s'affliger; ***t… take up with***, s'associer à.—*n.* prise pêche, quantité (*de poissons*); (*Cine.*) prise d… vue, *f.*
take-in ['teikin], *n.* duperie, attrape, *f.*
take-off ['teikɔ:f], *n.* caricature, charge, *f.* (*Av.*) décollage, *m.*
take-over ['teikouvə], *n.* (*Fin.*) rachat (*d'entre… prise*), *m.*; ***take-over bid***, offre de rachat, *f*
taking ['teikiŋ], *a.* attrayant, séduisant (*colloq.*) contagieux (*maladie*).—*n.* prise arrestation, *f.*; (*pl.*) recettes (*argent*), *f.pl.*
talc [tælk], *n.* talc, *m.*
talcum powder ['tælkəm'paudə], *n.* talc, *m.*
tale [teil], *n.* conte, récit, *m.*; histoire, *f.*
talent ['tælənt], *n.* talent, *m.*
talented ['tæləntid], *a.* de talent, habile, bien doué.
talisman ['tælizmən], *n.* talisman, *m.*
talk [tɔ:k], *v.t.* parler, dire; ***to talk over*** cajoler (*quelqu'un*); discuter (*quelque chose*). —*v.i.* parler (*de*); converser, causer; bavarder, jaser (*babiller*); ***to talk at***, haranguer.—*n.* entretien, *m.*, propos, *m.pl.*, conversation; causerie (*intime*), *f.*; bavardage, bruit (*racontar*), *m.*; ***small talk***, banalités, *f.pl.*
talkative ['tɔ:kətiv], *a.* causeur, bavard.

alker ['tɔ:kə], *n.* causeur, parleur, *m.*
alking ['tɔ:kiŋ], *a.* causeur, bavard.—*n.* conversation, causerie, *f.*
all [tɔ:l], *a.* grand (*personne*); haut (*chose*).
allboy ['tɔ:lbɔi], *n.* chiffonnier, *m.*; (haute) commode-secrétaire, *f.*
allness ['tɔ:lnis], *n.* grande taille, hauteur, *f.*
allow ['tælou], *n.* suif, *m.*
allow-candle ['tælou'kændl], *n.* chandelle, *f.*
ally ['tæli], *n.* taille; entaille, marque; étiquette (*à bagages*), *f.*—*v.i.* s'accorder; ***to tally with***, s'accorder avec, correspondre à.
ally-ho! [tæli'hou], *int.* (*Hunt.*) taïaut!
Talmud ['tælmʌd], *n.* talmud, *m.*
alon ['tælən], *n.* serre, griffe, *f.*
ambourine [tæmbə'ri:n], *n.* tambour de basque, *m.*
ame [teim], *a.* apprivoisé; domestique; (*fig.*) insipide.—*v.t.* apprivoiser; dompter (*dominer*).
amely ['teimli], *adv.* avec soumission; sans cœur.
ameness ['teimnis], *n.* apprivoisement, *m.*, domesticité; soumission; (*fig.*) faiblesse (*de style etc.*), *f.*
amer ['teimə], *n.* dompteur (*de bête sauvage*) *m.*
aming ['teimiŋ], *n.* apprivoisement, *m.*
amp [tæmp], *v.t.* bourrer, tamponner.
amper ['tæmpə], *v.i.* ***to tamper with***, se mêler (*de*); expérimenter (*avec*); jouer avec; fausser (*serrure etc.*).
ampering ['tæmpəriŋ], *n.* menées secrètes, *f.pl.*
an [tæn], *n.* tan; tanné (*couleur*); hâle (*de la peau*), *m.*—*v.t.* tanner; bronzer (*la peau*).
andem ['tændəm], *n.* tandem (*bicyclette*), *m.*
ang [tæŋ], *n.* goût, *m.*, saveur, *f.*
angent ['tændʒənt], *n.* tangente, *f.*
angerine [tændʒə'ri:n], *n.* mandarine, *f.*
angible ['tændʒibl], *a.* tangible, palpable.
Tangier(s) [tæn'dʒiə(z)]. Tanger, *m.*
angle [tæŋgl], *n.* enchevêtrement, *m.*—*v.t.* embrouiller, enchevêtrer.
angled [tæŋgld], *a.* embrouillé.
ango ['tæŋgou], *n.* tango, *m.*
ank [tæŋk], *n.* réservoir; (*Mil.*) char (d'assaut), *m.*
ankard ['tæŋkəd], *n.* chope, *f.*
anker ['tæŋkə], *n.* bateau citerne, *m.*
anner ['tænə], *n.* tanneur, *m.*
annery ['tænəri], *n.* tannerie, *f.*
anning ['tæniŋ], *n.* tannage, *m.*; (*fam.*) rossée, *f.*
antalize ['tæntəlaiz], *v.t.* tantaliser, tourmenter.
antalizing ['tæntəlaiziŋ], *a.* tentant, torturant.
antamount ['tæntəmaunt], *a.* équivalent (*à*).
antrum ['tæntrəm], *n.* mauvaise humeur, *f.*
Tanzania [tænzə'ni:ə]. la Tanzanie, *f.*
ap (1) [tæp], *n.* robinet (*bain*); comptoir (*bar*), *m.*; cannelle (*de baril*), *f.*; taraud (*outil*), *m.*; ***on tap***, en perce.—*v.t.* tirer (*liquide*); mettre en perce (*baril*); inciser (*arbre*); tarauder (*vis etc.*); (*Surg.*) faire la ponction à.
ap (2) [tæp], *n.* tape, *f.*, petit coup (*à la porte etc.*), *m.*—*v.t.* taper, frapper doucement.—*v.i.* taper, frapper.
ape [teip], *n.* ruban (de fil), *m.*; ganse (*sur habit*); bande (magnétique), *f.*; ***red tape***, (*fig.*) routine administrative, *f.*
tape-measure ['teipmeʒə], *n.* mètre ruban, *m.*
taper ['teipə], *n.* bougie effilée, *f.*; (*Eccles.*) cierge, *m.*
tape-recorder ['teipriko:də], *n.* magnétophone, *m.*
tape-recording ['teipriko:diŋ], *n.* enregistrement magnétique, *m.*
tapering ['teipəriŋ], *a.* effilé.
tapestry ['tæpistri], *n.* tapisserie, *f.*
tape-worm ['teipwə:m], *n.* ver solitaire, *m.*
tapioca [tæpi'oukə], *n.* tapioca, *m.*
tapir ['teipiə], *n.* tapir, *m.*
tappet ['tæpit], *n.* taquet (*de soupape*), *m.*
tapping (1) ['tæpiŋ], *n.* taraudage (*de vis*), *m.*; mise en perce (*de baril*); incision (*d'arbre*); (*Surg.*) ponction, *f.*
tapping (2) ['tæpiŋ], *n.* tapotement, *m.*
tar [tɑ:], *n.* goudron; loup de mer (*matelot*), *m.* —*v.t.* goudronner.
tarantella [tærən'telə], *n.* tarentelle (*danse*), *f.*
tarantula [tə'ræntjulə], *n.* tarentule, *f.*
tardily ['tɑ:dili], *adv.* tardivement, lentement.
tardiness ['tɑ:dinis], *n.* lenteur; tardiveté (*de fruit*), *f.*
tardy ['tɑ:di], *a.* lent; en retard, tardif.
tare (1) [tɛə], *n.* tare (*poids*), *f.*
tare (2) [tɛə], *n.* (*Script.*) ivraie; (*pl.*) (*Agric.*) vesce, *f.*
target ['tɑ:git], *n.* cible, *f.*; but, objectif, *m.*
tariff ['tærif], *n.* tarif, *m.*
tarmac ['tɑ:mæk], *n.* macadam, *m.*; (*Av.*) piste d'envol, *f.*—*v.t.* goudronner.
tarn [tɑ:n], *n.* petit lac (de montagne), *m.*
tarnish ['tɑ:niʃ], *v.t.* ternir; (*fig.*) souiller, flétrir.—*v.i.* se ternir.
tarpaulin [tɑ:'pɔ:lin], *n.* (*Naut.*) prélart, *m.*, bâche, toile goudronnée, *f.*
tarry (1) ['tɑ:ri], *a.* goudronneux, bitumeux.
tarry (2) ['tæri], *v.i.* rester, tarder.
tart (1) [tɑ:t], *n.* tarte, tourte, *f.*
tart (2) [tɑ:t], *a.* acide, âcre; (*fig.*) aigre.
tartan ['tɑ:tən], *n.* tartan, *m.*
tartar ['tɑ:tə], *n.* (*Chem.*) tartre, *m.*
tartaric [tɑ:'tærik], *a.* tartrique.
tartish ['tɑ:tiʃ], *a.* aigrelet.
tartly ['tɑ:tli], *adv.* avec aigreur; (*fig.*) vertement, sévèrement.
tartness ['tɑ:tnis], *n.* acidité; (*fig.*) aigreur, *f.*
task [tɑ:sk], *n.* tâche, *f.*; devoir (*leçon*); pensum (*punition*), *m.*; ***to take to task***, réprimander, semoncer.
taskmaster ['tɑ:skmɑ:stə], *n.* chef de corvée, *m.*
Tasmania [tæz'meinjə]. la Tasmanie, *f.*
Tasmanian [tæz'meinjən], *a.* tasmanien.—*n.* Tasmanien (*personne*), *m.*
tassel [tæsl], *n.* gland, *m.*
taste [teist], *v.t.* goûter; (*fig.*) savourer, éprouver.—*v.i.* goûter (*de*); avoir un goût (*de*).—*n.* goût; soupçon (*trace*), *m.*
tasteful ['teistful], *a.* de bon goût.
tastefully ['teistfuli], *adv.* avec goût.
tasteless ['teistlis], *a.* fade, insipide.
tastelessly ['teistlisli], *adv.* insipidement, fadement.
taster ['teistə], *n.* dégustateur, *m.*
tasting ['teistiŋ], *n.* dégustation, *f.*
tasty ['teisti], *a.* (*colloq.*) de bon goût; savoureux.

tatter ['tætə], *n.* haillon, lambeau, *m.*, guenille, *f.*
tattered ['tætəd], *a.* déguenillé, en haillons (*personne*); en lambeaux, tout déchiré (*vêtements etc.*).
tatting ['tætiŋ], *n.* frivolité (*dentelle*), *f.*
tattle [tætl], *n.* babil, caquet, *m.*—*v.i.* bavarder.
tattler ['tætlə], *n.* babillard, bavard, *m.*
tattling ['tætliŋ], *a.* babillard, bavard.
tattoo [tə'tu:], *v.t.* tatouer.—*n.* tatouage, *m.*; (*Mil.*) fête militaire, *f.*
taunt [[tɔ:nt], *n.* injure, *f.*, reproche amer, *m.* —*v.t.* tancer, reprocher à, injurier.
tauntingly ['tɔ:ntiŋli], *adv.* injurieusement.
Taurus ['tɔ:rəs]. (*Astron.*) le Taureau, *m.*
taut [tɔ:t], *a.* raide, tendu; enflé (*voile*).
tautology [tɔ:'tɔlədʒi], *n.* tautologie, *f.*
tavern ['tævən], *n.* taverne, *f.*; cabaret, *m.*
tawdry ['tɔ:dri], *a.* criard, de mauvais goût, prétentieux.
tawny ['tɔ:ni], *a.* fauve.
tawse [tɔ:z], *n.* martinet, *m.*
tax [tæks], *n.* impôt, *m.*, taxe; (*fig.*) contribution, *f.*; ***income-tax***, impôt sur le revenu; ***purchase tax***, taxe de luxe; ***tax evasion***, fraude fiscale, *f.*; ***surtax***, surtaxe, *f.*—*v.t.* imposer, taxer; (*fig.*) accuser (*de*).
taxable ['tæksəbl], *a.* imposable.
taxation [tæk'seiʃən], *n.* taxation, *f.*
tax-free ['tæks'fri:], *a.* exempt d'impôts.
taxi ['tæksi], *n.* taxi, *m.*
tax-payer ['tækspeiə], *n.* contribuable, *m.*, *f.*
tea [ti:], *n.* thé, *m.*; tisane (*infusion*), *f.*; goûter (*repas*), *m.*
tea-caddy ['ti:kædi], *n.* boîte à thé, *f.*
tea-cake ['ti:keik], *n.* brioche, *f.*
teach [ti:tʃ], *v.t. irr.* enseigner, instruire; apprendre (*à*).—*v.i.* enseigner, professer.
teachable ['ti:tʃəbl], *a.* disposé à apprendre, docile; enseignable (*chose*).
teacher ['ti:tʃə], *n.* maître, instituteur; professeur (*de lycée*), *m.*
tea-chest ['ti:tʃest], *n.* caisse à thé, *f.*
teaching ['ti:tʃiŋ], *n.* enseignement, *m.*
tea-cup ['ti:kʌp], *n.* tasse à thé, *f.*
teak [ti:k], *n.* (*Bot.*) teck, tek, *m.*
teal [ti:l], *n.* (*Orn.*) sarcelle, *f.*
team [ti:m], *n.* attelage, *m.*, (*Spt.*) équipe, *f.*
teapot ['ti:pɔt], *n.* théière, *f.*
tear (1) [tiə], *n.* larme, *f.*, pleur, *m.*
tear (2) [tɛə], *v.t. irr.* déchirer; (*fig.*) arracher; ***to tear asunder***, déchirer en deux.—*v.i.* se déchirer.—*n.* déchirure, *f.*; ***wear and tear***, usure, *f.*
tear-drop ['tiədrɔp], *n.* larme, *f.*
tearful ['tiəful], *a.* tout en larmes.
tearfully ['tiəfuli], *adv.* les larmes aux yeux.
tearing ['tɛəriŋ], *n.* déchirement, *m.*
tease [ti:z], *v.t.* taquiner, tourmenter; carder (*laine*).—*n.* taquin, *m.*
tea-service ['ti:sə:vis], *n.* service à thé, *m.*
teasing ['ti:ziŋ], *a.* taquin.—*n.* taquinerie, *f.*
teaspoon ['ti:spu:n], *n.* cuiller à thé, *f.*
teaspoonful ['ti:spu:nful], *n.* petite cuillerée, *f.*
tea-strainer ['ti:streinə], *n.* passe-thé, *m.*
teat [ti:t], *n.* mamelon, tétin, *m.*; tette, *f.*
tea-table ['ti:teibl], *n.* table à thé, *f.*
tea-time ['ti:taim], *n.* l'heure du thé, *f.*
tea-tray ['ti:trei], *n.* plateau à thé, *m.*
tea-urn ['ti:ə:n], *n.* fontaine à thé, *f.*

technical ['teknikl], *a.* technique, de l'ar
technical school, école professionnelle,
technicality [tekni'kæliti], *n.* caractère tec nique; terme technique (*mot*), *m.*; (*fig* formalité, *f.*
technically ['teknikli], *adv.* techniquement
technician [tek'niʃən], *n.* technicien, *m.*
technique [tek'ni:k], *n.* technique, *f.*
technologist [tek'nɔlədʒist], *n.* technologu *m.*, *f.*
technology [tek'nolədʒi], *n.* technologie, *f.*
teddy ['tedi], *n.* ***teddy bear***, ours en peluch *m.*
tedious ['ti:diəs], *a.* ennuyeux, fatigant.
tedium ['ti:diəm], *n.* ennui, *m.*
tee [ti:], *n.* dé (*au golf*), *m.*
teem [ti:m], *v.i.* être fécond (*en*); ***to tee with***, abonder en.
teeming ['ti:miŋ], *a.* fécond, fertile, surabor dant (*de*).
teenager ['ti:neidʒə], *n.* adolescent, *m.*
teens [ti:nz], *n.pl.* l'âge de treize à dix-neu ans, *m.*; ***to be in one's teens***, n'avoir pa vingt ans.
teeth [TOOTH].
teethe [ti:ð], *v.i.* faire ses dents.
teething ['ti:ðiŋ], *n.* dentition, *f.*
teetotal [ti:'toutl], *a.* de tempérance.
teetotal(l)er [ti:'toutlə], *n.* buveur d'eau, *m.*
teetotalism [ti:'toutəlizm], *n.* abstinence d boissons alcooliques, *f.*
telegram ['teligræm], *n.* télégramme, *m* dépêche, *f.*
telegraph ['teligrɑ:f, -græf], *n.* télégraphe *m.*; ***telegraph office***, bureau télégraphi que, *m.*—*v.t.*, *v.i.* télégraphier.
telegraphic [teli'græfik], *a.* télégraphique.
telegraphist [ti'legrəfist], *n.* télégraphiste, *m* *f.*
telegraph-post ['teligrɑ:fpoust], **telegraph pole** ['teligrɑ:fpoul], *n.* poteau télégraphi que, *m.*
telegraph-wire ['teligrɑ:fwaiə], *n.* fil télé graphique, *m.*
telegraphy [ti'legrəfi], *n.* télégraphie, *f.* ***wireless telegraphy***, télégraphie sans fil
telepathy [ti'lepəθi], *n.* télépathie, *f.*
telephone ['telifoun], *n.* téléphone, *m.*; ***tele phone exchange***, central téléphonique, *m* —*v.t.*, *v.i.* téléphoner.
telephonic [teli'fɔnik], *a.* téléphonique.
telephonist [ti'lefənist], *n.* téléphoniste, *m.* *f.*
teleprinter ['teliprintə], *n.* téléimprimeur télétype, *m.*
telescope ['teliskoup], *n.* (*Astron.*) télescope *m.*; longue vue, *f.*
telescopic [teli'skɔpik], *a.* télescopique.
televiewer ['telivju:ə], *n.* téléspectateur, *m.*
televise ['telivaiz], *v.t.* téléviser.
television [teli'viʒən], *n.* télévision, *f.*; ***tele vision-set***, téléviseur, appareil de télé vision, *m.*
tell [tel], *v.t. irr.* dire; faire part de; raconte (*réciter*); montrer, indiquer (*expliquer*) révéler, dévoiler; énumérer (*compter*), avouer (*confesser*); reconnaître (*à*); savoi (*deviner*).—*v.i.* dire; faire son effet, porte (*influer*); juger (*interpréter*).
teller ['telə], *n.* diseur; raconteur; (*Am.*, *Sc.* caissier (*de banque*); (*Parl.*) scrutateur, *m.*

elling ['teliŋ], *a.* qui porte; expressif.—*n.* récit, *m.*, narration, *f.*
ell-tale ['telteil], *a.* rapporteur; (*fig.*) révélateur.—*n.* rapporteur, *m.*
emerity [ti'meriti], *n.* témérité, *f.*
emper ['tempə], *n.* tempérament, *m.*, disposition; humeur; colère (*rage*), *f.*; sang-froid (*équanimité*), *m.*; trempe (*d'acier etc.*), *f.*; ***to lose one's temper***, se mettre en colère.—*v.t.* tempérer (*de*); détremper (*couleurs*); tremper (*acier etc.*); (*fig.*) adoucir.
emperament ['tempərəmənt], *n.* tempérament, *m.*
emperamental [tempərə'mentl], *a.* capricieux, instable.
emperance ['tempərəns], *n.* tempérance, *f.*
emperate ['tempərit], *a.* modéré; tempéré (*climat*).
emperature ['tempritʃə], *n.* température, *f.*
empest ['tempist], *n.* tempête, *f.*
empestuous [tem'pestjuəs], *a.* orageux, tempétueux.
emplar ['templə], *n.* templier, *m.*
emple [templ], *n.* temple, *m.*; (*Anat.*) tempe, *f.*
emplet ['templit], *n.* patron, gabarit, *m.*
emporal ['tempərəl], *a.* temporel; (*Anat.*) temporal.
emporarily ['tempərərili], *adv.* temporairement.
emporary ['tempərəri], *a.* temporaire, provisoire.
emporization [tempərai'zeiʃən], *n.* temporisation, *f.*
emporize ['tempəraiz], *v.i.* temporiser.
empt [tempt], *v.t.* tenter (*de*); pousser (*à*).
emptation [temp'teiʃən], *n.* tentation, *f.*
empter ['temptə], *n.* tentateur, *m.*
empting ['temptiŋ], *a.* tentant, séduisant, attrayant; appétissant (*nourriture*).
emptress ['temptris], *n.* tentatrice, *f.*
en [ten], *a.* dix.—*n.* dix, *m.*; une dizaine (*dix environ*), *f.*
enable ['tenəbl], *a.* soutenable.
enacious [ti'neiʃəs], *a.* tenace.
enaciously [ti'neiʃəsli], *adv.* d'une manière tenace, obstinément.
enacity [ti'næsiti], *n.* ténacité, *f.*
enancy ['tenənsi], *n.* location, *f.*
enant ['tenənt], *n.* locataire, *m.*, *f.*
ench [tentʃ], *n.* (*Ichth.*) tanche, *f.*
end [tend], *v.t.* garder, soigner.—*v.i.* tendre (*à*); se diriger vers.
endency ['tendənsi], *n.* tendance, disposition, *f.*
ender (1) ['tendə], *n.* offre (*proposition*); (*Comm.*) soumission, *f.*; ***legal tender***, monnaie légale, *f.*—*v.t.* offrir.—*v.i.* ***to tender for***, soumissionner pour.
ender (2) ['tendə], *n.* (*Naut.*) allège, *f.*; (*Rail.*) tender, *m.*
ender (3) ['tendə], *a.* tendre; sensible (*vulnérable*).
ender-hearted ['tendə'hɑːtid], *a.* sensible, au cœur tendre.
enderly ['tendəli], *adv.* tendrement.
enderness ['tendənis], *n.* tendresse; sensibilité (*vulnérabilité*); sollicitude, *f.*
endon ['tendən], *n.* tendon, *m.*
endril ['tendril], *n.* (*Bot.*) vrille, *f.*
enement ['tenimənt], *n.* habitation, maison, *f.*
tenet ['tiːnit, 'tenit], *n.* principe, *m.*
tenfold ['tenfould], *a.* décuple.—*adv.* dix fois.
tennis ['tenis], *n.* tennis; *jeu de paume, *m.*
tennis-court ['teniskɔːt], *n.* court de tennis, tennis; *jeu de paume, *m.*
tennis-racket ['tenisrækit], *n.* raquette de tennis, *f.*
tenor ['tenə], *n.* (*Mus.*) ténor, *m.*
tense (1) [tens], *n.* (*Gram.*) temps, *m.*
tense (2) [tens], *a.* tendu, raide.
tensile ['tensail], *a.* ductile (*métal*).
tension ['tenʃən], *n.* tension, *f.*
tent [tent], *n.* tente, *f.*; ***bell-tent***, tente conique.
tentacle ['tentəkl], *n.* tentacule, *m.*
tentative ['tentətiv], *a.* tentatif, d'essai.
tentatively ['tentətivli], *adv.* en guise d'essai.
tenter-hook ['tentəhuk], *n.* clou à crochet, *m.*; ***to be on tenter-hooks***, être sur des épines.
tenth [tenθ], *a.* dixième; dix (*du mois, roi etc.*). —*n.* dixième (*fraction*), *m.*; (*Eccles.*) dîme, *f.*
tenuous ['tenjuəs], *a.* délié, mince, ténu.
tenure ['tenjuə], *n.* tenure, *f.*
tepid ['tepid], *a.* tiède.
tercentenary [təːsen'tiːnəri], *a.* de trois siècles.—*n.* tricentenaire, *m.*
term [təːm], *n.* terme, *m.*; limite; (*Law*) session, *f.*; (*Sch.*) trimestre, *m.*; (*pl.*) conditions, *f.pl.*; prix, *m.*—*v.t.* nommer, appeler.
termagant ['təːməgənt], *n.* mégère, *f.*
terminable ['təːminəbl], *a.* terminable.
terminal ['təːminl], *a.* terminal.—*n.* (*Elec.*) borne, *f.*; ***air terminal***, gare aérienne, aérogare, *f.*
terminate ['təːmineit], *v.t.* terminer, finir.
termination [təːmi'neiʃən], *n.* fin, terminaison, *f.*
terminology [təːmi'nɔlədʒi], *n.* terminologie, *f.*
terminus ['təːminəs], *n.* terminus (*gare*), *m.*; tête de ligne, *f.*
tern [təːn], *n.* sterne, *m.*, hirondelle de mer, *f.*
ternary ['təːnəri], *a.* ternaire.
terrace ['teris], *n.* terrasse, *f.*
terraced ['terist], *a.* étagé en terrasse.
terra-cotta ['terə'kɔtə], *n.* terre cuite, *f.*
terra firma ['terə'fəːmə], *n.* terre ferme, *f.*
terrestrial [tə'restriəl], *a.* terrestre.
terrible ['teribl], *a.* terrible.
terribly ['teribli], *adv.* terriblement; (*colloq.*) diablement.
terrier ['teriə], *n.* terrier, chien terrier, *m.*
terrific [tə'rifik], *a.* terrible, épouvantable; (*fam.*) formidable.
terrify ['terifai], *v.t.* terrifier.
territorial [teri'tɔːriəl], *a.* territorial.
territory ['teritəri], *n.* territoire, *m.*
terror ['terə], *n.* terreur, *f.*; effroi, *m.*
terrorism ['terərizm], *n.* terrorisme, *m.*
terrorist ['terərist], *n.* terroriste, *m.*, *f.*
terrorize ['terəraiz], *v.t.* terroriser.
terse [təːs], *a.* net, concis; bien tourné, élégant.
tersely ['təːsli], *adv.* nettement; d'une manière concise.
terseness ['təːsnis], *n.* netteté, *f.*
tertian ['təːʃən], *a.* tierce.
tertiary ['təːʃəri], *a.* tertiaire.
tessellated [tesə'leitid], *a.* tessellé.

test [test], *n.* épreuve, *f.*; test; essai, *m.*; pierre de touche, *f.*—*v.t.* éprouver, mettre à l'épreuve, tester; (*Metal.*) coupeller.
testament ['testəmənt], *n.* testament, *m.*
testator [tes'teitə], *n.* testateur, *m.*
testicle ['testikl], *n.* testicule, *m.*
testify ['testifai], *v.t.* témoigner; (*Law*) déposer (*de*).—*v.i.* (*Law*) déposer.
testimonial [testi'mouniəl], *n.* témoignage; certificat, témoignage d'estime, *m.*
testimony ['testiməni], *n.* témoignage, *m.*
testiness ['testinis], *n.* humeur, irritabilité, *f.*
testing ['testiŋ], *n.* épreuve, *f.*, essai, *m.*
test-tube ['testtju:b], *n.* éprouvette, *f.*
testy ['testi], *a.* irritable, susceptible.
tetanus ['tetənəs], *n.* tétanos, *m.*
tether ['teðə], *n.* longe, *f.*; ***to be at the end of one's tether***, être à bout de forces.—*v.t.* mettre à l'attache, attacher (*à*).
tetrahedron [tetrə'hi:drən], *n.* tétraèdre, *m.*
tetrarch ['tetrɑ:k], *n.* tétrarque, *m.*
Teuton ['tju:tən], *a.* teuton.—*n.* Teuton (*personne*), *m.*
Teutonic [tju:'tɔnik], *a.* teutonique.
text [tekst], *n.* texte, *m.*
text-book ['tekstbuk], *n.* manuel, livre de classe, *m.*
textile ['tekstail], *a.* textile.—*n.* tissu, textile, *m.*, étoffe, *f.*
textual ['tekstjuəl], *a.* textuel.
texture ['tekstʃə], *n.* tissu, *m.*; contexture (*d'écrits etc.*), *f.*
Thai [tai], *a.* thaïlandais.—*n.* thaïlandais (*langue*); Thaïlandais (*personne*), *m.*
Thailand ['tailænd]. la Thaïlande, *f.*, le Siam, *m.*
Thames [temz], **the**. la Tamise, *f.*
than [ðæn], *conj.* que; de (*between* more *or* less *and a number*); que de (*before an infinitive*).
thank [θæŋk], *v.t.* remercier (*de*); rendre grâces à.
thankful ['θæŋkful], *a.* reconnaissant (*de*).
thankfully ['θæŋkfuli], *adv.* avec reconnaissance.
thankfulness ['θæŋkfulnis], *n.* reconnaissance, *f.*
thankless ['θæŋklis], *a.* ingrat; oublié (*non reconnu*).
thanklessness ['θæŋklisnis], *n.* ingratitude, *f.*
thank-offering ['θæŋkɔfəriŋ], *n.* sacrifice d'actions de grâces, *m.*
thanks [θæŋks], *n.pl.* remercîments, remerciements, *m.pl.*, grâces, *f.pl.*
thanksgiving ['θæŋksgiviŋ], *n.* actions de grâces, *f.pl.*
that [ðæt], *dem.a.* (*pl.* **those** [ðouz]) ce, cet, *m.*, cette, *f.*; (*emphatically*) ce . . . -là, cet . . . -là, *m.*, cette . . . -là, *f.*—*dem.pron.* celui-là, *m.*, celle-là (*that one*), *f.*; cela, (*colloq.*) ça, *m.*—*rel.pron.* qui, que, lequel, *m.*, laquelle, *f.*, lesquels, *m.pl.*, lesquelles, *f.pl.*—*conj.* que.
thatch [θætʃ], *n.* chaume, *m.*—*v.t.* couvrir de chaume.
thatcher ['θætʃə], *n.* couvreur en chaume, *m.*
thaw [θɔ:], *n.* dégel, *m.*—*v.t.* dégeler; (*fig.*) fondre, attendrir.—*v.i.* dégeler, se dégeler; (*fig.*) fondre, s'attendrir.
the [ðə], *before vowel* [ði], *def. art.* le, l', *m.*, la, l', *f.*, les, *pl.*
theatre ['θiətə], *n.* théâtre, *m.*
theatrical [θi:'ætrikl], *a.* de théâtre, théâtral.
theatricals [θi:'ætriklz], *n.pl.* spectacle, *m.*

***thee** [ði:], *pron.* (*also Poet.*) toi; te.
theft [θeft], *n.* vol, *m.*; ***petty theft***, larcin, *m*
their [ðɛə], *poss.a.* leur, leurs, *pl.*
theirs [ðɛəz], *poss.pron.* le leur, *m.*, la leur, les leurs, *pl.*, à eux, *m.pl.*, à elles, *f.pl.*
theism ['θi:izm], *n.* théisme, *m.*
theist ['θi:ist], *n.* théiste, *m.*, *f.*
theistic [θi:'istik], *a.* théiste.
them [ðem], *pron.* eux, *m.pl.*, elles, *f.pl.*; (*ob*j.) les; (*dat.*) leur, *pl.*
theme [θi:m], *n.* thème, sujet, *m.*
theme-song ['θi:msɔŋ], *n.* chanson leit-mot*i*f, *f.*
themselves [ðem'selvz], *pron.* eux-mêmes, *m.pl.*, elles-mêmes, *f.pl.*; (*reflexive*) se, *pl.*
then [ðen], *adv.* alors; ensuite, puis (*après*); dans ce cas (*puisqu'il en est ainsi*); donc; ***but then***, par contre; ***by then***, alors, déjà; ***now and then***, de temps en temps.—*con*j. donc.
thence [ðens], *adv.* de là, en; dès lors.
thenceforth [ðens'fɔ:θ], **thenceforwar**d [ðens'fɔ:wəd], *adv.* dès lors, depuis lors, à partir de ce moment-là.
theocracy [θi:'ɔkrəsi], *n.* théocratie, *f.*
theocratic [θi:ə'krætik], *a.* théocratique.
theodolite [θi:'ɔdəlait], *n.* théodolite, *m.*
theologian [θi:ə'loudʒiən], *n.* théologien, *m*
theological [θi:ə'lɔdʒikl], *a.* théologique.
theology [θi:'ɔlədʒi], *n.* théologie, *f.*
theorem ['θi:ərəm], *n.* théorème, *m.*
theoretic [θi:ə'retik], **theoretical** [θi:ə'rekəl], *a.* théorique.
theorist ['θi:ərist], **theorizer** ['θi:əraizə], *n.* théoricien, *m.*
theorize ['θi:əraiz], *v.i.* théoriser.
theory ['θi:əri], *n.* théorie, *f.*
therapeutic [θerə'pju:tik], *a.* thérapeutiqu*e*.
therapeutics [θerə'pju:tiks], *n.pl.* thérapeut*i*que, *f.*
therapist ['θerəpist], *n.* praticien, *m.*
therapy ['θerəpi], *n.* thérapie, *f.*
there [ðɛə], *adv.* là, y; (*impers.*) il; en cela; voilà; ***here and there***, çà et là; ***ove*r *there***, là-bas; ***there and then***, séance tenante; ***there he comes!*** le voilà qui vient! ***there is*** or ***there are***, il y a.
thereabout [ðɛərə'baut], **thereabouts** [ðɛər'bauts], *adv.* par là, près de là; à peu près, environ (*plus ou moins*).
thereafter [ðɛər'ɑ:ftə], *adv.* après, d'après cela, ensuite.
thereat [ðɛər'æt], *adv.* par là, à cet endroit; (*fig.*) là-dessus, à cela.
thereby [ðɛə'bai], *adv.* par là, par ce moyen.
therefore ['ðɛəfɔ:], *adv.* donc, par conséquent.
therefrom [ðɛə'frɔm], *adv.* de là, en.
therein [ðɛər'in], *adv.* là-dedans, en cela; y.
thereof [ðɛər'ɔv], *adv.* en, de cela.
thereon [ðɛər'ɔn], *adv.* là-dessus.
Theresa [tə'ri:zə]. Thérèse, *f.*
thereto [ðɛə'tu:], **thereunto** [ðɛər'ʌntu:], *adv.* y, à cela; à quoi.
thereupon [ðɛərə'pɔn], *adv.* là-dessus, sur cela, sur ce.
therewith [ðɛə'wið], *adv.* avec cela, de cela, en.
therm [θə:m], *n.* thermie, *f.*
thermal ['θə:məl], *a.* thermal.
thermometer [θə'mɔmitə], *n.* thermomètre, *m.*

ermometrical [θəːmoˈmetrikl], *a.* thermométrique.
ermonuclear [θəːmoˈnjuːkliə], *a.* thermonucléaire.
ermos [ˈθəːməs], *a.* (*reg. trade mark*) ***thermos flask***, bouteille Thermos *ou* isolante, *f.*
ermostat [ˈθəːməstæt], *n.* thermostat, *m.*
ese [ðiːz], *a.* ces, ces . . . -ci, *pl.*—*pron.* ceux-ci, *m.pl.*, celles-ci, *f.pl.*
esis [ˈθiːsis], *n.* thèse, *f.*
espian [ˈθespiən], *a.* tragique, de la tragédie.
ew [θjuː], *n.* tendon, muscle, nerf, *m.*
ey [ðei], *pron.* ils, eux, *m.pl.*, elles, *f.pl.*; (*followed by a relative*) ceux, *m.pl.*, celles, *f.pl.*; (*impers.*) on (*les gens*); ***they say***, on dit.
ick [θik], *a.* épais; gros (*tuyau*); fort, solide (*porte etc.*); trouble (*boisson*); dru, serré (*touffu*); indistinct (*prononciation*); (*fam.*) intime.—*n.* fort, *m.*; ***in the thick of***, au (plus) fort de.—*adv.* (*also* **thickly** [ˈθikli]) épais; dru (*vite*); en foule (*l'un après l'autre*).
icken [θikn], *v.t.* épaissir; lier (*sauce*).—*v.i.* s'épaissir; augmenter; se lier (*sauce*).
ickening [ˈθikniŋ], *n.* épaississement, *m.*; liaison (*d'une sauce*), *f.*
icket [ˈθikit], *n.* fourré, hallier, taillis, *m.*
ick-headed [ˈθikˈhedid], *a.* sot, bête, stupide.
ickly [THICK].
ickness [ˈθiknis], *n.* épaisseur; consistance (*composition*), *f.*
ick-set [ˈθikset], *a.* touffu; trapu (*personne*).
ick-skinned [ˈθikˈskind], *a.* (*fig.*) peu sensible.
ief [θiːf], *n.* (*pl.* **thieves** [θiːvz]) voleur; larron, *m.*
ieve [θiːv], *v.i.* voler.
ieving [ˈθiːviŋ], *n.* vol, larcin, *m.*, rapine, *f.*
ievish [ˈθiːviʃ], *a.* adonné au vol; voleur.
ievishly [ˈθiːviʃli], *adv.* en voleur; par le vol.
ievishness [ˈθiːviʃnis], *n.* penchant au vol, *m.*, habitude du vol, *f.*
igh [θai], *n.* cuisse, *f.*
igh-bone [ˈθaiboun], *n.* fémur, *m.*
imble [θimbl], *n.* dé, *m.*
imbleful [ˈθimblful], *n.* un plein dé, *m.*
in [θin], *a.* mince; maigre (*décharné*); élancé, délié (*svelte*); peu nombreux (*gens*); clair; clairsemé, rare (*arbres etc.*); grêle, faible (*son etc.*).—*adv.* d'une manière éparse, clair.—*v.t.* amincir, allonger (*sauce etc.*); éclaircir; raréfier.
thine [ðain], *pron.* le tien, *m.*, la tienne, *f.*, les tiens, *m.pl.*, les tiennes, *f.pl.*; à toi.
ing [θiŋ], *n.* chose, *f.*, objet, *m.*, affaire, *f.*; être, *m.*; (*pl.*) affaires, *f.pl.*, effets, *m.pl.*
ink [θiŋk], *v.t. irr.* penser; croire (*tenir pour vrai*); imaginer, songer (*avoir l'idée*); trouver, juger (*considérer*).—*v.i.* penser; croire; s'imaginer; songer (*à*); s'aviser (*de*); avoir une idée *ou* opinion (*de*); ***to think over***, réfléchir à; ***to think up***, inventer.
hinker [ˈθiŋkə], *n.* penseur, *m.*
hinking [ˈθiŋkiŋ], *a.* pensant, qui pense, réfléchi.—*n.* pensée, *f.*; jugement, avis, *m.*
hinly [ˈθinli], *adv.* légèrement (*vêtu*); clairsemé, de loin en loin (*répandu*).
hinness [ˈθinnis], *n.* ténuité; fluidité; rareté, *f.*, petit nombre (*quantité*), *m.*; maigreur (*du corps*), *f.*
thin-skinned [ˈθinˈskind], *a.* à la peau mince; (*fig.*) irritable, chatouilleux, susceptible.
third [θəːd], *a.* troisième; trois (*mois, roi etc.*).—*n.* tiers (*fraction*), *m.*; (*Mus.*) tierce, *f.*
thirdly [ˈθəːdli], *adv.* troisièmement.
thirst [θəːst], *n.* soif, *f.*; ***to quench one's thirst***, se désaltérer.—*v.i.* avoir soif (*de*).
thirstily [ˈθəːstili], *adv.* avidement.
thirstiness [ˈθəːstinis], *n.* soif, *f.*
thirsty [ˈθəːsti], *a.* qui a soif; altéré.
thirteen [θəːˈtiːn], *a.* and *n.* treize, *m.*
thirteenth [θəːˈtiːnθ], *a.* treizième; treize (*rois etc.*).—*n.* treizième (*fraction*), *m.*
thirtieth [ˈθəːtiiθ], *a.* trentième; trente (*du mois*).—*n.* trentième (*fraction*), *m.*
thirty [ˈθəːti], *a.* and *n.* trente, *m.*
this [ðis], *a.* (*pl.* **these** [ðiːz]) ce, cet, *m.*, cette, *f.*; ce . . . -ci, cet . . . -ci, *m.*; cette . . . -ci, *f.*—*pron.* celui-ci, *m.*, celle-ci (*this one*), *f.*; ceci, *m.*
thistle [θisl], *n.* (*Bot.*) chardon, *m.*
thistly [ˈθisli], *a.* plein de chardons.
thither [ˈðiðə], *adv.* là, y; ***hither and thither***, çà et là.
thong [θɔŋ], *n.* courroie, lanière, sangle, *f.*
thoracic [θoˈræsik], *a.* thoracique.
thorax [ˈθɔːræks], *n.* thorax, *m.*
thorn [θɔːn], *n.* épine, *f.*
thorn-bush [ˈθɔːnbuʃ], *n.* buisson épineux, *m.*
thorny [ˈθɔːni], *a.* épineux.
thorough [ˈθʌrə], *a.* entier, complet; achevé, parfait; vrai (*véritable*).
thoroughbred [ˈθʌrəbred], *a.* pur sang (*cheval*); (*colloq.*) consommé.
thoroughfare [ˈθʌrəfɛə], *n.* voie de passage, *f.*, passage, *m.*; artère, *f.*; ***no thoroughfare***, passage interdit.
thoroughgoing [ˈθʌrəgouiŋ], *a.* résolu; achevé, consommé.
thoroughly [ˈθʌrəli], *adv.* tout à fait, entièrement; à fond.
thoroughness [ˈθʌrənis], *n.* caractère achevé, *m.*, perfection, *f.*
thorough-paced [ˈθʌrəpeist], *a.* achevé, franc, fieffé.
those [ðouz], *a.* ces; ces . . . -là, *pl.*—*pron.* ceux-là, *m.pl.*, celles-là, *f.pl.*
thou** [ðau], *pron.* tu; ***than thou, que toi.
though [ðou], *conj.* quoique, bien que (*with subj.*); quand même (*même si*).—*adv.* cependant, pourtant.
thought (1) [θɔːt], *past* and *p.p.* [THINK].
thought (2) [θɔːt], *n.* pensée; idée, *f.*; sentiment (*opinion*), *m.*
thoughtful [ˈθɔːtful], *a.* pensif, réfléchi; rêveur, méditatif; inquiet (*troublé*); attentif, soucieux (*prévenant*).
thoughtfully [ˈθɔːtfuli], *adv.* pensivement, avec attention.
thoughtfulness [ˈθɔːtfulnis], *n.* méditation, *f.*, recueillement, *m.*; sollicitude, prévenance (*attentions*), *f.*
thoughtless [ˈθɔːtlis], *a.* irréfléchi, insouciant.
thoughtlessly [ˈθɔːtlisli], *a.* avec insouciance; sans réfléchir.
thoughtlessness [ˈθɔːtlisnis], *n.* insouciance, négligence, *f.*
thousand [ˈθauzənd], *a.* mille; mil (*dates*).—*n.* mille; millier, *m.*, (*pl.*) milliers, *m.pl.*

thousandth ['θauzəndθ], *a.* millième.—*n.* millième (*fraction*), *m.*
thraldom ['θrɔːldəm], *n.* esclavage, asservissement, *m.*
thrall [θrɔːl], *n.* esclave, *m., f.*; esclavage, *m.*
thrash [θræʃ], *v.t.* battre, rosser (*quelqu'un*); [THRESH].
thrasher ['θræʃə], [THRESHER].
thrashing ['θræʃiŋ], *n.* rossée, *f.*; [THRESHING].
thrashing machine [THRESHING MACHINE].
thread [θred], *n.* fil; filet (*de vis*), *m.*—*v.t.* enfiler; traverser (*faire son chemin à travers*).
threadbare ['θredbεə], *a.* râpé; (*fig.*) rebattu.
threat [θret], *n.* menace, *f.*
threaten [θretn], *v.t.* menacer (*de*).
threatening ['θretniŋ], *a.* menaçant; de menaces.—*n.* menaces, *f.pl.*
threateningly ['θretniŋli], *adv.* avec menaces; d'un air menaçant.
three [θriː], *a.* and *n.* trois, *m.*
three-cornered ['θriːkɔːnəd], *a.* à trois cornes; ***three-cornered hat***, tricorne, *m.*
threefold ['θriːfould], *a.* triple.
three-master ['θriːmɑːstə], *n.* trois-mâts, *m.*
three-ply ['θriːplai], *a.* à trois épaisseurs; ***three-ply wood***, contreplaqué, *m.*
threescore ['θriːskɔː], *a.* soixante.—*n.* soixantaine, *f.*
thresh [θreʃ], *v.t.* (*Agric.*) battre (*en grange*).
thresher ['θreʃə], *n.* batteur en grange, *m.*
threshing ['θreʃiŋ], *n.* (*Agric.*) battage, *m.*
threshing machine ['θreʃiŋmə'ʃiːn], *n.* batteuse, *f.*
threshold ['θreʃould], *n.* seuil; (*fig.*) début, *m.*
thrift [θrift], **thriftiness** ['θriftinis], *n.* épargne, économie, *f.*
thriftily ['θriftili], *adv.* avec économie.
thriftiness [THRIFT].
thriftless ['θriftlis], *a.* dépensier, prodigue.
thriftlessly ['θriftlisli], *adv.* en prodigue, follement.
thriftlessness ['θriftlisnis], *n.* prodigalité, *f.*, gaspillage, *m.*
thrifty ['θrifti], *a.* ménager, économe, frugal.
thrill [θril], *v.t.* faire frissonner, faire tressaillir (*de*).—*v.i.* frémir, tressaillir (*de*).—*n.* tressaillement, frisson, *m.*
thriller ['θrilə], *n.* (*fam.*) roman *ou* film à sensation, *m.*
thrilling ['θriliŋ], *a.* saisissant, poignant, palpitant.
thrive [θraiv], *v.i. irr.* prospérer; réussir.
thriving ['θraiviŋ], *a.* florissant, vigoureux.
throat [θrout], *n.* gorge, *f.*; gosier, *m.*
throaty ['θrouti], *a.* guttural (*voix*).
throb [θrɔb], *v.i.* battre; palpiter.—*n.* battement, *m.*
throbbing ['θrɔbiŋ], *a.* palpitant, vibrant; lancinant (*douleur*).—*n.* battement; ronflement (*de moteur*), *m.*
throes [θrouz], *n. pl.* douleurs, angoisses, *f.pl.*
thrombosis [θrɔm'bousis], *n.* thrombose, *f.*
throne [θroun], *n.* trône, *m.*
throng [θrɔŋ], *n.* foule, multitude, *f.*—*v.t.* remplir.—*v.i.* accourir en foule, se presser.
thronged [θrɔŋd], *a.* serré (*personnes*); comble (*salle*).
throstle [θrɔsl], *n.* (*Orn.*) grive chanteuse, *f.*
throttle [θrɔtl], *v.t.* étrangler; étouffer.—*n.* gosier; (*Motor. etc.*) papillon, *m.*
through [θruː], *prep.* à travers; au travers de; par; dans; par suite de (*à cause de*).—direct (*train, billet etc.*).—*adv.* directeme droit (*sans s'arrêter*); de part en part; d' bout à l'autre (*dans toute sa longueur*); j qu'à la fin, jusqu'au bout; complèteme ***to be wet through***, être trempé jusqu'a os; ***to fall through***, manquer, écho (*projet*); ***to go through with*** (*som thing*), ***to see*** (*something*) ***throu*** mener (quelque chose) à bonne fin.
throughout [θruː'aut], *prep.* dans tout, tout.—*adv.* d'un bout à l'autre; entiè ment.
throw [θrou], *v.t. irr.* jeter; lancer; renvers tordre (*soie*); démonter, désarçon (*cavalier*); ***to throw aside***, jeter de côté; ***throw away***, jeter, rejeter; gaspiller; ***throw off***, se défaire de, ôter (*vêtemen* —*n.* jet, coup; (*fig.*) élan, *m.*
thrower ['θrouə], *n.* jeteur, lanceur, *m.*
thrush [θrʌʃ], *n.* (*Orn.*) grive, *f.*
thrust [θrʌst], *v.t. irr.* pousser, enfonc fourrer; presser.—*v.i.* porter une botte *ou* coup (*à*); se fourrer.—*n.* coup, *m.*; (*Fen* botte; (*Arch. etc.*) poussée, *f.*
thud [θʌd], *n.* bruit sourd; son mat, *m.*— faire un bruit sourd.
thug [θʌg], *n.* bandit, *m.*
thumb [θʌm], *n.* pouce, *m.*—*v.t.* man gauchement; feuilleter; salir (avec pouces).
thumbnail ['θʌmneil], *a.* en raccour minuscule.
thumb-screw ['θʌmskruː], *n.* vis à ailettes, poucettes (*supplice*), *f.pl.*
thumbstall ['θʌmstɔːl], *n.* poucier, doigti *m.*
thump [θʌmp], *v.t.* frapper du poing, cogn —*n.* coup, *m.*, bourrade, *f.*
thunder ['θʌndə], *n.* tonnerre, *m.*; (*fi* foudre, *f.*—*v.i.* tonner; (*fig.*) fulminer.
thunderbolt ['θʌndəboult], *n.* foudre, *f.*
thunder-clap ['θʌndəklæp], *n.* coup tonnerre, *m.*
thundering ['θʌndəriŋ], *a.* tonnant, fo droyant; (*colloq.*) énorme.
thunderous ['θʌndərəs], *a.* orageux; à to rompre (*applaudissements*).
thunderstorm ['θʌndəstɔːm], *n.* orage (a compagné de tonnerre), *m.*
thunderstruck ['θʌndəstrʌk], *a.* foudroy (*fig.*) atterré.
thundery ['θʌndəri], *a.* orageux.
Thursday ['θəːzd(e)i]. jeudi, *m.*
thus [ðʌs], *adv.* ainsi; ***thus far***, jusqu'ici.
thwack [θwæk], *n.* coup, *m.*—*v.t.* frapp rosser, battre.
thwacking ['θwækiŋ], *n.* roulée de cou raclée, *f.*
thwart [θwɔːt], *v.t.* traverser; (*fig.*) co trarier.—*adv.* en travers.—*n.* banc rameurs, *m.*
***thy** [ðai], *poss.a.* (*also poet.*) ton, *m.*, ta, tes, *pl.*
thyme [taim], *n.* thym, *m.*
thyroid ['θairɔid], *a.* thyroïde.
***thyself** [ðai'self], *pron.* (*also poet.*) toi-mêm toi; (*reflexive*) te.
tiara [ti'ɑːrə], *n.* tiare, *f.*
Tibet [ti'bet]. le Tibet, *m.*
Tibetan [ti'betn], *a.* tibétain.—*n.* tibéta (*langue*); Tibétain (*personne*), *m.*

bia ['tibiə], *n.* (*Anat.*) tibia (*os de la jambe*), *m.*
c [tik], *n.* tic, *m.*
ck (1) [tik], *n.* tic-tac (*bruit*), *m.*; marque, *f.* —*v.t.* marquer; ***to tick off***, pointer.—*v.i.* faire tic-tac, battre (*horloges etc.*).
ck (2) [tik], *n.* coutil (*de matelas*), *m.*
cket ['tikit], *n.* billet; ticket, *m.*; étiquette, *f.*; ***return ticket***, billet d'aller et retour; ***season ticket***, carte d'abonnement, *f.*; ***single ticket***, billet simple.—*v.t.* étiqueter, numéroter.
icket-collector ['tikitkəlektə], *n.* contrôleur, *m.*
icket-office ['tikitɔfis], *n.* bureau des billets, guichet, *m.*
icking (1) ['tikiŋ], *n.* tic-tac, battement (*de montre etc.*), *m.*
icking (2) ['tikiŋ], *n.* coutil, *m.*, toile à matelas, *f.*
ickle [tikl], *v.t.*, *v.i.* chatouiller.
ickling ['tikliŋ], *n.* chatouillement, *m.*
icklish ['tikliʃ], *a.* chatouilleux; critique, délicat.
idal [taidl], *a.* de marée; ***tidal harbour***, port à marée, *m.*; ***tidal wave***, raz de marée, *m.*
ide [taid], *n.* marée, *f.*; courant (*flot*), *m.*; (*fig.*) époque, *f.*
idily ['taidili], *adv.* proprement, en bon ordre.
idiness ['taidinis], *n.* propreté, netteté, *f.*, bon ordre, *m.*
idings ['taidiŋz], *n.pl.* nouvelles, *f.pl.*
idy ['taidi], *a.* rangé, bien arrangé, en ordre, propre, net.—*v.t.* mettre en ordre; ranger; arranger (*papiers etc.*).
ie [tai], *v.t.* lier, attacher; nouer, faire (*un nœud*).—*v.i.* se lier, se nouer; être à égalité. —*n.* lien; nœud (*knot*); cordon (*de chaussure*), *m.*; cravate; (*Mus.*) liaison; (*Games*) partie nulle, *f.*
ier [tiə], *n.* rang, *m.*; rangée, *f.*
ierce [tiəs], *n.* (*Cards*) tierce, *f.*
iff [tif], *n.* petite querelle, pique, *f.*
iffany ['tifəni], *n.* gaze de soie (*tissu*), *f.*
tiger ['taigə], *n.* tigre, *m.*
tiger-lily ['taigəlili], *n.* (*Bot.*) lis tigré, *m.*
tiger-moth ['taigəmɔθ], *n.* arctie, *f.*
tight [tait], *a.* serré; raide, tendu (*corde*); trop étroit (*vêtements*); imperméable; ***air-tight*** or ***water-tight***, imperméable à l'air *ou* à l'eau.
tighten [taitn], *v.t.* serrer; tendre (*contraindre*); (*fig.*) resserrer.
tight-fisted ['tait'fistid], *a.* serré, ladre.
tightly ['taitli], *adv.* ferme, fortement; étroitement serré.
tightness ['taitnis], *n.* raideur; étroitesse (*des vêtements*), *f.*
tight-rope ['taitroup], *n.* corde raide, *f.*; ***tight-rope walker***, funambule, danseur de corde, *m.*
tights [taits], *n.pl.* collant, maillot, *m.*
tigress ['taigris], *n.* tigresse, *f.*
tile [tail], *n.* tuile, *f.*; carreau (*for flooring*), *m.* —*v.t.* couvrir de tuiles; carreler (*une pièce*).
tiler ['tailə], *n.* couvreur (en tuiles), *m.*
tile-works ['tailwə:ks], *n.* tuilerie, *f.*
till (1) [til], *prep.* jusqu'à.—*conj.* jusqu'à ce que (*with subj.*).
till (2) [til], *n.* caisse, *f.*
till (3) [til], *v.t.* labourer, cultiver.
tillable ['tiləbl], *a.* labourable.
tillage ['tilidʒ], *n.* labourage, *m.*
tiller (1) ['tilə], *n.* laboureur, *m.*
tiller (2) ['tilə], *n.* (*Naut.*) barre du gouvernail, *f.*
tilt (1) [tilt], *n.* bâche, banne (*toile*), *f.*
tilt (2) [tilt], *n.* joute; inclinaison, *f.*—*v.t.* incliner, faire pencher.—*v.i.* jouter; incliner, pencher.
tilth [tilθ], *n.* labourage, *m.*, culture, *f.*
timber ['timbə], *n.* bois de construction, *m.*—*v.t.* boiser.
timbering ['timbəriŋ], *n.* boisage, *m.*
timber-work ['timbəwə:k], *n.* charpente, *f.*
timbrel ['timbrəl], *n.* tambour de basque, tambourin, *m.*
time [taim], *n.* temps, *m.*; saison, époque, *f.*; terme (*période*), *m.*; heure (*de la journée*), *f.*; moment, *m.*; occasion; fois (*répétition*); époque, *f.*, siècle (*d'histoire*), *m.*; mesure, *f.*; (*Drilling*) pas, *m.*; ***at times***, parfois, de temps à autre; ***in no time***, en un clin d'œil; ***in time***, à temps; (*Mus.*) en mesure.—*v.t.* faire à propos; fixer l'heure de; (*Spt.*) chronométrer; ***ill-timed***, inopportun; ***well-timed***, opportun, à propos.
time-bomb ['taimbɔm], *n.* bombe à retardement, *f.*
time-fuse ['taimfju:z], *n.* fusée à temps, *f.*
time-honoured ['taimɔnəd], *a.* vénérable; séculaire.
time-keeper ['taimki:pə], *n.* surveillant, contrôleur, *m.*
time-lag ['taimlæ:g], *n.* décalage, retard, *m.*
timeliness ['taimlinis], *n.* opportunité, *f.*, à-propos, *m.*
timely ['taimli], *a.* opportun, à propos.
time-piece ['taimpi:s], *n.* pendule, *f.*
time-sheet ['taimʃi:t], *n.* feuille de présence, *f.*
timetable ['taimteibl], *n.* indicateur, horaire; (*Sch.*) emploi du temps, *m.*
time-worn ['taimwɔ:n], *a.* usé par le temps.
timid ['timid], *a.* timide, craintif, peureux.
timidity [ti'miditi], *n.* timidité, *f.*
timing ['taimiŋ], *n.* ajustement, règlement; réglage (*de montre etc.*), *m.*
timorous ['timərəs], *a.* timoré, timide.
timorously ['timərəsli], *adv.* craintivement.
timorousness ['timərəsnis], *n.* timidité, *f.*
tin [tin], *n.* étain, *m.*; boîte (*de conserve*), *f.*—*v.t.* étamer.
tincture ['tiŋktʃə], *n.* teinture, *f.*, extrait, *m.*; (*fig.*) nuance, *f.*—*v.t.* teindre (*de*).
tinder ['tində], *n.* amadou, *m.*
tinder-box ['tindəbɔks], *n.* boîte à amadou, *f.*, briquet à silex, *m.*
tinfoil ['tinfɔil], *n.* feuille d'étain, *f.*
tinge [tindʒ], *n.* teinte, nuance, *f.*; soupçon (*goût*), *m.*—*v.t.* teindre.
tingle [tiŋgl], *v.i.* tinter; picoter, cuire (*douleur*).
tingling ['tiŋgliŋ], *n.* tintement (*son*); picotement, *m.*
tinker ['tiŋkə], *n.* rétameur, *m.*—*v.t.* rétamer; raccommoder.
tinkle [tiŋkl], *v.t.* faire tinter.—*v.i.* tinter.—*n.* tintement, *m.*
tinkling ['tiŋkliŋ], *n.* tintement, *m.*
tinny ['tini], *a.* qui abonde en étain; grêle (*son*).
tin-plate ['tinpleit], *n.* fer-blanc, *m.*

tinsel ['tinsəl], *a.* de clinquant; (*fig.*) faux.—*n.* clinquant; (*fig.*) faux éclat, *m.*
tinsmith ['tinsmiθ], *n.* ferblantier, *m.*
tint [tint], *n.* teinte, nuance, *f.*—*v.t.* teinter, nuancer (*de*).
tin-tack ['tintæk], *n.* semence étamée, *f.*
tinware ['tinwεə], *n.* ferblanterie, *f.*
tiny ['taini], *a.* tout petit, minuscule.
tip (1) [tip], *n.* bout, *m.*; extrémité, pointe, *f.*—*v.t.* garnir le bout.
tip (2) [tip], *n.* tape (*coup léger*), *f.*; pourboire (*gratuity*); dépotoir (*débris*); (*Spt.*) tuyau, *m.* —*v.t.* donner un pourboire à; décharger (*véhicule*); (*Spt.*) tuyauter.
tippet ['tipit], *n.* pèlerine, palatine (*fourrure*), *f.*
tipple [tipl], *v.i.* boire, pinter.—*n.* boisson, *f.*
tippler ['tiplə], *n.* buveur, *m.*
tippling ['tipliŋ], *n.* ivrognerie, *f.*
tipstaff ['tipstɑ:f], *n.* huissier, *m.*
tipster ['tipstə], *n.* (*Spt.*) tuyauteur, *m.*
tipsy ['tipsi], *a.* gris, ivre.
tiptoe ['tiptou], *n.* pointe du pied, *f.*; ***on tiptoe***, sur la pointe des pieds.
tip-top ['tip'tɔp], *a.* (*colloq.*) excellent.—*n.* comble, sommet, *m.*
tirade [ti'reid, tai'reid], *n.* tirade, diatribe, *f.*
tire ['taiə], *v.t.* lasser, fatiguer; ennuyer (*moralement*).—*v.i.* se fatiguer, se lasser.
tired ['taiəd], *a.* las, fatigué; ennuyé.
tiredness ['taiədnis], *n.* fatigue, lassitude, *f.*
tiresome ['taiəsəm], *a.* fatigant; ennuyeux (*assommant*).
tiresomeness ['taiəsəmnis], *n.* nature fatigante, *f.*; ennui, *m.*
tiro [TYRO].
tissue ['tiʃju:, 'tisju:], *n.* tissu, *m.*—*v.t.* tisser, broder.
tissue-paper ['tiʃju:peipə], *n.* papier de soie, *m.*
tit (1) [tit], *n.* mésange (*oiseau*), *f.*
tit (2) [tit], *n.* ***tit for tat***, un prêté pour un rendu.
titanic [tai'tænik], *a.* titanique, titanesque.
titbit ['titbit], *n.* morceau friand, *m.*
tithe [taið], *n.* dîme, *f.*, dixième, *m.*—*v.t.* dîmer.
titillate ['titileit], *v.t.*, *v.i.* chatouiller, titiller.
titillation [titi'leiʃən], *n.* titillation, *f.*, chatouillement, *m.*
titlark ['titlɑ:k], *n.* alouette des prés, *f.*
title [taitl], *n.* titre; (*fig.*) droit, document, *m.*
titled [taitld], *a.* titré.
title-deed ['taitldi:d], *n.* titre (de propriété), *m.*
title-page ['taitlpeidʒ], *n.* titre, *m.*
titmouse ['titmaus], *n.* (*pl.* **titmice** ['titmais]) mésange, *f.*
titter ['titə], *v.i.* rire tout bas.—*n.* petit rire étouffé, *m.*
tittle [titl], *n.* point, iota, *m.*
tittle-tattle ['titltætl], *n.* caquetage, bavardage, *m.*—*v.i.* jaser, bavarder.
titular ['titjulə], *a.* titulaire.
titulary ['titjuləri], *a.* de titre.—*n.* titulaire, *m.*, *f.*
to [tu], *prep.* à, de (*before infinitive*); pour, afin de (*dans le but de*); à (*un endroit*); en (*before names of countries of the feminine gender and those of the masculine gender beginning with a vowel*), au (*before those of the masculine gender beginning with a consonant*); dans (*followed by* le, la, *etc.*); vers (*un endroit*); contre (*pari*); près de (*cour royale etc.*); outre, en addition à (*en plus de*); pour (*faire quelque chose*); en comparaison de, auprès de (*à côté de*); jusqu'à (*telle ou telle limite*); envers (*à l'égard de*).
toad [toud], *n.* crapaud, *m.*
toadish ['toudiʃ], *a.* de crapaud.
toadstool ['toudstu:l], *n.* champignon vénéneux, *m.*
toady ['toudi], *n.* flagorneur, *m.*—*v.t.* flagorner, aduler.
toadyism ['toudiizm], *n.* flagornerie, servilité, *f.*
toast [toust], *n.* rôtie, tranche de pain grillé, *f.*; toast (*bu à la santé de quelqu'un*), *m.*—*v.t.* rôtir, griller; porter un toast à.
toaster ['toustə], *n.* grille-pain, *m.inv.*
toasting-fork ['toustiŋfɔ:k], *n.* fourchette à rôties, *f.*
toast-master ['toustmɑ:stə], *n.* préposé aux toasts, *m.*
toast-rack ['toustræk], *n.* porte-rôties, porte-toasts, *m.inv.*
tobacco [tə'bækou], *n.* tabac, *m.*
tobacco-box [tə'bækoubɔks], *n.* boîte à tabac, *f.*
tobacco-jar [tə'bækoudʒɑ:], *n.* pot à tabac, *m.*
tobacconist [tə'bækənist], *n.* marchand de tabac, *m.*; ***tobacconist's shop***, bureau de tabac, *m.*
tobacco-pouch [tə'bækoupautʃ], *n.* blague à tabac, *f.*
toboggan [tə'bɔgən], *n.* toboggan, *m.*; luge, *f.* —*v.t.* luger.
tocsin ['tɔksin], *n.* tocsin, *m.*
today [tə'dei], *adv.* aujourd'hui.
toddle [tɔdl], *v.i.* trottiner.
toddler ['tɔdlə], *n.* tout petit enfant, *m.*
to-do [tə'du:], *n.* tapage, éclat, *m.*, (*fam.*) histoire, *f.*
toe [tou], *n.* orteil, doigt de pied; devant du sabot, *m.*, pince (*de cheval*), *f.*; bout (*de bas*), *m.*
toe-nail ['touneil], *n.* ongle de pied, *m.*
toffee, toffy ['tɔfi], *n.* caramel au beurre, *m.*
toga ['tougə], *n.* toge, *f.*
together [tə'geðə], *adv.* ensemble, à la fois, en même temps (*simultanément*); de concert (*entre eux*); de suite (*consécutivement*).
Togo ['tougou]. le Togo, *m.*
Togolese [tougo'li:z], *a.* togolais.—*n.* Togolais (*personne*), *m.*
toil [tɔil], *n.* travail dur, labeur, *m.*; peine, *f.* (*pl.*) piège, *m.*—*v.i.* travailler fort, se fatiguer.
toiler ['tɔilə], *n.* travailleur, *m.*
toilet ['tɔilit], *n.* toilette, *f.*; les toilettes (*dans les hôtels etc.*), *f.pl.*
toiling ['tɔiliŋ], *n.* travail, labeur, *m.*, peine, *f.*
toilsome ['tɔilsəm], *a.* pénible, laborieux, fatigant.
toilsomeness ['tɔilsəmnis], *n.* difficulté, *f.*
token ['toukən], *n.* marque, *f.*; gage (*témoignage*); jeton (*jeux de cartes, téléphone etc.*), *m.*; ***book token***, bon de livre, *m.*; ***token strike***, grève d'avertissement, *f.*
tolerable ['tɔlərəbl], *a.* tolérable, passable (*assez bon*).
tolerably ['tɔlərəbli], *adv.* passablement, assez.
tolerance ['tɔlərəns], *n.* tolérance, *f.*
tolerant ['tɔlərənt], *a.* tolérant.

erate ['tɔləreit], *v.t.* tolérer; supporter.
eration [tɔlə'reiʃən], *n.* tolérance, *f.*
l (1) [toul], *n.* péage; droit; octroi (*impôt municipal*), *m.*
l (2) [toul], *n.* tintement, glas (*de cloche*), *m.* —*v.t.*, *v.i.* sonner, tinter (*cloche*).
l-bar ['toulbɑ:], **toll-gate** ['toulgeit], *n.* barrière de péage, *f.*
l-bridge ['toulbridʒ], *n.* pont à péage, *m.*
l-gatherer ['toulgæðərə], *n.* péager, *m.*
l-house ['toulhaus], *n.* bureau de péage, *m.*
ling ['touliŋ], *n.* tintement, *m.*
mahawk ['tɔməhɔ:k], *n.* tomahawk, *m.*; hache de guerre, *f.*
mato [tə'mɑ:tou], *n.* tomate, *f.*
mb [tu:m], *n.* tombeau, *m.*; tombe, *f.*
mboy ['tɔmbɔi], *n.* garçon manqué, *m.*
mbstone ['tu:mstoun], *n.* pierre tombale, *f.*
m-cat ['tɔmkæt], *n.* matou, *m.*
me [toum], *n.* tome, volume, *m.*
mfool [tɔm'fu:l], *n.* sot, bête, niais, *m.*
mfoolery [tɔm'fu:ləri], *n.* sottise, bêtise, niaiserie, *f.*
mmy-gun ['tɔmigʌn], *n.* mitraillette, *f.*
morrow [tə'mɔrou], *adv.* demain.
mtit ['tɔmtit], *n.* (*Orn.*) mésange bleue, *f.*
m-tom ['tɔmtɔm], *n.* tam-tam, *m.*
n [tʌn], *n.* tonne (*poids*), *f.*, tonneau (*capacité*), *m.*
ne [toun], *n.* ton; accent, timbre (*de voix*), *m.*—*v.t.* donner le ton à, régler; (*Mus.*) accorder; (*Phot.*) virer; ***to tone down***, adoucir, pallier.
neless ['tounlis], *a.* sans éclat, sans chaleur (*voix*).
ngs [tɔŋz], *n.pl.* pincettes; (*Tech.*) tenailles, pinces, *f.pl.*
ngue [tʌŋ], *n.* langue, *f.*; ***to hold one's tongue***, se taire.
ngued [tʌŋd], *a.* à langue.
ngue-tied ['tʌŋtaid], *a.* qui a la langue liée; (*fig.*) réduit au silence, muet.
nic ['tɔnik], *a.* and *n.* (*Med.*) tonique, fortifiant, *m.*
night [tə'nait], *n.* cette nuit, *f.*, ce soir, *m.*
nnage ['tʌnidʒ], *n.* tonnage, *m.*
nsil [tɔnsl], *n.* (*Anat.*) amygdale, *f.*
nsil(l)itis [tɔnsi'laitis], *n.* amygdalite, *f.*
nsure ['tɔnʃə], *n.* tonsure, *f.*—*v.t.* tonsurer.
o [tu:], *adv.* trop, par trop; aussi, de même, également (*pareillement*); d'ailleurs, de plus; ***too much*** or ***too many***, trop.
ol [tu:l], *n.* outil, instrument; (*fig.*) agent, *m.*
ol-chest ['tu:ltʃest], *n.* boîte à outils, *f.*
oth [tu:θ], *n.* (*pl.* **teeth** [ti:θ]) dent, *f.*; ***set of teeth***, râtelier, *m.*; ***wisdom tooth***, dent de sagesse.—*v.t.* denteler.
othache ['tu:θeik], *n.* mal de dents, *m.*
othbrush ['tu:θbrʌʃ], *n.* brosse à dents, *f.*
othed [tu:θt], *a.* à dents; (*Tech.*) denté.
othless ['tu:θlis], *a.* sans dents, édenté.
oth-paste ['tu:θpeist], *n.* pâte dentifrice, *f.*, dentifrice, *m.*
ooth-pick ['tu:θpik], *n.* cure-dents, *m.inv.*
ooth-powder ['tu:θpaudə], *n.* poudre dentifrice, *f.*
oothsome ['tu:θsəm], *a.* agréable au goût, savoureux, friand.
oothsomeness ['tu:θsəmnis], *n.* goût agréable, *m.*
op (1) [tɔp], *a.* premier, principal, extrême.—*n.* haut, sommet, *m.*; cime (*de montagne etc.*), *f.*; faîte (*d'édifice*), *m.*; (*Naut.*) hune, *f.*; dessus (*de table*), *m.*—*v.t.* couronner, surmonter (*de*).
top (2) [tɔp], *n.* toupie (*jouet*), *f.*
topaz ['toupæz], *n.* topaze, *f.*
top-boots ['tɔpbu:ts], *n.pl.* bottes à revers, *f.pl.*
top-coat ['tɔpkout], *n.* pardessus, *m.*
tope (1) [toup], *v.i.* (*colloq.*) pinter, boire.
tope (2) [toup], *n.* chien de mer, *m.*
toper ['toupə], *n.* ivrogne, *m.*, *f.*
top-hat ['tɔp'hæt], *n.* chapeau haut de forme, *m.*
topic ['tɔpik], *n.* matière, *f.*, sujet, *m.*
topical ['tɔpikl], *a.* d'actualité; (*Med.*) topique.
topmast ['tɔpmɑ:st], *n.* mât de hune, *m.*
topmost ['tɔpmoust], *a.* le plus haut, le plus élevé.
top-sail [tɔpsl], *n.* hunier, *m.*
topographer [tə'pɔgrəfə], *n.* topographe, *m.*
topographic [tɔpə'græfik], **topographical** [tɔpə'græfikəl], *a.* topographique.
topography [tə'pɔgrəfi], *n.* topographie, *f.*
topple [tɔpl], *v.i.* tomber, dégringoler.
topsy-turvy ['tɔpsi'tə:vi], *adv.* sens dessus dessous.
torch [tɔ:tʃ], *n.* torche, *f.*, flambeau, *m.*, lampe de poche, *f.*
torch-bearer ['tɔ:tʃbɛərə], *n.* porte-flambeau, *m.*
toreador [tɔriə'dɔ:], *n.* toréador, *m.*
torment (1) ['tɔ:ment], *n.* tourment, *m.*, torture, *f.*; supplice, *m.*
torment (2) [tɔ:'ment], *v.t.* tourmenter, torturer.
tormentor [tɔ:'mentə], *n.* tourmenteur, bourreau, *m.*
tornado [tɔ:'neidou], *n.* tornade, *f.*, ouragan, cyclone, *m.*
torpedo [tɔ:'pi:dou], *n.* torpille, *f.*—*v.t.* torpiller.
torpedo-boat [tɔ:'pi:doubout], *n.* torpilleur, *m.*
torpid ['tɔ:pid], *a.* engourdi, torpide, inerte.
torpor ['tɔ:pə], *n.* torpeur, apathie, *f.*
torrefaction [tɔri'fækʃən], *n.* torréfaction, *f.*
torrefy ['tɔrifai], *v.t.* torréfier.
torrent ['tɔrənt], *n.* torrent, *m.*
torrential [tɔ'renʃl], *a.* torrentiel.
torrid ['tɔrid], *a.* brûlant, torride.
torridness ['tɔridnis], **torridity** [tɔ'riditi], *n.* chaleur brûlante, *f.*
torsion ['tɔ:ʃən], *n.* torsion, *f.*
torso ['tɔ:sou], *n.* torse, *m.*
tortoise ['tɔ:təs], *n.* tortue, *f.*
tortoise-shell ['tɔ:təsʃel], *a.* d'écaille.—*n.* écaille de tortue, écaille, *f.*
tortuous ['tɔ:tjuəs], *a.* tortueux, sinueux.
tortuousness ['tɔ:tjuəsnis], *n.* tortuosité, *f.*
torture ['tɔ:tʃə], *n.* torture, *f.*; supplice, *m.*—*v.t.* torturer; (*fig.*) faire souffrir.
torturer ['tɔ:tʃərə], *n.* bourreau, *m.*
toss [tɔs], *n.* jet, lancement, *m.*; ***to win the toss***, gagner (à pile *ou* face).—*v.t.* lancer *ou* jeter (*en l'air*); ballotter; secouer.—*v.i.* s'agiter.
tossing ['tɔsiŋ], *n.* secousse, *f.*; ballottement; hochement, *m.*
toss-up ['tɔsʌp], *n.* coup de pile ou face, *m.*
total [toutl], *a.* total, complet, entier.—*n.* total, montant, *m.*, somme, *f.*—*v.t.* se monter à.

totalitarian [toutæli'tɛəriən], *a.* (*Polit.*) totalitaire.
totalitarianism [toutæli'tɛəriənizm], *n.* totalitarisme, *m.*
totality [tou'tæliti], *n.* totalité, *f.*, montant, tout, *m.*
totalizator ['toutəlaizeitə], *n.* totalisateur, *m.*
totally ['toutəli], *adv.* totalement, tout à fait, entièrement.
totem ['toutəm], *n.* totem, *m.*
totter ['tɔtə], *v.i.* chanceler; (*fig.*) vaciller, trembler.
tottering ['tɔtəriŋ], *a.* chancelant, tremblant. —*n.* chancellement, *m.*
tottery ['tɔtəri], *a.* chancelant.
touch [tʌtʃ], *v.t.* toucher; toucher à (*s'ingérer dans*); émouvoir (*attendrir*); ***to touch up***, retoucher.—*v.i.* toucher; se toucher; ***to touch at***, aborder à (*navire*); ***to touch upon***, effleurer, (*fig.*) faire allusion à.—*n.* le toucher (*sens tactile*); attouchement (*contact*), *m.*; légère attaque (*d'une maladie*), *f.*; (*fig.*) soupçon (*trace*), *m.*; ***it was touch and go***, il s'en est fallu de bien peu; ***to get in touch with***, se mettre en rapports, entrer en contact avec; ***to keep in touch with***, garder le contact avec.
touchiness ['tʌtʃinis], *n.* irascibilité, *f.*
touching ['tʌtʃiŋ], *a.* touchant, émouvant.—*prep.* concernant, au sujet de.
touch-line ['tʌtʃlain], *n.* (*Ftb.*) ligne de touche, *f.*
touchstone ['tʌtʃstoun], *n.* pierre de touche, *f.*
touch-wood ['tʌtʃwud], *n.* amadou, *m.*
touchy ['tʌtʃi], *a.* irritable, susceptible.
tough [tʌf], *a.* dur, raide, résistant; coriace (*viande*); fort (*solide*); difficile.
toughen [tʌfn], *v.t.* durcir.—*v.i.* s'endurcir.
toughish ['tʌfiʃ], *a.* un peu dur.
toughly ['tʌfli], *adv.* durement; vigoureusement.
toughness ['tʌfnis], *n.* raideur; dureté, nature coriace (*viande etc.*); (*fig.*) difficulté, *f.*
tour ['tuə], *n.* tour, voyage, *m.*; randonnée, tournée, *f.*—*v.t.*, *v.i.* visiter (*un pays*); voyager dans (*un pays*); excursionner.
tourism ['tuərizm], *n.* tourisme, *m.*
tourist ['tuərist], *n.* touriste, *m.*, *f.*, voyageur, *m.*; ***tourist agency***, bureau de tourisme, *m.*
tournament ['tuənəmənt], *n.* tournoi; concours, *m.*
tourniquet ['tuənikei], *n.* garrot, *m.*
tousle [tauzl], *v.t.* tirailler, chiffonner; ***tousled hair***, cheveux ébouriffés, *m.pl.*
tout [taut], *v.i.* racoler.—*n.* racoleur, *m.*
touting ['tautiŋ], *n.* racolage, *m.*
tow [tou], *n.* filasse, étoupe (*chanvre*); remorque, *f.*; ***in tow***, à la remorque.—*v.t.* remorquer, touer, haler.
towage ['touidʒ], *n.* remorquage, touage, halage, *m.*
toward, towards [tu'wɔ:d(z)], *prep.* vers, envers; du côté de; à l'égard de (*par respect pour*); sur, environ, vers (*l'heure*).
tow-boat ['toubout], *n.* remorqueur, *m.*
towel ['tauəl], *n.* essuie-mains, *m.inv.*, serviette, *f.*
towelling ['tauəliŋ], *n.* toile pour serviettes, *f.*; tissu-éponge, *m.*

tower ['tauə], *n.* tour, *f.*—*v.i.* s'élever (
dessus de), dominer.
towering ['tauəriŋ], *a.* élevé; domin
violent.
towing ['touiŋ], *n.* remorque, *f.*; halage (
canal), *m.*
towing-boat ['touiŋbout], [TOW-BOAT].
tow(ing)-line ['tou(iŋ)lain], **tow(ing)-r**
['tou(iŋ)roup], *n.* cable de remorque,
remorque, *f.*
tow(ing)-path ['tou(iŋ)pɑ:θ], *n.* chemin
halage, *m.*
town [taun], *n.* ville, *f.*
town clerk ['taun'klɑ:k], *n.* secrétaire
mairie, *m.*
town council ['taun'kaunsl], *n.* conseil mu
cipal, *m.*
town councillor ['taun'kaunsilə], *n.* consei
municipal, *m.*
town hall ['taun'hɔ:l], *n.* hôtel de ville,
mairie, *f.*
town planning ['taun'plæniŋ], *n.* urbanis
m.
townsfolk [TOWNSPEOPLE].
township ['taunʃip], *n.* commune, *f.*
townsman ['taunzmən], *n.* (*pl.* **-men** [me
habitant de la ville, bourgeois, *m.*
townspeople ['taunzpi:pl], **townsfolk** ['ta
fouk], *n.* habitants (de la ville), citadins, *m*
tow-rope [TOW(ING)-LINE].
toxic ['tɔksik], *a.* toxique.
toxicology [tɔksi'kɔlədʒi], *n.* toxicologie, *f*
toy [tɔi], *n.* jouet, joujou, *m.*—*v.i.* jou
folâtrer, s'amuser (*avec*).
trace (1) [treis], *n.* trace, *f.*; tracé (*calq*
m.—*v.t.* tracer; calquer (*dessin*); suivre
trace de (*to track*); (*fig.*) remonter à l'orig
de.
trace (2) [treis], *n.* (*usu. pl.*) traits (*harna*
m.pl.
traceable ['treisəbl], *a.* que l'on peut trac
tracer ['treisə], *n.* traceur; traçoir (*inst*
ment), *m.*
tracery ['treisəri], *n.* (*Arch.*) réseau, *m.*
trachea [trə'ki:ə], *n.* (*Anat.*) trachée-artère
tracing ['treisiŋ], *n.* tracé, tracement; calq
m.; ***tracing-paper***, papier à calquer, *m*
track [træk], *n.* (*Spt.*) piste, *f.*, chemin (*rou*
m.; (*Hunt.*) piste; (*Rail.*) voie; (*Astro*
orbite, *f.*, sillage (*de bateau*), *m.*; ***bea***
track, sentier battu, *m.*; (*Cine.*) ***sou***
track, bande sonore, *f.*—*v.t.* suivre à
piste; haler, remorquer.
tracker ['trækə], *n.* traqueur, *m.*
tracking ['trækiŋ], *n.* action de suivre à
trace, *f.*
trackless ['træklis], *a.* sans trace; s
chemins.
tract [trækt], *n.* étendue; contrée; broch
(*petit livre*), *f.*
tractable ['træktəbl], *a.* traitable, maniab
tractile ['træktail], *a.* ductile.
traction ['trækʃən], *n.* traction, tension, *f.*
traction-engine ['trækʃənendʒin], *n.* loc
motive routière, *f.*
tractor ['træktə], *n.* tracteur, *m.*
trade [treid], *n.* commerce, trafic, négo
métier, *m.*, profession (*vocation*), *f.*; ***Boa***
of Trade, Ministère du Commerce, *n*
free trade, libre-échange, *m.*; (*Comm*
trade name, marque déposée, *f.*—
trafiquer, faire le commerce (*de*).

ade-mark ['treidmɑ:k], *n.* marque de fabrique, *f.*

ader ['treidə], *n.* négociant, *m.*

adesman ['treidzmən], *n.* (*pl.* **-men** [men]) marchand, boutiquier (*détaillant*); fournisseur, *m.*

ade(s)-union ['treid(z)'ju:njən], *n.* syndicat ouvrier, *m.*

ade-unionism ['treid'ju:njənizm], *n.* syndicalisme, *m.*

ade-unionist ['treid'ju:njənist], *n.* syndicaliste, *m., f.*

ade-winds ['treidwindz], *n.pl.* vents alizés, *m.pl.*

ading ['treidiŋ], *a.* marchand, de commerce.—*n.* négoce, commerce, *m.*

adition [trə'diʃən], *n.* tradition, *f.*

aditional [trə'diʃənəl], *a.* traditionnel.

aduce [trə'dju:s], *v.t.* diffamer, calomnier.

aducer [trə'dju:sə], *n.* calomniateur, *m.*

affic ['træfik], *n.* trafic; commerce, négoce, *m.*; circulation (*de voitures*), *f.*; (*Rail.*) mouvement, *m.*; ***traffic jam***, embouteillage, *m.*—*v.i.* trafiquer, commercer.

afficker ['træfikə], *n.* trafiquant, *m.*

affic-light ['træfiklait], *n.* feu, *m.*

agedian [trə'dʒi:diən], *n.* auteur tragique; tragédien, *m.*

agedy ['trædʒədi], *n.* tragédie, *f.*

agic ['trædʒik], **tragical** ['trædʒikəl], *a.* tragique.

agi-comedy ['trædʒi'kɔmidi], *n.* tragicomédie, *f.*

agi-comical ['trædʒi'kɔmikəl], *a.* tragicomique.

ail [treil], *n.* traînée; (*Hunt.*) piste, *f.*—*v.t.* suivre à la piste; traîner (*tirer après soi*).—*v.i.* traîner.

ailer ['treilə], *n.* remorque (*bicyclette, camion etc.*); (*Am.*) roulotte, caravane; (*Cine.*) bande de lancement, *f.*

ain [trein], *n.* (*Rail.*) train, *m.*; suite, *f.* cortège (*personnel*), *m.*; série, *f.*, enchaînement (*succession*), *m.*; traînée (*de poudre à canon*); queue, traîne (*de robe*), *f.*; ***breakdown train***, train de secours; ***excursion train***, train de plaisir.—*v.t.* former; exercer, instruire; dresser, entraîner (*cheval etc.*).—*v.i.* s'entraîner.

ain-bearer ['treinbɛərə], *n.* porte-queue, *m.*

ainee [trei'ni:], *n.* stagiaire, *m., f.*

ainer ['treinə], *n.* dresseur; entraîneur, *m.*

aining ['treiniŋ], *n.* éducation, instruction, *f.*; dressage (*de cheval*); entraînement (*de cheval de course*), *m.*

aining-ship ['treiniŋʃip], *n.* vaisseau-école, *m.*

rait [trei, treit], *n.* trait, *m.*

raitor ['treitə], *n.* traître, *m.*

raitorous ['treitərəs], *a.* traître, perfide.

raitorously ['treitərəsli], *adv.* en traître, perfidement.

raitress ['treitris], *n.* traîtresse, *f.*

rajectory [trə'dʒektəri], *n.* trajectoire, *f.*

tram(-car) ['træm(kɑ:)], *n.* tramway, *m.*

trammel [træml], *n.* tramail (*filet*), *m.*; entrave (*de cheval*), *f.*—*v.t.* entraver, empêtrer (*de*).

tramp [træmp], *v.t.* faire à pied, faire.—*v.i.* aller à pied, marcher lourdement.—*n.* randonnée (*à pied*), *f.*; bruit de pas (*marche pesante*); vagabond, *m.*

trample [træmpl], *v.t.* fouler (*aux pieds*).

trampling ['træmpliŋ], *n.* piétinement, bruit de pas, *m.*

trance [trɑ:ns], *n.* extase; (*Path.*) catalepsie, *f.*

tranquil ['træŋkwil], *a.* tranquille.

tranquillity [træŋ'kwiliti], *n.* tranquillité, *f.*, calme, *m.*

tranquillize ['træŋkwilaiz], *v.t.* tranquilliser, calmer.

tranquillizer ['træŋkwilaizə], *n.* calmant, *m.*

transact [træn'zækt], *v.t.* traiter, expédier.

transaction [træn'zækʃən], *n.* transaction, affaire, *f.*

transactor [træn'zæktə], *n.* négociateur, *m.*

transalpine [træn'zælpain], *a.* transalpin.

transatlantic [trænzət'læntik], *a.* transatlantique.

transcend [træn'send], *v.t.* dépasser, surpasser.

transcendence [træn'sendəns], **transcendency** [træn'sendənsi], *n.* excellence, transcendance, *f.*

transcendent [træn'sendənt], *a.* transcendant.

transcendental [trænsen'dentl], *a.* transcendantal.

transcribe [træn'skraib], *v.t.* transcrire, copier.

transcriber [træn'skraibə], *n.* copiste, *m., f.*, transcripteur, *m.*

transcript ['trænskript], *n.* copie, *f.*

transcription [træn'skripʃən], *n.* transcription, *f.*

transept ['trænsept], *n.* transept, *m.*

transfer [træns'fə:], *v.t.* transporter; (*Law*) transférer.—['trænsfə:], *n.* copie, *f.*; (*Law*) transfert, *m.*

transferable ['trænsfərəbl], *a.* transférable, transmissible.

transference ['trænsfərəns], *n.* transfert, *m.*

transfiguration [trænsfigju'reiʃən], *n.* transfiguration, transformation, *f.*

transfigure [træns'figə], *v.t.* transfigurer.

transfix [træns'fiks], *v.t.* transpercer.

transform [træns'fɔ:m], *v.t.* transformer, changer (*en*).—*v.i.* se transformer (*en*).

transformation [trænsfə'meiʃən], *n.* transformation, *f.*, changement, *m.*; ***transformation scene***, changement à vue, *m.*

transformer [træns'fɔ:mə], *n.* transformateur, *m.*

transfuse [træns'fju:z], *v.t.* transfuser.

transfusion [træns'fju:ʒən], *n.* transfusion, *f.*

transgress [træns'gres, trænz'gres], *v.t.* transgresser, enfreindre.—*v.i.* transgresser, pécher.

transgression [træns'greʃən], *n.* transgression, infraction, *f.*

transgressor [træns'gresə], *n.* pécheur, *m.* pécheresse, *f.*

tranship [træn'ʃip], *v.t.* transborder.

transience ['trænziəns], *n.* nature transitoire, courte durée, *f.*

transient ['trænziənt], *a.* passager, transitoire.

transistor [træn'zistə], *n.* transistor, transistron, *m.*

transit ['trænzit], *n.* passage, *m.*; ***in transit*** en transit.

transition [træn'ziʃən], *n.* transition, *f.*

transitional [træn'ziʃənəl], *a.* de transition.

transitive ['trænzitiv], *a.* qui passe; (*Gram.*) transitif.

transitoriness ['trænzitərinis], *n.* nature transitoire, courte durée, *f.*
transitory ['trænzitəri], *a.* transitoire, passager.
translatable [træns'leitəbl], *a.* traduisible.
translate [træns'leit], *v.t.* traduire; transférer (*évêque*).
translation [træns'leiʃən], *n.* traduction; translation (*d'un évêque*), *f.*
translator [træns'leitə], *n.* traducteur, *m.*
translucent [trænz'lju:sənt], *a.* translucide.
transmarine [trænzmə'ri:n], *a.* d'outremer.
transmigrate ['trænzmaigreit], *v.i.* passer d'un corps dans un autre; émigrer.
transmigration [trænzmai'greiʃən], *n.* transmigration; métempsyc(h)ose (*des âmes*), *f.*
transmissible [trænz'misibl], *a.* transmissible.
transmission [trænz'miʃən], *n.* transmission, *f.*
transmit [trænz'mit], *v.t.* transmettre, envoyer; (*Rad.*) émettre.
transmitter [trænz'mitə], *n.* (*Rad.*) émetteur, *m.*
transmutable [trænz'mju:təbl], *a.* transmuable.
transmutation [trænzmju'teiʃən], *n.* transmutation, *f.*; changement (*de couleur*), *m.*
transmute [trænz'mju:t], *v.t.* transmuer, convertir.
transom ['trænsəm], *n.* traverse (*de fenêtre*), imposte, *f.*
transparency [træns'pɛərənsi], *n.* transparence; (*Phot.*) diapositive, *f.*
transparent [træns'pɛərənt], *a.* transparent.
transparently [træns'pɛərəntli], *adv.* avec transparence; évidemment.
transpire [træns'paiə, trænz'paiə], *v.i.* transpirer; (*fig.*) avoir lieu, arriver.
transplant [træns'plɑ:nt, trænz'plɑ:nt], *v.t.* transplanter; (*fig.*) déplacer.
transplanting [træns'plɑ:ntiŋ, trænz'plɑ:ntiŋ], *n.* transplantation, *f.*
transport ['trænspɔ:t], *n.* transport, *m.*—[træns'pɔ:t], *v.t.* transporter; déporter (*forçat*).
transportation [trænspɔ:'teiʃən], *n.* transport, *m.*; déportation (*des forçats*), *f.*
transporter [træns'pɔ:tə], *n.* entrepreneur de transports; (pont) transbordeur, *m.*
transporting [træns'pɔ:tiŋ], *a.* ravissant, transportant.
transposal [træns'pouzl], *n.* transposition, *f.*
transpose [trænz'pouz], *v.t.* transposer.
transubstantiation [trænsəbstænʃi'eiʃən], *n.* transsubstantiation, *f.*
Transvaal ['trænzvɑ:l], **the.** le Transvaal, *m.*
transversal [trænz'və:sl], *a.* transversal.
transversely [trænz'və:sli], *adv.* en travers.
transverse [trænz'və:s], *a.* transverse, transversal.
trap [træp], *n.* trappe, *f.*, piège, *m.*; carriole (*véhicule*), *f.*—*v.t.* prendre au piège, attraper.
trap-door ['træpdɔ:], *n.* trappe, *f.*
trapeze [trə'pi:z], *n.* trapèze, *m.*
trapper ['træpə], *n.* trappeur, *m.*
trappings ['træpiŋz], *n.pl.* harnais, *m.*; (*fig.*) parure, *f.*, atours, *m.pl.*
traps [træps], *n.pl.* bagages, *m.pl.*
trash [træʃ], *n.* rebut, *m.*; camelote, *f.*; fatras (*écrits*), *m.*
trashy ['træʃi], *a.* de rebut, sans valeur.
travel [trævl], *v.t.* parcourir; faire (*distan*[ce] *etc.*).—*v.i.* voyager, être en voyage.—voyage, *m.*
traveller ['trævlə], *n.* voyageur; (*Comm*[.]) commis voyageur, *m.*; ***traveller's chequ***[e] chèque de voyage, *m.*
travelling ['trævliŋ], *a.* voyageur, de voyag[e] ambulant (*itinérant*); ***travelling expense***[s] frais de déplacement, *m.pl.*; ***travellin***[g] ***case***, nécessaire de voyage, *m.*—*n.* voyag[e] *m.*, voyages, *m.pl.*
travelogue ['trævələg], *n.* film de tourisme, [*m.*]
traverse ['trævəs], *a.* oblique.—*n.* traverse, [*f.*] —*v.t.* traverser; (*Law*) nier.
travesty ['trævəsti], *n.* travestissement, *m*[.] parodie, *f.*—*v.t.* travestir, parodier.
trawl [trɔ:l], *n.* chalut (*filet*), *m.*—*v.i.* pêch[er] au chalut.
trawler ['trɔ:lə], *n.* chalutier, *m.*
trawling ['trɔ:liŋ], *n.* pêche au chalut, *f.*
tray [trei], *n.* plateau, *m.*
treacherous ['tretʃərəs], *a.* traître, perfide.
treacherously ['tretʃərəsli], *adv.* en traître.
treachery ['tretʃəri], *n.* trahison, perfidie, *f*[.]
treacle [tri:kl], *n.* mélasse, *f.*
tread [tred], *v.t. irr.* fouler, écraser.—*v.*[*i.*] mettre le pied, marcher (*sur*); se pos[er] (*pieds*).—*n.* pas, *m.*; marche (*d'escalier*), *f.*
treading ['trediŋ], *n.* pas, *m.*; marche, *f*[.] foulage (*de raisins etc.*), *m.*
treadle [tredl], *n.* marche; pédale, *f.*
treadmill ['tredmil], *n.* *moulin de disciplin[e] *m.*
treason [tri:zn], *n.* trahison, *f.*; ***hig***[*h*] ***treason***, lèse-majesté, *f.*
treasonable ['tri:znəbl], *a.* de trahison.
treasonably ['tri:znəbli], *adv.* par trahiso[n] traîtreusement.
treasure ['treʒə], *n.* trésor, *m.*—*v.t.* garde[r] priser.
treasurer ['treʒərə], *n.* trésorier, *m.*
treasure-trove ['treʒətrouv], *n.* trésor trouv[é] *m.*
treasury ['treʒəri], *n.* trésor, trésor public *m.*, finances, *f.pl.*, trésorerie, *f.*
treat [tri:t], *n.* régal, festin, (*fig.*) plaisir, *m.*—*v.t.* traiter; régaler (*de*).—*v.i.* traiter (*de*) négocier.
treatise ['tri:tis], *n.* traité (de *ou* sur), *m.*
treatment ['tri:tmənt], *n.* traitement, *m.*
treaty ['tri:ti], *n.* traité, *m.*
treble [trebl], *a.* triple; (*Mus.*) de dessus soprano.—*n.* triple; (*Mus.*) dessus, soprano *m.*—*v.t.*, *v.i.* tripler.
trebling ['trebliŋ], *n.* triplement, *m.*
trebly ['trebli], *adv.* triplement, trois fois.
tree [tri:], *n.* arbre; embauchoir (*pour botte*) *m.*; (*fig.*) croix, *f.*
trefoil ['tri:fɔil], *n.* trèfle, *m.*
trellis ['trelis], *n.* treillis, treillage, *m.*
trellised ['trelist], *a.* treillissé.
tremble [trembl], *v.i.* trembler.
trembling ['trembliŋ], *a.* tremblant, tremblotant.—*n.* tremblement, *m.*
tremendous [tri'mendəs], *a.* terrible, épouvantable.
tremendously [tri'mendəsli], *adv.* terriblement.
tremor ['tremə], *n.* tremblement, *m.* secousse, *f.*

tremulous ['tremjuləs], *a.* tremblant, (*fig.*) craintif.
tremulously ['tremjuləsli], *adv.* en tremblant, en tremblotant.
tremulousness ['tremjuləsnis], *n.* tremblotement, *m.*
trench [trentʃ], *n.* fossé, *m.*, tranchée; rigole (*entre sillons etc.*), *f.*—*v.t.* creuser.
trenchancy ['trentʃənsi], *n.* causticité, *f.*
trenchant ['trentʃənt], *a.* tranchant, caustique.
trencher ['trentʃə], *n.* tranchoir, tailloir, *m.*
trencherman ['trentʃəmən], *n.* (*pl.* **-men** [men]) gros mangeur, *m.*
trend [trend], *n.* direction, tendance, *f.*—*v.i.* se diriger, tendre (*vers*).
trepan [trə'pæn], *n.* (*Surg.*) trépan, *m.*—*v.t.* trépaner.
trepanning [trə'pæniŋ], *n.* trépanation, *f.*
trepidation [trepi'deiʃən], *n.* trépidation, *f.*
trespass ['trespəs], *n.* violation de propriété, *f.*, délit, *m.*; (*Scripture*) offense, *f.*—*v.i.* violer la propriété; empiéter (*sur*); (*Scripture*) pécher; transgresser.
trespasser ['trespəsə], *n.* violateur du droit de propriété; (*Scripture*) pécheur, *m.*, pécheresse, *f.*
tress [tres], *n.* tresse, boucle, *f.*
trestle [tresl], *n.* tréteau, *m.*
trestle-bed ['treslbed], *n.* lit de sangle, *m.*
triad ['traiæd], *n.* triade, *f.*
trial ['traiəl], *a.* d'essai.—*n.* expérience, épreuve, *f.*, essai; (*Law*) procès, *m.*
triangle ['traiæŋgl], *n.* triangle, *m.*
triangular [trai'æŋgjulə], *a.* triangulaire.
tribal [traibl], *a.* tribal.
tribe [traib], *n.* tribu, peuplade; (*fig.*) race, *f.*
tribulation [tribju'leiʃən], *n.* tribulation, *f.*
tribunal [trai'bju:nl], *n.* tribunal, *m.*
tribune ['tribju:n], *n.* (*Rom. Hist.*) tribun, *m.*; tribune (*estrade*), *f.*
tributary ['tribjutəri], *a.* tributaire.—*n.* tributaire; affluent (*rivière*), *m.*
tribute ['tribju:t], *n.* tribut; (*fig.*) hommage, *m.*
trice (1) [trais], *n.* ***in a trice***, en un clin d'œil.
trice (2) [trais], *v.t.* (*Naut.*) hisser.
trick [trik], *n.* tour, artifice, *m.*; (*Cards*) levée; ruse, finesse, *f.*; tic (*habitude*), *m.*; ***nasty trick***, vilain tour; ***to play someone a trick***, faire une niche *ou* jouer un tour à quelqu'un.—*v.t.* duper; tricher (*en jouant*); ***to trick out***, parer, orner.
trickery ['trikəri], *n.* tromperie, fourberie, tricherie, *f.*
trickish ['trikiʃ], *a.* trompeur, fourbe, fin.
trickle [trikl], *v.i.* suinter, dégoutter.
trickling ['trikliŋ], *n.* écoulement, *m.*
trickster ['trikstə], *n.* fourbe, escroc, *m.*
tricky ['triki], *a.* fourbe, rusé; (*fig.*) compliqué; délicat (*à manier*).
tricolour ['traikʌlə], *n.* drapeau tricolore, *m.*
tricoloured ['traikʌləd], *a.* tricolore.
tricycle ['traisikl], *n.* tricycle, *m.*
trident ['traidənt], *n.* trident, *m.*
tried [traid], *a.* éprouvé.
triennial [trai'eniəl], *a.* triennal.—*n.* (*Bot.*) plante triennale, *f.*
triennially [trai'eniəli], *adv.* tous les trois ans.
trier ['traiə], *n.* (*Law*) juge; arbitre, *m.*; (*fig.*) épreuve, pierre de touche, *f.*
trifle [traifl], *n.* bagatelle; (*Cook.*) sorte de charlotte russe, *f.*—*v.i.* badiner; ***to trifle with***, plaisanter avec, se moquer de.
trifler ['traiflə], *n.* personne frivole, *f.*
trifling ['traifliŋ], *a.* de rien, insignifiant, frivole.—*n.* frivolité, *f.*, badinage, *m.*
trigamy ['trigəmi], *n.* trigamie, *f.*
trigger ['trigə], *n.* détente, *f.*
trigonometry [trigə'nɔmətri], *n.* trigonométrie, *f.*
trilateral [trai'lætərəl], *a.* trilatéral.
trill [tril], *n.* trille, *m.*—*v.i.* triller.
trillion ['triljən], *n.* (*since* 1948) trillion; (*before* 1948) quintillion, *m.*
trilogy ['trilədʒi], *n.* trilogie, *f.*
trim [trim], *a.* soigné, coquet, bien mis, bien arrangé.—*n.* bon ordre, *m.*; assiette (*de bateau*), *f.*; orientement (*des voiles*); arrimage (*de cale*), *m.*—*v.t.* arranger, mettre en ordre; garnir, parer (*de*); émonder, tailler (*couper*); (*Naut.*) arrimer (*cargaison*); orienter (*voiles*). —*v.i.* (*Polit. slang*) balancer entre deux partis.
trimly ['trimli], *adv.* bien, gentiment, proprement.
trimmer ['trimə], *n.* (*Polit.*) opportuniste, *m.*, *f.*; (*Naut.*) soutier, *m.*
trimming ['trimiŋ], *n.* garniture; semonce; (*pl.*) parure (*de viande*), *f.*
trimness ['trimnis], *n.* air soigné, bon ordre, *m.*
Trinidad ['trinidæd]. (Île de la) Trinité, *f.*
Trinity ['triniti], *n.* Trinité, *f.*
trinket ['triŋkit], *n.* petit bijou, *m.*, breloque. *f.*
trinomial [trai'noumiəl], *a.* and *n.* trinôme, *m.*
trio ['tri:ou], *n.* trio, *m.*
trip [trip], *v.t.* renverser, faire tomber.—*v.i.* trébucher, faire un faux pas; fourcher (*la langue*); courir légèrement.—*n.* croc-en-jambe, faux pas, *m.*; excursion, *f.*, tour, voyage, *m.*
tripe [traip], *n.* tripes, *f.pl.*
triple [tripl], *a.* triple.—*v.t.* tripler.
triplet ['triplit], *n.* (*Pros.*) tercet; (*Mus.*) triolet, *m.*; (*pl.*) triplés, *m.pl.*
triplicate ['triplikit], *a.* triplé.—*n.* triplicata (*copie*), *m.*
tripod ['traipɔd], *n.* trépied, *m.*
tripper ['tripə], *n.* (*colloq.*) excursionniste, *m.*, *f.*
tripping ['tripiŋ], *a.* agile, léger.—*n.* croc en jambe, faux pas, *m.*; erreur, *f.*; pas léger, *m.*
trireme ['trairi:m], *n.* trirème, *f.*
trisect [trai'sekt], *v.t.* couper en trois.
trisyllabic [traisi'læbik], *a.* trissyllabe.
trisyllable [trai'siləbl], *n.* trissyllabe, *m.*
trite [trait], *a.* usé, banal, rebattu.
triteness ['traitnis], *n.* nature banale, trivialité, *f.*
Triton ['traitən]. Triton, *m.*
triumph ['traiəmf], *n.* triomphe, *m.*—*v.i.* triompher.
triumphal [trai'ʌmfl], *a.* triomphal.
triumphant [trai'ʌmfənt], *a.* triomphant.
triumphantly [trai'ʌmfəntli], *adv.* en triomphe.
triumvir [trai'ʌmvə], *n.* triumvir, *m.*
triumvirate [trai'ʌmvərit], *n.* triumvirat, *m.*
trivet ['trivit], *n.* trépied, *m.*

trivial ['triviəl], *a.* banal, insignifiant, sans importance.
triviality [trivi'æliti], *n.* insignifiance; banalité, *f.*
troat [trout], *n.* bramement, *m.*—*v.t.* bramer, raire (*cerf*).
trochaic [tro'keiik], *a.* trochaïque.
trochee ['trouki], *n.* trochée, *m.*
Trojan ['troudʒən], *a.* troyen.—*n.* Troyen, *m.*
troll [troul], *v.t.* rouler, tourner.
trolley, trolly ['trɔli], *n.* fardier, chariot; (*Elec.*) trolley, *m.*; ***dinner trolley***, table roulante, *f.*
trolley-bus ['trɔlibʌs], *n.* trolleybus, *m.*
trollop ['trɔləp], *n.* souillon, *f.*
trombone [trɔm'boun], *n.* trombone, *m.*
troop [tru:p], *n.* troupe, bande, *f.*—*v.i.* s'attrouper, s'assembler.
trooper ['tru:pə], *n.* (*Mil.*) soldat à cheval, cavalier, *m.*
trophy ['troufi], *n.* trophée, *m.*
tropic ['trɔpik], *n.* tropique, *m.*
tropical ['trɔpikəl], *a.* tropical, des tropiques.
trot [trɔt], *n.* trot, *m.*—*v.i.* trotter, aller au trot; trottiner (*enfant*).
troth [trouθ], *n.* foi, *f.*; ***by my troth !*** ma foi!
trotter ['trɔtə], *n.* cheval de trot, trotteur, *m.*; (*pl.*) pieds de mouton, pieds de cochon, *m.pl.*
trotting ['trɔtiŋ], *a.* trotteur.—*n.* trot, *m.*
troubadour ['tru:bəduə], *n.* troubadour, *m.*
trouble [trʌbl], *v.t.* agiter; troubler, déranger (*gêner*); tourmenter, affliger (*faire souffrir*); inquiéter (*préoccuper*).—*v.i.* s'inquiéter, se donner la peine (*de*).—*n.* trouble, *m.*; peine (*effort*); affliction, *f.*, souci, chagrin (*tristesse*); ennui (*difficulté*), *m.*; ***it is not worth the trouble***, ce n'est pas la peine.
troubled [trʌbld], *a.* inquiet, agité; trouble (*eau etc.*).
troublesome ['trʌblsəm], *a.* ennuyeux, incommode; fatigant, fâcheux.
troublesomeness ['trʌblsəmnis], *n.* ennui, embarras, *m.*, gêne, *f.*
***troublous** ['trʌbləs], *a.* troublé, agité, orageux.
trough [trɔf], *n.* auge, huche, *f.*; (*Cook.*) pétrin; auget, abreuvoir (*pour boire*), *m.*
trounce [trauns], *v.t.* rosser, étriller.
trouncing ['traunsiŋ], *n.* raclée, *f.*, étrillage, *m.*
trouser-press ['trauzəpres], *n.* presse-pantalon, *m.*
trousers ['trauzəz], *n.pl.* pantalon, *m.*
trousseau ['tru:sou], *n.* trousseau, *m.*
trout [traut], *n.* truite, *f.*
trowel ['trauəl], *n.* truelle, *f.*
Troy [trɔi]. Troie, *f.*
troy-weight ['trɔiweit], *n.* troy (*poids de douze onces à la livre*), *m.*
truant ['tru:ənt], *n.* fainéant, vagabond, *m.*; ***to play truant***, faire l'école buissonnière.
truce [tru:s], *n.* trêve, *f.*
truck [trʌk], *n.* fardier, chariot (*charrette*); (*Am.*) camion; (*Rail.*) wagon, *m.*—*v.i.* troquer.
truckle [trʌkl], *n.* roulette, *f.*—*v.i.* ramper s'abaisser (*devant*).
truckle-bed ['trʌklbed], *n.* grabat, *m.*.
truckling ['trʌkliŋ], *n.* soumission, *f.*, abaissement, *m.*

truculence ['trʌkjuləns], *n.* férocité, truculence, *f.*
truculent ['trʌkjulənt], *a.* brutal, féroc farouche.
trudge [trʌdʒ], *n.* marche pénible, *f.*—*v.* clopiner, marcher péniblement.
true [tru:], *a.* vrai, véritable; fidèle (*véridique*); exact (*juste*); loyal (*honnête*); dro (*vertueux*); ***to come true***, se réaliser.—*in* c'est vrai! c'est juste!—*adv.* juste (*précisément*).—*v.t.* ajuster.
true-bred ['tru:bred], *a.* de bonne race, p sang; (*fig.*) accompli.
true-hearted ['tru:'hɑ:tid], *a.* au cœ sincère.
trueness ['tru:nis], *n.* fidélité; justesse, *f.*
truffle [trʌfl], *n.* truffe, *f.*; ***to stuff wit truffles***, truffer.
truism ['tru:izm], *n.* truisme, *m.*
truly ['tru:li], *adv.* vraiment, véritablement
trump [trʌmp], *n.* trompe, trompette, *f.* (*Cards.*) atout, *m.*—*v.t.* jouer atout, couper
trumpery ['trʌmpəri], *a.* sans valeur, mes quin.—*n.* rebut, *m.*, blague, *f.*
trumpet ['trʌmpit], *n.* trompette, *f.*—*v.* proclamer.—*v.i.* barrir (*éléphant*).
trumpet-call ['trʌmpitkɔ:l], *n.* coup d trompette, *m.*
trumpeter ['trʌmpitə], *n.* trompette, *m.*
truncate [trʌŋ'keit], *v.t.* tronquer.
truncheon ['trʌntʃən], *n.* bâton, *m.*; matraque *f.*
trundle [trʌndl], *v.t.* rouler.
trunk [trʌŋk], *n.* tronc, *m.*; malle (*boîte*) trompe (*d'éléphant etc.*), *f.*; (*Sculp.*) torse, *m*
trunk-call ['trʌŋkkɔ:l], *n.* (*Teleph.*) appe interurbain, *m.*
trunk-road ['trʌŋkroud], *n.* route à grand circulation, *f.*
trunnion ['trʌnjən], *n.* tourillon, *m.*
truss [trʌs], *n.* botte (*de foin etc.*), *f.*; paquet (*Surg.*) bandage herniaire, *m.*—*v.t.* trousse (*une poule*); lier (*foin*).
trust [trʌst], *n.* confiance (*en*), *f.*; dépôt, *m.* garde (*charge*), *f.*; crédit; (*Law*) fidéi commis; (*Comm.*) trust, syndicat, *m.*—*v.t* se fier à, se confier à; faire crédit à (*e matière d'argent*).—*v.i.* avoir confiance (*e* ou *dans*); s'attendre (*à*).
trust-deed ['trʌstdi:d], *n.* acte fiduciaire, *m.*
trusted ['trʌstid], *a.* de confiance.
trustee [trʌs'ti:], *n.* gardien, *m.*, dépositaire (*Law*) fidéicommissaire, *m.*, *f.*
trusteeship [trʌs'ti:ʃip], *n.* administration tutelle, *f.*, (*Law*) fidéicommis, *m.*
trustiness ['trʌstinis], *n.* fidélité, loyauté, *f.*
trusting ['trʌstiŋ], *a.* plein de confiance.
trustworthiness ['trʌstwə:ðinis], *n.* fidélité (*personne*); exactitude (*des nouvelles etc.*), *f.*
trustworthy ['trʌstwə:ði], *a.* digne de confiance; exact (*nouvelles*).
trusty ['trʌsti], *a.* sûr, fidèle, loyal.
truth [tru:θ], *n.* vérité, *f.*, vrai, *m.*; ***to tell the truth . . .***, à vrai dire . . . .
truthful ['tru:θful], *a.* véridique, vrai.
truthfully ['tru:θfuli], *adv.* véridiquement, avec vérité.
truthfulness ['tru:θfulnis], *n.* véracité, *f.*
try [trai], *v.t.* essayer; éprouver, mettre à l'épreuve; tenter (*se prêter à*); (*Law*) juger. —*v.i.* essayer, tâcher (*de*).—*n.* essai, *m.*

trying ['traiiŋ], *a.* difficile, pénible.
***tryst** [traist], *n.* rendez-vous, *m.*
Tsar [zɑ:], *n.* Tsar, *m.*
Tsarina [zɑ:'ri:nə], *n.* Tsarine, *f.*
tsetse ['tsetsi], *n.* mouche tsé-tsé, *f.*
tub [tʌb], *n.* cuve, *f.*, baquet; bain (*moderne*), *m.*—*v.t.* encuver; (*Gard.*) encaisser.
tuba ['tju:bə], *n.* tuba, *m.*; contrebasse à vent, *f.*
tubby ['tʌbi], *a.* gros, obèse.
tube [tju:b], *n.* tube; (*Anat.*) conduit, canal; (*Rail.*) métro, *m.*; ***inner tube***, chambre à air, *f.*
tuber ['tju:bə], *n.* tubercule, *m.*
tubercular [tju'bə:kjulə], *a.* tuberculeux.
tuberculosis [tjubə:kju'lousis], *n.* tuberculose, *f.*
tuberose ['tju:bərous], *a.* tubéreux.—*n.* tubéreuse, *f.*
tuberous ['tju:bərəs], *a.* tubéreux.
tubular ['tju:bjulə], *a.* tubulaire.
tuck [tʌk], *n.* pli, *m.*—*v.t.* plisser; serrer; retrousser.
tucker ['tʌkə], *n.* chemisette, collerette, *f.*
Tuesday ['tju:zd(e)i]. mardi, *m.*; ***Shrove Tuesday***, mardi gras.
tuft [tʌft], *n.* touffe (*d'herbe* ou *de cheveux*); huppe (*d'oiseau*), *f.*
tufted ['tʌftid], *a.* touffu; huppé (*oiseau*).
tug [tʌg], *v.t.* tirer avec effort; remorquer (*to tow*).—*n.* tiraillement; remorqueur (*bateau*), *m.*
tuition [tju'iʃən], *n.* instruction, *f.*, enseignement, *m.*
tulip ['tju:lip], *n.* tulipe, *f.*
tulle [tju:l], *n.* tulle, *m.*
tumble [tʌmbl], *n.* culbute, chute, *f.*—*v.t.* culbuter.—*v.i.* tomber; rouler (*descendre en roulant*); dégringoler (*se tourner*).
tumbledown ['tʌmbldaun], *a.* croulant, délabré.
tumbler ['tʌmblə], *n.* verre sans pied; gobelet; culbutant (*pigeon*), *m.*
tumblerful ['tʌmbləful], *n.* plein un grand verre, *m.*
tumbril ['tʌmbril], **tumbrel** ['tʌmbrəl], *n.* tombereau, *m.*
tumefaction [tju:mi'fækʃən], *n.* tuméfaction, *f.*
tumefy ['tju:mifai], *v.t.* tuméfier.—*v.i.* se tuméfier.
tumid ['tju:mid], *a.* enflé, gonflé; (*fig.*) boursouflé.
tumidity [tju'miditi], **tumidness** ['tju:midnis], *n.* enflure; (*fig.*) turgescence, *f.*
tumour ['tju:mə], *n.* tumeur, *f.*
tumular ['tju:mjulə], *a.* en monticule.
tumult ['tju:mʌlt], *n.* tumulte; trouble, *m.*
tumultuous [tju'mʌltjuəs], *a.* tumultueux, turbulent, agité.
tumultuousness [tju'mʌltjuəsnis], *n.* turbulence, *f.*
tun [tʌn], *n.* tonneau, fût, *m.*; cuve, *f.*
tunable ['tju:nəbl], *a.* accordable.
tundra ['tundrə], *n.* toundra, *f.*
tune [tju:n], *n.* air; accord, *m.*; (*fig.*) harmonie, humeur, *f.*; ***in tune***, d'accord; ***out of tune***, faux.—*v.t.* accorder, mettre d'accord.—*v.i.* (*Rad.*) ***to tune in***, accrocher (*un poste*).
tuneful ['tju:nful], *a.* harmonieux, mélodieux.
tuneless ['tju:nlis], *a.* discordant.
tuner ['tju:nə], *n.* accordeur, *m.*
tungsten ['tʌŋstən], *n.* tungstène, *m.*
tunic ['tju:nik], *n.* tunique, *f.*
tuning ['tju:niŋ], *n.* accord, *m.*, action d'accorder, *f.*
tuning-fork ['tju:niŋfɔ:k], *n.* diapason, *m.*
tuning-hammer ['tju:niŋhæmə], *n.* accordoir, *m.*
Tunisia [tju'niziə]. la Tunisie, *f.*
Tunisian [tju'niziən], *a.* tunisien.—*n.* Tunisien (*personne*), *m.*
tunnel [tʌnl], *n.* tunnel, passage souterrain, *m.*—*v.t.* percer un tunnel dans.
tunnelling ['tʌnəliŋ], *n.* construction de tunnels, *f.*
tunny ['tʌni], *n.* (*Ichth.*) thon, *m.*
turban ['tə:bən], *n.* turban, *m.*
turbid ['tə:bid], *a.* trouble, bourbeux.
turbidity [tə:'biditi], **turbidness** ['tə:bidnis], *n.* état bourbeux, état trouble, *m.*
turbine ['tə:bin, 'tə:bain], *n.* turbine, *f.*
turbo-prop ['tə:boprɔp], *a.* (*Av.*) à turbopropulseur.
turbot ['tə:bət], *n.* turbot, *m.*
turbulence ['tə:bjuləns], **turbulency** ['tə:bjulənsi], *n.* turbulence, *f.*, tumulte, *m.*
turbulent ['tə:bjulənt], *a.* tumultueux, turbulent.
turbulently ['tə:bjuləntli], *adv.* tumultueusement.
tureen [tju'ri:n], *n.* soupière, *f.*
turf [tə:f], *n.* gazon, *m.*; motte de gazon; tourbe (*combustible*), *f.*; (*fig.*) turf, *m.*—*v.t.* gazonner.
turfing ['tə:fiŋ], *n.* gazonnement, *m.*
turf-moss ['tə:fmɔs], **turf-pit** ['tə:fpit], *n.* tourbière, *f.*
turfy ['tə:fi], *a.* gazonné; tourbeux.
turgid ['tə:dʒid], *a.* gonflé; boursouflé.
turgidity [tə'dʒiditi], **turgidness** ['tə:dʒidnis], *n.* turgescence; (*fig.*) emphase (*de style*), *f.*
Turk [tə:k], *n.* Turc (*personne*), *m.*
Turkey ['tə:ki]. la Turquie, *f.*
turkey ['tə:ki], *n.* dindon, *m.*; ***hen-turkey***, dinde, *f.*
Turkish ['tə:kiʃ], *a.* de Turquie, turc.—*n.* turc (*langue*), *m.*
turmoil ['tə:mɔil], *n.* tumulte, *m.*, agitation, *f.*
turn [tə:n], *v.t.* tourner, faire tourner; faire pencher (*la balance*); retourner (*vêtement etc.*); changer, convertir (*transformer*); traduire (*en une autre langue*); soulever (*l'estomac*); émousser (*le tranchant*); (*fig.*) rouler (*dans la tête*); ***to turn aside***, détourner, écarter (*de*); ***to turn away***, renvoyer, congédier; ***to turn back***, faire retourner; ***to turn down***, rabattre (*un col*); refuser; ***to turn in***, tourner en dedans; ***to turn into***, changer en; ***to turn off***, couper (*vapeur*), fermer (*robinet*); ***to turn on***, donner (*vapeur*), ouvrir (*robinet*); ***to turn out***, mettre dehors; éteindre (*lumière*); ***to turn over***, retourner, feuilleter (*pages d'un livre*); ***to turn tail***, prendre la fuite; ***to turn up***, retrousser.—*v.i.* tourner, se tourner; se retourner (*vers*); se détourner (*s'écarter*); se changer (*en*); devenir, se faire; ***to turn back***, rebrousser chemin; ***to turn from***, s'éloigner de; ***to turn in***, se coucher (*aller au lit*); ***to turn round***, tourner, se

tourner, se retourner; ***to turn to***, s'adresser à; ***to turn up***, se retrousser; arriver (*se passer*).—*n.* tour; coude, détour (*tournant*); service; changement, *m.*; occasion; tournure (*d'esprit*), *f.*; trait (*de balance*), *m.*; ***a bad turn***, un mauvais tour; ***a good turn***, un service; ***by turns, in turns***, à tour de rôle.

turncoat ['tə:nkout], *n.* renégat, *m.*

turn-cock ['tə:nkɔk], *n.* fontainier, *m.*

turner ['tə:nə], *n.* tourneur, *m.*

turnery ['tə:nəri], *n.* art du tourneur, *m.*

turning ['tə:niŋ], *n.* tournant (*de route etc.*); (*Carp.*) tournage, *m.*

turning-lathe ['tə:niŋleið], *n.* tour, *m.*

turning-point ['tə:niŋpɔint], *n.* point décisif, moment critique, *m.*

turnip ['tə:nip], *n.* navet, *m.*

turnkey ['tə:nki:], *n.* guichetier, porte-clefs, *m.*

turn-out ['tə:naut], *n.* équipage, *m.*; tenue, *f.*

turn-over ['tə:nouvə], *n.* chiffre d'affaires; chausson (*pâte*), *m.*

turnpike ['tə:npaik], *n.* barrière de péage, *f.*, tourniquet, *m.*

turnspit ['tə:nspit], *n.* tournebroche, *m.*

turnstile ['tə:nstail], *n.* tourniquet, *m.*

turn-table ['tə:nteibl], *n.* plaque tournante; platine, *f.*

turn-up ['tə:nʌp], *n.* revers (*de pantalon*), *m.*

turpentine ['tə:pəntain], *n.* térébenthine, *f.*

turpitude ['tə:pitju:d], *n.* turpitude, *f.*

turquoise ['tə:kwɔiz], *n.* turquoise, *f.*

turret ['tʌrit], *n.* tourelle, *f.*

turreted ['tʌritid], *a.* garni de tourelles.

turtle [tə:tl], *n.* tortue de mer, *f.*; ***to turn turtle***, chavirer (*bateau*), capoter (*voiture*).

turtle-dove ['tə:tldʌv], *n.* tourterelle, *f.*

Tuscan ['tʌskən], *a.* toscan.—*n.* Toscan (*personne*), *m.*

Tuscany ['tʌskəni]. la Toscane, *f.*

tush! [tʌʃ], *int.* bah! fi donc!

tusk [tʌsk], *n.* défense (*d'éléphant*), *f.*; croc (*dent*), *m.*

tussle [tʌsl], *n.* lutte, bagarre, *f.*

tut! [tʌt], *int.* bah! allons donc!

tutelage ['tju:tilidʒ], *n.* tutelle, *f.*

tutor ['tju:tə], *n.* précepteur (*dans une famille*); (*Univ.*) maître-assistant, *m.*—*v.t.* instruire, enseigner.

tutorial [tju:'tɔ:riəl], *a.* de précepteur.

tutoring ['tju:təriŋ], *n.* instruction, *f.*

tutorship ['tju:təʃip], *n.* préceptorat, *m.*

twaddle [twɔdl], *n.* bavardage, caquetage, *m.*

***twain** [twein], *a.* and *n.* deux, *m.*

twang [twæŋ], *n.* son sec (*d'une corde qui vibre*); accent nasillard (*voix*), *m.*—*v.t.* faire résonner, faire vibrer.—*v.i.* résonner, nasiller.

tweak [twi:k], *v.t.* pincer (*en tordant*).

tweezers ['twi:zəz], *n.pl.* pinces à épiler (*pour poils*), *f.pl.*

twelfth [twelfθ], *a.* douzième; douze (*du mois, des rois etc.*), *m.*; ***Twelfth Night***, jour des Rois, *m.*—*n.* douzième (*fraction*), *m.*

twelve [twelv], *a.* and *n.* douze, *m.*; ***twelve o'clock***, midi (*noon*), minuit (*midnight*), *m.*

twelvemonth ['twelvmʌnθ], *n.* an, *m.*, année, *f.*

twentieth ['twentiəθ], *a.* vingtième; vingt (*du mois etc.*).—*n.* vingtième (*fraction*), *m.*

twenty ['twenti], *a.* and *n.* vingt, *m.*

twenty-first ['twenti'fə:st], *a.* vingt et unième vingt et un (*du mois etc.*).

twice [twais], *adv.* deux fois.

twig [twig], *n.* brindille, ramille, *f.*

twilight ['twailait], *a.* crépusculaire.—*n* crépuscule, *m.*

twill [twil], *n.* étoffe croisée, *f.*

twin [twin], *a.* jumeau; jumelé; (*Bot.*) double géminé.—*n.* jumeau, *m.*, jumelle, *f.*

twine [twain], *n.* ficelle, *f.*—*v.t.* retordre, enlacer.—*v.i.* s'entrelacer, s'enrouler.

twinge [twindʒ], *n.* élancement; remords (*de conscience*), *m.*—*v.i.* élancer; (*fig.*) torturer.

twinkle [twiŋkl], *v.i.* étinceler.

twinkling ['twiŋkliŋ], *a.* étincelant, scintillant.—*n.* scintillement, clignotement (*des yeux*), *m.*; ***in the twinkling of an eye***, en un clin d'œil.

twirl [twə:l], *v.t.* faire tournoyer; friser (*favoris*).—*v.i.* tournoyer, tourner rapidement.—*n.* tournoiement, *m.*; pirouette, *f.*

twist [twist], *v.t.* tordre; tortiller, retordre; cercler, entourer; enlacer (*entortiller*); (*fig.*) pervertir (*dénaturer*).—*v.i.* se tordre, s'entrelacer, s'enlacer, s'enrouler.—*n.* cordon, *m.*, corde, *f.*; tortillon (*de papier*), *m.*; carotte (*de tabac*), *f.*

twisted ['twistid], *a.* tordu; (*fig.*) perverti, défiguré, dénaturé.

twisting ['twistiŋ], *a.* tortueux.—*n.* tordage; tortillement, *m.*

twitch [twitʃ], *n.* saccade, *f.*; tic (*contraction spasmodique*); tiraillement (*de douleur*), *m.*—*v.t.* tirer brusquement; crisper.—*v.i.* se contracter nerveusement.

twitching ['twitʃiŋ], *n.* saccade, crispation (*des muscles etc.*), *f.*; tiraillement (*de douleur*), *m.*

twitter ['twitə], *v.t., v.i.* gazouiller.—*n.* gazouillement, *m.*

two [tu:], *a.* and *n.* deux, *m.*

two-edged ['tu:edʒd], *a.* à deux tranchants.

twofold ['tu:fould], *a.* double.—*adv.* doublement, deux fois.

two-stroke ['tu:strouk], *a.* à deux temps.

tycoon [tai'ku:n], *n.* taïcoun; (*fam.*) brasseur d'affaires, manitou, *m.*

type [taip], *n.* type; (*Print.*) caractère; (*pop.*) type, *m.*—*v.t.* [TYPEWRITE].

typewrite ['taiprait], *v.t.* écrire à la machine, dactylographier, taper.

typewriter ['taipraitə], *n.* machine à écrire, *f.*

typewritten ['taipritn], *a.* tapé à la machine.

typhoid ['taifɔid], *a.* typhoïde.

typhoon [tai'fu:n], *n.* typhon, *m.*, trombe, *f.*

typhus ['taifəs], *n.* typhus, *m.*

typical ['tipikl], *a.* typique.

typically ['tipikli], *adv.* d'une manière typique.

typify ['tipifai], *v.t.* symboliser.

typing ['taipiŋ], *n.* dactylographie, (*fam.*) dactylo, *f.*

typist ['taipist], *n.* dactylographe, (*fam.*) dactylo, *m., f.*

typography [tai'pɔgrəfi], *n.* typographie, *f.*

tyrannical [ti'rænikl], *a.* tyrannique.

tyrannically [ti'rænikli], *adv.* tyranniquement.

tyrannize ['tirənaiz], *v.i.* faire le tyran; ***to tyrannize over***, tyranniser.

tyranny ['tirəni], *n.* tyrannie, *f.*
tyrant ['taiərənt], *n.* tyran, *m.*
tyre ['taiə], *n.* pneu (*de roue*), *m.*
tyro ['taiərou], *n.* novice, débutant, *m.*
Tzar [TSAR].

U

U, u [ju:]. vingt et unième lettre de l'alphabet, *m.*
ubiquitous [ju'bikwitəs], *a.* omniprésent.
ubiquity [ju'bikwiti], *n.* ubiquité, *f.*
udder ['ʌdə], *n.* mamelle, *f.*, pis, *m.*
ugh! [u:x, u:h, ʌx, uf], *int.* pouah!
ugliness ['ʌglinis], *n.* laideur, *f.*
ugly ['ʌgli], *a.* laid, vilain.
Ukraine [ju'krein], **the.** l'Ukraine, *f.*
Ukrainian [ju'kreiniən], *a.* ukrainien.—*n.* Ukrainien (*personne*), *m.*
ukulele [ju:kə'leili], *n.* ukulélé, *m.*
ulcer ['ʌlsə], *n.* ulcère, *m.*
ulcerate ['ʌlsəreit], *v.t.* ulcérer.—*v.i.* s'ulcérer.
ulcerated ['ʌlsəreitid], *a.* ulcéré.
ulceration [ʌlsə'reiʃən], *n.* ulcération, *f.*
ulcerous ['ʌlsərəs], *a.* ulcéreux.
ullage ['ʌlidʒ], *n.* vidange, *f.*
ulterior [ʌl'tiəriə], *a.* ultérieur; ***without ulterior motive***, sans arrière-pensée.
ultimate ['ʌltimit], *a.* dernier; extrême.
ultimately ['ʌltimitli], *adv.* finalement, à la fin.
ultimatum [ʌlti'meitəm], *n.* (*pl.* **ultimata** [ʌlti'meitə]) ultimatum, *m.*
ultimo ['ʌltimou], *adv.* (*abbr.* **ult.** [ʌlt]) du mois dernier.
ultra ['ʌltrə], *n.* ultra, *m.*
ultramarine [ʌltrəmə'ri:n], *a.* d'outremer.—*n.* outremer, *m.*
ululate ['ju:ljuleit], *v.i.* ululer.
Ulysses [ju:'lisi:z]. Ulysse, *m.*
umber ['ʌmbə], *n.* (*Paint.*) terre d'ombre, *f.*
umbilical [ʌm'bilikl], *a.* ombilical.
umbrage ['ʌmbridʒ], *n.* ombrage, *m.*
umbrella [ʌm'brelə], *n.* parapluie, *m.*; ***umbrella-stand***, porte-parapluies, *m.inv.*
umpire ['ʌmpaiə], *n.* arbitre, *m.*—*v.t.*, *v.i.* arbitrer.
unabashed [ʌnə'bæʃt], *a.* sans être confus.
unabated [ʌnə'beitid], *a.* sans diminution.
unable [ʌn'eibl], *a.* incapable (*de*); ***to be unable to***, ne pas pouvoir.
unabridged [ʌnə'bridʒd], *a.* non abrégé; en entier.
unacceptable [ʌnək'septəbl], *a.* inacceptable.
unaccommodating [ʌnə'kɔmədeitiŋ], *a.* peu accommodant.
unaccompanied [ʌnə'kʌmpənid], *a.* seul, sans suite.
unaccountable [ʌnə'kauntəbl], *a.* inexplicable, inconcevable.
unaccountably [ʌnə'kauntəbli], *adv.* inconcevablement.
unaccustomed [ʌnə'kʌstəmd], *a.* inaccoutumé (*à*); peu habitué.
unacknowledged [ʌnək'nɔlidʒd], *a.* non reconnu; sans réponse (*lettre*).
unacquainted [ʌnə'kweintid], *a.* étranger (*à*); peu familier (*avec*).
unadopted [ʌnə'dɔptid], *a.* non adopté.
unadorned [ʌnə'dɔ:nd], *a.* sans ornement.
unadulterated [ʌnə'dʌltəreitid], *a.* pur, non frelaté.
unadvisable [ʌnəd'vaizəbl], *a.* peu sage, inopportun.
unadvised [ʌnəd'vaizd], *a.* malavisé; imprudent (*rash*).
unadvisedly [ʌnəd'vaizidli], *adv.* inconsidérément.
unaffected [ʌnə'fektid], *a.* sans affectation; insensible (*peu ému*).
unaffectedly [ʌnə'fektidli], *adv.* sans affectation.
unafraid [ʌnə'freid], *a.* sans peur.
unaided [ʌn'eidid], *a.* seul, sans aide.
unallayed [ʌnə'leid], *a.* non apaisé.
unallowable [ʌnə'lauəbl], *a.* non permis; inadmissible.
unalloyed [ʌnə'lɔid], *a.* pur, sans alliage, sans mélange.
unalterable [ʌn'ɔ:ltərəbl], *a.* inaltérable, invariable.
unalterably [ʌn'ɔ:ltərəbli], *adv.* immuablement.
unambitious [ʌnæm'biʃəs], *a.* sans ambition.
unanimity [ju:nə'nimiti], *n.* unanimité, *f.*
unanimous [ju'næniməs], *a.* unanime.
unanimously [ju'næniməsli], *adv.* unanimement, à l'unanimité.
unanswerable [ʌn'ɑ:nsərəbl], *a.* incontestable.
unanswered [ʌn'ɑ:nsəd], *a.* sans réponse.
unappeasable [ʌnə'pi:zəbl], *a.* implacable.
unappetizing [ʌn'æpitaiziŋ], *a.* peu appétissant.
unappreciated [ʌnə'pri:ʃieitid], *a.* inapprécié.
unapproachable [ʌnə'proutʃəbl], *a.* inaccessible, inabordable.
unarmed [ʌn'ɑ:md], *a.* sans armes.
unascertainable [ʌnæsə'teinəbl], *a.* qu'on ne peut constater.
unashamed [ʌnə'ʃeimd], *a.* sans honte.
unasked [ʌn'ɑ:skt], *a.* sans être invité; spontané.—*adv.* spontanément.
unaspiring [ʌnə'spaiəriŋ], *a.* sans ambition.
unassailable [ʌnə'seiləbl], *a.* hors d'atteinte; inattaquable, irréfutable.
unassisted [ʌnə'sistid], *a.* sans aide.
unassuming [ʌnə'sju:miŋ], *a.* sans prétention, modeste.
unattached [ʌnə'tætʃt], *a.* sans être attaché (*à*); en disponibilité.
unattainable [ʌnə'teinəbl], *a.* inaccessible.
unattended [ʌnə'tendid], *a.* seul, sans suite.
unattested [ʌnə'testid], *a.* non attesté.
unattractive [ʌnə'træktiv], *a.* peu attrayant, sans attrait.
unauthenticated [ʌnɔ:'θentikeitid], *a.* dont l'authenticité n'est pas prouvée.
unauthorized [ʌn'ɔ:θəraizd], *a.* sans autorisation; illicite, illégal (*chose*).
unavailable [ʌnə'veiləbl], *a.* non valable; inutilisable (*billet*); indisponible (*fonds, personne*); qu'on ne peut se procurer (*chose*).
unavailing [ʌnə'veiliŋ], *a.* inutile, inefficace.
unavenged [ʌnə'vendʒd], *a.* impuni, non vengé.

unavoidable [ʌnə'vɔidebl], *a.* inévitable.
unavoidably [ʌnə'vɔidəbli], *adv.* inévitablement.
unaware [ʌnə'wɛə], *a.* ignorant; ***to be unaware of***, ignorer.
unawares [ʌnə'wɛəz], *adv.* à l'improviste; à son insu (*sans s'en rendre compte*); ***to be taken unawares***, être pris au dépourvu.
unbalanced [ʌn'bælənst], *a.* mal équilibré.
unbearable [ʌn'bɛərəbl], *a.* insupportable, intolérable.
unbearably [ʌn'bɛərəbli], *adv.* insupportablement.
unbeatable [ʌn'bi:təbl], *a.* invincible.
unbeaten [ʌn'bi:tn], *a.* invaincu.
unbecoming [ʌnbi'kʌmiŋ], *a.* peu convenable, malséant; qui ne va pas bien (*vêtement*).
unbecomingly [ʌnbi'kʌmiŋli], *adv.* d'une manière peu séante.
unbefitting [ʌnbi'fitiŋ], *a.* qui ne convient pas, peu propre.
unbeknown [ʌnbi'noun], *a.* inconnu; ***unbeknown to me***, à mon insu.
unbelief [ʌnbi'li:f], *n.* incrédulité, incroyance, *f.*
unbelievable [ʌnbi'li:vəbl], *a.* incroyable.
unbeliever [ʌnbi'li:və], *n.* incrédule; sceptique, *m., f.*
unbelieving [ʌnbi'li:viŋ], *a.* incrédule; sceptique.
unbend [ʌn'bend], *v.t. irr.* (*conjug. like* BEND) détendre, relâcher; débander (*l'arc*); (*fig.*) délasser (*l'esprit*).—*v.i.* se détendre.
unbending [ʌn'bendiŋ], *a.* inflexible.
unbiased [ʌn'baiəst], *a.* sans prévention, impartial.
unbidden [ʌn'bidn], *a.* sans être invité.
unbind [ʌn'baind], *v.t. irr.* (*conjug. like* BIND) délier, détacher.
unbleached [ʌn'bli:tʃt], *a.* écru.
unblemished [ʌn'blemiʃt], *a.* sans tache.
unblushing [ʌn'blʌʃiŋ], *a.* qui ne rougit point, éhonté, sans vergogne.
unblushingly [ʌn'blʌʃiŋli], *adv.* sans rougir.
unbolt [ʌn'boult], *v.t.* tirer les verrous de, ouvrir.
unborn [ʌn'bɔ:n], *a.* encore à naître; futur, à venir (*chose*).
unbosom [ʌn'buzm], *v.t.* ***to unbosom oneself***, ouvrir son cœur.
unbound [ʌn'baund], *a.* délié; non relié (*livre*).
unbounded [ʌn'baundid], *a.* illimité, infini.
unbreakable [ʌn'breikəbl], *a.* incassable.
unbridled [ʌn'braidld], *a.* débridé; (*fig.*) effréné.
unbroken [ʌn'broukn], *a.* non rompu; continu (*ininterrompu*); indompté (*non vaincu*); intact (*non violé*); non dressé (*animal*).
unbrotherly [ʌn'brʌðəli], *a.* peu fraternel.
unbuckle [ʌn'bʌkl], *v.t.* déboucler.
unburden [ʌn'bə:dn], *v.t.* décharger; ***to unburden oneself***, ouvrir son cœur.
unburied [ʌn'berid], *a.* sans sépulture.
unbusinesslike [ʌn'biznislaik], *a.* peu pratique.
unbutton [ʌn'bʌtn], *v.t.* déboutonner.
uncalled [ʌn'kɔ:ld], *a.* sans être appelé; ***uncalled for***, sans être demandé; gratuit (*superflu*); peu convenable (*mal élevé*); non mérité (*injuste*).
uncanny [ʌn'kæni], *a.* mystérieux, surnaturel.
uncared-for [ʌn'kɛədfɔ:], *a.* négligé.
unceasing [ʌn'si:siŋ], *a.* incessant, sans cesse.
unceasingly [ʌn'si:siŋli], *adv.* continuellement, sans cesse.
uncensored [ʌn'sensəd], *a.* non expurgé.
unceremonious [ʌnseri'mouniəs], *a.* peu cérémonieux; sans façon.
unceremoniously [ʌnseri'mouniəsli], *adv.* sans cérémonie, sans façon.
uncertain [ʌn'sə:tin], *a.* incertain, peu sûr.
uncertainty [ʌn'sə:tinti], *n.* incertitude, *f.*
uncertificated [ʌnsə'tifikətid], *a.* non diplômé (*instituteur*).
unchain [ʌn'tʃein], *v.t.* déchaîner.
unchallenged [ʌn'tʃælindʒd], *a.* indisputé.
unchangeable [ʌn'tʃeindʒəbl], *a.* inaltérable, immuable.
unchanged [ʌn'tʃeindʒd], *a.* inchangé, toujours le même.
unchanging [ʌn'tʃeindʒiŋ], *a.* invariable, constant.
uncharitable [ʌn'tʃæritəbl], *a.* peu charitable.
uncharitableness [ʌn'tʃæritəblnis], *n.* manque de charité, *m.*
uncharitably [ʌn'tʃæritəbli], *adv.* sans charité.
uncharted [ʌn'tʃɑ:tid], *a.* inexploré.
unchaste [ʌn'tʃeist], *a.* incontinent, impudique.
unchecked [ʌn'tʃekt], *a.* non réprimé, sans frein; non vérifié.
unchivalrous [ʌn'ʃivlrəs], *a.* peu chevaleresque.
unchristian [ʌn'kristiən], *a.* peu chrétien.
uncircumcised [ʌn'sə:kəmsaizd], *a.* incirconcis.
uncivil [ʌn'sivil], *a.* malhonnête, impoli.
uncivilized [ʌn'sivilaizd], *a.* peu civilisé, barbare.
uncivilly [ʌn'sivili], *adv.* malhonnêtement, impoliment.
unclaimed [ʌn'kleimd], *a.* non réclamé.
unclasp [ʌn'klɑ:sp], *v.t.* dégrafer, défaire.
unclassified [ʌn'klæsifaid], *a.* non classé.
uncle [ʌŋkl], *n.* oncle, *m.*; (*slang*) ***at uncle's***, chez ma tante (*le prêteur sur gage*).
unclean [ʌn'kli:n], *a.* malpropre, sale; impudique (*obscène*); impur.
uncleanliness [ʌn'klenlinis], **uncleanness** [ʌn'kli:nnis], *n.* saleté; (*fig.*) impureté, *f.*
unclench [ʌn'klentʃ], *v.t.* ouvrir, desserrer.
uncloak [ʌn'klouk], *v.t.* dévoiler.
unclose [ʌn'klouz], *v.t.* ouvrir.
unclosed [ʌn'klouzd], *a.* non fermé, ouvert.
unclothe [ʌn'klouð], *v.t.* déshabiller.
unclothed [ʌn'klouðd], *a.* déshabillé, nu.
unclouded [ʌn'klaudid], *a.* sans nuage, serein.
uncock [ʌn'kɔk], *v.t.* désarmer (*fusil etc.*).
uncoil [ʌn'kɔil], *v.t.* dérouler.—*v.i.* se dérouler.
uncombed [ʌn'koumd], *a.* mal peigné, ébouriffé.
uncomfortable [ʌn'kʌmftəbl], *a.* peu confortable, incommode; gêné (*personne*).
uncomfortably [ʌn'kʌmftəbli], *adv.* peu confortablement; mal à l'aise.
uncommitted [ʌnkə'mitid], *a.* non commis; non engagé, libre.

uncommon [ʌn'kɔmən], *a.* peu commun; rare.
uncommonly [ʌn'kɔmənli], *adv.* rarement; infiniment (*singulièrement*).
uncommunicative [ʌnkə'mju:nikətiv], *a.* peu communicatif, réservé.
uncomplaining [ʌnkəm'pleiniŋ], *a.* sans plainte, résigné.
uncomplainingly [ʌnkəm'pleiniŋli], *adv.* sans se plaindre, sans plainte.
uncompleted [ʌnkəm'pli:tid], *a.* inachevé, incomplet.
uncomplimentary [ʌnkɔmpli'mentəri], *a.* peu flatteur.
uncompromising [ʌn'kɔmprəmaiziŋ], *a.* peu accommodant, intransigeant.
unconcern [ʌnkən'sə:n], *n.* insouciance, indifférence, *f.*
unconcerned [ʌnkən'sə:nd], *a.* indifférent, insouciant.
unconcernedly [ʌnkən'sə:nidli], *adv.* avec indifférence.
unconditional [ʌnkən'diʃənl], *a.* sans conditions, absolu.
unconditionally [ʌnkən'diʃənəli], *adv.* sans condition.
unconfined [ʌnkən'faind], *a.* libre; illimité.
unconfinedly [ʌnkən'fainidli], *adv.* sans limite.
unconfirmed [ʌnkən'fə:md], *a.* non confirmé.
uncongenial [ʌnkən'dʒi:niəl], *a.* désagréable; peu sympathique.
unconnected [ʌnkə'nektid], *a.* détaché, sans rapport (*avec*); décousu (*style*).
unconquerable [ʌn'kɔŋkərəbl], *a.* invincible.
unconquered [ʌn'kɔŋkəd], *a.* insoumis.
unconscionable [ʌn'kɔnʃənəbl], *a.* déraisonnable.
unconscionably [ʌn'kɔnʃənəbli], *adv.* déraisonnablement.
unconscious [ʌn'kɔnʃəs], *a.* ignorant (*de*); sans connaissance, insensible.—*n.* inconscient, *m.*
unconsciously [ʌn'kɔnʃəsli], *adv.* à son insu.
unconsciousness [ʌn'kɔnʃəsnis], *n.* inconscience, *f.*; évanouissement, *m.*
unconsecrated [ʌn'kɔnsikreitid], *a.* non consacré.
unconsidered [ʌnkən'sidəd], *a.* inconsidéré.
unconstitutional [ʌnkɔnsti'tju:ʃənl], *a.* inconstitutionnel.
unconstrained [ʌnkən'streind], *a.* sans contrainte; aisé (*style*).
unconstraint [ʌnkən'streint], *n.* aisance, *f.*
uncontaminated [ʌnkən'tæmineitid], *a.* sans souillure.
uncontested [ʌnkən'testid], *a.* incontesté.
uncontrollable [ʌnkən'trouləbl], *a.* irrésistible; fou (*rire*).
uncontrollably [ʌnkən'trouləbli], *adv.* irrésistiblement.
uncontrolled [ʌnkən'trould], *a.* irrésistible.
unconventional [ʌnkən'venʃənl], *a.* peu conventionnel.
unconverted [ʌnkən'və:tid], *a.* inconverti.
unconvinced [ʌnkən'vinst], *a.* non convaincu.
unconvincing [ʌnkən'vinsiŋ], *a.* peu convaincant.
uncooked [ʌn'kukt], *a.* non cuit, cru.
uncork [ʌn'kɔ:k], *v.t.* déboucher.
uncorrupted [ʌnkə'rʌptid], *a.* non corrompu (*par*); intègre.
uncouple [ʌn'kʌpl], *v.t.* découpler; débrayer.
uncouth [ʌn'ku:θ], *a.* bizarre; grossier; gauche.
uncouthly [ʌn'ku:θli], *adv.* rudement; gauchement.
uncover [ʌn'kʌvə], *v.t.* découvrir.
uncovered [ʌn'kʌvəd], *a.* découvert.
uncreasable [ʌn'kri:səbl], *a.* infroissable.
uncritical [ʌn'kritikl], *a.* sans discernement.
uncrowned [ʌn'kraund], *a.* non couronné.
unction ['ʌŋkʃən], *n.* onction, *f.*
unctuous ['ʌŋktjuəs], *a.* onctueux.
unctuously ['ʌŋktjuəsli], *adv.* onctueusement.
uncultivated [ʌn'kʌltiveitid], *a.* inculte.
uncultured [ʌn'kʌltʃəd], *a.* sans culture.
uncurl [ʌn'kə:l], *v.t.* dérouler; défriser (*cheveux*).—*v.i.* se dérouler; se défriser (*cheveux*).
uncustomary [ʌn'kʌstəməri], *a.* inaccoutumé.
uncut [ʌn'kʌt], *a.* non coupé; entier; non entamé (*pain etc.*).
undamaged [ʌn'dæmidʒd], *a.* non endommagé; intact (*réputation*).
undated [ʌn'deitid], *a.* sans date.
undaunted [ʌn'dɔ:ntid], *a.* intrépide.
undeceive [ʌndi'si:v], *v.t.* désabuser, détromper.
undecided [ʌndi'saidid], *a.* indécis.
undecipherable [ʌndi'saifərəbl], *a.* indéchiffrable.
undefeated [ʌndi'fi:tid], *a.* invaincu.
undefended [ʌndi'fendid], *a.* sans défense, non défendu; sans défenseur (*accusé*).
undefiled [ʌndi'faild], *a.* sans tache, immaculé.
undefinable [ʌndi'fainəbl], *a.* indéfinissable.
undefined [ʌndi'faind], *a.* indéfini.
undelivered [ʌndi'livəd], *a.* non délivré.
undemonstrative [ʌndi'mɔnstrətiv], *a.* peu démonstratif, réservé.
undeniable [ʌndi'naiəbl], *a.* incontestable.
undenominational [ʌndinɔmi'neiʃənl], *a.* laïque (*école*).
under ['ʌndə], *a.* de dessous, inférieur; sous, subalterne, subordonné (*rang*).—*prep.* sous; au-dessous de (*inférieur à etc.*); dans, en (*en état de*); avec, à (*ayant*); ***to be under obligations to***, avoir des obligations à; ***to be under way*** (*ship*), être en marche; ***under age***, mineur; ***under consideration***, à l'examen; ***under cover of***, sous prétexte de; ***under discussion***, en discussion; ***under the breath***, à demi-voix; ***under these circumstances***, dans ces circonstances.—*adv.* dessous, au-dessous; ***see under***, voyez ci-dessous.
under-carriage ['ʌndəkæridʒ], *n.* (*Av.*) train d'atterrissage, *m.*
underclothes ['ʌndəklouðz], *n.pl.* sous-vêtements, *m.pl.*
undercurrent ['ʌndəkʌrənt], *n.* courant inférieur, *m.*
undercut (1) ['ʌndəkʌt], *n.* filet (*de bœuf*), *m.*
undercut (2) [ʌndə'kʌt], *v.t. irr.* (*conjug. like* CUT) vendre meilleur marché.
under-developed [ʌndədi'veləpt], *a.* sous-développé.
under-dog ['ʌndədɔg], *n.* opprimé, *m.*
underdone [ʌndə'dʌn], *a.* peu cuit, saignant.

under-estimate [ʌndər'estimeit], *v.t.* sous-estimer.
under-exposed [ʌndəriks'pouzd] *a.* (*Phot.*) sous-exposé.
underfelt ['ʌndəfelt], *n.* thibaude, *f.*
underfoot [ʌndə'fut], *adv.* sous les pieds.
undergo [ʌndə'gou], *v.t. irr.* (*conjug. like* GO) subir; supporter, endurer.
undergraduate [ʌndə'grædjuət] *n.* étudiant, *m.*
underground ['ʌndəgraund], *a.* souterrain; clandestin.—*n.* (*Rail.*) métro, *m.*—[ʌndə 'graund], *adv.* sous terre.
undergrowth ['ʌndəgrouθ], *n.* broussailles, *f.pl.*
underhand ['ʌndəhænd], *a.* clandestin; sournois (*personne*).—[ʌndə'hænd], *adv.* sous main; en cachette.
underline [ʌndə'lain], *v.t.* souligner.
underling ['ʌndəliŋ], *n.* subalterne, *m., f.*
underlying [ʌndə'laiiŋ], *a.* fondamental.
under-manned [ʌndə'mænd], *a.* à court de personnel.
undermentioned [ʌndə'menʃənd], *a.* ci-dessous.
undermine [ʌndə'main], *v.t.* miner; (*fig.*) détruire.
undermost ['ʌndəmoust], *a.* le plus bas.
underneath [ʌndə'ni:θ], *prep.* sous, au-dessous de.—*adv.* dessous, au-dessous, par-dessous, en dessous.
under-nourished [ʌndə'nʌriʃt], *a.* sous-alimenté.
underpaid [ʌndə'peid], *a.* mal payé.
underpants ['ʌndəpænts], *n.pl.* caleçons, *m.pl.*
under-privileged [ʌndə'privilidʒd], *a.* non privilégié.
under-production [ʌndəprə'dʌkʃən], *n.* sous-production, *f.*
underrate [ʌndə'reit], *v.t.* sous-estimer, déprécier.
under-ripe [ʌndə'raip], *a.* pas assez mûr, vert.
under-secretary ['ʌndəsekrətəri], *n.* sous-secrétaire, *m., f.*
under-side ['ʌndəsaid], *n.* dessous, *m.*
undersigned ['ʌndəsaind], *a.* and *n.* sous-signé, *m.*
undersized [ʌndə'saizd], *a.* au-dessous de la moyenne.
understand [ʌndə'stænd], *v.t. irr.* (*conjug. like* STAND) entendre, comprendre; apprendre, entendre dire (*être informé de*); s'entendre (*à* ou *en*) (*savoir faire*).—*v.i.* comprendre.
understandable [ʌndə'stændəbl], *a.* intelligible; compréhensible.
understanding [ʌndə'stændiŋ], *n.* entendement, *m.*, intelligence; compréhension; entente (*accord*), *f.*
understudy ['ʌndəstʌdi], *n.* doublure, *f.*
undertake [ʌndə'teik], *v.t. irr.* (*conjug. like* TAKE) entreprendre, se charger (*de*); s'engager (*à*); promettre (*de*).
undertaker ['ʌndəteikə], *n.* entrepreneur des pompes funèbres, *m.*
undertaking [ʌndə'teikiŋ], *n.* entreprise, *f.*
undertone ['ʌndətoun], *n.* ton bas, *m.*; ***in an undertone***, à voix basse.
underwear ['ʌndəwεə], *n.* sous-vêtements, *m.pl.*
underworld ['ʌndəwə:ld], *n.* enfer, *m.*; (*fig.*) bas-fonds (*des criminels*), *m.pl.*
underwrite [ʌndə'rait], *v.t. irr.* (*conjug. like* WRITE) souscrire; (*Insurance*) assurer.
underwriter ['ʌndəraitə], *n.* assureur, *m.*
undeserved [ʌndi'zə:vd], *a.* immérité, non mérité.
undeservedly [ʌndi'zə:vidli], *adv.* à tort, injustement.
undesirable [ʌndi'zaiərəbl], *a.* peu désirable.
undetected [ʌndi'tektid], *a.* non découvert, inaperçu.
undetermined [ʌndi'tə:mind], *a.* indéterminé, indéfini.
undeterred [ʌndi'tə:d], *a.* sans être découragé.
undeveloped [ʌndi'veləpt], *a.* non développé.
undies ['ʌndiz], *n.pl.* (*fam.*) lingerie, *f.*
undigested [ʌndi'dʒestid], *a.* non digéré.
undignified [ʌn'dignifaid], *a.* sans dignité.
undiluted [ʌndai'lju:tid], *a.* non dilué.
undiminished [ʌndi'miniʃt], *a.* non diminué.
undiplomatic [ʌndiplo'mætik], *a.* peu diplomatique.
undisciplined [ʌn'disiplind], *a.* indiscipliné.
undisclosed [ʌndis'klouzd], *a.* non révélé, caché.
undiscovered [ʌndis'kʌvəd], *a.* non découvert.
undisguised [ʌndis'gaizd], *a.* sans déguisement.
undismayed [ʌndis'meid], *a.* sans peur, sans terreur.
undisputed [ʌndis'pju:tid], *a.* incontesté.
undistinguished [ʌndis'tiŋgwiʃt], *a.* (*fig.*) sans distinction.
undisturbed [ʌndis'tə:bd], *a.* tranquille, calme.
undivided [ʌndi'vaidid], *a.* sans partage, tout entier.
undo [ʌn'du:], *v.t. irr.* (*conjug. like* DO) défaire; délier, détacher (*dénouer*); ruiner, perdre (*détruire*).
undoing [ʌn'du:iŋ], *n.* ruine, perte, *f.*
undone [ʌn'dʌn], *a.* ruiné, perdu; défait, delié.
undoubted [ʌn'dautid], *a.* incontestable, certain.
undoubtedly [ʌn'dautidli], *adv.* sans aucun doute.
undress [ʌn'dres], *v.t.* déshabiller.—*v.i.* se déshabiller.—*n.* (*Mil.*) petite tenue, *f.*
undressed [ʌn'drest], *a.* déshabillé.
undrinkable [ʌn'driŋkəbl], *a.* imbuvable, non potable.
undue [ʌn'dju:], *a.* non dû; excessif.
undulate ['ʌndjuleit], *v.i.* onduler, ondoyer.
undulating ['ʌndjuleitiŋ], *a.* accidenté (*terrain*).
undulation [ʌndju'leiʃən], *n.* ondulation, *f.*
unduly [ʌn'dju:li], *adv.* indûment; à tort; trop.
undying [ʌn'daiiŋ], *a.* impérissable, immortel.
unearned [ʌn'ə:nd], *a.* qu'on n'a pas gagné; immérité; ***unearned income***, rentes, *f.pl.*
unearth [ʌn'ə:θ], *v.t.* déterrer.
unearthly [ʌn'ə:θli], *a.* surnaturel; (*colloq.*) infernal.
uneasily [ʌn'i:zili], *adv.* mal à son aise; difficilement, péniblement, avec gêne.

uneasiness [ʌn'i:zinis], *n.* malaise, *m.*, peine; inquiétude (*d'esprit*), *f.*
uneasy [ʌn'i:zi], *a.* inquiet, gêné.
uneatable [ʌn'i:təbl], *a.* immangeable.
uneconomical [ʌni:kə'nɔmikl], *a.* non économique.
uneducated [ʌn'edjukeitid], *a.* sans éducation.
unemotional [ʌni'mouʃənl], *a.* peu impressionnable; peu émotif.
unemployed [ʌnim'plɔid], *a.* sans travail, inoccupé; (*fig.*) inactif, oisif.—*n.pl.* ***the unemployed***, les sans-travail, les chômeurs, *m.pl.*
unemployment [ʌnim'plɔimənt], *n.* manque de travail, chômage, *m.*
unencumbered [ʌnin'kʌmbəd], *a.* non embarrassé (*de*); non hypothéqué (*biens*).
unending [ʌn'endiŋ], *a.* interminable.
unendurable [ʌnin'djuərəbl], *a.* insupportable, intolérable.
un-English [ʌn'iŋgliʃ], *a.* non anglais; indigne d'un Anglais.
unenlightened [ʌnin'laitnd], *a.* peu éclairé.
unenterprising [ʌn'entəpraiziŋ], *a.* peu entreprenant.
unenthusiastic [ʌninθju:zi'æstik], *a.* peu enthousiaste.
unenviable [ʌn'enviəbl], *a.* peu enviable.
unequal [ʌn'i:kwəl], *a.* inégal; au-dessous (*de*); ***unequal to the task***, pas à la hauteur de la tâche.
unequalled [ʌn'i:kwəld], *a.* sans égal, sans pareil.
unequivocal [ʌni'kwivəkl], *a.* non équivoque.
unequivocally [ʌni'kwivəkli], *adv.* sans équivoque.
unerring [ʌn'ə:riŋ], *a.* infaillible, sûr.
uneven [ʌn'i:vn], *a.* inégal; raboteux (*terrain*).
unevenly [ʌn'i:vinli], *adv.* inégalement.
unevenness [ʌn'i:vinnis], *n.* inégalité, *f.*
uneventful [ʌni'ventful], *a.* sans incidents, monotone.
unexaggerated [ʌnig'zædʒəreitid], *a.* nullement exagéré.
unexciting [ʌnik'saitiŋ], *a.* peu intéressant.
unexpected [ʌniks'pektid], *a.* inopiné, inattendu; imprévu.
unexpectedly [ʌniks'pektidli], *adv.* à l'improviste.
unexpired [ʌniks'paiəd], *a.* non expiré.
unexplained [ʌniks'pleind], *a.* sans explication, inexpliqué.
unexploded [ʌniks'ploudid], *a.* non éclaté.
unexplored [ʌniks'plɔ:d], *a.* inexploré.
unexposed [ʌniks'pouzd], *a.* non exposé.
unextinguished [ʌniks'tiŋgwiʃt], *a.* non éteint.
unfading [ʌn'feidiŋ], *a.* (*fig.*) impérissable, immortel.
unfailing [ʌn'feiliŋ], *a.* inépuisable; infaillible (*certain*).
unfair [ʌn'fɛə], *a.* injuste; (*Spt.*) pas de jeu.
unfairly [ʌn'fɛəli], *adv.* injustement.
unfairness [ʌn'fɛənis], *n.* injustice, *f.*
unfaithful [ʌn'feiθful], *a.* infidèle.
unfaithfulness [ʌn'feiθfulnis], *n.* infidélité, *f.*
unfaltering [ʌn'fɔ:ltəriŋ], *a.* ferme, assuré; résolu (*actions etc.*).
unfamiliar [ʌnfə'miljə], *a.* peu familier (*avec*); peu connu.
unfashionable [ʌn'fæʃənəbl], *a.* démodé.
unfasten [ʌn'fɑ:sn], *v.t.* ouvrir, détacher, défaire.
unfathomable [ʌn'fæðəməbl], *a.* insondable.
unfavourable [ʌn'feivərəbl], *a.* peu favorable.
unfed [ʌn'fed], *a.* mal nourri.
unfeeling [ʌn'fi:liŋ], *a.* insensible, dur, cruel.
unfeigned [ʌn'feind], *a.* vrai, sincère.
unfeignedly [ʌn'feinidli], *adv.* sincèrement.
unfelt [ʌn'felt], *a.* qu'on ne sent pas.
unfenced [ʌn'fenst], *a.* sans clôture.
unfetter [ʌn'fetə], *v.t.* ôter les fers à; (*fig.*) délivrer.
unfettered [ʌn'fetəd], *a.* libre, sans entraves.
unfilial [ʌn'filiəl], *a.* peu filial.
unfinished [ʌn'finiʃt], *a.* inachevé.
unfit [ʌn'fit], *a.* peu propre; impropre (*à*); incapable (*de*); en mauvaise santé.
unfitting [ʌn'fitiŋ], *a.* inconvenant.
unfix [ʌn'fiks], *v.t.* détacher.
unfixed [ʌn'fikst], *a.* mobile; indécis.
unflagging [ʌn'flægiŋ], *a.* infatigable.
unfledged [ʌn'fledʒd], *a.* sans plumes; (*fig.*) novice.
unflinching [ʌn'flintʃiŋ], *a.* ferme, déterminé.
unfold [ʌn'fould], *v.t.* déplier, déployer; révéler.—*v.i.* se déployer, se dévoiler.
unforeseen [ʌnfɔ:'si:n], *a.* imprévu.
unforgettable [ʌnfə'getəbl], *a.* inoubliable.
unforgiving [ʌnfə'giviŋ], *a.* implacable.
unforgotten [ʌnfə'gɔtn], *a.* pas oublié.
unfortified [ʌn'fɔ:tifaid], *a.* non fortifié, ouvert.
unfortunate [ʌn'fɔ:tʃənit], *a.* infortuné, malheureux.
unfortunately [ʌn'fɔ:tʃənitli], *adv.* malheureusement.
unfounded [ʌn'faundid], *a.* sans fondement.
unframed [ʌn'freimd], *a.* sans cadre.
unfrequented [ʌnfri'kwentid], *a.* peu fréquenté, solitaire.
unfriendliness [ʌn'frendlinis], *n.* disposition peu amicale, *f.*
unfriendly [ʌn'frendli], *a.* peu amical (*personne*); malveillant (*chose*).
unfrock [ʌn'frɔk], *v.t.* défroquer.
unfruitful [ʌn'fru:tful], *a.* infertile, stérile.
unfulfilled [ʌnful'fild], *a.* non accompli.
unfurl [ʌn'fə:l], *v.t.* déferler, déployer.
unfurnished [ʌn'fə:niʃt], *a.* non meublé.
ungainly [ʌn'geinli], *a.* maladroit.
ungenerous [ʌn'dʒenərəs], *a.* peu généreux.
ungentlemanliness [ʌn'dʒentlmənlinis], *n.* impolitesse, *f.*
ungentlemanly [ʌn'dʒentlmənli], *a.* de mauvais ton.
ungodliness [ʌn'gɔdlinis], *n.* impiété, *f.*
ungodly [ʌn'gɔdli], *a.* impie.
ungovernable [ʌn'gʌvənəbl], *a.* ingouvernable; effréné.
ungraceful [ʌn'greisful], *a.* peu gracieux.
ungracious [ʌn'greiʃəs], *a.* peu gracieux, déplaisant.
ungrammatical [ʌngrə'mætikl], *a.* incorrect.
ungrateful [ʌn'greitful], *a.* ingrat (*envers*).
ungratefully [ʌn'greitfuli], *adv.* avec ingratitude.
ungrudging [ʌn'grʌdʒiŋ], *a.* de bon cœur.
ungrudgingly [ʌn'grʌdʒiŋli], *adv.* volontiers, de bon cœur.
unguarded [ʌn'gɑ:did], *a.* sans défense; imprudent, irréfléchi (*inconsidéré*).

unguardedly [ʌn'gɑːdidli], *adv.* imprudemment.
unguent ['ʌŋgwənt], *n.* onguent, *m.*
unhallowed [ʌn'hæloud], *a.* non sanctifié.
unhampered [ʌn'hæmpəd], *a.* non embarrassé (*par*).
***unhand** [ʌn'hænd], *v.t.* lâcher.
unhappily [ʌn'hæpili], *adv.* malheureusement.
unhappiness [ʌn'hæpinis], *n.* malheur, *m.*
unhappy [ʌn'hæpi], *a.* malheureux.
unharmed [ʌn'hɑːmd], *a.* sain et sauf.
unharness [ʌn'hɑːnis], *v.t.* déharnacher; dételer (*d'une charrette*).
unhatched [ʌn'hætʃt], *a.* non éclos.
unhealthy [ʌn'helθi], *a.* insalubre, malsain; maladif (*personne*).
unheard [ʌn'həːd], *a.* sans être entendu; ***unheard of***, inconnu, inouï (*extraordinaire*).
unheeded [ʌn'hiːdid], *a.* inaperçu, négligé.
unheedful [ʌn'hiːdful], **unheeding** [ʌn 'hiːdiŋ], *a.* insouciant; inattentif.
unhesitating [ʌn'heziteitiŋ], *a.* sans hésitation; résolu.
unhesitatingly [ʌn'heziteitiŋli], *adv.* sans hésiter.
unhewn [ʌn'hjuːn], *a.* brut; non taillé.
unhinge [ʌn'hindʒ], *v.t.* démonter.
unhitch [ʌn'hitʃ], *v.t.* décrocher; dételer (*cheval*).
unholy [ʌn'houli], *a.* profane, impie.
unhook [ʌn'huk], *v.t.* décrocher; dégrafer (*vêtements*).
unhoped [ʌn'houpt], *a.* inattendu; ***unhoped for***, inespéré.
unhorse [ʌn'hɔːs], *v.t.* désarçonner, démonter.
unhurried [ʌn'hʌrid], *a.* lent, sans précipitation.
unhurt [ʌn'həːt], *a.* sain et sauf, sans blessures.
unhygienic [ʌnhai'dʒiːnik], *a.* peu hygiénique.
unicorn ['juːnikɔːn], *n.* licorne, *f.*
unidentified [ʌnai'dentifaid], *a.* non identifié.
unification [juːnifi'keiʃən], *n.* unification, *f.*
uniform ['juːnifɔːm], *a.* and *n.* uniforme, *m.*
uniformity [juːni'fɔːmiti], *n.* uniformité, *f.*
uniformly ['juːnifɔːmli], *adv.* uniformément.
unify ['juːnifai], *v.t.* unifier.
unilateral [juːni'lætərəl], *a.* unilatéral.
unimaginable [ʌni'mædʒinəbl], *a.* inimaginable, inconcevable.
unimaginative [ʌni'mædʒinətiv], *a.* peu imaginatif.
unimpaired [ʌnim'pɛəd], *a.* inaltéré, intact.
unimpeachable [ʌnim'piːtʃəbl], *a.* irréprochable.
unimpeded [ʌnim'piːdid], *a.* sans empêchement.
unimportance [ʌnim'pɔːtəns], *n.* peu d'importance, *m.*, insignifiance, *f.*
unimportant [ʌnim'pɔːtənt], *a.* sans importance, insignifiant.
unimpressed [ʌnim'prest], *a.* sans être ému.
unimpressive [ʌnim'presiv], *a.* peu frappant.
uninformed [ʌnin'fɔːmd], *a.* non informé; ignorant.
uninhabitable [ʌnin'hæbitəbl], *a.* inhabitable.
uninhabited [ʌnin'hæbitid], *a.* inhabité.
uninitiated [ʌni'niʃieitid], *a.* non initié.
uninjured [ʌn'indʒəd], *a.* sain et sauf, sa blessures.
uninspired [ʌnin'spaiəd], *a.* non inspi terne.
uninspiring [ʌnin'spaiəriŋ], *a.* banal.
unintelligible [ʌnin'telidʒibl], *a.* inint ligible.
unintentional [ʌnin'tenʃənl], *a.* sans inte tion, involontaire.
unintentionally [ʌnin'tenʃənli], *adv.* f sans le vouloir, sans intention.
uninterested [ʌn'intristid], *a.* non intéres indifférent.
uninteresting [ʌn'intristiŋ], *a.* peu intér sant.
uninterrupted [ʌnintə'rʌptid], *a.* ininte rompu.
uninvited [ʌnin'vaitid], *a.* sans invitation.
uninviting [ʌnin'vaitiŋ], *a.* peu attrayar peu appétissant (*nourriture*).
union ['juːniən], *n.* union, *f.*; ***trade(s)-unio*** syndicat ouvrier, syndicat (corporatif), *m.*
unique [ju'niːk], *a.* unique.
uniquely [ju'niːkli], *adv.* d'une maniè unique.
unison ['juːnizn], *n.* unisson, *m.*; ***in uniso*** à l'unisson.
unit ['juːnit], *n.* unité, *f.*, bloc, élément, *m.*
unite [ju'nait], *v.t.* unir (*à* ou *avec*); joindr réunir (*efforts etc.*).—*v.i.* s'unir, se réunir; joindre (*à* ou *avec*).
united [ju'naitid], *a.* uni; réuni; join ***the United Kingdom***, le Royaume-Ur *m.*; ***the United States***, les États-Uni *m.pl.*
unity ['juːniti], *n.* unité; union, *f.*
universal [juːni'vəːsl], *a.* universel.
universally [juːni'vəːsəli], *adv.* universelle ment.
universe ['juːnivəːs], *n.* univers, *m.*
university [juːni'vəːsiti], *n.* université, *f* ***university degree***, grade universitai *m.*
unjust [ʌn'dʒʌst], *a.* injuste, inique.
unjustly [ʌn'dʒʌstli], *adv.* injustement.
unjustifiable [ʌn'dʒʌstifaiəbl], *a.* injus fiable.
unjustified [ʌn'dʒʌstifaid], *a.* sans justific tion.
unkind [ʌn'kaind], *a.* désobligeant; pe aimable; cruel.
unkindliness [ʌn'kaindlinis], *n.* désobl geance; malveillance, *f.*
unkindly [ʌn'kaindli], *a.* peu propice, défav rable.—*adv.* sans bienveillance; cruell ment, mal.
unkindness [ʌn'kaindnis], *n.* manque d'am bilité, *m.*, désobligeance; cruauté, dureté, *f*
unknowingly [ʌn'nouiŋli], *adv.* sans savoir, à son insu.
unknown [ʌn'noun], *a.* inconnu; ***unknow to me*** (*without my knowledge*), à mon insu
unlace [ʌn'leis], *v.t.* délacer, détacher.
unladylike [ʌn'leidilaik], *a.* peu digne d'un dame, de mauvais ton.
unlatch [ʌn'lætʃ], *v.t.* lever le loquet d ouvrir.
unlawful [ʌn'lɔːful], *a.* illégal; illicite.
unlawfully [ʌn'lɔːfuli], *adv.* illégalement illicitement.
unleash [ʌn'liːʃ], *v.t.* lâcher (*chien*).

unleavened [ʌn'levənd], *a.* sans levain; (*Scripture*) azyme.
unless [ʌn'les], *conj.* à moins que . . . ne (*with subjunctive*); à moins de (*followed by infinitive*); si . . . ne . . . pas (*followed by indicative*); si ce n'est, excepté que.
unlicensed [ʌn'laisənst], *a.* non autorisé; (*Comm.*) non patenté.
unlike [ʌn'laik], *a.* différent (*de*); qui ne ressemble pas (*à*).
unlikelihood [ʌn'laiklihud], *n.* invraisemblance, improbabilité, *f.*
unlikely [ʌn'laikli], *a.* improbable, invraisemblable, peu sûr.
unlimited [ʌn'limitid], *a.* illimité.
unlined [ʌn'laind], *a.* non doublé.
unlink [ʌn'liŋk], *v.t.* défaire, détacher.
unload [ʌn'loud], *v.t.* décharger; désarmer (*fusil*).
unlock [ʌn'lɔk], *v.t.* ouvrir.
unlooked-for [ʌn'luktfɔ:], *a.* inattendu, imprévu.
unloose [ʌn'lu:s], *v.t.* délier, détacher.
unloved [ʌn'lʌvd], *a.* pas aimé.
unluckily [ʌn'lʌkili], *adv.* malheureusement, par malheur.
unlucky [ʌn'lʌki], *a.* malheureux, infortuné; sinistre, de mauvais augure, de mauvais présagé.
unmade [ʌn'meid], *a.* défait; pas fait (*lit*); non empierré (*route*).
unmanageable [ʌn'mænidʒəbl], *a.* ingouvernable; rebelle.
unmanliness [ʌn'mænlinis], *n.* conduite indigne d'un homme, lâcheté, *f.*
unmanly [ʌn'mænli], *a.* indigne d'un homme, lâche; mou, efféminé.
unmannerliness [ʌn'mænəlinis], *n.* grossièreté, impolitesse, *f.*
unmannerly [ʌn'mænəli], *a.* grossier, mal appris, impoli.
unmarked [ʌn'mɑ:kt], *a.* non marqué (*de*); inaperçu.
unmarketable [ʌn'mɑ:kitəbl], *a.* invendable.
unmarried [ʌn'mærid], *a.* célibataire; ***unmarried man***, célibataire, *m.*; ***unmarried woman***, demoiselle, vieille fille, *f.*
unmask [ʌn'mɑ:sk], *v.t.* démasquer; (*fig.*) dévoiler.
unmastered [ʌn'mɑ:stəd], *a.* indompté.
unmatched [ʌn'mætʃt], *a.* dépareillé; (*fig.*) sans pareil.
unmentionable [ʌn'menʃənəbl], *a.* dont on ne parle pas.
unmerciful [ʌn'mə:siful], *a.* impitoyable, cruel.
unmercifully [ʌn'mə:sifuli], *adv.* impitoyablement, sans pitié.
unmerited [ʌn'meritid], *a.* immérité.
unmindful [ʌn'maindful], *a.* peu soucieux (*de*).
unmistakable [ʌnmis'teikəbl], *a.* évident, clair.
unmistakably [ʌnmis'teikəbli], *adv.* évidemment, clairement.
unmitigated [ʌn'mitigeitid], *a.* non adouci; (*colloq.*) fieffé (*gredin etc.*).
unmolested [ʌnmə'lestid], *a.* sans être molesté.
unmotherly [ʌn'mʌðəli], *a.* peu maternel.
unmounted [ʌn'mauntid], *a.* à pied (*sans cheval*); non collé (*photographie etc.*).
unmourned [ʌn'mɔ:nd], *a.* sans être pleuré.
unmoved [ʌn'mu:vd], *a.* immobile; (*fig.*) non ému.
unmusical [ʌn'mju:zikl], *a.* peu harmonieux; pas musicien (*personne*).
unmuzzle [ʌn'mʌzl], *v.t.* démuseler.
unnamed [ʌn'neimd], *a.* innommé; anonyme.
unnatural [ʌn'nætʃrəl], *a.* contre nature; dénaturé (*personne*).
unnavigable [ʌn'nævigəbl], *a.* innavigable.
unnecessarily [ʌn'nesəsərili], *adv.* sans nécessité, inutilement; par trop.
unnecessary [ʌn'nesəsəri], *a.* peu nécessaire, inutile.
unneighbourly [ʌn'neibəli], *a.* peu obligeant; de mauvais voisin.
unnerve [ʌn'nə:v], *v.t.* énerver; (*fig.*) décourager.
unnoticed [ʌn'noutist], *a.* inaperçu, inobservé.
unnumbered [ʌn'nʌmbəd], *a.* innombrable.
unobjectionable [ʌnəb'dʒekʃənəbl], *a.* irrécusable.
unobliging [ʌnə'blaidʒiŋ], *a.* désobligeant.
unobservant [ʌnəb'zə:vənt], *a.* peu observateur.
unobserved [ʌnəb'zə:vd], *a.* inaperçu.
unobtainable [ʌnəb'teinəbl], *a.* impossible à obtenir.
unobtrusive [ʌnəb'tru:siv], *a.* réservé, discret.
unobtrusively [ʌnəb'tru:sivli], *adv.* sans importunité, avec modestie.
unoccupied [ʌn'ɔkjupaid], *a.* inoccupé; libre, disponible (*temps etc.*); inhabité (*maison*).
unofficial [ʌnə'fiʃl], *a.* non officiel.
unofficially [ʌnə'fiʃəli], *adv.* non officiellement.
unopened [ʌn'oupənd], *a.* fermé; non décacheté (*lettre etc.*).
unopposed [ʌnə'pouzd], *a.* sans opposition.
unorganized [ʌn'ɔ:gənaizd], *a.* non organisé.
unoriginal [ʌnə'ridʒinəl], *a.* peu original.
unorthodox [ʌn'ɔ:θədɔks], *a.* peu orthodoxe.
unostentatious [ʌnɔsten'teiʃəs], *a.* sans faste; modeste.
unostentatiously [ʌnɔsten'teiʃəsli], *adv.* sans ostentation.
unpack [ʌn'pæk], *v.t.* déballer (*marchandises*); dépaqueter (*paquets*).
unpacking [ʌn'pækiŋ], *n.* déballage; dépaquetage (*de petits paquets*), *m.*
unpaid [ʌn'peid], *a.* non payé, sans paye.
unpalatable [ʌn'pælətəbl], *a.* désagréable (au goût).
unparalleled [ʌn'pærəleld], *a.* sans pareil; sans précédent.
unpardonable [ʌn'pɑ:dnəbl], *a.* impardonnable.
unparliamentary [ʌnpɑ:li'mentəri], *a.* peu parlementaire.
unpatriotic [ʌnpætri'ɔtik], *a.* peu patriotique (*sentiment*); peu patriote (*personne*).
unpaved [ʌn'peivd], *a.* non pavé.
unperturbed [ʌnpə'tə:bd], *a.* peu ému, impassible.
unphilosophical [ʌnfilə'sɔfikl], *a.* peu philosophique.
unpick [ʌn'pik], *v.t.* découdre.
unpicked [ʌn'pikt], *a.* non cueilli; décousu (*couture*).

unpin [ʌn'pin], *v.t.* défaire.
unpitied [ʌn'pitid], *a.* qu'on ne plaint pas.
unpitying [ʌn'pitiiŋ], *a.* sans pitié, impitoyable.
unplayable [ʌn'pleiəbl], *a.* injouable.
unpleasant [ʌn'plezənt], *a.* déplaisant, fâcheux.
unpleasantly [ʌn'plezəntli], *adv.* désagréablement.
unpleasantness [ʌn'plezəntnis], *n.* désagrément, *m.*
unploughed [ʌn'plaud], *a.* non labouré.
unpoetical [ʌnpo'etikl], *a.* peu poétique.
unpolished [ʌn'pɔliʃt], *a.* non poli; mat (*or etc.*); non ciré (*chaussures*); dépoli (*verre*); (*fig.*) grossier.
unpolluted [ʌnpə'lju:tid], *a.* non souillé; pur.
unpopular [ʌn'pɔpjulə], *a.* impopulaire.
unpopularity [ʌnpɔpju'læriti], *n.* impopularité, *f.*
unpractical [ʌn'præktikl], *a.* peu pratique.
unpractised [ʌn'præktist], *a.* inexpérimenté.
unprecedented [ʌn'presidəntid], *a.* sans précédent.
unprejudiced [ʌn'predʒudist], *a.* sans préjugés, impartial.
unpremeditated [ʌnpri'mediteitid], *a.* inopiné, improvisé, sans préméditation.
unprepared [ʌnpri'pɛəd], *a.* non préparé; ***to be unprepared for***, ne pas s'attendre à.
unpreparedness [ʌnpri'pɛəridnis], *n.* manque de préparation, *m.*
unprepossessing [ʌnpri:pə'zesiŋ], *a.* peu engageant.
unprincipled [ʌn'prinsipld], *a.* sans principes, sans mœurs.
unproductive [ʌnprə'dʌktiv], *a.* improductif; stérile (*terre*).
unproductiveness [ʌnprə'dʌktivnis], *n.* stérilité, *f.*
unprofessional [ʌnprə'feʃənəl], *a.* contraire aux règles d'une profession.
unprofitable [ʌn'prɔfitəbl], *a.* peu lucratif, sans profit; inutile.
unprofitably [ʌn'prɔfitəbli], *adv.* inutilement, sans profit.
unpronounceable [ʌnprə'naunsəbl], *a.* imprononçable.
unpropitious [ʌnprə'piʃəs], *a.* peu propice (*à*).
unprotected [ʌnprə'tektid], *a.* sans protection, sans défense; à découvert.
unprovided [ʌnprə'vaidid], *a.* dépourvu, dénué (*de*); ***we were unprovided for that***, nous ne nous attendions pas à cela.
unprovoked [ʌnprə'voukt], *a.* sans provocation; ***an unprovoked insult***, une insulte gratuite.
unpublished [ʌn'pʌbliʃt], *a.* inédit.
unpunished [ʌn'pʌniʃt], *a.* impuni.
unqualified [ʌn'kwɔlifaid], *a.* incapable (*de*), incompétent; (*fig.*) sans réserve; (*Law*) inhabile (*à*); non autorisé (*médecins etc.*).
unquenchable [ʌn'kwentʃəbl], *a.* inextinguible.
unquestionable [ʌn'kwestʃənəbl], *a.* incontestable, indubitable.
unquestionably [ʌn'kwestʃənəbli], *adv.* incontestablement; sans contredit.
unravel [ʌn'rævl], *v.t.* démêler, débrouiller. —*v.i.* se démêler, se débrouiller, s'effiler.
unreadable [ʌn'ri:dəbl], *a.* illisible.
unreadily [ʌn'redili], *adv.* lentement, contre-cœur.
unreadiness [ʌn'redinis], *n.* manque de pr paration *ou* de bonne volonté, *m.*
unready [ʌn'redi], *a.* mal préparé; lent.
unreal [ʌn'ri:əl], *a.* irréel; chimérique, imag naire.
unrealistic [ʌnri:ə'listik], *a.* peu réaliste.
unreality [ʌnri'æliti], *n.* défaut de réalité, *m*
unrealizable [ʌn'ri:əlaizəbl], *a.* irréalisable.
unreasonable [ʌn'ri:znəbl], *a.* déraisonnabl exorbitant.
unreasonableness [ʌn'ri:znəblnis], *n.* d raison; absurdité, extravagance (*de d mande*), *f.*
unreasonably [ʌn'ri:znəbli], *adv.* sar raison, à l'excès.
unrecognizable [ʌn'rekəgnaizəbl], *a.* mécor naissable.
unrecognized [ʌn'rekəgnaizd], *a.* sans êtr reconnu; (*fig.*) méconnu (*non apprécié*).
unrecompensed [ʌn'rekəmpenst], *a.* sar récompense.
unreconciled [ʌn'rekənsaild], *a.* irréconcili
unrecorded [ʌnri'kɔ:did], *a.* non enregistré.
unredeemable [ʌnri'di:məbl], *a.* irrache table.
unredeemed [ʌnri'di:md], *a.* non racheté.
unrefined [ʌnri'faind], *a.* non raffiné, brut (*fig.*) grossier.
unregistered [ʌn'redʒistəd], *a.* non en registré; non recommandé (*lettre etc.*).
unrelated [ʌnri'leitid], *a.* sans rapport (*avec*) ***who is unrelated to***, qui n'est pas paren de.
unrelenting [ʌnri'lentiŋ], *a.* inflexible, im placable.
unreliable [ʌnri'laiəbl], *a.* peu sûr; sur qui o sur quoi l'on ne peut compter.
unrelieved [ʌnri'li:vd], *a.* non soulagé; san relief.
unremitting [ʌnri'mitiŋ], *a.* incessant, infati gable.
unremunerative [ʌnri'mju:nərətiv], *a.* pe rémunérateur, peu lucratif.
unrepentant [ʌnri'pentənt], *a.* impénitent.
unrepresented [ʌnrepri'zentid], *a.* nor représenté.
unrequited [ʌnri'kwaitid], *a.* sans être récom pensé; qui n'est pas payé de retour (*amour*).
unreserved [ʌnri'zə:vd], *a.* sans réserve; absolu (*total*).
unreservedly [ʌnri'zə:vidli], *adv.* sans réserve.
unresisting [ʌnri'zistiŋ], *a.* qui ne résiste pas, soumis.
unresolved [ʌnri'zɔlvd], *a.* non résolu; irrésolu, indécis (*personne*).
unresponsive [ʌnris'pɔnsiv], *a.* peu sensible; froid.
unrest [ʌn'rest], *n.* inquiétude, agitation, *f.*
unrestrained [ʌnri'streind], *a.* non restreint; non réprimé; effréné, déréglé.
unrestricted [ʌnri'striktid], *a.* sans restriction.
unretentive [ʌnri'tentiv], *a.* peu tenace; peu fidèle (*la mémoire*).
unrevenged [ʌnri'vendʒd], *a.* non vengé.
unrevised [ʌnri'vaizd], *a.* non revu, non revisé.
unrewarded [ʌnri'wɔ:did], *a.* sans récompense.

nrewarding [ʌnri'wɔ:diŋ], *a.* peu rémunérateur.
nrig [ʌn'rig], *v.t.* dégréer.
nrighteous [ʌn'raitʃəs], *a.* injuste, inique.
nrighteousness [ʌn'raitʃəsnis], *n.* injustice, iniquité, *f.*
nripe [ʌn'raip], *a.* pas mûr, vert; (*fig.*) prématuré.
nrivalled [ʌn'raivəld], *a.* sans rival, sans égal.
nroll [ʌn'roul], *v.t.* dérouler, déployer.—*v.i.* se dérouler, se déployer.
nruffled [ʌn'rʌfld], *a.* tranquille, calme.
nruly [ʌn'ru:li], *a.* indiscipliné, insoumis, turbulent.
nsaddle [ʌn'sædl], *v.t.* desseller; débâter (*âne*); désarçonner (*cavalier*).
nsafe [ʌn'seif], *a.* peu sûr, dangereux, hasardeux.
nsaleable [ʌn'seiləbl], *a.* invendable.
nsalted [ʌn'sɔ:ltid], *a.* non salé, sans sel.
nsanctified [ʌn'sæŋktifaid], *a.* non consacré, profane.
nsatisfactorily [ʌnsætis'fæktərili], *adv.* d'une manière peu satisfaisante.
nsatisfactory [ʌnsætis'fæktəri], *a.* peu satisfaisant.
nsatisfied [ʌn'sætisfaid], *a.* peu satisfait.
nsavouriness [ʌn'seivərinis], *n.* insipidité, fadeur, *f.*; mauvais goût, *m.*
nsavoury [ʌn'seivəri], *a.* sans saveur, insipide; repoussant (*désagréable*).
nscarred [ʌn'skɑ:d], *a.* sans cicatrices.
nscathed [ʌn'skeiðd], *a.* sans blessures, sain et sauf.
nscholarly [ʌn'skɔləli], *a.* illettré, ignorant.
nscientific [ʌnsaiən'tifik], *a.* peu scientifique.
unscientifically [ʌnsaiən'tifikli], *adv.* peu scientifiquement.
unscrew [ʌn'skru:], *v.t.* dévisser.
unscrupulous [ʌn'skru:pjuləs], *a.* peu scrupuleux.
unscrupulously [ʌn'skru:pjuləsli], *adv.* sans scrupule.
unscrupulousness [ʌn'skru:pjuləsnis], *n.* manque de scrupule, *m.*
unseal [ʌn'si:l], *v.t.* décacheter; desceller.
unsealed [ʌn'si:ld], *a.* décacheté, ouvert.
unseasonable [ʌn'si:znəbl], *a.* mal à propos; indu (*heure*); pas de saison (*temps*).
unseat [ʌn'si:t], *v.t.* renverser; désarçonner (*d'un cheval*); (*Polit.*) invalider.
unseaworthy [ʌn'si:wə:ði], *a.* incapable de tenir la mer, innavigable.
unsecured [ʌnsi'kjuəd], *a.* sans garantie; mal fermé (*porte*).
unseeing [ʌn'si:iŋ], *a.* aveugle.
unseemliness [ʌn'si:mlinis], *n.* inconvenance, *f.*
unseemly [ʌn'si:mli], *a.* inconvenant; indécent.
unseen [ʌn'si:n], *a.* sans être vu, invisible.
unselfish [ʌn'selfiʃ], *a.* désintéressé.
unserviceable [ʌn'sə:visəbl], *a.* inutile, bon à rien.
unsettle [ʌn'setl], *v.t.* déranger; (*fig.*) troubler.
unsettled [ʌn'setld], *a.* mal fixé, mal établi; incertain (*temps etc.*); irrésolu (*personne*); dérangé, troublé (*esprit*); variable, changeant (*inconstant*).
unshackled [ʌn'ʃækld], *a.* sans entraves, libre.
unshaken [ʌn'ʃeikn], *a.* inébranlable, ferme.
unshapely [ʌn'ʃeipli], *a.* difforme, informe.
unshaved [ʌn'ʃeivd], **unshaven** [ʌn'ʃeivn], *a.* non rasé.
unsheathe [ʌn'ʃi:ð], *v.t.* dégainer.
unship [ʌn'ʃip], *v.t.* débarquer; démonter (*gouvernail etc.*); désarmer (*avirons*).
unshod [ʌn'ʃɔd], *a.* sans chaussures; déferré (*cheval*).
unshorn [ʌn'ʃɔ:n], *a.* non tondu.
unshrinkable [ʌn'ʃriŋkəbl], *a.* irrétrécissable.
unsightliness [ʌn'saitlinis], *n.* laideur, *f.*
unsightly [ʌn'saitli], *a.* laid, déplaisant.
unsigned [ʌn'saind], *a.* non signé.
unsisterly [ʌn'sistəli], *a.* peu digne d'une sœur.
unskilful [ʌn'skilful], *a.* inhabile, maladroit.
unskilled [ʌn'skild], *a.* inexpérimenté (*dans*); non qualifié; ***unskilled labour***, travail de manœuvre, *m.*; main-d'œuvre non spécialisée, *f.*
unsociable [ʌn'souʃəbl], *a.* insociable.
unsoiled [ʌn'sɔild], *a.* sans tache.
unsold [ʌn'sould], *a.* invendu.
unsoldierly [ʌn'sould3əli], *a.* indigne d'un soldat.
unsolicited [ʌnsə'lisitid], *a.* sans être sollicité.
unsolved [ʌn'sɔlvd], *a.* non résolu.
unsophisticated [ʌnsə'fistikeitid], *a.* qui n'est pas frelaté; pur, vrai.
unsought [ʌn'sɔ:t], *a.* non recherché; spontané.
unsound [ʌn'saund], *a.* défectueux, malsain; faux, erroné; mal établi (*crédit*); vicieux, pas sain (*cheval*); ***of unsound mind***, non sain d'esprit.
unsparing [ʌn'spɛəriŋ], *a.* libéral, prodigue; impitoyable (*sans pitié*).
unsparingly [ʌn'spɛəriŋli], *adv.* avec prodigalité; impitoyablement.
unspeakable [ʌn'spi:kəbl], *a.* inexprimable; indicible; ignoble, sans nom.
unspecified [ʌn'spesifaid], *a.* non spécifié.
unspoiled [ʌn'spɔild], *a.* non corrompu; bien élevé (*enfant*).
unspoken [ʌn'spoukn], *a.* non prononcé; tacite.
unsportsmanlike [ʌn'spɔ:tsmənlaik], *a.* indigne d'un chasseur *ou* d'un sportsman.
unspotted [ʌn'spɔtid], *a.* sans tache.
unstable [ʌn'steibl], *a.* irrésolu; inconstant; (*Mech.*) instable.
unstained [ʌn'steind], *a.* sans tache.
unstamped [ʌn'stæmpt], *a.* non timbré, sans timbre.
unsteadily [ʌn'stedili], *adv.* en chancelant; d'une manière irrégulière.
unsteadiness [ʌn'stedinis], *n.* instabilité, irrésolution, *f.*
unsteady [ʌn'stedi], *a.* chancelant; mal assuré, irrésolu, inconstant, irrégulier (*conduite*).
unstinted [ʌn'stintid], *a.* non restreint, abondant.
unstop [ʌn'stɔp], *v.t.* déboucher, ouvrir.
unstrengthened [ʌn'streŋθənd], *a.* non renforcé.
unstressed [ʌn'strest], *a.* inaccentué, atone.
unsubdued [ʌnsəb'dju:d], *a.* indompté.
unsubmissive [ʌnsəb'misiv], *a.* insoumis.

unsubmissiveness [ʌnsəb'misivnis], *n.* insoumission, *f.*
unsubstantial [ʌnsəb'stænʃl], *a.* peu substantiel; peu solide; (*fig.*) immatériel; chimérique.
unsuccessful [ʌnsək'sesful], *a.* qui n'a pas réussi, sans succès.
unsuccessfully [ʌnsək'sesfuli] *adv.* sans succès.
unsuitable [ʌn'sju:təbl], *a.* peu convenable, peu propre (*à*).
unsuited [ʌn'sju:tid], *a.* peu fait (*pour*), peu convenable (*à*).
unsullied [ʌn'sʌlid], *a.* sans souillure, sans tache.
unsung [ʌn'sʌŋ], *a.* non célébré.
unsupervised [ʌn'sju:pəvaizd], *a.* non surveillé.
unsupported [ʌnsə'pɔ:tid], *a.* non soutenu; (*fig.*) sans appui.
unsuppressed [ʌnsə'prest], *a.* mal contenu.
unsure [ʌn'ʃuə], *a.* peu sûr.
unsurpassed [ʌnsə'pɑ:st], *a.* non surpassé, sans égal.
unsuspected [ʌnsə'spektid], *a.* insoupçonné; non suspect.
unsuspecting [ʌnsə'spektiŋ], sans soupçon, confiant.
unsuspicious [ʌnsə'spiʃəs], *a.* sans méfiance, confiant.
unsustained [ʌnsə'steind], *a.* non soutenu.
unswayed [ʌn'sweid], *a.* qui ne se laisse pas influencer.
unswerving [ʌn'swə:viŋ], *a.* qui ne s'écarte pas, inébranlable.
unsymmetrical [ʌnsi'metrikl], *a.* asymétrique.
unsympathetic [ʌnsimpə'θetik], *a.* froid, peu compatissant.
unsystematic [ʌnsisti'mætik], *a.* peu systématique.
untainted [ʌn'teintid], *a.* non corrompu; frais (*viande*).
untamable [ʌn'teiməbl], *a.* indomptable.
untamed [ʌn'teimd], *a.* indompté, non apprivoisé.
untapped [ʌn'tæpt], *a.* inexploité (*ressources*).
untarnished [ʌn'tɑ:niʃt], *a.* non terni.
untaught [ʌn'tɔ:t], *a.* ignorant, illettré.
untaxed [ʌn'tækst], *a.* exempt d'impôts.
unteachable [ʌn'ti:tʃəbl], *a.* incapable d'apprendre.
untearable [ʌn'tɛərəbl], *a.* indéchirable.
untempered [ʌn'tempəd], *a.* non trempé (*métal*).
untenable [ʌn'tenəbl], *a.* insoutenable.
untended [ʌn'tendid], *a.* non gardé.
untested [ʌn'testid], *a.* inessayé.
unthanked [ʌn'θæŋkt], *a.* sans être remercié.
unthinking [ʌn'θiŋkiŋ], *a.* inconsidéré, étourdi.
unthinkingly [ʌn'θiŋkiŋli], *adv.* sans y penser.
untidily [ʌn'taidili], *adv.* sans ordre, sans soin.
untidiness [ʌn'taidinis], *n.* désordre, *m.*
untidy [ʌn'taidi], *a.* en désordre; négligé.
untie [ʌn'tai], *v.t.* délier, dénouer; défaire (*nœud*).
until [ən'til], *prep.* jusqu'à; avant.—*conj.* jusqu'à ce que, avant que.
untilled [ʌn'tild], *a.* inculte, en friche.
untimeliness [ʌn'taimlinis], *n.* inopportunité, *f.*
untimely [ʌn'taimli], *a.* prématuré, inopportun.—*adv.* avant terme, prématurément.
untiring [ʌn'taiəriŋ], *a.* infatigable.
untiringly [ʌn'taiəriŋli], *adv.* sans relâche.
***unto** ['ʌntu], *prep.* [TO].
untold [ʌn'tould], *a.* non raconté, non exprimé; sans nombre; inouï.
untouchable [ʌn'tʌtʃəbl], *a.* and *n.* hors caste, paria, intouchable, *m., f.*
untouched [ʌn'tʌtʃt], *a.* non touché; (*fig.*) non ému (*de*).
untoward [ʌn'tɔ:d, ʌn'touəd], *a.* insoumis, indocile (*rebelle*); fâcheux.
untraceable [ʌn'treisəbl], *a.* introuvable.
untrained [ʌn'treind], *a.* inexpérimenté (*inexpert*); indiscipliné; non dressé (*animal*).
untrammelled [ʌn'træməld], *a.* sans entraves.
untranslatable [ʌntrɑ:ns'leitəbl], *a.* intraduisible.
untravelled [ʌn'trævld], *a.* peu connu (*terre*); qui n'a pas voyagé (*personne*).
untried [ʌn'traid], *a.* non essayé; qui n'a pas encore été jugé.
untrimmed [ʌn'trimd], *a.* sans garniture; non émondé (*arbre*).
untrodden [ʌn'trɔdn], *a.* non frayé; immaculé (*neige*).
untroubled [ʌn'trʌbld], *a.* calme, tranquille.
untrue [ʌn'tru:], *a.* faux; inexact (*nouvelle etc.*); déloyal (*à*).
untrustworthiness [ʌn'trʌstwə:ðinis], *n.* inexactitude, fausseté, *f.*
untrustworthy [ʌn'trʌstwə:ði], *a.* indigne de confiance; inexact, mensonger (*nouvelle etc.*)
untruth [ʌn'tru:θ], *n.* contre-vérité, fausseté, *f.*
untruthful [ʌn'tru:θful], *a.* menteur; mensonger (*nouvelle etc.*); perfide, faux, déloyal (*traître*).
untruthfulness [ʌn'tru:θfulnis], *n.* fausseté, *f.*
untutored [ʌn'tju:təd], *a.* peu instruit, ignorant.
untwine [ʌn'twain], *v.t.* détordre; dérouler.
untwist [ʌn'twist], *v.t.* détordre, détortiller, défaire.
unused (1) [ʌn'ju:zd], *a.* non employé, inutilisé; inusité (*mot*).
unused (2) [ʌn'ju:st], *a.* inaccoutumé; ***unused to***, inaccoutumé à.
unusual [ʌn'ju:ʒuəl], *a.* peu commun, rare.
unusually [ʌn'ju:ʒuəli], *adv.* rarement; extraordinairement.
unutterable [ʌn'ʌtərəbl], *a.* inexprimable, indicible.
unuttered [ʌn'ʌtəd], *a.* non prononcé.
unvanquished [ʌn'væŋkwiʃt], *a.* indompté.
unvaried [ʌn'vɛərid], *a.* uniforme.
unvarnished [ʌn'vɑ:niʃt], *a.* non verni; (*fig.*) simple, naturel.
unvarying [ʌn'vɛəriiŋ], *a.* invariable, uniforme.
unveil [ʌn'veil], *v.t.* dévoiler; découvrir.
unventilated [ʌn'ventileitid], *a.* mal aéré.
unversed [ʌn'və:st], *a.* peu versé (*dans*).
unvisited [ʌn'vizitid], *a.* non visité, peu fréquenté.
unwarily [ʌn'wɛərili], *adv.* sans précaution, imprudemment.

unwariness [ʌn'wɛərinis], *n.* imprévoyance, imprudence, *f.*

unwarlike [ʌn'wɔːlaik], *a.* pacifique, peu belliqueux.

unwarrantable [ʌn'wɔrəntəbl], *a.* injustifiable.

unwarrantably [ʌn'wɔrəntəbli], *adv.* inexcusablement.

unwarranted [ʌn'wɔrəntid], *a.* non garanti; ***an unwarranted insult***, une insulte gratuite.

unwary [ʌn'wɛəri], *a.* inconsidéré, imprudent.

unwashed [ʌn'wɔʃt], *a.* non lavé, sale, malpropre.

unwavering [ʌn'weivəriŋ], *a.* résolu, inébranlable.

unwearable [ʌn'wɛərəbl], *a.* qu'on ne peut plus porter.

unwearied [ʌn'wiərid], *a.* non lassé, infatigable.

unwelcome [ʌn'welkəm], *a.* importun; fâcheux.

unwell [ʌn'wel], *a.* indisposé, souffrant, mal portant.

unwept [ʌn'wept], *a.* non pleuré, non regretté.

unwholesome [ʌn'houlsəm], *a.* malsain, insalubre.

unwieldy [ʌn'wiːldi], *a.* lourd, pesant, difficile à manier.

unwilling [ʌn'wiliŋ], *a.* peu disposé, mal disposé; ***to be unwilling to***, n'être pas disposé à.

unwillingly [ʌn'wiliŋli], *adv.* à contre cœur, sans le vouloir.

unwillingness [ʌn'wiliŋnis], *n.* mauvaise volonté, *f.*

unwind [ʌn'waind], *v.t. irr.* (*conjug. like* WIND) dévider; dérouler; (*fig.*) débrouiller. —*v.i.* se dévider.

unwise [ʌn'waiz], *a.* peu sage, malavisé, insensé.

unwisely [ʌn'waizli], *adv.* peu sagement, imprudemment.

unwished (for) [ʌn'wiʃt(fɔː)], *a.* non souhaité.

unwitnessed [ʌn'witnist], *a.* sans témoin, non certifié.

unwitting [ʌn'witiŋ], *a.* inconscient.

unwittingly [ʌn'witiŋli], *adv.* sans le savoir, inconsciemment.

unwomanly [ʌn'wumənli], *a.* indigne d'une femme.

unwonted [ʌn'wountid], *a.* inaccoutumé, rare.

unworkable [ʌn'wəːkəbl], *a.* impraticable.

unworked [ʌn'wəːkt], *a.* inexploité (*mine etc.*).

unworn [ʌn'wɔːn], *a.* non usé, non usagé.

unworthily [ʌn'wəːðili], *adv.* indignement, sans le mériter.

unworthiness [ʌn'wəːðinis], *n.* indignité, *f.*

unworthy [ʌn'wəːði], *a.* indigne (*de*), sans mérite.

unwrap [ʌn'ræp], *v.t.* défaire, désenvelopper.

unwrinkle [ʌn'riŋkl], *v.t.* dérider.

unwrinkled [ʌn'riŋkld], *a.* sans rides, uni.

unwritten [ʌn'ritn], *a.* non écrit; (*fig.*) oral, traditionnel.

unyielding [ʌn'jiːldiŋ], *a.* qui ne cède pas, inflexible.

unyoke [ʌn'jouk], *v.t.* ôter le joug à, dételer.

up [ʌp], *adv.* au haut, en haut, haut; en l'air; levé, sur pied (*pas au lit*); sur l'horizon; debout (*pas assis*); excité; en révolte, en insurrection; fini (*expiré*); élevé (*prix*); en hausse (*valeurs de Bourse*); ***it is up to us to do it***, c'est à nous de le faire; ***road up***, rue barrée; ***to be up to***, être au courant de; ***to make up to***, faire des avances à; ***up and down***, en haut et en bas, çà et là, de long en large, de haut en bas; ***up there***, là-haut; ***up to***, jusqu'à la hauteur de; ***up to date***, à la dernière mode; à jour; ***up to now***, jusqu'ici; ***up to then***, jusque-là; ***what's up?*** (*colloq.*) qu'est-ce qu'il y a donc?—*prep.* en haut de, au haut de; en montant; ***up hill*** or ***up stream***, en amont. —*n.* haut, *m.*; ***the ups and downs***, les hauts et les bas, *m.pl.*

upbraid [ʌp'breid], *v.t.* reprocher à; réprouver.

upbraiding [ʌp'breidiŋ], *n.* reproche, *m.*

upcast ['ʌpkɑːst], *n.* jet; coup, *m.*

upheaval [ʌp'hiːvl], *n.* soulèvement, *m.*

uphill ['ʌphil], *a.* qui monte; (*fig.*) ardu, pénible.—[ʌp'hil], *adv.* en côte, en montant.

uphold [ʌp'hould], *v.t. irr.* (*conjug. like* HOLD) soutenir, maintenir.

upholster [ʌp'houlstə], *v.t.* tapisser.

upholsterer [ʌp'houlstərə], *n.* tapissier, *m.*

upholstery [ʌp'houlstəri], *n.* tapisserie, *f.*

upkeep ['ʌpkiːp], *n.* entretien, *m.*

upland ['ʌplənd], *a.* élevé, des hautes terres.

uplands ['ʌpləndz], *n.pl.* terrain élevé, haut pays, *m.*, hautes terres, *f.pl.*

uplift [ʌp'lift], *v.t.* lever, élever, soulever. —['ʌplift], *n.* (*fig.*) inspiration, *f.*

uplifting [ʌp'liftiŋ], *n.* soulèvement, *m.*

upon [ə'pɔn], *prep.* sur; ***upon pain of***, sous peine de.

upper ['ʌpə], *a.* supérieur, d'en haut, de dessus, au-dessus; haut; ***the Upper House*** la Chambre Haute; ***upper circle***, troisièmes loges, *f.pl.*; ***upper deck***, pont supérieur, *m.*; ***upper hand***, dessus, *m.*, supériorité, *f.*

uppermost ['ʌpəmoust], *a.* le plus élevé; (*fig.*) le plus fort.

uppers ['ʌpəz], *n.pl.* empeignes (*de chaussures*), *f.pl.*; (*fam.*) ***to be on one's uppers***, être dans la débine.

Upper Volta ['ʌpə'vɔltə]. la Haute Volta, *f.*

uppish ['ʌpiʃ], *a.* fier, arrogant.

uppishness ['ʌpiʃnis], *n.* fierté, arrogance, *f.*

upraise [ʌp'reiz], *v.t.* soulever, élever.

upright ['ʌprait], *a.* droit, debout; d'aplomb, vertical; (*fig.*) honnête (*intègre*).—*adv.* tout droit.—*n.* montant, *m.*

uprightness ['ʌpraitnis], *n.* droiture, intégrité, *f.*

uprising [ʌp'raiziŋ], *n.* lever; soulèvement, *m.*

uproar ['ʌprɔː], *n.* tumulte, désordre; tapage, *m.*

uproarious [ʌp'rɔːriəs], *a.* bruyant; tumultueux.

uproariously [ʌp'rɔːriəsli], *adv.* avec un grand vacarme.

uproot [ʌp'ruːt], *v.t.* déraciner, extirper.

uprooting [ʌp'ruːtiŋ], *n.* déracinement, *m.*

upset [ʌp'set], *v.t. irr.* (*conjug. like* SET) renverser; (*fig.*) bouleverser.—*v.i.* se renverser;

verser (*véhicules*).—['ʌpset], *n.* bouleversement, *m.*
upshot ['ʌpʃɔt], *n.* résultat, *m.*, fin, *f.*, fin mot, *m.*
upside-down ['ʌpsaid'daun], *adv.* sens dessus dessous.
upstairs ['ʌpstɛəz], *a.* d'en haut.—[ʌp'stɛəz], *adv.* en haut.
upstanding [ʌp'stændiŋ], *a.* droit, debout.
upstart ['ʌpstɑ:t], *n.* parvenu, nouveau riche, *m.*
upsurge [ʌp'sə:dʒ], *n.* poussée, *f.*
upward ['ʌpwəd], *a.* dirigé en haut; ascendant.—*adv.* or **upwards** ['ʌpwədz], en haut; en montant; ***upwards of***, plus de.
Ural ['juərəl] **Mountains**. les Monts Ourals, *m.pl.*
uranium [ju'reiniəm], *n.* uranium, *m.*
urban ['ə:bən], *a.* urbain.
urbane [ə:'bein], *a.* qui a de l'urbanité, poli.
urbanely [ə:'beinli], *adv.* avec urbanité.
urbanity [ə:'bæniti], *n.* urbanité, *f.*
urbanize ['ə:bənaiz], *v.t.* urbaniser.
urchin ['ə:tʃin], *n.* gamin, polisson; (*colloq.*) mioche, gosse, *m.*; ***sea-urchin***, oursin, *m.*
urge [ə:dʒ], *v.t.* presser; pousser, exciter, porter (*à*); alléguer (*insister sur*); ***to urge on***, pousser en avant.—*n.* impulsion; poussée, *f.*
urgency ['ə:dʒənsi], *n.* urgence, *f.*
urgent ['ə:dʒənt], *a.* urgent, instant.
urgently ['ə:dʒəntli], *adv.* avec urgence, instamment.
urging ['ə:dʒiŋ], *n.* sollicitation, *f.*
uric ['juərik], *a.* urique.
urinal ['juərinl], *n.* urinoir; (*Med.*) urinal, *m.*; vespasienne (*urinoir public*), *f.*
urinate ['juərineit], *v.i.* uriner.
urine ['juərin], *n.* urine, *f.*
urn [ə:n], *n.* urne; fontaine (*à thé, à café etc.*), *f.*
Ursula ['ə:sjulə]. Ursule, *f.*
Uruguay ['juərugwai]. l'Uruguay, *m.*
Uruguayan [juəru'gwaiən], *a.* uruguayen.—*n.* Uruguayen (*personne*), *m.*
us [ʌs], *pron.* nous; ***for us Frenchmen***, pour nous autres Français.
usable ['ju:zəbl], *a.* utilisable, employable.
usage ['ju:zidʒ], *n.* usage, *m.*
use [ju:s], *n.* usage, emploi, *m.*; utilité, *f.*, avantage, profit, *m.*; habitude, *f.*; (*Law*) usufruit, *m.*; ***it is of no use***, cela ne sert à rien; ***of use***, utile; ***to make use of***, se servir de; ***what is the use of that?*** à quoi sert cela?—[ju:z], *v.t.* user de, faire usage de, employer, se servir de; utiliser; consommer.
used [ju:zd], *a.* usité (*mot etc.*), d'occasion (*voiture*); ***very little used***, qui a peu servi, presque neuf (*vêtement etc.*).—[ju:st] ***to be*** or ***get used to***, s'accoutumer à, s'habituer à.—[ju:st], *v. aux. in the expression* ***used to*** (*followed by inf.*) *usu. translated by the Imp. Tense in French*; ***he used to admire***, il admirait.
useful ['ju:sful], *a.* utile.
usefully ['ju:sfuli], *adv.* utilement, avec profit.
usefulness ['ju:sfulnis], *n.* utilité, *f.*
useless ['ju:slis], *a.* inutile; vain.
uselessly ['ju:slisli], *adv.* inutilement.
uselessness ['ju:slisnis], *n.* inutilité, *f.*
usher ['ʌʃə], *n.* huissier (*de cour de justice*); sous-maître, *m.*—*v.t.* faire entrer, introduire (*dans*); (*fig.*) annoncer.
usherette [ʌʃə'ret], *n.* (*Cine.*) ouvreuse, *f.*
usual ['ju:ʒuəl], *a.* usuel, ordinaire, habituel, accoutumé; d'usage; ***as usual***, comme d'habitude.
usually ['ju:ʒuəli], *adv.* ordinairement, d'ordinaire, d'habitude.
usurer ['ju:ʒərə], *n.* usurier, *m.*
usurious [ju:'zjuəriəs], *a.* usuraire.
usurp [ju'zə:p], *v.t.* usurper.
usurpation [ju:zə'peiʃən], *n.* usurpation, *f.*
usurper [ju'zə:pə], *n.* usurpateur, *m.*
usury ['ju:ʒəri], *n.* usure, *f.*
utensil [ju'tensil], *n.* ustensile, *m.*
uterine ['ju:tərain], *a.* utérin.
uterus ['ju:tərəs], *n.* utérus, *m.*
utilitarian [ju:tili'tɛəriən], *a.* utilitaire.
utilitarianism [ju:tili'tɛəriənizm], *n.* utilitarisme, *m.*
utility [ju:'tiliti], *n.* utilité, *f.*
utilizable ['ju:tilaizəbl], *a.* utilisable.
utilization [ju:tilai'zeiʃən], *n.* utilisation, *f.*
utilize ['ju:tilaiz], *v.t.* utiliser.
utmost ['ʌtmoust], *a.* extrême, le dernier, le plus haut, le plus grand; le plus élevé (*prix etc.*).—*n.* extrême, comble, *m.*; ***to do one's utmost***, faire tout son possible (*pour*).
Utopia [ju:'toupiə]. Utopie, *f.*
Utopian [ju:'toupiən], *a.* d'utopie, utopique.
utter (1) ['ʌtə], *a.* entier, complet; absolu; le plus profond (*extrême*); vrai; fieffé (*véritable*).
utter (2) ['ʌtə], *v.t.* pousser; proférer, prononcer; dire; émettre (*fausse monnaie*).
utterable ['ʌtərəbl], *a.* exprimable.
utterance ['ʌtərəns], *n.* énonciation, prononciation, parole, expression, *f.*
utterer ['ʌtərə], *n.* personne qui prononce, *f.* émetteur (*de fausse monnaie*), *m.*
utterly ['ʌtəli], *adv.* tout à fait, entièrement.
uttermost ['ʌtəmoust], *a.* extrême; le plus reculé.
uvula ['ju:vjulə], *n.* (*Anat.*) luette, uvule, *f.*
uvular ['ju:vjulə], *a.* uvulaire.
uxorious [ʌk'sɔ:riəs], *a.* uxorieux, esclave de sa femme.
uxoriousness [ʌk'sɔ:riəsnis], *n.* complaisance excessive pour sa femme, *f.*

V

V, v [vi:]. vingt-deuxième lettre de l'alphabet, *m.*
vacancy ['veikənsi], *n.* vacance, place vacante, *f.*; vide, *m.*; lacune (*trou*), *f.*
vacant ['veikənt], *a.* vacant, vide; libre (*inoccupé*); vide d'expression (*regard perdu*).
vacate [və'keit], *v.t.* laisser vacant, quitter.
vacation [və'keiʃən], *n.* vacation, *f.*, vacances, *f.pl.*
vaccinate ['væksineit], *v.t.* vacciner.
vaccination [væksi'neiʃən], *n.* vaccination, vaccine, *f.*
vaccine ['væksi:n], *a.* de vache.—*n.* vaccin, *m.*

vacillate ['væsileit], *v.i.* vaciller; (*fig.*) hésiter.
vacillating ['væsileitiŋ], *a.* vacillant, indécis.
vacillation [væsi'leiʃən], *n.* vacillation, indécision, *f.*
vacuity [və'kju:iti], *n.* vide, *m.*; vacuité, *f.*
vacuous ['vækjuəs], *a.* vide; (*fig.*) bête.
vacuum ['vækjuəm], *n.* vide, *m.*
vacuum-cleaner ['vækjuəm'kli:nə], *n.* aspirateur, *m.*
vade-mecum ['veidi'mi:kəm], *n.* vade-mecum, *m.*
vagabond ['vægəbənd], *a.* errant, vagabond.—*n.* vagabond, *m.*
vagary ['veigəri], *n.* caprice, *m.*, lubie, boutade, *f.*
vagina [və'dʒainə], *n.* (*Anat.*) vagin, *m.*
vagrancy ['veigrənsi], *n.* vagabondage, *m.*
vagrant ['veigrent], *a.* vagabond, errant.—*n.* vagabond, mendiant, *m.*
vague [veig], *a.* vague.
vaguely ['veigli], *adv.* vaguement.
vagueness ['veignis], *n.* vague, *m.*
vain [vein], *a.* vain; faux (*creux*); vaniteux, glorieux (*fier*); ***in vain***, en vain.
vainglorious [vein'glɔ:riəs], *a.* vain, vaniteux.
vainglory [vein'glɔ:ri], *n.* vaine gloire, gloriole, *f.*
vainly ['veinli], *adv.* en vain, vainement.
vainness ['veinnis], *n.* vanité, *f.*
valance ['væləns], *n.* frange de lit, *f.*
vale [veil], *n.* (*poet.*) vallon, *m.*, vallée, *f.*
valedictory [væli'diktəri], *a.* d'adieu.—*n.* discours d'adieu, *m.*
valet ['vælit], *n.* valet de chambre, *m.*
valetudinarian [vælitju:di'nɛəriən], *a.* and *n.* valétudinaire, *m.*, *f.*
valiant ['væliənt], *a.* vaillant, valeureux.
valiantly ['væliəntli], *adv.* vaillamment.
valid ['vælid], *a.* valide, valable.
validate ['vælideit], *v.t.* valider, rendre valable.
validity [və'liditi], **validness** ['vælidnis], *n.* validité, *f.*
validly ['vælidli], *adv.* validement.
validness [VALIDITY].
valise [və'li:z], *n.* valise, *f.*; sac de voyage, *m.*
valley ['væli], *n.* vallée, *f.*, vallon, *m.*
valorous ['vælərəs], *a.* valeureux.
valour ['vælə], *n.* valeur, vaillance, *f.*
valuable ['væljuəbl], *a.* précieux.
valuation [vælju'eiʃən], *n.* évaluation, *f.*
valuator ['væljueitə], *n.* estimateur, *m.*
value ['vælju:], *n.* valeur, *f.*; prix, *m.*—*v.t.* évaluer, estimer.
valued ['vælju:d], *a.* estimé, apprécié.
valueless ['væljulis], *a.* sans valeur.
valuer ['væljuə], *n.* estimateur, commissaire-priseur, *m.*
valve [vælv], *n.* soupape; valve; (*Rad.*) lampe, *f.*
valved [vælvd], *a.* à soupape; (*Bot.*) valvé, à valves.
valvular ['vælvjulə], *a.* (*Med.*) valvulaire.
vamp [væmp], *n.* empeigne; enjôleuse, femme fatale, *f.*—*v.t.* (*fig.*) raccommoder, rapiécer; (*Mus.*) improviser.
vampire ['væmpaiə], *n.* vampire, *m.*
van [væn], *n.* camionnette, voiture (*de déménagement*), *f.*; (*Rail. etc.*) fourgon, *m.*; avant-garde (*précurseur*), *f.*
vandal [vændl], *n.* vandale, *m.*, *f.*
vandalism ['vændəlizm], *n.* vandalisme, *m.*
vane [vein], *n.* girouette, *f.*
vanguard ['vængɑ:d], *n.* avant-garde, *f.*
vanilla [və'nilə], *n.* vanille, *f.*
vanish ['væniʃ], *v.i.* s'évanouir, disparaître.
vanishing-point ['væniʃiŋpɔint], *n.* point de fuite, *m.*
vanity ['væniti], *n.* vanité, *f.*
vanquish ['væŋkwiʃ], *v.t.* vaincre.
vanquisher ['væŋkwiʃə], *n.* vainqueur, *m.*
vantage ['vɑ:ntidʒ], *n.* avantage, *m.*, supériorité, *f.*
vapid ['væpid], *a.* fade, insipide; éventé (*boisson alcoolique*).
vapidity [væ'piditi], **vapidness** ['væpidnis], *n.* fadeur, insipidité, *f.*
vaporization [veipərai'zeiʃən], *n.* vaporisation, *f.*
vaporize ['veipəraiz], *v.t.* vaporiser.—*v.i.* se vaporiser.
vaporous ['veipərəs], *a.* vaporeux.
vapour ['veipə], *n.* vapeur; (*fig.*) fumée, *f.*
vapourish ['veipəriʃ], **vapoury** ['veipəri], *a.* vaporeux.
variability [vɛəriə'biliti], **variableness** ['vɛəriəblnis], *n.* variabilité; inconstance, *f.*
variable ['vɛəriəbl], *a.* variable; inconstant.
variance ['vɛəriəns], *n.* désaccord, *m.*
variation [vɛəri'eiʃən], *n.* variation, *f.*, changement, *m.*
varicose ['værikous], *a.* variqueux; ***varicose vein***, varice, *f.*
varied ['vɛərid], *a.* varié, divers.
variegate ['vɛərigeit], *v.t.* varier; nuancer.
variegated ['vɛərigeitid], *a.* varié, bigarré; (*Bot.*) panaché.
variegation [vɛəri'geiʃən], *n.* bigarrure, *f.*
variety [və'raiəti], *n.* variété, diversité, *f.*
various ['vɛəriəs], *a.* divers, différent.
variously ['vɛəriəsli], *adv.* diversement.
varnish ['vɑ:niʃ], *n.* vernis, *m.*—*v.t.* vernir; vernisser (*poterie etc.*).
varnisher ['vɑ:niʃə], *n.* vernisseur, *m.*
varnishing ['vɑ:niʃiŋ], *n.* vernissure, *f.*; vernissage, *m.*
vary ['vɛəri], *v.t.* varier; diversifier.—*v.i.* varier, changer.
varying ['vɛəriiŋ], *a.* changeant, qui varie, divers.
vascular ['væskjulə], *a.* vasculaire.
vase [vɑ:z], *n.* vase, *m.*
vaseline ['væsəli:n], *n.* (*reg. trade mark*) vaseline, *f.*
vassal [væsl], *n.* vassal, *m.*
vassalage ['væsəlidʒ], *n.* vasselage, *m.*; (*fig.*) servitude, *f.*
vast [vɑ:st], *a.* vaste, immense.—*n.* immensité, *f.*
vastly ['vɑ:stli], *adv.* immensément, excessivement.
vastness ['vɑ:stnis], *n.* vaste étendue, grandeur, *f.*
vat [væt], *n.* cuve, *f.*
vatful ['vætful], *n.* cuvée, *f.*
Vatican ['vætikən]. le Vatican, *m.*
vaudeville ['voudəvil], *n.* vaudeville, *m.*
vault [vɔ:lt], *n.* voûte, cave, *f.*; caveau (*lieu de sépulture*); saut (*bond*), *m.*—*v.t.* voûter.—*v.i.* sauter.
vaulted ['vɔ:ltid], *a.* voûté, en voûte.

vaulter ['vɔ:ltə], *n.* voltigeur, sauteur, *m.*, acrobate, *m.*, *f.*
vaulting ['vɔ:ltiŋ], *n.* construction de voûtes, *f.*; voûtes, *f.pl.*; voltige (*acrobatie*), *f.*
vaunt [vɔ:nt], *n.* vanterie, *f.*—*v.t.* vanter élever jusqu'aux nues.
vaunter ['vɔ:ntə], *n.* vantard, *m.*
vaunting ['vɔ:ntiŋ], *a.* plein de jactance.
vauntingly ['vɔ:ntiŋli], *adv.* avec jactance.
veal [vi:l], *n.* veau, *m.*
vedette [və'det], *n.* vedette, *f.*
veer [viə], *v.t.* virer (*bateau*).—*v.i.* tourner, changer de direction; virer (*bateau*).
vegetable ['vedʒitəbl], *a.* végétal.—*n.* végétal, légume, *m.*
vegetal ['vedʒitl], *a.* végétal.
vegetarian [vedʒi'tɛəriən], *a.* and *n.* végétarien, *m.*
vegetate ['vedʒiteit], *v.i.* végéter.
vegetation [vedʒi'teiʃən], *n.* végétation, *f.*
vegetative ['vedʒitətiv], *a.* végétatif, végétant.
vehemence ['vi:iməns], *n.* véhémence; (*fig.*) ardeur, *f.*
vehement ['vi:imənt], *a.* véhément, impétueux.
vehemently ['vi:iməntli], *adv.* avec véhémence, impétueusement.
vehicle ['vi:ikl], *n.* véhicule, *m.*, voiture, *f.*
veil [veil], *n.* voile, *m.*; voilette (*de dame*), *f.*—*v.t.* voiler; (*fig.*) déguiser.
vein [vein], *n.* veine; (*fig.*) humeur, *f.*—*v.t.* veiner.
veined [veind], **veiny** ['veini], *a.* veiné.
vellum ['veləm], *n.* vélin, *m.*
velocity [və'lɔsiti], *n.* vélocité, vitesse, rapidité, *f.*
velvet ['velvit], *a.* de velours; (*Bot.*) velouté. —*n.* velours, *m.*
velveteen [velvə'ti:n], *n.* velours de coton, *m.*
velvety ['velviti], *a.* velouté.
venal [vi:nl], *a.* vénal.
venality [vi:'næliti], *n.* vénalité, *f.*
vend [vend], *v.t.* vendre (*petits articles*).
vendee [ven'di:], *n.* acheteur, *m.*
vendetta [ven'detə], *n.* vendetta, *f.*
vendible ['vendibl], *a.* vendable.
vendor ['vendə], *n.* vendeur, *m.*
veneer [və'niə], *n.* feuille (*de bois etc.*); plaque, *f.*; (*fig.*) vernis, *m.*—*v.t.* plaquer (*de*).
veneering [və'niəriŋ], *n.* placage, *m.*
venerable ['venərəbl], *a.* vénérable.
venerableness ['venərəblnis], *n.* caractère vénérable, *m.*
venerate ['venəreit], *v.t.* vénérer.
veneration [venə'reiʃən], *n.* vénération, *f.*
venerator ['venəreitə], *n.* vénérateur, *m.*
venery ['venəri], *n.* chasse, vénerie, *f.*
Venetian [və'ni:ʃən], *a.* vénitien, de Venise; ***Venetian blind***, jalousie, *f.*; ***Venetian shutter***, persienne, *f.*—*n.* Vénitien (*personne*), *m.*
Venezuela [venə'zweilə]. le Vénézuéla, *m.*
Venezuelan [venə'zweilən], *a.* vénézuélien.—*n.* Vénézuélien (*personne*), *m.*
vengeance ['vendʒəns], *n.* vengeance, *f.*; ***with a vengeance***, furieusement, à outrance.
vengeful ['vendʒful], *a.* vindicatif.
venial ['vi:niəl], *a.* véniel, pardonnable.
veniality [vi:ni'æliti], *n.* vénialité, *f.*
Venice ['venis]. Venise, *f.*
venison ['venizn], *n.* venaison, *f.*
venom ['venəm], *n.* venin, *m.*
venomous ['venəməs], *a.* venimeux (*animal*) vénéneux (*plante*); (*fig.*) méchant.
venous ['vi:nəs], *a.* veineux.
vent [vent], *v.t.* donner issue à, exhaler décharger.—*n.* issue, *f.*, passage, cours; trou de fausse (*de baril*); soupirail (*pour l'air*) *m.*; ***to give vent to***, donner libre cours à.
ventilate ['ventileit], *v.t.* ventiler; aérer (*fig.*) discuter.
ventilation [venti'leiʃən], *n.* ventilation, *f.* ***ventilation shaft***, puits d'aérage, *m.*
ventilator ['ventileitə], *n.* ventilateur, *m.*
ventral ['ventrəl], *a.* ventral.
ventricle ['ventrikl], *n.* ventricule, *m.*
ventriloquism [ven'triləkwizm], *n.* ventriloquie, *f.*
ventriloquist [ven'triləkwist], *n.* ventriloque *m.*, *f.*
venture ['ventʃə], *n.* aventure, entreprise, *f.* —*v.t.* aventurer, risquer.—*v.i.* oser, se hasarder, s'aventurer; s'aviser de (*se permettre*).
venturer ['ventʃərə], *n.* personne aventureuse, *f.*
venturesome ['ventʃəsəm], *a.* aventureux, audacieux.
venue ['venju:], *n.* juridiction, *f.*; lieu de réunion, *m.*
Venus ['vi:nəs]. Vénus, *f.*
veracious [və'reiʃəs], *a.* véridique.
veracity [və'ræsiti], *n.* véracité, *f.*
veranda, **verandah** [və'rændə], *n.* véranda, *f.*
verb [və:b], *n.* verbe, *m.*
verbal ['və:bəl], *a.* verbal, littéral.
verbally ['və:bəli], *adv.* verbalement, mot à mot.
verbatim [və:'beitim], *adv.* mot pour mot.
verbena [və:'bi:nə], *n.* verveine, *f.*
verbiage ['və:biidʒ], *n.* verbiage, *m.*
verbose [və:'bous], *a.* verbeux, diffus, prolixe.
verbosity [və:'bɔsiti], *n.* verbosité, *f.*
verdant ['və:dənt], *a.* verdoyant, vert.
verdict ['və:dikt], *n.* verdict; (*fig.*) arrêt, *m.*
verdigris ['və:digri:], *n.* vert-de-gris, *m.*
verdure ['və:djə], *n.* verdure, *f.*
verge (1) [və:dʒ], *n.* bord, *m.*, bordure; lisière (*de forêt etc.*); verge (*baguette*), *f.*; ***on the verge of setting out***, à la veille de partir. —*v.i.* pencher (*vers*); ***to verge on***, toucher à.
verger ['və:dʒə], *n.* bedeau, huissier à verge, *m.*
verification [verifi'keiʃən], *n.* vérification, *f.*
verifier ['verifaiə], *n.* vérificateur, *m.*
verify ['verifai], *v.t.* vérifier.
***verily** ['verili], *adv.* en vérité, vraiment.
verisimilar [veri'similə], *a.* vraisemblable.
verisimilitude [verisi'militju:d], *n.* vraisemblance, *f.*
veritable ['veritəbl], *a.* véritable.
verity ['veriti], *n.* vérité, *f.*
vermicelli [və:mi'seli], *n.* vermicelle, *m.*
vermicule ['və:mikju:l], *n.* vermisseau, *m.*
vermilion [və'miljən], *a.* vermeil.—*n.* vermillon, *m.*
vermin ['və:min], *n.* vermine, *f.*
verminous ['və:minəs], *a.* vermineux.

vernacular [və'nækjulə], *a.* du pays, indigène. —*n.* langue vernaculaire, *f.*
vernal ['və:nəl], *a.* printanier.
veronica [və'rɔnikə], *n.* véronique, *f.*
versatile ['və:sətail], *a.* qui a des connaissances variées; qui se plie à tout.
versatility [və:sə'tiliti], *n.* souplesse, faculté d'adaptation, *f.*
verse [və:s], *n.* vers, *m.*, poésie; strophe (*stance*), *f.*
versed [və:st], *a.* versé (*dans*).
versification [və:sifi'keiʃən], *n.* versification, *f.*
versifier ['və:sifaiə], *n.* versificateur, rimailleur, *m.*
versify ['və:sifai], *v.t.* mettre en vers.—*v.i.* versifier.
version ['və:ʃən], *n.* version, *f.*
versus ['və:səs], *prep.* contre.
vertebra ['və:tibrə], *n.* (*pl.* **vertebræ** ['və:tibri]) vertèbre, *f.*
vertebral ['və:tibrəl], *a.* vertébral.
vertebrate ['və:tibrit], *a.* and *n.* vertébré, *m.*
vertex ['və:teks], *n.* (*pl.* **vertices** ['və:tisi:z]) sommet, zénith, *m.*
vertical ['və:tikl], *a.* vertical.
vertically ['və:tikli], *adv.* verticalement.
vertiginous [və:'tidʒinəs], *a.* vertigineux.
vertigo ['və:tigou], *n.* vertige, *m.*
verve [və:v], *n.* verve, *f.*
very ['veri], *a.* vrai, même, véritable.—*adv.* fort, bien, très.
vesper ['vespə], *n.* étoile du soir, *f.*; soir *m.*; (*pl.*) vêpres, *f.pl.*
vessel ['vesl], *n.* vase; vaisseau, bâtiment, navire, *m.*
vest [vest], *n.* tricot de corps; (*Am.*) gilet, *m.*—*v.t.* vêtir, revêtir; investir (*de*).—*v.i.* échoir (*à*).
vestal [vestl], *a.* vestale, de Vesta; (*fig.*) chaste.—*n.* vestale, *f.*
vestibule ['vestibju:l], *n.* vestibule, *m.*
vestige ['vestidʒ], *n.* vestige, *m.*, trace, *f.*
vestment ['vestmənt], *n.* vêtement (de cérémonie), *m.*; chasuble, *f.*
vestry ['vestri], *n.* sacristie, *f.*
vesture ['vestʃə], *n.* vêtements, *m.pl.*
Vesuvius [vi'su:vjəs]. le Vésuve, *m.*
vetch [vetʃ], *n.* vesce, *f.*
veteran ['vetərən], *a.* vieux, ancien, expérimenté.—*n.* vétéran, *m.*
veterinary ['vetərinri], *a.* vétérinaire; ***veterinary surgeon***, vétérinaire, *m.*, *f.*
veto ['vi:tou], *n.* veto, *m.*—*v.t.* mettre son veto à, interdire.
vex [veks], *v.t.* fâcher, vexer, contrarier.
vexation [vek'seiʃən], *n.* vexation, contrariété, *f.*, chagrin, *m.*
vexatious [vek'seiʃəs], *a.* vexatoire; irritant, fâcheux, ennuyeux.
vexatiousness [vek'seiʃəsnis], *n.* caractère vexatoire, *m.*
vexed [vekst], *a.* vexé, fâché; (*fig.*) épineux (*question*).
vexing ['veksiŋ], *a.* contrariant, vexant, ennuyeux.
via ['vaiə], *prep.* par, par voie de, via.
viability [vaiə'biliti], *n.* viabilité, *f.*
viable ['vaiəbl], *a.* viable.
viaduct ['vaiədʌkt], *n.* viaduc, *m.*
vial ['vaiəl], *n.* fiole, *f.*
viands ['vaiəndz], *n. pl.* aliments, *m.pl.*; mets, *m.*
viaticum [vai'ætikəm], *n.* viatique, *m.*
vibrate [vai'breit], *v.t.* faire vibrer.—*v.i.* vibrer, osciller.
vibration [vai'breiʃən], *n.* vibration, oscillation, *f.*
vibrating [vai'breitiŋ], **vibratory** ['vaibrətəri], *a.* vibrant, vibratoire.
vicar ['vikə], *n.* (*Engl. Ch.*) pasteur; (*R.-C. Ch.*) curé (*de paroisse*), *m.*; ***vicar-general***, vicaire, *m.*
vicarage ['vikəridʒ], *n.* cure, *f.*, presbytère, *m.*
vicarial [vi'kɛəriəl], *a.* de la cure, du curé.
vicarious [vi'kɛəriəs], *a.* vicarial, de vicaire; (*fig.*) de substitution.
vicariously [vi'kɛəriəsli], *adv.* par délégation, par substitution.
vice (1) [vais], *n.* vice, défaut, *m.*; ***vice squad***, brigade de mœurs, *f.*
vice (2) [vais], *n.* (*Tech.*) étau, *m.*
vice-admiral ['vaisædmirəl], *n.* vice-amiral, *m.*
vice-chancellor ['vaistʃɑ:nsələ], *n.* vice-chancelier; (*Univ.*) recteur, *m.*
vice-president ['vaisprezidənt], *n.* vice-président, *m.*
viceroy ['vaisrɔi], *n.* vice-roi, *m.*
vicinity [vi'siniti], *n.* voisinage, *m.*, proximité, *f.*, alentours, *m.pl.*
vicious ['viʃəs], *a.* vicieux; haineux.
viciously ['viʃəsli], *adv.* vicieusement; rageusement.
viciousness ['viʃəsnis], *n.* nature vicieuse, *f.*, vice, *m.*
vicissitude [vi'sisitju:d], *n.* vicissitude, *f.*
victim ['viktim], *n.* victime, *f.*
victimization [viktimai'zeiʃən], *n.* tyrannisation, *f.*
victimize ['viktimaiz], *v.t.* exercer des représailles contre, tromper.
victor ['viktə], *n.* vainqueur, *m.*
victorious [vik'tɔ:riəs], *a.* victorieux, de victoire.
victoriously [vik'tɔ:riəsli], *adv.* victorieusement, en vainqueur.
victory ['viktəri], *n.* victoire, *f.*
victual [vitl], *v.t.* approvisionner, ravitailler.
victualler ['vitlə], *n.* pourvoyeur, fournisseur (de vivres), *m.*; ***licensed victualler***, débitant de boissons, *m.*
victualling ['vitliŋ], *n.* ravitaillement, *m.*
victuals [vitlz], *n.pl.* vivres, *m.pl.*, provisions, *f.pl.*
vie [vai], *v.i.* rivaliser, lutter (*de*); le disputer (*à*).
Vienna [vi'enə]. Vienne, *f.*
Viennese [vi:ə'ni:z], *a.* viennois.—*n.* Viennois (*personne*), *m.*
Vietnam [vjet'næm]. le Vietnam, *m.*
Vietnamese [vjetnə'mi:z], *a.* vietnamien.—*n.* Vietnamien (*personne*), *m.*
view [vju:], *n.* vue, perspective, scène, *f.*; regard (*coup d'œil*); aperçu, examen (*exposé*), *m.*; intention, *f.*, dessein, *m.*; opinion, pensée, *f.*; ***in view of***, en considération de; ***on view***, ouvert au public; ***with a view to***, en vue de.—*v.t.* regarder; considérer; examiner, inspecter; explorer.
viewer ['vju:ə], *n.* spectateur; téléspectateur, *m.*
viewing ['vju:iŋ], *n.* examen, *m.*, inspection, *f.*

view-point ['vju:pɔint], *n.* point de vue, *m.*
vigil ['vidʒil], *n.* veille, veillée, (*Eccles.*) vigile, *f.*
vigilance ['vidʒiləns], *n.* vigilance, *f.*
vigilant ['vidʒilənt], *a.* vigilant, éveillé.
vigilantly ['vidʒiləntli], *adv.* avec vigilance.
vigorous ['vigərəs], *a.* vigoureux.
vigorously ['vigərəsli], *adv.* vigoureusement.
vigorousness ['vigərəsnis], **vigour** ['vigə], *n.* vigueur, *f.*
vile [vail], *a.* vil, abject, bas; détestable.
vileness ['vailnis], *n.* bassesse, *f.*
vilification [vilifi'keiʃən], *n.* diffamation, *f.*
vilifier ['vilifaiə], *n.* diffamateur, *m.*
vilify ['vilifai], *v.t.* vilipender, dénigrer.
villa ['vilə], *n.* villa, maison de campagne, *f.*
village ['vilidʒ], *n.* village, *m.*
villager ['vilidʒə], *n.* villageois, *m.*
villain ['vilən], *n.* scélérat, gredin; (*Theat.*) traître, *m.*
villainous ['vilənəs], *a.* vil, infâme.
villainy ['viləni], *n.* scélératesse, vilenie, *f.*
vindicate ['vindikeit], *v.t.* soutenir, défendre, justifier; venger.
vindication [vindi'keiʃən], *n.* défense, justification, *f.*
vindicator ['vindikeitə], *n.* défenseur, *m.*
vindictive [vin'diktiv], *a.* vindicatif.
vindictively [vin'diktivli], *adv.* d'une manière vindicative.
vindictiveness [vin'diktivnis], *n.* esprit de vengeance, *m.*
vine [vain], *n.* vigne, *f.*
vine-dresser ['vaindresə], *n.* vigneron, *m.*
vinegar ['vinigə], *n.* vinaigre, *m.*
vine-grower ['vaingrouə], *n.* viticulteur, *m.*
vine-growing ['vaingrouiŋ], *n.* viticulture, *f.*
vine-harvest ['vainhɑ:vist], *n.* vendange, *f.*
vine-prop ['vainprɔp], *n.* échalas, *m.*
vinery ['vainəri], *n.* serre à vignes, *f.*
vineyard ['vinjəd], *n.* vigne, *f.*; vignoble, *m.*
vinicultural [vini'kʌltʃərəl], *a.* vinicole.
viniculture ['vinikʌltʃə], *n.* viniculture, *f.*
vinous ['vainous], *a.* vineux.
vintage ['vintidʒ], *n.* vendange; vinée, récolte de vin (*cueillette*), *f.*; vendanges (*temps de la récolte*), *f.pl.*; ***a vintage wine***, un vin de marque, *m.*
vintager ['vintidʒə], *n.* vendangeur, *m.*
vintner ['vintnə], *n.* négociant en vins, *m.*
viny ['vaini], *a.* de vigne, de raisin; de vignoble.
viola (1) [vi'oulə], *n.* (*Mus.*) alto, *m.*; ***viola player***, altiste, *m.*, *f.*
viola (2) ['vaiələ], *n.* (*Bot.*) violette, *f.*
violate ['vaiəleit], *v.t.* violer, faire violence à; outrager.
violation [vaiə'leiʃən], *n.* violation, infraction, *f.*, viol (*d'une femme*), *m.*
violator ['vaiəleitə], *n.* violateur, *m.*
violence ['vaiələns], *n.* violence, *f.*; ***with violence*** (*of robbery*), à main armée.
violent ['vaiələnt], *a.* violent; atroce (*douleur*).
violently ['vaiələntli], *adv.* violemment, avec violence.
violet ['vaiəlit], *n.* violette (*plante*), *f.*; violet (*couleur*), *m.*
violin [vaiə'lin], *n.* violon, *m.*
violinist [vaiə'linist], *n.* violoniste, *m.*, *f.*
violist [vi'oulist], *n.* altiste, violiste, *m.*, *f.*
violoncellist [vaiələn'tʃelist], *n.* violoncelliste, *m.*, *f.*
violoncello [vaiələn'tʃelou], *n.* violoncelle, *m.*
viper ['vaipə], *n.* vipère, *f.*
viperish ['vaipəriʃ], **viperous** ['vaipərəs], *a.* de vipère; (*fig.*) venimeux.
virago [vi'rɑ:gou], *n.* virago, mégère, *f.*
virgin ['və:dʒin], *a.* vierge; virginal, de vierge.—*n.* vierge, *f.*
virginal ['və:dʒinəl], *a.* virginal, de vierge.
virginia-creeper [və'dʒinjə'kri:pə], *n.* vigne vierge, *f.*
virginity [və'dʒiniti], *n.* virginité, *f.*
viridity [vi'riditi], *n.* verdeur, fraîcheur, *f.*
virile ['virail], *a.* viril, mâle.
virility [vi'riliti], *n.* virilité, nature virile, *f.*
virtual ['və:tjuəl], *a.* virtuel; de fait.
virtually ['və:tjuəli], *adv.* virtuellement, de fait.
virtue ['və:tju:], *n.* vertu; (*fig.*) valeur, *f.* mérite, *m.*
virtuosity [və:tju'ɔsiti], *n.* virtuosité, *f.*
virtuoso [və:tju'ousou], *n.* (*pl.* **virtuosi** [və:tju'ousi]) virtuose, *m.*, *f.*
virtuous ['və:tjuəs], *a.* vertueux.
virtuously ['və:tjuəsli], *adv.* vertueusement.
virtuousness ['və:tjuəsnis], *n.* vertu, *f.*
virulence ['viruləns], *n.* virulence, *f.*
virulent ['virulənt], *a.* virulent.
virus ['vaiərəs], *n.* virus, *m.*
visa ['vi:zə], *n.* visa, *m.*—*v.t.* viser.
visage ['vizidʒ], *n.* visage, *m.*, figure, *f.*
viscera ['visərə], *n.pl.* viscères, *m.pl.*
viscid ['visid], *a.* visqueux.
viscosity [vis'kɔsiti], *n.* viscosité, *f.*
viscount ['vaikaunt], *n.* vicomte, *m.*
viscountess ['vaikauntis], *n.* vicomtesse, *f.*
viscountship ['vaikauntʃip], **viscounty** ['vaikaunti], *n.* vicomté, *f.*
viscous ['viskəs], *a.* visqueux, glutineux.
visibility [vizi'biliti], *n.* visibilité, *f.*
visible ['vizibl], *a.* visible; clair.
visibly ['vizibli], *adv.* visiblement, à vue d'œil.
vision ['viʒən], *n.* vision, vue, *f.*
visionary ['viʒənəri], *a.* and *n.* visionnaire, *m.*, *f.*
visit ['vizit], *n.* visite, *f.*; séjour (*a stay*), *m.*—*v.t.* visiter, aller, rendre visite à; ***I visit the theatre twice a week***, je vais au théâtre deux fois par semaine.—*v.i.* faire des visites.
visitant ['vizitənt], *n.* visiteur, *m.*
visitation [vizi'teiʃən], *n.* inspection; épreuve, *f.*
visiting ['vizitiŋ], *a.* en visite, de visite.—*n.* visites, *f.pl.*
visitor ['vizitə], *n.* visiteur; (*official*) inspecteur, *m.*; ***she has visitors***, elle a du monde.
visor ['vaizə], *n.* visière, *f.*
vista ['vistə], *n.* vue, perspective, *f.*
Vistula ['vistjulə], **the.** la Vistule, *f.*
visual ['viʒjuəl], *a.* visuel.
visualize ['viʒjuəlaiz], *v.t.* se représenter.
vital [vaitl], *a.* vital, de vie; (*fig.*) essentiel.
vitality [vai'tæliti], *n.* vitalité, *f.*
vitalize ['vaitəlaiz], *v.t.* vivifier; (*fig.*) animer.
vitally ['vaitəli], *adv.* vitalement.
vitals [vaitlz], *n.pl.* parties vitales, *f.pl.*
vitamin ['vitəmin], *n.* vitamine, *f.*

vitiate ['viʃieit], *v.t.* vicier; (*fig.*) corrompre.

vitiation [viʃi'eiʃən], *n.* viciation; (*fig.*) corruption, *f.*

vitreous ['vitriəs], *a.* vitreux; (*Anat.*) vitré.

vitrify ['vitrifai], *v.t.* vitrifier.—*v.i.* se vitrifier.

vitriol ['vitriəl], *n.* vitriol, *m.*

vitriolic [vitri'ɔlik], *a.* vitriolique.

vituperate [vi'tju:pəreit], *v.t.* vilipender, injurier.

vituperation [vitju:pə'reiʃən], *n.* reproches, *m.pl.*, invectives, *f.pl.*

vituperative [vi'tju:pərətiv], *a.* injurieux, hargneux.

vivacious [vi'veiʃəs], *a.* vif, vivace, animé.

vivaciously [vi'veiʃəsli], *adv.* vivement, avec vivacité.

vivaciousness [vi'veiʃəsnis], **vivacity** [vi'væsiti], *n.* vivacité, *f.*

vivary ['vivəri], *n.* vivier, *m.*

vivid ['vivid], *a.* vif, frappant.

vividly ['vividli], *adv.* d'une manière frappante, avec éclat.

vividness ['vividnis], *n.* vivacité, *f.*, éclat, *m.*

vivification [vivifi'keiʃən], *n.* vivification, *f.*

vivify ['vivifai], *v.t.* vivifier.

vivifying ['vivifaiiŋ], *a.* vivifiant.

viviparous [vi'vipərəs], *a.* vivipare.

vivisection [vivi'sekʃən], *n.* vivisection, *f.*

vivisector [vivi'sektə], *n.* vivisecteur, *m.*

vixen ['viksən], *n.* renarde (*bête*); mégère (*femme*), *f.*

vixenish ['viksəniʃ], *a.* de mégère, méchante.

viz. [viz] (*usu. read* namely), *adv.* à savoir.

vizier [vi'ziə], *n.* vizir, *m.*

vocabulary [vo'kæbjuləri], *n.* vocabulaire, *m.*

vocal [voukl], *a.* vocal, de la voix.

vocalist ['voukəlist], *n.* chanteur, *m.*, chanteuse, *f.*

vocalize ['voukəlaiz], *v.t.*, *v.i.* vocaliser.

vocally ['voukəli], *adv.* par la voix, vocalement.

vocation [vo'keiʃən], *n.* vocation; profession, *f.*

vocational [vo'keiʃənəl], *a.* professionnel.

vocative ['vɔkətiv], *n.* vocatif, *m.*

vociferate [və'sifəreit], *v.t.*, *v.i.* vociférer.

vociferation [vəsifə'reiʃən], *n.* vocifération, *f.*

vociferous [və'sifərəs], *a.* qui vocifère, bruyant.

vociferously [və'sifərəsli], *adv.* en vociférant.

vodka ['vɔdkə], *n.* vodka, *f.*

vogue [voug], *n.* vogue, *f.*

voice [vɔis], *n.* voix, *f.*; ***at the top of one's voice***, à tue-tête.—*v.t.* publier; exprimer.

void [vɔid], *a.* vide, vacant; (*Law*) nul, de nul effet.—*n.* vide, espace vide, *m.*—*v.t.* vider; (*Law*) annuler.

voidable ['vɔidəbl], *a.* annulable.

volatile ['vɔlətail], *a.* volatil; qui vole, volant; inconstant (*volage*).

volatility [vɔlə'tiliti], *n.* volatilité, *f.*

volcanic [vɔl'kænik], *a.* volcanique.

volcano [vɔl'keinou], *n.* volcan, *m.*

vole [voul], *n.* campagnol, *m.*

volition [və'liʃən], *n.* volition, volonté, *f.*

volley ['vɔli], *n.* décharge, salve (*de mousqueterie*); volée (*de canon*), *f.*—*v.t.* (*Ten.*) renvoyer (*la balle*) de volée.

volt [voult], *n.* (*Elec.*) volt, *m.*

voltage ['voultidʒ], *n.* voltage, *m.*

volte-face ['vɔltfɑ:s], *n.* volte-face, *f.*

volubility [vɔlju'biliti], *n.* volubilité, *f.*

voluble ['vɔljubl], *a.* délié (*langue*); facile (*débit*).

volubly ['vɔljubli], *adv.* avec volubilité.

volume ['vɔljum], *n.* volume; tome (*livre*), *m.*

voluminous [və'lju:minəs], *a.* volumineux.

voluminously [və'lju:minəsli], *adv.* d'une manière volumineuse.

voluminousness [və'lju:minəsnis], *n.* grosseur, *f.*

voluntarily ['vɔləntərili], *adv.* volontairement, spontanément.

voluntariness ['vɔləntərinis], *n.* spontanéité, *f.*

voluntary ['vɔləntəri], *a.* volontaire, spontané; libre; intentionnel.—*n.* (*Mus.*) improvisation, *f.*

volunteer [vɔlən'tiə], *n.* volontaire, *m.*, *f.*—*v.t.* offrir volontairement.—*v.i.* offrir ses services; s'engager comme volontaire.

voluptuary [və'lʌptjuəri], *n.* voluptueux, épicurien, *m.*

voluptuous [və'lʌptjuəs], *a.* voluptueux.

voluptuously [və'lʌptjuəsli], *adv.* voluptueusement.

voluptuousness [və'lʌptjuəsnis], *n.* volupté, *f.*

volute [və'lju:t], *n.* volute, *f.*

voluted [və'lju:tid], *a.* voluté.

volution [və'lju:ʃən], *n.* spirale, *f.*

vomit ['vɔmit], *v.t.*, *v.i.* vomir.—*n.* vomissement, *m.*

voodoo ['vu:du:], *n.* vaudou, *m.*

voracious [və'reiʃəs], *a.* vorace.

voraciously [və'reiʃəsli], *adv.* avec voracité.

voraciousness [və'reiʃəsnis], **voracity** [və'ræsiti], *n.* voracité, *f.*

vortex ['vɔ:teks], *n.* (*pl.* **vortices** ['vɔ:tisi:z]) tourbillon, *m.*

vortical ['vɔ:tikl], *a.* tourbillonnant, en tourbillon.

votaress ['voutəris], *n.* adoratrice, *f.*

votary ['voutəri], *n.* adorateur; (*fig.*) admirateur, *m.*

vote [vout], *n.* vote, *m.*; voix, *f.*—*v.t.*, *v.i.* voter.

voter ['voutə], *n.* votant, *m.*

voting ['voutiŋ], *n.* vote, *m.*; ***voting-paper***, bulletin de vote, *m.*

votive ['voutiv], *a.* votif, voué.

vouch [vautʃ], *v.t.* attester; affirmer.—*v.i.* témoigner (*de*), répondre (*de*).

voucher ['vautʃə], *n.* garant, *m.*, garantie; pièce justificative, *f.*; ***luncheon voucher***, bon de repas, *m.*

vouchsafe [vautʃ'seif], *v.t.* daigner, accorder.

vow [vau], *n.* vœu, *m.*—*v.t.* vouer.—*v.i.* faire un vœu; jurer.

vowel ['vauəl], *n.* voyelle, *f.*

voyage ['vɔiidʒ], *n.* voyage (*par mer*), *m.*

voyager ['vɔiidʒə], *n.* voyageur, passager, *m.*

vulcanite ['vʌlkənait], *n.* caoutchouc vulcanisé, *m.*, ébonite, *f.*

vulcanize ['vʌlkənaiz], *v.t.* vulcaniser.

vulgar ['vʌlgə], *a.* vulgaire, commun.

vulgarism ['vʌlgərizm], *n.* expression vulgaire, *f.*

vulgarity [vʌl'gæriti], *n.* vulgarité, grossièreté, *f.*; mauvais goût, *m.*

vulgarize ['vʌlgəraiz], *v.t.* vulgariser.

vulnerability [vʌlnərə'biliti], *n.* vulnérabilité, *f.*
vulnerable ['vʌlnərəbl], *a.* vulnérable.
vulpine ['vʌlpain], *a.* de renard; (*fig.*) rusé.
vulture ['vʌltʃə], *n.* vautour, *m.*

W

W, w ['dʌbəlju:]. vingt-troisième lettre de l'alphabet, *m.*
wad [wɔd], *n.* bourre (*armes à feu etc.*), *f.*; tampon, paquet (*faisceau*), *m.*—*v.t.* bourrer (*armes à feu etc.*); ouater (*vêtement etc.*).
wadded ['wɔdid], *a.* ouaté (*de*).
wadding ['wɔdiŋ], *n.* bourre (*armes à feu*); ouate (*rembourrage*), *f.*
waddle [wɔdl], *v.i.* se dandiner.
waddling ['wɔdliŋ], *n.* dandinement, *m.*
wade [weid], *v.t.* traverser à gué.—*v.i.* marcher (dans l'eau *ou* dans la vase).
wafer ['weifə], *n.* pain à cacheter, *m.*; gaufrette; (*R.-C. Ch.*) hostie, *f.*
waffle [wɔfl], *n.* gaufre, *f.*
waffle-iron ['wɔflaiən], *n.* gaufrier, *m.*
waft [wɔft], *v.t.* porter, transporter; faire flotter.
wag [wæg], *n.* badin, plaisant, farceur, *m.*—*v.t.* remuer, agiter.—*v.i.* s'agiter, remuer, se mouvoir.
wage [weidʒ], *v.t.* faire.—*n.* [WAGES].
wager ['weidʒə], *n.* gageure, *f.*, pari, *m.*—*v.t.* gager, parier.
wages ['weidʒiz], *n.pl.* gages (*de serviteur*), *m.pl.*; salaire, *m.*, paye (*d'ouvrier*), *f.*
waggery ['wægəri], *n.* espièglerie, plaisanterie, *f.*
waggish ['wægiʃ], *a.* badin, malin, facétieux.
waggishness ['wægiʃnis], *n.* badinage, *m.*, espièglerie, *f.*
waggle [wægl], *v.t.* remuer.—*v.i.* frétiller.
waggon, wagon ['wægən], *n.* charrette, *f.*, chariot; (*Mil.*) caisson, fourgon; (*Rail.*) wagon, *m.*
wagtail ['wægteil], *n.* hochequeue, *m.*
waif [weif], *n.* épave, *f.*
wail [weil], *v.t.* pleurer, lamenter.—*v.i.* pleurer, gémir, se lamenter.—*n.* (*also* **wailing** ['weiliŋ]) cri, *m.*, lamentation, plainte, *f.*
wain [wein], *n.* charrette, *f.*
wainscot ['weinzkət], *n.* lambris, *m.*, boiserie, *f.*
waist [weist], *n.* ceinture, taille, *f.*
waistband ['weistbænd], *n.* ceinture (*de pantalon etc.*), *f.*
waistcoat ['weis(t)kout], *n.* gilet, *m.*
wait [weit], *v.t.* attendre.—*v.i.* attendre; servir (*à table etc.*).—*n.* embuscade, *f.*, guet-apens, *m.*; attente, *f.*
waiter ['weitə], *n.* garçon, *m.*
waiting ['weitiŋ], *n.* attente, *f.*; service (*attentions*), *m.*; ***no waiting***, stationnement interdit, *m.*
waiting-maid ['weitiŋmeid], **waiting-woman** ['weitiŋwumən] (*pl.* **-women** [wimin]), *n.* femme de chambre; caméris (*de princesse etc.*), *f.*
waiting-room ['weitiŋru:m], *n.* salle d'attente, *f.*
waitress ['weitris], *n.* servante, fille de servic *f.*
waits [weits], *n.pl.* chanteurs de noëls, *m.p*
waive [weiv], *v.t.* écarter, mettre de côt abandonner, renoncer.
wake (1) [weik], *v.t. irr.* éveiller, réveiller.—*v.i.* veiller (*ne pas se coucher*); se réveiller (*sommeil*).—*n.* fête de village, *f.*
wake (2) [weik], *n.* sillage (*de navire*), *m.*; (*fig* suite, *f.*
wakeful ['weikful], *a.* éveillé; vigilant.
wakefulness ['weikfulnis], *n.* insomnie, *f.*
waken ['weikən], *v.t.* éveiller, réveiller.—*v.* s'éveiller, se réveiller.
waking ['weikiŋ], **wakening** ['weikniŋ], éveillé.—*n.* réveil, *m.*
wale [weil], *n.* marque (*de fouet*); côte (*tissu*); (*pl.*) (*Naut.*) préceinte, *f.*
Wales [weilz]. le Pays de Galles, *m.*
walk [wɔ:k], *v.t.* parcourir, traverser à pied faire à pied (*distance etc.*); mettre au pa (*cheval*).—*v.i.* marcher; aller à pied; s promener (*pour le plaisir*); aller au pa (*cheval*); ***to walk over***, traverser *ou* par courir à pied.—*n.* marche; promenade, *f* tour, *m.*; allée (*sentier*); démarche, allure, *f.* pas (*de cheval*), *m.*; (*fig.*) sphère, *f.*, chemin *m.*; ***at a walk***, au pas.
walker ['wɔ:kə], *n.* promeneur, marcheur piéton, *m.*
walkie-talkie ['wɔ:ki'tɔ:ki], *n.* (*fam.*) émetteur-récepteur portatif, *m.*
walking ['wɔ:kiŋ], *a.* ambulant; de marche.—*n.* la marche; promenade à pied, *f.*
walking-stick ['wɔ:kiŋstik], *n.* canne, *f.*
walk-over ['wɔ:kouvə], *n.* (*Spt.*) ***to have walk-over***, remporter une victoire facile gagner sans concurrent.
wall [wɔ:l], *n.* muraille, *f.*, mur, *m.*, paroi, *f.* espalier (*à fruits*), *m.*—*v.t.* entourer d murailles; ***to wall up***, murer.
wallet ['wɔlit], *n.* portefeuille, *f.*
wall-eye ['wɔ:lai], *n.* œil vairon, *m.*
wallflower ['wɔ:lflauə], *n.* giroflée jaune ravenelle, *f.*
wall-fruit ['wɔ:lfru:t], *n.* fruit d'espalier, *m.*
walling ['wɔ:liŋ], *n.* muraillement, *m.*; murs *m.pl.*
wallop ['wɔləp], *v.t.* rosser.
walloping ['wɔləpiŋ], *n.* rossée, volée de coups, roulée, *f.*
wallow ['wɔlou], *v.i.* se vautrer, se rouler.
wall-paper ['wɔ:lpeipə], *n.* papier peint, *m.*
walnut ['wɔ:lnʌt], *n.* noix, *f.*; noyer (*bois*), *m.*
walnut-tree ['wɔ:lnʌttri:], *n.* noyer, *m.*
walrus ['wɔ:lrəs], *n.* morse, cheval marin, *m.*
Walter ['wɔ:ltə]. Gauthier, *m.*
waltz [wɔ:l(t)s], *n.* valse, *f.*—*v.i.* valser.
waltzer ['wɔ:l(t)sə], *n.* valseur, *m.*
waltzing ['wɔ:l(t)siŋ], *n.* valse, *f.*
wan [wɔn], *a.* blême, pâle, pâlot.
wand [wɔnd], *n.* baguette, *f.*
wander ['wɔndə], *v.i.* errer; divaguer (*l'esprit*); délirer.
wanderer ['wɔndərə], *n.* vagabond, *m.*
wandering ['wɔndəriŋ], *a.* errant, vagabond; nomade (*tribu etc.*); (*fig.*) distrait.—*n.* course errante, divagation, *f.*; délire, *m.*

wanderlust ['wɔndəlʌst], *n.* manie des voyages, *f.*
wane [wein], *n.* déclin, *m.*; (*fig.*) décadence, *f.* —*v.i.* décroître (*lune*); (*fig.*) décliner.
wanly ['wɔnli], *adv.* avec pâleur.
wanness ['wɔnnis], *n.* pâleur, *f.*
want [wɔnt], *n.* besoin; manque, défaut (*absence*), *m.*; indigence, misère (*pauvreté*), *f.*; ***for want of***, faute de.—*v.t.* avoir besoin de; manquer de; vouloir, désirer (*avoir envie de*); demander (*réclamer*).—*v.i.* manquer (*de*).
wanting ['wɔntiŋ], *a.* qui manque, manquant.
wanton ['wɔntən], *a.* folâtre (*capricieux*); licencieux, libertin (*impudique*); gratuit (*sans cause*).—*n.* débauchée, *f.*—*v.i.* folâtrer.
wantonly ['wɔntənli], *adv.* en folâtrant; gratuitement.
wantonness ['wɔntənnis], *n.* légèreté, *f.*; libertinage, *m.*
war [wɔ:], *n.* guerre, *f.*—*v.i.* faire la guerre (*à*), lutter (*contre*).
warble [wɔ:bl], *v.t.*, *v.i.* gazouiller; (*fig.*) chanter.
warbler ['wɔ:blə], *n.* oiseau chanteur, *m.*; fauvette (*oiseau*), *f.*
warbling ['wɔ:bliŋ], *a.* mélodieux.—*n.* gazouillement, *m.*
ward [wɔ:d], *n.* pupille, *m.*, *f.*; tutelle (*protection*); garde (*de serrure*); salle (*d'hôpital*), *f.*; arrondissement (*de ville*), *m.*—*v.i.* ***to ward off***, parer, détourner.
warden [wɔ:dn], *n.* gardien; gouverneur, recteur (*d'université*); directeur (*de collège*), conservateur (*de jardin public*), *m.*
warder ['wɔ:də], *n.* gardien de prison, *m.*
wardress ['wɔ:dris], *n.* gardienne de prison, *f.*
wardrobe ['wɔ:droub], *n.* garde-robe; armoire (*meuble*), *f.*
ward-room ['wɔ:dru:m], *n.* (*Naut.*) carré des officiers, *m.*
ware [wɛə], *n.* (*collect.*) articles fabriqués, *m.pl.*; (*pl.*) marchandises, *f.pl.*
warehouse ['wɛəhaus], *n.* magasin; entrepôt, *m.*—*v.t.* emmagasiner.
warehousing ['wɛəhauziŋ], *n.* emmagasinage, *m.*
warfare ['wɔ:fɛə], *n.* la guerre, *f.*; les opérations, *f.pl.*
warily ['wɛərili], *adv.* prudemment, avec circonspection.
wariness ['wɛərinis], *n.* prudence, circonspection, *f.*
warlike ['wɔ:laik], *a.* guerrier, martial, belliqueux.
warlock ['wɔ:lɔk], *n.* sorcier, *m.*
warm [wɔ:m], *a.* chaud; (*fig.*) zélé, ardent; chaleureux (*accueil*).—*v.t.* chauffer; réchauffer (*ce qui s'était refroidi*); (*fig.*) échauffer.—*v.i.* chauffer, se chauffer, (*fig.*) s'animer.
warming ['wɔ:miŋ], *n.* chauffage, *m.*
warming-pan ['wɔ:miŋpæn], *n.* bassinoire, *f.*
warmly ['wɔ:mli], *adv.* chaudement; (*fig.*) vivement.
war-monger ['wɔ:mʌŋgə], *n.* belliciste, *m.*, *f.*
warmth [wɔ:mθ], *n.* chaleur; (*fig.*) ardeur, *f.*
war-office ['wɔ:rɔfis], *n.* ministère de la guerre, *m.*
warn [wɔ:n], *v.t.* avertir, prévenir (*de*); ***to warn against***, mettre en garde contre.
warning ['wɔ:niŋ], *n.* avertissement, avis, *m.*
warp [wɔ:p], *n.* chaîne (*tissage*), *f.*—*v.t.* ourdir (*tissage*); faire déjeter (*bois*); (*Naut.*) touer; (*fig.*) fausser, pervertir.—*v.i.* se déjeter, se déformer; gauchir; (*fig.*) dévier (*de*).
warping ['wɔ:piŋ], *n.* ourdissage (*tissage*); déjettement, gauchissement (*de bois*), *m.*
warrant ['wɔrənt], *n.* autorisation, garantie, *f.*; ordre, mandat; mandat d'amener, *m.*; (*fig.*) justification, *f.*—*v.t.* garantir, autoriser.
warrant-officer ['wɔrəntɔfisə], *n.* (*Mil.*) adjudant; (*Naut.*) premier maître, *m.*
warrantor ['wɔrəntə], *n.* (*Law*) garant, *m.*
warranty ['wɔrənti], *n.* garantie, *f.*
warren ['wɔrən], *n.* garenne, *f.*
warrior ['wɔriə], *n.* guerrier, soldat, *m.*
Warsaw ['wɔ:sɔ:]. Varsovie, *f.*
wart [wɔ:t], *n.* verrue, *f.*, poireau, *m.*
warted ['wɔ:tid], **warty** ['wɔ:ti], *a.* couvert de verrues; (*Bot.*) verruqueux.
wary ['wɛəri], *a.* avisé, prudent; défiant.
wash [wɔʃ], *n.* blanchissage, *m.*, lessive (*de linge*), *f.*; (*Paint.*) lavis; sillage (*de navire*), *m.*—*v.t.* blanchir (*linge*); (*fig.*) mouiller, laver.—*v.i.* se laver; faire la lessive (*blanchisseuse etc.*); ***to wash up***, faire la vaisselle.
washable ['wɔʃəbl], *a.* lavable.
washer ['wɔʃə], *n.* laveur, *m.*; machine à laver; (*Tech.*) rondelle, *f.*
washer-woman ['wɔʃəwumən], *n.* (*pl.* **-women** [wimin]) blanchisseuse, *f.*
wash-hand basin ['wɔʃhændbeisn], *n.* cuvette, *f.*
wash-house ['wɔʃhaus], *n.* lavoir, *m.*, buanderie, *f.*
washing ['wɔʃiŋ], *n.* lavage; blanchissage (*du linge*), *m.*
washing-machine ['wɔʃiŋməʃi:n], *n.* machine à laver, *f.*
wash-leather ['wɔʃleðə], *n.* peau de chamois, *f.*
wash-stand ['wɔʃstænd], *n.* toilette, *f.*; lavabo (*petit*), *m.*
wash-tub ['wɔʃtʌb], *n.* baquet, *m.*
washy ['wɔʃi], *a.* humide, mouillé; (*fig.*) fade.
wasp [wɔsp], *n.* guêpe, *f.*; ***wasps' nest***, guêpier, *m.*
waspish ['wɔspiʃ], *a.* irascible, irritable.
waspishness ['wɔspiʃnis], *n.* humeur irascible, *f.*
wastage ['weistidʒ], *n.* gaspillage, *m.*
waste [weist], *a.* de rebut; sans valeur; perdu (*inemployé*); inculte (*terre*).—*n.* perte (*mauvais emploi*), *f.*; déchet (*à nettoyer*); gaspillage; rebut, *m.*; terre inculte, *f.*—*v.t.* gaspiller; perdre (*employer mal*); gâcher (*faire sans soin*); ravager, dévaster (*piller*).—*v.i.* s'user, s'épuiser; ***to waste away***, dépérir, maigrir.
waste-book ['weistbuk], *n.* brouillard, *m.*
wasteful ['weistful], *a.* dissipateur, prodigue.
wastefulness ['weistfulnis], *n.* prodigalité, perte, *f.*, gaspillage, *m.*
waste-paper ['weist'peipə], *n.* papier de rebut, *m.*
waste-paper basket ['weistpeipə'bɑ:skit], *n.* corbeille à papier, *f.*
waste-pipe ['weistpaip], *n.* tuyau de dégagement; écoulement, *m.*
waster ['weistə], **wastrel** ['weistril] *n.* prodigue, *m.*, *f.*, gaspilleur, *m.*

wasting ['weistiŋ], *a.* qui épuise.—*n.* dépérissement, *m.*, consomption (*du corps*), *f.*
watch [wɔtʃ], *n.* montre; veille (*nocturne*); vigilance (*attention*); garde, *f.*; (*Naut.*) quart, *m.*—*v.t.* veiller sur, surveiller, regarder, épier.—*v.i.* veiller (*ne pas dormir*); prendre garde (*faire attention*); monter la garde; (*Naut.*) faire le quart.
watch-dog ['wɔtʃdɔg], *n.* chien de garde, *m.*
watcher ['wɔtʃə], *n.* surveillant, veilleur, *m.*
watch-fire ['wɔtʃfaiə], *n.* feu de bivouac, *m.*
watchful ['wɔtʃful], *a.* vigilant, attentif.
watchfulness ['wɔtʃfulnis], *n.* vigilance, *f.*
watching ['wɔtʃiŋ], *n.* surveillance, *f.*
watch-maker ['wɔtʃmeikə], *n.* horloger, *m.*
watch-making ['wɔtʃmeikiŋ], *n.* horlogerie, *f.*
watchman ['wɔtʃmən], *n.* (*pl.* **-men** [men]) gardien; veilleur de nuit, *m.*
watch-tower ['wɔtʃtauə], *n.* tour de guet, *f.*
watchword ['wɔtʃwə:d], *n.* mot d'ordre, *m.*
water ['wɔ:tə], *a.* d'eau, à eau; aquatique. —*n.* eau; marée (*flux*), *f.*, (*fig.*) ordre, rang, *m.*; ***drinking water***, eau potable; ***fresh water***, eau douce (*pas salée*).—*v.t.* arroser; donner à boire à, abreuver (*animal*); mettre de l'eau dans, couper (*diluer*); moirer (*étoffe*).
water-bottle ['wɔ:təbɔtl], *n.* carafe, *f.*; (*Mil. etc.*) bidon, *m.*; bouillotte (*pour chauffer le lit*), *f.*
water-carrier ['wɔ:təkæriə], *n.* porteur d'eau; broc (*à eau*), *m.*
water-cart ['wɔ:təkɑ:t], *n.* voiture d'arrosage, *f.*
water-closet ['wɔ:təklɔzit], *n.* toilettes, *f.pl.*, cabinet d'aisances, *m.*
water-colour ['wɔ:təkʌlə], *n.* aquarelle, *f.*
watercress ['wɔ:təkres], *n.* cresson, cresson de fontaine, *m.*
water-cure ['wɔ:təkjuə], *n.* hydrothérapie, *f.*
watered ['wɔ:təd], *a.* arrosé; moiré (*étoffe*).
waterfall ['wɔ:təfɔ:l], *n.* cascade; chute d'eau, *f.*
water-fowl ['wɔ:təfaul], *n.* oiseau aquatique, *m.*
waterfront ['wɔ:təfrʌnt], *n.* les quais, *m.pl.*, port, *m.*
water-hen ['wɔ:təhen], *n.* poule d'eau, *f.*
wateriness ['wɔ:tərinis], *n.* aquosité, *f.*
watering ['wɔ:təriŋ], *n.* arrosage (*plantes*), *m.*; irrigation (*terre*), *f.*; abreuvage (*animaux*); moirage (*étoffe*), *m.*
watering-can ['wɔ:təriŋkæn], *n.* arrosoir, *m.*
watering-place ['wɔ:təriŋpleis], *n.* ville d'eaux, station thermale, *f.*; abreuvoir (*pour animaux*), *m.*
water-jug ['wɔ:tədʒʌg], *n.* pot à eau, *m.*
water-level ['wɔ:təlevl], *n.* niveau d'eau, *m.*
water-lily ['wɔ:təlili], *n.* nénuphar, *m.*
water-line ['wɔ:təlain], *n.* ligne de flottaison, *f.*
water-logged ['wɔ:təlɔgd], *a.* envahi par les eaux.
watermark ['wɔ:təmɑ:k], *n.* étiage (*de rivière*); filigrane (*sur papier*), *m.*
water-melon ['wɔ:təmelən], *n.* melon d'eau, *m.*, pastèque, *f.*
water-mill ['wɔ:təmil], *n.* moulin à eau, *m.*
water-pipe ['wɔ:təpaip], *n.* tuyau d'eau, *m.*
water-plant ['wɔ:təplɑ:nt], *n.* plante aquatique, *f.*
water-polo ['wɔ:təpoulou], *n.* polo nautique, *m.*
water-power ['wɔ:təpauə], *n.* force hydraulique, *f.*
water-pressure ['wɔ:təpreʃə], *n.* pression d'eau, *f.*
waterproof ['wɔ:təpru:f], *a.* and *n.* imperméable, *m.*—*v.t.* rendre imperméable, cirer (*un tissu*).
water-rat ['wɔ:təræt], *n.* rat d'eau, *m.*
water-rate ['wɔ:təreit], *n.* taux d'abonnement aux eaux de la ville, *m.*
watershed ['wɔ:təʃed], *n.* versant, *m.*
waterspout ['wɔ:təspaut], *n.* trombe, *f.*; tuyau de descente, *m.*
water-tank ['wɔ:tətæŋk], *n.* réservoir à eau, *m.*, citerne, *f.*
water-tight ['wɔ:tətait], *a.* étanche.
water-works ['wɔ:təwə:ks], *n.pl.* établissement pour la distribution des eaux, *m.*, machine hydraulique, *f.*
watery ['wɔ:təri], *a.* aqueux; mouillé, plein d'eau; (*poet.*) humide.
watt [wɔt], *n.* (*Elec.*) watt, *m.*
wattage ['wɔtidʒ], *n.* (*Elec.*) wattage, *m.*
wattle [wɔtl], *n.* claie (*d'osier etc.*), *f.*—*v.t.* clayonner.
wave [weiv], *n.* vague, *f.*, flot, *m.*, lame, ondulation; (*poet.*) onde, *f.*; signe (*de la main*), *m.*; ***permanent wave***, permanente, indéfrisable, *f.*; ***long waves***, (*Rad.*) grandes ondes, *f.*; ***short waves***, petites ondes, ondes courtes, *f.pl.*—*v.t.* agiter, faire signe de (*la main*); onduler (*cheveux*).—*v.i.* ondoyer, onduler, flotter; faire signe (*à*).
waved [weivd], *a.* ondulé.
wave-length ['weivleŋθ], *n.* longueur d'onde, *f.*
waver ['weivə], *v.i.* hésiter, vaciller, balancer.
waverer ['weivərə], *n.* personne indécise, *f.*, esprit vacillant, *m.*
wavering ['weivəriŋ], *a.* indécis, vacillant, irrésolu.—*n.* hésitation, indécision, *f.*
waving ['weiviŋ], *n.* ondoiement, *m.*, ondulation (*blé etc.*), *f.*; geste (*de la main*), *m.*
wavy ['weivi], *a.* ondoyant, onduleux.
wax [wæks], *n.* cire; poix (*de cordonnier*); (*colloq.*) colère, *f.*—*v.t.* cirer, enduire de cire. —*v.i.* croître (*lune*), s'accroître; devenir.
wax-candle ['wæks'kændl], *n.* bougie, *f.*
waxen [wæksn], *a.* de cire; cireux.
wax-taper ['wæks'teipə], *n.* rat de cave; (*Eccles.*) cierge, *m.*
waxwing ['wækswiŋ], *n.* (*Orn.*) jaseur, *m.*
waxwork ['wækswə:k], *n.* ouvrage de cire, *m.*; (*pl.*) figures de cire, *f.*, *pl.*
waxy ['wæksi], *a.* cireux; (*colloq.*) en colère.
way [wei], *n.* chemin, *m.*, route, voie, *f.*; passage; côté, sens, *m.*, direction; manière, façon, mode, *f.*; moyen, *m.*, méthode, *f.*; état (*condition*), *m.*; ***a long way off***, loin, très loin; ***by a long way*** (*by far*), de beaucoup; ***by the way***, à propos.
way-bill ['weibil], *n.* feuille de route, *f.*
wayfarer ['weifɛərə], *n.* voyageur, *m.*
wayfaring ['weifɛəriŋ], *a.* qui voyage.
waylay [wei'lei], *v.t.* guetter, guetter au passage.
wayside ['weisaid], *a.* au bord de la route.—*n.* bord de la route, *m.*
wayward ['weiwəd], *a.* capricieux, entêté.

aywardness ['weiwədnis], *n.* humeur capricieuse, *f.*
e [wi:], *pron.* nous; (*indef.*) on; ***we Frenchmen***, nous autres Français.
eak [wi:k], *a.* faible, infirme, débile.
eaken [wi:kn], *v.t.* affaiblir; atténuer.—*v.i.* s'affaiblir.
eakening ['wi:kniŋ], *n.* affaiblissement, *m.*
eakling ['wi:kliŋ], *n.* être faible, faiblard, *m.*
eakly ['wi:kli], *a.* faible; infirme, débile.—*adv.* faiblement, sans force.
eak-minded ['wi:k'maindid], *a.* d'esprit faible.
eakness ['wi:knis], *n.* faiblesse; débilité, *f.*; (*fig.*) faible, *m.*
eak-spirited ['wi:k'spiritid], *a.* mou, sans courage.
eal [wi:l], *n.* bien, bien-être, bonheur, *m.*; marque (*sur la peau*), *f.*
ealth [welθ], *n.* richesse, *f.*, richesses, *f.pl.*; profusion, *f.*
ealthy ['welθi], *a.* riche, opulent.
ean [wi:n], *v.t.* sevrer; (*fig.*) détacher.
eaning ['wi:niŋ], *n.* sevrage, *m.*
eanling ['wi:nliŋ], *n.* enfant *ou* animal en sevrage, *m.*
eapon [wepn], *n.* arme, *f.*
ear [wɛə], *v.t. irr.* porter (*habits*); mettre (*enfiler*); ***to wear out***, user, (*fig.*) épuiser, lasser.—*v.i.* s'user (*s'élimer*); se porter (*habits*); (*fig.*) se conserver.—*n.* usage (*port*), *m.*; usure (*élimage*), *f.*
earable ['wɛərəbl], *a.* mettable.
earied ['wiərid], *a.* fatigué, las; (*fig.*) ennuyé.
earily ['wiərili], *adv.* péniblement, d'un air las.
eariness ['wiərinis], *n.* fatigue, lassitude, *f.*; (*fig.*) ennui, *m.*
earisome ['wiərisəm], *a.* ennuyeux; lassant.
earisomeness ['wiərisəmnis], *n.* nature ennuyeuse, *f.*
eary ['wiəri], *a.* fatigué, las, ennuyé; ennuyeux (*chose*).—*v.t.* lasser, fatiguer; ennuyer.
easel [wi:zl], *n.* belette, *f.*
eather ['weðə], *a.* du côté du vent.—*n.* temps, *m.*; (*fig.*) tempête, *f.*—*v.t.* résister à (*tempête etc.*); (*fig.*) tenir tête à.
eather-beaten ['weðəbi:tn], *a.* battu par la tempête; (*fig.*) fatigué; hâlé.
eathercock ['weðəkɔk], *n.* girouette, *f.*
eather-glass ['weðəglɑ:s], *n.* baromètre, *m.*
eather-proof ['weðəpru:f], *a.* à l'épreuve du (mauvais) temps, imperméable.
eather-report ['weðəripɔ:t], *n.* bulletin météorologique, *m.*
eather-ship ['weðəʃip], *n.* navire météorologique, *m.*
eave [wi:v], *n.* (*Tex.*) tissage, *m.*—*v.t.*, *v.i. irr.* tisser; tresser (*entrelacer*).
eaver ['wi:və], *n.* tisserand, *m.*
eaving ['wi:viŋ], *n.* tissage, *m.*
web [web], *n.* tissu, *m.*; sangle (*pour selle*); toile (*d'araignée*), *f.*
webbed [webd], **webby** ['webi], *a.* palmé.
webbing ['webiŋ], *n.* sangles (*de chaise, lit etc.*), *f.pl.*
web-footed ['webfutid], *a.* palmipède.
wed [wed], *v.t.* épouser, se marier avec.—*v.i.* se marier.
wedded ['wedid], *a.* marié (*à*); conjugal.
wedding ['wediŋ], *a.* de noces, de mariage.—*n.* noce, *f.*, noces, *f.pl.*, mariage, *m.*
wedding-ring ['wediŋriŋ], *n.* alliance, *f.*
wedge [wedʒ], *n.* coin, *m.*; cale (*pour tenir immobile*), *f.*—*v.t.* serrer; caler; coincer.
wedge-shaped ['wedʒʃeipt], *a.* en forme de coin, cunéiforme.
wedlock ['wedlɔk], *n.* mariage, *m.*
Wednesday ['wenzd(e)i]. mercredi, *m.*; ***Ash Wednesday***, mercredi des Cendres.
weed [wi:d], *n.* mauvaise herbe, *f.*; ***widow's weeds***, vêtements de deuil, *m.pl.*—*v.t.* sarcler; (*fig.*) nettoyer; ***to weed out***, extirper.
weeder ['wi:də], *n.* sarcleur (*personne*); sarcloir (*outil*), *m.*
weeding ['wi:diŋ], *n.* sarclage, *m.*
weed-killer ['wi:dkilə], *n.* herbicide, *m.*
weedy ['wi:di], *a.* plein de mauvaises herbes; (*fig.*) chétif.
week [wi:k], *n.* semaine, *f.*; ***this day week***, d'aujourd'hui en huit (*avenir*); il y a huit jours (*passé*).
weekday ['wi:kdei], *n.* jour ouvrable, jour de semaine, *m.*
week-end ['wi:k'end], *n.* fin de la semaine, *f.*, week-end, *m.*
weekly ['wi:kli], *a.* de la semaine; hebdomadaire (*revue*).—*n.* hebdomadaire, *m.*—*adv.* par semaine, tous les huit jours.
weep [wi:p], *v.t.*, *v.i. irr.* pleurer; ***to weep bitterly***, pleurer à chaudes larmes.
weeping ['wi:piŋ], *a.* qui pleure, éploré; (*Bot.*) pleureur; ***weeping-willow***, saule pleureur, *m.*—*n.* pleurs, *m.pl.*, larmes, *f.pl.*
weever ['wi:və], *n.* (*Ichth.*) vive, *f.*
weevil [wi:vl], *n.* charançon, *m.*
weft [weft], *n.* trame, *f.*
weigh [wei], *v.t.* peser; (*fig.*) juger; (*Naut.*) lever (*l'ancre*).—*v.i.* peser.
weigh-bridge ['weibridʒ], *n.* pont à bascule, *m.*
weighing ['weiiŋ], *n.* pesage, *m.*; ***weighing-machine***, bascule, *f.*
weight [weit], *n.* poids, *m.*; ***atomic weight***, masse atomique, *f.*
weighted ['weitid], *a.* chargé (*de*).
weightily ['weitili], *adv.* pesamment.
weightless ['weitlis], *a.* sans poids.
weightlessness ['weitlisnis], *n.* apesanteur, *f.*
weighty ['weiti], *a.* pesant, lourd; (*fig.*) important.
weir [wiə], *n.* barrage, déversoir, *m.*
weird [wiəd], *a.* fantastique, étrange.
weirdness ['wiədnis], *n.* étrangeté, magie, *f.*
welcome ['welkəm], *a.* bienvenu, agréable (*chose*); libre (*à profiter de quelque chose*).—*n.* bienvenue, *f.*, accueil, *m.*; ***to bid (someone) welcome***, souhaiter la bienvenue à (quelqu'un).—*int.* soyez le bienvenu.—*v.t.* souhaiter la bienvenue à, bien accueillir.
weld [weld], *v.t.* souder; (*fig.*) unir.—*n.* soudure, *f.*
welder ['weldə], *n.* soudeur, *m.*
welding ['weldiŋ], *n.* soudure, *f.*
welfare ['welfɛə], *n.* bien-être, bien, *m.*; ***Welfare State***, état providence, *m.*
well (1) [wel], *n.* puits, *m.*; (*fig.*) source, *f.*; ***ink-well***, encrier, *m.*—*v.i.* jaillir (*de*).
well (2) [wel], *a.* bien, en bonne santé; bon, heureux (*fortuné*); utile, profitable; ***to get well***, se rétablir; ***well off***, aisé (*riche*).—

adv. bien; très, fort; comme il faut; ***well!*** eh bien! ***well done!*** très bien! bravo! ***well, I never!*** pas possible!
well-being ['wel'bi:iŋ], *n.* bien-être, *m.*
well-informed ['welin'fɔ:md], *a.* instruit; bien renseigné.
wellingtons ['weliŋtənz], *n.pl.* demi-bottes, *f.pl.*
well-known ['welnoun], *a.* bien connu, célèbre.
well-meaning ['wel'mi:niŋ], *a.* bien intentionné.
well-meant ['wel'ment], *a.* fait à bonne intention.
well-nigh ['welnai], *adv.* presque.
well-timed ['wel'taimd], *a.* à propos, fait à propos.
well-to-do ['weltə'du:], *a.* très aisé, cossu.
well-wisher ['welwiʃə], *n.* ami, partisan, *m.*
Welsh [welʃ], *a.* gallois, du pays de Galles.—*n.* gallois (*langue*), *m.*; ***the Welsh***, les Gallois, *m.pl.*
Welshman ['welʃmən], *n.* (*pl.* **-men** [men]) Gallois, *m.*
welt [welt], *n.* bordure (*de gant*); trépointe (*de semelle*), *f.*
welter ['weltə], *n.* confusion, *f.*—*v.i.* se vautrer, se rouler.
wen [wen], *n.* loupe, *f.*; goitre, *m.*
wench [wentʃ], *n.* donzelle; (*pej.*) souillon, *f.*
wend [wend], *v.t.*, *v.i.* aller; ***to wend one's way***, se diriger (*vers*).
wer(e)wolf ['wə:wulf], *n.* loup-garou, *m.*
west [west], *a.* de l'ouest, occidental.—*n.* ouest, occident, couchant, *m.*—*adv.* à l'ouest.
westerly ['westəli], *a.* d'ouest.—*adv.* vers l'ouest.
western ['westən], *a.* de l'ouest, occidental, ouest, d'occident; à l'ouest (*vue*).—*n.* (*Cine.*) western, *m.*
westward ['westwəd], *adv.* à l'ouest.
wet [wet], *a.* mouillé, humide; pluvieux (*temps*); ***it is wet***, il pleut; ***to get wet***, se mouiller; ***wet through***, mouillé jusqu'aux os, trempé.—*n.* humidité; pluie, *f.* —*v.t. irr.* mouiller, humecter; arroser.
wetness ['wetnis], *n.* humidité, *f.*; état pluvieux, *m.*
wetting ['wetiŋ], *n.* trempage, *m.*
whack [hwæk], *n.* grand coup, *m.*; (*fam.*) part, *f.*—*v.t.* frapper, battre.
whale [hweil], *n.* baleine, *f.*
whalebone ['hweilboun], *n.* baleine, *f.*
whale-oil ['hweilɔil], *n.* huile de baleine, *f.*
whaler ['hweilə], *n.* baleinier, *m.*
wharf [hwɔ:f], *n.* (*pl.* **wharfs** [hwɔ:fs], **wharves** [hwɔ:vz]) quai, embarcadère, débarcadère; entrepôt (*pour marchandises*), *m.*
what [hwɔt], *a.* quel, *m.*, quelle, *f.*, quels, *m.pl.*, quelles, *f.pl.*—*pron.rel.* ce qui, ce que; qui, que; quoi.—*inter. pron.* qu'est-ce qui? que? qu'est-ce que? quoi? ***what!*** comment!
whatever [hwɔt'evə], **whatsoever** [hwɔtsou'evə], *pron.* and *a.* quoi que ce soit; quelque . . . que; tout ce qui, tout ce que (*all that*).
whatnot ['hwɔtnɔt], *n.* étagère, *f.*
whatsoever [WHATEVER].
wheat [hwi:t], *n.* blé, froment, *m.*
wheaten [hwi:tn], *a.* de froment.
wheedle [hwi:dl], *v.t.* cajoler, câliner.
wheedling ['hwi:dliŋ], *a.* cajoleur, câlin.—*n.* cajolerie, câlinerie, *f.*
wheel [hwi:l], *n.* roue, *f.*; volant (*pour conduire*); rouet (*pour filer*), *m.*; révolution, *f.*, tour, cercle (*rotation*); soleil (*feu d'artifice*), *m.*; ***driving wheel***, roue motrice, *f.*; ***fly wheel***, volant, *m.*—*v.t.* rouler, faire tourner; brouetter; voiturer.—*v.i.* rouler (*sur des roues*); tourner, se tourner (*en cercle*); tournoyer (*pirouetter*); (*Mil.*) faire une conversion; ***to wheel round***, faire volte-face.
wheel-barrow ['hwi:lbærou], *n.* brouette, *f.*
wheel-chair ['hwi:ltʃɛə], *n.* voiture de malade, *f.*, fauteuil roulant, *m.*
wheeled [hwi:ld], *a.* à roues.
wheeling ['hwi:liŋ], *n.* (*Mil.*) conversion, *f.* tournoiement (*d'oiseau*), *m.*
wheelwright ['hwi:lrait], *n.* charron, *m.*
wheeze [hwi:z], *v.i.* siffler en respirant.
wheezing ['hwi:ziŋ], *n.* sifflement, *m.*
wheezy ['hwi:zi], *a.* poussif, asthmatique.
whelk [hwelk], *n.* buccin, *m.*
whelp [hwelp], *n.* petit (d'un fauve), *m.*—*v.* mettre bas.
when [hwen], *conj.* quand, lorsque; que, où; ***the day when I saw him***, le jour où je l'ai vu.—*inter. adv.* quand est-ce que quand?
whence [hwens], *adv.* d'où.
whenever [hwen'evə], **whensoever** [hwensou'evə], *adv.* toutes les fois que, quand, n'importe quel moment que.
where [hwɛə], *adv.* où; là où.
whereabouts ['hwɛərəbauts], *adv.* où à peu près.—*n.* ***to know someone's whereabouts***, savoir où est quelqu'un.
whereas [hwɛər'æz], *adv.* au lieu que, tandis que; (*Law*) vu que.
whereat [hwɛər'æt], *adv.* à quoi, de quoi; sur quoi.
whereby [hwɛə'bai], *adv.* par lequel, par où.
wherefore ['hwɛəfɔ:], *adv.* pourquoi, c'est pourquoi.
wherein [hwɛər'in], *adv.* en quoi, dans lequel, où.
whereof [hwɛər'ɔv], *adv.* dont, de quoi, duquel.
whereon [hwɛər'ɔn], **whereupon** ['hwɛərə'pɔn], *adv.* sur quoi, sur lequel; là-dessus.
wheresoever [hwɛəsou'evə], [WHEREVER].
wherever [hwɛər'evə], *adv.* partout où, n'importe où.
wherewith [hwɛə'wið], *adv.* avec quoi; de quoi.
wherewithal [hwɛəwið'ɔ:l], *n.* ***to find the wherewithal to . . .***, trouver les moyens de . . . *ou* l'argent pour . . . .
wherry ['hweri], *n.* bachot, *m.*
whet [hwet], *v.t.* aiguiser, affiler; (*fig.*) stimuler.—*n.* aiguisement, repassage; (*fig.*) stimulant, *m.*
whether ['hweðə], *conj.* soit que; si, que; ***whether . . . or***, soit . . . soit, si . . . ou que . . . ou.
whetstone ['hwetstoun], *n.* pierre à aiguiser, *f.*
whey [hwei], *n.* petit lait, *m.*
which [hwitʃ], *a.* quel, *m.*, quelle, *f.*, quels, *m.pl.*, quelles, *f.pl.*; lequel, *m.*, laquelle, *f.* lesquels, *m.pl.*, lesquelles, *f.pl.*—*rel. pron*

qui, que, lequel, *m.*, laquelle, *f.*, lesquels, *m.pl.*, lesquelles, *f.pl.*; ce qui, ce que (*that which*), *m.*

whichever [hwitʃ'evə], *pron.* lequel, *m.*, laquelle, *f.*, lesquels, *m.pl.*, lesquelles, *f.pl.*; quelque . . . que; ***whichever you buy***, n'importe lequel que vous achetiez.

whiff [hwif], *n.* bouffée, haleine, *f.*—*v.t.* lancer en bouffées.

while [hwail], *n.* temps, *m.*; ***a little while ago***, il y a peu de temps; ***it is not worth while***, cela n'en vaut pas la peine.—*v.t.* passer, faire passer; ***to while away the time***, tuer le temps.—(*also* **whilst** [hwailst]), *conj.* pendant que (*au cours de*); tandis que (*par contraste*); tant que (*tout le temps que*); en, tout en (*suivi d'un participe présent*).

whilst [WHILE].

whim [hwim], *n.* caprice, *m.*

whimper ['hwimpə], *v.i.* pleurnicher.

whimpering ['hwimpəriŋ], *a.* pleurnicheur, geignard.—*n.* pleurnichement, *m.*

whimsical ['hwimzikl], *a.* fantasque; capricieux.

whimsically ['hwimzikli], *adv.* capricieusement, fantasquement.

whin [hwin], *n.* ajonc, genêt épineux, *m.*

whine [hwain], *v.i.* se plaindre, geindre, pleurnicher.—*n.* pleurnichement, *m.*

whining ['hwainiŋ], *a.* plaintif, dolent.—*n.* gémissement, geignement, *m.*; (*fig.*) plaintes, *f.pl.*

whinny ['hwini], *v.i.* hennir.—*n.* hennissement, *m.*

whip [hwip], *n.* fouet, *m.*, cravache (*de cavalier*), *f.*; (*Parl.*) secrétaire d'un parti, appel fait aux membres d'un parti, *m.*—*v.t.* fouetter; (*fig.*) battre.

whip-cord ['hwipkɔ:d], *n.* fouet; (*Tex.*) fil à fouet, *m.*

whip-hand ['hwiphænd], *n.* dessus, avantage, *m.*

whip-lash ['hwiplæʃ], *n.* mèche (de fouet), *f.*

whipper-in ['hwipər'in], *n.* piqueur, *m.*

whipper-snapper ['hwipəsnæpə], *n.* petit bout d'homme, *m.*

whippet ['hwipit], *n.* lévrier (de course), *m.*

whipping ['hwipiŋ], *n.* coups de fouet, *m.pl.*

whipping-top ['hwipiŋtɔp], *n.* sabot, *m.*

whir(r) [hwə:], *v.i.* tourner avec bruit; vrombir.—(*also* **whirring** ['hwə:riŋ]), *n.* bruissement, ronronnement, *m.*

whirl [hwə:l], *v.t.* faire tourner, faire tournoyer.—*v.i.* tournoyer, tourbillonner; pirouetter.—*n.* tournoiement; tourbillon (*de poussière etc.*), *m.*

whirligig ['hwə:ligig], *n.* tourniquet, *m.*; pirouette, *f.*

whirlpool ['hwə:lpu:l], *n.* tourbillon (d'eau), *m.*

whirlwind ['hwə:lwind], *n.* tourbillon, cyclone, *m.*

whirring [WHIR(R)].

whisk [hwisk], *n.* vergette, époussette, verge (*à œufs etc.*), *f.*—*v.t.* épousseter; fouetter (*crème*); battre (*œufs*).—*v.i.* passer rapidement.

whiskered ['hwiskəd], *a.* à favoris; à moustaches (*animal*).

whiskers ['hwiskəz], *n.* favoris, *m.pl.*; moustache (*de chat etc.*), *f.*

whisky, whiskey ['hwiski], *n.* whisky, *m.*

whisper ['hwispə], *n.* chuchotement, *m.*—*v.t.* chuchoter, dire à l'oreille.—*v.i.* chuchoter, parler tout bas.

whispering ['hwispəriŋ], *n.* chuchotement, *m.*

whist [hwist], *n.* whist, *m.*

whistle [hwisl], *n.* sifflet; coup de sifflet; sifflement (*du vent*); (*colloq.*) gosier, bec (*gorge*), *m.*—*v.t.*, *v.i.* siffler.

whistler ['hwislə], *n.* siffleur, *m.*

whistling ['hwisliŋ], *a.* sifflant.—*n.* sifflement, coup de sifflet, *m.*

whit [hwit], *n.* iota, point, atome, brin, *m.*

white [hwait], *a.* blanc; (*fig.*) sans tache, pur. —*n.* blanc; aubier (*de bois*), *m.*

whitebait ['hwaitbeit], *n.* blanchaille, *f.*

whiten [hwaitn], *v.t.* blanchir; (*Build.*) badigeonner.—*v.i.* blanchir.

whiteness ['hwaitnis], *n.* blancheur; pâleur, *f.*

whitening ['hwaitniŋ], *n.* action de blanchir, *f.*; [WHITING (1)].

whitewash ['hwaitwɔʃ], *n.* blanc de chaux, *m.* —*v.t.* blanchir à la chaux; badigeonner.

whither ['hwiðə], *adv.* où, par où.

whithersoever [hwiðəsou'evə], *adv.* n'importe où.

whiting (1) ['hwaitiŋ], **whitening** ['hwaitniŋ], *n.* blanc d'Espagne, *m.*

whiting (2) ['hwaitiŋ], *n.* (*Ichth.*) merlan, *m.*

whitish ['hwaitiʃ], *a.* blanchâtre.

whitlow ['hwitlou], *n.* panaris, *m.*

Whitsun ['hwitsən], *a.* de la Pentecôte; ***Whitsunday***, le dimanche de la Pentecôte.

Whitsuntide ['hwitsəntaid]. Pentecôte, *f.*

whiz(z) [hwiz], *v.t.* siffler.

whizzing ['hwiziŋ], *n.* sifflement, *m.*

who [hu:], *pron.* (*rel.*) qui; lequel; (*inter.*) qui ? qui est-ce qui ?

whodunit [hu:'dʌnit], *n.* (*colloq.*) roman policier, *m.*

whoever [hu'evə], *pron.* qui, quiconque; qui que ce soit; celui qui.

whole [houl], *a.* tout, entier, tout entier, complet; intégral; bien portant; en grains (*non moulu*).—*n.* tout, ensemble; total, montant, *m.*; somme, totalité, *f.*; ***on the whole***, en somme, dans l'ensemble.

whole-hearted [houl'ha:tid], *a.* sincère.

whole-heartedly [houl'ha:tidli], *adv.* sincèrement.

wholesale ['houlseil], *a.* en gros.—*n.* vente en gros, *f.*

wholesome ['houlsəm], *a.* sain, salubre; salutaire; utile.

wholesomeness ['houlsəmnis], *n.* salubrité, nature salutaire, *f.*

wholly ['houlli], *adv.* entièrement, complètement, tout à fait.

whom [hu:m], *pron.* (*rel.*) que, lequel; (*inter.*) qui ? qui est-ce que ?

whomsoever [hu:msou'evə], *pron.* qui que ce soit que.

whoop [hu:p], *n.* huée, *f.*; cri (*de guerre*), *m.*—*v.t.*, *v.i.* huer, crier.

whooping ['hu:piŋ], *n.* huées, *f.pl.*

whooping-cough ['hu:piŋkɔf], *n.* coqueluche, *f.*

whopper ['hwɔpə], *n.* (*slang*) chose énorme, *f.*; mensonge énorme, *m.*; bourde, *f.*

whose [hu:z], *pron.* (*rel.*) dont, de qui; duquel, *m.*, de laquelle, *f.*, desquels, *m.pl.*, desquelles, *f.pl.*; (*inter.*) à qui ?

whosoever [hu:sou'evə], *pron.* qui que ce soit qui.
why [hwai], *adv.* pourquoi?—*int.* eh bien, mais! tiens!
wick [wik], *n.* mèche, *f.*
wicked ['wikid], *a.* méchant, malin.
wickedly ['wikidli], *adv.* méchamment.
wickedness ['wikidnis], *n.* méchanceté, perversité, *f.*
wicker ['wikə], *a.* d'osier, en osier.—*n.* osier, *m.*
wicker-work ['wikəwə:k], *n.* clayonnage, *m.*; vannerie, *f.*
wicket ['wikit], *n.* guichet, *m.*
wide [waid], *a.* large, grand, ample, vaste, immense (*d'étendue*); ***three feet wide***, large de trois pieds; ***to open wide***, ouvrir tout grand.—*adv.* loin, au loin, largement; ***far and wide***, partout; ***wide apart***, écarté, espacé.
wide-awake ['waidə'weik], *a.* bien éveillé.
widely ['waidli], *adv.* au loin, loin; grandement; largement; ***widely known***, bien connu.
widen [waidn], *v.t.* élargir, étendre.—*v.i.* s'élargir, s'étendre.
wideness ['waidnis], *n.* largeur, étendue, *f.*
widening ['waidniŋ], *n.* élargissement, *m.*
wide-spread ['waidspred], *a.* répandu; général, universel.
widow ['widou], *n.* veuve, *f.*
widowed ['widoud], *a.* veuf, veuve; (*fig.*) privé (*de*).
widower ['widouə], *n.* veuf, *m.*
widowhood ['widouhud], *n.* veuvage, *m.*
width [widθ], *n.* largeur, étendue, *f.*
wield [wi:ld], *v.t.* manier, tenir.
wife [waif], *n.* (*pl.* **wives** [waivz]) femme, épouse, *f.*
wifely ['waifli], **wife-like** ['waiflaik], *a.* de femme, d'épouse, conjugal.
wig [wig], *n.* perruque, *f.*
wig-maker ['wigmeikə], *n.* perruquier, *m.*
wigged [wigd], *a.* à perruque, portant perruque.
wigging ['wigiŋ], *n.* (*colloq.*) savon, *m.*, semonce, *f.*
wiggle [wigl], *v.t.* agiter.—*v.i.* se dandiner.
wild [waild], *a.* sauvage; farouche (*non apprivoisé*); effaré, déréglé (*désordonné*); furieux (*de rage*); insensé, extravagant (*fou*); étrange, bizarre (*baroque*); ***wild beast***, fauve, *m.*; ***wild boar***, sanglier, *m.*; ***wild cat***, chat sauvage, *m.*—*n.*(*pl.*) désert, lieu sauvage, *m.*
wilderness ['wildənis], *n.* lieu désert, *m.*
wildfire ['waildfaiə], *n.* feu grégeois, *m.*; ***like wildfire***, comme l'éclair.
wildly ['waildli], *adv.* d'une manière farouche, d'un air effaré; étourdiment, follement; à tort et à travers.
wildness ['waildnis], *n.* état sauvage; dérèglement, désordre, *m.*, turbulence, licence, *f.*
wile [wail], *n.* (*usu. pl.*) artifice, *m.*, ruse, *f.*
wilful ['wilful], *a.* opiniâtre; obstiné, volontaire, prémédité.
wilfully ['wilfuli], *adv.* opiniâtrement; à dessein.
wilfulness ['wilfulnis], *n.* obstination, opiniâtreté, *f.*
will [wil], *n.* volonté, *f.*; vouloir; bon plaisir, gré (*inclination*); (*Law*) testament, *m.*—*v.t.* vouloir, ordonner; léguer (*par testa*[ment]).—*v. aux. irr.*, *when used to indicate th*[e] *future it is not translated*; ***he will come***, [i]l viendra; *when used emphatically it is trans*lated by **vouloir**; ***I will not do it***, je n[e] veux pas le faire.
William ['wiljəm]. Guillaume, *m.*
willing ['wiliŋ], *a.* bien disposé; de bonn[e] volonté; ***to be willing***, vouloir bien, êtr[e] disposé (*à*).
willingly ['wiliŋli], *adv.* volontiers.
willingness ['wiliŋnis], *n.* bonne volonté, *f.*, bon vouloir, *m.*; complaisance, *f.*
will-o'-the-wisp [wiləðə'wisp], *n.* feu follet *m.*
willow ['wilou], *n.* saule, *m.*
willy-nilly ['wili'nili], *adv.* bon gré mal gré.
wily ['waili], *a.* rusé, fin, astucieux.
win [win], *v.t. irr.* gagner (*bataille, argent etc.*); remporter (*prix, victoire etc.*).—*v.i.* gagner; remporter la victoire, triompher.
wince [wins], *v.i.* sourciller, tressaillir (d[e] douleur).—*n.* tressaillement, *m.*
winch [wintʃ], *n.* manivelle, *f.*, treuil (*cabestan*), *m.*
wind (1) [wind], *n.* vent; souffle, *m.*, respiration, haleine (*breath*), *f.*; (*Med.*) vents, *m.pl.* flatuosité, *f.*—*v.t.* faire perdre haleine à essouffler (*cheval*).
wind (2) [waind], *v.t. irr.* enrouler (*en peloton*); dévider (*soie etc.*); ***to wind up***, remonter (*pendule etc.*); terminer (*négociations*); (*Comm.*) liquider.—*v.i.* tourner; se rouler, s'enrouler, s'enlacer; faire un détour; serpenter (*route, rivière*).
wind-bag ['windbæg], *n.* (*fig.*) moulin à paroles, *m.*
winded ['windid], *a.* hors d'haleine, essoufflé; ***long-winded***, de longue haleine.
winder ['waində], *n.* dévidoir (*appareil*); remontoir (*de montre*), *m.*
windfall ['windfɔ:l], *n.* (*fig.*) bonne aubaine, *f.*
wind-gauge ['windgeidʒ], *n.* anémomètre, *m.*
winding ['waindiŋ], *a.* sinueux, tortueux; en spirale (*escalier*).—*n.* sinuosité, *f.*; (*Elec.*) enroulement, *m.*
winding-sheet ['waindiŋʃi:t], *n.* linceul, *m.*
wind-jammer ['winddʒæmə], *n.* (*Naut.*) voilier, *m.*
windlass ['windləs], *n.* treuil; (*Naut.*) guindeau, cabestan, *m.*
windmill ['windmil], *n.* moulin à vent, *m.*
window ['windou], *n.* fenêtre; glace (*de train, voiture etc.*); montre, vitrine, *f.*, étalage (*de magasin*), *m.*; (*pl.*) vitraux (*d'église*), *m.pl.*
window-box ['windoubɔks], *n.* jardinière, *f.*
window-cleaner ['windoukli:nə], *n.* laveur de carreaux, *m.*
window-dresser ['windoudresə], *n.* étalagiste, *m., f.*
window-dressing ['windoudresiŋ], *n.* art de l'étalage; (*fam.*) trompe-l'œil, *m.*
window-frame ['windoufreim], *n.* châssis de fenêtre, *m.*
window-pane ['windoupein], *n.* carreau, *m.*
window-shopping ['windouʃɔpiŋ], *n.* lèche-vitrine, *m.*
window-shutter ['windouʃʌtə], *n.* volet; contrevent, *m.*
window-sill ['windousil], *n.* rebord *ou* appui de fenêtre, *m.*
windpipe ['windpaip], *n.* trachée-artère, *m.*

ndscreen ['windskri:n], *n.* (*Motor.*) pare-brise, *m.*
nd-sock ['windsɔk], *n.* (*Av.*) manche à air, *f.*
nd-tunnel ['windtʌnl], *n.* (*Av.*) tunnel aérodynamique, *m.*
ndward ['windwəd], *adv.* au vent.—*n.* côté du vent, *m.*
ndy ['windi], *a.* du vent; venteux; ***it is windy***, il fait du vent.
ne [wain], *n.* vin, *m.*—*v.t.* ***to wine and dine***, fêter.
ine-bibber ['wainbibə], *n.* buveur, *m.*, ivrogne, *m.*, *f.*
ine-bin ['wainbin], *n.* porte-bouteilles, *m.*
ine-cellar ['wainselə], *n.* cave, *f.*
ineglass ['wainglɑ:s], *n.* verre à vin, *m.*
ine-growing ['waingrouiŋ], *a.* viticole.—*n.* viticulture, *f.*
ine-merchant ['wainmə:tʃənt], *n.* négociant en vins, *m.*
ine-press ['wainpres], *n.* pressoir, *m.*
ine-tasting ['wainteistiŋ], *n.* dégustation de vins, *f.*
ine-waiter ['wainweitə], *n.* sommelier, *m.*
ing [wiŋ], *n.* aile; (*Av.*) escadre; (*Theat.*) (*pl.*) coulisse, *f.*; ***on the wing***, au vol.—*v.t.* blesser à l'aile.
inged [wiŋd], *a.* ailé; (*fig.*) rapide; blessé à l'aile.
inger ['wiŋə], *n.* (*Ftb.*) ailier, *m.*
ing-span ['wiŋspæn], *n.* envergure, *f.*
ink [wiŋk], *n.* clin d'œil, *m.*, œillade, *f.*—*v.i.* cligner de l'œil; clignoter (*lumière*).
inking ['wiŋkiŋ], *a.* clignotant.—*n.* clignotement; clignement d'œil, *m.*
inkle [wiŋkl], *n.* (*Ichth.*) bigorneau, *m.*
inner ['winə], *n.* gagnant; vainqueur (*d'une course etc.*), *m.*
inning ['winiŋ], *a.* gagnant; (*fig.*) attrayant, séduisant.—*n.* (*pl.*) gain, *m.*
inning-post ['winiŋpoust], *n.* poteau d'arrivée, but, *m.*
innow ['winou], *v.t.* vanner.
inter ['wintə], *a.* d'hiver.—*n.* hiver, *m.*; ***in winter***, en hiver.—*v.i.* hiverner, passer l'hiver (*à*).
intry ['wintri], *a.* d'hiver, hivernal; (*fig.*) glacial.
ipe [waip], *v.t.* essuyer; ***to wipe off***, effacer; ***to wipe up***, nettoyer.
iper ['waipə], *n.* ***windscreen wiper***, essuie-glace, *m.*
ire ['waiə], *n.* fil métallique, fil de fer, *m.*; dépêche (*télégramme*), *f.*; ***barbed wire***, fil de fer barbelé.—*v.t.* attacher *ou* lier avec du fil de métal; griller; (*fig.*) télégraphier.
ire-cutters ['waiəkʌtəz], *n.pl.* cisailles coupe-fil, *f.pl.*
ire-haired ['waiəhɛəd], *a.* à poil dur (*chien*).
ireless ['waiəlis], *a.* sans fil.—*n.* radio, T.S.F., *f.*; ***wireless set***, poste de T.S.F., *m.*, radio, *f.*
ire-netting ['waiə'netiŋ], *n.* grillage, treillis métallique, *m.*
ire-rope ['waiə'roup], *n.* câble métallique, *m.*
iring ['waiəriŋ], *n.* (*Elec.*) canalisation, *f.*; câblage, *m.*
wiry ['waiəri], *a.* (*fig.*) nerveux, souple.
wisdom ['wizdəm], *n.* sagesse; prudence, *f.*
wise [waiz], *a.* sage; discret, prudent.—*n.* manière, façon, sorte, guise, *f.*
wise-crack ['waizkræk], *n.* bon mot, *m.*
wisely ['waizli], *adv.* sagement; prudemment.
wish [wiʃ], *n.* souhait, désir, *m.*, envie, *f.*—*v.t.*, *v.i.* souhaiter, désirer, vouloir; ***I wish I could***, je voudrais pouvoir; ***I wish I were . . .***, je voudrais être . . .; ***to wish well to***, vouloir du bien à.
wish-bone ['wiʃboun], *n.* lunette, fourchette, *f.*
wishful ['wiʃful], *a.* désireux (*de*).
wishy-washy ['wiʃi'wɔʃi], *a.* faible, pauvre.
wisp [wisp], *n.* bouchon de paille etc., *m.*; mèche (*de cheveux*), *f.*
wistaria [wis'tɛəriə], *n.* glycine, *f.*
wistful ['wistful], *a.* désireux; d'envie, de regret, pensif (*air, regard, sourire*).
wistfully ['wistfuli], *adv.* d'un air de vague regret.
wit [wit], *n.* esprit; entendement, jugement; (*fig.*) bel esprit; (*pl.*) esprit, *m.*, raison, tête, *f.*, sens, bon sens, *m.*; ***to be at one's wits' end***, ne savoir que faire.—*v.t.* savoir; ***to wit***, c'est-à-dire.
witch [witʃ], *n.* sorcière, magicienne, *f.*
witchcraft ['witʃkrɑ:ft], *n.* sorcellerie, magie noire, *f.*
witch-hazel ['witʃheizl], *n.* (*Bot.*) hamamélis, *m.*
with [wið], *prep.* avec; de, par (*au moyen de*); à, au, à la, aux (*in descriptive phrases*); chez, parmi (*en compagnie de*); auprès de (*de l'avis de*); malgré (*en dépit de*); ***angry with***, fâché contre.
withal [wið'ɔ:l], *adv.* avec tout cela, en outre.
withdraw [wið'drɔ:], *v.t. irr.* (*conjug. like* DRAW) retirer; rappeler; éloigner (*de*).—*v.i.* se retirer, s'éloigner (*de*).
withdrawal [wið'drɔ:əl] *n.* retraite (*des vaincus*), *f.*; retrait (*enlèvement*), *m.*
wither ['wiðə], *v.i.* se flétrir, se faner.
withering ['wiðəriŋ], *a.* écrasant (*sarcastique*).
withers ['wiðəz], *n.pl.* garrot (*de cheval*), *m.*
withhold [wið'hould], *v.t. irr.* (*conjug. like* HOLD) retenir; refuser.
within [wið'in], *prep.* dans, en; à moins de (*pas plus de*); ***within a pound or so***, à une livre près; ***within reach of***, à portée de.—*adv.* en dedans, à l'intérieur; à la maison, chez soi.
without [wið'aut], *prep.* sans (*manquant de*).—*conj.* à moins que, sans que (*unless*).—**adv.* en dehors, au dehors.
withstand [wið'stænd], *v.t. irr.* (*conjug. like* STAND) résister à, combattre.
withy ['wiði], *a.* d'osier.—*n.* osier, *m.*
witless ['witlis], *a.* sans esprit; sot.
witness ['witnis], *n.* témoin; témoignage (*preuve*), *m.*—*v.t.* témoigner; être témoin de.—*v.i.* témoigner, porter témoignage.
witticism ['witisizm], *n.* bon mot, *m.*
wittily ['witili], *adv.* spirituellement, avec esprit.
wittiness ['witinis], *n.* esprit, caractère spirituel, *m.*
wittingly ['witiŋli], *adv.* sciemment, à dessein.
witty ['witi], *a.* spirituel; plaisant (*facétieux*).
wives [WIFE].
wizard ['wizəd], *n.* sorcier, magicien, *m.*
wizened ['wizənd], *a.* ratatiné, ridé.
wobble [wɔbl], *v.i.* vaciller, ballotter.

wobbling ['wɔbliŋ], *a.* vacillant, branlant.—*n.* vacillation, *f.*; dandinement, *m.*
wobbly ['wɔbli], *a.* branlant, vacillant.
woe [wou], *n.* (*fig.*) peine, douleur, *f.*; malheur, *m.*
woebegone ['woubigɔn], **woeful** ['wouful], *a.* triste, malheureux, abattu.
woefully ['woufuli], *adv.* tristement.
wolf [wulf], *n.* (*pl.* **wolves** [wulvz]) loup, *m.*; ***she-wolf***, louve, *f.*
wolf-cub ['wulfkʌb], *n.* louveteau, *m.*
wolf-dog ['wulfdɔg], *n.* chien-loup, *m.*
wolfish ['wulfiʃ], *a.* de loup; (*fig.*) rapace.
wolves [WOLF].
woman ['wumən], *n.* (*pl.* **women** ['wimin]) femme, *f.*
woman-hater ['wumənheitə], *n.* misogyne, *m.*
womanhood ['wumənhud], *n.* état de femme, *m.*
womankind ['wumənkaind], *n.* le sexe féminin, *m.*; les femmes, *f.pl.*
womanly ['wumənli], *a.* de femme.
womanliness ['wumənlinis], *n.* fémininité, *f.*
womb [wu:m], *n.* (*Anat.*) matrice, *f.*; (*fig.*) sein, *m.*, flancs, *m.pl.*
women [WOMAN].
wonder ['wʌndə], *n.* étonnement, *m.*, surprise; merveille (*spectacle etc.*), *f.*, miracle, prodige, *m.*—*v.i.* s'étonner, être étonné; se demander; ***to wonder whether***, se demander si.
wonderful ['wʌndəful], *a.* étonnant, merveilleux.
wonderfully ['wʌndəfuli], *adv.* étonnamment, merveilleusement.
wonderment ['wʌndəmənt], *n.* étonnement, *m.*
wondrous ['wʌndrəs], *a.* merveilleux.
wondrously ['wʌndrəsli], *adv.* merveilleusement.
wont [wount], *a.* ***to be wont to***, avoir l'habitude de.—*n.* coutume, habitude, *f.*
wonted ['wountid], *a.* accoutumé, habituel.
woo [wu:], *v.t.* faire la cour à; courtiser.
wood [wud], *n.* bois (*matériel* ou *forêt*), *m.*
woodbine ['wudbain], *n.* chèvrefeuille, *m.*
woodcock ['wudkɔk], *n.* bécasse, *f.*
woodcut ['wudkʌt], *n.* gravure sur bois, *f.*
wood-cutter ['wudkʌtə], *n.* bûcheron, *m.*
wooded ['wudid], *a.* boisé.
wooden [wudn], *a.* de bois, en bois; (*fig.*) gauche (*mouvement etc.*).
woodland ['wudlənd], *a.* des bois, sylvestre.—*n.* pays boisé, bois, *m.*
woodman ['wudmən], *n.* (*pl.* **-men** [men]) garde forestier; bûcheron, *m.*
wood-nymph ['wudnimf], *n.* nymphe des bois, dryade, *f.*
woodpecker ['wudpekə], *n.* pic, *m.*; ***green woodpecker***, pivert, *m.*
wood-pigeon ['wudpidʒin], *n.* pigeon ramier, *m.*
wood-pulp ['wudpʌlp], *n.* pâte de bois, *f.*
wood-wind ['wudwind], *n.* (*Mus.*) les bois, *m.pl.*
woodwork ['wudwə:k], *n.* boiserie; menuiserie; charpente, *f.*
wood-worm ['wudwə:m], *n.* artison, *m.*
woody ['wudi], *a.* boisé; ligneux.
wood-yard ['wudja:d], *n.* chantier, *m.*
wooer ['wu:ə], *n.* amoureux, prétendant, *m.*
woof [wu:f], *n.* trame, *f.*; tissu (*texture*), *m.*
wooing ['wu:iŋ], *n.* cour, *f.*
wool [wul], *n.* laine, *f.*
woollen ['wulən], *a.* de laine, à laine.—*n.*(... tissus de laine, *m.pl.*, laines, *f.pl.*, lainag... *m.pl.*; ***woollen-cloth***, drap, *m.*; ***woolle... draper***, marchand de draps, *m.*; ***woolle... goods***, (*fam.*) ***woollies***, lainages, *m.pl.*
woolliness ['wulinis], *n.* nature laineuse; (*f*... imprécision, *f.*
woolly ['wuli], *a.* laineux.
Woolsack ['wulsæk], *n.* sac de laine (*siège ... Lord Chancellor*), *m.*
word [wə:d], *n.* mot, *m.*; parole (*prononc... f.*; avis, *m.*, nouvelle (*communication*), *f.*; ***word of mouth***, de vive voix; ***in a wo...*** en un mot; ***not a word!*** bouche close!... *v.t.* exprimer; énoncer; rédiger (*te... gramme*).
word-book ['wə:dbuk], *n.* vocabulai... lexique, *m.*
wordiness ['wə:dinis], *n.* prolixité, verbosi... *f.*
wording ['wə:diŋ], *n.* expression, *f.*; énor... (*d'un problème*), *m.*
wordy ['wə:di], *a.* verbeux, diffus.
work [wə:k], *v.t.* travailler; façonner (*o... vrager*); se frayer (*un chemin*); payer (*s... passage*) en travaillant; broder (*coudre*); fa... aller, manœuvrer (*machine etc.*); exploi... (*mine etc.*); ***to work off***, user; ***to work on... self up***, s'exciter; ***to work out***, résouc... (*problème*).—*v.i.* travailler; fonctionn... marcher, aller, jouer; opérer, avoir ... l'effet (*agir*); ***to work loose***, se desserrer.... *n.* travail; ouvrage, *m.*, besogne (*tâch...* (*fig.*) affaire; (*Lit.*) œuvre, *f.*; (*pl.*) méc... nisme (*de moteur*), *m.*; manœuvres (*d'u... machine*), *f.pl.*; (*Ind.*) fabrique, usine, ... (*Fort.*) travaux, *m.pl.*; mouvement (... *montre*), *m.*; ***road works ahead***, attentic... travaux! ***to be out of work***, chômer.
workable ['wə:kəbl], *a.* réalisable; exploitat... (*mine etc.*).
workaday ['wə:kədei], *a.* de tous les jours.
work-bench ['wə:kbentʃ], *n.* établi, *m.*
work-box ['wə:kbɔks], *n.* boîte à ouvrage, *f.*
worker ['wə:kə], *n.* travailleur; ouvrie... employé, *m.*
workhouse ['wə:khaus], *n.* maison d... pauvres, *f.*; hospice, *m.*
working ['wə:kiŋ], *a.* qui travaille, ouvrie... de travail (*vêtements*); ***hard-working***, lab... rieux; ***in working order***, en état ... fonctionnement; ***working capital***, capit... d'exploitation, *m.*; ***working man***, ouvrie... *m.*—*n.* travail, *m.*; marche, *f.*; fonctionn... ment, jeu (*de machine*), *m.*; opération; e... ploitation (*de mine etc.*), *f.*
working-class ['wə:kiŋ'kla:s], *n.* classe o... vrière, *f.*
working-day ['wə:kiŋ'dei], *n.* jour ouvrable, ...
workman ['wə:kmən], *n.* (*pl.* **-men** [men... ouvrier, artisan, *m.*
workmanlike ['wə:kmənlaik] *a.* bien fai... bien travaillé.
workmanship ['wə:kmənʃip], *n.* ouvrag... travail, *m.*
work-room ['wə:kru:m], **work-shop** ['wə:... ʃɔp], *n.* atelier, *m.*
world [wə:ld], *n.* monde; l'univers; (*fi...* monde, *m.*, vie, *f.*; ***all the world ove...***

dans le monde entier; ***a world of good***, un bien infini; ***the first world war***, la première guerre mondiale.
orldliness ['wə:ldlinis], *n.* mondanité; frivolité, *f.*
'orldly ['wə:ldli], *a.* mondain, du monde.
orldwide ['wə:ldwaid], *a.* universel, répandu partout.
'orm [wə:m], *n.* ver, *m.*; chenille, larve, *f.*; filet (*de vis*), *m.*—*v.t.* miner; ***to worm oneself into***, s'insinuer, se faufiler dans.
'orm-cast ['wə:mkɑ:st], *n.* déjection de ver (de terre), *f.*
'orm-eaten ['wə:mi:tn], *a.* rongé des vers, vermoulu.
'orm-screw ['wə:mskru:], *n.* tire-bourre, *m.*
'ormwood ['wə:mwud], *n.* armoise amère, *f.*; (*fig.*) fiel, *m.*
'orried ['wʌrid], *a.* tourmenté, harassé, ennuyé.
'orry ['wʌri], *n.* ennui, tracas, souci, *m.*—*v.t.* tourmenter, tracasser.—*v.i.* tracasser; ***don't worry!*** soyez tranquille!
'orse [wə:s], *a.* pire; plus mauvais; plus malade, plus mal (*santé*).—*n.* pire; plus mauvais, *m.*—*adv.* plus mal, pis; ***far worse***, bien pis, bien pire; ***so much the worse***, tant pis.
'orsen [wə:sn], *v.i.* empirer.
'orsening ['wə:sniŋ], *n.* aggravation, *f.*
'orship ['wə:ʃip], *n.* culte, *m.*, adoration, *f.*; honneur (*titre*), *m.*—*v.t.*, *v.i.* adorer.
'orshipful ['wə:ʃipful], *a.* honorable.
'orshipper ['wə:ʃipə], *n.* adorateur, *m.*
'orst [wə:st], *a.* le plus mauvais, le pire.—*adv.* le pis, le plus mal.—*n.* le plus mauvais, le pire, le pis.—*v.t.* battre, vaincre, défaire.
'orsted ['wustid], *a.* de laine peignée.—*n.* laine peignée, *f.*
worth [wə:θ], *a.* qui vaut, valant; qui mérite (*digne*); qui est riche de (*qui possède*); ***to be worth doing***, valoir la peine de faire.—*n.* valeur, *f.*; prix, *m.*; ***for all one's worth***, de toutes ses forces.
worthily ['wə:ðili], *adv.* dignement.
worthiness ['wə:ðinis], *n.* mérite, *m.*
worthless ['wə:θlis], *a.* sans valeur, qui ne vaut rien; ***worthless fellow***, vaurien, *m.*
worth-while ['wə:θ'hwail], *a.* qui vaut la peine (*de*).
worthy ['wə:ði], *a.* digne, honorable; (*colloq.*) brave.—*n.* (*colloq.*) brave homme; homme illustre, *m.*
would [wud], *v.aux. past* and *cond.* [WILL]. *When used emphatically* ***would*** *is translated by* ***vouloir***.
would-be ['wudbi:], *a.* prétendu soi-disant.
wound (1) [waund], *past* and *p.p.* [WIND (2)].
wound (2) [wu:nd], *n.* blessure; plaie, *f.*—*v.t.* blesser.
wounded ['wu:ndid], *a.* blessé.
woven [wouvn], *a.* tissé.
wrack [ræk], *n.* varech, *m.*; ruine, *f.*, débris, *m.*
wraith [reiθ], *n.* revenant, *m.*
wrangle [ræŋgl], *n.* dispute, querelle, *f.*—*v.i.* se disputer, se quereller.
wrangling ['ræŋgliŋ], *n.* dispute, *f.*, chamailleries, *f.pl.*
wrap [ræp], *v.t.* enrouler, envelopper.—*n.* châle, peignoir, *m.*
wrapper ['ræpə], *n.* enveloppe; toile d'emballage (*pour paquets*); bande (*pour journal*); couverture (*de livre*), *f.*
wrapping ['ræpiŋ], *n.* enveloppe, couverture, *f.*; ***wrapping-paper***, papier d'emballage. *m.*
wrath [rɔ:θ], *n.* courroux, *m.*, colère, *f.*
wrathful ['rɔ:θful], *a.* courroucé.
wreak [ri:k], *v.t.* exécuter, satisfaire.
wreath [ri:θ], *n.* guirlande, *f.*, feston, *m.*; couronne (*d'épouse etc.*), *f.*
wreathe [ri:ð], *v.t.* entrelacer, tresser (*de*).—*v.i.* s'entrelacer, s'enrouler.
wreathed [ri:ðd], *a.* entrelacé.
wreck [rek], *n.* naufrage; navire naufragé, *m.*, épave; (*fig.*) ruine, *f.*—*v.t.* faire faire naufrage à; (*fig.*) ruiner.
wreckage ['rekidʒ], *n.* débris de naufrage, *m.*, épaves, *f.pl.*
wrecked [rekt], *a.* naufragé; ruiné.
wrecker ['rekə], *n.* pilleur d'épaves, naufrageur, *m.*
wren [ren], *n.* (*Orn.*) roitelet, *m.*
wrench [rentʃ], *n.* torsion, *f.*, arrachement, *m.*; entorse (*des muscles*); clef (*outil*), *f.*—*v.t.* arracher (*à* ou *de*); se fouler (*cheville etc.*).
wrest [rest], *v.t.* arracher (*à*).
wrestle [resl], *v.i.* lutter.
wrestler ['reslə], *n.* lutteur, *m.*
wrestling ['resliŋ], *n.* lutte, *f.*; catch, *m.*; ***all-in wrestling***, lutte libre.
wretch [retʃ], *n.* malheureux, *m.*; misérable (*scélérat*), *m.*, *f.*; ***poor wretch***, pauvre diable, *m.*
wretched ['retʃid], *a.* malheureux, misérable; vilain, triste; pitoyable, à faire pitié.
wretchedly ['retʃidli], *adv.* malheureusement, misérablement; d'une manière pitoyable.
wretchedness ['retʃidnis], *n.* misère, pauvreté, *f.*
wriggle [rigl], *v.i.* se tortiller, se remuer.
wriggling ['rigliŋ], *n.* tortillement, *m.*
wring [riŋ], *v.t. irr.* tordre; arracher (*à*); presser, serrer (*étreindre*).
wringer ['riŋə], *n.* essoreuse (*à linge*), *f.*
wringing ['riŋiŋ], *a.* ***wringing wet***, trempé jusqu'aux os (*personne*); mouillé à tordre (*vêtement*).
wrinkle [riŋkl], *n.* ride (*à la figure etc.*), *f.*; pli, faux pli (*de vêtement*); (*slang*) tuyau (*renseignement*), *m.*—*v.t.* rider; plisser; ***to wrinkle one's brow***, froncer les sourcils. —*v.i.* se rider.
wrinkled [riŋkld], *a.* ridé; (*Bot.*) plissé.
wrist [rist], *n.* poignet, *m.*
wristband ['ristbænd], *n.* poignet, *m.*
wrist-watch ['ristwɔtʃ], *n.* montre-bracelet, *f.*
writ [rit], *n.* exploit, mandat, *m.*, ordonnance; (*Parl.*) lettre de convocation, *f.*
write [rait], *v.t.*, *v.i. irr.* écrire; ***to write off***, (*Comm.*) passer au compte des profits et pertes.
write-off ['raitɔf], *n.* annulation; non-valeur (*personne*), *f.*
writer ['raitə], *n.* écrivain; (*Comm.*) commis aux écritures, *m.*
writhe [raið], *v.i.* se tordre (*de douleur*); se crisper.
writing ['raitiŋ], *n.* écriture (*calligraphie*), *f.*; écrit (*chose écrite*); (*fig.*) ouvrage, document, *m.*; inscription, *f.*; ***in writing***, par écrit.
writing-case ['raitiŋkeis], *n.* papeterie, *f.*
writing-desk ['raitiŋdesk], *n.* pupitre, bureau, secrétaire, *m.*

writing-paper ['raitiŋpeipə], *n.* papier à écrire, *m.*
writing-table ['raitiŋteibl], *n.* table à écrire, *f.*
written [ritn], *a.* écrit, par écrit.
wrong [rɔŋ], *a.* faux, erroné, inexact (*pas vrai*); mal, mauvais; ***to be wrong***, avoir tort (*personne*), n'être pas à l'heure, aller mal (*montre*); ***what's wrong with you?*** qu'avez-vous ? ***wrong number***, (*Teleph.*) mauvais numéro, *m.*; ***wrong side***, envers, *m.*; ***wrong side up***, sens dessus dessous.—*adv.* mal, à tort, à faux.—*n.* mal, *m.*, injustice, *f.*, tort; dommage, *m.*—*v.t.* faire du tort à, nuire à.
wrongdoer ['rɔŋduə], *n.* pervers, méchant, *m.*
wrongdoing ['rɔŋduiŋ], *n.* le mal, *m.*
wrongful ['rɔŋful], *a.* injuste.
wrongfully ['rɔŋfuli], *adv.* à tort, injustement.
wrongly ['rɔŋli], *adv.* mal, à tort; ***rightly or wrongly***, à tort ou à raison.
wroth [rouθ], *a.* (*poet.*) en colère, irrité, courroucé.
wrought [rɔ:t], *a.* travaillé; façonné; ouvré (*tissu*); ***wrought iron***, fer forgé, *m.*
wry [rai], *a.* de travers, tordu, tors; ***to pull a wry face***, faire la grimace.

X

X, x [eks]. vingt-quatrième lettre de l'alphabet; X, dix, *m.*
Xerxes ['zə:ksi:z]. Xerxès, *m.*
Xmas ['krisməs]. (*abbr.* CHRISTMAS) Noël, *m.*
X-ray ['eksrei], *a.* radiographique; ***X-ray photograph***, radiographie, *f.*—*n.* (*pl.*) rayons X, *m.pl.*—*v.t.* radiographier.
xylophone ['zailəfoun], *n.* xylophone; (*slang*) claquebois, *m.*

Y

Y, y [wai]. vingt-cinquième lettre de l'alphabet; (l')i grec, *m.*
yacht [jɔt], *n.* yacht, *m.*
yacht-club ['jɔtklʌb], *n.* cercle nautique, *m.*
yachting ['jɔtiŋ], *n.* yachting, *m.*
yachtsman ['jɔtsmən], *n.* (*pl.* **-men** [men]) yachtman, *m.*
yak [jæk], *n.* (*Zool.*) ya(c)k, *m.*
yam [jæm], *n.* igname, *f.*
yank [jæŋk], *v.t.* (*fam.*) tirer brusquement.
Yankee ['jæŋki], *n.* Yankee, Américain, *m.*
yap [jæp], *v.i.* japper, aboyer.—*n.* jappement, *m.*
yard (1) [jɑ:d], *n.* cour, *f.*, préau, *m.*
yard (2) [jɑ:d], *n.* (*Naut.*) vergue, *f.*; (*Measure*) yard (*mètre 0·914383*), *m.*
yard-arm ['jɑ:dɑ:m], *n.* bout de vergue, *m.*
yarn [jɑ:n], *n.* fil; (*Naut.*) fil de caret; récit, conte (*histoire*), *m.*

yawl [jɔ:l], *n.* (*Naut.*) sloop, *m.*; (*Row.*) yo de mer, *f.*
yawn [jɔ:n], *n.* bâillement, *m.*—*v.i.* bâiller.
yawning ['jɔ:niŋ], *a.* qui bâille; (*fig.*) béant
***ye** [ji:], *pron.pl.* vous.
yea [jei], *adv.* oui; vraiment, en vérité.— vote affirmatif, *m.*
year [jiə], *n.* an (*unité de temps*), *m.*; anné (*particulière*), *f.*; ***every year***, tous les ans ***four times a year***, quatre fois par an ***new year***, nouvel an; ***next year***, l'a prochain.
year-book ['jiəbuk], *n.* annuaire, *m.*
yearling ['jiəliŋ], *a.* âgé d'un an.—*n.* poulain *m.*, *ou* pouliche, *f.*, d'un an.
yearly ['jiəli], *a.* annuel.—*adv.* tous les ans.
yearn [jə:n], *v.i.* ***to yearn after***, soupire après; ***to yearn to do something***, brûle de faire quelque chose.
yearning ['jə:niŋ], *n.* désir ardent, *m.*
yeast [ji:st], *n.* levure, *f.*
yell [jel], *n.* hurlement, *m.*—*v.i.* hurler pousser des hurlements.
yelling ['jeliŋ], *n.* hurlements, *m.pl.*
yellow ['jelou], *a.* jaune; (*slang*) poltron.—*n.* jaune, *m.*—*v.t.*, *v.i.* jaunir.
yellow-hammer ['jelouhæmə], *n.* (*Orn.* bruant jaune, *m.*
yellowish ['jelouiʃ], *a.* jaunâtre.
yellowness ['jelounis], *n.* couleur jaune, *f.*
yelp [jelp], *v.i.* glapir, japper.
yelping ['jelpiŋ], *n.* glapissement, jappement *m.*
Yemen ['jemən]. le Yémen, *m.*
Yemeni ['jeməni], *a.* yémenite.—*n.* Yémenit (*personne*), *m.*, *f.*
yeoman ['joumən], *n.* (*pl.* **-men** [men]) fermier-propriétaire, *m.*
yeomanry ['joumənri], *n.* fermiers-proprié-taires, *m.pl.*
yes [jes], *adv.* oui; si (*in reply to a negative*).
yes-man ['jesmæn], *n.* (*pl.* **-men** [men]) (*pop.*) Béni-oui-oui, *m.*
yesterday ['jestəd(e)i], *adv.* and *n.* hier, *m.*; ***the day before yesterday***, avant-hier; ***yesterday evening***, hier soir.
yet [jet], *conj.* pourtant, cependant, tout de même.—*adv.* encore, déjà; ***as yet***, jusqu'ici; ***not yet***, pas encore.
yew [ju:], *n.* (*Bot.*) if, *m.*
yield [ji:ld], *v.t.* produire, rapporter; livrer, céder (*au vainqueur*); ***to yield up***, rendre.—*v.i.* se rendre, céder (*à*); consentir (*à*).—*n.* rendement, produit, rapport, *m.*
yielding ['ji:ldiŋ], *a.* complaisant, facile.—*n.* reddition; soumission, *f.*
yoke [jouk], *n.* joug; attelage, *m.*, paire; palanche (*pour seaux*), *f.*; (*Dress.*) empiècement, *m.*—*v.t.* atteler, accoupler.
yokel [joukl], *n.* rustre, campagnard, *m.*
yolk [jouk], *n.* jaune (d'œuf), *m.*
yonder** ['jɔndə], *adv.* là, là-bas.—*a.* ***yonder castle, ce château-là.
***yore** [jɔ:], *adv.* autrefois, jadis.
you [ju:], *pron.* vous; (*to a child, relative, pet etc.*) tu, te, toi; (*indef.*) on.
young [jʌŋ], *a.* jeune; novice, neuf, inexpérimenté (*non éprouvé*); (*fig.*) naissant; ***young folks*** or ***young people***, jeunes gens, *m.pl.*; ***young lady***, demoiselle, *f.*—*n.pl.* les jeunes, les jeunes gens; les petits, *m.pl.*; ***with young***, pleine (*animal*).

ounger ['jʌŋgə], *a.* plus jeune; cadet (*de deux frères etc.*).
oungest ['jʌŋgist], *a.* le plus jeune.
oungish ['jʌŋiʃ], *a.* assez jeune.
oungster ['jʌŋstə], *n.* jeune homme; gamin, mioche, *m.*, gosse, *m., f.*
our [jɔ:], *a.* votre, (*pl.*) vos; (*to a child, relative, pet etc.*) ton, ta, tes; (*indef.*) son, sa, ses.
ours [jɔ:z], *pron.* le vôtre, *m.*, la vôtre, *f.*, les vôtres, *pl.*; à vous (*your property*); de vous (*by you*); (*to a child, relative, pet etc.*) le tien, la tienne, les tiens, les tiennes; à toi (*your property*); de toi (*by you*).
ourself [jɔ:'self], *pron.* (*pl.* **yourselves** [jɔ:'selvz]) vous-même, toi-même; (*pl.*) vous-mêmes; (*reflexive*) vous, te.
outh [ju:θ], *n.* jeunesse, adolescence, *f.*; jeune homme, adolescent (*personne*), *m.*; (*fig.*) jeunes gens, *m.pl.*
outhful ['ju:θful], *a.* jeune; de jeunesse.
outhfulness ['ju:θfulnis], *n.* jeunesse, *f.*
Yugoslav ['ju:go'slɑ:v], *a.* yougoslave.—*n.* Yougoslave (*personne*), *m., f.*
Yugoslavia [ju:go'slɑ:vjə]. la Yougoslavie, *f.*
Yule [ju:l], **Yule-tide** ['ju:ltaid], *n.* Noël, *m.*, fête de Noël, *f.*
Yule-log ['ju:llɔg], *n.* bûche de Noël, *f.*

Z

Z, **z** [zed, (*Am.*) zi:]. vingt-sixième lettre de l'alphabet, *m.*

Zambesi [zæm'bi:zi]. le Zambèze, *m.*
Zambia ['zæmbjə]. la Zambie, *f.*
zany ['zeini], *n.* zani, bouffon, *m.*
zeal [zi:l], *n.* zèle, *m.*
zealot ['zelət], *n.* zélateur, *m.*, fanatique, *m., f.*
zealous ['zeləs], *a.* zélé, zélateur.
zealously ['zeləsli], *adv.* avec zèle.
zebra ['zi:brə], *n.* zèbre, *m.*; ***zebra crossing***, passage clouté, *m.*
zenith ['zeniθ], *n.* zénith; (*fig.*) apogée, *m.*
zephyr ['zefə], *n.* zéphyr, zéphire, Zéphyre, *m.*
zero ['ziərou], *n.* zéro; (*fig.*) rien, *m.*; ***zero hour***, l'heure H, *f.*
zest [zest], *n.* goût, *m.*, saveur, *f.*; zeste (*d'orange, de citron*); (*fig.*) entrain, *m.*, verve, *f.*
Zeus [zju:s]. (*Myth.*) Zeus, *m.*
zigzag ['zigzæg], *a.* en zigzag.—*n.* zigzag, *m.* —*v.i.* aller en zigzag, zigzaguer.
zinc [ziŋk], *n.* zinc, *m.*—*v.t.* zinguer.
zinnia ['zinjə], *n.* (*Bot.*) zinnia, *m.*
Zion ['zaiən]. Sion, *m.*
zip [zip], *n.* sifflement (*de balle*), *m.*; énergie, verve, *f.*—*v.t.* siffler; ***zip fastener***, fermeture à glissière, *f.*
zither ['ziðə], *n.* cithare, *f.*
zodiac ['zoudiæk], *n.* zodiaque, *m.*
zone [zoun], *n.* zone, *f.*
zoo [zu:], *n.* jardin zoologique, (*fam.*) zoo, *m.*
zoological [zouə'lɔdʒikl], *a.* zoologique; ***zoological gardens***, jardin zoologique, *m.*
zoologist [zou'ɔlədʒist], *n.* zoologiste, zoologue, *m., f.*
zoology [zou'ɔlədʒi], *n.* zoologie, *f.*
zoom [zu:m], *n.* bourdonnement, ronflement, *m.*—*v.i.* vrombir.
Zulu ['zu:lu:], *a.* zoulou.—*n.* Zoulou, *m.*

French Verbs

1. All verbs not marked *irr.* in the French-English section of the Dictionary are either
(*a*) regular, and conjugated like AIMER, FINIR or VENDRE according to their endi
(see below) or
(*b*) anomalous, and conjugated like the verb in that group to which the user is referred.
2. The Imperfect Indicative, Conditional, Imperative, and Imperfect Subjunctive are not give
and may be assumed to be formed as follows:
Imperfect Indicative: by substituting for the final *-ons* of 1st Person Plural, Present Indicati
the endings *-ais, -ais, -ait, -ions, -iez, -aient* (except *être: j'étais*).
Conditional: by substituting for the endings of the Future those of the Imperfect Indicati
given above.
Imperative: (*a*) 2nd Person Singular, 1st and 2nd Person Plural, by using these forms

Infinitive	*Participles*	*Present Indicative*	*Past Historic*
REGULAR VERBS First Conjugation Infinitive in *-er*			
aim-*er*	aim-*ant* aim-*é*	aim-*e* aim-*es* aim-*e* aim-*ons* aim-*ez* aim-*ent*	aim-*ai* aim-*as* aim-*a* aim-*âmes* aim-*âtes* aim-*èrent*
Second Conjugation Infinitive in *-ir*			
fin-*ir*	fin-*issant* fin-*i*	fin-*is* fin-*is* fin-*it* fin-*issons* fin-*issez* fin-*issent*	fin-*is* fin-*is* fin-*it* fin-*îmes* fin-*îtes* fin-*irent*
Third Conjugation Infinitive in *-re*			
vend-*re*	vend-*ant* vend-*u*	vend-*s* vend-*s* vend vend-*ons* vend-*ez* vend-*ent*	vend-*is* vend-*is* vend-*it* vend-*îmes* vend-*îtes* vend-*irent*
ANOMALOUS VERBS			
amener	amenant amené	amène amènes amène amenons amenez amènent	amenai . . . amenâmes . . .
appeler	appelant appelé	appelle appelles appelle appelons appelez appellent	appelai . . . appelâmes . . .
assiéger	assiégeant assiégé	assiège assièges assiège assiégeons assiégez assiègent	assiégeai . . . assiégeâmes . . .

the Present Indicative without pronouns (*-er* verbs drop the final *s* of the 2nd Person Singular).

(*b*) 3rd Person Singular and Plural by using these forms of the Present Subjunctive.

Imperfect Subjunctive: from the 2nd Person Singular of the Past Historic by adding *-se, -ses, -^t, -sions, -siez, -sent.*

3. Exceptions to the above rules are indicated in footnotes.
4. Compound verbs (e.g. DEVENIR, REVENIR, etc.) are given only where they differ from the simple form (e.g. VENIR).
5. Defective verbs are marked † and all existing forms are given.

Future	*Present Subjunctive*	*English*
aimer-*ai* aimer-*as* aimer-*a* aimer-*on* aimer-*ez* aimer-*ont*	aim-*e* aim-*es* aim-*e* aim-*ions* aim-*iez* aim-*ent*	to like, to love
finir-*ai* finir-*as* finir-*a* finir-*ons* finir-*ez* finir-*ont*	fini-*sse* fini-*sses* fini-*sse* fini-*ssions* fini-*ssiez* fini-*ssent*	to finish
vendr-*ai* vendr-*as* vendr-*a* vendr-*ons* vendr-*ez* vendr-*ont*	vend-*e* vend-*es* vend-*e* vend-*ions* vend-*iez* vend-*ent*	to sell
amènerai... amènerons...	amène amènes amène amenions ameniez amènent	to bring
appellerai... appellerons...	appelle appelles appelle appelions appeliez appellent	to call
assiégerai... assiégerons...	assiège assièges assiège assiégions assiégiez assiègent	to besiege

French Verbs

Infinitive	Participles	Present Indicative	Past Historic
battre	battant battu	bats bats bat battons battez battent	battis . . . battîmes . . .
céder	cédant cédé	cède cèdes cède cédons cédez cèdent	cédai . . . cédâmes . . .
commencer	commençant commencé	commence commences commence commençons commencez commencent	commençai commenças commença commençâmes commençâtes commencèrent
dépecer	dépeçant dépecé	dépèce dépèces dépèce dépeçons dépecez dépècent	dépeçai dépeças dépeça dépeçâmes dépeçâtes dépecèrent
employer[1]	employant employé	emploie emploies emploie employons employez emploient	employai . . . employâmes . . .
manger	mangeant mangé	mange manges mange mangeons mangez mangent	mangeai mangeas mangea mangeâmes mangeâtes mangèrent
payer[1]	(See footnote)		
rapiécer	rapiéçant rapiécé	rapièce rapièces rapièce rapiéçons rapiécez rapiècent	rapiéçai rapiéças rapiéça rapiéçâmes rapiéçâtes rapiécèrent
rompre	rompant rompu	romps romps rompt rompons rompez rompent	rompis . . . rompîmes . . .
IRREGULAR VERBS			
† absoudre	absolvant absous, *m.*, absoute, *f.*	absous absous absout absolvons absolvez absolvent	

[1] All verbs in *-oyer* and *-uyer* change *y* to *i* before a mute *e*. With verbs in *-ayer*, *y* or *i* may

'uture	Present Subjunctive	English
attrai . . . attrons . . .	batte . . . battions . . .	to beat
éderai . . . éderons . . .	cède cèdes cède cédions cédiez cèdent	to yield
ommencerai . . . ommencerons . . .	commence . . . commencions . . .	to begin
lépècerai . . . lépècerons . . .	dépèce dépèces dépèce dépecions dépeciez dépècent	to cut up
emploierai . . . emploierons . . .	emploie emploies emploie employions employiez emploient	to employ, to use
mangerai . . . mangerons . . .	mange . . . mangions . . .	to eat
		to pay (for)
rapiécerai . . . rapiécerons . . .	rapièce rapièces rapièce rapiécions rapiéciez rapiècent	to patch
romprai . . . romprons . . .	rompe . . . rompions . . .	to break
absoudrai . . . absoudrons . . .	absolve . . . absolvions . . .	to absolve

be used. With *grasseyer y* is always used.

French Verbs

Infinitive	*Participles*	*Present Indicative*	*Past Historic*
† accroire	(used only in the infinitive in the phrase '*faire accroire*', to make o		
acquérir	acquérant acquis	acquiers acquiers acquiert acquérons acquérez acquièrent	acquis... acquîmes...
† advenir	advenant advenu	il advient	il advint
aller[1]	allant allé	vais vas va allons allez vont	allai... allâmes...
assaillir	assaillant assailli	assaille... assaillons...	assaillis... assaillîmes...
asseoir	asseyant *or* assoyant assis	assieds[2] assieds assied asseyons asseyez asseyent	assis... assîmes...
avoir[3]	ayant eu	ai as a avons avez ont	eus... eûmes...
boire	buvant bu	bois bois boit buvons buvez boivent	bus... bûmes...
bouillir	bouillant bouilli	bous bous bout bouillons bouillez bouillent	bouillis... bouillîmes...
† braire[4]	brayant brait	il brait ils braient	
† bruire[5]	bruissant bruit	il bruit ils bruissent	
† choir	chu	chois chois choit	chus... chûmes...
† clore	clos	clos clos clôt closent	

[1] 2nd pers. sing. Imperative: *va.*
[2] The forms in *-oi* (or *-eoi*) (same conjugation as *prévoir*) are accepted by the Académie Française but considered as familiar or even vulgar.

Future	Present Subjunctive	English
believe)		
acquerrai... acquerrons...	acquière acquières acquière acquérions acquériez acquièrent	to acquire
il adviendra	il advienne	to happen
irai... irons...	aille ailles aille allions alliez aillent	to go
assaillirai... assaillirons...	assaille... assaillions...	to assault
assiérai... *or* assoirai... assiérons... *or* assoirons...	asseye[2]... asseyions...	to set to seat
aurai... aurons...	aie aies ait ayons ayez aient	to have
boirai... boirons...	boive boives boive buvions buviez boivent	to drink
bouillirai... bouillirons...	bouille... bouillions...	to boil
il braira ils brairont		to bray
		to rustle
cherrai... *or* choirai... cherrons... *or* choirons...		to fall
clorai... clorons...	close... closions...	to close

[3] Imperative: *aie, ayons, ayez.*
[4] Imperfect Indicative: *il brayait, ils brayaient.*
[5] Imperfect Indicative: *il bruissait, ils bruissaient* or *il bruyait, ils bruyaient.*

French Verbs

Infinitive	*Participles*	*Present Indicative*	*Past Historic*
conclure	concluant conclu	conclus, -s, -t concluons...	conclus... conclûmes...
conduire	conduisant conduit	conduis, -s, -t conduisons...	conduisis... conduisîmes...
confire	confisant confit	confis, -s, -t confisons...	confis... confîmes...
connaître	connaissant connu	connais connais connaît connaissons connaissez connaissent	connus... connûmes...
coudre	cousant cousu	couds... cousons...	cousis... cousîmes...
courir	courant couru	cours,-s,-t courons...	courus... courûmes...
craindre	craignant craint	crains,-s,-t craignons...	craignis... craignîmes...
croire	croyant cru	crois crois croit croyons croyez croient	crus... crûmes...
croître	croissant crû, *m.*, crue, *f.*	croîs croîs croît croissons croissez croissent	crûs... crûmes...
cueillir	cueillant cueilli	cueille... cueillons...	cueillis... cueillîmes...
† déchoir[1]	déchu	déchois déchois déchoit déchoyons déchoyez déchoient	déchus... déchûmes...
devoir	devant dû, *m.*, due, *f.*, dus, *m.pl.*	dois dois doit devons devez doivent	dus... dûmes...
dire	disant dit	dis dis dit disons dites disent	dis... dîmes...
† échoir	échéant échu	il échoit ils échoient	il échut ils échurent

[1] No Imperfect Indicative.

uture	*Present Subjunctive*	*English*
onclurai . . . onclurons . . .	conclue . . . concluions . . .	to conclude
nduirai . . . onduirons . . .	conduise . . . conduisions . . .	to lead to drive
onfirai . . . onfirons . . .	confise . . . confisions . . .	to preserve
onnaîtrai . . . onnaîtrons . . .	connaisse . . . connaissions . . .	to know
oudrai . . . oudrons . . .	couse . . . cousions . . .	to sew
ourrai . . . ourrons . . .	coure . . . courions . . .	to run
raindrai . . . raindrons . . .	craigne . . . craignions . . .	to fear
croirai . . . croirons . . .	croie croies croie croyions croyiez croient	to believe
croîtrai croîtrons . . .	croisse . . . croissions . . .	to grow
cueillerai . . . cueillerons . . .	cueille . . . cueillions . . .	to gather
décherrai . . . décherrons . . .	déchoie déchoies déchoie déchoyions déchoyiez déchoient	to fall to lose
devrai . . . devrons . . .	doive doives doive devions deviez doivent	to owe to have to
dirai . . . dirons . . .	dise . . . disions . . .	to say
il échoira *or* écherra ils échoiront *or* écherront	il échoie *or* échée ils échéent	to fall due

French Verbs

Infinitive	*Participles*	*Present Indicative*	*Past Historic*
écrire	écrivant écrit	écris,-s,-t écrivons . . .	écrivis . . . écrivîmes . . .
envoyer	envoyant envoyé	envoie envoies envoie envoyons envoyez envoient	envoyai . . . envoyâmes . . .
être[1]	étant été	suis es est sommes êtes sont	fus . . . fûmes . . .
† faillir	faillant failli	faut[2]	faillis[3] . . . faillîmes . . .
faire	faisant fait	fais fais fait faisons faites font	fis . . . fîmes . . .
† falloir[4]	fallu	il faut	il fallut
† férir[5]	féru		
† forfaire (à)	forfait		
† frire	frit	fris fris frit	
fuir	fuyant fui	fuis fuis fuit fuyons fuyez fuient	fuis . . . fuîmes . . .
† gésir[6]	gisant	gît gisons gisez gisent	
haïr	haïssant haï	hais,-s,-t haïssons . . .	haïs . . . haïmes[7] . . .
lire	lisant lu	lis,-s,-t lisons . . .	lus . . . lûmes . . .
luire	luisant lui	luis,-s,-t luisons . . .	luis . . . luîmes . . .
maudire	conjugated like the regular verbs in *-ir*, e.g. *finir*, except for the past		
médire (de)	médisant médit	médis . . . médisons . . .	médis . . . médîmes . . .

[1] Imperfect Indic.: *j'étais*; Imperative: *sois, soyons, soyez.*
[2] Only in the phrase *le cœur me faut.*
[3] In current usage followed by an infinitive, *e.g. il faillit tomber*, he nearly fell.
[4] Imperfect Indic.: *il fallait.*

Future	*Present Subjunctive*	*English*
écrirai . . . écrirons . . .	écrive . . . écrivions . . .	to write
enverrai . . . enverrons . . .	envoie envoies envoie envoyions envoyiez envoient	to send
serai . . . serons . . .	sois sois soit soyons soyez soient	to be
faudrai *or* faillirai		to fail
ferai . . . ferons . . .	fasse . . . fassions . . .	to make, to do
il faudra	il faille	to be necessary
		to strike
		to be false (to)
frirai . . . frirons . . .		to fry
fuirai . . . fuirons . . .	fuie . . . fuyions . . .	to flee
		to lie
haïrai . . . haïrons . . .	haïsse . . . haïssions . . .	to hate
lirai . . . lirons . . .	lise . . . lisions . . .	to read
luirai . . . luirons . . .	luise . . . luisions . . .	to gleam
participle (*maudit*).		to curse
médirai . . . médirons . . .	médise . . . médisions . . .	to speak ill of

[5] The infinitive is used only in the phrase *sans coup férir,* without striking a blow. *Féru* is adjectival only (*féru d'amour*, lovesick).
[6] The Imperfect Indic., *je gisais*, etc., is used.
[7] The plural is written without a circumflex: *haïmes, haïtes.*

Infinitive	*Participles*	*Present Indicative*	*Past Historic*
mettre	mettant mis	mets,-s,-t mettons...	mis... mîmes...
moudre	moulant moulu	mouds mouds moud moulons moulez moulent	moulus... moulûmes...
mourir	mourant mort	meurs meurs meurt mourons mourez meurent	mourus... mourûmes...
mouvoir	mouvant [1]mû, *m.*, mue, *f.*, mus, *m.pl.*	meus meus meut mouvons mouvez meuvent	mus... mûmes...
naître	naissant né	nais nais naît naissons naissez naissent	naquis... naquîmes...
nuire (à)	nuisant nui	nuis,-s,-t nuisons...	nuisis... nuisîmes...
† oindre[2]	oint		
† ouïr[3]	oyant ouï		ouïs... ouïmes...
ouvrir	ouvrant ouvert	ouvre... ouvrons...	ouvris... ouvrîmes...
† paître	paissant	pais pais paît paissons paissez paissent	
plaire	plaisant plu	plais plais plaît plaisons plaisez plaisent	plus... plûmes...
† pleuvoir	pleuvant plu	il pleut	il plut
† poindre	poignant point	il point	
pourvoir	pourvoyant pourvu	pourvois,-s,-t pourvoyons,-yez,-ient	pourvus... pourvûmes...

[1] The past part. of *émouvoir* is *ému,* and of *promouvoir, promu* (no circumflex on the *u* of the masculine sing.).

uture	Present Subjunctive	English
ettrai... ettrons...	mette... mettions...	to put
oudrai... oudrons...	moule... moulions...	to grind
ourrai... ourrons...	meure meures meure mourions mouriez meurent	to die
ouvrai... ouvrons...	meuve meuves meuve mouvions mouviez meuvent	to move
aîtrai... aîtrons...	naisse... naissions...	to be born
uirai... uirons...	nuise... nuisions...	to harm
oindrai...		to anoint
ouïrai... ouïrons...		to hear
ouvrirai... ouvrirons...	ouvre... ouvrions...	to open
paîtrai... paîtrons...	paisse... paissions...	to graze
plairai... plairons...	plaise... plaisions...	to please
il pleuvra	il pleuve	to rain
il poindra ils poindront		to dawn to sting
pourvoirai... pourvoirons...	pourvoie... pourvoyions...	to provide

[2] Imperfect Indic.: *je oignais.*
[3] This verb is seldom used other than in the infinitive and in the compound tenses.

Infinitive	*Participles*	*Present Indicative*	*Past Historic*
pouvoir	pouvant pu	peux *or* puis peux peut pouvons pouvez peuvent	pus . . . pûmes . . .
prendre	prenant pris	prends prends prend prenons prenez prennent	pris . . . prîmes . . .
prévoir	prévoyant prévu	prévois,-s,-t prévoyons, -yez, -ient	prévis . . . prévîmes . . .
recevoir	recevant reçu	reçois reçois reçoit recevons recevez reçoivent	reçus . . . reçûmes . . .
résoudre	résolvant résolu *or* résous	résous résous résout résolvons résolvez résolvent	résolus . . . résolûmes . . .
rire	riant ri	ris,-s,-t rions . . .	ris . . . rîmes . . .
savoir[1]	sachant su	sais,-s,-t savons . . .	sus . . . sûmes . . .
sentir	sentant senti	sens,-s,-t sentons . . .	sentis . . . sentîmes . . .
† seoir	seyant	il sied ils siéent	
suffire	suffisant suffi	suffis,-s,-t suffisons . . .	suffis . . . suffîmes . . .
suivre	suivant suivi	suis,-s,-t suivons . . .	suivis . . . suivîmes . . .
surseoir[2]	sursoyant sursis	sursois,-s,-t sursoyons, -yez, -ient	sursis . . . sursîmes . . .
taire	conjug. like *plaire* except that there is no circumflex on the *i* of the 3rd		
tenir[3]	tenant tenu	tiens tiens tient tenons tenez tiennent	tins tins tint tînmes tîntes tinrent
† traire	trayant trait	trais,-s,-t trayons . . .	

[1] Imperative: *sache, sachons, sachez.*
[2] The Past Historic and the Imperfect Indicative are seldom used.

uture	*Present Subjunctive*	*English*
ourrai... ourrons...	puisse... puissions...	to be able
rendrai... rendrons...	prenne... prenions...	to take
révoirai... révoirons...	prévoie... prévoyions...	to foresee
ecevrai... ecevrons...	reçoive reçoives reçoive recevions receviez reçoivent	to receive
ésoudrai... ésoudrons...	résolve... résolvions...	to resolve
irai... irons...	rie... riions...	to laugh
saurai... saurons...	sache... sachions...	to know
sentirai... sentirons...	sente... sentions...	to feel to smell
il siéra ils siéront	il siée ils siéent	to become to suit
suffirai... suffirons...	suffise... suffisions...	to suffice
suivrai... suivrons...	suive... suivions...	to follow
surseoirai... surseoirons...	sursoie... sursoyions...	to delay to suspend
Pers. Sing. Pres. Indic.: *il tait.*		to keep silent about
tiendrai... tiendrons...	tienne tiennes tienne tenions teniez tiennent	to hold
trairai... trairons...	traie... trayions...	to milk

Imperfect Subjunctive: *tinsse, -es, tînt, tinssions, -iez, -ent.*

Infinitive	*Participles*	*Present Indicative*	*Past Historic*
vaincre	vainquant vaincu	vaincs vaincs vainc vainquons vainquez vainquent	vainquis... vainquîmes...
valoir	valant valu	vaux, -x, -t valons...	valus... valûmes...
vêtir	vêtant vêtu	vêts, vêts, vêt vêtons...	vêtis... vêtîmes...
vivre	vivant vécu	vis,-s,-t vivons...	vécus... vécûmes...
voir	voyant vu	vois,-s,-t voyons, -yez, -ient	vis... vîmes...
vouloir[1]	voulant voulu	veux veux veut voulons voulez veulent	voulus... voulûmes...

[1] Imperative: *veuille*, *veuillons*, *veuillez*.

uture	Present Subjunctive	English
incrai... incrons...	vainque... vainquions...	to conquer
udrai... udrons...	[2]vaille... valions...	to be worth
êtirai... êtirons...	vête... vêtions...	to clothe
ivrai... ivrons...	vive... vivions...	to live
errai... errons...	voie... voyions...	to see
oudrai... oudrons...	veuille... voulions...	to be willing to want, to wish

prévaloir: prévale, prévalions.

English Verbs

All verbs not marked *irr.* in the English-French section of the Dictionary come in one of t following categories:

(*a*) Regular verbs, conjugated like WORK or LIVE.

(*b*) Verbs ending in *-y* preceded by one or more consonants, e.g. DENY, REPLY, IMPL conjugated like CARRY (i.e. the *y* changes to *i* in the Past Tense and Past Participle).

(*c*) Verbs ending in a single consonant preceded by one or more vowels (but not a diphthor e.g. WAIT, or a double vowel, e.g. SEEM), which are monosyllabic or in which the stress fa on the last syllable, conjugated like DROP and PREFER (i.e. the final consonant is doubled in t Past Tense and Past Participle).

N.B. Apart from those which are irregular, all verbs ending in *-l* preceded by one or mo vowels (but not a diphthong, e.g. SAIL, or a double vowel, e.g. PEEL) double the *l* in the Pa Tense and Past Participle even if the stress does not fall on the last syllable, e.g. IMPERI DIAL.

* = obsolete. *A = obsolete, but still used adjectivally. † = becoming obsolete.

Infinitive	*Past Tense*	*Past Participle*	*French*
REGULAR VERBS (*a*)			
work	worked	worked	travailler
live	lived	lived	vivre
REGULAR VERBS (*b*)			
carry	carried	carried	porter
REGULAR VERBS (*c*)			
drop	dropped	dropped	laisser tomber
prefer	preferred	preferred	préférer
imperil	imperilled	imperilled	hasarder
dial	dialled	dialled	composer un numéro
IRREGULAR VERBS			
abide	abode	abode	demeurer
awake	awoke	awoken *or* awakened	éveiller
be *Pres. Indic.* am, art, is, are	was, were	been	être
bear	bore	borne *or* born[1]	porter
beat	beat	beaten	battre
beget	begot *begat	begotten	engendrer
begin	began	begun	commencer
bend	bent	bent	courber
bereave	bereaved *or* bereft	bereaved *or* bereft	priver (de)
beseech	besought	besought	supplier
bid	bade *or* bid	bidden *or* bid	ordonner

[1] *born* = né; *borne* = porté.

Infinitive	*Past Tense*	*Past Participle*	*French*
bind	bound	bound *A bounden[1]	lier
bite	bit	bitten	mordre
bleed	bled	bled	saigner
blow	blew	blown	souffler
break	broke	broken	casser
breed	bred	bred	élever
bring	brought	brought	apporter
build	built	built	construire
burn	burnt *or* burned	burnt *or* burned	brûler
burst	burst	burst	éclater
buy	bought	bought	acheter
Pres. Indic. can	could	——	pouvoir
cast	cast	cast	jeter
catch	caught	caught	attraper
choose	chose	chosen	choisir
cleave (*v.t.*)	cleft *clove	cleft *A cloven[2]	fendre
cling	clung	clung	s'attacher
come	came	come	venir
cost	cost	cost	coûter
creep	crept	crept	ramper
crow	crowed *or* †crew	crowed	chanter (coq)
cut	cut	cut	couper
deal	dealt	dealt	distribuer
dig	dug	dug	creuser
do	did	done	faire
draw	drew	drawn	tirer, dessiner
dream	dreamt *or* dreamed	dreamt *or* dreamed	rêver
drink	drank	drunk *A drunken[3]	boire
drive	drove	driven	conduire

[1] It is his *bounden* duty. [2] *Cloven* hoof. [3] A *drunken* brawl.

English Verbs

Infinitive	*Past Tense*	*Past Participle*	*French*
dwell	dwelt	dwelt	demeurer
eat	ate	eaten	manger
fall	fell	fallen	tomber
feed	fed	fed	nourrir
feel	felt	felt	sentir
fight	fought	fought	combattre
find	found	found	trouver
flee	fled	fled	fuir
fling	flung	flung	lancer
fly	flew	flown	voler
forbear	forbore	forborne	s'abstenir
forbid	forbade *or* forbad	forbidden	interdire
forget	forgot	forgotten	oublier
forsake	forsook	forsaken	abandonner
freeze	froze	frozen	geler
get	got	got *or* gotten[1]	obtenir, devenir
gird	girded *or* girt	girded *or* girt	ceindre
give	gave	given	donner
go	went	gone	aller
grind	ground	ground	moudre
grow	grew	grown	croître, devenir
hang[2]	hung	hung	pendre
have *Pres. Indic.* have, hast, has	had	had	avoir
hear	heard	heard	entendre
heave	heaved *or* hove	heaved *or* hove	soulever
hew	hewed	hewn *or* hewed	tailler
hide	hid	hidden	cacher
hit	hit	hit	frapper

[1] Ill-*gotten* gains; *gotten* is common in American usage.
[2] To suspend. In the meaning 'to execute by hanging', the verb is regular.

initive	*Past Tense*	*Past Participle*	*French*
d	held	held	tenir
rt	hurt	hurt	blesser
ep	kept	kept	garder
eel	knelt	knelt	s'agenouiller
ow	knew	known	savoir
	laid	laid	poser
d	led	led	conduire
n	leant *or* leaned	leant *or* leaned	pencher
p	leapt *or* leaped	leapt *or* leaped	sauter
rn	learnt *or* †learned	learnt *or* †learned	apprendre
ve	left	left	laisser, quitter
nd	lent	lent	prêter
:	let	let	laisser
[1]	lay	lain	être couché
ght	lit *or* lighted	lit *or* lighted	allumer
se	lost	lost	perdre
ake	made	made	faire
es. Indic. may	might	——	pouvoir (permission, probabilité)
ean	meant	meant	signifier
eet	met	met	rencontrer
ow	mowed	mowed *or* mown	faucher
ay	paid	paid	payer
ut	put	put	mettre
uit	quitted *or* quit	quitted *or* quit	quitter
ead	read	read	lire
end	rent	rent	déchirer
id	rid	rid	débarrasser
ide	rode	ridden	aller à cheval
ing[2]	rang	rung	sonner

[1] To recline. In the meaning 'to be untruthful', the verb is regular.
[2] (Of a bell). In the meaning 'to put a ring round', the verb is regular.

English Verbs

Infinitive	*Past Tense*	*Past Participle*	*French*
rise	rose	risen	se lever
rive	rived	riven *or* rived	fendre
run	ran	run	courir
saw	sawed	sawn	scier
say	said	said	dire
see	saw	seen	voir
seek	sought	sought	chercher
sell	sold	sold	vendre
send	sent	sent	envoyer
set	set	set	placer
sew	sewed	sewn *or* sewed	coudre
shake	shook	shaken	secouer
Pres. Indic. shall[1]	should[1]	——	——
shear	sheared	shorn *or* sheared	tondre
shed	shed	shed	verser
shine	shone	shone	briller
shoe	shod	shod	chausser
shoot	shot	shot	tirer (au fusil)
show	showed	shown *or* showed	montrer
shrink	shrank	shrunk *A shrunken	rétrécir
shrive	shrove	shriven	se confesser
shut	shut	shut	fermer
sing	sang	sung	chanter
sink	sank	sunk *A sunken[2]	sombrer
sit	sat	sat	être assis
slay	slew	slain	tuer
sleep	slept	slept	dormir
slide	slid	slid	glisser
sling	slung	slung	lancer

[1] Used as auxiliaries only. [2] *Sunken* cheeks.

finitive	*Past Tense*	*Past Participle*	*French*
nk	slunk	slunk	s'esquiver
t	slit	slit	fendre
nell	smelt *or* smelled	smelt *or* smelled	sentir
nite	smote	smitten	frapper
w	sowed	sown *or* sowed	semer
eak	spoke *spake	spoken	parler
eed	sped *or* speeded	sped *or* speeded	se hâter
ell	spelt *or* spelled	spelt *or* spelled	épeler
end	spent	spent	dépenser
pill	spilt *or* spilled	spilt *or* spilled	verser
pin	spun	spun	filer
pit[1]	spat	spit	cracher
plit	split	split	fendre
poil	spoilt *or* spoiled	spoilt *or* spoiled	gâter
pread	spread	spread	s'étendre
pring	sprang	sprung	s'élancer
tand	stood	stood	être debout
tave	staved *or* stove	staved *or* stove	crever
teal	stole	stolen	voler
stick	stuck	stuck	coller
sting	stung	stung	piquer
stink	stank	stunk	puer
strew	strewed	strewed *A strewn	répandre
stride	strode	stridden	marcher à grands pas
strike	struck	struck *A stricken[2]	frapper
string	strung	strung	ficeler
trive	strove	striven	s'efforcer
	swore	sworn	jurer
	swept	swept	balayer

...eing 'to put on a spit', the verb is regular.

English Verbs

Infinitive	*Past Tense*	*Past Participle*	*French*
swell	swelled	swollen *or* swelled	enfler
swim	swam	swum	nager
swing	swung	swung	se balancer
take	took	taken	prendre
teach	taught	taught	enseigner
tear	tore	torn	déchirer
tell	told	told	dire
think	thought	thought	penser
thrive	thrived *or* throve	thrived *or* thriven	prospérer
throw	threw	thrown	jeter
thrust	thrust	thrust	lancer
tread	trod	trodden	fouler
wake	woke *or* waked	waked *or* woken	éveiller
wear	wore	worn	porter (vêtements)
weave	wove	woven	tisser
weep	wept	wept	pleurer
wet	wetted *or* wet	wetted *or* wet	mouiller
will	would	——	vouloir
win	won	won	gagner
wind	wound	wound	enrouler
wring	wrung	wrung	tordre
write	wrote	written	écrire